THE HISTORY OF PARLIAMENT

THE HOUSE OF COMMONS 1509-1558

THE HISTORY OF PARLIAMENT

THE
HOUSE OF COMMONS
1509-1558

S. T. Bindoff

III
MEMBERS
N–Z

PUBLISHED FOR THE HISTORY OF PARLIAMENT TRUST
BY SECKER & WARBURG, LONDON
1982

First published in England 1982 by

Martin Secker & Warburg Limited

54 Poland Street, London W1V 3DF

© *Crown copyright 1982*

ISBN 0-436 04282 7

Printed in England for Secker & Warburg
by Willmer Brothers Limited, Rock Ferry, Merseyside

Contributors

T.F.T.B.	T. F. T. Baker
S.T.B.	S. T. Bindoff
C.J.B.	C. J. Black
M.B.	Muriel Booth
D.F.C.	D. F. Corcos
M.E.C.	M. E. Coyle
C.G.C.	C. G. Cruickshank
M.K.D.	M. K. Dale
A.D.	Alan Davidson
R.L.D.	R. L. Davids
A.J.E.	A. J. Edwards
P.S.E.	P. S. Edwards
N.M.F.	N. M. Fuidge
J.J.G.	J. J. Goring
A.H.	Alan Harding
A.D.K.H.	A. D. K. Hawkyard
T.M.H.	T. M. Hofmann
P.H.	Patricia Hyde
S.R.J.	S. R. Johnson
L.M.K.	L. M. Kirk
R.J.K.	R. J. Knecht
E.McI.	Elizabeth McIntyre
H.M.	Helen Miller
D.M.P.	D. M. Palliser
J.P.	John Pound
A.B.R.	A. B. Rosen
R.J.W.S.	R. J. W. Swales
M.J.T.	M. J. Taylor
S.M.T.	S. M. Thorpe
R.V.	Roger Virgoe

Abbreviations

In the preliminary paragraphs:

abp.	archbishop
abpric.	archbishopric
adm.	admission, admitted
adv.	advocate
apptd.	appointed
b.	born
bap.	baptized
bef.	before
bp.	bishop
bpric.	bishopric
bro.	brother
c.	circa
called	called to the bar
ch.	child(ren)
c.j.	chief justice
coh.	coheir
commr.	commissioner
c.p.	common pleas
ct.	court
cr.	created
d.	died
da.	daughter(s)
dep.	deputy
depr.	deprived
disp.	dispensation
div.	divorced
educ.	educated
fa.	father
fac.	faculty
gent. pens.	gentleman pensioner
gov.	governor
g.s.	grammar school
h.	heir

[I]	Ireland, Irish
illegit.	illegitimate
inf.	infant
inst.	installed
i.p.m.	inquisition post mortem
jt.	joint
j.p.q.	justice of the peace of the quorum
kntd.	knighted
l.c.j.	lord chief justice
lic.	licence
ld. lt.	lord lieutenant
m.	married
nom.	nominated
o.	only
PC	Privy Councillor
prob.	probably
rem.	removed
rest.	restored
ret.	retired
s.	son(s)
sec.	secretary
sis.	sister
suc.	succeeded
summ.	summoned
surv.	surviving
unm.	unmarried
w.	wife
wid.	widow
yr.	younger
yst.	youngest

In the footnotes:

Add.	Additional mss, British Library
admon.	admonition, letters of administration
AO	Archive Office
APC	*Acts of the Privy Council*
archs.	archives
BL	British Library
Bodl.	Bodleian Library, Oxford
Bull. IHR	*Bulletin, Institute of Historical Research*
Cal. Border Pprs.	*Calendar of Letters and Papers, Borders of England and Scotland*
Carew Pprs.	*Calendar of Carew Manuscripts, Archiepiscopal Library at Lambeth*
CCR	*Calendar of Close Rolls*
CChR	*Calendar of Charter Rolls*
CFR	*Calendar of Fine Rolls*
Ch.	Charter
CIPM Hen. VII	*Calendar of Inquisitions Post Mortem, Henry VII*
CJ	*Commons Journals*
consist.	consistory

corresp.	correspondence
Cott.	Cotton mss, British Library
CP and CR Ire.	*Calendar of Patent and Close Rolls, Ireland*
CPR	*Calendar of Patent Rolls*
CSP Dom.	*Calendar of State Papers, Domestic*
CSP For.	*Calendar of State Papers, Foreign*
CSP Ire.	*Calendar of State Papers, Ireland*
CSP Rome	*Calendar of State Papers, Rome*
CSP Scot.	*Calendar of State Papers, Scotland 1547–74* (4vv)
CSP Scot. ed. Thorpe	*Calendar of State Papers, Scotland 1509–1608* (2vv)
CSP Span.	*Calendar of State Papers, Spanish*
CSP Ven.	*Calendar of State Papers, Venetian*
DKR	*Deputy Keeper's Report*
DNB	*Dictionary of National Biography*
DWB	*Dictionary of Welsh Biography*
Dwnn, *Vis.*	*The Heraldic Visitation of Wales and Part of the Marches between 1586 and 1613 . . . by Lewys Dwnn* ed. S. R. Meyrick (Welsh Manuscript Society 1846)
EETS	Early English Text Society
Egerton	Egerton mss, British Library
EHR	*English Historical Review*
Griffith, *Peds.*	J. E. Griffith, *Pedigrees of Anglesey and Caernarvonshire Families*
Hamilton Pprs.	*Hamilton Papers. Letters and Papers illustrating the Political Relations of England and Scotland in the 16th Century*
Harl.	Harleian mss, British Library
HMC	*Historical Manuscripts Commission*
Lit. Rems. Edw. VI	*Literary Remains of Edward VI* (Roxburghe Club 1857)
LJ	*Lords Journals*
LP Hen. VIII	*Letters and Papers, Foreign and Domestic, Henry VIII*
MI	Monumental inscription
N. and Q.	*Notes and Queries*
NLW	National Library of Wales
NRA	National Register of Archives
n.d.	no date
n.s.	new series
OR	*[Official] Return of Members of Parliament*
PCC	Prerogative Court of Canterbury
PPC	*Proceedings and Ordinances of the Privy Council*
PRO	Public Record Office
PRO Lists	*Public Record Office Lists and Indexes*
Q. Sess.	*Quarter Sessions*
R̃.	R̃oyal
RCHM	*Royal Commission on Historical Monuments*
rep.	repertory, report
RO	Record Office
Rot. Parl.	*Rotuli Parliamentorum*
Royal	Royal mss, British Library
Sloane	Sloane mss, British Library
SP Hen. VIII	*State Papers, Henry VIII*
Statutes	*Statutes of the Realm* (1810)

Stowe	Stowe mss, British Library
TRHS	*Transactions of the Royal Historical Society*
Val. Eccles.	*Valor Ecclesiasticus*
VCH	*Victoria County History*
UCNW	University College of North Wales

MEMBERS
N–Z

NANCE see **TRENGOVE** alias **NANCE**

NANFAN, William (by 1485–1536/37), of London.

DORCHESTER 1529

b. by 1485, prob. illegit. s. of Sir Richard Nanfan† of Trethewel, Cornw. and Birtsmorton, Worcs. *m.* Agnes.[1]

Collector of bill money, Calais by 1506–9; clerk of the council, Calais 20 May 1520–3, of the peace, Cornw. 1531–6.[2]

Sir Richard Nanfan died in 1507 leaving no male heir. He provided in his will for one bastard son and William Nanfan was probably another, as Sir Richard's son-in-law John Flamank* called him 'brother'. Flamank and William Nanfan had been especially trusted by Sir Richard during his deputy-ship at Calais, partly as he said 'because you be next unto me', and partly because most of the officials in the pale had been appointed by his precursor as deputy and their loyalty was suspect. William Nanfan's childhood was spent in Cornwall where about 1490 he was given the rent from a house in Padstow, but he was no longer living in the county, perhaps because he had joined Sir Richard in Calais, on 3 Dec. 1491 when the deed for the rent was entrusted to another Cornishman to keep to his use. He became friendly with Wolsey when the future cardinal was Sir Richard's chaplain, and they remained on good terms after Wolsey's rise to power. In 1519 Nanfan wrote to Wolsey about the losses which the King suffered through corruption in the duchy of Cornwall and promised to enlarge on the matter at their meeting: evidently he put his ideas on paper for in 1531 Cromwell was instructed to look out 'Nanfan's book touching the duchy of Cornwall'. It was on Wolsey's recommendation that he was appointed clerk of the council at Calais, but as he exercised the office through a deputy the council approached Wolsey to replace him by a man of their choosing. In August 1523, therefore, the clerkship was regranted to Nanfan in survivorship with Adrian Dyer to whom not long after he sold his interest. Nanfan's sale was not to deter him later

from pressing a claim upon the clerkship against Dyer's successor, Thomas Derby*. The patent falsity of this suggests that he was of a dishonest inclination, an impression further borne out by a complaint made to Wolsey by Sir Richard Sach-everell*, alleging that after buying a bill of credit 'for little or nothing' he had begun an action for debt against Sacheverell.[3]

As a client of Wolsey, Nanfan may have sat in the Commons before 1529, but it is to be doubted whether the doomed minister could have done anything towards finding him a seat in the Parlia-ment of that year. Several officials in the duchy of Cornwall, including the receiver-general Sir John Arundell, are known to have been in agreement with Nanfan's proposals to reform the duchy, and it is likely that influence from that direction explains his return for Dorchester as the duchy owned the manor of Fordington on the outskirts of the town. Arundell's kinsman Sir Giles Strangways I, himself elected for the shire, may also have had a hand in the matter, either in his own right or through his brother-in-law Sir Thomas Trenchard of nearby Wolveton, who was perhaps already high steward of the town. In view of the King's request that the Members of this Parliament should be re-elected in 1536, Nanfan probably sat again in the Parliament which met that June. In 1531 he had obtained the clerkship of the peace for Cornwall and this appointment he kept until a few months before his death. He made his will on 18 Oct. 1536, asking to be buried in St. Paul's churchyard, 'where the cross standeth', with as little cost as may be, 'for so it is most expedient to be done'. He had already arranged for his lands to go to his wife while she lived, the relevant deeds being kept by her and his friend Thomas Treffry*, and he made her executrix of the will, which was proved on 9 Jan. 1537.[4]

[1] Date of birth estimated from first office. *LP Rich. III and Henry VII* (Rolls Ser. xxiv), i. 231–2; J. Maclean, *Trigg Minor*, i. 281; iii. 308; PCC 1 Dyngeley. [2] P.T.J. Morgan, 'The govt. of Calais 1485–1558' (Oxf. Univ. D. Phil. thesis, 1966), 304, 307; *LP Hen. VIII*, i, iii, x. [3] *CIPM Hen. VII*, iii. 365; Maclean, i. 281; iii. 308; *LP Rich. III and Hen. VII*, i. 231–2; *LP Hen. VIII*, i–v; C1/550/25, 569/3, 628/30, 31. [4] Information from G. Haslam; PCC 1 Dyngeley.

H.M.

NAPPER, Edward (by 1512–58), of Holywell, nr. Oxford.

KNARESBOROUGH 1554 (Apr.)

b. by 1512, yr. s. of John Napper of Swyre, Dorset by Anne, da. of John Russell of Swyre. *educ.* Oxf. BA 2 July 1526, determined 1527, fellow, All Souls 1527–33, MA 17 July 1531. *m.* (1) by Oct. 1536, Joan (*d.*1545), wid. of William Clare of Holywell; (2) by 1550, Anne, da. of John Peto of Chesterton, Warws., 2s. 4da.[1]

Estate agent of William Petre*, Oxon. and west country by 1540.[2]

Edward Napper came of a family long settled in Dorset and linked by descent and marriage with Sir John Russell*, 1st Earl of Bedford. Russell is not known to have promoted Napper's career unless by encouraging him to go to Oxford, where several kinsmen had preceded him. At Oxford Napper struck up a friendship with another fellow of All Souls, William Petre, who may have persuaded him to take up civil law. Napper's marriage to a grazier's widow put an end to his academic career but he retained his interest in his college and the university. In later life he seems to have been one of Petre's estate agents.[3]

In 1537 Napper leased the Civil Law School from the university. He also bought and leased land in Oxfordshire and elsewhere, his most notable purchase being that of the ancestral manor of Swyre, Dorset, in 1546. It was after he had helped Petre to muster a force against Wyatt's rebels that he was returned to Mary's second Parliament. Lacking personal ties with Knaresborough or with the duchy of Lancaster, which owned the honor, he doubtless owed his nomination to the principal secretary, with Petre's brother Richard perhaps intervening as prebendary of Knaresborough. Napper's Membership appears to have left no trace. In 1555 he was one of the witnesses to the deed implementing the foundation of St. John's College. It was as a sick man that he made his will on 8 Aug. 1558. Apart from providing for his family, he made bequests to churches in Dorset and Oxfordshire and endowed the three poorest fellows of All Souls out of lands in South Petherton, Somerset, and Wheatley, Oxfordshire. On 12 Aug. he added a codicil in favour of his two sons and of the Knights of St. John of Jerusalem and he died one or two days later. One of the executors, Philip Huckle, was to marry Napper's widow, and another Petre obtained the wardship of his son William. The second son George was to be executed as a seminary priest at Oxford in 1610.[4]

[1] Date of birth estimated from education. A. Wood, *Life and Times,* i (Oxf. Hist. Soc. xix), 192–3; *Vis. Dorset* (Harl. Soc. xx), 74; *Vis. Oxon* (Harl. Soc. v), 253–5; *Cath. Rec. Soc.* i. 133–7; Emden, *Biog. Reg. Univ. Oxf. 1501-40,* p. 412. [2] F. G. Emmison, *Tudor Sec.* 25, 171; *LP Hen. VIII,* xiv, xvi. [3] Emden, 412; *LP Hen. VIII,* xviii;

Oxf. Univ. Arch. T/S cal reg. chancellor's ct. box reg. GG, p. 35. [4] Emden, 412; *LP Hen. VIII,* xxi; G. Scott Thomson, *Two Centuries of Fam. Hist.* 340; *CPR,* 1558–60, pp. 385, 421; Emmison, 171, 304; *Essex Recusant,* iv. 93; *St. John's Coll. Oxf.* (Oxf. Hist. Soc. n.s. i), 378–80; PCC 18 Welles; E150/946/19; G. Anstruther, *Seminary Priests,* i. 243.

A.D.

NAUNTON, William (by 1511–52/53), of Alderton, Suff.

BOSTON 1547[1]

b. by 1511, 1st s. of Thomas Naunton of Alderton by 2nd w. Margery, da. of Richard Basiarde. *educ.* G. Inn, adm. 1525. *m.* Elizabeth, da. of Sir Anthony Wingfield* of Letheringham, 6s. 2da.[2]

Servant, household of Charles Brandon, 1st Duke of Suffolk by 1537, treasurer by 1540–5; j.p. Lincs. (Lindsey) 1539–44; commr. musters 1546, relief 1550; gent. at arms in Feb. 1547; marshal of the King's bench 1550–*d.*[3]

Thomas Fuller, wriing of William Naunton's grandson Sir Robert Naunton†, author of *Fragmenta Regalia,* noted the family's great antiquity, and the evidence of place names tends to confirm his statement. By the beginning of the 16th century, however, the Nauntons counted for little in Suffolk and when in 1550 Catherine, daughter of the 11th Lord Willoughby of Eresby and widow of the Duke of Suffolk, described William Naunton as her 'cousin' she was referring to the connexion arising from his own marriage to a second cousin of the duke.[4]

After a legal education Naunton entered the service of the Duke of Suffolk, who in 1537 rewarded him with a 99-year lease of two manors in the vicinity of Alderton, and a third part of the advowson there, at a rent of £6 12s.8d. In 1538 he leased Butley priory, Suffolk, with the rectories of Butley and Capel, but when two years later Suffolk asked Cromwell to allow Naunton to purchase the priory it went instead to the 3rd Duke of Norfolk. Naunton was by then beginning to serve in local administration in Lincolnshire, where he was also perhaps engaged in overseeing both the Willoughby inheritance and the vast properties which Suffolk had acquired after the rebellion of 1536. Naunton remained in Suffolk's service until the duke's death in 1545, but is not mentioned in his will.[5]

One of Suffolk's last acts had been to procure a borough charter for Boston with a large grant of property. Naunton's election to the Parliament of 1547 obviously reflects the influence wielded there by his widow, a forceful woman who, as Baroness Willoughby of Eresby in her own right, was a landowner to be reckoned with in the parts of Holland: a correspondent of the 2nd Earl of Rutland wrote about this time, 'In Leicestershire Lord [blank] and the Earl of Huntingdon have the rule, in Lincolnshire, Lady Suffolk'. Whether Naunton was elected in 1547 or by-elected later is not known, as the original return is lost and the Members' names are known only from a list revised in preparation for the session of 1552. The duchess's patronage of Naunton did not end with this election, for between April and November 1550 she wrote several times to Cecil for assistance to her 'friend' and 'cousin' in a dispute with Richard Fulmerston*: the matter at issue was to be decided by the Protector Somerset, whose wife, according to the duchess, had caused Naunton to fall under his displeasure. The dispute may have been over the marshalship of the King's bench, in which post Naunton succeeded Fulmerston on 14 Nov.[6]

Naunton died during or shortly after the final session of the Parliament, and his widow presented Boston with a bill for his wages. The town first offered to pay 40s. and finally, on 17 Jan. 1553, a week before the next parliamentary election, agreed on a compromise of £6 13s.4d. If Naunton had served throughout the Parliament he would have been entitled, at the standard rate of 2s. a day, to some £33: unless the town was prepared to make only a token payment, therefore, the figures suggest that he had been by-elected and had sat only during the later sessions. Even so, the demand was clearly unwelcome, and Boston was to take care in the future that no outsiders were paid.[7]

On 20 June 1548 Naunton and his wife purchased manors, lands and advowsons in Suffolk from Sir Thomas* and Sir William Woodhouse*, and on 2 Apr. 1550 they sold these properties, or most of them, to John Bacon. No transactions in Lincolnshire have been traced but Naunton's continued connexion with that county is shown by his appointment as an overseer of the third payment of the relief there in 1550. His will has not been found. It was probably to his son William that Sir Charles Brandon*, the Duke of Suffolk's illegitimate son, bequeathed £40 in his will of 1551.[8]

[1] Hatfield 207. [2] Date of birth estimated from education. *Vis. Suff.* ed. Metcalfe, 153; Harl. 1820; Add. 19143 ff. 20, 31v. [3] *LP Hen. VIII.* xiv-xvi, xx, xxi; *CPR*, 1549-51, p. 164; 1553, p. 355; Add. Ch. 909; LC2/2, f. 43; 2/3(1), p. 113 ex inf. W. J. Tighe. [4] *CSP Dom.* 1547-80, pp. 27-31; *Cal. Chs. Bodl. Lib.* ed. Turner, 420. [5] Add. Ch. 909; *LP Hen. VIII.* xiv, xv, xxi; *Wills from Doctors' Commons* (Cam. Soc. lxxxiii), 28-41. [6] St.Ch.3/8/18; *HMC 12th Rep.* iv(1), 32; *CSP Dom.* 1547-80, pp. 27-31; *CPR*, 1549-51, p. 164. [7] Boston min. bk. 1545-1607, ff. 12v-13. [8] *CPR*, 1548-9, p. 86; 1549-50, p. 199; 1553, pp. 74, 355; *APC*, iv. 226; *N. Country Wills*, i (Surtees Soc. cxvi), 216-17.

T.M.H.

NEALE, Robert (by 1531–?68 or later), of Streathayne in the parish of Colyton, Devon.

BRIDPORT 1554 (Apr.)

b. by 1531. *educ.* ?I. Temple, adm. 1548. *m.* 30 May 1552, Alice, da. of John Strowbridge of Streathayne

by Thomasin, da. of John Tudoll* of Lyme Regis, Dorset.[1]

Robert Neale's wife was the stepdaughter of William Pole; it was probably to this connexion that he owed his election for Bridport to Mary's second Parliament, since Pole had sat for the borough in her first. Neale may have moved Pole for a place in the House in order to press an action which he and his wife had begun the year before against his brother-in-law, John Strowbridge*, and several other kinsmen. It is possible that Neale was already acquainted with his fellow-Member, Edmund Prowte, since Prowte was to stand surety for a 'seceder' with another man from Colyton, Richard Calmady*. On the election indenture Neale was described as gentleman, but whether this style had substance is not known.[2]

Pole was a prominent figure at the Inner Temple and Neale's marriage gives some colour to his identification with a youth from Horncastle, Lincolnshire, admitted there in 1548. This man was still alive 20 years later when he petitioned Elizabeth for protection against his persecution 'for matters of religion' in Mary's reign. He may also have been a party to the lawsuit in 1558 over the title to a Lincolnshire manor which one Robert Neale had purchased from John Hastings, a Member for Bridport in the Parliament of 1563, and perhaps the pensioner in receipt of £6 from Edward Hastings*, Baron Hastings of Loughborough, in 1563. If this presumption is correct, Neale may have had the support of Bridport's patron, Christopher Smith*, who was also of Lincolnshire origin.[3]

[1] Date of birth estimated from marriage. *Colyton Par. Regs.* (Devon and Cornw. Rec. Soc. xiv), 15, 461. [2] *Colyton Par. Regs.* 15, 461; C1/1311/22. [3] *CSP Dom.* 1547-80, p. 325; Req.2/23/27; Lansd. 7(15), f. 31.

H.M.

NELSON, William (by 1462–1525), of York and Riccall, Yorks.

YORK 1504, 1510,[1] 1512,[2] 1515[3]

b. by 1462, 2nd s. of Thomas Nelson† of York. *m.* Joan, da. of John Norton of Bilbrough, at least 3s. 3da.[4]

Member, Corpus Christi guild, York 1483, senior chamberlain 1489-90, sheriff 1495-6, member of the Twenty-Four 1496, master, merchants' guild 1499-1500, alderman 1499-1517, mayor 1500-1; commr. subsidy 1512, 1514, 1515.[5]

William Nelson followed his father, a merchant who was twice mayor of York, by becoming a freeman in 1488-89 and master of the merchants' guild in 1499. He is known to have dealt in the Richmondshire lead which was shipped through York, while the taunt of 'false extortioner' may mean that he was also a money-lender. Having inherited some of his father's property in York and in neighbouring Poppleton, Riccall and Sherburn, in 1500 and again in 1503 he was adjudged eligible for knighthood as having a landed income of over £40 a year. It was in the course of a property dispute with the city in 1503–4 that he was fined for threatening the mayor, Sir John Gilliot†, and in 1503 he acquired further adjacent land at Acaster Malbis.[6]

Nelson's election to four Parliaments in succession—which no York Member was to repeat throughout the century—bespeaks his ascendancy in the city during these years. On the last occasion, however, he was chosen only after the delivery of Henry VIII's letter requesting the return of the previous Members, the city having first elected Alan Staveley and William Wright: Nelson replaced Staveley but the election of Wright was allowed to stand, perhaps because Nelson's former partner Thomas Drawswerd was mayor-designate. Yet all was not harmony in York. In 1504 the King sent Nelson and his fellow-Member Richard Thornton back from Parliament with instructions to the city to keep the peace after an election riot, and on their arrival they discussed the situation with Archbishop Savage, head of the council in the north, who was 'best acquainted' with them; it is also likely that Nelson's two journeys south after the dissolution of Parliament in 1514, one of them on the order of the Council, were connected with the disturbances in the city and its surroundings which called forth a proclamation in November of that year. In 1516 Nelson himself became involved in the aftermath of a contested aldermanic election, when he and Drawswerd, who had been on opposite sides, were summoned before the Council and he himself was committed to the Fleet. He was still in custody when, in January 1517, he was elected mayor, to the anger of the King who had the election annulled; later in the year Nelson, by then a free man, resigned his aldermanship. He seems to have taken no further part in civic life and may have retired to his country house at Riccall, although it was as a parishioner of St. Mary, Bishophill, that he was assessed for subsidy in 1524 on goods valued at 40 marks.[7]

Nelson prefaced his will of 21 Mar. 1525 with a vigorous declaration of his faith. He asked to be buried in Holy Trinity church, Micklegate, near his father; he had already endowed a chantry there to the tune of £100, and he made bequests to that church and to the York friaries, leper houses and maisons dieu, to the poor, and to certain guilds. He left to his wife and family four houses in the city and property at Acaster Malbis, Grimston, Kelfield, Riccall and 'Welehows'. He complained at length of the gifts, worth over £90, which he had made to William Gascoigne (perhaps one of the two sons of Sir William Gascoigne† so christened), who had married one of his daughters and then deserted her. He made his wife and his son and heir Christopher his executors and residuary legatees, and William Coke, priest, his supervisor. The will was proved on 12 Apr. 1525.[8]

[1] *York Civic Recs.* iii (Yorks. Arch. Soc. rec. ser. cvi), 31. [2] Ibid. 37; York archs. B9, f. 62. [3] *York Civic Recs.* iii.42–46. [4] Date of birth estimated from first reference. *HP*, ed. Wedgwood 1439–1509 (Biogs.), 625; *Reg. Corpus Christi Guild, York* (Surtees Soc. lvii), 114n; York wills 9, f. 305. [5] *Reg. Corpus Christi Guild, York*, 114, 184; *Reg. Freemen, York*, i (Surtees Soc. xcvi), 213; York archs. B6–B9 passim; E179/279/1 m. 7; *Statutes*, iii. 85, 112, 175. [6] *York Mercers and Merchant Adventurers* (Surtees Soc. cxxix), 323; York archs. B8, ff. 95, 103; B9, ff. 2v, 9, 10, 33; *York Civic Recs.* iii. 38; *Test. Ebor.* v (Surtees Soc. lxxix), 198n; *Yorks. Arch. Jnl.* xxxvi, 362, 364; *Yorks. Deeds*, x (Yorks. Arch. Soc. rec. ser. cxx), 8. [7] *York Civic Recs.* ii. 142–3, 145–65; iii. 3, 4, 28–51 passim; *Tudor R. Proclamations*, ed. Hughes and Larkin, i. 125–6; D. M. Palliser, 'York in the 16th cent.' (Oxf. Univ. D.Phil. thesis, 1968), 164; *Yorks. Arch. Jnl.* iv. 188. [8] York wills 9, f. 305; *Test. Ebor.* v. 198–201; York pub. lib. R. H. Skaife ms, civic officials, ii. 527–9; W. K. Jordan, *Charities of Rural Eng.* 370.

D.M.P.

NETHERMILL, John (by 1515–59), of Coventry, Warws.

COVENTRY 1553 (Oct.), 1559

b. by 1515, 1st s. of Julian Nethermill of Coventry by w. Joan. *m.* (1) Winifred, wid. of Richard Dod of Coventry; (2) settlement 18 Nov. 1550, Bridget, da. of Henry Over *alias* Waver* of Coventry, 1s. *suc.* fa. 11 Apr. 1539.[1]

Warden, Coventry 1543–4, sheriff 1547–8, mayor 1557–8.[2]

John Nethermill was a draper who inherited considerable wealth from his father and an estate in Exhall within the city liberties. Although he was less active in business and in civic affairs than the only two men of comparable wealth in Coventry, his relatives by marriage Christopher Warren* and Henry Over, Nethermill took his share in administration and in 1549 joined with John Milward in the purchase of Warwickshire chantry lands for £671. Shortly afterwards he was engaged in a series of chancery actions over his sister's jointure with her father-in-law Thomas Bracebridge.[3]

Nethermill's civic career followed the usual pattern from his election as warden in 1543: he attended the mayor's council with reasonable frequency and acted as feoffee for the city and as arbiter in diputes between citizens. His return to Mary's first Parliament thus answered to his standing and his service. Unlike his fellow-Member Thomas Bond he opposed the initial measures for the restoration of Catholicism, and whereas on 12 Dec. 1553, six days after the close of the Parliament, Bond received £6 14s., full payment at the statutory rate of 2s. a day, Nethermill received £4 16s.10d., sufficient to cover only the 44 days of the second session. He sat again in the first Parliament of the following reign and died on 31 Oct. 1559.[4]

[1] Date of birth estimated from age at fa.'s i.p.m., C142/65/16. Dugdale, *Warws.* i. 167; *Vis. Warws.* (Harl. Soc. xii) 253; CP40/1138, r. 433; Req.2/29/110; C142/170/14. [2] *Coventry Leet Bk.* (EETS cxxxiv), ii. 783; Coventry council bk. 1, p. 17; mayors' accts. 1542–61, p. 19. [3] E179/192/125, 130, 157, 178; PCC 6 Alenger; *CPR*, 1549–50, p. 21; 1553–4, p. 452; C1/1291/51, 1406/68, 1456/16. [4] Coventry mayors' accts. 1542–61, pp. 494 seq.; chamberlains' accts. 1, p. 232; treasurers' payments, pp. 25 seq.; *Coventry Leet Bk.* ii. 780, 789, 793–6, 803, 809; Shakespeare Birthplace Trust, Gregory Hood collection 164; Bodl. e Museo 17; C1/1471/10–14; 142/170/14.

S.M.T.

NETHERSOLE, Robert (by 1482–?1556), of Dover, Kent.

DOVER   1523,[1] 1529, 1536[2]

b. by 1482, 2nd s. of William Nethersole of Nethersole. *m.* at least 1s.[3]
    Jurat, Dover by 1503–?d., mayor 1505–6, 1508–9, 1512–13; bailiff to Yarmouth 1503.[4]

Robert Nethersole appears to have been baptized Richard but to have renamed himself Robert, the name by which he is known throughout his career. He was probably not a native of Dover but it was there that he established himself as a merchant shipowner and man of property. During the first quarter of the century he was prominent as both businessman and town official, capacities which tended to overlap: thus in 1514–15 he went to London to buy ordnance for Dover and in May 1520 he supplied three ships for the port's service.[5]

The war with France in 1523 involved Nethersole in large contracts with the central government and at the same time he made his first appearance in the House of Commons. The election writ, issued on 23 Jan. but forwarded by the lord warden only on 20 Feb., was accompanied by a letter calling for the return of 'discreet, expert and sufficient persons continually resident and inhabited there as now do or heretofore have exercised the office and administration of justice within the same'. By these criteria Nethersole was well qualified: a jurat of 20 years' standing and three times mayor, he had also represented Dover at the Brotherhood of the Cinque Ports since 1503, although in 1523 he and his fellows would be charged with contempt for non-appearance there. Since 1513 he had been involved in the great question of the liability of the ports to pay subsidy, a matter which was to engage him during his attendance at Parliament. He and his fellow Thomas Vaughan were in London throughout the first session in April and May, but Nethersole alone appears to have travelled up for the second, and even he started from Dover 12 days late for its opening and arrived back four days before its end. Such laxity was not without its compensation in

reducing the wages bill incurred by the town: in July the corporation sent letters and messengers to Faversham, Folkestone and the Isle of Thanet asking these 'limbs' to share the burden, but by September it had no option but to levy a tax to raise the money.[6]

The liability became heavier still when Nethersole represented Dover again, this time with John Warren, in the long drawn-out Parliament of 1529, especially as both Members seem to have attended throughout the greater part of its successive sessions. The town was none the less able to record in its accounts for 1536 that the Members were 'clear paid for this Parliament wages of all old debts and of all service that they have done since'. This service included their attention to a matter of great moment to Dover, the restoration of its harbour after the breach of an embankment in 1530. The Members acted as go-betweens, memorializing Cromwell and seeking statutory support for the rebuilding scheme. Re-elected with Warren, in accordance with the King's request for the return of the previous Members, to the brief Parliament of 1536, Nethersole was not to sit in any subsequent one. He might have done so but for his propensity to get himself involved in disputes even with close colleagues. Three weeks before his last election on 28 May 1536 he and John Warren were each bound over in 100 to keep the peace towards one another. Fresh trouble arose as soon as the Parliament was over, with the town refusing to meet Nethersole's wage-bill. This dispute had eventually to be remitted to two arbitrators drawn from the jurats, of whom Nethersole chose William Granger*; the settlement which followed included payments to Nethersole for coming from London to Dover twice 'with Mr. Gonstone [William Gonson, clerk of the King's ships] and three Frenchmen and also with Sergeant Plomer and his brother'.[7]

Nethersole is last mentioned in the local records on 25 Nov. 1555 when he handed over to the town two slings with three chambers from the cliff bulwarks which had been given to him by Sir Christopher Morrice. His name was crossed off the list of jurats for 1555–6 so that he presumably died in the latter year. No will has been found but Nethersole is known to have had at least one son, another Robert, who was chamberlain of Dover in 1547 and probably also captain of the Black Bulwark on the cliff until 1553.[8]

[1] Egerton 2093, f. 51. [2] Ibid. f. 139. [3] Date of birth estimated from first reference. *Vis. Kent* (Harl. Soc. lxxv), 138. [4] *Cinque Ports White and Black Bks.* (Kent Arch. Soc. recs. br. xix), 130; Egerton 2093, f.91v; 2094, ff.1, 7; Add. 29618, f.57. [5] C1/845/7–13; Egerton 2092, f. 510; 2093, ff. 4v–19, 48–49; Add. 29618, ff. 139, 148, 606. [6] *LP Hen. VIII*, iii, iv; add. 29618, ff. 187–92v; *Cinque Ports White and Black Bks.* 130–1, 152, 187–9; Egerton 2092, f. 538. [7] Add. 29617,

ff. 265v, 353; 29618, ff. 280v, 281–2, 289v, 292, 294, 296, 296v, 300v, 302v; S. P. H. Statham, *Dover*, 96–102. Egerton 2092, f. 538; 2093, ff. 92, 133, 136, 138, 139, 155v, 158; 2094, ff. 59, 79, 90v, 109v; C1/792/31–33, 845/7–13; Dover hundred ct. bk. ff. 225, 225v; J. Lyons, *Dover* (1813), i. 46–47, 135. [8] Egerton 2094, f. 140; Dover accts. 1547–58, ff. 1, 281v; *Cinque Ports White and Black Bks.* 223; *LP Hen. VIII*, xvi; Lansd. 156, f. 110.

P.H.

NEVILLE, Sir Anthony (by 1508–57), of South Leverton and Mattersey, Notts.

NOTTINGHAMSHIRE 1545

b. by 1508, ?s. of Alexander Neville of South Leverton. *educ.* G. Inn, adm. 1522. *m.* (1) by 1538, Mary, 1s; (2) Anne, da. of Thomas, 3rd Lord Burgh of Gainsborough, Lincs., wid. of John Bussy (*d.*31 Jan. 1542) of Hougham, Lincs.; at least 1s. 3da. Kntd. 11 May 1544.[1]

J.p. Notts 1538–*d.* q.1554, midland circuit 1540; commr. musters, Notts. 1539, chantries, Notts. and Derbys. 1548, relief, Notts. 1550, goods of churches and fraternities 1553; other commissions 1535–*d.*; esquire of the body by 1539; member, council in the north Feb. 1550–*d.*; sheriff. Notts. and Derbys. 1552–3.[2]

Anthony Neville's parentage has not been established, although it is clear that he belonged to the family settled at South Leverton and thus counted among his forbears Thomas Neville, recorder of Nottingham and Member for that town in 1472. He may have been the son of Alexander Neville, escheator of Nottinghamshire and Derbyshire in 1519–20, and the brother of Richard Neville whose elder son Thomas became dean of Canterbury and younger son Alexander† secretary to Archbishops Parker, Grindal and Whitgift.[3]

A lawyer by training, Neville was counsel to the 4th Earl of Shrewsbury, whose will he was to witness (and may have prepared) in August 1537. During the rebellion of the previous year he had been paymaster to the earl's retinue and when Shrewsbury was made responsible for defending Derby he used his 'friend' Neville to report to the King and to bear back the royal orders. Another patron was Cranmer, himself a Nottinghamshire man, who judged Neville a man 'of right good wisdom, experience and discretion' and recommended him to Cromwell in 1537 for the office of custos rotulorum. (It was, however, a namesake who was Cranmer's steward.) To his role in local government, especially in a judicial capacity, and his place at court, Neville added military duty in the north; in 1544 he was made surveyor general of victuals for the Earl of Hertford's campaign and was one of those knighted at Leith.[4]

His service under Hertford probably contributed to Neville's election as knight of the shire in the Parliament of 1545, when his fellow-Member was Hertford's brother-in-law Michael Stanhope, but he was in other respects well qualified for the seat. In 1539 he had been granted the dissolved priory of Mattersey, not far from South Leverton, and the manor of Mattersey and neighbouring properties. It must have been shortly afterwards that he made a prestigious second marriage to the widowed daughter of the 3rd Lord Burgh and so acquired a connexion with a future Queen in Catherine Parr, while he was closely associated with such leading local figures as Sir John Markham* and John Hercy*. Neville was not to be elected again, but as sheriff in 1552–3 he returned the knights for Nottinghamshire and Derbyshire to Edward VI's second Parliament and Mary's first. His choice as sheriff in 1552, and his earlier appointment to the council in the north, imply that he stood well with the Duke of Northumberland, but he probably shared the temporizing attitude of the 5th Earl of Shrewsbury, the president of the council, and he was to be retained on the bench under Mary.[5]

Neville's qualities were recognized by William Phillipot, a rich merchant and one of Newark's greatest benefactors, who appointed him supervisor of his will, 'to the intent that my said executors may the better and more be assisted by his good counsel in and about all my causes'; he and Phillipot were also among the executors of Thomas Magnus, archdeacon of the East Riding, who left his estate to charity. His second marriage made Neville the uncle of Richard Topcliffe†, who became his ward, but there is no reason to believe that Topcliffe's hatred of Catholics owed anything to the relationship. Neville's own resort to litigation was not to be compared with the legal battle in which his widow and elder son were to engage after his death. When he died on 3 Sept. 1557 he possessed lands in Mattersey, Rampton and Thorpe valued at £41 a year, the manor of South Leverton worth £10, and scattered properties in Nottinghamshire valued at £5 13s. By his will, dated eight days earlier, he bequeathed to his younger son George his lease of Laxton parsonage and certain lands and tenements, and gave all his servants a quarter's wages and subsistence until they found new employment. The heir Alexander was 19 years old when his father died.[6]

[1] Date of birth estimated from education. C1/1456/28–29; *LP Hen. VIII*, xiv; *Vis. Lincs.* ed. Metcalfe, 18; *Lincs. Peds.* (Harl. Soc. l), 216. [2] *LP Hen. VIII*, viii, xii–xvii, xx; *CPR*, 1547–8, pp. 75, 77, 88; 1548–9, p. 137; 1550–3, pp. 141, 395; 1553, pp. 357, 386, 415; 1553–4, pp. 22, 29; 1554–5, pp. 109, 110; R. R. Reid, *King's Council in the North*, 492. [3] *The Gen.* n.s. xxvii. 232; *DNB* (Neville, Alexander and Thomas). [4] NRA 9837, p. 8; PCC 13 Crumwell; *LP Hen. VIII*, xi, xiv, xvii, xix; *Cranmer* (Parker Soc.), ii. 348, 374; Strype, *Cranmer*, 610; *HMC Bath*, iv. 71–72, 75–76; *Hamilton Pprs.* ed. Bain, ii, 356. [5] *LP Hen. VIII*, xiv; Dugdale, *Mon. Angl.* vi(2), 965; *HMC Rutland*, iv. 267, 372; *HMC Middleton*, 317; PCC 28 Pynnyng. [6] C. Brown, *Newark*, ii. 210, 362; *LP Hen. VIII*, xxi; C1/1039/16–18, 1147/39–40, 1456/21–25, 26–30; 142/112/124; York wills 15(2), f. 107; *CPR*, 1557–8, p. 5.

C.J.B.

NEVILLE, George (by 1534–?92), of Babham End, nr. Cookham, Berks.

HELSTON 1555

b. by 1534, yr. s. of George Neville, 5th Lord Bergavenny. Prob. *unm.*[1]

Like that of his fellow-Member Thomas Mildmay, George Neville's name was inserted on the Helston indenture for 1555 in a different hand. That Neville was the younger son of Lord Bergavenny rather than one of many namesakes is suggested by the patronage which that young man could command. The warden of the stannaries, (Sir) Edward Hastings*, and the recent joint receiver-general for the duchy of Cornwall (who had kept an interest in the office after selling his share to John Cosworth*), Sir Edward Waldegrave*, were his kin and since they were political allies they may well have acted in concert to procure him the seat. This identification of Neville is given substance by the passage during the Parliament of an Act (2 and 3 Phil. and Mary, c.22) restoring the heirs of Sir Edward Neville, George Neville's uncle and Waldegrave's father-in-law, to the remainder of the barony of Bergavenny. Neville probably also met Mary's criterion that the Members chosen for her fourth Parliament should be 'grave men, and of good and honest behaviour, and especially of Catholic religion' in that he did not follow Sir Anthony Kingston's lead in opposing a government bill. Moreover, it may have been as one out of sympathy with the prevailing orthodoxy that he lived in relative obscurity in Berkshire throughout the reign of Elizabeth until his death, when he left £40 to be 'distributed among Catholic persons' by his cousin and executor Nicholas Waldegrave. His will, made on 2 June 1591 or 1592 and proved on 22 June 1592, also shows that he was related to his Berkshire neighbours, the Babhams and the Mores.[2]

[1] Presumed to be of age at election. PCC 56 Harrington. [2] C219/24/25; PCC 56 Harrington; *VCH Berks.* iii. 128–9.

A.D.K.H.

NEVILLE, Sir Henry (c.1520–93), of Billingbear, Berks.

BERKSHIRE 1553 (Mar.), 1559, 1563, 1571, 1584

b. c.1520, 2nd s. of Sir Edward Neville of Addington Park, Kent by Eleanor, da. of Andrew Windsor*, 1st Baron Windsor. *m.* (1) 1551/55, Winifred, da. of Hugh Loss of Whitchurch, Mdx., ?*s.p.*; (2) by 1561, Elizabeth (*d.*1573), da. of Sir John Gresham of Titsey, Surr., 4s. inc. Edward† and Henry† 2da.; (3) May 1578, Elizabeth (*d.*1621), da. of (Sir) Nicholas Bacon* of Redgrave, Suff., wid. of Sir Robert Doyley† of Greenlands, Bucks., *s.p.* Kntd. 11 Oct. 1551.[1]

Groom, the privy chamber by 1546, gent. by Oct. 1550; master of the harriers 1552–5; steward, Mote park, Windsor forest 1557, honor of Donnington and bailiff, crown lands. Newbury, Berks, 1562; j.p.q. Berks. 1558/59–*d.*, Wilts. 1573/74–*d.*, jt. (with (Sir) William Fitzwilliam*) ld. lt. Berks. 1559, (with (Sir) Thomas Parry*) 1560, dep. lt. c.1587; collector for loan, Berks, 1562; commr. eccles. causes 1572; sheriff, Berks. 1572–3; custos rot. by 1583–*d.*; high steward, New Windsor and Reading 1588.[2]

Sir Henry Neville's father was the third surviving son of George Neville, 4th Lord Bergavenny, and brother of the 5th Lord, whose vast estates were entailed in June 1535 on himself and his heirs, with remainder to the lines of his brothers (Sir) Thomas* and Sir Edward. Lord Bergavenny died in the same year and was succeeded by his only son, a boy of eight, but prospects of wealth for Sir Edward Neville's branch ended with his involvement in the destruction of the Courtenays and the Poles. His sister Jane had married Henry Pole, Lord Montagu, who was arrested with the Marquess of Exeter on 4 Nov. 1538 and condemned for treason a month later. Four more victims followed, including Neville himself, who was alleged to have called the King 'a beast and worse than a beast'; alone of the defendants he maintained his innocence, but he was beheaded, with Exeter and Montagu, on Tower Hill on 9 Jan. 1539.[3]

Unlike the sons of his fellow-sufferers, who were kept in the Tower, Neville's children were not penalized for long under his attainder. The eldest son, another Edward, secured his restoration in blood during the Parliament of 1542 (34 and 35 Hen. VIII, c.36), and an order of 1 Mar. 1537 for the payment of £20 a year to Henry Neville, the King's godson, was allowed to continue. In the original grant he had been described as being with the French ambassador, so that he may have been intended for a diplomatic career. In March 1546 he was given a further annuity of £20, to be paid out of the augmentations, and nine months later he was listed as a groom of the chamber in the King's will, and was bequeathed £100.[4]

Advancement came to Neville with the ascendancy of the reformers. As a gentleman of the privy chamber he was granted in October 1550 another £50 a year, and 12 months later, when John Dudley made himself Duke of Northumberland, he was knighted and given £100 on his departure to France with Admiral Clinton for the christening of the Duke of Angoulême. In March 1552 Neville succeeded the recently executed (Sir) Michael Stanhope* as master of the harriers. On 17 June 1553 he was licensed to retain 20 men besides his household attendants and official subordinates, and four days later he was among the signatories of Edward VI's letters patent devising the crown upon Lady Jane Grey.[5]

Neville's commitment to Northumberland laid

the basis of his position in Berkshire and so of his parliamentary career. By a grant of 22 Sept. 1551 he and Winifred Loss were to receive lands worth £115 a year: he was described as affianced to Winifred Loss, whose father was a surveyor of augmentations and a great speculator in ex-monastic property. The lands consisted of the manors of Billingbear, Culham, Waltham St. Lawrence, Warfield and Wargrave, with the advowsons of the churches there, all in Berkshire and recently extorted from John Ponet as the price of his appointment to the see of Winchester. A prebend and various livings in Yorkshire, formerly held by Sir Michael Stanhope and worth £84 a year, were added early in 1553. In the pardon roll of October 1553 Neville is described as 'alias of Sunninghill Park', a part of Windsor forest, so that he may already have been domiciled in Berkshire by virtue of an office connected with the forest, although he does not appear to have held land there before 1551. His attachment to Northumberland presumably secured his return as a knight of the shire in March 1553, when he sat with Sir William Fitzwilliam, likewise a newcomer to that honour.[6]

Nothing is known about Neville's part in the succession crisis of 1553 and the details of his career under Queen Mary are obscure. In December 1553 the two annuities of £20 each granted by Henry VIII were replaced by one of £40 and in May 1554 he was licensed to alienate his Yorkshire rectory of Wadsworth. He then went abroad, having granted letters of attorney to John Lovelace* and John Whitwood. Thomas Hoby met him at Padua in August 1554, but two years later John Brett, who had been sent by the Marian government with 'certain letters and commandments' to various of the exiles, including Neville, reported that he had already returned to England. He had, indeed, acquired a wardship in Nottinghamshire on 24 May 1555 and, although he surrendered the mastership of the harriers in 1555, he received the keepership of Mote park, with 4d. a day and attendant profits, in July 1557. The keepership may have been conferred because of a decision to restore Wargrave and other manors to the bishop of Winchester, after John White had succeeded Gardiner; compensation was usually given in such cases but there is no evidence that Neville was offered anything more substantial. An Act restoring the heirs of Sir Edward Neville to the remainder of the barony of Bergavenny (2 and 3 Phil. and Mary, c.22) was passed in the Parliament of 1555.[7]

Neville's past activities were enough to ensure that he would welcome the accession of Elizabeth. A more distinguished career was to follow, mainly in Berkshire where it seems unlikely that his candidature for the county seat was ever seriously challenged. He died on 13 Jan. 1593 and was buried in the church of Waltham St. Lawrence.[8]

[1] Date of birth estimated from family history and career. Vis. Berks. (Harl. Soc. lvii), 181; VCH Berks. iii. 183; PCC 29 More; Misc. Gen. et Her. (ser. 1), ii. 317-18; Vis. Suff. ed. Metcalfe, 109; CSP Dom. 1547-80, p. 35. [2] LP Hen. VIII, xxi; CPR, 1549-51, p. 222; 1550-3, p. 381; 1555-7, pp. 184, 252; 1560-3, pp. 234, 434, 523; 1563-6, pp. 39, 41-42; 1569-72, pp. 219, 221, 440-2; CSP Dom. 1547-80, p. 152; APC, iii. 416; NRA 6803, p. 52; E163/14/8; Osborn Coll. Yale Univ. Lib. 71-6-41; HMC Hatfield, i. 429, 443, 473 seq.; HMC Foljambe, 26; Reading Recs. i. 388, 410; Bodl. Ashmole 1126, f. 50. [3] DNB (Neville, Sir Edward); D. Rowland, Nevill Fam. table III, p. 140. [4] LP Hen. VIII, xvii, xxi; CPR, 1553-4, p. 61; Wealth and Power, ed. Ives, Knecht and Scarisbrick, 94. [5] CPR, 1549-51, p. 222; 1550-3, p. 381; 1553, p. 78; CSP Dom. 1547-80, p. 35; APC, iii. 416; Chron. Q. Jane and Q. Mary (Cam. Soc. xlviii), 100. [6] CPR, 1550-3, pp. 151-2, 406; 1553-4, p. 411; M. C. Rosenfield, 'The disposal of the property of London monastic houses' (London Univ. Ph.D. thesis, 1961), 298; VCH Berks. iii. 135. [7] CPR, 1553-4, pp. 61, 353; 1554-5, p. 308; 1555-7, pp. 184, 252; NRA 6803, p. 52; C. H. Garrett, Marian Exiles, 235-6; Cam. Misc. x(2), 116; Trans. R. Hist. Soc. n.s. xi. 129; VCH Berks. iii. 193. [8] C142/240/95.

T.F.T.B.

NEVILLE, Sir John I (1493-1543), of Snape, Yorks.

YORKSHIRE 1529*

b. 17 Nov. 1493, 1st s. of Richard Neville, 2nd Lord Latimer, by Anne, da. and h. of Sir Humphrey Stafford† of Grafton, Worcs. and Blatherwyk, Northants. m. (1) by 1520, Dorothy (d.7 Feb. 1527), da. of Sir George Vere, sis. of John, 14th Earl of Oxford, at least 1s. 1da.; (2) lic. 20 June 1528, Elizabeth, da. of Sir Edward Musgrave† of Hartley, Westmld. and Edenhall, Cumb.; (3) 1533, Catherine, da. of Sir Thomas Parr of Kendal, Westmld., wid. of Sir Edward Burgh. Kntd. 14 Oct. 1513; suc. fa. as 3rd Lord Latimer Dec. 1530.[1]

J.p. Yorks. (N. Riding) 1528-39, (liberty of Ripon) 1538, (W. Riding) 1538-41, (E. Riding) 1538-41; commr. to inquire into all misdeeds, Yorks. 1536, musters 1539; steward, Ripon in 1536, Galtres forest May 1542; member, council in the north June 1530.[2]

John Neville was a descendant of Ralph, 1st Earl of Westmorland, by his second wife Joan Beaufort, the daughter of John of Gaunt: thus he was not only a distant kinsman of Henry VIII but he was also connected by blood and marriage with many noble families. His immediate forbears had been protagonists in the feuding which preceded the Wars of the Roses and in 1469 his grandfather had fallen in the cause of Henry VI at Edgecote. The fortunes of this branch of the Nevilles were rescued after that disaster by a sympathetic relative, Cardinal Bourchier, who procured the wardship of the 2nd Lord Latimer and preserved his inheritance. Latimer grew up to become a figure of importance in the north.[3]

The first glimpse of his son John Neville is of a 20 year-old warrior accompanying Henry VIII to northern France in 1513 and being knighted after the taking of Tournai. By 1522 he was recognized as a spokesman for his father by the northern magnates and the heads of monastic houses, but it was not until six years later that he was first named to the Yorkshire bench for his native Riding. His return to the Parliament of 1529 as one of the knights for Yorkshire was a further step in his progress, even if he owed it to his father: the representation of the county was something of a family affair, Neville's fellow-knight being his cousin Sir Marmaduke Constable I, over whom he took precedence probably by reason of his noble lineage. He was not to be a Member of the Commons for long: his father died either a few days before the close of the first session or immediately after it and thenceforth he was to sit in the Lords. The resulting vacancy was not filled until three years later, when his kinsman and namesake of Chevet was chosen in his place.[4]

In 1530 the new Lord Latimer was appointed to the council in the north and signed the letter sent to Clement VII in favour of the King's divorce. The opening of the second session of the Parliament saw him take his place in the Lords: the loss of the Journal of that House for all but one of the sessions obscures his attendance save at the sixth, when he was regularly present, but his two letters of 1534 and 1536 to Cromwell asking for leave of absence show that he journeyed to Westminster for the prorogations and in 1532 he used his attendance in Parliament to sue out livery of his inheritance.[5]

Business in Worcestershire kept Latimer from the opening of the Parliament of 1536; he reappeared there soon afterwards but although this was a brief Parliament he evidently quitted it early as for the last week his name lacks the "p" which would have signified his presence. He may have returned to Worcestershire to complete his business there, but by the time the Pilgrimage of Grace began in the autumn he was back in Yorkshire. As the leading figure in Mashamshire, one of the centres of the revolt, he was urged to spare no effort to prevent it from spreading, but his house at Snape was not strong enough to be held and he could not rely on the support of his neighbours. By 16 Oct. he was reported with his brother-in-law Sir Christopher Danby* to have been taken captive, and his behaviour at the conference at York and later at Doncaster, where he put the Pilgrims' case to the 3rd Duke of Norfolk, prompted the suspicion that he secretly sympathized with his ostensible captors. Norfolk did not share this view and recommended Latimer's retention on the council in the north, but others were not so sure and Latimer was to spend the following year enlisting the aid of friends to clear his name. Cromwell still harboured doubts even after Sir Francis Bigod's* insurrection of January 1537 in

Yorkshire had given Latimer the chance to prove his loyalty by decisive action, and he cultivated the minister with an annuity of 20 nobles and perhaps by surrendering to him the Latimer house in London: he followed this up in 1538 by selling one Buckinghamshire manor to Cromwell's friend John Gostwick* and another to Cromwell himself, although these sales were also designed to pay for lands at Nun Monkton and elsewhere in Yorkshire which he bought about the same time.[6]

Latimer attended the Parliament of 1539 nearly every day, but he did absent himself on 19 May 1539, when the attainder of Thomas, Lord Darcy, for complicity in the Pilgrimage was made final, and during the final session a year later he missed the last week of May. The deterioration of relations with Scotland and the troubled state of the borders soon demanded his presence in the north, but he was able to attend the first session of the Parliament of 1542. By the summer he was back in the north fighting the Scots and advising the 1st Earl of Rutland on the conduct of the campaign. He prepared for the hazards of war by making a will on 12 Sept. 1542 in which he provided for his wife, family and servants, but he was not to die in the field. When the second session of the Parliament opened in the following January he did not make an appearance in the Lords, but he must have journeyed to London to attend the session for it was there that he died on 2 Mar. 1543 and in St. Paul's that he was buried. He was succeeded in the barony by his son John, then aged 23 years. His widow was sought in marriage by Sir Thomas Seymour II but in the following July she became the sixth wife of the King and only after his death did she marry Seymour.[7]

[1] Date of birth given in *Coll. Top. and Gen.* ii. 174. *CP*; *Vis. Yorks.* (Harl. Soc. xvi), 225; *Glover's Vis. Yorks.* ed. Foster, 628; *Test. Ebor.* iii (Surtees Soc. xlv), 374. [2] *LP Hen. VIII*, iv, x–xvii; R. R. Reid, *King's Council in the North*, 490. [3] R. L. Storey, *The Fall of the House of Lancaster*, 95 seq. [4] *LP Hen. VIII*, i; *Clifford Letters* (Surtees Soc. clxxii), 63–67; NRA 6160, p. 52. [5] *LP Hen. VIII*, v, vii, x, xi; *LJ*, i. 58–83. [6] *LJ*, i. 85–101; *LP Hen. VIII*, xi–xv; Elton, *Policy and Police*, 51; M. H. and R. Dodds, *Pilgrimage of Grace*, 184–6; R. B. Smith, *Land and Politics*, 173–4, 229, 241, 246. [7] *LJ*, i. 166–212; *LP Hen. VIII*, xvi–xviii; PCC 17 Spert.

L.M.K./A.D.

NEVILLE, Sir John II (by 1488–1541), of Chevet, Yorks., and Mile End, Stepney, Mdx.

YORKSHIRE 1529*

b. by 1488, 3rd s. of Sir John Neville (*d.*22 Oct. 1502) of Liversedge, Yorks, by Maud, da. of Sir Ralph Rither of Rither, Yorks. *m.* by Aug. 1509, Elizabeth, da. and coh. of William Bosvile of Chevet, wid. of Sir Thomas Tempest (*d.*1507) of Bracewell, Yorks., at least 4s. 4da. Kntd. 25 Sept. 1513.[1]

Yeoman of the horse by 1509; keeper, Old park, Wakefield, Yorks. 1509. Cotescue Park, lordship of Middleham, Yorks. 1532; warden, Selwood forest,

Som. 1515; numerous other forestry offices; constable, Tintagel castle, Cornw. 1516; sheriff, Yorks. 1518–19, 1523–4, 1527–8; receiver and surveyor, forfeited lands of 3rd Duke of Buckingham 1522, Holderness, Yorks. 1522, jt. 1527; commr. subsidy Yorks. (W. Riding) 1523, 1524, offences against clothing statutes Yorks. 1533, tenths of spiritualities, Leics. 1535, for survey of monasteries, Leics. 1536; j.p. Yorks. (N. Riding) 1532, (W. Riding) 1538–d.; knight of the body by 1533; steward and feodary, duchy of Lancaster, honor of Leicester, 1534; steward, forfeited lands of Lord Darcy 1538; gent. pens. 1540–d.[2]

John Neville was a courtier, soldier and administrator. He belonged to the prolific and powerful northern family but as a younger son of a cadet branch his early prospects cannot have been good. He presumably gained his footing in the Household through his relatives in the royal service.

The first traces of Neville date from 1509: he attended the funeral of Henry VII and obtained the wardship of his own stepdaughter. His marriage with a Yorkshire heiress, which had taken place by August 1509, established him in the West Riding, where he came to occupy the position once enjoyed by her forbears: to point his ascendancy he undertook the rebuilding of Chevet, which he was to boast made him no man's debtor. His local progress was matched by his advance at court. In 1513 he was in the army which besieged Tournai and on the city's fall he was knighted. His skill in arms served him not only on the battlefield but also at the lists, and in 1520 he was chosen to joust both at the Field of Cloth of Gold and at Gravelines. Three years later it was put to a severer test against the Scots, and the second shrievalty which followed shows that it had come through satisfactorily. This was an office which Neville prized, but after he had held it for the third time in 1527–8 his request for a fourth term was denied.[3]

Neville may have entered Parliament before 1529, the names of the Members of the earlier Parliaments of the century being mostly lost, but the addition of a proviso to the Act of 1523 (14 and 15 Hen. VIII, c.20) attainting the 3rd Duke of Buckingham which protected his receivership of the duke's forfeited Yorkshire lands, does not of itself imply that he sat in the Parliament which passed that measure. He was not one of the original Members of the next Parliament, but the succession of his kinsman and namesake as the 3rd Lord Latimer left vacant one of the knighthoods for Yorkshire. Latimer perhaps helped Neville to fill it on 3 Feb. 1533, but what probably settled the matter was his nomination by Cromwell and the suitability of his residence in the West Riding, Latimer being a man from the North Riding and the other knight Sir Marmaduke Constable I from the East. Nothing has come to

light about Neville's part in the work of this Parliament. Presumably he served for Yorkshire again in the following one, that of 1536, when the King asked for the re-election of the previous Members.[4]

When the Pilgrimage of Grace began, Neville was with the 4th Earl of Shrewsbury surveying monastic houses in Leicestershire. Three of his sons and two of his sons-in-law helped to restore order but his sister, who was married to Christopher Stapleton of Wighill, openly supported the insurgents. Neville assured Cromwell of his own loyalty and the minister approved his selection as a juror to try the rebels. His friendship with Cromwell did not yield him the monastic property that he coveted but equally the catastrophe of 1540 did not harm him. Neville's undoing was his failure in the next year to report a conspiracy in the West Riding: in April 1541 he was arrested, committed to the Tower and arraigned for treason. The Privy Council decided against his execution at the same time as the Countess of Salisbury's, which the conspiracy had precipated, and on 3 June ordered his removal to York, where he was put to death twelve days later. The French ambassador described Neville as 'a man well known at the court but of mediocre ability and wit'. His wife and heir sued out pardons in the month of his death, but it was not until 1552 that his children were restored in blood by a private Act (5 and 6 Edw. VI, no.29). His descendants continued to live at Chevet until the 18th century when the family died out.[5]

[1] Date of birth estimated from first reference. *Vis. Yorks.* (Harl. Soc. xvi), 228–9; *Dugdale's Vis. Yorks.* ed. Clay, ii. 155, 157; *Test. Ebor.* iv. (Surtees Soc. liii), 198–9; *LP Hen. VIII*, i. [2] *LP Hen. VIII*, i–xvi; Somerville, *Duchy*, i. 508, 564, 568, 570; *Statutes*, iii. 256. [3] *LP Hen. VIII*, i–iv; Hunter, *S. Yorks.*, ii. 394–5; *Yorks. Arch. Jnl.* xxxii. 326–30; J.Croft, *Excerpta Antiqua* (1797), 78–91. [4] *LP Hen. VIII*, vii. 56 citing SP1/82, ff. 59–62. [5] *LP Hen. VIII*, v–vi, xi–xvi; *Yorks. Arch. Soc. rec. ser.* xlviii. 26–27, 60–62, 65, 71–72, 74–75; R. B. Smith, *Land and Politics*, 227; *Yorks. Arch. Jnl.* xxxiv. 379–98; J. T. Cliffe, *Yorks. Gentry*, 170–1.

L.M.K./A.D.

NEVILLE, Thomas (by 1484–1542), of Mereworth, Kent and London.

?KENT 1515

b. by 1484, 5th s. of George, 4th Lord Bergavenny, by 1st w. Margaret, da. and h. of Hugh Fenne† of Sculton Burdeleys, Norf. and Braintree, Essex. *m.* Catherine, da. of Humphrey, 1st Lord Dacre of Gilsland, wid. of George, 8th Lord FitzHugh (*d.* 28 Jan. 1513), 1da.; (2) lic. 28 Aug. 1532, Elizabeth, wid. of Robert Amadas (*d.*1531/32) of London. Kntd. 8 Feb. 1515.[1]

Councillor to Henry VII and Henry VIII; under sheriff, London Nov. 1509–14; j.p. Kent, Surr., Suss. 1512–*d.*, Mdx. 1514–*d.*; commr. subsidy, Kent 1512–*d.*, Kent and Mdx. 1514, 1515, 1523, 1524, loan, Kent 1524, tenths of spiritualities 1535; other commissions,

London, Kent and Mdx. 1517–40; surveyor of liveries c.1514–d.[2]

Speaker of House of Commons 1515.

Thomas Neville was a Councillor to Henry VII and became a trusted servant of Henry VIII. About 1514 he began to assume a general supervision over the suing out of liveries by the heirs to the estates of any tenant-in-chief. He was probably appointed orally and to duties which were unspecified: it was only under his supervision that a definite office of liveries began to develop apart from the administration of wardships. In 1529 he was formally appointed to oversee all liveries of possessions in England, Wales and Calais. Associated with him in this grant and in later re-issues was an eminent lawyer, Robert Norwich. Neville remained the effective head of the office until the year of his death and of the merger of the office of liveries in the newly-established court of wards and liveries.[3]

On 8 Feb. 1515 Neville was presented to the King by the Lower House as their choice for Speaker; after the customary disabling speech had been rejected and Neville admitted to office he was knighted by the King in the presence of the assembled Lords and Commons, a mark of distinction thought to be without precedent. His constituency is unknown but it is likely to have been his native shire of Kent, where he had been named a subsidy commissioner in 1512 and 1514. If so, he had presumably sat for the same shire in the previous Parliament and perhaps earlier, but all that is known of his parliamentary experience before 1515 is that, as under sheriff of London, he had twice been asked to speak to his father about bills in which the City was interested. As Speaker, he had to face problems with the subsidy and over ecclesiastical rights of jurisdiction, but he appears to have handled them to the satisfaction of the King.[4]

Neville was one of the most frequent attenders at the Council between 1516 and 1527. He was one of the Councillors appointed to hear poor men's causes and sat in the Star Chamber as well as in the court of requests; in the division of subjects between Councillors ordered in 1526 he was put down to deal with matters of law. There is no record of his having had any formal legal education, but his post under Catherine of Aragon would suggest it; he received a fee of £3 6s.8d. as 'retained of the Queen's counsel'.[5]

In 1521 Neville's brother, the 5th Lord Bergavenny, fell into disgrace and was forced to sell his manor of Birling, Kent, to the crown: Sir Thomas and Sir Edward Neville and their wives formally gave their consent to the surrender. Neville was not otherwise involved in this family crisis and it made no difference to his career. He played an active part in the attack on the monasteries and was one of the commissioners who visited Malling abbey, Kent, for this purpose. He himself wanted to be high steward of Malling or, better still, after the Dissolution to receive a grant of the abbey: he offered Cromwell 500 marks for it, while his son-in-law, Robert Southwell*, added his persuasions to the suit. Southwell was personally interested, for his wife, Margaret, was Neville's only child but most of her father's lands would go to the heir male. Perhaps it was lack of land which frustrated Neville's earlier efforts to marry his daughter to Cromwell's son, Gregory*; but relations between the two fathers remained friendly, and Cromwell recommended Robert Southwell as a husband for Margaret. Neville did not get Malling, but in March 1539 he was granted, for £400, the manor of Shelwood in Surrey for his lifetime, with remainder to his daughter and son-in-law.[6]

Southwell was named overseer of Neville's will of 23 May 1542 and among the executors were Neville's cousin Sir Thomas Willoughby, chief justice of common pleas, and (Sir) John Baker I*. Neville died on 29 May 1542 and was buried in Mereworth church.[7]

[1] Date of birth estimated from mother's death and his having a younger brother, apparently of the whole blood. *DNB*; D. Rowland, *Nevill Fam.* ped. iii; *CP*; R. E. C. Waters, *Chesters of Chicheley*, i. 20; *Mar. Lic. London* (Harl. Soc. xxv), 8; *LJ*, i. 20. [2] *LP Hen. VIII*, i–v, viii, xii–xvi, add.; Lansd. 1, ff. 108–10; 12, ff. 124–30; City of London RO, Guildhall, jnl. 11, ff. 90v, 191v; W. C. Richardson, *Tudor Chamber Admin.* 301–2; *Statutes*, iii. 79, 112, 116, 168, 170; *Va. Eccles.* i. 107. [3] *LP Hen. VIII*, i, ii; *EHR*, lix. 209; Westminster abbey reg. 2, f. 67. [4] *LJ*, i. 19, 20; City of London RO, rep.2, ff. 148 171; *Bull. IHR*, xxxv. 138; J. S. Roskell, *The Commons and their Speakers, 1376–1523*, pp. 317–20. [5] *LP Hen. VIII*, iv, viii, xii. [6] Ibid. iii, iv, viii, xiv. [7] PCC 11 Spert; W. D. Belcher, *Kentish Brasses*, ii. 92.

H.M.

NEVILLE, William (by 1532–59 or later), of Torksey, Lincs.

CHIPPENHAM   1558

b. by 1532, yr. s. of Ralph Neville, 4th Earl of Westmorland by Catherine, da. of Edward Stafford, 3rd Duke of Buckingham. *m.* Elizabeth, da. of (Sir) Geoffrey Pole* of Lordington, Suss., at least 1da.[1]

William Neville, a younger son of the 4th and brother of the 5th Earl of Westmorland, is the only bearer of his not uncommon name likely to have commanded the influence to secure his return for Chippenham, where his name is inserted in the indenture in a different hand from that of the document. A namesake from the Latimer branch of the family, who had settled at Wick near Pershore in Worcestershire, both enjoyed similar family connexions and had various Wiltshire interests but had probably died even before his brother Sir John

Neville I*, 3rd Lord Latimer, made his will in 1543. Neville may have obtained his seat either through his brother Westmorland or through his wife's family, the Poles. Westmorland was in favour at court and was on friendly terms with the Wiltshire magnate William Herbert I*, 1st Earl of Pembroke, a marriage alliance between the two families being under consideration early in 1553. Little is known of Neville's own career but he described himself as of Torksey when in 1553 he sued out a pardon, and nine years earlier Sir Philip Hoby*, who was both a friend of Pembroke and a distant relative by marriage of Neville, had received a grant of monastic lands there. The date of Neville's marriage is unknown; his father-in-law had sat for Wilton in the Parliament of 1529 and was himself related by marriage to the Marvyns, a leading Wiltshire family.[2]

Nothing is known of Neville's role in the House and no explanation has been found for the circle which stands against his name, and those of 29 others, on a copy of the list of Members. In 1556 he had sued out a pardon after failing to appear to answer to a debt of 200 marks and in 1559 he procured a general pardon. Later in the same year his brother Westmorland granted him the manor of Torksey. This is the last certain reference found to him although the Lincolnshire tenants of the 4th Duke of Norfolk at his attainder included a William Neville for the manor of Lee. Neville had not joined in the conspiracy of his brothers-in-law, Arthur and Edward Pole and Anthony Fortescue, against Elizabeth and it may well have been death rather than an anticipation of his nephew the 6th Earl's Catholic exile that removed him from the Elizabethan scene: he is not mentioned in the 5th Earl's will of 1563.[3]

[1] Date of birth estimated from first reference. *Vis. Suss.* (Harl. Soc. liii), 89; *Vis. Salop* (Harl. Soc. xxviii), 132; *Chron. Eng. Canonesses, St. Monica's Louvain*, ed. Hamilton, ii. 117. [2] C219/25/138; *CP*, xii(2), 560–3, 688–9; *Coll. Top. et Gen.* ii. 174; *LP Hen. VIII*, vi, ix; *VCH Wilts.* viii. 236; *Surtees Soc.* cvi. 159–63; *CSP Span.* 1553, p. 44; *CPR*, 1553–4, p. 411. [3] Wm. Salt. Lib. SMS 264; *CPR*, 1555–7, p. 60; 1558–60, pp. 129, 169; Arundel castle ms G1/7; *Surtees Soc.* xxxviii. 1–6.

T.F.T.B./A.D.

NEWDIGATE, John (1514–65), of Harefield, Mdx.

MIDDLESEX 1547,[1] 1553 (Oct.), 1554 (Apr.), 1558

b. 9 Oct. 1514, 3rd but 1st surv. s. of John Newdigate of Harefield by Anne, da. and h. of Nicholas Hilton† of Cambridge; bro. of Francis†, Nicholas* and Robert†. *educ.* L. Inn, adm. 7 Aug. 1538, called 1548. *m.* (1) settlement 4 Feb. 1541, Mary, da. of Sir Robert Cheney of Chesham Bois, Bucks,. 2s. inc. John† 1da.; (2) 19 Nov. 1559, Elizabeth, da. of Thomas Lovett of Astwell, Northants., wid. of Anthony Cave of Chicheley, Bucks., 1s. *suc.* fa. 19 June 1545.[2]

Pensioner, L. Inn 1556–7, bencher 1557, Autumn reader 1558, treasurer 1561–2.

J.p. Mdx. 1547–*d.*; commr. relief 1550.[3]

John Newdigate was the eldest surviving son in his generation of a Middlesex family. A lawyer, he never rose to the eminence of his grandfather the serjeant, but he was a bencher and treasurer of his inn, where he read once only, paying a fine of £20 a few weeks before his death to be discharged of a further reading.[4]

When his father died Newdigate filled the vacancy on the Middlesex bench; from then on he was named to a variety of commissions in the county, and after the accession of Elizabeth he was authorized to survey the possessions of the bishopric of London and to raise funds for the rebuilding of St. Paul's. Other members of the family were more deeply involved in the upheavals of the age: his uncle Sebastian, a monk at the Charterhouse, was executed at Tyburn in 1535, and his brother Francis, who served the Protector Somerset, came near to sharing Somerset's fate but survived to marry his widow. As a knight of the shire for Middlesex in four Parliaments between 1547 and 1558 John Newdigate saw many changes but was not, so it appears, much affected by them; nor did he make, on the evidence of the Journal, any impact on the House, the only piece of information about his Membership being the marking of his name with a circle on the list of Members of the Parliament of 1558 as revised for its second session. Judged by the bishop of London to be a 'favourer' of religion in 1564, he died at his home at Harefield on 16 Aug. 1565. The administration of his goods was granted on 4 July 1566 to his son John, with the consent of his widow who took as her third husband Richard Weston*.[5]

[1] Hatfield 207. [2] Date of birth given in F. A. Crisp, *Vis. Eng. and Wales, notes*, vii. 34–35. C142/145/61; Burke, *LG* (1952), 1880. [3] *CPR*, 1553, p. 356; 1563–6, p. 24; *APC*, v. 187. [4] *Surr. Arch. Colls.* vi. 230, 236; *Black Bk. L. Inn*, i. 346; *Trans. London and Mdx. Arch. Soc.* xxi. 100–4; NRA 5622, p. 37, 8596 passim. [5] *CPR*, 1563–6, p. 126 *Cam. Misc.* ix (3), 60; *PCC Admins.* ed. Glencross, i. 71.

H.M.

NEWDIGATE, Nicholas (1520–64 or later), of Westminster, Mdx. and Oxhey Hall, Watford, Herts.

WESTMINSTER 1558

b. 6 Dec. 1520, 6th but 4th surv. s. of John Newdigate of Harefield, Mdx. by Anne, da. and h. of Nicholas Hilton† of Cambridge; bro. of John*, Francis† and Robert†. *educ.* Eton; King's, Camb. adm. 19 Feb. 1541.[1]

Surveyor, lands of Westminster abbey 2 Jan. 1557–8 or later; bailiff, Westminster Nov. 1558/Jan. 1559–60.[2]

Nicholas Newdigate received at his father's death in 1545 an annuity of £4 (to be increased to £5 when his mother died) 'until he be preferred by my son John to some living of better value'; the elder John

Newdigate also exhorted his wife and eldest son to 'set forth my son Nicholas to some good service as shortly as they can'. The first office Nicholas Newdigate is known to have obtained was that of surveyor of the lands of Westminster abbey, at a fee of 40s. a year, which he received in January 1557: 11 months later he was given a 21-year lease of some of the abbey's property in Tothill Street. His surveyorship is perhaps sufficient to account for his Membership of Mary's last Parliament but he could have received support from the same quarter as enabled his brother John to become one of the knights for Middlesex. As an officer of the abbey he presumably resisted the measures introduced during the first session abolishing sanctuary at Westminster, and it was perhaps he who moved the Speaker to summon Abbot Feckenham before the House to defend the right. Both Newdigate's name and his brother's are among those marked with a circle on the list of Members as revised for the second session, the significance of which has not been explained.[3]

If Newdigate's appointment as bailiff of Westminster at the accession of Elizabeth was meant as a reward for recent service in the House, it was also to augment his modest fee from the abbey as surveyor and 'upon colour to avoid Sir Edward North from the same'. The circumstances of the grant are obscure, being known only from allegations made several years later by his successor as bailiff William Bowyer[†], but Abbot Feckenham seems to have curried North's favour by offering him the bailiwick while allowing Newdigate to discharge it 'upon such conditions as he should challenge nothing thereby'. One of the duties performed by the bailiff was as returning officer at elections and this presumably barred his re-election in 1559 when Westminster abbey was dissolved. The Act for the dissolution (1 Eliz., c.24) safeguarded all grants of office and he continued to exercise his for another year, although Bowyer claimed the grant ' thereby void in law'. During 1560 Newdigate asked (Sir) Thomas Parry* as steward of the abbey's lands for preferment to the service of Sir Robert Dudley* and let Parry have his patent. Shortly before his death Parry sent the patent to the dean and chapter of Westminster with a new one with 'more granted' in Bowyer's name. Newdigate had understood his appointment to be for life, but despite his petition for redress Bowyer kept it. The loss of Newdigate's position at Westminster seems to have been followed, not by advancement with Dudley, but by a futher decline in fortune, if the only later reference to him found is any indication. On 28 May 1564 the Privy Council ordered the bishop of Chichester to send some of his

men to accompany two of the Queen's servants 'sent down with Nicholas Newdigate to recover a bag of money of the said Newdigate's, which he hath left in a place between Chichester and Sidlesham . . . that done, Newdigate to return hither in keeping of the Queen's men again'.[4]

[1] Date of birth given in F. A. Crisp, *Vis. Eng. and Wales*, notes, vii. 34-36. [2] Westminster Abbey 37730; C219/26/58; SP12/31/44. [3] London consist. ct. 77 Thirlby; Westminster Abbey 37730; reg. 4, f. 50; *CJ*, i. 49; *DNB* (Feckenham, John); Wm. Salt Lib. SMS 264. [4] SP12/31/44; Westminster Abbey 33198 DE; 37730; *CPR*, 1558-60, p. 209; *APC*, vii. 146.

H.M.

NEWDIGATE, William (1495–1530/31), of Chalfont St. Peter, Bucks. and London.

GREAT BEDWYN 1529*

b. 3 Feb. 1495, yr. s. of John Newdigate of Harefield, Mdx. by Amphelicia, da. and h. of John Neville of Sutton, Lincs. *m.* Anne, prob. da. of Sir Edward Darrell* of Littlecote, Wilts., at least 1da.
Officer in the royal stables by 1525; keeper, Maxstoke castle and park, Warws. 14 July 1530–?*d.*[1]

The Newdigate family probably derived its name from the Surrey village where its main, though less significant, line was settled. William Newdigate belonged to a cadet branch which had been at Harefield since the 14th century. He is said to have been born at Whitefriars, London, on 3 Feb. 1495, but the evidence for this statement has not been found.[2]

The probability that Newdigate married a daughter of Sir Edward Darrell, one of whose feoffees he was, rests on the couple's inclusion, between Darrell's daughters Elizabeth and Catherine, in his will of July 1528, and on Darrell's bequest to them of 100 marks, the sum which he also bequeathed to Catherine. It was doubtless Newdigate's father who procured this advantageous match, which may also have led to his introduction into the royal service: when this took place is not known, but it was as a member of the King's household that in January 1525 he was licensed, with Francis Sidney, also of the stables, to export 400 tuns of beer for two years, and that in July 1530 he was granted the keepership of Maxstoke castle and park.[3]

Darrell also had a hand in Newdigate's return to Parliament in 1529. As lord of the manor of Bedwyn he must have conveyed the nominations there even if he did not originate them, and his interest in the Wiltshire elections is shown by his own return as a knight of the shire and his son Edmund's as a Member for Marlborough. As Newdigate's election came shortly after the grant to him of the manor of Willingale, Essex, and was to be followed by that of the keepership of Maxstoke, the initiative could have lain with the King. In the House, besides his Darrell kinsmen, Newdigate would have sat with his brother-in-law Robert Dormer and with Sir Edward Chamberlain, whose son Leonard Chamberlain* married his sister Dorothy, but as it turned out, he was not to do so for long. In the absence of a will and of an inquisition post mortem his death cannot be dated with any precision but it presumably occurred between 14 July 1530, the day of the Maxstoke grant, and 18 Oct. 1531, when that office was given to William Paget. Newdigate therefore died at about the same time as Sir Edward Darrell, and their passing was recorded by the addition of 'mortuus' to their names on the list of Members which was revised in the spring of 1532. The vacancy at Great Bedwyn was almost certainly filled, probably by Thomas Polsted (q.v.), at a by-election held before the opening of the fifth session of the Parliament in February 1533, when the borough was in the King's gift following Darrell's death. Newdigate's only known issue was a daughter Johanne who is mentioned in the will of Richard Newdigate, probably his cousin, dating from 1545.[4]

[1] Date of birth given in F. A. Crisp, *Vis. Eng. and Wales*, notes, vii. 36. PCC 37 Porch, 18 Jankyn; *Vis. Surr.* (Harl. Soc. xliii), 27; *Vis. Warws.* (Harl. Soc. vii), 39; *Mdx. Peds.* (Harl. Soc. lxv), 67; *Mon. Brass Soc. Trans.* vi. 59; Mill Stephenson, *Mon. Brasses*, 301; *Wilts. Arch. Mag.* iv. 228; *Surr. Arch. Colls.* vi. 262; Egerton 2604, f. 3; *LP Hen. VIII*, iv, v. [2] *Surr. Arch. Colls.* vi. 227–67; Crisp, vii. 36. [3] *Wilts. Arch. Mag.* iv. 228; PCC 18 Jankyn; Egerton 2604, f. 3; *LP Hen. VIII*, iv. [4] *Surr. Arch. Colls.* vi. 262.

R.L.D.

NEWENHAM, William (by 1502–46), of Everdon, Northants. and Kirklington, Notts.

WARWICK 1529
NORTHAMPTONSHIRE 1542

b. by 1502, 1st s. of Edmund Newenham of Everdon by Elizabeth, da. of William Harpur of Rushall, Staffs. *m.* (1) settlement 19 May 1520, Audrey, da. of George Catesby of Ashby St. Ledgers, Northants, prob. 3s. 3da.; (2) Benedicta, da. of Sir Godfrey Foljambe, wid, of Sir John Dunham (*d.* 1535) of Kirklington, prob. 2 da. *suc.* fa. 28 May 1527. Kntd. 1 Nov. 1532.[1]

J.p. Northants. 1531–d.; sheriff, 1536–7, 1540–1, Lincs. 1538–9; commr. musters, Northants. 1546; other commissions 1535–d.[2]

William Newenham succeeded as a young man to a fair-sized estate in Northamptonshire and Warwickshire. Although his first marriage had also brought him Warwickshire connexions, he appears to have had none with the town of Warwick itself and he may have owed his election there in 1529 to Sir George Throckmorton, senior knight for Warwickshire in the same Parliament: three years later Throckmorton was to recommend Newenham, amongst others, to Cromwell as a suitable replacement for Sir William Spencer of Althorp as sheriff of Northamptonshire. Newenham was also related through his mother to Throckmorton's fellow-knight Sir Edward Ferrers. Nothing is known of his role in the House but that he enjoyed and no doubt earned the favour of the crown is shown by his knighting at Calais in 1532. (The list of Members as revised earlier in that year had erred in attaching 'miles' to his name.) He was probably returned again for Warwick in 1536, in accordance with the King's general request for the re-election of the previous Members, and perhaps also in 1539 when the names of the Warwick Members are unknown.[3]

Throckmorton's recommendations for the shrievalty of Northamptonshire were made against a background of strife within that shire, where Spencer's widow was attempting to withhold from the crown the valuable wardship of her husband's heir; a year later Sir William Parr* of Horton, who was himself related to Throckmorton, expressed to Cromwell his hope that neither the Knightleys, Edmund* and Richard*, who were supporting their sister Lady Spencer, nor any of their party, amongst whom he counted Newenham, would obtain the office. The Knightleys were also related to Throckmorton and their seat at Fawsley was, as Leland observed, within a mile of that of Newenham at Everdon. Whatever part Newenham played in these local factions, he was not hopelessly compromised; he did not achieve the shrievalty until 1536, but in October 1534 William Penison wrote to remind Cromwell of his promise to make Newenham sheriff and two years later Richard Cromwell *alias* Williams* sent advice to his uncle through Newenham. Even Parr praised Newenham to the minister for his exertions in the aftermath of the Lincolnshire rising: he served with Parr on the commission which tried a number of the rebels at Lincoln and was a juror for the trial of northern men. In 1540 he attended the reception of Anne of Cleves and in November 1541 was a juror for the trial of Thomas Culpeper and Francis Dereham. Having by 1542 twice enjoyed the shrievalty of his shire he was probably able to procure his own return as one of its knights that year, while as in 1529 profiting from the favour of Throckmorton and other friends and kin.[4]

Two years later Newenham served in the French campaign under the command of Sir John Russell*, Baron Russell, and took the precaution beforehand, on 1 June 1544, of making his will. In it he styled himself of Kirklington, a Nottinghamshire manor which formed part of his second wife's dower. This marriage, while considerably extending his sphere of influence, had involved him in a number of lawsuits. Several arose out of the execution of Sir John Dunham's will and one, a chancery suit by his brother Edmund, over the execution of their father's will, but he and his wife were also engaged in disputes with her son-in-law John Hasilwood over property rights in Ringesdon, Lincolnshire, and with Edith Marmion over Rippingale in the same county. In the course of the dispute with Edith Marmion the pair used the curious argument that they were strangers in a county of which shortly afterwards Newenham was to be sheriff.[5]

Newenham returned safely from France and in 1546 was instructed to attend the reception of the Admiral of France, but died on 8 June of that year. The estate which he left to his heir was not greatly enhanced by his own purchases, although he had acquired two granges in Nottinghamshire from the crown. It was worth, at his own valuation, £150 and more a year, and in the will which he had made two years previously he left it, after provision for his younger children and his wife's life interest, to his eldest son Thomas.[6]

[1] Date of birth estimated from age at fa.'s death, Baker, *Northants.* i. 293. Bridges, *Northants.* i. 36; *Cat. Anct. Deeds*, v. 453; Thoroton, *Notts.* iii. 97; *Vis. Notts.* (Harl. Soc. iv), 160; PCC 16 Populwell, ptd. in *N. Country Wills*, ii (Surtees Soc. cxvi), 195; C1/861/25–28; 142/75/38, 78. [2] *LP Hen. VIII*, v, viii, xii, xiii, xvi, xx, xxi. [3] Ibid. v; *Chron. Calais* (Cam. Soc. xxxv), 123; he is correctly styled in a list of the King's retinue for Calais in Oct. 1532, *HMC Bath*, iv. 2. [4] *LP Hen. VIII*, v–vii, xi, xii, xiv–xvi; Leland, *Itin.* ed. Smith, i. 10. [5] *LP Hen. VIII*, xviii, xix; PCC 16 Populwell; Leland, iv. 18; C1/753/33–37, 861/25–28, 862/16–21, 907/5–8, 921/44–47; Northants. RO, Finch-Hatton ms 605. [6] *LP Hen. VIII*, xvii, xxi; C142/75/38, 78.

S.M.T.

NEWMAN, William (by 1517–83/89), of Poole, Dorset.

POOLE 1553 (Mar.),[1] 1571

b. by 1517, 1st s. of John Newman of Salisbury, Wilts. by Dorothy. *m.* Alice, da. of Richard Haviland of Poole. *suc.* fa. Sept./Oct. 1519.[2]
Bailiff, Poole 1547–8, mayor 1554–5, 1568–9, 1575–6; commr. piracy 1583.[3]

William Newman came from a merchant family of moderate estate settled in Salisbury. It is not known whether his business interests or his marriage first took him to Poole: in May 1540 he witnessed a lease made by the mayor and corporation, and from the following year he was trading extensively through the port, importing a variety of goods and exporting cloth and lead. By 1547 his assessment of £15 on goods for the subsidy put him among the middle range of local taxpayers.[4]

Newman's election to the second Parliament of Edward VI's reign anticipated his first mayoralty but he took precedence over the ex-mayor Thomas White III, possibly because he benefited from the influence of his brother-in-law the customer John Harward, who had sat for Poole in the two previous Parliaments. After the Parliament was over Newman and White were paid £4 3s.4d. as the sum outstanding 'for their burgess-ship'. In his capacity as mayor

Newman presided over the parliamentary elections in the autumn of 1554, and a year later his name was singled out for mention as a voter on the indenture sent into Chancery. He played an increasingly important role in the town and enjoyed a second experience of Parliament under Elizabeth. His will made on 25 June 1583 was proved six years later.[5]

[1] Poole rec. bk. 1, p. 85. [2] Date of birth estimated from father's death and from his having two younger brothers. PCC 10 Stokton, 21 Ayloffe, 38 Leicester; H. P. Smith, *Poole*, ii. 16. [3] Poole rec. bk. 1, p. 75; Hutchins, *Dorset*, i. 34; C219/23/51. [4] PCC 21 Ayloffe; Poole recs. envelope 19; E122/122/4, 7, 21, 123/2, 207/6; 179/104/174; *LP Hen. VIII*, add. [5] Poole recs. envelope 4, rec. bk. 1, p. 85; Strype, *Eccles. Memorials*, ii(2), 64–66; Lansd. 3(19), f. 36; Smith, 16; J. Sydenham, *Poole*, 253; PCC 38 Leicester.

M.K.D.

NEWPORT, George (by 1532–58/60), of Droitwich, Worcs.

DROITWICH 1554 (Nov.), 1555

b. by 1532, ?s. of George Newport of Droitwich by Joan. *m.* by 1554, Elizabeth, da. of Peter Blount of Sodington Hall in Mamble, 4da.[1]
Bailiff, Droitwich 1553–4.[2]

George Newport came of a leading Droitwich family which had supplied the borough with bailiffs intermittently since 1485. The namesake who held office between 1487 and 1514 was probably his father or grandfather, and among his kinsmen were the Edward, John and Richard Newport listed in 1541 as holders of phates, or salt-pans, and the William Newport whose name stands first among the electors on the indenture of 3 Nov. 1554.[3]

Newport appears in the charter of April 1554 as the first of the two bailiffs whose term was to expire on the following 2 Oct.; he was therefore a natural choice as the senior of the two Members whom Droitwich elected to the Parliament of November 1554, the first to which it had sent representatives, as far as is known, since 1311. The responsibility did not weigh so heavily as to deter Newport from quitting the Parliament early without obtaining leave to do so. For this offence he was informed against in the King's bench in the following Easter term, but as no proceedings were taken against him the authorities must have satisfied themselves that his withdrawal had not been a gesture of dissent. That it did not cost him the support of his brethren is shown by his re-election, with the same fellow-Member, Robert Wythe, to the following Parliament. In that House, to judge from the list of the Members concerned, he did not follow the lead of Sir Anthony Kingston by voting against one of the government's bills.[4]

Little has come to light about Newport's life. It is not clear whether he was the 'Mr. Newport, a gentleman dwelling in the Wiche' who, as Leland recorded in the early 1540s, had begun but later abandoned salt-workings and had built a 'fair new house of timber' at the end of the town; nor whether the George Newport who in April 1542 was given a passport with Humphrey Coningsby* to travel abroad 'for their affairs there' was Coningsby's Worcestershire neighbour or one of the Newports of Essex and Hertfordshire. The Worcestershire musters for the army for France in 1544 included Edward, George and William Newport, but the last two names were cancelled.[5]

Newport died between 18 Dec. 1558 and 24 Apr. 1560, the dates of the making and probate of his will. It was very short, having been drawn up while he was sick. He wished to be buried in St. Augustine's churchyard by his grandfather, whom he did not name. He left to his wife four salt-pans then occupied by his cousin Mary Bedell (Roger Bedell had been his fellow-bailiff), and to Fulk Newport a lease. He named as his executors his brother Robert Newport and Gilbert Dedick and charged them to give sums of money to his daughters at their discretion.[6]

[1] Date of birth estimated from first reference. *VCH Worcs.* iii. 87; *Vis. Worcs.* (Harl. Soc. xxvii), 22; PCC 24 Mellershe. [2] *CPR*, 1553–4, p. 403. [3] *Habington's Worcs.* (Worcs. Hist. Soc. 1899), ii. 306–7; Worcs. RO, bulk accession 1006, ncs. 316–43; Nash, *Worcs.* i. 323; *VCH Worcs.* iii. 87; *CPR*, 1549–51, pp. 37–38; C219/23/138. [4] *CPR*, 1553–4, p. 403; KB29/188 rot. 48. [5] Leland, *Itin.* ed. Smith, v. 93–94; *LP Hen. VIII*, xvii, xix. [6] PCC 24 Mellershe; *Habington's Worcs.* 481.

M.K.D.

NEWPORT, John (by 1508–64), of Bridgwater, Som.

BRIDGWATER 1554 (Apr.), 1554 (Nov.),[1] 1558

b. by 1508, s. of Francis Newport of Worcs. *m.* by 1545, Emma, da. of John Selwood of Chard, Som., 4s. 4da.[2]

Mayor, Bridgwater in 1532, 1537–8, 1542–3, 1548–9, ?in 1556.[3]

John Newport was a merchant who became one of the most important men in Bridgwater. He is first glimpsed in 1529 when he bought a wardship for £10. By 1532 he had a flourishing business, mainly with Spain, exporting cloth and farm produce and importing a variety of goods. He also seems to have owned a ship. He laid out much of his acquired wealth on purchasing land including the manor of Pawlett, Somerset, and a number of houses and other property in Bridgwater.[4]

Newport's stature was recognized by his frequent terms of office as mayor and his three elections to Parliament under Mary. Early in 1555 he received £3 6s.8d. 'for business money of the Parliament' and during the prorogation in 1558 40s. 'for his fees at the Parliament'. He made his will on 28 Nov. 1564 and died two days later. He left £20 or so to each of his younger children and the residue to his wife and eldest son John, who were his executors. John was still under age and on 13 May 1566 his wardship and marriage were granted to John Colles, the value of the inheritance being £26 6s.4d. a year. On John Newport's premature death on 15 July 1566 his brother Emmanuel, himself still a minor, became his heir.[5]

[1] Huntington Lib. Hastings mss Parl. pprs. [2] Date of birth estimated from first reference. *Vis. Som.* ed. Weaver, 123; C142/141/17. [3] *LP Hen. VIII*, iv, xiii; S. Jarman, *Bridgwater*, 268–9; Bridgwater corp. mss 1446, 2067. [4] Jarman, 268–9; Bridgwater corp. ms 1437; *LP Hen. VIII*, xx; C142/141/17. [5] Bridgwater corp. mss 1457, 1459, 1535; C142/141/17; *CPR*, 1563–6, p. 396; 1566–9, p. 333.

R.V.

NEWPORT, Richard (by 1511–70), of High Ercall, Salop.

SHROPSHIRE 1547

b. by 1511, 1st s. of Thomas Newport of High Ercall by Anne, da. of Sir Robert Corbet of Moreton Corbet. *educ.* I. Temple, adm. 7 May 1525. *m.* 1545, Margaret, da. and h. of (Sir) Thomas Bromley I* of Eyton-upon-Severn, Wroxeter and Shrewsbury, 4s. inc. Andrew† and Francis† 4da. *suc.* fa. 1551. Kntd. 21 July 1560.[1]

Commr. relief, Salop 1550, goods of churches and fraternities 1553; sheriff 1551–2, 1557–8, 1568–9; j.p. 1554–?d.; member, council in marches of Wales by *d.*[2]

The family of Newport was one of the foremost in Shropshire. Richard Newport's father, whom Cromwell had included among nominees for a vacant knighthood of the shire in the Parliament of 1529, married into the powerful Corbet family, which furnished three knights for Shropshire in a 20-year period; he also inherited property in Kent from Henry, 7th and last Lord Grey of Codnor. That it was not he but his son who was to sit in Edward VI's first Parliament, despite the continuing activity which included his shrievalty in 1549–50, may have owed something to Richard Newport's recent marriage to the heir of Sir Thomas Bromley, a member of the council of regency: Bromley had acquired much of the land of Shrewsbury abbey, including the abbot's country house at Eyton-upon-Severn, and the marriage was to bring Newport lands in five western counties.[3]

Nothing is known of Newport's role in the House but in 1549 the Shrewsbury bailiffs' account records the payment to him of 13d. 'on his return from Norfolk', presumably after taking part, with his fellow-knight Sir George Blount, in the suppression of Ket's rebellion. Although his father held land in Warwickshire, it is more likely to have been his namesake of Hunningham, Warwickshire, a son-in-law of Sir Edward Ferrers* and grandfather of Sir William Hatton† (formerly Newport), who had earlier served in the French war and who held office in that shire. Newport himself was pricked sheriff of Shropshire by each of Henry VIII's children and like his father-in-law Bromley, who was made lord chief justice by Mary, seems to have acquiesced in their various changes of policy. As sheriff he took the lead in proclaiming Elizabeth in Shropshire. Two years later he was among the English captains 'who best served in Scotland under [the 13th] Lord Grey of Wilton' and was knighted by the 4th Duke of Norfolk at Berwick. In 1564 Bishop Bentham took his advice in drawing up the report to the Privy Council on the religious sympathies of the Shropshire gentry, and before his death he had become a member of the council in the marches of Wales.[4]

Newport died on 12 Sept. 1570, having made his will on the previous day. He named as executors his wife and his 13 year-old heir Francis and as supervisors his 'cousins' George* and Thomas Bromley II*; in the following year the wardship of the heir was granted to the widow and George Bromley. Of Newport's daughters, Elizabeth had already made the first of her two marriages into the Lawley family and Isabel was married to a son of Charles Foxe*, secretary of the council in the marches. Magdalen Newport, then 'of tender years', was later to marry Richard Herbert† of Montgomery Castle and become the mother of Edward Herbert†, Lord Herbert of Chirbury. Edward Herbert may have inherited some of his historical interests from his grandfather Newport who owned a copy of the chronicle written by Edward Hall I, a Member for two Shropshire boroughs and perhaps a native of Kinnersley, near High Ercall. Newport was buried, as he had asked to be, in Wroxeter church near his father-in-law. The Shrewsbury chronicle described him as 'a valiant knight of Shropshire and of a princely personage . . . for whose death there was much moan made in Shrewsbury'.[5]

[1] Date of birth estimated from education. *Vis. Salop* (Harl. Soc. xxix), 373; Wards 7/13/70; PCC 39 Holney, 15 Bucke. [2] *CPR*, 1550–3, p. 395; 1553, pp. 358, 415; 1553–4, p. 23; 1563–6, p. 26; *CSP Scot.* i. 438; *HMC De L'Isle and Dudley*, i. 332; P. H. Williams, *Council in the Marches of Wales*, 352–3. [3] *CP*, vi. 132–3; *LP Hen. VIII*, vii. 56 citing SP1/82, ff. 59–62; H. Owen and J. B. Blakeway, *Shrewsbury*, i. 287. [4] Owen and Blakeway, i. 342; PCC 15, 29 Bucke; Leland, *Itin.* ed. Smith, iii. 66; *LP Hen. VIII*, xix; *VCH Warws.* vi. 118; *Vis. Warws.* (Harl. Soc. xii), 203; *Trans. Salop Arch. Soc.* (ser. 1), vi. 111; *Cam. Misc.* ix(3), 44. [5] Wards 7/13/70; PCC 39 Holney; *CPR*, 1569–72, p. 269; Add. 10128; A. B. Grosart, *Works of George Herbert*, i. p. xxvii; *Trans. Salop Arch. Soc.* (ser. 1), iii. 269; Pevsner, *Salop*, 328.

A.H.

NICHOLAS, Richard (by 1532–79 or later), of Calne, Wilts.

CALNE 1558

b. by 1532. ?*m.* at least 1s.[1]
Burgess, Calne by 1553–79, guild steward 1563.[2]

Nicholas may have been related to the neighbouring family of Nicholas of Roundway, near Bishops Cannings, and if so he was perhaps named after the Richard Nicholas who succeeded to Roundway in 1502. He seems to have been assessed for subsidy only in 1560. Although Nicholas and Allen are entered under Calne on the Crown Office list for the Parliament of 1558, for an unascertained reason neither appears on the copy revised for the second session.[3]

It is probable that the Member had a son and namesake, since he is called Richard Nicholas the elder in the accounts which he rendered as joint guild steward, the highest office in Calne. Nothing else is known about him, except that in 1562/3 he was granted a lease for the winter of some of the town's common lands, in consideration of 10s. still owed to him for his attendance in Parliament. This item, the sole indication that Calne paid parliamentary expenses in the early 16th century, is an illustration of the burden which they imposed on smaller boroughs.[4]

[1] Date of birth estimated from first reference. *Wilts. Arch. Soc. recs. br.* vii. 5. [2] C219/21/177, 23/143; *Wilts. Arch. Soc. recs. br.* vii. pp. xxi, xxviii. [3] *Wilts. Vis. Peds.* (Harl. Soc. cv, cvi), 141–3; *VCH Wilts.* vii. 191; *Wilts. Arch. Soc. recs. br.* vii. 1–5; A. E. W. Marsh, *Calne*, 333; C193/32/2; Wm. Salt. Lib. SMS 264. [4] *Wilts. Arch. Soc. recs. br.* vii. 3; *VCH Wilts.* v. 114.

T.F.T.B.

NICOLLS, Thomas (by 1529–68), of the Rectory, Pytchley, Northants. and the Old Bailey, London.

GRAMPOUND 1553 (Mar.)

b. by 1529, 1st s. of William Nicolls of Great Billing and Ecton, Northants. *educ.* M. Temple. *m.* by 1552, Anne, da. of John Pell of Elkington, Northants., 4s. 3da.[1]
Bencher, M. Temple 1566, Autumn reader 1566.

It is not known whether Northamptonshire was Thomas Nicolls's native or adopted county. His father, who was born about 1480, came from the north of England and only settled in that county towards the end of his life, perhaps after his son had married into a Northamptonshire family and had begun to purchase land there. Nicolls entered the Middle Temple, established a reputation for himself and achieved high rank within the inn before his early death. When early in the next century the windows of the hall were adorned with the arms of notable Middle Templars, his were included. From 1550 he made regular purchases of land, chiefly in Northamptonshire, and in 1567 he obtained Hardwick, which was to become his descendants' principal seat.[2]

It was presumably as a step in his career that Nicolls sought election to the Parliament summoned at Northumberland's behest in the spring of 1553. He had no personal ties with Cornwall and probably obtained his seat for Grampound as the nominee of Sir John Russell*, 1st Earl of Bedford. Bedford was a substantial landowner in the east midlands and his steward Giles Isham* was a near neighbour of Nicolls there: the two families saw much of each other and Robert Isham, chaplain to Queen Mary, appointed Nicolls one of his executors. Nothing is known of Nicolls's part in the work of the House, and it is not clear why he did not sit again: the accession of Mary is unlikely to have proved a deterrent to him, and it may be that his flourishing law practice monopolized his attention.[3]

On 20 Mar. 1568 Nicolls made a will providing for his wife, children and father. He gave his father a lease on the manor of Hardwick for the maintenance and education of his children, and provided for the discharge of his debts by the sale of his house in the Old Bailey and his moiety of a Dorset manor. His assistant Edward Griffin received two law-books, and the remainder of his library was shared between his sons, Francis, later the governor of Tilbury fort, Augustine, the judge, Lewis and William. He forgave Edmund Mordaunt* the arrears of an annuity of £6 8s. 4d. granted to him by Mordaunt and his grandfather, and left his friends Francis Saunders*, Robert Bell† and John Hippisley* 20s. each for mourning rings. As his executors, he appointed his wife, eldest son, father and father-in-law. He died at Peterborough on the following 29 June and was buried at Pytchley. His 15 year-old heir Francis was to become the ward of his father, who survived Nicolls by eight years.[4]

[1] Date of birth estimated from first reference. *Vis. Northants.* ed. Metcalfe, 119; PCC 19 Babington. [2] *M. T. Bench Bk.* 435; *CPR*, 1549–51, p. 193; 1554–5, p. 56; 1555–7, p. 65; 1560–3, p. 606; 1566–9, p. 42; *VCH Northants.*, ii. 176. [3] *Northants. Rec. Soc.* xviii. 29–29; xix. 15; xxi, p. lxv. [4] *CPR*, 1566–9, p. 420; 1569–72, p. 424; *DNB* (Nicolls, Sir Augustine); *Notable Middle Templars*, 174; Mill Stephenson, *Mon. Brasses*, 384; Bridges, *Northants.* i. 372; ii. 95; iii. 142; PCC 19 Babington; C142/161/117.

A.D.K.H.

NORMAN, John (by 1483–1525), of York.

YORK 1523[1]

b. by 1483, s. of John Norman of York by Agnes. m. (1) Catherine; (2) aft. 1512, Jane; (3) 1525, Anne, da. of Richard Birley of Gateforth; at least 2s. 2da.[2]

Member, Corpus Christi guild, York 1512, senior chamberlain 1512–13, sheriff 1514–15, member of the Twenty-Four 1515, alderman 1517, 1521–d., mayor 1524–5.[3]

The son of a merchant who had come from New Malton, Yorkshire, and rose to be sheriff of York seven years before his death in 1497, John Norman entered the York merchants' guild in 1501 and became a freeman by patrimony in 1503–4. He was constable of the guild in 1507 and master in 1515–16, and in 1521–2 twice went to London on behalf of the city and its merchants to answer to the Council for complaints made by the Hanse. He was probably the John Norman who in 1519–20 paid custom at Hull on a variety of wares brought in from the Netherlands, and he is known to have had shares in overseas ventures, one of his partners being Thomas Burton*. When in 1524 he was assessed for subsidy on £40 in goods in the rich central parish of All Saints, Pavement, he was said to have 'decayed by chance of the sea' to the extent of £50 since the previous year; this would mean that in 1523 he was perhaps the sixth richest layman in York. In the year of his death he acquired the manor of South Duffield near York, being apparently the first York alderman to become lord of a rural manor.[4]

Norman's civic progress was interrupted when in 1516 his candidature as alderman, supported by Thomas Drawswerd* but opposed by William Nelson*, resulted in a tie with his opponent: the outcome was a riot and an order from the Council vetoing the appointment of either, and when in the following year the city compromised by electing both, the King had the election quashed. Four years later Norman was elected without opposition, and within the next four he was successively one of the city's Members of Parliament and its mayor. Of his Membership nothing is known save that he and Thomas Burton expended £16 5s.8d. on writings concerning the sale of wool, probably the monopoly of wool exports which York acquired about this time. The resulting conflict with the Merchants of the Staple was to be the principal feature of Norman's mayoralty.[5]

Norman made his will on 13 Nov. 1525. He asked to be buried in All Saints', Pavement, near his second wife and under a marble slab engraved with 'the image of a man and three women images with scriptures'. He left money to York friaries, hospitals and prisoners, and to a York anchoress to pray for him. He bequeathed all his property in Doncaster, Ripon and York to his younger son Anthony, appointed his other children, George, Jane and Anne, executors with his brother Thomas, a chantry priest of York minster, and Miles Newton the town clerk, and named his relatives and fellow aldermen John Thornton and John Rasyng supervisors. The will was proved on 1 Dec. 1525. Of the children, George Norman began as a York merchant, but moved out to Gateforth; Anthony was contracted in marriage to the future wife of Archbishop Holgate, who was thereby caused some embarrassment; and Jane took as her second husband Richard Goldthorpe, who sat for York in 1559.[6]

[1] *York Civic Recs.* iii (Yorks. Arch. Soc. rec. ser. cvi), 86. [2] Date of birth estimated from admission as freeman. *Test. Ebor.* v (Surtees Soc. lxxix), 213–15; York pub. lib. R. H. Skaife ms, civic officials, ii. 538–9. [3] *Reg. Freeman, York,* i (Surtees Soc. xcvi), 227; *Reg. Corpus Christi Guild, York* (Surtees Soc. lvii), 175, 192; York archs. B9, 10 passim. [4] *Test. Ebor.* v. 213n; *York Mercers and Merchant Adventurers* (Surtees Soc. cxxix), 117, 126, 323; *Bronnen tot de Geschiedenis van den Handel met Engeland, Schotland en Ierland,* ed. Smit, i. 277–80; *York Civic Recs.* iii. 72, 77, 79; *Yorks. Arch. Jnl.* iv. 176; *Tudor Feet of Fines,* i (Yorks. Arch. Soc. rec. ser. ii), 44. [5] *York Civic Recs.* iii. 51–61, 86, 90–104; York archs. B10, ff. 10, 68. [6] York wills 9, ff. 327–8; *Test. Ebor.* v. 213–15; *Reg. Freemen, York,* i. 249; A. G. Dickens, *Robert Holgate* (Borthwick Pprs. viii), 24–26, and *Lollards and Protestants in the Dioc. of York 1509–58,* p. 186.

D.M.P.

NORRIS, Henry (c.1525–1601), of Bray, Berks.

BERKSHIRE 1547
OXFORDSHIRE 1571

b. c.1525, 1st s. of Henry Norris of Bray by Mary, da. of Thomas Fiennes, 8th Lord Dacre of the South. *m.* by 1544, Margery, da. and event. coh. of Sir John Williams*, Lord Williams of Thame, 6s. inc. Edward†, Sir Henry†, Sir John† and William†, 1da. *suc.* fa. 17 May 1536. Kntd. 6 Sept. 1566; *cr.* Lord Norris 1572.[1]

Official of royal stables by 1546; gent. privy chamber by 1547; butler, port of Poole 1553; j.p. Berks. 1558/59, Oxon. 1561–91; sheriff, Oxon. and Berks. 1562–3; ambassador to France 1566–70; keeper of the armoury and porter of the outer gate, Windsor castle 1578; high steward, Abingdon c. 1580, Wallingford 1588; jt. ld. lt. Oxon. and Berks. c.1585–99; capt. of light horse, the Queen's bodyguard July 1588.[2]

The Norris family owed its eminence to Sir John Norris†, keeper of the great wardrobe to Henry VI. He acquired the manor of Yattendon through his wife and bought many neighbouring estates. These lands descended through his son Sir William† to his various grandchildren, of whom three died comparatively young, so that much of the inheritance was reunited under Sir John Norris, Sir William's eldest son by his second marriage. John had already received Yattendon, where he lived, while his younger brother Henry, father of the Member, was making his way at court. After attracting the King's favour, the elder Henry Norris rose rapidly, only to be arrested on 1 May 1536, on a charge of adultery with Anne Boleyn, and beheaded on the 17th. He left one son and one daughter by a wife who had died five years earlier.[3]

The early years of this son, the younger Henry, are obscure. His patrimony was restored to him by an Act of 1539 (31 Hen. VIII, c.22), and in December 1542 his uncle Sir John Norris of Yattendon, who was childless, was licensed to settle his estates in reversion on Henry, who was his ward, and on Margery, the younger daughter of Sir John Williams,

and their heirs. The couple must therefore have been betrothed by this date, and by 26 Aug. 1544 they were married. Norris was then described as a royal 'servant', and since Margery was to become the coheir of her wealthy father, who in the same year became treasurer of the court of augmentations, his prospects were bright. The couple received several properties, all but one formerly monastic, and as Williams was continuing to acquire land in Berkshire, as well as Rycote in Oxfordshire, the deaths of his uncle and father-in-law would greatly increase Henry Norris's already considerable wealth.[4]

These advantages notwithstanding, Norris's youth and inexperience made him an unusual choice as knight of the shire for Berkshire in 1547. He is not known to have been a partisan of the Duke of Somerset, although his cousin Sir William Wroughton* was described by the duke as a kinsman and had been a ward of Sir John Seymour*, and he seems to have taken no part in local administration under Edward VI and to have received no land or office. He is not known to have sat in the Parliament of March 1553, for which the names of many Members are lost, but on 21 June he was among the King's gentlemen who witnessed the device settling the crown upon Lady Jane Grey. After the succession crisis Mary did not hold this act against him as she approved his appointment as butler of Poole in the autumn, but he was to take little part in public affairs during her reign save for an interlude in 1554 when he is said to have helped to guard the Princess Elizabeth at Woodstock.[5]

Norris was to prosper under Elizabeth, who took the view that his father had died for his loyalty to Queen Anne and who bestowed her friendship on him and his wife. On the death of Lord Williams in 1559 he received much Oxfordshire property, and settled at Rycote, where he died on 27 June 1601.

[1] Date of birth given in *CP. DNB.* [2] *LP Hen. VIII,* xix, xxi; *CPR,* 1553–4, p. 276; *Bull. IHR,* v. 20–21; *APC,* xv. 118; xvi. 196; *CSP Dom.* 1595–7, p. 296. [3] C. Kerry, *Bray,* 113, 120; *VCH Berks.* iv. 4, 80, 127. [4] Camden, *Elizabeth* (1688), p. 636; *LP Hen. VIII,* xvii, xix. [5] *Chron. Q. Jane and Q. Mary* (Cam. Soc. xlviii), 100; *CPR,* 1553–4, p. 276.

T.F.T.B.

NORRIS, John (by 1502–77), of Fifield, Berks.

DOWNTON 1553 (Oct.), 1554 (Apr.)
TAUNTON 1554 (Nov.)
BODMIN 1558

b. by 1502, 1st s. of Edmund Norris of Fifield by Alice, da. of John Fowler of Fifield. *m.* by 1523, Mary, da. and coh. of Henry Staverton of Bray, 2s. inc. William* 5da.[1]

Gent. usher, the privy chamber by 1536, principal

gent. usher July 1553–8 or later; keeper, Foliejon park, Windsor park, Berks. 1536–d., Ashridge, Bucks. 1545; j.p. Berks. 1538–58/59; comptroller of works, Windsor castle 24 July 1538–d.; commr. relief, Berks. and Windsor 1550, chantries 1553, goods of churches and fraternities 1553; gent. usher of the Black Rod and the order of the Garter 1554–d.[2]

John Norris, the second of his line at Fifield, came of a cadet branch of the Norris family of Speke, Lancashire, and was a kinsman of Henry Norris* of Bray, Berkshire. Although the details of his career are obscured by the existence of several contemporary namesakes, its main outlines are clear. It was spent mainly in the royal household, of which he had probably been a member for some time before he appears as a gentleman usher in January 1536. During the next ten years he had a number of grants of lands and offices. Under Edward VI he remained an usher and was on a number of Berkshire commissions, including that of the peace.[3]

Norris corresponded with Lady Lisle during the late 1530s about the welfare of her son James Bassett*. Doubtless it was through Bassett, a trusted servant of Stephen Gardiner, bishop of Winchester that Norris obtained the clerkship of the episcopal castle at Taunton by September 1549 and that he was elected for Downton and Taunton, two of the bishop's boroughs, to Mary's first three Parliaments; his name was added to the indenture for Downton in March 1554 in a different hand. As Morris was one of the mourners at the funeral of Gardiner, who died while Parliament was in session, it is possible that Morris represented Taunton in the fourth Parliament of the reign, but in the absence of the original return this must remain a matter for speculation. According to Edward Underhill* he was a 'rank papist', and as such was promoted at Mary's accession to be principal gentleman usher of the privy chamber. In May 1554 he gained another mark of the Queen's personal favour by being made usher of the Black Rod. He was appointed gentleman usher to King Philip in June 1554, and helped to organize the royal wedding at Winchester. For his nomination at Bodmin he was probably indebted once more to Bassett since his fellow-Member, Sir Walter Hungerford, was Bassett's brother-in-law.[4]

On the accession of Elizabeth, Norris was summoned to Hatfield, perhaps to give advice on the new Household. He remained in the new Queen's service—at least in her first year—but took little further part in public affairs. He appears to have retired eventually to Fifield, and died on 30 Jan. 1577, leaving a house there and other property in Berkshire. Later in the same year his younger son Henry, then living at Bray, was reported as a Catholic.[5]

[1] Date of birth estimated from marriage. *Vis. Berks.* (Harl. Soc. lvi), 23, 131; (lvii), 55, 184; C142/176/2. [2] *LP Hen. VIII*, x–xii, xviii, xx; *CPR*, 1547–8, p. 81; 1550–3, p. 392; 1553, pp. 351, 413; 1553–4, pp. 17, 28, 113, 116; Stowe 571, f. 50v; E101/423/12, pt. 2, ff. 8, 12; *The King's Works*, iii. 415. [3] *LP Hen. VIII*, x, xii, xvi, xxi; *CPR*, 1550–3, p. 142 et passim; Stowe 571, ff. 30, 50v, 59–59v. [4] *LP Hen. VIII*, xv; *Letters of Stephen Gardiner*, ed. Muller, 514; Eccles. 2/155889, 155891; C219/22/93; *Chron. Q. Jane and Q. Mary* (Cam. Soc. xlviii), 128; *CSP Span.* 1554, p. 297; *APC*, v. 39. [5] *APC*, vii. 4; C142/176/2; *Cath. Rec. Soc.* xxii. 86.

R.V.

NORRIS, William (1522/23–91), of Fifield, Berks.

NEW WINDSOR   1554 (Nov.), 1555,[1] 1558

b. 1522/23, 1st s. of John Norris* of Fifield by Mary, da. and coh. of Henry Staverton of Bray. *educ.* G. Inn, adm. 1544. *m.* 1547/48, Mary, da. of Sir Adrian Fortescue of Shirburn and Stonor Place, Oxon., 6s. inc. John[†] 6da. *suc.* fa. 30 Jan. 1577.[2]

Gent. usher, the privy chamber by 1553; gent. pens. by May 1558–d. ?steward, Bray and Cookham, Berks. 1567; comptroller of works, Windsor castle, and keeper of Foliejon park, Berks. 30 Jan. 1577–d.; gent. usher of the Black Rod and the order of the Garter ?1577–d.[3]

William Norris, a well-connected courtier, had recently received a grant of the reversion to his father's offices at Windsor castle when he was returned for the town to the third of Mary's Parliaments. Unlike his fellow-Member Richard Ward I he was not numbered among those found absent when the House was called early in January 1555, and neither he nor Ward was among the opponents of a government bill in the Parliament which met later that year.[4]

On the accession of Elizabeth, Norris retained his place in the royal household, of which his wife's stepfather, (Sir) Thomas Parry*, became comptroller. It was, perhaps, his role as an usher appointed to attend upon Parliament that explains why Norris did not sit in the Elizabethan House of Commons. He died on 16 Apr. 1591, leaving lands in Berkshire and Oxfordshire to his eldest son John. A brass was set up by the widow in the church of St. Michael at Bray, showing Norris wearing the badge of the Garter, since the gentleman usher of the Black Rod was also usher of the order, and with an inscription recording that he had been 'ever of honest behaviour and good reputation'.[5]

[1] C219/24/6. *OR* gives 'Merryes'. [2] Aged 68 at death according to MI, Ashmole, *Berks.* iii. 11. *Vis. Berks.* (Harl. Soc. lvii), 184–6; W. H. St. J. Hope, *Windsor Castle*, i. 271, 274. [3] Stowe 571, f. 30v; *CPR*, 1553–4, p. 116; 1566–9, p. 125; E407/1/1–20, E351/542/18v, all ex inf. W. J. Tighe; *The King's Works*, iii. 415. [4] *CPR*, 1553–4, p. 116. [5] *APC*, vii. 4; Lansd. 3(89), f. 197v; E351/542/18v; C142/228/30; Ashmole, iii. 11–12.

T.F.T.B.

NORRIS, Sir William (1501–68), of Speke, Lancs.

LIVERPOOL   1554 (Apr.)

b. 1501, 1st s. of Henry Norris of Speke by Clemence, da. of Sir James Harington of Hornby, Lancs. and Wolfage in Brixworth, Northants. *m.* (1) settlement 1521, Ellen, da. of Rowland Bulkeley of Beaumaris,

Anglesey and Whatcroft, Cheshire, 1s. 6da.; (2) by 1535, Anne, da. and coh. of David Myddelton of Chester, Cheshire, wid. of Thomas Seton, 6s. 6da. *suc.* fa. 7 July 1524. Kntd. 1531.[1]

Sheriff, Lancs. 1544–5; j.p. Cheshire 1547; commr. relief, Cheshire, Lancs. 1550; other commissions 1535–65; mayor, Liverpool, Lancs. 1554–5; member, council of Edward Stanley, 3rd Earl of Derby by 1555.[2]

Speke is seven miles from Liverpool and Sir William Norris was much involved in the affairs of the town, though he seems to have avoided attempting to impose his own authority, and instead aided the municipal authorities against the Molyneux family. He also enjoyed the favour of the 3rd Earl of Derby, the dominant authority in Liverpool affairs. He had joined the earl with 103 men against the northern rebels in 1536 and was a member of his council by 1555, being present as such at the first examination of the Protestant martyr George Marsh on 24 Apr. 1555. It was thus as a local notable who enjoyed a magnate's support that he gained his single experience of the House of Commons. He was nominated but not pricked sheriff of Cheshire on six occasions between 1545 and 1552 and occasionally inhabited the 16th Earl of Oxford's manor house at Blacon near Chester.[3]

Norris took part in the Earl of Hertford's Scotch expedition and brought away with him as his loot (or part of it) a number of books. In one of these, an edition of one of Bartolus's commentaries dating from 1499, he wrote that he had got it at Edinburgh on 11 May 1544 and would leave it 'to remain at Speke for an heirloom'. He was a careful student of his own family deeds and on 9 June 1563 composed a 'genealogical declaration'. He did not profit from the Dissolution and he made relatively few changes in the property which he had inherited. He died on 30 Jan. 1568, shortly after he had been formally reconciled to Rome, and was buried at Childwall. His eldest son, William, had been killed in 1547 and his third but eldest surviving son Edward was now 28. His descendants remained Catholic until the mid 17th century and after they had conformed continued to sit for Liverpool.[4]

[1] Date of birth estimated from age at fa.'s i.p.m. and date of parent's marriage; *VCH Lancs.* iii. 135; *Top. and Gen.* ii. 377. *Vis. Lancs. 1567* (Chetham Soc. lxxxi), 84; J. B. Watson, 'Lancs. gentry 1529–58' (London Univ. M.A. thesis, 1959), 433; G. Ormerod, *Misc. Palatina*, 23 seq.; H. H. Leonard, 'Knights and knighthood in Tudor Eng.' (London Univ. Ph.D. thesis, 1970), 303. [2] *CPR*, 1547–8, p. 82; 1553, p. 360; *LP Hen. VIII*, viii, xiii; Somerville, *Duchy*, i. 322–3n; *Liverpool Town Bks.* ed. Twemlow, i. 16, 33, 278; *APC*, vii. 284; Foxe, *Acts and Mons.* vii. 41. [3] *Liverpool Town Bks.* 33, 112, 167, 221; Watson, 435; *LP Hen. VIII*, xi, xx; Foxe, vii. 41–42; *Chetham Soc.* xlix. 17; *CPR*, 1547–8, p. 82; 1553, pp. 317, 328, 349, 376, 387; *VCH Lancs.* iii. 135. [4] *Top. and Gen.* ii. 357–83; Watson, 435; *Ducatus Lanc.* i. 10, 24, 43; *Chetham Soc.* (ser. 3), xvii. 37; *Cal. Norris Deeds* (Lancs. and Cheshire Rec. Soc. xciii), pp. vii, 52, 206; *VCH Lancs.* iii. 135; J. S. Leatherbarrow, *Lancs. Eliz. Recusants* (Chetham Soc. n.s. cx), 29, 31; Strype, *Annals*, i(2), 259; C. Haigh, *Ref. and Resistance in Tudor Lancs.* 249–52.

A.D.

NORTH, Edward (c.1504–64), of Kirtling, Cambs., the Charterhouse, Mdx. and London.

CAMBRIDGESHIRE 1542, 1547, 1553 (Mar.)

b. c.1504, s. of Roger North of London by Christian, da. of Richard Warcup of Sinnington, Yorks. *educ.* St. Paul's; ?Peterhouse, Camb; L. Inn, adm. 1 July 1522. *m.* (1) c.1528, Alice (bur. 22 Aug. 1560), da. of Oliver Squire of Southby, Hants, wid. of John Brigandine of Southampton, Hants, and Edward Murfyn of London, 2s. inc. Roger* 2da.; (2) Margaret (*d.*2 June 1575), da. of Richard Butler of London, wid. of Andrew Francis and Robert Chertsey, both of London, and David Broke* of Horton, Glos. and London. *suc.* fa. Nov. 1509. Kntd. ?16 Jan. 1542; *cr* Lord North of Kirtling 1554.[1]

Steward, L. Inn 1528–30.

?Clerk of the council of the city of London in late 1520s; clerk of the Parliaments Feb. 1531–Sept. 1540; King's serjeant-at-law in 1536; j.p. Cambs. 1536–*d.*, Hunts. 1554–*d.*, I. o. Ely 1564, Mdx. and Suff. 1562–*d.*; sheriff, Cambs. and Hunts. 1542–3; treasurer, ct. augmentations Mar. 1540–Apr. 1544; jt. (with Sir Richard Rich) chancellor Apr.–July 1544, sole July 1544–Aug. 1548; commr. benevolence, Cambs. and Hunts. 1544/45, relief, Cambs., Hunts. and London 1550, for heresies 1557; other commissions 1535–*d.*; auditor, Queen Catherine Parr's accts. 1546; PC 12 Mar. 1547–July 1553; ld. lt. Cambs. and I. o. Ely 1557–*d.*; trier of petitions in the Lords, Parlts. of 1558, 1559 and 1563.[2]

Although Edward North's father Roger, a younger son, was settled in London at the time of his death, he had been born in Nottinghamshire where the less enterprising members of his family remained. Roger North made no mention of his three young children in the will which he made on 19 Nov. 1509 and which was proved 11 days later. Apart from two small bequests to the church of St. Michael in Quern, he left all his possessions to his wife Christian whom he appointed executrix. His only son Edward was sent to the newly-founded St. Paul's school, where his contemporaries and friends included Anthony Denny*, William Paget, Thomas Wriothesley and John Leland, who later addressed to North a 38-line Latin poem recalling their school-days together.[3]

Edward North may have continued his studies for a short time at Cambridge before being admitted to Lincoln's Inn in 1522; the suggestion that he attended Peterhouse lacks confirmation despite his later benefactions to that college. Until 1530 his name appears regularly in the records of his inn. It was probably at the instance of his brother-in-law, Alderman William Wilkinson, that he obtained employment in a legal capacity with the corporation of London. He may have been the Edward North described as of London, who in 1525 received a pardon from the King for some unknown offences, and was certainly the gentleman of that name who two years later was admitted to the Mercers' Company by redemption.[4]

While still at Lincoln's Inn North appears to have caught the attention of Sir Brian Tuke, treasurer of the chamber, a man of considerable learning and ability, who was the patron of many promising young men. It may have been such works as a poem he wrote about 1525 on the decay of the realm that first brought him to Tuke's notice. The poem, composed of stanzas of seven and written in English in the manner of Lydgate, condemned both the nobility and the clergy for a moral decline which only the grace of God and the nobility of the King and his Queen could arrest. North's appointment to the clerkship of the Parliaments was in survivorship with Tuke who had previously held the office undivided from 17 Apr. 1523. North was the junior partner on whom there should have fallen the work involved while Tuke busied himself with other duties. In a letter of 1 June 1539 to Cromwell, Tuke reported an outbreak of measles where he was staying and so excused himself from attendance at Parliament as he had 'no business but what Mr. North can do'. The 9th Lord la Warr asked Cromwell on 11 Jan. 1532 to send his leave of absence from Parliament straight to North; in the following year Sir Thomas Audley sent to North to obtain the Act of Annates so that he could make the ratification desired by the King; in 1534 copies of the protest against the bill of farms were supplied by him on demand; and in 1536 Cromwell obtained from him copies of the Acts concerning Wimbledon, Carnaby's lands and uses. Such recurrent applications to North, far from demonstrating his mastery of the business, may well point in a different direction. It appears that during North's clerkship (and beyond) no Acts of Parliament were enrolled in Chancery, a circumstance which, while it may be linked with changes in procedure, is also suggestive of neglect of duty.[5]

North's marriage to the widow of two merchants not only gave him financial security but permitted him the opportunity to speculate on the land market. On 1 Jan. 1533 he bought the manor of Kirtling, Cambridgeshire, which was to become his principal seat and the nucleus of his estates in East Anglia and the Fenlands. The title to Kirtling proved doubtful and North temporarily lost possession as the result of a lawsuit in 1534. Receiving the manor back from the King, North made certain of his ownership by an Act (28 Hen. VIII, c.40) passed during the Parliament of 1536 and shortly afterwards he began a splendid reconstruction of the house. About the same time the King acquired the manor of Edmonton, Middlesex, from North and William Browne, and it was probably in connexion with this sale that North agreed to forbear payment by the King till later. Grants in recognition of his services helped to consolidate North's gradually increasing properties.[6]

His work as clerk of the Parliaments brought North into close contact with Cromwell, for whom he was making confidential reports by 1535. This relationship was probably decisive in North's appointment to the court of augmentations in 1540. It was to be over three years before North was required to render an account as treasurer of that department: although this showed a balance due from him of almost £25,000, after his elevation to the joint chancellorship he paid over little more than £22,000 to his successor. When the King was informed of this discrepancy, he summoned North from his bed in the Charterhouse early one morning to defend his conduct; this North was able to do although at the price of an arrangement settling the matter by an exchange of lands favourable to the King. Although North had used his position to line his pocket and continued to do so throughout his connexion with the court, his financial reputation was unimpaired and he was frequently commissioned to audit accounts under Henry VIII, Edward VI and Mary. Secure in Henry VIII's esteem, North was confirmed in his office as chancellor on the eve of the King's death, was appointed an executor of his will, and was bequeathed £300.[7]

The beginning of the new reign saw North made a Privy Councillor and reappointed to the chancellorship, but he was soon to be antagonized by the Protector Somerset who in August 1548 connived at his being eased out of his office in favour of Richard Sackville II*. This act was to cost the Protector dear, for in the *coup d'état* against him a year later North was one of the first to join the dissident Councillors in London and to sign the letter listing the Protector's offences.[8]

North had been returned as one of the knights of the shire for Cambridgeshire to the Parliament of 1542, at the opening of which he was probably knighted along with a number of other royal officials; he may have sat in the Parliament of 1545, for which the return does not survive, and he did so in that of 1547. His name appears in the Act of 1543 (34 and 35 Hen. VIII, c.24) settling the payment of Cambridgeshire knights of the shire. Nothing further is known of his activities in the House until the second session of the Parliament of 1547, when on 12 Feb. 1549 he was one of those appointed to hear and determine, if they could, the bill against Nicholas Hare*. During the third session, the Acts for a general pardon, for a churchyard in West Drayton, for the restitution of William Hussey II*, and for the fine and ransom of the Duke of Somerset, were signed by North among others, and in the fourth, the original bill fixing the time for the sale of wool was committed to him and Sir Martin Bowes after its third reading on 18 Mar. 1552.[9]

As a partisan of the Duke of Northumberland North was recommended by the Privy Council to the sheriff and freeholders of Cambridgeshire for election to the Parliament of March 1553, and he was duly returned with the Council's other nominee, James Dyer. North witnessed the device to alter the succession, Edward VI's will, and the letter of 9 July 1553 in support of Queen Jane. There may, however, have been a measure of disagreement between North and Northumberland as the Charterhouse, which North had held since 1545 and which was apparently still his at the beginning of 1553, escheated to the crown on the duke's attainder later that year.[10]

As soon as it became clear that there was no support for Queen Jane, North joined the exodus from London of Privy Councillors to submit to Mary, who was a little distrustful of a man who had been so sympathetic towards Northumberland. His appointment as a Privy Councillor was not renewed, although he was raised to the baronage, the Charterhouse was restored to him, and he continued to serve on important commissions, including the one for heresy in 1557 and those connected with monetary reform. In 1554 he was one of the escort for Philip of Spain from Southampton to Winchester for his marriage in July, and he bore the sword before Philip at the reception of Cardinal Pole at Westminster in November. Foxe records the story, without giving it credence, of a woman living near Aldersgate in 1555 who claimed to have been approached by North to surrender her recently delivered baby to him at the time when the termination of the Queen's (false) pregnancy was expected.[11]

Immediately after Elizabeth's accession, she visited North at the Charterhouse between 23 and 29 Nov. 1558. This stay did not betoken the new Queen's confidence in him nor did it lead to North's taking a more important role in the country's affairs. Pardoned for general offences, he was employed to hear claims to do service at the coronation and to discover the extent of alienation of crown lands during the previous reigns. His opposition to several government-backed measures, including the Act of Uniformity, in the Parliament of 1559 must have destroyed any chance that he had of appointment. Elizabeth paid a second visit to the Charterhouse between 10 and 13 July 1561. Later in 1564 the bishop of Ely reported that in religion North was 'quite comfortable'.[12]

North made his will on 20 Mar. 1563 asking to be buried at Kirtling beside the body of his first wife. He left his second wife Margaret jewels, £500 and leases in Chertsey, London and Southwark, and provided for his children and grandchildren. His executors were to be (Sir) William Cordell* and Sir James Dyer and his supervisors the 4th Duke of Norfolk, Sir Robert Dudley*, Earl of Leicester, and (Sir) William Petre*. A third of his property in Cambridge and Huntingdonshire, Middlesex and Suffolk he bequeathed to the Queen; of the remainder nearly all was left to his son Sir Roger. By a codicil of 30 Dec. 1564 he ordered the Charterhouse to be sold to pay for his funeral expenses and Roger's debts. He died the following day at the Charterhouse and was buried at Kirtling early in the new year.[13]

[1] Aged 47 'or thereabouts' in 1551, Foxe, *Acts and Mons.* vi. 157-8; A. Collins, *Peerage*, iv. 454; Leland, *Coll.* ed. Hearne, v. 154-5; *DNB*; *CP*. [2] D. North, *Edward Lord North* (1658), 7; *LP Hen. VIII*, v, viii, x, xiii, xvi, xvii, xx; *CPR*, 1547-8, pp. 97, 297; 1553, pp. 351, 354, 361; 1553-4, p. 28; 1560-3, pp. 439, 442; 1563-6, pp. 29, 41, 274; W. C. Richardson, *Ct. Augmentations*, 330; E101/424/12, pt. i. f. 49; *LJ*, i. 514, 542, 581. [3] PCC 23 Bennett; Leland, v. 154-5. [4] *LP Hen. VIII*, iv; List of mercers, (T/S Mercers' Hall), 355. [5] Lansd. 858, ff. 25v-30; *LP Hen. VIII*, v-vii, ix, xi, xiv; *EHR*, lvii. 31-58, 202-26, 312-33; lxxiii. 78-85; C. G. Ericson, 'Parlt. as a legislative institution in the reigns of Edw. VI and Mary' (London Univ. Ph.D. thesis, 1974), 154 seq.; Elton, *Reform and Renewal*, 102 n. 14. [6] *LP Hen. VIII*, x, xi; Pevsner, *Cambs.* 339. [7] *LP Hen. VIII*, v, ix, xi, xix-xxi; *CPR*, 1553-4, pp. 176, 265, 302; 1554-5, p. 343; 1558-60, p. 66; 1560-3, p. 237; Richardson, 331; North, 10; Strype, *Eccles. Memorials*, ii(2), 19; *DKR*, x. 243. [8] NRA 0837, p. 2; *CPR*, 1547-8, pp. 184, 200; *Lit. Rems. Edw. VI*, 233, 237; W. K. Jordan, *Edw. VI*, i. 507. [9] House of Lords RO, Original Acts, 3 and 4 Edw. VI, nos. 24-25, 30-31; *CJ*, i. 8, 20. [10] Strype, ii(2), 65; *Chron. Q. Jane and Q. Mary* (Cam. Soc. xlviii), 72; *Machyn's Diary* (Cam. Soc. xlii), 30; Foxe, vii, 285-6, 288-9, 386; *CPR*, 1554-5, p. 207. [11] *CPR*, 1555-7, p. 282; Foxe, vii. 126; Strype, iii(1), 323. [12] *Wriothesley's Chron.* ii (Cam. Soc. n.s. xx), 142; Strype, *Annals* i (1), 19, 87, 93, 403; i(2), 391; *CPR*, 1558-60, pp. 71. 189; 1560-3, p. 237; *LJ*, i. 514, 542, 581; *Cam. Misc.* ix(3), 24. [13] PCC 7 Morrison; *Cat. Arundel Mss, Coll. of Arms*, 63; Pevsner, 338-9; C142/141/32.

A.D.K.H.

NORTH, John (by 1495-1558), of York.

YORK 1545, 1553 (Oct.)

b. by 1495, s. of Richard North of York. *m.* Agnes, da. of John Roger of York, at least 1s.[1]

Bridgemaster, Ouse bridge, York c.1523-4, junior chamberlain 1527-8, sheriff 1529-30, member of the Twenty-Four 1530/31, keeper, guild of SS Christopher and George by 1533, alderman 1534-*d.*, mayor 1538-9, 1554-5.[2]

John North came of a family of York craftsmen who were rising in status; his grandfather, a tilemaker and yeoman, was city chamberlain in 1497-8, and his father Richard, a tanner, was sheriff in 1513-14. Although North was to surpass them both, he continued to live in his father's unfashionable parish of St. Margaret's, Walmgate. Admitted to the freedom during 1515-16 as a tanner, he may have taken over his father's business, but he also dealt in corn and lime; in 1535 he was one of three York aldermen accused of raising the price of grain in the city by buying large quantities in Holderness and Lincolnshire. His material progress is reflected in his tax assessment: in 1524 this was 40 marks in goods, but by 1546-7 it had reached £100, and on this showing he was one of the four richest laymen in York. His wealth may not all have come from trade, for he married the daughter of one of the three richest citizens of the previous generation.[3]

As he moved up the civic ladder North also rose to prominence in the popular city guild of SS. Christopher and George. In 1533 he accompanied the mayor and other aldermen to London, where a dispute involving the guild had come before the Star Chamber. The affair seems to have rankled in York, and in 1536 North and John Hogeson*, who sided with him, were attacked in slanderous bills which evidently attracted wide sympathy; yet when in 1538 Mayor John Shaw died nine days after being installed it was North who was elected over an old guild adversary, Ralph Simson. The mayoralty was chiefly memorable for an outbreak of plague, probably the worst in York for 30 years. North and his colleagues levied a rate to help the infected, the earliest such levy known in England. By contrast, during the next serious plague in 1550 he was one of the aldermen who fled the city.[4]

North's Catholicism must have made the two Parliaments which he attended more congenial to him than he would have found either of the intervening ones; it was, indeed, one of the great reformist measures of the first Edwardian Parliament, the Chantries Act (1 Edw. VI, c.14), which brought him south again in 1549 on a deputation from York seeking to protect guild property from confiscation. As Members for York he and Robert Hall II seem to have been chiefly concerned with the promotion of the city's economic welfare, but in the first of Mary's Parliaments they showed their interest in the Catholic restoration by reporting to the council the Acts repealing attainders and treasons: they themselves were not among the Members noted as having 'stood for the true religion' against this legislation. When in 1554-5 North was again mayor, he and his brethren showed their loyalty to Queen and Church by offering prompt military aid at the time of Wyatt's rebellion, restoring the apocryphal plays about the Virgin to the city's Corpus Christi cycle and reviving three annual religious processions.[5]

North made his will on 28 July 1558, when York seems to have been suffering its worst epidemic of the century. He bequeathed his soul in the traditional way and asked for burial in St. Mary's choir (presumably in St. Margaret's church) 'where I sit most usually'. He left much property, mostly to his wife, son and granddaughters: in the city he had 19 houses, nine closes, two gardens, two orchards, a bowling alley and a dovecote, and outside it lands in Fulford and a lease of tithes in Skirpenbeck. (His religious sympathies had not stopped him from buying cheaply in 1549 the redundant York church of St. Peter-in-the-Willows.) North's charitable bequests included 6d. to every house in his parish. He named his son Richard executor and residuary legatee and his fellow-aldermen William Holme* and Richard Goldthorpe† supervisors. The will was proved on 23 Aug. 1558.[6]

[1] Date of birth estimated from admission as freeman. *Yorks. St. Ch. Procs.* ii. (Yorks. Arch. Soc. rec. ser. xlv), 32; *Reg. Corpus Christi Guild, York* (Surtees Soc. lvii), 300n; York wills 15(2), f. 289. [2] *Yorks. St. Ch. Procs.* ii. 32; York archs. B11-22 passim. [3] *Reg. Corpus Christi Guild, York*, 110n, 138n, 300n; *Yorks. St. Ch. Procs.* ii. 32; *Reg. Freemen, York*, i (Surtees Soc. xcvi), 237; York archs. B13, f. 29; *LP Hen. VIII*, ix; York Merchant Adventurers' archs. D82; *Yorks. Arch. Jnl.* iv. 182; *VCH York*, 132; E179/217/110, 111; York wills 11, f. 1. [4] *Yorks. St. Ch. Procs.* ii. 32; *York Civic Recs.* iii (Yorks. Arch. Soc. rec. ser. cvi), 163; iv (ibid. cviii), 10, 11, 27-38; v (ibid. cx), 43; York archs. B13, f. 127; D. M. Palliser, 'York in the 16th cent.' (Oxf. Univ. D.Phil. thesis, 1968), 120. [5] *York Civic Recs.* iv. 58-61, 63, 123, 133, 148-9; v. 4, 6-9, 92-96, 99-112; *VCH York*, 147. [6] York wills 15(2), f. 289.

D.M.P.

NORTH, Roger (1531-1600), of Kirtling, Cambs. and Mildenhall, Suff.

CAMBRIDGESHIRE 1555, 1559, 1563*

b. 27 Feb. 1531, 1st s. of Edward North*, 1st Lord North, by 1st w. Alice, da. of Oliver Squire of Southby, Hants. *educ.* ?Peterhouse, Camb. *m.* c.1547, Winifred, da. of Richard Rich, 1st Baron Rich, wid. of Sir Henry Dudley, 3s. inc. Henry† and John† 1 da. KB 15 Jan. 1559; *suc.* fa. as 2nd Lord North 31 Dec. 1564. Kt. banneret 1586.[1]

Member of Queen's chamber 1558; j.p. Cambs. 1558/59-d., Suff. and I. o. Ely 1579-d., Mdx. 1591; alderman, Cambridge 1568, high steward 1572; ambassador to Vienna 1568, France 1574; ld. lt. Cambs. 1569; commr. musters 1569; trier of petitions in the Lords, Parlts. of 1571, 1572, 1584, 1597; steward, duchy of Lancaster, Cambs., Norf. and Suff. 1572; custos rot. Cambs 1573/74-?d.; gov. Flushing June 1586, Utrecht and Harlingen July 1586; PC and treasurer of the Household Aug. 1596.[2]

Roger North was born in the same year that his father became clerk of the Parliaments. Little information survives about his boyhood and youth. He may have been a student of Peterhouse like his brother Thomas, the translator of Plutarch, but his admission to Gray's Inn in 1561 was probably honorary. The generally accepted date for his marriage is an error arising out of a confusion between two Henry Dudleys, both sons of the Duke of Northumberland. One died in 1544, the other in 1557; all North's children were born by 1556. Young North excelled at tilting, and at one tournament Princess Elizabeth rewarded him with a scarf of red silk, a token which figures proudly in a fine contemporary portrait. He became a member of

Elizabeth's Household upon her accession and was created knight of the Bath at her coronation.[3]

Doubtless his father's prestige and influence procured North's first election to Parliament in 1555 at the age of 24, when he was returned as senior knight of the shire for the county of Cambridge. Despite his father's standing at court, North voted against a government bill and his absence from the next Parliament may be attributable to this opposition. His Protestantism later took a Puritan form. In later life he was to remain an active magistrate in Cambridgeshire, and to become high steward of the borough, while winning national fame at court and on the battlefield. He died on 3 Dec. 1600.[4]

[1] Date of birth recorded by father, *EHR*, xxxvii. 566. *DNB*; *CP*, ix. 652-3, 726n. [2] Lansd. 3, f. 193; *CSP For.* 1572-4, pp. 560-2; *CSP Ven.* 1558-80, pp. 520-1; *LJ*, i. 667, 703; ii. 62, 191; Somerville, *Duchy*, i. 595; *CPR*, 1560-3, p. 435; 1563-6, pp. 20, 123; SP12/59, f. 190v; *Al. Cant.* i(3), 266; *Cambridge Chs.* ed. Maitland and Bateson, 103. [3] *Biog. Reg. Peterhouse*, i. 228; *LP Hen. VIII*, xx; *EHR*, xxxvii. 565-6; F. Bushby, *Three Men of the Tudor Time*, 45n. [4] Guildford mus. Loseley 1331/2; *Cam. Misc.* ix(3), 24.

T.M.H.

NORTHEY, Henry (by 1521–69), of Lambeth, Surr.

THETFORD 1553 (Mar.)

b. by 1521. *m.* lic. 18 June 1548, Elizabeth Payne, wid., 1s. 1da.[1]

Sec. to Robert Radcliffe, 1st Earl of Sussex, by 1542; steward, household of Henry Radcliffe, 2nd Earl of Sussex, by 1555.[2]

In view of his service to the earls of Sussex, who were great landowners in Essex, Henry Northey almost certainly came of one of the families of the name to be found in that shire, around Braintree and in Colchester. Nothing has been discovered of his education and he first appears as the 1st Earl of Sussex's secretary in the earl's will of 17 Oct. 1542 under which he was left, subject to certain charges, two Lancashire manors for 50 years and one of the earl's gowns. He remained in the service of the 2nd Earl, of whose will of 27 July 1555 he was an executor, and it was evidently to his master, then the leading magnate in East Anglia, that he owed his return for Thetford to the Parliament of March 1553 in which the earl's son Sir Thomas Radcliffe sat as knight of the shire for Norfolk.[3]

Having served the Radcliffes for two generations Northey may well have continued in the household of the 3rd Earl, his former parliamentary colleague, but all that has come to light of his later years is that by 1565 he had settled at Lambeth. By his will of 27 July 1569 he asked to be buried in Lambeth church 'in the aisle wherein I commonly sit' and left his house there to his wife for life with remainder to his son George. He also bequeathed George £160 out of the £280 due to him under the will of the 2nd

Earl of Sussex, dividing the remaining £120 equally between his wife and his daughter Anne. He named his wife executrix and two London vintners, Andrew and Francis Morgan, overseers. The will was proved on 29 Oct. 1569.[4]

[1] Date of birth estimated from first reference. *Mar. Lic. Fac. Off.* (Harl. Soc. xxiv), 13; PCC 21 Sheffelde. [2] PCC 1 Alen, 33 Wrastley. [3] Morant, *Essex*, i. 187; ii. 157; *The Gen.* iii. 172-3; *Vis. London* (Harl. Soc. xvii), 127; *VCH Essex*, ii. 502; *London Rec. Soc.* viii. 33 [4] *Lambeth Churchwardens' Accts.* (Surr. Rec. Soc. xl), 87, 89, 92; PCC 21 Sheffelde.

R.V.

NORTON, John (?1497–1561), of East Tisted, Hants.

HAMPSHIRE 1554 (Nov.),[1] 1555

b. ?1497, 1st s. of Richard Norton of East Tisted by Elizabeth, da. of William Rotherfield *alias* Lyndhurst of Rotherfield. *educ.* prob. L. Inn, adm. 12 Feb. 1516. *m.* by 1530, Anne, da. of George Puttenham of Sherfield, 7 or 8s. inc. Richard† 6da. *suc.* fa. 17 Feb. 1537.[2]

Recorder, Winchester by 1538–48; j.p. Hants 1538–47, q. 1554, western circuit 1540; commr. relief, Hants 1550, proclamations 1551, goods of churches and fraternities 1553, piracy 1556; sheriff 1556–7.[3]

John Norton, whose family was long established in Hampshire and also owned property in Essex, Surrey and Sussex, had many namesakes especially in Kent and Yorkshire, some of them better known than himself: one was involved in the administration of the Hampshire estates of Viscount Lisle. The nature of Norton's appointment presupposes a legal training, and he is probably to be identified with the member of Lincoln's Inn who had a chamber there in 1518 and was fined 40d. for a misdemeanour in the following year, rather than with the man admitted to the Inner Temple in 1519. After marrying within the county and succeeding his father, he took his place in local administration and on circuit and was for ten years recorder of Winchester. He was among those appointed for military service in the Netherlands in 1543 and was in the vanguard of the army which captured Boulogne. In 1545 he mustered and marched 600 men to Portsmouth when a French raid on the Isle of Wight was mistaken for the start of an invasion.[4]

Norton's father, to judge from his will, had been a man of exceptional piety, and the son was to cling to Catholicism. How early he became a follower of Stephen Gardiner is not known; East Tisted lies midway between Winchester and Farnham, and Norton probably saw Gardiner regularly and perhaps entertained him when he visited the diocese. In 1539 Sheriff Kingsmill noted his support of the bishop in the electoral contest of that year, and he may himself have entered the Commons before the death of Henry VIII: as a nominee of Gardiner's he could have been returned for one of the episcopal boroughs (Downton, Hindon and Taunton) to any or all of the last three Parliaments of the reign, for which the names in question are lost. When Gardiner was brought to trial in January 1551 Norton was one of those who testified for him. Although not removed from the bench under Edward VI, he was passed over in 1552 for the shrievalty, as he had been several times before. The quarrel which had earlier brought Norton into the Star Chamber against his fellow-justice George Rithe (q.v.) may not have been unconnected with religion.[5]

With Mary on the throne and Gardiner made chancellor, Norton could aspire to the knighthood of the shire. The senior place became the preserve of his neighbour Sir Thomas White, but Norton was twice returned as White's fellow-Member: he was helped by the absence of Sir John Mason as ambassador at Brussels, for Mason both preceded and followed him in the seat. The Journal does not mention him. In 1556 he achieved the shrievalty which had so long eluded him, but this was to be the climax of his career for in 1558-9 Elizabeth removed him from the Hampshire bench.[6]

Norton was well connected, especially within the circle of Gardiner's followers. Oliver Vachell, who sat for two of the bishop's boroughs, was his brother-in-law, and it was as Sir Richard Cotton's* 'well beloved' friend that in 1556 he was entrusted with the residue of Cotton's goods. Norton made his own will on 4 Jan. 1559, providing for his wife, children and grandchildren, but overlooking an alienation for which his widow had to secure a pardon in 1561. He appointed as executors his wife, his son Thomas and his sons-in-law Charles Bekinsau and William Knight, and the will was witnessed by another son, John, and by Henry Knight and Henry White*. Norton died on 5 July 1561, leaving the 31 year-old Richard Norton as his heir. He was buried in East Tisted church.[7]

[1] Huntington Lib. Hastings mss Parl. pprs. [2] Date of birth estimated from age at fa.'s i.p.m., C142/58/118, and at Gardiner's trial, Foxe, *Acts and Mons.* vi. 226-7. *Vis. Hants* (Harl. Soc. lxiv), 14; *VCH Hants*, iii. 31; PCC 4 Crumwell, 9 Streat. [3] *Black Bk. of Winchester*, ed. Bird, 161, 196; *LP Hen. VIII*, xiii, xv; *CPR*, 1547-8, p. 84; 1550-3, p. 142; 1553, pp. 353, 361; 1553-4, p. 19; NRA 10665; *APC*, v. 335. [4] *LP Hen. VIII*, vi, xviii, xx; *CPR*, 1550-3, p. 179; *Black Bk. L. Inn*, i. 185; *Cal. I.T. Recs.* i. 45. [5] PCC 4 Crumwell; *LP Hen. VIII*, xiv; Foxe, vi. 130; St.Ch.3/1/76; 4/89. [6] *PRO Lists*, ix. 56 mistakenly gives Norton as pricked sheriff in 1552. He was one of those nominated in that year, but he was passed over in favour of William Keilway, *CPR*, 1553, p. 387. [7] PCC 23 Ketchyn, 9 Streat; C142/131/184; *CPR*, 1560-3, p. 400; *VCH Hants*, iii. 31; Pevsner, *Hants*, 203.

A.D.K.H.

NORTON, Sir John (by 1512-57), of Northwood in Milton, Kent.

ROCHESTER 1553 (Mar.)

b. by 1512, o. s. of Sir John Norton of Faversham by 1st w. Jane, da. and coh. of John Northwood of Northwood. *m.* by 1533, Alice, da. and h. of Edward Cobbe of 'Cobbesplace', 1s. *suc.* fa. 8 Feb. 1534. Kntd. 22 Feb. 1547.[1]

V.-adm. Kent 1550; commr. relief 1550, goods of churches and fraternities 1553; other commissions 1541-*d.*; j.p. 1554.[2]

John Norton came of a long-established Kent family and succeeded to the lands both of his father and of his father-in-law in 1534: the elder Norton's first wife had also been an heiress and his second had been the widow of Sir Richard Fitzlewis*. Norton had many namesakes including one of East Tisted, Hampshire, who was with him on the French campaign of 1544 and who later sat for Hampshire in two Marian Parliaments, and another of Upchurch, Kent, who was active in shire administration.[3]

Norton evidently adopted his father's profession of soldiering; in the month after his knighthood he sued for the captaincy of Cap-Gris-Nez and at the same time his 'friend' William, 13th Lord Grey of Wilton, whose acquaintance he may have made in 1544 and who was governor of Boulogne, tried to obtain for him the office of marshal there. Apparently unsuccessful in both these suits, in September 1549 Norton replaced Sir Henry Palmer* at the castle of the Oldman, Boulogne. Earlier in 1549 he had raised a force of 300 soldiers and conducted 200 foot to Boulogne. In July 1550, however, when he received a reward of £400 from the crown he was said to have been 'maimed' on service and seven months later he was excused from going to Ireland because of sickness, although he was well enough to accompany the 9th Lord Clinton on an embassy to France in the winter of 1551. He probably owed his return for Rochester to the Parliament of March 1553 to the influence of Sir Thomas Cheyne*, whom he was to name overseer of his will, and perhaps also of his friend Lord Grey who was in favour with the Duke of Northumberland. If, like Cheyne and Grey, Norton supported the duke in the effort to alter the succession to the throne in the summer of 1553 he evidently made his peace with Mary and in 1554 he was for the first time appointed to the Kent bench. It may, however, have been another namesake of Norton Conyers, Yorkshire, who in the same year was described as the Queen's servant when he received a licence to export beer.[4]

By his will of 6 July 1557 Norton bequeathed £5 to the poor of Calais and 40s. to each of the six parishes of the hundred of Milton. He left his wife all his household stuff in England, Calais and Guisnes and 'the curtilage of Milton' and the rest of his lands and goods to his only son Thomas, then aged 23, naming him executor with a cousin Richard Norton. Norton died on 9 July 1557 and the will was proved on 20 Nov. 1558. His widow married John Brooke *alias* Cobham†.[5]

[1] Date of birth estimated from marriage. *Vis. Kent* (Harl. Soc. xlii), 79–80; *DNB*. [2] *HCA*25/1; *CPR*, 1553, pp. 355, 414; 1553–4, pp. 20, 28; *LP Hen. VIII*, xvi. [3] *Arch. Cant.* xli. 107–8; *LP Hen. VIII*, vii, xiii, xiv, xvi, xix. [4] *CSP For.* 1547–53, pp. 322–3, 354; *APC*, ii. 305, 314; iii. 89, 212; Strype, *Eccles. Memorials*, ii(1), 507; *CPR*, 1553–4, p. 330. [5] Canterbury prob. reg. A31, f. 163v; E150/506/4.

P.H.

NORTON, Thomas (by 1532–84), of London.

GATTON	1558
BERWICK-UPON-TWEED	1563
LONDON	1571, 1572

b. by 1532, 1st s. of Thomas Norton of London by Elizabeth, da. of Robert Mery of Northaw, Herts. *educ.* Michaelhouse, Camb., matric 1544 and 1545, MA 1570; I. Temple, adm. Nov. 1555. *m.* (1) by 1561, Margaret, da. of Thomas Cranmer, abp. of Canterbury, *s.p.*; (2) by 1568, Alice, da. of Edmund Cranmer, 4s. 2da. *suc.* fa. 10 Mar. 1583.[1]

Counsel to Stationers' Co. 1562; remembrancer, London 6 Feb. 1571–*d.*, ?garbler of spices 10 Mar. 1583–*d.*; commr. to examine Catholic prisoners 1574, 1578–83, for Guernsey 1579, for Sark 1583; solicitor to Merchant Taylors' Co. 1581; censor for bp. of London by 1581.[2]

Thomas Norton's father, who came of a yeoman family at Sharpenhoe in Bedfordshire, made his career as a grocer in London. On 24 Oct. 1542 the City made him its garbler of spices for life, but when four years later he asked for the office to be assured to him and his heirs for 40 years the common council turned down the request. In the first session of the Parliament of 1547 he exhibited a bill to this effect which received two readings in the Commons before he withdrew it at the request of the aldermen. After agreeing to abide by the decision of the committee chosen to reconsider the matter he enlisted the aid of the Protector Somerset, but when the committee recommended an extension for one year after Norton's death a further letter from Somerset in 1549 failed to obtain more than this nominal concession. This favour shown to the elder Norton by the Protector was perhaps linked with the younger Norton's joining Somerset's household as a tutor, although no reference has been found to his employment there before 1550. In that year Norton published his translation of the letter sent by Peter Martyr on Somerset's release from the Tower. After Somerset's death he assured Calvin that the duke's children were

> liberally educated and have no other attendants or governors but those to whom they were entrusted by their father in his lifetime. Philip Gilgate, a worthy gentleman, is their governor, and I retain my old office of instructing them.

A sonnet written while Norton was in Somerset's service was included by William Turner* in *A Preservative or triacle agaynst the poyson of Pelagius* in 1551 and his epitaph on Henry Williams* was printed in *The Songes and Sonnettes written by Henry Haward late Earle of Surrey and others* six years later.[3]

Norton seems to have remained tutor to the Seymour children until his admission to the Inner Temple. It was probably not he but his father whose action against a servant of (Sir) Edward Hastings* led to the issue of a writ of privilege by the Commons on 15 Nov. 1553. Norton's career at the Temple was marred by an affray in which he, Thomas Copley* and others took part at the Autumn reading in 1556. The offenders were committed to the Fleet but were pardoned after making humble submission. It was doubtless Copley who suggested Norton as his fellow-Member at Gatton, where his mother was the sole elector. Norton later won fame as a speaker in the Commons but it was Copley who focused attention upon himself in the Parliament of 1558. All that is known about Norton as one of its Members is that his name is among those marked with a circle on a copy of the Crown Office list: the significance of this annotation is unexplained. In 1558 he became a freeman of the Grocers' Company.[4]

In his Protestantism Norton inclined more to Calvin whose *Institutes* he translated than to Cranmer whose daughter and niece he married successively: his zeal for persecuting Catholics under Elizabeth earned him an unenviable reputation as 'rackmaster-general'. His fame today rests not on his faith nor his activity in the House, but on his writings, particularly his co-authorship with Thomas Sackville* of *The Tragedie of Gorboduc*. Norton died at Sharpenhoe on 10 Mar. 1584 and was buried at Streatley.[5]

[1] Date of birth estimated from age at fa.'s i.p.m., C142/203/12. *DNB*; *N. and Q.* (ser. 3), iv. 480; Harl. 1234, f. 113; 1547, f. 45v; *Her. and Gen.* iii. 276; *Vis. Herts.* (Harl. Soc. xxii), 80–81, 152; R. E. C. Waters, *Fams. Thomas Cranmer and Thomas Wood*, 22–23. [2] *Archaeologia*, xxxvi(1), 106, 115; Lansd. 33, f. 150; 48, f. 188 seq.; *APC*, viii. 319; xi. passim; xii. 62, 88–89, 264–5; xiii. 37, 144, 164–5; *CSP Dom.* 1581–90, p. 48. [3] Beds. RO, A BP/R 15, f. 52 ex inf. Miss Joyce Godber; City of London RO, Guildhall, rep. 10, f. 286; 11, ff. 385, 396, 397, 422v, 454v, 456(2), 478v, 479v; 12(1), f. 103v; jnl. 15, f. 269; M. L. Bush, *Govt. Pol. Somerset*, 110–11; *Zurich Letters* (Parker Soc.), iii. 339. [4] *CJ*, i. 30; *Cal. I.T. Recs.* i. 187; *Her. and Gen.* iii. 276 seq.; Wm. Salt Lib. SMS 264. [5] F. P. Wilson, *Eng. Drama 1485–1585*, pp. 132–7; C142/203/38; *VCH Beds.* ii. 382–3.

S.R.J.

NOSEWORTHY, John (by 1481–1530/32), of Ashburton and Exeter, Devon.

EXETER	1523[1]

b. by 1481, ?poss. s. of John Noseworthy of Ashburton.[2]

Churchwarden, Ashburton 1502–4; bailiff, Exeter

1502–3, member of the Twenty-Four by 1508, receiver 1516–17, mayor 1521–2; commr. subsidy 1523, 1524.[3]

John Noseworthy came of a family traceable in the locality of Widecombe since the 13th century but his parentage has not been established. Either he or a namesake (possibly his father) collected money for wax for candles in Ashburton church during 1496–7. He was to become churchwarden there after his admission as a freeman of Exeter in 1501–2 but before he settled in Holy Trinity parish, Exeter: on several occasions he was to represent Ashburton's interests in the city's courts.[4]

Noseworthy soon established himself as one of the chief spokesmen for his adopted city and frequently travelled to the capital on its business, but it was not until April 1516 that in succession to John Orenge* he became one of the city's fee'd counsellors. Long before then, however, he seems to have given up his private practice as a lawyer to devote himself to public affairs. His integrity and fairness combined with his charm and generosity made him 'honoured of the best, reverenced by the inferior and beloved by all'. During his mayoralty he reformed much of the administration of the city and it was he who ordered adequate storage for its records, thus earning him the gratitude of the antiquary John Hooker† who rated him among the best of Exeter's mayors. Before his many virtues were manifest he had stood for election to the Parliament of 1512 but gained only two votes at the poll. When 11 years later he stood again he was a proven man and as an ex-mayor he took precedence over his less experienced, but nevertheless outspoken, fellow-Member John Bridgeman. The pair received £8 before the opening and a further £10 before the second session, £2 being earmarked for civic business, presumably connected with the confirmation of a charter which they took with them. This was to be the high point of his career. Within three years his fee as a counsellor had ceased and he had largely withdrawn from Exeter affairs. Of his closing years all that is known is that he made donations regularly to the church at Ashburton until 1530–1. The will by which he left his 'private concerns' in Exeter for the advancement of the city was proved in the Guildhall there during 1531–2.[5]

[1] Exeter act bk. 1, f. 100. [2] Date of birth estimated from admission as freeman. [3] *Ashburton Churchwardens' Accts.* (Devon and Cornw. Rec. Soc. n.s. xv), 30, 31; R. Izacke, *Exeter* (1681), 104, 108, 111; Exeter act bk. 1, f. 1; *LP Hen. VIII*, iii, iv. [4] Exeter, Hooker's commonplace bk. f. 338; *Ashburton Churchwardens' Accts.* 23, 31; *Exeter Freemen* (Devon and Cornw. Rec. Soc. extra ser. i), 63. [5] Exeter act bk. 1, ff. 1–101v passim; receivers' accts. 1515–16 to 1525–6 passim; Hooker's commonplace bk. f. 338; *Tudor Exeter* (Devon and Cornw. Rec. Soc. n.s. xxii), 24, 44; J. Hoker, *The description of the citie of Excester* (Devon and Cornw. Rec. Soc. xi), passim; *Ashburton Churchwardens' Accts.* 52, 75, 80, 86; Izacke, 116.

M.B.

NOWELL, Alexander (1516/17–1602), of Westminster, Mdx. and London.

WEST LOOE 1553 (Oct.)*

b. 1516/17, 1st s. of John Nowell of Read, Lancs. by 2nd w. Elizabeth, da. of Robert Kay of Rochdale. *educ.* Middleton g.s. Lancs.; Brasenose, Oxf. matric. 1536, BA 29 May 1536, fellow 1536–8, determined 1537, MA 10 June 1540, D.Th. supp. 10 June 1578, cr. 1 Oct. 1595. *m.* (1) Jane (*d.*3 Aug. 1579), da. of Robert Mery of Northaw, Herts., wid. of Thomas Bowyer (*d.*13 Sept. 1558) of London, *s.p.*; (2) Elizabeth, da. of one Hast of Wyndham, Suss., wid. of Lawrence Ball and of Thomas Blount of London, *s.p.*[1]

Master, Westminster sch. 1543–55; canon and prebendary, Westminster 5 Dec. 1551–4, 21 June 1560–4, Canterbury 14 Feb. 1560–4, London 3 Dec. 1560–*d.*, Windsor 25 Apr. 1594–*d.*; archdeacon, Westminster Jan. 1560; rector, Saltwood, Kent 3 Feb. 1560, Much Hadham, Herts. Dec. 1562–89; commr. to visit dioceses of Lichfield, Lincoln, Oxford and Peterborough 1559, Canterbury and Rochester 1560; other commissions 1563–83; dean, St. Paul's 17 Nov. 1560–*d.*; eccles. commr. 1562, 1572; j.p.q. Herts. 1564–79; fellow, Manchester Coll. Lancs. by 1578; principal, Brasenose, Oxf. 6 Sept.–14 Dec. 1595.[2]

In old age Alexander Nowell recalled that he was 13 years old on going to Oxford and that he spent 13 years there before being made master of Westminster school. At Oxford he is said to have shared a chamber with John Foxe, the martyrologist, who thought him 'a man earnestly bent on the true worshipping of God'. At Westminster he instructed his pupils 'in pure language and true religion' and introduced the reading of Terence in Latin and St. Luke's gospel and the Acts of the Apostles in Greek. Appointed a canon and prebendary in the cathedral at Westminster in 1551, he received a licence to preach two years later but is not known to have done so before the death of Edward VI.[3]

Nowell had a hand in the by-election of his brother Robert to the Parliament of 1547. He himself was returned in September 1553 for the duchy of Cornwall borough of West Looe, presumably with the support of the 1st Earl of Bedford as steward of the duchy. His Membership was challenged and on 12 Oct. a six-man committee headed by Secretary Bourne was ordered to see whether he and John Foster II 'may be of this House'. On the following day the committee reported that 'Nowell being a prebendary in Westminster and thereby having a voice in the convocation house' could not sit in the Commons. This opinion being 'so agreed by the House', the Speaker asked for a writ 'to be directed for another burgess in that place', but with what result is not known.[4]

Following his exclusion from Parliament, Nowell lost his prebend but he kept his post at the school for another two years, whereupon possibly through fear of arrest he left for the Continent. By October 1556 he had settled at Frankfurt, living there until his return to England three years later. After being considered for the see of Coventry and Lichfield by Queen Elizabeth he was made dean of St. Paul's. Although rebuked several times by the Queen in the 1560s he became a leading exponent of the Anglican settlement. His numerous publications included three versions of the Anglican catechism, all in Latin. He withdrew from public affairs in 1588, made his will in 1592 and died in 1602. Nowell is remembered today not for his work as teacher and divine but for his passion for fishing; he appears in Izaak Walton's *Compleat Angler* as 'A dear lover, and constant practitioner of angling, as any age can produce'.[5]

[1] Date of birth estimated from Nowell's statement about age on entering Oxford. R. Churton, *Alexander Nowell*, app. 1; *Chetham Soc.* lxxxi. 36; A. B. Grosart, *The Spending of the Money of Robert Nowell*, pp. xxxviii–xliii; Emden, *Biog. Reg. Univ. Oxf. 1501–40*, pp. 419–21; *DNB*. [2] Churton, 9, 43, 50, 304; *CPR*, 1550–3, p. 111; 1553–4, p. 307; 1558–60 to 1569–72 passim; *CSP Dom.* 1581–90, p. 115. [3] Churton, 6, 9, 13–17; Foxe, *Acts and Mons.* vi. 272; J. F. Mosley, *John Foxe*, 16; Strype, *Eccles. Memorials*, ii (2), 277. [4] *CJ*, i. 27; Bodl. e Museo 17. [5] Churton, 20–38, 81–83, 103–4, 107, 109, 269–73, 280, 364; C. H. Garrett, *Marian Exiles*, 237; Strype, *Annals Ref.* i (1), 153; *Parker*, i. 193–4; A. G. Dickens, *Eng. Ref.* 293; P. Collinson, *Eliz. Puritan Movement*, 46, 61; *APC*, viii. 165; *CSP Dom.* 1547–80, pp. 382, 497; PCC 11 Montague.

A.D.K.H.

NOWELL, Andrew (by 1512–63), of Whitwell, Rutland and Old Dalby, Leics.

RUTLAND 1553 (Oct.)

b. by 1512, 3rd s. of James Nowell of Hilcote, Derbys. by da. of one Poole of Langley, Derbys. *m.* (1) Dorothy, da. of Reynold or Richard Conyers, wid. of Richard or Roger Flower of Whitwell, 1s.; (2) settlement Apr. 1551, Elizabeth, da. of John Hopton of Glos., wid. of Sir John Peryent (*d.*1551), 4s. 2da.[1] Feodary, Northants. and Rutland May 1533–*d.*, Leics. June 1534–*d.*, Lincs. Nov. 1535–*d.*; sheriff, Rutland 1536–7, 1550–1, 1556–7, Lincs. 1546–7; subsidy collector, Rutland 1543; commr. musters, Rutland 1546, contribution 1546, relief, Leics., Rutland 1550; j.p. Leics. 1558/59, Rutland 1561–*d.*[2]

A younger son of an unimportant gentleman, Andrew Nowell probably received some training in law, for the feodaryships which laid the foundation of his fortune called for legal knowledge. Under whose patronage he was appointed to them has not been discovered: since they were in the gift of the master of the wards it must have been either Sir William Paulet or Thomas Englefield, joint masters at the time, who were responsible or instrumental, but nothing has been found to link Nowell with them. Nowell was to derive from the offices more than their considerable financial rewards: he secured for his heir a wardship which led to an excellent match and to much of the family's future prosperity, and his own second wife was the widow of a former auditor of the wards.[3]

Nowell's acquisition of a landed estate began in 1544 with his purchase of Old Dalby manor from the crown; in 1546 he bought another ex-monastic manor, Stonesby, Leicestershire, from John Bellow* and Edward Bales, and in 1548 he completed the purchase of Brooke priory, Rutland, from Sir Anthony Cope. Within a few years he also acquired most of the non-monastic lands in Brooke, Dalby and Stonesby. These transactions gave him a stake in Leicestershire and may have enhanced his position in neighbouring Rutland, where he had also bought land. His return for that county to Mary's first Parliament cannot be explained, however, in terms of his landholding there, for despite its small size Rutland had men of far greater substance and much longer residence. In particular, Nowell's displacement of Anthony Colly, who with Kenelm Digby had represented the county in the three previous Parliaments and was to sit for it again in the next two, suggests that there were particular reasons for the change, although what these were can only be guessed at. Nowell's ward John Flower married a daughter of Colly's: if this marriage had taken place or been arranged by 1553 Colly could well have stepped down then in Nowell's favour. With his exceptional knowledge of land-ownership in the county Nowell may have appeared well qualified for a Parliament in which the future of church property might be raised, especially as his own estate was largely ex-monastic. In the event, Parliament was not yet called upon to face this issue, and in its restoration of Catholic doctrine Nowell was evidently ready to concur, his name being unmarked on the list which recorded those of his fellows who 'stood for the true religion'.[4]

Nowell died on 31 Jan. 1563, having made his will on 6 Dec. 1559. One of its executors was his brother-in-law Maurice Tyrrell*. He did not leave the customary third of his estates to John Nowell, his heir by his first marriage, and he instructed his cousin Robert Nowell† to explain the reasons for this to the Queen; the bulk of his property passed to his eldest son by his second wife, but although Robert Nowell, when he granted John Nowell a lease in 1563, exhorted him to come to an agreement with his stepmother, the will does not appear to have been formally disputed and it was proved on 4 Feb. 1563. John Nowell's share was the manor of Quadring, Lincolnshire, to which he was to add lands brought by his wife: their son was wealthy enough to purchase a viscountcy from James I.[5]

[1] Date of birth estimated from first reference. *Vis. Leics.* (Harl. Soc. ii), 3, 28, 114; *Vis. Rutland* (Harl. Soc. iii), 29; *CPR*, 1550–3, p. 85; PCC 6 Chayre. [2] *LP Hen. VIII*, vi, vii, ix, xxi; E179/281; *CPR*, 1553, pp. 356–7. [3] *LP Hen. VIII*, xiii, xviii, xix; H. E. Bell, *Ct. Wards and Liveries*, 10, 24, 38 seq.; *CPR*, 1547–8, p. 75; 1550–3, p. 101; 1555–7, pp. 288, 483; 1560–3, p. 84. [4] *LP Hen. VIII*, xix,

xxi; SC6/Edw. VI, 225; *CPR*, 1547–8, p. 338; CP40/33 Hen. VIII, m. 18v; C142/137/29. [5] C142/137/33; PCC 6 Chayre; Pevsner, *Leics. and Rutland*, 204.

S.M.T.

NOWELL, Robert (c.1520–69), of Gray's Inn, London, and Hendon, Mdx.

WESTMINSTER	1547[*1]
?SALTASH	1555
WESTMINSTER	1563

b. c.1520, 4th s. of John Nowell of Read, Lancs. by 2nd w. Elizabeth, da. of Robert Kay of Rochdale, Lancs.; bro. of Alexander*. *educ.* Middleton g.s. Lancs.; Brasenose, Oxf.; G. Inn, adm. 1544.[2] Autumn reader, G. Inn 1561.

Commr. eccles. causes, Canterbury, Chichester, Rochester and Winchester dioceses 1559, audit accts. Queen's household 1565; attorney, ct. wards 1561–*d.*; steward, dean and chapter of St. Paul's; j.p. Mdx. 1564–*d.*[3]

Robert Nowell replaced Sir George Blagge, who died in 1551, as Member for Westminster in the last session of the Parliament of 1547. He was then a young lawyer at Gray's Inn and presumably his election was the work of a contemporary there, Secretary Cecil, helped by his elder brother, Alexander Nowell, master of Westminster school: nothing is known about his role in this Parliament. If he was re-elected to its successor in March 1553, for which Cecil discussed the composition beforehand with the Duke of Northumberland, it was not for Westminster, but with Cecil's help then he could have been returned almost anywhere.[4]

The accession of Mary saw a downward turn in the fortunes of Nowell's family: the election of his brother Alexander of West Looe in the autumn of 1553 was declared invalid, and Alexander and another brother went into exile rather than acquiesce in the reunion with Rome. Although he shared his brothers' Protestantism, Robert Nowell remained in England and continued to practise as a lawyer: he is probably identifiable with the 'Mr. Nowell' employed in January 1555 as counsel by the Duchess of Suffolk for a private bill submitted to the Parliament of November 1554. The indenture for Saltash to the Parliament of 1555 is damaged and of the senior Member's name only the surname 'Nowell' and the style 'esquire' remain. Two considerations suggest that Robert Nowell was the Member concerned: the style signifies a legal training and only one other Nowell meets this qualification, a kinsman who entered Gray's Inn in 1549, when Cecil was acting as attorney for the 2nd Earl of Bedford, the most eminent landowner in the neighbourhood of the town, during the earl's absence abroad. Nowell may also have been able to rely on the support which two years before had

facilitated his brother Alexander's election for a nearby borough. 'Mr. Nowel' followed Sir Anthony Kingston's lead in voting against a government bill, and perhaps for this reason he did not secure a place in Mary's last Parliament. With the advent of Elizabeth, his family's circumstances improved and he obtained a lucrative post in the court of wards. Nowell sat in one further Parliament before his death on 6 Feb. 1569.[5]

[1] Hatfield 207. [2]. Date of birth estimated from that of his elder brother Alexander. A. B. Grosart, *The Spending of the Money of Robert Nowell*, pp. xxxi, xxxv–xxxvi. [3] *HMC 11th Rep. III*, 94; *CPR*, 1560–3, p. 6; Grosart, p. xxxvi. [4] Westminster abbey, reg. 5, f. 18v. [5] *DNB* (Nowell, Alexander); *CJ*, i. 27, 41; C219/24/32; Guildford mus. Loseley 1331/2; Grosart, pp. xxxvi–xxxvii.

H.M./A.D.K.H.

ONLEY, John (by 1498–1537), of London and Catesby, Northants.

CONSTITUENCY UNKNOWN 1536[1]

b. by 1498, s. of John Onley of Withington, Salop by Jane, da. of Thomas Pontesbury of Salop. *educ.* New Inn; I. Temple, adm. 25 Oct. 1514. *m.* (1) by 1519, Jane (*d.*Sept./Oct. 1529), da. of (?Henry) Smith of Sherborne, Warws., 4s. inc. Edward† and Thomas* 2da.; (2) by 1537, Elizabeth (*d.*3 Aug. 1556), wid. of William Whitlok (*d.*Aug. 1520), Thomas Lee (*d.*Aug. 1527), and Robert Wade (*d.*June 1529), all of London, *s.p.*[2]

Master of revels, I. Temple 1515, auditor 1527–8, attendant on reader 1529, 1532, 1536–7, Lent reader 1530.

Common serjeant, London 2 Apr. 1530–17 Mar. 1533, under sheriff 17 Mar. 1533–*d.*; commr. tenths of spiritualities 1535; solicitor, ct. augmentations 24 Apr. 1536–*d.*[3]

John Onley was probably born at Withington in Shropshire, where his parents were buried in 1512 and 1513, but his grandfather was the Sir Robert Olney (or Woneley) who had prospered as a wool merchant at Coventry, becoming mayor about 1480 and one of the town's Members in 1485. Although his first child was also born at Withington, it was his Warwickshire rather than his Shropshire affiliation which seems to have shaped Onley's upbringing and early career; he probably owed his early patronage by William Shelley* to Shelley's wife Alice Belknap, sister of Henry VII's fiscal henchman Edward Belknap, who was a Warwickshire man, and he was himself to marry Jane Smith of Sherborne (close to Warwick), the servant of hers to whom Alice Shelley was to give the manuscript known as the 'Belknap Hours'. If, as is likely, Onley had been under age when his father died, he could have been brought up in the Belknap household. He had older and younger namesakes, and perhaps kinsmen, at Pulborough, Sussex.[4]

At the Inner Temple, besides Shelley who had sponsored his entry, Onley was able to cultivate such promising senior members as Thomas Audley,

John Baker I* and John Baldwin*; the last was to stand godfather to one of Onley's younger children, Shelley having given his name to the first son. It was to Shelley and Baker, as successive under sheriffs and recorders of London, that Onley probably owed his appointments as common serjeant and then under sheriff, although the first of them presumably needed the assent of Richard Rich, who had been promised the next vacancy after he had failed to secure the office in 1526. The decision that Onley should be the first solicitor of the court of augmentations was no doubt Cromwell's, but both Audley, by then chancellor, in whose opinion he was 'a right honest discreet man', and Rich, the head of the new court, may have given their support; it was a signal mark of favour that, when the London court of aldermen called on him to resign as under sheriff, the King intervened to enable him to keep the office. Even during his brief time at the augmentations Onley seems to have made his mark there. Its business involved him in frequent travel, and although Lord Lisle's agent John Hussee, who judged him 'of small honesty', complained of his constant absences, Hussee conceded that nothing could be done without him. That he still found time for private practice appears from a chancery suit begun in Trinity term 1536 in which he wrongly advised Edward Elrington* and his wife.[5]

Onley's Membership of the Parliament of 1536 is to be inferred from the appearance of his name on the originals of two Acts which it passed, one withholding benefit of clergy from abjurors in certain cases, the other for continuing expiring laws: the names accompanying his own are those of lawyers all of whom are either known or can be presumed to have been Members at the time. The conclusion is strengthened by the passage in the same Parliament of an Act (28 Hen. VIII, c.28) assuring a moiety of the manor of Richard's Castle, Herefordshire; Onley had bought a moiety of this manor from the 2nd Lord Vaux in November 1535, but the conveyance was found to be defective and had to be replaced, and the Act secured Onley's title. (In March 1537 he used the moiety as part-payment for the dissolved nunnery at Catesby.) Onley was a natural choice for Membership of this Parliament: it was summoned three days after he was made solicitor of the augmentations, and the three other principal officers of the court, Rich, Thomas Pope and Robert Southwell, were all to sit in it, Rich himself becoming Speaker. For which borough Onley was elected is a matter for speculation. If, like Pope, he was nominated by Cromwell, he could have come in for any one of many and need not have had any personal connexion with the one chosen.[6]

Onley died in London on 22 Nov. 1537. Three weeks earlier he had chosen to pay a fine rather than read for a second time at his inn and he was a sick man when on 12 Nov. he made his will. He asked to be buried without pomp or pride in his parish church of St. John Zachary, London. As befitted one who had been assessed at £1,000 for the City's loan of the previous year to the King, he made ample monetary provision for his wife and children, of whom his two surviving sons Edward and Thomas were in their 'teens. Besides making charitable bequests to the prisons and friaries of London, Onley left Audley and Rich £6 13s.4d. each, and Pope and Southwell £3 6s.8d. apiece. He appointed his wife executrix and Baker and John Morris* overseers. Before the will was proved Elizabeth Onley fraudulently obtained from augmentations £5 in expenses previously claimed by her husband, but the truth came out.[7]

[1] House of Lords RO, Original Acts, 28 Hen. VIII, nos. 1, 9. [2] Date of birth estimated from marriage. *Vis. Northants.* ed. Metcalfe, 12, 38–39; *Vis. Salop* (Harl. Soc. xxix), 401, 403–4; *Cat. Lib. Maj. J. R. Abbey* (Sotheby and Co. 1 Dec. 1970), 30–31; C142/108/84; PCC 31 Ayloffe, 22 Porch, 8 Jankyn, 17 Dyngeley, 11 Ketchyn. [3] *Guildhall Misc.* ii. 386; *LP Hen. VIII*, viii, xiii. [4] Pevsner, *Salop*, 321; *Vis. Northants.* 12, 38–39; *Cat. Lib. Maj. J. R. Abbey*, 30–32; PCC 1 Fetiplace. [5] *LP Hen. VIII*, v, xi, xii; City of London RO, Guildhall, rep. 9, ff. 51, 100, 141v, 197, 206–7; *HMC 8th Rep.* pt. 2 (1881), 20–23; W. C. Richardson, *Ct. Augmentations*, 12, 42, 88, 92–93, 492; C1/783/10–12. [6] House of Lords RO, Original Acts, 28 Hen. VIII, nos. 1, 9; *LP Hen. VIII*, xii. [7] PCC 17 Dyngeley; C142/108/84; *LP Hen. VIII*, viii.

A.D.K.H.

ONLEY, Thomas (1523–89), of London.

BRACKLEY   1554 (Apr.), 1554 (Nov.), 1572

> *b.* 24 Nov. 1523, 4th but 2nd surv. s. of John Onley* of London and Catesby, Northants. by Jane, da. of (?Henry) Smith of Sherborne, Warws.; bro. of Edward†. *educ.* I. Temple, adm. Feb. 1550. *m.* by 15 Jan. 1559, Jane, da. and coh. of Thomas Rigges of Cumberworth, Lincs., wid. of Julian Morgan of Ilford, Essex, 1s. 3da.[1]

According to notes made by his father in the 'Belknap Hours', Thomas Onley's godfather was Thomas West, 8th Lord la Warr. Just over a dozen years later the dissolution of the monasteries was to arouse la Warr's hostility but to give John Onley employment, with what consequences to their relationship is not known. On the eve of his early death Onley left Thomas £300 on reaching 22 and entrusted the 'governance, order, rule and bringing up' of his two sons to his brother-in-law George Cotton of Combermere and nephew Richard Cotton* who was shortly to marry one of Onley's daughters. Onley seems to have meant Thomas to follow a career similar to his own, but although Thomas entered the Temple at the advanced age of 26 he is not known to have made any mark outside a small circle of friends and relatives. In 1553 he helped Richard Corbet* to buy a manor in York-shire and after the breakdown of the marriage of his cousin Mary Cotton to the 3rd Earl of Derby, Onley and his brother managed her affairs.[2]

Onley presumably owed his return at Brackley twice in 1554 to the Earl of Derby, assisted by his family's ties with Northamptonshire. His appear-ance for a second time that year as one of the borough's Members did not comply with the regime's preference for inhabitants, but it is likely that he met its religious criterion as he did not support his kinsman Sir Ralph Bagnall in refusing the papal absolution from Cardinal Pole. Onley sat for Brackley again under Elizabeth and died in 1589, being buried near his brother at Catesby in Northamptonshire.[3]

[1] Date of birth given in *Cat. Lib. Maj. J. R. Abbey* (Sotheby and Co., 1 Dec. 1970), 31; Belknap Hours (no. 2869 of preceding sale). Bridges, *Northants.* i. 35; *Vis. Northants.* ed. Metcalfe, 38–39, 121; St.Ch.4/1/13; *CPR*, 1558–60, p. 385. [2] PCC 17 Dyngeley; *CPR*, 1553, p. 60; 1558–60, p. 347; 1560–3, p. 333. [3] Northants. RO, Ellesmere mss box X 465.

S.M.T.

ONSLOW, Richard (1527/28–71), of the Inner Temple, London.

STEYNING	1558
ALDBOROUGH	1559
STEYNING	1563

b. 1527/28, 2nd s. of Roger Onslow of Shrewsbury, Salop by 1st w. Margaret, da. of Thomas Poyner of Salop. *educ.* I. Temple, adm. 1 July 1545. *m.* 7 Aug. 1559, Catherine, da. and coh. of William Harding of Knowle in Cranleigh, Surr., 2s. 5da.[1]

Bencher, I. Temple 1559, Autumn reader 1562, gov. 1564–6.

Member, council in the marches of Wales by 1560–*d.*; clerk of the council, duchy of Lancaster 1561–*d.*; j.p.q. Salop 1562–*d.*, Mdx. 1564; commr. eccles. causes 1562; recorder, London by 13 June 1563–June 1566; solicitor-gen. 27 June 1566–Mar. 1569; attorney, ct. wards 12 Mar. 1569–*d.*[2]

Speaker of House of Commons 1566.

Richard Onslow derived his surname from a lord-ship within the town of Shrewsbury, where his forbears can be traced from the late 13th century. His uncle Humphrey Onslow, custos rotulorum of Shropshire, was a municipal benefactor, but although Onslow himself held property in the parish of Holy Cross, Shrewsbury, he took little part in the affairs of the town or county.[3]

Onslow's career at the Inner Temple was marred by an affray in which he and others took part at the Autumn reading in 1556. The eight offenders were expelled from the fellowship and committed to the Fleet, but were pardoned and readmitted after making humble submission. Three of them, Thomas Copley, Thomas Lucas and Thomas Norton, all Protestants like Onslow, were to sit with

him in the Commons in 1558. To this, his first, Parliament Onslow was returned for Steyning, a borough usually represented by nominees of the 12th Earl of Arundel, many of them lawyers. No direct connexion has been traced between Onslow and Arundel, but the Inner Temple could have provided several indirect ones, either through Arundel's son-in-law the 4th Duke of Norfolk or through a local figure such as Sir Richard Sackville*. Of Onslow's part in the proceedings of the House all that is known is that on 22 Feb. 1558 he was licensed by the Speaker to ride to the assizes at Worcester where he was to appear as counsel. He may therefore have missed the speech which cost his associate Copley a spell of detention.[4]

Onslow's speedy rise under Elizabeth was to carry him to legal eminence as recorder of London and solicitor-general and to parliamentary distinction as Speaker in 1566. He died while on a visit to Shrews-bury on 2 Apr. 1571. His widow married Richard Browne†.[5]

[1] Aged 17 on admission to Inner Temple, *Surr. Arch. Colls.* xxxix. 65. *DNB; Vis. Salop* (Harl. Soc. xxix), 379; *Vis. Surr.* (Harl. Soc. xliii), 154; Manning and Bray, *Surr.* iii. 54; *CPR*, 1560–3, pp. 52, 117. [2] *Trans. Salop Arch. Soc.* (ser. 1), iii. 269–70; *Cam. Misc.* ix(3), 60; *CPR*, 1560–3, pp. 442, 523; 1563–6, p. 474; 1566–9, pp. 395, 396; Somerville, *Duchy*, i. 414; City of London RO, Guildhall, rep. 16, ff. 73v, 138v; H. E. Bell, *Ct. Wards and Liveries*, 22–23. [3] J. A. Manning, *Lives of the Speakers*, 230–5; *CPR*, 1548–9, p. 31; *Trans. Salop Arch. Soc.* (ser. 1), iii. 257–90. [4] *Cal. I.T. Recs.* i. passim; *CJ*, i. 50. [5] *Trans. Salop Arch. Soc.* (ser.1), iii. 269–70; A. J. Dasent, *Speakers*, 139.

R.J.W.S.

ORENGE, John (by 1480–1538 or later), of London, Exeter and Plymouth, Devon, and Wimborne Minster, Dorset.

EXETER	1504, 1510[1]
PLYMOUTH	1515[2]
WAREHAM	1529

b. by 1480, s. of John Orenge† of Exeter. *educ.* M. Templc. *m.* by 1531, Agnes, 2da.[3]

Bencher, M. Temple 1511, Autumn reader 1511, Lent 1517, assistant Lent 1513, Autumn 1518.[4]

Bailiff, Exeter 1506–7, member of the Twenty-Four by 1508–16, receiver 1510–11; j.p. Devon 1506, 1515, Dorset 1530–8.[5]

John Orenge did not enter his family's trading business but became a lawyer of some eminence whose services were sought in the south-west by magnates, religious foundations and corporations. He was already established in his calling by 1501 when he and several others were pardoned all trespasses involved in their enfeoffment of some land near Kingston-upon-Thames, Surrey. A petitioner in Chancery during the 1520s described him as 'an aged and ancient' man, but this was an *ex parte* statement and Orenge's career did not blossom until after the accession of Henry VIII.[6]

It was as John Orenge 'of London', the son of a former citizen, that he was admitted to the freedom of Exeter in 1503–4. The corporation was soon retaining his counsel and he became a member of the governing body, where several of his kinsmen were serving. An opportunity to sit in Parliament followed hard on his admission as a freeman, and he was doubtless helped to do so both in 1504 and 1510 by his senior colleague at the Middle Temple, Lewis Pollard†, who was the city's recorder. When Orenge stood for election in 1510 his name headed the poll with 17 votes out of an electorate of 21. Of his part in this Parliament nothing is known. He did not offer himself for election in 1512, probably because he had failed to render his account at the end of his term as receiver and the other members of the Twenty-Four were cool towards him. Relations were not improved by his many absences in London and his pursuit of his other interests, and on losing his fee as counsellor and his place on the Twenty-Four he moved his Devon residence from Exeter to Plymouth. He voted at the parliamentary elections at Exeter in 1512 and 1515 but on the second occasion he was himself returned for Plymouth. The King had asked that the Members of the Parliament of 1512 should be returned again, but the town's senior Member in that Parliament, Robert Bowring, had died not long after its dissolution and Orenge stepped into the vacant place. He had not yet made his home at Plymouth but his association with Bowring at the Temple probably helped him, as doubtless did the influence of Pollard, by now a judge and a power in Devon. He was evidently also content to serve without wages, for after the first session the town gave him the token sum of 13s.4d. for 'his labour and attendance'. By the time the next Parliament was called in 1523 Plymouth had been his home for several years and although the Members' names are lost it is likely that he was one of them. Six years later Orenge was living in Dorset, where he probably owed his seat for Wareham in the Parliament of 1529 to Sir Giles Strangways I, a fellow Middle Templar who was himself elected a knight of the shire.[7]

One of Orenge's daughters had married a Plymouth man, Henry Hereford. Standing bound in £40 for Hereford's good behaviour as customer of Plymouth, Orenge was sued in the Exchequer for the forfeit when Hereford was accused of malpractices in 1533; he appealed to Cromwell for judgment to be deferred and started a suit against Hereford in Chancery to recover his losses. Writing to Cromwell on 27 Jan. 1534 Orenge said that he had been ill for three months and was not able to travel to London before Easter: he may have been answer-ing an inquiry as to why he had not been present for the opening of the sixth session of Parliament 12 days earlier. Nothing else is known of his attendance or activity, but he was presumably re-elected, in accordance with the King's general wish to that effect, to the short Parliament of June–July 1536. While he lived in Devon, Orenge had been named only twice to the commission of the peace but he served on the Dorset bench continuously from December 1530 to July 1538. Since he was not named in the next commission, that of July 1539, he may have died during the intervening 12 months.[8]

1 Exeter act bk. 1, 10v. 2 Plymouth receiver's acct. bk. 1514–15. 3 Date of birth estimated from first reference. Exeter bk. 55, f. 67; C1/551/71; Vis. Devon, ed. Colby, 129; Vis. Dorset (Harl. Soc. xx), 50. 4 Dugdale, Origines Juridiciales, 215. 5 Exeter receiver's acct. 1506–7 to 1515–16 passim; CPR, 1494–1509, p. 636; LP Hen. VIII, ii, iv–xiii. 6 CPR, 1494–1509, pp. 232, 580; C1/588/26, 721/33; Val. Eccles. i. 427; Hutchins, Dorset, iv. 318; LP Hen. VIII, i. 7 Exeter Freemen (Devon and Cornw. Rec. Soc. extra ser. i), 64; Exeter bk. 55, f. 67; receiver's acct. 1506–7 to 1515–16 passim; act bk. 1, 61v, 71; Plymouth receiver's acct. bk. 1514–15; C1/551/71; E. W. Ives, 'Some aspects of the legal profession in the late 15th and early 16th cents.' (London Univ. Ph.D. thesis, 1955), app. i. a. 8 LP Hen. VIII, xii–xiv; C1/864/38.
H.M.

ORWELL see CAVELL

OVER alias WAVER, Henry (by 1509–67), of Coventry, Warws.

COVENTRY 1542[1]

b. by 1509. m. by 1530, Catherine, 1s. 2da.[2]
Warden, Coventry 1533–4, sheriff 1537–8, mayor 1544–5, alderman by 1557; subsidy collector 1545.[3]

The damaged election indenture of 1542 for Coventry no longer furnishes more than the christian name 'Henricus' of the second Member, but the entries for his wages in the mayor's accounts serve to identify him as Henry Over alias Waver: he was paid in full for the first session and for all but five days of the second but seemingly for only 21 days of the last. Of unknown origin, but presumably sprung from the Coventry family of Over, itself perhaps connected with the Warwickshire gentle family of Waver, Over was a grocer or mercer. He does not appear in the subsidy list of 1525 but by 1530 he was married and three years later he received his first civic office. During his year as sheriff the monastic visitor John London came to Coventry and found him a 'lively politic man'. It may have been London's recommendation to Cromwell of some reward for Over which led to his receipt shortly afterwards of a lease of monastic property; he took another such lease in 1540.[4]

Over's Membership of the Parliament of 1542 has left no trace, but three days after the close of the first session he completed a purchase of monastic lands on behalf of the corporation. The greater part of the money involved came from Sir Thomas White, the wealthy London alderman, who intended to devote the income to charity. The transaction was the first of a series between White, Over and Christopher Warren* for the benefit of Coventry. During the next 18 years Over and Warren borrowed further sums from White or at his direction for various civic purposes and negotiated agreements with him for the use of the capital and income; there also survive the accounts of these operations which they submitted to the mayor's council. Over added to these commitments a variety of official tasks, including numerous missions to the court, the Council and, down to 1553, John Dudley, Earl of Warwick and Duke of Northumberland. In view of the city's practice of re-electing its Members, Over might have been expected to sit again, unless it was that he could not be spared from his many duties.[5]

Over's private affairs probably gained rather than suffered from his public concerns, especially his raising and making of loans and his dealings in property. In 1551 the subsidy commissioners gave him the second highest assessment in the city, and at his death he owned considerable property, chiefly ex-monastic, within it and in such neighbouring places as Bedworth, Corley, Coundon and Fletchamstead. By his will, made on 24 June 1567, two days before he died, and proved on 24 Nov. following, he left much of his property in the city to the mayor and council for 12 years or until it should have yielded £500; of this sum £400 was to be used for loans to individuals and the remainder to be added to the town's poor chest. The property was afterwards to pass in specified parcels to a long list of named relatives, including his daughters' children. The residuary legatee and executor was Over's son Richard. His daughter Bridget had married John Nethermill*.[6]

¹ Only the christian name survives on a damaged indenture, C219/18B/103; surname supplied from Coventry mayors' accts. 1542–61, pp. 12, 17, 21. ² Date of birth estimated from marriage. C142/145/4, 147/210; PCC 32 Stonard. ³ *Coventry Leet Bk.* (EETS cxxxiv), ii. 714, 727, 769; E179/192/170. ⁴ *Coventry Recs.* ed. Jeaffreson, B.65; *LP Hen. VIII*, xiii–xv; Shakespeare Birthplace Trust, Gregory Hood collection 156. ⁵ E318/321, C1a; Coventry mayors' accts. 1542–61, pp. 3–510 passim; treasurers' payments, p. 6; chamberlains' accts. 1, p. 232; council bk. 1, pp. 1–17, 43; St. John's Coll. Oxford muniments xix 3, 4; C1/1150/6–11;St.Ch.4/3/48; *CPR*, 1550–3, p. 423. ⁶ E179/193/188; C1/1138/105–6, 1160/50–1; 142/145/4, 147/210; Coventry statute merchant rolls, 33–35, 38, 39, 53; NRA 5613, pp. 23, 29; *LP Hen. VIII*, xx, xxi; *CPR*, 1547–8, p. 54; 1549–51, p. 60; 1550–3, p. 430; 1553, p. 113; 1558–60, pp. 73, 89; *VCH Warws.* iv. 60; vi. 36, 52, 56, 89; viii. 85; PCC 32 Stonard.

S.M.T.

OVEREND, William (by 1508–58) of Lynn, Norf.

LYNN   1547*, 1554 (Apr.)

b. by 1508. *m.* (1) by 1534, Margaret, 1s.; (2) by 1543, Catherine.[1]

Chamberlain, Lynn 1535–6, common councilman 1537–40, alderman 1540–*d.*, mayor 1547–8, Jan.–May 1558; commr. sewers, Norf. 1554.[2]

William Overend was born at Bentham, probably the place of that name in the West Riding of Yorkshire. On 12 July 1529 he was admitted to the freedom of Lynn by purchase: he was then called a 'tiler' (which probably signifies a brickmaker), but although he continued to be so described for several years there is no evidence that he practised that craft. He owned several ships and had a share in others: these may have been meant to transport his products but he used them to bring coal, fish and other merchandise to Lynn. From 1540 onwards he was usually called merchant, but in his will he is styled gentleman. In 1545 an inquiry was held into his seizure of foreign vessels bound for Scotland: one of them belonged to a Dane who denied supplying arms to the Scots, and on his appearance before the Council Overend was ordered to pay its owner £42 in compensation and to restore his ship.[3]

Despite the frequency with which Overend was fined for breaking Lynn's trading regulations he became a leading figure there. The evidence given in a suit brought in the Star Chamber by Margery Grindal, ostensibly because he had broken into her house in 1541 but almost certainly because of the dissolution of a trading partnership, suggests that he was respected by his colleagues in the town's assembly, particularly by its clerk and Thomas Waters*. In 1546 he went with other aldermen to Norwich to testify before the commissioners surveying chantries and guilds as a prelude to their suppression. The town was alarmed at the prospect because the income from its guild lands was used to maintain the banks and dykes protecting it from the sea, and it fell to Overend, then mayor-elect, and the recorder, Thomas Gawdy I, to plead Lynn's cause as its Members in the Parliament of 1547. The government's bill to dissolve the chantries was introduced in the Lords on 6 Dec. 1547, but before it reached the Commons the Lynn Members brought in one for the town and its two chantries which, however, lapsed after its second reading. They also supported the objections raised by Henry Porter (q.v.), Christopher Warren (q.v.) and others to the dissolution bill, to such effect that its passage was endangered. The Protector Somerset was informed, and after a discussion in the Council he 'thought it better to stay and content them . . . by granting to them . . . their guild lands . . . than through their means, on whose importune labour and suggestion the greater part of the Lower House rested, to have the article defaced'. Rather than agree to provisos for Lynn and Coventry to be added to the bill and so encourage others to seek similar exemption, the Protector offered to grant the lands to the two towns after the bill's enactment on condition that their Members desisted from further opposition. The Council honoured its side of the bargain in May 1548 when Lynn procured the lease of its guild lands and the opportunity to buy lands worth £100 a year towards the upkeep of its sea defences. Overend's stand had displeased the government and during the second session he was replaced by George Amyas.[4]

In the succession crisis of 1553 Overend and Thomas Waters seem to have supported Sir Robert Dudley's* attempt to raise Lynn for Queen Jane. On 25 July Mary ordered their committal to the Marshalsea where they remained until their discharge on payment of a fine of £200. The decision by the town's assembly in September to raise the sum by a compulsory levy suggests that the pair had been made scapegoats. Their election to the Queen's second Parliament was both a vote of confidence in them and a snub to the regime. Nothing is known about Overend's part in the Commons on this occasion, but as a merchant he presumably objected to the two (unsuccessful) bills limiting imports. Before his return home he was sent £5 for his expenses. A year later the town contributed £160 towards the fine paid by him and Waters. On hearing this the Council summoned the pair to Westminster and later ordered the money to be given back. Despite the town's protests the Council insisted and on 16 Dec. 1556 the town gave way. This seems to have angered Overend who was first rebuked for 'certain opprobrious and contumelious words' and then deprived of his freedom. On 3 Jan. 1558 he submitted to the town's assembly and three days after this reconciliation he was elected mayor.[5]

Overend made his will on 28 May 1558, leaving small bequests to charity and to friends, servants and godchildren. He appointed his wife residuary legatee and sole executrix, provided she gave his son Thomas 20 marks a year 'for his exhibition one year in an inn of chancery and three years in an inn of court'. He died later the same day and his will was proved in the following month. At the inquisition held on 18 Sept. 1559 it was found that he had owned the manor of Hardwick, Norfolk, as well as houses and property in Lynn.[6]

[1] Date of birth estimated from admission as freeman. St.Ch.2/16/224; C142/119/134; PCC 30 Noodes; Blomefield, *Norf.* ix. 200. [2] Lynn congregation bks. 4, 5 passim; *CPR*, 1554–5, p. 108. [3] PCC 30 Noodes; Lynn congregation bk. 4, ff. 282, 288, 328; St.Ch.2/16/224–6, 20/122–3, 25/234, 244; *LP Hen. VIII*, xx; *APC*, i. 163, 263. [4] Lynn congregation bk. 4, ff. 288v, 328; 5, ff. 44v, 104v; *CJ*, i. 2, 3; W. K. Jordan, *Edw. VI*, ii, 184; *APC*, ii. 193–5; *CPR*, 1549–51, p. 344. [5] Lynn congregation bk. 5, ff. 192v, 206v, 222, 227v, 261v, 275, 306, 306v; *APC*, iv. 416. [6] PCC 30 Noodes; C142/119/134; NRA 15579 (Derbys. RO. T.485, 494).

R.V.

OVERTON, Guthlac (by 1478–1537), of London and Swineshead, Lincs.

WALLINGFORD 1529, 1536[1]

b. by 1478, s. of Thomas Overton of Swineshead. *m.* by 1521, Olive, ?sis. of Sir Edward Browne, prob. 1s. 1da. *suc.* fa. 4 Dec. 1533.[2]
Jt. auditor, duchy of Cornw. 1508–*d.*; feodary or dep. to feodary, duchy of Lancaster, south parts 1508–9; commr. and assessor for duchy of Cornw. lands in Cornw. and Devon 1521, 1525, 1528, 1535; commr. to collect subsidy from nobility 1524, stannaries 1532, tenths of spiritualities, Berks. 1535; auditor for order of St. John of Jerusalem by 1533; gent. usher extraordinary by 1533.[3]

The father and grandfather of Guthlac Overton are both described as 'generosus' in their inquisitions, although their family is not given a pedigree in any of the heralds' visitations of Lincolnshire. William Overton, who died in 1522, and his son Thomas both left property at Swineshead and elsewhere in Holland, Lincolnshire, which they held of Thomas Holland, Sir John Hussey*, Sir William Willoughby and other local magnates, as well as of the royal honor of Richmond: as nearly all these lands are also included in Guthlac Overton's inquisition, he was probably the only surviving son when he succeeded in 1533. His unusual christian name may indicate that he was born in a parish connected with Crowland abbey, whose patron was the Mercian St. Guthlac.[4]

Nothing is known of Overton's life before his appointment as joint auditor of the duchy of Cornwall, in survivorship, with effect from Michaelmas 1508. His colleague Robert Coorte had held that office alone since 1484 and was dead by May 1514, when it was regranted, again in survivorship, to Overton and John Turner: after this the two auditors were normally named together in commissions for assessing the lands and revenues of the duchy until Overton's death left Turner in sole occupation. In 1514 Overton and Sir John Sharp were granted, in survivorship, the 'tribulage' or poll-tax on tin-miners in the Cornish hundreds of Kirrier and Penwith and in the stannary there, and nine years later Overton acquired a 21-year lease of the toll of tin in the manor of Tywarnhaile, Cornwall. In February 1522 he also became tenant of the demesne lands of the manor of Mere in Wiltshire, another property of the duchy.[5]

Overton's work was not restricted to the duchy of Cornwall. He was fortunate to start his career when a growing number of revenues were being withdrawn from the Exchequer and placed under the control of the chamber; their auditing then fell to the King's general surveyors, whose powers were legalized by the establishment of a court of audit in

1512, the forerunner of the court of general surveyors. The number of crown auditors rose and under
Henry VIII special commissions were often set up
to audit important accounts. While remaining a
duchy official, Overton became concerned with
expenditure in many fields: in 1513 he made a
declaration of the accounts of the deputy serjeant of
the King's tents, in 1523 he audited the expenses of
the vice-admiral Sir Nicholas Poyntz* and in 1526
he took the accounts of the subsidy collectors. Like
other men who enjoyed a successful career in
administration, he secured an appointment in the
privy chamber.[6]

Overton also had a long association with the order
of St. John of Jerusalem. He had dealings with it as
early as 1510 and in October 1519 he became lessee
of its manor of Temple Rockley, Wiltshire. Shortly
afterwards he conveyed most of his rights there to a
local man, John Goddard, whom he later accused of
breaking the terms of their agreement. There were
closer ties than this with the order. By June 1533,
when he was admitted to the freedom of London, he
was its auditor and in the following year the prior
refused a request by Viscount Lisle for a lease of the
preceptory or manor of Swingfield in Kent, after
consulting both Overton and the commander there,
Sir Edward Browne, who was Overton's brother-in-
law.[7]

Neither Overton nor Sir Edward Chamberlain,
his fellow-Member for Wallingford in the Parliament of 1529, is mentioned in the corporation
minute book and neither seems to have owned any
property in the area. The honor of Wallingford was
part of the duchy of Cornwall but the borough was
not the parliamentary preserve of any particular set
of officials and in 1523 a royal letter had ordered the
return of local men. In 1529 the Members may have
been nominated by or on behalf of the King, who
was at Woodstock on 25 Aug. and again on 4 Sept.
Chamberlain promised to serve without wages and
his successor Thomas Denton signed a similar agreement in 1536, but there are no such quittances by
Overton. He could have afforded to give one, to
judge from his endowment of a chantry in 1510 and
his presentation of a doe and a hogshead of wine to
Lincoln's Inn, on his special admission in August of
the same year: moreover, when a subsidy was levied
on all members of the inns of court in November
1523 his goods were assessed at £100, a figure
matched by one and exceeded by only three of his
24 fellows at Lincoln's Inn who appear on the list
concerned. Yet he was not above demanding 40
marks in a chancery suit against the executors of
Sir John Sharp to pay for the board of Sharp's
nephew, Robert Browne. Overton's description of

himself in this case as Sharp's 'solicitor in all his
causes' presumably means that he practised law as
well as auditing accounts.[8]

Overton died on 20 Apr. 1537. Besides his lands
in Lincolnshire, he appears to have occupied
property in St. John's Street, in the parish of St.
Sepulchre, Holborn, which had belonged to the
order of St. John. He left no will, and his widow was
given the administration of the estate, to which the
heir was a 15 year-old son Edmund. This was perhaps the 'Mr. Overton' who was buried at St.
Michael Cornhill on 30 Mar. 1559.[9]

[1] Berks. RO, W/AE p. 3/1. [2] Date of birth estimated from age at
fa.'s i.p.m., E150/569/17, 571/24. *LP Hen. VIII*, vii, xix; *Lincs. Peds.*
(Harl. Soc. li), 542. [3] *CPR, 1494–1509*, p. 625; Somerville, *Duchy*, i.
626; *LP Hen. VIII*, i–v, viii, xi; PCC 2 Hogen. [4] E150/556/17, 569/
17, 571/24; *VCH Lincs.* ii. 105. [5] *CPR, 1494–1509*, p. 625; Somer-
ville, i. 623; *LP Hen. VIII*, i, iii, xii, xvi. [6] W. C. Richardson, *Tudor
Chamber Admin.* 176, 184, 413; *LP Hen. VIII*, i, iii, iv. [7] *LP Hen.
VIII*, i, vii, xi; *CPR, 1494–1509*, p. 238; *Feet of Fines, London and
Mdx.* ed. Hardy and Page, ii. 20; *Cat. Anct. Deeds*, ii. 163; C1/813/31;
City of London RO, Guildhall, rep. 9, f. 11. [8] *VCH Berks.* iii. 528;
Berks. RO, W/AE pp. 1, 2, 3/2; *LP Hen. VIII*, i; *Black Bk. L. Inn*,
i. 162; *Cal. I.T. Recs.* i. 459; C1/551/49, 657/56–58. [9] E150/571/24;
LP Hen. VIII, xix; *PCC Admins.* ed. Glencross, i. 4; PCC 34
Mellershe; *Reg. St. Michael Cornhill* (Harl. Soc. reg. vii), 79, 182.

T.F.T.B.

OWEN, George (by 1499–1558), of Oxford and
Godstow, Oxon.

OXFORDSHIRE 1558*

b. by 1499. *educ.* Merton, Oxf. BA 1519, fellow 1520,
MA 1521, MB 1525, MD 1528. *m.* (1) by 1532,
Lettice of Suff. wid.; (2) Mary; 3s. 2da. prob. by
1st w.[1]

Keeper of Bourgchier chest, Oxf. 1520–1, Chichele
and Audley chest in 1521, Danvers chest 1522–4; 1st
bursar, Merton, 1524–5, 3rd 1525–6; R. physician by
1537–*d.*; fellow, College of Physicians by Oct. 1538, an
elect 1552, pres. 1553–5; receiver-gen., duchy of
Lancaster 30 Sept. 1547–*d.*; j.p. Oxon. 1547, q. 1554;
commr. relief 1550.[2]

George Owen was born in the diocese of Worcester and educated at Oxford, where he settled. Of
obscure origin, he seems to have been destined for
the Church, but on his marriage he took up medicine
after first trying to trade as a white baker without
becoming a freeman of Oxford. He had been appointed one of Henry VIII's physicians by 1537 when he
was one of the six signatories to the letter informing
the Privy Council of the grave condition of Queen
Jane Seymour after the birth of Prince Edward. The
recipient of an encomium by Leland, he joined
Queen Catherine Parr in persuading Thomas Caius
to translate Erasmus's paraphrase of St. Mark's
gospel into English. He witnessed the will of Henry
VIII in which he was bequeathed £100. Edward VI
retained his medical services and he was present at
the young King's death, as he had been at his birth,
and was the last to speak to him. Following Mary's
accession he was elected president of the College of

Physicians and in that capacity he promoted the Act (1 Mary St. 2, c.9) for the enlargement of the college's powers. Two years later his proposals regulating admission to medical degrees at Oxford were ratified by Cardinal Pole as chancellor of the university. In 1554 he certified that Princess Elizabeth was well enough to answer the Queen's summons to London after Wyatt's rebellion, and later he was sent to Woodstock to attend Elizabeth during an illness. In the last year of his life he published the treatise *A meet Diet for The new ague*.[3]

Owen was generously treated by his successive royal patients. Henry VIII gave him New Hall and St. Alban Hall in Oxford and a fee of £100, and in 1537 he was able to purchase the manor of Yarnton, Oxfordshire. In November 1538 the abbess of Godstow wrote to Cromwell, 'We have obeyed your letters for the preferment of Dr. Owen to our demesnes and stock', and the nunnery itself thus gained a brief respite from suppression, but in March 1540 Owen purchased it for £558. In 1541 he paid £1,174 for the manors of Walton and Wolvercote and the house and site of Rewley abbey, and in October 1546 he joined with Dr. John Bridges to purchase for £1,300 lands at Cumnor. From 1547 he was apparently able to use the duchy of Lancaster's money as his own. Later acquisitions included the manor of Congresbury, Somerset, and Durham College, Oxford. Some of these he later resold. The appropriate conclusion to this accumulation of property was Edward VI's grant of arms to Owen.[4]

These grants made Owen the greatest landowner immediately to the north-west of Oxford and brought him into conflict with Sir John Williams* over rights in Wytham woods, and with the city over common rights and jurisdiction in the region of Port Meadow. Suits continued after Owen's death between the city and Richard Owen, and Richard Fiennes* was asked to arbitrate between them. But if he was on bad terms with the city, Owen was able to marry his children into one of the county's leading families. His eldest son married Mary, daughter of Sir Leonard Chamberlain*, Mary's leading supporter in Oxfordshire after Sir John Williams, and one of his daughters, first married to another duchy receiver Thomas Mathew*, later married Chamberlain's third son and eventual heir, John. Owen's second son, William, married a Fettiplace so that Owen could claim a connexion with John Denton* who as sheriff of Oxfordshire and Berkshire in 1557–8 returned him to Parliament. Such alliances must have made him acceptable to the Oxfordshire freeholders in 1558 and his position at court to the Queen. Nothing is known about his part in the work of the House and

he died of an intermittent fever on 18 Oct. 1558 during the prorogation, being buried in St. Stephen's, Walbrook, London, six days later. By a will made a month earlier he provided for his wife and family and named his son Richard, Secretary Boxall, Sir Leonard Chamberlain and Thomas Wendy* executors. At his death, Owen owed £3,265 to the duchy of Lancaster and on 26 June 1559 his widow Mary and two of his sons contracted to repay it by instalments; the sum being finally discharged in December 1580. No trace of a by-election to replace him in the brief, second session of the Parliament of 1558 has been found.[5]

[1] Date of birth estimated from first office. Emden, *Biog. Reg. Univ. Oxf. 1501–40*, pp. 426–7; *Vis. Oxon.* (Harl. Soc. v), 127–8; DL41/34/2 f. 70; PCC 11 Chaynay; *DNB*. [2] *LP Hen. VIII*, xii; G. Clark, *Coll. of Physicians*, i. 71; W. Munk, *Roll of R. Coll. of Physicians*, i. 36–37; Somerville, *Duchy*, i. 403; *CPR*, 1553, p. 357; *Rep. R. Comm. of 1552* (Archs. of Brit. Hist. and Culture iii), 18, 19, 103, 106. [3] *LP Hen. VIII*, v, xii, xxi; Oxf. Univ. Arch. B27, p. 3; *Oxf. Recs.* 61, 94; Strype, *Eccles. Memorials*, ii. (1), 46; *Lit. Rems. Edw. VI*, pp. cxcix, xx; Foxe, *Acts and Mons*. viii. 606, 617; *Norf. Arch.* iv. 181, 183, 186, 221, 223. [4] Lansd. 156 (28), ff. 105–6v; *LP Hen. VIII*, xiii–xvii, xx, xxi; *Oxf. Recs.* 163, 175, 217; *CPR*, 1547–8, p. 214; 1548–9, p. 191; 1553, pp. 260, 274–5, 305; 1557–8, p. 234; *CSP Dom.* 1601–3, *Add*, 1547–65, p. 427; *APC*, iv. 152; *VCH Oxon*. iii. 238. [5] *Oxf. Recs.* 111. 116, 177, 211–13, 225, 247–55; Bodl. Wood D18(3), f. 40; St.Ch.4/7/14; *ECP*, x. 117; *Machyn's Diary* (Cam. Soc. xlii), 177; PCC 11 Chaynay; C142/116/5; *CPR*, 1558–60, p. 98; DL41/34/2 f. 70; Somerville, i. 404.

A.H.

OWEN *see also* **AWEN**

OWGAN, Morgan (by 1525–57 or later), of Hereford.

HEREFORD   1555

b. by 1525.[1]
    Under collector of relief, Hereford 1550.[2]

Morgan Owgan lived in Widmarsh ward, Hereford, where in 1549 he was lessee of some ex-chantry property called the 'Parson's Close'. Three years earlier he had been assessed towards the subsidy on goods worth £8, but no trace has been found of his occupation and his only known civic assignment was as a collector of the relief in 1550. His election with Hugh Gebons to the Parliament of 1555 followed the city's receipt of a letter from the council in the marches asking it to choose Catholics. That the pair conformed to this requirement is implied by the absence of their names from the list of Members who opposed one of the government's bills, although they might in any case have wanted to avoid disfavour in the interest of the Act for rebuilding four mills on the river Wye near Hereford which they helped Thomas Kerry (q.v.) to secure (2 and 3 Phil. and Mary, c.14). One of the knights for Herefordshire, Stephen Parry, died during the Parliament and in June 1557 Owgan testified to the date of his death. Owgan is last glimpsed two or three months later when William Herbert I*, 1st Earl of Pembroke, president of the council in the marches, visited Hereford and he accommodated one of the suite in his house. If he made a will it has not come to light.[3]

[1] Date of birth estimated from first reference. [2] E179/117/207. [3] E179/117/162; CPR, 1549-51, p. 143; HMC 13th Rep. IV, 322-4; C142/107/57.

P.S.E.

OXENBRIDGE, Sir Robert (1508/9–74), of Brede, Suss. and Hurstbourne Priors, Hants.

EAST GRINSTEAD   1553 (Mar.)
SUSSEX   1554 (Apr.), 1555, 1558

b. 1508/9, 1st s. of Sir Goddard Oxenbridge of Brede by 2nd w. Anne, da. of Sir Thomas Fiennes of Claverham, Kent. m. by 1543, Alice, da. and coh. of Sir Thomas Fogge of Ash, Kent, wid. of Edward Scott, 1s. 2da. Kntd. by 18 Feb. 1553.[1]
Commr. musters, Suss. 1539, relief 1550; other commissions 1539-54; esquire of the body by 1541; bailiff, Rye 1541 (reversion)–64; j.p. Suss. by 1541–58/59, q. Hants 1561–2; constable, Pevensey castle, Suss. 1550–d.; sheriff, Surr. and Suss. 1551–2, Hants 1567–8; lt. the Tower 1556, constable 1557–8.[2]

The Oxenbridge family had lived in Sussex since at least the early 14th century. Robert Oxenbridge's grandfather Adam Oxenbridge sat for Rye in three Parliaments between 1484 and 1495, and his father was three times sheriff of Surrey and Sussex. Although Oxenbridge lived at Brede after his father's death in 1531, the house was not his until his cousin William Oxenbridge* bequeathed it to him in 1550; a dispute over William Oxenbridge's goods was settled by the Council in his favour.[3]

During the first part of his career Oxenbridge was largely concerned with his own part of East Sussex, although he had a place in the royal household and afterwards in Princess Elizabeth's. He does not seem to have served in war but his chief appointments were quasi-military, first the constableship of Pevensey castle and then the lieutenancy and constableship of the Tower. Pevensey belonged to the duchy of Lancaster, and it was for the duchy borough of East Grinstead that Oxenbridge was first returned to Parliament. That connexion apart, he was well befriended in the shire: he was related to the Pelhams of Laughton, the Gages of Firle and the Lords Dacre of the South, and the sheriff who returned him, Sir Anthony Browne*, was the son of his predecessor at Pevensey. Oxenbridge had himself served as sheriff in the previous year and it was perhaps then that he had been knighted: these marks of favour look like attempts by the Duke of Northumberland to win over one who was to be a lifelong Catholic. In the event it was under Mary that Oxenbridge reached the height of his career

with his three elections as knight of the shire and his appointment at the Tower: both indicated that the mantle of his kinsman Sir John Gage* had passed to him. Of his role in the Commons it is known only that in 1555 he did not vote with the opposition against one of the government's bills.[4]

Elizabeth did not reappoint Oxenbridge as lieutenant of the Tower and while his migration to Hampshire was followed by his transfer from the Sussex bench he was not to remain on that of Hampshire for long. He bought the manor and park of Hurstbourne Priors, near Whitchurch, in 1558 for more than £2,000, and during the next three years he parted with two Sussex manors and a London house in Trinity Lane; Brede he kept but let to the family of Devenish. The marriage arranged in 1565 between his heir Robert and a daughter of his fellow-Catholic (Sir) Thomas White II* of South Warnborough helped to establish him socially in his new county, but even after serving as its sheriff in 1567–8 he was not restored to the commission; the bishop of Winchester had written to Cecil advocating his exclusion. He does not appear to have been further penalized but after his death his stepson William Scott and nephew Andrew Oxenbridge D.C.L. were to be imprisoned for their religious beliefs.[5]

Oxenbridge made his will on 21 June 1574. He left Hurstbourne to his wife and the rest of his lands and goods to be shared between her and the heir. He named his wife and son executors and as overseers his nephew Andrew Oxenbridge and William Lawrence, probably the Member for Winchester. He gave £20 to his nephew and smaller sums or rings to his sister Lady Tyrwhitt (widow of Sir Robert Tyrwhitt I*), his daughter Catherine Tuck and daughter-in-law Anne Cheyne. Oxenbridge died on 17 Nov. 1574.[6]

[1] Aged 65 at death. Suss. Arch. Colls. viii. 231–2; Vis. Hants (Harl. Soc. lxiv), 153; C219/20/133. [2] LP Hen. VIII, xiv, xvi, xx; CPR, 1547–8, p. 90; 1553, pp. 350, 376; 1553–4, pp. 24, 28, 37; 1554–5, p. 108; 1555–7, pp. 403, 531; 1557–8, pp. 106, 380, 462; 1560–3, p. 442; 1563–6, pp. 42, 91; APC, vi. 44, 78; Somerville, Duchy, i. 615. [3] Suss. Arch. Colls. viii. 213 seq.; PCC 9 Coode. [4] LP Hen. VIII, xiv–xvi, xx, add.; Suss. Rec. Soc. xvi. 38; CPR, 1553, p. 363; Machyn's Diary (Cam. Soc. xlii), 108. [5] CPR, 1557–8, p. 462; 1560–3, p. 199; Harl. 608, f. 86; Suss. Rec. Soc. xix. 23, 172; VCH Hants, iv. 287–9; HMC Hatfield, i. 392; ii. 512; SP12/59, f. 162. [6] PCC 45 Martyn; C142/172/113.

R.J.W.S.

OXENBRIDGE (OXBRIDGE, UXBRIDGE), William (by 1498–1550), of Rye and Winchelsea, Suss., and London.

RYE   1542[1]

b. by 1498, prob. s. of William Oxenbridge.[2]
Page of the chamber by 1526, groom porter to the Queen by 1537; doorward, Holt castle, Denb. 1526–d.; jurat, Rye 1535-43 or later; commr. oyer and terminer

1539; paymaster, Winchelsea c.1539, Camber castle 1542–4; mayor, Winchelsea 1549–50.[3]

William Oxenbridge was a grandson of Adam Oxenbridge, four times mayor of Rye and thrice Member for the port between 1482 and 1495. His career in the Household can be traced from 1519, when he was paid for riding on royal business, until 1544/45, when he was a groom porter on the Queen's side, without bouche of court. It was doubtless their shared service to Anne Boleyn, as well as perhaps their common affiliation with Kent, which led Sir John Dudley to call Oxenbridge his 'fellow' when reporting to Cromwell in November 1535 the outcome of their joint investigation of a charge of treasonable utterances by the vicar of Rolvenden. From about 1540, when he was ceasing to reside at court, Oxenbridge was employed as paymaster for the new coastal defences in the south-east.[4]

His combination of gentle birth and royal service gained Oxenbridge first place in the list of jurats of Rye. It also doubtless accounts for his election to the Parliament of 1542, although he then took second place to John Fletcher, presumably because of Fletcher's long record of service. There was evidently no question of his forgoing parliamentary wages, and as the £17 6s. which he received seems to have been calculated at the standard rate the 173 days which it represented fell far short of the 261 consumed by the three sessions. Even so, Oxenbridge must have attended longer than Fletcher, and his absences may have been due to his concurrent responsibility as paymaster at Camber. Besides sitting in Parliament, he had spent 21 days at Michaelmas 1543 soliciting for the Cinque Ports, doubtless to secure their customary exemption from subsidy, and for this the Brotherhood paid him £3 6s.8d.[5]

By 1549, when he became mayor of Winchelsea, Oxenbridge had evidently settled there, and it was as of Winchelsea, esquire, that he made his will on 2 Jan. 1550. The absence of any mention of wife or children suggests that he was unmarried. He left to his cousin, Robert Oxenbridge* his principal manor house and all his lands in Brede, Sedlescombe and Udimore, and to his brother-in-law Robert Londones the lands and tenements in Rye which he had bought from Henry VIII (probably in 1542) and all his cattle and other livestock, save 300 sheep which were to be sold to cover his bequests. He named the same two his executors and residuary legatees. To William Wymond of Rye he bequeathed lands already given to him at Guestling, Icklesham and Pett, and an outstanding obligation of £30; to Thomas Jerman a house in the Butchery in Winchelsea; to John Stookes of London (probably John

Stokes*) all the goods in his chamber in London; to John Hall a silver-and-gilt cruse and a scarlet gown; and to William Egleston* a similar cruse. Before the will was proved on 23 Apr. 1550 there was trouble between the executors, for on 18 Feb. the Council, acting on a complaint by Robert Oxenbridge, ordered Robert Londones to deliver the dead man's goods to Oxenbridge and to appear to answer for himself in the matter.[6]

[1] Rye chamberlains' accts. 4, f. 388; 5, f. 42. [2] Date of birth estimated from first reference. *Suss. Arch. Colls.* viii. 230. [3] *LP Hen. VIII*, iv, xii, xiv–xvi, xviii; *CPR*, 1549–51, p. 237; Rye chamberlains' accts. 4, ff. 283 seq.; *Cinque Ports White and Black Bks.* (Kent Arch. Soc. recs. br. xix), 222, 230, 240. [4] *LP Hen. VIII*, iii–v, ix, xx; SP1/87, ff. 38–39 (*LP Hen. VIII*, vii. 1440 where misdated 1534). [5] Rye chamberlains' accts. 5, ff. 42, 42v, 75v; *Cinque Ports White and Black Bks.* 222, 229–30, 240. [6] PCC 9 Coode; *APC*, ii. 394.

H.M.

OXENDEN, William (c.1510–76), of Wingham, Kent.

HYTHE	1553 (Oct.)[1]
NEW ROMNEY	1554 (Nov.)

b. c.1510, s. of Edward Oxenden of Wingham by Alice Barton. *m.* Elizabeth, da. of one Hill, ?wid. of one Wildgoose, *s.p. suc.* fa. 1521 or soon after.[2]

Capt. of the Clay bulwark, near Deal by 1553; commr. sewers, Kent 1553; escheator Feb.–Nov. 1557.[3]

William Oxenden was named with his mother executor of his father's will of 1521, although then probably still a child. He should have succeeded on his mother's death to lands in Wingham and elsewhere in Kent, but his father had died in financial trouble, having been released from prison only on a promise to discharge his debts, and some land seems to have been sold to meet them; however, the Wingham estate remained intact for Oxenden to inherit.[4]

Oxenden was a servant of Sir Thomas Cheyne* from at least 1540. In February 1553 he was sent by Cheyne, who was lord warden of the Cinque Ports, to rebuke the men of Sandwich for ignoring his wishes at the election of their Members. His own election for Hythe in the following autumn Oxenden probably owed to Cheyne, and he was certainly Cheyne's nominee at Romney for the Parliament of November 1554, his name being inserted in the schedule in a different hand from that of the document. Unlike his fellow-Member Thomas Jekyn he was not among those who opposed the first steps towards the reunion with Rome in Mary's first Parliament, but he was one of over 100 Members who were informed against in the King's bench in 1555 for leaving her third Parliament before its dissolution without having been given leave to do so. No further action was taken against him until 1558, when he was three times distrained —of 2s., 5s. and 3s.4d.—for failing to appear to answer the charge; before the next law term began the Queen was dead and the process lapsed. The episode may help to explain why he did not reappear in Parliament under Mary, but it did not put an end to his employment by the crown. In April 1556 he was named to a commission on heretical books in the diocese of Canterbury, and in August the Privy Council instructed him and William Rastell* to investigate an escape of prisoners from Canterbury gaol. He also retained his captaincy of the Clay bulwark near Deal.[5]

Cheyne died in 1558, leaving Oxenden £10 in his will. Oxenden seems to have continued in the service of the new warden for he had a room in Dover castle at the time of his death. By his will, made on 26 Mar. 1576 and proved three months later, he asked to be buried near his accustomed place in Wingham church and made bequests to the poor of Staple and Wingham. Having had no children of his own but only two 'sons-in-law', that is, presumably, stepsons, he left his house and all his lands to his nephew Edward Oxenden for ten years. He made small bequests to his friends William Lovelace†, serjeant-at-law and the overseer of the will, William Crispe, lieutenant of Dover castle, Cyriak Petyt* and Vincent Engeham, and his brother Henry Oxenden, whom he named executor with his nephew Richard Hardres. Oxenden was buried at Wingham on 10 Apr. 1576.[6]

[1] Bodl. e Museo 17. [2] Date of birth estimated from fa.'s will, Canterbury prob. reg. OC83; *Vis. Kent* (Harl. Soc. lxxv), 140. [3] Stowe 571, f. 42; *CPR*, 1553-4, p. 36. [4] C1/551/77. [5] *LP Hen. VIII*, xvi; Sandwich little black bk. f. 31v; C219/23/184; KB27/1186-8, 29/188 rot. 48; *CPR*, 1555-7, p. 24; *APC*, v. 327; SP11/11/72, ff. 154v, 155v. [6] PCC 1 Chaynay; Canterbury prob. reg. C32, f. 218; *Arch. Cant.* vi. 279.

H.M.

PADYHAM, Simon (by 1515-68 or later), of New Romney, Kent.

NEW ROMNEY 1553 (Mar.),[1] 1558

b. by 1515, 1st s. of John Padyham of New Romney by 1st w. *m. suc.* fa. Apr. 1553/July 1555.[2]
    Chamberlain, New Romney 1552-3, jurat by 1558, bailiff 1561-2.[3]

Simon Padyham was probably a young man when in 1536 he exported oxen and sheep from New Romney to Boulogne. It was not until 1552 that he took any part in the government of Romney, of which his father was bailiff in 1544-5 and jurat thereafter. By his father's will of 7 Apr. 1553, which he proved on 26 July 1555, he received the lease of one house, half the proceeds from the sale of another, and the residue of goods.[4]

Padyham was not Romney's choice for the Parlia-

ment of March 1553. The town elected Richard Bunting* and William Tadlowe* but had them rejected by the lord warden, Sir Thomas Cheyne*; of Cheyne's nominees only Padyham is known. Romney paid him £3 6s.8d. for the 31-day Parliament, while putting on record that he was 'appointed burgess by our lord warden contrary to our election'; Tadlowe and Bunting were compensated with 20s. apiece. Whatever moved Cheyne to interfere, the episode did not affect the relations between the men involved, for both Bunting and Padyham witnessed Tadlowe's will three years later. Any ill will which Padyham incurred among others in the town was presumably dispelled by the spring of 1557 when he was one of those chosen by the combined Cinque Ports to go to London in defence of their liberties, and he was probably the town's own choice to sit in the Parliament of the following year. He was paid £5 2s. for 51 days but whether this was for the first session which had lasted 47 days (the few extra days being allowed for travelling) or was for an incomplete attendance in both sessions (60 days) is not known.[5]

Only occasional references have been found to Padyham's career under Elizabeth. In 1560 the Cinque Ports undertook to pay his costs in a private dispute with the archbishop of Canterbury over a matter of probate, his refusal to appear in the commissary's court being seen as a vindication of the ports' freedom from outside jurisdiction. It was probably his own interest in the basis of such privileges which led him to have a copy made in 1564 of the custumal of New Romney, in the translation prepared a few years earlier by the town clerk. At some time after August 1568 he was a plaintiff in the court of requests over a suit against him for debt in the sheriffs' court of London. This is the last reference found to him.[6]

[1] Romney chamberlains' accts. 1528-80, f. 80v. [2] Date of birth estimated from first reference. Canterbury prob. reg. C26, ff. 96, 149. [3] *Cinque Ports White and Black Bks.* (Kent Arch. Soc. recs. br. xix), 247, 256, 262. [4] F122/36/13; Romney chamberlains' accts. 1528-80, f. 57; Canterbury prob. reg. C26, f. 96. [5] Romney chamberlains' accts. 1528-80, ff. 80v, 113; Canterbury prob. reg. C26, f. 149; *Cinque Ports White and Black Bks.* 255. [6] *Cinque Ports White and Black Bks.* 260; *Arch. Cant.* li. 189; Req.2/37/31.

H.M.

PAGE, Edmund (by 1512-51), of Shorne, Kent.

ROCHESTER 1529*[1]

b. by 1512, 1st s. of Thomas Page of Shorne by Joan, da. of John Mungeam. *m.* Eleanor, da. and h. of John Herenden, 5s. inc. Thomas* 2da.[2]
    Commr. relief, Rochester 1550.[3]

Edmund Page lived at Shorne, between Graves-end and Rochester, where there had been Pages since at least the late 15th century. Nothing is known of his career outside Parliament beyond his appointment in 1550 as a commissioner: he was presumably of insufficient standing to be employed in local administration.[4]

Nicholas Hurleston, one of the Members for Rochester, is marked 'mortuus' on the Crown Office list as it was revised in the spring of 1532, and the vacancy is included in a list of Cromwell's concerned with the filling of such vacancies and drawn up later in the same year or early in 1533, where Rochester is annotated 'nota for Mr Attorney'. The person so designated was probably (Sir) Christopher Hales*, the attorney-general, whose main residence was near Canterbury but who was later to become steward of the lands of the see of Rochester and may already have been connected with the city. No direct link has been found between Hales and Page, but Page's daughter was to marry into the Kempe family, with whom Hales engaged in extensive land transactions. Page's Membership, however, is established by his appearance on another of Cromwell's lists, compiled in the spring of 1533, where 'Edmund Page of Rochester' follows Hurleston's fellow-Member Robert Fisher. The Members listed are thought to have been opposed to the bill in restraint of appeals, some out of apprehension at reprisals against the wool and cloth trades but others, like Fisher, on religious grounds. If Page was one of these, he is unlikely to have been a nominee of Hales, a close associate of Cromwell who was to conduct the prosecution of Bishop Fisher. It is thus to local conditions, and perhaps even the continuing influence of the bishop himself, that one must look for an explanation of Page's election; if he already leased the manor of Beckley from the neighbouring magnate George Brooke, 9th Lord Cobham, that too may have helped him. As Robert Fisher died before the last session of the Parliament, and is not known to have been replaced, Page may have represented Rochester alone during that session. If his opposition in 1533 was not held against him, he was presumably returned again to the Parliament of June 1536, in obedience to the King's general request for the re-election of the previous Members, and perhaps also to those of 1539 and 1542, when the Members for the city are unknown.[5]

It was as Edmund Page of Shorne, gentleman, that he made his will on 15 Jan. 1551. He left to his wife Eleanor nine acres of land in the parish of Shorne in fee simple and the income of all his lands, not otherwise willed, for her lifetime with remainder to his son Thomas; Thomas was also to allow his mother to occupy the manor of Beckley. Thomas Page was to inherit at once a house and lands in the parishes of Chalk, Gravesend, Higham and Milton next Gravesend, and the residue of all goods, real and personal, including apparel and books. He was also appointed executor and made responsible for the upbringing of the other children, four sons and two daughters, each of whom was to receive £26 13s.4d. at the age of 20, or earlier on reasonable grounds such as sickness or marriage. To every child of his brother James Page and his sister Faith Leffes the testator gave a silver spoon worth 6s.8d. and to a number of friends a gold ring each 'in a poor remembrance'. The will was proved on 20 Feb. 1551. Page was buried in Shorne church, where brasses commemorated him, his wife, his father-in-law Herenden and his son Thomas Page.[6]

[1] LP Hen. VIII, ix. 1077 citing SP1/99, p. 234. [2] Presumed to be of age at election. Vis. Kent (Harl. Soc. lxxv), 16; Rochester prob. reg. 11, f. 117v. [3] CPR, 1553, p. 362. [4] Hasted, Kent, iii. 455. [5] LP Hen. VIII, vii. 56 citing SP1/82, ff. 59–62; ix. 1077 citing SP1/99, p. 234. [6] Rochester prob. reg. 11, f. 117v; Hasted, iii. 451–2.

H.M.

PAGE, Thomas (c.1530–58/59), of Shorne, Kent.

ROCHESTER 1558

b. c.1530, 1st s. of Edmund Page* of Shorne by Eleanor, da. and h. of John Herenden. prob. unm. suc.. fa. Jan./Feb. 1551.[1]

Thomas Page must have been a young man when his father died in 1551, his brothers and sisters all being under 20 at the time. He was to be head of the family for less than eight years and as he died before his mother he never succeeded to the whole inheritance. His father had played a minimal part in local administration and he himself is not known to have taken any at all. His election to the last Marian Parliament thus presupposes influential patronage, and the most likely source of this was George Brooke, 9th Lord Cobham, a local magnate from whom Page held his manor of Beckley, especially as the sheriff, George Vane, came of a family closely linked with Cobham's own.

Page survived this Parliament, and the Queen who had summoned it, by only a few weeks; he may well have been a victim of the prevailing epidemic. By a will of 2 Dec. 1558 he left the gold ring which he wore on his finger to his mother, and other gold rings, worth 20s., to her, to her second husband John Allen, and to friends and relations. His cousin Bartholomew Page was to have the house and land lately bought from him, in return for specified payments to the testator's brother George, who was named sole executor and given £5 a year for life and all lands and goods not otherwise bestowed. The overseers of the will, which was proved on 13 Jan. 1559, were Page's cousin Walter Herenden and his stepfather Allen. Page was buried in the church at Shorne, where a brass plate commemorated him.[2]

[1] Date of birth estimated from father's will, Rochester prob. reg. 11, f. 117v. [2] Ibid. 12, f. 279v; Hasted, Kent, iii. 452.

H.M.

PAGET, Sir Henry (1536/37–68), of Beaudesert Park, Staffs., West Drayton, Mdx. and London.

ARUNDEL   1555
LICHFIELD   1559, 1563*

     b. 1536/37, 1st s. of William Paget, 1st Lord Paget of Beaudesert, by Anne, da. of Henry Preston of 'Preston' (?Preston Patrick or Preston Richard, Westmld.). *m.* 20 May 1567, Catherine, da. of Sir Henry Knyvet of East Horsley, Surr., 1da. KB 29 Sept. 1553. *suc.* fa. as 2nd Lord Paget 9 June 1563.[1]
     J.p.q. Staffs. 1563–*d.*[2]

Richard Cox, tutor to Prince Edward, suggested in December 1544 that his godson Henry Paget might join the household at Ashridge to be brought up with the prince. Nothing came of this, perhaps because of the reorganization of the prince's establishment later in the year, and Henry Paget was to have an indifferent education which left him with, among other shortcomings, poor French. The knighthood he received when hardly above 16, and the seat in the Commons found for him two years later, were a measure of his father's recovery of power on the accession of Mary. Paget went to the Netherlands with his father in 1554 and was entertained by Charles V at Brussels. Returned for a borough controlled by his father's close associate the 12th Earl of Arundel, Paget is predictably missing from the list of Members who voted against one of the government's bills. He was not re-elected to the next Parliament, but in 1559 and 1563 he sat for Lichfield, where his father wielded unchallengeable sway. Removed to the Lords for the session of 1566, he died on 28 Dec. 1568, leaving a four month-old daughter by his marriage of the year before. His widow married Edward Carey†.[3]

[1] Date of birth estimated from age at fa.'s i.p.m., C142/137/47. *CP*; *The Gen.* n.s. xiii. 237–8; S. R. Gammon, *Statesman and Schemer*: *William, 1st Lord Paget*, 200; PCC 11 Sheffelde. [2] *CPR*, 1563–6, p. 26. [3] *LP Hen. VIII*, xix, xx; Gammon, 112, 220–1, 248; Wards 7/11/77.

                                    R.J.W.S.

PAGET, William (by 1506–63), of Beaudesert Park and Burton-upon-Trent, Staffs., West Drayton, Mdx., and London.

CONSTITUENCY UNKNOWN   1529*[1]
MIDDLESEX   1545
STAFFORDSHIRE   1547*

     b. by 1506, 1st s. of John Pachett *alias* Paget of London. *educ.* St. Paul's; Trinity Hall, Camb., adm. by 1520, ?BCL 1526; Paris 1526–7. *m.* by 1536, Anne, da. of Henry Preston of 'Prescon' (?Preston Patrick or Preston Richard, Westmld.), 4s. inc. Henry* 1da. *suc.* fa. aft. 1530. Kntd. 1/19 Jan. 1544; KG nom. 17 Feb. inst. 23 May 1547, degrad. 22 Apr. 1552, rest. 27 Sept. 1553; *cr.* Lord Paget of Beaudesert 3 Dec. 1549.[1]
     Clerk, the signet by Nov. 1531, Privy Council 10 Aug. 1540–Apr. 1541, the Parliaments 15 July 1541–

Dec. 1549/July 1550; keeper, Maxstoke castle, Warws. 1531; j.p. Mdx. 1537–*d.*, Bucks. 1547–*d.*, Derbys. 1547, Staffs. 1547–*d.*; sec. to Queens Jane Seymour by 1537, Anne of Cleves 1540, Catherine Howard 1540; ambassador to France Sept. 1541–Apr. 1543; PC 23 Apr. 1543–*d.*; principal sec. 23 Apr. 1543–June 1547; jt. (with John Mason*) master, the posts 29 Sept. 1545; custos rot. Derbys. by 1545, Staffs. by 1545–*d.*; chancellor, duchy of Lancaster 1 July 1547–July 1552; high steward, Camb. univ. 1547–53, Aug. 1554–*d.*; comptroller, the Household 29 June 1547–3 Dec. 1549; commr. to visit Eton, Camb. univ. 1548, Winchester, Windsor, Oxf. univ. 1549, relief, Mdx., Staffs. 1550; steward for Thomas Seymour, Baron Seymour of Sudeley, unknown property by 1548; jt. ld. lt. Mdx., Staffs. 1551; trier of petitions in the Lords, Parlts. of Oct. 1553, ?Apr. 1554, Nov. 1554, 1555, 1558; ld. privy seal 29 Jan. 1556–Nov. 1558; numerous minor offices.[3]

William Paget's origins are obscure. According to Dugdale his father John was born at Wednesbury, Staffordshire, a county where a Pachett family is found in the early 14th century. A wealthy lawyer Thomas Pachett† died in 1465 in the adjacent county of Worcestershire, leaving a son John, then under age, who was to be apprenticed as a mercer in London, as well as a brother and a cousin of the same christian name. Between 1515 and 1518 one of the numerous John Pachetts was a suitor in Chancery for lands in Bromsgrove, Worcestershire, his claim being one which his grandson was making in vain 40 years later. The fact that Paget's father lent small sums of money, a pound or two at a time, to Bromsgrove residents suggests that he was related to the Worcestershire Pachetts.

John Pachett settled in London, where he appears to have been a jack-of-all-trades, being described in 1502 as a barber, in 1511 as a shearman and in 1530 as a clothworker. The Earl of Surrey's pejorative remarks of 1547 imply that John Pachett also served as a constable or bailiff. Dugdale says that he acted as a serjeant-at-mace to the sheriffs of London, a statement which is confirmed by an acquittance of 1511 in which he is referred to as 'serjeant of London'. His regular small loans to the inhabitants of Staffordshire and Worcestershire notwithstanding, his means were moderate: the visitation of Staffordshire of 1583 describes him as *mediocrae fortunae vir*.

The eldest son William Paget was educated at St. Paul's school, where he studied under William Lilly, the high master (1512–22) whom he was later to defend against Erasmus's friend William Gonell. Among school-fellows with whom he formed lasting friendships were Edward North*, Anthony Denny*, Thomas Wriothesley and John Leland, who wrote a 58-line Latin poem, *Encomia*, which is the principal biographical source for Paget's early life. Paget continued his studies at Trinity Hall, Cambridge, where he was apparently one of the deserving scholars maintained by Thomas Boleyn. His protestant sympathies were observed—he presented a contemporary with the works of Luther and other German divines, openly read Melanchthon, and supported the religious radicals at the university—but also tolerated by the master of the college, Stephen Gardiner, whose friend he became. On leaving Cambridge he went to Paris where he perfected his knowledge of languages: by June 1528 he had been brought by Gardiner into the service of the crown.

Paget probably accompanied Gardiner during the negotiations with Francis I in 1527 and 1528, as the French ambassador thought him well enough known in France to mention his bout of sweating sickness in a despatch of 1528. His appointment as clerk of the signet, one offering considerable administrative opportunity, he presumably owed to Gardiner, who in July 1529 had become secretary to the King. A chance to display his talents came when Cranmer proposed that the European universities should be canvassed about the divorce: in June 1530 Paget joined Edward Foxe, Reginald Pole and Sir Francis Bryan* at Paris, and a year later he obtained from Orleans a condemnation of the papal summons to Henry VIII to appear in Rome. In the following September he was sent to discuss with the Landgrave of Hesse English support for the Schmalkaldic League and to solicit the opinions of theologians there; he returned to Germany in 1532 to encourage the League and to consult with Melanchthon, going by way of France so that English and French policy could be co-ordinated. When Gardiner's opposition to the King's policy brought him into disfavour Paget swiftly deserted him for Cromwell, assuring that minister in February 1533, 'I speak without dissimulation, I esteem myself more bounden to your mastership than to all other.' Cromwell knew his skill in diplomacy and when the decision was taken to break with the papacy he was appointed to the mission sent to the German princes. Between February and June 1534 he visited Luneberg, Mecklenburg, Prussia and Poland.

By that time Paget had begun his career in Parliament. This is clear from the inclusion of his name in a list compiled by Cromwell on the back of a letter of December 1534 and thought to be of those Members particularly connected with the treasons bill then being debated, perhaps as belonging to a committee. Paget had presumably been returned at a by-election held before the beginning of the seventh session. Either the King or Cromwell could have nominated him, and his election may have signalled

his break with Gardiner: perhaps the obsequious letter he sent to Cromwell not long after the opening of the fourth session was part of its aftermath. Which constituency he represented is not known, but with such backing he could have been returned almost anywhere. His mission to northern Europe early in 1534 must have cut short his attendance during the sixth session, but later ones would not have done so to the same extent: in 1536 Edward Foxe asked for him to be sent to Germany again, but he is not known to have gone.[4]

Paget was probably returned to the Parliament of 1536 in accordance with the King's general request for the re-election of the previous Members, and as one who remained close to Cromwell he may also have sat in the following one, that of 1539. His diligence continued to commend him and he was rewarded with the secretaryship to Queens Jane Seymour and Anne of Cleves (later also to Catherine Howard) and numerous confidential tasks; his honorary admission to Gray's Inn was a measure of his growing stature. The fall of Cromwell did not adversely affect Paget's career. It is clear that before the end of 1539 his role as clerk of the signet was expanding, and amid the subsequent adjustments to the administrative machine, especially the Privy Council, came his appointment as the first regular full-time clerk of that body with responsibility for keeping its register. In the following year he became clerk of the Parliaments, but the duties of that office he seems never to have discharged in person: the surviving parliamentary records yield evidence of the work of others but none of his.

It was shortly after accompanying the King to York in 1541 for the proposed meeting with James V of Scotland that Paget replaced Lord William Howard as ambassador to France. The success with which Paget fulfilled his task of discovering French policies without divulging his own King's negotiations with the Emperor made him unacceptable to Francis I, especially after the defeat of the Scots at Solway Firth: he presented his letter of recall on 24 Feb. 1543 but was not allowed to depart until 18 Apr., when his exchange for the French ambassador in England was arranged. On his return Paget was appointed a principal secretary and admitted to the Privy Council: until his colleague Wriothesley's appointment as chancellor he was the junior of the two secretaries but with the advent of William Petre* it was Paget who became the senior and who began to be addressed as chief secretary. His embassy of 1541 presumably debarred him from election to the Parliament of the following year, but his recall may have enabled him to enter it at a by-election. It has been suggested that he replaced

Sir John Dudley as one of the knights for Stafford-shire, but no evidence has been found to corroborate this: even if he had done so, his mission to the Emperor during 1544 would have prevented him from being in the House for the only session, the third and final one, which he could have attended.[5]

As secretary, Paget gained the ear and confidence of the King so that in the closing years of the reign, apart from his five embassies, he was rarely per-mitted to go far from the court. Contemporaries observed the growth of his influence and increasingly directed their letters to him. His desire to see the King well served and the diligence of others rewarded, his experience in foreign affairs, his knowledge and understanding, all these were readily appreciated by the King, who with the onset of painful illness confided in him more and more: eventually Henry came to use Paget as the main intermediary not only between himself and the Council, but also between himself, the court and the kingdom.

In 1545 Paget was returned to Parliament as one of the knights of the shire for Middlesex: as principal secretary he also received a writ of assist-ance to the Lords. His proximity to the King might have been expected to leave many traces of his hand in the preparations for this Parliament, but in fact there are few, one of them being his letter to the deputy of Calais on behalf of Richard Blount (q.v.). He was also to play little part in the proceedings of the first session, for it had hardly begun when he departed on a mission to the Netherlands and had to be kept informed of its progress by Petre. On 27 Dec. he wrote to Petre regretting his absence from the Parliament and especially from 'the most godly, wise and kingly oration', which if he had heard his eyes

> would largely have uttered the affections of my heart, hearing it expressed *tam florida et viva voce* as I know his Majesty can, and I doubt not did, when the reading your recital but of a piece of it my heart doth yearn.

The second session of the Parliament coincided with the King's protracted final illness. Despite Henry VIII's supposed unwillingness to let him leave the royal presence, on 13 Jan. 1547 Paget served on the panel presiding over the Earl of Surrey's trial: when the jury appeared unwilling to condemn Surrey, he hastened to the King's bedside and returned to procure the verdict of guilty. After the King's death on 28 Jan. and Edward VI's arrival in London, Paget was one of those who went to the Parliament House on 31 Jan. to announce the death and acces-sion: after he had read the late King's will to the assembly, Parliament was dissolved.[6]

The direction of the wars with Scotland and France had absorbed much of Paget's time during the closing years of the reign. The military com-manders had come to depend on him for com-munication with the King while they were cam-paigning, and among them the Earl of Hertford, soon to be raised to the dukedom of Somerset, developed a relationship with Paget which was to be of great importance after the change of sovereign, when Paget became the Protector Somerset's constant companion. In February 1547 the imperial ambassador rated Paget 'the person most in author-ity', but this was an overestimate. True, he did stand at the centre of affairs, but the late King's will (of which Paget was perhaps at least part-author) is a surer guide to his position: he was not one of the principal beneficiaries, receiving only £300 in cash and lands worth 400 marks a year. It was the new King, or the Protector Somerset in his name, who gave Paget the Garter, and upon his resignation as secretary made him comptroller of the Household and chancellor of the duchy of Lancaster.[7]

While Somerset was with the army in Scotland during the summer of 1547 Paget was the effective head of the government and to him there fell the supervision of the elections to the Parliament sum-moned for the autumn. Although in this matter he was more an agent than a principal, the unusually large number of crown officials returned may reflect his intervention. His personal influence is most evident in the duchy of Lancaster boroughs and in Staffordshire, where he was responsible for the re-enfranchisement of Lichfield and where he himself was elected one of the knights of the shire. There is little trace of his role during the first session, but he presumably began to play the part of government manager and spokesman in the Commons, and liaison-officer with the Lords, which he was to continue in the second. Then the bill for cattle breeding was committed to him after its second reading on 16 Jan. 1549, as was that for abstaining from flesh on the following 25 Feb. and the 'new' bill for curriers, cordwainers and girdlers after its first reading on 13 Feb. He served on the committee to hear the matter against (Sir) Nicholas Hare (q.v.), carried bills up to the Lords on 16 Feb. and 10 Mar., and on 4 Mar. was ordered by the House to 'require the Lords, that, if necessity require to have the Lords come down, that upon a further suit they may come down' to the Commons. He resumed his activity in the third session until his elevation to the peerage, whereupon Sir Ralph Bagnall replaced him in the Commons. On 15 Nov. 1549 the bill for the continuance of the Act of sewers was committed to him after its first reading and on 30 Nov. he was ordered to attend the Lords for an answer to the petition for the relief, reporting back the King's pleasure and the permission to treat on it. In the Lords he was a fairly regular attendant for the remainder of the session and he was appointed to the committee for the bill concerning enclosures. The Acts for a general pardon and for the fine and ransom of the Duke of Somerset, passed during this session, were signed by Paget, and another (3 and 4 Edw. VI, no.25), introduced after he had left the Commons, enabled him to acquire the churchyard at West Drayton in exchange for other property.[8]

During 1548 Somerset became increasingly aloof from the Council, consulting only his closest supporters and minions. This estrangement alarmed Paget, who in June of that year wrote to the duke about the dangerous direction in which he was moving. Other warnings were to follow with growing frequency in the months that followed, and with Somerset's consulting him less often and less openly Paget recognized that he had become Somerset's Cassandra, an embarrassment to be avoided. His advice was none the less to the point, as in his exhortation of 12 Mar. 1549, 'for God's sake to end the Parliament'; he argued that the session had fulfilled its purpose once the subsidy (2 and 3 Edw. VI, c.36) had been granted and that the Members should return to their homes to maintain the peace and defend the realm, a recommendation which Somerset followed two days later. Despite his doubts Paget continued to cling to Somerset until the autumn of 1549 when the Protector was toppled from power: then the duke's decision to surrender to the Earl of Warwick was probably made on Paget's advice, and it was Paget who arrested him on Warwick's behalf. His role in the crisis brought Paget his peerage.[9]

Initially that role did not alter with the change of regime, but once Warwick's supremacy was assured Paget's support was no longer necessary and by the summer of 1551 he had almost ceased to have any say in affairs. Worse was to follow: at first directed to stay away from the court, when in the autumn Somerset's old supporters were rounded up he was confined to his house in the Strand, then transferred to the Fleet and finally put in the Tower. He escaped a charge of treason but was accused of malversation as chancellor of the duchy (the case appears to have been trumped-up, evidently being modelled on that against John Beaumont*), deprived of his offices and stripped of the Garter. On 31 May 1552 he signed a submission of guilt: two weeks later he made his confession orally before the Council and was then released from the Tower. On 20 June his fine was fixed at £8,000 and he was ordered to remove to

Staffordshire within six weeks, but before that time he secured permission to stay in the vicinity of London. The fine was later reduced to £4,000, a sum which the Council agreed to accept in land to a yearly value of £200, and in December he sued out a pardon. By February 1553 he had paid enough of the fine for the King to forgive the remainder; early in March he was allowed to kiss the royal hand in gratitude for his restoration to favour, and he took his place daily in the Parliament of that month, voting against two minor measures. Three months later he witnessed the King's will.[10]

The former Warwick, now Duke of Northumberland, sought Paget's support in the succession crisis which followed the death of Edward VI, and Paget put his name to the order sent to Richard Rich, Baron Rich, to hold Essex against Mary. Despite this initial show of solidarity it was Paget who rode to Framlingham to inform Mary of the Council's decision to recognize her as Queen. His recent degradation now redounded to his credit, the Queen completed his restoration and for the first weeks of the reign her government was virtually headed by Paget and the 12th Earl of Arundel. His championship of the Spanish marriage—for some unknown reason he accompanied the supporters of an English marriage when they waited on Mary—and his tireless negotiations at first earned him the Queen's trust, but this he was soon to forfeit. An opponent of extremism, he refused to support the religious settlement advocated by Gardiner, with whom he disagreed openly and violently in the Council, in Parliament and in public, to the detriment of the regime. King Philip interceded for him but the Queen could not be persuaded that Paget meant well: on Gardiner's death she refused to accept his nomination for the chancellorship but agreed to his becoming lord privy seal, an office which retained him in the government without making him one of its leaders. The appointment was not renewed at the accession of Elizabeth, but Paget remained a Privy Councillor and his advice was often sought in the last few years of life.[11]

Throughout his career Paget invested the profits of office in land. As early as 1534 he had secured from the 5th Earl of Northumberland a lease of Northumberland place in Aldersgate. Three years later he took a lease of a manor in West Drayton, Middlesex, which in later years he expanded into a large estate. At the Dissolution he acquired much property, including the site and nearly all the possessions of Burton abbey in Staffordshire. It was the late 1540s which saw his aggrandizement at its peak: during 1546 'his special good service' earned him from the crown six

Staffordshire manors including Beaudesert, and when in 1548 the bishop of Exeter was obliged to surrender his town house in the Strand to the King, Paget obtained it and renamed it after himself.

Paget was one of the more conscientious peers in attending the Lords during the reign of Mary, missing only the opening weeks of the Parliament of November 1554 while he was conducting Cardinal Pole to England, and the second session of the Parliament of 1558 from which he obtained leave of absence. On 23 Feb. 1554 he was one of the Councillors approached 'to consider what laws shall be established in this Parliament and to name men that shall make the books thereof', and shortly before the opening Mary asked him and several others to decide what was to be laid before Parliament. He was chosen to serve on the committees for bills in which the Queen had a personal interest, but angered by Gardiner's failure to consult him over religious legislation he encouraged his colleagues to reject the heresy bill and amended that to extend the protection of the treason laws to Philip. It was not uncommon for Paget to vote against private bills, but his opposition to legislation of official origin was unusual. Ill health prevented him from taking his place in the Lords in the Parliament opened in 1559 by Elizabeth and allowed him to make only a few appearances in the second Parliament of her reign.[12]

Paget did not show, even if he possessed, any strong religious convictions, and contemporary judgments of his beliefs varied. In 1545 Petre was sure that he was a Protestant; later Renard was convinced that he was deep with heretics, Soranzo called him an acknowledged anti-Catholic and the Jesuit Persons was certain that he had been a convert to Reform. On the other side, Foxe and Ponet were certain that he was a Catholic. Paget himself explained to Renard that one of the Henrician and Edwardian bishops had led him into error over transubstantiation but he had long since seen and renounced that heresy. What emerges is that Paget's faith was moderate, conservative and private.

Paget made his will on 4 Nov. 1560. He provided for his wife, children and kinswomen and gave £100 to be distributed among his servants. The lands assigned to his widow for life had been conveyed earlier in the year to Thomas Carus*, Richard Cupper*, George Freville* and Edmund Twyneho*, and about the same time other lands had been entrusted to James Bedell, Cupper, Freville and Twyneho to the use of Paget's son Sir Henry, whom he also made his residuary legatee and sole executor. As overseers he appointed Edmund and William Twyneho†, Cupper and Robert Jones. Paget lived for nearly three years after making his will, dying on 9 June 1563 at West Drayton where he was buried with considerable pomp nine days later. A cenotaph was erected in his honour by the 2nd Lord Paget in Lichfield cathedral. His descendants were to become earls of Uxbridge and marquesses of Anglesey. There remain several portraits of Paget from the last 20 years of his life.[13]

[1] LP Hen. VIII, vii. 1522(ii) citing SP1/87, f. 106v. [2] Date of birth estimated from admission to Cambridge. This biography rests on S. R. Gammon, Statesman and Schemer: William, 1st Lord Paget; CP; DNB. [3] EHR, lxxvii. 82; LP Hen. VIII, xv, xx; Somerville, Duchy, i. 394, 545, 612; C66/985 ex inf. J. C. Sainty; E163/12/17, nos. 38, 51, 54; LJ, i. 447, 464, 492, 513. [4] LP Hen. VIII, vii. 1552(ii). [5] Wm. Salt Arch. Soc. xxiii. 322-3. [6] SP1/210/126; C218/1. [7] Wealth and Power, ed. Ives, Knecht and Scarisbrick, 87–105. [8] CJ, i. 6, 8–12, 14–15; M. A. R. Graves, 'The Tudor House of Lords 1547–58' (Otago Univ. Ph.D. thesis, 1974), 336–8; House of Lords RO, Original Acts, 3 and 4 Edw. VI, nos. 24, 31. [9] The Letters of William, Lord Paget of Beaudesert, 1547–63 (Cam. Misc. xxv), 1–141; B. L. Beer, 'The Paget letter bk.', Manuscripta, xiv. 176–9; 'A critique of the Protectorate', HL Quarterly, xxxiv. 277–83; 'Sir William Paget and the Protectorate, 1547–9', Ohio Academy of Hist. Newsletter, ii. 2–9. [10] Graves, 337–8. [11] City of London RO, Guildhall, rep. 13(1), ff. 129, 206v, 213; Graves, 337–8; D. M. Loades, Two Tudor Conspiracies, 11–238 passim. [12] Graves, 336–8; LJ, i. 541–618. [13] PCC 27 Chayre; C142/137/47; Machyn's Diary (Cam. Soc. xlii), 309, 395–6; S. A. J. McVeigh, Drayton of the Pagets, passim; R. C. Strong, Tudor and Jacobean Portraits, 241–2.

A.D.K.H.

PAGMAN (PACKMAN, PAGENHAM, PAKENHAM), Robert (by 1497–1552), of Tooting Bec, Surr. and Kirkstall, Yorks.

GREAT BEDWYN   1547[1]

b. by 1497, s. of Hugh Pagman by Agnes, da. and h. of William Clement. m. Elizabeth, da. and h. of Maurice Berkeley of Wymondham, Leics., 5s.[2]

Clerk comptroller, the counting house by 1518; clerk of the accts. by 1543; clerk of the green cloth by 1547; surveyor within the dresser at the coronation of Anne Boleyn 1533; commr. to audit accts. of cofferer of Prince Edward Dec. 1541; member, household of Queen Catherine Parr 1543–8.[3]

Robert Pagman probably owed his advancement to the connexions which his family had built up through advantageous marriages: his cousins in varying degrees included John Dudley, Duke of Northumberland, and (Sir) Henry Sidney* and among his uncles was Sir William Fitzwilliam I*, Earl of Southampton. By 1518 he was an officer in the royal counting house and by 1547 clerk of the green cloth, an office which he kept until his death and in virtue of which he attended Henry VIII's funeral. The 'jewel set with stones which was my Lady Lovell's' that he was to leave to his wife perhaps signalized his friendship with another officer of the Household, Gregory Lovell, although it hints at the patronage of Sir Thomas Lovell I*. Other associations of Pagman's are reflected in the names of those with whom he was party to a deed of 1534 relating to Cockington, Devon: these included Leonard Chamberlain* and Hugh Paulet*.[4]

In 1544 Pagman was listed among those who were to go to France with the army and was ordered to supply two horsemen, four archers and five others. In November 1544 he was a master victualler to the army, disbursing £4,820 with Richard Esquyers, and reporting to the 3rd Duke of Norfolk that the wagons were imperfect. In the following year he was commanded by the Privy Council to go to Calais to view the victuals there and 'to hasten the furniture of Guisnes from thence'. He was to have expenses of 10s. a day, but when he returned from his mission after eight days to report a shortage only of vinegar and ale the Privy Council ordered him to be paid £10.[5]

Pagman's wife was heir to her brother John Berkeley, and in 1540 the couple received livery of her lands. In the same year Pagman secured from the court of augmentations a 21-year lease of the site of Kirkstall, abbey, Yorkshire. When in August 1548 lands were granted to John Dudley, Earl of Warwick, Pagman and his wife were included in that part of the patent relating to the manor of Tooting Bec. The inquisition taken after Pagman's death shows that Warwick had conveyed to them his interest in the manor within three days of its acquisition, perhaps in exchange for lands in Leicestershire which he received from Pagman at some unknown date.[6]

Pagman's return to the Parliament of 1547 for Great Bedwyn he presumably owed to the favour of either the Protector Somerset or his brother Admiral Seymour. With Somerset himself Pagman had no known connexion but as a member of the household of Queen Catherine Parr, who in 1544 and 1545 had given him New Year's gifts of black satin, he is likely to have enjoyed both her support and that of her new husband. The election to this Parliament of a Berkeley as knight of the shire for Somerset and another as Member for Hereford may also indicate that, in this respect as in others, Pagman was fortunate in his marriage.[7]

The will which Pagman made on 2 Sept. 1552, and the inquisition post mortem taken on 1 Feb. following, reveal that he had three grown up sons, Edmund, John and Anthony, and another, Robert, aged eight at the time of the inquisition, and that when he died on 5 Sept. 1552 his wife Elizabeth was 'great with boy'. He made provision for the first three, and for the unborn child, who were left all the lands which he had leased and purchased, but the younger Robert, unmentioned in the will, was to be named in the inquisition as his father's nearest heir. The nature of this arrangement is made more clear in the grant of general livery to the younger Robert on 20 June 1566, where it is stated that a third of his father's lands had descended to him. It is possible that the precedence as his father's heir which the

eight year-old Robert had been given over his elder brothers was a device to provide for his wardship which was granted to his second cousin Sir Henry Sidney on 24 May 1554.[8]

[1] Hatfield 207. [2] Date of birth estimated from first reference. *Vis. Suss.* (Harl. Soc. liii), 44–45; *Vis. Leics.* (Harl. Soc. ii), 2–3; *Lincs. Peds.* (Harl. Soc. lii), 748; PCC 32 Powell; Wards 7/6/109. [3] *LP Hen. VIII*, vi, xvi, xix; LC 2/2, f. 28; Add. 21116, f. 57; information from Susan Roberts. [4] *Vis. Surr.* (Harl. Soc. xliii), 6; *LP Hen. VIII*, ii, xviii; *Soc. Antiq.* (1790), 218; LC 2/4/1; *CPR*, 1553, p. 5; *Machyn's Diary* (Cam. Soc. xlii), 24–25; NRA 7028, nos. 1–4. [5] *LP Hen. VIII*, xix, xx. [6] *VCH Surr.* iv. 94–95; *LP Hen. VIII*, xvi; *CPR*, 1547–8, pp. 105–7; 1548–9, pp. 29–31; 1553–4, p. 474. [7] E101/423/12, ff. 8, 12. [8] PCC 32 Powell; Wards 7/6/109; 9/62/6, f. 159v; *CPR*, 1553–4, p. 81 giving incorrect date of death (1 Sept.).

R.L.D.

PAKINGTON, John (by 1488–1551), of Hampton Lovett, Worcs. and London.

GLOUCESTER 1515[1]
WORCESTERSHIRE 1539[2]

b. by 1488, 1st s. of John Pakington by Elizabeth, da. of Thomas Washborne of Stanford-le-Teme, Worcs.; bro. of Robert*. educ. I. Temple. m. by 1530, Anne, da. of Henry Dacres of London, wid. of Robert Fairethwatt of London, at least 1s. d.v.p. 2da. Kntd. 23 Nov. 1546/9 Feb. 1547.[3]

Christmas butler, I. Temple 1512, marshal 1515, auditor 1516–17, Lent reader 1520, 1528, treasurer 1528–33, gov. 1536.

Chirographer, c.p. 17 June 1509–d.; j.p. Glos. 1515–d., Mdx. 1524–d., N. Wales, Worcs. 1532–d., Herefs., Staffs. 1537–d., Cheshire, Salop 1539–d., Mon. 1543; commr. subsidy, Gloucester 1515, Mdx. 1523, 1524, chantries, Brec., Card., Carm., Glam., Rad. 1546, Herefs., Worcs. 1546, 1548, relief, Salop, Worcs. 1550; serjeant-at-law 1 Nov. 1531; member, council in the marches of Wales in 1534; sheriff, Herefs. 1538–9, Worcs. 1540–1; recorder, Worcester by 1539–d.; custos rot. Worcs. 31 Aug. 1540; justice, Brec., Glam. and Rad. 1541–50.[4]

Whether the John Pakington who obtained the lease of some property near Gloucester in June 1513 was the young lawyer or his father is not certain, but that it was the younger man who was chosen to serve for the town in the Parliament of 1515 is consonant with Pakington's appointment to the Gloucestershire bench in the same year and his remaining on it until his death. Between the Parliament's two sessions he and his fellow-Member Thomas Porter nominated the town's collectors for the recently granted subsidy. His Membership in 1515 may have marked the beginning of a parliamentary career of which, owing to the gaps in the evidence, we have only one further glimpse. He could have sat in 1523, a Parliament for which few names of Members survive, have been by-elected to the Parliament of 1529 and thus also have been returned again in 1536, and even have sat again for Worcestershire in 1545 (when the knights for that shire are unknown). The fact that, when elected in

1539, he was sheriff of the neighbouring county of Hereford may indicate not only that Cromwell wanted him in the House but also that he too was eager to sit there. One of the measures debated during the third session and enacted as the Statute of Fines (32 Hen. VIII, c.36) proved to concern him as chirographer of common pleas and on 19 May 1540 Bishop Rowland Lee appealed to Cromwell to protect his interests in that office.[5]

After 20 or more years of regular attendance at his inn and of practice both in London and the country, Pakington was exempted in 1529 from wearing his hat in the King's presence, taking the order of knighthood and being made a baron of the Exchequer or a serjeant-at-law. Two of these were, however, to be disregarded.[6]

In 1531 Cromwell acted as counsel in a case against Pakington and his brother Robert. Later that year Cromwell received a fine of £267 from him for an unspecified misdemeanour, which appears to have been the reason behind a temporary coolness between the two. Pakington's ability was such, however, that when Christopher Hales* recommended on 9 Nov. 1532 that he should be made justice of North Wales, Cromwell acquiesced. Within two years Pakington was also appointed to the council in the marches of Wales, of which he became an active member. Thereafter the two corresponded frequently on administrative and personal matters, Cromwell several times interceding with the King to compensate Pakington for his expenses in Wales.[7]

By marriage Pakington was well connected: his wife's brothers-in-law included Robert Cheseman*, George Rolle* and Robert Dacres, the Privy Councillor, while his brother's father-in-law was (Sir) John Baldwin*. From 1521, when he bought the manor of Extons, Pakington regularly purchased land in Worcestershire, where he had been born, until by the time of his death he owned a not insignificant estate. His most important acquisitions were the manor of Hampton Lovett in 1528 and the lease of Westwood priory in 1539. Pakington died at Hampton Lovett on 21 Aug. 1551, five days after making his will, and was buried in the chapel of St. Anne in the parish church despite his own wish to be interred in the chancel. He had made provision for his wife and his daughters, Bridget, wife of John Lyttleton*, and Ursula, wife of William Scudamore, and left numerous small bequests to kinsmen, friends and charities. Pakington's sons had predeceased him without issue so that he was succeeded by his nephew Thomas Pakington.[8]

[1] E179/279/3, m. 23. [2] E159/319, brev. ret. Mich. r. [1–2]. [3] Date of birth estimated from first office. *Vis. Worcs.* (Harl. Soc. xxvii), 102; *LP Hen. VIII*, xxi; *CPR*, 1547–8, pp. 11–12; C142/140/196; PCC 30

Bucke; *DNB*. [4] *LP Hen. VIII*, i–v, viii, xi–xv; *Cal. I.T. Recs.* i. 98; *Statutes*, iii. 171; *CPR*, 1549–51, pp. 211–12; 1553, pp. 358–9, 362; A. D. Dyer, *Worcester in 16th Cent.* 201. [5] *LP Hen. VIII*, i, xv; E179/279/3, m. 23. [6] *LP Hen. VIII*, iv. [7] Ibid. v–vii, x, xii, xiv, xv; Strype, *Eccles. Memorials*, ii(2), 161. [8] *VCH Worcs.* ii. 151; iii. 7, 16, 25–26, 39, 82, 128, 154, 156–7, 234, 262; iv. 228, 234; C142/93/102; Pevsner, *Worcs.* 183; PCC 30 Bucke.

A.D.K.H.

PAKINGTON, Robert (by 1489–1536), of London.

LONDON 1529*

b. by 1489, 2nd or 3rd s. of John Pakington by Elizabeth, da. of Thomas Washborne of Stanford-le-Teme, Worcs.; bro. of John*. *educ*. I. Temple, adm. 1520. *m*. (1) by 1520, Agnes, da. and coh. of (Sir) John Baldwin* of Aylesbury, Bucks., 2s. 3da.; (2) Catherine, wid. of Richard Collyer (*d*.1533) of London.[1]

Warden, Mercers' Co. 1527–8, 1536–*d*.; auditor, London 1534–6.[2]

Robert Pakington was born in the parish of Stanford-le-Teme where lands long held by the family of Washborne were brought to his own by his father's marriage to Elizabeth Washborne. His eldest brother was an Inner Templar and it was the same inn that he himself entered, although as a social rather than a professional step as he was pardoned all vacations and offices and was licensed to be in commons at his pleasure. By that time, indeed, he had already been a freeman of the Mercers' Company for ten years, having completed his apprenticeship in 1510, and had recently become a member of the livery. An exporter of cloth and an importer of sundry wares, he was one of the 'worshipful commoners' present at a general court of the Merchant Adventurers in 1516. Although he never became a merchant on the largest scale Pakington continued in a fair way of business; in 1535, for example, he shipped 75 long and 168 short cloths to the midsummer mart at Antwerp. His trade took him from time to time to the Netherlands, where in February 1534 he was one of the assistants of the Merchant Adventurers at Bergen-op-Zoom, and whither Stephen Vaughan* sent him to report on affairs to Cromwell in September 1535. In London he lived in the parish of St. Pancras, Needlers Lane, where he was assessed at £250 in goods for the subsidy of 1523 and at 500 marks for that of 1534.[3]

In preparation for the Parliament of 1523 Pakington and other Merchant Adventurers were elected by the Mercers' Company 'to devise such articles as should be thought necessary . . . as well for the enhancing and bringing up of the hanse concerning the Merchants Adventurers and for all other things . . . for the weal and profit of the said company': a few days later he received a similar charge from the City, being one of those chosen by the court of aldermen 'to devise what things be most necessary and behoveful for the common weal of this City to be moved at this next Parliament'. A number of Acts passed by the Parliament (14 and 15 Hen. VIII, cc.1, 2, 3, 4, 9, 11) may have owed something to these initiatives. Six years later Pakington was again called upon by his company to devise articles for presentation to Parliament by the City's Members. Of the five grievances they suggested for redress, one was to figure prominently in the proceedings of the House of Commons: it was

to have in remembrance how the King's poor subjects, principally of London, [have] been polled and robbed without reason or conscience by the ordinaries in probating of testaments and taking of mortuaries, and also vexed and troubled by citations, with cursing one day and assoiling the next, *et haec omnia pro pecuniis*.

Although thus early associated with the work of this Parliament, Pakington did not become a Member of it until he was elected to replace William Bowyer for its last two sessions: among his colleagues in the House was his father-in-law Sir John Baldwin. Pakington may have sat again in the Parliament of 1536, for which the names of the Members for London are lost but to which the King asked for the re-election of the previous Members. According to Edward Hall I*, who described Pakington as 'a man of a great courage, and one that both could speak and also would be heard', he spoke in Parliament 'somewhat against the covetousness and cruelty of the clergy'.[4]

This anti-clerical Londoner was nevertheless a daily worshipper in the church of St. Thomas of Acon across the road from his house in Cheapside. While on his way to mass there, early on the morning of Monday 13 Nov. 1536, he was shot and killed by an unknown assailant. All the accounts of the incident derive from Hall, who describes how the report of the gun was heard by neighbours and bystanders but the assassin hidden by a dense mist. His identity was never established, but there was no lack of speculation. Hall himself suggested that 'most like' Pakington had been murdered by a cleric, as Richard Hunne had been a generation earlier; Foxe went so far as to name the murderer as the dean of St. Paul's, Dr. Incent, who on his deathbed was said to have confessed 'that he himself was the author thereof, by hiring an Italian for 60 crowns or thereabouts to do the feat'. Eventually a less controversial, if less dramatic, sequel was recorded by Holinshed, who wrote that

at length the murderer indeed was condemned at Banbury in Oxfordshire to die for a felony which he afterwards committed, and when he came to the gallows on which he suffered, he confessed

that he did this murder, and till that time he was never had in any suspicion thereof.[5]

Pakington was buried in his parish church of St. Pancras (where a monument later commemorated him), and the sermon was preached by the Protestant Robert Barnes. He had made his will on 23 Nov. 1535, trusting to find salvation 'only by the merits of Jesus Christ'. He committed his 'little children' to the care of the executors, his wife and his brother Humphrey, and of the overseers, his brother John and the children's grandfather Sir John Baldwin. By the custom of London the children became orphans of the City, and on 20 Nov. 1537 the court of aldermen entrusted the care of the eldest, Thomas, to Baldwin. Nearly five years later Thomas, then presumably of age, acknowledged that he had received his share of his father's estate and in 1544 the younger son did likewise, after he had taken an oath that he was 21.[6]

[1] Date of birth estimated from first reference. *Vis. Worcs.* (Harl. Soc. xxvii), 102–3; C1/1050/2–5; 142/73/7; City of London RO, Guildhall, rep. 4, ff. 65–65v; 10, ff. 24, 260v; 11, f. 54v; PCC 4 Dyngeley, 24 Thower. [2] *Acts Ct. of Mercers' Co.* ed. Lyell and Watney, 748; Mercers' Co. acts of ct. 1527–60, f. 91; City of London RO, jnl. 13, ff. 422, 449v. [3] PCC 4 Dyngeley; *Habington's Worcs.* (Worcs. Hist. Soc. 1895), i. 382; Lits of mercers (T/S Mercers' Hall), 378; E122/81/8, 82/3, 7, 9 ex inf. Prof. P. Ramsey; 179/251/15v; *Acts Ct. of Mercers' Co.* 433, 511; SP1/33, f. 25; O. de Smedt, *De Engelse Natie te Antwerpen*, ii. 60, 429; *LP Hen. VIII*, ix. [4] *Acts Ct. of Mercers' Co.* 559–60; City of London RO, rep. 4, f. 145v; Mercers' Co. acts of ct. 1527–60, ff. 24v–25v; Hall, *Chron.* 824. [5] Hall, 824; *Wriothesley's Chron.* i (Cam. Soc. n.s. xi), 59; Foxe, *Acts and Mons.* v. 250; Holinshed, *Chron.* iii. 804. [6] *Stow's Survey of London*, i. 261; *LP Hen. VIII*, xi; PCC 4 Dyngeley; City of London RO, rep. 10, ff. 7, 24, 260v; 11, ff. 54v, 115v.

H.M.

PALLADY, Richard (1515/16–59/63), of St. Bride's, London and Ruscombe, Berks.

PETERBOROUGH   1547
HEYTESBURY   1559

b. 1515/16. *educ.* Eton c.1529; King's, Camb. adm. 18 Aug. 1533, fellow 1536–7. *m.* (1) by 1544, Catherine, da. of Guy Armston of Armston, Northants.; (2) Anne, da. of William Kirkby of Upper Rawcliffe, Lancs.[1]

Attorney, sheriff's ct. London 27 July 1540– 5 Mar. 1548; servant, Edward Seymour, Duke of Somerset by 1548; j.p. Berks. 1558/59[2].

At the opening of the 16th century there was a yeoman family named Pallady living at Irthlingborough in Northamptonshire, and as its sons were customarily baptized Richard, the Member so named was probably one of them. At about the time he was born Irthlingborough passed into the custody of Sir Nicholas Vaux*, afterwards Lord Vaux of Harrowden, who in 1515 secured the wardship of its young heir Elizabeth Cheyne; when she married his own heir Thomas, Irthlingborough became part of the Vaux estates and was long used as a family residence. By 1529, when Pallady entered Eton,

Thomas, 2nd Lord Vaux, was 19 and had perhaps spent some time at Cambridge, where four years later Pallady was to become a scholar of King's: it may well have been to the cultured Vaux that this humble neighbour owed his start in life. He was to become a servant of Edward Seymour, Earl of Hertford, whose steward (Sir) John Thynne* had earlier been a member of Vaux's household: Thynne had made the transition in 1536 and Pallady may have joined him within a year or two, although he is first met with in Hertford's service some ten years later. By then he had married and had been sued by his wife's kinsmen over the title to the manor of Armston in Kingsthorpe, Northamptonshire which had given her family its name: at one point the plaintiffs, Robert Kirkham (Pallady's cousin) and Thomas Henson, called Catherine Armston illegitimate. No decree survives, but an agreement may have been reached, for in 1546 Kirkham and Pallady sold the manor to a local gentleman, John Lane, who resold it in the following year to Edward Montagu.[3]

Although Pallady has been credited with the design of Somerset Place, the town mansion which Seymour began as Earl of Hertford and continued as Duke of Somerset, he was probably responsible solely for the accountancy of its construction: this was a task usually given to a financially experienced officer of the household concerned, and all that is known of Pallady suggests that this was his place in Somerset's establishment. It was doubtless as such that he was elected to the Parliament of 1547 for Peterborough. If, as is possible, the city was returning for the first time, Somerset probably took the initiative in its enfranchisement, at the same time nominating at least one of the Members: it lay on his route both to and from Scotland in the summer of 1547 and, as elsewhere, the matter may have been settled in his presence. A link with its high steward, Sir John Russell*, Baron Russell, who in the previous year had recommended Pallady for a stewardship to the aldermen of London, perhaps facilitated his election, while Pallady's local origin—Irthlingborough is some 30 miles from Peterborough—and connexions would have commended him. Nothing is known of his part in the proceedings during the first two sessions of the Parliament, but on the eve of the third he was one of the dependants of Somerset who followed the fallen Protector into the Tower: he was kept there for three months, thus missing the whole of the third session, and was then released with William Cecil, Richard Whalley* and Edward Wolf, in a recognizance of 4,000 marks to appear before the Council to answer charges. There is no evidence that these were ever brought, and in the absence of any indication to the contrary

on the list of Members as revised for the final session of January 1552 it is to be presumed that he avoided further trouble at the time of Somerset's trial and execution and resumed his seat in the House.[4]

It was while the duke was still in power that Pallady had joined Francis Foxhall, a London mercer, in paying £1,522 for property in London, Warwickshire and elsewhere in the midlands. The crown did not have undisputed title to all the property granted, for Pallady was obliged to sue the churchwardens of All Hallows the Less for at least one tenement; although the outcome of that suit is unknown, in April 1549 the treasurer of augmentations had a warrant to pay Pallady and Foxhall £462, probably because the title to property recently acquired from that court had proved to be defective. Whether Pallady retained these possessions is not known, and there are few indications of where or how he passed his remaining years. A lawsuit of 1555 against the dean and chapter of Worcester, from whom he had leased tithes at Warton in Lancashire, may be connected with his second marriage, but he does not appear to have settled in his wife's county: on the pardon roll of 1559 he is described as 'late of Ruscombe, Berkshire', and he seems to have ended his days at Buckland, Gloucestershire. His election to the Parliament of 1559 for Heytesbury suggests a continuing association with Sir John Thynne, by then a leading figure in west Wiltshire with an interest in that borough. Pallady died intestate before 27 Mar. 1563 when letters of administration were granted to his widow.[5]

[1] Aged 17 on admission to Cambridge. Bridges, *Northants.* ii. 418; *Vis. Lancs.* (Chetham Soc. lxxxi), 41. [2] City of London RO, Guildhall, rep. 10, f. 168v; 11, f. 429; Egerton 2815. [3] Northants. consist. ct. G41, Y176; C1/1020/52; 3/139/9; Peterborough cath. lib. 28, p. 37; G. Anstruther, *Vaux of Harrowden*, 25, 62, 94, 96; Bridges, ii. 418; Req.2/6/133, 7/120. [4] Egerton 2815; City of London RO, rep. 11, f. 311; *APC*, ii. 322, 372. [5] *CPR*, 1548–9, p. 25; 1558–60, p. 150; *APC*, ii. 273; *Ducatus Lanc.* 209, 298, 302; PCC admons. act bk. 1563, f. 59.

S.M.T.

PALMER

CONSTITUENCY UNKNOWN 1547[*1]

On 5 Nov. 1549 the House ordered Sir William Babthorpe*, John Cock II*, John Gwillim* and (Sir) Nicholas Hare* to 'excuse the appearance of Mr. Palmer, burgess, before the justices of the common pleas, returned in attaint'. The designation 'burgess' in the minute for the order in the Journal rules out the identification of this recipient of privilege with the John Palmer who was then a knight of the shire for Sussex, and as neither the returns nor the list of Members revised for the final session includes a namesake of the Sussex knight, the Journal entry furnishes the only evidence for a second Palmer elected to the Parliament of 1547.

As Palmer's name does not occur on the list of Members for the final session, it follows that he had been replaced as a Member by 1552, but whether withdrawal, ejection or death accounts for this is unknown. Leaving aside the possibilities of withdrawal or ejection, the commonness of his name renders any attempt to establish his identity from among those known to have died between 1549 and 1552 highly speculative. The same reservation attaches to any cases before the court of common pleas, and scrutiny of its plea roll for Michaelmas term 1549 for evidence of an action interrupted by the invocation of privilege has proved fruitless. Of the numerous Palmers then being sued in the court none was a resident of a parliamentary borough and most were of humble status. Only two of the cases relate to gentlemen, and both of these were cases which had extended over several years. The less significant concerned William Palmer of Mucking, Essex, accused of breaking into a nearby close and causing damage estimated at £5. The other involved John Palmer of Upper Lemington, Gloucestershire, who was being sued for a debt of £120 by Thomas Wenman* of Witney, Oxfordshire, as executor of the will of his father Richard Wenman (d.1534). Twice ordered to appear during Michaelmas term this John Palmer failed to respond and in November a further date was fixed for his appearance. If he answered the summons it is not recorded in the plea roll for the Hilary term. This case was almost certainly linked with another for the same amount brought by Thomas Onslow of London against Thomas Kynaston of Otley, Shropshire, in the same court, as is made clear by a third suit in which Onslow sued both Kynaston and Palmer for various smaller sums. A sheepowner, described by an adversary as a 'man of great possessions', John Palmer was allied to several families of importance in the marches and had been active in local affairs, albeit in a minor capacity, since the 1520s. At least two of his kinsmen, Sir Fulke Greville and George Willoughby, were Members of the Parliament of 1547. As a Gloucestershire man he could have enjoyed the patronage of the Protector Somerset or Admiral Seymour, as a relative of Willoughby that of the Earl of Warwick, and as a lessee of lands at Toddenham held by Secretary Petre that of Petre. With such sponsorship John Palmer could have obtained a seat almost anywhere at the elections in 1547 or at a by-election in the following two years. The main objection to his identification with the Member is that he did not die until 21 July 1553, so that he could not have been

removed from the list of Members as having died before the final session. No other reason for his withdrawal can be surmised unless it was that the matter of the privilege backfired on him, but this is unlikely.[2]

[1] CJ, i. 11. [2] CP40/1138, r. 242v, 1139, rr. 73, 607v, 611, 1140, 1141, r. 72, 1142, rr. 264, 295, 1143; LP Hen. VIII, iii, vi; Bristol and Glos. Arch. Soc. Trans. liv. 156; Vis. Glos. (Harl. Soc. xxi), 119; Vis. Warws. (Harl. Soc. xi), 171, 220, 222; VCH Glos. vi. 252; PCC 21 Hogen, 16 Tashe, 74 Noodes; C142/100/45.

A.D./A.D.K.H.

PALMER, Sir Henry (by 1496–1559), of London and Wingham, Kent.

BRAMBER   1554 (Apr.)

b. by 1496, 2nd s. of Edward Palmer of Angmering, Suss. by Alice, da. and h. of John Clement of Ightham Mote, nr. Sevenoaks, Kent; bro. of John*. m. by 1536, Jane, da. of Sir Richard Windebank of Guisnes, 3s. inc. Thomas†. Kntd. 30 Sept. 1544.[1]
Bailiff, Guisnes 1537–46, forester 1540–d., treasurer by 1543; master of the ordnance, Boulogne Sept. 1545, member of council Sept. 1545; commr. to hear and determine causes, criminal and civil, Guisnes 1546.[2]

'A gentleman born, though a younger son', as one of his contemporaries described him, Henry Palmer was to spend the greater part of his life in royal service overseas. He is first mentioned in the Calais accounts in 1528 as a spear in receipt of 18d. a day: the sole earlier reference found to him dates from 1527, when he was granted for life the reversion of the manor of Pollicott, Buckinghamshire, then held by Thomas Palmer*, doubtless an older kinsman. His uncle and younger brother both served at Calais, while his elder brother occupied the estate in Sussex.[3]

Palmer was patronized by Cromwell, whom he supplied with information on troop movements. After unsuccessfully approaching Cromwell in 1535 for the office of bailiff of Guisnes, Palmer was holding it by 1537 although not receiving his patent until 1540. He was a regular visitor to England as messenger or escort. In 1538 he travelled through the Netherlands with Thomas Wriothesley, who praised both his care and his fluency in French. With the outbreak of war Palmer was responsible for the strengthening of Guisnes and for collecting intelligence preparatory to the invasion of France. He took part in the capture of Boulogne and escorted the French commander back to the town after its surrender. In the skirmishing which followed, Palmer's house was destroyed and his sheep seized, but he had the consolation of being knighted by the King and in the following year of being made master of the ordnance and a member of the council at Boulogne. During his time there, however, he became increasingly critical of military short-comings and when in the summer of 1549 he withdrew from an outlying fortress which he thought untenable he was relieved of his command. The cession of Boulogne in the following year closed this chapter in his career.[4]

From 1551 Palmer began to acquire land in east Kent, first buying the house of Swingfield priory from Sir Anthony Aucher and then adding the reversion of St. Bartholomew's hospital outside Dover and Wingham college near Canterbury: it was as a parishioner of Wingham that he figured in a Star Chamber case under Mary against the perpetrators of a fraudulent scheme to raise money for the repair of the church. He was drawn into the orbit of the Duke of Northumberland by his brother Sir Thomas Palmer, and the relationship cost him arrest in July 1553 after the failure of the attempt to exclude Mary. It does not appear that he was implicated and in the following October he received a general pardon. His return to the Queen's second Parliament appears something of an excursus. As the holder of ex-monastic property he may have been exercised about its future; it is also possible that he hoped to do something in Parliament towards salvaging his dead brother's estate, for it was this Parliament which restored in blood the Marquess of Northampton, with whom Sir Thomas Palmer had been attainted. His seat for Bramber is suggestive of the 3rd Duke of Norfolk's patronage but his kinsman by marriage John Caryll*, who was steward of the barony of Bramber, is likely to have been instrumental in the election.[5]

Palmer served again in the war of 1557 and was wounded. Captured soon afterwards, he was ransomed with the help of Alderman Thomas Lodge of London, whom the Queen thanked for saving 'a gentleman whose service hath heretofor and may be hereafter very acceptable unto us'. He died on 15 Jan. 1559, apparently intestate. His property passed to his 17 year-old son Thomas.[6]

[1] Aged 60 'and above' in June 1556, CSP For. 1553–8, p. 230. Vis. Suss. (Harl. Soc. liii), 24; W. Berry, Co. Genealogies, Suss. (Comber's annotated copy at W. Suss. RO), 206; LP Hen. VIII, xi, xix; DNB (Palmer, Sir Thomas). [2] LP Hen. VIII, xi, xv, xxi; APC, i. 146, 241, 245. [3] LP Hen. VIII, iv, xvii; VCH Bucks. iv. 5. [4] LP Hen. VIII, ix–xiii, xvii–xix, xxi, add.; APC, i. 146, 241, 245, 348, 507; iii. 207, 216, 377; CSP For. 1547–53, p. 354; W. K. Jordan, Edw. VI, i. 303; CPR, 1550–3, p. 143. [5] CPR, 1550–3, pp. 80, 320; 1553, p. 81; 1553–4, p. 444; SP10/19, ff. 46, 58v; St.Ch.4/5/11; APC, iv. 303. [6] CSP For. 1553–8, pp. 325–6, 348; SP11/13, f. 110; C142/123/93.

R.J.W.S.

PALMER, John (by 1495–1563), of Angmering, Suss.

SUSSEX 1547

b. by 1495, 1st s. of Edward Palmer of Angmering by Alice, da. and h. of John Clement of Ightham Mote,

nr. Sevenoaks, Kent; bro. of Sir Henry*. m. (1) Joan (d.by 1528), da. of Thomas Hynde of London, wid. of Henry Tingleden of Reigate, Surr., 1s.; (2) by 1542, Mary, da. of William, 1st Lord Sandys of The Vyne, Sherborne St. John, Hants, wid. of Sir William Pelham of Laughton, Suss., 1s. Thomas†. suc. fa. 1516.[1]

Esquire of the body by 1528; j.p. Suss. 1529–d.; Sheriff, Surr. and Suss. 1533–4, 1543–4; commr. for dissolution of monasteries, Suss. 1537, musters 1539, relief 1550 church goods 1552.[2]

John Palmer came of the senior line of a family which had been settled at Angmering since the early 14th century. It was as a courtier, soldier and local administrator that he made his career. His modern notoriety as a gambler, to whom Henry VIII regularly lost at cards and at dice, rests on a mistaken identification, originating in Strype's Ecclesiastical Memorials. Although the privy purse expenses of the King reveal that between 1530 and 1532 he lost money to one 'Master Palmer', Edward Underhill's* autobiography shows this man to have been John Palmer's younger brother, later executed for supporting the Duke of Northumberland. The first trace of John Palmer comes in 1524, when he was assessed towards the recently granted subsidy at Angmering on goods worth £100. Four years later as a minor official at court he received a pardon from the King for hunting in the royal forests. In 1529 he was named to the Sussex bench and in the years that followed he played an increasingly important role in county affairs, being pricked sheriff for the first time in 1533. He was not one of the richest figures in the county and with Cromwell's assistance he obtained in February 1534 a warrant for £40 to defray the losses he would sustain in that office. Although he enjoyed Cromwell's favour on this occasion, he is probably not identifiable with the Palmer described later in the decade as one of the minister's servants: nor is he likely to have been the 'Master Palmer' who at More's trial was unable to testify as to More's interrogation by Richard Rich.[3]

Palmer was closely concerned with the dissolution of the lesser monasteries in Sussex. In 1536 he reported to Cromwell irregularities practised by the prior of Tortington, whereupon the prior was brought to the court for examination; later in the year Palmer received a grant of lands which the priory had owned in Lyminster. He profited from the suppression of Syon abbey, acquiring the manors of Ecclesdon, Hodford, Pipering and Wiggonholt in exchange for three manors purchased earlier from Sir Henry Owen. He also bought the manor of West Angmering and made its mansion, at one time the residence of the Syon bailiff, the home of his family and descendants. All these estates were still in Palmer's hands at his death, and to them he had added in 1547 the manor of Poling, in 1554 chantry property in East Angmering, and finally in 1562 the manors of Littlehampton and Tortington, for which he paid over £1,600.[4]

Between 1541 and 1547, Palmer was involved in a well-known enclosure suit when some copyhold tenants of his manor of Ecclesdon, living in West Angmering, brought a case into the Star Chamber alleging that on becoming lord of the manor in 1540 he had enclosed their pasture, seized the commons and made them into fishponds, destroyed houses and barns, warned tenants of houses near the sea to vacate their premises, and used violence after uttering the threat 'Do you not know that the King's grace hath put down all the houses of monks, friars and nuns? Therefore now is the time come that we gentlemen will put down the houses of such poor knaves as you be'. Palmer claimed that an exchange had been agreed ten years before, when he leased the manor from Syon abbey, and that he wished only to improve his estate and the lot of his tenants. Although the result of the case is unknown, he was charged on other occasions with wrongful eviction, at least once successfully.[5]

A second term as sheriff prevented Palmer from accompanying the King to France in 1544, but two years later he served at Boulogne, captaining a band of horse under the command of the Earl of Surrey: following one skirmish he could not be accounted for, but after Surrey had reported that his body had not been 'found amongst the slain' he reappeared alive and well. His association with Surrey evidently did not harm him when early in 1547 the earl was executed for treason. His military experience and mention in despatches perhaps brought him to the notice of another commander, the Earl of Hertford, who at the accession of Edward VI became Duke of Somerset and Protector. Palmer's experience made him a man whose presence in Parliament Somerset is likely to have welcomed, and in 1547 he entered the Commons as junior knight for Sussex with his 'cousin' Sir William Goring, a connexion of Somerset's brother. Nothing has come to light about his role in this Parliament: the Journal refers to a 'Mr. Palmer' excused during the third session from appearing in the common pleas, but as this Member is styled 'burgess' he cannot have been the knight for Sussex. Although there is no evidence that Palmer sat again, he may have done so in March 1553. Neither of the shire members for that Parliament is certainly known, though one was probably (Sir) Richard Sackville II (q.v.); but in view of his brother's pre-eminent position in the counsels of Northumberland, Palmer would have been a natural choice as junior knight of the shire. There were,

however, no favourable grants to John Palmer in the later years of Edward VI's reign.[6]

Palmer seems not only to have been out of favour during the following reign, but he may even have been suspected of complicity in the Dudley conspiracy by supporting Richard Uvedale. In a deposition dated 22 May 1556 he denied any recent contact with that conspirator, but admitted that Uvedale 'brought me word . . . in cleansing week last, that he would come to me shortly to give me thanks for my favour shown unto him at the sessions four or five years agone, which he said was more than any other justice of the shire had shown him'. No more than this glimpse of Palmer's behaviour at this time has been found. With the advent of Elizabeth he apparently made something of a recovery. In 1559 he was among a group of local gentlemen, including his cousin (Sir) Thomas Palmer* of Parham, ordered to examine the sexton of Chichester cathedral for his 'seditious words'. Three years later he helped to make an inventory of the bullion, plate and ornaments in Chichester cathedral.[7]

Palmer was a sick man when he made his will on 7 Jan. 1563 and he died before the day was out. After asking to be buried in the chapel at West Angmering he remembered his servants, family and friends, including John Caryll* to whom he left an annuity of £10. He named his son Thomas, then almost 21, executor and John Caryll, his son Edward Caryll, and John Paynett supervisors. A third of his lands were to be held by the Queen until Thomas came of age.[8]

[1] Aged 52 or thereabouts in February 1549, Req.2/17/65, f. 9, but younger brother Henry aged 60 'and above' in 1559. *Vis. Suss.* (Harl. Soc. liii), 24, 211; *Suss. Rec. Soc.* iii. 23; *LP Hen. VIII*, ii; H. H. Leonard, 'Knights and knighthood in Tudor Eng.' (London Univ. Ph.D. thesis, 1970), 322; PCC 5 Jankyn. [2] *LP Hen. VIII*, iv, v, vii, x, xiii, xiv, xvii; *Suss. Arch. Colls.* liii, 209; *CPR*, 1547-8, p. 90; 1550-3, p. 142; 1553, p. 359; 1554-5, p. 111. [3] *DNB* (Palmer, Sir Thomas); Strype, *Eccles, Memorials.* ii(1), 180; *Narr. Ref.* (Cam. Soc. lxxvii), 158n; *Privy Purse Expenses Hen. VIII*, ed. Nicolas, 32-33, 267, 270; *Suss. Rec. Soc.* lvi. 54; *LP Hen. VIII*, iv. vii, viii, xiii; Elton, *Policy and Police*, 410, 414-15; M. L. Robertson, 'Cromwell's servants' (Univ. California, Los Angeles Ph.D. thesis, 1975). 535-6. [4] *LP Hen. VIII*, x, xii, xiii, xvi, xvii; *Suss. Rec. Soc.* iii, 23-25; *CPR*, 1547-8, p. 227; 1560-3, p. 305. [5] St.Ch.2/6/181 ptd. *Tudor Econ. Docs.* ed. Power and Tawney, i. 19-29; *Suss. Rec. Soc.* xvi. 72; Req.2/20/65. [6] *LP Hen. VIII*, xxi; *CJ*, i. 11. [7] *APC*, vi. 19; *Suss. Rec. Soc.* lviii. 210. [8] PCC 6 Chayre; *Suss. Rec. Soc.* iii. 23-25; *CPR*, 1563-6, p. 117.

R.J.W.S.

PALMER, Thomas (by 1520-82), of Parham, Suss.

ARUNDEL	1553 (Mar.), 1553 (Oct.)
SUSSEX	1554 (Apr.)
GUILDFORD	1559

b. by 1520, 1st s. of Robert Palmer of London and Parham by 1st w. Bridget, da. and coh. of John Wesse or West of Millington, Yorks. *m.* (1) Bridget or Griselda da. of John Caryll of Warnham, Suss., 3da.; (2) by 1557, Catherine, da. of Sir Edward Stradling of St. Donats, Glam., 1 or 2s. *suc.* fa. May 1544. Kntd. 2 Oct. 1553.[1]

J.p. Suss. 1547–61, q. 1562–*d.*; commr. relief 1550, musters, Chichester 1580; other commissions Suss. 1554–65; collector for loan 1562; sheriff, Surr. and Suss. 1559-60; dep. lt. Suss. 1569-82.[2]

Thomas Palmer's father, an offspring of the family of Angmering, Sussex, bought the manor of Parham in 1540 and established a branch there. Palmer's early career is not easily disentangled from those of several namesakes. If his age was correctly stated at his father's inquisition he cannot have been the entrant of 1528 at Gray's Inn, but he was probably the servant of Cromwell's who carried letters to France and Calais in 1539 and who went to Winchester to hear a suspect preacher. He served in the Boulogne campaign of 1544 under his future master the 12th Earl of Arundel and alongside his cousin Sir Henry Palmer*. His succession to Parham, and his purchase of two manors once the property of Holy Trinity college, Arundel, were followed by his appointment to the bench in 1547. His religious conservatism notwithstanding, he was to retain his place on it for the rest of his life. He was admitted to the Mercers' Company in 1555.[3]

Palmer was clearly prepared to conform, but it was to the Earl of Arundel that he looked for immunity in times of stress and of advantage during the happier reign of Mary. In August 1553 Arundel sued to the Queen for Palmer's lease of a large area of marsh in east Sussex, and in 1555 the earl, as master forester of Petworth honor, appointed him keeper of River park and of all lodges in the honor; later in the reign Palmer bought Lurgashall manor and the lordship of Donnington, both of which formed part of the honor. He and Sir Thomas Stradling* acted for Arundel in a land transaction, and during the earl's absence at Calais in 1555 they managed his affairs: by 1557 he and Stradling had become brothers-in-law.[4]

It was as Arundel's nominee that Palmer sat in Parliament. The earl was released from his imprisonment as a supporter of the Protector Somerset in time to nominate Members for the Parliament of March 1553, in which Palmer sat for Arundel. His kinship with the Duke of Northumberland's henchman Sir Thomas Palmer may explain why a Catholic like Palmer was a Member of this hostile House. Re-elected to its more congenial successor, he was knighted by the earl, who had become lord steward of the Household, three days before the Parliament opened, although the return of 23 Sept. had styled him knight. Unlike his fellow-Member, the Norfolk lawyer Thomas Gawdy II, he did not oppose the initial measures towards reunion with Rome; nothing is known of his attitude towards the Act confirming the attainder of his dead cousin

(1 Mary st. 2, c.16). Six months later he achieved his only knighthood of the shire, but for the three remaining Parliaments of the reign he was evidently passed over in favour of other clients of the earl. His last appearance was in 1559 for Guildford, a town of which Arundel was high steward.[5]

Adjudged by Bishop Barlow in 1564 a 'faint furtherer' of religion, Palmer was unharmed by the subsequent misadventures of Arundel, and from 1569 he was a deputy lieutenant. He began to build Parham House in 1577 but did not live to see its completion, dying on or about 14 Apr. 1582. In the will which he had made on 24 Feb. 1580 he left small bequests to Parham church and Chichester cathedral, and to his sons-in-law John Leeds and Sir Thomas Palmer†. His lands and goods were divided between his wife and the 28 year-old son and heir William.[6]

[1] Date of birth estimated from age at fa.'s i.p.m., C142/70/46. *Vis. Suss.* (Harl. Soc. liii), 25; PCC 12 Pynnyng; Comber, *Suss. Genealogies (Horsham)*, 45; *Suss. Rec. Soc.* xix. 166. [2] *CPR*, 1547–8, p. 90; 1553, p. 359; 1553–4, pp. 24, 28, 37; 1554–5, p. 110; 1563–6, pp. 27, 38, 40, 42; Osborn coll. Yale Univ. Lib. 71.6.41; SP12/6, f. 133; *APC*, vii. 283; xii. 8; J.E. Mousley, 'Suss. country gentry in the reign of Eliz.' (London Univ. Ph.D. thesis, 1956), 641. [3] Mousley, 621; D. G. C. Elwes and C. J. Robinson, *Castles, Mansions and Manors of W. Suss.* 164; *Suss. Arch. Colls.* xxv. 18, 20; *LP Hen. VIII*, xiii, xiv, xix, xxi; List of mercers (T/S Mercers' Hall), 381. [4] *APC*, iv. 329; *CPR*, 1554–5, p. 305; 1555–7, p. 251; 1557–8, pp. 51, 370, 380; Harl. 606, f. 65; 608, f. 57v. [5] C219/21/151. [6] *Cam. Misc.* ix(3), 9; *VCH Suss.* ii. 25, 26; *APC*, x. 50; *HMC 6th Rep.* 345; R. B. Manning, *Rel. and Soc. in Eliz. Suss.* 79, 82–90, 92–94, 100; Nairn and Pevsner, *Suss.* 290–2; C142/197/60; PCC 18 Tirwhite.

R.J.W.S.

PALMER, Sir Thomas (by 1498-1544), of Pollicott, Bucks. and London.

GUILDFORD 1529

b. by 1498, prob. 3rd s. of John Palmer of Angmering, Suss. by Isabel, da. and h. of Edward Bitton of Suss. Kntd. by 1522.[1]

Overseer, petty customs, London Aug. 1519; surveyor, Henley-in-Arden June 1521; usher, receipt of the Exchequer, and custodian, Star Chamber July 1526.[2]

The identification of this Member rests chiefly on the dating of the only known list of Members of the Parliament of 1529. But for the evidence of that document there would be a strong case for identifying him with the Sir Thomas Palmer who served the King both at court and in the field and who in 1534 was made knight porter of Calais: alike in the royal household and in his military capacity Palmer came under the aegis of Sir William Fitzwilliam I*, who was almost certainly instrumental in procuring the return of both Members for Guildford. The main stumbling-block to this identification is the term 'miles' attached to the name as it appears on the list of Members, for the knight porter was dubbed only in November 1532, during the King's visit to Calais, whereas the list in question probably dates from several months earlier. Unless 'miles' was added to the name either in error (of which the list is not innocent) or later (which is unlikely), the senior Member for Guildford was already a knight at the time of his election—or at latest by the spring of 1532—and thus cannot have been the knight porter. There are, moreover, certain other considerations which tell against this identification, among them the fact that for most of the lifetime of the Parliament the knight porter was resident at Calais. Although such absences would not in themselves have excluded him from Membership, his return to Calais early in December 1534, after a stay of nearly a year in England, would have removed him mid way through the seventh session and in circumstances scarcely consonant with his being a Member.[3]

No such difficulties arise if the choice falls on a namesake and kinsman of the knight porter. This Sir Thomas Palmer, one of the Palmers of Angmering, Sussex, was perhaps a younger son of John Palmer and thus uncle to the knight porter and to his brothers John* and Sir Henry Palmer*: his kinship with them is reflected in the grant to Henry Palmer in 1527 of the reversion of the manor of Pollicott, Buckinghamshire, which Thomas had acquired in May 1522. Palmer's early career is not easy to distinguish from that of the future knight porter, although the first seems to have confined his activities to the court while the second was chiefly prominent as a soldier. From 1509 there are grants to Thomas Palmer of such offices as co-feodary of the honor of Richmond (1509), coroner of Usk, Llanvenethe and Trelleck, Monmouthshire, constable of Caerleon and Penrith castles (1511), and bailiff of Barton-upon-Humber, Lincolnshire (1517), but which man received which appointment it seems impossible to determine: on the other hand, the Thomas Palmer who appears in the revels accounts for the early years of the reign, who fought as one of the King's spears in 1513 and who served for a while at Tournai, was probably the future knight porter.[4]

From 1522 there is less scope for confusion since in that year, or perhaps shortly before it, the first Thomas Palmer was knighted. This honour seems to have been the climax to a series of favours to Palmer which had begun in August 1519 with his appointment as overseer of the petty customs of London, continued with a grant jointly to him and Robert Palmer, presumably his brother the London mercer, of presentations to two royal chantries at Chichester (made at Calais in July 1520, this followed his attendance on the King at the Field of

Cloth of Gold), and concluded with his appointment in June 1521 as surveyor of Henley-in-Arden and his receipt of an annuity of £20. Five years later, in July 1526, Palmer was to be given his most important, and doubtless his most lucrative, office, that of an usher at the Exchequer and custodian of the Star Chamber. Of the services thus rewarded the only indication comes from the years 1529–32. In January 1530 he received £338 10s. 'for so much money by the King's grace lost to him at game', and the £400 the King had given him 'in reward' in the previous March may have been in discharge of a similar debt; in company with the 3rd Duke of Norfolk he diced with the King (who was again the loser) at Calais in October and November 1532. The resources called for to sustain even successful gambling on this scale and in this company Palmer could scarcely have accumulated from his official emoluments. It was as a parishioner of All Hallows, Barking, that he was assessed at £1,000 for the loan of 1522; he was thus presumably already occupying the house in Mark Lane which he still had in 1539, and this domicile in the city, coupled with his fraternal tie with the Mercers' Company, suggests that he put his income to profitable use in the money-market.[5]

It was therefore as an intimate of the King as well as a figure at court familiar to Sir William Fitzwilliam that Palmer came to be returned for Guildford in 1529. Henry VIII may well have been personally responsible for Palmer's nomination as part of the electioneering which he conducted while at Windsor in August. That Palmer remained in favour during his Membership of the Commons is shown by his receipt of royal New Year gifts in 1532 and 1533, and by his attendance on the King on his visit to Calais in the autumn of 1532, but of his part in the proceedings of the House the sole indication dates from the end of 1534. It is then that, as 'Mr. Palmer', he is included in a list of Members drawn up by Cromwell on the back of a letter written in December: this list, which is believed to record the names of Members having a particular connexion with the treasons bill then passing through Parliament, includes a string of more than a dozen holders of household offices, and it is among these that Palmer appears.[6]

Palmer was doubtless returned for Guildford to the Parliament of 1536 in accordance with the King's request for the re-election of the previous Members, and he may possibly have sat again in 1539: on that occasion Fitzwilliam took charge of the nominations in Surrey and its neighbouring counties, and Palmer's description in 1538 as a servant of Cromwell's may reflect an attachment to the minister which could have earned him that powerful support. Of what else befell Palmer in his closing years little has transpired, and that little is once again subject to confusion following the conferment of a knighthood on his namesake of Calais. It was, however, Palmer of London and Pollicott who was a juror at the trial of Henry Norris in 1536 and almost certainly he who on 13 June 1542 was granted an annuity of £30. This grant also furnishes a clue to the date of Palmer's death which, in the absence of a will, has to be inferred from circumstantial evidence. A list of annuities payable by the augmentations includes, under the date 26 Mar. 1544, one to Sir Thomas Palmer with a note 'and nothing more *quia mortuus*'. The implication that the recipient died within a year of the date mentioned is borne out by a grant of the reversion of Pollicott, dated 6 June 1544, in which he is described as dead; as his brother Robert Palmer, making his will in May 1544, had forgiven him a debt of £140, we may with some confidence place the death at the end of May or the beginning of June 1544.[7]

[1] Date of birth estimated from first appointment. *Vis. Suss.* (Harl. Soc. liii), 24; *LP Hen. VIII*, iii. [2] *LP Hen. VIII*, iii, iv. [3] *DNB* (Palmer, Sir Thomas); *LP Hen. VIII*, v–vii. [4] *LP Hen. VIII*, i–iii, iv; C. G. Cruickshank, *Eng. Occupation of Tournai, 1513–19*, p. 93. [5] *LP Hen. VIII*, iii–v, x, xii, xiv; *Privy Purse Expenses of Hen. VIII*, ed. Madden, 17, 22. [6] *LP Hen. VIII*, v. vi; vii. 1522(ii) citing SP1/87, f. 106v; *HMC Bath.* iv. 2. [7] *LP Hen. VIII*, xiii, xviii–xx; PCC 12 Pynnyng.

S.R.J.

PALMES, Brian (by 1467–1519), of Naburn, Yorks.

YORK   1510[1]

b. by 1467, 1st s. of William Palmes of Naburn by Ellen, da. of Guy Roecliffe of Roecliffe. *educ.* M. Temple. *m.* (1) by 1488, Anastasia (?Heslerton); (2) lic. 15 Nov. 1493, Ellen, da. of John Acclom of Moreby, at least 1s.; (3) by 1506, Anne, da. of Sir Thomas Markenfield of Markenfield, wid. of Christopher Conyers of Sockburn, co. Dur.; at least 4s. 6da.[2] Bencher, M. Temple by 1504, Lent reader 1504.

J.p. Yorks. (E. Riding) 1494–1514, (W. Riding) 1501–14, liberties of Beverley and Ripon 1507, (N. Riding) 1514, Cumb., Northumb. and Westmld. 1514, York 1515, Lincs. (Holland) 1519; commr. musters, Yorks. (E. Riding) 1495, Yorks. 1511, (W. Riding) 1512, subsidy, Yorks., Kingston-upon-Hull and York 1512, 1514, 1515; other commissions, Northumb., Yorks. and Westmld. 1494–1516; recorder, York 23 Dec. 1496–1509; serjeant-at-law 1510; justice of assize, northern circuit 1514–15, midland circuit 1516–*d*.[3]

Brian Palmes came of a family which had held the manor of Naburn, near York, since at least the reign of John, but a provision in his will suggests that he was born at his mother's home at Roecliffe near Boroughbridge. It was probably about 1480 that he and his younger brother Guy entered the

Middle Temple, where both were to do well. In 1496 he became recorder of York in succession to Sir William Fairfax, and in the following year was made a freeman; he proved more diligent in attending the York council than some recorders, twice supervising elections when a mayor died in office. It was a measure of the city's satisfaction that in 1504 it appointed his brother, who was already a serjeant, to be 'of counsel' at 20s. a year. His and his first wife's membership of the city's Corpus Christi guild, and his own of the merchants' guild, suggest that he engaged in trade. When in December 1509 Palmes was elected to Parliament he at once resigned the recordership. The city rarely elected its recorder and the choice of Palmes may have been influenced by his recent despatch to London with two aldermen, one of them his fellow-Member William Nelson, on unspecified business. Unlike Nelson, he was not to be re-elected, perhaps because he was made a serjeant in 1510, but his continued standing in the city and shire is reflected in his appointment to nine subsidy commissions between 1512 and 1515. Little of a personal nature has come to light about his later years. In 1515 he presented his son George (later Wolsey's confessor and a canon of York) to the living of Sutton-upon-Derwent, Yorkshire, and in the following year he was named executor by his brother.[4]

In his own will of 31 Oct. 1519 Palmes asked to be buried in his parish church of St. George, York, whither his body was to be escorted by friars from the four York houses and by members of the Corpus Christi guild, and to have prayers said for him and his family locally for seven years and at Roecliffe for ever. He made numerous bequests of lands and goods to his family, and named as executors and residuary legatees his wife, Sir William Bulmer* and Sir Guy Dawny, Thomas Langton and James Duffelde, gentlemen, Richard Ellis, clerk, and William Marshall. The will was proved on 11 Jan. 1520 and an inquisition post mortem held at York castle on 27 (?)Apr. 1520 found that Palmes had died on 1 Oct. (*sic*) 1519 leaving as his heir a 20 year-old son Nicholas. At his death Palmes held the manors of Naburn and Gate Fulford, and lands, some of them acquired recently, scattered over a wide area of Yorkshire.[5]

[1] *York Civic Recs.* iii. (Yorks. Arch. Soc. rec. ser. cvi), 31. [2] Date of birth estimated from marriage. *Reg. Corpus Christi Guild, York* (Surtees Soc. lvii), 123n; *Test. Ebor.* v (Surtees Soc. lxxix), 103–6. [3] *CPR*, 1485–94, pp. 478, 506; 1494–1509, passim; *LP Hen. VIII*, i–iii; *Statutes*, iii. 85, 86, 112, 117, 175; *York Civic Recs.* ii. (Yorks. Arch. Soc. rec. ser. ciii), 128. [4] *Reg. Freemen, York*, i (Surtees Soc. xcvi), 221; *Test. Ebor.* v. 81, 104–6; *York Civic recs.* iii. 8, 11, 12, 25, 28, 31; York pub. lib. R. H. Skaife ms, civic officials, ii. 548. [5] York wills 9, ff. 90v–91; *Test. Ebor.* v. 103–7; C142/35/7; E150/222/10.

D.M.P.

PANTRE, William (by 1523–62 or later), of Oxford.

OXFORD 1555

b. by 1523. *educ.* Queen's, Oxf.[1]
Chamberlain, Oxford 1545–6, bailiff 1554–5.[2]

William Pantre was evidently a kinsman of John Pantre, provost of Queen's College from 1515, being described at one time as the provost's scholar and at another as his servant, and perhaps also of Thomas Pantre esquire, bedel of arts. John Pantre named William an executor of his will of October 1540 and left him £8 and the residue of his estate, but Thomas Pantre's will of May 1537 makes no mention of him.[3]

Pantre became a brewer and was admitted a freeman of Oxford in 1543–4. In 1545 he was assessed for subsidy on goods in the suburbs worth £20, two years later on goods in the south-west ward worth £9 and in 1559 on goods worth only £6. He played a full part in the civic life of Oxford and, like other leading citizens, he was assigned various duties which often took him to London. He was returned to Mary's fourth Parliament with John Wayte on 24 Sept. 1555, in the last week of his bailiffship, and on 14 Oct., shortly before the Parliament met, he and Wayte were authorized to proceed in a suit of *quo warranto* and in other cases then pending. Two days later Wayte at least, as mayor, attended the burning of Latimer and Ridley and at an unknown date Pantre 'received at Mr. Stanley's hand the sum of £40 for my lord Cranmer and others in the like case'.[4]

On 19 June 1562 Pantre and ten others were expelled the council for their support of John Cumber in his disobedience and on the same day, and presumably for the same cause, Pantre was bound over 'to behave himself honestly among his neighbours'. This is the last reference found to him.[5]

[1] Date of birth estimated from admission as freeman. Emden, *Biog. Reg. Univ. Oxf. 1501–40*, p. 430. [2] *Oxf. Recs.* 178, 221. [3] *Oxf. Univ. Arch.* B27, p. 2; T/S cal. chancellor's ct. reg. EEE, pp. 305, 509; PCC 6 Dyngeley. [4] *Oxf. Recs.* 174, 203, 221–3, 228, 233, 262, 268, 318; E179/162/240, 261, 318; Foxe, *Acts and Mons.* vii. 549. [5] *Oxf. Recs.* 289.

T.F.T.B.

PARIS, Robert (by 1487–1546 or later), of New Romney, Kent.

NEW ROMNEY 1523[1]

b. by 1487. *m.* Willmyne, 1s.[2]
Jurat, New Romney from 1508; bailiff to Yarmouth 1522.[3]

Robert Paris regularly attended the Brotherhood of the Cinque Ports between 1508 and 1536 as a jurat of Romney, but when he was chosen a bailiff to Yarmouth in 1522 he and two of his three colleagues—Thomas Cheseman *alias* Baker and Edmund Franke—were unable to make their report to the Brotherhood held the following Easter as they were Members of the Parliament then in session: the name of his fellow-Member is unknown. All that has come to light about Paris outside the record of his public life derives from his will of 20 Jan. 1546 in which he asked for burial in the churchyard of St. Martin's, Romney: to his wife Willmyne he left £4 to be paid in instalments, 'in the name of her dowry', household stuff and livestock, and to his son and executor Thomas his house and the four acres belonging to it. But the will bears no date of probate and, despite his evidently modest status, it is tempting to identify Paris with the gentleman of that name who on 9 Oct. 1550 was assaulted at Newbury, Berkshire by John Cheyne II* and others and who died of his wounds four days later. The murder victim was probably the second husband of Elizabeth Jackman whose first husband John Knight I* had died on 13 Jan. 1550.[4]

[1] *Cinque Ports White and Black Bks.* (Kent Arch. Soc. recs. br. xix), 185, 187. [2] Date of birth estimated from first reference. Canterbury prob. reg. C21, f. 45. [3] *Cinque Ports White and Black Bks.* 141 seq. [4] Ibid. 185, 187; Canterbury prob. reg. C21, f. 45; *CPR*, 1550–3, p. 239; *Vis. Berks.* (Harl. Soc. lvii), 166.

H.M.

PARKER, Henry (by 1509–51), of Berden, Essex.

BEDFORD 1545

b. by 1509. *m.* by Mar. 1537, Mary, *s.p.*[1]
Servant of Sir Francis Bryan* by 1530; member of the Household by 1537; groom of chamber by 1545.[2]

There were at least four men of this name in Henry VIII's household, but the identity of the Member for Bedford seems clear. Henry Parker 'of the Household' and his wife Mary received a lease of Berden priory in March 1537 and two years later a crown grant of the property in tail male with appurtenances elsewhere, including some in Clavering near Saffron Walden. In October 1550 William Smith of Woburn, Bedfordshire alienated his interest in Clavering rectory to Parker. The will of Henry Parker of Berden, made on 7 Aug. 1551, identifies Smith as his uncle and the Woburn connexion further points to Parker as the servant of Sir Francis Bryan. When Bryan was ambassador in France (1530–1) his servant carried letters between the English and French courts. An augmentations grant of 1544–5 to Parker, as groom of the chamber, of the keepership of the 'little park of Ampthill' in reversion after Bryan confirms the identification, for Parker of Berden's will was to mention 'stuff' at Ampthill.[3]

The will also deals with property at Bishop's

Stortford, Hertfordshire, part of a grant for which Parker and one Peter Grey of London had paid almost £400 in 1549 and which comprised land in 12 or more Bedfordshire parishes, including Milton Bryant, in Essex and elsewhere in Hertfordshire. Another grant to Grey and Parker, dated 1548, included the chantry house of Chalgrave, Bedfordshire: Grey and Smith had earlier acquired one of the manors in Chalgrave. These transactions suggest that Parker need not have been altogether an 'outsider' at the time of his election although he would still have needed a patron in a town where, so far as is known, he owned no property. The most likely patron was Bryan, but Henry Parker, 10th Lord Morley, who had married into the Bedfordshire family of St. John, could also have wielded influence. Parker called Morley's son, Sir Henry Parker*, his 'most loving and assured friend' in his will, left his children £50 and named him co-executor with the widow. The widow was to have the Bishop's Stortford property, everything at Berden, and the 'stuff' at London and Ampthill. Clavering parsonage was to be sold to pay debts and legacies but Parker's legal heir, his brother John, who was over 60 when he succeeded, contested the sale and was granted livery of one third of the parsonage. The will was proved on 7 Sept. 1551, the date given in Parker's inquisition post mortem as that of his death.[4]

[1] Date of birth estimated from first reference. PCC 24 Bucke; C142/93/84. [2] *LP Hen. VIII*, v. xiii, xx. [3] Ibid. v, xiii-xv, xviii, xx; *VCH Essex*, ii. 143. [4] *CPR*, 1549–51, pp. 221–2, 229; 1550–3, p. 216; 1553, pp. 370–1; *VCH Beds*. iii. 201, 346, 349; PCC 24 Bucke; C142/93/84.

N.M.F.

PARKER, Sir Henry (by 1514–52), of Morley Hall and Hingham, Norf., and Furneux Pelham, Herts.

HERTFORDSHIRE 1539,[1] 1547*

b. by 1514, s. of Henry Parker, 10th Lord Morley by Alice, da. of Sir John St. John of Bletsoe, Beds. *educ.* ?L. Inn, adm. 1516. *m.* (1) 18 May 1523, Grace, da. and h. of John Newport of Furneux Pelham, at least 2s. 1da.; (2) by 1549, Elizabeth, da. and h. of Sir Philip Calthrope of Erwarton, Suff., at least 1s. *d.v.p.* KB 31 May 1533.[2]

Commr. tenths of spiritualities, Herts. 1535, musters 1539, loan 1544, chantries, Essex and Herts. 1548, relief, Essex, Herts., Norf. and household of Princess Elizabeth 1550; other commissions 1538–51; sheriff, Essex and Herts. 1536–7; j.p. Herts. 1537–d.; custos rot. c.1547.[3]

Sir Henry Parker's father was a prominent courtier, an accomplished translator and author, and a close friend of Cromwell. One of his daughters married George Boleyn, Viscount Rochford, and Parker himself was to be connected, through his second marriage, with the Boleyn family. The

beginnings of Parker's career are obscure. The man of that name who was page of the chamber and gentleman usher from 1514 was probably a namesake, perhaps Henry Parker* of Berden, Essex.[4]

By his marriage to Grace Newport, who was only eight in 1523, Parker acquired the manors of Furneux Pelham and Stapleford, and in 1536 he procured a private Act (28 Hen. VIII c.20) settling his two Norfolk manors on himself and his wife, in lieu of the jointure that he had covenanted to make her on marriage. In 1541 the under sheriff of Essex and Hertfordshire was sued for abducting a 14 year-old ward, Jane Barenton, who had been contracted in marriage to the younger John Newport, presumably Parker's brother-in-law. Parker was apparently a party to the abduction, for his servants escorted the girl in her flight from her guardian and helped her to elude him in London.[5]

Parker was knighted at Anne Boleyn's coronation and served regularly on Hertfordshire commissions from 1535. It is possible that he sat in the short Parliament of 1536, for which the Hertfordshire returns have not survived; it was that Parliament which passed the Act relating to the settlement on Grace Parker, although such an uncontroversial measure hardly required Parker's presence in the Commons as well as his father's in the Lords. His election for Hertfordshire in 1539 is to be explained by his father's closeness to Cromwell and his own leading position in his county. In two letters to Cromwell (probably of 1536) Parker reported his imprisonment of two parsons who had disobeyed the royal injunctions against superstitious holy days, and begged Cromwell to help his chaplain, whom the bishop of London's surveyor was suing for no good reason. Parker explained that he knew 'the love and favour which . . . your lordship always hath borne to the word of God and to all them which endeavour to set forth the King's most godly and gracious injunctions' and interpreted the action against his chaplain as an attack by the conservative Bishop Stokesley on himself. He attended at court on ceremonial occasions, such as the christening of Prince Edward and the reception of Anne of Cleves. He was also called on for military service, his name appearing in lists of Hertfordshire gentlemen to serve against the northern rebels in 1536, and eight years later he was with the rearguard of the army in France. In April 1536 he had a grant from the crown of the dissolved priory of Latton, Essex, which he sold, with other land, five years later. He was assessed in Hertfordshire for the subsidy, his lands there being valued at £100 a year in 1546, which made him one of the county's ten or 12 richest men.[6]

Parker retained interests in Norfolk which

involved him in several Star Chamber cases. One of these concerned rights of common at Hingham, where he wished to pasture 500 sheep. His alleged enclosure of Hingham common was one of the grievances of the Norfolk peasantry at the time of Ket's rebellion in 1549, and Parker served with Northampton in his unsuccessful attempt to put down the rebellion in August.[7]

Under Edward VI Parker was appointed to most of the important commissions for Hertfordshire. He was not immediately chosen knight of the shire in 1547 but was elected on 24 Oct., less than a fortnight before the Parliament met, to fill the vacancy left by the death of Sir Anthony Denny on the previous 10 Sept. A bill 'for increase of trees and woods' was committed to him on 5 Nov. 1549, after its first reading. His parliamentary career ended before the following and last session of this Parliament began, for he died on 6 Jan. 1552. The Privy Council sent instructions on 19 Jan. following for a second by-election in Hertfordshire and recommended Sir Ralph Sadler as the fittest person; it was nevertheless John Cock II who was elected. Parker died during the lifetime of his father. The inquisition post mortem taken in Norfolk thus mentioned only the two manors settled on Parker and his first wife to provide her jointure and valued at £50 a year; the larger of these, Hingham, had been re-settled for the benefit of Parker's second wife, Elizabeth, who later married Sir William Woodhouse* and Dru Drury†. Parker's heir was his eldest son Henry, aged 20 years and 11 months at his father's death; he did not share his father's religious views, but fled to the Continent in Elizabeth's reign and became one of the leading English Catholic exiles there. No will of Parker's has been found.[8]

[1] E159/319, brev. ret. Mich. r. [1–2]. [2] Date of birth estimated from first commission. *CP*; *LP Hen. VIII*, vi. [3] *LP Hen. VIII*, viii, xii–xiv, xvi, xviii; *CPR*, 1547–8, pp. 76, 84; 1548–9, p. 135; 1550–3, p. 141; 1553, pp. 352, 354, 356, 363; C66/801; 193/12/1. [4] *DNB* (Parker, Henry); *LP Hen. VIII*, v, xiii, xvi; PCC 24 Bucke. [5] St.Ch. 2/24/107; C142/42/96. [6] *LP Hen. VIII*, viii, x–xii, xiv, xvi, xviii, xix, SP1/106, f. 229; E179/121/177. [7] St.Ch.2/10/113–18, 338, 338a, 27/55, 29/140; 3/6/30; S. T. Bindoff, *Ket's Rebellion* (Hist. Assoc. gen. ser. xii), 9; Holinshed, *Chron.* iii. 971. [8] C219/19/39, 44; *CJ*, i. 11; C142/96/34(2).

D.F.C.

PARKER, Thomas I (by 1519–58), of London and Notgrove, Glos.

CRICKLADE 1553 (Oct.), 1554 (Nov.)

b. by 1519, s. of Humphrey Parker. *m.* by 1546, Jane, da. of John Moore of Dunclent, Worcs., wid. of James Dingley and Michael Ashfield, 3s. 1da.[1]
Clerk of the treasury and auditor, Gloucester abbey, Glos. by 1540; clerk of the crown and of the peace, Glos. 1544, of the peace 1555–7; commr. sewers, Glos. and Worcs. 1554.[2]

Thomas Parker seems to have begun his admini-

strative career in the service of Gloucester abbey. He was probably the nephew of William Malvern *alias* Parker, the last abbot, who appears to have taken up residence with him at Notgrove after being denied a pension for refusing to accept the surrender of his house. Another uncle, also Thomas Parker, who died in 1538, had been chancellor of Salisbury and an important ecclesiastical officer in Hereford and Worcester dioceses. In 1549 the dean and chapter of Salisbury regained direct control of Abingdon Court, one of the manors in Cricklade, which they had previously leased to Thomas Seymour, Baron Seymour of Sudeley: it is probable that they influenced Parker's return to the Parliaments of October 1553 and November 1554. To this sponsorship Parker could have added his own landed interest in the neighbourhood of Cricklade. Of his part in the work of the Commons all that is known is that he was absent when the House was called early in January 1555. For this dereliction he was informed against in the King's bench in the following Easter term. A writ of *venire facias* was issued but no further action was taken against him.[3]

Some time before 1546 Parker had lived in London where he may have acquired legal training, but he later settled in Gloucestershire. In 1554 he was granted an exemption from going to the French wars, perhaps because he was then clerk of the peace and of the crown for the county; in February 1545 he was a tenant at Cirencester and Tewkesbury; in April 1546 he and his wife acquired the lease of the manor of Northleach, not far from Cricklade, which had belonged to Gloucester abbey; and some time during Henry VIII's reign he purchased the nearby manor of Notgrove. In 1549 he was involved in a dispute in the Star Chamber over the ownership of another manor in the district, at Farmington. In 1555 his name was included on a list of pensions payable to the former staff of Gloucester abbey.[4]

The nature of Parker's religious beliefs remains uncertain as the Catholic preamble to his will was written before the death of Queen Mary. Parker made this will on 16 Aug. 1558 at Notgrove and asked to be buried there or at Northleach. He left most of his lands to his eldest son Edmund, with the provision that his wife and executrix should enjoy the revenues during her life. He also left lands to his two younger sons, Thomas and Michael, and bequests of money and cattle to his stepchildren and other kinsmen. The exact date of his death is not known but as he described himself as 'somewhat sick' it is probable that he died within a few weeks of making his will which was proved on 15 Dec.[5]

[1] Date of birth estimated from first reference. PCC 56 Noodes; *Vis. Glos.* (Harl. Soc. xxi), 257; *Vis. Glos.* ed. Fenwick and Metcalfe, 128–9; *N. and Q.* (ser. 11), xi. 106. [2] *LP Hen. VIII*, xvi, xviii;

CPR, 1554–5, p. 107; Stephens, *Clerks of the Peace*, 58; *Bristol and Glos. Arch. Soc. Trans.* xxix. 106, 118; xlix. 110. ³ *Bristol and Glos. Arch. Soc. Trans.* vii. 34; ix. 123–4; PCC 56 Noodes, 4 Spert; C142/98/25; *LP Hen. VIII*, iv, x, xiii; Le Neve, *Fasti*, ii. *Hereford*, comp. Horn, 9, 23, 30; Emden, *Biog. Reg. Univ. Oxf. 1501–40*, p. 433; *VCH Wilts.* iii. 186–7; *Cricklade*, ed. Thomson, 17, 59; *Fac. Off. Reg. 1534–49*, ed. Chambers, 376; KB27/1176, 29/188. ⁴ *LP Hen. VIII*, xviii, xx, xxi; *Bristol and Glos. Arch. Soc. Trans.* xxix. 106, 118; xlix. 110. ⁵ PCC 56 Noodes.

E.McI.

PARKER, Thomas II (by 1527–80), of Ratton, Willingdon, Suss.

EAST GRINSTEAD 1558

b. by 1527, 1st s. of John Parker of Ratton by 1st w. Joan, da. of Richard Sackville† of Withyham. *m.* by 1547, Eleanor, da. of William Waller of Groomsbridge, Kent, 3s. inc. John† and Sir Nicholas† 1da. *suc.* fa. 9 Nov. 1557.[1]

J.p. Suss. 1558/59–?70; commr. for survey of bpric. of Chichester 1559, sewers, Suss. 1564, piracy 1565.[2]

Two of Thomas Parker's forbears had sat in Parliament for Lewes in 1417 and 1453, but he was the next of the family to do so. His election for East Grinstead, a duchy of Lancaster borough, Parker clearly owed to his family connexions: he was first cousin to (Sir) Richard Sackville II*, whose son Thomas was returned with him (although choosing to sit for Westmorland), and his sister married Sir John Gage's* eldest son Sir Edward. Shortly before the election, and perhaps in anticipation of it, Sir Edward Gage and Sir Richard Sackville visited Parker's father at Willingdon. John Parker had bequeathed the greater part of his property to his younger sons, and the object of the visit was to persuade him to entrust their 'rule and order' to their elder half-brother. The father explained that he did not mean to disinherit his eldest son, but 'only to bridle him and his wife withal, because of their stout stomach', and it was agreed that Thomas Parker should pay annuities of £20 and £40 to his younger half-brothers until they came of age, and an annuity for life of £20 to his stepmother.[3]

His father's depiction of Parker is borne out by the sobriquet of 'Parker the Wild, as he is counted in all Sussex', given him in the account of his capture of a Sussex heretic. Put on the bench at the beginning of Elizabeth's reign he was adjudged in 1564 a 'misliker of religion and godly proceedings' and the Thomas Parker who appears as a justice in 1569 and 1570 may have been his half-brother. Parker died on 16 Apr. 1580. No will or inquisition survives.[4]

¹ Date of birth estimated from age at fa.'s i.p.m., *Suss. Rec. Soc.* xiv. 177. *Vis. Suss.* (Harl. Soc. liii), 22; J. E. Mousley, 'Suss. country gentry in the reign of Eliz.' (London Univ. Ph.D. thesis, 1956), 644–7 where Parker's mother is mistakenly given as a daughter of Sir Richard Sackville. ² SP12/74, f. 107; *CPR*, 1558–60, p. 31; 1563–6, pp. 37–38, 40; *APC*, vii. 283. ³ Mousley, 644; *Suss. Arch. Colls.* lxxx. 137–9; Barbican House, Lewes, F.B. 143. Gage mss 21/11, 12; PCC 31 Noodes. ⁴ Foxe, *Acts and Mons.* viii. 337; *Cam. Misc.* ix(3), 10; Mousley, 646; R. B. Manning. *Rel. and Soc. in Eliz. Suss.* 245.

R.J.W.S.

PARR, Sir William (by 1484–1547), of the Blackfriars, London and Horton, Northants.

NORTHAMPTONSHIRE 1529, 1539[1]

b. by 1484, 2nd s. of Sir William Parr† (*d.*1483/84) of Kendal, Westmld. by 2nd w. Elizabeth, da. of Henry, 5th Lord FitzHugh. *m.* by 1511, Mary, da. and coh. of William Salisbury of Horton, 4da. Kntd. 25 Sept. 1513; *cr.* Baron Parr of Horton 23 Dec. 1543.[2]

Keeper, great and little parks, Brigstock, Northants. 1506; esquire of the body by 1507, knight 1512; steward, chancellor and receiver, King's lands, Pemb. 1509–33; commr. subsidy, Northants. 1512, 1515, 1523, 1524, tenths of spiritualities 1535; j.p. Northants. 1515–*d.*, Yorks. (N. Riding) 1525–36, (E. and W. Ridings) 1528–36, Cumb. 1530–6; sheriff, Northants. 1517–18, Feb.–Nov. 1522, 1533–4, 1537–8; keeper, Rockingham castle, Northants. 1523–44, 1546–*d.*; chamberlain, household of Henry Fitzroy, Duke of Richmond 1525–36, household of Queen Catherine Parr 1543–*d.*; steward, Crovland abbey's lands, Northants., Ramsey abbey's manor, Elton, Northants., Pipewell abbey's manors by 1535, forfeited lands of Sir John Hussey*, Lord Hussey, Northants. 1538.[3]

The younger son of a prominent northern knight, William Parr first appears at court as one of the King's spears in January 1506. Made an esquire of the body by Henry VII and knight of the body by Henry VIII, he soon began to receive local crown offices. It was during these years, too, that he and his elder brother Thomas married two Northamptonshire heiresses. Both marriages doubtless owed something to their mother, herself the daughter of a Northamptonshire nobleman, and to their stepfather Sir Nicholas Vaux*, a leading figure in the county. Vaux also enjoyed royal favour and under his aegis William Parr advanced rapidly. He was nominated as sheriff of his adopted county in 1510 and although not pricked on that occasion he was chosen seven years later in succession to Vaux. At court he excelled in the lists, where he was often chosen as an opponent for the King. In 1513 he went in Sir William Sandys's retinue on the campaign in France and was knighted at Tournai. It was probably about this time that he served at Calais, as a later deposition regarding the extent of the English pale records that he was present on certain occasions when the limits were settled by the English.[4]

After his return Parr probably spent much of his time at court or in London: in 1523 he was living at Blackfriars. He nevertheless strengthened his links with Northamptonshire. In 1518, just after his first term as sheriff, he arranged a marriage between his eldest daughter and the son and heir of William Lane, one of the county's leading gentlemen; he was soon to find husbands in the neighbourhood for his other daughters, one of whom married Thomas Tresham* and another a Digby, and in 1522 his stake in the county was increased by a grant of the valuable property there of the recently attainted 3rd Duke of Buckingham.[5]

In 1520 Parr accompanied the King to the Field of Cloth of Gold and to Gravelines, and on the outbreak of war he was sent north to serve under the Earl of Surrey: he commended himself by his valour and became one of Surrey's most trusted captains. His knowledge of the north probably helped to procure him the chamberlainship of the household set up in 1525 for the King's natural son, the Duke of Richmond, which was designed not only to serve and educate the young prince, a task especially entrusted to Parr, but also to govern the north. For the next ten years these were to remain Parr's principal duties, although he did not spend all his time in the north: indeed, Richard Croke, Richmond's first schoolmaster, complained that in two years Parr had been absent for 66 weeks. There was dissension in the household over status, authority over the young duke and expenditure. Extravagance was another of Croke's charges against Parr, who certainly seems to have become deeply indebted to the duke, but the King retained confidence in him and it was Croke, not Parr, who was removed: one advantage of Parr's sojourns in London to attend Parliament or the court was that they enabled him to act as a link between the councillors in the north and those at the centre.[6]

Whether between 1525 and 1533 he found time to act upon the Northamptonshire commissions to which he was appointed is doubtful, but in 1533 it was found advisable to reappoint him sheriff there, as one of the few men in the county powerful enough to prevent Sir William Spencer's widow and her relatives, the brothers Edmund* and Richard Knightley*, from carrying their intrigues concerning the wardship of Spencer's heir and lands to a conclusion detrimental to the crown. At the same time he was involved in family affairs, and Richmond's council was being reorganized as the council in the north, so that his attendance on it diminished considerably. With Richmond's death in 1536 Parr's association with the north ceased almost entirely; in 1535 he had petitioned for the captaincy of Berwick, but he did not obtain it.[7]

As a well-connected administrator and a courtier esteemed by the King, Parr was a natural choice for election to the Parliament of 1529. The list of Members is torn so that Parr's constituency and the beginning of his christian name are lost but that he sat for Northamptonshire is clear from the sequence of shires on the list. He may have sat in one or more of the earlier Parliaments of the reign, as he had been named to the Northamptonshire commissions for the subsidies granted in 1512, 1515 and 1523, and he was presumably re-elected to that of June 1536 when

the King asked for the return of the previous Members. The only indication of his activity in the House is the appearance of a proviso safeguarding his interests in a private Act (28 Hen. VIII, c.28) obtained by John Onley*. When the Lincolnshire rebellion broke out in the autumn of 1536 he set an example by the alacrity with which he answered the King's call to arms. He was one of those designated for command should the Duke of Suffolk be required elsewhere and he took a share in the punishment of the rebels, but he was to be disappointed in his hope of acquiring attainted lands or offices, especially a lease of the Lincolnshire abbey of Barlings where he was in charge of the suppression. For the next few years he was preoccupied with the preservation of law and order in the midlands. If the story of one parson is to be credited, he was perhaps over-zealous in his search for fomentors of disaffection. The rector concerned declared that Parr set him in the stocks for six hours without trial and before freeing him exacted a promise of a lease, a bond for its secure delivery and another bond for good behaviour; later, when the rector attempted to present his complaint to the King, Parr made great efforts to suppress it. Whether or not this was a fair sample of his behaviour, Parr remained in favour: he was granted leases of ex-monastic property, including the site of Pipewell abbey and several granges, and in 1539 he was elected to Parliament for the last time, being joined in the Commons on this occasion by his son-in-law Tresham. Early in August 1540, not long after the dissolution of this Parliament, he was written to about the subsidy which he had helped to pass.[8]

Parr's career culminated three years later when his niece Catherine, the widow of Sir John Neville I*, 3rd Lord Latimer, was married to the King: he became the chamberlain of her household and was raised to the peerage. He took his seat in the Lords on 17 Jan. 1544 and thereafter attended the House irregularly for nearly three weeks and then only once again before the dissolution. Later in the year Suffolk asked for his help in the new war against Scotland, but the King chose to make him one of the council appointed to advise the Queen during his own absence abroad. His advancing years, and perhaps ill-health, may explain this sedentary role: he became an infrequent visitor at court and he was absent from the Lords throughout the last Parliament of the reign. On 21 June 1546 he made a will in which he provided for his wife and relatives, including his grandson Ralph Lane* and his nephew (Sir) Nicholas Throckmorton*. As executors he named his wife and Throckmorton and as overseers his nephew William Parr, Earl of Essex, and his niece the Queen. Parr lived to see the advent of Edward VI, dying on 10 Sept. 1547. He was buried at Horton, where the inscription on his monument wrongly gives his year of death as 1546. His name was initially in the register of peers summoned to Parliament later in the same autumn, but three days after the opening it was removed.[9]

[1] E159/319, brev. ret. Mich. r. [1–2]. [2] Date of birth estimated from father s death. *CP*; Bridges, *Northants.* i. 367; *Vis. Northants.* ed. Metcalfe, 56, 159, 186; Baker, *Northants.* ii. 61. [3] *CPR*, 1494–1509, pp. 446, 550; 1550–3, p. 146; *LP Hen. VIII*, i–xxi; *Statutes*, iii. 88, 169; R. R. Reid, *King s Council in the North*, app.; *Northants. Rec. Soc.* xii. passim. [4] *LP Hen. VIII*, i, xvi. [5] *Northants.* RO, Gunning mss, box 1236; *LP Hen. VIII*, iii. [6] *LP Hen. VIII*, iii, iv. [7] Ibid. iv–vi. [8] Ibid. xi–xiii, xvi, add.; M. H. and R. Dodds, *Pilgrimage of Grace*, passim; St.Ch.2/32/16; Elton, *Policy and Police*, 307, 357, 368–9; E159/319, brev. ret. Mich. r. [1–2]; 371/309, r. 61(i). [9] *LP Hen. VIII*, xix–xxi; Bridges, i. 370; *LJ*, i. 236–64, 267–82, 284–90, 291–3; Fuller, *Worthies* (1670), 187; P. Glanville, 'The Parr Pot', *Arch. Jnl.* cxxvii. 147–55; Pevsner and Cherry, *Northants.* 263–4.

S.M.T.

PARRETT *see* PERROT

PARRY (AP HARRY), John (1517/18–84 or later), of Carmarthen.

CARMARTHEN BOROUGHS   1554 (Nov.), 1559

b. 1517/18. *m.* Cecily, da. of Hugh Vaughan of Kidwelly, 1s.[1]

    Comptroller of customs, Milford Haven, Pemb. 10 May 1559–84 or later; subsidy collector, Carmarthen 1562; bailiff, Carmarthen 1563–4.[2]

John Parry may have been a kinsman of William Parry, his precursor both as bailiff of Carmarthen and as its Member. It appears that in 1547 he and William Parry acquired the former Franciscan friary in Lammas Street, Carmarthen. The property had earlier been granted to Thomas Lloyd, precentor of St. David's cathedral, for use as a grammar school. When Lloyd died in 1547 he left lands for the staffing and upkeep of the school and the town promoted a bill for its foundation, but this failed and in February 1550 the two Parrys were granted a 21-year lease of the property. They were to be sued in Chancery by the town in 1562 for failing to establish the school. John Parry then denied some of the allegations but with what result is unknown.[3]

    Parry was first returned to Parliament when John Vaughan II*, whose sister he had probably already married, was mayor of Carmarthen, and his election accorded with the Queen's request for resident Members. He was not among those who quitted the Parliament without leave before its dissolution. His career was to be closely linked with Vaughan's, the two being fellow-officers in the customs at Milford Haven. It is in this capacity that Parry is last heard of in 1584.[4]

[1] Aged 55 in October 1573, E178/3345, m. 9v. Dwnn, *Vis. Wales*, i. 214. [2] E159/340, recognizances Easter 45; 179/264/10; *Welsh Port Bks.* (Cymmrod. rec. ser. xii); 329; NLW ms 5586B, p. 10. [3] E178/3345, m. 9v; *CPR*, 1550–3, p. 201; 1553–4, p. 367; *Trans. Carm.*

Antiq. Soc. vii. 52–53; viii. 23–24; xiii. 51 seq.; *LJ*, i. 309; C 3/33/51 [4] E159/340, recognizances Easter 45; 178/3345; *Welsh Port Bks.* 329

P.S.E.

PARRY (AP HARRY), Stephen (c.1505–55), of Rathangan, co. Kildare, Ireland; Rotherwas and Moorhampton, Herefs.

HEREFORDSHIRE   1553 (Oct.),[1] 1555*

b. c.1505, s. of John Parry of Herefs. by da. of one Gossington. *m.* (1) by 1532, Jane, da. of John Worlich of Wickhambrook, Suff., 2s. 1da.; (2) by Dec. 1540, Jane, da. of John York of Ramsbury, Wilts., wid. of Thomas Bodenham (*d.*12 May 1538) of Rotherwas.[2]

    Servant of Lord Leonard Grey 1519–40; gaoler, Dublin castle c.1535; constable, Rathangan castle c.1535; j.p. Herefs. 1541–*d.*; commr. musters 1542, relief 1550; sheriff 1545–6, 1555.[3]

The Parry family of Moorhampton, where it settled after Stephen Parry bought that manor from the crown in 1540, is not to be confused with its namesake of Poston, Herefordshire, and Llandefailog Tregraig, Breconshire, which furnished Queen Elizabeth with her maid of honour Blanche Parry.[4]

    Parry early became servant to Lord Leonard Grey, sixth son of the 1st Marquess of Dorset, who took him to Ireland. He was not to return permanently until Grey's own final recall in 1540. When he came under suspicion and was temporarily summoned back in 1536 he was described as the deputy's 'most intimate servant' and Grey let him go 'with grief', telling Cromwell of his 17 years' service and begging good treatment for him. Others were shocked by Parry's corruption; he was accused of having 'a fleece of all poor men that come from Ireland' and of using his position for bribery and extortion. At Grey's trial for treason in 1541 the bishop of Meath named Parry as one of the 'rabblement of light persons' who had ruled Grey and caused his downfall. Grey paid the penalty and Parry retired to Herefordshire, where he invested £300 of his gains in ex-monastic lands at Moorhampton.[5]

    Parry spent his remaining years establishing himself there. Nominated as sheriff four years in succession from 1539, he was pricked in 1545 and took his place on the bench in 1541. Unless he was elected for the shire to the Parliament of 1545, for which the Herefordshire names are lost (but which, coinciding with the beginning of his shrievalty, he is unlikely to have attended), it was the accession of Mary which gave Parry his opportunity to sit in Parliament. He may have welcomed this not only as a Catholic but as a holder of ex-monastic property. In his first Parliament he did not oppose the initial measures towards the restoration of Catholicism. On the second occasion he was elected with John Baskerville whose daughter his son John may already have married. During the Parliament, Parry was pricked sheriff for a second time but he did not live to take up the appointment or to see the dissolution, as he died on 27 Nov. 1555. He made his will on the same day, asking for burial in a 'Christian grave' where it should please his brother. After providing for his servants and for the settlement of debts he named his son John as residuary legatee and, with Baskerville, as executor. The witnesses included the two executors, John Garnons* and William Garnons. It was John Parry who on 6 Dec. following obtained probate of the will. The Queen chose Baskerville to replace Parry as sheriff, but it is unlikely that the vacancy in the House caused by his death was filled before the dissolution.[6]

[1] Bodl. e Museo 17. [2] Date of birth estimated from early career. Vis. Herefs. ed. Weaver, 6, 82; LP Hen. VIII, xvi; C142/60/77, 107/57; PCC 11 Crymes. [3] LP Hen. VIII, xi, xvi, xx; CPR, 1547-8, p. 84; 1553, p. 354; 1554-5, p. 20. [4] LP Hen. VIII, xvi; DKR, ix(2), 157. [5] R. Bagwell, Ireland under the Tudors, i. 189; CSP Ire. 1509-73, pp. 15, 22, 36, 40, 49; LP Hen. VIII, ix, xi, xii, xvi. [6] C142/107/57; PCC 37 More.

A.J.E.

PARRY (AP HARRY), Thomas (by 1515-60), of Welford and Wallingford, Berks., Hatfield, Herts. and Oakley Park, Glos.

WALLINGFORD 1547, 1553 (Mar.), 1555
HERTFORDSHIRE 1559

b. by 1515, 1st s. of Henry Vaughan of Tretower, Brec. by Gwenllian, da. of William ap Grene or Grono of Brecon, Brec. m. 1539/1540, Anne, da. of Sir William Reade of Boarstall, Bucks., wid. of Sir Giles Greville and of Sir Adrian Fortescue (d.1539) of Shirburn and Stonor Place, Oxon., 2s. inc. Thomas[†] 3da. Kntd. by 20 Nov. 1558.[1]
Servant of Thomas Cromwell by 1536-40; clerk of the crown and peace, Glos. 1537-43; jt. bailiff, manor of Welford, Berks. 1546; cofferer, household of Princess Elizabeth by 1548-58; woodward, ct. augmentations, Berks. and Oxon. in 1552; j.p. Bucks., Herts. and Hunts., q. Dorset 1554, Berks., Glos. and Herts. 1558/59; PC 20 Nov. 1558; comptroller, the Household 20 Nov. 1558; treasurer Jan. 1559; master, ct. wards Jan. or Apr. 1559; master, the game of swans Nov. 1559-d; steward, possessions of Westminster abbey 1559; steward, honor of Donnington and bailiff of crown lands, Newbury, Berks. by 1560; jt. (with Sir Henry Neville*) ld. lt. Berks. Apr. 1560.[2]

Thomas Parry was probably born and brought up in Wales, since he was known by his father's christian name. The latter came of an old marcher family, being the son of Sir Thomas Vaughan[†] who had been executed at Pontefract by Richard III. The Vaughans were very distantly related to the Cecils, for in 1582 Lord Burghley recalled that his great-grandfather had married into the family; the statesman then drily commended his messenger, Mr. Vaughan, since 'in the manner of Wales I account him my cousin'.[3]
Several of the Tudors' most famous servants had

Welsh blood, notably Cromwell, Sir John Williams*, and the Cecils, although Parry is the only one likely to have been born in the principality. If he was the Thomas Parry first mentioned in a letter of February 1536 to the secretary from Sir John Dudley, he seems to have been taken directly into Cromwell's personal service. A month later Parry and Thomas Lee I* were investigating a theft of jewels from Winchester cathedral and urging the appointment of William Basing as prior on the ground that he would double Cromwell's annuity. Later in the same year Parry was paid for his costs in the suppression of Bilsington, in Kent, and thereafter he was to visit many houses, from Gloucestershire to East Anglia, with instructions from Cromwell. By 4 May 1538 he was important enough to seek the abbot of Pershore's fee-farm at Hawkesbury, Gloucestershire, for a Mr. Butler of that county, an esquire of the body, and to be bribed by the abbot if he would abandon the suit. At the end of November 1538 he and John Millicent* were enfeoffed of the lordship of Oakham, Rutland, by Cromwell to the use of his son Gregory*.[4]

A further step in Parry's career, which brought him to Hertfordshire and perhaps into contact with Princess Elizabeth, was his marriage to Anne Reade. Her previous husband, the son of Sir John Fortescue by a daughter of Sir Geoffrey Boleyn and a great-aunt of Queen Anne, was included in the attainder of the Pole family and executed in July 1539. Soon after this his widow married Parry, but she quickly repented of it, for in August 1540 a commission was set up under the bishop of London to investigate Parry's complaint that she had left him. Husband and wife were brought together again, and some two years later a son was born to them. In October 1542 Anne Parry was granted 1,500 sheep in Gloucestershire, with other goods of her late husband, and in September 1546 the couple leased the manor of Welford, the rectory of Chieveley and other lands in Berkshire which had once belonged to Abingdon abbey. Although Parry now had property in Berkshire, he probably did not yet have any in Wallingford, for which he was returned with a townsman, Henry Huntley, to the Parliament of 1547. It is likely that Parry was in favour with the Protector Somerset, or with his brother the admiral, a relationship which may also explain Parry's earlier appointment as cofferer to Princess Elizabeth, perhaps while she was still living at Chelsea with Admiral Seymour and his wife Catherine Parr.[5]

The date of Parry's entry into the princess's household is uncertain, as it was only during the crisis over Seymour's designs on her that he first attracted attention as her cofferer. In the summer of 1548 Elizabeth left the admiral and his wife for

Hatfield, where she had an establishment of her own at the time of Seymour's arrest on 17 Jan. 1549. Four days after that event Parry and Catherine Astley, the princess's governess, were brought to the Tower, while Sir Robert Tyrwhitt I* was sent down to question their mistress. It is unlikely that the two had taken the initiative in anything so dangerous as a marriage between Elizabeth and Seymour; Elizabeth herself denied it, and although Tyrwhitt believed that all three had conspired to keep silent, Mistress Astley has never been adjudged guilty of more than indiscretion or Parry of being more than an accessory. The Council could unearth nothing until on 9 Feb. Parry was somehow induced to confess that he had met Seymour in London, before and after Christmas 1548; they had discussed the lands which Elizabeth was to receive under her father's will and the admiral had expressed the hope that these would be in the west, near his own. Parry also admitted to having talked with Elizabeth of a marriage and to having learned from Mistress Astley that the princess had left the Seymour household after being found by the former Queen in her husband's arms. The cofferer's breakdown earned him the scorn of the governess, who then followed suit with a similar confession; between them, although they revealed no plot, they sealed the admiral's fate.[6]

Parry's behaviour did not discredit him for long, either with the government or with Elizabeth. In September 1549 he was once more at Hatfield, apparently reinstated, and writing his first known letter to Cecil: in this he related a visit to the princess by the Venetian ambassador, which was to be reported to Somerset as a sign of Elizabeth's frankness, but the main historical interest of the letter lies in the choice of Cecil as its recipient. It may never be known if Parry deserves the credit for first drawing Elizabeth's attention to her future minister, but he took care to insert his own professions of friendship and, in a subsequent letter of July 1550, to assure Cecil that the princess was about to seal his patent as her surveyor. After Cecil had been won over by the Duke of Northumberland, Parry hastened to ask for advice from the new secretary of state on Elizabeth's behalf, and letters on routine matters continued until at least April 1553.[7]

In 1552 Parry ignored a command to collect two payments of a relief from Elizabeth's household, so that a new commission had to be directed to him on 11 Oct. He does not seem to have fallen into disgrace, but continued to acquire property in Berkshire and to establish himself at Wallingford. By December 1548 he had assumed joint custody of the bells of St. Nicholas's college, Wallingford, and about four years later he and his wife leased the clerk's lodgings

there; he had earlier been described as Thomas Parry alias Vaughan of Wallingford in a suit at common pleas. It is not known whether Parry accompanied Elizabeth on her sister's triumphal entry into London in August 1553, nor if he was at court with her in the autumn; when he sued out a pardon in October he was described as a resident of Hatfield.[8]

If there was any need for Parry to atone for his weakness in 1549 he did so in the equally dangerous days of 1554. In March Elizabeth was sent to the Tower, only to be escorted two months later to Woodstock and placed in the care of Sir Henry Bedingfield*. The cofferer had to provide for the princess's household but on 26 May, three days after her arrival at Woodstock, the Council told Bedingfield that there was no reason for Parry to stay there. Elizabeth's guardian, a conscientious man who sought safety by clinging to the letter of his instructions, communicated this decision to Parry, who baffled him by staying in the town. The cofferer now proceeded to make Bedingfield's life a misery. He first objected to the provisioning of his retinue out of Elizabeth's resources, until Bedingfield was commanded to supply them by a special warrant. This was simply a harassing tactic, for books were being conveyed to Elizabeth, some of which Bedingfield suspected of being seditious, and when Parry sent him two harmless ones he was forced to return them for want of explicit instructions. Bedingfield complained that he was helpless, as 'daily and hourly the said Parry may have and give intelligence', and once again the cofferer's position was referred to the Council. Early in July Parry was at the Bull inn, 'a marvellous colourable place to practise in', receiving every day as many as 40 men in his own livery, besides Elizabeth's own servants. At length the Council forbade such large meetings and, from Bedingfield's subsequent silence on the point, it seems that the order was obeyed. There survive among the Thynne Papers at Longleat several letters from Parry to (Sir) John Thynne* which provide a commentary on the cofferer's handling of the princess's affairs.[9]

The government's mild reaction to Parry's behaviour probably sprang from fear of arousing public opinion, but it may also have hoped that he would co-operate. Parry was not to be separated from Elizabeth for long, if at all, for it was from Hatfield that he was summoned at the end of October 1555, while King Philip was still in England, and in November 1558 the Spanish ambassador Feria described him in a despatch as 'a fat man whom your majesty will have seen at Hampton Court'. In 1555 Parry was able to sit again for Wallingford, when he seems to have toed the line to the extent of not appearing on the list of those who opposed one of the government's bills.[10]

Mary's death and Elizabeth's accession transformed Parry's fortunes. The new Queen was still at Hatfield when he was knighted and sworn in as comptroller of the Household and Privy Councillor. Both he and Cecil were shortly elected to Elizabeth's first Parliament. For the next two years they shared the Queen's secret counsels, although it is now known that Cecil's opinion soon began to carry more weight. Parry's claims on Elizabeth were those of a faithful servant rather than an adviser, but the position was to be obscured by his premature death on 15 Dec. 1560. A drawing of him by Holbein survives.[11]

[1] Date of birth estimated from first reference. *DNB*; *Vis. Berks.* (Harl. Soc. lvii), 191; E150/381/5. [2] *LP Hen. VIII*, x, xii, xviii, xxi; M. L. Robertson, 'Cromwell's servants' (Univ. California Los Angeles Ph.D. thesis, 1975), 538; J. E. Neale, *Eliz.* 31; *CSP Dom.* 1547-80, pp. 116, 128, 152-7; Stowe 571, f. 6; *APC*, ii. 240; vii. 3; *HMC Hatfield*, xiii. 40; *CPR*, 1550-3, p. 232; 1553-4 pp. 17, 18, 20; 1558-60, pp. 12, 43, 51, 60, 67, 71, 102, 119, 443; 1560-3, pp. 45, 212, 234. [3] Jones, *Brec.* iii. 175; C. Read, *Cecil*, 64 n. [4] *LP Hen. VIII*, x, xi, xiii. [5] Ibid. xv, xvii, xxi; E150/381/5; J. A. Froude, *Hist. England*, v. 132. [6] Neale, 31-35; F. A. Mumby, *Girlhood of Eliz.* 42, 45-49; *HMC Hatfield*, i. 67, 73; *CSP Dom.* 1547-80, pp. 13-14. [7] Mumby, 62, 75-77; *CSP Dom.* 1547-80, pp. 23, 28, 29, 45; *HMC Hatfield*, i. 101, 114-15. [8] *CPR*, 1550-3, pp. 232, 379; 1553-4, p. 444; 1557-8, p. 173; J. K. Hedges, *Wallingford*, ii. 312, 315; CP40/1139, r. 493v. [9] Neale, 49; *Norf. Arch.* iv. 155, 161, 171, 177, 180, 194, 196; Bath mss, Thynne pprs. 2, ff. 192-3v, 234-5v, 243-4. [10] *CSP Span.* 1558-67, p. 2; *CPR*, 1555-7, pp. 326, 343, 345-6; 1557-8, p. 197; *CSP Dom.* 1547-80, p. 116. [11] *APC*, vii. 3; Read, 221; E150/381/5; *CPR*, 1560-3, p. 249; *Holbein* (The Queen's Gallery, Buckingham Palace 1978-9), 109-10.

T.F.T.B.

PARRY (AP HARRY), William (by 1517-69 or later), of Carmarthen.

CARMARTHEN BOROUGHS   1553 (Mar.)

b. by 1517. *m.*[1]
    Bailiff, Carmarthen 1555-6; escheator, Carm. 1565-6; sheriff 1567-8; j.p. in 1568; under sheriff 1568-9.[2]

William Parry may have been related to John Parry (q.v.), with whom he leased the former Franciscan friary in Carmarthen. Described as of Carmarthen, he was sued in Chancery between 1533 and 1538 by a Londoner named Edward Blacknoll over a messuage and 20 acres of land in the town and fields of Cardigan. It was while serving as one of the town's bailiffs that he was summoned, with the mayor and his fellow-bailiff, to the Exchequer in Trinity term 1556 on an information laid by the attorney-general that they had taken it upon themselves to collect customs at Carmarthen and were wrongfully detaining a sum of £100; the case was one episode in a long drawn-out dispute between the merchants of Carmarthen and the crown searcher. Less impersonal was the grievance which Parry himself made the subject of a Star Chamber action when he was sheriff. He then charged a number of Carmarthen men with staging an armed incursion into St. Peter's church on Whit Sunday 1568, while he was attending

divine service in company with the mayor, aldermen and justices of the peace, assaulting him and disrupting the service; according to Parry one of the justices, Jenkin Dafydd ap Ieuan, was privy to the affair. The defendants claimed that Parry, who was a widower, had himself provoked the attack by threatening Dafydd and others when his suit to marry one of Dafydd's daughters was refused, and that they had gone to the church to protest to the mayor after Parry had harassed them earlier in the day.[3]

His mention as under sheriff in a Star Chamber case of 1569 is the last reference to Parry which has been found.[4]

[1] Date of birth estimated from first reference. St.Ch.5/P66/3. [2] *Cal. Sheriffs etc. of Carmarthen* (NLW ms 5586B), 9; St.Ch.5/B107/4. [3] C1/736/26; E159/336, Trin. 85; St.Ch.5/P66/3. [4] St.Ch.5/B107/4.

P.S.E.

PARTRIDGE (PATRICHE), Henry (by 1523-77 or later).

HEYTESBURY   1558

b. by 1523, s. of one Partridge by Anne. *m.* lic. 21 Nov. 1547, Alice, da. of one Merry (or Goodere) of Hatfield, Herts., wid. of James Nedeham (*d.*22 Sept. 1544) of Little Wymondley, Herts.[1]
    ?Member, household of Henry Fitzroy, Duke of Richmond by 1536; member, household of Prince Edward by 1544; equerry of the stable to Princess Elizabeth by 1547, in the Household by 1550-65 or later.[2]

Several gentle families named Partridge are to be found during the 16th century in counties stretching from East Anglia to the west country, but Henry Partridge cannot be placed in any of them. His mother, seemingly a widow by 1544, when she was the lessee of a house in the parish of St. Andrew by the Wardrobe, London, had a life annuity from Henry VIII which in 1557 she exchanged for one in survivorship with her son. This acknowledgment, and Partridge's own record of service, suggest that either he or his father had been the 'Harry Patriche' who was a member of the Duke of Richmond's household. His return with Christopher Sackville to Mary's last Parliament took place on the day after he had been granted by the crown a lease of Frostendon manor, Suffolk. Neither he nor Sackville had any known link with Heytesbury, but both were colleagues in the Household of Henry Wheeler, a gentleman of the privy chamber who was lord of the manor, and the sheriff who returned them, Sir Walter Hungerford*, was a gentleman pensioner. Nothing is known about Partridge's role in the Commons. In 1565 he was granted the reversion of a lease of lands in Crayford, Kent, and it was as 'an old servant' of Elizabeth that 12 years later he complained to the Privy Council of molestation by one

John Drake. The Council's order for an investigation is the last reference found to Partridge.[3]

[1] Date of birth estimated from first certain reference. *CPR, 1557–8*, p. 122; *Mar. Lic. Fac. Off.* (Harl. Soc. xxiv), 11; *Vis. Herts.* (Harl. Soc. xxii), 16, 77; J. Harvey, *Eng. Med. Architects*, 189–92; *The King's Works*, iii. 406; PCC 21 Pynnyng. [2] *LP Hen. VIII*, xi; E179/69/48; LC2/2/52, 4/20; *APC*, iii. 158; ix. 281; Lansd. 3(89), f. 198; 156(28), f. 98. [3] C219/25/133; *LP Hen. VIII*, xi, xii, xix; *CPR, 1557–8*, pp. 122, 141; *1563–6*, pp. 339–40; *APC*, ix. 281.

R.L.D.

PARVYN, John (by 1485–1531), of Northampton.

NORTHAMPTON 1523[1]

b. by 1485, ?s. of William Parvyn of Northampton. prob. *unm.*[2]

Bailiff, Northampton 1506–7, mayor 1509–10, 1524–5; commr. subsidy, Northants. 1512, Northampton 1515, 1523, 1524, gaol delivery 1513, 1514, 1516, 1518.[3]

John Parvyn may have been a son of William Parvyn, bailiff of Northampton in 1494–5, and his will suggests that, like Thomas Doddington his fellow-Member in the Parliament of 1523, he was a mercer by trade. He could have sat in one or more of the earlier Parliaments of the reign, especially in the light of his appointment to subsidy commissions in 1512 and 1515. Little else has been ascertained about him. Not long before his death he was involved in a chancery suit as alderman of the guild of the Holy Rood in the Wall in St. Gregory's, Northampton. By his will of 24 Mar. 1531 he asked to be buried in the Corpus Christi chapel of All Saints', Northampton, and made provision for the children of his brother Robert Parvyn but none for any of his own. He named his brother and his brother-in-law Edward Manreying executors and Lawrence Manley* overseer. The will was proved on 13 May 1531.[4]

[1] Bridges, *Northants.* i. 436. [2] Date of birth estimated from first reference. *Recs. Northampton*, ed. Cox and Markham, ii. 559; PCC 4 Thower. [3] *Recs. Northampton*, ii. 551, 559; *Statutes*, iii. 88, 169; *LP Hen. VIII*, i–iv. [4] C1/660/39; PCC 4 Thower.

S.M.T.

PASMORE, John (by 1505–44), of Sutton in Halberton, Devon and Lions Inn, London.

EXETER 1542*

b. by 1505, 1st s. of Thomas Pasmore of Sutton by Thomasie. *educ.* Lions Inn. *m.* by 1526, Cecily, da. of John Seman of Sutton, 7s. 3da.; 1s. illegit. *suc.* fa. Feb./Mar. 1529.[1]

J.p. Devon 1540–*d.*; escheator, Devon and Cornw. 1541–2.[2]

John Pasmore came of a cadet branch of a gentle family seated at Pasmorehayes in Tiverton. He had an uncle and a cousin of the same name, both of whom survived him, but as a lawyer whose counsel was retained by the city it was presumably he who was returned for Exeter in March 1543.[3]

Halfway through the second session of the Parliament of 1542 Pasmore and George Kirk replaced William Hurst (q.v.) and Thomas Spurway, who were said to be sick. Like Pasmore, Spurway came from near Tiverton and may have had a hand in his election. Alone among Members for Exeter in the early 16th century Pasmore was not a freeman; that he was not made one on election, as was the custom when non-freemen were chosen, was probably due initially to his absence in London and afterwards to his removal in favour of Hurst. His fellow-Member Kirk was to be superseded by Spurway before the second session was over and it was perhaps about the same time that Hurst displaced Pasmore, who had ceased to be one of the city's Members by the following session; early in 1544 he received from Hurst a token payment of 5s., and he and Spurway supervised the copying of one of the city's charters in the Exchequer. He may have accompanied Hurst back to Exeter, where on 25 Mar. the city's receiver paid him his quarterly fee. Four days later he was dead.[4]

By his will of 25 Aug. 1543 Pasmore asked to be buried at Halberton. After providing for his wife and children he left the income from his lands near Tiverton to maintain his children until they came of age and to educate the sons, and bequeathed to his mother-in-law all his possessions in Lions Inn and in several houses outside Temple Bar. He was succeeded by his 18 year-old son Denis who did not sue for livery until 1552. His widow married Richard Bidwell of Gatton in Shobrooke, Devon.[5]

[1] Date of birth estimated from marriage. *Vis. Devon*, ed. Colby, 166; *Vis. Devon* (Harl. Soc. vi), 207; *Vis. Devon*, ed. Vivian, 589; PCC 3 Jankyn, 8 Pynnyng. [2] *LP Hen. VIII*, xv, xvi, xviii, xx. [3] Ibid. iv; *CPR, 1547–8*, p. 263; *1553*, p. 383; *Trans. Dev. Assoc.* lxi. 199, 206; Exeter act bk. 2, f. 52v. [4] Exeter L28; receiver accts. 1542–3, 1543–4. [5] PCC 8 Pynnyng; C142/70/14; *CPR, 1553*, p. 383; CP 40/1142, r. 672.

A.D.K.H.

PASSEY, John (by 1514–?84), of Wigley in Stanton Lacy, nr. Ludlow, Salop.

LUDLOW 1553 (Oct.)

b. by 1514. *m.* ?1s. 1da.[1]

Bailiff, Ludlow 1539–40, 1546–7, 1557–8.[2]

Nothing has been discovered about the origins of John Passey beyond his claim to gentle status, although a mercantile background is suggested by his, or a namesake's, assessment for subsidy at Leominster in 1535 on goods worth £20 13s.4d. If Passey was not already domiciled at Ludlow he probably moved there following his lease in that year of a house from the hospital of St. John. It was after he had served the town twice as bailiff and had been to London on its business, perhaps over the renewal of its charter, that he was returned to Mary's first

Parliament with his kinsman by marriage Thomas Wheeler. Neither he nor Wheeler opposed the initial measures to restore Catholicism, but whatever his beliefs Passey seems to have been a good churchman, a pewholder close to the pulpit in his parish church and one of its benefactors. He was to do more business in London on the town's behalf in 1555 but he was not re-elected to Parliament. He died at some time before 12 Nov. 1584, when letters of administration were granted to his daughter. Another John Passey, perhaps his son, was steward of Corfton, near Ludlow, between 1587 and 1607.[3]

[1] Date of birth estimated from first reference. PCC admons. act bk. 1581–6, f. 122v. [2] Bodl. Gough Salop 1, ff. 276, 276v, 277v. [3] G. F. Townsend, *Leominster*, 54; Add. Ch. 41330; Salop RO, Ludlow bailiffs' accts. 1552–3, 1554–5; *Ludlow Churchwardens' Accts.* (Cam. Soc. cii), 45, 87, 133; PCC admons. act bk. 1581–6, f. 122v; Wm. Salt Lib. Aqualate ms ex inf. F. Stitt.

A.H.

PASTON, Erasmus (by 1508–40)

ORFORD 1529

b. by 1508, 1st s. of Sir William Paston of Caister and Oxnead, Norf. by Bridget, da. of Sir Henry Heydon † of Baconsthorpe, Norf.; bro. of Clement †, John* and Sir Thomas*. *m.* Mary, da. of Sir Thomas Wyndham of Felbrigg, Norf., 3s. 3da.[1]
Commr. sewers, Norf. 1538.[2]

A member of the prominent Norfolk family, Erasmus was the only Paston known to have sat for a Suffolk borough. His fellow-Member, Richard Hunt, was a municipal official of Orford and doubtless the town's nominee. The other seat, which in 1523 had been claimed by the 11th Lord Willoughby, may by 1529 have come under the sway of the Duke of Suffolk, who held the wardship of Willoughby's heir; however, Willoughby's brother Christopher was challenging his niece's claim to succeed to the family estates which included the castle and manor of Orford, and he may have tried to wield the patronage. What is likely to have been the decisive factor is that Paston's father Sir William was sheriff of Norfolk and Suffolk at the time of the election. Little more is known of Paston save that he was in the retinue of the 3rd Duke of Norfolk appointed to receive Anne of Cleves. He died in 1540 and was buried on 6 Nov. of that year in Paston church, where a monument was erected in his memory. If he made a will it has not been found. His title to the family estates passed to his son William, who succeeded his grandfather 15 years later, and founded in North Walsham the branch of the family from which the 1st Earl of Yarmouth was descended.[3]

[1] Presumed to be of age at election. *Vis. Norf.* (Norf. Arch.), 47–48; *Vis. Norf.* (Harl. Soc. xxxii), 216–17. [2] *LP Hen. VIII*, xiii. [3] *CPR*, 1554–5, p. 10; W. A. Copinger, *Suff. Manors*, i. 208; Pevsner, *N.E. Norf. and Norwich*, 298.

M.K.D.

PASTON, John (1510/12–75/76), of Paston, Norf. and Huntingfield, Suff.

NOTTINGHAM 1547

b. 1510/12, 3rd but 2nd surv. s. of Sir William Paston of Caister and Oxnead, Norf., and bro. of Clement †, Erasmus* and Sir Thomas*. *m.* (1) 1da.; (2) by 1565, Anne, da. of Christopher Moulton, wid. of one Arrowsmith of Huntingfield, 1da.[1]
Gent. waiter, household of Thomas Manners, 1st Earl of Rutland, by 1536–43, of Henry, 2nd Earl 1543–9 or later; gent. pens. from c.1542–69; keeper, Old Park, Wakefield, Yorks. 1542–62; steward, duchy of Lancaster, Cambs., Norf., Suff. 3 Nov. 1550–10 Nov. 1553, former lands of Vale Royal abbey in 1546.[2]

John Paston was presumably introduced at court by his father who held a minor appointment there. Although he never cut as important a figure as his younger brother Sir Thomas, he was to be remembered after his death as having been in youth 'a gallant courtier . . . with rarest virtues adorned, to courtiers all a glass.' He became a gentleman pensioner and it was in this capacity that he 'faithfully' served four successive monarchs. The first trace we have of him is not at court, but in the company of his brother-in-law the 1st Earl of Rutland at the meeting with the Pilgrims of Grace at Doncaster in 1536; when not required by the King he often joined the earl, and gifts of cloth to him as one of the earl's attendants are recorded in Rutland's household accounts. In 1544 he fought in France under Henry VIII's direction, and a year later the King rewarded him with an annuity of £20. In 1547 he was a mourner at the King's funeral and shortly afterwards he performed the happier duty of attending Edward VI's coronation.[3]

Paston's election to the young King's first Parliament was doubtless the work of his nephew the 2nd Earl of Rutland, who was constable of Nottingham castle; he took precedence over his fellow-Member, the town's recorder Nicholas Powtrell. One of his brothers-in-law, (Sir) Francis Leke, sat for Newcastle-upon-Tyne and another kinsman, Henry Leke, for Lyme Regis. Nothing has come to light about his activity in the Commons, but as Rutland's uncle and a household official he presumably helped the passage of a bill enacted during the first session assuring the King of certain lands from the earl. During the second prorogation he kept the earl informed about the unrest in the west and begged his nephew to obtain permission for him to leave the court and join the earl with the army in Scotland. It is possible that he sat in the second Parliament of the reign summoned on the Duke of Northumberland's advice, but in the absence of so many names his Membership in March 1553 is uncertain: he appears to have enjoyed Northumberland's favour as he succeeded to his brother's post in the duchy of Lancaster, but if he did reappear in the Commons it was not as one of the Members for Nottingham.[4]

On Mary's accession Paston and his brother Clement were ordered to stay with their father in Norfolk until the Queen's pleasure concerning them became known, with the result that the pair missed the funeral of Edward VI. Nearly a month later both brothers were summoned back to court and resumed their duties there. On 13 Oct. 1553 Paston sued out a pardon as 'of Paston, Norfolk, esquire', but this was almost certainly a general precaution rather than one relating to his behaviour in the succession crisis earlier in the year. Although his whereabouts then have not been traced, his loyalty may have been doubted as he lost his stewardship in the duchy of Lancaster to (Sir) Richard Southwell* and he was not to sit in Parliament again. His last known appearance at court was for the funeral of Mary, but he almost certainly continued to frequent it until his death, when a panegyric claimed that 'the court laments his end'. After his second marriage he settled in Suffolk and kept a flock of 1,200 sheep. Like his brother Clement he was drawn into the circle of Thomas, 4th Duke of Norfolk, and he became a regular visitor to Kenninghall. He lost his gentleman pensionership between 1 Jan. and 28 Sept. 1569, and on a list compiled in 1570 of alleged Catholics associated with the duke he was noted as indulging in 'too broad talk for religion'. He made his will on 4 Sept. 1575, providing for his wife and two daughters and remembering several kinsmen. He appointed his wife residuary legatee and sole executrix, with two lawyers to assist her, and his brother Clement and a nephew as overseers. In compliance with his wishes his body was buried in the chancel of the church at Huntingfield where a monument was erected to his memory. His will was proved on 30 May 1576.[5]

¹ Date of birth estimated from age at death according to MI. *Vis. Norf.* (Harl. Soc. iv), 216; Pevsner, *Suff.* 259; PCC 9 Carew. ² *HMC Rutland*, iv. 284; *LP Hen. VIII*, xvii, xx, xxi; E407/1/4, 5, ex inf. W. J. Tighe; *CPR*, 1563–6, pp. 278–9; Somerville, *Duchy*, i. 595. ³ Pevsner, 259; *LP Hen. VIII*, xix, xxi; *HMC Rutland*, iv. 279, 284, 287; LC2/2, f. 42. ⁴ M. A. R. Graves, 'The Tudor House of Lords' (Otago Univ. Ph.D. thesis, 1974), ii. 282; *HMC Rutland*, i. 36; M. L. Bush, *Govt. Pol. Somerset*, 85. ⁵ *APC*, iv. 306, 309, 330; *CPR*, 1553–4, p. 439; LC2/4/2; Pevsner, 259; *HMC Hatfield*, i. 438, 440; N. Williams, *Thomas Howard 4th Duke of Norfolk*, 188; PCC 9 Carew.

C.J.B.

PASTON, Sir Thomas (by 1517–50), of London.

NORFOLK   1545

b. by 1517, 4th but 3rd surv. s. of Sir William Paston of Caister and Oxnead, Norf., and bro. of Clement†, Erasmus* and John*. *m.* by 1544, Agnes, da. of Sir John Leigh of Stockwell, Surr., 2s. 1da. Kntd. 30 Sept. 1544.[1]

Gent. privy chamber by 1538–*d.*; keeper of armoury, Greenwich 1541–*d.*; jt. (with William Sharington*) steward and constable, Castle Rising, Norf. 1542–*d.*; steward, manors of Navestock, Pyrgo and Stapleford, Essex 1545–7; steward, duchy of Lancaster, Cambs., Norf. and Suff. 14 Mar. 1547–*d.*; j.p. Norf. 1547.[2]

Thomas Paston spent most of his comparatively short life at court. First found there in February 1538, when as a gentleman of the privy chamber he was granted an annuity of £46 13s.4d., he was probably the 'Mr. Paston' who in December 1539 accompanied the King to supper with the Earl of Hertford. He campaigned in France in 1544 and was knighted after the capture of Boulogne. The King bequeathed him £200 and, according to Paget, intended to make him steward for the duchy of Lancaster in Cambridgeshire, Norfolk and Suffolk; he received the appointment after the King's death and on his own it passed to his brother John. His services also yielded Paston, through grant or purchase, a considerable estate in Norfolk and elsewhere, chiefly from monastic sources. In 1545 he paid nearly £1,300 for the site and possessions of the college of St. Gregory at Sudbury, Suffolk, and in 1548 nearly £500 for a Suffolk chantry. The loss of the inquisitions for Norfolk and Suffolk makes it impossible to say which of these properties he retained; the surviving inquisition for Essex mentions only the manor of Bronden.[3]

Two of Paston's land transactions were the subject of Acts of Parliament: in the first session of the Parliament of 1542 an Act confirmed his exchange of a prebend of Salisbury cathedral, granted him in 1540, for the manor of Godalming, Surrey, and in the second session another registered an exchange of manors in Norfolk between him and the bishop of Norwich. The probability that Paston promoted these Acts from a seat in the Commons is strengthened by the appearance of his signature on the originals. If he was a Member, he could have been the second knight for Norfolk, whose name is lost, or if (Sir) Richard Southwell was re-elected on this occasion Paston could have sat for Thetford. A parliamentary apprenticeship in 1542–4 would also help to explain Paston's choice as first knight for Norfolk at the next election, when even his knighthood and his standing at court might otherwise have yielded to his brothers' seniority. He was connected by marriage with the 3rd Duke of Norfolk—his father-in-law John Leigh being a half-brother of Queen Catherine Howard—and his fellow-knight and kinsman Christopher Heydon was a son-in-law of the sheriff Sir William Drury*.[4]

In August 1547 Paston and (Sir) Thomas Pope* entered into recognizances on behalf of Paston's father-in-law who had recently been released from the Fleet prison and who three years later was to leave the Tower for Paston's house. He served with the Marquess of Northampton against the Norfolk rebels in the summer of 1549 and made his will on the following 7 Oct., adding a codicil on the day of his death, 4 Sept. 1550. He named his wife, to whom he left a life-interest in all his lands, executrix and his father-in-law, his brother Clement Paston (to whom he owed £230) and his cousin Richard Heydon* overseers. His heir Henry was aged five in December 1550; a second son Edward, not yet born, although provided for when the will was made and unnamed in the codicil, was to receive £100 under the will of his grandfather Leigh. Paston's daughter Catherine married Henry Newton† and his widow married Edward Fitzgerald† by whom she was the mother of the 14th Earl of Kildare.[5]

[1] Date of birth estimated from first reference. *Vis. Norf.* (Harl. Soc. xxxii), 216 which mistakenly gives Paston's only child as Sir William; PCC 25 Coode; *Misc. Gen. et Her.* i. 214, 246; *Surr. Arch. Colls.* li. 90–92. [2] *LP Hen. VIII,* xiii, xvi, xvii, xx; *CPR,* 1547–8, pp. 87, 113; 1549–51, p. 402; Somerville, *Duchy,* i. 595. [3] *LP Hen. VIII,* xiii–xxi; *HMC Bath,* iv. 341; *APC,* ii. 18; *CPR,* 1547–8, p. 113; 1548–9, p. 78; C142/90/85. [4] House of Lords RO, Original Acts 33 Hen. VIII, no. 40, 34 and 35 Hen. VIII, no. 45; *Vis. Surr.* (Harl. Soc. xliii), 20, 21. [5] *APC,* ii. 111–12, 142; iii. 54, 97, 118, 127, 301; Blomefield, *Norf.* iii. 239, 241; PCC 25 Coode; C142/90/85; *Suss. Arch. Colls.* li. 90–92.

R.V.

PATCHE, Thomas (by 1504–53), of Sandwich, Kent.

SANDWICH 1539,[1] ?1547,[2] 1553 (Mar.)[3]

b. by 1504. *m.* Susan.[4]
    Common councilman, Sandwich 1533–7, jurat 1537–*d.*, mayor 1539–40, bailiff 1543–*d.*; sewer of the chamber by 1543; bailiff to Yarmouth 1544; capt. of the Turf bulwark, nr. Sandwich by 1553.[5]

Thomas Patche had a house in Sandwich in 1525, but it was not until three years later that he was admitted to the freedom 'by reason of his free purchase', that is to say, his purchase of a free tenement. Although he held office in Sandwich from 1533 he did not play a prominent part in the life of the town, but he was chosen to go to the Brotherhood of the Cinque Ports on three occasions and to serve as Member of Parliament and as mayor. His election to the Parliament of 1539 may have been due chiefly to some outside interest (perhaps a military command) or to the influence of the lord warden of the Cinque Ports, Sir Thomas Cheyne*; he did not serve free of charge, however, being paid £5 as wages during 1540–1.[6]

In November 1543 Patche was appointed by the King bailiff of Sandwich. His office presumably accounts for his election to the two Parliaments of Edward VI's reign, although on the first occasion this was countermanded. He and Thomas Ardern, comptroller of the customs at Sandwich, were re-turned after the mayor had refused to seal the indenture naming Thomas Pinnock (q.v.) and John Seer (q.v.) as the Members, but the Council upheld the original election and the appearance of his and Ardern's names on the list of Members of this Parliament may indicate only that they sat in the House until the Council decided against them. It was perhaps to make amends for this rebuff that Patche was elected to the following Parliament. This time Cheyne disapproved of the choice of Thomas Menys as his fellow-Member and rebuked the port for not consulting him: Patche and William Oxenden*, whom the warden had favoured, informed the mayor and jurats of his displeasure, but Menys's election was allowed to stand. The Journal throws no light on Patche's activity in the Commons.[7]

Patche made his will on 17 May 1553, asking to be buried in the chancel of St. Mary's, Sandwich. After providing for his brother, he made his wife his sole executrix and left her all his movable goods and all his property in Richborough and Sandwich except the *White Hart* in Sandwich, which he gave to Thomas Gull, a kinsman. His 'well beloved friend' William Oxenden, appointed overseer, was one of the witnesses of the will, which was proved on 26 June 1553.[8]

[1] Sandwich old Red bk., f. 111. [2] Hatfield 207. [3] Sandwich little black bk., f. 31. [4] Date of birth estimated from first reference. Canterbury prob. reg. C25, f. 33. [5] Sandwich old red bk., ff. 13 seq.; little black bk., ff. 1 seq.; *LP Hen. VIII,* xviii; *CPR,* 1553, p. 78; Stowe 571, f. 42. [6] Sandwich white bk., f. 352; old red bk., ff. 13, 133v; treasurers' accts. Sa/Fac. 34; *Cinque Ports White and Black Bks.* (Kent Arch. Soc. recs. br. xix), 224, 233. [7] Sandwich little black bk., f. 31; old red bk., ff. 200v, 207; *APC,* ii. 536–7. [8] Canterbury prob. reg. C25, f. 33.

H.M.

PATE (PATES), Richard (1516–88), of Minster-worth, Glos. and London.

GLOUCESTER 1558, 1559, 1563, 1586

b. 24 Sept. 1516, poss. s. of Walter Pate of Cheltenham, Glos. *educ.* Corpus, Oxf. adm. 26 Sept. 1532; L. Inn, adm. 10 Aug. 1541, called 1558. *m.* Maud, da. of John Rastell of Gloucester, Glos., wid. of Henry Marmion and Thomas Lane* (*d.*2 Dec. 1544) of Gloucester.[1]
    Steward, reader's dinner, L. Inn 1562, Lent reader 1563, associate 1571.
    Under steward and keeper of lands formerly of Cirencester abbey 1544, Hailes abbey 1546; jt. (with Anthony Bourchier*) under steward, lands formerly of Tewkesbury abbey and keeper, borough cts. Tewkesbury 1546; commr. chantries, Glos., Bristol and Gloucester, 1547, relief, Glos. 1550, grain 1573, piracy 1577; j.p. Glos. 1547, q. 1558/59–*d.*, marcher and some Welsh counties 1564; escheator, Glos. 1548–9; recorder, Gloucester 1556–87; member, council in the marches of Wales in 1560; dep. justice, Glam. 1563; sheriff, Glos. 1580–1.[2]

Richard Pate's parentage has not been established but he was a nephew of his namesake the Marian bishop of Worcester. Trained as a lawyer, throughout his life he took an active part in the administration of Gloucestershire. He became an associate and friend of the diplomat Thomas Chamberlain†, with whom he invested money in ex-monastic property. In a letter to Paget of July 1545 Chamberlain suggested that Pate 'could shortly spy something meet' for Chamberlain or his friends. In 1547 Pate leased Abbot's Court Place (Hertpury manor) in Gloucester, but he must have made Minsterworth, three and a half miles from the city, his domicile before 1559.[3]

Pate may have owed his appointment as recorder of Gloucester in 1556 to Chamberlain's influence, although his marriage had given him a standing in the city and his precursor John Pollard* probably favoured the nomination since he had stayed at Pate's house when in Gloucester for the burning of Bishop Hooper. In 1557 Pate was among the more substantial citizens ordered to appear before the Privy Council for non-payment of the loan of £100. It was as the city's recorder that Pate was elected to Mary's last Parliament. On a copy of the Crown Office list for this Parliament, his name is one of those marked with a circle. During the first session of 29 Jan. 1558 he had committed to him the second reading of a bill for the fortifications of Melcombe Regis.[4]

Under Elizabeth the sphere of Pate's work widened, especially after he became law officer for the council in the marches of Wales. He died on 27 Oct. 1588 and was buried in the south transept of Gloucester cathedral, where there is an effigy.[5]

[1] Date of birth given in Emden, *Biog. Reg. Univ. Oxf. 1501-40*, p. 436. *DNB*; A. L. Browne, 'Richard Pate', *Bristol and Glos. Arch. Soc. Trans.* lvi. 201-25; PCC 20 Pynnyng; T. D. Fosbroke, *Gloucester*, 136. [2] *LP Hen. VIII*, xix, xxi; *CPR*, 1547-8, p. 84; 1548-9, p. 136; 1553, pp. 327, 354; 1558-60, p. 92; 1560-3. p. 437; W. H. Stevenson, *Cal. Recs. Gloucester*, 33; P. H. Williams, *Council in the Marches of Wales*, 274-5, 354-5; *APC*, viii. 158; x. 135; Gloucester Guildhall 1394, f. 60v. [3] *Bristol and Glos. Arch. Soc. Trans.* lvi. 201-7; *Hist. Jnl.* xx. 803; *LP Hen. VIII*, xx, xxi; *CPR*, 1547-8, p. 196; 1548-9, pp. 260-1; 1558-60, p. 184. [4] *Bristol and Glos. Arch. Soc. Trans.* lvi. 208-9; Gloucester Guildhall 1394, ff. 50-50v; Wm. Salt Lib. SMS 264; *CJ*, i. 48. [5] Fosbroke, 136.

M.K.D.

PATESHALL, John (by 1523-64 or later), of the Inner Temple, London and Ford in Pudleston, Herefs.

HEREFORDSHIRE 1558

b. by 1523, 1st s. of William Pateshall of Ford by Sybil, da. of (?John) Gomond of Byford, Herefs. *educ.* I. Temple. *m.* Eleanor, da. of James Tomkins of Weobley, Herefs., 2s. 1da. *suc.* fa. unknown.[1]

Commr. gaol delivery, Hereford 1554; j.p.q. Herefs. 1558/59-64.[2]

John Pateshall came of a gentle family which had owned property near Pudleston since the 14th century. His membership of the Inner Temple is known from the complaint which he addressed to Chancellor Audley between 1538 and 1544 about the vicar of Byford's failure to honour an agreement with him. He presumably owed his election to Mary's last Parliament to the same support as his fellow-knight and relative Gregory Price, with his distant kinsman Richard Monington assisting as sheriff. The Journal throws no light on Pateshall's part in the House. His appointment to the Herefordshire bench may have followed the accession of Elizabeth and in 1564 he was commended for his learning and his support of the Anglican settlement. This is the last reference found to him. His widow lived until 1582.[3]

[1] Date of birth estimated from first reference. *Vis. Herefs.* ed. Weaver, 54, 66. [2] *CPR*, 1553-4, p. 34; 1560-3, p. 438; 1563-6, p. 23. [3] C. J. Robinson, *Mansions and Manors of Herefs.* 7; C1/1049/2-3; *Vis. Herefs.* 33-34, 65, 66; *Cam. Misc.* ix(3), 13-14; NLW Hereford consist. ct. wills box 9 Pa(1).

A.J.E.

PAULET, Chidiock (by 1521-74), of Wade, Hants.

BRAMBER 1547*[1]
GATTON 1553 (Oct.)[2]

b. by 1521, 3rd s. of William Paulet, 1st Marquess of Winchester, by Elizabeth, da. of Sir William Capell* of London. *educ.* I. Temple, adm. 1535. *m.* (1) Elizabeth, da. of (Sir) Thomas White II* of South Warnborough, Hants, 1s. 3da.; (2) by 1562, Frances, da. of Sir Edward Neville of Aldington, Kent, wid. of Sir Edward Waldegrave* of Borley, Essex, 1s.[3]

Esquire of the stable by 1545; receiver, ct. augmentations, Glos., Hants, Wilts. by 1550-4; Exchequer 1554-*d.*; capt. Portsmouth May 1554-9; j.p.q. Hants 1558/59-*d.*; commr. subsidy 1563; treasurer, bp. Winchester 1566-*d.*[4]

Chidiock Paulet owed any success he achieved to his father. He attended the Inner Temple, where in 1535, at his father's request, he was pardoned all offices and vacations and received a licence to dine with the clerks. Soon after his father became steward of the Household he received a minor appointment there and a lease of the manor of Odiham, Hampshire, together with the bailiwick of its lordship. It was from Odiham that in the summer of 1545 Paulet led 200 men to Portsmouth during the threat of invasion by the French. In the following year the townsmen of Southampton provided him with a gallon of wine 'when he lay at Netley to see how far our guns would shoot'. His official duties concerned the defence of the Hampshire coast, and this responsibility became more particularly his in 1554 on his appointment as captain of Portsmouth.[5]

Paulet replaced (Sir) William Sharington (q.v.) in the Parliament of 1547 as one of the Members for Bramber, a Sussex borough with which he had no ties. The date of his by-election is not known, but his name 'Chidiocus Powlet miles Dominus Powlet' appears on the list of Members for the last session (1552). Paulet was presumably nominated by the

Council, of which his father was president, as a man who could be relied upon to comply with official intentions. He was not re-elected at Bramber for the following Parliament and is not known to have sat elsewhere, but after the accession of Mary he was returned to the first Parliament of her reign for Gatton, a borough owned by the Copley family. Either he or his father may have approached Thomas Copley*, a junior colleague at the Inner Temple, for his place on this occasion.[6]

Lacking his father's personality and talents, Paulet was prominent only in his native county, and his few appearances on the public stage were undistinguished, as an incident during Wyatt's rebellion indicates. As Sir Thomas Wyatt II* moved along the Strand towards the City after defeating a force at Charing Cross, 'certain of the lord treasurer's band to the number of 300 men, whereof the Lord Chidiock Paulet his son was captain, met them, and so going on the one side passed by them on the other side without anything saying to them'. Paulet was less ineffective at Portsmouth towards the end of Mary's reign, but despite the favourable impression he made there Elizabeth dismissed him in 1559 and appointed Sir Adrian Poynings in his stead. Poynings was to make himself unpopular with the townsmen for his overbearing attitude, but when Paulet was offered the post again in 1562 he declined it. Court gossip reported that Paulet had been 'mildly revoked', but no reason was given either for his dismissal or for his refusal of reinstatement.[7]

Paulet remained in the foreground of Hampshire politics, although in 1564 Bishop Horne of Winchester reported on his Catholicism. The Marquess of Winchester's influence kept him on the commission of the peace even after he had refused to sign a submission to the Act of Uniformity. Tactfully the bishop wrote that 'his lordship showeth himself otherwise an obedient and faithful subject, giving us thereby some hope of his good conformity in time to come'. Horne had good reason to know, for Paulet had succeeded his father-in-law, Sir Thomas White, as the bishop's treasurer three years before. After the death of Elizabeth White, Paulet married the widow of a prominent Marian, but unlike her first husband he did not suffer for his faith.[8]

Paulet left a large estate in Hampshire and some property in Buckinghamshire when he died on 17 Aug. 1574. He had acquired most of this property during Edward VI's reign. The will he made three days before his death omits his lands entirely. He bequeathed to his wife all the plate, hangings, bedding, brass and pewter he had received at their marriage in Borley, Essex, and all his household silver. His daughters Elizabeth and Susan received £900 between them, his son Thomas a £20 annuity, and his stepson Charles Waldegrave a horse. William Paulet, his son and heir, was appointed executor.[9]

[1] Hatfield 207. [2] Bodl. e. Museo 17. [3] Date of birth estimated from pardon in I. Temple. *Vis. Hants* (Harl. Soc. lxiv), 82; PCC 4 Stonard, 12 Pyckering. [4] *LP Hen. VIII*, xxi; LC2/4/7, f. 21v; Stowe 571, f. 10v; *CSP Dom.* 1547–80, p. 287; W. C. Richardson, *Ct. Augmentations*, 281. [5] *Cal. I.T. Recs.* i. 110; *LP Hen. VIII*, xx; *VCH Hants*, iv. 90; Soton RO, liber de finibus, 38 Hen. VIII–1 Edw. VI; *CPR*, 1553–4, p. 273; SP11/11, f. 151. [6] Hatfield 207. [7] *Chron. Q. Jane and Q. Mary* (Cam. Soc. xlviii), 50; Stow, *Annals* (1631), 621; SP11/9, f. 41, 13, ff. 117–18; 12/24, f. 95; *CSP For.* 1559–60, p. 138; 1562, p. 294. [8] *Cam. Misc.* ix(3), 56; SP12/59, f. 160; 15/25, f. 267; *Cath. Rec. Soc.* xiii. 89. [9] C142/172/120; *CPR*, 1549–51, p. 66; 1550–3, pp. 43, 246; 1557–8, p. 23; 1569–72, pp. 350, 460; PCC 12 Pyckering.

R.J.W.S.

PAULET, Hugh (by 1510–73), of Hinton St. George, Som.

SOMERSET   ?1529*, ?1536, 1539,[1] 1572*

b. by 1510, 1st s. of Sir Amias Paulet† of Hinton St. George by 2nd w. Laura, da. of William Keilway of Rockbourne, Hants. *educ.* M. Temple. *m.* (1) c.1530, Philippa, da. of Sir Lewis Pollard† of Kings Nympton, Devon, 3s. inc. Amias† 2da.; (2) settlement 12 Nov. 1560, Elizabeth, da. of Walter Blount I* of Blount's Hall, nr. Uttoxeter, Staffs., wid. of Anthony Basford of Bentley, Derbys. and of Sir Thomas Pope* of London and Tittenhanger, Herts. *s.p.* Kntd. July 1536; *suc.* fa. 11 Apr. 1538.[2]

J.p. Som. 1532–*d.*, western circuit 1540–*d.*, Devon 1547–*d.*, Dorset 1562–*d.*; steward, bp. Bath and Wells by 1534–72, jt. (with s. Amias) 1572–*d.*; sheriff, Som. and Dorset 1536–7, 1542–3, 1547–8, Devon 1541–2; member, council in the west 1539; commr. coastal defence, west country 1539, relief, Som. 1550, goods of churches and fraternities, Bath, Som. 1553, fortifications, Jersey 1562, musters, Som. 1569; surveyor, lands of Glastonbury abbey 1540; v.-adm., Som. and Dorset c.1540; treasurer, Boulogne 11 Oct. 1544–Oct. 1546; gov. Jersey 20 Mar. 1550–*d.*; v.-pres. council in the marches of Wales 8 Apr. 1559; custos rot. Som. c.1562–*d.*; chief steward, Taunton 1572–*d.*[3]

Hugh Paulet's forbears took their surname from a village near Bridgwater, which remained the family seat until Hinton St. George passed by marriage into its ownership during the 15th century. His father, who practised as a lawyer, figured prominently in county affairs and procured the influential post of steward to the bishop of Bath and Wells first for himself and on his resignation for his son. Paulet's succession to his father in this office suggests why, not long after achieving his majority, he was included on the Somerset bench, for which neither his descent nor his fortune pre-eminently qualified him. It was perhaps through his brother-in-law Richard Pollard* that he came to Cromwell's notice; they were apparently well known to each other by 1534 when Bishop Clerke hoped to clear himself of a malicious report when Cromwell mentioned it to Paulet, and thereafter his name occurs frequently among the minister's remembrancers.[4]

Paulet was knighted in July 1536, probably co-incidentally with Cromwell at the dissolution of the short Parliament of that summer. The timing of Paulet's accolade suggests that he had sat in that Parliament, and if he had he was also probably a Member of the previous one, as the King asked for the re-election of Members of that Parliament to its successor. If we assume that he had been by-elected within his own county, he may have replaced Sir William Stourton as one of the Somerset knights on his summons to the Lords as 7th Baron Stourton. If this surmise is true, Sir Hugh Paulet could look back on two parliamentary sessions when he took the senior knighthood in the Parliament of 1539. Of his role in this Parliament nothing is known, but after the dissolution in 1540 he and his fellow-knight Sir Thomas Speke received a letter about the collection of the subsidy that they had helped to grant.[5]

At the outbreak of the northern rebellion in 1536 Paulet was ordered to attend the King at Ampthill, Bedfordshire, and later he led a band of 300 men against the insurgents. This was the start of a varied military and administrative career. In 1544 he served at the siege of Boulogne, and on the town's surrender he became a member of its governing council, with special responsibility for its safety, and he resided there for the next two years. He is not known to have fought in either Edward VI's Scottish war or Mary's French one, but in 1549 he helped Sir John Russell*, Baron Russell to restore order in the west and when in 1562 the Huguenots handed over Le Havre to Elizabeth, he advised the Earl of Warwick on its control. Notwithstanding his links with the Protector Somerset to whom he lent money and commended men for service, he was named in 1550 the ex-Protector's replacement as governor of Jersey: Paulet had gone to the Channel Islands in the previous year to review their administration and defence. While governor he ordered the translation of the first Prayer Book into French: Strype's statement that he did this as governor of Calais must be an error, for Paulet is known to have encouraged and advanced the progress of the Reformation in the Channel Islands.[6]

The discharge of his obligations elsewhere did not prevent Paulet from taking part in the management of the south-west, but his absences from England doubtless explain the 30-year interval between his return for Somerset in 1539 and that in 1572. His suing out of general pardons in 1547, 1554 and 1559 seem to have been no more than a conventional precaution. Throughout his career he availed himself of the opportunity to expand his inheritance, acquiring lands by grant or purchase from the crown. He died on 6 Dec. 1573 and was buried in the church at Hinton St. George in the tomb which he had built to receive his first wife and himself.[7]

[1] E159/319, brev. ret. Mich. r. [1–2]. [2] Date of birth estimated from age at fa.'s i.p.m., C142/61/14. Vis. Som. ed. Weaver, 60; G. R. Balleine, Biog. Dict. Jersey, 622 seq.; PCC 18 Dyngeley, 8 Martyn; Collinson, Som. ii. 167. [3] LP Hen. VIII, v, viii, xi, xiii–xxi; CPR, 1547–8 to 1569–72 passim; Strype, Annals, i(1), 34; VCH Dorset, ii. 108; APC, vii. 81; C66/985 ex inf. J. C. Sainty; SP12/93. [4] DNB; HP, ed. Wedgwood 1439–1509 (Biogs.), 667–8; P. H. Hembry, Bps. Bath and Wells 1540–1640, pp. 46–47; LP Hen. VIII, vii–xiii. [5] Information from Dr. H. H. Leonard; E139/319, brev. ret. Mich. r. [1–2]. [6] LP Hen. VIII, xi–xiii, xviii–xxi; Strype, Annals, 548; Cranmer, 416, 1035; Collinson, ii. 81; The description of the citie of Excester (Devon and Cornw. Rec. Soc. xi), 95; Balleine, 662; Bath mss Thynne pprs. 2, ff. 70–71v, 127–8v, 141–2v; HMC Bath. iv. 109; W. K. Jordan, Edw. VI, i. 234–5; ii. 350; A. J. Eagleston, The Channel Islands under Tudor Govt. 12. [7] LP Hen. VIII, xiii–xviii, xx; W. C. Richardson, Ct. Augmentations, 135; CPR, 1547–8 to 1572–5 passim; Trans. Som. Arch. and Nat. Hist. Soc. lxxii. 33; C142/167/78.

A.D.K.H.

PAULET, Sir William (by 1488–1572), of Basing and Netley, Hants, Chelsea, Mdx. and London.

HAMPSHIRE 1529

b. by 1488, 1st s. of Sir John Paulet of Basing and Nunney, Som. by Alice, da. of Sir William Paulet of Hinton St. George, Som. educ. ?I. Temple. m. Elizabeth, da. of Sir William Capell* of London, 4s. inc. Chidiock* 4da. Kntd. 1523/25; KG nom. 23 Apr. 1543, inst. 6 May; suc. fa. 5 Jan. 1525; cr. Baron St. John 9 Mar. 1539, Earl of Wiltshire 19 Jan. 1550, Marquess of Winchester 11 Oct. 1551.[1]

Sheriff, Hants 1511–12, 1518–19, 1522–3; commr. subsidy 1512, 1515, 1523, 1524, musters 1512, 1514, Wilts. 1539, various counties 1545, survey, Calais 1535, 1540, coastal defence, Hants 1539, sale of crown lands 1544, 1546, 1554, 1559, benevolence, Hants 1544/45, relief, Hants, London and Household 1550, goods of churches and fraternities, Hants 1553; j.p. Hants 1514–d., Wilts. 1523–d., Som. 1531–d., all counties 1547–d.; Councillor by 1525; jt. (with Thomas Englefield) master, King's wards 3 Nov. 1526, sole 21 Dec. 1534–July 1540; steward, bpric. of Winchester by 1529–d.; surveyor-gen. wards' and widows' lands and gov. idiots and naturals 14 Jan. 1531; comptroller, the Household May 1532–Oct. 1537, treasurer Oct. 1537–Mar. 1539, chamberlain c.May 1543–Oct. 1545, gt. master by Nov. 1545–Feb. 1550; jt. (with Cromwell) surveyor, King's woods by 1533, keeper 23 June 1541; keeper, Pamber forest, Hants Feb. 1536, St. Andrew's castle, Hamble, Hants July 1547, Alice Holt and Woolmer forests, Hants July 1548, jt. (with s. John) Jan. 1561; trier of petitions in the Lords, Parlts. of 1539, 1542, 1545, 1547, Mar. 1553, Oct. 1553, Nov. 1554, 1555, 1558, 1559; master, ct. wards 26 July 1540, 18 Nov. 1542, ct. wards and liveries 20 Nov. 1542–54; gov. Portsmouth 1542; PC 19 Nov. 1542; ld. pres. Council by Nov. 1545–Feb. 1550; warden and c.j. forests south of Trent 17 Dec. 1545–2 Feb. 1550; custos rot. Hants c.1547; keeper of the great seal Mar.–Oct. 1547; ld. treasurer 3 Feb. 1550–d.; ld. lt. Hants May 1552, May 1553, May 1559, Nov. 1569, London and adjacent counties 1558, London and Mdx. 1569; capt. I.o.W. and Carisbrooke castle bef. 1560; high steward, Taunton, Som. at d.[2]

The Paulets of Basing, a cadet branch of the family of Hinton St. George, acquired their Hampshire residence in the early 15th century on the marriage of William Paulet's great-grandfather to a coheir of the last Lord St. John of Basing. Early in 1536 Paulet was granted the keepership of Pamber forest as heir (he was not, in fact, even the senior coheir) to Hugh, Lord St. John; later in the same year he was ranked among Councillors of noble blood in an answer to the northern rebels' charge that the Council was made up of new men; and in 1539 he was himself created Baron St. John.[3]

Trained as a lawyer Paulet made his career as a bureaucrat. No trace has been found of his admission to an inn of court but he was almost certainly the man of that name known to have been marshal of the Inner Temple between 1505 and 1507: his younger brother George was admitted there in 1507 and his own son Chidiock in 1535. Before being admitted to the King's Council 'for matters in law' he served a long apprenticeship in shire administration, being first nominated for the shrievalty of Hampshire in 1509; he also became steward of the bishopric of Winchester, probably during the episcopacy of Richard Fox (d.1528), although he first appears in office during the brief tenure of the see in commendam by Wolsey. His kinsman by marriage Thomas Arundell* was a member of Wolsey's household and as steward of the bishopric Paulet was responsible for the Membership in 1529 for Taunton of the cardinal's secretary Cromwell; on the eve of the Parliament Cromwell instructed his agent Ralph Sadler* to 'require' Paulet to name him 'one of the burgesses of one of my lord's towns of his bishopric of Winchester', but whether Paulet did so on instructions from Wolsey or out of friendship for Cromwell is not known. Paulet himself may have owed his return as knight for Hampshire to the intervention of the King, the writ being one of those which Henry VIII had sent to him at Windsor. This is the only Parliament in which Paulet is known to have sat in the Commons: he may have done so earlier in the reign (although his first and third shrievalties would have prevented his return for Hampshire in 1512 and 1523) and he was probably re-elected in 1536 in accordance with the King's general request to that effect.[4]

Paulet had been appointed joint master of the King's wards with Thomas Englefield in 1526, but the claims of Englefield's judgeship meant that Paulet was soon the sole effective master and early in 1531 he alone was made surveyor of wards' and widows' lands: this concentration of wardship offices was formalized in 1540 by the erection of the court of wards, later of wards and liveries, with Paulet as master. In May 1532 he succeeded the courtier Sir Henry Guildford* as comptroller of the Household, and later that year or early in 1533 he and his 'fellow

and friend' Cromwell assumed joint control of the King's woods. In October 1532 he was with the King at Calais and in the following spring he accompanied the 3rd Duke of Norfolk's embassy to France; in the winter he went with the Duke of Suffolk and others to reduce the household of Catherine of Aragon and in 1534 he joined with the Earl of Wiltshire to persuade Princess Mary to renounce her title. When in 1535 he was commissioned with Sir William Fitzwilliam I* to visit Calais he hoped before doing so to spend a fortnight in overseeing the construction he had undertaken at Basing: in October the King visited him there. In 1536 he was engaged in organizing the royal army at Ampthill, Bedfordshire.[5]

In the same month as he became a baron Paulet was involved with Fitzwilliam, now Earl of Southampton, in the defences of Hampshire and in the shire election for the Parliament of that year. Only a few glimpses can be caught of his own earlier career in the Commons. As 'Mr. Comptroller' he appears on a list drawn up by Cromwell on the dorse of a letter of December 1534 and thought to be of Members connected, perhaps as a committee, with the treasons bill then on its passage through Parliament: his placing next after the minister himself and Fitzwilliam, treasurer of the Household, bespeaks his importance. His name is also to be found on the dorse of a private Act passed during the last session of the Parliament concerning the heirs of Lord Willoughby de Broke, together with those of seven of his family and kinsmen, including his son John and John's wife Elizabeth Willoughby. It was probably his second son Thomas, rather than his younger brother of that name, who was included in a fragmentary list of boroughs and nominees seemingly prepared by Cromwell for the Parliament of 1536. The three boroughs named were those belonging to the bishop of Winchester, and Thomas Paulet is coupled with William Petre for Downton. Bishop Gardiner was abroad at the time and it is unlikely that such a nomination would have failed, but there is nothing to confirm Thomas Paulet's Membership. The only one of Paulet's children known to have sat in the Commons was his son Chidiock, although several of his near relatives did so, among them his cousin Hugh Paulet and his nephews Sir Henry Capell and John Zouche I, who was first returned for Hindon, another of the bishop of Winchester's boroughs. Paulet had ample opportunity to wield parliamentary patronage, whether on his own behalf or, as in 1539, on the crown's. Nicholas Hare probably owed his return for Downton in 1529 and Taunton in 1547 to his friendship with Paulet, while John Bekinsau, although doubtless acceptable to

Gardiner as a Member for Downton and Hindon in Mary's reign, was Paulet's neighbour in Hampshire. Michael Gore was returned as his servant to the Parliament of 1545 for Portsmouth, where Edmund Cockerell, one of his subordinates in the Exchequer, and John de Vic, his secretary, were also returned after Chidiock Paulet had become captain of Portsmouth, as was his friend Sir Richard Sackville II while Chidiock was captain-designate. As master of the wards and (probable) custodian of Henry Weston*, Paulet may have been responsible for the re-enfranchisement of Petersfield in 1547 when his younger brother George was sheriff of Hampshire.[6]

Paulet was an active member of the Lords, especially after he became lord treasurer. Regularly appointed a trier of petitions, he had a good attendance record and served on numerous committees; his signature appears twice on Acts for the Parliament of 1539, once for 1542, and seven times for 1547. On 7 Jan. 1550 he adjourned the House in the absence of Chancellor Rich and he presumably did the same after the death of Gardiner during the Parliament of 1555, which he later dissolved. On 14 Nov. 1558 he and Chancellor Heath headed the Lords' delegation to the Commons about the subsidy. In the following reign he took Bacon's place as Speaker on 4 Mar. 1559 and from 5 to 25 Oct. 1566, when 'the decay of his memory and hearing, griefs accompanying hoary hairs and old age' led to his retirement in favour of Sir Robert Catlyn.[7]

In 1540 Paulet had again been sent to Calais and four years later he served on the French campaign, being appointed with Sir John Gage* to see to the transport of the army overseas. In July the Duke of Suffolk described him as 'one of my hands' at Boulogne and in the following year the duke endorsed the King's choice of Paulet to take over the military government of Portsmouth. There he fell ill, the victim of a prevailing epidemic, and in September a servant reported that he was in danger of death but resolved to 'wear it out'. At about this time he became great master of the Household and also lord president of the Council: it was as the holder of these offices that in January 1547 he was appointed with three other peers to deliver the ailing King's assent to the Duke of Norfolk's attainder.[8]

Paulet was named as executor of Henry VIII's will, taking precedence after Archbishop Cranmer and the chancellor, and was one of the five Councillors to receive a bequest of £500. According to the testimony given by Secretary Paget as to the King's intentions, he was also to have had lands and an earldom, but he had to wait for promotion in the peerage until after the overthrow of the Protector Somerset. He had already added extensively to his inheritance by grant

and purchase and under Edward VI he obtained further lands in Dorset, Hampshire, Hertfordshire, Middlesex, Somerset and Wiltshire, being one of the five major recipients of crown lands by gift. For a few months in 1547 he served as lord keeper of the great seal after the dismissal of Wriothesley and was holding the office when the first Parliament of the reign was summoned. Shortly after his appointment he was one of the seven Councillors who signed a request to the young King for a commission empowering the Council to wield full authority during the minority. He was an assiduous attendant at Council meetings, several of which were held at his house in London and at Basing in 1549 and 1552.[9]

In 1549 Paulet gave his support to the Earl of Warwick against Somerset—whom, according to one account, he bluffed into financing the *coup* against himself. Created Earl of Wiltshire and given Somerset's office of lord treasurer in exchange for the great mastership of the Household he was advanced to the marquessate of Winchester when Warwick was created Duke of Northumberland in October 1551; in the previous month he had been appointed high steward for the trial of Somerset. He remained treasurer until his death but in his last years was effectively replaced by his eventual successor Cecil. Unlike his precursors Paulet was a conscientious administrator with a dislike for unnecessary expenditure and reservations about large-scale reforms. His bureaucratic conservatism led to frequent rumours about his imminent dismissal in the 1550s and to his exclusion from the revenue commission of 1552 and the council of finance set up in 1558. Elizabeth expressed doubts about his work in the recoinage, and it was only after Cecil had allayed these that she reconfirmed Paulet as treasurer: the extraordinary sequence of deaths in the winter of 1558–9 left her with little choice in the matter. His main objective from 1555 until retirement was to eliminate corruption from the receipt of the Exchequer and to improve efficiency by making it subordinate to his authority as treasurer, but a series of scandals during 1569–70 revealed the weaknesses inherent in his approach which was then scrapped without consulting him in favour of the more enlightened ideas of (Sir) Walter Mildmay*.[10]

In the struggle for the succession in the summer of 1553 Paulet was one of the Councillors who gave increasingly reluctant support to Northumberland and after a brief period of house-arrest in August he was retained in his offices by Mary. One of the four peers who gave the Queen in marriage 'in the name of the whole realm', he entertained the royal couple at Basing on the day after the wedding. It was perhaps a sign of the favour he enjoyed that his eldest son was summoned to the Lords for the last three Parliaments of the reign in Paulet's barony of St. John. As befitted one who, in the words of Sir Robert Naunton[†], was 'always of the King's religion, and always [a] zealous professor', and despite his uncharacteristic vote against the Act of Uniformity in 1559, he had no difficulty in accommodating himself to the Elizabethan settlement. Although he refused to take the oath incorporated in the Act of Succession he remained in the forefront of national affairs until the summer of 1570, when apparently on account of ill-health he withdrew to Basing. He absented himself from the Parliament of 1571 and was excused attendance at the trial of the 4th Duke of Norfolk early in 1572.[11]

Paulet died intestate on 10 Mar. 1572 at Basing and was buried there. He had spent lavishly on his building there and at Chelsea (where he had been granted Sir Thomas More's house in 1536) and at his death he owed over £34,000 to the crown and some £12,000 to individuals. Several portraits of Paulet survive. According to Naunton, Paulet ascribed his retention of high office under four sovereigns to his ability to bend (*Ortus sum ex salice, non ex quercu*) and (Sir) Richard Morison* saw in him one who had 'a tongue fit for all times, with an obedience ready for as many new masters as can happen in his days'. But many men were as ready as Paulet to trim to Tudor winds of change, and it was another hostile critic, John Knox, who came nearer the truth when, speaking of those who governed for Edward VI, he asked, 'Who could best dispatch business, that the rest of the Council might hawk and hunt, and take their pleasure? None like unto [Paulet]'.[12]

[1] Date of birth estimated from first reference. *CP*; *DNB*. [2] *Statutes*, iii. 89, 170; *LP Hen. VIII*, i–xxi; *CPR*, 1547–8, pp. 80–93, 177, 326; 1549–51, p. 177; 1550–3, p. 27; 1553, pp. 358, 360, 363, 415; 1553–4, pp. 175, 265; 1558–60, pp. 59, 119; 1560–3, pp. 186, 433–47, 1563–6, pp. 19–31; 1569–72, p. 364; Eccles. 2/155874 seq.; D. E. Hoak, *The King's Council in the Reign of Edw. VI*, 96–97; *LJ*, i. 103, 165, 267, 293, 430, 448, 465, 492, 513, 542; *APC*, i. 54; ii. 58, 70; iv. 49, 276; C66/801; 193/12/1 ex inf. J. C. Sainty; *CSP Dom.* 1547–80, p. 102; *HMC Hatfield*, i. 443. [3] *VCH Hants*, iv. 116; *LP Hen. VIII*, x, xi. [4] *Cal. I.T. Recs.* i. 2, 5, 6, 8, 10, 13, 110; information from Virginia Moseley; *LP Hen. VIII*, iv, add.; A. J. Slavin, *Pol. and Profit*, 19. [5] *LP Hen. VIII*, iv–ix, xi; J. Hurstfield, *The Queen's Wards*, 243–4; W. C. Richardson, *Tudor Chamber Admin.* 270; *HMC Bath*, iv. 2. [6] *LP Hen. VIII*, vii. 1522 (ii) citing SP1/87, f. 106v; xiv; House of Lords RO, Original Acts 27 Hen. VIII, no. 27; Cott. Otho C10, f. 218. [7] S. E. Lehmberg, *Later Parlts. of Hen. VIII*, 162, 182, 222–3; M. A. R. Graves, 'The Tudor House of Lords 1547–58' (Otago Univ. Ph.D. thesis, 1974), ii. 299–300; House of Lords RO, Original Acts, 31 Hen. VIII, nos. 16, 22; 33 Hen. VIII, no. 44; 1 Edw. VI, no. 21; 3 and 4 Edw. VI, nos. 22–25, 29, 31; *CJ*, i. 52; *LJ*, i. 558, 629, 637. [8] *LP Hen. VIII*, xv, xix–xxi. [9] *Wealth and Power* ed. Ives, Knecht and Scarisbrick, 88–90, 96, 101; *LP Hen. VIII*, xi, xiv, xv, xvii, xviii, xxi; *CPR*, 1547–8, pp. 42, 66–68; 1548–9, pp. 375, 386; 1549–51, p. 196; 1550–3, p. 139; W. K. Jordan, *Edw. VI*, i. 64, 73, 88, 89, 115–16; *Lit. Rems. Edw. VI*, 234n; *APC*, iv. 112, 124; Hoak, 35, 42, 47, 49, 51. [10] *EHR*, lxx. 604; Jordan, ii. 93; Elton, *Reform and Reformation*, 358; G. D. Ramsay, 'The City of London', 146 seq.; information from Dr. J. D. Alsop and C. H. D. Coleman; Hoak, 100, 104, 111, 121, 196, 211–13, 247, 252, 254–8, 263. [11] *Chron. Q. Jane and Q. Mary* (Cam. Soc. xlviii), 9, 15, 169; Graves, 303; R. Naunton, *Fragmenta Regalia* (Harl. Misc. ii), 87; Neale, *Commons*, i. 80; information from Coleman; Hoak, 215. [12] L. Stone, *Crisis of the Aristocracy*, 423–4,

496, 542, 554; *CPR*, 1569–72, pp. 405–6; N. Pevsner and D. Lloyd, *Hants*, 88; *VCH Hants*, iv. 117, 126; *LP Hen. VIII*, x; R. C. Strong, *Tudor and Jacobean Portraits*, 332; Naunton, 87; *Lit. Rems. Edw. VI*, pp. clxxi, ccxxvii.

A.D.

PAYCOCK, Robert (by 1513–70), of York.

YORK 1558

b. by 1513. *m.* (1) Anne (*d.*1557), da. of George Gale* of York; (2) Anne, wid. of Ralph Babthorpe of Osgodby; at least 5s. 2da.[1]

Junior chamberlain, York 1537–8, constable, merchant guild 1539–40, 1541–2, master 1542–3, 1563–5, sheriff 1540–1, member of the Twenty-Four 1541, alderman 1543–*d.*, mayor 1548–9, 1567–8.[2]

Robert Paycock, whose parentage has not been traced, was probably not a native of York, where he was admitted a freeman during 1533–4. His progress in civic office was matched by his rise in the city's merchant guild. His assessment for subsidy, as a parishioner of All Saints, Pavement, on £40 in goods in 1546 and £50 in the following year reveals him as one of the 12 richest York laymen. All but one of his recorded trading activities involved the shipment of lead either to London or overseas, and it was he who in 1550 secured for York an export licence for lead. To the yield of trade he added that of his first marriage, to a daughter of his wealthiest fellow-citizen.[3]

Paycock reached the bench of aldermen only ten years after becoming a freeman, and five years later he was elected mayor. His year of office saw the excision of Marian plays from the city's Corpus Christi cycle, as well as the uniting of many York parishes and the sale of redundant churches; in the next year, when his father-in-law was mayor, he obtained one such church very cheaply. When with William Holme he attended the first session of Mary's last Parliament, a valuable gift and tax concession were secured for the city. Neither was able to attend the second session, both being struck by the disease then afflicting York: Holme died but Paycock recovered. During his long service as alderman, he seems to have been involved in more quarrels with other councillors, and the subject of more slanders, than most aldermen, but the quarrels are difficult to follow—in 1562 'Proud Paycock' was taunted with cowardice, and in 1563 with being 'against the common wealth'. He died on 15 June 1570 and was buried, as he had asked to be, in All Saints' church, Pavement, where his brother William was rector.[4]

By his will of 10 July 1569 Paycock left to his wife and children various York properties, including his dwelling house in Coppergate, and houses in the Pavement, Peaseholme and the Water Lane. He named five of his six surviving children executors and residuary legatees, and his son William, his brother William and his 'cousin' Gregory Paycock[†] supervisors. His Protestant-sounding bequest of his soul to God the Father and Son in the hope of salvation only through the merits of Christ's passion, accords with the upbringing of the children of his first marriage but not with the archbishop of York's dismissal of him in 1564 as 'no favourer of religion' or the Catholicism which his second wife was to profess until she, too, conformed in 1581. The will was proved on 20 June 1570.[5]

[1] Date of birth estimated from admission as freeman. *Vis. North* (Surtees Soc. cxxii), 61; *Yorks. Par. Reg. Soc.* c.102; York wills 19, f. 118; *Reg. Corpus Christi Guild, York* (Surtees Soc. lvii), 301n; *Reg. Freemen, York*, ii (Surtees Soc. cii), 11; J. C. H. Aveling, *Cath. Recusancy in York 1558–1791* (Cath. Rec. Soc. monograph ii), 332–3. [2] York archs. B13–24 passim; *York Mercers and Merchant Adventurers* (Surtees Soc. cxxix), 136, 153–4, 167, 323–4. [3] *Reg. Freemen, York*, i (Surtees Soc. xcvi), 252; York pub. lib. R. H. Skaife mss civic officials, ii. 553; E179/217/110, 111; *APC*, iv. 149; *York Civic Recs.* v (Yorks. Arch. Soc. rec. ser. cx), 47. [4] *York Civic Recs.* iv (Yorks. Arch. Soc. rec. ser. cviii), 95, 97, 120, 170–83; v. 1–10, 17, 29, 67–68, 172, 189; vi (ibid. cxii), 45, 53, 120, 123–32; York archs. B22, ff. 121–2; *Yorks. Par. Reg. Soc.* c.104; York wills 19, f. 118; F. Drake, *Eboracum*, 294. [5] York wills 19, f. 118; Aveling, 332–3; *Cam. Misc.* ix(3), 72; J. J. Cartwright, *Chapters in Yorks. Hist.* 151; *Reg. Freemen, York*, ii. 3, 11.

D.M.P.

PAYNE, Giles (by 1519–70), of Winchcombe and Rodborough, Glos.

WOOTTON BASSETT 1554 (Apr.), 1554 (Nov.)

b. by 1519, 1st s. of John Payne of Rodborough by Rose, da. of Edward Halyday of Rodborough. *m.* Jane, da. of one Sydenham, *s.p. suc.* fa. 5 June 1541.[1]

Keeper, Sudeley park, Glos. temp. Edw. VI; commr. sewers, Glos. and Worcs. 1554.[2]

Little has come to light about Giles Payne beyond the facts of his birth, death and Membership of Parliament. He is mentioned in a Star Chamber case in Edward VI's reign as a servant of Sir Edmund Brydges, who also sat for Wootton Bassett (and whose grandfather's name Payne bore). The plaintiff accused Payne of supporting Brydges's threats on his life and of helping his master to conceal a murder and flout the authority of the council in the marches of Wales; two other Members, William Rede I and John Tunks, also adherents of Brydges, were involved in this case. It was thus doubtless under Brydges's patronage that Payne was returned to the two Parliaments of 1554. His withdrawal from the second of them without leave led to an information being laid against him in the King's bench in Easter term 1555 but no further proceedings were taken against him. In the information he was styled 'of Bristol', a city with which neither he nor Sir Edmund Brydges is known to have been connected. In view of the enthusiastic support of Mary by the Brydges family, Payne is unlikely to have absented himself as a gesture of dissent, but he was not to be returned again.[3]

Until his mother's death Payne lived at Winchcombe where in 1545 he was assessed towards the subsidy on £10. If he made a will it has not been traced, but the inquisition taken on 15 Dec. 1570 found that he had died at Rodborough on the previous 1 Sept. leaving his brother Walter heir to his lands in Gloucestershire. His widow Jane married one William Hampshire, perhaps his fellow-Member in the Parliament of November 1554.[4]

[1] Date of birth estimated from age at fa.'s i.p.m., C142/64/25. *Vis. Glos.* (Harl. Soc. xxi), 123; *Bristol and Glos. Arch. Soc. Trans.* lxi. 59–61; C142/155/153. [2] *CPR*, 1554–5, p. 107; St.Ch.3/5/21. [3] St.Ch.3/5/21; *CPR*, 1554–5, p. 52; KB27/1176 rex roll 17. [4] E179/114/247; C142/64/125; *VCH Glos.* xi. 223.

E.McI.

PAYNE, Thomas (by 1507–60), of Gloucester.

GLOUCESTER 1553 (Oct.),[1] 1554 (Apr.), 1558

b. by 1507. *m.* (1) or (2) ?sis. of John Soller.[2]

Sheriff, Gloucester 1528–9, 1533–4, alderman 1533–*d.*, master of St. Margaret's hospital 1535–6, 1548–9, mayor 1540–1, 1552–3, coroner 1548–9; clerk of the creeks and passages belonging to Bristol 30 Dec. 1556.[3]

Thomas Payne may have been a descendant of a Bristol namesake who dealt in wine in the late 15th century, and a kinsman of Anthony Payne, importer of wine in the 1540s. He was styled merchant in 1544 when he acquired the site of the Greyfriars, Gloucester. In 1556 he settled this property, where he was then living, upon Thomas Pirry and his wife, who were to lease it to him for 50 years at a rent of £10. Payne built the city's conduit for which he was paid £75 in 1551, and he was responsible for its maintenance until his death.[4]

Payne owed the experience of sitting in Parliament at the opening of Mary's reign to the mayoralty of Sir Thomas Bell who had established a lien on one of the city's seats, and to the provision of a seat elsewhere for the recorder, Sir John Pollard. He was first elected at the close of his own second mayoral year. Unlike his fellow-Member Thomas Loveday, he received payment in full for the Parliament of April 1554. In both these Parliaments Payne was appropriately returned as senior Member (he and Bell are often called 'the eldest aldermen' in the city's records), but on his third and last election in 1558 he took second place to the new recorder, Richard Pate.[5]

Payne made his will as a sick man on 7 Aug. 1559, asking to be buried in the choir of Christ Church near to his last wife. He left sums of money to the poor, and to a number of servants and others including his brother-in-law John Soller and his kinsman Thomas Barbour. To Thomas Pirry, overseer of the will, he left gowns, furniture and the instruments in his brewhouse, and to his kinsman

¹ Egerton 2093, f. 163v; Add. 29618, f. 316. ² Date of birth estimated from first reference. Canterbury prob. reg. C18, f. 4. ³ Add. 29617, ff. 262, 353; 29618, ff. 228, 296v, 300; *LP Hen. VIII*, iv; Egerton 2092, f. 312; 2093, ff. 156, 163v, 173v; *Cinque Ports White and Black Bks.* (Kent Arch. Soc. recs. br. xix), 222. ⁴ Add. 29617, f. 262; 29618, ff. 312v, 316v; *LP Hen. VIII*, vii, x; Egerton 2108, f. 25; 2092, ff. 461–1v; 2093, f. 152v.

P.H.

William Soller of London the site of the Greyfriars in tail male with remainder to the children of William Haserd, late alderman of Gloucester, whom he named executor. He died on 19 Mar. 1560.⁶

¹ Gloucester Guildhall 1394, f. 42; Bodl. e Museo 17. ² Date of birth estimated from first reference. PCC 53 Mellershe. ³ *LP Hen. VIII*, xiii, xvi; W. H. Stevenson, *Cal. Recs. Gloucester*, 23; *CPR*, 1555–7, p. 257; Gloucester Guildhall 1300; 1375, ff. 28, 30v. ⁴ *Overseas Trade of Bristol* (Bristol Rec. Soc. vii), nos. 144, 162; *APC*, i. 267, 296; *LP Hen. VIII*, xix; Stevenson, 1253–5; PCC 37 Blamyr, 23 Adeane; Gloucester Guildhall 1394, ff. 22v–71. ⁵ Gloucester Guildhall 1300, ff. 127v–32v; 1394, ff. 22–67; 1397, ff. 42–43v. ⁶ PCC 53 Mellershe; Gloucester Guildhall 1375, f. 30v.

M.K.D.

PAYNTOR, John (by 1482–1540), of Dover, Kent.

DOVER 1539¹

b. by 1482. m. Joan, 1s. 1da.²

Collector, half passage money, Dover 1517–28 or later, chamberlain 1525–6, jurat 1532–d., mayor 1534–5, 1535–6; bailiff to Yarmouth 1537.³

Taxed as an artificer in September 1503, John Payntor is next met with as a witness of a fight at Dover between Robert Nethersole* and Pers Young in February 1508; 30 years later, when Nethersole was in dispute with the town over his parliamentary wages, Payntor was one of the two jurats chosen to mediate between them. He had by then been in municipal life for upwards of 20 years and had represented Dover at four Brotherhoods of the Cinque Ports. When mayor in 1536 he had had some official correspondence with Cromwell. His Membership of the Parliament of 1539 was to be his last service to the town and he did not discharge it to the full. Elected with Thomas Vaughan on 23 Mar., he left Dover on 26 Apr., two days before the Parliament opened, was back there between 24 and 29 May during the first prorogation, and came home again on 10 June, 18 days before the close of the second session. For his attendance on 36 days, and the four journeys involved, 42 days in all, he was paid £4 4s. The third and last session, of April–July 1540, lasted 104 days, but as Payntor's widow was to receive a sum of £7 as payment for 90 days he again fell short of maximum attendance. He could have begun late, or have paid a visit to Dover during the session, but a more probable explanation is that he died in London before the Parliament ended or made for home a dying man. The only clue to the date of his death is the payment of £3 of the £7 due to his widow by September 1540, for the will which he had made on 26 July 1537 bears no date of probate. Payntor had asked to be buried in his parish church of St. Peter and had provided for masses to be said for a year. His son Thomas and daughter Joan were to have £20 each and to share half his movables, the residue passing to his wife, whom he named an executor.⁴

PEAKE, Nicholas (by 1505–58/59), of Sandwich, Kent.

SANDWICH 1539,¹ 1555

b. by 1505, s. of John Peake of Wye by Margaret, da. of Simon Anselm. m. Joan, da. of Roger Manwood I* of Sandwich, 3s. inc. Edward† 3da.²

Common councilman, Sandwich (St. Peter's parish) 1526–33, (St. Clement's parish) 1533–7, treasurer 1529–30, auditor in 1531, 1534, 1535, 1539, 1541–3, 1549, keeper of the common chest and of the orphans 1537–8, 1543–6, keeper of the common chest 1542–3, keeper of the orphans 1549–50, 1553–5, mayor 1537–8, 1544–6, jurat 1538–d., clerk of the market 1538–9, 1541–2; bailiff to Yarmouth 1541–2.³

Nicholas Peake was a merchant of Sandwich. In an investigation into the depredation of pirates he deposed that on 31 Oct. 1536 a Spaniard from Sluis stopped his crayer off the Kentish coast, broke both his topmasts, and stole goods worth 30s. In 1552 the Privy Council ordered him to supply the garrison at Guisnes with 40 quarters of wheat; in 1555 he is entered in the port book of Sandwich as sending wheat and malt to London.⁴

Peake was elected to Parliament for the first time in March 1539; the treasurers of 1540–1 paid him £7 for his parliamentary wages. He was a candidate for election in January 1553 and March 1554 and was elected for the second time on 4 Oct. 1555 to serve at the customary wage of 2s. a day. In this Parliament Peake's name is not to be found, as is his fellow-Member Sir John Perrot's, on the list of Members who voted against one of the government's bills. He had also been chosen to attend the coronation of both Edward VI and Mary. He went to the Brotherhood at Romney 19 times between 1525 and 1558, and in 1557 was appointed a solicitor for the Cinque Ports' suit in defence of their liberties challenged by a writ of *quo warranto*.⁵

Peake had several brushes with authority. Two months after Edward VI's coronation the Privy Council ordered his examination for allegedly using words 'sounding very evil against the King's majesty', and he was one of four Sandwich men summoned to appear before the Council, for what reason is unknown, in March 1551. He was again before the Council in October 1557, this time with his son-in-law Thomas Menys*, then mayor of Sandwich, about a letter sent by the town to Sir Thomas Cheyne*, lord warden of the Cinque Ports, which Cheyne must have resented; Peake and five others had to report daily to one of the clerks of the Council until further order.[6]

Peake made his will on 31 Dec. 1558. He asked to be buried in the churchyard of St. Clement's beside his late wife, with dirges or masses 'or such other service as at that time by authority shall be set out'. To his son Roger he left his dwelling house, malt-house, orchard and garden in Sandwich, and to his other surviving son Edward a house with a quay in Sandwich and his manor in the neighbouring parish of Ash. His daughters Agnes, widow of Thomas Menys, and Alice, wife of Matthew Menys, were to have £30 apiece, his daughter Christian 100 marks on marriage, and his 'cousins' Roger Manwood II*, John Manwood[†] and Thomas Manwood a horse each. Roger and Thomas Manwood were executors of the will, which was proved on 15 Mar. 1561.[7]

[1] Sandwich old red bk. f. 111. [2] Date of birth estimated from first reference. *Vis. Kent* (Harl. Soc. lxxv), 67, 141; PCC 10 Loftes. [3] Sandwich white bk. f. 367v; old red bk. passim; little black bk. passim. [4] *LP Hen. VIII*, xii; *APC*, iv. 35; E122/131/8. [5] Sandwich old red bk. ff. 111, 193; treasurers' acct. bk.; little black bk. ff. 31, 45v, 55v, 74; *Cinque Ports White and Black Bks.* (Kent Arch. Soc. recs. br. xix), 193–256 passim. [6] *APC*, ii. 468–9; iii. 235; vi. 189; Sandwich old red bk. ff. 220v, 222v–223; little black bk. f. 47v. [7] PCC 10 Loftes.

H.M.

PECKHAM, Sir Edmund (by 1495–1564), of the Blackfriars, London and Denham, Bucks.

BUCKINGHAMSHIRE 1553 (Oct.), 1554 (Nov.)

b. by 1495, 2nd s. of Peter Peckham of London and Denham by 2nd w. Elizabeth, da. of Henry Eburton of London. *m.* by 1516, Anne, da. of John Cheyne of Chesham Bois, Bucks., 4s. inc. Henry* and Sir Robert* 2da. Kntd. 18 May 1542.[1]

Clerk, counting house by 1520; treasurer, the chamber 1 May 1522–1 Jan. 1524; cofferer, the Household Jan. 1524–31 Mar. 1547; j.p. Bucks. 1525–43, Mdx. 1537–43, q. Bucks., Mdx. 1554–58/59; constable, Scarborough castle, Yorks. 1529–37; high treasurer, all the mints 25 Mar. 1544–d.; PC 6–30 Oct. 1549, 29 July 1553–Nov. 1558; commr. relief, Bucks., Mdx. 1550, goods of churches and fraternities 1553, subsidy, Bucks. 1558; receiver-gen. of the Exchequer 1 Dec. 1553.[2]

A younger son of a Londoner who acquired land in Buckinghamshire, Edmund Peckham was a clerk in the counting house when he attended Henry VIII at Gravelines in 1520. He rose by way of financial office in posts of the Household to become in 1544 high treasurer of all the mints in England and Ireland; this office, and the residence at Blackfriars which went with it, he was to hold until his death. Appointed at the beginning of the Great Debasement, he saw that process carried to its conclusion and then reversed by the reforms under Mary and Elizabeth. Through it all he was sustained in office by a combination of integrity in business and neutralism in politics. Henry VIII, whom he accompanied to France in 1544, named him one of the assistant

executors of his will and bequeathed him £200. Brought on to the Council at the political crisis of October 1549 but speedily removed from it, he took no other part in the politics of Edward VI's reign, when as a Catholic and a friend and relation by marriage of Thomas Wriothesley, Earl of Southampton, he was estranged from the wielders of power.[3]

Peckham's only positive intervention was designed to frustrate the exclusion of Mary: he was one of the men of Buckinghamshire who planned to move by way of William, Lord Paget's house at Drayton to seize the armoury at Westminster. For his service 'at Framlingham' he was given an annuity of £60. By August he had become a Privy Councillor and before the end of 1553 his eldest son Robert Peckham had also joined Mary's Council. When, late in that year, the revenue courts were re-organized, it was Peckham who became sole receiver of the Queen's revenue. A contemporary chronicle extolled his devotion to duty and his loyalty to the Queen: if, as is conjectured, that chronicle was written by an officer of the mint, such praise could be expected, but when in July 1554 Mary forwarded to the treasurer his request for a grant of land it was with the comment that he had deserved it and had received no recompense.[4]

Peckham had little to complain of. Since 1527, when he was assessed in the Household on lands at £126 a year, he had consolidated his position at Denham and bought Biddlesden abbey in north Buckinghamshire from Wriothesley as well as leasing manors in Cheshire; he had also been granted the keepership of Scarborough castle. His stake in Buckinghamshire and his ascendancy at court together qualified him for the knighthood of the shire in Mary's first Parliament. Unlike his dissentient son Henry, Peckham did not oppose the first steps towards the restoration of Catholicism, and he carried two of the bills passed in the Commons to the Lords. In the Parliament of April 1554 Peckham's place was taken by his son Robert, but six months later the father again shared the representation of the shire: this time he is predictably missing from the ranks of those who quitted the Parliament early without leave. Protestant influence appears to have prevailed in all the Buckinghamshire elections for the Parliaments of 1555 and 1558, but Peckham's disappearance from the House may also have reflected Henry Peckham's complicity in the Dudley conspiracy.[5]

Under Elizabeth, Peckham lost his seat on the Privy Council but was retained at the mint. His name appears on the pardon roll of the Queen's first year. He made his will on 12 May 1563, asking for his vile carcase to be buried without pomp. The only property he mentioned was the manor of Denham, left to his wife for life with remainder to his sons Robert and George, and lands in Halse, Northamptonshire, and Croydon, Surrey, left to his sons as executors. Peckham died on 29 Mar. 1564 and was buried in Denham church where a monument was erected to his memory.[6]

[1] Date of birth estimated from marriage. *DNB*; PCC 13 Vox, 16 Moone; *CIPM Hen. VII*, ii. 482; *Vis. Bucks.* (Harl. Soc. lviii), 153. [2] *Rutland Pprs.* (Cam. Soc. xxi), 57; *LP Hen. VIII*, iii–v, xi, xii, xiv, xv, xvii–xx; *CPR*, 1549–51 to 1558–60 passim; W. C. Richardson, *Tudor Chamber Admin.* 238, 485; D. E. Hoak, *King's Council in the Reign of Edw. VI*, 54, 58; Harl. Ch. 84C, nos. 29, 31, 34; *APC*, i–vi passim; Strype, *Eccles. Memorials*, ii. 160; *Brit. Numismatic Jnl.* xlv. 65. [3] *Rutland Pprs.* 57; *HMC Bath*, iv. 5, 115; *LP Hen. VIII*, xix, xxi; W. K. Jordan, *Edw. VI*, i. 72, 79, 80, 507; ii. 458, 527; Hoak, 54, 58; C. E. Challis, *Tudor Coinage*, passim. [4] S. R. Gammon, *Statesman and Schemer*, 194; *APC*, iv. 293 et passim; *CSP Dom.* 1547–80, p. 60; *Chron. Q. Jane and Q. Mary* (Cam. Soc. xlviii), 119, 178; *Original Letters*, ed. Ellis (ser. 2), ii. 251; Richardson, *Ct. Augmentations*, 249. [5] *LP Hen. VIII*, iv, xvi; E179/69/51; L. J. Ashford, *High Wycombe*, 104–6, 116–17; *First Wycombe Ledger Bk.* (Bucks. Rec. Soc. ii), 97; *VCH Bucks.* ii. 211; *CJ*, i. 31. [6] *CPR*, 1558–60, pp. 66, 226; 1563–6, p. 3; PCC 28 Stevenson; E150/54/3; *VCH Bucks.* iii. 261; Pevsner, *Bucks.* 103.

M.K.D.

PECKHAM, Henry (by 1526–56), of Denham, Bucks.

CHIPPING WYCOMBE   1553 (Mar.), 1553 (Oct.),
                    1554 (Apr.), 1555

b. by 1526, 2nd s. of Sir Edmund Peckham* of Denham by Anne, da. of John Cheyne of Chesham Bois; bro. of Sir Robert*. *m.* lic. 6 Nov. 1547, Elizabeth, da. of Robert Dacres of London and Cheshunt, Herts.[1]

Henry Peckham may have followed his father and elder brother into the service of the crown, for in an exchange of lands with Edward VI in 1550 he was called 'the King's servant'. His marriage to the daughter of a former Privy Councillor was almost certainly the work of his father and it was perhaps the influence of Elizabeth Dacres and her uncles (Sir) Anthony Denny* and (Sir) John Gates* that won him to Protestantism. In 1547 his father and elder brother settled upon Peckham the manor of Lavendon in Buckinghamshire and the remainder of some property in Dorset after the father's death. In 1550 Lavendon was leased to a Buckinghamshire man and Peckham exchanged the lordship with the King for the manor of Dartington with lands elsewhere in Devon. In 1550 also he acquired from Edward Fiennes, 9th Lord Clinton, rights for himself and his heirs in the manor of Lantian, Cornwall, and in the reversion of two manors in Sussex. Peckham was described as of Southland, which was part of the family estate at Denham, when in April 1552 he conveyed Dartington to John Aylworth*, a transfer presumably connected with the sum of £3,000 for which he was bound to Aylworth in the same month.[2]

Peckham's election as a Member for Chipping Wycombe in March 1553 with a kinsman John

Cheyne suggests that both were helped by Sir Edmund Peckham, who had some influence in the borough. Peckham, however, may have been put in on this occasion, not so much through his family's standing in south Buckinghamshire, but because as a Protestant kinsman of Sir John Gates he was more acceptable to the Duke of Northumberland than his father and brother who were Catholics. Unlike Gates, Peckham is not known to have supported Northumberland during the succession crisis later in the year, but rather he seems to have commanded some of the forces mustered by his father for Mary. He took part in resisting Wyatt's march through London in 1554, when he had charge of the approach to Ludgate gate under his father, but was absent at the moment of Wyatt's arrival, having 'belike gone to his father or to look to the water side'. For Peckham's loyalty on these occasions he was granted a manor in Gloucestershire in 1554 and another in Hertfordshire a year later.[3]

Despite his support for the Queen at her accession Peckham soon showed reservations about her plans. He was re-elected for Chipping Wycombe to three of her five Parliaments, only missing one before his death, that of November 1554 when Mary asked for inhabitants. He was returned for both Wycombe and the newly enfranchised borough of Aylesbury to the second Parliament of the reign, but evidently he preferred to sit for Wycombe as Humphrey Moseley (q.v.) took his place in the House for Aylesbury. In October 1553 Peckham 'stood for the true religion' against the initial measures to restore Catholicism. Two years later he attended the meetings at 'Harondayle's house' where the parliamentary opposition discussed its tactics, and he followed Sir Anthony Kingston's lead in voting against one of the government's bills. If his activities outside and within the House on this occasion cost Peckham a spell of imprisonment, as it did some others, it did not deter him from joining the Dudley conspiracy in 1556. Several meetings by the plotters were held in Peckham's lodgings at his father's home in the Blackfriars and it was proposed to store stolen bullion there. Peckham agreed to raise Buckinghamshire and it was he who persuaded Francis Verney* and several other kinsmen to join the plot. At Sir Anthony Kingston's instigation he prevailed on Edward Lewknor* to obtain a copy of Henry VIII's will, which he annotated for use in publicly defending the rising. Peckham was one of the first to be arrested and despite his elder brother's intervention and his own confession he was hanged on 7 or 8 July 1556. His widow was allowed to retain the manor of Tring, Hertfordshire, for life and she later married John Blount of London.[4]

[1] Date of birth estimated from marriage. *Fac. Off. Reg. 1534–49*, ed. Chambers, 300, 309; Harl. 1533, f. 75. [2] *CPR*, 1547–8, pp. 99, 199; 1549–51, pp. 349–50, 434; 1550–3, p. 224; A. Emery, *Dartington Hall*, 71; LC4/188, f. 52 ex inf. Dr. A. J. A. Malciewicz; *VCH Bucks.* iv. 384. [3] *CPR*, 1553–4, p. 9; 1554–5, p. 75; *Chron. Q. Jane and Q. Mary* (Cam. Soc. xlviii), 129. [4] Bodl. e Museo 17; SP11/8, no. 35. Guildford mus. Loseley 1331/2; D. M. Loades, *Two Tudor Conspiracies*, 189, 191, 196, 210, 212–14, 217–18, 224, 227, 231–2, 237, 267; *Verney Pprs.* (Cam. Soc. lvi), 59–76; *CSP Dom. 1547–80*, pp. 61, 64, 78, 81–84; *DKR*, iv(2), 254; *Machyn's Diary* (Cam. Soc. xlii), 109, 351n; *Wriothesley's Chron.* ii (Cam. Soc. n.s. xx), 136; *VCH Herts.* ii. 283.

M.K.D.

PECKHAM, Sir Robert (by 1516–69), of London, Biddlesden and Denham, Bucks.

BUCKINGHAMSHIRE 1554 (Apr.)

b. by 1516, 1st s. of Sir Edmund Peckham* of Denham by Anne, da. of John Cheyne of Chesham Bois, Bucks.; bro. of Henry*. *educ.* G. Inn, adm. 1533. *m.* c.1537, Mary, da. of Edmund, 1st Lord Bray, *d.v.p.* Kntd. 2 Oct. 1553; *suc.* fa. 29 Mar. 1564.[1]

Clerk comptroller, counting house by 1540–3; j.p. Bucks. 1542–7, q. 1558/59; commr. subsidy 1543, relief 1550; escheator, Beds. and Bucks. 1545–6; sheriff 1556–7; PC Aug. 1553–Nov. 1558.[2]

Robert Peckham began his career, as his father had done, in the King's counting house but rose no higher in the central administration. Perhaps married by 22 June 1537, when his father settled property in Denham on him and Mary Bray, to be followed in July 1542 by the manor of Weedon Pinkney, Northamptonshire, Peckham left the counting house in 1543 and withdrew, possibly to his father's recent acquisition, Biddlesden abbey, to pursue the studies which were later said to have impaired his health.[3]

Peckham probably joined his father's Buckinghamshire contingent in support of Mary in July 1553, for he was given an annuity of £60 for service 'at Framlingham'. On 5 Aug. he was appointed with two others to take an inventory of all plate and goods in the Earl of Hertford's house in Aldgate Street. His appearance as a Privy Councillor on 22 Aug. was followed by a knighthood conferred at the coronation; he attended council meetings with fair regularity throughout the reign. He sat in only one Parliament, as a knight for Buckinghamshire, seemingly in place of his father. When his brother Henry was condemned for his part in the Dudley conspiracy Peckham made a long statement on his behalf.[4]

In the general pardon which he obtained in 1559 Peckham was described as of Biddlesden *alias* of London. Removed from the Council and the bench, and adjudged by his bishop in 1564 as 'not fit to be trusted', he went abroad after his father's death for the sake of his health and his religion. After several years' journeying he reached Rome, only to die there on 10 Sept. 1569. He was buried in the church of San Gregorio Magno, but at his own request his heart was buried at Denham; there, too, an epitaph commemorates him both as a good neighbour and as 'a man studious in learning . . . having more than a mean judgment in most of the arts . . . not ignorant of the laws of this realm, but specially addicted to the study of divinity'. It was to Peckham that Sion Dafydd Rhys of Brecon dedicated his *De Italica Pronunciatione Libellus* published at Padua in 1569. Peckham's own library at Biddlesden was left to the sons of his brother George, to whom in default of heirs his landed property passed.[5]

[1] Date of birth estimated from age at fa.'s i.p.m., E150/54/3. *Vis. Beds.* (Harl. Soc. xix), 163; *LP Hen. VIII*, xvii. [2] *LP Hen. VIII*, xvi–xviii, xx, xxi; *CPR*, 1547–8, p. 81; 1553, p. 351; 1553–4, p. 29; E179/78/125; *APC*, iv–vi passim. [3] E150/54/3; Wards 7/12/114; *LP Hen. VIII*, xvii; *VCH Bucks.* iv. 154–5. [4] Lansd. 156(28), ff. 90, 92; *APC*, iv–vi passim; *HMC Laing*, i. 13; *CSP Dom. 1547–80*, p. 82; D. M. Loades, *Two Tudor Conspiracies*, 217, 224. [5] *CPR*, 1558–60, p. 234; *Cam. Misc.* ix(3), 32; *CSP For. 1564–5*, pp. 238, 431; *N. and Q.* (ser. 3), i. 259; *VCH Bucks.* iii. 261; Lipscomb, *Bucks.* iv. 451; *Recs. Bucks.* xix. 353–4; PCC 25 Sheffelde; Wards 7/12/114.

M.K.D.

PELHAM, Nicholas (by 1513–60), of Laughton, Suss.

ARUNDEL 1547
SUSSEX 1558

b. by 1513, 1st s. of Sir William Pelham of Laughton by Mary, da. of Sir Richard Carew of Beddington, Surr.; half-bro. of Edward Pelham[†]. *m.* by 1537, Anne, da. of John Sackville I* of Withyham and Chiddingly, Suss., 5s. inc. John[†] and Thomas[†] 3da. *suc.* fa. 1538/39. Kntd. 17 Nov. 1549.[1]

Commr. musters, Suss. 1543, benevolence 1544/45, relief 1550, goods of churches and fraternities 1553, loan 1557; j.p. 1544–*d.*; sheriff, Surr. and Suss. 1549–50.[2]

The fortunes of the Sussex branch of the Pelhams, a family originating in Cambridgeshire, were established in the early 15th century by Sir John Pelham[†], treasurer of England under Henry IV, and were enlarged by his son, another Sir John, who became chamberlain to Queen Catherine of Valois. Their descendants were men of substance, active in local affairs and at court. Sir William Pelham followed in this tradition, as the inclusion of his name on the Sussex bench and his second marriage to a daughter of William, 1st Lord Sandys, testify. So did his son Nicholas, although the execution of the younger Pelham's uncle Sir Nicholas Carew*, after whom he was presumably named, may have estranged him from the court, to which he was summoned only on occasions such as the French admiral's reception in 1546, and led him to pass his life mainly in his county.[3]

Pelham's marriage to the daughter of a local gentleman strengthened his Sussex connexions, particularly with the earls of Arundel, with whom his family had long been associated. His relations with his neighbours seem to have been smooth, although it was the accidental killing of one of his gamekeepers by Thomas Fiennes, 9th Lord Dacre of the South, in the spring of 1541 that first brought him into the public eye: Dacre and his companions were caught poaching in Pelham's park at Laughton and for fatally wounding one of their pursuers Dacre was executed. Three years later Pelham was named to the bench, but it was not as a justice that he was next to commend himself: when in 1545 the French raided the Sussex coast between Newhaven and Brighton, their attacks were met by the local militia under Pelham's command. This affair gave him a reputation for leadership in the field: in Mary's reign he was to be described as 'a gentleman of a good experience in the wars' and his prowess was commemorated on his tomb.[4]

The reign of Edward VI saw a fluctuation in Pelham's fortunes. In the autumn of 1547 he made what was probably his first appearance in Parliament as a Member for Arundel. The nearest borough to Pelham's home at Laughton was Lewes, which on this occasion returned two officials, Sir Walter Mildmay and Sir Anthony Cooke, and it was perhaps as an alternative that he turned to Arundel: in securing the necessary assistance of the 12th Earl, he was doubtless helped both by his father-in-law, who was sheriff, and by his stepfather John Palmer, himself one of the knights of the shire, while among Pelham's other kinsmen who sat with him were two of his brothers-in-law, John Sackville II and Richard Sackville II. Nothing is known of his part in the proceedings but in the autumn of 1549 he was pricked sheriff and a few days later knighted: as these marks of favour coincided with the Earl of Warwick's distribution of honours after his overthrow of the Protector Somerset they imply that Pelham had not sided with Somerset, and they were to be followed by a valuable grant of recently forfeited lands in Sussex. Yet two years later Pelham was to be imprisoned in the Tower with the ex-Protector and the Earl of Arundel: that the 'Pellam' then held 'for the conspiracy of the duke' was Nicholas and not his younger brother William, later lord justice of Ireland, is borne out by the will which he made on 21 Jan. 1552, the day before Somerset's execution. The will, which he wrote himself, provided for his daughters, sons, brothers and a sister and ended:

This for lack of learning I make to be my last will, and where it is not formable I will mine executors done (sic) make it according to the law changing no purpose, the residue of all my goods, my debts paid, I will to mine executors to bury me according to their discretion, whom I will shall be Anne Pelham, my wife.
by me Nycholas Pelham

Several of Pelham's fellow-prisoners were lawyers, but he may not have had access to them. How long he was kept in custody is not known, but he must have missed the opening of the fourth session of Parliament on 23 Jan. and may not have reappeared before the dissolution. Not surprisingly, he was not returned to the Parliament of March 1553, although two of his kinsmen, Thomas Palmer and Thomas Morley, sat in it for Arundel.[5]

Pelham may have looked for better times under Mary, when the Earl of Arundel stood high in favour, but although he was retained on the local bench he was not to sit in Parliament until the last year of the reign. The delay may perhaps be accounted for by his own inclination towards Protestantism and his brother William's involvement in Wyatt's rebellion, whereas in 1558 the threat of invasion doubtless put a premium on his military reputation and helped him to gain the knighthood of the shire with his second cousin, Sir Robert Oxenbridge. It must therefore have been the more galling when in the summer he refused to supply men for the war; his remissness earned for him first a rebuke from a Sussex magnate, Anthony Browne I*, 1st Viscount Montagu, and then a brief spell in the Fleet in the company of Thomas Morley. He was released on 5 Aug. upon promising to supply horsemen.[6]

Although not a leading landowner in Sussex, Pelham was a substantial one around Lewes, with an interest in rearing sheep for their wool. During the 1550s he purchased a house called the *White Hart* at Lewes, in 1557 the site for the future family mansion at Halland, and in 1558 lands in Hartfield from his brother-in-law Christopher Sackville*. There is no indication that he profited directly from the dissolution either of the monasteries or of the chantries. On 6 Feb. 1560 he made a new will in which he divided his property, goods and livestock between his wife and children. He named his eldest son John residuary legatee and executor and George Goring[†], William Morley[†] and John Leigh overseers. He did not die until the following 15 Sept. and he was buried in St. Michael's church, Lewes.[7]

[1] Date of birth estimated from first reference. *Vis. Suss.* (Harl. Soc. liii), 21; *LP Hen. VIII*, xiv; Add. 33137, f. 5; PCC 23 Dyngeley. [2] *LP Hen. VIII*, xx; *CPR*, 1547–8, p. 90; 1550–3, p. 142; 1553, pp. 359, 415; 1553–4, pp. 24, 28, 37; 1555–7, p. 124. [3] E. G. Pelham and D. Maclean, *Some Early Pelhams*, 57 seq.; *Suss. Arch. Colls.* lxix, 53 seq.; J. E. Mousley, 'Suss. country gentry in the reign of Eliz.' (London Univ. Ph.D. thesis, 1956), 650; *LP Hen. VIII*, xx. [4] *LP Hen. VIII*, vii, xvi; Mousley, 651; *Suss. Arch. Colls.* vii.88; SP11/2/17. [5] Add. 33137, ff. 7, 9–10v; *APC*, iii. 35; *CPR*, 1550–3, p. 14; SP10/19, f. 31; *DNB* (Pelham, Sir William); Harl. 249, f. 43. [6] D. M. Loades, *Two Tudor Conspiracies*, 60, 111; SP11/2/17; *APC*, vi. 354, 358, 363–4. [7] *Suss. Rec. Soc.* iii. 19–21; *Suss. Arch. Colls.* xciii. 6; Mousley, 651; *CPR*, 1557–8, p. 345. PCC 9 Streat; R. B. Manning, *Rel. and Soc. in Eliz. Suss.*, 264; Add. 33137, f. 11; Nairn and Pevsner, *Suss.*, 553.

R.J.W.S.

PELLATT, William (c.1514–58), of Charlton Court, Steyning, Suss.

STEYNING 1554 (Nov.)[1]

b. c.1514, 1st s. of Richard Pellatt of Steyning by Joan. *m.* by 1534, 2s. inc. Richard† 7da. *suc.* fa. 1532.[2] Churchwarden, Steyning in 1548.[3]

William Pellatt came of a family long resident at Steyning and by the 16th century of importance there. This the Pellatts derived from their lease of the manor of Charlton, bordering the borough and belonging to Syon abbey: held successively by Pellatt's grandfather and father, the lease was confirmed to him in 1539 at a rent of £34 a year. After the Dissolution the manor was annexed to the honor of Petworth, but in July 1557 Pellatt bought the freehold for £1,253. This, and his purchase in the same year for £34 of a scattering of lands in Sussex were his final additions to a patrimony which included the lease of a mill and buildings within the town. He combined sheep-farming with growing wheat and barley, and it is some indication of his affluence and aspirations that he sent his eldest son Richard to Cambridge and Gray's Inn.[4]

Before Pellatt's return to the Parliament of November 1554 the family's role in elections had been limited to that of elector or at most constable, and thus returning officer, of the borough: Pellatt's brother Thomas was constable at the election of 26 Sept. 1553 and signed the indenture. It was doubtless Mary's request in the autumn of 1554 for the return of resident Members which allowed Pellatt to secure a seat himself. He disregarded Chancellor Gardiner's admonition at the opening about attendance and was found to be absent at the call of the House early in January 1555. For this dereliction he was prosecuted in the King's bench: on his failure to appear in Michaelmas 1555 Pellatt was distrained 20s., and in the following Easter term he was fined 53s.4d.: his sureties were John Hyde of Lancing and his brother Thomas Pellatt.[5]

In his will of 22 Aug. 1558 Pellatt described himself as patron of Steyning church, where he wished to be buried beside his ancestors. He named his son Richard executor and residuary legatee and stipulated that his second son John should have £40 on coming of age and the lease of Steyning parsonage. Six of his daughters were to receive £46 13s.4d. each, and the seventh £30. The overseers were Pellatt's brothers Richard and Thomas and his cousin John Gratwycke of Cowfold, and among the witnesses was the vicar of Steyning, Stephen Green. As the will was proved in September 1558 Pellatt, a man not yet 50, must have made it when close to death, perhaps of the disease then widespread.[6]

[1] Huntington Lib. Hastings mss Parl. pprs. [2] Date of birth estimated from a lease of 1539 and from his being under 22 when his father made his will. *Suss. Arch. Colls.* xxxviii. 107; PCC 46 Noodes. [3] *Suss. Arch. Colls.* viii. 132. [4] Ibid. viii. 132; xxxviii. 101; E326/5643, 5666, 6359 ex inf. Dr. R. W. Dunning; Harl. 606, f. 42; *Chantry Recs.* (Suss. Rec. Soc. xxxvi), 110; *Ministers' Accts. Manor of Petworth* (ibid. lv), 63, 82; C142/121/158. [5] C219/21/153; KB27/1176, 1178; 29/188 rot. 48. [6] PCC 46 Noodes.

R.J.W.S.

PENRUDDOCK, George (by 1527–81), of Ivy Church and Compton Chamberlayne, Wilts., Broxbourne, Herts. and Clerkenwell, Mdx.

SALISBURY 1553 (Mar.)
WILTSHIRE 1558
DOWNTON 1571
WILTSHIRE 1572

b. by 1527, 3rd s. of Edward Penruddock of Arkleby, Cumb. by Elizabeth, da. of Robert Highmore of Armathwaite, Cumb.; bro. of Robert*. *m.* (1) Elizabeth, da. and h. of William Apryce of Faulstone, Wilts., 2s. Edward† and Robert†; (2) by 1 Apr. 1560, Anne, da. of Thomas Goodere of Hadley, Herts., wid. of John Cock II* (*d.*6 Sept. 1557) of London and Broxbourne, *s.p.* Kntd. 7 Aug. 1568.[1]

Servant of Sir William Herbert I*, 1st Earl of Pembroke, receiver-gen. by 1559; j.p. Wilts. 1554, q. 1558/59–*d.*, j.p. Herts. 1562–9, q. 1573/74–*d.*; sheriff, Wilts. 1562–3, Herts. 1567–8; esquire of the body by 1565; commr. subsidy, Wilts. and Salisbury 1576; other commissions, Wilts. and western circuit 1554–*d.*; dep. lt. Wilts.[2]

George Penruddock's grant of arms in May 1548 described him as of Penruddock in Cumberland. He and his brother Robert retained property in their native county but made their homes in the south. George Penruddock must have settled in Wiltshire and begun his association with the Earl of Pembroke by 1551, when he held a 21-year lease of the earl's manor of Broad Chalk. It was to his service with Pembroke that he owed his first seat in Parliament, for on 3 Feb. 1553 the city of Salisbury gave Pembroke the nomination of both its Members. Penruddock was the earl's standard-bearer by February 1554, when they served together against Wyatt's rebellion. In the following month Penruddock shared in the distribution of gifts made on the Emperor's behalf to leading personages at court and their retainers in the hope of gaining support for the proposed Spanish marriage; he received a gold chain and 100 crowns. His admission to Gray's Inn in 1555 was doubtless honorary.[3]

Penruddock was with Pembroke at St. Quentin in August 1557 and, as the earl's standard-bearer, distinguished himself in single combat against a French nobleman. (He is said to have earned the reward of a jewelled chain from Queen Catherine Parr for similar valour on an earlier occasion, presumably in Henry VIII's last war with France and Scotland, but the circumstances of that exploit are unknown.) His own martial fame, and his master's ascendancy, sufficed to gain for Penruddock a knighthood of the shire in Mary's last Parliament. Why he had not sat in any of her previous ones is unclear: it would have been natural for Pembroke to have wanted him in the House. He withdrew from the first session of the Parliament of 1558 a week before it ended, being given leave on 28 Feb., with three Members for Wiltshire boroughs, to attend the assizes in that county.[4]

Like his master Pembroke, Penruddock remained in favour under Elizabeth until his death on 8 July 1581.[5]

[1] Date of birth estimated from first reference. *Wilts. Vis. Peds.* (Harl. Soc. cv, cvi), 148–9; *CPR*, 1558–60, p. 455. [2] *CSP Dom.* 1547–80, p. 140; *Two Taxation Lists* (Wilts. Arch. Soc. recs. br. x), 63, 109; *EHR*, xxiii. 470–6; *CPR*, 1553–4, pp. 25, 28; 1560–3, pp. 438, 443; 1563–6, pp. 123, 145, 224, 226, 497; 1569–72, pp. 218–19; Req.2/30/78. [3] *Wilts. Arch. Mag.* ix. 228; xviii. 116; Hoare, *Wilts. Chalk,* 132; Salisbury corp. ledger B, f. 309v; Req.2/36/30; *Chron. Q. Jane and Q. Mary* (Cam. Soc. xlviii), 188; *CSP Span.* 1554, p. 159. [4] *Wilts. Arch. Mag.* xliv. 256; *Wilts. Vis. Peds.* 150; *CPR*, 1558–60, p. 231; *CJ*, i. 50. [5] C142/197/82.

D.F.C.

PENRUDDOCK, Robert (by 1525–83), of Hale, Hants.

CUMBERLAND 1554 (Apr.), 1554 (Nov.)

b. by 1525, 1st s. of Edward Penruddock of Arkleby, Cumb. by Elizabeth, da. of Robert Highmore of Armathwaite, Cumb.; bro. of George*. *m.* Joyce, da. of John Charnells of Wishaw, Warws., *s.p. suc.* fa. by 1543.[1]

Gauger, port of Poole Feb. 1551; surveyor, ct. augmentations, Dorset Aug. 1552; chief steward, Exchequer, Som. and Dorset Feb. 1561; j.p. Hants 1558/59, q. 1561–4, j.p. Wilts. 1573/74–d.[2]

Of old Cumbrian stock, Robert Penruddock and his younger brother George both moved south. Granted a lease for 21 years of the office of gauger in Poole, Dorset, in February 1551, he became in the following year surveyor for the augmentations in Dorset and in 1561 chief steward of lands in Somerset and Dorset which had been under that court before its absorption by the Exchequer; in 1554–5 he was auditor of the lordships of James Blount, 6th Lord Mountjoy, in the same two counties and elsewhere. By 1555 he enjoyed the patronage of the lord treasurer, William Paulet, Marquess of Winchester, who in July of that year sponsored the grant to him of former monastic property in Wimborne All Saints, Dorset. A Paulet connexion is also reflected in Penruddock's appearance on the pardon roll in 1559 as of Hale, for this property, later to be purchased by John Penruddock†, was from 1564 in the hands of Winchester's grandson, Lord Thomas Paulet. In June 1563 Penruddock was granted a lease of tithes in Morden, Dorset, partly in recognition of his service in that county.[3]

It was almost certainly Penruddock who sat for Cumberland in the two Parliaments of 1554, for his grandfather and namesake, if still alive, would have been at least in his mid 70s. Probably a kinsman both of his fellow-knight John Lee II and of Thomas Lee III*, the sheriff who returned them, Penruddock could also have commended himself as one well placed to represent the local holders of monastic property in the current uncertainty about its future. He was not to sit again under Mary and after 1558 his religion stood in the way of his doing so. Brought onto the Hampshire commission of the peace at the beginning of Elizabeth's reign, he was put off it after being adjudged in 1564 a 'misliker or not favourer' of the new orthodoxy, but was later appointed to the Wiltshire bench.[4]

Penruddock made his will on 10 Mar. 1579 when 'weak and sick in body'. Although still at Hale, he asked to be buried in the chancel of Broad Chalk, Wiltshire, where he was lessee of the parsonage and his brother Sir George of the manor belonging to the earls of Pembroke. His wife Joyce and his nephew and godson Robert† were to receive a delivery of wheat and barley every year for ten years out of the parsonage, but the lease itself went to another nephew, John, whom his uncle had already enfeoffed of all the Cumberland and Westmorland lands, subject to the widow's jointure. Joyce and Robert Penruddock were given the lease of Hale and made residuary legatees and executors, with Sir George and John Penruddock as overseers as well as executors for the collection of debts. Penruddock died in 1583 and the will was proved on 8 Apr. of that year.[5]

[1] Date of birth estimated from younger brother's and from first reference, *LP Hen. VIII*, xxi. *Vis. Cumb.* (Harl. Soc. vii), 2; *Wilts. Vis. Peds.* (Harl. Soc. cv, cvi), 148; *LP Hen. VIII*, xviii. [2] *CPR*, 1553, p. 374; 1560–3, pp. 181, 442; 1563–6, pp. 26, 42; *APC*, iv. 109. [3] *CPR*, 1553, p. 374; 1555–7, p. 98; 1558–60, p. 202; 1560–3, pp. 181, 493–4; *HMC Hastings,* i. 350; *VCH Hants,* iv. 578; *HMC Bath,* iv. 133. [4] *CPR*, 1550–3, p. 9; 1563–6, p. 510; Req.2/36/30; *Cam. Misc.* ix(3), 56. [5] PCC 17 Rowe; *VCH Hants,* iv. 578.

A.D.

PERCE *see* **TAYLOR**

PERCY, Henry (c.1532–85), of Alnwick, Northumb.

MORPETH 1554 (Nov.)[1]
NORTHUMBERLAND 1571

b. c.1532, 2nd s. of Sir Thomas Percy of Prudhoe by Eleanor, da. of Sir Guischard Harbottle of Horton; bro. of Thomas*. *m.* by 25 Jan. 1562, Catherine, da. and coh. of John Neville, 4th Lord Latimer, 8s. 3da. Kntd. 30 Apr. 1557; *suc.* bro. as 2nd Earl of Northumberland 22 Aug. 1572.[2]

Capt. Norham castle, Northumb. by Jan. 1558; constable, Tynemouth castle, Northumb. 1559, gov. 1560–83; member, council in the north Dec. 1558–Apr. 1571; j.p. co. Dur. 1558/59, Northumb. 1558/59, q. 1561–4, Cumb., Yorks. (E. and N. Ridings) 1569; sheriff, Northumb. 1562–3; commr. piracy 1565, to enforce Acts of Uniformity and Supremacy, province of York 1568; steward, former lands of Tynemouth priory, Northumb. 1570-?83.[3]

Henry Percy was about five years of age when his father, brother to the 5th Earl of Northumberland, was executed for his part in the Pilgrimage of Grace. With the bestowal of the Percy estates upon the crown and the death of the earl shortly afterwards, the family lost much of its importance, but the custody of its remaining representatives was a matter of concern; among their guardians was Sir Thomas Tempest*. Henry Percy received gifts in his grandmother the countess's will of 1542 and his stepfather Sir Richard Holland's of 1548. In the following year his brother was restored in blood.[4]

Percy had only recently come of age when he was returned for Morpeth to the third Marian Parliament. He had no known connexion with the borough and was probably the nominee of the 3rd Lord Dacre, the most influential figure there. His brother's election to the same Parliament as senior knight of the shire for Westmorland suggests that there was some agreement to give the two a start in the Commons together, although in the upshot neither was to have much future there, Thomas Percy being soon elevated to the Lords and Henry Percy reappearing only in 1571. As might be expected neither is to be found on the list of Members who quitted this Parliament without leave before its dissolution. On 30 Apr. 1557 Henry Percy was knighted and when on the following day his brother was created Earl of Northumberland it was with remainder to Percy in default of heirs. Both were soon engaged in border warfare, the new peer being made joint warden of the east march and his brother probably becoming his deputy. Percy bought the captaincy of Norham from Richard Norton, who was reprimanded by the crown for the transaction, and also appears to have obtained the custody of Tynemouth castle, though not made its governor until 1560.[5]

At first trusted by the Elizabethan government, Percy remained loyal in 1569 and was a Member of the Parliament of 1571 which attainted his brother and other leaders of the rebellion. He succeeded to the earldom on his brother's execution but was himself committed to the Tower on suspicion and did not take his seat in the Lords until 1576. Sent to the Tower again in 1584 in connexion with the Throckmorton plot, he died there of a shot from his own pistol on 20 June 1585.[6]

[1] Huntington Lib. Hastings mss Parl. pprs. The original return (C219/23/96) is damaged so that only the Member's surname and style survive. [2] CP, giving date of birth. DNB; E. B. de Fonblanque, Annals of the House of Percy, ii. 126; Arch. Ael. (ser. 3), i. 82-83; Northumb. Co. Hist. ix. 266; Vis. Suss. (Harl. Soc. liii), 138; Percy Bailiff's Rolls (Surtees Soc. cxxxiv), p. xiv; CSP Dom. 1547-80, p. 193. [3] CSP Dom. 1601-3, Add. 1547-65, pp. 468-9; Northumb. Co. Hist. viii. 160, 165; W. S. Gibson, Tynemouth Monastery, i. 239-41;

ii. 115-16; R. R. Reid, King's Council in the North, 186, 210, 493; CPR, 1566-9, pp. 172-3; 1569-72, pp. 223-4. [4] M. H. and R. Dodds, Pilgrimage of Grace, ii. 273-4; LP Hen. VIII, xii, xiii; Merriman, Letters, Thomas Cromwell, ii. 200; Test. Ebor. vi (Surtees Soc. cvi), 168, 193. [5] CPR, 1555-7, p. 495; CSP Dom. 1601-3, Add. 1547-65, pp. 463-4, 468-9, 474, 477, 480; APC, vi. 123, 143, 151, 209, 221, 345, 360, 366, 370, 374, 396, 399; Gibson, i. 239-40; E. Lodge, Illustrations, i. 310-13; Northumb. Co. Hist. viii. 160-1. [6] Northumb. Co. Hist. v. 64; viii. 163-5.

M.J.T.

PERCY, Thomas (1528-72), of Alnwick, Northumb., Topcliffe, Yorks., and Petworth, Suss.

WESTMORLAND 1554 (Nov.)[1]

b. 10 June 1528, 1st s. of Sir Thomas Percy of Prudhoe, Northumb., and bro. of Henry*. m. 12 June 1558, Anne, da. of Henry Somerset, 2nd Earl of Worcester, 1s. d.v.p. 4da. suc. fa. 2 June 1537. Kntd. and cr. Baron Percy 30 Apr. 1557, 1st Earl of Northumberland 1 May 1557; KG nom. 22 Apr. 1563, inst. 23 May 1563, degraded 27 Nov. 1569.[2]
Keeper, Prudhoe castle Mar. 1556; member, council in north May 1557; steward, liberty of Richmond, Yorks. 26 July 1557; jt. (with Thomas Wharton*, 1st Baron Wharton) warden, E. and Middle marches 2 Aug., sole warden 9 Aug. 1557-?Nov. 1559; j.p.q. Northumb. 1558/59-64, Yorks. (all Ridings) 1561-4; commr. musters, Yorks. 1569.[3]

Thomas Percy's father was executed in June 1537 and his uncle Henry, 5th Earl of Northumberland, died in the same month, having made over all his lands to the King. Brought up by guardians, who included for a time Sir Thomas Tempest*, Percy was restored in blood by an Act of 1549 (2 and 3 Edw. VI, no. 47). With his brother Henry he was in receipt of an annuity of 100 marks out of the lordship and manor of Prudhoe, and he eventually obtained possession of the castle. In January 1552 he received a grant of some former Percy properties in Northumberland.[4]

Percy's restoration was to be completed under Mary. His introduction to public life came with his election as senior knight of the shire for Westmorland to the Queen's third Parliament. Westmorland was not his own shire and he presumably owed his return to his cousin Henry, 2nd Earl of Cumberland, with perhaps the help of his uncle's former servant Thomas, 1st Baron Wharton. His brother Henry was returned to the same Parliament for Morpeth. Predictably, neither withdrew from it without leave before its dissolution. Percy's next appearance in Parliament was to be in the Lords, following his creation as Earl of Northumberland on 1 May 1557 and his restoration in the following August to the lost lands; these lay chiefly in Yorkshire, where were the chief residences, Cumberland, Northumberland and Sussex. Shortly after his creation the King and Queen recommended Percy to the 5th Earl of Shrewsbury as marshal of the field in the northern army; at the same time he was appointed to the council in the north and soon afterwards became warden of the east and middle marches. The war with Scotland prevented him from taking his seat in the Lords in the last Parliament of the reign, and early in 1558 he obtained leave of absence from the House.[5]

Elizabeth confirmed Northumberland in his offices and excused him from attending Parliament in 1559 on their account, but she removed him after allegations of misconduct and of partiality towards Mary Queen of Scots. He refused to receive his successor at Alnwick in 1560 or to act as host there to the proposed meeting between the two Queens two years later. On taking his place in the Lords in 1563 he spoke against measures curbing Catholicism. His receipt of the Garter several months later was intended as a gesture of conciliation, but he remained an outspoken critic of the regime and its church policy. His sympathy towards the Scottish Queen on her arrival in England annoyed the Council and his plan to set her free with Spanish support received papal approval. When a year later he declined a summons to London his arrest was ordered, but he eluded his captors and with the 6th Earl of Westmorland he proclaimed Mary Queen of England. After the failure of their rising he sought refuge in Liddesdale where the Laird of Ormiston delivered him to the Regent Moray. His wife escaped to the Continent, whence she tried unsuccessfully to ransom him. He and the other rebel leaders were attainted by the Parliament of 1571. In May 1572 the Scots surrendered him to Elizabeth and on 22 Aug. he was beheaded at York. For refusing to abandon his faith in return for his life Northumberland was beatified in 1895.[6]

[1] Huntington Lib. Hastings mss Parl. pprs. [2] Age and birth given on his portrait dated 1566, *Pictures at Petworth* (National Trust), 2. CP; DNB; *Arch. Ael.* (ser. 3), i. 82–83; *Northumb. Co. Hist.* ix. 266; *Vis. Suss.* (Harl. Soc. liii), 138. [3] *CPR*, 1555–7, p. 479; 1557–8, pp. 12, 71, 194; 1558–60, pp. 56, 58; 1560–3, pp. 436–7, 441; 1563–6, pp. 21–22; *CSP For.* 1558–9, p. 265; *CSP Dom.* 1547–80, p. 335; 1601–3, *Add.* 1547–65, p. 450. [4] G. Brenan, *House of Percy*, i. 251; *SP Hen. VIII*, v. 92, 118–19; Merriman, *Letters of Thomas Cromwell*, ii. 99–100; *CJ*, i. 8; *CPR*, 1550–3, pp. 118, 185; *APC*, iii. 222, 434; v. 206, 248–9. [5] *CPR*, 1555–7, p. 495; 1557–8, pp. 179–89; *Northern Hist.* i. 59, 67n; *Estate Accts. Earl of Northumberland* (Surtees Soc. clxiii), pp. xi seq.; *Arch. Ael.* (ser. 4), xxxv. 49; *Econ. Hist. Rev.* (ser. 2), ix. 434–5; *HMC Shrewsbury and Talbot*, i, ii passim; M. A. R. Graves, 'The Tudor House of Lords 1547–58' (Otago Univ. Ph.D. thesis, 1974), ii. 276; *The King's Works*, iii. 229. [6] *HMC Shrewsbury and Talbot*, i, ii passim; *CSP For.* 1558–9 to 1564–5 passim; *CSP Span.* 1558–67, pp. 293–4; *CSP Dom.* 1566–79, pp. 294, 424; 1601–3, *Add.* 1547–65, p. 567; H. Aveling, *Northern Catholics*, passim; *TRHS* n.s. xx. 177–8; *Memorials of the Rebellion of 1569*, ed. Sharp, 203–4, 212–13; D. Mathews, *Catholicism in England*, 39–40.

A.D.

PERNE, Christopher (by 1530–66 or later), of London.

?BOSSINEY	1555[1]
?PLYMPTON ERLE	1558
ST. IVES	1559
GRAMPOUND	1563*

b. by 1530, prob. yr. s. of John Perne of East Bilney, Norf. *educ.* Queens', Camb. adm. pens. Easter 1544. ?*m.* at least 3s.[2]

Christopher Perne was probably a younger brother of Andrew Perne, fellow of Queens' College, Cambridge, several of whose family attended either that college or, after Andrew Perne became master there, Peterhouse. Beginning as a defender of Catholic doctrine, Andrew Perne became a leading Protestant preacher under Edward VI. Christopher Perne evidently shared the same outlook: in 1552 he received a lease of several Yorkshire parsonages and early in the following reign he was indicted with others who had 'notably offended', presumably by their conduct during the succession crisis. Like Andrew Perne, he made his peace with the Marian government, suing out a general pardon in October 1553 as Christopher Perne of London, gentleman.[3]

Perne's parliamentary career probably began in 1555. A Ralph Perne, perhaps of the same family, sat for Dorchester in the Parliament of that year, but he is less likely than Christopher Perne to have been the 'Mr. Perne' who followed Sir Anthony Kingston's lead in opposing one of the government's bills: it was almost certainly for this offence that Christopher Perne was put in the Fleet on 11 Dec., two days after the dissolution. He was to owe his later returns to Francis Russell*, 2nd Earl of Bedford, whom he may have met in Cambridge, and if he enjoyed the same patronage in 1555 (exercised by Sir William Cecil in the earl's absence abroad) his constituency may well have been Bossiney, where the only Member known is Ralph Skinner, who also figures on the list of those who opposed the government's bill. On 24 Dec. the warden of the Fleet was instructed to allow Perne the liberty of the prison and to bring him and his fellow-prisoner Gabriel Pleydell (q.v.) before the Council on the following Friday. On 29 Dec. Perne was bound in a recognizance to appear weekly before the Council and released from custody. His sureties Sir William Fitzwilliam II* and Robert Warner* were both associates of Bedford, to whom Warner was to owe his return for Bossiney to the Parliament of 1559. Early in 1556 Henry Peckham* revealed details of the Dudley conspiracy to Perne who then made several of the plotters welcome in his house in the parish of St. Dunstan-in-the-west. On 30 May 1556 he was accordingly imprisoned and his two sureties were discharged. His name was coupled with that of Anthony Forster† on the controlment roll, but without any subsequent note of process, and he next appears in July 1557 as the recipient of a lease in reversion of the rabbit warren at Hamdon, Somerset. He may have owed his successful emergence from this latest crisis in part to the influence of Andrew Perne, whose acceptance of the Marian restoration of Catholicism was to be recognised in December 1557 by his appointment to the deanery of Ely.[4]

Despite his unsatisfactory record, Perne sought election to the Parliament of 1558, again evidently at the hands of Bedford. His name and that of Thomas Southcote appear on the Crown Office list as the Members for Plympton Erle (although they are among the 17 whose names are missing from a copy of the list), but on 5 Mar. 1558 the Journal records:

> For that Christopher Perne affirmeth, that he is returned a burgess for Plympton in Devon, and hath brought no warrant thereof to the House, nor returned hither by the clerk of the crown, by book or warrant, he is awarded to be in the custody of the serjeant, till the House have further considered.

The Parliament was prorogued two days later evidently before a decision could have been made, and on 17 Mar. Perne appeared before the Council and was told that within a week he should 'depart from the court and not come near thereunto by the space of seven miles, saving the first week of the next term to repair to London for such special suits as he hath to do in Westminster Hall, upon pain of forfeiture of £500'. This decree, if still in force, may have prevented Perne from attending the second session, even if his right to do so was admitted by the House, but there is no evidence of a by-election.[5]

The accession of Elizabeth brought little change in Perne's chequered career. He was returned to the first two Parliaments of the reign but shortly after the opening of the second he was committed to the Marshalsea 'for pickery' and when a new writ was issued for Grampound in October 1566 he was 'reported to be lunatic'. His subsequent history is unknown but he probably died before Andrew Perne made his will in 1588 and was perhaps the deceased brother mentioned in it who had sold all the lands and houses which he had inherited from their father.[6]

[1] Guildford mus. Loseley 1331/2. [2] Date of birth estimated from education. *Vis. Cambs.* (Harl. Soc. xli), 93; PCC 46 Leicester. [3] *DNB* (Perne, Andrew); Strype, *Eccles. Memorials* ii(2), 278; *APC*, iv. 86, 345; *CPR*, 1553-4, p. 449; 1566-9, pp. 369, 421; 1569-72, p. 164; 1572-5, pp. 28-29. [4] Guildford mus. Loseley 1331/2; *APC*, v. 203, 209, 214, 275; *CPR*, 1555-7, p. 453; 1557-8, p. 19; D. M. Loades, *Two Tudor Conspiracies*, 230, 235. [5] C193/32/2; Wm. Salt Lib. SMS 264; *CJ*, i. 51; *APC*, vi. 287. [6] Add. 5123, f. 16v; *CJ*, i. 75; PCC 46 Leicester.

A.D.K.H.

PERNE, Ralph

DORCHESTER   1555

No Ralph Perne, gentleman, has been traced in Dorchester or elsewhere in the mid 16th century, but the variant form Peryn was well known in the town. One Ralph Peryn witnessed a number of Dorchester deeds between 1538 and 1550, and was bailiff in 1549-50 and constable during the following year. By trade a glover he owned houses and land in the town which by his will made 'in or about' 12 Aug. 1551 he left to his eldest son, John Peryn. The text of the will has not survived, nor is the date of probate known: if Ralph Peryn was indeed the Member in 1555 he must have lived for some years after making his will and despite his trade and apparently modest circumstances been of gentle birth. There is no reference to him in the town records after 1551 until eight years later when a burgage lately in his tenure is mentioned.[1]

The election at Dorchester in 1555 of the former household officer, Robert Robotham, and Ralph Perne broke with the practice which was becoming established there of choosing Christopher Hole with another, preferably a townsman, as Members. As Perne took the junior seat which was usually allocated to the townsmen, the Member could be identifiable with the glover or a kinsman of his, but it is more likely that he had no personal ties with Dorchester, and that he was related to one of the 2nd Earl of Bedford's clients, Christopher Perne. The owner of some property in the town, the earl was to become its parliamentary patron under Elizabeth, and he could well have influenced the election there in 1555. The 'Mr. Perne' who joined Robert Robotham in opposing one of the government's bills may have been the Dorchester Member but is thought to have been Christopher Perne (q.v.).[2]

[1] C. H. Mayo, *Recs. Dorchester*, 322-61 passim; Req.2/61/97. [2] Guildford mus. Loseley 1331/2.

H.M.

PERROT (PARRET), John (1528/29-92), of Haroldston and Carew Castle, Pemb.

CARMARTHENSHIRE	1547*[1]
SANDWICH	1553 (Oct.),[2] 1555
WAREHAM	1559
PEMBROKESHIRE	1563
HAVERFORDWEST	1589

b. 1528/29, reputed illegit. s. of Henry VIII by Mary, da. of James Berkeley of Thornbury, Glos., w. of Thomas Perrot of Islington, Mdx. and Haroldston; half-bro. of Henry Jones I* and Richard Jones*. *educ.* St. Davids. *m.* (1) Anne (*d.*Sept. 1553), da. of Sir Thomas Cheyne* of Shurland, Kent, 1s. Thomas†; (2) by 1566, Jane, da. of Hugh Prust of Hartland, Devon, wid. of Sir Lewis Pollard of Oakford, Devon, 1s. 2da.; at least 1s. illegit. James† 2da. illegit. *suc.* Thomas Perrot 1531. Kntd. 17 Nov. 1549.[3]

Sheriff, Pemb. 1551-2; commr. goods of churches and fraternities, Pemb. 1553, concealed lands 1561, armour 1569, musters 1570, Denb. 1580, Haverfordwest 1581, piracy Card., Carm. 1575, Pemb. 1577; j.p. Pemb. 1555-8, q. Card., Carm., Pemb. 1558/59-*d.*, q. all Welsh counties 1579-*d.*, marcher counties 1582;

steward, manors of Carew, Coedraeth and Narberth, Pemb., and St. Clears, Carm. 1559, lordship of Cilgerran, Pemb. 1570; constable, Narberth and Tenby castles, Pemb. 1559; gaoler, Haverfordwest 1559; mayor, Haverfordwest 1560–1, 1570–1, 1575–6; custos rot. Pemb. by 1562; president of Munster 1570–3; member, council in the marches of Wales by 1574; ld. dep. Ireland 1584–8; dep. lt. Pemb. in 1587; PC 10 Feb. 1589.[4]

John Perrot was probably born at Haroldston, the home of the Perrot family since the 12th century. His mother had been, briefly, mistress of Henry VIII, and his paternity has been ascribed to the King whom he resembled in physique and colouring. After the death of Thomas Perrot his wardship was acquired by his stepfather Thomas Jones*, who then settled at Haroldston. As a boy John Perrot went to school at St. David's and later his stepfather procured him a place in the household of William Paulet, Baron St. John. He soon gained an unenviable reputation for violence. On one occasion he and Henry, 6th Lord Bergavenny fell out, and before they could be separated broke glasses 'about one another's ears' so that 'blood besprinkled . . . the chamber'. It was to a brawl with two yeomen of the guard that he owed his introduction to Henry VIII. Whether in acknowledgement of his birth or in admiration of his spirit the King promised him preferment, but died before giving it.[5]

The death of Sir Richard Devereux created a vacancy in the Commons several days after the opening of Edward VI's first Parliament. The date of Devereux's replacement by Perrot is not known, but if it occurred during the first session the newcomer was not yet 20. He had few personal links with Carmarthenshire, and his by-election was perhaps the work of Paulet as lord president of the Council, helped by his uncle, the reader in Greek to the young King, and by his stepfather, a leading figure in west Wales and himself a knight of the shire. Nothing has come to light about Perrot's role in this Parliament but as a Protestant he doubtless welcomed its ecclesiastical legislation. The timing of his knighthood suggests that he sided with the Earl of Warwick against the Protector Somerset. In 1551 he accompanied the Marquess of Northampton to France to negotiate the marriage of the King and the French Princess Elizabeth. During a hunt there he saved Henry II from a wounded boar which threatened his life. The King embraced him in gratitude but Perrot mistaking the gesture for a show of strength lifted Henry 'somewhat high from the ground, with which the king was nothing displeased but proffered him a good pension to serve'. Perrot declined the invitation and returned to England, where his extravagances forced him to mortgage his family lands. According to his anonymous biographer, Edward VI sympathised with his predicament and persuaded the Council to grant him £100 from concealed lands which he might discover, the grant coming two months before the King's death. As a favoured courtier he may well have sat in the second Parliament of the reign, but if he did it was not as the knight for Carmarthenshire, that place being taken by his half-brother Henry Jones. He could have replaced his stepfather for Pembrokeshire, as the return from that shire is defaced, or with the backing of his father-in-law Sir Thomas Cheyne have been returned for a Cinque Port, while Paulet's pervasive influence might have served him elsewhere.[6]

The Marian Restoration cannot have been to Perrot's liking and he soon incurred the displeasure of the new regime. In January 1554 he was held a prisoner in the Fleet for three days for assaulting several servants of the 3rd Earl of Worcester. Returned for Sandwich to two of Queen Mary's Parliaments, on both occasions because Cheyne disregarded the port's own choice of Members, Perrot aligned himself with the opposition: in 1553 he 'stood for the true religion' and in 1555 he supported Sir Anthony Kingston against a main government bill. For harbouring Protestants at Haroldston he was denounced by Thomas Cathern* and briefly imprisoned in the Fleet again. His refusal to assist Sir William Herbert I*, 1st Earl of Pembroke, in harrying his co-religionists led to a quarrel with Pembroke with whom he had recently become associated in local administration. This quarrel came to the notice of the Queen and imperilled his suit for Carew castle. In an effort to redeem himself he tried to beg Mary's forgiveness, but in doing so he stepped on her train and earned a rebuke. Mary referred his petition to the Council where Pembroke recommended the grant, although he felt Perrot's animosity to be such that he 'would at this time, if he could, eat my heart with salt'. The Council and the Queen followed the earl's advice, but if they hoped possession of the castle would win Perrot over they were to be disappointed, for it was not long afterwards that he gave his support to Kingston. He attended the meetings at which the parliamentary opposition discussed its tactics and he was presumably the 'Master Paretes, [Pembroke's] most favourite and familiar gentleman' who according to the Venetian ambassador quarrelled so violently with Pembroke for supporting Sir Edward Hastings's stand in the Commons that he was dismissed from Pembroke's London house and service. In April 1556 Perrot was arrested on suspicion of complicity in the Dudley conspiracy, but evidence against him was lacking and no proceedings were taken. He and Pembroke were reconciled by the following year when he served under the earl's command at St. Quentin. In January 1558 the Council excused him from service at sea. A month later he complained to the Council about Thomas Cathern, not long after Cathern's return to the Parliament of that year, and it is possible that he had been defeated at the Pembrokeshire election. He later broke into Cathern's house and took Cathern into custody at Carew castle. Both men appeared before the Council in June and when it was found that Perrot had 'exceeded his commission and misused himself' he was committed yet again to the Fleet. A month later he was bound over in a recognizance of £200 to keep the peace and on 1 Sept. commissioners were chosen to investigate the charge made against him by Cathern. The outcome of this enquiry is not known, but it probably lapsed with the Queen's death.[7]

Under Elizabeth, Perrot sat in Parliament again, served in Ireland and in the marches of Wales, and became a Privy Councillor. His choleric nature was to be his undoing. Imprisoned in 1591, he was attainted in the following year and died in the Tower while awaiting execution.

[1] Hatfield 207. [2] Bodl. e Museo 17. [3] Date of birth estimated from age at Thomas Perrot's i.p.m., Wards 9/129/164v. Dwnn, *Vis. Wales*, i. 89, 134; C142/119/114; *Lit. Rems. Edw. VI*, p. ccvii; *DNB*; *DWB* (Perrot fam. of Haroldston). [4] *CPR*, 1553, p. 418; 1558-60, p. 45; 1563-6, pp. 30, 31, 317; 1569-72, p. 252; *APC*, ix. 267-8; xii. 364; xvii. 76; *CSP Dom.* 1547-80, pp. 537-41, 615; R. Flenley, *Cal. Reg. Council, Marches of Wales*, 60, 122, 126, 132, 139-40, 172, 200, 213, 216, 234; P. H. Williams, *Council in the Marches of Wales*, 60-69; *Arch. Camb.* (ser. 3), xi. 195; *Cal. Haverfordwest Recs.* (Univ. Wales Bd. of Celtic Studies Hist. and Law ser. xxiv), 30, 184; *HMC Foljambe*, 26. [5] Wards 9/129/164v; *LP Hen. VIII*, vi; *Life of Sir John Perrott*, ed. Rawlinson, 17-27. [6] *Life of Sir John Perrott*, 29-34; *APC*, ii. 271; iv. 284; *Lit. Rems. Edw. VI*, 317, 384, 389. [7] *APC*, vi. 235, 270, 333, 344, 354, 386, 390; Bodl. e Museo 17; *Life of Sir John Perrott*, 37-42; *CPR*, 1554-5, pp. 299, 300; Guildford mus. Loseley 1331/2; D. M. Loades, *Two Tudor Conspiracies*, 210-11, 223, 233, 267; *HMC Foljambe*, 6-7.

P.S.E.

PERSALL *see* **PESHALL**

PERSELL *see* **PURCELL**

PERTE, John (by 1514-49/51)

CONSTITUENCY UNKNOWN   1547*[1]

b. by 1514, s. of John Perte of Tewkesbury, Glos. *m.* Anne, da. of Edward Tyndale of Pull Court, Worcs., at least 1s.[2]

Bailiff, Tewkesbury abbey's manors of Burnett, Som. and Pull, Worcs. by 1535; jt. auditor, ct. augmentations, all woods 16 Apr. 1545-*d.*, jt. (with Matthew Herbert and later with William Wightman*) receiver, S. Wales by 1547-*d.*, auditor, N. Wales by 1547-*d.*, woodward, S. Wales temp. Edw. VI; jt. bailiff, manor of Hartbury, Glos. 27 Apr. 1546-*d.*; servant of Thomas Seymour, Baron Seymour of Sudeley by 1549.[3]

The Commons Journal records that on 9 Jan. 1549 a bill for hats and caps was committed after its second

reading to 'Mr. Perte etc.'. This is the only evidence that the Parliament then in session included a Member of that name. His identification with John Perte, an official in the court of augmentations, presupposes that Perte must have died before the end of 1551, when the revised list of Members of the Parliament was drawn up, and in all probability that he was legally qualified, as Members to whom bills were committed customarily were. Although Perte's name has not been found in the records of any inn of court, his enjoyment of the style 'esquire' implies that he was a trained lawyer. The date of his death is also a matter of inference from somewhat confusing evidence. He was alive in the spring of 1549 but dead by 3 May 1553, when property which he had leased in Middlesex was sold by the crown. Between these dates there are to be found mentions of him in the report on the financial courts submitted at the end of 1552 and in another of 1 Sept. 1552 by the pension commissioners for Gloucestershire, stating that he had died in the August of the sixth year of Edward VI, that is, August 1552. Although the references in the first of these documents could have followed, and not preceded, his death, those in the second cannot be reconciled with his omission from the Members present during the final session of the Parliament, which ended on 15 Apr. 1552. In the absence of any discoverable namesake with whom he may have been confused, it appears likely that the regnal year is mistaken, the 'vi' perhaps being an error for 'iv', and that Perte was replaced in the Commons by 1551.[4]

Perte was of Gloucestershire origin and could claim gentle birth. Nothing is known about his upbringing or early career save for his receipt of a small legacy on the death of his father in 1523. The father is said to have been an official in the service of Tewkesbury abbey, but this may be to confuse father and son, as Perte had himself entered the abbey's service by 1535 and he married one of the daughters of the abbey's steward: he was also in receipt of an annuity from Winchcombe abbey, Gloucestershire. His services were presumably retained by the crown after the Dissolution, as were his father-in-law's, and in 1544 he signed a receipt of expenses incurred by some soldiers going with the King to France. In the same year he was party to several land transactions involving gentlemen of the west country; in March Maurice Denys* sold to him the ex-Augustinian friary in Bristol, which Perte soon resold, and in June William Sharington* conveyed to him and Henry Brouncker a manor in Berkshire.[5]

Perte's appointment, at the same time as a brother-in-law's, to the court of augmentations in 1545 may have been connected with his introduction to Queen

Catherine Parr, whose accounts he was helping Anthony Bourchier* to audit two years later, and to Catherine's last husband Thomas, Baron Seymour of Sudeley, who leased to him the site of the 'clarks' at Offley in Hertfordshire. It was doubtless to one or other of these patrons that Perte owed his election to the Parliament of 1547; he probably sat for a borough in Wiltshire (the returns for all of them being lost), where the couple's influence was extensive. After Seymour's fall Perte was one of his servants recommended to the Protector Somerset by (Sir) Hugh Paulet* and John Berwick* as suitable to enter the Protector's service, but with what result is unknown. His widow was to marry William Clerke*, another of the men so recommended, and his brother-in-law Thomas Tyndale* replaced him as the auditor in the court of augmentations for North Wales.[6]

[1] *CJ*, i. 6. [2] Date of birth estimated from first two appointments Worcester consist. ct. wills 1523; B. W. Greenfield, *Gen. Fam. of Tyndale* (1843) no pagination; PCC 9 Spence. [3] *Val. Eccles.* ii. 475, 480; W. C. Richardson, *Ct. Augmentations.* 110, 281, 494; *LP Hen. VIII*, xx, xxi; *HMC Bath*, iv. 109. [4] *CJ*, i. 6; *CPR*, 1553, p. 170; *Rep. Roy. Comm. of 1552* (Archs. of Brit. Hist. and Culture iii), 49, 61, 63; *Bristol and Glos. Arch. Soc. Trans.* xlix. 119, 120; *LP Hen. VIII*, xxi; *Vis. Glos.* (Harl. Soc. xxi). 170; *CPR*, 1553, p. 119. [5] Worcester consist. ct. wills 1523; *Bristol and Glos. Arch. Soc. Trans.* xlix. 119, 120; lix. 248; *LP Hen. VIII*, xix. [6] E163/12/17, nos. 31, 56; Bath mss, Seymour pprs. 9/245 ex inf. Julianna Marker; *HMC Bath*, iv. 109.

P.S.E./A.D.K.H.

PESHALL (PERSALL), John (1484/85–1564 or later), of Horsley, nr. Eccleshall, Staffs.

NEWCASTLE-UNDER-LYME 1529

b. 1484/85 1st s. of Humphrey Peshall of Horsley by Helen, da. of Humphrey Swynnerton of Swynnerton and Hilton. *m.* (1) by 1506, Catherine, da. of Thomas Harcourt of Ranton; (2) Ellen, 3s. 1da. *suc.* fa. 3 June 1489.[1]

Commr. oyer and terminer, Staffs. 1540; j.p. 1547, 1554.[2]

Early in John Peshall's life his sister Thomasin cited Thomas Harcourt in the court of requests for a rape of ward, alleging that he had been carried off on his father's death and married when under age to one of Harcourt's daughters. Harcourt maintained that the bishop of Coventry and Lichfield had acquired Peshall's wardship and marriage from the crown and that the bishop had sold both to him. Peshall's marriage involved him in the long-standing feud between the Harcourts of Ranton and those of Stanton Harcourt, Oxfordshire, and Ellenhall, Staffordshire, in which he was to figure prominently, often with recourse to litigation.[3]

In July 1535 Sir Simon Harcourt complained to Cromwell that Peshall had been most abusive towards him and his son, Sir John Harcourt*, and had fallen upon the latter's servants when they had refused him passage through a park in the previous summer: for this offence Peshall had been indicted but later pardoned by the King. Harcourt begged

Cromwell to write to the Staffordshire justices so that Peshall might be 'handled according to his demerits' at the next sessions, when Harcourt proposed to indict him for felony and riot. Cromwell complied and the indictment was successful, but in January 1536 Harcourt complained that Peshall still maintained 'unthrifty persons' about him and asked for Cromwell's support in a further action which he was bringing by subpoena in the Star Chamber. This case appears not to have come on until Michaelmas 1537, by which time Peshall had enlisted the aid of the 4th Earl of Shrewsbury, who in October wrote to Cromwell soliciting his favour for Peshall, described as an 'old friend', in his dispute with Harcourt 'about a highway'. The affair was still smouldering two years later, when Bishop Rowland Lee wrote to Cromwell in Harcourt's favour.[4]

Peshall's Membership of the Parliament of 1529 was perhaps intended to protect him from his enemies. The fact that he took precedence over his fellow Richard Grey, an illegitimate son of a minor nobleman, may mean that he had sat in an earlier Parliament for which the names are lost. His election was presumably favoured by his kinsman Edward Littleton, who was chosen one of the knights for Staffordshire, but it must have been due to a combination of support from the Earl of Shrewsbury, who held the duchy of Lancaster's stewardship of Newcastle-under-Lyme, and his family's influence in the town, of which his stepbrother had been mayor twice, his wife's uncle three times, and her grandfather four times. Peshall was later to claim that he attended Parliament every day from its opening until its dissolution except when he had been licensed to appear before the King's justices at Chester and the justices of the peace in Staffordshire to answer certain mistaken indictments against him: however, when in 1536–7 he claimed payment of his wages 'after the rate of 2s. by the day above the sum of £66', the mayor, Thomas Bradshaw, and his brethren objected, and when Peshall persuaded the sheriff to pursue the levy of his wages Bradshaw delayed the matter by taking it to Chancery.[5]

In the course of the proceedings Bradshaw cited the statute regulating parliamentary elections (23 Hen. VI, c.14) to show that Peshall had not been duly elected. He maintained that the sheriff, Sir Edward Aston, had complied with Peshall's request to return him to Parliament, although neither an election nor an indenture had been made. After Aston had made the return the mayor, Richard Robinson, had been chosen unanimously and had gone up to London but had failed to gain admittance to the Commons because of Peshall's obstructiveness. Bradshaw also claimed that Peshall had departed from Parliament without a licence, contrary to the statute of 1515 (6 Hen. VIII, c.16), and had thus forfeited his wages. Peshall contended that he should not suffer because a clerk had been neglectful and repeated that both he and Richard Grey had been duly returned. Bradshaw was concerned not so much perhaps with the invalidity of the return as with Peshall's demand for expenses, which was indeed excessive: the Parliament had lasted for 483 days, not for more than 600 (even allowing for travel) as his claim implies. Unfortunately the outcome of this interesting case is unknown, as is its possible effect upon the next election, that of 1536, when despite the King's request for the return of the previous Members the town may have decided to do without Peshall. It may be that the decision to contest Peshall's claim was in some way linked with his concurrent dispute with the Harcourts. A further lawsuit with a parliamentary flavour in which he was involved was one with Richard Bradbury, a London saddler, who accused Peshall of offering— although with the help of an inducement of 40s.—to speak to (Sir) William Coffin*, with whom he was travelling to London to attend a session, about an appointment in Queen Anne Boleyn's household. As the post did not come Bradbury's way, nor did Peshall return the douceur, he had Peshall arrested in London on a suit for the money, but Peshall regained his freedom by a writ of privilege out of Chancery. Bradbury then petitioned Chancellor Audley for remedy, but with what result is unknown.[6]

Peshall's landed income amounted to 100 marks. In the later part of his long life he was given a place in the local government of Staffordshire, even though his opponents had described him as a man inclined to violence. This tendency was twice put to the test on his country's behalf: in 1513 he served as a captain in the expedition which captured Tournai, and more than 30 years later he returned to French soil with 100 men for the defence of Boulogne. The last glimpse of Peshall dates from 5 May 1564 when he answered charges about tithes in Eccleshall.[7]

[1] Date of birth estimated from age at fa.'s i.p.m., C142/5/26. *Wm. Salt Arch. Soc.* iii(2), 95; v(2), 240; C1/1047/27; Req.2/4/206; *Staffs. Rec. Soc.* (ser. 4), viii. 138. [2] *LP Hen. VIII*, xv; *CPR*, 1547-8, p. 89; 1553-4, p. 24. [3] Req.2/4/206. [4] *LP Hen. VIII*, viii, x, xii, xiv; A. F. Pollard, 'An early parlty election petition', *Bull. IHR*, viii. 161-2. [5] *Bull. IHR*, 159-66; T. Pape, *Newcastle-under-Lyme*, 37; C1/862/11-12, 14. [6] C1/732/9, 862/11-14; *Bull. IHR*, 156. [7] *LP Hen. VIII*, i, xiv, xxi; Leland, *Itin.* ed. Smith, ii. 170; P. and M. H. Spufford, *Eccleshall*, 38; *Wm. Salt Arch. Soc.* (n.s.) 1907 (pt. i), 84-90; 1933, pp. 4-6; St.Ch.2/57/66; C1/1106/34-37.

L.M.K./A.D.K.H.

PETERSON, William (by 1517-78), of London.

LEWES   1558

b. by 1517, s. of John Peterson of Lewes, Suss. *m.* by 1549, Anne (*bur.* 30 July 1564), ?da. of Robert Morley of Lewes, 2s. 3da.[1]

William Peterson was a brother of Robert Peterson, last prior of the Cluniac house at Lewes: the name suggests that the family was of Netherlandish origin. In 1538, after the dissolution of the priory, Robert Peterson sought Cromwell's help for a lease of some lands near Lewes for his brother, but with what result is not known. By his will of 1555 he left the residue of his goods to his beloved brother William, 'merchant of London', who also acted as executor of the will after Richard Brydley, archdeacon of Lewes and late prior of the Lewes cell of Horton in Kent, had refused to do so. At the time of his own death William Peterson had two houses with lands and gardens in the barony of Lewes.[2]

A London haberdasher, Peterson had a house called the *Bell and Checker* in Fenchurch Street; he exported cloth to Antwerp and also traded with Lubeck. In 1563 he was among a group of merchants of London and Hull who petitioned the Queen to be allowed to impound goods belonging to Lubeck merchants after their own goods had been seized, as prize by men from that city. In the following year, on the incorporation of the Merchant Adventurers, Peterson was appointed one of the first assistants of the company. His election for Lewes to the last Marian Parliament answered to his combination of local standing with London residence and connexions, while his family tie with the priory suggests that he satisfied at least one of the criteria of the royal letter calling for the return of 'men given to good order, Catholic and discreet'.[3]

Peterson died in London on 3 Oct. 1578 and was buried in St. Dionis Backchurch five days later. By the will which he had made on 15 July previously he left his property in Lewes to his heir Robert, then rising 27, and the *Bell and Checker* valued at £10 a year, to his second son Daniel; Robert was also to receive £60 within one year of the father's death, a daughter Grace, wife of John Master gentleman, a gold chain and tablet of gold, and a friend Richard Hale, merchant taylor of London, a gold ring worth £3. Daniel Peterson was appointed executor of the will, which was proved before the end of 1578.[4]

[1] Date of birth estimated from first reference. *Suss. Arch. Colls.* xcii. 24; PCC 35 Langley, 15 Morrison; C142/186/22; *Regs. St. Dionis Backchurch, London* (Harl. Soc. Regs. iii), 74, 75, 189, 195. [2] *Chartulary, Lewes Priory* (Suss. Rec. Soc. lvi), 98; *Suss. Arch. Colls.* lxxxvi. 178-82; *LP Hen. VIII*, xiii; PCC 35 Langley. [3] Lansd. 7(47), f. 107; SP12/6, f. 112; *CPR*, 1558-60, p. 191; 1563-6, p. 179. [4] C142/186/22; *Regs. St. Dionis Backchurch, London*, 195; PCC 35 Langley.

R.J.W.S.

PETHEBRIDGE, John, of Liskeard, Cornw.

LISKEARD   1554 (Nov.)

John Pethebridge was a merchant. His election with John Connock to the third Parliament of Mary's reign complied with her directive for the return of residents. Neither man was found to be present when the House was called early in January 1555, and for this dereliction Pethebridge was informed against in the King's bench during the following Easter term: a writ of *venire facias* was sent to the sheriff of Cornwall, but no further process was taken against him. The last glimpse of Pethebridge is four years later when in 1559 he contributed 8*s*.4*d*. to the subsidy on the basis of goods worth £5.

KB27/1176; E179/87/218.

J.J.G.

PETRE, John I (by 1526–71), of Dartmouth, Exeter and Hayes, Devon.

DARTMOUTH 1554 (Nov.)

b. by 1526, yr. s. of John Petre of Tor Newton in Torbryan by Alice, da. of John Collinge of Woodland; bro. of Robert† and William*.[1]
    Collector of customs, Dartmouth and Exeter 22 Nov. 1547–?*d*.[2]

Of the two men named John Petre who sat in the Parliament of November 1554 the Member for Dartmouth came of the family settled at Torbryan, between Newton Abbot and Totnes. He had other namesakes, including an elder brother, from whom he cannot always be distinguished, but he was almost certainly the John Petre who was appointed customer of Dartmouth in 1547 and died in 1571, and may have been the Dartmouth merchant of that name who was bailiff there in 1540 and receiver in 1544. His customership he probably owed to his brother Sir William, by then principal secretary, and the same influence may have smoothed his purchases of monastic property, in 1552 the manor of Norton in East Allington, and early in 1553 the manor in Kingkerswell which he bought with John Ridgeway*, whose daughter married his brother John. During the western rebellion of 1549 Petre narrowly escaped death when struck by an arrow loosed by his best friend, a Catholic named Richard Taylor.[3]

There is no evidence that Petre married or had children. He was living at Exeter when he made his will, in which he called himself 'esquire', on 3 Feb. 1571. He left most of his lands to his nephew William, son of John Petre of Exeter, and made bequests to various other kinsmen. He died nine days later and the will was proved on the following 22 May. At the inquisition held at Exeter on 10 Mar. 1571 his brother Sir William was found to be his heir.[4]

[1] Date of birth estimated from first reference. *Vis. Devon*, ed. Colby, 169. [2] *CPR*, 1553, p. 314; 1560–3, p. 99. [3] *Trans. Dev. Assoc.* xlv. 417–30; Exeter city lib. Dartmouth mss 1982, f. 197v; 2002,

f. 19v; 2003, f. 6; *Devon Monastic Lands* (Devon and Cornw. Rec. Soc. n.s. i), 108–9; J. Hoker, *The description of the citie of Excester* (Devon and Cornw. Rec. Soc. xi), 755. [4] PCC 26 Holney; C142/156/18.

R.V

PETRE, John II (by 1517–81), of Exeter and Bowhay, Devon.

EXETER 1554 (Nov.)

b. by 1517, prob. s. of Otes Petre of Exeter and Bowhay. *m.* (1) by 1538, Wilmot, da. of John Petre of Tor Newton in Torbryan, 4s. 1da.; (2) Alice, da. of Walter Smith of Totnes, wid. of John Hurst (*d*.1555), 4s. 3da.[1]
    Bailiff, Exeter 1553–4, member, the Twenty-Four Sept. 1554–?*d*., receiver 1555–6, sheriff 1556–7, mayor 1557–8, 1562–3, 1575–6; gov. merchant adventurers 1560–1.[2]

John Petre's parentage is variously stated in the visitations, but that of 1620, which makes him the son of Otes Petre, receives some support from the recurrence of this unusual christian name among the Petres of Compton, Devon, to whom he was closely related and to whose properties in various places his own were adjacent. With their and his namesakes of Torbryan he was also connected, perhaps more remotely, before he married one of them and so became the brother-in-law of John Petre I*, Robert Petre† and (Sir) William Petre*. Of Petre's career before becoming a freemen of Exeter in 1553 nothing else has come to light.[3]

A merchant whose business included the import of Gascon wine, Petre was one of the founder members of the Exeter merchant adventurers in 1559 and became their first governor. His second wife was the widowed daughter-in-law of the Exeter merchant William Hurst* and sister of Bernard Smith* of Totnes. He made regular purchases of land, including the manor of Polisloe from Sir Arthur Champernon* in 1554 and the manor of Charleston from William Herbert*, 1st Earl of Pembroke, in 1561, and he is said to have rebuilt his house at Bowhay. His single election to Parliament came early in his civic career; coinciding as it did with the return of John Petre I it may have owed something to his other brother-in-law the secretary of state. He was not one of the Members who quitted this Parliament without leave before its dissolution.[4]

Petre died on 3 Oct. 1581 and was buried two days later in St. Mary Arches. His heir was his son Otes, aged 30 years and more, his eldest son having predeceased him. By his will, made on 8 Dec. 1579 and proved on 4 Nov. 1581, he made bequests to the surviving children of his two marriages for whom he had not already made provision, and to several others of his kin.[5]

¹ Date of birth estimated from marriage. *Vis. Devon* (Harl. Soc. vi), 210; *Vis. Devon*, ed. Colby, 169; *Vis. Devon*, ed. Vivian, 592; *Trans. Dev. Assoc.* xlv. 429; C142/198/41. ² R. Izacke, *Exeter* (1681), 52, 127–8, 130, 135; *CPR*, 1558–60, p. 427; Exeter act bk. 2, ff. 134, 146, 156. ³ *Trans. Dev. Assoc.* xlv. 417–30; *Exeter Freemen* (Devon and Cornw. Rec. Soc. extra ser. 1), 79. ⁴ *CPR*, 1557–8, p. 66; 1558–60, pp. 52, 427; 1560–3, p. 146; 1566–9, p. 436; *CSP Dom.* 1547–80, p. 217; *Trans. Dev. Assoc.* xliv. 207–8; xlv. 425. ⁵ C142/198/41; PCC 36 Darcy.

A.D.K.H.

PETRE, William (1505/6–72), of Ingatestone, Essex, and Aldersgate Street, London.

?DOWNTON   1536[1]
ESSEX   1547
?ESSEX   1553 (Mar.)[2]
ESSEX   1553 (Oct.), 1554 (Apr.), 1554 (Nov.),[3] 1555, 1558, 1559, 1563

b. 1505/6, s. of John Petre of Tor Newton in Torbryan, Devon by Alice, da. of John Collinge of Woodland, Devon; bro. of John I* and Robert†. *educ.* Oxf. adm. by 1519; fellow, All Souls 1523; BCL and BCnL 1526; DCL 1533; adv. Doctors' Commons 8 Mar. 1533. *m.* (1) ?Feb. 1534, Gertrude (*d.*28 May 1541), da. of Sir John Tyrrell of Warley, Essex, 1s. *d.v.p.* 2da.; (2) by Mar. 1542, Anne (*d.*10 Mar. 1582), da. of William Browne of Flambards Hall, Essex and London, wid. of John Tyrrell (*d.*1540) of Heron in East Thorndon, Essex, 4s. inc. Sir John† 2da. Kntd. Jan. 1544.[4]

Proctor, ct. chancellor, univ. Oxf. by 1527–8; principal, Peckwater Inn, Oxf. Jan. 1530–Feb. 1534; clerk in Chancery by 1533, master 1536–41; official principal and commissary to Cromwell as vicegerent 13 Jan. 1536–40; canon of Lincoln and prebendary of Langford Ecclesia Nov. 1536–Apr. 1537; receiver of petitions in the Lords, Parlts. of 1539, 1542; King's Councillor 5 Oct. 1540; principal sec. 21 Jan. 1544–Mar. 1557; j.p. Essex by 1544–*d.*; PC by 1545–*d.*; custos rot. Essex 1547–*d.*; keeper, seal *ad causas ecclesiasticas* 18 Aug. 1548; treasurer, ct. first fruits and tenths 22 Oct. 1549–25 Jan. 1553; commr. relief, Essex 1550, chantries 1553; gov. Chelmsford g.s. 1551; chancellor, order of the Garter 27 Sept. 1553.[5]

William Petre came of a family of Devon yeomen, his father being a farmer and tanner assessed at £40 in goods for the subsidy of 1523. Petre was probably the second son and he was fortunate to be sent to Oxford, where he early distinguished himself by his learning. He is said to have been engaged by the Earl of Wiltshire as tutor to his son George Boleyn at some time between 1526 and 1529, and in June 1529 he received his first royal appointment, being nominated one of the King's two proctors or advocates in the trial before the papal legates, Campeggio and Wolsey, of the validity of Henry VIII's marriage to Catherine of Aragon. Petre was one of the lawyers sent by the King to the Continent in 1530 to obtain opinions from universities on the marriage; the Earl of Wiltshire was in the same year sent ambassador to Charles V at Bologna but it is not known whether Petre travelled with his patron or on a separate mission. By 1535 he had commended himself to Cromwell, for in November of that year the minister proposed him to Archbishop Cranmer for the post of dean or presiding judge of the court of arches: Petre did not obtain the post, but in January 1536 he was appointed deputy in ecclesiastical matters to Cromwell, by then vicegerent to Henry VIII, and in that capacity he presided over an important session of Convocation on 16 June 1536 in St. Paul's cathedral. In the same year he was appointed one of the visitors of the monasteries, an appointment which was to occupy most of his time for several years. On the surviving evidence it can be said that Petre worked hard and conscientiously in the Dissolution, avoiding both the financial dishonesty and the disreputable behaviour of which some other visitors were accused. He received for his services a grant of the priory and manors of Clatercote and certain adjoining lands, worth about £70 a year in all; in addition various monastic houses before their dissolution granted him annuities or pensions, the total of which by 1540 amounted to over £100 a year.[6]

Petre married into the Essex family of Tyrrell, but when not abroad or on monastic visitations he first seems to have made his home in London. In 1537 he acquired lands in south Essex from monastic and private owners and in May 1538 he took from the convent of Barking a lease of the manor of Ging Abbess, which became the nucleus of a large estate at what is now Ingatestone. In 1539 and 1540 he purchased, through the court of augmentations, further lands in Essex, Oxfordshire and Somerset. It has been calculated that by the end of 1540 Petre had laid out over £1,600 on the purchase of lands and that they yielded him in rents and sales some £500 a year. As a visitor Petre would have had the detailed knowledge of monastic lands necessary for prudent buying. After his first wife's death in 1541 he married again within a year: his new wife brought him, in addition to a marriage portion of 400 marks, lands in Cambridgeshire, Essex and Hampshire worth £280 a year.

From 1536 to 1541 Petre served as one of the 12 masters in Chancery, and as such was one of three persons appointed in November 1536 to receive, examine and burn papal bulls, licences and dispensations. By 1539 or 1540 he was one of those empowered to hear cases in the court of requests; although he took some part in the court's work, most of it was probably dealt with by the two or three 'ordinary' or full-time masters. Petre also sat in at least one case in the court of Admiralty, perhaps as coadjutor, for he does not seem to have been a regular judge there. He took part in the examination of Robert Aske in the Tower in 1537 after the failure of the Pilgrimage of Grace, and was one of the six administrators of the estate of Queen Catherine of Aragon whose appointment was intended to enable the King to appropriate her possessions with some show of legality. In April 1539 he was one of the commissioners who drafted the bill which later became the Act of Six Articles, but when in September Cromwell recommended him to Cranmer as master of the faculties in the consistory court at Canterbury, Cranmer had already promised the post to another. Like the earlier suggestion that he might be made dean of the court of arches, the proposal may mean that Petre was inclined to exchange political life for a career as a civilian. In the struggle for power that preceded Cromwell's fall in 1540 he seems to have been useful to each side without becoming involved: he examined Tunstall in the Tower, searched Cromwell's house by warrant from the King and was appointed a commissioner to test the validity of the marriage to Anne of Cleves. His own emergence from the crisis was signalized by his admission to the Council, and when he was straightway accused before that body by a former monk of Christchurch, Canterbury, of concealing treasons alleged against the prior, the matter was held to be 'false and malicious' and he was absolved. During Sir John Gage's* absence in the north in 1543–4 he was deputy keeper of the seal of the duchy of Lancaster.[7]

In January 1544 Petre was knighted and appointed one of the King's two principal secretaries, the other being William Paget; a member of the Privy Council *virtute officii*, he attended its meetings regularly. He was one of the six persons authorized to sign documents with a stamp of the King's signature and one of the five appointed to advise Queen Catherine Parr during her regency in July 1544. Petre drafted most of the letters sent by the Council while the King was in France and Paget also abroad; in the following April he himself went to Brussels to negotiate a settlement of commercial disputes, returning in July. In common with well-nigh all his colleagues at the centre of affairs during these years, Petre was content to execute decisions made by the King; not for him More's advice to Cromwell to advise the King what he should do rather than what he could, and the Earl of Surrey's complaint that 'the kingdom has never been well' since 'mean creatures' were in government was probably as much a criticism of this limited conception of ministerial duty as of the social origins of those who held it. Petre was actively concerned in the raising of money for the French war by securing loans from foreign bankers and by his membership of commissions for the sale of crown lands, chiefly ex-monastic; in September 1546 he and the dean of St. Paul's were sent to France to negotiate the settlement of a dispute between the

two countries about an outstanding French debt, but they were not successful in their mission.[8]

It is not known for certain that Petre sat in the Commons during Henry VIII's reign, but his connexion with Cromwell and his later advancement make it likely that he did, and the supposition receives some support. There is first a list, believed to be in Cromwell's hand, of the names of three boroughs normally in the gift of the bishop of Winchester, with corresponding names of persons several of whom were Members later; one of the names is Petre's and it appears against the borough of Downton. The document is undated but is included among papers of 1536, and as Stephen Gardiner was abroad at the time of the elections for the Parliament of that year, Cromwell may have nominated Members for these episcopal boroughs and Petre have begun his long parliamentary career as a Member for Downton in the brief Parliament of 1536. For his Membership of its successor in 1539, which on general grounds is highly probable, the circumstantial evidence is less strong. He was named one of the receivers of petitions and was also involved in the preparation of the Act of Six Articles, but neither of these assignments implies that he sat in the Commons: if he did so, it must have been for a borough, as the names of the knights of the shire, and of the representatives of most cities, are known. For the Parliament of 1542 more names have survived, but not those for Essex or either of its boroughs; it seems to have been on this negative evidence that Browne Willis included Petre as knight of the shire for Essex, but his guess is weakened by the fact that Petre did not sit for the county in the next Parliament. On that occasion, however, Petre was present in the House of Lords. By an Act of 1539 (31 Hen. VIII, c.10) the principal secretaries, among others, had been given the right to sit in the Lords, and in 1545 Petre was among those who received writs of assistance to that effect. He had probably already made his appearance there in the third session of the previous Parliament, following his appointment, although if a writ was issued it has not survived. It was presumably as one of the secretaries that he attended the prorogation of the first session of the Parliament of 1545 by Henry VIII; he afterwards summarized the King's speech for Paget who was abroad, sent him a schedule of the new enactments and concluded

The bill of books, albeit it was at the beginning set earnestly forward, is finally dashed in the Common House, as are divers others, whereas I hear no[t] his Majesty is much miscontented. The book of colleges etc. escaped narrowly and was driven [over] to the last hour, and yet then passed only by a division of the House.[9]

Petre was reappointed principal secretary on the accession of Edward VI. He had not been named an executor of Henry VIII's will but only an assistant, and he was the only person in either group who was not left a legacy, although he apparently contrived to secure payment of £200, the standard amount for an assistant executor, by October 1547. As an assistant Petre did not immediately rejoin the Privy Council; a month elapsed before he and the other assistants did so. In August 1547 the Protector Somerset entrusted to Petre the royal seal for ecclesiastical causes; he had become sole principal secretary two months earlier, when Paget was appointed chancellor of the duchy of Lancaster, but Paget continued to take the lead in deciding questions of policy. In April 1548 (Sir) Thomas Smith I* was appointed second principal secretary, to act jointly with Petre, but was replaced, after Somerset's fall in 1549, by Nicholas Wotton, and he in turn by William Cecil. His secretarial duties seem to have occupied Petre's time fully for most of the next two years. He was on the commission to visit Oxford and reform the university's statutes, but he did not take much part in the work: in August 1549, with Cecil and Smith, he was appointed by the Council to examine all printed books before publication, a censorship which he carried on alone for the rest of the reign.[10]

In the manoeuvrings of October 1549 which led to Somerset's fall, Petre was careful not to identify himself clearly with the protagonists until the issue of their struggle was beyond doubt. Being with Somerset and the King at Hampton Court on 5 Oct. 1549 when the conflict seemed imminent, he was sent to London and arrived there the next day to demand of the Earl of Warwick and the other Councillors the purpose of their assembly and of their proposed journey to Hampton Court, and to warn them that 'If they meant to talk with the Protector, they should come in a peaceable manner'. Arrived in London, Petre found that the majority of the Council supported Warwick and he accordingly remained with them, to draft their letters in the epistolary war which followed. Petre insured himself against a charge of defection by including in the Council's letter the phrase: 'Almost all your Council being now here we have for the better service of your Majesty caused your secretary to remain here with us'; whether Petre did so under duress cannot be known. On 8 Oct. Secretary Smith, who remained with Somerset, wrote a personal appeal to Petre to help in securing honourable terms: 'Now is the time', he wrote, 'when you may show yourself to be of that nature whereof I have heard you and, as I think, worthily, glory, that is no seeker of extremity nor blood but of moderation in all things'. In the

event Petre did not exercise any moderating influence on Warwick; the proclamation drafted by Petre and issued by the Council in answer to Somerset's own was a flat rejection of the pleas for moderation and a demand for unconditional surrender. Petre also drafted the two letters sent on 10 Oct., one to Somerset and the King, the other to Cranmer, Paget and Smith, which carried conflicting messages designed to secure Somerset's apprehension without bloodshed. His conduct can be defended only on the assumption that he believed Somerset's instant removal necessary to avert civil war. Somerset went to the Tower with his followers, including Smith, whose secretaryship was given to Wotton. Petre seems to have been honest, even generous, in the share of the secretary's fees which he paid to Smith on his release.[11]

Petre not only retained his secretaryship but was also given, on 20 Oct., the treasurership of the court of first fruits and tenths. Warwick appointed him one of the four ambassadors to negotiate peace with France in return for the cession of Boulogne in January 1550, and he is said to have been chiefly instrumental in saving England 200,000 crowns during the negotiations; he was also, with three others, deputed in May to complete the signing of the peace on England's behalf. From April 1550 Petre was absent from Council meetings for several months, being seriously ill in Essex. Some of his tasks, for example his part in the lengthy trials of Bonner and Gardiner, Petre evidently owed to his training in the civil law. He was also the man most frequently employed to bear the government's messages to Princess Mary forbidding her to have mass celebrated in her houses. These frequent and doubtless unpleasant missions were a strain on his health; he was ill again in August 1551, after a visit with Richard Rich, 1st Baron Rich, and Sir Anthony Wingfield* which Mary ended with the words: 'I pray God to send you to do well in your souls and bodies too, for some of you have but weak bodies'. When in the early part of 1553 the King worked out a project for dividing the Council into three separate bodies dealing with different branches of its work Petre is known to have revised and systematized the scheme, presumably in consultation with the King.[12]

It was as first knight of the shire for Essex that Petre sat in the Parliament of 1547, as he was to do in every Parliament until 1563: he also had a writ of assistance to the Lords. The traces of his part in the business of the Commons begin in the second session, when on 26 Jan. 1549 a bill about precontracts for marriage was committed to him after its first reading; he was also one of five Members deputed to try a case brought by bill against (Sir)

Nicholas Hare*. In later sessions five bills were committed to him, among them those on ecclesiastical jurisdiction, the dean of Wells's answer to a bill against him, and a bill 'for fantastical prophecies'; the preponderance of religious subjects doubtless reflects Petre's knowledge of church law. Two of the Acts passed during the third session, for a churchyard in West Drayton and for the fine and ransom of the Duke of Somerset, bear his signature. The returns for Essex to Edward VI's second Parliament are incomplete, but the mention of Petre in the Journal as having an apparel bill committed to him shows that he sat in this Parliament, almost certainly as a knight of the shire.[13]

Petre was among the Councillors who secured the assent of the judges to the device altering the succession. In June 1553 (Sir) John Cheke* had been appointed third principal secretary, and it was rumoured that Petre intended to resign, but he did not do so. He took the oath of allegiance to Lady Jane Grey after Edward VI's death and was among the Councillors confined in the Tower by the Duke of Northumberland to ensure their loyalty to her, but when on 19 July 1553 a number of them escaped from the Tower and declared for Mary, Petre was among them. He remained in London to carry on the Council's business when most of his colleagues went to make their submission to Mary. His secretaryship had been brought to an end by Edward VI's death, but Mary re-appointed him and he was sworn of her Council on 30 July. His second wife, a firm Catholic, was a friend of the Queen's and rode with her in procession upon her entry to London; she may have helped to smooth Petre's path back to favour. He prepared a plan for reforming abuses in government and with Gardiner he reviewed the national finances, but his principal concern was with foreign relations, of which for the next four years he was to have almost sole direction. Although the Council under Mary became even larger than it had been under Edward VI, the decision-making body was a group of six or eight Councillors, of whom Petre was invariably one.

Petre avoided committing himself in the matter of the Queen's marriage; once it was settled he helped to conclude the marriage treaty and his support was rewarded by a pension of £250 when Philip came to England. He raised a substantial force from his Essex estates to serve against Wyatt's rebels and may have seen action himself. He took part in the interrogation and trial of rebels both in London and Essex, and was one of those appointed in March 1554 to examine Princess Elizabeth in the Tower about her supposed complicity. He was evidently on good terms with the Earl of Devon, some of whose pos-

sessions he planned to purchase after the earl's departure for Italy although the transaction fell through. It appears that by September 1554 Petre would have liked to resign his secretaryship in favour of Cecil. He took no direct part in the proceedings against Protestants, although a member of the Council which directed and of the Parliament which authorized them. His own religious views remain a matter of conjecture. The papal bull of November 1555—so far as is known, the only one obtained by an Englishman—confirming his title to his ex-monastic lands was a piece of insurance which probably owed less to any particular regard for the sanctions of the Church than to inside information about the Pope's intentions. In June 1555 Paul IV had issued a bull ordering the restoration of church lands which was never published in England, being replaced by another which confirmed the owners of such property in their possession: according to Pole, no-one in England knew about the first bull 'except the Queen's secretary'. During the later part of 1556 Petre was again in poor health and this probably explains his resignation of the secretaryship in March 1557, although dislike of the government's policy both at home and abroad may have come into it. Yet he remained an active member of the Council. He was one of the standing committee appointed to devise means of raising money, among them a revision of the customs system.[14]

In the frequent Parliaments of the reign Petre came rapidly to the fore. During the first of them he had a bill 'for certain artificers to dwell in towns' committed to him and on two occasions he carried bills to the Lords. Before the next one met in April 1554 he was on the committee appointed by the Council 'to consider what laws shall be established in this Parliament and to name men that shall make books thereof'; in the course of the Parliament itself he carried bills from the Commons to the Lords six times. In the Parliaments of November 1554 and of 1555 Petre was evidently recognized as a leading official figure. He carried bills to the Lords four times and had two bills committed to him. The Treasons Act of 1555 (1 and 2 Phil. and Mary, c.10) furnishes a rare glimpse of Petre at work on the drafting of an important bill; he was one of those who, on the Queen's instructions, consulted with the imperial ambassador about the form of the bill introduced in the Commons after a similar bill originating in the Lords had been rejected there. As principal secretary it fell to Petre to act as the Queen's spokesman in the Commons; on 27 Nov. 1554 he transmitted instructions for the House to attend the court to hear Pole's explanation of his legatine mission and on 31 Oct. 1555 he informed the House that the

Queen was 'contented to refuse' the two fifteenths they had voted her. He was one of 20 Members chosen 'to devise articles for aid to the Queen's majesty' in October 1555, one of six chosen to consult with the Lords on the privilege question raised in December 1555 by the case of Gabriel Pleydell*, and one of four sent in November 1555 to tell the young 4th Duke of Norfolk, who had made a personal appearance in the House with his lawyers to demand the furtherance of a bill, that the House would consider his case. An entry in the Journal for 26 Oct. 1555 reads 'Arguments for execution of laws —S. Petre', which suggests that he took a leading part in the debate. In the following Parliament, the last of the reign, he was appointed to the committee to examine the sanctuary rights claimed by Westminster abbey, and the bill placing an embargo on the import of French wines was committed to him after its second reading.[15]

Mary appointed Petre one of the executors of her will and bequeathed him 500 marks, a legacy which he never received because Elizabeth did not allow the provisions of the will to be carried out. He remained a Councillor under Elizabeth and during Cecil's absence in the north in 1559 he was recalled to act as secretary. Elizabeth liked him personally and in July 1563 she passed a few days at Ingatestone, but age, ill health and deafness limited his usefulness. He died on 13 Jan. 1572 at Ingatestone and was buried there. The surviving portraits confirm the impression of a man of high intelligence but aloof and calculating.[16]

[1] LP Hen. VIII, x. 40(ii) citing Cott. Otho C10, f. 218. [2] CJ, i. 25. [3] Huntington Lib. Hastings mss Parl. pprs. [4] Date of birth estimated from age given on portrait, R. C. Strong, Tudor and Jacobean Portraits, 246–7. This biography draws largely on F. G. Emmison, Tudor Sec., individual references to which are not given. DNB; Emden, Biog. Reg. Univ. Oxf. 1501–40, pp. 445–6. [5] Emden, 445; LP Hen. VIII, xx, xxi; CPR, 1547–8, p. 83; 1553–4, p. 160; LJ, i. 103, 165. [6] Bull. IHR, xlvi. 102–6; EHR, lxxxi. 225–35; Elton, Policy and Police, 167, 248; Reform and Renewal, 134–5; D. Knowles, Rel. Orders in Eng. 375; J. E. Oxley, Ref. in Essex, 54, 101, 115, 130, 132. [7] Select Cases in Ct. Requests (Selden Soc. xii), pp. xviii, xix, cv; Sel. Pleas in Ct. Admiralty (Selden Soc. vi), p. lix; Strype, Eccles. Memorials, i(2), 254–5; Somerville, Duchy, i. 394. [8] APC, i. 246; F. M. G. Evans, Principal Sec. of State, 29. [9] Cott. Otho C10, f. 218; C218/1, m. 3; LP Hen. VIII, xx. [10] W. C. Richardson, Ct. Augmentations, 248. [11] Tytler, Edw. VI and Mary, i. 228–30; Cam. Misc. xxv. 136; W. K. Jordan, Edw. VI, i. 506–17. [12] Cam. Misc. xxv. 81–97; Elton, Tudor Rev. in Govt. 230; Bull. IHR, xxxi. 203–10. [13] CJ, i. 7–8, 11, 13–14, 16, 18, 25; House of Lords RO, Original Acts, 3 and 4 Edw. VI, nos. 25, 31. [14] D. M. Loades, Two Tudor Conspiracies, 14n; CSP Span. 1554, p. 315; APC, iv. 398; Oxley, 184–5. [15] CJ, i. 28, 31–36, 38–40, 42–44, 46, 49; W. J. Fitzgerald, 'Treason legislation in Eng. 1547–1603' (London Univ. M.A. thesis, 1963), 52–63, 147; C. G. Ericson, 'Parl. as a legislative institution in the reigns of Edw. VI and Mary' (London Univ. Ph.D. thesis, 1973), 211; Knowles, iii. 375. [16] PCC 1 Petre; Pevsner, Essex, 250; R. C. Strong, The Eng. Icon, 127; Tudor and Jacobean Portraits, 246–7.

D.F.C.

PETTIFER, George (by 1489–1558/59), of Chipping Wycombe, Bucks.

CHIPPING WYCOMBE 1510[1]

b. by 1489, s. of John Pettifer of Chipping Wycombe by Catherine. m. Agnes, 3s. 1da. suc. fa. Feb./Mar. 1505.[2]

Mayor, Chipping Wycombe 1526–7, 1532–5, 1538–9, 1541–2, 1551–2.[3]

George Pettifer was a weaver of an established family in Chipping Wycombe, one of whom was bailiff there in 1490. He must have become a leading freeman by the date of his election to Parliament with Richard Birch, another townsman; both were elected on condition that they served without wages. Pettifer could afford to do so: he owned a fulling mill in the town and in 1524 he was one of the three men to be assessed for subsidy on goods worth £40, only one other being more highly rated, at 200 marks. Pettifer appears to have owned a house called the Antelope in the High Street, from which in 1556 he assigned a rent of 53s.4d. to the mayor and other burgesses. His will was made on 2 Feb. 1558 and proved on 27 Apr. in the following year by his widow Agnes and his son Christopher. He left to two of his sons, Christopher and Rowland, three tenements and meadows which probably included the mill held by Christopher in October 1559.[4]

[1] First Wycombe Ledger Bk. (Bucks. Rec. Soc. xi), no. 61. [2] Presumed to be of age at election. PCC 27 Holgrave; Bucks. RO, D/A/WE/11/270. [3] First Wycombe Ledger Bk. nos. 88, 98; St.Ch.2/32/119; T. Langley, Hundred of Desborough, 79. [4] First Wycombe Ledger Bk. passim; HMC 5th Rep. 564, 565; VCH Bucks. iii. 118, 123; PCC 2 Pynnyng; Subsidy Roll for Bucks. 1524 (Bucks. Rec. Soc. viii), 28; Bucks. RO, D/A/WE/11/270.

M.K.D.

PETYT, Cyriak (by 1517–91), of Boughton under Blean, Kent.

WINCHELSEA 1554 (Apr.)
CHIPPENHAM 1554 (Nov.)*

b. by 1517, s. of William Petyt of Brabourne by a da. of one Gladwines of Herts. m. by 1552, Florence, da. of Robert Charnocke of Holcot, Beds., 5s. 4da.[1]

Servant of John Baker I* by 1543; under steward, manors of Langport, Littlebourne, Minster, Newington Belhouse, Newington Fee, Stodmarsh, Tirlingham and Waltham, Kent 1545; commr. relief, Kent 1550, for heretical books, diocese of Canterbury 1556, division of crown lands, Kent 1557, to survey lands of abpric. of Canterbury 1560; j.p. Kent 1554; surveyor of lands for Cardinal Pole in 1556–7.[2]

Cyriak Petyt, who came of a gentle but relatively undistinguished family, may have been a lawyer. His cousin, John Petyt, a baron of the Exchequer, was of Gray's Inn and although there is no record of the Member's attendance at an inn of court, it was probably he with whom one Dr. Willoughby claimed involvement during the prebendaries' plot against Cranmer, saying that he had never 'reasoned with Pettyd or any other lawyer touching indictments, or any such matter': there was, however, at least one other of Petyt's surname involved in the plot. More-over, he was a friend of John Webbe* of Faversham, Kent, a Catholic lawyer who joined him in purchas-ing a lease at Boughton under Blean and who left him a gelding, two gowns and £5; Petyt also often acted as a feoffee and as an overseer of wills, including those of Webbe himself, of Nicholas Crispe* and of his father (Sir) Henry Crispe*.[3]

The earliest reference to Petyt concerns his lease in November 1538 of tithes at Stockbury and Borden, late of St. Augustine's abbey, Canterbury. He may have inherited a link with this monastery, as the *valor ecclesiasticus* of 1535 recorded that its manor and rectory at Selling were let to William Petyt, 'generosus'. Presumably Cyriak Petyt was a man of some importance by March 1539, when he was admitted a freeman of Canterbury and, for reasons unspecified, excused from paying for the privilege. In the following year he acquired a grain rent from the farm of Ickham manor and the lease of a meadow at Westbere.[4]

Petyt's role in the prebendaries' plot reveals his conservative sympathies. At Easter 1543 a group of Cranmer's clergy denounced the archbishop's allegedly excessive zeal for reform in a petition which was presented to Henry VIII with the approval of Sir John Baker and the bishop of Win-chester. The King, instead of punishing Cranmer as a heretic, appointed him judge in his own cause by ordering him to conduct an inquiry. The resulting depositions show that Petyt, who was identified as Baker's servant, had helped to draw up the charges and that his confederates had included Speaker Moyle. Although Cranmer's accusers were forced to sue for his pardon, there were no setbacks to the careers of Baker or Moyle, either of whom might have assisted Petyt's advancement. In September 1544 Petyt paid £476 for former monastic property in Canterbury and London, in the following year he was given charge of eight Kent manors belonging to the court of augmentations, and in 1547 he attended the funeral of Henry VIII as an esquire. He pur-chased no further lands under Edward VI, during whose reign he is recorded on only one commission, but in November 1554 Petyt and John Webbe paid £80 for the remainder of a lease at Boughton under Blean, which had reverted to the see of Canterbury (whose temporalities were then in the Queen's hands) on the suicide of Sir James Hales, son of John Hales I*. That the lease was thus forfeit was un-successfully disputed by Hales's widow in the cele-brated lawsuit, *Hales v. Petit*. Petyt and his family were living at Boughton by May 1557, when they acquired further lands at Faversham and Graveney.[5]

Mary's reign saw Petyt become more active in public life. On 11 Mar. 1554 it was agreed at Winchelsea 'by the whole assent and consent of all the commons that the lord warden shall have the nomination of the burgesses for the Parliament for this time'. The lord warden, Sir Thomas Cheyne*, a conservative and Nicholas Crispe's father-in-law, must therefore have been responsible for the return of Petyt and Joseph Beverley to Mary's second Parliament. One of the Members for Winchelsea in the previous Parliament had been Sir Thomas More's son-in-law William Roper, whose brother Christopher Roper* was Petyt's neighbour. Petyt must have been well known to the More family circle, several of whom had been involved in the prebendaries' plot. William Roper figures largely in John Webbe's will and his own will of 1577 refers to lands let to a Mr. Petyt. On 3 Nov. 1554 Sir Thomas Moyle was returned for Chippenham to the third Parliament of the reign, but after deciding to sit for Lynn, where he had also been elected, Petyt replaced Moyle at Chippenham on 20 Nov., eight days after the opening of Parliament. As all his property lay in the capital or in Kent, Petyt must have owed his election to official favour: this may have been secured through Moyle or Sir John Baker, who continued to hold high office and with whom he sat on many local commissions, including those for the punishment of heretics. Petyt was not one of those who 'seceded' from this Parliament.[6]

Petyt's engagement in local affairs may have pre-vented him from seeking election to Mary's later Parliaments and his Catholicism explains his later obscurity. There are few further notices of him. In February 1560 he was released from the forfeiture of a marriage and annuity due under the wardship of the son and heir of John Newland, which he had been granted in 1548 but for which he had no patent. A similar release was made to him in October 1562, concerning the wardship of the son and heir of Robert Browne, a citizen and grocer of Canterbury, granted to him in June 1545.[7]

In his will Petyt asked to be buried next to his wife at Boughton. He left his manor of Colkyns in Boughton and other lands to be held by his eldest son Henry and Henry's wife Mary for their two lives, with remainder in tail male and further remainder to the testator's younger sons, John and Thomas. He also mentioned two daughters, Eliza-beth, wife of John Dryland, and Anne, wife of Thomas Hawkins of Nash Court, Boughton, by whom she was the mother of the three literary brothers, Henry, John and Sir Thomas. In 1588 one of Petyt's sons, presumably Henry, and his wife with these two daughters and their husbands had appeared on a list of Kent recusants. Petyt was buried at Boughton on 15 Oct. 1591, where a brass was erected to his memory, and his will was proved on 4 Apr. 1592.[8]

[1] Date of birth estimated from first reference. *LP Hen. VIII*, xiv; *Vis. Kent* (Harl. Soc. lxxv), 19–20; *CPR*, 1555–7, p. 379; *Vis. Beds.* (Harl. Soc. xix), 12; *Boughton under Blean Regs.* ed. Boodle, 70; *Arch. Cant.* xxii. 189; Mill Stephenson, *Mon. Brasses*, 211. [2] *LP Hen. VIII*, xviii, xxi; *CPR*, 1553, pp. 355, 361; 1553–4, pp. 21, 36; 1555–7, p. 24; 1557–8, pp. 364, 398; 1558–60, p. 422; SP11/11, f. 130v. [3] *LP Hen. VIII*, xviii; L. W. Abbott, *Law Reporting in Eng.* 225 describes him as of Gray's Inn; *CPR*, 1550–3, p. 70; 1554–5, p. 102; PCC 8 Wrastley, 41 Pyckering, 1 Martyn. [4] *LP Hen. VIII*, xiv, xv; *Val. Eccles.* i. 21; Canterbury accts. Mich. 1538–9. [5] *LP Hen. VIII*, xviii, xix, xxi; LC2/2, f. 68v; *CPR*, 1554–5, p. 102; 1555–7, p. 379; E. Plowden, *Commentaries* (1779), 253–64; Abbott, 226. [6] Winchelsea hundred ct. bk. f. 56; *Arch. Cant.* xlv. 207–8; PCC 27 Langley; Foxe, *Acts and Mons.* vii. 292, 295. [7] *CPR*, 1558–60, p. 343; 1560–3, p. 251. [8] Canterbury prob. reg. C24, f. 24; *Kentish Wills*, ed. Clarke, 94–95; *Boughton under Blean Regs.* 79; *DNB* (Hawkins, Henry, John and Sir Thomas); *London Recusant*, ii. 1–11; *Cath. Rec. Soc.* xxii. 122; Mill Stephenson, loc. cit.; W. D. Belcher, *Kentish Brasses*, i. 16; ii. 22.

T.F.T.B.

PETYT, John (by 1464–1532), of London.

LONDON 1529*

b. by 1464, s. of Nicholas Petyt of Dent-le-Dale, Yorks. *m.* (1) by 1485; (2) 1521, Lucy (*d.*28 Nov. 1558), da. of John Wattes of London, at least 1s. 2da.[1] Warden, Grocers' Co. 1519–20; auditor, London 1523–5, 1529–31.[2]

John Petyt came from the town of Dent-le-Dale, Yorkshire. Both he and his father were there styled yeomen, but a connexion between them and the gentle family of Kent is shown by the bequest of 40s. made in 1485 by Valentine Petyt, esquire, of the Isle of Thanet, to 'John Petyt the younger, of London, grocer, and to his wife'. In the pedigree drawn up on the heralds' visitation of Kent in 1574 John Petyt, 'alderman of London' (which Petyt never was), appears as Valentine Petyt's son: he may have been a nephew.[3]

Petyt dwelt in London for some 50 years, but not until late in life did he rise to any prominence. During the first decade of the 16th century—but apparently not thereafter—he exported cloth in considerable quantity: for the rest his career is sparsely documented until 1520, when he began to be employed in city government. In that year he was among those named by the court of aldermen to consider a petition of Billingsgate porters for the foundation of a fraternity of St. Christopher, in 1521 he was one of those charged with drawing up new rates for the admission of freemen by redemption, in 1522 he shared in the assessment of aldermen for the loan of £20,000 to the King, and in 1523 he and others were asked 'to devise what things be most necessary and behoveful for the common weal of this City to be moved at this next Parliament'. In 1529 he was himself elected to Parliament by the commonalty of London.[4]

From this point all the evidence for his career comes from a single source, the account of 'an ancient Protestant called Mr. John Petyt' sent by the archdeacon of Nottingham to John Foxe in 1579. The archdeacon, John Louthe, was not writing from his own knowledge, for he was still a child at the time of the events he recounted, and although his story ended 'teste ipsius uxore Lucia Petyt', Petyt's widow had died 21 years before Louthe sent his manuscript, written in his own hand, to Foxe. Louthe may well have acquired his information from Lucy Petyt, who after her third marriage lived at Worksop, Nottinghamshire, but the account as it stands contains too many inconsistencies to be a transcription of a first-hand narrative. Foxe for his part used only a fraction of the material sent to him by Louthe, perhaps because he had good cause to doubt the accuracy of another of Louthe's narratives, an embellished version of the examination of Anne Askew originally printed by Foxe himself.[5]

Louthe's account begins:

This John Petyt was one of the first that with Mr. Frith, Bilney and Tyndale caught a sweetness in God's word. He was 20 years burgess for the city of London, and free of the grocers, eloquent and well spoken, exactly seen in histories, song and the Latin tongue. King Henry VIII would ask in the Parliament time, in his weighty affairs, if Petyt were of his side; for once when the King required to have all those sums of money to be given him by Act of Parliament which afore he had borrowed of certain persons, John Petyt stood against the bill, saying, 'I can not in my conscience agree and consent that this bill should pass, for I know not my neighbours' estate. They perhaps borrowed it to lend the King. But I know mine estate, and therefore I freely and frankly give the King that I lent him'.

Petyt was elected for the first and only time in 1529, to the Parliament summoned in the 21st year of Henry VIII's reign. He was thus a Member of the Parliament which during its first session released to the King all sums of money previously raised by loan (21 Hen. VIII, c.24) and could have made this speech in the debate upon the bill: whether his remarks had the effect upon Henry VIII which Louthe ascribed to them is a matter for conjecture.[6]

'This burgess', the account continued, 'was sore suspected of the lord chancellor and the prelacy of this realm, that he was a fautor of the religion that they called new, and also a bearer with them in printing of their books. Therefore Mr. [Thomas] More cometh upon a certain time to his house at Lion's Quay, then called Petyt's Quay, and knocking at the door, Mrs. Petyt came toward the door and seeing that it was the lord chancellor she whipped in haste to her husband, being in his closet at his prayers, saying, 'Come, come, husband, my lord chancellor is at the door, and would speak with you'. At the same word the lord chancellor was in the closet at her back. To whom Mr. Petyt spoke with great courtesy, thanking him that it would please his lordship to visit him in his own poor house;

but, because he would not drink, he attended upon him to the door, and, ready to take his leave, asked him if his lordship would command him any service. 'No', quoth the chancellor, 'you say you have none of these new books?' 'Your lordship saw', said he, 'my books and my closet'. 'Yet', quoth the chancellor, 'you must go with Mr. Lieutenant. 'Take him to you', quoth the chancellor to the lieutenant. Then he was laid in a dungeon upon a pad of straw, in close prison.

Although More did not see it, there was a New Testament in the forbidden translation under Petyt's desk, but the 'little old priest' who had been ready to testify that Petyt possessed Tyndale's Testament and had helped in its publication, at the last denied all knowledge of Petyt, who was thereupon released. During his imprisonment, however, he had 'caught his death' and he died immediately after his return home. He was replaced in the Commons by William Bowyer.[7]

The role of the chancellor in this story—personally arresting on suspicion of heresy one of London's Members—seems designed to discredit More, although a Member's privilege of freedom from arrest gave no protection against the crown. The improbabilities are compounded by 'a strange thing or two' which Louthe added to the main story, of how John Frith, while a prisoner in the Tower visited Petyt at his home, by the connivance of the keeper, and how Petyt himself while in the Tower was allowed to dine with Bilney in the cell above. Bilney was never in the Tower after 1529, when Petyt was certainly still at liberty, but was condemned and burnt for heresy at Norwich in 1531. Frith went to the Tower at some date between 25 July and 21 Oct. 1532, and could therefore have been allowed out to visit Petyt, who died in August 1532, only during a short period if Petyt's death followed 'immediately' upon his release.[8]

Petyt had made his will on 22 Aug. 1531, 12 months before he died, leaving the lease of his house and quay to his wife and dividing his goods between her and his children. He was not a rich man (his assessment to the subsidy of 1523 was only £200 in goods) 'albeit', as the archdeacon's account has it, 'he had great riches by his first wife (being his mistress and a widow) and especially by his second wife'. His comparative poverty was ascribed to the fact that the chancellor, 'of a popish charity', made him pay the forfeit for the non-appearance of a sick friend for whom he stood surety, and to the generosity of his gifts to the poor, 'specially to poor preachers, such as then were on this side the sea and beyond the sea', debts which he entered in his accounts as 'lent unto Christ'. Petyt's estate at his death therefore amounted to no more than £160, beside his house in the city and lands in Shoreditch

and Walthamstow. His title to some of this property, moreover, was being contested at the time of his death. The lands in Shoreditch were of the inheritance of his second wife and her mother disputed his right to them, while the lease of his house and quay, held of the chamber of London, had expired and was sought by an alderman, Richard Choppyn. In this matter Lucy Petyt, who in her husband's lifetime had appealed for assistance to Cromwell, secured the minister's support. Writing to the mayor and aldermen on 9 Oct. 1532, Cromwell asked for the renewal of Petyt's lease at the old rent in favour of the widow, since Petyt was 'a true and loving citizen and from time to time exceeding painful in the procurement of your common affairs'. On the widow's marriage to John Parnell, however, Choppyn evicted her.[9]

[1] Date of birth estimated from first reference. LP Hen. VIII, i; Narr. Ref. (Cam. Soc. lxxvii), 28, 299; PCC 12 Maynwaryng, 36 Milles. [2] Wardens of Grocers' Co. ed. Grantham, 16; City of London RO, Guildhall, jnl. 12, ff. 244v, 293v; 13, ff. 153v, 238. [3] C67/57; PCC 36 Milles; Vis. Kent (Harl. Soc. lxxv), 20–21. [4] E122/79/12, 80/2, 4, 5 ex inf. Prof. P. Ramsey; City of London RO, rep. 4, ff. 58, 84v, 145v; jnl. 12, ff. 118v, 188; 13, f. 149v (where in the record of his election to Parliament he is described as grocer, not common pleader as in Beaven, Aldermen of London, i. 274. The common pleader was the John Petyt who later became a baron of the Exchequer). [5] Narr. Ref. 7, 14, 40n, 299. [6] Ibid. 25–26. [7] Ibid. 26–27. [8] Ibid. 27. [9] Ibid. 28, 296; E179/251/15; C1/875/8–10, 707/38–40, 866/23; LP Hen. VIII, vii; City of London RO, rep. 8, f. 242.

H.M.

PEYTON, Edmund (by 1518–?58), of Calais.

CALAIS 1553 (Oct.), 1555

b. by 1518, s. of (?Richard) Peyton by Alice, da. of one Layson. prob. unm.[1]

Customer of the Lantern gate, Calais 11 Apr. 1541–12 May 1552; jt. (with Thomas Fowler*), waterbailiff, Calais 9 Aug. 1546–Mar. 1556 or later, sole by July 1556–8, alderman by 1553, mayor 1554–5.[2]

Edmund Peyton was of gentle birth and belonged to the family at Isleham in Cambridgeshire, his father being almost certainly Richard, the younger brother of Edward*, John* and Robert Peyton I*. Richard Peyton was provided for in a family settlement of 1514 but little else is known about him apart from his death in the early 1520s; that he left a widow and an heir is inferred from the marriage of Edmund Peyton's mother to Thomas Fowler by 1527 and from the interest shown by the childless Edward Peyton in Edmund's well-being. Edmund Peyton seems to have been brought up by his stepfather, whose orthodoxy he shared, but he is first glimpsed in 1539 as one of his uncle Edward's deputies as customer of the Lantern gate at Calais, serving under Thomas Broke*. After Broke's attack on the mass in the Parliament of 1539 Peyton gave evidence in London against him. According to Foxe, Peyton acted 'out of love' for the customership 'rather than the truth of the matter ... through frailty of youth' but later regretted it; in return he gained the reversion of his uncle's post after Broke had been deprived of it. He and Broke were to be reconciled, but Peyton kept the customership until the reorganization of Edward VI's reign.[3]

In 1546 Peyton joined his stepfather as water-bailiff of Calais and after Fowler's death ten years later he held the post alone until the fall of the town. He was chosen to sit in the first Marian Parliament by the deputy and his council and in the third by the mayor and town council; on both occasions he was joined in the House by his uncle John Peyton. Neither of the Peytons opposed the initial measures to restore Catholicism but the 'Mr. Peyton' who voted against one of the government's bills in 1555 was probably the uncle. Edmund Peyton's end is obscure. The final meeting of the council of Calais was held in his house on the market place in the early hours of 7 Jan. 1558, but no further trace of him has been found. As he was not mentioned when the settlement of 1514 was invoked on his uncle John's death in the following autumn he may be presumed to have died earlier in the year, but whether in action at Calais or from natural causes is not known.[4]

[1] Date of birth estimated from first reference. PCC 10 Ketchyn. [2] *LP Hen. VIII*, xvi, xxi; *Rep. R. Comm. of 1552* (Archs. of Brit. Hist. and Culture iii). 164; *CPR*, 1550–3, p. 296; C219/21/211; Egerton 2094, f. 129. [3] *Vis. Cambs.* (Harl. Soc. xli), 4–5, C142/121/104; PCC 6 Populwell, 10 Ketchyn; *LP Hen. VIII*, xiii, xv; Foxe, *Acts and Mons.* v. 509–10; *Rep. R. Comm. of 1552*, p. 167. [4] *LP Hen. VIII*, xx, xxi; *CPR*, 1550–3, p. 404; P. T. J. Morgan, 'The govt. of Calais, 1485–1558' (Oxf. Univ. D. Phil. thesis, 1966), 264; C142/121/104.

A.D.K.H.

PEYTON, Edward (by 1501–48), of London and Calais.

MALDON   1529

b. by 1501, 3rd *s.* of Sir Robert Peyton of Isleham, Cambs. by Elizabeth, da. of Sir Robert Clere[†] of Ormesby, Norf.; bro. of John* and Robert I*. *unm.*[1]

Gent. usher, the chamber by 1522; bailiff, manor of Desning, keeper, Comby and Southwold parks, Suff. 1522; receiver, duchy of Lancaster, Cambs., Norf. and Suff. Jan. 1526–7; customer of the Lantern gate, Calais 1530–Apr. 1541.[2]

The Peyton family owned extensive lands in Essex, Kent and Suffolk but had its principal seat in Cambridgeshire. Of the two contemporary Edward Peytons one was a younger brother and the other the third son of Sir Robert Peyton, who died in 1518. It is likely that the Member was the son, for the brother was an elderly man who had made no mark, while his younger namesake was a courtier who had a brother, another Robert, in the Parliament of 1529. Granted the reversion of the office of customer at one of the gates of Calais on 16 Jan. 1522, he succeeded to it in 1530 but need not have let it interfere with his attendance at court, as such an office could be farmed and Peyton is known to have dealt with his in this way. The farmer he chose, Thomas Broke*, was not a success, for in January 1540 he was reported to Sir William Fitzwilliam I*, Earl of Southampton, for defrauding the crown of 20*d.* in every £1 of customs revenue received; later he was also accused of heresy, by Peyton among others if his own statement is to be trusted. As Peyton was probably in attendance at court he could have attended Parliament at small expense, and the impoverished borough of Maldon must have been glad to be served by one in favour with the King and unlikely to expect wages. Peyton was given the freedom of Maldon on 18 Oct. 1529, as his fellow-Member Thomas Tey had been two weeks earlier. Despite the King's general request for the re-election of the Members of the previous Parliament, Peyton and Tey were not returned for Maldon in 1536, possibly because they were thought to be partisans of Anne Boleyn.[3]

Little else has come to light about Peyton's life. He remained in the King's favour after his spell in Parliament, for in 1540 he was granted an annuity of 20 marks out of the revenues of a Suffolk manor. He made his will and died at Knowlton, Kent, in 1548, between 27 Apr. and 15 May. Most of his property he left to Anne Cawnton, whom he made his executrix, and he bequeathed an annuity to his nephew Edmund Peyton*, who had succeeded him in the customership at Calais in April 1541.[4]

[1] Date of birth estimated from first reference. *Vis. Cambs.* (Harl. Soc. xli), 4; C142/33/1, 12, 109. [2] *LP Hen. VIII*, iii, iv, xiii; Somerville, *Duchy*, i. 597; P. T. J. Morgan, 'The govt. of Calais, 1485–1558' (Oxf. Univ. Ph.D. thesis, 1966), 302. [3] *LP Hen. VIII*, xiv, xv; Morant, *Essex*, ii. 159, 180; *Colchester Oath Bk.* ed. Benham, 142; Essex RO, D/B3/1/2, f. 78. [4] *LP Hen. VIII*, xv, xvi; PCC 6 Populwell; C142/121/104.

D.F.C.

PEYTON, John (by 1500–58), of Knowlton, Kent.

HASTINGS   1553 (Oct.),[1] 1554 (Nov.)
WINCHELSEA   1555

b. by 1500, 2nd *s.* of Sir Robert Peyton of Isleham, Cambs. by Elizabeth, da. of Sir Robert Clere[†] of Ormesby, Norf.; bro. of Edward* and Robert I*. *m.* by 1539, Dorothy, da. of Sir John Tyndale of Hockwold, Norf., 3s. inc. John[†] 2da.[2]

Commr. relief, Kent 1550; *j.p.* 1554.[3]

In 1554 John Langley of Knowlton settled his property in Kent on his wife Jane with remainder to her nephews John, Edward* and Richard Peyton. Jane Langley took as her second husband Sir Edward Ryngeley*, who died at Knowlton in 1543, and in the following year she conveyed most of her interest in Langley's property to John Peyton, who then took up residence at Knowlton. His return for two of the Cinque Ports was the work of the lord warden, Sir Thomas Cheyne*, who on the second occasion had his name inserted in a blank space left by Hastings on its indenture at Cheyne's bidding. In 1555 Hastings re-elected Thomas Rodes, Peyton's previous fellow-Member, but Peyton transferred to Winchelsea, presumably to make way for Roger Manwood II who had himself been displaced at Sandwich by Cheyne's son-in-law Sir John Perrot. Peyton was one of the Members found absent without leave when the House was called shortly before the dissolution of the Parliament of November 1554 and was accordingly informed against in the King's bench during Easter term 1555, but no further action was taken against him until 1558 when his non-appearance earned him three distraints totalling 10s.4d. If his withdrawal was a gesture of dissent, it serves to identify him, and not his nephew Edmund, with the 'Mr. Peyton' who followed Sir Anthony Kingston's lead in opposing one of the government's bills in 1555, and the two episodes may have cost him Cheyne's support at the next election. Peyton died intestate on 22 Oct. 1558 and on the following day three neighbours put in their claim on the estate for debts of £50. Administration of his goods was granted to his widow three weeks later and the wardship of his son Thomas to Thomas Ludwell in 1560.[4]

¹ Bodl. e Museo 17. ² Date of birth estimated from younger brother Edward's. *Vis. Cambs.* (Harl. Soc. xli), 4-5; *Vis. Kent* (Harl. Soc. lxxv), 142. ³ *CPR*, 1553, p. 355; 1553-4, p. 20. ⁴ C142/121/104; 219/23/184; *Arch. Cant.* xvi. 58; Romney chamberlains' accts. 1528-80, f. 88; KB27/1186-8; 29/188 rot. 48; Guildford mus. Loseley 1331/2; Canterbury prob. reg. A15, f. 61; *CPR*, 1558-60, p. 342.

H.M.

PEYTON, Robert I (by 1498-1550), of Isleham, Cambs.

CAMBRIDGESHIRE   1529

b. by 1498, 1st s. of Sir Robert Peyton of Isleham by Elizabeth, da. of Sir Robert Clere† of Ormesby, Norf.; bro. of Edward* and John*. *m.* by Nov. 1520, Frances, da. and h. of Francis Haselden of Guilden Morden, Cambs. and Chesterford, Essex, 6s. inc. Robert II* 2da. *suc.* fa. 17 Mar. 1518. Kntd. aft. 3 Nov. 1529.[1]

Commr. subsidy, Cambs. 1523, 1524, tenths of spiritualities, Cambridge and Cambs. 1535, musters, Cambs. 1546; other commissions 1530-d.; j.p. Cambs. 1524-d., q. 1547; sheriff, Cambs. and Hunts. 1525-6, 1535-6.[2]

Robert Peyton inherited land in four counties from his father and became for a short time a royal ward; the family had built up estates by marriage with heiresses and Peyton's own marriage brought him and his descendants four entailed Cambridgeshire manors and land in Essex. The names of Peyton Hall manor, Boxford, Suffolk, and of Payton Hall, Alphamstone, Essex, bore witness to the family's long residence in those places; Isleham had become its principal seat in Richard III's reign.[3]

Peyton's wealth and ancestry assured him from early manhood a place on all Cambridgeshire commissions and may have secured him election to the Parliament of 1523, the names for which are lost. He was knighted during the first session of the Parliament of 1529, but as he was pricked sheriff towards its close he presumably did not sit in its short successor of 1536, although he may have done so again in 1545. He performed other duties appropriate to his station, serving at Anne Boleyn's coronation in 1533 and attending the christening of Prince Edward in 1536 and Anne of Cleves's reception in 1540. He was ordered to raise 80 men for service against the northern rebels in 1536 and probably served in 1544 with the vanguard of the army which captured Boulogne, a campaign for which he provided 20 footmen.[4]

Most of Peyton's time was probably spent in the management of his estates, which he seems to have concentrated in Cambridgeshire and Suffolk. In February 1550 Peyton obtained a licence for himself and his immediate family to eat meat during Lent; his will, made in the following July, has a preamble mildly Protestant in tone. After small charitable gifts, he left money to his younger children and divided his purchased Cambridgeshire lands and Isleham manor between them in the event of his eldest son Robert's failing to honour his (unspecified) arrangements as to Wicken manor. He directed his wife, the executrix to pay his debts and bring up their younger sons; Robert was to receive £50 a year for 14 years from the income of Wicken manor, valued in the inquisition post mortem at only £40 a year. Peyton died at Isleham on 1 Aug. 1550, the day after he made his will, and was buried in the church there.[5]

¹ Date of birth estimated from age at fa.'s i.p.m., C142/33/1. *Vis. Cambs.* (Harl. Soc. xli), 4; C1/554/25-26. ² *LP Hen. VIII*, iii-v, viii, xii-xviii, xx, xxi; *CPR*, 1547-8, pp. 75-76, 81; E371/350 r. 31. ³ C142/33/1, 12, 91; *Cat. Arundel mss in Coll. of Arms*, 60c; C1/554/25-26; St.Ch.2/29/137; Morant, *Essex*, ii. 267. ⁴ *LP Hen. VIII*, vi, xi, xii, xiv, xix. ⁵ *LP Hen. VIII*, xi; PCC 27 Coode; C1/554/25-26; 142/93/9; St.Ch.2/29/137; *CPR*, 1549-51, p. 189; Mill Stephenson, *Mon. Brasses*, 63.

D.F.C.

PEYTON, Robert II (by 1523-90), of Isleham, Cambs.

CAMBRIDGESHIRE   1558, 1563*

b. by 1523, 1st s. of Robert Peyton I* of Isleham by Frances, da. and h. of Francis Haselden of Guilden Morden, Cambs. and Chesterford, Essex. *educ.* Jesus, Camb. 1535-6. *m.* by 1550, Elizabeth, da. of Richard Rich, 1st Baron Rich, 3s. inc. John† 3da. *suc.* fa. 1 Aug. 1550.[1]

Commr. relief, Cambs. and Cambridge 1550, goods of churches and fraternities, Cambridge 1553, loan, Cambs. 1562; sheriff, Cambs. and Hunts. 1553-4, 1567-8, 1586-7; j.p. Cambs. 1558/59-d., q. by 1569, I.o.Ely 1564; dep. lt. Cambs. 1569.[2]

Robert Peyton inherited large estates in Cambridgeshire, Essex and Suffolk and, as the son-in-law of Baron Rich and brother-in-law of Roger North*, was eminently fitted to serve a turn as knight of the shire. He was an active local official but his career was otherwise undistinguished, not to say obscure. Nothing has come to light about his life between his education and his succeeding his father. His marriage in or before 1550 might have looked like the prelude to a political career, but Peyton was to rise no higher than the shrievalty. What, if anything, he did when the succession to the throne was contested so near his home we do not know, although his appointment as Queen Mary's first sheriff of Cambridgeshire and Huntingdonshire implies his loyalty to the new regime. It was during this year of office that five prisoners escaped from Cambridge castle gaol, an escape for which Peyton was legally answerable and in respect of which he obtained a pardon in July 1554. He was described as 'conformable' in religion in 1564 and his will, made a week before his death on 19 Oct. 1590, has a long religious preamble.[3]

[1] Date of birth estimated from age at fa.'s i.p.m., C142/93/9. *Vis. Cambs.* (Harl. Soc. xli), 4; PCC 74 Drury; *CPR*, 1549-51, p. 189. [2] *CPR*, 1550-3, p. 395; 1553, pp. 351, 417; 1554-5, p. 109; 1558-60, p. 31; 1560-3, p. 435; 1563-6, pp. 20, 29, 41; 1569-72, p. 215; Osborn Coll. Yale Univ. Lib. 71.6.41. [3] *CPR*, 1553-4, p. 128; *Cam. Misc.* ix(3), 25; PCC 74 Drury; C142/228/76.

D.F.C.

PHAER (FAYRE), Thomas (by 1514-60), of Carmarthen, Carm.; Forest, Cilgerran, Pemb.; and London.

CARMARTHEN BOROUGHS 1547[1]
CARDIGAN BOROUGHS 1555, 1558, 1559

b. by 1514, s. of Thomas Phaer of Norwich, Norf. by Clara or Elery, da. of Sir Richard or Sir William Goodere of London. *educ.* ?L. Inn; Oxf. MB and MD 1559. *m.* (1) at least 1da.; (2) June 1548/Dec. 1551, Agnes, da. of Thomas Walter of Carmarthen, wid. of John Revell (*d.*23 Apr. 1547) of Forest, 2da.[2] Constable and forester, Cilgerran 9 Dec. 1548, steward 1549-*d.*; crown searcher, Milford Haven by May 1556-*d.*, collector, customs 23 Aug. 1559; crown solicitor, council in the marches of Wales by 1558; j.p. Carm. 1555, q. Card., Carm. and Pemb. 1558/59; custos rot. Pemb.[3]

When Thomas Phaer moved to Wales is unknown. On his own showing he was a protégé of William Paulet, later Marquess of Winchester, through whom he first entered the royal service; it was probably Paulet who obtained for him the office of solicitor in the court of the council in the marches at Ludlow. Phaer acknowledged his debt to Paulet, his 'first bringer-up and patron', in the dedication to Queen Mary of his translation of a part of the *Aeneid* in 1558.

Phaer is said to have been in his youth both a student at Oxford and a member of Lincoln's Inn,

but neither statement can be verified. It was, however, with a law book that he first appeared in print. This was his *Natura brevium* published in 1535 and followed eight years later by *A newe boke of presidentes*, a comprehensive formula book of legal documents. Within a year he had broken fresh ground, and there appeared an edition of three short medical works with his translation of *Lentretenement de vie* by Jehan Goevrot, under the title, *The regiment of lyfe*. His declared aim was to make medicine, in particular paediatrics, intelligible to Englishmen in their own language. Why Phaer should have waited until 1559 for the degree of bachelor of medicine can only be guessed at, but a month after receiving the MB (and leave to practise) he gained his doctorate in medicine. He was also a classical scholar of some note, his greatest achievement being his translation into English of the *Aeneid*. Phaer had taught himself Latin, and in 1558 he was granted by Queen Mary the sole right to print and sell the first seven books of the epic which came out that year. He was the first Englishman to attempt a translation of the whole poem, but death prevented its completion: his friend, William Wightman*, saw to the publication of the first nine books and as much of the tenth as could be found at Cilgerran. Phaer himself was a poet in his own right. He wrote a commendatory poem for Peter Betham's translation of Jacopo di Porcia's *The preceptes of warre* (1544) and his 'How Owain Glyn Dwr seduced by false prophecies took upon him to be Prince of Wales' was published in *A myrrour for magistrates* (?1555).[4]

In the late 1540s Phaer was living at Carmarthen where he was assessed for taxation at St. Mary's Street in 1549, his goods being valued at £20. He must have become an important townsman, perhaps making his living in medicine or law, or both, and it was for Carmarthen Boroughs that he first sat in Parliament in 1547. Whether as cause or effect of his establishment there he married a daughter of one of the leading townsmen and widow of a Haverfordwest merchant who had his main residence at Forest. In November 1549 Phaer took a 21-year lease of 110 acres of demesne lands of the lordship of Cilgerran. Cilgerran lies just over the border from the town of Cardigan, and the demesne lands of the lordship may well have extended into Cardiganshire; thus although officially in Pembrokeshire, Phaer was a neighbour of Cardigan and it is from this time that his association with the borough can be dated: his three further appearances in the Commons were all as Member for Cardigan Boroughs. In the reign of Edward VI he and his wife, as administrators of the will of Thomas Revell of Haverfordwest, appeared in Chancery as plaintiffs against Revell's son-in-law,

Richard Howell*, for embezzlement. In the early 1550s Phaer prepared a report on the harbours and customs administration in Wales on the orders of Treasurer Winchester: this was enrolled after Phaer's death on the Queen's remembrancer's memoranda roll for Hilary term 1562. In 1552 Phaer was nominated for the shrievalty of Cardiganshire but was passed over.[5]

During Queen Mary's reign Phaer was active as crown searcher in the port of Milford Haven. In 1556 his duties involved him in a dispute over the cargo of a Breton ship with a number of Carmarthen merchants, including Gruffydd Done*. The *periculum Karmerdini* which Phaer mentioned at the conclusion of his translation of book five of the *Aeneid*, penned on 4 May 1556, must be a reference to this affair. In June of the same year Phaer and his wife obtained the wardship of her son Thomas Revell[†], a grant made eight years earlier to Agnes alone having been left uncompleted. Phaer was evidently in favour under Mary, but the accession of Elizabeth brought no alteration in his fortunes. He made his will on 12 Aug. 1560, requesting George Ferrers* to supply a passage of scripture for his tomb at Cilgerran, and died shortly afterwards, being succeeded as steward there by John Vaughan II* on 26 Sept. following. Phaer's widow married William Jenkins.[6]

[1] Hatfield 207. [2] Date of birth estimated from first reference. Dwnn, *Vis. Wales*, i. 148, 150 where the Gooderes are described as of Herefs.; Fenton, *Pembs.* 505; Emden, *Biog. Reg. Univ. Oxf. 1501–40*, pp. 446–7; PCC 23 Loftes; *DNB*; *DWB*; CP40/1142, r. 491; J. Cule, 'Thomas Phaer MD of Cilgerran', *Trans. Cymmrod. Soc.* 1979, pp. 105–28. [3] *Trans. Cymmrod. Soc.* 1979, p. 109; *CPR*, 1557–8, p. 363; Stowe 571, f. 74v; E159/336, Trin. 23; *Welsh Port Bks.* (Cymmrod. rec. ser. xii), 329–30; J. R. Phillips, *Cilgerran*, 98–102; SP11/5/6; Dwnn, i. 150. [4] Wood, *Ath. Ox.* ed. Bliss, i. 316–18; *CPR*, 1557–8, p. 309; *Trans. Cymmrod. Soc.* 1979, pp. 113, 116–21. [5] E179/263/35; *CPR*, 1553, p. 387; 1557–8, p. 363; C1/1255/13–14; *Bull. Bd. of Celtic Studies*, xxiv. 485–503. [6] E159/336, Trin. 23, Easter 12; *CPR*, 1555–7, p. 74; PCC 23 Loftes ptd. *Shakespeare Soc. Pprs.* iv. 1–5.

P.S.E.

PHELIPS, John (by 1533–58 or later), of Montacute, Som.

WEYMOUTH 1554 (Nov.)[1]
POOLE 1555

b. by 1533.[2]

John Phelips evidently owed his returns for Weymouth and Poole to his kinsman Richard Phelips, himself knight of the shire for Dorset in Mary's third Parliament. Both quitted the House prematurely and without leave and were on that account informed against in the King's bench during Easter term 1555. A writ of *venire facias* was soon afterwards directed to the sheriff of Somerset and Dorset, but no further process was taken against John Phelips until Michaelmas 1558 when he was fined 53s.4d. and gave as his sureties Richard

Fitzjames of Redlynch, Somerset, and one of Richard Phelips's servants, Andrew Horde*. In the meantime Phelips had sat for Poole in the Parliament of 1555 where he is thought to have joined in the opposition to a government bill: a 'Mr. Fillips' appears on the list of opponents to the measure, and the similarity of the spelling used further down the list for his kinsman Thomas Phelips [Mr. Thomas Fillips] creates the presumption that it was he and not a namesake, Richard Philipps, the Member for Pembroke Boroughs, who was meant.[3]

Little else has come to light concerning Phelips. Either he or a namesake was a servant of the Marquess of Exeter in the early 1530s at a time when Richard Phelips was surveyor for the marquess in the southwest. In January 1554 a John Phelips witnessed the will of William Hodges of Ilchester, Somerset, in which sums of money were left to 'Mr. Phelips of Montacute', his wife and children; this John Phelips was named first bailiff of Ilchester in 1556.[4]

[1] C219/282/13; Huntington Lib. Hastings mss Parl. pprs. [2] Presumed to be of age at election. [3] KB27/1176, 1188; Guildford mus. Loseley 1331/2. [4] *LP Hen. VIII*, xiii; PCC 1 More, 38 Drury; *CPR*, 1555–7, p. 528.

M.K.D.

PHELIPS, Richard (by 1488–1558) of Poole and Charborough, Dorset, Southwark, Surr. and London.

POOLE 1512,[1] 1515[2]
MELCOMBE REGIS 1529
?WAREHAM or WEYMOUTH 1553 (Mar.)[3]
DORSET 1554 (Nov.)

b. by 1488, ?s. of Thomas Phelips of Montacute, Som. by Joan. *m.* (1) by 1514, Emily, 4s. inc. Thomas* 2da.; (2) Emma, wid. of John Spring (*d.*1533) of Bristol, Glos.[4]

Yeoman the chamber by 1509; butler, Lyme Regis and Weymouth 1510–13; collector of customs, port of Poole 1511–14, 1520–7; escheator, Som. and Dorset 1520–1; commr. subsidy, Dorset 1523, 1524, 1533, benevolence 1544/45, relief 1550; j.p. Dorset 1523–*d.*, Som. 1536–47; under sheriff, Dorset 1531–2.[5]

The pedigree of Phelips of Montacute starts in the early 16th century with two brothers Richard and Thomas said to have been the sons of Thomas Phelips, escheator of Somerset and Dorset from 1471 to 1479. This Thomas was probably also a collector of customs in Bridgwater; he owned property in Montacute where he died early in 1501 after making a will providing only for a wife and witnessed by a Richard Phelips.[6]

Richard Phelips began his career in the household of Henry VII: he was present at the King's funeral and at Henry VIII's coronation. His prospects were soon furthered by appointments in the customs administration of Dorset, perhaps through the influence of the Uvedales, who held the comptroller-ship of Poole during the first quarter of the century: Phelips was to stand bail for William Uvedale in a land transaction of 1518 and to be associated with him in the collection of the subsidy of 1523. As butler in the Dorset ports Phelips was deputy to Sir Robert Southwell, chief butler of England. After his first term as customer of Poole he obtained a pardon in which he was described as late of London, Montacute, Poole and Southwark. He may by then have been living at Sock Dennis in Tintinhull, a mile-and-a-half north of Montacute; about 1525 a moiety of this manor was held on lease from the 1st Marquess of Dorset (d.1501) during the lives of Phelips, his wife Emily and their sons Bertram and Thomas.[7]

His final accounts for the customership brought Phelips into difficulties with the Exchequer. In 1527 his cousin John Witcombe of Somerset named him executor, provided he discharged himself from the troubles which he then had 'against the King'. This Phelips succeeded in doing by way of a pardon in the next year, a deliverance to which he referred when writing to Cromwell in 1529 to thank him for the care he had taken and to ask him to intercede with Wolsey. Phelips had occasion to thank Cromwell again in 1533 and 1534 for helping his son Thomas, accused of breaking into the gaol at Ilchester, and to his gratitude he then added an offer of £20 if Cromwell would take Thomas into his service. Phelips may also have been obliged to the minister for his servitorship at the coronation of Anne Boleyn.[8]

Active in local administration, Phelips improved his status as a minor gentleman. Some time after 1522 he obtained from Sir John Russell* the right to the tolls of Poole, and in the 1540s he received from the townsmen there a fee of 20s. a year. In 1539 his daughter Edith married as her second husband the son of (Sir) John Horsey* of Clifton Maybank, who named Phelips overseer of his will with a number of Dorset magnates; Phelips was also a feoffee, and overseer of the will dated 1535, of Sir John Rogers of Bryanston. Less propitious was the record of his service from 1524 as surveyor to Cecily, Marchioness of Dorset, and her son the 2nd Marquess for all their manors in Cornwall, Dorset, Somerset and Wiltshire. His forceful discharge of his duties brought complaints not only from the tenants but also, before 1530, from the marchioness herself. In a Star chamber suit she complained that Phelips and Nicholas Chauntrell, far from re-establishing good order on her estates after complaints of earlier extortions, had conspired to replace old tenants by new ones from whom they took for themselves large en-trance fines, and in other ways had vexed her tenantry. There was more trouble to follow from the same quarter: during the 1540s the 3rd Marquess addressed a bill to Chancellor Wriothesley against Thomas Phelips and another for withholding the deeds of the manor of Sock Dennis.[9]

Phelips's first investment in Dorset property was his purchase in May 1522 from Richard Wykes of the remainder of the manor of Charborough; he gained possession in October 1531. Five or six years later he took a 50-year lease of the manor of Canford Priory. He was not officially concerned with the suppression of the monasteries in Dorset, but in 1538 a letter from Edward Seymour, Earl of Hertford, gave him custody of Muchelney abbey, some seven miles from Montacute. His estates were rounded off by the acquisition in 1540 of the manor of Corfe Mullen from Leonard Chamberlain*. His home was then at Charborough, where he was assessed for the subsidy of 1545 at £76 in land, fees and annuities.[10]

Phelips's Membership of the Parliaments of 1512 and 1515 is disclosed by the record of payments of 20s. made to him on 25 Feb. 1512, on 20 Jan. 1513 and on a day not specified in February 1515. His election points to government influence since Ralph Worsley, his fellow-Member in 1512 and perhaps again in 1515, was also a customs official: the intermediary may have been Henry Uvedale[†], a court official at that time comptroller of Poole. It is likely enough that Phelips sat again in 1523 but the loss of most of the names makes this a matter of conjecture. In 1529 Phelips found a seat at Melcombe Regis, where his fellow was Oliver Lawrence who had succeeded him as customer at Poole: their election doubtless owed something to John Horsey, lord of one of the three manors in Melcombe and himself one of the knights for Dorset in this Parliament. His association with the foremost families of the county, notably those of Horsey and Strangways, might have been expected to provide Phelips with a seat in the later Henrician and Edwardian Parliaments, but he is not known for certain to have been returned again until the reign of Mary. He probably sat in the Parliament of 1536, when the King asked for the re-election of the previous Members, and may have done so in its successors of 1539 and 1542, when most of the Dorset names are again lost; but he did not secure his own election in either 1545 or 1547, although his son Thomas was returned on both these occasions. He may have reappeared in the second Parliament of Edward VI's reign, when a Richard whose surname is lost was Member for Wareham or Weymouth.[11]

It was in the following year that Phelips for the

first and only time attained the knighthood of the shire. The opportunity may have arisen from the outlawry for debt during that summer of Sir Giles Strangways II, who during these years enjoyed a virtual monopoly of one of the Dorset seats; if it did, Phelips's combination of connexions, experience and interest in Parliament, the last reflected in his many nominations for Dorset boroughs, would have made him an obvious alternative. The same occasion saw Melcombe comply with his request by returning his son, and Weymouth elect a kinsman in John Phelips. For all three the Parliament was to mean trouble. When on its dissolution those Members who had absented themselves without leave were prosecuted in the King's bench they were all involved: Phelips himself was distrained for non-appearance in every successive term until his death, and at the next shire election, in 1555, when Strangways was returned again, Phelips's role was limited to that of an elector. It was not his only brush with the government: the fines for offences by 'old Phillips and his son' which were referred by the Privy Council to the Star Chamber in May 1558 probably arose out of his conviction for carrying off Joan Camans, a ward already married, and for re-marrying her to one of his sons.[12]

Phelips made his will on 24 Jan. 1557. After thanking God for his long life and begging forgiveness for his sins he asked to be buried at Charborough or elsewhere without pomp. Masses were to be said for six years for himself and his first wife. He remembered the poor at Charborough, Montacute and elsewhere. His physician Francis Lamme received household goods and a gown for care during his illness and his servants Richard and Margery Knollys recognition of their services. Andrew Horde*, his trusted servant for many years, was repaid with an annuity. To his son and daughter-in-law William and Mary Phelips he left £20 a year from lands in Corfe and Poole on surrender of previous annuities made to them; their daughter Elizabeth was to have £20 on marriage. Phelips avowed his special trust in his own son Thomas, appointed him sole executor without an overseer and left him the interest in the property at Charborough. Thomas was also charged with assigning dower and household goods to Phelips's second wife Emma; their marriage had raised contention, still unsettled, with one John Maye who claimed her as his wife upon a pre-contract. In a codicil to the will Phelips named Sir John Horsey and Horsey's wife, his own daughter Edith, as co-executors, but this he revoked on 28 Oct. 1557 when Thomas was re-appointed sole executor. (Horsey then owed Phelips £193 and three nests of silver gilt goblets valued at £80 which had been pledged on Horsey's behalf.) Phelips did

not mention his sons Bertram, who had probably died young, and Henry, the black sheep of the family, who after being a student for 20 years had robbed his parents and fled to the Continent, and among other discreditable actions was to betray Tyndale to the imperial authorities at Antwerp in 1535. Phelips died between Trinity term 1558, when he was distrained 6s.8d. for non-appearance in the King's bench, and the following Michaelmas term when his death was noted beside his name on the controlment roll of the court. His will was proved on 26 Nov. 1560 and on 27 Nov. a sentence concerning the codicils was pronounced on behalf of the executor.[13]

[1] Poole rec. bk. 1, p. 26. [2] Ibid. 1, p. 1. [3] C219/282/7. [4] Date of birth estimated from first certain reference: his brother Thomas was born in 1483–4, Som. Rec. Soc. xxvii. 101. PCC 56 Mellershe, 38 Drury; Vis. Som. (Harl. Soc. xi), 85; Burke, LG (1957), 2018; C1/1126/29. [5] Poole rec. bk. 1, p. 1; C67/62, m. 3; LP Hen. VIII, i, iii, iv, vi, xiii, xv–xvii, xx, xxi; CPR, 1547–8, p. 76; 1550–3, p. 435; 1553, p. 352; 1553–4, p. 18. [6] CFR, 1471–85, nos. 8, 10, 12, 83, 93, 149, 458; CPR, 1476–85, p. 335; sede vacante wills, Canterbury F, f. 22; Vis. Som. 85; Hutchins, Dorset, iii. 357. [7] Poole rec. bk. 1, p. 1; C67/62, m. 3; LP Hen. VIII, i, iv; E315/385, f. 29v. [8] LP Hen. VIII, iv, vi, vii; Som. Rec. Soc. xxvii. 273, n. 2; E122/120/6–8, 121/1–6, 207/1–2, 215/20. [9] LP Hen. VIII, v, ix, xii; J. Sydenham, Poole, 388; G. Scott Thomson, Two Cents. of Fam. Hist. 146; Poole rec. bk. 1, pp. 71–72, 87; PCC 8, 40 Alen; St.Ch.2/12/310, 30/69; C1/924/20–21, 1126–29, 1165/52–56, 1167/30–32. [10] Hutchins, iii. 301; LP Hen. VIII, xiii; C1/1167/32; CP40/1107, m. 10; E179/104/156. [11] Poole rec. bk. 1, pp. 1, 26; E122/121/7, 9, 207/3–5; Hutchins, iv. 426; C219/282/7. [12] Weymouth and Melcombe Regis ms misc. deeds, v. 1; KB27/1176–83; 29/188, r. 48v; APC, vi. 316; Harl. 2143, f. 11. [13] PCC 56 Mellershe; LP Hen. VIII, ix, xiv; DNB (Tyndale, William); KB27/1183; 29/188, r. 48v.

M.K.D.

PHELIPS, Thomas (by 1514–90), of Sock Dennis by Montacute, Som.

WAREHAM	1545
MELCOMBE REGIS	1547[1]
WAREHAM	1553 (Oct.)
MELCOMBE REGIS	1554 (Nov.)[2]
WAREHAM	1555
POOLE	1558

b. by 1514, 1st s. of Richard Phelips* of Poole and Charborough, Dorset; Southwark, Surr. and London by 1st w. Emily. m. by 1535, Elizabeth, da. of Matthew Smith of Bristol, Glos., at least 4s. inc. Edward†. suc. fa. 1558/60.[3]

Member, household of Queen Catherine Parr 1543; hayward, manor of Shapwick, Dorset 1547.[4]

During the 1520s Richard Phelips leased a moiety of the manor of Sock Dennis for the lives of himself, his wife, and his sons Thomas and Bertram. By the time that Phelips obtained this lease, he was probably settled in Dorset permanently, and it was left to his eldest son Thomas to take up residence: Thomas Phelips, his wife and young children were living at Sock when his errant brother wrote from Louvain asking him to intercede with their parents on his behalf. Thomas Phelips's decision to live at Sock was perhaps influenced by his family's long association with Montacute, in which parish the hamlet was situated and where his uncle Thomas 'the elder' (1483/84–1565) and his shortlived cousin 'the younger' Thomas (d. by 1565) had their home. Thomas Phelips of Sock was sometimes described as of Montacute, and his contemporaries did not often distinguish between him, his uncle and his cousin, so that attribution of the numerous references to the three namesakes is problematic. After an early period at court the uncle's sphere of interest appears to have been restricted to his native shire, and this suggests that it was his nephew, the servant of Catherine Parr, whose parliamentary career began in 1545 with the help of his father Richard Phelips. After 1547 there are no certain references to Thomas Phelips 'the younger', so that the senior Member for three different Dorset boroughs over a span of 13 years is presumed to have been the son of Richard Phelips.[5]

In March 1533 Thomas Arundell* asked Cromwell to continue his goodness to 'young Phelips', for whom his father was probably seeking a place at court. This attempt to advance his career was jeopardised several months later when he was accused of instigating a prison break at Ilchester. When the inquiry was unduly drawn out, his father protested about the manner of his treatment and begged Cromwell not to end his favour towards the young man. In the following year, when Phelips had thrown himself on the King's mercy in the matter, Arundell wrote again to Cromwell evidently with success, as not long afterwards Richard Phelips was to ask the minister to take Thomas into his service. Thomas Phelips did not enter Cromwell's household but instead found employment with several of the more important families in the south-west. One of the families with which Phelips and his father had dealings was that of Seymour, and this business link could explain his admission to the household of Catherine Parr on her marriage to Henry VIII.[6]

As one close to Queen Catherine and himself returned as a knight for Dorset in 1545 Arundell presumably promoted Phelips's return for Wareham, but his nomination there as it was elsewhere later was almost certainly the work of his father. Arundell doubtless played a similar role two years later when Phelips was chosen for Melcombe Regis, a borough amenable to the influence of his brother-in-law, Sir John Horsey*, and when the returning officer, John Sydenham*, was one of his co-lessees with Edward Napper* of Montacute priory from (Sir) William Petre* four years previously. In the autumn of 1554 he was re-elected at Melcombe at 'the contemplation' of his father who undertook to pay his wages. Phelips joined the opposition to a government measure in

1555, and may have done so again in 1558 when his name is one of those marked with a circle on the copy of the list of Members in use during the second session of the Parliament of that year. Along with his father and his kinsman John Phelips he was found to be absent at the call of the House early in January 1555 and for this dereliction he was informed against in the King's bench during the following Easter term. He was distrained for non-appearance for a year when he was fined 53s.4d. and gave as a surety Thomas Phelips of Montacute, esquire. His father died shortly before the accession of Elizabeth, and with his death Phelips lost his parliamentary patron and maybe the urge to sit in the Commons. He did not cut much of a figure in the remaining 30 years of his life.[7]

By his will made on 25 Sept. 1588 he asked to be buried without pomp and provided for his family. As his three elder sons had proved unsatisfactory, it was his youngest son Edward whom Phelips made his executor and to whom he left his house at Montacute, instructing him to pay £650 for it to his eldest brother. Thomas Phelips died on 28 May 1590, and Edward Phelips justified his father's choice by becoming an eminent lawyer and Speaker of the House of Commons.[8]

[1] Hatfield 207. [2] Huntington Lib. Hastings mss Parl. pprs.; Weymouth and Melcombe Regis ms misc. deeds, v. 1. [3] Date of birth estimated from marriage. Burke, LG (1957), 2018; Vis. Som. (Harl. Soc. xi), 23; Vis. Dorset (Harl. Soc. xx), 76; Collinson, Som. ii. 292; Hutchins, Dorset, iii. 357; LP Hen. VIII, ix; PCC 38 Drury. [4] E101/423/12 pt. ii, ff. 8, 40; C1/1461/34–35. [5] E315/385, f. 29v; C1/1167/30–32; LP Hen. VIII, ix. [6] LP Hen. VIII, vi, vii; Elton, Policy and Police, 112; M. L. Robertson, 'Cromwell's servants' (Univ. California Los Angeles Ph.D. thesis, 1975), 539; HMC Bath, iv. 124–332 passim; E101/423/12 pt. ii. f. 8. [7] C1/1456/8; Bodl. e Museo 17; Weymouth and Melcombe Regis, misc. deeds, v. 1; KB27/1176–8; Guildford mus. Loseley 1331/2; CPR, 1557–8, p. 347; Wm. Salt Lib. SMS 264. [8] PCC 38 Drury; C142/228/6.

M.K.D.

PHILIPPS, Richard (by 1534–61), of Picton, Pembs.

PEMBROKE BOROUGHS 1555[1]

b. by 1534, 2nd or 3rd s. of John Philipps of Picton by 2nd w. Elizabeth, da. of Sir William Gruffydd of Penrhyn, Caern.; bro. of William†. unm.[2]

Richard Philipps's family claimed princely descent and was connected with the leading families in Pembrokeshire where it had settled on moving from Carmarthen in the late 15th century. Under his father's will of 1549 Philipps inherited a share in property in the lordship of Llanstephan and at St. Clears. His return to the Parliament of 1555 reflected his connexions and preceded that of his brother William for the shire four years later. He was joined in the House by his equally youthful 'cousins', Sir Henry Jones, Richard Jones and Sir John Perrot, and by his uncle Sir Rhys Gruffyd. In view of the opposition of two of his cousins to a government bill it is tempting to identify Philipps with the 'Mr. Fillips' on the list of opponents to the measure, but the Member concerned is thought to have been John Phelips (q.v.). Little else has come to light about Philipps. With the encouragement of the bard Gruffydd Hiraethog, and perhaps also of his own kinsman Gruffydd Done*, he began a collection of Welsh proverbs, prose and poetry which was unfinished at his death in late September 1561.[3]

[1] C219/330/28, pt. i. [2] Presumed to be of age at election. Dwnn, *Vis. Wales*, i. 115. [2] *DWB* (Philipps fam. of Picton); D. Miles, *Sheriffs, Pembs.* 15; PCC 14 Powell ptd. *W. Wales Hist. Recs.* vii. 161–4; Guildford mus. Loseley 1331/2; *HMC Welsh*, i. 937, 982; *DWB* erroneously gives the year of death as 1551, ex inf. M. Helen Davies, Dept. Mss and Ptd. Recs., NLW.

A.D.K.H.

PICKERING, Sir William (1516/17–75), of London, and Byland and Oswaldkirk, Yorks.

WARWICK 1547

b. 1516/17, 1st s. of Sir William Pickering of London, Byland and Oswaldkirk by Eleanor, da. of William Fairfax. *educ.* Camb. *unm.* 1da. illegit. *suc.* fa. 1542. Kntd. 22 Feb. 1547.[1]

Gent. of the chamber by 1550; keeper, Sheriff Hutton park, Yorks. and constable of the castle by 1551; ambassador to France 1551–3; j.p. Mdx. 1562.[2]

William Pickering's father, knight marshal to Henry VIII, acquired considerable monastic property in Yorkshire and other counties. At Cambridge Pickering was tutored by John Cheke* and his scholarship was sufficient for him to be considered worthy of mention in a list of those who had adopted Cheke's new pronunciation of Greek.[3]

In 1538 Pickering was suggested as 'one of those most meet to be daily waiters' upon the King and 'allowed in his house', but it is not known if this suggestion was acted upon. Of his career and activities nothing further has been traced until 2 Feb. 1543, when he went with several other young bloods led by Henry Howard, Earl of Surrey, on a nocturnal spree in London, smashing windows and firing crossbows at passers-by. A week later Surrey was brought before the Council on a composite charge of eating flesh in Lent and breaking the King's peace, and among his principal associates were named Pickering, Sir John Clere*, Thomas Clere and Sir Thomas Wyatt II*, all noted Protestants. When Wyatt and Pickering were called before the Council they claimed to be licensed for the flesh-eating and denied the window-breaking: both were committed, Wyatt to the Compter and Pickering to the Porter's Lodge, and on the following day they were confronted by one of the Cleres, who had confessed, whereupon they admitted their guilt. They spent a month in the Tower before being released on recognizances of

£200. Surrey tried to maintain that the group's antics were intended to remind the citizens of the suddenness of God's judgment, but he, too, found it prudent to retract and to attribute it to the reckless folly of youth: he employed Pickering as an envoy to the Council to ask for mercy.[4]

Before the reign ended, and with it Surrey's life, Pickering had exchanged that perilous attachment for a more promising one. His new patron was John Dudley, Viscount Lisle and Earl of Warwick, under whose aegis he was knighted at Edward VI's coronation and elected by the borough of Warwick as its senior Member in the King's first Parliament, the only man from outside the county to be chosen there throughout the period. (Although the Journal throws no light upon his activity in the House, Pickering is known to have sympathized with Wyatt's scheme for a militia authorized by Parliament.) But the largest dividend was to accrue three years later when, after Warwick's seizure of power from the Protector Somerset, Pickering was appointed to replace Sir John Mason* as envoy to France. The imperial envoy Scheyfve promptly wrote him off as a creature of Warwick's, about 30 years old, unlettered and a zealous Protestant, and Warwick's use of a novice in diplomacy on so important a mission reflects his overriding need for loyalty in its discharge.[5]

The surrender of Boulogne by the treaty of May 1550 had brought the Anglo–French war to an end and Pickering's task was to smooth the way for a marriage alliance between Edward VI and the French Princess Elizabeth. After a brief sojourn with Mason in February and March 1551, from which he returned on urgent private business (the nature of which does not appear), he went back in May with the embassy despatched to invest the King of France with the Garter and to negotiate the marriage: the Garter ceremony was performed before the end of May but the treaty was not concluded before the middle of July. Pickering was then left as resident ambassador in France, where he was to remain until after the death of Edward VI. In measure as that event, and with it the lapse of the treaty, were foreshadowed during these two years his importance diminished and his treatment worsened. When he was recalled, soon after Mary's accession and at the end of an embarrassing month in which he had received no instructions, his debts were such that he had difficulty in leaving Paris.[6]

His absence abroad had prevented Pickering from attending the last session of the Parliament of 1547— on the list of Members as revised for that session he is marked 'extra regnum'—or from sitting in that of March 1553: it also saved him from involvement in the struggle over the succession, but he was soon engaged in activities which justified the new government's mistrust of him. In October 1553 Renard, the imperial ambassador in England, reported to the Queen that Pickering had talked over two hours with Princess Elizabeth, 'and I suppose their conversation had something to do with the French ambassador'. Pickering was soon conspiring against the Spanish marriage with his old associate Wyatt, and although he did not take part in the rising he was indicted after he had fled to France. In March 1554 he and Sir Peter Carew* arrived at Caen to organise ships with which, it was said, they hoped to intercept the Spanish fleet bringing Prince Philip to England. For the provision of the ships they relied on the French King, to whom Pickering was to be envoy, but Henry II immediately disavowed any connexion with the project and even promised Wotton, the new English ambassador, to apprehend the plotters. This promise notwithstanding, in April Pickering and Carew were living openly in Paris and Wotton was writing home about Pickering's familiarity with the English diplomatic cipher, which had to be changed. By this time, however, Pickering was veering round and he revealed to Wotton what he claimed to be the French King's plan to land the conspirators in Essex or the Isle of Wight towards the end of the summer. With Cecil's cousin, Thomas Dannett†, he then fled to Italy for fear of revenge but when Carew soon afterwards followed suit this fear was removed. By March 1555 Pickering had received a royal pardon and was in Brussels awaiting favourable tidings to embark for England: he finally arrived in July and retired into private life for two years. In January 1558 the Queen called on him to recruit mercenaries in the Netherlands and Germany for the French war; after he had engaged in protracted negotiations the transaction was countermanded, but not before it had involved him in financial commitments which were still outstanding five years later when a commission was issued to view and settle his accounts.[7]

The accession of Elizabeth brought Pickering a last flash of notoriety. Unmarried, reputedly successful with women, and a Protestant, he was for a time spoken of as a candidate for the Queen's hand. Ambassadors reported his secret visits to the Queen; he had taken up residence at court, entertained lavishly and showed extravagant tastes; he dined alone with music playing, had made his way into the royal chapel reserved for the nobility—to the fury of the 12th Earl of Arundel said to be his rival in the Queen's favour—and had challenged the 2nd Earl of Bedford to a duel for having spoken ill of him. The truth is probably that Pickering never considered himself a suitor: the Queen, he told ambassadors,

'would laugh at him and at all the rest of them as he knew she meant to die a maid'.[8]

Apart from a place briefly on the Middlesex bench and a commission of lieutenancy for London at the time of the rebellion of 1569, Pickering received no further appointments, ending his days in semi-retirement and literary recreations. In his will made on 31 Dec. 1574 part of his land was left to found a free school and maintain students at Oxford. Most of his property, which he had settled securely on trustees to the performance of his will, he bequeathed to his illegitimate daughter, Hester, who was to be brought up by his friend Thomas Unton. His extensive library and armoury, with the exception of certain books on antiquities, globes and compasses which he gave to Cecil, were to be kept intact for his daughter's husband. He made bequests to his heir, his sister, and to numerous friends, including his executors, John Astley*, his cousin Thomas Heneage*, Thomas Wotton* and Dru Drury†, and his supervisors Cecil and (Sir) Nicholas Bacon*. He died in his London house, in the parish of St. Andrew Undershaft, on 4 Jan. 1575, and in accordance with his wishes he was buried in the church of St. Helen within Bishopsgate. Strype called Pickering 'the finest gentleman of his age, for his worth in learning, arts and warfare'.[9]

[1] Date of birth estimated from age at fa.'s i.p.m., C142/65/63. *DNB*; PCC 15 Spert, 1 Pyckering. [2] Stowe 571, f. 69v. [3] *LP Hen. VIII*, xvii, xviii; *HMC Bath*, iv. 2; NRA 6160, no. 4837; C. Peers, *Byland Abbey*, 4; Strype, *Eccles. Memorials*, ii(1), 574; *Cheke*, 435. [4] *LP Hen. VIII*, xviii; *APC*, i. 104–5, 125–6. [5] *Pprs. Geo. Wyatt* (Cam. Soc. 4th ser. v), 57; B. L. Beer, *Northumberland*, 110–11; W. K. Jordan, *Edw. VI*, i. 232; *CSP Span.* 1550–2, p. 218. [6] Jordan, ii. 88, 127, 145, 158, 160, 167; *Lit. Rems. Edw. VI*, 304–464 passim; E. Lavisse, *Histoire de France*, v(2), 147–50; *CSP For.* 1547–53 passim; 1553–8, p. 5; *CSP Span.* 1550–2 passim; *APC*, iii, iv passim; *HMC Hatfield*, i. 85; Lansd. 3(30), ff. 59–60. [7] Hatfield 207; *CSP Span.* 1553, p. 314; 1554, passim; 1554–8, pp. 380, 389, 404; *CSP For.* 1553–8, passim; *CSP Dom.* 1547–80, pp. 100, 103; *CSP Dom.* 1601–3, *Add.* 1547–65, p. 466; D. M. Loades, *Two Tudor Conspiracies*, 15–16, 24, 50, 92n, 96, 158; *CPR*, 1554–5, p. 177; 1558–60, p. 71; *APC*, vi. 242, 310, 314–15, 320; Lansd. 8(70), ff. 163–4; *HMC Hatfield*, i. 257. [8] *CSP For.* 1558–9, no. 729; *CSP Span.* 1558–67 passim; *CSP Ven.* 1558–60 passim; Strype, *Annals*, i(2), 491; *Parker*, i. 164. [9] *CSP Span.* 1558–67, p. 337; PCC 1 Pyckering; C142/170/32, 171/73; Strype, *Annals*, ii(1), 530.

S.M.T.

PIERREPONT, George (1510–64), of Whaley, Derbys. and Holme Pierrepont, Notts.

NOTTINGHAM 1539[1]

b. 16 July 1510, 1st s. of Sir William Pierrepont of Holme Pierrepont by Joan, da. of Sir Richard Empson† of Easton Neston, Northants. educ. ?I. Temple. m. (1) 25 Nov. 1532, Elizabeth (d.1543), da. of (Sir) Anthony Babington* of Dethick, Derbys. and Kingston-on-Soar, Notts., 1da.; (2) 20 Nov. 1544, Winifred, da. and h. of Sir William Thwaites of 'Mallowtree' (?Manningtree), Essex, 2s. inc. Henry† 2da. suc. fa. 29 Aug. 1533. Kntd. 22 Feb. 1547.[2]

?Butler, I. Temple 1544.

Commr. musters, Derbys. 1546, relief, Derbys. and Notts. 1550, goods of churches and fraternities, Notts.

1553; j.p. Derbys. 1547, Notts. 1547–*d.*; recorder, Nottingham 1555–*d.*; sheriff, Notts. and Derbys. 1558–9.[3]

George Pierrepont was born when his mother's father was awaiting the traitor's death which came to him a month later. This natal misfortune was to have no discernible effect on his career—unless it contributed to his somewhat belated entry into local administration—but it may help to explain the interest which Cromwell took in Pierrepont's prospective inheritance from his mother. Pierrepont was by then married to Elizabeth Babington, from nearby Kingston-on-Soar. Her father was prominent at the Inner Temple, where Pierrepont almost certainly had his training, as did others of his family, and with Babington's other son-in-law John Markham he was charged with supervising Babington's will of February 1534.[4]

Pierrepont is known to have sat in only one Parliament, that of 1539, but it is possible that he had come in for Nottingham in 1536: his father-in-law seems to have been re-elected by the town on that occasion, and if Nicholas Quarnby (q.v.) was no longer available Babington might well have secured Pierrepont the vacancy. By 1539, with Babington dead, Pierrepont must have relied on his own standing in the town, where he owned property, and the favour of his fellow-Member Sir John Markham, whose son was married to his sister-in-law Catherine Babington. The evidence of contact between Pierrepont and Cromwell is too slight to warrant any suggestion of ministerial support, although Markham was the local champion of government policy. Nothing is known of Pierrepont's part in the work of the Commons, but his purchase in July 1540 of local monastic property for over £600 may not have been unconnected with his Membership. His earlier acquisition of Cotgrave manor, adjoining Holme Pierrepont, reflected the Babington connexion, for it had formerly belonged to the order of St. John of Jerusalem, of which his wife's uncle Sir John Babington had been turcopolier and his father-in-law for a time the prior's steward. In July 1544 Pierrepont bought more monastic land for upwards of £400.[5]

It is a matter of surprise that, unless Pierrepont was one of the two knights of the shire for Nottinghamshire in 1542—when the sheriff was Sir Henry Sacheverell, whose daughter was married to Pierrepont's brother-in-law Thomas Babington—he was not to sit again despite his increasing activity in local administration and his appointment to the recordership of Nottingham during the reign of Mary, when his Catholic sympathies would have further fitted him for Membership. He sued out a pardon in 1553

as of Holme Pierrepont, late of Whaley, and contributed £100 to the loan of 1557. In March 1559, while sheriff, he fell ill but he did not die until 21 Mar. 1564. Only a part of his will is preserved in his inquisition post mortem of the following 24 May: he asked to be buried in Holme Pierrepont church and appointed as executor his friend and neighbour (Sir) Gervase Clifton* who later married his widow. His elder son Henry Pierrepont, then aged 17, was to sit in the Parliament of 1572, despite his Catholicism.[6]

[1] C60/352, m. 18. [2] Date of birth given in *HMC 9th Rep.* pt. 2, p. 375. *Vis. Notts.* (Harl. Soc. iv), 50–51 (where Pierrepont's father is wrongly given as Sir Nicholas), 56; Thoroton, *Notts.* ed. Throsby, 176; Mill Stephenson, *Mon. Brasses*, 244; Strype, *Eccles. Memorials*, ii (2), 328. [3] *LP Hen. VIII*, xxi; *CPR*, 1547–8, pp. 82, 88; 1550–3, pp. 141, 393; 1553, pp. 352, 357, 415; 1553–4, p. 22; 1560–3, p. 440; 1563–6, pp. 25, 38; *Nottingham Bor. Recs.* iv. 115, 117, 417. [4] *LP Hen. VIII*, vii; *Cal. I.T. Recs.* i. 43, 48, 49, 52, 100, 139, 140, 146; PCC 39 Hogen. [5] *LP Hen. VIII*, xiv, xv, xix; T. Bailey, *Annals Notts.* (1853) 478. [6] Strype, iii (1), 277; iii (2), 78; *CPR*, 1553–4, p. 422; C142/140/153.

A.D.K.H.

PINNOCK, Thomas (by 1523–56 or later), of Sandwich, Kent.

SANDWICH 1547[1]

b. by 1523, 4th s. of Thomas Pinnock of Sandwich.[2] Common councilman, Sandwich (St. Clement's parish) 1544–7, jurat 1547–56, mayor 1548–9, keeper of the common chest 1548–9, of the orphans 1548–9, 1550–2, auditor 1550, 1551, 1553.[3]

Thomas Pinnock was perhaps a draper, the trade followed by his father and other members of his family. He and John Seer* were elected jurats at Sandwich on 7 Mar. 1547, although it was more usual for new jurats to be chosen at the annual election of officers in December. On the same day a servant of Archbishop Cranmer was made a freeman of the port at the suit of the archbishop. In November 1546 another of Cranmer's servants had also been made free at his master's suit, and his sureties had included Seer. It is possible, therefore, that the election of Pinnock and Seer to the juratship was promoted by Cranmer. (On the day of the election, for some unknown cause Pinnock came to blows with John Lee III* in the council chamber.) In the following September the same pair were chosen Members of the forthcoming Parliament, with wages of 2s. a day each, but their election was set aside by the mayor who proceeded to hold another and to return Thomas Patche and Thomas Ardern (qq.v.) as Members. After an appeal, the Privy Council decided in favour of the first election and ordered that Pinnock and Seer should be allowed 20s. for being 'put to business and charges without reason'. Late in 1551 they were instructed to solicit for the furthering of the work on the haven when they went up to London for the session due to open on 23 Jan., but if the Parliament were prorogued to a later date it was Pinnock and the mayor who were to do this. It was during this session, which began on the day expected, that the validity of Pinnock and Seer's election was again raised; they were asked to absent themselves from the House until it had been settled, but the outcome is not known.[4]

During Edward VI's reign Sandwich tried to obtain help for the improvement of its harbour, and the intermediary chosen to further its suit with the Protector was Cranmer and not, as was customary, the lord warden of the Cinque Ports, Sir Thomas Cheyne*. Pinnock played a leading part in the campaign, to which, as he reported early in 1548, Cranmer 'like an honourable prelate granted his aid and help'. In the spring he and several others were appointed to solicit the cause; a petition was laid before the Protector and in August a commission of inquiry was issued to the archbishop and others. In the following December Pinnock was elected mayor, and as such he attended the Brotherhood of the Cinque Ports at Romney in July 1549. It was undoubtedly as a 'solicitor' that his services were most in demand. In March 1551 he and the then mayor moved Cheyne and other Privy Councillors for an answer 'touching as well the payments of the workmen working upon the haven, and victuallers of the town, as also for the proceedings thereof'. The last instructions given to him in the matter appear to have been those he shared with John Seer during the final session of the Parliament of 1547.[5]

Within a year or two this spate of activity was brought to an end. In October 1554 Pinnock was an unsuccessful candidate in the election at Sandwich for the third Parliament of Mary's reign. Two months later he was ordered to be committed to ward, as soon as he could be found, for assaulting Nicholas Peake*, while Peake was on the bench with the mayor and jurats. After this he is not recorded as attending any assembly of the mayor and jurats, nor does he appear on the list of jurats for December 1555: it was not until the following 13 July, however, that he was deprived of his juratship 'for divers urgent and necessary' (but unspecified) causes. In view of Pinnock's association with Cranmer, the coincidence in time between Cranmer's downfall and Pinnock's demotion is suggestive, but the connexion cannot be documented. The last reference found to Pinnock comes in a letter from the Council to the mayor and jurats on 18 Nov. 1556 restoring to him goods committed to a townswoman on (Sir) John Guildford's* instructions.[6]

[1] Sandwich old red bk. ff. 197v, 251. [2] Date of birth estimated from first reference. *Vis. Kent* (Harl. Soc. lxxv), 108. [3] Sandwich old red bk. passim; little black bk., passim. [4] Sandwich old red bk. ff. 21v, 187, 194v, 195, 197v, 207; Canterbury prob. reg. A6, f. 70; 8, f. 74v; *APC*, ii. 536–7; *CJ*, i. 17. [5] Sandwich old red bk. ff. 204, 206v, 208, 209, 211v, 243, 251; W. Boys, *Sandwich* (1792), ii. 732–5; *Cinque*

Ports White and Black Bks. (Kent Arch. Soc. recs. br. xix), 240. [6] Sandwich little black bk. ff. 55v, 61–62, 92v; *APC*, vi. 18.

H.M.

PINNOCK, William (by 1509–55), of Hanley Castle, Worcs.

WARWICK 1545

b. by 1509, s. of one Pinnock of Upton-on-Severn. *m.* by Mar. 1541, Elizabeth, wid. of Roger Badger of Hanley Castle, *s.p.*[1]

Rent collector, manor of Warwick 1530–6 or later; jt. receiver-gen. Salisbury's lands, Cornw., Devon, Dorset, Hants, Som., Wilts., Warwick's lands, Leics., Staffs., Warws., Worcs. 13 Feb. 1539–?d.; receiver-gen. Countess of Somerset's lands by Sept. 1541–?d.; gent. usher by 1543; escheator, Worcs. 1547–8; commr. enclosures, Beds., Berks., Bucks., Leics., Northants., Oxon., Warws. 1548, relief, Worcs. 1550; j.p. Worcs. 1554.[2]

William Pinnock was of humble birth but by service to the crown and by marriage to a moderately rich widow he gained position and property in his native Worcestershire. Nothing has been learnt about his life before his appointment in 1530 as collector of manorial rents for the crown at Warwick. By 1537 he was acting as receiver-general with Richard Bream for two forfeited estates administered for the crown by the court of general surveyors, although another two years passed before he was officially named as Bream's partner, and by 1541 he was sole receiver-general for another estate managed by the general surveyors. His promotion in the administration of crown lands was reflected by a minor post in the Household and his Membership of the Parliament of 1545. While the opening of the Parliament stood postponed he signed the letter of inquiry from the leading figures in Worcestershire about the force to be sent to Portsmouth in the event of an invasion, and during the prorogation in 1546 he reported to the Council on repairs to Warwick castle. Although he was not re-elected to Parliament he was named escheator, commissioner and justice in Worcestershire and served with John Hales II* on the commission to investigate the extent of enclosure in the midlands. By a will made on 11 Dec. 1554 he divided his property between his wife, brother, sisters, nephews and nieces and provided for his stepson and other kinsmen. He died on 1 Jan. 1555, when he was succeeded by his brother John then aged 42 years and more, and his will was proved on 18 May following by his widow, brother and godson William Lygon.[3]

[1] Date of birth estimated from first reference. PCC 25 More, 3 Wrastley; *LP Hen. VIII*, xvi. [2] SC6/Hen. VIII, 3700–6, ex inf. Dr. R. W. Dunning; *LP Hen. VIII*, xiv, xviii, xix; *CPR*, 1547–8, p. 419; 1553, p. 360; 1553–4, p. 26. [3] PCC 25 More, 3 Wrastley; *VCH Worcs.* iii. 555; iv. 101, 126, 215, 516; *LP Hen. VIII*, xvi, xix–xxi; *CPR*, 1548–9, pp. 191, 302; 1563–6, pp. 166–7; C142/106/81.

S.M.T.

PLEYDELL, Gabriel (by 1519–90/91), of Midgehall in Lydiard Tregoze, Wilts.

WOOTTON BASSETT   1553 (Mar.)[1]
MARLBOROUGH   1555
WOOTTON BASSETT   1563

b. by 1519, 4th s. of William Pleydell of Midgehall and Coleshill, Berks. by Agnes, da. and coh. of John or Robert Reason of Corfe Castle, Dorset; bro. of John†. *m.* (1) Anne, da. and coh. of Henry Stocks (Stokes) of Suss., 1s. *d.v.p.* 1da.; (2) by 17 Nov. 1563, Elizabeth, *s.p.* (3) Jane, *s.p.*[2]

Chief ranger and keeper, Savernake forest, Wilts. by ?1554; receiver-gen. for Anne, Duchess of Somerset, in 1554.[3]

A younger son of a Berkshire man who had settled in Wiltshire, Gabriel Pleydell had presumably come of age by 1540, when he was holding land at Eisey, near Cricklade, from Sir Anthony Hungerford*. In 1545 he was assessed at Midgehall to pay 26s.8d. towards the benevolence and four years later his father was licensed to settle on him the remainder of the manor of West Ilsley, Berkshire. Under his father's will, proved in May 1556, he received the remainder of a 95-year lease of Midgehall, which eventually passed to him after his mother and next elder brother Virgil had died and 11 years after his eldest surviving brother Tobias had settled at Chipping Faringdon, Berkshire.[4]

Pleydell's three elections to Parliament are explained in part by his standing as a local landowner. Midgehall lay one mile north of Wootton Bassett, where Pleydell was to buy and sell property under Elizabeth, and although his christian name alone survives on the return to the Parliament of March 1553 it was a sufficiently uncommon one to leave no doubt that he was the man elected. He was likewise no stranger to Marlborough: in 1559, while his mother still occupied Midgehall, he sued out a pardon as of Chippenham *alias* of Preshute, a parish on the outskirts of that town, where his father may have had interests earlier. To this contiguity Pleydell could add influential connexions. The link with the Seymours, known from several cases in the Star Chamber under Mary, may have been of long standing; Pleydell's father held lands at Eastrop and elsewhere of Thomas Seymour, Baron Seymour of Sudeley, who had also alienated lands at Eisey to his younger brother Zachary in 1541. The Protector Somerset's widow appointed him chief ranger of Savernake forest in succession to John Berwick*. He also attached himself to Somerset's former steward (Sir) John Thynne*, a rising figure in the county whom he was to support in a contest for the knighthood of the shire in 1559.[5]

Pleydell was seldom out of the courts. Towards the end of Edward VI's reign he brought a suit in the Star Chamber against a number of defendants who had expelled him from the Gloucestershire manor of Withington which he had leased. There followed a series of actions before the same court, Pleydell being usually a defendant. He was accused of helping John Berwick to expel the occupant of Somerset's former manor of East Grafton in the autumn of 1553 and of procuring an amenable jury at Marlborough which found that there had been no breach of the peace; he claimed to have acted on the orders of the duchess and denied interfering with the jury. At about the same time he was sued for forcible entry and seizure of goods at Little Bedwyn and for similar offences at Collingbourne Ducis, where he maintained that he was only distraining for unpaid rent.[6]

It may have been on one of these charges, or on yet another, that in Michaelmas term 1555 Pleydell and other defendants were found guilty in the Star Chamber. His accomplices in what was described as a riot were presumably sentenced forthwith, but Pleydell, who was then sitting in Parliament for Marlborough, claimed privilege and was bound in £500 to appear as soon as Parliament was dissolved. This recognition by the court of a Member's immunity from legal proceedings—at least at suit of party, as the case against Pleydell must have been—was evidently outweighed in the minds of at least some of his fellow-Members, when the decision was reported to the House, by the suspicion that it was meant to intimidate Pleydell and, by implication, other figures in the parliamentary opposition. On 6 Dec. the House resolved to send a deputation, headed by Sir Robert Rochester, to declare to the Lords the opinion that the court had infringed Pleydell's privilege. After the Lords had replied by requiring six Members to attend to receive the answer, Rochester, Sir William Petre and four others unnamed heard, and reported to the House, that the chief justices, the master of the rolls and the serjeants held the recognizance to be no breach of privilege. Although this was undoubtedly correct in law, the fact that the Commons, to judge from the Journal, took the matter no further does not imply that they were satisfied with the ruling; it may mean only that further action was blocked by the dissolution which followed three days later.[7]

Pleydell had supported Kingston in the House and his committal on the morrow of the dissolution suggests that he too was regarded as a ringleader. Kept in the Fleet until after Christmas, he was released on 28 Dec. after giving another bond for £500 to attend the Star Chamber on the first day of the following term. This he appears to have done, being then fined £40 with £5 costs, but he also spread it abroad 'that he was not punished in the Fleet at his last being there for any matter depending in the court of Star Chamber but for speaking his conscience in the Parliament in a bill concerning the commonwealth'. True as this may have been, it was an impudence which the Star Chamber treated as a slander to be inquired into, although with what result is unknown. The proceedings may have been overlaid by the next case against Pleydell, that arising from his alleged protection of two of his servants in the rangership of Savernake after one of them had been convicted of murder and the other of abetting a robbery. Here his opponent was his former associate John Berwick, with whom he was in perpetual conflict over rights in Savernake forest. In spite of being under recognizance to appear regularly before the Council, in July 1557 Pleydell secured a commission from the Star Chamber empowering William Button*, Henry Clifford*, Griffith Curteys* and John Hooper* to examine his own and Berwick's witnesses, and then appeared at Marlborough with a list of 240 articles and a host of people to be examined on behalf of his two servants. For this attempt to 'deface' the Queen's justices and abuse the Star Chamber 'by colour of a commission . . . to try a riot', he was indicted in that court by Edward Griffin, the attorney-general, in Michaelmas term 1557. The court sent him to the Tower and fined him 1,000 marks by forfeiting the recognizance which he had given to that amount. On 19 Dec. 1557 he was allowed to leave the Tower for the house of Thomas Garrard, a merchant taylor, after entering into a further bond of £1,000 for his good behaviour.[8]

Pleydell always replied to his local accusers that he acted within the law as receiver-general for the Duchess of Somerset or as ranger of Savernake forest. Possibly he was in part the victim both of those who hoped to encroach on the Seymours' rights and of the jealousy of Berwick, the previous ranger. None the less he came from a family enriched by monastic spoils, he opposed Mary's government in the Commons and rashly claimed that he had been victimized for this. The revival of his fortunes after Elizabeth's accession, perhaps aided by Sir John Thynne, was to be followed by his second term for Wootton Bassett and by his implication in the alleged forgery of the will of Andrew Baynton*. This charge and a further series of lawsuits, while confirming for Gabriel Pleydell a niche in parliamentary history, detract still further from his reputation. He died between 19 Dec. 1590 and 3 Feb. 1591, the dates of the making and proving of his will.[9]

[1] C219/282/11. [2] Date of birth estimated from first reference. *Wilts. Vis. Peds.* (Harl. Soc. cv, cvi), 153; *Wilts. N. and Q.* v. 175; PCC 12 Sainberbe. [3] St.Ch.4/1/33, 5/13, 8/48. [4] *LP Hen. VIII*, xv; *Two Taxation Lists* (Wilts. Arch. Soc. recs. br. x), 21; *CPR*, 1548–9, p.

240; *Wilts. N. and Q.* v. 89–90, 129–3; *VCH Berks.* iv. 33; *Vis. Berks.* (Harl. Soc. lvi), 47. [5] *Wilts. N. and Q.* iv. 505, 559, 561–2; v. 175; *CPR*, 1558–60, p. 149; *LP Hen. VIII*, xvi; Marlborough corp. gen. entry bk. 1553–4, f. 1; *Cat. Anct. Deeds*, i. 358. [6] St.Ch.3/2/22. 4/1/33, 8/48, 49. [7] *APC*, v. 202, 210; Harl. 2143, ff. 3–3v; *CJ*, i. 46. [8] Guildford mus. Loseley 1331/2; *APC*, v. 202, 209, 210; vi. 67–68, 75, 125, 165, 217–19; Harl. 2143, ff. 3–3v, 7; St.Ch.4/3/72, 5/13, 96. [9] PCC 12 Sainberbe.

T.F.T.B.

PLOWDEN, Edmund (1519/20–85), of the Middle Temple, London; Plowden, Salop; Shiplake, Oxon. and Burghfield, Berks.

WALLINGFORD	1553 (Oct.)
READING	1554 (Nov.)
WOOTTON BASSETT	1555

b. 1519/20, 1st s. of Humphrey Plowden of Plowden by Elizabeth, da. of John Sturry of Rossall, Salop, wid. of William Wollascott. *educ*. ?Camb. and Oxf.; M. Temple. *m*. Catherine, da. of William Sheldon* of Beoley, Worcs., 3s. 2da. *suc*. fa. 10 Mar. 1558.[1]

Autumn reader, M. Temple 1557, Lent 1560, treasurer 1561–70.

Steward, manor of Greenham, Berks. 1550; member, council in the marches of Wales 1553; dep. chief steward, duchy of Lancaster, south parts 1557, under steward 1558–*d*.; j.p.q. Glos., Herefs., Salop, Worcs. 1554; j.p. Berks. 1558/59, q. 1561, rem. 1569; other commissions, Berks. etc. 1564–76.[2]

The Plowden family, which claimed Saxon descent, had held land at Plowden, near Bishop's Castle in the south-west of Shropshire, at least since the reign of Richard I. Despite this lineage, Edmund Plowden's father played little part in local affairs and the son's own early life is obscure. He is said to have studied at both universities and even to have been admitted to practise 'chirurgery and physic' at Oxford in 1552, 14 years after the traditionally accepted date for his entry into the Middle Temple, a date based on his own claim to have begun the study of law in his 20th year. He was named a trustee by John Winchcombe *alias* Smallwood* in a family settlement of 1548, perhaps as a lawyer, and may then already have resolved to make his own home in Berkshire; his acquisition two years later of the stewardship of Greenham in the Winchcombe parish of Thatcham was the first step he took to establish himself there. The choice was probably prompted by the Englefields, a leading Berkshire family which owned land in Shropshire at Up Rossall, near the home of Plowden's mother; Sir Francis Englefield* is said to have confided the administration of these estates to Plowden, who secured a lease there for his brother-in-law, Richard Sandford.[3]

Plowden's parliamentary career was over before he became prominent in Berkshire. Wallingford, where the castle and honor had been transferred from the duchy of Cornwall to the royal manor of Ewelme in 1540, was a decaying town, often open to intruders, so that its return of Plowden to Mary's first Parliament was not necessarily a sign of his local standing. Reading, with a stronger tradition of independence, normally returned one townsman with one figure prominent in the county, and in November 1554 John Bourne filled the first role. Confusion has arisen over whether Edmund Plowden or his younger brother Edward was the Reading Member, probably because the christian name in the return is represented by an ambiguous abbreviation and because Edward would conveniently fill the gap if Edmund was also returned, as some authorities claim, for Wootton Bassett, although the Crown Office list shows that borough as represented by Giles Payne and William Hampshire. The return for Wootton Bassett is defaced, but a comparison of the abbreviation in that for Reading with other, known, names, together with the entry in the corporation diary and the fact that only the elder brother is known to have lived at any time in Berkshire, all indicate that it was the elder brother who was chosen for Reading: he was certainly returned for Wootton Bassett in 1555 when his name was inserted in the indenture over an erasure and in a different hand from that of the document. Sir Francis Englefield was steward of Reading in 1554 and was granted the lordship of Wootton Bassett early in 1555, so it is likely that Plowden rose under Mary with his help, which he was afterwards to repay. Plowden was later to be favoured by the Wiltshire magnate Sir William Herbert I*, 1st Earl of Pembroke, who may also have helped to secure his return in 1555.[4]

In Mary's first Parliament there were no Berkshire Members among those marked as opposing the reunion with Rome. The numerous local duties which then fell to Plowden show that the Queen held him to be one of the 'wise, grave and Catholic sort' whom she wished to see returned to Parliament in November 1554 and it is at first sight surprising to find him included with those who were absent without licence when the House was called early in January 1555. Informations for contempt were laid by the attorney-general against a first batch of 'seceders', including Plowden and his friend Richard Ward I, a Member for Windsor. Six submitted to their fines but Plowden 'took a traverse full of pregnancy' and was the only one known to have pleaded that he had not been absent. Eventually the information against him in the King's bench was withdrawn. A fellow-Member of the Parliament of November 1554, Andrew Tusser, had acted as his attorney, and Plowden for his part may have advised or encouraged his relative George Leigh (q.v.) to plead in the same fashion. Although he failed to find a seat in the last Parliament of the reign, during its first session he appeared before the House with John Story* and the abbot of

Westminster over the abbey's right of sanctuary. In October 1558 the abbot granted Plowden a retainer of £4. In the same month Plowden was among those summoned to take the degree of serjeant-at-law in the following Easter term, but Mary died within three weeks and her successor omitted his name from her writs, so that he never achieved the dignity which some later writers have allowed him.[5]

A career in politics was now closed to Plowden but he could still exercise a weighty conservative influence by defending followers of the old order. He pleaded for Edmund Bonner, the deprived Marian bishop of London, who had refused to take the oath of supremacy, and in 1566 he appeared before the Commons as counsel for Dean Goodman of Westminster to argue for the exclusion of Westminster abbey from the scope of the bill (later defeated on a division) for the abolition of sanctuaries for debt. Twelve years later the Catholic prisoner Francis Tregian was permitted 'to use the advice of Mr. Serjeant [Francis] Gawdy† and Mr. Plowden'. One of several unlikely explanations for the expression that has become proverbial, 'The case is altered, quoth Plowden', is that the words were spoken in the lawyer's defence of a man accused of attending mass, when it was revealed that the supposed priest was a layman and an informer. Another, even less credible, is that it was Plowden himself who had been present at the mass. He was, indeed, known to be a Catholic. In 1564 Bishop Jewell said that he was 'as it is supposed a hinderer' and in 1569 he was the only Berkshire justice who refused to subscribe to the Act of Uniformity, although he claimed that he had hitherto been as dutiful in church attendance as any man 'of his profession in the common law and having as much business as he hath had in term time and out of the term'. He was then bound in 200 marks to be of good behaviour for a year and to appear before the Council when required. In 1577 he was accused of not attending church since the northern rebellion with the result that the Middle Temple was 'pestered with papists', and a list of Catholics in the capital a year later included 'Mr. Plowden who hears mass at Baron Brown's, Fish Street Hill'.[6]

Although Plowden was debarred from promotion his services continued to be in demand. He retained his office in the duchy of Lancaster and was one of those assembled early in Elizabeth's reign to discuss the 'great case of the duchy', relating to the sovereign's rights therein. He also appeared as arbitrator at one stage in a long-standing dispute between the boroughs of Weymouth and Melcombe Regis in 1575 and it is probable that, if his own name seldom appears in legal cases under Mary and Elizabeth, he can be identified with the 'apprentice of the Middle

Temple' who features in his own reports. A sign of the respect in which he was held was the justification given by William Lovelace † for a legal opinion, 'that Mr. Plowden's hand was first unto it, and that he supposed he might in anything follow St. Augustine'.[7]

Plowden acted for such leading figures as the earls of Leicester and Pembroke and it was Pembroke who in 1567 obtained for him and (Sir) Edward Saunders* the much coveted wardship of Francis, son of John Englefield of Wootton Bassett and nephew and heir presumptive of Sir Francis. Plowden was thus never entirely without influence. He is even said to have been offered the lord chancellorship by the Queen and to have made a dignified refusal on the ground that, as one who found 'no reason to swerve from the Catholic faith', he could never 'countenance the persecution of its professors'. If the offer was ever made, it must have been after the death of (Sir) Nicholas Bacon* in February 1579 and before the elevation of Thomas Bromley II* two months later or, more probably, in the period between Bacon's death and Bromley's admission to the Privy Council during March. Catholic or conservative sympathies might not have barred Plowden but he was by then known as a recusant.[8]

Plowden's reputation rests not on the attainment of high office but on his compilation of the important cases which he attended from 1550 to 1579, a work which has 'come to be regarded as the most accurate and painstaking collection of its kind produced in the 16th and 17th centuries'. *Les Comentaries, ou les reportes de Edmunde Plowden* were first printed privately, at the author's own expense, in 1571, but they were reprinted with a second part, seven years later. In a preface of 1578, the lawyer, as a 'man of simple understanding and of weak memory', disclaimed any intention of publishing, until he found that the private circulation of his work had led to clerks and others inaccurately transcribing 'day and night' and until the justices of both benches had joined with the barons of the Exchequer to urge publication.[9]

Plowden also wrote a treatise in support of Mary Stuart's claim to the English throne and against that produced by John Hales II* in favour of Lady Catherine Grey. Plowden's thesis, a '*locus classicus* . . . for the theory of the King's two bodies', was later adopted by Anthony Browne II* and Bishop Leslie. According to a dedication to James I written by Plowden's son Francis for one of the surviving copies of the treatise, during the Parliament of 1566 the 4th Duke of Norfolk asked for the lawyer's opinion 'by way of discourse in speech' and the work was ready for printing when the Treasons Act of 1571 (13 Eliz. c.1) inhibited discussion of the succession. This account does not square with other surviving prefaces and the projected publication may have been connected with the Ridolfi plot, although no other evidence has been found of Plowden's involvement therein.[10]

The will of Humphrey Plowden had been proved on 6 May 1558 and the lawyer was licensed to enter on his father's Shropshire property on 23 Feb. 1559. His younger brother Edward, who had been left £40 and an annuity of 40s., apparently lived on the ancestral estate, for his will of 1 Apr. 1575 describes him as 'of Plowden' and he asked to be buried in the nearby church of Lydbury North, as their father had also requested. Edmund Plowden did not neglect the chance of adding to his patrimony, for in May 1554 he paid £91, and a London merchant, John White, paid £252 for the reversion of the manor of Lydbury North, which White was to enjoy for life and which was then to go to Plowden. At the same time, they bought the manor of Frimley, Surrey. In Berkshire, Plowden acquired the manor of Wokefield and land at Stratfield Mortimer, Sulhampstead Banister and Sulhampstead Abbots, but he lived at Shiplake, where the Thames divides Oxfordshire from Berkshire, and at Burghfield. Shiplake had belonged to the Englefields for some 300 years before its seizure and Plowden, who first began to live there as guardian of the young Francis, was granted a lease of the house, rectory and various lands there for £3 a year in 1574. When his ward came of age, the Englefield estates were surrendered to him by Plowden, who none the less still kept his lease of Shiplake Court from the Queen. Bishop's Castle was granted a charter in 1574 and Plowden was named one of the head burgesses together with his nephew Andrew Blunden. He probably helped to secure the borough's enfranchisement ten years later and the first two Members, John Cole and Thomas Jukes, were his relatives and seem to have sat on his nomination.[11]

When Plowden made his will on 2 Jan. 1582, he gave his residences as Shiplake and Burghfield. Always restrained, he made no defiant declaration of faith and left his executor to decide the funeral expenses 'which I would not have great', asking to be buried in the Middle Temple if he should die in London. His wife Catherine already lay there and today there stands an imposing, canopied tomb against the north wall, with a recumbent effigy of the lawyer and a brief epitaph. Plowden's eldest son and executor, also Edmund, was at least 22 when his father died on 6 Feb. 1585. The younger Edmund, however, died unmarried in August 1587 and was succeeded by his brother Francis, to whom the lawyer had left, among other similar bequests, £6 13s.4d. out of a lease he held at Burghfield from John

Talbot of Grafton: Francis Plowden married the daughter of Thomas Fermor*. Plowden provided for the marriage of his daughter Mary but left it to the discretion of his son-in-law Francis Perkins, Thomas Vachell II*, William Wollascott and Andrew Blunden to increase or decrease the sum suggested as they saw fit: in his own will, Edmund Plowden the younger laid it down that the sum provided should be £1,000. In the meantime, the elder Plowden entrusted Mary to the care of Mrs. Englefield, presumably the mother of his ward Francis, his sister-in-law Philippa, daughter of William Sheldon and widow of Anthony Pollard, and his married daughter Anne Perkins. Mary later married Richard, eldest son of George White* of Hutton, Essex. Andrew Blunden was overseer of the will and secured a lease of Shiplake Court. A portrait at Plowden and a bust and a coat of arms in the Middle Temple hall also commemorate a man who was acknowledged as the greatest and most honest lawyer of his day.[12]

[1] Aged 19 on entry into M. Temple. Plowden, *Commentaries* (1779), preface p. iii. B. M. Plowden, *Plowden Fam.* 16; *Vis. Salop* (Harl. Soc. xxix), 448; PCC 20 Noodes, 54 Brudenell; *Trans. Salop Arch. Soc.* lii. 179, 183; *Recusant Hist.* xiii. 172 n. 1; *DNB*; information from G. de C. Parmiter. [2] E315/221/308; *CPR*, 1553–4, pp. 19, 20, 23, 26; 1560–3, p. 434; Somerville, *Duchy*, i. 432; *HMC 11th Rep. VII*, 224; *APC*, ix. 311–12; R. O'Sullivan, *Edmund Plowden* (Autumn reading, M. Temple 1952), 13. [3] O'Sullivan, 2, 3; Burke, *LG* (1952), 2043; J. B. Blakeway, *Sheriffs Salop*, 132, 222; C142/115/161; *LP Hen. VIII*, xvii; Mill Stephenson, *Mon Brasses*, 429; Cooper, *Ath. Cant.* i. 501–3; Wood, *Ath. Ox.* ed. Bliss, i. 503; *CPR*, 1548–9, pp. 89–90; *VCH Berks.* iii. 319. [4] *VCH Berks.* iii. 528; *Reading MPs*, 40; J. B. Hurry, *Reading Abbey*, 36; C219/23/4, 6, 24/187; *Reading Recs.* i. 242; *CPR*, 1554–5, p. 52; *VCH Wilts.* ix. 191. [5] E. Coke, *Institutes*, iv (1671), 18–20; KB27/1176, rex roll 16; 1180, rex roll 36; *CJ*, i. 49; *HMC 10th Rep. IV*, 409; H. W. Woolrych, *Serjeants-at-law*, i. 101–31. [6] *CJ*, i. 74, 76, 79; *APC*, x. 249; *CSP Dom.* 1547–80, pp. 355, 689; *Add.* 1566–79, p. 550; *Cam. Misc.* ix(3), 38; SP12/144/45, 46; E. Rose, *Cases of Conscience*, 38; H. Foley, *Jesuit Recs.* iv. 540–2. [7] Plowden, 212–23; Somerville, i. p. xiii; *APC*, ix. 312, 368; O'Sullivan, 10–11; L. W. Abbott, *Law Reporting in Eng.* 203, 206; E. J. Climenson, *Shiplake*, 207–9; Blakeway, 223; *CPR*, 1566–9, p. 242; *Vis. Salop* (Harl. Soc. xxviii), 49; *Recusant Hist.* xiii. 159–77; xiv. 9–25; *Trans. Salop Arch. Soc.* (ser. 2), ix. 122–45. [8] *Downside Rev.* xc. 251–9; xcii. 62–67. [9] Abbott, 198–239. [10] *HL Quarterly*, xxxvii. 209–26; *The Queen's Two Bodies*, passim; M. Levine, *The Early Eliz. Succession Question*, 92–94, 111–15; W. K. Jordan, *Edw. VI*, i. 55n; Bodl. Don. c.43. [11] PCC 20 Noodes, 39 Carew; *CPR*, 1553–4, pp. 268–9; 1558–60, p. 76; 1572–5, pp. 14–15, 491; *VCH Berks.* iii. 425; Climenson, 202–3, 207–8; E310/22/119, m. 42 ex inf. G. de C. Parmiter. [12] PCC 54 Brudenell; Climenson, 203–6, 214–17; C142/206/13, 221/123; *VCH Worcs.* iv. 14; *VCH Berks.* iii. 245; Camden, *Eliz.* (4th ed.), 304.

T.F.T.B.

PLYMPTON, John (by 1514–55/58), of Wincanton, Som. and Shaftesbury, Dorset.

SHAFTESBURY 1554 (Nov.)[1]

b. by 1514, ?s. of John Plympton by Edith, wid. of John Hody of Stowell, Som. *m.* Cecily, da. of Robert Mayo of Dinton, Wilts., 2s. 1da.[2]

Auditor, commission for tenths of spiritualities, Som. 1535.[3]

John Plympton was settled at Wincanton in Somerset but he seems also to have been an occasional resident of Shaftesbury over the county border in Dorset. He was mustered at Shaftesbury as an archer in 1542 and witnessed a deed signed there in July 1550. He probably owed his return for Shaftesbury in 1554 to the lord of the borough, (Sir) William Herbert I*, 1st Earl of Pembroke, from whom he leased a house in Stoke Trister, the parish adjoining Wincanton. The earl's steward Robert Grove* was also a tenant and officer there and Grove's son William* was to marry Cecily Plympton's niece.[4]

No will or inquisition post mortem has been found, but Plympton was dead (perhaps a victim of the prevailing epidemic) before 21 Feb. 1558 when his widow and daughter, together with Nicholas Swanton (whom the widow was to marry), took out a new lease on the house in Stoke Trister.[5]

[1] Huntington Lib. Hastings mss Parl. pprs. [2] Date of birth estimated from first reference. *Vis. Wilts.* (Harl. Soc. cv, cvi), 128–9; C142/80/50; PCC 53 Harrington. [3] *LP Hen. VIII*, viii; *Val. Eccles.* i. 206–21 passim. [4] E36/29, p. 132; C. H. Mayo, *Shastonian Recs.* 82; *Pembroke Survey* (Roxburghe Club cliv), 421. [5] *Pembroke Survey*, 421.

H.M.

POLE, Geoffrey (1501/5–58), of Lordington, Suss.

WILTON 1529

b. 1501/5, 4th s. of Sir Richard Pole (*d.*20 Dec. 1505) of Ellesborough, Bucks. by Margaret (Countess of Salisbury 1513), da. of George, Duke of Clarence. *m.* by 1528, Constance, da. and coh. of Sir Edmund Pakenham of Lordington, 5s. 5da. Kntd. aft. 3 Nov. 1529.[1]

J.p. Hants, Suss. 1531–8; commr. sewers, Suss. 1534, 1538; jt. keeper, Slindon park, Suss. in 1553.[2]

The favour of Henry VIII made the first half of his reign an Indian summer for the Pole family. Geoffrey Pole's mother, widowed in 1505, was restored to her father's earldom of Salisbury and granted large estates in Essex, Hampshire, Wiltshire and the west; soon afterwards her eldest son Henry was created Lord Montagu, and in 1527 the second, Reginald, who had been educated at the King's expense, returned after five years' study abroad to be made dean of Exeter. Sir Richard Pole had been gentleman of the bedchamber to Prince Arthur, and hence the christian name of another of his sons, who died not long after marrying Jane Lewknor. He also bequeathed to Margaret Pole his association with Catherine of Aragon; this developed into the lifelong friendship between the two which, cemented by the countess's appointment as governess to Princess Mary, helped to shape the Poles' disastrous attitude towards the divorce and the breach with Rome.[3]

Geoffrey Pole lived at Lordington, in the west Sussex parish of Racton, where his father was once mistakenly thought to have held the manor: this was in fact inherited from Sir Edmund Pakenham in 1528, together with a moiety of the manor of

Gatcombe in the Isle of Wight. Geoffrey Pole is mentioned only once in his father-in-law's will, in the bequest to his wife of the £10 already paid to him 'for his interest that I had by him in the farm of Gatcombe'. Pakenham seems to have thought more highly of his other son-in-law Edmund Marvyn, the future judge, who received a number of personal gifts and was made an overseer of the will. Perhaps Pole was already showing signs of extravagance: in May 1530 he wrote to Master Frynd, a schoolmaster at Chichester, begging the loan of £6 until Michaelmas, and a few years later, when the family lay under the King's suspicion, Lord Montagu was persuaded to pay off Pole's heavy debts by the fear that he might otherwise flee and so precipitate disaster.[4]

Pole was at odds with some of his neighbours. In a suit before the court of requests he was accused of conspiring with his mother-in-law and Edmund Marvyn to draw the income of lands at Bosham from which they had forcibly expelled the occupier on Christmas eve 1529. Shortly afterwards he was himself the plaintiff in a series of actions in the Star Chamber over trespasses on his lands at Lordington and the destruction of hedges. The defendants were all humble men, but in one of the cases Pole claimed that he and his wife had recently begun to enclose part of a wood until on the night of 1 May 1531 their hedge was pulled down by some 60 armed men at the command of the 11th Earl of Arundel. Later there was a contest with the Fitzalans over the keepership of Slindon park, for in 1536 Pole took possession of it and Cromwell had to order the 9th Lord de la Warr to enforce the King's decision in favour of Arundel's heir, Lord Mautravers.[5]

At Wilton, Pole was clearly nominated to the Parliament of 1529 by his mother, who had held the borough since 1513, and whose connexion with the threatened Queen seems to have been no obstacle to such patronage. As for Pole himself, it is possible that he sought a place in the Commons less on political or social grounds than as a protection against creditors. He certainly behaved circumspectly enough to be given a knighthood in the course of the first session, and for a time he appears to have acquiesced in the march of events: thus his name is not to be found on the list of Members drawn up by Cromwell in 1533 and thought to be of those opposed to the bill in restraint of appeals. By contrast, on 20 Apr. 1533 he wrote to Cromwell thanking him for past favours and trusting in his goodness. When Anne Boleyn was crowned on 1 June 1533 he was among those who served at her coronation banquet, and in 1534 he was paid £40 by a servant of Cromwell.[6]

Pole was none the less being drawn into the ranks of the opposition. In January 1532 his brother Reginald, who had declined the see of York and refused to countenance the divorce, was allowed to leave England, and in the following autumn, when the King went to Calais to seek the approval by Francis I of his proposed marriage, Lord Montagu secretly took his younger brother with him: Pole, in disguise, gathered intelligence sufficient to send Montagu to Queen Catherine with an assurance that Francis would never recognise Anne Boleyn. In the next year, when the Countess of Salisbury was dismissed for refusing to surrender Mary's jewels, the new Queen's coronation did not prevent Montagu, Pole and others from dining with the princess at Otford five days later. George Croft, the chancellor of Chichester who was to be tried with him in 1538, testified that when Pole returned to Sussex from sessions of Parliament he often voiced dislike of its proceedings, notably of the rejection of papal supremacy.[7]

Early in November 1534 Chapuys informed Charles V that Pole and many others never tired of urging him to tell the Emperor how easily England might be conquered; he added that Pole had warned his brother Reginald not to come home and had made the countess write to the same effect. In March 1535 Chapuys advised Pole, for the sake of his relatives, not to flee to Spain, and on the eve of Queen Anne's arrest the ambassador learned from Pole at dinner that the King had been inquiring about the validity of his marriage to her. Although Pole's association with Chapuys must have betrayed his discontent, nothing so damning as incitement to invasion was to be cited at his trial. The fall of Anne must have gratified the family: the countess reappeared at court and Pole himself may have been re-elected to the Parliament which completed the Queen's destruction.[8]

It was the raising of his brother to the cardinalate which preluded Pole's and his family's downfall. He was the first to lapse into disfavour, perhaps because of his debts. On 1 Feb. 1537 he was warned that John Gostwick*, treasurer of the first fruits and tenths, 'looks for you for the King's money', and when Prince Edward was christened in the following October the King refused to receive him at court. In a letter to Chancellor Audley, written from Lordington probably on 5 Apr. 1538, he voiced his distress at the humiliating prospect of visiting London on legal business after Cromwell and others had warned him not to wait upon the King: he may have spared himself, for a week later he joined his fellow justices in examining suspected thieves at Chichester. As late as 9 July he was reappointed to commissions of the peace but at the end of August he was arrested in

Sussex and lodged in the Tower: according to Chapuys, he was suspected of having corresponded privately with the cardinal.[9]

Pole remained in prison for nearly two months, while Cromwell was hearing an improbable story that the cardinal had secretly visited England to confer with his relatives. On 26 Oct. 1538 the first of seven interrogations was conducted by Sir William Fitzwilliam I*, Earl of Southampton. Although Southampton was less concerned with Pole's views than with those of greater figures, two days later John Hussee reported to his master Viscount Lisle that Pole had hurt himself badly in an attempt at suicide, and it was perhaps soon after this, when he was rumoured to be in a frenzy, that Lord Montagu countered his wife's fears with the reply that it did not matter what a madman said. His kinsmen had indeed but little confidence in him: the cardinal had urged him not to meddle and in the summer of 1538 Montagu had sent to his house to destroy incriminating letters. The government had shrewdly picked on the weakest of its suspects: Pole revealed enough for Montagu and the Marquess of Exeter to be arrested and for a string of confessions to be wrung from their friends and servants.[10]

By 12 Nov. Pole's own interrogations were over and his mother's about to begin. Having thrown himself on the King's mercy, he was tried at Westminster on 4 Dec. with Sir Edward Neville, a mariner named Hugh Holland, and two priests, John Collins and George Croft. He was accused of having praised the cardinal to Montagu in 1536, of treasonably corresponding with the exile through the seaman Holland, and of declaring that he would make only a formal appearance in arms against the northern rebels. Clearly he would have fled abroad if Holland had agreed to take him, although he denied any intention of joining his brother. The messages he had sent to Reginald included a warning against the King's plans for assassination and the bleak prediction: 'The world in England waxeth all crooked, God's law is turned upsodown, abbeys and churches overthrown . . . and I think they will cast down parish churches and all at the last'. All the defendants were found guilty and sentenced to death. The sting of Pole's confession had lain in the rash statements he attributed to Montagu and Exeter, condemned on the two previous days, and propagandists made play of Montagu's conviction out of the mouth of his brother. Exeter, Montagu and Neville were beheaded on 9 Jan. 1539, when Chapuys wrote that their accuser had tried to suffocate himself and might escape with life imprisonment: he had in fact been pardoned a week earlier and by April he seems to have been back in Sussex, where his name was included on a muster certificate.[11]

The rest of Pole's life was a melancholy epilogue. In June 1539 he wrote to Cromwell from Lordington to seek help for a lawsuit brought by his wife, who for a time had been kept with him in the Tower, and in December the minister sent him £20. In the following May he was used to convey a royal command to the local justices of peace but he was clearly still in a wretched state. Early in September Southampton wrote from Cowdray that Pole had assaulted John Gunter, once a fellow magistrate, for having disclosed private conversations to his inquisitors: considering 'the ill and frantic furious nature of the unhappy man', the earl feared that to arrest him might cause a dangerous relapse, while 'no man of wit will become his surety'. The Privy Council replied by insisting that the culprit should be publicly committed, and he was pardoned, although banished from court, only at his wife's intercession. In April 1541, a month before his mother's execution, he was found to have incited his chaplain to make a malicious accusation against the parson of Racton, but on this occasion no action seems to have been taken. In May 1543 the King granted to Pole and his wife the manor of Grandisons in Kent, with the profit from Michaelmas 1537; although it had belonged to the countess, the new owners alienated it a year later to (Sir) Thomas Moyle*. As a final favour, in December 1545 Pole secured a licence to export 1,000 dickers of leather.[12]

In 1548, having quitclaimed Lordington to Edmund Ford* and his wife, Pole fled from England. After the cardinal had taken him to receive absolution from the pope, he led a restless existence in France, the Netherlands and Germany. By the summer of 1550, as he told Sir John Mason* at Poissy, he longed to return, and in the following May he sought—in vain—an interview at Malines with Nicholas Wotton, the English ambassador to the Emperor. His wife shared a great-grandfather with John Dudley, Duke of Northumberland, whose ascendancy may have encouraged Pole. In December 1552 he wrote to the Privy Council from Liége, thanking Northumberland and others for their kindness to his dependants, and enclosing a letter to his wife whom he pined to see after four years; he rejoiced that his son Arthur was out of prison and in the service of 'his grace'. His plea was unavailing, for he and his brother were among those specifically excluded from the general pardon granted in the Parliament of March 1553 (7 Edw. VI, c.14).[13]

It was Mary's accession which allowed Pole to return. He was made joint keeper of Slindon park and granted an annuity of £50 for life, but the past was not forgotten. Exeter's son Edward Courtenay, freed from the Tower and restored to his father's earldom of Devon, swore to kill Pole in revenge for the slaughter of his kin. The affair took on political importance, for in September 1553 the imperial ambassadors reported that Pole was being specially guarded and in October the Emperor himself referred to the feud in warning the pope that the time was not yet ripe for Cardinal Pole to go home. After this last flicker of notoriety Pole disappears, probably to spend his last years in rural seclusion. He died shortly before his brother in November 1558 and was buried in the church of Stoughton near Chichester, where his widow also asked to be laid in her will of 12 years later.[14]

Pole's royal blood and religious dissidence continued to haunt his children. Two of his sons, Arthur and Edmund, embarked on a futile conspiracy in 1562 and disappeared as prisoners in the Tower, and the second son Thomas inherited Lordington only to die without issue, the manor passing to another brother Geoffrey, a recusant who alienated it before his death in exile.[15]

[1] Date of birth estimated from father's death and elder brother Reginald's birth. *CIPM Hen. VII*, iii. 876; PCC 36 Porch; *Vis. Suss.* (Harl. Soc. liii), 89; *DNB.* [2] *LP Hen. VIII*, v, vii, xiii; E371/300/49; Stowe 571, f. 55. [3] *CP*, ix. 96n. [4] *Suss. Arch. Colls.* xxi. 75–76; *VCH Suss.* iv. 116; *VCH Hants*, v. 247; PCC 36 Porch; *LP Hen. VIII*, iv, xiii. [5] Req.2/2/182; *Suss. Rec. Soc.* xvi. 48–50; St.Ch.2/19/306, 315, 334, 337, 20/176, 285, 25/260; *LP Hen. VIII*, xi. [6] *VCH Wilts.* vi. 28; *LP Hen. VIII*, vi. [7] *LP Hen. VIII*, vi, xiii. [8] *CSP Span.* 1534–5, pp. 325, 471; 1536–8, p. 107. [9] *LP Hen. VIII*, xii, xiii. [10] Ibid. xiii. [11] Ibid. xi, xiii, xiv; Hall, *Chron.* 827. [12] *LP Hen. VIII*, xiv–xvi, xviii–xx. [13] *Suss. Feet of Fines* (Suss. Rec. Soc. xix), 281; *CSP For.* 1547–53, pp. 52, 106, 108; *VCH Hants*, v. 247; *HMC Hatfield*, i. 104–5. [14] *CPR*, 1554–5, p. 351; Stowe 571, f. 55; Lansd. 156 (28), ff. 95–99; *CSP Span.* 1553, pp. 241–2, 274, 287; PCC 28 Lyon. [15] *DNB* (Pole, Arthur); *Suss. Arch. Colls.* xxi. 74; *Suss. Feet of Fines*, 281; H. Foley, *Jesuit Recs.* iii. 791–2.

T.F.T.B.

POLE (POWLE, POLEY), William (1515–87), of Colyford and Shute, Devon and the Inner Temple, London.

LYME REGIS	1545
BRIDPORT	1553 (Oct.)
WEST LOOE	1559

b. 9 Aug. 1515, s. and h. of William Pole by 2nd w. Agnes, da. of John Drake of Ash, Devon. *educ.* I. Temple. *m.* (1) 19 Nov. 1548, Thomasin, da. of John Tudoll* of Lyme Regis, Dorset, wid. of John Strowbridge (*d.*1539) of Streathayne in the parish of Colyton, Devon, and of William Beaumont (*d.*1547), *s.p.*; (2) by 1559, Catherine, da. of Alexander Popham* of Huntworth, Som., 5s. inc. William† 2da.[1]

Bencher, I. Temple 1556, Autumn reader 1557, Lent 1562, treasurer 1564–5.

J.p. Dorset 1558/59–*d.*, Devon 1562–*d.*; counsellor to Lyme Regis by 1564.[2]

In the sheriff's schedule of the Members elected in Dorset to the Parliament of 1545 the names of those for Lyme Regis were added in a different hand

from the rest; and in Bridport's indenture for Mary's first Parliament William Pole's name was inserted in a blank space left for the second Member. As early as 1541 Pole held a judicial appointment in Lyme, being then 'a young justice' whose behaviour was criticized by one who declared himself to be 'a gentleman as Mr. Pole was (putting aside his office) and as well born as he'. Possibly there was opposition to his election in 1545 although later his advice was often sought by the town and he was retained of counsel by 1564. With Bridport he had no direct link; but John Paulet, Lord St. John, was high steward of both Lyme Regis and Bridport in 1553, and his deputy at Bridport, Robert Tytherleigh the younger, was a near relative of Pole.[3]

The family residence, Shute, in the parish of Colyton, formerly the property of Henry Grey, Duke of Suffolk, was acquired by Pole from (Sir) William Petre*, to whom it had been granted after Suffolk's attainder. There Pole died on 15 Aug. 1587.[4]

[1] Date of birth given in MI. Polwhele, *Devonshire*, iii. 3111; *Vis. Devon*, ed. Vivian, 603; *Colyton Par. Regs.* (Devon and Cornw. Rec. Soc. xiv), 20–21, 459, 579–82; St.Ch.4/3/10. [2] Lyme Regis, finance I, p. 60. [3] C219/18C/36, 21/56; Lyme Regis, fugitive pieces, I, no. 6; Bridport doom bk. 213. [4] W. Pole, *Description of Devonshire* (1791), 137–8; C142/213/72; PCC 62 Spencer.

H.M.

POLEY, Thomas (by 1523–64), of London and Ware, Herts.

MELCOMBE REGIS	1545
IPSWICH	1554 (Apr.)
RIPON	1555

b. by 1523, 2nd s. of Edmund Poley (*d.*31 Dec. 1548) of Badley, Suff. by Mirabelle, da. of John Garneys or Garnish of Kenton, Suff. *m.* Mary.[1]

Jt. (with Maurice Denys*) receiver, rents of former lands of the order of St. John of Jerusalem Oct. 1544–*d.*; member, household of Princess Mary by 1549; equerry, the stable by Nov. 1553–*d.*; bailiff of manor and keeper of park, Ware 7 Nov. 1553–*d.*[2]

The christian name Thomas was a common one in the Poley family but the most likely bearer of it to have sat for three widely separated boroughs between 1545 and 1555 was a younger son in the branch seated at Badley. This Thomas Poley may have owed his advancement to the marriage of his elder brother John to a daughter of Sir Thomas Wentworth I*, 1st Baron Wentworth, which had taken place by 1544. Poley himself is first glimpsed in April 1544 when, as a resident of London, he bought Manton manor, Suffolk, from Edward Elrington* and Humphrey Metcalfe. In October of the same year he was appointed joint receiver of the former lands of the order of St. John, an office which gave him an official tie with Sir Thomas Arundell*, his most likely patron at Melcombe Regis in 1545.

He was not the port's own choice since his name and that of his fellow, another East Anglian, Anthony Cokett, appear over an erasure on the sheriff's schedule.[3]

By 1549 Poley had joined the household of Princess Mary. Accused in that year of participating in disorders in Suffolk, he was exonerated by the princess who said that 'Poley remained continually in her house and was never doer among the commons nor came into their company'. She admitted, however, that she had another servant of the name living in Suffolk. Poley remained in Mary's service after she became Queen and was rewarded with the office of bailiff of Ware in November 1553. He sat in her second and fourth Parliaments, in April 1554 for Ipswich, a Suffolk town not five miles from the chief seat of the Wentworths, and in 1555 for Ripon, a duchy of Lancaster borough where he and John Holmes II were said to have been 'appointed' by Sir Robert Rochester*, chancellor of the duchy, who was familiar with Poley from their time in the Queen's service while princess. Poley's name was inserted on the indenture for Ripon, and at this and his earlier returns he was styled esquire.[4]

Under Elizabeth Poley continued to hold his post of equerry and may have been returned to her first Parliament for Thetford. The Thetford Member has been identified as a namesake of Icklingham, Suffolk, but Poley's kinsman Nicholas Rookwood had sat for the borough in three Marian Parliaments and his nephew, another Thomas Poley, was probably to do so in 1586. For the first payment of the subsidy of 1563 he was assessed in Ware at £20 on lands and fees. Within a year he died intestate and his widow Mary took out letters of administration of his estate.[5]

[1] Date of birth estimated from first reference. *Vis. Suff.* ed. Metcalfe, 58–59; *Vis. Suff.* ed. Howard, i. 274–5, 301–4; Add. 40138; PCC 31 Populwell. [2] *LP Hen. VIII*, xx; *CPR*, 1553–4, p. 325; Lansd. 3(89), f. 198. [3] PCC 35 Bucke; *LP Hen. VIII*, xix, xx; C219/18C/36. [4] Strype, *Eccles. Memorials*, ii(1), 276–7; Coll Arms, Talbot m.ss P, f. 267; *HMC Shrewsbury and Talbot*, ii. 349; C219/24/63. [5] E179/121/202; PCC admons. act bk. 1564, f. 78.

M.K.D.

POLLARD, John (by 1508–57), of Plymouth, Devon; London, and Nuneham Courtenay, Oxon.

PLYMOUTH   1529, 1536[1]
OXFORDSHIRE   1553 (Oct.), 1554 (Apr.), 1554 (Nov.)
CHIPPENHAM   1555

b. by 1508, 1st s. of Walter Pollard of Plymouth by Avice, da. of Richard Pollard of Way, Devon. *educ.* M. Temple. *m.* Mary, da. and coh. of Richard Grey of London, *s.p. suc.* fa. ?1527. Kntd. Oct. 1555/Apr. 1557.[2]
?Bencher, M. Temple by 1535, Lent reader 1546. J.p.q. Oxon. 1536–*d.*, Devon 1538–47, Glos., Herefs., Salop, Worcs. 1554–*d.*; of counsel to Plymouth by 1538–51 or later; commr. musters, Oxon. 1539, relief, Oxon. and Oxford 1550, goods of churches and fraternities, Oxford 1553; under steward, duchy of Lancaster, south parts 15 Jan. 1543–*d.*; serjeant-at-law ?Jan. 1547–21 Oct. 1550; member, council in the marches of Wales June 1550, v.-pres. by Feb. 1552; justice, Brec., Glam. and Rad. 23 Nov. 1550–*d.*, Chester and Flint, Denbigh and Montgomery 8 Apr. 1557–*d.*; recorder, Gloucester 1553–6, Oxford by Apr. 1554–*d.*[3]
Speaker of House of Commons Oct. 1553, 1555.

On his father's side John Pollard had as forbears three generations of merchants and mayors of Plymouth, but his mother came from the family at Way which had produced a notable lawyer in Sir Lewis Pollard[†], a justice of common pleas during Pollard's early years at the Middle Temple, and another patron in Richard Pollard*, client of Cromwell and a power in the west country, who was to make Pollard his executor in 1542.[4]

Pollard's return for Plymouth in 1529 is sufficiently explained by his combination of local and legal standing, for the town was perhaps already retaining him as one of its counsel. Their relationship was not to be a smooth one. By January 1535 Pollard and his fellow-Member Thomas Vowell had quarrelled so badly with a part of the corporation that their opponents complained to Cromwell of the misdeeds of 'certain seditious persons', among them Pollard and Vowell, whom they described as 'men without substance and unfit to rule this town'. Pollard at least was substantial enough to have served in Parliament for no more than the 13s.4d. he had originally, if rashly, agreed to accept, and the charge of unfitness was unlikely to be sustained against a man of his connexions. The entry in the Plymouth accounts for 1536–7 of a payment of 20s. to Pollard 'for his attendance at the late Parliament' can thus probably be taken to mean that the town complied with the King's request for the return of the previous Members to the Parliament summoned for June 1536: if so, the corporation doubtless acted on the advice of Sir Peter Edgecombe* and Andrew Hillersdon the recorder, whom it had consulted in the matter.[5]

This was the end of Pollard's occupancy of a seat for Plymouth, and although he was to be named to the Devon bench in 1538, remaining on it until 1547, and to continue as one of Plymouth's counsel longer still, his main interests shifted elsewhere. It is not known whether his translation to Oxfordshire was the cause or the result of his marriage with Mary Grey, stepdaughter to Sir William Barentyne*, a leading gentleman of that county. In July 1538 Pollard was recommended to Cromwell as a suitable under steward of the lordship of Abingdon, being called by the bailiff, John Welsborne*, 'an honest gentleman, well learned in law and the Latin tongue, a man of judgment and substance'. Four years later the 1st Earl of Sussex, chief steward of the south parts of the duchy of Lancaster, made Pollard his deputy, and in January 1543 he was formally appointed under steward: he was to be succeeded at his death by Edmund Plowden*, another Middle Templar and a relation of his by marriage.[6]

Pollard's association with Plowden, who preserved some of his dicta in the *Commentaries*, raises the question how far his career was affected by his evident conservatism in religion. His absence from the remaining Henrician Parliaments (in so far as their Membership is known) may have been connected with his removal to Oxfordshire, although a successful lawyer such as he had become need scarcely have lacked a seat, and before the first Edwardian Parliament was summoned he had been made a serjeant, an achievement which the corporation of Plymouth, old scores seemingly forgotten, celebrated with a present of wine. Whether he cut any figure in the upheavals of 1549, either in his native county or at court, is not known, but in June 1550 he was given a seat (afterwards becoming vice-president) on the council in the marches of Wales and later in the year he was released from his serjeancy and made justice of the counties of Brecon, Glamorgan and Radnor in place of (Sir) John Pakington*. It may be that in forsaking the prospect of a judgeship at Westminster Pollard thought it too remote to cling to, there being a string of serjeants ahead of him, but perhaps he also preferred to remove himself from an atmosphere he found uncongenial. In the event he probably evaded the dilemma in which so many of his brethren were to find themselves two-and-a-half years later, and it is not surprising that he seems to have been absent from the Parliament of March 1553 which prefaced the succession crisis of that summer.[7]

If his attitude before July 1553 remains obscure, Pollard clearly welcomed the Marian regime and in turn enjoyed its confidence. He was by then firmly based in Oxfordshire. He had inherited property in Exeter and Plymouth and his wife brought him land at Kingston-upon-Thames and in London. He had probably owned a house in Oxfordshire since 1536, and in 1543 and 1544 he bought further property in that county, including the manor of Nuneham Courtenay, some five miles south of Oxford, for £818. In the following year he and William Byrte paid over £1,600 for former monastic property in Gloucestershire and Wiltshire, and in partnership with George Rithe* he added numerous parcels of land in Oxfordshire and elsewhere. Many of these properties he must have sold or released to his

partner; his own he concentrated around Nuneham Courtenay.[8]

Thus qualified by property and residence to gain the knighthood of his adopted shire, Pollard must have owed his election in the autumn of 1553 to the support of the crown, which had chosen him for the Speakership. When the House assembled on 5 Oct. 1553 Sir Thomas Cheyne nominated him; he is said to have made an 'excellent oration' on 9 Oct. and appears to have acquitted himself well in the session which followed. On 17 Nov. the House ordered that Councillors who were Members should have 'copies of the articles whereof Mr. Speaker made relation to the Queen's highness by word' and on 2 Dec. the Speaker was required to obtain such documents as would further the passage of the bill revoking the attainder of the 3rd Duke of Norfolk. Re-elected for Oxfordshire to the next two Parliaments, Pollard had a number of bills committed to him. It was doubtless he, and not his namesake the Member for Barnstaple, who in April 1554 handled a bill for the election of university scholars and was called upon with another Member to attend to a case of privilege raised by William Johnson I*. In the next Parliament Pollard had no namesake, and it was indubitably he who made a vehement speech in defence of King Philip on a bill, which the House nevertheless rejected, to punish those who wrote or spoke against the King and Queen. His loyalty, ability and experience led the Council to take the unusual course of nominating him as Speaker for the second time in the autumn of 1555. In what looks like a gesture of protest by the freeholders of Oxfordshire Pollard was on this occasion denied the knighthood of that shire and a seat had to be found for him at Chippenham, almost certainly after an attempt in the meantime to have him elected at Gloucester. Yet on the first day of the Parliament he was chosen Speaker 'by the entire voice' and made an oration which was considered excellent by James Bassett* and by Cardinal Pole, who wrote a few days later to King Philip expressing the hope that the Commons would 'show the same mind in matters relating to religion and the honour and advantage of the crown as evinced by their Speaker'. On the contrary the House was to prove practically unmanageable, with a group of Members doing their utmost to block the government's measures. High-handed action was necessary to secure the passage of a bill renouncing the crown's right to first fruits, but Pollard was in turn coerced into abetting the defeat of the bill threatening Protestant refugees abroad with heavy penalties. The knighthood conferred on him, probably at the close of the session, seems less a reward than a consolation.[9]

In April 1557 Pollard was appointed justice of

Chester and Flint for life and of two other Welsh counties during pleasure, but by the summer he had been taken ill, perhaps with the infection then widespread, and on 2 Aug. he made a second and final will. As he had no children his property was to descend in tail male, on the death of his wife and the extinction of her life interest in Nuneham Courtenay, to his much younger brother and heir Anthony, who had already had certain lands settled on him at his marriage six years earlier to Philippa, daughter of William Sheldon*; in the event of Anthony's death without male issue the inheritance would pass to William, younger son of Sir Richard Pollard, whom the executors were to 'find to learning in Latin' for two more years and then to put to some good master. To his wife Pollard left the household stuff at Nuneham, with farm stock, money and plate, to his brother Anthony his books, a sum of £20 and all his apparel at Ludlow, and to kinsfolk and friends, including his mother, smaller bequests: the residue was to go to pay debts and damages and to support charities. The executors were his brother, Ralph Ferne and Thomas Mynd*, and the overseer Sir John Williams*, Lord Williams of Thame.[10]

Pollard died on 12 Aug. 1557 and was buried in London on the 25th. His wife, who by 1561 had married one Thomas Norris, outlived him by nearly half a century and Anthony Pollard, despairing of getting possession of Nuneham Courtenay, entered into an agreement in 1577, the year of his own death, by which his interest passed to the sons of Sir Richard Pollard.[11]

[1] Plymouth receivers' acct. bk. 1536–7. [2] Date of birth estimated from first reference. *Vis. Devon*, ed. Vivian, 597; *Vis. Oxon.* (Harl. Soc. v), 305; Plymouth black bk. f. 135v; *CPR*, 1555–7, pp. 214, 468. [3] Plymouth receivers' acct. bk. 1538–9 to 1549–50; *CPR*, 1547–8, p. 75; 1549–51, pp. 211–12, 228; 1550–3, pp. 395, 423; 1553, p. 357; 1555–7, p. 468; Williams, *Oxford M.Ps*, 41; Gloucester Guildhall 1394, ff. 41–54; *Oxf. Recs.* 216, 267; Somerville, *Duchy*, i. 432; *LP Hen. VIII*, xiv. [4] R. N. Worth, *Plymouth*, 212–13; *CIPM Hen. VII*, iii. 705; J. A. Youings, 'The disposal of monastic property in land in the county of Devon 1535–58' (London Univ. Ph.D. thesis, 1950), 109–10; Foss, *Judges*, v. 228; PCC 27 Pynnyng. [5] *LP Hen. VIII*, viii; Plymouth receivers' acct. bk. 1530–1, 1535–6, 1536–7. [6] *LP Hen. VIII*, xiii; Somerville, i. 432. [7] E. Plowden, *Commentaries* (1816), 17–18; Plymouth black bk. f. 135v; PCC 37 Wrastley; *VCH Oxon.* v. 241; *LP Hen. VIII*, xix, xx; E150/821/6. [9] *CJ*, i. 27, 30, 32, 35, 38, 40–42, 44; *CSP Span.* 1554–8, p. 125; *CSP Ven.* 1555–6, pp. 225, 233, 283. [10] PCC 37 Wrastley. [11] E150/821/6; *Machyn's Diary* (Cam. Soc. xlii), 148; *VCH Oxon.* v. 241.

R.V.

POLLARD, Sir John (1527/28–75), of Forde Abbey, Dorset, Horton, Glos., Trelawne, Cornw., and Bishopsgate, London.

PLYMPTON ERLE	1553 (Mar.)
BARNSTAPLE	1554 (Apr.)
EXETER	1555, 1559
GRAMPOUND	1563

b. 1527/28, 1st s. of (Sir) Richard Pollard* of Putney, Surr., London and Forde Abbey by Jacquetta, da. of John Bury of Colliton, Devon. *m.* Catherine, at least 3da.; at least 1s. illegit. *suc.* fa. 10 Nov. 1542. Kntd. 10 Nov. 1549.[1]

J.p. Devon 1558/59–*d.*, q. by 1569, j.p. Som. by 1569; commr. eccles. causes 1559; visitor, diocese of Exeter 1559; pres. council of Munster 1568.[2]

John Pollard's father provided for his boyhood governance by his uncles Sir Hugh Pollard and (Sir) Hugh Paulet*, but in August 1543 his wardship and marriage were granted to Sir John Russell*, Baron Russell. Russell's defection from the Duke of Somerset was followed by Pollard's knighting on the same day as his friend Arthur Champernon*; the wardship grant was formally cancelled in December 1550 but Pollard was not licensed to enter upon his inheritance until nine days before the death of Edward VI.[3]

Pollard had by then sat in his first Parliament as senior Member for Plympton Erle. One of his relatives, the archdeacon of Barnstaple, was lessee of some property there from the family of the other Member, Richard Strode II, but Russell, now Earl of Bedford, was doubtless responsible for his nomination. His next appearance was in Mary's second Parliament when with another of the earl's protégés, George Ferrers, he sat for Barnstaple. His grandfather had been, and his uncle Sir Hugh Pollard still was, recorder of the borough, while he had more than one marital link with (Sir) John Chichester*, its chief patron. As the owner of property there he also went some way towards satisfying the crown's request for resident Members, although he is to be distinguished from a kinsman and namesake who lived at Barnstaple. It was doubtless yet another John Pollard, then knight of the shire for Oxfordshire and Speaker in the Parliaments of October 1553 and 1555, who in April 1554 was concerned with a bill for the election of university scholars and with a case of privilege raised by William Johnson I*.[4]

Neither noble patronage nor local ties procured Pollard a seat in the second Parliament of 1554, but in the following year he was elected senior Member for Exeter. Not without connexions there, for the recorder was his cousin and an uncle was a prebendary in the cathedral, he must again have been a nominee, especially as he did not meet the city's recent requirement that only resident freemen could be elected. The new Earl of Bedford was abroad, so that the nomination was probably made by Cecil, whom Bedford had empowered to act for him during his absence. The corporation did what it could to regularize Pollard's position by making him a freeman immediately after his election. It was in this Parliament that he sat under the Speakership of his namesake, to whose difficulty in controlling the House he made his contribution. A member of Cecil's parliamentary dinner-party and of the group which met to discuss the tactics of opposition, he voted against one of the government's bills.[5]

Pollard seems to have remained in London after the Parliament was dissolved and by mid February 1556 he is known to have become involved in the Dudley conspiracy. He was one of those sent to the Tower on 29 Apr. but it was not until 4 Nov. that he was indicted and within another month he was released. His service in the French campaign of the following year doubtless helped him to obtain a pardon on 30 Jan. 1558 and to recover some of his property. While abroad he had witnessed the will of Sir William Courtenay II*, who had been imprisoned and freed with him.[6]

The description of Pollard in the pardon as 'late of Forde, Dorset *alias* late of Horton, Gloucestershire' may reflect losses of property otherwise than by escheat. Forde itself had passed to his cousin Amias Paulet† by 1558 and other possessions were sold piecemeal to meet debts which had probably originated with the wardship. Pollard's lease of the manor of Trelawne, Cornwall, in 1561 gave him his new home. He sat in the first two Elizabethan Parliaments and it may have been the ill-health that prevented him from taking up his appointment to the presidency of Munster which kept him out of the next two. He did not die, however, until 1575.[7]

[1] Date of birth estimated from age at fa.'s i.p.m., C142/65/25. *Vis. Devon*, ed. Vivian, 598; PCC 27 Pynnyng, 47 Pyckering. [2] *CPR*, 1560-3, p. 345; 1566-9, p. 350; 1569-72, pp. 222-3; N. M. Fuidge, 'Personnel of the House of Commons of 1563-7' (London Univ. M.A. thesis, 1950), 269; *CSP Ire.* 1509-73, pp. 392-3, 410, 429. [3] *LP Hen. VIII*, xviii, xxi; *CPR*, 1553, p. 7; PCC 27 Pynnyng; Docquet bk. f. 21. [4] NRA 4154, p. 156; *LP Hen. VIII*, xviii; PCC *Admins.* ed. Glencross, i. 107; N. Devon Athenaeum, Barnstaple, 1712; 3972, ff. 20v, 42(2), 45(2), 55(2) et passim; *CJ*, i. 35. [5] *HMC Exeter*, 362; *Trans. Dev. Assoc.* lxi. 194; *Exeter Freemen* (Devon and Cornw. Rec. Soc. extra ser. i), 81; Exeter act bk. 2, ff. 142v, 143; F. Peck, *Desiderata Curiosa*, i. 19; SP11/8/7, 35; Guildford mus. Loseley 1331/2. [6] Strype, *Eccles. Memorials*, iii(1), 488; *Machyn's Diary* (Cam. Soc. xlii), 104; *CSP Dom.* 1547-80, p. 84; *CPR*, 1555-7, p. 456; 1557-8, p. 89; D. M. Loades, *Two Tudor Conspiracies*, 223-34. Loades, 212 and C. Read, *Cecil*, 109-10 confuse him with the Speaker. [7] *CPR*, 1557-8, p. 89; 1560-3, pp. 153, 368; *Devon and Cornw. N. and Q.* xxix. 302-4.

A.D.K.H.

POLLARD, Richard (by 1505-42), of Putney, Surr., London, and Forde Abbey, Dorset.

?TAUNTON   1536[1]

DEVON   1539,[2] 1542[3]

b. by 1505, 2nd s. of Sir Lewis Pollard† of Kings Nympton, Devon by Agnes, da. of Thomas Hext of Kingston, nr. Totnes, Devon. *educ.* M. Temple, adm. 4 July 1519. *m.* by 1528, Jacquetta, da. of John Bury of Colliton, Devon, 3s. inc. Sir John* 1da. Kntd. 16 Jan. 1542.[4]

Autumn reader, M. Temple 1535, ?bencher by 1535.[5]

Servant of Sir William Courtenay I* by 1532; j.p. Devon 1532, Mdx. 1537-d., western circuit 1540-d.; King's remembrancer May 1536-d.; third gen. surveyor, office of gen. surveyors Feb. 1537, second 1539; sheriff, Devon 1537-8; member, council in the

west 1539; steward, late possessions of Henry, Marquess of Exeter 1539-d.; second gen. surveyor, ct. gen. surveyors of the King's lands May 1542-d.[6]

Richard Pollard began his career as a practising lawyer; he had chambers above the gateway to the Middle Temple, received annuities from Cornish and Devonshire abbeys, and served on the council of the south-western magnate, Sir William Courtenay. The employment by Courtenay, which included accompanying him on monastic visitations, brought Pollard to the attention of Cromwell, for whom he was working before Courtenay's death. In the summer of 1535, at Cromwell's request and in company with other common lawyers, he met several doctors from the court of arches to discuss spiritual jurisdiction. Afterwards he wrote to Cromwell about the unsatisfactory nature of the meeting, and suggested:

> if it may stand with the King's grace's pleasure and yours, it were better to devise a remedy that the temporal judges may hereafter have jurisdiction of all such crimes and causes as the ecclesiastical judges have had jurisdiction heretofore, and by that means we shall have but one law within this realm, which I think better in my poor mind than to have several laws.

Although his radical proposal was not adopted, Pollard continued in favour and his name appears often in Cromwell's remembrances. His experience suggests that he was the 'Pollarde' who supplied a series of entries found appended to a set of law reports made by Justice John Spelman.[7]

The suggestion that Pollard was returned for Taunton to the Parliament of 1536 rests on the appearance of his name on a list, seemingly of nominees for the bishop of Winchester's boroughs, written by Cromwell on a document probably of that year. Cromwell had sat for Taunton in the Parliament of 1529 (with William Portman, who also appears on the above list for that borough), but he presumably transferred to a knighthood of the shire in 1536, although there is no evidence for this. In the next two Parliaments Pollard sat for Devon: his knighthood of that shire was a measure of his local and official standing, and it was amplified by his being knighted in the parliament chamber at the opening of Parliament on 16 Jan. 1542. Two weeks later, together with his fellow-Members Richard Catlyn, John Caryll and Sir Roger Townshend, Pollard was approached by the city of London to sponsor a bill for cleaning the Fleet ditch. Pollard's brother-in-law, Sir Hugh Paulet*, was sheriff on the occasion of his second election for the county.[8]

As a royal surveyor, Pollard was concerned with the suppression of the lesser Kent, Surrey, Sussex and Yorkshire monasteries in 1537, as well as of Glastonbury and Reading abbeys between the parliamentary sessions of 1539. He supervised the defacement of the shrines at Bury St. Edmunds, Winchester and Canterbury, where he was described as so busy night and day 'in prayer with offering unto St. Thomas' that he had 'no idle worldly time' to spare until his 'spiritual devotion' was completed. The recipient of numerous gifts and annuities (in 1541 he was assessed for subsidy in London at £230 in lands and fees), Pollard acquired his greatest prize with the grant in 1540 of Forde abbey—then in Devon—which he had leased the previous year. He was nominated as a founder member of the council in the west in 1539 with permission to attend at his pleasure or when summoned.[9]

The fall of Cromwell did not arrest Pollard's progress: he was one of the outstanding civil servants of the period, and when the new court of general surveyors was instituted he was appointed its joint first officer. His death on 10 Nov. 1542 removed the prospect of yet higher office and of the establishment of his family in greater state. It is not known who replaced him for the last two sessions of the Parliament of 1542. He had made his will on 31 Mar. 1541, providing for his wife, children and servants. The upbringing of his children was confided to his wife, his elder brother and his brother-in-law Paulet. To Sir William Fitzwilliam I*, Earl of Southampton, and Sir John Russell*, Baron Russell, he left rings, and to Sir Richard Rich (the overseer) a salt. He named his cousins John Pollard* and Humphrey Colles* executors.[10]

[1] LP Hen. VIII, x. 40 (ii) citing Cott. Otho C10, f. 218. [2] E159/319, brev. ret. Mich. r. [1-2]. [3] C219/18B/159. [4] Date of birth estimated from education. Vis. Devon, ed. Vivian, 598; PCC 27 Pynnyng; Hutchins, Dorset, iv. 527. [5] LP Hen. VIII, ix; Reps. of Sir John Spelman, i (Selden Soc. xciii), p. xxv. [6] LP Hen. VIII, v-xvii. [7] Ibid. v-xiv; L. Snell, Suppression of Rel. Foundations of Devon and Cornw. 66; J. Youings, Dissolution of the Monasteries, 54; SP1/95, f. 121; G. R. Elton, Reform and Renewal, 133-4; Reps. of Sir John Spelman, i, p. xxv. [8] Cott. Otho C10, f. 218; Wriothesley's Chron. i (Cam. Soc. n.s. xi), 133; City of London RO, Guildhall, rep. 10, f. 242v. [9] W. C. Richardson, Tudor Chamber Admin. 258; LP Hen. VIII, viii-xvii; Devon Monastic Lands (Devon and Cornw. Rec. Soc. n.s.i.), xxi, 13; RCHM, W. Dorset, 240-66; DKR, x(ii), 25; E179/144/120. [10] W. C. Richardson, Ct. Augmentations, 78; PPC, vii. 113-280 passim; C142/65/25; PCC 25 Pynnyng.

A.D.K.H.

POLLE, John (b. by 1531–56 or later), of Leominster, Herefs.

LEOMINSTER 1553 (Oct.)

b. by 1531, prob. s. of John Polle of Leominster by Maud.[1]
Capital burgess, Leominster 1554, bailiff 1555-6.[2]

John Polle's place in his family, a leading one at Leominster, is not altogether clear. His return to the first Marian Parliament as John Polle 'senior' distinguishes him from his namesake who appears on subsidy rolls and elsewhere as 'baker' and suggests that he was the elder of the two sons of that name who were mentioned in the will of John Polle 'the

elder', made on 3 June 1550 and proved on 30 Apr. 1552: John Polle 'baker' was an overseer of this will. The elder of these sons was bequeathed a Leominster burgage on condition that he 'apply himself to help me and my wife in our business and trouble when he shall be required and so that he do not disturb nor disquiet my executors'. It was evidently this testator who had been assessed as John Polle senior on £15 in goods for the subsidy of 1543 but nine years later it was probably the two brothers who, as John Polle senior and junior, were each assessed on £10 in goods. There is nothing to show which of these brothers (if either) was the John Polle of Leominster who made his will on 25 May 1578.[3]

Little else is known of Polle, although his leading place in the borough under Mary suggests that he was the 'Mr. Polle', merchant, who in the reign of Edward VI acted for Leominster in negotiations with the city of Gloucester over free passage on the river Severn. Neither Polle nor his fellow-Member William Strete 'stood for the true religion' against the initial measures to restore Catholicism.[4]

[1] Date of birth estimated from subsidy assessment. PCC 12 Powell. [2] CPR, 1553-4, p. 396; G. F. Townsend, Leominster, 293. [3] C219/21/72; PCC 12 Powell; Townsend, 54, 71, 76, 83, 258; E179/117/218, 237/40; NLW Hereford consist. ct. wills box 10, Po(1). [4] Townsend, 50-52.

P.S.E.

POLLINGTON, Ralph (by 1519–87), of Wallingford, Berks.

WALLINGFORD 1547*,[1] 1558

b. by 1519, s. of Thomas Pollington of Wallingford. m. (1) by 1546, Joan, at least 2s.; (2) Agnes, 4s. 3da; at least 1 ch. illegit.[2]
Mayor, Wallingford 1549, 1552, 1555, 1557, 1558, 1568.[3]

During the first half of the 16th century, the family of Pollington was rivalled in Wallingford only by that of à Deane. Ralph Pollington's father was a mercer who had been a freeman at least since 1507, and first became mayor in 1513, after which he and William à Deane practically monopolized this office for 30 years. At first William à Deane the elder was assessed as the richer man, but by 1525 Pollington headed the list. He remained the wealthiest townsman until his death in the summer of 1547 after which Ralph increased the family's pre-eminence.[4]

Pollington followed his father into trade and dealt in cloth. It is probable that he was the eldest son, for he was his father's residuary legatee and sole executor, receiving all the property in Wallingford. There were, however, both a brother called John, who was left some lands in Oxfordshire, and several other children, to each of whom Ralph was enjoined to pay £20. He himself had already started to accumulate property. In 1540 he bought a cottage and garden at Wallingford and in 1542 several orchards and crofts at Fawley, Buckinghamshire: this second purchase involved him in a chancery suit shortly before the death of Henry VIII. In December 1546 he and one John Petyt were licensed to acquire the neighbouring manor of Wyfold in Oxfordshire.[5]

After his father's death, Pollington became more prominent in borough affairs. It is likely that a man as prominent as his father had sat in one or more of the early Parliaments of Henry VIII, for which no returns have survived, and his son was an obvious choice if a townsman was to replace Henry Huntley, whose Membership of Edward VI's first Parliament was cut short by his death in 1549. The appearance of Pollington's name on the list of Members revised for the last session of that Parliament shows that he was indeed by-elected to it. With but a single session to his credit, he might have expected to be returned to the next Parliament. On that occasion, however, both Wallingford seats went to non-townsmen, and Pollington was not to sit again until 1558.[6]

It is possible that his landed interests and the lawsuits arising from them made Pollington reluctant to continue as a Member. His lease of a fulling mill from the royal manor of Ewelme in 1549 brought no trouble, but his purchases at Fawley were the subject of further proceedings. Preparations were made to try the case locally, which so alarmed Pollington that he petitioned the chancellor to transfer it to London. Among other reasons for this adjournment he explained that he 'is now daily attendant at this present Parliament . . . and cannot therefore attend the trial of the said issue with such diligence as is therein requisite'. In the first year of Mary's reign he again invoked the law, when trying to evict a widow from her tenement on his manor of Wyfold: the court of requests finding that the defendant had forfeited it by being 'incontinent of her living' since her husband's death. This was a triumph for property but not for morality, for Pollington was himself to leave an illegitimate child. His attitude to the Catholic restoration is not known, but he was to be mayor of Wallingford three times under Mary.[7]

Pollington was not re-elected to Parliament after 1558, but he was to serve once more as mayor and remained active in local affairs until his death on 19 Dec. 1587. By his will made on 3 May 1585 and styling him gentleman he asked to be buried in St. Peter's church, Wallingford, and provided for his family. Further to an earlier settlement in favour of his two elder sons, John and Ralph, he gave them £10 apiece, with the injunction not to contest the will as 'either of them will answer before God at the

dreadful day of judgment'. Agnes, his second wife and executrix, had to support the younger children under a bond of £300 to the overseers, Thomas Farmer[†] and Michael Molyns[†].[8]

[1] Hatfield 207. [2] Date of birth estimated from first reference. PCC 45 Alen, 80 Spencer; C1/1312/56; 142/217/130. [3] Berks. RO, W/AC a1, ff. 59v, 60v, 71v, 72v; J. K. Hedges, *Wallingford*, ii. 228. [4] Berks. RO, W/AC a1, ff. 1, 8, 15v, 18, 21, 24; E179/73/128, 156, 74/216. [5] Berks. RO, W/AC a1, f. 52v; C1/1152/27; *LP Hen. VIII*, xxi. [6] Hedges, ii. 312. [7] *CPR*, 1558–60, p. 393; C1/1312/56–57; Req. 2/22/32, 75/2. [8] Berks. RO, W/AC a1, f. 68; C142/217/130; PCC 80 Spencer.

T.F.T.B.

POLSTED, Henry (by 1510–55), of Albury, Surr.

BLETCHINGLEY	1547*,[1] 1553 (Oct.)[2]
GUILDFORD	1554 (Nov.), 1555

b. by 1510, 2nd s. of Thomas Polsted of Stoke by Agnes; bro. of Thomas*. *educ.* ?Guildford g.s. *m.* 18 May 1539, Alice, da. of Robert Lord *alias* Lawerde, 1s. Richard[†] 1da.; at least 1 ch. illegit.[3]

Bencher, I. Temple 1552.

Receiver to Cromwell by 1533; under steward, ct. augmentations, north of Trent May 1538–June 1540; commr. benevolence, Surr. 1544/45, chantries, Surr., Suss. and Chichester 1548, relief, Surr. and Suss. 1550, goods of churches and fraternities, Surr. 1553; other commissions 1551–4; j.p. Essex 1547, Surr. 1547–*d.*, q. 1554, Suss. 1547; escheator, Surr. and Suss. 1549–50.[4]

Although there had been Polsteds in Surrey since the 12th century, no doubt deriving from Polsted manor in the parish of Compton near Guildford, the first of the name to achieve prominence were Henry Polsted and his elder brother Thomas. In 1509 their father was appointed a trustee of property bequeathed to establish a grammar school in Guildford and it is likely that Henry Polsted was a pupil there: on 1 July 1550 he gave the school two houses in Guildford, and Nicholas Elyot, who is thought to have been headmaster of the school, claimed kinship with him.[5]

The first mention of Polsted occurs in his father's will of March 1529, of which he was an executor. In 1531 he purchased two houses in Guildford and in the same year was associated with his brother Thomas in a property transaction in the county. Unlike his brother, Henry does not seem to have received any legal training, but by 1533 he had become Cromwell's receiver and he was to display considerable talent for administration; four years later Richard Cromwell *alias* Williams* wrote to his uncle, 'I have not seen a man of his order so gentle to entertain suitors; such men deserve promotion'. Although it is not known how Polsted came to Cromwell's notice, his father's connexion with Wolsey, whose bailiff the elder Polsted was at Wargrave, Berkshire, suggests that he effected the introduction.[6]

Polsted's services to Cromwell were of a varied

nature. He was present when Bishop Fisher was questioned in the Tower, helped to take the surrenders of monastic houses in Kent and Sussex and reported to Cromwell on their condition; he examined suitors to his master and accounted for the issues of the Rolls office. In September 1535, on Cromwell's direction, he attempted to influence the nomination of the under sheriff of Middlesex and at the same time he was busy negotiating with the bishops elect of Rochester and Worcester for the payment of their first fruits and tenths; it was, however, probably his brother who took part in the discussions of August 1535 with ecclesiastical lawyers on the jurisdiction of church courts.[7]

As receiver of Cromwell's private possessions Polsted clearly stood close to the minister: he frequently advised Cromwell on legal problems arising from property transactions and acted as his feoffee. A hint of ruthlessness is revealed in a letter of his to Cromwell in February 1538: after reminding the minister to call upon the dissolution commissioners to make their returns of surrendered monasteries, he suggested that 'if one that were found faulty were put in the Fleet, the residue would be more diligent'. When in May 1538 Cromwell was appointed chief steward of all augmentation lands north of the Trent, Polsted became his deputy and did the work of the office, at a salary of £20 paid by the court. Although Polsted does not appear to have been seriously compromised by his master's fall, Cromwell's successor as chief steward, Thomas Audley, Baron Audley, appointed John Lucas* as his deputy. In August 1540 Polsted was appointed overseer of Cromwell's possessions.[8]

It is less clear what Polsted did afterwards. He was described as the King's servant when in June 1543 he was granted an annuity of £40 upon his surrender of one of the same value granted to him by Cromwell in March 1538, and shortly afterwards he became active in local affairs; after the death of (Sir) Christopher More* in August 1549 he called Cecil's attention to the scarcity of justices of the peace (of which he was now one) in Surrey, recommending suitable persons and asking for money for a county gaol. Part of his time he devoted to business in Guildford, where in April 1545, and again in the following May, he was among millers of the town fined for occupying the High Street throughout the year with their horses and mares. Bishop Parkhurst, who had been born in Guildford and held Calvinist views, wrote a complimentary verse in Latin to his 'fellow country-man' Polsted, whom he thus distinguished from less upright justices:

But you not the least celebrated in the law speak the truth

You, oh shining constellation and inspiration of your people
You assist the poor with words, experience and advice
You expound the difficult knots of law, the deep meanings, with a sense of beauty in these matters
You think with judgment and decide fairly . . .

In February 1552 the Inner Temple, his brother's inn, called Polsted to its bench on payment of £6 13s.4d. and the condition that 'it shall be no precedent to any other hereafter to be called to the bench because he never exercised any office in this house'. It appears that Polsted had learned his law outside the professional schools but had done well enough to be honoured by one of them.[9]

During his service with Cromwell, Polsted had been well placed to obtain a seat in Parliament, but the loss of so many names of Members in 1536 and 1539 leaves it uncertain whether he did so: his brother Thomas almost certainly sat at least twice during these years. In March 1539 Sir William Fitzwilliam I*, Earl of Southampton, was attempting to procure the return of suitable Members from Hampshire, Surrey and Sussex; he approved Guildford's choice of Daniel Mugge, assuring Cromwell that Mugge was 'an honest man' and 'a kinsman of Henry Polsted'. If Polsted was himself found a seat in this Parliament, his attendance must have been subject to interruption: thus on 4 May 1539, during the first session, John Hussee wrote that Polsted and (Sir) John Baldwin* would meet Viscount Lisle at Dover nine days later (Lisle's crossing being, however, postponed at the last minute), and on 13 June, during the second session, Polsted was at Cromwell's house at Halden, Kent.[10]

The first Parliament of which Polsted is known to have been a Member was that of 1547: he replaced Sir Thomas Cawarden at Bletchingley. It was probably during the second session that Cawarden exchanged his borough seat for the knighthood of the shire and Polsted's by-election doubtless followed soon after. Cawarden himself controlled the borough and he too was connected with the Mores of Loseley. In the following Parliament Polsted may have found a seat at Guildford, the Members for that borough being unknown, but in the first Parliament of Mary's reign he was re-elected for Bletchingley. He was not among those who in the course of that Parliament 'stood for the true religion', that is, for Protestantism. In November 1554 and again in 1555 he was returned for his native Guildford, where by his acquisition of Albury manor he had also become one of the largest local landowners. On both occasions he sat with his friend and associate William More. Neither of them 'seceded' from the first of these Parliaments and only More is known to have opposed a government bill in the second. More's father called Polsted his 'cousin', and Polsted was related to Daniel Mugge, Sir Christopher More's brother-in-law. Polsted appointed William More an executor of his will and in 1567 his son Richard was to marry More's daughter Elizabeth. Polsted was himself an executor of the will of his cousin Thomas Elyot, Member for Guildford in 1545 and 1547.[11]

In May 1539 Polsted had married the daughter of a colleague, Robert Lord, servant to (Sir) John Gostwick*, the treasurer of first fruits and tenths. (The ascription to him of an earlier marriage in the Surrey visitation of 1623 probably arose from a confusion of Polsted with his uncle and namesake of Purley, a merchant taylor of London.) In August 1536, nearly three years before his marriage, Polsted had written to Cromwell that his hope of advancement in marriage was clearly gone 'by his late evil chance'; he did not specify the trouble, but it may have been an episode revealed in a Star Chamber complaint against him dating from between 1533 and 1542. The plaintiff, John Crowe, alleged that Polsted had forcibly entered his house near Temple Bar, had over a long period committed adultery with Crowe's wife Maud, who bore a child by him, had driven Crowe from his wife and home, and had embezzled goods to the value of 200 marks. Polsted's reply to the charges has not survived and the outcome of the case is unknown.[12]

One of the most noticeable features of Polsted's career is his large accumulation of monastic and chantry property. In February 1540 he paid £540 for the priory of Bicknacre, Essex, and in August 1548, with William More, £382 to augmentations for former chantry property in Berkshire, Hampshire, London, Surrey and Sussex. In December 1548, again with More, he purchased for £2,035 chantry lands in Kent, Surrey and Sussex and in the following March, with Sir Anthony Aucher, he paid £2,745 into augmentations for lands in Essex, London, Surrey and Sussex. He had inherited some property in Guildford and its neighbourhood from his father, but alienated much of it before his death.[13]

In his will of 1 Aug. 1555 Polsted asked that there should be no pomp at his burial and that only his wife, his other executors (William More and John Brace*) and four of his servants should wear mourning. His rents and leases he left to his wife Alice, until his son Richard, then a boy of ten, should come of age, provided she remained unmarried and paid for the children's upbringing. She was also to enjoy a life interest in the manors of Albury and Wildwood, the chantry house in Shere and all its property

in Albury, Alford, and Shere, and, in consideration of her dower and his 'benevolence', former chantry property in Kent, London, Surrey and Sussex. Polsted's nephew, Anthony Elmes, was given a manor and lands in Worthing, Sussex, and his daughter received a 'barn and a close' in Reading, Berkshire. Polsted divided much of his property into portions, creating entails for various relatives in the event of his dying without issue. He granted the Queen an annuity of 50 marks for six years from his manors of Catford, Kent, and Hall Place, Surrey. Four lawyers were appointed to resolve any obscurities in the will, and to emend it if need be, each receiving a gold ring worth 40s. for his pains; another distinguished lawyer, John Caryll*, was named among the overseers. Polsted died on 10 Dec. 1555 and the will was proved on 16 May 1556.[14]

[1] Hatfield 207. [2] Bodl. e Museo 17. [3] Date of birth estimated from purchase of property in 1531. PCC 5 Jankyn, 6 Ketchyn; Surr. Arch. Colls. ii. ped. section; VCH Surr. ii. 165; LP Hen. VIII, xiv. [4] M. L. Robertson, 'Cromwell's servants' (Univ. California Los Angeles PhD. thesis, 1975), 544-5; W. C. Richardson, Ct. Augmentations, 222; Surr. Arch. Colls. iv. 10; LP Hen. VIII, ix, xx; CPR, 1547-8, pp. 83, 90; 1548-9, p. 135; 1549-51, p. 301; 1550-3, pp. 141, 395; 1553, pp. 338, 357, 359, 415; 1553-4, pp. 24, 29, 35; 1554-5, p. 107. [5] Manning and Bray, Surr. i. 75; VCH Surr. ii. 165; iii. 21; LP Hen. VIII, i, iv, xiv; add. 6167, f. 199v. [6] PCC 5 Jankyn; Cal. I.T. Recs. i. 49, 102, 104; LP Hen. VIII, iv; Surr. Feet of Fines (Surr. Rec. Soc. xix), 190, 226; VCH Berks. iii. 192. [7] Elton, Tudor Rev. in Govt. 199-200, 304; LP Hen. VIII, viii, ix, xi-xiv. [8] LP Hen. VIII, viii, ix, xi-xiii, xv; Richardson, 222, 494. [9] LP Hen. VIII, xviii; APC, iv. 146; CSP Dom. 1547-80, p. 21; Guildford Bor. Recs. (Surr. Rec. Soc. xxiv), 81, 121; Johannis Parkhursti Ludicra sive Epigrammata Juvenilia (1578), 25; Cal. I.T. Recs. i. 163. [10] LP Hen. VIII, xiv. [11] VCH Surr. iii. 73; Guildford mus. Loseley 346/3, 347/17, 19, 1-2; 2021; HMC 7th Rep. 597; PCC 6 Ketchyn; CSP Dom. 1547-80, p. 21; LP Hen. VIII, xv; E150/1102/2; Surr. Feet of Fines, 827; PCC 24 Populwell. [12] Surr. Feet of Fines, 263; Elton, 197, n. 3; LP Hen. VIII, xi; Vis. Surr. (Harl. Soc. xliii), 83; Manning and Bray, ii. 576; St.Ch.2/11/82. [13] LP Hen. VIII, xiv, xv; CPR, 1547-8, pp. 60, 280; 1548-9, p. 282; 1549-51, pp. 199, 232; VCH Surr. iii. 105; iv. 89; Manning and Bray, i. 170, 173; Feet of Fines, London and Mdx. ed. Hardy and Page, ii. 81; PCC 6 Ketchyn; Surr. Fines, 264, 309, 357, 433, 530, 580, 800, 806, 827, 1029; E150/505/3, 1102/2; 315/219, f. 131, 224, f. 292; Richardson, 293, 294; C142/106/56. [14] PCC 6 Ketchyn; C142/106/56.

S.R.J.

POLSTED, Thomas (by 1505-?41), of Guildford, Surr. and London.

?GREAT BEDWYN 1529*[1]

b. by 1505, 1st s. of Thomas Polsted of Stoke, and bro. of Henry*. educ. I. Temple, adm. 1519. suc. fa. 15 Mar. 1529.[2]

Bencher, I. Temple 1537.

King's attorney, ct. wards 3 Aug. 1540-7 Feb. 1541.[3]

It was A. F. Pollard who suggested that Thomas Polsted was by-elected to the Parliament of 1529 about the year 1533. Pollard's scrutiny of a list of over 30 names preserved among the State Papers revealed that 26 or 27 of them were those of Members elected in 1529 and that all the names appeared in a topographical order identical with that adopted in Crown Office lists until after that date: he concluded that the remaining names were those of men returned at by-elections held after

1529 but before the date of the list in question. Among the seven or eight names concerned is that of Thomas Polsted 'of Guildford'. Nineteen of the men named are thus attached to places, which almost certainly represent residences and not constituencies: thus four of those listed are marked 'of Chelsea'. The Polsted on the list may therefore be identified with the eldest son of Thomas Polsted of Stoke-next-Guildford, Surrey, who died in March 1529, leaving the bulk of his property to his son and namesake.[4]

With regard to the constituency Polsted's name occurs in the list between those of Members known to have sat for Wiltshire boroughs since 1529, Thomas Chaffyn I for Salisbury and John Poyntz for Devizes. Of the four Wiltshire boroughs whose names usually appear between Salisbury and Devizes, namely Malmesbury, Cricklade, Great Bedwyn and Marlborough, the only one for which a vacancy is known to have arisen is Great Bedwyn; one of the Members returned there in 1529, William Newdigate, had been marked 'mortuus' on a list dating from the spring of 1532, and the vacancy is confirmed by a list of unfilled seats compiled by or for Cromwell, probably before the end of 1532, which includes Great Bedwyn but no other Wiltshire borough. There can thus be little doubt that Polsted was returned for Great Bedwyn, or that, as the list dates from the fifth session of the Parliament, the by-election took place in December 1532 or January 1533.[5]

Polsted was then perhaps in his early thirties. His career has to be distinguished from that of his cousin and namesake, a merchant taylor of London: in a fine made in 1535 the first is called 'senior, and the second 'junior', but as feoffees for Cromwell in the same year they are not so qualified. Their differing avocations warrant the identification of the Member with the lawyer who entered the Inner Temple in 1519 and in 1537 reached the bench there: moreover, this Thomas Polsted's record at the inn was marred by derelictions of duty such as might well have been occasioned by the demands of his public life. How early he became associated with Cromwell is not known, but his younger brother Henry Polsted was the secretary's receiver by 1533, and as their father had been one of Wolsey's bailiffs the connexion may have been formed by 1529. (The Polsteds' link with Wolsey did not, however, prevent him as chancellor from ruling against them, in June 1529, when the father was already dead, in a suit brought by Magdalen College, Oxford.) Of the scattered appearances of the name before that year it is hard to say whether they denote the father or the son: the most tantaliz-

ing, especially in view of Polsted's seeming doubts about royal policy in 1533, is the ambiguous reference, in an account of the perambulation in March 1525 of the waste and common of Shere, Surrey, a manor then held by Catherine of Aragon, to Thomas Polsted as either one of the Queen's servants or one of the neighbouring residents taking part.[6]

Whatever his affiliations before the close of 1532, Polsted can scarcely have owed his by-election to anyone but Cromwell, although perhaps through the agency of Sir William Essex*. Formerly under the patronage of Sir Edward Darrell*, the lord of the manor, Bedwyn had come, since Darrell's death in 1531, into the custody of Essex. That the King himself intervened is unlikely: true, the daughter of one of his physicians, Balthazar Gwercye, was to marry a Thomas Polsted, but this was almost certainly the merchant taylor, whose personal and marital record accords well with such an alliance, and unless the King's interest had been solicited in this roundabout way Polsted could not have looked elsewhere than to the secretary for nomination at a borough with which he himself had no known connexion. Of Polsted's role in the Commons there is but a solitary glimpse —yet an unexpected one. It is afforded by the same list as furnishes the evidence of his Membership. If, as is believed, this list records the names of Members opposed to the bill in restraint of appeals to Rome, Polsted's appearance on it means that his entry into the House under Cromwell's sponsorship did not prevent him from taking an independent line there. He would not have been the only lawyer to do so: his name is followed on the list by those of William Whorwood, a future law officer of the crown, and of Thomas Bromley I, a future chief justice (and a colleague of Polsted's at the Inner Temple). And just as neither Whorwood's nor Bromley's career was to be blighted by their opposition at this juncture, so Polsted's clearly did not suffer. How much he owed to his brother we cannot say, but although their names are regularly conjoined in the service of the minister, as when in June 1537 they sent him 'bridgements' of the correspondence between Sir John Neville I*, 3rd Baron Latimer, and Sir Francis Bigod*, Thomas Polsted is also found acting individually, especially in Cromwell's legal business and interests: it is thus likely that he, and not his brother, took part in the discussions of August 1535 with ecclesiastical lawyers on the jurisdiction of church courts. He also acted for other notables, one of them being the 9th Lord la Warr, whose conservatism in religion he may well have shared. Whether it was he, or the merchant taylor, who carried a letter from Bernardino Sandro at Padua to Thomas Starkey is not known.[7]

Polsted's connexion with Cromwell makes it probable that he was returned again for Bedwyn to the Parliament of 1536, in accordance with the King's request for the re-election of the previous Members: he may even have sat in that of 1539, another Parliament for which the names of most of the Members, including those for Bedwyn, are missing. If he did so, it was presumably again with the support of Cromwell. That he was not beholden only to the minister, however, appears from his first, and it may be his sole, appointment, that of King's attorney of the court of wards. His patent for this (in which he is again called 'senior') is dated 3 Aug. 1540, ten days after the Act establishing the court (32 Hen. VIII, c.46) had received the royal assent, and six days after the execution of Cromwell. Even if, as may well have been the case, Polsted had been involved in the business of wardship before the erection of the court, it is unlikely that he would have obtained the post if he had clung to the fallen giant: Cromwell's overthrow was to cost Henry Polsted the deputy stewardship of augmentations north of the Trent. Polsted's professional qualifications, if adequate, were in themselves hardly good enough to account for his appointment. The attorneyship was, or was to become, the preserve of lawyers who had already become double readers and benchers at their inns. Polsted had been called to the bench in February 1537 (although it is not clear whether he had read) but the subsequent disappearance of his name from the records of the inn suggests that he took little or no part in its affairs: only if this withdrawal coincided with his first involvement in wardship administration could the years in question have strengthened his claim. It is thus to support from within that administration rather than from outside it that Polsted may have looked. At the head of it, both before and after 1540, stood Sir William Paulet, whose path Polsted's had crossed at several points, at the Inner Temple, in the House of Commons, at court, and perhaps in their neighbouring counties of Hampshire and Surrey. Then there were the surveyor-general, John Hynde, another ex-Member of the Parliament of 1529, and the auditor, Sir John Peryent, whose nephew Henry was later to acquire the wardship of a younger Thomas Polsted, the son and namesake of the merchant taylor.[8]

The questions posed by Polsted's appointment to the attorneyship are matched by those which arise from his loss of it. On 7 Feb. 1541, after a tenure of only six months, he was replaced by John Sewster, the terms of whose patent give no reason for the change. Among possible explanations, the most obvious, that Polsted was dead, seems incapable of proof. In the absence of a will or inquisition post mortem, the date of his death can only be inferred from evidence which is itself inconclusive. Thus, if he is to be identified with the 'Master Polsted' who on 2 May 1546 was assessed for a fifteenth at 10d. for 20 acres of land in Trinity parish, Guildford, he had survived the end of his attorneyship by more than five years, and if, further, with the Thomas Polsted who was escheator of Surrey and Sussex in a year believed to be 1547 he did so for somewhat longer. Yet the second of these references may be to the merchant taylor, who in later life acquired various lands in Surrey and Kent, and the first to his brother Henry, who both had property in Guildford and was prominent in its affairs. The only other pointer to the date of Polsted's death is the omission of his name from his brother's will of 1 Aug. 1555, a will in which several more distant relatives are remembered. If it was not death which cut short his attorneyship, Polsted must have surrendered it voluntarily or have been compelled to do so. As nothing has come to light suggestive of either *dénouement*, an untimely death, perhaps from the 'sickness' which renewed its appearance at the inns about that time, remains the likeliest solution. There is no contemporary evidence that Polsted had married or procreated, but in the visitation of Surrey taken in 1623 it is stated that he died without issue.[9]

[1] *LP Hen. VIII*, ix. 1077 citing SP1/99, p. 234. [2] Date of birth estimated from education. PCC 5 Jankyn; *Surr. Arch. Colls.* ii. peds. (unpaginated) at end vol.; li. 94–95; Manning and Bray, *Surr.* i. 178. [3] J. Hurstfield, *Queen's Wards*, 224; *LP Hen. VIII*, xv. [4] *Bull. IHR*, ix. 31–43; *LP Hen. VIII*, ix. 1077; SP1/99, p. 234. [5] *LP Hen. VIII*, vii. 56 citing SP1/82, ff. 59. 62. [6] *CPR*, 1549–51, p. 199; *Surr. Rec. Soc.* xix. 33; *LP Hen. VIII*, iv, viii, add.; *Cal. I.T. Recs.* i. 49, 99, 100–2, 104, 115; Manning and Bray, i. 522–3. [7] *Surr. Arch. Colls.* ii. peds. (unpaginated) at end vol.; *London IPMs* (Brit. Rec. Soc. xv), i. 145; C142/113/55; *CPR*, 1557–8, p. 225; *LP Hen. VIII*, viii, ix, xii, xiii; Elton, *Reform and Renewal*, 133. [8] *LP Hen. VIII*, xv; W. C. Richardson, *Ct. Augmentations*, 222–3; H. E. Bell, *Ct. Wards and Liveries*, 20, 22–24; *Cal. I.T. Recs.* i. 110; *CPR*, 1557–8, p. 225. [9] *LP Hen. VIII*, xvi, xxi; *Surr. Rec. Soc.* xxiv. 135; PCC 6 Ketchyn.

R.L.D.

POLWHELE, John (by 1523–72 or later), of Polwhele in St. Clement, Cornw.

CORNWALL 1558

b. by 1523, s. of John Polwhele of Polwhele by da. and h. of John Tresawell of Probus. *m.* Grace, da. of Nicholas Lower of Trelaske, 2s. 1da.[1]

Commr. gaol delivery, Cornw. 1554; reeve, Moresk 1558–9, 1564–5; j.p.q. Cornw. 1562–4.[2]

The Polwheles had been seated at a place of that name about two miles from Truro since the reign of Edward III. In 1526 John Polwhele's father was described, perhaps conventionally as 'a gentleman of great power, well kinned and allied', but apparently he was never regarded as qualified to sit on the

Cornish bench. When in 1540 either Polwhele or his father, or perhaps both, quarrelled with Thomas Trevethen, it was Sir John Russell* 1st Baron Russell, and Sir Thomas Arundell* who were involved in settling the dispute. Four years later, when his father was almost certainly dead, Polwhele helped John Cosworth* to partition Nicholas Carminowe's inheritance. The two were associated again in 1548, when Sir John Arundell of Trerice appointed them feoffees for his bastard son Robert: this transaction was open to different interpretations, and Sir John Arundell referred his disagreement with Polwhele over it to Chancery for arbitration.[3]

It was in the 1550s that Polwhele came into prominence in Cornish affairs. Accused in the Star Chamber of depriving Thomas Fuidge, vicar of Lawannack, of church property, he was praised some years later in the same court for preventing Henry Trengove *alias* Nance's* son from killing a duchy of Cornwall official at Truro. In February 1553 and October 1554 his name figures among the electors for the knights of the shire, and in 1558 he was himself returned to the last Parliament of Mary's reign. A number of considerations were in his favour: the duchy of Cornwall was doubtless prepared to look kindly on him after the incident at Truro; his partner John Arundell I came from a family with which he had business links; he was a kinsman by marriage of the powerful Thomas Treffry I*; and he was a Catholic. Nothing is known about Polwhele's part in the work of the Commons, but his Membership was probably the high point of a career which took a downward turn with the advent of Elizabeth. In 1564 the bishop of Exeter wondered why such 'an extreme enemy' of the Anglican settlement should be a justice, and on his recommendation Polwhele was removed from the bench. The remaining years of his life are obscure: in 1569 he obtained a grant of arms and three years later he was assessed at Polwhele towards the subsidy. The date of his death has not been discovered, but he was succeeded by his son Digory, who died in 1615.[4]

[1] Date of birth estimated from first reference. *Vis. Cornw.* ed. Vivian, 299, 376. [2] *Duchy Cornw.* RO, 131, m. 11; 137, m. 11; *CPR*, 1554–5, p. 106; 1560–3, p. 435; 1563–6, p. 20. [3] *Vis. Cornw.* 376; St.Ch.2/17/84; *LP Hen. VIII*, xv, add; C3/2/64, 178/1; *Gent. Mag.* (1829), ii. 216. [4] St.Ch.4/1/48, 8/35; C219/20/21. 23/19; *Cam. Misc.* ix (3), 69; *Grantees of Arms* (Harl. Soc. lxvi), 202; E179/88/229, m. 2v; *Vis. Cornw.* 376.

J.J.G.

POOLE, Sir Giles (by 1517–89), of Sapperton, Glos.

GLOUCESTERSHIRE   1554 (Apr.), 1559, 1571

b. by 1517, 1st s. of Leonard Poole of Sapperton by

Catherine, da. of Sir Giles Brydges of Coberley; bro. of Henry Poole I*. *m.* (1) Elizabeth (*d.*18 Sept. 1543), da. of Thomas Whittington of Pauntley, at least 1s. Sir Henry†; (2) Eleanor, da. of Edward Lewknor of Kingston Buci, Suss., wid. of Sir William Wroughton* (*d.*4 Sept. 1559) of Broad Hinton, Wilts., ?*s.p. suc.* fa. 30 Sept. 1538. Kntd. 28 Sept. 1547.[1]

Gent. pens. 1540–c.51; j.p. Glos. 1547–61 or later, q. 1564–*d.*; commr. relief, Glos. 1550, grain 1573, eccles. causes, diocese of Gloucester 1574; provost marshal [I] 1558; sheriff, Glos. 1565–6.[2]

Sir Giles Poole's grandfather, Richard Poole† owned several manors in Gloucestershire, Oxfordshire and Wiltshire, of which Elmbridge and Sapperton in Gloucestershire passed to his son and heir Leonard in 1517 and from Leonard to Giles in 1538. Leonard Poole had been a gentleman usher extraordinary, but Giles Poole probably owed his post at court more to his maternal uncle, Sir John Brydges*, as his cousin Edmund Brydges* was appointed a gentleman pensioner at the same time.[3]

Poole attended the reception of Anne of Cleves, and in 1542 as the King's 'beloved servant' he obtained the reversion of the rents and site of the manor of Hunlacy and Torleton by Coates in Gloucestershire. He served with the army in France during 1544 and in the north between 1547 and 1548. A letter written by him during the Scottish campaign to (Sir) John Thynne* suggests that he might be identifiable with a 'Mr. Poole' who was in Thynne's household earlier in the decade. In 1550 his court pension was increased to £50, for services to Henry VIII and in recompense for a grant of another annuity which he had been promised but had not received. His annuity from Henry VIII was apparently during pleasure or for a term of years and his court appointment may not have continued, since his name does not appear under the pensioners, lists for the funerals of Edward VI and Mary.[4]

Poole was returned to Mary's second Parliament doubtless as a safe Catholic who, like his uncle, had supported her cause in the preceding summer. Sir John Brydges received his barony at the beginning of this Parliament and Poole may have been chosen in the place of his cousin Sir Edmund, who in the previous Parliament had opposed the restoration of Catholicism. In 1558, the year in which he became provost marshal for Ireland, Poole obtained, for a sum of money and in consideration of his service, the reversion of the lease of Haselden in Gloucestershire. Under Elizabeth his circle included leading men of court and county but he was not called upon for more than the normal local duties. He died on 24 Feb. 1589.[5]

[1] Date of birth estimated from livery of inheritance. *Vis. Glos.* (Harl. Soc. xxi), 125; *Bristol and Glos. Arch. Soc. Trans.* xxxi. 11; *Misc. Gen. et Her.* (ser. 5), iii. 206–9; *LP Hen. VIII*, xiv; *Lit. Rems.*

Edw. VI, 216; Mill Stephenson, Mon. Brasses, 154. [2] E179/69/63, 64, ex inf. W. J. Tighe; LP Hen. VIII, xiv, xv; LC2/2, f. 42; CPR, 1547-8, p. 84; 1553, p. 354; 1553-4, p. 19; 1563-6, p. 22; APC, vi. 370. [3] PCC 26 Holder, 25 Dyngeley; C142/33/123, 79/294; LP Hen. VIII, ii. [4] LP Hen. VIII, xiv, xv, xvii, xix, xx; APC, ii. 487; Bath mss, Thynne pprs. 2, ff. 22-23v; CPR, 1549-51, p. 310; LC2/4/1, 2; Stowe 571, f. 316; Add. 30198. [5] CSP Dom. 1547-80, p. 110; CPR, 1557-8, p. 123; C142/222/45; Bristol and Glos. Arch. Soc. Trans. 1. 209-10; PCC 31 Leicester.

M.K.D.

POOLE, Henry I (by 1526–80), of Ditchling, Suss.

WOOTTON BASSETT 1553 (Oct.)

b. by 1526, 2nd s. of Leonard Poole of Sapperton, Glos. by Catherine, da. of Sir Giles Brydges of Coberley, Glos.; bro. of Sir Giles*. m. Margaret, da. of George Neville, 5th Lord Bergavenny, wid. of John Cheyne (d.1544), 6s.[1]

Gent. pens. in reversion by 1547, gent. pens. by Apr. 1549–1561/4; commr. relief, Wilts. 1550; j.p. Suss. 1564.[2]

Poole is to be distinguished both from his namesake who sat for Leicestershire in the Parliament of April 1554 and, more specifically, from his own uncle of Chelworth near Wootton Bassett. Like his brother Giles, he probably owed his start at court to his uncle Sir John Brydges*.[3]

Although after his marriage he was to settle in Sussex, Poole had inherited an interest in Minety and Oaksey near Wootton Bassett, and as late as 1573 Giles Poole and Thomas Wroughton† conveyed to him the manor of Broad Hinton in the same neighbourhood, apparently by way of a mortgage. To his standing there and at court he could add his connexions, especially with his uncle Brydges, soon to be created Baron Chandos, and with his brother-in-law Edward Baynard†, sheriff of Wiltshire at the time of his election. Although a 'Mr. Poole' (possibly Giles) had earlier been in (Sir) John Thynne's* household it is unlikely that Thynne's help was necessary. Poole was not among the Members who 'stood for the true religion' against the initial measures to restore Catholicism and 11 years later, when he had only just been placed on the Sussex bench, Bishop Barlow was to describe him as a 'misliker of religion and godly proceedings'.[4]

By that time Poole had already settled at Ditchling, although it was not until 1576 that his brother-in-law Henry, 6th Lord Bergavenny, granted him a lease of the park there. He and his wife also held land in Keymer and elsewhere in Sussex and in 1568 he sold lands in Kent to Sir Henry Cheyne(y)†. Poole made his will on 28 Jan. 1580 and died on the following 28 Mar. Besides lands already mentioned, he left property in the Blackfriars, London, and a manor in Somerset. He bequeathed his best armour and a saddle to Lord Bergavenny and rings to various relatives and friends including Sir John

Pelham† whom he named one of the overseers of the will. He was buried in Ditchling church, where in accordance with his wishes a mural monument was erected to his memory.[5]

[1] Date of birth estimated from first appearance as a gentleman pensioner. Misc. Gen. et Her. (ser. 5), iii. 207-8; Vis. Oxon. (Harl. Soc. v), 201; Vis. Berks. (Harl. Soc. lvii), 104; Arch. Cant. xxiv. 122-3; PCC 15 Arundell. [2] LC2/2, ff. 41-3; 2/3(1), p. 113; E 179/69/62, 407/1/2, 3 ex inf. W. J. Tighe; CPR, 1553, p. 359. [3] St.Ch.4/7/21; LP Hen. VIII, xiii; Misc. Gen. et Her. (ser. 5), iii. 212; LC2/2, f. 42v, 4/1, 2. [4] PCC 25 Dyngeley; CPR, 1572-5, p. 172; Bath mss, Thynne pprs. 2, ff. 22-23v; HMC Bath, iv. 116, 118; Cam. Misc. ix(3), 10; R. B. Manning, Rel. and Soc. in Eliz. Suss. 244. [5] VCH Suss. vii. 104-5, 108, 179; Suss. Rec. Soc. xxxiv. 3, 32; CPR, 1566-9, p. 296; PCC 15 Arundell; Suss. Arch. Colls. xxviii. 134-5.

A.D.

POOLE, Henry II (by 1507–59), of Kirk Langley, Derbys. and Withcote, Leics.

LEICESTERSHIRE 1554 (Apr.)

b. by 1507, 1st s. of Henry Poole of Chesterfield, Derbys. by Ursula, da. and h. of Thomas Twyford of Kirk Langley. m. Dorothy, da. of Richard Cave of Stanford, Northants., wid. of John Smith (d.1545) of Withcote; 1s. 1da. illegit.[1]

Member, order of St. John of Jerusalem 23 July 1528, lt. turcopolier 1534, preceptor, Dalby, Leics. 1535–40; j.p. Leics. 1538–d.; commr. musters 1539, 1546, relief 1550; sheriff, Warws. and Leics. 1558–d.[2]

Henry Poole came of a cadet branch of the family seated at Radbourne, Derbyshire. He appears to have been the heir to his father's lands but none the less chose to make his career in the order of St. John of Jerusalem which he entered on 23 July 1528. In 1533 he was a witness in the controversy over Sir Clement West's deposition from the office of turcopolier and in 1534 he succeeded Edward Bellingham* as lieutenant turcopolier. In 1535, while in Malta, he was appointed preceptor of Dalby and on his return he engaged in a dispute with the lessee of the demesne, Humphrey Babington, whom he wished to evict. He was soon facing the much graver problem of the future of the order in England and, with it, of his own position, but on its suppression in 1540, he received an annuity of 200 marks out of its Leicestershire properties. He appears to have continued to live at Dalby for some time, even after it was first leased, and in 1544 sold, to his cousin Andrew Nowell*: he still had some interest in the parish at his death.[3]

Poole had already begun to take part in local administration, and in 1544 he led a contingent from Leicestershire in the war with France: at this time he was generally styled knight as he had been in the order. It was almost certainly his namesake, a Member for Wootton Bassett in the Parliament of October 1553, who was the gentleman pensioner at the funerals of Henry VIII, Edward VI and Mary. It is not known when he married Dorothy Smith, sister of his fellow-hospitaller Sir Ambrose Cave*, but it was this which took him to Withcote, 'one of the fairest houses in Leicestershire', of which she enjoyed a life tenancy. It remained his principal residence although he engaged in building at Kirk Langley, leaving £100 in his will for the completion of the work: he sued out a pardon in October 1553 as of Withcote. The Cave connexion probably accounts for his election as second knight of the shire to the Parliament of April 1554, the returning officer Robert Throckmorton* being one of his kinsmen. Nothing is known of Poole's activity in the House.[4]

In the autumn of 1558 Poole was himself pricked sheriff and after his death on 3 Feb. 1559 his term of office was completed by his brother-in-law Brian Cave. He had made his will on the previous 18 Apr., providing for his wife, his stepchildren, his own two illegitimate children and his many brothers (one of whom succeeded him at Kirk Langley) and nephews; his son Henry Poole *alias* Carter was still a schoolboy and his daughter Elizabeth was married to John Bussy of Haydor, Lincolnshire, whom he named executor with his brother William Poole. Amongst those to whom he left mourning rings were Sir Ambrose Cave and Andrew Nowell, whom he named as supervisor. His annuity was in arrears and he left one of the two payments of £66 13s.4d. outstanding 'to answer the Queen's privy seal for the hundred marks I must lend her grace'; he was also owed £55 by the crown purveyors. The will was proved on 17 Feb. 1559. Poole was buried in the church at Kirk Langley where his tomb bears the incised effigies of himself and his wife and an inscription identifying him as the church's patron.[5]

[1] Date of birth estimated from first reference. J. C. Cox, *Derbys. Churches*, iv. 268–74; *Vis. Leics.* (Harl. Soc. ii), 66; Nichols, *Leics.* ii. 393; PCC 42 Pynnyng, 39 Welles. [2] H. P. Scicluna, *Eng. Tongue 1523–97*, pp. 23, 33, 34, 44; C1/732/38; *LP Hen. VIII*, xiii–xv, xx, xxi; *CPR*, 1547–8, p. 85; 1553, p. 356; 1553–4, p. 21. [3] Scicluna, 44; *LP Hen. VIII*, vii, xvi; C1/732/38; *Statutes*, iii. 778; Nichols, iii. 249. [4] *LP Hen. VIII*, xix; Nichols, iii. 387; Pevsner, *Leics. and Rutland*, 266; *CPR*, 1553–4, p. 432. [5] Cox, iv. 273; PCC 39 Welles; *Lincs. Peds.* (Harl. Soc. l), 217; Pevsner and Williamson, *Derbys.* 261.

A.D.

POPE, Thomas (1506/7–59), of Clerkenwell, London and Tittenhanger, Herts.

BUCKINGHAM 1536[1]
BERKSHIRE 1539[2]

b. 1506/7, 1st s. of William Pope of Deddington, Oxon. by 2nd w. Margaret, da. of Edmund Yate of Standlake, Oxon. *educ.* Banbury sch.; Eton c.1520–4. *m.* (1) ?Elizabeth Gunston (div. 11 July 1536); (2) 17 July 1536, Margaret (*d.*1538), wid. of Sir Ralph Dodmer of London, 1da.; (3) Elizabeth, da. of Walter Blount I* of Blount's Hall, nr. Uttoxeter, Staffs. and Osbaston, Leics., wid. of Anthony Basford (*d.*1 Mar. 1538) of Bentley, Derbys., *s.p. suc.* fa. 16 Mar. 1523. Kntd. Oct. 1537.[3]

Clerk of the writs, Star Chamber 1532, jt. clerk 1534–*d.*; warden of the mint, the Tower of London 1534–6; treasurer, ct. augmentations 1536–40; master of the woods, south of the Trent by 1545–53; clerk of the crown in Chancery by July 1537, jt. (with John Lucas*) Feb. 1538–44; j.p. Oxon., Surr. 1541–7, q. Kent, Oxon., Surr. 1554; commr. benevolence, Surr. 1544/45, contribution 1546, chantries, Surr., Suss. and Southwark 1546, Surr. 1549, of Admiralty in Nov. 1547, relief, Herts., Oxon., Surr. and Southwark 1550, heresy 1557; PC by July 1544–?47, 4 Aug. 1553–?58; custos rot. Surr. c.1547; sheriff, Essex and Herts. 1552–3, 1557–8.[4]

William Pope was a small landowner whose ancestors had moved from Kent to Oxfordshire at the beginning of the 15th century. He held property at Hook Norton and Whitehill which had been vested in feoffees and which on his death was divided between his widow and his eldest son. Thomas Pope was also left £100, while £40 was given to each of his three sisters, but there is no mention of the second son John.[5]

In the statutes of his foundation of Trinity College, Oxford, Pope was to refer to his own education at Banbury school. Thomas Warton, the 18th-century author of a colourful biography, says that his hero was destined for the law, although there is no evidence that Pope was admitted to an inn of court. His bequest of a gown to Master Croke, his 'old master's son', probably means that he was articled to Richard Croke, comptroller of the hanaper and chief of the Six Clerks in Chancery who served Chancellor More. More has been credited with furthering Pope's early career but he had resigned the great seal by October 1532, when Pope first obtained office. Two-and-a-half years later More is said to have been visited in the Tower by his former underling and to have replied cheerfully when told that he was shortly to be executed. Such an ambiguous service was to be typical of Pope's career.[6]

More's successor Audley certainly favoured Pope, who is described as his 'servant' in March 1536; later, Pope was to receive a grant of land jointly with the chancellor and to be named his executor. Further advancement needed the help of Cromwell, for whom Pope was negotiating land purchases in September 1534. Audley himself cultivated the minister and Pope followed suit, swearing that he had no other friend. His rise was signalized on 26 June 1535 by a grant in arms, which are still borne by his college, and by a knighthood in 1537. In March 1540 the chancellor thanked Cromwell for his kindness to Pope, who had just resigned the treasurership of augmentations, and promised that he would requite it; three months later Cromwell fell, but Audley and Pope escaped unhurt.[7]

Pope must have had exceptional ability to be singled out when so young. The court of augmentations had been set up to deal with the property of suppressed religious houses. Sir Richard Rich became its chancellor and Pope, a man of about 28 and of far less experience, its treasurer and second officer. The court's officers, although politic, were not always subservient to Cromwell, and on one occasion Pope incurred the minister's anger over the manor of Drayton Bassett, Staffordshire, which the treasurer bought from Sir John Dudley and leased to George Robinson, when Cromwell wanted it for himself. Henry Polsted*, Cromwell's servant and deputy steward north of the Trent, told his master that Pope knew of Cromwell's interest and rejected Pope's claim to have lost money on the transaction. Pope importuned others to intercede for him, including Thomas Wriothesley and John Gostwick*, who wrote on his behalf to Cromwell's nephew. The minister promised to bear no ill will if Pope would let him buy Drayton and in the same year the treasurer sought his favour against a young Oxfordshire landowner named Billing, who was protesting that he had been under age when Pope acquired some property from him. Cromwell seems to have kept his word, for the lands, at Ardley, remained with Pope, who also held the manor there when he died. In September 1536 Pope joined his colleague Robert Southwell* in support of a charge of profiteering brought against Rich by Christopher Lascelles (q.v.).[8]

Another debt of Pope's to Cromwell was his return to Parliament for Buckingham in 1536. On 19 May George Gifford II, his fellow-Member, wrote to the minister from Northamptonshire, where he was visiting religious houses, that he and Pope had been duly elected, in accordance with Cromwell's letters to the town. Unlike Gifford, Pope had no family ties with Buckinghamshire, sat on no commissions there and held no property in the county; he was an official nominee and he and Gifford were made an exception to the general directive calling for the re-election of the previous Members. His return for Berkshire in 1539 with Sir Richard Brydges was probably also Cromwell's work, although in this case there is no evidence of such intervention, for Pope's connexion with this county was equally tenuous.[9]

If Cromwell suspected Pope of being both selfish and devious, others were sure of it. Viscount Lisle was obliged to bribe him as treasurer of augmentations to secure payment of an annuity. Corruption may help to explain Pope's wealth but calculation was the key to his survival. He was on a list of Surrey gentlemen who were to supply men, probably to crush the Pilgrimage of Grace in 1536, and perhaps saw in the troubles a chance to rise higher by discrediting others. When the 3rd Duke of Norfolk was subduing the north, John Freeman, a receiver in the augmentations, reported at dinner in Pope's house that the duke had spoken sympathetically to the rebels at Doncaster. His host made Freeman write down his allegations on the spot and tried without success to persuade the other guests to do likewise. In May 1537 Norfolk was forced to refute this and other slanders in a letter to the King.[10]

Pope's own attitude to the rebellion was naturally dictated by his office. He was not yet a justice of the peace, but the chancellor and treasurer of the augmentations both helped to examine the Lincolnshire rebels. Although not a regular commissioner for suppressing the monasteries, on 5 Dec. 1539 he received the surrender of St. Albans. In many cases, annuities were extracted from religious houses and then confirmed by the court; Pope, who often signed warrants granting pensions to the inmates, was enjoying four such annuities, according to his own account as treasurer for the year ending Michaelmas 1539. In 1543 the number is recorded as five, compared with 11 which had been granted to Cromwell and 13 to Rich.[11]

Pope resigned as treasurer in favour of Edward North* in March 1540, probably at his own request. A new post, the mastership of the woods south of the Trent, was instituted in 1543 and perhaps at once given to Pope; he was master in 1545 and was confirmed in office when the court of augmentations was reformed, to include that of general surveyors, on 2 Jan. 1547. He was now only the fourth officer in the court but a man of much greater substance, for these were his busiest years in buying and, less frequently, selling property; he now played a fuller part in local affairs and could supply 50 men at a muster of the Surrey gentry in 1544. A member of the Council by July of that year, he was involved in secret diplomacy, for in April 1545 the Protestant 3rd Earl of Cassillis sent him a letter in cypher from Edinburgh which he passed on to Secretary Petre. In the following year he advertised his orthodoxy by joining Norfolk and others in witnessing the recantation of Dr. Crome, who had offended against the Six Articles.[12]

Too much has been made of Pope's withdrawal from affairs under Edward VI. True, he was no longer a member of the Council, and he is said to have been out of sympathy with the Reformers, but he continued as master of the woods in the augmentations until the court's abolition in 1553. Grants of land continued and on 23 July 1547, in accordance with an indenture of the late King, he and his wife received the house and park of Titten-hanger, which became his chief residence. He would hardly have been pricked sheriff in 1552 if the Duke of Northumberland had seriously distrusted him, but he was not among those who signed the King's letters devising the crown upon Jane Grey or who otherwise abetted Jane during her brief reign.[13]

Pope must have been quick to rally to Mary, with whom he was later reported to have had great influence. On 29 July 1553 the Council ordered him to arrest (Sir) Francis Russell* and other suspects, on 4 Aug. he was sworn in as a Councillor and on 4 Oct. he obtained a general pardon. In February 1554 he was among those who watched Wyatt's rebels surging along Fleet Street to Ludgate Hill; he later joined in the baiting of prisoners taken to the Tower, where for over a week he sat with (Sir) Richard Southwell* and others to examine them. Chosen in 1556 as custodian to Princess Elizabeth, Pope probably spent only a short time with her at Hatfield, although Warton lists a series of festivities supposedly given by him in her honour; in April 1558 he was deputed to broach with her a marriage proposal from Eric XIV of Sweden. In 1557 he had been named to the commission which was to punish heresy, nonconformity, vagrancy and neglect or misuse of church property. His surprising absence from all the Parliaments of the reign may have reflected either a desire to avoid the limelight or a growing preoccupation with the plan for a new college at Oxford.[14]

The dissolution of the monasteries had helped to make Pope one of the richest commoners of his time. In July 1537 he had complained to Cromwell 'I have no gain in office but my fee, above which I must spend yearly 200 marks', but already his accumulation of lands in many midland counties had begun. Thenceforward he acquired or exchanged monastic property almost every year, most of it in Oxford-shire, where it extended into 15 parishes, or in the suburbs of London. At Bermondsey he pulled down the old priory to make way for Bermondsey House, which he sold to (Sir) Robert Southwell* in 1555, and he established another town residence at Clerkenwell. Large sums changed hands in the process: among scores of lesser transactions between 1540 and 1554 four large purchases cost him nearly £6,000.[15]

Apart from his wife Pope had no one to provide for; his brother was also a rich man and Pope's only child, Alice, had died in infancy. Accordingly, on 20 Feb. 1555 he bought the site of the former Durham College, Oxford, which had passed into private hands. Royal letters of 8 Mar. licensed him to establish a new college dedicated to the Trinity; he

was also given leave to found a free school at Hook Norton, but this intention was afterwards abandoned in favour of four scholarships to the college. Although his foundation provided for masses and traditional observances, his aims were not primarily religious and his statutes followed other codes of the day, being notable only for their avoidance of detailed rules governing elections. He also presented 93 volumes to the library, with furnishings and plate. The lands settled on the college were barely adequate, in view of the many charges specified in the statutes, especially as Pope's property was mostly let to relatives or friends on 99-year leases. There were to be financial and religious difficulties which he did not live to see, but most of the original endowment is still held by the college.[16]

Pope made a long will on 6 Feb. 1557, adding a codicil on 12 Dec. 1558. The many personal and charitable bequests included sums to the nuns of Syon and the friars of Smithfield. A family settle-ment had left most of his estates to his brother, who was to be the ancestor of the earls of Downe, but Clerkenwell, Tittenhanger and certain Derbyshire properties went to the widow, with remainder to the sons of her first marriage. The widow, her brother William Blount and Nicholas Bacon* were named executors and Sir Thomas Cornwallis*, Sir Francis Englefield* and the brothers Sir Richard and Sir Robert Southwell overseers. Pope died in his house at Clerkenwell on 29 Jan. 1559, probably of the prevailing epidemic, and a week later his coffin was borne to St. Stephen's Walbrook as he had requested. His widow married (Sir) Hugh Paulet*.[17]

Pope's memorial was to be Trinity College, in whose chapel his widow erected a handsome tomb, with alabaster effigies of her husband and herself, to which his remains were transferred in 1567. The president's lodgings contain one of several portraits of him, painted in middle life, but the stolid and rather fleshy features are not revealing. He cannot have been a commonplace man, but he owed his fame to his benefaction rather than to his career.[18]

[1] *LP Hen. VIII*, x. 916. [2] E159/319, brev. ret. Mich. r. [1–2]. [3] Date of birth estimated from age at fa.'s i.p.m., C142/40/56. *DNB*; H. E. D. Blakiston, *Trinity Coll. Oxf.* 35. [4] *LP Hen. VIII*, v, vii, xi, xiii, xv–xxi; W. C. Richardson, *Ct. Augmentations*, 71, 304–5, 331n, 492; C66/801; 193/12/1; *CPR*, 1547–8, pp. 88, 90; 1548–9, p. 115; 1550–3, p. 141; 1553, pp. 354, 357, 362; 1553–4, pp. 20, 23–24, 35, 138, 176, 195–6, 265, 302, 507; 1554–5, pp. 90–91, 107, 343; 1555–7, p. 281; Manning and Bray, *Surr.* iii. 115; *Rep. R. Comm. of 1552* (Archs. of Brit. Hist. and Culture iii), 76; C. E. Challis, *The Tudor Coinage*, 30, 84; HCA 14/2. [5] C142/40/56; Blakiston, 30; T. Warton, *Sir Thomas Pope* (1780), 4, app. 1 and 2. [6] Blakiston, 30–31; Warton, 6–7, 10. [7] *LP Hen. VIII*, vi, x, xv, xviii, xix; *Grantees of Arms* (Harl. Soc. lxvi), 202; Blakiston, 52. [8] Richardson, 71–72; Challis, 160–1; Blakiston, 32; *LP Hen. VIII*, xiii; *VCH Oxon.* vi. 9–10. [9] *LP Hen. VIII*, x; E159/319/1–2. [10] *LP Hen. VIII*, xi–xiv; R. B. Merriman, *Letters, Thos. Cromwell*, ii. 235–6. [11] Richardson, 85; *LP Hen. VIII*, xii, xiv, xviii. [12] Richardson, 330; *LP Hen. VIII*, xix–xxi. [13] PCC 10 Chaynay; *CPR*, 1547–8, p. 116; 1548–9, p. 139. [14] Strype, *Annals*, i(1), 46; *APC*, vi. 148, 354; *CPR*, 1553–4, p. 421;

1555-7, p. 281; *Chron. Q. Jane and Q. Mary* (Cam. Soc. xlviii).
51-52, 65; D. M. Loades, *Two Tudor Conspiracies*, 94n; Blakiston, 34,
15 *LP Hen. VIII*, v, xii, xv, xx, xxi; Richardson, 492; G. W. Phillips,
Bermondsey, 6-7, 15; E. J. Ward, *Clerkenwell*, 32; *CPR*, 1547-8,
p. 116; 1553-4, pp. 139-40; M. C. Rosenfield, 'The disposal of the
property of London monastic houses' (London Univ. Ph.D. thesis,
1961), 290; Req.2/18/135; Copinger, *Suff. Manors*, iv. 124; *Misc.
Gen. et Her.* (ser. 5), v. 381. 16 Blakiston, 36, 37; *CPR*, 1554-5,
pp. 90-91; A. Wood, *Hist. Coll. Oxf.* (1786), 517-20; *VCH Oxon.*
iii. 20, 244. 17 PCC 10 Chaynay; *Vis. Herts.* (Harl. Soc. xxii), 129;
C142/124/53; *Machyn's Diary* (Cam. Soc. xlii), 188. 18 *VCH Oxon.*
iii. 245; Blakiston, 38; Richardson, 1, 2; Sherwood and Pevsner,
Oxon. 205.

T.F.T.B.

POPHAM, Alexander (by 1504-56), of Huntworth, Som.

BRIDGWATER 1545, 1547[1]

b. by 1504, 1st s. of John Popham of Huntworth by
Isabel, da. of Thomas Knolle. *educ.* ?M. Temple. *m.* by
1530, Joan, da. of Sir Edward Stradling (*d.*1535) of St.
Donat's, Glam., 4s. inc. Edward* and John* 3da. *suc.*
fa. 17 Feb. 1536.[2]

Escheator, Som. and Dorset Apr.-Nov. 1536,
1551-2; j.p. Som. 1538-*d.*; recorder, Bridgwater by
1541-*d.*; commr. benevolence, Som. 1544/45, relief
1550.[3]

Everything in Alexander Popham's career points
to his having had a legal training but his name does
not appear in the registers or books of any of the
inns. Since he was almost certainly the 'Mr. Popham
of the Middle Temple' who oversaw the will of his
father-in-law, Sir Edward Stradling, he may be
confidently assigned to that inn which many of his
descendants also attended. In 1536, during his term
as escheator, he had the unusual duty of holding the
inquisition following his own father's death and of
finding himself to be the heir. He was soon afterwards put on the Somerset bench and served on a
variety of other commissions during the next
20 years.[4]

His home being only two miles from Bridgwater,
Popham was naturally brought into contact with the
town as indeed his forbears had been. The
returns made by Bridgwater do not survive for
Henry VIII's previous Parliaments, but presumably he sat for the borough in the Parliament of
1542 since he already held the recordership. If he
had succeeded a previous holder, Baldwin Malet,
after Malet's death in 1533, he may also have sat in
the Parliament of 1529, replacing Henry Thornton,
and the two following ones. It is not clear why he did
not sit again after 1547, but several of the Members
chosen by Bridgwater before his death were apparently favoured by Popham. There is no indication
that he had noble or government connexions, but
he was a familiar figure among the Somerset gentry,
appearing frequently as executor or supervisor of
their wills.[5]

Popham had inherited from his father only the
manor of Huntworth but he took advantage of the

Dissolution to acquire other lands. Some of these he
re-sold, but at his death he held the manors of
Buckland and Huntworth, and 60 houses in
Bridgwater. He made his will on 1 June 1556. After
asking to be buried in North Petherton church
Popham provided for several charities, his children
and his servants. He left annuities to Lady Margaret
and Lady Eleanor Bourchier, and to his kinsman
(Sir) William Portman* a mare. The executors were
Sir Robert Stradling, Bartholomew Combe and
Humphrey Walrond (Popham's brother-in-law)
with Portman and Richard Michell, Popham's son-
in-law, as overseers. Popham died ten days later and
the will was proved early in the following month.[6]

[1] Hatfield 207. [2] Date of birth estimated from age at fa.'s i.p.m.,
C142/58/81. *Vis. Som.* (Harl. Soc. xi), 125. [3] *LP Hen. VIII*,
xiii-xxi; *CPR*, 1553, p. 359; Bridgwater corp. ms 1449. [4] *LP Hen.
VIII*, xiii, xv; C142/58/81. [5] Bridgwater corp. mss 1449; 1456;
1533; *Som. Med. Wills* (Som. Rec. Soc. xxi), 63, 68, 112, 126.
[6] *LP Hen. VIII*, xix, xx; PCC 10 Ketchyn; C142/108/104.

R.V.

POPHAM, Edward (by 1530-86), of Huntworth, Som.

GUILDFORD 1558
HYTHE 1563
BRIDGWATER 1571, 1572, 1584

b. by 1530, 1st s. of Alexander Popham* of Huntworth
by Joan, da. of Sir Edward Stradling of St. Donat's,
Glam.; bro. of John*. *m.* settlement 1 July 1551, Jane,
da. of Richard Norton of Abbots Leigh, Bristol, Glos.
7s. inc. Alexander† 9da. *suc.* fa. 11 June 1556.[1]

Subsidy collector, Som. 1553; escheator, Som. and
Dorset 1560-1; recorder, Bridgwater by 1572-*d.*;
j.p.q. Som. 1573/74-*d.*; commr. piracy 1577, musters
1583.[2]

Edward Popham was almost certainly trained at
the Middle Temple, of which his father, his brother
John and his sons Alexander, Ferdinand and John
were all members in their time. In July 1551 his
father settled on him and his wife lands worth £18
a year, and on his father's death five years later he
succeeded to a considerable patrimony in and
around Bridgwater. In 1558 he brought a Star
Chamber case against two Salisbury merchants and
two Londoners for their alleged attempt to dispossess
him of the manor of Milton, Somerset, which he had
recently bought: among those who gave evidence
were two of Popham's servants and his brother
John, and he probably won the case as he was
holding the manor when he died.[3]

Although both brothers were to sit in the Parliament of 1558, neither did so for Bridgwater, which
chose two townsmen. Edward Popham's return for
Guildford, a borough with which he had no known
tie and where his name is inserted in the indenture
in a different hand from that of the document, he
must have owed to his kinship with Sir Thomas

Stradling*, whose master the 12th Earl of Arundel exercised patronage there. Popham supplanted the Protestant William More to join a local Catholic, William Hammond; his own connexion with the conservative Stradlings suggests that, at least under Mary, Popham conformed without difficulty. He was to sit in four Elizabethan Parliaments and died on 24 Jan. 1586.[4]

[1] Date of birth estimated from age at fa.'s i.p.m., C142/108/104. *Vis. Som.* (Harl. Soc. xi), 87–88, 125, where he is incorrectly shown as the third son; C142/211/56. [2] E179/169/140; Lansd. 56, f. 168; 146, f. 19v; *VCH Som.* ii. 254n. [3] *M.T. Recs.* i. 165, 261, 273; C142/108/104; PCC 10 Ketchyn; *CPR*, 1555–7, p. 242; St.Ch.2/20/283, 22/265, 26/314; 3/9/88; 4/7/29. [4] C142/211/56; 219/25/109.

S.R.J.

POPHAM, John (1532/33–1607), of Wellington, Som. and London.

LYME REGIS   1558
BRISTOL   1571, 1572

b. 1532/33, 2nd s. of Alexander Popham*, and bro. of Edward*. *educ.* Balliol, Oxf.; M. Temple. *m.* by Jan. 1549, Amy, da. and h. of Hugh Adams of Castleton, Glam., 1s. Francis[†] 6da. Kntd. 1592.[1]

Autumn reader, M. Temple 1568, Lent 1573, treasurer 1580–8.

Recorder, Bridgwater 1571–2, Bristol 1571–80; j.p.q. Som. 1573/74–d., Mdx. 1583, Bucks., Norf., Wilts. 1594, Beds., Cambs., Hunts., Suff. 1600; serjeant-at-law 1579; solicitor-gen. 1579–81; attorney-gen. 1581–9; 2nd justice, Lancaster 1581–9; j.c.p. 1589–92; l.c.j. KB 1592–d.; receiver of petitions in the Lords, Parlts. of 1593, 1597, 1601, 1604; custos rot. Som. by 1594; commr. eccles. causes, Salisbury diocese 1599, chancellorship of duchy of Lancaster 1601; PC 1599.[2]

Speaker of House of Commons 1581.

John Popham married very young, apparently when no more than 17; his wife, who was heir to the manor of Castleton in Glamorganshire, may have been a ward of his father, from whom John was to inherit property in Bridgwater, Somerset. According to Aubrey it was not until he was 30 years old that Popham was persuaded by his wife to concentrate on his legal studies. He had earlier been put out of commons by his inn, where in November 1556 he was restored on paying a fine of 40s.; and it was not until the 1560s that he began that progress which brought him to the top of his chosen profession.[3]

Popham's election to the Parliament of 1558 by Lyme Regis may have been the work of his brother-in-law William Pole, who sat for the town in 1545 and who was to become its legal counsellor. Nothing is known of Popham's role in Mary's last Parliament although his name is marked with a circle on a copy of the list of its Members in use for the second session: the significance of the circle has yet to be explained.[4]

After a long and distinguished career under Elizabeth, Popham died on 10 June 1607, and was buried in the church at Wellington. Several portraits of him in middle age survive.[5]

[1] Aged 25 on 15 May 1558, but allegedly 76 at death according to MI, St.Ch.3/9/88; Collinson, *Som.* ii. 483. *Vis. Som.* (Harl. Soc. xi), 125; *CPR*, 1553, p. 326. [2] W. Barrett, *Bristol*, 115; Dugdale, *Chronica Series*, 95, 97–98; *APC*, xxix. 738; *LJ*, ii. 168, 191, 226, 263; Somerville, *Duchy*, i. 396–7; C66/1421; SP 13 case no. 11. [3] *CPR*, 1553, p. 326; Manning, *Speakers*, 247; C142/108/104; *M.T. Recs.* i. passim. [4] Wm. Salt Lib. SMS 264. [5] Collinson, ii. 483; *Cat. Boughton House State Rooms and High Pavilion*, 1, 2.

H.M.

PORTE, John (by 1514–57), of Etwall, Derbys.

DERBYSHIRE   1539,[1] 1553 (Oct.)

b. by 1514, s. of Sir John Porte of Etwall by Joan, da. of John Fitzherbert. *educ.* Brasenose, Oxf. adm. c.1524; I. Temple, adm. 3 Feb. 1528. *m.* (1) by 1538, Elizabeth, da. of (Sir) Thomas Giffard* of Caverswall and Chillington, Staffs., 2s. *d.v.p.* 3da.; (2) Dorothy, da. of Sir Anthony Fitzherbert of Norbury, Derbys. *suc.* fa. Mar. 1540. KB 20 Feb. 1547.[2]

Commr. benevolence, Derbys. 1544/45, musters 1546, relief 1550, goods of churches and fraternities 1553, heresy 1557, loan 1557; j.p. 1545–d.; escheator, Notts. and Derbys. 1546–7; sheriff 1553–4.[3]

The brief ascendancy of the Porte family in Derbyshire was based upon the successful pursuit of the law. Born into a merchant family of Chester, John Porte's father and namesake the judge married into the shire and by his death was an outstanding figure there; it was he who bought Etwall in the south-west of the county.[4]

John Porte the younger's career was less distinguished but more varied. A fellowship at Brasenose on his father's foundation, and a special admission to the Inner Temple as the son of a judge were followed by a period of service with Cromwell and a recommendation to the service of the crown. His knighthood of the shire in 1539, when comparatively short of years and experience, he owed to his father's standing, with perhaps the support of the minister in his campaign for a 'tractable' Parliament. Before it ended both his father and his patron were dead, but during the next dozen years he established his own position in the shire; he added substantially to his inheritance to become the largest landowner in Derbyshire, and he was knighted at Edward VI's coronation. The Catholicism which he shared with his relatives made him an appropriate choice as the senior knight in Mary's first Parliament and as her first sheriff of Nottinghamshire and Derbyshire. Unlike his fellow-Member Richard Blackwell he did not oppose the initial measures to restore Catholicism. Porte spent much of the Parliament successfully negotiating the purchase of two manors in Derbyshire. He delivered a letter of recommendation from the 5th Earl of Shrewsbury to Stephen

Gardiner who passed it on to Speaker Pollard; although Pollard was unable to intervene personally, things went well and on his return to Etwall Porte sent Shrewsbury a dish of wildfowl. Later in the reign he was to help Shrewsbury to raise troops for the war against Scotland.[5]

By his will of 9 Mar. 1557 Porte left lands in Derbyshire and Lancashire to found a grammar school either at Etwall or Repton; it was established at Repton and maintained under the direction of the Harpur family. He also discharged a wish of his father's by bequeathing £200 to his old college to establish lectureships in philosophy and in humanity. His many other charitable bequests included the endowment of an almshouse in Etwall and the distribution of alms to poor people in the county gaol and of marriage gifts to 60 poor young women in Cheshire and Derbyshire. To the church at Etwall he gave a 'cope and one vestment of cloth of gold' embroidered with his and his wife's arms, and to four neighbouring churches silk vestments similarly embroidered. His five executors, who included his father-in-law Sir Thomas Giffard and his cousin Richard Harpur, were directed to enter into an obligation of £3,000 with his overseers, Francis Curzon*, (Sir) Thomas Fitzherbert* and William Fitzherbert*, for the performance of the will. The inheritance was divided between Porte's three daughters, who married Sir Thomas Gerard†, the 4th Earl of Huntingdon and Sir Thomas Stanhope†.[6]

[1] E159/319, brev. ret. Mich. r. [1–2].   [2] Date of birth estimated from admission to I. Temple. His fellowship at Oxford beforehand was one endowed by his father and it is likely that the usual age of admission was waived in his favour. *DNB*; Emden, *Biog. Reg. Univ. Oxf. 1501–40*, p. 458; PCC 4 Alenger.   [3] *LP Hen. VIII*, xx, xxi; *CPR*, 1547–8, p. 82; 1550–3, p. 394; 1553, pp. 352, 414; Strype, *Eccles. Memorials*, iii(2), 15.   [4] *LP Hen. VIII*, i, xiv, xv.   [5] Ibid. xiii, xiv, xix, xxi; M. L. Robertson, 'Cromwell's servants' (Univ. California Los Angeles Ph.D. thesis, 1975), 545–6; E179/91/118; College of Arms, Talbot ms P, f. 197; *HMC Shrewsbury and Talbot* ii. 46, 47, 350; C1/1053/48.   [6] PCC 20 Wrastley; E150/1052/5; Pevsner, *Notts*. 134.

C.J.B.

PORTER, Arthur (by 1505–59), of Newent and Alvington, Glos.

GLOUCESTERSHIRE   1554 (Nov.)
GLOUCESTER   1555
AYLESBURY   1559

b. by 1505, 1st or o. surv. s. of Roger Porter of Newent by Margaret, da. of John Arthur of Clapton-in-Gordano, Som. *educ.* L. Inn, adm. 14 Feb. 1524. *m.* (1) by Feb. 1524, Alice, da. of John Arnold of Churcham, Glos., at least 12ch. inc. Sir Thomas†; (2) Isabel, da. of Sir William Denys of Dyrham, Glos. by Anne, da. of Maurice, *de jure* 3rd Lord Berkeley, wid. of Sir John Berkeley (*d.c.*1548) of Stoke, Som., *s.p. suc.* fa. 1523.[1] Escheator, Glos. and Welsh marches 1526–7; feodary, duchy of Lancaster, Glos. and Herefs. 1529–30, 1559; j.p. Glos. 1537–47, q. 1554–*d.*; commr.

musters 1542, chantries 1548, relief 1550; sheriff 1548–9.[2]

The Porter family, originally from Somerset, was settled in Newent, Gloucestershire, by the mid 15th century. Arthur Porter's legal training was influenced by his marriage into the Arnold family. It was as son-in-law to John Arnold, prothonotary and clerk of the crown in Wales, that he was admitted with Arnold's son Nicholas* to Lincoln's Inn to use Arnold's chamber there.[3]

Porter may have practised as a lawyer but little is known of his activities apart from his connexion with the duchy of Lancaster and work on the local bench. He was called the King's servant when appointed receiver of the lands of Llanthony priory by Gloucester in 1539 and also in 1542. He attended the reception of Anne of Cleves in 1539 and served in the army against France in 1544. He was to be appointed an executor of the will of Sir John Brydges* in 1556.[4]

Porter's lands lay a few miles south of Gloucester and also north-west of the city at Newent. He does not appear always to have resided at his family seat; two of his children were buried in 1538 at Quedgeley, where he is credited with the rebuilding of the manor house, and six others later at Hempstead. His receivership of monastic lands in 1539 led to his grant a year later of the site and lands of Llanthony priory and also the chief messuage of the manor of Alvington, which he made one of his two chief residences. In 1544 he acquired Pitchcombe manor in Painswick. During the summer of 1547 Porter was named as one who had not compounded for knighthood. His local status was such that, although he served as sheriff only once, he was put forward for that office in 1545, 1547, and 1552.[5]

By his second marriage Porter strengthened his relationship with Sir Nicholas Arnold, his new wife being Arnold's sister-in-law; she also brought him a connexion with the Berkeley family. These two affiliations may have influenced his election for Mary's third Parliament, when his fellow-knight, William Rede I, was also related to the Arnolds. In the following Parliament Porter found a seat at Gloucester where he had a joint interest in 25 houses. His election on 1 Oct. 1555 was, however, not easily secured; the recorder, Sir John Pollard, who had earlier in his term of office been returned for Oxfordshire, had apparently been defeated there, after which he probably approached the corporation to have the recorder's place in the Parliament. As a pillar of the regime Pollard was an unpopular figure with many in the city and its locality; the mayor of Gloucester lost control of the election, and Pollard was forced to seek a seat elsewhere. Porter and his fellow-Member William Massinger, voted against a government bill when Sir Anthony Kingston closed the door of the House against Pollard's wish.[6]

Porter was not re-elected to Mary's last Parliament but secured a seat in Elizabeth's first which he survived by little more than three weeks, dying on 31 May 1559.[7]

[1] Date of birth estimated from first appointment. *Bristol and Glos. Arch. Soc. Trans.* xxi. 30, 340; xxv. 128; xxxi. 8; *Vis. Glos.* (Harl. Soc. xxi), 4, 8; Mill Stephenson, *Mon. Brasses*, 152. [2] Somerville, *Duchy*, i. 639; *LP Hen. VIII*, xii, xiv–xviii, xx; *CPR*, 1547–8, p. 83; 1548–9, p. 136; 1553, p. 354; 1553–4, pp. 19, 27; 1554–5, pp. 106–7, 111. [3] *Bristol and Glos. Arch. Soc. Trans.* xxi. 340; C67/49, m. 28; *LP Hen. VIII*, i–iii; Somerville, i. 639; PCC 7 Bodfelde; *Black Bk. L. Inn*, i. 208, 227. [4] *LP Hen. VIII*, xiv–xvii, xix; PCC 16 Wrastley. [5] Mill Stephenson, 152, 154; *LP Hen. VIII*, xv, xvi, xix, xx; SP10/11/97; *CPR*, 1553, pp. 316, 387; *VCH Glos.* x. 218. [6] Guildford mus. Loseley 1331/2. [7] C142/122/74.

M.K.D.

PORTER, Baldwin (by 1487–1560/65), of Coventry, Warws.

COVENTRY 1539[1]

b. by 1487, s. of John Porter of Coventry; bro. of Henry*. *educ.* New Inn; I. Temple, adm. 29 Jan. 1514. *m.* at least 3s. 4da. *suc.* fa. by 1527.[2]

Attorney, Coventry in 1516, steward and town clerk by 1524–52 or later, subsidy collector 1545; j.p. Warws. 1524–52 or later; commr. tenths of spiritualities, Coventry and Warwick 1535, relief, Warws. 1550; escheator, Leics. and Warws. Nov. 1532–Feb. 1534.[3]

Baldwin Porter came of a line of Warwickshire lawyers which included the Thomas Porter who was knight of the shire between 1431 and 1447 and his son Baldwin who was brother-in-law to the eminent judge Sir Thomas Littleton. This older namesake was probably Porter's grandfather and the John Porter who was steward and town clerk of Coventry from 1507 to 1521 his father. First mentioned as a feoffee in 1507–8, and thus probably of age by that time, Porter was described as of New Inn when admitted to clerks' commons at the Inner Temple in January 1514 and pardoned certain offices, his sponsor being William Shelley*. In 1519 he and another were assigned a chamber in the inn, but he is not again mentioned in its records. When, three years earlier, Coventry had appointed him its attorney, its grant of the 'whole office' and whole fee suggests that he was already sharing the office, perhaps with his father. The civic career thus begun was to last for some 40 years and was to include a 30-year tenure of the offices of steward and town clerk, and one known election to Parliament which has passed unrecognized in the local history. That he was not returned on other occasions probably reflects the town's preference for choosing its recorder and keeping its chief executive officer at his post, but he was given a vicarious interest in other Parliaments through the election of his

brother. Until the Dissolution his services were retained by several religious houses in Warwickshire and as long as he was steward and town clerk of Coventry he had a place on the county bench.[4]

Porter inherited from his father the manor of Eastcote Hall, near Solihull, Warwickshire, and the leasehold of other property in the locality. In November 1530 he himself took a lease for 21 years of the manor of Fletchamstead, less than three miles from Coventry; the rent was £21 a year, but he was allowed a reduction of 20s. a year 'for a fee for his counsel in the law' given to his landlord Sir Walter Smith. The lease was the subject of litigation between 1538 and 1544, Porter alleging wrongful expulsion from the premises, withholding of his counsel's fee and numerous breaches by Smith of the terms of the lease, Smith counterclaiming for payment of the rent due. Porter drew his own bill of complaint, the sum in dispute being £24 plus costs. Probably the action was amicably settled and Porter granted a new lease, for his brother Henry settled at Fletchamstead and it was there that Henry died in 1555. He himself lived in the Spoon Street ward at Coventry, where his assessment of 20 marks for subsidy in 1550 reflects prosperity but not conspicuous wealth by the city's standards.[5]

Following the death of his son and heir-apparent Robert in Mary's reign, Porter sued his daughter-in-law Alice for the recovery of the title deeds of the manor of Eastcote where she had continued to live after her marriage to a servant of his; during 1560–1 he brought an action in Chancery against Richard Aglionby for allegedly dispossessing him of a field at Eastcote. In a grant of January 1565 he is referred to as the former lessee of tithes at Fletchamstead; since the lease had been made in his name for 45 years in 1532, this wording suggests that he was dead by January 1565. If he made a will it has not been found.[6]

[1] E159/319, brev. ret. Mich. r. [1–2]. [2] Date of birth estimated from first reference. C1/1459/84; 3/145/5; PCC 20 Ketchyn. [3] *Coventry Leet Bk.* (EETS cxxxviii), 650, 686–800 passim; E179/192/170; *LP Hen. VIII*, iv, v, viii, xii–xiv, xvi, xvii, xx; *CPR*, 1548–9, p. 90; 1553, p. 360. [4] Dugdale *Warws.* ii. 983; *Warws. Feet of Fines*, iii (Dugdale Soc. xviii), 224; *Cal. I.T. Recs.* i. 29, 48; *Bailiffs' Accts. of Monastic and Other Estates* (Dugdale Soc. ii), 46. [5] C1/872/52–55; 3/145/5; *LP Hen. VIII*, xvi; *CPR*, 1555–7, p. 311; E179/193/188. [6] C1/1459/84; 3/145/5; *CPR*, 1555–7, p. 116; 1563–6, p. 205.

D.F.C.

PORTER, Henry (by 1501–55/56), of Fletchamstead and Coventry, Warws.

COVENTRY 1545, 1547, 1555

b. by 1501, yr. s. of John Porter of Coventry; bro. of Baldwin*. prob. *unm.*[1]
Steward, Coventry by 1553.[2]

Little has come to light about Henry Porter. Like

his brother Baldwin, he may have received a legal education, for the plaintiff in a chancery suit brought against him as steward of the mayor's court described him as 'learned in the law'. According to the certificate of musters taken in 1522, he was then a tenant in Smithford Street ward, Coventry. In July 1524 he obtained a 40-year lease of the manor and tithes of Sherborne, Warwickshire, from the Knights of St. John and it may thus well have been he who (then said to be resident in London) assisted Sir George Throckmorton (q.v.) five years later in ejecting Martin Dowcra from the commandery of Balsall. (Throckmorton's son John was to be Porter's fellow-Member in the Parliament of 1555.) In 1537 and 1539 Porter acquired leases of the rectory of Harbury and the tithes of the rectory of Offchurch.[3]

Porter sat with Christopher Warren in the Parliaments of 1545 and 1547. On 12 Dec. 1545 he received £3 10s. for his charges 'by 37 days', a generous allowance for the 32 days of the first session of the Parliament of 1545 which, however, did not end until 24 Dec., and early in the following reign he had £2 8s. for his attendance at the second session. The first session of the Parliament of 1547 lasted 51 days but Porter was paid £6 8s. for 64 days, this time at the statutory rate of 2s. a day, and a further £3 for his other charges. The next payment made to him on 15 Feb. 1549 was of £5 and a year later he received £9 3s.2d., of which £7 14s. was for his attendance at the third session (at the beginning of which he had also shared £6 11s. with Warren) until 16 Jan. 1550, just over a fortnight before its close. His additional expenses during the first session and his prolonged sojourn in London may have arisen out of the Coventry Members' vigorous opposition to the bill for the dissolution of the chantries. 'None were stiffer nor more busily went about to impugn' the inclusion of guild lands in this measure than the Coventry Members and their colleagues from Lynn. Coventry's case was that of the two churches in the city serving 11 or 12,000 people one was dependent on the revenues of guild lands, and it asked, successfully, for a promise of a new grant of the lands. Although in May 1548 the Privy Council agreed, it was not until September 1552 that the grant was made, and then at a cost to the city of £1,315. The bill 'for the city of Coventry' introduced into the second session concerned the related matter of Bond's hospital but after Thomas Bond (q.v.) had been questioned about his grandfather's bequest no more is heard of the bill.[4]

Porter made his will on 5 Aug. 1555 but was presumably still in good health when on 8 Oct. he was returned to Parliament for the third and last time. Nothing is known of his attendance or role in the House: the two Mr. Porters appearing on the list of those who opposed a government bill were the Members for Gloucester and Grantham. His will shows that he had settled at Fletchamstead, a manor less than three miles from Coventry which his brother had leased 25 years earlier. He asked to be buried there, provided £40 for alms to the poor and left a further £40 to his 'ghostly father'. Other bequests included £20 each to his nephews Henry and William Porter and £10 each to his four nieces, and he left the residue of his goods (no lands are mentioned) to 'poor householders decayed and to young setters up' in Coventry. His brother Baldwin was an overseer of the will which was proved on 2 Nov. 1556: the date of Porter's death is otherwise unknown.[5]

[1] Date of birth estimated from first reference. PCC 20 Ketchyn; C1/1459/84. [2] C1/1321/50. [3] Ibid.; Coventry accts. various 18, f. 12v; CPR, 1566–9, pp. 361–2, 395; St.Ch.2/17/401; LP Hen. VIII, x; VCH Warws. vi. 198. [4] Coventry mayors' accts. 1542–61, pp. 30, 35, 43, 49, 494, 496; APC, ii. 193–5; W. K. Jordan, Edw. VI, ii. 184–5; CPR, 1550–3, pp. 337–43; CJ, i. 5–7. [5] PCC 20 Ketchyn; VCH Warws. vi. 235; C1/872/52–55.

S.M.T.

PORTER, Thomas (by 1482–1522), of Gloucester.

GLOUCESTER   1515[1]

b. by 1482.[2]
    Sheriff, Gloucester 1503–4, 1509–10, mayor 1511–12, alderman 1516–d.; commr. subsidy 1512, 1514.[3]

The christian name Thomas was a popular one in the Porter family of Gloucestershire, and this Member is not to be confused with a namesake of Newent, who was the grandfather of Arthur Porter* and died before 1510. Thomas Porter of Gloucester was a minor beneficiary under the will dated 1503 of Thomas Lane's* father. Otherwise, little has been discovered about his career. Between the two sessions of the Parliament, Porter and his fellow-Member John Pakington appointed the collectors for the subsidy which they had helped to grant. Porter died on 22 Mar. 1522.[4]

[1] E179/279/3, m.23. [2] Date of birth estimated from first reference. [3] S. Rudder, New Hist. Glos. 115; T. D. Fosbroke, Gloucester (1819), 208; Statutes, iii. 82, 118; Gloucester Guildhall 1375, f. 28. [4] Bristol and Glos. Arch. Soc. Trans. iv. 223; lxxxvii. 198; PCC 9 Holgrave; E179/279/3, m. 23; Gloucester Guildhall 1375, f. 28.

A.D.K.H.

PORTER, William (by 1526–?93), of Gray's Inn, London, and Grantham, Lincs.

GRANTHAM   1555
BLETCHINGLEY   1559
HELSTON   1563

b. by 1526, 2nd s. of Augustine Porter of Belton, Lincs. by Ellen, da. of one Smith of Withcote, Leics. educ. G. Inn, adm. 1540. m. by 1569, Jane, da. of John Butler of Aston-le-Walls, Northants., by Margaret, da. and coh.

of John Dudley of Aston-le-Walls, 8s. 2da. *suc.* bro. John 23 Oct. 1575.[1]

Commr. sewers, Cambs., Hunts., I. of Ely, Lincs., Northants., Notts. 1555; alderman, Grantham in 1559.[2]

The younger son of a Lincolnshire gentleman, William Porter entered Gray's Inn in the same year as William Cecil. His early career was probably divided between London and his native county. His return to the Parliament of 1555 for Grantham, of which he was a near neighbour at Belton and was to be alderman in 1559, probably owed something to Cecil, himself senior knight of the shire in this Parliament and doubtless responsible for the nomination of the other Grantham Member, George Williams. Both Williams and Porter (although not Cecil) appear on the list of Members who voted against one of the government's bills, Porter being styled 'of Grays Inn' to distinguish him from Arthur Porter of Gloucester, who also appears on the list, and Henry Porter of Coventry, who does not. He seems to have been unrelated to either, and among the various contemporary William Porters the only one with whom he could be plausibly identified is the tenant of John Broxholme and John Bellow* living at Lincoln in 1545.[3]

Porter sat in Parliament twice more under Elizabeth. In 1564 Bishop Bentham rated him as 'earnest in religion' and as one upon whom the regime could rely, but despite this recommendation Porter was never named to the bench. He is said to have been buried at Grantham on 7 Dec. 1592, but his inquisition post mortem gives the month of his death as January 1593.[4]

[1] Date of birth estimated from education. *Lincs. Peds.* (Harl. Soc. lii), 791–2; *Vis. Northants.* ed. Metcalfe, 8; Bridges, *Northants.* 101. [2] *CPR*, 1554–5, p. 109; *R. Chs. Grantham*, ed. Martin, 90–91. [3] Guildford mus. Loseley 1331/2; *LP Hen. VIII*, xx. [4] *Cam. Misc.* ix(3), 27; *Lincs. Peds.* 791–2; C142/236/106.

T.M.H.

PORTMAN, William (by 1498–1557), of Orchard Portman, nr. Taunton, Som. and London.

TAUNTON   1529, ?1536[1]

b. by 1498, 1st s. of John Portman of Orchard Portman by Alice, da. of William Knoyle of Sandford Orcas, Dorset. *educ.* M. Temple, adm. 19 May 1517. *m.* by July 1521, Elizabeth, da. of John Gilbert, wid. of Giles Brent, 1s. 1da. *suc.* fa. 5 July 1521. Kntd. 6 Feb. 1547.[2]

Bencher, M. Temple 1532, Autumn reader 1532, Lent 1539.

J.p. Som. 1524–*d.*, Devon 1541, Berks., Glos., Herefs., Mon., Oxon., Salop, Staffs., Worcs. 1542–*d.*; member, council in the west Apr. 1539; serjeant-at-law 1540; King's serjeant 23 Nov. 1540; j.KB 14 May 1546, c.j. 16 June 1555–*d.*; custos rot., Som. c.1547; commr. relief Bath, Som. 1550, goods of churches and fraternities 1553, chantries 1553; receiver of petitions in the Lords, Parlts. of Mar. 1553, Oct. 1553, Apr. 1554, Nov. 1554, 1555.[3]

Like his father, William Portman was by profession a lawyer, and his career is epitomised in the list of his offices and duties. He spent an average length of time in study and practice of the law before becoming a serjeant, but his advance in the next six years through the grade of King's serjeant to the bench, and his subsequent appointment as chief justice, suggest either outstanding ability, or the enjoyment of favour, or both. Although Cromwell, his fellow-Member for Taunton in 1529, can have had little influence on his later career, he and Portman must have known each other well, for Portman was probably legal counsel to Wolsey as bishop of Winchester, as he was later to Wolsey's successor Gardiner. Apart from this connexion with the bishop, who was lord of Taunton, Portman himself had extensive property there and he may have had some part in the nomination of Cromwell on the eve of the meeting of Parliament in November 1529. Portman's name appears twice on Acts passed by that Parliament, on the dorse of the Act regulating the keeping of sheep which was passed in its sixth session and on the front of that concerning Sir Piers Dutton and Corpus Christi college passed in its eighth. In the Parliament of 1536 he was called on by Cromwell to draft a bill, a summons which suggests, even if it does not prove, that Portman sat in this Parliament, as indeed he is likely to have done in the light of the King's request for the return of the previous Members and of the appearance of his name for Taunton on a list drawn up by Cromwell, seemingly of nominees for the bishop of Winchester's boroughs. He may have sat once again, in 1539, but thereafter, as King's serjeant or judge, he received a writ of assistance to the Lords, where he was to be regularly named a receiver of petitions. He was knighted at the accession of Edward VI.[4]

Portman was frequently cited by reporters, especially Dalison and Plowden, and he took part in several notable trials, including those of the Duke of Somerset in 1551 and of (Sir) Nicholas Throckmorton* in 1554. His main interest seems to have remained in the west country, where besides performing judicial duties he served on a number of local commissions. He added considerably by purchase to his landed inheritance in Somerset and at his death he left several manors and extensive property in and around Taunton.[5]

By Portman's will, dated 25 Jan. 1557, these lands descended, together with the residue of his goods, to his son and executor Henry. He gave his daughter Mary £200 besides sheep and clothes, and made small bequests to his sister, brother and mother. He named among his overseers (Sir) John Baker I*, Nicholas Halswell* and (Sir) Nicholas Hare*. He died on 5 Feb. 1557 and was buried with great pomp at St. Dunstans-in-the-West, London.[6]

[1] *LP Hen. VIII*, x. 40 (ii) citing Cott. Otho C10, f. 218. [2] Date of birth estimated from age at fa.'s i.p.m., C142/37/112. *Vis. Som.* ed. Weaver, 126; *Wriothesley's Chron.* i. (Cam. Soc. n.s. xi), 181; C142/108/112. [3] *LP Hen. VIII*, iv–xxi; *CPR, 1547–8 to 1557–8* passim; Foss, *Judges*, v. 387–9; *Rep. R. Comm. of 1552* (Archs. of Brit. Hist. and Culture iii), 113; *LJ*, i. 430, 447, 464, 492; C66/801; 193/12/1; W. K. Jordan, *Edw. VI*, i. 61. [4] Eccles. 2/155877, 155886–7; C142/108/94; House of Lords RO, Original Acts, 25 Hen. VIII, no. 13, 27 Hen. VIII, no. 53; *LP Hen. VIII*, xi; Cott. Otho C10, f. 218; C218/1. [5] Howell, *State Trials*, i. 870–902; Jordan, ii. 93; L. W. Abbott, *Law Reporting in Eng.* 120, 223; *LP Hen. VIII*, iv, xix, xx; *CPR, 1547–8 to 1557–8* passim. [6] PCC 5 Wrastley; C142/108/94; *Machyn's Diary* (Cam. Soc. xlii), 125.

R.V.

PORTWAY, Thomas (by 1524–57), of Dover, Kent.

DOVER 1553 (Mar.)[1]

b. by 1524. *m.* Alice, 1s. 2da.[2]
Common councilman, Dover 1546–7, jurat 1548–?d., mayor 1550–1, bailiff 4 June 1552–d.[3]

A victualler and hackneyman, Thomas Portway engaged in such sizeable operations as shipping the £100 worth of foodstuffs from London to Calais which a Netherlander captured in 1544–45 and bringing soldiers home from Boulogne in 1551 at a cost of £400, while at the other end of the scale he paid 13s.4d. for the lady chapel roof of Dover priory and 12s. for its gravestones. The part of St. Martin's 'church and yard' which he rented for 20s. a year was probably a depot. After a brief municipal career leading to the mayoralty in succession to Thomas Warren (q.v.), he became deputy bailiff to Edmund Mody*, whom he quickly succeeded, continuing to represent Dover at Brotherhoods of the Cinque Ports until 1556. In October 1552 he was one of four chosen by the town to inform the Privy Council about the state of the harbour, in February 1554 he was again before the Council as one of a group which faced the charge that Dover had been passive during Wyatt's rebellion, and in June 1556 he headed a list of those ordered to make Dover defensible against the French.[4]

Portway was first elected for Dover on 29 Jan. 1553. His fellow-Member Henry Crispe was clearly the nominee of the lord warden, Sir Thomas Cheyne*, whereas Portway was presumably chosen by the town. Given 40s. on his departure, he presented a bill on his return for 31 days' attendance and four days' travel at 2s. a day, with an additional '2s. placing and 4s. to the clerk', and was paid the balance of 36s. on 15 Apr. He might well have been re-elected to the Parliament summoned on the following 19 June, but by the time the writ reached Dover on 10 July Edward VI was dead and the summons lapsed. Two months later Dover elected him and Thomas Colly to the first Parliament called by Mary. If by doing so the town hoped to forestall

intervention by the warden it was quickly undeceived, for two days after the election the mayor and jurats indemnified the commonalty for breach of the relevant statutes and had their choice set aside in favour of two men nominated by the warden, Joseph Beverley and John Webbe. At the next election the town succeeded in choosing one of the Members, but its choice fell on Colly, who unlike Portway had not sat before, and Portway was not to be re-elected to either of the two further Parliaments called before his death.[5]

Portway died between 11 Sept. 1557, when he made his will, and the following 24 Oct., when he was succeeded as bailiff of Dover by Sir Thomas Cheyne. By his will he left lands in Kent and elsewhere to his wife for life, with remainder to his son Thomas and two daughters, Mary and Catherine. As his executrix his widow proved the will on 15 Mar. 1558; she also returned to the town a silver mace which he had used in office. Her own will was to become the subject of arbitration in April 1562 by John Malin, William Hannington* and Thomas Warren.[6]

[1] Add. 34150, f. 139. [2] Date of birth estimated from first reference. Canterbury prob. reg. C27, ff. 64v–65. [3] Dover accts. 1547–58, f. 4; Egerton 2094, ff. 25, 27, 31, 37, 45, 51; *CPR, 1550–3*, p. 321. [4] Add. 29618, ff. 308, 322; Egerton 2092, f. 494v; 2093, f. 190; 2094, ff. 36, 58, 166; *Bronnen tot de Geschiedenis van den Handel met Engeland, Schotland en Ierland*, ed. Smit, i. 607, 658n *APC*, iii. 7, 291; iv. 393; *Arch. Cant.* xlvii. 142; Dover accts. 1547–58, f. 160; *Cinque Ports White and Black Bks.* (Kent Arch. Soc. recs. br. xix), 226–54 passim. [5] Dover accts. 1547–58, ff. 198v, 199; Egerton 2094, ff. 89, 90v. [6] Canterbury prob. reg. C27, ff. 64v–65; *CPR, 1557–8*, p. 122; Egerton 2094, ff. 174v, 224.

P.H.

POTY, Richard (by 1517–45/46), of Orford and Woodbridge, Suff.

ORFORD ?1536,[1] ?1539,[2] ?1542[3]

b. by 1517, prob. 3rd s. of Nicholas Poty of Walberswick. *m.* Alice, 2s. 2da.[4]
Constable, Woodbridge in 1538.[5]

It is only known that Richard Poty was a Member for Orford from evidence given in a suit between the inhabitants of that town and Sir William Willoughby*, 1st Baron Willoughby of Parham, about parliamentary and other rights. John Harrison testified that since 1523 the town had always had two Members and that John Harman and 'young Poty' had been chosen several times; another made clear that the second of these was Richard Poty. If the meaning was that the two had sat together, the Parliaments concerned could only have been those of 1536 and 1539, but as the name of one of the Members is also unknown for 1542 Poty could have sat in that Parliament as well. John Culham of Dunwich who had lived in Orford until 1536 recalled 18 years later that after his departure from the town Poty had been elected Member and had 'served in the Parliament accordingly' but could not recall the name of Poty's partner. The evidence given by Harrison, Culham and others is open to interpretation but Culham's statement about Richard Hunt (q.v.) creates the presumption that Poty was returned in 1536.[6]

Poty's father was probably the Nicholas Poty of Walberswick mentioned in the will of a relative, Robert Poty, a shipowner of Walberswick, in 1513. Richard Poty owned lands and tenements in Woodbridge as well as property in Orford. In March 1538, as constable of Woodbridge, he was one of the principal signatories to a letter to Cromwell about wheat taken to the King's use from a Spanish vessel, part of which was being held in Poty's house there. In 1544 he acquired the manor of Bacon *alias* Davelers in Pettistree, Suffolk, from John Ball* and Francis Noone.[7]

Poty died between 28 May 1545 when he made his will and 19 May 1546 when it was proved. His lands, all in Suffolk, were left to his wife and children. To his wife he bequeathed the manor of Bacon, with remainder to his daughter Alice, to his elder son John lands and tenements in Woodbridge, to his younger son Robert a tenement in Orford on the widow's death, and to his daughter Margaret a tenement and lands in Dallinghoo. He also made bequests to Orford church where he asked to be buried. He named his wife and eldest son executors.[8]

[1] E111/48. [2] Ibid. [3] Ibid. [4] Date of birth estimated from constableship. PCC 17 Fetiplace; Suff. archdeaconry ct. 15, f. 203. [5] *LP Hen. VIII*, xiii. [6] E111/48. [7] PCC 17 Fetiplace; CP25(2)/41/280, no. 27. [8] Suff. archdeaconry ct. 15, f. 203.

                                      M.K.D.

POUNTE, Jasper (by 1515–61 or later), of London.

LYME REGIS   1555, 1558*[1]

b. by 1515, s. of one Pounte by Mary. *m.* 28 Jan. 1542, Clement Woodland.[2]
    Servant of Sir Richard Rich c.1537; messenger, ct. augmentations by 1539; clerk of the compter in Bread Street, London by 1544.[3]

In the late 1520s Jasper Pounte was living with his mother within the precincts of the priory of St. Helen, Bishopsgate, London. The prioress, from whom Pounte's stepfather Thomas Parker, a London ironmonger, rented the house, complained bitterly of the behaviour of the whole family—of Pounte for abusing the porter. Pounte, when he had his own establishment, lived in a new house in the parish of St. Mary Aldermanbury. Although he lived and worked in London, Pounte also had interests in Dorset. In the 1530s he laid claim unsuccessfully to the manor of Axnoll in Beaminster, bought by his mother, of which he and other feoffees

had been dispossessed, and in the early 1550s he bought the farm of Wotton in Dorset.[4]

No link between Pounte and Lyme Regis has been discovered and he appears to have owed his elections there to his former connexions in augmentations; one of these, Matthew Colthurst*, was a figure of some influence in the south-west and an associate of the 1st Earl of Pembroke. Pounte was chosen for Lyme Regis in 1555 at the same time as a superior, John Foster III, was returned for Shaftesbury, not far from Colthurst's residence. Three years later Lyme elected Foster and John Popham to Parliament, but Foster, who had also been returned for Hertfordshire, preferred the knighthood of that shire: a writ was therefore issued on 24 Jan. for a fresh election at which, three days later, Pounte replaced him. Pounte's name does not appear on the original Crown Office list for the Parliament of 1558 but is on the copy made during its course.[5]

In 1561 Pounte tried to obtain possession of a house and mills in Somerset and was hindered (as he thought) by the partiality of the under sheriff, Richard Fitzjames. No further reference to him has been found.[6]

[1] Wm. Salt Lib. SMS. 264. [2] Date of birth estimated from mother's second widowhood in 1517, St.Ch.2/17/217. C1/876/55; *Reg. St. Mary Aldermanbury* (Harl. Soc. xli), i. 5. [3] Information from Mary E. Coyle; *LP Hen. VIII*, xiv; City of London RO, Guildhall, rep. 12(1), f. 127v; *London Consist. Ct. Wills* (London Rec. Soc. iii), 128. [4] St.Ch.2/17/217, 24/228, 25/185; *CPR*, 1549–51, p. 410; C1/876/55, 1355/12–14, 1370/84–85; 78/9/70. [5] C193/30/2; 219/25/32, 39–40; Wm. Salt Lib. SMS. 264. [6] St.Ch.2/34/25, 3/9/90.

POWELL (APOWELL), Adam (by 1496–1546), of Gloucester.

GLOUCESTER   1529

b. by 1496. *m.* Mary, 2s. 1da.[1]
    Sheriff, Gloucester 1517–18, 1525–6, alderman 1529–d., coroner 1536–7, master of the guild of Holy Trinity 1536–7.[2]

Adam Powell remains a shadowy figure. No evidence has been found to support the surmise that he was the son of Philip ap Howell and his wife Joan, who was nurse to Henry VII, and the enigmatic epithet 'very severe' applied to him in a letter of 1519 is the only known fragment of information about his personality. Powell was assessed for the subsidy in 1523 at 40s. and in 1544 on goods worth £40. He was said in 1542 to be the tenant of a messuage in the city which had belonged to Derehurst priory. His election to the Parliament of 1529 was a measure of his standing in the city. He may have sat in that of 1523, for which the names of the Gloucester Members are unknown, and almost certainly did so in that of June 1536 in accordance with the King's request for the return of the previous Members: the only other Parliament in which he could have sat is that of 1542, when the names are again lost. Ten days before his death on 5 Mar. 1546 Powell made a will, asking to be buried in the chancel of St. Michael's church, Gloucester. He left beds to his two sons, one of whom was under 21, and to his daughter Elizabeth Machyn who was presumably the wife of one of the supervisors, John Machyn.[3]

[1] Date of birth estimated from first reference. Gloucester consist. ct. wills 1545. [2] Gloucester Guildhall 1300; 1375, ff. 27v–28. [3] *CPR*, 1485–94, pp. 95, 365; *LP Hen. VIII*, iii, xiii, xvii, xix; E179/113/214, 114/245; Gloucester consist. ct. wills 1545; Gloucester Guildhall 1375, f. 28.

L.M.K./M.K.D.

POWELL (APPOWELL), Edmund (by 1506–58/59), of New Windsor, Berks. and Sandford-on-Thames, Oxon.

LUDGERSHALL   1553 (Oct.), 1554 (Apr.)
OXFORDSHIRE   1555

> *b.* by 1506, s. of Morris ap Hywel of 'Guernon', Card. by Gille, da. of William Phillips. *m.* by 1542, Isabel, da. of (?Henry) Banester (?of Chesterton, Oxon.), 2s. 1da.[1]
>
> Under steward, manor of Ewelme, Oxon. in 1537; j.p. Oxon. 1541–*d.*, q. by 1554; commr. relief 1550; escheator, Oxon. and Berks. 1554–5.[2]

Edmund Powell's pedigree shows the descent of his mother back three generations but not that of his father. Morris ap Hywel was probably of humble origin and in all likelihood may be identified with the man who sued out a pardon on Henry VIII's accession as 'Maurice Flood or Lloyd of London, *alias* Maurice Walshman late of Elsing, Norfolk, *alias* Maurice Appowell late of—, Oxfordshire, yeoman'. His father's mobility and yeoman status, combined with the use of several *aliases*, would help to explain the obscurity of Edmund Powell's early years, and a domicile in Oxfordshire his later acquisition of property in that county.[3]

The earliest reference to Powell occurs in the grant of a pension made to him on 29 June 1527 by the priory of Maiden Bradley, Wiltshire; for his 'good and laudable counsel', which suggests that he had a legal education, he was to receive 20s. a year for life out of the manor of Babington, Somerset. The John Phillips who leased Babington in the following year was probably related to Powell's mother. In 1530 Powell, described as a gentleman of New Windsor, Berkshire, was granted by the priory an 88-year lease, in reversion after the death of the life-tenant, of a house in North Tidworth, Wiltshire. By 1537 he had found employment as under steward of the royal manor of Ewelme, Oxfordshire. Until his attainder in 1536 Henry

Norris had been keeper of Ewelme and in 1538 Sir Francis Bryan* was granted the office; Powell probably used his connexions with one or both of these prominent courtiers to further his own advancement. A lesser courtier, the wardrobe official Edward Lloyd (q.v.), may have been Powell's kinsman.[4]

By March 1541 Powell was already of sufficient stature in Oxfordshire to be included on the commission of the peace. In January 1542 he was granted, in exchange for his property in New Windsor and for £388, the manor of Sandford in Oxfordshire and other lands in Gloucestershire, Oxfordshire and Somerset, some of which he disposed of almost immediately. He may have been speculating on a small scale in the land market for in 1542 he purchased the rectory and advowson of Evenley, Northamptonshire, and sold it a month later. He made his second major purchase in 1544, paying £222 for scattered parcels of land in Gloucestershire and Oxfordshire and a house in London which he immediately alienated to Robert King, perhaps a cousin. He consolidated his estate at Sandford in 1548 when he acquired the neighbouring priory of Littlemore from Sir John Gresham and Sir John Williams*.[5]

Williams* may also have been Powell's kinsman by marriage and such a connexion would help to explain Powell's return for Oxfordshire in 1555. He does not otherwise seem to have been of sufficient standing, although he was known to the sheriff, (Sir) Richard Brydges*. He had already sat in the two previous years for Ludgershall under Brydges's patronage and on the first occasion with Brydges as his fellow-Member: his elder son was to enter Brydges's inn, the Middle Temple, in June 1554 and his property at North Tidworth lay about two miles from Ludgershall. Moreover, like Brydges, Powell was probably a Catholic: he opposed neither the reunion with Rome in Mary's first Parliament nor a government bill in her fourth.

Little else is known of Powell's career under Mary: he was associated with John Rastell of Gloucester in a lease of property in the city of Gloucester, and in 1555 he attended Cranmer's trial at Oxford. In the first year of Elizabeth's reign Powell and his sister-in-law, Margaret Worthington, brought a suit in the court of requests complaining of arrears owing on an annuity which Henry Banester of Chesterton, Oxfordshire, perhaps Powell's father-in-law, had agreed to pay Margaret in 1546. Banester had since died and had committed all his goods to two Londoners, who refused to pay arrears. In 1550 another Henry Banester had accused an Oxford scholar in the chancellor's court there of defaming his sister, Isabel Powell, and her husband. Powell was appointed to the first commission of the peace issued in Elizabeth's reign but must have died shortly afterwards as his elder son, also Edmund, was in possession of Sandford in 1559. It was probably this son who was the Edmund Powell imprisoned in 1571 for complicity in planning the escape of Mary Queen of Scots. The family remained Catholic until in the 18th century the male line expired in two Franciscan friars.[6]

[1] Date of birth estimated from first reference. *Vis. Oxon.* (Harl. Soc. v), 287-8; *LP Hen. VIII*, xvii; C142/240/80. [2] *LP Hen. VIII*, xii, xvi, xvii, xx; *CPR*, 1547-8, p. 88; 1553, p. 357; 1554-5, pp. 23, 27. [3] *LP Hen. VIII*, i. [4] E315/240, ff. 157-8; Hoare, *Wilts.* Mere, 104; *LP Hen. VIII*, x. [5] *LP Hen. VIII*, xvii, xix; *DKR*, x. 255; *VCH Oxon.* v. 81, 270; *VCH Glos.* vi. 67; *CPR*, 1547-8, p. 302; F. G. Lee, *Thame Church*, 385. [6] E315/180, f. 95; Strype, *Cranmer*, 1072; Req.2/254/70; Oxf. Univ. Arch. T/S cal. chancellor's ct. reg. GG, p. 77; C142/240/80; *CSP Dom.* 1547-80, pp. 436, 471; *HMC Hatfield*, i. 535, 537-9, 544-6, 549, 550, 553, 571-2; *VCH Oxon.* v. 274; *Cath. Rec. Soc.* xxii. 97 and n.

S.R.J.

POWELL (AP HYWEL, AP HOWELL), John (by 1524-91/93), of Cardigan, Llangoedmor and Pen-yr-Allt, Card.

CARDIGAN BOROUGHS   1554 (Apr.)

b. by 1524. *m.* at least 1s.[1]
  Yeoman, household of Prince Edward by 1545-7; yeoman of the guard temp. Edw. VI-temp. Eliz.; commr. subsidy, Card. 1553, armour 1569, musters 1570, victuals 1574, tanneries 1574; j.p. 1555-*d*.; escheator 1563-4, 1567-8; sheriff 1568-9.[2]

Nothing has come to light about the parentage of John Powell, who is variously described as of Cardigan and its neighbour Llangoedmor, or of Pen-yr-Allt near Aberporth. He is less often met with under the Welsh patronymic ap Hywel than is Edward ap Hywel, who sat for Cardigan Boroughs a year before him and may have been his brother.[3]

Powell's career as a royal servant can be traced from before the death of Henry VIII until after the accession of Elizabeth and in county administration from the middle of Mary's reign until late in Elizabeth's. It was while a yeoman of the guard under Edward VI that he was a suitor in the court of requests against Thomas ap Hywel, a student at Oxford and probably his kinsman, in a dispute over the parsonage of Llandovery, Carmarthenshire. Later in the reign he charged the burgesses of Cardigan with failing to use the mill at Cenarth which he had leased, with two neighbouring ones, in May 1550. Another suit, this time in Chancery, arose out of his lease of the parsonage of Llanbadarn Trefeglwys in Cardiganshire: he accused his factor John Gwyn* of failing to account for two years' receipts of the parsonage, amounting to some £30.[4]

Powell was nominated as sheriff in 1553 but not pricked, so that he was free to sit for the Cardigan-

shire Boroughs in the first Parliament of the following year. He did not sit again, although two years later he gained a place on the bench which he was to keep for more than forty. Its continuity, and his choice as sheriff in 1568, show that the change of regime gave him no difficulty; at Elizabeth's accession he sued out a general pardon as of Llangoedmor and in 1575 he was certified as a resident in the commote of Troed-yr-Aur in which that parish lay. In a Star Chamber action he and his servant Thomas Walter claimed to have been wounded by about 40 assailants at Cilgerran, near his home, when the portreeve of Cilgerran, Thomas Revell[†], 'departed smiling away'.[5]

Powell may have begun in trade at Cardigan and later become a landed proprietor. At the end of Henry VIII's reign he had been assessed in the town on goods worth £10, but at his death he was said to have owned lands in Cardiganshire and Pembrokeshire worth between £13 and £16 a year. He died between 1591 when he was last named to the bench and 1593 when the guardianship of his son John became the subject of a Star Chamber action brought by Richard Parry of Carmarthen, who claimed that the boy, his ward, had been abducted from his house. The boy must have been the offspring of a late marriage, of which no other trace has been found.[6]

[1] Date of birth estimated from first reference. St.Ch.5/P31/16. [2] E179/69/48, 219/74; 321/27/64; LC2/2/54v; Req.2/14/111; *Augmentations* (Univ. Wales Bd. of Celtic Studies, Hist. and Law ser. xiii), 44; *CPR*, 1558-60, p. 206; R. Flenley, *Cal. Reg. Council, Marches of Wales*, 60, 69, 109, 126, 138, 213. [3] J. R. Phillips, *Sheriffs, Card.* 5; *HMC Welsh*, i(1), 128; *CPR*, 1558-60, p. 209. [4] Req.2/14/111; *CPR*, 1553, p. 377; 1557-8, p. 106; 1572-5, p. 371; E321/27/64; *Augmentations*, 44, 243, 245; C1/1257/50. [5] *CPR*, 1558-60, p. 209; *HMC Welsh*, i(1), 128; St.Ch.5/W82/5. [6] St.Ch.5/P31/16; E179/263/37.

P.S.E.

POWLE see POLE

POWNSAR, John (by 1477-1517), of Reading, Berks.

READING   1515[1]

b. by 1477. *m.* Isabel, *s.p.*[2]
  Member of guild, Reading 1498, tax collector 1498, on inner council of burgesses 1511, assessor 1512, mayor 1514-15.[3]

John Pownsar, who sought entry into the Reading merchants' guild on 22 Feb. 1498, had no relatives of whom anything is known, although a Nicholas Pounsar was a yeoman of the king's guard in 1509 and 1512. Described in 1509 as a draper, Pownsar reached the list of three candidates for the mayoralty by 1507. Although he is not recorded as a partisan of his fellow-draper Richard Cleche* in the town's struggle with Reading abbey, for five successive years (1509–13) he failed to secure the abbot's nomination as mayor, to be finally chosen in September 1514. While in office he was elected to the Parliament of 1515 as junior Member with a lawyer and outsider, Edmund Knightley; the return by Reading of its mayor had a recent precedent in that of William Gifford and was to be repeated with Nicholas Hyde, before becoming customary in the 1550s. The word 'mortuus' against Pownsar's name on a list of 1514 must have been added later.[4]

Pownsar was one of the wealthiest townsmen. His contributions of a 10s. fine to the abbot in 1509, of 20s. towards the renewal of the town's charters in 1510 and of one bow and one man to the King in 1513 were larger than those of any other townsman who sat in Parliament, save William Justice and, in 1510, Richard Cleche and Richard Smith. A debt of 53s.4d. to the guild in 1513 does not seem to have been outstanding at his death and, during his lifetime, Pownsar gave 3s.4d. towards candlesticks for St. Lawrence's, where he was to be buried, as well as presenting the church with altar cloths and curtains. From 1512 to 1513 he was a warden of the mass of Jesus there, a chantry to which he was to bequeath £10. Houses in Reading High Street and Cheese Row are mentioned in the will, made on 28 June and proved on 9 Dec. 1517, in which he left the bulk of his property to his wife and executrix, with remainder to the overseer, John Barfote, and Barfote's son.[5]

[1] *Reading Recs.* i. 130. [2] Date of birth estimated from first reference. PCC 1 Ayloffe. [3] *Reading Recs.* i. 95, 96, 121, 124, 128. [4] Ibid. i. 95, 102, 104, 111, 115, 122–4, 128, 130, 133, 145; *LP Hen. VIII*, i; PCC 1 Ayloffe. [5] *Reading Recs.* i. 111, 114, 126, 127; C. E. Kerry, *St. Lawrence, Reading*, 32, 37, 106, 173–4, 187; PCC 1 Ayloffe.

T.F.T.B.

POWTRELL, Nicholas (by 1517–79), of Egmanton, Notts.

NOTTINGHAM 1545, 1547, 1554 (Nov.)

b. by 1517, 2nd s. of John Powtrell of West Hallam, Derbys. by Margaret, da. and coh. of John Strelley of Strelley, Notts.; bro. of Thomas*. *educ.* G. Inn, adm. 1531. *m.* (1) or (2) Anne, da. of Walter Rodney of Stoke Rodney, Som.[1]

Commr. chantries Derbys., Notts. 1546, array, Derbys. 1546, relief, Notts. 1550; recorder, Nottingham 1546–55; j.p.q. Notts. 1554–d., Yorks. and border counties 1562–4; serjeant-at-law 1558; justice itinerant and of assize, Durham and Sedbergh 1559; 2nd justice at Lancaster, duchy of Lancaster 1559–62, chief justice 1562–d.[2]

An ancient Nottinghamshire family settled at Thrumpton, the Powtrells established themselves in Derbyshire after the acquisition in 1467 of the manor and advowson of West Hallam by Nicholas Powtrell's grandfather. In Powtrell's generation

each shire was to provide the setting for one of the brothers, Nicholas basing himself on Nottinghamshire and his elder brother Thomas on Derbyshire. Nicholas Powtrell was to strengthen his connexion with Nottinghamshire by his purchase before 1554 from Sir Edward Stanhope of part of the manor of Egmanton, where he built a large hall which he emparked.[3]

Nothing has been discovered about Powtrell's career in the 15 years after his entry to Gray's Inn, but his appointment in 1546 to the recordership of Nottingham must reflect a successful pursuit of the law. The office in turn accounts for his parliamentary career, which began shortly before he obtained it and came to an end after he quitted it. Of his part in the first two Parliaments in which he sat there is no trace, but in the Parliament of November 1554 he was one of the large number of Members prosecuted in the King's bench for absenting themselves without licence. Informed against in Easter term 1555, he failed to appear and was distrained in each of the following terms until Hilary 1557 when he was fined 53s.4d.; Anthony Forster* was one of his sureties. The record of the prosecution implies that Powtrell's absence was held to be deliberate and inexcusable, and there are other grounds for thinking that it was: not only did his public career show no advancement during the remainder of Mary's reign, but the laying of the information against him coincided with his vacating of the recordership.[4]

The reign of Elizabeth opened well for Powtrell: he was made a serjeant-at-law and a judge at Lancaster, and for several years he was kept busy on commissions both in his home county and further north. This spate of activity seems to have ended abruptly about 1565 and thereafter he disappeared almost completely from public life. He was not yet an old man, but he could have been an ailing one, although he had a dozen more years to live. Whether he again paid the penalty of dissent, this time not on his own account but on his family's, it is impossible to say—in 1564 the archbishop of York omitted to categorize him—but his life cannot have been made easier when his nephew's house at West Hallam became a refuge for Catholic priests: Edmund Campion was to stay there not long after Powtrell's death.[5]

During his earlier career Powtrell had been closely associated with leading local families, notably the Willoughbys of Wollaton, from whom he was receiving an annuity of 20s. in 1547 and again in 1572, and the Manners, earls of Rutland. Although not one of the 2nd Earl's household servants, Powtrell performed services for him, as when in 1557 the earl's servants and tenants in Yorkshire had to be made ready as light horsemen for the wars. In March 1554 Powtrell had sent to the earl in London a horse which apparently did not meet with his approval: Powtrell's letter on the subject includes a claim for £20 for his services in Nottinghamshire.[6]

In his will, made on 1 Sept. 1579, Powtrell recited an indenture, drawn up in the previous year, by which he had leased the manor of Egmanton and lands in Laxton, Tuxford and Weston to his niece Julian and her husband William Mason, two of his executors; he had afterwards granted these properties to a group of feoffees, including his cousin Thomas Markham*, to his own use and on his death to that of Markham and his heirs. He had made a similar arrangement for the disposal of other lands in north Nottinghamshire, intending at that time to disinherit his nephew Walter Powtrell, because of 'the untrue and slanderous reports and of the unnatural dealing that he and his wife have and do daily use towards me'. In his will, however, Powtrell declared his 'readiness . . . to die in charity towards them and all the world', and in the hope that his nephew's son would prove 'more wise, honest . . . and of better judgment' he granted these lands to Thomas Markham to the use of Walter and his heirs. His household goods, articles of silver and other valuables Powtrell left to relatives, including his nephews the Masons and the Stringers, and he made several monetary bequests to his servants. William Dabridgecourt and Thomas Markham were appointed supervisors.[7]

Powtrell died on 29 Oct. 1579. His attempt to disinherit his nephew in favour of Thomas Markham provoked a dispute between Walter Powtrell and the executors; on 20 June 1584 the administration of the will was granted to Walter Powtrell, as next of kin, but on 27 Mar. 1587 the decision was revoked and probate was granted to the executors. He was buried in the chancel of Egmanton church.[8]

[1] Date of birth estimated from education. *The Gen.* n.s. viii. 68; *Trans. Thoroton Soc.* vi. 80; Thoroton, *Notts.* ed. Throsby i. 30. [2] *LP Hen. VIII*, xxi; *CPR*, 1547–8, p. 416; 1553, p. 357; 1553–4, p. 22; 1558–60, p. 65; 1560–3, pp. 31, 57, 187–8, 435–7, 440–1, 443, 445–7; 1563–6, pp. 20–22, 25, 27, 29, 37, 42, 105, 124; *Trans. Thoroton Soc.* xvi. 123; *CSP Dom.* 1547–80, p. 122; Somerville, *Duchy*, i. 471, 473; *Nottingham Bor. Recs.* iv. 15, 416–17. [3] Thoroton, i. 30; Notts RO, Torre ms, Egmanton 2. [4] KB27/1176–81. [5] J. C. Cox, *Derbys. Churches*, iv. 220; *APC*, ix. 216; xiii. 197; *Cath. Rec. Soc.* lx. 5–9; *Cam. Misc.* ix(3), 73. [6] *HMC Middleton*, 317, 433; *HMC Rutland*, i. 61, 68; iv. 205. [7] PCC 21 Spencer. [8] E150/772/6; *Trans. Thoroton Soc.* vi. 80; PCC admons. act bk. 1581–6, f. 110.

C.J.B.

POWTRELL, Thomas (by 1514–57), of West Hallam, Derbys.

DERBYSHIRE 1547, 1554 (Apr.)

b. by 1514, 1st s. of John Powtrell of West Hallam, and bro. of Nicholas*. *educ.* G. Inn, adm. 1528. *m.* (1) Dorothy, da. and coh. of William Bassett of Muskham, Notts., 2da.; (2) by June 1544, Elizabeth, da. of Walter Rodney of Stoke Rodney, Som., 2s. 1da. *suc.* fa. Nov. 1543.[1]

J.p. Derbys. 1537–*d.*; commr. musters Derbys. 1539, benevolence 1544/45, array 1546, relief 1550, goods of churches and fraternities 1553; escheator, Notts. and Derbys. 1549–50.[2]

The insignificant career of Thomas Powtrell's father was offset by the careers of his two sons. Both Nicholas and Thomas Powtrell were educated at Gray's Inn, but whereas Nicholas rose to become a serjeant and judge, Thomas combined the roles of landowner and magistrate, serving on the bench continuously from 1537 until his death and on many other commissions in the county. Both brothers inherited land in Nottinghamshire, but whereas Nicholas chose to consolidate his position in that county Thomas extended his holdings in neighbouring Derbyshire; in June 1544 he purchased for £102 the former monastic properties of Stanley Grange and lands in Dale and Spondon.[3]

Although Thomas Powtrell enjoyed the local standing without which he could scarcely have hoped to represent the shire in Parliament, his choice in 1547 may well have owed something to his legal connexions and in particular to the rising importance of his brother Nicholas, who had sat for the borough of Nottingham in 1545 and accompanied him in the same capacity to the Parliament of 1547. Powtrell's only other appearance in the Commons, in the first Parliament of 1554, need not have reflected any special sympathy with the Marian regime, since although his son and daughter-in-law and their descendants were to become recusants, his own career was apparently unaffected by the religious upheavals of his own day and his will, drawn up in June 1557, gives no indication of enthusiasm.[4]

Thomas Powtrell died on 12 Aug. 1557. He had appointed as executors his wife Elizabeth, his brother Nicholas, in whom he placed his 'especial trust', and Sir John Chaworth, who was to have his second best gelding. Bequests to relatives and servants included 'my chain and one half of all my plate' to his son Walter, £100 to his daughter Frances, £200 to his daughter Mary, and a black coat to each of his yeoman servants. The wardship of his heir Walter, aged 12 years, was purchased by his wife for £100.[5]

[1] Date of birth estimated from education. *The Gen.* n.s. viii. 68; Wards 7/1/118; E150/765/1. [2] *LP Hen. VIII*, xii–xviii, xx, xxi; *CPR*, 1547–8, p. 82; 1550–3, p. 394; 1553, pp. 352, 414; 1553–4, p. 18. [3] *LP Hen. VIII*, xviii, xix; *CSP Dom.* 1601–3, *Add.* 1547–65, p. 458. [4] J. C. Cox, *Derbys. Churches*, iv. 220; Lichfield consist. ct. will 109. [5] E150/765/1; Lichfield consist. ct. will 109; Index 10217(1), f. 66.

C.J.B.

POYNINGS, Sir Edward (1459–1521), of Westenhanger, Kent.

?KENT 1512

b. autumn 1459, o. s. of Robert Poynings † of Maidstone by Elizabeth, da. of Sir William Paston of Paston, Norf.; half-bro. of Sir Matthew Browne†. *m.* by 1485, Elizabeth or Isabel (*d.*1528), da. of Sir John Scott† of Scot's Hall, Smeath, Kent, 1s. d.v.p.; 3s. 4da. illegit. *suc.* fa. 17 Feb. 1461. Kntd. 7 Aug. 1485, KG 1493, banneret Aug. 1513.[1]

Councillor 1485; j.p. Kent 1485; knight of the body by 1488; dep. lt. Calais 1493; dep. [I] 1494–6; lt. Dover castle by 1496, constable 1504–*d.*; dep. warden, Cinque Ports 1505–9, warden 1509–*d.*; comptroller, the Household by 1509–19 or later, treasurer 1519–*d.*; commr. subsidy, Kent 1512, 1514, 1515, royal household 1515; other commissions, London and Kent 1489–*d.*; lt. Tournai Sept. 1513–Jan. 1515.[2]

Robert Poynings was killed at St. Albans in 1461, and Edward was brought up by his mother and his stepfather, Sir George Browne† of Betchworth, Surrey. He took part in the Kentish rising of 1483 in support of the 2nd Duke of Buckingham's rebellion against Richard III and was attainted, as 'Edward Ponyngs late of Marsham, esquire', in the Parliament of January 1484. He made his escape from England, joined Henry Tudor and returned with him in August 1485, being knighted after the landing at Milford Haven; when Parliament met in November his attainder was reversed.[3]

The Parliament of 1485 in its turn attainted the followers of Richard III, among them Humphrey Stafford†, and in September 1488 Poynings was granted seven of Stafford's manors, in Buckinghamshire, Leicestershire, Northamptonshire and Warwickshire. He had already become active in the administration of Kent, where he had his chief seat. Most of his time, however, was spent either abroad or at court. In August 1488 he was commissioned to view the armaments at Calais, Guisnes and Hammes. Four years later he commanded 12 ships sent in support of the Emperor to besiege Sluys and after its capitulation he joined Henry VII at Boulogne. Appointed the King's deputy lieutenant at Calais, Poynings was in July 1493 sent with William Warham to the Netherlands in a vain attempt to discredit Perkin Warbeck, maintained there by Margaret of Burgundy.[4]

Henry VII next turned to Ireland, where in the summer of 1494 a new landing by Warbeck was daily expected. In September of that year the King made his four year-old son Henry lieutenant of Ireland, with Poynings as his deputy, to suppress the 'savage Irish' and bring them under the same laws as those within the pale. Poynings succeeded in routing the Yorkist faction in Ireland and subordinating Anglo-Irish and Irish alike to the authority of England in

the famous 'Poynings's law', passed by the Parliament which he had summoned to meet at Drogheda on 1 Dec. 1494. Attempts at financial reform were less successful and, the crisis past, in 1496 Henry VII reverted to the policy of ruling through the Anglo-Irish aristocracy: Poynings was recalled and the 8th Earl of Kildare appointed deputy of Ireland.[5]

The Cinque Ports at their Easter Brotherhood in 1496 were awaiting the return from Ireland of Poynings, now lieutenant of Dover castle. Presumably he had been appointed to this office before his departure, possibly in October 1494 when Prince Henry was made constable of the castle and lord warden of the Cinque Ports. In 1509 Poynings himself was formally admitted at the court of Shepway as lord warden. During his wardenship he was elected to the Parliament of 1512, almost certainly as knight of the shire for Kent, and led the delegation of the Commons which announced its choice of Speaker to the chancellor in the Lords. He was presumably re-elected in 1515 in compliance with the general directive for the return of previous Members, and could well have sat in earlier Parliaments for which the returns are lost. There is no direct evidence that he used his office as lord warden to secure parliamentary nominations in the Cinque Ports.[6]

A trusted servant of Henry VII, Poynings was appointed one of the additional feoffees of crown lands under the King's last will in 1504. He stood even closer to Henry VIII, whose coronation he attended as comptroller of the Household, an office he retained until May 1519, when, or soon afterwards, he was promoted to treasurer. The intention seems to have been that he should retain the new position only until his services were rewarded with a barony, but he died in 1521 still holding it and still a commoner. His illegitimate son Thomas was later ennobled.[7]

In the early years of the reign Poynings had often gone abroad in the King's service. In June 1511 he was appointed admiral of the expedition sent to assist Prince Charles of Castile in suppressing a revolt in Guelderland and in December 1512 he was one of the four commissioners to treat for a coalition against France; with Sir Richard Wingfield he was responsible for the negotiations in the Netherlands, where he arrived early in 1513. He served in the campaign that took Tournai and was named its first governor. His duties at Tournai prevented him from attending the third session of the Parliament of 1512 where he obtained an Act (5 Hen. VIII, c.18) annulling all suits and processes harmful to his landed possessions which had been or might be decided against him in his absence. He did not return to England until his replacement as governor by the 4th Lord Mountjoy early in 1515. Later in the year he hoped to go on pilgrimage to Rome, but on 7 May he was appointed ambassador to Prince Charles and arrived in Bruges on 23 May. He came back to England in the autumn. Early in 1516 he returned to the Netherlands to conclude a treaty with Charles.[8]

This was the last of Poynings's diplomatic missions apart from a visit to Calais in May 1517 to settle disputes between English and French merchants and to deal with all violations of the treaty; in London in October 1518 he was one of the many signatories to the treaties of marriage and universal peace with France. His duties as warden of the Cinque Ports and comptroller of the Household—presumably more often than not exercised by deputy during these busy years—now occupied him. As warden he was called on to provide ships to transport Henry VIII and his retinue to Calais in 1520, and as a household officer he attended upon the King at the Field of Cloth of Gold and at the meeting with the Emperor at Gravelines.[9]

His 'laudable service' in two reigns did not bring Poynings much material reward. The grant of Stafford's manors in 1488 was the only such grant which he is known to have received throughout his life, although it was supplemented in 1497 by the wardships of Henry Pympe and Humphrey Stafford. Another wardship, that of his grandson Edward Fiennes, 9th Lord Clinton, cost him nearly £135 in 1518. Poynings's only child by his wife predeceased him but he left seven illegitimate children. He provided for them in his will of 27 July 1521, leaving Westenhanger to the eldest son Thomas. To his wife he left £80 a year, together with silver and household stuff and 200 sheep. He named his servant Edward Thwaytes executor and the prior of Christchurch, Sir John Norton and James Digges overseers. Poynings died on 22 Oct. 1521 and the will was proved on the following 19 Dec. His heir was Henry Percy, 4th Earl of Northumberland, but the former Stafford manors (granted to Poynings in tail male) were reoccupied after his death by Humphrey Stafford, restored to his inheritance by an Act of 1515 (5 Hen. VIII, c.13).[10]

[1] Date of birth estimated from age at fa.'s i.p.m., quoted *Paston Letters*, ed. Gairdner, ii. 329. *DNB*; *Suss. Arch. Colls.* xv. 16; *Arch. Cant.* xxxvii. 116; Mill Stephenson, *Mon. Brasses*, 212; H. H. Leonard, 'Knights and knighthood in Tudor Eng.' (London Univ. Ph.D. thesis, 1970), 220n. [2] Hall, *Chron.* 424, 465–6, 524; *CPR*, 1485–94, p. 250, 1494–1509, pp. 12, 62, 427; Rymer, *Foedera*, v(4), 69; *Cinque Ports White and Black Bks.* (Kent Arch. Soc. recs. br. xix), 119–20; *LP Hen. VIII*, i–iii; *Chron. Calais* (Cam. Soc. xxxv), 8; *Statutes*, iii. 79, 112, 168, 172. [3] *Paston Letters*, ii. 329; iii. 33; *Rot. Parl.* vi. 245, 273. [4] *CPR*, 1485–94, p. 250; *Materials for Reign of Hen. VII*, ii. (Rolls ser. lx), 344; Hall, 452–3, 465–6; Rymer, v(4), 69. [5] *CPR*, 1494–1509, pp. 12, 62; A. Conway, *Hen. VII's Relations with Scotland and Ireland, 1485–98*, pp. 61–63, 80, 87, 92, 137, 142; Elton, *Tudor Constitution*, 33. [6] *Cinque Ports White and Black Bks.* 119–20; *CPR*,

1494–1509, pp. 26, 427; *LP Hen. VIII*, i; Sandwich white bk. f. 173; *LJ*, i. 11. [7] *Rot. Parl.* vi. 522; *LP Hen. VIII*, i, iii; [8] *LP Hen. VIII*, i, ii; Hall, 524; *Chron. Calias*, 8; C. G. Cruickshanks, *Eng. Occupation of Tournai*, 1513–19, passim; *The King's Works*, iii. 326; *CSP Span.* 1509–25, p. 247; Add. Ch. 1521. [9] *LP Hen. VIII*, ii, iii. [10] *CPR*; 1494–1509, pp. 84, 105, 338; *LP Hen. VIII*, ii; Index 10217(1), f. 3v; *CP*, vii. 690; PCC 21 Maynwaryng; C142/36/14, 38/39, 39/85, 81/193, 194, 197; Mill Stephenson, 212.

H.M.

POYNTZ, John (c.1485–1544), of Alderley, Glos.

DEVIZES 1529

b. c.1485, 2nd s. of Sir Robert Poyntz of Iron Acton by Margaret, illegit. da. of Anthony Wydevill, 2nd Earl Rivers. *m.* (1) by 1528, Elizabeth, da. of Sir Matthew Browne† of Betchworth Castle, Surr., 4s. inc. Matthew† 3da.; (2) settlement 1 May 1544, Margaret, da. of Nicholas Saunders of Charlwood, Surr.[1]

Sewer to Queen Catherine of Aragon in 1520; commr. for surrender of Kingswood abbey, Glos. in 1538, musters, Glos. 1542; j.p. 1539–*d.*[2]

When Sir Robert Poyntz made his will on 19 Oct. 1520 he left to his brother Thomas a life interest in the manor of Alderley, with its appurtenances in Hillesley, Kilcott and Tresham, all of which were afterwards to pass to John Poyntz and his heirs. As these lands lay in southern Gloucestershire, to the east of Wotton-under-Edge and a few miles from the western border of Wiltshire, it might be inferred that John Poyntz of Alderley is more likely to have represented a Wiltshire borough than is his namesake and remote kinsman of North Ockendon, Essex.[3]

His return for Devizes, however, owed less to Poyntz's geographical propinquity than to his official connexions. Like its neighbour Marlborough, Devizes formed part of the jointure of queens consort and in 1529 its parliamentary patronage was clearly exercised by Catherine of Aragon's vice-chamberlain, Sir Edward Darrell* of Littlecote. Poyntz's connexion with the Queen's household, begun by his father's vice-chamberlainship to Catherine before her second marriage, had been maintained by his own appointments in her service, first as a sewer, the office which he held when he attended her at the Field of Cloth of Gold, and later as a receiver, with his son William, of some of her lands. (It is, however, more likely to have been John Poyntz of Ockendon who was to act as receiver for both Anne Boleyn and Catherine Parr.) Through his first marriage, Poyntz also acquired kinship with Sir Henry Guildford*, comptroller of the King's household: in 1528 he acted as a feoffee for Guildford and four years later witnessed his will. Another friend was Sir Thomas Wyatt I* who, probably in 1536, addressed a satire on the courtier's life to 'mine own John Poyntz'.[4]

If in 1529 Darrell had thus not far to look for one of his nominees to the Queen's two Wiltshire boroughs, Poyntz's election gave Devizes a Member familiar with clothmaking, which was the mainstay both of the town and of his own village, as he was later to inform the visiting Leland. It may thus have been as much his concern for that industry as his connexion with the unfortunate Queen which led to the inclusion of his name on a list of Members drawn up early in 1533 and believed to indicate those who, on grounds either of religion or of trade, were opposed to the bill in restraint of appeals to Rome. It is uncertain whether Poyntz, perhaps for this reason a marked man, sat again in 1536, following the King's general request for the return of the previous Members, or in 1539, when the names of borough Members are for the most part unknown.[5]

In 1533 Poyntz took a 21-year lease of the manor of Symonds Hall, near Alderley, and in 1541 he was licensed to alienate his manor of Sturden to John Smith, a Bristol merchant. He joined his nephew Sir Nicholas Poyntz* in accepting the surrender of the neighbouring abbey of Kingswood in 1538 and in granting pensions to the monks; they also arrested a suspect friar at Wotton, and John Poyntz later warned Sir William Kingston* that there was unrest in the district.[6]

Poyntz made his will on 1 June 1544 and added a codicil six days later, before leaving with the army for the invasion of France. He asked to be buried without any pomp and besought Sir Nicholas Poyntz, to whom he bequeathed a silver-gilt cup, to be good to his young children. Henry the eldest son was to be cared for by his mother, who could use the rents from the former Kingswood property to 'see him honestly kept and found during his life because he is not able, by reason of his weakness, to govern himself'. The bulk of the property was left to the second son Matthew and his heirs, with remainder to the third and fourth sons Robert (later a distinguished Catholic divine) and William; three daughters, Frideswide, Elizabeth and Alice, were to receive £40 each on their coming of age or marriage. Poyntz's widow, who later married James Skinner* of Reigate, was joined as executrix by the parson of Alderley and another resident there, but the will was placed in the care of John Anderden of the Middle Temple, who had been given an annuity of 13s.4d. and who was to assist the testator's 'cousin' Charles Bulkeley* and Thomas Saunders* in resolving any ambiguities. Poyntz seems to have perished on the ensuing expedition, or shortly after his return from it, for an inquisition found that he died on 29 Nov. 1544, leaving the 16 year-old Henry as his heir. A painting and a drawing of Poyntz by Holbein survive.[7]

[1] Date of birth estimated from those of elder and younger brother, *DNB* (Poyntz, Sir Francis). *Vis. Glos.* (Harl. Soc. xxi), 129; *Vis. Essex* (Harl. Soc. xiii), 270; PCC 19 Pynnyng; C142/70/27. [2] *LP Hen. VIII,* iii, xiii–xvii, xx. [3] PCC 28 Ayloffe. [4] *LP Hen. VIII,* iii, iv, vii, xix; *Sir Thomas Wyatt. The Complete Poems,* ed. Rebholz, 186–92. [5] Leland, *Itin.* ed. Smith, iv. 111, 116; v. 95; *LP Hen. VIII,* ix. 1077 citing SP1/99, p. 234. [6] *LP Hen. VIII,* vi, xiii, xv, xvi. [7] PCC 19 Pynnyng; *DNB* (Poyntz, Robert); C142/70/27; *Holbein* (The Queen's Gallery, Buckingham Palace 1978–9), 87.

T.F.T.B.

POYNTZ, Sir Nicholas (by 1510–56), of Iron Acton, Glos. and London.

GLOUCESTERSHIRE	1547[1]
CRICKLADE	1555

b. by 1510, 1st s. of Sir Anthony Poyntz of Iron Acton by Elizabeth, da. and coh. of Sir William Huddesfield† of Shillingford, Devon. *m.* 24 June 1527, Joan, da. of Thomas, *de jure* 5th Lord Berkeley, 5 or 6s. inc. Sir Nicholas† 3da. *suc.* fa. Sept. 1532/Feb. 1533. Kntd. Apr. 1535/Oct. 1536.[2]

Keeper, Kingswood forest, Glos., Flywood forest, Som. 1531–*d.*, New Park, Berkeley, Glos. 1531–5, Michaelwood chase, Whitcliff park, Glos. 1533; steward, bp. of Worcester's lands, Glos. 1533–40, manors of Kingswood abbey, Glos. 1537; j.p. Glos. 1537–9; commr. for surrender of Kingswood abbey 1538, musters, Glos. 1542, 1546, of Admiralty in Nov. 1547, relief 1550; groom, the bedchamber 1539; sheriff, Glos. 1539–40, 1545–6; capt. *Gret Calais* 1544; v.-adm. of the western seas 1544; bailiff, the seven hundreds of Cirencester, Glos. by 1547.[3]

Nicholas Poyntz came from a family which had been established in Gloucestershire for over 200 years. His grandfather, Sir Robert Poyntz, had been successively vice-chamberlain and chancellor to Catherine of Aragon, and his father, while making his reputation as a soldier and commander, also held office in the royal household.[4]

Nicholas Poyntz's marriage into the Berkeley family involved him in frequent litigation with his wife's kinsmen over her claim to certain property. He was also sued in the Star Chamber for assault and for poaching and in 1533, as steward to the bishop of Worcester in Gloucestershire, he was accused of holding courts and taking fines without his master's permission. In spite of his allegedly wayward character, he had influential friends. Sir Richard Rich appealed to Cromwell in 1538 to favour 'my friend Sir Nicholas Poyntz' in the purchase of former monastic lands. In the following year Richard Cromwell *alias* Williams* appealed to his uncle in the same cause, saying that Poyntz was 'in very ill case, having with great reproach in his country, sold his lands to pay' for them, and adding that he himself 'would rather lose much of his living' than that Poyntz should suffer. Poyntz was summoned before the Council in October 1541 to answer to charges preferred against him by the council in the marches and imprisoned in the Fleet;

he was not released until June 1542 after his wife had appeared before the Council to plead for him. Before he was set free, Poyntz was required to make an agreement with James Higgs over the manors of Ozleworth and Wotton Combe, Gloucestershire. Their quarrel was not, however, settled and Higgs sued him in the courts of Chancery, requests and Star Chamber during the reign of Edward VI for the illegal distraint of the same manors.[5]

Poyntz had become a soldier at an early age. In 1534 he fought in Ireland under his 'cousin', Sir John St. Loe*. In 1536 he served under Sir William Kingston* during the northern rebellion: early in 1543 he was assigned to go with (Sir) Robert Bowes* to the Netherlands, but by July he was in command of a patrol guarding the Bristol Channel and its approaches. During 1544 he was active on land and at sea; in March his ship was among those of the lord admiral's squadron which were delayed by a storm off Tynemouth; in May he took part in the Earl of Hertford's raid on Kinghorn; in June Sir John Russell*, Baron Russell, asked the Council to allow Poyntz to remain at Calais because he was a good officer; and in July he distinguished himself in an action before Hardelot castle. In the following year he was employed against pirates. His military career was to continue after his election to Parliament, for in 1549 he commanded a company against the western rebels, probably working in close association with his relative and fellow-Member, Sir Anthony Kingston.[6]

After 1532 when he went to Calais with the King, Poyntz was often present at court for important state occasions, such as the christening of Prince Edward, the arrival of Anne of Cleves, and the welcoming of the Admiral of France in 1546. In 1540 and in 1545 he purchased lands in Gloucestershire formerly belonging to Kingswood abbey for nearly £1,000, but by 1546 he was in debt and was forced to surrender part of his property to the King for arrears of rent.[7]

Local influence alone might account for the return of Poyntz as knight for Gloucestershire in 1547, when his uncle Nicholas Wykes* was sheriff, but as a distinguished soldier he probably had government support as well as the particular favour of the Seymour family with whose members he had dealings earlier in the decade. Poyntz's connexion with the Seymours was strengthened at an unknown date by the marriage of his daughter to an illegitimate brother of the Protector Somerset. Evidently Poyntz was a close adherent of Somerset for on 26 Oct. 1551, ten days after the Protector's arrest, Poyntz was sent to the Tower, where he remained until 4 Mar. 1552 when he was brought before the Council. As his servant was granted privilege on the following 9 Apr., it appears that he had returned to his seat in the House by that date. On the list of Members compiled for the fourth session, Poyntz's name was at first deleted and noted as 'extra Regnum' but this marginalia was later struck through and 'stet' entered by his name. There is no other record of Poyntz's absence from the kingdom at this time, so it is possible that the clerk was in error.[8]

Poyntz maintained his connexions with the Seymour family. On 19 July 1553 he reported the rumour of Queen Mary's acclamation in London to St. Loe who was then at Longleat. Poyntz was apparently loyal to Mary at first, since he had ignored Jane Grey's order to take arms against Mary's supporters, but it is doubtful whether he remained so. He has been identified with the Sir Nicholas Poynings mentioned as an 'assistant at the Tower' during Wyatt's rebellion. While posted there he was supposed to have offered suggestions for the defence of London to the Queen. According to the imperial ambassador, however, Wyatt, with whom Poyntz had business and family ties, admitted Poyntz's complicity in the rebellion. His cousin (Sir) Gawain Carew* was arrested for his support of Wyatt but the Council left Poyntz alone. In 1556 he was 'vehemently suspected' for the Dudley conspiracy, of which Sir Anthony Kingston was one of the leaders. In the meantime Poyntz had sat in the Parliament of 1555 as a Member for Cricklade, where the Berkeleys had influence, and had followed Kingston's lead in opposing a government bill.[9]

Poyntz was again left unmolested but died shortly afterwards on 27 or 28 Nov. 1556, leaving his wife as guardian of his four younger sons. His will, made earlier the same year on 26 Feb., provided against his eldest son, Nicholas, denying the others their inheritance. He also mentioned £200 which he owed John Seymour 'so that he assure my daughter Jane a living'. He did not bequeath any money to charity or the Church. His religion, if any, was probably Protestant as he is said to have built his house at Ozleworth with the 'stones pulled from the crosses in the parishes thereabouts'. He had witnessed the Protestant dean of Westbury's attempt to imprison Anne Berkeley's priest for playing games on Sunday and for reading popish books. Several paintings of Poyntz after a drawing by Holbein survive.[10]

[1] Hatfield 207. [2] Date of birth estimated from first office. *Cricklade*, ed. Thomson, 139; *Vis. Glos.* (Harl. Soc. xxi), 128–9; J. Smyth, *Berkeleys*, ii. 235; iii. 225; E315/239/24; PCC 37 Horne. [3] J. Maclean, *Mems. Poyntz Fam.* 71; Stowe 571, ff. 56v–7; E315/239/24; Worcs. RO, 009:1 BA 2636/178 92517 ex inf. C. Dyer; Dugdale, *Monasticon*, v. 428; *Wilts. Arch. Mag.* xxviii. 313; *LP Hen. VIII*, v, vi, viii, xii, xiv, xvii, xviii, xx, xxi; *CPR*, 1553, p. 354; SC6/Edw. VI,

187, f. 12; HCA 14/2. [4] *VCH Wilts.* viii. 37; *DNB* (Poyntz, Sir Francis); *LP Hen. VIII*, i, vii. [5] *Bristol and Glos. Arch. Soc. Trans.* xxi. 28; lxviii. 48; lxxix. 306; *LP Hen. VIII*, vi, xiii, xiv; Smyth, ii. 235, 262–5, 268–9; St.Ch.2/4/221–4, 6/270, 3/6/39; *PPC*, vii. 250–1, 263, 276, 286, 288; *APC*, i. 5, 8–9; Req.2/16/18. [6] *LP Hen. VIII*, vii, xi, xviii, xix, xxi; *APC*, i. 250; Maclean, 71; *HMC Hatfield*, ix. 205. [7] *HMC Bath*, iv. 2; *LP Hen. VIII*, ix, xii, xiv, xv, xvii, xx, xxi; *DKR*, x. 256; *Bristol and Glos. Arch. Soc. Trans.* lxxiii. 150, 189–91. [8] *Wriothesley's Chron.* ii. (Cam. Soc. n.s. xx), 58; Hatfield 207; *CJ*, i. 22; *HMC Bath*, iv. 377. [9] *Wilts. Arch. Mag.* viii. 310; Strype, *Cranmer*, 913; Maclean, 72; *Chron. Q. Jane and Q. Mary* (Cam. Soc. xlviii), 51; *LP Hen. VIII*, xix; D. M. Loades, *Two Tudor Conspiracies*, 92n, 210–11; *Wilts. N. and Q.* iv. 158; Guildford mus. Loseley 1331/2. [10] Smyth, iii. 307; *Bristol and Glos. Arch. Soc. Trans.* xi. 213–14; PCC 22 Wrastley; C142/107/51; *Holbein* (The Queen's Gallery, Buckingham Palace 1978–9), 92–93.

E.McI.

PRESTALL, Thomas (by 1503–51), of Poling and Houghton, Suss. and London.

ARUNDEL 1529

b. by 1503, s. of Ellis Prestall of Poling by Jane, da. of Richard Brocas, wid. of Thomas Purvocke. *educ.* I. Temple. *m.* c.1534, Margaret (?Ingler), 1s. 1da. *suc.* fa. 1524/27.[1]

Servant of William Fitzalan, 11th Earl of Arundel; bailiff, Arundel rape, Suss. by 1528; receiver-gen. Arundel coll. by Dec. 1529.[2]

The family of Prestall was not of old Sussex stock and may have migrated from Lancashire. Between 1536 and 1538 Thomas Prestall fought a chancery case over lands in Sussex granted in 1514 by the abbot of Tewkesbury to his uncles Edward and Nicholas, both of whom had died without issue: Edward Prestall had been described on the pardon roll of 1513 as 'of Ferring, Sussex, husbandman, *alias* late of Manchester, Lancashire, yeoman'.[3]

Thomas Prestall was assigned a chamber at the Inner Temple on 27 June 1517. Appointed master of the revels there in 1519, he was frequently proposed as marshal or butler during the 1520s and 30s, was fined £5 for refusing the butlerage in January 1535 and four years later was similarly fined over the marshalcy. The records of the inn contain nothing more about him, but he must have set store by his legal training to have instructed his wife that their son John was to be supported 'in his learning' at the inns of court or chancery.[4]

On his deathbed in 1524 Thomas, 10th Earl of Arundel, remembered his servant Ellis Prestall, and it is likely that Thomas Prestall (perhaps named after the earl) began his career with the family before that date: within a few years of it his services were certainly retained by the 11th Earl to whom he must also have owed his seat in the Parliament of 1529 with another Fitzalan client, Richard Sackville I. Nothing is known about his part in the affairs of this Parliament, but during 1530–1 he and Sackville were pitted against each other in a wrangle over lands belonging to Arundel college. He doubtless sat for Arundel again in 1536, in compliance with the King's request for the re-election of the previous

Members, and he may have done so again in 1539, 1542 and 1545, Parliaments for which the names of the borough's Members are lost.[5]

Prestall's legal knowledge was called upon to safeguard his property, particularly 600 acres at Sullington, which his father had leased from Arundel college and which various people attempted to wrest from him, but after a prolonged legal battle, intervention by the earl and bribing of the master of the college, Prestall received a new lease of it in 1541. This success proved to be short lived, for eight years later he was in court again against a local justice, John Ledes of Steyning, who had seized the land: Ledes braved an order from the Council to yield it up, used all possible means to discredit Prestall, and in a final bid to win the case replaced his first attorney by John Sulyard*. From this three-year struggle Prestall emerged the victor only months before death, and such was the hostility aroused that within two more years his widow was to be dispossessed of much of her property.[6]

Prestall usually dwelt at Poling, but it was at Houghton that he made his will on 30 Sept. 1551. Apart from his lease at Sullington left to Margaret for life, he had property in seven Sussex villages. His wife was to administer the estate, and if she remarried his children John and Joan, the wife of William Cheyne, were to receive the profits of his land under the watchful eye of his 'cousin' Thomas Ingler*. The will was proved early in the following December.[7]

[1] Date of birth estimated from education. C1/436/26, 530/27, 1313/72; PCC 35 Bucke. [2] C1/701/9, 875/70. [3] C1/875/70; 67/61, n. 7. [4] *Cal. I.T. Recs.* 40, 49, 86, 96, 101, 108–9; PCC 35 Bucke. [5] PCC 28 Bodfelde. [6] Req.2/17/65; C1/1313/72. [7] PCC 35 Bucke.

R.J.W.S.

PRESTWOOD, Thomas (by 1500–58), of Exeter, Devon.

EXETER 1547*

b. by 1500, s. of Reginald Prestwood of Worcester, Worcs.; bro. of Richard[†]. *m.* by 1532, Alice, da. of Thomas Gale of Kirton in Crediton, Devon, wid. of John Bodley of Exeter, 3s. 1da.[1]

Bailiff, Exeter 1530–1, member of the Twenty-Four 26 Aug. 1534–*d.*, receiver 1539–40, sheriff 1542–3, mayor 1544–5, 1550–1; commr. goods of churches and fraternities 1550, 1553.[2]

As a boy Thomas Prestwood so impressed his father by his 'pregnant wit and forwardness' that he was sent from Worcester, where he had been born, to be apprenticed to a rich London mercer, Thomas Hynde. After his admission to the Mercers' Company in 1521 Prestwood continued to work for Hynde and it was while doing so that he first came to Exeter and met John Bodley's wealthy widow.

With Hynde's consent he married her and settled in Exeter, where he soon had a flourishing business of his own. Admitted by fine to the freedom of the city during 1528–9 he rose to be its mayor and interested himself greatly in its welfare: the repair of the crumbling walls and the improvement of the river Exe were both begun on his initiative.[3]

During the western rebellion of 1549 Prestwood, a Protestant, both helped to defend Exeter and, with two of his relations, also merchants, put money at the disposal of Sir John Russell*, Baron Russell, the royal commander, thus enabling him to take the offensive. This timely loan, which was probably arranged by Russell's secretary, John Gale*, a kinsman of Prestwood, resulted in a close friendship between him and Russell as well as in Russell's solicitude for the interests of the city. It was shortly after this crisis that Prestwood entered the House of Commons: on the death of John Hull II, he was chosen at a by-election held on 29 Oct. 1549 and sat as a Member for Exeter during the last two sessions of the Parliament then in being. Before the end of the third session Russell wrote on 20 Jan. 1550 to the mayor that he had asked Prestwood and Griffith Ameredith, his fellow-Member, who had 'behaved themselves very thankfully in the service' of the city, not to remain at Westminster during Russell's absence in France, but to repair there on his return 'for the more sure furthering of the city's suits'. Prestwood missed the opening of the final session on 23 Jan. 1552 as he did not leave Exeter until two days later, but having arrived at the Parliament he stayed there until its dissolution, returning home on 18 Apr. following.[4]

Prestwood was rated at £4, on goods assessed at £80, for the relief which he had helped to grant in the session of 1549–50, but gradually in his later years he forsook business for property. He was one of the consortium of Exeter merchants who bought much of the former monastic property in Exeter on behalf of the corporation, to whom it was later sold, and at the time of his death he owned the manors of Butterford, Tynacre and Venny Tedburn, besides a tin-blowing mill, a fulling mill and eight large houses in Exeter. He made his will on 16 Sept. 1558 and died the next day. He asked to be buried in the churchyard of St. Petrock's without pomp or pride and for a sermon to be preached at his funeral by 'some virtuous, discreet and learned man' to the 'edification of the congregation and testimony of my undoubted and assured faith in the infallible promises of God in his scripture'. After his debts had been discharged and several charitable bequests and small legacies to relatives performed, his property was to be shared between his widow

and his only surviving son. The overseers were William Strode and Richard Prestwood, a brother who had followed in his footsteps to Exeter and who had married his stepdaughter.[5]

[1] Date of birth estimated from admission to the Mercers' Co. *Vis. Devon*, ed. Vivian, 615; *Vis. Devon*, ed. Colby, 174.   [2] Exeter act bk. 2, ff. 34, 44; Exeter receiver's accts. 1530–1; R. Izacke, *Exeter* (1681), 122; *Trans. Dev. Assoc.* lxi. 206; *CPR*, 1550–3, p. 396; 1553, p. 416.   [3] *The description of the citie of Excester* (Devon and Cornw. Rec. Soc. xi), 658; *Eliz. Govt. and Soc.* ed. Bindoff, Hurstfield and Williams, 166–7; *Exeter Freemen* (Devon and Cornw. Rec. Soc. extra ser. i), 71; E122/201/1; W. T. MacCaffrey, *Exeter 1540–1640*, pp. 225–6; List of Mercers (T/S Mercers' Hall), 378.   [4] Hoker, 82–83; F. R. Troup, *Western Rebellion of 1549*, pp. 182, 239–40; HMC Exeter, 22; Exeter act bk. 2, f. 118.   [5] E179/99/319; HMC Exeter, 291; *Eliz. Govt. and Soc.* 175–6; Hoker, 410–25; PCC 50 Noodes; C142/120/46.

A.D.K.H.

PRICE, Ellis (by 1514–94), of Plas Iolyn and Ysbyty Ifan, Denb.

MERIONETH 1558, 1563

b. by 1514, 2nd s. of Robert ap Rhys of Plas Iolyn by Margaret, da. of Rhys Lloyd of Gydros, Merion. *educ.* St. Nicholas Hostel, Camb., BCL 1533, DCL 1534. *m.* (1) Catherine, da. of Thomas Conway of Bodrhyddan, Flints., 1s.; (2) Ellyw, da. of Owain Pool, rector of Llandecwyn, Merion., 2s. 4da.; at least 2s. illegit.[1]

Visitor to monasteries, Wales 1535; chancellor, dioceses of St. Asaph c.1537–8, Bangor 1560; commissary gen. St. Asaph in 1538; j.p.q. Merion. 1543, 1555–d., Denb. 1555–d., Caern. 1561–d., Anglesey, Mont. 1564, most Welsh counties by 1575, all Welsh counties and Mon. by 1579; sheriff, Denb. 1548–9, 1556–7, 1568–9, 1572–3, Merion. 1551–2, 1555–6, 1563–4, 1567–8, 1573–4, 1578–9, 1583–4, Caern. 1558–9, Anglesey 1577–8, 1585–6; commr. for visitation of St. David's diocese 1549, relief, Merion. 1550, eisteddfod, Caerwys, Flints. 1568, musters, Denb., Merion. 1570, 1580; custos rot. Merion. 1558/59–77 or later; member, council in the marches of Wales 1560–d.; steward, Earl of Leicester's Denbigh lordship from c.1564; master in Chancery extraordinary.[2]

Ellis Price's grandfather Rhys ap Meredydd fought under Henry Tudor at Bosworth and his father Robert ap Rhys prospered as chaplain and crossbearer to Wolsey. After a successful academic career which gave him the name by which he became known throughout Wales, Y Doctor Coch (the Red Doctor), Price may have profited from this connexion with the cardinal to enter the service of Thomas Cromwell who in 1535 placed him on the commission to visit religious houses in Wales. His colleagues Adam Bekinsau and John Vaughan complained that his immorality and arrogance unfitted him for such employment and despite the intervention of Bishop Lee, president of the council in the marches, he was dismissed. He was not long in disgrace, becoming chancellor and commissary general of the diocese of St. Asaph. About 1537 or 1538 he was sued in Chancery by the vicar of

Llanarmon, Denbighshire, who complained that John Lloyd of Llanarmon, aided and abetted by his kinsman Price had misappropriated tithes. Lloyd and Price were again confederates in an assault upon the Welsh scholar William Salusbury of Llanrwst, Denbighshire, who was Price's brother-in-law.[3]

As commissary general of St. Asaph, Price was engaged during 1538 in the destruction of images and the eradication of superstitious practices; he seems to have relished the work, reporting to Cromwell on 6 Apr. that

> I have done my diligence and duty for the expulsing and taking away of certain abusions, superstitions and hypocrisies used within the said diocese . . . [but] there is an image of 'Darfel Gardarn' within the said diocese, in whom the people have so great confidence, hope and trust that they come daily a pilgrimage unto him.

By the end of the month Price had seen to the dismantling of the image and sent it to London despite the offer of a £40 bribe to leave it alone. It was used at Smithfield to fulfil the prophecy that it would one day set a forest on fire—the Franciscan martyr John Forest.[4]

By 1549, when Cranmer commissioned him to visit the vacant diocese of St. David's, Price had also become involved in secular administration as a justice of the peace and sheriff, the first of his 14 shrievalties in four counties. Said to have at first favoured Jane Grey in 1553, Price made such a prompt change of allegiance, himself proclaiming Mary, that he remained a trusted servant of the crown. No evidence has been found to support the statement that he was returned for Merioneth to the Parliament of 1555, but he certainly sat in Mary's last Parliament. On 25 Feb. 1558 he was licensed by the Speaker 'to be absent for the Queen's affairs for musters'.[5]

Price's nephew John Wyn ap Cadwaladr sat for Merioneth in the first Parliament of the new reign and Price himself was returned to that of 1563, being again granted leave of absence on 15 Mar. 1563. By this time he had become a member of the council in the marches and he was soon the leading agent for the Earl of Leicester in Denbighshire and Merioneth. He died on 8 Oct. 1594.[6]

[1] Date of birth estimated from first reference. Dwnn, *Vis. Wales*, ii. 344; Griffith, *Peds.* 204; C1/878/22–23; *DNB*; *DWB*. [2] *LP Hen. VIII*, ix; C1/789/30; 193/12/1; *HMC De L'Isle and Dudley*, i. 323; *Cal. Wynn (of Gwydir)*, *Pprs. 1515–1690*, p. 339; *CSP Dom. 1547–80*, p. 586; 1581–90, pp. 586, 657; *CPR*, 1553, p. 363; 1563–6, pp. 30–31; Strype, *Cranmer*, i. 274; *HMC Welsh*, i(1), 291; R. Flenley, *Cal. Reg. Council, Marches of Wales*, 60, 109, 125, 127, 132, 135, 146, 179, 200, 212; E. G. Jones, *Cymru a'r Hen Ffydd*, 13–14; NLW 9080 E, f. 17; SP11/5/6; 12/93/6. [3] SP1/08/6, 99/63; *LP Hen. VIII*, ix; C1/789/30, 878/22–23; St.Ch.2/29/178. [4] Cott. Cleop. E4(37), f. 72; *LP Hen. VIII*, xiii; *Arch. Camb.* (ser. 4), v. 152–6. [5] *HMC Welsh*, ii(1), 89; E. Breese, *Kalendars of Gwynedd*, 116; *CJ*, i. 50. [6] *CJ*, i. 69; P. H.

Williams, *Council in the Marches of Wales*, 239; *Arch. Camb.* (ser. 6), xv. 120.

P.S.E.

PRICE, Gregory (1535–1600), of Hereford.

HEREFORDSHIRE   1558
HEREFORD   1572, 1584, 1586, 1589, 1593, 1597

b. 6 Aug. 1535, 1st s. of Sir John Price* of Brecon, Brec. and Hereford by Joan, da. of John Williams *alias* Cromwell of Southwark, Surr.; bro. of Richard[†]. *m.* (1) by Nov. 1559, Mary, da. of Humphrey Coningsby* of Hampton Court, Herefs., 1s.; (2) by 1598, Grissel, da. of Walter Roberts of Glassenbury, Kent, wid. of Gervase Gebons, 1da.; 2s. 1da. illegit. *suc.* fa. 15 Oct. 1555.[1]

J.p. Herefs. 1564, q. by 1573/74–d., Brec. 1591–d.; sheriff, Herefs. 1566–7, 1575–6, 1595–6, Brec. Feb.–Dec. 1587, 1594–5, commr. musters, Herefs. 1570, tanneries, Hereford 1574, subsidy, Herefs. 1580, 1591–2; mayor, Hereford 1573–4, 1576–7, 1597–8; dep. lt. Brec. 1587.[2]

According to the commonplace book kept by his father, Gregory Price was born on 6 Aug. 1535, some ten months after John Price's marriage to Cromwell's niece; he was named after Gregory Cromwell*. Price had not come of age when he inherited his father's lands in Herefordshire; the smaller Breconshire properties, including Brecon priory, passed by will to his brother Richard, with whom he shared most of their father's books. Price was licensed to enter into his patrimony in November 1557. Two months earlier he and Thomas Kerry* had paid £950 for the manor and priory of Monmouth, four other manors in Herefordshire, Monmouthshire and Suffolk, and a brewhouse in Hereford, all former church property.[3]

Price's election as senior knight for Herefordshire to the last Marian Parliament was a rare distinction for a youngster of 22 whose inexperience was not offset by impressive lineage: it is all the more striking in that he never achieved it again. He presumably owed his election in 1558 to two previous knights of the shire: Thomas Havard, whom Price's father had named an executor of his will, was a relative of the sheriff, and Humphrey Coningsby was perhaps already Price's father-in-law. Nothing has come to light about Price's part in the House on this occasion. Although he lacked his father's ability he was to be prominent in marcher affairs until his death on 19 Mar. 1600. His widow married Sir John Poyntz[†].[4]

[1] Date of birth recorded by father, *Brycheiniog*, viii. 102. *DWB*; *Vis. Herefs.* ed. Weaver, 58; *CPR*, 1560–3, p. 133; J. Maclean, *Fam. Poyntz*, 88; PCC 39 More, 45 Chaynay, 28 Wallop; C142/261/24. [2] *CPR*, 1563–6, p. 23; R. Johnson, *Anct. Customs, Hereford*, 233–4; Duncumb, *Herefs.* i. 367; J. Price, *Hereford*, 258; R. Flenley, *Cal. Reg. Council, Marches of Wales*, 60; *HMC Foljambe*, 26; *APC*, xx. 23. [3] *Brycheiniog*, viii. 102; PCC 39 More; *NLW Jnl.* ix. 255–61; *CPR*, 1555–7, p. 242; 1557–8, p. 269. [4] PCC 39 More, 28 Wallop; C142/261/24.

P.S.E.

PRICE, John I (by 1523–50 or later), of Whitton, Rad.

RADNORSHIRE 1542*

b. by 1523.[1]
    Escheator, Rad. Jan.–Dec. 1545; commr. relief 1550.[2]

John Price claimed gentle birth, but his parentage has not been established. His domicile not far from the borders of Radnorshire with Herefordshire and Shropshire suggests that he was a member of the family settled in the locality which was to share the representation of the county with their kinsfolk the Lewises of Harpton by the end of Mary's reign. He may have had some grounding in the law as he was styled esquire on being returned to the Parliament of 1542. The death of John Baker IV after the opening of the final session led to the by-election on 19 Feb. 1544 at which Price was elected. Presumably he had the support of James Price of Monaughty near Bleddfa, whose name appears second among the electors on this occasion, but his return seems to have been the work of the sheriff Richard Blike* acting on behalf of the council in the marches or of Blike's kinsmen the Bakers. Although Price was not to be re-elected the experience of sitting in the House may have qualified him for a part in local administration, as in 1545 he was named escheator and five years later a commissioner to collect the relief. In 1549 he leased some property at Knucklas and elsewhere in Radnorshire from the crown, and in December 1550 he bought from Sir John Williams (whose acquaintance he had perhaps made while a Member) the grange of Monaughty Poeth near Knucklas, where one of his tenants was his presumed kinsman James Price of Monaughty. No trace of him after 1550 has been found.[3]

[1] Presumed to be of age at election. [2] *CPR*, 1553, p. 364. [3] C219/18B/141; *Augmentations* (Univ. Wales Bd. of Celtic Studies, Hist. and Law ser. xiii), 213; *CPR*, 1549–51, p. 244.

P.S.E.

PRICE (AP RICHARD AP DAFYDD LLOYD RHYS), John II (by 1532–84), of the Inner Temple, London and Gogerddan, nr. Aberystwyth, Card.

CARDIGANSHIRE 1553 (Oct.), 1554 (Apr.), 1563, 1571, 1572

b. by 1532, 1st s. of Richard ap Rhys ap Dafydd Lloyd of Gogerddan, by Elliw, da. and coh. of William ap Jenkin ap Iorwerth. *educ.* I. Temple, adm. Feb. 1550. *m.* (1) Elizabeth, da. of Thomas Perrot of Islington, Mdx. and Haroldston, Pemb., 2s. Richard† and Thomas† 1da.; (2) Bridget, da. of James Price of Monaughty, Rad., 1s. *suc.* fa. Sept. 1553 or later.[1]
    Bencher, I. Temple 1568–71.
    J.p. Card. 1555, q. 1558/59–*d.*, Merion. 1573/74–9, many Welsh and marcher counties 1579; custos rot.

Card. 1558/59–79; commr. piracy, Card. 1565, armour 1569, musters 1570, victuals 1574, tanneries, Aberystwyth 1574; sheriff, Merion. 1579–80, Card. 1580–1; member, council in the marches of Wales by 1579–81.[2]

When he was first elected to Parliament John Price was entered on the return under his patronymic John ap Richard ap Rhys Dafydd Lloyd, but he was usually called Price. Born into a family which claimed descent from Gwaethfoed, lord of Ceredigion, and which had been established for the last two generations at Gogerddan, Price was trained to the law. It was his consequent absence from the shire which was to be the subject of a prosecution following his first election. On 15 Nov. 1553, while Parliament was in session, the attorney-general brought an action in the Exchequer against the sheriff, Owen Gwyn (q.v.), for returning Price although at the time he was not resident in the shire. It was presumably a defeated opponent who had laid the information, but who this was is unknown. Gwyn met it by declaring that Price had been born and had always lived in the shire, at his father's house at Gogerddan, and that although on 20 July his father had sent him to London on business (*circa negotia*) he had returned by 6 Sept., three weeks before the election. The proceedings continued into the Easter term of 1554 and the record ends with Gwyn asking for the case to be dismissed. By then Price had been re-elected, Gwyn's successor as sheriff, (Sir) Henry Jones I*, perhaps already being Price's brother-in-law. Presumably it was Price as knight for Cardiganshire who introduced the measure for the county court to alternate between Aberystwyth and Cardigan enacted not long after the start of the prosecution (1 Mary st.2, no.23).[3]

It was probably not Price, but his namesake the Member for Hereford, who on 27 Oct. 1553 was appointed with two civilians to examine the validity of a return, but as a common lawyer he could well have been entrusted in the course of the next Parliament with a bill to prohibit the use of dags, or handguns. The only other indication of his part in the proceedings of either Parliament is the absence of his name from those who in the first of them voted against the initial measures towards the restoration of Catholicism. This suggests that he did not share the Protestantism of (Sir) John Perrot*, whose stepsister he married, although he was afterwards to come to terms with the Elizabethan regime, which he served in a variety of capacities.[4]

Price died on 15 May 1584. His descendants retained Gogerddan until the present century.[5]

[1] Presumed to be of age at election. Dwnn, *Vis. Wales*, i. 44-45.
[2] *CPR*, 1560-3, p. 446; *Welsh Port Bks.* (Cymmrod. rec. ser. xii), 310; R. Flenley, *Cal. Reg. Council, Marches of Wales*, 60, 69, 109, 126, 132; P. H. Williams, *Council in the Marches of Wales*, 354-5.   [3] *DWB*; *Cal. Wynn (of Gwydir) Pprs. 1515-1690*, p. 3; E159/333, Mich. 83.
[4] *CJ*, i. 29, 35.   [5] C142/208/242.

P.S.E.

PRICE, Sir John (1501/2-55) of Brecon and Hereford.

BRECONSHIRE	1547[1]
HEREFORD	1553 (Oct.)
LUDLOW	1554 (Apr.)
LUDGERSHALL	1554 (Nov.)[2]

b. 1501/2, 1st s. of Rhys ap Gwilym ap Llywelyn of Brecon by Gwenllian, da. of Hywel Madoc. *educ.* Oxf.; Camb. BCL 1535/36. *m.* 11 Oct. 1534, Joan, da. of John Williams *alias* Cromwell of Southwark, Surr., 6s. inc. Gregory* and Richard† 5da.; 1 da. illegit. Kntd. 22 Feb. 1547. *suc.* fa. unknown.[3]

Servant of Cromwell by 1530; registrar, bpric. of Salisbury Dec. 1534; jt. registrar-gen. in ecclesiastical matters by 1534; public notary by 1536; sec. council in the marches of Wales 27 Sept. 1540-*d.*; sheriff, Brec. 1542-3, Herefs. 1553-4; j.p. Herefs., Mon., Salop, Welsh counties 1543, Cheshire, Glos., Worcs. 1545-7; commr. subsidy, Brec. 1543, chantries, Wales 1545, relief, Brec. 1550, goods of churches and fraternities Herefs., Hereford 1553; bailiff, Brecon 1544-5.[4]

John Price was descended from Dafydd Gam, a renowned hero of Agincourt. After studying civil law at Oxford he had by 1530 come within the orbit of Thomas Cromwell. In May 1534 he was one of the agents who secretly searched Tunstall's palace in Durham because of the bishop's attitude towards the royal divorce and the ecclesiastical changes which accompanied it. In the following year he was present at the coronation of Anne Boleyn as one of the servitors at the dresser. The King rewarded him with the registrarship of the bishopric of Salisbury which he obtained despite a prior claim on it by Richard Watkins*. In the dispute as to who was entitled to the registrarship Cromwell supported Watkins, but the minister's line does not suggest animosity towards Price. Cromwell followed his advice on how to proceed in argument against the bishops, and made him one of the family; on 11 Oct. 1534 Price married Cromwell's niece at the minister's home in Islington, he being at that time 32 and his bride 18. Their firstborn son was to be named Gregory after Cromwell's eldest boy.[5]

Among the activities for which Price is chiefly remembered is his part in the visitation of the monasteries launched by Cromwell early in 1535. Little good has ever been said of the visitors, but Price for one should not be judged too harshly. A sincere Reformer, he had no patience with the superstitions enshrined in decadent religious houses, but his sense of history gave him some respect for the monastic ideal. He also deplored the behaviour of Thomas Lee I (q.v.), whom he usually accompanied on visitation. Price's instinct to be fair and humane was perhaps out of place in an operation designed not to assess the spiritual worth of the monasteries but to find reasons for their destruction. He was next to find employment as a public notary during the examinations and interrogations of the rebels of 1536, both in London and in their homelands. During 1539 he was a commissioner for the surrender of the monasteries in a number of counties, mainly in the west of England, and in 1540 he was prothonotary during the process of nullification of the marriage of Henry VIII and Anne of Cleves.[6]

Price furnished Cromwell with a great deal of information about Wales, although there is no evidence for the suggestion that he was the author of the petition to the crown for the Union. He was a tireless worker. In a letter written in his own hand to Cromwell in 1538 he listed the 'examinations, writing of professions, instruments touching his grace's marriage, minutes of leagues, riding on his grace's affairs and such other simple services as I have done his highness'; he had been diverted into this multiplicity of tasks by 'the decay of his office [of registrar] which chiefly consisted in election of abbots and priors now abolished', and to make up for this he petitioned for the purchase of the former priory at Hereford or for the ratification of his lease of the priory. If his activities were not lucrative in themselves, they put him in a good position with respect to the new crown property. In May 1538 he leased the rectory of the parish church of Brecon, in 1540 the grange of Dereham in Norfolk and in 1542 the sites of Brecon and Hereford priories and lands elsewhere.[7]

Price's peripatetic activities came to an end with the fall of Cromwell. In September 1540 he was appointed to the council at Ludlow as its secretary. He was straightway involved in a dispute with Charles Foxe*, who with his brother Edmund Foxe* held the post of clerk of the signet and clerk of the council, over their respective functions. Price complained to the Privy Council, and after both men had been summoned to appear at Westminster an order was made on 13 Sept. that all matters of variance between them 'should now be ended'. This resolution proved too sanguine, for 18 months later Price and Foxe were again at Westminster, this time with Edmund Foxe as well. It was then decided that Price should be given the signet but that the clerkship and secretaryship of the council should be further considered and the fees meanwhile held by the president: how the matter was finally resolved does not appear. His duties on the council and elsewhere earned Price exemption from military service in France in 1544 but brought him a knighthood at Edward VI's coronation.[8]

The new reign also saw the beginning of Price's parliamentary career: his election for Breconshire in 1547 answered to his standing in a shire of which he had been sheriff five years earlier. Although as an enthusiast for the Edwardian Reformation, which he was to propagate in Wales, he might have been expected to sit again in March 1553, he is not known to have done so (the names of nearly all the Members for the Welsh and border constituencies are known, except those for Hereford, Herefordshire, Leominster, New Radnor Boroughs and Radnorshire, for any of which he might have been returned), but he was to appear in the first three Marian Parliaments. In October 1553 he sat for Hereford, near which he had his main residence. His election was shortly followed by his appointment as sheriff, a mark of the Queen's confidence which he perhaps reciprocated by not opposing the first measures passed in this Parliament for the restoration of Catholicism. It was also at this time that he wrote his treatise on the restoration of the coinage, which he dedicated to the Queen.[9]

When at the next election his shrievalty compelled Price to look elsewhere for a seat, he used his position and connexions at Ludlow to provide him with one, although perhaps not without competition, for the indenture bears an alteration suggestive of a contest. Six months later he scraped into what was to prove his last Parliament only by filling a casual vacancy much further afield. This arose when Anthony Browne II, who had been returned at both Maldon and Ludgershall, chose to sit for Maldon: at a by-election on 19 Nov. 1554, seven days after the Parliament had begun, Price replaced him at Ludgershall. All that is clear about this curious episode is that Price must have owed his nomination to (Sir) Richard Brydges*, the patron of Ludgershall. Whether he had tried and failed to secure election in Wales, and why he turned to Brydges, are alike unknown: the two were almost certainly divided in religion, and there seems to be nothing to connect them save the incidental fact that Price's county of Herefordshire was among those of which Brydges was joint receiver for the duchy of Lancaster. Not the least interesting aspect of the affair is Price's evident eagerness to find a seat. The Parliament was to see the Marian Restoration reach its climax with the repeal of the Act of Supremacy; although this was a betrayal of all that Price stood for, he was not one of those found to be absent without leave at the calling of the House early in January 1555. He was

presumably the 'Mr. Price' appointed on 27 Oct. 1553 with two other civilians, David Lewis and Sir John Tregonwell, to examine the validity of John Foster II's return, but it is less certain whether he or John Price II was the recipient in the following April of the unsuccessful bill prohibiting the use of handguns.[10]

Throughout his life Price was an active scholar. A student of history, he wrote the *Historiae Britannicae Defensio* to defend the Arthurian legend against the attacks made on it by Polydore Vergil. In his will he urged his son Richard to print those works 'that I have made against Polydore's *Story of England*, and to annex to the same some piece of antiquity that is not yet printed out of the written books of histories that I have in my house, as William Malmesbury's *De Regibus Anglorum* or Henry of Huntingdon'. Loyal to his father's wish, Richard Price saw to the publication of the *Defensio*, which appeared in 1573. Price's other works were the *Description of Cambria*, published as part of the *Historie of Cambria* by David Powell (1584), and *Fides Historiae Britannicae*, another attack on Polydore Vergil. He was also versed in theology, bequeathing his 'written books of divinity' to Hereford cathedral and St. Augustine's works to the vicar of Bromyard, Herefordshire. His interest in spreading the reformed faith in Wales led him to undertake the publication in 1547 of the first printed book in Welsh, *Yny Lhyvyr hwnn*, which contained translations of the Creed, the Ten Commandments and the Lord's Prayer; in the preface he advocated worship in the vernacular. He was also a noted collector of Welsh manuscripts, which he left to one Thomas Vaughan of Glamorgan.[11]

Price made his will on 6 Oct. 1555. In it he recorded that he had delivered 1,000 marks to the keeping and custody of Thomas Havard*, 'whereof £500 is in gold and fine silver and locked in a coffer or chests under three locks, the three keys whereof I will that three of my executors hereafter named do have the keeping'. His numerous bequests included money for the marriages of his daughters. As executors he named Thomas Havard, (Sir) William Petre* and Sir Robert Townshend. Price died nine days later, possessed of lands worth about £135 a year.[12]

[1] Hatfield 207. [2] Huntington Lib. Hastings mss Parl. pprs. supplies the surname missing from the damaged by-election indenture, C219/23/157. [3] Aged 32 on marriage. Jones, *Brec.* ii. 139; *Vis. Herefs.* ed. Weaver, 33–34, 58; Emden, *Biog. Reg. Univ. Oxf. 1501–40*, pp. 463–4; *Brycheiniog*, viii. 101–2; PCC 39 More; *NLW Jnl.* ix. 255–61; *DNB; DWB.* [4] *LP Hen. VIII*, iv, vii, ix, xi, xii, xiv, xvi, xx, xxi; E179/219/29; C193/12/1; 219/18C/165; *CPR*, 1547–8, pp. 82–84, 86, 88, 91; 1550–3, pp. 394, 397; 1553, pp. 364, 376, 414, 416; Strype, *Eccles. Memorials*, ii(2), 163; St.Ch.4/3/33. [5] Emden, 463–4; Jones, ii. 139; *LP Hen. VIII*, iv–vii; M. L. Robertson, 'Cromwell's servants' (Univ. California Los Angeles, Ph.D. thesis, 1975), 549–50; J. J. Scarisbrick, *Hen. VIII*, 331; Merriman, *Letters, Thomas Cromwell*, i.

115–16, 143n; *Brycheiniog*, viii. 101–2; D. Knowles, *Rel. Orders in Eng.* iii. 272–3. [6] SP1/98, ff. 19–20; *LP Hen. VIII*, xi, xii, xv; Knowles, 280–8, 288–9, 300, 342. [7] *Brycheiniog*, viii. 101–2; SP1/157, ff. 156–8; *Augmentations* (Univ. Wales Bd. of Celtic Studies, Hist. and Law ser. xiii), 200; *LP Hen. VIII*, xvi, xvii. [8] *LP Hen. VIII*, xvi, xix; *PPC*, vii. 31, 35, 322. [9] C. E. Challis, *The Tudor Coinage*, 116. [10] Hereford cathedral mun. chapter act bk. 1512–66, f. 92v; *CJ*, i. 29, 35. [11] N. R. Ker, 'Sir John Prise', *The Library* (ser. 5), x. 1–24; PCC 39 More; W. Spurrell, *Carmarthen*, 27; *Brycheiniog*, viii. 97–98. [12] PCC 39 More; *NLW Jnl.* ix. 255–61; C142/105/83, 134/70.

P.S.E.

PRICE, Leisian (by 1527–88), of Neath and Briton Ferry, Glam. and London.

CARDIFF BOROUGHS 1558

b. by 1527, 1st s. of Rhys ab Ifan of Ynys-y-Maerdy and Cwrt-y-Carnau, Glam. by Elizabeth, da. of David Mansell of Gower, Glam. *educ.* I. Temple, adm. Feb. 1549. *m.* Maud. da. of David Evans* of The Great House, Neath, 6s. 3da.[1]

Escheator, Glam. 1560–1; j.p. 1561–*d.*; commr. subsidy 1574; recorder, Carmarthen, Carm. by 1581–3 or later.[2]

Leisian Price had begun to practise law before his admission to the Inner Temple, for in the previous autumn he had appeared as an attorney at the great sessions at Cardigan. He continued to do so at both Cardigan and Pembroke while a student at the Temple and about 1550 he leased a house at Baglan near Neath. He twice gave offence at the Temple, being fined in 1555 for defying the ban on beards and a year later being expelled for a time following a misdemeanour during the Autumn reading; both incidents were closed by his humble submission and he lived them down. In 1562 he served as steward at the Lent reader's dinner, but when six years later he was called to the bench his repeated refusal led to his discharge in 1571 at the cost of a £10 fine.[3]

Price's return to Mary's last Parliament was a step in his local progress. He held property in Cardiff from the crown but he probably owed his election to his neighbour David Evans, one of whose daughters he was to marry. The Journal throws no light on his part in the Commons, but as a justice of the peace under Elizabeth he was to sue for assault and wounding in the head while making an arrest at Bridgend in 1563 and was himself later to be charged by the customer of Cardiff with corruption and abuse of authority. In 1586 he laid an information in the Exchequer against the heirs of (Sir) Edward Mansell* for challenging his lease of coal mines on the manor of Millwood. He died on 1 Jan. 1588 possessed of lands in Glamorganshire worth £7 a year, in which he was succeeded by his son William, a minor.[4]

[1] Date of birth estimated from first reference. G. T. Clark, *Limbus Patrum Morganiae*, 84. [2] *CPR*, 1563–6, p. 29; R. Flenley, *Cal. Reg. Council, Marches of Wales*, 142, 213; E179/221/26; C. Spurrell, *Carmarthen*, 179. [3] NLW ms 18/8–10; 27/7; *Augmentations* (Univ.

Wales Bd. of Celtic Studies Hist. and Law ser. xiii), 413; E159/334, Mich. recognizances 7; *Cal. I.T. Recs.* i. 179, 188, 220, 224, 249–50, 259. [4] St.Ch.5/P66/34; *Exchequer* (Univ. Wales Bd. of Celtic Studies Hist. and Law ser. iv), 299; Flenley, 231; C142/216/81.

P.S.E.

PRICE, Stephen (by 1522–62), of Pilleth, Rad.

RADNORSHIRE 1555

b. by 1522, 2nd s. of Ieuan ap James ap Rhys of Monaughty by Margaret, da. of Sir Edward Croft of Croft Castle, Herefs. *m.* Sybil, da. and h. of Gruffydd ap Meredydd Fychan, 3s. 4da.[1]

J.p. Rad. temp. Edw. VI–1560, q. 1561; sheriff 1555–6; commr. subsidy 1558; escheator 1561–*d.*[2]

A younger son in one of the leading Radnorshire families, Stephen Price had settled at Pilleth by 1543, being assessed at £8 in goods there for the subsidy of that year. In 1555 he was perhaps the second member of his family to be elected knight of the shire, a John Price having been by-elected to the Parliament of 1542. While a Member, Price was pricked sheriff, but he is not known to have obtained leave of absence to execute the office. He had been returned as 'armiger' but in 1559 he sued out a pardon as of Pilleth, 'gentleman' *alias* of Nant-y-Groes, 'yeoman'. He died midway through his term as escheator of Radnorshire, a new appointment being made on 19 June 1562. The Stephen ap Rhys of Old Radnor who made his will on 6 July 1562 must therefore have been a namesake.[3]

[1] Date of birth estimated from first reference. Dwnn, *Vis. Wales*, i. 252. [2] NLW ms Wales 26/6,7; SP11/5/6; E179/224/567. [3] *Trans. Rad. Hist. Soc.* xxi. 42; xxix. 46; xxxvii. 42–43; E179/224/536, 568; NLW ms Wales 26/4, m. 12v; *CPR*, 1553, p. 338; 1558–60, p. 219.

P.S.E.

PRICE (AP RHYS AP HYWEL), William (c.1520–74 or later), of Beaumaris, Anglesey.

BEAUMARIS 1558, 1559, 1563

b. c.1520, 1st s. of Rhys ap Hywel ap Rhys of Bodowyr in Llanidan by Alice, da. of Dafydd ap Ieuan ap Matto. *suc.* fa. 1540.[1]

Capital burgess, Beaumaris 1562.[2]

In the will of Rhys ap Hywel, written in Welsh and Latin and proved in 1540, William Price is mentioned as the eldest son. Although of an old Welsh family from the south of Anglesey and kin to several unsympathetic to the Bulkeleys, he was to identify himself with the Bulkeley interest. His father named one William Bulkeley (probably the Member of that name, living at Llangefni) as protector of his wife and executrix, and a generation later Price was the lessee of ten acres from Richard Bulkeley. On the first two occasions that he was returned for Beaumaris the knight for the island was his cousin Rowland ap Meredydd and on the third Richard Bulkeley. After 1559 Price rarely used the

Welsh form of his name, but it was by his patronymic that he was entered on the tenancy list in 1574. This is the last reference found to him.[3]

[1] Date of birth estimated from fa.'s will, PCC 17 Crumwell. Griffith, *Peds.* 51, 83. [2] *CPR.* 1560–3, p. 347. [3] C. E. M. Evans, 'Medieval Beaumaris and the commote of Dindaethwy' (Univ. Wales M.A. thesis, 1949), iii. 96.

P.S.E.

PRICE *see also* AP RHYS

PRIDEAUX, John (by 1520–58), of Upton Pyne, Devon and the Inner Temple, London.

PLYMOUTH   1547[1]
DEVON   1554 (Apr.)

b. by 1520, 1st s. of Thomas Prideaux of Ashburton, Devon by Joan. *educ.* I. Temple, adm. 15 Nov. 1537. *m.* by 1549, Mary, da. of Sir Hugh Stukeley of Trent, Som., 3s. 3da. *suc.* fa. 22 Jan. 1548.[2]

    Bencher, I. Temple 1550, Summer reader 1551, Lent 1552, Autumn 1555.

    Commr. chantries, Devon 1546, 1548, relief 1550; counsel to Exeter 20 Oct. 1548; j.p.q. Devon 1554; serjeant-at-law 1555; King and Queen's serjeant-at-law 23 Jan. 1558.[3]

John Prideaux the serjeant had a number of contemporary namesakes but it was certainly he who was knight of the shire for Devon in 1554. Whether he also sat for Plymouth in the Parliament of 1547 is less clear: it is possible that he was the John Prideaux assessed towards a subsidy at Plymouth during 1543–4 on goods worth 20s., but although the serjeant was related to the influential Edgecombes he is not known to have had a more personal link with the town. The Roger Prideaux who sat in this Parliament for Totnes was doubtless related to him: it is not clear which of them was the 'Mr. Prideaux' to whom a bill for decayed houses was committed after its first reading on 30 Jan. 1550, but John Prideaux was presumably the 'Mr. Pridioke skilled in the law' consulted at the Temple by the advisers of the 16th Earl of Oxford over the measure which became the Act for frustrating assurances to the Duke of Somerset made by the earl (5 and 6 Edw. VI, no. 35).[4]

With Exeter, Prideaux did have a close connexion: in 1548 as 'John Prideaux of Bramford Pyne' he was granted an annual fee of 20s. for his counsel. He progressed steadily at his inn and became involved in local administration in Devon. He was caught up in an affair of greater moment when in January 1554 he and Sir Thomas Denys*, the sheriff, got wind of the plot to raise Exeter against the Spanish marriage: the declaration which he made on 24 Jan. is the chief source of information on the episode. It can hardly be a coincidence that two months later he was elected, for the only time in his career, one of the

knights of the shire for Devon: his friend Denys was doubtless of help to him as sheriff, but the court may well have intervened on behalf of so trusty a watchdog. Twelve months later he was made a serjeant, and with his promotion to King and Queen's serjeant in January 1558 he was clearly heading for the bench before his death on the following 29 Sept. A knell was rung for him at Ashburton, whose churchwardens he had advised in legal matters for many years.[5]

Prideaux had added considerably to his patrimony. The chantry lands in Herefordshire worth £55 a year which he and Roger Hereford had bought in 1549 he divided with Hereford, and a year before his death he and his wife paid nearly £1,200 for the reversion of a number of Devon manors held by the Duchess of Suffolk for life. Not only did he buy property himself but he also advised others about their land transactions. Prideaux left no will and administration was first granted to Thomas Stukeley, his brother-in-law, who was also granted the wardship of his son and heir Thomas. Thomas Prideaux had licence to enter on the lands on 17 May 1571 and 12 months later shared administration of the goods with a sister.[6]

[1] C219/282/2; Hatfield 207. [2] Date of birth estimated from age at fa.'s i.p.m., C142/84/29. *Vis. Devon*, ed. Vivian, 624. [3] St.Ch.3/2/14; *CPR*, 1548–9, p. 135; 1553, p. 352; 1553–4, pp. 18, 59; 1557–8, p. 1. [4] E179/97/237; C1/1253/48–56; *CJ*, i. 16; information from Susan Flower. [5] Exeter mayor's ct. bk. 1545–7, f. 99; *Cal. I.T. Recs.* i. 157–76 passim; *CSP Dom.* 1547–80, p. 57; D. M. Loades, *Two Tudor Conspiracies*, 35–38; *Ashburton Churchwardens' Accts.* (Devon and Cornw. Rec. Soc. n.s. x), 121, 139, 140; C142/122/31. [6] *CPR*, 1548–9, p. 258; 1550–3, p. 248; 1555–7, p. 479; 1558–60, pp. 19, 227; 1569–72, p. 245; J. E. Kew, 'The land market in Devon 1536–58' (Exeter Univ. Ph.D. thesis, 1967), 23; W. K. Jordan, *Edw. VI*, i. 455; C142/122/31; PCC *Admins.* ed. Glencross, ii. 6.

R.V.

PRIDEAUX, Roger (by 1524–82), of Soldon, Devon and London.

TOTNES   1545, 1547[1]

b. by 1524, 3rd s. of Humphrey Prideaux of Thuborough, Devon, by Joan, da. of Richard Fowell of Fowelscombe, Devon; half-bro. of Thomas Prideaux*. *educ.* ?I. Temple. *m.* settlement 10 Feb. 1549, Phillippa (*d.*1597), da. of Richard Yorke, wid. of Richard Parker, 2s. inc. Nicholas[†] 2da.[2]

    Escheator, Cornw. and Devon 1550–1, 1561–2; commr. sewers, Devon 1554, maritime causes 1578; steward, Exchequer, Devon 1561–*d.*; j.p. Devon 1561, q. 1564–*d.*; sheriff 1578–9.[3]

Roger Prideaux's career suggests that he was a lawyer by training, but unless he was the 'Master Predyeux the younger', so called at the Inner Temple in 1546 to avoid confusion with John Prideaux*, he cannot be traced at an inn. The practice of the law could also help to explain why Prideaux, who was to receive nothing under his father's will, is found engaging in land transactions at an early age. In 1546 he and John Wollacombe bought for £422 a Dorset manor which they immediately sold and two Cornish manors which Prideaux gave to his wife for her dower. In 1549 he and his uncle Nicholas Prideaux acquired for £1,438 lands in Devon and Dorset, most of which they kept for themselves, and in 1553 he joined with Richard Chamond*, the principal mover, in buying for £1,406 the manor of Launcells, Cornwall, and scattered properties in Essex, Devon and Somerset. Supplemented by regular small purchases from neighbours and others, these acquisitions produced a valuable set of properties which Prideaux's descendants were to consolidate.[4]

Prideaux's family had long been connected with Totnes, a town not far distant from its residence, and several of his maternal ancestors had sat in Parliament, but his election there in 1545 at so early an age implies his enjoyment of influential support: whence this could have come is not known, but its channel may have been the sheriff, Sir Hugh Stukeley, whose daughter was, or was to be, married to John Prideaux. When he was re-elected in 1547 Roger Prideaux was to sit in the House with this kinsman, so that it is not clear which of them was the 'Mr. Prideaux' to whom a bill for decayed houses was committed after its first reading on 30 Jan. 1550. That was to be the end of Prideaux's parliamentary career, although not of his local one: the next 30 years were to see him brought onto the Devon bench and eventually pricked sheriff.[5]

By his will of 13 May 1579 Prideaux left instructions that he was to be buried without pomp or pride. His widow received for life the use of his property and house at Soldon which at her death reverted to his elder son Nicholas. His two sons were each left £100 and his unmarried daughter £200. As overseer he named his son-in-law John Peryam.[†] He added a codicil on 2 Jan. 1582 and six days later he died. Probate was granted on 8 Feb. 1582, and at his inquisition his lands were given an annual value of upwards of £88.[6]

[1] C219/282/2; Hatfield 207. [2] Presumed to be of age at election. Vis. Devon (Harl. Soc. vi), 228–9; Vis. Devon, ed. Vivian, 621; J. Maclean, Trigg Minor, ii. 365. [3] CPR, 1553, p. 348; 1554–5, p. 108; 1560–3, pp. 181, 436; 1563–6, p. 21; J. Hoker, The description of the citie of Excester (Devon and Cornw. Rec. Soc. xi), 584–97. [4] Cal. I.T. Recs. i. 145; LP Hen. VIII. xxi; CPR, 1548–9, pp. 226, 362; 1553, pp. 12–13, 269; 1554–5, p. 5; 1558–60, p. 405; 1560–3, p. 553; 1563–6, p. 167; PCC 15 Coode. [5] CJ, i. 16. [6] PCC 7 Tirwhite; C142/198/37.

P.S.E./A.D.K.H.

PRIDEAUX, Thomas (by 1532–59 or later), of London.

BARNSTAPLE	1553 (Mar.)
NEWPORT IUXTA LAUNCESTON	1554 (Apr.)
CAMELFORD	1558

b. by 1532, 1st s. of Humphrey Prideaux of Thuborough, Devon by 2nd w. Edith, da. of William Hatch of Aller, Devon; half-bro. of Roger Prideaux*. m. ?1da.[1]

Apart from his service in Parliament, very little has come to light about the career of Thomas Prideaux. Sprung from a family of gentle standing in south Devon, Prideaux received a small bequest under the will made in 1549 by his father who 12 years earlier had settled several leases on him and two other children in survivorship. Presumably he sought election to Parliament after his father's death with a view to promoting his career. For his return in the spring of 1553 as the junior Member for Barnstaple, where his name was inserted on the indenture in a different hand, he was doubtless indebted to his brother Roger, who in 1549 had purchased with an uncle some former chantry property in the town, later sold to Roger Apley* and another townsman acting for the municipal authorities. A year later Prideaux seems to have been returned for three Cornish boroughs; his brother had business dealings with Richard Chamond* and many other leading figures in the county, and he may have been favoured by the steward of the duchy, the 1st Earl of Bedford. He evidently preferred to sit for one of the two Launceston constituencies and was replaced at Bodmin by John Sulyard and at Grampound by Sir Thomas Cornwallis. In 1557 he acquired a 21-year lease from the crown of property in Cornwall, and a year later he took the senior place for another Cornish borough. Early in Elizabeth's reign he assigned this lease to Walter Kestell who in 1567 replaced it by a lease of his own. By then Prideaux may have been dead—in March 1566 Roger Prideaux had substituted the names of two of his own children for those of his brother and sister in their father's settlement of 1537—or he could have been the Mr. Prideaux known to have been in Spain between 1563 and 1572 and the Thomas Prideaux who wrote from that country in 1574 commending his wife and daughter to his brother Richard.[2]

[1] Presumed to be of age at election. Vis. Devon, ed. Vivian, 618; CSP Dom. 1547–80, p. 486. [2] PCC 15 Coode; CPR, 1548–9, p. 362; 1555–7, pp. 489–90; 1563–6, p. 390; 1566–9, p. 105; C193/32/1; 219/282/3; R. Inst. Cornw., Truro, HL/1/1; Strype, Annals, i(2), 54; ii(1), 495; CSP Dom. 1547–80, p. 486.

A.D.K.H.

PRINCE, Richard (by 1530–98), of Shrewsbury, Salop.

LUDLOW	1558
BRIDGNORTH	1559

b. by 1530, o. s. of John Prince of Shrewsbury by Alice, da. of John Bradley of Wenlock. educ. I. Temple, adm. Nov. 1553. m. (1) Margaret (d.1584), da.

of Geoffrey Manchester of Manchester, Lancs., *s.p.*; (2) Dorothy, da. of William Leighton of Plaish, Salop, 4s. 5da.; 1da. illegit. *suc.* fa. 20 July 1557.[1]

Counsellor-at-the-bar, ct. of the council in the marches of Wales, temp. Eliz.; feodary, Salop by 1562–73; commr. musters 1577.[2]

Richard Prince's father was a shoemaker and master of the hospital of St. Giles in the Abbey Foregate at Shrewsbury, the street in which lay the property he left to his son. Styled 'literatus' when in 1551 he was made a freeman of Shrewsbury, Prince had probably already begun his legal training, although the Inner Temple gave him special admission only in November 1553. His connexion with the council in the marches is known only from his reinstatement by the Privy Council in 1577 after he had been dismissed for lack of the necessary qualification, but it was clearly as a legal officer of the council that he was returned to two Parliaments in succession: the boroughs concerned were both meeting places of the council. In the election indenture for Ludlow his name was inserted over an erasure, perhaps replacing John Allsop's*: as Allsop was town clerk, his supersession would imply that Prince was imposed upon the borough in his stead. Prince afterwards prospered at Shrewsbury, where the house which he built still stands. He died on 4 Oct. 1598.[3]

[1] Date of birth estimated from admission as freeman. *Vis. Salop* (Harl. Soc. xxix), 410; H. Owen and J. B. Blakeway, *Shrewsbury*, ii. 140; *Trans. Salop Arch. Soc.* (ser. 4), v. 47; viii. 122–5. [2] P. H. Williams, *Council in the Marches of Wales*, 173; *APC*, ix. 379; *CPR*, 1560–3, p. 449; 1572–5, pp. 154, 354; C. A. J. Skeel, *Council in the Marches of Wales*, 255. [3] *Shrewsbury Burgess Roll*, ed. Forrest, 244; C210/25/89; Williams, 190; *HMC 15th Rep. X*, 19, 24, 52, 59; Owen and Blakeway, i. 387, 562; Pevsner, *Salop*, 286; C142/252/41.

A.H.

PROCTOR, John (?1520–58/59).

CHIPPENHAM 1554 (Nov.)

?b. Apr./May 1520. *educ.* Corpus, Oxf., adm. Jan. 1537; All Souls fellow 1540–7; BA 1540, determined 1541, MA 1545. ?m. Elizabeth.[1]

?Headmaster, Tonbridge sch., Kent 1553–8 or later.[2]

No John Proctor seems to have been connected with Chippenham, where strangers were frequently returned, nor with any other place in Wiltshire. If the Member was an outsider, he was at any rate presumably a known supporter of the government. It is therefore possible that he was the Catholic apologist who became the first headmaster of Tonbridge, where the London skinner Sir Andrew Judd secured a royal grant for his foundation in May 1553. One of his pupils was a kinsman of (Sir) John Thynne*, but the Member is more likely to have owed his return to the Kentish lawyer and former Speaker Sir Thomas Moyle, who although

he chose to sit for Lynn had also been elected for Chippenham: Moyle was replaced at Chippenham by Cyriak Petyt, another Kentishman. Proctor was not among those who 'seceded' from this Parliament.[3]

The headmaster is said by Wood to have come from Somerset, but nothing is known about his forbears. His first book, *The fal of the late Arrian*, published in 1549 and dedicated to Princess Mary, was followed in 1554 by *The historie of Wyates rebellion* and two years later by a translation from the Latin, *The Waie home to Christ and Truths*. The two later works were also dedicated to Mary and the second earned a notice from Strype, who saw Proctor as 'another of these well-wishers to the pope's religion'. He had played a small part himself during the Wyatt rebellion, carrying news to (Sir) Robert Southwell*, a service which Southwell reported to the Privy Council.[4]

The assumption, followed by the *Dictionary of National Biography*, that Proctor, after 20 years of total obscurity, was in 1578 presented to the rectory of St. Andrew, Holborn, and died some six years later, is based on a misapprehension, the rector's christian name being James not John. On the other hand, the belief that the headmaster was buried at Tonbridge on 3 Oct. 1558 appears to arise from a misreading of the parish registers, for a Mrs Joan Proctor was buried there on that date. But the registers, which mention the baptism and burial of a William Proctor in 1554, also record the marriage on 12 July 1559 of Elizabeth Proctor, widow, to one Harry Stubberfield, and John Proctor's death at the end of Mary's reign or the beginning of Elizabeth's is the most likely explanation of his failure to make any further mark in any of his various fields of activity. Such an early death may also cast doubt on the further assumption that the poet Thomas Proctor was the headmaster's son.[5]

Others of the name include a gentleman of Wisbech, Cambridgeshire, who helped to secure the town's incorporation in 1549 and whose will was proved in 1583, and a man from Cowper Cote in the West Riding of Yorkshire who bought property nearby and died on 24 Sept. 1597. The Yorkshireman left a son aged at least 38 and seems to have had a forbear of the same name, but there is nothing apart from chronology to suggest that the Member came from this family.[6]

[1] The John Proctor admitted to Corpus in 1537 was then aged 16 years 9 months, Emden, *Biog. Reg. Univ. Oxf. 1501–40*, p. 465. Wood, *Ath. Ox.* ed. Bliss, i. 235; *DNB*. [2] S. Rivington, *Tonbridge Sch.* 18, 125–6. [3] *CPR*, 1553, p. 223. [4] Strype, *Eccles. Memorials*, iii(1), 271; *Arch. Cant.* iv. 235–6; D. M. Loades, *Two Tudor Conspiracies*, 16. [5] Emden, 465; *Novum Repertorium Parochiale Londinense*, ed. Hennessy, 90; *Reg. Tonbridge Sch.* ed. Hart, 18; *Burials at Tonbridge Church 1547–1837*, trans. Wall (Soc. of Genealogists), 6, 9; *Marriages* (ibid.), 1; *Baptisms* (ibid.), 2. [6] *CPR*, 1548–9, pp. 339–40; PCC 24

Rowe; *APC*, v. 174; T. D. Whitaker, *Craven*, ed. Morant, 233, 420, 502, 519; C142/252/58.

T.F.T.B.

PROWTE, Edmund (by 1533–89/90), of Litton Cheney and Melbury Osmond, Dorset.

BRIDPORT   1554 (Apr.)

b. by 1533. *m.* (2); at least 1s. 2da.[1]

In the 1550s Edmund Prowte lived at Litton Cheney, five miles south-east of Bridport, but his own standing is not sufficient to explain his return for the borough. His election could have been favoured by Sir Giles Strangways II, his neighbour at Melbury Osmond, who himself sat for the county in the same Parliament, or by the influential Phelips family. One of his daughters married a Thomas Phelips and in 1558 Prowte and Richard Calmady* stood surety for Richard Phelips's* servant Andrew Horde, when he was fined for quitting the third Marian Parliament without leave. Through Calmady, Prowte may have been connected with Robert Neale, his fellow-Member at Bridport. When he was returned to Parliament and when he stood surety, Prowte was described as a gentleman, but in his will of 17 Dec. 1589 he claimed no higher status than that of yeoman. He was then living at Melbury Osmond but he left 20s. to the poor of Litton as well as to the poor of his own parish. He bequeathed a bullock to Elizabeth Morris, 'my last wife's goddaughter', a piece of gold worth 10s. to each of his son-in-law Phelips's children, and half his goods to an unmarried daughter; the residuary legatee and executor was his son and namesake. The will was proved on 9 Mar. 1590.[2]

[1] Presumed to be of age at election. PCC 17 Drury.   [2] KB27/1188; PCC 17 Drury.

H.M.

PRYSELEY, William (by 1499–1540 or later), of Calais.

CALAIS   1536[1]

b. by 1499.[2]
     Alderman, Calais by 1520, mayor 1520–1; commr. sewers 1532, defence 1535, oyer and terminer 1540.[3]

William Pryseley occupied a house outside the walls of Calais, between the Water and Lantern gates. The vulnerability of his domicile and his representation on the town council of a ward where the only Englishmen were soldiers engendered a concern with the problems of defence. Early in 1536 he was reassured about his status in Calais by Sir William Fitzwilliam I* who advised him to continue the King's loyal subject. As the promoter of the Act (27 Hen. VIII, c. 63) enfranchising the town Fitzwilliam may have proposed him as the first representative of the mayor and aldermen to be returned to Parliament. He left the town for the assembly after the departure of his fellow-Member Thomas Boys, taking with him fresh instructions concerning the water-defences which were under review by the Council. On 17 June 1536 he and Boys informed the deputy, Viscount Lisle, about the discussions on the defences which they held each day with Fitzwilliam and others 'after doing our duties in the Parliament House', and early in July the pair raised the matter successfully with Cromwell during a sitting of the House. His antipathy towards the Protestantism abroad at Calais may have prevented his re-election in 1539 when Thomas Broke was chosen by the mayor and aldermen. When after Broke's speech on the eucharist a commission into heresy was ordered, Pryseley ingratiated himself with Lisle by testifying against Broke. Following Lisle's imprisonment in 1540 he was named to the commission of oyer and terminer issued in November. This is the last reference found to Pryseley. If he made a will it has not been traced.[4]

[1] *LP Hen. VIII*, x. 1086.   [2] Date of birth estimated from first reference.   [3] P. T. J. Morgan, 'Govt. Calais, 1485–1558' (Oxf. Univ. D. Phil. thesis, 1966), 301; *LP Hen. VIII*, vi, xvi, app.; C1/418/21.   [4] *LP Hen. VIII*, iii, vi, x–xii, xiv.

A.D.K.H.

PULESTON, John (by 1492–1551), of Caernarvon, Caern. and Bersham, Denb.

CAERNARVON BOROUGHS   1542
CAERNARVONSHIRE   1545, 1547*

b. by 1492, 1st s. of John Puleston of Hafod Y Wern and Bersham by 1st w. Ellen, da. of Robert Whitney of Whitney, Herefs. *m.* (1) by 1526, Gaynor, da. of Robert ap Meredydd ap Hwlcyn Llwyd of Glynllifon, Caern., 4s. inc. Robert* 5da.; (2) Sioned, da. of Meredydd ap Ieuan ap Robert of Dolwyddelan and Gwydir, Caern., wid. of Edmund Gruffydd of Porthyr-Aur, Caern., 1s. 3da.; 1s. illegit. *suc.* fa. c.1523. *Kntd.* by 20 Dec. 1546.[1]
     Sewer, the chamber by 1513; serjeant-at-arms 1513–d.; constable, Caernarvon castle 1523–d.; *ex officio* mayor, Caernarvon 1523–d.; dep. sheriff, Merioneth bef. 1533; sheriff and escheator 5 May 1533–40; steward, lands of Bardsey abbey by 1535–d.; commr. tenths of spiritualities, diocese of Bangor 1535, coastal defence N. Wales 1539, musters, Merion. 1539, relief, Caern. 1550; v.-adm. N. Wales by 1539; j.p. Caern. 1540–d.; sheriff, Denb. 1542–3, Caern. 1543–4; ?chamberlain, N. Wales in 1547.[2]

The Pulestons of Caernarvon were an offshoot of the family of Bersham in Denbighshire, itself sprung from the main line at Emral, Flintshire; the name derived from Puleston or Pilston near Newport, Shropshire. John Puleston's father and namesake had fought for Henry VII at Bosworth and served in the royal household: he was made constable of Caernarvon castle in 1506 and receiver of the lordship of Denbigh in 1519. John Puleston the younger saw service in Henry VIII's first French war as a member of Viscount Lisle's retinue, and it was on his return from France in November 1513 that he was made a serjeant-at-arms. Ten years later he succeeded his dead or dying father as constable of Caernarvon castle and ten years after that was made sheriff and escheator of the old county of Merioneth in the principality of North Wales.[3]

Puleston's relations with Sir Richard Bulkeley, the joint chancellor and chamberlain of North Wales until his death in 1547, were far from happy. During a dispute in 1535 Bulkeley described Puleston and his son-in-law Edward Gruffydd of Penrhyn as his old adversaries, and both parties thought it expedient to write to Cromwell. Two years later Puleston and Bulkeley were at loggerheads again when Bulkeley sent his brother William Bulkeley I* to put Cromwell's nephew Gregory Williams in possession of the benefice of Llandwrog, of which Puleston and another were patrons but which Cromwell wanted for his nephew. The pair had sometimes to work together, as when in 1539 they were commissioned to inspect the coastal defences in the region; at the time Puleston was vice-admiral of North Wales. In 1538 he and a fellow serjeant-at-arms, John ap Richard, had leased the ex-priory at Conway with various lands and the rectory at Eglwys Rhos.[4]

Following the death of Edward Gruffydd in 1540, Puleston supported his daughter in her quarrel with her brother-in-law Rhys Gruffydd* over the descent of the Penrhyn estates. Puleston maintained that Edward Gruffydd's lands should descend to his three daughters, the eldest of whom was six, Rhys Gruffydd that he should inherit. In July 1542 Chancellor Audley and Sir William Paulet awarded lands to the value of £33 to Rhys Gruffydd and the rest to the daughters, but even that was not the end of the affair. In June 1544 Puleston purchased the wardship and marriage of his three grand-daughters; it was one of several such deals, including the wardships of William Lewis* of Presaddfed, Anglesey, and of the daughters of Robert Salusbury of Llanrwst, Denbighshire.[5]

In 1539 Puleston was fearful that the new order in Wales would diminish his authority, but at the Union he emerged as one of the chief figures in the region: he was among the first justices for Caernarvonshire, was sheriff of that county and Denbighshire, and was knighted. He also sat in the first three Parliaments to which Wales sent Members, in 1542 for Caernarvon Boroughs, where his constableship made him supreme, and in 1545 and 1547 for the shire. In 1545 the sheriff who returned him was his

brother-in-law and ally John Wynn ap Meredydd*, who was to replace him as knight of the shire on his death during the prorogation between the third and fourth sessions of the Parliament of 1547. In that Parliament Puleston's son Robert sat for the Boroughs.[6]

Puleston made his will on 14 Jan. 1551, leaving his lands in Denbighshire to Robert Puleston and those in Caernarvonshire mainly to a younger son. His bequests of cattle and other livestock show that he must have farmed on a considerable scale, while silver articles and featherbeds witness to a comfortable home in Caernarvon. He was also well befriended, his executors including Paulet, then Earl of Wiltshire, (Sir) John Salusbury II*, and John Wynn ap Meredydd. The will was proved in the following month.[7]

[1] Date of birth estimated from first reference. Griffith, *Peds.*, 275; *DWB* (Puleston fam.); E. Breese, *Kalendars of Gwynedd*, 127; *Cal. Caern. Q. Sess. Recs.* ed. Williams, 33; *LP Hen. VIII*, iv. [2] *LP Hen. VIII*, i, viii, xiii, xiv; Breese, 70, 126–7; P. R. Roberts, 'The Acts of Union and the Tudor settlement of Wales' (Camb. Univ. Ph.D. thesis, 1966), 40, 172; *Cal. Caern. Q. Sess. Recs.* 31, 38–39, 53, 55–56, 60–61; HCA 13/3, f. 182; *CPR*, 1553, p. 363. [3] Breese, 126–7; *LP Hen. VIII*, i, iv; NLW ms Wales 20/3, m. 22. [4] *LP Hen. VIII*, viii, ix, xi, xiv. [5] Req.2/6/210; *LP Hen. VIII*, xv, xvii, xix; Wards 7/4/1, 3, 100/4, 8; 9/131/169. [6] *Cal. Caern. Q. Sess. Recs.* 33(5); *CPR*, 1547–8, p. 307. [7] PCC 7 Bucke.

P.S.E.

PULESTON, Robert (by 1526–83), of Caernarvon, Caern. and Bersham, Denb.

CAERNARVON BOROUGHS 1547
DENBIGHSHIRE 1553 (Mar.), 1571

b. by 1526, 1st surv. s. of (Sir) John Puleston* of Caernarvon and Bersham by 1st w. *m.* Ellen, da. of William Williams of Cochwillan, Caern., 6s. 2da. *suc. fa.* Jan./Feb. 1551.[1]
Commr. goods of churches and fraternities, Denb. 1553, for the Exchequer, Merion. 1561, piracy, Denb. 1565, Caerwys eisteddfod, Flints. 1568, victuals 1574, musters, Denb. 1580; j.p. Denb. 1555–61, q. 1562–*d.*; sheriff, Denb. 1558–9, 1569–70, Mont. 1571–2; j.p. Caern. 1573/74–*d.*[2]

Of Robert Puleston's life little has been discovered before his father's death early in 1551. He had then been for upwards of three years a Member of Edward VI's first Parliament for Caernarvon Boroughs, an apprenticeship clearly arranged by his father, constable of Caernarvon castle and knight of the shire in the same Parliament.

Under Sir John Puleston's will Robert Puleston inherited most of the family's lands in Denbighshire and with them the ancestral home at Bersham; the bulk of the Caernarvonshire land went to a younger brother, but Puleston received some property there, including a house in Caernarvon. It was, however, with Denbighshire that Puleston was to be chiefly concerned and at Bersham that he was to settle. (The Robert Puleston, 'gentleman', appearing in the

Caernarvonshire quarter sessions records in 1552 both as a plaintiff and as a juryman need not have been Puleston of Bersham, for Sir John Puleston had left an illegitimate son of the same christian name who was then living in Caernarvon.) He was to be a justice in Denbighshire for nearly 30 years, was to serve twice as sheriff and was to represent the shire in two Parliaments. On both occasions on which Puleston was returned for Denbighshire, to the Parliaments of March 1553 and 1571, the sheriff making the return was his ally Edward Almer*: his elections there were perhaps also assisted by his cousin Sir John Salusbury (q.v.) who was one of the leading figures in the county. Puleston died on 15 Aug. 1583 and was succeeded by his son John.[3]

[1] Presumed to be of age at election. Griffith, *Peds.* 275; A. N. Palmer, *Country Townships of Wrexham,* app. p. 63; Dwnn, *Vis. Wales,* ii. 359; PCC 7 Bucke. [2] *CPR,* 1553, p. 419; 1560–3, p. 446; *APC,* vii. 286; *HMC Welsh,* i(1), 291; R. Flenley, *Cal. Reg. Council, the Marches of Wales,* 109, 133, 200–1, 205, 212. [3] PCC 7 Bucke; *Cal. Caern. Q. Sess. Recs.* ed. Williams, 66, 88, 91, 110, 237; Dwnn, ii. 359.

P.S.E.

PULLEY, John (by 1526–83), of Bridgnorth, Salop.

BRIDGNORTH 1547

b. by 1526. *m.* Isabel Taylor of Bridgnorth.[1]
   Bailiff, Bridgnorth 1566–7, 1573–4, town clerk c.1566.[2]

John Pulley remains unidentified, but he is taken to be the 'John Pulley, senior' who was buried in St. Leonard's church, Bridgnorth, on 28 Jan. 1583, and whose will shows him to have been a draper with property in Bewdley, Worcestershire, as well as at Bridgnorth, and a relation by marriage of the Lutwich family of Lutwyche Hall, six miles west of the borough. The testator's widow and executrix died soon after her husband, and in April 1584 the administration of his remaining goods was granted to his brother, Richard Pulley.[3]

[1] Presumed to be of age at election. PCC admons. act bk. 1581–6, f. 100v. [2] Add. 28731, f. 10. [3] Shrewsbury pub. lib. transcript of St. Leonard's reg.; PCC 23 Rowe; *Vis. Salop* (Harl. Soc. xxix), 345–7; PCC admons. act bk. 1581–6, f. 103.

A.H.

PURCELL, Nicholas (by 1503–59), of Dinthill, Salop.

SHREWSBURY   1539,[1] 1545, 1553 (Mar.), 1553 (Oct.), 1554 (Apr.), 1555, 1558

b. by 1503, 1st s. of Richard Purcell of Shrewsbury by Anne, da. of John Gittons *alias* Lloyd† of Shrewsbury. *m.* (1) by 1526, Anne, da. of Randolph Beeston of Shrewsbury, 3s. inc. Richard† 1da.; (2) Gwen, da. of Maurice ap Gwilym ap Gruffydd Decwas, 1s. 1da.; 2s. 3da. illegit. *suc.* fa. 1524.[2]
   Bailiff, Shrewsbury 1532–3, 1536–7, 1540–1, 1544–5, 1550–1, 1554–5, alderman 14 Sept. 1534–*d.*; master, drapers' co. 1545–6; j.p. Mont. in 1544, 1558/59; commr. relief 1550; sheriff 1554–5.[3]

Sprung from a cadet branch of an ancient Shropshire family, Nicholas Purcell inherited lands in or near Shrewsbury which made him a leading townsman there, and others in Montgomeryshire, where in 1549 he was himself to add the manor of Talerddig, qualifying him to play a part in the administration of that shire. He followed his father, who had also been bailiff of Shrewsbury, into the drapers' company in 1524 and it was evidently to further his trade that in 1536 he joined with others in claiming the right of foreign burgess-ship in Welshpool, Montgomeryshire: nine years later, having served as steward and assistant to the wardens, he was elected master of the drapers'. He sat in seven of the ten Parliaments summoned between 1539 and 1558 but all that is known of his activity in the Commons is that in April 1554 he and his partner Richard Mytton were asked by the Vintners' Company to support the repeal of the Licensing Act of 1553 (7 Edw. VI, c. 5).[4]

Purcell sued out a pardon early in 1559 as of Dinthill, near Shrewsbury, and on 28 June he added a codicil to the will he had made when ill on 20 Aug. 1556. He probably died on the same day and the will was proved on the following 29 Aug.[5]

[1] Salop RO, 215/56. [2] Date of birth estimated from first reference. *Vis. Salop* (Harl. Soc. xxix), 413; PCC 22 Bodfelde, 40 Chaynay. [3] *Trans. Salop Arch. Soc.* (ser. 1), iii. 255–64; (ser. 4), ix. 269–77; x. 193, 195, 198; xii. 183–4; Shrewsbury Guildhall 75(4); *CPR,* 1553, p. 363. [4] W. V. Lloyd, *Sheriffs Mont.* 69–80; *Mont. Colls.* ii. 429; *LP Hen. VIII,* xvi, xxi; *CPR,* 1553, pp. 376, 387; *Trans. Salop Arch. Soc.* (ser. 4), iii. 146, 234; iv. 207, 215, 229–30; xii. 183; *Guildhall Studies in London Hist.,* i. 48–49. [5] *CPR,* 1558–60, pp. 201, 360; PCC 40 Chaynay. Only the day of death (28th) can be read on Purcell's i.p.m. C142/127/24.

A.D.K.H.

PURSLOW (PURSELAW), Nicholas (by 1533–63), of the Inner Temple, London.

APPLEBY   1558
MORPETH   1559

b. by 1533, 1st s. of Robert Purslow of Sidbury, Salop by Margaret, da. and h. of William Sparke. *educ.* I. Temple, adm. by 1547, called. *m.* Margaret, da. of Thomas Williams of Willaston or Wollaston, Salop, *s.p.*[1]
   Bencher, I. Temple by 1563.

Nicholas Purslow came of a gentle family long established in Shropshire and by the 16th century settled near Bridgnorth. A lawyer who before his early death bought property in the south-west of the county, he presumably owed both his appearances in the Commons to John Eltoftes, his colleague at the Temple and in the service of the northern aristocracy; Eltoftes was his fellow-Member on the first occasion and Purslow was not to be returned again after Eltoftes's death. Nothing has come to light about his part in the Commons. He made his will on 5 July 1563, commending his wife to his father's care and ordering the payment of debts amounting to £80. He died on the following 8 Aug. and his heir was his brother Robert, then aged 27.[2]

[1] Date of birth estimated from education. *Trans. Salop Arch. Soc.* (ser. 4), iii. 111; C142/142/79; *Vis. Salop* (Harl. Soc. xxix), 415, 442, 507. [2] *Trans. Salop Arch. Soc.* (ser. 4), iii. 112; PCC 35 Mellershe; *CPR*, 1558-60, pp. 6, 10; 1560-3, p. 72; C142/142/79.

D.F.C.

PURVEY, John (by 1525–83), of Wormley, Herts.

HUNTINGDON	1553 (Oct.)
HORSHAM	1554 (Nov.)
HERTFORDSHIRE	1558
HIGHAM FERRERS	1559, 1563

b. by 1525. *m.* (1) lic. ?July 1547, Anne, da. and coh. of William Woodleaf of London, 1s.; (2) by 1564, Magdalen, da. of Peter Cheke of Cambridge, Cambs., wid. of Lawrence Earsby or Eresby (d.?1564), of Louth, Lincs., *s.p.*[1]
Auditor, duchy of Lancaster, south parts 1546–*d.*; commr. relief, Herts. 1550; other commissions 1554–*d.*; j.p. Herts. 1554, q. by 1558/59–*d.*, Lincs. (Lindsey) 1569–*d.*; feodary, Herts. by 1562; warden of Louth 1568, 1573, 1582.[2]

John Purvey's parentage has not been discovered. No connexion has been found between him and the Buckinghamshire family of Purefoy, but his marriage to the daughter of a London mercer, himself possibly of Buckinghamshire origin, suggests he may have been related to another London merchant, John Purvey of Southwark, who died in 1554.

Purvey began his career as a clerk to Robert Heneage of Lincoln, auditor for the south parts of the duchy of Lancaster. This office, surrendered to Purvey in 1546, was held by him for life and afterwards came to his son William. By his first marriage Purvey acquired the manor of Wormley in Hertfordshire and some lands in Norfolk. He already owned six houses in Paternoster Row and Warwick Lane in London, but added little to his estates before Elizabeth's reign. Put on the Hertfordshire bench in 1554, he also sat on several inquisitions post mortem with William Tooke*, whose son married the second of William Woodleaf's daughters. The Tooke and Purvey families were patrons of Wormley church, and the wardship which Purvey acquired in 1554 he probably owed to William Tooke as auditor of the court of wards and liveries.[3]
Purvey sat in Parliament three times during Mary's reign. He owed his election at Huntingdon to his position in the duchy, to which the borough belonged, and his return for Horsham, if not attributable to his fellow-Member, William Tooke, may also have been due to this connexion. His patron there could have been either the 12th Earl of Arundel, steward of duchy lands in Sussex, or

John Caryll*, a prominent Sussex Catholic living very close to Horsham and attorney-general to the duchy. In June 1555 Purvey was to receive, jointly with Caryll, a lease of the duchy greenwax. Firmly established in Hertfordshire, Purvey was returned a knight of the shire there in 1558. He did not oppose the initial measures towards reconciliation with Rome in 1553, and he was to be noted by his bishop in 1564 as 'a hinderer of religion'.[4]
Re-elected to Parliament twice under Elizabeth, Purvey became an ally by marriage of Secretary Cecil in the early 1560s. He remained active in duchy and local administration until his death on 21 Apr. 1583.[5]

[1] Date of birth estimated from first reference. *VCH Herts.* iii. 488; *Mar. Lic. Fac. Off.* (Harl. Soc. xxiv), 10; *CPR*, 1553, p. 370; *Vis. Essex* (Harl. Soc. xiii), 177; C142/201/71; PCC 19 Butts. [2] *CPR*, 1553, p. 354; 1553-4, p. 20; 1560-3, pp. 400, 438; 1563-6, pp. 43, 123; SP11/5, f. 36; Somerville, *Duchy*, i. 443; *Louth Old Corp. Recs.* ed. Goulding, 19. [3] Clutterbuck, *Herts.* ii. 235, 237; *CPR*, 1553-4, pp. 7, 303; 1563-6, p. 308; *VCH Herts.* iii. 488. [4] Somerville, i. 408; *Cam. Misc.* ix(3), 30. [5] C142/201/71.

R.J.W.S.

PURY, William (by 1489–1537 or later), of New Windsor, Berks.

| NEW WINDSOR | 1510[1] |

b. by 1489. *m.* ?Margaret.[2]
Jt. warden, guild of the Holy Trinity, Windsor by 1513–14; town clerk by 1514–?*d.*, mayor 1518–19, 1522–3.[3]

William Pury was probably a kinsman, if not a son, of Edmund Pury, mayor of Windsor in 1466, and he was perhaps also related to John Pury†, a household officer who held land in Windsor at about the same time. The antiquarian Elias Ashmole's extracts from the Windsor corporation records, of which many of the originals have disappeared, include a reference to Pury as a Member of the Parliament of 1510, in which the high steward, Sir Andrew Windsor*, secured a rent from a fee-farm for the town in an Act (1 Hen. VIII, c. 16) for the royal household. There is no evidence that Pury's parliamentary expenses were paid, but the same source frequently mentions his wages as town clerk, the first payment, one of 6s.8d. 'for writing', being dated 13 Jan. 1514; a book of chamberlains' accounts which does survive records many similar payments for later years, the last of them occurring in the account heard at the guildhall on 16 Oct. 1537.[4]
Pury must have been a substantial townsman to have belonged, as did his fellow-Member John Welles, to the guild of the Holy Trinity. The brethren of this guild monopolized local offices, one of which had evidently been bestowed on Pury when in 1519 a sum of £3 18s.5d. was delivered to

him for various repairs at the market place, the butts and in St. Mary's church. He was also paid 5s.8d. in 1517 'for his costs riding to London divers times to Master Windsor for the subsidy', and he received the normal fee of 20s. after each of his years as mayor. An indication of his financial standing is furnished by two indentures for subsidy assessments, dated 1 June 1524 and 2 Jan. 1525, in both of which he was rated at 20s. on goods worth £20; although this was small compared with the £200 worth of goods recorded for Andrew Bereman and Thomas Bennet, only these two exceptionally rich men, and four others ranging from £50 to £100, stood above Pury, and his name preceded those of dozens of poorer men, including a John Pury with goods valued at 20 marks.[5]

It was presumably this John Pury, a warden of the Trinity guild in 1520, who received 6s.8d., 'being clerk for his fee', every year from 1538 until 1544, the year in which he was mayor, and was then replaced by Thomas Butler II*. As William Pury is not to be found in the next subsidy assessment, that of 1540, in which John appears with goods worth £20 and a Margaret 'Pery', widow, with the same, it appears that the Member had a kinsman—whether son, brother or nephew we cannot say—who succeeded him as town clerk but who did not hold that office long or enter the House of Commons in virtue of it.[6]

[1] R. R. Tighe and J. E. Davis, *Windsor Annals*, i. 500. [2] Presumed to be of age at election. E179/73/153; Bodl. Ashmole 1125, f. 25v. [3] Bodl. Ashmole 1115, f. 40; 1126, f. 23; Windsor recs. Wi/FA c.1, ff. 11, 18v, 41v. [4] *VCH Berks.* iii. 316-17; E. Cust, *Cust. Fam.* i. 273-4, 293; *Vis. Oxon.* (Harl. Soc. v), 189; Tighe and Davis, i. 500; Bodl. Ashmole 1126, f. 23; Windsor recs. Wi/FA c.1, ff. 7-41v. [5] *VCH Berks.* iii. 59-60; Windsor recs. Wi/FA c.1, ff. 10, 12, 12v, 19v; E179/73/130, 137. [6] Windsor recs. Wi/FA c.1, ff. 41v, 42v-48; E179/73/153.

T.F.T.B.

PYCTO, Thomas

DUNWICH 1558

Thomas Pycto may have been descended from the landed family of that name in Staffordshire, but his immediate antecedents were probably in Norfolk, where a man of this name was a member of the common council of Norwich from 1520 to 1524 and perhaps also surveyor of the streets there in 1545. If the surveyor was the Thomas Pycto whose will was proved at Norwich in 1548, another Thomas Pycto was admitted to the Norwich guild of St. George in 1550 or the following year, and had property (perhaps in right of his wife Alice) at Eccles, some ten miles from Thetford. In 1557 or 1558 he disposed of land near Thetford to Richard Fulmerston*, treasurer to the 4th Duke of Norfolk. It was possibly this connexion that gained Pycto his

seat; the duke and his agents were active patrons in East Anglian elections to the Parliament of 1558.

CPR, 1553-4, p. 471; 1558-60, p. 304; *LP Hen. VIII*, xix; *Wm. Salt Arch. Soc.* (n.s.) 1906, pp. 8-9; Norwich ass. procs. 2, ff. 104v, 121, 186v; Norwich consist. ct. 210-12 Wymer; NRA 8282, no. 23 (1-11).

M.K.D.

PYMME alias FRYER, Thomas (by 1524-66), of Chipping Wycombe, Bucks.

CHIPPING WYCOMBE 1554 (Apr.), 1558

b. by 1524. educ. M. Temple. m. Agnes, 2s. 3da.[1]
Comptroller of the pipe roll by 1545–Sept. 1562; mayor, Chipping Wycombe 1555-6; baron of the Exchequer 30 Sept. 1562–d.[2]

Thomas Pymme alias Fryer was perhaps a grandson of Thomas Pymme, mayor of Wycombe in the reign of Henry VIII, whose son and namesake was apposer of the foreign receipts of the Exchequer from 1516. The apposer died in 1549, leaving houses in Wycombe and Islington, Middlesex, to his wife, with remainder to his 'cousin' Thomas Pymme alias Fryer. Edward Frere*, whose grandfather had migrated to Oxford from Wycombe in 1525, was also a 'cousin' of the apposer but the exact relationship between the two families, and with it the explanation of Pymme's alias, has not come to light.[3]

After studying at the Middle Temple, Pymme presumably owed his introduction to the Exchequer to his kinsman the apposer. A list of fees in 1545 describes the comptroller of the pipe roll as Thomas Pymme junior. Only Thomas Pymme senior was assessed for subsidy at Wycombe in that year but in 1550 the younger man held land and cottages there and five years later he was elected mayor. Whatever his standing in the town, however, Pymme may have owed his returns to the second and fifth of Mary's Parliaments rather to his professional tie with Sir Edmund Peckham*, whose son Henry was his fellow-Member in the spring of 1554.[4]

Pymme was present as one of the aldermen and late mayors in June 1566 when the arms of Wycombe were ratified. He made his will on 20 Oct. 1566 and died soon afterwards, being replaced at the Exchequer on the following 12 Nov. He asked to be buried in Wycombe church, in the chapel beside his pew, and left copyholds there and in Islington to his wife and executrix, who was to pay for the education of his sons Timothy (recently admitted to the Middle Temple) and Henry. The will was proved on 13 Mar. 1567.[5]

[1] Date of birth estimated from first reference. PCC 8 Stonard. [2] E405/115/47v, 117/25, 39, 121/22v, 26; Stowe 571, f. 6; *First Wycombe Ledger Bk.* (Bucks. Rec. Soc. xi), no. 99; *CPR*, 1560-3, p. 248. [3] *First Wycombe Ledger Bk.* nos. 55, 56, 67-70, 76; Bucks. RO, D/A/WE/1/203; *LP Hen. VIII*, ii; PCC 1 Coode; *Oxf. Recs.* 54. [4] E179/78/32, 125; 405/115/8v, 9, 47v; *CPR*, 1550-3. p. 3. [5] *HMC*

5th Rep. 565; Vis. Bucks. ed. Harvey, 49; PCC 8 Stonard; CPR, 1563–6, p. 483.

M.K.D.

PYNE, Henry (1504/5–56 or later), of Ham in Morwenstow, Cornw.

LISKEARD 1529

b. 1504/5, s. of Thomas Pyne of Ham by Margaret, da. of Oliver Wise of Sydenham, Devon. m. Catherine, da. of Christopher Tredeneck of Tredinnick in St. Breock, Cornw., 1da. suc. gd.–fa. 23 Apr. 1510.[1]

Under sheriff, Cornw. 1531–2; sewer, the chamber by 1538; keeper, Liskeard park, Cornw. 1538.[2]

The Pynes had been seated at Ham in the extreme north of Cornwall since the early 15th century. Thomas Pyne died not long after Henry Pyne's birth, whereupon a life interest in part of his property went to his wife. She married William Kendall, who in February 1511 became her son's guardian. Kendall belonged to a family with estates near Liskeard and was himself the chief agent in Cornwall of the Marquess of Exeter, high steward of the duchy of Cornwall. It was doubtless his influence which procured Pyne's election to the Parliament of 1529 for Liskeard with the equally youthful James Trewynnard. Both were presumably returned again to the Parliament of 1536 in accordance with the King's request for the re-election of the previous Members, but before its successor met in 1539 the Marquess of Exeter had disappeared from the scene and Kendall with him: in the absence of the names of the Liskeard Members for this and the following Parliament we cannot say whether the loss of his patron cost Pyne his seat, but we do know that he was not to reappear in the Commons from 1545.[3]

Shortly before the arrest of the marquess, Pyne received a grant in survivorship of Liskeard park; he was soon to become its sole holder and remained so until about 1556 when the ground was disparked. Some years before this appointment he had obtained from the duchy of Cornwall a 21-year lease of lands in the park: this he sold to Sir John Arundell of Trerice (whom he served as under sheriff) in return for a reconveyance of the Northground and an annuity of 40s. As Arundell seems not to have observed the agreement, Pyne complained of his behaviour in Chancery in 1547. Arundell for his part had earlier sued Pyne for debt before the lord mayor and sheriffs of London and had him arrested in the City. Although Pyne had obtained livery of the family lands in November 1526, and had acquired a further 1,300 acres on the death of his mother eight years later, he appears to have been in chronic and at times desperate financial trouble. In the summer of 1532, as under sheriff of Cornwall, he tried to obtain £40 by offering to free two prisoners in Launceston gaol. From being a man described as 'strong in the county' he probably lost importance as he grew older: some time after 1536 he sold the manor of Ham, perhaps his most important single asset, to Sir John Wyndham, and he lost a lawsuit with his cousin over the title to a Devon manor. His death occurred after the park at Liskeard had been converted to other uses: he was survived by his wife, who married again, and by a daughter who took as her second husband Robert Mordaunt†.[4]

[1] Date of birth estimated from age at grandfather's i.p.m., C142/25/148. Vis. Devon, ed. Vivian, 632, 791; Vis. Cornw. ed. Vivian, 457; Gilbert, Cornw. ii. 242–3. [2] St.Ch.2/10/283; LP Hen. VIII, xiii. [3] LP Hen. VIII, i, iv; Vis. Cornw. 258; C1/666/36; A. L. Rowse, Tudor Cornw. 169. [4] LP Hen. VIII, iv, xiii; CPR, 1557–8, p. 142; Duchy Cornw. RO, 228, m. 3v; C1/666/36, 1046/55, 1182/53, 1282/62; 142/25/132, 148, 82/120; St.Ch.2/10/283; Rowse, 237–8; Vis. Cornw. 383, 457.

J.J.G.

PYNE, John (by 1500–31/32), of London.

LYME REGIS 1529*

b. by 1500, s. of Roger Pyne of Plymouth, Devon. m. by 1521, Joan (?Hall), at least 2s.[1]

The John Pyne returned by Lyme Regis to the Parliament of 1529 appears to have been a stranger to the town, although he had a contemporary there named Robert Pyne who was succeeded in 1539 by a son John. By that year, however, the Member was dead, and it is the note to this effect on the list of Members as it was revised in the spring of 1532 which suggests an identification with a London scrivener whose will, originally made in 1521, was revised on 29 July 1531 and proved on the following 9 Aug. This John Pyne came of Devon stock and had been born in Plymouth. In his will he referred to another west countryman, George Rolle*, as his 'master' and he may have been Rolle's deputy as keeper of the records of common pleas; he had business connexions with Sir Thomas Denys, one of the knights for Devon in 1529, and was a neighbour of Rowland Hill* whom he appointed with Rolle an executor of his will. He may also have been one of the feoffees of the parish church of Axmouth, Devon, who started two suits in Chancery between 1515 and 1518 to recover the deeds of property at Colyford; their counsel was William Wadham†, steward of Lyme Regis, who himself died in 1522 but whose kinsman Sir Nicholas Wadham was to be one of the knights for Somerset in 1529. (Dorset and Somerset shared a sheriff, who would thus have been responsible for returning both Wadham and Pyne.) The scrivener or his eldest son could also have been the man described as an attorney of the court of common pleas in two undated Star Chamber cases over property in Somerset. Pyne may have been replaced in the Commons by John Tudoll (q.v.) for the remaining sessions of the Parliament.[2]

[1] Date of birth estimated from date of will. [2] PCC 7 Thower; C1/398/1–2, 558/26; Lyme Regis ct. recs. 1437–1508, no. 17; rec. bk. 6; St.Ch.2/34/120; 3/9/93.

H.M.

QUARNBY, Humphrey (by 1513–65/66), of Nottingham.

NOTTINGHAM 1553 (Oct.), 1554 (Apr.), 1563*

b. by 1513, s. of Thomas Quarnby of Derby by Elizabeth, da. and coh. of Henry Tickhill. *m.* Elizabeth, da. and h. of Robert Mellors (*d.*1515 or later) of Nottingham, at least 3s. 3da.[1]
  Sheriff, Nottingham 1534–5, alderman by 1541, mayor 1542–3, 1549–50, 1555–6, 1562–3, j.p. by 1552.[2]

Humphrey Quarnby was by trade a bell-founder. His family did not make its mark in Nottingham until Quarnby's appointment as sheriff in 1534 was followed by the election of his uncle Nicholas Quarnby to fill a vacancy in the town's representation in Parliament. Their ascendancy doubtless owed something to a double alliance with the influential Mellors family, the uncle marrying Robert Mellors's widow and the nephew his daughter and heir. The younger Quarnby succeeded to Mellors's bell-foundry and to his municipal position. He bought metal from the dissolution commissioners, including a bell from the Nottingham Greyfriars, and among the bells he cast were those commissioned for Worksop priory during the reign of Mary. He became a warden of the Nottingham free school, which two generations of Mellors had patronized.[3]

Privileged to hold 'a greyhound to chase' and to hunt hares and foxes in Sherwood forest, Quarnby possessed property in various parts of Nottingham, his own house being on Swine Green. He was involved in considerable litigation, notably with kinsmen of his wife over her inheritance. As a townsman and municipal dignitary he was a natural choice for one of Nottingham's seats at the opening of Mary's reign. Unlike his fellow-Member in October 1553, Thomas Markham, he did not oppose the initial measures towards the restoration of Catholicism. The will which he was to make a dozen years later bears out his religious conservatism; this did not however prevent his election to Elizabeth's second Parliament, of which he was a Member at his death in 1565 or 1566.[4]

[1] Date of birth estimated from first reference. Thoroton, *Notts.* ed. Throsby, ii. 40–41; *Nottingham Bor. Recs.* iv. 395. [2] *Nottingham Bor. Recs.* iii. 465; iv. 101, 416–18. [3] Ibid. iii. 194; iv. 108; *VCH Notts.* ii. 368. [4] *Nottingham Bor. Recs.* iii. 215; iv. 395, 396; C1/741/241, 1172/32, 1183/1; *N. Country Wills*, ii (Surtees Soc. cxxi), 43–44.

C.J.B.

QUARNBY, Nicholas (by 1502–35 or later), of Nottingham.

NOTTINGHAM 1529*

b. by 1502, 2nd s. of Thomas Quarnby of Derby. *m.* Julian, da. and h. of one Mapurley, wid. of Robert Mellors (*d.*1515 or later) of Nottingham.[1]

Of Derby origin, Nicholas Quarnby married the widow of an influential Nottingham freeman, whose own family, the Mapurleys, had supplied a Member for the town in 1478. Unlike his nephew Humphrey Quarnby* he did not make use of his marriage to enter the governing body of Nottingham although he appears to have had no property or other interests elsewhere. He was involved in several chancery suits before Wolsey, one as plaintiff against William Hyton for retaining the title deeds to his land in Nottingham, and another as defendant in a similar action brought against him by one of his wife's kinsmen; he also sued Oliver Rigby, the parson of Cossall church, for giving to another the tithe corn promised him in 1523. In 1533 he was himself successfully sued in the Exchequer for a debt of £40 by the widow of a London alderman.[2]

Quarnby's return for Nottingham at the by-election held on 29 Jan. 1535, only four days after the death of one of the Members, Henry Statham, he probably owed to his nephew William Mellors, then one of the sheriffs of the borough and as such debarred from election. Two other members of the Mellors family were among the electors. This is the last reference found to Quarnby, who may not have survived to sit in the Parliament of 1536 in accordance with the King's general request for the return of the previous Members.[3]

[1] Date of birth estimated from first reference. Thoroton, *Notts.* ed. Throsby, ii. 41. [2] C1/438/3, 540/34–6, 560/2; E13/211, m. 19. [3] C219/18A/10 gives 29 Jan., not 25 Jan. as ptd. in *OR*.

C.J.B.

RADCLIFFE, Cuthbert (by 1491–1545), of Cartington and Dilston, Northumb.

NORTHUMBERLAND 1529

b. by 1491, 1st s. of Sir Edward Radcliffe of Cartington by Anne, da. and h. of Sir John Cartington[†] of Cartington. *m.* lic. 6 Jan. 1515, Margaret, da. of Henry, 10th Lord Clifford, 4s. 3da. Kntd. Nov. 1530/June 1534; *suc.* fa. c.1537.[1]
  J.p. Northumb. 1512–*d.*, marches of Scotland ?1532; escheator, Northumb. 1513–14; sheriff Jan.–Nov. 1526, 1530–1, 1539–40; 'learned steward' of 5th Earl of Northumberland's estates in Northumb. 1529–*d.*; commr. redress of injuries in west march 1531, musters Northumb. 1539; other commissions 1534–41; esquire of the body in 1533; member, council in the marches by 1537; constable and chief forester, Alnwick, Northumb. 1539–*d.*; chief steward, Tynemouth 1539; dep. warden, middle march 1540–3;

dep. steward, Hexham 1543; capt. Berwick-upon-Tweed castle 1544-5.[2]

Sir Edward Radcliffe, a younger son in the family seated at Derwentwater, Cumberland, settled in Northumberland on his marriage to an heiress, although it was his son Cuthbert who eventually inherited Dilston under the will which his grandmother, Lady Cartington, made in February 1522. Radcliffe's father had been a fee'd man of the Percys but he himself began the shedding of that allegiance which, a Clifford marriage notwithstanding, was to be continued by his son: he served the 4th Earl of Northumberland as steward and counsellor-at-law but he was also warden of the middle march and an esquire of the body.[3]

It seems likely, in view of his father's legal training and the offices he was to hold, that Cuthbert Radcliffe received some training in the law, although he cannot be traced at an inn of court. He first achieved prominence in border warfare: in 1520 he was rewarded for his services in the destruction of Scottish fortresses and three years later, after taking part in a similar expedition under the 2nd Lord Dacre, he and four others formulated a scheme for the better government of the middle march. In 1525 he was party to an agreement by prominent Northumbrian gentry for keeping watches on the east march: at about the same time Archdeacon Magnus recommended his promotion to the quorum of the bench as a means of strengthening it, with what result is unknown. His inclusion in 1528 in the body of fee'd men in the county was part of a process whereby the crown, by the granting of annuities, enlisted the services of local gentlemen for the wardens of the marches.[4]

Radcliffe's election as senior knight of the shire to the Parliament of 1529 reflected his local standing and his own and his family's record of public service. He was appointed to the shrievalty for a second term while a Member, and although the date of his knighthood is unknown he is first so styled on 1 June 1534. The appointment and the honour alike reflect the confidence reposed in him and there can be little doubt that he was returned again to the Parliament of 1536 in accordance with the King's general request for the re-election of the previous Members; he may also have sat in one or both of the following Parliaments, those of 1539 and 1542, for which the names of the Northumberland knights are unknown. Although the wording of the grant of 1530 making him 'learned steward' of the Earl of Northumberland's estates in Northumberland implies that he was being confirmed in a post which he already held, there is nothing to suggest, as there is in the case of his father, that Radcliffe was spying for the crown

in the Percy household: he does not appear, however, to have stood close to the 5th Earl, and unlike numerous officers in the north he was not provided for in the Act (27 Hen. VIII, c.47) assuring the Percy inheritance to the crown in 1536.[5]

In 1532 Radcliffe was appointed one of the arbitrators between Sir John Delaval and Sir Philip Dacre and in 1534 he was a juror at the trial of the 3rd Lord Dacre on a bill of treason. It was probably two years later that he was one of the petitioners to the King on behalf of former sheriffs and escheators of Northumberland for pardon for failing to account annually at the Exchequer, a dereliction which according to the petition had begun in the first year of Edward IV. Radcliffe himself had been proceeded against for failing to make his proffer at Michaelmas 1531, and when at Easter 1532 he had still not rendered account he was fined £20. He seems to have done all in his power to avoid accounting at the Exchequer (although as a Member he must have been often in its vicinity), and his successor as sheriff was ordered to distrain him and to appear with him on a given day: this summons too was ignored, but Radcliffe did eventually appear and he then confessed that every sheriff pocketed £120 a year from the profits of the shire. The petitioners of 1536 pleaded in extenuation the time-honoured practice of not accounting and the extraordinary demands of the office in Northumberland. When Radcliffe became sheriff for the third time, the warden of the east march was granted a writ of *dedimus potestatem* to receive his oath for the faithful performance of his office and the recognizances of two persons willing to be his sureties under a penalty of 200 marks each. Radcliffe was clearly one of the sheriffs whose contumacy prompted the Act of 1549 (2 and 3 Edw. VI, c.34) ordering future sheriffs of Northumberland to account annually and to give surety for their conduct. He had also been lax in his handling of writs: he was prosecuted for failing to return 66 exchequer writs by Michaelmas 1533 and fined £10 by that court. There was another side to the picture: Radcliffe's protest of 1539 to Cromwell over the non-payment of sums due to him helps to explain his own and his fellows' laxity, as perhaps does his absence from the shire as a Member during two-and-a-half months of his second shrieval year.[6]

Radcliffe was not involved in the Pilgrimage of Grace. He may have been one of the gentlemen compelled to take the rebel oath at the meeting convened by Sir Ingram Percy ostensibly to see to the border country. He does not appear to have been with the 'King's party' barricaded in Chillingham, but he did enter into the calculations of the rebels, for at their conference at York in November 1536 he was chosen as one of the three representatives of Northumberland to meet the royalists at Pontefract, although there is no evidence that he was present or even knew that he had been chosen. His inactivity in the rebellion was rectified by his industry for the crown and the cause of order after its failure. He was in attendance on the 3rd Duke of Norfolk in Northumberland, and with other prominent figures he drew up in July 1539 the plans for dealing with Tynedale and Redesdale which were sent to the King. He was commissioned to survey Langley castle as part of the review of frontier defences undertaken in 1538 by the council in the north.[7]

The crown's acquisition of former monastic property in Northumberland, and its tightened grip on the Percy property and following in the shire in 1537, opened the way to Radcliffe for further service with the crown. He had probably had custody of Alnwick since 1537 but his formal appointment as constable to succeed Sir Ingram Percy two years later may mean that the crown kept the office vacant for some time after the disgrace of the Percy family. Apart from the fact that Radcliffe had already been involved with the Percy inheritance, the grant of this office may be connected with his appointment shortly afterwards as deputy warden of the middle march: the constableship of Alnwick was a valuable aid to the warden, giving him the leadership of the men of that lordship. Some care was taken over Radcliffe's appointment as deputy warden, both as to suitability and willingness, for Norfolk was sounded on these matters by the Privy Council. In July 1541 the Council of Scotland acknowledged that Radcliffe's occupancy of that office had conduced to the preservation of peace.

In August 1542 Radcliffe was captured when the expedition of (Sir) Robert Bowes* was thrown into disarray by the Scots at Haddon Rig. He was taken into the custody of the bishop of Glasgow, and his release was delayed because he was one of the prisoners 'meet for the King's purpose'. By April 1543 some doubt was cast by Admiral Lisle on Radcliffe's competence as deputy warden and in August the 2nd Earl of Rutland and the council in the marches were sounding opinion about a replacement. This may be explained by the changing nature of the office after 1541, for Radcliffe appeared to have no great aptitude for the raids and counter raids which became increasingly important: in a list of fee'd men in Northumberland drawn up between 1537 and 1540 a crown agent had described Radcliffe as 'a wise man well learned and well minded to justice but no adventurer to the field'. His appointment soon afterwards as captain of Berwick suggests no waning of confidence in him on the part of the crown, but during his tenure Berwick was insufficiently manned, organised and furnished with ordnance.[8]

Amid his public service Radcliffe did not neglect his estates. Although there is no record of any grants or leases from the crown he seems to have benefited to a small extent from the redistribution of ex-monastic and also perhaps ex-Percy property. He was involved in disputes with his family and other Northumbrians. No will of his has been found but by a deed of settlement of February 1534 Dilston was to devolve upon his wife and after her death upon his heir George. When Radcliffe died on 20 July 1545 George succeeded to the other Northumberland properties. The Radcliffes, who remained a Catholic family, became earls of Derwentwater in the reign of James II, only to lose the title on the attainder of the Jacobite 3rd Earl[9]

[1] Date of birth estimated from first reference. *Vis. Northumb.* ed. Foster, 88–89; *Northumb. Co. Hist.* x. 280; *Vis. of the North* (Surtees Soc. cxxii), 38–41. [2] *LP Hen. VIII,* i, ii, iv, v, viii, xi–xvi, xviii, xix, add; M. H. and R. Dodds, *Pilgrimage of Grace,* ii. 232; Alnwick castle mss letters and pprs. 2, f. 27; *Northumb. Co. Hist.* viii. 215. [3] *CPR 1494–1509,* pp. 200, 213, 487; *LP Hen. VIII,* i; *Northumb. Co. Hist,* x. 264–5, 280; M. E. James, *A Tudor Magnate and the Tudor State* (Borthwick Pprs. xxx), 17–18. [4] *LP Hen. VIII,* iii, iv; *HMC Bath,* iv. 48. [5] *LP Hen. VIII,* i, vii. [6] *Northumb. Co. Hist.* ix. 82–83; *LP Hen. VIII,* vii, xiv; E368/305/1, 11, 306/16; Hodgson, *Northumb.* i(1), 364. [7] M. H. and R. Dodds, i. 199–201; *LP Hen. VIII,* xi–xiv. [8] *LP Hen. VIII,* xii, xiv–xviii, xx; Hodgson, ii(3), 232; Cott. Calig. B6(234), f. 432. [9] Wards 7/2/47; C1/425/14; St.Ch.2/18/216; *Northumb. Co. Hist.* x. 265–6, 280; *Vis. of the North,* 40–41; Admiralty, Greenwich Hosp. deeds 75/81.

M.J.T.

RADCLIFFE, Sir Henry (by 1533–93).

MALDON	1555
CHICHESTER	1559
HAMPSHIRE	1571
PORTSMOUTH	1572

b. by 1533, 2nd s. of Henry Radcliffe, 2nd Earl of Sussex, by 1st w. Elizabeth, da. of Thomas Howard, 2nd Duke of Norfolk; bro. of Sir Thomas*. *m.* lic. 6 Feb. 1549, Honor, da. and coh. of Anthony Pound (*d.*1547) of Drayton in Farlington, Hants, 1s. Kntd. 2 Oct. 1553; *suc.* bro. as 4th Earl of Sussex 9 June 1583; KG nom. 22 Apr. inst. 19 Dec. 1589.[1]

MP [I] 1560.

Sewer by 1556; PC [I] 1557; lt. Leix and Offaly 1557–64; constable, Portchester castle and lt. Southbere forest 14 June 1560; jt. steward, crown possessions in Essex 1561; warden and capt. Portsmouth May 1571–d., high steward 9 Sept. 1590–d.; j.p.q. Hants 1573/74, commr. musters by 1576, jt. (with William Paulet†, 3rd Marquess of Winchester) ld. lt. 1585–d.; trier of petitions in the Lords, Parlts. of 1586, 1589, 1593.[2]

Henry Radcliffe can have been scarcely of age when Edward VI died but he was already married, for in May 1553 his wife and her sister came into their inheritance in Hampshire. He and his father early declared their support for Mary and he was knighted at her coronation. The earl, a great land-owner in Essex, obtained one of the Maldon seats in the Queen's first Parliament for his servant John Raymond, and undoubtedly did the same for his son two years later. As a Member of this Parliament Radcliffe is not listed as having voted against one of the government's bills, as did his uncle Sir Humphrey Radcliffe, but both were doubtless concerned with the unsuccessful bill for the Countess of Sussex's jointure. In July 1556 Radcliffe was granted by the Queen an annuity of 50 marks for his services, and in the following year he went to Ireland in the service of the lord deputy, his brother Thomas, Earl of Sussex since the death of their father in February 1557. The two brothers returned to attend Elizabeth's coronation and to sit in her first Parliament, but then went back to Ireland, from which Radcliffe came home for good in 1565. He was to sit twice more in the Commons and after succeeding to the earldom he took his place in the Lords. He died on 14 Dec. 1593.[3]

[1] Date of birth estimated from age at brother's i.p.m., C142/210/84. *CP*. [2] *CPR*, 1555-7, p. 516; 1558-60, p. 390; *CSP Dom.* 1547-80, p. 413; 1581-90, pp. 245-6; 1591-4, p. 418; *Cal. Carew Pprs.* 1515-74, passim; *CSP Ire.* 1509-73 passim; R. East, *Extracts from Portsmouth Recs.* 133, 137; Lansd. 4, f. 156; 56, ff. 168 seq.; *LJ*, ii. 113, 145, 169. [3] *CPR*, 1553, p. 6; 1555-7, p. 516; *Chron. Q. Jane and Q. Mary* (Cam. Soc. xlviii), 5; *CJ*, i. 44-46; *CSP Ire.* 1509-73, pp. 136, 138, 167 et passim; *Cal. Carew Pprs.* 1515-74, pp. 266, 272, 279; PCC 19 Dixy.

D.F.C.

RADCLIFFE, Sir Humphrey (1508/9-66), of Elstow, Beds. and Beddington, Surr.

BEDFORDSHIRE	1553 (Mar.), 1554 (Apr.), 1554 (Nov.), 1555,[1] 1558
MALDON	1559

b. 1508/9, 3rd s. of Robert Radcliffe, 1st Earl of Sussex, by 1st w. Elizabeth, da. of Henry Stafford, 2nd Duke of Buckingham; half-bro. of Sir John Radcliffe*. *m.* Elizabeth or Isabel, da. and h. of Edmund Harvey of Elstow, 2s. Edward† and Thomas† at least 3da. Kntd. by June 1536.[2]

Gent. pens. 1540-52, lt. 1552-5 or later; j.p. Beds. 1554, q. 1561-*d.*; sheriff, Beds. and Bucks. 1558-9; steward, manor of Elstow 1563-*d.*[3]

Named after his maternal great-grandfather, Humphrey Radcliffe was introduced at court by his father, the 1st Earl of Sussex. As a boy he was contracted to marry one of the two daughters of John Marney*, 2nd Baron Marny, but in the event Catherine Marney married his brother George and he the daughter of a courtier. In 1536 he took part in the celebrations marking the King's marriage to Jane Seymour and he seems to have been one of the young men knighted then by Henry VIII. A year later he attended the christening of Prince Edward

and not long after the funeral of the Queen. Appointed to the new bodyguard set up in 1540 he was present at the reception of Anne of Cleves and all the main state occasions throughout the 1540s and early 50s. He served in the expedition which took Boulogne, but he is not known to have fought in either Edward VI's Scottish war or Mary's French one.[4]

On his marriage Radcliffe settled in Surrey, where his father-in-law, Edmund Harvey, was keeper of the Carew property at Beddington following the execution of Sir Nicholas Carew*, but on receiving the manor of Elstow from Harvey in July 1553 he migrated to Bedfordshire. By that time he had already sat in the previous Parliament as one of the knights for the shire, having been returned in opposition to a directive from the Privy Council in support of Sir John St. John and Lewis Dyve. Dyve was elected, but St. John was passed over in favour of Radcliffe. Why St. John, who had sat for the county at least twice before, should have been replaced this time is a matter for speculation, as is the choice of Radcliffe, a man 20 years younger than St. John and without experience of local management or of the House. His position at court may have commended him although he lacked government support. (It may not be without significance that his nephew Thomas Radcliffe, Lord Fitzwalter, was not summoned to the Lords on this occasion, as were the heirs to other earldoms, but also sat as a knight of the shire.) His local affiliation, standing at court and noble kin explain his repeated election as one of the knights for Bedfordshire in all but one of Mary's Parliaments. His regular appearance in the House does not seem to have brought him into prominence there. The only mention of him in the Journal concerns a grant of privilege on 28 Oct. 1555 to one of his servants who had been arrested by the sheriff of Middlesex, but before the year was out he is known to have joined the opposition in defeating a government bill. Queen Mary put him on the Bedfordshire bench but replaced him as lieutenant of the pensioners.[5]

Edward Underhill* thought that Radcliffe 'always favoured the gospel', but the only evidence he adduced was that as lieutenant of the pensioners Radcliffe had seen to it that Underhill continued to receive his wages while in disfavour with the Marian regime, and had further defended him before the steward of the Household, a course of conduct which looks as much like the reaction of a commanding officer to an attack on one of his subordinates as it does that of a co-religionist. In 1564 he was rated 'indifferent' to the Anglican settlement. Re-elected in 1559 for a borough amenable to his family's influence, he failed to find a seat three years later and died on 13 Aug. 1566.[6]

[1] *CJ*, i. 42. [2] Aged 57 at death according to MI, *Beds. N. and Q.* i. 126–7. Doyle, *Baronetage*, iii. 481; *Vis. Beds.* (Harl. Soc. xix), 48, 65; *CPR*, 1558–60, p. 2; *Beds. N. and Q.* i. 90; *LP Hen. VIII*, xv. [3] *LP Hen. VIII*, iv, x, xiv(2) 783; LC2/2, f. 41v; *Rep. R. Comm. of 1552* (Archs. of Brit. Hist. and Culture iii), 94; *Chron. Q. Jane and Q. Mary* (Cam. Soc. xlviii), 128; *Narr. Ref.* (ibid. lxxvii), 161, 168; *CPR*, 1553–4, p. 17; 1560–3, p. 518; information from W. J. Tighe. [4] *LP Hen. VIII*, vi, xii, xiv–xvi, xix; *Archaeologia*, xii. 389; *Lit. Rems. Edw. VI*, pp. ccc, 1; Add. 34320, f. 84v; *CP*, vi. 184. [5] Strype, *Eccles. Memorials*, ii(2), 65; *LP Hen. VIII*, xiv, xvi; *VCH Beds.* iii. 281, 293; *CPR*, 1550–3, pp. 458–9; 1553, p. 232; 1558–60, p. 2; 1560–3, p. 518; *CJ*, i. 42; Guildford mus. Loseley 1331/2. [6] *Narr. Ref.* 161, 168; *Cam. Misc.* ix(3), 28; *Beds. N. and Q.* i. 126–7; Pevsner, *Beds., Hunts. and Peterborough*, 84.

N.M.F.

RADCLIFFE, Sir John (1539–68), of Old Cleeve, Som.

CASTLE RISING 1558
GRAMPOUND 1559

bap. 31 Dec. 1539, 4th s. of Robert Radcliffe, 1st Earl of Sussex, by 3rd w. Mary, da. of Sir John Arundell of Lanherne, Cornw.; half-bro. of Sir Humphrey Radcliffe*. *m.* Anne, *s.p.* Kntd. 22 Feb. 1547.[1]

The 1st Earl of Sussex died three years after the birth of his youngest son John Radcliffe, who was brought up by his mother and her second husband Henry, 12th Earl of Arundel. It was as the son, half-brother and stepson of three earls that Radcliffe was knighted, when only in his eighth year, at the coronation of Edward VI. He received the manor of Cleeve from his father or half-brother and when he was 15 his stepfather was licensed to grant him Northam manor in Devon. His precocious election to Mary's last Parliament he must likewise have owed to these two kinsmen: Castle Rising belonged to the dukes of Norfolk, and the 4th Duke was Arundel's son-in-law and Sussex's cousin. This was the first occasion on which the borough returned Members and Norfolk may have secured its enfranchisement to provide his servant Sir Nicholas Lestrange with a seat. Nothing is known of Radcliffe's role in the House but he was presumably interested in the Act for the assurance of the Countess of Sussex's jointure (4 and 5 Phil. and Mary, no.13) passed during the first session. He was re-elected at Castle Rising to the next Parliament but was replaced by the duke's stepfather Thomas Steyning and sat instead for Grampound, where he presumably owed his return to one of his mother's family. His half-brother Sir Humphrey Radcliffe also sat in both Parliaments. Radcliffe died on 9 Nov. 1568.[2]

[1] Baptism given in H. B. Wilson, *St. Laurence Pountney*, 129. *CP*, xii(1), 519–20; PCC 21 Babington; *DNB* (Radcliffe, Robert) incorrectly gives the earl's second wife as Sir John's mother. [2] Collinson, *Som.* iii. 512; *CPR*, 1553–4, p. 372; 1563–6, p. 8; *Reg. St. Olave, Hart St.* (Harl. Soc. xlvi), 108, 120.

R.V.

RADCLIFFE, Sir Thomas (1525/26–83), of Woodham Walter, Essex.

NORFOLK 1553 (Mar.)

b. 1525/26, 1st s. of Henry Radcliffe, 2nd Earl of Sussex, by 1st w. Elizabeth, da. of Thomas Howard, 2nd Duke of Norfolk; bro. of Sir Henry*. *m.* (1) ?Mar. 1545, Elizabeth (*d.*Jan. 1555), da. of Thomas Wriothesley, 1st Earl of Southampton, 1da. *d.v.p.*; (2) lic. 26 Apr. 1555, Frances (*d.*1589), da. of Sir William Sidney of Penshurst, Kent. Kntd. 30 Sept. 1544; *summ.* to Lords in fa.'s barony as Baron Fitzwalter 14 Aug. 1553; *suc.* fa. as 3rd Earl of Sussex 17 Feb. 1557, KG nom. 23 Apr. 1557, inst. 9 Jan. 1558.[1]

Warden and capt. Portsmouth 24 Nov. 1549–Apr. 1551; commr. relief, Norf. and Norwich 1550; carver by 1553; gent. privy chamber to King Philip June 1554; j.p. Essex, Norf. 1554, q. Suff. 1564; trier of petitions in the Lords, Parlts. of 1555, 1559, 1571, 1572; ld. dep. [I] 27 Apr. 1556–60, ld. lt. 6 May 1560–Oct. 1565; warden and c.j. forests south of Trent 3 July 1557; capt. gent. pens. 1557–*d.*; pres. council in the north July 1568–Oct. 1572; PC 30 Dec. 1570; ld. chamberlain, the Household July 1572–*d.*; steward, New Hall (Beaulieu), Essex July 1572, Maldon, Essex at *d.*[2]

Thomas Radcliffe probably received the greater part of his education in the household of Stephen Gardiner, bishop of Winchester; there is no basis for the statement that he was at Cambridge and Gray's Inn. From November 1542, when his father succeeded to the earldom, he bore the title of Lord Fitzwalter, which he retained until his own succession 15 years later. The marriage arranged for him in January 1543 with Elizabeth Wriothesley probably took place in 1545, after he had served in the Boulogne campaign and had been knighted. In 1546 he accompanied Gardiner on a mission to the Netherlands and John Dudley, Viscount Lisle, on one to France, and he was one of the canopy-bearers at Henry VIII's funeral.[3]

The fall of the Howards in 1546 had left Fitzwalter's father the leading nobleman in East Anglia, although he counted less in national affairs. For Fitzwalter himself the new reign first brought the setbacks of Gardiner's imprisonment and the dismissal of his father-in-law Wriothesley, but luck was on his side at Pinkie, where he narrowly escaped death, and he was to share in Wriothesley's temporary return to favour when Dudley rose to power. It was to Wriothesley that he clearly owed his first office, the captaincy of Portsmouth, which he was to surrender after Wriothesley's death, and before accompanying the Marquess of Northampton on his mission to France in 1551. Less easy to interpret is Fitzwalter's election for Norfolk to the Parliament of March 1553. He was eligible because, unlike the heirs to the earldoms of Bedford and Shrewsbury and the Dudley dukedom of Northumberland, he was not summoned to the Lords. Whether—and, if so, why—he was passed over at the instance of Northumberland, there seems to be no way of determining, but it could scarcely have been by coincidence that his fellow-knight was the duke's second son Robert Dudley. A stranger to the county, Dudley had been by-elected for Norfolk to the previous Parliament, and the decision that Fitzwalter should take the other seat, instead of appearing in the Lords, could have been an answer to the intrusion: the two men were to become bitter rivals in the reign of Elizabeth. That the Radcliffes, father and son, were not reckoned among Northumberland's firm supporters is implied by their omission from a list of those expected to rally certain shires to Jane Grey, and although both of them signed the instrument providing for her succession, on the King's death they and the younger son Henry declared for Mary and joined her with their following at Framlingham. Fitzwalter attended Edward VI's funeral as a carver.[4]

Under Mary, Fitzwalter came rapidly to the fore. Granted an annuity of £133, probably for his service against Wyatt's rebellion, he took the news of its suppression to the Emperor, to whom the imperial ambassador Renard commended him as an able and learned man. Although he was said to have opposed the Spanish marriage, he accompanied the 1st Earl of Bedford on the mission to escort Philip to England and was to become a favourite with the King, who gave him a jewelled sword and was present at his second marriage. In 1555 he was appointed to a mission to France to announce that the Queen was thought to be pregnant, and early in the following year he was sent to the new Emperor. He had also been summoned in his father's barony to the first four Parliaments of the reign. There is no surviving Lords Journal for the Parliament of October 1553 and he was unable to attend that of April 1554 because of his mission to Spain, but he was present for slightly less than half the Parliament of November 1554 and some three-quarters of that of 1555. In 1555, when his younger brother sat in the Commons for Maldon, he was appointed a trier of petitions for Gascony and two bills, for the punishment of exiles and for the re-edifying of decayed houses of husbandry and for the increase of tillage, were committed to him; he also voted against the bill to deprive Bennet Smith of benefit of clergy and the bill to re-edify four mills near Hereford and must have been concerned with the unsuccessful bill for the divorced Countess of Sussex's jointure.[5]

Before the next Parliament Radcliffe had both succeeded to the earldom of Sussex and been appointed lord deputy of Ireland, but after spending a year and a half in that country he was licensed to return to England and was able to attend the first session of Mary's last Parliament, during which the bill granting the 1st Baron Rich's honor of Rayleigh to the Queen was committed to him and a measure for his own wife's jointure was enacted (4 and 5 Phil, and Mary, no. 13). He went back to Ireland two weeks after the prorogation and although on 31 Oct. 1558 he was licensed to return 'to confer upon the state and affairs of that realm' he was still there when Parliament met again in November and did not leave until after the Queen's death. He had been named an executor of her will and was apparently present at her funeral as captain of the gentlemen pensioners: by hereditary right he served as chief sewer at the coronation of Elizabeth. Although reappointed to his Irish post, he attended the first Parliament of the new reign and thereafter was regular in his appearances in the Lords, missing only the first session of the Parliament of 1563, and had many bills committed to him: he also exercised parliamentary patronage in the borough of Maldon. During the second session of the Parliament of 1563 he spoke against the bill on the consecration of bishops and voted with the Catholic party against it: another opponent of this measure, William Stanley*, 3rd Lord Monteagle, named Sussex as his proxy in 1580. Notwithstanding this indication of nonconformity, Sussex was unfailingly loyal to the Elizabethan regime and after his service against the northern rebellion of 1569—when, however, he came briefly under suspicion for his leniency and because his half-brother Egremont Radcliffe had joined the rebels—he was appointed to the Privy Council. He died on 9 June 1583 at his house in Bermondsey and was buried a month later at Boreham, Essex. His brother Sir Henry Radcliffe succeeded him as 4th Earl of Sussex.[6]

[1] Aged 57 at death. CP; LP Hen. VIII, xviii; Mar. Lic. London (Harl. Soc. xxv), 16; Susan M. Doran, 'Pol. career of Thomas Radcliffe, 3rd Earl of Sussex' (London Univ. Ph.D. thesis, 1977); DNB. [2] CPR, 1549–51, p. 115; 1553, pp. 351, 361; 1553–4, pp. 19, 22; 1555–7, pp. 56, 318; 1563–6, p. 27; 1569–72, pp. 361–2; APC, iii. 261; Stowe 571, f. 30v; CSP Span. 1554, p. 297; LJ, i. 492, 542, 667, 703. [3] LP Hen. VIII, xiv, xxi; Ath. Cant. i. 462; Strype, Eccles. Memorials, ii(2), 298. [4] Holinshed, Chron. iii. 876, 879; CSP For. 1547–53, p. 123; M. A. R. Graves, 'The Tudor House of Lords 1547–58' (Otago Univ. Ph.D. thesis, 1974), i. 149–51; Lansd. 103, art. 1; Chron. Q. Jane and Q. Mary (Cam. Soc. xlviii), 99; LC2/4/1, f. 19v. [5] Lansd. 156, f. 97; CSP Span. 1553, p. 441; 1554, pp. 86, 93, 96, 149 seq.; PCC 52 Brudenell; CSP Ven. 1555–6, p. 58; APC, v. 27, 54, 126; CSP For. 1553–8, p. 220; Graves, ii. 294–6. [6] Graves, ii. 294–6; LC2/4/2; LJ, i. passim ex inf. Susan M. Doran; CSP Span. 1558–67, p. 596.

R.V.

RAGG, Robert (by 1517–53 or later), of Derby.

DERBY 1547, 1553 (Mar.)

b. by 1517, poss. s. of William Ragg of Wirksworth.[1] Bailiff, Derby 1538–9, 1546–7.[2]

Robert Ragg was usually styled gentleman, but his enemies called him yeoman. He may have been the son of the William Ragg, described as a yeoman of Wirksworth, who in 1503 was pardoned for aiding and abetting Roger Vernon in the abduction and rape of Margaret Kebell: before the suppression of Darley abbey a William Ragg had purchased the next presentation to Mackworth church, and in 1543 by virtue of a prior arrangement with the abbot Robert Ragg appointed a new incumbent to the living.[3]

Whatever his chief occupation, Robert Ragg probably derived part of his income from coal mining. It appears that before the Dissolution the abbot of Darley had leased to him for £5 a year certain coal pits and mills at Ripley and had allowed him timber to work the pits. Ragg retained the pits until at least 1542, but in the course of the following five years he sold his interest to Thomas Sutton, who was to be his fellow-Member in 1547. By March 1545 Ragg was the tenant of property called St. Helen's in Derby. From the prveious until at least April 1549 he and Oliver Thatcher, his fellow-bailiff during 1538–9, leased the tithes and certain tithe barns in Derby, altogether worth £33 12s.5d.: these were still held by Ragg in May 1553. He appeared before the Exchequer on two occasions during 1546 on charges of keeping a dicing house and a bowling alley in Derby: a day was appointed for the allegations to be heard before a local jury but no further process is recorded.[4]

Ragg's Membership of Parliament was presumably the natural extension of his municipal career. If the allegations made against him in the previous year had been substantiated, the honour of representing his home town in 1547 may have come second in his mind to the freedom from arrest that it conferred, a privilege which perhaps also throws some light on his return to the following Parliament, when his name was inserted over an erasure on the town's indenture. Nothing is known about Ragg's part in either Parliament, and the date of his death has not been discovered.[5]

[1] Date of birth estimated from first reference. [2] W. Hutton, *Derby*, 80. [3] C219/19/26; *CPR*, 1494–1509, p. 336; J. C. Cox, *Derbys. Churches*, iv. 286. [4] C1/1156/85; *LP Hen. VIII*, xvii, xix; *CPR*, 1548–9, pp. 405–6; 1553, p. 11; E159/324/rec. Hil. r. 37, 325/rec. East rr. 14, 33. [5] C219/20/40.

C.J.B.

RAILTON, Richard (by 1522–75), of Canterbury, Kent.

CANTERBURY   1554 (Nov.)[1]

b. by 1522. *m.* Catherine, 2s. 2da.[2]
    Common councilman, Canterbury 1552–5 or later, alderman by 1557–70, mayor 1562–3.[3]

Richard Railton was styled yeoman when he was admitted to the freedom of Canterbury by redemption in 1543, but he seems to have had legal training: in 1552 he was referred to as attorney with one Christopher Scott against the city in a land dispute, and in 1569 he was granted a fee of 40s. a year for his 'pains, travail and counsel' for the city. His first service to it appears to have been in 1550–1 when he was repaid 3s.4d. by the chamberlain 'that he laid out when the trial of our custumal was at Westminster'.[4]

Railton was a common councilman and perhaps already an alderman when he sat in his only Parliament. He did not see it out, for both he and his fellow-Member Nicholas Fish were found absent when the House was called early in 1555 and were consequently informed against in the King's bench in the following Easter term. As no further process was taken against either of them it is likely that their absence was not regarded as a gesture of opposition. On 15 Jan., the day before the dissolution, Railton was present at a Canterbury burmote which resolved that no future Member for the city should be paid out of its chamber and that any mayor, alderman or councillor attempting to transgress this rule should be fined £10. This resolution confirmed, with the addition of the penal clause, one passed in the previous year, and although neither of them excluded payment by special levy Railton's decision in 1570 to release the city from what it owed him for his service in Parliament shows that he had not been paid.[5]

Railton's civic career under Elizabeth was not unaffected by controversy. His term as mayor followed the disputed mayoral election of 1561 when the two candidates named, as was customary, by the outgoing mayor and his brethren were rejected by the commonalty because they were 'perversely given to further the order of religion established'; as Railton was one of the two 'discreet men' chosen to replace those rejected he may be presumed to have been inoffensive in religion. Eight years later he was himself in trouble for neglect of his aldermanic duties. Warned in December 1569 that this might cost him banishment or a fine, in the following July he was deprived of the aldermanship; after being referred with his consent to two of the city's counsel, Robert Alcock[†] and William Lovelace[†], this decision was confirmed by the burmote with the proviso that he should never again be an alderman,' although the threat of banishment was lifted and the fine suspended. When in October he remitted the fee of 40s. granted him ten months earlier the burmote declared itself well pleased.[6]

For all this, Railton styled himself one of the

aldermen of Canterbury when he made his will on 6 July 1575. He left his house in the parish of St. Andrew to his wife, with remainder to his sons Robert and Richard and his two daughters. To Robert he left £5 and to Richard £3 on completion of his apprenticeship, and when Robert inherited the house he was to give Richard £30 as a stock. The daughters, both married, were given two silver spoons each, and the wife had the residue of goods and was named executrix. The will was proved on 22 Oct. 1575.[7]

[1] Huntington Lib. Hastings mss Parl. pprs. [2] Date of birth estimated from admission as freeman. Canterbury prob. reg. A42, f. 22. [3] Canterbury chamberlains' accts. 10, 11 passim; burmote bk. 1542–78 passim. [4] *Freemen of Canterbury*, ed. Cowper, col. 295; Canterbury burmote bk. 1542–78, ff. 68v, 232; chamberlains' accts. 1550–1. [5] KB29/188, r. 48; Canterbury burmote bk. 1542–78, ff. 83v, 90v, 247. [6] Canterbury burmote bk. 1542–78, ff. 150–1, 163, 240, 245, 247. [7] Canterbury prob. reg. A42, f. 22.

H.M.

RALEGH, Adam (c.1480–1545 or later), of Fardel and Plympton St. Mary, Devon; London, and Southwark, Surr.

TOTNES   1529
PLYMPTON ERLE   1545

b. c.1480, 2nd s. of Walter Ralegh (*d.*by 1486) of Fardel by Margaret. *m.* Elizabeth.[1]

A branch of the Ralegh family had been established at Fardel since at least the mid 15th century. His elder brother Wymond's marriage made Adam Ralegh a kinsman of Sir Peter Edgecombe*. The marriage was the outcome of the acquisition by Edgecombe's father in 1486 of the wardship and marriage of Wymond Ralegh, and it sealed the already close association between the families: in 1519 Adam Ralegh was to be one of a group which assured to the King an annuity from Edgecombe's Cornish manors. When he sued out a pardon on 8 Feb. 1510 Ralegh was styled of Cornwood and Fardel, Devon, London, and Southwark, Surrey; his house at Fardel, with its 15th-century chapel, still remains.[2]

It was doubtless to his powerful connexions that Ralegh owed his two or more spells of Membership of the Commons. At the time of the elections to the Parliament of 1529 Edgecombe, who held the manor and castle of Totnes, was sheriff of Devon: Ralegh was also related, through the Edgecombes, to Sir William Courtenay I, who on this occasion was returned as senior knight of the shire. His Membership of this Parliament probably ensured Ralegh's re-election in 1536, when the King asked for the return of the previous Members. Whether he sat again in 1539 we cannot say as the names of the Members for Totnes are lost, but in 1545 he reappeared in the Commons as one of the two representatives of Plympton Erle. He was by then living at Plympton St. Mary (some miles west of Fardel), where in the same year he was assessed at 20*s.* towards the subsidy, and to this residential qualification he could again add the support of the Edgecombe family. Following the attainder of the Marquess of Exeter, who had held the manor and castle of Plympton, Sir Peter Edgecombe and his son Peter had been given custody of many of the forfeited estates; they also had a seat at West Stonehouse, not far from Plymouth, which Ralegh's brother had frequented. Nothing further has been found about Ralegh.[3]

[1] Date of birth estimated from elder brother's, c.1475, M. J. G. Stanford, 'A hist. of the Ralegh fam. of Fardel and Budleigh in the early Tudor period' (London Univ. M.A. thesis, 1955), 114. *Vis. Devon*, ed. Vivian, 639 corrected by *Vis. Devon*, ed. Colby, 180 and Stanford, clxxiv. [2] Stanford, 114; *LP Hen. VIII*, i; Lansd. 16(55), f. 121. [3] E179/98/271; *Trans. Dev. Assoc.* xxxii. 438; M. R. Westcott, 'The estates of the earls of Devon 1485–1538' (Exeter Univ. M.A. thesis, 1958), 83, 197, 244, 294; Stanford, 131.

L.M.K./A.D.K.H.

RALEGH, Walter (1504/5–81), of Hayes Barton in the parish of East Budleigh, Devon.

WAREHAM   1558

b. 1504/5, s. of Wymond Ralegh of Fardel by Elizabeth, da. of Sir Richard Edgecombe† of Cotehele, Cornw. *m.* (1) by 1528, Joan, da. of John Drake of Exmouth, Devon, 2s.; (2) da. of one Darrell of London, 1da.; (3) Catherine, da. of Sir Philip Champernon of Modbury, Devon, wid. of Otes or Otho Gilbert (*d.*10 Feb. 1547) of Compton and Greenway, Devon, 2s. Carew† and Walter† 1da. *suc.* fa. 7 July 1512.[1]

J.p. Devon 1547; commr. relief 1550; dep. v.-adm. 1555–8; churchwarden, East Budleigh in 1561.[2]

Walter Ralegh was a child of seven when his father died, a matter which his relatives clearly hoped might be kept from the authorities. No inquisition post mortem was held on Wymond Ralegh until July 1514, and then the jury alleged that the son and heir Walter was 12 years old and that Wymond Ralegh had parted with all his lands in Devon to Sir Peter Edgecombe*. Fardel, the family residence, was held of Sir Nicholas Vaux*, who was determined to have the wardship. In July 1515 Vaux entered into a recognizance to pay £200 for it, and the same month a second inquisition was ordered, to be taken this time by special commissioners, not by the escheator. Their return was closer to the truth: Walter Ralegh was ten, and Sir Peter Edgecombe held the lands not as his own, but to the use of Wymond Ralegh and his heirs. A month later Edgecombe undertook to give up both the lands and the boy: in April 1516 the wardship was granted to Vaux and in May Edgecombe's recognizance was cancelled, the condition being fulfilled. In November 1526 Walter Ralegh, having come of age, was granted livery of his lands.[3]

Ralegh lived most of his life at Hayes Barton, near Exmouth, a property which he leased from Richard Duke*, and where he was assessed for the subsidy in 1545 on lands worth £60. Sailors from Exmouth rescued him during the western rebellion from people near Exeter whom he had threatened with dire penalties if they disobeyed the new religious observances. Ralegh's attitude in 1549 apparently did not prevent his conforming under Mary or holding local office during her reign. His only known election (he was so powerfully allied that he could have sat earlier) came when the war against France was causing anxiety. Presumably he was chosen at Wareham because he was an admiralty man, but his own motive appears to have been personal rather than political. On 5 Feb. 1558, in the third week of the Parliament, four Members were appointed to consider a writ issued by the court of Admiralty for his arrest: three days later the House authorized Ralegh to obtain a writ of privilege, and it was not until a year later that he appeared in court to answer. He was found guilty of depriving the plaintiff of £200 by restoring a prize to its owner (although the Privy Council had ordered the ship to be returned) and sentenced to pay half the costs, but he was not made to compensate the plaintiff. The case appears to have been considered mainly as an exercise in the perennial dispute between the Admiralty and the Council. Between the two sessions of the Parliament Ralegh served as a petty captain for the defence of Devon and was ordered with a ship to join the fleet at Portsmouth.[4]

If Ralegh was the loser in 1559, at other times he undoubtedly profited from his office. In August 1557 his ship the *Katherine Raleigh* of Exmouth captured a Portuguese vessel which he pretended was a prize from the French, a ruse which did not deceive the admiralty officers. Since 1544 he had been actively (if not personally) engaged in privateering and piracy. In February 1553 he was committed to the Fleet on a charge arising from these pursuits but released in the following month after giving bonds to the admiralty judge to appear before him when called. Early in 1554 he aided the rebel Sir Peter Carew* by providing him with a boat in which to escape from England.[5]

Ralegh seems to have retired to a quieter life about the time of the accession of Elizabeth but he must, even in his old age, have given a stimulus to the seafaring exploits of his son and namesake, and of his stepson, Sir Humphrey Gilbert†. By 1569 he had left Hayes Barton and was living mainly at his house in Exeter, but he died at Colaton Raleigh on 19 Feb. 1581 and was buried at Exeter four days

later. His eldest son inherited the manors of Fardel and Withycombe Raleigh; the two other manors which Ralegh had inherited from his father he had entailed upon his third wife with remainder to his sons.[6]

[1] Date of birth estimated from age at fa.'s second i.p.m., C142/30/45. *Vis. Devon*, ed. Vivian, 639; M. J. G. Stanford, 'A hist. of the Ralegh fam. of Fardel and Burleigh in the early Tudor period' (London Univ. M.A. thesis, 1955), 140–1. [2] *CPR*, 1547–8, p. 83; 1553, p. 352; Stanford, 256, 271, 273. [3] C82/467; 142/29/60, 30/45; *LP Hen. VIII*, ii, iv; Stanford, 144–7. [4] *The description of the citie of Excester* (Devon and Cornw. Rec. Soc. xi), 62–63; Stanford, 144–7, 165, 229, 271, 273, 283–99; *CJ*, i. 48; SP11/12/70. [5] Stanford, 180, 276–8; *APC*, iv. 223, 237; *CSP Dom.* 1547–80, p. 59. [6] Stanford, 333–4, 341–2; C142/194/2.

H.M.

RAND, Nicholas (by 1503–58/59), of Northampton.

NORTHAMPTON 1529, 1555

b. by 1503. *m.* Alice, 3s. 1da.[1]
Bailiff, Northampton 1524–5, mayor 1534–5, 1551–2.[2]

Nicholas Rand was a Northampton draper, whose descendants were to establish themselves at Great Billing, a village in the locality. His election to the Parliament of 1529 was evidently an extension of his municipal career and anticipated his first mayoralty. On the list of Members revised in the spring of 1532 his name appears as 'Rous', but as no family of that name can be traced in Northamptonshire A. F. Pollard's suggestion that this was a copyist's error is to be accepted. Nothing has come to light about Rand's role in this Parliament, although he evidently absented himself from part of the fourth session. On 11 May 1532 the mayor of Northampton acknowledged an order from the Council to fine him and two other freemen for disregarding one of the town's charters, but all three refused payment to the King's officers as they had appealed 'to the law' against the imposition. Cromwell rebuked the mayor for the 'sinister' support given by the townsmen to their colleagues, but the outcome of the affair is not known. It is possible that Rand's offence and his wish to evade punishment for it lie behind his election in 1529. Presumably he served for the town in the following Parliament, that of 1536, when the King asked for the re-election of the previous Members, and perhaps again in 1539, 1542 and 1545, Parliaments for which the names of the town's Members are unknown. In Mary's reign he was again returned to Parliament, this time taking the senior place. Neither he nor his fellow John Balgye could have commended himself to the government by their conduct in the House for both men joined the opposition led by Sir Anthony Kingston to a government bill. While he was in London for this

Parliament he pressed for the renewal of several leases held by the town.[3]

Rand made his will on 18 Dec. 1558, providing for his wife, children, kinsmen and friends. He appointed his wife executrix and John Long and John Balgye overseers of the will, which was proved on 16 Jan. 1559.[4]

[1] Date of birth estimated from first reference. PCC 29 Welles. [2] Recs. Northampton, ed. Cox and Markham ii. 551, 559. [3] LP Hen. VIII, v, add. Recs. Northampton, i. 157, 170–1; Northampton ass. bk. 30, 43, 52, 147, 301, 315; APC, iii. 465; Guildford mus. Loseley 1331/2; Bridges, Northants, i. 406. [4] PCC 29 Welles.

S.M.T.

RANDALL (RANDOLPH), Nicholas (by 1519–61/62), of Truro, Cornw.

TRURO 1547,[1] 1553 (Mar.), 1553 (Oct.), 1555, 1558, 1559

b. by 1519. ?m. Alice.[2]

Constable, Trematon castle, Cornw. Sept. 1542–d.; havener, duchy of Cornw., Sept. 1542–d.; bailiff, Aylewarton and Penzance, Cornw. Apr. 1543; comptroller and collector of customs, duchy of Cornw., 1554/55–d.[3]

Nicholas Randall was described as a yeoman of Truro when in 1540 he obtained a 21-year lease of all the lands in Cornwall formerly belonging to the Black Friars of Truro, together with their former conventual buildings in the town. Six years later he received a lease of the duchy of Cornwall manor of Tybesta in Creed at the suit of a brother of Robert Heneage, joint auditor of the duchy. His residence in Truro and his position as a minor duchy official well qualified him to sit for the borough in Parliament, and he did so six times, but as he was not chosen for either the second or third Parliament of Mary's reign his election was not a foregone conclusion. Little is known about his part in the House: he did not support the Protestant opposition in 1553, but two years later (when his name was inserted in a different hand on the indenture) he voted with many other west-country Members against a government bill.[4]

Randall died during the 12 months preceding May 1562 since the duchy accounts record his death during the 16th year of his tenure of Tybesta. The Anne Randall living in Truro after 1562 may have been his widow.[5]

[1] Hatfield 207. [2] Date of birth estimated from first reference. C3/119/90. [3] LP Hen. VIII, xvii, xviii; Duchy Cornw. RO, 228/3v; E6.1/23v. [4] LP Hen. VIII, xvi, xxi; E315/212, f. 137v; Guildford mus. Loseley 1331/2. [5] Duchy Cornw. RO, 134, m. 4v; 225, m. 4v; C3/119/90.

J.J.G.

RANDALL (RENDALL), Richard (by 1520–58 or later), of London.

DORCHESTER 1547[1]

b. by 1520. educ. I. Temple. m. by Aug. 1555, Isabel Beake of Haddenham, Bucks., wid. of Edward Weldon* (d.25 May 1551) of Bray, Berks.[2]

Richard Randall was a London lawyer, possibly a relative of the Robert Randall who was living in Dorchester in 1547. He obtained a lease from augmentations of some property in Gloucestershire in 1541, and four years later he and a colleague in the Inner Temple, Robert Keilway II*, bought a manor in Kent. In August 1548 Randall received a large grant of monastic and chantry land in Dorset, London and Wiltshire, for which he paid £661; the grant included two burgages in Dorchester which had formerly belonged to the fraternity of St. Mary. When in the same month the rest of the property of this chantry was granted to the freemen of Dorchester, it is likely that Randall, then the town's junior Member, negotiated the deal.[3]

Randall probably owed his seat in the first Edwardian Parliament to Keilway, who was known to the high steward of Dorchester, Sir Thomas Trenchard, and who also stood close to the Protector Somerset. If Randall enjoyed Seymour support for his election in 1547, he may have been similarly favoured on the previous occasion, from which many returns do not survive. By 1553 the Seymour family was in eclipse, and Randall is not known to have sat in the second Edwardian Parliament. He was active in the affairs of his inn during the 1550s although he had refused to be elected a bencher in 1541. Since he last appeared at the Inner Temple parliament on 26 June 1558, he may have died in the epidemic of that year.[4]

[1] Hatfield 207. [2] Date of birth estimated from first reference. PCC 31 More. [3] C. H. Mayo, Recs. Dorchester, 333; LP Hen. VIII xvi, xx; CPR, 1547–8, p. 309; 1548–9, pp. 44–46. [4] Cal. I.T. Recs. i. 129 seq.

H.M.

RANDALL, William, of Weymouth, Dorset.

WEYMOUTH 1554 (Nov.)[1]

William Randall was chosen by his fellow-townsmen to be their junior Member in the third Parliament of Mary's reign; one of Weymouth's two bailiffs (the returning officers for the election) was one Robert Randall, presumably a kinsman. Randall and his fellow-Member John Phelips, left the Parliament early without having first obtained permission, and during the Easter term of 1555 they were informed against in the King's bench. A writ of venire facias was directed to the sheriff of Somerset and Dorset, but no further process is recorded. Both on the election indenture and in the indictment Randall is styled 'the younger' to distinguish him from a namesake in the town, a merchant, who had held municipal office earlier and who was perhaps his father. Nothing more has come to light about Randall; his experience at Westminster did not apparently lead to other duties at Weymouth although men of that name continued to hold office in the town during the next few decades.[2]

[1] Huntington Lib. Hastings mss Parl. pprs.; C219/282/13. [2] KB27/1176 rex roll 16; C219/24/55, 25/38, 282/13; St.Ch.2/32/95; *LP Hen. VIII*, vi; LR6/12/1; E122/122/5.

H.M.

RANDOLPH, Thomas (1522/23–90), of St. Peter's Hill, London and Milton, Kent.

ST. IVES or NEW ROMNEY	1558
GRANTHAM	1559
ST. IVES	1572
MAIDSTONE	1584, 1586, 1589

b. 1522/23, 2nd s. of Avery Randolph of Badlesmere, Kent by Anne, da. of Sir John Gaynsford of Crowhurst, Surr. *educ.* Canterbury sch.; Christ Church, Oxf., BA 1545, BCL 1548, suppl. DCL 1566, 1574. *m.* (1) 1571, Anne, da. of Thomas Walsingham[†] of Chislehurst, Kent, *s.p.*; (2) by 1575, Ursula, da. of Henry Copinger of Buxhall, Suff., 3s. prob. 3da.[1]

Notary public by Apr. 1548; principal, Broadgates Hall 21 Nov. 1549–14 Oct. 1553; envoy to Germany 1558, Scotland 1559–66, Russia 1568–9, Scotland 1570, 1572, France 1573, 1576, Scotland 1578, 1581, 1586; master of the posts 1567–*d.*; constable (by assignment from Sir Robert Constable[†]), Queenborough castle, Kent 1567–*d.*; steward, manors of Merden and Milton, Kent 1567–*d.*; chamberlain, the Exchequer 14 May 1572–*d.*; j.p. Kent 1573/74–*d.*; commr. musters, Kent c.1584.[2]

Thomas Randolph's career at Oxford came to an end shortly after Mary's accession. He then went abroad with his brother Edward and resumed his studies at Paris, where he stayed on after Edward's return to England. He was still in France in the spring of 1557, when the English ambassador Sir Nicholas Wotton, referred to a letter from him, but in the following June he may have accompanied Wotton when the ambassador was recalled on the outbreak of war. In 1558 Randolph was returned by two boroughs, a recently enfranchised Cornish one and a Cinque Port. At St. Ives he could have been sponsored by the lord lieutenant for the south-west, Francis Russell*, 2nd Earl of Bedford, with whom he was soon to be close and whose will he was to witness: as Bedford was an associate of the warden of the Cinque Ports, Sir Thomas Cheyne*, he may also have had a part in the nomination at New Romney, but Randolph's father was a friend of Cheyne's, who in 1558 bequeathed him £10, and his brother-in-law William Crispe was lieutenant of Dover castle. Which of the two boroughs Randolph preferred is not known: his name appears beside both on the two lists of Members for this Parliament, but on the second of these it is marked under

Romney with a circle, possibly an indication that he was absent during the second session, in the course of which he is known to have been abroad again. In September 1558 Wotton returned to France to negotiate for peace, and it was perhaps on his recommendation that Randolph was employed as an English agent in Germany. Some years later Henry Killigrew* recalled that in 1558 Randolph acted both on Queen Mary's instructions and with Princess Elizabeth's knowledge.[3]

It is not certain that Randolph had originally gone abroad because of his Protestantism. Years afterwards, in Scotland, 'his banishment in France for religion' was recalled, with regret that the 'fraternity of religion' then established had since withered; Randolph himself referred to it simply as a time when he had travelled. What is clear is that the accession of Elizabeth brought him new opportunities: the erstwhile scholar, who in his journeyings had met many people and perhaps acquired a taste for diplomacy, was to make his career as an ambassador and a royal official, and to sit in five Parliaments, before his death on 8 June 1590.[4]

[1] Aged 67 at death, Wood, *Ath. Ox.* ed. Bliss, i. 563. Emden, *Biog. Reg. Univ. Oxf. 1501–40*, p. 474; *Vis. Surr.* (Harl. Soc. xliii), 12; CSP Dom. 1547–80, pp. 301, 424; *CSP For.* 1569–71, pp. 176, 529; *London IPMs* (Brit. Rec. Soc. xxxvi), 146–7; *Vis. Suff.* ed. Metcalfe, 129; PCC 75 Drury. [2] Emden, 474; *CSP Dom.* 1547–80, p. 301; 1581–90, p. 672; *CSP Dom. Add.* 1566–79, p. 453; *CPR*, 1566–9, p. 144; 1569–72, p. 448. [3] *CSP For.* 1553–8, p. 299; 1558–9, pp. 5–6, 21–23; 1561–2, p. 631; C. H. Garrett, *Marian Exiles*, 266–7; PCC 1 Chaynay, 45 Windsor; C142/173/91; 193/32/2; *APC*, vi. 13; Wm. Salt Lib. SMS 264; A. C. Miller, *Sir Henry Killigrew*, 23; L. Howard, *A Coll. of Letters from Orig. Mss* (1753), 184; Lansd. 106, f. 31; SP52/6/82. [4] *Melvil's Mems.* (3rd ed.), 231; *CSP For.* 1561–2, pp. 380–2.

H.M./A.D.K.H.

RANDOLPH *see also* RANDALL

RASTELL, John (by 1468–1536), of London.

DUNHEVED	1529

b. by 1468, s. of Thomas Rastell of Coventry, Warws. *educ.* ?M. Temple. *m.* by 1504, Elizabeth, da. of Sir John More of London, 2s. inc. William* 2da.[1]

Coroner, Coventry 1507–9; servant of Sir Edward Belknap by 1512; commr. tenths of spiritualities, Mdx. 1535.[2]

John Rastell was the son of a leading Coventry citizen and Warwickshire justice of the peace. Although he is said to have been born in London, he was admitted in 1489 to the guild of Corpus Christi, Coventry. He was probably the Rastell mentioned in 1503 as an utter barrister of the Middle Temple, for in his early manhood he was busy with legal affairs in Coventry. The city was a centre of Lollardry and in 1507 Rastell was named overseer in the will of an ex-mayor whose bequests included a 'bible in English'. It was soon after his term as coroner that Rastell moved permanently to

London. His marriage into the More family does not necessarily imply earlier residence there, for the Mores probably had connexions with Coventry, but it is doubtless to be numbered with Coventry's wide-ranging business interests among the influences which took Rastell to London and afterwards further afield. In London he entered the service of Sir Edward Belknap, whose many charges in the King's service included the royal works, and thus exchanged the practice of the law for the supervision of carpenters and labourers.[3]

Rastell's duties in this capacity included the preparation of state occasions and the entertainment of the King, his guests and the court. In April 1520 he and Clement Armstrong were employed to make and garnish the roofs of the great banqueting hall built at Guisnes for the Field of Cloth of Gold 'so that no living creature might but joy in the beholding thereof'. These roofs earned high praise from the chronicler Edward Hall I*, as did a pageant devised by Rastell two years later for the King and the Emperor on their way to St. Paul's cathedral, where 'there was builded a place like heaven, curiously painted with clouds, orbs, stars and hierarchies of angels' and with 'a fair lady' issuing out of the clouds to the playing of minstrels and the voices of the angels. More terrestrial was the pageant called the 'Father of Heaven' which Rastell made at Greenwich in 1527 for the reception of the French ambassadors; on this occasion the roof was 'like a very map or chart' of 'the whole earth environed with the sea'. Rastell's combination of artistic creativeness with enthusiasm for geography may have owed something to his brother-in-law Thomas More. It was not long after the publication of Utopia in 1516 that Rastell set off in the Barbara of Greenwich on a voyage of discovery to North America. The expedition was thwarted by his seamen, who refused to go further than Waterford: he went ashore there and may have spent the next two years in Ireland. His advocacy of exploration and interest in pageantry were in turn served by his main occupation from about 1512, that of printing; the most famous of his printer's devices shows the Father of Heaven, the Merman and the Mermaid, the heavenly bodies, and under all the Four Elements. Memories of the medieval pageants of Coventry probably coloured Rastell's literary projects, but the influence most evident at the beginning of his printing venture was his legal training. He embarked on an ambitious scheme of law-printing, employing the small secretary type which he had seen in use at Rouen: in 1516 he completed La Grande Abbregement de le Ley by Anthony Fitzherbert, recorder of Coventry. Among important non-legal books which he printed were The Mery Gestys of the Widow Edith (1525), The Hundred Mery Talys (1526) and Necromantia (n.d.).[4]

Rastell's first press was at 'the Abbot of Winchcombe's place' by the Fleet bridge; later he had a shop on the south side of St. Paul's and finally, in 1519, he moved to Paul's Gate in Cheapside. He also acquired a country residence: in January 1515 he leased a house at Monken Hadley, near High Barnet and not far from Sir John More's. There he did a considerable amount of building, clearing and planting, and 'entertained Master Cromwell . . . at a shooting, running and other games'. In 1524 he leased more land and built himself a house in Finsbury Fields, where he erected the earliest recorded Tudor stage. His property involved Rastell in much litigation, an activity to which he seems to have been prone. In October 1515 Belknap secured for him a grant of the lands and goods of the heretic Richard Hunne and the wardship of Hunne's two daughters; Rastell undertook to pay the crown the girls' dowry but he defaulted on this payment and in May 1523 Hunne's property and Rastell's deeds and debts were granted to another, although in 1529 he was probably still in possession of the estate.[5]

From soon after 1526 Rastell was printing works of his own authorship which give him an important place in the history of Tudor drama. Two plays, Of gentylnes and nobylyte and The IIII Elements, may with fair certainty be attributed to him, while a third, Calisto and Melibea, shows signs of his workmanship. The purpose of The IIII Elements is to awaken interest in natural science and discovery. In Of gentylnes and nobylyte, largely a dialogue between a ploughman and a knight, the evils of inheritance are attacked and it is argued that nobility is not a matter of birth. Both plays present the notion of the 'commonweal', and the third, Calisto and Melibea, concludes with a moralizing address on his other theme, that natural knowledge and reason are aids to, not enemies of, religion. Rastell's chronicle The pastyme of people (1529) is a paraphrase of Fabyan's, but it includes comments which imply a view of Wolsey akin to Edward Hall's. Like Hall, Rastell looked for improvement to King, Parliament and good laws; he had particular praise for the statutes of Edward I and also showed interest in the history of coinage and the changing value of money. His interests and ideas well qualified Rastell for election to the Parliamant summoned in the autumn of 1529, when Wolsey's power was broken and opposition to him erupted. Several weeks before the Parliament opened Wolsey lost the chancellorship to More, who probably utilized his new authority to procure his brother-in-law's return for a borough in Cornwall with which Rastell had no personal links: a possible intermediary was Bishop Veysey of Exeter, who as a native of Sutton Coldfield may well have known Rastell. Rastell was to prove a most active and enthusiastic Member. He first inclined to moderation in his views and eschewed those of the reforming party: he published More's *Dialogue* on a number of contemporary issues including the veneration of images, and in 1530 he came to More's aid with *A new boke of Purgatory,* in which he defended the doctrine by 'natural reason and good philosophy'. It was a visit to France, perhaps to canvass support for the King's divorce, that led to his conversion and to a break with More and his circle. A bill drafted in 1531 calling for the bible in English, and deriving from Christopher St. German (like Rastell a Middle Templar), has been associated with Rastell, who may have been its advocate in the Commons. Two years later a bill to set up an office 'for the true making of legal instruments' in London named Rastell and another lawyer as the first holders of the appointment, but nothing came of this.[6]

The most interesting glimpse of Rastell in the Commons is connected with its discussion of the treasons bill of 1534. This was a measure in which he could hardly fail to have been especially interested, whether as a professed student of the law or as the brother-in-law of its greatest potential victim, and such an interest found fitting expression in his appearance on a list of Members which Cromwell compiled at the time and which may indicate the proposed or actual composition of a committee on the bill. The probability that Rastell was thus closely involved with the measure adds significance to what his son, Judge William Rastell, was later to write about the opposition to it in the Commons and the insistence that the word 'maliciously' should be inserted as a qualification necessary to make words treasonable; it is likely that the younger Rastell was here drawing upon his father's testimony. Not that John Rastell can have been an outright opponent of the bill, for by this time he had both embraced Protestantism and attached himself to Cromwell.[7]

In the spring of 1535 he went daily to the London Charterhouse to convert the monks, who treated his visits with derision. He submitted to Cromwell a book compiled with the help of Francis Bigod* and others, 'for a charge to be given at sessions by the ustices for the instruction of the learned as well as for the people at large to withdraw all confidence from the pope'. This Cromwell returned for revision, but apparently in an encouraging way, for Rastell then urged that at least 10,000 copies should

be printed and that he should be given a monopoly. Claiming that he had 'leaned' towards Cromwell 'more than any other of the King's Council this four or five years', during which he had spent all his time 'compiling books in furtherance of the King's causes and opposing the pope', he declared that he had a primer of prayers ready for issue, suggested a committee of masters in Chancery to assist the chancellor in matters of heresy and another of learned men to compose sermons for publication, and proposed that 'before Parliament meets' pamphlets should be printed against clerical celibacy, the honouring of images and prayers for the dead, and that five bills should be introduced into Parliament against these practices and for the reform of the common law. So radical had his views become by 1536 that they were noted among the heresies which the Pilgrims of Grace wished to suppress.[8]

It was over the question of the exactions of the clergy, which had brought Hunne to his death, that Rastell's zeal brought him into conflict with authority. Although a proclamation of February 1535 had ordered the payment of tithes in London under a settlement made by Cranmer between the clergy and the citizens, Rastell denied the clergy's right to tithes. Brought before Cranmer, he protested that not only were the poor depressed instead of relieved by the curates, 'but also the rich have [by the payment of tithes] . . . a watergate to stop up the plenteousness of their hearts'; in support of his views he 'sung again his old song of which the archbishop . . . was weary', that is to say, he appealed to 'the law of nature, of man, and of God'. Perhaps on account of his outspokenness during this examination Rastell was imprisoned and so presumably missed the last session of the Parliament: he was certainly in custody on 20 Apr. 1536, six days after the dissolution, when he made a will providing for his wife and children. He left legacies to Cromwell to enlist his good services and to Chancellor Audley to speed his suit, and to raise money for these bequests he ordered that his books should be sold. He continued:

> And because I am most in danger to the King's grace by bonds and orders of his common law, I make his grace and my poor neighbour Ralph Cressey mine executors not because he is able to match with his most noble grace but because he knoweth many secrets of mine which be necessary for his grace to know.

He was still in prison when Cromwell became lord privy seal on the following 1 July and it was in this capacity that the minister received a letter from Rastell, 'oppressed by extreme poverty and long imprisonment, forsaken by his kinsmen, destitute of friends', claiming that he had not offended the King or done anything contrary to law. This was probably Rastell's farewell utterance for his will was proved on 13 July.[9]

Rastell had earlier enjoyed some support from Cromwell, with whom and others he had in 1533 shared the grant of mining rights on Dartmoor. The minister also nominated Rastell's son John to fill the vacancy in Parliament for Tavistock caused by the death of William Honychurch, but his esteem was not sufficient to free Rastell from captivity in 1536.[10]

[1] Date of birth estimated from first reference. This biography draws largely on A. W. Reed, *Early Tudor Drama*. [2] *Dugdale Soc.* xix, 14, 172; *LP Hen. VIII*, i. [3] *LP Hen. VIII*, i, iii, iv, viii, xiv; *Coventry Leet Bk.* (EETS cxxxviii), pp. li, 603, 605, 619; C1/439/10–12, 560/47–48, 1253/20–23. [4] S. Anglo, *Spectacle, Pageantry and Tudor Policy*, 164–7; 'The imperial alliance and the entry of the Emperor Charles V into London', *Guildhall Misc.* ii. 131–55; *LP Hen. VIII*, i–iv; J. A. Williamson, *Voyages of the Cabots*, 244–8; B. Winchester, *Tudor Fam. Portrait*, 41; C1/562/13, 880/7–9, 883/8; L. W. Abbott, *Law Reporting in Eng.*, 14, 23n, 171. [5] *LP Hen. VIII*, iii, vii; C1/560/47–48, 50–51. [6] S. E. Lehmberg, *Ref. Parlt.* 121–2. [7] *LP Hen. VIII*, vii. 1522(ii) citing SP1/87, f. 106v; N. Harpsfield, *Life of More* (EETS clxxxvi), 229; R. W. Chambers, *Thomas More*, 320. [8] G. R. Elton, *Reform and Renewal*, 62, 68, 127, 139; *Studies in Tudor and Stuart Pol. and Govt.*, ii. 63–64; *Econ. Hist. Rev.* xiv. 70–73. [9] *Tudor R. Proclamations*, ed. Hughes and Larkin, i. 224; *LP Hen. VIII*, x, xi; PCC 3 Crumwell. [10] *LP Hen. VIII*, vi, vii, x; SP1/82, f. 59v.

A.H.

RASTELL, William (c. 1508–65), of London.

HINDON	1553 (Oct.)
RIPON	1554 (Apr.)
CANTERBURY	1555

b. c.1508, yr. s. of John Rastell* of London by Elizabeth, da. of Sir John More of London. *educ.* Oxf. c.1525; L. Inn, adm. 12 Sept. 1532, called 1539. *m.* 1544, Winifred, da. of John Clement, *d.s.p.*[1]

Pens. L. Inn 1545, bencher 1546, Autumn reader 1547, keeper of black bk. 1548, treasurer 1549, 1554–5. Serjeant-at-law Oct. 1555; commr. heresy 1557; j. KB 27 Oct. 1558.[2]

According to Anthony Wood, William Rastell was sent to Oxford 'in 1525 or thereabouts, being then in the year of his age 17', and there laid 'a considerable foundation in logic and philosophy' although leaving without a degree. He was already assisting his father, whom in 1527 he helped devise a pageant at Greenwich for the entertainment of ambassadors from France, but it was his father's printing business which chiefly claimed him until in 1529 he set up his own press, publishing *The supplycacyon of soulys* by his uncle Sir Thomas More. The year 1533 was Rastell's most productive year as a printer, but in 1534, two years after his admission to Lincoln's Inn and when he was perhaps seeking a career less hazardous to an opponent of the Reformation, he turned instead to the law.[3]

Rastell became an active member of his inn, but his progress was cut short by his flight overseas during the reign of Edward VI. By an inquisition taken at Guildhall it was found that he had departed without licence for Louvain with his household on 21 Dec. 1549 and his house, *Skales Inn*, and two messuages in Maiden Lane, seven other messuages in London and all his household goods were accordingly forfeit to the crown. In February 1550 he was also fined £10 for quitting the country without leave of the governors of Lincoln's Inn and he was to be specifically excluded from the general pardon granted in the Parliament of March 1553 (7 Edw. VI, c.14). He remained at Louvain until after the accession of Mary, compiling and preparing for the press his edition of More's English works which was later printed by Richard Tottel. In July 1553 Rastell's wife, a daughter of More's adopted daughter Mary Giggs and John Clement (a physician who also took refuge at Louvain in the reigns of Edward VI and Elizabeth), died and was buried in the church of St. Pierre, Louvain: in the following year Rastell supplied the chapel of Lincoln's Inn with various altar furnishings on condition that prayers should be said for her soul.[4]

Rastell probably owed his return for Hindon to Mary's first Parliament to his proved Catholicism and his membership of the More circle rather than to any personal connexion with the patron Bishop Gardiner. As chancellor, Gardiner may have secured his return to the succeeding Parliament for Ripon, where his fellow-Member John Temple was the bishop's servant, perhaps with the help of Sir Robert Rochester*, chancellor of the duchy of Lancaster. In the spring of 1554 Rochester nominated Rastell's brother-in-law John Heywood for Lancaster and in the autumn, with Heywood finding a seat at Hindon and Rastell perhaps preoccupied with resuming his legal career, another kinsman, Thomas More II, was returned for Ripon. In the following year Rastell's fellow-Member and probable patron at Canterbury was Sir Thomas More's son-in-law William Roper, also of Lincoln's Inn; on 14 Sept. 1555, a week-and-a-half after the writs had gone out, the burmote agreed that the two men should be admitted and sworn freemen of the city 'freely, of the gift and benevolence of the mayor and commonalty', thus qualifying them for their election some three weeks later. In 1556 Rastell, by then a serjeant-at-law, was retained of counsel by Canterbury at an annual fee of 40s. As might be expected, he neither 'stood for the true religion' against the initial measures for the restoration of Catholicism in Mary's first Parliament nor opposed one of the government's bills in her fourth and his last. In each of these Parliaments he had bills committed to him, one for the continuance of divers Acts on its second reading on 30 Nov. 1553, another touching absence of knights and burgesses in the Parliament-time on its third reading on 26 Oct. 1555 and a third dealing with the proclamation of outlawries on its second reading on 7 Nov. 1555; only the first was enacted (1 Mary st.2, c.13).[5]

In 1557 Rastell was named a commissioner for heresy and in the following year he was active as a justice of assize in the north. His appointment on 27 Oct. 1558 as a justice of the King's bench was renewed by Elizabeth, but on 3 Jan. 1562 he again fled to Louvain where he remained until his death on 27 Aug. 1565: he was buried beside his wife. He had filed an autograph copy of his will with the registrar at Antwerp and probate was granted on 5 Oct. 1565 to his father-in-law John Clement and his nephew Ellis Heywood. He made this nephew his heir, leaving him the rents which he apparently still drew from lands and houses in North Mimms bought in 1542 and part of an annuity of 780 florins purchased from the city of Antwerp, the rest going either to Bartholomew More (a grandson of the chancellor) while he remained an exile from Protestant England or to charity. The goods, including books, which Rastell had left at Serjeants' Inn and forfeited by his second departure, were valued by commissioners at £48. It appears to have been during this second exile that he wrote a life of Sir Thomas More, of which only those parts survive which relate to Bishop Fisher, including an account of the Parliament of 1529 in which Rastell's father had sat for Dunheved.[6]

[1] Aged 17 on entry to Oxford, Wood, *Ath. Ox.* ed. Bliss, i. 343. PCC 3 Crumwell; Emden, *Biog. Reg. Univ. Oxf. 1501–40*, p. 475; A. W. Reed, *Early Tudor Drama*, 86; *DNB*. [2] *CPR*, 1554–5, p. 59; 1555–7, p. 281; 1557–8, p. 457. [3] Reed, 74–76, 79, 82. [4] *CPR*, 1550–3, pp. 171–2; *Black Bk. L. Inn*, i. 293, 308–9; Reed, 87–88. [5] Canterbury burmote bk. 1542–78, ff. 96v, 102v; *CJ*, i. 32, 42, 43. [6] *CPR*, 1555–7, p. 281; 1557–8, pp. 350, 457; 1558–60, pp. 65, 77, 231; 1560–3, pp. 31, 57, 87, 187; E178/1076; Reed, 85, 91, 92; N. Harpsfield, *Life of More* (EETS clxxxvi), pp. ccxv–xix, 219–52, 350–2; Neale, *Commons*, 282.

H.M.

RATCLIFFE *see* RADCLIFFE

RAWLINS, John (by 1493–1532), of Gloucester.

GLOUCESTER   1529*

b. by 1493, ?s. of Robert Rawlins of Gloucester.[1]
    Sheriff, Gloucester 1514–15, 1518–19, alderman 1519–*d.*, mayor 1524–5; commr. subsidy 1523, 1524.[2]

John Rawlins, who was assessed at £4 10s. for the subsidy of 1523, seems to have come of a family long resident in Gloucester and was probably a son of a former mayor. He was perhaps a kinsman of Hugh Rawlings *alias* Williams, the parson of Holy Trinity, Gloucester, whose advocacy of reform so disturbed Thomas Bell*. As mayor, Rawlins welcomed Princess Mary to Gloucester on 12 Sept.

1525. He died on 10 Oct. 1532, several months after the end of the fourth session of the Parliament. It is not known who was by-elected in his place.[3]

[1] Date of birth estimated from first reference. Williams, *Glos. MPs*, 188. [2] *LP Hen. VIII*, iii, iv; Gloucester Guildhall 1375, f. 28; E179/113/214. [3] *LP Hen. VIII*, i; *HMC 12th Rep. IX*, 442; Elton, *Policy and Police*, 121–3, 364; Gloucester Guildhall 1375, f. 28.

L.M.K./A.D.K.H.

RAY, Alexander (by 1529–92), of Cambridge, and Saffron Walden, Essex.

CAMBRIDGE   1553 (Mar.)[1], 1555

b. by 1529, o. s. of John Ray of Cambridge by Catherine. *m.* by 1572, Elizabeth, da. of John Lawe, at least 1s. *d.v.p.*[2]
    Alderman, Cambridge, mayor 1550–1, 1566–7; j.p. 1556; commr. gaol delivery 1561.[3]

Alexander Ray's father had combined, or pursued successively, scholarship and business, being both a fellow of King's College, Cambridge, and a mercer and draper. Ray himself followed the second of these callings without, so far as is known, any similar educational advantage. He lived in Great St. Mary's parish, Cambridge, where he was a churchwarden from 1563 to 1565. He was one of the chief supporters of Robert Ray in his various and sometimes violent disputes with Edward Slegge* and his sons in the time of Queen Mary, but the two Rays do not seem to have been closely related. Seniority in borough government rather than religion was probably the important qualification for Cambridge Members in this period, for Ray was returned to Parliament under both Edward VI and Mary; his name does not appear as one of those opposing a government bill in the Parliament of 1555. He served his second term as mayor two years after the bishop of Ely had named him as one of the borough officers whom he 'misliked' for their religious views. In November 1564 Ray was chosen one of the three arbitrators on the borough's side for the settlement of disputes with the university.[4]

Ray must have owned one of the largest houses in Cambridge, for the 4th Duke of Norfolk lodged with him when the Queen visited Cambridge in the same year. His position as an alderman probably helped him in trade; the borough's largest single expense when called on to raise troops in 1563 was a payment of £6 13s.4d. to Ray 'towards the setting forth of the soldiers'. By 1564 he owned the *Hand* inn, which he was said to have acquired on mortgage from Robert Ray, refusing then either to let him the inn or to accept repayment of the mortgage money. Ray purchased *Paul's* inn, St. Michael's parish, in 1572 jointly with his wife; it was in her right that he acquired, for a term of 40 years, a manor or grange at Saffron Walden, where he evidently retired in middle or old age. This acquisition led to his involvement in at least two lawsuits in the court of requests, one of which seems to have dragged on. Their outcome is not known, nor has any will or inquisition post mortem for Ray been found. He died in 1592 and was buried in Great St. Mary's church, Cambridge; his widow continued to live at Saffron Walden until her death in 1596.[5]

[1] The christian name, torn from the indenture (C219/20/15), is supplied by C. H. Cooper, *Cambridge Annals*, ii. 82. [2] Date of birth estimated from first reference. Camb. Univ. Arch. vicechancellor's ct. wills 1, ff. 59 and v; Req.2/68/13; C. H. Cooper, *Cambridge Memorials*, iii. 352n; *PCC Admins*. ed. Glencross, ii. 106. [3] Cooper, *Annals*, ii. 108; F. Blomefield, *Coll. Cant.* 224–5; *CPR*, 1560–3, p. 406. [4] *Churchwardens' Accts., Great St. Mary's, Cambridge*, ed. Foster, 149, 155; St.Ch.4/2/56; *Cam. Misc.* ix(3), 25; *APC*, vii. 161. [5] Cooper, *Annals*, ii. 178, 205; *Memorials*, iii. 352n; *CPR*, 1560–3, p. 269; Req.2/68/13, 157/359; C3/150/11, 154/116, 164/94; *APC*, xiii. 360; *Churchwardens' Accts. Great St. Mary's*, 226; Essex RO, 253/CW/3.

D.F.C.

RAYDON see ROYDON

RAYMOND, John I

READING 1529, 1536,[1] ?1539[2]

Of the 23 men who represented Reading in Parliament between 1510 and 1558 three cannot be identified, and John Raymond is one of them. In the early years of Henry VIII the town almost invariably returned residents but in 1529, with the King at Windsor intervening in the elections, Reading may have been persuaded to accept at least one nominee. Raymond and his fellow, Thomas Vachell I, were to be re-elected to the next Parliament, in accordance with the King's general request to that effect, on 2 June 1536: although both were then given the customary designation 'burgesses', neither is ever found among the membership of the guild or the town oligarchy and neither held municipal office. Vachell was a neighbouring landowner and agent of Cromwell, who as high steward of Reading is likely to have procured his further re-election in 1539, when the Members' names are unknown, but Raymond's return on that occasion is open to more doubt. That the corporation had been under pressure to accept two 'strangers' is shown by its resolution of 11 Apr. 1539 that in future at least one Member should be a burgess, by which was presumably meant a member of the guild. The fact that on this occasion—the only one during the century—no record of the election itself appears in the corporation diary, may mean either that the names of nominees were as yet unknown in the borough or that as a form of silent protest they were not entered. The terms of the resolution, however, leave no doubt that neither can have fallen within its

definition, which was the case with both Vachell and Raymond; but whereas Vachell, who was to be returned to the next two Parliaments, may be presumed to have sat in this one also, Raymond had no parliamentary future and was perhaps passed over this time in favour of a more obvious nominee.[3]

Although he stood outside the municipal oligarchy Raymond was probably not unknown in Reading. In 1530 a notary public of that name, with two others, witnessed the exemption from municipal office of Richard Barnes; in 1542 both a John Raymond 'gentleman' and a 'Master Raymond' contributed to the cost of the Scottish campaign, and in 1560 a John Raymond was holding, but not occupying a tenement and garden, as well as two more tenements which he held with, amongst others, Thomas Vachell II*. The presence in or near the town of one family of the name, if not two, is also shown by the christening at St. Mary's of a John in 1538, followed by an Alice and a Dorothy, as well as by the bequests made in 1544 by a vicar of Thatcham, himself bearing the well known local surname Justice, to his cousins John, Leonard and Thomas Raymond. Nothing that has come to light, however, explains the election of a local man who was not a burgess, while the few John Raymonds found elsewhere are in the main even more hypothetical. The purveyor at Calais in 1520 might have been connected with Richard Smith I, Member for Reading in 1512 and himself sometime a customer of Calais, but only their name draws attention to either the merchant taylor of London who died about 1557 or the man of Dorset who did so in 1575. By contrast, it can be said with confidence that John Raymond II, Member for Maldon in 1536 and in October 1553 was a different man.[4]

[1] *Reading Recs.* i. 166–7. [2] C. Coates, *Reading*, App. xiii. [3] *Reading Recs.* i. 167, 172. [4] Ibid. i. 157, 180; *Reading Chs.* ed. Pritchard, 39, 40, 44; S. Barfield, *Thatcham*, ii. 76–77; *Reg. of St. Mary's Reading*, ed. Crawfurd, 1, 2; *LP Hen. VIII*, iii; PCC 20 Noodes; C142/173/34.

T.F.T.B.

RAYMOND, John II (by 1510–60), of Little Dunmow, Essex.

MALDON 1536,[1] 1553 (Oct.)

b. by 1510, 1st s. of William Raymond. *m.* by 1530, Margaret, da. of one Barker, at least 5s. 1da.[2] Auditor to 1st and 2nd Earls of Sussex; dep. chamberlain, the Exchequer by 1534–51; ?writer of the counter roll 1543–6; commr. tenths of spiritualities, Colchester and Essex 1535.[3]

John Raymond was one of the most trusted servants of both the 1st and 2nd Earls of Sussex, who were great landowners in Essex, particularly in the neighbourhood of Maldon. It must have been the 1st Earl who procured Raymond's return for

Maldon in 1536, for the borough almost certainly expected its Members to serve without payment, and unlike his fellow-Member William Harris II he was then a man of modest means: in 1547 he was to be assessed for subsidy at £24 in lands, although at £95 'for lands appointed to the will of the earl', that is, the 1st Earl of Sussex, who died in 1542. An executor of the will, Raymond was given a legacy of £20 and annuities totalling £5 6s.8d. a year. It was to this Earl that he also owed his appointment in the Exchequer for at the time Sussex was one of the two chamberlains; Raymond was to retain the office under the next chamberlain, Thomas Wriothesley. The 2nd Earl, who died in 1557, also appointed Raymond one of his executors and left him 'a goblet gilt without a cover'. He presumably secured Raymond's re-election for Maldon in October 1553; the Members elected in 1539 and 1542 had undertaken to serve without wages and the same condition must have applied in 1553. As a Member of this Parliament Raymond was not one of those who 'stood for the true religion' against the initial measures to restore Catholicism. Nothing further is known of his role in the Commons but he was doubtless concerned with the unsuccessful bill against the 2nd Earl of Sussex's divorced wife.[4]

Little has come to light about Raymond's parentage or personal life. He may have been a native of Little Dunmow or have settled there when he took service with Sussex, who owned the site and lands of the dissolved priory of Dunmow and was thus landlord as well as master to Raymond, a lessee of some of the priory lands as early as 1531. As John Raymond gentleman he held land at Harlow and Sheering in 1548 and in October 1550 bought land at Fairsted, which he resold by fine for £100 in 1556; under Edward VI and Mary he spent £220 on the purchase of land in Essex by fine. By his will of 7 Mar. 1560 proved on the following 25 June he asked to be buried 'without any pomp or sumptuous funeral' and left legacies of varying sums up to £20, among the beneficiaries being several grandchildren and three sons, George, Giles and Francis; three sons so named were among the children born to Raymond before his being made a Member and freeman of Maldon in 1536. The testator did not mention the earls of Sussex, but he did bequeath by his will 'one gilt cup with a cover glass fashion', perhaps the one left him by the 2nd Earl three years before.[5]

¹ Essex RO, D/B3/1/2, f. 112. ² Date of birth estimated from first reference. *Vis. Essex* (Harl. Soc. xiii), 95; Essex RO, D/B3/1/2, f. 112. ³ PCC 1 Alen, 33 Wrastley; E405/115/29; E405/202-4, 210; *LP Hen. VIII*, viii. ⁴ Strype, *Eccles. Memorials*, iii(1), 503; PCC 1 Alen, 33 Wrastley; E179/110/320; *CJ*, i. 31-32. ⁵ C24/36/32; NRA 5232, p. 34; *CPR*, 1548-9, pp. 74, 387; 1549-51, p. 228; Essex RO,

D/B3/1/2 passim; D/ABR2, ff. 37-40; CP25(2)/57/423 nos. 52, 56; 70/581 no. 38, 583 no. 13, 585 no. 33.

D.F.C.

RAYNSFORD (RAINFORTH), Sir John (by 1482-1559), of Bradfield, Essex.

COLCHESTER 1529

b. by 1482, o. s. of Sir John Raynsford of Bradfield by Anne, da. and coh. of Sir Humphrey Starkey of Wouldham, Kent. *m.* (1) by 1503, Elizabeth or Isabel (*d.*1508), da. and h. of Edward Knyvet of Suff.; ?(2) Alice; (2) or (3) Winifred, da. and h. of John Pympe of Nettlestead, Kent, *d.s.p. suc.* fa. 1521. Kntd. 1 July 1523.[1]

J.p. Essex 1523-30, 1536-*d.*; commr. subsidy 1524, benevolence 1544/45, musters 1546, relief 1550, goods of churches and fraternities, Colchester 1553; other commissions 1530-54; sheriff, Essex and Herts. 1537-8; bailiff, manors of Kirby, Thorpe and Walton, Essex by 1545; keeper, Clacton, Weeley and Wix parks, Essex by 1553.[2]

The elder Sir John Raynsford, of an established Essex family, was successively esquire and knight of the body to Henry VII; he served both Henry VII and Henry VIII as a captain in the French wars and was liberally rewarded for his services with grants of lands and privileges. It was probably in his retinue that his son and namesake saw service as a captain of foot in the war of 1513, and thenceforward the younger Raynsford devoted himself to the profession of arms.[3]

Raynsford had been married by 1503 to the only daughter and heir presumptive of Edward Knyvet, an extensive landowner in East Anglia, but Knyvet died in that year leaving the greater part of his lands in trust for her stepmother Catherine for life, with remainder to his own heirs. This settlement greatly reduced the Raynsfords' prospects, for Catherine, a daughter of Sir Henry Marney†, was a youngish woman who was to be married again in 1509, this time to Thomas Bonham*, and to survive until 1535. Raynsford's own position was still further weakened when his wife died in February 1508 leaving him childless and thus without even a life interest in the lands which her heirs had already sought to make sure of by petitions in both Chancery and Star Chamber. Hostilities between the rival claimants continued for a number of years and provoked several more chancery suits, but a compromise may have been reached eventually with Raynsford in receipt of an annuity of £20 and a life interest in two of the Knyvet manors. He may also have married again before 1518, for among the King's payments in that year was one of £15 for a half-year's fee to 'Alice, wife of John Raynsford'; she could, however, have married a different man of that name who was later a gentleman usher. On his father's death, about the end of 1521, Raynsford had again to bear with the extensive and elaborate provision made for his stepmother and his two sisters, one of whom married Sir Thomas Darcy*, a ward of his father's and a notable beneficiary by the will.[4]

In 1523 Raynsford was knighted for his part in the capture of Morlaix and made his first appearance on the Essex bench, having evidently cleared himself of serious charges brought shortly before in the Star Chamber. His accuser was a rascal named Richard Vynes, an ex-servant of the abbot of Colchester, who had earlier fallen foul of Raynsford's father and whose grudge against the family led him to accuse Raynsford of committing a murder within the sanctuary of Colchester abbey. Raynsford's answer to the circumstantial evidence against him was that he had been conversing with the victim when two men entered and killed him after a struggle in which Raynsford's efforts to protect him failed because he was unarmed at the time; not realizing the seriousness of his wounds, Raynsford had tried to succour him and was thus found with the body. Vynes further charged Raynsford with having harboured in his retinue at Tournai a tailor who had previously committed a murder in London. This was not the first time Raynsford had been accused of murder: he had faced that charge in the King's bench in 1511 but had evidently been acquitted or pardoned. Guilty or not on these occasions, he seems to have been of a violent disposition. The principal Raynsford manor, Bradfield Hall, was held in chief of the earls of Oxford, and Raynsford's father and the 14th Earl had been joint stewards of the Barking abbey lands in 1520. In 1524 Raynsford accompanied the earl on his armed expedition into Lavenham park against the countess, but perhaps not surprisingly the friendship did not last, and ten years later Raynsford was petitioning Cromwell for protection against the 15th Earl. In the meantime he had satisfied a private grudge against a neighbour, Henry Wilcox, who described Raynsford as 'a very dangerous man of his hands and one that delighteth much in beating, mayheming and evil entreating your subjects'.[5]

Raynsford was to sit in the Parliament of 1529 for Colchester. Its nearness to his home at Bradfield made it the obvious borough for him to represent, but as its tradition of electing townsmen had to be satisfied by his admission as an out-burgess his nomination probably owed less to his particular standing there than to his prestige and connexions in the county and at court. He might, indeed, have aspired to the knighthood of the shire, but that was shared on this occasion by two lawyers and officials, the Speaker-designate Thomas Audley and Rayns-

ford's relation by marriage Thomas Bonham; to both of these he was socially superior but they commanded the greater support. Raynsford's fellow-Member at Colchester, Richard Rich, another lawyer, owed his nomination to the Earl of Oxford, and Raynsford may still have been close enough to the earl to enjoy his backing. Raynsford's Membership of this Parliament, about which nothing but the fact is known, may not have been the limit of his experience in the Commons: he is unlikely to have sat before 1529 but was probably returned again for Colchester in 1536, in accordance with the King's request for the re-election of the previous Members, and could have sat in either or both of the Parliaments of 1539 and 1542, for which the names of the Colchester Members are lost.[6]

Although Raynsford was no reformer, to judge from his removal in 1526, with Bishop Tunstall's consent, of the host from Bradfield church to a specially built chapel at Bradfield Hall so that it should be safe from desecration, he was not averse to sharing in the distribution of monastic lands while lacking the touch needed for success. It was probably early in 1539 that he wrote to Cromwell asking for a lease of either the Whitefriars in Ipswich or the Greyfriars in Colchester, but in a blustering fashion which could have done nothing to advance his suit, and without any hint of a gift for the expected favour: in the event the Greyfriars was leased to Francis Jobson*, and Raynsford's only consolation seems to have been a grant of the herbage and pannage of Grinsted and Weeley parks, of which Cromwell had been keeper, after the minister's attainder and execution. In 1539 he was busy preparing the Essex coastal defences against the expected invasion. He had raised 100 men for the King at the time of the northern rebellion, and had been among those summoned to the christening of Prince Edward in October 1537 and the reception of Anne of Cleves two years later. During the summer of 1541 the King stayed with him at Bradfield, and about this time he acquired for £500 the ex-monastic manor of Manningtree, Essex, and lands in Devon and Suffolk, although not without a hitch: his former parliamentary colleague Rich, now chancellor of augmentations, had the grant stayed 'because the money was not paid', but by March 1541 it had gone through. Raynsford raised 100 men for the expedition to the Netherlands under Sir John Wallop in the summer of 1543 and himself took part in the war as one of the army's five captains of foot; he served again in France in the following year, when he was in the King's 'battle'. One of the Essex gentlemen appointed to attend the reception of the French ambassador at court in 1546, he was excused this duty, possibly because of illness.[7]

Raynsford remained in favour under Edward VI, perhaps through the influence of his erstwhile brother-in-law Thomas Darcy*, by then Baron Darcy of Chiche and chamberlain of the royal household. He retained the keepership of Weeley park and the stewardship of the manor, which his father had held before him, and he consolidated his lands by the sale of his Suffolk properties in 1549 and the purchase of more lands at Bradfield and Manningtree in the following year. In June 1553 he bought other lands around Mistley in Essex worth £20 a year; as Mistley was only a mile or two from Bradfield, his principal seat, this last purchase was perhaps the outcome of a successful appeal to the Duke of Northumberland earlier in the year, when the duke had written on Raynsford's behalf to the commissioners for the sale of crown lands 'for the old acquaintance that hath been between him and me . . . [and] considering his old service'.[8]

Although he was one of the witnesses to the letters patent altering the succession to the crown, Raynsford is not known to have played any active part during the brief reign of Queen Jane and he did not forfeit favour under Mary. In 1555 he was ordered to lend his servants to help Rich at the execution of Protestant heretics in Essex and received the thanks of the Council for doing so: the Council at the same time asked him to look to the affairs of the county, especially with regard to the punishment of 'disordered persons'. When in August 1556 the same body bound Raynsford in 1,000 marks to stay within two miles of his London house, it is less likely that he was politically suspect than that he had become involved in another of his escapades, perhaps the one which led to a sword fight in London between a servant of his and one of the 16th Earl of Oxford's. Two years later he was again ordered to appear, this time to explain his delay in providing a horseman for the Queen's service. Of the various chancery cases in which he had been involved since the time of Edward VI only one yielded a known result, and that went against Raynsford: it concerned his seizure of the person and lands of an infant whom he claimed as his ward by knight-service and it cost him £60 in damages.[9]

A man of over 70 who had less than a year to live when Elizabeth came to the throne, Raynsford made a last appearance before the Council for refusing to yield a house in Chelmsford to his old associate Rich, who planned to occupy it at the time of the shire election to the Queen's first Parliament. He struck a happier note—if Bacon's account of the incident is to be trusted—when, on the morrow of her coronation he was egged on by other courtiers to

ask the Queen to include among the prisoners to whom the ceremony would bring their liberty, the apostles Matthew, Mark, Luke and John, who had been too long imprisoned in the Latin tongue and should be free to go abroad in English: 'the Queen answered, with a grave countenance; it were good, Raynsford, they were spoken with themselves, to know of them, whether they would be set at liberty?' This was one of a string of stories which were to circulate after Raynsford's death, some of them to be preserved in Sir John Harington's 'Epigrams', and which enshrine his reputation as a swashbuckling and lecherous humorist. His own last contribution to his fame was the elaborate military display at his burial in St. Catherine Creechurch, London, on 20 Sept. 1559. By his will, made 12 days earlier, he had left his disposable lands and goods for division between nine persons, among them his cousins Thomas Raynsford and Richard Starkey, the latter being also one of the executors. As supervisor he named his 'especial and singular friend' Francis Russell*, 2nd Earl of Bedford, to whom he left his best gown. His widow, who had brought him lands in Kent worth £65 a year, had become insane long before his death.[10]

[1] Date of birth estimated from marriage. *Vis. Essex* (Harl. Soc. xiii), 96; *CPR*, 1494–1509, p. 321; *LP Hen. VIII*, ii; PCC 31 Bennett, 21 Maynwaryng; C142/127/3. [2] *LP Hen. VIII*, iii, iv, viii, xi, xii, xiv–xvii, xx, xxi; *CPR*, 1547–8, p. 83; 1550–3, pp. 141, 396; 1553, pp. 352, 416; 1553–4, pp. 19, 27; Stowe 571, f. 50; SC6/900, m. 6v. [3] *CPR*, 1494–1509, pp. 39, 319, 588; *LP Hen. VIII*, ii. [4] C1/298/50, 392/38; *CIPM Hen. VII*, ii. 417; iii. 457, 537; J. Hurstfield, *Queen's Wards*, 134, 137; *CPR*, 1494–1509, p. 321; *LP Hen. VIII*, i, ii; St.Ch.2/20/143; W. S. Holdsworth, *Hist. English Law*, iii. 185; *Essex Feet of Fines*, iv. ed. Reaney and Fitch, 271; *Chron. Calais* (Cam. Soc. xxxv), 177; *N. and Q.* cxlviii. 132; PCC 31 Bennett, 21 Maynwaryng. [5] *LP Hen. VIII*, iii, iv, add.; St.Ch.2/18/61, 294, 20/26, 22/216, 23/130, 25/159; W. M. Sturman, 'Barking abbey' (London Univ. Ph.D. thesis, 1961), 215; KB9/458, nos. 57–60. [6] *Colchester Oath Bk.* ed. Benham, 154; *Cal. Colchester Ct. Rolls*, ed. Harrod, 65–66. [7] J. E. Oxley, *Ref. in Essex*, 16; *LP Hen. VIII*, xi–xvi, xviii, xix, xxi. [8] *CPR*, 1549–51, pp. 55, 404; 1550–3, p. 396; 1553, pp. 99, 286, 416; Harl. 284, f. 123. [9] *Chron. Q. Jane and Q. Mary* (Cam. Soc. xlviii), 100; *APC*, v. 141, 153, 328; vi. 351, 355; St.Ch.4/10/53; C1/1201/55–57. 1427/37; C78/7, mm. 24–25. [10] *APC*, vii. 38; F. Bacon, *Apophthegms Old and New* (1625), 13–14; J. Harington, *Epigrams*, bk. ii. no. 45; bk. iii. no. 41; J. Craig, *The Mint*, 113; *Machyn's Diary* (Cam. Soc. xlii), 211; PCC 42 Chaynay; C142/126/88.

D.F.C.

REDE, Edward (by 1476–1544), of Norwich, Norf.

NORWICH 1529

b. by 1476, 3rd s. of John Rede of Norwich by Joan Ludlowe. *m.* (1) Elizabeth Lyston *alias* London; (2) a da. of William Stanley, prob. of Beccles, Suff., 3s. 2da.; (3) Isold Woodles (*d.*13 Sept. 1523), wid. of Thomas Wemble of Harwich, Essex, 1da.; (4) Anne Cranmer, 1s.[1]

Common councilman, Norwich 1502–8, keeper of the keys 1503–5, chamberlain's council 1503, 1506, 1520, 1533–6, chamberlain 1505, alderman 1508–*d.*, sheriff 1508–9, auditor 1513, 1522, 1525–9, 1531, 1534, 1537–9, 1541–3, mayor 1521–2, 1531–2, 1543–4, coroner 1524; commr. subsidy 1512, 1514, 1515, 1523, 1524, gaol delivery 1515, musters 1539.[2]

Edward Rede, mercer, was admitted a freeman of Norwich on 3 May 1497, during his father's mayoralty, and elected to the common council five years later. In the year before his death he served for the third time as mayor and in the intervening 40 years he had filled nearly every office in the city, some of them repeatedly. In 1516 he was threatened with expulsion for his 'monstrous contumelies' if he did not submit to the mayor; he evidently did so and in 1519 was himself a candidate for the mayoralty. Two years later he achieved the office and found himself responsible for the city's affairs at a critical point in its dispute with the prior of the cathedral. Between October 1520 and May 1521 he rode four times to London on this business and in 1524 he was one of those who bound the city to submit to Wolsey's judgment.[3]

Rede may well have sat in the Parliament of 1523, for which the names of the Norwich Members are lost: when he did so in that of 1529 he was clearly one of the 'city fathers'. Nothing is known of his part in the proceedings of the Commons, but when after the close of the second session he was again elected mayor he was brought into prominence by the outstanding event of his year of office, the trial and execution for heresy of Thomas Bilney in August 1531. On the following 1 Oct. Rede called some of the aldermen who had been present to a meeting at the council house. He told them that he would shortly be going up to Parliament (which, in the event, was further prorogued until January 1532) and that since he expected to be questioned on the affair he wished to take a true account of it, signed by all and sealed with the city seal. He then read his own version which was approved by everyone except Alderman John Curatt, who complained that Rede had not mentioned Bilney's reading of a bill of revocation at the stake. On 9 Nov. Curatt testified before the King's Council as to Bilney's death and its aftermath, and on 1 Dec. Rede himself admitted that he had seen a bill of revocation drawn up but could not tell if it was the one read by Bilney, whose subsequent words to the people did not agree with it. He had refused to exemplify the bill brought to him after the execution because many had objected that it was not what Bilney said. He had himself drawn up the account which he had handed to the clerk of the Council but there were two other versions by Norwich citizens. On further examination Rede admitted to having been present at Bilney's trial and said that when Bilney had appealed to the King and charged Rede, as mayor, to take him into custody, he had referred this invocation of the Supreme Headship to the ecclesiastical judge for decision. He further testified that Bilney

had asked for absolution at his execution but did not recall that he had submitted to the Church or revoked his errors. The tenor of Rede's evidence implies sympathy with the martyr's views and a determination, clearly shared by some of his fellow citizens, to deprive the Church of the benefit of a recantation. He was doubtless one of those who, as Sir Thomas More admitted, wrote from Norwich that Bilney had not forsworn his opinions and who, when forced to agree with most of the official version, watered it down with their own additions. More, who examined the witnesses, believed Curatt's story and—although fiercely attacked by Foxe on the matter—was probably right to do so.[4]

Although Rede's will shows no sign of religious fervour it is likely that he was anti-clerical, especially after his experience of disputes with the cathedral. He probably supported the policy pursued in the Parliament of 1529 and he was certainly one of the prime movers in the acquisition of monastic property by the city. On 31 Aug. 1538 the assembly agreed that Rede and Augustine Steward* should ride to the 3rd Duke of Norfolk for his opinion on the city's projected petition for a grant of the Blackfriars and five days later Rede was a signatory to a letter to Cromwell on the subject. Three years earlier Norfolk had complained to Cromwell that Norwich had under-assessed itself for a tax and undertook to have Rede, Steward and Reginald Lytilprowe* bring him the false certificate: these three appear to have been the leading citizens at the time or at least those who could be most relied on. Lytilprowe had been Rede's fellow-Member and unless he was already dead by the summer of 1536 he and Rede probably sat again in the Parliament of that year in deference to the King's general request for the return of the previous Members: three years later one of the seats went to Steward.[5]

Rede was probably approaching 70 when he was elected mayor for the third and last time. A few months after his term had ended, on 25 Oct. 1544, he made his will and he died the next day. He asked to be buried in St. Peter Mancroft 'by my beloved wife' and ordered 100 masses to be said for his soul at or soon after his funeral. He left houses to provide money for St. Peter's bell to be rung for 20 years and his house in St. Peter's parish to his son. His other property in Norfolk and Suffolk he left to his wife for life, as well as £100 and jewels, apparel and household stuff. The reversion of the land and some of the movables went to his second son. Peter Rede, Augustine Steward (his niece's husband), John Sutton and John Rede were named executors and John Corbet II* supervisor.[6]

[1] Date of birth estimated from admission as freeman. *Vis. Norf.*

(Harl. Soc. xxxii), 227–8. ² Norwich ass. procs. passim; *Statutes*, iii. 81, 113, 174; *LP Hen. VIII*, ii–iv, xiv. ³ Norwich ass. procs. 2, ff. 26, 90v, 100, 107v, 110, 113, 115v; *LP Hen. VIII*, i, ii, iv, v. ⁴ *LP Hen. VIII*, v; T. More, *English Works*, 349; Foxe, *Acts and Mons.* iv, 643; J. Gairdner, *Lollardy and the Ref.* i. 395–423. ⁵ Norwich ass. procs. 2, f. 165v; *LP Hen. VIII*, ix, xiii. ⁶ PCC 27 Pynnyng; Cott. Galba B10, f. 187; C142/75/29; Blomefield, *Norf.* iv. 200–1.

R.V.

REDE, John I (by 1509–57), of Westminster, Mdx.

WESTMINSTER 1547

b. by 1509. m. (1) by 1531, Joan, wid. of John Trower of Westminster; (2) Alice Bentley, wid. of Richard Mody (d.Jan./Feb. 1550) of London.¹
   Keeper of the wardrobe, York Place 1530, Westminster 1533–d.²

Nothing has been discovered about John Rede's life before 1530, when he is found acting as keeper of the wardrobe at York Place a few months after the house had come into the King's hands by the attainder of Cardinal Wolsey; in 1533 he received a patent of appointment to the same office in the palace of Westminster and this he retained until his death.³

Having himself sat in Parliament for Westminster from 1547 to 1552, Rede was present at the Westminster election for the Parliament of March 1553 and the Middlesex and Westminster elections for the first, second and fourth Parliaments of Mary's reign. In December 1548 he and a Hampshire gentleman received a grant of land in Hampshire and Westminster, some of which they sold two months later. In August 1553 he sent two of his servants to assert his right to a manor in Kentish Town against John Story, who had been one of his fellow-Members before being expelled. The manor was attached to a prebend at St. Paul's and Story claimed it under a lease of the present holder, John Feckenham, Rede under a former grant by Richard Layton. Rede was removed from possession by a writ of restitution and forced to answer Story's suits in Star Chamber and Chancery: he appears to have lost the case for he made no mention of the property in his will.⁴

By that will, dated 16 Sept. 1557, Rede left to his wife Alice his capital messuage, formerly the hospital of Our Lady of Rounceval, near Charing Cross, and to his nephew, Robert Rede, two tenements in the parish of St. Martin in the Fields. Robert's three sons were to inherit four new tenements next to their father's when they were 21, until which time the rent was to be spent on their education by Rede's executors, his wife and William Gyes*. The overseer of the will was Sir Richard Rede, whose relationship to John Rede is unknown. Rede died on 27 Sept. 1557 and was buried in St. Martin in the Fields. His widow was sued by Robert Rede for

failure to pay the first instalment due to his sons, a suit which Alice Rede, 'an aged woman', declared vexatious, 'whereby her days are like to be shortened'; she did die in September 1558, but not before she had been ordered to fulfil the terms of her late husband's will and had lost another dispute over her inheritance.⁵

¹ Date of birth estimated from first reference. *Cat. Anct. Deeds*, v. 514; PCC 51 Wrastley, 3 Coode. ² *LP Hen. VIII*, v, vi; PCC 51 Wrastley. ³ *LP Hen. VIII*, v, vi. ⁴ C1/1469/80; 219/20–22, 24; *CPR*, 1548–9, pp. 77–78, 169; St.Ch.4/4/40. ⁵ PCC 51 Wrastley, 48 Noodes; *St. Martin in the Fields, Churchwardens' Accts.*, ed. Kitto, 161; Req.2/23/40, 61, 31/57.

H.M.

REDE, John II (by 1530–70), of Bristol and Boddington, Glos. and the Inner Temple, London.

CRICKLADE 1554 (Nov.)

b. by 1530, 2nd s. of Richard Rede (d.18 July 1544) of Boddington by Joan, da. of William Rudhale† of Rudhall, Herefs. educ. I. Temple. m. by 1560, Margaret, da. of John Pauncefoot by Bridget, da. of Robert Tate of London. suc. bro. 24 Feb. 1570.¹
   Commr. sewers, Glos., Worcs. 1553–4.²

John Rede was a lawyer with a largely west-country clientele. Although a younger son of a Gloucestershire family with a modest estate he was well connected and could number among his kin the families of Berkeley and Brydges. It was presumably their sponsorship which explains his return for Cricklade, but to such powerful backing he could have added his own family's interest in the locality, his elder brother William holding property at Ashton Keynes, Haydon and Leigh. His election was doubtless approved by his uncle William Rede I who had served for the borough earlier and who in 1554 joined him in the House as one of the knights for Gloucestershire. Both uncle and nephew were found to be absent at the call of the House early in January 1555. As John Rede 'of Bristol, gentleman' he was informed against on this account in the King's bench and as John Rede 'of London, gentleman' he was fined 53s.4d. during Hilary term 1556, at which time two fellow-Inner Templars stood surety for him.³

Apart from his practice and Membership little has come to light about Rede. In 1544 he inherited an annuity of £4 from his father; four years later he was involved in a Star Chamber case concerning trespass and the theft of some hawks on his elder brother's manor of Redgrove. A man of his name, but perhaps a namesake, swore allegiance to Mary at Framlingham on 14 July 1553. On the death of his elder brother he succeeded to 'the most part' of the family property but he did not enjoy it for long. It was at the family house at Boddington that he made his will on 20 July 1570, asking to be buried near his father in the parish church, providing for his wife (the executrix) and remembering other relatives. Rede died just over two weeks later on 3 Aug.[4]

[1] Date of birth estimated from age at brother's i.p.m. C142/153/59. *Vis. Herefs.* ed. Weaver, 93; *VCH Berks.* iv. 165; PCC 1 Holney. [2] *CPR,* 1553–4, p. 37; 1554–5, p. 107. [3] *CPR,* 1547–8, p. 402; 1553, p. 152; KB27/1176–7; 28/188; St.Ch.3/2/5. [4] *APC,* iv. 429; St.Ch.3/2/5, 6/12; SP12/67/30; PCC 59 Chaynay, 9 Lyon, 1 Holney.

E.McI.

REDE, William I (c.1500–58), of Mitton, Worcs. and Tewkesbury, Glos.

CRICKLADE   1529
GLOUCESTERSHIRE   1554 (Nov.)

b. c.1500, 2nd s. of William Rede (*d.*10 Aug. 1508) of Boddington, Glos. by Margaret, da. of Richard Beauchamp†, 2nd Baron Beauchamp of Powick. *m.* by 1530, Catherine, da. of Richard Rowdon of Gloucester, Glos. by Cecily Arnold, 2s. 3da.[1]
  Servant of the Brydges family c.1540; escheator, Glos. 1553–4; j.p. 1554.[2]

William Rede was connected by descent with a number of the principal families in the Welsh marches and the west midlands, and his own marriage allied him further with those in his native county of Gloucestershire. His father, a servant of the 2nd Baron Beauchamp of Powick, had married one of his master's younger daughters and thereby gained a small estate in north Gloucestershire and adjoining areas.

It is not certain to which kinsman Rede owed his election to the Parliament of 1529, to his stepfather Thomas, *de jure* 5th Lord Berkeley, who was to mention both Rede and his wife in his will, or to Sir John Brydges*, one of Berkeley's associates whose service Rede may already have entered. If Rede was, or was related to, the man who in 1548 held the lease of some property in Ashton Keynes, Wiltshire, four miles from Cricklade, this may have determined his constituency. Presumably he was re-elected in 1536 in compliance with the general directive for the return of the previous Members. It was doubtless Brydges who secured Rede's return in 1554 as junior knight of the shire to Mary's third Parliament: he was then styled 'senior' on the indenture to distinguish him from his nephew, William Rede, 'junior', of Boddington. He was to be informed against in the King's bench, along with another nephew, John Rede II, for quitting this Parliament prematurely without leave, but as no further process was taken against him he may have cleared himself. In 1556 he was named an executor of Brydges's will. He, or his nephew and namesake, is probably to be identified with the gentleman

pensioner, as several others appointed at the setting up of the company of pensioners were kinsmen or clients of Brydges, and either of the pair may have been the esquire in the household of Anne of Cleves.[3]

As a younger son Rede did not inherit much property but he appears to have acquired a substantial estate. It was probably he who in July 1544 purchased crown lands valued at £212; in the following September he was granted lands formerly belonging to Tewkesbury abbey, including the abbot's own house called the *Vineyard*; and in 1552, with his nephew John, he purchased part of another manor that had belonged to the abbey for £387. On acquiring the 'Vineyard' he moved to Tewkesbury from Mitton, where until then he had lived.[4]

It is not known whether Rede received a grounding in the law, but several of his relatives and friends, including (Sir) David Broke* and Thomas Williams II*, and his nephew John Rede, were lawyers. He appeared as a litigant in the court of requests and the Star Chamber, and in Edward VI's reign he was to be accused of abetting his 'cousin' (Sir) Edmund Brydges* in contempt of the council in the marches.[5]

Rede made his will on 20 Aug. 1557, asking to be buried in the chancel of Bredon church, near his wife and eldest son. After providing for his daughters and several nieces, he left the 'Vineyard' to his nephew John and the bulk of his possessions to his surviving son Giles, whom he made an executor with his nephew and namesake and his 'good friend' Arthur Porter*. Rede died on 3 Nov. 1558, and in June the following year the wardship and marriage of Giles Rede, then aged 18, was granted to (Sir) Thomas Russell*.[6]

[1] Date of birth estimated from elder brother's, E150/344/1. *CPR,* 1558–60, p. 33; *Bristol and Glos. Arch. Soc. Trans.* xiv. 230; J. Smyth, *Berkeleys,* ii. 180; Duncumb, *Herefs.* ii. 71; PCC 3 Hogen, 59 Chaynay; C142/118/55. [2] *The Gen.* n.s. xxx. 101; *CPR,* 1554–5, p. 19; St.Ch.3/5/21. [3] *Cricklade,* ed. Thomson, 138; *Bristol and Glos. Arch. Soc. Trans.* xiv. 113; xliii. 26; lxxxiv. 137; *The Gen.* n.s. xxx. 101; Smyth, ii. 229–30; *CP,* ii. 47, 136–7; xii(2), 686–8; PCC 3 Hogen, 16 Wrastley; *CPR,* 1547–8, p. 402; KB 27/1176 rex roll r. 16, 29/188; LC2/2, f. 67. [4] *Bristol and Glos. Arch. Soc. Trans.* xiv. 230; xlvi. 327; *VCH Worcs.* iii. 287, 506–7; *LP Hen. VIII,* xiv, xvi, xix; *CPR,* 1547–8, p. 402; 1553, p. 152. [5] St.Ch.3/5/21; PCC 59 Chaynay; Req.2/249/25. [6] *Bristol and Glos. Arch. Soc. Trans.* lv. 26; PCC 59 Chaynay; C142/118/55; *CPR,* 1558–60, p. 33; Req.2/249/25.

E.McI.

REDE, William II (by 1529–69 or later), of Devizes, Wilts.; Yate, Glos. and the Middle Temple, London.

DEVIZES   1553 (Oct.)[1]

b. by 1529, s. of Thomas Rede (*d.*1529) by Joan. *educ.* M. Temple. *m.* by 1558, Maud, da. of Walter Bailey of Devizes, at least 1s.[2]
  Subsidy collector, Wilts. 1552; escheator, Hants and Wilts. 1564–5.[3]

Since Devizes normally returned townsmen under Mary, William Rede was probably a son of Thomas Rede, the wealthy clothier who was assessed for the subsidy in 1525 on goods in St. John's parish worth £100, the second largest sum recorded for the borough; apparently a younger son, William received £40 by Thomas's will. Although William Rede was never assessed for subsidy in Devizes, his family background makes it likely that he was the William Rede of Yate, in southern Gloucestershire, who married a daughter of Walter Bailey, another rich clothier of Devizes; Bailey left small bequests to his son-in-law William Rede and his 'godson' Edward Rede, both of whom witnessed his will on 1 Mar. 1559.[4]

Rede was admitted to the Middle Temple between 1524 and 1550, a period for which the entries are missing, and he was followed there by his son Edward. He could have been the attorney of that name in the common pleas in the late 1540s. If his career lay in London it is less surprising that the Devizes records, which exist in a fragmentary state from 1555, do not mention him. He seems none the less to have retained links with the town; the subsidy collector of 1552 is described as 'William Reade of the Devizes, gentleman', a similar style is given to the escheator of Hampshire and Wiltshire 12 years later and property in Devizes was sold by Rede and his wife in 1560–1. During the Easter law term of 1569 the same couple sold more lands, this time in Chippenham and Titherton Lucas. It is also likely that he was the man so named who had been steward of Calstone manor, near Calne, in 1562, when it was owned by Thomas Long.[5]

Rede's return to Parliament reflected his own local standing and may have been intended to promote his career. Of his part in the work of the House all that is known is that he did not oppose the restoration of Catholicism. When he obtained a pardon in June 1554 he was styled as 'late of London, *alias* of the Middle Temple, *alias* of Bristol'. That he was some-time a resident of Bristol suggests that he may have been a kinsman of William Rede I*, whose mother, Lady Berkeley, lived there. The Berkeley family had a lease of the manor of Yate where Rede lived.[6]

[1] Bodl. e Museo 17.   [2] Date of birth estimated from father's will, PCC 7 Jankyn. *Wilts. Vis. Peds.* (Harl. Soc. cv, cvi), 160; PCC 13 Mellershe. [3] E179/198/265. [4] E179/197/156; PCC 7 Jankyn, 13 Mellershe. [5] *M.T. Recs.* i. 154, 156, 171; CP40/1140, r. 453; E179/198/265; *Wilts. N. and Q.* iv. 456; vi. 355; vii. 305; Wilts. RO, 212b/967/12.   [6] *CPR*, 1553–4, p. 429; *Bristol and Glos. Arch. Soc. Trans.* xxi. 11.

T.F.T.B.

RESKYMER, John (c.1499–1566), of Merthen in Constantine and Tremayne, Cornw.

CORNWALL   1547[1]

b. c.1499, s. of John Reskymer of Merthen by 2nd w. Catherine, da. of John Tretherffe of Tretherffe in Ladock *unm.* 3s. 1da. illegit. by Margaret Greber. *suc.* fa. c.1504.[2]

Servant, household of Cardinal Wolsey by 1523; esquire of the body by 1535; sheriff, Cornw. 1535–6, 1539–40, 1556–7; j.p. 1536–64; reeve, Grampound, Cornw. 1541–2; commr. musters, Cornw. 1546; church goods 1549, relief 1550; bailiff, Helston, Cornw. 1549–50.[3]

John Reskymer belonged to a family seated at Merthen since the early years of the 15th century. His father died when he was about five years old, whereupon, in his own words, his body 'was seized and sold during his minority to divers hands and then at last came by sale unto the hands of one John Skewys', who had married his mother. This trans-action probably took place in or shortly before 1514, the year in which William Lytton and Sir William Trevanion brought an action against Skewys for ravishing the boy, whom they claimed as their ward. On coming of age Reskymer had difficulty in obtaining his inheritance. His complaint that his stepfather held on to it for 15 or 16 years is borne out by the fact that as late as 1537 the annual homage payment for Merthen was being charged to feoffees, as though the manor was still held by a minor. Not until the following year, when he was almost 40, was Reskymer himself asked to pay this sum, a demand which he evidently ignored as in 1544 proceedings were begun against him for seven years' arrears.[4]

It was some compensation for this ill usage that Skewys, who was on good terms with Wolsey, pro-cured for his stepson a place in the cardinal's house-hold. From this vantage-point Reskymer and Richard Antron petitioned Wolsey for the reversal of the attainder of Sir Henry Bodrugan and for the restoration of his estates to them as the next of kin; alleging that Bodrugan had been attainted on the perjured evidence of Sir Richard Edgecombe[†], they wanted the lands restored by Act of Parliament and to this end they offered the King and his minister 1,500 marks, but without avail. Wolsey's fall did not harm Reskymer and during the 1530s he received several marks of favour from the King. A familiar figure at court, he was immortalized in that setting by Holbein's portrait. During his first term as sheriff of Cornwall he was entrusted with raising the Cornish levy against the northern rebels: chosen sheriff again in 1539, he was perhaps for that reason absent from the reception for Anne of Cleves. His relations with his stepfather, never good, worsened before Skewys's death. In January 1543, abetted by William Carnsew* and William Cavell*, Reskymer occupied Skewys's manor of Polrode: about the same time Skewys was complaining that some of his deeds had passed into Reskymer's possession.[5]

When war came in 1543 Reskymer explained to the King that he could provide only six men for the army in France because most of his tenants were mariners or tinners. His own peak of activity was reached three years later when he was given the command of 300 Cornishmen for the defence of Boulogne: he set out for Dover with 100 of them but on the way he received fresh orders to join the lord admiral and spent the closing months of the war with the fleet in the Channel. This experience, combined with his place at court and his local ascendancy, made Reskymer a natural choice as one of the knights for Cornwall in 1547, when he was returned with another Sir Richard Edgecombe, grandson of the man he had once disparaged. (He may have sat in Parliament before, but in the absence of most of the returns to the Parliaments of Henry VIII, this remains uncertain.) Nothing is known about Reskymer's role in the House.[6]

Although he was not to sit in Parliament again, even when the accession of Mary restored the Church to which he remained faithful, Reskymer was prominent in Cornish affairs until shortly before his death. In 1564 Bishop Alley of Exeter rated him 'an extreme enemy' of the Elizabethan settlement and thought him unfit to remain on the bench, not only by reason of his Catholicism but also because he kept a mistress at Tremayne. It was to secure the succession to his estates of his eldest illegitimate son that in June 1555 he appointed Thomas Treffry I*, John Trelawny* and others as trustees in tail male of all his lands in Cornwall. After his death at Tremayne on 28 June 1566 all the property, with the exception of the Tretherffe estates, passed to this son, John Reskymer *alias* Greber.[7]

[1] Hatfield 207. [2] Aged 'five or thereabouts' at fa.'s death, C3/175/19. C. G. Henderson, *Constantine*, 98, 101; J. Maclean, *Trigg Minor*, i. 555. [3] E179/281; *LP Hen. VIII*, ix, x, xxi; *CPR*, 1550-3, p. 141; 1553, p. 351; 1560-3, p. 435; 1563-6, p. 20; Duchy Cornw. RO, 123, m. 11v; *CSP Dom.* 1601-3, *Add.* 1547-65, p. 398; information from G. Haslam. [4] Henderson, 95, 101; C3/175/19; Duchy Cornw. RO, 120, m. 15; 122, m. 16v; 223, m. 2. [5] *DNB* (Skuish or Skewes, John); Req.2/3/377; C1/1068/18-22; SP1/233, ff. 189-90; *Holbein* (The Queen's Gallery, Buckingham Palace 1978-9), 60-62; *LP Hen. VIII*, xi. [6] Henderson, 106; *LP Hen. VIII*, xi, xix, xxi; SP1/184, f. 101v; *APC*, iii. 504. [7] *Cam. Misc.* ix(3), 69; Henderson, 105-7; Truro mus. HA13/32, Henderson transcripts, 6, f. 299.

J.J.G.

RESTWOLD, Anthony (by 1517-55/60), of The Vache, Bucks.

NEW WOODSTOCK 1554 (Nov.)
AYLESBURY 1555

b. by 1517, 3rd but 1st surv. s. of Edward Restwold of The Vache by Agnes, da. of John Cheyne of Drayton Beauchamp, *s.p. suc.* fa. 1547.[1]
Servant of Lord Mautravers in 1541.[2]

The Restwold family was of Berkshire origin and had long been prominent in that and neighbouring counties. It also had links with the north of England; three of its five earlier Members had sat for Cumberland and Westmorland, and in 1542 Anthony Restwold's father sold the castle of Highhead in Cumberland shortly after buying the Buckinghamshire manor of Monks Risborough. He also held the manors of The Vache and Hedsor in Buckinghamshire and lands in Berkshire and Wiltshire. By a will which was proved on 12 Nov. 1547 two thirds of all this property went to his widow, who in 1549 married Thomas Waterton I*, and one third to Anthony.[3]

Anthony Restwold's wife had attended Catherine Howard before her marriage and was involved in her disgrace and downfall. She was first questioned about her former mistress on 5 Nov. 1541 and on 22 Dec. pleaded guilty to misprision of treason as having concealed the facts of the Queen's behaviour. The conviction and sentence, forfeiture of goods and life imprisonment, were confirmed by Parliament (33 Hen. VIII, c.21) in the following February, but within a few weeks she received a pardon. Her husband appears only once during this crisis. On 27 Nov. the Privy Council at Westminster asked the deputy governor of Calais, Lord Mautravers, to excuse the absence of his servant Anthony Restwold, detained because of his wife's examination. In 1544 Mautravers succeeded as 12th Earl of Arundel and Restwold may have stayed in his service, since nothing is known of his career until he was returned to Parliament.[4]

Arundel was not Restwold's only link with the adherents of Mary. The executors of Edward Restwold's will were his wife and her brother-in-law Sir Edmund Peckham*, and the witnesses included Doctor Feckenham, the future abbot of Westminster, then domestic chaplain to Bishop Bonner. Peckham's estate at Denham made him a neighbour of the Restwolds in Buckinghamshire, where in 1549 he bought Hedsor from Anthony Restwold and where he took the lead in proclaiming Mary four years later. Through Peckham Restwold was distantly related to another leading Marian, Sir Leonard Chamberlain*, who presumably secured his return for New Woodstock in the autumn of 1554, perhaps on the recommendation of Peckham, once Chamberlain's colleague at the Tower. Peckham himself was probably responsible for Restwold's election at Aylesbury in 1555. These official connexions notwithstanding, Restwold was one of those (Peckham's son Henry being another who opposed one of the government's bills in the Parliament of 1555.[5]

Neither will nor inquisition post mortem survives for Restwold, but on 1 Jan. 1560 his sisters and coheirs, together with their husbands (who included Richard Bunny*, Robert Lee† and Thomas Waterton II*) and their cousin John Babham, had licence to alienate Monks Risborough to Thomas Fleetwood*.[6]

[1] Date of birth estimated from age at fa.'s i.p.m., C142/86/5. *Misc. Gen. et Her.* ii. 135; *Vis. Bucks.* (Harl. Soc. lviii), 153. [2] *LP Hen. VIII*, xvi. [3] *Trans. Cumb. and Westmld. Arch. Soc.* n.s. xii. 25-28; *LP Hen. VIII*, xvi; PCC 48 Alen. [4] *LP Hen. VIII*, xvi, xvii; *DKR*, iii. 264-6. [5] *VCH Bucks.* iii. 55; *APC*, ii. 332; Guildford mus. Loseley 1331/2. [6] *CPR*, 1558-60, p. 376; *VCH Bucks.* iii. 188.

T.F.T.B.

REYNBALD, William (by 1488-1556), of Ipswich, Suff.

IPSWICH 1545

b. by 1488. *m.* Anne, 4s. 3da.[1]
Portman, Ipswich 1539-*d.*, bailiff 1542-3, 1549-50, 1555-6, j.p. 1542-5, 1546-7, 1549-50, 1553-4, 1555-6.[2]

William Reynbald came of a family at Norwich, where his brother Robert was a grocer. Acquiring a comfortable fortune from overseas trade, he is found lending Bishop Nykke of Norwich £80, and his subsidy assessment in 1545, of £60 on goods, was among the highest at Ipswich. Like other Ipswich merchants, he engaged in the Icelandic trade, where he and they were able to pay far higher wages to their crews than could the merchants of the smaller towns: Reynbald offered a skiff-master £7 for a single voyage.[3]

From the early 1540s until his death Reynbald served Ipswich almost continuously, either as bailiff or justice of the peace, and he clearly owed his return to the Parliament of 1545 to his municipal standing. He died between 23 Sept. and 29 Oct. 1556, the date of his will and its probate. His property, all in Ipswich and including a house lately called the *Greyfriars*, was left to his wife and son William. Two ships were to be sold, with preference of purchase to his sons Robert and William. The other two sons and his three daughters received generous bequests of money. He named as executors his son William, his brother Robert and his son-in-law Thomas Richmond and as supervisor his 'trusty friend Edmund Stuard, clerk'.[4]

[1] Date of birth estimated from first reference, 1509, E122/53/19. [2] N. Bacon, *Annals Ipswich*, 214-43 passim. [3] P. Millican, *Freemen of Norwich*, 71; E122/53/19; 179/181/280; *LP Hen. VIII*, x; J. G. Webb, *Great Tooley of Ipswich*, 77-78, 142. [4] PCC 19 Ketchyn.

J.P.

REYNOLD, John

BATH 1539[1]

John Reynold remains unidentified. The name was a common one, and none of those who bore it was either so prominent nationally or so clearly linked with Bath as to be accepted without question. The best case can be made for a resident of Keynsham who made his will in March 1553 providing for a wife and two daughters and died before the following July when it was proved. Keynsham lies between Bristol and Bath, although nearer the first, and this John Reynolds was a man of means who left three gowns, two of them furred, to different beneficiaries. He may have been the John 'Reignold' who in May 1551 was tenant of a house and 100 acres of land at (the unlocated) 'Kington Maundefeld', Somerset, but the inquisition taken in Devon in April 1548 must be that of another John Reynold, who owned land in that county worth £18 a year. The Reynold who was a yeoman of the crown between 1539 and 1545 could have been either of these or yet another, and such a court connexion might explain the election of an outsider, whereas the possibility of episcopal influence would arise if the Member was the 'Mr. Raynold' who was host in 1540 to a household servant of John Clerke, bishop of Bath and Wells. There is nothing to be said in favour of John Reynolds *alias* John ap Rhydderch, who probably entered Gray's Inn in 1530 and was clerk of the peace and of the crown in Anglesey and Merioneth between 1542 and 1546; his identification by a modern authority with the yeoman of the crown is probably wrong.[2]

[1] E159/319, brev. ret. Mich. r. [1-2]. [2] Wards 7/4/53; PCC 15 Taske; *LP Hen. VIII*, xiii, xviii, xx; *CPR*, 1550-3, p. 36; *Som. Med. Wills* (Som. Rec. Soc. xxi), 60; E. Stephens, *The Clerks of the Counties, 1360-1960*, p. 125.

D.F.C.

REYNOLDS, George (by 1518-77), of Rye, Suss.

RYE 1547,[1] 1563

b. by 1518, poss. s. of George Reynolds of Rye. *m.* (2).[2]
Chamberlain, Rye 1539-40, 1543-4, jurat 1546-77, mayor 1551-3, 1556-7, 1564-6, dep. mayor 1571-3; bailiff to Yarmouth 1554.[3]

George Reynolds's first Membership of Parliament was a landmark in his career. As a local official he was already known to Sir Thomas Cheyne*, the lord warden of the Cinque Ports, and in 1544 he had conducted men to Dover for Cheyne's use. It is possible that his return to the Parliament of 1547 was Cheyne's work. The indenture is lost, but a list compiled from the collections of a 17th-century lieutenant of Dover castle (who had access to manuscripts no longer extant) suggests that Rye reelected its two previous Members, Alexander Welles and Robert Wymond. Although payments of wages to Welles and Reynolds are recorded for the last three sessions, none has been traced for the opening session. As Wymond was released from service as a jurat in the summer of 1548 on account of ill-health, he may have been replaced at the same time as one of the town's Members, but it is more likely that Cheyne had overridden Rye's apparent choice in the previous year as he did there and elsewhere in the Cinque Ports on other occasions. Reynolds assisted Welles in soliciting advice and support for three bills in which the town was interested and in enforcing the ecclesiastical reforms which they had helped to pass.[4]

Although not elected again until 1563, Reynolds made an appearance in Parliament during Mary's reign. At a mayoral meeting held at Rye on 24 Nov. 1554 he was made 'solicitor to the Parliament for the repealing of a certain statute made for the delivering of herring at the town of Great Yarmouth in the time of the free fair there'. He was thus preferred to the town's two Members John Holmes I and Thomas Smith II, neither of whom was a jurat, when it came to a matter of which first-hand knowledge was desirable, and rightly so for he was at that time bailiff to Yarmouth. There is no knowing what influence he had on the course of the bill 'for buying of herrings upon the sea in the coasts of Norfolk and Suffolk' which passed the Commons but which failed after two readings in the Lords.[5]

Reynolds kept a tavern. In January 1555 he obtained a patent licensing him, 'forasmuch as the house in Rye in which he dwells is by reason of his great costs in building and repairing a meet place for subjects and strangers to resort to', to keep a tavern in this house or any other in Rye which he might inhabit in future; he was also pardoned for all offences against the Act (7 Edw. VI, c.5) fixing the retail price of wine and forbidding the keeping of any tavern without licence.[6]

A year later the Council asked Rye to choose as mayor George Reynolds, the Queen's servant, and the port complied. In the following year the Council wrote again, saying that whereas they had previously 'recommended' Reynolds they now, being informed that he had acquitted himself well in office and was likely to do so again, 'required' the mayor and jurats to take order for his re-election. This time, however, the Council's instruction, which was brought down by Reynolds himself, was ignored and his friend, colleague and possibly kinsman Welles elected. At a Guestling held earlier in 1557 he and Welles had been chosen as Rye's solicitors in the suit against the writ of *quo warranto* directed to the Cinque Ports: the expenses were borne by the town, Reynolds being paid £6 13s.4d. during the spring when he went to London on this business.[7]

Reynolds made his will on 17 Sept. 1577 and died two weeks later. The will was proved on 4 Oct.[8]

[1] Rye chamberlains' accts. 5, ff. 184, 185v; Hatfield 207. [2] Date of birth estimated from first reference. E. Suss. RO, Lewes archdeaconry wills A7, ff. 67v–69; *Vis. Kent* (Harl. Soc. lxxv), 119. [3] Rye chamberlains' accts. 4–8 passim; *Cinque Ports White and Black Bks.* (Kent Arch. Soc. recs. br. xix), 250; *Rye Shipping Recs.* (Suss. Rec. Soc. lxiv), 13. [4] Rye chamberlains' accts. 5, ff. 91v, 184, 185v, 186, 190, 218, 218v, 219, 222: 6, f. 39; churchwardens' accts. 1513–70, f. 114; Add. 34150. [5] Rye hundred ct. bk. 1546–56, f. 31; *CJ*, i. 38–39; *LJ*, i. 477–8. [6] *CPR*, 1554–5, pp. 236–7. [7] *APC*, v. 327; vi. 112; Rye chamberlains' accts. 6, ff. 129, 147v; hundred ct. bk. 1556–61, ff. 5, 6v; *Cinque Ports White and Black Bks.* 225. [8] E. Suss. RO, Lewes archdeaconry wills A7, ff. 67v–69.

H.M.

REYNOLDS, Owen (c.1519–76/77), of Melcombe Regis, Dorset.

MELCOMBE REGIS   ?1553 (Mar.),[1] 1553 (Oct.),1571

b. c.1519, prob. yr. s. of John Reynolds of Melcombe Regis. *m.* Emma, 4s. 4da.[2]
    Mayor, Melcombe Regis 1553–4, 1558–9, 1560–2, 1566–7, Weymouth and Melcombe 1575–6; customer, port of Weymouth by 1562–*d.*; chamberlain, Weymouth and Melcombe 1570–1.[3]

Owen Reynolds's grandfather was born in Somerset at Langport, but on his appointment as customer of Weymouth he had settled at Melcombe Regis. The tie between his family and the customs, established by his grandfather, lasted for several generations, and some 50 years after his grandfather had enjoyed the office Reynolds was customer himself. Reynolds was one of the leading figures in Melcombe, where he was mayor five times before its union with Weymouth and once afterwards, and thus he was a natural choice as one of the town's Members. He is first known to have been elected to Parliament on 11 Sept. 1553. At Michaelmas he succeeded Thomas Samways II* as mayor of Melcombe and on 1 Oct. he acknowledged receipt of 47s.4d. from Samways and others towards his parliamentary wages: this payment may have been a (somewhat unusual) contribution in advance or a discharge of the town's debt to Reynolds if he had sat with John Wadham in the Parliament of March 1553. During the first Parliament of Mary's reign there was an inevitable conflict of opinion in the House, and Reynolds was one of those noted as having 'stood for the true religion', that is to say for the Protestant cause.[4]

Reynolds was never described as a merchant, and his name rarely appears in the customs accounts, but in November 1558 Henry Newman and he, acting together, imported Gascon wine, salt and paper. Under Elizabeth he played a leading part in Melcombe's controversy with Weymouth over the harbour which the two ports shared and was returned to the Parliament which settled the issue by amalgamating the two. He died between the completion of his only mayoralty of the two united towns and September 1577 when his house in St. Thomas's

Street was granted by the corporation to his widow for her life, with remainders to their four sons and four daughters.[5]

[1] Weymouth and Melcombe Regis mss Sherren pprs. 16. [2] Aged 50 'or thereabouts' in 1569, E134/11 Eliz., Easter 3. *Vis. Dorset*, ed. Colby and Rylands, 42–43; Weymouth and Melcombe Regis ms M 2, f. 9. [3] Weymouth and Melcombe Regis mss M 2, f. 3, Sherren pprs. 29–31, 34; St.Ch.5/M30/14. [4] *LP Hen. VIII*, i; Weymouth and Melcombe Regis mss Sherren pprs. 16; Bodl. e Museo 17. [5] E122/123/2; St.Ch.5/M30/14; Weymouth and Melcombe Regis ms M 2, f. 9.

H.M.

RICE, William (by 1522–88), of Medmenham Bucks.

AYLESBURY 1554 (Nov.), 1555
LANCASTER 1558

b. by 1522, s. of one Rice by Eden, da. of Thomas Saunders. *m.* by Nov. 1553, Barbara ?Fuller.[1]

Sewer, the chamber by 1543; bailiff, manors of Kingsland and Much Marcle, Herefs. Feb. 1543; gent. the privy chamber by Nov. 1553; bailiff and collector of former lands of St. Mary's abbey, York in Cumb., Lincs., Yorks. and Westmld. 1553–?*d*.[2]

William Rice claimed gentle birth but his parentage has not been traced. He is first glimpsed in 1543 when already established as a minor household officer he obtained the bailiwick of two Herefordshire manors. Of his progression at court nothing has been found until Mary made him a gentleman of the privy chamber and gave him an annuity of £20 in reward for his support during the succession crisis of 1553. A more substantial grant to him and his wife Barbara, for good service, was made on 7 Nov. 1553, comprising the manors of Backnoe in Thurleigh, Bedfordshire and Medmenham. Later royal grants included manors in Kent and Somerset, and a moiety of some former Dudley properties in the midlands. Barbara Rice is sometimes identified with the Mistress Rice to whom during her last illness Queen Mary confided that when she died Calais would be found 'lying' on her heart, but this is more likely to have been Beatrice ap Rhys who had been in Mary's service since at least 1525.[3]

Rice doubtless owed his return for Aylesbury in 1554 and 1555 to his post in the Household and his establishment in Buckinghamshire. He obviously satisfied the religious criterion then being applied. Why he was not re-elected for Aylesbury in 1558 remains a matter for speculation, but a seat was found for him at Lancaster by the duchy presumably in response to official prompting. The Journal does not mention him. At the accession of Elizabeth he withdrew from court and played no part in national or local affairs. In April 1561 he was imprisoned in the Tower 'for the mass', but although he implored pardon he is not known to have accepted the Anglican settlement. He was a sick man when on 22 July

1588 he made a will providing for his wife and three of his sisters and naming his wife and two friends executors. He died at Chipping Wycombe a week later. At the inquisition, not taken until 1596, it was found that the manor of Medmenham had been settled in July 1588 on his nephew William Rice, but by 1596 there were no heirs on his father's side, and his nearest kinsman was his maternal cousin, William Saunders.[4]

[1] Date of birth estimated from first reference. C142/246/107. [2] *LP Hen. VIII*, xviii; *CPR*, 1553–4, p. 284; LC2/4/2. [3] A. H. Plaisted, *Manor and Par. Recs. of Medmenham*, passim; *CPR*, 1553–4. pp. 45, 53, 259, 281, 501–2; 1554–5, pp. 168, 175; 1557–8, pp. 89, 407; C142/246/107; Holinshed, *Chron.* iv. 137; *VCH Bucks*. iii. 9, 12–14; *Privy Purse Expenses of Princess Mary 1536–44*, ed. Madden, 38, 55. [4] *CSP Dom.* 1601–3, *Add.* 1547–65, p. 510; 1547–80, p. 180, (the letter calendared under 1570 in *CSP Dom.* 1547–80, p. 403 was almost certainly written much earlier, probably in 1561, SP12/75/75) and cf. SP12/75/75); *Cath. Rec. Soc.* i. 45, 49–52, 55; Strype, *Parker*, i. 218–19; PCC 10 Leicester; C142/246/107.

M.K.D.

RICH, Richard (1496/97–1567), of West Smithfield, Mdx., Rochford and Leighs, Essex.

COLCHESTER 1529
?ESSEX 1536[1]
ESSEX 1539[2]
?ESSEX 1542[3]
ESSEX 1545

b. 1496/97, s. of John Rich of Penton Mewsey, Hants by Agnes. *educ.* Camb.; M. Temple, adm. ?5 Feb. 1516. *m.* by May 1536, Elizabeth, da. of William Gynkes or Jenks of London, at least 3s. 9 or 10da.; 1s. illegit. *suc.* fa. ?1509. Kntd. 12 June 1536; *cr.* Baron Rich 16 Feb. 1547.[4]

Master of revels, M. Temple 1516; butler 1519–20, Autumn reader 1529.

J.p. Essex, Herts. 1528–*d.*; member, council of 15th Earl of Oxford by 1529; commr. subsidy, London 1540, relief, Essex 1550, goods of churches and fraternities 1553; other commissions 1529–*d.*; clerk of recognizances 22 Mar. 1532–7 Dec. 1548; attorney-gen. for Wales 13 May 1532–28 June 1558; dep. chief steward, duchy of Lancaster, south parts, 1532–6; recorder, Colchester 30 Sept. 1532–44; solicitor-gen. 10 Oct. 1533–13 Apr. 1536; chirographer, ct. common pleas 27 July 1535–3 July 1537; surveyor of the liveries 20 Apr. 1536–14 Mar. 1537; chancellor, ct. augmentations 24 Apr. 1536–24 Apr. 1544, jt. (with (Sir) Edward North*) chancellor 24 Apr.–1 July 1544; groom, privy chamber in 1539; PC by Aug. 1540–Nov. 1558; treasurer, French war 1 May–Dec. 1544; bailiff, manor of Northwold May 1546; ld. chancellor 23 Oct. 1547–21 Dec. 1551; trier of petitions in the Lords, Parlts. of Oct. 1553, Nov. 1554, 1559, 1563; chief steward, honor of Rayleigh 4 July 1558.[5]

Speaker of House of Commons 1536.

Richard Rich was born at Basingstoke, Hampshire. A tradition deriving from Stow links him with a family prominent in the affairs of London and of the Mercers' Company during the 15th century, but the genealogies illustrating this line of descent date from the 17th century and contain numerous variations and some errors. He was the son of one John Rich of

Penton Mewsey, who in 1509 left a house in Islington, Middlesex, to a son Richard, on condition that he was obedient to his mother. When during the trial of John Philpot, the Edwardian archdeacon of Winchester, Philpot stated that he was a son of Sir Peter Philpot of Hampshire, Rich remarked that Sir Peter was his near kinsman, wherefore he was the more sorry.

Like many of his contemporaries in the service of the crown, Rich owed his initial advancement to his legal training. He is probably to be identified with one 'Master Shreche' who entered the Middle Temple in February 1516; by 1529 he was sufficiently advanced to be chosen Autumn reader. He first tried to establish himself in public life by seeking office in the city of London, but he lost the election to the common serjeantship in 1526 to the crown's nominee, William Walsingham, although he was promised the office at the next vacancy. Two years later he sought to bring himself to the attention of Wolsey by expressing interest in the chancellor's proposed reform of the common law; again he failed to secure an office, although his letter to Wolsey may have influenced his appointment to the Essex and Hertfordshire commissions of the peace in December 1528.

Rich owed his return for Colchester to the 15th Earl of Oxford, of whose council he was a member. However, as another servant of the earl's, Richard Anthony, had already been elected by the time that Oxford preferred Rich for the seat, which Anthony then resigned, it is probable that the earl had yielded to persuasion to make the change, although from what quarter can only be guessed: one of Rich's friends, Thomas Audley, had already been designated as Speaker and chosen knight of the shire, and he could well have been the intermediary in Rich's favour. Three years later Audley, now chancellor, may have helped Rich to obtain his first important office, that of solicitor-general. In this capacity Rich followed Audley into the House of Lords and on 20 Dec. 1534 a warrant was issued to pay him £20 for his attendance there. He has been shown to have shared in the drafting of several bills passed during this Parliament, among them those forbidding appeals to Rome, dissolving the lesser monasteries and establishing the court of augmentations. Ten days after the dissolution of Parliament on 14 Apr. 1536 he was appointed first chancellor of augmentations, a post for which he was probably in mind when it was created: his occupancy of it was to move the French ambassador Marillac to call Rich 'the most wretched creature . . . the first inventor of the destruction of the abbeys and monasteries [and] the general confiscation of church property', a stigma which has continued to tarnish his memory.[6]

Still greater obloquy attaches to Rich's part in the state trials of these years. As solicitor-general he had to prosecute those who denied the validity of the King's second marriage or the royal supremacy. He prepared the indictment against the Nun of Kent and her associates in 1533, and in the following year he took part in the examination of the priors of Bevell in Nottinghamshire and of the Charterhouse in Axholme, Lincolnshire, who refused to accept the King as Supreme Head. He also helped to examine Bishop Fisher, but was probably not responsible for the unscrupulous tactics ascribed to him in Hall's 'Life' of the bishop. It was, however, Rich's testimony which was the gravamen of the indictment against Sir Thomas More and his evidence at the trial which was decisive in securing a conviction: in Roper's account More retaliated by denouncing Rich as a perjurer, and for good measure as an idler and a gambler, epithets which the circumstances of their origin have helped to make synonymous with Rich's name. By contrast, his scarcely less decisive part in the condemnation of Cromwell five years later is seldom held against him.[7]

It was a different kind of demonstration of his subservience to the crown that Rich gave in the Parliament of 1536, to which he was probably returned as one of the knights for Essex. Asked to choose a Speaker by the second day of the Parliament, the Commons had to beg for more time before deciding on Rich on the third day: whether this means that his election encountered opposition we cannot tell. His opening oration compared the King to Solomon for prudence and justice, to Samson for strength and bravery, and to Absalom for beauty. Equally extravagant was his concluding address likening the King's care for his subjects to the sun's influence upon the world. Next to nothing is known about his part in the preparation and management of the legislative programme, but Bishop Gardiner later recalled that he and Rich had advised on the drafting of a bill enacted giving authority to such as should succeed to the crown of the realm (28 Hen. VIII, c.17). After the dissolution Rich was paid the customary fee of £100 as Speaker.[8]

Rich was returned to the Parliaments of 1539 and 1545 as senior knight for Essex, with Sir Thomas Darcy as his junior colleague. Darcy, who had married a daughter of the Earl of Oxford, had probably first entered the Commons at a by-election following the death of Thomas Bonham in 1532 and had thus almost certainly been Rich's fellow-knight at the Parliament of 1536. During the Parliament of 1539 Rich obtained a private Act (31 Hen. VIII, c.23) to assure him certain lands and in the last session signed another (32 Hen. VIII, c.77) concerning the King and Sir Thomas Wyatt I*. Although no indenture survives to furnish the names of the Essex knights in 1542, Rich and Darcy were doubtless returned again; Rich's signature appears at the foot of four Acts, all passed during its final session, for exchanges of lands between the King and several of his subjects, and he bore a message from the Commons on 4 Feb. 1544 to the Lords for a conference on the King's style.[9]

By 1540, when the last monastic houses had been dissolved, Rich was presiding over the largest of the revenue courts and was, consequently, an important member of the Privy Council. An able administrator, he acquiesced in the policy of alienating land to meet the financial needs of the crown which began with a commission to Cromwell and Rich in 1539 to sell lands to the annual value of £6,000. During his chancellorship of the augmentations Rich was able to build up a considerable estate in Essex, chiefly through purchase; his principal gift, made by the King in 1536, was the small priory at Leighs, which Rich shortly rebuilt, and four other small manors worth £26 a year. As chancellor Rich had to defend himself against several charges of corruption before the King and Privy Council, and when under Mary the court was merged with the Exchequer further accusations were brought against him of faulty drafting of indentures in exchanges of land and in sales of wood and lead. None of these attacks issued in formal prosecution.

In his final months at the augmentations Rich joined Sir Thomas Wriothesley in mobilizing financial resources for the forthcoming French campaign and on 1 May 1544 he became treasurer for the French war. He crossed the Channel in July and for five months was in charge of pay, supplies and transport. His final account does not seem to survive, but a memorandum puts his outgoings from 1 May to 18 Oct. 1544 as £424,692, a figure greatly in excess of his own and Wriothesley's forecast of the previous spring. The King 'marvelled' at several of the discrepancies and it may not have been illness alone which caused Rich's resignation and return in November. For the last three years of the reign he held no major appointment but he continued his association with the war effort, serving on special commissions for meeting its costs and for examining the royal revenues.

As the reign drew to its close Rich became increasingly identified with the conservative faction in the Privy Council. In 1546 he was involved in Bishop Bonner's attempt to put down heresy in the diocese of London, especially in Rich's adopted county of Essex, and according to Foxe it was

Wriothesley and Rich who racked Anne Askew in order to discover her sympathisers at court. Yet he remained on good terms with Edward Seymour, Earl of Hertford, who at one stage recommended him for an appointment at Boulogne. He also connived at the destruction of the 3rd Duke of Norfolk and the Earl of Surrey, being one of the Councillors deputed to examine the duke. Henry VIII appointed him to be an assistant to the execution of his will and bequeathed him £200 for his pains.[10]

On the accession of Edward VI Rich was created a baron. He supported the assumption of the Protectorship by Hertford, now Duke of Somerset, and helped to engineer the removal of Wriothesley from the chancellorship. He himself was not the Protector's immediate choice to hold the great seal, for William Paulet, Baron St. John, succeeded Wriothesley in March 1547, but in October, before the opening of the first Edwardian Parliament, he became chancellor. In this capacity he was instrumental in securing the passage of Somerset's legislation during the first session. The bill repealing the Treason Acts of Henry VIII was committed to him after its first reading in the House of Lords and again after the fifth reading when he annexed certain provisos to it; when this bill was rejected by the Commons Rich was a member of the committee of both Houses which discussed the new bill introduced there. During the same session an Act was passed for the assurance of certain lands to Rich and (Sir) William Shelley* (1 Edw. VI, no. 13). Both membranes of the Act for the King's general pardon were signed by Rich and six other Privy Councillors.[11]

At first Rich put the power and dignity of the chancellorship behind the Council's policy of gradual Reformation. He ordered the bishops to adopt the new rite ordained by the Prayer Book of 1549 and commanded the justices to ensure the conformity of lay people. He also confirmed the sentences of deprivation passed against Bonner and Gardiner. An enemy of religious extremism, he suppressed Protestant conventicles in Essex; in 1551 he was a reluctant witness at the trial of Gardiner. Although he spent considerable time presiding over Chancery in person, he could not avoid the factional strife within the Council. He took the formal lead in prosecuting Admiral Seymour, and in the *coup d'état* of October 1549 he joined the Councillors against the Protector and used his good relations with the mayor and aldermen of London to win their support: a contemporary witness also judged that Rich's use of letters under the great seal to countermand the Protector's appeals for assistance to sheriffs and justices was decisive in securing the Council's victory. His signature is to be found on four Acts, including one for the fine and ransom of Somerset, passed during the third session of Parliament in the autumn of 1549.[12]

Rich did not support John Dudley, Earl of Warwick, in his political manoeuvring during 1551. He sealed the warrants for the arrest and trial of Somerset and, when he fell ill, established a commission to hear causes in Chancery in his absence. The illness may have been genuine but it was also timely in that Rich retained office while avoiding the final conflict between Somerset and Warwick. Yet it was not enough to save him. Following a rumour that Somerset, taught by the experience of 1549, had attempted to obtain the great seal, Rich was visited on 31 Dec. at his house in Smithfield by Dudley, newly created Duke of Northumberland, and had the seal taken from him. It was to be almost a year before he attended another meeting of the Council, and he was never to hold great office again. One of his last acts as chancellor had been to sign a bill for the city of London which was to be enacted in the fourth session of Parliament, which met early in 1552.[13]

Rich was one of those who subscribed on 21 June 1553 to the device settling the crown on Lady Jane Grey. Three days later he received the honor of Rayleigh, clearly a reward for his acquiescence and an attempt to ensure his support. It failed of its purpose, for on Edward VI's death he quickly declared for Mary. He was confirmed as a Privy Councillor and one of his first tasks was as a commissioner of claims for the Queen's coronation. He appears to have attended Council meetings infrequently during Mary's reign, but even if in Parliament he opposed one ecclesiastical measure probably for fear it would cost him his monastic properties, as a justice in Essex he enforced the Catholic restoration so ruthlessly that Strype denounced him as a 'severe persecutor'. With the 16th Earl of Oxford and other Essex notables he supervised the burning of heretics, and in 1556 he served on the commission inquiring into the property of those who fled the realm on religious grounds. Rich's primary concern in breaking up conventicles and suppressing heresy among the artisans of Essex seems to have been for the preservation of order and the maintenance of authority: he was more interested in conformity than in theology. One of his daughters is said to have entered the revived Bridgettine house at Syon as a nun. During the first session of the Parliament of 1558 the bill whereby he granted the manor of Rayleigh to the Queen was debated and enacted (4 and 5 Phil. and Mary, no. 11). He was obliged to surrender further properties but to compensate him for their loss he

was soon afterwards made steward of the manor.[14]

At the accession of Elizabeth, Rich accompanied her on her leisurely progress to London. The new Queen did not confirm his appointment as a Privy Councillor but she retained his services and he continued to be styled Councillor until his death. It is possible that at one time he was nominated to the order of the Garter, for on a licence of January 1563 he is styled KG. In the new conditions he was able to repurchase several of the properties surrendered earlier, notably St. Bartholomew's priory for which he had originally paid £1,605 in 1544 and which he had surrendered in December 1555 without compensation. Excluded from authority at the centre Rich played a prominent role in Essex, where he had become a principal landowner. He was an active justice of the peace and intervened in parliamentary elections, as when in 1563 he sought unsuccessfully to have his heir Robert chosen a knight of the shire. In the Parliament of 1559 Rich voted against the Act of Uniformity, and in 1566 he was a member of a delegation from both Houses which addressed the Queen on the subject of her marriage and the succession.

Rich died at Rochford on 12 June 1567 and was buried at Felstead on 8 July. By the terms of his will, dated 12 May 1567 but with two codicils added nearly a month later, he devised most of his estates upon his surviving son Robert. His nine surviving daughters, all married, were to share the movable goods. An illegitimate son Richard was also provided for, with a stipulation that he was to be brought up in the study of the common law. The will arranged for the establishment of an almshouse in Rochford, but Rich had already made his principal benefactions. On the death of his eldest son Hugh he had founded a chantry at Felstead, licensed in April 1555, and a perpetual Lenten herring dole for the poor of Felstead and neighbouring parishes: in conformity with the Elizabethan settlement the chantry was converted into a grammar school and an almshouse established. Drawings of Rich and his wife made by Holbein survive.[15]

[1] *LJ*, i. 84–86. [2] E159/319, brev. ret. Mich. r. [1–2]; *LJ*, i. 124; [3] House of Lords RO, Original Acts, 35 Hen. VIII, nos. 19, 21–23; *LJ*, i. 243. [4] Aged 54 in Jan. 1551, Foxe, *Acts and Mons.* vi. 175–6. This biography rests on M. E. Coyle, 'Sir Richard Rich, 1st Baron Rich (1496–1567): a political biog.' (Harvard Univ. Ph.D. thesis, 1967) and E. McIntyre, 'Some aspects of the life and political career of Sir Richard Rich' (Aberdeen Univ. M. Litt. thesis, 1968). [5] *LJ*, i. 448, 465, 542, 580. [6] *EHR*, lxvi. 176; *Pprs. Geo. Wyatt* (Cam. Soc. ser. 4, v), 159. [7] Elton, *Policy and Police*, 343, 404, 408, 410–16. [8] Hargrave 388, f. 135. [9] *LJ*, i. 124, 243; House of Lords RO, Original Acts, 32 Hen. VIII, no. 73; 35 Hen. VIII, nos. 19, 21–23. [10] *Wealth and Power*, ed. Ives, Knecht and Scarisbrick, 90, 101. [11] M. A. R. Graves, 'The Tudor House of Lords' (Otago Univ. Ph.D. thesis, 1974), ii. 340–5. [12] House of Lords RO, Original Acts, 3 and 4 Edw. VI, nos. 23, 24, 30, 31. [13] Ibid. 5 Edw. VI, no. 21. [14] Graves, ii. 340–5. [15] *Holbein* (The Queen's Gallery, Buckingham Palace 1978–9), 114–16.

M.E.C./A.D.K.H.

RICHERS, Robert (by 1524–87/89), of Lincoln's Inn, London and Wrotham, Kent.

REIGATE 1547, 1554 (Apr.), 1554 (Nov.)
GRAMPOUND 1558

b. by 1524, 2nd s. of Henry Richers of Swannington, Norf. by Cecily, da. of Robert Tills of Runhall, Norf. *educ.* L. Inn, adm. 3 June 1538, called 1544. *m.* by Nov. 1553, Elizabeth, da. of Edmund Cartwright of Ossington, Notts. by Agnes, da. of Thomas Cranmer of Sutton, Notts., wid. of Reginald Peckham (*d.*21 July 1551) of Yaldham, Kent, 1s. 5da.[1]
Associate of the bench, L. Inn 1567; reader, Furnival's Inn 1567.
J.p. Kent 1558/59–*d.*

A younger son in an old Norfolk family, Robert Richers was set to the law. His youthful indiscretions merited a rebuke by the elders of Lincoln's Inn; they were not otherwise held against him but, once he had become a barrister, his inattention to the details of the inn's administration displeased his colleagues. His education there was barely finished when he entered the Commons in 1547. He was a stranger to Reigate. With the 3rd Duke of Norfolk a prisoner in the Tower, the patronage of the borough may have been exercised by the Council or by the duke's half-brother, Lord William Howard, with whom perhaps Richers was already acquainted; if Richers needed conciliar endorsement on this occasion, his later connexion by marriage with Archbishop Cranmer may explain how he got it. During 1553 Howard was in Calais and his absence was perhaps the reason why Richers was not returned to either of the Parliaments held in that year: in the spring Howard alienated several manors in Suffolk to him and in the autumn his counsel was retained by the Duke of Norfolk over the bill reversing his attainder. By the following year Howard had returned to England and had become a Privy Councillor, and Richers's reappearance in the Commons was presumably his doing. Howard's influence was pervasive, and even though Richers did not sit for Reigate again he may have received support elsewhere. In the absence of so many returns his Membership in 1555 is hypothetical—it was the year of Cranmer's burning—but in 1558 he must have used one of the numerous links between Lincoln's Inn and Cornwall to sit for a Cornish borough. If he was not to reappear in the House, it was presumably for lack of inclination rather than because of religious dissidence; in 1564 he was rated 'conformable' by Archbishop Parker and for the last 30 years of his life he was a leading figure in Kent.[2]

Richers's practice prospered and early in his career he made numerous purchases in East Anglia. On his marriage to Elizabeth Cranmer he settled in Kent and his acquisitions in middle life were mainly in his adopted county. He made his will on 4 May 1587. He left the details of his funeral to the discretion of his wife and son, who were to be his executors, only requesting that there should be 'no pomp or vain glory'. His brother Henry was to be supervisor. He left £5 to 'the most poor and needy people, sturdy beggars and vagabonds as much as may be avoided', and 16*s.*8*d.* to be distributed each Good Friday for seven years following his death to the poor in three parishes. He gave a silver bowl to each of his three married daughters, and £10 to his granddaughter. His two unmarried daughters received £100 each and all his property in Devon. His wife was to enjoy a life estate of all his property in Norfolk and Kent and to share with her son John the residue of his goods. The date of Richers's death is not known, but the will was proved on 12 Feb. 1589.[3]

[1] Date of birth estimated from education. [2] *Black Bk. L. Inn*, i. 260, 305; *CPR*, 1553, pp. 73, 111; *CJ*, i. 32; *Cam. Misc.* ix(3), 57–58. [3] *CPR*, 1547–8, p. 337; 1549–51, pp. 52, 57; 1553–4, p. 89; Blomefield, *Norf.* viii. 183, 303; E150/503/3; Hasted, *Kent*, v. 14, 16; PCC 25 Leicester.

S.R.J.

RIDER (RYTHER), Thomas (by 1479–1525 or later), of New Windsor, Berks.

NEW WINDSOR 1512,[1] 1515[2]

b. by 1479.[3]
Mayor, New Windsor 1512, 1524–5; commr. subsidy 1515.[4]

The first mention of Thomas Rider shows that in 1500 he paid a rent of 4*s.* to the guild of the Holy Trinity, Windsor, presumably for some property in the borough. He was almost certainly a townsman, since the chamberlains' accounts between 1515 and 1522 contain several payments to him for the annual 'upping of swans', when the swan mark of the corporation was placed on their bills. A Thomas Rider was among the surveyors of the hall in the King's household between 1509 and 1524, but there is nothing but the name to connect him with the Member for Windsor.[5]

Rider appears only once in the chamberlains' book as mayor, when he heard the accounts at the guildhall in October 1524. He is known, however, to have held the office in 1512, for Ashmole's extracts from the corporation records include a note that he was mayor in the fourth year of Henry VIII. Ashmole also noted payments to Rider as a Member of the Parliament of 1512, although he seems to have copied these from the chamberlains' accounts, which still exist and which sometimes yield different sums. The dates and amounts are the same as those recorded for Rider's fellow-Member John Welles, save that between April 1515 and April 1516 a sum of 13*s.*4*d.*

was delivered to Rider alone 'in full payment of 40s.'; he also received 6s.8d. 'for the commission of the subsidy of the town of Windsor'. It is difficult to relate these payments to any particular parliamentary session. Rider may have sat again in 1523 when the names of the Windsor Members are unknown. In 1524 he was assessed for subsidy on goods worth £50, which makes him one of the half-dozen wealthiest townsmen, and his last appearance in the chamberlains' accounts is in the following October, when he received a fee of 20s. for his recent term of office. A year later William Symonds* was paid for keeping the swans, so it seems that Rider died at about this time, and his name with him.[6]

[1] R. R. Tighe and J. E. Davis, *Windsor Annals*, i. 465; Windsor recs. Wi/FA c.1, f. 6v. [2] Tighe and Davis, i. 473–4; Windsor recs. Wi/FA c.1, ff. 7v, i, 9v. [3] Date of birth estimated from first reference. [4] Windsor recs. Wi/FA c.1, f. 7, 20v; *LP Hen. VIII*, i; Tighe and Davis, i. 515. [5] Bodl. Ashmole 1126, f. 16v; *VCH Berks.* iii. 60; Windsor recs. Wi/GA c.1, ff. 8–17; *LP Hen. VIII*, i, iv. [6] Windsor recs. Wi/FA c.1, ff. 6v, 7v, 8, 9v, 20v, 23, 25; Tighe and Davis, i. 515; *LP Hen. VIII*, i; Bodl. Ashmole 1126, f. 23; E179/73/130, 137.

T.F.T.B.

RIDGEWAY, John (by 1517–60), of the Middle Temple, London, and Newton Abbot, Abbotskerswell and Tor Mohun, Devon.

DARTMOUTH   1539,[1] 1545
EXETER   1553 (Oct.), 1554 (Apr.)

b. by 1517, s. of Michael Ridgeway of Newton Abbot. *educ.* M. Temple. *m.* by 1542, Elizabeth, da. of John Wendford of Newton Abbot, 1s. Thomas† 2da.[2]

Jt. feodary, Devon 3 June 1538; jt. chief steward for Torre abbey, Devon 1538–9; jt. receiver-gen. Devon, Dorset and Som. for Syon abbey 1538–9; j.p. Devon 1540–d., q. 1554; commr. relief 1550; escheator, Devon and Cornw. 1554–5; recorder, Totnes by 1554.[3]

The son of a Newton Abbot brewer, John Ridgeway became a lawyer and his grandson Thomas was to be ennobled. No explanation has been found of the *alias* Peacock which was added to his name in the pedigree supplied at the heraldic visitation four years after his death but which has been found nowhere else. At the Temple he shared chambers with John Southcote, presumably his neighbour at Bovey Tracey and Member for Lostwithiel, not the Elizabethan judge: Ridgeway's son later strengthened the ties between the families by marrying one of Southcote's granddaughters.[4]

The year 1538 saw Ridgeway embarked on his local career, the crown appointing him feodary, Dartmouth retaining his services and two monasteries giving him posts. During the following year he received a number of appointments and pensions from religious houses in Devon, but as a Member of the Parliament of 1539 he helped to pass the Act (31 Hen. VIII, c.31) dissolving them. He may have been responsible for the inclusion of Dartmouth in the Act for the re-edification of towns westwards (32 Hen. VIII, c.19), which gave the places concerned temporary relief from certain payments to the crown, for the £8 13s.4d. which Dartmouth paid him, although below the statutory rate, was almost three times as much as his fellow-Member William Holland received. It was, however, Holland whom the town re-elected to the next Parliament and when Ridgeway was returned to its successor he appears not to have been the first choice, his name being inserted over an erased one on both the return for the shire and the sheriff's schedule. According to the town accounts for 1546–7 he was paid 46s.8d. 'for his wages for the Parliament this year at 8d. a day'; since only the second session fell within this financial year, and that lasted for 18 days, the difference between the bill thus incurred, which even if it included six days' travel would have amounted to 16s., and the amount paid must mean either that Ridgeway was being paid for both sessions (totalling, with travel time, 60 days and thus costing £2) or that he was receiving a substantial addition for fees or other expenses.[5]

It was during and shortly after his first Parliament that Ridgeway made his first purchases of ex-monastic land, including Abbotskerswell which he bought in December 1540 and which he made his home. He was called upon to furnish men for the French campaign of 1544 and victuals for the Scottish one three years later. Nothing has come to light about his part during the western rebellion in 1549 but when five years later the Carews joined Wyatt's conspiracy he kept the sheriff Sir Thomas Denys* and the Council informed about unease in the county. He reappeared in Parliament twice under Mary, sitting on both occasions for Exeter with his friend Richard Hart. He had advised the city and many of its leading merchants, but he probably owed his adoption there to the support of Secretary Petre whom he assisted in land transactions and whose estate accounts for the south-west he audited; in compliance with the civic ordinance governing Membership he was admitted to the freedom four days after his first election. Of his role in these two Parliaments all that is known is that he did not oppose the restoration of Catholicism, but he presumably supported the bill introduced in the first of them to bring the terms of apprenticeship in Bristol and Exeter into agreement with those in London. He was doubtless excluded from re-election in the autumn of 1554 by the Queen's request for the return of residents and he was not to sit again before his death at Tor Mohun on 24 Apr. 1560. Under his will, which is known only from extracts quoted in his inquisition post mortem, he provided for his widow, children and servants, remembered the poor and named among his executors Richard Hart and Thomas Southcote*. He was buried at Tor Mohun where a monument was later erected to his memory.[6]

[1] Exeter city lib. Dartmouth ms 2002, f. 13v. [2] Date of birth estimated from first reference. J. E. Kew, 'The land market in Devon 1536–58' (Exeter Univ. Ph.D. thesis, 1967), 347–8; *Vis. Devon*, ed. Colby, 183; *Vis. Devon*, ed. Vivian, 647; Wards 7/8/48. [3] *LP Hen. VIII*, xiii, xv, xvi, xviii, xx; *CPR*, 1553, p. 352; 1553–4, p. 18; *Devon Monastic Lands* (Devon and Cornw. Rec. Soc. n.s. i), passim; Devon RO, 1579/A1v. [4] Kew, 347–8; *Vis. Devon*, ed. Colby, 183; *M.T. Recs.* i. 92; *Trans. Dev. Assoc.* lvi. 221. [5] *LP Hen. VIII*, xiii; Exeter city lib. Dartmouth ms 2002, ff. 13v, 16v, 17v, 18v, 22v; C219/18C/32, 33. [6] *LP Hen. VIII*, xv–xx, add; *Devon Monastic Lands*, passim; Kew, 203, 311; L. S. Snell, *Suppression of Rel. Foundations in Devon and Cornw.* 155, 164; E315/340/12; St.Ch.2/32/134; C1/1058/70; *APC*, ii. 188; D. M. Loades, *Two Tudor Conspiracies*, 37, 45; *Archaeologia*, xxviii. 147; *CSP Dom.* 1547–80, p. 57; Exeter act bk. 2, ff. 115v, 126; NRA 9466 sec. iii passim; 9546, pp. 8–11; *Exeter Freemen* (Devon and Cornw. Rec. Soc. extra ser. i), 80; *CPR*, 1558–60, p. 164; Wards 7/8/48; W. G. Hoskins, *Devon*, 501.

R.V.

RIDLEY, Thomas (by 1509–80), of Caughley, Willey and The Bold, nr. Kinlet, Salop.

MUCH WENLOCK 1555

b. by 1509. *m.* by 1554, Agnes, da. of Sir John Blount* of Knightley, Staffs. and Kinlet, wid. of Richard Lacon (*d.*1542) of Willey, 1s. *d.v.p.* 1da.[1]
Bailiff, Much Wenlock 1554–5; escheator, Salop 1559–60.[2]

There were two families of this name in Shropshire but Thomas Ridley is not to be found in the pedigree of either the Ridleys of Bouldon (which includes a namesake who settled at Ely and was probably the father of Thomas Ridley[†]) or those of Alkington. His association with Reginald Ridley, probably the younger son of Owen Ridley of Alkington, suggests that he came from that family: in 1541 the two shared in a lease of an iron smithy at Much Wenlock. Thomas Ridley, who had been admitted to the freedom of Much Wenlock in 1530, was then living at nearby Caughley, where in 1542 he acted as feoffee for John Mounslowe. He moved to Willey on his marriage to Agnes Blount and seems to have remained there until his stepson Roland Lacon[†] came of age. It was doubtless to this alliance with two leading families that he owed his advancement in the borough and his return while bailiff to Mary's fourth Parliament with his brother-in-law Sir George Blount. The fact that Ridley, like Blount, opposed one of the government's bills suggests that it was not he but a namesake who shortly afterwards was in receipt of a crown annuity of £40.[3]

Ridley served as escheator early in the reign of Elizabeth but although he survived until 1580 he made no further mark either in the shire or the borough. He made his will on 12 Aug. 1580 as of The Bold and asked his wife and executrix, Sir George Blount and his cousin Robert Wollaston to see to its safe transfer to his daughter Cecily. He left small sums of money to the daughters of his brother William Ridley and his cousin Wollaston. He was buried at Stottesdon on the following 1 Sept.[4]

[1] Date of birth estimated from admission as freeman. *Trans. Salop Arch. Soc.* (ser. 1), vi. 110, 124; (ser. 3), ii. 313–14; *Vis. Salop* (Harl. Soc. xxviii), 54. [2] Much Wenlock min. bk. f. 239; C219/23/110, 24/132. [3] *Vis. Salop* (Harl. Soc. xxix), 417, 419–20; *LP Hen. VIII*, xvii; *CPR*, 1554–5, pp. 21–22; 1557–8, pp. 378–9; Much Wenlock min. bk. f. 79; C219/24/132; Guildford mus. Loseley 1331/2; E405/121, mm. 21, 82; Lansd. 156(28), f. 96. [4] NLW Hereford consist. ct. wills, box 10; *Trans. Salop Arch. Soc.* (ser. 3), ii. 314.

A.H.

RIGMAYDEN, John (1515/16–57), of Wedacre in Garstang, Lancs.

LANCASHIRE 1553 (Oct.)

b. 1515/16, 1st s. of Thomas Rigmayden of Wedacre by Jane, ?da. of Sir Richard Langton of Newton. *?unm. suc.* fa. 10 Oct. 1521.[1]
J.p. Lancs. 1538–*d.*; commr. subsidy 1542, 1545, relief 1550, chantries, Lancs. and Bowland forest 1552, Lancs. and Yorks. 1553; dep. forester, Quernmore and Wyresdale 1540–1, master forester 1545.[2]

Several John Rigmaydens can be traced in the early 16th century but it may be safely inferred that the head of the family domiciled at Wedacre and a member of the Lancashire bench for almost 20 years was the knight of the shire returned to the first Parliament of Mary's reign, being styled on the indenture 'the elder, esquire'. His election in 1553 is almost certainly to be ascribed to the favour of the 3rd Earl of Derby: his fellow knight of the shire, Sir Richard Sherborn, was a 'right beloved servant' of the earl. Although no such direct connexion can be established for Rigmayden, the suggestion of the pedigrees that his mother took as her second husband Thurstan Tyldesley* would provide a link, for Tyldesley was a servant of Derby's. Whether or not Rigmayden was Tyldesley's stepson, they may have lived under the same roof, for the Tyldesley home contained a room called 'Rigmayden's chamber'. Rigmayden was not one of the Members who opposed the restoration of Catholicism. Although not re-elected to Parliament he remained active in local affairs until his death in 1557, when he was succeeded by his cousin and namesake. If he made a will it has not been found. The family remained Catholic until it died out at the beginning of the 17th century.[3]

[1] Aged five at father's death, *VCH Lancs.* vii. 317. Chetham Soc. cv. 215; *DKR*, xxxix. 559; *Vis. Lancs.* (Chetham Soc. lxxxi), 55; *Ducatus Lanc.* i. 25; J. B. Watson, 'Lancs. gentry 1529–58' (London, Univ. M.A. thesis, 1959), 465. [2] Watson, 465; E179/130/148, 167(1); *CPR*, 1553, p. 360; *VCH Lancs.* ii. 97; Somerville, *Duchy*, i. 508–9; *LP Hen. VIII*, xix. [3] Chetham Soc. xxxiii. 112; cv. 217; *Cam. Misc.* ix(3), 77; *Cath. Rec. Soc.* iv. 170; C. Haigh, *Ref. and Resistance in Tudor Lancs.* 250–1, 260–1, 283; *Ducatus Lanc.* i. 38.

A.D.

RITHE, Christopher (by 1531–1606), of Lincoln's Inn, London.

PETERSFIELD 1555, 1558
HASLEMERE 1584

b. by 1531, yr. s. of Marlyon Rithe of Totford, Hants.; bro. or half-bro. of George Rithe*. *educ.* L. Inn, adm. 13 Nov. 1556, called 1563. *m.* Catherine, da. of John Gedney of Bag Enderby, Lincs., 3s. inc. Marlyon† 2da.[1]

Pensioner, L. Inn 1570.
J.p. Mdx. 1569–?*d.*, q. by 1573/74.

Christopher Rithe was almost certainly the younger brother of George Rithe. The pair married two sisters, both were members of Lincoln's Inn, to which a Christopher Rithe, described as the brother of George Rithe, was specially admitted in 1556, and by his will of 1557 George Rithe left his brother Christopher a gold signet ring bearing his arms. As Christopher Rithe was to practise law it was presumably he, and not a namesake admitted in 1547, who was called to the bar in 1563.[2]

By 1552 Rithe was holding a chapel and garden in Petersfield, but his two elections for that borough he probably owed chiefly to his brother, who had preceded and was to follow him as one of its Members. On both occasions he sat with the lord of the manor, the young Henry Weston. The appearance of his name over an erasure on the indenture of 1555 is to be regarded as the product of error rather than as evidence of his having superseded a rival, since both names are unaltered earlier in the document; the name erased may have been that of John Vaughan II, who had been returned for Petersfield with Weston to the two previous Parliaments but who in 1555 sat for Bletchingley. Rithe was not among the Members of this Parliament whose names are listed as opponents of one of the government's bills.[3]

Rithe was not to sit in an Elizabethan Parliament until 1584, his brother's death in 1561 having presumably cost him the chance of re-election at Petersfield. He prospered sufficiently to be able to acquire an estate at Twickenham, Middlesex, which became his residence, and a house at Chiswick which he left to his wife when he died in November 1606.[4]

[1] Date of birth estimated from first reference. *Mdx. Peds.* (Harl. Soc. lxv), 28; *Vis. Surr.* (Harl. Soc. xliii), 197; *Lincs. Peds.* (Harl. Soc. li), 396; PCC 92 Stafford. [2] *LP Hen. VIII*, xxi; PCC 35 Loftes; *L.I. Adm.* i. 57, 63. [3] *CPR*, 1550–3, p. 372; C219/24/139. [4] PCC 92 Stafford.

P.H.

RITHE, George (by 1523–61), of Lincoln's Inn, London and Liss, nr. Petersfield, Hants.

BRAMBER   1553 (Mar.)
PETERSFIELD   1553 (Oct.), 1559

b. by 1523, s. of Marlyon Rithe of Totford, Hants; bro. or half-bro. of Christopher Rithe*. *educ.* L. Inn, adm. 25 Feb. 1537. *m.* c.1542, Elizabeth, da. of John Gedney of Bag Enderby, Lincs., wid. of Thomas Rigges of Cumberworth, Lincs., 2s. inc. Robert†.[1]

Autumn reader, L. Inn 1556, keeper of black book 1556–7, treasurer 1558–9, gov. 1560–1.

J.p. Hants 1547–*d.*, Wilts. 1558/59–*d.*; escheator, Hants and Wilts. 1549–50; commr. relief, Hants 1550.[2]

George Rithe came of a Hampshire family which probably also gave rise to the line of heralds and thus to Thomas Wriothesley, 1st Earl of Southampton, whose negotiations for the purchase of Beaulieu abbey in 1537–8 were conducted through a 'Mr. Rythe', presumably one of the family. The christian name Marlyon, borne by George Rithe's father and handed down to his nephew who sat in an Elizabethan Parliament, had originated with his grandmother Malyne or Malene. Both his grandfather and father were of Totford in Northington, near Winchester, and had lands at Petersfield and elsewhere in Hampshire.[3]

George and Christopher Rithe, who were almost certainly brothers or half-brothers, both became lawyers. In 1545–6 George Rithe made two large purchases of monastic land, the first for over £600 with the Middle Templar John Pollard* and the second for nearly £1,600 with a fellow member of Lincoln's Inn Thomas Grantham*: both transactions included many scattered items intended for re-sale—licences to dispose of some of them were to be granted soon afterwards—but Rithe retained lands at Liss, near Petersfield. The standing which they gave him was recognized by his appointment to the Hampshire bench in 1547 and doubtless accounts for his election with Sir Anthony Browne to the first Marian Parliament for Petersfield. He probably owed his return to the preceding Parliament for Bramber to Browne as sheriff of Surrey and Sussex, perhaps by way of a bargain whereby Rithe stood down at Petersfield in Browne's favour. His religion made him a more conformable Member then than it did six months later, when he was one of those who 'stood for the true religion' against the initial measures for the restoration of Catholicism. He was not to sit again under Mary, although Christopher Rithe did so for Petersfield in the Queen's last two Parliaments.[4]

Religion may have entered into some of the quarrels which brought Rithe into the court. Soon after he was made a justice of the peace he and his fellow justice John Norton* complained in the Star Chamber of each other's conduct at the sessions; they were members of the same inn, but as a follower of the imprisoned Stephen Gardiner Norton was unlikely to see eye to eye with the Protestant-inclined Rithe. Another Catholic opponent was Edmund Ford (q.v.), who accused Rithe of fomenting trouble against him by abetting his brother Thomas Rithe to sue Ford in Chancery and one of Ford's tenants to do the same in the court of requests. There was presumably no religious element in the series of cases which Rithe contested on behalf of his wife when she was accused of having forged her first husband's will.[5]

The pious will which Rithe made on 20 Aug. 1557 was perhaps prompted by fear of the current epidemic. He survived it by some four years, probate being granted on 18 Nov. 1561.[6]

[1] Date of birth estimated from education. *Vis. Surr.* (Harl. Soc. xliii), 197; *Lincs. Peds.* (Harl. Soc. li), 396; St.Ch.4/1/13; *CPR*, 1548–9, p. 160; PCC 35 Loftes. [2] *CPR*, 1547–8, p. 84; 1553, p. 358; 1553–4, p. 19. [3] *LP Hen. VIII*, xiii, add.; *VCH Hants*, iii. 394–6; information from A. C. Cole. [4] *LP Hen. VIII*, xx, xxi; *CPR*, 1547–8, pp. 98, 335, 361; Bodl. e Museo 17. [5] St.Ch.3/1/76, 4/89, 9/35; 4/1/13, 3/76; C1/1351/35, 1428/35, 1466/74; Req.2/21/22, 23/98. [6] PCC 35 Loftes; *Black Bk. L. Inn*, i. 331–3.

P.H.

ROBERTON *see* **ROBOTHAM**

ROBERTS, John (1531–73), of Cranbrook, Kent and Ticehurst, Suss.

STEYNING 1554 (Nov.)[1]

b. 6 Aug. 1531, 3rd s. of Thomas Roberts of Glassenbury, nr. Cranbrook by Elizabeth, da. of Sir James Framlingham of (? Debenham), Suff. *m.* Elizabeth, da. of Robert Pigott of Colwick in Waddesdon, Bucks., at least 3s. 1da.[2]

The identity of the senior Member for Steyning in the third Marian Parliament has not been established beyond question. If his election conformed with the Queen's request for the return of townsmen, as his fellow-Member William Pellatt's clearly did, he could scarcely have been other than the John Roberts of Steyning who had inherited his father Henry Roberts's lands there in 1544, was a lessee of chantry property called Woslands in Steyning in 1548 and at his death in January 1556 was holding about 200 acres in Steyning, including a house called 'The Nashe', as well as lands in neighbouring Ashurst and West Grinstead; some of these Roberts leased from Francis Shirley*, in whose favour he had deposed during Shirley's dispute with the 9th Lord la Warr in 1552. Of sufficient local standing to have been elected with Pellatt (although not to have taken precedence over him on the return), this John Roberts could nevertheless hardly have been the target of the legal proceedings aimed at the Member for Steyning, along with many other Members, Pellatt included, after the Parliament was over, in particular the outlawry pronounced in 1558, nearly three years after the Steyning man's death. It seems to follow that the borough conformed with the Queen's request only in respect of Pellatt, and that his fellow-Member was not John Roberts of Steyning but a namesake from Kent.[3]

This John Roberts, a younger son in a family settled near Cranbrook, owed his advancement to a connexion with his eminent neighbour (Sir) Walter Hendley*. It was probably his father whom Hendley named overseer of his will and his elder brother Thomas was to become the fourth husband of Hendley's widow. She had been born Margery Pigott, and in her will of 1587 she was to call John Roberts's widow her niece; the two were living together when Roberts made his own will in August 1573. It is Roberts's kinship with Margery Hendley which furnishes the most likely explanation of his election for Steyning, for her stepdaughter Anne married, not long before his death in 1547, Richard Covert of Slaugham and thus became the daughter-in-law of John Covert. As one of the 3rd Duke of Norfolk's servants in Sussex, and a man of independent standing there, John Covert sat in several Parliaments, including that of November 1554, and could well have been instrumental in procuring his kinsman's return on that occasion, as he probably was to be when Walter Hendley's servant Robert Byng came in for Steyning a year later.[4]

The case for regarding this John Roberts as the Member is strengthened by the course of events which arose out of this Parliament. Both Members for Steyning were prosecuted in the King's bench for quitting it without leave before its dissolution, but the proceedings against them differed in significant ways. Whereas Pellatt, described in the information laid by the attorney-general as 'of Steyning, in the county of Sussex, gentleman', was first distrained for non-appearance and then made his fine in Easter term 1556, Roberts is described in the information merely as of Sussex, gentleman, the blank left for his domicile remaining unfilled, and after neither appearing nor being distrained he was eventually outlawed on 13 Oct. 1558. Not only is it hard to believe that he and Pellatt would have been handled so differently if both had belonged to Steyning, but Roberts's treatment by process leading to outlawry instead of by distraint—in this respect he was unique among all the defendants—implies that he either had, or was represented as having, no property in Sussex on which distraint could be levied. By what looks like more than a coincidence the sheriff who was first called upon to serve the writ of *venire facias* upon the defaulting Sussex Members was John Covert. If Covert had endorsed the writ for Roberts *non inventus*, thus professing himself unable to find Roberts within his area of jurisdiction, he could have spared his kinsman the burden of distraint at the deferred cost of setting in motion the process which issued, 13 law-terms and three-and-a-half years later, in the outlawry; and this ultimate retribution, exacted five weeks before the Queen's death, brought to an end all the cases still outstanding, Roberts could have evaded either by suing out a pardon (of which no record has been found) or by simply ignoring it.[5]

Roberts's settlement at Ticehurst, where his brother Thomas and Margery Hendley also established themselves, may have followed his marriage 'on St. Andrew's day' in a year unknown. It was probably he who in February 1568 was granted a 21-year lease of the manor of Snave, near New Romney, and adjacent lands at a rent of £76 a year; as the manor itself had been one of those bought from the crown in 1539 by Walter Hendley. By his will of 11 Aug. 1573 Roberts left his lands in Hawkhurst and Ticehurst to his wife so long as she and Margery Hendley lived together, but stipulated that part of the income should be used to maintain his son Thomas; after Lady Hendley's death this son was to receive other benefits and his mother to occupy the house at Boarzell in Ticehurst. Roberts also provided for his daughter Marjorie, gave to Walter Hendley, Sir Walter's nephew, an annuity of £10, and named his wife and her brother Francis Pigott executors. He died in 1573, was buried at Ticehurst and the will was proved in November 1576.[6]

[1] Huntington Lib. Hastings mss Parl. pprs. [2] Date of birth given in W. Suss. RO, Comber pprs. 23, pp. 71–72. *Vis. Kent* (Harl. Soc. lxxv), 24–25; *Vis. Beds.* (Harl. Soc. xix), 46. [3] PCC 7 Pynnyng; *CPR*, 1547–8, p. 282; C142/110/145; *Suss. Rec. Soc.* liv. 191; SP10/14/62(i). [4] Comber pprs. loc. cit.; PCC 10, 30 Coode, 37 Carew. [5] KB29/188 rot. 48. [6] Comber pprs. loc. cit.; *CPR*, 1566–9, p. 193; *LP Hen. VIII*, xiv; PCC 37 Carew.

R.J.W.S.

ROBINS, Henry (by 1515–62 or later), of Caernarvon, Caern.

CAERNARVON BOROUGHS 1553 (Oct.), 1554 (Apr.)

b. by 1515, s. of William Robins. *m.* Angharad, da. of Ifan Lloyd ap Iorwerth of Llangwnadl, at least 1s.[1]
Commr. subsidy, Caernarvon 1546, relief 1549; bailiff, Caernarvon c.1548, 1554–5.[2]

Henry Robins was of English ancestry, the family being of Fletleton Hall in Lancashire, but it is not known when any of its members moved into Caernarvonshire. The John Robins, clerk, living in Caernarvon in 1546 may have been a brother, and the James and Hugh Robins who were bailiffs of Caernarvon and Conway respectively were probably also related to Henry.[3]

The earliest trace found of Robins is his supply to the Exchequer at Caernarvon in 1536 of green cloth, lighting fuel, peat, hay and straw on the occasion of an audit. He was one of the jury for the town at the quarter sessions at Epiphany 1542, and gave similar service in the following years. After being present at the election of the Member for the Caernarvon Boroughs in the Parliaments of 1545, 1547 and March 1553 he was himself returned to the first two Marian Parliaments. Of his part in them all that is

known is that he did not oppose the initial measures towards the restoration of Catholicism. He was again present at the election of his successor in the autumn of 1554. Robins's failure to appear, with Gruffydd Davies*, in the common pleas at the suit of a Beaumaris merchant, to whom they had sold but not delivered a quantity of leather, led to their being outlawed, but on 6 Oct. 1557 they sued out pardons. Assessed at Caernarvon in 1560 as owning lands worth £10 a year, Robins is last found in June 1562 leasing property in the town. No will or inquisition has survived.[4]

[1] Date of birth estimated from first reference. Griffith, *Peds.* 207; Dwnn, *Vis. Wales*, ii. 114. [2] *Cal. Caern. Q. Sess. Recs.* ed. Williams, 120–1, 132, 136, 140; E179/220/135, 140. [3] E179/220/135; *Cal. Caern. Q. Sess. Recs.* 129, 138; *CPR*, 1569–72, p. 250. [4] SC6/Hen. VIII, 5478 m. 7v; *Cal. Caern. Q. Sess. Recs.* 13, 66, 108–9, 115, 185; C219/18C/173, 19/151, 20/183, 23/193; *CPR*, 1557–8, p. 347; E179/220/139; *Augmentations* (Univ. Wales Bd. of Celtic Studies, Hist. and Law ser. xiii), 298.

P.S.E.

ROBINSON, William (by 1515–55/58), of Worcester.

WORCESTER 1553 (Mar.)

b. by 1515. *m.* Eleanor, 3s. 2da.[1]
Bailiff, Worcester 1536–7, 1538–9; commr. musters 1539.[2]

William Robinson was a mercer who also dealt in pewter; he sometimes used the *alias* Mercer. His assessment on £25 in goods for the subsidy of 1546 made him one of the wealthiest men in his ward. Nothing is known of his parentage although he may well have been related to John Robins, a London mercer whose will of 1512 shows that he held property in Worcester, and perhaps also to George Robinson, another London mercer, who leased lands in Warwickshire from Sir John Dudley, under whose aegis as Duke of Northumberland the Parliament of March 1553 was summoned. Among Robinson's many namesakes one of the most distinguished was a third London mercer, an alderman who died in 1552.[3]

As bailiff of Worcester in the late 1530s and during the episcopacy of Latimer, Robinson shared in measures against Catholic disaffection in the area and signed several reports to Cromwell, but no indication has been found that these activities represented his personal sympathies unless his Membership of Edward VI's second Parliament is to be counted as one: his will, on the other hand, has a conventional Catholic preamble. He and his fellow-Member Edward Brogden were paid for 36 days at the statutory rate of 2s. a day having set out for the Parliament on 27 Feb. and returned on 3 Apr. Robinson was named second in the list of 24 capital citizens when Worcester obtained a confirmation of its charter in April 1555, and in the following month he made a will leaving £10 to each of his children and the residue of his estate to his wife who proved the will in June 1558. The inventory taken of his goods valued them at some £170.[4]

[1] Date of birth estimated from first reference. Worcs. RO, 008.7/BA 3585/17. [2] Nash, *Worcs.* ii. App. cxii; *LP Hen. VIII*, xiv. [3] A. D. Dyer, *Worcester in 16th Cent.* 86–87, 108; E179/200/166; C1/772/57, *Machyn's Diary* (Cam. Soc. xlii), 28, 328. [4] *LP Hen. VIII*, xii–xiv; Worcester Guildhall, chamber order bk. 1540–1601, f. 46; *CPR*; 1554–5, p. 81; Worcs. RO, 008.7/BA 3585/17.

D.F.C.

ROBOTHAM, Robert (by 1522–70/71), of London, Hartington, Derbys. and Raskelf, Yorks.

REIGATE	1553 (Mar.)
DORCHESTER	1555
READING	1563

b. by 1522. *m.* Sept. 1551, Grace, da. of one Paget, wid. of Robert Bull of London, 2s. 3da.[1] Gent. household of Prince Edward by 1543; groom of the wardrobe by Jan. 1548; yeoman of the robes by Sept. 1549; comptroller of customs, Newcastle-upon-Tyne, Northumb. Aug. 1551–*d.*; parker, St. John's Wood, Mdx. May 1552–*d.*, Berry Pomeroy, Devon June 1552.[2]

Robert Robotham's origin and parentage are unknown, although one visitation pedigree, taken in 1634, states that his brother came from 'the northern parts of England'. Robotham himself acquired a coat of arms in 1560, the grant of which recites his 'true and faithful service' to Edward VI.[3]

No trace of Robotham has been found earlier than 1543 when he was already in the service of Prince Edward. The accession of his young master to the throne in 1547 led to his employment in the royal household and by the autumn of 1549 he was a yeoman of the robes and closely associated with Richard Cecil*. He attracted the occasional notice of the Council but it was not until after the fall of the Protector Somerset that he received any mark of favour. The sequence of grants he then enjoyed, of lands in Yorkshire, a wardship, a lucrative post in the customs, and several minor positions elsewhere, suggests that he supported the King's new minister, the Earl of Warwick. It was probably to Warwick, by then Duke of Northumberland, that he owed his return for Reigate to the Parliament of March 1553, perhaps on the recommendation of Secretary Cecil, son to Robotham's colleague in the robes. The borough was in the control of Lord William Howard, but he was preoccupied with the deputyship of Calais, and neither Robotham nor his fellow-Member Henry Fisher seems to have had any link with him.[4]

Nothing is known of any part Robotham may have played in this Parliament or in the succession crisis

which followed in the summer of 1553. He attended the funeral of Edward VI, and despite his Protestantism he remained in the Household. On 25 Dec. 1553 Mary awarded him an annuity of £23 5s., to take effect from the following June, presumably to compensate him for the loss of his office in the wardrobe, a change which may have been intended as the first stage of his removal from court. Robotham was soon in trouble: on 12 Jan. 1554 the Council ordered his committal to the Fleet for his 'lewd talk that the King's majesty should be yet living'. The outcome is unknown, but Robotham appears to have taken up residence not long afterwards in Derbyshire where he acquired some property in June 1554. This and other lands leased from the duchy of Lancaster became a bone of contention which was several times referred to the duchy courts in Mary's and early in Elizabeth's reigns. Simultaneously he was a litigant in the courts of Chancery and requests over the estate of his wife's first husband. Evidently he was not deprived of his yeomanry of the robes since he went to Mary's funeral in that capacity and he was the recipient of an annuity from her chamberlain, Edward Hastings*, Baron Hastings of Loughborough.[5]

In 1555 Robotham was elected senior Member for Dorchester, where his surname appears on the (damaged) indenture as 'Roberton'. His colleague Ralph Perne may have been equally strange to the borough and their election broke with its practice of returning Christopher Hole with another, preferably a townsman. Perne and Robotham probably owed their choice to the patronage of the 2nd Earl of Bedford, as exercised during his absence abroad by Sir William Cecil. 'Mr. Robothim' followed Sir Anthony Kingston in opposition to a government bill, as did 'Mr. Perne', either his fellow-Member Ralph Perne or Christopher Perne (q.v.).[6]

At the accession of Elizabeth, Robotham was confirmed in his offices and once more became prominent in the Household. He had a further spell in Parliament, and died a wealthy man within a year of making his will on 30 Apr. 1570. Its overseers were three notable Protestants: the 3rd Earl of Huntingdon, (Sir) Walter Mildmay* and Sir Henry Neville*.[7]

[1] Date of birth estimated from first reference. *Vis. Herts.* (Harl. Soc. xxii), 87; C1/1394/7. [2] E179/69/35; 315/220, f. 34, 224, f. 315; 403/2449, f. 60; *CPR*, 1553, p. 374; *Lit. Rems. Edw. VI*, p. cccxii; PCC 46 Populwell. [3] *Vis. London* (Harl. Soc. xvii), 208; *Vis. Herts.* 87; *Misc. Gen. et Her.* (ser. 2), i. 260. [4] E179/69/35; 315/221.f. 350, 222, f. 34, 224, f. 315; 403/2449, f. 60; *Lit. Rems. Edw. VI*, p. cccxii; *Vis. Herts.* 87; *CPR*, 1550–3, p. 229; 1553, p. 374; *APC*, iv. 94, 197; Strype, *Eccles. Memorials*, ii(2), 164, 283–5; PCC 47 Holney. [5] *CPR*, 1553–4, p. 317; *APC*, iv. 383; DL1/4/36, R.i.a, b, 34, R6, 38, H27, 40, R16, 43, N2.a, R.i–g passim, 46, R5–5a; 3/79, H.i. a–z passim; LC2/4/2; C1/1314/47, 1383/48, 1394/7; C78/7; Req. 2/6/47, 14/77, 121; Lansd. 7(15), f. 34. [6] C219/24/58; Guildford mus. Loseley 1331/2. [7] *CPR*, 1558–60, p. 427; 1560–3, pp. 80, 357; 1569–72, p. 261; PCC 47 Holney.

S.R.J.

ROCHE, William (by 1478–1549), of London and Havering atte Bower, Essex.

LONDON 1523,[1] 1542

> *b.* by 1478, prob. s. of John Roche of Wickersley, Yorks. *m.* (1) by 1520, Juliana (*d.*1526), 1s. 4da.; (2) 1531, Elizabeth, wid. of Thomas Cropp of London; (3) by 1541, Margaret, wid. of John Long (*d.*1538) of London. Kntd. 1540/41.[2]
>
> Warden, Drapers' Co. 1512–13, 1520–1, master, 1531–2, 1535–6, 1540–1, 1543–4, 1545–6, 1548–9; auditor, London 1519–21, 1541–3, sheriff 1524–5, alderman 1530–*d.*, mayor 1540–1.[3]

William Roche was bound apprentice in the Drapers' Company in 1492. When he sued out a pardon in 1509 he was described as of London, late of Wickersley, Yorkshire, and Norton Disney, Lincolnshire. His brother Brian Roche, serjeant of the acatery in the Household, possessed lands in Wickersley, which had probably been their childhood home: the village lies a few miles from Roche abbey, which may have given the family its name.[4]

In 1502–3 Roche exported 100 cloths from London. He rose to prominence in the Spanish trade, exchanging cloth for oil, iron and other goods; one of his apprentices was Thomas Howell, whose ledger gives a detailed account of the trade. Among Roche's imports were salt and wheat. At one time he had so much bay salt stored in a rented house at Rotherhithe that the owner complained of damage; later the court of aldermen bargained with him for a supply of salt to the City. He also furnished the City with wheat: in 1527–8 he laid out £3,000 on its behalf, a sum which he had great difficulty in recovering. When in 1531 his second marriage yielded him 'great plenty of wines' and he sought permission to retail wine, his servants were allowed to sell the existing stock but no more, since an alderman might not retail victuals.[5]

Roche was first returned to Parliament in 1523 as one of the Members elected by the commonalty of London. He was not re-elected in 1529 and although it was once thought possible that he sat in the Parliaments of 1536 and 1539, the aldermanic Members in 1539 are now known to have been two other men and his election in 1536 would have run counter to city practice. He had been an alderman only since 1530, and had not yet served as mayor, a duty from which he had been dispensed for five years after his election as alderman; and no alderman who had not been mayor had been elected to Parliament since 1491, unless Sir Richard Gresham* had provided a precedent in 1536. Roche's mayoralty followed in 1540. Early in his year of office he was knighted—a year or two earlier he had been fined £13 6s.8d. in distraint of knighthood—and in June 1541 his grant of arms was confirmed. As mayor he

was appointed a commissioner for heresies within the City and was present at the execution of the Countess of Salisbury at the Tower. He was also expected to use his formal presentation to the King as an occasion to further the City's suit for the four dissolved houses of friars in London, his fellow-aldermen advising him on his reply if Henry VIII should accuse the citizens of being 'pinch pence'. The negotiation proceeded successfully enough for Roche to continue to be used in it after the end of his mayoral year.[6]

In 1542 Roche was elected to Parliament by the aldermen, who in February 1544 agreed to ask the City's Members to oppose a bill against deceitful packing of woollen cloth. On 19 Jan. 1545 he was re-elected to a Parliament originally summoned for that month and then prorogued until November, but a week later he was sent to the Fleet 'for words of displeasure taken by the King's Council' when it sat at Baynard's Castle to assess Londoners for a benevolence of 2s. in the pound. While he was in prison a writ was issued for a by-election and on 9 Feb. the aldermen elected Sir William Forman, who was a close friend of Roche and was perhaps chosen for that reason. Roche was released on Passion Sunday, 22 Mar., but although before Parliament met Forman resigned his Membership on the ground of ill-health he was succeeded not by Roche but by Sir Richard Gresham. It is not surprising if Roche jibbed at a demand for the equivalent of half a subsidy. He had himself been assessed at £750 in goods for the subsidy of 1523 and 2,000 marks for that of 1540, he had been ordered to contribute 3,000 marks to a loan in 1535 or 1536, and he had been a Member of the Parliament which had cancelled all debts incurred by the King by way of loan or privy seal since 1 Jan. 1542 (35 Hen. VIII, c.12). Yet he was ready enough to lend to the crown; within five months of his release from prison he joined Forman and two others in a loan of £900 on the security of a grant, to take effect if the loan were not repaid within a year, of three manors in Surrey.[7]

By the 1520s Roche had acquired lands in Hornchurch and Havering atte Bower, Essex. He buried his first wife at Hornchurch and in 1541 he enfeoffed the dean of St. Paul's and others of the manor of Up-Havering to the use of himself and his third wife. At the time of his death he also held the manor of Nelmes with its appurtenances in Havering atte Bower. He made his will on 12 July 1549 and died in London on the following 11 Sept. He left a third of his goods each to his wife and his only son John, whom he named executors and residuary legatees, and £50 to the children of his only surviving daughter who was married to a London goldsmith. John

Roche, who was said to be aged 24 and more when his father's inquisition post mortem was taken in April 1550, had been licensed to marry the daughter of Sir William Forman in January 1549. Although Roche had stipulated that his burial was 'to be done reasonably', he was given an impressive funeral in his parish church of St. Peter the Poor, a standard with his crest and a pinion of his arms being carried before him, and his coat armour borne by a herald.[8]

[1] City of London RO, Guildhall, jnl. 12, f. 213v; rep. 4, f. 144v. [2] Date of birth estimated from apprenticeship. J. Weever, *Funeral Monuments* (1767), 402; *Trans. Essex Arch. Soc.* n.s. vi. 321; xi. 328; PCC 3 Thower, 19 Dyngeley, 42 Populwell; C142/90/91; City of London RO, rep. 8, f. 194v; A. H. Johnson, *Company of Drapers*, ii. 257. [3] Johnson, ii. 468–70; City of London RO, jnl. 12, ff. 15, 67, 293v; 14, ff. 232v, 273, 339v; rep. 8, f. 131v. [4] P. Boyd, *Roll of Drapers' Co.* 156; *LP Hen. VIII*, i; PCC 33 Fetiplace. [5] E179/79/12, 80/2, 5, 81/8, 82/3, 9 ex inf. Prof. P. Ramsey; G. Connell-Smith, *Forerunners of Drake*, 63, 69; C1/642/34, 645/16; City of London RO, rep. 4, f. 157v; 7, ff. 228v, 252; 8, ff. 186v, 194v–5, 209, 228v; 10, f. 274v; 11, ff. 127 and v. [6] J. Noorthouck, *London* (1773), 898; Beaven, *Aldermen*, i. 274; City of London RO, jnl. 13, f. 254; rep. 10, ff. 200, 227v; *LP Hen. VIII*, xiii, xvi; *Vis. Essex* (Harl. Soc. xiii), 477. [7] City of London RO, rep. 11, ff. 38, 244; *Wriothesley's Chron.* i (Cam. Soc. n.s. xi), 151–2; E179/110/335, m. 4, 144/120, 145/174, m. 13, 251/15v; Cott. Cleop. F 6, f. 344v; *LP Hen. VIII*, viii, xix. [8] Req.2/5/222; PCC 42 Populwell; C142/90/91; City of London RO, rep. 12(1), f. 36v; *Stow's Survey of London*, ed. Kingsford, i. 177; Johnson, ii. 102–3; *Trans. Essex Arch. Soc.* n.s. xi. 328.

H.M.

ROCHESTER, Sir Robert (c.1500–57), of Stansted, Essex.

ESSEX 1553 (Oct.), 1554 (Apr.), 1554 (Nov.), 1555

b. c.1500, yr. s. of John Rochester of Terling by Griselda, da. and event. coh. of Walter Writtle† of Bobbingworth. *unm.* KB 29 Sept. 1553; KG nom. 23 Apr. 1557.[1]

Member, council of 16th Earl of Oxford in 1542, receiver by 1542, supervisor 1546–7; member, household of Princess Mary by Apr. 1547, comptroller by May 1550; commr. relief, Essex and household of Princess Mary 1550, rebel fines 1553, marriage treaty 1554, sale of crown lands 1554, augmentations 1554; other commissions 1553–*d.*; comptroller, the Household 5 Aug. 1553–*d.*; PC 1553–*d.*; chancellor, duchy of Lancaster and constable, Pleshey castle, Essex by Sept. 1553–*d.*; j.p. Essex and Suff. 1554; chief steward, crown lands, Essex May 1554; temporary keeper, privy seal 1555; under steward, Westminster Jan. 1555–*d.*; bailiff and under steward, St. Alban's liberty, Herts. Dec. 1556–*d.*; keeper, Beaulieu, Essex and bailiff, manors of Boreham, Essex and Hunsdon, Herts. July 1557–*d.*[2]

The Rochester family had long been settled in Essex. Robert Rochester's father died young and although his mother had taken a second husband, Thomas West, before the death of his grandfather and namesake in May 1508, and a third, Edward Waldegrave, by June 1509, it is possible that he was brought up in the household of the earls of Oxford. The elder Robert Rochester had been comptroller to the 13th Earl and in the late 1530s the 15th Earl gave the younger man land in Stapleford Abbots, Essex, which had belonged to Wivenhoe chantry. It was probably from the 16th Earl, whose receiver

Rochester had become by 1542, that he received the bailiffship of Lavenham, Suffolk.[3]

Rochester was supervisor of Oxford's lands in 1546 but by the following April he had transferred to the service of Princess Mary. It may have been the earl who persuaded the Council to agree, while Mary could be trusted to welcome the brother of a Carthusian martyr. Rochester may have been her comptroller from the outset and was certainly so by the summer of 1550, when he advised her not to try to escape overseas on the ground that whether the attempt succeeded or failed she would be compromised. The despatch of (Sir) John Gates* to thwart the scheme was followed by a fresh effort to make Mary conform in which Rochester, his nephew Edward Waldegrave* and Sir Francis Englefield* were the hapless go-betweens. Their eventual refusal to compel her not to attend mass brought them in August 1551 to the Tower; they remained there, or in custody elsewhere, until March 1552, when they were allowed home, and in the following month they resumed their places in Mary's household.[4]

All that is known of Rochester's role in the succession crisis of 1553 is that he conferred secretly with the imperial ambassadors, who reported that he was doing good and true service. The Queen made him a knight of the Bath and Privy Councillor, comptroller of the Household and chancellor of the duchy of Lancaster, but his lack of political acumen was to bring him close to retirement before the year was out. A supporter of Bishop Gardiner, who was to appoint him an executor, he favoured the Queen's marriage to Edward Courtenay, Earl of Devon, with whom his friendship had probably ripened while both were in the Tower, and although by December he realized that the Spanish marriage was inevitable he told Renard that the Queen no longer treated him with the same confidence as before. He added that if he had known of Mary's affection for Philip he would have acted otherwise himself and would have countered the parliamentary opposition to the marriage. His conversion was symbolized by his membership of the commission to arrange the marriage treaty and rewarded by a Spanish pension of 1,000 crowns, the largest of them all save Secretary Petre's.[5]

Rochester was to have been one of an inner council of six members proposed early in 1554, and although excluded from a similar body envisaged later he was regular in his attendance at the Council until the late summer of 1556; thereafter attendance upon the Queen and perhaps declining health kept him away. After the 1st Earl of Bedford's death in 1555 he acted as keeper of the privy seal, and the forced loan of the following year was raised through him as comptroller instead of through the treasurer. He was one of the four Councillors to whom the Queen first disclosed her resolve to restore church lands still in the hands of the crown, and his patronage of the Carthusians, whom he housed for a while in the hospital of the Savoy before enabling them to settle at Sheen, bespeaks his solicitude for Catholicism. It is less certain that he favoured a rigorous attitude towards religious or political dissent. In his official capacity he attended the execution of the first Protestant martyr John Rogers and served on the commission of inquiry into the Dudley conspiracy, but he is said to have argued for clemency after Wyatt's rebellion and later to have intervened in favour of Courtenay and Princess Elizabeth. It is hard to say whether the 3rd Duke of Norfolk's naming of Rochester as an executor was a measure of the duke's esteem or of his insensitiveness, for Norfolk had presided over the trial of John Rochester in 1537.[6]

Rochester's parliamentary career may have begun under Henry VIII. If the knighthoods of the shire for Essex in the later Henrician Parliaments appear to have been the preserve of Rich and Sir Thomas Darcy, a seat for Colchester in 1542 could have come his way as it did on other occasions for servants of the earls of Oxford. Excluded from the two Edwardian Parliaments by his allegiance to Princess Mary, he was to be returned to the four Marian Parliaments summoned before his death, taking precedence each time over his fellow-Councillor Sir William Petre. He confirmed his position in Essex by acquiring land there, and not long before his death he made his principal residence at Stansted, of which he bought the freehold reversion for £1,634 in November 1556. He was also able to wield parliamentary patronage elsewhere, especially as chancellor of the duchy of Lancaster. The Journal provides occasional glimpses of the part he played in the Commons. He spoke in the debate on the bill for the repeal of the Treasons Act on 16 Oct. 1553. With his fellow Petre he was among the 20 Members chosen 'to devise articles for aid to the Queen's majesty' in October 1555 and, again with Petre, among the six ordered to confer with the Lords concerning the case of Gabriel Pleydell (q.v.) in the following December. On 12 Nov. 1554 he helped conduct Clement Heigham to the Speaker's chair and on 7 Dec. 1555 he announced the forthcoming dissolution of the Queen's fourth and his own last Parliament. He was often charged with the carrying of bills to the Lords.[7]

Rochester was nominated a knight of the Garter on 23 Apr. 1557 but he had not been installed before his death on the following 28 Nov. As he was unmarried, a third of his lands passed to his elder

brother William, and by his will of 27 May 1557 he left the greater part of the remainder to the Carthusians at Sheen. He also made provision for the chantry at Terling for which he had recently received a licence and left annuities of £20 and £5 to the nuns of Langley and Syon. His nephew Waldegrave, who later succeeded him as chancellor of the duchy, was to have his bailiffship of Lavenham and he gave £100 to the Queen 'as a poor witness of my humble heart duty and service to the same'. His executors included Bishop Baynes of Coventry and Lichfield, Waldegrave and William Cordell*, and his overseer was Chancellor Heath. He was buried at Sheen on 4 Dec. 1557, attended by Clarencieux and Lancaster heralds, and his will was proved on 13 Dec. 1558.[8]

[1] Date of birth estimated from elder brother's, *CIPM Hen. VII*, iii. 534. *Vis. Essex* (Harl. Soc. xiii), 280; *DNB* where he is incorrectly described as the eldest son. [2] Information from Susan Flower; Essex RO, D/DPr/60–61; Harl. Roll N5; *APC*, ii. 86; *CSP Span.* 1550–2, p. 84; 1554, p. 2; *Machyn's Diary* (Cam. Soc. xlii), 39; Somerville, *Duchy*, i. 395, 612; *CPR*, 1553, pp. 352, 363; 1553–4, pp. 19, 24, 36–37, 76, 88, 265, 300; 1554–5, pp. 107–8, 220; 1555–7, pp. 284, 509, 554. [3] Morant, *Essex*, ii. 127; *CIPM Hen. VII*, iii. 534; *LP Hen. VIII*, i, xvii, add.; Essex RO, T/B124, D/DPr/60–61; *VCH Essex*, iv. 225; Harl. Roll N5. [4] *APC*, ii. 86; iii. 187, 333, 337, 341, 350, 352, 508; iv. 20; D. Knowles, *Rel. Orders in Eng.* iii. 439; *CSP Span.* 1550–2, passim; W. K. Jordan, *Edw. VI*, ii. 256–64. [5] *CSP Span.* 1553, 1554, 1554–8 passim; *CSP Ven.* 1555–6, p. 88; PCC 3 Noodes. [6] *APC*, iv–vi passim; F. G. Emmison, *Tudor Sec.* 188, 207n; E. M. Thompson, *Carthusian Order in Eng.* 463–5, 501–2, 507; D. M. Loades, *Two Tudor Conspiracies*, 176; PCC 14 More. [7] *CJ*, i. 28, 29, 31, 32, 34, 37, 39–42, 45, 46. [8] *Machyn's Diary*, 160; PCC 15 Welles; *CPR*, 1555–7, pp. 363–4.

D.F.C.

RODES, Thomas

HASTINGS 1553 (Oct.),[1] 1554 (Nov.),[2] 1555

Bailiff, Hastings 1554–5, 1555–6.[3]

Although he was presumably related to at least some of the bearers of his surname in Sussex, including John Rothes or Rotes who sat for Bramber in 1491, nothing has been discovered about the origins of Thomas Rodes. His career is also obscure. He is unlikely to have been the Thomas Rodes who appeared in July 1533 at a Brotherhood of the Cinque Ports as chamberlain for Winchelsea, but may well have been the Thomas Roodes 'of the guard' who 12 years later was captain of the *Mary Fortune* and perhaps also the man who for services unspecified was granted in November 1550 a fee of 6d. a day for life, to be paid by the treasurer of the chamber. Employment by the crown could account for Rodes's return to three Marian Parliaments for Hastings and would be consistent with the absence of his name from any of the 'opposition' lists.[4]

Rodes may have continued to serve the crown under Elizabeth for in May 1574 Thomas Rootes, deputy vice-admiral of Sussex, was summoned to appear before the admiralty court at Southwark to account for the revenues of the office of vice-admiral: when he failed to appear his arrest was ordered and in July he entered into a recognizance to appear at the next session of the court. In the following April Thomas Rootes, gentleman, deputy bailiff of Pevensey (a limb of Hastings) was present at a special Brotherhood of the Cinque Ports. Since the Thomas Rhodes of Chichester who made his will in April 1585 was apparently a man of humbler station this is the last reference found which may relate to the Member.[5]

[1] Bodl. e Museo 17. [2] C219/23/184; *OR* gives Thomas Rede. [3] *Cinque Ports White and Black Bks.* (Kent Arch. Soc. recs. br. xix), 249, 251–2. [4] *Cinque Ports White and Black Bks.* 216; *LP Hen. VIII*, xx, add.; Royal 18C, 24, f. 9v. [5] Guildford mus. Loseley 1591, 1740/1, 2; *Cinque Ports White and Black Bks.* 299; W. Suss. RO, orig. will J14.

P.H.

ROGERS, Edward, of Kingston-upon-Hull, Yorks.

KINGSTON-UPON-HULL 1545

Prob. s. either of William Rogers or of James Rogers of Kingston-upon-Hull.

The identification of an obscure townsman with the Member for Kingston-upon-Hull is preferred to one with his namesake, the Protestant courtier. Although the latter could have been nominated for the borough by its governor, (Sir) Michael Stanhope*, no link has been found between him and Stanhope, the brother-in-law of Edward Seymour, Earl of Hertford; he was not a client of the Seymours and his quarrel with Sir Thomas Seymour II earlier in the decade tells against the suggestion. The Member was thus probably the Edward Rogers who was assessed in the White Friars ward of the town during the mid 1540s on goods worth 20s. A Rogers family seems to have been important in the town: James Rogers had been a town chamberlain in the 1530s and had served as mayor during 1543–4, and William Rogers had been mayor in 1532–3 and 1536–7. Of the life of Edward Rogers the Member nothing further has emerged, probably because the municipal records from the late 1540s onwards are missing.

E179/203/216; T. Gent, *Kingston-upon-Hull* (1869), 109, 115; L. M. Stanewell, *Cal. Anct. Deeds, Kingston-upon-Hull*, 155–6. 375; J. Tickell, *Kingston-upon-Hull*, 186.

P.S.E.

ROGERS, Sir Edward (1498/1502–68), of Cannington, Som.

TAVISTOCK 1547[1]

SOMERSET 1553 (Mar.),[2] 1553 (Oct.), 1558, 1559, 1563

b. 1498/1502, 1st s. of George Rogers of Langport by Elizabeth. *m.* by 1528, Mary, da. and coh. of Sir John Lisle of I.o.W. 1s. George† ?3da. *suc.* fa. 9 Sept. 1524. Kntd. 22 Feb. 1547.[3]

?Servant of the Courtenay fam. c.1525; esquire of the body by Dec. 1534; bailiff, Hammes and Sangatte

17 Dec. 1534–Oct. 1540; j.p. Dorset 1538–40, Som. 1538–53 or later, q. 1558/59–*d.*; sewer, the chamber by 1540, carver by 1544, one of the four principal gent. 15 Oct. 1549–Jan. 1550; v.-chamberlain, the Household Nov. 1558–Jan. 1559, comptroller 21 Jan. 1559–*d.*; PC Nov. 1558–*d.*; commr. ordnance 1568.[4]

Edward Rogers was given livery by the Marquess of Exeter in 1525 and may have been in the service of the Courtenays, to whom he was distantly related, for some time previously. A year later he was in serious trouble, and with George Carew* and Andrew Flamank he took refuge in France, but in April 1527, as 'Edward Rogers of Martock and Langport, Somerset, *alias* of London, *alias* of Powderham, Devon', he secured a pardon.[5]

Within the next few years Rogers obtained a position in the royal household, and thenceforward his career lay largely in that sphere. If he discharged the office of bailiff of Hammes in person, his absence did not check his career in the Household and by 1540 he was a sewer to the King. In that year he quarrelled with Sir Thomas Seymour II and had to enter into recognizances of £1,000 to keep the peace. Already he seems to have become associated with the Protestant group at court and in April 1543 he was one of those reprimanded for eating meat in Lent. These episodes did not tell against him, and in 1544 he went to France as captain of the men-at-arms in the King's personal troop.[6]

Rogers's growing power and prestige in the west country mirrored his rise at court. His landed inheritance was quite small but he took full advantage of the opportunities presented by the Dissolution. In March 1537 he obtained a lease of Cannington priory, which a year later he converted into a grant, and in 1541–2 he leased a considerable amount of other Somerset property, including Buckland abbey, of which within a few years he likewise purchased the reversion in fee or tail male.[7]

Rogers was knighted at Edward VI's coronation. It was with the Russells, rather than the Seymours, that he seems to have been most closely connected, and his first parliamentary seat, for Tavistock in 1547, he probably owed as much to Sir John Russell*, Baron Russell, as to his own Devon connexions. It was presumably he as a member of the Household, and not his namesake, one of the knights for Dorset, who was the 'Mr. Rogers' to whom the redrafted bill prohibiting the sale of pensions was committed after its second reading on 7 Feb. 1549. Not until the Protector's fall in October 1549 did he receive further promotion in the Household, but he held his new post, as one of the King's principal gentlemen, for only a few months before being dismissed and put under house arrest in January 1550. The reason for this temporary disgrace, which coincided with the dismissal of the Earls of Arundel and Southampton from the Council, remains unknown. Rogers soon returned to favour and on 29 June 1550 he was granted a pension of £50, presumably to replace that attached to his lost post.[8]

Having sat for his shire in the Parliament of March 1553, Rogers signed the device settling the crown upon Jane Grey, but nothing has come to light about his part in the succession crisis. He was, however, a strong Protestant, and his re-election, with his earlier colleague Sir Ralph Hopton, to Mary's first Parliament suggests that many of the Somerset freeholders shared his views. In this Parliament he was one of those who 'stood for the true religion' by opposing one of the measures for the restoration of Catholicism. His Protestantism and his old tie with the Courtenays soon involved him in plots against the Spanish marriage. Late in November 1553 he and others were accused of conspiring to seize the Tower, and on their return from Westminster he and Hopton planned an insurrection in Devon to coincide with Wyatt's rebellion.[9]

On the premature outbreak of the rising in Kent Rogers's complicity in the movement was taken for granted, and on 24 Feb. 1554 he was sent to the Tower. Wyatt accused him of bringing messages from the Earl of Devon, and on 7 Apr. 1554 he and others were indicted before a special commission of oyer and terminer. He does not seem to have been brought to trial and he shared in the Queen's clemency. Although his property was formally confiscated, he was held prisoner in the Tower for less than a year, being released in January 1555 with Sir Gawain Carew* and Sir Edward Warner* after entering into recognizances of £1,000 'for good order and fine at pleasure'. At his appearance before the Privy Council in April he compounded for the £709 worth of his goods already seized and was released of all his bonds and other penalties. In July 1555 he was granted a full pardon. He is then said to have gone into exile for a time but he had returned by the beginning of 1558 when Somerset again showed its Protestant leaning by returning him as senior knight of the shire. In February he was bold enough to petition the Privy Council for recompense for his losses during the time of his imprisonment. An amendment proposed by Rogers and two others on the morning of the prorogation of the first session saved the bill for musters by limiting the raising of aids to pay troops to the current invasion scare.[10]

On the accession of Elizabeth, (Sir) Nicholas Throckmorton* recommended Rogers for the comptrollership of the Household, and after a short period as vice-chamberlain he succeeded Sir Thomas Parry* in January 1559. For the next few years he was one of the most trusted and active members of the Privy Council. He died on 3 May 1568, leaving a will by which most of his goods and all his lands descended to his only son.[11]

[1] C219/282/2; Hatfield 207. [2] C219/282/5. [3] Date of birth estimated from age at fa.'s i.p.m. C142/41/1, and that given on portrait, R. C. Strong, *Tudor and Jacobean Portraits*, i. 268; *Vis. Som.* (Harl. Soc. xi), 128; C142/41/1, 56; PCC 11 Babington. [4] *LP Hen. VIII*, iv, vii, xv, xvi; *The Gen.* n.s. xxx. 19; Lansd. 2, f. 34; *APC*, ii. 345; *CSP Span.* 1558-67, p. 6; *CPR*, 1558-60, p. 56; Strype, *Annals*, i(2), 390. [5] *LP Hen. VIII*, iv. [6] Ibid. vii, xi, xix; *PPC*, vii. 34; *APC*, i. 114. [7] C142/41/1, 56; *LP Hen. VIII*, xiii, xvi, xvii, xix, xx; K. S. H. Wyndham, 'The redistribution of crown land in Somerset by gift, sale and lease 1536-72' (London Univ. Ph.D. thesis, 1976), 78-79. [8] PCC 4 Holder; *HMC Rutland*, i. 55; *CJ*, i. 7; *CPR*, 1549-50, p. 307. [9] *Chron. Q. Jane and Q. Mary* (Cam. Soc. xlviii), 100; Bodl. e Museo 17; *CPR*, 1554-5, p. 293; SP11/2/33; D. M. Loades, *Two Tudor Conspiracies*, 15 seq. [10] Loades, 15 seq.; *CSP Span.* 1554, pp. 106, 126; *Chron. Q. Jane and Q. Mary*, 65; *DKR*, iv(2), 246-7; *APC*, v. 90, 111; vi. 270; Strype, *Cheke*, 95; *CJ*, i. 51; C. G. Ericson, 'Parlt. as a legislative institution in the reigns of Edw. VI and Mary' (London Univ. Ph.D. thesis, 1973), 280-1, 518. [11] *EHR*, lxv. 93; C142/148/28; PCC 11 Babington.

R.V.

ROGERS, James (by 1504-58), of Coventry, Warws.

COVENTRY 1553 (Mar.)

b. by 1504, 1st s. of Henry Rogers of Coventry by Elizabeth. *m.* Alice, 5s. 4da. *suc.* fa. Nov. 1518.[1]
Warden, Coventry 1534-5, sheriff 1540-1, mayor 1547-8.[2]

James Rogers inherited property in Coventry and Kenilworth, Warwickshire, from his father, who was mayor of Coventry in 1517-18, and himself became an influential member of the mayor's council, employed in the oversight of the corporation's lands and on its business at court and in London. Like his father a vintner by trade, he was assessed for subsidy on £10 in goods in 1525 and on £40 in 1550. During his mayoralty he entertained the Earl of Warwick and the 3rd Marquess of Dorset in his house and early in 1549 he provided a dinner for Warwick at a cost to the town of 57s.4d.: later that year the earl granted Coventry a lease of the manor of Cheylesmore. The Parliament of March 1553 was summoned under the aegis of Warwick as Duke of Northumberland but there is no evidence that he had any hand in the election of Rogers or of his fellow-Member John Talonts, whom the town had sent to deliver the payment for the lease. Rogers and Talonts had also been active in the affair of Bond's hospital and were among those sued in Chancery for withholding the deeds of the inheritance of Thomas Bond's* wife. Both were paid parliamentary wages but whereas Talonts received £3 16s.4d., full payment at the statutory rate of 2s. a day for the 31 days of the Parliament, Rogers was allowed £6 18s.4d., having evidently incurred other expenses. Nothing is known of his role in the House but he may well have taken a personal interest in the Act to avoid the great price and excess of wines (7 Edw. VI, c.5).[3]

Rogers died between the making of his will on 12 July 1558 and its probate on the following 24 Sept. He asked to be buried beside his parents in the Corpus Christi chapel of Holy Trinity church. He had added to his inheritance and he provided for his younger sons out of his purchases; his wife was to have a third of his goods and property in Coventry and was to keep his tavern for two years, after which it was to pass to his eldest son William. The executors were his sons-in-law Richard Smith and John Fitzherbert.[4]

[1] Date of birth estimated from first reference. PCC 11 Ayloffe, 47 Noodes. [2] *Coventry Leet Bk.* (EETS cxxxiv), ii. 718, 742, 781. [3] Ibid. 651; E179/192/130, 193/188; Coventry council bk. 1555-1634, unpaginated; mayors' accts. 1542-61, pp. 15, 19, 21, 43, 44, 47, 70, 494; B. L. Beer, *Northumberland*, 180; C1/1199/42. [4] PCC 47 Noodes.

S.M.T.

ROGERS, Sir John (by 1507-65), of Bryanston, Dorset.

DORSET 1545, 1547,[1] 1555, 1559

b. by 1507, 2nd s. and h. of Sir John Rogers by 1st w. Elizabeth, da. of Sir William Courtenay of Powderham, Devon. *m.* lic. 27 Jan. 1523, Catherine, da. of Sir Richard Weston* of Sutton Place, Surr., 16s. (11 *d.v.p.*) inc. Richard† and Thomas† 4da. (2 *d.v.p.*). *suc.* fa. June 1535/Feb. 1536. Kntd. July 1538/Jan. 1540.[2]

J.p. Dorset 1528-*d.*; steward, duchy of Lancaster, Dorset 1531-*d.*, hundred of Kings Somborne, Hants. by 1561; steward, Blandford Forum, Dorset by 1565; commr. musters, Dorset 1544, 1546, benevolence 1544/45, chantries, Dorset, Som. 1548; sheriff, Som. and Dorset 1552-3.[3]

John Rogers was granted livery of his father's lands in February 1536. He was executor of his father's will, drawn up on 9 June 1535, the overseers being his father-in-law, Sir Richard Weston, and Richard Phelips*. As John Rogers junior he had been on the commission of the peace for Dorset since 1528 but it was only after his succession to his inheritance that he became prominent in the county, his new importance being recognized and enhanced by the knighthood which came to him by 1540.[4]

In 1536 Rogers was called upon to help suppress the northern rebellion. A year later he attended Prince Edward's christening and in 1540 the reception of Anne of Cleves. In 1544 he went with the Dorset contingent to the siege of Boulogne. His services to the King were rewarded by a grant, for £739, of the dissolved house of the Black Friars in Melcombe Regis and other former monastic property in Dorset; in May 1546 he received a further grant, of a lordship in Dorset forfeited by the Marquess of Exeter, for which he paid £514 and in 1552 a lease of the lordship of Street in Somerset. He

had a large family to provide for and seems to have fallen into difficulty, selling or mortgaging sizeable properties to Thomas White III* of Poole, Robert Oliver of London and others. His troubles were to worsen and he was to die insolvent.[5]

Roger's parliamentary career spread intermittently over three reigns and 14 years. His election as junior knight of the shire in 1545 and 1547, on both occasions with the powerful Sir Thomas Arundell, answered to his own combination of court favour and local standing. The 'Mr. Rogers' to whom a bill was committed in the second session of the Parliament of 1547 is thought to have been his namesake Sir Edward Rogers. His choice as sheriff of Somerset and Dorset in the autumn of 1552, although implying that he stood well with the Duke of Northumberland, barred his return to both the Parliament called in the spring of 1553 and that summoned by Queen Mary in the following autumn. Whether Rogers as sheriff wavered in the intervening succession crisis we do not know. His subsequent readiness to join with his fellow-justices in proclaiming as traitors those who rebelled against the Spanish marriage seems to reflect his loyalty to the new regime, but it may well have been a grudging loyalty; not only did he become less active in local government but in 1555, on his next appearance in the House of Commons, he was one of more than 100 Members who opposed a government bill. In so doing he went along with kinsmen and colleagues: his son-in-law John Buller whose seat at Weymouth Rogers had probably procured, another relative by marriage, Roger Fowke, who sat for Bridport, and his friends Sir Giles Strangways II, feoffee of his lands, and Clement Hyett, his deputy in the stewardship of the hundred of Kings Somborne, all joined him in this protest. For a protest of another kind, abusing the subsidy collector who called upon him, Rogers was committed to the Fleet in the Easter term of 1556: as this episode followed a crop of arrests of political suspects both his behaviour and its consequence may have had ulterior significance.[6]

Re-elected to Parliament in 1559, Rogers died in July 1565 while staying at Beck, Berkshire. His body was brought back to Blandford Forum for burial in the parish church, where a monument later commemorated him, his wife and their 20 children.[7]

[1] Hatfield 207. [2] Date of birth estimated from first commission. Hutchins, *Dorset*, i. 250; *Mar. Lic. London* (Harl. Soc. xxv), 3; *LP Hen. VIII*, x. [3] *LP Hen. VIII*, iii-xxi; Somerville, *Duchy*, i. 628-30; Hutchins, i. 225; *Ducatus Lanc.* iii. 243; *CPR*, 1548-9, p. 136. [4] *LP Hen. VIII*, ix; PCC 8 Alen. [5] *LP Hen. VIII*, xi, xii, xv, xvii, xix, xxi; E315/224, f. 217; PRO T/S 'Cal. deeds enrolled in CP'. [6] Harl. 2143, f. 4; *CSP Dom.* 1547-80, p. 58; Guildford mus. Loseley 1331/2; D. M. Loades, *Two Tudor Conspiracies*, 149, seq. [7] Hutchins, i. 225; E150/454/1; *PCC Admins.* ed. Glencross, i. 67.

H.M.

ROGERS, William (1497/98–1553), of Norwich, Norf.

NORWICH 1542

b. 1497/98. *m.* Catherine, ?*s.p.*[1]

Common councilman, Norwich 1527–31, keeper of the keys 1530–1, sheriff 1531–2, alderman 1532–*d.*, auditor 1532–5, 1546, 1548, 1551, chamberlain's council 1541–6, mayor 1542–3, Nov. 1548; commr. relief 1550.[2]

William Rogers, grocer, an apprentice of Alderman Robert Jannys (who was to name him executor), was sworn a freeman of Norwich on 6 Dec. 1525. Elected to the common council at Easter 1527, he progressed rapidly in wealth and civic status; within ten years he was able to lend money to the corporation for the erection of a council chamber. His election to the Parliament of 1542 was quickly followed by his first mayoralty, which he signalized by obtaining from the assembly for himself and his successors the power to dismiss city officials who were negligent in their duties. In the Commons he doubtless helped to procure the Act of 1542 protecting the Norwich worsted industry (33 Hen. VIII, c.16). It may have been his concern for the public good which gained for Rogers the support of the commonalty when in November 1548 the mayoralty became vacant through death; although the aldermen held aloof, fearing (to follow Blomefield) that opposition would precipitate an outburst, Rogers was elected. In the event, when the outburst came with Ket's rebellion in the following summer he fared no better than his fellows: although he was no longer mayor, the rebels took him prisoner. He survived the experience by four years, during which he continued to render the city a variety of services.[3]

Rogers acquired much land in and around Norwich, including the manor of Thelveton, valued at his death at £40 a year. By his will he left to the corporation of Norwich, 'to the use of God's House to the relief of the poor', the manor of 'Pakemans' and other lands in Shropham hundred; among the payments which were to be made from the endowment was one of 50s. a quarter to the schoolmaster of Aylsham. He prefaced the will, made on 10 Mar. 1552 while in sound health, with a renunciation of all such good works, 'show they never so glorious in man's sight as touching my redemption', and submitted himself 'wholly to the mere mercy of Christ who suffered for our sins alone'. He desired 'a godly preacher' to preach for him every Sunday or holiday in St. Andrew's church 'or elsewhere in the city where I have lived', the preacher to have £8 a year and board with Rogers's wife for five years. Seemingly childless, he made small bequests to relatives, including his godson William Rogers of London and his 'sister' Beatrice Lambard, but the bulk of his movable property he left to charity. The largest bequest was a sum of £300 to be loaned in units of £5, £10 and £20 'to the relief of merchants and other inhabitants of Norwich' at the discretion of his widow and, on her death, of the mayor and three justices of the peace; the proviso that if they would not carry out its terms the legacy should go to the towns of Yarmouth and Lynn was to prove unnecessary, for in April 1556 the widow and the city agreed on its administration. The residue of his property Rogers gave to his wife, whom he made sole executrix, with the assistance of serjeants Thomas Gawdy I* and Richard Catlyn*, and his kinsman Robert Rogers of Calton (?Yorkshire). Rogers died on 25 May 1553, and the will was proved on the following 4 June.[4]

[1] Aged 53 in July 1551, *Norwich Depositions*, ed. Rye, 37. PCC 12 Tashe. [2] Norwich ass. procs. 2 passim; *CPR*, 1553, p. 361. [3] Norwich ass. procs. 2, ff. 122, 127, 170, 208, 229, 240v; chamberlains' accts. 1536–7, f. 150; *LP Hen. VIII*, vii; Blomefield, *Norf.* iii. 222, 238; Harl. 1576, f. 254v. [4] Blomefield, i. 149; Norwich ass. procs. 2, f. 122; 3, f. 23; PCC 12 Tashe; C142/101/88.

R.V.

ROKEWOOD *see* **ROOKWOOD**

ROLFE, Thomas (by 1518–66/67), of Sandwich, Swingfield and Canterbury, Kent.

SANDWICH 1542[1]

b. by 1518. *m.* Mary, da. and coh. of John Somer* (*d.*1526) of Sandwich, ?*s.p.*[2]

Auditor, office of gen. surveyors 1539; collector of customs, port of Sandwich 1540–7; jurat, Sandwich 26 Dec. 1541–3; esquire of the body by 1544.[3]

Nothing has come to light about Thomas Rolfe's family and origins save that his brother John was a clerk in Canterbury by 1547: his marriage to the daughter of a Sandwich merchant presumably followed on his appointment as customer there. His first appointment in June 1539, at the suit of Sir John Dauntesey* and Richard Pollard*, was as auditor of the possessions of the dissolved abbey at Woburn, Bedfordshire, and other forfeited lands at an annual fee of £20; five years later he and Francis Southwell*, were granted the more profitable auditorship of the lands of Margaret Pole, Countess of Salisbury, and Richard Fermor*, which they surrendered in November 1548 in exchange for an annuity of £100. He may have been the Thomas Rolfe admitted to Gray's Inn in 1543.[4]

Rolfe evidently owed his return for Sandwich to his customership: he was admitted a jurat on 26 Dec. 1541, the day of his election, and sworn again a year later, but he was only once entered as present at any other assembly of the mayor and jurats. In 1547 he was accused in the exchequer court of concealing goods and fined £185, thrice the value of the merchandise concerned, but his supersession as customer at the end of the year by Simon Linch* had been arranged earlier, Linch compounding with him for the office; not until April 1550 did he receive his final discharge from all liabilities. From 1543 he was also engaged with Thomas Wingfield* in victualling the King's ships in the Straits of Dover and he was thus brought into association with the admiral, John Dudley, Earl of Warwick, from whose son he was later to lease lands in Kent.[5]

Rolfe took advantage of his official contacts to build up an estate in Kent. In 1543-4 he purchased the house and site of the Greyfriars in Canterbury from Thomas Spilman, an augmentations receiver, and in 1547 with his brother John he acquired Lydcourt manor, near Sandwich, from (Sir) Richard Southwell*, a brother of his fellow-auditor, and Edward Bashe*, surveyor of victuals for the navy. On the accession of Elizabeth he sued out a pardon as of Swingfield, near Folkestone, and Canterbury. Possession of Lydcourt brought him into conflict with Sandwich over the highway between that port and Deal which ran through his land. An affray over the right of way was followed by Rolfe's imprisonment in the town gaol and in 1564 he sued the port authorities in the Star Chamber: early in 1566 the arbitrators appointed by the court, Archbishop Parker and (Sir) Richard Sackville II* ruled that the way must be kept open but with 'no straggling nor ranging' beyond it.[6]

By his will of 16 Feb. 1566 Rolfe left all his possessions to his executors John Dudley (possibly the Member for Carlisle and Helston) and William Lovelace†, to be disposed of 'as by my writings I have required them'. By one such indenture, made on the same day as his will, Rolfe granted the Greyfriars in Canterbury to Lovelace and others to be given to his widow in compensation for her dower, and this was done in November 1567. Nevertheless she contested the will and it was not until 18 May 1568, after Dudley had testified that Rolfe was of whole mind at its making, that administration was granted to Lovelace.[7]

[1] Sandwich old red bk. f. 141v.   [2] Date of birth estimated from first reference. *Vis. Kent* (Harl. Soc. xlii), 68.   [3] *LP Hen. VIII*, xiv, xix, xx; *CPR*, 1549–51, p. 292; 1553, p. 314; Sandwich old red bk. ff. 141v, 151.   [4] *CPR*, 1547–8, p. 73; *LP Hen. VIII*, xiv, xix; E403/2448, f. 8.   [5] Sandwich old red bk. ff. 141v, 151; *LP Hen. VIII*, xviii–xxi; *CPR*, 1549–51, p. 292; 1553, p. 314; E159/362, mm. 39–40; *APC*, ii. 169; iii. 294, 305; NRA 8388 (Essex RO, Lennard mss D/DL, T6/30).   [6] *Arch. Cant.* xxxiv. 90–91; *CPR*, 1547–8, p. 73; 1558–60, p. 150; St.Ch.2/26/291 (misdated temp. Hen. VIII); Sandwich little black bk. ff. 224–5, 253, 290–1, 298v.   [7] PCC 10 Babington; *Arch. Cant.* xxxiv. 91n.

H.M.

ROLLE, George (by 1486–1552), of Stevenstone, Devon and London.

BARNSTAPLE   1542,[1] 1545

b. by 1486. *m.* (1) Elizabeth, da. of one Ashton; (2) by 1522, Eleanor, 2nd da. of Henry Dacres of London, 6s. 5da.; (3) by 23 June 1551, Margery, wid. of Henry Brinklow and Stephen Vaughan* (*d.*25 Dec. 1549) both of London.[2]
   Keeper, recs. c.p. by 1507–*d.*; j.p. Devon 1545–*d.*; commr. relief 1550; bailiff, duchy of Cornw., hundred of Stratton, Cornw. in 1545–*d.*[3]

George Rolle was probably of Dorset origin. His illegitimate kinsman Thomas Rolle, who died in 1525 leaving the residue of his estate to Rolle himself and to an uncle William Rolle, parson of Wichampton, Dorset, had been born at Wimborne Minster in that county. Rolle was to make his career in London, where he owned and leased property, but although Dorset was one of the four western counties in which he acquired property it was in Devon, at Stevenstone near Torrington, that he built his country house, a 'fair brick building' noted by Leland.[4]

No trace has been found of Rolle's legal education, but it yielded him a clientele which included several monastic houses in Devon. The most prominent person to retain his services was Arthur Plantagenet, Viscount Lisle, whom he served as legal counsel until Lisle's death in 1542. Rolle figures largely in Lisle's affairs in Devon, notably in the protracted dispute of the 1530s with Henry Daubeney, afterwards Earl of Bridgwater, over Lady Lisle's property; in 1539 Rolle deterred Lisle from seeking a settlement of the matter in Parliament.[5]

Rolle makes a striking first appearance in the parliamentary history of the time as the beneficiary from a private Act (14 and 15 Hen. VIII, c.35) of 1523. This unusual measure secured for him a life tenure of the office of keeper of the writs and rolls of the common pleas. It had probably been occasioned by the appointment of Sir Robert Brudenell as chief justice of common pleas in 1521, for Rolle had entered office during Brudenell's earlier spell in the common pleas, before his removal to the King's bench in 1507, and the Act pointed to his 'long good and perfect knowledge and experience' of it in justification of the life appointment. The loss of so many Members' names leaves it in doubt whether Rolle was able to promote this bill himself or through friends in the house: the most useful of these would have been John Pakington*, who besides being his colleague in the common pleas was—or was to become—his sister-in-law's husband, while he was similarly linked with two other legal administrators in Robert Cheseman* and Robert Dacres. With one Member of the Commons of 1523,

Thomas Cromwell, Rolle was to be associated later, and if he had already attached himself to Sir Arthur Plantagenet he could have hoped for support in the Lords, where Plantagenet took his seat upon being created Viscount Lisle soon after the Parliament opened.[6]

Rolle was not returned at the next general election in 1529 and unless he was by-elected to that Parliament he is unlikely to have sat in its successor of 1536. The loss of most of the names for the next, that of 1539, including those for Barnstaple, leaves his Membership again open to doubt, nor would it be known that he was elected for Barnstaple in 1542 but for the payment by the town in 1543-4 of 20s. for his 'burgesship in Parliament'; the mayor's transmission to him in 1541-2 of 26s.8d., and the expenditure of 2s. for his entertainment by Roger Worth*, doubtless also related to his Membership. In 1545 he owed his reappearance in the House for Barnstaple to its new recorder, Sir Hugh Pollard, to whom the town entrusted the nominations and who chose Rolle and George Haydon: Rolle's association with Pollard's more distinguished younger brother (Sir) Richard* during the 1530s was perhaps remembered by the recorder, but Pollard's choice of the two lawyers is more likely to have been influenced by the pair's local connexions and partnership in the purchase of ex-monastic lands. Rolle was not re-elected in 1547 when two followers of the Protector Somerset sat for Barnstaple and by the next Parliament he was dead.[7]

By his will made on 11 Nov. 1552 Rolle instructed his wife to bury his body in such place as he should die at and provided for his three unmarried daughters whom he entrusted to the care of their brother George and their stepmother. He left the wardship and marriage of a Cornish heiress to his son and namesake and the residue of his goods to his wife whom he named executrix. He died nine days later, a month before his eldest son John's 30th birthday. His widow, who was to marry Sir Leonard Chamberlain*, obtained a limited probate on his will on 9 Feb. 1553 and probate *caetorum* on a slightly different version four months later: in 1573, after the death of his son George, Rolle's daughter Jacquetta received a grant of his goods.[8]

[1] N. Devon Athenaeum, Barnstaple, 3972, f. 54. [2] Date of birth estimated from first reference. *Vis. Devon*, ed. Colby, 184; *Vis. Devon*, ed. Vivian, 652; *Vis. Devon* (Harl. Soc. vi), 244; *Trans. Dev. Assoc.* lxxii. 252; C142/98/3; City of London RO, Guildhall, rep. 12(2), f. 349; 13(1), f. 235v. [3] *LP Hen. VIII*, iii, xx; *CPR*, 1553, p. 352; Duchy Cornw. RO, 127, m. 17v. [4] PCC 2 Porch, 3 Tashe; *Trans. Dev. Assoc.* lxxii. 252; *LP Hen. VIII*, iv, xiv, xvi, xviii; *DKR*, x. 262; *Devon Monastic Lands* (Devon and Cornw. Rec. Soc. n.s. i), pp. xxii–xxiii, 34, 47, 68–71, 128; J. E. Kew, 'The land market in Devon 1536–58' (Exeter Univ. Ph.D. thesis, 1967), 129–30, 224–7; N. Devon Athenaeum 1098; Leland, *Itin.* ed. Smith, i. 173, 300. [5] *Cal. I.T. Recs.* i. 462; Kew, 203; *LP Hen. VIII*, vi–xiv; M. L. Bush, 'The Lisle-Seymour land disputes', *Historical Jnl.* ix. 255–74. [6] *LP*

Hen. VIII, v, xiv. [7] N. Devon Athenaeum 3972, ff. 50(2), 54, 55(2); *LP Hen. VIII*, xi. [8] PCC 3 Tashe; C142/98/3.

A.D.K.H.

ROLSTON, James (by 1501–54/55) of Mayfield, Staffs.

NEWCASTLE-UNDER-LYME   1547, 1553 (Oct.),[1] 1554 (Apr.)

b. by 1501, 2nd s. of Thomas Rolston (*d.*1529) of Mayfield by Elizabeth, da. of John Turvill of New Hall, Leics. *unm.*[2]

Servant of Francis Talbot, 5th Earl of Shrewsbury by 1538–*d.*; commr. in local dispute, Staffs. 1551.[3]

Little is known of James Rolston. He came from a cadet branch of the gentle family which had lived at Rolleston in Staffordshire 'time out of mind'. His father had entailed his lands before making his will on 13 Aug. 1528, which contains no indication of James Rolston's inheritance, if any; but Rolston, described in his own will as of Mayfield, is known to have held property there, at nearby Ashbourne in Derbyshire and at Farley. The Mayfield property may have been that for which James had obtained a 40-year lease from the prior of Tutbury on 11 Sept. 1522: he shared the lease with his brother Christopher, who predeceased him, and it passed to his elder brother Francis. The prior of Tutbury had been one of the overseers of Thomas Rolston's will.[4]

Rolston was of an age with the 5th Earl of Shrewsbury whose service he had entered by the end of 1538. He evidently helped to run the earl's estates and towards the end of his life he loomed large in the earl's financial transactions. Presumably it was to Shrewsbury that he owed his three appearances in the Commons, as he had no personal links with Newcastle-under-Lyme and the earl was steward of the manor there belonging to the duchy of Lancaster: a family connexion with the influential Peshalls was perhaps of assistance in commending him to the borough. The Journal throws no light upon his role in the Commons, but there is some reason to believe that he toed the same parliamentary line as his master: two days after his return in 1554 he acknowledged a letter from Shrewsbury asking him to wait upon the earl at Oxford while the Parliament was meeting there, Rolston being then unaware that several days before, on 15 Mar., the Parliament had been prorogued to Westminster. The making of his will on 2 Nov. 1553 during the preceding Parliament suggests that he took the opportunity of being in the capital to do this. The markedly Catholic tone of the will probably indicates Rolston's attitude towards the overthrow of the Edwardian Reformation begun during his first Membership of the Commons, and this would accord with the absence of his name among those Members opposed to the reunion with Rome. After remembering his brother Francis (the supervisor), three godsons, servants and the poor, he left leases and money to 'my priest' Thomas Mansfield and to William Woodward and his wife for the upbringing of their children. He also bequeathed £20 to his nephew Thomas Peshall towards his education at Cambridge. The will was proved at Lichfield on 11 Sept. 1555 by Rolston's executors Thomas Mansfield and William Woodward, who valued his estate at £301.[5]

[1] Bodl. e Museo 17. [2] Date of birth estimated from first reference. *The Gen.* n.s. viii. 74; J. C. Wedgwood, *Staffs. Parl. Hist.* (Wm. Salt Arch. Soc.), i. 324–5; T. Pape, *Newcastle-under-Lyme*, 39–40. [3] *LP Hen. VIII*, xiii; *Wm. Salt. Arch. Soc.* (ser.3) 1912, p. 181. [4] Erdeswick, *Staffs.* 537; Wedgwood, i. 325; PCC 14 Jankyn; *Wm. Salt Arch. Soc.* (ser. 3) 1929, p. 165; *Staffs. Rec. Soc.* 1938, p. 165. [5] *LP Hen. VIII*, xiii; *HMC Shrewsbury and Talbot*, i. 15; ii. 303; Somerville, *Duchy*, i. 543; Wedgwood, i. 325.

A.D.

ROOKWOOD, Brice (by 1523–70 or later), of Halvergate, Norf.

LOSTWITHIEL 1554 (Apr.), 1555

b. by 1523, 4th s. of Edmund Rookwood of Euston, Suff. by 2nd w. of William London; half-bro. of Nicholas Rookwood*. *educ.* L. Inn, adm. 26 Jan. 1548. *m.* (1) by 1547, Amy, da. of William Salter of South Wootton, Norf., wid. of Henry Prentice; (2) Margaret, da. of Sir Edmund Bedingfield of Oxburgh, Norf., wid. of Thomas Garneys.[1]

Commr. gaol delivery, western counties 1544–55.[2]

Brice Rookwood sat in Parliament twice during Mary's reign for Lostwithiel, the administrative centre of the duchy of Cornwall: on both occasions he served with members of the Southcote family, in 1554 with George and a year later (when his name was inserted on the indenture in a different hand) with John I. Since he was a commissioner of gaol delivery whose circuit included Launceston castle, Rookwood may have been able to rely on his own links with Cornwall to obtain election, but he probably owed his nomination to his kinship with the Privy Councillor, Sir Henry Bedingfield*, presumably acting through the agency of the duchy. All that is known about his part in the House is that he did not join the protest led by Sir Anthony Kingston in 1555, perhaps because like so many of his family he was Catholic. The successive deaths of his elder brother Nicholas, of his mother who had outlived her third husband, Thomas, 3rd Lord Burgh, and of Queen Mary, and the waning of Bedingfield's influence on the accession of Elizabeth, left Rookwood's prospects in middle age somewhat bleak. He appears to have retired to East Anglia, and it is as the principal resident of Halvergate in 1570 that he is last glimpsed addressing the Queen on the conduct of her steward there.[3]

[1] Date of birth estimated from first commission. *Vis. Norf.* (Harl. Soc. xxxii), 235; *CP*, ii. 423; C1/1154/53–54. [2] *LP Hen. VIII*, xx, xxi; *CPR*, 1547–8, p. 74; 1553–4, pp. 30–32; 1554–5, p. 105. [3] C219/24/28; *CPR*, 1554–5, p. 105; Req.2/110/10; *APC*, x. 310–12; H. Foley, *Jesuit Recs.* iii. 785–6.

J.J.G.

ROOKWOOD, Nicholas (by 1511–57), of Lincoln's Inn, London and Euston, Suff.

THETFORD 1554 (Apr.), 1554 (Nov.),[1] 1555

b. by 1511, 2nd s. of Edmund Rookwood of Euston by 1st w.; half-bro. of Brice Rookwood*. *educ.* L. Inn, adm. 20 Nov. 1525. *m.* by 1554, Elizabeth, da. of George Peryent of the diocese of Norwich, wid. of Sir Humphrey Style (*d.*1552) of Beckenham, Kent, 1s.[2]

Chief prothonotary c.p. by May 1533–*d.*; commr. gaol delivery, western circuit 1537–*d.*, clerk of assize by 1552; j.p.q. Kent, Suff. 1554–*d.*[3]

Sprung from a well connected family of East Anglia, Nicholas Rookwood became a lawyer. It was as chief prothonotary of the common pleas that in 1533 he obtained his predecessor's chambers at Lincoln's Inn and as a kinsman of Bishop Nikke of Norwich that he had the entry fee remitted. The city of London retained his services as its attorney in the common pleas, but most of what is known about his career refers to his work as a commissioner of gaol delivery or to land transactions in East Anglia. In 1537 he bought the family seat at Euston from his elder brother, who had no son, and he was to acquire other property in the locality. His marriage to a widow of a Kentish knight gave him a say in local administration in Kent as well as in Suffolk.[4]

During Wyatt's rebellion Rookwood was wounded in the nose by an arrow while denying the rebels entry to Lincoln's Inn; his honourable scar may have helped to commend him for a seat in Parliament, which for the rest he could have owed to his local standing, Thetford being only four miles from Euston, and to his ties with Sir Henry Bedingfield* and with officials of the duchy of Lancaster. Predictably, he is not to be found among the opponents of the government in the House. Rookwood made his will at Euston on 13 Sept. 1557 and died that day. After providing for his wife, he remembered his relatives and left rings to the attorney-general, William Cordell* and (Sir) Clement Heigham*. John Sulyard* witnessed the will, which was proved on the following 23 Oct. by Rookwood's executors, his widow and his stepmother Lady Burgh. His son Edward, who was aged three on 31 Oct. 1557, was to die a Catholic.[5]

[1] Huntington Lib. Hastings mss Parl. pprs. [2] Date of birth estimated from education. *Vis. Norf.* (Harl. Soc. xxxii), 235; *Vis. Norf.* (Norf. Arch.), i. 140–2; *Vis. Herts.* (Harl. Soc. xxii), 156; C142/112/146. [3] *Black Bk. L. Inn*, i. 235; *LP Hen. VIII*, xii–xviii, xx; *CPR*, 1547–8, p. 78; 1550–3, p. 249; 1553–4, p. 30; 1554–5, p. 103; 1555–7, p. 418. [4] *Black Bk. L. Inn*, i. 235; City of London RO, Guildhall, rep. 13(2), f. 541; *LP Hen. VIII*, xii–xxi; Coppinger, *Suff. Manors*, i. 292; Blomefield, *Norf.* i. 144. [5] *Chron. Q. Jane and Q. Mary* (Cam. Soc. xlviii), 132; Bath mss, Thynne pprs. 2, ff. 191–91v;

PCC 39 Wrastley; C142/112/146; A. H. Smith, *County and Ct.*, 202, 218.
                                                                    R.V.

ROOS (ROS), Robert (1510–83), of Ingmanthorpe, Kirk Deighton, Yorks.

Thirsk 1555

b. May/June 1510, 1st s. of Robert Roos of Ingmanthorpe by 1st w. Mary, da. of Sir James Strangways (*d.*1521) of West Harlsey. *m.* Elizabeth, da. of Sir Nicholas Fairfax* of Gilling Castle and Walton, 1da. *suc.* fa. May 1530.[1]

The Roos family of Ingmanthorpe was a cadet branch of the baronial family. In 1512 the Roos barony passed to the Manners, earls of Rutland, who were chief lords of the manor of Ingmanthorpe, and about 1532 the 1st Earl presented to the benefice of Kirk Deighton upon wrong information that Robert Roos was still under age. Roos was an executor of his father's will of 25 Oct. 1529.[2]

To his patrimony Roos added the claim derived through his mother to a share in the Strangways inheritance, which included property formerly belonging to the Scropes of Masham. Following the death of Sir James Strangways the younger in 1541 an award of June 1543, confirmed by an Act of 1544 (35 Hen. VIII, c.24), gave Roos as one of the claimants, and in consideration of his costs in the litigation involved, Upsall and other manors in Northumberland, and Yorkshire, the reversion of further manors in those counties, and two advowsons in Leicestershire. He received livery of these lands in January 1545 but disputes continued: thus in October 1549 the 3rd Lord Dacre, another of the claimants, informed the 5th Earl of Shrewsbury that Roos had at length been ejected from Leonard Dacre's* house at Upsall. By then Roos had begun to part with his lands: in 1541 he sold North Deighton to William and Elizabeth Scrymgeour, in 1545 he mortgaged a fifth part of five manors to Robert Curzon* and (Sir) Thomas Pope* (a transaction which led to a chancery suit which was reported by Edmund Plowden*), in 1547 he sold Potto to William Tancred*, and in 1557 and 1558 other manors went to Christopher Lascelles* and Christopher Wray*.[3]

What significance should be attached to Roos's election to the Parliament of 1555 is a matter for speculation. Already on the road to ruin, he may have had an interest in visiting London under the protection of privilege or merely have wished to enjoy an experience befitting his station. His property at Upsall gave him a local standing at Thirsk, but he probably owed his adoption there to his connexions, notably his marriage to Elizabeth Fairfax; his fellow-Member Christopher Lascelles, who had a lien on one of the seats for Thirsk, may also have had a hand in his nomination. Neither Roos nor Lascelles appears on the list of Members of this Parliament who opposed one of the government's bills, and if Roos shared the Catholicism which was later to bring trouble to James Roos of Ingmanthorpe, who was presumably his brother, it was not disaffection which kept him out of other Marian Parliaments.[4]

Early in Elizabeth's reign Roos sought financial salvation by surrendering his remaining lands to the 2nd Earl of Rutland

> to the end his debts should be paid and he have some exhibition during life, which seemeth was not much, for he had a chamber wherein he lay in South Deighton and had his diet sent every mealtime from Mr. Manners's table, who then lived at the parsonage house there.

The transaction took place during Rutland's presidency of the north, and it may account for the second licence to enter on the Strangways inheritance which was granted to Roos in March 1562. The remainder of his life was passed in obscurity. On his death in 1583 he left a daughter Bridget who was to sink even lower: married to a kinsman, Peter Roos of Laxton, Nottinghamshire, she was reduced to such poverty that, so tradition has it, she was one of those who gleaned corn in the field there.[5]

[1] Date of birth estimated from age at fa.'s i.p.m., C142/81/302. *CP*, iv. 68; *Vis. Yorks.* (Harl. Soc. xvi), 300; *Yorks. Arch. Soc. rec. ser.* xxxiv. 32; *VCH Yorks* (N. *Riding*), i. 336. [2] *CP*, xi. 117–19; *LP Hen. VIII*, xii; *Test Ebor.* v (Surtees Soc. lxxix), 276–8. [3] *LP Hen. VIII*, xix, xx; *Yorks. Arch. Jnl.* vii. 492; *HMC Shrewsbury and Talbot*, ii. 344–5; NRA 11614 (Ingilby recs., Ripley Castle, Harrogate, Yorks. nos. 359, 843–4, 846); *VCH Yorks.* (N. *Riding*), i. 346, 408; ii. 28, 291, 313–14; *Yorks. Arch. Soc. rec. ser.* ii. 117, 131, 207, 211; L. W. Abbott, *Law Reporting in Eng.* 339–40. [4] *Leeds Phil. and Lit. Soc. Procs.* x, 277; *Biog. Studies* (now *Recusant History*), iii. 83–84. [5] *Yorks. Arch. Soc. rec. ser.* xxxiv. 32; *CPR*, 1560–3, p. 362; *Vis. Notts.* (Harl. Soc. iv), 111–12; *VCH Yorks.* (N. *Riding*), i. 336; Thoroton, *Notts.* ed. Throsby, iii. 209.
                                                                    A.D.

ROPER, Christopher (1508/9–58/59), of Lynsted, Kent.

Rochester 1553 (Mar.)

b. 1508/9, yst. s. of John Roper of St. Dunstan's, Canterbury and Eltham by Jane, da. of Sir John Fineux† of Faversham and Herne; bro. of William*. *educ.* Corpus, Oxf. 2 July 1524; G. Inn, adm. 1528. *m.* Elizabeth, da. of Christopher Blore of Rainham, 3s. 5da.[1]

Escheator, Kent and Mdx. 1550–1; commr. relief, Kent 1550; j.p.q. 1554.[2]

Christopher Roper was his mother's youngest and favourite son. If she had had her way he and not the eldest, William, would have inherited the Ropers' old home in Canterbury, but in 1524 her husband left this to her for life and then to William. He provided for Christopher out of the family's other residence at Eltham, from which his mother was to receive £13 6s.8d. for his maintenance and education until he was 24, and feoffees were to pay him initially a further £20 a year and then the entire yield. This arrangement was doubtless one of the issues in the dispute over the will which had to be resolved by a private Act of Parliament in 1529 (21 Hen. VIII, c.23): it was there laid down that each of the younger sons should receive lands worth £26 13s.8d. a year, and in the event Christopher Roper was to inherit the lodge at Lynsted which his mother had brought to her marriage.[3]

The decision that Roper should enter Gray's Inn, instead of following his father and brother at Lincoln's Inn, must also have been his mother's, for it was there that her own father the lord chief justice had learned his law; it was she, too, who would later cultivate the connexion with another member of the inn, Thomas Cromwell. Roper was in Cromwell's service by 1535, the year which saw the death of William Roper's mentor Sir Thomas More, and three years later he was included in a list of the minister's servants considered suitable for advancement by the King. It was a judgment at variance with his mother's admission that in his youth he preferred pleasure to profit, and there is no evidence that it was acted upon; a dozen years were to pass before Roper was named to his only office as escheator of Kent. His Commons career was to be correspondingly brief, being limited to the 31 days of the Parliament of March 1553. Lacking any personal claim to sit for Rochester beyond a marital connexion with the village of Rainham, some miles east of the city, Roper could have done so only because his brother William, one of the Rochester Members in at least the two previous Parliaments, was on this occasion not re-elected. It is doubtful whether there was more to the exchange than fraternal goodwill, for if the younger Roper's Cromwellian background may have told in his favour under the Duke of Northumberland, he was to yield nothing to his brother in his subsequent loyalty to Mary. When Sir Thomas Wyatt II* sought to raise Kent in rebellion, Roper was taken prisoner for proclaiming him a traitor, a service later rewarded by a lease of Maidstone rectory and other former church property in the county. This, with his lease of the manor of Tonge, near Lynsted, from Jane Seymour in 1537 (renewed by the crown in 1540) and his purchase or lease of Panthurst Park, near Sevenoaks Weald, from (Sir) George Harper* and Thomas Culpeper in 1556, seem to have been his only additions to his inheritance.[4]

Roper's will of 20 May 1558 was Catholic in tone and content, with its provision for a light to burn night and day for a year before the sacrament in Lynsted church and its bequests to the Observant Franciscans of Greenwich and to the Dominicans in Smithfield, London. His lands he bequeathed to his wife and executrix while she lived, with remainder successively to his three sons and to William Roper, the loving eldest brother whom he named overseer. He died between 18 June 1558, when he and William acquired the wardship of Elizabeth Parke (who was to marry his son John), and 18 Apr. 1559 when the will was proved. In 1616 John Roper was created 1st Baron Teynham.[5]

[1] Aged 15 years 6 months on admission to Corpus, Emden, *Biog. Reg. Univ. Oxf. 1501–40*, p. 491. *Vis. Kent* (Harl. Soc. xlii), 82–83; Add. 34812, ff. 6v, 7, 9v.   [2] *CPR*, 1553, p. 355; 1553–4, pp. 20, 28, 36.   [3] *LP Hen. VIII*, iv, v; *Arch. Cant.* ii. 153–74.   [4] *LP Hen. VIII*, viii, ix, xi–xiii, xv; M. L. Robertson, 'Cromwell's servants' (Univ. California Los Angeles Ph.D. thesis, 1975), 552; J. Proctor, *The Historie of Wyates rebellion* (1554), 6, 7, 56; D. M. Loades, *Two Tudor Conspiracies*, 56; *CPR*, 1554–5, pp. 43–44; NRA 8388 (Essex RO, Lennard mss D/DL, T5/69).   [5] PCC 3 Chaynay; *CPR*, 1557–8, p. 1.

H.M.

ROPER, Thomas (1533/34–98), of Eltham, Kent.

NEW SHOREHAM	1553 (Oct.)
NEWPORT IUXTA LAUNCESTON	1558

b. 1533/34, 1st s. of William Roper* of St. Dunstan's, Canterbury and Eltham, Kent and Chelsea, Mdx. by Margaret, da. of Sir Thomas More of London and Chelsea. *educ.* L. Inn. *m.* by 1557, Lucy, da. of Sir Anthony Browne* of Cowdray, Suss., 5s. 5da. *suc.* fa. 4 Jan. 1578.[1]

Prothonotary, KB 1574–*d.*[2]

Thomas Roper was a student at Lincoln's Inn barely out of his teens when he took the senior place for one of the 3rd Duke of Norfolk's boroughs in Mary's first Parliament: his fellow-Member was his older kinsman Thomas Elrington. His father's association with the duke, which dated back as early as 1529, could account for their election, but if Roper himself was already married the returning officer, Sir Anthony Browne, was his brother-in-law. At Newport it was presumably another of his brothers-in-law, James Bassett*, who enlisted the powerful support of his Grenville kinsmen: his fellow-Member Thomas Hungate was a former dependant of the Browne family. Roper did not support the Protestant opposition in 1553 and the 'Mr. Roper' mentioned in the Journal for 1558 was undoubtedly his father.[3]

Roper lacked the literary talent of his sister Mary, an expert classical scholar who contributed to the cost of printing the first edition of More's English works in 1557, and his Catholicism precluded him from a public career in his mature years. In 1574 Roper's father passed on to him the prothonotary-ship of the King's bench, which he had held for over 50 years, but shortly afterwards his family's troubles began. Three years later Lincoln's Inn made a return of recusants stating that William Roper and his two sons had been sequestered from the inn 'for suspicion had of their religion'. Early in the following year Thomas Roper was given until its last council before Easter 'to conform to the religion that is now preached', but despite the threat a year later to deprive him of his chambers, he did not comply and his name disappears from the records of the inn. When his house was searched in 1581, vessels for use in the mass were found and he was imprisoned in the Fleet with his steward, a priest named Francis Thompson. A month later he was released after he had agreed to attend services at Orpington church. During his remaining years he exercised the prothonotaryship mainly through a deputy. Roper died on 21 Jan. 1598, having refused to make a will on his deathbed since he was unable to do any more for his younger children than he had already done, and referring his servants to his eldest son whom he said 'should have all and hang all'. The inquisition following his death found he had held manors at Eltham and Redbroke, a house outside the west gate of Canterbury, over 1,500 acres near Whitstable and lands in Staffordshire, all of which were valued at £238.[4]

[1] Aged 30 in 1564, W. Roper, *Life of More* (EETS cxcvii), p. xxxi. *Vis. Kent.* (Harl. Soc. lxxv), 26. [2] PRO Index 1342. [3] *CJ*, i. 48–49. [4] N. Harpsfield, *Life of More* (EETS clxxxvi), 83, 333; M. Blatcher, *Ct. K.B. 1450–1550*, p. 153; *Cath. Rec. Soc.* xxii. 11; H. Foley, *Jesuit Recs.* ii. 589; *APC*, xiii. 147–8, 158, 196; PCC 13 Lewyn; C142/255/178.

R.J.W.S.

ROPER, William (1495/96–1578), of St Dunstan's, Canterbury and Eltham, Kent and Chelsea, Mdx.

BRAMBER   1529
ROCHESTER   1545, 1547[1]
WINCHELSEA   1553 (Oct.)[2]
ROCHESTER   1554 (Apr.), 1554 (Nov.)
CANTERBURY   1555, 1558

b. 1495/96, 1st s. of John Roper of St. Dunstan's, Canterbury and Eltham by Jane, da. of Sir John Fineux† of Faversham and Herne, Kent; bro. of Christopher*. *educ.* ?Oxf.; L. Inn, adm. 25 Dec. 1518, called 1525. *m.* lic. 2 July 1521, Margaret, da. of Sir Thomas More of London and Chelsea, 2s. inc. Thomas* 3da. *suc.* fa. 7 Apr. 1524.[3]

Bencher, L. Inn 1535, gov. 1553–69/70.

Prothonotary, KB 1524–74; j.p. Kent 1526–54, Mdx. 1543–58/59; abp. Canterbury's steward, Maidstone, Kent by 1535; commr. relief, Mdx. 1550, heresy, diocese of Canterbury 1556, home counties 1557; other commissions 1530–68; steward, Faversham, Kent 1546–66 or later; sheriff, Kent 1554–5.[4]

William Roper had a legal ancestry on both his parents' sides. According to tradition he studied at one of the universities, perhaps Oxford where his brother attended Corpus Christi, before entering Lincoln's Inn. It was probably in 1518 that he

joined the household of Sir Thomas More, for in that year he and More shared a fee from the city of London for the 'making of a book' and he was to recall his residence in More's house 'by the space of 16 years and more'. At the time of his marriage into More's family Roper was inclined to Lutheranism, and at length became so enthusiastic in his talk that he was charged with heresy before Wolsey, who, out of respect to More, dismissed him with a friendly warning. More himself, after long reasoning with his son-in-law, saw that he was not able to 'call him home' by argument and decided to rely on prayer; and Roper, who during this period had taken a dislike to his father-in-law, soon afterwards returned to his faith and his friendship with More. These two loyalties were to shape his life; it is as More's 'son Roper' and hagiographer that he is remembered.[5]

Roper's parliamentary career perhaps began in 1523 when More was Speaker, but in the absence of the returns his Membership is uncertain. In 1529 More replaced Wolsey as chancellor shortly before the opening of the new Parliament and presumably he helped Roper to secure election for a Sussex borough controlled by his friend the 3rd Duke of Norfolk: Roper's partner Henry See was in chambers with him at Lincoln's Inn. An Act (21 Hen. VIII, c.23) passed in the first session settled the five year-old dispute which the will of Roper's father had given rise to and established his right to the greater part of the inheritance. Four sessions later, early in 1533, Roper and See were listed by Cromwell as opposed on religious or economic grounds to the bill in restraint of appeals then passing through Parliament. In the next session, when More was directly threatened by a bill to attaint him and others of misprision of treason in concealing the activities of the nun of Kent, it was to Roper, meeting him in the Parliament house, that Cromwell gave the message that More's name had been taken out of the bill. The respite was shortlived. Roper was doubtless among those of the Commons who in the autumn of 1534 'stuck' to have the word 'maliciously' inserted into the Act (26 Hen. VIII, c.13) making it treason to deny the royal supremacy, in the hope of limiting its scope, but their stand was to avail nothing, and in July 1535 More was executed. Roper may have served for Bramber again in the following Parliament, that of June 1536, when the King asked for the return of the previous Members, and possibly for a third time in 1539, a Parliament for which the names of the Members are lost: his Membership in 1539 receives some colour from the inclusion of his name in the preamble to the Act for changing the custom of gavelkind (31 Hen. VIII, c.3) passed during the first session of that Parliament.[6]

Roper's career did not apparently suffer by his father-in-law's fate. He continued to be prothonotary of the King's bench, an office in which he had succeeded his father, who had obtained it for him at 'no little charge' after the two had worked in it from at least 1519, and which Roper was in turn to pass on in 1574 to his son Thomas. Yet there was always a lurking danger. Early in 1543 Roper was imprisoned in the Tower and fined £100: his offence was 'relieving by his alms a notable learned man', John Bekinsau*, with whom he was involved in the prebendaries' plot against Cranmer.[7]

In 1545 Roper was elected a Member for Rochester, where he was doubtless well known as a magistrate with several minor posts in the locality, and presumably was required to take the oath of supremacy. He was re-elected to the first Parliament of Edward VI's reign by the same city, but he is not known to have sat in that King's second Parliament, in which the Duke of Northumberland's influence was paramount, although his brother Christopher did so for Rochester. Roper himself was a Member of all five of Mary's Parliaments. To the first of these, summoned for October 1553, he was returned for Winchelsea by Sir Thomas Cheyne*, lord warden of the Cinque Ports, although he had not been elected by the port itself, which had chosen William Egleston* and (Sir) John Guildford*. For the next two Parliaments Roper reverted to Rochester, but in 1555 his shrievalty barred him from election there and he was returned for Canterbury, which as a city was independent of the sheriff of Kent. The Ropers, who had long owned St. Dunstan's, outside the west gate of the city, were a family of great local renown, and William Roper probably needed no extraneous influence to secure his election: indeed, he seems to have seen to it that the second seat went to a friend of his, More's nephew William Rastell. The election had clearly been decided beforehand: on 14 Sept. 1555, 11 days after the writs for a new Parliament had gone out, the burmote agreed that Rastell and Roper should be admitted and sworn freemen of the city 'freely, of the gift and benevolence of the mayor and commonalty', and thus the statutory obligation to elect citizens could be observed at the election some three weeks later. In the Parliament of 1558 Roper was again a Member for Canterbury, this time serving with his former partner for Winchelsea, Sir Henry Crispe: the names of both men were inserted in a different hand on the indenture.[8]

Roper's addiction to the House of Commons—he is known to have sat in eight Parliaments and may have done so in three or four more—was perhaps not unconnected with his headship of the administra-tion of the court of King's bench. If, as has been suggested, he had a good deal to do with perfecting the procedural devices which at this time brought a much needed revival of business in that court, although amid mounting criticism from outside it, especially from the court of common pleas, he could well have judged it necessary to belong to the only assembly which was capable of interfering in his court's conduct of its affairs. Thus when the Parliament of 1547 debated a bill 'for the reformation of the common laws of the realm', which probably sought to deal with these innovations of procedure, we may be sure that Roper, and doubtless other stalwarts of the King's bench, would have bestirred themselves to protect an institution which was also their livelihood. This speculation apart, little trace remains of Roper's activities in the Commons. During the second session of the Parliament of 1547 his aid was enlisted by Thomas Jolye* to block a bill depriving the 2nd Earl of Cumberland of an hereditary shrievalty, and in the following session, on 15 Nov. 1549, a bill allowing beneficed priests to be non-resident in time of sickness was committed to him. In February 1558 he was one of those assigned to consider the issue of a writ of privilege for Walter Ralegh* and, later in the same month, to peruse the grants of sanctuary in Westminster which the abbot alleged were infringed by a new sanctuary bill. Outside Parliament Roper cut a figure in local government, his activities increasing markedly during Mary's reign. He was appointed to the commission which heard the appeal of Bishop Bonner of London against his deprivation under Edward VI and to two commissions for the discovery of heresy, the first limited to the diocese of Canterbury. He also received, in consideration of his service, a licence to found a chantry in the church of St. Dunstan, Canterbury.[9]

So enthusiastic a Marian was unlikely to commend himself to Elizabeth. Roper was immediately removed from the Kent bench and only briefly retained on the Middlesex one, and he did not reappear in Parliament. On 8 July 1568 he submitted himself to the Privy Council for having assisted with money (unnamed) persons who had left England to print books against the Queen's supremacy; he promised 'from henceforth to obey all her Majesty's laws and ordinances set forth by her Majesty's authority, in all matters of religion and orders ecclesiastical'. Yet the next year, when commissioners came down into Kent to take the oath of all justices or former justices, Roper, being as he said 'a man very aged and likewise subject to great infirmities and diseases', besought them to be suitors to the Queen and Council 'to bear with him touching his conscience';

and instead of signing a subscription to the Act of Uniformity, he was allowed to bind himself in 200 marks to be of good behaviour to the Queen and her people 'according to the form of the statute in that case had and provided' and to appear before the Privy Council when summoned. By January 1570 he was no longer a governor of Lincoln's Inn, an office which he had held every year since 1553, but he still held his prothonotaryship in the King's bench. In 1577 he was reported as a non-communicant and an absentee from church. All the same he appears to have been left in peace, although directly after his death his London house was searched and vestments for the mass found.[10]

Roper made his will on 10 Jan. 1577 asking to be buried at Chelsea, 'in the vault with the body of my dearly beloved wife (whose soul our Lord pardon), where my father-in-law Sir Thomas More (whose soul Jesus bless) did mind to be buried'. Thomas, his elder son, inherited lands in Kent, and Anthony, his younger, lands in London, Middlesex and Oxfordshire. His executors included Dr. James Good, in whose house he had a room, Edmund Plowden* and (Sir) Christopher Wray*. He died on 4 Jan. 1578 and was buried, not in Chelsea, but if his epitaph there is to be believed, in St. Dunstan's, Canterbury. About 1538 he and his wife were painted in miniature by Holbein, who had earlier included Margaret Roper in his celebrated depiction of More's family.[11]

[1] Hatfield 207. [2] Bodl. e Museo 17. [3] Aged 82 at death according to MI. *Vis. Kent* (Harl. Soc. xlii), 82; *Mar. Lic. London* (Harl. Soc. xxv), 2. [4] Index 1331, 1342; *LP Hen. VIII*, iv–xxi; *CPR*, 1547–8 to 1555–7 passim; 1569–72, p. 220; *Val. Eccles.* i. 5; Faversham wardmote bk. 43–112 passim. [5] Wood, *Ath. Ox.* ed. Bliss, i. 89; City of London RO, Guildhall, bridge accts. 1509–25, ff. 163, 186; W. Roper, *Life of More* (EETS cxcvii), 3, 84–88; Elton, *Policy and Police*, 410–12, 417, 419. [6] *Black Bk. L. Inn*, i. 203; Roper, 71; *LP Hen. VIII*, viii; ix. 1077 citing SP1/99, p. 234. [7] *Statutes*, iii. 311; Index 1331, 1342; M. Blatcher, *Ct. KB 1450–1550*, pp. 146, 150; *LP Hen. VIII*, xvii, xviii; N. Harpsfield, *Life of More* (EETS clxxxvi), 89; Strype, *Cranmer*, i. 169. [8] Winchelsea hundred ct. bk. 2, f. 55; Canterbury burmote bk. 1542–78, f. 96v; C219/25/143. [9] Blatcher, 103–6; *Clifford Letters* (Surtees Soc. clxxii), 102–4; *CJ*, i. 11, 48–49; *LP Hen. VIII*, iv–xxi; *CPR*, 1550–3 to 1555–7 passim. [10] SP12/47/7, 59/37; *Black Bk. L. Inn*, i. 306–362 passim; Index 1342; *Cath. Rec. Soc.* xxii. 11, 101; *APC*, x. 143. [11] PCC 27 Langley; C142/181/122; R. C. Strong, *Tudor and Jacobean Portraits*, 345–8.

H.M.

ROSCARROCK, Francis

NEWPORT IUXTA LAUNCESTON	1553 (Mar.)
CAMELFORD	1553 (Oct.)
LISKEARD	1554 (Apr.)
CAMELFORD	1554 (Nov.)

Nothing has been discovered about Francis Roscarrock 'gentleman' beyond his Membership of four consecutive Parliaments. He was presumably a member of the family of that name in Cornwall as he sat for boroughs where it or its kin were influential. The head of the family, Richard Roscarrock, twice joined him in the House as one of the knights for the shire and Richard's brother Thomas once as a Member for Liskeard. When returned for Camelford in the autumn of 1554 Roscarrock's name was inserted in a different hand on the indenture.

C219/23/30.

J.J.G.

ROSCARROCK, John (by 1520–64 or later).

LISKEARD 1545

b. by 1520, s. of John Roscarrock of Roscarrock in St. Endellion, Cornw. by 2nd w. Mary, da. of Nicholas Cavell of Treharrock in St. Kew; half-bro. of Richard Roscarrock* and William Roscarrock*. *educ.* L. Inn, adm. 8 Jan. 1534, called 1539.[1]
  Butler, L. Inn 1553–5.
  Under steward, stannary ct. Kerrier and Penwith, Cornw. by 1563.[2]

Soon after John Roscarrock had been called to the bar, his advice was sought by his kinswoman, Viscountess Lisle: an important letter from the viscountess in 1539 was entrusted to George Rolle* for its delivery to Roscarrock in the south-west, and several months later another servant was sent unsuccessfully to his inn to seek him out. The fall of Viscount Lisle in 1540 probably blighted Roscarrock's early hopes of advancement, and nothing has been discovered about his career in the years immediately following, until his return in 1545 as the senior Member for Liskeard, a borough where his family had property. Roscarrock presumably stood for election in the hope of commending himself to the King or another patron by service in the House, and in this he evidently had the backing of his superior at Lincoln's Inn, Sir Thomas Arundell*, who supervised the elections in the south-west on this occasion, as well as his own Cornish connexions; he was related to both of the knights of the shire in 1545, John Beauchamp and Richard Chamond, and to the returning officer, Sir Richard Grenville. Roscarrock's practice in Cornwall flourished during the middle years of the century and from 1546 onwards he received occasional employment, often in association with Henry Chiverton*, from the crown in matters of local administration. A dispute over some cattle with Martin Trewynnard in 1564 brought him and John Killigrew† into Chancery as plaintiffs: this is the last certain reference found to Roscarrock. He may be identifiable with the man who held the manor of Trehane in Trevalga during the 1570s and who probably died during the following decade, leaving his property to a namesake who lived until 1606.[3]

[1] Date of birth estimated from education. *Vis. Cornw.* ed. Vivian, 440. [2] St.Ch.5/T22/12. [3] *LP Hen. VIII*, xiv; Duchy Cornw. RO, 491, m. 21v; C1/1367/82; St.Ch.2/16/22A; 3/6/89; *APC*, ii. 204; E. Coke, *Institutes*, iv. 230; J. Maclean, *Trigg Minor*, iii. 295.

J.J.G.

ROSCARROCK, Richard (c.1507–75), of Roscarrock in St. Endellion, Cornw.

CORNWALL 1553 (Oct.), 1554 (Apr.)

b. c.1507, 1st s. of John Roscarrock of Roscarrock by 1st w. Agnes, da. of Sir Thomas Grenville of Stowe in Kilkhampton; bro. of William* and half-bro. of John Roscarrock*. *m.* by Feb. 1528, Isabel, da. and coh. of Richard Trevenor *alias* Denny of Lamorran, 6s. inc. Thomas* 3da. *suc.* fa. 26/27 Oct. 1537.[1]

Reeve, Camelford, Cornw. 1541–2; bailiff, Trigg hundred 1541–4, 1566–7, 1568–9, 1575; sheriff 1550–1, 1561–2; j.p. 1554–64.[2]

Richard Roscarrock was described in a dispute, perhaps conventionally but not without truth, as 'a man of great worship, wealth and substance, and well friended' in Cornwall: he was connected by descent or marriage with the leading families in the county, and among his closest kinsmen were numbered Arthur Plantagenet, Viscount Lisle, Sir John Arundell*, Richard Chamond* and (Sir) Richard Grenville I*. No trace has been found of Roscarrock's career before 1541 when he obtained a minor post in the duchy of Cornwall. For the next quarter-of-a-century he figured prominently in local affairs and enjoyed some esteem: in the 1540s his name was put forward six times running for the shrievalty before the office came his way. His behaviour during the rebellion of 1549 is not recorded, but after its suppression some doubt attached to him and he was bound by Sir Ralph Hopton* to appear before the Privy Council on the following 12 Nov.: when he did so he evidently cleared himself, for in the following year he was pricked sheriff for the first time.[3]

The reign of Mary saw the burgeoning of Roscarrock's career. He gained the second knighthood of the shire in her first Parliament, where he was not one of those who opposed the restoration of Catholicism, and his acquiescence doubtless paved the way for his return to the next, held in the spring of 1554, when he shared the representation of the shire with his kinsman Sir John Arundell. In the same year he began his service on the Cornish bench, which was to last until his removal in 1564 as 'a very enemy' of the Anglican settlement. Apart from his occasional recourse to law Roscarrock's closing years are obscure, but it is known that in December 1569 he subscribed to the Act of Uniformity as an ex-justice. He was a sick man when on 28 May 1575 he made his will. After providing for one unmarried daughter, remembering the poor and making amends for tithes forgotten, he bequeathed the residue of his estate to his wife and eldest son, whom he appointed his executors. Roscarrock lived for another two-and-a-half years, dying on 26 Oct. 1575.[4]

[1] Date of birth estimated from age at fa.'s death, J. Maclean, *Trigg*

Minor, i. 562–3. *Vis. Cornw.* ed. Vivian, 400; Gilbert, *Cornw.* ii. 357; *Paroch. Hist. Cornw.* i. 331. [2] Duchy Cornw. RO, 123, mm. 12v, 14; 222, m. 16; information from G. Haslam; *CPR*, 1553–4, p. 17; 1563–6, p. 20. [3] C3/30/48; *APC*, ii. 356; A. L. Rowse, *Tudor Cornw.* 289; F. Rose-Troup, *Western Rebellion*, 355; *LP Hen. VIII*, xx, xxi; *CPR*, 1553, pp. 317, 328, 339, 349. [4] *Cam. Misc.* ix(3), 69; SP12/60, ff. 83v–84; PCC 22 Carew; C142/173/9; Maclean, i. 558, 562–3.

J.J.G.

ROSCARROCK, Thomas (by 1532–87), of Pentire in St. Minver and Roscarrock in St. Endellion, Cornw.

LISKEARD 1553 (Oct.)

b. by 1532, 1st s. of Richard Roscarrock*. *m.* Jane, da. and h. of William Pentire of Pentire, 6s. 5da. *suc.* fa. 26 Oct. 1575.[1]

Sheriff, Cornw. 1585–6.

Thomas Roscarrock was rising 21 when returned as one of the Members for Liskeard to the first Parliament of Mary's reign. Family interest accounts for his return: the Roscarrocks owned some property in the town and his father secured his own election as one of the knights for Cornwall. Neither father nor son opposed the initial measures towards the reintroduction of Catholicism in 1553, but the son was not re-elected with the father in 1554. If his early introduction to Parliament stimulated an interest in public service, he was not given a second opportunity to prove himself in that respect until after his father's death 20 years later. Although never put on the bench he was then pricked sheriff and named to several inquiries into piracy. While sheriff he himself was charged with piracy following the boarding of a Venetian galleon called *Il Lombardo* off Cape St. Vincent by the crew of his ship, the *Roscarrock*, but the Council accepted his explanation. In 1576 he tried to buy the manor of Colquite in St. Mabyn, but to no avail. Within a few years he was in debt to Thomas Cock of Bodmin, 'a man of carnal disposition and a great usurer', to the sum of about £700, and he died on 3 Feb. 1587 'leaving . . . his son and heir deeply indebted as well to divers others' as well as to Cock, the money outstanding to Cock alone amounting to £1,100.[2]

[1] Date of birth estimated from age at fa.'s i.p.m., C142/173/9. *Vis. Cornw.* ed. Vivian, 400. [2] Duchy Cornw. RO, 491, m. 21v; Cornw. RO, Liskeard mayor's accts. 1575–6, m. 1; 1582, f. 1; *CSP Dom.* 1581–90, pp. 29, 310, 316–17; *APC*, xiv. 64–65; 74, 85; xv. 244–5; SP12/187, ff. 33, 177; J. Maclean, *Trigg Minor*, i. 562–3; ii. 481 n.; Req.2/121/6, 124/52; C142/216/86.

J.J.G.

ROSCARROCK, William (c.1512–55 or later).

BOSSINEY 1554 (Apr.)

b. c.1512, 2nd s. of John Roscarrock of Roscarrock in St. Endellion, Cornw. by 1st w. Agnes, da. of Sir Thomas Grenville of Stowe in Kilkhampton; bro. of Richard* and half-bro. of John Roscarrock*.[1]

William Roscarrock is an obscure figure; apart

from his Membership of Mary's second Parliament all that is known about him is that in 1555 he attended the tin coinage at Truro. When he entered the Commons in 1554 he did so in the company of his brother Richard as one of the knights for Cornwall: the other knight, Sir John Arundell, was constable of Tintagel castle, which overlooked Bossiney, and he presumably added his authority there to Richard Roscarrock's to ensure William Roscarrock's election. It is a fair inference that Roscarrock shared the orthodoxy of his brother and of Arundell.[2]

[1] Date of birth estimated from elder brother's. *Vis. Cornw.* ed. Vivian, 400. [2] E101/275/8, m. 6.

J.J.G.

ROSE *see* ROOS

ROTHERAM, William (by 1519–59), of Lincoln.

LINCOLN 1554 (Apr.)

b. by 1519, ?s. of William Rotheram of Lincoln. *m.* Alice (?Broxholme), 1s. 2da.[1]
Sheriff, Lincoln 1545–6, alderman by 1551–9, mayor 1554–5, j.p. by 1559.[2]

William Rotheram's parentage has not been traced but he could have been the son of William Rotheram, sheriff of Lincoln in 1529. About 1540 he made a bid for the Blackfriars at Lincoln, but the property went instead to John Bellow* and John Broxholme, whom Rotheram was to describe in his will as his brother-in-law. In 1551, with three other aldermen including William Alanson*, Rotheram tried to establish cloth-finishing at Lincoln by setting up a mill and dyehouse; their aim was to relieve unemployment but the scheme was not a success.[3]

Rotheram's election to the second Marian Parliament has the appearance of an interlude in the representation of Lincoln by George St. Poll, its recorder, and Robert Farrar, secretary to the 2nd Earl of Rutland. Why on this occasion Rotheram replaced St. Poll is not clear, but as in 1555 St. Poll was to gain a knighthood of the shire he may have sought this unsuccessfully in the spring of 1554 and thus cleared the way for Rotheram. (Whether Rotheram benefited similarly in 1555 is not known, since the only name which has survived from that election is Farrar's; if Rotheram was re-elected he did not align himself with Farrar in opposing one of the government's bills.) As an alderman and the city's next choice as mayor Rotheram satisfied the council's 'remembrance' of 1553 that only those who had served in either capacity were eligible for election, and his contribution to the cloth-finishing project showed him to have the city's welfare at heart. It was a measure of his standing that at about the same

time the common council granted Rotheram a lease of the parsonage of Surfleet, Lincolnshire. In 1557 he and Thomas Grantham* sold their manor of Wickenby to Gilbert Dighton.[4]

The closing weeks of Rotheram's life were marred by controversy. On 25 Feb. 1559 the common council voted to expel him from his office of justice of the peace and from the council and aldermanship, to disfranchise him and to debar him from readmission: his offences were that he had behaved himself contemptuously towards the mayor and had broken out of the ward to which he had been committed. On the same day the council sent a representative to London to solicit the discharge of a subpoena that Rotheram had brought against the mayor. It quickly became evident that the council had overreached itself. On 14 Mar. a justice of assize, acting under instructions from the lord keeper, ordered the disfranchisement to be annulled and four days later Rotheram was readmitted; although the ban on his reappointment to office was reaffirmed, this was to be robbed of its effect by his early death.[5]

Rotheram had made his will on 30 Apr. 1556 and it was proved on 31 May 1559. He asked to be buried in the cathedral, and among other bequests he left £200 to each of his daughters.[6]

[1] Date of birth estimated from first reference. *Associated Architectural Societies' Reps. and Pprs.* xxxix. 243; PCC 12 Chaynay. [2] *Associated Architectural Societies' Reps. and Pprs.* xxxix. 217 seq.; J. W. F. Hill, *Tudor and Stuart Lincoln*, 67; HMC *14th Rep. VIII*, 50–51. [3] *Associated Architectural Societies' Reps. and Pprs.* xxxix. 243; Hill, 63, 67. [4] HMC *14th Rep. VIII*, 47; CPR, 1557–8, p. 334; 1560–3, pp. 545–6. [5] HMC *14th Rep. VIII*, 50–51. [6] PCC 12 Chaynay.

T.M.H.

ROUPE, Gilbert (by 1514–75/78), of Dartmouth, Devon.

DARTMOUTH 1553 (Mar.)

b. by 1514; prob. bro. of Nicholas*. *m.* 3da.[1]
Receiver, Dartmouth 1544–5, mayor 1551–2, common councilman by 1558.[2]

Gilbert Roupe could claim gentle descent but it was as a merchant trading from Dartmouth that he made his career. In 1535 he sued another merchant in the town's court on behalf of Christopher Savery* for damage done to a boat. His election with Nicholas Adams *alias* Bodrugan to the Parliament of March 1553 followed immediately on his mayoralty and represented a return to the port's policy of choosing a townsman with a local lawyer: in the following Parliament Adams was to sit with Nicholas Roupe. Although Gilbert Roupe was not re-elected to Parliament he remained active in municipal affairs until his death. By his will made on 17 Apr. 1575 and proved on 17 Nov. 1578 he asked for burial in St. Saviour's church in Dartmouth, provided for his daughters, two of whom Dorothy and Thomasin were unmarried, and named Dorothy executrix.[3]

[1] Date of birth estimated from first reference. PCC 43 Langley. [2] Exeter city lib. Dartmouth ms 2002, ff. 19v, 28, 60v; Add. 24773, ff. 94, 95v. [3] E122/201/13; 179/99/321; Exeter city lib. Dartmouth mss 2002, ff. 20v, 52–55, 60v; 2003, ff. 11, 17; PCC 43 Langley.

R.V.

ROUPE, Nicholas (by 1506–55 or later), of Dartmouth, Devon.

DARTMOUTH 1553 (Oct.)

b. by 1506; prob. bro. of Gilbert*.[1]
    Constable, Dartmouth 1534–5, receiver 1535–6, 2nd bailiff 1536–7, churchwarden, St. Saviour's 1537–8, 1st bailiff 1538–9, common councilman by 1541, mayor 1547–8, 1554–5.[2]

Nicholas Roupe was a Dartmouth merchant who traded with Spain. In 1527 his partnership with Nicholas Seymour broke down over a dispute about raisins imported from Malaga. As one of the richest townsmen he was assessed towards the subsidy in 1550 at 20s. on goods, 5s. more than Gilbert Roupe, who was probably his brother. His election to Mary's first Parliament came after Gilbert's to the previous one. Unlike his fellow-Member, Nicholas Adams *alias* Bodrugan, he did not oppose the restoration of Catholicism and he seems to have been a good churchman, serving as warden and as a caretaker of church property. The last trace found of him is during his second mayoralty in 1554–5.[3]

[1] Date of birth estimated from first reference. [2] Exeter city lib. Dartmouth mss 1982, ff. 194v, 207; 2002, f. 8v; 2003, ff. 6–6v; H. R. Watkin, *Pre-Reformation Dartmouth*, 178, 187, 293; Add. 24773, f. 93v; C219/23/43. [3] Exeter city lib. Dartmouth ms 1982; E179/99/321; Watkin, 268, 293.

R.V.

ROUS, Anthony (by 1502–46), of Dennington and Henham, Suff.

SUFFOLK 1545*

b. by 1502, 1st s. of Sir William Rous* of Dennington by Alice, da. of Sir John Sulyard† of Wetherden; bro. of Sir Edmund*. *m.* by 1523, Agnes, da. of Sir Thomas Blennerhasset of Frenze, Norf., 2s. *suc.* fa. 1538/39. Kntd. 23/25 Nov. 1545.[1]
    Treasurer to 3rd Duke of Norfolk by Jan. 1536, of King's works at Guisnes Apr. 1541–?Sept. 1542; j.p. Suff. 1537–*d.*; various commissions, Suff. and Calais 1538–*d.*; comptroller, Calais Oct. 1542–Apr. 1544; treasurer of the King's jewels May 1544–Nov. 1545, of the chamber and ct. gen. surveyors Nov. 1545–*d.*[2]

Nothing is known of the education and early career of Anthony Rous. He may have followed the family tradition of attachment to the Duke of Norfolk's household and have served a long apprenticeship there before promotion to the office of treasurer. He was well trusted by the 3rd Duke, who used him constantly as a messenger on private as well as on public business. He was with Norfolk in Yorkshire for the suppression of Bridlington priory and Jervaulx abbey in the summer of 1537, and was left behind to help survey their lands and to 'put things in order'. In August of the following year the duke sent him to Cromwell to report on action taken against 'seditious bruit' and to further the cause of Norfolk's daughter, the Duchess of Richmond. In September, when Norfolk could not take the surrender of the Grey Friars in Ipswich on account of illness, he was replaced by Rous and others of his council.[3]

During the years 1536 to 1539 Rous had thus become known as a man of ability. Richard Southwell*, writing to Cromwell in January 1536 about the circumspect behaviour of Sir John Cornwallis and Rous in safeguarding the records of the recently deceased bishop of Norwich, spoke of them as men 'whose honest dealings it were too long to declare'. Rous himself, writing to Cromwell from Framlingham this year, expressed the wish that 'you will accept Mr. Richard Southwell as a witness of my desire to serve you'. Rous's brother George was then in Cromwell's service and was later to be employed in Calais as a man-at-arms. From his position as a member of Norfolk's council, Rous was to become a man of substance in his own right. He had married into a leading family of Norfolk and must have succeeded his father sometime after May 1538, the last date at which Sir William's name appears on a commission. In 1539 he enlarged his inheritance in Suffolk by purchasing four manors there and in the following year he made a larger acquisition in the form of leases of ex-monastic property for £1,679.[4]

Rous appears to have left Norfolk's service in 1539, for in that year under the arrangements for defending the coast he was assigned to provide victuals for Calais, Guisnes and Hammes, and the duke, writing from Hexham, had to ask Cromwell to order Rous to send him a supply of wheat. This was the beginning of Rous's involvement in the organisation and defence of the English possessions across the Channel. He now began to move in a different sphere: he exchanged books with the scholar-courtier Richard Morison*, and was one of the esquires at the reception of Anne of Cleves in 1540. He was nominated sheriff of Norfolk and Suffolk in November 1540, but was not pricked; instead, he was summoned to court to discuss supply, and it was on this business that he arrived at Calais in February 1541, to be appointed within two months treasurer of the works at Guisnes.[5]

For the next three years Rous discharged this office

and other responsibilities in a manner which earned the esteem of those with whom he worked. Promoted to the comptrollership of Calais, he took part in the campaign of 1544 with a personal troop of 12 horsemen and 20 footmen. While still answerable for certain payments in Calais, he was brought into closer association with Henry VIII by his appointment in May 1544 as keeper of the jewel house. Together with Walter Mildmay* he was responsible for the transport of plate, jewels and 'books of wars' to the Tower of London in November 1544. In the following year Rous purchased further property in Suffolk from the crown, including Henham Hall which became the family seat. His election for Suffolk to the Parliament of 1545 answered to his standing in the county and at court and may have been occasioned by his first-hand experience of the French war, as the Parliament, originally summoned to meet in January 1545, had been called to meet its costs. Two days after the Parliament opened on 23 Nov. Rous was appointed treasurer of the chamber and of the court of general surveyors in succession to Sir Brian Tuke and at about the same time he was knighted.[6]

Rous's career and further prospects were cut short by his death at Boulogne on 8 Feb. 1546. Occurring six weeks after the end of the first session of the Parliament, his death created a vacancy which perhaps remained unfilled during the brief second session of January 1547. No will has been found, but a letter about Rous's affairs was sent to Boulogne by Sir William Paget and 'the other executors', one of whom, his son and heir Thomas Rous, then aged 22, had recently married Catherine, daughter of Giles Hansard of Lincolnshire. His father's sudden death was to involve Thomas Rous in financial difficulties which may account for the delay of more than three years before he received licence to enter upon his inheritance. Among debtors to the court of augmentations on its dissolution in 1547, Sir Anthony Rous was said to have owed £6,090: since Thomas Rous successfully claimed a deduction of £1,737 for money spent by his father on fortifications, this large sum had presumably accumulated through Rous's public responsibilities and did not represent money owing for land transactions.[7]

[1] Date of birth estimated from marriage. Vis. Suff. ed. Metcalfe, 62; LP Hen. VIII, xiii, xx; H. H. Leonard, 'Knights and knighthood in Tudor Eng.' (London Univ. Ph.D. thesis, 1970), 184n. [2] LP Hen. VIII, x, xii–xiv, xvi–xx. [3] Ibid. x–xiii; CIPM Hen. VII, i. 804; CP25(2), 40/266, no. 31. [4] LP Hen. VIII, x, xii–xv, xvii; Wards 7/4/31; Copinger, Suff. Manors, iii. 28–29; iv. 22, 32, 239; Vis. Suff. 44; DKR, x(2), 262–3. [5] LP Hen. VIII, xiv–xviii; PCC 29 More. [6] LP Hen. VIII, xvi–xx; PPC, vii. passim; APC, i. passim; Copinger, ii. 85; J. A. Froude, Hist. Eng. iv. 98–99; W. C. Richardson, Tudor Chamber Admin. 110, 244, 485, 489. [7] Wards 7/4/31; LP Hen. VIII, xxi; CPR, 1549–51, p. 64; C1/1227/27, 28, 1260/28; Mar. Lic. Fac. Off. (Harl. Soc. xxiv), 1160; W. C. Richardson, Ct. Augmentations, 264 and n.

M.K.D.

ROUS, Sir Edmund (by 1521–69 or later), of Dunwich, Suff.

GREAT BEDWYN	1554 (Apr.)
DUNWICH	1554 (Nov.)[1]
DOVER	1555[2]
DUNWICH	1559

b. by 1521, yr. s. of Sir William Rous*, and bro. of Anthony*. m. Mary, da. and coh. of one Paynell of Lincs., 1da. Kntd. Dec. 1550/Sept. 1552.[3]
J.p. Suff. 1543–7; commr. relief 1550; v.-treasurer [I] by Dec. 1553–?55.[4]

Edmund Rous probably began his career as a servant of the 3rd Duke of Norfolk. In January 1537 Norfolk told Cromwell that followers of Sir Arthur Hopton* had taken from the duke's ground at Sibton four horses belonging to his servant Edmund Rous, who was then assisting him in the north after the Pilgrimage of Grace. On the duke's downfall, or perhaps earlier, he transferred to the service of Admiral Seymour, on whose behalf he received money from Seymour's Shropshire estates in 1548.[5]

At various times from 1542 Rous owned or leased considerable estates in Suffolk, including ex-monastic property in Dunwich and the manors of Badingham, Middleton, Okynghall, Rendham and Westleton; in Kent he had property in the Medgrove and Shulford district. Between 1549 and 1554 he sold several Suffolk manors, and early in Mary's reign he delivered Kentish property valued at £87 to the crown in payment of a debt. He also became involved in chancery suits over his lands in Dunwich and elsewhere in Suffolk.[6]

The exact dates of Rous's Irish service have not come to light but his appointment there may have been, like the annuity of £40 which he was granted 'for service at Framlingham', a reward for his loyalty in the succession crisis of 1553. He is first found in Ireland in October of that year and was vice-treasurer by December. He was in England during the following March, when he was summoned before the commissioners for Irish accounts. In the same month he was returned to Parliament for Great Bedwyn, where his patron was probably (Sir) John Thynne* to whom he could have been recommended either by his cousin Andrew Baynton* or by his fellow-Member Richard Fulmerston, a former servant of the 3rd Duke of Norfolk. Later in the year he was elected at Dunwich, where his local influence was evidently sufficient to gain him the seat. He was to be returned there again at the beginning of Elizabeth's reign and later claimed £19 4s. for wages and travelling expenses in the two Parliaments. The town challenged this demand in Chancery maintaining that Rous, a resident who knew of its impoverishment, had agreed to serve without wages.

Notwithstanding this demand, Rous was found absent without leave when the House was called early in January 1555 and was accordingly informed against in the King's bench in the following Easter term. A writ of *venire facias* was issued but apart from a solitary distraint of 12*d*. for non-appearance in Easter term 1558 no further action was taken against him and in the meantime he was returned to Mary's fourth Parliament for Dover on the nomination of Sir Thomas Cheyne*, lord warden of the Cinque Ports. Despite being a nominee and an outsider, Rous was paid in full (though with no allowance for travelling) for his attendance in this Parliament, during which one of his servants was granted privilege after being arrested for debt.[7]

Rous's financial difficulties under Elizabeth suggest that the debt of 1555 was his own. The date of his death is unknown but he may still have been alive in 1572.[8]

[1] Huntington Lib. Hastings mss Parl. pprs.   [2] Dover accts. 1547–58, f. 271v; Egerton 2094, f. 136.   [3] Date of birth estimated from first certain reference. *Vis. Suff.* ed. Metcalfe, 62, 174; *HMC 7th Rep.* 662; Suckling, *Suff.* ii. 366 (where his wife is said to have been a Bacon); *CPR*, 1550–3, p. 428; 1553, p. 358.   [4] *LP Hen. VIII*, xviii, xx; *CPR*, 1547–8, p. 89; *APC*, iv. 378.   [5] *LP Hen. VIII*, x–xii; SC6/Edw. VI, 773, D5, 7; E323/6, f. 40v.   [6] *LP Hen. VIII*, xvii; Copinger, *Suff. Manors*, ii. 125, 196, 272; iii. 175, 177; v. 159; *CPR*, 1547–8, pp. 145, 245; 1549–51, p. 321; 1550–3, p. 428; 1560–3, p. 308; 1563–6, p. 386; C1/1259/38–40.   [7] *APC*, iv. 358 seq., 378, 430; v. 4 seq., 61, 117, 183; *CSP Ire.* 1509–73 passim; *CPR*, 1554–5, p. 103; 1555–7, p. 107; Lansd. 156(28), f. 92, C3/56/91; KB27/1176, 1186, 29/188; *CJ*, i. 43.   [8] *CSP Dom.* 1547–80, p. 318; *CPR*, 1566–9, p. 413; Arundel castle ms G1/7, f. 7v.

P.H.

ROUS, Sir William (by 1471–1538/39), of Dennington, Suff.

DUNWICH 1529

b. by 1471, 1st s. of Henry Rous of Dennington by Agnes, da. of one Denton of Oxon. *m.* Alice, da. of Sir John Sulyard[†] of Wetherden, Suff., 3s. inc. Anthony* and Sir Edmund* 2da. *suc.* fa. 21 Sept. 1492. Kntd. 9 Sept. 1513.[1]
    Commr. subsidy, Suff. 1523, 1524, tenths of spiritualities 1535; j.p. 1531–*d*.[2]

The Crown Office list for the Parliament of 1529 gives Sir Robert Rous as the first Member for Dunwich, but no knight of this name has been traced. Several Robert Rouses were living at that time in East Anglia; one of them, a mercer of Colchester, witnessed to the treason of Abbot Marshall in 1539; another, a prosperous clothier of Nayland who died between 1535 and 1538, was linked by marriage with a group of London merchants; and a third was the Robert Rice (Royse) of Preston, a gentleman of modest means, who for the last seven years before his death in 1544 served on the Suffolk bench. As none of these men was of sufficient standing to take precedence over so well-established a lawyer as Christopher Jenney, it is con-

cluded that the list is in error here and that the Member was Sir William Rous, a Suffolk gentleman who owned property in Dunwich and whose family supplied the borough with one of its representatives through at least five generations.[3]

The family can be traced back to the early 14th century, when it was already settled at Dennington. Several of its members had been in the service of the Mowbray dukes of Norfolk, whose castle of Framlingham lay only two miles from Dennington, and William Rous may have begun his career under the Mowbrays' successors in the dukedom, the Howards: his only brother was in Howard service and two, or perhaps all three, of his sons belonged to the 3rd Duke's household, Anthony becoming his treasurer. If he received a legal education it was probably at Lincoln's Inn where his father-in-law had been a leading light, but nothing has been discovered about his life before 1513 when he fought at Flodden under Thomas Howard, Earl of Surrey, and was knighted; a year later he accompanied Princess Mary to France for her marriage to Louis XII. His appointment to the commissions to supervise the collection of the subsidy of 1523 suggests that he may have sat in the Parliament which granted it, as indeed he is likely to have done in one or more of the earlier ones of the century. His election in 1529 anticipated his appointment as a justice of the peace, but his own standing may have sufficed to procure it: if he needed help he could have looked in more than one direction, to his old patron, now Duke of Norfolk and a power in the land, to Princess Mary's second husband the Duke of Suffolk, or perhaps to the locally influential Willoughby family. Of his role in the proceedings of this Parliament nothing is known: his designation to take the oaths of his Suffolk neighbours to the succession, in accordance with the Act of 1534 (25 Hen. VIII, c.22), was no more than a logical consequence of his Membership, and the 'Mr. Ruse' whose name appears on the back of the Act for flax and hemp passed during the previous session was probably not Rous, but Thomas Rush. Rous may have sat for Dunwich again in the Parliament of June 1536, in compliance with the King's request for the return of the previous Members, but if he did it was to be his last spell in the House, for by the time the following Parliament met he was almost certainly dead. The date of his death has not been established, as neither will nor inquisition survives, but whereas in the course of 1538 he was appointed to several commissions in Suffolk, by May 1539 his name had been removed from the county bench, and he may thus be thought to have died earlier in that year.[4]

[1] Date of birth estimated from age at fa.'s i.p.m., *CIPM Hen. VII*, i. 804. *Vis. Suff.* ed. Metcalfe, 61–62; Suckling, *Suff.* ii. 366; *Vis. Norf.* (Harl. Soc. xxxii), 238.   [2] *LP Hen. VIII*, iii, iv, vii, viii, xii,

xiii. [3] *Colchester Oath Bk.* ed. Benham, 152; Elton, *Policy and Police*, 157–9; *Suff. Green Bks.* x. 7; PCC 26 Ayloffe, 16 Dyngeley, 13 Pynnyng; *LP Hen. VIII*, xii–xviii, xx; *Vis. Suff.* 205. [4] *Diary of John Rous* (Cam. Soc. lxvi), v; *Suff. Green Bks.* ix(2), 54; *LP Hen. VIII*, i, iii, xiii, xiv; *Reg. Butley Abbey, Suff. 1510–35*, ed. Dickens, 62; House of Lords RO, Original Acts, 24 Hen. VIII, no. 6.

M.K.D./A.D.K.H.

ROUS see also RAND

ROWLAND, John (by 1512–49), of Windsor, Berks.

Winchelsea 1547[*1]

b. by 1512. *m.* da. of Richard Raynolde.[2]
Page of the robes by 1542–*d.*; keeper of Hundon park, Suff. 1543–*d.*; comptroller of customs, Chichester by 1546–*d.*[3]

The first reference found to John Rowland relates to the coronation of Anne Boleyn in 1533, when he was appointed an almoner to attend at the table of the lord mayor: if this points to a London origin it has not been traced. As page of the robes in the royal household Rowland was to win the regard of the King, who left him £50 in his will and also bequeathed him clothes and rings: the keepership of a park in Suffolk and a customs post at Chichester were doubtless also marks of royal favour. In 1544 he had accompanied his royal master to northern France on the expedition which took Boulogne.[4]

Rowland was to survive the King less than three years but during that time he attended his only Parliament. The fact that he was returned for Winchelsea with John More, a colleague in the customs at Chichester, can only mean that both were nominated at the Cinque Port, but by whom is a matter for conjecture. The Protector Somerset himself, who as treasurer was head of the customs administration, may have intervened: another and more interesting possibility is that his brother Admiral Seymour used his position to secure the return of two port officials, one of whom also stood close to the young King whose devotion Seymour was already seeking to win. Of Rowland's role either in the Commons or at court during the next two years nothing is known, and almost all the remaining information about him comes from his will.

Rowland prepared this long document when he was already sick and it is dated 5 Sept. 1549. He commended his soul to God, 'trusting that for the passion and merit of Jesu Christ, in whom is my only belief and trust, I shall be one of them that shall rest in the kingdom of Abraham, Isaac and Jacob'. Then, 'for a token of obedient love', he left the King a sum of £6 13s.4d. remaining in the hands of John More. The articles which Henry VIII had left to him Rowland now in turn bequeathed: to

Philip Lenthall he gave 'a white satin doublet which was the King's that dead is' and to a Mrs. Weyser 'a ring of gold set over with a fine spark of a sapphire, which was the King's'. To his 'natural mother, desiring her of her blessing and that it may please her to pray for me', he left the house where she lived with its appurtenances 'both above and beneath and the two smith's shops rent free'; he also left her his rents and tenements in Windsor, with remainder to his sister Alice and her husband Robert Smart, swordbearer of London, for life, and then to their daughter Catherine. He had also a nephew, Robert Rowland, to whom he left £4, and a father-in-law, Richard Raynolde, who received 20s. and a nightgown, but he made no mention of a wife.

The rest of the bequests were to friends and servants, the former including (Sir) Thomas Cawarden*, Robert Robotham*, yeoman of the King's robes and Thomas Weldon*, master of the King's household. Many less highly placed or well known friends at Windsor were also remembered. A servant, Nicholas Snow, was to have the lands at Eton leased to him and others at Blewbury, Berkshire. Robert and Alice Smart were to be the executors and John Stokes the overseer. As Rowland's will was proved on 29 Dec. 1549 he had probably died shortly after making it, perhaps before the opening of the third session of Parliament on 4 Nov. It is not known who replaced him in the Commons.[5]

[1] Hatfield 207. [2] Date of birth estimated from first reference. PCC 46 Populwell. [3] *LP Hen. VIII*, xvii, xviii; *CPR*, 1553, p. 331; E122/37/1, 2. [4] *LP Hen. VIII*, vi, xix; *APC*, iii. 220; *HMC Bath*, iv. 7. [5] PCC 46 Populwell; *CPR*, 1560–3, p. 157.

P.H.

ROWLETT, Sir Ralph (by 1513–71), of Holywell House, St. Albans, Herts.

Hertfordshire 1547

b. by 1513, 1st s. of Ralph Rowlett of London and St. Albans by 1st w. Jane Knight. *educ.* ?G. Inn, adm. 1533. *m.* (1) by 1544, Dorothy (*d.*1557), da. of John Bowles of Wallington, Herts.; (2) 27 June 1558, Margaret (*d.*3 Aug. 1558), da. of Sir Anthony Cooke* of Gidea Hall, Essex, *s.p. suc.* fa. 4 Mar. 1543. Kntd. by 23 Sept. 1547.[1]
?Escheator, Essex and Herts. 1540–1; j.p. Herts. 1547–*d.*, q. 1562; commr. relief 1550; sheriff, Essex and Herts. 1559–60.[2]

Sir Ralph Rowlett's father established the fortune of the family; he was a member of the Goldsmiths' Company of London, a merchant of the staple, and one of the two deputy masters of the mint from 1533. It was probably he and not his son who served as sheriff of Essex and Hertfordshire in 1541–2. When he died in March 1543 the son inherited seven Hertfordshire manors, and land and houses in St. Albans, of a total assessed value of over £150 a year.

The elder Rowlett had been assessed for subsidy in 1540 at the very large sum of 500 marks, while the son's estate was then valued at £26 13s.4d.[3]

In June 1543 Rowlett had livery of his inheritance, and in 1551 he and the other executors of his father's will secured the discharge of a recognizance of £3,000 in which the elder Rowlett had been bound in 1530, probably as security for the proper performance of his duties at the mint. It was probably he, not his father, who had served as escheator in 1540–1, but otherwise he seems to have held no public office under Henry VIII. It was Edward VI who knighted Rowlett and made him a justice of the peace. He is known to have been Protestant in sympathy in Elizabeth's time, and may have been so earlier; if so, his religious stance perhaps helped to secure his election to Parliament in 1547 in preference to rivals of older family or higher standing in Hertfordshire; the other knight of the shire was Sir Anthony Denny, a strong Protestant. Like Denny, Sir Richard Lee* and Sir Henry Parker*, Rowlett served with the Marquess of Northampton in his unsuccessful expedition of August 1549 against the Norfolk rebels. William Cecil listed Rowlett as one of those who was to have transacted affairs in Hertfordshire on behalf of Queen Jane's government, but there is nothing to suggest that he was actively involved in the succession crisis of 1553. He sued out a pardon after Queen Mary's accession.[4]

Rowlett remained on the commission of the peace, but otherwise took no part in either local or national affairs under Mary. Family matters appear to have occupied him, for between 1556 and 1558 he made two separate settlements of his extensive lands. The first created an entail for the issue of himself and his first wife and may have been prompted by the birth of children who failed to survive. The second, in April 1558, was made in contemplation of his short-lived marriage to Margaret Cooke, a maid in waiting to the Queen. In December 1556 and January 1557 Rowlett sold three large parcels of land, one including the manor of Gorhambury, Hertfordshire, acquired through the agency of certain third parties by Sir Nicholas Bacon*, a brother-in-law of Rowlett's, who made it his main seat. Rowlett divested himself in 1565–6 of much of his remaining land by settlements for the benefit of his heirs-apparent, since it was by then evident that he would die childless.[5]

Rowlett was involved in a good deal of litigation. About 1554 another brother-in-law, Thomas Skipwith, alleged that Rowlett had accepted £270 to transfer by fine four of the family's principal manors to Joan Skipwith, Rowlett's sister, retaining only life interests for himself and his wife, but that Rowlett afterwards denied receiving the money and refused to make the transfer. The chief witness against Rowlett was his rival for social primacy in St. Albans, Sir Richard Lee. Relations between the two men worsened and in January 1565 the Privy Council commissioned certain persons to try a dispute between them and, in the following month, took the drastic step of removing both from the Hertfordshire bench. Further details are lacking, but Rowlett had been restored to the bench by the following September.[6]

Rowlett had been admitted a freeman of the Goldsmiths' Company in 1551, but he does not appear to have followed his father's trade or to have taken any part in the company's affairs. It can hardly have been for the purpose of trade that he was licensed in 1566 to remain overseas, a licence renewed in May 1567 and again, for two years, in July 1568. He was presumably home again by July 1570, when he was accused of vexing tenants at Wheathampstead in their rights of common, and certainly when death came to him on 20 Apr. 1571, for his body was buried eight days later in St. Alban's abbey. Apart from some lands in Leicestershire and Northamptonshire, Rowlett was then possessed only of Hallywell park and three manors, valued at about £115 a year. The rest of the family lands had been transferred by 1566 to his heirs, four nephews and two nieces, children of his five sisters, whose inheritances were ratified in his will of 28 July 1566. He left sums of money to various relatives and friends, and to charities, among them £100 to St. Albans School. Most of his disposable realty he divided between his nephews, but he left to Chief Justice Sir Robert Catlyn a life interest in Hallywell, and to Bacon the freehold of considerable land in Hertfordshire and adjoining counties. The executors were Bacon, Catlyn, Gilbert Gerard* and John Southcote II*, with Cecil as overseer. The mayor and corporation of St. Albans contested the will, alleging that the original made no mention of the executors, but the prerogative court of Canterbury, not surprisingly, pronounced in favour of a will exhibited by such an eminent quintet.[7]

[1] Date of birth estimated from age at fa.'s i.p.m., C142/68/40. *Machyn's Diary* (Cam. Soc. xlii), 160, 169–70, 364n; *LP Hen. VIII*, xix; *Misc. Gen. et Her.* (ser. 5), viii. 88; C219/19/42. [2] *LP Hen. VIII*, xxi; *CPR*, 1547–8, p. 84; 1553, p. 354; 1560–3, p. 438; 1563–6, pp. 23, 42, 123. [3] J. Craig, *The Mint*, 100–1; C. E. Challis, *The Tudor Coinage*, 20–84 passim, 311, 312; Mill Stephenson, *Mon. Brasses*, 193; St.Ch.2/32/120; E179/120/148. [4] *LP Hen. VIII*, xviii; W. C. Richardson, *Ct. Augmentations*, 242n; *CPR*, 1549–51, p. 226; 1553–4, p. 452; Lansd. 103(1), ff. 1–2; Holinshed, *Chron.* iii. 971. [5] *Machyn's Diary*, 160, 169–70; *CPR*, 1555–7, pp. 130–1, 331–2, 337; 1557–8, p. 330; 1560–3, p. 72; C142/206/3; PCC 33 Holney. [6] C1/1055/135–6; 3/49, 89, 122/26; 24/34, n. 29; *APC*, vii. 183, 194, 257. [7] W. S. Prideaux, *Goldsmith's Co.* i. 56; NRA 10873, p. 262; C142/206/3; PCC 33 Holney, 30 Martyn; *St. Albans Par. Reg.* ed. Brigg, 183.

D.F.C.

ROYDON (RAYDON), Thomas (c.1521–c.1565), of Truro, Cornw.

TRURO 1553 (Mar.), 1554 (Nov.), 1555,[1] 1558

b. c.1521. *m.* by 1546, Anne, 1s.[2]
Peiser of tin, Truro coinage c.1552; woodward, duchy of Cornw., Cornw. 1560–2.[3]

Thomas Roydon was a prosperous tin merchant who owned several mines in Cornwall. Early in his career he was associated with John Hull II* who undertook in 1545 to invest £300 in his business, but only paid £130: Roydon alleged that this breach of contract had left him 'destitute of money to perform such bargains as (he) had made' and 'in great slander amongst his creditors'. He further complained that, on 30 May 1546, Hull and three servants had come armed to his house in Truro and had demanded the repayment of the £130 and the surrender of his part of the indenture. Later he became a partner in a lease of the King's 'prerogative of the sale of all the whole tin as well of Devon as Cornwall'. Although this grant was revoked in December 1553, Roydon continued to play a prominent part in the commerce of the region. To the coinage held at Truro in July 1554 he brought over 6,000 lbs. of the metal, the fifth largest amount submitted. Such large quantities of tin involved him in the payment of heavy dues to the duchy: in 1556 he was owing £176 10s.4d. and ten years later, just after his death, his executors were faced with a demand for unpaid dues amounting to £866 13s.4d.[4]

Roydon's commercial standing made him an obvious candidate for election, and he was chosen as the junior Member for Truro four times before his early death. He entered the House in the second Parliament of Edward VI's reign, when he was rising 30, and he may have enjoyed the support on this occasion of his close acquaintance, Sir William Godolphin, himself a knight for Cornwall. Roydon usually sat with Nicholas Randall but in the autumn of 1554 his partner was John Melhuish. Both he and Melhuish quitted this Parliament without permission and were informed against for that dereliction in the King's bench. A writ of *venire facias* was issued but Roydon failed to appear; distrained 12d. in Michaelmas 1555, he incurred the same penalty each term until the end of 1558 when the case lapsed.[5]

Roydon died at Truro, probably in 1565. By his will, which no longer survives, he appointed his wife his executrix. She appears to have inherited all his possessions with the exception of some miscellaneous goods and 20 gallons of tin, which passed into the hands of Roydon's mine-manager by the 'crafty dealings' of one of her servants. Her execution of the will was disputed by her son Anthony

Roydon, a London merchant, who claimed to be the rightful inheritor of some houses and gardens in Redruth and Truro of a yearly value of £6 13s.4d.[6]

[1] 'Thomas Ro . . .' is legible on the indenture, C219/24/21: *OR* gives Thomas [Randall?]. [2] Aged '35 or thereabouts' in 1556, St.Ch.4/1/48. St.Ch.3/2/10; C3/149/47. [3] St.Ch.4/1/48; Duchy Cornw. RO, 133, m. 46; 134, m. 47v. [4] St.Ch.3/2/10; Harl. 6380, f. 5; E101/275/11, mm. 7v, 8v; Duchy Cornw. RO, 230, m. 6v; 235, m. 9; C3/155/77; Truro mus. HP 1/3. [5] KB27/1176–84; St.Ch.4/1/48. [6] C3/148/90, 149/47.

J.J.G.

ROYNON, Walter (by 1529–64 or later), of Chichester, Suss.

CHICHESTER 1554 (Nov.)

b. by 1529.[1]

Walter Roynon's origins are unknown. The only established family of the name lived in Somerset, and the 'Chilchester', Hampshire, from which the first of them to appear in the family pedigree is said to have come was probably Silchester. Roynon's Somerset contemporary John Roynon, fifth in descent from their ancestor, was a well connected servant of Princess Elizabeth.[2]

In 1550 Roynon, described as of Chichester, gentleman, paid Robert Trigges* £56 for a lease of the mansion house of Waltham prebend, late of Bosham collegiate church, and it was as citizens and residents of Chichester that Roynon and John Digons were returned to Mary's third Parliament. The city had elected nominees of the 12th Earl of Arundel to the three preceding ones and the reversion to local men might be seen as an acceptance of the Queen's request both in that respect and in the matter of religion, for the return certified that the Members would answer for Chichester in all matters concerning 'the honour of God'. Roynon, although not Digons, was to quit the Parliament without leave before its dissolution and to be prosecuted for this dereliction in the King's bench. When he failed to appear he was distrained 40s. in Michaelmas term 1555, but in Trinity 1556 he asked for a day to be appointed for his answer. No further process is recorded.[3]

Roynon was still living in Chichester in June 1564 when he leased a tenement and garden there from the cathedral chapter, but no later trace of him has been found.[4]

[1] Date of birth estimated from first reference. [2] *Vis. Som.* (Harl. Soc. xi), 95–96; *Som. Wills*, ed. Brown, vi. 67–68; *CSP Dom.* 1547–80, pp. 29, 118, 521; *CPR*, 1560–3, p. 475. [3] C1/1478/51; 219/23/127; KB27/1176, 1179. [4] *Suss. Rec. Soc.* lviii. 44.

R.J.W.S.

RUDHALE, John (1498–1530), of Rudhall, Herefs.

HEREFORDSHIRE 1529*

b. 1498, 1st s. of William Rudhale† of Rudhall by Anne, da. and coh. of Simon Milborne of Tillington,

Herefs. and Icomb, Glos. *educ.* I. Temple, adm. 7 Feb. 1516. *m.* Isabel, da. of Richard Whittington, at least 2s. 4da. *suc.* fa. 22 Mar. 1530.[1]

J.p. Worcs. 1524, 1526, Herefs. 1525, 1528.[2]

The well established family of Rudhale took its name from Rudhall, near Ross, where it had been settled since at least the early 14th century. John Rudhale's father, who had been steward of Hereford in 1511–13, was prominent as a bencher of the Inner Temple: he presided over the parliament there which admitted John Rudhale to masters' commons in 1516 and which assigned him a chamber with his father 'next the fig tree'. The family's improvement of its estates incurred the displeasure of Bishop Booth of Hereford, who thought that they were being augmented at the expense of the bishopric.[3]

Rudhale's election as junior knight for Herefordshire in 1529 doubtless owed something to his father, who had preceded him in that capacity nearly 40 years earlier, but it could hardly have been uninfluenced by his kinship with Sir Richard Cornwall, his senior colleague, who had married his aunt. Rudhale was not to enjoy his Membership for long. Although when he made his will on 13 May 1530, barely two months after his father's death, Rudhale professed himself 'whole in mind and in body', his own death followed swiftly and the will was proved on the same day, 27 July, as his father's. It reveals him as a conscientious son and father in his limitation of his funeral expenses to 40s. so that his own father's debts could be paid and his six or more young children provided for. His wife, who is not mentioned, may have predeceased him; his executors were his mother and a cousin, and another relative, his 'master' Sir Thomas Englefield, judge of the common pleas and joint master of the wards, was appropriately entrusted with the wardship of the heir.[4]

The vacancy created by Rudhale's death was filled by the election of John Scudamore, who married, as his second wife, Rudhale's sister Joan.

[1] Date of birth given in Duncumb, *Herefs.* iii. 165. *Vis. Herefs.* ed. Weaver, 91, 93; Williams, *Herefs. MPs*, 36.   [2] *LP Hen. VIII*, iv.   [3] Duncumb, iii. 153–60; *Cal. I.T. Recs.* i. 36; *Reg. Caroli Bothe* (Canterbury and York Soc. xxviii), 45–54.   [4] PCC 26 Jankyn.

A.J.E.

RUDSTON, Robert (1514/15–90), of Boughton Monchelsea, Kent.

STEYNING   1547

b. 1514/15, 1st s. of Sir John Rudston of London by 2nd w. Ursula, da. of Sir Robert Dymoke of Scrivelsby, Lincs. *m.* by 1549, Anne, da. of Sir Edward Wotton of Boughton Place, Boughton Malherbe, Kent, 2s. 1da. *suc.* fa. 1531.[1]

Servant of the Wyatt family by 1539; j.p. Kent 1547,

1558/59–*d.*; commr. relief 1550, goods of churches and fraternities 1553, Rochester bridge 1561, 1571.[2]

Robert Rudston's family was of Yorkshire origin, but his father, a draper, settled in London where he became an alderman. Sir Robert Constable of Flamborough, Yorkshire, purchased Rudston's wardship and marriage shortly before he reached his majority, but although Constable was executed for treason in 1537 Rudston's prospects do not seem to have been harmed. His mother had taken as her second husband Sir Edward Wotton, a courtier and administrator esteemed by Henry VIII, and presumably it was Wotton who introduced his stepson (who by 1549 was also his son-in-law) to his neighbour and colleague, Sir Thomas Wyatt I*. Rudston joined Wyatt on his embassy to the Emperor and during 1539–40 he travelled with the imperial court from the Netherlands to Spain, being employed by his master as a courier to Paris and London. On Wyatt's recall he returned to England, but the termination of the embassy and Wyatt's death two years later did not bring to a close Rudston's link with the family, for his services continued to be used by Wyatt's son Thomas. Rudston was later to be recalled as one of the younger Wyatt's 'companions in the profession . . . of arms', so that he probably served with Wyatt at Boulogne.[3]

On the accession of Edward VI, Sir Edward Wotton became a Privy Councillor and doubtless it was he who recommended Rudston for election to the first Parliament of the reign. The patronage of Steyning had passed on the imprisonment of the 3rd Duke of Norfolk to another Privy Councillor, Admiral Seymour, whom Wotton presumably approached for the nomination: Rudston's election may also have been encouraged by his uncle Sir Edward Dymoke and by Sir Thomas Wyatt II, both of whom sat in this Parliament. Although the Journal throws no light on Rudston's activity in the House, he is known to have supported the proposal submitted by Wyatt to the Privy Council for the establishment of a militia. By the following Parliament Sir Edward Wotton was dead and Rudston is not known to have been re-elected; he was not to sit again in the Commons during the 37 years which remained to him.[4]

Rudston shared Wyatt's distaste for Queen Mary's Spanish marriage and in January 1554 he joined Wyatt's rebellion. Excluded from the general pardon offered to the rebels, he helped to muster their forces at Brentford, Middlesex, for an attack upon London and on 7 Feb. he took a leading part in that luckless enterprise. Within two days of the repulse he had been committed to the Tower, and on 13 Feb. he was tried, found guilty and sentenced. It was through the intercession of his kinsman, Nicholas Wotton, the Queen's ambassador in France, that he was reprieved, to be released shortly afterwards and pardoned on 1 Apr. About the middle of May he entered into an obligation with William Cromer † to pay £500 for their movables and the Council wrote to (Sir) Robert Southwell* to effect this restitution: two months later his confiscated estates were returned to him on a 21-year lease at a fixed rent. In 1555 Cromer and Rudston entered into a joint obligation of 4,000 marks for the return of their lands in full ownership, thus bringing their total indebtedness to over £3,000. This sum they paid off in half-yearly instalments of £166 13s.4d. until June 1558, when they entered into separate obligations for the amounts outstanding. Rudston continued to pay reduced instalments until in 1560 the residue was remitted.[5]

When Elizabeth came to the throne Rudston was restored to the Kent bench; in 1564 he was rated 'meet' and he remained a justice until his death. On 12 Apr. 1588 he made his will, remembering the poor and providing for his wife and surviving children. He appointed his wife and one of his sons as executors and his nephew Edward Wotton †, his 'son-in-law' William Cromer and his 'loving friend' William Lambarde † as overseers. On 4 Feb. 1590 Rudston completed the division of his property between his sons and he must have died not long afterwards as an inquisition was held on the following 18 June.[6]

[1] Aged 73 on making will, PCC 12 Drury. *Vis. Kent* (Harl. Soc. lxxv), 27; PCC 7 Thower. [2] *LP Hen. VIII*, xiv; *CPR*, 1547–8, p. 85; 1553, pp. 355, 414; 1560–3, p. 438; 1569–72, pp. 225, 278; *Arch. Cant.* xvii. 216. [3] *LP Hen. VIII*, ix, xiv, xv, xxi; *DNB* (Constable, Sir Robert and Wotton, Sir Edward); D. M. Loades, *Two Tudor Conspiracies*, 50; *Pprs. Geo. Wyatt* (Cam. Soc. ser. 4, v), 57. [4] *Pprs. Geo. Wyatt*, 57. [5] Loades, 71, 108, 113, 117, 199, 120, 127, 254; *Chron. Q. Jane and Q. Mary* (Cam. Soc. xlviii), 53; *CPR*, 1553–4, pp. 261, 331; 1554–5, p. 272. [6] *APC*, ix. 274; *Cam. Misc.* ix(3) 58; PCC 12 Drury; C142/227/206.

R.J.W.S.

RUDSTON, Thomas (by 1507–56), of Swaffham Bulbeck, Cambs.

CAMBRIDGESHIRE 1542

b. by 1507, prob. s. of William Rudston of I. of Ely. *educ.* G. Inn, adm. 1521. *m.* (1) by 1528, Dorothy, prob. da. of Nicholas Hughson (?Hewson or Huston); (2) Anne, da. of William Mordaunt, wid. of Humphrey Torrell and of one Fowler; 2s. 4da.[1]

J.p. Cambs. 1530–*d.*, q.1547, Cambridge 1537, Norfolk circuit 1540; commr. for tenths of spiritualities Cambridge and Cambs 1535, musters Cambs. 1546, relief 1550, goods of churches and fraternities 1553; other commissions 1540–*d.*; escheator, Cambs. and Hunts. 1536–7, 1542–3.[2]

Rudstons were prominent in London and Yorkshire, but Thomas Rudston is not known to have been connected with either place. His father was

perhaps the William Rudston, who became secretary to Bishop West of Ely: this was a locality in which he and his descendants were to hold land and offices, and it was probably he who acted for John Goderyk of Ely (presumably Bishop Goodrich's elder brother) and tricked the citizens of Ely in 1539.[3]

In 1527–8 the Cambridge corporation paid Rudston a fee of 13s.4d., evidently as a retainer for legal service; similar annual payments, mostly of 20s., followed until 1539, then again from 1550–2 and perhaps later. He is named in Cromwell's remembrances and like other lawyers was instructed to keep order in his county at the time of the Pilgrimage of Grace in the expected absence of the leading gentry. At some time before its dissolution Rudston was bailiff of Swaffham Bulbeck priory; it was claimed by his executor in 1560 that he had pasturage for 400 sheep on the land of Swaffham Prior manor, under a lease granted in 1545 and probably itself the renewal or extension of an earlier monastic grant.[4]

Rudston was of insufficient status to be elected knight of the shire without some powerful support; his fellow-Member Sir Edward North may have helped him (although no connexion between the two men has been found), as may Sir Giles Alington, a landowner in Rudston's own district who had sat for Cambridgeshire in the previous Parliament. By a fine of 1540 Rudston had purchased land at Swaffham Bulbeck from his then or future brother-in-law Edmund Mordaunt (perhaps the contemporary at the Middle Temple of the Member of that name) and in 1549 he paid £100 to (Sir) John Brocket*, probably also a kinsman, for a further 1,600 acres, the moiety of three manors and houses in Swaffham Bulbeck, Swaffham Prior and other villages in Cambridgeshire. He was among the Cambridgeshire gentry called upon to raise troops for the French war of 1544 and he supplied six footmen for the vanguard of the army, probably accompanying them to France. It is not known whether he was one of the many gentlemen taking part in that war who sat in the Parliament of 1545, as the names of the knights for Cambridgeshire are missing.[5]

In a court of requests case of Henry VIII's or Edward VI's reign, the plaintiff complained that Rudston, his stepfather, had broken his agreement to pay his second wife's children £20 a year between them, notwithstanding 'the preferment of living which hath grown to him by his said wife'. Rudston's social and political advancement would explain why his name was first included (although later deleted) in the list ascribed to Cecil of men of standing in Cambridgeshire who might be looked to for support for Queen Jane in the summer of 1553. Nothing is known of Rudston's part during the succession crisis.

The pardon which he obtained in December 1553 does not imply any political misadventure, and he was to be thanked by the Privy Council in June 1555 for his help in looking after the county's government.[6]

Rudston made his will on 13 Sept. 1556 and died before the following 6 Nov., when it was proved. He ordered 'that no pomp or great cost be made or done for me at my burial' but left generous legacies in corn and money to the poor of a number of Cambridgeshire villages. Among numerous legacies to friends and relatives he left 100 marks and much movable property to his wife, £10 each to four named sons-in-law and £100 to each of his two sons to buy land, appointing supervisors specially to deal with the last legacy. No inquisition post mortem has been found, but the will, dealing only with the land the testator was free to devise, disposed of unspecified manors and land in Ely and 14 towns or villages in Cambridgeshire and Suffolk. The elder son was appointed sole executor and the younger was to be brought up 'in virtuous learning and discipline with convenient exhibition at the law'. All disputes arising from the will were to be settled by (Sir) James Dyer*.[7]

[1] Date of birth estimated from education. *Vis. Cambs.* (Harl. Soc. xli), 100; *Feet of Fines, Cambs.* ed. Palmer, 35; Req.2/8/261; PCC 21 Ketchyn; E. Hailstone, 'Swaffham Bulbeck' (printer's proofs in Camb. Univ. Lib., Cam. bb. 892, 1), 41, 44–45. [2] *LP Hen. VIII*, iv, viii, xii, xv–xvii, xxi; *CPR*, 1547–8, pp. 75–76, 81; 1553, pp. 352, 414; 1553–4, p. 17; E371/350, r. 31. [3] *Al. Cant.* i(3), 497; *VCH Cambs.* iv. 41. [4] C. H. Cooper, *Cambridge Annals*, i. 360–1; Downing Coll. Camb., Bowtell mss Liber Rationalis 1510–60, 1527–8 acct., f. 23 and later accts. s.d.; *LP Hen. VIII*, vi, xi; *Cambs. Antiq. Soc. Procs.* xxxi. 51; C3/151/22. [5] *LP Hen. VIII*, xviii, xix; Hailstone, loc. cit. [6] Req.2/8/261; Lansd. 103, ff. 1–2; *CPR*, 1553–4, p. 422; *APC*, v. 150. [7] PCC 21 Ketchyn.

D.F.C.

RUGGE, Robert (by 1503–59), of Norwich, Norf.

NORWICH 1545

b. by 1503, yr. s. of William Rugge of Northrepps, by Agnes. *m.* (1) Elizabeth, da. of Robert Wood of Norwich, 5s. inc. Francis† 3da.; (2) Alice (*d.*1566), da. of William Wayte of Tittleshall, wid. of William Hare of Beeston, ?*s.p.*[1]

Common councilman, Norwich 1529–31, alderman 1533–*d.*, sheriff 1537–8, chamberlain's council 1539–44, auditor 1551, mayor 1545–6, 1550–1.[2]

Of a family which had settled at Northrepps in the 14th century, Robert Rugge was a much younger brother of William Rugge or Repps, who in 1536 became bishop of Norwich. By then a freeman of 12 years' standing, a prosperous merchant and an alderman, in the following year Rugge was to be elected sheriff, an office he had twice before evaded, and seven years later was a candidate for the mayoralty. Although passed over on that occasion, before the year was out he was elected with Richard Catlyn to the Parliament summoned for January

1545, and during the interval before its postponed meeting in October he became mayor. It was not the first time that one of the city's current Members had been chosen—both its Members in the Parliament of 1529 had served as mayor during that Parliament's lifetime—but in thus enhancing Rugge's status the city added weight to its representation in the Commons. His kinship with the bishop must have been a political liability rather than an asset, in view of William Rugge's low reputation, but materially he did well out of it, with a grant of the manor of Greengate and leases of two others belonging to the see helping to swell the landed interest which he amassed in and around Northrepps.[3]

In 1549 Rugge was one of the two 'chiefest citizens', the other being Augustine Steward*, whom the rebel leader Robert Ket used as intermediaries with the royal commander the Earl of Warwick. After his second mayoralty in 1550–1 his evident wish to avoid another led the Norwich assembly to exempt him from the office for six years, an interval which he did not survive. He made his will on 24 Dec. 1558 and died on the following 18 Feb. He gave his wife Alice a life interest in certain lands and a house, furnishings and plate, and divided the remaining lands between his elder sons William and Francis. To the third son John, a priest who had gone into exile under Mary, spending some time in Italy with Thomas Wyndham (probably a son of (Sir) Edmund Wyndham*), his father left £4 a year, with the proviso that if on his return he remained in the ministry this should be exchanged for the advowson of the archdeaconry of Sudbury. The executors were William and Francis Rugge, and the supervisors two sons-in-law, Robert Flint (possibly the Member for Thirsk in 1547) and George Thimblethorpe. Rugge was buried in St. John's, Maddermarket, Norwich, where a brass bears his merchant's mark but styles him esquire. His will was proved on 26 June 1559.[4]

[1] Date of birth estimated from admission as freeman. Blomefield. *Norf.* iv. 292; vii. 247; viii. 151–2; xi. 35; *Vis. Norf.* (Harl. Soc, xxxii), 229; *Vis. Norf.* (Norf. Arch.), ii. 72. [2] Norwich ass. procs. 2 passim. [3] Blomefield viii. 151–2; xi. 35, 39; Norwich ass. procs. 2, ff. 120, 156, 158, 186v; *DNB* (Rugg or Reppes, William); W. Rye, *N. Erpingham Hundred*, 16. [4] Holinshed, *Chron.* iii 977; Norwich ass. procs. 3, f. 13v; Norwich consist. ct. 447 Colman; *Norf. Arch.* xiv. 63–69; C. H. Garrett, *The Marian Exiles*, 274–5; *Merchants' Marks* (Harl. Soc. cviii), unpaginated; Pevsner, *N.-E. Norf. and Norwich*, 245.

R.V.

RUSH, Thomas (by 1487–1537), of Sudbourne, Suff.

IPSWICH 1523,[1] 1529

b. by 1487. *m.* (1) by 1509, Anne, da. and h. of John Rivers of Ipswich, wid. of William Wimbill† (*d.*1487) and Thomas Alvard† (*d.*1504), both of Ipswich, 5s. 1da.;

(2) Christine, wid. of Thomas Baldry* (*d*.1524/25) of Ipswich. Kntd. 1 June 1533.[2]

Serjeant-at-arms 1508; commr. subsidy, Suff. 1512, 1514, 1515, 1523, 1524, loan 1524, tenths of spiritualities 1535, survey of monasteries, Norf. and Suff. 1536; other commissions, E. Anglia 1525–*d*.; customer, Ipswich, sole 1515–21, jt. (with Thomas Alvard*) 1521–9 or later; j.p. Suff. 1524–*d*.; knight of the body by 1533; sheriff, Norf. and Suff. 1533–4.[3]

Thomas Rush's origins are obscure but there is reason to believe that he came of a Lincolnshire family. Early in Henry VIII's reign he received a general pardon as of Lincolnshire and Suffolk; two of the domiciles mentioned, Eresby and Parham, are suggestive of a connexion with the influential family of Willoughby, and in April 1511 Rush was associated with John Willoughby in maintaining the sea-banks near Boston. It may thus have been under Willoughby's patronage that he first went to court; he was already in the King's service when he became a serjeant-at-arms, in which capacity he attended the funeral of Henry VII, the coronation of Henry VIII and in 1514 the marriage of Princess Mary to Louis XII of France.[4]

The last of these occasions must have brought Rush into renewed association with Charles Brandon, Duke of Suffolk, who led an embassy to France at this time and who in the previous year commanded the vanguard of the army in which Rush served as a captain. In May 1515, some months after Suffolk had married the widowed Queen of France, Rush was one of those, among them the duke's uncle Sir Robert Brandon†, who were granted pardon for an unspecified offence, perhaps one connected with that daring marriage.[5]

Rush's association with Ipswich perhaps dated from his marriage to the widow of two prominent townsmen there, but it was probably to his position at court that he owed the customership of the town. By 1517 he had become a freeman of Orford and had acquired property at nearby Sudbourne, where in 1524 he was assessed for the subsidy on goods valued at 200 marks. These local connexions notwithstanding, Rush was not a typical townsman Member for Ipswich, where he and his colleague Humphrey Wingfield appeared in person on the day of their election to the Parliament of 1523 and took the oath as freemen. Wingfield was a client of Wolsey, who almost certainly had a hand both in his election and in Rush's. His seat in this Parliament may explain why Rush did not join Suffolk's army in France; in the previous year he had been responsible with Thomas Hungerford for the supply of provisions to Calais. Among his local appointments at this time was the receivership of the 11th Lord Willoughby's lands in Norfolk and Suffolk.[6]

Rush's friendship with Cromwell must also have ripened during these years. In 1526 they acted together in two legal disputes in East Anglia, and they were soon to collaborate in the building of Wolsey's college at Ipswich, Rush being appointed in 1528 the cardinal's attorney for this purpose. In that and the following year he was closely involved in the affairs of local monasteries, including Bromehill priory which was suppressed, and he supervised the transfer of some of their lands to Wolsey's foundation at Oxford. By 1529 Rush and his stepson Thomas Alvard were sufficiently close to Cromwell to be given legacies in the will he made in that year, Rush's being £10. It was to Rush, too, that Ralph Sadler* first turned when on the eve of the Parliament of that year Cromwell sought a seat in the Commons, in the mistaken belief that Rush could find him one at Oxford. Rush was himself re-elected for Ipswich, with his stepson for his fellow-Member. Of his part in this Parliament all that is known is that he was probably the 'Mr. Ruse' whose name is one of four on the dorse of the Act passed during the fifth session for the sowing of flax and hemp. It was, however, after the close of the first session in December 1529 that he rode home with Thomas Audley I as far as Colchester. Reporting to Cromwell Audley's belief that the King would take the property of monasteries recently suppressed, so voiding all leases, he asked leave to 'sue a remedy', a request which implies that he himself was already a lessee. Six months later Rush was put on a commission to inquire into Wolsey's Suffolk lands, and in December 1530 he took a joint lease with Alvard of the manors of Aldeburgh and Snape.[7]

By this time Rush was inseparably linked with Cromwell, whom he was to serve diligently for the last few years of his life and to whose favour he doubtless owed the knighthood which he received in 1533. He audited the accounts of priests in Ipswich and reported on offerings made to the Virgin Mary at Borne and Ipswich. In June 1534 he informed the minister about seditious words spoken in the county. The final phase of Rush's career came with the dissolution of the smaller monasteries in 1536. In July and August of that year he helped to suppress the houses at Bruisyard and Butley. When rebellion broke out in Lincolnshire he was first called on to attend the King with 60 men but afterwards left to help maintain order in Suffolk: the ague from which he was suffering may have prevented him from taking a more active part. He was involved in the examination of some of those fomenting unrest and in May 1537 he was appointed one of the jurors to deal with the rebels.[8]

This was his last official duty: he probably died

shortly before 13 June 1537, the day on which his son Arthur sent his will to Cromwell as one of the executors, only to die himself within a month. A summary list of Rush's goods preserved among Cromwell's remembrances gives some indication of his wealth. The plate was valued at over £180 and livestock at nearly £300; debts due to him came to £364, with a further £150 owed for corn and sheep. The total value of the assets was about £1,050, of which £424 went towards legacies and £448 to the payment of debts. A flock of 500 sheep and a herd of 20 cows, together valued at £48, were claimed by his wife and remained at Snape. Rush was clearly a man of considerable landed wealth but in the absence both of the will itself and of an inquisition post mortem the extent of his lands cannot be determined. In November 1537 Thomas Manning, suffragan of Ipswich, wrote to inform Thomas Wriothesley that his servants had been given a copy of the court rolls for the lands held by Rush at Chillesford, Iken, Orford and Sudbourne, these having passed into the custody of Wriothesley with the wardship and marriage of Anthony Rush, the grandson and heir. Rush was buried in St. Stephen's church, Ipswich.[9]

[1] Ipswich ct. bk. 8, p. 116. [2] Date of birth estimated from first reference. N. Bacon, *Annals Ipswich*, 203n; *Vis. Suff.* ed. Metcalfe, 3, 63. [3] *CPR*, 1494–1509, p. 605; *LP Hen. VIII*, ii–viii; Ipswich ct. bk. 8, pp. 41, 286. [4] *LP Hen. VIII*, i, ii; *CPR*, 1494–1509, p. 605. [5] *LP Hen. VIII*, i, ii; C67/62, m.2. [6] Bacon, 108, 203; Add. 19147, f. 306; *Suff. Green Bks.* x. 269; *LP Hen. VIII*, ii, iv. [7] *LP Hen. VIII*, iii, iv; Elton, *Tudor Rev. in Govt.* 77–79; House of Lords RO, Original Acts, 24 Hen. VIII, no. 6. [8] *LP Hen. VIII*, v–ix, xi, xii; Elton, *Policy and Police*, 360. [9] *LP Hen. VIII*, xii; Bacon, 203n.

J.P.

RUSSELL, Francis (1527–85), of Amersham and Chenies, Bucks. and Russell (Bedford) House, the Strand, Mdx.

BUCKINGHAMSHIRE 1545, 1547

b. 1527, o.s. of Sir John Russell*, 1st Earl of Bedford, by Anne, da. of Sir Guy Sapcotes of Hunts. *educ.* King's, Camb. *m.* (1) Margaret (*d.*27 Aug. 1562), da. of Sir John St. John* of Bletsoe, Beds., wid. of William Gostwick (*d.*Dec. 1545), of Willington, Beds., 4s. inc. Sir Francis[†], John[†] and William[†] 3da.; (2) settlement 25 June 1566, Bridget (*d.*12 Jan. 1601), da. of Sir John Hussey*, Lord Hussey, wid. of Sir Richard Morison* (*d.*20 Mar. 1556) of London and Cassiobury, Herts. and of Henry Manners, 2nd Earl of Rutland (*d.*17 Sept. 1563), *s.p.* Kntd. 20 Feb. 1547. *summ.* to Lords in fa.'s barony as Baron Russell 1 Mar. 1553; KG nom. 23 Apr. 1564, inst. 15 May 1564. *suc.* fa. as 2nd Earl of Bedford 14 Mar. 1555.[1]

J.p. Bucks. 1547–*d.*, Beds., Cornw., Devon, Dorset, Northants, Som. 1558/59–*d.*; sheriff, Beds. and Bucks. 1547–8; custos rot. Bucks. c.1547–*d.*; commr. relief Bucks. 1550, goods of churches and fraternities 1553, eccles. causes, dioceses of Lincoln and Peterborough 1571; trier of petitions in the Lords, Parlts. of 1558, 1559, 1563, 1571; ld. lt., Cornw., Devon, Dorset 1558–*d.*; PC 21 Nov. 1558–*d.*; ld. warden of the

stannaries 1559–80; ambassador to France 1559, 1561; gov. Berwick-upon-Tweed, Northumb. and warden, east marches 1564–25 Aug. 1568; lt. gen., the north 1 Aug. 1565; high steward, duchy of Cornw. 13 Apr. 1572–*d.*; c.j. in eyre, south of the Trent 1584–*d.*; numerous minor offices.[2]

Francis Russell owed his place in Tudor society and government to his father's success. Nothing is known of his childhood and early education, nor of the duration of his study at Cambridge, but his connexion with that university was to set the direction of his religious beliefs. As a boy he was drawn by Holbein and while yet a stripling he served under his father in the French campaign of 1544. It was probably in 1546 that he married Margaret St. John, whose first husband had died in December 1545. Francis Russell received from his father a marriage allowance of £200 a year and doubtless lived at his manor of Amersham, for that was to be named in 1553 as his late place of domicile. In 1551 he obtained a number of offices scattered throughout the midlands which had recently been surrendered by his father, and a year later a licence to have 50 persons in his livery, over and above his household.[3]

Russell was no more than 17 when elected to the Parliament of 1545, but a birthday intervened between its delayed opening and his election: he was not to be included in local commissions for another two years. His fellow-knight for the shire was the royal favourite, Sir Francis Bryan, who had been returned for the county to at least two previous Parliaments: Russell's place could only have been procured for him by his father, who was by then lord privy seal. At the election of 1547, in spite of his youth and thanks to his parentage, Russell stood first on the return before Sir Anthony Lee, an older man of great wealth and standing in Buckinghamshire. A doubt as to Russell's eligibility to remain in the Commons on his father's creation as Earl of Bedford was settled by an order on 21 Jan. 1550 that he should abide in the Lower House 'in the state he was before', and on the list of Members as revised for the fourth session he was entered as 'Sir Francis Russell Lord Russell'. It was during that session, in March 1552, that he had committed to him a bill concerning pewterers and tin, and another about leases, and that a month later he was required by the House, together with Sir Robert Dudley* and (Sir) John Cheke,* to intercede with the Duke of Suffolk on behalf of Ralph Ellerker after Ellerker's discharge for assaulting Sir Robert Brandling (q.v.). In Edward VI's second Parliament he was summoned to the Lords on 1 Mar. 1553 as Baron Russell: despite his youth he made an immediate impact upon the House, and his attendance there was exemplary, with only two absences.[4]

Russell was among the peers' sons who on 16 June 1553 signed the letters patent settling the crown on Lady Jane Grey, but he doubtless soon afterwards followed his father in supporting Mary's title. Imprisoned in the Fleet with others on 29 July, he was specially favoured by being removed into the custody of the sheriff of London and allowed visits from his mother. He was soon released, but freedom did not entail the restoration of his seat in the Lords, and he was not to be summoned again as Baron Russell. He fought with his father against the Kentish rebels early in 1554 and was a royal envoy to receive the Prince of Piedmont: none the less, he continued to display his Protestantism. He corresponded with the reformers John Bradford and Edward Underhill* in prison: Underhill, to whom he also sent money, had saved him from drowning in the Thames and was later to be described as 'familiar with him in matters of religion as well across the seas as at home'. The preacher Thomas Becon, once the Duke of Somerset's chaplain, named Russell in the dedication of works entitled 'The monstrous merchandise of the Roman bishops' and 'The Christian knight'. His father's death was the occasion of his seeking and receiving permission to travel abroad for two years. Now an earl and the owner of great possessions, he gave power of attorney to his friend Sir William Cecil (q.v.) to administer his affairs in his absence: it appears that this gave Cecil a share in the Russell patronage in parliamentary elections. Bedford's licence, dated 20 Apr. 1555, was ostensibly given to enable him to gain experience, especially as a visitor to the Emperor at Brussels. This duty discharged reluctantly but meticulously, he was allowed by the Emperor to proceed to Italy, where he travelled as far south as Naples. Between August 1556 and the spring of 1557 he visited Zurich where he began lasting friendships with Bullinger and other reformers. He held a command at the battle of St. Quentin in August 1557, and then returned to England to take up the lord lieutenancy of the south-western counties. He did not establish a residence there but his interest in his forbears led him to buy the ancestral manor of Kingston Lacy in south Dorset. He took his place in the Lords as an earl for the first time in the Parliament of 1558, and his appearance there was no less impressive than it had been before, in his father's shadow. For the remainder of his life he was one of the leading figures in the House.[5]

Bedford was to serve Elizabeth in many spheres. An active Privy Councillor, he added to the lieutenancy of the south-west important military and administrative responsibilities in the north. His gifts of languages and polished manners were valuable on missions abroad and at home he earned a reputation for great piety. He followed his father's example by wielding extensive parliamentary patronage. Bedford died at Russell House in the parish of St. Clement Dane on 28 July 1585 but was buried at Chenies only on 14 Sept. An alabaster tomb supporting coloured effigies of the earl and his first wife, and bearing a lengthy inscription, was erected in the family chapel. His will, made on 7 Apr. 1584, was proved on 30 Sept. 1586 by among others (Sir) Thomas Bromley II*; Sir Robert Dudley*, Earl of Leicester; Charles Morison†; Henry Neville† and Sir Francis Walsingham† as executors. It included provision for 20 sermons at Chenies and elsewhere, for the endowment of the two universities with £40 for poor students of divinity and of University College, Oxford with £20 for two poor students to be known as 'the Earl of Bedford's scholars', the last not being carried out. To Lord Burghley, one of his overseers, Bedford left, besides a rich jewel, his 'ancient written English books of Wycliffe's works' in his closet at Russell House; all his Latin and Italian manuscripts and books passed to his heir. As Bedford's three eldest sons predeceased him, he was succeeded by Edward, only son of his third son Francis, then aged 13.[6]

[1] Date of birth estimated from parents' marriage and from age (28) at fa.'s i.p.m. (C142/102/80) and (58) at own death. *CP; DNB;* H. P. R. Finberg, *Gostwicks of Willington* (Beds. Hist. Rec. Soc. xxxvi), 72n, 76, 89 establishes that Margaret 2nd Countess of Bedford was the daughter-in-law, not the wife, of Sir John Gostwick* as given in *CP.* [2] *CPR,* 1547–8, pp. 81, 419; 1550–3, pp. 141, 393; 1553, pp. 351, 413; 1563–6, p. 259; 1566–9, p. 201; 1569–72, pp. 476–7; *APC,* iv. 49, 277; G. Scott Thomson, *Lds. Lt.* 39, 46, 48; information from J. C. Sainty; *LJ,* i. 514, 542, 580, 667; Arundel castle mss autograph letters 1513–85, no. 29. [3] *Al. Cant.* iii. 499; *Ath. Cant.* ii. 532; G. Scott Thomson, *Two Cents. of Fam. Hist.* 204; *Holbein* (The Queen's Gallery, Buckingham Palace 1978–9), 111–12; *CPR,* 1550–3, pp. 145, 302; 1553–4, p. 282. [4] C142/102/80; *CJ.* i. 15, 19, 23; M. A. R. Graves, 'The Tudor House of Lords 1547–58' (Otago Univ. Ph.D. thesis, 1974), ii. 256–7. [5] *APC,* iv. 305, 314; v. 37; *Machyn's Diary* (Cam. Soc. xlii), 38; *Chron. Q. Jane and Q. Mary* (Cam. Soc. xlviii), 15, 99; *Two Cents. of Fam. Hist.* 204–5, 207–10, 219; D. M. Loades, *Two Tudor Conspiracies,* 93; *The Writings of John Bradford* (Parker Soc.), 77, 138; *Narr. Ref.* (Cam. Soc. lxxviii), 145–6; *DNB* (Bradford, John; Becon, Thomas); *Orig. Letters Relating to the Eng. Ref.* (Parker Soc.), i. 138; *Cam. Misc.* x. 120; *CSP Ven.* 1555–6, p. 145; *CSP For.* 1553–8, no. 488 ex inf. K. Bartlett; Graves, ii. 256–7; *CSP Dom.* 1547–80, p. 94 et passim; *CPR,* 1558–60, p. 277; *Lds. Lt.* 39. [6] Neale, *Commons,* passim; *CSP Ven.* 1557–8, p. 1554; J. A. Froude, *Eliz.* i. 44; Lipscomb, *Bucks.* iii. 257; *VCH Bucks.* iii. 202; PCC 45 Windsor; *Rev. Eng. Studies,* vii. 385–405; Pevsner, *Bucks.* 85.

M.K.D.

RUSSELL, John I (1493/94–1556), of Strensham, Worcs.

WORCESTERSHIRE 1529, 1539[1]

b. 1493/94, 1st s. of Robert Russell of Strensham by Elizabeth, da. of Thomas Baynham of Clearwell, Glos. *m.* settlement 11 Jan. 1519, Edith, da. of Sir Thomas Unton† of Wadley, Berks., 1s. Thomas*. *suc.* fa. 28 June 1502. Kntd. aft. 3 Nov. 1529.[2]

Jt. (with s. Thomas and John Gostwick*) supervisor, lands of bpric. of Worcester by 1523, sole 1533–40; commr. subsidy, Worcs. 1523, 1524, loan

1524, musters 1539, 1546, relief 1550, goods of churches and fraternities 1553; other commissions 1533–47; j.p. Worcs. 1531–*d.*, Glos. 1532; sheriff, Worcs. Mar.–Nov. 1538, 1541–2, 1546–7.[3]

The Russells had held Strensham since the late 13th century and one of them had represented Worcestershire in Parliament as early as 1365. John Russell's inheritance, of which he had livery in May 1516, included, besides Strensham and other Worcestershire lands, property in Buckinghamshire, Derbyshire and Gloucestershire.[4]

As Habington was to observe, the name of Russell was 'somewhat common' and the Worcestershire knight had several contemporary namesakes. One of these, the Member for Westminster in the Parliament of 1545, is readily distinguished from John Russell of Strensham, with whom his career and background had no point of contact except the fact that Strensham was held of the abbot of Westminster. On the other hand, Sir John Russell, knight of the shire for Buckinghamshire in 1529 and later 1st Earl of Bedford, could have been confused, at least in the earlier stages of his career, with the younger knight and the two were accordingly distinguished in some contexts as 'senior' and 'junior' and in others, notably in the accounts of the royal household, by the addition of a territorial label to the younger man's name. Kinship was later claimed and acknowledged by both families: as early as 1533 Russell of Strensham wrote that he had sought the future earl's assistance in a suit, and his grandson, born in 1551, was to be brought up in the household of Francis Russell*, the 2nd Earl. None the less, the connexion is not discernible except perhaps through the marriage of the 1st Earl's grandfather into a Worcestershire family, while the arms of the two families are quite distinct. A third namesake and more probable kinsman, who settled at Little Malvern, Worcestershire, after a career as secretary to the 3rd Duke of Buckingham, to Princess Mary and to the council in the marches of Wales, was never knighted and so is only liable to be confused with Russell of Strensham before his own knighting. It was probably the secretary who was placed on the Herefordshire bench in 1528 and on the Shropshire one early in 1529: Russell of Strensham did not become a justice in Worcestershire until 1531 but he did hold two of his Worcestershire manors of the Cornwalls of Herefordshire and acted as a feoffee for Sir Richard Cornwall*.[5]

Russell's youth and relative inexperience make it probable that his parliamentary career opened in 1529, although he could have sat in 1523 when the names of the knights of the shire are lost. He was knighted at York Place in the course of the first session and seems also to have gained a foothold at court: by the following New Year's Day he and his wife begin to appear in the accounts of the royal household and he was later to attend the coronation of Anne Boleyn and the reception of Anne of Cleves. After the sixth session Russell and his fellow-knight Sir Gilbert Talbot sued out a writ *de expensis* from Chancery and claimed £160 for their combined wages for 400 days, that is, presumably for the 365 days so far consumed by the Parliament, with 35 days added for the 12 journeys they had made to and from it. When payment was withheld by Sir Edward Ferrers*, the sheriff of Worcestershire, they brought an action against him in the Exchequer, claiming damages of £40: whether they succeeded is not known. In the next session Russell's name appears on a list drawn up by Cromwell on the dorse of a letter of December 1534 and thought to be of Members with a particular, but unknown, connexion with the treasons bill then on its passage through Parliament. He was to sit for the shire again in 1539 and doubtless did so in the intervening Parliament of 1536, when the King asked for the return of the previous Members; he did not reappear in the Commons thereafter unless perhaps in 1545 (when the names of the Worcestershire knights are unknown), although his re-election on that occasion is unlikely in view of his son Thomas's return to the previous Parliament at a by-election held on 27 Dec. 1542 after the death of Russell's former colleague Sir Gilbert Talbot.[6]

Russell enjoyed Cromwell's confidence and it was from him that the minister sought information in 1535 when the King heard of the disputes at Worcester priory, where charges of treason had been brought against one of the monks; Russell replied that he had already been consulted by the subprior and had advised him to inform the council in the marches. This seeming reluctance to become involved may have been prudent in view of Cromwell's failure to sustain any charge: Russell had been similarly cautious in his earlier handling of a Worcestershire person accused of speaking against the King. Although nothing is known of Russell's own religious sympathies, two or possibly three of his family were Knights of St. John, his brother Giles attaining the high rank of turcopolier in the order. Russell's own experience as an episcopal administrator may have swayed him towards conservatism. As early as 1523, during the episcopate of the Italian Ghinucci, he had been appointed joint supervisor of the lands of the bishopric of Worcester and ten years later he reminded Cromwell of a promise to favour his suit to regain it. This he did and 30 years later the office was held by his son, who as an infant had shared it with him and John Gostwick in 1523. In 1534 Russell took the oath of fealty from the abbot of Tewkesbury and in the following year he served on the commission for tenths of spiritualities in the county as well as the city of Worcester. He was summoned to attend the King with 100 men at the time of the northern rebellion and in March 1538 he was named to complete William Walshe's term as sheriff, later accounting for the whole shrieval year. Early in 1540 he assisted at the surrender of Pershore abbey and three years later he was mustered to serve in the French campaign.[7]

Russell died on 15 Aug. 1556, three days after making a will in which he named his son executor and noted that his wife Edith was 'visited with such infirmity as she is not well able to govern herself'. He was buried in Strensham church where a mural brass was erected to his memory.[8]

[1] E159/319, brev. ret. Mich. r. [1–2]. [2] Date of birth estimated from age at fa.'s i.p.m., *CIPM Hen. VII*, ii. 562, 587, 651, 654, 655. *Vis. Worcs.* (Harl. Soc. xxvii), 119; C142/108/128; *Habington's Worcs.* (Worcs. Hist. Soc. 1895), i. 389. [3] Worcs. RO, 009:1 BA 2636/178 92517 ex inf. C. Dyer; *LP Hen. VIII*, iii-viii, xii, xiv-xvi, xx, xxi; *CPR*, 1547-8, p. 75; 1553, p. 359; 1553-4, p. 25. [4] *VCH Worcs.* iv. 204; *LP Hen. VIII*, ii; *Habington's Worcs.* i. 389. [5] *VCH Worcs.* iii. 450; iv. 204; *LP Hen. VIII*, ii, iv, vi; *Habington's Worcs.* i. 389; G. Scott Thomson, *Two Cents. of Fam. Hist.* 102, 336; R. S. Thomas, 'Pol. career, estates and connexions of Jasper Tudor, Earl of Pembroke and Duke of Bedford' (Swansea Univ. Ph.D. thesis, 1971), 274-5; C. Rawcliffe, *The Staffords, Earls of Stafford and Dukes of Buckingham 1394-1521*, passim; C142/55/33. [6] *LP Hen. VIII*, iv, vi, vii. 1522(ii) citing SP1/87, f. 106v, xiv; E13/214/11v. [7] *LP Hen. VIII*, iii, vi-xii, xvi, xix; Elton, *Policy and Police*, 124-7, 355-6; *Vis. Worcs.* 119; W. Porter, *Knights of Malta*, 724. [8] C142/108/128; PCC 17 Ketchyn; Mill Stephenson, *Mon. Brasses*, 540; Pevsner, *Worcs.* 273.

A.D.

RUSSELL, John II (by 1501-66), of Westminster, Mdx. and London.

WESTMINSTER 1545

b. by 1501, 2nd s. of Richard Russell (*d.*14 May 1517) of Westminster by Constance. *m.* by Mar. 1531, Christian, da. of Humphrey Coke of London, 2s. 2da.[1] Master carpenter, the King's works 1 Oct. 1532–*d.*, jt. with William Clement 1532–40 and with John Colbrand 8 Feb. 1565–*d.*; junior warden, Carpenters' Co. 1538–9, senior warden 1540–1, master 1541–2, 1549–50, 1557–8, 1565–*d.*; surveyor of the works, Westminster abbey by 1555–*d.*[2]

Whereas his elder brother William became a waxchandler, John Russell followed their father into carpentry. Although the father was never appointed royal master carpenter—a post held by Russell himself for nearly 34 years and before that by Russell's father-in-law—he was chief carpenter at Westminster abbey and master carpenter of the royal works at King's College chapel in Cambridge and of Wolsey's works at York Place and Hampton Court. By his will made in 1514 and proved three years later he left his lease of the *Bell* in Westminster to his wife for life, directing that upon her death it was to go to their son William. This came about in

January 1522 and two years later the property was divided between William, his brother John and their two sisters. In 1531 the brothers assigned the remaining years of their leases to Cromwell for the King's use as part of an agreement whereby Russell obtained the post of master carpenter in succession to James Nedeham who not long afterwards was promoted to the surveyorship.[3]

Russell is first met with in 1515 as an apprentice-carpenter working under his father's direction at York Place: three years later he had joined the staff responsible for the maintenance of Westminster abbey and its properties. During the 1530s he undertook repairs to various royal manors, but apart from those at Otford, St. Albans and Whitehall between 1541 and 1548 and minor ones at Westminster from 1551 to 1558 his only later known work for the crown was the reconstruction of the Poor Knights' Lodgings at Windsor and the building of a conduit there in 1557–8. From 1555 or earlier he was surveyor of the works at Westminster abbey, a post held by his brother until 1543, and he was consulted over a number of major building projects. He and the Westminster victualler Robert Smallwood were the Members elected by the city to the Parliament of 1545, when it is first known to have returned Members. Nothing is known about Russell's part in the House, but while the opening of the Parliament was postponed he led a number of carpenters to Boulogne. He assisted at subsequent elections for Westminster and Middlesex in February 1553 and signed the Westminster election indentures in October 1554 and 1555.[4]

Russell was a sick man when he made his will on 19 Dec. 1564. He provided for his children and left his wife an inn called the *Christopher*, which had been her father's, an adjacent tenement which he had bought from Henry VIII, and another in the Little Sanctuary, which he had bought from Edward VI: his wife was also to enjoy the remaining years of his leases, including that of the rectory of St. Margaret's, Westminster. He recovered from his illness, but in the following year he surrendered his patent as master carpenter in favour of a new one for himself and John Colbrand who succeeded him in the office at his death on 1 July 1566. He was buried in the church of St. Martin-in-the-Fields three days later and his will was proved by his widow before the end of the month.[5]

[1] Date of birth estimated from apprenticeship. D. R. Ransome, 'Artisan dynasties in London and Westminster in the 16th cent.', *Guildhall Misc.* ii. 236-47. [2] *The King's Works*, iii. 408; *Recs. Carpenters' Co.* ed. Marsh, iii. 211; Westminster abbey 37557v. [3] *Guildhall Misc.* ii. 240-6; J. H. Harvey, *Eng. Med. Architects*, 233; Westminster abbey, reg. 2, ff. 38, 109, 183v, 207v; London consist. ct. Thirlby; *Cat. Anct. Deeds*, v. 441-2, 506; *The King's Works*, iii. 10, 41. [4] *Guildhall Misc.* ii. 242; Harvey, 231; *The King's Works*, iii. 3, 31-32, 41, 56, 318-19; *LP Hen. VIII*, v, xiv, xvii-xxi

Westminster abbey 37045, 37557v, 37923, 38005–8; C219/20/79, 80, 23/85, 24/105. ⁵ PCC 21 Crymes, 5 Thower; Westminster abbey 37777, 38644; *CPR*, 1563–6, p. 255; *Recs. Carpenters' Co.* iii. 211; *St. Martin-in-the-Fields*: *Churchwardens' Accts.* ed. Kitto, 226.

H.M.

RUSSELL, Sir John (c.1485–1555), of Berwick, Dorset; Russell House, the Strand, Mdx. and Chenies, Bucks.

BUCKINGHAMSHIRE 1529

b. c.1485, s. of James Russell of Berwick by Alice, da. of John Wise of Sydenham, Devon. *m.* spring 1526, Anne (*d.*14 Mar. 1559), da. of Sir Guy Sapcote of Hunts., wid. of John Broughton (*d.*1517/19) of Toddington, Beds. and of Sir Richard Jerningham (*d.*1525/26) of London, 1s. Francis*. *suc.* fa. 20 July 1505. Kntd. 2 July 1522; KG nom. 24 Apr. 1539, inst. 18 May 1539; *cr.* Baron Russell 9 Mar. 1539, Earl of Bedford 19 Jan. 1550.[1]

Gent. the privy chamber 1507; knight marshal, the Household 1523–7; knight of the body by 1527; sheriff, Som. and Dorset 1527–8; j.p. Beds., Bucks., Herts., Hunts., Northants. 1533–*d.*, Cornw., Devon, Dorset, Som. 1539; PC 1536–*d.*; comptroller, the Household 18 Oct. 1537–9; pres. council in the west 1539; high steward, duchy of Cornw. 4 July 1539–*d.*, univ. Oxf. 1543–*d.*; ld. warden of the stannaries 4 July 1539–*d.*; commr. coastal defences, south-western counties 1539, relief, Beds., Bucks., London 1550; trier of petitions in the Lords, Parlts. of 1539, 1542, 1545, 1547, Mar. 1553, Oct. 1553, ?Apr. 1554, Nov. 1554; ld. admiral 28 July 1540–17 Jan. 1543; ld. privy seal 3 Dec. 1542–*d.*; steward, manor of Stamford, Lincs. 1543–7, 1548–*d.*; ld. lt. Devon, Cornw., Som., Dorset 1545, 1549–53, Bucks. 1552.[2]

John Russell came from a Dorset family of moderate standing whose estates had been acquired gradually during the 14th and 15th centuries from the profits of trade and the fortunes of marriage. His grandfather, another John, who broke with family tradition by making a career in the service of the crown, had been a knight of the shire for Dorset in 1472 and had died in 1505 leaving a son and heir James who did not long survive him. Of John Russell's early life nothing is known for certain, but in the 17th century Thomas Fuller heard that he had been 'bred beyond the seas', an upbringing which would accord with his command of foreign languages. When early in 1506 the fleet taking the Archduke Philip to Spain was driven by a storm into Weymouth Bay, the gentlemen of Dorset were ordered to entertain him and escort him to Henry VII at Windsor; it was Russell's linguistic fluency on this occasion which saved Sir Thomas Trenchard and other gentlemen from embarrassment and which probably commended him to the King, who shortly afterwards gave him a place at court.

Russell's appointment in the privy chamber was confirmed by Henry VIII, his junior by some six years. In 1513 he fought in the campaign in northern France and after the capture of Tournai he received an administrative post there. He became a familiar figure in the city during its occupation, often serving as an intermediary between its council and Wolsey and once being involved in a scheme to capture, or even to assassinate the Yorkist claimant to the throne Richard de la Pole. In 1514 he went to Paris for the marriage of Louis XII to Princess Mary and four years later he accompanied the King to the Field of Cloth of Gold. In 1522 his valour at the siege of Morlaix cost him an eye but gained him a knighthood. Wolsey employed him as an agent between 1523 and 1527 in a search for alliances against Francis I and during his journeys he witnessed the battle of Pavia and narrowly escaped the sack of Rome. His travels came to an end shortly before he was pricked sheriff of Somerset and Dorset: the appointment may have been intended in part to reimburse him for the expenses he had incurred, for he had been obliged to dispose of some of his Dorset property. These years were nevertheless rewarding ones for Russell: he had made his mark with both King and cardinal, and he had married an heiress who brought him an interest in Buckinghamshire, where he was to settle.[3]

In the spring of 1529 Russell was appointed to go to the French court, but his mission was countermanded before he set out. Wolsey's position was becoming precarious and he relied on Russell as his spokesman with the King. That Russell was not compromised by the cardinal's fall is shown by his election to the Parliament of 1529 as a knight of the shire for his adopted county: the writ for Buckinghamshire was one of those called for by the King when he was at Windsor in August. His Membership of this Parliament was probably not Russell's first experience of the Commons, for he may have sat earlier for a Dorset borough where his standing at court combined with his family connexions could have procured him a place. Early in 1530 he defended Wolsey before the King and in so doing incurred the wrath of Anne Boleyn, whose continuing hostility to him may have impeded his progress: of Henry VIII's marriage to Jane Seymour in 1536 he was to remark, 'The King hath come out of hell into heaven for the gentleness of this [Queen] and the cursedness and unhappiness in the other'. In compliance with the King's request Russell doubtless sat in the Parliament which opened nine days after the marriage: its purpose, to complete the destruction of Anne Boleyn, was one which he must have applauded. It was not until then that he became a Privy Councillor. In 1532 he had gone to Calais with the King and a year later had been offered, but did not accept, the deputyship of the town.

Russell distinguished himself during the suppression of the Lincolnshire rebellion and the Pilgrimage of Grace, and as he grew closer towards Cromwell he was clearly a candidate for high office. The opportunity came with the establishment of the council in the west. The execution of the Marquess of Exeter had created a political vacuum in Devon and Cornwall which the King would not suffer to be filled by another magnate of doubtful loyalty. Russell had proved his worth, his family links with the region were an added qualification, and a patrimony reduced by sale and neglect could be augmented to match the dignity of the office. He received substantial grants of land in the south-west, the high stewardship of the duchy of Cornwall and the lord wardenship of the stannaries (both previously held by Exeter), the Garter and a peerage. The council came into being in 1539 but failed to establish itself, perhaps because its president was often needed at court and there was no natural successor to Exeter. Yet Russell's personal ascendancy in the south-west was to remain unchallenged for the rest of his life.

Russell survived Cromwell's fall, as he had done Wolsey's, and in the redistribution of offices which followed he secured the admiralty. Two years later the 3rd Duke of Norfolk recommended him to succeed Sir William Fitzwilliam I*, 1st Earl of Southampton as lieutenant in the north, but this command went to the Earl of Hertford, and Russell received another of Southampton's offices, that of lord privy seal: his failure to take Montreuil, when he was called upon to campaign in 1544, suggests that he had been rightly passed over. He spent the late summer of 1545 in a tour of inspection of coastal defences in the south-west, but otherwise he was rarely absent from the King's side during the last years of the reign: an ambassador described him as 'not only of great authority in the Council but also one who always eats and talks with his majesty'. In 1542 he entertained the King at Chenies, and five years later he received £500 under Henry VIII's will, of which he was an executor.

According to Secretary Paget the King had at first meant to promote Russell in the peerage but although he suffered no loss of power under Edward VI he did not benefit from the dispersal of honours at the opening of the new reign, perhaps on account of an earlier disagreement with the Protector Somerset. On the outbreak of the Prayer Book rebellion of 1549 he was commissioned to restore order. This he was initially expected to do without adequate supplies or reserves, and until the Council met his demands he moved with caution: his dilatoriness was adversely criticized by the Protector and it was said

that during the summer he 'lived in more fear than he was feared'. Russell's strategy, perhaps influenced by his experience earlier in the north, may not have inspired confidence but the rising was suppressed and any recrudescence prevented. He was still in the west when the *coup d'état* was staged against the Protector: Somerset called upon him and (Sir) William Herbert I* for support, but they halted at Andover whence they informed him on 8 Oct. of their support for the Earl of Warwick. Their defection sealed Somerset's fate and Russell was rewarded with the earldom of Bedford and more lands in the south-west and the east midlands, including a reversionary grant of Woburn abbey. He was among those charged to attend upon the King 'for the honourable education of his highness . . . in learning and virtue', he went abroad in 1550 to negotiate peace with the French, and in the following year he attended the discussions in London about the eucharist. In June 1553 he signed the device which put Lady Jane Grey on the throne and swore allegiance to her, but as soon as the Duke of Northumberland left London he quitted the Tower with other Privy Councillors and helped to proclaim Mary. Retained as a Councillor, Bedford opposed the Spanish marriage and supported the petition for an English one, but he did not long persist in this stand, rallying to the Queen's side during Wyatt's rebellion and regaining her confidence and a leading place in her counsels. She entrusted him with the embassy to conduct Philip from Spain, and it was perhaps on his advice that Philip landed at Southampton instead of in the west country where feeling was strong against the marriage.[4]

Bedford was as diligent in attending the House of Lords as he was the Privy Council. He missed the last weeks of the third session (1549–50) of the Parliament of 1547 through his mission to France, and almost the whole of the second Parliament of Mary's reign while on embassy to Spain. His other notable absence from the Lords, during the Parliament of March 1553, is not so easily explained: whether through illness, or because he suspected Northumberland's schemes, after the first two weeks he did not attend the House until the last day of the Parliament. Presumably he was an important government spokesman, but little trace has been found of his contribution to the business of the Upper House save in the first Edwardian Parliament, when in the first session he signed the bill for the King's general pardon and in the third six others including that for the fine and ransom of the Duke of Somerset, and when he twice adjourned the Lords in the absence of Chancellor Rich.[5]

So eminent a figure would have followed affairs in

the Commons no less keenly than those in the Lords. Bedford showed a lively interest in the membership of the Commons, making use of his authority to procure the return of those amenable to himself and to the crown. Although he supported kinsmen, clients and young lawyers (especially those from Lincoln's Inn where in 1529 he had been made an honorary member), he did not disregard local interests, a policy which was to be maintained by his son the 2nd Earl. The extent of his intervention can be deduced from the number of those connected with him who were returned for constituencies in the south-west during the 1540s and early 1550s. Both in 1539 and 1545 he spent some time in the area, and his hand is more in evidence in the elections to the Parliaments of those two years than on occasions when he was unable to exert such direct influence. In the case of Edward VI's first Parliament he was probably responsible for the enfranchisement of seven boroughs in Cornwall since their first Members were nearly all known to him and they were to remain in his patronage until his death. Bedford's hold on the south-west was temporarily shaken when Mary came to the throne, but once he regained her trust his authority revived and was not to be challenged.

At the beginning of 1555 Bedford fell ill: he made his last appearance in Council on 11 Jan. and his will is dated 2 Feb. He provided for his wife, son, grandchildren, kinsmen and servants. He died on 14 Mar. at Russell House and was buried with pomp six days later at Chenies where a monument was erected to his memory. In the west country his death was marked by the tolling of bells and other signs of public mourning. Several portraits of Bedford from the last 20 years of his life survive.[6]

[1] This biography rests on G. Scott Thomson, *Two Cents. of Fam. Hist.* and D. Willen, 'The career of John Russell, 1st Earl of Bedford: a study in Tudor politics' (Tufts Univ. Ph.D. thesis, 1972). G. Scott Thomson's estimate of Russell's date of birth has been adopted. PCC 4 Adeane, 17 Ayloffe, 9 Porch; C142/33/120, 40/28, 48, 46/25. [2] *LJ*, i. 103, 165, 267, 293, 430, 447, 464; Stamford hall bk. 1461–1657, ff. 138, 146; G. Scott Thomson, *Lds. Lt.* 19–21; I. Temple, Petyt ms 538, vol. 46, f. 442v; *APC*, iii. 6, 258–9; iv. 49, 276. [3] C. G. Cruickshank, *The Eng. Occupation of Tournai 1513–19*, pp. 210–11 corrects the *DNB* entry where the John Russell active at Tournai is distinguished from the future earl. [4] *Wealth and Power*, ed. Ives, Knecht and Scarisbrick, 88–90, 96, 101; D. E. Hoak, *The King's Council in the Reign of Edw. VI*, passim. [5] *LJ*, i. 103 seq.; M. A. R. Graves, 'The Tudor House of Lords 1547–58' (Otago Univ. Ph.D. thesis, 1974), ii. 254–5; House of Lords, Original Acts, 1 Edw. VI, no. 21, 3 and 4 Edw. VI, nos. 22–23, 25, 29, 30–31. [6] PCC 5 Ketchyn; *Machyn's Diary* (Cam. Soc. xlii), 83; *RCHM Bucks.* 88–91; Pevsner, *Bucks.* 85–88; *Holbein* (The Queen's Gallery, Buckingham Palace 1978–9), 59–60; R. C. Strong, *Tudor and Jacobean Portraits*, 21.

A.D.K.H.

RUSSELL, Thomas (1519/20–74), of Strensham and Witley, Worcs.

WORCESTERSHIRE 1542*, 1547,[1] 1553 (Oct.), 1559, 1571

b. 1519/20, o.s. of John Russell I*. *educ.* G. Inn, adm. 1544. *m.* (1) by 1544, Frances, da. and coh. of Sir Roger Cholmley* of London and Highgate, Mdx., 1s. John† 1da.; (2) Margaret, da. of William Lygon of Madresfield, Worcs. 1s. Kntd. 17 Nov. 1549; *suc.* fa. 15 Aug. 1556.[2]

Jt. (with fa. and John Gostwick*) supervisor, lands of bpric. of Worcester 1523, supervisor or surveyor in 1564; sheriff, Worcs. 1551–2, 1559–60, 1569–70; commr. goods of churches and fraternities, Worcs. 1553, to enforce Acts of Uniformity and Supremacy 1572, musters, Worcs. 1573; j.p. 1558/59–*d.*, q. by 1562; steward, manor of Martley, Worcs. by 1570, of lands formerly of Great Malvern and Pershore abbeys, Worcs. at *d.*; custos rot. Worcs. by 1573/74.[3]

Appointed in infancy joint supervisor of the lands of the bishopric of Worcester, Thomas Russell is mentioned in 1535 as the bearer of letters to his father from Cromwell concerning the affairs of Worcester priory. His next appearance is as a knight of the shire, by-elected on 27 Dec. 1542 to replace Sir Gilbert Talbot who had died on the previous 22 October. This distinction, while still in his early twenties and before he had exercised any public office, he evidently owed to his father, who had then just completed his second term as sheriff. The sheriff at the time of the by-election, Sir George Throckmorton*, who shared an interest in the estates of the bishopric of Worcester with the Russells, probably lent his support.[4]

Russell may have sat again in 1545, when the Worcestershire knights are unknown, and was probably returned before the opening of the Parliament of 1547, when his father was again sheriff, although his Membership is known only from the Crown Office list drawn up for the fourth session. During this Parliament he was one of six knights, including the Duke of Lüneburg and Ambrose Dudley, a younger son the Earl of Warwick, dubbed at Westminster in November 1549 and two years later he was pricked sheriff for the first time. He should not be confused with a namesake who served as provost marshal in 1549 and who had earlier been engaged in provisioning Boulogne and Calais. Nothing is known of Russell's role within the House or of any part he may have played in the conflicts of the reign. He may have attached himself to Sir John Russell*, created Earl of Bedford early in 1550, with whom the Russells of Strensham claimed kinship and in the household of whose son Sir Thomas Russell's own elder son, born in 1551, was to be brought up. Since Bedford supported the Duke of Northumberland, however, this leaves unexplained Russell's failure to sit for his shire in the Parliament of March 1553. Whatever the reason for that absence, he was again returned to the first Parliament of the new reign but was one of those Members of it who opposed the restoration of Catholicism. His Protestantism, thus evidenced and later underlined by his friendship with Bishop Sandys whom he assisted in the compilation of the return of 1564, accounts for his failure to sit again before 1559, but he was not entirely excluded from favour, being employed early in 1558 to raise men in Worcestershire for the relief of Calais. In October 1557 his father-in-law Sir Roger Cholmley (who had been imprisoned at the beginning of Mary's reign for his role in the succession crisis) was licensed to grant his manors of Broad Campden, Gloucestershire and Over Strensham, Worcestershire, to the Russells.[5]

Russell died on 9 Apr. 1574, six days after making his will. His widow and executrix married Henry Berkeley† of Somerset.[6]

[1] Hatfield 207. [2] Date of birth estimated from parents' marriage and age at fa.'s i.p.m., C142/108/128. *Vis. Worcs.* (Harl. Soc. xxvii), 119; PCC 11 Pynnyng. [3] *LP Hen. VIII*, iii; *Cam. Misc.* ix(3), 4; *CPR*, 1550-3, p. 396; 1553, p. 415; 1560-3, p. 444; 1569-72, p. 440; 1572-5, p. 243; *CSP Dom.* 1547-80, p. 460; Lansd. 56, f. 170; *Habington's Worcs.* (Worcs. Hist. Soc. 1899), ii. 196; SP 12/93 ex inf. J. C. Sainty. [4] *LP Hen. VIII*, ix. [5] *Lit. Rems. Edw. VI*, p. cccvii; *APC*, ii. 351; *LP Hen. VIII*, xx; G. Scott Thomson, *Two Cents. of Fam. Hist.* 102, 336; Bodl. e Museo 17; *Cam. Misc.* ix (3), 1, 4-7; *EHR*, xxiii. 658; *CPR*, 1557-8, p. 337. [6] C142/172/163; PCC 8 Pyckering.

A.D.

RUST, John (by 1516-69), of Cambridge.

CAMBRIDGE 1545,[1] 1547*,[2] 1554 (Apr.)

b. by 1516. *m.* Elizabeth, at least 2s.[3]
Mayor, Cambridge 1548-9, alderman 1556; commr. goods of churches and fraternities 1553, heresy 1555, gaol delivery in 1561; j.p. 1555.[4]

A chandler by trade, John Rust lived in Great St. Mary's parish, where he was a churchwarden from 1537 to 1539 and again in the 1550s. His first return to Parliament preceded his mayoralty by three years and followed the death of Thomas Brakyn* during the postponement of the Parliament of 1545. Brakyn's death was presumably announced at the assembly of the Parliament late in November 1545 as Rust was chosen his replacement at an election held at Cambridge on 2 Dec. following. Rust's second Membership resulted from the death of John Fanne in 1551 while the next Parliament stood prorogued. His re-election in 1554 was thus as a man with experience of sitting in the Commons for three sessions. Although nothing is known about Rust's part in the work of the House, his involvement in the long drawn-out feud between town and gown is well documented from 1546, when he was thrice singled out for mention by the vice-chancellor of the university in a complaint against the borough, until his death 23 years later.[5]

Rust was mayor at the time of the anti-enclosure riots on 10 July 1549, and he went to Barnwell with the town's force to keep order; he apparently improved the occasion by picking a quarrel with the vice-chancellor. He also sometimes quarrelled with townsmen: thus, in the reign of Mary, he was the principal 'bearer' and abettor of Robert Ray's hostilities with Edward Slegge (q.v.) and his sons. Rust admitted to having said 'that he [Roger Slegge] and such other as will sue forth process for such matters as be determinable within the town of Cambridge is not worthy to enjoy the liberty of the same', a view in accordance with the terms of the freemen's oath, although the Slegges clearly had grounds for complaining of bias against them in the mayor's court and for appealing to a higher tribunal.[6]

In October 1558 Rust purchased Cotton Hall manor for £200; the manor house was already long derelict by 1549, when it was stated to have 80 acres of land attached to it, presumably in demesne, which were let for £5 a year. In November 1564 Rust performed his last known municipal service as one of the Cambridge aldermen commissioned jointly with representatives of the university to settle differences between the two bodies. He made his will on 19 June 1569, leaving Cotton Hall manor to his wife for life, with remainder to his two sons. The will, although lengthy, casts no light on his character or religious outlook, but deals entirely with his extensive house and shop property; he was living at Barnwell and left his house there to his wife, who may have been a sister of the town clerk Edward Ball, 'my brother Ball', as Rust calls him. He died within a day or two of making the will and was buried on 23 June in St. Benet's church, Cambridge.[7]

[1] C. H. Cooper, *Cambridge Annals*, i. 440 and n. [2] Hatfield 207; Cooper, ii. 65. [3] Date of birth estimated from first reference. Cooper, ii. 39 n. A namesake succeeded before 1526 to part of the manor of Garnons, Essex, as kinsman and heir of John Fermor, *LP Hen. VIII*, iv, xx; C142/40/117, 62/69. [4] Cooper, ii. 108, 110; *CPR*, 1548-9, p. 240; 1553, p. 417; 1560-3, p. 406. [5] *Churchwardens' Accts. of St. Mary the Great, Cambridge*, ed. Foster, 84, 90, 118, 120-1; J. Lamb, *Letters from ms Lib. of C.C.C. Cambridge*, 75-76; Downing Coll. Camb. Bowtell mss Liber Rationalis 1510-60, 1515 acct. [6] Cooper, ii, 36, 43; St.Ch.4/2/56; C1/1382/25, 27. [7] *APC*, vii. 161; Cooper, ii. 39-40; J. M. Gray, *Notes on Camb. Mayors*, 25; Cambridge Guildhall reg. bk. 1539-82, ff. 235-8v.

D.F.C.

RUTHALL, Thomas (by 1506-54 or later), of Moulsoe, Bucks.

PRESTON 1554 (Apr.)

b. by 1506, 1st s. of Richard Ruthall of Moulsoe by Agnes, da. and h. of William Hobbes. *educ.* L. Inn, adm. 12 May 1526. ?*m.* Elizabeth, da. of John Barnard of St. Helen's, London. *suc.* fa. 1525/28.[1]

Thomas Ruthall's father was an officer of the bishopric of Durham under his brother Thomas, who was bishop from 1509 until his death in 1523. The family came from Gloucestershire, but Richard Ruthall settled at Moulsoe in Buckinghamshire; he was escheator for Bedfordshire and Buckinghamshire in 1524–5, and died at Moulsoe soon after-wards. His widow died on 20 July 1528 and her inquisition post mortem, taken a year later, records an agreement, dated 19 Aug. 1528, whereby Thomas Ruthall disposed of all his interest in Moulsoe and Stony Stratford to the father of John Marshe*. Thomas Ruthall is said to have been his uncle's heir as well, but this lacks confirmation. During his father's lifetime Ruthall was appointed a trustee for the lands of John, 4th Lord Lumley, along with various Durham notables.[2]

Little else has come to light about Thomas Ruthall. He was specially admitted to Lincoln's Inn early in 1526 and a year-and-a-half later he and two others were each fined 10s. for ravishing a woman at the *Antelope* in Holborn during Lammas vacation. In May 1549 he received a 21-year lease of the former endowment of St. Nicholas's chantry at Halsall, in Lancashire, and it was presumably this interest combined with the marriage of his sister Mary into the Charnock family of Charnock Hall that accounts for his return for Preston to the second Marian Parliament. The Journal does not mention Ruthall. If he made a will it has not been found.[3]

[1] Date of birth estimated from age at mother's i.p.m., C142/80/89. *Vis. Bucks.* ed. Metcalfe, 38; *Vis. Bucks.* (Harl. Soc. lviii), 208–9; *Vis. Glos.* (Harl Soc. xxi), 203; *Recs. Bucks.* iii. 167n. [2] W. Hutchinson, *Durham,* i. 400n; *LP Hen. VIII,* i, iii; *DNB* (Ruthall, Thomas); Sheahan, *Bucks.* 569; C142/80/89; *CPR,* 1553–4, p. 157. [3] *Black Bk. L. Inn,* i. 218; J. B. Watson, 'Lancs. gentry 1529–58' (London Univ. M.A. thesis, 1959), 563; Pink and Beaven, *Parl. Rep. Lancs.* 142; *PRO Lists,* xiv. 31; *VCH Lancs.* iii. 191n.

A.D.

RUTTER, William (by 1488–1541), of Southwark, Surr.

EAST GRINSTEAD 1529

b. by 1488. *m.* Elizabeth (?Lowe), 1s. 2da.[1]
Yeoman of the chandry by 1509; churchwarden, St. Margaret's, Southwark 1516–18; serjeant of the scullery by 1520.[2]

William Rutter's origins and early life are obscure. He had entered the Household by the death of Henry VII, whose funeral he attended as a yeoman, as he did the subsequent coronation. He made his career in the Household for the next two decades; he accompanied Henry VIII to the Field of Cloth of Gold but appears not to have done so 12 years later to the meeting with Francis I, perhaps because he had by then given up his post. In 1534 he leased, from Bishop Capon of Bangor, the *Tabard* in Southwark, where he had been living for some time, and he passed the remainder of his life as an innkeeper: as well as the *Tabard* he had an interest in a property called the *Horse's Head.* It is tempting to imagine that he accommodated some of his parliamentary colleagues at either or both of these estab-

lishments. His daughter Agnes was to marry William Harris II*, a Member for Maldon in the Parliament of 1536.[3]

Rutter's election to the Parliament of 1529 may have been the work of the King's brother-in-law, the Duke of Suffolk, who had a house in Southwark. Although he was not a stranger to the Sussex borough that returned him, as he owned a house in East Grinstead and his brother Thomas lived there, such personal links would hardly have sufficed to procure his election in a borough belonging to the duchy of Lancaster: he may have been helped by George Payne, an influential local gentleman and servant to Sir John Gage, one of the knights for Sussex in 1529, who was apparently to be charged with Rutter's wages. Presumably Rutter sat for East Grinstead again in 1536, in accordance with the King's request for the re-election of the previous Members, and if so he doubtless supported the bill for the enlargement of St. Margaret's churchyard, Southwark, enacted in that Parliament (28 Hen. VIII, c.31): earlier in the reign he had been a churchwarden of St. Margaret's and more recently he had contributed towards the purchase of Lord Ferrer's Place as an extension of the churchyard. Whether he reappeared in the Commons in 1539 is not known, as most of the names of the Members are again lost.[4]

Rutter made his will on 22 Oct. 1540, leaving his place of burial to the discretion of his wife. After several small bequests he left to his son William, who was to remain in her custody until he came of age, a sum of £50 and property in Oxfordshire and East Grinstead: he also made provision for his wife, two married daughters, sons-in-law, kinsmen and servants. His brother Thomas was to receive 20s., a horse and several small sums owing to Rutter, who added 'Also I will that the executors of George Payne [who had died in 1538] do pay to my brother Thomas Rutter 10s. for my wages when I was burgess'. He appointed his wife executrix and his 'brother' Edward Lowe (or in his absence John Smith of the *Vine*) overseer of the will, which was proved on 8 Oct. 1541, seven days after Rutter's burial at St. Saviour's, Southwark. His son may have been the William Rutter committed to the Marshalsea for uttering seditious words against the future bishop of Bath and Wells, Gilbert Bourne, at a sermon preached by Bourne at Paul's Cross in August 1553.[5]

[1] Date of birth estimated from first reference. PCC 34 Alenger. [2] *LP Hen. VIII,* i, iii, iv; *Surr. Arch. Colls.* xiii. 28–35. [3] *LP Hen. VIII,* i, iii, iv; *Surr. Arch. Colls.* xiii. 28–35; PCC 34 Alenger. [4] *Suss. Rec. Soc.* lvi. 136; *Surr. Arch. Colls.* xiii. 28–35; PCC 34 Alenger. [5] PCC 34 Alenger; Greater London RO, P 92/SAV/359; SP11/13, f. 119.

R.J.W.S.

RUYNON (REYNION), Richard *alias* **Robert** (by 1478–?1521), of Shepton Mallet and Wells, Som.

WELLS 1512,[1] 1515[2]

b. by 1478.[3]

Jt. (with John Pole †) bailiff, liberties of bp. of Bath and Wells, Som. and bp.'s bailiff, Wells Dec. 1499–1511, sole 1511–?*d.*; keeper, Evercreech park, Som. Dec. 1499; member of the Twenty-Four, Wells 1512–*d.*[4]

Nothing has been discovered about Richard Ruynon's parentage. The chief branch of a family of his name was established at Bickford in Compton Martin after moving from Axbridge in the 15th century. Although Richard Ruynon was not mentioned in the will of William Ruynon of Compton Martin, who died in 1512, he may have been a younger brother or at least a kinsman, since he lived and worked in the same part of the county.[5]

Ruynon had become an administrative official in the service of the bishop of Bath and Wells before the turn of the century. He may have owed his appointment to the favour of John Pole with whom he shared his two bailiwicks, since the Ruynon family owned property near Pole's home in West Harptree; the terms of the grant ensured that Ruynon was Pole's assistant, forbidding him to act without Pole's consent or to take any fees or profits as long as Pole lived (perhaps by way of compensation, he received the parkership of Evercreech at the same time). In 1501 Ruynon acted as attorney to deliver seisin of Goathurst manor and property in Wells in a settlement on behalf of John and Mary Paulet. It was in an official capacity that he witnessed the wills of Bishop King in 1503 and of Thomas Beaumont, archdeacon of Wells, four years later. At that date Ruynon was living at Shepton Mallet where in 1505 he was to be associated with other leading inhabitants in founding a guild of the Holy Trinity, St. Mary and St. John. In the general pardon which he obtained in 1510 he was described as Richard Ruynon *alias* Robert Ruynon, gentleman, of Shepton Mallet, Emborrow, and Wells.[6]

The death of Pole in 1511 marked the beginning of greater opportunities for Ruynon. On 9 Jan. 1512, as bailiff of Wells, he was admitted to the freedom and elected to a vacancy in the Twenty-Four: at the same time, having presented the sheriff's precept for the election, he was himself chosen to sit in the Parliament of 1512 at the town's usual wage of 12*d.* a day. In 1513, a year in which there was no session of Parliament, Ruynon was ordered by the Twenty-Four to reply to articles against him under penalty of expulsion. Whatever the nature of his offence, it did not prevent him from being elected for Parliament again in 1515 in response to the King's letter asking

for the return of the same men as before. Ruynon died before 13 Sept. 1521 when another was elected to the Twenty-Four in his place.[7]

[1] Wells act bk. 2, p. 266. [2] Ibid. 2, p. 280. [3] Date of birth estimated from first reference. [4] Wells act bk. 2, p. 266; *HMC Wells*, ii. 157. [5] *Vis. Som.* (Harl. Soc. xi), 95–96; *Som. Med. Wills* (Som. Rec. Soc. xix), 155; *Som. Wills from Exeter* (Som. Rec. Soc. lxii), 137. [6] *HMC Wells*, ii. 157, 183, 236; *CCR, 1476–85*, no. 109; 1500–9, no. 146; *CPR, 1494–1509*, p. 418; *Som. Med. Wills*, 46, 113; *LP Hen. VIII*, i; Collinson, *Som.* ii. 133, 141, 157; P. H. Hembry, *Bps. Bath and Wells 1540–1640*, p. 23. [7] *Som. Med. Wills*, 155; Wells act bk. 2, pp. 266, 279, 304.

M.K.D.

RYNGELEY, Sir Edward (by 1497–1543), of Knowlton and Sandwich, Kent.

DUNHEVED 1529

b. by 1497, s. of one Ryngeley of (?Tipton), Staffs. *m.* by 1518, Jane, da. of Thomas Peyton, wid. of John Langley of Knowlton, *s.p.* Kntd. 1 July 1522.[1]

Gent. usher by Dec. 1521; master of the ordnance 1523; bailiff, Sandwich 1524–30; j.p. Kent 1526–*d.*; marshal, Calais 22 Nov. 1530–6 Oct. 1535, comptroller 29 Apr. 1539–*d.*; commr. coastal defences, Kent 1539.[2]

Sir Edward Ryngeley's parentage is unknown. As he came from a minor Staffordshire family he may have been a son of William Ryngeley, gentleman, of Tipton, who witnessed a deed in 1506. He was also perhaps a protégé of a magnate powerful in both Staffordshire and Kent, the 3rd Duke of Buckingham, since his career was to be linked with those of two of Buckingham's sons-in-law, George Neville, 6th Lord Bergavenny, and Thomas Howard, Earl of Surrey and later 3rd Duke of Norfolk. Ryngeley established himself in Kent through his marriage with the widow of a local gentleman and through purchase of land. In 1521 he obtained the reversion of the stewardship of Dover castle, and of the keepership of a nearby warren, but on the death of their holders his entry was stopped by Sir Edward Guildford*, the warden of the Cinque Ports, who claimed letters patent granting the offices to himself; for six years Ryngeley was in his own view wrongfully dispossessed before he took the matter to the Star Chamber, with what result is not known. His appointment to another post in the gift of the crown, the bailiwick of Sandwich, went no more smoothly, for a series of disputes with the townsmen prevented him from exercising it, and in 1530 he agreed to sell it to them for £100.[3]

In 1520 Ryngeley accompanied Henry VIII to the Field of Cloth of Gold and jousted at the tournament held in honour of Francis I at Guisnes. Two years later he served with some distinction in Brittany under Surrey's command and was knighted by him on the capture of Morlaix: he served again under Surrey in the following year, this time on the northern marches against Scotland, where his skill in mining and gunnery brought him to the notice of Wolsey. In 1528 he was put on an important commission to survey the defences of Calais and he signed the reports submitted to the Council. His employment on this commission and his connexion with Surrey, now Duke of Norfolk, made Ryngeley a likely choice for election to Parliament in 1529, but his disputes with Sir Edward Guildford and at Sandwich doubtless precluded his return for a constituency in Kent: his place in the House for a Cornish borough, to which he was a complete stranger, he may have owed to one of the knights for Cornwall on this occasion, Richard Grenville I, whose family possessed interests both there and in Calais. Barely a year after his election Ryngeley was appointed marshal of Calais, doubtless with the approval if not at the instance of Norfolk and his brother-in-law the 2nd Lord Berners, the deputy of the town. As the office was not one to be exercised by deputy, Ryngeley must have been often absent from Parliament: it was probably on account of Berners's fatal illness in the spring of 1534 that he missed the whole of the sixth session. In 1535 he handed over the marshalship to Grenville and so was able to attend the final session (Feb.–Apr. 1536) in the course of which legislation for Calais was enacted: two weeks before the session opened he wrote to Cromwell of his intention to cross to England, presumably to speak in the House on the bill, and he probably did so as he is known to have been in the country on the day the Parliament was dissolved. He was also available for its successor of June 1536, to which he is likely to have been elected again for Dunheved in accordance with the King's request for the return of the previous Members.[4]

Ryngeley had got on well with Berners, whose will he witnessed, but he was not so fortunate in the new deputy, Viscount Lisle, with whom he soon quarrelled. The antagonism between the two may have influenced Ryngeley's decision to sell his office to Grenville, who was related to Lisle, and to quit Calais for Kent. He thanked Lisle for saying that he was not a little sorry to see Ryngeley go, but he was not sorry himself: 'My blunt fashion has served me enough hitherto, and I trust it will do as long as I live. If I have been blunt to you at any time, it has been for your honour, for I never meant worse to you than to myself'. Lisle was not alone in his dislike of Ryngeley's plain speaking; his factor summed it up by saying that the marshal had a large mouth. Cranmer, however, had formed a favourable opinion of him and was able to work with him in Kent. In 1539 Ryngeley was entrusted with the erection of new fortifications on the Downs and during that summer he obtained the comptroller-

ship of Calais, to the consternation of Lisle, whose dislike of him had not lessened with separation: on the other hand, Cromwell's regard for Ryngeley had progressed in step with his doubts about Lisle, and it was as Cromwell's man that Ryngeley returned to Calais. He may have had a further taste of Parliament that year—most of the Members' names are lost—but if he was elected his duties on the Downs and at Calais must have made him again mainly an absentee. He survived the downfall of Cromwell and retained the comptrollership until his death. He is not known to have sat in the last but one of Henry VIII's Parliaments, that of 1542, when his earlier association with Cromwell and Norfolk might have told against him.[5]

That Ryngeley had not shared Cromwell's religious outlook is suggested by his treatment of the sacramentaries at Calais. This earned him the censure of Foxe, whose charge that he did not know 'a B from a battledore, nor even a letter of the book' was not unfair comment on one who admitted that he could neither read nor write: after his rough handling of her, Thomas Broke's* wife told him 'the King's slaughterhouse found wrong when you were made a gentleman', and his death three years later was hailed by some as divine retribution. Ryngeley made his will on 24 July 1543, providing for his wife, kinsmen and servants, and naming Thomas Boys*, whose brother his sister had married, one of the executors and Cranmer supervisor. He died not long after making his will, for Anthony Rous* succeeded him as comptroller on 28 Aug. Ryngeley was buried, as he had wished to be, at Sandwich.[6]

[1] Date of birth estimated from marriage. *Vis. Kent* (Harl. Soc. xlii), 66; *Kent Recs.* vii. p. xii; Req. 2/11/188; C1/563/40; *Chron. Calais* (Cam. Soc. xxxv), 31. [2] *LP Hen. VIII*, ii, iv, v, viii, xiii, xiv, xvi–xviii; P. T. J. Morgan, 'The govt. of Calais 1485–1558' (Oxf. Univ. D.Phil. thesis, 1966), 295, 296. [3] *Wm. Salt Arch. Soc.* xii. 53; xv. 6, 29, 107; (ser. 3) 1928, p. 115; *LP Hen. VIII*, iii–xix; St.Ch.2/32/135. [4] *LP Hen. VIII*, iii–x; *Chron. Calais*, pp. xli, 31–32, 164. [5] *Chron. Calais*, 138, 164, 196; *LP Hen. VIII*, xi–xix. [6] Foxe, *Acts and Mons.* v. 516, 519–20; *LP Hen. VIII*, xix, xx; Canterbury prob. reg. C19, ff. 7v–12 ptd. *Test Cant.* ed. Duncan, 285–6.

A.D.

RYTHER (RYDER), John (by 1514–52), of London.

COLCHESTER 1547

b. by 1514, prob. s. of Nicholas Ryther ?of Castle Hedingham, Essex by w. Margaret. *educ.* ?Queens', Camb. pens. 1517–21. *m.* (1) Margaret; (2) Mary, at least 3s. 3da.[1]

Commr. tenths of spiritualities, Suff. 1535, subsidy, royal household 1547, relief 1550; comptroller, household of Elizabeth, dowager Countess of Oxford by 1537, of 16th Earl of Oxford in 1542; receiver, forfeited possessions of Cromwell 1540; cofferer, household of Prince Edward by 1541–7, royal household 1547–d.; receiver and chamberlain, ct. gen. surveyors of the King's lands by 1545.[2]

John Ryther came of an old established Yorkshire family, which took its name from its main seat at Ryther in the West Riding. It is probable that he was the son of Nicholas Ryther, a servant of John de Vere, 13th Earl of Oxford, in 1490, and of Margaret Ryther 'the elder', servant to the earl's widow. In 1537 the countess left the elder Margaret Ryther, 'for the true and faithful service that she of long continuance hath done to me', 100 marks, two silver-gilt salts and much linen and tapestry. To her comptroller of household John Ryther she left silver worth £11 6s.8d., to his wife Margaret some linen and bedding, to her goddaughter Elizabeth Ryther £5 and to a younger John Ryther the same sum; Margaret Ryther the elder and John Ryther were among the executors of the will. By her own will of 1542 this Margaret Ryther, then a widow, appointed her son John sole executor: she made bequests of silver and linen to other named relatives and charitable gifts to churches in Wakefield, Yorkshire, and at Castle Hedingham and Earls Colne, Essex, the last two being seats of the De Vere family.[3]

Nothing is known of Ryther's early years. Of an age with the 14th Earl, he was doubtless reared to service in the household and may have been the 'John Rider' who was a pensioner at Queens' College, Cambridge from 1517 to 1521. The year 1537, which saw the death of the countess and the birth of Prince Edward, was the occasion of Ryther's entry into the royal service as well as of his growing employment in public affairs. In 1539 he was commissioned to report to Cromwell on the alleged embezzlement by one of the abbot's servants of the jewelry of Colchester abbey; it was perhaps as a consequence of this assignment that he himself purchased £25 worth of the abbey's 'household stuff' at the end of that year. The fall of the minister in the following one brought Ryther his first important post: in August 1540 he was appointed receiver of all Cromwell's forfeited possessions and keeper of his principal house. His fee for this office was upwards of £35 a year plus one per cent of the 'issues', and in 1543 he received an additional £200, perhaps as a gratuity on the completion of a long and difficult assignment. The John Ryther who raised a company of eight billmen to serve in the French war of 1544 was probably a namesake, for he himself must have been fully occupied with the day-to-day financing of the expedition as one of the five persons authorized in May to purchase provisions for the army on the strength of bills which the treasurer for the war, Sir Richard Rich, was instructed to honour.[4]

In 1544 Ryther bought land in Essex from the Earl of Oxford and the crown and in the following year a good deal more in Suffolk, some of which he soon resold. His appointment as cofferer of the Household on Edward VI's accession was followed by considerable rewards in land and money, including an annuity of 50 marks granted in July 1550. It also brought him a seat in Parliament, the choice being evidently dictated by his own and his family's long connexion with the earls of Oxford. He owned only a small amount of property in Essex, but the 16th Earl could certainly dispose of at least one of the Colchester seats and Ryther would not have lacked support from the court: he was, for instance, a 'most especial friend' of the Protector Somerset's brother-in-law (Sir) Clement Smith*, who named him an executor. In the Commons Ryther presumably looked after the crown's financial interest, but neither of the bills committed to him, to diswarren common land and to prevent regrating, forestalling and engrossing, was of much consequence.[5]

Ryther made his nuncupative will on 5 Oct. 1552 and died six days later. He left £100 to each of five named children and provided for the marriage of his two eldest sons to the two daughters of a Worcestershire landowner, John Pritchard, both of whose wardships he had purchased in 1551. Among the executors were his second wife Mary and John Wiseman* of Great Canfield. Ryther's eldest son John was about 19 at the time of his father's death: in recognition of the dead man's services to the crown the son was granted his own wardship and marriage as free gifts and in the following reign he was awarded an annuity of £37.[6]

On the list of Members of the Parliament of 1547 as revised for the final session of January 1552 Ryther's name is erased and marked 'mortuus'. As he did not die until the following October, after the Parliament had been dissolved, the emendation must have been made late in 1552 or early in 1553 and is probably to be connected with the nomination of Members to Edward VI's second Parliament.[7]

[1] Date of birth estimated from first certain reference. *Dugdale's Vis. Yorks.* ed. Clay, ii. 458; PCC 8 Spert, 31 Powell. [2] *LP Hen. VIII*, viii, xvi, xx; *CPR*, 1553, p. 367; information from Susan Flower; *Lit. Rems. Edw. VI*, p. xxxii; E315/523, passim; *APC*, ii. passim; W. C. Richardson, *Ct. Augmentations*, 275n. [3] *Household Bks. of John Duke of Norfolk and Thomas Earl of Surrey* (Roxburghe Club), passim; *Trans. Essex Arch. Soc.* n.s. xx. 9–16; *Archaeologia*, lxvi. 319; PCC 8 Spert. [4] *LP Hen. VIII*, xiv, xv, xvii, xix. [5] Ibid. xix, xx; *CPR*, 1547–8, p. 202; 1549–51, p. 292; 1550–3, pp. 40, 439; 1553, p. 137; *CJ*, i. 16–17. [6] PCC 31 Powell; *CPR*, 1553–4, pp. 89–90. [7] Hatfield 207.

D.F.C.

SABINE, William (by 1491–1543), of Ipswich, Suff.

IPSWICH 1539[1]

b. by 1491, s. of John Sabine. *m.* (1) Alice; (2) Margaret, wid. of James Cole.[2]

King's armourer by 1512–*d.*; capt. *Sabine* 1512, *Rose Galley* 1514, *Les Bark* 1529; serjeant-at-arms 1518–*d.*; weigher, port of Ipswich 1525–9, member of the Twenty-Four 1531, bailiff 1536–7, 1540–1, j.p. 1536–7, 1540–1, portman 1537–*d.*[3]

Little is known about William Sabine's origins or upbringing. By his own admission to Wolsey, he was 'a poor secretary', but whatever he perhaps lacked in literacy was no bar to his career as a ship-owner, naval commander, merchant and municipal figure. Either he or a namesake was the master of an Ipswich vessel in 1504. He is first certainly glimpsed eight years later when he captained a boat of his own called the *Sabine* in a patrol to keep the Straits of Dover free from enemy shipping. In 1513 he served in the operations off the coast of Brittany and it was he who reported Admiral Howard's death to Wolsey. After then helping to transport the royal army to France he was sent north to Scotland where he was recruited with other seamen into the Earl of Surrey's hastily mustered force and fought at Flodden. Stationed in the Channel again in 1514 he took part in the landings near Cherbourg. With the armistice with France he was named to escort Princess Mary there for her marriage to Louis XII and given the captaincy of the *Rose Galley*, but not long after he was redirected to Scottish waters as part of a show of force in support of Queen Margaret of Scotland. Henry VIII used him in 1519 to negotiate the return of the *Black Bark* from the French and when Sabine's authority to do so was queried the King wrote confirming the power of his 'well beloved' servant to act in the matter. On the outbreak of war in 1522 he was given the command of a squadron to harry the Scots. An attack led by him on Leith was successful but other engagements at sea later in the 1520s were not. The 3rd Duke of Norfolk complained to the Council in 1542 of the poor quality of the grain supplied by Sabine to the troops at Newcastle-upon-Tyne, but this complaint seems to have been the only serious blot on a war record stretching over 30 years. His service at sea was rewarded by posts at court, grants of land and other marks of royal favour.[4]

Admitted a freeman of Ipswich in 1519 Sabine co-operated with a number of other merchants there, particularly with Henry Tooley, in ventures to Bordeaux, the Baltic and Iceland. He combined trade with his discharge of the crown's weighership in the town and of municipal offices. His Membership of the Parliament of 1539 answered to his position at Ipswich, but it may well have been sponsored by the Duke of Norfolk who in that year assured Cromwell of the return of such men in

Suffolk as 'I doubt not shall serve his highness according to his pleasure'. Sabine's friendship with Ralph Sadler*, soon to be one of the principal secretaries, perhaps also promoted his return. Nothing is known about Sabine's part in the work of this Parliament which was to assent to the palace revolution from which the Howards emerged victorious. While bailiff for the second time he offered the King £41 for the former house of the Ipswich Black Friars but the sale was not completed until his term was over.[5]

By his will made on 25 Mar. 1543 Sabine bequeathed the greater part of his goods and property in Suffolk and elsewhere to his 'nephew' and heir male William Atwood, the rest being left to his wife with remainder to his sister and heir general Elizabeth. To meet various minor bequests he ordered the sale of his ship the *James* of Ipswich but she was to remain in use until then. He named Thomas Atwood *alias* Smith and William West executors and Sir Ralph Sadler supervisor: among the witnesses were Richard Bryde *alias* Byrde* and John Gosnold*. Sabine died on 11 Apr. following and his widow married Thomas Maria Wingfield*.[6]

[1] N. Bacon, *Annals Ipswich*, 213. [2] Date of birth estimated from first certain reference. *Vis. Suff.* ed. Metcalfe, 2; J. G. Webb, 'Henry Tooley, merchant of early Tudor Ipswich' (London Univ. M.A. thesis, 1953), 29–32; *LP Hen. VIII*, ii; PCC 16 Alen. [3] Bacon, 205–17 passim; *LP Hen. VIII*, i, iv, xvi; C1/935/33–34. [4] *LP Hen. VIII*, i, ii, iv, xiii, xvii; J. G. Webb, *The Great Tooley of Ipswich*, 22; *Mariner's Mirror*, xli. 209–21; Add. 24435, f. 127; *Navy Recs. Soc.* x. pp. xii–xiii, xlv, 128 n1, 141–4, 154–61, 163–6. [5] *Mariner's Mirror*, xli. 218–19; C1/1175/52; I. E. Gray and W. E. Potter, *Ipswich Sch.* 31–35; *LP Hen. VIII*, xiii, xvi. [6] C1/935/33–34.

J.P.

SACHEVERELL, Sir Richard (by 1469–1534), of Newarke College, Leicester, Leics. and Ratcliffe-upon-Soar, Notts.

b. by 1469, 2nd s. of Ralph Sacheverell (*d.*28 Aug. 1488) of Morley, Derbys. by Joan, da. of John Curzon of Kedleston, Derbys. *m.* 1 May 1509, Mary, *suo jure* Baroness Botreaux, Hungerford and Molyns, da. and h. of Sir Thomas Hungerford, wid. of Edward Hastings, 2nd Lord Hastings (*d.*Nov. 1506), *s.p.* Kntd. 25 Sept. 1513.[2]

Receiver-gen. to Edward, Lord Hastings by 1498; j.p. Leics. 1509–*d.*, Bucks. 1514, Oxon. 1515; commr. subsidy, Leics. 1512, 1514, 1515, 1523, 1524, Leicester 1523; other commissions 1507–31; jt. surveyor, King's woods 1521–30; steward, master forester, feodary, duchy of Lancaster, honor of Leicester 29 June 1529–*d.*; jt. c.j. in eyre, royal forests, south of Trent 1530–*d.*[3]

Richard Sacheverell was born in Derbyshire and migrated to Leicestershire at about the time of his father's death. He is thought to have had some legal training: in 1502 he shared with several midland lawyers a grant of the wardship of Walter, son of Thomas Kebell, serjeant-at-law, and a little later he acted as trustee for a small Leicestershire landowner at Barrow, where the Hastings family held a manor.[4]

From 1498, and probably earlier, Sacheverell had been receiver-general to Lord Hastings, who died in November 1506: less than three years later Sacheverell married his widow. As stepfather to George, 3rd Lord Hastings and later 1st Earl of Huntingdon, he thus became the senior representative of the most powerful family in Leicestershire. His wife, a considerable heiress in her own right, held the baronies of Hungerford and Molyns through her father and that of Botreaux through her great-grandmother: a woman of aristocratic bearing, she aroused unfavourable comment by using her own title in preference to her late husband's, and she was generally to be found at Sacheverell's side, sharing alike in his sports and his quarrels.[5]

The quarrels were chiefly with the Greys, marquesses of Dorset, who had risen, as had the Hastings, in the service of the House of York. Both factions retained more men in arms than the law permitted and in 1516 Wolsey himself intervened by summoning the principals to appear in the Star Chamber to give bonds for good behaviour. Early in 1519 he ordered the parties to discharge their forces and to avoid the county courts and quarter sessions which were occasions for lawlessness: although this did not prevent an action for murder against Sacheverell's servants, for two years neither party attended the courts, to the great amelioration of justice. The lull was ended, according to the Greys, when Sacheverell resumed his attendance, or sent his servants in his absence, and in 1524 a riot at Leicester, a town traditionally loyal to Hastings, forcibly ejected several of the 2nd Marquess of Dorset's men. There followed a series of clashes over forest and hunting rights, and accusations of embracery, so that in 1526 the whole business reappeared in the Star Chamber. Trouble had also arisen between the Sacheverells and Lord George Grey, dean of Newarke College, which Sacheverell and his wife had made their home from well before 1525. Grey accused Sacheverell of profiting from the sale to the college of the manor of Ashley in Wiltshire and of obtaining leases without fine in the dean's absence. The matter was taken to the Council but its settlement was remitted to Bishop Longland of Lincoln: the judgement is lost but Sacheverell and his wife appear to have gone on living there until their deaths.[6]

One of the witnesses at Longland's inquiry said that Sacheverell and his friends in the last Parliament had been responsible for the college's exemption from the provisions of the Subsidy Act of 1523 (14 and 15 Hen. VIII, c.16) and another added that Roger Wigston disclaimed credit for it with the words, 'Give thanks to Master Sacheverell, for albeit I and Master [Ralph] Swillington* did as much as we might therein, it had not been gotten but by Master Sacheverell'. Swillington and Wigston had sat for Leicester; Sacheverell's own constituency is unknown but he was almost certainly a knight of the shire for Leicestershire. During the Parliament he also obtained the passage of an Act (14 and 15 Hen. VIII, c.26) to ensure his possession of Ratcliffe-upon-Soar, which he had purchased from the 3rd Duke of Buckingham in 1520 but which had come into the hands of the crown following an inquest of office after the duke's attainder. Sacheverell seems to have been on good terms with Buckingham as it was through him that the duke had transmitted a proposal for a double marriage alliance with the 4th Earl of Shrewsbury in 1516.[7]

Sacheverell may have sat in earlier Parliaments, especially those of 1512 and 1515 when he was a subsidy commissioner. His return in 1529 with Sir William Skeffington, an adherent of the Greys, may have resulted from an agreement to share the representation, but it may also have been approved by the King. In the summer of 1529 Sacheverell had given evidence in favour of the divorce before the legatine court and during the Parliament he was one of five Members who signed the petition to Pope Clement in its support.[8]

Sacheverell's career had also taken him into the field. He was treasurer of the war in 1513, when he went to France with the Earl of Shrewsbury, and in 1521, and he commanded a considerable body of horse in the north in 1522. Both he and his wife were prominent at court, and he was present at the Field of Cloth of Gold in 1520 and at the Emperor's reception in England in 1522. By that time he had also been appointed with Sir William Fitzwilliam of Milton, Northamptonshire, to the new office of surveyor of woods. His most important local appointment, to the stewardship of the honor of Leicester, came to him shortly before his election to Parliament in 1529 and must have strengthened his claim to represent the shire.[9]

Sacheverell took advantage of his ascendancy to obtain various profitable leases and tenancies from both monastic and lay landlords, to some of which his title was disputed. By his will dated 29 Mar. 1534 (the last day but one of the sixth session of Parliament) he left his lands to his kinsfolk, and in particular his sisters' children, for whom he seems to have been solicitous, arranging a marriage for one of them with the wealthy Christopher Nele of Barrow and bestowing the two others on his own leading supporters John Turvile and George Vincent*. To these nieces and to a nephew he left equal shares in his property in tail male, with reversion first to the heirs of two of the nieces, Elizabeth Nele and Jane Vincent, and then to Mary Turvile's brothers, George and William Fyndern, and to another nephew, Ralph Sacheverell. Sacheverell died on 14 Apr. 1534, and was buried beside his wife, who had predeceased him by little more than a year, in Newarke College. It is not known by whom the vacancy left in the Commons was filled unless it was by William Ashby (q.v.).[10]

[1] A. H. Thompson, *Hosp. Newarke*, 157, 172. [2] Aged 60 and more in 1529, *LP Hen. VIII*, iv. *Vis. Notts.* (Harl. Soc. iv), 163; *CIPM Hen. VII*, i. 423; *Som. Rec. Soc.* xxvii. 177-8; *CP*, vi. 375; PCC 15 Hogen. [3] C1/569/3; *CPR, 1494-1509*, p. 561; *LP Hen. VIII*, i-v; *Statutes*, iii. 84, 115, 168; W. C. Richardson, *Tudor Chamber Admin.* 260, 261, 265; Somerville, *Duchy*, i. 564, 568, 570. [4] *LP Hen. VIII*, iv.; *CPR, 1494-1509*, p. 279; *CIPM Hen. VII*, ii. 852. [5] Thompson, 143-5, 171-2 et passim. [6] *LP Hen. VIII*, ii, iii; *HMC Shrewsbury and Talbot*, ii. 3; St.Ch.2/12/260 seq.; Thompson, 143-96 passim. [7] Thompson, 157, 172; C. Rawcliffe, *The Staffords, Earls of Stafford and Dukes of Buckingham 1394-1521*, pp. 136, 142; *HMC Shrewsbury and Talbot*, ii. 338. [8] *LP Hen. VIII*, iv. [9] Ibid. i-v. [10] C1/622/25; 142/56/35; St.Ch.2/3/266 seq.; *HMC Hastings*, i. 26, 95; *LP Hen. VIII*, iii; G. F. Farnham, *Leics. Med. Peds.* 66; *VCH Leics.* iv. 429; PCC 15 Hogen.

S.M.T.

SACKVILLE, Christopher (by 1519-58/59), of Albourne and Worth, Suss.

HEYTESBURY 1558

b. by 1519, 2nd s. of John Sackville I* of Withyham and Chiddingly by 1st w. Margaret, da. of Sir William Boleyn of Blickling, Norf.; bro. of John II* and Richard Sackville II*. *m.* by 1541, Constance, da. of Thomas Culpeper of Bedgebury, Kent, at least 2s. inc. John† 1da.[1]

Gent. pens. 1540-d.[2]

Christopher Sackville perhaps owed his appointment at court to kinship with William Baron Sandys, who died not long after the establishment of the gentlemen pensioners. Most of what has come to light about Sackville refers to his household duties, for which he received £46 13s.4d. a year and, from 1551, an annuity of £10. In 1544 he served in Henry VIII's last French war and in the following reign he presumably fought in Scotland. In 1547 he leased 240 acres in Hartfield, Sussex, with one of his brothers-in-law, John Ashburnham I*, and 11 years later he granted his share to another, (Sir) Nicholas Pelham*. In 1551 he acquired from his father-in-law a manor in Kent which he straightway conveyed to George Sydenham, but the lands settled on him by his father in 1552 remained in his possession and passed to his descendants. Five years later his father left him the contents of Buckhurst in remainder, but he did not live to enjoy them.[3]

Sackville sat with his nephew Thomas in the last Parliament of Mary's reign. He may have hoped for a nomination at East Grinstead, but five days before the election there he was returned for Heytesbury. His election with Henry Partridge, another Household officer, was probably the work of the sheriff, Sir Walter Hungerford*, until recently a gentleman pensioner like Sackville; and of Henry Wheeler, a gentleman of the privy chamber who was lord of the manor. Nothing is known about Sackville's part in Parliament, but during its prorogation he and Jerome Fermor† gave surety in £50 that Robert Eyre of Gray's Inn should surrender to the Fleet at the beginning of the Michaelmas term. Two weeks later, on 27 Aug., Sackville made his will, naming his wife executrix and Sir Nicholas Pelham overseer. He presumably attended the second session of the Parliament, as he was present at Queen Mary's funeral on 14 Dec., but he must have died shortly afterwards, probably of the disease then widespread, as his will was proved on 28 Feb. 1559. He was buried in St. Sepulchre, Holborn.[4]

[1] Date of birth estimated from first reference. *Vis. Suss.* (Harl. Soc. lxxxix), 95; *Vis. Kent* (Harl. Soc. lxxv), 95; C. J. P. Phillips, *Sackville Fam.* i. 122. [2] *The Gen.* xxx. 21; xxxiv. 81; Stowe 571, f. 31v; LC2/4/2; E407/1/1. [3] *LP Hen. VIII*, xix, xx; *CPR, 1550-3*, p. 8; 1557-8, p. 345; Phillips, i. 125; Hasted, *Kent*, v. 328; PCC 48 Chaynay. [4] *APC*, v. 328; PCC 46 Welles; LC2/4/2; *Vis. Suss.* 95.

R.L.D.

SACKVILLE, John I (by 1484-1557), of Mount Bures, Essex, Withyham and Chiddingly, Suss.

EAST GRINSTEAD 1542

b. by 17 Mar. 1484, 1st s. of Richard Sackville† of Withyham by Isabel, da. of John Digges of Barham, Kent; bro. of Richard Sackville I*. *m.* (1) by 1507, Margaret, da. of Sir William Boleyn of Blickling, Norf., 3s. Christopher*, John II* and Richard Sackville II* 3da.; (2) by 1534, Anne, da. of Humphrey Torrell of Willingale Doe, Essex, *s.p. suc.* fa. 28 July 1524.[1]

J.p. Essex 1513-24, Suss. 1524-d.; commr. subsidy, Essex 1523, 1524, Suss. 1546, loan, Essex 1524, musters, Suss. 1539, relief 1550; other commissions 1530-d.; sheriff, Surr. and Suss. 1527-8, 1540-1, 1546-7.[2]

John Sackville's father held lands in both Sussex and Essex, but Sackville's early domicile and public service in Essex probably arose from his marriage into the Boleyn family. From 1524, when he came into his inheritance, he lived in Sussex and his career was thereafter confined to that county and Surrey. The John Sackville of Calais, 'late soldier, late of Withyham, Sussex', pardoned in 1509, was his uncle.[3]

Sackville's return for a Sussex borough to the Parliament of 1542 followed immediately on the end of his second term as sheriff. The suggestion made in the *Official Return* that the borough was East Grinstead is borne out by the appearance among the electors' names on the indenture concerned (which is fragmentary and lacks the name of the other Member) of one which is found on several later indentures for East Grinstead. It was there, too, that Sackville, as the leading gentleman of the district, could have been expected to find a seat. The loss of returns leaves it in doubt whether Sackville had sat for the borough in 1539 or would do so again in 1545, but the shrievalty which kept him out of the first Edwardian Parliament he doubtless used on behalf of his sons John II*, who came in for East Grinstead, and Richard II*, elected at Chichester, as well as for his son-in-law Nicholas Pelham, who sat for Arundel.[4]

Apart from sharing with his brother-in-law Sir Thomas Boleyn in the presentation to a prebend of St. Stephen's chapel, Westminster, Sackville seems to have derived no benefit from his first marriage, and he did little on his own account to augment his inheritance. It is thus tempting to see behind some transactions of the 1540s the acquisitiveness for which his son Richard was to become notorious. In 1541 the pair bound themselves to perform an award made by Thomas Bromley I* and William Whorwood* governing the manumission of one John Selwyn of Friston, Sussex, gentleman, whom they claimed as their bondman; a year later they sold to Selwyn for £6 13s.4d. the wardship and marriage of the heir of John Bray of Westdean, Sussex, and the custody of the manor of Westdean which was held of the elder Sackville by knight's service. Their acquisition in 1544 for over £900 of ex-monastic property in Surrey, Sussex, London and elsewhere, and the profitable disposal of parts of it within the next two years, certainly fore-shadowed Richard Sackville's own operations in the land market.[5]

After making settlements of his property Sackville passed his closing years at Chiddingly, and it was there that he made his will on 1 July 1556. He bequeathed sums to the poor of five Sussex villages, and of Mount Bures in Essex, and asked for candles at his funeral, a requiem mass for himself and prayers for his parents. His wife was to have the household goods at Chiddingly, with remainder to the three daughters, all his livestock, including sheep, which she could give 'to those that she findeth the most friendship in', and the contents of Buck-hurst, the house at Withyham of which only the gatehouse survives. The executors were the widow and Sir Nicholas Pelham. Sackville died on 27 Sept. 1557 and was buried at Withyham on 5 Oct. The execution of the will was to be successfully chal-lenged by Sir Richard Sackville who, for what reason is unknown, had not been mentioned in it;

he was granted the administration in October 1559.[6]

[1] Birthday given as St. Edward's eve (17 Mar.) in will: year of birth estimated from age at fa.'s i.p.m., C142/42/128. Collins, *Peerage* (1812), ii. 103–7; C142/116/75; *Vis. Essex* (Harl. Soc. xiii), 116; Mill Stephenson, *Mon. Brasses*, 141. [2] *LP Hen. VIII*, i–v, vii–ix, xiii, xiv, xx, xxi; *CPR*, 1547–8, p. 76; 1553, p. 359; 1553–4, pp. 28, 37. [3] *LP Hen. VIII*, i, iv. [4] C219/18B/98. [5] *LP Hen. VIII*, iv, xx, xxi; *Suss. Arch. Colls.* xl. 21; NRA 10279 (Suss. Arch. Soc. Holman mss CH 315–19). [6] PCC 48 Chaynay; C142/116/75; *Machyn's Diary* (Cam. Soc. xlii), 153–4, 360.

R.J.W.S.

SACKVILLE, John II (by 1523–47/52)

EAST GRINSTEAD 1547*

b. by 1523, 3rd s. of John Sackville I* by 1st w., and bro. of Christopher* and Richard Sackville II*. *educ.* I. Temple, adm. 11 Feb. 1540.[1]

John Sackville was admitted to the Inner Temple at the suit of his brother Richard and was pardoned all offices and vacations on payment of 40s. It is possible that he was intended to occupy the family estates in Essex, as his father had once done: in 1544 he joined his father in buying from Richard Duke* a property in the county called 'Le Almarye' in West Bergholt. Three years later, after the acces-sion of Edward VI, Sackville made a brief incursion into public life when, together with his brother Richard and his brother-in-law Nicholas Pelham, he entered the first Parliament of the reign. His election at East Grinstead was undoubtedly the work of his father, who was sheriff at the time and whose home at Withyham was some six miles from the borough, which he himself had represented in the last Parliament but one. The career thus begun was to be cut short by death, although how quickly is not known. A terminal date is provided by the list of Members as revised for the final session of the Parliament, which began in January 1552: on this list he is replaced by George Darrell. No will has been found and it is not known whether Sackville had married.[2]

[1] Date of birth estimated from purchase of property in 1544. C. J. Phillips, *Sackville Fam.* i. 119, 126–50; *Vis. Essex* (Harl. Soc. xiii), 29. [2] *Cal. I.T. Recs.* i. 126; *LP Hen. VIII*, xix; Hatfield 207.

R.J.W.S.

SACKVILLE, Richard I (by 1501–45/46), of Westhampnett, Suss.

ARUNDEL 1529

b. by 1501, 2nd s. of Richard Sackville†, and bro. of John I*. *educ.* G. Inn. *m.* Agnes, da. of Thomas Thatcher of Westhampnett, 1da.[1]
Lent reader, G. Inn 1529.
Commr. subsidy, Suss. 1523, 1524; j.p. 1524–*d.*; steward, Arundel college, Arundel, Suss. by 1531; high steward, Arundel castle 1536; steward, Suss. lands of William Fitzalan, 11th Earl of Arundel 1536.[2]

Richard Sackville was a lawyer. As a young man he assisted his father in estate management and county affairs, while his elder brother resided on the family estates in Essex. In 1522 he became an 'ancient' of Gray's Inn and two years later he was named to the Sussex bench, on which he remained active until his death. He was closely associated with Thomas and William Fitzalan, 10th and 11th Earls of Arundel, from whom he received a succession of offices in their gift. His origin and connexions made him a natural choice for a seat in Parliament, and his election in 1529 was probably not his first, although the loss of names for preceding Parliaments leaves this in doubt. His return in 1529 may have been encouraged from another quarter, for through his brother's marriage he was related to the Boleyns. He probably sat for Arundel again in the next Parliament, in June 1536, when the King asked for the return of the previous Members, and may have continued to do so in succeeding cnes for which the names of the Members are lost. Nothing is known of his part in the proceedings of the House.[3]

In 1529 Sackville's fellow-Member was another Fitzalan client, Thomas Prestall, with whom he was soon on bad terms. Early in the life of the Parliament he took Prestall to court in an attempt to break a lease of 600 acres of land which Prestall held from Arundel college. The master and fellows had made a lease to Sackville on the understanding that he would invalidate Prestall's interest in the property. This he failed to do, and it was perhaps in an attempt to recoup his costs that he sold the valueless lease to Thomas Devenish, from whom it passed to a John Ledes who in 1549 was still seeking to establish its validity. In 1537 Sackville had lost a dispute with Devenish over property at Westhampnett which was leased from the Earl of Arundel and which may have been part of Devenish's payment to him for the disputed college lease.[4]

Sackville was gradually eclipsed in local affairs by his more eminent nephew and namesake from whom he is not easy to distinguish in that context after 1540. He was still alive at the beginning of April 1545, but within a year he had been replaced as the 12th Earl of Arundel's steward by Thomas Carpenter*. Sackville was buried at Westhampnett, where a monument was erected to his memory. His widow married John Ledes, and it may have been at her instigation that Ledes took up the matter of the college lease against Prestall. Sackville died intestate and it was not until 1587 that administration of his goods was granted to Henry Shelley of Warminghurst, who had married his only child Elizabeth.[5]

[1] Date of birth estimated from first reference. Comber, *Suss. Genealogies (Lewes)*, 286; D.G.C. Elwes, *Castles and Manors of W. Suss.* 110. [2] *LP Hen. VIII*, iii–v; C1/1291/1. [3] *G. Inn Pension Bk.* 408; *LP Hen. VIII*, xiii; C1/1292/1; E315/101, f. 55v. [4] Req.2/17/65. [5] *LP Hen. VIII*, ix–xix; Chichester corp., Recs. Three city cts. 1491–1537, ff. 41v–47v; L. Fleming, *Pagham and Suss.*, 415;

Comber, 286; Nairn and Pevsner, *Suss.* 373; W. Suss. RO, admins. B45v.

R.J.W.S.

SACKVILLE, Richard II (by 1507–66), of Ashburnham and Buckhurst, Suss. and Westenhanger, Kent.

CHICHESTER	1547
?SUSSEX	1553 (Mar.)[1]
PORTSMOUTH	1554 (Apr.)
SUSSEX	1559, 1563*

b. by 1507, 1st s. of John Sackville I* by 1st w., and bro. of Christopher* and John II*. *educ.* Camb.; I. Temple. *m.* by 1536, Winifred, da. of (Sir) John Brydges* of London, 3s. inc. Thomas* 1da. Kntd. by 17 Feb. 1549; *suc.* fa. 27 Sept. 1557.[2]
Gov. I. Temple 1558–*d.*
Escheator, Surr. and Suss. 1541–2; steward, abp. of Canterbury's Suss. manors 1544, duchy of Lancaster lands in Suss. 1549–53, 1561–*d.*; commr. chantries, Suss. 1546, 1548, relief 1550; j.p. Suss. 1547, Essex, Kent, Surr. Suss. 1558/59–*d.*; chancellor, ct. augmentations Aug. 1548–Oct. 1553, 20–23 Jan. 1554; custos rot., Suss. 1549–*d.*; ld. lt. Suss. 1550; PC 20 Nov. 1558–*d.*; under treasurer, the Exchequer Feb. 1559–*d.*[3]

Richard Sackville was nicknamed 'Fill-Sack, by reason of his great wealth and the vast patrimony which he left to his son'. On his own showing his success owed little to education, for he told Roger Ascham that before he was 14 his schoolmaster drove him 'with fear of beating from all love of learning', and although he went up to Cambridge he left without taking a degree to enter an inn of court. It was as a lawyer that he began his career and entered local administration, but as most of the references to a Richard Sackville active in Sussex during the 1530s and early 1540s are to his uncle and namesake, a servant of the earls of Arundel, little can be established about his early progress. His hard-headedness is perhaps to be discerned in the manumission of a bondman by his father and himself in 1541, as in their subsequent exploitation of their claim to knight's service; and their joint purchase in 1544 of over £900 worth of property in London, Surrey, Sussex and elsewhere, some of which they disposed of profitably in the following two years, was certainly a portentous operation, for the younger man was to make his career and fortune in the administration and disposal of ex-monastic lands.[4]

Sackville was rising 40 when he was returned as the senior Member for Chichester to the first Parliament of Edward VI's reign. Although from east Sussex, his family was well known at Chichester, where his uncle had been prominent at the local sessions, and it is possible that he had sat for the city before the death of Henry VIII; but in 1547 he enjoyed the great advantage of being the son of the sheriff, who was also a follower of the 12th Earl of Arundel. Nothing has come to light about his part in the first two sessions of this Parliament, but it was presumably as a client of Arundel's that in 1548 he was chosen to replace (Sir) Edward North* as chancellor of augmentations and about the same time given a knighthood. He did not go to the Protector Somerset's assistance during the *coup d'état* in the autumn of 1549, and was rewarded by the Earl of Warwick with increased powers in his court and with lands and a lord lieutenancy: he had probably been disturbed by the unrest in Sussex which Arundel had pacified, and it may not be without significance that it was to him as 'Mr. Chancellor' that during the next session of Parliament the bill for repressing unlawful assemblies and risings was committed after its second reading. On the arrest of the ex-Protector and the Earl of Arundel for treason in 1551, the custody of Arundel's heir with his schoolmasters and servants was entrusted to Sackville.[5]

In July 1552 Edward VI noted in his diary that Sackville had been asked to 'surcease' his chancellorship of augmentations, but the request was evidently withdrawn as he kept the office until the court was dissolved under Mary. The decision may have been the Duke of Northumberland's as part of his quest for support in his political manoeuvring. Sackville seems to have been a Member of the Parliament which Northumberland caused to meet in March 1553, for 'Mr. Chancellor' again had a bill committed to him, this time the bill that clothiers and handicraftmen should dwell in boroughs and towns, which went to him after its second reading on 17 Mar. 1553. He cannot have sat for Chichester, or for any Sussex borough, as the names of their Members are known, but as lieutenant for the county he would have been a likely choice as one of the knights of the shire whose names are lost.[6]

Sackville was prepared to follow Northumberland to the point of signing the device for the alteration of the succession, and it was probably this political misjudgment, rather than the allegations of corruption against him, which accounted for his dismissal from office in October 1553. He was compensated with an annuity of £300. Early in the following year he was briefly recalled to supervise the winding-up of the court, but this summons did not indicate a return to favour. He was, however, returned to the Parliament of April 1554 for Portsmouth, where he presumably owed his election to William Paulet, 1st Marquess of Winchester, whose son Chidiock*, captain-designate of the garrison there, had been a receiver under Sackville in augmentations: Winchester was to be one of the overseers of

Sackville's will and his heir would marry Sackville's widow. How Sackville conducted himself in this Parliament has not come to light: it was to be his only appearance there during the reign, but in 1558 he was to have a son sitting in the House.[7]

Sackville was to resume his political career under Elizabeth: appointed a Privy Councillor before the new Queen set out for London, he figured prominently in her administration until his death on 21 Apr. 1566.[8]

[1] *CJ*, i. 25. [2] Date of birth estimated from age at fa.'s i.p.m., C142/42/128. C. J. Phillips, *Sackville Fam.* i. 126–50. *Suss. Arch Colls.* xxxiii. 55–57; *Vis. Essex* (Harl. Soc. xiii), 29; *CPR*, 1548–9, p. 181; *DNB.* [3] *CPR*, 1547–8, pp. 90, 297; 1548–9, p. 181; 1553–4, p. 243; 1558–60, p. 56; Lambeth Palace, ct. rolls 1401; Somerville, *Duchy*, i. 621; W. C. Richardson, *Ct. Augmentations*, 189, 193–4; *Rep. R. Comm. of 1552* (Archs. of Brit. Hist. and Culture iii), pp. xxviii, 75. [4] R. Naunton, *Fragmenta Regalia*, ed. Arber, 55; *LP Hen. VIII*, xix–xxi. [5] *CJ*, i. 12; *CPR*, 1548–9, p. 181; *APC*, iv. 64. [6] *Lit. Rems. Edw. VI*, 432; Richardson, 339; Roy. 18C, xxiv, f. 134; *CJ*, i. 25; C219/20/125, 126. [7] *CPR*, 1554–5, p. 24; Elton, *Tudor Rev. in Govt.* 240–1; Lansd. 156(28), ff. 108–10; PCC 14 Crymes. [8] *APC*, vi. 230; C142/145/11.

R.J.W.S.

SACKVILLE, Thomas (1535/36–1608), of London.

WESTMORLAND	1558
EAST GRINSTEAD	1559
AYLESBURY	1563

b. 1535/36, prob. 1st s. of Richard Sackville II*. *educ.* 'Sullington' (?Lullington) g.s.; ?Hart Hall, Oxf.; ?Jesus, Camb.; I. Temple, adm. 1 July 1555, called; Camb. MA 1571; Oxf. incorp. 1592. *m.* 1555, Cecily, da. of (Sir) John Baker I* of London and Sissinghurst, Kent, 4s. inc. Robert† 3da.; ?1s. illegit. *suc.* fa. 21 Apr. 1566. Kntd. 8 June 1567; KG nom. 22 Apr., inst. 18 Dec. 1589. *cr.* Baron of Buckhurst 8 June 1567, Earl of Dorset 13 Mar. 1604.

J.p. Kent, Suss. 1558/59–*d.*; feodary, duchy of Lancaster, Suss. 1561; jt. ld. lt. Suss. 1569; ambassador to France 1571–2, 1591, to the Netherlands 1586, 1598; trier of petitions in the Lords, Parlts. of 1572, 1584, 1586, 1589, 1593, 1597; custos rot. Suss. 1573/74–*d.*; chief butler, England 1590; high steward, Winchester c.1590; jt. commr. of great seal Nov. 1591–May 1592; chancellor, Oxf. Univ. 1591; ld. treasurer May 1599–*d.*[2]

His father's exclusion from office under Mary did not significantly delay Thomas Sackville's entry upon public life for it was not long after his coming of age that he sat in his first Parliament. His election at the beginning of 1558 for East Grinstead, where his father wielded great influence, has the appearance of a safeguard against his failing to carry off the knighthood for Westmorland; after he had done so and entered the House as junior knight for that shire, the vacancy at East Grinstead was filled by another Sackville nominee, Thomas Farnham. The circumstances of Sackville's election for Westmorland are not made easier of explanation by the damaged state of the return, on which the surname is represented only by the fragment 'Sa...' A century ago the name was read as 'Salkeld'. The accuracy of this reading is borne out by the appearance of that name, afterwards erased and replaced by 'Sackvell', on one of the two remaining copies of the Crown Office list; the other and later copy has 'Sackveld' alone. It is thus possible that a Thomas Salkeld, presumably of the prominent Westmorland family of that name, was elected but was afterwards superseded by Sackville. What is more likely, however, is that Sackville was elected and that instead of his unfamiliar name its near counterpart was entered on the return, to be copied on the Crown Office list and only corrected when Sackville appeared in the House. Who procured his election is a matter of speculation. Neither he nor his fellow-knight Anthony Kempe, another Sussex man, had any standing in Westmorland, but both could claim a marriage connexion with the 2nd Earl of Cumberland, hereditary sheriff of the county, and with his father-in-law the 3rd Lord Dacre of Gilsland; Cumberland must also have had dealings with both Sackville's father, an ex-chancellor of augmentations, and his father-in-law Sir John Baker, one of whom doubtless made the approach. For Sackville, as for Kempe, a knighthood of the shire was not to recur: he was to sit as a burgess in the first two Elizabethan Parliaments and in the third he took his seat in the Lords.[3]

Sackville had appeared on the pardon roll in October 1553 as of London. On 8 Mar. 1557, together with Thomas Swynton, he purchased various properties in Kent and Sussex for £1,221. In co-operation with Thomas Norton* he wrote *The Tragedie of Gorboduc*, but he handed over his other literary project *A myrroure for magistrates* to George Ferrers* and William Baldwin after completing the 'Induction'. His career took Sackville to the treasurership and an earldom before he died at the council table on 19 Apr. 1608. Several portraits of him in old age survive.[4]

[1] Aged 72 at death, G. Abbott, *Funeral Sermon* (1608), 16. *Vis. Suss.* (Harl. Soc. lxxxix), 95; *DNB*; *CP*; J. E. Mousley, 'Suss. country gentry in the reign of Eliz.' (London Univ. Ph.D. thesis, 1956), 692; C. J. Phillips, *Sackville Fam.* i. 151, 242. [2] Somerville, *Duchy*, i. 619; G. Scott Thomson, *Lds. Lt.* 50; *LJ*, i. 703; ii. 62, 113, 145, 168, 191; SP12/93 ex inf. J. C. Sainty; C66/1682 ex inf. J. C. Sainty; *APC*, xiv. 3; *CSP Dom.* 1581–90, p. 702; Hants RO, Winchester 1st bk. of ordinances ex inf. Dr. Adrienne Rosen. [3] C193/32/2; 219/25/28, 113, 116; Wm. Salt Lib. SMS 264; *CJ*, i. 47. [4] *CPR*, 1553–4, p. 442; 1555, p. 473; F. P. Wilson, *Eng. Drama 1485–1585*, pp. 132–7; C. H. Wilson, 'Thomas Sackville: an Elizabethan poet as citizen', *Ten Studies in Anglo–Dutch Relations* (Pbls. Sir Thomas Browne Inst. Leiden, gen. ser. v), 30–50; R. C. Strong, *Tudor and Jacobean Portraits*, 67–68; *The Eng. Icon*, 260.

A.D.

SACKVILLE, William (by 1509–56), of Bletchingley and Dorking, Surr.

BLETCHINGLEY 1542

b. by 1509, 1st s. of Edward Sackville of Bletchingley

by Jane, da. of Sir Roger Kynaston of Myddle and Hordley, Salop. *m.* (1) 1535, Rose (*d.*1545), da. of Sir John Gaynesford of Crowhurst, Surr., wid. of Sir George Puttenham of Sherfield, Hants, 2s. 1da.; (2) disp. 15 Feb. 1546, Eleanor, da. of Thomas Shirley* of West Grinstead, Suss., wid. of Henry Browne of Betchworth, Surr. *suc.* fa. 1535.[1]

Yeoman, the chamber by 1530, sewer by 1544–53; escheator, Surr. and Suss. 1544–5; j.p. Surr. 1547–*d.*; commr. relief 1550; Queen's trainbearer 1554.[2]

William Sackville's father, a younger brother of Richard Sackville[†] of Withyham, Sussex, was a substantial landholder at Bletchingley, being assessed there for the subsidy of 1523 at £30 a year. It may have been Sir Nicholas Carew*, the lord of Bletchingley manor, who launched Sackville on the career in the royal household which was to last until his death; if so, his selection for the Surrey jury which in 1539 found Carew guilty of treason was perhaps based on more than geography. With Carew's successor as the local magnate, Thomas Cawarden*, Sackville was to engage in a feud which eventually brought them into the Star Chamber. To judge from his record of litigation Sackville was as prone to quarrel as was Cawarden, whom he may have regarded as an upstart. The two of them were returned for Bletchingley in the Parliament of 1542 but whether as friends or enemies cannot be said; both combined local standing with court connexion, and Sackville at least may have sat in 1539, when the names are lost. The hostilities which took them to law arose from Sackville's acquisition in 1544 of the ex-monastic manor and rectory of Caterham and Cawarden's enclosure of part of these lands in his capacity of keeper of Anne of Cleves's manor of Bletchingley; the affair and its ramifications lasted for several years and reached the Star Chamber only towards the close of Edward VI's reign. By then Sackville had disposed of all his property in Bletchingley and had gone to live at Dorking in a house belonging to his second wife.[3]

The names of both Members for Bletchingley in 1545 are lost, but Sackville's service in the King's entourage on the French campaign of 1544, and the subsequent grant to him of the reversion of ex-monastic lands in Essex and Surrey and the bailiffship of others, may be thought to have favoured his re-election unless Cawarden was able to block it. He was not to sit under either Edward VI or Mary, although he served both monarchs at court and in his shire; his further purchases of monastic lands, including an agglomeration drawn from a dozen counties for which in May 1553 he paid nearly £2,000 'in ready money' (presumably the yield of his Bletchingley sales), may have been smoothed by his kinship with Richard Sackville II*, the chancellor of augmentations. (His earlier acquisition, with another yeoman of the chamber, John ap Robert Lloyd (q.v.), of a lease of two Welsh townships had led their inhabitants to charge him before the court of general surveyors with having evicted them.) He is not known to have played any part in the local episodes provoked by Cawarden's subversive activities under Mary.[4]

Sackville died intestate on 19 May 1556. He seems to have owed a good deal of money, for his widow cited his debts to the Queen and others in seeking a reversal of judgment for debt against him in the common pleas. His son John, who was rising 20 at Sackville's death, also went to Chancery about part of his inheritance in Cardiganshire.[5]

[1] Date of birth estimated from first reference. C. J. Phillips, *Sackville Fam.* i. 108; *Vis. Salop* (Harl. Soc. xxix), 295; *Vis. Surr.* (Harl. Soc. xliii), 9, 93–94; Manning and Bray, *Surr.* i. 592; iii. p. cxxi; *Fac. Off. Reg. 1534–49*, ed. Chambers, 270; U. Lambert, *Bletchingley*, ii. 493–5; C142/110/148. [2] *LP Hen. VIII*, v, xix, xx, CPR, 1547–8, p. 90; 1553, p. 357; 1553–4, p. 24; 1554–5, p. 357; Stowe 571, f. 30v. [3] *Surr. Arch. Colls.* v. 265; *LP Hen. VIII*, xiv, xix; St.Ch.2/29/151; 3/3/49; Req.2/9/2, 10/228, 15/71; *CPR*, 1549–51, p. 108; 1553, pp. 115, 272; *Surr. Fines* (Surr. Rec. Soc. xix), 83, 84, 93. [4] *LP Hen. VIII*, xix, xx; *Archaeologia*, xii. 379; *CPR*, 1553, p. 286; *Augmentations* (Univ. Wales Bd. of Celtic Studies, Hist. and Law ser. xiii), 5. [5] C1/1469/1, 1473/6; 142/110/148.

S.R.J.

SADLER, Ralph (1507–87), of Hackney, Mdx., Standon, Herts. and Lesnes, Kent.

?HINDON	1536[1]
MIDDLESEX	1539[2]
HERTFORDSHIRE	1542
PRESTON	1545
HERTFORDSHIRE	1553 (Mar.), 1559, 1563, 1571, 1572, 1584, 1586

b. 1507, 1st s. of Henry Sadler, prob. of Warws. and Hackney. *m.* bigamously by 1535, Ellen, da. of John Mitchell of Much Hadham, Herts., w. of Matthew Barr, at least 3s. inc. Henry† and Thomas† 4da. Kntd. 18 Apr. 1538, banneret 10 Sept. 1547.[3] Clerk of the hanaper 1535–*d.*; gent. the privy chamber by May 1536; ambassador to Scotland 1537, 1540, 1542; jt. (with John Godsalve*, Gregory Railton and Francis Kempe*) prothonotary, Chancery 1537–?*d.*; principal sec. Apr. 1540–Apr. 1543; PC 1540–53, 1566–*d.*; master of gt. wardrobe 1543–53; j.p. Herts. 1544–7, 1558/59–61, Glos. 1547, q. Herts. 1562–*d.*; chamberlain or receiver, ct. gen. surveyors by 1545; commr. musters, Herts. 1546, loan 1546, 1562, goods of churches and fraternities 1550, relief, Herts. and London 1550, eccles. causes 1572; duchy of Lancaster steward of Hertford and constable of Hertford castle Dec. 1549–54, 1559–87; warden of the east and middle marches 1559–60; custos rot. Herts. by 1562–*d.*; chancellor, duchy of Lancaster 1568–*d.*; ld. lt. Herts. 1569.[4]

Ralph Sadler's father was probably a Warwickshire man, like his master Sir Edward Belknap, and only acquired his house at Hackney in 1521, after Belknap's death and at about the time he became the 2nd Marquess of Dorset's steward at Tilty, Essex. Cromwell was already acting as Dorset's attorney by 1522, but his acquaintance with Henry Sadler probably began earlier. The inscription on Ralph Sadler's tomb states that he 'was brought up with Thomas Cromwell', and Sadler himself in later life spoke of Cromwell as 'him that hath hitherto from the years of discretion nourished brought up and advanced' him. No evidence of Sadler's education at a university or inn of court has been found, but he clearly had a good education, for he knew French and Latin and had some Greek and a working knowledge of the law. By 1526 he had become a valuable agent for Cromwell and by 1529 was sufficiently intimate with his master to be appointed an executor and beneficiary of his will. In the same year it was Sadler who successfully negotiated in London to secure Cromwell a seat in Parliament. Like Cromwell, Sadler stood by Wolsey and in June 1530 Cromwell urged Wolsey to thank him for his support.[5]

Sadler's only master for the next four or five years was Cromwell. His work was not only secretarial but included assistance with routine legal business and the running of Cromwell's household. His part in writing the enormous mass of Cromwell's letters, drafts and tracts gave him a knowledge of his master's, and hence of national, affairs which his own talents later enabled him to turn to advantage. By 1534 Sadler's position was important enough for that inveterate suitor Viscount Lisle to seek his favour and for him in return to recommend a friend to Lisle for a post at Calais. In May 1534 Sadler obtained his first grant of public office, the reversion to the office of prothonotary in Chancery. Appointed gentleman of the privy chamber in May 1536, Sadler had become known at court as Cromwell's messenger. On 10 Nov. 1535 John Whalley reported to Cromwell a conversation with Henry VIII, 'Mr. Sadler standing by', and on 11 Jan. 1536 Sadler himself wrote from the court at Greenwich to Cromwell reporting a long conversation of his own with the King.[6]

In March 1536 Sadler received a reversionary lease for 40 years of a manor at Walthamstow, Essex, the first of the many grants which came his way under Henry VIII and which were to make him one of the richest commoners in the kingdom by 1547. A letter of Sadler's to Cromwell, probably dating from 1537, confirms the assumption that Sadler owed his appointment as gentleman of the privy chamber to Cromwell's desire to increase the number of his agents at court. The inclusion of Sadler's name for Hindon in a list of boroughs and nominees prepared by Cromwell, seemingly in anticipation of the Parliament of 1536, makes it likely that he then began a parliamentary career that was to extend over half a century. The three boroughs belonged to the see of Winchester and in 1536 Bishop Gardiner was ambassador to Paris. It was probably also Cromwell's backing which secured Sadler his seat in the Parliament of 1539. When in 1542 he was first returned for Hertfordshire, Sadler was already principal secretary, holder of other important offices and a considerable land-owner in the county. On his appointment with Thomas Wriothesley as secretary in April 1540 he was able to continue his attendance in the Commons during the last session of the Parliament of 1539 (and to seek election to that of 1542) because the King set aside the recent Act (31 Hen. VIII, c.10) requiring the secretary to sit in the Lords and allowed them to sit alternate weeks in the Commons. In 1545 it was probably royal favour that secured him the nomination for Preston, a duchy of Lancaster borough. He had been in Scotland or the northern marches for most of that year and may not have had time to make arrangements for his candidature in Hertfordshire, where the senior knight was his friend Sir Richard Lee. Perhaps Sadler did not intend to sit in Parliament in 1545 at all, but was constrained to do so in order to forward the private Act for regularizing his marriage.[7]

Sadler's most important service was in diplomatic missions to Scotland under Henry VIII, of which he has left voluminous and often vivid record in his correspondence. His first mission to that kingdom, during which he was given audience by Queen Margaret, took place in January and February 1537. His charge performed to the King's satisfaction, Sadler was despatched in March to France, where he remonstrated on the King's behalf with James V at the way his mother was treated in Scotland; Sadler was apparently back in London by 15 Apr. He visited Scotland again in the summer of 1537 and possibly in 1538, and instructions were prepared for him to go there in April 1539. He would have missed the first session of the Parliament of 1539 if he had gone but his wife's illness caused a change of plan and he was with her in Kent on 28 May. His next mission, in 1540, was the result of the seizure in England of the papers of a French envoy to Scotland, including an anti-English letter of Cardinal Beaton, and Sadler was instructed, *inter alia*, to try to weaken the cardinal's influence. He arrived in Edinburgh on 17 Feb. 1540 but the negotiation was foredoomed to failure, as Sadler recognized in his reports to Cromwell. He was not blamed for this but his appointment as joint princi-

pal secretary in April 1540 brought an interruption in his series of missions abroad.[8]

Sadler's last and most important mission to Scotland under Henry VIII began in March 1543, against the background of the King's journey to York in 1541 for the meeting with James V which never took place, the war of 1542 and Arran's temporary deposition of Beaton. He was instructed to secure a peace treaty that should include the marriage of Prince Edward and Mary, heir to the throne of Scotland. The virtual failure of this mission was ensured by Sadler's own partiality to the Scottish Protestants and his mistrust of all Catholics on principle. He shared Henry VIII's false optimism about the prospect of the proposed marriage and under-estimated the extent to which dislike of subjection to England cut across fractional differences in Scotland. A treaty was concluded on 25 Aug. 1543 but was repudiated by the Scots in December; by that time England was actually at war with France and virtually so with Scotland. Sadler's position degenerated from that of ambassador to that of enemy agent and he became the victim of popular feeling against England; several attempts were made on his life before he was extricated on 10 Nov. from Edinburgh.[9]

Appointed steward of royal lands at Anstey, Hitchin and Standon, Hertfordshire, probably after the death of Jane Seymour, Sadler was living at Standon by September 1539. He became keeper of Standon manor and park three months later, and obtained first an estate tail in the property, in December 1540, and finally the fee simple, for £450, in 1544. Other important grants were Stratford priory, Middlesex, in February 1539; the huge complex of Yorkshire lands that had belonged to Selby abbey in August 1540, part of a complicated transaction that resulted in their sale shortly afterwards; and in March 1542 a block of lands in Bedfordshire and Hertfordshire centred on Temple Dinsley, and formerly the possession of the Knights of St. John. Sadler asked Cromwell, probably in April 1539, to obtain for him Robertsbridge abbey in Sussex, but it was already promised to another. The last favours he owed directly to his former master were his appointment as principal secretary and his knighthood.[10]

Cromwell went to the Tower in June 1540 and, according to Foxe, Sadler alone dared to carry to the King his letter begging for mercy. Sadler himself was imprisoned in the Tower on 17 Jan. 1541 but six days later he attended a Privy Council meeting, having presumably cleared himself. He is generally believed to have been of the Protestant party in the Council and certainly took a leading part in the examination of Catherine Howard and her relatives in November 1541. The exceptional size of the grants obtained by him in 1541–3 suggests that his skill, his knowledge of affairs and his leading position as secretary made his support valuable to the rival factions in the Council. He sold Lesnes, Kent, which seems at one time to have been his principal residence, in February 1541. During the earlier part of 1541 he was with the Council in London and probably lost influence at court, but his position improved after November. Much of 1542 he spent in Hertfordshire, occupied in raising the benevolence. He was in Scotland in 1543, and lost the secretaryship in April; the keepership of the great wardrobe granted him in May was perhaps meant to compensate him materially for the loss of political influence thus sustained. In December 1543 Sadler asked to be recalled from Scotland, but he remained there, or in the border regions, perhaps with some intervals, until April 1545. Appointed treasurer for the Scottish war in February 1544, he was a signatory with the 5th Earl of Shrewsbury and Bishop Tunstall to numerous despatches to the Council in London; he also worked closely with Hertford, as he had earlier done with Lisle, and it was in his name that the King intrigued with Scots nobles for the murder of Cardinal Beaton. When Sadler attended meetings of the Privy Council in October 1545, it was after an absence of more than two years. He shared in the rising influence of the Protestant party at court in the last two years of Henry VIII's reign, and was one of the assistants appointed by the King's will to advise the Councillors of Edward VI, receiving a legacy of £200. His close acquaintance and former service in the north with the Protector Somerset and the Earl of Warwick might have been expected to assure him a leading part in government under Edward VI; in fact, his active political career seems to have been interrupted before Henry VIII's death, and was not to be resumed until after Elizabeth's accession.[11]

During the last six years of Henry VIII's reign, Sadler was named to various commissions, for taking the accounts of officials, for the sale of crown lands, the survey of the crown jewels, and the like. Perhaps the most important was that of December 1545, when he was appointed with Richard Rich (q.v.) to examine the procedure and the officers of the revenue courts and to collect debts due to the crown. The findings of this commission, and of another appointed soon after, led to the reorganisation in January 1547 of the courts of augmentations and of general surveyors; Sadler was a chamberlain or receiver of the latter court by 1545. A modern historian of these courts states that neither Rich nor Sadler 'was imbued with the zeal of the reformer'. It is hardly surprising that Sadler was not, for he was himself the arch-pluralist of his time and his position made it easy for him to purchase land from the crown. By Henry VIII's death he had become one of the largest landowners in Hertfordshire, with property in 24 other counties in England and Wales. He was assessed for the subsidy of 1546 on an annual income of £356.[12]

In 1545 Matthew Barr, whose apparent widow Sadler had married by 1535, reappeared and claimed his wife. Sadler was therefore obliged to have his children legitimized by a private Act (37 Hen. VIII, c.30). The archbishop of Canterbury and two bishops were commissioned on 28 Nov. 1545 to inquire into the validity of the marriage. After its introduction in the Commons by Sadler, the original bill was read twice in the Lords before a modified version was given a reading there on 15 Dec. and another four days later. It was then sent back to the Commons whence it was redelivered on 21 Dec. after which it was passed, becoming law on 24 Dec. (On 22 Dec. Sadler himself carried five bills to the Lords.) The Act, which also voided Ellen Sadler's interest in the great complex of lands at Westbury-on-Trym, Gloucestershire, Sadler's last major purchase under Henry VIII, makes it clear that she remained the lawful wife of Barr. Months, or even years, may have elapsed before Sadler was able to regularize his marital status, and this perhaps helps to explain the relative obscurity in which he lived for the ensuing two reigns. 'Master Sadler took his matter very heavily', Wriothesley reported to Secretary Paget in November 1545.[13]

Sadler remained a member of the Privy Council under Edward VI; he was treasurer for the wars in August 1545 and fought with great distinction at Pinkie, where he was created a knight banneret. Although Sadler is said to have been on better terms with Warwick than with Somerset, he never, so far as is known, became one of the former's confidants. Either service in the north or lack of inclination kept him out of the Parliament of 1547. His standing in Hertfordshire may have been affected by the trouble about his marriage; the Council ordered the sheriff in January 1552 to arrange Sadler's election as 'the most fittest of any other person thereabouts' to replace the deceased Sir Henry Parker, but he was not chosen. Sadler signed the warrant for Admiral Seymour's execution in March 1549 and in August he served with the Marquess of Northampton against the Norfolk rebellion. In November he sided with Warwick against Somerset and in the following month was rewarded with two appointments in the duchy of Lancaster. He attended the Privy Council's meetings regularly from October 1549 to May 1550 but after that his attendances became desultory. His last two attendances, at Westminster on 25 and 28 Mar. 1553, were perhaps the result of his presence in London for the Parliament of March 1553. He was returned, for only the second time, for Hertfordshire, presumably because Warwick, now Duke of Northumberland, was sure he could be relied on for support and would do nothing to risk his vast fortune; he carried bills to the Lords on 29 Mar. He signed the device settling the crown on Jane Grey, and was noted by Cecil as one of those expected to act on her behalf. He made one large purchase during these years, paying £4,041 in December 1550 to the crown for lands scattered throughout the country, but he probably sold as much, including in July 1547 the lands of Waltham abbey, Essex, and land around Coventry, to (Sir) Anthony Denny* and John Hales II*. Hales later stated that Sadler had suffered very great losses through the fraud and craft of Northumberland. It is possible that Sadler did so suffer, by forced loans or sales to the duke, but he remained a very wealthy man until his death.[14]

After the resolution of the succession struggle in Mary's favour, Sadler was confined to his house on 25 July 1553 but five days later he was ordered to present himself before the 12th Earl of Arundel. He sued out a pardon on 6 Oct., but later in the month he lost his mastership of the wardrobe to Sir Edward Waldegrave* and in the following May his duchy of Lancaster offices at Hertford to Sir John Mordaunt*. He seems to have retained his clerkship of the hanaper, accepting Francis Kempe* as joint holder in 1557, and he was employed as a commissioner for the loan in 1557. On Elizabeth's accession he was immediately restored to favour, attending the first meeting of her Privy Council on 20 Nov. 1558. During the reign he again served in Anglo-Scottish diplomacy and in May 1568 secured his last major office, that of chancellor of the duchy of Lancaster.[15]

Sadler made his will on 27 Apr. 1584 and died on 30 Mar. 1587.[16]

[1] *LP Hen. VIII*, x. 40 (ii) citing Cott. Otho C10, f. 218. [2] E159/319, brev. ret. Mich. r. [1–2]. [3] Date of birth given in A. J. Slavin, *Pol. and Profit: a Study of Sir Ralph Sadler 1507–47*, upon which much of this biography is based. Clutterbuck, *Herts.* iii. 28, 226–8; *DNB*; *LP Hen. VIII*, xx. [4] *Bull. IHR*, xxxviii. 31–47; *LP Hen. VIII*, xv, xviii–xxi; *CPR*, 1547–8, pp. 83–84; 1550–3, pp. 141, 394; 1553, pp. 354, 361; 1553–4, p. 326; 1563–6, pp. 226, 497; 1569–72, pp. 440–2; Somerville, *Duchy*, i. 324n, 604; Osborn Coll. Yale Univ. Lib. 71.6.41. [5] *Sadler Pprs.* i. p. iii; Merriman, *Letters, Thos. Cromwell*, i. 60, 329. [6] *LP Hen. VIII*, vi, vii, ix, x, xii. [7] Ibid. x, xii, xv; Cott. Otho C10, f. 218; Elton, *Tudor Constitution*, 120–3, [8] *Hamilton Pprs.* i and ii passim. [9] Ibid. [10] *LP Hen. VIII*, xii, xiv, xv; *EHR*, lxxix. 778–83; *Yorks. Arch. Jnl.* xliv. 170–2. [11] Foxe, *Acts and Mons.* v. 401–2; *LP Hen. VIII*, xvi, xviii–xxi. [12] W. C. Richardson, *Ct. Augmentations*, 111–14; *LP Hen. VIII*, xx, xxi. [13] *HL Quarterly*, xxviii. 131–43; *LP Hen. VIII*, xx; *LJ*, i. 273–5, 278–80, 282; Req.2/20/14. [14] *APC*, ii. 120, 338, 408; iii. 39, 151, 231, 316, 403 seq., 458–9; iv. 3, 5, 6, 52–56, 157, 243–5; *CPR*, 1547–8,

p. 225; 1549–51, pp. 265–73; 1555–7, pp. 191–2; *Troubles conn. with the Prayer Bk. of 1549* (Cam. Soc. n.s. xxxvii), 85, 93; *Chron. Q. Jane and Q. Mary* (Cam. Soc. xlviii), 100; Lansd. 103(1), 1–2; Somerville, i. 604; *CJ*, i. 26; Holinshed, *Chron.* iii. 971. [15] *APC*, iv. 307, 416; vi. 189; vii. 3; *CPR*, 1553–4, pp. 326, 421; 1555–7, p. 517; 1558–60, p. 380; Somerville, i. 395. [16] PCC 23 Spencer; C142/215/259.

D.F.C.

ST. AUBYN, William (by 1526–58/71), of Mawgan in Meneage, Cornw.

HELSTON	1554 (Apr.), 1554 (Nov.)
WEST LOOE	1555
CAMELFORD	1558

b. by 1526, 2nd s. of Thomas St. Aubyn of Clowance by Mary, da. of Sir Thomas Grenville of Stowe in Kilkhampton, wid. of Richard Bluett of Holcombe Rogus, Devon. *educ.* L. Inn, adm. 27 June 1540. *m.* Elizabeth, da. of Walter Borlase of Newlyn, Cornw., 1s.[1]

William St. Aubyn came from a Cornish family of gentle standing related by marriage and descent with the Grenvilles and the Arundells of Lanherne. He received a legal education at Lincoln's Inn where his kinsman, Sir Thomas Arundell*, was a prominent figure, but he is not known to have practised as a lawyer. In the spring of 1554 Arundell's brother Sir John procured his own return as a knight for Cornwall and presumably he favoured St. Aubyn's election at Helston, a constituency some four miles from St. Aubyn's home. Later in the same year Queen Mary asked for the return of local men, and Helston complied by choosing him for a second time. He had no personal links with either West Looe or Camelford, but in 1555 the sheriff was Sir John Arundell and Camelford was amenable to Arundell's influence; as West Looe was until the death of Mary almost a preserve for Lincoln's Inn men, he may have owed the seat to his connexion with the inn. The Journal does not mention him. Apart from his Membership little else is known about St. Aubyn's life. As he was not re-elected after Elizabeth's accession, St. Aubyn may have died in 1558 or 1559, a victim of the epidemic current at the time: he was certainly dead by 1571 when his son was assessed at Mawgan for the subsidy.[2]

[1] Date of birth estimated from education. *Vis. Cornw.* ed. Vivian, 437–8; W. C. Borlase, *Fam. Borlase*, 80. [2] *Paroch. Hist. Cornw.* 283; *Vis. Cornw.* 437–8; E179/88/232, m.2.

J.J.G.

SAINTCLERE, John (1506/7–68/71), of East Budleigh and Ashburton, Devon.

WEST LOOE	1555

b. 1506/7, 1st s. of Gilbert Saintclere of East Budleigh by Joan, da. of John Strowbridge of Streathayne in the parish of Colyton. *m.* by 1540, Joan, da. of John Ford of Ashburton, prob. 1s. *suc.* fa. 15 Nov. 1525.[1]

Capt. *Jesus of Lubeck* 1545; commr. musters, Devon 1546, relief 1550; j.p. 1547–53.[2]

The Saintcleres had been seated at Tidwell in East Budleigh since the first half of the 15th century. John Saintclere's father died seised of the manors of Clyst Hydon and Kennerleigh together with 360 acres in Clyst Hydon and Tidwell. His mother was left a life interest in Tidwell, and under his father's will Saintclere received an 'iron-bound wain with eight oxen', 100 sheep and a featherbed. He added considerably to his modest patrimony: he married a local heiress, and acquired by purchase other lands near Budleigh from Richard Duke* and elsewhere in Devon from the 3rd Marquess of Dorset.[3]

After his marriage Saintclere made his principal home at Ashburton. In 1546 he obtained an 80-year lease of the manor and borough from Bishop Veysey of Exeter. Two years later he supported the claim of the townsmen that the exercise of the town's market belonged to them and not to the guild of St. Lawrence. The issue was a crucial one because John Prideaux*, one of the chantry commissioners for Devon, argued that the lease of the market, as a possession of the dissolved guild, was the property of the crown. Prideaux referred the issue to the quarter sessions held at Exeter that October, but evidently lost his case. Saintclere and the townsmen were probably helped by his family's friendship with Sir Thomas Denys*, the presiding justice, but their principal champion at Exeter was Nicholas Adams *alias* Bodrugan*, a lawyer, who argued that Ashburton market was not affected by the terms of the Chantries Act (1 Edw. VI, c. 14).[4]

Saintclere relied on Adams's counsel in several more personal matters, and in 1549 as a justice of the peace he evicted rival claimants to some of Adams's property near Dartmouth. This relationship may help to explain his Membership of Parliament for a Cornish borough in 1555 as Adams had been one of West Looe's original representatives, but he probably owed his election to the duchy of Cornwall through his tin-mining interests and his position as the leading figure in a stannary town: his fellow-Member William St. Aubyn was related to the Bluett and Grenville families with whom he had worked during the French wars of the 1540s. Saintclere did not follow Sir Anthony Kingston's lead in helping to defeat a government bill, but his support for the measure did not facilitate his re-election to Parliament or his restoration to the Devon bench from which he had been discharged at Mary's accession.[5]

In July 1557 Saintclere was bound by the Council in a recognizance for £500 to help Robert Carey* and Sir John Chichester* in their investigations into mining in Cornwall. Little trace has been found of him in the remaining years of his life: he was still alive in 1568 when he and his wife received the rent for some property in Ashburton, but in the following year his wife was the sole recipient and in 1571 she was described as 'widow'. He was succeeded by Gabriel Saintclere, who was probably his son Within a few years this prodigal had wasted much of the family substance in riotous living and pulled down the house at Tidwell.[6]

[1] Date of birth estimated from age at fa.'s i.p.m., C142/45/62. *Vis. Devon*, ed. Vivian, 349; PCC 2 Porch. [2] *LP Hen. VIII*, xx, xxi; *CPR*, 1547–8, p. 83; 1553, p. 352. [3] C142/29/133, 45/162; PCC 2 Porch; *Trans. Dev. Assoc.* xxii. 284; *Devon Monastic Lands* (Devon and Cornw. Rec. Soc. i), 31; *LP Hen. VIII*, xxi. [4] *Trans. Dev. Assoc.* xxviii. 213; St.Ch.3/2/14. [5] St.Ch.2/20/290; *LP Hen. VIII*, xx, xxi. [6] *APC*, vi. 133; *Ashburton Churchwardens' Accts.* (Devon and Cornw. Rec. Soc. n.s. xv), 108, 128, 157, 159, 161; E179/100/367, m. 4v, 369, m. 3v; *Trans. Dev. Assoc.* xxii. 284.

J.J.G.

SAINTHILL, Peter (by 1524–71), of Bradninch, Devon.

GRAMPOUND 1547[1]
SALTASH 1554 (Apr.)

b. by 1524, s. of Richard Sainthill (*d.*29 Dec. 1525), of Moreton Hampstead by Joan, da. of Richard Mayne of Exeter. *educ.* ?M. Temple. *m.* (1) by 26 Nov. 1552, Catherine, da. and coh. of Sir Humphrey Browne, wid. of Richard Townshend (*d.*by Nov. 1551), of Brampton, Suff., *s.p.*; (2) 1560, Julian, da. of William Shine of Bradley, Berks., wid. of Stephen Wilford and Alexander Writhington, 2s. 1da.[2]

Commr. relief, Devon 1550, sewers, London 1554; dep. steward, manor of Bradninch by 1559–*d.*[3]

Peter Sainthill came of a gentle family which had been settled in the neighbourhood of Moreton Hampstead since the 14th century. He inherited a small estate in Moreton but evidently preferred to make his home at Bradninch. He was probably a Middle Templar, for his first wife was the daughter of one of that inn's luminaries, his friends and colleagues seem to have been largely drawn from its members, and his son was to be admitted there. In 1546 he supported a successful claim to a coat of arms with the declaration that he had 'long continued in virtue and in all his acts and other his demeaning hath discreetly and worshipfully guided and governed himself'. Such virtue had not been its own reward, for in the previous year he had bought former monastic land to the tune of £600 and he would go on to make regular, if smaller, purchases and to rebuild his house at Bradninch.[4]

In 1547 Sainthill entered the Commons for a recently enfranchised borough. He had no personal link with Grampound and he probably owed his return there to Admiral Seymour: on the previous 11 May he had visited Seymour House on admiralty business and when on 17 Sept. he wrote to the admiral from Hamworthy, Dorset, about a vessel driven ashore on the Isle of Wight, he professed himself 'your friend assured'. By the time of the next Parliament, in March 1553, both Seymour and his elder brother, the Duke of Somerset, had disappeared and it was not the moment for a former client of their family to be helped to obtain a seat in the Commons. Sainthill did not reappear there until the spring of 1554, when he was returned for another Cornish constituency, his fellow being Humphrey Cavell, a member of the 1st Earl of Bedford's circle. Although this was to be his last experience of Parliament, he did not lose all connexion with it: in 1557 he and Richard Calmady* stood surety for John Evelegh, when Evelegh was fined for quitting the Parliament of November 1554 prematurely without leave.[5]

After Sainthill had secured for himself the deputy stewardship of the duchy of Cornwall's manor of Bradninch, his right to the office was disputed by John Haydon*, who had been deputy steward there under Bedford and who had retained rent rolls, court rolls and other muniments; Sainthill brought actions against Haydon in both Chancery and Star Chamber, complaining that his precursor was causing 'much contention . . . between the copyholders and the Queen's highness', and succeeded insofar as he retained the office. In the autumn of 1566, however, he became insane, and he seems to have remained so afflicted until his death on 19 Nov. 1571.[6]

[1] Hatfield 207. [2] Date of birth estimated from first reference. *Vis. Devon*, ed. Vivian, 663; *Vis. Norf.* (Harl. Soc. xxxii), 291; A. St. Hill, *Sainthill Fam.* i. 13–14; *CPR*, 1550–3, p. 333; C142/45/80. [3] Duchy Cornw. RO, 131, m. 22; *CPR*, 1553, p. 352; 1553–4, p. 37. [4] St. Hill, 5; *CPR*, 1550–3, p. 333; 1563–6, p. 300; C1/1270/25–26; 142/147/203; *Misc. Gen. et Her.* (ser. i), i. 281–2; *LP Hen. VIII*, xx; *Devon Monastic Lands* (Devon and Cornw. Rec. Soc. i), 59–60. [5] HCA 1/34, f. 64; 14/2; KB 27/1184. [6] Duchy Cornw. RO, 130, m. 23v; 131, m. 22; St.Ch.3/6/32; 5/S29/26; C3/158/9; 142/147/203, 160/7; St. Hill, 13–14; *CPR*, 1569–72, p. 329.

J.J.G.

ST. JOHN, John (c. 1505–76), of Lydiard Tregoz, Wilts., Farley Chamberlayne, Hants and Ewell, Surr.

BLETCHINGLEY 1529

b. c.1505, 1st s. of John St. John of Lydiard Tregoz by Joan, da. and h. of Sir John Ewerby of Farley Chamberlayne. *m.* (1) by 1526, Margaret, da. of Sir Richard Carew of Beddington, Surr., 1s. Nicholas*; (2) by Nov. 1535, Elizabeth, da. of Sir Richard Whethill of Calais, 2s. inc. William†. *suc.* fa. 1 Sept. 1512.[1]

Esquire of the body extraordinary by 1533; j.p. Wilts. 1554–*d.*; sheriff 1555–6, 1572–3; commr. sewers, Berks., Hants, Wilts. 1564, 1568, oyer and terminer, western circuit 1564.[2]

When John St. John was about seven years old his father died while serving at Fuenterrabia, Spain,

leaving him heir to the estates of the junior branch of the ancient St. John family. The freehold property comprised land in Essex, the midlands and Wiltshire, and its annual value, excluding the income from Essex, was reckoned in his father's inquisitions at £78. He was later to inherit from his mother, who was still alive in 1549, manors in Hampshire and Surrey. Sir Richard Carew acquired the wardship of the young St. John, who by 1526 was married to one of Carew's daughters; the two families were already connected, St. John's maternal grandmother, Sanchia Carew, being Sir Richard's first cousin. Although nothing is known of St. John's education, his connexions suggest that he may have gone early to court: he shared a common ancestor with Henry VII, for Sir Oliver St. John's wife, Margaret Beauchamp, had married secondly John Beaufort, Duke of Somerset, while his brother-in-law Nicholas Carew* was an intimate of the young Henry VIII.[3]

It was to this brother-in-law, who owned Bletchingley manor, that St. John clearly owed his return to the Parliament of 1529: his fellow-Member, Nicholas Leigh, was another brother-in-law of Carew's. The names 'Mr. St. John' and 'Mr. Lee' are found in conjunction on a list of Members drawn up by Cromwell on the back of a letter of December 1534. Those listed are thought to have been Members with a particular, but unknown, connexion with the treasons bill then on its passage through Parliament, and with no other clue to their identification the appearance of these two names together suggests that the bearer of the first was John St. John of Lydiard and not the head of the senior branch of the family, Sir John St. John of Bletsoe (q.v.), who may by this time have been by-elected to the House. In September 1533 another namesake had been appointed a serjeant-at-arms, 'to be specially attendant upon the King's person outside the time of Parliament, and in the time of Parliament to be attendant on the Speaker elected by the Commons'. It is likely that St. John sat again for Bletchingley in the Parliament of 1536, in accordance with the King's general request for the re-election of the previous Members, but as the returns for Bletchingley to the next Parliament, that of 1539, have been lost it is not possible to say whether he was returned on that occasion, immediately after Carew's conviction for treason.[4]

In 1533 St. John acted as a servitor at the coronation of Anne Boleyn. At his death in 1535 the bishop of Rochester owed one John St. John £20, but no direct connexion has been discovered between Bishop Fisher and the Member, although a Sir John St. John, presumably the father of Sir John of Bletsoe, had been chamberlain to Lady Margaret Beaufort and a fellow-executor with Fisher of her will. It was probably Sir John of Bletsoe, and not his cousin of Lydiard, who was in the household of Princess Mary at the time of Catherine of Aragon's death in January 1536. In the previous year St. John had married as his second wife a daughter of Sir Richard Whethill. He disagreed with his new brother-in-law over the provision of Whethill's will, of which he was an assistant overseer, and in March 1537 he journeyed from Calais to England to make his case to Cromwell and the Council. St. John appears to have been peripatetic, as his family's scattered estates may have encouraged him to be: in a grant of July 1545 he is described as of Farley Chamberlayne, a property of his mother's (where he was also probably living a year earlier when called upon to provide eight foot soldiers for the war), whereas in a settlement which he had made of his property in the previous month he is described as of Ewell, where his mother held the manor of Fitznells. His inclusion on the Wiltshire commission of the peace in 1554 seems to imply that he had finally settled at Lydiard Tregoz.[5]

In 1545 St. John purchased the manor of Littleton for his son Nicholas. The tenants of Littleton quarrelled with the two St. Johns over the rents and dues of the manor, and in Edward VI's reign they brought suits in the courts of Star Chamber and requests. They alleged that the St. Johns had forcibly entered the property and done at least £500 worth of damage, a charge denied by the elder St. John who claimed that he and his son had distrained legally for rent on 6 Dec. 1550 or 1551: Nicholas St. John for his part explained how his father had acquired two of the lessees' shares in the manor. In 1548 Nicholas obtained a writ of partition from Chancery which was unsuccessfully challenged by the tenants in common pleas. The outcome of these suits is not known, but John St. John was able to bequeath the property to his son William.[6]

In 1564 St. John was described by the bishop of Salisbury as 'no hinderer' to the Elizabethan settlement. He made his will ten years later on 24 Apr. 1574. Besides Littleton, William was to have the manor and advowson of Farley Chamberlayne, some household furnishings and '400 wether sheep which I left in stock there'. The youngest son, John, received the manor of Bincknoll, Wiltshire, and all the cattle, crops, and household stuff at Littleton unless his brothers paid him a stipulated amount for them. By a codicil of 2 Dec. 1575 William and John also received gifts of plate, bedding, a chain of gold and four horses. Nicholas, the heir, was appointed sole executor and had the residue of all the goods.

St. John died on 5 Apr. 1576 and probate was granted on the following 9 Nov.[7]

[1] Date of birth estimated from age, variously given, at fa.'s i.p.m., C142/27/57, 28/35, 40, 86, 27/52. *Wilts. Vis. Peds.* (Harl. Soc. cv, cvi), 167–9; C142/175/99; PCC 5 Dyngeley; *LP Hen. VIII*, ix. [2] *LP Hen. VIII*, ii; *CPR*, 1553–4, p. 25; 1563–6, pp. 38, 39, 42; 1569–72, p. 219. [3] *VCH Surr.* iii. 280; iv. 182; *VCH Hants.* iv. 443; J. G. Taylor, *Our Lady of Batersey*, 148; *Surr. Arch. Colls.* liv. 101. [4] *LP Hen. VIII*, vi; vii. 1522(ii) citing SP1/87, f.106v; *CPR*, 1554–5, p. 224. [5] *LP Hen. VIII*, vi, viii, x, xii; M. Macklem, *God have Mercy: Life of Fisher*, 25; PCC 5 Dyngeley; LC2/2; C142/175/99; *VCH Surr.* iii. 280; *VCH Hants.* iv. 443. [6] St.Ch.3/2/32; Req.2/14/71; PCC 32 Carew. [7] *Cam. Misc.* ix(3), 38; PCC 32 Carew; C142/175/99.

S.R.J.

ST. JOHN, Sir John (by 1495–1558), of Bletsoe, Beds.

BEDFORDSHIRE   ?1529*,[1] 1539,[2] 1542

b. by 1495, 1st s. of Sir John St. John of Bletsoe by Sybil, da. of Rhys ap Morgan. *m.* (1) by 1521, Margaret, da. of Sir William Waldegrave† of Smallbridge, Suff., 5s. inc. John† and Oliver* 4da.; (2) Anne, da. of Thomas Neville of Cotterstock, Northants., 1s. 4da. illegit. bef. m. *suc.* fa. 30 Mar. 1525. Kntd. Feb./Nov. 1526.[3]

Commr. subsidy, Beds. 1523, 1546, musters 1539, 1546, benevolence 1544/45, chantries, Beds. and Bucks. 1546, 1548, relief, Beds. and Hunts. 1550, goods of churches and fraternities, Beds. 1553; other commissions 1530–54; j.p. Beds. 1528–d., Hunts. 1528–47; sheriff, Beds. and Bucks. 1529–30, 1534–5, 1549–50; knight of the body by 1533; 'custos' to Princess Mary in 1536; yeoman forester, Farming Woods, Northants. 1539–44; chamberlain, household of Princess Elizabeth date unknown.[4]

Head of the senior branch of his family, Sir John St. John could trace his descent to Normandy before the Conquest, although there is no firm evidence of settlement in England until after 1100. His great-grandmother, Margaret Beauchamp, had considerably increased the family's wealth by her inheritance of the manors of Lydiard Tregoz, Wiltshire, and Bletsoe, Bedfordshire, and its standing by her second marriage to John Beaufort, Duke of Somerset, thus linking the St. Johns with the house of Tudor. The Wiltshire property descended to the junior branch of the family.[5]

St. John's monumental inscription is probably correct in stating that he was brought up by Margaret Beaufort, and as he was on the threshold of manhood when she died in 1509 his entry to the court of her grandson would have been a natural sequel. In 1521 he was among 50 gentlemen who accompanied Wolsey to Calais. In the same year his father made a marriage settlement of the greater part of his inheritance—the manors of Bletsoe and Keysoe, Bedfordshire, and Paulerspury, Northamptonshire—to the use of St. John and his wife: its annual value was estimated in 1525 at £130. In 1526 St. John leased his other freehold property, a

Dorset manor worth £13 a year, to William Uvedale for 21 years.[6]

St. John was knighted at some time between February 1526 and the following autumn, when he was nominated, but not pricked, sheriff of Bedfordshire and Buckinghamshire. In July 1527 he again accompanied Wolsey to Calais. His inclusion in the commissions of the peace for Bedfordshire and Huntingdonshire in 1528 marks the beginning of his continuous participation in local affairs. He was pricked sheriff of Bedfordshire and Buckinghamshire in 1529, after the election of knights of the shire for which, if he had cherished any hope of being chosen, he had evidently been passed over. Either St. John or John Gostwick*, whose son married St. John's daughter Margaret, may have been by-elected in place of George Acworth, who died in 1530; their names appear against Bedfordshire in a list of vacancies which had occurred between the opening of Parliament and the second half of 1532. As St. John was to be nominated sheriff in 1533 and 1534, and pricked on the second occasion, it may well have been he who succeeded Acworth, although the 'Mr. St. John' included in a list of Members drawn up by Cromwell probably in December 1534 is more likely to have been John St. John (q.v.) of Lydiard Tregoz. If St. John did join the Parliament of 1529 he was probably also returned to that of 1536, for which the King requested the return of the previous Members. In the meantime he had been discharging the honourable duties of his station, accompanying the King to Calais in 1532 and attending Anne Boleyn at her coronation in 1533 as a servitor of the dresser. In 1532 he purchased the manor of Lawrence in Riseley, Bedfordshire.[7]

St. John was to be described on his tomb as at one time 'custos' to Princess Mary. No record of this appointment has been found but it appears to be corroborated by a letter written immediately after the death of Catherine of Aragon on 7 Jan. 1536. Addressed to Cromwell by 'John St. John', the letter contains a request to the King to excuse the writer's wife from being a mourner at the ex-Queen's funeral, both because she was recovering from a pregnancy and because the writer, 'being in service with my Lady Princess', could not furnish the horses and servants needed for the occasion. Although Princess Mary had been officially deprived of that title since 1533, there can be little doubt that the reference is to her and not to her mother: if the writer had been attendant on Catherine at Kimbolton he could readily have brought his wife from nearby Bletsoe, whereas this would have been more difficult to arrange from Eltham where Mary was staying. It thus appears that St. John was discharging this duty at the beginning of 1536, but since when he had done so, and how long he continued to, are alike unknown: it is, however, probable that the assignment interfered to some extent with his attendance in Parliament.[8]

St. John took a leading part in putting down the northern rebellion of 1536. He was appointed to attend the King personally with a retinue of 100 men, and with Sir Francis Bryan* and Sir William Parr* he led the 'best' men of Bedfordshire, Buckinghamshire and Northamptonshire northwards. He appears to have acted as a liaison between the Duke of Suffolk and others who were helping to put down the rebellion. That St. John was an able soldier is suggested by his appointment in July 1543 as one of four counsellors to Sir John Wallop for his expedition against the French; a letter of 13 Aug. from Wallop and others to Henry VIII, describing their actions in the Netherlands, bears St. John's signature. He was again abroad in the following July when he signed a letter from the 3rd Duke of Norfolk to the Council, giving details of the war. In both campaigns he supplied men for the army.[9]

His martial prowess notwithstanding, St. John was, in Bryan's words, 'a man of gentle nature'. In a letter to Cromwell of October 1537 Bryan asked that St. John might have the manor of Bushmead, which the King had already leased to him. The request came too late, for Sir William Gascoigne* had already been granted the reversion of Bushmead, but St. John retained his 21-year lease of the property at a rent of £21. He prospered greatly by the Dissolution. In 1540 he paid £305 for the manor of Keysoe and Keysoe Grange, as well as other property in the neighbourhood. In the following year he paid £469 and surrendered his manor and advowson of Paulerspury, Northamptonshire, for three manors in Huntingdonshire, one manor in Bedfordshire, some land in Glamorganshire, and a London house. He quickly alienated the Glamorganshire property and in 1543 settled the rest on the marriage of his eldest son Oliver.[10]

In October 1537 St. John had attended Prince Edward's christening and, in the following month, the funeral of Queen Jane Seymour. In December he was suspected with two others of hunting without permission in the 5th Lord Mountjoy's park at Abthorpe, Northamptonshire, which lay near his own manor of Paulerspury: among Cromwell's remembrances are notes 'to examine St. John and Sir Henry Parker* for hunting' and 'to speak for' them. Whatever the outcome, St. John's career does not appear to have suffered: he was reappointed to the commission of the peace for Huntingdonshire in 1538, helped to receive Anne of Cleves in 1539 and in 1546 was one of four Bedfordshire representatives summoned to court to welcome the French ambassador. His return to the Parliament of 1539 may have owed something to Cromwell, but if so he must have retained the seat three years later by reason of his position at court and his standing in the county. He probably procured his son Oliver's knighthood of the shire in 1547 by standing down himself. If so, it was his last success in the parliamentary sphere, for he was not to be returned again nor any of his near kin elected until after his death.[11]

The last ten years of St. John's life are only occasionally illuminated. Their most interesting episode dates from the beginning of 1553, when he and Lewis Dyve were recommended by the Privy Council to the sheriff of Bedfordshire as suitable for election as knights of the shire in the forthcoming Parliament: Dyve was elected, but St. John was not, the second seat going to Sir Humphrey Radcliffe. Why St. John was nominated is less hard to explain than why he was passed over. His earlier custody of Mary suggests that he already veered towards the Protestantism which can be read between the lines of his will, a tendency which may well have been strengthened by his daughter's marriage some years before to Francis Russell*, heir to the earldom of Bedford. Russell was himself to be summoned to the Lords in the Parliament of March 1553, and his father, a leading Councillor, could well have taken the lead in St. John's nomination: for his part St. John seems to have stood well with John Dudley, Duke of Northumberland, the chief 'manager' of the elections, having served with Dudley against the Norfolk rebels in 1549 and been pricked sheriff immediately after Dudley overthrew the Protector Somerset in the following autumn. Why so well befriended a man, who had already represented the shire in Parliament, should have had to yield to one 20 years his junior and a stranger to the House is a mystery: if it smacks of local resentment at the Council's intervention there remains the question why it was St. John, and only he, who was given the rebuff.[12]

Whereas both the 1st Earl of Bedford and his son Francis were implicated in the succession crisis which followed, there is nothing to show that St. John took any part in it. He did figure in a local disturbance in August 1553, when it appears that a group of anti-enclosure rioters tried without success to enlist his support: it is not clear whether the eight prisoners in Bedford gaol (including a woman committed for seditious words against the Queen) whom St. John and the 1st Lord Mordaunt were commissioned on 26 Aug. to deal with had taken part in the affair, but St. John's employment on this occasion, like his reappointment to the Bedfordshire bench in the following February, implies that the new Queen had nothing against him save perhaps a lingering grudge for his earlier role as her custodian. None the less, if the testimony of his monumental inscription is once again to be accepted, it was not to Queen Mary but to Princess Elizabeth that he was to be most directly attached during these years, for he is there described as having been *camerarius* to Elizabeth both as Princess and Queen. As with the custody of Mary no evidence has come to light of St. John's appointment to Elizabeth's household nor, in this case, is there any reference to him in this capacity: perhaps, like John Thynne*, he was one of those whom she named in 1555 but who did not in practice serve her. His death within a month of her accession may have robbed him of the reward he might have expected, but the speedy ennoblement of his son Oliver was perhaps a mark of royal gratitude.[13]

St. John made his will on 6 Apr. 1558. After commending his soul to God, he appointed as executors his second wife Anne, his sons Oliver and John, and a son-in-law Edmund Elmes, and as overseers his son-in-law Bedford, Henry 11th Lord Morley and John Zouche, the last perhaps the knight of the shire for Derbyshire at the time. From the profits of his manors of Fonmon and Penmark, spread over a period of 12 years, the executors were to pay sums of money totalling £372 to his children and grandchildren, to provide rings for his daughters, to give £27 to the parishes within two miles of Bletsoe and to give what was left over from £480 to his heir Oliver St. John. Two of his daughters were to receive goods and money worth altogether 400 marks, his son John was to have his gold chain, and his plate was to be shared equally between Anne and Oliver. St. John died on 19 Dec. 1558 and the will was proved on 27 Feb. 1559. The annual value of all his Bedfordshire property, excluding that settled on Oliver in 1543, was reckoned in his inquisition to be £226.[14]

[1] *LP Hen. VIII*, vii. 56 citing SP1/82, ff. 59–62. [2] E159/319, brev. ret. Mich. r. [1–2]. [3] Date of birth estimated from age at fa.'s i.p.m., C142/44/160, 161. *Vis. Beds.* (Harl. Soc. xix), 53; PCC 45 Welles; *LP Hen. VIII*, iv; *CPR*, 1550–3, p. 410. This biography owes much to information from F. T. Smallwood transmitted personally and in *Rep. Friends of Lydiard Tregoz*, vii. 1–86 passim; x. 24–31. A biography of St. John in *Sel. Cases St. Ch.* (Selden Soc. xxv), 25–27 confuses his father and grandfather and supposes him to have died in the reign of Edw. VI. [4] *LP Hen. VIII*, ii–v, vii, x, xi, xiii–xxi; *CPR*, 1547–8, pp. 75, 76, 80, 85; 1548–9, p. 137; 1550–3, pp. 140, 393; 1553, pp. 339, 351, 354; 1553–4, pp. 17, 29. [5] J. G. Taylor, *Our Lady of Batersey*, 142 seq.; *CP*, xi. 333–4. [6] C142/43/ 16, 44/160–1; *LP Hen. VIII*, ii; *Chron. Calais* (Cam. Soc. xxxv), 98; *CPR*, 1550–3, p. 410. [7] *LP Hen. VIII*, ii–iv, vi, vii. 56, 1522(ii); *VCH Beds.* iii. 158; *Vis. Beds.* 53; *Chron. Calais*, 39, 42. [8] *LP Hen. VIII*, x. [9] Ibid. xi, xvii–xix. [10] Ibid. xii, xv–xviii, xxi; *CPR*, 1553–4, p. 252; *VCH Beds.* iii. 125; *Sel. Cases Ct. Requests* (Selden Soc. xii), 64 seq.; St.Ch.3/3/22, 7/34. [11] *LP Hen. VIII*, xii–xiv, xxi. [12] *CPR*, 1548–9, p. 137; 1550–3, p. 393; *APC*, v. 66, 242. [13] *Chron. Q. Jane*

and Q. Mary (Cam. Soc. xlviii), 15; *APC*, iv. 332; *CPR*, 1553–4, pp. 17, 29.   [14] PCC 45 Welles; C142/120/12.

S.R.J.

ST. JOHN, Nicholas (by 1526–89), of Lydiard Tregoz, Wilts.

CAMELFORD	1553 (Mar.)
?SALTASH	1555[1]
CRICKLADE	1563
GREAT BEDWYN	1571
MARLBOROUGH	1572

b. by 1526, 1st s. of John St. John* by 1st w., and half-bro. of William St. John[†]. *m.* c.1548, Elizabeth, da. of Sir Richard Blount* of Mapledurham, Oxon., 3s. inc. Oliver[†] 2da. *suc.* fa. 5 Apr. 1576.[2]

Gent. pens. by 1552–60 or later; porter, Wallingford castle, Berks. 1552; steward, lands formerly of Wallingford priory 1552; j.p. Wilts. 1573/74–*d.*; sheriff 1579–80.[3]

Nicholas St. John's home was only a few miles from Wootton Bassett, but if he aspired to election there, he was to be disappointed. Although in middle life he was to procure his return for boroughs in his native Wiltshire, as a young man he had to look outside the county for a seat. He had his first experience of the House in Edward VI's second Parliament, summoned under the aegis of the Duke of Northumberland, and almost certainly in the company of Robert Huick, who had served for Wootton Bassett in the previous Parliament: presumably St. John owed his seat for a Cornish borough to his post in the royal household and more specifically to his association with Sir Francis Knollys, the constable of Wallingford castle and one of Camelford's first two Members. St. John's Protestantism, which doubtless commended him to both Knollys and to Northumberland, became after Mary's accession a liability and probably explains his absence from the Commons until opinion began to turn against the regime. If he is to be identified with one of the Members for another Cornish borough in 1555, he did not join his fellow, Robert Nowell, in supporting Sir Anthony Kingston by voting against a government bill.[4]

Under Elizabeth, St. John at first sat regularly in Parliament and often figures in the Journal as a committeeman. After his father's death his obligations as head of the family and member of the Wiltshire bench became his chief concern and he disappeared from the parliamentary ranks. He made his will on 1 Nov. 1589 and died seven days later.[5]

[1] The indenture is mutilated and only 'Nic . . .' of the junior Member's christian name is legible, C219/24/30.   [2] Date of birth estimated from age at fa.'s i.p.m., C142/175/99. *Wilts. Vis. Peds.* (Harl. Soc. cv, cvi), 168; *CPR*, 1547–8, p. 377.   [3] *CPR*, 1550–3, p. 294; 1558–60, p. 430; Lansd. 3(89), f. 197.   [4] *CPR*, 1550–3, p. 294; A. L. Rowse, *Tudor Cornw.* 300.   [5] *CJ*, i. 89–122 passim; PCC 3 Drury; C142/227/208.

J.J.G.

ST. JOHN, Oliver (by 1522–82), of Bletsoe, Beds.

BEDFORDSHIRE	1547

b. by 1522, 1st s. of Sir John St. John* of Bletsoe by 1st w., and bro. of John[†]. *m.* (1) by Feb. 1543, Agnes, da. of Sir John Fisher, gd.-da. and h. of Sir Michael Fisher (*d.*Feb. 1549) of Clifton, Beds., 4s. inc. John II[†] and Oliver II[†] 6da.; (2) by 28 Aug. 1572, Elizabeth, da.of Geoffrey Chamber of Stanmore,Mdx., wid. of Sir Walter Stonor (*d.*1551) of Stonor, Oxon., of Reginald Conyers (*d.*1560) of Wakerley, Northants., and of Edward Griffin (*d.*1569) of Dingley, Northants. *suc.* fa. 19 Dec. 1558. *cr.* Baron St. John of Bletso 13 Jan. 1559.[1]

Gent. waiter extraordinary, household of Prince Edward by 1547, royal household 1547; commr. relief, Beds. 1550, musters 1560, eccles. causes, dioceses of Lincoln and Peterborough 1571, 1575; sheriff, Beds. and Bucks. 1551–2; j.p. Beds. 1554–8, q. 1558/59–*d.*, Cambs., Hunts. 1562–*d.*; custos rot. Beds. 1558/59; ld. lt. 1569.

Oliver St. John began his career in the household of Prince Edward, and on the accession of his master he entered the royal household. His own court connexion combined with his father's influence explain his return as one of the knights for Bedfordshire to the first Parliament of the reign, although as yet he had no experience of local affairs. The designation 'junior' on the election indenture leaves no doubt that it was he and not his uncle and namesake who was then returned. All that is known of his part in the Commons is that on 21 Feb. 1549 he was licensed to be absent for three days, presumably on account of problems arising from his wife's succession to the Fisher inheritance in the midlands. If he was re-elected to the King's second Parliament, it was not for Bedfordshire, but he could have obtained a seat for almost any borough. From 1550 he figured increasingly in county administration and from 1554 he served as a magistrate.[3]

Ennobled shortly after his father's death St. John demonstrated his allegiance to Elizabeth in both public and private matters. His second marriage to a widow well provided for by two of her three previous husbands further enriched him. He made his will on 20 Apr. 1582 and died the following day.[4]

[1] Date of birth estimated from marriage. *Vis. Beds.* (Harl. Soc. xix), 53–55; *CP*; *VCH Beds.* ii. 277, 323; *CSP Dom.* 1595–7, p. 359; PCC 19 Mellershe, 22 Tirwhith; R. J. Stonor, *Stonor*, 216; C142/120/12.   [2] Roy. 7, C16, f. 94; LC2/2, f. 53v; *CPR*, 1553, p. 351; 1553–4, p. 17; 1560–3, pp. 433, 435, 437; 1569–72, pp. 277–8; 1572–5, p. 551; *Coll. State Pprs.* ed. Haynes, i. 559–60; *State Trials*, ed. Howell, i. 957.   [3] *CJ*, i. 8.   [4] *APC*, iv, v, vii, x, xiii; *CPR*, 1558–60, p. 74; 1563–6, pp. 43, 361; PCC 5 Bucke, 19 Mellershe, 32 Holney; *HMC Var.* iii. 87–88; *Selden Soc.* xii, 64 seq.; St.Ch.3/3/22, 7/34; C142/198/1; PCC 22 Tirwhite.

N.M.F.

ST. LEGER, Sir John (by 1516–93/96), of Annery in Monkleigh, Devon.

DARTMOUTH	1555
DEVON	1559

ARUNDEL   1563
DEVON   1571, 1572
TREGONY   1584

b. by 1516, 1st s. of Sir George St. Leger of Annery by Anne, da. of Edmund Knyvet. *m.* by June 1535, Catherine, da. of George Neville, 5th Lord Bergavenny, at least 2s. 4da. *suc.* fa. 1533/37. Kntd. 1544/1 Oct. 1547.[1]

Commr. relief, Devon 1550, musters 1569; j.p. 1554, q. 1558/59–*d.*; dep. lt. Devon and Cornw. 1558, Devon 1569; sheriff, Devon 1560–1.[2]

John St. Leger was only a boy when his father and grandmother arranged that he should marry a daughter of the wealthy royal favourite Sir William Compton; the bride was to bring a dowry of £2,346 and both families were to settle lands on the couple. The marriage did not take place, seemingly because Catherine Compton died, and it was replaced by a match with Catherine Neville, a granddaughter of the 3rd Duke of Buckingham. St. Leger was married by 1535 and within two years he had livery of an inheritance comprising lands in nine counties. He served in the French campaign of 1544. According to Sir William Paget, Henry VIII on his deathbed chose St. Leger for creation as a baron, but the Council revised the King's plan after his death.[3]

It was not until he was about 40 that St. Leger entered the Commons but he was to sit in every Parliament save one for the 30 years which followed. His election in 1555 may have owed something to the prominent part he had played in the rounding up of the Carew rebels at the beginning of the previous year; this had earned him the thanks of the Queen and a place on the Devon bench. Himself linked by marriage with the Carew and Courtenay families, and returned for Dartmouth with the outgoing sheriff James Courtenay, St. Leger is likely to have enjoyed most support from James Bassett, the court favourite who sat in this Parliament as one of the knights of the shire. The names of Courtenay and St. Leger are conspicuously absent from the list of Members, among them many 'western' men, who voted against one of the government's bills. For the rest of Mary's reign St. Leger was an active local official, and when early in 1558 Francis Russell*, 2nd Earl of Bedford was made lord lieutenant of Devon and Cornwall, Sir Thomas Denys* and St. Leger became his deputies.[4]

St. Leger had both added to and consolidated his possessions in Devon, especially through grants of ex-monastic lands, but in later life he parted with much of his property and he died in the mid 1590s a poor man.[5]

¹ Date of birth estimated from livery of inheritance in 1537. *Vis. Kent* (Harl. Soc. lxxv), 69; *Vis. Devon*, ed. Colby, 10, 22, 91; *Trans. Dev. Assoc.* xlix. 213; PCC 35 Hogen; *CPR*, 1547–8, p. 52. ² *CPR*,

1553, p. 358; 1553–4, p. 18; *CSP Span.* 1554–8, p. 369; *CSP Dom.* 1547–80, p. 341; *Add.* 1566–79, p. 130. ³ C142/53/3, 55/2, 4; PCC 35 Hogen; *LP Hen. VIII*, xii, xix; *Wealth and Power*, ed. Ives, Knecht and Scarisbrick, 96. ⁴ D. M. Loades, *Two Tudor Conspiracies*, 42–43, 105; *APC*, v. 6; vi. passim. ⁵ *LP Hen. VIII*, xviii, xix; *CPR*, 1547–8, pp. 52, 263; 1554–5, pp. 136, 140; 1560–3, pp. 72, 551; Devon RO, Tingey mss 840, 850, 852, 865, 885–7; *HMC Hatfield*, xvii. 500; J. A. Youings, 'The disposal of monastic property in the co. of Devon, 1536–58' (London Univ. Ph.D. thesis, 1950), 259, 282; *Devon Monastic Lands* (Devon and Cornw. Rec. Soc. n.s. i), 25–27, 91.

R.V.

ST. LOE, Sir John (1500/1–59), of Sutton Court, Bishops Sutton, Som. and Tormarton, Glos.

SOMERSET   1545
?SOMERSET   1555[1]
GLOUCESTERSHIRE   1559*

b. 1500/1, 1st s. of Nicholas St. Loe of Sutton Court by Eleanor, da. of Sir Thomas Arundell of Lanherne, Cornw. *m.* by 1518, Margaret, da. of Sir William Kingston* of the Blackfriars, London, and Elmore and Painswick, Glos., 2s. Edward† and Sir William† 1da. *suc.* fa. 1 Sept. 1508. Kntd. by Nov. 1528.[2]

Jt. (with Sir William Kingston) constable, Thornbury castle, Glos. 1528–40, sole 1540–*d.*; j.p. Som. 1532–*d.*, Glos. 1547; chief steward, Portbury, Som. 1533; marshal of the army [I] 1535–6; sheriff, Glos. 1536–7, Som. and Dorset 1551–2; commr. benevolence, Som. 1544/45, musters 1546, chantries, Dorset, Som. 1548, relief, Glos., Som. 1550.[3]

Only seven years old at his father's death, John St. Loe became the ward of Sir William Kingston, with whom he was to remain closely associated throughout his life and whose daughter he was to marry. It was presumably under Kingston's wing that he gained the military experience which seems to have earned him his early knighthood.[4]

St. Loe was sent on active service to Ireland in 1534 and on the following 30 Apr. the King appointed him marshal of the rather unruly army there. He was recalled in 1536 and fought against the northern rebels. Thereafter he seems to have lived mainly on his Somerset estates, although he was present at court on ceremonial occasions such as the christening of Prince Edward and the reception of Anne of Cleves, and in 1544 he commanded a troop of foot in France.[5]

Although until the 1540s a considerable part of the St. Loe patrimony remained with Sir Edward Wadham, who had married the widow of St. Loe's grandfather, St. Loe had inherited the manor of Stoke, Somerset in 1522 and after the Dissolution he purchased or leased other property in the county: thus in May 1550 he obtained a long lease of the manor of Keynsham and other lands in Somerset. Together with what fell to him on the death of Wadham, which included Tormarton manor, these made him a considerable, though not a great, landowner in Gloucestershire and Somerset and helped to qualify him for the knighthood of the latter shire in the Parliament of 1545 when he and his cousin and fellow-knight, Sir Thomas Speke, doubtless benefited from the support of their kinsman, Sir Thomas Arundell*, Queen Catherine Parr's chancellor. In spite of this achievement and of his Protestant sympathies, reflected in his association with Sir Anthony Kingston* and the marriage of his son, William, to a daughter of Sir Edward Baynton*, he is not known to have sat in either of Edward VI's Parliaments; he was, however, put on a number of local commissions, served a term as sheriff and had licence to retain 60 men. In June 1549 he was ordered to Ireland with 300 men but the expedition was postponed, and probably cancelled, by the western rising.[6]

The succession crisis of 1553 faced St. Loe with a hazardous decision. On 18 July Jane Grey and her Council wrote to him and Sir Anthony Kingston ordering them to muster forces and march to Buckinghamshire in her support. Three or four days later St. Loe was at Longleat, whither he had gone presumably to concert action with Sir John Thynne*, and there received from his cousin Sir Nicholas Poyntz* intelligence that Queen Mary had been proclaimed in London. Whatever course of conduct the two may have envisaged, the news that Jane had been repudiated in London left them no choice: Thynne proclaimed Mary at Warminster and St. Loe doubtless hastened into Somerset with a similar resolution. The new regime at first left him unscathed: he was even reappointed to the Somerset bench. Both he and his sons, however, stood suspect and were to be penalized in turn. In February 1554 Sir William St. Loe was arrested in connexion with Wyatt's rebellion, and in May 1556, suspicion of their complicity in the Dudley plot earned his younger brother a spell in the Fleet and his father house-arrest under a recognizance of £1,000. St. Loe had, indeed, done nothing to mollify the Queen and Council by his behaviour in the Parliament of 1555, his election to which, probably for Somerset again in company with another dissentient, Sir Ralph Hopton, was in itself something of a challenge: both he and Hopton followed the lead of Sir Anthony Kingston in opposing a government bill in the Commons.[7]

St. Loe did not long survive the advent of a more congenial regime. Elected to Elizabeth's first Parliament for Gloucestershire, where he had now probably made his main home, he died on 20 Mar. 1559 while it was still in session.[8]

[1] Guildford mus. Loseley 1331/2. [2] Date of birth estimated from age at fa.'s i.p.m., *CIPM Hen. VII*, i. 355. *LP Hen. VIII*, iv. xii, xiii. [3] *LP Hen. VIII*, iv, vi, viii, xvi, xvii, xxi; *CPR*, 1547-8 to 1558-60 passim, [4] *LP Hen. VIII*, i, iv, xiii, xvi. [5] Ibid. viii, ix, xi, xii, xiv. [6] Ibid. i, iii, xiii; Collinson, *Som.* ii. 403; *CPR*, 1550-3, pp. 7, 396; 1553, p. 354; *CSP Ire.* 1509-73, p. 105. [7] *Chron. Q. Jane and*

Q. Mary (Cam. Soc. xlviii), 65, 108; *Wilts. Arch. Mag.* viii. 310; *APC*, v. 270; Guildford mus. Loseley 1331/2. [8] E150/46/37; PCC 4 Chaynay; *Machyn's Diary* (Cam. Soc. xxxii), 191.

R.V.

ST. POLL (SAMPOLL), George (by 1499–1558/ 59), of Louth Park, Lincoln, North Carlton, and Snarford, Lincs. and Lincoln's Inn, London.

LINCOLN	1542*,[1] 1545, 1547, 1553 (Oct.), 1554 (Nov.)[2]
LINCOLNSHIRE	1555
LINCOLN	1558

b. by 1499, 3rd s. of John St. Poll of Snarford by Helen, da. of Sir Richard Thimbleby of Poolham, Lincs. *educ.* L. Inn, adm. 1523. *m.* Jane, da. of Sir William Askew* of Nuthall, Notts. and Stallingborough, Lincs., 2s. inc. Thomas† 2da. *suc.* bro. 1556.[3] Autumn reader, L. Inn 1540.

Commr. tenths of spiritualities, Lincs., Lincoln 1535, musters, Lincs. (Lindsey) 1539, relief, Lincs. (Holland, Lindsey), Boston 1550, goods of churches and fraternities, Boston 1553; member, council of Charles Brandon, Duke of Suffolk 1537–45; j.p. Lincs. (Lindsey) 1538–d.; recorder, Lincoln 1542–d.; jt. (with William Cordell*) steward, duchy of Lancaster, Bolingbroke honor, Lincs. Dec. 1553; serjeant-at-law 1555.[4]

George St. Poll was descended from a substantial Lincolnshire family. Although he was a third son, he eventually inherited the family estates at Snarford, but by then he was nearing 60 and had long since made his own way through his profession of the law. After training at Lincoln's Inn and early practice, he became counsel to the Duke of Suffolk. In 1546 St. Poll testified to having had 'the doings of all his causes in and at the laws of the realm by the space of nine years past' and five years earlier the duke had acknowledged St. Poll's 'good counsel' by making him steward of a string of manors in Lincolnshire at a fee of £6 13s.4d.[5]

After the Lincolnshire rebellion of 1536 the common council of Lincoln had agreed to grant Suffolk the nomination of the city's recorder. When Suffolk's first nominee, Anthony Missenden*, died in 1542, the duke named St. Poll, who was made recorder on 7 Sept. He also succeeded to Missenden's seat in the Parliament which then stood prorogued. No return survives, but as the writ for the by-election was issued on 8 Nov. 1542 St. Poll was probably elected in time to take his seat at the opening of the second session in January. On the following 23 Aug. he remitted to the city his wages for that session, but as the amount involved was £8 14s. the claim which he forwent was either for attendance at 87 out of its 111 days at the standard rate of 2s. a day, or for a longer period at a reduced rate: he may therefore have missed part of the session on his own or on the duke's affairs. St. Poll was to sit for Lincoln in almost every subsequent Parliament until 1558: apart from that of March 1553 (when the Members for the city are not known), the only exceptions were the Parliaments of April 1554 and 1555, in the second of which he was a knight of the shire. Despite his long service in the Commons there is little trace of his contribution there: in the second session of the Parliament of 1547 he was enlisted to speak on behalf of the 2nd Earl of Cumberland in a debate concerning the hereditary shrievalty of Westmorland, and in the first session of Mary's (and his own) last Parliament a bill on payments to receivers and collectors was committed to him after its first reading, and the proposal to limit the raising of aids to pay soldiers to the current emergency, put forward by him with Richard Grafton and Sir Edward Rogers, saved the musters bill from loss on its return from the Lords on the morning of the prorogation.[6]

Until Suffolk's death in 1545 St. Poll engaged in extensive property transactions both on the duke's behalf and on his own. In 1539 he acquired Westlaby grange from Suffolk, and in 1543 he purchased Swallow manor from John Bellow* and Robert Brokelsby. In the augmentations accounts for 1545-6 St. Poll is described as Suffolk's deputy in his office of high steward of suppressed and attainted lands beyond the Trent: he had played a similar role in at least one abbey before the Dissolution, that of Newsham, of whose Lincolnshire manors he was made under steward in January 1537. During most of the 1540s St. Poll lived at Louth Park; in the pardon roll of 1547 he is described as of Lincoln and Louth Park, *alias* of Lincoln's Inn. In 1551 some land in his tenure at Spalding was granted to (Sir) John Cheke*, and in 1556 he acquired various properties at Gainsborough from the 9th Lord Clinton; in the same year he succeeded to the family estates at Snarford after the death of his two elder brothers.[7]

In 1556-7 St. Poll headed the list of justices of peace in Lindsey whom the Privy Council ordered to take an inventory of the goods of John Bellow and to put them under custody while Bellow's conduct in various transactions and affrays was under investigation. Possibly connected with this affair is a letter from St. Poll to the mayor of Grimsby concerning the indictment of a certain prisoner there, with a postscript that reads: 'And I pray you have me commended to Mr. Bellow and so far as concerning such matters as he wrote to me of as concerning Mr. Chancellor, I made Mr. Chancellor no such promise nor I did not conveniently forbear it; I intend to speak with Mr. Chancellor shortly in the same'. Probably the reference is to the chancellor of augmentations as Bellow's troubles appear to have

derived in part from his surveyorship of augmentations in the East Riding.[8]

Amid his various activities St. Poll had not forgotten the law. He read at his inn in 1540, served on several commissions of oyer and terminer from 1547 and was called to be serjeant in 1555: if both he and Queen Mary had lived longer he might have attained the bench, but he died soon after her. He made his will on 30 Dec. 1558 and it was proved on the following 22 Feb. Describing himself as of North Carlton, Lincolnshire, he asked to be buried at Snarford. The religious convictions expressed or reflected in the will are not easy to interpret: if the testator's trust in God 'by the merits of his only Son . . . to have forgiveness of all my sins and to be in the number of those whom he by his Holy Spirit hath sanctified to everlasting life' may be (as it has been) held to stamp him as a Protestant, his provision for a priest to pray for his soul hardly supports that conclusion: no more does the absence of St. Poll's name from the lists of parliamentary opponents of the Marian regime. Of the effect upon him of the martyrdom of his sister-in-law Anne Askew there appears to be no trace, but her family figures prominently in the will, of which Francis Askew was a supervisor with Christopher Wray*.[9]

[1] *HMC 14th Rep. VIII*, 38; Lincoln min. bk. 1541-64, ff. 16, 24. [2] Huntington Lib. Hastings mss Parl. pprs. [3] Date of birth estimated from age at elder brother's death, *Lincs. Peds.* (Harl. Soc. lii), 844-5. [4] *LP Hen. VIII*, viii, xii-xiv, xvi, xx; *APC.* vi. 49; C1/1161/8; *HMC 14th Rep. VIII*, 38; *CPR, 1547-8 to 1555-7 passim*; *Lincoln Rec. Soc.* liv, p. lxxv et passim; Somerville, *Duchy*, i. 577. [5] *Black Bk. L. Inn*, i. passim; C1/1161/8; NRA 5789, p. 479. [6] J. W. F. Hill, *Tudor and Stuart Lincoln*, 51; Lincoln min. bk. 1511-42, f. 258v; 1541-64, ff. 16, 24; *HMC 14th Rep. VIII*, 38; *Clifford Letters* (Surtees Soc. clxxii), 33-34, 102; *CJ*, i. 48, 51; C. G. Ericson, 'Parlt. as a legislative institution in the reigns of Edw. VI and Mary' (London Univ. Ph.D. thesis, 1973), 280-1, 518. [7] Hill, 63; *LP Hen. VIII*, xiv, xviii-xxi; NRA 5789, p. 481; *CPR*, 1548-9, pp. 154, 226; 1550-3, p. 138; 1553-4, p. 90; 1554-5, p. 120; 1555-7, pp. 376, 393. [8] *APC*, v. 243; vi. 49, 106; *CPR*, 1554-5, p. 59; *HMC 14th Rep. VIII*, 254 citing Gt. Grimsby AO, loose corresp. [9] PCC 43 Welles; D. Wilson, *A Tudor Tapestry*, 160.

T.M.H.

SALESBURY, John (1533-80), of Rûg, nr. Corwen, Merion. and Bachymbyd, nr. Ruthin, Denb.

MERIONETH	1553 (Oct.)
DENBIGH BOROUGHS	1554 (Apr.), 1558
DENBIGHSHIRE	1559

b. 1533, 1st s. of Robert Salesbury of Rûg and Bachymbyd by Catherine, da. of John ap Madog of Bodfel, Llanor, Caern. *educ.* G. Inn, adm. 1550. *m.* by 1566, Elizabeth, da. of (Sir) John Salusbury II* of Lleweni, Denb., 3s. inc. Robert† 2da. *suc.* fa. 28 Sept. 1550.[1]

Jt. steward, manor of Ruthin, by 1557-69 or later; sheriff, Merion. 1558-9, 1577-8; commr. Caerwys eisteddfod, Flints. 1568, musters, Denb. 1570, 1580, tanneries, Denb. 1574, felons, Merion., Mont. 1575; j.p. Denb., Merion. 1577, q. 1579.[2]

The Salesbury family of Rûg and Bachymbyd

was founded in the late 15th century by John Salesbury, fourth son of Thomas Salusbury of Lleweni (*d.*1471), and acquired the lordship of Rûg by marriage in the next generation. Quickly adopting the variant spelling of its name, the family made Rûg the more important of its residences but continued to be active in Denbighshire.[3]

It was as a minor that in 1548 John Salesbury received from his father the manors of Rûg and Glyndyfyrdwy, Merioneth, and Dinmael, Denbighshire, and he was still under age when his father died in 1550. Either deliberately or through ignorance he concealed his minority from the court of wards and did not sue out his livery when he came of age. The situation had come to light by 30 May 1554 when the wardship and marriage were granted to Philip Mainwaring, but it was only later that the court dealt with the delinquency: it exonerated Salesbury from the arrears due since he became 21 and contented itself with the livery charge itself. Concurrently with this episode he was called upon to discharge his father's and his own debts to the crown, an obligation which led to his being repeatedly summoned to appear before the council in the marches at Ludlow. It was not until 22 Feb. 1557 when he was almost 24 that he obtained livery of his inheritance.[4]

Salesbury's election to Mary's first Parliament was perhaps not unconnected with these circumstances: it would have enabled him to go to London, perhaps with the idea of reaching some accommodation, under the protection of his Membership. Rising 20, he must have enjoyed powerful backing, and this is most likely to have come from the 1st Earl of Pembroke as president of the council in the marches, whose servant he described himself to be at the time of his return. Pembroke was no longer president when Salesbury was returned for Denbigh Boroughs to the following Parliament, but as the holder of several offices in the county he was well placed to promote Salesbury's candidature. The Membership of the Boroughs was virtually controlled by Salesbury's kinsman, and later father-in-law, Sir John Salesbury: with a domicile near Ruthin, Salesbury was well known in at least one of the contributory boroughs and a neighbour, and perhaps already a brother-in-law, of Simon Thelwall who had been the Member for the Boroughs in 1553. Pembroke was president once more when Salesbury was re-elected for the Boroughs in 1558 and a year later when he entered the House as knight for the shire Thelwall was Member for the Boroughs. Nothing is known about his part in the Commons, but it was perhaps while a Member in 1553 or 1554 that he brought an action in Chancery

for the recovery of lands in Creigiog, near Llanarmon Yn Yale, which had belonged to his father. If his Catholicism stood him in good stead when returned to Parliament during the 1550s it did not debar him from a say in local affairs after the Anglican settlement, even though in 1571 he was defeated on standing for re-election for Merioneth. He died on 16 Nov. 1580. His widow married (Sir) Henry Jones I*.[5]

[1] Date of birth estimated from age at fa.'s i.p.m., Wards 9/135, f. 312v, and from grant of wardship and marriage in 1554. Griffith, *Peds.* 59; Dwnn, *Vis. Wales*, ii. 331–2; *Salusbury Corresp.* (Univ. Wales Bd. of Celtic Studies, Hist. and Law ser. xiv), tables i, ii; Req.2/23/66. [2] SC2/225/7–13; *HMC Welsh* i(1), 291; R. Flenley, *Cal. Reg. Council, Marches of Wales*, 69, 127, 146, 200–1, 205. [3] *Salusbury Corresp.* 13; *DWB* (Salusbury, Salesbury fam. of Rûg and Bachymbyd). [4] *CPR*, 1547–8, p. 374; 1553–4, p. 12; 1555–7, p. 243; Wards 7/6/4; 9/103, ff. 135, 221, 229, f. 312v; J. Hurstfield, *Queen's Wards*, 179. [5] *CPR*, 1557–8, p. 31; C1/1363/62, 1385/9; Wards 7/20/173.

P.S.E.

SALUSBURY (SALESBURY), George

DENBIGH BOROUGHS 1545

s. of Robert Salusbury of Denbigh, Denb. by Ellen. m. Gwen, da. of Eden Lloyd.[1]

The description of George Salusbury, on the indenture recording his election, as son and heir of Robert Salusbury of Denbigh does little towards locating him in the luxuriant tree of the Salusbury family; it also hints at the existence of at least one namesake from whom he needed to be distinguished. It may have been either he or this namesake who, having been deputed by Robert Heneage to survey and sell royal timber in Denbighshire, in 1542 brought a suit in the augmentations against Roger and Henry Salusbury of Denbigh for abuses in the local forests, and another against Henry Salusbury, who alleged in reply that the plaintiff was animated by spite against him for having deserted his wife, who was the plaintiff's cousin. Since the two defendants in this case were sons of John Salusbury I*, the dominant figure in the shire, it may be thought unlikely that their adversary should have been elected so soon afterwards for a constituency where their father wielded such influence. There is more to be said for identifying the Member with the George Salusbury of Erbistock, lying on the border of Denbigh and the detached part of Flintshire, who was described in a chancery case of 1545 as being 32 years of age and a servant of Sir Anthony Wingfield*. Although Wingfield was not to succeed John Salusbury I as chancellor and chamberlain of Denbighshire until 1549, both were courtiers of long standing, and Salusbury's nephew John Salusbury II* had served with Wingfield in the campaign of 1544; a servant of Wingfield's would thus have been a likely recruit to a Parliament in which Wingfield himself sat for Horsham and the younger John Salusbury for Denbighshire.[2]

The further career of George Salusbury is correspondingly difficult to trace. If he was the resident at Erbistock he survived until at least 1587/88 when he litigated against the widow of Richard Myddelton, who had sat for Denbigh Boroughs in 1542. He had probably been one of those who elected John Salusbury II for the shire to the first Marian Parliament, but it is not clear whether he was the inhabitant of Ruthin assessed at £10 in goods in 1552, the man of Llandyrnog (near Denbigh) pardoned with more than 40 others, among them Simon Thelwall*, for a double murder in 1555, or the suitor at the manorial courts of Ruthin and Dyffryn Clwyd between 1547 and 1582.[3]

[1] SC2/225/3, m. 2; C1/894/45; NLW ms Wales 21/20, m. 17. [2] *Augmentations* (Univ. Wales Bd. of Celtic Studies, Hist. and Law ser. xiii), 73; E321/33/70; C1/894/6, 45; 24/11. [3] St.Ch.3/6/64; 5/M19/3; *Augmentations*, 100; C2/Eliz.M5/58; *CPR*, 1547-8, p. 93; 1555-7, p. 42; C219/21/29; E179/220/173; SC2/225/3, 10, 20, 26.

P.S.E.

SALUSBURY, John I (by 1485-1547/49), of Denbigh.

DENBIGHSHIRE 1542

b. by 1485, 4th s. of Sir Thomas Salusbury (*d.*1505) of Lleweni by Sionet, da. of William Gruffydd of Penrhyn, Caern. *m.* at least 2s.[1]

Groom, the chamber by 1506, sewer by 1509; forester and master of the game, lordship of Denbigh 1506; parker, Cors Nodiog, nr. Denbigh 1513; constable, Conway castle, Caern. by 1526; esquire of the body by 1530; steward, Denbigh by 1530; jt. (with bro. Thomas Salusbury) steward and custos rot., lordship of Denbigh and constable, Denbigh castle June 1530–6; member, council of Ireland in 1535; chancellor and chamberlain, Denb. Aug. 1536–*d.*; commr. defence, N. Wales 1539, subsidy, Denb. 1547; sheriff, Denb. 1540–1; j.p. and custos rot. Denb. and Mont. 1543–*d.*[2]

The Salusburys were of English origin, probably sprung either from Herefordshire or Lancashire, but had settled at Lleweni by 1334. They increased in wealth and power throughout the 15th century and then sealed their success by their support of the Tudor dynasty. Thomas Salusbury was knighted at Blackheath and appointed steward of the lordship of Denbigh and his fourth son John, nicknamed Sion y Bodiau (John of the Thumbs), was found a place in the royal household.[3]

It was as a groom of the chamber that John Salusbury was granted his first Welsh office, that of forester and master of the game in the lordship of Denbigh, in succession to his father. He attended the funeral of Henry VII and continued in the service of Henry VIII. On the death of his eldest brother Sir Roger Salusbury in 1530 he became the effective head of the family during the minority of his nephew John Salusbury II*, and although his brother's offices of steward and custos rotulorum of the lordship of Denbigh were granted to a Mr. Radcliffe of the privy chamber before Salusbury could reach the King, he was able to purchase Radcliffe's interest for 400 marks: his brother Thomas Salusbury of Leadbrook, Flintshire, was joined in the patent but on condition that he should receive none of the fees during Salusbury's lifetime. It was largely through the profits of office that Salusbury became the wealthiest man in Denbighshire, assessed for subsidy in the hundred of Isaled on lands worth 300 marks a year and goods valued at 440 marks. As steward, he maintained his brother's quarrel with Robert Dolben over the recordership of Denbigh and between 1530 and 1534 appeared as plaintiff against him in the court of requests. Dolben, who argued that the recordership was separate from the stewardship and who had been supported by Wolsey, claimed that Salusbury and 'his eldest brother before him and their father and friends afore them have had the rule and offices in that country, thereby have deceived the King of his right sundry wise and hurt the town and the country such as pleased them'. In 1538 Piers Lloyd of Henllan, father of Fulk Lloyd (q.v.), further accused Salusbury in the Star Chamber of having abused his power in defence of his two sons against whom Lloyd had commenced a suit before the council in the marches.[4]

In 1534 Salusbury went to Ireland as a captain of 250 foot in the army sent to suppress the Geraldine rebellion and by August 1535 he was a member of the council there. In the following May he expressed his concern to Cromwell on hearing 'that Denbighland is a shire enacted by Parliament' and his hope that 'the said Act [27 Hen. VIII, c.26] shall not hurt nor diminish me of my said room and fees'. His fears proved groundless for in August 1536 he was appointed chancellor and chamberlain of the new shire, with the same fees he had enjoyed as steward, and granted the appointment of a baron of the exchequer at Denbigh. Three years later he wrote to Cromwell as a commissioner for the defence of North Wales to ask whether he should 'come up and wait upon the King and your lordship the said Parliament time, or else tarry at home and do my devoir according to the said commission', a request which has been mistakenly taken to mean that Salusbury was a Member of the Parliament of 1539. He was returned in 1542 as the first knight for Denbigh by his nephew and namesake who had followed him as the shire's second sheriff: he was distinguished in the return from the younger man by the suffix 'senior'.[5]

The date of Salusbury's death has not been found but he served on his last commission in May 1547 and was succeeded in his Denbighshire offices by Sir Anthony Wingfield* in December 1549.[6]

[1] Date of birth estimated from first reference. Dwnn, *Vis. Wales*, ii. 331; Griffith, *Peds.* 222; St.Ch.2/23/169. [2] *CPR*, 1494–1509, p. 483; *LP Hen. VIII*, i, ii, iv, ix, xi, xiv; C193/12/1, ff. 44, 45; E179/220/171. [3] *Salusbury Corresp.* (Univ. Wales Bd. of Celtic Studies, Hist. and Law ser. xiv), 1–7. [4] *I.P Hen. VIII*, x; E179/220/169; Req. 2/12/60; St.Ch.2/23/167. [5] *LP Hen. VIII*, ix, xi, xiv; SP1/103/217, 150/165; *Salusbury Corresp.* 7; *DWB* (Salusbury of Lleweni); C219/18B/125. [6] E179/220/171; *CPR*, 1549–51, pp. 163–4.

P.S.E.

SALUSBURY, John II (by 1520–78), of Lleweni, Denb.

DENBIGHSHIRE 1545, 1547,[1] 1553 (Oct.), 1554 (Apr.), 1554 (Nov.), 1558[2]

b. by 1520, 1st surv. s. of Sir Roger Salusbury of Lleweni by 2nd w. Elizabeth, da. of John Puleston of Hafod Y Wern. *m.* Jane, da. and coh. of David Myddelton of Chester, Cheshire, at least 1s. 1da. *suc.* fa. 1530. Kntd. 22 Feb. 1547.[3]

Sheriff, Denb. 1541–2, 1574–5, Flints. 1548–9; j.p.q. Denb. 1543–*d.*; commr. benevolence, Denb. 1544/45, chantries, N. Wales 1548, subsidy, Denb. 1547, relief, Denb., Herefs., Mont. 1550, goods of churches and fraternities 1553, musters 1557, armour 1569; alderman, Denbigh in 1545; jt. chancellor and chamberlain in survivorship with the Protector Somerset, N. Wales 28 May 1547–*d.*; receiver, ct. augmentations, N. Wales in survivorship with the Protector Somerset 28 May 1547–54, Exchequer 1554–30 Sept. 1568; custos rot., Denb. by 1558/59–64 or shortly afterwards.[4]

John Salusbury was perhaps a minor on succeeding to his patrimony in 1530, as it was another ten years before he began to cut a figure in Denbighshire. During that time the family influence was wielded by his uncle and namesake, from whom he was usually distinguished by the suffix 'junior' until his knighthood. He followed his uncle as sheriff and as such returned him as the first knight for the shire to the Parliament of 1542. In 1544 he served in the rearguard of the army invading France and in the following year he took his place in the Commons for the first time. He may have remained in London when this Parliament was dissolved by Henry VIII's death, for he was knighted in the following month at the coronation of Edward VI. His standing in North Wales was soon enhanced by three appointments there conjointly with the Protector Somerset, whom in the next two years he was to approach through (Sir) John Thynne* for the purchase of Ruthin college and to whose cofferer he delivered money in 1550. The patronage of the Protector, which must have ensured his election to the first

Edwardian Parliament, may also explain his absence from the second, when his cousin Robert Puleston sat for Denbighshire. It is, indeed, likely that he was implicated in the events which led to Somerset's execution: a year later the crown was in possession of property 'by the attainder of Sir John Salusbury' and in the spring of 1553 the Council agreed to his trial as an accessory to murder. He did not, however, forfeit any of his offices, and by May 1553 he was sufficiently restored to be named to the commission to survey church goods.[5]

Nothing has come to light about Salusbury's role in the succession crisis of 1553, but he was to sit in all but one of Mary's Parliaments and in the first of them he was not among the Members who were noted as having 'stood for the true religion', that is, for Protestantism. The only other possible clue to his public attitude—although its significance is not apparent—is the appearance of a circle against his name on the list of Members for the second session of the Queen's, and his own, last Parliament. In the course of the reign he became involved in several protracted lawsuits with a vicar of Northop, Flintshire, over tithes, with Rhys Gruffydd of Caernarvon for allegedly accepting bribes while levying troops for the St. Quentin campaign, and with Bishop Goldwell over the presentation to the archdeaconry of St. Asaph: the outcome of the first two cases is not known but judgment went against him in the last.[6]

On 24 June 1558 the Council ordered Salusbury to pay Sir Richard Bulkeley* the money levied more than a year earlier for the maintenance of soldiers billeted at Beaumaris. His suing out of a general pardon at the accession of Elizabeth may have been more than the conventional precaution, for evidence of financial mismanagement began to accumulate. In April 1560 he recognized a debt of £4,000 to the crown and promised 'from henceforth well and truly [to] behave himself' in his receivership as long as he continued to hold it. Four years later Henry Norris told his father Sir William Norris* that Salusbury was 'far behindhand and especially his deputies (for whom he is answerable) in as ill a case or rather worse, which causeth him to shift his hands of the same office' and that he had 'bonds of great value forfeited in the Exchequer touching that office, not as yet cleared or answered as they must be'. It is not known whether he surmounted these difficulties, but in 1568 he was replaced in the receivership by Edward Hughes, a client of Sir Robert Dudley*, Earl of Leicester.[7]

The incursion of Leicester into North Wales marked the end of Salusbury's ascendancy there: besides the receivership he lost the office of custos rotulorum in his shire and his hold on the town of Denbigh. By his will of 15 Mar. 1578 he provided for his wife and family, and appointed as executors his wife and his grandson and heir Thomas. He was buried in St. Marcel's church, Denbigh, and his will was proved on 11 June following. Thomas Salusbury, who was brought up by Leicester, was to be executed for complicity in the Babington plot.[8]

[1] Hatfield 207. [2] Wm. Salt. Lib. SMS 264. [3] Date of birth estimated from first appointment. Dwnn, *Vis. Wales*, ii. 331; PCC 26 Langley. [4] C219/18C/176; *CPR*, 1547–8, pp. 93, 163; 1548–9, p. 137; 1553, pp. 354, 363, 376, 419; 1563–6, p. 39; R. Flenley, *Cal. Reg. Council, Marches of Wales*, 60; W. C. Richardson, *Ct. Augmentations*, 223 n. 25, 281; *Rep. R. Comm. of 1552* (Archs. of Brit. Hist. and Culture iii), 63, 186; St.Ch.4/3/19; E179/220/166, 169. [5] *LP Hen. VIII*, xix; H. M. C. Jones-Mortimer, *Sheriffs, Denb.*, 47; Bath mss. Thynne pprs. 2, ff. 25–25v, 101–2v; Egerton 2815; *APC*, iii. 184, 249. [6] Wm. Salt. Lib. SMS 264; C1/1354/27, 1431/26–27, 1432/54; St.Ch.4/3/19. [7] *Salusbury Corresp.* (Univ. Wales, Bd. of Celtic Studies, Hist. and Law ser. xiv), 24; *APC*, vi. 288; *CSP Dom.* 1547–80, p. 154; Add. 36926, ff. 8–9; *CPR*, 1566–9, p. 207; Req. 2/201/50. [8] NRA 14045, p. 3; *HMC Bath*, v. forthcoming; Flenley, 74; PCC 26 Langley; SP12/99/55; *EHR*, lix, 353–5.

P.S.E.

SALUSBURY, Thomas (by 1518–61 or later), of Flint.

FLINT BOROUGHS 1545

b. by 1518, ?illegit. s. of Thomas Salusbury of Flint. ?*m.* Jane, da. of Robert Massey of Coddington, Cheshire.[1]
   Commr. i.p.m., Cheshire and Flints. 1539, Flints. 1554, relief 1550, goods of churches and fraternities 1553; escheator 1547–8; mayor, Flint 1553; j.p. Flints. 1555.[2]

Thomas Salusbury cannot be placed with confidence in the prolific family of that name. All that is known for certain is that he was a nephew of John Vain Salusbury of Denbigh and thus a grandson of that uncle's father Thomas Salusbury of Denbigh. His father could have been the Thomas Salusbury of Flint who died in December 1530 leaving as heir an 11 year-old daughter Agnes, for this Thomas had a bastard son and namesake whose illegitimacy could have arisen from the father's divorce from Margaret Pennant *alias* Salusbury in or after 1529. It appears that the inheritance, consisting of manors and lands in and around Flint and at Hawarden, Flintshire, first passed to another daughter Margaret, who in May 1555 undertook to convey it to Agnes; in the following month it was valued preparatory to its delivery. If Agnes's illegitimate brother was the Thomas Salusbury who three months later sold lands in the Wirral and at Hawarden to Sir John Salusbury* he had evidently been well provided for, and on this foundation he could have built the career at Flint and in the shire which probably included election for the Flint Boroughs to the Parliament of 1545.[3]

The Thomas Salusbury then elected can hardly have been other than Robert Massey's brother-in-law of that name, for Massey was to follow him at Flint in 1547 and later. It was with John Massey and George Salusbury (probably his colleague in 1545) that Salusbury was to be accused a few years later by William Aldersey* of stealing from a barn at Coleshill £30 worth of tithe corn belonging to Aldersey as rector of Holywell; Salusbury was himself lessee of the commote of Coleshill, in which lay the town of Flint, and the corn may have been destined for the flour mill at Flint which at about this time Edward Stanley II* charged Salusbury with erecting in breach of his own monopoly of grinding corn in the town.[4]

The last reference found to Salusbury is his mention in his uncle John Vain Salusbury's will of January 1561.[5]

[1] Date of birth estimated from first reference. NRA 14045, p. 2; *Vis. Cheshire* (Lancs. and Cheshire Rec. Soc. lviii), 176. [2] *LP Hen. VIII*, xiv; *CPR*, 1553, pp. 363, 419; 1553–4, p. 303; C1/1433/47; 219/20/190; SP11/5/6. [3] Dwnn, *Vis. Wales*, ii. 331; C1/1473/7; *LP Hen. VIII*, xv; PCC 8 Loftes; NRA 14045, pp. 2, 25, 79. [4] St.Ch. 3/6/64; *Augmentations* (Univ. Wales Bd. of Celtic Studies, Hist. and Law ser. xiii), 100; SC6/Hen. VIII, 5136, m. 2; C1/1069/1–2. [5] PCC 8 Loftes.

P.S.E.

SALUSBURY, William (by 1519–59), of Barnstaple, Devon.

BARNSTAPLE 1554 (Nov.), 1558

b. by 1519, 1st s. of John Salusbury of Barnstaple by Catherine, wid. of one Couch. *m.* by 1539, Lettice, da. of Richard Gay of Barnstaple, 5s. 3da. *suc.* fa. 1549/52.[1]
   Alderman, Barnstaple 1543–*d.*, mayor 1557–8.[2]

William Salusbury's great-grandfather had been a younger son in the family of Salusbury of Denbighshire, and he was thus a distant cousin of his namesake the lexicographer and translator. His grandfather, a physician, had settled in Barnstaple, where his father and uncles played a part in municipal affairs as he was to do in his turn. He was made a gift of sugar and spices worth 3s.4d. by the town in 1541/42 and elected alderman in 1543. Assessed at 13s.4d. for the subsidy of 1543, he obtained a lease of chantry lands two years later and in 1549 acted as feoffee with his father in the purchase of the chapel of St. Anne from Roger Prideaux*; he was later appointed a trustee of the chapel school. He appears as one of the capital burgesses in the borough's charter of 1557 and his re-election to Parliament occurred while he was mayor. Nothing is known of his role in the Commons save that he was not among those who left the Parliament of November 1554 without leave before its dissolution. He was buried in the parish church of Barnstaple on 26 Nov. 1559.[3]

[1] Date of birth estimated from first marriage. *Vis. Devon*, ed. Vivian, 667; N. Devon Athenaeum, Barnstaple, D. Drake ms 'MPs Barnstaple', 28. [2] N. Devon Athenaeum, D. Drake ms. op. cit. 28; 2520; 3330. [3] N. Devon Athenaeum, 512; 602; 2520; 3972, f. 52(2);

D. Drake ms. op. cit. 28; *DNB* (Salisbury, William); *CPR*, 1548-9, p. 380; 1555-7, p. 391.

A.D.K.H.

SALVEYN, John (by 1531-70/71), of London.

MAIDSTONE 1553 (Mar.)

b. by 1531, yr. s. of Gerard Salveyn of Croxdale, co. Dur. by Joan. *educ.* L. Inn, adm. 14 Feb. 1545, called 1552. *m.* (1) Martha; (2) Elizabeth, da. of Thomas Wheler; ?at least 1s. *d.v.p.*[1]

Pens. L. Inn 1558-9, butler 1560, bencher 1562, Autumn reader 1564, Lent 1569, keeper of black bk. 1564-5, treasurer 1566-7, gov. 1570-d.

John Salveyn was a younger son in an established Durham family. His career as a lawyer began badly for in the spring of 1551 he and Robert Monson* were expelled from Lincoln's Inn for breaking the window of William Roper*; both were re-admitted in the following November and called to the bar early in 1552. He probably owed his return for Maidstone to his fellow-Member William Wotton (q.v.), who had entered Lincoln's Inn in 1547. Maidstone had been incorporated in 1549 but the charter made no mention of its parliamentary representation and on 21 Mar. 1553, three weeks after the opening of Parliament, the Commons deputed two Members, Robert Broke and Richard Morgan, to examine the charter and in the meantime ordered Salveyn and Wotton to withdraw from the House: the borough did not return Members again until 1563 when it did so under a new charter.[2]

Salveyn, unlike Wotton, did not sit again and little has come to light concerning him apart from his steady progress at Lincoln's Inn. Before his second reading in 1569 the Privy Council wrote to remind him of the obligation to take the oath of supremacy. His family was Catholic—his brother Anthony Salveyn, a former master of University College, Oxford, was deprived of his office as vicar general of the bishop of Durham at the accession of Elizabeth and his nephew George Birket or Birkhead was to become the second of the Catholic archpriests—but nothing is known of his own religious sympathies although the circumstances of his return for Maidstone suggest that he was then expected to support the Duke of Northumberland. He made his will on 10 Dec. 1570 and asked to be buried in the parish church, next to his wife Martha, if he should die while resident 'here in the parish of St. Margaret's in Lothebury'. He left to his nephew Gerard Birkhead £20, a black nag 'going at Mr. Temple's at Burton Dassett', Warwickshire (presumably John Temple of Lincoln's Inn, father of Thomas Temple†) and all the debts owing to him from his eldest brother Gerard Salveyn. He gave a gold ring to his sister Isabel Birkhead, all his books

and a gold ring to his brother-in-law Richard Wheler, who had been admitted to Lincoln's Inn in 1566, and gold coins to three godsons (one of them the son of Thomas Wilbraham†, recorder of London, with whom Salveyn had acted as feoffee for Sir Thomas Chaloner* in 1565), his wife's three sisters and their parents. He also bequeathed his father-in-law, a London draper, his gelding 'going at Mr. Wotton's', a legacy which suggests that he had maintained his friendship with the family of his fellow-Member who had died in 1556. He left the residue of all his goods to his wife and named her and his father-in-law executors. The will was proved on 7 Mar. 1571.[3]

[1] Date of birth estimated from education. Surtees, *Durham*, iv. 118-19; PCC 12 Holney. Although Salveyn may have been older than 14 when admitted to Lincoln's Inn—his eldest brother was born by 1513—he can hardly have been the John Salwey who in 1526 was licensed to marry Martha Nelson of St. Gregory's, London, *Mar. Lic. London* (Harl. Soc. xxv), 5. [2] *Black Bk. L. Inn*, i. 297, 298, 300; *CJ*, i. 25. [3] *Bull. IHR*, sp. supp. 11, p. 9; Emden, *Biog. Reg. Univ. Oxf. 1501-40*, p. 503; G. Anstruther, *Seminary Priests*, i. 35; PCC 47 Bakon, 11 Holney.

H.M.

SAMMES, William (by 1491-1542 or later), of Lincoln.

LINCOLN 1529

b. by 1491.[1]

Common councilman, Lincoln 1512-d., alderman, 1513-31, c.1535-d., mayor 1515-16; commr. subsidy 1512, 1515; j.p. 1515-16, 1519.[2]

William Sammes (the form 'Scoumys' in the *Official Return* is a misreading) appears to have been a native of Lincoln, although his parentage has not been traced. In 1518 he was granted a lease for 60 years of a strip of highway alongside his tavern door at the head of 'Bawershyll', but it is less likely that he was a tavern keeper by trade than that he was trained in the law. The place-name Bowers Hill has disappeared, but it is thought to have lain in the parish of St. Michael on the Mount, just below the cathedral precincts.[3]

Sammes was chosen one of the common council at the first recorded election of 3 Jan. 1512; to qualify for election he must have previously served as chamberlain of one of the wards, but there is no record of his occupancy of that office. In 1513 he was elected alderman and allowed three years respite before being elected mayor, 'that he may prepare himself for the office': this notwithstanding, he was nominated for the mayoralty in the next year and elected in 1515. As mayor Sammes sponsored numerous civic reforms. During his term a confirmation of the city's charter was obtained and arrangements set on foot for new chartering of the city guilds; the panel of aldermen, three short of the proper number, was filled by a special election;

ordinances were passed against the pulling down of houses; an attempt was made to tidy up the accounts of monies owing to the city and to revive the cloth trade by attracting a clothier to Lincoln; and an ordinance for registering apprentices produced 33 registrations, more than in any five years combined. The city had been in the habit of selling exemptions from the burdensome office of sheriff; Sammes tried to break this and even managed to persuade one freeman to surrender his discharge and to serve for the next year.[4]

In the following year, 1516–17 Sammes served as graceman of the guild of St. Anne, the most prosperous guild in the city and one whose affairs and finances were largely governed by the common council; it was customary for the outgoing mayor to serve in this capacity for a year, with his sheriffs as the guild's chamberlains. Among Sammes's other duties were the assessing of taxes and auditing of accounts, and the viewing and valuing of lands. In 1513 he joined with the recorder, Richard Clerke*, to represent the city in Chancery, the Council and the duchy chamber in a dispute over the election of a sheriff. Sammes was also involved himself in various disputes. In 1518 a Lincoln goldsmith, George Browne, accused him in the common council of detaining some of his goods, and the matter grew so heated that both were committed to ward, Sammes for 'contumelious words and seditious countenance'. A more serious affair began in 1519 when, as a justice for the city, he bribed and threatened one of the sheriffs 'to be good and favourable to John Brampston which hath killed Robert Cootes'. Brampston had his case removed from Lincoln by writ of *certiorari*, and its outcome is not known, but the common council decided that Sammes had 'behaved him wrong and contrary against his oath'. Finally, on 26 Sept. 1531 the common council resolved that he 'shall be none of the said number [of common councilmen] for divers causes by them considered', and for a few years his name disappears from the list of aldermen.[5]

These blots on his civic record had not deterred the city from electing Sammes as one of its Members to the Parliament of 1529, although the fact that he was not re-elected in 1536 may reflect his demotion in 1531. The city was scrupulous in its payment of his parliamentary wages and by 19 Aug. 1535 he had received £45 4s.0d.; like his fellow-Member Vincent Grantham he had thus presumably been diligent in his attendance, although of his part in the proceedings of the House nothing is known. The cost of its two Members was a staggering burden for the city, exceeding even the fee-farm paid to the 1st Earl of Rutland during those years. Sammes's

differences with the city were eventually resolved and during the closing years of his life he was restored as an alderman, finally disappearing from the minute books between October 1542 and October 1543. Presumably he was dead by the latter date, but no will or inquisition post mortem has survived.[6]

[1] Date of birth estimated from first reference. [2] Lincoln min. bk. 1511–42, ff. 4, 5v, 43, 46v, 67v, 96v, 222; *Statutes*, iii. 88, 172; *DKR*, x. app. ii, 118; *LP Hen. VIII*, xvi. [3] Lincoln min. bk. 1511–42, f. 79v; J. W. F. Hill, *Medieval Lincoln*, 360. [4] Lincoln min. bk. 1511–42, ff. 4, 5v, 46–66v passim. [5] Ibid. ff. 4v–5, 17–18v, 68v, 78, 89–90, 103v–104, 219, 222; C1/568/3; 891/10–12. [6] Lincoln min. bk. 1511–42, ff. 216, 219v–20, 228v, 230v, 246, 249v–50.

T.M.H.

SAMWAYS (SAMUYS), Thomas I (by 1523–53 or later), of Weymouth, Dorset.

WEYMOUTH 1553 (Oct.)[1]

b. by 1523. *m.* prob. at least 1s.[2]
Subsidy collector, Weymouth 1545.[3]

Thomas Samways was probably a kinsman of Thomas Samways II* of Melcombe Regis. In the musters of 1539 the Weymouth Samways, described as an archer, appeared with a bow, a sheaf of arrows and a harness, the Melcombe Samways with a bow and a sheaf of arrows. In July 1545 each was appointed subsidy collector in his own town; and in 1550 and again in 1552 Samways of Weymouth was assessed at £20 in goods to the other's £10. One or other, or both, frequently exported and imported goods through Weymouth, which was also Melcombe's outlet. In 1559 the necessity of sharing the port led to friction between the two towns, and the mayor of Melcombe, Owen Reynolds*, complained in the Star Chamber against Thomas Samways and Henry Newman, at that time the bailiffs of Weymouth. It may have been the former Member who had to contest this case, but it was probably a younger namesake who was to play an important, if factious, part in the life of Weymouth up to the 1580s. This Thomas Samways making his will in 1588, asked to be buried in the church at Wyke Regis 'on the north side of the tombstone under which my father lieth buried'.[4]

Samways took the senior place for Weymouth along with another townsman, John Jordan *alias* Blancombe, in Mary's first Parliament. Neither had filled high municipal office, but in Jordan's case, at least, this was to follow. Unlike the Members for Melcombe, John Leweston and Owen Reynolds, the two did not overtly display Protestant sympathies in the House.

[1] Bodl. e Museo 17. [2] Date of birth estimated from appearance at musters. [3] E179/104/156. [4] SP2/S; E122/122/4, 7, 21; 179/104/156, 195, 200; St.Ch.5/M30/14; H. J. Moule, *Cat. Docs. Weymouth and Melcombe Regis*, passim; PCC 46 Rutland.

H.M.

SAMWAYS (SAMWISTE), Thomas II (by 1522–68/70), of Melcombe Regis, Dorset.

MELCOMBE REGIS 1554 (Apr.)

b. by 1522. *m.* 1s.
Bailiff, Melcombe Regis 1543–4, mayor 1545–6, 1552–3, 1554–5; subsidy collector 1545.

Thomas Samways was a merchant of Melcombe Regis; already a resident, he bought three burgages in the town in 1544. He may have been the grandson of Geoffrey Samways of Dorchester who in 1486 left his eldest son, William, a burgage in both Melcombe and Weymouth. Geoffrey's sons included two Thomases, two Henrys and two Roberts and the nominal confusion in the family apparently outlasted this generation: at all events there was throughout the mid 16th century a namesake Thomas Samways I* in Weymouth as well as in Melcombe. Thomas Samways of Melcombe was an important municipal official and was still living in Melcombe in 1568; two years later his name was not included in a list of past mayors of the town and he may be presumed dead with the more certainty since his son, also Thomas, was then no longer designated junior.

In the spring of 1554 Melcombe, an impoverished port easily won over by candidates ready to forego their statutory wages, complied with the Queen's wish by electing two townsmen, Robert Michell and Samways, to Parliament. This compliance was probably unintentional, arising only from the chance that the captains of the two royal forts nearby, John Leweston and John Wadham, previous representatives of the borough in the House, were this time elected elsewhere. Samways's decision to stand may have been influenced by his namesake's Membership of the previous Parliament, which his own appearance at Westminster was perhaps meant to emulate.

Date of birth estimated from first reference. Weymouth and Melcombe Regis mss Sherren pprs. 34; E179/104/156; PCC 4 Milles; Harvard pf. ms Eng. 757, pp. 3, 19.

H.M.

SANDELL, Leonard (by 1533–70), of Hatfield Peverel, Essex.

?ORFORD 1554 (Nov.)[1]

b. by 1533. *educ.* I. Temple, adm. 1548 or 1550. *m.* Elizabeth, da. of John Roper of St. Dunstan's, Canterbury, and Eltham, Kent, wid. of John Pilborough (*d.*1548), *s.p.*[2]
Jt. (with Miles Sandys†) clerk of the crown and King's attorney KB 1559–*d.*[3]

Leonard Sandell appears to have been returned for Orford to Mary's third Parliament, although on the list of Members of that Parliament his name has been struck through. Since his fellow-Member John Harman, whose name has also been deleted,

is known to have been prosecuted for quitting the Parliament early without leave, it is likely that both deletions were made in error and that Sandell also sat. If so, he probably owed his return, as did Harman, to the patron of Orford, William Willoughby*, 1st Baron Willoughby of Parham; he may already have been related to Willoughby through the Tyrrells of Little Warley, Essex, or have been brought into contact with him through a brother-in-law, (Sir) Edward Madison*. Sandell's legal training could have been a recommendation, as Willoughby was to introduce a bill into this Parliament to confirm his title to the inheritance of the Duchess of Suffolk if she died childless. On 16 Jan. 1555 this bill was defeated in the Commons on a division, Sandell being doubtless one of its 73 supporters.[4]

Apart from the grant of his office in the King's bench, little has come to light about Sandell's career. In 1561 he bought the manor of Woodham Mortimer, Essex, from Sir Andrew Corbet*, but less than three years later he sold it. In 1562 a list of names for a crown loan included him among the 'new' men who had not contributed to a previous one under Mary but were judged capable of lending to Elizabeth. Details of his family are found in his will, drawn up in August and proved in November 1570. In a devout preamble he dedicated his soul to the Trinity and looked towards a joyful resurrection. He left legacies to the poor in a large number of Essex parishes and 40s. to those at Fairford, Gloucestershire, 'where I was born'. He bequeathed 20s. to each of five London prisons, smaller sums to his household servants, and money, rings or clothes to six of his wife's children by her former husband and to his own brothers Edmund and Robert. Several leases in Essex were to go to his brothers and other relatives. His widow and residuary legatee was joined in the executorship with John Ivie, 'secondary of my office', and Thomas Ivie, 'my clerk'.[5]

[1] Huntington Lib. Hastings mss Parl. pprs. [2] Presumed to be of age at election. *I.T. Adm.* 5, 9 (Leonard Randell of Hatfield Peverel); PCC 33 Lyon; Foss, *Judges*, v. 317. [3] *CPR*, 1558–60, p. 107. [4] *CJ*, i. 41. [5] *CPR*, 1560–3, p. 137; 1563–6, p. 135; Osborn collection. Yale Univ. Lib. 71.6.41; Morant, *Essex*, i. 341; PCC 33 Lyon.

N.M.F.

SANDYS, Sir Richard (by 1488–1538/39).

HAMPSHIRE 1529

b. by 1488, yr. s. of Sir William Sandys (*d.*26 Oct. 1496) of The Vyne, Sherborne St. John, Hants by Margaret, da. of John Cheyne of Shurland, Isle of Sheppey, Kent. *m.* (1) 1s.; (2) 1534, Denise, wid. of Walter Champion of London. Kntd. 1 Nov. 1523.[1]
Gent. usher by 1509, to Princess Elizabeth 1536; bailiff, scunage of Calais and islands of Coulogne in marches of Calais 1521–*d.*; commr. subsidy, Hants 1523, 1524; other commissions 1530–5; jt. lt. Claren-

don forest, Hants and Wilts. 1524–*d.*; j.p. Hants 1529–*d.*; knight of the body by 1533.[2]

Sir Richard Sandys doubtless owed his election to the Parliament of 1529 either directly or indirectly to the King. The writ for Hampshire was one of those which Henry VIII had sent to him at Windsor, where Sandys may well have been in attendance. Both in his own right, and as the brother of William, 1st Baron Sandys, one of the King's favourite courtiers, he was a natural choice for the knighthood of a shire in which his family held a leading place.[3]

Although Richard Sandys succeeded to all the lands which his father had purchased, he seems not to have had an establishment of his own but to have lived in his brother's household. He was a gentleman usher at Henry VII's funeral. In 1513 he accompanied his brother on the expedition to France, and in the following January the two were at Portsmouth preparing for a French attack. From 1517 Lord Sandys was frequently at Calais, and Richard was probably there with him: both served under Suffolk in the expedition of 1523 and Richard was one of those knighted at its close. In that year he was named a subsidy commissioner for Hampshire, but was 'beyond the sea in the King's wars' when his own assessment came to be made. He was at Calais during Wolsey's visit in 1527 and the King's in October 1532.[4]

Nothing is known of Sandys's part in the proceedings of the Parliament, but during its lifetime he remained closely associated with his brother. On 6 May 1533 he and his son John were granted the office of bailiff of the scunage of Calais which he had held alone since 1521: when his right to the office was challenged by the mayor of Calais, Lord Sandys wrote on his behalf to the deputy, Viscount Lisle, assuring him that Sir Richard had long been bailiff both of the scunage and of Coulogne. In January 1535 the same writer informed Cromwell in an indignant letter that his brother had been attacked the day before in the Queen's park of Stratfield Mortimer, Berkshire, by 'young Trapnell', son-in-law to Sir Thomas Englefield*, and six of his servants, an assault for which he demanded redress. This was a reversal of the role imputed to Sandys in a Star Chamber case in Wolsey's time, when Francis Digneley* complained of an attack by him in Alice Holt forest, Sussex.[5]

Sandys probably sat in the Parliament of 1536 in accordance with the King's request for the re-election of the previous Members. During the northern rebellion he was one of the gentlemen appointed to attend upon the King. In the same year he became a gentleman usher to Princess Elizabeth and he was present at the christening of

Edward VI on 15 Oct. 1537 and the funeral of Queen Jane a month later. He was alive on 3 June 1538, when he witnessed a deposition against a priest who looked forward to the end of the royal supremacy, but was dead by 23 June 1539, when Lord Sandys wrote to Cromwell about a dispute with his widow. Sandys's marriage to this lady, the widow of a rich alderman of London, had greatly improved his financial position. After his death she complained to Cromwell that 'she was like to go a begging' because her husband and Lord Sandys had between them 'consumed and expended of her goods above £7000': this her brother-in-law denied, claiming that although not obliged to do so he had agreed to give her £80 a year for life, an offer which she had first accepted and then refused.[6]

[1] Date of birth estimated from first reference. *Test. Vet.* ed. Nicolas, ii. 432; *CP*, xi. 441; *LP Hen. VIII*, iii, vi, vii. [2] *LP Hen. VIII*, i–vi. [3] Ibid. iv. [4] *Test. Vet.* ii. 432; *LP Hen. VIII*, i. iii; SP1/29, f. 7; *Chron. Calais* (Cam. Soc. xxxv), 39, 42. [5] *LP Hen. VIII*, iii, iv, vi, viii; St.Ch.2/13/241. [6] *LP Hen. VIII*, x–xiii; SP1/156, ff. 169–70; 2/Q, ff. 31–35.

P.H.

SAPCOTE, Edward (?1489–1547), of Burley, Rutland.

RUTLAND 1539[1]

> *b.* ?1489, 1st s. of Thomas Sapcote† of Burley by Joan, da. and coh. of Sir John Frauncey of Foremark, Derbys., wid. of William Staveley (*d.*1488) of Bignell, Oxon. *educ.* ?I. Temple. *m.* settlement 6 Sept. 1514, Jane, da. of Thomas Quadring of Careby, Lincs., *s.p. suc.* fa. c.1503. Kntd. 22 Feb. 1547.[2]
>
> Sheriff, Rutland 1510–11, 1527–8, 1531–2, 1535–6, 1542–3, 1546–7; commr. subsidy 1512, 1523, 1524, musters 1546; j.p. 1524–*d.*, Lincs. (Holland) 1543; esquire of the body by 1539; steward, honor of Richmond in 1540–1.[3]

Edward Sapcote's father, who was probably a younger brother of the eminent Sir John Sapcote† of Devon, acquired Burley in right of his wife, whose mother Isabel Plessington of Burley had married Sir Richard Sapcote of the same place. Sapcote was a young man, and his father recently dead, when he first served as sheriff; he had sued out a pardon at the accession of Henry VIII. His marriage may be placed at about 1514, the date of a settlement for Joan Quadring, whose father was later to make Sapcote both an executor and a beneficiary: the lease of North Rawesby grange which he then inherited cost him a chancery suit against its landlord, Swineshead abbey, when the abbot refused to acknowledge it.[4]

Sapcote was a near neighbour at Burley of John Harington I, one of the two magnates of the county, and it was with Harington that he was to be elected a knight of the shire in 1539. As a landowner whose subsidy assessment of £100 a year in 1540 was second only to Harington's in Alstoe hundred, and as an administrator with four shrievalties to his name, Sapcote could well expect his turn to come, but that it did so at this time may reflect the ascendancy of Sir John Russell* (created Baron Russell a week after the summoning of the Parliament), a relation by marriage who had been one of the trustees in a settlement made by Sapcote in 1527 and whom he was to call in his will his 'singular good lord'. Although his contacts with Cromwell appear too slight to warrant any suggestion of ministerial support, his joint report with Sir Everard Digby* on their interrogation of a priest whose form of service and public prayers breached the Act of Supremacy (26 Hen. VIII, c.1) betokens his acceptance of the new order in religion.[5]

Sapcote served in the rearguard of the army in France in 1544, when Russell commanded the van, and discharged two more shrievalties, during the second of which he made the return to Edward VI's first Parliament. He died at Burley on 14 Dec. 1547. By his will made earlier in the month he made a number of gifts to churches and the poor in Burley and in Lincolnshire, and gave a life interest in Burley house and its contents to his wife, while directing that all 'harness, bills, bows, spears, javelins and all other my ustelments [furnishings] of war shall remain at Burley as heirlooms'. He named his heirs (including his nephew Robert Brokesby†) his executors and Russell his supervisor, and remitted any doubts about the will to his 'trusty friend' Edward Griffin, the solicitor-general, who was to have 40s. for his pains. Since Sapcote left no issue the manor of Burley, which was valued at his death at over £100 a year, was eventually sold. The mansion, embellished by George Villiers, Duke of Buckingham, was destroyed in the Civil War.[6]

[1] E159/319, brev. ret. Mich. r. [1–2]. [2] Date of birth estimated from death of his mother's first husband and from his first shrievalty. VCH Rutland, ii. 115; Wards 7/5/5; Lit. Rems. Edw. VI, p. ccci. [3] LP Hen. VIII, iii, iv, xiv, xvi, xx, xxi; Statutes, iii. 85. [4] VCH Rutland, ii. 115; LP Hen. VIII, i; Wards 7/5/5; Lincoln Wills, ii (Lincoln Rec. Soc. x), 75–77; C1/709/20. [5] E179/165/123; LP Hen. VIII, v, xiii–xv; PCC 6 Populwell; NRA 8679 passim. [6] LP Hen. VIII, xix; PCC 6 Populwell; Wares 7/3/91, 5/5, 8; VCH Rutland, ii. 112; Pevsner, Leics. and Rutland, 289.

D.F.C.

SARGER, Walter (by 1488–1535), of Wells, Som.

WELLS 1512,[1] 1515,[2] 1523[3]

b. by 1488, s. of John Sarger (d.1490/91) of Taunton ?by Isabel. m. by June 1507, Maud, da. of Nicholas Trappe† of Wells, at least 2 ch.[4]

Auditor, Wells 1509–d., constable 1510–11, member of the Twenty-Four, 18 Sept. 1511–d., master 1511–12, 1516–17, 1523–4, keeper, altar of St. Catherine 1515–17, rent collector 1523–4; commr. subsidy, Som., Wells. 1523.[5]

Walter Sarger came from a family of Taunton,

where his father, or perhaps his uncle, John Sarger the younger, had been constable between 1470 and 1485. This John Sarger's elder brother and namesake appears to have been a rich man; he died leaving a large quantity of silver and plate to his son Walter, his daughter Anastasia and his brother whom he appointed executor.[6]

Nothing is known of Walter Sarger's inheritance other than in these goods. In September 1509 he was admitted to the freedom without an entry fine because he was married to the daughter of a freeman, and two years later he joined the governing body of the Twenty-Four but paid 20s on refusing to undertake the office of rent collector. Sarger's first term as master began in the autumn of 1511, and he was elected to Parliament on the following 9 Jan. He also sat in the Parliament of 1515, doubtless in accordance with the King's letter to Wells requesting the return of the same two Members as before, and again in 1523. For his service at Westminster and the Blackfriars on each of these occasions he received the city's usual payment of 12d. a day. For the subsidy of 1523 he was assessed (as living in the High Street) on goods valued at £50.[7]

Sarger must have died shortly before 5 July 1535, the date on which another citizen was chosen to fill his place among the Twenty-Four. A deed of 1544 describes him as late tenant of 12 acres of land belonging to the manor of Wookey.[8]

[1] Wells act bk. 2, p. 266. [2] Ibid. 2, p. 280. [3] Ibid. 2, p. 312. [4] Date of birth estimated from admission as freeman. PCC 37 Milles, 21, 34 Bennett; CPR, 1467–77, p. 72. [5] Wells act bk. 2, pp. 257–382 passim; LP Hen. VIII, iii. [6] PCC 37 Milles; Som. Arch. and Nat. Hist. Soc. lv. 54. [7] Wells act bk. 2, pp. 254–312 passim; E179/169/156. [8] Wells act bk. 2, p. 382; T. S. Holmes, Wookey, 57.

M.K.D.

SAUNDERS, Drew (by 1525–79), of Hillingdon, Mdx.

BRACKLEY 1558

b. by 1525. m. Anne, ?sis. of John Hutton, 1s. prob. d.v.p. 1da.[1]

Drew Saunders was evidently a kinsman, perhaps a brother, of his fellow-Member Robert Saunders. He was a merchant of the staple who appears in 1546 in the correspondence of Robert Saunders's brother-in-law Otwell Johnson, with whom he joined in making a loan to the treasurer of Calais. His business must have suffered from the loss of Calais, although in the years which followed he was among the merchants licensed to export wool to Bruges. By then he was shifting his interest elsewhere, having become a charter member of the Russia Company: among his associates in this enterprise was Blase Saunders, a younger brother of Robert. A suit brought in the court of requests by

John Hutton, his brother-in-law and fellow-stapler, against Henry Chapman, his son-in-law and executor, shows Saunders trading in 1570 through Hamburg and maintaining a factor there; Chapman, in his rebuttal, mentioned the 'multitude of the accounts and books of reckonings which came to his hands from the said Drew having so great dealings in merchandise'.[2]

In 1558 Saunders acquired Cowley Hall and its appurtenances in Hillingdon (where the earls of Derby, lords of Brackley, were principal landowners and occasional residents) from Robert Hutton, and he was to make his will on 21 June 1577 when living in a house called Moorcroft in that parish. No relationship has been found between Drew Saunders and Thomas Saunders of nearby Uxbridge, whose son Nicholas sat in several Elizabethan Parliaments. Saunders left 100 marks to his wife together with her jewelry and four rooms in Moorcroft. The will was proved on 23 June 1579, the year in which his brass in Hillingdon church states that he died.[3]

[1] Date of birth estimated from first reference. Req.2/99/18; Mill Stephenson, *Mon. Brasses*, 304; PCC 26 Bakon. [2] *LP Hen. VIII*, xxi, add.; *CPR*, 1554-5, p. 56; 1557-8, p. 300; 1558-60, pp. 24, 411; T. S. Willan, *Muscovy Merchants of 1555*, pp. 52-53, 121-2; PCC 44 Mellershe; Req.2/99/18. [3] *VCH Mdx.* iv. 62, 71, 73, 89, 91; PCC 26 Bakon.

S.M.T.

SAUNDERS, Edward (1506-76), of Whitefriars, London; Westminster, Mdx. and Weston-under-Wetherley, Warws.

COVENTRY   1542*[1]
SALTASH   1553 (Mar.)

b. 4 Apr. 1506, 1st surv. s. of Thomas Saunders of Sibbertoft, Northants. by Margaret, da. of Richard Cave of Stanford, Northants.; bro. of Robert*. *educ.* Camb.; M. Temple, adm. 3 May 1524. *m.* (1) by 1540, Margery (*d.*11 Oct. 1563), da. of Sir Thomas Englefield of Englefield, Berks., wid. of George Carew (*d.*1538) of (?Bury St. Edmunds) Suff., 1da.; (2) by 1566, Agnes, da. of one Hussey. *suc. fa.* 8 Mar. 1528. Kntd. 27 Jan. 1555.[2]

Autumn reader, M. Temple 1539, bencher 1539. Servant of Cromwell by Dec. 1537; j.p. Northants. 1539-*d.*, Warws. 1544-*d.*, Cumb., Yorks. (W. Riding) 1554-8, Leics. 1554-*d.*, Berks., Glos., Herefs., Oxon., Salop 1562-*d.*; serjeant-at-law 1540-7; recorder, Coventry 1541-53; King's serjeant 1547-53; j.c.p. 4 Oct. 1553-7; c.j. Lancaster 1554; c.j.KB 1557-9; retained of council, duchy of Lancaster 1558-*d.*; receiver of petitions in the Lords., Parlts. of 1558, 1559, 1563, 1571, 1572; chief baron of the Exchequer 29 Jan. 1559-*d.*[3]

Edward Saunders came of a minor Northamptonshire family, connected by descent and marriage with some of the leading families in the midlands. He was not the first-born, but his elder brothers did not survive childhood: Thomas Saunders gave him

lands worth 20 marks a year with a reversionary interest in the lands left to his mother. As a lawyer Edward Saunders showed early promise and his services were enlisted by Cromwell in return for a fee: he was never an established member of the minister's household but was expected to answer Cromwell's call. In 1538 he signed a letter to Cromwell about the rights of the townsmen of Saltash and perhaps with Cromwell's approval he married the daughter of a leading light of the Middle Temple. As one who stood close to the minister he may have sat in Parliament during the 1530s, but in the absence of nearly all the returns this remains hypothetical.[4]

Saunders's advancement suffered no setback on Cromwell's fall from power. In the autumn of 1540 he became a serjeant-at-law and in the following year he succeeded Roger Wigston* as recorder of Coventry. In the Parliament of 1542 Wigston took the senior seat for Coventry as he had done on previous occasions, but he died on 27 Nov. 1542, two months before the second session opened. Saunders may have filled the vacancy during that session but he is not known to have done so until the third (1544), for which he received payment. Coventry expected its recorders to take a lease of a house there and to be frequent in their visits: Saunders complied with the first condition, but pressure of business in London prevented him from appearing as often as the corporation wished. It was perhaps for this reason that he was not re-elected for the city during his recordership, although in 1545 a link with Queen Catherine Parr, through his kinsmen the Throckmortons, may have helped him to obtain a seat elsewhere. In 1544 he had campaigned with the King in northern France.[5]

On the recommendation of the chancellor, Saunders was promoted early in 1547 to King's serjeant. The Protector Somerset may have taken exception to him as one of the last recipients of Chancellor Wriothesley's favour and he did not find a seat in the Commons later in the same year, although as a King's serjeant he received a writ of assistance to the Lords; he brought a number of bills from there to the Commons and in the first session he served on the Lords committee to scrutinize the bill for vagabonds. The extensive property owned by the duchy of Cornwall in Coventry may explain his return for a duchy borough to the second Edwardian Parliament, but it is more likely to have been the work of Sir John Russell*, 1st Earl of Bedford at the request of Humphrey Cavell, a colleague at the Temple: Cavell was to sit twice for the borough a year later. As an assistant in the Lords in this Parliament Saunders may not have taken his place in the Commons, but he appeared there as the bearer of bills at least twice, bringing down three on 21 Mar. and six days later another for the restitution of Sir Edward Seymour.[6]

Saunders did not sign the document by which Jane Grey succeeded to the throne, and he proclaimed Mary Queen at Coventry. His movements at this point are not certain, but before Mary left Framlingham he had sworn allegiance to her. The Queen gave him an annuity worth £20 and made him a judge, whereupon he relinquished his recordership in favour of John Throckmorton I*. He was to become a prominent figure on the bench during the reign, presiding over the trials of Sir Peter Carew*, Archbishop Cranmer, Guildford and Ambrose Dudley, Jane Grey and (Sir) Nicholas Throckmorton*. He heard the case brought in the common pleas disputing the return made for Anglesey in the autumn of 1553 and gave judgment in favour of Sir Richard Bulkeley*. He does not appear to have been compromised by the arrest for heresy of his younger brother Lawrence, to whom he wrote in prison urging him to

> reform your error in the opinion of the most blessed and our most comfortable sacrament of the altar the accustomable using whereof I am fully professed unto during my life, and to give more faith unto the confessions of holy Bernard than to Luther . . . for that the antiquity, the universality of the . . . Church and the consent of all saints and doctors do confirm the same.

Two days before his brother was arraigned, Saunders was knighted by King Philip. As a judge he was summoned to the Lords in each Parliament of the reign and in 1558 he served for the first time as a receiver of petitions.[7]

Elizabeth initially confirmed Saunders in his appointments, but following a dispute with an admiralty judge and an appearance before the Privy Council he was removed as chief justice within a few weeks of her accession and transferred to the Exchequer, where he remained until his death. Although she thus eliminated a possible source of embarrassment, Elizabeth did not neglect Saunders's proven abilities, frequently calling on his advice. One of the first cases referred to him at the Exchequer was the dispute over the election of the knights for Monmouthshire in 1558, although this was settled at the assizes. His judgements were highly thought of in the profession and were widely reported.[8]

Saunders made his will on 10 Nov. 1576, asking to be buried at Weston. He made provision for his wife, children and kinsmen, remembered his servants and tenants, and left money to relieve paupers in Coventry. He appointed his friends Humphrey Duke, Laurence Eyton, (Sir) Walter Mildmay* and Edmund Plowden* as executors. He died two days later and was buried at Weston, where a monument was erected to his memory.[9]

[1] Coventry mayors' accts. 1542–61, f. 21. [2] Date of birth given at fa.'s i.p.m., C142/48/136. Vis. Northants. ed. Metcalfe, 11; Vis. Warws. (Harl. Soc. xii), 371; Vis. Berks. (Harl. Soc. lvi), 7; Vis. Suff. ed. Metcalfe, 187; CPR, 1548–9, p. 9; PCC 31 Porch, 41 Carew; Mill Stephenson, Mon. Brasses, 525–6; VCH Warws. vi. 252, 254 C142/182/32(2); Machyn's Diary (Cam. Soc. xlii), 342; DNB. [3] M. L. Robertson, 'Cromwell's servants' (Univ. California Los Angeles Ph.D. thesis, 1975), 555–6; Stowe 571, f. 18v; CPR, 1547–8, p. 182; 1553–4, p. 71; 1555–7, p. 363; 1558–60, pp. 58, 65; CSP Dom. 1547–80, p. 61; Somerville, Duchy, i. 320 n. 3, 456, 470; LJ, i. 513, 542, 580, 666, 703. [4] PCC 31 Porch; LP Hen. VIII, xiii, xiii; Elton, Policy and Police, 337. [5] Coventry mayors' accts. 1542–61, p. 21; letters i. 63–64; treasurers' accts. 14, 19, 23, 28; council bk. 17; statute merchant rolls 43, 49; LP Hen. VIII, xix. [6] APC, ii. 25; C218/1; LJ, i. 295, 302–4, 371, 402, 404–5, 409, 411, 436, 438, 440, 442; CJ, i. 13–14, 19, 20, 25–26; information from G. Haslam. The tradition cited in DNB that Saunders sat for Lostwithiel in the Parliament of 1547 is unfounded. [7] Dyer, Reps. ii. 113v; Coventry annals 1553; State Trials, ed. Howell, i. passim; APC, iv. 21; v. 22; vi. 187, 296, 310, 419; Foxe, Acts. and Mons. vi. 636; Machyn's Diary, 342. [8] Select Pleas Ct. Admiralty (Selden Soc. xi), pp. xii–xvi, 22–23; T. W. Whitley, Parl. Rep. Coventry, 49; APC, vii. 12–397 passim; E159/333, Mich. 86; Plowden, Reps. passim; Dyer, passim; L. W. Abbott, Law Reporting in Eng. 144. [9] PCC 41 Carew; C1/1472/8–9; 142/180/32(2); Req. 2/4/105; VCH Warws. vi. 252, 254.

S.M.T.

SAUNDERS, Francis (1513/14–85), of Welford, Northants.

BRACKLEY   1547, ?Mar. 1553[1]

b. 1513/14, s. of William Saunders of Welford by w. Dorothy, da. of John Young of Crome D'Abitot, Worcs.; half-bro. of Walter Haddon*. educ. M. Temple. m. (1) Elizabeth, da. of George Carew of (?Bury St. Edmunds) Suff., 2s. 1da.; (2) Helen, da. of Roger Chaloner of London, wid. of Thomas Farnham* (d.4 Sept. 1562) of Stoughton and Quorndon, Leics. and London, prob. 1s.; (3) Frances, da. of one Pope, 1s. 4da.[2]

Bencher, M. Temple by 1575.

J.p. Northants. 1554–77; jt. (with Robert Saunders*) steward, Brackley in 1558.[3]

As a younger son Francis Saunders was to inherit only a modest estate at Welford and he made his career in the law. For most of his life he had a chamber at his inn and he supervised the training there of a number of young relatives and friends. In 1559 he was fined for failing to be Autumn reader but he ended his career as a bencher.[4]

Branches of the Saunders family customarily maintained close ties, members of different ones executing each other's wills and making marriages which appear to reflect a common policy. It is thus not surprising that Francis Saunders shared the stewardship of the 3rd Earl of Derby's borough of Brackley with his cousin Robert Saunders. This joint appointment, known to have been in force in 1558 when the question of its cancellation was mooted, may have been of some years' standing and thus explain Francis Saunders's election there in 1547, as it doubtless does his cousin's successive ones later; but Saunders had other useful connexions, including one by marriage with the sheriff, Thomas Cave. His own first marriage was into the Carew family: its date is unknown but by 1540 Elizabeth Carew had become the stepdaughter of Edward Saunders*, Robert's elder brother, and the fact that her cousin Sir Wymond Carew sat in this Parliament for Peterborough until his death in 1549 gives a family flavour to Francis Saunders's Membership. He was probably re-elected to the following Parliament with his cousin: the indenture is in poor condition and the name of the junior Member cannot be fully made out, but the christian name appears to be Francis and the first letter of the surname could be either 'B' or 'S'. Of Saunders's part in the proceedings of the Commons nothing is known.[5]

Saunders was not to sit again but during the remaining 40 years of his life he consolidated his position in his shire. Under Mary he was put on the commission of the peace and used for other local purposes. By then he had evidently acquired an interest in his mother's property, although she did not die until the early 1570s, for in November 1553 he and her stepson Paul Darrell[†], who was also Saunders's brother-in-law, were licensed to alienate land in Cold Ashby to their cousin Walter Young: this was almost certainly a stage in the settlement of the inheritance, for the property eventually returned to Saunders. His second and third marriages further strengthened his links with the leading families in the region and his purchase of the manors of Hardwick and Shangton in Leicestershire in 1563 enlarged his property. In 1564 he was adjudged by the bishop of Peterborough 'indifferent' in religion and so qualified for retention on the Northamptonshire bench; the Francis Saunders imprisoned in the Tower two years earlier may have been a Suffolk namesake. In 1567-8 Saunders settled three manors to his own use by fine and in 1573 he entailed his mother's lands in Cold Ashby upon his eldest son as part of a marriage settlement.[6]

Saunders died on 20 June 1585. By his will of 26 Oct. 1584 he left Hardwick and Shangton, a good third of his property, to Matthew, his only son by his last marriage, after a life tenancy to his wife. Yelvertoft went to his third son Francis, his patrimony of Welford to his second son William, who was to be his executor; and the residue, including the entailed Cold Ashby, to his heir Edward. The provisions of the will were scrupulously carried out, and his sons, two of whom were knighted, founded several more branches of the family in Leicestershire and Northamptonshire.[7]

[1] C219/20/89. [2] Aged 71 at death according to MI, Mill Stephenson, *Mon. Brasses*, 391. *Vis. Northants*. ed. Metcalfe, 44, 131; *Vis.*

Worcs. (Harl. Soc. xxvii), 153; Lipscomb, *Bucks*. iii. 32; *CPR*, 1558-60, p. 324; C142/63/24, 211/193; PCC 35 Brudenell. [3] *CPR*, 1553-4, p. 22; Northants. RO, Ellesmere mss box X 464. [4] *M.T. Recs.* i. 113, 118, 120, 123-4, 127, 131, 136, 161, 208. [5] Baker, *Northants*. i. 153, 293. [6] *CPR*, 1553-4, p. 362; 1554-5, p. 106; Lipscomb, iii. 38; C3/111/22, 172/6; 142/166/57; Northants. RO, Isham (Lamport) collection, nos. 1470, 1472, 1474-5, 1479, 1479A, 1598, 1606-7, 1668-9, 1681, 1683-4, 1699, 1707-8, 1716, 1742, 1795, 1804, 2177, 2191, 2273, 2285, 2290, 2292, 2302, 2307, 2311, 2364; *Cam. Misc.* ix(3), 36; *APC*, vii. 126; *CSP Dom.* 1547-80, pp. 196, 206. [7] C142/211/193; PCC 35 Brudenell; Northants. RO, Isham (Lamport) collection, no. 2364.

S.M.T.

SAUNDERS, Nicholas (c. 1530-87), of Ewell, Surr.

BLETCHINGLEY 1554 (Apr.)

b. c.1530, 1st s. of William Saunders* of Ewell by 1st w. Jane, da. and coh. of William Marston. *educ.* I. Temple, adm. Nov. 1556. *m.* (1) 1560, Isabel, da. of Nicholas Carew of Beddington, 3s. inc. Nicholas[†] 3da.; (2) Margaret, da. of Nicholas Bostock of Newington, wid. of Richard Blount[†] of London and Williton, Som. and Jasper Fisher* (*d.*1579) of London. *suc.* fa. 1570/71.[1]

The Nicholas Saunders returned for Bletchingley to Mary's second Parliament was almost certainly not the Catholic controversialist, then a civilian at Oxford, but his kinsman from the Ewell branch of the family. A man in his twenties at the time of the election and with his entry to the Inner Temple still to come, this Nicholas Saunders could have looked for a nomination both to his father, a knight for Surrey in three Marian Parliaments, and to his cousin (Sir) Thomas Saunders*, sheriff on the occasion. The seat at Bletchingley doubtless became available through the temporary eclipse of (Sir) Thomas Cawarden*, who usually controlled the borough, following his suspected complicity in Wyatt's rebellion. William Saunders took a leading part in sequestering Cawarden's armoury and was also at odds with him over the incumbent of Bletchingley, where Saunders held the manor of Pendell: to see his son returned for the borough must have been as satisfying to Saunders as it was galling to Cawarden.[2]

The Catholicism which made the younger Saunders acceptable to the Marian regime was to become a liability under Elizabeth, excluding him from public life and costing him and his brother Erasmus a spell in the Fleet prison in 1578. The month and the day are omitted from the will which Saunders made in 1587; it was proved on 18 Jan. 1588. Among family bequests he gave substantial marriage portions to each of his three daughters on condition that they married with the 'consent and liking' of the executor, his son Nicholas. 'The poor ancient householders of Ewell and Epsom' were left 40s. a year and 100 quarters of corn for five years after his death, but he made no bequest to any local church, although the vicar of Malden was to have £1.

Saunders's recusancy gives point to his choice of Burghley as an overseer; the other was his brother-in-law Sir Francis Carew. Saunders also commended his heir to Burghley's favour, perhaps with the result that Nicholas Saunders changed his religion.[3]

[1] Date of birth estimated from his parents' marriage, the birth of their fourth child in 1535 and Saunders's Membership. *Vis. Surr.* (Harl. Soc. xliii), 69; Manning and Bray, *Surr.* i. 459. [2] *DNB* (Sanders, Nicholas); *Loseley Mss*, ed. Kempe, 140–4; *HMC 7th Rep.* 608, 610; *Surr. Arch. Colls.* liv. 83. [3] *Surr. Arch. Colls.* liv. 94–96; PCC 7 Rutland.

S.R.J.

SAUNDERS, Robert (c. 1514–59), of Flore, Northants.

BRACKLEY 1553 (Mar.), 1553 (Oct.), 1558, 1559

b. c.1514, 2nd surv. s. of Thomas Saunders of Sibbertoft by Margaret, da. of Richard Cave of Stanford; bro. of Edward*. *educ.* ?M. Temple. *m.* (1) Margaret, da. and h. of Thomas Stanton of Stanton, Mon., 2s. 1da.; (2) by Oct. 1558, Joyce, da. of Sir John Goodwin of Upper Winchendon, Bucks. at least 1s.[1] Jt. (with Francis Saunders*) steward, Brackley in 1558.[2]

Robert Saunders must have been well under age in March 1528 when his father bequeathed him 100 marks and entrusted him to his mother for 'convenient' learning. He is therefore to be distinguished from the namesake who was in the service of Sir Thomas Lovell I* in 1522 and from the entrant to the Middle Temple of 1518, although as this was his elder brother's inn he may have gone there later. Saunders assisted his brothers-in-law John and Otwell Johnson in buying wool. By 1558 he was joint steward of the borough of Brackley with his first cousin Francis Saunders, and he frequently appears on the borough court rolls suing various local merchants for minor debts. His official standing doubtless explains his return to Parliament for the borough, even though his ties with the 3rd Earl of Derby, its patron, do not seem to have extended beyond his stewardship. His Membership of the Parliament of March 1553 may have been in conjunction with his cousin Francis, one of the two original representatives for Brackley in 1547, and was perhaps favoured by his brother Edward who on this occasion was returned for Saltash. Of Saunders's part in the Commons all that is known is that he opposed the reintroduction of Catholicism in the Parliament of October 1553: this gesture of defiance to the Marian regime and his younger brother Lawrence's Protestantism may have cost him his seat in the next three Parliaments of the reign, but it did not prevent him from supporting his kinsman Thomas Boughton's election in 1555. When Saunders reappeared for Brackley in 1558 his fellow-Member was a relative, Drew

Saunders, and the pair were joined in the House by one of his wife's cousins Sir John Spencer as a knight for Northamptonshire. The sickness which induced Saunders to make his will on 3 Oct. 1558 perhaps kept him away from the second session which came to an end with Queen Mary's death. Saunders recovered sufficiently to sit in the first Parliament of Elizabeth's reign but died on 13 Nov. 1559, being buried at Flore. His widow married Anthony Carleton[†].[3]

[1] Date of birth estimated from reference to him in fa.'s will, PCC 31 Porch. Baker, *Northants.* i. 153, 293; Bridges, *Northants.* i. 509; *Vis. Northants.* ed. Metcalfe, 11, 57; B. Winchester, *Tudor Fam. Portrait*, 17. [2] Northants. RO, Ellesmere mss box X 464. [3] PCC 31 Porch, 27 Jankyn; *LP Hen. VIII*, add.; Northants. RO, Ellesmere mss box X 449; Bodl. e Museo 17; *DNB* (Saunders, Lawrence); *Vis. Bucks.* (Harl. Soc. lviii), 64; PCC 44 Mellershe; Bridges, i. 509.

S.M.T.

SAUNDERS, Thomas (by 1513–65), of London and Charlwood, Surr.

GATTON 1542
SURREY 1553 (Mar.)
REIGATE 1553 (Oct.)[1]
SURREY 1558

b. by 1513, 3rd but 1st surv. s. of Nicholas Saunders of Charlwood by Alice, da. of John Hungate of (?Saxton), Yorks. *educ.* I. Temple, adm. 1527. *m.* settlement 6 June 1539, Alice (*d.*21 May 1558), da. of Sir Edmund Walsingham* of Scadbury, Chislehurst, Kent, 3s. 2da. Kntd. ?1550. *suc.* fa. 29 Aug. 1553.[2] Attendant on Lent reader, I. Temple 1546, 1547, Summer 1546, Autumn reader 1546, 1547, treasurer 1556–8, gov. in 1557. Solicitor, household of Queens Anne of Cleves and Catherine Howard 1540; j.p. Surr. 1541–58, q. 1558/59–*d.*; commr. chantries, Surr., Suss. and Chichester 1548, relief, Surr., Suss. 1550, goods of churches and fraternities, Surr. 1553, musters 1557, conventicles 1557, subsidy 1563; King's remembrancer, the Exchequer Aug. 1549–*d.*; sheriff, Surr. and Suss. 1553–4.[3]

The will of Thomas Saunders's great-uncle Henry Saunders suggests that he was a third son, but when his father died in 1553 he was left heir to extensive property in Surrey. Both his great-uncle, the father of William Saunders*, and his uncle William, father of Nicholas Saunders the Catholic controversialist, may have been members of other inns, but he established the family's connexion with the Inner Temple, where on his admission in 1527 he was pardoned all vacations and offices and allowed to be out of commons at his pleasure. His long upward progress there received occasional checks: his refusal to read in the summer of 1547 cost him temporary demotion from the bench, and in 1560 his work as treasurer was challenged and he was called upon to re-account. No such setbacks appear in his government career. Appointed solicitor of the Queen's household in 1540, originally for Anne of Cleves but then for Catherine Howard, he obtained the reversion of the office of King's remembrancer in 1545 and the office itself in 1549. Its previous holder was (Sir) Christopher More*, a fellow Inner Templar who had settled in Saunders's own county; in February 1547 Saunders indemnified More against any harm resulting from his visits to the Exchequer 'to see and peruse the records and process there for his learning and knowledge of the course of the said office'. He was to retain the post until his death. Similar continuity marked Saunders's record in local administration: for the last 24 years of his life he served every regime in turn.[4]

Saunders sat in the Commons under three successive monarchs and at intervals over a span of 16 years. His return for Gatton to the Parliament of 1542 he must have owed to Sir Roger Copley, described in the indentures as 'burgess and only inhabitant of the borough', but whether as Copley's near neighbour at Charlwood or through an intermediary like Copley's father-in-law (Sir) William Shelley* it is impossible to say. In the first session he shared in the passing of the Act (33 Hen. VIII, c.21) attainting his mistress the Queen. Whether he unsuccessfully sought a seat at the two following elections is not known, but when on 1 Feb. 1552 the Council sent a writ for the election of a knight for Surrey to replace either Sir Christopher More, or more probably More's successor, it was accompanied by an instruction to the sheriff, Sir Robert Oxenbridge*, to 'prefer' Saunders. This may well have been done on the initiative of William Paulet, 1st Marquess of Winchester: as treasurer, Winchester was Saunders's departmental chief, and he had probably engineered Saunders's knighthood in 1550 shortly after his own promotion. In the event the Council's recommendation was ignored and the sheriff returned John Vaughan I. Twelve months later the Council prepared to intervene again; this time it favoured the re-election of Vaughan and the other previous Member Sir Thomas Cawarden, but whereas Cawarden was chosen Vaughan was passed over in favour of Saunders. What lay behind this reversal can only be guessed at: the implied assertion of shire independence may have been more apparent than real and the explanation lie in an amicable adaptation to circumstances.[5]

Saunders was not to regain the knighthood of the shire until 1558; at three of the intervening elections it was his ultra-Catholic cousin William Saunders who replaced him, once during Saunders's shrievalty. Still he was elected for Reigate, where his patron was probably the lord of the manor, Lord William

Howard from whom, he held property there. Unlike some other Members from Surrey he did not oppose the initial measures for the restoration of Catholicism, and it was in the course of the second session that he was pricked sheriff. He had presumably won the Queen's confidence by ignoring the attempt of the Council, as soon as Edward VI was dead, to secure Surrey for Jane Grey, and his conduct during Wyatt's rebellion justified his choice. The invidious duty of sequestering Cawarden's goods and, with William Saunders, of removing Cawarden's weapons he appears to have carried out efficiently but humanely, afterwards sending Lady Cawarden a letter of apology and 'a token of your own', and he may not have been wholly to blame for the failure to return all the goods with which Cawarden was later to charge him.[6]

Before succeeding his father at Charlwood in August 1553 Saunders had himself acquired the manors of Flanchford and Hartswood in 1539 and in the following year had had three manors in Sanderstead and Warlingham settled on him by his father on his marriage to Alice Walsingham. In 1543 he took a 21-year lease of a house in the Blackfriars, which presumably became his London residence; from 1550 his landlord there was his Surrey neighbour Cawarden. This transaction apart, Saunders did not interest himself in monastic property. His legal standing made him a suitable choice as an overseer of wills, and among those who named him in this capacity were his father-in-law Walsingham and one of his successors as Member for Gatton, John Tingleden. Saunders's own will, which he drew up himself, was meticulous in its provisions and requirements. His wife was to have a life interest in most of his property but if she remarried she would have to give the heir written sureties against despoiling of woods or furnishings; the rest of the property was divided among the younger children. Anxious that at least one of his sons should study law, Saunders promised his law books to whichever of them did so. His care for learning showed itself in his ample provision for 'an honest parish clerk at Charlwood that can play the organ and teach children, for maintenance of God's service', and the bequest of his 'books of humanity and stories in Latin or French' to his own children. Although he made the will on 7 Mar. 1563, Saunders did not die until 18 Aug. 1565, probate following on 7 July 1566.[7]

[1] Bodl. e Museo 17. [2] Date of birth estimated from education. *Vis. Surr.* (Harl. Soc. xliii), 18; *Surr. Arch. Colls.* iv. 10; xi. 18; C142/141/25; City of London RO, Guildhall, rep. 12(1), f. 177; *CPR, 1553*, p. 357. [3] *LP Hen. VIII*, xvi, xvii, xx; *CPR, 1547–8*, p. 90; 1549–51, p. 135; 1550–3, p. 395 1553, pp. 357, 415; 1560–3, pp. 441,

485; 1563-6, p. 137; HMC 7th Rep. 607; The Gen. n.s. xxx. 26; Guildford mus. Loseley 1074; City of London RO, rep. 12(1), f. 177; Manning and Bray, Surr. ii. 190. [4] Manning and Bray, ii. 190; VCH Surr. iii. 185; PCC 15 Ayloffe; Cal. I.T. Recs. i. passim; The Gen. n.s. xxx. 26; LP Hen. VIII, xx; Guildford mus. Loseley 1128/20. [5] APC, iii. 470-1; Strype, Eccles. Memorials, ii(2), 65-66. [6] VCH Surr. iii. 237; Wards 7/10/117; HMC 7th Rep. 608-11, 614, 615. [7] VCH Surr. iii. 237; iv. 239, 336; Wards 7/10/117; Guildford mus. Loseley 1074; Manning and Bray, ii. 190; Surr. Arch. Colls. xvii. 14; LP Hen. VIII, xviii; PCC 25 Coode, 30 Bucke, 19 Crymes.

S.R.J.

SAUNDERS, William (by 1497–1570), of Ewell, Surr.

?GATTON   1529
SURREY   1553 (Oct.),[1] 1554 (Nov.), 1555

b. by 1497, 1st s. of Henry Saunders of Ewell by Joan, da. of John Lepton of Yorks. m. (1) Jane (d.1539), da. and coh. of William Marston of Horton, Surr., wid. of Nicholas Mynn (d.1528) of London and Norf., 3s. inc. Nicholas* at least 1da.; (2) Joan, wid. of Thomas Gittons (d.c.1544) of London, 4da. suc. fa. 1518.[2]

Receiver, ct. augmentations, Surr. and Suss. 1540-48; j.p. Surr. 1541-64; commr. musters 1544, chantries, Surr., Suss. and Southwark 1546, relief, Surr. 1550, goods of churches and fraternities 1553, loan 1562; other commissions 1541-68; escheator, Surr. and Suss. 1548-9; sheriff 1555-6; surveyor of crown lands, Surr. and Suss. in 1562-3.[3]

It is possible, but unlikely, that the William Saunders who sat for Gatton in 1529 was a cousin of the later Member of that name and an uncle of Thomas Saunders* of Charlwood. This William Saunders, who belonged to a prosperous Surrey family, was probably resident in that county at the time (his son Nicholas, the famous Catholic controversialist, being born at Charlwood in the following year), and was presumably of an age to have been returned to Parliament; he may also have been a member of the Middle Temple. Yet he seems to have owned no land in Surrey and to have taken no part in its affairs, he is described by some writers as resident in Aston, a place-name which cannot be located in Surrey, and it thus seems likely that he left the county after Nicholas's birth. Failing him, the Member for Gatton can only have been his cousin and namesake who was to sit again under Mary, and this is the conclusion adopted here.[4]

Little is known about Saunders's early life, and this little has been confused both by the statement, based upon a misreading of Henry Saunders's will, that he was a second son, and by the inference from his signature on a copy of the Pendell rent rolls that he was acting as his own lawyer in 1520. The will makes it clear that he was the eldest son, and the fact that his brother Nicholas had then been married for at least four years suggests that he was well over age at his father's death. He was bequeathed

considerable landed property, part of which, however, was to be administered by trustees while he received an annuity of £5; this arrangement lasted until April 1529, when the trustees conveyed the property to him. Neither his probable age nor his subsequent career makes it likely that he was the William Saunders who graduated BA at Cambridge in 1524-5. He must have married his first wife soon after 1528, the year in which her first husband died, as their fourth child Erasmus was born in 1535: it is not known whether his five daughters were all by this wife, who was to die in 1539. His return to Parliament in 1529 would thus have coincided with his marriage and his entry upon his inheritance, but apart from his proximity to Gatton there is nothing to connect him with Sir Roger Copley, the owner of that borough and clearly the man responsible for the choice of both its Members. Nothing is known of Saunders's part in the proceedings of this Parliament, nor is it more than a probability that he sat again in its successor of 1536 in accordance with the King's general request for the re-election of the previous Members. He may have been returned a third time in 1539, when the names of the Gatton Members are unknown, but from then until 1553 he did not reappear in the House.[5]

It is in 1537 that Saunders makes his first appearance in local affairs as a collector of rents for the manors of Ewell and Kingswood, the property of Merton priory: he was already a lessee of another of the priory's manors, Chessington, of which in January 1536 he had succeeded Richard Rogers in a 21-year lease. If it was he, and not his cousin, who appears in a list of 1538 he had by then attached himself, if somewhat tenuously, to Cromwell: a William Saunder was one of the 'gentlemen not to be allowed in my lord's household aforesaid but when they have commandment or cause necessary to repair hither'. In the same year he was a member of the Surrey jury which returned an indictment of the Marquess of Exeter and Lord Montagu at Southwark. On 1 Feb. 1539 he was given the next vacancy as one of the 17 particular receivers of the court of augmentations, and within 18 months he was established in that office, which carried a salary of £20 a year and other recognised emoluments. In 1541 he became a member of the Inner Temple by special admission; there he joined his second cousin Thomas Saunders, already a lawyer of repute. When war came in 1543 his name was included among those of Surrey gentlemen required to provide men for the army overseas, his quota being three foot-soldiers. On the dissolution of the first court of augmentations in 1547 he lost his receivership without apparently being given an appointment in the new court: he was, however, amply compensated on 15 May by a life annuity of £80.[6]

His later enthusiasm for the Catholic cause notwithstanding, Saunders aided the progress of the Reformation in Surrey by his work for the court of augmentations and his membership of the commissions for chantries, for taking possession of the deanery of Hastings and for the sale of church goods in east Surrey: in March 1549 he was busy certifying the inventories of the village churches near Ewell. In 1553, however, he emerged as an ardent supporter of the new Queen. Although the claim that he became cofferer of her household is not supported by the accounts for the reign, which show that the office was held in turn by Thomas Weldon*, Sir Richard Friston, Michael Wentworth* and Richard Ward I*, his name does appear on a list of annuities granted by the Queen 'for service at Framlingham in her lifetime' and he may therefore have served in her household, perhaps in a financial capacity. He was certainly active against religious dissidents: according to a list of sheriffs of Surrey and Sussex 'that did burn the innocents, with a list of such whom they burned', Saunders burned the highest number, 14. It is thus not surprising to find him returned as knight of the shire to three Marian parliaments, on the last occasion as the senior Member, although his replacement in 1558 by the more moderate Sir Thomas Saunders (who had been sheriff at the time of his cousin's second return for the county) may reflect some dislike of him for his share in the persecution, a consideration which would have told even more heavily against him if he had sought, in his old age, to sit in the Elizabethan House.[7]

Saunders was brought repeatedly into conflict with that doughty Protestant (Sir) Thomas Cawarden*. When on the outbreak of Wyatt's rebellion Lord William Howard ordered the seizure of Cawarden's armoury at Bletchingley, Sir Thomas Saunders as sheriff called on his cousin for help and together they made an inventory of the arms and arranged for their despatch. (In a brief transcript of one of the many documents relating to this episode William Saunders is described as Cawarden's servant, but this must be a mistake). Cawarden was afterwards to complain to Queen Elizabeth that the inventory was incomplete, and that although the sheriff had been ordered to return everything only a few items had been restored. Another occasion of ill feeling was Queen Mary's grant of Nonsuch Palace to the 12th Earl of Arundel. Henry VIII had granted Cawarden several offices at Nonsuch, and it was with evident relish that Saunders aided John, Baron Lumley, the earl's son-in-law, to evict

Cawarden from the premises. Bletchingley, where Saunders's ownership of the manor of Pendell made him a close neighbour of Cawarden, was yet another battleground between them. In 1547 Cawarden chose a new rector, William Wakeling, married with six children and a firm Protestant; he was replaced in 1554 by a Catholic, Robert Harvey, but restored probably soon after Mary's death. Wakeling appears to have claimed the freehold of part of Pendell, for at a manorial court held in November 1562, before a full attendance of 22 homagers, Saunders produced the rent rolls of 1451 and 1491 and triumphantly refuted Wakeling's claim.[8]

It is clear from a Star Chamber suit in which he was involved that Saunders could inspire hostility in others than Cawarden. In 1547 one William Warner had sold him the manor of Parrock with an iron mill near Hartfield in Sussex, and after Warner's death a claim by his son that the sale was not complete had been rejected in Chancery. The Warners' lessee of the mill, Denise Bowyer, complained that Saunders had interfered with her use of the forge there, but it is not known how the case was decided as Denise Bowyer had only a 10-year lease and by 1564 Saunders was in possession of the mill: in 1577 the Warners formally abandoned their claim to the manor.[9]

Under Elizabeth the Saunders of Ewell became one of the leading recusant families in Surrey. Saunders's sons Nicholas and Erasmus were Catholic stalwarts and several of his daughters married into recusant families in Norfolk. When Roger Castell of Raveningham, Norfolk, contracted to marry Elizabeth Saunders he did so both with Saunders and with Thomas, 4th Duke of Norfolk, and among other Catholic peers with whom Saunders was intimate was Lord Lumley, whom he appointed overseer of his will. In 1542 Saunders had himself been appointed executor to Elizabeth Lady Carew, widow of Sir Nicholas Carew*, and in 1560 his eldest son Nicholas married their daughter Elizabeth.[10]

Although his father had been a younger son Saunders both inherited and acquired considerable property. From his father he received the manor of Batailles and other lands in Chessington, Epsom and Ewell after the expiry of successive life interests to his mother and sister-in-law Joan; he also came into the mansion at Ewell, a water-mill and lands in Chessington, Epsom and Ewell not belonging to Batailles manor, and a string of properties held by feoffees which included Pendell in Bletchingley and the *Three Crowns* inn, Southwark. Some of these Saunders sold, a house in Southwark for £140 in 1537 and land in Charlwood for 50 marks in 1544, but he more than offset them by buying the manors of Cardens in Kent, Chessington in Surrey and Parrock in Sussex.[11]

By his will of 2 Oct. 1570, proved on the following 10 Nov., Saunders asked to be buried without pomp. He left farm animals, corn, household fittings and plate to his wife Joan, who was also to have a life interest in the manor of Cardens if she chose to live there. To his son Erasmus he gave his 'cross of gold with a pearl in the end thereof', his best doublet, a sum of £100 and a share with the third son Francis of Harsing marsh in Kent; Francis himself received jewelry, clothes, household goods, annuities totalling £25, a lease of property in Ashstead, Surrey, and lands in Cliffe, Kent. After small bequests to his daughters, his grandchildren, his stepson Oliver Gittons and his servants, Saunders bequeathed the rest of the estate to his eldest son Nicholas.[12]

[1] Bodl. e. Museo 17. [2] Date of birth estimated from father's will, PCC 15 Ayloffe. Manning and Bray, *Surr.* i. 459; PCC 23 Spert; *Surr. Arch. Colls.* xxi. 128; liv. opp. 102; *Vis. Surr.* (Harl. Soc. xliii), 53; C142/71/82. [3] *LP Hen. VIII*, xiii, xiv, xvi, xvii, xx, xxi; *CPR*, 1547–8, p. 90; 1553, pp. 327, 357, 406; 1553–4, p. 24; 1560–3, pp. 325,441; 1563–6, pp. 26, 36, 39; 1569–72, p. 220; Guildford mus. Loseley 1074; W. C. Richardson, *Ct. Augmentations*, 50; Manning and Bray, iii. 664; Osborn coll. Yale Univ. Lib. 71-6-41; *Surr. Arch. Colls.* iv. 136; viii. 302. [4] PCC 15 Ayloffe; *Surr. Archs. Coll.* liv. opp. 102; *DNB* (Sanders, Nicholas). [5] *Surr. Arch. Colls.* xiii. 145; liv. 85; Surr. RO, Pendell rentals; PCC 15 Ayloffe, 35 Porch; Add. Ch. 23411, 23412; C142/71/82; U. Lambert, *Bletchingley*, i. 297–8. [6] LC2/190, f. 123; *VCH Surr.* iii. 684; A. Heales, *Recs. Merton Priory*, cxxvi; *LP Hen. VIII*, xiii, xviii, xix, xxi; M. L. Robertson, 'Cromwell's servants' (Univ. California Los Angeles Ph.D. thesis, 1975), 556; E315/218, f. 26; *Cal. I.T. Recs.* i. 128; Richardson, 281. [7] *Surr. Arch. Colls.* xxi. 35–55, 60–62, 66, 74–76; liv. 87, opp. 102; E351/1795, mm. 6–11; Lansd. 156(28), ff. 90–94; *DNB* (Sanders, Nicholas); *HMC 7th Rep.* 614; G. A. Carthew, *Hundred of Launditch*, i. 185. [8] *Loseley Mss*, ed. Kempe, 140–4; *HMC 7th Rep.* 608, 610, 611; *Surr. Arch. Colls.* liv. 88; Lambert, ii. 416. [9] *Surr. Arch. Colls.* liv. 89–90; *Suss. Rec. Soc.* xvi. 61–64; E. Straker, *Wealden Iron*, 241–2; St.Ch.2/24/36. [10] Strype, *Annals*, ii(2); *HMC Hatfield*, iv. 267, 272; *Surr. Arch. Colls.* liv. 91–92; *Vis. Norf.* (Norf. Arch.), i. 12, 35, 253; Carthew, i. 185; Arundel Castle ms G1/7; PCC 42 Holney; *The Voyage of Sir Nicholas Carewe to the Emperor Charles V, 1529* (Roxburghe Club), i. [11] PCC 42 Holney; *Surr. Feet of Fines* (Surr. Rec. Soc. xix), 266, 415; *Surr. Arch. Colls.* liv. 89, 90. [12] PCC 42 Holney.

S.R.J.

SAVAGE, Francis (by 1524–57), of Elmley, Worcs.

WORCESTERSHIRE 1553 (Mar.)

b. by 1524, 1st s. of Christopher Savage of Elmley by Anne, da. of Sir Richard Lygon of Worcs. *m.* lic. 26 Nov. 1546, Anne, da. of William Sheldon* of Weston, Warws. and Beoley, Worcs., 4s. 2da. *suc.* fa. 23 Nov. 1545.[1]

J.p. Worcs. 1554–d.; receiver, crown lands in Herefs., Leics., Northants., Rutland, Salop, Staffs., Warws. and Worcs. 28 Mar. 1555–d.[2]

A younger branch of the Savage family of Cheshire was established by Francis Savage's grandfather at Elmley, where in 1544 his father, an esquire of the body, bought the castle and manor jointly with (Sir) William Herbert I*, who in the same year relinquished his claim. With this property Francis Savage inherited Chipping Campden and five other

Gloucestershire manors which descended from his grandfather as kinsman of Thomas Savage, archbishop of York; to these he was to add ex-monastic land in the same county, which he and George Wall acquired from Herbert in 1548, and the manor of Tysoe in Warwickshire, bought some five years later from Edward Aglionby II*.[3]

Savage's election, while he was still young and untried, looks like the work of his father-in-law William Sheldon, himself knight of the shire in the previous Parliament, with perhaps the aid of Herbert, by then Earl of Pembroke and president of the council in the marches, and even of the Duke of Northumberland, whose son the Earl of Warwick counted Aglionby, also a Member of this Parliament, among his servants. Although Savage was to sue out a pardon at Mary's accession, neither he nor Sheldon can have been seriously compromised by the events which preceded it, for in 1554 he joined Sheldon on the Worcestershire bench. In the following year he bought his father-in-law's office of receiver in the augmentations for eight midland counties, including Warwickshire and Worcestershire.[4]

Savage was 'sick in body' when he made his will on 17 Aug. 1557 and he died two days later. In fulfilment of his father's will he left annuities to his five brothers, including one who was a London apprentice. To his two infant sons he bequeathed 100 marks each and to his two daughters 200 marks. He left his lease of the manor of Hardwick, Worcestershire, to his mother for life, with remainder to his brother Thomas, and his wife Anne was similarly to enjoy the house at Elmley and one-third of the manor of Aston Subedge, Gloucestershire. He included in the will a list of all his tenants with the value of their holdings. He named his wife and his father-in-law executors and directed them to pay £300 for the dissolved chantry in Elmley for his son William. The will was proved on 4 July 1558.[5]

[1] Date of birth estimated from age at fa.'s i.p.m., C142/72/101. *Vis. Worcs.* (Harl. Soc. xxvii), 125; *Fac. Off. Reg.* 1534–49, ed. Chambers, 285; PCC 32 Noodes. [2] *CPR*, 1553–4, p. 26; 1554–5, p. 77; 1557–8, p. 205. [3] *Vis. Cheshire* (Harl. Soc. xviii), 203–4; *VCH Worcs.* iii. 340–2; C142/33/132, 72/101; *LP Hen. VIII*, xiv, xix, xxi; *CPR*, 1547–8, pp. 276, 358; 1553, p. 113. [4] *CPR*, 1553–4, p. 422; 1554–5, p. 77. [5] PCC 32 Noodes; C142/112/168; *CPR*, 1557–8, p. 69.

M.K.D.

SAVERY, Christopher (by 1502–60), of Totnes, Devon.

TOTNES 1553 (Mar.), 1553 (Oct.), 1554 (Nov.)

b. by 1502, 1st s. of John Savery of Harberton; bro. of Richard*. *m.* by 1525, Catherine, 3s. 3da.[1]
Mayor, Totnes 1535–7, 1548–9, 1556–7.[2]

Said to be of Breton origin, the Savery family can be traced at Totnes from the 13th century and at Dartmouth from the 15th. Christopher Savery shared in the government of Totnes from 1525, serving regularly as a juror at the manor court. In the year of his first election as mayor he sued for damage done to his boat at Dartmouth, and in 1545 he formed a partnership with, among others, John Wotton* to build the *George of Totnes*, which first served with the royal fleet and then as a privateer; Savery and Wotton were also partners in the *Trynitie*, which the Privy Council denounced for robbing Spanish as well as French and Scottish ships, and then and later Savery's own *Christopher* was another privateer. He was one of the Totnes merchants included in a pardon of September 1560 for offences against various statutes governing trade; in the previous year he had obtained a general pardon. Savery was assessed for subsidy in 1523–4 on goods worth £70 and in 1550–1, by which time he had begun to acquire property, on goods worth £3 6s.8d. In February 1550 he was licensed to use a crossbow.[3]

Savery sat for Totnes in three of the four Parliaments summoned in 1553 and 1554. With nearly 30 years of municipal service behind him, he exemplified the borough's electoral independence in the face of pressures from outside, as did his fellow-Members John Wotton and his younger brother Richard Savery. The town was perhaps encouraged to return the two Saverys in November 1554, after what looks like the intrusion of patronage at the preceding election, by the Queen's call for resident Members. They may also have satisfied her preference for Catholics since the elder Savery had not opposed the measures to restore Catholicism passed by the Parliament of October 1553. Soon after Elizabeth's accession Savery was reported to have used 'lewd words' which the Privy Council instructed (Sir) Richard Edgecombe* to inquire into, but whether they were aimed at the approaching Anglican settlement is not known.[4]

Savery made his will on 2 Apr. 1558. After several small bequests to the corporation, charities, servants, godchildren and grandchildren, he left to his wife his property in Brixham, his household stuff and plate, and £200; to his eldest son Alan the parsonage at Dartington and the residue of his lands, a sum of £400 and a further £200 on certain conditions; to his second son Stephen £800; and to his two unmarried daughters 400 marks towards their marriages. He died on 18 Apr. 1560 and was buried in Totnes church. Alan Savery was 34 when he was licensed to enter upon his lands in the following November.[5]

[1] Date of birth estimated from younger brother Richard's. *Vis. Devon* (Harl. Soc. vi), 253; *Vis. Devon*, ed. Colby, 186; *Vis. Devon*, ed. Vivian, 670; PCC 27 Mellershe. [2] H. R. Wilkins, *Totnes Priory*, ii. 939; *Western Antiq.* ix. 125, 149. [3] *Devon and Cornw. N. and Q.* xxviii. 285; P. Russell, *Totnes*, 47; Exeter city lib. Dartmouth ms 1982, f. 188v; R. M. S. Tugwood, 'Piracy and privateering from Dartmouth and Kingswear, 1540–58' (London Univ. M.A. thesis, 1953), 87, 142, 183; *LP Hen. VIII*, xx; Devon RO, 1597/L6; 1597A/BM33; L. M. Nicholls, 'The trading communities of Totnes and Dartmouth late 15th and early 16th cents.' (Exeter Univ. M.A. thesis, 1960), 12; E122/201/9, 3; 179/99/321; *CPR*, 1549–51, pp. 179–80; 1558–60, pp. 183, 334. [4] *APC*, vii. 51–52. [5] PCC 27 Mellershe; C142/125/23; *CPR*, 1560–3, p. 120.

A.D.K.H.

SAVERY, Richard (by 1503–72), of Totnes and Staverton, Devon.

TOTNES 1554 (Nov.)

b. by 1503, 2nd s. of John Savery of Harberton; bro. of Christopher*. *m.* by 1527, Agnes, da. of one Buckington or Darkington, 3s. 1da.[1]

When Richard Savery was elected to his only Parliament it was with his elder brother Christopher who had sat twice before. The less prominent and successful of the two, Savery none the less prospered as a merchant, often in association with his brother; in 1523–4 he was assessed for subsidy on goods worth £31 13s.4d. and in 1550–1 he paid £3 on goods. Like his brother he sued out a general pardon at Elizabeth's accession and in September 1560 both were among the merchants of Totnes pardoned for breaches of statutes governing trade. Savery purchased many properties in and around Totnes, among them the manor of Little Totnes for which he paid the 2nd Earl of Bath 800 marks in 1542; it was perhaps his landed wealth which prompted him to style himself 'gentleman', and he took pains in the division of his property among his kin.[2]

By his will of 1 Sept. 1571 Savery asked to be buried in Totnes church, made several bequests to local charities and provided for his wife and children. An inquisition held at Exeter on 20 Oct. 1572 found that Richard Savery the elder (thus distinguished from his nephew and namesake) had died on the previous 4 Feb. and that his heir was his son Nicholas aged 45 and more.[3]

[1] Date of birth estimated from first reference. *Vis. Devon* (Harl. Soc. vi), 253; *Vis. Devon*, ed. Colby, 186; *Vis. Devon*, ed. Vivian, 670. [2] L. M. Nicholls, 'The trading communities of Totnes and Dartmouth in the late 15th and early 16th cents.' (Exeter Univ. M.A. thesis, 1960), 12, 83; E179/99/221; *CPR*, 1547–8, pp. 288–9; 1558–60, pp. 183, 334; 1566–9, p. 44; *LP Hen. VIII*, xix; J. E. Kew, 'The land market in Devon, 1536–58' (Exeter Univ. Ph.D. thesis, 1967), 176. [3] PCC 19 Daughtry; C142/160/2.

A.D.K.H.

SAVILE, Henry (1517/18–69), of London, Barrowby, Lincs. and Lupset, Yorks.

GRANTHAM 1558
YORKSHIRE 1559

b. 1517/18, 1st s. of John Savile of Lupset by Anne, da. of William Wyatt. *educ.* ?Oxf. BCL 1535. *m.* (1) 1545, Margaret, da. and coh. of Henry Fowler or Fuller, *?s.p.*; (2) by 1551, Joan, da. and h. of William Vernon of Barrowby, Lincs., wid. of Sir Richard Bozom of Long Clawson, Leics., 3s. inc. George† 4da.; (3) Dorothy, da. of Richard Grosvenor of Eaton, Cheshire, wid. of Richard Wilbraham* (*d.*1558), *s.p. suc.* fa. 16 Jan. 1530.[1]

J.p. Yorks. (W. Riding) 1547, 1558/59–*d.*, (E. and N. Ridings) 1562–*d.*, Lincs. (Kesteven) 1554–*d.*; commr. chantries, Yorks. (W. Riding) 1548, relief, Lincs. (Kesteven), Yorks. 1550, to enforce Acts of Uniformity and Supremacy, province of York 1561; surveyor, ct. augmentations, Yorks. (N. Riding) by 1552–4, Exchequer 1554–*d.*; keeper, New Park, Wakefield, Yorks. 1554; escheator, Lincs. 1555–6; member, council in the north by Dec. 1558; sheriff, Yorks. 1567–8.[2]

Henry Savile was rising 12 when his father died and in 1531 his wardship was granted to Edmund Copyndale. In the absence of a more likely namesake he may be presumed to have been the Henry Savel or Sayvell who took a BCL at Oxford in July 1535 and who in the following April acted as proctor in the chancellor's court there. Of his progress thereafter a glimpse is provided by his description on the pardon roll of 1553 as 'of Barrowby . . . *alias* late of Lupset . . . *alias* late of the city of London'. His domicile at Barrowby, two miles west of Grantham, resulted from his second marriage, which brought him considerable property there in addition to his inheritance at Lupset. How he had occupied himself in London has not been discovered, but if he was the civil lawyer he could have engaged in the legal side of commerce.[3]

Savile's return for Grantham to the last Marian Parliament is probably to be explained by his own local standing, although he may also have enjoyed the support of either the 6th Earl of Shrewsbury, one of whose daughters his heir was to marry, or of the 2nd Earl of Rutland, who was his neighbour at Belvoir. It was presumably Shrewsbury's influence which gained Savile a knighthood for Yorkshire in the succeeding Parliament at the same time as he became a member of the council in the north. Adjudged a favourer of the Anglican settlement in 1564 Savile continued to serve in the north until his death early in 1569.[4]

[1] Date of birth estimated from age at fa.'s i.p.m., C142/51/106. *Vis. Yorks.* (Harl. Soc. xvi), 275–6; *Glover's Vis. Yorks.* ed. Foster, 341; *Lincs. Peds.* (Harl. Soc. l), 167, (ibid. lii), 859–60; Emden, *Biog. Reg. Univ. Oxf. 1501–40*, p. 505; *Yorks. Arch. Jnl.* xxv. 16 seq. [2] *CPR*, 1547–8, p. 92; 1548–9, p. 136; 1553, pp. 353, 355; 1553–4, pp. 21, 238; 1560–3, pp. 436–7, 439, 573; 1563–6, p. 24; 1566–9, p. 172; *Inventories of Church Goods* (Surtees *Soc.* xcvii), 109; Stowe 571, f. 11v; *Rep. R. Comm. of 1552* (Archs. of Brit. Hist. and Culture iii), 55; *CSP For.* 1558–9, p. 55; J. J. Cartwright, *Chapters in Yorks. Hist.*, 19n; R. R. Reid, *King's Council in the North*, 493. [3] Emden, 505; *CPR*, 1553–4, p. 433. [4] *Cam. Misc.* ix(3), 70; PCC 11 Sheffelde.

T.M.H.

SAVILE, Sir Henry (1498/99–1558), of Thornhill, Tankersley, and Elland, Yorks.

YORKSHIRE 1539[1]

b. 1498/99, 1st s. of Sir John Savile of Thornhill and Tankersley by 2nd w. Elizabeth, da. of Sir William Paston† of Norwich, Norf. and London. *m.* 29 Aug. 1517, Elizabeth, da. and h. of Thomas Soothill of Soothill, Yorks., 2s. 1da.; 2s. illegit. by Margaret, da. of Peter Barkston. *suc.* fa. 16 Mar. 1505. KB 30 May 1533.[2]

J.p. Yorks. (W. Riding) 1528, rem. 1530, rest. by 1534–*d.* (E. and N. Ridings) 1544–*d.*, northern circuit 1539–*d.*; steward, duchy of Lancaster, Pontefract honor 4 Nov. 1537–27 Nov. 1549, jt. (with George, 6th Earl of Shrewsbury) 27 Nov. 1549–*d.*; sheriff, Yorks. 1537–8, 1541–2; capt. Pontefract castle in 1539, Bamborough castle, Yorks. in 1546; member, council in the north in 1542–9, by 1552–*d.*; commr. benevolence, Yorks. (W. Riding) 1544/45, relief, Yorks. (E. N. and W. Ridings) 1550.[3]

The young Henry Savile's wardship passed successively to his stepfather Sir Richard Hastings and the 4th Earl of Shrewsbury before being bought early in 1517 by Thomas Soothill; seven months later Savile married Soothill's daughter and heir, and within another four years he had livery of his lands. The marriage was to prove a stormy one, with Savile fathering two sons by one of his wife's gentlewomen, but it survived her persistent attempts at a divorce and she was to benefit under his will.[4]

His marital discord was one of the issues in the feud between Savile and Thomas, Lord Darcy of Temple Hurst, and Darcy's kinsman Sir Richard Tempest*, which ended only with his opponents' deaths in 1537. From 1523, when the Earl of Surrey tried to reconcile him with Tempest while they were serving together against the Scots, until 1534, when both risked expulsion from the Yorkshire commissions in the interest of order, their antagonism defined all efforts to allay it. Savile was the more successful in soliciting the support of higher authority, and his creation as a knight of the bath at Anne Boleyn's coronation foreshadowed the outcome of the rebellion of 1536. Where Darcy and Tempest fatally compromised themselves, Savile justified the rebels' proscription of him by his refusal to parley with them, and he was soon reaping his reward. In the autumn of 1537 he succeeded Darcy as steward of Pontefract and was pricked sheriff, an office which he discharged to the admiration of Bishop Holgate, president of the council in the north, and in the spring of 1539 he was elected first knight of the shire. His second shrievalty excluded him from re-election in 1542 but he could have been returned to the last Parliament of the reign, the Yorkshire names being lost. Brought onto the council in the north in 1542, he fought in all the Scottish campaigns of the following years and spent much time in garrison duty on the border.[5]

Early in 1549 Savile was replaced as a member of the council in the north by Sir Charles Fairfax but within three years he had been renamed to the council. By his will made on 15 Feb. 1556 he left lands to his daughter Dorothy, the only child for whom until then he had made no provision, and remembered his wife. After his death on 20 Apr. 1558 he was buried in accordance with his wishes at Thornhill, his widow married Richard Gascoigne of Barnborough in Yorkshire, and his brother-in-law Richard Corbet* replaced him on the council in the north. His son and heir Edward who had been affianced to a daughter of Sir Richard Lee* during Savile's lifetime was mentally unstable, and although adjudged sane about 1560 he sought the protection of the earls of Shrewsbury with whom he resided until his death in 1603, whereupon his estates passed to a kinsman Sir George Savile† of Lupset.[6]

[1] E159/319, brev. ret. Mich. r. [1–2]. [2] Date of birth estimated from age at fa.'s i.p.m., *CIPM Hen. VII*, ii. 803. *Vis. Yorks.* (Harl. Soc. xvi), 275; *Glover's Vis. Yorks.* ed. Foster, 185. [3] *LP Hen. VIII*, iv, xii, xv, xvi, xx, xxi; R. B. Smith, *Land and Pol.* 148, 158; *CPR*, 1547–8, pp. 75, 91; 1553, pp. 353–4; Somerville, *Duchy*, i. 515–16; C60/355, m. 4; R. R. Reid, *King's Council in the North*, 490ff; *HMC Shrewsbury and Talbot*, ii. 28; Strype, *Eccles. Memorials*, ii(2), 161. [4] *Glover's Vis. Yorks.* 185; *LP Hen. VIII*, i, iii–v; *Test. Ebor.* iv (Surtees Soc. liii), 170; Smith, 58, 217; C142/116/43. [5] *LP Hen. VIII*, iii–xxi; *Yorks. Arch. Jnl.* xxxix. 123; *Yorks. Arch. Soc. rec. ser.* xli. 178–80, 189; Elton, *Policy and Police*, 304–5; *HMC Bath*, iv. 58, 66, 71; *Plumpton Corresp.* (Cam. Soc. iv), 246–7. [6] *HMC Shrewsbury and Talbot*, ii. 28, 43, 76, 99, 404; C142/116/43; *Test. Ebor.* v (Surtees Soc. lxxix), 82.

A.D.K.H.

SAWYER *see* **SAYER**

SAXMUNDHAM, George (by 1520–72), of Dunwich, Suff.

DUNWICH 1555

b. by 1520. *m.* by 1541, Margaret, 2s. 4da.[1]
Bailiff, Dunwich in 1549, 1551, 1556, 1557, 1565, 1566, alderman in 1555.[2]

George Saxmundham was a prosperous Dunwich fisherman, assessed in the parish of St. Peter on goods worth £7 for the subsidy of 1568. His Membership of Mary's fourth Parliament was an episode in his municipal advancement. He made his will on 10 Apr. 1572, leaving the greater part of his property, including three tenements in Dunwich, to his wife and executrix. Other bequests included 'three of my best lines in the tackle house' and 20s. to his apprentice, Henry May; the tackle house itself to William Wodde on payment of £7 to Margaret Saxmundham; and small sums to servants. Saxmundham was buried on 30 May 1572 and the will was proved on the following 4 Nov.[3]

[1] Date of birth estimated from marriage. Suff. archdeaconry ct. 24, f. 180; Add. 34561, ff. 22–23v, 58v. [2] T. Gardner, *Dunwich*, 82; C210/24/147. [3] *Suff. Green Bks.* xii. 65; Suff. archdeaconry ct. 24, f. 180; Add. 34561, f. 62v.

J.P.

SAYER, George (by 1515–77), of Colchester, Essex.

COLCHESTER 1554 (Nov.)

b. by 1515, s. of Thomas Sayer of Colchester. *m.* (1) by 1540, Agnes (*d.*Nov. 1556), da. of Thomas Wesden, 4s. 3da.; (2) Frances (*d.*29 Apr. 1570), da. of Thomas Salmon.[1]
Chamberlain, Colchester 1537–8, bailiff 1540–1, 1546–7, 1552–3, 1555–6, 1559–60, 1563–4, 1567–8, alderman by 1541; commr. subsidy 1557.[2]

George Sayer came of a wealthy family long established in the parish of St. Peter, Colchester. In the earliest references to Sayer he is described as a clothmaker and this was probably his family's business before him. His father does not seem to have taken much part in municipal affairs, but his grandfather was probably the John Sayer, alderman and bailiff, commemorated by a fine brass in St. Peter's church. Evidence is lacking for the statement that Sayer inherited the patrimony when his elder brother Richard, a Protestant, fled to the Netherlands in 1537. He added to his inheritance by acquiring much ex-monastic property outside the borough; between 1545 and 1548 he bought from Henry Fortescue*, Sir Francis Jobson* and others lands in Essex worth £540 a year.[3]

Sayer may have owed his only election to Parliament to Queen Mary's directive on that occasion for the return of resident Members, perhaps even to direct intervention by the crown designed to exclude such dissidents as William Cardinall and Sir Francis Jobson who had represented Colchester six months earlier. (With Cardinall, however, Sayer's relations were cordial enough for the one's son to marry the other's daughter.)[4]

Sayer's will, made on 22 Jan. 1573, vouches for his wealth; he left 200 marks each to two granddaughters, subject to their not marrying under 22 except with their father's consent, and £200 and 100 marks respectively to two grandsons. He died on 19 May 1577 and was buried in St. Peter's, Colchester, where a mural monument commemorates him with details of his life and family and a long laudatory epitaph in English. A group of almshouses was erected in Colchester at Sayer's expense in 1570, but he left no endowment to maintain them, and they were pulled down before the beginning of the 18th century.[5]

[1] Date of birth estimated from admission as freeman in 1536, Colchester town hall, Benham mss 22, p. 23. Morant, *Colchester*, ii. 111; *Trans. Essex Arch. Soc.* n.s. xiii. 47. [2] Colchester town hall, Benham mss 22, p. 23; *Colchester Oath Bk.* ed. Benham, 158–61, 165,

170, 174, 180, 182; *APC*, vi. 163.   ³ F. Chancellor, *Essex Mons.* 366; Anon. *Searstan Fam. of Colchester, Eng.* 8–9; *Colchester Oath Bk.* 158; *LP Hen. VIII*, xxi; *Feet of Fines, Essex*, iv, ed. Reaney and Fitch, 285, 297; *CP* 25(2)/57/418, m. 17.   ⁴ PCC 25 Daughtty. ⁵ PCC 25 Daughtry; Pevsner and Radcliffe, *Essex*, 137; Morant, ii. 171.

D.F.C.

SAYER, John (by 1499–1562), of Southwark, Surr.

SOUTHWARK   1547*,[1]   1553 (Mar.),   1553 (Oct.),[2]
1554 (Apr.),   1554 (Nov.)[3]

b. by 1499, prob. s. of Thomas Sayer (*d.*1505) of Southwark by Alice. *m.* settlement 20 Oct. 1520, Margaret, da. of Harry Boys of Tavistock, Devon, 2s. 1da.[4]

Gov. St. Thomas's hosp. Southwark 1552–3, 1558, 1560–*d.*[5]

There was a Yorkshireman called John Sayer in the mid 16th century, but the Member chosen five consecutive times for Southwark was doubtless the resident there. He was returned at a by-election to the Parliament of 1547 following Sir John Gates's election as a knight for Essex. Sayer was an obvious choice for election, being a merchant, clothier and innkeeper whose goods were assessed at £30 or £40 for the subsidies of the period. The Journal does not refer to him. He was probably the son of a man who had been bailiff of Southwark although the bailiff did not mention any children in his will. Sayer presumably met his wife through the household of the Duke of Suffolk, whose brother-in-law, Sir John Shilston*, came from Devon. Her dowry was fixed at 40 marks, but Sayer had received only £5 when his father-in-law died and to obtain the balance he had to sue her relatives in Chancery.[6]

Sayer was a sick man on 29 Nov. 1562 when he made his will, and in accordance with his wishes he was buried in St. Saviour's, Southwark on the following 3 Dec. He left his 30-year lease, which he had evidently obtained from the heirs of Humphrey Colet*, of 'that messuage called the sign of the *George* wherein I now dwell' to his daughter and son-in-law, and he charged his estate with a perpetual payment of 20s. 'towards maintenance of the new grammar school' of which he was a founder. He named his sons executors and residuary beneficiaries, and after his death they brought actions in requests against Lady Sandys for goods worth £750 sold to her. The overseers included Thomas Cure†, William Evenson and John Jeffrey†.[7]

¹ Hatfield 207.   ² Bodl. e Museo 17.   ³ Huntington Lib. Hastings mss Parl. pprs.   ⁴ Date of birth estimated from marriage. Req.2/265/ 7, 266/10; C1/567/92; PCC 42 Holgrave, 4 Chayre.   ⁵ City of London RO, Guildhall, rep. 12(2), f. 478; 14, ff. 73, 391v, 465. ⁶ *LP Hen. VIII*, iv, ix, xviii, xx; City of London RO, jnl. 10, ff. 238v, 299–9v; rep. 13(2), f. 309v; PCC 42 Holgrave; C1/567/92, 1267/10– 13; E179/185/223, 230, 232, 257, 266, 286; *Procs. Huguenot Soc. London*, xix. 72.   ⁷ PCC 4 Chayre; Greater London RO, P92/SAV/ 356; Req.2/265/7, 266/10; *CPR*, 1560–3, p. 268.

D.F.C.

SCOTT, Sir John (by 1484–1533), of Scot's Hall, Smeeth, Kent.

NEW ROMNEY   1512[1]

b. by 1484, 1st s. of Sir William Scott† of Scot's Hall by Sybil, da. of Sir Thomas Lewknor† of Trotton, Suss. *m.* by 1507, Anne, da. of Reginald Pympe of Nettlestead, nr. Maidstone, Kent, 5s. 6da. Kntd. 1511; *suc.* fa. 24 Aug. 1524.[2]

Commr. subsidy, Suss. 1512, 1514, 1515, Kent 1523, 1524; sheriff, Kent 1527–8; j.p. 1531–*d.*; knight of the body by 1533.[3]

John Scott's grandfather and father were both prominent figures at court, in the Cinque Ports and at Calais, and both had sat in Parliament for Kent. To his advantages of birth Scott could add the lustre of his part in the expedition led by his uncle Sir Edward Poynings* to the Netherlands in 1511, which gained him a knighthood from Prince Charles, the future Emperor, subsequently transmuted by Henry VIII into a knighthood of the body. His return to the Parliament of the following year for Romney, one of the two Cinque Ports nearest to his family's chief residence, doubtless owed something to Poynings, who as lord warden made the return and himself sat in this Parliament, probably for Kent. What is less clear is why, unlike his fellow-Member, the townsman Clement Baker, Scott was not re-elected for Romney to the next Parliament, in accordance with the King's request for the return of the previous Members. He was presumably in England at the time, for the campaign of 1514, in which he led an 80-strong following, had ended with a peace treaty in August. A possible explanation is that he was re-elected, but not for Romney. Although both knighthoods of the shire were probably bespoke, one for the Speaker-designate Thomas Neville and the other for Poynings himself, Scott could have been nominated either for Hythe, the other port nearest his home, or for Hastings, where the names of the Members are lost, although the previous Members for both these boroughs were available for re-election; it is perhaps a point in favour of Hastings that Scott was included in the Sussex subsidy commissions of 1514 and 1515.[4]

During the remainder of his comparatively short life Scott went to war again in 1523, discharged courtly duties such as attending Wolsey at the reception of Charles V, whose baggage he was responsible for transporting from Dover to Canterbury, and took his part in local administration. If he was able to obey the summons to act as servitor at Anne Boleyn's coronation in May 1533 it was his last ceremonial occasion, for he died on the following 7 Oct. His eldest son was then 26 years old.[5]

¹ Romney assessment bk. 1492–1516, f. 162; Add. 34150, f. 136. ² Date of birth estimated from age at fa.'s i.p.m., C142/44/102.

Fam. Min. Gent. (Harl. Soc. xl), 1301–3; J. R. Scott, *Mems. Scott Fam. of Scot's Hall*, 252 table; Hall, *Chron.* 524. ³ *Statutes*, iii. 83, 114, 168; *LP Hen. VIII*, ii–iv. ⁴ Hall, 524. ⁵ *LP Hen. VIII*, i, iii, vi; *Chron. Calais* (Cam. Soc. xxxv), 15, 16, 34; C142/55/107.

H.M.

SCOTT *see also* **WILLIAMS**

SCOUMYS *see* **SAMMES**

SCRIVEN, John (by 1525–60), of Poole, Dorset.

POOLE   1553 (Oct.)
WAREHAM 1559

    b. by 1525. *m.* by Sept. 1546, Agnes, da. of William Biddlecombe* of Poole, 2s. 3da.[1]
    Bailiff, Poole 1549–50, mayor 1557–8.[2]

John Scriven was a merchant trading from various Dorset ports from 1547 until his death. As he remembered the children of Thomas Scriven, cofferer of the Household between 1552 and 1554, in his will, he was perhaps like the cofferer of west midland origin. One of his name was a yeoman in the Household during the 1540s, and apparently another a Shaftesbury baker said to be 'of evil name and fame, using and keeping a house of bawdry'. The baker and his wife Maud had left Shaftesbury by 1546 whereupon they may have moved to Poole, but if the merchant and the baker are one and the same Maud Scriven must have died sometime before September 1546 when William Biddlecombe made his will naming his son-in-law, the merchant, an executor.[3]

    Scriven's return for Poole to the first Marian Parliament was a stepping-stone in his municipal career and was presumably to be explained by his marriage into the Biddlecombe family of which he was effective head during the minority of William Biddlecombe's children; Anthony Dillington, his fellow-Member in 1553, later married into the Biddlecombes. Neither Scriven nor Dillington opposed the initial measures towards the restoration of Catholicism. Scriven is one of the electors named on the indenture for Poole dated 1 Nov. 1554. After his mayoralty in 1557–8 he was returned for the nearby borough of Wareham early in Elizabeth's reign. He died between 8 Dec. 1560 when he made his will and the 14th when it was proved.[4]

¹ Date of birth estimated from marriage. PCC 28 Alen, 60 Mellershe. ² Poole recs. envelope 6; Hutchins, *Dorset*, i. 34. ³ E122/122/4, 7, 21, 123/2; 179/104/185; 315/439, f. 15v; *LP Hen. VIII*, xvii; PCC 60 Mellershe; C1/1066/6–11, 1404/39–42; Req.2/10/133; C. H. Mayo, *Shastonian Recs.*, 81. ⁴ C219/23/51; PCC 60 Mellershe.

D.F.C.

SCROPE, Ralph (by 1529–72), of Hambleden, Bucks., Doncaster Yorks. and Cockerington, Lincs.

KNARESBOROUGH 1553 (Oct.) 1554 (Nov.)[1]

    b. by 1529, 2nd s. of John Scrope of Spennithorne, Yorks. and Hambleden by Phyllis, da. of Ralph Rokeby of Mortham, Yorks. *educ.* L. Inn, adm. 4 July 1543, called 1548–9. *m.* by July 1560, Elizabeth, da. of William Windsor*, 2nd Lord Windsor, wid. of Henry Sandys (*d.c.*1555) and Sir George Paulet, at least 3s. 1da.[2]
    Pens. L. Inn 1558, marshal 1559, keeper of Black Bk. 1561, treasurer 1564, gov. 1570, 1571.
    J.p.q. Bucks. 1558/59–*d.*

Ralph Scrope was a cadet of the noble family of Scrope of Masham and Bolton. His career at Lincoln's Inn was punctuated by reproofs for evading promotion: in 1549 he risked the loss of his commons for not taking up his call to the bar and in June 1558 he was expelled for similar reluctance when made a bencher. Having put this right by the following November, he was named Autumn reader in 1560 and either Lent or Autumn reader, alternating with Robert Kempe*, in 1561, but he did not read, being discharged from the duty in May 1562 at a cost of £40.[3]

    Scrope probably owed his two elections for Knaresborough, which belonged to the duchy of Lancaster, not to any personal link with the duchy but to his web of family connexions. These included relationships with the 2nd Earl of Cumberland, chief steward of the honor of Knaresborough, and the 5th Earl of Shrewsbury, president of the council in the north and the leading parliamentary patron in Yorkshire, as well as with the Rokeby family, prominent both in the north and at Lincoln's Inn, and with Marmaduke Wyvill, one of the first two Members for Ripon at the same time as Scrope filled that role at Knaresborough. The marriage of his sister to Thomas More II, with whom he was to sit in the third Marian Parliament, brought Scrope into the More circle, and he may also have been connected with John Long (q.v.), who sat for Knaresborough in the second Parliament and for Hedon in the third. Scrope was one of the Members found absent without leave when the House was called early in January 1555 and he was accordingly informed against in the King's bench in the following Easter term. That his dereliction, however, was not regarded as subversive is implied by his avoidance of further process, especially as his brother-in-law More, for whom he stood surety, was fined for the same offence.[4]

    Although when standing surety Scrope was described as of Doncaster, he was to settle and to be buried at Hambleden, long a Scrope property. It was to the Buckinghamshire bench that he was named at Elizabeth's accession; he kept his place on it despite his censure as a 'hinderer of religion' in 1564, but five years later the bishop of Winchester urged Cecil not to allow him, among others, to be put on the Hampshire commission. Scrope's will was witnessed on 1 Sept. 1572 and he died on 28 Oct. 1572. His executors included his brothers, John, Adrian and Robert. His son and heir, another Adrian, was then aged nine years nine months and 15 days. A memorial was erected on the south wall of the tower of Hambleden church.[5]

[1] Huntington Lib. Hastings mss Parl. pprs. [2] Date of birth estimated from education. *Dugdale's Vis. Yorks.* ed. Clay, ii. 5, 6; *Test. Vet.* ed. Nicolas, ii. 722–3; *Vis. Yorks.* (Harl. Soc. xvi), 268–9; *CP*, xi. 444–5; *CPR*, 1558–60, pp. 329–30; PCC 40 Daper. [3] *Black Bk. L. Inn*, i. 287–8, 290–1, 323–5, 331, 333–4, 336; Dugdale, *Origines Juridiciales*, 252. [4] *DNB* (Rokeby, John and Ralph); *Test. Vet.* ii. 752–7; KB27/1176. [5] *Lincoln Rec. Soc.* ii. 49, 251; *Cam. Misc.* ix(3), 32; *HMC Hatfield*, i. 392–3; PCC 40 Daper; C142/164/121, 180/18; *CPR*, 1572–5, p. 164; *VCH Bucks.* iii. 52.

A.D.

SCUDAMORE (SKYDMORE), John (by 1503–71), of Holm Lacy, Herefs.

HEREFORDSHIRE 1529*[1]

b. by 1503, s. of William Scudamore of Holm Lacy by Alice, da. of Richard Mynors of Treago. *m.* (1) Sybil, da. of Walter Vaughan of Hergest, 4s. 5da.; (2) Joan, da. of William Rudhale† of Rudhall, wid. of Richard Rede (*d.*18 July 1544) of Boddington, Glos., *s.p.*[2]

Gent. usher, the chamber by 1524–35, esquire of the body ?1535; sheriff, Herefs. 1524–5, 1536–7, 1543–4, 1552–3; steward, duchy of Lancaster, Glos. and Herefs. 1524–*d.*; j.p. Herefs. 1528–*d.*, Worcs. 1532–58/59, Oxford circuit 1540, Glos. 1554–58/59, Salop 1554; receiver, diocese of Hereford 1535, ct. of augmentations, Herefs., Salop, Staffs. and Worcs. Apr. 1536–54; commr. musters, Herefs. 1542, 1546, chantries, north and central Wales 1546, goods of churches and fraternities, Herefs. 1553; other commissions 1530–48; member, council in the marches of Wales 1553–?*d.*; custos rot. Herefs. by 1561; steward, Hereford and high steward, Archenfield, Herefs. in 1564.[3]

The Scudamores of Holm Lacy were a cadet branch of the family settled at Kentchurch: they had acquired Holm Lacy by marriage in the mid 14th century and John Scudamore was himself to augment it. He also built a house there on a site which, according to tradition, had been the dwelling-place of Walter de Lacy and his heirs. Further additions were to be made to the estate by the marriage of Scudamore's son William with the heiress of (Sir) John Pakington* of Hampton Lovett, Worcestershire.[4]

John Scudamore had early combined service in the royal household with duties in local administration. In 1534 he and his fellow-justices were asked by the mayor of Hereford to examine Richard Stopes *alias* Pewterer, a report of whose treasonable words went to Cromwell. That Scudamore had early found favour with Cromwell is shown by a letter of July 1534 from Scudamore to Alderman Ralph Warren, in which he deplored a fight which had taken place

between 'a lewd boy of mine' and a servant of Cromwell's, 'a good master of mine', and promised to put the offender in prison for a year if he caught him. Cromwell appointed Scudamore to make leases of the lands of the bishopric of Hereford after the death of Bishop Booth in 1535. He also seems to have ignored Bishop Rowland Lee's objections to Scudamore when the president of the council in the marches sought to prevent his promotion in those parts, 'as he is a gentleman dwelling nigh the welshry and kinned and allied in the same'. Scudamore's opinion of the Welsh clearly differed from Lee's, for he asked Cromwell whether he should not treat those parts of the marches annexed to the county as shire ground, adding that 'the people are not well furnished but seem willing to serve the King if need be'.[5]

Scudamore's Membership of the Parliament of 1529 is revealed by a lawsuit which arose out of it. In 1535 he brought a case in the Exchequer against Sir Edward Croft, who had been sheriff of Herefordshire in 1533–4. (A similar case was brought in Chancery against Croft by the executors of Sir Richard Cornwall, another knight of the shire for Herefordshire.) Scudamore claimed that on 2 Apr. 1534—three days after Parliament was prorogued—he had obtained a writ *de expensis* which he had delivered to Croft at Hereford on 20 June, and which the sheriff had executed at Ross on 20 Oct.: since then, however, Croft had refused to pay him the sum due and had caused him damages which he estimated at £20. As the amount involved, £30 16*s.*, represented his wages for the 154 days which he had spent in going to, attending and returning from the fifth and sixth sessions of the Parliament, it is clear that he had been by-elected in place of John Rudhale, whose sister he was later to marry. His choice had evidently owed something to Cromwell, who had placed a circle against his name on a list of nominees to vacancies. Scudamore's name next appears on another of Cromwell's parliamentary lists written on the back of a letter of December 1534 and thought to be of Members having a particular, but unknown, connexion with the treasons bill then on its passage through Parliament; he was also the 'Mr. Skydmore' who served on a committee for the Act regulating the keeping of sheep which was passed during the sixth session. He may have sat again in the short Parliament of 1536, in accordance with the King's general request for the return of the previous Members, but it is unlikely that he did so thereafter, except perhaps in 1545 when the names of the Herefordshire knights are lost. As the result of his suit against Croft is unknown, we cannot say whether financial considerations deterred him from seeking to prolong his parliamentary career, but its comparative brevity may have been due simply to the shire's evident predilection at this time for regular change in its representation, few of its Members sitting more than once.[6]

Scudamore was no stranger to the administration of ecclesiastical property when in April 1536 he became augmentations receiver for Hereford and the neighbouring counties. Although Edward Fox had received the temporalities of the see of Hereford in the previous September, Scudamore had continued to administer them because of the bishop's pre-occupation with the King's business in Germany: in a letter of 31 Aug. 1535 Fox had thanked him for his diligence and had referred all suitors to him. In January 1536 he is described as 'farmer of the parsonage of Bridstow', and in the following month the 3rd Lord Ferrers received his fee of £5 as the bishop's steward over the signature of Scuadamore as 'receiver of the bishop's lands'. The receivership was well paid but Scudamore had to work hard in it at least until the court of augmentations was reconstituted in 1547. He was then one of seven out of the original 29 receivers who were reappointed. As an augmentations official he was able to benefit considerably from the Dissolution, his major acquisition being the house and lands of Abbey Dore, Herefordshire, which he purchased in 1540 for £379.[7]

During the northern rebellion of 1536 Scudamore was appointed to attend upon the King with 40 men and eight years later he served in the army against France. Shortly before the dissolution of the court of augmentations in 1554 he was made a member of the council in the marches of Wales, an appointment which he may have owed to his Catholicism but from which he was not removed on the accession of Elizabeth. It was as a member of the council, custos rotulorum and steward of Hereford that in 1564 he headed Bishop Scory's list of those in authority in Herefordshire who were unfavourable to the Elizabethan settlement: if his religion did not prevent his continued employment, he himself was sufficiently accommodating to subscribe to the Act of Uniformity.[8]

Scudamore's will, made on 20 July and proved on 17 Nov. 1571, was nevertheless as firmly Catholic as that of the more intransigent Thomas Havard*, who had refused to subscribe. He bequeathed his soul to God, the Virgin Mary and the company of heaven and gave £20 to the poor to pray for his soul; a further £100 was to be bestowed on his funeral if he died at or near Holm Lacy but otherwise was to be 'distributed amongst poor people to pray for my soul

and all Christian souls and in amending of highways'. His eldest son William had died before 1560 but he still had a large family to provide for, including several grandchildren. Of his daughters, Jane was then married to (Sir) William Devereux* of Merevale, Warwickshire. The residuary legatee was Scudamore's grandson and heir, John, who was to serve in six Elizabethan Parliaments as junior knight for Herefordshire: he was named executor together with Edward Cooper, archdeacon of Hereford, with Richard Seborne* as overseer. Scudamore died on 25 Sept. 1571 and was buried beside his first wife at Holm Lacy, the inscription on their altar-tomb praying passers-by 'of their charity to say for their souls a paternoster and an ave'.[9]

[1] E13/214/11; House of Lords RO, Original Acts, 25 Hen. VIII, no. 13. [2] Date of birth estimated from first reference. *Vis. Herefs.* ed. Weaver, 63; C. J. Robinson, *Mansions and Manors of Herefs.* 174; C142/153/59. [3] Somerville, *Duchy*, i. 637, 640; *Coll. Top. et Gen.* iv. 256; *LP Hen. VIII*, iv, v, vii, xi–xviii, xxi; *CPR*, 1547–8, pp. 75, 76, 84, 91, 372; 1548–9, p. 137; 1553, p. 416; 1553–4, pp. 19, 20, 23, 26; 1569–72, p. 225; *Cam. Misc.* ix(3), 12; W. C. Richardson, *Ct. Augmentations*, 47, 49; P. H. Williams, *Council in the Marches of Wales*, 356–7. [4] Robinson, 138–41. [5] *LP Hen. VIII*, vii, viii, xi; Elton, *Policy and Police*, 65. [6] E13/214/11; *LP Hen. VIII*, vii. 56 citing SP1/82, ff. 59–62, 1522(ii) citing SP1/87, f. 106v; House of Lords RO, Original Acts, 25 Hen. VIII, no. 13. [7] *LP Hen. VIII*, ix, x, xiii–xv; Richardson, 47. [8] *LP Hen. VIII*, xi, xix; *Cam. Misc.* ix(3), 12. [9] PCC 44 Holney; C142/161/80; *Coll. Top. et Gen.* iv. 256.

A.J.E.

SEBOURNE, Richard (by 1524–84), of Sutton St. Nicholas, Herefs.

HEREFORDSHIRE 1554 (Nov.)

b. by 1524, s. of John Sebourne of Sutton St. Nicholas by a da. of John Parrott of Moreton. *educ.* I. Temple. *m.* by 1545, Elizabeth, da. of William Elton of Ledbury, 1s. 6da.[1]
    Bencher, I. Temple 5 Feb. 1550.
    J.p. Herefs. 1547, q. 1554–77, j.p.q. Cheshire 1558/59, 1564–82, Mon. 1558/59, 1564–77, Salop 1564–77, Welsh counties 1558/59, 1564–77; commr. relief, Herefs. 1550, to survey lands of bpric. of Hereford 1559; other commissions 1554–*d.*; dep. justice of Anglesey, Caern. and Merion. Mar. 1559; member, council in the marches of Wales 1560–77 or later.[2]

Richard Sebourne was of gentle birth but modest patrimony and his study of the law was probably intended to qualify him for its practise or for office-holding. By 1555, when his inn called on him to read, he was well launched on his local career and may already have come into his inheritance, so that he probably did not grudge the £40 which it cost him to evade the obligation; thereafter he is not known to have held office at the inn.[3]

Although by 1554 Sebourne was a justice of some years standing, his election in the autumn of that year as first knight of the shire smacks of official intervention: the names of both knights were inserted over erasures on the return. Whether or not Bishop Heath, president of the council in the marches, supported Sebourne as he clearly did the other knight, Thomas Havard, the man best placed to influence the outcome was Sir John Price*, secretary to the council and sheriff on the occasion. Price's friendship with Havard is not known to have extended to Sebourne, but the two were near neighbours outside Hereford and it was from Price that Sebourne had bought the manor of Rushock on his marriage in 1545. Like both Price and Havard, Sebourne attended the Parliament until its dissolution and so avoided the prosecution which awaited the Members who withdrew from it early without leave.[4]

Sebourne's employment under Elizabeth, notably as a member of the council in the marches, shows that he conformed to the new order in religion as he had done to the old, even if Bishop Scory's judgment of him in 1564 as 'unfavourable' implies that he shared the Catholicism for which other members of the family were noted. There is no hint of dissent in the will which he made on 18 May 1584 and which was proved on the following 7 July. He asked to be buried beside his parents in the chancel of Sutton church and left 100 marks for distribution to the poor at the discretion of his son and heir John, whom he named executor. His wife had predeceased him and three of his six daughters were unmarried at his death.[5]

[1] Date of birth estimated from first reference. *Vis. Herefs.* ed. Weaver, 26, 64; Williams, *Herefs. MPs.* 39. [2] *CPR*, 1547-8, p. 84; 1553, p. 354; 1553-4, pp. 34, 35, 37; 1558-60, pp. 31, 422; 1560-3, pp. 283, 438; 1563-6, pp. 23, 26, 28, 29-31, 41-42; 1569-72, p. 225; P. H. Williams, *Council in the Marches of Wales*, 356-7; R. Flenley, *Cal. Reg. Council, Marches of Wales*, 52, 96, 102, 111, 125; SP12/121, f. 3v; Hatfield 223/7. *CPR*, 1553-4, p. 20 gives John Sebourne as j.p. Herefs. 1554 probably in error for Richard Seborne who was certainly on the bench at this time, Hereford pub. lib., city muniments, bag 8, no. 14. [3] *Cal. I.T. Recs.* i. 187, 194. [4] C219/23/59; *LP Hen. VIII*, xx. [5] *Cam. Misc.* ix(3), 12; *Cath. Rec. Soc.* lvii. 44; lxi. 31; G. Anstruther, *Seminary Priests*, i. 305; SP12/247/8; Williams, 98, 285; *CPR*, 1566-9, p. 114; PCC 15 Watson.

A.J.E.

SECKFORD (SAKFORD), Thomas (1515/16–87), of Gray's Inn, London.

RIPON	1554 (Nov.)[1]
ORFORD	1555, 1558
IPSWICH	1559, 1563
SUFFOLK	1571
IPSWICH	1572

b. 1515/16, 2nd s. of Thomas Seckford of Seckford Hall, Great Bealings, Suff. by Margaret, da. of Sir John Wingfield of Letheringham, Suff.; bro. of Thomas†. *educ.* Camb.; G. Inn, adm. 1540, called 1542. *m.* lic. 18 Jan. 1567, Elizabeth (*d.*28 Nov. 1586), da. of Thomas Harlowe, wid. of William Billingsley and Sir Martin Bowes* (*d.*4 Aug. 1566) both of London, *s.p.*[2]

Ancient, G. Inn 1547, Lent reader 1556, treasurer 1565.

Dep. chief steward, duchy of Lancaster, northern parts 6 Sept. 1558; master of requests 9 Dec. 1558; j.p.q. Mdx. and Suff. 1558/59; steward, Marshalsea ct. by 1559–?70; commr. eccles. causes 1559; other commissions, London and E. Anglia; steward, bp. of Ely's liberty, Suff. 1563; surveyor, ct. wards 1579.[3]

The Seckfords had held one of the two manors in Great Bealings since the end of the 12th century and were related by descent and marriage to the leading families in Suffolk. A younger son, Thomas Seckford made his way in the law. Early in 1554 he became reversioner of a minor duchy of Lancaster post under Sir William Willoughby*, 1st Baron Willoughby of Parham, and this appointment accounts for his return for the duchy borough of Ripon later in the year, as does his link with Willoughby for Orford to the next two Parliaments. Presumably as one connected with Willoughby he supported the measure settling the Duchess of Suffolk's inheritance on Willoughby which was rejected on a division in the Commons on 16 Jan. 1555. Later in the same year he helped defeat a government bill and on 28 Feb. 1558 the bill for confirmation of letters patent was committed to him after its first reading.[4]

After his appointment as a master of requests at the beginning of Elizabeth's reign Seckford became increasingly active in local and national affairs, and was re-elected to Parliament four times. He used the considerable wealth he acquired in building himself a 'great house' at Ipswich and in founding the Seckford almshouses at Woodbridge. He died on 19 Dec. 1587.[5]

[1] Huntington Lib. Hastings mss Parl. pprs. [2] Aged 67 in 1583 according to parents' MI at Great Bealings. C142/175/69; pprs. on Seckford family read by P. Chandler to Soc. of Antiqs. 2 June 1923; *Mar. Lic. London* (Harl. Soc. xxv), 35; Wards 7/23/57; *Vis. Suff.* ed. Metcalfe, 64. [3] *APC*, vii. 17; Somerville, *Duchy*, i. 427; *CPR*, 1558-60, pp. 19, 28, 118; 1563-6, pp. 126, 184, 257, 488; 1566-9, p. 132; 1569-72, pp. 34, 217-18, 224, 440-2; Lansd. 104, f. 53; Exchequer deposition, Mich. 44-45 Eliz. 39, at Woodbridge; J. Hurstfield, *Queen's Wards*, 224. [4] Copinger, *Suff. Manors*, iii. 6; iv. 325; V. B. Redstone, *Seckfords of Seckford Hall* (Suff. Inst. Arch. ix), 359-69; Guildford mus. Loseley 1331/2; *CJ*, i. 50. [5] Wards 7/23/57.

M.K.D.

SEDBOROUGH, Silvester (1515/16–51), of Porlock, Som.

| BATH | 1545 |

b. 1515/16, 1st s. of William Sedborough of Porlock by Joan (*d.*27 Sept. 1537), sis. and coh. of Jerome Bratton of Porlock. *m.* (1) Anne Staveley, 1s. 2da.; (2) by 1550, Mary. *suc.* fa. 2 Mar. 1527.[1]

The Sedborough family originated from north Devon and it was the marriage of William Sedborough to an heiress that brought him into Somerset. Silvester Sedborough may have owed his unusual christian name to either his family's veneration of St. Silvester, who had only one church in England dedicated to him and that in Devon, or less probably to a connexion with Silvestro de' Gigli, bishop of Worcester (1499–1521). Little has been discovered of Sedborough's life beyond the information given incidentally by Star Chamber cases in which he was to be involved. The most important of these was the result of a dispute with his stepfather Robert Coke of Tiverton, Devon, upon whom his mother had settled all the Bratton lands for life. When she died in 1537 Sedborough seems to have been out of England and he later pleaded that he was also under age, although this seems to have been untrue. For whatever reason, it was not until 1545 that he challenged his stepfather's possession of the lands. On 8 May of that year he distrained on Coke's tenants and cattle. Coke pleaded that because of such 'unlawful bearing and maintenance as he hath within the said county of Somerset' Sedborough could not be restrained by normal process, and the Star Chamber granted an injunction ordering the return of the distrained beasts and commanded Sedborough's appearance. It is clear from Sedborough's answer and depositions that he was legally in the wrong. No result of the case is given, but a compromise seems to have been reached whereby Coke leased the land to Sedborough for 60 years or his life. An inquisition post mortem for Sedborough's Devon lands is extant: he was found to have had property near Tiverton, which he had conveyed in 1550 to Richard Michell, Alexander Popham* and Sir Thomas Speke* for the use of himself and his wife Mary for life.[2]

Sedborough's Somerset lands were in the west of the county near Minehead and he can have exerted little personal influence on the residents of Bath to secure his election in 1545. Who was responsible for this and for the 'maintenance' that was complained of is not clear, but it may have been Queen Catherine Parr's chancellor, Sir Thomas Arundell*, as Sedborough's widow was to marry a William Arundell. His Membership seems to have been the only public service Sedborough performed before his early death on 20 Aug. 1551. His heir, aged about nine years, was his son Robert, on whose behalf William Arundell brought a chancery case against Bartholomew Staveley, his uncle to whom Sedborough seems to have alienated his lands just before his death.[3]

[1] Date of birth estimated from age at fa.'s i.p.m., C142/46/116. Healey, *West Country*, 331–3; C1/1381/23–25. [2] F. Arnold-Foster, *Studies in Church Dedications*, i. 294; iii. 86, 447; Healey, 329–30; *Som. Rec. Soc.* xxvii, 121, 239–42; C1/1381/23–25; 142/95/36. [3] Healey, 336; C1/1381/23–25; 142/95/36.

R.V.

SEE, Henry (by 1496–1537), of Herne, Kent and Lincoln's Inn, London.

BRAMBER 1529

b. by 1496, 1st s. of Robert See of Herne. *educ.* L. Inn, adm. 16 Feb. 1520, called 1525. *m.* settlement 8 May 1531, Elizabeth, wid. of Richard Crompton (*d.*1528/30) of London, 1s. 3da.[1]

Reader, Thavies's Inn 1529; bencher, L. Inn 1534, Autumn reader 1535.

J.p. Kent 1531; commr. sewers 1531; solicitor to the city of York by 1535.[2]

Henry See was one of the more distinguished members of an ancient yeoman family living at Herne in Kent, and his comparatively early death cut short a most promising career in the law. See was among a group of young men fined at Lincoln's Inn in August 1520 for seizing a doe, but the colleagues with whom he was later to work inspired a zeal for the law which brought rewards. Before November 1522 he had lived in chambers over the old gate with the father of Henry Heydon*, but for some years thereafter he occupied chambers with George Barratt and William Roper*, who became his closest friend. See and Roper were called to the bar at the same time and in 1527 he was offered a chamber 'in the new building next the kitchen' where Roper also lived and practised.[3]

See perhaps owed his seat in the Parliament of 1529 for the 3rd Duke of Norfolk's borough of Bramber to his friendship with Roper, his fellow-Member, whose father-in-law More then stood close to the duke. It was, however, not Roper but See who took precedence; the reason for this may lie either in some earlier parliamentary experience of which we have no other trace or a personal link with the duke through Alfred Berwick* and Henry Hussey*, with whom 12 years before he had been associated as an attorney in a fine and settlement of the manor of Denne in the ducal borough of Horsham, Sussex. During the first session a bill against the recognition of protections was committed to See, Cromwell and three others, but perhaps because they thought it ill advised it did not pass. Cromwell classed See with Roper, William Dauntesey and John Latton as 'of Chelsea', that is, of the circle of Sir Thomas More, on a list thought to be of Members opposed on religious or economic grounds to the bill in restraint of appeals to Rome which was passed during the fifth session. More's execution in 1535 may have briefly threatened See's prospects, but if so, rather than efface himself, he seems to have sought by his diligence both in and out of Parliament to commend himself to the regime. In the final session (Feb.–Apr. 1536) he was instrumental in procuring an Act (27 Hen. VIII, c.32) to

reduce the fee-farm paid by the city of York to the
1st Earl of Rutland, and he and three other lawyers
signed the Act for the heirs of Sir Hugh Dutton
(27 Hen. VIII, c.43). Presumably he sat for
Bramber again in the following Parliament, in June
1536, after the King had asked for the re-election of
the previous Members.[4]

See's marriage to the widow of a young London
mercer trading with the Netherlands was an
advantageous one: it brought him substantial
property in Somerset belonging to his wife and ready
money amongst her first husband's effects in
London and Antwerp. (It may also have given him
an insight into the cloth trade which could have
helped to turn him against the appeals bill, with its
threat of economic reprisals abroad.) The Somerset
lands were claimed by Sir William Fitzwilliam, a
leading mercer, but after See had brought a box of
deeds to the Chancery in 1534 Fitzwilliam admitted
his full right to the property. It was known in 1535
that See was in the market for land, probably using
his wife's resources: in November Sir Reynold
Carnaby, a servant of the 5th Earl of Northumberland, wrote to the earl's attorney in London that he
was selling some lands in Kent and that See should
have preference if he wanted them.[5]

See was a sick man when he made his will, which
is undated. His wife, whom he appointed sole
executrix, was charged with the distribution of his
estate under the guidance of William Roper,
Nicholas Rookwood*, See's brother William and
his clerk William Pattyn. On 7 July 1537 he settled
the manor of Buckland in Kent upon his father and
other feoffees to the use of himself and his heirs, and
died three days later, perhaps a victim of the
epidemic abroad in London. At the inquisitions
following his death he was found to have been
possessed of land in Devon, Kent and Somerset and
to have left as his heir a son Anthony then aged five
or six. Anthony See evidently died without leaving
issue as later heraldic visitations call Henry See's
daughters Millicent, Mary and Elizabeth his
coheirs.[6]

[1] Date of birth estimated from appearance as an attorney 1517. *LP
Hen. VIII*, ii; E150/492/2; PCC 24 Jankyn, 12 Dyngeley. [2] *LP
Hen. VIII*, v, ix. [3] *Black Bk. L. Inn*, i. 194–216 passim. [4] *Suss.
Rec. Soc.* xix(1), 125; *LP Hen. VIII*, ix. 1077 citing SP1/99, p. 234;
House of Lords RO, Original Acts, 27 Hen. VIII, no. 53; *York Civic
Recs.* iii (Yorks Arch. Soc. rec. ser. cvi), 138–74 passim; iv (ibid. cvii),
4, 13. [5] E150/492/2, 926/15; C1/891/20; City of London RO,
Guildhall, rep. 8, f. 165; *LP Hen. VIII*, ix. [6] E150/178/2, 492/2,
926/15; PCC 12 Dyngeley; *Vis. Kent* (Harl. Soc. lxxiv), 93; *Vis.
London* (Harl. Soc. xv), 163; Hasted, *Kent*, vi. 398; x. 240.

R.J.W.S.

SEER, John (by 1512–52/53), of Sandwich, Kent.

SANDWICH 1547[1]

b. by 1512. *m.* Agnes, 1s. 1da.[2]

Common councilman, Sandwich (St. Clement's
parish) 1533–4, 1537–47, (St. Peter's parish) 1534–7,
treasurer 1536–7, auditor 1540, 1547, 1548, constable
of the 12th ward 1537–41, jurat 1547–*d.*; bailiff to
Yarmouth 1551–*d.*[3]

John Seer was a baker. He usually absented himself from the assizes of bread held at Sandwich, and
on the only occasion he is known to have attended a
breadweighing he was fined 5s. for forestalling and
regrating five bushels of barley. He did not cut
much of a figure in the port: although he served as a
constable of one of its wards from 1537 to 1541 and
attended the Brotherhood of the Cinque Ports at
Romney on five occasions, he was never mayor. The
apex of his career was undoubtedly his Membership
of Parliament: this followed half-a-year after his
election as a jurat and appears to have been the work
of Archbishop Cranmer, for one of whose servants he
had stood surety in 1546. The mayor refused to
seal the indenture naming Seer and Thomas
Pinnock (q.v.) as Members and returned Thomas
Patche (q.v.) and Thomas Ardern (q.v.) instead,
but the Privy Council overruled the mayor and
further ordered the port to pay Seer and Pinnock
20s. compensation. As a Protestant Seer doubtless
welcomed the Edwardian Reformation, but nothing
has come to light about his part in the proceedings
of the Commons: he must have missed part of the
third session when on 14 Dec. 1549 he attended a
breadweighing at Sandwich, and during the fourth
session, when he had been instructed to help
Pinnock in the matter of Sandwich harbour, the
pair were ordered to leave the House until the
validity of their Membership had been settled.[4]

Seer made his will on 4 May 1551, ordering that
no prayers should be said at his burial but that a
sermon should be preached then and at his month's
mind and year's mind. After remembering the poor
he left his son Thomas, born on 28 May 1545, £20
on reaching 21, and his daughter Elizabeth £20
when she became 18 or married. He made his wife
residuary legatee and sole executrix and appointed
as overseers John Broke, Thomas Cotton and
Thomas Harflete, asking them 'to see my children
brought up in the informance of the Lord and to
defend my wife from wrongs'.

The last reference to Seer in the records of
Sandwich occurs on 5 Oct. 1552 when a boy was
apprenticed to him to learn 'the craft of bakership.'
His will was proved twice, on 18 Jan. and 13 Mar.
1553. On 21 Jan. 1553 his widow was fined 5s. for
failing to keep the assize of bread.[5]

[1] Sandwich old red bk., f. 197v, 251. [2] Date of birth estimated
from first reference. Canterbury prob. reg. A29, f. 7. [3] Sandwich
old red bk., passim; little black bk., f. 1; *Cinque Ports White and
Black Bks.* (Kent Arch. Soc. recs. br. xix), 244, 247. [4] Sandwich old
red bk., ff. 94, 102, 112, 128, 187, 194v, 197v, 207, 251; *Cinque Ports*

White and Black Bks., 222, 237–9, 244, 247; *APC*, ii. 536–7; *CJ*, i. 17.
[5] Canterbury prob. reg. A29, ff. 7, 313; Sandwich little black bk., ff. 21, 30v.

H.M.

SELBY, Odinel (by 1500–55), of Berwick-upon-Tweed and Tweedmouth, Northumb.

BERWICK-UPON-TWEED 1539,[1] 1547,[2] 1554 (Apr.)

b. by 1500. *m.* Janet, ?da. of one Fowberry of Fowberry, 3s. 2da.[3]
Mayor, Berwick-upon-Tweed 1536–7, 1540–1, 1551–2; ?yeoman extraordinary in 1547.[4]

Odinel Selby was probably the leading resident of his time in Berwick and he was also a small landowner in the neighbourhood of the town. Virtually nothing is known of the Selby family before him, but by the second quarter of the 16th century branches were established in northern Northumberland at Branxton, Grindon Rigg and Twizell, and Selby may have come from one of these. In the middle of the century several men of this name were prominent in the affairs of Berwick, and John Selby, a 'faithful and trusty friend' of Odinel Selby, was porter of the town. The Selbys of Berwick may also have been related to their namesakes the influential merchants of Newcastle.[5]

Selby was closely connected with the guild and with the regulation of trade in Berwick. He had probably become one of the Twelve sometime before his first mayoralty in 1536. His main interest as a merchant, to judge from his inventory, was in the salmon trade, one of Berwick's two main trades. In 1521 he shared in the lease of a fishery belonging to the town. At the time of his death he was both owed and owing various quantities of salmon and he was in debt to various men in London, perhaps the stockfishmongers much engaged in trade with Berwick in this period; he also owed £5 5s. to Henry Anderson* of Newcastle. He was on several occasions involved in legal proceedings with fellow merchants. In 1533 a Norfolk shipowner ordered by the treasurer of Berwick to bring corn to the town was arrested in connexion with a dispute over a wrongful action for debt. The case was brought before a court of the bishop of Durham and was later referred to Cromwell; Selby secured the backing of an influential local gentleman, Sir William Eure. He was also cited in a chancery suit for keeping deeds relating to a tenement in Berwick which William Hamcottes, a London stockfishmonger, rightfully owned. Later it was claimed in the Star Chamber that Selby while mayor ordered his officers to arrest Hamcottes, and a certain Lawrence Fober (?Fowberry) at the instigation of Selby commenced actions against Hamcottes at Berwick and Newcastle and took his ship, goods and merchandise. A further

charge was made against Selby's exercise of his authority, for in another chancery case about the sending of barrels of salmon to London without payment, John Goldsmith, a London fishmonger, claimed that George Lordysman of Berwick had been 'greatly friended and favoured within the same' by the mayor and others. The outcome of all these cases is unknown.[6]

Selby was also involved in border affairs; he filed numerous bills at days of truce in 1536 and the following year. The extent of his involvement in the plot of 1538 to murder Sir Thomas Clifford, captain of Berwick, is not clear. The leading conspirators were members of the Grey family, and Edward Bradford and some of the Selby family were implicated. According to Thomas Grey* the plot eventually failed because Clifford heard rumour of it through the 'babbling' of the 'foolish fellow' Odinel Selby.[7]

It was probably in 1537 that Selby's absence from Berwick led the Twelve to compel him to reside in the town by a specified date. By the following year he was chosen one of the six persons through whom the fish trade with London, which had been causing some difficulty, was to be conducted. In 1539 Selby was chosen by the Twelve to sit in Parliament and, he was allowed 2s.8d. a day. It was doubtless his prominence in the town both as a merchant and a magistrate which secured his return. As a Member Selby may have been involved in Berwick's dispute with Newcastle about the shipping of wools, hides and woolskins, for in April 1539 the captain of Berwick informed Cromwell that the Members intended to discuss their grievance in Parliament; no further reference to the matter has been found. Selby continued to figure prominently in the affairs of the town until his death and he was returned to Parliament on two further occasions. If he was the man of his name who attended Henry VIII's funeral—and the unusual christian name makes this likely—he must before that date have been given the minor court appointment of yeoman extraordinary.[8]

It is not clear when Selby acquired the property at Tweedmouth which was situated on the other side of the river from Berwick, but it may have been after 1542 since in a survey of that year no owner is named of the tower of Tweedmouth which Selby later bequeathed to his wife. Selby also mentioned in his will property at 'Crabwater' and the tithe corn of Goswick, and in his inventory it is noted that Ralph Grey of Chillingham owed him certain rent for the half tithe of South Middleton. At the Dissolution he leased the tithes of Akeld, Lanton and Shotton. He seems to have engaged in small farming, for he mentioned in his will a barn, a byre, a henhouse, a plough, oxen and nags at Tweedmouth. Selby made his will on 6 May 1555 and died later in the same year. After bequeathing his soul to God he requested that his body should be buried in Tweedmouth church. He left much of his property to his wife on condition that she remained single but provided that if she remarried she should have one-third of this legacy; he also made numerous bequests to his relatives. His son William was his heir.[9]

[1] Berwick guild bk. 1508–68, unfoliated. [2] Hatfield 207. [3] Date of birth estimated from first reference. *Wills and Inventories*, i (Surtees Soc. ii), 142–5; *Northumb. Co. Hist.* xiv. 223. [4] J. Scott, *Berwick*, 479; LC2/2, f. 72. [5] *Arch. Ael.* (ser. 4), xiv. 63–64; Scott, 445; Raine, *N. Durham*, 315, 338; Berwick guild bk. 1508–68 GMI; NRA 8992 (Northumb. RO, Haggerston (Harelaw) mss. nos. 1, 3–5). [6] Berwick guild bk. 1508–68, GMI; *LP Hen. VIII*, iii, vi, vii; C1/414/40, 994/12; St.Ch.2/35/84. [7] *LP Hen. VIII*, xiii; *Northumb. Co. Hist.* i. 263, 267. [8] Berwick guild bk. 1508–68 GMI; SP1/150/167–8; LC2/2, f. 72. [9] Raine, 25, 244–5; *Wills and Inventories*, i. 142–5; *Northumb. Co. Hist.* xi. 118–19.

M.J.T.

SENTHIELL see SAINTHILL

SENTPOLL see ST. POLL

SEYMOUR, David (by 1522–57/58), of London.

WAREHAM	1547[1]
GREAT BEDWYN	1555

b. by 1522, ?s. of Robert Seymour* of Ivy Church, Wilts. and London. *m.* June 1546/June 1550, Mary, da. of Nicholas Odell or Woodhill of Odell, Beds. by 2nd w. da. of Sir William Parr*, Baron Parr of Horton, 2s. 1da.[2]

Gent. usher of the chamber by 1546; gent. at arms in Feb. 1547; capt. *Tigre* 1557.[3]

David Seymour was a relative of the Protector Somerset, perhaps the son of Somerset's uncle Robert Seymour, as he inherited an annuity granted earlier to Robert Seymour by the Hungerford family and enjoyed another from Amesbury abbey where Robert Seymour had been a lay official. The career followed by David Seymour was not unlike Robert Seymour's, only the younger man made a splendid match with a kinswoman of Queen Catherine Parr; both men entered the royal household and both distinguished themselves in warlike action on land and at sea. As a young man David Seymour incurred displeasure by eating flesh during Lent 1543. He remained on good terms with a fellow-offender on this occasion, Sir John Clere*, under whose naval command he served towards the end of Mary's reign, and perhaps earlier. Henry VIII gave Seymour a pension of £6 13s.4d. two months before he died, and this was followed by one of 40 marks a year from Edward VI which Seymour exchanged in 1550 for one out of the ugmentations worth £75 a

year for himself and his wife in survivorship. He died not long after being sent into northern waters on convoy duty in 1557, for on 18 Jan. 1558 his widow released to the Clothworkers' Company the house in Fenchurch Street which had been granted to him by the Company in 1546, in succession to his father (unnamed) who had had it for life.[4]

It was doubtless as the nominee of the Protector or his brother Admiral Seymour that Seymour was returned as senior Member for Wareham to the first Edwardian Parliament. He is not known to have been involved in the Protector's fall from power in the autumn of 1549, but on Somerset's second arrest in October 1551 he was sent to the Tower. He was soon released on condition of remaining in custody in his own house pending interrogation, but this evidently yielded nothing and he probably took his place for the final session (1552) of the Parliament. His exoneration seems to be reflected on the list of Members in use for this session, his name being struck out but then marked 'stet'. He is not known to have been returned to the succeeding Parliament, of which his name and connexion would have made him an unlikely Member, nor to the first three of Mary's reign, but in 1555 he came in for the Seymour borough of Great Bedwyn; both his name and his fellow-Member Henry Clifford's were inserted on the election indenture. He and Clifford alike opposed a government bill in this Parliament. Through an oversight the compiler of the list of opponents in 1555 appears to have entered his name twice, first as 'Mr. David Seymer' and later as 'Mr. Semar', presuming, that is, he did not have a namesake sitting in the House.[5]

[1] Hatfield 207. [2] Date of birth estimated from first reference. *Vis. Northants.* ed. Metcalfe, 56, 159; *APC*, iii. 53, 58; *CPR*, 1553–4, p. 220. [3] *LP Hen. VIII*, xxi; SP11/11/35; LC2/2, f. 43, 2/4(1) p. 113 ex inf. W. J. Tighe. [4] *LP Hen. VIII*, xviii, xxi; Hoare, *Wilts.*, Ambresbury, 165; SP11/11/35, 38; *APC*, iii. 53, 58; *CPR*, 1553–4, p. 220; Lansd. 156(28), f. 108v; Clothworkers' Co., orders of ct. 1536–58, ff. 187, 189, 288v. [5] *Wilts. Arch. Mag.* vi. 295–6; Tytler, *Edw. VI and Mary*, ii. 4, 37; *APC*, iii. 426; C219/24/189; Guildford mus. Loseley 1331/2.

H.M.

SEYMOUR, Sir Henry (by 1503–78), of Marwell, Hants.

HAMPSHIRE	1547

b. by 1503, 3rd s. of Sir John Seymour* of Wolf Hall, Wilts. by Margery, da. of Sir Henry Wentworth† of Nettlestead, Suff.; bro. of Sir Thomas II*. *m.* by 1559, Barbara, da. of Morgan Wolfe, 3s. inc. John† 7da. KB 20 Feb. 1547.[1]

Keeper, Taunton castle, Som. by 1526–d., Bridgwater castle, Som. 1544, Marwell park, Hants by 1547–51; sewer extraordinary, the chamber by 1533; bailiff, manor of Hampstead Marshall, Berks. 1536–d., Romsey, Hants by 1546–d.; steward, manors of Bierton with Broughton, Whaddon and Wendover, Bucks. 1536–d., Wyrardisbury, Bucks. and Kings

Langley, Herts. 1536–39; gen.-receiver, manors of Bierton with Broughton, Claydon, Swanbourne, Wendover and Whaddon, Bucks., Berkhampstead, Herts. and Finmer, Oxon. 1536–40; capt. *Lyon of Hamburgh* 1544; carver, household of Queen Anne of Cleves 1540, of Queen Catherine Parr by 1545; commr. relief, Hants 1550, goods of churches and fraternities 1553; j.p. 1554–*d*.; sheriff, Hants 1568–9.[2]

Unlike his two brothers, Edward, Duke of Somerset, and Thomas, Baron Seymour of Sudeley, Henry Seymour lacked the ability, the ambition and the will to govern: he was a nonentity who passes unnoticed in his nephew Edward VI's diary. He held no office of importance and reaped little reward. His brothers died on the block; he outlived them by nearly 30 years to die in his bed.

Seymour was probably the 'Harry Seymor', living in St. John's parish, Winchester, who was assessed on 10 marks in wages for the subsidy in 1524: the appearance of his name among those of men known to have been servants or members of the bishop's household suggests that he was in the service of Richard Fox. He had doubtless owed his introduction there and at court to his father and to the example of his brother Edward, but he is not known to have progressed until the King married his sister, whereupon he was appointed to several offices mainly connected with the administration of her estates. Some of these he lost at her death, although she bequeathed him several valuable chains. In 1544 he served under his brother Thomas's command in the navy. While on patrol in the Channel in the autumn of that year his ship was driven by a storm into the Dart estuary and wrecked: he was held culpable and was given no further military or naval command. Shortly afterwards he ceased to be a member of the household of Queen Catherine Parr, his name not being found in the relevant lists after 1545. By the end of the reign he appears to have been living in Hampshire, discharging minor duties for his younger brother and the bishop of Winchester.[3]

The accession of his nephew and the ascendancy of the Protector momentarily brightened Seymour's prospects: he took part in the coronation, was made a Knight of the Bath and in the autumn of 1547 was elected a knight of the shire for Hampshire, but his only appointments were in the government of that county. His brother's neglect may help to explain his failure even to answer the Protector's letter of 5 Oct. 1549 calling on him to muster forces against the Council in London. For this passive complicity in Somerset's overthrow he was rewarded by John Dudley, Earl of Warwick, with grants of land in Buckinghamshire and Hampshire, and he was to receive from Dudley, who was bent on retaining his

support, the attention never forthcoming from his brother. It produced as little result as the earlier treatment had done.[4]

Seymour pursued his inconspicuous course under Mary and Elizabeth: the first made him a justice of the peace and the second gave him a term as sheriff. In 1564 he was described as a 'favourer' of religion. A sick man when he made his will on 28 Mar. 1578, he was able to make more than adequate provision for his wife and children, his daughters receiving £1,000 each. He appointed as his executors his nephews the Earl of Hertford and Henry Ughtred†. He died on 5 Apr. at his house in Winchester, leaving a son and heir John who was just over 18 years old.[5]

[1] Date of birth estimated from first reference. H. St. Maur, *Annals of the Seymours*, ped. opp. p. 1. [2] *LP Hen. VIII*, ii, vi, xii, xiv, xvi, xix, xx; *CPR*, 1550–3, pp. 151, 395; 1553, pp. 358, 415; 1553–4, pp. 19, 252; *The Gen.* n.s. xxx. 24; Stowe 571, f. 576; SC6/190/21; Eccles. 2/155674, 155888A–9; E179/69/48. [3] *LP Hen. VIII*, xii, xv, xix; *CSP Hen. VIII*, i. 780; E179/174/287; A. A. Locke, *Seymour Fam.*, 29. [4] *CSP Dom.* 1547–80, pp. 23, 345; *APC*, iii. 138, 310, iv. 153, 221, 242, 338; *Black Bk. Winchester* ed. Bird, 180; W. K. Jordan, *Edw. VI*, i. 35–36, 508. [5] *Cam. Misc.* ix(3), 55; PCC 20 Langley; C142/183/64.

A.D.K.H.

SEYMOUR, John I (by 1523–67), of Great Marlow, Bucks.

GREAT BEDWYN 1545

b. by 1523. *educ.* I. Temple. *m.* by 1544, Alice, wid. of John Purce of St. Albans, Herts., *s.p.*[1] Under clerk of the Parliaments 1547–67; j.p. Bucks., Herts. 1547; escheator, Beds. and Bucks. 1548–9; commr. relief, Bucks., Herts. 1550; clerk of the peace, Bucks. by 1555–9 or later.[2]

It was A. F. Pollard who distinguished the John Seymour returned for Bedwyn in 1545 from two namesakes elected to the succeeding Parliament, and who correctly identified him with the under clerk of the Parliaments. This conclusion rests on the fact that the last Parliament at which Seymour officiated, that of 1563, ended within 12 months of the proving of the will of John Seymour 'of Great Marlow, in the county of Buckingham, gentleman', the style and domicile given on the return of 1545.[3]

Seymour's parentage is unknown, but it is almost certain that he was descended from the John 'Semer' of Great Marlow who in 1425 left to his grandson Thomas the remainder in a lease of the manor of Seymours belonging to Muchelney abbey, Somerset. At the Dissolution the lands of the abbey were granted to Edward Seymour, Earl of Hertford, who according to the local historian Thomas Langley, citing deeds in his father's possession, leased the manor of Seymours for 100 years to a John Seymour on 4 Sept. 1541; the lease was to be confirmed in 1549 by the dean and chapter of Bristol, to whom the crown granted the lands at

Marlow in 1542 after having recovered them from Hertford by means of an exchange. It was probably the same John Seymour who received an annuity of £20 from the earl in 1542 and who is found acting for him in land transactions in 1544 and 1548. The legal training implied by such employment is known to have come the way of the under clerk, who in May 1547 was admitted a fellow of the Inner Temple, a status which normally presupposed three years of study; his simultaneous discharge, at the cost of 20s., of all offices and his freedom to be out of commons were to be confirmed in 1560, when they were said to have been granted 'having regard as well to the building of his chamber as that he was clerk of the Parliament house'.[4]

It must have been to Hertford that Seymour owed his return for Bedwyn to the Parliament of 1545: Bedwyn was one of the manors, previously held by Sir Edward Darrell* and his heir Edmund Darrell*, which had been granted to Hertford a few months before the election. It was presumably also on Hertford's, now Somerset's, nomination that he became under clerk of Parliament. The date of this appointment is left in doubt by the patent of 10 May 1548 which directed Seymour 'to attend upon the Commons of the realm of England thereto convoked, from Michaelmas'. That the Michaelmas referred to was 29 Sept. 1547 is shown by the Privy Council's warrant of 27 Mar. 1549 for a reward to Seymour for 'his diligent attendance given at both the last assessments of the Parliament', and by payments made to him from the Exchequer and by the corporation of London in respect of the year 1547–8. It is therefore certain that he was under clerk from the opening of Edward VI's first Parliament. Although he held the office during pleasure, he was not to be deprived of it either at Somerset's fall from power or at the duke's trial and execution, which cost him no more than a summons before the Privy Council in December 1551; he was evidently not close enough to Somerset to be judged dangerous and the value of his services to the Commons may have been already apparent.[5]

Seymour had his patent renewed by both Mary and Elizabeth; the first took the opportunity to cut his salary from £10 to £5 and the second to restore it to the old rate. He also received a reward from the crown at the end of each parliamentary session, in 1549 one of 40 marks, increased in 1550 and 1552 to 50 marks, as well as gifts from the city of London which, starting at £5 in 1548, fell to 5 marks in 1549 and to four in 1550 and 1552, to £5 for the two Parliaments of 1553 and to 40s. apiece thereafter. In 1549 the corporation minuted that although under clerks had their accustomed fee which they had

'heretofore commonly used to have at every session of the Parliament', such payment was a 'free gift' for Seymour's 'gentle behaviour and good will' and not one that he 'ought of right' to have. On only one occasion is Seymour known to have received payment from the City for a specific service: the £5 he received in 1548 was partly in payment 'for his pains taken in writing of the book in parchment to have been enacted by Parliament for the assurance of the late hospital of little St. Bartholomew in West Smithfield and of the lands thereto belonging'. Seymour appears to have acted on his own initiative in starting the Commons' Journal as we know it: during his 20 years of keeping it he shaped its form for centuries to come.[6]

In the will which he made on 7 Oct. 1565, and which was proved on 12 Dec. 1567, Seymour affirmed his trust 'to be of the number that shall inhabit the Kingdom that is prepared for the chosen people of God'. The direction that if he should chance to die at Marlow he should be buried in Great Marlow church near his wife's pew may indicate that he made the will in expectation of an earlier resumption of the Parliament of 1563 than in fact took place. Evidently childless, Seymour bequeathed his house at St. Albans to his wife Alice for life, after which it was to pass to Edward Grace, whom elsewhere he calls 'my boy'; the remainder of his 'farm' (presumably his lease of Seymours) he left to his wife for 39 years, with reversion to his executor Hugh Dawson, cook, in the event of her marriage or death. His charitable bequests included one of £1 a year for 60 years towards the repair of Marlow bridge.[7]

[1] Date of birth estimated from marriage. C1/1062/28. [2] M. F. Bond, *Recs. Parlt.* 305; *CPR*, 1547–8, pp. 81, 84; 1548–9, p. 3; 1553, pp. 327, 351, 354; 1553–4, p. 262; 1558–60, p. 56; E. Stephens, *Clerks of the Counties*, 58. [3] A. F. Pollard, 'Under clerks and the Commons' Jnls. 1509–58', *Bull. IHR*, xvi. 144–67; PCC 36 Stonard. [4] PCC 3 Luffenam; *VCH Bucks.* iii. 68, 73–74; *LP Hen. VIII*, xvii; T. Langley, *Desborough Hundred*, 105–6; *Two Cartularies of the Abbeys of Muchelney and Athelney* (Som. Rec. Soc. xiv), 1; *HMC Bath*, iv. 98–99, 125, 210; *CPR*, 1547–8, p. 371; *Cal. I.T. Recs.* 149, 206; E. W. Ives, 'Some aspects of the legal profession in the late 15th and early 16th centuries' (London Univ. Ph.D. thesis, 1955), 24; Egerton 2819; *APC*, iii. 433, 452, 460, 461; *Bull. IHR*, xvi. 154. [5] *Bull. IHR*, xvi. 144–69; Neale, *Commons*, 333; *CPR*, 1548–9, p. 3; *APC*, ii. 270; City of London RO, Guildhall, rep. 11, f. 415; E405/484, f. 10v. [6] *Bull. IHR*, xvi. 144–69; *CPR*, 1553–4, p. 262; 1558–60, p. 56; Lansd. 156(28), ff. 111–12; E405/119, m. 6, 484, ff. 18v, 33; *APC*, iii. 270, 389; iv. 48; Neale, *Commons*, 340–1; 'The Commons' Jnls. in the Tudor period', *Trans. R. Hist. Soc.* (ser. 4), iii. 141; City of London RO, rep. 12(1), ff. 6, 217v; 12(2), f. 488; 13(1), ff. 103v, 145v, 167; 13(2), f. 353; 14, ff. 13v, 101v. [7] PCC 36 Stonard.

R.L.D.

SEYMOUR, John II (by 1518–52), of London.

WOOTTON BASSETT 1547[1]

b. by 2 Dec. 1518, 1st s. of Edward Seymour, later Duke of Somerset, of Wolf Hall, Wilts. by 1st w. Catherine, da. of Sir William Fyloll of Woodlands, Dorset. *educ.* ?G. Inn, adm. 1537.[2]

John Seymour is first mentioned in a settlement of his maternal grandfather's estates made when his mother was in her twentieth year. How early her behaviour gave rise to scandal is not known, but the provision which her father made for her in his will of 1527 was conditional upon her leading a virtuous life. By then she had been repudiated by her husband, who doubted the paternity of at least her first born, although it was not until 1540 that he procured the Act (32 Hen. VIII, c.78) disinheriting both John Seymour and the younger brother Edward in favour of the offspring of his second marriage.[3]

The future Protector disposed of much of Catherine Fyloll's inheritance but did not ignore her sons: after the battle of Pinkie he gave Edward Seymour a knighthood and either he or his brother Admiral Seymour nominated John Seymour for election to Parliament. The borough of Wootton Bassett, then in the hands of the Queen dowager Catherine Parr, was clearly amenable to Seymour influence, and although the election return does not survive and there is no trace of Seymour in the Commons before the fourth session in 1552, it may be presumed that he was elected in 1547, when the Protector was at the peak of his power, and not later, when decline was followed by disaster.

The fall of Somerset does not seem to have implicated the son whom he had first disowned and later favoured. It was not this John Seymour, but a namesake, the duke's illegitimate brother and a leading figure in his household, who in October 1551 joined his master in the Tower. A month earlier he had been by-elected at Reading in place of the deceased William Grey II, one of Somerset's chief supporters, but when he was imprisoned the election was cancelled and in the following January, on the eve of the new session, the borough chose Sir John Mason in his stead. The episode had a momentarily confusing sequel, for the clerk who shortly afterwards revised the list of Members, under the impression that it was the Member for Wootton Bassett who was in the Tower, struck through his name and added the explanatory phrase 'in Turrem'; only when he, or another, realized his mistake was it rectified by the further addition 'stet'.[4]

Not only did Seymour keep his seat in Parliament but he turned the death of Somerset to advantage by seeking the restitution of his mother's inheritance. On 3 Mar. 1552 he exhibited in the Commons a bill, signed by the King, to repeal the Act of 1540, and at the close of the session this received the royal assent as the Act touching the limitation of the late Duke of Somerset's lands (5 and 6 Edw. VI, no. 37). A month later the chancellor was ordered to establish a committee to consider his claim and the implementing of the Act. In the autumn of 1552 he received some property from Edward VI and a sum of £20 towards his costs; Treasurer Winchester was also empowered to restore his inheritance, but this Seymour did not live to enjoy. He was a sick man when on 7 Dec. 1552 he made a brief will appointing his brother Sir Edward executor and residuary legatee after the discharge of a number of bequests: the John Seymour who witnessed the will was presumably the erstwhile prisoner in the Tower, who had received a pardon three months earlier. Within a few days the testator was dead and on 19 Dec. he was buried in the hosptial of the Savoy. Sir Edward Seymour, who was to be restored in blood by the Parliament of March 1553 (7 Edw. VI, no. 16), reaped the benefit of his brother's efforts over the inheritance, but it was not until the 18th century that his descendants achieved the dukedom of Somerset.[5]

[1] Hatfield 207. [2] Date of birth estimated from a reference to Seymour in a settlement of his grandfather's estates, C142/46/25. [3] A. A. Locke, *Seymour Fam.*, 32–33. [4] Hatfield 207; *Machyn's Diary* (Cam. Soc. xlii), 10; *APC*, iii. 391, 397; *HMC Bath*, iv. 98–377 passim; Egerton 2815; *CPR, 1547–8*, p. 371; C1/1316/39; *Reading Recs.* 218–20, 222. [5] *CJ*, i. 19; *APC*, iv. 55, 120; PCC 9 Tashe; *CPR, 1550–3*, pp. 278–9, 410; 1553, pp. 76–77; *Machyn's Diary*, 27; *CP*, xii(1), 65; Hoare, *Wilts. Mere*, 113–14.

A.D.K.H.

SEYMOUR, Sir John (1473/74–1536), of Wolf Hall, Wilts.

HEYTESBURY 1529

b. 1473/74, 1st s. of John Seymour of Wolf Hall by Elizabeth, da. of Sir George Darrell of Littlecote; bro. of Robert*. m. Margery, da. of Sir Henry Wentworth† of Nettlestead, Suff., 6s. inc. Sir Henry* and Sir Thomas II* 4da. suc. fa. 26 Oct. 1491. Kntd. 17 June 1497, banneret 1513.[1]

Warden, Savernake forest, Wilts. Oct. 1491; sheriff, Wilts. 1498–9, 1507–8, 1518–19, 1524–Jan. 1526, Som. and Dorset 1515–16, 1526–7; j.p. Wilts. 1499–d.; steward, 3rd Duke of Buckingham's lands, Wilts. by 1503; knight of the body by 1509; constable and doorward, Bristol castle, Glos. Aug. 1509, jt. (with s. Edward) July 1517; under captain, *Dragon of Greenwich* 1512; commr. subsidy, Wilts. 1512, 1514, 1515, Wilts. and Salisbury 1523, musters, Wilts. 1513, loan 1524; other commissions 1502–d.; steward, manor of Kingston Lisle, Berks. bef. 1513; forester, Grovely, Wilts. Feb. 1526; groom of the bedchamber 1532.[2]

Although the Seymours were already of some substance in Wiltshire, it was a combination of timely demise, good fortune and royal favour which established them early in the 16th century as one of the leading families in the shire. Sir John Seymour's great-grandfather and namesake had inherited both the Seymour-Beauchamp fortunes and a great part of the lands of Sir William Sturmy†; it was also he who secured Wolf Hall.[3]

By its size and provenance the Seymour inheritance was bound to provoke rivalry and litigation. Even Wolf Hall was not free from dispute: at some time between 1518 and 1529 one Thomas Bruyn petitioned in Chancery for half of the manor as 'cousin and heir' of Sturmy's elder daughter Agnes. The impression of Seymour as lawless and overbearing given by one plaintiff in 1502 is confirmed by litigation over Easton priory and Grafton manor. In 1514 Seymour himself complained that the bishop of Salisbury's servants had killed deer in Savernake forest, which the bishop denied.[4]

Seymour's behaviour does not seem to have impaired his relations with the crown. He was regularly employed as a royal official in Wiltshire, was a knight of the body and groom of the chamber to Henry VIII, and in 1535 and 1536 entertained that monarch at his houses in Hampshire and Wiltshire. He attended the funeral of Henry VII in 1509 and that of Prince Henry two years later, and took part in Henry VIII's meetings with Francis I and Charles V and other state occasions. According to one pedigree he was knighted 'on account of his gallant and conspicuous conduct at the Battle of Blackheath', and after the battle of the Spurs in 1513 he was made knight banneret. Nine years later he was again in the field, this time with Suffolk's army of invasion in France.[5]

As a leading figure in Wiltshire Seymour may well have sat in one or more of Henry VIII's early Parliaments, for which the names of the Members are lost. He was certainly an obvious choice in 1529 and he could perhaps think himself unlucky to yield to Sir Edward Darrell (his brother-in-law) and Sir Edward Baynton for the knighthood of the shire. As it was, he and his brother Robert were returned for Heytesbury. This was not a borough which lay within the family's sphere of influence and the appropriation of both seats was something of an achievement: perhaps Seymour's role as a feoffee in the conveyance by Walter Hungerford of the manor of Heytesbury to Thomas Westley on 2 Oct. 1529, shortly after the election, reflects his standing there. Of his part in the proceedings of the Commons nothing is known. It is likely, however, that he was re-elected in 1536, in accordance with the King's request for the return of the previous Members.[6]

By then it was clear that the King intended to marry Seymour's daughter Jane, with whom he had been dallying for nearly two years. The marriage took place on 30 May, nine days before the opening of the Parliament which attainted the dead Anne Boleyn and revised the succession to the throne. That Seymour himself, unlike his elder sons, appears to have received no mark of royal favour may or may not be indicative of his feelings in the matter. He was not to live to see the marriage vindicated, and his daughter sacrificed, by the birth of his royal grandson, for he died on 21 Dec. 1536. Buried in Easton priory, he was to be reinterred by his grandson, when half-a-century later that church lay derelict, in his own parish church of Great Bedwyn. In the absence of a will or an inquisition post mortem, the disposition of his property cannot be established, but it is known that his heir, the future Protector, inherited lands to the annual value of £275.[7]

[1] Date of birth estimated from age at fa.'s i.p.m., *CIPM Hen. VII*, i. 767–72. A. A. Locke, *Seymour Fam.* 5–6; Earl of Cardigan, *Wardens of Savernake Forest*, 131–4; *Wilts. Arch. Mag.* li. 329–39, 500–20; H. St. Maur, *Annals of the Seymours*, 18. [2] *LP Hen. VIII*, i–v, viii; *CPR, 1494–1509*, pp. 287, 665; *Statutes*, iii. 80, 113, 169; C. Rawcliffe, *The Staffords, Earls of Stafford and Dukes of Buckingham, 1394–1521*, p. 211. [3] *Wilts. Arch. Mag.* li. 329–39, 500–20. [4] C1/464/48, 472/59, 631/6; Req.2/5/73; *Wilts. Arch. Mag.* xxix. 58–99, 156–84; St.Ch.2/14/153–7, 17/331; *LP Hen. VIII*, i. [5] C1/506/1; SP1/68/145; *Rutland Pprs.* (Cam. Soc. xxi), 32, 46; *Wilts. Arch. Mag.* li. 514; *Wilts. N. and Q.* iii. 258; *HMC Bath*, iv. 2; *VCH Hants*, iv. 75; *LP Hen. VIII*, i–iii, ix. [6] *LP Hen. VIII*, iv. [7] *Coll. Top. et Gen.* v. 21–23; J. Smyth, *Lives of the Berkeleys*, ii. 235–8; *HMC Bath*, iv. 324, 377; *Wilts. Arch. Mag.* li. 515; Harl. 1529, f. 38.

R.L.D.

SEYMOUR, Robert (c. 1480–1545 or later), of Ivy Church, Wilts. and London.

HEYTESBURY   1529

b. c.1480, 3rd s. of John Seymour of Wolf Hall, Wilts. by Elizabeth, da. of Sir George Darrell of Littlecote, Wilts.; bro. of Sir John*.[1]

Member, council of Tournai 1517; capt. *Crist* 1522; sewer by 1526; steward, lordship and hundred of Amesbury, lordship of Winterbourne Earls and hundred of Alderbury, Wilts. 1526–?*d*.; sheriff, Anglesey 1527–34; gent. usher, the chamber by 1528; warden, Melchet forest, Wilts. 1530–1; capt. Newnham Bridge 1533–9.[2]

Since his fellow-Member was Sir John Seymour of Wolf Hall, Robert Seymour may be taken to have been Sir John's younger brother and not one of the insignificant Robert Seymours of Lincolnshire. His election is to be ascribed to a combination of royal favour and local standing: he may also have enjoyed a personal connexion with Walter Hungerford, lord of the manor of Heytesbury, who in June 1536 was to grant him an annuity. Of Seymour's parliamentary career nothing is known. It is likely that he was returned again in 1536 in accordance with the King's request for the re-election of the previous Members, and it may have been his homecoming from that Parliament (which ended on 18 July) which prompted the purchase a week earlier of sugar and spices for his nephew Edward's kitchen 'against the coming down of Mr. Robert Seymour'. This was probably the last the Commons saw of him, for in 1539 he was serving at Calais and there is no trace of him in the Parliament of 1542.[3]

On his own showing, Seymour had entered the royal service at about the time of Henry VIII's accession, and he seems to have been chiefly engaged in overseas military duties. In 1515 he received payment as a footman after the Tournai campaign and he remained there as one of the council. When war came again in 1522 he was at first captain of the *Crist*, but later in that year Sir William Sandys told the King of his part in overcoming resistance during the Picardy campaign and in 1523 he served in the Duke of Suffolk's expedition across the Somme. In 1532 he was to have been in the King's retinue at the meeting with Francis I at Calais, but William Raynsford's name was substituted for his on the list of those so designated: no royal displeasure need be suspected, for upon the King's return to Dover he drew £4 13s.4d. to play at the tables with Seymour.[4]

In 1535 Seymour went to Calais to deliver letters from Cromwell to Sir Thomas Palmer, his precursor as captain of Newnham Bridge. His attachment to Cromwell continued, for in 1536 he was back in England on the minister's business: it was at this time, too, that he sought Cromwell's protection for his chaplain and successfully contended for his favour with John Tregonwell* over the priory of Ivy Church. Later, it was to his own rising nephew Edward Seymour that he looked for support, as he did in 1539 in his unsuccessful effort to retain his office at Newnham Bridge: it was then that he spoke of his 30 years in royal service.[5]

Seymour's closing years can be traced only from fragments of evidence and his death dated only approximately. In October 1543 he was still receiving (from its new owner, his nephew Edward) his fee of £5 6s. 8d. for the stewardship of Amesbury, and he is last heard of in a land transaction in April 1545. His death before November 1546 is probably to be inferred from the grant then made to David Seymour* of an annuity of £6 13s.4d., a similar grant having been made to Robert Seymour by Sir Walter Hungerford in 1536; and if (which is not certain) David Seymour was his son, he had died before 23 July 1546. He is thus almost certainly to be distinguished from the Robert Seymour who figures in a Star Chamber case for forcible expulsion in Wiltshire in May 1547, as well as the man of thes ame name who in 1551 was compensated for the non-ransoming of prisoners he had taken.[6]

¹ Date of birth estimated from eldest brother's. H. St. Maur, *Annals of the Seymours*, ped. opp. p. 1. ² Lansd. 1(62), f. 201; Strype, *Eccles. Memorials*, i. 11; *VCH Hants*, iv, 541; Egerton 2604; *LP Hen. VIII*, iv, v, xiv, xvi; P. T. J. Morgan, 'The govt. of Calais, 1485–1558' (Oxf. Univ. D. Phil. thesis, 1966), 297. ³ *LP Hen. VIII*, xxi; *HMC Bath*, iv. 329. ⁴ *LP Hen. VIII*, ii, iii, xiv; *HMC Bath*, iv. 2; *Privy Purse Expenses of Hen. VIII*, ed. Nicolas, 273. ⁵ *VCH Wilts*. iii. 294; *LP Hen. VIII*, ix, xii, xiii–xv; SP1/144/19. ⁶ *LP Hen.*

VIII, xix–xxi; LC2/2; St.Ch.3/6/76; *APC*, iii. 290; *HMC Bath*, iv. 129, 333; Clothworkers' Co. orders of ct. 1536–58, f. 187.

R.L.D.

SEYMOUR, Sir Thomas I (by 1476–1535/36), of London, Saffron Walden, Essex, and Hoxton, Mdx.

LONDON 1529*

b. by 1476, s. of John Seymour of Saffron Walden by Christian. *m.* by 1515, Mary, wid. of Robert Imber (*d*.1512); 1da illegit. Kntd. June 1520.[1]
    Warden, Mercers' Co. 1509–10, master 1517–18, 1525–6; alderman, London 1515–*d*., auditor 1515–17, 1526–8, sheriff 1516–17, mayor 1526–7; mayor, staple of Calais 1523, staple at Westminster 1530; commr. subsidy, London 1523, 1524; j.p. Essex 1530–*d*., Herts. 1531–*d*.[2]

Thomas Seymour's father was a London stock-fishmonger with property in Saffron Walden. Seymour himself lived in Walden before coming to London, where after serving his apprenticeship he was made free of the Mercers' Company in 1497, became a merchant of the staple of Calais and a merchant adventurer, and set up house in the parish of St. Stephen's, Walbrook. In March 1502 he exported 40 sacks of wool in nine different ships bound for Calais and on 27 June he shipped 9 more sacks of wool and 2,000 wool fells. In 1506–7 he exported 132 cloths and in 1512–13 80 cloths; in 1509 he and two other London merchants were licensed to export wool and cloth through the Straits of Gibraltar. As both a stapler and merchant adventurer he was a suitable go-between in the conflicts of the two companies: thus in December 1509 the mercers authorized him to speak to Sir John Tate*, the mayor of the staple, for the settlement of one such dispute, and in April 1512 he was chosen by the staplers to present their case against their rivals.[3]

When Seymour was a warden of the Mercers he was prominent in a quarrel between the merchants of London and the government over the levy of customs. Early in August 1509 the Mercers heard from him of a Council order forbidding the import of goods free of custom. He and his fellow-wardens of the company thereupon joined with the wardens of other companies to take counsel's opinion, which was that, as the grant of customs had been made to Henry VII for life, merchants need not pay tonnage and poundage to his son and successor unless these duties were given him by Act of Parliament. In reporting this opinion to his fellow-mercers, Seymour 'bade every man do as they should think best'. There the matter rested until the approach of Parliament, when Seymour called on the company to consider 'what things be to be remembered for the general wealth of this realm and specially of this city of London', in order that 'the burgesses may be clearly instructed and advised whereof they shall speak or desire anything that may be for all our wealths'. The matter being of such general interest, the Mercers decided to consult other companies and on 10 Jan. 1510 a joint meeting of 'divers fellowships adventurers' elected 17 men to 'study and devise what things be necessary to be sued for at the said Parliament'.[4]

Parliament opened on 21 Jan., and two weeks later Seymour, although not a Member, 'perceived well that it was the King's mind to have the subsidy [of tonnage and poundage] granted at this Parliament' and added that as 'the most part of the Parliament' were gentlemen, who would be unaffected by the grant, it would certainly pass unless action were taken to stop it. The next day, therefore, the Merchant Adventurers decided on a petition to the King; Seymour meanwhile, with the mayor, the City's legal counsel and 'certain burgesses of the Parliament', drew up provisos to be added to the Act by the Commons, deferring its date of commencement (except in the case of the staplers) until Michaelmas 1510 and providing for payment at the old rate of Henry VII's first year, not the enhanced rate of the end of his reign. By 12 Feb. it was obvious that the grant would be made retrospective to the first day of the reign, but the merchants still hoped that something might be done about the rate, and agreed to present a book of rates of 4 Hen. VII to the King and the Lords for inclusion in the Act. Two days later, however, it passed with no concessions, and on 16 Feb. Seymour advised the Merchant Adventurers to sue to the King for a remission of all payments from the first day of his reign until the day of the grant, as under Henry VII. Seymour and others presented the petition to the King on the following morning as he came from mass; ten days later Seymour reported the Council's request that the suit should be for Londoners only, not for the whole country, but in the conclusion finally reached in October the Merchant Adventurers were pardoned only one third of the payments due.[5]

Seymour was considered for election to the next Parliament, but was not chosen; on 19 Jan. 1512, however, he was appointed by the court of aldermen 'to hear matters' for the Parliament, due to begin in two days' time. By a similar arrangement before the Parliament of 1515, he and ten others were appointed to discuss possible reforms and 'to have the examination of all such bills as shall be exhibited to this Parliament, before that they be presented to the same'. Later in 1515 Seymour was committed to

ward by the court of aldermen for refusing to give up custody of his stepdaughter: he was not long in disgrace, and before the end of the year, after five nominations since February, he was elected alderman. In 1516 he was the mayor's choice for sheriff and thus held office at the time of 'evil May day': ten years later, when he was elected mayor, his behaviour during the riot was still held against him and the commons unsuccessfully opposed him. In the meantime he had received his knighthood from the King at Calais.[6]

Within a few days of becoming mayor Seymour was summoned to the Star Chamber to hear a peremptory demand from Wolsey for the election of John Scott as recorder of London in place of William Shelley*. The court of aldermen agreed to stand firm against this encroachment and elected one of the under sheriffs of London, John Baker I*. A few months later the City again defended its privileges when the King called for the discharge of Paul Withypoll* from the aldermanship to which he had been unwillingly elected: this time the mayor and aldermen were less successful, a series of visits to the cardinal and a deputation headed by Seymour to the King proving of no avail. These episodes brought Seymour into unfortunate prominence at court and may have conduced to his later difficulties, although they were without immediate consequences.[7]

In 1529 Seymour was elected senior Member for London. Before Parliament met the mayor and aldermen asked the city companies to suggest topics for consideration there, and the wardens and six liverymen of the Mercers (not including Seymour) drew up five 'articles' of grievances particularly affecting London. On 20 Nov., after two and a half weeks of the session, Seymour reported to the Mercers that the Lords and Commons, 'for certain high considerations them moving', had remittted to the King the loan recently advanced to him by his subjects,

which his grace accepteth and taketh right thankfully, declaring that unless right urgent causes move him (which shall be evident to all his said subjects) his grace will never demand penny of them during his life natural; and further, in case they could study anything that might be for the public wealth of this his realm and city of London, his grace would right gladly condescend thereunto.

When the whole company heard Seymour's account of the proceedings, 'they all admitted the same to be very well done, and prayed God to save his grace and send him prosperous fortune and long life'.[8]

By 1532, however, Seymour was 'in the King's danger' for illegal acts committed during his mayoralty of the staple; it was said that the 'causer of his trouble' was Cromwell. The offences included the liberation of prisoners on bail, illegal export of goods and breaches of statutes relating to the staple. Seymour was eventually pardoned but fined £2,000: he paid 500 marks at once and bound himself to pay the rest in instalments over five years, a fellow-mercer, Rowland Hill*, being associated with him in the obligation.[9]

Seymour was not to live to discharge his bond. In June 1535 the court of aldermen decided to ask him whether he would agree to retire; in July they renewed the request by letter, insisting that he should reside in London and fulfil his aldermanic duties or be replaced. He had evidently given up his house in London, where he had been assessed for the subsidy of 1523 at £3,500 in goods, but he promised that 'as soon as God shall send him health' he would 'provide him of a house within this city' and attend to his duties as an alderman. On 2 Dec. 1535, in 'extreme sickness', he sent word that he was willing to vacate his seat in Parliament: it is doubtful whether he had attended recent sessions, for when in January 1534 his three fellow-Members were granted their accustomed wages and fees there was no mention of Seymour. On 11 Dec. 1535 the testament which Seymour had made on 14 May 1533 was read over to him in the presence of witnesses. He bequeathed £10 for the maintenance of the almshouse at Walden, £40 to his poor kinsfolk living in or near Walden, and £600 to other charities: his executors were his wife and his 'trusty friend' Rowland Hill, and his overseers John Baker and Henry White, then the under sheriff. On the same day, or soon after it, Rowland Hill, who 'knew much of the intent and purpose' of Sir Thomas Seymour, seeing that he had not provided for his only child, an illegitimate daughter, asked him if it were not his intention that all his lands should descend eventually to her: Seymour, stricken with palsy and unable to speak, signified his assent by raising his hand.[10]

The testament was proved on 31 Jan. 1536 but the provisions of the will were contested by Seymour's nephew and namesake: he claimed the remainder to all the lands after the death of the widow, whereas she supported the daughter, Grace, and her husband Edward Elrington*. Rowland Hill described the circumstances in which the will had been made, and the court of Chancery found for the defendants, ordering the young Thomas Seymour to pay their costs. The estate was considerable: the manor of Widdington, four miles south of Walden, and two other manors in Essex, the manor of Hoxton in Middlesex, one manor in Gloucestershire and three in Lancashire. All were to go to Lady Seymour until her death and then, with the exception of the capital messuage at Hoxton, which Sir

Thomas bequeathed to Rowland Hill for life, to Grace Elrington and her heirs. Hoxton had been Seymour's home in his later years and he was buried in the parish church of St. Leonard, Shoreditch; Lady Seymour, when she made her will in 1555, asked for burial in the same church.[11]

[1] Date of birth estimated from admission to freedom of Mercers' Co., List of mercers (T/S Mercers' Hall), 445. PCC 31 Hogen, 28 Fetiplace; City of London RO, Guildhall, rep. 3, f. 18; C1/887/14. [2] *Acts. Ct. of Mercers' Co.* ed. Lyell and Watney, 325, 446, 698; City of London RO, rep. 3, f. 61v; 7, f. 143; jnl. 11, ff. 227, 265v; 12, f. 354v; 13, f. 32; *LP Hen. VIII*, iii–v. [3] List of mercers (T/S Mercers' Hall), 445; *LP Hen. VIII*, i; C67/62 m. 1; E122/79/9, 80/4, 82/9 ex inf. Prof. P. Ramsey; E179/251/15v; *Acts Ct. of Mercers' Co.* 344, 401. [4] *Acts. Ct. of Mercers' Co.* 326–7, 345–6. [5] Ibid. 346–53, 380–1. [6] City of London RO, rep. 2, ff. 125v, 127, 205v; 3, ff. 4v, 6, 18, 47v, 53, 60v; jnl. 11, f. 265v; *Grey Friars Chron.* (Cam. Soc. liii), 33. [7] City of London RO, rep. 7, ff. 145, v, 148, 171v–80. [8] Ibid. rep. 8, f. 66; Mercers' Co. acts of ct. 1527–60, ff. 25v–26. [9] SP1/69, f. 270; *LP Hen. VIII*, v, vi, viii. [10] City of London RO, rep. 9, ff. 41v, 110, 116v, 117v, 141v; jnl. 13, f. 446v; E179/251/15v; PCC 31 Hogen; W. K. Jordan, *London Charities*, 93, 327; C1/783/13. Beaven, *Aldermen of London*, ii. 24 gives 11 Dec. as date of death but without citing evidence. [11] PCC 31 Hogen, 13 Ketchyn; C1/783/7–13, 887/14–18; *Stow's Survey of London*, ii. 75.

H.M.

SEYMOUR, Sir Thomas II (by 1509–49), of Bromham, Wilts., Seymour Place, London, and Sudeley Castle, Glos.

WILTSHIRE 1545

b. by 1509, 4th s. of Sir John Seymour*, and bro. of Sir Henry*. *m.* May 1547, Catherine, da. of Sir Thomas Parr of Kendal, Westmld., wid. of Sir Edward Burgh, Sir John Neville I* 3rd Lord Latimer, and Henry VIII, 1da. *cr.* Baron Seymour of Sudeley 16 Feb. 1547. Kntd. 18 Oct. 1537, KG nom. and invest. 17 Feb. inst. 23 May 1547.[1]

Servant to Sir Francis Bryan* by 1530; master forester, Enfield Chase, Mdx. 9 Aug. 1532–*d.*; gent. the privy chamber 1536–46 or later; capt. *Sweepestake* 1537, *Peter* 1544; jt. master steward, Chirk and Holt castles, Denb. 1537; ambassador to Hungary June 1542, the Netherlands 30 Apr. 1543; keeper, Farleigh Hungerford castle and park, Wilts. 11 Mar. 1544; master of the ordnance 18 Apr. 1544–26 Mar. 1547; steward, duchy of Lancaster, Essex, Herts. and Mdx. 28 May 1544–*d.*; admiral 1544; commr. benevolence, Wilts. 1544/45, array, Kent 1545, chantries, Wilts. 1546, musters, Wilts. 1546, of Admiralty in Nov. 1547; PC 23–28 Jan., 2 Feb. 1547–18 Jan. 1549; ld. adm. 17 Feb. 1547–18 Jan. 1549; j.p. Berks., Devon, Essex, Glos., Hants, Herefs., Herts., Kent, Mdx., Salop, Suss., Wilts. and Worcs. 1547; master, St. Katharine's hospital by 1548; numerous minor offices.[2]

Nothing has been discovered about the early life and education of Thomas Seymour; since he was literate, it may be inferred that he received private tuition. He seems to have attained some fluency in French, but this may have been a product of his early career rather than his upbringing. Probably through his father's preferment Seymour was, by 1530, employed in the service of his 'cousin' Sir Francis Bryan, then English ambassador in France, as a messenger to and from the King. In August 1532 he obtained the master forestership of Enfield

Chase, but he seems to have secured no further advancement before the marriage of his sister Jane to the King in May 1536, when he became a gentleman of the privy chamber and shared a grant of the stewardship of two castles in the Welsh marches and of the adjoining lordships in Wales. From these inauspicious beginnings, early in 1537, he received his first command in the navy, which he was to make virtually his own much in the same way as his brother Edward was to do with the army. After helping to patrol the Channel and taking part in the action against four French ships in Mount's Bay, he returned to court for the christening of his nephew Prince Edward and three days later he was knighted, while his brother was raised to the earldom of Hertford. The death of the Queen in the following week did nothing to impair the advancement of either brother.[3]

Seymour had the ear of Henry VIII. During the Easter Law vacation of 1538 he told the King that Archbishop Cranmer was misusing his income but retracted on learning his information was wrong. That this episode did not harm him is shown by what happened next. In July of that year the 3rd Duke of Norfolk suggested to the King that Seymour should marry his daughter (the King's widowed daughter-in-law) the Duchess of Richmond, but despite the King's approval nothing came of the match. In the following autumn he accompanied Sir Anthony Browne* to France as a member of Browne's embassy to Francis I. Over the next year or so he acquired the manor of Coleshill in Berkshire, the commandery of Baddesley in Hampshire and the sites and lands of the abbeys of Coggeshall in Essex and Romsey in Hampshire. An exchange of lands between Sir Richard Long* and himself was confirmed by a private Act (31 Hen. VIII, no. 24) in the Parliament of 1539. In December 1539 he went to Calais as one of the dignitaries to meet Anne of Cleves and escort her to London, and six months later he was one of the challengers at the tournaments held in her honour at Westminster palace and who on 28 May 'feasted all the knights and burgesses of the Common House'. It may have been a fracas excited by these festivities which caused Edward Rogers* to be bound on 12 Sept. in £1,000 to keep the peace towards Seymour. He returned to Calais in May 1541 with William Fitzwilliam I*, Earl of Southampton, and while there visited Ardres in disguise. He was presumably the 'Mr. Seymour' entrusted with Catherine Howard's jewels following her arrest later in the year. In June 1542 the King named him ambassador to the court of Ferdinand of Hungary and while there he observed the unsuccessful attempt to recapture Pesth from the Turks.

On completing his embassy in the autumn he was ordered to hire German mercenaries for the army but failed.[4]

In May 1543 Seymour went with Nicholas Wotton as ambassador to the Regent of the Netherlands to Brussels where he remained until the declaration of war against France. Appointed marshal of the field and second-in-command to Sir John Wallop he served in the campaign in the Netherlands. His outspokenness about Charles V's failure to give the promised support to the English force led the Emperor to remark that Seymour had shown himself more dry and difficult than Wallop, but Henry VIII showed his satisfaction with Seymour by making him master of the ordnance for life in the spring of 1544 with a salary more than four times that of his predecessor, Sir Christopher Morres. By virtue of his new office he supplied the guns and munitions for the campaign to capture Boulogne. After taking part in the storming of the town he was made an admiral with orders to victual the garrison left there and to harry the French in the Channel. His failure to execute those orders brought a sharp rebuke from the Council, but his explanation was accepted by the King. During the spring and summer of 1545 Seymour combined his duties as admiral and master of the ordnance with those of the lord warden of the Cinque Ports while Sir Thomas Cheyne* was indisposed; his energies in each capacity were directed by the Council towards the defence of England which at the time was threatened by invasion from France. In September he was instructed to patrol the Straits of Dover. When the Parliament postponed from January assembled in November he took his place in the House as the senior knight for Wiltshire. His election in the previous January reflected his growing prestige and his family's standing in the county. No evidence has been found that Seymour exercised any patronage at the elections to this Parliament. It is possible that he had sat in one or more of the Parliaments between 1536 and 1542 for which the names of most of the Members are lost. Nothing is known about his work in the House. During the first session he obtained Hampton Place from the King, which he renamed Seymour Place[5]

In January 1546 Seymour began a land transaction with Andrew Baynton*, by which, it was decided in Mary's reign, the latter had been swindled out of his inheritance. In March Seymour joined his brother Hertford in Calais while the earl was lieutenant-general of the army there. Hertford's closeness to Seymour at this time is shown by his use as a confidential messenger between the earl and the Council. Such a close relationship between the two

Seymour brothers is of much interest occurring as it does near the end of the reign and the fall of the Howards. In June, the Duke of Norfolk asked the King once again to help him arrange a marriage between his daughter, the Duchess of Richmond, and Seymour. The proposed marriage is said to have been frustrated this time by the opposition of the duchess and her brother the Earl of Surrey. It may be, however, that Seymour was already contemplating marriage with Princess Elizabeth; Catherine Astley is reported in 1549 to have said that if Henry VIII had lived Seymour would have married the princess and she herself admitted that she was then encouraging the match. Five days before the King's death Seymour was sworn a member of the Privy Council on Secretary Paget's declaration that this was Henry VIII's desire, but according to the Earl of Warwick later in the year the King had said 'No, no', on being told of Seymour's admission to the Council. Henry VIII named Seymour one of the assistants to the executors of his will.[6]

Misinformed by Warwick that it had been secretly agreed that Hertford was to be Protector of the realm and Seymour governor of Edward VI, Seymour interrupted a meeting of the Council on 2 Feb. to demand proper recognition. Without answering him the Council 'straight . . . rose up and departed'. Hertford was irritated by the episode but to conciliate his brother he seems to have obtained Seymour's readmission to the Council even though he had not been one of those designated by the late King to advise Edward VI until he became of age. On 6 Feb. 1547 Paget announced that it had been Henry VIII's intention that Seymour should be a peer and admiral of England, first with £300 and then £500 a year in land, and within two weeks he had been made Baron Seymour of Sudeley, admiral and a knight of the Garter. At the coronation he helped to bear the royal train and was among the challengers at the jousts. It was he who early in March received the great seal from Chancellor Wriothesley, some eight days before his elder brother, now Duke of Somerset, was confirmed as Protector and Governor; Seymour was not one of the eight signatories. Another two months elapsed before Seymour began to cut much of a figure in the new regime.[7]

According to the act of attainder, Seymour tried, soon after Henry VIII's death, to marry the 13 year-old Princess Elizabeth, but the Council would not allow it. Whatever the truth of this, in May 1547 he secretly married the princess's guardian, Queen Catherine Parr, for whose hand he had been a contender before Henry VIII chose her for his own wife. By his marriage to Catherine, Seymour may have forfeited his creation as Duke of Richmond and Norfolk, the rumour of which advancement the French and Spanish ambassadors had relayed to their masters earlier in the year. It also marked a further straining in his relationship with the Protector. Evidently, however, the prestige this match brought him was of greater consequence to Seymour than such considerations. 'He spared no cost his lady to delight, or to maintain her princely royalty'. He made alterations at Sudeley towards which (Sir) William Sharington* claimed to have given him £1,100 and he kept 120 gentlemen and yeomen about his wife. She, for her part, generously provided him with cash, according to her accounts totalling some £2,000 during their 16-month union. The chronicler Ellis Gruffydd gives an interesting sidelight on Seymour's 'slothfulness to serve' by observing that 'his devotion was such that he would not leave her palace except to come to court'. Unlike Princess Mary, Elizabeth stayed on in Catherine Parr's care after the marriage, and there occurred those familiarities, doubtless at first more imprudent than serious, which are said to have caused Catherine, although she at first condoned them, to send the princess away and which spiced the rumours surrounding Catherine's death and her husband's projected marriage with the princess.[8]

In August 1547, with the 9th Lord Clinton in charge of the fleet, the Protector Somerset went on campaign in Scotland leaving Seymour as lieutenant-general of the south and one of the custodians of the King's person. Resentful that he had not been given the custody of the King before 'so drunken a fool as Sir Richard Page was', Seymour seems to have considered abducting Edward VI. According to Sharington it was in the following month 'that he wished the King were at home in his house'. It was about the same time that he began to provide John Fowler (q.v.) with money for Edward VI's use and to encourage his nephew to 'bear rule, as other kings do'.[9]

The elections to the Parliament of 1547 gave Seymour a unique opportunity to influence the composition of the new House and he appears to have intervened on a considerable scale. He may have been prompted to do so by his wife's example, for both as Queen in 1544–5 and as dowager Queen in 1547 Catherine was instrumental in the return of her household officers and other dependants, notably for the Wiltshire boroughs forming part of her jointure. In July 1547 three of these boroughs, Chippenham, Cricklade and Devizes passed in reversion to Seymour (the other two, Marlborough and Wootton Bassett, going to his brother the

Protector), and he quickly added to them four of his own in Sussex: in August he received among the lands granted to him in accordance with the late King's supposed intention the barony and borough of Bramber, the manors and boroughs of Horsham and New Shoreham, and the borough of Lewes. In acquiring these properties he can scarcely have overlooked their scope for parliamentary patronage any more than he did when as bailiff of the liberty of Cirencester in Gloucestershire he was almost certainly behind the restoration of that borough's franchise. If to this proprietary interest are added the various constituencies open to his influence as admiral, Privy Councillor, uncle to the King and brother to the Protector, it is not surprising that his hand can be seen, or at least divined, behind many elections. Precision is made the more elusive by an at least partial fusion between his own and his wife's patronage; thus while the Queen may be thought to have nominated, either directly or through her brother-in-law the 1st Earl of Pembroke, both Members for Cardiff, Devizes and Westbury, and one each for Camelford, Lewes, Penryn, Shoreham, Wilton and Wootton Bassett, the remaining Members for the boroughs under her control are more readily associated with Seymour himself or his brother. With Seymour's own boroughs we are on firmer ground: he appears to have chosen both Members for Bramber, Cirencester and Horsham, and one each for Lewes and Shoreham. Further afield, two of his dependants were elected for Grampound and Pembroke respectively. He could thus have engineered the return of a dozen or more Members, who with an equivalent number of his wife's nominees would have constituted the largest such group in the House which the period has to show.[10]

Himself summoned to the Lords in 1547 Seymour was a regular attendant there until his arrest on 17 Jan. 1549. He resented not being 'placed in the parliament house as one of the King's uncles' and his irritation was intensified by quarrels with the Protector over the precedence to be accorded to Catherine Parr and over the jewels given her by Henry VIII. He tried to use Parliament as an instrument of his resentment. He 'thought to have made suit to the Parliament' for his own appointment as regent 'and he had the names of all the Lords, and totted them whom he thought he might have to his purpose to labour them'. To this end he asked the King to write desiring the Parliament 'to be good unto the said Lord Seymour in such suits and matters as he should open and declare unto them'. He meant 'not only in his own person to have brought [it] into the Nether House of . . . Parlia-

ment, but also to have likewise opened the same in the Higher House, having in both Houses laboured, stirred and moved a number of persons to take part and join with him in such things as he would set forth and enterprise'. He swore that if his plans were rejected he would make it 'the blackest Parliament that ever was in England', and the Council was later to accuse him of planning to disrupt the business of the Commons. He voted against the bill for the confirmation of letters patent for certain lands following the addition of a proviso in the Commons. In 1548 he planned to obstruct a measure then under consideration by the government for a subsidy in the form of a levy on sheep if it was introduced in the second session of the Parliament.[11]

The improvement in Seymour's relations with the Protector noted by observers late in 1547 did not last for long and by mid February 1548 the two had quarrelled publicly. The Protector adversely criticized Seymour's behaviour in a number of matters in the following months but in September he was able to congratulate his brother on the birth of a daughter. Catherine Parr died on 7 Sept., eight days after the birth. As she had been surrounded by attendants during the confinement little credence can be given to the gloss made in the act of attainder on the deposition of one of them, Elizabeth Tyrwhit, that Seymour had murdered his wife 'to haste forward his other purposes'. Seymour's immediate reaction was one of resignation and he contemplated disbanding Catherine's household and let Jane Grey return to her father. Within a few days he regretted the decision to allow Jane's departure and he wrote to her father to regain custody of her with a promise to promote her marriage to the King.[12]

By Christmas 1548 there 'was a full report everywhere that the Lady Elizabeth should be married to the Lord Admiral' and it was rumoured that she was already expecting his child. He did little to allay the rumours; besides his discussions about Elizabeth's marriage he indulged himself in wild statements about the Protector and the Council. In mid January 1549 he learnt from one of his servants that the 2nd Earl of Rutland had given evidence against him and he refused to attend the Council unless Sir John Russell*, Baron Russell, and Sir William Paget stayed at his house as pledges against his return. The Marquess of Dorset's brother Thomas dissuaded him from such a course and when (Sir) John Baker I* and (Sir) Thomas Smith I* came with Sir Ralph Hopton* and his men at eight o'clock in the morning on 17 Jan. to arrest him he did not resist. He said to John Harington II* 'I am sure I can have no hurt, if they do me right;

they cannot kill me, except they do me wrong'.[13]

During the five weeks following his arrest Seymour was twice brought before the Council and 33 articles 'of high treason and other misdemeanours' were drafted. With the exception of the charges relating to his connivance at piracy and such suppositions as his intending the King's death, these articles closely follow the evidence given in the depositions collected by the Council. When faced with the articles on 23 Feb. Seymour resolutely refused to make any answer 'except he had his accusers brought before him, and except he were brought in open trial of arraignment, where he might say before all the world what he could say for his declaration'. The Council, in their turn, refused to leave the articles with him. Seymour was entitled to trial by his peers, a course which would have necessitated his accusers facing him, but even before examining Seymour the Council had persuaded the King that 'Parliament should have the determination and order' of the case 'according to the order of justice and the custom of the realm in like cases'. On 25 Feb. a bill of attainder against him was introduced into the Lords and given its first reading. Two readings later it was sent to the Commons where it

> was very much debated and argued; and at last the minds of the lawyers [were] asked and [they] declared that the said offences of the Lord Admiral for divers causes were in the compass of high treason; when no man was able to say to the contrary, being divers times provoked thereunto by the Speaker, the Nether House being marvellous full almost to the number of 400 persons [370 were returned to the Parliament] not 10 or 12 at the most [the Spanish ambassador said 2 or 3] giving their nays thereunto, the bill was there likewise passed and consented unto the 5th of March.[14]

Five days later the Council obtained the King's approval to deal with Seymour without troubling him further and after another five days it sent the bishop of Ely to prepare Seymour for death. Before his execution on 20 Mar. he asked if his daughter might be brought up by the Duchess of Suffolk. The Act (2 and 3 Edw. VI, c.18) was repealed less than a year later when his daughter was restored in blood (3 and 4 Edw. VI, c.14). Mary Seymour died in infancy. Several portraits of Seymour survive.[15]

---

[1] Date of birth estimated from first reference. This biography rests on Maclean, *Sir Thomas Seymour* and the notes of Julianna Marker on Seymour bequeathed to Prof. S. T. Bindoff. H. St. Maur, *Annals of the Seymours*, ped. opp. p. 1; *CP*; *DNB*. [2] *LP Hen. VIII*, v, xi–xxi; *CPR*, 1547–8 to 1549–51 passim; HCA 14/2; Somerville, *Duchy*, i. 604, 606, 612; D. E. Hoak, *The King's Council in the Reign of Edw. VI*, 47, 49, 51, 278; C. Jamison, *R. Hospital of St. Katharine*, 61–62; *HMC Bath*, iv. 336. [3] *LP Hen. VIII*, v, xii. [4] *Narr. Ref.* (Cam. Soc. lxxvii), 260–3; *EHR*, lxvi, 19–20; *LP Hen. VIII*, xiii, xiv, xvi, xvii; *Chron. Calais* (Cam. Soc. xxxv), 168; *London Topographical Rec.* x. 107–8. [5] *LP Hen. VIII*, xviii–xx, add.; E. Lodge, *Illustrations* i. 135–6. [6] *LP Hen. VIII*, xxi; Hoak, 233, 345 n. 9; *Wealth and Power*, ed. Ives, Knecht and Scarisbrick, 91; Add. 48126, ff. 6–6v.

[7] *Wealth and Power*, 88, 90, 91, 102; *LP Hen. VIII*, xxi; Hoak, 41–43, 45, 232–4. [8] *CSP Span.* 1547–8, pp. 88–89; Add. 5841, f. 250; *Wilts. Arch. Mag.* xviii. 93; *Archaeological Jnl.* lxx. 178; SP 12/19/21; E315/384/169; *HMC Hatfield*, i. 61–73. [9] *APC*, ii. 115–19, 130–1; *HMC Hatfield*, i. 54. [10] *Wealth and Power*, 102–3; *CPR*, 1547–8, pp. 25–33; *Suss. Rec. Soc.* xxxvi. 66–76 passim; *Wilts. Arch. Mag.* xxxviii. 428; *HMC Bath*, iv. 376; SP 10/6/13, f. 35; E318/1933, mm. 23–26. [11] M. A. R. Graves, 'The Tudor House of Lords 1547–58' (Otago Univ. Ph.D. thesis, 1974), ii. 347–50; SP 10/6/13, f. 36; *APC*, ii. 20–21. [12] *Coll. State Pprs.* ed. Haynes, 163–4; E. Dent, *Annals of Winchcombe and Sudeley*, 173; SP 10/6/13, f. 36; SP 10/6/16; *Orig. Letters*, ed. Ellis, ii. 154–5; *HMC Hatfield*, i. 55–56, 61–73; A. F. Pollard, *Eng. under Protector Somerset*, 185. [13] *Grey Friars' Chron.* (Cam. Soc. liii), 58; *CSP Span.* 1547–9, pp. 332–3, 340–1. [14] *APC*, ii. 248–58; *Select Pleas in Ct. Admiralty* (Selden Soc. xi), p. xi; *CSP Span.* 1547–9, p. 343; *Coll. State Pprs.* 59–60, 62–67; *HMC Hatfield*, i. 61–73. An Act (2 and 3 Edw. VI, c.6) ending payments to the Admiralty by seamen and merchants going abroad passed through both Houses at the same time as the attainder; Seymour is said to have been unsympathetic to the measure. [15] *APC*, ii. 261–2; *Grey Friars' Chron.* 58; J. Harington, *Nugae Antiquae*, 259–60; R. C. Strong, *Tudor and Jacobean Portraiture*, 357–9.

R.L.D./A.D.K.H.

SHAKERLEY, Robert (by 1510–69 or later), of Little Longstone and Chesterfield, Derbys.

HEDON   1553 (Mar.), 1553 (Oct.)

b. by 1510, s. of Robert Shakerley of Little Longstone. *m.* Elizabeth, da. of John Peto of Chesterton, Warws., 2s. 3da.[1]

Treasurer, household of Francis, 5th Earl of Shrewsbury.[2]

The Shakerley family of Little Longstone was a cadet branch of the Cheshire house, Robert Shakerley's grandfather having bought the manor shortly after 1474. Of Shakerley himself little trace has been found before his first election for Hedon. It was doubtless a namesake who served as a gunner at Guisnes in 1540 and possibly another who acknowledged the settlement of a debt due to him and Nicholas King in 1549 and who appears with Roger Heigham* as a deputy chamberlain of the Exchequer in 1552–3. By contrast, Shakerley's return to the two Parliaments summoned in 1553 can be confidently ascribed to the patronage of the 5th Earl of Shrewsbury, perhaps reinforced on the second occasion by the Queen's. Although the first reference found to Shakerley as Shrewsbury's servant dates from October 1560, when he attended the earl's funeral as treasurer of the household, the two had been associated since the 1530s and related since at least 1547 through the earl's marriage to Shakerley's sister Grace. To the link thus established, or strengthened, with the earl, and through him with Princess Mary, Shakerley may have been able to add another connexion with the princess, who had a Mistress Shakerley in her service. Thus whereas at both elections in 1553 the earl, as president of the council in the north, was instrumental in Shakerley's nomination, at the second of them, when he had his name inserted on a blank return, it may have been at the prompting of the countess, then acting as her husband's representative with the Queen.[3]

Shakerley's disappearance from the Commons after 1553 remains unexplained; he can hardly have failed to welcome the Catholic restoration, which as a Member of Mary's first Parliament he had not opposed, and he may simply have yielded place to Shrewsbury's many other clients. After the 5th Earl's death he remained a dependant of the new one, with whom he corresponded between April 1562 and February 1563, and at whose orders he was examined in 1565 about an infanticide at Youlgreave Hall, Derbyshire. Although he is not mentioned in his brother Rowland Shakerley's will of March 1565 he was still living at Chesterfield in 1569 and early in the following year a 'Mr. Shakerley' entertained one of the 6th Earl's servants engaged on a survey in that neighbourhood.[4]

[1] Date of birth estimated from first reference, 1531. J. C. Cox, *Derbys. Churches*, ii. 100; *The Gen.* n.s. viii. 77–78, the two pedigrees given here differ as to whether Shakerley was a son of his father's first or second marriage. [2] J. Hunter, *Hallamshire*, ed. Gatty, 78. [3] Cox, ii. 100; *LP Hen. VIII*, xiii, xvi; *CPR*, 1548–9, p. 228; Stowe 571, f. 6v; *Privy Purse Expenses of Princess Mary 1536–44*, ed. Madden, 21; C219/21/59; *HMC Shrewsbury and Talbot*, ii. 24, 348; E. Lodge, *Illustrations*, i. 227; E315/161, f. 212. [4] *HMC Shrewsbury and Talbot*, i. 16, 17, 148; ii. 91, 538; J. P. Yeatman, *Recs. Chesterfield*, 135; PCC 10 Morrison; *The Gen.* n.s. viii. 78.

A.D.

SHARINGTON, William (c. 1495–1553) of Lacock, Wilts.

HEYTESBURY	1545
BRAMBER	1547*
WILTSHIRE	1547*

b. c.1495, 1st s. of Thomas Sharington of Norfolk by Catherine, da. and h. of William Pyrton of Little Bentley, Essex. *m.* (1) Ursula, illegit. da. of John Bourchier, 2nd Lord Berners; (2) Eleanor, da. of William Walsingham; (3) 1542, Grace, da. of one Farrington of Devon, wid. of Robert Paget of London. KB 20 Feb. 1547.[1]

Page of the robes by 1539, groom 1540; page of the privy chamber 1541, groom 1542; jt. (with Thomas Paston*) steward and constable, Castle Rising, Norf. Nov. 1542; member, household of Queen Catherine Parr by 1544–5 or later; under treasurer, Bristol mint 25 Mar. 1546–25 Dec. 1548; j.p. Wilts. 1547–*d.*; commr. to inquire into the mints 1547, of Admiralty in Nov. 1547, chantries, Glos., Gloucester and Bristol 1548, for sale of Boulogne 1550, goods of churches and fraternities, Wilts. 1553; sheriff, Wilts. 1552–*d.*[2]

Nothing has come to light about William Sharington during the first 30 years of his life, but by 1538 he was in the retinue of Sir Francis Bryan*, poet, soldier and diplomatist. He could claim kinship with Bryan through his marriage to a natural daughter of the 2nd Lord Berners, who was Bryan's brother-in-law, and this may have had a bearing on his clientage: as Bryan was a frequent visitor to Calais, the marriage of Sharington's

sister to the comptroller of the garrison there was also perhaps a by-product of the Bryan connexion. It was, however, not Bryan himself but another of his servants, Sir Thomas Seymour II, who was to determine Sharington's further career: as Seymour's fortunes rose in the years from 1536 Sharington's rose with them, only to crash in the fatal winter of 1548–9.[3]

The twin agencies of this process were the Dissolution and the Great Debasement. In January 1539 William Petre* informed Cromwell that he had taken the surrender of Lacock abbey which he proposed to leave in Sharington's care: 18 months later the abbey was granted to Sharington for £783. This was his first property in Wiltshire and he was probably encouraged by Seymour to make his home in what was rapidly becoming the Seymours' chief territory, although he had (or was to have) a family connexion there, his second wife's cousin being married to Edward Baynton of Lackham. The purchase of Lacock was the prelude to a sustained intervention in the land market. A lease of the demesne of the lordship of Heytesbury in 1541 was closely followed by the bestowal of over £2,000 on ex-monastic land in Berkshire, Gloucester and Wiltshire, of which all but the Wiltshire properties were sold and their yield applied to the purchase of more land in that county. Sharington spent more than £1,000 in 1543 and over £2,800 in 1548, by which time he owned 14 manors in Wiltshire and others in Dorset, Gloucestershire and Somerset. In 1550 he was to pay £12,867 for his restoration in blood and lands, although over £4,000 of this was said to represent a debt to the crown. He continued to buy land in Wiltshire until the month of his death.[4]

Sharington also engaged in overseas trade. On the King's recommendation he was made an honorary freeman of London in 1542 and four years later he himself successfully recommended a London brewer for the same honour: his own marriage in 1542 to the widow of a London alderman (perhaps a kinsman of William Paget) may have quickened his interest in trade. In 1549 he claimed that he had a £2,000 interest in the Antwerp trade and he is known to have bought wool from all over Wiltshire: a few years earlier he had received a licence to import 300 tons of French wares and he owned several ships trading from Bristol. It is also clear that by the time of his attainder he had gone in for moneylending on a large scale.[5]

Landowner and merchant, Sharington was also a man of culture. When he obtained Lacock he found the abbess's lodging on the west of the cloister had recently been modernized. In his remodelling of the property he kept the sacristy, chapter house and warming house, the dormitory on the east side, the refectory and the kitchen. Of the extensions made by him there survives only an octagonal tower. The alterations and improvements incorporating many renaissance and mannerist features were then to the forefront of fashion in England and have justly become famous. Much of the building stone may have come from the ruins of Devizes castle, then owned by Seymour, which had also been used by Sir Edward Baynton* in the construction of Bromham House. Sharington employed expert masons and they were in great demand. A fortnight before his death he wrote to (Sir) John Thynne* at Longleat apologizing for not sending a workman. Seymour employed Sharington's men at Sudeley and Bromham where over £2,500 was spent on improvements, and in May 1551 the Council asked Sharington to spare for a few more months a workman of his engaged on the royal works in the Scilly Isles.[6]

Early in 1546 Sharington was appointed under treasurer of the mint at Bristol where he proceeded to make a substantial profit not only for the King but also for himself and for Seymour. It was doubtless to Seymour, then admiral, that he owed both his knighthood at Edward VI's coronation and his seat in the Parliament of 1547 as a Member for Bramber. He had sat in the previous Parliament for Heytesbury, where if he had needed any reinforcement of of his position as lessee of the demesne he could have looked for it either to Seymour or to Queen Catherine Parr, from whom as a member of her household he received New Year's gifts of satin in 1544 and 1545. Of his part in either Parliament no trace has been found until his implication in the downfall of Seymour. On 19 Jan. 1549 Sharington joined his patron in the Tower. A fortnight earlier Seymour's brother the Protector had sent three men to examine the accounts at Bristol. They called at Lacock on the way and under Lady Sharington's supervision they collected writings, money, plate and jewels which they sealed in chests and left in the charge of four servants. At Bristol they learned that James Paget, a teller there (who may well have been a relative of Lady Sharington), had come from London and taken away all Sharington's papers: they advised his arrest and reported their intention of keeping the mint at work to avoid suspicion of their purpose.[7]

A Welsh-speaking Bristol shoemaker named Jenkin Dee declared under examination that it was Thomas Barro, an officer at the mint, who had revealed Sharington's fraud, but there can be no doubt that both Paget and Thomas Dowrishe,

Sharington's deputy, were aware that he had coined testons in defiance of the prohibition of April 1547. Sharington claimed to have done this so that he could buy silver at the great Bristol fair at St. James's tide, the mint being under pressure to provide money for Ireland: this requirement was certainly true, but Sharington had clearly profited from debased coin ever since his appointment at Bristol and on his own admission had made £4,000 in three years and embezzled large sums for the admiral. Seymour may have thought he had a right to money from Bristol for he seems to have believed that his brother was making a personal fortune from the mint at Durham Place.[8]

On 14 Feb. 1549 Sharington was tried at Guildhall, found guilty of counterfeiting and embezzling the King's money and sentenced to death; early in March an Act of attainder was passed against him (2 and 3 Edw. VI, c.17). He had, however, already written to the earls of Shrewsbury and Southampton begging them to intercede with the Protector to spare his life, even if he had to pass it in perpetual imprisonment. His plea was granted, but at the price of his giving information sufficient to destroy the admiral. Eight months later, when Thomas Seymour's execution had been followed by his brother's overthrow, the way was clear for Sharington's rehabilitation: in November 1549 he was pardoned and in January 1550 an Act restored him to his estates and goods (3 and 4 Edw. VI, c.13). His swift recovery of favour is shown by his membership of the commission appointed in March to collect 200,000 crowns from the French, the first half of their purchase money for Boulogne. In a sermon delivered before the King in Lent 1550 Latimer praised Sharington as 'an honest gentleman and one that God loveth. He openly confessed that he had deceived the King and made open restitution . . . It is a token that he is a chosen man of God and one of his elected'.[9]

Sharington's attainder cost him his seat in Parliament. Although there appears to be no record of its forfeiture, it had been filled before the opening of the final session in January 1552 by Chidiock Paulet, who had presumably been by-elected in time to sit in the previous one of 1549–50. With the reversal of the attainder, however, Sharington was eligible for re-election and an opportunity presented itself when in October 1551 Sir William Herbert was made Earl of Pembroke: three months later, on the eve of the meeting of Parliament, Sharington was by-elected to the vacant knighthood of the shire for Wiltshire. This signal token of his rehabilitation was to be followed, in the autumn of the same year, by his being pricked sheriff. His discharge of this office, which evidently excluded him from Membership of the Parliament of March 1553, would, if he had lived long enough, have faced him, on the death of Edward VI, with the choice of proclaiming either Jane Grey or Mary Tudor. As it was, he died three days after the King, and the decision passed to others.[10]

If any of his three wives had borne him children they did not long survive and he was succeeded by his brother Henry, then over 36 years of age, who was living with him. Because he had no children of his own, Sharington had left 500 marks for the dowry of his first cousin Parnell which Henry later refused to pay. This is the only detail known of Sharington's missing will. A drawing of him by Holbein survives.[11]

[1] *DNB* giving date of birth; *The Gen.* n.s. xii. 241; *LP Hen. VIII*, xvii. [2] *LP Hen. VIII*, xiii, xv–xvii, xxi; *Brit. Numismatic Jnl.* xlv. 68; *CPR*, 1547–8, pp. 91, 116; 1548–9, p. 136; 1549–51, p. 335; 1553, p. 387; HCA 14/2. [3] *LP Hen. VIII*, xiii. [4] *Wilts. Arch. Mag.* xxvii. 160; xxxiii. 375–6; *LP Hen. VIII*, xv–xix; SP 10/19, ff. 15, 57v; *CPR*, 1547–8, pp. 337, 375, 401; 1549–51, pp. 188, 199; 1550–3, p. 62; 1553, pp. 109, 164. [5] City of London RO, Guildhall, rep. 10, f. 264; *LP Hen. VIII*, xi–xxi; *Wilts. Arch. Mag.* xxvii. 169. [6] *Wilts. Arch. Mag.* xxvii. 229; xxxviii. 426–34; li. 9; E. Mercer, *Eng. Art 1553–1625*, pp. 60–72; J. Summerson, *Architecture in Britain 1530–1830*, pp. 42–44; M. Whinney, *Sculpture in Britain 1530–1830*, pp. 8–9; Pevsner and Cherry, *Wilts.* 284–9, 651; J. Wright, *Med. Floor Tiles*, 153–4. [7] *HMC Hatfield*, i. 58; E101/423/12, ff. 8, 40; C. E. Challis, *The Tudor Coinage*, 255. [8] *HMC Hatfield*, i. 59, 61, 67, 68, 70; *Coll. State Pprs.* ed. Haynes, 92, 105; Challis, 100–3, 259, 287. [9] *HMC Hatfield*, i. 70; *APC*, ii. 246, 335; S. Seyor, *Bristol Mems.* i. 228; W. K. Jordan, *Edw. VI*, i, 373–4, 382–5; *Sermons of Hugh Latimer* (Parker Soc.), i. 263. [10] C142/101/121; Hatfield 207. [11] C1/1482/56; *Holbein* (The Queen's Gallery, Buckingham Palace 1978–9), 103.

R.J.W.S.

SHARPE, Richard, of Grantham, Lincs.

GRANTHAM   1554 (Nov.)

Save that he was not among those who quitted Mary's third Parliament without leave before its dissolution, nothing of interest has been ascertained about Sharpe.

C219/23/80; Huntington Lib. Hastings mss Parl. pprs.; *LP Hen. VIII*, xiv, xviii; *CPR*, 1553–4, p. 336; 1554–5, pp. 124, 276; 1555–7, p. 20; 1557–8, p. 184; *Cal. Lincs Wills*, i. 281.

T.M.H.

SHARRARD *see* **SHERARD**

SHAW, Richard (by 1533–63 or later), of Langton Matravers, Dorset.

POOLE   1554 (Apr.)
MELCOMBE REGIS   1558, 1559
WAREHAM   1563

b. by 1533, ?s. of Peter Shaw by Elizabeth.[1]
    Subsidy collector, Pimperne hundred, Dorset 1559–60.[2]

Richard Shaw was a client of Sir John Rogers*, the most eminent figure in west Dorset during the middle years of the 16th century: the village where

he had his home belonged to Rogers. Shaw doubtless owed his nomination at Poole to his master who, although he had no personal links with the borough, would have been able to rely on the support of one of its patrons, his colleague, Richard Phelips*. Phelips may have introduced Shaw to Melcombe Regis where his son-in-law, Sir John Horsey*, was powerful, but it was to Rogers that Shaw was obliged since Rogers entered into an agreement with the townsmen on 11 Jan. 1558 for the election of Richard Shaw 'yeoman' as one of their Members in return for Rogers's paying his parliamentary expenses. His two further appearances in the Commons were also at the instance of Rogers.[3]

Apart from his dependence on Rogers (presumably he was in Rogers's service since all that is known about him implies such a relationship) little trace has been found of Shaw, and none of the references after Rogers's death in 1565 to men of the same name in other parts of the county can certainly be attributed to him. Shaw is, however, probably to be identified with a litigant in Chancery during the 1560s over the title to property in Dorset and Sussex.[4]

[1] Presumed to be of age at election. C3/165/3, 167/55. [2] Dorset mus. 6267/2. [3] Harvard pf. ms Eng. 757, p. 17; Hutchins, *Dorset*, i. 284, 287. [4] Wards 9/199, f. 280; C3/165/3, 167/55, 142/125/15.

M.K.D.

SHEFFIELD, Sir Robert (by 1462–1518), of the Inner Temple, London, West Butterwick, Lincs. and Chilwell, Notts.

LONDON   1495, 1497, 1504
?LINCOLNSHIRE   1512, 1515

b. by 1462, 1st s. of Robert Sheffield† of South Cave, Yorks. and West Butterwick by Jane, da. of Alexander Lounde of West Butterwick. *educ.* I. Temple. *m.* (1) by 1485, Ellen (*d.*1509 or later), da. of Sir John Delves† of Doddington, Cheshire, 1s. 4da.; (2) by 1518, Anne. Kntd. 17 June 1497; *suc.* fa. 18 Aug. 1502.[1]
    Gov. I. Temple 1511–?*d.*
    Commr. sewers Lincs. 1485–*d.*, oyer and terminer, London 1495, 1503, benevolence 1500, subsidy Lincs. 1504, 1512, 1514, 1515, London 1504; other commissions Lincs., Yorks. and London 1495–*d.*; steward, bp. of Durham's liberty of Howden, Yorks. Mar. 1493, manor of Stoke Bardolph and others in Notts. Feb. 1508–*d.*, manor of Kirton, Lincs. and crown lands in Kingston-upon-Hull and elsewhere in Yorks. 20 July 1509–*d.*; recorder, London by 21 Sept. 1495–Apr. 1508; j.p. Lincs. 1495–7, 1510–16 or later, Notts. 1511–16 or later; jt. keeper, Lincoln castle 10 Feb. 1501–*d.*; 'councillor' in 1508; custos rot. Lincs. (Lindsey) by 1516.[2]
    Speaker of House of Commons 1512.

Robert Sheffield followed, with added success, the path trodden by his father and grandfather, as lawyer, local administrator, landed proprietor and

Member of Parliament. It was as recorder of London that he sat in Henry VII's last three Parliaments. Even after he ceased to be recorder, and thus one of the London Members, the City continued to look to Sheffield to promote its interests: when in the Parliament of 1510 the City opposed the grant of tonnage and poundage to the new King, Sheffield was one of those asked by the Merchant Adventurers to support their request for the maintenance of the old book of rates—this approach suggests that he was a Member of that Parliament, although he did not sit in it for London —and after he had been made Speaker in 1512 the City raised from 40s. to five marks the annuity it had paid him since he gave up the recordership.[3]

As Speaker-designate of this Parliament Sheffield was doubtless returned for a shire to accord with that distinction: that he sat for Lincolnshire, rather than one of the other counties, Nottinghamshire and Yorkshire, with which he was connected is suggested by his appointment as a subsidy commissioner there, and if so he was presumably re-elected for the shire in 1515 when the King asked for the return of the previous Members. He had been presented as Speaker within two days of the opening of the Parliament of 1512, but of his role in that Parliament all that is known is that on 9 Feb. 1514 London decided to give him £5 'for the expedition of certain causes of the City in Parliament', one of which may have issued in the Act (5 Hen. VIII, c.5) for juries in London. In January 1513 the treasurer of the Chamber paid him £200 for the first two sessions but it was not until April 1515 that he received his fee for the third and final session. This delay has given rise to the belief that he was chosen Speaker again in 1515, but it was Sir Thomas Neville whom in February 1515 he presented to the King as his successor.[4]

In 1515 Sheffield helped Wolsey to redraft the measure which became the Resumption Act (6 Hen. VIII, c.25), but such co-operation soon gave place to hostility. When the bill renewing the Act denying benefit of clergy to men not in holy orders (4 Hen. VIII, c.2) was defeated in the Lords Sheffield led a delegation from the Commons urging the King's spiritual advisers to discuss the subject with Church representatives. His comments to the King two years later suggest that he supported a further bill to the same effect passed by the Commons but rejected by the Lords after a single reading. In giving a lead to the anti-clerical forces in the House he incurred the cardinal's displeasure and he soon paid the price. Within a year or so of the dissolution he was charged before the Star Chamber with negligence as a justice of the peace for Lincoln-

shire and Nottinghamshire; bound over in 29 recognizances, in November 1516 he sued out a pardon. Eight months later he was committed to the Tower for complaining to the King about Wolsey. Brought before Star Chamber again, he confessed to having obtained the pardon without permission and given asylum to criminals, and asserted that if the temporal lords had been of one mind in the last Parliament 'my lord cardinal's head should have been as red as his coat'. On 13 Feb. 1518 he cut up the pardon while kneeling before Wolsey and besought the King's mercy, but he seems to have been kept in the Tower until his death six months later on 10 Aug.[5]

By a will made two days before he died, and proved on the following 28 Feb., Sheffield asked to be buried beside his first wife in the church of the Austin Friars in London and provided for his wife Anne and his unmarried daughters. He left Wolsey a silver gilt statue in the hope that the cardinal would be gracious to his widow and children, and named his son Robert and brother Sir Thomas Sheffield (a knight of the order of St. John at Rhodes) executors and Sir Thomas Lovell I* supervisor: among the witnesses was Henry Barley*. On 1 Sept. 1518 Sir Thomas Burgh replaced Sheffield as steward of the manor of Kirton and two months later the Council ordered the cancellation of his bonds for good behaviour. His son Robert married the King's second cousin Jane Stanley and their son Edmund was created Baron Sheffield at the accession of Edward VI.[6]

[1] Date of birth estimated from age at fa.'s i.p.m., *CIPM Hen. VII*, ii. 566. *DNB*; *LP Hen. VIII*, i; *Gt. Chron. of London*, ed. Thomas and Thornley, 277; *Stow's Survey of London*, ed. Kingsford, 179; PCC 15 Ayloffe; C142/54/85. [2] *CPR*, 1485–94 and 1494–1509 passim; *LP Hen. VIII*, i–iii; *Statutes*, iii. 89, 119, 172; *Rot. Parl.* vi. 534, 542; Somerville, *Duchy*, i. 583; B. Andrew, *Historia Regis Henrici Septimi* (1858 ed.), 115. [3] *Bull IHR*, xxxv. 128–49; J. S. Roskell, *The Commons and their Speakers in Eng. Parlts. 1376–1523*, p. 96; City of London RO, Guildhall, rep. 2, f. 130. [4] *LP Hen. VIII*, i; *LJ*, i. 10–11, 20; *Bull IHR*, xxxv. 136–7; *Gt. Chron. of London*, 379; Cit6 of London RO, Guildhall, rep. 2, f. 171v; *Cal. I.T. Recs.* i. 2;y Roskell, 316. [5] Roskell, 320; A. F. Pollard, *Wolsey*, 45, 52n; *LP Hen. VIII*, ii; E. Lodge, *Illus.* i. 32; Elton, *Reform and Reformation*, 64; C142/33/57; J. A. Guy, *The Cardinal's Ct.* 76–78. [6] PCC 15 Ayloffe summarised in *Test Vet.* ed. Nicolas, ii. 556–7; Roskell, 321; *LP Hen. VIII*, ii.

A.D.K.H.

SHELDON, Thomas (by 1520–46 or later), of Worcester.

WORCESTER 1542, 1545[1]

b. by 1520, 2nd or 3rd s. of Ralph Sheldon of Beoley by Philippa, da. and coh. of Baldwin Heath of Fordhall in Wootton Wawen, Warws.; bro. of William*. *m.* Elizabeth, da. of one Rawlins, 2s. 1da.; ?(2) Eleanor, da. of Sir John Huddleston of Millom, Cumb. and Southam, Glos.[2]

Low bailiff, Worcester 1544–5.[3]

A younger son in a leading Worcestershire family,

Thomas Sheldon had settled in Worcester by 1541 when he was associated with (Sir) John Russell I* of Strensham in business relating to Pershore abbey: his wife Elizabeth Rawlins may have been related to the Brogdens of Worcester. By a will of 28 Mar. 1545, proved on 11 Feb. 1546, his father Ralph Sheldon left him a life interest, with remainder to his own sons Ralph and Thomas, in lands in Worcester itself and in Pershore, North Piddle, Wyre Piddle, Upton-on-Severn, Walcot and Weatheroak Hill, all in Worcestershire, and Oldbury, Shropshire. He was also to receive £200, part of which was to be used to pay his debts, and the lease of a parsonage on condition that he did not live in Worcester: no explanation is given of this requirement unless the reference to Sheldon's debts means that he had failed in business there. All that is known of his business activities is that, like his elder brother William, he speculated in monastic lands, joining with Lawrence Poyner of Tewkesbury in 1544 to purchase property in Tewkesbury, Worcester and elsewhere for £413, some at least of which they resold in the same year.[4]

Sheldon probably owed his return to the last two Parliaments of Henry VIII less to his own standing than to his family's; his elder brother William was one of the knights for Worcestershire in 1542 and perhaps in 1545 and on the first occasion the sheriff was Sheldon's former associate Russell. Between the two Parliaments Sheldon was elected low bailiff of Worcester and in that capacity he was named captain of 50 men in the King's service in July 1545. His Membership of the Parliament of 1545 is known only from the payment of wages to him and his fellow Richard Calowhill. On 31 May 1546 they were allowed £7 4s. at the statutory rate of 2s. a day for the 32 days of the first session, with four days' travelling expenses, but only Calowhill was paid for the short second session of January 1547. By then Sheldon may have been dead. The last reference found to him is in his mother's will, which is undated but was proved in January 1549, and he does not appear in his brother Baldwin Sheldon's will of June 1548. Eleanor Huddleston, who in the absence of a will or inquisition post mortem is identified as Sheldon's second wife only by inference from a deed of May 1555, had by then married Kennard Delabere by whom she was the mother of two future Members. Sheldon's daughter married a Calowhill, possibly his fellow-Member in 1545, his elder son Ralph married a daughter of Sir Richard Lygon and his second son Thomas a daughter of Sir Henry Delves*.[5]

[1] Worcester Guildhall, chamber order bk. 1540–1601, f. 20.
[2] Date of birth estimated from first reference. *Vis. Worcs.* (Harl. Soc.

xxvii), 127–8; E. A. B. Barnard, *The Sheldons*, 5; *Trans. Bristol and Glos. Arch. Soc.* l. 295–7. [3] Nash, *Worcs.* ii. app. cxii. [4] *LP Hen. VIII*, xvi, xix; PCC 28 Alen; *VCH Worcs.* iii. 469; iv. 261; *Habington's Worcs.* (Worcs. Hist. Soc. 1895), i. 396, 431, 444. [5] Worcester Guildhall, chamber order bk. 1540–1601, ff. 13, 20; PCC 23 Populwell; *Trans. Bristol and Glos. Arch. Soc.* l. 295–7; *Vis. Cheshire* (Harl. Soc. xviii), 78.

A.D.

SHELDON, William (by 1511–70), of Weston, Warws. and Beoley, Worcs.

WORCESTERSHIRE   1542,[1] 1547,[2] 1554 (Apr.), 1555

b. by 1511, 1st s. of Ralph Sheldon of Beoley, and bro. of Thomas*. educ. M. Temple, rem. to I. Temple 1528. m. (1) Mary (d.25 Jan. 1553), da. and coh. of William Willington of Barcheston, Warws., 2s. inc. Ralph† 4da.; (2) Margaret, da. of (Sir) Richard Broke* of London, wid. of William Whorwood* (d.28 May 1545) of Putney, Surr., 1s. suc. fa. 11 Sept. 1546.[3] Marshal, I. Temple 1542, 1544, steward 1553.

J.p. Worcs. 1532–d., Warws. 1554–58/59; commr. musters, Worcs. 1539, chantries, Salop, Staffs. and Shrewsbury 1546, Herefs., Worcs., Hereford and Worcester 1548, relief, Worcs. 1550, to survey lands of bpric. of Worcester 1560; other commissions 1535–64; solicitor to Queen Catherine Parr by May 1544; receiver, ct. augmentations, Herefs., Leics., Northants., Rutland, Salop, Staffs., Warws. and Worcs. May 1547–53, Exchequer 1553–5; sheriff, Worcs. 1547–8, 1556–7, 1567–8; steward for Thomas Seymour, Baron Seymour of Sudeley, unknown property by 1548; custos rot. Worcs. by 1558/59; collector for loan, Worcs. 1562.[4]

William Sheldon's uncle purchased the manor of Beoley in the reign of Edward IV and, dying without issue, was succeeded there by William's father. It was probably his training in the law which accounts for Sheldon's nomination to the Worcestershire bench before he himself held any property in the shire and seemingly before his father's appointment to it. His marriage to one of the coheirs of a wealthy merchant of the staple may have prompted and perhaps enabled him in 1535 to purchase a residence of his own at Weston, where he lived until his father's death and which he made the second seat of his family. His six sisters-in-law married into such prominent local families as Greville, Holte and Mountford.[5]

Ralph Sheldon was nominated but not pricked sheriff of Worcestershire in 1541, 1542 and 1544, and he may therefore have been of sufficient standing to secure his eldest son's election as knight of the shire to the Parliament of 1542 and perhaps also to that of 1545, for which the Worcestershire knights are unknown: on both occasions Ralph's younger son Thomas sat for Worcester. William Sheldon was probably also an original Member of the Parliament of 1547, although his Membership is known only from the Crown Office list drawn up for the fourth session; by 1547 he was the head of his family and established in the service of the crown. He had been mustered in 1544 for service in the expedition against France and in 1547 he was to be pricked sheriff for the first time.[6]

Sheldon had also entered the market in monastic lands: in January 1544, with his brother Francis, he bought property in Worcestershire for £1,804, most of which they resold, and in February 1544, with his father-in-law Willington, he purchased the manor of Packwood, Worcestershire, for £876, selling it to Robert Burdett*, of whose will he was to be chief executor. Later in 1544 he received two further grants from the crown and by May 1545 he had arranged further purchases which for the most part he was to retain, although various small parcels were sold to friends and relatives. His appointment in the augmentations ought to have put him in a favourable position for making forther acquisitions, but although he continued to buy lands none of his purchases was from the crown, with the possible exception of the advowson of Grimley and Hallow, Worcestershire, and most of them were not of former monastic property.[7]

About this time Sheldon's private life was marred by an unseemly quarrel which eventually found its way to the Star Chamber, and which modifies the impression of domestic harmony created by his epitaph. His young sister Mary had been placed in the household of Ursula, widow of (Sir) Edmund Knightley*, and while there had engaged herself to one of Lady Knightley's servants named Silvester, by whom she was with child. Sheldon and his mother took the girl away and sent her to live with a relative but she returned to Lady Knightley's house and there married her lover. Lady Knightley, charged with abduction, retaliated with accusations of 'unmannerliness' in Mary and cruelty on her mother's part. The result of the suit is unknown, but Mary was later married, more suitably, to a younger son of Sir Edward Ferrers*.[8]

Sheldon's preoccupation with his duties as receiver may account for his absence from the Parliament of March 1553, when he doubtless helped his son-in-law Francis Savage to be elected junior knight of the shire. There is no sign that his earlier connexion with the Seymours persuaded him to stand down. His relationship with the Dudley family, arising out of his second marriage (Margaret Broke's stepdaughter had been the first wife of Ambrose Dudley, later Earl of Warwick), had yet to be established and was presumably to be more helpful to his son Ralph under Elizabeth. In 1556 Margaret Broke's other stepdaughter, Margaret, married Ralph Sheldon's brother-in-law Thomas Throckmorton II*.

When the court of augmentations was dissolved in 1553 Sheldon evidently retained his post in the Exchequer court which replaced it, for in 1555 he was licensed to sell his office of receiver, with its fees of £100 plus portage, to Savage. His two further elections for Worcestershire and his second shrievalty testify to his standing during the new reign although he was excused the knighthood of the bath at the Queen's marriage 'in consideration of his small ability and living'. He was not among those Members who opposed a government bill in the Parliament of 1555 and in the same year he was one of several gentlemen instructed to watch Richard Tracy* for signs of nonconformity. In 1558 he was granted the wardship of his grandson William Savage. He had sued out a pardon at the beginning of the reign as of Beoley, Weston the Wocestershire manor of Tredington and the Inner Temple, and in 1559 he obtained another as of Beoley, Weston, Putney and London.[9]

Sheldon did not sit in any Elizabethan Parliament but his elder son was junior knight of the shire in 1563. In the following year he was among those described by Bishop Sandys as 'indifferent in religion or else of no religion' but was also said to be fit to remain on the bench and to serve as sheriff, which he did for a third time in 1567. It was in these years that he occupied himself with the work that was to bring him widespread renown, the fostering of tapestry weaving in England. Sheldon had long been actively engaged in the wool trade but it was apparently Richard Hicks of Barcheston who, while travelling as tutor to Sheldon's son Ralph in 1554 or 1555, first became interested in the art of tapestry and was instructed in it in Flanders; Sheldon described Hicks in his will as 'the only author and beginner of this art within this realm'. The enterprise was a great success and was much admired as a practical method of providing employment for the poor: the Earl of Leicester, when visiting Warwick in 1570, recommended the townsmen to follow Sheldon's example in their own efforts to re-establish the town's fortunes. Less admirable was the series of disputes which arose from the settlement of his father-in-law's estate in which Sheldon was accused of failing to pay legacies, terrorizing his mother-in-law and in other ways abusing his position as executor.[10]

Sheldon died on 24 Dec. 1570 at Skilts, Warwickshire, and was buried in Beoley church where his son erected an elaborate monument with a fulsome epitaph describing him as a peacemaker and benefactor to friends, servants and kinsmen. Sheldon did indeed leave a considerable amount of property and made a very long and complex will on 3 Jan. 1570 to govern it. His executors, who included his elder son

Ralph and two of his sons-in-law, Edmund Plowden* and Anthony Pollard (a younger brother of Sir John*), received the greater part of the estate for six years to pay debts and legacies. Most of the freehold was then to pass to the heir, provided he allowed it to be encumbered with various annuities and life grants to his mother and sisters. Frampton in Gloucestershire, and various other small properties, including mines in Coleorton, Leicestershire, were left to his younger son William. The leasehold property was divided among his daughters' sons with numerous reversions and provisos.[11]

[1] C219/18B/108. [2] Hatfield 207. [3] Date of birth estimated from first commission. Vis. Worcs. (Harl. Soc. xxvii), 127–8; Nash, Worcs. i. 64–66; Dugdale, Warws. i. 584; E. A. B. Barnard, The Sheldons, 5; Habington's Worcs. (Worcs. Hist. Soc. 1895), i. 71. [4] LP Hen. VIII, v, viii, xii–xiv, xvi, xvii, xx, xxi; CPR, 1548–9, p. 137; 1553, p. 359; 1553–4, pp. 25, 26; 1554–5, pp. 76–77; 1558–60, p. 422; 1563–6, pp. 28, 41; E101/423/15, f. 8; 163/12/17, nos. 38, 51, 54; 315/161/38; W. C. Richardson, Ct. Augmentations, 281; Stowe 571, f. 10v; Osborn Coll. Yale Univ. Lib. 71.6.41. [5] Dugdale, i. 584, 601; Nash, i. 66; VCH Warws. v. 55; LP Hen. VIII, xx. [6] LP Hen. VIII, xvi, xvii, xix, xxi. [7] Ibid. xix–xxi; Habington's Worcs. i. 431; ii. 170; VCH Worcs. iii. 269, 414, 489; CPR, 1548–9, p. 386; 1549–50, p. 199; 1550–3, p. 59; Dugdale, i. 553; ii. 784. [8] St.Ch.2/20/94, 25/197. [9] CPR, 1553–4, p. 457; 1554–5, pp. 76, 262; 1557–8, p. 69; 1558–60, p. 176; APC, v. 50, 145. [10] Cam. Misc. ix(3), 4–7; Barnard, 13–16, 23–24; J. Humphreys, Eliz. Sheldon Tapestries. [11] Habington's Worcs. i. 69–73; C142/159/87; PCC 8 Holney.

S.M.T.

SHELLEY, Richard (1513/14–87).

GATTON 1547

b. 1513/14, 3rd s. of (Sir) William Shelley* of Michelgrove, Suss. by Alice, da. and event. coh. of Henry Belknap of Knell, Beckley, Suss. unm. Kntd. May 1555/Jan. 1557.[1]

Aid of the chamber to King Philip June 1554; turcopolier, order of St. John of Jerusalem 1557, grand prior Sept. 1561–d.[2]

A younger son of the eminent judge, Richard Shelley received the training of a diplomat and courtier. At the age of 21 he carried letters from Thomas Starkey in London to Richard Morison* in Padua, where he probably joined Reginald Pole's household. It seems that he had earlier spent some time in France, and certainly his knowledge of French was much praised by his contemporaries. Shelley left Padua, probably after the break-up of Pole's household there in 1536, and went to Bologna. By October 1538 he was in Venice whence he wrote to Morison of his studies (which included Greek and Latin authors) and of one Donato, who was Pole's host in Venice.[3]

In May 1539 Shelley, proclaiming himself weary of 'this scholastical life', set out for Constantinople in the train of the Venetian ambassador; the journey, he said, was 'for his promotion', and he told his father that he would look out for Greek books and for trade openings between England and Turkey. As far as Shelley knew he was the first Englishman to visit the Ottoman court. By March 1540 he was back in Venice and by January 1541 he had entered the service of the deputy of Calais, Lord Mautravers, later 12th Earl of Arundel. In 1543 Shelley took part in a tournament held at Calais and about this time he received a gift of black satin from Queen Catherine Parr. From 1546 he was employed on various diplomatic missions, for which he was well qualified by his proficiency in languages and knowledge of foreign customs. In June 1546 he attended, with his old friend Morison, an Italian ambassador to the court, and in the following month he joined the English embassy to France, perhaps on the recommendation of his first cousin, Dr. Nicholas Wotton, recently appointed resident ambassador there.[4]

Described on the return as 'of the court', Shelley owed his election to the Parliament of 1547 to his brother-in-law Sir Roger Copley, whom the indenture called 'burgess and only inhabitant of the borough and town of Gatton'. With one possible exception all Shelley's diplomatic postings at this time occurred between the four sessions of the Parliament and he would probably not have required leave of absence from the House: nothing, however, is known of his part in its proceedings, although an Act for the assurance of certain lands to Sir Richard Rich and Shelley's father (himself present in the Lords) was passed during the first session (1 Edw. VI, no. 13). In May 1549 Shelley was sent as a special envoy to the French court to complain of an attack on the Boulonnais, in the following October he accompanied the French ambassador to Dover, and in the summer of 1550, with his future antagonist Thomas Stukeley, he escorted a French hostage to Scotland and back. In October 1550 Sir John Mason*, the new ambassador to the King of France, suggested to the Council that Shelley should be sent over as a special commissioner to negotiate with the French, but it is not known whether he went. In November 1551 Shelley and Edward Dudley escorted Mary of Guise, Queen Dowager of Scotland, on her return from France to Scotland.[5]

On 21 Feb. 1552, while Parliament was in its last session, Shelley was appointed ambassador to the imperial court, and on 12 June the Council issued a warrant authorizing payment to him of £250 'towards the furniture of [his] journey beyond the sea'. It is not certain, however, that Shelley went on this embassy: his role in the succession crisis of the following year, when he seems to have been a tool in the Council's hands, suggests that he did not. Despatched on 15 July 1553 to the Emperor to explain the accession of Jane Grey, he was refused audience, while the correspondence of the imperial ambassadors does not imply that he was already known at their court. On hearing of Shelley's appointment in 1552 one of them, Scheyfve, had written: 'we hear he is of the new religion and has studied in Germany, where the late King employed him.' Shelley is not otherwise known to have served Henry VIII in Germany, and if an attachment to Reform would help to explain his role in the crisis it can only have been a passing one.[6]

Shelley quickly won favour with Queen Mary, who in December 1553 sent him as ambassador to the King of the Romans. In the following June he was named one of three aids of the chamber to King Philip and in May 1555 sent to inform the King of Portugal of the Queen's supposed pregnancy. He must have been knighted after this mission but before January 1557, when he is so styled in a report of his appointment as ambassador to the Duchess of Parma, and it was perhaps at the same time that he was given an annuity of £50 for life. In 1557 the order of St. John of Jerusalem was re-established in England on the initiative of Cardinal Pole, who may also have influenced the crown's choice of Shelley as turcopolier of the English 'Tongue'. Shelley had not, as the office demanded, been a professed knight for 15 years: he was not named among the knights who were granted pensions on the dissolution of the order in 1540. As to his having ever been at Malta, it was reported in 1853 that two letters from him to Henry VIII, in which he complained of the King's treatment of the order, were missing from the library in Malta: he could have joined the order as a young man before embarking upon his studies and he almost certainly visited the island in the course of his travels. His uncle Sir John had been one of the knights killed at the siege of Rhodes in 1522, and he had at least one other kinsman in the order at the time, Edward Bellingham, who later became a trusted Henrician diplomat—and so perhaps turned Shelley in that direction—and sat for Gatton in the Parliament of 1545.[7]

Summoned to Malta in 1558, Shelley fell sick at Brussels and remained there on hearing of Queen Mary's illness. In December he returned to England to greet the new Queen. Religious scruples, however, prevented him from remaining long, and in the spring of 1560 he set out for Spain without a royal licence, much to the displeasure of Elizabeth, who ordered him to return. From the first Shelley protested his complete loyalty, saving his conscience, and throughout his chequered career in exile he was at pains to convince the English government of his patriotism. He entered or, rather, remained in the service of Philip II, who thought highly of the abilities and religious devotion of one whom he described as his 'taster'—perhaps one of Shelley's

duties as an aid of the chamber. In 1561 he obtained a licence to go to Malta to attend to his duties as turcopolier: before setting out he informed (Sir) Thomas Chaloner* that the furtherance of the English order's affairs was Philip's only motive in employing him, and some 20 years later he told Cecil that he had asked for leave of absence because of the growing enmity between England and Spain. He had only reached Genoa when he was recalled by Philip to go as ambassador to Persia; this mission was, however, cancelled. Meanwhile Shelley had been elected, at the instance of his brother Sir James Shelley, grand prior of the order in place of Sir Thomas Tresham*.[8]

Shelley served Philip II for the next three years but refused his offer of naturalization. The Turkish attack on Malta in 1565 drew him thither, but he was delayed at Naples and afterwards spent some time in Rome, not taking his seat in the council at Malta until September 1566. He quarrelled with the prior of Messina on a point of precedence and, although judgment was awarded in Shelley's favour in October of the following year, he left Malta some two years later after the prior had succeeded la Valette as grand master.[9]

In 1570 Shelley was said to be hoping to become a cardinal. Two years later he was in Venice where he greatly impressed the papal legate, who suggested that the pope might employ him on business concerning England. In 1575 he journeyed from Venice to Rome where he joined a group of English Catholics in a discussion of the conversion of England. Such was their esteem for Shelley that many of them wished him to be created a cardinal. Before 1575 the Venetian seignory proposed to send Shelley as their ambassador to Russia and Persia to enlist aid against the Turk. In 1581 the pope ordered Shelley to leave Rome following a dispute with a rival group of English Catholics led by Sir Thomas Stukeley.[10]

Shelley retired to Venice where, according to a friend, 'the chief nobles wonder at him for his learning and good life'. He refused to take his Spanish pension because of the deterioration in relations between England and Spain. An undated list of Philip II's pensioners includes 'Master Shelley, who is called lord great prior of England. He hath not any pension, but doth maintain himself by making knights of the order of Malta'. He made himself useful to the English government by supporting the suit of some English merchants in the Senate, and corresponded frequently with Burghley and Walsingham. His services not only earned him in 1583 a passport to return, which he never used, but also strengthened his successful plea for the life of his nephew, William Shelley of Michelgrove, sentenced to death for treason in 1586. Shelley died in Venice on 15 July 1587.[11]

Shelley won the admiration of his contemporaries by his learning, his knowledge of Europe, his uprightness of character and the sacrifice he made for his religion. His 'virtue' was such, wrote a friend to Cecil, that he was fit to serve any prince in the world. Shelley had a strong sense of personal mission concerning the conversion of England. He addressed the pope in 1561 and 1566, deprecating the use of force but urging that otherwise no pains should be spared. He aspired to be a mediator between England and the papal see, and for this reason (according to the papal nuncio in Venice) tried to commend himself to the English government; although the Queen, wrote the nuncio, 'counts not on him for her and her side, as she would wish, yet he is not so odious to her as the other exiles that are her professed enemies'. The mission, however, never took place, and when in his exile in Venice from 1581 Shelley asked to be allowed to return home his motives seem to have been more personal and less religious than formerly. Perhaps his failure to make use of his passport arose from a suspicion that he would not be allowed the religious freedom which had been promised. Shelley's cautious viewpoint enraged Sir Thomas Stukeley, who favoured the use of force, and Father Robert Persons had to intervene to save Shelley from the Inquisition. Persons believed that Shelley hoped to be made a cardinal and 'by that means to deal peaceably with the Queen'. It was this argument, and another concerning the English College in Rome, which prompted the pope's decision to send Shelley to Venice in 1581.[12]

[1] Aged 68 in August 1582, *CSP For.* 1582, p. 288. C. Read, *Sir Francis Walsingham*, iii. 288; *Vis. Suss.* (Harl. Soc. liii), 37; *CSP Ven.* 1556–7, p. 914; *CSP For.* 1553–8, p. 172; *DNB.* [2] *CSP Span.* 1554, p. 297; H. P. Scicluna, *Eng. Tongue* 1523–67, p. 52. [3] *LP Hen. VIII,* ix, xiii, xv; W. G. Zeeveld, *Foundations of Tudor Policy,* 44, 108–9. [4] *LP Hen. VIII,* xiv, xviii, xxi; *PPC,* vii. 111; E101/423/12, f. 12; *DNB* (Wotton, Nicholas). [5] *Vis. Suss.* 37, 111; *APC,* ii. 281, 329; iii. 26, 54, 404, 405, 409, 481, 482; *CSP Span.* 1547–9, pp. 376, 382; *CSP For.* 1547–53, pp. 59, 191; *CJ,* i. 3. [6] *Lit. Rems. Edw. VI,* 491; *APC,* iv. 76; *CSP Span.* 1550–2, p. 468; 1553, pp. 88, 91, 99, 130. [7] Egerton 2790, f. 141v; *CSP Span.* 1554, pp. 154, 297; *APC,* v. 66, 126, 152; *CSP Ven.* 1556–7, p. 793; *CSP For.* 1553–8, pp. 50, 172; Lansd. 155(28), f. 98; *N. and Q.* (ser. 1), viii. 190; *VCH Mdx.* i. 194, 196; R. Vertot, *Kts. of Malta,* i. 160; E. J. King, *Kts. of St. John,* 85 seq.; *Statutes,* iii. 778–81. [8] *CSP For.* 1558–9, pp. 28, 30; 1559–60, pp. 594, 596; 1560–1, pp. 489n, 542; 1561–2, p. 520; *Letters of Sir Richard Shelley,* 1–3, 6–12; Scicluna, 52; *CSP Rom.* 1558–71, pp. 36, 70. [9] *CSP For.* 1562, pp. 372, 382, 394, 482–4; 1564–5, pp. 418, 502; *CSP Rom.* 1558–71, p. 190; *Letters of Sir Richard Shelley,* 6–12; A. Mifsud, *Kts. Hosp. of Eng. Tongue,* 213. [10] *CSP For.* 1569–71, p. 209; *CSP Rom.* 1572–8, pp. 4, 193; *Letters and Memorials of Card. Allen,* ed. Knox, 267–8; *Cath. Rec. Soc.* ii. 64, 162, 163. [11] *CSP For.* 1581–2, pp. 389–90; 1582, pp. 287–9; 1583–4, pp. 586–7, 635–6; 1584–5, pp. 144, 145, 182; 1586–8, p. 161; *Recs. Eng. Caths.* ed. Knox, 302; Read, iii. 288; R. B. Manning, *Rel. and Soc. in Eliz. Suss.* 164n. [12] Leland, *Coll.* v. 147; *CSP Rom.* 1558–71, pp. 60, 185; 1572–8, pp. 81, 198, 206–7; *CSP For.* 1564–5, p. 502; *Letters and Memorials of Card. Allen,* 267–8.

S.R.J.

SHELLEY, William (by 1479–1549), of London and Michelgrove, Suss.

LONDON 1523[1]

b. by 1479, 1st s. of John Shelley† by Elizabeth, da. and h. of John Michelgrove *alias* Fauconer† of Michelgrove. *educ.* I. Temple. *m.* by 1508, Alice, da. and event. coh. of Henry Belknap of Knell, Beckley, Suss., 7s. inc. Richard* 7da. *suc.* fa. 3 Jan. 1527. Kntd. aft. 3 Nov. 1529.[2]

Lent reader, I. Temple 1518, gov. 1520–1.

J.p. Suss. 1512–*d.*, Warws. 1512–15, Surr. 1522–38, numerous other counties from 1528; commr. subsidy, Warws. 1512, Coventry 1512, 1514, musters, Suss. 1512, benevolence 1544/45; other commissions 1520–*d.*; recorder, Coventry 15 July 1512–12 Feb. 1515; under sheriff, London 27 June 1514–20, recorder 10 May 1520–6; serjeant-at-law 1521; j.c.p. 1526–*d.*; receiver of petitions in the Lords, Parlts. of 1539, 1542, 1545, 1547; custos rot. Suss. by 1547–*d.*[3]

According to his son Richard, William Shelley was, as an eldest son, 'put to the inns of court but to learn to understand his own evidence'; in the event he became a lawyer and rose high in his profession. His first appointment was to the recordership of Coventry for which he was recommended both by the retiring recorder, Anthony Fitzherbert, who described him as 'a gentleman of good conscience and well learned in the law of the land', and by letters from the King and 'divers great lords' which he may have obtained through his brother-in-law Sir Edward Belknap, himself connected with Coventry through his servant John Rastell*. Shelley resigned the recordership within three years because, like Fitzherbert before him, he could no longer 'give his attendance . . . as he ought to do': in June 1514 he had been appointed an under sheriff of London, and as judge in the sheriff's court and legal counsellor to the City he was expected to attend upon the mayor and aldermen at their twice-weekly meeting unless engaged on their behalf in the law courts at Westminster.[4]

Service as under sheriff was often followed by election to the recordership and on the resignation of that office by Richard Broke* in 1520 Shelley succeeded him. In the following year he was made a serjeant-at-law, a promotion which threatened to deprive him of his office under an ancient rule of the City that the recorder should be no more than an apprentice of the law. But Broke had retained office after taking the coif and Shelley's petition to the mayor and aldermen to be allowed to do the same was granted. The recorder was frequently employed as an intermediary between the City and the crown. In June 1521 Shelley went to see Cardinal Wolsey about the City's right to appoint to the office of common weigher in London which was disputed by the King. Wolsey reported that the

King was 'highly displeased' over this matter and, still more, over reports of discontent in London at the execution of the 3rd Duke of Buckingham, and that he intended 'to punish the City with such sharp and grievous punishment which they be not nor shall be able to bear'. At a meeting of the court of aldermen in the following month, Shelley put forward the City's suggestions for the prevention of insurrection: either there should be watch kept continually in London for a whole year or all the harness within the City should be removed to safe custody, at the choice of the King. Henry VIII insisted on both precautions and after a long debate Shelley was authorized to 'pacify and please the King's grace' by reporting the willingness of the aldermen to give up their own harness but their inability to 'promise for all the City'. In 1522 another sharp conflict arose. On 16 May Shelley reported to a special meeting of the court of aldermen the cardinal's request, revealed two days earlier to Sir John Brydges* and himself, for a loan of £100,000. Six days later he delivered the City's offer of £14,000 and the cardinal eventually agreed to accept £30,000, to be paid in three instalments, the third to be remitted if no longer needed. The City interpreted this as a loan of £20,000 and in the following month Shelley concluded the negotiations by obtaining Wolsey's agreement to the terms of its repayment.[5]

As recorder Shelley was elected by London to the Parliament of 1523. The dispute over the right to appoint to certain offices within the City being still unsettled, Shelley and five aldermen were sent to sue to Wolsey for the offices 'to be granted by the King's grace to the City and to be ratified by Parliament', and on 16 May the court of aldermen agreed that 'a bill of petition made and devised by Mr. Broke and Mr. Recorder to be exhibited to the Parliament concerning certain offices within this City, with a proviso concerning the office of common weigher, shall be exhibited and put up as it is'. But the bill met with no success in a Parliament preoccupied with the demands made upon it for a large subsidy. Before the next Parliament met, Shelley had been made a judge, and from 1529 until his death he was personally summoned to each Parliament by writ of assistance. From 1539 he was regularly appointed a receiver of petitions and was called upon to advise on bills; during the first session of the Parliament of 1547—in which his son Richard sat for Gatton—an Act (1 Edw. VI, no. 13) was passed for the assurance of certain lands to him and Sir Richard Rich.[6]

During the first session of the Parliament of 1529 Shelley was sent to Wolsey to take formal possession of York Place for the King; that task performed he was knighted by Henry VIII in York Place. Soon afterwards, according to his son, he fell out of favour and suffered 'great loss' during the ascendancy of Cromwell, and it was not until the end of the reign that the King 'made much of him again'. If this was indeed so, it can scarcely have arisen from any differences over public policy, for although Shelley was to die a Catholic and his children to become prominent recusants he did not resist the Henrician Reformation and was active as a judge in the prosecution of its opponents. What does give some colour to his son's allegation is that Shelley was forced by Cromwell to sell to the King the lordship of Knell in Beckley, the ancient residence of the Belknaps, which had been his wife's dowry, and that in 1541 he was recompensed—'liberally', as his son conceded, and with poetic justice—by the grant of two manors in Essex forfeited by Cromwell. When in London Shelley lived in the parish of St. Sepulchre, where he was assessed at 300 marks in goods to the subsidy of 1523; his lands, in an assessment of lawyers to this subsidy, were valued at £140 a year. On the death of his father in 1527 he succeeded to considerable estates in Hertfordshire, Kent and Sussex and took up residence at Michelgrove, in the parish of Clapham. Here he entertained Henry VIII and rebuilt the medieval house into a large mansion, said to have been one of the finest in the county.[7]

In his will of 6 Nov. 1548 Shelley asked to be buried in Clapham church if he died in the neighbourhood, 'without any pomp or costly ceremonies', and provided for the saying of 100 masses. Only three of his younger sons were still alive: he left the manor of Mapledurham and other Hampshire lands to Thomas, £20 a year to Richard and 100 marks to James. Richard Shelley might have received a larger legacy but his father had 'been at great charges with the finding of him in Italy': he was, however, to have the £100 owed to Shelley by Henry VIII's executors (whom the judge had advised), 'for I lent it to our said late sovereign lord at his being at the siege of Boulogne' —an allusion which shows that Shelley, after being summoned to raise soldiers for the campaign of 1544, had accompanied the King to France. He named his heir John sole executor but provided that in the event of John's death—and he survived his father by less than two years—that task should be undertaken by his cousin Henry White (q.v.), his daughter Elizabeth Copley and his friend and servant Thomas Bishop*. Elizabeth Shelley's marriage to Sir Roger Copley and her brother Thomas's to Sir Roger's sister Mary led to the

return for Gatton of several of Shelley's family as
well as of his servant Bishop; another daughter,
Catherine, married Henry Browne of Betchworth
Castle, Surrey, several of whose family sat for
Gatton after the flight overseas of Shelley's grandson Thomas Copley*. John Shelley's marriage to
Mary Fitzwilliam renewed his family's relationship
with Sir Anthony Cooke*, a descendant of Henry
Belknap, who had married her half-sister. In a
codicil to his will of 29 Dec. 1548 Sir William
Shelley forgave debts owing to him, including those
of Leonard West*. He died six days later. A tomb
with figures in Clapham church commemorates
him, his wife and their 14 children.[8]

[1] City of London RO, Guildhall, jnl. 12, f. 213v; rep. 4, f. 144.
[2] Date of birth estimated from age at fa.'s i.p.m., C142/46/14. Vis.
Suss. (Harl. Soc. liii), 36–37; Suss. Arch. Colls. xxiii. 148–9; xxvi. 215;
Hasted, Kent, ii. 102; DNB. [3] LP Hen. VIII, i–v, x, xii, xiii, xx;
CPR, 1547–8, pp. 74, 75, 77, 82, 85–88, 90; 1548–9, p. 181; Statutes,
iii. 82, 85, 116; Coventry Leet Bk. (EETS cxxxviii), 635, 646; City of
London RO, jnl. 11, f. 191v; rep. 4, f. 52v; 7, ff. 145, 147; LJ, i. 103,
165, 267, 293. [4] Letters of Sir Richard Shelley, 15; Coventry Leet Bk.
635, 646; City of London RO, rep. 3, ff. 245, 247v. [5] City of London
RO, Liber Dunthorne, f. 459v; rep. 5, ff. 191, 199v, 204v, 288, 290,
291 and v, 296v, 297. [6] Ibid. rep. 6, ff. 32, 36v; C218/1; Rymer,
Foedera, vi(3), 5, 74; LJ, i. 118, 273, 295, 301–3. [7] G. Cavendish,
Wolsey (EETS ccxliii), 116–17; Letters of Sir Richard Shelley, 15; LP
Hen. VIII, viii, x, xii–xiv, xvi; E179/251/15v; Cal. I.T. Recs. i. 465
where his christian name is given as John; C142/46/14, 40, 92; Suss.
Arch. Colls. lv. 284. [8] PCC 25 Populwell; APC, ii. 42; LP Hen.
VIII, xix; Vis. Suss. 111; M. E. Finch, Five Northants. Fams.
(Northants. Rec. Soc. xix), ped. at end vol.; C142/88/78; Suss. Arch.
Colls. xxiii. 149; xxvi. 215.

H.M.

SHELTON, Sir John (by 1503–58), of Shelton, Norf.

NORFOLK   1554 (Nov.)

b. by 1503, 1st s. of Sir John Shelton of Carrow by
Anne, da. of Sir William Boleyn of Blickling. educ. L.
Inn, adm. 1 Mar. 1517. m. c.1530, Margaret, da. of
Henry Parker, 10th Lord Morley, 2s. 3da. suc. fa. 21
Dec. 1539. Kntd. 22 Feb. 1547.[1]
   J.p. Norf. 1543–d.; commr. relief 1550; PC 1553–5;
sheriff, Norf. and Suff. 1554–5.[2]

John Shelton's mother was an aunt of Anne
Boleyn, on whose accession she was given the
custody of Princess Mary at Hatfield. Shelton was
doubtless seen at court while his cousin was Queen
but thereafter he was in the main to confine himself
to his county. His father, 'a man of great possessions',
sought to evade the Statute of Uses in their transmission, but after the elder Shelton's death the
matter came to light, the lawyers involved, who
included William Coningsby* and (Sir) Nicholas
Hare*, were punished, and an Act was passed in
1541 (33 Hen. VIII, c.26) annulling the 'crafty
conveyances' resorted to. The legal aftermath was to
be troublesome for Shelton but he did not suffer
politically: he joined the Norfolk bench in 1543 and
after serving in the Boulogne campaign he was
knighted at Edward VI's coronation. Yet it was

only with the accession of Mary that he came
briefly to the fore: his prompt adherence to her
cause brought him an annuity of £60 and a seat on
the Council, which he attended with some regularity
until March 1555. His election for Norfolk to the
third Parliament of the reign must have been
approved and was probably supported by the crown,
and it was immediately followed by his appointment
as sheriff. Predictably, Shelton was not among the
Members who quitted this Parliament without leave
before its dissolution.[3]

Shelton had evidently withdrawn from affairs at
the centre by March 1556, when the Council
thanked him for sending news from Norfolk and
told him to report in future to the 2nd Earl of
Sussex. He made his will on 12 Feb. 1558 and died
on the following 15 Nov., two days before the Queen.
His inquisition post mortem mentions only his
manor of Carrow, so that he must have disposed of
his other lands. He was succeeded by his son Ralph,
who married a daughter of Sir William Woodhouse*,
himself Shelton's kinsman through his wife Elizabeth Parker.[4]

[1] Date of birth estimated from education. Vis. Norf. (Norf. Arch.),
ii. 345–6, 391; DNB (Parker, Henry). [2] LP Hen. VIII, xx; CPR,
1547–8, p. 87; 1553, p. 356; 1553–4, pp. 22, 27; APC, iv and v
passim. [3] P. Friedmann, Anne Boleyn, i. 267, 271–2; Blomefield,
Norf. v. 267; Hall, Chron. 837; LP Hen. VIII, xix, add.; APC, i. 14;
iv. 430 et passim; v passim; Chron. Q. Jane and Q. Mary (Cam. Soc.
xlviii), 5; Lansd. 156, ff. 90–94. [4] APC, v. 316; PCC 37 Welles;
C142/119/127.

R.V.

SHERARD, George (by 1499–1575), of Stapleford, Leics.

LEICESTERSHIRE   1558

b. by 1499, 1st s. of Thomas Sherard† of Stapleford by
Margaret, da. and h. of Sir John Helwell. educ. L. Inn,
adm. 22 Nov. 1514. m. by 1537, Rose, da. of Sir
Thomas Pulteney of Misterton, 2s. 6da. suc. fa. 6 Mar.
1538.[1]
   Escheator, Warws. and Leics. 1537–8; sheriff,
Rutland 1544–5, 1554–5, 1562–3, Leics. 1567–8; j.p.
Rutland 1547–62, Leics. 1558/59–d.; commr. relief
Leics. and Rutland 1550, goods of churches and
fraternities, Rutland 1553; other commissions
1538–59.[2]

George Sherard came of a family which had been
established at Stapleford for over a hundred years.
His father, a merchant of the staple, had been
several times sheriff and had represented Leicestershire in Parliament in 1491–2. He sent his eldest
son to acquire some knowledge of the law, and in
this George Sherard may have acquired some
proficiency, for in later years he was to serve
regularly on commissions of gaol delivery and oyer
and terminer. He led a modest contingent to the
war in France in 1544 and added to his estate by
buying the rectory and tithes of Stapleford and

adjoining parcels there, and two manors in Scalford.[3]

Sherard was to die a firm Protestant, declaring in his will that he had 'no confidence in masses, trentals, dirges or in any ceremonial things or rites, or in any Romish or popish customs or such like'. If he had already reached this conclusion in middle life, his election to Mary's last Parliament may have been something of a protest against the regime. He may, indeed, have been patronized by the 2nd Earl of Rutland, whose support would have reinforced a claim based on local standing and connexions with families such as Digby, Pulteney and Turpin. Of his role in the Commons we know nothing but as he was not to reappear there in the more congenial atmosphere of the years ahead it is likely to have been a modest one.[4]

Under Elizabeth, Sherard remained active locally and he was nearly 70 when pricked sheriff for the fourth time. He died on 6 Aug. 1575 and was buried at Stapleford. By his will, made on 14 July in that year, he had left all his lands in tail male to his elder son Francis, with reversion in default of issue to his five daughters, who also received a life interest in the manor of Wissendon. His descendants became earls of Harborough.[5]

[1] Date of birth estimated from age at fa.'s i.p.m. C142/59/114. *Vis. Leics.* (Harl. Soc. ii), 10; PCC 15 Dyngeley. [2] *CPR*, 1547–8, p. 88; 1553, pp. 356–7, 415; 1553–4, p. 23; 1560–3, p. 439; *LP Hen. VIII*, xiii, xv, xvi. [3] *CPR*, 1553–4, pp. 381, 499; 1554–5, pp. 106, 151, 290, 415; 1558–60, p. 278; *LP Hen. VIII*, xiii, xv, xix; G. F. Farnham, *Leics. Med. Village Notes*, iv. 5n. [4] PCC 34 Pyckering. [5] C142/171/65.

S.M.T.

SHERBORN, Sir Richard (by 1522–94), of Stonyhurst, Lancs.

LANCASHIRE 1553 (Oct.)
PRESTON 1554 (Nov.)
LIVERPOOL 1555
PRESTON 1558

b. by 1522, 1st s. of Thomas Sherborn of Stonyhurst by Joan, da. of Sir John Towneley of Towneley. *m.* (1) 1538, Maud (*d.*10 Nov. 1588), da. of Sir Richard Bold of Bold, 5s. 3da.; (2) 1588, Isabel Wood, 1s. 2da. illegit. bef. *m.*; also 1s. illegit. by Grace Ryddynge. *suc.* fa. 22 Sept. 1536. Kntd. 11 May 1544.[1]

Dep. steward, duchy of Lancaster, Blackburn hundred, Lancs. 1543, steward and master forester, Bowland and Quernmore 1554–*d.*, dep. master forester, Amounderness 1560–1 and 1586–7; commr. chantries, Lancs. 1552, 1554, eccles. causes, diocese of Chester 1562, to survey crown lands, Lancs. 1576, musters 1577, 1580; servant of earls of Derby by 1555, member, council by 1561; butler, Lancs. 1559; searcher, port of Liverpool 1559; lt. I.o.M. in 1561; j.p. Lancs. by 1564–83 or later; member eccles. comm. in 1568; clerk of the market and feodary, Bowland and Lancs. 1582; dep. lt. Lancs. by 1585–*d.*[2]

Richard Sherborn's father died in 1536 while sheriff of Lancashire. Sir Thomas Holcroft*

acquired Richard's wardship in June 1538 and shortly afterwards married him to Maud Bold: guardian and ward were knighted together at Leith in 1544. By then Sherborn had already been involved in an attempt to overthrow the liberties of the town of Clitheroe, four miles from Stonyhurst. He had licence to enter on his lands without proof of age and without livery in February 1544 and in the same year he obtained Holcroft's interest in the lease of Wigglesworth in Yorkshire, formerly in the possession of Sir Stephen Hamerton, and he was probably helped by his former guardian in the scramble for monastic lands. He purchased Wigglesworth and certain former properties of Whalley abbey for £712 in 1558.[3]

Of much greater significance in Sherborn's career, however, was his connexion with the earls of Derby. He followed his father into their service and held many offices under the 3rd and 4th Earls; he was an executor of the 3rd Earl's will and his son, another Richard, was to marry Catherine Stourton, whose mother was a Stanley. Sherborn's parliamentary career mirrored this noble patronage. His election as first knight of the shire to Queen Mary's first Parliament, when he had barely turned 30 and before he had taken any significant part in local administration, was a striking tribute both to his own standing with the 3rd Earl and to that magnate's early and notable support of the new monarch; and even though he could not hope to retain so exalted a place—which would be occupied on the next three occasions by the earl's younger son— Sherborn owed it to the same pervasive influence that he was to reappear in three subsequent Parliaments. In two of these he sat for Preston, a borough monopolized by nominees, and in the third for Liverpool, where Derby's influence was especially strong: Sherborn was, indeed, styled on the return for Liverpool 'knight and steward to the noble earl Lord Edward Earl of Derby'. Nothing is known about Sherborn's part in the work of the House.[4]

Sherborn was to continue in the Stanleys' service after 1558 but he did not sit in any Elizabethan Parliament, presumably because of his reservations about the Anglican settlement. In 1561 he was one of the members of Derby's council who sat in judgment on a dispute at Liverpool; described in the municipal records as the earl's chief councillor, he was said to be a friend of the town. He accompanied Derby on his visit there in 1566 and his name appears on the burgess roll in 1572 and 1589. In 1562 he was mentioned as having taken, as Derby's officer, £80 in duties from a Portuguese shipowner. In 1578 he was acting as Lady Derby's agent in a dispute over Neroche forest in Somerset. He was deputy to the 3rd and 4th Earls as master forester of Amounderness. In July 1555 the 3rd Earl had granted him the custody of Greenhalgh castle and park, and in July 1567 the earl added the stewardships of Bolton in Lonsdale and of the wapentake of Ewcross with the master forestership of the chase of Ingleborough in Yorkshire. He was to have accompanied the 4th Earl to France in 1585 as his treasurer, but was apparently prevented by illness.[5]

Sherborn was more than a trusted servant of the Stanleys. If he served them as lieutenant of Man, he also served the crown as deputy lieutenant of Lancashire when the 4th Earl of Derby was lord lieutenant. He received so many instructions from the central authorities to inquire into local disputes that he has been called 'almost a special investigator'; one such dispute concerned Richard Houghton (probably the bastard son of Sir Richard Houghton*) and Sir Robert Dudley*, Earl of Leicester. In June 1563 Sherborn purchased the manor of Leagram from Dudley for £1,619; it had once been leased to his father Thomas and was closely connected with his stewardship of Bowland.[6]

If Sherborn's religion did not exclude him from active local service, especially as a deputy lieutenant of his county at a time of threatened invasion, it does seem that his sympathies were Catholic. He was judged unfavourable as a justice of the peace in 1564 and in or about 1588 he was delated as a Catholic and a generally obnoxious person. The accusations seem to have had no effect and Sherborn remained in office. He is even said, most implausibly, to have been so favoured by Elizabeth that he was allowed to maintain a priest. The earls of Derby could no doubt have protected him but they could scarcely have secured him the offices he held if his Catholic sympathies had been pronounced. Four years after being thought unfavourable as a justice he was a member of the ecclesiastical commission and in July 1568 sat in judgment on eight leading recusants at Lathom. In 1585 he was one of the signatories to a document on 'the enormities of the sabbath', a document apparently of a Puritan nature although Sir Richard may have signed as one concerned rather with public order than with theology. Certainly there was no special significance in his signing the Lancashire Bond of Association. Shortly before Sherborn's death his son's second wife Anne, daughter of Henry Kighley and widow of Thomas Houghton, was summoned before the Privy Council as a recusant; on that occasion she conformed but the Sherborn family was later recusant. Sherborn had been one of those who reported on the affray in which Thomas Houghton was killed.[7]

Sherborn died on 26 July 1594, having made his will on the previous 2 Oct. Amongst the legatees was Richard, eldest son of his daughter Mary and Thomas Fleetwood, himself the son of John Fleetwood† of Penwortham. Sir Richard Shuttleworth, chief justice of Chester and a Sherborn connexion by marriage, was supervisor of the will. A memorial in the church at Mitton lists several of Sherborn's chief offices, but does not mention his having sat in Parliament. He had begun the rebuilding of his home before his death and the work was completed by his son Richard. The house passed into the ownership of the English College from Liege in 1794 and is now a Catholic public school.[8]

[1] Date of birth estimated from first reference, but said to be ten at fa.'s death. *Vis. Lancs.* (Chetham Soc. lxxxi), 58; (lxxxviii), 264; C. D. Sherborn, *Sherborn Fam.* 27 seq.; *Chetham Soc.* lx. 267; *VCH Lancs.* vii. 5. [2] *VCH Lancs.* ii. 97–98; vii. 5; *CPR*, 1560–3, pp. 280–1; 1572–5, p. 92; *Chetham Soc.* n.s. lxxii. 24; *APC*, xii. 8; xviii. 386; *Cam. Misc.* ix(3), 77; *HMC Foljambe*, 25; *DKR*, xliii. 274; Somerville, *Duchy*, i. 467n, 491, 501; *CSP Dom.* 1591–4, p. 402. [3] *LP Hen. VIII*, xiii, xix; *Lancs. and Cheshire Rec. Soc.* xxxv. 171; *DKR*, xxxix. 559; *CPR*, 1554–5, p. 330; 1557–8, p. 174. [4] PCC 38 Daper; *Liverpool Town Bks.* ed. Twemlow, i. 52a. [5] Twemlow, i. 165, 169, 313; ii. 831, 838; *APC*, vii. 107; xi. 49; *Chetham Soc.* n.s. xix. 76; lxxii. 30; *Lancs. and Cheshire Hist. Soc.* xcii. 51, 53. [6] J. B. Watson, 'Lancs. gentry 1529–58' (London Univ. M.A. thesis, 1959), 478; *APC*, xi. 89, 163, 191; *CPR*, 1560–3, pp. 538, 581; *Chetham Soc.* n.s. lxxii. 2, 12, 27. [7] *VCH Lancs.* vii. 5, 131; *Cam. Misc.* ix(3), 77; *CSP Dom.* 1591–4, pp. 159–60, a document tentatively dated 1591 but see H. H. Leonard, 'Knights and knighthood in Tudor Engl.' (London Univ. Ph.D. thesis, 1970), 256n; *Cath. Rec. Soc.* iv. 178–9; J. Croston, *Samlesbury*, 104–5; J. S. Leatherbarrow, *Lancs. Eliz. Recusants* (Chetham Soc. n.s. cx), 27, 32, 99; Harl. 1926, f. 80; *APC*, xxiv. 281, 334, 410; *Lancs. and Cheshire Rec. Soc.* lxxxviii. 45. [8] *Chetham Soc.* lx. 267; T. D. Whitaker, *Whalley* (3rd ed.), 467; *Ducatus Lanc.* i. 161; Pevsner, *N. Lancs.* 239–40.

A.D.

SHILSTON, Sir John (by 1491–1529/30), of Wood, Devon, and Southwark, Surr.

SOUTHWARK 1529*

b. by 1491, yr. s. of Robert Shilston of Devon. *m.* Anne, da. of Sir William Brandon. Kntd. bef. Nov. 1513.[1]

Keeper and bailiff, manor of Dartington, Devon 1514; j.p. Devon 1515; sheriff 1515–16; commr. loan, Anglesey 1522; under steward, manor of Bromfield, Salop 1522; 'justice', N. Wales.[2]

John Shilston came of a family long established in Devon. As a younger son he enjoyed only the profits during life of houses and 740 acres in the county settled on him by his elder brother, but military service evidently brought him to the attention of Charles Brandon, Lord Lisle, whose sister he was to marry, and this in turn probably led to appointments both in Devon and in North Wales where Lisle was chamberlain. Shilston had been one of the captains on the expedition to Guienne in 1512, and again in the campaign against Tournai during the following year. He also saw action in France in 1522 and 1523.[3]

Shilston was the defendant in a court of requests case probably of 1523–4 over his alleged abuse of his power as under steward of Bromfield. The plaintiff had obtained judgment against him before the commissioners for the marches of Wales, but complained that Shilston had ignored this and had said 'in open audience if there came an hundred such commandments to him he would not obey': Shilston further promised him that 'if he tarried or dwelled in Bromfield the space of seven years he would tread on his skirts for his busy suit making', a threat he had already made good by false imprisonment and menace of assault since the litigation began. Some years later, when Shilston was summoned before Chancellor More he demanded, 'What is [it] for me to be steward of Bromfield if the King's commissioners should break any order that I had made?', to receive the reply, 'The King's commissioners be set there to order you and all other great officers and all the King's subjects in those parts'.[4]

In 1529 Shilston's brother-in-law, now Duke of Suffolk, was a leading Councillor, and it was doubtless at his nomination that Shilston was chosen for Southwark, where he may have lodged in Suffolk's house. He can only have attended the first session: he made his will on 10 Dec. 1529 and died not long after, a writ of *diem clausit extremum* being issued on 23 Jan. 1530. After asking to be buried in St. George's Southwark, Shilston divided most of his property between his wife, whom he made sole executrix, a great-niece Elizabeth, to whom he left £90 and a gold chain worth £80, and 'one Jane which was given to me [as a ward] and now remaineth with my sister Coffin'. His Devon lands comprised some four houses and 250 acres of land, held jointly with his wife, and over ten tin mines. Shilston's death was noted when the list of Members came to be revised in the spring of 1532, and his place was later filled by Thomas Bulla. His widow married Gawain Carew*.[5]

[1] Date of birth estimated from first reference. C142/31/34; *Vis. Devon*, ed. Vivian, 135; *LP Hen. VIII*, i. [2] A. Emery, *Dartington Hall*, 71; *LP Hen. VIII*, i–iii; *Cal. Wynn (of Gwydir) Pprs. 1515–1690*, pp. 239–40; Req.2/12/154. [3] Polwhele, *Devonshire*, ii. 461n; *Trans. Dev. Assoc.* lxxvi. 227–8; C1/573/33; *LP Hen. VIII*, i; Req.2/12/154. [4] Req.2/12/154. [5] PCC 3 Thower; C142/51/89; SP1/56, ff. 2–10 (the 'mortuus' is omitted in *OR*).

D.F.C.

SHIRLEY, Francis (c. 1524–78), of West Grinstead, Suss.

NEW SHOREHAM 1555

b. c.1524, 1st s. of Thomas Shirley* of West Grinstead by Elizabeth, da. and coh. of Marmaduke Gorges *alias* Russell of Gloucester, Glos. *m.* by 1555, Barbara, da. of Sir Richard Blount* of Mapledurham, Oxon. and Dedisham, Suss., 2s. inc. Thomas † 2da. *suc.* fa. 28 Apr. 1544.[1]
Collector of customs, Southampton, Hants in 1553–4; j.p. Suss. 1564–*d.*; sheriff, Surr. and Suss. 1573–4.[2]

According to the inquisition taken on his father's lands in January 1545 Francis Shirley was then of age, yet in May 1546 it was as 'a minor in the King's hands' that he was granted custody of Buddington manor in Wiston, Sussex, and his own wardship and marriage. In view of his mother's suppression of his father's will his age may have been misrepresented in 1545 in an effort to safeguard his interest. When she died in August 1557 Francis Shirley was a prisoner in the Fleet for a debt to the crown of £507 shared by Henry Carey*, James Hardwick of Derbyshire, and Henry Peckham* but he had instructed his wife and servants to enter the West Grinstead house and lands, which his mother had retained; they did so, and his wife sold some plate to maintain the household. His brother William Shirley, as administrator of their mother's estate, then took the dispute to Chancery and at the same time sued the constable of West Grinstead and two of Francis Shirley's servants in the Star Chamber for theft and violence, but Francis Shirley was to remain in possession of West Grinstead for the rest of his life. Among his other conflicts was one with the 9th Lord la Warr in 1552 over the title to East Court, a house in West Grinstead, which Shirley defended by force at the cost of a reprimand from the Council but which (Sir) Richard Sackville II* as official arbitrator awarded to la Warr. Shirley's conduct in this episode and his attempt to evict a Steyning merchant from 50 acres of land in Wiston may exemplify a disposition to lawlessness which could account for his exclusion from county administration until after the accession of Elizabeth.[3]

If la Warr had not died in 1554 Shirley would scarcely have been returned to the Parliament of the following year, for both the Shoreham seats in that of April 1554, the last to be summoned before la Warr's death, had gone to his nominees. Although Shirley's father had held property in the borough and his own lands at Wiston were not far away, Shirley was himself almost certainly a nominee, his name and Thomas Hogan's being inserted on the indenture probably in the same hand. With the 3rd Duke of Norfolk in his grave and his grandson a minor, the patron is hard to identify, but the dead duke's follower John Covert* was sheriff and his brother George Covert had been a servant of la Warr. La Warr's nephew William West, who was claiming the title, was another possible patron; Shirley's father-in-law Sir Richard Blount, who had sat for Steyning in March 1553 but was out of favour under Mary, is unlikely to have wielded any influence. It was to be Shirley's only spell in the Commons and all that is known of it is that he was not among the Members who voted against one of the government's bills. He was, indeed, returned for Bramber to Elizabeth's first Parliament but on 26 Jan. 1559 (three days after the Parliament had met) 'that pretended return' was revoked by the town in a letter which announced the election of Robert Buxton and Sir Henry Gates. It is more likely that the patron, the 4th Duke of Norfolk, had changed his mind than that there was an election contest.[4]

Before he died on 24 Mar. 1578 Shirley had attained the Sussex bench and served a term as sheriff. His heir Thomas, aged 23, inherited the manor of Buddington, the house at West Grinstead, lands in Horsham, Lancing and Steyning, and a manor in Somerset. Shirley is not known to have left a will, but in his own will of 1606 Thomas Shirley was to ask for a monument to be raised to his parents and grandparents in West Grinstead church, which appears not to have been done.[5]

[1] Date of birth estimated from age at fa.'s i.p.m., C142/183/63, amended by *LP Hen. VIII*, xxi. *Suss. Arch. Colls.* v. 11.   [2] SP12/74, f. 106v.   [3] C1/1355/39, 1471/21–25; E111/1/56; *Suss. Rec. Soc.* xvi. 91–93; Barbican House, Lewes, Knole ms cal. Kn. 1/8; SP10/14/62; *APC*, iv. 121.   [4] C219/24/162; Loseley Pk. Loseley letters, box I, no. 6.   [5] *CPR*, 1558–60, pp. 131, 263; *APC*, viii. 350; *Suss. Rec. Soc.* iii. 112; PCC 3 Hudleston.

R.J.W.S.

SHIRLEY, Sir Richard (by 1477–1540), of Wiston, Suss.

SUSSEX   1529

b. by 1477, 1st s. of Ralph Shirley of Wiston by Joan, da. of Thomas Bellingham[†] of Lyminster; bro. of Thomas*. *m.* (1) by 1498, Alma, da. of John Shelley[†] of Michelgrove, 4s. 6da.; (2) Elizabeth, da. of Sir Richard Guildford[†] of Cranbrook and Rolvenden, Kent, wid. of Thomas Isley of Sunridge, Kent. *suc.* fa. 1510. Kntd. 1526.[1]
  J.p. Suss. 1512–*d.*; commr. array 1512, subsidy 1512, 1514, 1515, 1523, 1524, musters 1539; sheriff, Surr. and Suss. 1513–14, 1526–7; knight of the body by 1533.[2]

The Shirley family, which had owned Wiston since the early 15th century, only made it their residence after the death of Richard Shirley's grandfather in 1466. His father built up a reputation in the county, served Henry VII as an esquire of the body and was pricked sheriff of Surrey and Sussex in 1503. Shirley's own career mirrored that of his father. He served the crown on local commissions and as a justice of the peace, and was pricked twice as sheriff, but he rarely looked beyond Sussex for adventure or gain. During the French campaign of 1514 Shirley, as sheriff, mustered 55 men and led them to Canterbury to join the retinue of the 5th Lord Bergavenny. In 1526 the King made a progress through the southern counties and appears to have knighted Shirley while he was in Sussex. In 1536 Shirley was ordered to supply troops and

march against the northern rebels, but his services were not required in the field and he remained to keep order in Sussex; three years later he was asked to survey the county's coastal defences against the threatened French invasion. He was an occasional visitor at court and it was presumably as a knight of the body that he attended the reception of Anne of Cleves in 1540.[3]

Like his father Shirley derived part of his income from farming: he is known to have exported tallow and leather from Shoreham but whether he also sent wool by sea the scanty customs accounts do not indicate. In 1524 he was assessed at £120 in lands at Wiston and in January 1527 he bought property in Ashington, Chiltington, Grinstead and Washington for £35. He assisted Sir Roger Lewknor with the administration of his estates and in 1526 he was sued in the Exchequer to account for money he had collected as receiver of Lewknor's lands in Sussex.[4]

As a justice of long standing and a recent sheriff Shirley was well qualified for a knighthood of the shire in the Parliament of 1529 even if he had not sat in an earlier House of Commons, as he may well have done. Yet he probably owed his election to the sheriff, Richard Bellingham, who was his cousin, while the fact that his fellow-Member Sir John Gage was his wife's brother-in-law cannot but have helped. It is likely that he and Gage shared the same outlook on the great issue of the divorce when it confronted them in the House. Early in 1533 Shirley's name was one of those included by Cromwell on a list of Members who are thought to have been opposed, either on grounds of conscience or of economic expediency, to the bill in restraint of appeals to Rome then being debated in the Commons: if this is indeed the basis of the list, Gage's name would doubtless also have been on it if he had not by then retired from court, and probably also from Parliament, as a gesture of disapproval of the divorce proceedings. Close on two years later both men's names do appear on another of Cromwell's lists. This one, dating probably from December 1534, appears to relate to the treasons bill then in passage, the Members named perhaps constituting, or being considered for, a committee on that bill: if so, Gage and Shirley may be thought of as belonging to the group of 'opposition' Members included in the total. That Shirley did not forfeit the King's favour is implied by his retention of his appointment as a knight of the body: probably for him, as for Gage and others, the death of Catherine of Aragon in January of that year helped to relieve the tension and the fall of Anne Boleyn a few months later eased the situation still further. There is thus no reason to doubt that he reappeared in the Parliament of

June 1536 in accordance with the King's request for the return of the previous Members.[5]

Shirley made his will on 21 Oct. 1540. Professing himself 'to be a true Christian Catholic man and in full and perfect belief of Christ's Church intending through God's mercy in the same to die', he asked to be buried in the chancel of Wiston church before the image of St. Anne, where masses would be said for his soul. He provided for his wife and three unmarried children, and appointed his son William executor: his overseers included his cousins Richard Bellingham, Sir John Gage and (Sir) William Shelley*, and his brother Thomas Shirley. Shirley died on the following 16 Nov., and was succeeded by William, then rising 42.[6]

[1] Date of birth estimated from marriage. *Vis. Suss.* (Harl. Soc. liii), 7, 159; *Suss. Arch. Colls.* v. 1–13. [2] *LP Hen. VIII*, i–v, xiii–xv; *Statutes*, iii. 84, 113, 169; *Suss. Rec. Soc.* lvi. 62. [3] *LP Hen. VIII*, i, xi, xiv, xv; H. H. Leonard, 'Knights and knighthood in Tudor Eng.' (London Univ. Ph.D. thesis, 1970), 163, 319, 324. [4] E122/36/1; *Suss. Rec. Soc.* lvi. 62; Barbican House, Lewes, Knole ms cal. Kn. 1/1, 2. [5] *LP Hen. VIII*, vii. 1522(ii) citing SP1/87, f. 106v; ix. 1077 citing SP1/99, p. 234. [6] PCC 22 Alenger; C142/67/91; Nairn and Pevsner, *Suss.* 382.

R.J.W.S.

SHIRLEY, Thomas (by 1489–1544), of West Grinstead, Suss.

STEYNING 1529

b. by 1489, yr. s. of Ralph Shirley of Wiston, and bro. of Sir Richard*. *m.* Elizabeth, da. and coh. of Marmaduke Gorges *alias* Russell of Gloucester, Glos., 2s. inc. Francis* 4da.[1]

J.p. Suss. 1524–*d.*; commr. subsidy 1524, sewers 1534, tenths of spiritualities 1535; collector of customs, Southampton by 1542–*d.*[2]

Thomas Shirley, who inherited lands in Buckinghamshire as well as at Beeding and Broadwater in Sussex, founded a branch of the family at West Grinstead. In 1510 he acquired the wardship and marriage of Elizabeth and Maud Gorges, and he afterwards married Elizabeth. Nine years later he shared the wardship and marriage of Francis Dawtrey, heir of Sir John Dawtrey†, Shirley's predecessor in his customs post. For the subsidy of 1524 he was assessed at £40 in lands and £66 13s. 4d. in goods.[3]

Shirley's Membership of the Parliament of 1529 was doubtless the work of his elder brother Sir Richard, whose home was not far from Steyning and who in 1529 obtained his own election as one of the knights for Sussex. The names of both appear on a list compiled by Cromwell on the back of a letter of December 1534 and thought to be of Members connected, perhaps as a committee, with the treasons bill then on its passage through Parliament. Shirley was probably re-elected in 1536, in accordance with the King's general request for the return of the previous Members, and he may have been so

again in 1539, when the names of the Members for Steyning are lost.[4]

On 26 Oct. 1535 he and Thomas Michell* obtained a 60-year lease of lands belonging to Rusper priory. Shortly before his death Shirley bought some former monastic property in Grinstead, Shoreham, Steyning and Wiston. He made his will on 21 Sept. 1534, some two weeks before the opening of the seventh session of the Parliament of 1529. After several small bequests to local churches, he provided for his wife, children, kinsmen and servants and named his wife executrix and Sir Edward Bray*, his 'son' Henry Browne and Richard Lister supervisors. Almost ten years later, on 28 Apr. 1544, he added a codicil devising his recently acquired property on his two sons and died the same day. His widow suppressed the will and took all his goods (valued at £600) into her hands. She also refused to honour his debts, including one of £52 owed to John Michell II* from the profits taken of his lands during his minority. In August 1557 Elizabeth Shirley died intestate and William, her second son, was appointed to administer his father's will and his mother's estate, itself valued at £200. Thus Thomas Shirley's will was not proved until September 1557.[5]

[1] Date of birth estimated from first reference. Comber, *Suss. Genealogies* (Lewes), 260. [2] *LP Hen. VIII*, iv, v, vii, viii, xix; E122/209/3; *Suss. Rec. Soc.* lvi. 59. [3] D. W. Davies, *Elizabethans Errant*, 1–3; *Suss. Arch. Colls.* v. 10 seq.; *LP Hen. VIII*, i–iii; *Suss. Rec. Soc.* lvi. 59. [4] *LP Hen. VIII*, vii. 1522(ii) citing SP1/87, f. 106v. [5] Ibid. x, xii, xvii; PCC 34 Wrastley; *Suss. Rec. Soc.* xvi. 91–92; C1/1142/84; 142/75/67.

R.J.W.S.

SHOYSWELL, Thomas (by 1506–33), of Hastings, Suss.

HASTINGS 1529

b. by 1506, prob. 2nd s. of John Shoyswell of Shoyswell.[1]

Jurat, Hastings 1527–*d.*, bailiff 1530–1; bailiff to Yarmouth 1527.[2]

Thomas Shoyswell was a younger son in a family long settled at the manor of that name on the Sussex–Kent border north of Hastings. He is missing from the pedigree included in the Sussex visitation, the namesake appearing there at this time being the son and heir of Roger Shoyswell, the Member's elder brother who died in 1524–5.[3]

It may be presumed that Shoyswell made a career in trade at Hastings, where in 1528–9 he is found importing salt. He was a jurat by 1527 and in that year he first attended the Brotherhood of the Cinque Ports. His return to Parliament in 1529, after only a few years' municipal experience, marked his rising status, as did his election as bailiff in the following year: both may have owed something to his gentle birth and resulting connexions. Although nothing is known of his role at Westminster, there are glimpses of his activity nearer home: the choice of him as one of the auditors of the 'book of Sandwich' on the occasion of a dispute between that port and Sir Edward Ryngeley, its powerful bailiff, may not have been unconnected with Ryngeley's concurrent Membership of Parliament.[4]

Shoyswell attended the Brotherhood at its Easter meeting in 1533: he was asked to tell the new lord warden, Lord Rochford, that he could have a third of all 'findals' for life but that he was to keep the grant secret so as not to create a precedent in a matter which nearly always provoked dispute. Three months later Shoyswell was appointed deputy to the bailiff, Richard Lane, but thereafter he disappears from the scene. That this connotes his death is shown by the advent, on a list of Members of Parliament of later compilation, of the names of John Durrant and John Taylor as representatives of Hastings. Shoyswell's fellow-Member Richard Calveley had died soon after the Parliament began and was perhaps already replaced; his own death, occurring after the close of its fifth session in April 1533, created the further vacancy. In the absence of a will it is not known whether Shoyswell was married.[5]

[1] Date of birth estimated from first reference. *Misc. Gen. et Her.* (ser. 5), iii. 185. [2] *Cinque Ports White and Black Bks.* (Kent Arch. Soc. recs. br. xix), 202–3, 205, 210–11, 213, 215–16. [3] *VCH Suss.* ix. 215; PCC 38 Bodfelde. [4] E122/200/5; *Cinque Ports White and Black Bks.* 202, 211, 214. [5] *Cinque Ports White and Black Bks.* 215–16; Add. 34150, f. 137.

P.H.

SIDNEY, Henry (1529–86), of London and Penshurst, Kent.

BRACKLEY 1547
KENT 1553 (Mar.), 1563, 1571, 1572

b. 20 July 1529, 1st s. of Sir William Sidney of Penshurst by Anne, da. of Sir Hugh Pagenham, wid. of Thomas Fitzwilliam. *m.* 29 Mar. 1551, Mary, da. of John Dudley, Earl of Warwick, later Duke of Northumberland, 3s. inc. Philip† and Robert† 4da. Kntd. 1551, KG nom. 23 Apr., inst. 14 May 1564; *suc.* fa. 1553.[1]

Henchman of Henry VIII c. 1538; royal cupbearer 1550; gent. of privy chamber by 1551; keeper, Richmond park by 1552; high steward, honor of Otford and Knole park, master of otterhounds 1553; v.-treasurer [I] 1556–9, ld. justice 1557, 1558; pres. council in marches of Wales 1559–d.; j.p.q. Kent 1561–d.; ld. dep. [I] 1565–71, 1575–8; PC 1575.[2]

In 1538 Henry Sidney's father was appointed chamberlain of the household to Prince Edward. The young Sidney became intimate with the prince, who after succeeding to the throne gave him a number of court offices. As late as 1583 Sidney still wrote of Edward as 'my dear king and master', and recalled that it was in his arms that the young king had died.[3]

In addition to his duties in the royal household Sidney was twice chosen, in 1551 and the following year, to go on special embassies to France. Before the first of these, which was intended to arrange the betrothal of Edward to Princess Elizabeth of France, he was privately married to Mary Dudley, the public wedding being postponed until his return at Whitsun. During this period, when he was in higher favour at court than at any other time of his life, he and his father received large grants of land from the crown, including the manors of Penshurst in Kent and Tyburn, Middlesex, and the lordship of Southwell, Nottinghamshire. He also sat in both Edwardian Parliaments. At Brackley, which appears to have returned Members for the first time in 1547, he was doubtless a nominee of the lord of the borough, the 3rd Earl of Derby, to whom he may have been recommended by the King, and in Kent he must have had the support of his father-in-law the Duke of Northumberland. Sidney signed the letters patent limiting the succession to Jane Grey but took no further part in the crisis of 1553 and was pardoned by Mary for his complicity before the end of July 1553. In October he sued out a general pardon; in the same month he surrendered to the Queen the lordship of Southwell, but in November 1553 he was confirmed in possession of the other lands and offices granted to him by Edward VI.[4]

Mary's acceptance of Sidney was not merely formal. Early in 1554 he was chosen to accompany the commissioners on their voyage to Spain to bring Prince Philip to England, and in the following November Philip stood godfather to his eldest son. When the Queen was thought to be with child in the summer of 1555 he was instructed to be ready to carry the news of the birth to the King of the Romans; nine months later he was appointed vice-treasurer, receiver-general and treasurer of the wars in Ireland, offices which he held until July 1559. As lord deputy of Ireland in the 1560s and 1570s and as president of the council in the marches of Wales he served Queen Elizabeth until his death at Ludlow on 5 May 1586. He was buried at Penshurst.[5]

[1] Date of birth given in inscription on portrait at Petworth House. A. Collins, *Mems. Sidneys*, i. 82–83, 96; *CSP Dom.* 1547–80, p. 35; *DNB.* [2] SP12/159/1; *CPR*, 1549–51, p. 174; 1553, p. 201; 1555–7, p. 82; 1558–60, p. 120; 1560–3, p. 438; *APC*, iii. 271; iv. 242–3; ix. 11; Stowe 571, f. 53v; R. Flenley, *Cal. Reg. Council, Marches of Wales*, 11 et passim; *CSP Ire.* 1509–73, pp. 141, 265, 441; 1574–85, pp. 77, 142. [3] *LP Hen. VIII*, xiii; SP12/159/1; B. L. Beer, *Northumberland*, 128; W. K. Jordan, *Edw. VI*, ii. 519. [4] Beer, 139, 146; Jordan, ii. 174–5; *APC*, iii. 271; iv. 196, 267; *CPR*, 1550–3, p. 358; 1553, p. 60; 1553–4, pp. 215, 467; *Chron. Q. Jane and Q. Mary* (Cam. Soc. xlviii), 13, 100. [5] *Chron. Q. Jane and Q. Mary*, 68; Collins, i. 96, 98; *APC*, v. 126; *CPR*, 1555–7, p. 82; 1558–60, p. 120.

H.M.

SIMON, John (by 1458–1524), of Exeter, Devon.

EXETER 1512,[1] 1515[2]

b. by 1458. *m.* (1) Alison (*d.* aft. Jan. 1519), 1s.; (2) Agnes.[3]

Bailiff, Exeter 1483–4, member of the Twenty-Four by 1496–*d.*, receiver 1499–1500, mayor 1512–13, 1523–*d.*; churchwarden, St. Petrox's, Exeter 1487–90, 1502–4; collector of customs, ports of Exeter and Dartmouth 4 Oct. 1492–?*d.*, gauger 12 Feb. 1508–?*d.*; constable of the staple, Exeter 1501–2, 1505–6; commr. subsidy, Devon 1512, 1513, 1515, Exeter 1523, 1524.[4]

John Simon was an Exeter merchant who was remembered as a wise gentleman. After his admission to the freedom during 1478–9 he combined trade with local administration and service to the crown. His Membership was an episode in his civic career and could have had official support since as a customer he helped to victual the armies sent to Spain and northern France; at the election held in 1512 he polled 19 votes out of a possible 21. During the prorogation of that year he and his fellow-Member Richard Hewet agreed to defer submitting their claim for wages until the Parliament was dissolved, and after their uncontested re-election in 1514, in compliance with the call for the return of the previous Members, they seem to have made a similar arrangement for that Parliament: the pair were eventually paid in full at the standard rate of 2s. a day.[5]

Simon died during his second mayoralty. He was a sick man when on 26 Sept. 1524 he made his will asking for burial in St. Petrox's church near his first wife. He left money to the Black Friars to form a cortege for the funeral and £40 to his second wife on condition that she paid for masses for his soul for four years. After making several small bequests he left the residue of his estate to his son William whom he named executor. He died on the following day and it was then decided by the members of the Twenty-Four that Thomas Hunt should take his place until the new mayor, William Hurst*, was sworn in. The vacancy on the Twenty-Four caused by his death was not filled for another year and his will not proved until 24 Jan. 1526.[6]

[1] Exeter act bk. 1, f. 26. [2] Ibid. 1, f. 57. [3] Date of birth estimated from his admission as freeman. Exeter act bk. 1, f. 59v; PCC 1 Porch. [4] R. Izacke, *Exeter* (1681), 91, 103, 107 (where erroneously given as Richard Symons), 113; Exeter act bk. 1 passim; *Trans. Dev. Assoc.* xiv. 433; *CPR*, 1494–1509, pp. 213, 425; *CFR*, 1485–1509, nos. 448–50, 907; *LP Hen. VIII*, i, iii, iv; *Statutes*, iii. 80, 117, 174; B. Wilkinson, *Med. Council, Exeter*, 92–97. [5] Exeter, Hooker's commonplace bk. f. 339; act bk. 1, ff. 26, 32v, 57; receivers' accts. 1514–15; *Exeter Freemen* (Devon and Cornw. Rec. Soc. extra ser. i), 58; *The description of the citie of Excester* (Devon and Cornw. Rec. Soc. xi), 612, 791–2, 863; *LP Hen. VIII*, i. [6] PCC 1 Porch; Exeter, Hooker's commonplace bk. f. 339; act bk. 1, ff. 105, 111.

M.B.

SKEFFINGTON, William (by 1521–71), of Skeffington, Leics.

LEICESTERSHIRE 1555

b. by 1521, 1st s. of Thomas Skeffington of Skeffington by Margaret, da. and h. of Edmund Stanhope of West Markham, Notts. *m.* by 1547, Mary, da. of Thomas Cave of Stanford, Northants. 2s. 3da. *suc.* fa. 1543.[1]

J.p. Leics. 1547–*d.*; commr. relief 1550; other commissions 1555–*d.*; sheriff, 1560–1.[2]

William Skeffington was a grandson of Sir William Skeffington*. His father had married an heiress who predeceased him, and had also purchased from the 1st Earl of Rutland seven messuages in Skeffington, so that William Skeffington succeeded to a much augmented estate. He continued the consolidation of the family property, buying small pieces of land in Billesdon and Skeffington, and selling messuages in Foxton and Great Bowden. He also settled the long dispute in which his uncle and his father had engaged over property left to the uncle in Sir William Skeffington's will.[3]

Active in local administration, Skeffington was frequently called upon to act as trustee or supervisor for friends and relatives, and in 1551 he was granted the wardship of William Belgrave, one of his Leicestershire neighbours. His single appearance in the Commons, as junior knight of the shire, answered to his position as a man of medium estate. His ties of kinship with the Cave and Stanhope families were apparently not strong enough to procure his re-election in 1558 or under Elizabeth.[4]

Skeffington died on 22 Sept. 1571 leaving an estate sufficient to give his daughters handsome dowries and to provide for his younger son and his brother Francis, without encroaching on the main body of the property at Skeffington, which descended to his son Thomas. He also left various legacies to kin and servants, amounting in all to nearly £200. He was buried at Skeffington beside his wife.[5]

[1] Date of birth estimated from age at fa.'s i.p.m. E150/1145/9. *Trans. Leics. Arch. Soc.* xvi. 100–1; *Vis. Leics.* (Harl. Soc. ii), 10. [2] *CPR*, 1547–8, p. 85; 1553, p. 356; 1553–4, p. 21; 1554–5, p. 106; 1558–60, p. 60; 1560–3, p. 439. [3] C142/161/97; *Trans. Leics. Arch. Soc.* xvi. 124. [4] *CPR*, 1550–3, p. 54; *Quorndon Recs.* ed. Farnham, 259. [5] C142/161/97; PCC 15 Daper; *CPR*, 1569–72, p. 377.

S.M.T.

SKEFFINGTON, Sir William (by 1467–1535), of Skeffington and Groby, Leics.

LEICESTERSHIRE 1529*

b. by 1467, 1st s. of Thomas Skeffington of Skeffington by w. Mary. *m.* (1) Anne, da. of Sir Everard Digby† of Tilton, Leics. and Stoke Dry, Rutland, 3s. 2da.; (2) Anne, da. of Sir John Digby of Kettleby, Leics. 2s. 3da. *suc.* fa. by 1496. Kntd. May 1509/14.[1]

J.p. Leics. 1501–*d.*; commr. subsidy 1514, 1515; sheriff, Warws. and Leics. 1515–16, 1521–2; master of the ordnance 1515–34; ld. dep. [I] 1530–2, 1534–*d.*[2]

William Skeffington is first mentioned in two cases concerning landed rights in Skeffington and

Keythorp in 1488 and 1496. A supporter of the Greys, he was an executor of the will of the 1st Marquess of Dorset, who died in 1501. He may have served with Dorset in France, as he was to do with the 2nd Marquess, when he was given command of the ordnance. It was thus as an experienced artillery-man that he replaced Sir Sampson Norton as master of the ordnance in 1515. With the return of peace the work may have been at first less demanding, and by 1522 Skeffington had served twice as sheriff and had discharged various other local duties; but when in 1526 he testified in the dispute between Dorset and Sir Richard Sacheverell* he admitted that he had not been in his county for four years. As well as performing ceremonial duties he had served on various commissions relating to Calais and had spent most of his time either there or at the Tower, the two principal ordnance depots. In 1523 he had also been charged with supplying victuals to the army in the field, and his frequent voyages between Calais and London also made him a useful liaison officer. His admission to the Inner Temple in 1523 was evidently honorific.[3]

Skeffington was a natural choice for the knight-hood of the shire in 1529; to the local support of the Greys he could add the prestige of his position at court. As both these conditions had already been present in 1523, he may well have been returned to that Parliament (for which the names are lost) as was the case with his fellow-knight of 1529, Sir Richard Sacheverell. Skeffington's attendance in the Com-mons must, however, have been intermittent. In July 1529, shortly before the Parliament was sum-moned, he had been appointed deputy to the Duke of Richmond, newly created lieutenant of Ireland. As his patent was not issued until May 1530 and he did not reach Ireland until early in the following August, he could have been present for the first session in 1529, but he missed those of 1531-2 and although in England when the fifth and sixth ses-sions were held early in 1533 and 1534 he had left again for Ireland before the seventh opened in the following November. His death left a vacancy for the final session, but whether or by whom it was filled is not known unless it was by William Ashby (q.v.).[4]

Skeffington was to achieve great military, but little political, success in Ireland. The resentment of the 9th Earl of Kildare at his own supersession as lord deputy was not assuaged by Skeffington's adherence to the Grey family, into which Kildare had married; from the first he treated Skeffington as a subordinate and in 1532 he crossed to England and induced the King to renew his own patent. Skeffing-ton's convocation of an Irish Parliament in 1531 to strengthen the country's laws had come to nothing

in the face of Kildare's intransigence. When, after Kildare had overreached himself and re-entered the Tower, Skeffington was preferred to the 3rd Duke of Norfolk, with whom he was at odds, as the man to put down the ensuing Geraldine rebellion, it was with Cromwell's backing but also at the price of having to take several of Cromwell's servants with him as well as Lord Leonard Grey, another former associate turned enemy. Not surprisingly Skeffing-ton, now elderly and in uncertain health, was less than enthusiastic to be gone; he made the most of his difficulties in collecting troops, guns and supplies, and only a peremptory order from the King finally sent him across in October 1534. Once in the field, however, he again proved himself a vigorous and ruthless commander and in two campaigns he brought the rebels to submission. His success out-weighed the complaints brought against him, not-ably by his marshal Leonard Grey, and the King had resolved to maintain him as deputy when a second Irish winter overcame him. He died at Kilmainham on 31 Dec. 1535 and was buried in St. Patrick's cathedral.[5]

Skeffington died in debt, and it is likely that he had long been in financial difficulty. His salary as master of the ordnance was not large, even when augmented by an annuity of equal value. It was for debts to the crown that he gave bonds to Sir John Dauntesey* and Sir Brian Tuke in 1526, and later ones to Robert Amadas appear to relate to further debts. True, Skeffington was granted wardships and lands, including part of the 3rd Duke of Bucking-ham's estates, and Cromwell helped him to acquire further lands in Skeffington, but these were appar-ently insufficient to meet his outgoings. The result-ing situation helps to explain the repeated accusa-tions of covetousness levelled at him and the fre-quency of lawsuits over property in which he was involved. The number of claims for debt brought against his widow as his executrix may account for the stay of execution of the will (dated 1 June 1522) ordered by Cromwell; for her part she had great trouble in recovering outstanding dues from the crown, and was evidently frustrated and acrimoni-ous. Skeffington died possessed of considerable estates in the east midlands and Kent, and his arrangements for the endowment and marriage of his younger children appear to have been carried out.[6]

[1] Date of birth estimated from first reference. *Vis. Leics.* (Harl. Soc. ii), 7; St.Ch.1/1/7; *Arch. Cant.* x. 39-45; *LP Hen. VIII*, i. [2] *LP Hen. VIII*, ii, iv-vii; *Statutes*, iii. 115, 168. [3] KB 23/906, m. 252; G. F. Farnham, *Leics. Med. Peds.* 40.; *LP Hen. VIII*, i-iv; CP40/1016, r. 333; *Leics. Recs.* ed. Bateson, iii. 13; St.Ch.2/12/266. [4] R. Bagwell, *Ireland under the Tudors*, i. 153 seq.; Elton, *Reform and Reformation*, 207-8. [5] *LP Hen. VIII*, iii-x. [6] Ibid. ii, iii; C1/1060/27-32; St.Ch.2/21/222, 23/50, 55, 26/183; Req.2/3/244, 7/84; PCC 10 Dyngeley.

S.M.T.

SKINNER, James (by 1489-1558), of Reigate, Surr.

REIGATE 1542, 1554 (Nov.)

b. by 1489, 2nd s. of John Skinner† of Reigate by ?Catherine; bro. of John I*. *educ.* I. Temple, adm. 11 Feb. 1518. *m.* (1) by 1513, Catherine, da. of one Green; (2) Elizabeth (*d.* 1549), wid. of one Bacon; (3) Margaret, da. of Nicholas Saunders of Charlwood, wid. of John Poyntz* (*d.* 1544) of Alderley, Glos.; *d.s.p.*[1]

Under steward, Southwark priory, Surr. by 1535; j.p. Surr. 1538-41, 1543-7 or later, q. 1554-*d.*; commr. musters, Surr. 1539, 1544, benevolence, Surr. 1544/45, chantries, Surr., Suss. and Southwark 1546, Surr., Suss. and Chichester 1548, relief 1550, goods of churches and fraternities, Surr. 1553, conventicles, Surr. 1557; escheator, Surr. and Suss. 1547-8.[2]

James Skinner shares with his elder brother John Skinner I* the confusion as to their parentage arising from discrepancies between the family pedigrees, and the brothers themselves are usually indistinguishable in the records of the Inner Temple. When James Skinner was admitted there he was a married man in his late 20s—he had been associated with his father in a land transaction in 1510—and his maturity was recognized by his exemption from certain offices and from attendance in vacations; in July 1519 he was assigned a chamber with Baldwin Porter*. He remained a member of the inn, from time to time holding office, until at least January 1556, when his discharge 'from all duties now due' on payment of 33s. 4d. may have marked his retirement. Like his brother, Skinner held local office for religious houses: he was under steward to Sir Nicholas Carew* for Southwark priory, collected rents at Shalwood for Merton priory and had a life annuity of 40s. from Newark priory chargeable on the parish of Leigh.[3]

Skinner seems to have adhered to the Howard interest in Surrey. It was probably his connexion with Lord Edmund Howard which led Howard's rival Sir Matthew Browne to ask Cromwell to have him put off the commission within a year of his joining it in 1538. The elections to the Parliament of 1542 took place under the shadow of the disgrace of Catherine Howard, and the return for Reigate of two of the Skinner family, James and his nephew John II, is probably to be explained by its own standing in the borough rather than by Howard patronage— James Skinner may indeed have sat for Reigate in the previous Parliament, for which the names of the Members are lost—and he was not compromised by the episode unless his summons before the Privy Council in May 1542 and his temporary disappearance from the commission of the peace five months later were part of its aftermath. Restored to the

bench in 1543, during the years which followed he discharged a variety of local duties, collecting oxen and carts for the war in 1545, dealing with a Scottish suspect in 1546 and dissolving chantries and confiscating church goods under Edward VI. He may have been re-elected for Reigate to the Parliament of 1545, the names being again lost, but he was not to sit again until Mary's third Parliament. That was after he had helped Lord William Howard to arrest his Protestant neighbour (Sir) Thomas Cawarden (q.v.) at the time of the rebellion of his kinsman Sir Thomas Wyatt II* and had temporarily lodged Cawarden in his own house at Reigate. With Howard now wielding patronage in the borough, and with Skinner's new brother-in-law Sir Thomas Saunders serving as sheriff, it is not surprising that Skinner was re-elected in 1554. Nothing is known about Skinner's part in the work of the House.[4]

To the lands which he inherited, chiefly from his mother, Skinner made a number of additions, notably the rectory and advowson of Reigate, for which he paid £458 in cash in December 1552; it had once belonged to Southwark priory and yielded £20 a year. Himself childless, he settled most of his property on his great-nephew (and son-in-law) John Skinner†. He made his will on 28 July 1558 and died two days later; the will was proved on the following 7 Dec. It opens with a lengthy preamble on the transitoriness of the world and the evils of dying intestate. Skinner asked to be buried in Reigate church between his 'two hearty beloved wives Catherine and Elizabeth'. He left portions for his unmarried female relatives and sums of money to his nephews and the husbands of several step-daughters: each of the seven daughters of Thomas Ingler*, who had married Skinner's niece Catherine Cooper, were to receive £20 on the day of their marriage. Skinner appointed his wife sole executrix and his nephew John Skinner II* his overseer.[5]

[1] Date of birth estimated from first reference. *Vis. Surr.* (Harl. Soc. xliii), 59, 112; *Vis. Essex* (Harl. Soc. xiii), 270; Harl. 897, f. 140; *Surr. Feet of Fines* (Surr. Rec. Soc. xix), 78; *Surr. Arch. Colls.* xxxii. 69; Manning and Bray, *Surr.* 623; PCC 10 Welles. [2] *LP Hen. VIII*, xiii, xiv, xvi, xx, xxi; *CPR*, 1547-8, pp. 76, 90; 1548-9, p. 135. 1550-3, p. 459; 1553, pp. 316, 357; 1553-4, p. 24; *Surr. Arch. Colls*; xxiii. 50; xxiv. 15; Lansd. 2(10), f. 32; Guildford mus. Loseley 1074; *Val. Eccles.* ii. 50. [3] *Cal. I.T. Recs.* i. 47, 52, 56, 65, 96, 111, 122; *Surr. Feet of Fines*, 78; *Surr. Arch. Colls.* xxxii. 67; *LP Hen. VIII*, xv, xvii; St.Ch.2/24/29. [4] *LP Hen. VIII*, xiv, xvii, xviii, xxi; H. C. M. Lambert, *Banstead*, i. 623; A. Heales, *Recs. Merton Priory*, p. cxxv; W. Hooper, *Reigate*, 116; *HMC 7th Rep.* 603, 611; *Surr. Arch. Colls.* iv. 99, 107, 110-13, 119, 127, 129, 130, 133, 175. [5] *Surr. Feet of Fines*, 703; *LP Hen. VIII*, xxi; *CPR*, 1550-3, p. 312; *VCH Surr.* iii. 33, 225, 239; PCC 10 Welles, 22 Stevenson; E315/217, f. 177; C142/204/123(1); *Vis. Surr.* 112.

S.R.J.

SKINNER, John I (by 1486-?1543), of Reigate, Surr.

REIGATE 1529

b. by 1486, 1st s. of John Skinner† of Reigate by ?Catherine; bro. of James*. *educ.* I. Temple. *m.* c. 1510, Catherine (*d.* 1545), da. of one Barley, 3s. inc. John II*. *suc.* fa. 8 Mar. 1517.[1]

Clerk of the peace, Surr. 1507–22; commr. subsidy 1523, 1524, tenths of spiritualities 1535, musters 1539; j.p. 1524–*d.*; ?under steward, lordship of Banstead in 1533; steward, cts. of Tandridge priory by 1536; under steward, lands of Reigate priory by 1536.[2]

The parentage of John Skinner and his younger brother James is differently recorded in two pedigrees of the family, as is the identity of John Skinner's wife. According to the Visitation of 1623 their father was of Reigate and of Havering atte Bower (although his wife, born Jane Gainsford, is not shown as their mother), and John Skinner married Catherine, daughter of one Barley of Albury (perhaps a kinswoman of Henry Barley*), whereas the other pedigree, probably of the late 16th century, gives their mother's name as Catherine and adds that 'Barley of Clavering, Essex, married a daughter of Gainsford of Surrey and had issue . . . Dorothy, wife to John Skinner of Reigate in Surrey'. That John Skinner's wife was named Catherine seems to be established by the death of a widow of that name in 1545, but in default of evidence the identity of his mother cannot be determined.[3]

Skinner's career also gives rise to a problem of identification, as he shared his baptismal name with both his father and his son. It was in 1507 that he succeeded his father as clerk of the peace, an office which the elder man had held since 1488, but the John Skinner who served as a justice of the peace from 1505 to 1517 was the father, not the son: the one died on 8 Mar. 1517 and the other was first included on the commission in 1524. Less easy to disentangle is Skinner's career at the Inner Temple. Although there is no record of his entry he was presumably one of the two 'Skinners' fined in May 1520 for being out of commons and may also have been the 'Skinner the elder'—so called to distinguish him from either his brother or his son—who was chosen as butler in June 1530: but it seems impossible to say whether it was he or his brother who was fined in January 1521 for not keeping the Christmas vacation or who in the following November was among those ordered to 'keep their vacations of their entry to the masters' commons'.[4]

In 1523 Skinner was appointed a commissioner to collect the subsidy in Surrey and from this date he served regularly in local administration. It is not always clear whether he or his son held certain offices, but with one exception no evidence has been found of the son's occupying these, or being regranted them, after 1543. It was probably the father who was steward of the courts of Tandridge priory in 1536 and under steward of the courts of Reigate priory in the same year, both offices being granted for life. If it was also he who was described in a will of 1533 as under steward of the lordship of Banstead, his son must have succeeded him in that office, for there are three accounts by a John Skinner, deputy to (Sir) Ralph Sadler* as the King's bailiff of Banstead, dating from 1540, 1542 and 1546: the last two of these show that the charge included the manors of Nonsuch and Walton-on-the-Hill.[5]

Skinner doubtless owed his return for Reigate to the Parliament of 1529 both to his forbears' long connexion with its representation and to its patron the 3rd Duke of Norfolk; he may already have been under steward at Reigate to Lord Edmund Howard, the duke's brother. Of his part in the proceedings of the House nothing is known. He was probably re-elected in 1536 in accordance with the King's general request for the return of the previous Members, and may have sat again in 1539, when the names of the Reigate Members are lost. It was perhaps his own advancing years and the progress of his younger son's career at court which in 1542 led this son to take the seat in his stead.[6]

In 1536 Skinner's name appears on a list of Surrey gentlemen to whom it was apparently proposed to write in connexion with the northern rebellion: another list of names with numbers attached, probably indicating the size of retinues, also includes Skinner's followed by the figure five. From March to April 1539 he was busy as a commissioner for musters in the hundreds of Blackheath, Reigate and Wotton: the return for Reigate of 1 Apr. shows that he had six servants. In the following January he was among the Surrey gentlemen who assembled to greet Anne of Cleves as she passed through Blackheath. It may have been either he or his son who was instructed by the Council on 28 Sept. 1542 to help in inquiries into 'the conveyance away of the King's timber in Bristowe's charge' and who was a commissioner of oyer and terminer on the home circuit in January 1543. If one or other of these duties was laid on Skinner it was probably his last: in the absence of better evidence the note on one of the pedigrees that he died in 1543 is to be taken as correct, for he was marked 'mortuus' on a list drawn up in the following year of Surrey gentlemen expected to provide troops for France. If he made a will it has not been traced.[7]

[1] Date of birth estimated from first reference. *Vis. Surr.* (Harl Soc. xliii), 50, 59; Harl. 897, f. 140; *Surr. Arch. Colls.* xxxii. 67, 68, [2] E. Stephens, *Clerks of the Counties*, 165; *LP Hen. VIII*, iii–v, viii. xii–xiv, xvi–xviii, xx; H. C. M. Lambert, *Banstead*, i. 168; E371/300 m. 47. [3] *Vis. Surr.* 59; Harl. 897, f. 140; *Surr. Arch. Colls.* xxxii. 68. [4] Stephens, 165; J. E. Smith, *Parl. Rep. Surr.* 30–31; *LP Hen. VIII*, i, ii; *Surr. Arch. Colls.* xxxii. 67; *CPR, 1495–1509*, p. 660; E372/352 item Suss.; *Cal. I.T. Recs.* i. 52, 65, 96. [5] Lambert, i. 168; *HMC 7th*

Rep. 602, 603. ⁶ VCH Surr. iii. 233; Manning and Bray, Surr. i. 298. ⁷ LP Hen. VIII, xi, xiv, xvii, xix; Harl. 897, f. 140.

S.R.J.

SKINNER, John II (by 1509–71), of Reigate, Surr.

REIGATE 1542
SURREY 1555, 1558

b. by 1509, 1st s. of John Skinner I* of Reigate by Catherine, da. of one Barley. *m.* settlement 1530, Anne, da. of Thomas or Walter Newdigate, 1s. John† 5da. *suc.* fa. ?1543.[1]

Servant of Sir Anthony Browne* by 1540; clerk of the avery by 1541; under steward, lordship of Banstead, Surr. by 1546; commr. relief, Surr. 1550, musters 1557, conventicles 1557, subsidy 1563; j.p. 1554, q. by 1558/59–64; collector of loan 1557; clerk of the green cloth by 1564–*d.*; usher and crier, KB by *d.*[2]

Nothing is known for certain of John Skinner's upbringing and his early career is not easily disentangled from the last phase of his father's. He is unlikely to have been the Oxford graduate of 1521 but he could have spent some time at the Inner Temple. When first heard of at court in 1540 he was in the service of Sir Anthony Browne, master of the horse. Since that office had earlier been held by Sir Nicholas Carew*, a neighbour and friend of the Skinners, it may have been from Carew's service that Skinner passed to Browne's and so to the King's; Carew was one of the trustees named by the elder John Skinner when he gave Anne Newdigate a life interest in certain property on her marriage to his son.[3]

By the close of 1541 Skinner was clerk of the avery in the royal stables. He was so described when in December of that year the council attendant on the King recommended that he should be given charge of Lord William Howard's house at Reigate after Howard had been sent to the Tower for suspected complicity in Catherine Howard's treason; the Council's letter, written by (Sir) Ralph Sadler*, was signed by, among others, Sir Anthony Browne. At the parliamentary elections in Surrey which immediately followed, Browne was returned for the shire and Skinner for Reigate. Both may be thought to have had crown support, but Skinner's election, with his uncle James Skinner, also answered to the family's standing in the borough; his father had been returned for it in 1529 and probably since, and it was evidently thought prudent to identify the new Member by the addition of 'junior' to his name. He may have been re-elected to the next Parliament, for which the names of the Reigate Members are lost; he had probably succeeded to his patrimony in 1543, had accompanied the King to France in the follow-

ing year and had bought a house and lands in Reigate.[4]

Under Edward VI Skinner appears to have made little headway. The 30-year lease of all the attainted 3rd Duke of Norfolk's property in and near Reigate which he obtained in March 1547 did not secure him a seat in the Parliament of that year and his only local promotion was to the relief commission in 1550; the John Skinner named in October 1551 as one of the commissioners to reform the canon law was almost certainly a namesake, doubtless the registrar of the ecclesiastical commission of 1559. In July 1553 Skinner attended the funeral of Edward VI as second averer in the stable. The reign of Mary first brought him into prominence. His appointment to the Surrey bench followed, and perhaps rewarded, his steadfastness during the rebellion of his kinsman Sir Thomas Wyatt II*, when he and his uncle helped Lord William Howard to arrest Sir Thomas Cawarden*, and towards the close of the reign he was to be much in evidence in the county, especially as a collector of the loan of 1557; but his most notable achievement was to sit in the last two Marian Parliaments as second knight of the shire, even though this was made easier for him by the eclipse of Cawarden. As could be expected, he does not appear on the list of Members of the Parliament of 1555 who supported Sir Anthony Kingston in opposing one of the government's bills.[5]

Skinner conformed as readily under Elizabeth as he had under Mary. Retained on the commission of the peace, in which capacity he was adjudged 'indifferent' (that is, impartial) in 1564, he improved his standing in the royal household by his appointment as clerk of the green cloth. Although he did not sit in Parliament again, his son did so for Reigate. Skinner's lands in Reigate, all held of the manor there, included a house called Dodds; he also had property in Charlwood and Horley, and in 1565 he bought from Lord William Howard the manors of Billeshurst and Lingfield. By his will of 27 Aug. 1570 he asked to be buried in Reigate church near his grandfather John Skinner†, left his wife a life interest in Dodds and in her settled lands, made gifts to his married daughters, their husbands and his own servants, and provided an annuity for an unmarried daughter. He named his wife and his heir executors, and his overseers were his brother (the vicar of Reigate), his brother-in-law Richard Elyot and his cousin-by-marriage Thomas Ingler*. He died on 16 Nov. 1571 and the will was proved on 16 Feb. 1572.[6]

¹ Date of birth estimated from marriage. *Vis. Surr.* (Harl. Soc. xliii), 59; Harl. 897. ff. 41, 140, 141; PCC 6 Daper. ² *LP Hen. VIII*, xvi; *CPR*, 1553, p. 357; 1553–4, p. 24; 1560–3, p. 441; 1563–6, pp.

26, 184, 480; 1569–72, p. 375; 1572–5, p. 81; *APC*, iii. 382; Guildford mus. Loseley 1074; *HMC 7th Rep.* 602, 603, 613; H. C. M. Lambert, *Banstead*, i. 68. [3] Emden, *Biog. Reg. Univ. Oxf. 1501–40*, p. 518; *LP Hen. VIII*, xvi; Manning and Bray, *Surr.* i. 301; Lambert, ii. 148. [4] *LP Hen. VIII*, xvi, xix, xx; Lambert, i. 168; *VCH Surr.* iii. 233; *HMC 7th Rep.* 602; C219/18B/86v, 89. [5] *Surr. Feet of Fines* (Surr. Rec. Soc. xix), 458; *CPR*, 1550–3, p. 3; 1558–60, p. 119; E315/218, f. 23; Elton, *Tudor Constitution*, 224; LC2/4/1; *HMC 7th Rep.* 611, 613. [6] *Cam. Misc.* ix(3), 56–57; C142/204/123(1); *CPR*, 1563–6, p. 273; PCC 6 Daper; Harl. 897, f.140.

S.R.J.

SKINNER, Ralph (1513/14–63).

LEICESTER	1547
PENRYN	1553 (Oct.)
?PENRYN	1554 (Apr.) [1]
BOSSINEY	1555
WESTBURY	1559

b. 1513/14. *educ.* Winchester, adm. 1528; New Coll. Oxf. adm. 23 Dec. 1531, BA 1536, fellow 1531–8, MA by 1551. ?*m.* c. 1538, Elizabeth, da. of one Ellis, *s.p.* [2]

Lay rector, Broughton Astley, Leics. 1550–3; pro-warden, New Coll. 1551–3; warden, Sherburn hosp. Durham 7 Nov. 1559–*d.*; dean of Durham 1 Mar. 1560–*d.*; chancellor and receiver-gen. palatinate of Durham c. 1561; member, council in the north Jan. 1561–*d.*; commr. eccles. causes, province of York 1561; j.p.q. Yorks. (N. Riding) and diocese of Durham 1561–*d.*; rector, Sedgefield, co. Dur. 1562–*d.* [3]

Nothing is known of Ralph Skinner's parentage. He came to Winchester from Feltham, Middlesex, and went on to Oxford in the customary way. It is not known why he vacated his fellowship in 1538; he may already have been showing signs of the Protestantism which he later adopted and have resigned or been dismissed on that account by Bishop Gardiner, the college visitor, or he may have departed on marriage, for a Ralph Skinner appears in the augmentations records in 1540 as the husband of Elizabeth Ellis. [4]

It was probably about this time that Skinner came under the patronage of Henry Grey, 3rd Marquess of Dorset, who was interested in scholarship, and Dorset's influence is the most likely explanation of his first appearance in the Commons, where he sat for Leicester, a town with which he had no known personal tie. He presumably greeted with enthusiasm the progressively reformist legislation of that Parliament and during its lifetime he received preferment, being given in 1550—as a layman—the rectory of Broughton Astley and in the next year the office of pro-warden of New College, after Gardiner had been sent to the Tower. Of his role in the events of 1553 which led to the downfall of his patron, now Duke of Suffolk, nothing has been discovered; he did not sit in the Parliament of March 1553, which formed part of the prelude to those events, or seemingly find it prudent to sue out a pardon on Queen Mary's accession. The change of regime did, however, cost him both his rectory and his pro-warden-ship, which he resigned on Gardiner's restoration. [5]

Skinner's career under Mary is obscure save for his Membership of three of her Parliaments. In the first of these he was returned for Penryn, and almost certainly this result was repeated seven months later—he is known to have sat, and Penryn is one of the only two boroughs for which the names of the Members in this Parliament are unknown. He may have enjoyed the patronage of Ralph Couche I*, lessee of the borough of Penryn. In 1555 Skinner sat for another Cornish borough, Bossiney; here he is likely to have benefited by the patronage of Francis Russell*, 2nd Earl of Bedford, which was probably wielded at this time, while the earl was abroad, by Sir William Cecil.

Whatever uncertainty may attach to the means by which Skinner reached Westminster, the part he was to play there is more than ordinarily clear: he consistently opposed the Marian government. In the Parliament of October 1553 he was one of those who 'stood for the true religion', that is, against the initial measures towards reunion with Rome. In April 1554 he made a notable intervention in the debate on the bill declaring that the Queen enjoyed all the prerogatives of her masculine predecessors. Voicing the widespread suspicion in the Commons that the bill had a hidden meaning, he warned the House to look well to it, but despite his anxiety the measure was engrossed after the debate and passed and sent to the Lords the following day. Missing from the second Parliament to assemble that year, he returned in 1555 to be numbered among the 100 and more Members who, under the leadership of Sir Anthony Kingston, voted against another government bill. This was the limit of his parliamentary resistance, for he was not to sit in Parliament again until after Elizabeth's accession. [6]

Although Skinner appears to have confined his displays of opposition to the parliamentary forum, his persistence in them suggests that he enjoyed the protection of a magnate similarly aligned, who may also indeed have furnished his livelihood; but who this was remains a matter of speculation. With Elizabeth's accession, however, he could expect ampler provision, and it was soon forthcoming in the deanery of Durham, to which he was appointed on 20 Dec. 1560, having been ordained in the previous January. He did not long enjoy his preferment, for he died in January 1563 and was buried at Sedgefield, where he had become rector the year before. [7]

[1] G. Burnet, *Hist. Ref.* ii. 447–8. [2] Aged 14 on admission to Winchester. Emden, *Biog. Reg. Univ. Oxf. 1501–40*, p. 518; *LP Hen. VIII*, xvii. [3] Emden, 518; *CPR*, 1558–60, pp. 5, 390; 1560–3, pp. 61, 170–1, 341, 437; NRA 6229, no. 97; R. R. Reid, *King's Council in the North*, 494. [4] *LP Hen. VIII*, xvii. [5] Strype, *Annals*, ii(2), 497. [6] Bodl.

e Museo 17; Burnet, ii. 447–8; Guildford mus. Loseley 1331/2.
[7] Strype, *Grindal*, 73; *Parker*, i. 173; *CSP Dom.* 1547–80, p. 161;
CPR, 1560–3, pp. 341, 493; Le Neve, *Fasti*, ed. Hardy, iii. 299.

S.M.T.

SKINNER, Richard (by 1506–75), of Barnstaple, Devon.

BARNSTAPLE 1558

b. by 1506. *m.* Agnes (*d.* July 1567), 1s. 3da.[1]
    Mayor, Barnstaple 1537–8, 1550–1, alderman by
1546–*d.*[2]

As an ex-mayor Richard Skinner took precedence
over the current mayor, William Salusbury, when
they were elected for Barnstaple to the last Marian
Parliament; he had recently been named one of the
capital burgesses in the town's new charter. First
heard of as the lessee of the Luppingcote garden in
Barnstaple in 1526–7, he later took leases of several
properties from chantries within the parish church;
for the subsidy of 1540 he was assessed at 10s. It is
not known what was the nature of the variance
'betwixt the town and Richard Skinner' which in
1531–2 was referred to the recorder, Hugh Pollard.
Skinner was buried in Barnstaple church on 12 Aug.
1575.[3]

[1] Date of birth estimated from first reference. N. Devon Athenaeum,
Barnstaple, D. Drake ms 'MPs Barnstaple', 29. [2] J. B. Gribble,
Barnstaple, 200–1; T. Wainwright, *Barnstaple Recs.* i. 158; ii. 225.
[3] Wainwright, i. 190, 206; ii. 28, 32; *CPR*, 1548–9, p. 363; 1549–51,
p. 169; 1555–7, p. 391; E179/97/214; N. Devon Athenaeum, 1141;
1142; 3972, f. 50; D. Drake ms op. cit. 29.

A.D.K.H.

SKINNER, Walter (by 1515–54 or later), of Plympton, Devon and Dulverton, Som.

NEWPORT IUXTA LAUNCESTON 1545

b. by 1515. *m.* Dorothy, da. of Roger Elford[†] of
Sheepstor, Devon.[1]
    Messenger, Chancellor Audley by Feb. 1536, ct.
augmentations Apr. 1536.[2]

Walter Skinner, whose origins are obscure, was a
minor government employee. Presumably he owed
his appointment in augmentations by the King in
person to his first known master Thomas Audley,
with whom he had gained a reputation for conscientiousness in the performance of his duties:
Skinner's persistence was not always admired, for in
the summer of 1536 Cromwell was 'not half pleased'
with him because he had been 'so busy' on behalf of
the deputy of Calais, Viscount Lisle. It may have
been through Lisle and his Grenville wife, if not
Audley and his protégé John Grenville*, that
Skinner made the acquaintance of the marshal of
Calais, (Sir) Richard Grenville I*, with whom he
soon became closely associated. In 1537 Lisle's
factor told his master that Sir Richard Grenville
'did your errand to Walter Skinner who is very

much vexed'. It was Grenville for whom Skinner
appeared in the Exchequer in the spring of 1545 to
claim compensation for the loss of an office, and for
whom he acted in the purchase of woods formerly
belonging to Buckland abbey: after Grenville's
death he claimed that he had never been reimbursed
for his expenses in acquiring the Buckland woods,
but Grenville's executors answered that he had
never produced proof of these and that he had
always been accounted 'a subtle and crafty merchant'. When Skinner was elected to the last
Parliament of Henry VIII's reign Grenville's
nephew Richard was his fellow-Member and Grenville himself the returning officer; Skinner may have
had a link with the constituency as one Robert
Skinner occupied a house in Launceston during
1543–4. He utilized his post in augmentations to
acquire the lease of several rectories in Somerset. He
lived in south Devon after his marriage to Dorothy
Elford—her kinsman alleged that the marriage was
invalid since he already had a wife living in the
north of the county at Barnstaple—but by the time
he sued out a general pardon in May 1554 he had
settled in Somerset. No further trace of Skinner has
been found, and the date of his death is unknown.[3]

[1] Date of birth estimated from first reference. *Vis. Devon*, ed.
Vivian, 329; C1/1265/30. [2] *LP Hen. VIII*, x. [3] Ibid. x–xiii, xxi; W. C.
Richardson, *Ct. Augmentations*, 46 n. 45, 493; C1/1265/30, 1270/49–
50; Launceston mayor's accts. 1543–4; *DKR*, xxx. 190; *CPR*,
1553–4, p. 429.

J.J.G.

SKIPWITH, William (by 1487–1547), of South Ormsby, Lincs.

LINCOLNSHIRE ?1529*,[1] 1539[2]

b. by 1487, 1st s. of Sir John Skipwith of South
Ormsby by Catherine, da. of Sir Richard Fitzwilliam
of Aldwark, Yorks. *m.* (1) c.1505, Elizabeth (*d.*c.1515),
da. of Sir William Tyrwhitt* of Kettleby, Lincs., 1s.
Sir William*; (2) c.1517, Alice (*d.*29 June 1550), da.
and coh. of Sir Lionel Dymoke of Mareham-on-the-
Hill, Lincs., 4s. inc. Henry[†] 7da.; 1s. 1da. illegit. by
Agnes. *suc.* fa. 5 Jan. 1518. Kntd. 31 May 1533 / 26
June 1534.[3]
    J.p. Lincs. (Lindsey) 1520–*d.*; commr. subsidy,
Lincs. 1523, 1536, loan 1524, musters 1542, 1546,
contribution 1546; other commissions. 1530–*d.*;
sheriff, Lincs. 1526–7; servitor at coronation of Anne
Boleyn 1533.[4]

William Skipwith, a descendant of the 14th-
century judge Sir William de Skipwith, and the head
of a prosperous Lincolnshire family connected by
marriage with more important neighbours, was
active in the affairs of the county. During the rising
of 1536 he acted for the King, not without jeopardy
to his life. Taken prisoner at Louth by the insurgents, he yielded to pressure and signed the letters
expounding grievances to the King; but on the

advance of the Duke of Suffolk to put down the rebellion he managed to evade his captors on 14 Oct. and submitted to Suffolk five or six days later.[5]

The ennoblement, towards the end of 1529, of Sir John Hussey and Sir Gilbert Tailboys, the two knights of the shire for Lincolnshire in the Parliament of that year, had created two vacancies which were left unfilled until Cromwell intervened in 1532 or 1533. From a prepared list of three names Cromwell, perhaps after consultation with the King, chose Skipwith and his brother-in-law Sir Robert Tyrwhitt, against whose names he placed a circle, in preference to Robert Hussey, younger brother of Lord Hussey. Although there is no evidence that either Skipwith or Tyrwhitt was by-elected, Skipwith's knighthood, which may have been conferred during the sixth session early in 1534, would have suitably recognized his representation of the shire in Parliament. If he did join it in that or the previous year, he was doubtless re-elected to its successor in 1536, in accordance with the King's general request for the return of the previous Members. He was certainly chosen again in 1539, when he may be thought to have had a share in the Act (31 Hen. VIII, c. 16) for his daughter Margaret's jointure on her marriage to George, 2nd Lord Tailboys. It was during the second session of the same Parliament, on 10 June 1539, that the house and site of the suppressed abbey of Markby, Lincolnshire, from which he had earlier drawn a fee, were leased to Skipwith, the reversion being granted to the Duke of Suffolk: the £100 he was owing to the King three years later may have been arrears of payment for this lease.[6]

Skipwith died at Ormsby on 7 July 1547, apparently intestate.[7]

[1] *LP Hen. VIII*, vii. 56 citing SP1/82, ff. 59–62. [2] E159/319, brev. ret. Mich. r.[1–2]. [3] Date of birth estimated from age at fa.'s i.p.m., C142/33/21. *Lincs. Peds.* (Harl. Soc. lii), 889, 895; *Vis. Lincs.* ed. Metcalfe, 64; *Holles' Church Notes* (Lincoln Rec. Soc. i), 120; Mill Stephenson, *Mon. Brasses*, 280; C142/91/94; W. O. Massingberd, *Ormsby*, 94, 391; *LP Hen. VIII*, vi, vii; *Lincs. Wills, 1500–1600*, p. 16. [4] *LP Hen. VIII*, iii–viii, xi, xiv, xvi, xvii, xx, xxi. [5] *LP Hen. VIII*, iii, iv, xi. [6] SP1/82, ff. 59–62; *LP Hen. VIII*, xiv, xvii; *Lincs. Peds.* 895; *Vis. Lincs.* 40–41. [7] C142/87/26.

A.D.K.H.

SKIPWITH, Sir William (by 1510–86), of South Ormsby, Lincs.

LINCOLNSHIRE 1547

b. by 1510, 1st s. of Sir William Skipwith* of South Ormsby by Elizabeth, da. of Sir William Tyrwhitt* of Kettleby; half-bro. of Henry Skipwith†. *educ.* G. Inn, adm. 1527. *m.* by 1534, Elizabeth (bur. 7 Apr. 1573), da. of Sir Richard Page of Beechwood, Herts., 1s. 5da.; 1s. illegit. Edward† by Anne, da. of John Tothby of Tothby, Lincs. *suc.* fa. 7 July 1547. Kntd. 28 Sept. 1547.[1]

Gent. pens. 1540–47/49; feodary, duchy of Lancaster, Bolingbroke honor 1544–5; commr. relief, Lincs. 1550; other commissions, north midlands 1554–*d.*; sheriff, Lincs. 1552–3, 1563–4; j.p. Lincs. (Lindsey) 1554–72, q. 1573/74–*d.*[2]

William Skipwith began to take part in the affairs of his native county from about 1530, and the frequency with which his name appears from then onwards in local transactions and assignments calling for legal expertise suggests that his admission to Gray's Inn had not been a formality. Presumably it was with the help of his kinsmen the Tyrwhitts, and particularly of his father-in-law, that he obtained a post in the new royal guard of gentlemen pensioners. In this capacity he attended the funeral of Henry VIII and fought in the Scottish campaign of 1547, being knighted for his military service by the Protector Somerset. Skipwith's father had died during the summer of that year, so it was as head of the family that he was elected to the first Edwardian Parliament, together with his relative Sir Edward Dymoke. He might have been expected to support the Protector, but nothing has been discovered about his whereabouts during the *coup d'état* of 1549 and he seems to have commended himself to Somerset's successor the Duke of Northumberland, for in 1552 he was pricked sheriff. Two Parliaments were summoned during his year of office from which he was for that reason excluded. His role in the succession crisis of 1553 remains obscure, but he emerged from it unscathed. Mary appointed him to the Lincolnshire bench, and it was in the maintenance of order and the administration of his estates that the remaining 32 years of his life were to be mostly spent.[3]

Under Elizabeth, Skipwith enjoyed a second term as sheriff, but apparently he showed no desire for re-election to Parliament; this was not out of distaste for the Anglican settlement, for in 1564 he was noted as 'earnest in religion', that is to say, in the reformed faith. Following the rising of the northern earls he sued out a general pardon, but this was doubtless as a precaution rather than a necessity. He was living with his friend George Metham at Hanby when on 4 June 1584 he made his will providing for his children and appointing as executors George Metham and Andrew Gedney. He was not to die until 17 Oct. 1586, being buried at South Ormsby on the following day.[4]

[1] Date of birth estimated from age at fa.'s i.p.m., C142/87/26. *Lincs. Peds.* (Harl. Soc. lii), 889, 895; *Lit. Rems. Edw. VI*, 219; W. O. Massingberd, *Ormsby*, 102, 391. [2] Somerville, *Duchy*, i. 582; *The Gen.* n.s. xxx. 21; CPR, 1553 to 1569–72 passim; information from W. J. Tighe. [3] *Lincs. Wills, 1500–1600*, pp. 7, 15–16; *Lincs. Wills* (Lincoln Rec. Soc. xxiv), 45; LC2/2, f. 41v. [4] *Cam. Misc.* ix(3), 27; C67/49; 142/214/235; *Lincs. Wills, 1500–1600*, p. 112; Massingberd, 103.

A.D.K.H.

SLANNING, Nicholas (1523/24–83), of Plymouth, Devon.

PLYMOUTH 1558, 1559

b. 1523/24, 1st s. of Nicholas Slanning of Ley in Plympton St. Mary by Elizabeth, da. of Thomas Maynard of Sherford. *m.* by 1564, Margaret, da. of William Amadas, wid. of John Heath, 1da. *suc.* fa. 1560/68.[1]

Town clerk, Plymouth by 1546–50 or later, coroner by 1552, mayor 1564–5.[2]

Nicholas Slanning seems to have been meant to follow his father into the service of Plympton priory; in 1538 he joined his father as bailiff of its manor and grange at Plympton, but its dissolution put an end to this phase of his career. His appointment as town clerk of Plymouth in succession to James Horswell* doubtless owed something to the standing of both his father and his uncle John Slanning, a rising lawyer and local landowner. His marriage with a granddaughter of John Amadas* was to link Slanning with several leading families in the town, notably those of Buttockshide and Hawkins, and such ties would have reinforced his official claim to be one of its Members. Nothing is known of his part in the Commons. After his father's death he settled at Bickleigh, which his uncle John had bought, and it was there that he died on 8 Apr. 1583, four days after making his will.[3]

[1] Aged 59 at death according to MI, *Trans. Dev. Assoc.* xix. 454. *Vis. Devon*, ed. Colby, 2, 189; *Vis. Devon*, ed. Vivian, 687; C142/200/11(2). [2] Plymouth receivers' acct. bk. 1546–50; *CPR*, 1550–3, p. 435; 1558–60, p. 409; R. N. Worth, *Plymouth Recs.* 213. [3] *Devon Monastic Lands* (Devon and Cornw. Rec. Soc. n.s. i), passim; J. E. Kew, 'The land market in Devon' (Exeter Univ. Ph.D. thesis, 1967), 187; *Trans. Dev. Assoc.* xix. 452–4; E150/181/2; 179/99/321; NRA 4154, pp. 128, 157; Plymouth receivers' acct. bk. 1546–50; black bk. f. 297v; PCC 63 Noodes, 18 Rowe; *CPR*, 1558–60,pp. 75, 76, 242; C142/200/11(2); Mill Stephenson, *Mon. Brasses*, 89.

R.V.

SLEGGE, Edward (by 1494–?1558), of Cambridge.

CAMBRIDGE 1542[1]

b. by 1494, s. of one Slegge by Joan. *m.* Alice Cockerell of Suff., 2s. inc. Roger†.[2]

Treasurer, Cambridge 1521, bailiff 1524, coroner 1527, mayor 1528–9; j.p. 1537; commr. gaol delivery 1540, relief, Cambs. 1550; serjeant-at-arms 1535–c.1555.[3]

Edward Slegge must have been of gentle birth to achieve the office of serjeant-at-arms but nothing is known of him before his admission to the freedom of Cambridge in 1514–15 save that his mother's name was Joan. Shortly after he had attained his first municipal office, that of treasurer in 1521, he was appointed an executor of the will of John Bury*. If other leading townsmen held him in the same esteem at this time—although his performance of his duties as executor was to involve him in two chancery cases—he may have been chosen to represent the town in the Parliament of 1523 for which the names of the Cambridge Members are unknown.[4]

In 1529 Slegge made a vigorous effort as mayor to determine his successor and, when defeated in that attempt by Thomas Brakyn*, to control the ensuing parliamentary election by holding it without warning on the last day of his year of office. The ruse failed and the two men chosen a week later were Brakyn and his supporter in the earlier disturbances, Robert Chapman: Slegge and five aldermen of his party sued Brakyn in the Star Chamber, with unknown result, and Chapman was appointed to bring proceedings, which were however not sustained, against Slegge in the mayor's court. Brakyn and Slegge seem to have been reconciled.[5]

At the time of these disputes Slegge was also under sentence of excommunication by the vice-chancellor of the university, and although he never again achieved the mayoralty he often represented the town in its disputes with the university and with other towns. He was thus well qualified to serve Cambridge in Parliament. He is known only to have attended the last session of the Parliament of 1542, and since his receipt of 20s. on 19 Feb. 1544 'when he went up to London to the Parliament' and later of 22s. 'for his whole Parliament money' exactly matches, at the town's then customary rate of 1s. a day, attendance for the remainder of the session of 1544 with three days' travelling time, it is almost certain that he was returned at a by-election held after the opening of that session. Whom he replaced is not known: only Brakyn received wages for an earlier session and the town's return in 1542 is lost. Slegge is remembered today neither for his defence of his town's interest nor for his Membership but for his part in bringing the succession crisis of 1553 to an end when in Queen Mary's name he arrested the Duke of Northumberland on 22 July.[6]

In February 1550 Slegge obtained a crown lease for 21 years of land at Comberton, Cambridgeshire, which involved him in further quarrels and lawsuits. Three years later he joined with another man to buy ex-chantry lands in Cambridgeshire, Staffordshire and elsewhere for £1,539: the pair promptly resold the Staffordshire lands. His effort to purchase some freehold land leased to him near Cambridge was thwarted by one Robert Ray and led to the forfeiture of his lease in 1554 and a series of lawsuits, in one of which he was called 'a very froward perverse and malicious man following the most devilish counsel of his two sons'. The only indication found of the date of Slegge's death comes from a chancery suit of 1596, in which his grandson stated that he had died 'about the last year of the reign of Queen Mary'; he was perhaps a victim of the epidemic of that time.

No will has been found although he is said to have made at least two; one of these he entered 'in a book wherein he usually wrote his debts, receipts and reckonings', but it was the other, written on paper, which was pronounced valid in a court of wards action soon after his death.[7]

[1] C. H. Cooper, *Cambridge Annals*, i. 415. [2] Date of birth estimated from admission as freeman. C2/S13/58; St.Ch.4/2/19, 20. [3] Cooper, i. 306, 310, 325; F. Blomefield, *Coll. Cant.* 224; *LP Hen. VIII*, viii, xii, xiii, xv, xvi; *CPR*, 1553, p. 352; St.Ch.4/2/55. [4] Stowe 669, f. 1; *Cambridge Bor. Docs.* ed. Palmer, i. 46; C1/615/47-8, 819/32, 1382/26, 28; PCC 5 Bodfelde. [5] St.Ch.2/26/178. [6] Cooper, i. 331, 391, 415; C142/93/9; Downing Coll. Camb. Bowtell ms Liber Rationalis 1510-60, 1537-38 acct. 27-30, 1543-4 acct. 9; Stow, *Annales* (1631), 612; *Chron. Q. Jane and Q. Mary* (Cam. Soc. xlviii), 10n; Cooper, ii. 76n; C. Sturge, 'The life and times of John Dudley, Earl of Warwick and Duke of Northumberland' (London Univ. Ph.D. thesis, 1927), 245. It cannot have been the mayor, who had no right of entry or jurisdiction in King's College, who made the arrest as stated by the imperial ambassador, *CSP Span.* 1553, p. 112. [7] *CPR*, 1553, pp. 218-21, 343; *LP Hen. VIII*, xiii; St. Ch.2/17/34, 21/58; 3/3/40; 4/2/19, 20, 54-56; C1/1382/25-28; 2/S13/58; Req.2/24/26; Cambridge Guildhall reg. bk. 1539-82, ff. 166v, 167; Cooper, ii. 98.

D.F.C.

SMALLWOOD, Robert (by 1509-?59), of Westminster, Mdx.

WESTMINSTER 1545, 1553 (Oct.)

b. by 1509. *m.* (1) ?Margaret (*d.*1552), 1da.; (2) 14 Apr. 1554, Joan Henbury, 2s. 1da.[1]

Robert Smallwood's origin and parentage have not been traced. His surname, found in the parish registers of Winchcombe, Gloucestershire, was originally borne by John Winchcombe of Newbury who also sat in the Parliament of 1545, but no connexion has been established between Smallwood and this famous clothier or his son John*. Smallwood did, however, resemble the Winchcombes in his attainment of gentility: in his younger days he was a beer brewer, but from 1547 he was regularly styled gentleman, and although remaining a member of the London company until his death he had by then leased his implements, carts and horses to another brewer. His elder daughter married a knight's son and his widow took as her second husband Oliver St. John of Lambeth.[2]

A resident in Westminster since before 1530, when he leased from the abbey six tenements in Long Ditch, Smallwood was elected for the city, with John Russell II, to the Parliament of 1545, the first to which Westminster is known to have returned Members. At the next seven elections he helped to choose either the knights of the shire or the Members for the city or both, and at the third of them he was himself re-elected, this time with William Gyes. Of his part in the proceedings of the Commons all that is known is that he did not oppose the measures to restore Catholicism passed by Mary's first Parliament.[3]

Smallwood made his will on 11 Nov. 1558. He left a diamond and ruby ring to his married daughter and a 'table' (panel) carved with the King's arms to her father-in-law Sir William Norris*; his younger children were to receive £100 each on coming of age. He named his wife executrix and gave her all his landed property; his overseers included Nicholas Newdigate* and Richard Hodges*. Smallwood was buried in St. Margaret's Westminster on 8 Jan. 1559.[4]

[1] Date of birth estimated from first reference. *Reg. St. Margaret's Westminster*, ed. Burke, 15, 276, 391; PCC 35 Welles. [2] London consist. ct. 35 Wymesley; St.Ch.2/27/172; PCC 35 Welles, 27 Street; *Reg. St Margaret's Westminster*, 278. [3] Westminster abbey, reg. 2, f. 262v; C219/19/128, 20/79, 80, 21/98, 22/48, 23/85, 24/104 25/71. [4] PCC 35 Welles; *Reg. St. Margaret's Westminster*, 402.

H.M.

SMALLWOOD see also WINCHCOMBE

SMART, Richard (by 1507-60), of Ipswich, Suff.

IPSWICH 1545, 1555

b. by 1507. *m.* 1528, Catherine, wid. of William Shreve of Ipswich, 5s. inc. William† 2da.[1]

Treasurer, Ipswich 1537-9, 1549-50, claviger 1541-6, 1547-9, 1555-7, portman 1552-*d.*, bailiff 1547-8, 1551-2, 1558-9, j.p. 1547-8, 1551-3, 1554-5, 1557-60.[2]

Elected to the freedom of Ipswich in 1528, Richard Smart, draper, became one of its wealthiest residents. In 1545 he was assessed for the subsidy on £50 in goods and in 1550 on £80—the highest assessment in the town. At his death he owned three manors in north-east Essex and one in Suffolk, with extensive property in Ipswich.[3]

Smart's return to the Parliaments of 1545 and 1555 reflected his local standing. Although in June 1543 he had paid the borough £20 to be permanently exempted from the offices of bailiff and portman, he was at the time of his first election serving as claviger or keeper of the keys of the town chest. In September 1547 he agreed to serve as bailiff, and when he was chosen for the office a second time in 1551 he redeemed the £20 which he had earlier paid to avoid it. Whatever his personal views, he conformed to the prevailing policy over religion. In 1556, according to Foxe, he denounced the wife of a tailor for not attending church since the Queen's accession, and two years later at the burning of two Protestants he complied with the sheriff's order to shorten their prayers with the words, 'On, on, have done. Make an end. Nail them to the stake'. This persecuting zeal was to evaporate on Mary's death, for thereafter Smart (in Foxe's words) 'rendered his life in godly repentance, protesting that if God should suffer him to live, he would never be the man he had been before, what laws soever should come again'.[4]

Smart died on 25 Aug. 1560, six days after making his will. In addition to lands and plate he left some £355 in money. His wife was to receive a third part of his lands and tenements in Essex and Suffolk, £100 in money and much of her husband's silver, and his eldest son William two manors, one in Essex and one in Suffolk, together with a house in Ipswich and a share of the silver. From this bequest William was expected to provide 100 marks for each of his sisters, one of whom, Thomasine, was left an additional 100 marks. The remainder of Smart's lands were shared by his younger sons. His wife and two of the sons were named executors and the will was proved on 16 Oct. 1560.[5]

[1] Date of birth estimated from admission as freeman. *Suff. Rev.* i. 7; PCC 48 Mellershe; Ipswich ct. bk. 8, p. 246. [2] N. Bacon, *Annals. Ipswich*, 210, 212, 231–51 passim. [3] E179/181/299. [4] Bacon, 234; Foxe, *Acts and Mons.* viii. 223, 496. [5] PCC 48 Mellershe.

J.P.

SMART *see also* **HARVEY**

SMETHWICK, William (by 1515–55 or later)

PENRYN	1547[1]
GRAMPOUND	1553 (Oct.)
BLETCHINGLEY	1555

b. by 1515.[2]
 In royal household by 1536; sewer of the chamber to Queens Anne of Cleves, Catherine Howard and Catherine Parr, 1540–7.[3]

Although details of William Smethwick's political career are plentiful nothing has come to light about his parentage, early life, marriage (if he made one) or death. His name is not noted in the pedigree of the main branch of the Smethwick family seated in Cheshire nor in those of junior branches established in Hertfordshire and Staffordshire. He may have sprung from obscure west-country stock: in a papal grant of 1555 he was described as an esquire of the diocese of Bath, and from 1546 until 1567 a namesake was the incumbent of Berkley, Somerset. In 1548 one Joan Smethwick, widow, was paying 2s. a year for meadows in Marston, Somerset.[4]

The first glimpse of Smethwick comes in 1536 when he obtained a lease of the conventual buildings of the recently dissolved priory of Rosedale, Yorkshire. He was already the holder of a minor appointment in the Household, possibly 'on the Queen's side' for it was there that he was employed during the closing years of the King's reign. Catherine Parr survived her royal husband and it was presumably she who procured a place for Smethwick in the first Parliament of the new reign: Sir Thomas Arundell* was not only her chancellor but also receiver-general of the duchy of Cornwall, and doubtless she enlisted Arundell's aid to ensure Smethwick's return as senior Member for a recently enfranchised Cornish borough. In the spring of 1547 the Queen married Thomas Seymour, Baron Seymour of Sudeley, and although his hand cannot be discerned in Smethwick's election in the autumn the two men were evidently to come together, as is attested by the replies given by (Sir) William Sharington* on his arrest in 1549. When the second session of the Parliament opened on 24 Nov. 1548, Sharington recalled,

> As I was going thitherwards, I met with Smethwick who took me aside advising me friendly that I should not come to my Lady Elizabeth. I asked him but he said no more to me.

Soon afterwards Sharington saw Seymour:

> I told him I was warned by Smethwick that I should not come to my Lady Elizabeth, and thereupon I said unto him, 'Have you anything to do there? I take it that I am warned not to meddle in any such matter and no more I will.' Whereunto the admiral [Seymour] answered that he had nothing to do there, but said he, 'Why should not the King's daughter be married within the realm?'

Although Smethwick was clearly aware of Seymour's matrimonial ambitions following the death of Catherine Parr, he is not known to have been interrogated about Seymour or to have suffered for his dependence on the admiral: he remained a Member and his name appears on a list of the Commons for the last session of the Parliament. He is not known to have found a seat in the following Parliament, where his connexion with the Seymours would have made him unwelcome.[5]

Smethwick reappeared in Parliament at the accession of Mary. He sat for another Cornish constituency and probably owed his return to his colleague in the House on this occasion, Sir Thomas Smith, with whom he was on excellent terms. Unlike Smith he joined the Protestant opposition and after the dissolution of Parliament he became involved in Wyatt's rising. For this he was sent to the Tower on 7 Feb. 1554 and remained there until the following 23 June, when his transfer to the Fleet was ordered: while in the Tower he was questioned in the hope that he would turn Queen's evidence against Princess Elizabeth who was also a prisoner there. The date of his release is not known, but he did not stay in the Fleet for long, as he wrote to (Sir) John Thynne* on 8 Dec. that Elizabeth was well and might soon have her liberty. In 1555 Smethwick used the links which he had maintained with the Seymour family during its eclipse, and his other connexions at court, to obtain a seat in the Parliament of that year: he was a stranger to Bletchingley, where his name was inserted on the indenture in a different hand, but his religious convictions would have commended him to its patron, Sir Thomas Cawarden*. His fellow-Member John Vaughan I had been his contemporary in the Household and both men incurred displeasure by voting against a government bill.[6]

In 1555 Smethwick obtained a papal indulgence for himself and 'any five of his friends whom he should nominate (excepting regulars), such as were married and their children of both sexes': he named Sir Thomas Smith as one of the friends to be covered. No trace has been found of Smethwick later than 1555 nor of the rewards which he might have expected from Elizabeth after her accession: possibly he did not long survive his last appearance in the Commons and succumbed to the epidemic which marked the close of the reign.[7]

[1] Hatfield 207. [2] Date of birth estimated from first reference. [3] E179/69/47; 315/209, f. 9; *LP Hen. VIII*, xx; *The Gen.* n.s. xxx. 25. [4] *Vis. Cheshire* (Harl. Soc. xviii), 208; *Vis. Herts.* (Harl. Soc. xxii), 21; *Vis. London* (Harl. Soc. xvii), 247; *Som. Incumbents*, ed. Weaver, 24; *Som. Chantries* (Som. Rec. Soc. ii), 97; Strype, *Smith*, 47. [5] *Wilts. Arch. Mag.* xxvii. 163. [6] Bodl. e Museo 17; *Chron. Q. Jane and Q. Mary* (Cam. Soc. xlviii), 53, 71; *APC*, v. 46; Foxe, *Acts and Mons.* viii. 619; Bath mss, Thynne pprs. 2, ff. 214–15v.; C219/24/153; Guildford mus. Loseley 1331/2. [7] Strype, 47.

S.R.J.

SMITH, Bernard (by 1522–91), of Totnes, Devon.

TOTNES 1558

b. by 1522, s. of Walter Smith of Totnes. *m.* by 1547, at least 1da. *suc.* fa. 1555.[1]
Mayor, Totnes 1549–50, ?1565–6; escheator, Devon and Cornw. 1567–8.[2]

Bernard Smith claimed gentle birth but like his father he was brought up in trade. His seizure of a Spanish vessel and its cargo in 1545 led to the intervention of the Privy Council and an order to restore both to their owner. He partnered the brothers Christopher* and Richard Savery* in several business ventures but a quarrel resulted in his charging them in the Star Chamber under Elizabeth with assault and theft. His father bought Totnes priory and some of its lands at the Dissolution, and in 1544 conveyed these to trustees for his own and Smith's use. Smith made further purchases, and by exchanges and litigation, sometimes with the corporation of Totnes, he built up a sizeable estate which made his only surviving child an heiress much sought in marriage. His election to Mary's last Parliament was presumably as much in recognition of past service as a gesture of conciliation after the lawsuit following his cutting off of the water supply for the castle mills. Nothing is known about his part in the House but during the second session he had an agreement between himself and his brother-in-law John Petre II* enrolled in the common pleas. After the accession of Elizabeth he and George Yeo, the son of his fellow-Member, were engaged to

receive a deed from George, 10th Lord Zouche, presumably in connexion with the town's acquisition of the manor from Sir Richard Edgecombe*. Smith gradually withdrew from municipal affairs, perhaps because his responsibility in county matters increased. He died in Totnes on 16 July 1591 and was succeeded by his daughter Eleanor, then married to John Wray. If he made a will it has not been found.[3]

[1] Date of birth estimated from first reference, 1543, *LP Hen. VIII*, xviii. *Vis. Devon*, ed. Colby, 48; C142/236/59; Pevsner, *S. Devon*, 297. [2] *Western Antiq.* ix. 150; *Trans. Dev. Assoc.* xii. 326. [3] *LP Hen. VIII*, xviii–xx; *APC*, ii. 250; J. C. Roberts, 'Parl. rep. Devon and Dorset, 1559–1601' (London Univ. M.A. thesis, 1958), 218; L. S. Snell, *Suppression of Rel. Foundations in Devon and Cornw.* 155, 156, 164; *Trans. Dev. Assoc.* xii. 326; P. Russell, *Totnes*, 47, 48, 58–59; Devon RO, 1579/25, A1; Totnes deeds; *CPR*, 1547–8, p. 288; 1558–60, p. 202; C142/236/59.

A.D.K.H.

SMITH, Christopher (by 1510–89), of London and Annables, Herts.

SALTASH   1547[1]
BRIDPORT   1553 (Oct.)
ST. ALBANS   1559

b. by 1510, yr. s. of Robert Smith of Waltham, Lincs. by Eleanor, da. and coh. of William Lilbourne of Fenby, Lincs. *m.* c.1540, Margaret, da. of John Hyde of Aldbury, Herts., 2s. 4da.[2]
?Servant of Henry, Marquess of Exeter in 1532; clerk of the Exchequer by 1545, of the pipe by 1551–*d.*; j.p. Herts. 1562–*d.*[3]

Christopher Smith's father-in-law was clerk of the pipe in the Exchequer from the late 1520s until his death in 1545. Smith married his daughter about 1540, but he had probably known Hyde some years before this and could himself have been working in the Exchequer in the 1530s: he stood as surety to Hyde in an undated grant which has been assigned to 1531. He may have been the Christopher Smith, servant to the Marquess of Exeter, who was admitted to the freedom of London in 1532. Although Hyde's chief residence was in Hertfordshire he also had a house in Dorset, at Hyde near Bridport, and a connexion between Smith and this borough may be seen as early as 1545 when he delivered into Chancery the findings of the inquisition held at Bridport after the death of William Chard*.[4]

Smith used his alliance with the Hyde family to influence parliamentary elections at Bridport. He seems not to have thought at first of his own election there, but he probably had a hand in the return of Richard Watkins in 1545 and of Henry Gates in 1547. He himself was elected in 1547 by Saltash, a borough which had not hitherto returned Members. He had no ties with Saltash, but as a clerk in the Exchequer he presumably had the backing of Somerset as treasurer. Early in 1553 Smith and

Thomas Hyde (who as the son of John Hyde had inherited his father's property in Dorset) wrote to their 'very loving friend' John Alford*, one of the bailiffs of Bridport, on behalf of Peter Osborne† of the Exchequer, who was prepared to serve without wages. In the absence of a return for Bridport it is not known whether their nominee was chosen, but later in the same year Smith himself sat for the town. He was not to do so again, but in 1558 (when two outsiders were chosen at Bridport) he appears initially to have found himself a seat for Scarborough; his name was one of the two entered for that borough in the Crown Office list, although it was afterwards struck out and Richard Josselyn's inserted. Josselyn may have been adopted as a neighbour of Smith's kinsmen in Hertfordshire.[5]

Smith had bought the manor of Annables in that county in 1555. It became his chief residence and he seems to have given up his London house, bought from Sir Nicholas Lestrange* in 1548, to which he made no reference in his will. He may have passed it on to his elder son, who succeeded him as clerk of the pipe, an office which Smith in his old age probably exercised by deputy.[6]

[1] Hatfield 207. [2] Date of birth estimated from first reference. Cussans, *Herts.* Dacorum Hundred, 356. [3] City of London RO, Guildhall, rep. 8, f. 263; *LP Hen. VIII*, xx; *CPR*, 1548–9, pp. 8–9; 1560–3, p. 438; E405/117, m. 17. [4] *LP Hen. VIII*, xxi; C142/71/184. [5] *LP Hen. VIII*, xviii; PCC 36 Pynnyng; *HMC 6th Rep.* 497; C193/32/2; Wm. Salt Lib. SMS 264. [6] Cussans, 356; *CPR*, 1547–8, p. 279; PCC 60 Leicester.

H.M.

SMITH, Clement (by 1515–52), of Little Baddow and Rivenhall, Essex.

MALDON   1545, 1547

> *b.* by 1515, 2nd s. of Thomas Smith of Rivenhall by 2nd w. Isabel, da. and h. of William Foster of Little Baddow. *m.* Dorothy, da. of Sir John Seymour* of Wolf Hall, Wilts. 3s. 4da. Kntd. 22 Feb. 1547.[1]
> Lord treasurer's remembrancer in the Exchequer, Dec. 1539; j.p. Essex 1541–*d.*; commr. relief, Essex and household of Princess Mary 1550.[2]

The Smiths of Rivenhall, near Witham, were a county family of little distinction: the manor of Little Baddow, where Clement Smith for the most part lived, may have come through his mother, an heiress there. In 1513 Smith's elder brother John had become reversioner or assistant to Edmund Denny in the important office of lord treasurer's remembrancer in the Exchequer and in 1539, when he was probably already at work there, perhaps as his brother's subordinate, he obtained the reversion of the same office. He was admitted and took the oath on 2 Dec. in the presence of Cromwell as chancellor of the Exchequer: the office, which had to be exercised in person, carried a fee of £64 2s. a year. The provision in Smith's will that his sons

should be trained by 'auditors or other officers toward the laws' may reflect a hope that one of them might in turn hold it.[3]

It was probably several years before 1539 that Smith had married Sir John Seymour's youngest daughter, whose sister was to become Henry VIII's third Queen and whose eldest brother Duke of Somerset and Protector. The alliance was not to yield him much advantage beyond the knighthood which he received a few days after his nephew's coronation. He acquired a little property in Essex, in 1540 by leasing some of the forfeited lands of the 3rd Duke of Buckingham, and four years later by buying from the augmentations the mansion of Bourchiers and its appurtenances at Coggeshall, but the second of these at least cost him the full price, without any hint of favour. His lease of Bradwell manor from Queen Catherine Parr hints at a connexion which may have contributed more to his two elections at Maldon (a borough five miles away from Little Baddow) than his Seymour one, for the Queen's brother was a considerable landowner there and one of Smith's fellow-Members, Nicholas Throckmorton, was a servant of William Parr.[4]

That Smith was to profit so little from the Seymour ascendancy is to be ascribed, at least in part, to his lack of sympathy with the religious changes which accompanied it. A staunch Catholic, he was once reprimanded by Edward VI himself for hearing mass and in April 1550 he spent a few weeks in the Fleet for the same offence. A year earlier he had been in trouble on another score, this time for offending Somerset's rival and successor the Earl of Warwick. In April 1550 Smith was summoned before the Council to answer for his 'presumption and lewdness' in subscribing his name to a writ issued by the Exchequer against Warwick for a debt due to the crown. The writ had been issued as a matter of course by Smith in the process of collecting crown revenue, and there is no indication of his appearance in answer to the summons.[5]

Smith died on 26 Aug. 1552. His will is instinct with Catholic feeling, from its long preamble to its final prayer to God for forgiveness, if anything in it 'for lack of great knowledge and learning be contrary unto His will and word or unto the Church Catholic'. The greater part of it is concerned with arrangements for repaying Smith's debts and with provisions for the education and marriage of his younger children. He left nothing to his wife, 'which she or her friends might think an unkindness in me other than I would they should or than I mean or is true'; his explanation was that 'the King's Majesty hath given [her] fair lands which with the poor jointure and other such lands as I have put her in jointly with me for term of her life . . . and her dowry be double as much as all my lands manors and tenements'. Among the five executors Smith named his 'most especial friends' Robert Rochester* and John Ryther*. Although the will bears the date 13 July 1552 it must have been drawn up earlier, for one of the supervisors was the Duke of Somerset who had been executed in the previous January; the other was Smith's surviving brother-in-law Sir Henry Seymour*.[6]

Dorothy Smith was granted a pension of 100 marks a year towards her expenses in the maintenance of her niece, the Protector's daughter Lady Elizabeth Seymour. She did not long remain a widow, marrying Thomas Laventhorpe before November 1553. Smith's children stuck to Catholicism and one of his sons, Sir John Smith, won distinction as a soldier in the reign of Elizabeth.[7]

[1] Date of birth estimated from first reference, 1536, Essex Feet of Fines, iv. ed. Reaney and Fitch, 204. Vis. Essex (Harl. Soc. xiii), 173–4; PCC 28 Powell; Strype, Eccles. Memorials, ii(2), 327–8. [2] LP Hen. VIII, xiv, xvi, xvii, xx; CPR, 1547–8, pp. 76, 83; 1550–3, pp. 352, 363. [3] LP Hen. VIII, xiv; PCC 28 Powell; Elton, Tudor Rev. in Govt. 115; E405/205, 210. [4] LP Hen. VIII, xv, xix; Strype, ii(1), 451; E315/340, f. 6v. [5] W. K. Jordan, Edw. VI, ii. 253; Lit. Rems. Edw. VI, 310; APC, iii. 8. [6] PCC 28 Powell; J. E. Oxley, Ref. in Essex, 260. [7] CPR, 1553–4, p. 170; APC, iv. 362; DNB (Smith, Sir John).

D.F.C.

SMITH, Edmund (by 1508–36), of Cressing Temple, Essex.

HELSTON 1529

b. by 1508, 1st s. of Sir John Smith of Cressing Temple by 1st w. Anne, da. and h. of Edward Wood of London; half-bro. of Francis Smith*. m. by 1530, Barbara, da. and h. of Sir John Hampden of Theydon Mount, Essex, 1da.[1]
Esquire of the body by 1533.[2]

Edmund Smith probably owed his return to the Parliament of 1529 to the influence of his father, a prominent financial official who rose to be a baron of the Exchequer. Smith himself may have held a minor post in the Exchequer, for in September 1533 he obtained the reversion of the remembrancership there in succession to his father, but the few glimpses of him suggest that he was a minor, but favoured, servant at court. Evidently he was held in some regard, for Archbishop Cranmer sent him a buck in the summer of 1533.[3]

Smith made his will on 30 Mar. 1536, 12 days after his fellow-Member John Holdiche had died and two weeks before the King dissolved Parliament. He left all his property in Essex, Kent and London to his only daughter, who was then about six years old. He appointed his brothers Thomas and Edward his executors and ordered them to pay his debts. He died soon afterwards, the will being proved on the following 26 June. By that time the new Parliament, summoned for the early summer, had been in session for over two weeks, and as the King had asked that the previous Members should be returned again it is possible that before he died Smith was again chosen at Helston.[4]

[1] Presumed to be of age at election. Vis. Essex (Harl. Soc. xiii), 175, 459; Morant, Essex, ii. 156. [2] LP Hen. VIII, vi. [3] Ibid. vi. [4] PCC 33 Hogen; C1/1184/41.

J.J.G.

SMITH, Francis (by 1516–1605), of Ashby Folville, Leics. and Wootton Wawen, Warws.

TRURO 1545
STAFFORD 1553 (Mar.)

b. by 1516, 1st s. of Sir John Smith of Cressing Temple, Essex, by 2nd w. Agnes, da. and coh. of Sir William Harwell of Wootton Wawen; half-bro. of Edmund Smith*. m. (1) 15 Apr. 1537, Mary (d. 30 Mar. 1550), da. and h. of John Moreton of Ashby Folville, 1s.; (2) Elizabeth, da. of Sir Thomas Brudenell of Deene, Northants., s.p.[1]
Sec. to Walter Devereux, 1st Viscount Hereford by 1558; j.p. Leics. 1558/59–64, q. 1569–84/87; sheriff, Warws. and Leics. 1566–7.[2]

Francis Smith was a stranger to both the boroughs for which he served in the Commons. His return as senior Member for Truro to Henry VIII's last Parliament suggests that in 1545 he had the backing of the receiver-general of the duchy of Cornwall, Sir Thomas Arundell*, who supervised the elections in the south-west. Smith's father was a baron of the Exchequer whom Arundell may have wished to please, and his own business dealings with Lord John Grey, a kinsman of Arundell, could also have helped. By the beginning of 1553 both Arundell and Sir John Smith were dead, and Francis Smith evidently turned to his master Viscount Hereford and to the Giffard family of Chillington for a seat at Stafford in the Parliament summoned on the initiative of the Duke of Northumberland: Hereford's son William Devereux was returned on that occasion as one of the knights for the county. In 1558 Smith was to witness Hereford's will under which he received clothes and an annuity of 40s.[3]

After his first marriage Smith occupied his wife's house at Ashby Folville, but his mother's death in 1562 led him to settle at Wootton Wawen. At the accession of Elizabeth he was named to the Leicestershire bench, on which he remained until old age, despite having been reported in 1564 'an adversary of true religion'; he was even pricked sheriff of Warwickshire and Leicestershire in 1566, the last man to hold the joint office. By 1586 two of his fellow-justices could assure the Council that he was not a recusant, being 'a good and dutiful' subject who attended church regularly. In his will of 10 Jan. 1605 he asked to be buried in the church at Wootton 'before the place were I have usually sat'. After several bequests to his grandson and to his great-grandchildren, he left £1,000 to be divided between three granddaughters and the residue of his property to his only son George. He appointed his 'loving kinsmen' John Giffard* and Thomas Throckmorton II* overseers. Smith died on 3 Sept. 1605 and was buried on the same day at Wootton, where a fine tomb still marks his grave.[4]

¹ Date of birth estimated from marriage. *Vis. Essex* (Harl. Soc. xiii), 175–6; *Vis. Warws.* (Harl. Soc. xii), 71; W. Cooper, *Wootton Wawen*, 21; *CPR*, 1553, p. 377. [2] PCC 47 Noodes; *CPR*, 1563–6, p. 24; 1569–72, p. 226. [3] PCC 42 Alen; Morant, *Essex*, ii. 114; *VCH Staffs.* iv. 81; *VCH Warws.* iii. 197–8. [4] *LP Hen. VIII*, xii; *CPR*, 1558–60, p. 135; *VCH Warws.* iii. 197–8, 205; Cooper, 21–24; *Cam. Misc.* ix(3), 8; *CSP Dom.* 1581–90, p. 319; C142/293/70; Pevsner and Wedgwood, *Warws.* 481.

J.J.G.

SMITH, Hugh (by 1531–81), of Long Ashton, Som.

WAREHAM 1554 (Nov.)

b. by 1531, 1st s. of John Smith of Bristol, Glos. by Joan, da. of John Parr; bro. of Matthew*. *educ.* I. Temple, adm. 1550. *m.* 1556, Maud, da. and coh. of Hugh Biccombe of Crowcombe, Som., 1da. 2 other ch. *suc.* fa. 1 Sept. 1556.[1]

J.p. Som. 1573/74–8.[2]

Hugh Smith's father bought Long Ashton, three miles from Bristol, of Sir Thomas Arundell* in 1545, and it was as of Long Ashton *alias* of Bristol that the son sued out a general pardon at the accession of Elizabeth. Smith also inherited the manors of Ashton-Meriet and Durleigh; in 1556 he and his mother, just widowed, bought the manor of Mark; and as part of his marriage settlement he obtained the manor of Broomfield. In May 1560 he and his wife were licensed to create a use in part of his property, the feoffees being Richard Michell*, Thomas Phelips*, John Popham* and Francis Stradling; if they had no son the beneficiary was to be Smith's brother Matthew.[3]

Smith was in his early twenties when he had his brief experience of Parliament. As his name was inserted over an erasure on the indenture for Wareham he was evidently not the townsmen's own choice. He had no personal link with the town, but his uncle by marriage Thomas Phelips had already sat for it at least twice, and when in the autumn of 1554 Phelips was elected for Melcombe Regis one of the Wareham seats was left free for Smith. Both he and his fellow-Member Roger Gerard joined Phelips in quitting the Parliament early without leave, and all three were informed against in the King's bench for doing so. In Smith's case a writ of *venire facias* was directed to the sheriff, but no further process is recorded.[4]

It is not known why in June 1556 Smith and his father were summoned before the Council, where they were 'to be remitted to the commissioners of examinations', but the reason may have been one of the son's outbursts of ill temper. By nature arrogant and given to violence, he had been put out of commons at the Inner Temple in 1552 for striking a barrister who had counselled the arrest of his brother for debt. Later in life, and more seriously, he was involved in a long drawn-out dispute with his neighbours in Somerset which culminated in his removal from the commission of the peace and his commitment for a few weeks to the Fleet.[5]

Smith made his will on 27 Feb. 1581 asking to be buried in Long Ashton church, 'where I have two children buried', and appointing as overseers John Popham and (Sir) William Wynter†. He died three days later leaving an only daughter, Elizabeth, married to Edward Morgan†, and Long Ashton went to his brother and heir Matthew Smith, whom he had named his executor.[6]

¹ Date of birth estimated from age at fa.'s i.p.m., C142/108/109, 110/173. Collinson, *Som.* i. 72; ii. 292. [2] *APC*, x. 292. [3] Collinson, i. 72, 79; ii. 292, 298; *CPR*, 1555–7, p. 246; 1558–60, pp. 154, 262–3. [4] C219/23/50; KB27/1176 rex roll 16. [5] *APC*, v. 290; viii. 387; x. 230–2, 243, 291–2, 361, 390–1; xi. 292; xii. 276; *Cal. I.T. Recs.* i. 165; SP12/132/48, 165/51. [6] PCC 9 Darcy; C142/193/87.

H.M.

SMITH, John I (by 1489–1561), of Newcastle-under-Lyme, Staffs.

NEWCASTLE-UNDER-LYME 1542

b. by 1489, s. of Richard Smith of Newcastle-under-Lyme. *m.* by 1516, Ellen, 3s. inc. John II* and Richard Smith II* 3da. *suc.* fa. 1518 or later.[1]

Churchwarden, St. Giles, Newcastle-under-Lyme in 1510; bailiff for commonalty 1519–20, for the Twenty-Four 1521–2, constable 1520–1, receiver 1522–3, mayor 1523–4, 1524–5, 1535–6, 1539–40, 1541–2, 1543–4, 1550–1.[2]

John Smith, yeoman, was returned to the Parliament of 1542 with Henry Broke, with whom four years earlier he had leased the ex-Dominican friary at Newcastle. His identification with the townsman of that name is established by a second lease made in favour of Smith and his son Richard on 4 May 1540, for although in the new grant John Smith was erroneously called yeoman of the guard Richard Smith of Newcastle was to hold the friary after his father John's death in 1561. The date of the second lease suggests that Smith could have been a Member of the Parliament of 1539 then in session, for which the names of Newcastle's representatives are lost. As mayor in 1542 he returned himself to Parliament. Nothing is known about his part in the Commons, but his recollection of the experience may have led him to nominate his sons John and Richard for election after he himself had withdrawn from an active part in municipal affairs. His name appears after that of the mayor on the indentures for the town to the Parliaments of 1545 and April 1554.[3]

Smith followed his father Richard, who had been mayor four times, in the service of Newcastle. Nothing has come to light about his trade or profession unless his assessment at 40s. on lands and fees suggests legal knowledge or service to a local magnate. Either conjecture could be further supported by the designation esquire used by him on making his will, but this may only reflect his social aspirations after enlarging his modest inheritance: two of his sons and his descendants were to go a stage further by claiming gentle birth. By his will made on 8 Mar. 1561 and proved on 5 May following he asked to be buried in the Lady chapel in Newcastle church and left his daughter Catherine £50 and his wife Ellen a life interest in his lands with the consent of his son Richard whom he named co-executor with Ellen.[4]

¹ Date of birth estimated from first reference. *Wm. Salt Arch. Soc.* iii(2), 130; Lichfield consist. ct. wills 1561. ² T. Pape, *Newcastle-under-Lyme*, 8, 180–2, 186, 188, 191. William Sneyd was mayor in 1544–5 (C219/18C/107) and not Smith as listed in Pape, 188. J. C. Wedgwood, *Staffs. Parlty. Hist.* (Wm. Salt Arch. Soc.), i. 313 mistakenly gives Smith his son's mayoralty in 1555–6. ² *VCH Staffs.* iii. 272–3; *LP Hen. VIII*, xiv; C219/18C/107, 22/70. ⁴ Pape, 8, 38. E179/177/143; *LP Hen. VIII*, xiv; Lichfield consist. ct. wills 1561.

N.M.F.

SMITH, John II (by 1531–81/83), of Newcastle-under-Lyme, Staffs.

NEWCASTLE-UNDER-LYME 1553 (Mar.)

b. by 1531, 2nd s. of John Smith I* of Newcastle-under-Lyme by Ellen; bro. of Richard Smith II*. *m.* Margaret, da. of Ralph Pickman of Middlewich, Cheshire, 3s. *suc.* bro. 1581.[1]

Mayor, Newcastle-under-Lyme 1555–6; churchwarden, St. Giles, Newcastle-under-Lyme 1566–7.[2]

The ties between Newcastle-under-Lyme and the 1st Viscount Hereford, and the election of Hereford's son William Devereux for Staffordshire and of Hereford's secretary Francis Smith for Stafford, might suggest that John Smith owed his return to the viscount, but his kinship with the secretary, who was of Essex origin, is doubtful and on the indenture he is described as 'of Newcastle aforesaid, junior, gentleman'. His father and namesake who had sat for the town in the Parliament of 1542 was still alive, although no longer as active as before, and it was to distinguish between the pair that until his father's death in 1561 he was called junior; his later description of 'beyond water' seems to imply that he dwelt on the far side of the Castle Pool. His Membership preceded that of his elder brother Richard whom during his mayoralty in 1555 he was to return to Parliament. In the autumn of 1552 he had bought

the silver formerly used in the Lady chapel of the parish church for £3, but whether he agreed with the spoliation of the churches is not known: under Elizabeth his father was to ask for burial in that chapel and he himself was to be one of the churchwardens. In September 1561 he obtained confirmation of his arms from Garter King of Arms. Six years later he and his brother Thomas both enlarged their houses and in 1581 he succeeded Richard to the family property. He was dead by December 1583 when the heralds visiting Staffordshire allowed his son Ralph the use of a coat of arms different from that of 1561.[3]

¹ Date of birth estimated from first reference. *Wm. Salt Arch. Soc.* iii(2), 130. ² T. Pape, *Newcastle-under-Lyme*, 192, 196. ³ C219/20/112; Pape, 28, 42, 196, 197; *Grantees of Arms* (Harl. Soc. lxvi), 233–4.

N.M.F.

SMITH, Sir Lawrence (1515/16–82), of Chester and Hough, Cheshire.

CHESHIRE 1545, 1555
CHESTER 1558, 1559

b. 1515/16, 1st s. of Sir Thomas Smith of Chester by Catherine, da. of Sir Andrew Brereton of Brereton. *m.* (1) by 1546, Agnes, da. of Sir Thomas Foulshurst of Crewe, 3s.; (2) Jan. 1561, Jane, da. of Sir Peter Warburton of Arley, wid. of Sir William Brereton* of Brereton, 1 or 2da. *suc.* fa. 1538. Kntd. 11 May 1544.[1]

Mayor, Chester 1540–1, 1558–9, 1563–4, 1570–1, alderman 1544; j.p. Cheshire 1543–*d.*, q. by 1564; commr. benevolence, Chester 1544/45, musters, Cheshire 1545, 1569, 1570, relief, Cheshire and Chester 1550, goods of churches and fraternities, Chester 1553; sheriff, Cheshire 1551–2, 1566–7; commr. and dep. to council in marches of Wales 1553.[2]

Lawrence Smith may have been the goldsmith of that name mentioned in the Chester records in 1543. The son of a civic dignitary noted for his integrity and philanthropy, he was himself to offer to pave the Blackfriars at his own expense. His election as one of the first two knights known for Cheshire following its enfranchisement in 1543 he probably owed to his possession of two qualifications: his mother was a Brereton and he had gained a knighthood in the Earl of Hertford's Scottish campaign of 1544. Ten years later he was re-elected first knight of the shire to Mary's fourth Parliament and he then followed the lead of Sir Anthony Kingston by voting against one of the government's bills; he may have already taken the stand in religion which was to earn his bishop's approval in 1564. His Membership of the next two Parliaments as one of the citizens for Chester coincided with his mayoralty. In the first of them a bill limiting tanners to boroughs and market towns was committed to him on 29 Jan. 1558 after its second reading; he was also one of the Members of this Parliament whose names are marked with a circle on a copy of the Crown Office list, an annotation so far unexplained. Smith died on 23 Aug. 1582.[3]

[1] Aged 66 at death, Ormerod, *Cheshire*, iii. 503. PRO, Chester 3/67/113, 80/19; *Vis. Cheshire* (Harl. Soc. xviii), 209; (lix), 212; *Chetham Soc.* li. 21. [2] Chester RO, A/B/1/74v; M/L/5/3; Ormerod, i. 213; *Cheshire Sheaf* (ser. 1), ii. 184; Chester mayor's bk. 1541–5, f. 3; G. L. Fenwick, *Chester*, 534; *LP Hen. VIII*, xix, xx; *CPR*, 1547–8, p. 81; 1550–3, p. 397; 1553, pp. 360, 361, 416–17; SP11/5/6; B. Coward, 'Stanley fam. c.1385–1651' (Sheffield Univ. Ph.D. thesis, 1968), 201; *APC*, vii. 284. [3] Chester RO, A/B/1/185; *LP Hen. VIII*, xix; *HMC Bath*, iv. 59, 66, 70, 72; Guildford mus. Loseley 1331/2; *Cam. Misc.* ix(3), 73, 76; *CJ*, i. 48; Wm. Salt. Lib. SMS 264.

N.M.F.

SMITH, Matthew (by 1537–83), of the Middle Temple, London.

WAREHAM 1558

b. by 1537, 2nd s. of John Smith of Bristol, Glos. by Joan, da. of John Parr; bro. of Hugh*. *educ.* M. Temple. *m.* Jane, da. and coh. of Thomas Tewther of Ludlow, Salop., wid. of Bartholomew Skerne of Lincs., 1s. 1da. *suc.* bro. 2 Mar. 1581.[1]
Treasurer, M. Temple 1570–4.
J.p. Som. 1582–*d.*

Both Matthew Smith and his elder brother Hugh received a legal education, one at the Inner Temple, the other at the Middle Temple, the elder in preparation for the life of a country gentleman, Matthew as the start of his career as a lawyer. Matthew Smith was admitted in December 1551 to the chamber of John Mawdley II*, treasurer of the Middle Temple. He was never called to the bar, being specifically exempted in 1563, and was never a reader, but he undertook the treasurership in four consecutive years and eventually became one of the masters of the bench. It was as an aspiring man of the law that he was returned as senior Member for Wareham to the last Marian Parliament; he owed this single appearance in the House (as had his brother earlier) to his uncle Thomas Phelips who had sat for the borough on several previous occasions but who in 1558 procured his election at Poole, thus leaving a place vacant at Wareham for Smith.[2]

Smith was bequeathed a manor in Gloucestershire and a house in Bristol by his father in 1556. The lands which he bought himself all lay (except for a manor in the city of Gloucester) in Somerset. On the death of his brother he inherited Long Ashton and other manors in Somerset and in 1582 he became a justice of the peace there. He died on 10 June 1583. In his will, dated nine days earlier, he asked for burial in Long Ashton church, stipulating that 'no heralds be hired to be thereat' and that the funeral should not cost more than 200 marks. He provided generously for his wife, left his daughter £2,000, and offered the master of the wards £50 if the wardship of his young son and heir were given to his over-

seers, Roger Kemish, John Popham* and (Sir) William Wynter†.[3]

[1] Presumed to be of age at election. Collinson, *Som.* ii. 292–3. [2] *M.T. Recs.* i. 84–264 passim. [3] *CPR*, 1555–7, p. 412; 1560–3, p. 615; Collinson, ii. 81, 372, 422, 425, 441; C142/201/120; PCC 9 Butts.

H.M.

SMITH, Richard I (by 1453–1516), of London and Reading, Berks.

READING 1497, 1504, 1512[1]

b. by 1453. *m.* by 1509, Agnes, wid. of Henry Justice; 1s. illegit.[2]
Member of guild, Reading 1474, guardian of the old ward 1476, tax assessor, London ward 1481, cofferer 1487; yeoman of the robes by 1486–*d.*; bailiff, manor of Caversham, Berks. 1493, jt. (with Richard Justice*) 1510–15; bailiff, Swallowfield, Berks. 1509–*d.*; steward, lordship of Caversham 1509–*d.*; customer, Calais 25 June 1509, jt. customer 1513–*d.*[3]

It is not known whether Richard Smith was born at Reading but he was an active member of the merchants' guild there before he rose in the King's service and he played some part in municipal affairs until his death. Five out of the nine Reading Members between 1478 and 1504 had been royal servants, although not necessarily strangers to the town, but under Henry VIII, apart from Smith himself, only Nicholas Hyde and Smith's stepson Richard Justice were to continue this tradition.[4]

Richard Smith of Reading and London, gentleman or clothier, was pardoned with his wife Agnes on the accession of Henry VIII and was soon confirmed in his offices. In May 1509 he was named keeper and paler of the park and bailiff or collector of the Queen's lordship of Swallowfield for life, and steward of the lordship of Caversham, in place of Edmund Dudley†. He also appeared as a groom at Henry VII's funeral and a yeoman at the coronation before being appointed in June 1509 customer of Calais. Four years later he was regranted this office jointly with a fellow-yeoman, John Sharpe, while receiving with him two corrodies in Abingdon abbey previously held by Sharpe alone.[5]

There is no sign in the corporation diary that Smith held office in Reading after 1487, although he has been described as mayor in 1504–5. His duties elsewhere can have left him little time for his home town but in 1510 he is twice listed as a townsman, first as one who paid 40s. towards a renewal of its charters—this being twice as much as anyone else, even the wealthy William Justice†—and then as a 'generosus'. He sat in the Parliament of 1512 as junior Member with another gentleman, William Gifford, but is not on the list of townsmen who in the following year contributed to the cost of the French war. It was as a yeoman of the robes that he was paid in March 1514 for going to Tournai. As Swallowfield is only six miles from Reading, and Caversham, across the river, still nearer, his royal service may sometimes have taken him home. He is marked 'mortuus' on a corporation list of 1514 but this must have been a later entry, as it was in the case of John Pownsar†, for he was still active as a wardrobe official in May 1516.[6]

In his will dated 18 July 1515 and proved on 15 Aug. 1516 Smith's many pious bequests included sums for the repair of all three parish churches in Reading, as well as those at Caversham and Swallowfield. He asked to be buried in St. Lawrence's, Reading, and left to the mass of Jesus there three houses which he owned in the town: in 1505 he had helped Richard Cleche* and the corporation to secure royal approval for the endowment of this chantry and he now stipulated that the wardens should spend 20s. a year on his dirge and mass, on pain of forfeiting the property to the abbot of Abingdon. A fourth Reading house was left to Richard Justice, who was to pay £10 to the mass of Jesus, while another in London went to Richard Weston*. A bastard son Richard received £10 and some goods, while various unnamed godchildren and many friends or colleagues were remembered, including John Pownsar. Smith's wife, who was the principal legatee, and Thomas Justice, vicar of St. Lawrence's, her son by her previous marriage, were appointed executors, and the overseers included Thomas Englefield, the Speaker's son, and John Heron, treasurer of the chamber.[7]

[1] *Reading Recs.* i. 124. [2] Date of birth estimated from first reference. PCC 22 Holder. [3] *Reading Recs.* i. 69, 74, 79, 84; *CPR*, 1485–94, pp. 99, 421; *LP Hen. VIII*, i, ii. [4] *Reading MPs*, 31–34. [5] *LP Hen. VIII*, i, ii. [6] *HP*, ed. Wedgwood, 1439–1509 (Biogs.), 778; *Reading Recs.* i. 114, 116, 133; *LP Hen. VIII*, ii. [7] PCC 22 Holder; *CPR*, 1494–1509, pp. 351, 452; *LP Hen. VIII*, ii; C. E. Kerry, *St. Lawrence, Reading*, 46.

T.F.T.B.

SMITH, Richard II (by 1516–81), of Newcastle-under-Lyme, Staffs.

NEWCASTLE-UNDER-LYME　1554 (Nov.),[1] 1555

> *b.* by 1516, 1st s. of John Smith I* of Newcastle-under-Lyme by Ellen; bro. of John II*. *m.* Margaret, da. of John Dodde of Cloverley, Salop, *s.p. suc.* fa. 1561.[2]
> Bailiff for commonalty, Newcastle-under-Lyme 1537–8, church reeve 1538–9, mayor 1547–8, 1549–50, alderman by 1555.[3]

Richard Smith of Newcastle had several better-known namesakes elsewhere, but his identification with the Member for that borough in November 1554 is all but certain in view of Mary's request for the election of townsmen and entirely so a year later when it was Richard Smith 'alderman' who was returned. His fellow-Members were the brothers Sir Ralph and Sir Nicholas Bagnall, who took precedence over him on the returns as their family did over his in the town. If it is not surprising that Smith did not follow Sir Ralph Bagnall's solitary example in refusing the absolution pronounced by Cardinal Pole in November 1554, his omission from the list of those who withdrew prematurely from that Parliament may imply that it was not he, but Thomas Smith II, who was the 'Mr. Smythe' listed among Sir Anthony Kingston's followers in the next. In any case, he appears to have been a good churchman, serving as church reeve and obtaining in 1563 a pew in Newcastle church for his own use and that of future owners of his house called the 'Hart's Head'.[4]

In 1540 Smith shared with his father the grant from the crown of the ex-Dominican friary at Newcastle and 11 years later he obtained the reversion of the lease of the hospital of St. John the Baptist there. After the death of his father he bought Tunstall Court near Eccleshall in Staffordshire from John, 2nd Baron Sheffield and he was drawn into litigation over the ownership of several properties. His relations with his fellow-townsmen were not always cordial and in 1574 as joint lessee of the castle mills he brought an action against several of them for withdrawing their custom from the mills, but the frequency with which he was named executor or overseer in wills suggests that his reputation was unharmed. He was buried in Newcastle church on 22 May 1581 and was succeeded by his brother John.[5]

[1] Huntington Lib. Hastings mss Parl. pprs. [2] Date of birth estimated from first reference. *Wm. Salt Arch. Soc.* iii(2), 130; J. C. Wedgwood, *Staffs. Parl. Hist.* (Wm. Salt Arch. Soc.), i. 347. [3] T. Pape, *Newcastle-under-Lyme*, 9, 186–7, 190–1; C219/24/143. [4] Guildford mus. Loseley 1331/2; Pape, 42. [5] *LP Hen. VIII*, xvi; *VCH Staffs.* iii. 273, 289; viii. 8, 48; *Wm. Salt Arch. Soc.* 1931, p. 30; Wedgwood, 347.

A.D.K.H.

SMITH, Robert

CARLISLE　1545

Robert Smith's identity is uncertain. His return for Carlisle in 1545 with Catherine Parr's clerk of the council Hugh Aglionby suggests that he also owed his Membership to royal intervention. No Robert Smith has been traced in the Queen's household, but a man of that name was bailiff for some property belonging to Admiral Seymour after his marriage to the Queen. Either he or a namesake had acted as an attorney for the 4th Earl of Westmorland with the Queen's kinsman William Burgh in the purchase of some Yorkshire property in 1536, and the links between the Burghs and Lincolnshire create the presumption that he was the searcher of the port of Boston appointed in 1548. If the Member was not a dependant of the Queen, he may have been a nominee of Thomas Wharton I*, 1st Baron Wharton, to whom as warden of the west marches Carlisle was amenable. A Smith family of gentle descent lived at Kirkby Stephen in Westmorland, not far from Wharton's home, and Robert was a baptismal name favoured by the family: the exchequer official named an executor of the will of John Hasilwood* in 1544 seems to have come from this family, and it was perhaps he who as a resident of Bray in Berkshire in 1584 provided for his wife Margery and stepsons George and Richard Depuppe and remembered his Westmorland kin.

E163/12/17, nos. 37, 50, 54; 405/115, m. 6; *LP Hen. VIII*, xi, xiii; *CPR*, 1550–3, p. 321; PCC 6 Pynnyng, 41 Watson.

A.D.

SMITH, Roger (by 1522–62), of Morville, Salop.

BRIDGNORTH   1547, 1553 (Mar.)

b. by 1522, s. of Richard Smith of Morville by Mary Gery of Clive. *m.* Frances, da. of Richard Cresset of Upton Cressett, 3s. at least 2da.[1]

Sewer of the chamber by 1543; porter and keeper of prisoners, council in the marches of Wales Apr. 1543; bailiff, Bridgnorth 1545–6, 1548–9, 1551–2, coroner 1549–50; escheator, Salop. 1560–1.[2]

Morville is only three miles from Bridgnorth, but Roger Smith was the first of his family to make any mark in the borough records, and the Smith pedigree recorded at the visitation of 1623 goes back only to his father, of whom nothing more than his name is known. Roger Smith himself created the fortunes of his family. It is not clear whose patronage brought him office in the Household and, nearer home, in the council in the marches: the second office, combined with the steady acquisition of new lands in the neighbourhood, gave him an important position in Bridgnorth, where the council sometimes met and which its officials sometimes represented in Parliament.[3]

At the time of Smith's appointment the Porter's Lodge at Ludlow was said to be 'such a strait place of punishment as the common people termed it a hell', but it soon became 'no terror of punishment of the body but a gulf through fees to suck up a mean man'. Smith's own upward progress was certainly marked. In 1545 he was granted by John Dudley, Viscount Lisle the reversion of the cell or grange of Morville, once the property of Shrewsbury abbey and till 1558 occupied by the last abbot in lieu of a pension. In the same year he had the unusual experience of being chosen bailiff of Bridgnorth just after being admitted a freeman there: he was to hold the office twice more during the next reign. The standing thus acquired, and doubtless the support of the council, of which Dudley was for a time president and Sir Robert

Townshend, father-in-law of Ambrose Gilberd, Smith's fellow-Member in 1553, vice-president, resulted in his election to the Parliaments of 1547 and March 1553. His return on the second occasion, and his disappearance from the parliamentary ranks thereafter, alike imply his dependence on Dudley, then Duke of Northumberland, as does his appointment in August 1553, after the duke's overthrow, to a commission to deal with the misappropriation of some of the fallen magnate's forfeited goods.[4]

Smith's continued acquisition of church property in Bridgnorth alarmed the corporation. In 1550 he obtained a prebend in the royal free chapel of St. Mary Magdalen, in 1557 (Sir) John Perrot* granted him some lands of the hospital of St. James, and about the same time he bought the remainder of a lease of chantry lands in the town. In the third year of Elizabeth's reign it was alleged in the borough court that he 'prevented the town of the chantry of St. Leonard's', had 'gotten into his hands the hospital of St. James', and had occupied and forcibly held land belonging to the town: he was sentenced to 'have no benefit of his burgess-ship'. Despite further sanctions Smith kept the hospital, and the inquisition post mortem of his son George at the beginning of the next century shows property stretching right round the southern edge of the town and across the Severn to the hospital's important site on the east bank.[5]

Smith died on 25 June 1562. The wardship of George Smith, then aged 16, was granted to (Sir) Henry Sidney*, president of the council in the marches. A will dated the day of Smith's death and witnessed amongst others by William Acton*, his kinsman by marriage, provided that £80 should go to each of his two younger sons on their apprenticeship, and the house at Morville and one third of the lands to his wife Frances. She took three more husbands and the last, William Clench of Bridgnorth, another officer of the council in the marches, claimed the Morville property. The council supported Clench, but George Smith secured the protection of the Privy Council by proving the will a forgery, and there is a note to this effect, dated July 1584, in the margin of the probate register.[6]

Whether or not he began it, Morville Hall, an Elizabethan house, is a monument to Smith's success; it was built by the same craftsmen who worked upon the house of his wife's family at nearby Upton Cressett.[7]

[1] Date of birth estimated from first reference. *Vis. Salop* (Harl. Soc. xxix), 439; PCC 7 Chayre. [2] *LP Hen. VIII*, xviii; Bridgnorth ms 9(2), ff. 395, 557, 560–1, 565. [3] J. F. A. Mason, *Bridgnorth*, 17. [4] P. H. Williams, *Council in the Marches of Wales*, 169; *LP Hen. VIII*, xxi; *Trans. Salop Arch. Soc.* li. 7–9; *APC*, iv. 316. [5] *CPR*, 1548–9, p. 386: 1569–72, p. 471; *VCH Salop*, ii. 100n, 126; *Trans. Salop*

Arch. Soc. (ser. 4), viii. 56–57; li. 7–9; Bridgnorth ms 9(2), f. 437. [6] C142/135/10; *CPR*, 1560–3, p. 613 where 1563 is incorrectly given as Smith's date of death; PCC 7 Chayre; *Vis. Salop* (Harl. Soc. xxviii), 115; *APC*, xiv. 49–50. [7] Pevsner, *Salop*, 206.

A.H.

SMITH, Thomas I (1513–77), of Anderwyke, Bucks., and Hill Hall, Theydon Mount, Essex.

MARLBOROUGH	1547[1]
GRAMPOUND	1553 (Oct.)
LIVERPOOL	1559
ESSEX	1571, 1572*

b. 23 Dec. 1513, 2nd s. of John Smith (*d.* 1557) of Saffron Walden, Essex by Agnes, da. of one Charnock of Lancs. *educ.* Queens', Camb. 1526, fellow 1530, BA 1530, MA 1532, LlD and DCL 1542. *m.* (1) 15 Apr. 1548, Elizabeth (*d.*1552), da. of William Carkeke of London, *s.p.*; (2) 23 July 1554, Philippa (*d.*1578), da. of Henry Wilford of London, wid. of Sir John Hampden of Theydon Mount, *s.p.*; 1s. illegit. Kntd. Apr. 1549.[2]

King's scholar, Camb. 1532/33, reader in nat. philosophy and Greek, Camb. 1533–50, public orator 1533, regius prof. of civil law 1540; v.-pres., Queens'; v.-chancellor, Camb. 1543–4; chancellor, bp. of Ely Jan. 1545; sec. to Edward Seymour, Duke of Somerset 1547; clerk to the Privy Council Mar. 1547–Apr. 1548; provost of Eton 29 Dec. 1547–12 July 1554; sec. of state 17 Apr. 1548–Oct. 1549, 13 July 1572–*d.*; dean of Carlisle June 1548–54, 1559–*d.*; commr. heresy 1548, 1550, 1559, visit Eton and Cambridge 1548; envoy to Antwerp 1548, France 1550, 1562–6, 1567, 1571–2; j.p. Bucks., Essex 1558/59–*d.*; PC Mar. 1571–*d.*; chancellor, order of the Garter 1572; ld. privy seal by May 1573.

Thomas Smith was the precocious but sickly son of a small sheepfarmer. Although it is not known who introduced him to Cambridge, he would have had to leave after taking his master's degree but for the royal physician William Butts, who probably obtained King's scholarships both for him and John Cheke*. At Cambridge he won praise for his learning and for his command of language, but he also showed aptitude for more worldly affairs: he joined Cheke in attracting Henry VIII's notice with a dissertation on the King's marriage in 1539, successfully undertook a journey through France to Padua in 1540–2 with the aim of increasing his prestige, and as vice-chancellor proved himself a methodical administrator and a valuable advocate for the university. His inaugural lectures as professor were notably self-congratulatory and his first book, *De Recta et Emendata Linguae Graecae Pronuntiatione*, exaggerated his own share, at the expense of Cheke's, in introducing the new and controversial pronunciation of Greek. It was once thought that Smith had been ordained, but this was not the case: the provostship of Eton was conferred only after a royal command to the fellows to disregard the fact that he was a layman.

The rapidity of Smith's rise after he reached the court in February 1547 testifies to his ability and perhaps also to the reputation which he had already gained. He joined the Duke of Somerset's household at the same time as his pupil Cecil, and when another of his pupils, Roger Ascham, was helping Cheke to teach Edward VI. He was already receiving £40 a year as professor of civil law, a post which he continued to hold, as well as annuities of £50 as chancellor to the bishop of Ely and £36 from a benefice which he had acquired at Leverington in the Isle of Ely. In March 1547 he became a clerk to the Privy Council, with £40 a year and his diets, and he also acted as the master of Somerset's unofficial court of requests until succeeded by Cecil in June 1548. The deanery of Carlisle was burdened with a pension to its former holder, but the provostship of Eton brought him a further £50 a year, with allowances of some £200; the secretaryship of state, in which he succeeded Paget in April 1548, raised his income by a further £200 a year, with perquisites that added thousands. The wealth thus suddenly accruing called for swift investment. In October 1547 Smith paid £300 for the reversion of the manor and advowson of Yarlington, Somerset, and in the following year 200 marks for the lease of a house in Cannon Row, Westminster; the date of this second transaction, 3 May 1548, seems to connect it with the dowry of 1,000 marks which had been brought by his 19 year-old bride, the daughter of a London printer, whom he married on 15 Apr. of that year. Twelve months later, in nominal association with Henry Needham, Smith paid some £700 for the late royal free chapel in the church of All Saints, Derby, with other property there and tithes.[3]

Smith's long, if intermittent, career in the Commons began with his return as the senior Member for a Wiltshire borough: this he undoubtedly owed to the Protector Somerset, who presumably commended him to Queen Catherine Parr, lord of the borough. The indenture for Marlborough has not survived but Smith's is one of the two names of its representatives appearing on a list of Members revised in 1552 and there is no reason to doubt that he and Humphrey Moseley had served from the beginning of the Parliament: he was, indeed, afterwards to refer to an attack made upon him 'at the first Parliament', that is, during the first session, by Bartholomew Traheron*. As a confidant of Somerset, Smith was probably one of the government's leading spokesmen and managers during the first two sessions: his hand has been seen in more than one of the Acts then passed, notably the Act of Repeal, the Treasons Act and the Vagabonds Act (1 Edw. VI, cc. 6, 11, 12), he was entrusted with the draft of the first Prayer Book after it had been read, and bills were committed to him dealing with the leather trade and with schools. On his appointment as secretary of state he may have also attended in the Lords, even though he is not known to have received a writ of assistance. He took no significant part in the next session which opened soon after Somerset's fall and his own dismissal from the secretaryship, but during the last session the bill against bigamy was committed to him after its second reading.[4]

The eloquence which had won fame for Smith at Cambridge might have made him a powerful advocate of ecclesiastical and other changes in the Commons, but while interest and perhaps inclination had aligned him with reform he was impervious to any religious enthusiasm and so invited attacks from every quarter. In a letter of 1549 to the Duchess of Somerset he recalled the accusation of indifference made by Traheron, 'whom yet I never spoke unto of it, for I had rather by deeds convince such men than by words'; he had always, he maintained, taken his stand openly, 'in the university before all the learned men . . . in the Parliament before all the lords and commons, and yet now they will make me a neutral, which I never yet was, since I was born'. Even his frankness could give offence, as it did to conservative-minded bishops and Councillors when he concluded a discussion on the eucharist by saying that the communion bread 'could not be the true body, or else He must want His head or His legs.' In 1549 he incurred the reproaches of Bishop Ridley by proposing, as an absentee member of a commission to visit the university, that Clare and Trinity halls should become a college of civil law at Cambridge; Ridley's recall from the commission, at Smith's instigation, did not prevent Parliament from rejecting a bill to unite the two halls. Both his friendship with Gardiner and his lay pluralism made Smith suspect to Protestants, while his high-handed action in imprisoning Bishop Bonner of London without reference to Cranmer brought almost universal condemnation.

Indifference was not the only ground for complaint. Smith successfully urged a suspension of all trade with Antwerp until the privileges of the English merchants were restored, but his criticism of (Sir) William Damsell's* raising of loans there brought a rebuke from Paget. When complaints of his behaviour reached the Duchess of Somerset he first enlisted the help of (Sir) John Thynne* to refute his detractors, but then had to address himself personally to the duchess. He denied accusations of being haughty, 'a severe and extreme man' in litigation, 'a great purchaser' and 'a great chopper and

changer of lands', as well as a 'neutral' in religion. He supplied details of his income to rebut charges of his harshness as a landlord and his indulgence in speculation and corruption; he had joined the ducal household with £300 saved from his wages at Cambridge, and apart from Yarlington and the lands in Derby his only property was the house in Cannon Row, which was sublet to Paget, and one, yet to be paid for, in Philpot Lane where he himself lodged with a brother. Smith's presumably unsuccessful application through Thynne early in June 1549 for a vacant customership is an interesting commentary both on his financial position and on his notion of what was his due.[5]

Despite his well attested faults, Smith was a hard-working and efficient secretary of state. His duties ranged from the interrogation of Somerset's brother Admiral Seymour and (Sir) William Sharington* to the literary justification of the duke's Scottish policy in *An Epitome of the Title that the King's Majesty of England hath to the Sovereignty of Scotland*. It was after he had failed to convince the Protector of the necessity for monetary reform that he retired temporarily to Eton where he composed the 'Discourse of the Commonweal' in which the debased coinage was for the first time held responsible for rising prices and social unrest. He was summoned back to court in September 1549, only to share in his master's fall. On 5 Oct. he drew up a proclamation against 'the painted eloquence' of the duke's enemies, 'come up but late from the dunghill', and a few days later he sent the Earl of Warwick's party a defiant letter, which was also signed by Cranmer and Paget. After being arrested with Somerset at Windsor castle, Smith was sent to the Tower as one of the Protector's 'principal instruments and counsellors', and on 15 Oct. Nicholas Wotton replaced him as secretary of state.

Smith was saved from further punishment, including the loss of his chair, by Warwick's leniency. Released in February 1550 on giving a bond of £3,000 to be of good behaviour, he busied himself with his private comfort and non-political concerns. He paid over £400 in part exchange for four manors, on one of which Ankerwyke, near Eton, he built a house where he lived until after Mary's accession, devoting himself to the improved financial administration of Eton and to the life of a scholar and gentleman. He did not renew his ties with Somerset and so escaped implication in the duke's tragic end. Attempts to bind him to the new order early in 1551, when he was appointed a commissioner to examine offences against the Prayer Book, were rebuffed by his refusal to incriminate Gardiner, brought to trial for a sermon preached after Smith had tried to persuade him to conform. Although he was the most active member of the embassy to negotiate peace with France in 1551, Smith was given no further public employment by Somerset's supplanters.

His retirement spared Smith prosecution as an opponent of Mary but he was deprived as dean of Carlisle and provost of Eton. Bonner, restored to his see, hoped for vengeance and was probably cheated of it only by Gardiner, the new lord chancellor. It was probably Gardiner who secured Smith's return for Grampound with William Smethwick on 8 Sept. 1553, as well as the grant of a pension of £100 a year on 12 May 1554. (Smith did not join the Protestant opposition in the House on this occasion, although his name was for a short time mistakenly noted among those standing 'for the true religion'.) If, as has been suggested, it was Smith who about this time wrote the 'Memorandum for the Understanding of the Exchange' (alternatively ascribed to a later date and to different authorship, including Sir Thomas Gresham's), this treatise could be regarded as a service proffered to Gardiner, who was much concerned with the monetary problem: the attribution derives some colour from the fact that Smith is not known to have sat in Mary's second Parliament and could therefore have assumed, as does the writer of the 'Memorandum', that the sumptuary bill introduced in that Parliament became an Act, whereas it was in fact lost by the sudden dissolution of 5 May 1554. Assured of the chancellor's goodwill Smith welcomed John Taylor, the deposed bishop of Lincoln, at Ankerwyke, received the 16th Earl of Oxford's heir into his household and successfully answered accusations that as dean of Carlisle he had embezzled alms for the poor. Widowed in 1552, he married in July 1554 the daughter of another Londoner and thus acquired the extensive manor of Theydon Mount; in the following March he was granted a 30-year lease of the manor of Wyrardisbury, near Ankerwyke, as satisfaction for unpaid expenses on his French embassy.[6]

After his second marriage Smith left the imposing residence at Ankerwyke for Hill Hall, one of two houses which he was to rebuild at Theydon Mount. He spent the last years of Mary's reign in outward conformity and in retirement: the first came easily to one of his secular outlook, but his renewed activity after 1558 shows how hard it must have been for him to turn his back on public life. His services to Elizabeth were rewarded in 1571 by a place on her Privy Council and in the following year he regained the secretaryship which he had lost nearly a quarter of a century before. He made his last appearance at a Council meeting early in 1576

and after a long illness he died at Hill Hall on 12 Aug. 1577.

[1] Hatfield 207. [2] This biography rests on M. Dewar, Sir Thomas Smith and J. G. Nichols, 'Some additions to the biographies of Sir John Cheke and Sir Thomas Smith', Archaeologia, xxxviii. 98–127. [3] Bath mss, Thynne pprs. 2, ff. 12–18v. [4] Hatfield 207; C. S. L. Davies, 'Slavery and Protector Somerset, The Vagrancy Act of 1547', EHR (ser. 2), xix. 533–49; W. J. Fitzgerald, 'Treason legislation in Eng. 1547–1603' (London Univ. M.A. thesis, 1963), 20, 40; CJ, i. 5–6, 21; M. L. Bush Govt. Pol. Somerset, 52. [5] Thynne pprs. 2, f. 74. [6] Bodl. e Museo 17; Econ. Hist. Rev. (ser. 2), xvi. 481–4, 486.

T.F.T.B.

SMITH, Thomas II (1522–91), of London, Ashford and Westenhanger, Kent.

?TAVISTOCK	1553 (Oct.)
AYLESBURY	1554 (Apr.)
RYE	1554 (Nov.)
WINCHELSEA	1555
PORTSMOUTH	1563

b. 1522, 2nd s. of John Smith of Corsham, Wilts. by Joan, da. of Robert Brouncker of Melksham, Wilts. *m.* c.1554, Alice, da. of Sir Andrew Judd of London and Tonbridge, Kent, 7s. inc. John†, Richard† and Thomas† 6da.[1]
Collector, tonnage and poundage, London 1558–69; j.p.q. Kent 1577–*d.*; treasurer for repair of Dover haven 1580; master, Haberdashers' Co. 1583.[2]

Thomas Smith, later known as Customer Smith, came from a yeoman family of Wiltshire. His father was a clothier and small landowner, most of whose property descended in 1538 to his eldest son John. The second son Thomas received only one farm in Amesbury hundred worth £20 a year and had his own way to make in life, probably after experience in the cloth trade at the family mill near Corsham. The dates of his settling in London and his admission to the livery of the Haberdashers' Company are not known. As a haberdasher he secured the favour of Sir Andrew Judd, a wealthy London merchant, whose daughter he married. In 1552 he contracted to deliver lead to Sir Thomas Gresham in the Netherlands, and three years later he was named among the Merchant Adventurers in their grant of privileges.[3]

With so common a surname the account of Smith's parliamentary career can only be tentative. He may well have been the man returned for the 1st Earl of Bedford's borough of Tavistock to Mary's first Parliament with Richard Wilbraham, a household officer equally strange to Tavistock. Both names appear to have been inserted by a different hand on the indenture. In the following spring Smith may more readily be identified as the gentleman returned for Aylesbury, a newly enfranchised borough in the patronage of Sir Thomas Pakington, son-in-law of Sir Thomas Kitson, who belonged to the merchant community of London and was likely to be well acquainted with Smith. The name Thomas Smith was originally omitted on the return for Rye in the autumn of 1554 and interlineated in a different hand. The first Member, John Holmes I, received parliamentary wages and the fact that the second was unpaid bears out the supposition that one nomination was made by Sir Thomas Cheyne*, lord warden of the Cinque Ports: Smith with a domicile at Westenhanger was presumably known to Cheyne who was keeper of the manor there belonging to the crown. The same influence probably accounted for Smith's election for Winchelsea to the Parliament of 1555, in which, in company with his fellow-Member John Peyton, he is likely to have voted against one of the government's bills, although the presence of his namesake the Member for Newcastle-under-Lyme leaves some doubt in the matter. It is also uncertain whether he was the Thomas Smith who sat for Wigan in 1558, but this is taken to have been Thomas Smith IV (q.v.).[4]

Smith's official career began when he succeeded Philip Cockram as collector of the petty custom in the port of London in July 1558, an office for which he is said to have paid a fine of £2,500. He pursued wide commercial interests, which included mineral works and a monopoly of the sale of alum in England, and was an original member of the Russia and Levant Companies. Although not all Smith's ventures were successful, he became a very rich man: his landed property alone consisted of 12 manors in Kent (partly of his wife's inheritance), London and Wiltshire.[5]

Smith died on 7 June 1591 and was buried in Ashford church. His grandson and namesake was created Viscount Strangford in 1628.[6]

[1] This biography rests on L. L. S. Lowe, 'Mr. Customer Smythe' (Oxf. Univ. B. Litt. thesis, 1950). *Arch. Cant.* xvii. 193; xx. 76; *Vis. Kent* (Harl. Soc. xlii), 113–14. [2] *CSP Dom.* 1547–80, p. 671. [3] E. Veale, *Eng. Fur Trade in Later Middle Ages*, 188; *Recs. Skinners of London* ed. Lambert, 183–4, 187; Beaven, *Aldermen*, ii. p. lv; *APC*, iv. 145–6; *CPR*, 1554–5, p. 57; PCC 58 Noodes, 54 Welles; T. S. Willan, *Muscovy Merchants of 1555*, p. 122. [4] *LP Hen. VIII*, vi, x; *APC*, ii. 85; iv. 361; v. 537; C219/21/46, 22/9, 23/184; Guildford mus. Loseley 1331/2. [5] *APC*, vi. 173, 369; *Arch. Cant.* xvii. 193. [6] C142/229/142.

M.K.D.

SMITH, Thomas III

CHIPPENHAM 1554 (Apr.)

This Member bore so common a name that his identity is uncertain. He and his equally obscure partner William Smith are known only from the Crown Office list in the absence of the original returns. Since neither is given any style or description, this Thomas Smith is unlikely to have been the former secretary of state, who had been knighted by Edward VI and who moreover is thought not to have attended Mary's second Parliament

even though he had sat in her first. Nor is there anything to associate Thomas Smith IV who sat for Wigan in 1558 with Chippenham. It is not even known whether the two Members for Chippenham were related. Neither paid taxes there, although a Philip Smith senior was assessed for subsidy on goods worth £80 in 1523 and shortly afterwards Christopher, John and Robert Smith paid smaller sums. Philip Smith is again recorded between 1534–35 and 1552, and John appears under Edward VI. They were perhaps related to the Smiths of nearby Corsham, among whom John, Philip and Robert were popular christian names. Smith's namesake who joined him in the House as one of the Members for Aylesbury was a cadet of this prolific family.[1]

Whether or not the Member belonged to the Smiths of Corsham, he may have been the testator whose will was proved on 24 May 1568 or one of two namesakes who died in 1576. The first, Thomas Smith of Knighton, in the parish of Chalke, was a man of moderate wealth, who left 100 marks to one daughter, £50 to another, a lease at 'Vyford' to his young son Thomas, and £100 to his widow; the four friends who acted as supervisors included George Penruddock and Charles Vaughan†, whose own families were prominent in the parliamentary history of Wiltshire, and Robert Grove*, a servant of the earls of Pembroke. The second was a resident of Tockenham Wick, a few miles to the east of Chippenham, whose largest bequest was one of £30 to an unmarried daughter; his sole connexion with Chippenham is the possession of land in the neighbourhood and there is no sign of a possible patron. The third was a gentleman of Mitcham, Surrey, who held much property in and around London and in Essex; he is the man most likely to have enjoyed official support, since by 1557 he was a clerk of the kitchen and in 1575, as a clerk of the green cloth, he acquired an interest in Wiltshire by leasing the manor of Monkton Farleigh.[2]

[1] *Econ. Hist. Rev.* (ser. 2), xvii. 481–2; E179/197/151, 155, 178, 209, 244a, 245; 198/256a, 265, 267; *Wilts. Vis. Peds.* (Harl. Soc. cv, cvi.), 32, 180–1; *Vis. Kent* (Harl. Soc. xlii), 113–14. [2] PCC 22, 32 Carew, 11 Babington; *CPR*, 1555–7, p. 360; 1557–8, p. 368; *VCH Wilts.* vii. 67.

T.F.T.B.

SMITH, Thomas IV (1525/26–94), of Blackmore, Essex.

WIGAN 1558

b. 1525/26, 1st s. of John Smith of Blackmore by Elizabeth, da. of William Trymnell of Orley Hall, Worcs. *m.* (1) one Colshill, 1s.; (2) settlement 28 Oct. 1562, Margaret, da. and h. of John Turner of Cressinghall, Essex, 3s. 3da. *suc.* fa. 1544.[1]

There is at least one among the many Thomas

Smiths of gentle status during the early 16th century who can be connected with the duchy of Lancaster. He was Thomas, son of John Smith of Blackmore, Essex, and nephew of (Sir) Clement Smith*. One of the 'most especial friends' whom Sir Clement appointed executors of his will dated 13 July 1552 was Robert Rochester*, later chancellor of the duchy. Rochester died in 1557 and was succeeded as chancellor by his nephew Sir Edward Waldegrave*, although the chancellorship was vacant at the time of the election for the Parliament of 1558. This identification of the Member for Wigan accords with the pattern by which a number of Essex gentlemen connected with Rochester, Waldegrave, or both, were returned for duchy boroughs during Mary's reign, and is thus to be preferred to the suggestion that it was a namesake who seems to have sat in all the previous Parliaments of the reign. It is even less likely, against this background, that the Member should have been, as has been suggested, of an obscure local family. Thomas Smith of Blackmore was presumably, like Sir Clement Smith, a Catholic, and his being so, while an advantage in 1558, might also account for his later obscurity.[2]

John Smith, who had been Cromwell's auditor, had property in Berkshire, Gloucestershire, London, Norfolk and Worcestershire, as well as in Essex, much of it held on lease. In his will of 10 May 1543 he provided that his children and wards should be 'brought up honestly and diligently at school till they and every of them shall have convenient learning in the Latin tongue and after that by the discretion of my executors to learn the laws of this realm or with some auditor or in some other offices toward the law whereby they may be the better able for to live honestly according unto the laws of God'. Thomas Smith's wardship, with an annuity of £20 out of lands in Blackmore and Ingatestone, was granted to the father of Sir Thomas Lovell II* in June 1546. Smith obtained livery of his inheritance a year later. Nothing has come to light about his part in the succession crisis of 1553 but in the autumn he sued out a general pardon as Thomas Smith of Blackmore, esquire. Apart from his sale of the Ingatestone property in 1565 to (Sir) William Petre* and an unsuccessful attempt to demolish the nave of the former priory church at Blackmore while building a new house on the site of the priory, it is difficult to disentangle his career from those of an indeterminate number of contemporaries of the same name. In 1592 Smith and his second wife witnessed the will of their son Thomas who predeceased them. Two years later he died and was buried in the priory church where a funeral monument with recumbent alabaster effigies was subsequently erected in the south chapel to the memory of him and his wife.[3]

[1] Under age in June 1546 but of age a year later. *Vis. Essex* (Harl. Soc. xiii), 173, 303, 487–8; *Vis. Worcs.* (Harl. Soc. xxvii), 137, although, according to this, Elizabeth Trymnell married Thomas Smith; PCC 21 Pynnyng. [2] PCC 28 Powell; J. B. Watson, 'Lancs. gentry 1529–58' (London Univ. M.A. thesis, 1959), 564. [3] PCC 21, 26 Pynnyng ptd. *Trans. Essex Arch Soc.* iii. 55–63; M. Dewar, *Sir Thomas Smith*, 2n; *LP Hen. VIII*, xvi, xxi; *CPR*, 1547–8, p. 142; 1553–4, p. 414; 1560–3, p. 404; 1563–6, pp. 265, 307; Arundel Castle ms G1/7; C. S. Simmons, *Priory Church of St. Lawrence, Blackmore*, unpag.; Pevsner, *Essex*, 89; *RCHM Essex*, ii. 17; Essex RO, D/AEW, 10/92.

A.D.

SMITH, William

NEWPORT IUXTA LAUNCESTON 1553 (Oct.)
CHIPPENHAM 1554 (Apr.)

This Member had so many namesakes that he cannot be identified. It is not even certain that the same man represented Newport iuxta Launceston and Chippenham, although this was probably the case, since the returns were made to successive Parliaments and no other borough is known to have elected a William Smith during the early Tudor period. Newport, which had been attached to the duchy of Cornwall after the surrender of Launceston priory, was accustomed to be represented by a mixture of local gentry, lawyers and officers of the duchy. Chippenham likewise had fallen under royal influence since the forfeiture of the manor and hundred by the Hungerford family in 1540, although the hundred had been acquired by (Sir) William Sharington* in June 1553. Both Chippenham and Newport iuxta Launceston often returned royal officials, but at both places a number of Members had local connexions.[1]

William Smith is described as a gentleman on the indenture for Newport, as is his fellow-Member John Gayer, a landowner whose estates lay at the farther end of Cornwall and who may have been elected through his connexion with the sheriff. Unlike Gayer, however, Smith was not listed among those Members who 'stood for the true religion' in Mary's first Parliament. He is given no style on the Crown Office list which records his return for Chippenham, where at least one townsman had been elected to Mary's first Parliament, and it is conceivable that he belonged to a neighbouring family of prosperous clothiers, the Smiths of Corsham. The same might be true of his fellow-Member, Thomas Smith III, but neither man has been identified as such and they are not known to have been related to each other. A William Smith was left 20 marks by the will (made in 1547) of an earlier Chippenham Member, William Button I.[2]

It therefore seems likely that William Smith was

a royal official who rose in favour under Mary and who held no property in either of the boroughs where he was elected. If so, he may have been the William Smith, esquire, whom Mary made a clerk of the Council in July 1553, in return for his services at Framlingham. Smith and Francis Allen*, who was similarly rewarded, received annuities of £50, which exceeded the previous wages of their office, and in October 1558 the former was also granted for life 'the office of clerk of Hell', otherwise called the clerkship of the treasure-house of the common pleas. Neither will nor inquisition survives for this man, which makes it even more difficult to distinguish his career from those of his many namesakes. In 1565 he obtained a lease of the Dorset manor of Gillingham and on 23 Dec. 1566, the last occasion when he is recorded as a clerk of the Council, he secured a lease of the rectory of St. Austell, his only known link with Cornwall. He was dead by 24 Feb. 1568, when his son William wrote in Latin to Cecil complaining that he had been left destitute and seeking admission as a Queen's scholar.[3]

It is uncertain whether the clerk of the Council can be identified with the younger of two William Smiths who were already landowners in Bedfordshire. A William Smith had served as a commissioner for the subsidy there in 1524 but it seems to have been a younger namesake who was recorded in the visitations as the first of a modest family of gentry in that county. Presumably it was the second William Smith who was a client or servant of Sir Richard Rich and who in 1534 was made a clerk of the writs in the Star Chamber. He bought monastic property in London for resale under Rich's auspices and by 1545 he was paying rent to Sir Francis Bryan* for the site of Woburn abbey, where he was living two years later. In 1547 he became a justice of the peace in Bedfordshire, where he was augmentations surveyor of crown lands under George Wright*, and by 1548 he was steward of Dunstable and Woburn; he was appointed escheator of Bedfordshire and Buckinghamshire in 1550 and joined the elder Smith in considerable purchases of chantry property which he had earlier helped to survey. In October 1550 he sold his interest in Clavering rectory to Henry Parker*. No Smith was living at Woburn in 1560 and the surveyor's office was granted to George Fish in the following year; Smith may have lived on elsewhere in the county, however, since his son and heir George, who continued the line, is described in the visitation as a resident of Biggleswade. No other children are recorded but this does not exclude the possibility that there was an impecunious younger son named William, who might have been Cecil's correspondent. If on the other hand William Smith

of Bedfordshire was not the clerk of the Council, his activities under Edward VI and the promotion of the clerk under Mary make it more likely that it was the latter who was returned to Parliament.[4]

[1] R. and O. B. Peter, *Launceston and Dunheved*, 35, 54–56; A. F. Robbins, *Launceston, Past and Present*, 96; *Chippenham Recs.* ed. Goldney, pp. xix, 295–7; *CPR*, 1553, p. 109. [2] *Wilts. Vis. Peds.* (Harl. Soc. cv, cvi), 180–1; PCC 49 Alen. [3] *CPR*, 1554–5, p. 189; 1557–8, p. 459; 1560–3, p. 340; 1566–9, p. 67; *APC*, iv. 419; vi. 419; Lansd. 10(14), ff. 77–78, 156(28), f. 103. [4] *LP Hen. VIII*, iv, v, xii, xiii, xviii; *Vis. Beds.* (Harl. Soc. xix), 139; *Trans. R. Hist. Soc.* (ser. 4), xvi. 147, 149–50; *CPR*, 1547–8, p. 81; 1548–9, pp. 137, 194–5; 1549–51, pp. 41, 229; 1550–3, p. 1; 1553, pp. 348, 351; 1560–3, p. 96.

T.F.T.B.

SMITH *alias* **DYER, John** (1498/99–1571), of Ipswich, Suff.

IPSWICH   1547, 1553 (Mar.), 1554 (Nov.)[1]

b. 1498/99. *m.* Jan. 1546, Catherine Coppyn, prob. a wid., 3s. 4da.[2]

Chamberlain, Ipswich 1541, member of the Twenty-Four 1543, constable 1545, bailiff 1546–7, 1551–2, 1557–8, 1560–1, 1566–7, j.p. 1546–9, 1551–3, 1557–62, 1564–5, 1566–70.[3]

Nothing has been discovered about the origins of John Smith *alias* Dyer, but his late appearance in the Ipswich records suggests that he was not a native of that town, although he could have been the merchant of Ipswich who was involved in two chancery suits relating to land between 1529 and 1538. For the subsidy of 1545 he was assessed on goods worth £40, showing him to have been among the wealthier townsmen; in 1568 his assessment was on £30. This local standing was reflected in Smith's return to three Parliaments between 1547 and 1554; early in 1553 he and Richard Bryde *alias* Byrde were elected despite a recommendation from Edward Grimston† in favour of a crown official, William Honing*. Smith also made journeys to London on the town's business. In 1562 he went with others at the request of (Sir) Nicholas Bacon* for proceedings in the 'compromise concerning Mr. Tooley's mortmain'. Five years later he was called upon to give evidence in a Star Chamber case between the corporation and Edmund Withypoll*.[4]

By a will made on 12 Sept. 1571 Smith left two houses in Ipswich, a mortgage on Elton Hall and a lease of Brook's Hall there to be divided between his wife and his sons, two named William, and John. He also made bequests to his sons-in-law John Blowers, John Coppyn (probably a stepson), Thomas Kennington and William Saunders and left books to his sons including 'Paraphrases upon the epistles of St. Paul', Bullinger 'upon the Apocalypse' and a bible 'of the Geneva translation'. 'Mr. Keyes, preacher' received a gown and money. The will was proved on 2 Oct. 1571 by the executors, Smith's sons William the elder and John. The latter may have been the John Smith lodging by the London Bridewell to whom Edward Dyer[†] (possibly a relative) wrote on 2 Aug. 1571 as 'my very friend' suggesting that he should come to court, the Earl of Leicester having recommended him to the Queen.[5]

[1] Huntington Lib. Hastings mss Parl. pprs. [2] Aged 68 in 1567. PCC 38 Holney, 16 Carew; Add. 37226, p. 194; N. Bacon, *Annals Ipswich*, 277n. [3] Bacon, 216, 221 et passim. [4] C1/667/9, 758/12; E179/181/270; *Suff. Green Bks.* xii. 166; Ipswich central lib. letters, accession 2672, no. 4; Bacon, 262, 277n; *Walthamstow Antiq. Soc.* xxxiv. 45. [5] PCC 38 Holney; Lansd. 13, ff. 117–18.

J.P.

SMITH see also GOLDSMITH

SMOTHYE, William (by 1516–57 or later), of Hereford.

HEREFORD 1554 (Nov.)

b. by 1516. *m.* by 1547, Joan, da. of John Hosier of Hereford.[1]
  Mayor, Hereford 1553–4.[2]

William Smothye was a merchant of Hereford who in 1551 was assessed for taxation in Bystreets ward on goods worth £16. In 1537 he shared the presentation to Catherine's hospital in Ledbury with Richard Warnecombe* and several other citizens. During the closing years of Henry VIII's reign he was sued in Chancery by his stepsons for withholding their inheritances. His Membership followed his mayoralty and satisfied Queen Mary's preference for townsmen, as well as perhaps for Catholics, and the fact that it did not comply with the request to Hereford from Bishop Heath, president of the council in the marches, to re-elect Thomas Havard and Thomas Bromwich, is to be explained by Havard's return as a knight of the shire; the two weeks which elapsed between that election and the city's would have sufficed to secure Heath's consent to the substitution of Smothye and Leonard Boldyng, both of whom were to conduct themselves to his and the government's satisfaction by not withdrawing from the Parliament without leave before its dissolution. In May 1555 Smothye testified against the vicar of St. Peter's church in Hereford for removing vestments and ornaments. Mentioned as the lessee of property in Hereford in August 1557, Smothye may have died before the 1st Earl of Pembroke visited the city later that year as he does not appear to have helped entertain the earl.[3]

[1] Date of birth estimated from first reference. C1/1133/51–52. [2] R. Johnson, *Anct. Customs, Hereford*, 233. [3] E179/117/219; Hereford cathedral muniments, chapter act. bk. 1512–66, f.80v; pub. lib., city muniments, bag 8, nos. 9, 12, 14, 15; C1/1133/51–52; *HMC 13th Rep. IV*, 318–19, 322; Johnson, 157, 159; *CPR, 1553*, p. 128; 1557–8, p. 135.

P.S.E.

SMYTHWYKE see SMETHWICK

SNELL, Nicholas (by 1515–77), of Kington St. Michael, Wilts.

CHIPPENHAM   1555
WILTSHIRE   1558
CHIPPENHAM   1559, 1563
MALMESBURY   1571, 1572*

b. by 1515, o.s. of Richard Snell of Kington St. Michael by Joan, da. of Nicholas Marsh of Easton. *m.* (1) by 1537, Alice, da. of John Pye of Rowdon, 3s. inc. John[†] 5da.; (2) Mary, da. of William Cleveood of Wilts., *s.p. suc.* fa. 1547.[1]
  ?Servant to abbot of Glastonbury by 1540; commr. relief, Wilts. 1550; j.p. 1554–58/59, q. 1561–*d.*; servant to earls of Pembroke by 1555–*d.*; sheriff, Wilts. 1566–7.[2]

Either Nicholas Snell or his father Richard, a yeoman of the crown, was in the service of the last abbot of Glastonbury. Possibly both men were, for in 1534 the father obtained the grant of a corrody in the abbey and six years later the son took a crown lease of the tithes of hay and corn of a rectory in Wiltshire belonging to it; the lease for 21 years at £10 a year was granted on the surrender of an earlier lease by the abbot, but it is not known whether Snell himself was the original lessee. In 1536 Snell and his father leased the manor or chantry of West Hatch and eight years later Snell purchased the manor of Kington St. Michael, formerly a grange of Glastonbury, from the crown for some £800. In the years following his father's death he added considerably to his lands in Wiltshire. His knowledge of the ex-monastic land in the county must have put him in a favourable position as a purchaser, and may also have been the first cause of his connexion with another buyer, William Herbert I*, 1st Earl of Pembroke, whose steward he became. According to the visitation of 1523 his first wife Alice was a daughter of George Pye of Oxford, but no such person has been traced, whereas John Pye of Rowdon was a Wiltshire gentleman of similar standing to the Snells and, like Richard Snell, a yeoman of the crown: 'Oxford' is probably a misreading for 'Hereford', the Pyes' native city[3].

Snell had recently been placed on the bench and was lessee of Chippenham hundred and a considerable landowner in Wiltshire when returned to Parliament for Chippenham, where his name was inserted on the indenture in a different hand. He was not one of the Members who opposed a government bill in 1555 but his name is one of those marked with a circle on a copy of the list of Members for 1558; the significance of this annotation has yet to be explained. Like his master Pembroke, Snell must have been adaptable in his religious views, to which his will of 20 Dec. 1576 furnishes no clue. He died on 31 Mar. 1577.[4]

[1] Date of birth estimated from first certain reference. *Wilts. Vis. Peds.* (Harl. Soc. cv, cvi), 183; *The Gen.* n.s. xii. 242; C142/179/99; PCC 27 Alen. [2] *Aubrey, Wilts. Topog. Colls.* ed. Jackson, 133; *CPR*, 1553, p. 359; 1553-4, p. 25; 1560-3, p. 443; 1563-6, pp. 28, 38, 39; 1569-72, p. 219; *CSP Dom. Add.* 1566-79, p. 455. [3] *LP Hen. VIII*, vii, xv, xix, xx; Wilts. RO, 473/12(58), 15(81), 41(228, 230); *CPR*, 1547-8, p. 53; 1551-3, p. 396; 1553, p. 415; 1553-4, pp. 288, 453; 1563-6, pp. 250-1; *Wilts. N. and Q.* ii. 305, 368; iii. 126, 373, 461, 558; iv. 120, 157, 213, 264, 266; *Wilts. Arch. Soc. recs. br.* x. 27; *Vis. Berks.* (Harl. Soc. lvi), 270. [4] C219/24/188; Wm. Salt. Lib. SMS 264; *Cam. Misc.* ix(3), 38; PCC 17 Daughtry; C142/179/99.

S.T.B.

SNEYD, Richard (by 1523-54/55), of the Inner Temple, London and Chester, Cheshire.

CHESTER 1547,[1] 1553 (Mar.), 1553 (Oct.), 1554 (Apr.), 1554 (Nov.).

b. by 1523, 2nd s. of Richard Sneyd of Bradwell, Wolstanton, Staffs. and Chester by Anne, da. of Sir Robert Foulshurst of Crewe, Cheshire. *educ.* I. Temple. *unm.*[2]

Auditor, I. Temple 1550.
Alderman, Chester in 1544, recorder by 1550-*d.*[3]

Richard Sneyd's family was of north Staffordshire origin and can be traced back to the 14th century. By purchase and by inheritance it had acquired a small estate in Cheshire which gave its members a position there, particularly in Chester, although its chief seat remained in Staffordshire. Sneyd's father spent £2,000 in buying property and by his death in 1537 he had doubled his inheritance. He had been recorder of Chester, an attorney to the council in the marches during Princess Mary's presidency and later the King's attorney in North Wales.[4]

Sneyd, too, was a lawyer and recorder of Chester. In 1541 he was fined 6s. 8d. for his part in an affray at the Inner Temple and five years later he was briefly suspended from its commons, almost certainly for owing money. It was during his elder brother's mayoralty that on 21 Apr. 1544 he was made a freeman of Chester, presumably as a step to becoming recorder. The first reference found to him in this office dates from 1550, but he had probably obtained it before being made an alderman six years earlier. If so, he may well have sat for Chester in the Parliament of 1545, for which the names of the city's Members are lost, and thus have helped in the passage of the Act for the amendment of the highways beside Chester (37 Hen. VIII, c. 37) in which both the city and his kinsman Sir Hugh Calverley (q.v.) were interested. His services were certainly called for in the Parliament of 1547, when several bills were introduced relating to Chester. Two of these failed but two were enacted, one for the taking of recognizances (2 and 3 Edw. VI, c. 31) and the other for removing weirs in the river Dee (3 and 4

Edw. VI, no. 26): a proviso for the city was also added to the Act for the relief of the poor (5 and 6 Edw. VI, c. 2). It is possible, but unlikely, that Sneyd was the 'Mr. Recorder' to whom the weirs bill was committed after its second reading on 5 Dec. 1549: as used in the Journal the term invariably connotes the recorder of London, and the holder of that office, Robert Broke, to whom many bills were committed, may have had an interest in this one arising from his Shropshire origin and connexions. Of Sneyd's attitude towards the larger issues raised in this and succeeding Parliaments there is only the negative evidence that he was not among those who 'stood for the true religion' in the first Marian Parliament and that he did not choose to absent himself from the third before its dissolution. He may, indeed, not have lived to witness this episode, for although the date of his death is unknown his successor as recorder, William Gerard II*, was made a freeman of Chester only six days after that Parliament was dissolved. It may thus be that Sneyd was unable to take action on the letter which had been sent to him and his fellow-Member Thomas Massey, after the Parliament opened, on the harm done by the incorporation of the merchant adventurers at Chester which had been recently secured by William Aldersey*.[5]

Sneyd died unmarried and seemingly intestate. The reference in a land sale of 1550 to Richard Sneyd of Chester and his wife Margaret is to a namesake, a kinsman and wealthy draper who by that time had been dead for over eight years.[6]

[1] Hatfield 207. [2] Date of birth estimated from admission as freeman. *Vis. Cheshire* (Harl. Soc. lix), 215. [3] Chester RO, mayor's bk. 1543-5, f.3; R. H. Morris, *Chester*, 204. [4] J. W. Blake, 'The Sneyds of Keele c. 1530-1949', *N. Staffs. Jnl. of Field Studies*, ii. 11-25. [5] *Cal. I.T. Recs.* i. 128, 141; *Freemen, Chester* (Lancs. and Cheshire Rec. Soc. li), 24; *CJ*, i. 1-4, 8, 9, 12, 13, 15; Chester RO, letters M.L. 5, no. 265. [6] *Students, I. Temple*, 9; *CPR*, 1549-51, p. 6; Morris, 543, 582; Chester RO, mayor's bk. 1541-3, f. 2; sheriff's bk. 7A, ff. 5, 7v, 135; J. Beck, *Tudor Cheshire*, 98; *Jnl. Chester and N. Wales Arch. and Hist. Soc.* n.s. xxxviii. 53, 54.

P.S.E.

SOMER, John (by 1484-1526), of Sandwich, Kent and Calais.

SANDWICH 1523[1]

b. by 1484, s. of one Somer of 'Hennyswell'. *m.* Alice, da. of one Haman or Harman of Crayford, Kent, 8da.[2]
Common councilman, Sandwich (St. Clement's parish) 1505-6, jurat 1506-*d.*, auditor 1510, 1519, mayor 1512-13, 1514-15, 1523-4, 1524-5, clerk of the market 1525-*d.*; bailiff to Yarmouth 1515.[3]

John Somer was one of the merchants of the staple pardoned in November 1505 for breaking trading regulations. He was admitted to the freedom of Sandwich 'by purchase' on 4 Dec. 1505, when his sureties included John Cock I*. A year later he was elected jurat. For refusing to accept office he was committed briefly to gaol but it was not until April 1508 that he submitted and was sworn in. Although his erratic attendance at council meetings led to his demotion being considered in 1511 he assured the town authorities that henceforth he would not be so lax, and not long afterwards he was chosen mayor for the first time. As mayor in 1513 he took part in the discussions about transporting the army to France. He was thrice re-elected mayor, on the last occasion being allowed to travel overseas if necessary and to appoint a deputy, and he frequently represented the town at the Brotherhood of the Cinque Ports at New Romney and the guestling at Dover. In 1520 he received 30s. for helping to convey the King to the meetings with Francis I and the Emperor. Five years later he administered the oath to the incoming lord warden Sir Edward Guildford* on behalf of the Cinque Ports.[4]

To judge from the town records Somer was an irascible man. In an argument on the quayside with John Westcliff* in 1516 he detained his opponent by force; in a fracas with James Hobard* two years later he hit Hobard and on drawing his knife was himself attacked and wounded by two of Hobard's sons; and in 1519 he provoked Vincent Engeham* into striking him with a knife. Despite these incidents and a series of disputes where violence seems to have been avoided Somer loomed large in Sandwich and its locality. His return to the Parliament of 1523 was an extension of his municipal career. He and his fellow-Member Roger Manwood I were instructed at their departure to report an escape from the Sandwich gaol to the King's bailiff for the town, Brian Tuke. After Tuke's replacement by Sir Edward Ryngeley* he acted as one of the town's spokesmen against Ryngeley and it was as a fund-raiser to take the new bailiff to law that he is last glimpsed on 8 Mar. 1526. By a will made on 16 Feb. 1522 and proved on 27 June 1526 he left money for masses to be said for his soul in St. Clement's church, Sandwich and for that of his father at 'Hennyswell'. He stipulated that his part in three ships and houses in Calais and elsewhere should be sold and the proceeds divided between his wife and children. He also remembered his brother-in-law Thomas Browne, several nieces and nephews and his 'gossip' Thomas Iden, whom he named executor with Browne. His widow married John Boys*.[5]

[1] Sandwich white bk. f. 315. [2] Date of birth estimated from first reference. PCC 8 Porch; *Vis. Kent* (Harl. Soc. xlii), 39; Berry, *Kent Peds.* 440–1. [3] Sandwich white bk. ff. 138–359v passim; *Cinque Ports White and Black Bks.* (Kent Arch. Soc. recs. br. xix), 157–201 passim; W. Boys, *Sandwich* (1792), 418. [4] *CPR*, 1494–1509, p. 448; Sandwich white bk. ff. 140v–323v passim; treasurers' accts. Sa/FA t. 20, 25; *Cinque Ports White and Black Bks.* 193. [5] Sandwich white bk. ff. 242, 261v–2, 268v, 315, 316v, 360v–1; PCC 8 Porch.

R.J.K.

SOMERSET, Francis (by 1532–63), of Chepstow, Mon. and London.

MONMOUTHSHIRE 1558

b. by 1532, 3rd s. of Henry Somerset, 2nd Earl of Worcester by 2nd w. Elizabeth, da. of Sir Anthony Browne; bro. of Charles† and Thomas*. *unm.* 1s. 1da. illegit.[1]

On 3 Jan. 1553 Francis Somerset obtained a pardon for burglary and other crimes and the restoration of the lands that he had forfeited in punishment. He was to make his name as a soldier and his Membership was an interlude in his career. His return to Mary's last Parliament was disputed by William Herbert IV who claimed that he and William Morgan had been re-elected. The attorney-general acted upon the information laid by Herbert, but the sheriff Henry Lewis failed to appear before the Exchequer to answer the allegation until Trinity term 1559. Because no jury travelled up with Lewis the case went on *nisi prius* to the Monmouthshire assizes, where the validity of Somerset's election was upheld, but since this verdict was not reached until eight months after the dissolution it merely confirmed the right to sit which he had probably exercised. In 1557 Somerset had served in France as a captain under his brother the 3rd Earl of Worcester and during the prorogation a year later he conducted 300 men from Guisnes to the Scottish border where his action in the field earned him Mary's thanks. His command was renewed by Elizabeth and it was during an attack upon Le Havre that he died on 22 July 1563. He had made his will two months earlier dividing most of his possessions between his brothers Charles and Thomas. He left his black armour to his cousin the 13th Lord Grey of Wilton and his portrait to his mistress. Thomas Somerset proved the will on 5 Jan. 1564.[2]

[1] Date of birth estimated from first reference. Bradney, *Mon.* ii(1), 26; PCC 3 Stevenson. [2] *CPR*, 1550–3, p. 402; E159/338, Easter 48; *HMC Foljambe*, 6; *APC*, vi. 337, 396; *CSP Scot.* 1547–63, nos. 487, 759, 778, 839, 848; *CSP For.* 1558–9, nos. 527, 974; 1559–60, nos. 276 (2, 3), 327(1), 1088; 1560–3, nos. 421 (1, 2), 471(9), 476, 484(4), 537(3), 599, 966, 1563, nos. 226, 282, 289, 391(4), 664, 896(1), 1045(2); *CSP Dom.* 1601–3, *Add.* 1547–65, p. 481; PCC 3 Stevenson.

P.S.E.

SOMERSET, Thomas (by 1529–86).

MONMOUTHSHIRE 1553 (Oct.), 1554 (Nov.)

b. by 1529, 2nd s. of Henry Somerset, 2nd Earl of Worcester, by 2nd w. Elizabeth, da. of Sir Anthony Browne; bro. of Charles† and Francis*. ?*unm.* at least 1s. 1da. illegit.

Member, household of Stephen Gardiner, bp. of Winchester by 1550–5; bailiff, manor of Highclere, Hants by 1551–5; j.p.q. and custos rot. Mon. by 1558/59–62; jt. (with Thomas Seckford†) porter and keeper of prison, council in the marches of Wales 1563–*d.*[2]

Thomas Somerset was probably brought up in the household of Stephen Gardiner, whose servant he then became. In 1551 Gardiner named Somerset as one of the proctors to appear for him at his trial. It was presumably to Gardiner as much as to his family's ascendancy in south-east Wales that Somerset owed his return to two of Mary's Parliaments. He may have promoted the unsuccessful bill in 1553 for county days in Monmouthshire to be held at Usk, because that town lay not far from the home of his brother, the 3rd Earl of Worcester, at Raglan and was more amenable to the earl's influence than either Monmouth or Newport where the county court was required to meet alternately under the Act of Union (27 Hen. VIII, c.26). Somerset was not among the opponents of the initial measures to restore Catholicism in 1553, but he was one of over 100 Members prosecuted in the King's bench for withdrawing from Parliament prematurely a year later. Worcester did not attend the Lords on this occasion, and the reason behind the earl's absence may also account for Somerset's, since no further process was taken against him. Somerset continued in Gardiner's service until his master's death in November 1555 when he received a small legacy and bore a banner at the funeral. Although he was not re-elected to Parliament after Gardiner's death, his two younger brothers were to be returned for the shire in 1558, 1571 and 1572.[3]

Somerset did not welcome the accession of Elizabeth nor her religious settlement. To signify his disapproval he translated from the French *The Oration of the most noble and reverende father in God the Lorde Cardinelles grace of Lorrain made and pronounced in thassemblie at Poyssi . . . the sixtene daye of Septembre In the yeare of our Lorde 1561*. For publishing this without approval he was committed to the Fleet in 1562 and for refusing to make a submission before the Council he was removed from the Monmouthshire bench. It was perhaps to compensate him for this loss that Worcester obtained for him the gaolership of the council in the marches of Wales. Unchastened by this setback he corresponded with the leading Catholic exiles, helped William Allen to raise funds for the establishment of the college at Douai and sent his illegitimate son and nephew there. In 1580 he was summoned before the ecclesiastical commissioners but released upon bond. During his last six years he was kept under observation by the regime and on suspicion of complicity with Mary Queen of Scots he was imprisoned in the Tower in 1585. It was there that he died on 6 Apr. 1586. On his deathbed he signified that his brother Worcester and nephew Edward Lord Herbert should order his affairs, pay his debts

and remember his attendants and warder. His nuncupative will was proved on the following 27 May.[4]

[1] Date of birth estimated from first reference. Bradney, *Mon.* ii(1), 26. [2] *Letters of Stephen Gardiner*, ed. Muller, 518; Eccles. 2/155890, 155894; *CPR*, 1560–3, p. 444; *CSP Dom.* 1547–80, p. 457; R. Flenley, *Cal. Reg. Council, Marches of Wales*, 230. [3] *Letters of Stephen Gardiner*, 506, 507, 510, 516; Foxe, *Acts and Mons.* vi. 120, 121, 130, 134, 135; *CJ*, i. 30; KB29/188, r. 48; M. A. R. Graves, 'The Tudor House of Lords' (Otago Univ. Ph.D. thesis, 1974), ii. 301; PCC 3 Noodes. [4] *APC*, vii. 108; xiii. 336, 407–8; information from Katharine F. Pantzer of Harvard College Lib.; *Cath. Rec. Soc.* i. 49; xxi. 126; *CSP Dom.* 1547–80, p. 457; 1581–90, pp. 249, 278; 1601–3, add. 1547–65, p. 524; K. E. Kissack, *Monmouth*, 32; L. Hicks, *An Eliz. Problem*, 47, 164; Harl. 360, f.49; SP12/186/61; PCC 28 Windsor; Flenley, 230.

P.S.E.

SONE (SOONE), Francis (by 1523–61), of Wantisden, Suff.

ORFORD 1545, 1558, 1559

b. by 1523, 1st s. of John Sone of Wantisden. *educ.* G. Inn, adm. 1537. *m.* (1) Alice, da. of Sir John Spelman of Narborough, Norf.; (2) Margaret, da. of Sir Anthony Wingfield* of Letheringham, Suff., 2s. 3da.; 1s. *suc.* fa. 1552.[1]

J.p.q. Suff. 1558/59–*d.*

In May 1544 Francis Sone and his father acquired the manor, rectory and advowson of Wantisden. On his father's death he inherited considerable property in Suffolk, including the manors of Boville and Peche in Alderton and of Campsea and Chillesford, some of which he sold in February 1553 to Robert Vesey. In the autumn of that year he levied a fine against Francis Harman for houses and pasture in east Suffolk, and three years later he acquired lands in Sudbury from Roger Warren, perhaps the brother-in-law mentioned in his will. Sone's return for Orford on three occasions may have reflected the influence of the Willoughbys or Wingfields, but as a landowner in the neighbourhood with some legal training he could well have been the town's own choice. He was brother-in-law to George Jerningham, Member for Orford and Dunwich under Mary. The Protestant leanings expressed in his will may explain his absence from most of the Marian Parliaments and his belated appointment to the Suffolk bench.[2]

Sone died on 11 Nov. 1561.[3]

[1] Date of birth estimated from education. *Vis. Norf.* (Harl. Soc. xxxii), 264–5; C142/97/74; Copinger, *Suff. Manors*, v. 119. [2] *LP Hen. VIII*, xix; C142/97/74; CP25(2)/79/666, no. 15; *CPR*, 1555–7, p. 129; 1557–8, p. 364; 1558–60, pp. 271, 341; PCC 41 Pyckering. [3] C142/132/43.

J.P.

SOOLLE see LLOYD

SOOME, Robert (by 1468–1522/24), of Lynn, Norf.

LYNN 1515[1]

b. by 1468, yr. s. of John Soome† of Lynn. *m.* Christiana.[2]

Chamberlain, Lynn 1489–90, common councilman 1491–1508, constable 1498–1506, jurat 22 Sept. 1508–*d.*, coroner 1509–10, j.p. 1512, mayor 1514–15.[3]

Lynn complied only in part with the King's request that the Members of the Parliament of 1512 should be re-elected to its successor of 1515: the town re-elected Thomas Wythe but replaced Francis Monford by the serving mayor Robert Soome. The change may have been imposed by Monford's adoption on this occasion by the city of Norwich, but Soome was an obvious choice both as mayor and as one of the delegation—Wythe being another—appointed by Lynn in November 1514 to contest the bishop of Norwich's claims to jurisdiction in the town. Whether he or Wythe pursued the matter during their attendance in the Commons is not known, but Soome informed the town assembly of the proceedings on his return after its prorogation and eventual dissolution.[4]

Soome followed his father and elder brother Edmund into trade. He was admitted a freeman in 1489 and immediately made chamberlain. His municipal life followed the usual progression. Early in his career he combined a post in the customs with his own business and town affairs and it was as 'merchant, late customer' that in 1510 he sued out a general pardon. In 1506 he leased the water of the Kettlemill from the town authorities for use in his brewhouse in the messuage called the *Swan* on the Grassmarket. After September 1522 his name ceases to be listed among the jurats of Lynn and during 1523–4 the rent for the Kettlemill water was paid by his widow. If he made a will it has not been found.[5]

[1] Lynn congregation bk. 4, f. 151. [2] Date of birth estimated from admission as freeman. PCC 13 Vox; Lynn chamberlains' accts. 1523–4. [3] Lynn congregation bk. 3, p. 563; 4, ff. 18v, 75v, 88, 91v, 142v; *LP Hen. VIII*, i. [4] Lynn congregation bk. 4, ff. 146v, 151, 152v, 171. [5] PCC 13 Vox; Lynn congregation bks. 3 and 4 passim; chamberlains' accts. 1523–4; *Lynn Freemen* (Norf. Arch.), 68; *LP Hen. VIII*, i.

R.V.

SOTHERTON, Thomas (by 1525–83), of Norwich, Norf.

NORWICH 1558, 1559

b. by 1525, 1st s. of Nicholas Sotherton of Norwich by Agnes Wright; bro. of George†. *m.* Elizabeth, da. of Augustine Steward* of Norwich, 4s. 4da. *suc.* fa. 10 Nov. 1540.[1]

Common councilman, Norwich prob. 1547–54, common speaker 1554, 1555, auditor 1547, 1550, 1555, 1558, 1560, 1569, sheriff 1556–7, alderman 1557–*d*, mayor 1565–6.[2]

Thomas Sotherton, grocer, was admitted to the freedom of Norwich on 22 Dec. 1546 as the son of a citizen and alderman. Under his father's will of six

years before he had been given the reversion of the family house in Norwich on his mother's death and £100 when he reached the age of 24. His early civic career is liable to confusion with his uncle's of the same name, but he was probably a councilman from 1547, auditor in that and later years and twice common speaker. At the close of his term as sheriff in 1557, during which he had served with his brother Leonard, he was granted 'his two free men', that is, two nominations to the freedom, 'as is accustomed to the sheriffs'. As sheriff he had to play his part in the Marian persecution.[3]

Sotherton was connected by marriage with many leading citizens: he and his brother John each married a daughter of Augustine Steward, whose will he was to supervise and who left him £10, and his sister married John Aldrich*. It was during Aldrich's mayoralty that Sotherton was first elected to Parliament. Of his part in that or the succeeding Parliament nothing has come to light. He died in 1583.[4]

[1] Date of birth estimated from admission as freeman. *Misc. Gen. et Her.* (ser. 5), ix. 129–31; *Vis. Norf.* (Harl. Soc. xxxii), 269; Blomefield, *Norf.* iv. 291; PCC 21 Alenger; Norwich consist. ct. 122 Bate. [2] Norwich ass. procs. 2 and 3 passim. [3] Ibid. 2, f. 197v; 3, f. 36; PCC 21 Alenger. [4] PCC 43 Holney; Norwich consist. ct. 122 Bate.

R.V.

SOUTH, Robert (by 1494–1540), of Salisbury, Wilts.

SALISBURY 1536,[1] 1539*[2]

b. by 1494, ?2nd s. of Robert South of Salisbury by w. Alice. *m.* by 1512, Beatrice, 3s. 2da.[3]

Collector in Market ward, Salisbury 1515, assessor 1522, member of the Forty-Eight by 1522, of the Twenty-Four 1528, mayor 1528, auditor 1528, 1533, 1535–6; commr. for vagabonds 1532, gaol delivery 1540; j.p. 1540.[4]

Robert South and his elder brother William of West Amesbury, Wiltshire, are the first of their family to be included in the heralds' visitation. They may have been the sons of Robert South, who figures in the accounts of the churchwardens of St. Edmund's, Salisbury, from 1468 until 1510–11 and who crowned an active civic career by becoming mayor in 1506. The elder Robert either inherited or acquired the status of gentleman, for he was so described in 1499–1500 when the great bell of St. Edmund's church was tolled for his wife Alice; his son William was given this style when assessed for subsidy at West Amesbury in 1545, and the younger Robert is called gentleman in his will. Both brothers held property in Salisbury in 1525, when William was assessed for subsidy on goods worth £50 and Robert on goods worth £80.[5]

South's Membership of two Parliaments was the natural culmination of his civic career but he probably owed his first election in 1536, when the King had asked for the return of the previous Members, to the poor health of one of them, Thomas Chaffyn I. Between then and his second return in 1539 South was active in the city's opposition to its reforming bishop, Nicholas Shaxton. John Madowell, the bishop's chaplain, writing in the spring of 1537 to complain of the city's papist sympathies, mentioned that 'Mr. South' had criticized the royal proclamation relaxing the Lenten fast. In October 1537 South was paid 42s. 6d. for journeying to London on the city's business, and in the following January he was one of the four men appointed to present its case against Shaxton to the Privy Council. The dispute sprang from the citizens' desire to assert their independence no less than from their conservatism, so that it is hard to assess the motives of those who took part. South helped Chaffyn and others to investigate rumours of a pilgrimage at Salisbury in August 1538.[6]

South made his will on 29 Apr. 1540, during the third and last session of the Parliament to which he had been elected on 31 Mar. 1539. He asked to be buried in the hospital of the Savoy, 'if it shall please God to call me to his mercy in the present sickness that I am now in'. His lease of Winterbourne Earls, and that of the parsonage of Pitton and Farley held of the treasurers of Salisbury cathedral, he bequeathed to his eldest son Thomas; to the younger, Robert, he left property at Stratford-sub-Castle, held of the cathedral's succentor and known as Subchanter's Farm, and a lease of the gaol at Fisherton Anger, held of Sir John Hampden. Both these sons, who were appointed executors, appear to have been of age by 1533–34, since the younger was to claim in the Star Chamber that they had then acquired a tenement at West Harnham. The widow received £100 and goods from the dwelling house in Salisbury, with leases in the hundred of Downton and at Fisherton Anger, and a share in her husband's plate. A daughter Sybil, who later married Thomas Chaffyn II*, was to have £100 and her sister Joan 100 marks. South presumably died in London, as the will was proved on 11 May 1540; there is no record that a by-election was held during the ten weeks which elapsed before the dissolution of the Parliament.[7]

[1] Salisbury corp. ledger B, f. 281. [2] Ibid. f. 289; E159/319, brev. ret. Mich. r. [1–2]. [3] Date of birth estimated from first reference. Ledger B, f. 233v; Wilts. Vis. Peds. (Harl. Soc. cv, cvi), 187; Churchwardens' Accts. of St. Edmund and St. Thomas, Sarum (Wilts. Rec. Soc. 1896), 51; St.Ch.2/32/35; PCC 5 Alenger. [4] Ledger B, ff. 233v, 249v, 263, 264, 271v, 276, 280, 282; LP Hen. VIII, v, xv. [5] Churchwardens' Accts. of St. Edmund and St. Thomas, Sarum, 10, 12, 26, 28, 37, 39, 51, 56; Ledger B, ff. 107, 215v; Two Taxation Lists (Wilts. Arch. Soc. recs. br. x), 1; E179/197/154. [6] Ledger B, ff. 281, 285, 286; LP Hen. VIII, xii, xiii; Elton, Policy and Police, 101. [7] PCC 5 Alenger; VCH Wilts. vi. 182, 202.

T.F.T.B.

SOUTHCOTE, George (by 1533–89), of the Middle Temple, London, and Calverleigh, Devon.

LOSTWITHIEL 1554 (Apr.)
TAVISTOCK 1558

b. by 1533, 2nd s. of John Southcote I* of Bovey Tracey, Devon by 1st w. Joanna, da. of one Hankford; bro. of Thomas*. educ. M. Temple, adm. 10 Nov. 1551. m. by 1561, Frances, da. and coh. of William Robins of London, 4s. 5da.[1]

Clerk of the peace and the crown, Devon 14 Sept. 1556–d.[2]

George Southcote's admission to the Middle Temple was sponsored by two lawyers from Devon, his cousin John Southcote II* and John Ridgeway* with whom he was allowed to share chambers in 1553; he was to marry his cousin's sister-in-law, the daughter of a London alderman. Southcote was probably in his early twenties when he was returned to the second Marian Parliament for Lostwithiel, a Cornish town which retained his father's counsel. He was not elected again until after his father's death, when he almost certainly owed his seat at Tavistock to his elder brother's association with the 2nd Earl of Bedford, the lord of the borough. In 1543 his father had obtained for him the succession to his clerkship of the peace and crown, but Southcote had held office for less than three months in 1556 when he was ejected by the custos rotulorum, Sir Thomas Denys*, in favour of Richard Hart*. He brought an action in Chancery to establish his interest and was presumably successful since he was exercising the clerkship in 1559 and retained it until his death. In 1558 he purchased Calverleigh, which he made his home, from (Sir) Gawain Carew* and on the accession of Elizabeth he sued out a general pardon. Nothing has come to light about his remaining 30 years outside his official duties: he made his will on 8 Oct. 1589 providing for his wife and children and died on the following 11 Nov.[3]

[1] Presumed to be of age at election. Vis. Devon ed Vivian, 697; PCC 12 Drury; C142/224/34. [2] LP Hen. VIII, xviii; C1/1467/29. [3] M.T. Recs. i. 83, 93; J. Morris, Troubles of Our Catholic Forefathers, i. 365; LP Hen. VIII, xviii; C1/1467/29–31; 142/224/34; CPR, 1557–8, p. 339; 1558–60, p. 196; PCC 12 Drury.

R.V.

SOUTHCOTE, John I (by 1504–56), of Bovey Tracey, Devon.

LOSTWITHIEL 1547,[1] 1554 (Nov.), 1555

b. by 1504, 1st s. of Nicholas Southcote by Margaret, da. and coh. of John Bossam of Bossam Sayle. educ. ?M. Temple. m. (1) by 1528, Joanna (d. 11 Apr. 1546), da. of one Hankford, wid. of one Sydenham, 2s. George* and Thomas* at least 1da.; (2) Agnes, wid. of Gilbert Kirk* of Exeter.[2]

Clerk of the peace and the crown, Devon 8 Aug. 1525–d.; auditor, commission for tenths of spiritualities 1535; steward, dean and chapter of Exeter cathedral temp. Mary.[3]

John Southcote I must be distinguished from his more eminent namesake and nephew, the Elizabethan judge, who sat in Parliament for two Sussex boroughs in 1553. He presumably received his own legal education at the Middle Temple, the inn later attended by his younger son and nephew. Early in his career he was in the service of religious foundations in south Devon, employment which perhaps helps to account both for his inclusion in the important tithes commission of 1535 and for his successful accumulation of property from 1540 until his death, when the yearly income from his lands in the Teign valley was put at £144. He was exempted from serving in the French campaign of 1544 and on the death of Henry VIII he sued out a general pardon. In 1546 the corporation of Lostwithiel retained him in a case against Lawrence Courtenay and William Lower*, and this link with the borough explains his own and his son George's successive elections there under Edward VI and Mary. He could also have been the man whose name was erased, save for its concluding 'ote', on the Lostwithiel indenture of 1545 in favour of that of Anthony Browne II (q.v.). If Southcote was one of the pair originally chosen by the town on that occasion, the occurrence of a similar replacement there in the autumn of 1553, when the original name was obliterated in favour of Christopher Dauntesey's, suggests that Southcote, or perhaps his son, was the man supplanted on that occasion. In what circumstances, whether friendly or otherwise, these changes were made does not transpire, but it is of interest that in 1555 both Southcote's name, and his fellow Brice Rookwood's, were inserted on the indenture in a different hand. Nothing is known about Southcote's part in the Commons. He made his will (known only from a reference to it in his inquisition) on 20 Aug. 1555 and died on 14 Sept. 1556.[4]

[1] Hatfield 207. [2] Date of birth estimated from first reference. *Vis. Devon* ed. Vivian, 697; C142/107/14. [3] *LP Hen. VIII*, iv–viii; C11/1467/29–31; J. E. Kew, 'The land market in Devon 1536–58' (Exeter Univ. Ph.D. thesis, 1967), 202. [4] *LP Hen. VIII*, iv, v, viii, xv–xix; Kew, 183, 202, 299, 311; D. H. Pill, 'The diocese of Exeter under Bp. Veysey' (Exeter Univ. MA thesis, 1963), 200; St.Ch.3/2/39; C142/107/14; 219/18C/21, 21/30, 24/28; *CPR*, 1548–9, p. 158.

R.V.

SOUTHCOTE, John II (1510/11–85), of London and Witham, Essex.

LEWES　　　1553 (Mar.)
STEYNING　1553 (Oct.)

b. 1510/11, s. of William Southcote by Alice, da. of one Tregonwell. *educ.* M. Temple. *m.* by 1555, Elizabeth,

da. and coh. of William Robins of London, 13ch. inc. 1s. 3da.[1]

Autumn reader, M. Temple 1556, Lent 1559.

Under sheriff, London in 1553–59 or later; justice, sheriff's ct. London in 1553; j.p. Mdx. 1554, q. Mdx. 1558/59–d., Essex 1564–d., Herts., Kent, Suss. 1564, Surr. 1564–79; serjeant-at-law 27 Oct. 1558; commr. to enforce Acts of Supremacy and Uniformity 1559, eccles. causes 1572; j.KB 10 Feb. 1563; justice assize, Essex 18 June 1571; trier of petitions in the Lords, Parlt. of 1572.[2]

John Southcote's early career overlapped the close of his uncle's of the same name, but in their Membership of Parliament the two are readily distinguishable. Until he became a serjeant the nephew was usually styled gentleman whereas the uncle was called esquire or armiger, and the man returned to the two Parliaments of 1553 was designated gentleman on both election indentures. A month before his return to the first of these Parliaments, and again within a fortnight after the opening of the second, Southcote was employed to prepare bills for the city of London, although neither measure is known to have been introduced into the House. These services, however, may have contributed to his election, for which he could also have had the support of another uncle, the eminent civilian John Tregonwell, who joined him in the House in the autumn of 1553: on that occasion Southcote had in his fellow-Member David Lewis, a colleague of Tregonwell and perhaps already a friend of his own. If Tregonwell was Southcote's sponsor (Sir) Anthony Browne I* as sheriff may have been instrumental in his election: Browne was the son-in-law of Sir John Gage, whose servant Thomas Gravesend was Southcote's fellow-Member in the spring. Southcote did not oppose the initial measures to restore Catholicism passed during Mary's first Parliament.[3]

Southcote was probably the John Southcote of Bodmin who in 1544 helped Tregonwell to buy and sell land in the south-west: in 1549 he was to be of similar assistance to Henry Chiverton*. He bought land himself near London and late in life settled in Essex. Mary promoted him serjeant and Elizabeth made him a judge, in which capacity he revised the bill settling the form of consecration for bishops before its enactment in 1566 (8 Eliz. c.1) and took part in the conference in 1577 on how to deal with recusancy. According to his descendants he shared their Catholicism and resigned his office rather than condemn a priest, retiring to his house at Merstham in Surrey 'where for three years he led a penitential life and happily ended his days'; this, however, conflicts with evidence of his continuing to serve as a judge until a year before his death at Witham. His son John was reported as having attended mass in

1584 and his daughters married into Catholic families, but his own conformity is borne out by his retention as a justice of the peace in all the home counties after 1564.[4]

By his will of 4 Aug. 1580 Southcote provided for his wife, children and other relatives, including his brother-in-law and cousin George Southcote*. He named his wife, his son and the clerk of assize John Glascock executors and (Sir) Christopher Wray* and (Sir) Thomas Bromley II* overseers. Three years later he added a codicil leaving rings to, amongst others, David Lewis, Alexander Nowell*, Sir John Petre† and Edmund Plowden*. Eleven days before his death on 18 Apr. 1585 he named his son sole executor and the will was proved a year later. Southcote was buried at Witham where a monument showing him in judge's robes was erected. He was remembered as 'a good natured man . . . governed by his wife'.[5]

[1] Aged 74 at death according to MI. This biography draws on P. R. P. Knell, 'The Southcott fam. in Essex, 1575–1642', *Essex Recusant*, xiv. 1–38, and A. Davidson, 'Southcott daughters', ibid. xiv. 88–101. *DNB*; *Vis. Essex* (Harl. Soc. xiii), 491–2; Wards 7/21/74. [2] Foss, *Judges*, v. 541–2; City of London RO, Guildhall, rep. 14, f. 110v; jnl. 15, f. 215; *CPR*, 1553–4, p. 22; 1557–8, p. 457; 1558–60, pp. 65, 118; 1560–3, pp. 279–80, 440, 469; 1563–6, pp. 22–27; 1569–72, pp. 211, 440–2; *LJ*, i. 703. [3] C219/20/128, 21/153; City of London RO, rep. 13(1), ff. 12v, 86v. [4] *LP Hen. VIII*, xix; *CPR*, 1548–9, p. 177; 1549–51, p. 53; St.Ch.5/C27/38; Strype, *Annals*, i(2), 230; J. Morris, *Troubles of Our Catholic Forefathers*, i. 384. [5] PCC 24 Windsor; Wards 7/21/74; Pevsner and Radcliffe, *Essex*, 429.

R.J.W.S.

SOUTHCOTE, Thomas (by 1528–1600), of Shillingford St. George and Bovey Tracey, Devon.

TAVISTOCK 1555
PLYMPTON ERLE 1558
DARTMOUTH 1559

b. by 1528, 1st s. of John SouthcoteI* of Bovey Tracey by 1st w. Joanna, da. of one Hankford; bro. of George*. *m.* (1) settlement May 1541, Grace (*d.*1547), da. and h. of John Barnhouse of Devon, 1s. 2da.; (2) Susan, da. of Thomas Kirkham of Blagdon in Paignton, 4s. 6da.; (3) Elizabeth, da. of George Fitzwilliam of Mablethorpe, Lincs., 8s. inc. George† and Richard† 4da. *suc.* fa. 14 Sept. 1556.[1]

Sheriff, Devon 1558–9, 1570–1; jt. surveyor, Exchequer, Devon and Exeter 16 Oct. 1560–2 June 1598; j.p.q. Devon 1561–*d.*[2]

Thomas Southcote is likely to have owed his return for Tavistock in 1555 to the influence of his family, either on its own account or on behalf of Francis Russell*, 2nd Earl of Bedford, during his absence abroad. Southcote may already have been the earl's tenant for the mansion house of Cowick which had belonged to Tavistock abbey. Although in 1564 he was to be one of six gentlemen consulted by the bishop of Exeter on the religious sympathies of their neighbours, he was not among those

Members of the Parliament of 1555 who followed Sir Anthony Kingston's lead in opposing one of the government's bills. By 1558, when his younger brother George sat for Tavistock, Southcote was head of the family and may not have needed Bedford's support to secure the senior seat for Plympton Erle. He was friendly with the locally important family of Strode, and he and his brother were joined in the House by his brothers-in-law George Kirkham and Walter Staplehill: he was also related to the sheriff, (Sir) Robert Denys*. Nothing is known of Southcote's role in this House, but he and his colleague Christopher Perne are among the 17 Members whose names are missing from a copy of the Crown Office list. Two of his sons were to sit for Plympton Erle before his death on 10 Aug. 1600.[3]

[1] Date of birth estimated from age at fa.'s i.p.m. C142/107/14. *Vis. Devon*, ed. Vivian, 697; *Lincs. Peds.* (Harl. Soc. l), 357–8; (lii), 913; *LP Hen. VIII*, xvi. [2] *CPR*, 1558–60, p. 429. [3] J. A. Youings, 'The disposal of monastic property in land in the county of Devon 1535–58' (London Univ. Ph.D. thesis, 1950), 271 n. 1; *Cam. Misc.* ix(3), 67–68; PCC 66 Wallop; Wm. Salt Lib. SMS 264.

R.V.

SOUTHWELL, Francis (c.1510–81), of Hertingfordbury, Herts. and Islington, Norf.

HERTFORDSHIRE 1554 (Apr.)
ST. ALBANS 1558

b. c.1510, 3rd s. of Francis Southwell (*d.*1512) by Dorothy, da. and coh. of William Tendring† of Little Birch, Essex; bro. of Richard* and Robert*. *m.* (1) by 1545, Alice, da. of William Standish, *s.p.*; (2) 6 Aug. 1560, Barbara, da. of John Spencer of Rendlesham, Suff., wid. of Richard Catlyn* (*d.*1556) of Norwich and Honingham, Norf. and Serjeants' Inn, London, 2s. 1da.[1]

Auditor, Exchequer 1542–?*d.*, jt. (with Walter Mildmay*), prests, ct. gen. surveyors of the King's lands, May 1543–7; receiver, ct. augmentations, Herts. 1547; commr. subsidy, Herts. 1544, chantries, Oxon., Northants., Rutland 1546, Herts. 1548, relief, Herts. 1550; j.p. 1547, q. 1554.[2]

Francis Southwell's career was uneventful compared with those of his older and more distinguished brothers Sir Richard and Sir Robert, but it brought him a respectable income and good standing in his adopted county of Hertfordshire. Nothing is known of his early years, but as his father died in 1512 he must have been brought up by a relative or guardian. In September 1536 Richard Southwell was one of the royal commissioners to value religious houses in Norfolk and Suffolk, and presumably he arranged that Francis should ride with the commissioners' certificate of their findings from Wood Rising, Norfolk, to Grafton, Northamptonshire, a journey for which the younger man claimed his costs from the crown. In January 1538 Francis Southwell witnessed the surrender of West Acre priory,

Norfolk, to his brother Robert, then attorney to the court of augmentations. A series of minor but lucrative royal leases and commissions followed, beginning with a reversionary appointment in February 1539 to the auditorship of royal castles and lordships in South Wales and elsewhere. Southwell obtained two crown leases of Pembrokeshire lands in 1540 and 1541, when both his elder brothers were officials of the court of augmentations. In October 1540 he was one of the surveyors of crown lands in South Wales and in November 1542, after a few commissions of survey and audit, came his first permanent appointment, as one of the exchequer auditors, at a fee of £10 a year. This was followed in May 1543 by a joint auditorship of the prests in the court of general surveyors; the fee was £40 a year, although when Southwell surrendered his moiety of the post in 1547 he obtained a crown pension of £53 6s. 8d. More profitable still was the auditorship of the lands forfeit to the crown by the attainders of the Countess of Salisbury and Richard Fermor*; this, too, was a joint appointment, conferred on Southwell and Thomas Rolfe* in May 1544 and surrendered by them in November 1548 in return for an annuity of £100. Southwell's inclusion in commissions to survey chantries in 1546 marked his recognition as a man of consequence outside the sphere of royal revenue administration.[3]

By 1544 Southwell was established at Hertingfordbury; he was one of the subsidy commissioners for the hundreds of Braughing and Hertford and was himself assessed at £120 in goods that year, and at £80 in 1546, being rated on each assessment as one of the county's wealthiest men. In February 1545, probably by way of marriage settlement, Southwell's father-in-law purchased Gaulden manor, Somerset, from the crown for £212, Southwell and his wife having a remainder in tail after Standish's life interest. He was probably the Francis Southwell admitted a member of Lincoln's Inn in December 1544, but he does not seem to have studied law or had chambers there. As a newcomer in Hertfordshire, Southwell could hardly have been returned as knight of the shire to the second and last Marian Parliaments without royal recommendation, which in turn he doubtless owed to his brothers, both high in favour under Mary.[4]

Southwell took a crown lease of Hertfordshire land in October 1549, for 21 years at a rent of £18 15s. a year. He may not have owned freehold land in the county and perhaps purchased Islington manor, Norfolk, in September 1565 in anticipation of the expiry of his Hertfordshire lease; a few months earlier he had transferred Gaulden, probably to a relative of his first wife. Withdrawn from public affairs under Elizabeth, he probably lived in Norfolk for the last ten years of his life; from 1563 his name is absent from the Hertfordshire subsidy rolls. He made his will on 6 Oct. and died on 19 Nov. 1581, leaving an 18 year-old elder son Miles as his heir. He left each of his children a large amount of silver and plate, and gave £666 13s.4d. to his daughter and £300 to each son.[5]

[1] Date of birth estimated from elder brothers'. *Vis. Norf.* (Harl. Soc. xxxii), 260–1, 263; *Vis. Norf.* (Norf. Arch.), i. 125–6. [2] *LP Hen. VIII*, xvii, xviii, xxi; *CPR*, 1547–8, p. 84; 1548–9, p. 135; 1553. p. 354; 1553–4, pp. 20, 29; 1569–72, p. 177; W. C. Richardson, *Ct. Augmentations*, 118, 148; E179/121/157; 403/2448, ff. 81–82. [3] Richardson, *Tudor Chamber Admin.* 458–62; *Ct. Augmentations*, 149n; *LP Hen. VIII*, xii–xix, xxi; E403/2448, f. 8; 405/212. [4] E179/121/157, 177; *LP Hen. VIII*, xx, xxi; *Black Bk. L. Inn*, i. 128–9, 271; PCC 19 Stevenson; *CPR*, 1555–7, p. 191. [5] *CPR*, 1550–3, p. 184; 1563–6, pp. 228, 270; C142/197/76; PCC 9 Tirwhite.

D.F.C.

SOUTHWELL, Richard (1502/3–64), of London and Wood Rising, Norf.

NORFOLK 1539,[1] ?1542,[2] 1553 (Oct.), 1554 (Apr.), 1554 (Nov.)[3]

b. 1502/3, 1st s. of Francis Southwell by Dorothy, da. and coh. of William Tendring† of Little Birch, Essex; bro. of Francis* and Robert*. *educ.* L. Inn, adm. 3 Feb. 1526. *m.* Thomasin, da. of Roger Darcy of Danbury, Essex, 1da.; (2) Mary (*d.* by July 1561), da. of Thomas Darcy of Danbury, wid. of Robert Leeche of Norwich, Norf., 1da. also 2s. illegit. inc. Richard Southwell *alias* Darcy* 2da. illegit. bef. *m. suc.* fa. 2 Sept. 1512; uncle 30 Mar. 1514. Kntd. Feb./Aug. 1540.[4]

J.p. Norf. 1531–54; sheriff, Norf. and Suff. 1534–5; receiver, ct. augmentations, Norf. and Suff. 24 Apr. 1536–17 Jan. 1542; commr. for survey of monasteries, Norf. and Suff. 1537, for suppression 1539, of Admiralty in Nov. 1547, relief, Norf. and Norwich 1550; other commissions from 1535; custos rot. Norf. by Feb. 1537; gen. surveyor, office of gen. surveyors by Feb. 1542; second gen. surveyor, ct. gen. surveyors of the King's lands 16 Nov. 1542–7; v.-treasurer of the wars July 1544, treasurer Aug. 1544; PC 12 Mar. 1547, Aug. 1553–Nov. 1558; steward, duchy of Lancaster, Cambs., Norf. and Suff. 1553–58/59; keeper of the armoury, Greenwich and Tower 19 Sept. 1553–31 July 1559; master, the Ordnance 11 May 1554–31 July 1559.[5]

Of Suffolk origin, the Southwells acquired Wood Rising through the marriage of Richard Southwell's grandfather and namesake, Member for Yarmouth in 1455. His father, an auditor of the Exchequer, was a younger son, but on the death of his uncle Sir Robert Southwell, a friend and servant of Henry VII, Southwell succeeded to a considerable estate. Early in 1515 his wardship was sold to Sir Robert's widow and William Wotton, but four years later it passed to Sir Thomas Wyndham who presumably arranged the marriage of his ward to his stepdaughter, a sister of Sir Thomas Darcy*, later 1st Baron Darcy of Chiche. Nothing further is known of Southwell's education and upbringing until his entry into

Lincoln's Inn (where he retained chambers as late as 1545) when already of age, but his family had long been clients of the dukes of Norfolk and it is possible that he was brought up in the ducal household. He seems to have been well educated for when put in charge of Cromwell's son he is said to have personally instructed the young man in pronunciation and etymology.[6]

Southwell was placed on the commission of the peace in 1531 but in the same year he was involved with two of his brothers in the murder of Sir William Pennington and in 1532 he was obliged to pay £1,000 for a pardon which was later confirmed by Act of Parliament (25 Hen. VIII, c.32). Cromwell seems to have helped Southwell in this affair and by 1535 he was one of the minister's trusted agents in East Anglia. It was to Cromwell's patronage that Southwell and his younger brother Robert owed their advancement in augmentations. Southwell was particularly active in the Dissolution, although his conservative sympathies appear in his appeal of March 1536 on behalf of Pentney priory. During the Pilgrimage of Grace the Earl of Surrey reported to his father the 3rd Duke of Norfolk that he had taken counsel from 'my friend Mr. Southwell' in the raising of forces in Norfolk.[7]

Southwell's career in the Commons may have begun with the Parliament of 1536, when he would have been a likely successor to Sir James Boleyn as one of the knights for Norfolk if the disgrace of Anne Boleyn had involved her uncle's exclusion from the King's general request for the re-election of the previous Members. At the next election Southwell and Edmund Wyndham were returned for the shire on the strength of a royal nomination, although not without a challenge from Sir Edmund Knyvet (q.v.); the resulting quarrel brought both Knyvet and Southwell before the Star Chamber and led Southwell to complain to Cromwell at being made to suffer for doing his duty to the King. In the event both men seem to have been consoled, Knyvet by being pricked sheriff in 1539 and Southwell by his knighthood. The damaged state of the return for Norfolk in 1542 leaves one of the names illegible, but as Southwell was a signatory of the Act for an exchange of lands between the King and the Duke of Norfolk he was probably the knight concerned; if so, he again sat with his younger brother Robert, returned for Surrey and knighted at the opening of the Parliament, as he had done in 1539 and perhaps in 1536. After the close of the first session Southwell was sent to view the fortifications of Berwick and his appointment to an embassy to Scotland in January 1543 probably made him miss at least part of the second session. Neither brother

is known to have sat in Henry VIII's last Parliament, although one or both may have done so for a borough whose Members' names are lost; that Richard Southwell was passed over for Norfolk could have reflected the county's desire for a change.[8]

Between the close of Henry VIII's reign and the accession of Mary, Southwell's propensity for time-serving brought him little reward. His part in the destruction of the Earl of Surrey may have owed something to the personal friction between them during their service at Boulogne, but it was essentially a move to ingratiate himself with the King and the rising house of Seymour, to which he was related by marriage. Named by Henry one of the assistants to the executors of his will, Southwell was brought on to the Privy Council by the Protector Somerset on 12 Mar. 1547. As a Catholic and a sheepmaster, however, he had little sympathy with the Protector's religious and social policies: by July 1548 he had been put off the full Council, being bracketed with the 'assistants', and in the following year he joined other conservatives in an alliance with the Earl of Warwick to overthrow the Protector. Southwell did not long maintain his restored position and when Warwick turned on the conservative party he was committed to the Tower and fined £500 'for certain bills of sedition written with his hand'. He sat in neither of Edward VI's Parliaments but as a Privy Councillor he signed Acts for the restitution of (Sir) William Hussey II* and for the fine and ransom of the Duke of Somerset during the third session of the Parliament of 1547.[9]

Southwell also signed the limitation of the crown in favour of Jane Grey and his name appears on a list thought to be of those expected to support her, but in the event he rallied to Mary who gave him charge of her armoury and restored him to the Privy Council. He attended its sittings regularly until December 1555 after which he seems to have retired into Norfolk until early in 1557 when he resumed attendance. A supporter of Bishop Gardiner, he was described by Renard as the prime mover of the plan to marry the Queen to the Earl of Devon, and (Sir) Nicholas Throckmorton* was to recall at his trial hearing Southwell (one of his judges) speak against the Spanish marriage in the Commons. He was returned for Norfolk to the first three Parliaments of the reign, taking precedence over his fellow-Councillors Sir Henry Bedingfield and Sir John Shelton. As a Councillor, it was probably he rather than his younger brother who was the 'Sir R. Southwell' appointed to the committee to determine whether John Foster II and Alexander Nowell were eligible to sit in the Parliament of

October 1553 and to whom on 28 Nov. 1553 the bill for the confirmation of letters patent was committed on its second reading. A year later, on 26 Nov., the bill for seditious rumours was committed to him and at about the same time, when the Queen was supposedly pregnant, he is said to have burst out in the Lords, 'Tush, my masters, what talk ye of these matters? I would have you take some order for our young master that is now coming into the world apace, lest he find us unprovided'. He carried two bills to the Lords on 17 Dec. 1554. His subsequent disappearance from the Commons may have been due to ill health or to a loss of favour at court or of influence in his shire, where both the knights in 1555 were men of Protestant sympathies.[10]

Southwell was not reappointed to the Privy Council on the accession of Elizabeth and in July 1559 he surrendered his offices in exchange for an annuity of £165. He had added considerably to his inheritance, making full use of his opportunities as a surveyor and receiver, and by 1546 held over 30 manors in Norfolk alone. The succession to his property was complicated since most of his children, including his two sons, were born before his marriage to their mother, a kinswoman of his first wife, and while she was married to the Norwich alderman Robert Leeche: the heir male was thus Thomas, son of Sir Robert Southwell. Southwell had settled lands on his elder son as early as 1545 and in his will of 24 July 1561 he made no distinction between his children on the score of legitimacy. The only child of his first marriage, Elizabeth, was married to George Heneage* and the only child born after his second, Catherine, was then the wife of Thomas Audley of Berechurch, Essex. Southwell bequeathed over 10,000 sheep to members of his family and left his personal armour to his 'cousin and friend' Sir Henry Bedingfield and other armour to the young 4th Duke of Norfolk, whom he named an executor: despite his betrayal of Surrey the 3rd Duke had appointed Southwell an executor of his will of 1554. Although he had not had the strength to sign his name in 1561, Southwell survived until 11 Jan. 1564 and his will, to which he had added a codicil on the day of his death, was proved on 22 June by Norfolk, Sir Thomas Cornwallis* and Francis Gawdy†. Several portraits of Southwell survive.[11]

₁ LP Hen. VIII, xiv(1), 808 citing SP1/150/160–1; E159/319, brev. ret. Mich. r.[1–2]. [2] House of Lords RO, Original Acts, 35 Hen. VIII, no. 22. [3] Huntington Lib. Hastings mss Parl. pprs. supplies the full name, which is barely legible on the return, C219/23/89. [4] Date of birth estimated from age at fa.'s i.p.m., C142/79/183, and that given on portrait of 1536. Vis. Norf. (Harl. Soc. xxxii), 259–61; PCC 19 Stevenson; C142/29/15; LP Hen. VIII, xv; E159/319, brev. ret. Mich. r.[1–2]; DNB. [5] LP Hen. VIII, v, viii, xii–xvii, xix–xxi; CPR, 1547–8, pp. 87, 97; 1553, p. 356; 1553–4, pp. 22, 108, 199; W. C. Richardson, Ct. Augmentations, 50; Rep. R. Comm. of 1552 (Archs. of Brit. Hist. and Culture iii), 14; APC, ii. 71; iv–vi passim; Somerville, Duchy, i. 595; A. H. Smith, County and Ct. 65; HCA 14/2. [6] LP Hen.

VIII, ii, iii, viii; Index 10217(1), f. 1; Vis. Essex (Harl. Soc. xiii), 186; PCC 3 Bodfelde; Black Bk. L. Inn, i. 271. [7] LP Hen. VIII, v, viii–xii, xiv; Elton, Policy and Police, 144–6, 410, 414; Richardson, 12. [8] SP1/146/242, 274, 150/155, 160; LP Hen. VIII, xvii; House of Lords RO, Original Acts, 35 Hen. VIII, no. 22. [9] APC, i. 239; ii. 19; LP Hen. VIII, xxi; N. Williams, Thomas Howard, 4th Duke of Norfolk, 14–15; CPR, 1547–8, p. 97; 1549–51, p. 297; D. E. Hoak, King's Council in the Reign of Edw. VI, 49 (where it is argued that Southwell was not made a full councillor at this time), 246–7; W. K. Jordan, Edw. VI, i. 72 and n, 79–80 and n, 507 and n; ii. 28, 31; Lit. Rems. Edw. VI, 232n, 246; House of Lords RO, Original Acts 3 and 4 Edw. VI, nos. 30, 31. [10] Chron. Q. Jane and Q. Mary (Cam. Soc. xlviii), 100; Lansd. 103, ff. 1–2; APC, iv. 314; CSP Span. 1553, pp. 310, 312, 399, 471; 1554, pp. 151, 220; D. M. Loades, Two Tudor Conspiracies, 94 and n; State Trials, ed. Howell, i. 875; CJ, i. 27, 31, 38, 39; Foxe, Acts and Mons. vi. 580. [11] CPR, 1547–8, pp. 72, 73, 222, 373; 1553–4, p. 63; 1558–60, p. 279; LP Hen. VIII, xiv, xix–xxi; Blomefield, Norf. ii. 343, 359; vi. 108; Add. 5947; Stowe 775; CSP Span. 1554, pp. 295, 316; H. Spelman, Hist. of Sacrilege (1895 ed.), 152–4; PCC 19 Stevenson; C. Devlin, Robert Southwell, 7–9; C142/140/142; Holbein (The Queen's Gallery, Buckingham Palace 1978–9), 54.

R.V.

SOUTHWELL, Robert (c.1506–59), of London and Mereworth, Kent.

LYNN	1529*,[1] 1536,[2] 1539[3]
SURREY	1542
SOUTHAMPTON	1547[4]
WESTMINSTER	1553 (Mar.)
KENT	1553 (Oct.), 1555
PRESTON	1558

b. c.1506, 2nd s. of Francis Southwell (d.1512) by Dorothy, da. and coh. of William Tendring† of Little Birch, Essex; bro. of Francis* and Richard*. educ. M. Temple, called. m. 1535, Margaret, da. and h. of Sir Thomas Neville* of Mereworth, 4s. 3da. Kntd. 16 Jan. 1542.[5]

Autumn reader, M. Temple 1540.

Common serjeant, London 1535–6; solicitor, ct. augmentations 1536–7, attorney 1537–40; j.p. Kent, Norf. 1538–54, Surr. 1541–d., Suff. 1544–d., Suss. 1544–d., Essex 1547–54; Councillor 1540; master of requests 1540; master of rolls 1541–50; receiver of petitions in the Lords, Parlts. of 1542, 1545 and 1547; various commissions, largely in Kent 1550–6; sheriff, Kent 1553–4.[6]

Robert Southwell was still a boy when his father died and in 1517 or the following year his wardship was sold for £66 13s.4d. to Sir Robert Wingham; the wardship of his elder brother Richard, heir to a considerable fortune, had been secured by their aunt in 1515 for over £330. Robert Southwell became a lawyer: there is no record of his admission to any inn of court but in 1547 he was described as late of the Middle Temple and he was undoubtedly the 'Mr. Southwell' who gave the autumn reading there in 1540.[7]

Early in 1535 Richard Southwell was acting as tutor to Gregory Cromwell* and Robert was in Thomas Cromwell's service. When the negotiation for Gregory Cromwell's marriage to the only child of Sir Thomas Neville broke down it was Robert Southwell who with Cromwell's approval secured the heiress; she was then 15 and their first son was born in December 1535. The marriage brought Southwell the house called Jotes Place in Mereworth, Kent, which he made his chief residence after the death of his father-in-law in 1542. It was probably at Cromwell's request that on 1 June 1535 the King wrote to the mayor and aldermen of London asking for Southwell's election as common serjeant, an office which the King declared him well suited to 'both for his learning, discretion and other his good qualities': he was elected on the following day. To Cromwell, too, he doubtless owed his entry to the House of Commons: on 15 Oct. 1535 he was elected by the mayor and corporation of Lynn 'in lieu and place of Richard Bewcher'. The town must have been well pleased to have his support in its suit to the crown for a new grant of liberties, and he was to be twice re-elected one of its Members.[8]

In April 1536 Southwell entered the service of the crown, giving up his office in London to become solicitor of the court of augmentations. The financial loss which, as he told Cromwell, he suffered by this change he made the ground of his suit for the dissolved priory of Rochester. He also pointed out, this time to Ralph Sadler*, that he now needed a London house, his living quarters in the Temple being a good mile from where the chancellor of augmentations was, with a consequent wastage of time every day in travelling: he coveted a little house formerly belonging to Elsingspittle priory, and as it was already let he offered £30 to redeem the lease, hoping at the cost of 100 marks to have it ready for himself and his wife before the winter. In September 1536 he joined his colleague Thomas Pope* in support of charges of profiteering brought by Christopher Lascelles (q.v.) against Sir Richard Rich. Southwell's duties were not confined to London: he undertook a number of tasks elsewhere, notably in surveying monasteries and taking their surrender. In July 1537 he was in Lancashire and in 1538 successively in Norfolk, Northamptonshire and Kent; in November 1538 he was commissioned to take surrenders in Hampshire, Wiltshire and Gloucestershire, whence in January 1540 he moved into Worcestershire, finishing his business there on 27 Jan. at Evesham.[9]

Southwell surrendered his augmentations office in March 1540. A few days afterwards a warrant was delivered into Chancery for the payment to him of an annuity of £100 'for his office last given him', with the further endorsement, 'Mr. Robert Southwell to be admitted of the Council in Mr. Hare['s] room with the fee of £100'. Southwell thus became a member of the King's 'Ordinary Council' and replaced Sir Nicholas Hare* as one of the masters of requests. Almost immediately he was sent up to the sessions in York to assist the president and council in the north. While he was away the death of (Sir) Christopher Hales* made vacant the mastership of the rolls, to which Southwell was appointed in July 1541; on surrendering his patent for this office in December 1550 he retired from regular government service. In September 1541 he and (Sir) John Baker I* were instructed to survey lands at Calais; on 3 Nov. their report was read to the Council.[10]

As master of the rolls Southwell received a writ of assistance to the Parliaments of 1542, 1545 and 1547, in all three of which he acted as a receiver of petitions in the Lords. In 1542 and 1547 (and probably in 1545, a Parliament for which the names are incomplete) he was also returned to the House of Commons. His knighthood of the shire for Surrey in 1542 he may have owed to his fellow-Member Sir Anthony Browne, with whom he could claim distant kinship through his wife, or to the 6th Lord Bergavenny, his wife's first cousin: it was signalized by his being knighted by the King on the first day of the Parliament. During the third session he was joined by Sir John Baker and Sir Richard Rich in the delegation from the Commons to the Lords to ask for a conference on the King's style. Southwell's return in 1547 for Southampton, a town which normally confined its representation to residents, also presupposes powerful patronage, presumably that of his friend Thomas Wriothesley, 1st Earl of Southampton, and governor of the castle there. In the last session of this Parliament two bills, one concerning 'affrays in churches or churchyards' and the other for rearing calves, were committed to Southwell after their second reading in the Commons, and he was one of those nominated to investigate the legal situation governing the lands of the late Protector Somerset, bringing 'copies and notes' before the House on 12 Mar.[11]

During his years in government service Southwell accumulated a considerable landed estate. Before 1540 he obtained large grants of monastic property in Kent, London, Norfolk, Suffolk, Surrey and Sussex, some of which he disposed of during the 1540s. In 1543 he paid over £1,500 for the lordship, manor and hundred of Hoxne, Suffolk, formerly owned by the bishop of Norwich. Other property which he acquired between 1544 and 1550, much of it for re-sale, included the manors of Chippenham and Rowden, Wiltshire, former monastic manors in Kent, Norfolk and Suffolk, and two Essex manors by exchange with the crown.[12]

Although Southwell resigned the mastership of the rolls in 1550 it was apparently not because of any dissension between him and the Edwardian regime.

He continued to be named on local commissions and on 11 Nov. 1551 the Privy Council wrote asking him to come up to court as quickly as he could 'for such causes as wherein the King mindeth to use his service'. His election to the Parliament of March 1553 bespeaks official patronage, but he was no stranger to Westminster, where he had property in his wife's right. If the Duke of Northumberland had a hand in Southwell's return on this occasion he was supporting one who was to forsake him during the succession crisis a few months later. Although Southwell witnessed the device vesting the succession in Jane Grey, he quickly gave his allegiance to Mary, signing the letter of 19 July in her support subscribed by a number of Kent gentry. The 'Mr. Southwell' to whom two bills had been committed in March 1553, one for tanning and the other for artificers, was probably Sir Robert rather than his nephew Richard Southwell *alias* Darcy, but the 'Sir R. Southwell' who was appointed to the committee to inquire into the eligibility for Membership of Alexander Nowell and John Foster II in October 1553, and to whom a bill was committed in the following month, is more likely to have been his elder brother, then a Privy Councillor.[13]

As sheriff of Kent Southwell showed his loyalty during the rising led by Sir Thomas Wyatt II* early in 1554. For his 'great expenses and labours' in the Queen's service during the rebellion he and his wife were granted the lordship of Aylesford in Kent and all its lands, except the site of the priory, forfeited by Wyatt on his attainder. Southwell nevertheless sued out a pardon for all treasons committed between 10 Jan. and 1 Apr. 1554, all heresies and murders, and all omissions in the performance of his duties as sheriff. The inclusion of heresy among the derelictions of which he might be accused probably means little: in April 1556 he was included in a commission to investigate cases of heresy in the diocese of Canterbury, although admittedly the fact that he had been given a similar commission by Edward VI argues some flexibility in his religious position.[14]

Southwell was twice knight of the shire for Kent during the reign of Mary and in her last Parliament he sat for Preston, a borough belonging to the duchy of Lancaster; on this occasion his name is one of those missing from a copy of the Crown Office list. Whether he sought a place in Elizabeth's first Parliament is not known but if so he did not obtain one. He died on 26 Oct. 1559. Making his will on the previous 24 Aug., he bequeathed to his eldest son Thomas the goblet which Henry VIII, 'mine old master', had given him as his last New Year's gift, and the manors of Chickering and Hoxne in Suffolk. He made provision for his younger sons and gave

£500 each to his two unmarried daughters. His goshawk he left to Sir Henry Jerningham* and rings to Sir Henry Bedingfield* and (Sir) Edmund Wyndham*. The executors were his eldest son Thomas, his brother Sir Richard and John Thruston of Hoxne, and the supervisors his wife and (Sir) Nicholas Bacon*. Southwell was buried in Kent, presumably at Mereworth, on 8 Nov. 1559: his widow married William Plumbe of Middlesex.[15]

[1] Lynn congregation bk. 4, f. 301. [2] Ibid. 4, f. 302v. [3] Ibid. 4, f. 320. [4] Hatfield 207. [5] Date of birth estimated from elder and younger brothers'. *Vis. Norf.* (Harl. Soc. xxxii), 260–1; *Wriothesley's Chron.* i (Cam. Soc. n.s. xi), 133. [6] City of London RO, Guildhall, jnl. 13, f. 444v; 14, f. 13; *LP Hen. VIII*, xiii, xv, xvi; *PPC*, vii. 112; *APC*, iii. 412; *CPR*, 1549–51, p. 329; 1550–3, p. 355; 1554–5, pp. 67–69; 1555–7, pp. 24, 191. [7] Index 10217(1), ff. 1, 3; *LP Hen. VIII*, ii; *CPR*, 1548–9, p. 142; Dugdale, *Origines Juridiciales*, 216. [8] M. L. Robertson, 'Cromwell's servants' (Univ. California Los Angeles Ph.D. thesis, 1975), 563–5; *LP Hen. VIII*, viii; Mill Stephenson, *Mon. Brasses*, 201; C142/128/55; City of London RO, jnl. 13, ff. 444v, 445v; Lynn congregation bk. 4, ff. 301, 302, 302v, 304v, 320. [9] *LP Hen. VIII*, xii, xiii, xv. [10] Ibid. xv, xvi; *PPC*, vii. 74, 112, 167, 266; *CPR*, 1549–51, p. 329. [11] *LJ*, i. 165, 243, 267, 293; *LP Hen. VIII*, xvi; C218/1; *Wriothesley's Chron.* i. 133; *CJ*, i. 19, 20. [12] *LP Hen. VIII*, xiii–xvi, xviii, xix; *CPR*, 1547–8, pp. 98, 226, 228; 1548–9, pp. 86, 239; 1549–51, pp. 229, 318; 1554–5, p. 137. [13] *APC*, iii. 412; *Chron. Q. Jane and Q. Mary* (Cam. Soc. xlviii), 100; Add. 33320, f. 21; *CJ*, i. 25, 27, 31. [14] *CPR*, 1550–3, p. 355; 1554–5, pp. 67–69; 1555–7. pp. 24, 191; D. M. Loades, *Two Tudor Conspiracies*, 58–59, 78. [15] C142/128/55; PCC 53 Mellershe; *Machyn's Diary* (Cam. Soc. xlii), 217; Wm. Salt Lib. SMS 264.

H.M.

SOUTHWELL *alias* DARCY, Richard (by 1531–1600), of Lincoln's Inn, London; Horsham St. Faith, Norf. and Gatton, Surr.

GATTON 1553 (Mar.)

b. by 1531, 1st illegit. s. of (Sir) Richard Southwell* of London, and Wood Rising, Norf. by Mary, da. of Thomas Darcy of Danbury, Essex. *educ.* Corpus, Camb. matric. 1545; L. Inn, adm. 4 Feb. 1547. *m.* (1) by Dec. 1555, Bridget (*d.*1583 or later), da. of Sir Roger Copley of Gatton, 3s. 4da.; (2) by Oct. 1589, Margaret, da. of John Styles of Ellingham, Norf., 2s. 3da.[1]

In 1589 the Jesuit Robert Southwell exhorted his father Richard Southwell *alias* Darcy to return to Catholicism, reminding him that 'the world never gave you but an unhappy welcome, a hurtful entertainment, and now doth abandon you with an unfortunate farewell'. The elder Southwell was the first of four children borne by Mary Darcy to Sir Richard Southwell before their marriage. Most of Sir Richard Southwell's estates passed at his death in 1564 to his nearest legitimate male heir, his nephew Thomas Southwell, but under a settlement of September 1545 Richard Southwell inherited the manor of Horsham St. Faith and other property in Norfolk. This settlement was presumably made at the time of his engagement, or perhaps at his brother Thomas's, to Audrey Malte, the illegitimate daughter of the King's tailor, who after the breaking of the engagement married John Harington II (q.v.), leaving him free to espouse the bookish servant of Princess Elizabeth, Bridget Copley. He was tutored by the Protestant John Lowth in Latin and 'the laws civil and municipal' before a spell at Cambridge and admission to Lincoln's Inn where Lowth continued his instruction. Of Lowth his father remarked, 'He will make the boy like himself, too good a Latinist and too great a heretic.' By 1550 Southwell was an 'inner barrister' of his inn and eight years later it was ordered that he should be called to the bar upon his examination at the next moot. He was described as 'late of Lincoln's Inn' when Sir Richard Southwell made his will on 24 July 1561 leaving him 'all my books of scripture, prophecy, stories and other Latin authors and my books of law and statute books'. His name does not occur in the records of the inn after 1558 and no trace has been found of him practising as a lawyer. As Bridget Copley remained in the service of Elizabeth until her own death and his son was to accuse him of prodigality in maintaining an appearance at court he may have spent much of his life in attendance on the Queen.[2]

Southwell's single Membership of Parliament was a by-product of his betrothal or marriage to Bridget Copley, whose mother had a life-interest in the manor of Gatton, and it may have been helped by his kinsman Sir Anthony Browne* who as sheriff returned him: his fellow-Member Leonard Dannett was a distant relative of Lady Copley. He was joined in the House by his uncle Sir Robert Southwell, who is the more likely to have been the 'Mr. Southwell' to whom two bills were committed. Before the dissolution he and his father obtained a licence to sell some property in London.[3]

After Thomas Copley's* flight abroad in 1569 Southwell and his wife made their home at Gatton until Cecil ordered them to leave, but he continued to manage his brother-in-law's affairs and he was to be an executor of Copley's will. In May 1576 he was imprisoned in the Marshalsea on suspicion of having spoken against the Queen while staying at his sister's house at Berechurch in Essex. Although he was released within a month for lack of evidence, the charge brought against him was perhaps not groundless as his sister was a known Catholic, and while he lay in prison his son Robert arrived at Douai to start training for the priesthood. Unwise financial dealings by another son, Thomas, forced him to mortgage Horsham St. Faith and his other property to Henry Hobart† in an effort to pay off Thomas's creditors. This worthy action earned for him a rebuke from Robert who thought the money better used to promote Catholicism and took the opportunity to denounce Southwell's second marriage. Although Robert complained about the

indecent haste of this union, it was probably not that which irked him but the calling of Margaret Styles's father as a minister in the Anglican Church. If Robert lacked filial respect, Southwell did not fail in parental responsibility on his son's arrest in 1592. His intercession with the Queen led to the ending of Robert's interrogation under torture and the meagre comfort allowed the prisoner until execution three years later was the father's work. This compassion was almost certainly his own undoing for he remained under suspicion after 1595 and it was while a prisoner in the Fleet (for what reason has not been found) that he died in June 1600. By his will made on 17 Oct. 1596 he remembered the poor at Horsham St. Faith and left his wife an annuity of £80. A year later he had added a codicil making better provision for his wife and shortly before his death he confirmed these arrangements. According to Father Garnet, writing on 1 July 1600, Southwell died a Catholic.[4]

[1] Date of birth estimated from education. *Vis. Norf.* (Harl. Soc. xxxii), 259; *Vis. Norf.* (Norf. Arch.), i. 124–6; C. Devlin, *Robert Southwell*, 7; H. Spelman, *Hist. of Sacrilege* (1895 ed.), 152–4; *Letters of Sir Thomas Copley* (Roxburghe Club 1897), pp. xix, 169. [2] Add. 34395, f. 36 seq.; *DNB* (Southwell, Robert); Devlin, 8, 202; *LP Hen. VIII*, xx; Emden, *Biog. Reg. Univ. Oxf. 1501–40*, p. 364; *Narr. Ref.* (Cam. Soc. lxxvii), 45; Strype, *Eccles. Memorials*, i(i), 595; *Black Bk. L. Inn*, i. 288, 291–3, 296, 318, 323; PCC 19 Stevenson. [3] *CJ*, i. 25; *CPR*, 1553, p. 272. [4] *Copley Letters*, 97, 169, 182; PCC 13 Brudenell, 56 Wallop; H. Foley, *Jesuit Recs.* i. 303, 358; Devlin, 201–3, 289, 290.

S.R.J.

SOUTHWORTH, Richard

LANCASTER 1529

This Member has not been identified. He may have been a younger brother of Sir Thomas Southworth of Samlesbury, who died in 1546, or a member of another, more obscure, family of Southworth seated at Highfield, Lancaster; but Southworth was a common name in Lancashire and Richard a not uncommon christian name to find with it. In 1495–96 a Richard Southworth, son of Nicholas, granted the reversion of Blake Hall in Ellel, Cockerham parish, to George Stanley, 9th Lord Strange, and in 1517 a namesake of Shenstone, son and heir of Henry, released his lands in Croft, Winwick parish, to Sir Thomas Southworth at a yearly rent.[1]

The Member may be identifiable with the Richard Southworth who was one of the two bailiffs of Lancaster accused of levying an illegal toll in 1529. He could also have been the man who, together with Gilbert and Evan Southworth and Thomas Holden, was accused of unlawfully attempting to impress two men in 1522 to serve against the Scots and imprisoning them when they refused. A

Richard Southworth was assessed at Lancaster on goods worth £5 in 1543.[2]

[1] Pink and Beaven, *Parl. Rep. Lancs.* 107; Hornyold-Strickland, *Lancs. MPs* (Chetham Soc. n.s. xciii), 90; J. B. Watson, 'Lancs. gentry 1529–58' (London Univ. M.A. thesis, 1959), 481–2, 485; *VCH Lancs.* iv. 170n; viii. 36–37, 100n; *Lancs. and Cheshire Rec. Soc.* xxxv. 235–6. [2] DL1/5/H12, 12a, 12b, 12c; *Ducatus Lanc.* ii. 136; *Lancs. and Cheshire Rec. Soc.* xxxv. 245–6; Watson, 485.

L.M.K./A.D.

SPARKE, John (by 1502–66), of Plympton St. Maurice, Devon.

PLYMPTON ERLE 1554 (Apr.)

b. by 1502, s. of one Sparke of Nantwich, Cheshire. *m.* Jane (bur. 29 Dec. 1583), da. of one Moore of Devon, 4s.[1]

Collector subsidy, Plympton Erle 1523; mayor (bailiff) 1554–5.[2]

It is not known what led John Sparke, who was born in Cheshire, to settle in Plympton St. Maurice, nor is he easily distinguished from a number of contemporary namesakes. His election to Mary's second Parliament and his mayoralty later in the same year marked the culmination of his municipal career. Assessed at 5s. on his goods towards the subsidy of 1546, he may have been an overseas merchant as his sons and grandsons were later to be. He was probably the tenant who appears in rentals of the Strode estate during the 1540s, but further identification is more doubtful, whether it is with the servant of Arthur Plantagenet, Viscount Lisle, who was rewarded with 13s.4d. when Lisle's household was broken up in 1542, the servant of William Gibbes whom Richard Pollard* called an arrant thief in 1538, or the co-defendant to a charge of assault in an undated Star Chamber case.[3]

Sparke was buried in the church of Plympton St. Maurice on 11 July 1566.[4]

[1] Date of birth estimated from first reference. *Vis. Devon*, ed. Vivian, 856; *Vis. Cornw.* (Harl. Soc. ix), 205. [2] E179/281; C219/23/42, 24/44. [3] E179/98/271; PCC 29 Pyckering; NRA 4154, pp. 158, 166; *LP Hen. VIII*, xiii–xv; St.Ch.2/30/65. [4] J. B. Rowe, *Plympton Erle*, 248–9.

A.D.K.H.

SPARROW, John (by 1516–45/46), of Ipswich, Suff.

IPSWICH 1542

b. by 1516, 1st s. of Thomas Sparrow of Somersham by Elizabeth, da. of Walter Snelling of Elmsett. *m.* (1) Elizabeth, da. of John Bacon of Hessett; (2) Emma, wid. of William Drought *alias* Sampson of Ipswich, ?1s.[1]

Treasurer, Ipswich 1537–9, portman 1537–*d.*, bailiff 1540–1, j.p. 1541–2, 1545–*d.*, claviger 1541–*d.*[2]

John Sparrow was born into a family which had settled in Ipswich by 1419. His father lived at Somersham, several miles from the town, but Sparrow himself was an Ipswich mercer and clearly owed his seat in Parliament to his municipal standing. He owned considerable property in the town, including maltings and tanneries. In 1538 he was concerned with Robert Daundy* and other officials in dealing with the misdeeds of James Crawford, the priest in charge of the Daundy chantry. Two years later, as bailiff, he was required to ride to London with the town clerk to sue to the court of augmentations for the 'half-market' of Woodbridge.[3]

Sparrow's will, made on 15 Nov. 1545, shows him to have been a moderately wealthy man and, if his donations to the poor of Ipswich and as many as 15 villages are an indication, a pious one. He disposed of almost £220, in addition to his property in Ipswich, the greater part of which he left to his wife. His sister, Elizabeth Peckiswell, was to receive £40 and an additional £6 13s.4d. with all the timber, boards and planks 'in the late Whitefriars' with which to build a house where she thought fit. Her four children were bequeathed between them a total of £40, of which £20 and a house were to go to Joan Peckiswell. Other money and property went to Sparrow's two brothers Nicholas and Thomas, godchildren, servants and friends. John Holland the elder and Elizabeth Peckiswell were appointed executors and Robert Sparrow supervisor. The will was proved on 21 May 1546.[4]

[1] Date of birth estimated from first reference. N. Bacon, *Annals Ipswich*, 215n.; Add. 19149, pp. 320–3; Ipswich ct. bk. 6, pp. 36, 68. [2] Bacon, 210–24; *LP Hen. VIII*, xvi. [3] Bacon, 215n, 216; *LP Hen. VIII*, xiii. [4] PCC 9 Alen.

J.P.

SPARROW, Robert (by 1459–1528), of Winchelsea, Suss.

WINCHELSEA 1510,[1] ?1512, ?1515,[2] 1523[3]

b. by 1459, poss. s. of Thomas Sparrow of Winchelsea by Margaret. *m.* by 1522, Joan, wid. of Robert Borraunt, 2s. 2da.[4]

Jurat, Winchelsea 1496–*d.*, mayor 1501–2, 1511–12, 1517–18, 1524–5, dep. mayor in 1505, 1512, 1516, 1518; bailiff to Yarmouth 1497, 1509, 1521.[5]

Robert Sparrow probably sat for Winchelsea in four consecutive Parliaments with Thomas Ashburnham and Ashburnham's son John as his fellow-Members. His election with John Ashburnham is known only from a 17th-century list of Members where it is dated 'Henry VIII' without a regnal year. The names of the port's representatives are known for five Henrician Parliaments, leaving those of 1512, 1515, 1536 and 1539 unaccounted for, but as Sparrow and Ashburnham were dead by 1528 they can only have sat together in the first two of these: that they did so in both is likely in view of the King's call for the re-election in 1515 of the previous

Members. Nothing is known about Sparrow's part in the House, but in April 1514 the Brotherhood of the Cinque Ports directed him and John Warren* of Dover, both of whom seem to have remained in London after the dissolution of the Parliament of 1512, to deposit with the nominees of the lord warden money collected towards the recent subsidy until a dispute over the assessment was settled; a year later, while the Parliament of 1515 stood prorogued, the Brotherhood asked the same pair to sue for the discharge of the assessors. For their efforts in obtaining a verdict favourable to the ports they were paid 30s. each in 1516 and allowed £5 4s.4d. towards disbursements made to 'learned men' in the court of Exchequer. Sparrow was later involved in the dispute between Winchelsea and Sandwich over the allocation of the relief conceded by the Exchequer.[6]

Sparrow was a Winchelsea merchant who imported wine, raisins and other commodities. His parentage has not been traced, but he may have been the son of Thomas Sparrow described in the customs account for 1485–6 as a 'native' of the town. For 33 years from 1492 he was active in municipal affairs and often represented the port at the Brotherhood. In 1519 he excused himself from being elected bailiff to Yarmouth for a third time as he was in his 60s, but two years later he agreed to undertake the journey to Norfolk: he subsequently accepted election to Parliament in 1523 and to the mayoralty for a fourth time in 1524. By his will made on 24 June 1528 he asked to be buried in the churchyard of St. Thomas the Martyr in Winchelsea. After providing for his wife he left his son William £10 on completing his apprenticeship, his son Joseph the same amount but without the same proviso, his daughter Joan £13 6s.8d. and her sister Agnes £10 on reaching 20. He named his wife executrix and Thomas Ensing overseer of the will, which was proved on the following 25 Aug.[7]

[1] Add. 34150, f. 135. [2] Ibid. f. 138. [3] Ibid. f. 136. [4] 'Above 60 years' in July 1519, Cinque Ports White and Black Bks. (Kent Arch. Soc. recs. br. xix), 176; Rye chamberlains' accts. 4, f. 112; PCC 36 Porch. [5] Cinque Ports White and Black Bks. 121–91 passim. [6] Ibid. 155, 158, 161–3, 165. [7] E122/34/30, 35/5, 11, 18; C1/510/45; Cinque Ports White and Black Bks. 183; PCC 36 Porch.

P.H.

SPECOTE, Humphrey (by 1532–89 or later), of Thornbury, Devon.

PLYMOUTH 1558

b. by 1532, 1st s. of Edmund Specote of Thornbury by Jane, da. of Roger Grenville of Stowe in Kilkhampton, Cornw. m. by 1561, Elizabeth, da. of John Walter of Broxbourne, Herts., wid. of John Arscott* (d.1558) of Tetcott, Devon, 3s. inc. Sir John[†] 1da. suc. fa. 24 Apr. 1557.[1]

Commr. i.p.m. Cornw. 1564; j.p. Devon 1582–3.[2]

Humphrey Specote's family took its name from the manor which it owned in the parish of Merton in north Devon. His marriage to the widow of a wealthy neighbour augmented his patrimony which in the 1590s was said to yield £20 a year. He inherited a burgage in Plymouth but his election there to Mary's last Parliament and his admission as a freeman at about the same time were probably promoted by his kinsmen: he was joined in the House by his 'cousin' James Bassett, his uncle John Grenville and one of his father's trustees Thomas Browne alias Bevill, all sitting for Devon constituencies. Nothing is known about Specote's part in the Parliament but he may have used the occasion to arrange his marriage as his wife's first husband is thought to have died near London shortly before it opened. Little else has come to light about Specote apart from his role in county affairs under Elizabeth. He assisted the widow of Roger Prideaux* in a dispute over her title to some of her husband's lands and from his petition to the court of requests on the widow's behalf he is known to have been still alive late in 1589. He may have died shortly afterwards as during 1592–3 he was named to the quorum of the Devon bench, from which he had been removed nine years before, but was immediately struck off.[3]

[1] Date of birth estimated from age at fa.'s i.p.m., C142/113/11. Vis. Devon, ed. Colby, 190; Vis. Devon (Harl. Soc. vi), 272; Vis. Devon, ed. Vivian, 706; Al. Ox. 1395. [2] CPR, 1563–6, p. 334. [3] C142/113/11; Plymouth receivers' acct. bk. 1538–9; black bk. f. 297v; Req.2/61/48; Hatfield 278.

R.V.

SPEKE, Sir Thomas (1508–51), of White Lackington, Som. and London.

SOMERSET 1539,[1] 1545

b. 25 Mar. 1508, 1st s. of John Speke of White Lackington by Alice, da. of Sir Thomas Arundell of Lanherne, Cornw. m. (1) by 1530, Anne, da. of Richard Berkeley of Stoke, Som., 1s. George[†] 1da.; (2) 1549, Elizabeth, wid. of William Willoughby, 1da. suc. fa. 6 Dec. 1524. Kntd. bef. July 1538.[2]

J.p. Som. 1532–d.; sheriff, Som. and Dorset 1539–40, 1549–50; keeper, Neroche Forest, Som. Dec. 1539–Apr. 1542, Eltham park, Kent 1547–d.; sewer, the chamber by 1540, gent. by 1544; surveyor, ct. augmentations, Som. c.1540–d.; chief steward, lands formerly of Glastonbury abbey 1540, East and West Greenwich, Kent c.1547; commr. benevolence, Som. 1544/45, chantries, Dorset, Som. 1548, relief, Kent, Som. 1550; supervisor of kerseys, London, Southampton June–Nov. 1549.[3]

Originally of Devon, the Speke family had acquired considerable lands in Somerset during the 15th century and Sir John Speke[†], grandfather of Thomas, had made his main seat at White Lackington. On reaching his majority in 1529 Thomas Speke succeeded to rich estates in both counties, as also to the lands and half the goods of his uncle Sir George Speke. For a few years he seems to have resided quietly at White Lackington; between January and March 1535 he spent some weeks at Calais with his friend Viscount Lisle the deputy there, but on his return he seems again to have devoted himself mainly to local affairs.[4]

It was from 1538 that Speke's career gathered momentum. His knighthood in that year was succeeded early in the next by his election to Parliament for his shire. He probably began his career at court at about the same time, and his attendance there, and in the Commons, meant that the shrievalty which quickly followed must have been largely discharged, in his absence, by the under sheriff. Following the dissolution of the monasteries and the attainder of the Marquess of Exeter in 1539 he obtained lucrative posts under the new augmentations office in Somerset; he seems, however, to have purchased little land himself. He probably continued to live much at court, where he was clearly a favourite of the King. He may have sat in the Parliament of 1542 (for which the names of the Somerset knights are unknown), and certainly did so in that of 1545; his combination of royal favour and local prestige must have conduced to his ascendancy. In 1544 he led a troop of horse on the campaign in France and in November 1545 he was licensed to retain 40 persons in his livery. Like his brother-in-law Sir Maurice Berkeley* he was included in the King's will, receiving a legacy of 200 marks. Speke was one of the challengers at the tournaments in honour of Edward VI's coronation, and although not elected to the new Parliament appears to have remained in favour; he was made steward of several royal manors in north-west Kent and obtained a lease of Eltham manor and other property there. In December 1549 he bought from the bishop of Exeter the manor and borough of Paignton, Devon, although a month earlier, on the fall of the Protector Somerset, he had vacated the post of surveyor of kerseys in Southampton and London granted to him in June 1549.[5]

On 10 July 1551 Speke was struck down by the 'sweating sickness' which also carried off a number of his fellow-courtiers in that month. Having made his will on the 11th, he died the day after at his house in Chancery Lane and was buried at St. Dunstan's in the West. He left to his son all his lands, leases, jewels and cash, to his wife £240 'in old gold', half his household stuff and the manor of Dawlish for life, and to his two daughters 500 marks each at their marriage. He asked that all leases and copyholds which he had made but not yet confirmed should be fulfilled. As executors he appointed his son and wife, and among the overseers were (Sir) William Herbert I*, Sir Thomas Cheyne*, (Sir) Hugh Paulet (his fellow-knight in 1539) and Alexander Popham*. The will was proved on 18 July 1551 by his son, and by sentence of 14 Nov. 1552 was pronounced valid except for the bequests to the widow, which were nullified by her adultery.[6]

[1] E159/319, brev. ret. Mich. r.[1–2]. [2] Age and birthday given in fa.'s i.p.m., C142/44/119. Collinson, *Som.* i. 67; *Devon N. and Q.* xxi. 151 seq.; C142/95/38; *LP Hen. VIII*, xiii. [3] *LP Hen. VIII*, v–xxi; *The Gen.* n.s. xxx. 19; *CPR*, 1547–8, p. 184; 1548–9, pp. 136, 337; 1553, pp. 355, 359; *APC*, iii. 436; PCC 18 Bucke. [4] PCC 39 Porch; C142/50/121; *LP Hen. VIII*, viii, ix. [5] *Som. Rec. Soc.* xxvii. 216–25; *LP Hen. VIII*, xiv–xvi, xix–xxi; *Lit. Rems. Edw. VI*, p. ccci; *CPR*, 1547–8, pp. 184, 188; 1548–9, p. 337; 1549–50, p. 50. [6] *Machyn's Diary* (Cam. Soc. xxxii), 7; Strype, *Eccles. Memorials*, ii(1), 493; PCC 18 Bucke, 32 Powell; C142/95/38.

R.V.

SPENCER, Sir John (1524–86), of Althorp, Northants. and Wormleighton, Warws.

NORTHAMPTONSHIRE 1554 (Apr.), 1558

b. 1524, o.s. of Sir William Spencer of Althorp and Wormleighton by Susan, da. of Sir Richard Knightley of Fawsley, Northants. educ. ?M. Temple. m. by Oct. 1545, Catherine, da. of Sir Thomas Kitson of London and Hengrave, Suff., 5s. inc. John[†], Richard[†] and William[†] 6da. suc. fa. 22 June 1532. Kntd. 2 Oct. 1553.[1]

Sheriff, Northants. 1551–2, 1558–9, 1571–2, 1583–4; j.p. 1554, q. 1561–d.; dep. lt. 1560, 1586; collector for loan 1562; commr. musters by 1569.[2]

The Spencers first appear as Warwickshire graziers in the late 15th century and the family was still deriving much of its wealth from sheep after ennoblement in the reign of James I. The founder of its fortunes was the first Sir John Spencer, who purchased Wormleighton in 1506 and Althorp two years later.[3]

This Sir John Spencer's grandson and namesake was a child of eight when his father died leaving an estate which at his majority was valued at £454 a year. His uncles Edmund and Richard Knightley (qq.v.) joined with his mother in an attempt to defraud the King of the wardship, and this was not granted to (Sir) Giles Alington* until December 1539. Spencer may have entered the Middle Temple, to which his uncles belonged and which his eldest son was to join in 1564. His marriage to a daughter of the wealthy merchant Thomas Kitson, although less profitable than the one he was to arrange between his eldest son and a kinswoman, the only daughter of chief justice Sir Robert Catlyn, was a step in the social advance of the family, for three years later Lady Kitson became the Countess of Bath and married another of her daughters to the earl's heir apparent.[4]

Spencer served his first term as sheriff in the reign of Edward VI, but his knighting at Mary's coronation implies that he had declared for her in the previous summer, perhaps following the lead of Sir Thomas Tresham* in Northamptonshire. Two of his brothers-in-law, Richard Brydges and John Cotton, were knighted at about the same time and all three were to serve as knights of their shires in Marian Parliaments. Spencer's two elections answered to his standing in Northamptonshire, where he was related to most of the leading families, whereas his disappearance from the Commons after 1558 is doubtless to be explained by his Catholicism and by the virtual monopoly of the shire's representation by Privy Councillors. In 1564 Bishop Scambler judged him a 'great letter [hinderer] of religion' and ten years later Mary Stuart's agent accounted him a Catholic, yet he was sufficient of a conformist to play a leading part in shire administration. Only the family of his third son William was to remain intermittently Catholic.[5]

Spencer was a careful steward of his inheritance, which he augmented by judicious purchases, and he was able to settle estates on his three surviving younger sons and to provide generous dowries for his six daughters. All the daughters married well and his sons-in-law included Sir George Carey[†], later 2nd Baron Hunsdon, Sir William Stanley*, 3rd Lord Monteagle, and Ferdinando Stanley, later 5th Earl of Derby. He named Carey and another son-in-law Thomas Leigh of Stoneleigh, Warwickshire, overseers of his will of 4 Jan. 1586 and his three younger sons executors. He bequeathed £40 in plate to William Cecil, Lord Burghley, and £20 to (Sir) Walter Mildmay, his fellow-Member in the Parliament of 1558. He died on 8 Nov. 1586 and was buried, according to his request, with his wife in Brington church where his epitaph listed his sons, his daughters and all their husbands.[6]

[1] M. E. Finch, *Five Northants. Fams.* (Northants. Rec. Soc. xix), ped. at end of vol. which gives date of birth. [2] *CPR*, 1553–4, p. 22; *HMC Montagu*, 9; *Northants. Lieutenancy Pprs.* (Northants. Rec. Soc. xxvii), pp. xviii, 2, 15; Osborn coll. Yale Univ. Lib. 71.6.41; *CSP Dom.* 1547–80, p. 345. [3] Finch, 38–65, 171–2; W. K. Jordan, *Edw. VI*, i. 403; Pevsner, *Northants.* 71–75. [4] Finch, 39, 50–51; *LP Hen. VIII*, v, vii, xiii, xiv, xx; *DNB* (Kytson, Sir Thomas); *M.T. Recs.* i. 145. [5] *Cam. Misc.* ix(3), 36; *Cath. Rec. Soc.* xiii. 94; Finch, 175. [6] Finch, 57–63, 173–8; Bridges, *Northants.* i. 45, 105, 108, 117, 130, 330–1, 472–6, 479, 484; PCC 1 Spencer; C142/215/258.

S.M.T.

SPENCER, William (by 1473–1529 or later), of Ipswich, Suff.

IPSWICH 1510[1]

b. by 1473, poss. yr. s. of James Spencer of Naughton Hall, Rendlesham.[2]
Member of the Twenty-Four, Ipswich 1497, customer 1497–8, 1500–1, ?1503–4, ?1505–6, portman 1505, bailiff 1508–9, j.p. 1509–10; comptroller of customs, port of Ipswich 1501–6.[3]

William Spencer's origins are uncertain. A mercer by trade, he was living in Bury St. Edmunds when he was admitted a freeman of Ipswich on 6 Jan. 1494, a condition of entry being that he should live in the town. He soon became a member of its governing body and in 1506 he was elected bailiff but discharged on the instructions of Henry VII 'by reason that he is our officer and customer of the said port'. Two years later, no longer customer, he was again elected to the bailiffship and his term of office was followed by his return to the Parliament of 1510. He was paid 40s. in wages and 6s. 8d. for his expenses 'in procuring writs to the bailiffs for the same'.[4]

Little else has come to light concerning Spencer. In 1524 he was assessed for subsidy on £100 in goods and four years later he supplied oaks for the building of Wolsey's college at Ipswich. He is last glimpsed as plaintiff in a chancery suit brought against the bailiffs of Ipswich between 1529 and 1532.[5]

[1] Ipswich ct. bk. 7, p. 196. [2] Date of birth estimated from admission as freeman. N. Bacon, *Annals Ipswich*, 180–1; *Vis. Suff.* ed. Metcalfe, 67. [3] Bacon, 177, 180–1; *CPR*, 1494–1509, p. 254; *PRO Lists and Indexes, Exchequer Customs Accounts*, i. [4] Bacon, 167, 185; Ipswich ct. bks. 3, p. 9; 4, p. 55; 5, p. 49; 7, p. 196. [5] *Suff. Green Bks.* x. 415; *LP Hen. VIII*, iv; *ECP*, vi. 160.

J.P.

SPICER, Thomas (1502/3–59 or later), of Orford, Suff.

ORFORD 1555

b. 1502/3. ?*m.* Helen, 2s. 1da.[1]
Servant of Sir William Willoughby*, later 1st Baron Willoughby of Parham ?1537–54 or later; bailiff, manor of Orford by 1554.[2]

Thomas Spicer was probably a descendant of a namesake and mayor of Orford against whom the townsmen drew up an unspecified complaint in the reign of Henry VI. Nothing has come to light about his own life until in his mid 30s he entered the service of William Willoughby; as Willoughby's servant he collected the rents for 'stall boats' in Orford haven due to Lady Mary Willoughby until her death and then to his master as lord of the manor. Willoughby made Spicer his bailiff there. The Willoughby lordship of Orford was contested by the townsmen and Spicer's dependence on the family was to involve him in the clashes between the townsmen and Willoughby. During the uprisings of 1549 he was taken prisoner by the townsmen headed by Robert Pawling, one of their constables, and put in the stocks for three days. Early in January Spicer tried to arrest Pawling in Orford church on a writ of *non omittas* but Pawling denied his authority to do so, claiming it infringed the liberties of the town. Others came to Pawling's help and Spicer was only spared a second spell in the stocks by reason of their being broken. This episode, together with two other complaints against him of ploughing up a local highway and removing timber from a collapsed market stall, led to a series of suits and counter charges in the Chancery, Exchequer and Star Chamber, in which the Willoughby interest was again put to the test. Among the many deponents who in the autumn answered interrogatories relating to these suits before Sir William Drury* and Clement Heigham* were Spicer and his brother-in-law John Cook (q.v.). Spicer's own return to Parliament a year later has the appearance of being an affirmation of Willoughby's authority as well as a vindication of Spicer's own conduct. Like his fellow-Member Thomas Seckford he followed the lead of Sir Anthony Kingston in opposing a government bill.[3]

In January 1559 he sued out a general pardon from Elizabeth as Thomas Spicer, yeoman, late of Orford, and after his difficult term as bailiff he could well have moved away from the neighbourhood. If so, he may be identifiable with the man of this name assessed for the subsidy of 1568 on goods worth £6 in Lakenheath, Suffolk. This Thomas Spicer, by a will proved on 13 July 1579, left his lands there to his wife and son Mark, and his mares to two grandsons, the children of his son Thomas and daughter Joan Walker respectively. His executors were his son Mark and his son-in-law Edward Walker.[4]

[1] Aged 51 in Oct. 1554, C1/1392/35. Norwich consist. ct. 209 Woodstocke. [2] C1/1392/35; E111/48. [3] HMC Var. iv. 274; NCA 13/5; C1/1392/34, 35; St.Ch.4/10/52, 53, 76; E111/48; information from Dr. D. MacCulloch; Guildford mus. Loseley 1331/2. [4] CPR, 1558–60, p. 246; Suff. Green Bks. xii. 171; Norwich consist. ct. 209 Woodstocke.

M.K.D.

SPURWAY, Thomas (1481/83–1548), of Exeter, Devon.

EXETER 1542*

b. 1481/83, 2nd s. of John Spurway of Spurway in Oakford by Anne, da. of one Sherron. m. (1) da. of Geoffrey Lewis of Exeter; (2) Anne, da. of one Gale of Kirton in Crediton; at least 2s. 2da.[1]

Receiver-gen. to Edward 8th Earl of Devon by 1507–9, William 9th Earl of Devon 1511, Henry 10th Earl of Devon and Marquess of Exeter 1511–39, Catherine Dowager Countess of Devon by 1523–7; bailiff, Exeter 1529–30, member of the Twenty-Four by Oct. 1534–d., receiver 1535–6, mayor 1540–1; bailiff, manor of Exe Island by Oct. 1536–9 or later; receiver, lands of Queen Catherine Howard, Devon by 1542; jt. (with John Grenville*) particular-receiver, lands of Queen Catherine Parr, Devon and Dorset by 1548.[2]

According to John Hooker[†], Thomas Spurway was 'a reasonably tall man of stature, well compact of body, wise [of] nature and discreet, willing to

please and loath to offend any man'. He was born at Tiverton, of a gentle family with a tradition of service to the Courtenay earls of Devon, and this he followed until 1539 when the Marquess of Exeter was arrested for treason. His 'great credit' with the marquess did not harm him, for he was put in charge of the forfeited estates: he was also given the administration of some of the lands of two queens.[3]

It was after his marriage to the daughter of a former mayor of Exeter that Spurway was made a freeman, and on his father-in-law's death he went to live in Lewis's house in St. Martin's parish. For a number of years he reconciled the demands of a civic career with his position as the marquess's representative, but he was no longer filling the second when he was elected to Parliament. Both he and William Hurst (q.v.) were replaced during the second session, ostensibly on account of ill health, but on 12 Apr. 1543, only 16 days after the by-election, Spurway left Exeter to attend the remainder of the session; on the following day his replacement Gilbert Kirk returned there and had his account settled. It was Spurway, not Kirk, who accompanied Hurst to the third and last session a year later; while in the capital he was party to the copying of one of the city's charters in the Exchequer. He may have had a hand in the election for Exeter to the next Parliament of his colleague in Catherine Parr's service John Grenville.[4]

Despite his alleged sickness in 1542 Spurway is not known to have curtailed his activities before his death in 1548, two years after that of his temporary replacement in the House. By his will, made on 29 Mar. 1548 and proved on the following 8 May, he asked to be buried in St. Nicholas's churchyard at Exeter. After leaving money towards the maintenance of St. Martin's church where he was a parishioner, he provided for his wife and children, instructing his elder son Thomas to abide in the custody of his friend John Haydon* and to set himself to learning in London. His widow married Walter Staplehill*.[5]

[1] Aged 56 in 1538 or 1539, SP1/138, f. 130. PCC 6 Populwell; Vis. Devon (Harl. Soc. vi), 274; Vis. Devon, ed. Vivian, 724. [2] SP1/138, f. 130; LP Hen. VIII, iii, iv, vi, ix, xix, xx; Exeter act bk. 1, f. 139v; 2, f. 96v; R. Izacke, Exeter (1681), 115, 118, 130; Trans. Dev. Assoc. lxx. 415; information from W. Harwood; E315/340, f. 4v. [3] Exeter, Hooker's commonplace bk. f. 346; SP1/138, f. 130; M. R. Westacott, 'The estates of the earl of Devon, 1485–1538' (Exeter Univ. MA thesis, 1958), 52, 83; LP Hen. VIII, xix, xx. [4] Exeter Freemen (Devon and Cornw. Rec. Soc. extra ser. i), 69; Exeter, Hooker's commonplace bk. f. 346; act. bk. 2, f, 57v; J. Hoker, The description of the citie of Excester (Devon and Cornw. Rec. Soc. xi), 897. [5] PCC 6 Populwell.

A.D.K.H.

STAFFORD, Edward (1536–1603), of London.

BANBURY 1554 (Nov.)[1]

STAFFORD 1558, 1559

b. 17 Jan. 1536, 4th s. of Henry Stafford, 1st Baron Stafford by Ursula, da. of Sir Richard Pole of Ellesborough, Bucks.; bro. of Sir Henry* and Walter†. *m.* by Nov. 1566, Mary, da. of Edward Stanley, 3rd Earl of Derby, 2s. 2da. *suc.* bro. as 3rd Baron Stafford 1566.[2]

J.p.q. Glos., Salop, Staffs. by 1573/74, Mont. by 1591; v.-adm. Glos. 1587; member, council in marches of Wales 1601.[3]

Little is known of Edward Stafford's youth. His admission to the Middle Temple in 1565 and his MA at Oxford in 1566 came too late to be more than honorary distinctions. He may have finished his education in Europe, where his elder brothers Henry and Thomas travelled widely between 1550 and 1553. In Mary's reign Edward Stafford 'late of London', his father and a number of their retainers were accused in the Star Chamber of forcibly expelling Edward Stanford from an orchard at Forebridge, Staffordshire. The only other reference to Stafford about this time concerns his appearance before the Privy Council on 3 May 1557, shortly after his brother Thomas had failed in an ill-planned attempt to seize Scarborough castle. There is nothing to connect his brother's treason with Stafford, who was simply ordered to return to his father's home and await further orders.[4]

Banbury was incorporated and enfranchised in January 1554 by the 'labour and diligent suit' of Baron Stafford and Thomas Denton*, the first of whom may have been high steward of the borough. It is thus clear that at Banbury, as at Stafford, Stafford owed his return to his father: he was only 18 when elected for Banbury. His replacement of his uncle at Stafford in 1558 and his brother Sir Henry's failure to sit in the same Parliament may have had something to do with the divided religious allegiance of the Staffords. His uncle had opposed the initial measures towards the restoration of Catholicism in Mary's first Parliament and both uncle and brother may have been tainted by Thomas Stafford's treason, whereas Edward Stafford seems to have remained a Catholic. Yet if it was this which made him more acceptable than others of his family in 1558 it did not prevent his return in 1559, and his later career seems to have been more affected by his character than his religion.[5]

Stafford died intestate on 18 Oct. 1603.[6]

[1] Huntington Lib. Hastings mss Parl. pprs. [2] *CP* giving date of birth; *Staffs. Peds.* (Harl. Soc. lxiii), 213; *CPR*, 1569–72, pp. 35, 245. [3] R. Flenley, *Cal. Reg. Council, Marches of Wales*, 216; P. H. Williams, *Council in the Marches of Wales*, 358–9; *APC*, xv. 254. [4] St.Ch.4/4/38; *APC*, vi. 83. [5] A. Beesley, *Banbury*, 222; *Cath. Rec. Soc.* liii. 125, 230. [6] PCC admons. act bk. 1604, f. 190.

T.F.T.B.

STAFFORD, Henry (by 1520–55 or later), of Pickering, Yorks.

STAFFORD 1545, 1547, 1553 (Oct.), 1555

b. by 1520, illegit. s. of Edward Stafford, 3rd Duke of Buckingham.[1]

Steward of Henry, Baron Stafford's lordship of Essington in Holderness, Yorks. 30 Nov. 1541; commr. sewers. Yorks. (E. Riding) 1555.[2]

The identity of the Henry Stafford who was returned four times for the borough of that name has to be established by a process of elimination. Were it not for the fact that on each occasion the style 'armiger' is appended to the name there would be a case for distinguishing the man who sat in the first two Parliaments from his namesake in the two remaining ones: the earlier might then have been the Duke of Buckingham's heir Henry Baron Stafford and the later in all probability Stafford's son and namesake. As one tainted in blood by his father's condemnation Baron Stafford was eligible to sit in the Commons and as recorder of Stafford since 1532 he would have had a lien on that borough: only after his restoration in blood during the first session of the Parliament of 1547 would it have been necessary to replace him in the Commons, and his 20 year-old son Henry (the second so christened, after an earlier one had died in infancy) would have been at hand for the purpose. To this dual identification, however, the repeated use of 'armiger' is a stumbling-block, not only because it implies that the same individual was concerned throughout, but also because the style itself was hardly appropriate to either Henry Baron Stafford or his son. For his part the former, although he could have been properly so described, invariably appears as Baron Stafford, while his son could not have retained the style after his knighting in October 1553.[3]

No such difficulties arise in the case of a third Henry Stafford, an illegitimate son of the 3rd Duke of Buckingham and base brother of Henry Baron Stafford. This Henry Stafford is first heard of in 1541 when his brother granted him the stewardship of the family lands in Holderness. His association with Yorkshire makes it likely that he was the Henry Stafford who in 1544 led some horsemen from Bridlington to fight against the Scots, and this in turn suggests that it was he who some five years later was taken prisoner in Scotland and was rewarded by the Council with Scottish prisoners to the value of £200 as a contribution towards his own ransom of £700. While in the north in 1549 he was sued in the common pleas for £20 owed by him to a London mercer. He is, however, almost certainly to be distinguished from the Henry Stafford who in May 1547 despoiled a French ship off Rye and was being sued in the court of Admiralty for this offence three-and-a-half years later. By that time the

Member for Stafford was a seasoned parliamentarian. It is not certain whether he or Sir William Stafford was the 'Stafford, burgess' given leave of absence on 22 Feb. 1552 when suffering from measles, but he may have played a part in the restoration of Henry Baron Stafford in 1547, and a bill introduced, but not passed, during the same session for bakers at Stafford and elsewhere could have engaged his attention. In the first Parliament of Mary's reign he was one of the Members who 'stood for the true religion', that is, for Protestantism, but two years later he did not follow the lead of Sir Anthony Kingston in voting against one of the government's bills.[4]

It is not easy to trace Stafford's subsequent career but he may have gone to Ireland: a Henry Stafford gentleman was party to a fishing agreement there in 1556 and a man of the same name was appointed constable of the castle and honor of Dungarvan, Waterford, on 17 July 1559. In that case he is likely to have numbered among his kinsmen, perhaps as descendants, bearers of his name in south-east Ireland, including Sir Thomas Stafford, the reputed author of *Pacata Hibernia*.[5]

[1] Date of birth estimated from first reference. J. C. Wedgwood, *Staffs. Parlt. Hist.* (Wm. Salt Arch. Soc.), i. 317. [2] Wedgwood, i. 317; *CPR*, 1554–5, p. 110. [3] C219/18C/108, 19/92, 21/142, 24/142; Hatfield 207; Bodl. e Museo 17; Wedgwood, i. 315–16; *CP*. [4] Wedgwood, i. 317; *HMC 4th Rep.* i. 326; *HMC Bath*, iv. 70; *HMC. Shrewsbury and Talbot*, ii. 30; *APC*, iii. 149, 197; CP 40/1141, rr. 291, 465; *CJ*, i. 2, 18; Bodl. e Museo 17. [5] *APC*, v. 259; *CPR*, 1558–60, p. 92; *DNB* (Stafford, Sir Thomas).

A.D.

STAFFORD, Sir Henry (by 1527–66)

SHROPSHIRE   1555

b. by 1527, 2nd but 1st surv. s. of Henry Stafford, 1st Baron Stafford, by Ursula, da. of Sir Richard Pole of Ellesborough, Bucks.; bro. of Edward* and Walter†. *educ.* travelled 1551. *m.* by Sept. 1557, Elizabeth, da. of John Davy of Holbeach, Lincs., *d.s.p.* Kntd. 2 Oct. 1553; *suc.* fa. as 2nd Baron Stafford 30 Apr. 1563.[1] J.p. Salop 1554, q. Mont., Salop and Staffs. 1564; keeper of records, Tower temp. Eliz.[2]

Henry Stafford is chiefly memorable for having failed to secure election as knight for Staffordshire to both the Parliaments of 1553. Nothing is known of what went wrong on the first occasion, when William Devereux and Walter Aston were returned although according to Baron Stafford his son was 'chosen by the whole shire, no man saying the contrary'. Despite this setback Baron Stafford, who stood well with the Marian government, put his son forward confidently in the autumn, leaving it to his friends Sir George Griffith* and Humphrey Welles* to manage the election, but whereas Sir Thomas Giffard was returned unopposed Henry Stafford was again beaten, this time by Edward Littleton (q.v.).[3]

Stafford's knighting at Mary's coronation, which serves to distinguish him from the illegitimate son of his grandfather Edward, 3rd Duke of Buckingham, who sat four times for Stafford, may have helped towards his election for Shropshire in 1555. His family owned Cause castle and his appointment to the county bench in the previous year suggests that he was himself resident in the shire, as does his quarrel at Shrewsbury during 1556–7 with Edward Herbert*. He could also count on the support of his kinsman the 12th Earl of Arundel, a leading Shropshire landowner. Nothing is known of his role in the Commons save that he is not to be found on the list of those who opposed one of the government's bills, nor is he known to have been involved two years later in the rebellion of his brother Thomas. His father was a Catholic and on friendly terms with Cardinal Pole, who in 1551 had pressed his nephew, then travelling in Italy, 'to return to Christ's laws', but in 1564 the son was to be accounted favourable to the Elizabethan settlement. If he did not share his father's religion, his appointment as keeper of the records in the Tower early in Elizabeth's reign suggests that he shared his antiquarian interests. Even in this he was not left undisturbed for in January 1564 he complained to Cecil that he had been forcibly deprived of his office by William Bowyer†. Stafford died intestate on 1 Jan. 1566 and on 11 Apr. 1567 letters of administration were issued to Richard Tise of Southwark, a merchant taylor. He was succeeded in the barony by his brother Edward Stafford.[4]

[1] Date of birth estimated from position in a list of his father's children in order of birth, dated 1534, Add. 6672, f. 193. *CP*; *CSP For.* 1547–53, pp. 70–71; *Vis. Yorks.* (Harl. Soc. xvi), 93; *Lincs. Peds.* (Harl. Soc. l), 291. [2] *CPR*, 1553–4, p. 23; 1563–6, pp. 41–42; Stowe 543, f. 60. [3] *EHR*, lxxviii. 227–9. [4] *VCH Salop*, viii. 311; *Trans. Salop Arch. Soc.* (ser. 4), iv. 54; *CSP For.* 1547–53, pp. 70–71; *Cam. Misc.* ix(3), 16, 42; Stowe 543, f. 60.

A.H.

STAFFORD, Sir William (by 1512–56), of Chebsey, Staffs., Rochford, Essex, and London.

HASTINGS   1547[1]

b. by 1512, 2nd s. of Sir Humphrey Stafford of Blatherwycke and Dodford, Northants. by Margaret, da. of Sir John Fogge† of Ashford, Kent. *m.* (1) 1533/34, Mary (*d.*30 July 1543), da. of Thomas Boleyn, Earl of Wiltshire and Earl of Ormond, wid. of William Carey (*d.*22 June 1528), of Aldenham, Herts., *s.p.*; (2) by 1552, Dorothy (*d.*23 Sept. 1603), da. of Henry Stafford, 1st Baron Stafford, 3s. inc. Edward† and John† 1da. Kntd. 23 Sept. 1545.[2] Esquire of the body by 1541; gent. pens. 1540; standard bearer, gent. pens. by 20 May 1550–3.[3]

William Stafford could boast royal descent, but as the younger son of a midland family whose fortunes had been depleted during the previous century he had little hope of advancement before his marriage to Mary Boleyn, an ex-mistress of Henry VIII. He attended the coronation of Queen Anne Boleyn as a servitor and this may have been the occasion of his meeting with her sister whom he could have known, however, through his Kentish relatives. Their marriage displeased the King and Queen, as well as Cromwell, and Mary Boleyn told the minister that love had triumphed over reason and that although she 'might have had a greater man of birth and higher' she was content to lead 'a poor honest life' with her youthful husband. It was perhaps the Queen's coolness towards the pair which protected them when disaster struck her and her brother Lord Rochford: in the event they were gainers, for between 1539 and 1542 Mary Stafford was to inherit in succession her father's lands, those held in jointure by Rochford's widow and those of her grandmother the Countess of Ormond. Although the bulk of this property was to pass to the children of her first marriage, she was able to give her husband several manors in Essex, including Rochford which they made their home. In 1541 Stafford acquired the manor of Hendon in Kent from the crown but several months later he exchanged it for more valuable property in Yorkshire and London. After Mary's death he inherited the manor of Abinger, Surrey, which he later sold to Edward Elrington* and his cousin Thomas*.[4]

In 1543 Stafford was committed to the Fleet together with Sir John Clere* and others for eating meat on Good Friday. After his release and a rebuke from the Privy Council he served on the campaign of that year in the Netherlands. In 1544 he fought in France and in 1545 in Scotland, where he was knighted by Edward Seymour, Earl of Hertford. It was doubtless as a Protestant courtier and a soldier known to Hertford (by then Protector and Duke of Somerset) that he was returned to the Parliament of 1547: the electors of Hastings had no part in the matter, for the indenture was evidently returned to the lord warden, Sir Thomas Cheyne*, bearing one name only, that of John Isted, and it was Cheyne who added Stafford's. He was to be joined in the Commons by his stepson Henry Carey, one of the Members for Buckingham, and by his stepdaughter's husband Sir Francis Knollys, who sat for Camelford. Nothing is known of Stafford's role in the House, but if his second marriage had either taken place or was in contemplation he may have supported the Act for the restitution of Baron Stafford (1 Edw. VI, no. 18) passed during the first session, and it was either he or Henry Stafford who in the last session was licensed on 22 Feb. 1552 to be absent when suffering from measles. He was not harmed by

the Protector's fall: in 1550 Somerset's rival the Earl of Warwick granted him an annuity of £100 for his services to Henry VIII and entrusted him with the custody of three noble French hostages from Dover to London. In 1551 he accompanied the 9th Lord Clinton to Paris for the christening of one of Henry II's sons and on his return he took part in the New Year's tournament at court. He showed his loyalty to Northumberland by reporting a servant's allegation that the Protector had been innocent of the charges laid against him. Whether this act assured Northumberland of his support is not known, nor whether he sat in the next Parliament summoned early in 1553 under the duke's aegis: John Isted was re-elected for Hastings but the name of his fellow-Member on this occasion has not been discovered. A brawl with Adrian Poynings[†] in the previous November had reduced his standing in the Council's esteem and had led to a brief recommittal to the Fleet.[5]

Although Stafford's second marriage linked him more closely to the peerage, it brought him no wealth. In the early 1550s he disposed of much of the property given him by Mary Boleyn, and mounting debts induced him in 1552 to exchange his annuity for £900 in cash. It was perhaps as much fear of his creditors as of religious persecution that drove him into exile shortly after Queen Mary's accession. Accompanied by his wife, children, sister, cousin and servants, he settled in Geneva in March 1554, being known there as Lord Rochford. He soon became embroiled in its disputes and on returning there after the uprising of 1555 he was nearly killed in an affray. It was perhaps against a possible repetition of this incident that, as 'excellent personnage, homme de bien et de cognoissance', he was allowed to carry a sword. When the English congregation was set up he joined it and his son John was the first child to be baptized on 4 Jan. 1556, Calvin standing as godfather. Stafford died there on 5 May 1556, but the Privy Council was unaware of this when ten days later it ordered that 'no payment of money by exchange or otherwise' was to reach him. Calvin claimed the custody of his son John and forbade his widow to leave with him. She appealed to Stafford's younger brother and the threat to invoke French aid persuaded Calvin to yield. She then moved to Basle, remaining there until January 1559, when she returned to England. Queen Elizabeth, whom she outlived, appointed her mistress of the robes.[6]

[1] Hatfield 207. [2] Date of birth estimated from first reference. *The Gen.* n.s. xxxi. 177; *Her and Gen.* iv. 40; *Arch. Cant.* xxviii. 196. [3] *LP Hen. VIII*, xvi, xix; Stowe 571, f. 31; S. Pegge, *Curialia* (1791), 43; information from W. J. Tighe. [4] *LP Hen. VIII*, vi. vii, xv–xviii; PCC 14 Alen; C142/72/86(1); *CPR*, 1549–51, p. 247; 1553–4, p. 414;

APC, iv. 120. ⁵ *APC*, i. 106, 114, 125; iii. 5; iv. 179, 185; *LP Hen. VIII*, xviii, xix; Add. 34150; *CJ*, i. 18; *CPR*, 1549–51, p. 306; *Lit. Rems. Edw. VI*, pp. clxviii, 260, 349, 384; W. K. Jordan, *Edw. VI*, ii. 432–3; B. L. Beer, *Northumberland*, 136. ⁶ *CPR*, 1549–51, p. 247; 1553–4, p. 352; *APC*, iv. 79, 188; v. 257, 271; W. C. Richardson, *Ct. Augmentations*, 350; C. Martin, *Les protestants anglais réfugiés à Genève, 1550–60*, pp. 55–58, 335, 337; C. H. Garrett, *Marian Exiles*, 296.

P.H.

STAFFORD *see also* **STOWFORD**

STANFORD, Thomas (by 1480–1532), of Rowley, Staffs.

STAFFORD 1529*

b. by 1480, 3rd s. of Robert Stanford of Rowley by Margery, da. of one Fisher of Rowley. *m.* by 1501, da. of William Henshaw of Gloucester, 1s. 3da.; 1s. illegit.[1]

Little has come to light about Thomas Stanford. Although he lived in the neighbourhood, he was apparently not a freeman of Stafford. His election could have owed something to the constable of Stafford castle, Edward Littleton, who in 1529 was returned as a knight of the shire. Stanford's marriage into the family of a bell-founder and mayor of Gloucester suggests that his career may have begun in the service of Edward Stafford, 3rd Duke of Buckingham (*d.*1521), whose principal residence had been in Gloucestershire; his mother's forbears had served the Stafford family and owed to it their property in Rowley. After Stanford's death the capital messuage there was to be the subject of a dispute between his heir and Buckingham's heir Baron Stafford, who claimed that the property had been restored to him with the barony in 1531.[2]

Stanford died on 13 Jan. 1532, two days before the opening of the third session of the Parliament, and was buried in the church at Castle Church. At the inquisition held at Stafford on the following 5 Feb. it was found that he had some property in the locality and that his son and heir William (not to be confused with a namesake, Stanford's nephew, who was to be returned for Stafford to the last two Henrician Parliaments) was aged 31 years and more. Thomas Stanford's death was noted a month or two later when the list of Members of the Parliament was revised, and at the by-election which followed he was replaced by Sampson Erdeswick.[3]

¹ Date of birth estimated from marriage. *Wm. Salt Arch. Soc.* iii(2), 133, 136. ² Ibid. iii(2), 133; (1912), 24; *VCH Staffs.* v. 80; *Trans. Bristol and Glos. Arch. Soc.* xxvi. 45. ³ *Wm. Salt Arch. Soc.* iii(2), 133; viii(2), 89; SP1/56/9; C142/53/32; E150/1038/5.

L.M.K./A.D.K.H.

STANFORD (STAMFORD, STAMPFORD, STAUNFORD), William (1509–58), of Hadley, Mdx. and London

STAFFORD	1542, 1545
NEWCASTLE-UNDER-LYME	1547

b. 22 Aug. 1509, 2nd s. of William Stanford of London by Margaret, da. and h. of one Gedney of London. *educ.* Oxf.; G. Inn, adm. 1528, called 1536. *m.* Alice, da. of John Palmer of Kentish Town, Mdx., 6s. inc. Robert† 5da. Kntd. 27 Jan. 1555.[1]

Autumn reader, G. Inn 1544, Lent 1551.[2]

Attorney, ct. gen. surveyors of the king's lands 1542–28 Dec. 1546; commr. sale of crown lands 1543, benevolence, Mdx. 1544/45, chantries, London, Westminster, Mdx. 1546, contribution, Mdx. 1546, of Admiralty in Nov. 1547, relief, Mdx. and Westminster 1550, eccles. law 1552, goods of churches and fraternities, Westminster 1553, survey crown possessions 1557; other commissions 1553–55; j.p. Mdx. 1543–*d.*, Cornw., Devon, Dorset, Hants, Som., Wilts. 1554; serjeant-at-law 17 Oct. 1552; Queen's serjeant 19 Oct. 1553; j.c.p. by June 1554; receiver of petitions in the Lords, Parlt. of 1558.[3]

William Stanford's father, a London mercer, was a younger son of Robert Stanford of Rowley, Staffordshire. The 'spirit of retraction of one to his native country' led William Stanford to acquire property in Staffordshire, but his birthplace remained his home, Hadley on the borders of Middlesex and Hertfordshire.[4]

Stanford entered Gray's Inn after a spell at Oxford and was called to the bar in 1536. He was chosen Autumn reader in 1544 but had to postpone his lectures, said to have been on Glanvill, until the following year on account of the plague. His patent of appointment as attorney of the newly-erected court of general surveyors is dated 1 May 1542, but he had by then been discharging the duties for some months: on 24 Apr. he was given a receipt for £850 which he had paid into the court in February. The office, which was third in rank in the court, carried a fee of £40 a year and when he surrendered his patent on 28 Dec. 1546 he received an annuity of £90. Sometimes described as general attorney or attorney general to the court, he has on this account been wrongly said to have succeeded William Whorwood* as attorney general in 1545.[5]

Stanford's parliamentary career began coincidentally with his attorneyship and was doubtless connected with it: his chief friend at court, Sir Thomas Wriothesley, who had followed him at Gray's Inn and was now one of the two principal secretaries, was much involved in the elections of 1542. Locally, it must have been with the consent of Henry Stafford, later 1st Baron Stafford, that Stanford was returned for the borough of that name: Stafford held the castle and manor there and was heavily indebted to Stanford. It was probably also Stafford, a relation by marriage of the locally powerful 5th Earl of Shrewsbury, who procured Stanford's return for Newcastle (where his name was inserted in the indenture in a different hand from that of the document and over an erasure), while Stanford himself may have recommended his fellow-lawyer Richard Forsett and Edward Colbarne at Stafford in 1547 and 1553. Although Stanford was described in the returns of 1542 and 1545 as of London, it was at this time that he began to nourish his Staffordshire roots by investment. In 1545 he leased woodland and in the following year he joined with William Wyrley in buying the manor of Perry Barr; ten years later he bought Sir John St. Leger's* manor of Handsworth. It was, however, probably his cousin and namesake of Rowley who in 1537 leased 'the manor place of the castle of Stafford', who was involved in the dissolution of the Grey Friars and Austin Friars there in 1538 and whose signature appears on the record of an interrogation about a debt to the last abbot of Glastonbury; it was this cousin, too, who was co-defendant in a suit of 1549 over the property of the late deanery of Stafford.[6]

Stafford's Membership of the Commons came to an end in 1552, but under Mary he was to be summoned to the Lords by writ of assistance, first as a Queen's serjeant and then as a judge. There appear to be few traces of his part in the proceedings of either House. In the Parliament of 1542 he was one of the five Members, all royal officials, who signed the Act for an exchange of lands between the King and the 3rd Duke of Norfolk which was passed in the third session, and in March 1552, during his own last session in the Commons, he was one of the committee which drafted the Treasons Act (5 and 6 Edw. VI, c.11). In the Lords, in the course of Mary's third Parliament, the bill for punishment of seditious words and rumours was committed to him for the adding of a proviso. It was after he had ceased to sit in the Commons that an unexpected tribute was paid to his speeches there. It came from Sir Nicholas Throckmorton*, whom he helped to prosecute for treason in April 1554 and who rebutted his arguments with what he had 'remembered and learned of you master [Sir Nicholas] Hare*, and you master Stanford in the Parliament House, where you did sit to make laws, to expound and explain the ambiguities and doubts of law sincerely, and that without affections': Stanford could only answer that if he had known that the prisoner would be 'so well furnished with book cases' he would have come better provided himself. As a judge Stanford heard at least one case which may have stirred memories: this was the leading case in electoral law, Sir Richard Bulkeley (q.v.) versus Rhys Thomas, in which one of the issues was the validity of a parliamentary election 'by the greater number', without indication of the number of electors. Stanford held that the sheriff could make such a return, and his fellow-judges, among them Sir Robert Broke*, concurred.[7]

During Edward VI's reign Stanford did not share in the eclipse of his friend Wriothesley (who in 1550 named him an executor) but succeeded in reconciling his Catholicism with service to the increasingly Protestant regime. His call as serjeant in October 1552 shows that neither he nor Broke, another Catholic included in the call, was discriminated against and his place on the commission to try Bishop Tunstall that he was trusted: he was even included among the bishops, divines and civil and common lawyers charged with reforming the canon law. It was left to Mary, however, to promote him to Queen's serjeant and judge. His only mention by Foxe relates to his time as Queen's serjeant and depicts him as befriending a Protestant, Richard Bertie[†]. One of Stanford's assignments was to question Sir Anthony Kingston after his committal to the Tower for his obstreperous behaviour in the Parliament of 1555. He has secured a place in legal history chiefly by his writings. He is said to have prepared the first printed edition of Glanvill's *Tractatus*, and his own *Les Plees del Coron* (1560) and *Exposicion of the Kinges Prerogative* (1567) became standard works and went into several editions. As a judge he was a recognized expert on interpretation: in 1556 he lent his authority to the rules which should govern the construction of a deed.[8]

Stanford made his will on 4 Apr. 1558, leaving his soul to God and his body to be buried in Hadley, Handsworth or Islington. He left 200 marks' worth of household goods to his wife Alice, to whom he had already assured for life all his lands and tenements in London and Middlesex. The rest of his household goods, to the value of £100, went to his heir Robert. Three daughters each received 200 marks, and four sons £100. He named his wife executrix and his fellow-judge (Sir) James Dyer* overseer. Stanford died at Hadley on 28 Aug. 1558, when his heir Robert was 18 years old. The widow, who later married Roger Carew[†], received a grant of Robert's wardship in April 1559. Robert Stanford settled in Staffordshire and sat for the county in the first Jacobean Parliament. It may have been his religion that kept him out of the Commons under Elizabeth: his brother Ralph was a seminary priest.[9]

[1] Date of birth given in *DNB*. *Wm. Salt Arch. Soc.* v(2), 279–80; Harl. 897, f. 18; Lansd. 874, f. 60; Emden, *Biog. Reg. Univ. Oxf. 1501–40*, p. 535. No evidence has been found for the statement in Shaw, *Staffs.* ii. 108 that Stanford married Elizabeth Comerford. [2] Dugdale, *Origines Juridiciales*, 293. [3] *LP Hen. VIII*, xvii, xviii, xx, xxi; *CPR*, 1547–8, p. 86; 1550–3, pp. 354–5, 396; 1553, pp. 186, 356, 361, 417; 1553–4, pp. 17–19, 21, 23, 25, 28, 30, 32, 162; 1554–5, p. 105; 1555–7, p.313; *APC*, iii. 382; *Machyn's Diary* (Cam. Soc. xlii) 26–27; *LJ*, i. 513; HCA 14/2. [4] Fuller, *Worthies*, ii. 323. [5] G. H. G.

Hall, *Glanvill*, p. lxiii; *LP Hen. VIII*, xvii; *CPR*, 1553–4, p. 10; W. C. Richardson, *Ct. Augmentations*, 258–9; Foss, *Judges*, v. 390. [6] *LP Hen. VIII*, xiii, xiv, xix–xxi; J. C. Wedgwood, *Staffs. Parl. Hist.* (Wm. Salt Arch. Soc.), i. 311; A. D. Tucker, 'Commons in Parlt. of 1545' (Oxf. Univ. D. Phil. thesis, 1966), 552; C219/19/91; *CPR*, 1554–5, pp. 136, 140; *VCH Staffs.* v. 85, 90; Richardson, 394. [7] C218/1, mm. 1–11; *APC*, v. 22; House of Lords RO, Original Acts, 35 Hen. VIII, no. 22; *CJ*, i. 20; W. J. Fitzgerald, 'Treason legislation 1547–1603' (London Univ. M.A. thesis, 1963), 42; *LJ*, i. 474; *State Trials*, ed. Howell, i. 869 seq.; Strype, *Eccles. Memorials*, ii(1), 554; L. W. Abbott, *Law Reporting in Eng.* 223–4. [8] T. Tanner, *Bibl. Brit. Hib.* (1748), 691; *APC*, iii. 382; v. 202; *CPR*, 1553–4, p. 76; Foxe, *Acts and Mons*, viii. 570; W. S. Holdsworth, *Hist. Eng. Law*, iii. 460; v. 392; Wood, *Ath. Ox.* ed. Bliss, i. 263; Abbott, 229. [9] PCC 53 Noodes; C142/115/1; *CPR*, 1558–60, p. 103; G. Anstruther, *Seminary Priests*, i. 330–1; *Cath. Rec. Soc.* liv. 258–9; lv. 615–16.

A.D.

STANHOPE, Michael (by 1508–52), of Shelford, Notts., Kingston-upon-Hull, Yorks. and Beddington, Surr.

NOTTINGHAMSHIRE 1545, 1547*

b. by 1508, 2nd s. of Sir Edward Stanhope of Rampton, Notts. by Adelina, da. of Sir Gervase Clifton[†] of Clifton, Notts. *m.* by Nov. 1537, Anne, da. of Nicholas Rawson of Aveley, Essex, 7s. inc. Edward Stanhope I[†], Edward Stanhope II[†], John Stanhope[†], Michael[†] and Sir Thomas[†] 4da. *suc.* bro. 21 Jan. 1529. Kntd. Sept. 1545/Feb. 1546.[1]

Servant of Thomas Manners, 1st Earl of Rutland by 1532; j.p. Notts. 1537–*d.*, Yorks. (W. Riding) 1543–*d.*, (E. and N. Ridings) 1544–*d.*; (? yeoman) of the stable by 1538–40; keeper, Knessall park., Notts. 1538, Hundon park., Suff. June 1542–Dec. 1543, Beddington House, Surr. 1547–*d.*; bailiff, lordship of Knessall 1538, former estates of Lenton priory, Notts. 1539; esquire of the body 1540; lt. Kingston-upon-Hull 17 Feb. 1542–*d.*, gov. by Sept. 1544–*d.*; steward, ct. augmentations, Earl of Northumberland's lands by 1544; commr. benevolence, Yorks. (E. Riding) 1545, relief, Notts. 1550; custos rot. Notts. in 1547; groom of the stole 24 Aug. 1547–25 Mar. 1549; master of the King's harriers July 1548–*d.*; chief gent. the privy chamber by 1549.[2]

Michael Stanhope was born into a well established Nottinghamshire family. His father, who fought at Stoke in 1487 and at Blackheath ten years later, was afterwards a knight of the body, constable of Sandal castle and steward of the town and lordship of Wakefield: he died in 1511 and was succeeded by his eldest son, whose own death without male issue in 1529 gave Michael Stanhope the patrimony. Stanhope was in the Earl of Rutland's service by 1532, when he received a livery on the earl's behalf, but it was the marriage of his half-sister Anne to the royal favourite Sir Edward Seymour which set the course of his career. His first post in the royal stables was a modest one but from 1540, when he became an esquire of the body, his rise was swift.[3]

In October 1536 Stanhope met the 4th Earl of Shrewsbury in Sherwood Forest to help prevent the rebellion in Lincolnshire from spreading to neighbouring counties. His decisiveness on this occasion earned him a place on the Nottinghamshire bench and several offices in the locality, as well as enabling him to secure much ex-monastic property. His most important acquisition was Shelford priory, which he bought with some neighbouring manors in November 1537; it was followed two years later by leases of Lenton priory and of all the booths and profits of Lenton market, and appointment as bailiff of the lordship. In 1540 he bought Shelford manor and other lands nearby as well as rectories in Nottinghamshire, Lincolnshire and Derbyshire formerly appropriated to Shelford priory.[4]

Stanhope's appointment first as lieutenant of the Hull garrison and then as governor of the town he must have owed to his brother-in-law, by then Earl of Hertford; as well as carrying responsibility for the town's defence the offices involved him in supplying ships and provisions for Berwick. His manner of carrying out these duties soon brought him into conflict with the townsmen of Hull, whose 'lewd behaviour' he complained of in 1546 to the Privy Council, but despite the countervailing complaints of his own high-handedness he was kept in office. The downfall of his brother-in-law weakened his position, but the issue was only to be resolved by his death.[5]

Stanhope had reached the peak of his career with the accession of Edward VI and Hertford's elevation to the dukedom of Somerset and the Protectorate. As groom of the stole he controlled the King's privy purse and by 1549 he was recognized as the leading figure in the royal entourage: it was to circumvent Stanhope that Somerset's brother, Admiral Seymour, used John Fowler* as intermediary in his dealings with the King. With enhanced status went material benefits and influence. In 1548 Stanhope purchased, with John Bellow*, large parcels of chantry land in various counties, the main body being in the East Riding of Yorkshire. In the previous year he had acquired the hospital of St. Sepulchre near Hedon and all its possessions within the borough, and it was clearly at his suit that Hedon was straightway re-enfranchised. Neither of the Members returned to the Parliament of that year was a resident, and one of them, Robert Googe, had sat for Hull in 1545, doubtless also as Stanhope's nominee.[6]

Stanhope himself sat in the Parliament of 1547 as one of the knights for Nottinghamshire: he had done so in its precursor and may have been first returned for the shire in 1542, when the names have not been preserved. Nothing is known of his role in the Commons, but his knighting at Hampton Court almost certainly took place while he was attending the first session of the Parliament of 1545. He probably missed the whole of the third session of the following Parliament on account of his captivity in the Tower and the terms of his release from it. He had accompanied the Protector to Windsor during the *coup d'état* of 1549, and for his share in Somerset's 'ill-government' he was sent to the Tower a month before the session opened. Somerset was released on 6 Feb. 1550, and although an order of 17 Feb. for Stanhope's custody without servants or visitors seemed to presage his continued detention he too was freed five days later upon entering into a bond of £3,000 to 'be from day to day forthcoming and to abide all orders'. The renewed attack on Somerset a year-and-a-half later saw Stanhope's re-entry to the Tower, this time with his half-sister the duchess, as an accomplice in the alleged conspiracy against the Duke of Northumberland. On 26 Jan. 1552 he and Sir Miles Partrych were indicted for having 'feloniously' instigated Somerset to insurrection and for 'holding rebellious assemblies, for the purpose of taking imprisoning and murdering' Northumberland, the Marquess of Northampton and the 1st Earl of Pembroke. At his trial he pleaded not guilty, but the court convicted him of felony and sentenced him to be hanged. In the event Stanhope was beheaded on 26 Feb. His attainder was confirmed by Act (5 and 6 Edw. VI, no.37) and his death was noted on the list of Members then in use, but there is no evidence that he was replaced in the Commons before the dissolution nearly two months later.[7]

On 2 Mar. 1552 (Sir) Richard Sackville II* was ordered to eject Stanhope's widow from her house at Beddington and to provide her with alternative accommodation; on 13 Mar. she received a grant of Lenton priory, the demesne lands and other lordships in Nottinghamshire, and it was there that she 'brought up all the younger children in virtue and learning . . . and kept continually a worshipful house' until her death in 1587. Stanhope's lands were restored to his heir Thomas by an Act for his restitution in blood (1 Mary st. 2, no. 26) passed in Queen Mary's first Parliament. Thomas Stanhope was the ancestor of the earls of Chesterfield.[8]

[1] Date of birth estimated from age at brother's i.p.m., C142/47/17. *Vis. Notts.* (Harl. Soc. iv), 7; *APC*, iii. 484; *DNB*. [2] *HMC Rutland*, iv. 271; *LP Hen. VIII*, xii–xiv, xvii–xxi; W. C. Richardson, *Ct. Augmentations*, 52n, 53; *CPR*, 1547–8, pp. 88, 91–92, 274; 1550–3, p. 381; 1553, pp. 137, 357; *APC*, ii. 394; E351/2932. [3] *Trans. Thoroton Soc.* vii. 38 seq.; *CPR*, 1494–1509, p. 303; *HMC Rutland*, iv. 271; *LP Hen. VIII*, xvi, xxi. [4] *LP Hen. VIII*, xi–xv. [5] Ibid. xvii–xx; *Hamilton Pprs.* ii. 329(2); *APC*, i. 533; iii. 102, 196, 203. [6] E351/2932; *CPR*, 1547–8, p. 170; 1548–9, pp. 37–39, 204–8; *HMC Bath*, iv. 374. [7] *HMC Bath*, iv. 112; W. K. Jordan, *Edw. VI*, i. 520, 521; ii. 32, 91–92, 97, 110; R. S. Gammon, *Statesman and Schemer*, 167; *Lit. Rems. Edw. VI*, 234, 355, 361, 385, 394; *APC*, ii. 343, 393, 398; iii. 102, 391, 397, 484; *DKR*, iv(2), 231–2; B. L. Beer, *Northumberland*, 130–1; *CJ*, i. 23; Hatfield 207. [8] *Trans. Thoroton Soc.* vii. 38 seq.; *APC*, iii. 495, 506; Pevsner, *Notts.* 157.

C.J.B.

STANLEY, Edward I (by 1513-64 or later), of Harlech, Merion.

MERIONETH 1542

b. by 1513, 2nd s. of Peter Stanley of Flint, by Janet, da. of Sir Thomas Butler. ?*educ.* Oxf. BA 2 July 1526. *m.* Ellen, illegit. da. of Meredydd ap Ievan ap Robert of Dolwyddelan and Gwydir, Caern.[1]

Dep. constable, Harlech castle by 1534–51, constable 26 Mar. 1551–?*d*.; bailiff, commote of Arduwy, Merion. in 1534; j.p.q. Merion. 1543–64 or later; sheriff 1544–5, 1552–3, 1559–60; commr. benevolence 1544/45, relief 1550, goods of churches and fraternities 1553, subsidy 1556.[2]

On 17 Dec. 1541 Rowland Lee, president of the council in the marches, wrote to John Wynn ap Meredydd* recommending Richard Mytton* as knight of the shire for Merioneth in the Parliament due to assemble in the following month, but it was Wynn's brother-in-law Edward Stanley who was to be chosen on 3 Jan. 1542, while Mytton was elected with his father for Shrewsbury. Stanley perhaps had the support of a more influential figure than Lee in the person of the King's favourite Sir Francis Bryan, whose deputy he was at Harlech castle: Bryan himself sat for Buckinghamshire on this occasion. Although Bryan lived until 1550 Stanley did not reappear in Parliament: in 1545 he was debarred by his shrievalty and by 1547 Bryan had ceased to be a favourite. As sheriff Stanley returned his neighbour Rhys Vaughan I to Parliament in 1544 and Lewis ab Owen and John Salesbury seven years later.[3]

Stanley's father had been a pillar of the Tudors in north Wales, and in addition to offices in Denbighshire and Flintshire he had held the shrievalty of Merioneth and the constableship of Harlech castle until his death during 1520–1: after Bryan's death Stanley himself succeeded to the constableship. He may be identifiable with the student at Oxford in the early 1520s, but nothing is otherwise known about his life before 1534, by which time he was an established figure in Merioneth. At the Union he was named to the county bench and he was thrice pricked sheriff. He remained active in local affairs until 1564, but after that date nothing more is heard of him. If he made a will it has not been found.[4]

[1] Date of birth estimated from first reference. Dwnn, *Vis. Wales*, ii. 284, 316; Griffiths, *Peds.* 280; Emden, *Biog. Reg. Univ. Oxf. 1501–40*, p. 535. [2] SC6/Hen. VIII, 5457, mm. iv, 5v; Stowe 571, f. 75; E. Breese, *Kalendars of Gwynedd*, 133; C193/12/1; E179/222/314, 316, 323; *CPR*, 1553, pp. 363, 419; 1563–6, p. 31. [3] *Cal. Wynn (of Gwydir) Pprs. 1515–1690*, p. 1. [4] Breese, 70, 133; SC6/Hen. VIII, 5457, 5471, 5473–5, 5477.

P.S.E.

STANLEY, Edward II (1521/22–?1609), of Ewloe and Cilcain, Flints.

FLINT BOROUGHS 1553 (Mar.), 1553 (Oct.), 1555

b. 1521/22, 1st s. of Peter Stanley of Flint, by Jane

Parker. *m.* by 1553, Margaret, da. of Sir James Stanley of Cross Hall, Lancs., 7s. 3da. *suc.* fa. 1539.[1]

Subsidy collector, Flints. temp. Edw. VI; j.p. 1555, q. 1558/59; escheator 1562–3.[2]

Edward Stanley belonged to the Hooton branch of an old Cheshire family, and his forbears had long been prominent in Flint. His father died when Stanley was rising 17, but with the aid of his uncle and namesake he was able to buy his own wardship and marriage, and on reaching his majority he sued out livery of his inheritance in June 1543. He had to defend it against encroachments by kinsmen and others, among them Thomas Salusbury* who infringed his monopoly of grinding corn at Flint by erecting another mill nearby. His Membership of three Parliaments in quick succession may have been connected with these disputes; it is unlikely that he sat in April 1554 as Robert Massey's (q.v.) replacement at Flint Boroughs, since Massey was related by marriage to his opponent Salusbury. All that is known about Stanley's part in the Commons is that he did not join the opposition to the Marian regime in 1553 or 1555.[3]

Stanley was named to the local bench shortly before his last appearance in the House and he was placed on the quorum at Elizabeth's accession. Doubts as to his fitness were first raised by his detractors and then conceded by his friends, and he was not reappointed to the bench on completing his term as escheator. In May 1569 he suffered a mental breakdown from which he never recovered although he enjoyed lucid spells until his death 40 years later. An inquisition held in 1574 found that during his madness he had sold land worth £16 a year and recommended that his remaining property should be transferred to his son Robert. During one of his last spells of lucidity five years later Stanley set up a trust to provide for his daughters. He continued to engage in litigation, and in 1585 he made a fine in the Exchequer for his sloth in collecting the subsidy under Edward VI. He was buried at Hawarden near Ewloe in January 1609.[4]

[1] Date of birth estimated from age at fa.'s i.p.m., E150/1223/11. H. Taylor, *Flint*, 122; Dwnn, *Vis. Wales*, ii. 316. [2] *Exchequer* (Univ. Wales Bd. of Celtic Studies, Hist. and Law ser. xv), 191; SP11/5/6. [3] Taylor, 101, 106–7; *CPR*, 1485–94, p. 196; 1494–1509, p. 486; 1549–51, p. 76; *LP Hen. VIII*, iv, viii, xviii; Wards 9/149, f. 161; *Augmentations* (Univ. Wales Bd. of Celtic Studies, Hist. and Law ser. xiii), 95, 99, 104; E159/334, Easter 74. [4] C1/1474/44–46; *Cat. Mss Wales* (Cymmrod. rec. ser. iv), 603; Wards 7/14/79; Harl. rolls E15; *Exchequer*, 191; Taylor, 122; Ches. 3/77/26, 90/21.

P.S.E.

STANLEY, Thomas (1511/13–71), of Dalegarth, Cumb. and London.

LIVERPOOL 1547
BOSSINEY 1558

b. 1511/13, 3rd s. of Thomas Stanley of Dalegarth by Margaret, da. of John Fleming. *educ.* ?G. Inn, adm. 1537. *m.* by 1552, Joyce, da. of John Barrett of Belhus in Aveley, Essex, wid. of Sir James Wilford* (*d.*Nov. 1550) of Hartridge, Kent, 1da.[1]

Assay master, Tower I mint Mar. 1545–Mar. 1552, comptroller Mar. 1552–Sept. 1561, under treasurer Sept. 1561–*d.*; warden, Goldsmiths' Co. 1555–6, 1560–1, prime warden 1565–6; commr. sewers, Kent 1553, 1555; j.p. 1562, q. 1569.[2]

It has been customary to identify the senior Member for Liverpool in the Parliament of 1547 with the Sir Thomas Stanley, second son of the 3rd Earl of Derby, who was to sit as knight of the shire for Lancashire in three Marian Parliaments. Yet the earl had been married not long before February 1530 and his eldest son born in September 1531, so that in the autumn of 1547 his son Thomas could have been barely 15, an age at which even an earl's son could scarcely have been elected. Much to be preferred is the identification of the Member of 1547—and of 1558—with Thomas Stanley of the mint.[3]

Although this Thomas Stanley inherited 'the first and most ancient family possessions of Greysouthen, Embleton and Brackenthwaite in Cumberland', and was himself to add to them, he spent his life in and around London. He may have prefaced his apprenticeship as a goldsmith by a spell at Gray's Inn, where a Thomas Stanley was admitted in 1537: the style 'esquire' appended to his name both on the election indenture of 1547 and on the pardon roll of the same year could have owed something to legal attainment. It was, however, as a goldsmith that Stanley qualified himself for his career. Trained under Sir Martin Bowes*, whose second wife's sister he later married, Stanley was admitted to the livery of the Goldsmiths' Company during March 1545 on the eve of becoming an assay master in the mint, where following its recent reorganization Bowes was already established as under treasurer. On the accession of Edward VI he sued out a pardon as a citizen and goldsmith of London *alias* of Dalegarth, esquire.[4]

Election to the first Parliament of the new reign would have followed naturally from such a progression. With the ill effects of the Great Debasement under attack and the Protector himself holding the office of treasurer, the mint seems to have been well represented in the Commons, amongst others Bowes sitting for London. Enjoying such patronage, and with his name and distant kinship to the Earl of Derby to commend him, Stanley was suitably placed at Liverpool, where indeed a colleague at the mint Francis Goldsmith may have been originally named as his fellow, only to be superseded by Francis Cave. Of Stanley's part in the work of this Parliament the only trace is the committal to him, on 7 Mar. 1549, of a bill 'for the continuance of divers Acts' which, however, did not survive the prorogation a week later, but presumably he took an active interest in the Act regulating the exchange of gold and silver (5 and 6 Edw. VI, c.19) passed in the final session of 1552. By what must be taken for an error—perhaps arising from an attempt to explain what may have appeared a double occupancy of the second Liverpool seat—Stanley's name is suffixed by the adjective 'mortuus' on the list of Members which was annotated in preparation for that session: he had another 20 years of life ahead of him, and no other Thomas Stanley is known to have died about this time.[5]

Towards the end of his Membership in the Parliament of 1547 Stanley was consulted about the new coinage then under review by the Duke of Northumberland and exchanged the office of assay master at the Tower for that of comptroller. On the downfall of the Protector the treasurership had passed to the 1st Marquess of Winchester, and Stanley's promotion with Winchester's approval is unlikely to have had political significance. In the absence of so many returns to the Parliament he is not known to have been re-elected early in 1553 when his expertise would have proved invaluable in the passage of the Act reviving earlier measures controlling the export of gold and silver (7 Edw. VI, c.6). Both Winchester and Stanley retained their offices under Mary, and Stanley had his salary increased from 100 marks to £100 a year. His growing prosperity had already shown itself in his acquisition of land. In January 1549 he had paid close on £150 for a chantry in the parish church of Kirkby Ireleth, a property which while it gave him a stake in Lancashire was geographically an outlier of his Cumberland patrimony, while his subsequent securing of three wardships in his native county reflects his continued interest in its affairs. It was, however, his position at the mint which dictated his principal purchases, beginning in 1548 with a house at Woolwich bought from Sir Edward Dymoke*. On 1 July 1553 he obtained the wardship of his stepson, Thomas Wilford, with custody of Thomas's inheritance in Kent. Four years later he sold some Kentish property to John Robinson, one of his Cumberland wards, but he bought more in the county in 1558 and 1565, and in May 1562 Robinson, who also became a goldsmith, had licence to alienate to him certain manors in Cumberland.[6]

Problems arising from the reorganization of the mint and schemes to reform the coinage were to take up most of Stanley's time under Mary. At first he shared the control of the Tower mint with Thomas

Egerton* but after Egerton's dismissal in 1555 the responsibility was his alone. The proposals submitted by him late in 1557 for the revaluation of the coinage presumably account for his Membership in 1558 when as Thomas Stanley 'armiger' he was returned for Bossiney. As his name was inserted on the election indenture over an erasure, the replacement of Stanley's earlier style of 'esquire' need not tell against the identification, while the translation from Lancashire to Cornwall is less unlikely than it might appear. Treasurer Winchester's pervasive influence apart, Sir John Arundell* of Lanherne could have provided the necessary link. Arundell had sat for Preston in 1555, doubtless at the instance of the Earl of Derby, one of whose daughters, the widowed Lady Stourton, he was afterwards to marry, and in 1558 he was to secure a knighthood of the shire for Cornwall: as another client of Derby's, Stanley may well have enjoyed Arundell's backing at Bossiney, a borough which was used to returning such stranger-nominees. Nothing is known about his part in this Parliament.[7]

Retained in office by Elizabeth, Stanley sued out a pardon in 1559 and he was further promoted in 1561 to under treasurer; the recoinage considered for over a decade was then achieved under his supervision. This task brought him into conflict with his subordinates at the mint and his manner of executing it seems to explain the clash between him and the Goldsmiths not long after his term as prime warden of the company. The ostensible quarrel with the Goldsmiths over the delivery of bullion and its repayment within two weeks led to an information being laid against him in the Exchequer early in 1571 and the confiscation of some of his Cumberland property in October following his failure to render a complete account for the reign of Mary. The process against him was terminated by his death two months later, on 15 Dec., apparently intestate. The new reign had seen him increase his standing in Kent, where his acceptance of the Anglican settlement earned him in 1564 a certificate of fitness to retain the place on the county bench which he had achieved two years before. His social advancement was reflected in the marriage of his only child Mary to Edward Herbert[†], by whom she became the mother of William Herbert[†], 1st Baron Powis.[8]

[1] Age given as 50 on a medal dated only 1562, M. B. Donald, *Eliz. Monopolies*, pl. 2. *Vis. Cumb.* (Harl. Soc. vii), 10; C142/161/111. [2] *Brit. Numismatic Jnl.* xlv. 68; *LP Hen. VIII*, xx; *CPR*, 1550–3, p. 320; 1553–4, pp. 36, 86; 1554–5, p. 110; 1560–3, pp. 17, 438; 1563–6, p. 23; 1569–72, p. 225. [3] *CP*; C219/19/50; H. Hornyold-Strickland, *Lancs. MPs* (Chetham Soc. n.s. xciii), 95; Pink and Beaven, *Parl. Rep. Lancs.* 63–64; *Liverpool Town Bks.* ed. Twemlow, i. 216, 383, 582; J. B. Watson, 'Lancs. gentry 1529–58' (London Univ. M.A. thesis, 1959), 618; J. Craig, *The Mint*, 113–14 where the knighthood bestowed on the official presumably arises out of con-

fusion with the earl's son. [4] Hutchinson, *Cumb.* i. 587; Nicolson and Burn, *Westmld. and Cumb.* ii. 587; C219/19/50; *CPR 1547–8*, p. 358; Hatfield 207; *CJ*, i. 10. [5] *CJ*, i. 10; Hatfield 207. [6] C. E. Challis, *The Tudor Coinage*, 107; *CPR, 1547–8* to 1563–6 passim. [7] Challis, 111, 117; C193/32/2; 219/25/22; Wm. Salt Lib. SMS 264. [8] *CPR, 1558–60*, p. 154; Challis, 36, 115, 122, 127–34; C142/161/111; *Cam. Misc.* ix(3), 58.

A.D./A.D.K.H.

STANLEY, Sir Thomas (1532/33–76), of Winwick, Lancs. and Tong, Salop.

LANCASHIRE   1554 (Apr.), 1554 (Nov.), 1555

b. 1532/33, 2nd s. of Edward Stanley, 3rd Earl of Derby, by Dorothy, da. of Thomas Howard, 2nd Duke of Norfolk. *m.* Margaret, da. and coh. of (Sir) George Vernon* of Haddon, Derbys., 2s. Kntd. 2 Oct. 1553.[1]
?Commr. goods of churches and fraternities, Lancs. 1552, musters 1569; lt. I.o.M. in 1562; mayor, Liverpool 1568–9.[2]

It was to his father that Sir Thomas Stanley owed his knighthood of the shire in three successive Parliaments while still in his early twenties: on each occasion he was the senior knight, and in 1555 his fellow-Member was his kinsman Sir William Stanley, later 3rd Lord Monteagle.

Stanley's marriage to Margaret Vernon brought him Tong in Shropshire and other estates. In October 1563 he received a 99-year lease of the rectory of Winwick at a rent of £120 from one of his Monteagle kinsmen, Thomas Stanley, bishop of Sodor and Man; the Earl of Derby and the bishop of Chester were consenting parties to the lease. The earl himself gave his son a life interest in various manors and lands in Cheshire, Devon, Oxfordshire and Warwickshire, of which the most important was probably Eynsham in Oxfordshire. Stanley was a freeman of Liverpool and Preston in the 1650s.[3]

The earls of Derby adhered more or less faithfully to 'the religion that had most good luck', but many other members of the Stanley family remained Catholic after the accession of Elizabeth. Although described as meet to be a justice of the peace in 1564, Sir Thomas Stanley was among these, as befitted one whom his Catholic stepmother Margaret Barlow called 'the good Stanley'. He was in communication with Mary, Queen of Scots, in 1566 and although he had been active in suppressing the northern rebellion in 1569 he was arrested in 1571 for conspiring with Thomas Gerard[†] and others to procure Mary's escape by conveying her to the Isle of Man. He was still in prison in 1572.[4]

Stanley made a nuncupative will on 14 Dec. 1576, leaving everything equally between his wife Margaret and his surviving son Edward. Letters of administration were granted to Margaret on the following 22 Dec. The son erected 'a magnificent monument' to his father in Tong church, one further distinguished by its bearing of two epitaphs attributed to William Shakespeare.[5]

[1] Date of birth estimated from elder brother's and from presumption that he was of age at election. *CP*; P. Draper, *House of Stanley*, 52; J. B. Watson, 'Lancs. gentry 1529–58' (London Univ. M.A. thesis, 1959), 617–18. [2] *VCH Lancs.* ii. 97; Watson, 618; *Liverpool Archs. 13th–17th Cent.* ed. Picton, 34; *Liverpool Town Bks.* ed. Twemlow, i. 224, 383. [3] Shaw, *Staffs.* i. 401; *CPR, 1566–9*, p. 11; *VCH Lancs.* iv. 127–8n; *Oxon. Rec. Soc.* xviii. 41–42; Watson, 618; *Liverpool Town Bks.* i. 477. [4] J. Croston, *County Fams. Lancs. and Cheshire*, 48; J. S. Leatherbarrow, *Lancs. Eliz. Recusants* (Chetham Soc. n.s. cx), 43; *Cam. Misc.* ix(3), 77–78; *Palatine Note Bk.* iv. 229; *APC*, viii. 37; *HMC Hatfield*, i. 339, 505–76 passim; C. Haigh, *Ref. and Resistance in Tudor Lancs.* 253–4; Lansd. 14, art. 16; *CSP Dom. 1547–80*, p. 442; *Trans. Salop Arch. Soc.* (ser. 2), ii. 236. [5] PCC 39 Carew; *Trans. Salop Arch. Soc.* xlix (1937–8), 251–64; Pevsner, *Salop*, 303.

A.D.

STANLEY, Sir William (1528–81), of Hornby Castle, Lancs.

LANCASHIRE   1555

b. 1528, 1st s. of Thomas Stanley, 2nd Lord Monteagle, by 1st w. Mary, da. of Charles Brandon, 1st Duke of Suffolk. *m.* (1) Anne, da. of Sir James Leyburn* of Cunswick, Westmld., 2da.; (2) by 15 Sept. 1575, Anne, da. of Sir John Spencer* of Althorp, Northants. Kntd. 22 Feb. 1547; *suc.* fa. as 3rd Lord Monteagle 25 Aug. 1560.[1]
?Commr. chantries, Notts. and Derbys. 1548; musters, Lancs. 1573, Lancaster 1580; j.p.q. Som. 1564–77 or later.[2]

As heir to the barony of Monteagle, Sir William Stanley can have needed no other recommendation than that of his lineage to become junior knight of the shire in 1555; the senior seat went to his kinsman, Sir Thomas Stanley, a younger son of the head of the family, Edward, 3rd Earl of Derby. Of Sir William Stanley's brief career in the Commons all that has come to light is that on 20 Nov. 1555 the House ordered that his servant Thomas Bosseville, who had been attached in London for debt at the suit of John Ayer, should have privilege.[3]

Early in 1558 the 2nd Lord Monteagle was ordered to levy 150 men to be sent as a reinforcement to Berwick under the command of his son. On 14 Feb. 1558 father and son were rebuked by the Privy Council for levying this force as far as Somerset and Devon; the Council had intended that they should be drawn only from such shires as were under the lieutenancy of the north. Later in 1558 Stanley took part in a raid into Scotland.[4]

The Monteagle interest in Somerset and Devon accrued from the 2nd Lord's marriage to Mary Brandon. On 12 Dec. 1553 Henry and Frances Grey, Duke and Duchess of Suffolk, Lady Margaret Clifford (later wife of the 4th Earl of Derby), and Sir William Stanley had licence as coheirs to enter upon the lands of Henry Brandon, Duke of Suffolk;

the greater part of Stanley's share seems to have lain in Lincolnshire but there were properties, including advowsons, scattered throughout the country. On 20 June 1561, as Lord Monteagle, he had livery of his father's lands. Soon afterwards, and mainly in May 1563, Monteagle and his wife received a large number of licences to alienate property, chiefly in Lincolnshire. Most of these licences related to the Suffolk inheritance but Monteagle also disposed of part of his patrimony. He had begun to do so before his father's death and apparently without his consent: this may explain why he is not mentioned in the father's will.[5]

One such Monteagle estate was sold to the crown in consideration of a debt of £417. This is one of the few indications of the reason for these sales. In 1571 the Privy Council began to press Monteagle to pay an annuity of 40 marks which he had promised John Pistor *alias* Baker† on Pistor's yielding his pensioner's office to Monteagle's brother-in-law Richard Zouche of Stavordale, Somerset; four years later the Council was ordering him to pay the annuity to Pistor's daughter Grace. The Monteagle inheritance itself was not a very rich one: it has been classed in the next to lowest of eight income-groupings of the peerage in 1559. Perhaps Monteagle's failure to hold office or to sit on more than a handful of commissions was due to some defect in his personality, although nothing of this sort appears to have been recorded. Like most of the Stanleys he was a Catholic, but that would have favoured his employment in Mary's reign and not seriously hindered it in the early years of Elizabeth's. He was to attend the House of Lords regularly until 1576, when he appointed as his proxy first Lord Burghley and then, in 1580, Thomas Radcliffe*, 3rd Earl of Sussex. Little is known of his activity there but he voted against the bill for the consecrating of bishops in 1566 and had a bill concerning tenancy committed to him in 1572. On 10 Dec. 1560, 5 Sept. 1562, and 28 Nov. 1571 he received protections.[6]

Monteagle died on 10 Nov. 1581. When his inquisition post mortem was taken a year later his only surviving child Elizabeth was aged 24 or more and married to her kinsman Edward Parker, 12th Lord Morley. His widow married Henry Compton†, 1st Lord Compton, and after his death Robert Sackville†, 2nd Earl of Dorset.[7]

[1] Date of birth from fa.'s i.p.m. and date of parents' marriage, *CP. Vis. Yorks.* (Harl. Soc. xvi), 293; J. B. Watson, 'Lancs. Gentry 1529–58' (London Univ. M.A. thesis, 1959), 617. [2] *CPR*, 1548–9, p. 137 1563–6, p. 27; Watson, 617; *APC*, xii. 8. [3] *CJ*, i. 45. [4] *APC*, vi. 244 268; *CSP Dom.* 1601–3, *Add.* 1547–65, p. 475. [5] *CPR*, 1553–4, p. 5; 1555–7, p. 439; 1560–3, pp. 118, 204, 489–90, 549–50, 552–3, 557, 562, 581–2, 584–5, 600, 602; 1563–6, pp. 47, 137, 200; 1566–9, p. 330; 1569–72, pp. 295, 455; *VCH Lancs.* viii. 98n; *Surtees Soc.* xxvi. 113–16. [6] *CPR*, 1558–60, p. 323; 1560–3, p. 265; 1563–6, p. 200; 1569–72, p. 446; *APC*, viii. 9, 137, 239, 320, 331; L. Stone, *Crisis of*

the *Aristocracy*, 729, 760; *Cath. Rec. Soc.* xiii. 90; *CSP Dom. Add.* 1566–79, p. 286; *LJ*, i. 582 seq. [7] C142/198/55.

A.D.

STAPLEHILL, Walter (by 1510–63), of Exeter, Devon.

EXETER 1558

b. by 1510, 1st s. of Thomas Staplehill of Bromley. *m.* (1) 24 Nov. 1539, Elizabeth, da. of John Southcote I* of Bovey Tracey, 1s.; (2) autumn 1548, Anne, da. of one Gale of Kirton in Crediton, wid. of Thomas Spurway* of Exeter, 1s.; at least 2s. 1da. *suc.* fa. 22 Apr. 1557.[1]
Bailiff, Exeter 1550–1, member of the Twenty-Four 6 Nov. 1552–*d.*, receiver 1553–4, sheriff 1554–5, 1563–4, mayor 1556–7.[2]

Walter Staplehill was born at Trusham, Devon. His grandfather William Staplehill had sat for Dartmouth in the Parliament of 1491. In November 1526 his father promised him in marriage to one of the daughters of John Southcote I and 13 years later he married Elizabeth Southcote. In 1530–1 he had been admitted a freeman of Exeter after his apprenticeship with Richard Martin there, and had then embarked upon his successful career as a merchant. He was to be one of the founders of the merchant adventurers in 1560. He won praise from John Hooker† for his interest in the city's welfare: many reforms of its ordinances derived from him both when he was in and out of office. Although 'not zealous for God and the true religion' but 'much blinded in popery', he did not denounce those of contrary beliefs when he might have done so but remained 'friendly and loving'.[3]

Staplehill's discharge of his parliamentary duties in 1558 is well documented. He left the city on 15 Jan. for the first session and returned on 12 Mar. He took with him £46 13s. 4d. in bills 'for city affairs', on which he had been given instructions; the 'laying in of the writs of Parliament' cost 4d. and the drafting of a bill for apprentices (rejected after its second reading in the House) 5s. 8d., but most of the money was spent on armaments, including £6 1s. 6d. for bows and £17 9s. for gunpowder. Besides his wages for the session, which at 3s. 4d. a day for 57 days amounted to £10, he was paid 53s. 4d. for the hire of a horse 'in the city's affairs at the Parliament'. Shortly before leaving for the second session he was asked to approach Queen Mary on the city's behalf for the butlerage and prisage of Barnstaple, Dartmouth and Exeter, or else 'for Ruxston towards the maintenance of the castle and also for the statute of the staple'. For the second session, which took him away from 3 to 29 Nov., he received £4 10s. in wages and 18s. 4d. for the hire of another horse.[4]

Staplehill made his will on 7 June 1561. Styling

himself gentleman, he declared his acceptance of all 'that God and the Holy Catholic Church willeth and commandeth me to believe'. After several charitable bequests, he left to his wife and executrix a life interest in the property which he had inherited from his father, to his wife's two daughters by her first marriage £20 each, and to his own children £10 each. As overseer he appointed Geoffrey Tothill[†]; one of the witnesses was Richard Hart*. Staplehill probably died early in 1563, the will being proved on 19 Mar. 1563, but the vacancies caused by his death were not filled until 21 Sept., when Simon Knight[†] was elected to the Twenty-Four and John Peryam[†] was made alderman.[5]

[1] Date of birth estimated from admission as freeman. *Vis. Devon* (Harl. Soc. vi), 275; *Vis. Devon*, ed. Vivian, 697-8; C142/113/8. [2] R. Izacke, *Exeter* (1681), 52, 124, 126-7; Exeter act bk. 2, ff. 120, 126; *Trans. Dev. Assoc.* xliv. 223. [3] Exeter, Hooker's commonplace bk. f. 351v; mayor's ct. bk. 5, f. 88v; *CPR*, 1558-60, pp. 427-8; *HMC Exeter*, 372; *Exeter Freemen* (Devon and Cornw. Rec. Soc. extra ser. 1), 72, 78; J. E. Kew, 'The land market in Devon 1536-58' (Exeter Univ. Ph.D. thesis, 1967), 164; *The description of the citie of Excester* (Devon and Cornw. Rec. Soc. xi), 870. [4] Exeter act bk. 2, ff. 158v, 161v, 345; C. G. Ericson, 'Parlt. as a legislative institution in the reigns of Edw. VI and Mary' (London Univ. Ph.D. thesis, 1973), 529 noting that CJ ms, f. 173v gives the reading on 21 Feb. 1558 as a second although both printed editions call it a first. [5] PCC 14 Chayre; *Trans. Dev. Assoc.* xlv. 421; Exeter, Hooker's commonplace bk. f. 351v erroneously gives Staplehill's date of death as '28 Feb. 1557'.

A.D.K.H.

STAPLETON, Anthony (by 1514-74), of the Inner Temple, London.

EAST GRINSTEAD 1554 (Apr.)

b. by 1514, 3rd s. of George Stapleton of Rempstone, Notts. by Margaret, da. and coh. of William Gasgill of Rolleston, Notts. *educ.* I. Temple. *m.* (1) lic. 14 Aug. 1544, Joan, da. of Sir Michael Dormer of London, wid. of James Bolney (*d.*1536) of London and of Edward Borlase (*d.*1544) of London, 2s.; (2) Alice, da. of Francis Roos of Laxton, Notts., ?wid. of Brian Stapleton of Burton Joyce, Notts.[1]

Summer reader, I. Temple 1543, Autumn 1544, Lent 1553, treasurer 1555-7, gov. 1555, 1566.

Recorder, Colchester, Essex in 1544; j.p. Mdx. 1547-55 or later, q. 1558/59-*d.*, I. o. Ely 1564; member, council of 16th Earl of Oxford by 1550-4 or later; town clerk, London 24 July 1570-*d.*[2]

A younger son of a younger son in an old Yorkshire family, Anthony Stapleton became a successful lawyer: in 1537 Elizabeth, dowager Countess of Oxford, left him £10 'towards his learning in the law'. During a lifetime of activity at the Inner Temple he rarely missed a parliament, was three times reader and held the highest offices. Among his early clients were the 5th Earl of Northumberland and his uncle Sir Brian Stapleton; later he acted for the 16th Earl of Oxford, whose will he signed in 1548 and who paid him an annuity of £13 6s. 8d., and for the dean and chapter of Westminster at a retainer of 40s. a year and such fees as the 5s. he earned 'for making a bill against Sir Andrew

Dudley* in 1549. He held court in Southwark for the corporation of London in 1550-1 and probably at other times, but his quest for London office was a long one: recommended by Cromwell in 1539 for the posts of town clerk and common serjeant, he obtained the reversion of the clerkship in 1544 only to wait 26 years before entering upon the office. It was as town clerk that in 1572 he signed a letter which was carried to York by the Members for that city acknowledging the right of their fellow-citizens to bring goods to London without payment of toll.[3]

Stapleton might have been expected to sit in more than one Parliament and for a borough other than East Grinstead. His service with the Earl of Oxford, to whom he presumably owed the recordership of Colchester, might have yielded him a seat in Essex or his northern connexions one in that area—his distant cousin William Stapleton was returned for Carlisle to the Parliament of 1542 and his nephew John Eltoftes for Appleby three times under Mary— while his marriage to a daughter of Sir Michael Dormer could have had the same result in Buckinghamshire. As it was, his Dormer kinsfolk may have elicited official support for his election to Mary's second Parliament, but if they did so at East Grinstead it is likely to have been through the Bolney family who held land there. Less circuitously, Stapleton's friendship with Sir Richard Sackville* could have yielded him the seat. Like his fellow-Member Richard Whalley, Stapleton was associated with Sir Thomas Holcroft* with whom he had recently served on a commission to try some of Wyatt's followers. Nothing is known of his part in the Commons, but it is unlikely that he welcomed the restoration of Catholicism, for ten years later Bishop Grindal reported favourably on his attitude towards the Elizabethan settlement and Bishop Cox of Ely, who rated him the leading justice in the Isle of Ely, thought him meet to be of the quorum.[4]

Stapleton's connexion with Ely arose through his second marriage. It was his second wife to whom in the will which he made on 20 Oct. 1569 he left his Nottinghamshire manor of East Leake, with remainder to their issue, and whom he appointed executrix, with her brother Peter Roos supervisor. He must have died early in 1574 from the illness for which the City then gave him leave of absence; his successor was admitted on 25 May 1574 and his will was proved on 12 Oct. 1575. His widow married Thomas Leke of Derbyshire.[5]

[1] Date of birth estimated from first reference, 1535. *Vis. Yorks.* (Harl. Soc. xvi), 296; York wills 19, f. 690; *Marr. Lic. Fac. Off.* (Harl. Soc. xxiv), 2. [2] Colchester town hall, Benham ms 23; *CPR*, 1547-8, p. 86; 1553-4, p. 22; 1560-3, p. 400; 1563-6, pp. 24, 29; Essex RO, D/DPr/140-1; *Guildhall Misc.* iii. 61. [3] Information from Susan Flower; *LP Hen. VIII*, viii, ix; St.Ch.2/25/47; Westminster Abbey 9789; 33178A; 33193 37404; 37619. City of London RO,

Guildhall, rep. 10, ff. 106v, 111v; 12(2), f. 381; jnl. 16, f. 83v. [4] PCC 14 Crymes; *CPR*, 1554–5, p. 94; *Cam. Misc.* ix(3), 25, 60. [5] *Vis. Cambs.* (Harl. Soc. xli), 119; York wills 19, f. 690; *Guildhall Misc.* iii. 61.

R.J.W.S.

STAPLETON, George (by 1519–61/68), of Barnstaple, Devon.

BARNSTAPLE 1555

b. by 1519. *m.* by 1547, Agnes, 3da.[1]
Mayor, Barnstaple 1556–7, 1560–1.[2]

George Stapleton's parentage has not been established, although in his will he was to style himself gentleman. He is likely to have been of Devon stock, but he could have entered the county in the service of Bishop Veysey of Exeter; in 1540 he took delivery at Crediton on the bishop's behalf of the archdeaconry of Cornwall's quota of the subsidy and later in London he handled papers relating to that archdeaconry. There is no reason to identify him with Anthony Stapleton's* brother of the same name.[3]

By 1548, when the eldest of his three daughters was baptized, Stapleton was living in Barnstaple, where in the following year he leased property formerly belonging to the chantry of St. Anne in the parish church. His residence there may not have been unconnected with the fact that the nearby manor of Tawton belonged to the see of Exeter, but it was as leading townsmen that he and Robert Apley were elected to the Parliament of 1555. Apley was later to recount their efforts on the town's behalf and to complain that their expenses remained unpaid. Unlike so many western Members they do not appear on the list of those who supported Sir Anthony Kingston in opposing one of the government's bills.[4]

Stapleton made his will on 26 Oct. 1558. He left his place of burial to the discretion of his wife, his sole executrix, but he gave 3s. 6d. to the high altar of Kenton, near the home of the Courtenays at Powderham. To his only surviving daughter he bequeathed his best standing cup, his silver salt, a gilt cup with a cover, the bed that 'my lord my master' had given him, and £20. The lease of his mills and the residue of his property he left to his wife, with reversion to his daughter. He appointed as supervisors his brother Anthony Stapleton and Roger Worth*. The date of Stapleton's death has not been discovered, but it must have been between the autumn of 1561, when he ended his second mayoralty, and 26 Oct. 1568, when his will was proved.[5]

[1] Date of birth estimated from first reference. N. Devon Athenaeum, Barnstaple, D. Drake ms 'MPs Barnstaple', 29. [2] *CPR*, 1555–7, p. 391; T. Wainwright, *Barnstaple Recs.* i. 222. [3] F. Rose-Troup, *The Western Rebellion*, 62–63. [4] N. Devon Athenaeum, D. Drake ms op. cit. 1135, 1139; Wainwright, i. 190. [5] PCC 19 Babington.

A.D.K.H.

STAPLETON, William (c.1495–1544), of Wighill, Yorks. and London.

CARLISLE 1542

b. c.1495, 5th s. of Sir Brian Stapleton of Wighill by Jane, da. of Sir Lancelot Threlkeld of Threlkeld, Cumb. *m.* Margaret, at least 1s.[1]
Feodary, lands in Yorks. of Henry Percy, 5th Earl of Northumberland 1533.[2]

William Stapleton was a lawyer, but where he trained for the profession is not known: his distant cousin Anthony Stapleton* was to attain prominence at the Inner Temple and his nephew Brian Stapleton entered Gray's Inn. In 1533 he was appointed attorney, at a fee of £10, to the 5th Earl of Northumberland and later in the same year he became the earl's feodary in Yorkshire, but his career was also influenced by his kinship with Thomas Wharton I*, who married his sister by 1518: in August 1531 Wharton sought Cromwell's goodwill in certain causes which Stapleton would lay before him. It was as 'Master Stapleton of London, brother-in-law to Sir Thomas Wharton' that Stapleton provided John Leland with information about the north. His relationship to Wharton doubtless told in Stapleton's favour when he appeared before the council at York after his involvement in the northern rebellion of 1536. On his own confession he had been forced by a rebel multitude at Beverley, Yorkshire, where he was visiting his bedridden brother Christopher, to become their captain and as such to join Robert Aske and to preside over the siege of Hull, returning to Wighill when the King's conciliatory attitude led Aske to disband his forces. In his defence he maintained that he had acted under duress, had saved property by preserving discipline and had tried to aid Wharton to escape danger in Westmorland by procuring him a safe-conduct into Yorkshire, of which, however, Wharton made no use. (How far his conduct had reflected his brother Christopher's marriage-connexion with Aske is a matter of conjecture.) Stapleton's explanation was accepted and he was to benefit by Wharton's speedy advancement. In the winter of 1537–8 he persuaded Cromwell to accept the claim of his nephew Robert Stapleton, whose father Christopher had succumbed to his illness, to be of age and to receive livery of the inheritance. Wharton may have procured Stapleton's return for Carlisle to the Parliament of 1539, the names of the Members being lost, and must certainly have done so at the next election held after he had become governor of the town. On this occasion Wharton and his son were themselves probably returned for Cumberland, and Stapleton's election would have been convenient alike to his brother-in-law, himself and the town, which was presumably not called upon to reimburse Stapleton, a practising lawyer, for his residence in London.[3]

Stapleton barely saw out the Parliament, for it was as a sick man that he made his will on 30 Mar. 1544, two days after it ended, and he was dead by the following 7 May, when the will was proved. He besought 'the holy Church to pray for me as God hath appointed it after the manner as it is set forth by the King's book to God's glory', left his son (still a minor) one third of his goods and the rest to his wife Margaret, and asked his 'very good lord my lord Wharton' (who had been elevated a few weeks earlier) and his 'cousin' Thomas Wharton II* to join with his nephew Robert Stapleton in caring for them. One of the witnesses, John Stokes, may have been the groom of the chamber of that name and perhaps the Member for Westbury in 1547.[4]

[1] Date of birth estimated from that of eldest brother Christopher (b. c.1485). *Dugdale's Vis. Yorks.* ed. Clay, i. 170–1. [2] M. E. James, *Change and Continuity in Tudor North* (Borthwick Pprs. xxvii), 13 and n; R. B. Smith, *Land and Politics*, 141. [3] James, 13n; *LP Hen. VIII*, v, viii, ix, xi–xiii; Leland, *Itin.* ed. Smith, v. 2; M. H. and R. Dodds, *Pilgrimage of Grace*, i. passim; *Trans. E. Yorks. Antiq. Soc.* x. 80–106; H. E. Chetwynd-Stapleton, *Chron. Yorks. Fam. of Stapleton*, 24–27; Smith, 182–3. [4] PCC 6 Pynnyng.

P.S.E.

STARKEY, John (by 1503–54), of Canterbury, Kent.

CANTERBURY 1539[1]

b. by 1503, s. of Thomas Starkey of Canterbury. *m.* Agnes, 1s.[2]
Common councilman, Canterbury by 1529, sheriff 1529–30, alderman by 1534, chamberlain 1534–7, mayor 1538–9; commr. relief 1550.[3]

John Starkey, yeoman, was admitted to the freedom of Canterbury by redemption in 1524. His career in the city followed the normal pattern, from common councilman to alderman, chamberlain and mayor. It was when he was chamberlain that he was first elected to Parliament, but as an official letter—opened, so the sheriff reported to Cromwell, only after this election—asked for the return of John Bridges and Robert Darknall, who had sat in the later sessions of the previous Parliament, Canterbury was forced to comply by holding a second election. The city took the earliest opportunity of compensating Starkey for this rebuff by electing him in 1539 during his mayoralty. In 1539–40 he received £4 0s.4d. in parliamentary wages for an unspecified number of days' attendance, probably during the first and second sessions which together lasted 56 days. It was perhaps during the second session, in the summer of 1539, that he sought Cromwell's aid for the furthering of a petition from Canterbury to the King: in November 1539 he wrote to Dr. Bellasis, to whom on Cromwell's order he had delivered the petition, to remind him of it and to ask

him when he should come up to discuss it. Starkey went to London again on the city's business in 1540–1, 1543–4 and 1548–9, his expenses being paid by the chamberlains of those years. During the Catholic reaction of the early 1540s Starkey and his wife had been momentarily at risk. In the autumn of 1543 he was reported to have said that 'the rood light' in his parish church 'should not be lighted but when it pleased him, and although the King had suffered light before the rood yet he gave no commandment to light them'; he and his wife were also named as present in the church when John Toftes openly read the Bible in English, and Mrs. Starkey was alleged to have said—although she denied doing so—that it was idolatry to creep to the cross on Good Friday. Robert Serles, whose accusations had touched off the inquiry into heretical opinion in Kent, declared that Starkey and Toftes were men of evil fame in Canterbury.[4]

The common clerk of Canterbury, George Toftes, was a witness to Starkey's will, made on 3 Aug. 1554, and he and Richard Railton*, the overseer, were left the testator's lands and tenements in Harbledown for six years, in order that they might pay John Bush of London his annuity of £6; this property was then to go to Starkey's wife Agnes until his son John came of age. Starkey bequeathed to his wife his dwelling-house in the parish of St. Mary of Northgate, and the residue of his goods; as executrix she proved the will on 11 Sept. 1554. He also left 40s. to the chamber of Canterbury, evidently as a refund of two payments of the annuity of 20s. which the city had granted him in May 1553 for life as an alderman of the city who had fallen into 'decay and poverty'.[5]

[1] E159/319, brev. ret. Mich. r.[1–2]; Canterbury chamberlains' accts. 1539–40. [2] Date of birth estimated from admission as freeman. Canterbury prob. reg. A13, f. 92; A29, f. 82. [3] Canterbury chamberlains' accts. passim; *CPR*, 1553, p. 361. [4] *Freemen of Canterbury*, ed. Cowper, col. 302; *LP Hen. VIII*, x, xiv, xviii; Canterbury chamberlains' accts. 1539–40, 1540–1, 1543–4, 1548–9. [5] Canterbury prob. reg. A29, f. 82; burmote bk. 1542–78, f. 77; chamberlains' accts. 1552–3, 1553–4.

H.M.

STARKEY, Lawrence (by 1474–1532), of Lancaster, Lancs. and London.

LANCASTER ?1523, 1529*

b. by 1474, prob. yr. s. of Geoffrey Starkey of Stretton, Cheshire by Joan, da. and coh. of Roger Darby of Chester, Cheshire and Liverpool, Lancs. *m.* (1) 1da.; (2) c.1519, Anne, da. of Sir Thomas Butler of Bewsey, Lancs., wid. of (?John) Radcliffe (?of Radcliffe Tower, Lancs.) and George Atherton of Atherton, Lancs., 1da.; 1s. illegit.[1]
Mayor, Lancaster 1495, 1523; dep. or acting sheriff, Lancs. 1497–1523 and 1524–?d.; bailiff, serjeanty of Halton fee in 1501–2; receiver, duchy of Lancaster, Lancs. and Cheshire July 1509–23;

commr. subsidy, Lancs. 1512, 1514, 1515; attorney-gen. for city of London in duchy of Lancaster 1515.[2]

An earlier identification of this Member with the son of James Starkey of Huntroyde and Simonstone, Lancashire, and the suggestion that he was a duchy receiver and mayor of Lancaster but not under sheriff of Lancashire, are alike refuted by the evidence of a number of actions brought in the duchy of Lancaster courts, which show that all three offices were held by the same man and that he came of a different family. In one of these suits, brought before Henry Marney[†], 1st Baron Marny, probably in 1523, the plaintiff William Tunstall described Starkey as mayor of Lancaster and under sheriff of Lancashire, and in another heard before Sir Richard Wingfield probably later in the same year he called Starkey the father-in-law of William Banester*, who is known to have married Lawrence Starkey's elder daughter Margaret. Finally, in an action brought before Sir William Fitzwilliam I* after Starkey's death, his younger daughter Etheldreda and her husband Humphrey Newton of Newton and Pownall, Cheshire, described him as receiver. Although it cannot be claimed with quite the same certainty that this Lawrence Starkey was the Member for Lancaster, his ubiquitousness in local administration and his close association with the borough clearly point to him, whereas Lawrence of Huntroyde, first son of a marriage assigned to 1506–7, would have lacked both the years and the standing called for in a candidate for election in 1529.[3]

A further indication of Starkey's position in Lancaster is provided by the second of Tunstall's suits. He accused Starkey of having first had his son-in-law Banester made a freeman of the borough 'and incontinent after caused him to be chosen a burgess of Parliament' in order to protect him against this action. Banester replied that he had been 'freely by the desire and good minds of the burgesses of the said town chosen burgess'. At what must have been the election of 1523 Banester's fellow-Member was probably Starkey himself, who is known to have been in London during the Parliament.[4]

Starkey was a servant and friend of his kinsman by marriage Edward Stanley, 1st Lord Monteagle. For many years he was Monteagle's deputy as sheriff of Lancashire, an office to which the then Sir Edward Stanley had been appointed for life in October 1485, and he also became a feoffee of his master's lands. In 1523 Monteagle appointed Starkey one of his executors, with Richard Bank, Thomas Lord Darcy, Sir John Hussey* and Sir Alexander Radcliffe: Starkey was to have 'all his plate which lies in pledge in mine hands for £40, and to be dis-charged of the said £40 as my bequest', to enjoy all such grants as Monteagle had made to him and to be deputy steward of Cockersand abbey. Monteagle died in April 1523 and Starkey proved the will on 25 Aug. 1524. He became involved in disputes with the other executors, which are reflected in a number of letters, mostly addressed to Darcy. On 6 July 1523 Hussey wrote from London to Darcy: 'Starkey hath been here and hath made very short tarriance. He is home again, as I suppose, to make men ready for to go with my lord treasurer and to gather the King's money [presumably the Amicable Loan] which is yet ungathered.' Starkey must therefore have been absent from London during at least part of the second session of the Parliament of that summer, but he was back there by 17 July when he wrote from London to tell Darcy that adversaries of the new Lord Monteagle, a minor whose interests he was defending or at least claiming to defend, had been praying the King to remove Starkey from his office of under sheriff, which here as elsewhere he significantly calls that of sheriff. He was absent again during the third session, writing from Lancaster on 12 Aug. to inform Richard Bank that Starkey's brother-in-law Thomas Butler had been appointed to lead the Monteagle tenants in war during the minority of the heir. In a letter to Darcy of 25 Apr. 1524, again from Lancaster, Starkey announced his appointment as 'sheriff', through the influence of Sir Richard Wingfield, and his hope that young Monteagle would have the office when of age.[5]

Starkey had received a pardon on 24 May 1509 under the comprehensive designation of Lawrence Starkey of London and Lancaster and Hornby, Lancashire, and 'Falley' (?Fawley), Buckinghamshire, gentleman or draper, late mayor of Lancaster. Hornby connects him with Monteagle, and 'Falley' may have been a property of his first wife, who left a tenement in Henley-on-Thames to her daughter. A Peter Starkey was a citizen and draper of London at this time and Lawrence Starkey adopted the same style in 1515 when he made a successful application for the post of attorney-general for the City in the duchy of Lancaster.[6]

Starkey died on 24 July 1532 leaving, besides his daughters, an illegitimate son Oliver (conceivably a cousin of Oliver Starkey*, the illegitimate son of a London mercer). He had acquired property in Bolton-le-Sands, Broughton, Lancaster and Preston, Lancashire, and also in Cheshire, Staffordshire and Yorkshire. The distribution of these estates, favouring the younger daughter as a Butler, led to more litigation. It has been suggested that the lack of a legitimate male heir and the consequent failure to found a 'noteworthy line' may be 'the reason why historians have identified Lawrence Starkey of Huntroyde with the public figure of Henry VIII's reign'.[7]

[1] Date of birth estimated from first reference. *Trans. Hist. Soc. Lancs. and Cheshire*, lxxiii. 188, 192, 194–5. [2] Ibid. lxiii. 176; lxxiii. 190, 193; Somerville, *Duchy*, i. 462, 495, 513; *Statutes*, iii. 87, 118, 171; City of London RO, Guildhall, jnl. 11, f. 208v. [3] Pink and Beaven, *Parl. Rep. Lancs.* 107; H. Hornyold-Strickland, *Lancs. MPs* (Chetham Soc. n.s. xciii), 96–97; Somerville, i. 495; *Trans. Hist. Soc. Lancs. and Cheshire*, lxxiii. 190, 193, 196; Ormerod, *Cheshire*, i. 641; J. B. Watson, 'Lancs. gentry 1529–58' (London Univ. M.A. thesis, 1959), 608. [4] *Trans. Hist. Soc. Lancs. and Cheshire*, lxxiii. 193–4; Watson, 609. [5] *Surtees Soc.* cxvi. 111–16; *LP Hen. VIII*, iii, iv; SP1/28, p. 106; *Lancs. and Cheshire Rec. Soc.* lxxi. 69. [6] *LP Hen. VIII*, i; *Trans. Hist. Soc. Lancs. and Cheshire*, lxxiii. 192, 195–6; C1/442/28. [7] *Trans. Hist. Soc. Lancs. and Cheshire*, lxxiii. 188, 192, 195–6; Watson, 609.

L.M.K./A.D.

STARKEY, Oliver (c. 1523–83/86).

ST. ALBANS 1554 (Apr.), 1554 (Nov.)

b. c.1523, illegit. o.s. of Roger Starkey of London by Elizabeth of Antwerp. *educ.* Louvain; I. Temple.[1]
Member, order of St. John of Jerusalem, commander Quenington, Glos. 1558, lt. turcopolier Feb. 1560, Latin sec. to grand master bef. 1565–?8, titular bailiff of Eagle, Lincs. 1569.[2]

Oliver Starkey's parentage is set out in the depositions of witnesses in a chancery case begun by him in 1546, soon after his father's death. He was born in Antwerp, where his father was in the service of Sir Thomas Baldry, 'at which time the said Roger kept the mother of the said Oliver as his harlot not being at any time married together'. Soon after Oliver's birth Roger Starkey gave up the woman, 'whose name was Bedkyn and in English Elizabeth', and she went to live with another man. The boy took his mother's domicile and was educated on the Continent. His father died in 1545 worth, according to one estimate, £3,000 in land and goods; two years earlier he had obtained a grant of arms and he acknowledged his son by leaving him £300 in his will and by naming him its executor. Oliver Starkey obtained a grant of probate on 14 Nov. 1545 but renounced it six days later; the chancery case between Starkey and his first cousin Thomas Starkey turned on the reasons for this renunciation and the intentions of Roger Starkey in making the will.[3]

Thomas Starkey, the chief beneficiary under the will, was found by jury to be the heir and as such entitled to property in London and Middlesex. According to his witnesses, Roger Starkey had left him most of the land unconditionally and had given him authority to alter the will before proving it. Oliver Starkey had been offered, and had accepted, £300 to renounce the executorship, explaining to the judge of the prerogative court 'that he would not let [hinder] his learning to be about the business of it'. Since his bill starting the case has not been found, it is not clear whether he received £600 in all or whether the £300 offered was inserted into the will as a legacy after his agreement to renounce the executorship. His own witnesses asserted that Roger Starkey had left his entail to his nephew on an express but unwritten trust that it should be transferred to his son 'within three months after the said Oliver should fortune to be made denizen'; had Roger left his land to Oliver, a Flemish subject, it would have been forfeit to the crown. The crucial weakness in Starkey's case, and the reason for its probable failure, was his inability to produce a bond said to have been given him by his cousin during their negotiation or to explain why he should have surrendered it before its condition had been performed. A reference in 1565 to Starkey's 'patrimony' suggests that he invested some of his £300 or £600 in the purchase of land, but it is not known where.[4]

Many of the London Starkeys were mercers (although Humphrey Starkey of the previous generation had been chief baron of the Exchequer), but other branches were seated as gentry in Cheshire and Lancashire. Oliver Starkey could thus probably claim gentle birth, despite the bastardy which should have disqualified him for membership of the order of St. John. Another disqualification was his birth outside the limits of the English 'Tongue', but between the order's dissolution in England in 1540 and its re-establishment in 1557 recruiting almost stopped; one man was admitted in 1545 (on Cardinal Pole's certification) without proof of noble birth and another in 1547 despite his being born a Scot, so that Starkey no doubt benefited from similar laxity, for he cannot have been admitted to the order before 1544. (It is, however, unlikely that the Oliver Starkey who married a Lincolnshire woman in or before 1551 was the knight, even though in 1545 English knights had been allowed to marry; this was probably a namesake from Caton, Lancashire.) Starkey was doubtless naturalized after his father's death but before he began the chancery suit or joined the order. He may have used his legacy to continue his education and he had some reputation as a poet and Latin scholar. He is credited by Warton with a translation of the Book of Ecclesiastes into (presumably Latin) verse and a translation of Sallust, but the only work of his known to survive is an elegant Latin verse epitaph on Grand Master la Valette, who died in 1568.[5]

Cardinal Pole was chiefly responsible for the re-establishment of the order of St. John in England, projected in 1554 although not accomplished till 1557. Starkey must have owed his appointment to Quenington commandery to Pole, who was in Brussels in January 1554 and was perhaps introduced to Starkey by Richard Shelley* or his brother James, who was to be appointed a commander in 1558; Starkey, James (and perhaps Richard) Shelley, and the new prior, Sir Thomas Tresham*, were the only knights in 1558 who had not been admitted before the dissolution in 1540. A former servant of Pole's, Thomas Starkey, author of the 'Dialogue between Pole and Lupset', came of the Wrenbury, Cheshire, branch of the family and this connexion may also have helped Starkey. Tresham also sat (for Northamptonshire) in both the Parliaments for which Starkey represented St. Albans, a conjunction which suggests that legislation to re-establish the order and to restore its lands was contemplated in 1554, and that Tresham and Starkey were returned as spokesmen for the order, whose professed members were probably debarred by their religious status from sitting in the Commons. Starkey had no known connexion with St. Albans or Hertfordshire and must have been a crown nominee. In the event the order was re-established by letters patent and was granted only the land which still remained in the crown's ownership.[6]

Starkey left for Malta with other knights of the order soon after April 1558 and no certain trace of him in England after that time has been found. He was in Malta in November 1558, presumably to undergo the training of several years that was obligatory for new knights. He remained there after Elizabeth had again confiscated the order's property in England, although without abolishing it. Unlike most of the knights Starkey was evidently without private means and dependent on the revenues of his commandery; his indigence kept him in Malta and also brought him rapid promotion in the order, for all the other English knights, except Starkey and James Shelley, had either remained in or returned to England by February 1560, when Starkey became lieutenant turcopolier. He may have subsisted for a time on a legacy of Pole's to the English 'Tongue', but by April 1562 he was begging Cardinal Moroni, the protector of England, to secure him a pension from the revenues of the English pilgrims' hospice in Rome. A second plea in July was reinforced by a testimonial from the order's legate to the Holy See, but it too was probably unsuccessful. In April 1565 Sir Thomas Smith*, while at Marseilles on his French embassy, wrote of Starkey:

> men doth give him a very good report for wisdom and also for valiantness. But he is very poor and not able without more help than he has of the order there to maintain his estate. It is no news to hear *Probitas Laudatur et Alget*. I perceive yet he is (as naturally all men be) desirous to return home to his country and very fain would know the Queen's Majesty's pleasure

touching his commandery and that her Highness would not be offended with him for tarrying there [Malta] being not commanded to the contrary . . . He hath also beside the commandery some other patrimony in England of which he hath long time had no profit. By that I can perceive if he do come home he can be content to conform himself to our religion . . .

The beginning of the great siege of Malta in May 1565 probably changed Starkey's outlook.[7]

As Latin secretary to Grand Master la Valette Starkey was probably in constant attendance on him; he took part in the council called by la Valette when the siege began and had command of the English post at Borgo, with a force of Maltese and Greeks stationed there in the absence of any other Englishmen. The post was a strong one, and Starkey's secretarial duties probably occupied more of his time than fighting; he is not mentioned by the chroniclers of the siege as taking part in any of its principal battles or incidents. He was granted a pension by the order and continued to live in the English lodge in Borgo and later, presumably, in Valletta. He took part in several of the precedence disputes that seemed to constitute the main business of the knights in peacetime, and became titular bailiff of Eagle, Lincolnshire, in 1569. He composed the Latin epitaph on la Valette's tomb in 1568, and is said to have been—but was almost certainly not—buried in the grand masters' crypt 20 years later. He had probably remained in Malta and perhaps supplemented his pension from the order, as did James Shelley, by acting as agent for English merchants. Neither the date nor the place of Starkey's death is known; he was certainly in Malta in December 1583, but died before April 1586, when a new bailiff of Eagle was appointed.[8]

[1] Date of birth estimated from evidence in lawsuit, C24/9, no. 31; 24/12. PCC 41 Pynnyng; information from K. J. Brookes. [2] *CPR*, 1557–8, p. 313; H. P. Scicluna, *Eng. Tongue 1523–67*, p. 50; G. Bosio, *Mil. di S. Giov. Gierosalemitano* (2nd imp.), iii. 840b; E. J. King, *Kts. of St. John*, 116. [3] C24/9, no. 31; 24/12; PCC 41 Pynnyng; C33/4, f. 50v; Harl. 1507(96), f. 441. [4] C24/9, no. 31; 24/12. [5] C1/1263/49–54; DL1/22, f. 30; Ormerod, *Chester*, ii. 188; Scicluna, pp. xxiv, xxvi; J. P. Rylands, *Starkie Fam.* 3–4; Bosio, 364a; *N. and Q.* (ser. 12), x. 43; Add. 5844, ff. 51–52. [6] E. J. King, *Docs. relative to Restoration of Grand Priories*, 4–6; *CPR*, 1557–8, pp. 313 seq. [7] King, *Docs.* 8; Scicluna, 37, 50; *Arch. Storico di Malta*, n.s. vii (fasc. ii), 220; *CSP Rom.* 1558–71, 78, 96; SP70/77/908; E. Bradford, *Great Siege*, 58. [8] Bradford, 63, 228; Harl. 6993(15), f. 28; F. Balbi de Correggio, *La Verdadera Relacion* (1568), 29; *Arch. Storico di Malta*, n.s. vii (fasc. ii), 219; Scicluna, *Church of St. John, Valletta*, plate cxxx.

D.F.C.

STATHAM, Henry (d. 1535).

NOTTINGHAM 1529*

The Henry Statham returned as junior Member for Nottingham to the Parliament of 1529 with the recorder, Sir Anthony Babington, could have been either of two men. One was a son of Robert Statham of London and of Bleasby, Nottinghamshire, the other the son and heir of John Statham of Gonalston, Nottinghamshire. Coming from the same part of the shire and both having interests in Nottingham itself, the two were probably related, and although nothing has been discovered to show whether they were connected with the ancient Derbyshire family of the same name, the second of them is known to have held land within eight miles of that family's seat at Morley. Nicholas Statham, a younger son in the Morley family, who sat in two Parliaments during the 15th century, had been a distinguished lawyer of Lincoln's Inn and one or other of the men in question was probably the Henry Statham who had become a butler of Lincoln's Inn by February 1505 and who four years later was admitted to the fellowship of the inn.[1]

A Henry Statham is to be found at work in Nottingham during the 1520s: in 1523 he acted as surety for Henry Shepherd at his admission to the freedom, five years later he was named an overseer of the will of John Rose, an influential alderman, who left £10 to be spent upon the highways under Statham's direction, and in the following year he was an executor of the will of John Williamson. A later will, that of John Plough, made in July 1538, refers to his earlier (but undated) appointment as a feoffee of Henry Statham, who was the mayor's clerk at the time but who had since been replaced in office. Statham had also been auditor for Lenton priory and in 1541 his executors Edmund Knightley and Henry Parker were found to be in arrears with the rent of property that had previously belonged to the priory. Knightley was probably the Member for Wilton in the Parliament of 1529, a Middle Templar, and there had been a Henry Parker at Lincoln's Inn in 1516, perhaps the son of Lord Morley who sat in Parliament for Hertfordshire in 1539 and 1547.[2]

Of the two men thus far undifferentiated, the first, Henry Statham of Bleasby, married the daughter of a Nottingham merchant and is known to have had a claim to a tenement in that town called the *White Hart*. He was a son of Robert Statham, a London mercer who acquired property in Nottinghamshire, which may have been his native shire, and who settled at Bleasby, 11 miles to the north east of Nottingham. Two of this mercer's sons, Robert and William, followed the same trade. Henry Statham was evidently holding Bleasby by 1502, when he quarrelled with the vicar. His father was buried in the neighbouring Thurgarton abbey and both his brothers, who died early in the 1520s, left bequests to Bleasby church.[3]

The second Henry Statham is even more obscure: all that is known for certain of him is that in July 1530, styled of Nottingham and described

as the son and heir of the late John Statham of Gonalston, he sold lands in Derbyshire to Thomas Mellors, then mayor of Nottingham. He may have been the man commissioned, together with Sir Anthony Babington and Richard Simon, by Chancellor More to investigate a local dispute, being then described as of Nottingham, perhaps to distinguish him from his namesake of Bleasby. No will or inquisition post mortem has been discovered for either man but the Member is known to have died on 25 Jan. 1535, a little more than a month after the close of the seventh session, and to have been immediately replaced by Nicholas Quarnby, who had married into the Mellors family.[4]

With nothing on which to base a confident choice between the two, preference may be given to the Henry Statham who was at one time the mayor's clerk and who may well also have been the former butler of Lincoln's Inn. His Derbyshire holdings, in so far as they provide a connexion with the earlier Nicholas Statham, suggest that the butler was Henry Statham who sold land to Thomas Mellors in 1530. Moreover, it was presumably he who appeared in 1522–23 as a feoffee with one of the Coffin family and who was also a trustee for Sir Roger Mynors'* wife. Since Nottingham was one of the boroughs for which the King had asked for the election writ to be sent to him, such connexions might well help to explain the choice of Henry Statham.[5]

[1] *Derbys. Chs.* ed. Jeayes, 66; *Black Bk. L. Inn*, i. 134, 153. [2] *Nottingham Bor. Recs.* iii. 161, 174; *Test. Ebor.* v (Surtees Soc. lxxix), 266, 280; *N. Country Wills*, i. (Surtees Soc. cxvi), 157; J. T. Godfrey, *Lenton*, 178; *LP Hen. VIII*, xvi. [3] C1/443/34; *Test. Ebor.* iv (Surtees Soc. liii), 63–64; PCC 32 Bodfelde, 26 Maynwaring; H. L. Williams, *Bleasby*, 8–9. [4] *Derbys. Chs.* 66; C1/741/24; C219/18A/10. [5] C142/64/156; *Derbys. Arch. Soc. Jnl.* xv. 39.

C.J.B./A.D.

STAUFFORD *see* **STOWFORD**

STAVELEY, John (by 1523–59), of Southampton.

SOUTHAMPTON 1558

b. by 1523. *m.* Joan, at least 2s.[1]
Steward, Southampton 1544–5, water bailiff 1546–7, ct. bailiff 1550–1, sheriff 1552–3, mayor 1554–5.[2]

John Staveley was a grocer who had a house and a shop in Holyrood parish, Southampton. He traded on occasion in oil and 'images' and may have been the merchant stapler who was pardoned in 1559 for shipping wool from London to Bruges instead of to Calais. From 1548 he acted as attorney for a number of people, taking and delivering seisin of their property. During his mayoralty he sought to check absenteeism among members of the sisterhood of woolpackers by decreeing that after an absence of three months they should re-enter the sisterhood only with the permission of the mayor. His election to the last Marian Parliament accorded with the town's practice of choosing an ex-mayor to accompany the recorder. In 1559 he was one of those who received directions from the ecclesiastical commissioners for the ordering of religious affairs in the town.[3]

Staveley was present at a town meeting on 2 Oct. 1559 but was dead by 15 Nov., when his goods were valued at £236 in an inventory drawn up according to his instructions. He had made an elaborate will on 28 Dec. 1557, that is, after his election to Parliament, but his failure to name an executor meant that his property was eventually administered as that of an intestate. He had provided for a fourfold division of his household goods, his wife taking one part and his children the rest; his wife was also to have his stock and leases and to bring up the children, to whom the mayor and his brethren were asked to act 'as fathers'. Staveley bequeathed to the town a piece of plate worth 40s.[4]

[1] Date of birth estimated from first reference. Hants RO, wills 1560. [2] *Third Bk. of Remembrance*, i (Soton Rec. ser. ii), app. i; ii (ibid. iii), app. i. [3] *Black Bk.* iii (Soton Rec. Soc. vii), 91, 95, 105–11, 117; *CPR*, 1558–60, pp. 24, 412; *HMC 11th Rep. III*, 94. [4] *Third Bk. of Remembrance*, ii. 74n; Hants RO, wills 1560; *Black Bk.* iii. 106–11; C. Platt, *Med. Southampton*, 213.

P.H.

STAVERTON (STAFFERTON), Christopher (by 1517-57 or later), of Aldenham, Herts. and London.

PORTSMOUTH 1542

b. by 1517, 2nd s. of Ralph Staverton of Stroud Hall, Bray, Berks. by Agnes, da. of William Rogers of Bradford, Wilts. *educ.* G. Inn, adm. 1531.[1]

Staverton, a younger son in a well connected Berkshire family, probably owed his return for Portsmouth to his relationship to William Fitzwilliam*, Earl of Southampton. The relationship, arising out of the marriage of John Norris* to a Staverton, was a distant one but the sale in 1554 by Anthony Browne*, 1st Viscount Montagu, of the Hampshire manor of Eversley, part of his inheritance from Southampton, to Staverton's nephew suggests that it was none the less acknowledged and effective. Bray is not far from Windsor, where Southampton held office, and Staverton's elder brother Richard was a member of the royal household, of which until 1539 Southampton had been treasurer. Richard Staverton, moreover, was closely associated with Sir Richard Weston* (although he does not seem to have been, as claimed in the Staverton pedigrees, Weston's son-in-law), a friend of Southampton and steward of Bray and Cookham until his death in 1541. Staverton was also related

through his mother to Sir Thomas Lisle, the junior knight for Hampshire in 1542.[2]

In June 1546 a lease to William Honing* of Gobions in North Mimms, Hertfordshire, described the manor as then in the tenure of Christopher Staverton, whose cousin Richard Staverton had been Sir Thomas More's brother-in-law, and by 1550 Staverton was resident at Aldenham, Hertfordshire. Nothing has been found to suggest that he was otherwise a member of the More circle, several of whom sat in Marian Parliaments, nor is there any indication of his religious sympathies although two of his great-nephews were to be seminary priests. In December 1557 land in Romney Marsh held by Christopher Staverton of London, gentleman, was granted to Sir Richard Sackville*. No further reference has been found to Staverton.[3]

[1] Date of birth estimated from education. *Vis. Berks.* (Harl. Soc. lvi), 130–1; *Vis. Hants* (Harl. Soc. lxiv), 68–70. [2] *VCH Berks.* iii. 106; *VCH Hants*, iv. 34; *LP Hen. VIII*, x, xi, xvi, xvii; PCC 13 Spert, 19 Populwell. [3] *LP Hen. VIII*, xxi; CP40/1139, rot. de attorn. 24v; G. Anstruther, *Seminary Priests*, i. 330; *CPR*, 1557–8, p. 139.

P.H.

STEMPE, John (by 1530-82 or later), of Lewes, Suss.

LEWES 1554 (Nov.)

b. by 1530, o. s. of John Stempe of Lewes. *m.* Anne, prob. at least 1s. 1da. *suc.* fa. July/Nov. 1553.[1]
Constable, Lewes 1555–6, 1563–4, 1572–3; subsidy collector, Southover 1560.[2]

From his father and namesake, a burgess of Southover and constable of Lewes, John Stempe inherited property in Fletching and Lewes, armour and silver spoons. His election to the Parliament of November 1554 with John Morley, the constable whom he was to succeed in the following year and with whom he had served as a feoffee in 1551, accorded with the Queen's request for resident Members; their receipt from the town of £6 10s. between them represented a wage of 1s. a day each for their 66 days of attendance. Stempe's further services to the town included a successful visit to London in 1557 as a trustee of its grammar school, to contest the crown's appropriation of the income which maintained the school, and a contribution of 10s. in 1564 towards the cost of a market hall.[3]

In 1564 Stempe leased lands in Falmer, near Brighton, and by 1580 he had obtained possession of the manor of Southover, once (like Falmer) held by Anne of Cleves and granted to John Kyme III* and Richard Kyme in 1557; in 1582 Stempe and his wife sold it to Thomas Sackville*, Baron Buckhurst. No further reference has been found to him but he was probably the father of the Anne Stempe who married Herbert Springett of Lewes and of the

William Stempe elected constable of Lewes in 1598.[4]

[1] Date of birth estimated from first reference. PCC 20 Tashe; *Suss. Rec. Soc.* xlviii. 45; *Vis. Suss.* (Harl. Soc. liii), 145. [2] *Suss. Rec. Soc.* xlviii. 9, 14, 21; *Suss. Arch. Colls.* xlviii. 20. [3] *Suss. Rec. Soc.* xix. 164; xxxvi. 138-9; xlviii. 2, 8, 15; lvi. 96. [4] *CPR*, 1557-8, pp. 198-9; 1569-72, p. 330; *Suss. N. and Q.* xii. 69; *VCH Suss.* vii. 48, 224; *Suss. Rec. Soc.* xx. 412; xlviii. 45; *Vis. Suss.* 145.

R.J.W.S.

STEPNETH (STEPNEY), Robert (by 1513-57), of West Ham, Essex, and Aldenham and St. Albans, Herts.

St. Albans 1555

b. by 1513, 1st s. of Thomas Stepneth of St. Albans; half-bro. of Alban Stepneth†. *m.* Alice, at least 4s. 1da.[1]
Bailiff and collector, former lands of Holy Trinity priory, Aldgate, London, and Stratford-at-Bow priory, Essex 1546-d.[2]

One Thomas Stepneth is named in the accounts of St. Alban's abbey for 1529-30 as the abbey's solicitor and a John Stepneth was one of the city's wealthier townsmen in 1523. There was thus a family connexion with the city, even though Robert Stepneth did not live there, so far as can be discovered, until the last few years of his life.[3]

Of the two half-brothers so named, the elder who died in 1557 was probably the Member. It was almost certainly he who in 1544 took a crown lease of Monkwick mansion outside Colchester for 21 years at a yearly rent of £22. John Dudley, Earl of Warwick and later Duke of Northumberland, had a crown grant of the freehold reversion of Monkwick in June 1547, but sold it to his dependant and relative by marriage Sir Francis Jobson*, who in turn must have acquired the leasehold interest from Stepneth, for he made Monkwick his principal residence and died there in 1573. Stepneth's will clearly shows the connexion between the two men, which probably dated back to 1544 and may have prompted Stepneth to take his lease as Jobson's nominee, perhaps in return for favours from Jobson as receiver for Essex and Hertfordshire to the court of augmentations. Stepneth's advancement, and in particular his return to Parliament, are only to be explained by some influential connexion, such as that with Jobson; his younger brother, who is not known to have enjoyed any such connexion, is much less likely to have earned a comparable reward.[4]

Stepneth also took a lease in 1544 of land at West Ham that had earlier belonged to Stratford-at-Bow priory. Both this lease and Stepneth's offices as collector for the lands of two dissolved monasteries he perhaps also owed to Jobson's influence; after his death they passed to a namesake, probably the younger brother. Styled a gentleman, Stepneth lived at West Ham at least until 1548, when he acquired from a distant cousin, Ralph Stepneth, the Hertfordshire manor of Aldenham; one-third of the manor came to Stepneth as heir at law, the other two-thirds were bequeathed to him for life, with remainder to his younger son Ralph, presumably the testator's godson. Robert Stepneth was involved in at least one chancery case, and his descendants in several more, against other cousins who tried, apparently without success, to prove that his grandfather had not been the firstborn but had had an elder brother, whose descendants, the claimants, should have inherited the land.[5]

On Mary's accession Sir Francis Jobson suffered temporary imprisonment for his support of Queen Jane, but he did not lose the lands he had accumulated with Northumberland's help or fail to sit in two Marian Parliaments. He did so in 1555, and presumably also supported Stepneth's candidature at St. Albans. He may have foreseen that bills to be introduced into this Parliament would concern him personally, and so felt the need of a reliable supporter in the House. Somewhat surprisingly, the only known roll of 'opposition' Members in the Commons of 1555 does not include the names of either Stepneth or Francis Jobson. Stepneth, for his part, had already run into some unspecified trouble with authority. He was one of four persons bound by the Privy Council on 1 Feb. 1554 in the sum of 50 marks each to appear when summoned 'and in the meantime to behave themselves like true subjects'. The offence does not sound a very serious one, and the exhortation suggests a recourse to violence, perhaps as an accompaniment of some lawsuit, or as an aftermath of the political crisis of the preceding year.[6]

Unlike Jobson, Stepneth had no opportunity to sit again, for he died between 11 Feb. 1557, when he made his will, and the following 24 Apr., when his offices were granted to another of the same name. He provided for his wife by leaving her land in St. Albans for life, and also 'my office of the collection-ship within the town of St. Albans with the yearly fee of £10 8s.' and 'all such debts and duties' as Jobson then owed him. Alice Stepneth was also left a crown annuity *pur autre vie* of 50s., perhaps granted to her husband in return for the surrender of the stewardship of Hertford priory, which he is known to have held earlier. After directing the sale of his house in Hart Street, London, Stepneth provided for his four sons from lands in Essex and Hertfordshire; each son also received £20 in cash and an unmarried daughter £80. He also remembered his brother Robert and a number of more distant relatives, and named his wife executrix and Sir Francis Jobson overseer.[7]

[1] Date of birth estimated from age at cousin's i.p.m., C142/88/72. *St. Albans and Herts. Arch. Soc.* (1933–5), 320–2; PCC 12 Wrastley. [2] *LP Hen. VIII*, xxi; *CPR*, 1555–7, pp. 293–4. [3] E315/274, ff. 24v, 80, 85v. [4] *LP Hen. VIII*, xix; *CPR*, 1547–8, pp. 204, 254; 1555–7, pp. 293–4; PCC 24 Populwell. [5] *St. Albans and Herts. Arch. Soc.* loc. cit.; C1/1217/46–47; 2 Eliz./516/56; 3/168/9; 142/88/72; *LP Hen. VIII*, xix, xxi. [6] *APC*, iv. 391. [7] Clutterbuck, *Herts.* i. app. 21; PCC 12 Wrastley.

D.F.C.

STERNHOLD (STERNELL), Thomas (by 1517–49), of Westminster, Mdx.

PLYMOUTH   1545

b. by 1517. *educ.* ?Oxf. *m.* by 1546, Agnes, prob. da. of one Horswell, 2da.[1]

Servant of Cromwell by 1538; groom of the robes 1540–*d.*; receiver-gen. ct. gen. surveyors of the King's lands, attainted lands, Yorks., Jan. 1545; j.p. Glos. 1547; master, St. Bartholomew's hospital, Gloucester Sept. 1547–*d.*; commr. chantries, Glos., Bristol and Gloucester 1548.[2]

Thomas Sternhold, the versifier of the psalms, is said by both Bale and Holinshed to have been a Hampshire man—Holinshed says that he was born at Southampton—but a much later account has it that he was born at Awre in Gloucestershire and lived there as a neighbour of his fellow-translator John Hopkins. There is no evidence that the two were ever acquainted or that Hopkins had any connexion with Gloucestershire but there were Sternholds in the shire and towards the end of his life Thomas Sternhold was appointed to commissions there and granted the mastership of a hospital in Gloucester, although most of the land which he obtained lay in Cornwall and Hampshire.[3]

Sternhold's education at Oxford rests on the unsupported statement of Wood and his first appearance is as a servant of Cromwell: like many of his fellows he secured a post in the royal household on the minister's fall. In 1543 he was one of the group of Protestants in the Household who were imprisoned for their involvement with one of the Windsor Martyrs but were soon pardoned and restored to favour: Henry VIII, indeed, left Sternhold 100 marks in his will. He was to act as feoffee and as surety for one of his fellow-prisoners, Sir Philip Hoby*, and his widow was almost certainly 'that worthy Sternhold's wife' who married Hoby's brother William Hoby of Hursley, Hampshire. He was also a feoffee for the poet William Grey II* who belonged to the same Protestant circle. He served in the French campaign of 1544 and in the following year was returned to Parliament for Plymouth. He was a friend and probably a relative by marriage of James Horswell*, a local Protestant and former client of Cromwell who may, however, have died before the election, and he must have known his fellow-Member George Ferrers, a writer who had also passed from Cromwell's service to the King's.

Ferrers's return for Cirencester in 1547 at the hands of Admiral Seymour may have owed something to Sternhold, an annuitant of Catherine Parr and a man of influence in that town.[4]

In 1541 Sternhold obtained a 21-year lease of Bodmin priory, Cornwall, from the crown, converting it into a grant in fee three years later when he also leased the Hampshire manor of Merdon; he later purchased another Hampshire manor, Slackstead, from Sir Ralph Sadler*. By his will of 22 Aug. 1549, made the day before his death and proved on the following 12 Sept., he left two thirds of his lands in Bodmin and Slackstead to his wife and executrix for life together with all his goods and chattels. One of the witnesses, Edward Whitchurch, was presumably the Protestant publisher who had printed the first edition of Sternhold's version of the psalms: the date of publication is unknown but the dedication was to Edward VI who, Sternhold said, had taken pleasure in hearing him sing them.[5]

[1] Date of birth estimated from first reference. Emden, *Biog. Reg. Univ. Oxf. 1501–40*, p. 539; PCC 37 Populwell; I. Gray, 'The Sternhold mystery', *Bristol and Glos. Arch. Soc. Trans.* lxxxvii, 209–12; *CPR*, 1548–9, p. 245; *DNB*. [2] *LP Hen. VIII*, xiii, xiv, xvi, xx, add.; *CPR*, 1547–8, pp. 84, 193; 1548–9, pp. 136, 244. [3] Gray, 209–12. [4] M. L. Robertson, 'Cromwell's servants' (Univ. California Los Angeles Ph.D. thesis, 1975), 566; *APC*, i. 97; ii. 244; *LP Hen. VIII*, xviii, xix, add.; *Test. Vet.* ed. Nicolas, i. 44; *CPR*, 1547–8, p. 224; 1549–51, p. 312; Gray, 210; *Vis. Worcs.* (Harl. Soc. xxvii), 80; SC6, Edw. VI/726, ff. 21v, 25; *Bristol and Glos. Arch. Soc. Trans.* xi. 119. [5] *LP Hen. VIII*, xvi, xix; *VCH Hants*, iv. 444; PCC 37 Populwell; C142/88/12; *Lit. Rems. Edw. VI*, pp. lv–lvi and n; *CPR*, 1553–4, p. 298.

R.V.

STEWARD, Augustine (1491–1571), of Norwich, Norf.

NORWICH   1539,[1] 1547[2]

b. 1491, s. of Geoffrey Steward of Norwich by Cecily, da. of Augustine Boys of Norwich. *m.* (1) Elizabeth, da. of William Rede of Beccles, Suff., 2s. 6da.; (2) Alice, da. of Henry Repps of Marshland, Norf., 1s. 2da.[3]

Common councilman, Norwich, 1522–6, auditor 1525, 1528–9, 1531–3, 1535–7, 1540–1, 1543–5, 1547–8, 1554–5, 1557, 1560, 1564, alderman 1526–*d.*, sheriff 1526–7, mayor 1534–5, 1546–7, 1556–7; commr. relief 1550, goods of churches and fraternities 1553, sewers 1566.[4]

Augustine Steward was a mercer who had been born and christened in the parish of St. George's Tombland, Norwich. He was admitted a freeman of the city on 12 Mar. 1516 and after serving for some years on the common council was elected an alderman in 1526, a position he was to retain until his death. In 1535 he was one of the men with whom the 3rd Duke of Norfolk discussed the under-assessment of Norwich towards the subsidy recently granted; he evidently agreed with the duke's proposal that the city's contribution should be increased, for in the following year he was described as 'the chief advancer of the King's profit there'. After the death of Reginald Lytilprowe* he became the government's leading supporter in Norwich, and his 'good services' to the King earned him the praise of the duke and of Sir Roger Townshend* and commended him to Cromwell.[5]

Steward's standing with these magnates made him a valuable agent in the city's efforts to benefit from the Reformation. It was during his first mayoralty that negotiations were begun between the corporation and the cathedral authorites for a revision of Wolsey's settlement of a longstanding dispute between them. Steward continued to pursue the matter, approaching Cromwell in May 1537 for his favour and later asking the minister to reverse Wolsey's judgment placing the cathedral outside the city's jurisdiction. Early in 1539 he was one of the attorneys appointed to argue the case before the King and on 6 Apr. letters patent were granted in the city's favour. In the meantime he had also become the moving spirit in the attempt to anticipate the dissolution of the house of the Blackfriars by acquiring it for the city. In 1538 he and his kinsman Edward Rede*, after consultation with the duke, asked Cromwell for his assistance to this end, and when the house was suppressed it was granted to the city on 1 June 1540, Steward himself paying the £81 required.[6]

Steward's Membership of Parliament was a natural extension of his civic services. His first election in 1539, several years after his first mayoralty, was also doubtless favoured by both Norfolk and Cromwell: he and another (unknown) citizen had already been chosen when Cromwell asked the city to return John Godsalve (q.v.), and despite its demurrer Steward had Godsalve as his fellow-Member and as his colleague in supervising the collection of the subsidy they had helped to grant. It was during the third session of this Parliament that Steward helped to bring the suit for the Blackfriars to its conclusion. Although it has been stated that Steward was re-elected to the following Parliament the return in question, which survives in a damaged condition, has a 'Joh. . . . .' as second Member for Norwich with William Rogers. Steward was next returned, with the local lawyer Richard Catlyn, towards the close of his second mayoralty in 1547: any doubt as to the propriety of his thus returning himself is likely to have been offset by the connexion with the Protector Somerset which the marriage of his daughter to Somerset's cofferer John Pykerell had given him, but it was probably as a consequence of his election that he was replaced by John Aldrich* as one of the commissioners to survey the suppressed hospital at Nor-

wich. Although he is not mentioned in the Journal he is likely to have been interested in two Acts of this Parliament, one for the weaving of worsted (1 Edw. VI, c.6) passed during its first session and the other for the making of hats, dornick and coverlets in Norwich and Norfolk (5 and 6 Edw. VI, c.24) passed during its final one. While attending the session of 1552 he acted as one of the city's attorneys in a case heard before the court of wards.[7]

During Ket's rebellion Steward was made acting mayor after the insurgents had taken the mayor prisoner. As one of the richest citizens he had much at stake and it must have been with relief that on the Marquess of Northampton's arrival he presented the city's sword and entertained the marquess to dinner. But Northampton quickly withdrew and when the rebels entered Norwich they forced their way into his house, 'took him, plucked his gown beside his back, called him traitor and threatened to kill him', and then ransacked the house. On the approach of the Earl of Warwick the rebels sent Steward and Robert Rugge* to negotiate on their behalf, but on being taken to Warwick the two revealed to him how his troops could retake the city. Despite his harrowing experience and a rebuke from Warwick for pusillanimity, Steward retained his standing in Norwich and was regularly in office for a further 15 years.[8]

Little has come to light about the commercial activity which yielded Steward such wealth, but there is a reference to a venture of about 1530 in which, with his father-in-law Reginald Lytilprowe and others, he had a factor at Danzig freight a ship to a value of 800 marks for a voyage to Yarmouth. Part of his profits went into Norfolk land: in 1530 he bought the manor of Welborne, and in 1548 the manor of Barton Buryhall, which 12 years later he settled on his son-in-law Robert Wood. He made his will on 9 Oct. 1570, asking to be buried in St. Peter's Hungate 'where my well beloved wives are buried'. After bequests to churches and to St. Giles's hospital, Norwich, he divided his property between his children. He appointed as executors two sons and as supervisors six 'sons-in-law', including John Aldrich*, Thomas Layer[†] and Thomas Sotherton*. He attended his last meeting of the Norwich assembly early in 1571, but he was replaced as one of the aldermen in April of that year and his will was proved in the following November.[9]

[1] E159/319, brev. ret. Mich. r.[1–2]. [2] Norwich ass. procs. 2, f. 203; Hatfield 207. [3] Aged '79 years and a half' on 9 Oct. 1570, PCC 43 Holney. Vis. Norf. (Harl. Soc. xxxii), 268–9. [4] Norwich ass. procs. 1–3 passim; CPR, 1550–3, p. 396; 1553, p. 351; 1569–72, pp. 218–20; Norwich Census of the Poor (Norf. Rec. Soc. xl), app. viii. [5] PCC 43 Holney; B. Cozens-Hardy and E. A. Kent, Mayors of Norwich, 48; Merchants' Marks (Harl. Soc. cviii), unpaginated; Norwich old free bk., f. 60v; chamberlains' bk. 1531–7, ff. 63v, 102v, 132; LP Hen. VIII, ix, xi–xiii. [6] Norwich chamberlains' bk. 1531–7, f. 82; ass.

procs. 2, ff. 165v, 166, 171v, 177v, 179v.; *LP Hen. VIII*, xii, xiv, xv, add. [7] Norwich mayors' ct. bk. f. 152 ex inf. Dr. J. Miklovich; ass. procs. 2, f. 203; 3, f. 20; E159/319, brev. ret. Mich. r.[1–2]; *LP Hen. VIII*, xv; Blomefield, *Norf.* iii. 222; C219/18B/58; *CSP Dom.* 1547–80, p. 125. [8] Holinshed, *Chron.* 971–9; N. Sotherton, *The Commoyson in Norfolk, 1549* (Jnl. Med. and Ren. Studies vi), 87–97; Norwich ass. procs. 2, f. 229; 3, f. 20; *APC*, vi. 82. [9] *LP Hen. VIII*, add.; Blomefield, ii. 454; *CPR*, 1547–8, p. 373; 1558–60, p. 265; PCC 43 Holney; Norwich ass. bk. 3 passim.

R.V.

STOCKDALE, Alexander (by 1509–63), of Kingston-upon-Hull, Yorks.

KINGSTON-UPON-HULL 1553 (Mar.), 1554 (Apr.)

b. by 1509. *m.* Grace, da. of Thomas Estofte of Eastoft, 1s. 1da.[1]

Chamberlain, Kingston-upon-Hull 1530–1, sheriff 1540–1, mayor 1544–5, 1551–2, 1558–9; commr. sewers 1543.[2]

Alexander Stockdale's parentage has not been established. He was perhaps related to the West Riding family headed by Christopher Stockdale, who died in 1554 leaving a son and heir Anthony; another Christopher Stockdale was an alderman of Hull in 1563. By profession a merchant, Stockdale appears in the customs accounts for March 1541 as an importer of mixed goods, paying for iron, soap, nuts, prunes, grey paper, oil and herrings carried in one ship from the Netherlands and for madder and alum in another. During his first mayoralty he was one of those who reported to the 5th Earl of Shrewsbury on the impact of the war on shipping at Hull; he himself owned a half-share in a ship when he died. His assessment of £80 on goods for the subsidy of 1547 shows him to have been one of the wealthiest men in the town. He had by then acquired a number of properties within and outside it, including the manor of Lockington; to these he was to add chantry lands (which in 1560 he was absolved in the Exchequer of concealing), and a share in the Charterhouse at Hull and in the manor of Sculcoates bought from Thomas Dalton*.[3]

Stockdale's two elections to Parliament placed him among the small group of Hull magnates who sat more than once for the town, including his fellow-Members William Johnson and John Thacker. In April 1554 the Vintners' Company solicited his support in its unsuccessful attempt to repeal the Act of 1553 (7 Edw. VI, c.5) controlling the sale of wine. His suing out of a pardon at the accession of Elizabeth was probably a conventional piece of insurance. The will which he made on 20 Sept. 1563, the day before he died, contains no profession of faith. He asked to be buried in the church of St. Mary, Hull, and gave a life-interest in his house and one-third of his lands (excluding Sculcoates) to his wife, rents and a sum of £300 to his daughter and the residue to his son Robert; he named his wife and daughter executrices and his

wife's uncle Christopher Estofte[†] and her brother Thomas Estofte supervisors. The will was proved on 29 Dec. 1563 and in July 1565 Grace Stockdale and Christopher Estofte obtained the wardship of Robert Stockdale, then still a minor. In a subsequent dispute over Sculcoates the Estofte family alleged that Robert was a lunatic.[4]

[1] Date of birth estimated from first reference. *Yorks. Peds.* (Harl. Soc. xciv), 170–1; *Lincs. Peds.* (Harl. Soc. l), 335–6; York wills 17, f. 307. [2] L. M. Stanewell, *Cal. Anct. Deeds, Kingston-upon-Hull*; M479(81); T. Gent, *Kingston-upon-Hull* (1735), 112, 116, 118, 120; *LP Hen. VIII*, xx. [3] C142/102/41, 117/52; York wills 17, f. 307; *Bronnen tot de Geschiedenis van den Handel met Engeland, Schotland en Ierland*, ed. Smit, i. 524–5; *LP Hen. VIII*, xix; E179/203/233; *Yorks. Fines*, i (Yorks. Arch. Soc. rec. ser. ii), 68, 88, 121, 128–9; *Yorks. Suppression Pprs.* (ibid. xlviii), 121; Stanewell, D623, 628, M45; *VCH Yorks.* (*E. Riding*), i. 288, 468–9. [4] *Guildhall Studies in London Hist.* i. 48–49; *CPR*, 1558–60, p. 163; 1563–6, p. 248; York wills 17, f. 307; *VCH Yorks.* (*E. Riding*), i. 468–9.

M.K.D.

STOKES, John

WESTBURY 1547[1]

Of the several namesakes traceable in the mid 16th century the most distinguished and the one most likely to have been the Member for Westbury was an attorney practising in the court of common pleas. During the late 1540s the attorney acted in the court on behalf of a west-country clientele, including among others John Perte*, Nicholas Poyntz* and Thomas Tyndale*. In 1559 Sir Edward Rogers* and Sir Thomas Throckmorton* named him with Sir Maurice Berkeley*, Sir Giles Poole*, Sir John Thynne* and others in a settlement made on the marriage of Throckmorton's son and Rogers's daughter. Of the parties to this settlement four had been Members of the Parliament of 1547 and Throckmorton and Thynne had sat for Wiltshire constituencies. As Stokes's partner was another Throckmorton the patronage operating for that group could account for Stokes's own Membership. In its turn Kenelm Throckmorton's kinship with Catherine Parr suggests that Stokes is identifiable with a man assessed in 1545 and 1546 on £20 in goods as a member of the Queen's household. This John Stokes or perhaps a namesake had been a groom of the chamber in 1540.[2]

To his own business links with Wiltshire Stokes the attorney may well have been able to add those of birth and descent. A family of that name lived within ten miles of Westbury at Seend where a clothier John Stokes died in 1498. By his wife Alice the clothier had three sons, two of whom were christened John, and the third son, Robert, also had two sons so named: yet another John, the second son of the clothier's elder son John, had a son Edmund who married a daughter of Nicholas Snell[†] and founded a landed family in the county. One of these John Stokes was perhaps the man living at Langley

Burrell, near Chippenham, who was required to pay 26s.8d. towards the benevolence of 1545 and who— or whose namesake—was assessed on £3 for subsidy in 1576 at the same place. The modesty of these assessments does not accord with his being the attorney, who suffixed himself gentleman but whether by birth or advancement is not known.[3]

[1] Hatfield 207. [2] CP40/1140–2; C142/149/30; LP Hen. VIII, xx; The Gen. n.s. xxx. 26; Soc. Antiq. (1790), 170. [3] Wilts. N. and Q. ii. 577; v. 349, 350, 393; Misc. Gen. et Her. (ser. 2), ii. 25 seq.; (ser. 3), ii. 133; E. Kite, Mon. Brasses Wilts. plate x; E179/69/47, 48, m.2; Wilts. Arch. Soc. recs. br. x. 28, 56.

N.M.F.

STONARD (STONER), James (by 1497–1558), of Southampton.

SOUTHAMPTON   1553 (Mar.), 1554 (Nov.)

b. by 1497, 2nd s. of Peter Stonard of Southampton.[1] Steward, Southampton 1530–1, water bailiff 1532–3, ct. bailiff 1534–5, sheriff 1535–6, mayor 1546–7, alderman by 1553.[2]

James Stonard followed his father into trade and was admitted a freeman of Southampton on 16 Feb. 1518. His municipal career followed the usual course and by the time of his first Membership of Parliament he was the leading alderman in the town. As a supplier of victuals, munitions and building materials to the garrison on Alderney during 1549– 51 he was doubtless known to John Dudley, Duke of Northumberland, under whose aegis the Parliament of March 1553 was called. His re-election 18 months later satisfied Queen Mary's preference for townsmen. Unlike his partner on this occasion James Brande, he was not found to be absent without leave at the call of the House early in January 1555. The payment of 20s. made by John Staveley* as mayor during 1554–5 to Stonard, 'upon his allowance being burgess of the Parliament', was perhaps a contribution towards his expenses on both occasions. On the outbreak of war with France in 1557 he was entrusted with a sector of the South- ampton defences. He presumably died at his house on Simnel Street, which he had occupied since leasing it in 1548, as he was buried in St. Michael's church nearby on 2 Feb. 1558. If he made a will it has not been found.[3]

[1] Date of birth estimated from admission as freeman. Soton RO, bk. of oaths and ordinances, f. 8v. [2] Third Bk. of Remembrance, i (Soton Rec. ser. ii), app. i; C219/20/168. [3] Soton RO, bk. of oaths and ordinances, f. 8v; liber de finibus 1554–5; Third Bk. of Remembrance, i. 50n; ii (Soton Rec. ser. iii), 9n, 20, 36n, 57, 57n; APC, ii. 288, 292, 293, 300, 326, 351, 401; iii. 184, 291; La Société Guernesiaise, xvi. 230, 257, 264–5.

P.H.

STOPFORD, William (by 1522–84), of Bispham and Wrightington, Lancs.

LIVERPOOL   1558

b. by 1522, prob. s. of John Stopford. m. Blanche, da. of Henry Twiford of Kenwick, Salop, at least 1s.[1] Commr. in local disputes 1553, 1578.[2]

The Earl of Derby and the duchy of Lancaster customarily shared the nomination of the Liverpool Members. In 1558 George White, an Essex gentle- man, was clearly the nominee of the duchy, and William Stopford was recommended by the earl. A payment to Stopford 'for the church goods bought before' Edward Stanley, 3rd Earl of Derby, at Lathom is recorded in the Prescot churchwardens' accounts for 1553–4; in 1562 he received a fee of 53s.4d. from the earl and ten years later he was named an executor of the earl's will. Other Stop- fords were also members of the Derby household. Robert Bootle, who died about 1631, was married to the daughter of a Stopford who was secretary to the 4th Earl of Derby (d. 1593); whether this was the Member or one of his kinsmen is not known, as no pedigree has been found.[3]

Stopford first appears in 1543 as the purchaser of property in Wrightington. He engaged in a number of lawsuits, both as plaintiff and defendant, over his interests in Bispham, Eccleston, Mawdesley, North Meols, Wrightington and elsewhere in Lancashire. Stopford died in 1584 and according to his tomb- stone in Eccleston churchyard was buried on 18 June. As a servant of the earls of Derby he may have been a Catholic, but his relationship, if any, with the Marian priest Francis Stopford and with the 'Mr. Stopford' at whose Lancashire house mass was said has not been discovered. His widow married Robert Hesketh† and in 1601–2 John Stopford, claiming by conveyance from his father William, brought a suit against the Heskeths and William Ashehurst over property in Bispham and elsewhere. By about 1600 the Stopfords had settled at Ulnes Walton in Lancashire and they later moved to Saltersford in Cheshire. Their descendants became earls of Courtown.[4]

[1] Date of birth estimated from first reference. VCH Lancs. vi. 173n; Vis. Lancs. (Chetham Soc. lxxxv), 135. [2] Lancs. and Cheshire Rec. Soc. xl. 148; APC, x. 299. [3] Lancs. and Cheshire Rec. Soc. civ. 30; Lancs. RO, Stanley pprs. DDK/6/3, p. 17; J. B. Watson, 'Lancs. gentry 1529–58' (London Univ. M.A. thesis, 1959), 566; PCC 38 Daper; Vis. Lancs. (Chetham Soc. lxxxiv), 45. [4] Add. 32104, arts. 1366, 1390; VCH Lancs. vi. 173n.; Ducatus Lanc. ii. 176, 284; iii. 268, 348, 353; iv. 5, 94, 100, 112, 188, 218, 484; R. C. Shaw, Lancs. Fam. 156; Lancs. and Cheshire Rec. Soc. xl. 148; APC, x. 299; Trans. Hist. Soc. Lancs. and Cheshire, lxiii. 56; Strype, Annals, ii(2), 661; iv. 261; Trans. Lancs. and Cheshire Antiq. Soc. xxxiii. 206.

A.D.

STORY, John (c.1504–71)

SALISBURY	1545[1]
HINDON	1547*[2]
EAST GRINSTEAD	1553 (Oct.)
BRAMBER	1554 (Apr.)
BATH	1554 (Nov.)[3]

LUDGERSHALL   1555
DOWNTON   1559

b. c.1504, s. of Nicholas Story of Salisbury, Wilts. by Joan. *educ.* Hinxsey Hall, Oxf., BCL 1531, DCL 1538; adv. Doctors' Commons 1539. *m.* by 1549, Joan Watts, 1da. and 4 other ch.[4]

1st regius lecturer and prof. civil law, Oxf. 1535, reappointed 7 Oct. 1553, principal, Broadgates Hall 1537–9; vicar-gen. London diocese Nov. 1539–c.July 1540; chancellor, London and Oxford dioceses Jan. 1554–9; j.p.q. Mdx. 1554; Queen's proctor at the trial of Cranmer 1555; commr. heresy 1557–8; master in Chancery by 1558.[5]

A native of Salisbury, John Story may have received his early education at the cathedral school before going up to Oxford. It is said that he became a Franciscan lay brother, or perhaps a tertiary of the order, but whether early or late in life is not stated. His student career was a stormy one. In October 1530 he was first sentenced to imprisonment for insolence to the principal of his own hall and then to banishment for insolence to the judge who had heard his case. Reconciled with the principal (who was himself soon afterwards ordered to prison for similar behaviour), Story transferred to Broadgates Hall but quickly returned to Hinxsey. There he again stirred up trouble to the point where, in November 1533, he had his name struck off the books and was given leave to go elsewhere. So he went back to Broadgates, where in 1537 he became principal. None of this interfered with his study of civil law, in which his reputation became so great that the King appointed him first lecturer in civil law before he had taken his doctorate. The appointment was to be confirmed for life in 1544 in recognition of his skilful administration of the court of the earl marshal during the expedition to Boulogne. Meanwhile he had entered the college of advocates and was for a short time vicar-general of the London diocese under Bonner, himself a former student of Broadgates Hall.[6]

Story's return for his native city of Salisbury to the Parliament of 1545 was probably the work of the conservative Bishop Salcot. In January the city assembly had elected a local lawyer, Robert Keilway II*, and a citizen, Edmund Gawen, but Parliament was postponed until November and in the interval the lawyer had chosen to sit for Bristol and the citizen had fallen ill. To fill the vacancies there came Story and Thomas Gawdy I, but the assembly, which valued the city's independence, stipulated that the election of these 'outsiders' was not to set a precedent. For the following Parliament Story therefore found a seat at Hindon, one of the bishop of Winchester's boroughs. Stephen Gardiner was a prisoner in the Fleet at the time of the elections and it was doubtless his steward William Paulet, Baron

St. John, who procured Story's election, as he was to do again in 1559. Towards the end of the second session (1548–9) of this Parliament Story spoke against the Prayer Book with the lament 'Woe unto thee England when the king is a child'. The House took grave exception to the speech and on 24 Jan. 1549 Story was committed to the Tower, to be released in early March after an apology from himself and a petition to the House from his wife. Outraged by the Edwardian Reformation, Story travelled to Louvain where he entered the university. Here he made a will in which he prayed God to restore England to the unity of the Catholic Church and enjoined his wife to return there only when this had been achieved. The phrase 'extra regnum' appears beside his deleted name on the list of Members for the fourth session of the Parliament he had offended; his place was regarded as vacant and was filled by John Zouche I.[7]

Story came back after the accession of Mary and he sat in the first four of her Parliaments, on each occasion for a different borough. A fellow-Catholic, John Caryll, probably found Story his places for Sussex constituencies since he too had sat for one of the bishop of Winchester's boroughs in 1547 and was re-elected in the autumn of 1553; Caryll was attorney-general to the duchy of Lancaster which owned East Grinstead (where Story's name was inserted together with Sir Thomas Stradling's on the indenture), as well as steward of the barony of Bramber where Story sat with one of Caryll's kinsmen, Sir Henry Palmer. In the first of Mary's Parliaments Story served on the committee to examine the validity of the return of Alexander Nowell and John Foster II. His Membership for Bath he owed to the new bishop Gilbert Bourne, a former chaplain to Bonner. On the Crown Office list compiled for this Parliament Story's name was initially entered against Old Sarum as well as Bath, but this mistake was soon corrected when his name was struck through for the Wiltshire borough and replaced by John Tull's. The influence which provided Story with a seat for Ludgershall is uncertain, although Sir Richard Brydges*, the patron of the borough and a duchy of Lancaster receiver, may have obliged Caryll. It was in this Parliament that Story again offended the House. When he was one of the deputation to the Queen, led by the Speaker, which heard Mary's decision not to accept first fruits and tenths, he informed her that the Commons wanted papal licences to be restrained. His intervention, an affront to the Speaker, was pardoned by the Commons because he spoke 'of good zeal'; it may nevertheless help to explain why he did not find a seat in the Queen's last Parliament.

During the first session, however, he made an appearance in the House together with Edmund Plowden* and the abbot of Westminster as counsel over the abbey's right of sanctuary.[8]

As Chancellor of the London diocese under Bonner from January 1554 Story incurred the hatred of his Protestant contemporaries and of later writers for his alleged cruelty to heretics. Foxe, who thought him 'in summa worse than Bonner', describes how he came straight from a burning to the lord mayor's table to boast that as he had despatched one so would he all the rest. He certainly had few scruples as to the methods to be employed: as he wrote to Courtenay in 1555, 'Now the sharpness of the sword and other corrections have begun to bring forth that the word in stony hearts could not do'. He denounced the gentle treatment accorded to noblemen and gentlemen, and (as Father Persons relates) 'stormed publicly one day before the bishops and Privy Council ... complaining grievously of the abuse'. In a speech to the Commons in 1559 Story regretted that he and his colleagues had 'laboured only about the young and little twigs, whereas they should have struck at the root'. When himself on the scaffold Story denied the charge of cruelty, declaring that as a layman he could not give judgment and claiming that he had been responsible for the pardon of 27 poor and ignorant heretics.[9]

Story's execution followed several years in exile with the help of a pension from Philip of Spain and of the post of inspector of incoming ships at Antwerp, where he watched for heretical literature. Kidnapped by English sailors and brought to England, he was charged with having supported the rebellion of 1569 and encouraged Alva to invade; his refusal to plead, on the ground that he was a subject of Philip II, did not impede his conviction. He was executed on 1 June 1571 after making a long speech in which he justified his actions under Mary, extolled the virtues of his wife and ended with the peroration: 'every man is free-born and he hath the whole face of the earth before him to dwell and abide in where he liketh best; and if he cannot live here, he may go elsewhere'.[10]

[1] Salisbury corp. ledger B, f. 300v. [2] Hatfield 207. [3] Huntington Lib. Hastings mss Parl. pprs. [4] Date of birth given in DNB. Harl. Misc. (1808), iii. 105 seq.; I. Temple, Petyt mss 538 vol. 47, f. 66; CJ, i. 7; B. Camm, Eng. Martyrs under Eliz. 16; Emden, Biog. Reg. Univ. Oxf. 1501-40, p. 544; G. D. Squibb, Doctors' Commons, 148. [5] Wood, Ath. Ox. ed. Bliss, i. 386-7; CPR, 1553-4, pp. 21, 395; 1555-6, p. 281; London Guildhall Lib. Bonner's reg. ff. IV, 3; Strype, Cranmer, i. 533; E101/520/17. [6] J. Dyer, Reps. (1672), 300; Wilts. Arch. Soc. recs. br. x. 11; CPR, 1553-4, p. 395; Camm. 15; Oxf. Univ. Arch. T/S cal. chancellor's ct. EEE, pp. 205-6, 212, 220, 315, 468. [7] Salisbury corp. ledger B, f. 300v; Burnet, Hist. Ref. ii. 518; CJ, i. 6-7, 9; Hatfield 207. [8] C219/21/154; Huntington Lib. Hastings mss Parl. pprs.; CJ, i. 27, 44-45, 49. [9] Strype, Annals, ii. 296-7; Examinations and Writings of Archdeacon Philpot (Parker Soc.), 4-13, 47-48; R. Persons, A temperate watchword to ... Sir Francis Hastings (1599), 32-33; CSP Ven. 1555-6, p. 110. [10] CSP Span. 1558-67, pp. 322-3;

Strype, Parker, ii. 366-7; CSP Dom. 1547-80, pp. 389-415; State Trials, ed. Howell, i. 1087-95.

R.V./R.J.W.S.

STOUGHTON, Thomas (1521-76), of Stoughton, Surr. and West Stoke, Suss.

GUILDFORD	1547*[1]
CHICHESTER	1553 (Mar.), 1553 (Oct.), 1554 (Apr.)
GUILDFORD	1559
CHICHESTER	1563
GUILDFORD	1572*

b. 25 Mar. 1521, 1st s. of Lawrence Stoughton of Stoughton by Anne, ?da. of Thomas Combes of Guildford, Surr. educ. I. Temple. m. (1) Anne, da. of Francis Fleming of London, s.p.; (2) 27 Feb. 1553, Elizabeth, da. of Edmund Lewknor of Tangmere, Suss., 2s. Adrian[†] and Lawrence[†] 2da. suc. fa. 1571.[2] Bencher, I. Temple.

Comptroller, household of the 12th Earl of Arundel; under steward, crown lands in Suss.; j.p. Surr. 1558/59-d., Suss. 1558/59, 1573/74-d.; commr. musters, Surr. in 1560.[3]

The Stoughton family had held the manor of that name in the parish of Stoke-next-Guildford since at least the 12th century and was holding it direct from the crown by 1345. Members of the family had sat for the borough of Guildford since 1419.[4]

Like his grandfather Gilbert Stoughton[†], Thomas Stoughton was educated at the Inner Temple. His father is not known to have sat in Parliament and despite the family's long association with the borough and its friendship with the locally powerful Mores of Loseley, Stoughton probably owed his seat in the Parliament of 1547, in place of the deceased Thomas Elyot, to his master the Earl of Arundel, with whom he was to record about 1569 that he had lived for 20 years. Elyot, a servant of Sir Anthony Browne*, had died between September 1548 and 31 Jan. 1549, a month and a half before the closing of the second session, and Stoughton was presumably returned before Arundel's fall from grace early in 1550 and perhaps on the occasion of the earl's visit to Surrey in 1549 to prevent insurrection: Arundel was in Guildford on 29 June.[5]

Before the next Parliament the Marquess of Northampton had succeeded to Browne's post as keeper of Guildford park and apparently to his influence in the borough. Stoughton turned to Chichester, a borough seven miles from Arundel's manor of Stanstead (where Stoughton was himself resident in 1564 and 1569) and then more firmly under the earl's control: Stoughton's fellow-Member for Chichester in three Parliaments, Thomas Carpenter, was surveyor of the earl's lands in Sussex. The borough's willingness to accept

Arundel's nominees may have arisen out of a desire to obtain his support for a private bill to demolish the bishop's fishgarths in the harbour, although in the event the measure was not introduced until the following Parliament when it proceeded no further than its second reading: both the Members chosen had legal knowledge and previous parliamentary experience. Stoughton may have had other claims on the borough: in the reign of Henry VIII his father had been in the household of Thomas, 9th Lord la Warr, at nearby Halnaker, and his second wife's family was also connected with the la Warrs. His brother-in-law, Richard Lewknor[†], was to be recorder of Chichester from 1588 to 1600, when he was succeeded by Stoughton's younger son Adrian. Stoughton was on good terms with other Chichester Members: in 1565 Thomas Carpenter left him '20 angels besides the discharge of my book' and in 1568 Lawrence Ardren bequeathed 'to my friend Master Thomas Stoughton an old angelet'.[6]

Stoughton was not among the Members of the Parliament of October 1553 who 'stood for the true religion', that is, Protestantism; indeed, in 1564 he was to be described by the bishop of Chichester as 'a misliker of godly orders' and 'a stout scorner of godliness'. At first sight, therefore, it is difficult to account for his disappearance from the parliamentary scene after Mary's third Parliament and his reappearance in Elizabeth's first; the explanation seems to be that Chichester, in obedience to the Queen's circular letter asking for the return of Catholic residents, reverted to the practice of electing local men. Stoughton sat in Elizabeth's first Parliament for Guildford, where Arundel had become high steward, and did not sit again for Chichester until after his acquisition in 1560 of the neighbouring manor of West Stoke.[7]

Remaining in Arundel's service, Stoughton became involved in quarrels with Sussex gentlemen on the earl's behalf and, at least to the extent of knowing what was afoot, in his plotting with the 4th Duke of Norfolk. In 1572, despite the earl's disgrace, Stoughton was returned again for Guildford, where he had recently succeeded to his father's estate, and after his death on 26 Mar. 1576 the seat was filled by his elder son Lawrence.[8]

[1] Hatfield 207. [2] Add. 6174, ff. 127v–8 giving date of birth; Manning and Bray, Surr. i. 171; Vis. Surr. (Harl. Soc. xliii), 86–87; Surr. Arch. Colls. xii. ped.; VCH Surr. iii. 371. [3] HMC Hatfield, i. 436; CPR, 1563–6, pp. 26, 38–40; SP10/3/14, f. 114. [4] Manning and Bray, i. 38. [5] LP Hen. VIII, v; HMC Hatfield, i. 436; VCH Surr. i. 369–70; CSP Dom. 1547–80, p. 19. [6] VCH Suss. ii. 25; CJ, i. 28, 29; SP2/5, f. 206; PCC 31 Pynnyng; W. Suss. RO, wills 2. f. 21; original will C102. [7] Cam. Misc. ix(3), 10; CPR, 1558–60, pp. 319–20. [8] J. E. Mousley, 'Suss. country gentry in the reign of Eliz.' (London Univ. Ph.D. thesis, 1956), 777; CSP Dom. 1547–80, p. 153; Add. 6174, ff. 127–8; APC vii. 189, 193, 197, 200–1; viii. 261–2, 267, 275; E150/1108/8.

R.J.W.S.

STOURTON, Arthur (by 1525–58), of Westminster, Mdx.

WESTMINSTER 1553 (Mar.), 1555

b. by 1525, 3rd s. of William Stourton*, 7th Baron Stourton, by Elizabeth, da. of Edmund Dudley[†] of Atherington, Suss.; bro. of William*. m. Anne, da. of Henry Macwilliam of Stambourne, Essex, 2s.[1]

Jt. (with Richard Cupper*) bailiff, manor of Kenilworth, Warws. 1546; jt. (with Sir Andrew Dudley*) keeper of jewels and robes at Westminster 5 Jan. 1551–3; keeper of palace of Westminster 1553–d.[2]

Arthur Stourton was a nephew of John Dudley, successively Earl of Warwick and Duke of Northumberland. It was doubtless to this relationship that he owed his appointment in January 1551, with his uncle Sir Andrew Dudley, as keeper of the jewels and robes in the palace of Westminster, and both kinship and office would have helped to procure him one of the city's seats in the Parliament of March 1553, to which Andrew Dudley was returned as a knight for Oxfordshire. Yet Stourton, like his fellow-Member Sir Robert Southwell, was to avoid implication in the succession crisis which followed. We do not know whether he obeyed the warrant directed to him by Jane Grey on 10 July 1553, the day on which she was proclaimed Queen, for the delivery of 20 yards of crimson velvet, but a month later he received one for velvet for Queen Mary's coronation and it is clear from the patent of 12 Dec. 1554 appointing him keeper of the palace for life that there had been no break in his discharge of his previous office: the new fees and allowances, just over £100 a year, were made payable from 25 Mar. 1553, Dudley's patent evidently being held to have lapsed on the demise of the crown. On 28 Mar. 1555 Stourton was granted an annuity of 100 marks also dated from March 1553.[3]

It was with a fellow-official in Westminster, Richard Hodges, that Stourton was elected to Mary's fourth Parliament. Despite his dependence on the crown he may have been the 'Mr. Sturton' who appears on the list of Members voting against one of the government's bills; his brother William Stourton, who sat for Newport, was a catholic and unlikely to have taken this line. That neither was to be elected to the next Parliament may reflect the disgrace of their brother the 8th Baron Stourton's execution for murder in March 1557, but Arthur Stourton himself barely survived its opening. His burial at St. Martin in the Fields on 11 Feb. 1558, two days after he had made his will, may indicate that he was a victim of the epidemic then at its height. He named William Stourton an executor and left all the goods remaining after the payment of his debts to his two sons.[4]

[1] Date of birth estimated from first reference. Charles, Ld. Mowbray, *Noble House of Stourton*, 312, 314–15; *Vis. Dorset* (Harl. Soc. xx), 86; Morant, *Essex*, ii. 356. [2] *LP Hen. VIII*, xxi; *CPR*, 1549–51, p. 299; 1554–5, pp. 181–2; 1557–8, p. 74. [3] H. O. Coxe, *Catalogus Codicum Mss Coll. et Aul. Oxon.* i. 117; *CPR*, 1554–5, pp. 72, 181–2. [4] Guildford mus. Loseley 1331/2; *Machyn's Diary* (Cam. Soc. xlii), 165; PCC 20 Chaynay.

H.M.

STOURTON, Roger (by 1509–51), of Rushton, Dorset.

WEYMOUTH 1545

b. by 1509, 3rd but 2nd surv. s. of Edward Stourton, 6th Baron Stourton by Agnes, da. of John Fauntleroy of Marsh, nr. Sherborne; bro. of Sir William*. *m.* settlement 1–2 Jan. 1530, Jane, da. of one Bures of Suff.[1]

J.p. Dorset 1537; commr. musters 1539, 1542, relief 1550; escheator, Som. and Dorset 1539–40.[2]

Edward, Baron Stourton, making his will in November 1535, left to his son Roger £3 6s.8d., 'a hoop of gold, and half my raiment'; he had already, in January 1530, granted to Roger the manor of Up Cerne, Dorset. Roger Stourton, however, lived at Rushton, at the other end of the county, near Wareham, where he was assessed at £20 in lands in 1545. As the younger son of a peer of no great fortune, Stourton had a modest patrimony, but at the time of his death he owned at least 1,000 sheep at Up Cerne and another flock at Langford, Wiltshire, as well as corn and cattle on the Bures' manor of Brook Hall in Essex.[3]

Stourton's career in local administration began after the death of his father and flourished under the favour which his elder brother, the 7th Baron, enjoyed with Henry VIII. He was an occasional visitor at court, and in 1539 attended the reception of Anne of Cleves. His only known appearance in the House (he may have entered it earlier than 1545, when the returns are largely missing) was doubtless on the nomination of his elder brother, a leading figure in Dorset: Baron Stourton was the brother-in-law of John Dudley, Viscount Lisle, on whose influence in the past as lord admiral he could probably have relied. He was not re-elected in 1547, perhaps because his brother's duties at Ambleteuse absorbed his interests and limited his patronage at home.[4]

Stourton made his will on 28 Jan. 1551, leaving to his wife his manor house at Rushton, Up Cerne and all sheep and cattle not otherwise bequeathed. They had no children and the heir to Stourton's property was his nephew Charles, 8th Baron Stourton, appointed overseer of the will with Sir John Rogers*. Roger Stourton died three days after making the will. His widow and executrix was soon at loggerheads with Baron Stourton. She complained to the King in 1553 of a series of minor persecutions which she had

suffered at the hands of his servants since the death of her husband, when she had been left 'unfriended' in the county, having come to Dorset from Suffolk, the county of her birth. Jane Stourton, supported by her brother Robert Bures, had also to fight a running battle for the possession of Rushton with George Percy and his wife, the sister of Sir Henry Ashley*, but the court of Star Chamber decided in her favour and in May 1557 the sheriff reinstated her.[5]

[1] Date of birth estimated from marriage. Charles Lord Mowbray, *Noble House of Stourton*, 299. [2] *LP Hen. VIII*, xii, xiv, xvii; *CPR*, 1553, p. 352. [3] PCC 31 Hogen, 7 Bucke; Hutchins, *Dorset*, iv. 151; E179/104/156. [4] *LP Hen. VIII*, xiv, xv. [5] PCC 7 Bucke; C142/93/41; St.Ch.4/4/10, 9/31.

H.M.

STOURTON, William (by 1529–90), of Worminster, Som. and Marsh, nr. Sherborne, Dorset.

NEWPORT IUXTA LAUNCESTON 1555

b. by 1529, 4th s. of William Stourton*, 7th Baron Stourton, by Elizabeth, da. of Edmund Dudley† of Atherington, Suss.; bro. of Arthur*. *m.* (1) by 1550, Thomasin, da. of Sir John Fitzjames of Redlynch, Som., *s.p.*; (2) Mary, da. and coh. of John Wogan of Silvinch, Som., wid. of Robert Morgan of Mapperton, nr. Beaminster, Dorset, *s.p.*[1]

Servant of Thomas Seymour, Baron Seymour of Sudeley by 1549; steward, manor of Maiden Bradley, Wilts. by 1556.[2]

William Stourton's career began in the service of the Protector Somerset's ambitious younger brother Baron Seymour of Sudeley, and on his master's execution he was recommended by John Berwick* and Sir Hugh Paulet* to the Protector's service. Whether this advice was followed is not known, but in 1550 Stourton purchased a manor in west Dorset from two men close to Somerset, Lawrence Hyde† and Sir John Thynne*. Little trace has been found of his activities until after Mary's accession when he sued out a general pardon, although he is not known to have sympathised with his uncle the Duke of Northumberland or, apart from his lease of Portland, to have benefited from that kinship. He was returned to the fourth Parliament of Mary's reign as the senior Member for a Cornish borough where he had no personal links and where his name was inserted on the indenture in a different hand; presumably he was encouraged by his elder brother, the 8th Baron Stourton, but it was probably to the sheriff of Cornwall, his distant kinsman Sir John Arundell* of Lanherne, that he owed his seat. A 'Mr. Sturton' joined the opposition to a government bill in this Parliament, but since many of the Members concerned were of Protestant inclination as well as of west-country origin, whereas Stourton was to remain a Catholic, this is more likely to have been his brother Arthur. The opprobrium incurred by the family following the execution of the 8th Baron for murder in 1557 may have debarred Stourton from election to Mary's last Parliament and under Elizabeth his Catholicism was an even greater impediment.[3]

In 1559 Stourton sued out a general pardon and for the next 20 years he led an uneventful life in the south-west. His last years were troubled by suspicion of 'his disobedience in matter of religion' but he was still at liberty when he made his will on 12 Mar. 1590. After providing for his wife, he left a silver basin and ewer valued at £40 to his nephew, the 9th Baron Stourton, and various items of household stuff to his stepsons William and Christopher Morgan. He named his wife executrix and Thomas Chaffyn, John Fitzjames† and Christopher Morgan overseers. He died within a few hours of signing the will and was buried at nearby Folke.[4]

[1] Date of birth estimated from first land transaction. Hutchins, *Dorset*, ii. 158; *Vis. Som.* ed. Weaver, 106; *HMC Wells*, ii. 251, 270; Charles, Lord Mowbray, *Noble House of Stourton*, 321. [2] *HMC Bath*, iv. 109; Mowbray, 321. [3] *HMC Bath*, iv. 109; Hutchins, ii. 258; *CPR*, 1553–4, p. 451; 1563–6, p. 385; Guildford mus. Loseley 1331/2. [4] *CPR*, 1558–60, p. 234; *APC*, xii. 167–8; xvii. 415–16; PCC 18 Drury; C142/242/13; Mowbray, 321–2.

J.J.G.

STOURTON, Sir William (by 1505–48), of Stourton, Wilts.

SOMERSET 1529*

b. by 1505, 2nd but 1st surv. s. of Edward Stourton, 6th Baron Stourton, by Agnes, da. of John Fauntleroy of Marsh, nr. Sherborne, Dorset; bro. of Roger*. *m.* by 1524, Elizabeth, da. of Edmund Dudley† of Atherington, Suss., 7s. inc. William* and Arthur* 2da.; 1da illegit. Kntd. 1 Nov. 1523; *suc.* fa. as 7th Baron Stourton 13 Dec. 1535.[1]

Servant of Charles Brandon, Duke of Suffolk by 1520; j.p. Dorset 1528–*d.*, Som., Wilts. 1529–*d.*; commr. benevolence, Som., Wilts. 1544/45, musters Wilts. 1546; lt. army in Scotland Oct. 1545; dep. Newhaven (Ambleteuse) June 1546–*d.*[2]

William Stourton began his career in the household of the Duke of Suffolk and his wife, 'the French Queen'. In 1523 he went with Suffolk's army to France and was knighted at Roye. When in 1524 his father succeeded as 6th Baron Stourton, he became heir to estates in Dorset, Somerset and Wiltshire. Made a justice in these three counties in 1528–9, in the autumn of 1529 he was a natural choice as one of the knights of the shire for Somerset. His Membership was, however, to prove a heavy commitment, and on 31 Dec. 1531 he wrote to Cromwell asking that both his father, an aged and feeble man, and he should be excused attendance at the third session. Four years later he succeeded to the barony and took his seat in the Lords for the last session of this protracted Parliament. Whether he was replaced in the Commons is not known.[3]

Beyond leading 200 men against the northern rebels in 1536, bearing the towel at the christening of Prince Edward and giving regular attendance in the Lords, he is not known to have taken much part in public affairs during the late 1530s and 40s. He was probably a conservative in religion, for he was a friend of Viscount Lisle and in July 1539 he wrote in favour of the abbot of Glastonbury before his execution. He seems to have been foremost a soldier. On the outbreak of the war with Scotland in 1544 he joined the Earl of Hertford with the Wiltshire levies and fought in the Border campaigns of that and the following year. Commended for his good service by the commander, in 1546 he followed Hertford to France, where he was soon appointed deputy of Newhaven. His letters reflect his diligence and thoughtfulness in this office, which he was still holding when he died there on 16 Sept. 1548.[4]

The Stourtons were not among the wealthiest or most powerful of noble families but they loomed large in their own country. Between 1541 and 1545 the 7th Baron made large purchases of lands in Dorset, Somerset and Wiltshire, for which he paid some £4,500 to the crown and the 3rd Lord Ferrers. He was not on good terms with either his wife or his eldest son, whom in 1539 he angrily described to Cromwell as a 'false hypocrite' and worthy of the King's Bench or Marshalsea, a verdict which fell short of the 8th Baron's eventual fate. By his will of 8 Sept. 1548 he left nothing to his wife or to his younger sons, and little to his eldest, whom none the less he named executor. The greater part of his goods and household stuff he bequeathed to his mistress Agnes Rice, daughter of Catherine, Lady Bridgewater, by her first husband: Agnes, who bore him a daughter, claimed that a legal marriage had taken place between them, even though Stourton's wife was living, but this was rejected in several legal actions and the will itself was quashed by probate act of 1548. Administration of his father's goods was then granted to Charles, the new Baron Stourton.[5]

[1] Date of birth estimated from age at fa.'s i.p.m., Charles, Lord Mowbray, *Noble House of Stourton*, 299; *CP*; C142/87/36; *Wilts. Arch. Mag.* viii. 242 et passim. [2] *LP Hen. VIII*, ix–xxi. [3] Ibid. v, xiv; *CP*, xii(1), 305 note m. [4] *LP Hen. VIII*, xiv, xx, xxi; *LJ*, i. 87–312 passim; M. A. R. Graves, 'The Tudor House of Lords 1547–58' (Otago Univ. Ph.D. thesis, 1974), 353–4; *APC*, ii. 437–8, 444, 519; *CSP For.* 1547–53, pp. 294–346 passim; C142/87/36. [5] *LP Hen. VIII*, xix, xx; *Wilts. Arch. Mag.* viii. 275–80, 287–89; PCC 17 Populwell; C142/87/36.

R.V.

STOWELL, John (by 1517–50/51), of Exeter, Devon.

CONSTITUENCY UNKNOWN 1547*[1]

b. by 1517, s. of Richard Stowell of Exeter. *m.* Elizabeth, 1s.[2]

Servant of John Hull II* by 1538; v.-adm. Devon 4 Dec. 1545.[3]

John Stowell's Membership of the Parliament of 1547 has to be deduced from an entry in the Commons Journal. This records that on 17 Dec. 1547 an unsuccessful bill for buying of wool in Devon and Cornwall was delivered after its third reading to 'Mr. Stowell'. Since the known Members of this Parliament do not include anyone bearing that name, the questions of his identity and of his constituency have to be considered together. As to the first, the starting-point is the fact that he must have been dead by the end of 1551—otherwise his name would have been included in the list of Members which was revised at that time. In the matter of his constituency, this is most likely to have been within one or other of the two counties affected by the bill which was committed to him. Out of the four knights and 40 city or borough Members returned there in 1547, only the two knights for Devon and 12 of the Devon city or borough Members are known by name from returns made at the time: the names of the Members for Exeter are known from a by-election return, payments of wages and other references in the city's records as well as in the Journal, but those of the Cornish Members occur only on the list of Members produced towards the end of 1551 in preparation for the fourth session. It follows that 'Mr. Stowell' could have been elected in 1547 for any of the Cornish constituencies without his name having survived on the later list, and it is for one of them that he must be presumed to have been returned: his presence in the House during the first session may equally be taken to eliminate the possibility that he was by-elected.[4]

The man who best suits the requirements is John Stowell, a merchant of Exeter. When he became a freeman of the city in December 1538 he was described as a servant of John Hull II. A lawyer sprung from a merchant family of Exeter, Hull was a client of Cromwell and at the time customer of Exeter and Dartmouth. It was evidently on the maritime side of his activities that Hull employed Stowell, for by 1545 Stowell had become vice-admiral of Devon. (In earlier years he has to be distinguished from his namesake, a justice of the peace for Somerset, but this John Stowell died in 1543.) Within Exeter Stowell appears to have seized the opportunity of the western rebellion to pillage churches, for in August 1552 an inquiry was held into the church goods 'taken away in the commotion time by one John Stowell of Exeter now deceased'.[5]

The Cornish boroughs present too wide a field of possibility to be considered individually. No less than seven of them returned Members for the first time in 1547 and a number of the men elected appear to have been clients of Admiral Seymour. If, as is likely, Stowell was still vice-admiral of Devon at the time of his election, he could well have been nominated by his chief who might have nominated at any of the new Cornish boroughs.

Stowell sat for only the first three sessions of the Parliament. He made his will on 28 Sept. 1550, during the prorogation between the third and fourth sessions. He left £10 to his son John, who was still a minor. His wife Elizabeth was to have his house during her widowhood: she was also left all his goods and made sole executrix, the overseers including Stowell's father. The will was proved on 29 Sept. 1551.[6]

[1] *CJ*, i. 3. [2] Date of birth estimated from admission as freeman. PCC 26 Bucke. [3] *Exeter Freemen* (Devon and Cornw. Rec. Soc. extra ser. i), 74; *LP Hen. VIII*, xx; R. M. S. Tugwood, 'Piracy and privateering from Dartmouth and Kingswear' (London Univ. M.A. thesis, 1958), 44. [4] *CJ*, i. 3. [5] CP40/1142, r. 300; *LP Hen. VIII*, xiii–xxi; *Edwardian Inventories for Exeter* (Alcuin Club Colls. xx), 77–78, 80. [6] PCC 26 Bucke.

P.S.E.

STOWFORD (STAFFORD), George (by 1525–60 or later), of Ottery St. Mary, Devon.

CAMELFORD 1554 (Apr.)

b. by 1525, s. of William Kelloway *alias* Stowford of Ottery St. Mary by da. of William Hilling. *m.* Joan. da. of Richard Mercer of Ottery St. Mary, 1s. 3da.[1]

Auditor, Ottery St. Mary by 1546, under steward by 1559.[2]

George Stowford belonged to a branch of the north Devon family of Kelloway which by the beginning of the 16th century had generally come to be known by the name of Stowford, an estate in the parish of Dolton. This gentle family had some Cornish connexions—Stowford's uncle had married a Menwennick and one of his daughters was the wife of John Melhuish*—but these would not have sufficed to explain Stowford's election for a Cornish borough, which is probably to be ascribed to two of his neighbours who held administrative posts in the duchy, John Evelegh*, co-lord of Ottery, and John Haydon*, an official of the manor and Stowford's precursor as under steward.[3]

Apart from his one spell at Westminster and his manorial offices little has come to light about Stowford. In 1559 he was accused of expelling a man from some land in Ottery and in the lawsuit which followed he was described, perhaps conventionally, as one 'of great substance and well friended and allied'; the case went against him and possession was awarded to the plaintiff. A year later he obtained the wardship and marriage of a local heir. No later reference to Stowford has been discovered and the date of his death is unknown: he was succeeded by his son George who was still alive in 1620.[4]

[1] Date of birth estimated from first reference. *Vis. Devon*, ed. Vivian, 510, 712; Req. 2/76/34. [2] *Devon Monastic Lands* (Devon and Cornw. Rec. Soc. i), 81; Req.2/191/53. [3] *Vis. Devon*, 510; Req.2/76/34, 191/53. [4] Req.2/76/34, 191/53; *CPR*, 1558–60, p. 328.

J.J.G.

STOWFORD, Paul (*d.* 1555/57), of (?Exeter), Devon.

MITCHELL 1554 (Nov.)

Paul Stowford was of gentle birth and presumably a kinsman of George Stowford*. He lived by trade and his business links, which explain his single appearance in the Commons, stretched from Devon and Cornwall to London. His interest in tin took him occasionally to Truro and on his way to the coinage there he probably passed through Mitchell. One of the producers from whom he bought tin was John Beauchamp*: Beauchamp was a figure in the borough and may have been the returning officer at the election. Stowford heeded the chancellor's remarks about attendance and he did not follow the example of so many of his colleagues from the west country in absenting himself before the dissolution. His conscientiousness was not rewarded by re-election a year later and by 1558, when the next Parliament was called, he was dead. He was a sick man when he made his will on 30 Oct. 1555. He named the men who owed him money, including John Beauchamp and Valentine Dale*, and several London merchants to whom he himself was in debt. He asked his executor, his 'brother' William Maynard of London, to settle his debts and made Maynard his residuary legatee. The will was witnessed by several Exeter citizens and was proved on 8 Jan. 1557.

C219/23/27; PCC 1 Wrastley.

J.J.G.

STRADLING, David (by 1537–75 or later), of Glam.

ARUNDEL 1558

b. by 1537, 2nd s. of Sir Thomas Stradling* of St. Donats, Glam. by Catherine, da. of Sir Thomas Gamage of Coity, Glam.; bro. of Edward*. *educ.* I. Temple.[1]

David Stradling was probably a student at the Inner Temple when he was returned, with his elder brother, to Mary's last Parliament. The brothers owed their seats to their father's connexion with the 12th Earl of Arundel, the owner of the borough. For David Stradling the Parliament marked the beginning and the end of his public career. It is not known how soon after Elizabeth's accession his Catholicism drove him abroad, but he had probably gone before his father's bequest to him in December 1566 of a sum of money deposited at a friend's house in London. His sister Damascin had accompanied Jane Dormer, Countess of Feria, to the Netherlands and Spain in 1559–60 and another of his sisters went to Louvain. Scattered references suggest that during the 1570s Stradling moved between the same two countries; the last of them, an anonymous inquiry from Brussels to Sir Thomas Shirley[†] asking what had happened to him, may indicate that he was dead.[2]

[1] Presumed to be of age at election. PCC 21 Holney; *Cal. I.T. Recs.* i. p. lv. [2] PCC 21 Holney; *CSP For.* 1572–4, p. 451; *Cath. Rec. Soc.* xiii. 119; *HMC Hatfield*, ii. 87; *Stradling Corresp.* ed. Traherne, 232; SP15/23, f. 158v.

R.J.W.S.

STRADLING, Edward (1528/29–1609), of St. Donats, Glam.

STEYNING 1554 (Apr.)
ARUNDEL 1558

b. 1528/29, 1st s. of Sir Thomas Stradling* of St. Donats by Catherine, da. of Sir Thomas Gamage of Coity; bro. of David*. *educ.* Oxf.; I. Temple, adm. Feb. 1552; travelled. *m.* settlement 20 Jan. 1567, Agnes, da. of Sir Edward Gage of Firle, Suss., 1s. *d.v.p.* suc. fa. 27 Jan. 1571. Kntd. Oct. 1573.[1]

J.p. Glam. 1555, j.p.q. 1573/74–?*d.*; sheriff 1573–4, 1582–3, 1595–6; commr. piracy 1578, 1586; dep. lt. Pemb. 1590–4, Glam. 1595.[2]

Edward Stradling owed his Membership of two Marian Parliaments to his father's association with the 12th Earl of Arundel, the patron at both the boroughs concerned. That he was not to reappear in the Commons after 1558 is to be explained partly by Stradling's own and his family's Catholicism and partly by his love of Wales and his devotion to its culture. Although himself a conformist, during the early years of the new reign his father's recalcitrance at home and his brother's abroad kept Stradling under suspicion, and after he shook this off to become sheriff and deputy-lieutenant he was probably disinclined to challenge the Herbert domination of his shire. By then he was immersing himself in the studies of Welsh history and genealogy on which his fame rests and which were to be acknowledged by David Powel in his *Historie of Cambria* of 1584. No less memorable was his shouldering of the cost of printing Siôn Dafydd Rhys's Welsh grammar of 1592.[3]

Stradling's marriage into the Gage family of Firle helped to prolong the connexion with Sussex begun by his father; prominent among his many friends were Thomas Sackville*, Baron Buckhurst, Anthony Browne*, 1st Viscount Montagu, and a fellow-scholar, John Lord Lumley, whom he was to appoint overseer of his will. The will, dated 10 May 1609, is notable for its reference to his collections of arms and armour, books and manuscripts, and ancient coins. His only child having died in infancy, Stradling adopted as his heir a great-nephew John. He died on 15 May 1609.[4]

[1] Aged 80 at death, *DNB*; *DWB*; Barbican House, Lewes, Gage ms 21/46, 47, 49. [2] SP11/5/6, f. 61; *APC*, x. 331; xiv. 143; xix. 248; xxv. 14. [3] SP12/66, f. 59; *CSP For.* 1577-8, p. 536; *Stradling Corresp.* ed. Traherne, 30, 31, 233, 234-5; *CSP Dom.* 1581-90, p. 379; *HMC Hatfield*, iii. 214; *Cath. Rec. Soc.* xiii. 93; Wood, *Ath. Oxon.* ed. Bliss, ii. 50-51. [4] *Stradling Corresp.* passim; PCC 97 Dorset; G. J. Clark, *The Castle of St. Donat's, Glam.* 31.

R.J.W.S.

STRADLING, Sir Thomas (by 1495-1571), of St. Donats, Glam.

EAST GRINSTEAD 1553 (Oct.)
ARUNDEL 1554 (Apr.)

b. by 1495, 1st s. of Sir Edward Stradling of St. Donats by Elizabeth, da. of Sir Thomas Arundell of Lanherne, Cornw. *m.* settlement 20 Aug. 1516, Catherine, da. of Sir Thomas Gamage of Coity, Glam., 2s. David* and Edward* 5da. *suc.* fa. 8 May 1535. Kntd. 17 Feb. 1549.[1]

Sewer, the chamber 1525; j.p. Glam. 1536, 1555, q. 1558/59, Dorset 1538-40, Som. 1538-44, Glos., Herefs., Salop, Worcs. 1554; commr. musters, Glam. 1545, relief 1550, heresy 1557; sheriff, Glam. 1547-8; muster master July 1553.[2]

Thomas Stradling was on the threshold of middle age when he succeeded to an inheritance which stretched from its base in Glamorgan across to Somerset and Dorset. It was doubtless through his mother's kinsman Thomas Arundell*, a leading supporter of Wolsey, that Stradling had joined the royal household in 1525 and that he was later to attach himself to Arundell's kinsman by marriage the 12th Earl of Arundel. Although he made no further headway at court under Henry VIII, probably because of his conservatism in religion, after his father's death he was put on the bench in the three shires where his property lay and in the King's last year he was nominated for the shrievalty of Glamorgan.[3]

From 1547 Stradling's fortunes fluctuated with those of the 12th Earl of Arundel, in whose honor of Petworth he established himself by acquiring the manor of Binderton from Sir Thomas Smith I* in 1550. His knighting in February 1549, during the overthrow of Admiral Seymour, may have been a move of Arundel's to bind him to the Protector Somerset; shortly afterwards he and Sir Thomas Arundell stood surety for Arundell's brother Sir John*, who was suspected of complicity in the western rebellion, but what part he played in the crises of that summer and autumn has not been

discovered. He was not imprisoned with the two Arundells in January 1550 but when the Earl of Arundel was sent to the Tower in November 1551 Stradling joined him there. Arundel was released in December 1552 and Stradling probably somewhat later; he afterwards stated that he was freed 'not long before' Edward VI's death and he was certainly out by May 1553.[4]

Arundel's restoration to favour under Mary brought Stradling a widening of local responsibility and a brief career in the Commons. His election for East Grinstead, a duchy of Lancaster borough, to the first Parliament of the reign he owed to Arundel's stewardship of the duchy's lands in Sussex, and his seat in the second to the earl's lordship of the borough from which he took his title. Predictably, Stradling was not among the Members of the first Parliament who opposed the initial stages of the restoration of Catholicism; early in the second session he had a bill 'for one measure to be through England' committed to him after its second reading. He may have been excluded from the following Parliament out of deference to the Queen's request for resident Members and in 1555 as a consequence of the earl's absence in Calais, during which he shared responsibility for Arundel's lands; in the last Parliament of the reign he evidently stood down in favour of his sons Edward and David. That he was not returned in Glamorgan is to be ascribed to the strength of the Herbert interest in that shire. In 1557 Stradling brought an action in the Star Chamber against William Herbert V (q.v.) for extortion and bribery in the levy of men for the French war; he justified his choice of court by the argument that no lawyer would appear against Herbert at Cardiff, one which was borne out by the number and tone of the depositions. Stradling's purchase in the following year of the Glamorgan manor of Sully from Herbert's uncle the 1st Earl of Pembroke may have been a piece of reconciliation after this episode.[5]

After 1558 there was no future for Stradling in public life but unlike three of his children he did not take refuge abroad. Sent to the Tower (where he joined John Story, his fellow-Member at East Grinstead) in May 1561, apparently for having used 'the miraculous cross of St. Donats' to further the Catholic cause, he was released in October 1563 but remained irreconcilable. By December 1569, when he refused to subscribe to the Act of Uniformity, he was said to be bed-ridden although earlier in the year he seems to have visited Bath. Stradling died at St. Donats on 27 Jan. 1571. By his will of 19 Dec. 1566 he had placed sums of money in trust at a friend's house in London for his second son and two of his daughters, all of whom were probably abroad; by a codicil added on 11 Jan. 1571 David Stradling was also to receive all his apparel and his great chain of gold. He made charitable bequests to over 20 parishes in Glamorgan and left one cow to each of 17 young married couples 'so long as they be no town dwellers'. His lands and the residue of his goods passed to his elder son Edward. The executors were Dr. John Gibbon* and Hugh Griffith, one of the six clerks in Chancery, and the overseers Sir Thomas Palmer*, Stradling's brother-in-law, and John, Lord Lumley. The will was proved on 4 Mar. 1572.[6]

[1] Date of birth estimated from marriage; said to be 'above' 71 on 21 Dec. 1569, *Arch. Camb.* (ser. 3), xi. 47–48. *DNB*; *DWB*; C1/442/51; 142/57/68; *Cartae et Alia Munimenta de Glam.* 1797–1801; PCC 21 Holney. [2] *LP Hen. VIII*, iv, x, xiii–xvi, xviii, xx; SP11/5/6, f. 61; *CPR*, 1553, p. 364; 1553–4, pp. 19, 20, 23, 25; 1555–7, p. 281; *APC*, iv. 300. [3] C1/890/69, 894/69; *Cartae et Alia Munimenta de Glam.* 1909–10; *LP Hen. VIII*, iv, xxi. [4] *CPR*, 1549–51, p. 352; *APC*, ii. 304; iii. 411, 433; iv. 185; *Lit. Rems. Edw. VI*, 365; C1/1380/68; Harl. 249, f. 40v. [5] Somerville, *Duchy*, i. 617; *CJ*, i. 29; *CPR*, 1553, p. 268; 1554–5, pp. 146, 305; 1557–8, pp. 51, 369; *Suss. Rec. Soc.* xix. 166; *Cardiff Recs.* ed. Matthews, i. 462; St. Ch. 4/4/29; Harl. 608, f. 39v. [6] SP12/17, f. 37v; 18, f. 7; 24, f. 72; 66, f. 60; *EHR*, i. 513–17; *Cath. Rec. Soc.* i. 45, 52, 55–56; J. A. Williams, *Bath and Rome*, 7; C142/157/76; PCC 21 Holney; G. J. Clark, *The Castle of St. Donat's, Glam.* 22–24.

R.J.W.S.

STRANGMAN, John (by 1492–1527).

MALDON 1515[1]

b. by 1492, 1st s. of John Strangman of Hadleigh, Essex by Cecily, da. and h. of one Sandford of Rayleigh, Essex. *m.* by 1519, Mary, da. and event. h. of Robert Ingowe of Barking, Essex, 2s.[2]
?Commr. subsidy, Essex 1523, 1524; escheator, Essex and Herts. Nov. 1524–Feb. 1526.[3]

The Strangmans were copyholders in Essex in the reign of Edward IV and probably owed their rise in status to the profitable marriages of John Strangman and his eldest son and namesake. It was the younger Strangman who was returned for Maldon to the third Parliament of Henry VIII, for at his subsequent admission to the freedom of the borough he was described as childless. That this formality was needed shows that he was being elected for the first time, but no explanation has been found why the town failed in his case—his fellow-Member's name is lost—to comply with the King's request for the re-election of the previous Members, unless one of them had been Thomas Hintlesham*, who may have been dead or incapacitated by 1514. There seems to have been a connexion between the Strangmans and Sir Richard Fitzlewis, a kinsman of the 13th Earl of Oxford who had been returned for Maldon to at least two earlier Parliaments, for the elder John Strangman was to mention his goddaughter Joan Fitzlewis in his will, but the son's most likely patron was the courtier and

soldier Sir John Raynsford, constable of Hadleigh castle, who was also connected with the earls of Oxford. John Strangman junior was involved with Raynsford in land transactions between 1517 and 1520 and it was probably he who in November 1513 had received payment on behalf of Raynsford after the French campaign and who was described as Raynsford's servant in a Star Chamber case of 1519 or 1520: he was also named an executor of Raynsford's will.[4]

He is probably also to be identified with the John Strangman specially admitted to Lincoln's Inn in February 1516 but if so his subsequent career there has evidently been confused with that of the Thomas Strangman (perhaps his younger brother) admitted in 1520: Strangman's nephew Edward Bury, who sat for Maldon in 1542, followed them there in 1528. In 1524 Strangman and his wife Mary purchased the manor of Westhall with houses and 620 acres in Canewdon and Great Stambridge, Essex, and three years later it was probably he who acted as a feoffee for Thomas Audley, the future lord chancellor. Audley was another of Raynsford's executors and in his own will of April 1544 he left to Raynsford's son (the Member for Colchester in the Parliament of 1529) the money owed him by Edward and Thomas Strangman, the executors (and presumably the younger brothers) of John Strangman, for the goods and chattels of the elder Raynsford.[5]

Strangman's own will has not been found. He died in December 1527 and his inquisition post mortem shows that he held lands in Rayleigh, Rochford and elsewhere in Essex, mostly in right of his wife who had predeceased him. Strangman himself predeceased his father who by his will of 28 Apr. 1528 set aside certain lands for the performance of the son's will in accordance with an agreement made earlier. Strangman's heir William, a boy of eight in 1527, married a niece of Audley's first wife Christina Barnardiston.[6]

[1] Essex RO, D/B3/1/2, f. 78. [2] Date of birth estimated from probable first reference. *Vis. Essex* (Harl. Soc. xiii), 73, 103–5; Essex RO, D/AER4, ff. 53v–56; E150/311/6; Morant, *Essex*, i. 280. [3] *LP Hen. VIII*, iii, iv. [4] *Trans. Essex Arch. Soc.* n.s. xii. 299–302; *LP Hen. VIII*, i, iii; *Essex Feet of Fines*, iv. ed. Reaney and Fitch, 138; St.Ch.2/4/86–89; PCC 21 Maynwaring. [5] *Black Bk. L. Inn*, i. 178; *Essex Feet of Fines*, iv. 153, 166; PCC 1 Alen; *Trans. Essex Arch. Soc.* n.s. ii. 366. [6] E150/311/6; Essex RO, D/AER4, ff. 53v–56; *Lincs. Peds.* (Harl. Soc. l), 91–93.

D.F.C.

STRANGWAYS, Sir Giles I (1486–1546), of Melbury Sampford, Dorset.

DORSET 1529, 1539[1]

b. 4 May 1486, 1st s. of Henry Strangways of Melbury Sampford by 1st w. Dorothy, da. of Sir John Arundell of Lanherne, Cornw. *educ.* M. Temple, adm. 5 Nov. 1504. *m.* Joan, da. of Sir John Mordaunt[†] of Turvey,

Beds., 1s. 2da.; 1s. illegit. *suc.* fa. 10 Mar. 1504. Kntd. Feb./Oct. 1514.[2]

Esquire of the body by 1509, knight by 1534; j.p. Dorset 1509–*d.*, Som. 1514–21, western circuit 1540; sheriff, Som. and Dorset 1512–13, 1517–18, 1524–5, 1533–4, 1541–2; commr. subsidy, Dorset 1512, coastal defence, south-western counties 1539, benevolence, Dorset 1544/45, musters 1546, chantries 1546; v.-adm. Dorset c.1526–36; particular receiver, duchy of Cornw., Dorset c.1530; steward, duchy of Lancaster, Dorset 1530–1; member, council in the west 1539; high steward, Lyme Regis, Poole by 1546; numerous local offices.[3]

Giles Strangways's grandfather was the first of the family to settle in Dorset, having been persuaded to leave Yorkshire by Thomas Grey, 1st Marquess of Dorset. Melbury Sampford, which became the family residence, was acquired by Giles's father Henry through his second marriage to the widow of William Browning of Melbury; five years after Henry's death his son had a house in London and property in eight counties and the Isle of Wight. The estates in Dorset were to be further increased by a grant in 1543 of the dissolved abbey of Abbotsbury and the manors of Abbotsbury and East Elworth, for which Strangways paid nearly £2,000.[4]

Described in this grant as the King's servant, Strangways had indeed spent a lifetime in the service of the crown, both in the west country and in attendance upon the King. He served in the French campaign of 1514, was present at the Field of Cloth of Gold in 1520 and at the reception of Charles V at Canterbury in May 1522, and in the late summer of 1522 and again in 1523 was on active service in France. In 1536 he was summoned to assist the King against the northern rebels, bringing with him 300 men, the largest retinue demanded of any Dorset gentleman. In 1544 he was again in France with the army, this time in company with his son Henry, who died at the siege of Boulogne.[5]

Strangways was a justice of the peace in Dorset by the age of 23; three years later he began the first of his five terms as sheriff. His early ascendancy in local affairs provoked envy. Sir Edward Willoughby, an unsuccessful contender for the sheriffdom, complained bitterly of two men—one of them evidently Strangways—who ruled all the shire 'after their fantasies, against all justice'. Others denounced a series of robberies committed by his servants between 1527 and 1529 but never punished because of 'the great bearing and maintenance of the said Sir Giles Strangways'; these allegations received some support from the confession of one of the accused men. Yet Strangways's power in his county, if sometimes abused, was generally to the King's advantage, and in 1539 it secured him a place on the newly created council in the west under the presidency of

Sir John Russell*, Baron Russell. It had also procured him the knighthood of the shire. Although he is known to have sat in only two Parliaments, these were separated by another, that of 1536, in which he almost certainly did so in accordance with the King's request for the return of the Members of its precursor; he may also have been returned to one or more earlier Parliaments, perhaps sitting as far back as the first or second Parliament of the reign, when he made his start in local administration. On the other hand, it is unlikely that he reappeared in 1542, for although the names of the knights for Dorset on that occasion are lost, as sheriff he was ineligible within his own shire and could only have been elected for a borough in a neighbouring one. Of his part in the proceedings of the Commons there is but one glimpse: his name appears on a list of Members written by Cromwell on the back of a letter of December 1534 and thought to be of those having some particular connexion with the treasons bill then under consideration.[6]

Many minor rewards came to Strangways in the shape of stewardships and leases. In 1528 the King asked his natural son the Duke of Richmond to make Strangways steward of his manor of Canford, near Poole; the duke had already appointed Sir William Parr*, but some years later Strangways was viewing storm damage at Poole with Richmond and in 1537, when the manor was again in Henry VIII's hands, the stewardship was granted to him. In 1530 he was appointed steward of the duchy of Lancaster lands in Dorset, but had to surrender his grant in the following year, Sir John Rogers* claiming the office. In 1539 he became steward of the lordship of Cranborne and keeper of Blagdon park, Dorset, in 1540 he obtained a lease of the manor of Sydling, and in 1541 (two years before the grant of it) he had a lease of Abbotsbury abbey.[7]

The premature death of Strangways's son left him at the age of nearly 60 with a 16 year-old grandson, another Giles Strangways*, as his heir. He was not the only one to foresee the possibility that he would die within the next five years and the King thereupon claim rights of wardship and marriage over his heir; when in August 1546 he was rumoured to be dying, Sir Richard Rich secured a grant of the wardship directly from the crown. In the event Strangways lived long enough to arrange his grandson's marriage and to set up a trust in part of his lands for the young man and his wife; when he died, on 11 Dec. 1546, he left an heir still under age but protected against the worst risks of wardship. By his will, made on 20 Sept. 1546, Strangways also provided for his two daughters, his younger grandson and grand-daughters, and his bastard son

Thomas Symonds. He bequeathed £6 13s. 4d. a year for two years for a priest to say mass for the repose of his soul and the souls of his wife and son, £20 to Baron Russell and £10 each to Sir John Horsey (his fellow-knight in 1529 and 1539) and John Tregonwell* to help the executors and overseers of his will. He was buried at Melbury Sampford, where an inscription commemorates him and his wife.[8]

[1] E159/319, brev. ret. Mich. r.[1–2]. [2] Date of birth given in fa.'s i.p.m., *CIPM Hen. VII*, iii. 1126. PCC 24 Alen; Hutchins, *Dorset*, ii. 662; *LP Hen. VIII*, i. [3] *LP Hen. VIII*, i–xxi; *EHR*, xxiii. 741; information from G. Haslam; Somerville, *Duchy*, i. 628; Lyme Regis rec. bk. 1514–1687, f. 14; SC2/170/130, m. 4. [4] Hutchins, ii. 659, 661; *LP Hen. VIII*, i, xviii. [5] *LP Hen. VIII*, i, iii, xi, xix; *Chron. Calais* (Cam. Soc. xxxv), 31–33; Mill Stephenson, *Mon. Brasses*, 100. [6] *LP Hen. VIII*, iv; vii. 1522(ii) citing SP1/87, f. 106v; xi, xiv; St.Ch.2/31/4. [7] *LP Hen. VIII*, iv, vii, xii, xiv–xvi; Somerville, i. 628. [8] J. Hurstfield, *The Queen's Wards*, 137; *EHR*, lxviii. 34; C142/84/34; PCC 24 Alen; Mill Stephenson, 100; Newman and Pevsner, *Dorset*, 278.

H.M.

STRANGWAYS, Sir Giles II (1528–62), of Melbury Sampford, Dorset.

DORSET 1553 (Oct.), 1554 (Apr.), 1555, 1558, 1559

b. 13 or 20 Apr. 1528, s. and h. of Henry Strangways by Margaret, da. of George Manners, 11th Lord Ros. *educ.* Corpus, Oxf. 1541. *m.* Oct./Nov. 1546, Joan (*d.*1603), da. of John Wadham of Merrifield, Som., 4s. 2da. *suc.* gdfa. Sir Giles Strangways I* 11 Dec. 1546. Kntd. 11 Nov. 1549.[1]

Commr. relief, Dorset 1550, goods of churches and fraternities 1553; warden, Neroche forest, Som. 1551; j.p. Dorset 1554–*d.*[2]

Giles Strangways was 16 years of age when his father's death at the siege of Boulogne in 1544 made him heir apparent to his grandfather Sir Giles Strangways. A few weeks before Sir Giles's death in December 1546 the young heir was married to Joan Wadham; a profitable wardship, which Sir Richard Rich had been granted prematurely in August 1546, was thus deprived of much of its market value and Giles Strangways saved from a marriage arranged by a commercially-minded guardian. In July 1549, when he had come of age, he was licensed to enter upon his inheritance, and within a few months, following the Earl of Warwick's successful *coup d'état* against the Protector Somerset, he was knighted. Appointments in local government soon followed, although he was not named to the Dorset bench until Mary's accession. Since as a young man he apparently enjoyed the favour of Warwick, by now Duke of Northumberland, Strangways may have sat for the county in the second of Edward VI's Parliaments, for which the Dorset returns are lost.[3]

It was at the early age of 25 that Strangways was elected knight of the shire to the first Parliament of Mary's reign, a seat he retained at every election

save one until his death. His repeated appearance in Mary's Parliaments did not mean that he embraced her policy; in the Parliament of October 1553 he 'stood for the true religion' and two years later he opposed a government bill. He demonstrated his loyalty during the first Parliament of 1554 when he attended the execution for treason of Sir Thomas Wyatt II*, and after the disclosure of the Dudley conspiracy his arrest was followed by his speedy release. His absence from the second Parliament of 1554 may not have been from choice; in that year he was outlawed for non-appearance in the common pleas to answer a charge of debt and it was not until he had surrendered himself at the Fleet that he was pardoned in June 1555. He did not go unnoticed in the last Parliament of Mary's reign for his name was marked with a circle on a copy of a list of its Members.[4]

In 1557 Strangways saw active service in command of 50 men in the army led by the 1st Earl of Pembroke. Before setting off for France he made his will, leaving a horse and harness to each of his servants 'as came from my house with me and do go with me . . . in my journey beyond the seas . . . being soldiers in my band and retinue'. His lands and goods he bequeathed for the most part to his wife until his son should come of age; to his daughter Anne he left 1,000 marks for her marriage. Appointed an executor of the will which the dying Sir William Courtenay II* made after the siege and battle of St. Quentin, Strangways himself returned safely from the war and twice made additions to his own will as his family increased, providing in 1558 for a second son and on 11 Apr. 1562, the day of his death, for two more. He made his wife the sole executrix but named 13 overseers to assist her. The eldest son was only six when his father died; the wardship which the father had so narrowly escaped claimed the son. The boy lived with his mother for some years, but she failed to secure his wardship which was granted in 1565 to Pembroke. Sir Giles Strangways was buried at Melbury Sampford; his widow was buried in Bristol cathedral with her second husband Sir John Young*.[5]

[1] Date of birth given (uncertainly) at gd.-fa's i.p.m., C142/84/34. Hutchins, *Dorset*, ii. 662; Corpus, Oxf., visus bk. no fo. [2] *CPR*, 1550–3, p. 195; 1553, pp. 352, 414; 1553–4, p. 18. [3] C142/84/34; *EHR*, lxviii. 34. [4] Bodl. e Museo 17; Guildford mus. Loseley 1331/2; *Chron. Q. Jane and Q. Mary* (Cam. Soc. xlviii), 74; D. M. Loades, *Two Tudor Conspiracies*, 223; *CSP Ven*. 1555–6, p. 422; *CPR*, 1554–5, p. 259; Wm. Salt Lib. SMS 264. [5] *HMC Foljambe*, 5; PCC 17 Street; C142/136/7; *CSP Dom. Add*. 1566–79, p. 1; *CPR*, 1563–6, p. 302; Mill Stephenson, *Mon. Brasses*, 100; Hutchins, ii. 664.

H.M.

STRELLEY, Robert (by 1518–54), of Great Bowden, Leics.

LEICESTERSHIRE 1553 (Oct.)

b. by 1518, poss. s. of Sir Nicholas Strelley of Strelley, Notts. by 2nd w. Ellen, da. of Thomas Gresley. *m.* Frideswide, da. of John Knight of Spaldington, Yorks., *s.p.*[1]

Prob. steward, duchy of Lancaster, Essex, Herts., Mdx. bef. 1540; member, household of Princess Mary by 1553; chamberlain, the Exchequer 2 Nov. 1553–*d.*[2]

It is surprising, in view of the abundant genealogical information contained in Robert Strelley's will, that there should be a doubt about his own parentage. He does not appear in any of the Strelley pedigrees, which are in any case confused. In the pardon roll of 1548 he is styled '*alias* Tebbe late of Linby, gentleman', a description which would fit a base son of Sir Nicholas Strelley of Linby, Nottinghamshire, whose heirs were his sisters; such an origin would also account for Robert Strelley's acquisition, in the last year of his life, of an augmented coat of arms. Against this must be set the mention in his will of 'brothers' who can be identified as sons of Sir Nicholas Strelley of Strelley by his third wife, a description compatible with Robert's being this Sir Nicholas's son by an earlier wife and his omission from the pedigrees because he had died without issue in his father's lifetime. The circumstance that Robert Strelley died not only without issue but without heirs could be explained by the non-inheritance of the half blood, for Sir Nicholas appears to have had no relatives of the full blood for four generations and Frideswide Strelley's relatives of the full blood would have been almost equally distant. The augmentation of arms was to be effected by the addition of a border representing part of the arms of Gresley, the family from which Sir Nicholas's second wife descended. Finally, Robert Strelley's acquisition of lands in Linby may have been due solely to family solidarity, enhanced perhaps by his early residence with his cousins.[3]

Strelley was to spend most of his life in Mary's household, and hence the scarcity of references to him in the records of the time, except in connexion with his land transactions: it was, however, probably he who before 1540 was steward for the duchy of Lancaster of lands in Essex, Hertfordshire and Middlesex. In 1539 he received a crown lease of five watermills in Northampton; in 1545 he began to add to the quarter manor in Great Bowden which he had received from Sir Nicholas Strelley of Strelley and which, thus increased, he left at his death to his wife Frideswide; in 1547 he acquired the manor of West Langton. Frideswide was one of Princess Mary's favourite ladies-in-waiting, and upon the marriage the crown settled on the pair further lands in Great Bowden and Harborough, and the site of the abbey of Egglestone in Yorkshire. Under Edward VI Strelley added to his holdings in

Bowden the third part of the manor which had belonged to Laurence Asshe, another portion from Ralph Rolston and William Skeffington*, and property formerly belonging to Nicholas Purfrey. At the beginning of Mary's reign, therefore, he was a substantial gentleman whose service to the Queen at Framlingham and close attachment to her person would make him a suitable nominee for the knighthood of the shire.[4]

Their mistress's accession promised Robert and Frideswide Strelley a brilliant future and brought Robert notable early advancement. Without royal intervention he could not have secured the senior knighthood for Leicestershire in the first Parliament of the reign, especially when it conferred precedence over Sir Thomas Hastings. Both the achievement and the hopes were to prove short-lived: before the Parliament ended Strelley was a sick man—he is marked 'infirmus' on the Crown Office list for this Parliament—and he died on 23 Jan. 1554. By his will of 17 Jan. 1554 Strelley made bequests to various members of his family besides his wife, who by a codicil of 23 Jan. was appointed sole executrix. William Cordell*, Sir Edmund Peckham*, and others previously appointed executors, were asked to assist her. She received a grant of that part of the property which should have escheated to the crown and remained in the Queen's service, attending her funeral as a gentlewoman of the privy chamber.[5]

[1] Date of birth estimated from first reference. *CPR*, 1548–9, p. 126; *Yorks. Peds.* (Harl. Soc. xcvi), 457. [2] Somerville, *Duchy*, i. 604n; *CPR*, 1553–4, pp. 4, 193. [3] *Derbys. Arch. Soc.* xiv. bet. pp. 72–73, 85–86; C142/103/2, 6; E150/247/28; *CPR*, 1548–9, p. 150; 1555–7, pp. 266–7. [4] *LP Hen. VIII*, xv, xix, xxi; *VCH Leics.* v. 197; Somerville, i. 604n; J. M. Stone, *Mary I*, 351; H. F. M. Prescott, *Mary Tudor*, 271, 310; C1/1066/53, 54, 1158/53; *CPR*, 1548–9, p. 126; 1553–4, p. 193; *Derbys. Arch. Soc.* xiv. 86. [5] Bodl. e Museo 17; C142/103/2, 6; PCC 28 Tashe; *CPR*, 1555–7, pp. 266–7; 1563–6, p. 286; C1/1474/58 60; LC2/4/2.

S.M.T.

STRETE, Henry (by 1481–1535/36), of London and Devon.

PLYMOUTH   1510[1]

b. by 1481. *m.* by 1511, Richard.[2]

Yeoman of the crown by 1502, of the guard bef. 1509; keeper, Stockenham park, Devon 28 June 1508; yeoman usher, the chamber by June 1509–May 1513; bailiff, manor of Exe Island 3 June 1509–*d.*, earldom of Devon's lands, Hayridge hundred, Devon 3 Nov. 1509; serjeant-at-arms 18 May 1513–?*d.*; coroner, Devon by 1514–24 or later.[3]

Henry Strete claimed gentle birth but his parentage has not been established. He may have been a Devonian since a John Strete 'of Devonshire' died in 1495 and he himself made his home in the county about 1510 after living in London. On the death of the 8th Earl of Devon in 1509 the King granted Strete during pleasure two administrative offices in the estates which passed to the crown by reason of the attainder of the earl's son and heir: his tenure of both posts was confirmed for life two years later on the eve of the reversal of the attainder. Although the appointments were ostensibly in reward for service in the Household he had perhaps held them before the earl's death, and thus the pattern of his later life combining duties at court with employment by the Courtenay family may have been fixed from the outset of his career. Courtenay interest may explain Strete's election at Plymouth, for the family patronized Plympton priory which owned nearly all the land in the port: it could also have been favoured by his colleague in the Household, John Stile, who had sat for Plymouth in the previous Parliament but who in 1509–10 was on embassy to the Queen of Castile. After the dissolution Strete sued out a general pardon and received moneys towards his expenses from his fellow-Member John Bryan (q.v.). Not all the names of the Members for Plymouth and Plympton are known for the next three Parliaments, so that Strete may have been one of those whose names are lost. As a dependant of the Courtenays and coroner of the shire he was to play an important part in local affairs during Henry VIII's reign. In 1527 he witnessed the sealing of the dowager Countess of Devon's will. He accounted for the manor of Exe Island for the last time at Michaelmas 1535 but by October 1536 he had been replaced as bailiff by Thomas Spurway*.[4]

[1] Plymouth receivers' acct. bk. 1509–10. [2] Date of birth estimated from first reference. Devon RO, Exe Island ct. roll 1510–11, ex inf. W. Harwood. [3] CPR, 1494–1509, pp. 261, 358; LP Hen. VIII, i, ii; add. roll 13907; SC6/Hen. VIII, 527; Devon RO, CR532; E372/359, 367, 369, ex inf. Harwood. [4] HP, ed. Wedgwood, 1439–1509 (Biogs.), 822; LP Hen. VIII, i; Plymouth receivers' acct. bk. 1509–10; Devon RO, 1508M/London/Test. pprs. 1, ex inf. Harwood.

R.V.

STRETE, William (by 1525-54/57), of Leominster, Herefs.

LEOMINSTER 1553 (Oct.)

b. by 1525.[1]
Woodward, Ashwood in lordship of Leominster 15 May 1546; capital burgess, Leominster 1554.[2]

The Strete family was prominent at Leominster, and William Strete, who in 1553 was assessed for subsidy there on £10 in goods, was doubtless related to the Humphrey Strete named bailiff in the charter of 1554. He had been granted the woodwardship of Ashwood at the suit of its previous holder, the town's benefactor Sir Philip Hoby*, and it may have been to Hoby as well as to his own local standing that he owed his return to Mary's first Parliament; he could have sat in the previous Parliament for which the Leominster Members are unknown. Yet Strete does not seem to have shared Hoby's Protestant sympathies since neither he nor his fellow John Polle 'stood for the true religion' against the initial measures to restore Catholicism. The date of Strete's death is unknown but it had taken place before 30 Nov. 1557 when his interest in Ashwood was leased to Humphrey Coningsby*.[3]

[1] Date of birth estimated from first reference. [2] LP Hen. VIII, xxi; CPR, 1553–4, p. 396. [3] E179/117/218; CPR, 1566–9, pp. 139–40.

P.S.E.

STRINGER, George

DERBY 1554 (Apr.)

George Stringer almost certainly belonged to the family of that name which under the Tudors furnished three bailiffs of Derby as well as providing one of the town's Members in the Parliament of 1495 and another in four Elizabethan Parliaments. Although during that time no George Stringer appears among the holders of leading office in Derby, the lack of evidence about other municipal posts leaves open the possibility that it was one of their occupants who was elected to the Parliament of April 1554. By that date the George Stringer who had been admitted to Gray's Inn in 1547 could have been rendering legal services to the town and would presumably have been content with less than the statutory wage. In May 1558 a George Stringer, gentleman, of Bridgford, Nottinghamshire (some ten miles east of Derby), sold his property in Greenlane, near Derby, to a yeoman for £6 6s.8d.; that two leading townsmen, William More III* and Arthur Ireton, acted as his attorneys suggests that he was the recent Member. It is less clear whether the same applies to George Stringer of Breadsall, a village two and a half miles north of Derby, the lessor of a cottage and garden in St. Mary Gate, Derby, and to George Stringer, commissioner in 1573 for two Derbyshire inquisitions post mortem. In the absence of a will or inquisition post mortem there is no indication of the death of any local bearer of the name.

[1] W. Hutton, Derby, 79–81; PCC 10 Ayloffe, 35 Bennett; Harl. 5809, f. 15; Derby Lib. Derbys. deeds 596, 2171; CPR, 1572–5, pp. 150, 353.

C.J.B.

STRODE, Richard I

PLYMPTON ERLE 1512[1]

Subsidy collector, Devon 1512; commr. subsidy 1512, 1514, 1515, ?1523, ?1524; ?j.p. 1512–15 or later; ?escheator, Devon and Cornw. 1520–1.[2]

Richard Strode's Membership of the Parliament of 1512 is known from, and commemorated by, the Act which that Parliament passed in his favour (4 Hen. VIII, c.8). The genesis of the Act, as recited in its 'preamble', was Strode's co-operation with other, unnamed, Members in putting forward bills against the damage being done by tinworks to ports and estuaries in Devon, as well as other bills 'for the common weal' of that county. This initiative he and his associates must have taken in the first session of the Parliament, held in February and March, since it was during the ensuing prorogation that he was punished by his fellow-tinners for breach of a stannary ordinance of September 1510 by fines amounting to £160 at the four stannary courts of Devon. This was followed by his imprisonment in Lydford castle, a punitive measure which Strode himself blamed on one John a Gwyllam, to whom £20 of the fine had been assigned by the duchy of Cornwall, but which the duchy records explain as a necessary consequence of his not possessing lands or goods in Devon of sufficient value to meet the fine. Of the nature of the imprisonment there is only Strode's version, which describes his incarceration in a loathsome dungeon, at first in irons before he paid his gaoler to take them off, and on a diet of bread and water.[3]

Strode was still a prisoner, or had only just been released, when Parliament reassembled on 4 Nov. 1512, so that on the strength of his own statement that he was detained for more than three weeks his imprisonment must have begun early in October. It produced two lines of action, each of which was to leave its mark on the statute book. The first was taken by Thomas Denys*, the deputy warden of the stannaries, on whose responsibility Strode had been taken into custody; Denys now referred the matter to the King's Council, the supreme authority in stannary jurisdiction, which responded by ordering an inquiry to determine whether Strode was guilty and if so to award a *fieri facias* against him for the amount of the fine. Although this process was in due course to be recorded as a schedule to Strode's Act, it was evidently overtaken by the proceedings set in motion by Strode himself. Unable to seek redress in Parliament while it stood prorogued, he took advantage of his status as a subsidy collector to sue out a writ of privilege from the Exchequer (which was in session from 30 Sept.), and it was that court which effected his release, although only after Denys had extracted from him a bond for £100 designed to limit his freedom of action. However, before his release—or at least before news of it reached Westminster—the reassembly of Parliament swung that body into action. On 4 Nov., the opening day of the session, two writs were issued to Sir Henry Marney†, the lord warden of the stannaries, and to his deputy or deputies, 'by petition in Parliament': the first, a writ of *habeas corpus*, ordered

Marney to deliver Strode 'safe and sound' to Parliament in the octave of St. Martin, that is, by 18 Nov., under a penalty of £1,000, while the second, a writ of *supersedeas*, removed the case to the jurisdiction of Parliament, thus eliminating all other jurisdictions, whether the stannary courts, the Exchequer or even the Council. Since Marney was in all probability a Member of this Parliament the two writs should have been easy to deliver, but the first was to prove unnecessary: it is not known when Strode reappeared in the House but he had certainly done so before the *habeas corpus* expired.[4]

Strode now elaborated the petition which had moved Parliament to intervene into a 'bill containing within itself the form of an act'; it is this bill, accompanied by the schedule recording the Council's proposed action, which constitutes the Act bearing his name. The Act thus consists, in effect, of a preamble, three clauses and the schedule. The preamble recounts Strode's ordeal and the first clause seeks the annulment of the judgment against him as well as of the bond for his release. The second and third clauses apply both to Strode and to those who had acted with him: if any of them is to be proceeded against for their speeches or actions in this or any future Parliament such proceedings are to be null and void, while they themselves are given the right to sue anyone who vexes or troubles them on this account. The apparent contradiction between these safeguards and the promise of the schedule that Strode's conviction is to be inquired into, and if upheld put into execution, is explained by the place of the Council's action in the story. That the Act did annul the conviction is shown by the terse marginal against it in the duchy records: *Exoneratur per actum parliamenti pro eodem Ricardo in causa edicta.*[5]

In framing the bill which the Act reproduced, neither Strode nor—if he had their assistance—his friends had any other known purpose than his own exoneration and the protection of them all. (Thus the Act, and hence doubtless the bill, did not seek to punish Strode's judges or captors, or any future imitators, this being left to the person wronged to procure by civil suit.) If, therefore, the Act gave its authors what they wanted, there is nothing to show what use they made of it. In accordance with the King's request to that effect, Strode was presumably re-elected to the succeeding Parliament, with some at least of his associates, but there is no indication that the matter of the tinworks was raised there again, although the Act concerning cloth-making in Devon passed in 1515 (6 Hen. VIII, c.8) would have fallen within the definition of measures 'for the common weal' of the county.

Of Strode himself nothing has been established

beyond what is revealed by the documents in his case, that he was a tinner who lived in Devon where if the official reason for his imprisonment is to be accepted he possessed little property, although of sufficient standing to be a subsidy collector. Styling himself 'gentleman', he must have belonged to the well known family of Ermington and Newnham in Plympton St. Mary, but he cannot be confidently identified with either the younger son of the Richard Strode who had sat for Plympton in 1437 and 1447 or with a grandson of the same name, for the elder of these (who was dead by 1518) is likely to have been a man of some property and the younger was to inherit the estate at Newnham. As a member of a younger branch of the family he could have been one of the two Richard Strodes named in the Devon subsidy commissions of 1523 and 1524, the other being Richard Strode of Newnham, and as such he had perhaps been again re-elected to the Parliament of 1523, for which the names are lost. The younger namesake who was to sit for Plympton in March 1553 and 1559 was the grandson of Richard Strode of Newnham.[6]

[1] *Statutes*, iii. 53–54. [2] Ibid., iii. 53, 80, 117, 174; *LP Hen. VIII*, i–iv. [3] *Statutes*, iii. 53; Duchy Cornw. RO, 215, ff. 19, 26v. [4] Harl. 6849, ff. 48–49, inadequately calendared in *LP Hen. VIII*, i. 1474; G. R. Lewis, *Stannaries*, 87, 159. [5] Duchy Cornw. RO, 215, f. 26v. [6] *Vis. Eng. and Wales, Notes*, xii. 121; St.Ch.2/8/276–8, 15/77–80, 30/156; Req. 2/3/313, 10/5; C1/443/19, 570/1–16, 1063/78–79, 1136/32–34, 1158/36–38; 142/33/6, 95/20; E179/98, 271, 100/328; *LP Hen. VIII*, iii, iv, xviii, xx; *CPR*, 1549–51, p. 107.

A.D.K.H.

STRODE, Richard II (1528–81), of Newnham in Plympton St. Mary, Devon.

PLYMPTON ERLE   1553 (Mar.), 1559

b. 22 May 1528, 1st s. of William Strode of Newnham by Elizabeth, da. and h. of Philip Courtenay of Molland; bro. of William[†]. *m.* 11 Nov. 1560, Frances (*d.*7 Feb. 1562), da. of Gregory Cromwell*, 1st Baron Cromwell, 1s. William[†]. *suc.* fa. 5 May 1579.[1]
Escheator, Devon and Cornw. 1565–6.

Richard Strode's grandfather and namesake (who was almost certainly not the Member for Plympton Erle in 1512) survived until 1551 and his father until 1579; when he himself died on 5 Aug. 1581 the greater part of the family lands were still in his mother's possession. His father was presumably the 'William Strowd, of Newnham . . . esquire' who had been imprisoned in Exeter upon suspicion of heresy in the 1530s. Richard Strode's own religious views are unknown; if the fact that he was not returned during Mary's reign suggests that he too was a Protestant, he was to sit only once in the following reign in spite of connexions which included his own marriage to a peer's daughter and his sister's to

Edward Yarde[†], the 2nd Earl of Bedford's west country agent.[2]

[1] Date of birth given in Burke, *LG* (1939), 2173; *Vis. Eng. and Wales, Notes*, xii. 121; *Vis. Devon* ed. Vivian, 718–19; *Vis. Devon* (Harl. Soc. vi), 278; NRA 4154, pp. 135–6; C142/192/12. [2] C142/95/20; E179/100/328; Foxe, *Acts and Mons*. v. 18.

D.F.C.

STROWBRIDGE (TROWBRIDGE), John (by 1523–94), of Streathayne in the parish of Colyton, Devon.

LYME REGIS   1555

b. by 1523, s. of John Strowbridge of Streathayne by Thomasin, da. of John Tudoll* of Lyme Regis, Dorset. *m.* (1) 1541, Joan (*d.*1556), da. of William Coxhed of Chulmleigh, Devon, 4s. 4da.; (2) 1558, Dorothy, da. of Sir John Gaynsford of Crowhurst, Surr., wid. of one Cawarden. *suc.* fa. 1539.[1]

John Strowbridge inherited from his father the house at Streathayne in which he lived. He also owned one in Lyme, where his sister was married to a prominent merchant and his grandfather lived until his death in 1548. Strowbridge's father and his uncle (also John) frequently exported tin and cloth through the port of Lyme, but the younger John Strowbridge, described as gentleman at his election to Parliament, appears not to have engaged in trade. He was a stepson of the lawyer William Pole, a near neighbour at Colyford in Devon and one of Lyme's Members in 1545. Another neighbour, Secretary Petre, with whom Strowbridge was to have property dealings, may have favoured his return in 1555 as he had probably done that of Thomas Goodwin in the two previous years.[2]

In January 1547 the tenants of Colyton, who had held their lands of the crown since the attainder of the Marquess of Exeter, were allowed to purchase their holdings for a joint sum of £1,000: Strowbridge was one of the tenants chosen to negotiate this grant. The right to a market at Colyton on three days of the week was vested, with the powers of clerk of the market, in Strowbridge and other residents.[3]

Strowbridge lived to a great age. He made his will on 30 Jan. 1594, leaving to his wife all the goods she brought with her on marriage and an annuity from John Mallock*, and making bequests to his daughter Margaret Lowde and her children, his cousins Jane and Thomasin Strowbridge, and his son Adrian, whom he named executor and residuary legatee. He appointed as overseers of the will, which was proved on 2 Mar. 1594, his friend William Weston and his wife's son-in-law John Carpenter, minister, whom he asked to preach at the funeral. Strowbridge died and was buried at Colyton on the same day on which he made the will.[4]

[1] Date of birth estimated from tenure of a property in 1544, *LP Hen. VIII*, xix. PCC 2 Alenger, 26 Dixy; *Colyton Par. Regs.* (Devon

and Cornw. Rec. Soc. xiv), 4–5, 10, 12, 14–16, 457, 459, 463, 568, 572, 575, 599. [2] PCC 2 Alenger; *LP Hen. VIII*, xix; Lyme Regis, fugitive pieces, 2, no. 16; E122/121/7, 8, 207/2; NRA 9466 (Devon RO 123M/E1022–3). [3] *CPR*, 1554–5, p. 175; 1558–60, p. 410. [4] PCC 26 Dixy; *Colyton Par. Regs.* 595, 599.

H.M.

STROWBRIDGE, William

PLYMPTON ERLE   1554 (Nov.)

Younger sons in the family of Strowbridge were frequently christened William and it has not proved possible to determine which of them was the Member for Plympton, but he is likely to have been the man of that name who was receiver-general to Bishop Veysey of Exeter until Veysey's resignation in 1551 and who may also have served the Duke of Somerset, lord of the borough of Plympton from 1547 until his overthrow. That in spite of Queen Mary's request for townsmen Strowbridge was a nominee appears from the insertion of his name on the indenture, but it is doubtful whether Veysey, who had been restored by Mary, was involved because he was to die, aged almost 90, on the day after the indenture was sealed. Strowbridge may have owed the nomination to the joint support of Richard Calmady, his fellow-Member, and John Evelegh, elected one of the knights for Devon; Calmady was perhaps already Evelegh's son-in-law and he was to settle at Colyton, the home of Strowbridge's family. As Members of this Parliament neither Calmady nor Strowbridge quitted it early without leave, although Evelegh did. Nothing further has come to light about any contemporary William Strowbridge.

Vis. Devon, ed. Colby, 128, 172; PCC 2 Alenger, 54 Wrastley; *CPR*, 1550–3, p. 37; Req. 2/8/225; Egerton 2815; C219/23/42.

A.D.K.H.

STUMPE, Sir James (by 1519–63), of Malmesbury and Bromham, Wilts.

WILTSHIRE   1553 (Mar.)[1]
MALMESBURY   1555

b. by 1519, 1st s. of William Stumpe* of Malmesbury by 1st w. Joyce, da. of James Berkeley of Bradley, Glos.; bro. of John Stumpe†. *m.* (1) by 1542, Bridget, da. of Sir Edward Baynton* of Bromham, 1da.; (2) Isabel, da. of Sir John Leigh of Stockwell, Surr., wid. of Sir Edward Baynton (*d.*27 Nov. 1544). Kntd. 1549 or later; *suc.* fa. 22 July 1552.[2]

Keeper, Little Vastern park, Wilts. 1546, Braydon forest, Wilts. by 1563; sheriff, Wilts. Aug.–Nov. 1552, 1560–1; commr. oyer and terminer 1554; j.p. 1558/59–*d.*; steward, Hungerford manor, Berks. 1560–*d.*[3]

The life of Sir James Stumpe shows how rapidly the family of a rich Tudor clothier could be assimilated into the landowning class. Although his father may have been known to Henry VIII, it was probably Stumpe's relationship to the Bayntons which brought him the keepership of Little Vastern on 25 May 1546 at the suit of 'Mr. Seymour'. Vastern formed part of the jointure of Queen Catherine Parr, whom Sir Edward Baynton had served as vice-chamberlain and who continued for a time to be attended by his widow, Stumpe's future wife; 'Mr. Seymour' was presumably Sir Thomas Seymour II* later Baron Seymour of Sudeley. Perhaps if Stumpe had been an older man he would have been returned to Parliament in 1547 under Seymour's auspices; on the other hand it is possible that no place could be found for him, since William Stumpe and a prominent royal official, Sir Maurice Denys, represented his native borough of Malmesbury.[4]

William Stumpe showed in his will that he wanted his younger sons to continue as clothiers, while his heir was to take his place in the shire. The favour of William Herbert*, 1st Earl of Pembroke, who had succeeded the Seymours as the dominant power in Wiltshire, may now have furthered Stumpe's career. On 3 Aug. 1552 he was nominated to complete the remainder of his father's term as sheriff, and on the following day Pembroke wrote to Sir William Cecil from Wilton asking that Stumpe should become under steward of Malmesbury, where his father had been named steward in 1545. The stewardship of Hungerford manor was probably also secured at the request of the earl, who had succeeded Sir Edward Baynton as steward of the lands of the duchy of Lancaster in Wiltshire and whose own heir was to be granted Stumpe's office in 1564. Pembroke may have been responsible for the return of the clothier's son as a knight of the shire to the Parliament of March 1553, when he himself was in close alliance with the Duke of Northumberland, although Stumpe's candidature was doubtless also furthered by the sheriff, (Sir) William Sharington*, a kinsman of the Bayntons. In November 1552 Stumpe had bought from Northumberland four Wiltshire manors.[5]

Four days before this transaction Stumpe sold the manor of Througham and lands at Bisley, in the Gloucestershire Cotswolds, to Matthew King*, a Malmesbury clothier whose daughter married Stumpe's younger brother at about this time; in January 1553 he sold a fulling mill and a corn mill at Woodchester, Gloucestershire. None the less he had not yet entered on the lands of his father, who had continued to buy property until the year of his death and whose estate was burdened with provisions for his widow and the infant son of his third marriage. On 6 June 1553 Stumpe was promised special livery, after agreeing with the court of wards that an auditor could check the property and that there would be no abuses or evasions, and ten days later he was at last licensed to enjoy his inheritance. A number of lands and rents in Gloucestershire and Wiltshire were afterwards sold. William Stumpe's house within the precincts of Malmesbury abbey ceased to be the main residence of the head of the family: Sir James Stumpe is described as of Little Vastern in a deed of June 1558, as 'late of Malmesbury, *alias* of Oddington' when pardoned in January 1559, and as of Bromham in his will.[6]

Stumpe was among the Wiltshire gentry who were ordered to proclaim Mary at Warminster on 14 July 1553, and two days later he joined (Sir) John Bonham*, (Sir) John Thynne* and Sir William Wroughton* in a dutiful reply to the new Queen. Their proceedings brought protests from Charles, 8th Baron Stourton, on the ground that Mary had already named him lord lieutenant, and Stumpe was associated with his colleagues in denouncing Stourton to the Council on 24 July, although he does not figure in the later stages of this dispute. He cannot have been harmed by an order from the Council in April 1554 for the arrest of his servant Richard Cove and of Sir Anthony Hungerford's* man Thomas Cove, for in the following month he was appointed a commissioner of oyer and terminer. Although not assessed for subsidy in the borough, Stumpe retained property there and so was probably able to arrange his own return in 1555, when his name was inserted on the indenture in a different hand from that of the document. He may have been involved in earlier elections of Matthew King, his kinsman by marriage and fellow-Member.[7]

Opposition to a government bill in 1555 could have prevented Stumpe's re-election in 1558 and although in favour under Elizabeth he was not to sit in her first Parliament. He exchanged New Year gifts with the Queen in 1562; this may have led to the marriage of his only child, Elizabeth, a fortnight after his death, to Henry Knyvet†, whose wounding in the Scottish wars had excited the Queen's sympathy. Much of Stumpe's time, however, must have been taken up by a series of lawsuits over his wife's inheritance or his father's estate, and he did not live long enough to perpetuate a tradition of family representation at Malmesbury. His heirs were to sell property there, although his younger brother John was to remain active in municipal life for most of the reign and in 1584 was to represent the borough in Parliament with Sir Henry Knyvet.[8]

The extent of Stumpe's wealth is indicated by the will which he made on 28 Apr. 1563, the day before he died. His lands in Gloucestershire and Wiltshire were estimated to be worth 500 marks a year in rent and to have been leased for 700 marks; the plate and the household goods were valued

at £1,000, and the livestock included 1,800 sheep and 300 cattle. Stumpe also recorded that the Queen owed him £100 and two London mercers, Thomas Egerton* and Henry Saxey, £600 and £300 respectively; he himself had incurred debts of £100 apiece to Sir Giles Poole* of Sapperton, Gloucestershire, and Richard Roberts of London. His widow, who was assured of rents totalling £100 for her jointure, also received the interest in Bromham and Edington which she had brought to Stumpe on her marriage, together with 1,000 sheep, the household stuff at Edington and all her husband's plate, jewels, corn and cattle. Stumpe's daughter Elizabeth was left the remainder of the lease at Edington, 800 sheep and the household stuff at Bromham, in addition to the bulk of the inheritance as residuary legatee. Further bequests included £100 to the testator's 'trusty friend' Sir John Leigh, £40 to John Young, perhaps the former Member for Old Sarum, £20 to Stumpe's brother John, the same sum to every son of their uncle, another John Stumpe, and numerous legacies to servants. The executors were the widow and Sir John Leigh, and the supervisor the daughter, who was aged at least 20 when an inquisition was taken on 2 August.[9]

Stumpe must have spent his last days in London, for he had asked to be buried in St. Margaret's, Westminster. Machyn records that on 10 May 1563 two heralds accompanied the impressive funeral procession from Channel Row to St. Margaret's, where the lady chapel was hung with black. Henry and Elizabeth Knyvet were to be survived only by three daughters, who transmitted the blood and fortune of Wiltshire's most successful clothier to the dynasties of their respective husbands, the Earls of Lincoln, Rutland and Suffolk.[10]

[1] C219/20/138. [2] Date of birth estimated from age at fa.'s i.p.m., C142/95/91. *Wilts. N. and Q.* viii. 393, 448; *Wilts. Vis. Peds.* (Harl. Soc. cv, cvi), 7. [3] *LP Hen. VIII*, xxi; *CPR*, 1553, p. 412; 1553-4, p. 28; 1554-5, p. 52; 1560-3, pp. 443, 491; Somerville, *Duchy*, i. 627. [4] G. D. Ramsay, *Wilts. Woollen Industry in 16th and 17th Cents.* 36; *LP Hen. VIII*, xxi. [5] Ramsay, 36; *CSP Dom.* 1547-80 p. 43; *CPR*, 1550-3, p. 258; 1553, p. 412; Somerville, i. 627. [6] *CPR*, 1550-3, pp. 258-9; 1553, p. 259; 1557-8, p. 329; 1558-60, p. 153; 1560-3, pp. 89, 367; Wilts. RO, 88 : 30, 34-40; *Wilts. N. and Q.* iv. 119, 160, 311, 403; viii. 445-6. [7] *Wilts. Arch. Mag.* viii. 311-3; *APC* v. 14; *CPR*, 1553-4, p. 28; Ramsay 39; *CSP Dom.* 1601-3, *Add.* 1547-65, p. 509. [8] Guildford mus. Loseley 1331/2; J. Nichols *Progresses Eliz.* i. 115, 125; E. M. Richardson, *The Lion and the Rose*, i. 294; C3/105/64, 109/19, 157/78, 173/82; *CPR*, 1563-6, p. 135. [9] PCC 23 Chayre; *Wilts. N. and Q.* viii. 445-6. [10] *Machyn's Diary* (Cam. Soc. xlii), 308, 395; *Wilts. N. and Q.* viii. 447; Ramsay, 37.

T.F.T.B.

STUMPE, William (by 1498–1552), of Malmesbury, Wilts.

MALMESBURY 1529, 1547[1]

b. by 1498, ?s. of one Stumpe of North Nibley, Glos. m. (1) by 1519, Joyce, da. of James Berkeley of Bradley, Glos., 2s. Sir James* and John Stumpe†; (2) Tibbalda, wid. of William Billing (d.28 Aug. 1533) of

Deddington, Oxon.; (3) 1551, Catherine, wid. of Richard Mody (d.8 Nov. 1550) of Garsdon, Wilts., 1s.[2]

Receiver, ct. augmentations, N. Wales 1536–52; j.p. Wilts. 1538–d., Glos. 1539–44; commr. musters, Wilts. 1539, subsidy 1549, 1552, relief, Glos. and Wilts. 1550, goods of churches and fraternities, Wilts. 1553; bailiff, steward and collector, manors and hundreds of Chedglow, Malmesbury and Startley 1545; high collector of subsidy, Chippenham, Malmesbury and neighbouring hundreds 1545; escheator, Glos. 1545–6; sheriff, Wilts. 1551–d.[3]

William Stumpe, the richest and most famous Wiltshire clothier of his century, was of obscure and humble origin. His father is said to have been a weaver and at one time parish clerk of North Nibley in east Gloucestershire, where Stumpe's brother Thomas still described himself as a 'husbandman' in his will of 1551. North Nibley is not far from Berkeley castle, and Stumpe's marriage to a daughter of James Berkeley, a scion of the ancient baronial house who lived at neighbouring Bradley, may have been his first step towards fame and fortune.[4]

Stumpe is first recorded as a resident of Malmesbury in 1524, when the assessments for subsidy show him as already one of the town's four richest inhabitants. Nothing is known of him in the next decade save for his representation of Malmesbury in the Parliament of 1529, itself a sign of continuing prosperity. In 1535, according to the *valor ecclesiasticus*, he was paying 63s. a year to the abbey of Malmesbury as tenant of Winyard Mill in Whitchurch, in November of that year he paid £200 for all Sir Roger Tocotes's property in Malmesbury and elsewhere, and in December he took a 60-year lease in reversion of another of the abbot's mills.[5]

It is not clear whether Stumpe had been elected to Parliament simply as a prominent townsman, or whether he already enjoyed wider patronage, but by 1536 he had attracted enough notice to be appointed one of the 17 particular receivers of the newly established court of augmentations, with £20 a year, 'profits' and a travel allowance; out of the 29 receivers appointed during the life of the first court, he was to be one of seven to retain office after its reorganization in 1547. In view of the crown's request that the former Members should be returned again in 1536, it is likely that Stumpe was re-elected to the Parliament of that year, the writs for which were tested on 27 Apr., three days after his appointment as receiver; he may well have been chosen again in 1539, 1542 and 1545, when the names of the Malmesbury Members are again missing, for by this time he could add his court connexion to his ever-growing local importance. Although not granted arms until 1549, he was one of four gentlemen assessed on lands in the borough in 1541; four years

later he contributed £3 6s.8d. towards the benevolence, the next highest sum being the 53s.4d. paid by John Hedges*, and he was jointly assessed as the richest resident in 1549, on goods worth £100, and in 1552, on goods worth £40.[6]

The best known tribute to William Stumpe's industrial enterprise was paid by Leland, who visited Malmesbury about 1542. Those buildings of the abbey deemed worthy of preservation had been entrusted to Sir Edward Baynton*, while the less valuable ones were soon occupied by Stumpe, perhaps as Baynton's deputy. Leland made a natural mistake when he implied that the entire site had already been bought by Stumpe and turned into a workshop where 'every corner of the vast houses of office' was filled with looms, and the plan to create 'a street or two' for the artisans on vacant plots of abbey land within the town walls was apparently never carried out. Yet the size of the undertaking was impressive: Stumpe was to bequeath ten broad looms to his second son and yet more to his youngest, so that he must have amassed an exceptional number. Such concentrations were to dwindle after 1555, when an Act (2 and 3 Phil. and Mary, c.11) protected the poorer weaver by forbidding country clothiers to own more than one loom or weavers more than two, but Stumpe's operations may have brought social as well as economic advantages, with an estimated output of 3,000 cloths a year. The corporation of Oxford saw a chance to benefit the neighbourhood when negotiating, albeit unsuccessfully, with Stumpe in 1546 over the grounds, mills and empty buildings of Osney abbey; among other conditions, he was to find work for 2,000 people in clothmaking 'for the succour of the city of Oxford and the country about it'. Stumpe even provided employment in London, for he was sued in the court of requests over an agreement of 1541 whereby 32 red woollen cloths were to be sold for him there by Ralph Porter.[7]

Between 1538 and 1544 Ralph Porter, a clothier of Cherington, Berkshire, also sued Stumpe in the Star Chamber and, for non-appearance there, in Chancery; he claimed that Stumpe had supplied cloths that were 'not so good and substantial' as promised, thus abusing his authority as a magistrate. Stumpe for his part brought a suit against the townsmen of Tetbury over the tolls of their market, which he claimed to enjoy by virtue of a lease during the minority of Henry, 7th Lord Berkeley. William Mayo, late bailiff of Tetbury for the year ending Michaelmas 1544, pointed out that the borough, one of the best markets for wool and yarn in Gloucestershire, was only about three miles from Malmesbury, and that it was clearly Stumpe's intention, 'if he might obtain and get the tolls and weights of the said town of Tetbury in his own hands, so to use the said tolls that by his crafty means he would utterly destroy the said market at Tetbury'. This may have been an exaggeration, but the case does show how Stumpe waged war on smaller manufacturers by forcing local weavers to buy only his wool and yarn.[8]

Stumpe's success, however achieved, is reflected in his extensive acquisitions of property during the last 15 years of his life. Lands of the former abbey at Conway were leased to him from the augmentations in 1537–8, soon after he had become the court's receiver in that area, and a grant of 1557 shows that he had once been bailiff of the north Wales lordship and manor of Cymmer. Most of his purchases, however, were concentrated in the Cotswold area of east Gloucestershire and north-west Wiltshire and in the lowlands stretching from Tewkesbury southwards to Wootton Bassett and from Woodchester eastwards to Warminster. Probably his largest single transaction was the purchase of the site of Malmesbury abbey, in the centre of this belt, with the manor of Brinkworth and lands in Rodbourne and elsewhere; for these he paid £1,518 in November 1544. He also bought from such local magnates as (Sir) Anthony Kingston* and Sir Richard Long*.[9]

Litigation throws some light on Stumpe's public position and personal affairs. It was as one 'greatly kinned, allied and friended' in Wiltshire, and 'borne and maintained there both by the gentlemen and the freeholders', that he was sued in Chancery, in Audley's time, by Richard Vaughan for possession of five ex-monastic mills at Lower Barns farm and Bushford bridge; Vaughan, who lived in Essex and had been powerless to withstand Stumpe, claimed the mills by virtue of a grant from George Monoux*, whereas Stumpe rested his case on an earlier grant by Monoux. Two further actions in Chancery, brought against Stumpe by evicted copyholders at Brinkworth and Brokenborough, suggest that as a landlord he displayed the harshness attributed to so many of the newly rich, while the charge that he conspired with his second wife to defraud her son John Billing of £400 and plate bequeathed by Billing's father implies sharp practice even within his family circle.[10]

Stumpe's greatest achievement was to win for himself a place in the ranks of those who monopolized local government: a justice of the peace from 1538, he figured among the Wiltshire gentry who mustered for the French war in 1544 and he was to die while sheriff of that county. He built a house at Malmesbury, the Abbey House, and saved the superb nave of the abbey by presenting it to the town and procuring Cranmer's licence for its conversion into a parish church. It was presumably at his residence that there worked the French priest Oliver Boweseke, 'a good gardener', who became a denizen in 1544 after sojourning with him for a dozen years. Stumpe may even have been patronized there by Henry VIII, for Fuller has a story of the King's unexpected visit to him after hunting in Braydon forest and of his royal entertainment, at the expense of the host's workpeople who had to fast that the court might be fed.[11]

When Stumpe made his will on 15 Oct. 1550 he evinced no interest in the place or manner of his burial but he manifested his Protestantism by committing his soul to Christ, through whose passion 'I do verily trust to be saved . . . and by none other means nor ways that ever was or that ever I did say or do'. To his second son John he gave the leases of three houses at Charlton, with £500 and ten looms, to his brother Thomas's three sons £10 apiece, to every woman servant 20s. and to every manservant 40s. Five months after making the will he prepared for his impending marriage to Catherine Mody by entailing much of his property upon its offspring, although the abbey and other buildings in Garsdon and Malmesbury were excluded from this arrangement; the bequests in his will, of which the eldest son and residuary legatee was sole executor, were also unaffected and they were confirmed on the day of his death, 22 July 1552. He then left his remaining looms to William, his infant son by Catherine, forgave all his debtors, including the humble Thomas Stumpe and his sister Agnes Lyppet, and set aside the handsome sum of £40 for the poor of Malmesbury. His heir, Sir James Stumpe, was appointed to serve out his term as sheriff and when sued in Chancery by Christopher Dysmars*, clerk of the peace, for £11 16s. which Dysmars claimed was owing to him for the delivery of prisons, made the surprising rejoinder that he had not enough of his father's goods to meet the claim.[12]

[1] Hatfield 207. [2] Date of birth estimated from marriage. G. D. Ramsay, *Wilts. Woollen Industry in 16th and 17th Cents.* 30, 32, 36; J. Smyth, *Berkeleys*, i. 267; E150/805/3; *Wilts. N. and Q.* viii. 390–5. [3] W. C. Richardson, *Ct. Augmentations*, 47, 50; Ramsay, 35; *LP Hen. VIII*, xiii–xviii, xx; *CPR*, 1547–8, p. 91; 1548–9, p. 252; 1550–3, p. 396; 1553, pp. 259, 354, 359, 376, 415; E179/108/255a, 270; *Wilts. Arch. Soc. recs. br.* x. 20. [4] *Aubrey, Wilts. Topog. Colls.* ed. Jackson 47, 60; *Wilts. N. and Q.* viii. 531; Smyth, i. 267. [5] E179/197/153; Ramsay, 32; *Val Eccles.* ii. 121; Wilts. RO, Acc. 88/22, 23. [6] Richardson, 47, 50; *Foster's Grantees of Arms* (Harl. Soc. lxvi), 241; *Wilts. Arch. Soc. recs. br.* x. 29; E179/197/186, 198/255a, 270. [7] Leland, *Itin.* ed. Smith, i. 132; *Wilts. Arch. Mag.* xxxviii. 462–3, 496–7; Ramsay, 17, 33; *Oxf. Recs.* 185; Req.2/11/60. [8] St.Ch.2/17/374; C1/1049/43; Req.2/3/276. [9] *LP Hen. VIII*, xiii, xvii, xix–xxi; Ramsay, 32; *Wilts. N. and Q.* iii. 86, 373; iv. 28, 60, 61; *CPR*, 1549–51, p. 356; 1550–3, p. 239; 1555–7, p. 483. [10] C1/948/85–7, 1080/26–31, 1111/19–21, 1319/63–5; PCC 18 Hogen. [11] Ramsay, 34–35; SP1/184, f.195; *Wilts. Arch. Mag.* i. 250; *Letters of Denization 1509–1603* (Huguenot Soc. Pubs. viii) 28; Fuller, *Worthies* iii. 337. [12] PCC 26 Powell; *Wilts. N. and Q.* viii. 390–3; *CPR*, 1550–3 p. 66.

T.F.T.B.

STUPPENY, Richard (by 1487–1540), of New Romney, Kent.

NEW ROMNEY 1515[1]

b. by 1487. *m.* Joan, ?wid. of one Bunting, 2s. 2da.[2]

Jurat, New Romney 1510–*d.*, chamberlain 1519–20; bailiff to Yarmouth 1514; commr. subsidy, New Romney 1523, 1524.[3]

Richard Stuppeny, who was born at 'Kenerton', probably Kenardington, Kent, was admitted to the freedom of Romney on 22 Mar. 1512. His parentage is unknown but he was probably related to Robert Stuppeny who had been made a freeman in 1474 and to a namesake, admitted in 1509, from whom he was generally distinguished by the suffix 'senior' or 'the elder'. Richard Stuppeny, senior, was already a jurat and had begun his regular attendance at the meetings of the Brotherhood of the Cinque Ports.[4]

At the election held on 26 Dec. 1514 for the Parliament of 1515 Romney first chose Clement Baker and William Wodar, but Wodar was evidently unable or unwilling to go to Westminster—a few years later he was described as old and poor—and his name was crossed out in the record and Richard Stuppeny's substituted. Stuppeny received £3 5s.6d. wages for an unspecified number of days' attendance in two payments of 26s.8d. and 38s.10d. He may have been returned again in 1523 when the name of only one of the Members for Romney is known. In 1524 the Brotherhood employed him with Edmund Jacklin *alias* Bocher* on a mission to seek exemption from the loan by way of a gift: at Easter 1524 they were each allowed 20s. for the ten days they had spent travelling to Leeds castle to enlist the support of the comptroller of the Household Sir Henry Guildford* and then to London and to the court at St. Albans.[5]

Elected a jurat for the last time on 25 Mar. 1540, Stuppeny made his will on the following 4 May as Richard Stuppeny the elder of the parish of St. Nicholas, New Romney: it was proved on 28 Nov. 1540. He left his wife £20, a silver goblet and spoons and half the goods in his house called 'Clyderowes', the other half going to his unmarried daughter. His son Clement was to receive at 21 all the belongings in his messuage and brewhouse in Lydd and his second son Lawrence all his sheep and all the profits of his farm lands. Among the minor beneficiaries were his wife's daughter Margaret Bunting and several members of the Stuppeny family, whose relationship to the testator was not given: Richard Bunting* was one of the witnesses. Stuppeny asked to be buried in St. Stephen's chancel on the south side of the church of St. Nicholas and willed his executors to 'buy a stone to lay upon my grave, pictured with me, my wife and

my children; and to be laid so that it may be two feet above the foundation'. Such a tomb survives, 'new erected for the use of the ancient meeting and election of mayor and jurats of this port' by Stuppeny's great-grandson in 1622, but without the engravings and with the inscription of 1622 recording the death in 1526–7 of Richard Stuppeny, 'jurat of this town in the first year of King Henry VIII': the date of death may be that of Stuppeny's younger namesake, although it appears that he was never a jurat.[6]

[1] Romney assessment bk. 1492–1516, f. 183. [2] Date of birth estimated from that of younger namesake (born by 1488). Canterbury prob. reg. C17 f. 68. [3] Romney assessment bk. 1448–1526, ff. 162 seq.; 1516–22 ff. 87 seq.; chamberlains' accts. 1528–80, ff. 20 seq.; *Cinque Ports White and Black Bks.* (Kent Arch. Soc. recs. br. xix) 156; *LP Hen. VIII*, iii, iv. [4] Romney assessment bk. 1448–1526 ff. 70, 117, 119v; *Cinque Ports White and Black Bks.* 145–222 passim. [5] *HMC 5th Rep.* 550, 553; Romney assessment bk. 1492–1516 f. 183; 1516–22, f. 91v; *Cinque Ports White and Black Bks.* 191. [6] Romney chamberlains' accts. 1528–80, f. 38v; Canterbury prob. reg. C17 f. 68; *Arch. Cant.* xiii. 475n.

H.M.

STURE, Edmund (1509/10–60), of Bradley in North Huish, Devon and the Middle Temple, London.

PLYMPTON ERLE	1545
TOTNES	1547[1]
DARTMOUTH	1554 (Apr.)
EXETER	1555

b. 1509/10, 1st s. of Henry Sture of Bradley by Elizabeth, da. of Edmund Fortescue. *educ.* M. Temple. *m.* Elizabeth, *s.p. suc.* fa. 3 Mar. 1534.[2]

Bencher, M. Temple 1549–*d.*, Autumn reader 1549, Lent reader 1557, assistant to Autumn reader 1558.[3]

J.p.q. Devon 1547–*d.*; commr. relief 1550; counsel to Exeter Apr. 1554.[4]

Edmund Sture came of a minor landowning family, inheriting from his father a number of messuages and other property in the villages to the west of the river Dart. He became a lawyer, and it is clear from his will and inquisition that he added appreciably to the family estates, although there is no indication that he bought land from the crown.[5]

Sture's practice probably lay mainly in the west country. On 2 Apr. 1554 the Exeter city council appointed him standing counsel to the city, with a fee of £20 a year, on condition that he took up residence there and performed his duties whenever required: he was at the same time granted the reversion of the office of recorder. Although the city elected him as one of its Members in the Parliament of 1555, he does not seem to have carried out his legal duties, perhaps owing to illness, and after 1556 his fee was not paid. In October 1558 he was 'sick and impotent', and his duties were undertaken by John Charles. Sture had probably owed his return for Plympton Erle in 1545 and Totnes in 1547 to Sir Richard Edgecombe, who was influential in both boroughs: the fact that on the first occasion his name was written over an erasure on the county return suggests that he had not been the electors' choice, but in 1554 he was in receipt of fees from Totnes. His return for Dartmouth to the Parliament of April 1554 may reflect a similar situation.[6]

Sture was probably a Catholic. He was a friend of James Courtenay,* whom he had made an overseer of his will, and in 1557 was appointed a feoffee for the lands of Arthur, nephew of James Bassett*: his fellows on this occasion included (Sir) Anthony Browne I*, Viscount Montagu, (Sir) William Cordell*, William Rogers*, Sir Edward Waldegrave* and Bishop White, all Catholics. It is thus not surprising that he took no part in the parliamentary opposition to the Marian Restoration. In May 1557 he was a feoffee for Griffith Ameredith*. By his will, dated 12 Feb. 1560, Sture left most of his goods and an annuity to his wife Elizabeth, together with a life interest in Ermington park; he made bequests to the poor and to servants, and gave various leases to his nephew Henry Luscombe. The bulk of his landed property passed to his brother and heir Philip. Sture died at Bradley on 22 Feb. 1560.[7]

[1] C219/282/2; Hatfield 207. [2] Date of birth estimated from age at fa.'s i.p.m., C142/56/7. *Vis. Devon*, ed.Vivian, 725; PCC 19 Mellershe. [3] Dugdale, *Origines Juridiciales*, 217. [4] *CPR*, 1547–8, p. 83; 1553, p. 352; 1553–4, p. 18; Exeter act bk. 2 f. 139v. [5] C142/56/73, 125/36; PCC 19 Mellershe. [6] Exeter act bk. 2 f. 139v; receivers accts. 1555–6, 1556–7, 1557–8; C219/18C/32, 33; *Trans. Dev. Assoc.* xii. 328. [7] *CPR* 1555–7, p. 404; 1558–60, p. 448; NRA 11978 (Devon RO, 484 M/F4(1)); PCC 19 Mellershe; C142/125/36.

R.V.

STURGEON, John (by 1498–1570/71), of London.

LONDON   1542, 1545
HINDON   1547[1]

b. by 1498, 1st s. of Henry Sturgeon of London, by w. Joan. *m.* by 1522, at least 3s. 2da. *suc.* fa. Aug. 1526.[2]
Auditor, London 1537–8, 1542–4, bridgemaster 1547–8, chamberlain 1550–63; gov. Merchant Adventurers 1545, 1548–50.[3]

John Sturgeon may have been related to two 15th-century namesakes, a London mercer who sat in Parliament for the City and his more distinguished son who was knight of the shire for Hertfordshire. The latter held Gatesbury, Hertfordshire, and in his will of 1526 Sturgeon's father, a London ironmonger, mentions a kinsman at nearby Ware. Sturgeon did not follow his father's trade, being a member of the company of haberdashers by 1519 at about which time he imported haberdashery to the value of £248, but he lived in his father's parish of St. Benet Gracechurch, where (as his father had done) he served as churchwarden.[4]

Sturgeon was common councilman for Bridge ward in London by 1535. On 27 Jan. 1536 he was one of a number of commoners appointed by the court of aldermen to discuss 'such matters as shall be profitable for the common wealth of this city' at the coming session of Parliament. Later, when he was himself a Member of Parliament, he and the other Members for London were enjoined to consult among themselves about the City's parliamentary programme before the beginning of the session of 1543, and on 21 Feb. 1544 the court of aldermen agreed that they should oppose a bill 'against merchants, for packing of woollen cloths'. He had been named a commissioner in the Act for the partition of Wapping marsh (35 Hen. VIII, c.9). Later in 1544 he was imprisoned 'for his wilful disobedience' and only released by the court after Chancellor Wriothesley had sent letters in his favour. In June 1545 he was employed to convey money overseas for the King, and when in November he showed the aldermen a letter from Sir Edward Bray* 'concerning certain provision to be made for conveying of wood to this City' the Members were told to 'use their discretion therein as they shall think good at the Parliament'.[5]

On 26 Nov. 1547 Sturgeon was appointed by the common council of London to assist in the preparation of an answer to a bill introduced four days earlier into the Lords 'against the City' for the river Thames: whether or not the answer was completed no more was heard of the bill. Sturgeon's employment in this matter may mean that he sat in the Parliament of 1547 from the outset, but it is more likely that his experience in the two previous Parliaments, not current Membership, accounts for his inclusion in the 28-strong committee. His later Membership of the Parliament is known from a list revised for its final session in 1552 where his name is struck through and erroneously marked 'mortuus'. Unlike John Story, whose name precedes his and is also deleted, Sturgeon is not known to have been replaced in the Commons. The notice of his death some 18 years prematurely was perhaps a simple clerical error, but it could be that Sturgeon's name had been confused with that of John Croke (q.v.) and that he himself was Croke's replacement. Whenever he was returned for Hindon he presumably owed his election to the Privy Council and perhaps especially to the influence of Cranmer. As early as 1536 letters which Sturgeon wrote to a friend at Calais, evidently on religious matters, were prudently burnt by the recipient, whose reply of June 1536 reveals that Sturgeon was then a friend of Hugh Latimer and a Protestant sympathizer. William Morice, whose brother was Cranmer's secretary and who had known Latimer since 1532, sat for the nearby borough of Downton in the same Parliament. The imprisonment and deprivation of

Bishop Gardiner during Edward VI's reign left the episcopal boroughs of Downton, Hindon and Taunton open to intervention.[6]

Sturgeon was elected one of the bridgemasters of London in 1547 against eight other candidates; re-elected in the following year, he was replaced in October following his election as governor of the Merchant Adventurers. He had served as governor once before, in 1545, when he and other Englishmen at Antwerp were arrested, 'but in a gentle manner', in retaliation for the arrest in England of subjects of the Emperor. During his second term he represented the company at the entry of Philip of Spain into Antwerp in the summer of 1549. In November 1550 nine men disputed the chamberlainship of London. The contestants were reduced to two by vote of the court of aldermen, and Sturgeon was elected by the commonalty, although his rival Henry Fisher*, a London skinner, was supported by a letter from the King. He held the office for 13 years, and was thus again involved in the reception of Philip of Spain as well as making payments on behalf of the City to such men as Speaker Pollard. He retired in 1563 'by reason of his great age and weakness of body' and had by then begun to settle his estate, giving to London plots of land in Finsbury field and Newgate; early in 1569 he granted to his parish church a yearly rent of 40s. which he had been left for this purpose. He died in 1570 or early in 1571 and was buried in St. Benet Gracechurch.[7]

[1] Hatfield 207. [2] Date of birth estimated from first reference. PCC 10 Porch; City of London RO, Guildhall, rep. 15, f. 409v. [3] City of London RO, jnl. 14, ff. 45v, 339v; 15, ff. 46, 320, 375; rep. 11, f. 509v; 12(2), f. 288-88v; 15, f. 278-78v; O. de Smedt, De Engelse Natie te Antwerpen, ii. 90. [4] HP, ed. Wedgwood, 1439-1509 (Biogs.), 825-6; PCC 10 Porch; City of London RO, rep. 5, f. 4; 7, f. 115v; E122/81/8 ex inf. Prof. P. Ramsey. [5] City of London RO, jnl. 13, f. 435; rep. 9, f. 150; 10, f. 299; 11, ff. 38, 107, 205v, 220v, 222v, 247. [6] Ibid. jnl. 15, f. 339; LP Hen. VIII, x; Hatfield 207. [7] City of London RO, jnl. 15, ff. 320, 375; rep. 11, f. 509v; 12(2), f. 288; 13(1), ff. 92, 162v, 167, 251; 15, f. 278v; husting roll, 256(28); LP Hen. VIII, xx; de Smedt, ii. 174; Cal. Wills, Ct. of Hustings, ii (2), 678, 680, 684; Church-warden's accts. St. Benet Gracechurch, Guildhall Lib. 1568, ff. 109v, 110; Stow's Survey of London i. 213.

H.M.

SULYARD, John (by 1518-75), of Wetherden, Suff.

IPSWICH	1553 (Oct.)
BODMIN	1554 (Apr.)
PRESTON	1554 (Nov.)
IPSWICH	1555
CHIPPENHAM	1558

b. by 1518, 1st s. of John Sulyard of Wetherden by Margaret, da. of Robert Baker of Wetherden. educ. Clifford's Inn. m. (1) Elizabeth, da. of Sir Edmund Bedingfield of Oxborough, Norf., 1da.; (2) by 1541, Elizabeth, da. of Sir John Jerningham of Somerleyton, Suff., 2s. 2da.; (3) Alice, da. of Humphrey Carvell of Wiggenhall St. Mary, Norf., s.p. suc. fa. 20 Mar. 1540. Kntd. Mar. 1557/Jan. 1558.[1]

J.p. Suff. 1554-61; sheriff, Norf. and Suff. 1555-6; standard bearer, gent. pens. late 1553-late 1558; commr. sewers, Norf. and Suff. 1566.[2]

John Sulyard was a devout Catholic lawyer whose public career seems to have begun with the accession of Mary. He was one of a number of East Anglians who early in July 1553 hastened to her aid at Framlingham: his services then were rewarded by an annuity of 40 marks, which he later exchanged for a grant of the manor of Haughley, Suffolk. His loyalty was further recognised by his appointment, while still in his thirties and apparently only a year after his first appearance on the Suffolk commission of the peace, as sheriff of Norfolk and Suffolk. The surviving records of his term show him as having nothing more serious to contend with than the illegal export of corn, the troublesome behaviour of gypsies and the activities of a notorious highway-man.[3]

Sulyard's two elections at Ipswich were doubtless helped by his relationship to Sir Henry Jerning-ham and Sir Henry Bedingfield, knights of the shire for Suffolk and Norfolk respectively in Sulyard's first Parliament; the sheriff at the election of September 1553 was his relative by marriage Sir Thomas Cornwallis*. He was not re-elected for the town to the following Parliament, when Clement Heigham, the crown's choice as Speaker, and the court official Thomas Poley were returned, but he was found a seat in Cornwall. He was not Bodmin's original choice, but Thomas Prideaux whom it had elected got himself returned also at Grampound and Newport iuxta Launceston: Prideaux opted for Newport and presumably with the help of Beding-field Sulyard replaced him at Bodmin and Cornwallis at Grampound. At Preston in November 1554 his patron was probably the chancellor of the duchy of Lancaster, Sir Robert Rochester*, and at Chippen-ham in 1558 it was perhaps the sheriff of Wiltshire, Sir Walter Hungerford*, a former gentleman pen-sioner to whom the lordship of Chippenham had recently been restored and who himself sat for Bodmin in this Parliament. Sulyard must also have been known in the area through his kinship with Sir Edward Baynton*, and as standard-bearer of the gentlemen pensioners he had doubtless gone to France in 1557 with the Wiltshire magnate William Herbert*, 1st Earl of Pembroke; it may have been during the St. Quentin campaign that he received his knighthood. Although the Journal throws no light on his part in the business of the House, he is not surprisingly missing from the ranks of the opposition in 1553 and 1555.[4]

Mary's death brought Sulyard's public career virtually to a close. In 1574 his name stands sixth on a list of English knights who remained firm in their

Catholicism, but he seems to have caused no trouble to the government. He died on 4 Mar. 1575, leaving his eldest son Edward as heir to his lands in Suffolk. Both Edward and his widowed mother were to become well-known recusants after Sir John Sulyard's death.[5]

[1] Date of birth estimated from age at fa.'s i.p.m., C142/62/97. Vis, Suff. ed. Metcalfe, 70, 168; Req.2/17/65; C142/175/85. [2] CPR. 1553-4 pp. 24 27; 1569-72, p. 217; LC 2/4(2) f. 28, 2/4(3), p. 96, ex inf. W. J. Tighe; E405/121, m. 62v; Lansd. 156, f. 103. [3] Req.2/17/65; City of London RO, Guildhall, rep. 13(1), f. 108; Chron. Q. Jane and Q. Mary (Cam. Soc. xlviii), 5; CPR, 1555-7 pp. 308-9; APC, v. 198, 231, 264. [4] C193/32/1; CPR, 1555-7, p. 458. [5] Cath. Rec. Soc. xiii. 90; xxii. 55 and n.; Lansd. 5, f. 109; C142/175/85; Bodl. Tanner 118, f. 128 seq.

J.J.G.

SUTTON, Ambrose (1530–92), of Burton nr. Lincoln and Butterwick, Lincs., and London

GREAT GRIMSBY 1554 (Apr.)

b. 3 Feb. 1530, 3rd but 1st surv. s. of Henry Sutton (d.6 Jan. 1538), of Wellingore, Lincs. by Margaret, da. of Sir Robert Hussey of Linwood in Blankney, Lincs. m. Faith, da. of Sir William Tyrwhitt of Scotter, Lincs. 2s. suc. gd-fa. Nov. 1545.[1]
Commr. sewers, Cambs., Hunts., I. of Ely, Lincs., Northants., and Notts. 1555, Lincs. 1564.[2]

The Sutton family had furnished Members for Lincolnshire or Lincoln to several Parliaments in the 14th century. Ambrose Sutton's father, grandfather and two elder brothers all died while he was a minor, and nine months after his coming of age on 3 Feb. 1551 he had livery of an inheritance which included the manors of South Hykeham and Market Stainton. It must have been shortly after this that he and Edward Sutton, probably his cousin the 4th Lord Dudley, launched Star Chamber suits against each other for assault on servants and tenants in the course of forcible entry on some of these lands. There was a happier outcome to a claim made by Sutton and Thomas Hussey (probably the Member for Peterborough) to the disused church of St. Andrew, Lincoln; although rejecting their claim, the city corporation offered them the church for £53 in recognition of favours received from Sutton's forbears and in expectation of his own and Hussey's future goodwill.[3]

It is not immediately apparent why Sutton, whose influence focussed on Lincoln, should have attended his only Parliament as one of the Members for Grimsby. The explanation is probably to be found in the fact that he was returned there only after his uncle Thomas Hussey I, who had been elected for both Grimsby and Grantham, chose to sit for Grantham; Hussey had been nominated at Grimsby by the sheriff, Sir Francis Askew, whose help he may well have enlisted to secure his replacement by Sutton, to whom Hussey was to bequeath a silver-

gilt saltcellar. Of Sutton's part in the proceedings of this brief Parliament nothing is known, and the only reference found to him in a religious context is an ambiguous one. During Cardinal Pole's visitation of Lincoln, Sutton was presented for eating fish in Lent; to his explanation that the pope had dispensed him on medical advice Pole replied that he did not exhibit any infirmity and he was made to do penance. He may have been led astray by his uncle, who had been similarly accused some 15 years earlier.[4]

Sutton sued out general pardons in 1554 and 1559, presumably as precautionary measures. The few later references found to him are all suggestive of financial stress: in 1560 and 1566 he was pardoned of outlawry for debts of £70 and £25 to London tradesmen, in 1563 he sold his lands in Market Stainton and in 1566 he was licensed to sell his share in a house at Willoughton, also in Lincolnshire, to Nicholas Sutton. If he shared ancestry with Thomas Sutton the philanthropist, who came from the same part of Lincolnshire, he sank into an obscurity as great as the other's fame. The visitation of Lincolnshire in 1592 records an Ambrose Sutton of Burton one of whose sons, Robert, had already died without issue while the other, Hamon, was a lunatic. Since Faith Sutton took as her second husband Laurence Meres†, whose will was proved in May 1593, her first one, if alive in 1592, could hardly have survived that year.[5]

[1] Became 21 on 3 Feb. 1551, CPR, 1553, pp. 369-70. Lincs. Peds. (Harl. Soc. lii), 938-9. [2] CPR, 1554-5, p. 109; 1563-6, p. 40. [3] CPR, 1553, pp. 369-70; St.Ch.3/5/79, 80, 7/91; HMC 14th Rep VIII, 46. [4] Lincs. Wills 1500-1600, ed. Maddison, 51; Strype Eccles. Memorials, iii(2), 393-4. [5] CPR, 1553-4, p. 415; 1558-60, p. 227; 1560-3, pp. 89, 552; 1563-6, pp. 355, 416; Vis. Lincs. ed. Metcalfe, 68; Lincs. Peds. 939.

T.M.H.

SUTTON, Nicholas (by 1465-1532/33), of Rye, Suss.

RYE 1497,[1] 1510,[2] 1512,[3] 1515,[4] 1529*

b. by 1465, o. surv. s. of John Sutton† of Rye. m. 3s. ?at least 2da. suc. fa. 1506.[5]
Jurat, Rye 1495-1503, 1504-32 or 33, mayor 1509-11, 1516-17, 1519-20, July-Aug. 1529, 1531-2; bailiff to Yarmouth 1496; commr. subsidy, Rye 1514.[6]

Nicholas Sutton was the only son mentioned in his father's will of 1506. John Sutton was then about 80 years old and his son had been married long enough to have three sons of his own, James, Thomas and Richard, and, it seems, daughters for whom their grandfather made provision. Nicholas Sutton had attended his first Cinque Ports Brotherhood in 1486, and scattered entries in the customs accounts—in 1508 he shipped out six cows and in 1531 brought in some wine—reflect his perhaps limited involvement in trade.[7]

First chosen a jurat in 1495, when John Cheseman† was mayor, Sutton was not re-elected in 1503 by Richard Berkeley*; he was restored in the following year and when he became mayor for the second time in 1516 he turned the tables on Berkeley by displacing him from the juratship. This temporary demotion was the only check to his municipal progress and from 1514 he regularly headed the list of jurats, having started at the bottom; his precedence, however, he owed to length of service, not to status, for he was never styled 'esquire' as his father had always been. Between 1486 and 1520 he represented Rye at Brotherhood assemblies a score of times, although he only once acted as bailiff to Yarmouth. In 1514 he was one of two commissioners for Rye appointed by the crown to levy the subsidy granted in the last session of the Parliament of 1512. Although the Cinque Ports were specifically exempted from all charges by a proviso to the Subsidy Act (5 Hen. VIII, c.17), some of the inhabitants were assessed; there followed a long struggle with the Exchequer to uphold the ports' immunity, which they eventually won.[8]

The little that is known about Sutton's parliamentary career relates chiefly to his record of attendance. In his first three Parliaments he performed well in this respect, to judge by the days he claimed and was paid for, at the standard rate of 2s. a day. His attendance began to fall off in 1515, when he was paid for only 76 days out of the 101 consumed by the two sessions, and after his last election in 1529 it became progressively more erratic. The task of tracing it is complicated by the practice which the town's chamberlains began to adopt—perhaps as much through prudence as through economy—of paying Sutton by instalments, but he is known to have missed the first 30 days of the second session early in 1531, and the total amount he received for that and the first session (£8 12s. 8d. out of the maximum payable, £13 12s.) represents a loss of 50 days in all. This was nothing, however, to the tale of 1532: for the two sessions of that year Sutton received only 10s. and 20s. respectively, and as both payments were made in arrear and as the number of days was specified on each occasion it seems to follow that Sutton made no more than these two brief appearances at Westminster. His absenteeism may have more than one explanation. It occurred while Sutton was serving his fifth term as mayor, and although Rye several times returned its mayor to Parliament—Sutton himself had been returned in 1510—on this occasion he may have found the combination burdensome. He was at least in his late sixties and perhaps already an ailing man. As he was still alive in August 1532 it was probably not his last

fleeting visit to London which cost him his life from the epidemic which struck down several of his fellow-Members that summer: yet it may well have been plague which killed him between then and the following August when, after nearly 30 years of unbroken appearances there, his name is no longer found on the jurat list. He received no payment for the parliamentary session of February–April 1533 but whether because he was already dead, or too ill to attend, is not clear. His place was filled by Richard Inglet (q.v.). Sutton apparently died intestate, unlike his namesake, a gentleman of Osbaston, Leicestershire, the subject of many contemporary references, who died on 31 Dec. 1530.[9]

[1] Add. 34150, f. 135. [2] Ibid. f. 135. [3] Ibid. f. 136. [4] Rye chamberlains' accts. 4, f. 11v. [5] Date of birth estimated from first reference. PCC 13 Adeane. [6] Rye chamberlains' accts. 3, 4 passim; *Cinque Ports White and Black Bks.* (Kent Arch. Soc. recs. br. xix), 120; *LP Hen. VIII*, i. [7] PCC 13 Adeane; E122/35/18, 200/8. [8] Rye chamberlains' accts. 3, ff. 23, 143, 157, 252; *Cinque Ports White and Black Bks.* passim; *LP Hen. VIII*, i. [9] Rye chamberlains' accts. 3, ff. 43v, 46, 248, 278v, 294, 315; 4, ff. 11v, 21v, 22v, 190v, 192, 205–6, 207v, 222, 226; C142/52/78. The days for which Sutton was paid are as follows, the number of days in each Parliament or session being placed in brackets: 1497, 66(57); 1510, 44(34); 1512(i), 67(55); (ii), 36(47); (iii), 40(41); 1515(i), 42(60); (ii) 34(41).

H.M.

SUTTON, Thomas (by 1514–70/71), of Over Haddon and Kingsmead, Derby, Derbys.

DERBY 1542, 1545, 1547, 1553 (Oct.)

b. by 1514, s. of Alan Sutton of Over Haddon by Alice, da. of one Bridge of Bridgehall, Cheshire. *m.* (1) by 1543, Agnes, da. of Richard Barnard of London, 4s.; (2) Frances, 2s. 1da. *suc.* fa. 1528 or later.[1]

Commr. gaol delivery, Oxford circuit 1537–44, Derby 1542, midland circuit 1543–54, array, Derbys, 1546, relief 1550, goods of churches and fraternities 1553; j.p. Derbys. 1541–62, q. 1562–d.; recorder, Derby by 1545–53 or later; dep. steward, duchy of Lancaster, honor of Tutbury 1551; attorney, council in the north by 1556–8; comptroller, household of the earls of Shrewsbury by 1560.[2]

Thomas Sutton came of a gentle family of Cheshire origin but settled at Over Haddon since the reign of Henry VI. Nothing has come to light about his upbringing, but the appearance of his name on commissions of gaol delivery at the outset of his career and his drafting of his own bill of complaint against neighbours at Over Haddon for withholding some deeds allegedly belonging to him during Mary's reign suggest that he received a legal education. It was perhaps while a student at one of the inns of court that he married Agnes Barnard, 'being a poor maid but well and virtuously brought up'. It was probably his legal ability and connexion with the earls of Shrewsbury which procured for Sutton the recordership of Derby, an office which he was holding in 1545, and this which in turn accounted for his Membership of four Parliaments. It is possible that he also sat in the Parliament of 1539, for which the town's Members are unknown, and that he was the man superseded by Robert Ragg (q.v.) before the opening of the second Parliament of Edward VI's reign in March 1553.[3]

Sutton held land in Derby from 1537 when he leased the site of Kingsmead priory from the crown. In April 1543 he bought the leasehold of the priory from the 5th Earl of Shrewsbury to whom it had been granted by the King, and later in the same year he paid £94 for demesne lands once belonging to the priory in the town. It was as recorder that he was attacked by John Sharpe in the common hall at Derby in 1545. Sharpe and several other townsmen were concerned at the amount of enclosure of common land allowed by the bailiffs and common council, and it was Sutton's own enclosure of the Nun's Meadow which provoked Sharpe's 'seditious attempt' to deprive him of the recordership and to disfranchise the two bailiffs. In the hope of forestalling Sharpe he agreed to surrender the deed authorizing him to enclose the meadow, and at a common hall held shortly before Parliament opened he renounced it. Despite this Sharpe and his associates remained dissatisfied. Once the first session of the Parliament was over Sutton and his fellow-Member William Allestry were summoned with Sharpe before the Privy Council: on learning of his renunciation the Council let Sutton return home but ordered the others to remain near London while the Earl of Shrewsbury had time to 'perceive the inclination of the inhabitants of Derby and restore order'. Despite the earl's efforts Sutton and Sharpe remained on bad terms, and the suit brought against Sutton in the Star Chamber by William Bainbridge* during Edward VI's reign over depasturing a close in Bakewell seems to have been instigated by Sharpe.[4]

It is likely that Sutton had served the Talbots from at least 1538. During the last two years of Mary's reign he was employed as attorney to the council in the north under the 5th Earl's presidency; for this he received a yearly fee of £20, which he took from fines and forfeitures, but apparently without rendering account. He was also Shrewsbury's deputy steward for the honor of Tutbury, and it was as comptroller of his household that he attended the earl's funeral in 1560. He then passed into the service of the 6th Earl, who in May 1570 commended 'his old servant Sutton' to Cecil as one whom few could match in experience.[5]

In 1564 Bishop Bentham judged Sutton 'meet' to remain on the Derbyshire bench, and five years later he was one of the justices who signed the favourable reply to the Council on the state of religion in the county. Within two years more he was

dead: the will which he drew up on 2 Dec. 1570 was proved on the following 27 Apr. Among the lands which he bequeathed to his wife Frances for life were those recently purchased from Godfrey Foljambe* which were to revert to her eldest son Nicholas. To Alan, his eldest son by his first marriage, Sutton left a house, three closes of pasture and all his arable land in Derby, on condition that Alan paid £20 to his brother Thomas, £40 to Bartholomew, whom his father 'would have better advanced' if it had been possible, and £20 to the youngest brother Rowland, an 'unthrifty child who has been much to his cost'. George, Thomas's second son by Frances, was to receive £50 for his preferment, a further £20 at the age of 21 years and an annuity of £3 which Sutton had enjoyed from Sir John Zouche*. Sutton's wife and his only daughter Gertrude were his residuary legatees and executrices, and William Bainbridge one of the witnesses to the will.[6]

[1] Date of birth estimated from his tenure of a messuage in Over Haddon in 1535, *Derbys. Chs.* ed. Jeayes, no. 1331. J. C. Cox *Derbys. Churches*, iv. 89; Harl. 5809, f. 10; PCC 18 Holney; *Duchy of Lancaster's Estates in Derbys.* (Derbys. Arch. Soc. rec. ser. iii), 60. [2] *LP Hen. VIII*, xii–xviii, xx, xxi; *CPR*, 1547–8. pp. 76, 77, 82; 1550–3, p. 395; 1553, pp. 352, 417; 1553–4, pp. 18, 29; 1560–3, p. 435; 1563–6, pp. 20–21; St.Ch.2/25/129; Somerville, *Duchy*, i. 541; SP70/20/42; J. Hunter, *Hallamshire*, 78. [3] Cox, iv. 89; C1/1473/66; PCC 18 Holney. [4] *LP Hen. VIII*, xiii, xix; *APC*, i. 304; C66/721, m. 5; St. Ch.2/25/11, 129; 3/1/87. [5] *LP Hen. VIII*, xiii; SP70/20/424; *HMC Shrewsbury and Talbot* i. 138; ii. 360, 363; *CPR*, 1566–9 p. 317. [6] *Cam. Misc.* ix(3), 43; J. C. Cox, *Derbys. Annals*, 237; PCC 18 Holney.

C.J.B.

SUTTON *see also* DUDLEY

SWILLINGTON, George (by 1508-58/60), of Sutton Bonnington, Notts., and Liddington, Rutland.

LEICESTER 1547, 1553 (Mar.)

b. by 1508, s. of one Swillington of Driffield, Yorks. *educ.* M. Temple. *m.* settlement 1539, Anne, da. of William Turvile of Aston Flamville, Leics., 3da. *suc.* fa. by 1520.[1]

Servant of Cromwell by 1538, of the 3rd Marquess of Dorset by 1544; commr. subsidy, Rutland 1543, relief, Leics. and Rutland 1550; j.p. Leics. 1547, Rutland 1547–*d.*[2]

George Swillington was a descendant of the family long established at Driffield, Yorkshire. His grandfather had four sons, of whom Peter became a cleric, Robert a citizen and draper of London, and Ralph Swillington* recorder of Leicester and Coventry; all three died without issue, leaving property or money to their nephew George, whose father, unnamed in any of the wills, had presumably died earlier. George Swillington, when he died, no longer possessed any of the property in Yorkshire which had been bequeathed to him, but his most prominent uncle's long connexion with the midlands, and his own marriage into a Leicestershire family, are sufficient to explain his removal from his native county.[3]

The date of Swillington's entry into the Middle Temple is unknown, but his first appointment there, as marshal for Christmas 1551, must have come late in his career, for he had first appeared in 1529 acting with a number of other Leicestershire lawyers in a property transaction with the 1st Earl of Rutland. He had then attached himself to Cromwell, who in 1535 wrote to the bishop of Lincoln requiring him to grant Swillington the lease of the prebend of Liddington, which he eventually, although reluctantly, did. Swillington must have proved a satisfactory servant, for he was placed on the panel to try the leaders of the Pilgrimage of Grace, and about the same time Cromwell described him as a man of sufficient freehold in London for any service. In 1538 he was named one of Cromwell's gentlemen 'meet to be preferred to the King's service', but nothing came of this, and after the minister's fall he entered the service of the 3rd Marquess of Dorset, in whose train he went with the army to France in 1544.[4]

By this time Swillington was a modest landowner, for he had acquired by marriage and by purchase both parts of the manor of Sutton Bonnington in Leicestershire. He had also successfully defended a lawsuit brought by his nearest neighbour, Francis Shirley, over fishing and manorial rights, a success which enhanced the value of the property. It was not, however, his own standing in two neighbouring counties which accounts for Swillington's successive returns to Parliament for Leicester under Edward VI: these he owed to his master Dorset, whose ascendancy there was signalized by the bestowal of the stewardship of the honor of Leicester in 1551, and in some measure perhaps also to the repute of his uncle the late recorder. Dorset's advancement, which led by way of the dukedom of Suffolk to his daughter's designation as Edward VI's successor, put other opportunities in Swillington's way, notably in the acquisition of further land: he increased his estate at Sutton Bonnington and was granted ex-monastic property at Normanton-upon-Soar. His attachment to the duke survived the *débacle* of July 1553 for in December of that year he received from Suffolk, probably as a feoffee, the manor of Over Locko, Derbyshire; but from Suffolk's fatal attempt, a few weeks later, to raise Leicestershire and War-wickshire against the government Swillington evidently held aloof. He had already sued out his pardon from the Queen and his retention as a magistrate throughout her reign bespeaks his

acceptability. In July 1554 he took a lease from the crown of a portion of his attainted master's property in Loughborough. With the eclipse of the Grey faction in Leicestershire, however, Swillington's parliamentary career came to an end.[5]

Swillington's date of death has not been discovered; he appeared on the first Elizabethan commission of the peace but in October 1560 his surviving daughters had licence to enter on their inheritance. His widow made a will on 30 Oct. 1562 (proved on 5 June 1567) asking to be buried by her husband in the chancel of Liddington church.[6]

[1] Date of birth estimated from first reference. Farnham *Leics. Med. Peds.* 6; *Vis. Leics.* (Harl. Soc. ii), 55; C1/568/54, 1071/61; *CPR*, 1558-60, p. 447; PCC 19 Stonard. [2] M. L. Robertson, 'Cromwell's servants' (Univ. California Los Angeles Ph.D. thesis, 1975), 568-9; E179/281; *CPR*, 1547-8, pp. 85, 88; 1553, pp. 356-7; 1553-4, p. 23; *LP Hen. VIII*, xix. [3] PCC 3 Porch, 26 Ayloffe, 26 Alen, 29 Alenger. [4] *M.T. Recs.* i. 82; *LP Hen. VIII*, xii, xix. [5] St.Ch.2/29/5, 10, 82/83; C142/127/37; *CPR*, 1553-4, p. 350; 1557-8, p. 177; D. M. Loades, *Two Tudor Conspiracies*, 25-34. [6] *CPR*, 1558-60 p. 447; PCC 19 Stonard; *Vis. Warws.* (Harl. Soc. xii), 11.

S.M.T.

SWILLINGTON, Ralph (by 1485–1525), of the Inner Temple, London and Stivichall, nr. Coventry, Warws.

COVENTRY 1523[1]

b. by 1485, s. of William Swillington of Driffield, Yorks. *educ.* I. Temple. *m.* Elizabeth, da. and h. of William Babthorpe of Ellistown, Leics., wid. of Thomas Essex (*d.*c.1500) of Walham Green, Mdx., *s.p.*[2]

Lent reader, I. Temple 1514, 1523, treasurer 1523-4, gov. 1524-5.

J.p. Leics. 1509-*d.*, Mdx. and Warws. 1524-*d.*; recorder, Leicester 1510-*d.*, Coventry 1515-*d.*; commr. subsidy, Leics. and Leicester 1512, 1514, 1515; other commissions 1506-*d.*; dep. chamberlain, Exchequer c.1521; steward, manor of Cheylesmore, Warws. July 1522-*d.*; apprentice-at-law retained by duchy of Lancaster 1523-4; attorney-gen. Apr. 1524-*d.*[3]

Ralph Swillington was born at Driffield into the illegitimate but only surviving branch of an old Yorkshire family and his marriage brought him an interest in Leicestershire and Warwickshire, although his wife's inheritance in these and three other shires was entailed on William Essex*, her son by her first marriage. Swillington was appointed to the Leicestershire bench and became recorder of Leicester but in 1515, on being chosen recorder of Coventry, he contracted to spend the greater part of the year in that city—a promise from which he was released on becoming attorney-general—and took up residence in the neighbouring parish of Stivichall: in the certificate of musters taken at Coventry in 1522 he was said to be worth 400 marks in goods, and in the following year he was assessed for subsidy on £200 in goods there and at the Inner Temple.[4]

The Members for Coventry in the three Parliaments preceding 1523 are unknown but it is unlikely that Swillington, who evidently owed his election in 1523 to his recordership, was one of them. On the other hand, he may well have sat in the Parliaments of 1512 and 1515 for Leicester as its recorder, especially as he was appointed a subsidy commissioner there in both years: his nephew George Swillington sat for Leicester in both the Parliaments of Edward VI. On Swillington's return to Coventry after the Parliament of 1523 he and his fellow-Member Richard Marler reported on the work of the Parliament and received the thanks of the city.[5]

Swillington received increasing recognition of his ability as a lawyer in the last two or three years of his life when his employment by the duchy of Lancaster was followed by his appointment to the attorney-generalship. As attorney-general he initiated a successful suit against the feoffees of the 3rd Earl of Kent who had refused to surrender lands which the earl had sold to Henry VII. In July 1524 he was appointed to the commission for the redress of grievances in the north, but the time was inopportune and in the following month Cardinal Wolsey recalled him. In 1525 he spent some time in Coventry suppressing an insurrection; he was said to have kept the people of Coventry 'well in awe'. His forceful character is illustrated by a quarrel with Thomas Carminowe which came into the Star Chamber about 1521.[6]

Swillington was dead by December 1525. By his will of 11 July 1525, proved on 14 Feb. 1526, he left land he had purchased in Driffield to his nephew George Swillington, with 100 marks and £40 for the purchase of certain lands, and 100 marks to his niece Elizabeth. He named as executors his wife and his brother Peter Swillington, a priest. He asked to be buried in the Temple church but made arrangements for the erection of a memorial at Driffield to his father and brothers.[7]

[1] LP Hen. VIII, iv. app. 1. [2] Date of birth estimated from first reference. Farnham Leics. Med. Peds. 24; C1/355/46. [3] LP Hen. VIII i–iv; Recs. Leicester, ed. Bateson, iii. 15, 25, 459; Coventry Leet Bk. (EETS cxxxiv), 654; Statutes, iii. 80, 84, 113, 115, 168; CPR, 1494–1509, pp. 507, 561; St.Ch.2/24/76; Coventry Recs. ed. Jeaffreson, B.57; Somerville, Duchy, i. 453. [4] PCC 3 Porch; Thoresby Soc. xv. 210–11; C1/355/46; Coventry Leet Bk. 654, 688; VCH Warws. viii. 93; Coventry accts. var. 18, f. 111v; E179/192/125; Cal. I.T. Recs. i. 458. [5] LP Hen. VIII iv. app. 1. [6] C1/567/16; LP Hen. VIII, iv; St.Ch.2/24/76, 32/77. [7] LP Hen. VIII iv; PCC 3 Porch.

S.M.T.

SWINBURNE (WYNBORNE), John (by 1526–77 or later), of Chopwell, co. Dur.

NORTHUMBERLAND 1554 (Apr.)

b. by 1526, s. of John Swinburne of Chopwell by Anne, da. of Sir John Clavering of Callaley, Northumb., wid. of Sir Robert Raymes of Shortflat, Northumb. *m.* Anne, da. of George Smith of Nunstainton, co. Dur., 2s. *suc.* fa. c.1546.[1]

J.p. Northumb. 1547–64; escheator 1548–9, 1553–4; commr. enclosure upon the middle marches 1552/53; servant of Henry Neville, 5th Earl of Westmorland, by 1555; steward, baronies of Bolbec and Bywell for 5th and 6th Earls of Westmorland by 1562–9.[2]

On the list of Members for Mary's second Parliament both the knights returned for Northumberland are styled 'miles'. As neither John Swinburne nor Robert Horsley is known to have been knighted, the suffix was perhaps an error made in the compilation of the list. In the absence of the return it cannot be determined if the compiler had repeated a mistake on that document.[3]

The Swinburnes had been prominent in the north-east since the 13th century and under the Tudors were described as 'gentlemen of great friendship, kindred and alliance with most of the honourable and worshipful in Northumberland'. Of the two John Swinburnes who can be traced in the region during the 1550s the son of George Swinburne of Edlingham was the less distinguished, although he belonged to a senior branch of the family and his sister Marion was married to George Heron who sat for the shire in 1555. The knight of the shire of April 1554 was almost certainly not John Swinburne of Edlingham but his better known namesake in local administration who lived at Chopwell on the border of Durham with Northumberland. John Swinburne of Chopwell obtained a grant of arms in 1551 and the freehold of the manor of Chopwell from John Dudley, Duke of Northumberland, a year later. His father and namesake had been a servant of the 4th Earl of Westmorland and he himself became steward to the 5th and 6th Earls. His single experience of Parliament was presumably favoured by the 5th Earl, who although not a considerable landowner in Northumberland could through kinship with the Percys draw on their traditional support in the county; two months before the election the earl let his lands near Hexham to Swinburne. A dispute between Swinburne and the earl's brother-in-law Sir Roger Cholmley*, referred to the council in the north early in 1555, seems to have strained his relationship with the earl for several months and may account for his failure to be re-elected to the second Parliament of 1554.[4]

Swinburne was perhaps an experienced soldier by the beginning of Mary's Scottish war. (The captain of his name taken prisoner by the Scots and ransomed in 1546 was probably his father, who died not long after making his will on 20 Sept. 1545.) He helped to victual the Protector's army against Scotland and the forts erected during 1547 and 1548, and when he assisted Westmorland and Thomas

Percy*, 1st Earl of Northumberland, in the defence of the borders his reports were forwarded to the 5th Earl of Shrewsbury. After the accession of Elizabeth he loaned Northumberland £23 and served on the commission to survey his property in the county. Swinburne's connexions with the Percys were not always happy: he quarrelled with several of their followers and in 1568 with the earl's brother (Sir) Henry Percy*. Disagreements with the bishop of Durham and others gave rise to litigation and to judge from his opponents' remarks he was a detested figure. It was not, however, his personal short-comings but his Catholicism which led to his removal from the bench. Bishop Pilkington informed the Council in 1564 that Swinburne had been fined for keeping a priest in his house to say mass and five years later Cecil received information about his being 'evil in religion'. Swinburne was one of the few 'gentlemen of value' in the north who joined the rising of 1569 in favour of Mary Queen of Scots. After its failure he escaped to the Netherlands with the 6th Earl of Westmorland, with whom he was attainted by the Parliament of 1571. Philip II granted him a pension on his arrival in Madrid in 1573, but he seems not to have settled in Spain and it is as a refugee in Namur during 1577 that he is last glimpsed.[5]

[1] Date of birth estimated from first reference. *Vis. of the North*, i (Surtees Soc. cxxii), 53, 182–5; Surtees, *Dur.* ii. 278. [2] *CPR*, 1547–8, p. 87; 1553, p. 327; 1553–4 p. 22; 1560–3, p. 441; 1563–6, p. 25; Hodgson, *Northumb.* i. 360; *Northumb. Co. Hist.* vi. 82, 229. [3] C193/32/1, f. 4v. [4] *Northumb. Co. Hist.* vi. passim; vii. 132–3; *Arch. Ael.* (ser. 4), xii. 128; *Vis. of the North*, i. 53; *Grantees of Arms* (Harl. Soc. lxvi), 247; *CPR*, 1550–3, p. 231; *HMC Talbot and Shrewsbury*, i. 28. [5] *LP Hen. VIII*, xxi; *APC*, i. 393; Surtees, i. p. lxxvi; ii. 276–8; York wills 29, f. 149; *Northumb. Co. Hist.* iii. 77–78; iv. 53, 55; vi. 82, 86, 120, 133, 229, 281, 367, 379; ix. 85; x. 189; xii. 165; *HMC Shrewsbury and Talbot*, ii. 60; *HMC Rutland*, i. 38–39; *CSP Dom. Add.* 1566–79, pp. 90–91, 95, 113, 177, 185, 191–2, 468; 1601–3, *Add.* 1547–65, p. 350; *Northumb. Estate Accts.* (Surtees Soc. clxiii), 41, 50; B. N. Wilson, 'Changes of the Ref. period in Dur. and Northumb.' (Durham Univ. Ph.D. thesis, 1939), 412, 475, 479, 483–6, 519–21, 525; *Cam. Misc.* ix(3), 65–67; *Memorials of the Rebellion of 1569*, ed. Sharp, 8, 33, 45, 197–9, 229–30, 264; E164/38/202–7; Northumb. RO, Swinburne mss 1/183, 184, 189; *CPR*, 1572–5, passim.

M.J.T.

SWYNNERTON, Humphrey (by 1516–62), of Swynnerton and Hilton, Staffs.

STAFFORD   1554 (Apr.)

b. by 1516, 1st s. of Thomas Swynnerton of Swynnerton and Hilton, by Alice, da. of Sir Humphrey Stanley† of Pipe Ridware and Clifton Campville. *m.* by 1540, Cassandra (bur. 7 Jan. 1570), da. of Sir John Giffard* of Chillington, 2da. *suc.* fa. ?1541.[1]

Bailiff, former estates of Brewood priory, Staffs. by 1537; steward, Cannock forest, Staffs. 24 June 1541–*d.*; escheator, Staffs. 1559–60.[2]

In June 1541 Humphrey Swynnerton entered upon a landed inheritance of which the chief component, at Hilton north of Wolverhampton, was assessed for subsidy four years later at 40s. on an annual value of £20. He also added a number of his father's local offices to his own as bailiff of Brewood, one which he had retained after the purchase of that priory by (Sir) Thomas Giffard*, whose sister he had probably already married. Of his outlying properties, he sold the manors of Great and Little Barrow, Cheshire, in 1555 to Sir John Savage, who had long claimed them.[3]

It was the Giffard connexion which gave Swynnerton his only spell in the Commons: the sheriff who returned him was his brother-in-law and his fellow-Member was his youthful nephew John Giffard. He shared the Giffards' religious conservatism and doubtless supported the Catholic restoration. His piety found expression in his rebuilding of Shareshill church and in his preservation of a breviary disposed of by Lichfield under Edward VI and returned there by him on Mary's accession.[4]

It was as 'late of Swynnerton *alias* of Hilton' that Swynnerton sued out a general pardon in January 1559 but at Swynnerton that he made his will on 6 July 1561. He invoked the aid of the Virgin Mary and the company of heaven to attain salvation, asked to be buried, if he died at Swynnerton, in the lady chapel before the place where her image had stood, or if at Hilton (where he was to die) in the chancel of Shareshill where the image of St. Luke had stood, and left 3s. 4d. to the priests at Hampton to pray for his soul. After the expiry of his wife's life interest in his lands and goods they were to be divided equally between his daughters, whose husbands Henry Vernon* and Francis Gatacre he remembered with rings. According to the inscription formerly at Shareshill, Swynnerton died on 25 Aug. 1562. No inquisition has been found, although a writ was issued on 17 Oct. 1562, but the will was proved on 9 Feb. 1563 and the deed allotting Swynnerton to Elizabeth Gatacre (the widow of William Fitzherbert*) and Hilton to Margaret Vernon was drawn up on 8 May 1564.[5]

[1] Date of birth estimated from first reference. J. C. Wedgwood, *Staffs. Parl. Hist.* (Wm. Salt Arch. Soc.), i. 340; *LP Hen. VIII*, xvi; *Wm. Salt Arch. Soc.* vii(2), 56, 59. [2] *LP Hen. VIII*, xvi. [3] NRA 6242, p. 28; *LP Hen. VIII*, xv, xvi, xxi; E179/177/137; *Wm. Salt Arch. Soc.* vii(2), 57. [4] *VCH Staffs.* iii. 168–9; v. 179. [5] *CPR*, 1558–60, p. 163; 1560–3, p. 448; *Wm. Salt Arch. Soc.* vii(2), 57; 1926, pp. 119–20; PCC 8 Chayre; Pevsner, *Staffs.* 234.

A.D.K.H.

SYDENHAM, Sir John (by 1493–1557), of Brimpton, Som.

SOMERSET   1554 (Apr.)

b. by 1493, 1st s. of John Sydenham of Brimpton by Elizabeth, da. of Sir Humphrey Audley. *m.* by 1527, Ursula, da. of Sir Giles Brydges of Coberley, Glos., 6s. 3da. *suc.* fa. 6 Dec. 1542. Kntd. 3 Nov. 1549.[1]

J.p. Som. ?1541, 1543–*d.*, commr. benevolence 1544/45, musters 1545–6, relief 1550, goods of churches and fraternities 1553; sheriff, Som. and Dorset 1546–7, 1554–5.[2]

The Sydenhams, a prolific and widespread family in Tudor Somerset and Dorset, played a surprisingly small part in the politics of the period, preferring to live quietly on their estates. Sir John Sydenham is the only member of the family known to have sat in Parliament during the century.[3]

He is unlikely to have been the John Sydenham (probably his younger brother) in the service of Cromwell and the King between 1538 and 1542, and nothing has come to light about his career until 1542, when he succeeded to his father's considerable estates in the south-east of Somerset: it may have been the father who was named to the county bench in 1541. Sydenham served in the French campaign of 1544 and received payment for 100 men in the following year. His knighthood following the fall of the Protector Somerset in 1549 was perhaps a reward for support given to the Earl of Warwick during the *coup d'état* against the Protector, but it could have been a douceur for a man experienced in local administration in an area dominated by the Seymours. If Sydenham was a supporter of Warwick's he is not known to have sat in the Parliament of March 1553. His return a year later in April 1554 is likely to have been the work of his influential brother-in-law Sir John Brydges*, created Baron Chandos of Sudeley shortly after the Parliament opened. On 1 May the bill to make Glastonbury the shire town of Somerset was committed after its second reading to Sydenham: whether he had anything to do with its fate, for it got no further before the dissolution four days later, is not known. Pricked sheriff for a second term in the autumn he figured in county affairs for the remaining two-and-a-half years of his life.[4]

Sydenham made his will on 8 Apr. 1557. By it he divided some of his recently purchased lands among younger sons and left 400 marks for the marriage of his daughter Anne and certain lands in East and West Coker to his wife. The rest of his lands eventually fell to his eldest son after many had been settled on his wife for her life. He died eight days later and his widow, sole executrix and residuary legatee, proved the will in the following month.[5]

[1] Date of birth estimated from age at fa.'s i.p.m., C142/70/9. *Vis. Som.* ed. Weaver, 76; G. F. Sydenham, *Sydenham Fam.* 117–18. [2] *LP Hen. VIII,* xvi, xviii–xxi; *CPR,* 1547–8, to 1555–7 passim. [3] Sydenham, 117–18. [4] *LP Hen. VIII,* xiii–xxi; M. L. Robertson, 'Cromwell's servants' (Univ. California Los Angeles Ph.D. thesis, 1975), 569; *CJ,* i. 36. [5] C142/114/23; PCC 15 Wrastley.

R.V.

SYLLARDE *see* **SULYARD**

SYLSTERNE *see* **SHILSTON**

SYMONDS, William (c.1480–1547 or later) of New Windsor, Berks.

NEW WINDSOR   1529, 1542[1]

   b. c.1480, s. of Andrew Symonds *alias* Beerman of New Windsor by Joan. *educ.* ?I. Temple. *suc.* fa. 1540.[2]
   Member of guild, New Windsor 1519, bailiff 1520, mayor 1528–9, 1529–30, 1541–2; commr. subsidy 1524, 1540, 1541.[3]

An analysis of the many references to men of the time who bore the name William Symonds suggests that there were three whose careers may be distinguished with some clarity. The first, a son of John Simon* of Exeter, was a minor official in the royal household who served as a victualler and captain in the navy during the French wars of 1513 and 1522 and later followed his father into customs administration, both in Devon and at Southampton: he died in 1537. Then there was a lawyer of Warwickshire origin, whose career can be traced at the Inner Temple between 1530 and 1559, when he died shortly after his summons to become a serjeant. Although neither of these men is to be thought of in connexion with the seat at New Windsor, the first of them was probably Cromwell's nominee in 1532 to fill the vacancy at Lyme Regis caused by the death of John Pyne.[4]

It is William Symonds, the son of Andrew Symonds *alias* Beerman of Windsor, who may be taken to have sat in the Commons for that borough. Andrew Symonds, a rich brewer who had been mayor of Windsor in 1517, made his will on 12 June 1540. Of his two sons William was probably the elder as his brother Simon, who had been admitted to King's College, Cambridge, from Eton in 1505 at the age of 17, entered the Church. But the terms of the will suggest that William, although the heir, may not have continued in his father's business. Andrew Symonds left an alehouse to his daughter Christian Aley, who had married into another prosperous family of the town, and a beerhouse to his godson Andrew Aley, with lands in the parish of Burnham, while William Symonds received three tenements in Windsor, with an inn called the *Saracen's Head*, and six more tenements 'at the town's end', so long as he should not contest the will; all movables were bequeathed to Christian and Andrew Aley, who were to be executors, with Simon Symonds as an overseer. If William Symonds did not follow his father's trade he could have been the lawyer who was pardoned all offices and vacations at the Inner Temple in 1533 and whose designation as 'the elder' distinguishes him from the Warwickshire lawyer. On the subsidy rolls for 1524–5 William Symonds had been assessed to pay only 9s. on goods worth £18; in October 1540, after his father's death, the sum rose to 23s. on lands worth £23. He was the only townsman to be assessed on lands rather than goods in 1540 and again in 1542.[5]

The prominence of Andrew Symonds made his son a fitting choice for the Parliament of 1529 with Thomas Ward I, who held offices at the castle and estates in the neighbourhood. William Symonds, with ten years of municipal life behind him, and as mayor at the time of the election, was doubtless known to the King. He was active on behalf of the corporation, receiving £5 4s.2d. in 1530 'for divers parcels of charges at Westminster' and a further 2s. for riding to Wallingford; at the same time the mayor's annual fee of 20s. was trebled and paid to him for the expenses of his previous year's term of office. In 1531 a payment to Symonds of 40s. 'for his costs at the Parliament the 29th day of Apr. in the 23rd year of . . . King Henry VIII' presumably refers to the second session, which had in fact ended on 31 Mar. 1531; if so, it represents a rate of only some 6d. a day for that session. The fact that no payment was made to his colleague suggests that Symonds was a local choice, balancing that of Ward, the office holder.[6]

Although clearly not the man suggested by Cromwell for Lyme Regis, William Symonds of Windsor appears on two other lists drawn up by Cromwell in the course of the Parliament. Of these, the first may represent the opposition, both religious and economic, to the bill in restraint of appeals to Rome. The second list, which dates probably from December 1534 and includes Symonds's fellow-Member Thomas Ward, represents a wider range of opinion and may have been connected with an attempt to reach a compromise over the treasons bill then under consideration. Thus if the first list may be taken as a pointer to Symonds's religion, the second may illustrate his standing as a Member. He was to sit for Windsor again in the Parliament of 1542, when he was paid £4 by the borough for his expenses, and may also have sat in 1536 and 1539.[7]

Although there is no evidence of such a connexion as that enjoyed by William Symonds of Devon, his namesake seems to have had some influence with Cromwell. His brother Simon, a King's chaplain, was appointed to canonries at Lichfield and Windsor on 7 July 1535, and on 18 Aug. William wrote from Windsor with thanks for this preferment but asking that Simon should also have the hospital of St. Nicholas at Salisbury, whereupon he would trouble the minister no more. This disclaimer notwithstanding, he wrote again 12 months later, with grateful reference to the appointments at Lichfield, Salisbury and Windsor, followed by a reminder that the archdeaconry of Suffolk was likely to fall vacant

through death; in order that Simon should be able to keep due hospitality at Windsor his brother solicited this for him also. His preferment was not to make Simon Symonds a wholehearted supporter of the new ecclesiastical policy, for a sermon he preached at Paul's Cross on 6 Aug. 1536 was sent with a complaint to the minister, and in the following spring the bishop of Rochester, discussing the proposed preachers for Easter Week, advised Cromwell to admonish Dr. Symonds, in the belief that he would then do well. His appointment to the archdeaconry suggests that he did.[8]

William Symonds gave less satisfaction with the leading part that he played in the trial of the Windsor martyrs in 1543. Foxe describes the persecutor-in-chief as a lawyer, and although the better known lawyer of this name was the Warwickshire one already mentioned, not only does Foxe make it clear that the offender was a Windsor man but it is hard to believe that the other would have lived down such an episode and have received promotion in 1559. Foxe's description thus lends colour to the identification of Symonds with the Templar exempted from offices and vacations in 1533. According to Foxe, Symonds had campaigned against the three eventually burnt.[9]

Another defendant, the lawyer Robert Bennet, had been saved from trial by sickness. A Thomas Bennet shared with Andrew Symonds the highest subsidy assessment in Windsor, and Foxe says that Robert Bennet and William Symonds were 'the greatest familiars and company keepers that were in all Windsor' and 'cleaved together like burrs' in all matters save religion, where one was a reformer and the other 'a cankered papist'. The friendship moved Symonds to procure Bennet's release with the help of the bishops of Salisbury and Winchester, but this intervention did not lessen his unpopularity after the trial. Foxe saw evil meet its deserts when the King, told of the conspiracy behind the charges, ordered the arrest of Dr. John London, Symonds and the clerk to the court; all three were sentenced to the pillory and to ride about Windsor, Reading and Newbury with paper caps on their heads, facing their horses' tails. That the hounding of Symonds persisted is shown by a Privy Council letter of 23 Jan. 1547 commanding the people of Windsor to cease vexing him for his past misconduct.[10]

At the time of the trial Symonds was in trouble of his own at Windsor over some property claimed by David Mathew, in the right of his wife Elizabeth. A suit was brought in Chancery against William Symonds 'gentleman', alleging wrongful detention of deed, to which he replied that he had enjoyed the premises for 18 years past, having received them from a London baker long before Elizabeth Mathew's supposed father had acquired any claim. He added that the town bailiffs, at Mathew's instigation, had barred him from the house and later arrested him for trespass. Amidst all this disgrace William Symonds disappears from view. He is last recorded on a subsidy roll in 1543, and after his third mayoralty in 1541 he is mentioned in the chamberlain's accounts only once, when paid 8s. for an unspecified purpose in 1547. Then in his sixties, he may have quitted Windsor for a less hostile milieu or have succumbed under the obloquy heaped upon him.[11]

[1] Windsor recs. Wi/FA c.1, f. 46. [2] Date of birth estimated from that of supposedly younger bro., *Al. Cant.* i(4), 78; R. R. Tighe and J. E. Davis, *Windsor Annals*, i. 515-16; PCC 13 Alenger. [3] Windsor recs. Wi/FA c.1, ff. 12, 13, 28v, 29v, 45v; E179/73/130, 153, 158v. [4] *LP Hen. VIII*, i, iii, iv, vi–ix, xii–xiv, xxi, add.; *Cal. I.T. Recs.* i. 95, 201; *APC*, vii. 18; *Dugdale Soc.* iv. 72; PCC 36 Mellershe. [5] PCC 13 Alenger; *Al. Cant.* i(4), 78; *Cal. I.T. Recs.* i. 102; E179/73/153, 158. [6] Windsor recs. Wi/FA c.1, ff. 31, 33. [7] *LP Hen. VIII*, vii. 1522(ii) citing SP1/87, f. 106v; ix. 1077 citing SP1/99, p. 234; Windsor recs. Wi/FA c.1, f. 46. [8] *LP Hen. VIII*, viii, ix, xi–xiii. [9] Foxe, *Acts and Mons.* v. 464-94. [10] Ibid. v. 494-6; *APC*, i. 567-8. [11] C1/1143/17-21; Windsor recs. Wi/FA c.1, f. 53; E179/73/170.

T.F.T.B.

TADLOWE, George (by 1505–57), of London.

PETERSFIELD	1547[1]
GUILDFORD	1554 (Apr.)
GRAMPOUND	1554 (Nov.)
CAMELFORD	1555

b. by 1505. *m.* (1) Joan; (2) Anne; at least 1s. 2da.[2]
Searcher of woollen cloths, London 3 Sept. 1552; gov. Christ's hospital, London 6 Oct. 1552; master, St. Bartholomew's hospital by 1557.[3]

George Tadlowe's parentage has not been established, but presumably his father was of Kentish origin as Tadlowe's uncle William Tadlowe* was born at Canterbury and made his career at New Romney. He received an education (perhaps at St. Paul's) which enabled him to move with ease in cultivated circles, even though his Latin was 'not so well seen'. He appears not to have attended either a university or an inn of court, but as a young man he set himself up as a haberdasher in the capital and plied that trade until his death: by 1526 he valued his stock of feathers and caps at £100, but the consortium of merchants who took it over claimed that it was worth only a quarter of that sum. He traded in a large way with the Continent and imported wine from Bordeaux as well as haberdashery from the Netherlands and Spain. In 1534 a dispute over money brought Tadlowe and his factor at Bordeaux to the notice of Cromwell and in the following year the minister heard of him again, when he took sanctuary at Westminster to evade his creditors. His difficulties arose from the loss 'of his substance beyond the sea and in the sea by divers misfortunes

of shipwrecks as well as by divers evil debtors'; while in sanctuary he reached an agreement which one of the creditors, so he alleged, broke by suing him in the sheriffs' court. Tadlowe's business enterprises were punctuated by such proceedings: he was often obliged to go to law for his money and on other occasions he was himself sued for debt. Nevertheless he seems to have prospered. He acquired a little property in the City and took a lease of the *White Horse* tavern in Langborn ward; in 1541 he was rated for subsidy on goods worth £40 in the parish of St. Mary Wolnoth. He helped set up St. Bartholomew's and Christ's hospitals during Edward VI's reign, and retained an active interest in both foundations until his death.[4]

Tadlowe's return to Parliament in 1547 is not easy to explain: in what appears to have been his first experience of the Commons he was chosen by a recently enfranchised Hampshire borough. As Petersfield was famous for its serges and new draperies, Tadlowe may have been able to rely on business connexions for his election there, especially as his fellow-Member was another London merchant (and one of his debtors), Laurence Elveden *alias* Cattaneo. Yet it is likely that he was also beholden to William Paulet, Baron St. John, a Hampshire magnate prominent both on Edward VI's Council and in the City: St. John had an interest in the borough during the minority of its lord, Henry Weston*, and in 1547 the sheriff of Hampshire was his brother George Paulet. It is London which seems to have taken most advantage of Tadlowe's Membership. When early in the first session a bill for the river Thames was introduced in the Lords, the City asked him to draw up arguments against it: it is not without interest that St. John was on the Lords committee for the bill, and that Tadlowe himself was afterwards deputed to defend the City's interest in the river before the Middlesex justices of sewers.[5]

Tadlowe did not re-enter the House until after Mary's accession, when St. John was lord treasurer and Marquess of Winchester, and this nobleman's hand can again be discerned behind his three further appearances at Westminster during the reign. He must have been almost as unknown at Guildford as he had been at Petersfield, yet he once more took the first place and in doing so ousted William More II, who had brought displeasure on himself in the previous House. Since More shared the patronage of Guildford with the 12th Earl of Arundel, a connexion by marriage of Winchester's and at this time an enthusiastic Marian, it is likely that Arundel used his position to replace More by Tadlowe, a man more acceptable to the Queen: in this he may have been supported by Henry Weston, now out of his wardship and installed at Sutton Place, who was himself returned on this occasion for Tadlowe's former borough. At the next election More could evidently not be kept out again, and Tadlowe's patrons there turned to Cornwall for a seat, probably enlisting the help of their kinsmen the Arundells of Lanherne: that Tadlowe was not the choice of the electors at Grampound is shown by the insertion of his name, like that of his fellow-Member Robert Vaughan II on the indenture over an erasure. His experience was put to use by his colleagues when on 3 Dec. 1554 a bill for Welsh linen and cotton was committed to him; his scrutiny may have killed it for it is not heard of again. Tadlowe was not among the Members of this Parliament who left early and without leave, and the next general election saw him returned for another Cornish borough by the sheriff, Sir John Arundell* of Lanherne. This time, however, he was to compromise himself by voting with the opposition, led by Sir Anthony Kingston, against a government bill. His conduct could not have been unexpected, for he was an acquaintance of Cecil's and a hanger-on of Protestant groups. Whether it would have meant his exclusion from the Queen's last Parliament we cannot say, as before this was summoned he was dead.[6]

Tadlowe is remembered less as a parliamentarian than as the man who persuaded Ralph Robinson to complete his translation of *Utopia*. In the dedication of that work to Cecil, Robinson reveals his esteem for Tadlowe,

a man of sage and discreet wit, and in wordly matters by long use well experienced . . . an honest citizen of London, and in the same City well accepted, and of good reputation at whose request . . . I first took upon my weak and feeble shoulders the heavy and weighty burden of . . . this great enterprise. This man . . . ceased not by all measures possible continually to assault me, until he had at the last, what by the force of his pithy arguments and strong reasons, and what by his authority so persuaded me, that he caused me to agree and consent to the imprinting hereof. He therefore, as the chief persuader, must take upon him the danger, which upon this bold and rash enterprise shall ensue.

This lesser Maecenas was a sick man when he made his will on 28 Apr. 1557. He revoked his earlier wills and before providing for his second wife, his children and the poor, he asked to be buried beside his first wife in the church of St. Magnus and left seven silk banners to the church where he worshipped. He was buried in accordance with his wishes on the following 12 May.[7]

¹ C219/19/84; Hatfield 207. ² Date of birth estimated from first reference. PCC 22 Wrastley. ³ City of London RO, Guildhall, rep. 12(2), f. 525; E. H. Pearce, *Annals Christ Church*, 14; *Machyn's Diary* (Cam. Soc. xlii), 136. ⁴ Canterbury prob. reg. C26, f. 149;

More, *Utopia* (1556), address of translator to reader; C1/821/41–43, 910/1, 1077/3; *LP Hen. VIII*, iv, vii, xiv, add.; E179/144/120; Pearce, 14, 23; N. Moore, *St. Bartholomew's Hosp.* ii. 194. ⁵ Egerton 2094, f. 76; City of London RO, Guildhall jnl. 15, f. 339, rep. 12(1), f. 219v; *LJ*, i. 300. ⁶ C219/23/29; *CJ*, i. 38; Guildford mus. Loseley 1331/2. ⁷ More, *Utopia* (1551), title-page, dedication; *DNB* (Robinson, Ralph); PCC 22 Wrastley; *Machyn's Diary*, 136.

P.H.

TADLOWE, William (by 1495–1556), of New Romney, Kent.

NEW ROMNEY 1539,[1] 1542,[2] 1547*,[3] 1553 (Oct.)[4]

b. by 1495. *m.* (2) Elizabeth Rocke; 1s. 1da.[5]
Bailiff, New Romney 1523, 1540–1, jurat 1531–*d.*, chamberlain 1531–3, 1538–9; commr. subsidy 1523, 1524; bailiff to Yarmouth 1532.[6]

William Tadlowe, born at Canterbury, was admitted to the freedom of New Romney on 9 Dec. 1516. From 1518 to 1520 he was deputy to the bailiff of New Romney, at that time appointed by the archbishop of Canterbury; by 1523 he had become bailiff, and as such headed the list of subsidy commissioners appointed for Romney.[7]

Tadlowe was paid at least £36 by the chamberlains of New Romney for his attendance at four Parliaments. The port itself elected him five times, the third time on 6 Feb. 1552 as replacement for the deceased John Dering, but Sir Thomas Cheyne*, lord warden of the Cinque Ports, refused to return him to the Parliament of March 1553; Tadlowe was given 20s. by Romney in compensation for being 'put away by our lord warden from his election'. Before the next election he and Richard Bunting*, who had likewise been chosen by Romney and superseded, went to see the warden to 'require his favour concerning the election of burgesses', and this time Tadlowe was returned and attended throughout the session. He also represented New Romney at Mary's coronation on 1 Oct. 1553, four days before the opening of Parliament.[8]

Tadlowe was prominent in the assemblies of the Cinque Ports from 1531. In 1542 he was among those chosen to petition the King for relief from the fifteenth and tenth, and in 1547, after the accession of Edward VI, Tadlowe, Nicholas Ballard and Lawrence Elveden *alias* Cattaneo* were given an allowance of 2s. a day for further negotiations about taxation and the renewal of the port's charter. In 1554 the latest charter, reissued by Mary, was committed to Tadlowe's charge; in July 1556 it was transferred to the custody of John Cheseman*, probably when Tadlowe died.[9]

Tadlowe's will, made on 14 Apr. 1556, was proved on the following 9 Oct. He asked to be buried in the parish churchyard, next to his late wife. To his second wife, his executrix, he left the house in which he lived, and another house in New Romney, all his household stuff, sheep and cattle, corn and grain, and to her son, John Rocke, £6 and a cow. He also provided for his son Thomas and his married daughter, and made a bequest to his brother's son, George Tadlowe* of London. The will was witnessed by Richard Bunting, John Cheseman, Gregory Holton* and Simon Padyham*.[10]

[1] Romney chamberlains' accts. 1528–80, ff. 37, 39v. [2] Ibid. f. 53. [3] Romney ct. bk. 1552–9, f. 1v. [4] Bodl. e Museo 17. [5] Date of birth estimated from admission as freeman. Canterbury prob. reg. C26, f. 149. [6] Romney chamberlains' accts. 1528–80, ff. 12 seq., 38v; *LP Hen. VIII*, iii, iv; *Cinque Ports White and Black Bks.* (Kent Arch., Soc. recs. br. xix), 214. [7] Romney assessment bk. 1516–22, ff. 71, 117v, 131; *Cinque Ports White and Black Bks.* 176; *HMC 5th Rep*, 550. [8] Romney chamberlains' accts. 1528–80, ff. 37, 39v, 53, 55v, 56, 59, 70, 80v, 81. [9] *Cinque Ports White and Black Bks.* 212, 228–9, 236, 238, 240–1, 251, 253. [10] Canterbury prob. reg. C26, f. 149.

H.M.

TAILBOYS, Sir Gilbert (by 1500–30), of Kyme, Lincs.

LINCOLNSHIRE 1529*

b. by 1500, 1st s. of Sir George Tailboys, *de jure* 9th Lord Kyme (*d.*21 Sept. 1538), by 2nd w. Elizabeth, da. of Sir William Gascoigne of Gawthorpe, Yorks. *m.* by 1522, Elizabeth (*d.*1539/41), da. of (Sir) John Blount* of Kinlet, Salop, 2s. 1da. Kntd. May/Nov. 1524; *cr.* Lord Tailboys, adm. Lords 1 Dec. 1529.[1] Commr. sewers, Lincs. 1521, subsidy, Lincs. (Lindsey) 1523; j.p. Lincs. (Lindsey) 1522–*d.*, (Holland, Kesteven) 1528–*d.*; sheriff, Lincs. Jan.–Nov. 1526; bailiff and keeper of castle, Tattershall, Lincs. 1525; gent. the chamber in 1527.[2]

The Tailboys family, originally of Durham and Northumberland, acquired its Lincolnshire estates, together with the Northumberland lordship of Redesdale and a claim to the barony of Kyme and the earldom of Angus, through a 14th-century marriage into the house of Umfraville. Sir Luke Tailboys was knight of the shire for Northumberland in 1300 and Sir Gilbert Tailboys was the fourth of his line to serve as knight for Lincolnshire. In or about 1499 his father, who had been sheriff of both Lincolnshire and Northumberland, contracted 'the land evil', which enfeebled his mind, at Berwick while lieutenant of the east and middle marches. Although badly enough stricken to be thought a lunatic, he made a temporary recovery which enabled him to renew his service to the crown: a knight of the body in December 1509, when he was licensed to appoint justices in Redesdale, he fought in the French campaign of 1513. Within four years, however, he was again a sick man and in March 1517 the custody of his person and lands was entrusted to Cardinal Wolsey, whom Tailboys had first known as dean of Lincoln, and to eight of his Lincolnshire relations and neighbours, several of whom had been named executors in his will of five years before. These guardians appear to have been chosen in accordance with at least the spirit of an agreement made with the crown at the time of the first illness.[3]

Wolsey evidently took an interest in Gilbert Tailboys, who was presumably the man of that name listed among the cardinal's servants in 1517, and it was probably at his suggestion (as one of his critics was later to claim), if also with the King's approval, that Tailboys was married to Elizabeth Blount, once a maid of honour to Queen Catherine and more recently the mother of the King's son Henry Fitzroy. The marriage is usually assigned to 1519, the year of the boy's birth, but the first reference found to the pair is a grant made to them in June 1522 of the Warwickshire manor of Rokeby. By that time Tailboys had been appointed to the commission of the peace in Lincolnshire and had shared with Wolsey and others in a grant of the wardship of George Vernon*, later his brother-in-law. In 1523 he received the first of three nominations for the shrievalty of Lincolnshire, although he was not pricked, and despite his youthfulness he may have sat for the shire in the Parliament of that year: the name of only one of the knights, Sir John Hussey, is known, and he was to be returned with Tailboys in 1529 and then raised to the peerage with him. It was this Parliament, too, which saw the passing of an Act (14 and 15 Hen. VIII, c.34) to ensure a life estate in certain Tailboys manors to Elizabeth Tailboys: ostensibly a response to a petition from Sir George Tailboys and his son, moved by gratitude for the 'great sums' and 'many benefits' brought to them by the marriage, the Act may have resulted either from the King's wish to make further provision for his ex-mistress or from Gilbert Tailboys's to remove some of the family property from the control of his father's guardians. Five years later Tailboys's mother complained to Wolsey that she could not meet all her son's demands as well as maintain her household and bestow her four daughters in marriage: of these, Anne took as her first husband Sir Edward Dymoke*, Margaret became the wife of George Vernon, and Elizabeth married Sir Christopher Willoughby, to whom she bore the Sir William who sat for Lincolnshire in 1545. Lady Tailboys also reminded Wolsey that her son already had lands worth £343 a year, a figure which contrasts sharply with the £66 13s.4d. at which he had been assessed for the previous year's subsidy as a member of the King's chamber.[4]

Returned to the Commons in the autumn of 1529, Tailboys was one of four Members promoted to the Lords before the close of the first session. Unlike his fellow-knight Hussey he had done little to deserve the honour. If he was not unsuited to it by lineage— his father had sued out a pardon in 1509 as lord of

Kyme and Redesdale and Earl of Angus—his real claim arose from his peculiar relationship to the King: his stepson Richmond was being groomed for greatness, although he seems to have had no part in the boy's upbringing. It is not known who replaced Tailboys in the Commons although late in 1532 or early in 1533 three names, those of Robert Hussey, William Skipwith* and Sir Robert Tyrwhitt, were put forward.[5]

Tailboys survived his translation for no more than four months; he died on 15 Apr. 1530, apparently intestate, and was buried at South Kyme. His three children succeeded in turn to the barony of Tailboys, which became extinct on the death some 30 years later of Elizabeth Lady Tailboys. His widow, whose hand had been sought with apparent ardour by Lord Leonard Grey, married Edward Fiennes, 9th Lord Clinton.[6]

[1] Date of birth estimated from first commission. *CP; DNB; Lincs. Peds.* (Harl. Soc. lii), 945. [2] *LP Hen. VIII*, iv. [3] *LP Hen. VIII*, iii, iv. [3] *VCH Durham*, iii. 286–8; *Soc. Antiq. Newcastle-upon-Tyne rec. ser.* i. 170; *Northumb. Co. Hist.* xv. 383–4, 475–6; *CIPM Hen. VII*, i. 971, 1037, 1043–5, 1048, 1050, 1053–4; *CPR, 1494–1509*, pp. 176, 611; *LP Hen. VIII*, i, ii; *N. and Q.* (ser. 8), iv. 482. [4] *LP Hen. VIII*, ii–iv; *Cam. Misc.* ii(4), pp. xi, xii. [5] *LP Hen. VIII*, i. [6] *Lincs. Church Notes* (Lincoln Rec. Soc. i), 186; Mill Stephenson, *Mon. Brasses*, 287; *LP Hen. VIII*, v.

A.D.

TALBOT, Sir Gilbert (by 1479–1542), of Grafton, Worcs.

WORCESTERSHIRE 1529, 1542*

b. by 1479, 1st s. of Sir Gilbert Talbot[†] of Grafton by Elizabeth, da. of Ralph, 5th Lord Greystoke, wid. of Thomas, 5th Lord Scrope of Masham. *m.* (1) by 1505, Anne, da. and coh. of William Paston[†] of Norwich, Norf. and London by Anne, da. of Edmund Beaufort, 1st Duke of Somerset, 3da.; (2) Elizabeth, da. of Sir John Hungerford of Down Ampney, Glos., wid. of Roger Winter (*d.*1534) of Huddington, Worcs.; 2s. 2da. illegit. Kntd. 14 Oct. 1513; *suc.* fa. 16 Aug. 1517.[1]

J.p. Worcs. 1506–*d.*; commr. subsidy 1512, 1514, 1515, 1524, benevolence, Salop 1529, musters Worcs. 1539; other commissions 1530–39; knight of the body by 1533; sheriff, Worcs. 1539–40.[2]

The elder Sir Gilbert Talbot, a younger son of the 2nd Earl of Shrewsbury who during the minority of his nephew wielded the power of the earldom, had joined Henry Tudor before Bosworth and commanded the right wing in the battle. The Worcestershire manors of Grafton and Upton Warren, forfeited by Humphrey Stafford[†] and granted to Talbot in tail male in July 1486, formed part of his reward; the grant was confirmed to his son by an Act of 1542 (33 Hen. VIII, c.41). In 1507 he was appointed lieutenant of Calais and his son evidently served under him, joining with him in several recognizances made to the King. At a time when the father was very ill his son commanded a force of 100 men in the campaign of 1513 under his cousin

Shrewsbury, and was knighted at Lille. In the following year Talbot sued out a pardon, perhaps as a precaution against any proceedings that might be brought against him in connexion with an act of piracy committed in 1513 by a man using his name. When his father died in August 1517 he inherited a widespread estate which included, besides the principal lands in Shropshire and Worcestershire, the manor of Burghfield in Berkshire, property in Nayland, Suffolk, and a house with 117 acres in Calais, which he was to visit again in 1520 in attendance upon the King. His marriage had already brought him lands in Norfolk.[3]

As a great landowner in Worcestershire, with extensive interests elsewhere and a claim on the King's favour, Talbot may well have begun his parliamentary career before his return on 12 Aug. 1529 as knight of the shire with John Russell I. Nothing is known of his part in the proceedings of the House but between the seventh and eighth sessions he and Russell brought an action in the Exchequer against Sir Edward Ferrers*, sheriff of Worcestershire, for withholding payment of their combined wages of £160 for 400 days' service, claiming damages of £40. A writ *de expensis* had been obtained on 2 Apr. 1534, three days after the end of the sixth session, and had been promptly delivered to Ferrers who executed it on the following 20 Aug. The wages claimed were evidently for the 365 days of the Parliament to date, with an allowance of 35 days for 12 journeys to and from Parliament. The outcome of the case is unknown. The two were presumably returned again in 1536, in accordance with the King's general request for the re-election of the previous Members, but three years later Russell moved into the senior place and the junior one was taken by John Pakington, a distinguished lawyer whom Cromwell may have wished to see in the House. There is no reason to suppose that Talbot was out of favour: he had continued to render service, dealing firmly with the loose-tongued vicar of Crowle in September 1536, shortly afterwards being summoned to attend upon the King with 100 men for the suppression of the northern rebellion, and fulfilling his only term as sheriff during the lifetime of the Parliament of 1539 itself. It is not impossible that he had a hand in Pakington's election, as it was about this time that his grandson John Lyttelton* married Pakington's daughter.[4]

Talbot was again senior knight in the Parliament of 1542, when he doubtless sponsored the private Act confirming his possession of his father's manors, but he died on 22 Oct. 1542, between the first and second sessions, and was replaced by Thomas Russell, the son of his former colleague. He had

made his will three days before his death. He asked
to be buried, as his father had been, at Whitchurch,
Shropshire, beneath a marble tomb, and his provision for a chantry there is the only indication that
he shared the religious sympathies of his father, 'a
friend to churchmen and religious', and his half-
brother, who was to found a family of recusants.
Two of Talbot's daughters by his first wife, and the
third daughter's eldest son, John Lyttelton, were
later found to be his heirs, but he also provided for
four other children, two sons and two daughters,
who must have been illegitimate although not so
described in the will: Eleanor, one of the daughters,
was married to Geoffrey Dudley, a younger brother
of John, 3rd Lord Dudley. Her brother Humphrey
was appointed executor, with Talbot's half-brother
Sir John, who was left a London lease and upon
whom Burghfield, Grafton and Upton Warren had
earlier been settled; the supervisor was the bishop
of Worcester.[5]

¹ Date of birth estimated from age at fa.'s i.p.m., C142/39/96. *Vis.
Worcs.* (Harl. Soc. xxvii), 133–4, 148, 272; *Vis. Yorks.* (Harl. Soc.
xvi), 310; *Vis. Norf.* (Harl. Soc. xxxii), 216; PCC 22 Spert;
C1/1079/6–7, 142/65/13. The identity of Talbot's mother has been
questioned, D. Biddle, *A Gen. Puzzle*; *CP*, xi. 569 has been followed
here. ² *CPR*, 1494–1509, p. 666; *LP Hen. VIII*, i–v, xii–xiv; *Statutes*,
iii. 86, 112, 173. ³ *CPR*, 1485–94, p. 111; *CCR*, 1500–9, p. 361; *LP
Hen. VIII*, i, ii, iv, xvii; *VCH Berks.* iii. 401; Copinger, *Suff. Manors*,
iv. 202; *Chron. Calais* (Cam. Soc. xxxv), 21, 23; Blomefield, *Norf.*
v. 20; *Bristol and Glos. Arch. Soc. Trans.* lx. 278–80. ⁴ E13/214/11;
LP Hen. VIII, xi, xii; Merriman, *Letters Thos. Cromwell*, ii. 30–31.
⁵ C142/65/13; PCC 22 Spert, abstracted *Test. Vet.* ed. Nicolas, 695;
Trans. Salop Arch. Soc. (ser. 4), xi. 27; *Wm. Salt Arch. Soc.* v(2),
107n; *HMC Var.* ii. 309.

A.D.

TALBOT, Sir Thomas (prob. 1507/8–58), of
Bashall, Yorks., Rishton and Lower Darwen,
Lancs.

LANCASHIRE   1558*

b. prob. 1507/8, 1st s. of Edmund Talbot of Bashall by
Anne, da. of John Hart and sis. of Sir Percival Hart of
Lullingstone, Kent. *m.* by 1533, Cecily, da. of William
Venables of Kinderton, Cheshire, 1s. 1da.; also 1s.
illegit. *suc.* fa. 20 Feb. 1520. Kntd. 11 May 1544.[1]
   Sheriff, Lancs. 1551–2; commr. chantries 1554,
?1555, to survey woods and game, Leagram park and
Bowland forest 1555/56; steward, duchy of Lancaster,
Blackburn hundred 1554–6, jt. 1556–*d.*, master fores-
ter, Bowland 1554–6.[2]

Although Bashall is in Yorkshire, the Talbots of
Bashall are said to have 'inclined more to Lancashire
than to Yorkshire'. They were related to the earls of
Shrewsbury. After his father's death Thomas
Talbot's mother married Sir James Stanley of Cross
Hall, Lancashire, a union which later involved
Talbot in the marital and extra-marital affairs of
Ralph Rishton of Ponthalgh, Lancashire, which
have been chosen to illustrate the view that 'in
practice, if not in theory, the early 16th century
nobility was a polygamous society'. Rishton formed

a connexion, perhaps amounting to marriage, with
Talbot's half-sister Anne Stanley, and Lady Stanley
and her son Talbot combined to seize Anne and
force her into a 'marriage' with John Rishton of
Dunkenhalgh. His relationship to the Stanleys (Sir
James was the uncle of Edward, 3rd Earl of Derby)
may have helped to procure Talbot's election as
senior knight of the shire in 1558.[3]

Talbot had considerable experience in the field. In
1536 he joined the 3rd Earl of Derby with 16 men
and in May 1544 was knighted by the Earl of Hertford at Leith. He held a command in Blackburn
hundred in 1553, and in 1557 he again joined Derby,
this time with 200 men. On 7 Oct. 1557 the 5th Earl
of Shrewsbury wrote to Thomas Percy*, 1st Earl of
Northumberland, that he had sent Talbot with 200 or
300 men towards Berwick. He commended Talbot
'as a well willing friend of mine, whom I have
required to be at your lordship's commandment'
and asked Northumberland 'to be his good lord, and
to favour him according to his worthiness, whom as
soon as any man living, in case of need, I would have
been right glad to have had about mine own person'.[4]

Talbot made his will in September 1557. He left
Bashall and his Blackburn lease to his daughter Anne
and leases which he held of Sir Ralph Assheton to
his illegitimate son John. Anne Talbot married
William Farrington (son of Sir Henry*), whom
Talbot made executor of his will. Talbot's son and
heir Henry, who was aged 25 and more at his father's
death, married Millicent, daughter of Sir John
Holcroft, Talbot's fellow-Member in 1558. Talbot
died on 1 Aug. 1558, thus missing the second session
of the Parliament. If, as is likely, his death was not
reported until the House reassembled on 5 Nov.,
he was probably not replaced before the Queen's
death on 17 Nov. terminated the Parliament.[5]

¹ Date of birth estimated from age at fa.'s i.p.m. *Chetham Soc.* xcix.
150, but according to *VCH Lancs.* vi. 278 he was only three at his
fa.'s death. *Vis. Lancs.* (Chetham Soc. xcviii), 40n; J. B. Watson,
'Lancs. gentry 1529–58' (London Univ. M.A. thesis, 1959), 492; *LP
Hen. VIII*, xix. ² *VCH Lancs.* ii. 98; *APC*, vi. 365; *Ducatus Lanc.* iii.
189; Somerville, *Duchy*, i. 501, 508. ³ Watson, 492; *Chetham Soc.*
xcix. 150; ciii. pp. xxiv–xxix; *VCH Lancs.* vi. 278; *Vis. Lancs.*
33–34n; L. Stone, *Crisis of the Aristocracy*, 663. ⁴ *LP Hen. VIII*, xi,
xix; *VCH Lancs.* ii. 220; Strype, *Eccles. Memorials*, iii(2), 92; T. D.
Whitaker, *Whalley* (3rd ed.), 547. ⁵ Watson, 494; Preston RO,
Farington of Worden Deeds 2419; *Chetham Soc.* li. 211–13.

A.D.

TALONTS (TALOUGH, TALLANS), John (by
1510–63), of Coventry, Warws.

COVENTRY   1553 (Mar.), 1558

b. by 1510. *m.* Joan, at least 2da.; 1s. illegit.[1]
   Chamberlain, Coventry 1531–2, sheriff 1536–7,
mayor 1545–6, 1562–3.[2]

John Talonts was a goldsmith who became a
wealthy man and a leading citizen of Coventry. A

resident in Trinity parish, he supplied both the church and the corporation with crucifixes, plate and other articles. He is not known to have been a regular money-lender, but he lent £200 to Edward, 4th Lord Dudley, and smaller sums to George Kebell of Stanford, Northamptonshire. His first mayoralty was troubled by a dispute with the Warwickshire commission of array over musters within the city, when his firmness and tact were praised by Edward Saunders*. He made several journeys to London for the corporation in the matter of Bond's hospital, and in 1549 he delivered to John Dudley, Earl of Warwick, the payment for the lease of Cheylesmore park. He was one of those responsible for discovering the flaw in the grant of the Whitefriars to John Hales II* which enabled the city to oust him.[3]

It was with another ex-mayor, James Rogers, that Talonts was returned to the Parliament of March 1553. This was held under the aegis of the Duke of Northumberland, with whom as Earl of Warwick he had had dealings over Cheylesmore, but there is no evidence that Northumberland intervened in the election. Talonts's receipt of £3 16s.4d. includes the statutory wage of 2s. a day for the 31 days of the Parliament. Five years later he was re-elected with the recorder John Throckmorton I. It is not known what part he played in procuring the Act of 1558 for the payment of tithes in Coventry (4 and 5 Phil. and Mary, c.14).[4]

Although no Coventry citizen was obliged to serve a second term as mayor, Talonts again accepted this burdensome office in 1562. During his first mayoralty he had been accused in Chancery of using his authority to evict a poor man from his cottage and on another occasion he was charged in the Star Chamber with taking bribes as a juror; he had himself been the plaintiff in several chancery suits in the 1530s. He died on 27 Nov. 1563 shortly after completing his year of office and nine days after making his will. He named as his executor his illegitimate son Francis Justice alias Talonts. He had made some provision for this son five years earlier and later joined with him in the purchase of land from Henry Over alias Waver*; he now in effect recognized him as his heir while also providing for his wife and two grandsons and making generous bequests to his servants and to charity. The will was proved on 15 Feb. 1564 and two years later the wardship of one of his grandsons, Michael Samborough or Sandbroke, was granted to the widow.[5]

[1] Date of birth estimated from first reference. PCC 5 Stevenson; CPR, 1563–6, p. 433; C142/140/194. [2] Coventry Leet Bk. (EETS cxxxiv), ii. 706, 724, 778; B. Poole, Coventry, 371. [3] E179/192/157, 193/188, 190; Coventry statute merchant rolls 38, 41, 47; Coventry Trinity Deeds, T/S ed. Dormer Harris, nos. 71, 74, 76; Poole, 246; Coventry mayors' accts. 1542–61, passim; council bk. pp. 2–4, 8, 21,

45; letters, i. 63; T. Sharpe, Coventry, 161; C1/1199/42. [4] Coventry mayors' accts. 1542–61, p. 70. [5] C1/905/1–2, 907/9–15, 910/5–8, 1151/3, 1512/31; St.Ch.2/31/17; C142/140/194; PCC 5 Stevenson; NRA 5613 (Lincoln AO, Jarvis mss I/B/1/19, 3/7); CPR, 1560–3, p. 89; 1563–6, p. 433.

S.M.T.

TANCRED (TANKERD), William (by 1508–73), of Boroughbridge, Yorks.

YORK   1539[1]
BOROUGHBRIDGE   1553 (Oct.)

b. by 1508, s. of Hugh Tancred of Boroughbridge. educ. L. Inn, adm. 31 Jan. 1522, called 1527. m. by 1530, Anne, da. of John Pulleyn of Killinghall, 3s. 1da.[2]

Bencher, L. Inn 1537.
Recorder, York 1537–d.; j.p. Yorks. (W. Riding) 1538–47 or later, (N. Riding) 1547, 1569, (E. Riding) 1569, q. (W. Riding) 1554–72, Cumb. 1569; commr. relief, Yorks. (W. Riding) 1550; ?bailiff, Boroughbridge in 1555; member, council in the north 1566–72.[3]

William Tancred was born at Boroughbridge and made that town his home, but the greater part of his career was spent in the service of the city of York. First appearing in the York records in 1533, when as a 'learned man' he was sent to London on civic business, he may have got his start there through his father-in-law John Pulleyn, whom he succeeded as recorder in 1537, or his brother-in-law Miles Newton, for over 40 years the city's common clerk. It was with Newton that Tancred lodged when he was in York.[4]

Although Tancred is said to have been involved in the Pilgrimage of Grace as a Percy retainer, his only known action appears to have been the summoning of a meeting at Topcliffe 'about certain matters in variance among the townsmen', and his appointment to one of the Yorkshire benches in 1538 implies that he was not seriously compromised. His election as second Member for York in the Parliament of 1539 is easier to understand than the fact that it was not to be repeated throughout the remaining 34 years of his recordership. It may be that his non-residence told against his re-election; in 1550 his fee as recorder was withheld until he paid a promised visit to view the bounds of the city. In general, however, he appears to have carried out his duties to the city's satisfaction: they included acting as its spokesman on Henry VIII's arrival there in 1541 and spending considerable time in London on civic business between 1547 and 1549. (He was there in January 1549 when Thomas Jolye* mentioned him in a letter to the 2nd Earl of Cumberland.) Until 1548 his remuneration was limited by Sir Richard Page's retention of an annuity of £12 out of the recorder's annual fee of £13 6s. 8d. and clothing; when he was first given the full amount the corporation acknowledged the 'great charges' he had sustained, and during his later years of office he received additional rewards such as the hogshead of claret given him in 1567.[5]

Tancred's election as one of the first two Members for Boroughbridge in the autumn of 1553 answered to his standing as a leading resident and legal officer of the honor of Knaresborough, but as at York it was not to be repeated, whereas his fellow-Member, and colleague at Lincoln's Inn, Christopher Wray was to retain his seat throughout Mary's reign. Tancred's acceptance of the Catholic restoration is not implied by his omission from the Members of this Parliament noted as having opposed it, since Boroughbridge is one of the three boroughs missing from the list concerned, but he remained on the Marian bench and although sufficiently conformable under Elizabeth to be retained on it, and at Archbishop Young's suggestion even brought on to the council in the north, his restoration to the commission, after he was put off it in 1572 when 'aged and sickly', was opposed by the president of the council, the 3rd Earl of Huntingdon, in terms which leave no doubt that he remained a Catholic.[6]

Tancred died on 13 Aug. 1573 at Boroughbridge and was buried there. He died intestate but the inquisition post mortem taken on 26 Oct. at Wetherby shows him as owning the manors of Farnham, Hornby and Newsholme, the reversion of a moiety of Hewick, and many scattered properties in the North and West Ridings. His heir was his eldest son Thomas, then aged 43.[7]

[1] York archs. B14, f. 6; E159/319, brev. ret. Mich. r.[1–2]. [2] Date of birth estimated from education. York pub. lib. R. H. Skaife ms civic officials, iii. 729. [3] York archs. B13–25; *LP Hen. VIII*, xiii–xx; *CPR*, 1547–8, p. 92; 1553, p. 353; 1553–4, p. 26; 1560–3, p. 436; 1563–6, p. 21; 1569–72, p. 224; C210/24/62; R. R. Reid, *King's Council in the North*, 210–11. [4] York pub. lib. R. H. Skaife ms civic officials, iii. 729; *York Civic Recs.* iii (Yorks. Arch. Soc. rec. ser. cvi), 163; York archs. B13, f. 100; *N. Country Wills*, i (Surtees Soc. cxvi), 210. [5] Reid, 196; *LP Hen. VIII*, xii, xvi; *York Civic Recs.* iv (Yorks. Arch. Soc. rec. ser. cviii), 68–70, 85, 157, 167, 170–1, 174; v (ibid. cx), 3, 9, 48, 119; vi (ibid. cxii), 38, 121, 130, 143; vi (ibid. cxv), 6; York archs. B14, f. 6; *Clifford Letters* (Surtees Soc. clxxii), 33–34. [6] Somerville, *Duchy*, i. 525; Reid, 184 n. 75, 196, 198, 210, 211 n. 9; Lansd. 10(2), f. 4; *Cam. Misc.* ix(3), 70, 72; J. T. Cliffe, *Yorks. Gentry*, 242; T. Lawson-Tancred, *Recs. Yorks. Manor*, 174. [7] York pub. lib. R. H. Skaife ms civic officials, iii. 729; E150/260/24; *VCH Yorks.* (*N. Riding*), i. 199; ii. 28, 314.

D.M.P.

TATE, Sir John (by 1444–1515), of London.

LONDON 1504,[1] 1510[2]

b. by 1444, 2nd s. of Thomas Tate of Coventry, Warws. by one Poers; bro. of Robert†. *m.* Magdalen (Maud), da. of one Harpenden of Wales, 3s. Kntd. 17 June 1497.[3]

Warden, Mercers' Co. 1480–1, master 1486–7, 1492–3, 1500–1, 1508–9; alderman, London 1485–*d.*, sheriff 1485–6, auditor 1491–3, mayor 1496–7, June–Oct. 1514; mayor, staple of Calais 1505, 1509; justiciary for Hanse merchants in London 1511; commr. subsidy, London 1504, 1512, 1514.[4]

John Tate was the son of a Coventry mercer, himself a near relative of the John Tate, mercer and alderman of London, to whom his young namesake was apprenticed. Tate was admitted to the freedom of the company in 1465 and seven years later sued out the general pardon offered to merchants of the staple of Calais. In 1475 he and his elder brother Robert Tate, both living in Tower ward, were among the London merchants said to be worth £10 a year in lands or £100 in goods: at this time the two were trading jointly into the Netherlands. John Tate became an important stapler, exporting wool and wool fells in nine different ships bound for Calais in March 1502 in preparation for the Easter mart. In 1497 he bought a tenement in St. Nicholas parish, Calais, and the moiety of a hospice in Maisondieu Street; he acquired further property when his factor at Calais, his wife's half-brother, fell into debt and appealed to him for assistance, offering in return lands and tenements in Calais and four small houses in Faringdon, Berkshire. In London he lived first in the parish of All Hallows by the Tower and later in the parish of St. Dionis Backchurch.[5]

As a warden of the Mercers Tate was chosen on 24 Apr. 1483 to ride to meet Edward V on his entry into London, and two days later was elected by the common council of the City to assist the chief butler at the coronation, which in the event became the coronation of Richard III. An alderman of London from March 1485, he was among those charged with defence precautions in July 1485; two years later, after Henry VII had overcome the first rebellion of the reign, Tate was sent on a deputation to the King at Kenilworth. The Cornish rising of 1497 touched London more nearly, and when Henry VII rode into the City after Blackheath he knighted Tate, then mayor, for his services in the 'well guiding' of the City and the victualling of the royal army. Thereafter Tate was frequently employed on city business. Thus in March 1503 he reported to the King the widespread opposition to the new charter granted to the Merchant Taylors and in May was one of those appointed to negotiate with the monarch for the confirmation of London's charter, which the City hoped to see accompanied by the withdrawal of the Merchant Taylors'; in the same year he was empowered to discuss with the corporation of Exeter a dispute over scavage, and in December he was directed to take evidence on the subject.[6]

Both these issues were to come up in the next Parliament, to which Tate was elected on 30 Dec. 1503, after the death of Sir John Shaa†. The first was by implication decided in favour of the Merchant Taylors by an Act (19 Hen. VII, c.7) removing from the mayor and aldermen control over all companies' ordinances; the second was dealt with by an Act (19 Hen. VII, c.8) restricting scavage to goods sold by foreigners, but with the proviso that the City might levy the duty on denizens' goods with the assent of the King and Council. In 1510, when Tate was again a Member, his company made a determined attempt to limit the new Act (1 Hen. VIII, c.20) of tonnage and poundage made necessary by the accession of Henry VIII; although this passed without the desired amendments it did contain a special proviso for merchants of the staple. Tate was not re-elected in 1512, but he presided over the court of aldermen which approved the sending of a deputation, in which all the companies except the Merchant Taylors had agreed to take part, in support of a bill then before Parliament, 'that all crafts shall hereafter be under the rule of the mayor and aldermen'; during the second session he was assigned to speak to the 3rd Duke of Buckingham and the lord privy seal in favour of this bill, which nevertheless failed.[7]

After his second mayoralty in 1514, when he replaced William Brown who had died in office, Tate asked the court of aldermen what his 'anciency or preeminence' should be as the oldest alderman and the youngest to have been mayor twice. He did not long enjoy the distinction. In a long will, dated 3 Jan. 1515 and proved 18 days later, he asked to be buried in the collegiate church of St. Antholin, which he had rebuilt at his own cost, directed that 1,000 requiem masses should be said for him within two months of his death, and made charitable bequests totalling £1763 to religious houses in Coventry and London and to prisoners, the sick and the poor. He left to his wife, his executrix, the residue of his goods and all his lands in Berkshire, Calais, Essex and London, with remainder to his younger surviving son Bartholomew Tate. The exclusion of the elder son, to whom he left 'little or nothing', gave rise to contention and was criticized by the widow in her own will. Bartholomew Tate was the father of the Elizabethan Member of that name.[8]

[1] City of London RO, Guildhall, rep. 1, f. 150. [2] City of London RO, jnl. 11, f. 90. [3] Date of birth estimated from admission to freedom of Mercers' Co. Harl. 1504, f. 116; 1546, f. 64 (the first marriage ascribed to Tate in HP, ed. Wedgwood 1439–1509 (Biogs.), 841, was his nephew's); Gt. Chron. of London, ed. Thomas and Thornley, 277. [4] Acts Ct. of Mercers' Co. ed. Lyell and Watney, 138, 229, 244, 294, 316, 344; City of London RO, jnl. 9, f. 71; 10, f. 79; 11, f. 190; letter bk. L, 225, 281, 289; CPR, 1494–1509, p. 447; LP Hen. VIII, i; Statutes, iii. 83, 118. [5] Coventry Leet Bk. (EETS cxxxiv), i. 246; PCC 4 Holder; List of mercers (T/S Mercers' Hall); CPR, 1467–77, p. 315; Acts Ct. of Mercers' Co., 79; Bronnen tot de Geschiedenis van den Handel met Engeland, Schotland en Ierland, ed. Smit, ii. 1847; E122/79/9; CCR, 1485–1500, no. 992; C1/272/12–14. [6] Acts Ct. of Mercers' Co., 138, 147; City of London RO, jnl. 9, ff. 21v, 71, 82, 150v; 10, ff. 281, 285v; rep. 1, ff. 129, 147v; Gt. Chron. of London, 277. [7] Acts Ct. of Mercers' Co. 346 seq.; City of London RO, rep. 2, ff. 146, 148. [8] City of London RO, rep. 1, f. 136v; 2, ff. 178v, 197v; PCC 4, 35 Holder; W. K. Jordan, Charities of London, 1480–1660, p. 352.

H.M.

TAVERNER, Richard (1505/6–75), of London, Norbiton, Surr. and Wood Eaton, Oxon.

?LIVERPOOL 1547[1]

b. 1505/6, 1st s. of John Taverner of North Elmham, Norf. by Alice, da. of Robert Silvester of North Elmham; bro. of Robert* and Roger*. educ. Corpus Christi, Camb. adm. 1520; Cardinal, Oxf. adm by 1527, BA 21 June 1527, determined 1528; Gonville, Camb. incorp. 1529–30, MA 1529–30, pens. 1530–2; Strand Inn, adm. 1533; I. Temple, adm. 1534. m. (1) Aug. 1537, Margaret (bur. 31 Jan. 1563), da. of Walter Lambert of Chertsey, Surr. 4s. 3da.; (2) Mary, da. of Sir John Harcourt* of Stanton Harcourt, Oxon. and Ellenhall, Staffs. 1s. 1da.[2]

Marshal, I. Temple 1553–4.

Lecturer in Greek, Camb. ?1531–2; commr. relief, Surr. 1550; clerk of the signet by 1537–53; j.p. Surr. 1547, Oxon. 1558/59–d.; reeve, borough of Lydford, Devon by 1553–5 or later; sheriff, Oxon. 1569–70.[3]

According to his great-grandson the antiquary Anthony Wood, Richard Taverner was born at Brisley in Norfolk where the Taverners had property. After showing early promise at Cambridge he transferred to Oxford and obtained a petty canonry at Cardinal College before graduating. As against the possibility that Wolsey, anxious to attract talent to his foundation, engineered the move it may be suggested that Taverner joined the college because his Lincolnshire kinsman John Taverner had become master of the choristers there; Taverner shared the choirmaster's Protestantism and after his kinsmen's detention for owning heretical works he first returned to Cambridge and then went abroad to study. The death of an (unknown) benefactor in 1530 left him penniless but his appeal to Cromwell led to his being mentioned to the King and given a pension by the 3rd Duke of Norfolk; in return Taverner dedicated to Cromwell his translation of Erasmus's *Encomium Matrimonii* published under the minister's 'noble protection'. Two years later another of Erasmus's translators suggested that Cromwell should refer his work to Taverner for appraisal. Soon after this Taverner left Cambridge for London, where he studied at Strand Inn before entering the Middle Temple. After working privately for Cromwell he was recommended in 1536 for the King's service and within a year was made one of the clerks of the signet.[4]

It was 'at the impulsion and commandment' of Cromwell that Taverner undertook a series of translations designed to promote reform. *The confessyon of the fayth of the Germaynes exhibited to the most victorious Emperour Charles the V in the council of Augusta 1530* (1539) was followed by *Commonplaces of Scripture orderly set forth* (1538), *The new testament in Englysshe* (1539), *The most sacred bible newly recognized by R. Taverner* (1539), *An epitome of the psalmes* (1539), *A catechisme or institution of the christen religion* (1539), three volumes of *The garden of wysdome* (1539), *Mimi Publiani* (1539), *Flores aliquot sententiarum ex variis collecti scriptoribus* (1540) and *Catonis disticha moralia ex castigatione D. Erasmi* (1540). This spate of writings ended with Cromwell's downfall.[5]

Late in 1541 Taverner was briefly imprisoned in the Tower for failing to pass on a report that Anne of Cleves was with child by the King after their divorce, but he did not forfeit his clerkship. In 1544 he both served in the French campaign and acquired, besides the manor of Wood Eaton in Oxfordshire, various properties near Kingston-upon-Thames, Surrey, including a house at Norbiton; he strengthened his title to the manor of Hartington in Kingston by a series of conveyances with the Earl of Hertford. He also joined his younger brothers Robert and Roger in the speculative land market; during 1544–5 they sold property to Sir Thomas Seymour II.[6]

Taverner appears as a Member of only one Parliament, and then in circumstances which are far from clear. On the Crown Office list of the Parliament of 1547, as revised for the last session (1552), he is named as one of the Members for Liverpool, his partner being Thomas Stanley. Since the indenture of 1547 gives the names of Stanley and Francis Cave (q.v.) for Liverpool, it is natural to infer that Taverner had replaced Cave. Yet Cave had neither died nor, so far as is known, done anything to incur expulsion, so that his replacement by Taverner during the life of the Parliament would be hard to account for. (By a gratuitous complication Stanley is marked on the list as 'mortuus', but he no more than Cave had qualified for the adjective in 1552 and it was not he whom Taverner replaced.) It is less difficult to imagine that, despite the appearance of his name on the indenture, Cave had not become a Member in 1547 but had been supplanted by Taverner. There is certainly no lack of explanation of Taverner's claim to a seat at this time. His record as a Protestant publicist could not have failed to commend him and he enjoyed many valuable connexions. He was known to the brothers Seymour as well as to the Earl of Warwick, and as a clerk of the signet he was a former colleague of Sir William Paget, whose chancellorship of the duchy of Lancaster carried a share in the patronage of Liverpool with the Stanley earls of Derby. One of Taverner's current colleagues, William Honing, sat in this House for Winchester, and Honing's father-in-law Nicholas Cutler had done so in its precursor for Liverpool. It appears that Cave himself had been intruded into the place previously given to another, and Taverner would have been an eminently suitable

beneficiary of a similar change at the last minute. Unfortunately, there is no mention of Taverner in the Journal such as would clinch the matter.

After the dissolution in 1552 Taverner received a licence to preach and he did so several times before Edward VI. As a government official known to Northumberland he may have been returned to the Parliament of March 1553, for which many returns are missing. Nothing has come to light about his part in the succession crisis. He welcomed Mary's accession with 'An Oration gratulory' but she dismissed him from the signet office and removed him from the Surrey bench. In the first Parliament of the new reign he and another exhibited a bill preserving their interest in some lands while the measure repealing the attainder of the Duke of Norfolk was under review in the Commons, and after securing a copy of it the two were ordered to appear with their counsel to argue the matter on the following day.[7]

During the 1550s Taverner lived mainly at Norbiton while rebuilding the house at Wood Eaton, but with the work complete he settled in Oxfordshire. Named to the Oxfordshire bench by Elizabeth but declining a knighthood from her, he was active in local administration until his death on 14 July 1575. By a will made a month earlier he asked to be buried beside his first wife at Wood Eaton, provided for his family and named three of his sons executors. His widow Mary married Cromwell Lee.[8]

[1] Hatfield 207. [2] Date of birth given by his great-grandson, A. Wood, *Ath. Ox.* ed. Bliss, i. 419–23. *DNB*; *Vis. Norf.* (Harl. Soc. xxxii), 280; *Vis. Oxon.* (Harl. Soc. v), 159, 175, 179, 308; Emden, *Biog. Reg. Univ. Oxf. 1501–40*, pp. 557–8. [3] *LP Hen. VIII*, vi. xii; Elton, *Tudor Rev. in Govt.* 305–6; *CPR*, 1547–8, p. 90; 1553, p. 357; 1560–3, p. 441; 1563–6, p. 25; Duchy of Cornw. RO, 128/25; 227/2; Stowe 571, f. 21. [4] *Ath. Ox.* i. 419–23; G. Zeeveld, *Foundations of Tudor Policy*, 28, 73, 74; *LP Hen. VIII*, v, vi; Elton, *Reform and Renewal*, 18, 61–62; *Tudor Rev. in Govt.* 305–6. [5] Elton, *Reform and Renewal*, 35; *Policy and Police*, 424; Zeeveld,148, 152. [6] *APC*, i. 279; *LP Hen. VIII*, xvi, xix–xxi; *CPR*, 1547–8, pp. 3, 222; 1548–9, p. 369; 1549–51, pp. 65, 169, 229, 351; 1553–4, pp. 266, 373; 1554–5, pp. 164, 254; E210/D4819, 9789, 9958, 10499. [7] Hatfield 207; *Ath. Ox.* i. 424; *CJ*, i. 32. [8] PCC 32 Pyckering; C142/175/9; Req.2/97/26.

S.M.T.

TAVERNER, Robert (by 1523–56), of Lambourne, Essex.

DUNHEVED 1545

b. by 1523, yr. s. of John Taverner, and bro. of Richard* and Roger*. *m.* by 1556, Elizabeth, da. of Brian Newcomen of Saltfleetby, Lincs., 1s.[1]

Reeve, manor of Boyton, Cornw. by 1555–*d.*; bailiff, manor of Stapleford Abbots, Essex by 1556.[2]

Robert Taverner 'gentleman' took the junior place for a Cornish borough in the last Parliament of Henry VIII's reign. The election, which saw his return with William Cordell, was held at Dunheved on 20 Sept. 1545, eight months after the meeting of the county court at nearby Launceston castle to choose the two knights for Cornwall and long after most constituencies had decided on their representatives: probably the hand of Sir Thomas Arundell*, receiver-general for the duchy and chancellor of Queen Catherine Parr, can be discerned in this delay for on this occasion he supervised the elections in the south-west. Since Cordell was presumably Arundell's nominee, Taverner may have been as well. His only known experience of the House perhaps anticipated his lease of the prebend of St. Endellion which he held with Edmund Bedingfield at least by 1548, and his reeveship of a manor not far from Dunheved. His elder brother Richard, the translator of the Bible, who was clerk of the signet, may have promoted his nomination.[3]

The first glimpse of Taverner is in June 1544 when he acquired property in several counties from augmentations for just over £600. In the following ten months in conjunction with two of his brothers he bought land worth over £4,200, much of which they soon alienated, and he continued to make joint purchases with these two brothers in the closing years of Henry VIII's life and throughout the reigns of Edward VI and Mary until his death. He was able to buy and consolidate a small estate for himself in the neighbourhood of Lambourne and it was there that he made his will on 30 Apr. 1556, providing for his wife and recently born son Thomas, and appointing his mother, wife and brother Roger as executors. Taverner died not long afterwards as the will was proved on 30 May, although when his widow obtained the wardship of their son on 8 Mar. 1557 it was stated that he had died on 10 Oct. 1556. She took as her second husband William Hulcote*.[4]

author of a number of tracts which circulated privately on the problems of debasement and dearth, but his masterpiece was his 'Arte of surveyinge' (1565), which remained a standard text for a generation. He was concerned with land throughout his career: he assisted his brothers in the property market during the 1540s and 1550s and occasionally acted independently of them, but his predominant interest seems always to have been that of a surveyor. He deputized for Sir Francis Jobson* as surveyor in the court of augmentations and later in the Exchequer, and after Jobson's death he corresponded with Burghley on matters within his competence. Taverner may have owed his place in the second Marian Parliament to Jobson, who was concerned to defend his interest in the dismantled bishopric of Durham which the Queen wished to restore, but he also shared a disputed interest in the neighbourhood of Launceston with his brother Robert, who had sat for the town's other constituency on an earlier occasion.[3]

Taverner made his will on 6 Jan. 1578 committing his soul to God and asking that his funeral should be conducted under 'the rites according to the custom of the realm'. As he had already provided for his eldest son, for whom he had obtained the reversion of Jobson's surveyorship, he left the residue of his estate to his two younger sons whom he appointed executors. On the following 18 Sept. he wrote to Burghley in answer to a query from the minister, but he was dead by 5 Feb. 1582, when his will was proved.[4]

[1] Date of birth estimated from first reference. *Vis. Essex* (Harl. Soc. xiii), 499; *The Gen.* iv. 260; C142/109/154. [2] Duchy Cornw. RO, 128/39; 129/43; 130/37v; *CPR, 1555-7*, p. 300. [3] *L.P. Hen. VIII*, xix, xx; Duchy Cornw. RO, 128/39; E6.1/18v; *DKR*, x(2), 283-6; *DNB* (Taverner, Richard). [4] *LP Hen. VIII*, xx, xxi; *CPR, 1547-8* to 1555-7 passim; *VCH Essex*, iv. 77-81; PCC 7 Ketchyn, 25 Pyckering; C142/109/154.

S.M.T.

[1] Date of birth estimated from first reference, 1544. *Vis. Essex* (Harl. Soc. xiv), 499; *Vis. Herts.* (Harl. Soc. xvi), 95; PCC 10 Rowe. [2] *HMC Hatfield*, ii. 203; *CPR, 1569-72*, p. 341; Lansd. 43(66), f. 154. [3] Bodl. Wood F31, f. 38; *DNB* (Taverner, Richard); *LP Hen. VIII*, xx, xxi; *CPR, 1547-8* to 1555-7 passim; 1569-72, p. 341; W. C. Richardson, *Ct. Augmentations*, 308; Duchy Cornw. RO, 129/39, 43; 130/38; 131/38; E6.1/18v; *HMC Hatfield*, ii. 203; Lansd. 43(66), f. 154. [4] PCC 10 Rowe.

S.M.T.

TAVERNER, Roger (by 1523-78/82), of Upminster, Essex.

NEWPORT IUXTA LAUNCESTON   1554 (Apr.)

b. by 1523, yr. s. of John Taverner, and bro. of Richard* and Robert*. educ. ?Corpus, Camb. m. ?da. of one Hulcote, 3s.[1]
Dep. surveyor of woods, south of Trent, ct. augmentations by 1551-3, Exchequer 1553-73.[2]

According to a family tradition recorded by the antiquarian Anthony Wood, Roger Taverner followed his elder brother, the translator of the Bible, by going to Cambridge, but since Wood confused the careers of several members of the family in his sketch of Taverner this is untrustworthy. Taverner was certainly a lettered man: he was the

TAYLARD, John (by 1469-1528), of Upwood, Hunts.

HUNTINGDONSHIRE   1510[1]

b. by 1469, yr. s. of William Taylard† (d.1505) of Diddington by Elizabeth, da. of John Anstey† of Stow cum Quy, Cambs. educ. I. Temple. m. Alice, d.s.p.[2]
J.p. Hunts. 1506-14; commr. subsidy 1512, 1515; other commissions 1508-13; escheator, Cambs. and Hunts. 1513-14.[3]

John Taylard, a nephew of William Alington, Speaker in 1478, was the third of his family to serve as knight for Huntingdonshire. His own return is revealed by a plea of debt brought before the Exchequer in 1511 by which his fellow-knight John Wynde (q.v.) accused the ex-sheriff of delay in paying their wages of £8 each: he could also have sat in one or more of the next three Parliaments, for which the names of the Huntingdonshire knights are unknown. He had apparently followed the family tradition by training for the law but the only record of his attendance at the Inner Temple is his relinquishment of membership there in 1510. In 1490 he shared with three of his brothers in a grant of the manors of Clairvaux and Denes in Upwood from their brother-in-law Gerard Stuckley and was then described as John Taylard the younger to distinguish him from his uncle of Potton, Bedfordshire, who was to die in 1506. The Upwood manors passed into Taylard's hands and for the subsidy of 1524 he was assessed there on lands, goods and chattels at the substantial sum of £60.[4]

By his will of 10 Sept. 1528 Taylard left his wife for life his lands in Hail Weston, Huntingdonshire, according to his father's will, as well as three tenements in St. Ives. He named his wife, his brother Dr. William Taylard and Anthony Mallory executors and the will was proved on the following 2 Oct. His heir was his nephew Lawrence Taylard*.[5]

[1] E13/187, m. 30. [2] Date of birth estimated from first reference. *Vis. Hunts.* (Cam. Soc. xliii), 88–90; *The Gen.* n.s. xix. 160. [3] *CPR*, 1494–1509, pp. 507, 581, 644; *LP Hen. VIII*, i; *Statutes*, iii. 82, 175. [4] *VCH Hunts.* ii. 240; *CIPM Hen. VII*, iii. 890; E179/122/91. [5] Hunts. RO, Huntingdon archdeaconry wills 3, ff. 58–60; C142/50/160.

M.K.D.

TAYLARD, Lawrence (1498/99–1573), of Diddington, Hunts.

HUNTINGDONSHIRE 1529, 1553 (Oct.)

b. 1498/99, 2nd but 1st surv. s. of Walter Taylard of Diddington by Alice, da. and coh. of Robert Forster of London. *educ.* M. Temple, adm. 2 Nov. 1520. *m.* (1) Margaret, da. of Edmund Mordaunt, 10s. 4da.; (2) Dorothy, da. of Thomas Roberds of Willesden, Mdx., wid. of Alan Horde (*d.*1554) of the Middle Temple, London and Ewell, Surr. *s.p. suc.* fa. 1515. Kntd. 4 Feb. 1531/16 Feb. 1532.[1]

J.p. Hunts. 1522–45, 1554–*d.*; escheator, Cambs. and Hunts. 1523–4; commr. subsidy, Hunts. 1524, musters 1541, benevolence 1544/45, relief 1550; other commissions 1534–69; sheriff, Cambs. and Hunts. 1546–7, 1555–6.[2]

Taylards of Diddington had practised law and sat in Parliament for almost a century before Lawrence Taylard began to do so. By the close of the 15th century his forbears had acquired all three manors at Diddington as well as property in the south of Huntingdonshire and in Bedfordshire and Cambridgeshire: they remained, however, well below the first rank of local landowners and their continued prominence in the area rested more on their legal attainments than on their wealth.[3]

Lawrence Taylard's father died in 1515 and his mother three years later, whereupon he became the ward of his uncle William Taylard, a doctor of law and rector of Offord Darcy near Diddington. Another uncle who took an interest in him, and whose heir he became, was John Taylard of Upwood, Huntingdonshire, an Inner Templar who had sat in Henry VIII's first Parliament, but it was to the Middle Temple that Taylard was admitted in 1520. Within four years he was named a justice of the peace for his native county, its escheator and one of its subsidy commissioners. He may also have sat in the Parliament of 1523 for Huntingdon, which lies a few miles north of Diddington, and thus have been able to add experience of the Commons to the qualifications which six years later were to secure him the junior knighthood of the shire. His achievement on that occasion perhaps owed something to the current paucity of candidates from the leading county families, a situation in which Taylard's own standing could have sufficed for his election: already in Wolsey's time he was described by an opponent in Chancery, although not perhaps without some conventional exaggeration, as 'a great man of power and friends' in the shire.[4]

Of Taylard's part in the proceedings of the Parliament of 1529 nothing is known for certain, but two facts may throw indirect light on it. The first is the knighthood which was conferred on him at an early stage in that Parliament's lifetime. Coinciding as it probably did with the knighting of Nicholas Harvey, his fellow-Member for Huntingdonshire, Taylard's promotion may look like the counterpart of Harvey's but it must also imply satisfaction with his conduct both at Westminster and elsewhere. By contrast, the appearance of his name on a list of Members drawn up by Cromwell early in 1533 suggests something quite different, for this list is thought to record the names of known or putative opponents of the bill in restraint of appeals and Taylard stands second on it and next to such well-known dissidents as Sir William Essex, Sir Richard Shirley and Sir George Throckmorton. It may be that Taylard's initial acquiescence in what was demanded of this Parliament gave way to disenchantment and that the change did not escape official notice: by this time he was almost certainly married, and the strongly Catholic Mordaunts could well have influenced both his outlook and his fortunes. Such an interpretation of the meagre evidence gains some colour from Taylard's record in local government: named to a variety of commissions, and nominated for sheriff five times between 1532 and 1541, he was passed over at each pricking and not chosen until 1546. His parliamentary career exhibits a similar pattern: it is not known whether he was returned to the Parliament of June 1536, in accordance with the

King's request for the re-election of the previous Members, but he did not sit again for the shire (save, perhaps, in 1545, when the names of the Members are lost, or in the spring of 1553, when the name of only one Member is known) until the reign of Mary.[5]

What looks like Taylard's partial withdrawal or exclusion from public affairs under Henry VIII was to become more evident in the following reign. Put off the commission of the peace for his shrieval year in 1546-7 he was not restored to it nor employed, as before, on judicial ones: only three such appointments came his way. His demotion is not surprising in view of a clash between him and the Protector Somerset in October 1547. When one Dowve and certain others of St. Neots, which lies not far from Diddington, carried out the injunctions of that year to remove 'certain images of abuse' from the church there, Taylard, who was still sheriff, and Oliver Leder*, the steward of St. Neots, tried to make them restore the images and, when they failed in this, so maltreated Dowve as to cause a tumult. Dowve complained to the Protector, who was then passing through from Scotland, and Somerset told Taylard and Leder in friendly fashion to stop molesting the image-breakers, but no sooner had he left than the two started making fresh trouble for Dowve. They were then summoned before the Council and again ordered by Somerset to behave themselves, 'upon pain, if they were found any more culpable in that part, to be therefor sharply punished'.[6]

With the accession of Mary, Taylard resumed full public activity: he was restored to the commission of the peace, served again for oyer and terminer and gaol delivery, and had another term as sheriff. With his comrade Oliver Leder he reappeared in the House of Commons, which had probably not seen him for 17 years; not surprisingly, the Members who 'stood for the true religion', that is, for Protestantism, did not enlist his support. Yet neither then nor later can he have distinguished himself by his zeal for Catholicism, for the Elizabethan settlement was not to interfere with his public life as the Edwardian Reformation had done: in 1564 the bishop of Lincoln categorized him as 'indifferent' in religion and he kept his place on the commission of the peace. He was included in that of 1573/74 but apparently died in 1573 when letters of administration were issued for his estate. His eldest son had predeceased him and the heir was a granddaughter Catherine, who married into the Catholic family of Brudenell and whose son Thomas became the 1st Earl of Cardigan.[7]

[1] Date of birth estimated from age at grandmother's and brother's i.p.m.s, E150/68/3, 71/4. *Vis. Hunts.* (Cam. Soc. xliii), 89-90; Mill

Stephenson, *Mon. Brasses*, 487; *Vis. Surr.* (Harl. Soc. xliii), 52, 222-3. [2] *LP Hen. VIII*, iii-v, vii, viii, x, xii, xiii, xv-xviii, xx, xxi; *CPR*, 1547-8, pp. 75, 76, 292, 369; 1550-3, p. 141; 1553, p. 354; 1553-4, pp. 20, 29, 34; 1563-6, pp. 22-23, 41, 491; 1569-72, p. 220. [3] *VCH Hunts*. ii. 265, 270-1; Harl. 2044, f. 113 (formerly 89); E150/10/4, 68/2, 3; 179/122/91, 99, 109. [4] *Vis. Hunts.* 89-91; *VCH Hunts*. ii. 240, 327; C1/541/55. [5] *LP Hen. VIII*, v-vii; ix. 1077 citing SP1/99, p. 234; xi, xvi, xix, xxi. [6] *APC*, ii. 140-1. [7] *APC*, vii. 58; *Cam. Misc.* ix(3), 29; *Hunts. Wills* (Index Lib. xlii), 149; *Surr. Arch. Colls.* xxviii. 69; J. Wake, *Brudenells of Deene*, 47.

T.M.H.

TAYLOR, John I (by 1493-1547 or later), of Hastings, Suss.

HASTINGS 1529*,[1] ?1536

b. by 1493. *m.* Jane Bell, 1s.[2]

Commoner, Hastings 1514, chamberlain 1521, jurat 1522-46, bailiff 1524-5, 1528-9, 1534-5; bailiff to Yarmouth 1526, 1529, 1535, 1545.[3]

In his younger days John Taylor was the master of a small trading vessel, but he later engaged in brewing: he lived in the parish of St. Clement, where his mother had been buried. Once he had become a commoner of Hastings he frequently attended Brotherhoods of the Cinque Ports. On 4 June 1524, when bailiff, he made a mark in acknowledgment of £60 paid to him by Sir John Dauntesey* for transporting various noblemen and servants of the Emperor from Calais to Dover. In his same year of office he answered by indenture for the payment of subsidy by aliens living at Hastings, and when bailiff again in 1528 he was ordered by the Brotherhood to raise a levy of £7 on fishermen of Hastings for alleged breach of the regulations governing the Yarmouth fair.[4]

Taylor was by-elected for Hastings to the Parliament of 1529, but in the absence of any record both the date and the occasion are uncertain. The two Members returned at the general election died during the course of the Parliament, Richard Calveley in the winter of 1529-30 and Thomas Shoyswell in the spring or summer of 1534; Calveley may have been replaced by 1532 or his seat have remained vacant until Shoyswell's death, which would then have left the port unrepresented. Thus of the two men who, according to a list of Members of later compilation, sat for Hastings from 1534 either Taylor or John Durrant may have done so since 1532 or both have come in together two years later; in the first of these cases Taylor's slight seniority in municipal office makes him the likelier to have taken precedence. Both continued in the House until the dissolution of April 1536 and were then almost certainly re-elected to the Parliament called two months later: Hastings could be counted on to comply with the King's request for the return of the previous Members, as did all the Cinque Ports whose Members are known. To the question whether both Members, or either of them, served again in the Parliament of 1539 no answer can be given.

Taylor made his will on 5 Apr. 1547, but it bears no date of probate. He asked to be buried near his mother. His wife was to have his maltmill and brewhouse and the residue of his goods, and was to be the executrix; on her death a shop at the pier was to pass to his brother-in-law William Bell. His son John received only a gown furred with fox; Richard Godfrey and his wife Agnes were to have four silver spoons; his grandson, another John, four silver spoons, a 'great spit' and 'a brass pot with a broken brim'; and Richard Godfrey and his wife another four silver spoons.[5]

¹ Add. 34150, f. 137. ² Date of birth estimated from first reference. Lewes archdeaconry ct. A1, f. 140. ³ *Cinque Ports White and Black Bks.* (Kent Arch. Soc. recs. br. xix), 154, 182, 186, 191, 198, 205, 207, 209, 217, 220, 234. ⁴ E122/36/1; *LP Hen. VIII*, iv; *Lay Subsidy Rolls 1524-5* (Suss. Rec. Soc. lvi), 165; *Cinque Ports White and Black Bks.* 200, 203, 207. ⁵ Lewes archdeaconry ct. A1, f. 140.

P.H.

TAYLOR, John II (by 1533–68), of Burton-upon-Trent, Staffs.

LICHFIELD 1554 (Apr.)

b. by 1533. *m.* (1) by 1554, Alice; (2) settlement 1 Oct. 1567, Helen, da. of Ralph Okeover of Okeover, by Maud, da. of Sir William Bassett* of Blore, Staffs. and Meynell Langley, Derbys., 1da.[1]
Escheator, Staffs. 1555–6; commr. i.p.m. Francis Meverell* 1566.[2]

John Taylor, gentleman, had many namesakes in Staffordshire and elsewhere. Among them were the yeoman of the chamber who died not long after his appointment in June 1564 as woodward of Iverley wood, Staffordshire; the messenger of the receipt of the Exchequer appointed to that office in May 1545 and reappointed to it in survivorship with his son in July 1555; the translator of Valerius Maximus who was born in 1536 at Amberley, Sussex; a receiver for the duchy of Lancaster in London and the home counties who lived at Enfield, Middlesex, and who in 1585 petitioned the Queen for the relief of his poverty; a London Skinner of Staffordshire origin who died in 1592; and the John Taylor who sold property in the parish of St. Clement Danes, Middlesex, to William Paget, Lord Paget in May 1556.[3]

It was clearly at Paget's nomination that Taylor was returned for Lichfield to the Parliament of April 1554. The first reference found to the connexion between them dates from the previous January, when Richard Cupper* had recently repaid Taylor a sum of £4 owed to him by Paget. In December 1554 Taylor and his wife acquired from Paget the manor of Appleby Magna in Derbyshire and Leicestershire, and Caldon chapel in Staffordshire;

Taylor afterwards leased from Paget other Staffordshire properties at Burton and Horninglow. Between 1555–6 and 1557–8 Taylor appears as bailiff of several of Paget's manors in Staffordshire, and in March 1559 Paget wrote to Taylor as bailiff of his property at Burton. That the Member was this servant of Paget's, and not a forbear of the Taylors found at Lichfield in the later 16th century, is all but proved by the absence of a John Taylor from the subsidy rolls for the city and by the fact that John Taylor of Burton had no son. An inquisition held on 2 Sept. 1569 found that he had died on 13 Nov. 1568 leaving a three-week-old daughter named Maud as heir to an estate valued at £6 a year. She was the child of his second marriage to the granddaughter of a prominent Staffordshire gentleman.[4]

¹ Date of birth estimated from first reference. J. C. Wedgwood, *Staffs. Parl. Hist.* (Wm. Salt Arch. Soc.), i. 342–3; *CPR*, 1554–5, p. 135; C142/151/21. ² *CPR*, 1563–6, p. 30; 1569–72, p. 9. ³ C193/32/1; *LP Hen. VIII*, xvi, xx; *CPR*, 1554–5, p. 255; 1555–7, pp. 32, 86; 1563–6, pp. 90, 118, 323; 1569–72, p. 270; *Al. Cant.* iv. 205; PCC 89 Harrington. ⁴ Staffs. RO, D(W) A34/3/4/26(1); 1734/3/4/34; Paget mss 139/53 ex inf. C. J. Harrison; *CPR*, 1554–5, p. 135; C142/151/21.

A.D.K.H.

TAYLOR, Richard (by 1517–73 or later), of Haverfordwest, Pemb.

HAVERFORDWEST 1553 (Oct.)

b. by 1517, s. of Philip Taylor of Haverfordwest. *m.* by 1551, Elizabeth.[1]
Mayor, Haverfordwest 1538–9, 1546–7, member, town council by 1539–46 or later; commr. relief 1550, goods of churches and fraternities 1553; j.p. 1555–64 or later, q. 1573/74.[2]

Richard Taylor was a merchant living in St. Martin's parish, Haverfordwest, where his goods were assessed at £40 in 1545. The few glimpses of his progress derive from lawsuits. The first of these arose out of his being accosted, when he was mayor in 1539, by the servants of John Wogan* as he was on his way to St. Bartholomew's fair. Two cases heard at the Pembrokeshire great sessions in September 1551 concerned his property: in the first he alleged dispossession of a freehold tenement in Haverfordwest, in the second he charged a husbandman with cutting his grass and killing his sheep, crimes for which the defendant was executed. Another disputed title to a messuage in Haverfordwest brought Taylor into Chancery while Gardiner held the great seal; he had earlier been in that court with Richard Howell* and two other Haverfordwest merchants, following a deal between them and a Breton merchant for the supply of bell metal from the dissolved religious houses of Haverfordwest and St. Dogmael's.[3]

Taylor was only once elected to Parliament, and then, according to the defeated candidate Hugh

Carne of Haverfordwest, because the sheriff, Lewis Eynon, returned him illegally. Carne appeared in person before the barons of the Exchequer on 13 Oct. 1553, the eighth day of the session, but to what effect is not known since the record ends with Carne's seeking process against the sheriff. If, as is likely, Taylor retained his seat he acquiesced in the measures passed in this Parliament towards the restoration of Catholicism.[4]

Taylor continues to appear on the Haverfordwest commission of the peace until 1573/74 but no trace has been found of him thereafter.

[1] Date of birth estimated from first reference. C1/1386/1; NLW ms Wales 25/9, m. 2. [2] NLW Haverfordwest recs. 2139, ff. 2–5; *Cal. Haverfordwest Recs.* (Univ. Wales Bd. of Celtic Studies, Hist. and Law ser. xxiv), 19–21; C219/19/60; *CPR*, 1553, pp. 364, 419; 1563–4, p. 31. [3] E179/223/438; NLW Haverfordwest recs. 2139, f. 2; ms Wales 25/9, mm. 2, 10; C1/1214/1–2. [4] E159/333, Mich. 88.

P.S.E.

TAYLOR alias PERCE (PEERS, PERES), Peter
(by 1512–59 or later), of Marlborough, Wilts.

MARLBOROUGH 1554 (Nov.)

b. by 1512, ?s. of Peter Taylor of Marlborough.[1]
Member, mayor's council, Marlborough by 1542.[2]

The name Peter Taylor first appears in the general entry book of Marlborough corporation for 1532–3, where an older and a younger man who bore it are listed among the freemen. It was presumably the younger one who recurs in the next surviving book, for 1536–7, and who was by 1542 one of the mayor's 19 councillors. He was among the 47 taxpayers in the parish of St. Mary and St. Peter in 1544–5, when he was assessed at the modest sum of 8s. towards the benevolence; six years later he was called upon to pay 20s. on goods worth £20 in the Barley ward, nearly twice as much as was required of John Broke I*, with whom he was to sit in Parliament.[3]

The earliest reference to Taylor's *alias* 'Perce' is on the parliamentary return of 31 Oct. 1554; it reappears in the record of his prosecution as a 'seceder' in the following year, where he is called a tailor by trade, and in his grant of a pardon at Elizabeth's accession, where he is described as an innholder. The implied insufficiency of the name Taylor for such purposes suggests that it was an occupational one and that its bearer's family name was Perce. In the form Peers this name was borne by at least two other Marlborough men christened Peter: a Peter Peers and his father and namesake were party to a suit settled in the mayor's court in 1525, the younger of them was shortly afterwards arrested for brawling at night, and either he or another so named was the barber who in 1557 occupied a messuage in High Street belonging to Geoffrey Daniell*. It is possible that Peter Taylor

and Peter Peers were one and the same, more probable that they were members of the same family.[4]

In electing Taylor and Broke to the third Marian Parliament the borough deferred to the Queen's request for the return of townsmen, but in Taylor's case the result belied the hope that such Members would prove amenable. Found absent when the House was called early in January 1555 he was prosecuted in the following Easter term, distrained 40s. for non-appearance but later allowed time to answer, which he evidently failed to do before the Queen's death put an end to the proceedings. The court's restraint in dealing with him may imply that he was not regarded as a serious offender, but it was doubtless to consign the episode to oblivion that he sued out a pardon in 1559. No further trace of him has been found.[5]

[1] Date of birth estimated from first reference. [2] Marlborough corp. gen. entry bk. 1542–3, f. 2. [3] Ibid. 1532–3, f. 1; 1537–8, f. 1; *Two Taxation Lists* (Wilts. Arch. Soc. recs. br. x), 25; E179/198/257. [4] KB 27/1176, 1180; 29/188, f. 48v; *CPR*, 1557–8, p. 243; 1558–60, p. 227; *Wilts. Arch. Mag.* xix. 81–83; *Two Taxation Lists*, 92; Marlborough corp. gen. entry bk. 1542–3, ff. 25–34, 35. [5] KB 27/1176, 1180; 29/188, f. 48v; *CPR*, 1558–60, p. 227.

T.F.T.B.

TEDLOWE see TADLOWE

TEMPEST, Sir Richard (c.1480–1537), of Bracewell and Bowling, Yorks.

APPLEBY 1529

b. c.1480, 1st s. of Nicholas Tempest of Bracewell by Cecily or Margaret, da. of Sir John Pilkington† of Pilkington, Lancs. and Sowerby, Yorks. *m.* settlement 13 July 1497, Rosamund (*d.*1 Feb. 1554), da. and h. of Tristram Bolling (*d.*30 May 1502) of Bowling, at least 5s. 1da. *suc.* fa. 1483, uncle 1 July 1507. Kntd. 25 Sept. 1513.[1]
Steward, duchy of Lancaster, Bradford 1505–?*d.*, Blackburn hundred 1511–*d.*, Rochdale in 1527, Barnoldswick by 1537, master forester, Bowland by 1526–*d.*, keeper, Quernmore park in 1527; esquire of the body by 1509, knight by 1521; j.p. Yorks. (W. Riding) 1511–21, Yorks. 1530, (E. Riding) 1532, 1536, (N. Riding) 1536; commr. musters, Yorks. (W. Riding) 1511, 1512, subsidy Yorks. 1512, 1514, 1515, (W. Riding) 1524, for redress of outrages, west marches 1531; other commissions 1530–5; feodary, Yorks. 1514; sheriff 1516–17; receiver, 3rd Earl of Derby's lands in Lancs. in 1523; steward, Wakefield and constable, Sandall castle by 1530.[2]

Richard Tempest's father was a younger son in a leading Yorkshire family who were tenants and kinsmen of the great baronial house of Clifford. On his father's death Tempest was probably entrusted to the guardianship of his uncle Sir Thomas Tempest who arranged his marriage to an heiress and bequeathed him the family seat at Bracewell, where Richard Tempest is said to have built a new house. It may have been to another relative, Thomas Lord

Darcy of Temple Hurst, that he owed his advancement in the service of the crown and at court: Tempest was later to say that he would take Darcy's part against any lord in England. He received his first office, a duchy of Lancaster stewardship, as early as 1505, attended the funeral of Henry VII as an esquire of the body, apparently fought in the French campaign of 1513 and was knighted at Tournai (although according to some accounts he had also fought at Flodden earlier in the same month), and seven years later attended the Field of Cloth of Gold, where he was one of three knights charged with scouting the countryside in the interests of security; he was also present at the meeting of Henry VIII and the Emperor at Gravelines. In 1527 the Duke of Richmond expressed his gratification with Tempest as one 'at all times ... ready to do unto me all the pleasure he can'. Less satisfactory were his constant feuds and quarrels with his neighbours: in 1523, when he was serving against the Scots, the Earl of Surrey tried to reconcile him with Sir Henry Savile, and in November 1530 at Cawood the fallen Wolsey made a similar attempt to make peace between Tempest and Brian Hastings, 'between whom was like to ensue great murder'.[3]

Tempest evidently owed his return to the Parliament of 1529 to Henry Clifford, 1st Earl of Cumberland. Nothing is known of his role in the Commons but he may have taken advantage of his presence there to commend himself to Cromwell: in June 1532 he thanked the minister for being good to his son-in-law Thomas Waterton I*, and among the matters on which they corresponded was Tempest's continuing feud with Sir Henry Savile, which in 1534 reached such a pitch that both men risked removal from the Yorkshire bench. His involvement in border warfare caused Tempest to miss at least the beginning of the fifth session (1533) of the Parliament, and on 3 Nov. 1534, the day the seventh session opened, he was still at Bowling. He was probably returned for Appleby again in 1536, in accordance with the King's general request for the re-election of the previous Members, but the 'Mr. Tempest' whose name appears with three others on the dorse of an Act concerning expiring laws which was passed by this Parliament is likely to have been his kinsman Sir Thomas Tempest, a lawyer and servant of the crown.[4]

On the outbreak of the northern rising of 1536 Tempest offered to join Lord Darcy at Pontefract against the rebels, but Darcy (who was to be executed for his behaviour in the crisis) told him to stay at Wakefield. When Tempest did come to Pontefract it was to join the rebellious commons and in November he was among their captains at York. He was to be described as 'neither good first nor last' and was certainly less committed than his younger brother Nicholas, but his failure to rally to the crown contrasted ill with the vigour he had shown in the previous year when faced with a smaller insurrection in Craven. Nicholas Tempest was executed on 25 May 1537 and a week later the 3rd Duke of Norfolk thanked Cromwell for advising him of the King's suspicion of Sir Richard Tempest and John Nevill*, 3rd Lord Latimer. Summoned to court to answer the charges brought against him, Tempest was imprisoned in the Fleet. His plea to Cromwell to be released on bail for fear of infection was not entertained but was evidently justified, for he died on 25 Aug. 1537. He had made a will on 6 Jan. 1536, presumably before setting out to attend the last session of the Parliament of 1529, and had then asked to be buried in Bradford church if he died in the parish. According to John Gostwick* he willed before his death that his heart should be taken north and buried in the place he had prepared for himself and his wife, whom he had appointed executrix. Tempest's heir was his son Sir Thomas, then 40 years of age, and the will was proved on 29 Jan. 1538.[5]

[1] Date of birth estimated from age (variously given) in uncle's i.p.m., *CIPM Hen. VII*, iii. 362, 506. *Yorks. Arch. Jnl.* xi. 246; *Test. Ebor.* vi (Surtees Soc. cvi), 60–62; C142/59/11. [2] Somerville, *Duchy*, i. 498, 501, 506, 508, 522, 532; *LP Hen. VIII*, i–viii; *Statutes*, iii. 86, 117, 175. [3] *Yorks. Arch. Jnl.* xi. 247–8; xviii. 370, 379; *Northern Hist.* i. 51, 55; *LP Hen. VIII*, i, iii, iv, xi; *Bradford Antiquary*, n.s. i. 494; *Chron. Calais* (Cam. Soc. xlii), 22; *Rutland Pprs.* (Cam. Soc. xxi), 33, 42–43, 101; *Cam. Misc.* iii(4), p. lii; R. R. Reid, *King's Council in the North*, 96; G. Cavendish, *Wolsey* (EETS ccxliii), 144–6; M. H. and R. Dodds, *Pilgrimage of Grace*, i. 56, 61; Elton, *Policy and Police*, 304, 348–9. [4] *LP Hen. VIII*, iv–viii; House of Lords RO, Original Acts 28 Hen. VIII, no. 6. [5] M. H. and R. Dodds, i. 172, 235, 250, 312, 314; ii. 144, 218; R. B. Smith, *Land and Pol.* 134, 175, 189–90, 194, 199–202; *Northern Hist.* i. 47; *LP Hen. VIII*, xi, xii; C142/59/11 and E150/236/18, giving the date of death incorrectly as 20 Aug.; *Test. Ebor.* vi. 60–62.

A.D.

TEMPEST, Sir Thomas (c.1476–1543/44), of Holmside, co. Dur.

NEWCASTLE-UPON-TYNE 1529, ?1536[1]

b. c.1476, yr. s. of Robert Tempest of Holmside by Anne, da. of Thomas Lambton of Lambton. *educ.* Clare, Camb. BA 1493, fellow 1494; L. Inn, adm. 1496. *m.* (1) Elizabeth, da. and coh. of Sir William Brough of East Hauxwell, Yorks., 1da.; (2) 1530, Anne, da. of Thomas Lenthall of Latchford, Oxon. Kntd. 25 Sept. 1523.[2]

Butler, L. Inn 1506–7, pens. 1507–8, marshal 1512, Autumn reader 1513, Lent 1517, gov. 1517–18, bencher 1519–20.

J.p. bpric. Dur. 1507–23, Yorks. (N. Riding) 1511–?d., (E. Riding) 1525–?d., (W. Riding) 1525–?d., Northumb. 1525–38, Cumb. 1525–42, Westmld. 1525–37, Yorks. 1530, ?Lincs. (Holland)1537–?d.; steward, bpric. Dur. 1510–d., comptroller by 1522; commr. musters, Yorks. 1511, (N. Riding) 1511, 1512;

other commissions in northern counties 1509–*d.*; under marshal, Tournai 1515; recorder, Newcastle by 1517–36 or later; steward, manor of Northallerton, Yorks. by 1523; member, council of Duke of Richmond and comptroller of household 1525–36; esquire of the body 1526; member, council in the north 1530–*d.*; ?sheriff, Yorks. 1542–3.[3]

A cadet branch of the Tempests of Bracewell had been settled at Holmside since Sir Robert Umfraville, himself one of the cadet line of a great house, chose as his heir the Tempest husband of one of his four great-nieces. Thomas Tempest, who must be distinguished from several kinsmen and namesakes both in the palatinate and at Bracewell, was in his own words 'born to no lands and of mean substance', but his education at a university and an inn of court was to prove a sufficient endowment. Although he never reached the summit of his profession—there seems to be no evidence of his having become, as has been claimed, a serjeant—he was in middle life a leading figure at Lincoln's Inn and a rising administrator in the bishopric of Durham. As befitted a northern gentleman he also saw some military service, and during his time at Tournai he earned the respect of the lieutenant, Lord Mountjoy, who offered unsuccessful resistance to Wolsey's demand for his replacement by one of the cardinal's own men. He also made his way at court and in 1517 assisted at the banquet held at Greenwich for the French Queen and the imperial ambassador.[4]

From 1517 Tempest devoted himself almost wholly to affairs in the north. References to him as recorder of Newcastle in 1517 and 1536 show that he held the office throughout the intervening years: his connexion with Holmside gave him a residence close to the town. Of his military experiences he was to tell Cromwell in 1537 that he had served the King since the beginning of his reign in all his notable wars in the north, always with upwards of 100 persons without wages. In 1522 he was praised for his diligence in mustering the bishopric's forces to meet the Scots, and when in 1523 the Earl of Surrey reported to Wolsey that the burning of Jedburgh had been entrusted to two sure men, Sir William Bulmer* and Thomas Tempest, the earl claimed that 'no journey made into Scotland in no man's day living with so few a number is recounted to be so high an enterprise as this both with those countrymen and Scottish men'. The raid earned Tempest his knighthood, and six years later the two comrades-in-arms made a marital alliance by matching his only child with Bulmer's grandson.[5]

Tempest's growing stature in the north was reflected in his inclusion from 1525 in commissions of the peace for four northern counties: he also progressed at court, being made an esquire of the body, and he is found in association with leading private households. In 1526 his kinsman Thomas Lord Darcy paid him fees probably for legal services, and he may have counselled Darcy's stepson the 4th Earl of Westmorland: his second wife, whom he married in 1530, was described in the licence as of Brancepeth, the earl's seat, and in 1538 he was involved in land transactions between the crown, the earl and Sir Christopher Danby*. Chosen a member of the newly-formed Duke of Richmond's council, he was active in its judicial work as well as being comptroller of the duke's household. When the council's authority in the marches failed he was one of the three councillors sent to aid the new warden, the 4th Earl of Northumberland, in the government of the borders. In 1528 he was a commissioner to negotiate a treaty of peace with Scotland.[6]

As the town's recorder, and a man who enjoyed the confidence of the crown, Tempest was a natural choice to sit for Newcastle in the Parliament of 1529. (He may well have sat six years earlier, the names of the Newcastle Members on that occasion being unknown.) He presumably played a part in securing the passage during the first session of the Act (21 Hen. VIII, c.18) which confirmed the town's monopoly in the loading and unloading of goods in the area of the Tyne; the measure was partially directed against the bishop's rights and may have been occasioned by the vacancy in the see following its surrender by Wolsey. The only other hint of Tempest's role in the House during this Parliament is the inclusion of his name in a list drawn up by Cromwell on the back of a letter of December 1534 and thought to be of Members with a particular, but unspecified, connexion with the treasons bill then on its passage through the Commons. In the intervals of his attendance in Parliament he remained active in the north, serving on a number of commissions, including the inquiry into Wolsey's goods in the bishopric and those into tenths of spiritualities in the palatinate, Cumberland and Northumberland. While engaged on the last of these he corresponded with Cromwell and his request to the minister for a commission to investigate two chantry priests who were failing in their duties may reflect a solicitude for the state of such foundations. It was presumably he and not his kinsman Sir Richard Tempest whose name appears, as 'Mr. Tempest', with three others on the dorse of an Act for continuing expiring laws passed during the Parliament of 1536. To this Parliament he had doubtless been returned again for Newcastle in accordance with the King's general request for the re-election of the previous Members: he may also have sat in one or both of the

Parliaments of 1539 and 1542, for which the names of the Newcastle Members are unknown.[7]

Tempest's career was jeopardised by his conduct during the Pilgrimage of Grace. He appears, after only a slight show of resistance, to have placed himself with Sir William Eure and Robert Bowes* at the head of the revolt in Durham. He accordingly attended the council of the Pilgrims held at York late in November 1536, but he was not present at the meeting of its representatives with the King at Doncaster because he had caught a cold: the disability may have been genuine for he seems to have suffered from persistent ill-health. He transmitted some opinions on the rebel cause to its leader Robert Aske through his friend Robert Bowes: what they were is not known, although Aske said later that they were in favour of the reformation of certain statutes by Parliament and of the keeping of good order at Doncaster. There is little to be said for the suggestion that he was the author of an anonymous paper bitterly attacking Cromwell and Parliament.[8]

Tempest's survival of the crisis probably owed much to the 3rd Duke of Norfolk. At the time of the Doncaster meeting he was said to have been of old 'much acquainted' with Norfolk and in February 1537 he hailed the duke's arrival in the north as a 'great comfort to all good subjects'. He was appointed to Norfolk's advisory council, attended him throughout his northern progress and was made much use of in the reordering of the north. In March he was busy with the trial of offenders at Durham, but in the following month he and Robert Bowes were charged with conducting certain prisoners to London for trial, including Sir John Bulmer, his daughter's father-in-law. With the Percy estates in the hands of the crown, he was given custody of the sons of the attainted Sir Thomas Percy. Norfolk described Tempest in a letter to Cromwell as 'at more charge than his fee will bear'; Tempest himself took up the theme in his correspondence with the minister, but he also lent his support to the duke's plea to be released from the northern assignment and when he was at court in 1537 he explained his patron's position. Before leaving the north the duke had Tempest brought onto the reconstituted council in the north; he was to remain an active member, particularly with respect to the border, until just before his death. It is not clear whether Tempest was sheriff of Yorkshire in 1542–3: he had the necessary qualifications of property and standing but he was ageing and in poor health, so that the man chosen may have been his younger namesake of Bracewell.[9]

His complaints of financial stringency notwithstanding, Tempest was a man of some substance. The extent of his property in Durham is not known, but he may have succeeded to Holmside when his father and elder brother died of plague in 1522. His property in Yorkshire came through his wife and her sister, a widow who in 1518 vested her patrimony in trustees for the benefit of Tempest and his wife. Tempest died between 11 Aug. 1543, when he was said to be permanently ill, and September 1544 when the writ was issued for an inquisition post mortem. No will has been discovered. His heir was his daughter Anne, the wife of Sir Ralph Bulmer.[10]

[1] House of Lords RO, Original Acts 28 Hen. VIII, no. 6. [2] Date of birth estimated from education. Surtees, *Durham*, ii. 324–5. [3] Hutchinson, *Durham*, i. 384, 389, 401, 408–9, 443–4; *LP Hen. VIII*, i–v, viii, xi–xvii; J. Brand, *Newcastle*, ii. 215; R. R. Reid, *King's Council in the North*, 103–4, 113, 150; *Tudor R. Proclamations*, ed. Hughes and Larkin, i. 144. [4] Surtees, ii. 324–5; Burke, *LG*, ii. 1372; *Arch. Aeliana* (ser. 4), xiv. 56–57; *LP Hen. VIII*, ii, xii; *Black Bk. L. Inn*, i. passim; Reid, 103; C. G. Cruickshank, *English Occupation of Tournai*, 93–94. [5] *LP Hen. VIII*, iii, xii; NRA 3811, p. 57. [6] R. Welford. *Newcastle and Gateshead*, ii. 88; A. R. Laws, *Schola Novocastrensis*, i. 25–27; *LP Hen. VIII*, iv, xiii; Reid, 103–4 et passim, 138; *Reg. Bp. Tunstall* (Surtees Soc. clxi), 33. [7] J. R. Nef, *Rise of Coal Industry*, i. 140 et passim; *LP Hen. VIII*, iv. 1522(ii) citing SP1/87, f. 106v; viii; House of Lords RO, Original Acts 28 Hen. VIII, no. 6. [8] Reid, 137; *LP Hen. VIII*, xi, xii; M. H. and R. Dodds, *Pilgrimage of Grace*, i. 357–8, 366, 368, 373. [9] *LP Hen. VIII*, xi–xvi, xviii; Merriman, *Letters, Thos. Cromwell*, ii. 100; *Northumb. Co. Hist.* iii, 228–30. [10] *LP Hen. VIII*, iii, xii, xvii; E150/241/11; *VCH Yorks.* (N. Riding), ii. 412.

M.J.T.

TEMPLE, John (1518/19–58 or later).

| RIPON | 1554 (Apr.) |
| GREAT BEDWYN | 1558 |

b. 1518/19.[1]
Servant, household of Stephen Gardiner, bp. of Winchester by 1538–55; clerk of the enrolments, Chancery 26 Sept. 1554–22 Sept. 1556.[2]

John Temple had namesakes throughout the country, one of whom was in the royal service, but he alone claimed gentility. He is not to be found in the pedigrees of the armigerous family of Temple Hall, Leicestershire, the only ones of that name to survive for the 16th century. A possible clue to his origin is his patronage by Stephen Gardiner, who helped promote the careers of many from near his birthplace in East Anglia. Temple had entered Gardiner's service by early 1538 when he accompanied his master on an embassy to France and his mockery of the French and imperfect command of the language were reported to Thomas Wriothesley. He shared in Gardiner's downfall during Edward VI's reign, testifying on Gardiner's behalf at his trial and losing an annuity of £6 13s.4d. out of the bishopric of Winchester, and later in the bishop's restoration under Mary, when he regained the annuity. His appointment as clerk of the enrolments and his Membership of Mary's second Parliament were alike his master's doing, with the 2nd Earl of Cumberland perhaps acting as an intermediary at Ripon. The Queen's request for townsmen may have prevented his re-election there to the following

Parliament (although in the event the borough failed to comply with it) and by the autumn of 1555 the chancellor was a sick man. Temple witnessed Gardiner's will and bore Our Lady's banner at the interment at Southwark. Within a year he had surrendered his clerkship in favour of a nominee of Chancellor Heath.[3]

Temple presumably owed his second spell in the Commons to links formed while in Gardiner's service, as he had no known ties with Wiltshire. The sheriff Sir Walter Hungerford* was brother-in-law to Temple's ex-colleague James Bassett* and a kinsman of the Hungerford family which had a lien on Great Bedwyn; one of the members of that family, Edward Hungerford, who had sat for the borough in the Parliament of November 1554, had probably been Temple's companion in France; and Sir Anthony Hungerford's* son-in-law Henry Clifford, who had sat for Bedwyn in the intervening Parliament, was a distant relative of the Earl of Cumberland. The Journal does not refer to Temple's part in the House, and it is not clear what significance attaches to the omission of his name from a copy of the Crown Office list of Members for the Parliament of 1558.[4]

No trace of Temple has been found after 1558. If he survived into the reign of Elizabeth his Catholic background would presumably have told against him. The man from whom Sir Anthony Cooke* sought the restoration of cattle in 1569 was a namesake born about 1542 who founded the family at Stowe.[5]

[1] Aged 'a little above' 19 in 1538, *LP Hen. VIII*, xiii. [2] *LP Hen. VIII*, xiii; *Letters of Stephen Gardiner* ed. Muller, 506; *CPR*, 1554-5, p. 32; 1555-7, p. 521. [3] *Vis. Leics.* (Harl. Soc. ii), 167; Add. 5524, f. 162; *LP Hen. VIII*, xiii; *Letters of Stephen Gardiner*, 506; Foxe, *Acts and Mons.* vi. 130, 136, 248; PCC 3 Noodes. [4] Wm. Salt Lib. SMS 264. [5] T. Prime, *Temple Fam.* 12.

R.L.D.

TEMPLEMAN, Nicholas (by 1478–1515 or later), of Dover, Kent.

DOVER 1512,[1] 1515[2]

b. by 1478, ?s. of John Templeman of Dover. *m.*[3]
    Chamberlain, Dover 1505–6, jurat 1510–?*d.*, mayor 1510–11.[4]

Nicholas Templeman was an executor of the will made by his brother John in 1513 and the John Templeman who was mayor of Dover in 1486–7 may have been their father. An artificer by trade, Templeman held property in several of Dover's wards. He represented Dover at the Brotherhood of the Cinque Ports in 1499 and 1511. His Membership of the Parliaments of 1512 and 1515 is known only from his receipt of parliamentary wages and expenses in respect of them. These are preceded in the accounts by a payment in 1511–12 of £3 'in part of his pay-

ment for being burgess of Parliament' which may mean that, like John Warren, his fellow-Member in 1512 and 1515, he had also sat in 1510. For the first session of the Parliament of 1512 he was paid £6 2s. for 61 days' attendance, which included six days for travel; he received other payments for unspecified days' attendance at the later sessions and £3 6s. for only 33 days of the first session of the Parliament of 1515, which lasted 60 days, whereas Warren was paid in full for both its sessions. Templeman's poor attendance at the first and apparent absence from the second may have been due to illness and death: his name disappears from the list of jurats after September 1515 and a survey of Dover taken about 1520 shows that his widow had by then married one John Pysker.[5]

[1] Add. 29618, f. 55v; Egerton 2092, f. 90. [2] Add. 29618, f. 104v; Egerton 2092, f. 107. [3] Date of birth estimated from first reference. Add. 29617, f. 14; Egerton 2093, ff. 4v–13. [4] Add. 29617, f. 297; 29618, f. 33; Egerton 2092, passim. [5] Canterbury prob. reg. C11, f. 69; Add. 29617, ff. 262, 341v; 29618, ff. 53v, 55v, 59v, 104v; Egerton 2092, ff. 62, 90; 2093, ff. 4v–13; 2094, ff. 17–22; *Cinque Ports White and Black Bks.* (Kent Arch. Soc. recs. br. xix), 124, 147.

P.H.

TEMYS (TEMMYS, TEMSE), Thomas (by 1508–75), of Shorwell, I.o.W. and West Ashling, Suss.

WESTBURY 1529

b. by 1508, 5th s. of William Temys of Rood Ashton, Wilts. by Joan, da. of Robert Baynard† of Lackham, Wilts. *m.* by 1545, Elizabeth, da. of one Bowes of London, at least 1s. 1da.[1]
    Auditor and steward, manor cts. of Lacock abbey by 1535; ?servant of Cromwell c.1538; centenier, I.o.W. in 1545.[2]

The youngest of five sons, Thomas Temys might have had little prospect of advancement but for the fact that he was the brother of Joan Temys, the last abbess of the Augustinian nunnery at Lacock. She succeeded to that office, so it appears, shortly before 1516 and was to surrender the abbey to the crown in July 1539. She recruited her two youngest brothers to her service, Christopher as steward of her household and Thomas as a leading official of the abbey. The town of Westbury, near which lay the Temys family home, was within 15 miles of the main abbey lands. It is not known what influence his connexion with the abbey had on Temys's election in 1529, although the fact that its chief steward was the influential Sir Edward Baynton, himself returned as one of the knights for Wiltshire, is suggestive; his mother's family, the powerful Baynards of Lackham, may also have helped him. Of his part in the Commons' proceedings there is only one indication, but that a striking one. It dates from April 1532, when the House received a delegation of peers, headed by Chancellor More, which asked for a grant towards the fortification of the Scottish border. After two Members had argued that this was unnecessary, the best fortifications being the maintenance of justice at home and of friendship abroad, Temys fastened on the second of these aims of policy and, in the words of the chronicler Hall, who probably heard him, 'moved the Commons to sue to the King, to take the Queen again into his company, and declared certain great mischiefs, as in bastarding the Lady Mary, the King's only child, and divers other inconveniences'. What effect Temys's words had on the House we do not know, but the King, when they were reported to him, took the initiative by raising the matter when the Commons waited on him on 30 April. After expressing surprise that 'one of the parliament house' should have spoken openly of his separation from the Queen, 'which matter was not to be determined there, for he said it touched his soul', he described the 'grudge of conscience' which had assailed him over the marriage. The tone of the King's words, as reported by Hall, was one of sorrow rather than anger, but they vetoed any further discussion of the subject in Parliament.[3]

Whether they silenced Temys is not known, although when, less than 12 months later, Cromwell drew up what is believed to be a list of Members opposed to the bill in restraint of appeals his name was not included, and this despite the fact that Temys sat for one of the centres of the west country cloth trade, which was well represented by other names on the list. It is possible that he had ceased to attend regularly, but even if Westbury paid him wages no evidence has survived which might have thrown light on the point. In the same way, the loss of the names of the Westbury Members for the three succeeding Parliaments rules out any check of Temys's attitude based on his reappearance or disappearance as a Member.[4]

There are, however, hints that in course of time he came to terms with the regime. A list dating from 1538 of those in waiting on Cromwell includes his name among the 'gentlemen not to be allowed [that is, required and probably paid] in my lord's household . . . but when they have commandment or cause necessary to repair there': it was perhaps only a foot in the door, but it was not banishment. Two years later a 'Thomas Thame' attended the reception of Anne of Cleves. That Temys was the man concerned is the less improbable by reason of his employment in local administration. In March 1538 he and six others had taken depositions at Shorwell about local rumours that Queen Anne Boleyn had been 'boiled in lead'. Shorwell was a manor of which in September 1529 Temys had received an 80-year lease from Lacock abbey and

which in February 1544, some years after the Dissolution, he and his wife were to be granted in fee, at a cost of nearly £300. In June 1546 Temys leased much of his Shorwell property to a local man, John Lovibond: if Lovibond's statement in a chancery petition is to be believed, Temys had promised to do this before he bought the manor, in return for a loan of £82 from Lovibond towards the purchase price.[5]

Although Temys was to retain Shorwell until his death, his leasing of it in 1546 seems to have ended his active interest in the Isle of Wight in favour of Wiltshire and, later, Sussex. To judge from another lawsuit of about this time the reason may have been, at least in part, a far from creditable one. Meeting Temys at Portsmouth, a local butcher named Ireland assaulted him, declaring

> that at the taking of the French men and French ships in the Isle of Wight I stood in the King's garrison like a man when thou as a traitor and coward fleddest out of said Isle with thy wife and conveyest then all thy plate and thy money with thee as the King's untrue subject.

That Temys was there, or was supposed to be there, in July 1545 is clear from the inclusion of his name among those providing men for the Hampshire forces, but there is no way of testing the accusation, which Temys himself denied. Yet his seeming withdrawal from the island so soon after it had suffered its worst invasion of the century prompts the suspicion that the moral courage which Temys had once shown in the House was not matched by his physical courage in the field.[6]

It was at Temys's house called 'Le Pryorye' at Chitterne, Wiltshire, that the lease of Shorwell called for rent to be paid. The manor of Chitterne Temys had bought in 1543 from Sir John Williams* and another, but he had had an interest there since 1538, when he paid Lacock abbey £150 for a large flock of sheep which was kept at Chitterne. When Lacock was dissolved and acquired by (Sir) William Sharington* (Temys's relative by marriage) Temys was kept on there, at least for a time, as auditor and steward of the courts at his previous salary. His own most important acquisition from Lacock was the manor of Bishopstrow. The abbess had leased the manor there for 99 years to her sister and brother-in-law, Elizabeth and Robert Bath (a Bishopstrow clothier), and it was subject to this lease that in 1544 Temys bought the manor from the crown for £506. However, completion was unaccountably slow: Temys appears to have paid the first £250 in November 1544 and the balance by September 1546, but it was not until 1 May 1550 that a patent was issued which after stating that Henry VIII had been 'prevented by death' from making the grant, described the property as now indisputably his.[7]

Although Temys was not to die until 12 Feb. 1575, next to nothing has transpired about the last 25 years of his life. His earlier championship of Princess Mary seems to have found no echo when she came to the throne and he was never put on the bench. It is not known at what stage he moved from the Isle of Wight to Sussex, where he was resident at his death: the last known transaction in which he was involved, dating from May 1570, shows him and Giles Estcourt† selling the manor of Whitley and other lands in or near Calne, Wiltshire, to one William Jordan. His son John, who continued to live chiefly in Sussex, sold Bishopstrow in 1577 or 1578.[8]

[1] Presumed to be of age at election. *VCH Wilts.* iii. 313; C142/172/160; *The Gen.* n.s. xiii. 24; *Wilts. N. and Q.* vi. 554–6. [2] *Val. Eccles.* ii. 117; *LP Hen. VIII*, xx; M. L. Robertson, 'Cromwell's servants' (Univ. California Los Angeles Ph.D. thesis, 1975), 571. [3] W. L. Bowles and J. G. Nichols, *Annals of Lacock Abbey*, 281–2, 291–2; *VCH Wilts.* iii. 313, 314; Hall, *Chron.* 788; P. Hughes, *Ref. in England* (1963 ed.), i. 236; *LP Hen. VIII*, v. [4] *LP Hen. VIII*, ix. 1077 citing SP1/99, p. 234. [5] Ibid. xiii, xiv, xix, xxi; C1/1028/46. [6] St.Ch.2/31/121; *LP Hen. VIII*, xx. [7] *LP Hen. VIII*, xviii; *VCH Wilts.* iii. 314; Bowles and Nichols, 291–2, 311, 313–14; *CPR, 1550–3*, pp. 20–21. [8] C142/172/160; *VCH Wilts.* viii. 6; *CPR, 1569–72*, p. 141; *1572–5*, p. 537.

N.M.F.

TENNANT, Henry (by 1533–?1604), ?of Cleatop, nr. Giggleswick, Yorks.

HASTINGS 1558

b. by 1533, ?s. of Robert Tennant of Cleatop.[1]
Sec. to Sir Thomas Cheyne* by 1554–8; ?gov., Giggleswick g.s. by 1592–d.[2]

The Henry Tennent who appears on the Crown Office list as the second Member for Hastings in 1558 was clearly the nominee of the lord warden, Sir Thomas Cheyne. His dependence on Cheyne appears from two contemporary references: on 9 Sept. 1554 the common assembly of Dover resolved that 'Mr. Henry Tenett, secretary to my lord warden', should be given 40s. as 'solicitor', and in his will of 6 Dec. 1558 Cheyne bequeathed to 'Henry Tennante my servant one yearly rent of £4 by year during his life if sickness be not the cause of his absence from me': as Cheyne had then less than three weeks to live, Tennant presumably came into the legacy. During the lifetime of the Parliament which had ended with Queen Mary's death in the previous month he had doubtless been in attendance on his master, either in London or in Kent helping to prepare for the expected invasion following the fall of Calais.[3]

Of Tennant's origin, introduction to Cheyne and career after Cheyne's death, nothing has been established. Styled gentleman on the list of Members, he could have come of a family settled at Giggleswick in the West Riding and have been the Henry Tennant of that town whose petition, made jointly with the King's chaplain John Nowell and other inhabitants, led to the refounding of Giggleswick grammar school in May 1553. A connexion with Nowell and a concern for education would accord with the secretaryship to Cheyne, who was also linked with the Craven district through his cousin Elizabeth Sandys's marriage to Thomas Lord Darcy after the death of Darcy's first wife, the heir to Giggleswick. If Cheyne's servant was Henry Tennant of Giggleswick he survived his master by nearly half-a-century, during which time no trace of him has been found. He was 'weak in body by reason of old age' when, as Henry Tennant of Cleatop, he made his will on 5 July 1604 and was dead before the last day of that month when the will was proved. He asked for burial in the chancel of Giggleswick church and for a sermon at his funeral, provided for his relatives, godchildren and servants, gave lands worth £100 to send local boys to Cambridge and left his books, apart from a great English bible, to the school. His executors were one of his nephews and the vicar of Giggleswick and his overseers two neighbours, with serjeant Richard Hutton to assist them.[4]

[1] Date of birth estimated from first reference. York wills 29A, ff. 342–5. [2] Egerton 2094, f. 107; *Yorks. Schools*, ii (York. Arch. Soc. rec. ser. xxxiii), 251–4, 261. [3] C193/32/2, f. 8; Egerton 2094, f. 107; PCC 1 Chaynay. [4] *CPR* 1553, p.68; York wills 29A, ff. 342–5.

TEY, Thomas (1486 or 1488–1543), of Layer de la Haye, Essex.

MALDON 1529

b. 31 Oct. 1486 or 1488, 1st s. of William Tey of Layer de la Haye by Elizabeth or Isabel Bassett. *m.* by 1520, Jane, da. of one Harleston, at least 1s. 1da. *suc.* fa. 1500 or 1502.[1]
Servant of earls of Oxford; j.p. Essex 1532–d.; commr. tenths of spiritualities, Essex, Colchester 1535, gaol delivery, Colchester 1536–d.[2]

The Teys were one of the oldest families in Essex. The senior branch was settled at Marks Tey, Essex, and Brightwell Hall, Suffolk, and had as its head Sir Thomas Tey, one of the courtiers who attended Henry VIII at the Field of Cloth of Gold. Thomas Tey came from a cadet branch seated since the early 15th century at Layer de la Haye. In common with most Essex families the Teys were in the service of the earls of Oxford: in 1513 the 13th Earl bequeathed annuities of 53s.4d. to two men named Thomas Tey, one being probably the future Sir Thomas, who was knighted before 1526, and the other his distant cousin of Layer de la Haye.[3]

It was doubtless to his position in the household of the 15th Earl of Oxford that Tey owed his election in 1529, the borough admitting him as a freeman on 4 Oct. of that year: five years later he was to be one of the witnesses to the earl's will. He and Robert Rochester* were the chief counsellors and agents of the 16th Earl in his dispute of the early forties with Thomas Josselyn over the keepership of Oxford's park at Stansted Mountfitchet: although right was clearly on Josselyn's side and his brother-in-law John Gates* prevailed on Henry VIII to order Oxford to admit Josselyn, the earl is said to have hit upon the expedient of disparking to deprive Josselyn of the keepership.[4]

Tey was a beneficiary to the extent of £20 under the will of his cousin John Tey, another Oxford retainer who died in the house of the countess at Wivenhoe after a long illness there. Thomas Tey himself died on 20 Apr. 1543. He had planned to marry his son to a daughter of Edward Denny, one of the barons of the Exchequer, but this project failed despite his resort to Chancery. Tey's will is lost but from his inquisition post mortem it is known that he named as executors a neighbour who had been town clerk of Colchester and another faithful servant of Oxford's, Richard Anthony, whom the earl had nominated for election at Colchester in 1529 but had afterwards ordered to stand down in favour of Richard Rich.[5]

[1] He became 13 on the All Hallows Eve preceding his father's death, which took place, according to the probate of his will (PCC 16 Blamyr), in 1500 but, according to his i.p.m. (C142/16/62), on 8 June 1502. *Vis. Essex* (Harl. Soc. xiii), 297; Essex RO, D/B3/1/2, f. 78. [2] *LP Hen. VIII*, v, vii, viii, xi, xiii–xvii. [3] Morant, *Essex*, ii. 202; *LP Hen. VIII*, iii; *Archaeologia*, lxvi. 319. [4] Essex RO, D/B3/1/2, f. 78; *LP Hen. VIII*, vii, add. [5] PCC 17 Hogen; C1/582/40; 142/69/231; *Cal. Colchester Ct. Rolls* ed. Harrod, 65–66.

D.F.C.

THACKER, John (by 1520–56/57 or later), of Kingston-upon-Hull, Yorks.

KINGSTON-UPON-HULL 1547, 1553 (Oct.), 1554 (Apr.)

b. by 1520.[1]
Sheriff, Hull 1541–2, mayor 1546–7, 1552–3, alderman in 1553; commr. goods of churches and fraternities 1553.[2]

Although he bore a name that was fairly common in Yorkshire and Lincolnshire, nothing has come to light about the personal life of John Thacker. Described on the pardon roll of 1553 as a merchant *alias* alderman of Hull, he may well have been the John Thacker who was among the men from Yorkshire and Lincolnshire summoned in 1546 by Privy Council letters before a commission appointed to settle disputes between German and English merchants. The John Thecher, draper, to whom John Gates* owed £3 14s. in 1542 was probably a different man, although another Member for Hull,

Thomas Dalton, later had business relations with (Sir) Henry Gates*.[3]

Little has come to light about Thacker's role in the Commons save that in April 1554 his help was sought for the unsuccessful attempt to repeal the Licensing Act of 1553 (7 Edw. VI, c.5), but he evidently continued his trading ventures while in attendance there. It was on 26 Nov. 1548, two days after the opening of the second session of the Parliament of 1547, that he and two partners shipped wool from London to Calais: one of the partners was John Tredeneck*, a Cornishman whose marriage to a Lincolnshire woman reflects his connexion with Thacker's part of England. The session was still in progress when, on the following 8 Feb., the consortium acknowledged that they owed the King £244 in customs on the shipment: when this remained unpaid the manor of Salford, Warwickshire, belonging to the third partner Anthony Littleton, was seized by the crown, but whether Thacker or Tredeneck was penalized does not appear.[4]

The last references found to Thacker date from about 1556. Shortly before February of that year he sued Robert Hall of Tuxford, Nottinghamshire, for a debt of £10 18s., and about the same time he bought two messuages in Hull in partnership with Simon, younger brother of Robert Kemsey, who had sat for Hull in 1539. It is not known whether he was the John Thatcher, gentleman, required in July 1557 to take an inquisition post mortem in Yorkshire and other counties on Thomas Lee III*.[5]

[1] Date of birth estimated from first reference. [2] T. Gent, *Kingston-upon-Hull* (1735), 117–18; L. M. Stanewell, *Cal. Anct. Deeds. Kingston-upon-Hull*, D. 598. [3] *Guildhall Studies in London Hist.* i. 48–49; *CPR*, 1553–4, p. 423; *LP Hen. VIII*, xxi, add.; *APC*, i. 535. [4] *CPR*, 1553–4, p. 502. [5] Ibid. 1555–7, p. 143; 1557–8, p. 112; *Yorks. Arch. Soc. rec. ser.* ii. 181.

A.D.

THATCHER (THACKER), James (by 1536–65), of Derby.

DERBY 1558

b. by 1536.[1]
Bailiff, Derby 1557–8.[2]

A mercer by profession, James Thatcher was probably a member of the local family of that name, two of whom had served as bailiffs of Derby before him. He was a bailiff at the time of his election to Mary's last Parliament. On 13 June 1558, during the prorogation, he witnessed the sealing of the indenture of sale by George Stringer* to William Wandell, a former bailiff, of property in the town. When on his return for the second session in November he reported to the Commons that Derby was 'sore infected' he was given leave of absence from the House. He himself survived that visitation only to meet a violent end seven years later. On 12 Sept. 1565, in the course of a quarrel with a fellow-mercer, Ralph Haughton, he received a blow which resulted in his death on the following 30 Nov.; Haughton was indicted for manslaughter, but pleaded that he had acted in self-defence and was pardoned.[3]

[1] Date of birth estimated from first reference. [2] W. Hutton, *Derby*, 80. [3] Ibid. 79–80; Derby Lib. Derbys. deeds 596; *CJ*, i. 51; *CPR*, 1563–6, p. 427.

C.J.B.

THELWALL (THELOAL), Simon (1525/26–86), of Plas y Ward, Llanynys, Denb.

DENBIGH BOROUGHS	1553 (Mar.), 1553 (Oct.), 1559
DENBIGHSHIRE	1563
DENBIGH BOROUGHS	1571

b. 1525/26, 1st s. of Richard Thelwall of Plas y Ward by Elizabeth, da. of Thomas Herle of Stanton Harcourt, Oxon. and Aberystwyth, Card. *educ.* I. Temple, adm. Nov. 1555, called 1568. *m.* (1) Alice, da. of Robert Salesbury of Rûg, Merion. and Bachymbyd, Denb. 4s.; (2) Jane, da. of Thomas Massey* of Broxton and Chester, Cheshire, 1s. 2da.; (3) Margaret, da. of Sir William Gruffydd of Penrhyn, Caern., wid. of Sir Nicholas Dutton, *s.p. suc.* fa. 1568.[1]

Steward, reader's dinner, I. Temple 1579.

Commr. piracy, Denb. 1565, tanneries, Ruthin 1574, musters, Denb. 1580; sheriff, Denb. 1571–2; j.p. 1575–*d.*, steward, Ruthin manor 1575–*d.*; dep. justice, Chester circuit 1576, 1579, v. justice 1580, 1584; member, council in the marches of Wales c.1577.[2]

The Thelwall family had been established in the Ruthin area from about 1380, when John Thelwall arrived as a follower of Reginald de Grey, Lord of Ruthin; the Denbighshire home was acquired when his son married the heiress of Plas y Ward.[3]

Apart from his appearance on the subsidy list of 1544, when he was assessed at Llanynys on goods worth 46s.8d., nothing has come to light about Simon Thelwall before his two elections to Parliament in 1553. These are to be accounted for both by his family's standing at Ruthin, a contributory borough which is known to have taken part in the voting on both occasions, as it was to do in 1559 when Thelwall was re-elected, and by his connexions with leading local figures. Of these Sir John Salusbury, whom Thelwall later served as attorney, and Salusbury's cousin Robert Puleston in turn joined Thelwall in the House as knights of the shire, while Puleston's ally Edward Almer* was sheriff at both elections: another Member of the first Marian Parliament, John Salesbury, may already have become Thelwall's brother-in-law. Thelwall was not among the Members of the Parliament who 'stood for the true religion', although he was later to be known as an earnest Protestant. He may have moved in that direction during his years at the Inner Temple, which he entered at the comparatively advanced age of about 30 in November 1555, two months after being one of the 40 and more men of Denbighshire and Flintshire, among them perhaps George Salusbury*, pardoned for a double murder. Under Elizabeth he was to become a notable figure in his shire and a member of the council in the marches. He died on 18 Apr. 1586.[4]

[1] Aged 60 at death, Dwnn, *Vis. Wales*, ii. 113n, 336; Griffith, *Peds.* 274; *Vis. Oxon.* (Harl. Soc. v), 231; *Vis. Cheshire* (Harl. Soc. xviii), 175–6. [2] *APC*, vii. 286; xi. 243; SC2/225/14, 23; Add. Ch. 41406; P. H. Williams, *Council in the Marches of Wales*, 144, 358–9; W. R. Williams, *Welsh Judges*, 71; R. Flenley, *Cal. Reg. Council, Marches of Wales*, 127, 133, 200, 212. [3] *DWB* (Thelwall fam.). [4] E159/340, Trin. 28–29; 179/220/166; C219/20/187, 21/230; *CPR*, 1555–7, p. 43; NLW Bachymbyd deeds and docs. 543; J. W. Y. Lloyd, *Powys Fadog*, iii. 128–43; PCC 55 Windsor; *HMC Welsh*, i(2), 682.

P.S.E.

THOMAS, John I (by 1490–1540/42), of Cornw.

TRURO	1529

b. by 1490.[1]

Yeoman of the guard by 1511; serjeant-at-arms May 1513–*d.*; constable, Trematon castle, Cornw. May 1515–*d.*; comptroller and collector of customs, duchy of Cornw. May 1515–July 1517; havener, duchy of Cornw. May 1515; commr. subsidy, Cornw. 1523, stanneries 1532; auditor, commission for tenths of spiritualities, Cornw. 1535.[2]

John Thomas was a not uncommon name in Cornwall in the early 16th century, but only one man who bore it was of much consequence; he held several offices at court and in the duchy, he was prosperous (in 1523 his goods were valued at £120, more than four times as much as his next wealthiest namesake) and he lived in the hundred of Powder, in which Truro lay. On all these grounds he is to be identified with the junior Member returned by Truro to the Parliament of 1529. It is true that in 1533 Cromwell noted a vacancy at Truro which was to be filled at 'the King's pleasure', and that as Thomas's fellow-Member Roger Corbet did not die until 1538 an identification with one who was himself still alive in 1540 may appear faulty. It appears likely, however, that Cromwell wrote Truro in mistake for Lostwithiel, the borough which immediately precedes Truro on the list of Members of this Parliament and which itself had a vacancy following the death of Richard Bryan *alias* Croker; in that case there would be no reason to doubt that Thomas outlived the Parliament.[3]

If Thomas remained a Member until this long-drawn-out Parliament was dissolved he probably sat in its brief successor of June 1536, in accordance with the King's request for the re-election of the previous Members, and may have done so in 1539 and 1542, two Parliaments for which the names of the Truro Members are lost. Of his part in the proceedings of the House nothing is known, but there are glimpses of his activity outside it. In 1531 he was ordered to keep watch on a servant of the Marquess of Exeter, four years later he assisted the important commission for tithes, and in 1538 he and others accepted on the crown's behalf the movable effects of the suppressed house of Black Friars at Truro. Thomas was still alive early in 1540, when the havernership of the duchy was granted in reversion to another, but was dead by 22 Sept. 1542, when Nicholas Randall* became constable of Trematon.[4]

[1] Date of birth estimated from first reference. [2] *LP Hen. VIII*, i-iii, viii; Duchy Cornw. RO, 100, mm. 14, 15v; 496, m. 1. [3] E179/87/128, m. 1; 315/78, ff. 136, 160v, 161v, 162v; *LP Hen. VIII*, vii. 56 citing SP1/82, ff. 59-62. [4] *LP Hen. VIII*, v, viii, xiii; F. Rose-Troup, *Western Rebellion*, 24.

J.J.G.

THOMAS, John II (c.1531-81/90), of the Middle Temple, London and Constantine, Cornw.

MITCHELL 1555

b. c.1531, s. and h. of John Thomas of Lelant, Cornw. by (?Elizabeth) da. and h. of one Rosmell of Bodmin, Cornw. *educ.* M. Temple, adm. 6 May 1552. *m.* da. and h. of John Godolphin of Gwennap, Cornw., 2s. *suc.* fa. by Nov. 1547.[1]

John Thomas came of a gentle family who had lived at Lelant for several generations. In 1547 he accused an Elizabeth Thomas widow, perhaps his mother, in Chancery of wrongfully withholding various properties, including Lelant, from him. The outcome of this suit is not known, but judgment probably went against him as he settled at Constantine, where in 1530 one James Thomas, presumably a kinsman, had leased a small estate from the Arundells of Trerice. A connexion with this family (strengthened by later marriage alliances) would explain Thomas's return in 1555 with John Arundell II for Mitchell, where his name was inserted on the indenture in a different hand. If Thomas sought election to Parliament with an eye to his legal career, he was probably encouraged to do so by two professional associates, Henry Chiverton, one of the knights for Cornwall on this occasion, and Ralph Couche I, who sat for another Cornish borough. He did not, however, emulate Chiverton in opposing a government bill in the House.[2]

Thomas practised as an attorney in the court of common pleas: he was himself an enthusiastic litigant as well as the 'helper and solicitor' of others. The last glimpse of him comes in 1581 when he was interrogated in a Star Chamber case. The date of his death has not been found, but his will, which is no longer extant, was proved in 1590.[3]

[1] Aged about 50 in April 1581, St.Ch.5/C27/38. *Vis. Cornw.* ed. Vivian, 449; C1/1272/11-12. [2] C. G. Henderson, *Constantine*, 188; *Vis. Cornw.* 25, 449; C3/182/57; 219/24/22; St.Ch.5/C27/38. [3] *CPR*,

1557-8, p. 233; 1563-6, p. 287; C3/178/31; St.Ch.5/C27/38; *Devon and Cornw. Wills* (Index Lib. lvi), 319.

J.J.G.

THOMAS, William (by 1524-54), of London and Llanthomas, Brec.

OLD SARUM 1547*[1]
DOWNTON 1553 (Mar.)[2]

b. by 1524, ?s. of one Thomas of Llanthomas. ?*educ.* Oxf. *m.* ?(1) by 1544, Margaret, ?da. of one Watkins of Hereford, Herefs.; (2) by 1553, Thomasin, da. of Thomas Mildmay of Chelmsford, Essex, wid. of Anthony Bourchier* (*d.*13 July 1551) of London and Barnsley, Glos., 1da.[3]

?Clerk of the peace and of the crown, Brec., Mont. and Rad. 1542; servant of Sir Anthony Browne* by 1545; clerk, the Privy Council 1550-52/53; sec. to embassy to France 1551; ?coroner, Glos. 1552.[4]

Despite his fame as a scholar, nothing is known for certain about William Thomas before the last ten years of his life. It has been tentatively suggested that he was William, son of Thomas ap Philip ap Bleddyn of Llanigon in east Breconshire, and so brother to the Elizabeth who married Richard Seysallt and thereby perhaps became a kinswoman of William Cecil; or alternatively that he could have been a son of Cromwell's follower Walter Thomas of Crickhowell, who died in 1542. The first of these suggestions is at odds with chronology, for whereas William ap Thomas was born not later than 1494 William Thomas was described by two writers in 1545 as a young man; the second appears to be mere conjecture. More worthy of consideration is the origin mentioned in a grant of arms of 1 Feb. 1552 to William Thomas of Llanthomas, gentleman, 'descended of a noble house undefamed': if, as is highly probable, the recipient was the clerk of the Council, then at the height of his fortune, he must have been related in some way to the Thomases of Llanigon, whose seat was at Llanthomas in that parish.[5]

This pedigree, although respectable, was not distinguished enough to ensure advancement. The possibility that William Thomas attended Oxford university rests not on the admission of someone of his name as a bachelor of canon law in 1529, for this man was then already in priest's orders and in any case the author of the *Peregryne* was to deny that he was a canonist, but on the fact that he somehow attained a mastery of Latin. His name was too common to make it clear whether his first surviving letter is one sent from London on 19 May 1540 to John Scudamore* of the augmentations about pensions paid to former nuns at Limebrook and Wormsley, Herefordshire, in which the writer asks that payment for his labour should be made to his mother-in-law at Hereford. He can doubtless be distinguished from namesakes who were tenants at Oxford and Romsey in 1544 and he was certainly not the William John Thomas who sat on the first of several commissions in Monmouthshire in the previous year; but he could have been the William Thomas who became clerk of the peace in Radnorshire and neighbouring counties early in 1542, the man who received the next presentation to a Dorset vicarage in 1543 or the buyer and seller of the reversion of Beedon manor, Berkshire, at the beginning of 1544. He was almost certainly the grantee of a 21-year lease of the rectory of Hay in May 1540, Hay being only two miles from Llanthomas, and probably the tenant in September 1544, with his wife Margaret, of a house in St. Saviour's parish, Southwark, adjoining the former priory of St. Mary Overey and belonging to Sir Anthony Browne whose service William Thomas had entered by the following year.[6]

It is from early in 1545 that conjecture gives place to fact. On 13 Feb. of that year Stephen Vaughan*, the royal agent at Antwerp, reported the passage of one of the Earl of Hertford's servants sent after Thomas, who had run away with money. The fugitive, who was also sought in Germany, arrived in Venice on 10 Apr., the day that letters about him from the Council reached the English ambassador Edmund Harvel, to whom he at once confessed that 'folly and misfortune of play' had caused him to abscond with some bills of exchange issued by the Vivaldi company of Genoa. After having Thomas imprisoned and stopping payment of the bills, Harvel was moved by the culprit's plight and wrote on 3 May that he seemed penitent. At the end of the month the Council instructed Harvel to return a bill of exchange which Thomas had obtained with Sir Anthony Browne's money from Acelyne Salvage, an Italian merchant in London, so that Browne might be indemnified.[7]

Thomas's flight was the prelude to three years in Italy. How long he spent in prison and how he earned a living during the remainder of his exile are alike unknown, although there were wealthy Italian merchants who entertained him. He learned of Henry VIII's death when at Bologna in February 1547 on his way north from Florence to the freer atmosphere of Venice; there he probably wrote his first work, the *Peregryne*, a political dialogue in defence of the late King, with a scathing attack on the monks and a flattering portrait of Edward VI. He then moved south again, to pass the Christmas of 1547 at Rome, and soon afterwards he was commissioned to draw up his *Principal rules of the Italian grammar* by a Mr. Tamworth, probably John Tamworth[†], Cranmer's kinsman and like Thomas a future brother-in-law of (Sir) Walter Mildmay*. The grammar, perhaps composed in

Padua, was despatched from there to Tamworth with a covering letter on 3 Feb. 1548. Tamworth may have sent the author money for his journey home, for Thomas had never been outlawed and his political propaganda must have found favour with Edward VI's advisers. A new work, *The historie of Italie*, was finished after his return to England, via Strasbourg, in the late spring or early summer of 1548; the earliest English book on Italy, this was published by the King's former printer, the Welshborn Thomas Berthelet, in 1549.[8]

The next two years of Thomas's life are obscure, since he cannot be distinguished from others of the same name until his appointment as one of the clerks of the Privy Council on 19 Apr. 1550. His reappearance at home was probably not unconnected with the death on 28 Apr. 1548 of his former master Browne, whose will makes no mention of him. Thomas was almost certainly the Member for Old Sarum whose presence in Edward VI's first Parliament is known from the list of Members as revised for the final session in 1552: none of his namesakes was of a standing to enter the House of Commons. Whether he may be thought to have done so before his flight abroad depends upon a consideration of what is undoubtedly the most interesting passage in the *Peregryne*. In this Thomas argued that the Acts against Rome had been passed only after mature deliberation, 'for in the Parliament the law permitteth all men without danger to speak, as well against as with the King': decisions were therefore not unanimous, 'for the judgment in the parliament house cases is given by dividing all the persons, all that say yea on the one side of the house and all that say nay on the other side; and the most number do always attain the sentence'. With the exception of the dividing of the House by the King himself in March 1532, as reported by the imperial ambassador Chapuys, this is the earliest known description of a parliamentary division, and it would clearly gain in authority and interest if it could be regarded as based on first-hand knowledge rather than hearsay. Unfortunately, Thomas's Membership at an earlier date must be accounted possible rather than probable. The possibility arises from the loss of most of the names for the Parliament of 1539 and of many for that of 1542, but it would become a probability only if Thomas could be shown to have acquired the necessary patronage. Thus if he had entered Browne's service before the end of 1541 he could have been returned for one of several seats in Sussex, and even if the connexion had begun a year or two later he could have been by-elected in time to take his seat for the final session at the beginning of 1544; alternatively, it is not out of the question that

Thomas sat for a Welsh borough in this, the first Parliament which included Members for the principality.[9]

The circumstances of Thomas's by-election to the first Edwardian Parliament are scarcely less obscure. By-elected he must have been, for when the Parliament was summoned in 1547 he was still in Italy, but how soon after his return to England he entered the House, and under whose auspices, it is hard to say. His earlier service with Browne may have brought him to the notice of the Protector Somerset, who had secured Browne's assent to his assumption of that office and who as Earl of Hertford had sent one of his servants to pursue Thomas abroad in 1545. Yet Thomas could not have owed his clerkship of the Council to Somerset since he was granted that office when the duke, newly released from the Tower, was politically powerless. Thomas's appointment was followed by the admission of his precursor Sir John Mason* as a Privy Councillor and by Mason's promotion two months later to the clerkship of the Parliaments; as Sir William Paget, who preceded Mason, had likewise risen from one clerkship to the other, Thomas could aspire to a similar career. Although no previous connexion between Mason and Thomas has come to light, Mason supported Somerset's rival the Earl of Warwick, and it was to Warwick that Thomas dedicated The historie of Italie on 20 Sept. 1549, just when Warwick was poised to overthrow Somerset. Warwick was to secure Mason's return for Reading at a by-election in January 1552 and Thomas could well have been returned for Old Sarum at about the same time; he is styled 'armiger' on the list of Members and he was granted arms on 1 Feb. 1552.[10]

A third magnate who appears to have extended his favour to Thomas was William Herbert I*, Earl of Pembroke, the ally of every ruler in turn. It was to Pembroke's first wife, 'the lady Anne Herbert of Wilton', the sister of Queen Catherine Parr, that Thomas dedicated a short politico-moral treatise, The vanitee of this World, which was printed by Berthelet in 1549. In that year the future earl had leased from the bishop of Salisbury the manor of Milford, which adjoined the borough of Old Sarum, and with it seems to have acquired the patronage there: if, as is likely, this transaction preceded Thomas's election, Herbert was almost certainly responsible for that result. The other Member, John Young, previously a follower of Somerset, also came under Herbert's wing. By what may be more than a coincidence Young had been in Italy early in 1548 on a mission for Somerset, and it is tempting to speculate that he had met Thomas there and perhaps had a part in smoothing the exile's return.[11]

On the day after Thomas's appointment as a clerk of the Council he was made solely responsible for entering its proceedings in a new register and was accordingly discharged from all other business. A patent for the office for life was granted on 20 May, with annual wages of 50 marks, although it was again to be granted to him during pleasure, with £40 a year, on 12 May 1552; in addition, half-yearly expenses of £6 13s.4d. for books and paper were paid on 16 Aug. 1550. It was once assumed that Thomas himself transcribed his rough notes into the council book from 19 Apr. 1550 until 24 Sept. 1551, when his successor Barnard Hampton took over, but Thomas's own entries cease at the end of August 1550; a different hand has been detected from 3 Sept. 1550 until 5 Apr. 1551, a third hand from then until 5 July, when the second hand briefly reappears, and a fourth from 19 Aug. 1551 until Hampton's accession. The second writer may well have been Thomas's secretary, who could have accompanied his master to France in April 1551, in which case Thomas must have retained an active interest at least until the final disappearance of the second hand in August 1551. He was still nominally a clerk of the Council as late as 16 Nov. 1551 but had surrendered the office altogether by 31 Mar. 1553.[12]

Thomas's release from secretarial work coincides with his emergence as a mentor of Edward VI, to whom he dedicated his translation of the Persian embassy of the Venetian Giosafat Barbaro, as a New Year's gift, perhaps at the beginning of 1551. This new role was foreshadowed by an undated letter in which he offered instruction in the principles of statecraft, suggesting 85 'politic questions'. The King limited his interest to specific subjects, transmitted through (Sir) Nicholas Throckmorton*, and Thomas replied with at least five 'discourses'; the best known of these contained a plan for reforming the currency, criticisms of which were vigorously rebutted in a subsequent letter to the King. The discourses, whose chronology is disputed, were accompanied by several 'common-places of state', all of them military in character. In addition, Thomas translated the 13th-century De Sphaera for Henry Brandon, Duke of Suffolk, including in his preface a famous plea for the teaching of English. It was probably also at this time that he finished his translation of the Peregryne into Italian; the work was begun while he was still busy as a clerk of the council and was published abroad in 1552, for circulation in Italy, as Il Pellegrino Inglese.[13]

The frequency with which Edward VI recorded his interest in the coinage led Froude to suggest that Thomas might even have had a hand in composing the royal Journal. The nature and extent of his influence over the King are nevertheless hidden, since in his introductory letter secrecy was counselled from the start. Perhaps he was at odds with the King's tutor (Sir) John Cheke*, for it was to Cheke that Bishop Ridley appealed on 23 July 1551, when Thomas was trying to obtain a prebend of St. Paul's called Cantlers which was said to be worth over £34 a year. The King, to whom the late incumbent William Layton* had surrendered his interest, had promised the preferment to Thomas in June 1550, although the bishop hoped to collate Edmund Grindal, the future archbishop of Canterbury. Eventually Ridley had been browbeaten by the Council into promising that the vacancy would not be filled without reference to the King, and he was now indignant that Thomas had renewed his 'ungodly enterprise' by persuading certain Councillors to announce that Cantlers would be appropriated to the use of the royal stable. The protest must have had some effect, for neither Thomas nor Grindal secured the prebend which on 24 Oct. 1551 was bestowed on another of the bishop's protégés.[14]

A different request by Thomas, for the auditorship of Sussex, was rejected by the Council on 13 July 1551; it was then agreed that no more of these offices were to be granted until further notice, although Thomas should have the first vacancy thereafter. He was already a considerable landowner, having paid £279 in January 1551 for two manors in Herefordshire and Sussex. In October he obtained a second manor in Herefordshire with other rents there, and soon afterwards, in recompense for £17 6s.8d. a year and a debt of 500 marks which he had surrendered to the crown, the rectory of Presteigne; this rectory was later granted at his request to John Bradshaw I* of Ludlow, from whom at some unknown date he bought the site of Wigmore abbey. At the end of the year Thomas also secured in reversion several tolls and customs in the marches of Wales, with salt-houses at Droitwich and an annuity of 40 marks from the fee-farm of Hereford. This accumulation of property in Thomas's native country was furthered by his marriage to Thomasin, the widow of Queen Catherine Parr's auditor Anthony Bourchier. The wardship of his stepson Thomas Bourchier was granted to him on 31 Mar. 1553, with the custody of property in Berkshire, Buckinghamshire and Gloucestershire.[15]

During his active months as a clerk of the Council and throughout the rest of the reign Thomas performed a number of extra duties, for which he was often well paid. On 12 July 1550 he accompanied two Councillors to see the 12th Earl of Arundel, who had been forbidden the court, on 16 Aug. he

was given 66s.8d. for two journeys 'in post' and on 30 Aug. he was appointed to join Sir Andrew Dudley* and Sir Walter Mildmay in business connected with the King's wardrobe; on 7 Jan. 1551 the Council ordered that he should have £248 as a reward for unspecified services. In the spring of that year Thomas went as secretary to the embassy under the Marquess of Northampton to Henry II of France. Before the embassy set out he received £100 towards his expenses; during June he returned to England to obtain fresh instructions, after which a further £200 was granted to him on going back to France. It is not clear whether he was the William Thomas who was a coroner in Gloucestershire in January 1552 but it was certainly the clerk of the Council who, writing on the Earl of Pembroke's affairs from Wilton on 14 Aug. 1552, told Sir William Cecil that he would like to be sent to Venice, and who, when at Salisbury on 27 Aug., asked Chancellor Goodrich for a commission to try pirates in the Cinque Ports. His re-election in 1553 to Edward VI's second Parliament presumably had the backing of Pembroke as well as of the Duke of Northumberland (the former Earl of Warwick), but he himself may have approached Bishop Ponet, the patron of Downton, directly for the nomination: his fellow-Member Robert Warner was a client of Pembroke's. After the dissolution of the Parliament he accompanied Bishop Thirlby of Norwich on an embassy to the Emperor, with the object of ending the war with France; once again he was sent home while the talks were in progress, for on 15 June the imperial ambassador Scheyfve reported that he had spoken with Thomas in London. Edward VI's fatal illness and the upheaval which followed may have kept Thomas in England for some two months. After the new regime had decided to reinforce Thirlby's embassy he accompanied Sir Thomas Cheyne* and others to the imperial court, where they spent eight days before returning home. This was the last official activity undertaken by Thomas, for there is no record that he was reappointed a clerk of the Council, although he was accorded this title by the preacher Thomas Hancock in October and by Scheyfve's successor Renard in the following February.[16]

Thomas became involved in plans to prevent the Queen's Spanish marriage. It is not clear whether, as was to be alleged against him, he hoped to have Mary assassinated and thereby to render unnecessary the rebellion envisaged by Sir Thomas Wyatt II*. On 27 Dec., perhaps after his own suggestion had been rejected, he left London for Mohun's Ottery in Devon, the home of Sir Peter Carew*, who was supposed to head a rising in the west. A few weeks afterwards Thomas was sought by the Council. Sir John St. Leger*, wrote from Exeter on 29 Jan. that Thomas was nowhere to be found, and again reported failure on 4 Feb., after Carew had embarked for France, but surmised that he had escaped to Wales. The fugitive arrived at Bagendon parsonage, near Cirencester, accompanied by his brother-in-law David Watkins, and learned that his property had been seized in London, presumably after the Council had ordered his arrest by the sheriff of Gloucestershire on 12 Feb. Three days later Thomas set out in disguise for the capital, only to be taken near Henley and committed to the Tower on 20 Feb., 'there to remain apart in secret custody'. He was kept in prison for longer than most of his confederates. On the night of 25–26 Feb. he tried to kill himself with a bread-knife, but on 1 Mar. Renard told the Emperor that he had survived to inculpate himself in a plot against the Queen's life. A special commission for his trial was issued on 1 May and (Sir) Nicholas Arnold* deposed that on the previous 21 and 22 Dec. Thomas had discussed the Queen's death with him in London. The defendant was brought to Guildhall on 9 May, when his protest that an esquire should not be tried by a jury of common merchants was overruled. After his conviction Thomas was dragged from the Tower to Tyburn on 18 May and, after declaring that he died for his country, was hanged and dismembered; his head was set on London Bridge and three of his quarters over Cripplegate, near the house where he had plotted and where presumably he had lived.[17]

Thomas is remembered not for his life but for his writings, which reveal him as an early disciple of Machiavelli and also as the first to insist that English should be properly taught for its own sake rather than treated as a mere medium for instruction in the classics. In spite of his assertion that 'riches deserve not to be esteemed', when discussing the struggle of the body with the soul in *The vanitee of this World*, Thomas appears to have been as covetous as he was learned. Not all his material gains were wasted, for on 13 Dec. 1554 the Queen granted to his widow all his goods, with the manor of Garway and other lands in Herefordshire, and on the same day another Herefordshire manor was bestowed on her son Edward Bourchier for life. The grant to Thomasin, however, included the Herefordshire prebend of Nunnington, over which she was sued in Chancery before Archbishop Heath by the lord chancellor's chaplain Henry Welsh, who claimed that he had been promised the next vacancy. Thomas's daughter Anne was restored in blood in 1563 and three years later, was granted

Garway from the time of her mother's death, after which she passes into obscurity.[18]

[1] Hatfield 207. [2] C219/330/35 ex inf. Margaret Condon. [3] Date of birth estimated from first certain reference. *LP Hen. VIII*, xix, xx; P. J. Laven, 'Life and Writings of William Thomas' (London Univ. M.A. thesis, 1954), 16; *Vis. Essex* (Harl. Soc. xiii), 251; PCC 20 Bucke; *CPR*, 1553, p. 4; *LJ*, i. 591. [4] *LP Hen. VIII*, xvi, xx; *Lit. Rems. Edw. VI*, 258, 582; *CPR*, 1550–3, p. 220; *CSP Dom.* 1601–3, *Add.* 1547–65, p. 425. [5] *Tudor Studies* ed. Seton-Watson, 133–4; Dwnn, *Vis. Wales*, i. 159; Laven, 16, 19, app. G 361–2. [6] Emden, *Biog. Reg. Univ. Oxf.* 1501–40, p. 563; *Works of William Thomas* ed. D'Aubant (1774), 118; Laven, 20–21; *LP Hen. VIII*, xv, xviii, xix. [7] *LP Hen. VIII*, xx; *APC*, i. 176. [8] Laven, 29–34, 153; C. H. Garrett, *Marian Exiles*, 302; M. H. Merriman 'Eng. and Fr. intervention in Scot. 1543–50' (London Univ. Ph.D. thesis, 1975), 254–5. [9] PCC 10 Coode; *Works*, 45–46. [10] Tytler, *Edw. VI and Mary*, i. 169; *LP Hen. VIII*, xx; *APC*, i. pp. xii, xv; iii. 457; Hatfield 207. [11] Laven, 36, 113; *CSP Dom.* 1547–80, p. 43. [12] *APC*, iii. 3–4, 107, 183; *CPR*, 1549–51, p. 187; 1550–3, pp. 264, 285; 1553, p. 4; Laven, 43–48. [13] Strype, *Eccles Memorials*, ii(1), 156–65; ii(2), 315–27; *Lit. Rems. Edw. VI*, pp. clxii–clxiv, cccxxxv; Laven, 48–54, 56, 87–88; W. K. Jordan, *Edw. VI*, i. 415–19; C. E. Challis, *The Tudor Coinage*, 240. [14] J. A. Froude, *Hist. England*, v. 349; *Works of Nicholas Ridley* (Parker Soc. 1843), 331–2; *APC*, iii. 53, 58. [15] *APC*, iii. 316; iv. 153; *CPR*, 1549–51, p. 421; 1550–3, pp. 47, 129, 264; 1553, p. 4; 1553–4, p. 290. [16] *APC*, iii. 71, 115, 186, 269, 326; *CSP For.* 1547–53, pp. 123, 133; *CPR*, 1550–3, p. 220; *CSP Dom.* 1547–80, pp. 43–44; *CSP Span.* 1553, p. 56; 1554 (Jan.–July), p. 94; *Travels and Life of Sir Thomas Hoby* (Cam. Misc. x), 96; *Narr. Ref.* (Cam. Soc. lxxvii), 83–84; Laven, 60. [17] D. M. Loades, *Two Tudor Conspiracies*, 16, 19, 95, 98, 105, 108, 127, 143; *DKR*, iv(2), 248–9; J. Vowell *alias* Hooker, *Life and Times of Sir Peter Carew*, ed. Maclean, 168, 170; Laven, 61, 63, 69–70; *APC*, iv. 392, 395; *Chron. Q. Jane and Q. Mary*, (Cam. Soc. xlviii), 65, 69, 76; *CSP Span.* 1554 (Jan.–July) 130, 261; *State Trials*, ed. Howell, i. 884–6; Dyer, *Rep.* i (1794), 99b; *Machyn's Diary* (Cam. Soc. xlii), 63; Laven, 71–73. [18] *Tudor Studies*, 153–60; Laven, 74, 113, 136; *CPR*, 1554–5, p. 177; 1563–6, p. 383; Loades, 125; C1/1480/4, 1484/44–45; *LJ*, i. 591, 603.

T.F.T.B.

THORNEFF (THORNEY), Francis (c.1515–66 or later), of Stamford, Lincs.

STAMFORD 1555, 1558, 1563

b. c.1515, 2nd s. of John Thorneff (*d.*11 Mar. 1521) of Stamford by Edith.[1]

Member of the second Twelve, Stamford 1552–8, of the first Twelve 1558–63, alderman 1557–8; yeoman of the chamber by Feb. 1555.[2]

Francis Thorneff's parentage is disclosed by a chancery suit brought against him between 1547 and 1551 by his nephew William Thorneff: the nephew's claim to 12 messuages in Stamford as part of his inheritance from Christopher, the eldest son of John Thorneff, was met by Francis Thorneff's contention that by the custom of borough English the property should pass to him as the younger son. It was as an innholder *alias* yeoman that Thorneff sued out a pardon in October 1553, but by February 1555, when he was licensed to keep a tavern in his house during his lifetime, he was styled an ordinary yeoman of the chamber and the grant made in consideration of service; two years later he was described as a servant of the King and Queen when he acquired a wardship. The difficulty of distinguishing the final consonant of his name makes it likely that he was the Francis Thornesse, gentleman, late of Grantham, who was sued for debt in 1553 by William Rotheram* of Lincoln, and the man of the same name who unsuccessfully bargained with Reginald Warcop for the weighership of Boston in 1557 or 1558.[3]

Thorneff was one of the 'second Twelve' at Stamford when he was elected to the fourth Marian Parliament and was serving as 'alderman' (that is, mayor) when re-elected to its successor. He thus satisfied the Queen's preference for resident Members as well as enjoying his own court connexion; support is also likely to have been forthcoming from Sir William Cecil, whose influence was reflected in the election of his servant Francis Yaxley as the other Member in 1555. Both Members were presumably involved with the bill for the town and river of Stamford which passed both Houses in that Parliament but was not enacted. Thorneff's appearance on the list of Members of the same Parliament who voted against one of the government's bills is less surprising in a follower of Cecil than in an officer of the royal household, but this show of opposition neither cost Thorneff his post nor debarred him from re-election.[4]

After Elizabeth's accession Thorneff retained his standing at court and in the borough. The date of his death has not been established, but he probably did not survive for more than ten years of the new reign.[5]

[1] Date of birth estimated from elder brother's, E150/1222/8. C1/1272/17-19. [2] Stamford hall bk. 1461-1657, ff. 153v, 169, 182; J. Drakard, *Stamford*, 101; *CPR*, 1554-5, p. 180. [3] C1/1272/17-19; 3/178/172; *CPR*, 1553-4, p. 452; 1554-5, p. 180; 1555-7, p. 457; 1557-8, p. 63; E159/333, m. 111. [4] *CJ*, i. 44-45; Guildford mus. Loseley 1331/2. [5] Lansd. 3, f. 193; Stamford hall bk. 1461-1657, ff. 183 seq.

M.K.D.

THORNES, Robert (by 1518-49 or later), of London.

SHREWSBURY 1539[1]

b. by 1518, 3rd s. of Roger Thornes* of Shrewsbury, Salop by Jane, da. of Sir Roger Kynaston of Myddle and Hordley, Salop. *m.* Elizabeth, da. of Thomas Porte of Bridgnorth, Salop, 2s.[2]

Little has come to light about Robert Thornes, who married a kinswoman of judge Sir John Porte. Like Porte he could have been a lawyer, but it is more likely that he was reared to trade: his younger son Thomas became a London clothmaker. That it was he who was returned for Shrewsbury in 1539, and not either of his elder brothers who were important figures in the town, is presumably to be ascribed to Porte as a member of the council in the marches. Porte died before the dissolution of the Parliament of 1539 and Thornes is not known to have been re-elected to any of its successors. In 1543 he acted on behalf of his brother John in the transfer of a meadow at Hencote in Shropshire. The last

glimpse of him comes six years later when he is mentioned as the lessee of some property at Bridgnorth, presumably in right of his wife. If he made a will it has not been found.[3]

[1] Salop RO, 215/56. [2] Presumed to be of age at election. *Vis. Salop* (Harl. Soc. xxix), 459. [3] *DNB* (Port, Sir John); City of London RO, Guildhall, rep. 9, f. 75; *LP Hen. VIII*, xviii; C. A. J. Skeel, *Council in the Marches of Wales*, 69; *CPR*, 1549-51, p. 82.

A.D.K.H.

THORNES, Roger (by 1469-1531/32), of Shrewsbury.

SHREWSBURY 1510[1]

b. by 1469, s. of Thomas Thornes of Shrewsbury by Mary, da. of Sir Roger Corbet† of Moreton Corbet. *m.* Jane, da. of Sir Roger Kynaston of Myddle and Hordley, 3s. inc. Robert* 2da. *suc.* fa. by 1503.[2]

Bailiff, Shrewsbury 1497-8, 1505-6, 1509-10, 1515-16, 1521-2, 1525-6, 1530-1, alderman by 1509, coroner 1514-15; commr. subsidy 1514, 1515; escheator, Salop 1517-18.[3]

Members of Roger Thornes's family were bailiffs of Shrewsbury 22 times between 1363 and 1535, and four of them besides himself sat in Parliament for the borough. A joint lessee with his father of a tenement at Hencote, Shropshire, from the crown in 1490, Thornes had succeeded to the inheritance by 1503, but four years later he sold the Staffordshire portion and he seems to have resided chiefly at his Shrewsbury house, Thornes Place in Raven Street; his tenement in High Pavement Street he leased for 11s. a year. It was during his third term as bailiff that he was elected, with his fellow-bailiff Thomas Knight, to Henry VIII's first Parliament. Qualified by both residence and office, Thornes was also fortunate in his connexions with the leading local families of Corbet and Kynaston; he had recently been joined with his cousin Sir Robert Corbet and his brother-in-law Thomas Kynaston* in their release from a recognizance for debt to Henry VII. The payment to Thornes and Knight of 'expenses' totalling £10 between them which appears in their own accounts (as bailiffs) for 1509-10 is considerably more than might have been expected for a Parliament lasting 34 days.

Thornes's later municipal career is reflected in such references as his appearance in Chancery, during his fifth term as bailiff and with his fellow Thomas Hosier, to certify the number of Frenchmen dwelling in Shrewsbury, and a mission to the council of the marches at Bewdley with 'Mr. Lyster', presumably the well known lawyer, about a dispute between Shrewsbury and Worcester over the water of the Severn. He appears to have died intestate, but according to the Shrewsbury Chronicle

This year 1531 died Master Roger called the wise Thornes of Shrewsbury for that both town and country repaired to him for advice; he guided this town politically and lieth buried in St. Mary's church.[4]

¹ Shrewsbury Guildhall 438, ff. 1–5; *HMC 15th Rep. X*, 31. ² Date of birth estimated from first reference. *Vis. Salop* (Harl. Soc. xxix), 458–9. ³ H. Owen and J. B. Blakeway, *Shrewsbury*, i. 530–1; Shrewsbury Guildhall 66, f. unnumbered; 75(1), f. unnumbered; *Statutes*, iii. 119, 174. ⁴ H. E. Forrest, 'Thornes fam. of Thorne Hall', *Trans. Salop Arch. Soc.* (ser. 4), viii. 260–6; *CFR, 1485–1509*, no. 313; *Trans. Salop Arch. Soc.* (ser. 2), vi. 330; xii. 108; *LP Hen. VIII*, i; *HMC 15th Rep. X*, 31, 48; Shrewsbury Guildhall 438, ff. 1–5; Shrewsbury sch. Taylor ms 35, f. 56.

M.B.

THORNHILL, Hugh (by 1525–58), of Saundby, Notts.

NOTTINGHAM   1555
NOTTINGHAMSHIRE 1558*

b. by 1525, yr. s. of Hugh Thornhill of Walkeringham by Joan. *educ.* I. Temple. *m.* (1) Elizabeth, wid. of William Mering of Saundby; (2) by May 1558, Elizabeth, da. of Anthony Staunton of Staunton, wid. of Roger North (*d.*9 Apr. 1557) of Walkeringham, *d.s.p.*[1]

Steward's auditor, I. Temple 1550, 1553, 1557, treasurer's 1554, 1555, attendant on reader 1557, 1558.

Escheator, Notts. and Derbys. 1552–3; feodary, Notts. and Nottingham temp. Edw. VI and Mary; commr. sewers, north-east region 1555.[2]

A younger son in a family which had taken no part in the affairs of its shire, Hugh Thornhill inherited some of his father's lands at Walkeringham and acquired some of William Mering's at Clayworth, but the foundation of his prosperity was a successful career in the law. His entry to the Inner Temple has not been traced but by April 1546 he was sufficiently established there to stand pledge at another admission. In the same year he joined his brother in purchasing for £1,400 monastic lands in four counties, the bulk of them being properties in Nottinghamshire formerly belonging to Worksop priory and Darley abbey. In 1553 he paid the crown more than £450 for the capital messuage of Beckingham and lands and tithes of the prebend of Southwell then held by Roger North, whose widow he was to marry. By the time of his death Thornhill owned a string of properties in north Nottinghamshire between East Retford and Gainsborough.[3]

Thornhill's election to the last two Marian Parliaments was probably a reflection of his professional standing and in particular his connexion with the 2nd Earl of Rutland. By 1555 the borough of Nottingham had accustomed itself to the election of nominees, and the choice of Thornhill may have owed as much to the earl's influence as to his own legal services to the town, especially as his fellow-Member, John Bateman, was Rutland's secretary. His election as knight of the shire in the next Parliament was doubtless also to the earl's satisfaction as well as being acceptable to the local gentlemen, with a number of whom Thornhill evidently stood well;

one of them, (Sir) John Hercy*, he named supervisor of his will. Of his part in the proceedings of the Commons all that is known is that he was not listed among the Members who opposed one of the government's bills in 1555.[4]

The date of Thornhill's will, 24 Oct. 1557, suggests that it was made under the shadow of the disease then widespread. If so, its premonition was to be fulfilled, for Thornhill died in the following year, although on what date and whether in Nottinghamshire or London is not known; the addition of 'mortuus' to his name on a copy of the official list of Members seemingly made for the second session may indicate that he died during the prorogation, that is, between March and November. He had asked to be buried at Saundby and had made bequests both to that church and to the vicar of Beckingham. With no child of his own, he made his cousin William Thornhill his chief legatee while also providing for his niece Dorothy and for his Mering stepchildren; his 'abridgements and a book of entries' he left to the Inner Temple library. The will was proved on 18 Apr. 1559.[5]

¹ Date of birth estimated from first reference. Torre ms, Walkeringham church 17; E150/765/15; Thoroton, *Notts.* ed. Throsby, i. 309; iii. 326; *CPR, 1557–8*, pp. 362–3. ² C. J. Black, 'Admin. and parlty. rep. Notts. and Derbys. 1529–58' (London Univ. Ph.D. thesis, 1966), 184, 451; *CPR, 1554–5*, p. 110. ³ E150/765/15; *Cal. I.T. Recs.* i. 139; *LP Hen. VIII*, xxi; *CPR*, 1553, p. 194; C1/1272/20–21. ⁴ *Nottingham Bor. Recs.* iv. 397; *HMC Rutland*, i. 67; *N. Country Wills*, ii (Surtees Soc. cxxi), 2–3. ⁵ *N. Country Wills*, ii. 2–3; Wm. Salt Lib. SMS 264.

C.J.B.

THORNHILL, William (by 1500–57), of Thornhill in Stalbridge, Dorset.

POOLE 1529

b. by 1500, 1st s. of Thomas Thornhill of Thornhill by Joan, da. of Thomas Hussey† of Shapwick. *educ.* M. Temple. *m.* (1) by 1526, da. of William Chauncy of Charlton, Wilts., 2s. 3da.; (2) by Feb. 1550, Joan, da. of Henry Brydges* of Newbury, Berks., wid. of John Gifford.[1]

Marshal, M. Temple by 1551–*d.*

Escheator, Som. and Dorset 1521–2, 1528–9, Hants and Wilts. 1531–2; j.p. Dorset 1530–*d.*; commr. musters 1542, 1544, benevolence 1544/45. relief 1550; feodary, duchy of Lancaster, Dorset, Hants, Som., Wilts. by 1541–*d.*, jt. (with Richard Brydges*) receiver, Berks., Bucks., Dorset, Glos., Hants, Herefs., Oxon. and Wilts. 1541–*d.*[2]

According to Leland there were Thornhills of Thornhill long before the Conquest, and recorded evidence exists for the main line of the family from the early 13th century. William Thornhill's immediate forbears were gentry of moderate estate: his father inherited the manor of Thornhill and six tenements in Folke, and was active in local government, serving on the Dorset bench until 1528, the probable year of his death. Thornhill followed in the steps of his maternal grandfather and became a lawyer whose services were retained by several magnates and monasteries in the south-west. The date of his admission to the Middle Temple is not known, but he may have been the Thornhill (whose christian name is not given) who was master of the revels and held other minor offices between 1519 and 1524.[3]

Thornhill's public career began with his appointment as escheator in 1521, and it was while serving in this office for a second term that he was returned to Parliament. His entry into the Commons (if he had not already sat there in 1523) probably followed his father's death and preceded his own nomination as a justice of the peace. One of the knights of the shire for Dorset, Sir Giles Strangways I, was also a Middle Templar and may have favoured Thornhill's election, as may his kinsman Sir John Russell*, who was sheriff at the time, but such connexions were perhaps less important than his family's long association with Poole, which members of it had represented in several earlier Parliaments. Thornhill's profession must have made him particularly useful to the borough during the course of this Parliament, when William Biddlecombe, his fellow-Member, was entrusted with its charters for a suit to the King and Council. In January 1534, at the opening of the sixth session, he received through Biddlecombe what must have been a token payment of 26s.8d. 'for his time' in the Parliament. He was probably returned again by Poole to the next Parliament, that of June 1536, in accordance with the King's general wish to that effect, and he may have sat in 1539, when the Poole names are again lost. His progress in Dorset brought him within sight of its shrievalty, for which he was nominated, although not pricked, in 1535.[4]

Thornhill added considerably to his property by the purchase of monastic lands in Dorset: in 1539 he obtained the manor of Wolland for about £653, in 1541 he bought land in Gillingham, to which he later added a lease of mills and a fishery, and in 1546 he converted his lease of Upton in Osmington into ownership. The estates in Thornhill, Alverstone in Folke and Stalbridge, comprising some 1,400 acres, were settled upon himself and his wife in tail male early in 1550, probably soon after his marriage to the sister of a fellow-receiver in the duchy of Lancaster. His standing in Dorset is reflected in his appearance as a freeholder on the election indenture for the shire in the autumn of 1553.[5]

Thornhill's will, made on 8 July 1548, reflects his local ties, for he left money to the curates, and a dole of 1d. or 2d. to every poor man, of eight parishes in

Dorset and of two in Wiltshire. He bequeathed 12d. each Friday for a year to those confined in the bishop of Salisbury's prison, and 66s. 8d. towards the repair of the highway between Sherborne and Shaftesbury. He provided for his eldest daughter Alice £100 on marriage, and for her sisters Grace and Elizabeth, who were both under 21, 200 marks; the stock upon Upton manor, which in 1552 was leased to his younger son Matthew, he left towards the marriages of his older son Robert's children, should there be any. To his wife and executrix he bequeathed a lease of the parsonage of Stourpaine and all cattle and sheep on his manor of Charnhull. His best horse he gave to Sir William Paget. The overseers of the will were Sir William Portman*, Robert Coker and Thornhill's brother Robert. Thornhill died on 21 Aug. 1557 and his widow a few months later.[6]

[1] Date of birth estimated from first reference. Hutchins, *Dorset*, iv. 417; PCC 10 Bodfelde, 38 Wrastley; *Vis. Hants* (Harl. Soc. liv), 16; E150/944/13. [2] *LP Hen. VIII*, iv, xi–xviii, xx; *CPR*, 1547–8 to 1554–6 passim; Somerville, *Duchy*, i. 624, 626. [3] Leland, *Itin.* ed. Smith, iv. 142; Hutchins, iv. 417–18; *CIPM Hen. VII*, iii. 389; PCC 29 Adeane, 40 Alen; Somerville, i. 626; *LP Hen. VIII*, i, iii, iv, xiii; *Val. Eccles.* i. 277; *M.T. Recs.* i. 60–61, 71, 74. [4] Somerville, i. 624; *LP Hen. VIII*, iv, ix, xiv; Hutchins, iii. 162–3; G. Scott Thomson, *Two Cents. of Fam. Hist.* 118–19; Poole rec. bk. 1, pp. 2, 58; SP1/184, f. 169; *APC*, v. 264, 289. [5] *LP Hen. VIII*, xiv, xvi, xxi; Hutchins, iv. 418; E150/944/13; C219/21/52. [6] PCC 38 Wrastley, 9 Noodes; E150/944/13.

M.K.D.

THORNTON, Henry (by 1484–1533), of Buckland, Som.

BRIDGWATER 1529*

b. by 1484. *m.* 2da.[1]
     Yeoman of the crown by 1505, of the chamber by 1509; keeper, Ilchester gaol, Som. by 1505; bailiff and parker, Curry Mallet, Som. 1509–23; serjeant-at-arms 1513–*d.*; comptroller of customs, Bridgwater bef. 1529; j.p. Som. 1531–*d.*[2]

Henry Thornton's parentage and place of origin are unknown but he was probably from Somerset. He is first heard of on 28 Nov. 1505 when as keeper of Ilchester gaol and a yeoman of the crown he had a pardon for all escaped prisoners. He was no longer keeper when in 1512 he took out a general pardon as yeoman *alias* gentleman *alias* pardoner, but he was still a yeoman of the chamber when granted in 1509 the bailiwick and parkership of Curry Mallet. Four years later he was promoted to be one of the serjeants-at-arms, and the next 20 were to see him become a fairly wealthy and influential man in Somerset.[3]

The return of two customs officials in Thornton and Hugh Trotter for Bridgwater in 1529 was probably favoured by the town's recorder, Baldwin Malet, who was unable to take the recorder's accustomed place in the House owing to his appointment during the summer as solicitor-general. Neither Member appears to have lived in the town and Thornton, at least, was a crown agent who was later to be closely in touch with Cromwell over the election of his nominee as abbot of Muchelney. If the 'Mr. Paulet' mentioned in the Bridgwater receiver's accounts during the 1530s was the courtier Sir William Paulet, then Thornton who moved in similar circles and who owned property near Paulet's seat may have been able to rely on his support to take the senior place. On 21 Nov. 1530 Thornton was licensed to perform his comptrollership by deputy. The last year of his life was mainly taken up with the dispute over the abbey of Muchelney which he seems to have taken very seriously as affecting his whole position and prestige in the county; he enlisted Cromwell's influence to procure the election of his candidate, who however had to pay a large sum for the privilege.[4]

Thornton made his will on 1 Apr. 1533. The only land mentioned is the farm at Buckland, but Thornton also had leases of Ashe manor near Basingstoke, Hampshire, and of the manor of Halse, Somerset, belonging to the order of St. John. The principal legatees were Thomas Tynbry, Thornton's son-in-law, and his children, and Thornton's surviving daughter, her husband and children. There were small bequests to Thornton's nephew and niece, to John Portman, Humphrey Walrond, and servants. The Tynbrys were executors and residuary legatees, with Sir John Fitzjames[†], William Portman*, and Guthlac Overton*, auditor of St. John's, as overseers.[5]

To judge from the witnesses Thornton made his will in London where the fifth session of the Parliament was approaching its close: as the will was to be proved on 23 Apr. 1533 he may have died before the session ended on 7 Apr., perhaps a victim of the epidemic which claimed at least six Members. There is no record of a by-election, although it is possible that Alexander Popham* was chosen to take Thornton's place.

[1] Date of birth estimated from first reference. PCC 2 Hogen. [2] CPR, 1494–1509, p. 461; LP Hen. VIII, i, v; E122/27/9. [3] CPR, 1494–1509, p. 461; LP Hen. VIII, i–v. [4] LP Hen. VIII, iv, v; Bridgwater corp. ms 1437. [5] PCC 2 Hogen; LP Hen. VIII, v; Req.2/5/148.

R.V.

THORNTON, John (by 1529–1601), of Kingston-upon-Hull, Yorks.

KINGSTON-UPON-HULL 1554 (Nov.), 1563, 1571, 1584

b. by 1529, prob. s. of John Thornton (d.1540) of Kingston-upon-Hull by Margaret. m. Joan, da. and coh. of Ralph Constable of St. Sepulchre's in Holderness, at least 1s.[1]

Alderman, Hull by 1550, mayor 1555–6, 1566–7, 1577–8; commr. sewers, Hull 1565, musters 1569, eccles. causes, province of York c.1568, 1573, concealed lands, Hull 1584; gov. Hull fellowship of merchants 1577.[2]

John Thornton was probably the son of a Hull merchant; he is not to be confused with a namesake of Birdforth near Thirsk who came of the family at York which had supplied that city with a Member of Parliament in 1504. Already an alderman of Hull by 1550, and then resident in the city's north ward, Thornton profited from the revival of Hull's trade at this period and by 1555 was sufficiently known and respected as a merchant to receive a power of attorney from Denmark to settle a dispute with the Hull authorities over a ship seized in the Humber. Early in 1556, in partnership with James Clerkson (his fellow-Member in the Parliament of 1571), he leased the cloth hall in the High Street; throughout his life he was to add to his property in and near the town. It was probably at about the same time that he married into a cadet branch of the Constables of Burton Constable, for in 1562 he was to be entrusted by Thomas Aldred*, whose wife was Joan Constable's sister, with the upbringing of Aldred's elder son John: guardian and ward were to be returned together to the Parliament of 1584. Thornton's first election 30 years earlier had registered his standing in a town which preserved a large measure of electoral independence. Nothing is known of his role in that Parliament save that unlike his fellow Walter Jobson he was not among those who absented themselves without leave before its dissolution.[3]

Thornton was to be re-elected to three Elizabethan Parliaments and on several occasions he acted for Hull on other business in the capital and in negotiations with York. He died in 1601.[4]

[1] Date of birth estimated from first reference. Yorks. Arch. Soc. rec. ser. xi. 178, 238; Glover's Vis. Yorks. ed. Foster, 57–58, 144, 146. [2] J. M. Lambert, Two Thousand Years of Gild Life, 173, 236; T. Gent, Kingston-upon-Hull (1735), 120, 122, 125; CPR, 1566–9, pp. 172–3; 1569–72, p. 216; 1572–5, p. 169; L. M. Stanewell, Cal. Anct. Deeds, Kingston-upon-Hull, 105, 318. [3] E122/65/11, ff. 1v, 9v; 179/203/233; VCH Yorks. (E. Riding), i. 123, 142; Stanewell, 90–92, 96, 98, 101, 112, 164; York wills 17, f. 142. [4] CSP Dom. 1581–90, p. 130; Stanewell, 158–60; Surtees Soc. cxxix. 194, 212–15; Yorks. Arch. Soc. rec. ser. xxiv. 194; cxix. 162–3.

S.M.T.

THOROLD (THARROLDE), Anthony (by 1520–94), of Marston and Blankney, Lincs.

GRANTHAM 1558
LINCOLN 1559

b. by 1520, 1st s. of William Thorold of Marston and Hougham by 1st w. Dorothy, da. of Thomas Leke of Halloughton, Notts. educ. G. Inn, adm. 1537. m. (1) Margaret, da. of Henry Sutton of Wellingore, Lincs., 4s. inc. William[†] 2da.; (2) Anne, da. and coh. of Sir John Constable* of Kinoulton, Notts., wid. of George

Babington, 1da. *suc.* fa. 20 Nov. 1569. Kntd. 6 May 1585.[1]

Commr. relief, Lincs. (Kesteven) 1550, subsidy (Holland) 1563, musters, Lincoln 1580; other commissions from 1552; recorder, Grantham by c.1551–?d., Lincoln 1559–70; j.p.q. Lincs. (Kesteven) 1554–d., j.p. (Holland) 1554–84/87, q. by 1564, j.p.q. Notts. 1558/59; Queen's attorney in the north 1561–70; commr. eccles. causes, dioceses of Lincoln and Peterborough 1571, diocese of Lincoln 1575; sheriff, Lincs. 1571–2, dep. lt. 1587–d.; steward of Edward, 1st Earl of Lincoln in 1582.[2]

Of Yorkshire origin, the Thorold family had been settled at Marston, near Grantham, since the 14th century. Anthony Thorold's father, a merchant of the staple, was sheriff of Lincolnshire in 1558–9 and a leading figure at Grantham. Of Thorold's own early career nothing is known save that it included the professional training which equipped him for legal office. His first appointment, as recorder of Grantham, he appears to have received soon after 1550. In 1581 he explained to his fellow justices how throughout his time as recorder the borough had delegated its subsidy assessment to certain approved persons, a task which, he added, 'for almost 30 years past either Mr. Carre [presumably Robert Carr†] and I, or my father and I whilst he lived, have from time to time executed'. That the recordership was not more quickly followed by Thorold's election to Parliament may reflect the competition for seats between townsmen and nominees. When his own turn came in the Parliament of 1558 he could doubtless add to his municipal standing the support of the 2nd Earl of Rutland: it was Rutland who was to procure him a seat for Lincoln in the following Parliament as well as the recordership of the city. In August 1558 he was named an executor by Thomas Grantham*, who had just completed his year as mayor of Lincoln.[3]

Adjudged 'earnest in religion' in 1564, Thorold was to remain active in Lincolnshire until his death on 26 June 1594. He rebuilt Marston Hall, where his descendants still live.[4]

[1] Date of birth estimated from age at fa.'s i.p.m., C142/155/167. *Lincs. Peds.* (Harl. Soc. lii), 982–3. [2] *CPR*, 1553, p. 355; 1553–4, p. 21; 1554–5, p. 109; 1560–3, p. 439; 1563–6, pp. 24, 40; 1569–72, pp. 277–8; 1572–5, pp. 551–2; *Lincoln Rec. Soc.* liii. 53–54; liv. p. lxxviii; *HMC Ancaster*, 10; J. W. F. Hill, *Tudor and Stuart Lincoln*, 69–71; *HMC Hatfield*, iii. 297; *APC*, xii. 56; xxv. 25; R. R. Reid, *King's Council in the North*, 489; H. G. Wright, *Life and Works of Arthur Hall of Grantham*, 101. [3] Hill, 69–71; *HMC Ancaster*, 10; *HMC 14th Rep. VIII*, 49; PCC 41 Welles. [4] *Cam. Misc.* ix(3), 26; PCC 80 Dixy; C142/239/113; *Country Life*, cxxxviii (1965), 612–15; Pevsner and Harris, *Lincs.* 603–4.

T.M.H.

THRALE, Michael (*b.* by 1514), of Luton, Beds.

BEDFORD 1542

b. by 1514. *educ.* Queens', Camb. 1528.[1]

There had been Thrales in and around Luton at least since the 14th century. Prosperous yeomen, they were of local importance partly through their connexion with the guild of the Holy Trinity in the town: in 1483 and in 1509 one of the family was master of the guild.[2]

Of Michael Thrale very little has come to light, and no connexion has been traced between him and the borough which he represented in Parliament. A presumed relative, George Thrale, married into the landed family of Franklyn of Thurleigh, Bedfordshire, one of whom, William, had been closely associated, as archdeacon of Durham, with Wolsey and was by 1542 dean of Windsor and in favour at court. Sir William Gascoigne* had owed his position in Wolsey's household largely to Franklyn and when his son Sir John Gascoigne was returned as a knight of the shire for Bedfordshire to the Parliament of 1542 Michael Thrale was one of the electors.[3]

In 1535 Thrale was one of the witnesses to a land conveyance between two local families over a croft and land at West Hyde, in Luton. Two years later he leased from Richard Fermor* the manor of Luton Hoo, a mill at Stapleford and appurtenances in the Luton district; the lease was for 30 years, and he may still have held it when the ownership of the manor changed hands in January 1552. The only later reference found to him, early in Elizabeth's reign, leaves it doubtful whether he had died before this date: if he was still living, he had apparently left Luton, for a legal process of May 1564 described him as 'late of Luton'. No will or inquisition post mortem is known.[4]

[1] Date of birth estimated from education. [2] *Beds. Hist. Rec. Soc.* xxix. 92–93; *N. and Q.* cxciii. 495 seq.; W. Austin, *Luton*, i. 158, 203, 205–6; PCC 3 Jankyn, 13 Peter, 75 Leicester. [3] *Vis. Beds.* (Harl. Soc, xix), 3, 31; F. A. Blaydes, *Gen. Bedford*, 441; *DNB* (Franklyn, William); C219/18B/2. [4] *LP Hen. VIII*, iii; NRA 6970 (Beds. RO. Acc. no. 2059, item 3389), 7811 (Beds. RO, Luton Hoo Estates DW 6, 8); *CPR*, 1563–6, p. 119.

N.M.F.

THRELKELD, Thomas (by 1527–1598/1603), of Burgh by Sands, Cumb.

CUMBERLAND 1555[1]

b. by 1527, s. of William Threlkeld of Burgh by Sands. *m.* (1) at least 1s.; (2) Magdalen, at least 1s. 1da.[2]

Bailiff, Burgh by Sands ?1564–d.[3]

Only the christian name Thomas and the opening 'Th' of the surname survive on the return as clues to the identity of the first knight of the shire for Cumberland in the fourth Marian Parliament. It was Browne Willis who first suggested that he was Thomas Threlkeld, and what has come to light about Threlkeld makes this the most acceptable of several such guesses. One of the Threlkelds of Melmerby, a branch of the better known family

settled at Threlkeld, he was a younger son of a
bailiff of Burgh by Sands who died in or before 1564
and his own tenure of the office probably began at
that time; in October 1566 he and three others
obtained a lease for 21 years of the rectory of Burgh.
The manor of Burgh belonged to the Dacre family,
and Threlkeld could have been returned in 1555 at
the instance of William, 3rd Lord Dacre, whereas
his fellow-knight Henry Curwen was a client of
Thomas Wharton*, 1st Baron Wharton. Neither he
nor Curwen appears on the list of Members of this
Parliament who opposed one of the government's
bills.[4]

Threlkeld was one of the tenants of lands in and
around Newbiggin, near Penrith, bought in December 1548 by a London scrivener, Thomas Brende.
This was shortly after his brother John Threlkeld
had been captured by the Scots while commanding
the horsemen of the barony of Burgh; Wharton's
description on this occasion of the Threlkelds, father
and sons, as poor men may have been meant to
discourage hopes of a large ransom. Another brother,
Edward, rose in the Church to become archdeacon
of Carlisle and chancellor of Hereford; by his will of
1588 he bequeathed property in Burgh and Holme
Cultram to his nephews Richard and William,
Thomas Threlkeld's sons by his two marriages, with
remainder to their father. Threlkeld made his own
will on 24 Aug. 1598. Describing himself as bailiff of
Burgh, he made his wife Magdalen and his daughter
Elizabeth the chief legatees and appointed them
executrices. It was his widow who proved the will on
23 June 1603, Elizabeth being still a minor.[5]

[1] C219/24/36; Browne Willis, *Notitia Parl.* iii(2), 48. [2] Date of
birth estimated from first reference. W. Jackson, *Pprs. and Peds.*
(Cumb. and Westm^ld. Antiq. and Arch. Soc.), ii. 322–5, ped. bet.
pp. 328–9. [3] Ibid. 324. [4] Ibid. 282 seq., 296, 305, 312–13, 320; *CPR*,
1563–6, p. 462. [5] *CPR*, 1548–9, p. 70; *CSP Dom.* 1601–3, *Add.*
1547–65, p. 374; *Al. Cant.* i(4), 238; Jackson, 322–5; PCC 9 Leicester.

A.D.

THROCKMORTON, Clement (by 1515–73), of
London; Claverdon and Haseley, Warws.

WARWICK	1542
DEVIZES	1545
WARWICK	1547, 1553 (Mar.), 1553 (Oct.)
SUDBURY	1559
WARWICKSHIRE	1563
WEST LOOE	1571
WARWICKSHIRE	1572*

b. by 1515, 3rd s. of Sir George Throckmorton* of
Coughton, Warws. by Catherine, da. of Sir Nicholas
Vaux*, 1st Lord Vaux of Harrowden; bro. of Anthony†,
George*, John I*, Kenelm*, Nicholas* and Robert*.
educ. M. Temple. *m.* by 1545, Catherine, da. of Sir
Edward Neville of Aldington, Kent, 6s. inc. Job† 7da.[1]
Receiver, lands formerly of Evesham abbey 15 Dec.

1540; servant of Sir Richard Rich by 1541; surveyor,
ct. augmentations, Warws. by Apr. 1542–53, Exchequer 1553–67; cupbearer, household of Queen
Catherine Parr by 1544–8; commr. chantries, Leics.
and Warws. 1546, 1548, relief Warws. 1550, loan,
Warws. 1557; particular receiver for Queen Catherine
Parr, Leics. and Warws. by 1547–8; j.p. Warws.
1547–72, q. 1573; constable, Kenilworth castle,
Warws. 19 Sept. 1553–d.; member, High Commission
1572.[2]

Clement Throckmorton's upbringing and early
life appear to have left little trace, but by 1541 he was
in the service of Sir Richard Rich, with whom he had
a family connexion through a great-grandmother,
Catherine Rich. His activities during the years that
followed were largely dictated by his master's
chancellorship of the augmentations: they involved
much travel, particularly with a view to ensuring
that houses designated for the King's progresses
were fit for the purpose. The work was evidently
rewarding both materially and in terms of patronage:
in 1545 Throckmorton made his first purchase of
monastic lands and he continued to buy property
regularly until his death, in 1552 receiving a legacy
of £400 from his father for land purchases. His
rapid ascendancy in Warwickshire owed as much to
his family's standing there and his surveyorship in
the augmentations as to the marriage of his cousin
Catherine Parr to Henry VIII, an appointment in
her household and his own marriage into a noble
family.[3]

Throckmorton's election to the last but one of
Henry VIII's Parliaments he doubtless owed to his
father, perhaps assisted by his master Rich; the
town of Warwick was amenable to Sir George
Throckmorton's influence and a number of Rich's
dependants were returned on this occasion almost
certainly to smooth the passage of measures
relating to the royal estates. Throckmorton was to
sit for Warwick again, but in the next Parliament
it was his brother Kenelm who was elected there
while he transferred to Devizes, which formed part
of Catherine Parr's jointure as Queen. In the first
Parliament of the new reign another brother, Sir
Nicholas, sat for Devizes and Clement returned to
Warwick; he was to be re-elected there to the two
following Parliaments, in March 1553 with his
brother John. That this sequence of elections was
broken in 1554 is probably to be attributed to
Throckmorton's Protestant leanings—in Mary's
first Parliament he was one of those who 'stood for
the true religion'—and to the implication of his
brother Nicholas and kinsman John Throckmorton
II* in plots against the government, although the
family's hold on Warwick was strong enough for
two other brothers, George and Kenelm, to be

elected there in turn. Throckmorton himself remained loyal to Mary: in February 1554 he helped to arrest the fugitive Duke of Suffolk and then rode to court to announce the capture to the Queen. Retained on the bench and appointed constable of Kenilworth, he was an important figure at both Warwick and Coventry. In 1555 he was one of the founder members of the Russia Company and in the following year he undertook the rebuilding of his house at Haseley in a style befitting his wealth and position.[4]

With the accession of Elizabeth, Throckmorton resumed his career in the Commons, sitting in every Parliament summoned before his death. The adherence of his eldest brother Robert to Catholicism compromised the senior branch of the family and enhanced his own influence as one who was described in 1564 as 'a favourer of true religion'. Throckmorton died on 14 Dec. 1573 and was buried at Haseley.[5]

[1] Date of birth estimated from younger brother Nicholas's. *Vis. Warws.* (Harl. Soc. xii), 88–89; *Vis. Oxon.* (Harl. Soc. v), 120; Dugdale, *Warws.* 655; C142/172/143. [2] *LP Hen. VIII*, xvi, xxi; E163/12/17, no. 30; 314/22, nos. 1–5; 315/218, f. 15; LC2/2, f. 43; *CPR*, 1547–8, pp. 90, 136; 1553, p. 360; 1553–4, p. 25; 1555–7, p. 180; 1560–3, p. 444; 1566–9, p. 82; *EHR*, xxiii. 77; Somerville, *Duchy*, i. 561, 563n; W. C. Richardson, *Ct. Augmentations*, 337 n. 30; R. G. Usher, *Rise and Fall of High Commission*, 359. [3] E314/22, nos. 1–5; *LP Hen. VIII*, xvi–xxi; A. L. Rowse, *Ralegh and the Throckmortons*, 10; *VCH Warws.* iii. 44, 73, 104, 106, 117, 139, 143, 144, 151, 194; iv. 223; v. 162; vi. 199, 222; *CPR*, 1553–4, p. 366; 1554–5, p. 109; 1555–7, p. 180; 1558–60, p. 423; PCC 22 Tashe; Coughton Ct. mss boxes 1–33, 54. [4] Bodl. e Museo 17; *CPR*, 1548–9, p. 135; *VCH Warws.* iii. 104; viii. 491; *Narr. Ref.* (Cam. Soc. lxxii), 163; *Chron. Q. Jane and Q. Mary* (Cam. Soc. xlviii), 129; Coventry chamberlain's accts. 1554–5, p. 232; Warwick accts. 1546–69, mm. 24v, 37v, 70v; Pevsner and Wedgwood, *Warws.* 308; T. S. Willan, *Muscovy Merchants of 1555*, p. 125. [5] *Cam. Misc.* ix(3), 7; C142/172/143; E. W. Badger, *Mon. Brasses Warws.* 27; Pevsner and Wedgwood, 308.

S.M.T.

THROCKMORTON, George (by 1523–73 or later); of London; and Great Alne and Fulbrook, Warws.

WARWICK 1554 (Apr.)

b. by 1523, yr. s. of Sir George Throckmorton*, and bro. of Anthony†, Clement*, John I*, Kenelm*, Nicholas* and Robert*. *m.* Frances, da. of Sir John Brydges*, 1st Baron Chandos of Sudeley, 2s. 3da.[1]

Gent. at arms by 1544, gent. pens. in reversion by Feb. 1547; gent. pens. by Apr. 1549–61/4; commr. musters, Warws. 1546; comptroller of petty customs, London 12 Sept. 1553; gov. household of Anne of Cleves 1554; master of Queen's hawks in 1570.[2]

George Throckmorton was one of the three Throckmorton brothers who obtained court office after the marriage of their kinswoman Catherine Parr to Henry VIII. Like the other two, Clement and Nicholas, he was probably a Protestant— Nicholas Throckmorton was to recommend him to Elizabeth as a suitable replacement for the Catholic Sir Leonard Chamberlain* as governor of Guernsey

—but his religion did not prevent his remaining a gentleman pensioner throughout Mary's reign: he attended the funerals of Henry VIII, Edwar VI and Mary.[3]

Throckmorton has to be distinguished in his early years from a kinsman and namesake of Deerhurst, Gloucestershire, who died in 1548. He served at the siege of Boulogne and when taken prisoner by the French was ransomed for the large sum of £1,000; in 1548 he was a captain at Boulogne when Sir John Brydges was deputy governor and lieutenant. His father had conveyed the lease of the manor of Great Alne to him by September 1550 when the Privy Council ordered an abatement of rent in reward 'for his good service'. He spent part of Edward VI's reign abroad, being in Venice in 1551 and 1552 to learn the language and gain worldly experience. If he was one of the four Throckmorton brothers who are said to have sent word to Mary of Edward's death, the comptrollership of petty customs, forfeited by (Sir) Henry Gates*, may likewise have been a reward for good service. He was returned for Warwick, at this time largely controlled by his family, when one of his brothers was sheriff and another a prisoner in the Tower.[4]

In 1559 Throckmorton accused his wife of attempting to poison him, but after her family had complained that he had been tampering with the witnesses a further inquiry found that she had been guilty of nothing more serious than an indiscreet and evidently unsuccessful use of potions to win her husband's love. How the couple fared after this has not been discovered and the date of Throckmorton's eventual death is unknown: the last reference found to him is in 1573 when his eldest brother granted him the wardship of a cousin.[5]

[1] Date of birth estimated from first reference. *Vis. Warws.* (Harl. Soc. xii), 87 gives him as seventh son but this is the position in the family accorded to John Throckmorton I on his MI, Dugdale, *Warws.* 754; *CPR*, 1553–4, p. 439. [2] A. L. Rowse, *Ralegh and the Throckmortons*, 10; LC 2/2/ff. 41–43; 2/3(1), p. 113; E179/69/62; 407/1/2, 3, all ex inf. W. J. Tighe; Stowe 571, f. 31v; E407/1/1, 2; Lansd. 3(89), f. 197; *LP Hen. VIII*, xxi; *CPR*, 1553–4, p. 1; *APC*, v. 29; *CSP Dom.* 1547–80, p. 367. [3] *EHR*, lxv. 95; LC2/2, f. 42v, 4/1, 2. [4] *Vis. Glos.* (Harl. Soc. xxi), 163; C142/86/90; Rowse, 10–11; *LP Hen. VIII*, xix; *CSP For.* 1547–53, pp. 110, 345; *APC*, iii. 110; *CSP Ven.* 1534–54, p. 370; Lansd. 3(2), f. 3. [5] *CSP For.* 1558–9, pp. 500, 509; *CSP Dom.* 1547–80, pp. 137, 142; Rowse, 29; Coughton Ct. mss box 40.

S.M.T.

THROCKMORTON, Sir George (by 1489–1552), of Coughton, Warws.

WARWICKSHIRE 1529

b. by 1489, 1st s. of Sir Robert Throckmorton of Coughton by Catherine, da. of William Marrow† of London. *educ.* M. Temple, adm. 1 May 1505. *m.* by 1512, Catherine, da. of Sir Nicholas Vaux*, 1st Lord Vaux of Harrowden, 8s. inc. Anthony†, Clement*,

George*, John I*, Kenelm*, Nicholas* and Robert* 11da. *suc.* fa. 1519. Kntd. 1523.[1]

J.p. Warws. 1510–*d.*, Bucks. 1525–32, Worcs. 1531–44; esquire of the body by 1511, knight by 1533; commr. subsidy, Warws. 1512, 1523, Worcs. 1512, 1514, Bucks. 1524, loan, Warws. 1542, benevolence, Warws. and Coventry 1544/45, musters, Warws. 1546, relief, Warws., Worcs. and Coventry 1550, goods of churches and fraternities, Warws., Worcs. and Coventry 1553; other commissions 1523–*d.*; steward or keeper, Brandon, Warws. 1512–*d.*, Yardley, Worcs. 1512, Berkswell, Claverdon, Lighthorne, Moreton, Warws. by 1513–45, Harlington, Newton Closenfield, Bucks. 1514–*d.*, Evesham abbey 1527, Halton and Haseley, Warws. 1529, Tamworth, Warws. 1530–44, Maxstoke, Wroxall, Warws. 1535–*d.*, Balsall, Warws. 1539–*d.*; King's spear by 1513; sheriff, Warws. and Leics. 1526–7, 1543–4, Worcs. 1542–3; steward, lands of bpric. of Worcester in Warws. and Worcs. 1528–40, for Thomas Seymour, Baron Seymour of Sudeley, unknown property by 1548; custos rot. Warws. in 1547.[2]

The Throckmortons took their name from a manor in the parish of Fladbury, Worcestershire, where in the 12th century they were tenants of the bishop of Worcester: they acquired Coughton, Warwickshire, by marriage in the early 15th. George Throckmorton was born in Worcestershire and was to claim when seeking office there that the greater part of his inheritance lay in that shire, but his father seems to have made Coughton the family seat and George was to be the first of his line to sit in Parliament as knight of the shire for Warwickshire; his grandfather and great-grandfather had done so for Worcestershire. Sir Robert Throckmorton, soldier, courtier and Councillor to Henry VII, sent his eldest son to the Middle Temple, which George entered on the same day as a Northamptonshire kinsman, Edmund Knightley*; before his death in Italy while on pilgrimage to the Holy Land, Sir Robert had seen his son launched at court and in local government and in enjoyment of numerous leases and stewardships. This early advancement may have owed something to Throckmorton's marriage to a daughter of another courtier, Sir Nicholas Vaux, whose stepson Sir Thomas Parr, comptroller of the Household to Henry VIII, was further related to him by marriage. Throckmorton served with his father in the French war of 1513 as captain of the *Great New Spaniard*. Seven years later he was present at the Field of Cloth of Gold, which had been in part devised by his father-in-law. Vaux appointed Throckmorton one of his executors and as such in September 1523 he was commissioned to deliver Guisnes to the 1st Baron Sandys.[3]

During the 1520s Throckmorton seems to have attached himself to Wolsey although the first notice of their connexion does not suggest a happy relationship; in July 1524 Throckmorton, styled of Olney,

Buckinghamshire, was bound in £100 to appear before the Council and to pay whatever fine the cardinal should impose. The connexion may have been made through his uncle Dr. William Throckmorton, a trusted servant of the cardinal whose name appears on important papers relating to embassies and treaties and who was a master in Chancery by 1528. The younger Throckmorton engaged in some land transactions with Wolsey. Thus when in 1525 Wolsey had licence to dissolve several small and decayed monasteries in order to endow his new college at Oxford, one of them, the Buckinghamshire priory of Ravenstone (three miles from Olney), passed on a 100-year lease to Throckmorton for a rent of 100 marks. As Wolsey was seeking further land and Throckmorton a reorganization of his estates—in particular he had his eye on Sir William Gascoigne's* manor of Oversley, Warwickshire—he suggested to the cardinal an exchange of several manors, including Ravenstone, for Oversley and some neighbouring manors: the plan did not materialise, but in May 1528 Throckmorton sold Ravenstone to Wolsey at 20 years purchase. He evidently felt that he had deserved well of the cardinal, for in April 1528 on the death of Sir Giles Greville—and, curiously, at a time when his own imminent death was rumoured—he asked for Greville's office of comptroller to Princess Mary, and three months later, on the death of Sir William Compton, he sought to become sheriff and custos rotulorum of Worcestershire, steward of the see of Worcester and (as his great-grandfather Sir John Throckmorton[†] had been) under treasurer of England. Although the shrievalty went to Sir Edward Ferrers, later Throckmorton's fellow-knight for Warwickshire, he was successful in respect of the stewardship.[4]

Wolsey also employed Throckmorton to deal with local disputes. When the prior of the Knights of St. John disputed a lease of the commandery of Balsall made by his predecessor Thomas Dowcra to his brother Martin Dowcra, Wolsey empowered Throckmorton to seize the property pending a settlement. According to Throckmorton this was easier said than done, for when on 7 Oct. 1529 he and his servants arrived to occupy the property Dowcra fortified the house and manned it with 'sanctuary men' who were thieves and murderers. Throckmorton then set a watch on the house and later captured most of these men, whom he sent to Warwick gaol. As Wolsey had not instituted proceedings against Dowcra in Chancery or elsewhere, this was high-handed behaviour and it was to form one of the charges against the cardinal on his downfall; Dowcra also pursued Throckmorton for it in the

Star Chamber and Chancery. It may, indeed, have been because he was involved that the commandery was so bitterly disputed, for his father had once leased and later fortified it against the order's attempts at repossession. Neither this episode nor his other relations with Wolsey were to implicate Throckmorton in the cardinal's fall: he served on the Warwickshire commission of enquiry into Wolsey's goods.[5]

Throckmorton's election in 1529 as senior knight of his shire answered to his standing there and at court: he may well have sat previously, the names of the Warwickshire knights in the earlier Parliaments of the reign being unknown. Of his role in the Commons there is but one glimpse in the documentation of the Parliament itself: this is his appearance at the head of a list of Members drawn up by Cromwell early in 1533 and thought to be of those opposed to the bill in restraint of appeals. But his imprisonment in October 1537 called forth a detailed, if not wholly lucid, confession of his part in the Catholic opposition. In the course of this he related how, before the Parliament began, he had been sent for to Lambeth by his cousin William Peto, the Observant Franciscan and future cardinal, with whom he had a long conversation about the King's proposed marriage to Anne Boleyn. Peto alleged that the King had 'meddled' with both Anne's mother and her sister and advised him if he were in the parliament house 'to stick to that matter as I would have my soul saved'.[6]

Throckmorton's next revelation was more confused. Shortly after the beginning of the Parliament, when he had, he said, 'reasoned to' the bill in restraint of appeals (a statement which gives colour to the interpretation of the list mentioned above), he was summoned by Chancellor More to a private meeting in the parliament chamber. More then said:

> I am very glad to have the good report that goeth of you and that you be so good a catholic man as you be; if you do continue in the same way that you began and be not afraid to say your conscience, you shall deserve great reward of God and thanks of the King's grace at length, and much worship to yourself.

However faithfully he may have recalled these words—and he himself added the rider, 'or words much like to these'—the circumstances of the conversation cannot be as he described them, since More was no longer chancellor when the appeals bill was debated and was thus unlikely to have had the use of parliamentary premises: even if Throckmorton confused that measure with the annates bill, that itself had been debated in the third session and not shortly after the opening of the Parliament. Similarly, it cannot have been, as he says it was,

'shortly after' receiving this tribute from More that he discussed the Acts of Annates, Appeals and Supremacy, and the Petrine claims, with Bishop Fisher, who referred him to Nicholas Wilson, once the King's confessor, although it may well have been after the Act of Supremacy (26 Hen. VIII, c.1) that he made his own confession to Richard Reynolds, 'the Angel of Syon'. (Throckmorton had at least one other connexion with the Bridgettines, his kinswoman Clemence Tresham, sister of Sir Thomas*, having entered the order by 1518.) Both Fisher and Wilson conceded that if he were sure nothing was to be gained by his speaking out in Parliament, 'then I might hold my peace and not offend', but Reynolds added that he could not know beforehand whether others might not follow his example if he should 'stick in the right way'.[7]

It was, however, his conversation with Sir Thomas Dingley, a Knight of St. John, which was eventually to prompt Throckmorton's confession. Again, he ascribed this to a period six or seven years before October 1537, yet it related to the passage of the Act in restraint of appeals (24 Hen. VIII, c.12) in April 1533. When Dingley marvelled at the easy passage of such Acts, Throckmorton replied:

> that it was no marvel, for that the Common House was much advertised by my lord privy seal [Cromwell, who was holding that office in 1537], and that few men there would displease him. And the said Sir Thomas said, "I hear say ye have spoken much in divers matters". And I said, "True it is. I have spoken something in the Act of Appeals, whereupon the King's grace did send for me and spake with me in divers matters".

He had, so he told Dingley, repeated Friar Peto's insinuation about the female Boleyns to the King, who replied 'Never with the mother', to which Cromwell, who was present, added 'Nor never with the daughter either'. Throckmorton also admitted to reporting this conversation to his brother-in-law Sir Thomas Englefield at Serjeants' Inn as well as, he believed, to Sir William Barentyne and Sir William Essex. He had been in the habit of meeting with Barentyne, Essex and other Members, including Sir Marmaduke Constable I and Sir John Giffard (whose son Thomas* married Throckmorton's sister Ursula), at the *Queen's Head* to discuss parliamentary affairs.[8]

Throckmorton's experiences were to be recalled in the House half a century later. When in the Parliament of 1586 another Thomas Cromwell led the Commons' protest against the imprisonment of Peter Wentworth and four other Members for challenging Queen Elizabeth's veto on their discussion of church reform, he collected a series of precedents designed to prove that the crown had no right to imprison Members for their words or actions in the House. One of these precedents ran thus:

> It is reported that Sir George Throckmorton in the Lower House impugned a bill which the King was desirous to have pass. The King sent for him and shewed him the reasons which moved him to desire the passing of the said bill but could get no other answer from him than that it became him not to argue with the King in that place: but the next day without making mention of the King opened all those reasons in the House and answered them in such sort. And yet was not committed or misliked of the King for so doing.

To this Robert Beale, clerk of the Privy Council, added a marginal note on his copy of Cromwell's document, 'I have heard that the cause was touching the denouncing of Queen Catherine Dowager first wife to King Henry the 8th'. It is interesting to speculate on the source of Cromwell's (and Beale's) knowledge of the episode. During the interval of 50 years no less than a dozen of Throckmorton's descendants sat in the Commons, although only one of them, his grandson Job Throckmorton, was a Member in 1586. At the time of Cromwell's intervention Job Throckmorton was himself in deep trouble for having maligned James VI of Scotland in a speech to the House, a misfortune which could well have revived the memory of his grandfather's brush with an earlier monarch. There was even one Member in 1586, Sir Francis Knollys, whose career in the Commons had begun in the Parliament of 1529 (to which he had been by-elected by 1533) and who could have remembered the episode. Whatever its source, Cromwell's reference to the affair is not surprisingly unspecific and Beale's gloss hardly less so, but for what they are worth they seem to point to the Appeals Act.[9]

His revelations of what took place in the spring of 1533 explain Throckmorton's letter of the following October to Cromwell advising the minister that, as Parliament was prorogued, he would not come to London unless to speak with Cromwell and promising to follow his advice to 'stay at home and meddle little in politics'. The two had known each other since before the Parliament, and though they came into conflict over lands their relationship may at first have helped to protect Throckmorton from worse things. Whether Throckmorton obeyed the summons to the coronation of Anne Boleyn we do not know; he appears to have missed the next (sixth) session of Parliament, but he was there for the seventh, when he doubtless helped to oppose the treasons bill, although his name does not appear on a list of Members drawn up by Cromwell on the back of a letter of December 1534 and thought to be of those with a particular, but unknown, connexion with that measure. Early in the following year he heard that the King was again displeased with him and asked Sir Francis Bryan* to procure an audience for him, according to a promise the King had given at the last prorogation. Whatever the outcome, he was obliged in the following autumn to defend himself to Cromwell for not attending the King during his progress in the midlands: this Cromwell regarded as a sign of disaffection in spite of Throckmorton's protest that he had never found himself within 50 miles of the King and had been much occupied with the tithes commission. What is clear is that, besides local administration, quarrels with his neighbours had absorbed his attention: in particular his involvement in the affairs of the Knightleys can have done little to commend him to the minister. In the circumstances, it would be of special interest to know (which it is unlikely we ever shall) whether Throckmorton sat in the Parliament of 1536, in accordance with the King's general request for the return of the previous Members: Cromwell's desire to be rid of a trouble-maker may have been offset by his certainty that Throckmorton would yield to none in his rejoicing at the fate of Anne Boleyn. If he did reappear, it was probably for the last time: he was not re-elected for any shire and is unlikely to have been so for a borough.[10]

Before 1536 was out, however, Throckmorton was in worse trouble. He had come to London in November to transact legal business and falling in with an old friend, Sir John Clarke, had rashly discussed the demands of the rebels in the north; whereas Throckmorton had only seen the printed answer to the Lincolnshire rebels, Clarke had a manuscript account of Aske's new demands and sent Throckmorton a copy of it. Throckmorton next met Sir William Essex at the Queen's Head and lent him the demands so that he might take a further copy: this was a blunder, for Essex's servant Geoffrey Gunter, unknown to his master, took yet another copy for himself which he later circulated amongst a circle of disaffected priests at Reading. While on the way to keep an appointment with Sir Anthony Hungerford* at Essex's house in Berkshire, Throckmorton met Thomas Vachell I* who convinced him of the danger of possessing the document, which he thereupon burned at Reading. Passing the night at Englefield, he received a further warning and then went on to Essex's house where he learned the full story of Gunter's foolhardiness. Both he and Essex were soon in the Tower.[11]

Cromwell set himself to collect all possible evidence of their treasonable behaviour. The distribution of Aske's demands was a good start, but it was followed by an accusation that Throckmorton had failed the King against the northern rebels by declaring that if the 4th Earl of Shrewsbury joined them he would follow suit, a step which two of his soldiers had actually taken. To this charge Throckmorton replied that at the first insurrection he had come with 300 men to Ampthill and that the leaders there had discharged 200 of them. For a while both his life and Essex's hung in the balance: on 14 Jan. 1537 John Hussee reported as much to Viscount Lisle, and one of Throckmorton's family was later to write that his foes 'gaped to joint his neck'. But on 25 Jan. both were released, presumably because the charges could not be sustained. The threat lingered, however, as Cromwell was to show in the following October, when he was provoked by the defection of Throckmorton's younger brother Michael, who had been sent to spy on Cardinal Pole but had instead become his loyal servant. Cromwell then wrote to warn him that 'the least suspicion' thereafter should be 'enough to undo the greatest' of his family at home. Next Sir Thomas Dingley, whose execution two years later makes him accounted a Catholic martyr, revealed what Throckmorton had told him of the earlier episodes. When Throckmorton was again taken into custody, his wife appealed for advice to her half-brother Sir William Parr*, who may have persuaded him to make a confession. Declaring that he had perceived his errors through reading the New Testament and *The Institution of a Christian Man*, he claimed that at Grafton the King had given him a full pardon for his behaviour in Parliament. He remained in prison for some weeks but by the end of the year his release was at least under consideration. What saved him is a matter of guesswork: he had many influential relations but there is no hint that he made any such abject bargain with the crown as was later to rescue (Sir) Geoffrey Pole*. Nor did his brush with death, as did Pole's, mark the virtual end of his career. As early as July 1538 his kinsman Richard Rich could suggest that he should receive building materials from the dissolved abbey of Bordesley, Worcestershire; a year-and-a-half later he was summoned to attend the reception of Anne of Cleves, in the early 1540s he was twice pricked sheriff, and he was mustered for the French campaign of 1544. The King's marriage to Catherine Parr in 1543, greatly as it was to the advantage of his sons, came too late to explain his own return to favour. His part in the toppling of Cromwell in 1540 is too obscure, and may have been too small, to be given much weight: it is glimpsed only in the fallen minister's protest to the King that he

never spoke with the chancellor of the augmentations [Rich] and Throckmorton together at one time. But if I did I am sure I spoke never of any such matter and your grace knoweth what manner of man Throckmorton hath ever been towards your grace and your proceedings.

More important was the change in the religious climate, which not only Throckmorton, but his old comrades of the opposition found refreshingly congenial: not until his closing years did the wind of doctrine begin to blow chill.[12]

The fall of Cromwell did enable Throckmorton to acquire several properties which he had long coveted, including Oversley, and so to continue the consolidation of his estates which had been one of his principal concerns since his succession. He also built up extensive leasehold interests and acquired several valuable wardships, including that of Richard Archer whose execution for murder gave Throckmorton the opportunity to buy from the crown his most valuable property, Tamworth.[13]

Throckmorton lived to see some of his younger sons occupy high office in the state and others comfortably established. During his lifetime he settled small freehold estates on most of his younger sons and by his will of 20 July 1552 he left Kenelm an annuity of £40, Nicholas and Clement annuities of £20 each, and Clement a further £400 for land purchase. The eldest son Robert had control of part of his inheritance, the manors of Sheldon and Solihull, from his second marriage in 1542, and by the will he obtained a full third of the estate and the reversion of two manors after the executors had held them for three years for the payment of debts: the residue was settled on the widow for life. At his death, Throckmorton is said to have had 116 living descendants, including among his grandsons such diverse figures as Job Throckmorton and William Gifford, Archbishop of Rheims and first Peer of France.[14]

Throckmorton died on 6 Aug. 1552 and was buried in the stately marble tomb which he had prepared for himself in Coughton church. The most impressive monument which he left, however, was the gatehouse of Coughton court. Throckmorton spent most of his life rebuilding the house: in 1535 he wrote to Cromwell that he and his wife had lived in Buckinghamshire for most of the year, 'for great part of my house here is taken down'. In 1549, when he was planning the windows in the great hall, he asked his son Nicholas to obtain from the heralds the correct tricking of the arms of his ancestors' wives and his own cousin by marriage Queen Catherine Parr. The costly recusancy of Robert Throckmorton and his heirs kept down later rebuilding, so that much of the house still stands largely as he left it.[15]

[1] Date of birth estimated from first commission. *Vis. Warws.* (Harl. Soc. xii), 87; C142/33/14, 43, 46, 47. [2] *LP Hen. VIII*, i–v, vii, viii, xii, xvii, xx, xxi; *CPR*, 1547–8, p. 90; 1550–3, pp. 396–7; 1553, pp. 360–1; *Statutes*, iii. 85, 86, 112; Coughton Ct. mss boxes 1–33, no. App. 188; box 59; Worcs. RO, 009:1, BA2636/177 92509; 178 92517 ex inf. C. Dyer; E163/12/17, nos. 38, 51, 54. [3] *VCH Worcs.* iii. 355, 357; *LP Hen. VIII*, i–iv. [4] *LP Hen. VIII*, iv, vii, add.; Emden, *Biog. Reg. Univ. Oxf. 1501–40*, p. 566. [5] *LP Hen. VIII*, iv; St.Ch.2/12/236, 17/401; C1/627/11; *VCH Warws.* ii. 101. [6] *LP Hen. VIII*, ix. 1077; xii(2), 952; SP1/99, pp. 234–5; *Bull. IHR*, xli. 29. [7] *Bull. IHR*, xli. 30–31; *Northants. Past and Present*, v. 91–93. [8] *LP Hen. VIII*, iv, p. cccxxix. [9] Northants. RO, Finch-Hatton 16, ff. 549v–50. [10] *LP Hen. VIII*, iv–ix. [11] Ibid. xi. [12] Ibid. xi–xv, xix; A. L. Rowse, *Ralegh and the Throckmortons*, 7; Merriman, *Letters, Thos. Cromwell*, ii. 88–89, 265; *Vis. Warws.* 69. [13] *LP Hen. VIII*, iii, vi, xiii, xvi–xviii, xxi; Coughton Ct. mss boxes 1–33, nos. 716, 721, 725–9, 731, 733–47, 749, 753–4, 756–7, 775, App. 190–2; box 49; *VCH Warws.* iii. 14, 22, 24, 30, 63, 64, 70, 81, 98, 115; iv. 203, 219; v. 168, 210; vi. 38; *Trans. Birmingham Arch. Soc.* lxv. 95–97; Index 10217(1), ff. 4v, 6v, 8. [14] PCC 22 Tashe; C142/98/75; Rowse, 16. [15] *LP Hen. VIII*, ix; C142/98/75; Coughton Ct. mss box 61; *VCH Warws.* iii. 85; E. W. Badger, *Mon. Brasses Warws.* 17.

S.M.T.

THROCKMORTON, John I (by 1524–80), of Feckenham, Worcs.

LEICESTER	1545
CAMELFORD	1547[1]
WARWICK	1553 (Mar.)
OLD SARUM	1553 (Oct.)
COVENTRY	1554 (Nov.), 1555, 1558, 1559

b. by 1524, 7th s. of Sir George Throckmorton*, and bro. of Anthony†, Clement*, George*, Kenelm*, Nicholas* and Robert*. *educ.* M. Temple. *m.* Margaret, da. of Robert Puttenham of Sherfield-upon-Loddon, Hants, wid. of one Dockwray, at least 4s. 2da. Kntd. 1565.[2]

Attorney, council in the marches of Wales 1550–4, member of council 1558–*d.*, v.-pres. 1565–9; steward, manor of Feckenham 1552–*d.*; under steward of Westminster 1557–*d.*; master of requests 1553–9; recorder, Coventry 1553–*d.*, Worcester 1559–*d.*, Ludlow, Shrewsbury by 1560; j.p.q. Warws. 1554–79 or later, Welsh and marcher counties 1558/59–79 or later; justice of Chester, Denb. and Mont. 1558–79, of Denb. 1566; commr. eccles. causes, diocese of Chester 1562, piracy, Cheshire 1565.[3]

John Throckmorton's mother was an aunt by marriage to Queen Catherine Parr, and several of his brothers, especially Nicholas Throckmorton, were to be involved in affairs of state: thus although he had little material expectation from his father he was not without prospects. He pursued them by going to court, where he may for a time have held a position in Catherine Parr's household. He also received training at the Middle Temple which was to help him in his official career. When he came to marry, his bride supplied a link with the Grey family, powerful in Leicestershire.[4]

Any or all of these connexions may have helped to procure Throckmorton's return to Parliament in 1545. (He had possibly sat for Leicester in 1542, an election for which the name of the second Member is missing.) To judge from the number of her dependants elected, the Queen was an active patron

in 1545 and her support of Throckmorton may have been decisive; his youth would have been offset by the economy arising from his London domicile— there is no evidence that either he or his fellow-Member was paid. It was to prove, however, the only occasion on which he sat for Leicester. In the first Parliament of Edward VI he sat for Camelford and in the second for Warwick. At Camelford the Queen's influence, now shared by her fourth husband Admiral Seymour, was probably again wielded on his behalf, but this support disappeared with their deaths and at Warwick in March 1553 it is to the Throckmorton interest that attention first turns: two of John Throckmorton's brothers had sat for the borough in the three previous Parliaments and one of them was returned with him on this occasion. Yet his Membership of this Parliament, designed to buttress the Duke of Northumberland's regime, and for a borough located within the 'heartland' of the duke's territories, raises the question of John Throckmorton's attitude towards Northumberland and what the duke stood for.

It seems clear that Throckmorton prospered during Northumberland's years of power, as indeed is implied by his continuing association with Northumberland's leading supporters, among them his own cousin the Marquess of Northampton: as well as engaging in land transactions with Northumberland, Throckmorton received his first public appointment, as attorney to the council in the marches of Wales. What his role was during the succession crisis would be simply a matter for speculation but for the testimony of two men. Both Sir William Cecil, in his own justification of his behaviour during the crisis, and his servant Roger Alford*, in a later report based upon conversations with Cecil, describe Cecil's refusal to draft the proclamation of Queen Jane, a task which was therefore passed to John Throckmorton, 'whose conscience', Cecil himself added 'I saw was troubled therewith, misliking the matter'. Apart from the anachronism of Throckmorton's being called master of requests, an appointment which he received only from Queen Mary, there is nothing intrinsically improbable about the episode. If Throckmorton discharged the unwelcome and fruitless task, he must have exculpated himself even more completely than Cecil managed to do. He appears, indeed, to have joined Mary while she was still at Framlingham, a gesture for which he was granted an annuity. This was followed by the mastership of requests in exchange for his surrender of his post with the council in the marches.[5]

It was not only the memories of 1553 which Throckmorton had to rise above, it was the hazardous doings of kinsmen and friends and the treason of a namesake. As early as August 1553 he interceded with the Queen for the release of Edward Underhill, with whom he had sat in the Parliament of the previous March; six months later his brother Sir Nicholas Throckmorton was arrested for complicity in Wyatt's rebellion and only escaped conviction by magnificent self-defence at his trial; and in the spring of 1556 John Throckmorton II* (with whom he has sometimes been ludicrously confused) was executed for his part in the Dudley conspiracy. None of this appears to have shaken Throckmorton's position or diminished his activity. As master of requests he had much business referred to him by the Privy Council, including the examination of conspirators; the recordership of both Coventry, where he was expected to reside for part of the year, and Worcester added to the burden; and in 1557 he also heard pleas in the Marshalsea during a vacancy in the stewardship of the Household. It is not surprising that when nominated Autumn reader by the Middle Temple in 1558 he preferred to pay a substantial fine; he could doubtless well afford to do so, especially after the Queen had granted him the manor of Feckenham in fee-farm and had leased him that of Redfern, Warwickshire, valued between them at over £150 a year.[6]

Throckmorton was returned to four out of the five Marian Parliaments: there is no obvious explanation of his absence from the second, when following his appointment as recorder of Coventry he might have been expected to have sat for that city, as he would do regularly from November 1554. His first Marian appearance, however, had been for Old Sarum, where his fellow-Member was his Protestant brother Sir Nicholas Throckmorton; the brothers presumably owed the nomination to their kinsman William Herbert I*, 1st Earl of Pembroke. It appears that John Throckmorton had also been returned to this Parliament for Scarborough but had chosen Old Sarum and been replaced at Scarborough by Sir John Tregonwell; both Tregonwell, who was a master in Chancery, and Throckmorton are likely to have enjoyed government support.[7]

There are some glimpses of Throckmorton's part in the business of the House. The first of these, which promises to be the most interesting, is also unfortunately the most puzzling. It is the note set against his name, in the Crown Office list of Members of the Parliament of October 1553, that he voted 'with the last act and against the first'; since the names marked on this list (including Throckmorton's) are those of Members who 'stood for the true religion', the inference is that he displayed some opposition to the new government's religious

policy. Such an attitude would be difficult to reconcile, however, with his official standing and favour (even though his brother and fellow-member Sir Nicholas was certainly one of the opponents of the policy), and it is possible that the note was intended to apply to his namesake, who appears almost immediately after him in the list and whose tragic career it could well have foreshadowed. This conundrum apart, the evidence of Throckmorton's parliamentary activity is of a matter-of-fact kind: not surprisingly the list of Members who opposed a government bill in the Parliament of 1555 omits his name, and his nomination on 4 Dec. 1555, during its critical closing days, to carry bills from the Commons to the Lords bespeaks his attachment to the government's side. In the Parliament of 1558 he was one of four prominent Members deputed to investigate the legal basis of the Westminster sanctuary.[8]

One of the witnesses of Queen Mary's will, Throckmorton at first adapted himself without apparent difficulty to the changes which followed her death. From about 1570, however, his fortunes declined by reason of his own shortcomings as a lawyer and administrator and the recusancy of his family, and in 1579 he was heavily fined in the Star Chamber, and for a time kept in the Fleet, for giving a judgment in favour of a relation. He died within a few months of this disgrace. His will reveals heavy indebtedness which made his hoped-for provision for his daughter and younger sons a speculative matter. Four years later came the even worse disaster of his heir's execution for treason.[9]

[1] Hatfield 207. [2] Date of birth estimated from that of brother Nicholas. Nash, *Worcs.* i. 453; *Vis. Hants* (Harl. Soc. lxiv), 18; PCC 52 Arundell. [3] *CPR,* 1549-51, p. 299; 1550-3, p. 236; 1553-4, p. 269; 1557-8, pp. 461-2; 1560-3, pp. 280-1; 1563-6, pp. 41-42; P. H. Williams, *Council in the Marches of Wales,* 359-60; Westminster abbey reg. 4, f. 10v; *APC,* iv. 324; vii. 284; *Coventry Leet Bk.* (EETS cxxxiv), ii. 806; B. Poole, *Coventry,* 384; Dugdale, *Warws.* 149-50; A. D. Dyer, *Worcester,* 201; Ormerod, *Cheshire,* i. 63. [4] Strype, *Annals,* iii(2), 211; iv. 139. [5] *CPR,* 1547-8, p. 210; 1553, p. 272; 1553-4, pp. 65, 269-70; *CSP Dom.* 1601-3, *Add.* 1547-65, p. 574; Strype, iv. 487; Read, *Cecil,* 97; Lansd. 156, f. 94. [6] *APC,* iv. 324, 388; v. 88; vi. 75, 124, 247, 256, 270, 278; *Narr. Ref.* (Cam. Soc. lxxvii), 324; *Chron. Q. Jane and Q. Mary* (Cam. Soc. xlviii), 55; G. Goodman, *Mem. Ct. of James,* i(1), 116-18; *CPR,* 1554-5, p. 155; 1557-8, pp. 75, 376, 420; Somerville, *Duchy,* i. 562; St.Ch.2/20/193; Strype, *Eccles. Memorials,* iii(1), 488; *Machyn's Diary* (Cam. Soc. xlii), 102, 104; *CSP Dom.* 1547-80, pp. 78-79; *CSP Ven.* 1555-6, p. 466; M. T. *Recs.* i. 113, 116. [7] Bodl. e Museo 17. [8] Ibid.; Guildford mus. Loseley 1331/2; *CJ,* i. 46, 49. [9] A. L. Rowse, *Ralegh and the Throckmortons,* 25; *CSP Dom.* 1601-3, *Add.* 1547-65, p. 574; *APC,* vii. 371; xi. 193; *Trans. Birmingham Arch. Soc.* lix. 123-42; Williams, passim; PCC 52 Arundell; C142/191/114.

S.M.T.

THROCKMORTON, John II (c. 1529-56), of London.

WOOTTON BASSETT 1553 (Oct.)

b. c.1529, 4th s. of William Throckmorton of Tortworth, Glos. by Margaret, da. and coh. of Sir David

Mathew of Radyr, Glam.; bro. of Thomas I*. *unm. s.p.*[1]

'A man of spirit and ability', John Throckmorton had been left £100 by his father in 1537 but no lands. Nothing is known about his upbringing, although after his arrest he was noted as 'well learned in all sciences and especially in philosophy.' According to the Venetian ambassador he spent some time in Italy and at Venice, perhaps in the company of his kinsman George Throckmorton* who visited the city during 1551 and 1552. While in Rome he received a letter written late in November 1551, almost certainly from George's brother Sir Nicholas* but possibly from Sir William Cecil, warning him against another kinsman, Michael Throckmorton, who was in Cardinal Pole's household.[2]

Throckmorton's contact with Pole perhaps favoured his return to Mary's first Parliament. He had no personal links with Wootton Bassett and as his name is written over an erasure on the indenture he is unlikely to have been the electors' choice. His fellow-Member Henry Poole I was brother-in-law to the sheriff Edward Baynard†, but Throckmorton probably owed his seat to his kinsmen Sir Nicholas and John Throckmorton I, who were elected on the same day for another Wiltshire borough: to distinguish Throckmorton from his namesake of Feckenham in Worcestershire he was described on the indenture as 'of county Gloucester'. Because the two John Throckmortons were second Members for their boroughs, which follow one another on the Crown Office list for this Parliament, whoever marked on that list the names of the Members opposing the government's religious legislation may have confused them, and his comment 'with the last act but against the first' should perhaps apply to the Member for Wootton Bassett: the attitude implied would better fit what is known of him than the position then taken by his namesake.[3]

The extent of Throckmorton's complicity in Wyatt's rebellion is not known but on the arrest of its ringleaders, including his kinsman Sir Nicholas Throckmorton, he fled to France where he enlisted as a mercenary. After Sir Nicholas's acquittal he approached Nicholas Wotton, the English ambassador in Paris, for a pardon but five months elapsed between Wotton's intercession with the Queen and the pardon granted on 3 Dec. 1554. The description of him on the pardon as 'of Tortworth *alias* Corseland [Corse], county Gloucester' is misleading as these were his elder brother Thomas's homes. In 1556 his brother Anthony's wife was to testify that he had 'lain in their house [in St. Martins Orgar, London] these seven years, having a chamber to himself', and it was there that as part

of Dudley's conspiracy he planned the removal of bullion from the Exchequer. On the discovery of the plot he was committed to the Tower. Under torture he refused to implicate others but his efforts to inspire them with like fortitude failed. He was convicted of treason on 21 Apr. 1556 and executed at Tyburn a week later.[4]

[1] Aged less than 28 in 1556; *CSP Ven.* 1556–7, no. 466. *Vis. Glos.* (Harl. Soc. xxii), 163. [2] *CSP Ven.* 1556–7, no. 466; PCC 7 Dyngeley; SP15/3/84. [3] C219/21/172; Bodl. e Museo 17. [4] C. H. Garrett, *Marian Exiles*, 305; *CSP For.* 1553–8, p. 96; *CPR*, 1554–5, p. 195; 1555–7, pp. 318, 400–1, 453, 465; *CSP Ven.* 1556–7, nos. 466, 477; SP11/7/24, 30, 32, 33, 37, 40, 66, 8/3, 7, 14, 21, 29, 53; KB8/33, 34; *DKR*, iv. 252–3; D. M. Loades, *Two Tudor Conspiracies*, 188–267 passim; *Machyn's Diary* (Cam. Soc. xlii), 102, 104; *Wriothesley's Chron.* ii (Cam. Soc. n.s. xx), 135.

E. McI.

THROCKMORTON, Kenelm (by 1514–83/87), of London and Little Easton, Essex.

WARWICK 1545
WESTBURY 1547[1]
WARWICK 1555

b. by 1514, 2nd s. of Sir George Throckmorton*, and bro. of Anthony†, Clement*, George*, John I*, Nicholas* and Robert*. *educ.* M. Temple. *m.* 6s. 5da.[2] Servant of Thomas Cromwell by 1538, Sir William Parr, Earl of Essex and later Marquess of Northampton by 1547–80; keeper, Little Easton park, Essex by 1552; j.p. Essex 1558/59–82, q. 1583.[3]

Kenelm Throckmorton is one of the more obscure members of a prominent and prolific family. The date of his admission to the Middle Temple is unknown but he may already have been there by November 1531 when his father replied to Cromwell about a matter on which Kenelm had conveyed Cromwell's displeasure to Sir George. He was in London in July 1534 when his father used him as an intermediary with Cromwell over a local dispute. Early in the following year Sir George sought the minister's help towards a marriage for him. The lady in question was the daughter of Thomas Hunckes of Gloucestershire and the recently widowed partner of Thomas Littleton, whom Sir George called a countryman of his and who was perhaps a kinsman of John Lyttleton* of Worcestershire: no match resulted, however, and Throckmorton was to marry elsewhere, although the name of his wife, who was to add substantially to the number of Sir George's grandchildren, remains unknown.[4]

By about 1538 Throckmorton had gained a place in Cromwell's household: in a list assigned to that year he is numbered among the gentlemen 'most meet to be daily waiters' upon the minister and 'allowed in his house'. He was not to enjoy the position for long and after Cromwell's fall he transferred to the suite of his cousin William Parr, afterwards

Earl of Essex and Marquess of Northampton. It was while he and his brother Nicholas were serving with some distinction on the Scottish border that his new master's sister Catherine became Henry VIII's sixth Queen. He was thus well placed to benefit from the distribution of monastic lands and in August 1544 he partnered Sir William Barentyne, his father's old parliamentary colleague, and Henry Aveton in the purchase for £671 of Newcastle nunnery and lands in several counties: the nunnery they promptly sold to the Newcastle merchant Robert Brandling* and one of the Warwickshire properties soon afterwards passed to Clement Throckmorton. At court Throckmorton moved in Protestant circles and in 1546 he and his brother Nicholas visited Anne Askew in prison.[5]

Throckmorton's parliamentary career began with his return for Warwick to Henry VIII's last Parliament. His father had long wielded influence in the borough and between 1542 and 1554 Throckmorton's brothers Clement, George and John I all sat for it in turn. In 1545 he had three of his brothers in the House, Clement sitting for Devizes, John I for Leicester and Nicholas for Maldon; two years later the quartet reappeared, although with a re-arrangement of seats, and were joined by their cousin Thomas Throckmorton I. In this Parliament it was Clement who sat for Warwick and Kenelm who migrated to the Wiltshire borough of Westbury. His election there marks an exception to the rule by which Westbury was represented throughout the period either by townsmen or by gentlemen living within easy reach of the town; it is therefore to be explained only by the intrusion of a powerful influence from outside, and that influence can scarcely have originated elsewhere than in the circle of Catherine Parr and her new husband Admiral Seymour. Its exercise in favour of Throckmorton is to be accounted for by his dependence upon the Queen's brother.

Throckmorton's Membership of these two Parliaments, which earned him no mention in the Journal or elsewhere (although he presumably assisted the bill of 1552 confirming his master's second marriage), may have been followed by his re-election to the next, that of March 1553. Northampton stood close to the Duke of Northumberland, under whose aegis this Parliament was held, and four of the Throckmorton brothers sat in it, Clement and John I for Warwick, Nicholas for Northamptonshire and Robert for Warwickshire. As the Members for Westbury are unknown Kenelm may again have been one of them, or he could have been returned for another of the many boroughs for which the names of the Members are lacking. It is not known

whether he was involved in the succession crisis of the following summer, which cost Northampton his honours and almost his life, nor is his name mentioned in connexion with the conspiracies of the reign of Mary in which his brother Nicholas and his kinsman John Throckmorton II* were involved. If he did share Northampton's eclipse, Throckmorton was evidently sure enough of himself to sit in the Parliament of 1555, this time for Warwick again. As before, he had brothers among his fellow-Members, John I sitting for Coventry and Robert as knight for Warwickshire, as well as his relative Thomas Throckmorton. Of these four it is only the last who is listed as having opposed a government bill towards the close of this Parliament and Kenelm may thus be thought to have aligned himself with his brothers in an innocuous attitude.[6]

This was to prove Throckmorton's last appearance in the Commons although he had some 30 years of life still before him. It was at the close of Mary's reign that he began to build up the estate in Essex which qualified him for appointment to the bench of that county: in doing so he was following his master, who had lands and offices there and who for two years had been Earl of Essex. Throckmorton had already parted with the lands in Warwickshire which he had either inherited or acquired and had thus cut his links with his native county. Judged by the Bishop of London in 1564 to be a 'favourer' of religion, he was spared the troubles which their recusancy was to bring to others of his family and continued to be re-appointed to the Essex bench until his death, becoming a member of the quorum in 1583. He died between that year and 1587 when his name was removed from the *liber pacis* for Essex.[7]

[1] Hatfield 207. [2] Date of birth estimated from younger brother Nicholas's. *Vis. Warws.* (Harl. Soc. xii), 88–89; *Vis. Oxon* (Harl. Soc. v), 120. [3] *LP Hen. VIII*, xii; *CPR*, 1547–8, p. 212; 1569–72, p. 224; Stowe 571, f. 50; M. L. Robertson, 'Cromwell's servants' (Univ. California Los Angeles Ph.D. thesis, 1975), 573. [4] *LP Hen. VIII*, v. vii, viii; *Vis. Worcs.* (Harl. Soc. xxviii), 81–82. [5] *LP Hen. VIII*, xiii, xviii, xx; A. L. Rowse, *Ralegh and the Throckmortons*, 12; Warwick castle ms 2539; *CPR*, 1547–8, p. 212; 1553, p. 28; 1553–4, p. 374; *VCH Warws.* iii. 144, 172, v. 175; *Narr. Ref.* (Cam. Soc. lxxxvii), 42. [6] D. M. Loades, *Two Tudor Conspiracies*, 95–97, 188–230. [7] Morant, *Essex*, ii. 431, 457; *CPR*, 1558–60, p. 244; 1560–3, pp. 173, 476; 1563–6, p. 139; *CSP Dom.* 1547–80, p. 380; Coughton Ct. mss box 46; *Cam. Misc.* ix(3), 62; C142/205/197; E163/14/8.

S.M.T.

THROCKMORTON, Nicholas (1515/16–71), of London and Paulerspury, Northants.

MALDON	1545
DEVIZES	1547[1]
NORTHAMPTONSHIRE	1553 (Mar.)
OLD SARUM	1553 (Oct.)
LYME REGIS	1559
TAVISTOCK	1563

b. 1515/16, 4th s. of Sir George Throckmorton*, and bro. of Anthony†, Clement*, George*, John I*, Kenelm* and Robert*. *m.* by 1553, Anne, da. of Sir Nicholas Carew* of Beddington, Surr., 10s. inc. Arthur† and Nicholas† 3da. Kntd. Jan./May 1551.[2]

Page, household of Henry Fitzroy, Duke of Richmond by 1532–6; servant, household of William, Baron Parr, later Earl of Essex and Marquess of Northampton by 1543; sewer, household of Queen Catherine Parr by 1544–7 or 8; gent. privy chamber by 1549–53; under treasurer, Tower II mint 25 Dec. 1549–24 June 1552; keeper, Brigstock park, Northants. 14 Sept. 1553–d.; j.p. Northants. 1558/59–d.; ambassador to France 1563–4, to Scotland 1565, 1567; chamberlain, the Exchequer 21 June 1564–d.; chief butler, Eng. and Wales 28 Nov. 1565–d.[3]

As 'a brother fourth and far from hope of land' Nicholas Throckmorton began his career in the service of Henry VIII's illegitimate son the Duke of Richmond, presumably with the help of his uncle Sir William Parr*, who was Richmond's chamberlain. In 1532 he accompanied Richmond to France for the meeting of the King with Francis I at Calais and stayed on there with his master for nearly a year, learning French 'though nothing readily'. After Richmond's death in 1536 Throckmorton's prospects were slender until his mother persuaded Parr's nephew and namesake to take him into service: it was under the younger Parr that he served on the Scottish border in 1543. He had obtained a small annuity from Pipewell abbey before the Dissolution, and when his cousin Catherine Parr married the King he and his brother Clement received appointments in her household. In 1544 he returned to France, this time as a captain in the army which took Boulogne. His election to the Parliament of the following year he doubtless owed to the Queen, who was the principal landowner in the neighbourhood of Maldon. It was also through her favour that in 1546 he was granted a lease of two Hertfordshire manors. At court he moved increasingly in Protestant circles, becoming acquainted with Anne Askew whom he visited in prison.[4]

In 1547 Throckmorton fought under the Protector Somerset's command in Scotland and for bringing the news of Pinkie to Edward VI he received an annuity of £100. According to a family tradition he gained the young King's affection, and his knighting early in 1551 shortly before going on an embassy to France was the occasion for one of the King's rare outbursts of high spirits. In the first Parliament of the reign he sat for Devizes, which formed part of Queen Catherine's jointure and which had returned his brother Clement to the previous Parliament. Catherine's death in September 1548, and the subsequent downfall of her husband Admiral Seymour, did not harm Throckmorton, who had openly disapproved of Seymour's conduct and

stood closer to his own master, now Marquess of Northampton. He also appears not to have been compromised by the fall of Somerset; on the contrary, his appointment in the privy chamber and his under treasurership of the mint look like a reward for his part in that episode. The Commons Journal does not mention Throckmorton, but he was later to remind Nicholas Hare and William Stanford that he had heard them expound to the House 'the ambiguities and doubts of [the treason] law sincerely, and without affectations'; he presumably assisted in the passage of the private Act confirming the legality of Northampton's second marriage (5 and 6 Edw. VI, no. 30), and another likely to have interested him was the Act for the restoration in blood of Francis Carew, who was perhaps already his brother-in-law (2 and 3 Edw. VI, no. 42). In June 1552 Throckmorton, in company with a number of other officials there, gave up his appointment at the mint, for which he was shortly afterwards recompensed by a further annuity of £100. His acceptability to the Northumberland regime is borne out by the inclusion of his name in the Council letter recommending selected gentlemen for return to the Parliament of March 1553: he was put forward as knight of the shire for Northampton and was duly elected.[5]

Throckmorton's conduct during the succession crisis is not easy to determine. He signed the device settling the crown upon Lady Jane Grey, and when during her brief reign she agreed to be godmother to Edward Underhill's* son Anne Throckmorton acted as her deputy. On the other hand, he is supposed to have sent word of the King's death to Mary, and when he challenged Sir Thomas Tresham's* proclamation of Mary at Northampton it may have been on the ground that Tresham was not sheriff. There was certainly no immediate sign of disfavour: on 24 July he was appointed to conduct the Queen on her progress to London, and on 14 Sept. he was granted the keepership of the parks at Brigstock, Northamptonshire, forfeited by the Marquess of Northampton's attainder. In the Parliament of October 1553 he and his brother John sat for Old Sarum, presumably on the nomination of their kinsman William Herbert I,* 1st Earl of Pembroke. During this Parliament the Act legalising Northampton's second marriage was repealed (1 Mary st. 2, no. 30): neither brother is known to have opposed this measure, which had the Queen's approval, but Sir Nicholas Throckmorton joined the opposition to the reintroduction of Catholicism, being noted on the list of Members as having 'stood for the true religion'. Some months later he recalled hearing Sir Richard Southwell speak against the Spanish marriage in the Commons, where 'I did see the whole consent of the realm against it, and I, a hearer, but no speaker'.[6]

Even if Throckmorton did not speak against the marriage in the House, he was thought to be active against it outside and to have conspired with Sir Thomas Wyatt II* to prevent it. On 1 Jan. 1554 he was bound over in a recognizance of £2,000 to be of good conduct, and on the following 20 Feb., after the failure of Wyatt's rebellion, he was committed to the Tower. On 17 Apr. he was indicted of treason at Guildhall and brought to trial on a charge of being the 'principal deviser, procurer and contriver of the late rebellion: and that Wyatt was but his minister'. To the discomfiture of the crown he put up such a masterly defence that he was acquitted, but in the expectation that a further charge could be brought against him he was not released until 18 Jan. 1555, when he retired to his home in Northamptonshire. On the discovery of the Dudley conspiracy he feared that he would again be suspected, and on 20 June 1556 he fled to France. He protested his innocence to the English ambassador and gave some colour to this by not mixing with refugees known to have supported the conspiracy. During the autumn the Queen allowed his wife to send him some money, and on 1 May 1557 she pardoned him and restored to him the property confiscated on his flight. Later in the year he served under the Earl of Pembroke at the battle of St. Quentin. On his return to England he started a correspondence with Princess Elizabeth, and on the death of Queen Mary he presumed to advise her successor on ministerial appointments.[7]

Elizabeth shared (Sir) Richard Morison's* belief that Throckmorton was a 'Machiavellist', and although her reign saw his fortunes take an upward turn he never attained high position and his prospects were again clouded in 1569 by his suspected complicity with the 4th Duke of Norfolk. He died in London on 12 Feb. 1571 and was buried in the church of St. Catherine Cree, Aldgate.[8]

[1] Hatfield 207. [2] Aged 35 at Gardiner's trial in Jan. 1551, Foxe, *Acts and Mons.* vi. 148, and 46 in 1562, R. G. Strong, *Tudor and Jacobean Portraits*, 311. *Vis. Warws.* (Harl. Soc. xii), 87; *Vis. Northants.* ed. Metcalfe, 200; Add. 5841, p. 200; *DNB*; PCC 9 Daper. [3] Add. 5841, p. 252 seq.; *Soc. Antiq.* (1790), p. 167; *LP Hen. VIII*, xvi; *Brit. Numismatic Jnl.* xlv. 69; *APC*, iv. 76, 77, 84; *CPR*, 1549–51, p. 137; 1553, p. 9; 1563–6, pp. 118, 234; *CSP Dom.* 1601–3, *Add.* 1547–65, pp. 503, 561. [4] A. L. Rowse, *Ralegh and the Throckmortons*, 9–12; Add. 5841, p. 252 seq.; *LP Hen. VIII*, xvi, xviii, xix; *Narr. Ref.* (Cam. Soc. lxxvii), 42. [5] *CPR*, 1550–3, p. 104; Add. 5841, p. 252 seq.; Rowse, 12–19; *HMC Hatfield*, i. 61; *Lit. Rems. Edw. VI*, 317, 359; *CSP Span.* 1550–2, pp. 212, 302; *APC*, iii. 271; W. K. Jordan, *Edw. VI*, ii. 82, 104, 417. [6] Jordan, ii. 524; *Narr. Ref.* 12, 13, 100; *Chron. Q. Jane and Q. Mary* (Cam. Soc. xlviii), 63; Bodl. e Museo 17; Holinshed, *Chron.* iv. 31; *State Trials*, ed. Howell, i. 869 seq.; Strype, *Eccles. Memorials*, ii(1), 554; A. G. Dickens, *Eng. Ref.* 257; Add. 5841, p. 252 seq. [7] Rowse, 20–25; D. M. Loades, *Two Tudor Conspiracies*, 16, 18, 95–97, 158–9, 210, 214, 236; *Narr. Ref.* 63, 75; Foxe, vi. 349; *Machyn's Diary* (Cam. Soc. xlii), 60, 80; *DKR*, iv(2), 63; *Chron. Q. Jane and Q. Mary*, 75; *CPR*, 1555–7, p. 476; *CSP Dom.* 1547–80, p. 78; *CSP For.* 1553–8

passim; Add. 5841, p. 252 seq.; *EHR*, lxv. 91. [8] *EHR*, lxv. 91–98; C142/137/104; Pevsner and Cherry, *London*, i. 161.

S.M.T.

THROCKMORTON, Robert (by 1513–81), of Coughton, Warws. and Weston Underwood, Bucks.

WARWICKSHIRE 1553 (Mar.), 1553 (Oct.), 1555

b. by 1513, 1st s. of Sir George Throckmorton*, and bro. of Anthony†, Clement*, George*, John I*, Kenelm* and Nicholas*. *educ.* ?M. Temple. *m.* (1) 1527, Muriel, da. of Thomas, 5th Lord Berkeley, 3s. inc. Thomas II* 4da.; (2) 1542, Elizabeth (*d.* 23 Jan. 1554), da. of Sir John Hussey*, Lord Hussey, wid. of Walter, Lord Hungerford, at least 2s. 5da. *suc.* fa. 6 Aug. 1552. Kntd. by 25 Sept. 1553.[1]

Jt. (with fa.) steward, Evesham abbey 1527, Claverdon, Warws. 1531, Maxstoke, Warws. 1535, Balsall, Warws. 1539; bailiff, Warwick 1544–5; j.p. Warws. from 1547, q. 1561–4, rem. 1570; commr. relief 1550, loan 1557, musters 1569; sheriff, Warws. and Leics. 1553–4; constable, Warwick castle Sept. 1553–8; steward, lands of bp. of Worcester in 1564.[2]

Robert Throckmorton may have trained at the Middle Temple, the inn attended by his father, at least three of his younger brothers and his own eldest son, but as the heir to extensive estates he had little need to seek a career at court or in government. He was joined with his father in several stewardships from 1527 and was perhaps the servant of Robert Tyrwhitt*, a distant relative by marriage of the Throckmortons, who in 1540 took an inventory of Cromwell's goods at Mortlake. He attended the reception of Anne of Cleves and with several of his brothers served in the French war of 1544. Three years later he was placed on the Warwickshire bench and was thus suitably qualified for the knighthood of the shire which fell to him almost as though it were a part of his inheritance in March 1553: three of his brothers sat in the same Parliament, Nicholas as knight for Northamptonshire.[3]

Throckmorton's role in the succession crisis of 1553 is unknown but his standing with Queen Mary is shown by her reputed answer to the news of Edward VI's death sent her by four of his brothers: 'If Robert had been there she durst have gaged her life and hazarded the hap'. In the autumn of 1553 Throckmorton was knighted and appointed constable of Warwick castle and only his shrievalty prevented him from continuing to sit for the shire until in 1558 he gave way to his eldest son. His Catholicism explains his disappearance from the Commons in the new reign, although the most Catholic of his brothers, Anthony Throckmorton, was to sit in the Parliament of 1563. Judged an 'adversary of true religion' in 1564, Throckmorton remained active in Warwickshire until his refusal to subscribe to the Act of Uniformity led to his removal from the commission of the peace.[4]

In 1577 the bishop of Worcester listed Throckmorton as a Catholic and reckoned him to be worth 1,000 marks a year in lands and £1,000 in goods. He died on 12 Feb. 1581, six days after making a will in which he styled himself of Weston Underwood but asked to be buried at Coughton, where an alabaster and marble tomb was accordingly erected to his memory: there is a portrait at Coughton. He named as executors his eldest son Thomas and his sons-in-law Sir John Goodwin and Ralph Sheldon[†], and as overseers another son-in-law Sir Thomas Tresham and his 'loving friend' Edmund Plowden*.[5]

[1] Date of birth estimated from age at fa.'s i.p.m., C142/98/75. Dugdale, *Warws.* 755; *Vis. Warws.* (Harl. Soc. xii), 87–88; Coughton Ct. mss boxes 1–33, no. 764. [2] Coughton Ct. mss boxes 1–33, no. App. 188; box 59; *LP Hen. VIII*, v; C219/18C/124; *CPR*, 1547–8, p. 90; 1553, p. 360; 1553–4, pp. 199–200; 1563–6, p. 28; *CSP Dom.* 1547–80, pp. 95, 343, 366; *Cam. Misc.* ix(3), 4. [3] *LP Hen. VIII*, xiv, xv, xix, add. [4] A. L. Rowse, *Ralegh and the Throckmortons*, 18; *Cam. Misc.* ix(3), 4, 7; Lansd. 8(18), f. 81; *CSP Dom.* 1547–80, p. 366. [5] *Cath. Rec. Soc.* xxii. 65; C142/193/89; PCC 12 Darcy; *VCH Warws.* iii. 85; Pevsner and Wedgwood, *Warws.* 245; R. C. Strong, *Tudor and Jacobean Portraits*, i. 312; C. O. Moreton, *Waddesdon and Over Winchendon*, 131; *CPR*, 1553–4, p. 84.

S.M.T.

THROCKMORTON, Simon (by 1526–85), of Brampton, Hunts.

HUNTINGDON   1554 (Apr.)
HUNTINGDONSHIRE 1559

b. by 1526, 3rd s. of Richard Throckmorton of Higham Ferrers, Northants. by Joan, da. of Humphrey Beaufo of Whilton, Northants. *m.* by 1547, 2s.[1]

Simon Throckmorton's father, a younger brother of Sir George Throckmorton*, settled at Higham Ferrers, where he was steward for the duchy of Lancaster; he was also duchy receiver for Northamptonshire and neighbouring counties. Of Throckmorton's own career little has been discovered. It must have been an older namesake who was practising as an attorney in 1520, probably the member of the Suffolk family who died in 1527. Throckmorton is not known to have held office of any kind, but whereas his eldest brother became a groom of the chamber and receiver of Kenilworth and the other two were bailiffs for the Cromwell family, there is little doubt that he attached himself to Sir Robert Tyrwhitt I (q.v.). It was in 1550, two years after Tyrwhitt's purchase of Leighton Bromswold, that Throckmorton bought Fosters manor in Brampton, which he was to make his home; lying on the outskirts of Huntingdon, it was equidistant from Leighton Bromswold and Kimbolton, of which Tyrwhitt was custodian. Throckmorton's two elections to Parliament clearly reflect Tyrwhitt's patronage: on both occasions Tyrwhitt himself sat

for the shire and on the first Throckmorton had as his fellow-Member Tyrwhitt's stepson Thomas Maria Wingfield. Both were to disappear in the Commons after 1559, when despite his Protestantism Tyrwhitt was out of favour with the new Queen; there seems to be no means of judging whether Throckmorton was of the same religious persuasion. At his death on 27 Mar. 1585 he was succeeded by his 37 year-old son Robert.[2]

[1] Date of birth estimated from marriage. *Vis. Hunts.* (Cam. Soc. xliii), 123–4; Baker, *Northants.* i. 232; Burke, *Peerage* (1959), 2226; *Vis. Warws.* (Harl. Soc. xii), 203; C142/210/93. [2] Somerville, *Duchy*, i. 562, 587–8, 590–1, 593, 601; *LP Hen. VIII*, xx; Add. 5841, f. 191; *Val. Eccles.* iv. 273–4; Add. Roll 34286; *VCH Hunts.* iii. 15; E179/122/146; *CPR*, 1549–51, p. 245; 1553–4, p. 3; 1558–60, p. 142; *Cal. Feet of Fines, Hunts.* ed. Turner, 139, 149; C142/210/93.

M.K.D.

THROCKMORTON, Thomas I (by 1516–68), of Corse Court, Corse and Tortworth, Glos.

HEYTESBURY 1547[1]
WESTBURY   1555

b. by 1516, 1st s. of William Throckmorton of Tortworth by Margaret, da. and coh. of Sir David Mathew of Radyr, Glam.; bro. of John II*. *m.* by 1538, Margaret, da. and coh. of Thomas Whittington of Pauntley, Glos., 2s. inc. Sir Thomas[†] 2da. *suc.* fa. by May 1537, uncle George Throckmorton 16 Oct. 1548. Kntd. 2 Oct. 1553.[2]

Commr. sewers, Glos. 1543, musters 1546, chantries 1548, relief 1550; escheator 1546–7; j.p. 1547–63, q. 1564–*d.*; servant of Edward Seymour, Duke of Somerset by 1548; sheriff, Glos. 1558–9; member, council in the marches of Wales 1560–*d.*[3]

Thomas Throckmorton belonged to a cadet branch of the well known family of that name. His father, who was sheriff of Gloucestershire in 1529–30, acquired Tortworth by marriage and made it the family seat. Throckmorton inherited his substantial patrimony when he was in his early twenties and within a dozen years he was to add to it his own further inheritance from an uncle and his wife's as a coheir.[4]

By 1547 Throckmorton had served his apprenticeship in local government and had seen some military service against France and Scotland. It may have been his soldiering which brought him within the orbits of Edward Seymour, Duke of Somerset, and Somerset's right-hand man John Thynne*: in a grant of December 1548 Throckmorton is described as a servant of the Protector and in the following April he addressed Thynne as 'my master'. It was with Thynne that he was coupled in May 1549 in a grant of ex-chantry lands in Gloucestershire and other counties which cost them £4,340. There can be little doubt that Throckmorton's return for Heytesbury to the first Edwardian Parliament was a by-product of this relationship, especially as his fellow-Member Thomas Eynns was both an uncle of Thynne's and a connexion by marriage of Throckmorton's, whose kinsman Clement Throckmorton had married Eynns's sister-in-law Catherine Neville. Clement was one of the four Throckmortons of Coughton, Warwickshire, who also sat in this Parliament. Of Thomas Throckmorton's part in its proceedings nothing is known, but until the fall of Somerset, and with it the temporary disgrace of Thynne, he was doubtless a supporter of the regime both within and outside the House. A justice of the peace for Gloucestershire from 1547, he was regularly nominated for the shrievalty from 1548, although he was not to be pricked until ten years later.[5]

The reign of Mary began auspiciously for Throckmorton with the knighthood conferred on him on 2 Oct. 1553. As this took place three days before the opening of the Queen's first Parliament, it might be inferred that he had come up to take a seat in the Commons, but unless his name was confused with that of his younger brother John, who is recorded as sitting for Wootton Bassett, he does not appear to have been elected. Two years later he was returned, this time for Westbury, where it is likely that he again owed his nomination to Thynne. In this Parliament he was among the Members who under the leadership of his Gloucestershire neighbour Sir Anthony Kingston voted against one of the government's bills. This seems to have been the limit of his overt opposition to the Marian regime, but it was otherwise with his brother John, who took part in the Dudley conspiracy and was executed for treason in April 1556. Throckmorton himself did not escape suspicion and his services seem to have been little used for the rest of the reign: it was not he but his younger namesake of Coughton who sat in the Parliament of 1558.[6]

The picture changed with the accession of Elizabeth: within a week of that event Throckmorton was pricked sheriff of Gloucestershire and within two years he was put on the council in the marches. During his remaining years he was a leading figure in his shire, serving on many commissions and being active in suppressing recurrent disorders. In 1564 he advised Bishop Cheyney as to the suitability of his fellow-members of the Gloucestershire bench to continue in office. Throckmorton expanded and reorganized the family estates. Apart from his acquisitions through his wife and uncle and his purchases with Thynne, he bought property in Walton from the crown and the remainder of the manor of Tortworth from Thomas Morgan. Some of the chantry lands he soon alienated and he also sold part of his patrimony. The Gloucestershire

estates on his death were more compact, consisting of two groups of manors, one in the north of the county and the other in the south west: at his inquisition they were valued at rather more than £120 a year. By his will he left his daughter Margaret a dowry of 500 marks; his wife's jointure had been fixed after her marriage as the manors of Corse Court, Haw and Turley. The manor of Tortworth was assured to his executors for 40 years to pay debts, legacies and annuities, but with this proviso it and all the other properties were to pass to his eldest son Thomas, on condition that he paid his mother an additional annuity of £20. Throckmorton appointed his wife and George Huntley* executors. He died on 1 Mar. 1568—not, as is stated in many works on Gloucestershire, in 1586: contemporary references to 'Sir Thomas Throckmorton' between 1568 and his son's knighting in 1574 were made in error. He was buried in the church at Tortworth where a monument was erected to his memory.[7]

[1] Hatfield 207. [2] Date of birth estimated from livery of inheritance in May 1537, *LP Hen. VIII*, xii. *Vis. Glos.* (Harl. Soc. xxi), 162; C142/149/130. [3] *LP Hen. VIII*, xviii, xxi; *CPR*, 1547-8, p. 84; 1548-9, p. 267; 1553, p. 354; 1563-6, p. 22; P. H. Williams, *Council in the Marches of Wales*, 358-9. [4] *LP Hen. VIII*, xii; C142/86/90. [5] *LP Hen. VIII*, xviii, xix, xxi; *Bristol and Glos. Arch. Soc. Trans.* ix. 84; Bath mss Thynne pprs. 2, ff. 43-43v, 161-161v; *CPR*, 1548-9, p. 329; 1553, pp. 328, 339, 348, 376, 387. [6] Guildford mus. Loseley 1331/2; D. M. Loades, *Two Tudor Conspiracies*, 188-230 passim. [7] *Bristol and Glos. Arch. Soc. Trans.* viii. 306; x. 212; lix. 119, 148; *APC*, vii. 241; *VCH Warws.* iii. 112; *LP Hen. VIII*, xviii; *CPR*, 1555-7, pp. 95, 96; 1557-8, pp. 97-98; 1560-3, p. 394; 1563-6, p. 135; *Cam. Misc.* ix(3), 32; C142/149/130; PCC 8 Babington; D. Verey, *Glos.: the Vale and Forest of Dean*, 389.

S.M.T.

THROCKMORTON, Thomas II (by 1536-1615), of Coughton, Warws. and Weston Underwood, Bucks.

WARWICKSHIRE	1558
WARWICK	1559

b. by 1536, 1st s. of (Sir) Robert Throckmorton* of Coughton by 1st w. Muriel, da. of Thomas, 5th Lord Berkeley. *educ.* M. Temple, adm. 20 Mar. 1555. *m.* by 14 Feb. 1556, Margaret, da. and coh. of William Whorwood* of Putney, Surr., 3s. 5da. *suc.* fa. 12 Feb. 1581.[1]

J.p. Warws. 1564, rem. 1570.

It was to a quasi-hereditary knighthood of the shire that Thomas Throckmorton was elected in 1558; his grandfather Sir George had sat for Warwickshire in the Parliament of 1529 and his father Sir Robert three times between 1553 and 1555. In the circumstances it is hardly surprising that the writer of the election indenture should have styled him knight, an error which was only corrected after it had been repeated in the Crown Office list of Members. Then in his early twenties, Throckmorton had become a substantial landowner in his own county and elsewhere by his recent marriage to one of the two daughters of a former attorney-general; her wardship had passed in 1553 to (Sir) Henry Sidney*, from whom it was presumably acquired by Sir Robert Throckmorton.[2]

Elected for the borough of Warwick to Elizabeth's first Parliament and afterwards put on the county bench, Throckmorton later paid for his adherence to Catholicism by his exclusion from public life and the erosion of his wealth. He died on 13 Mar. 1615.[3]

[1] Date of birth estimated from age at fa.'s i.p.m., C142/193/89; according to his MI erected c. 1688 he was 81 at death. Nash, *Worcs.* i. 453; *Vis. Warws.* (Harl. Soc. xii), 88.   [2] C193/32/2; 219/25/119; on the copy of the Crown Office list in the Wm. Salt Lib. SMS 264, Throckmorton's name was mistakenly marked with a circle, afterwards struck out in the same hand; *CPR*, 1553, p. 1.   [3] A. L. Rowse, *Ralegh and the Throckmortons*, 190; C142/367/100.

S.M.T.

THYNNE, John (1512/13–80), of London and Longleat, Wilts.

MARLBOROUGH	?1539,[1] ?1542,[2] 1545
SALISBURY	1547[3]
WILTSHIRE	1559
GREAT BEDWYN	1563
WILTSHIRE	1571
HEYTESBURY	1572*

b. 1512/13, 1st s. of Thomas Thynne of Church Stretton, Salop by Margaret, da. of Thomas Eynns of Church Stretton. *m.* (1) settlement Jan. 1549, Christian, da. of Sir Richard Gresham* of London, 3s. 3da.; (2) 1566/67, Dorothy, da. of Sir William Wroughton* of Broad Hinton, Wilts., 5s. Kntd. 10 Sept. 1547.[4]

Servant of the 2nd Lord Vaux of Harrowden in 1535; steward of the household to Edward Seymour, Viscount Beauchamp and later Earl of Hertford and Duke of Somerset 1536–50; surveyor, ct. augmentations, Wilts. by 1545–53, Exchequer 1554–*d.*; common packer, London Aug. 1547; commr. chantries, Wilts. and Salisbury 1548, musters, Wilts. 1569, loan 1570, subsidy 1576; sheriff, Som. and Dorset 1548–9, Wilts. 1569–70; high steward, Warminster, Wilts. in 1553; j.p.q. and custos rot. Wilts. 1558/59–*d.*[5]

John Thynne was probably drawn to London by his uncle William Thynne, chief clerk of the King's kitchen by 1526 and a master of the Household from 1540, who is remembered as an editor of Chaucer. William Thynne accumulated many offices, some of which show that he retained links with his native Welsh border country; in 1529 he was appointed receiver-general of the earldom of March in reversion and in May 1546, shortly before his death, a fresh grant, made at the request of the Earl of Hertford, included John Thynne in the reversion.[6]

An account book kept by the steward of Lord Vaux of Harrowden includes John Thynne among the 46 persons 'ordinary of household' who attended Vaux's family at Harrowden, Northamptonshire, from 2 Aug. until 28 Oct. 1535. Within less than a

year Thynne had found preferment, for his first account as steward of the household to Edward Seymour, Viscount Beauchamp, opens on 17 July 1536. Coinciding as it did with Vaux's sale to Seymour of his only crown office, the governorship of Jersey, Thynne's exchange of service was from a master who was financially embarrassed and politically negligible to one who stood on the threshold of greatness. The birth of Prince Edward carried Seymour across that threshold, and by October 1537 Thynne was distributing gifts among the royal officers at Windsor on the occasion of Seymour's elevation to the earldom of Hertford. In the following year he was involved in litigation with his former master: between March and the end of November 1538 Thynne, described as Hertford's servant, brought an action in Chancery over the Northamptonshire parsonage of Wilby, from which he claimed to have been excluded by Vaux.[7]

When Thynne had entered Hertford's service, royal favour was already making the Seymours the foremost family in Wiltshire. He had no previous ties with that county, and was still described as resident in London on 11 Apr. 1539 when he received a 21-year lease of the Devon rectory of Clawton. A year later Sir John Horsey* sold Thynne the site of Longleat priory, with its appurtenances in three adjoining parishes on the borders of Wiltshire and Somerset; other possessions of Longleat and Hinton, in the same neighbourhood, were later granted by the crown to the Earl of Hertford, who on 25 June 1541 transferred them to Thynne. Here, close to his master's former monastic estate at Maiden Bradley, lay the centre of Thynne's domains, which were to expand until they rivalled those of the Seymours.[8]

During the closing years of Henry VIII's reign, Thynne's attendance upon Hertford cannot have allowed him to spend much time in Wiltshire. He appears to have penned the earl's letter to the Council from Alnwick on 29 Nov. 1542, reporting the murder of Somerset Herald, and he probably took part in the ensuing battle of Solway Moss. In March 1544 he was paid 40s.10d. for repairs at Newcastle and on 29 July 1545 Hertford wrote from the same town to Secretary Paget, asking him to hasten the return of Thynne, who had been sent south to move private business of the earl's with the King.[9]

Thynne's parliamentary career poses a number of problems, the first being when it began. Although he is not known to have been elected before 1545 he could well have sat in either or both of the Parliaments, those of 1539 and 1542, which followed his entry into Hertford's service, and if so he is most likely to have been returned for a borough within his master's sphere of influence in Wiltshire. An early historian of Marlborough, James Waylen, does indeed name Thynne as one of that borough's Members on two occasions before 1545, and although Waylen's ascription of the first of these to the year 1534 is almost certainly wrong, if this can be seen as an error for 1539, and his second date of 1541 be read as 1542, the resulting claim becomes credible on more than one ground. Marlborough formed part of the jointure of successive queens consort, but in 1539 there was no queen to wield patronage and in 1541-2 Catherine Howard could certainly not have done so. In these circumstances no one was better placed than Hertford to nominate the Members, and the names of Thynne and 'Barwicke', that is, John Berwick, in 1539 certainly bespeak the earl's influence, as does Thynne's three years later, although his fellow on this occasion, William Barnes I, is not so readily connected with Hertford. Thynne's representation of Marlborough in these two Parliaments may also be reflected in the bond for £33 from the corporation which he was holding early in March 1544: that sum approximates to the total of his parliamentary wages (at 2s. a day) for the three sessions of the Parliament of 1539 and the first two of that of 1542.[10]

If no such doubt attaches to Thynne's return for Marlborough in 1545, the circumstances of that election are not entirely clear. It appears from the indenture that on 20 Jan. 1545 Thynne was returned with John Berwick but that Berwick's name was later erased and replaced, in a different hand, by that of Andrew Baynton, Berwick's name nevertheless remaining unchanged a few lines below. The alteration, which implies some misunderstanding, or even dispute, about the identity of the second Member, is perhaps also a pointer to the patronage in operation. At the time of the election, and for some months before it, Hertford was fully occupied in fighting and negotiating abroad, and it may well be that Berwick and Thynne procured their own nomination at Marlborough without his personal intervention; moreover, as Hertford was to return from France only to leave soon afterwards for the north, the substitution of Baynton, which could have taken place some time after the original election (the Parliament having already been prorogued until the autumn), may also have owed nothing to Hertford himself. Alternative sources of support for Baynton are not far to seek: one was Sir Thomas Seymour II, with whom he was then exchanging lands, another, Queen Catherine Parr, since 1543 lord of Marlborough, whom Baynton's father had served as vice-chamberlain. Either, or both, of these powerful figures could have brushed aside the comparatively

humble Berwick: that Thynne survived the intervention he perhaps owed to his friendship with the Queen, who used to send him New Year gifts, as well as to his higher standing in the Seymour entourage.[11]

Attachment to Hertford brought increased rewards after the accession of Edward VI, when the earl became Protector and Duke of Somerset. On 2 Aug. 1547 'one Mr. Cycell' brought royal letters to the common council of London, demanding that Thynne should be given the 'packership of strangers' goods', although this post had already been filled 24 hours before. On the next day Thynne became a freeman of the City, as a member of the Mercers' Company (to which he had gained special admission in the course of the year), and it was agreed that he should be packer, although on condition that he should exercise the office only by the City's grant and should seek assurances that the King and Protector would never 'write any more such letters to this house for the said room or office'. Civic rights were further safeguarded by provisos that Thynne should pay the usual fine of £6 13s.4d. for the freedom—although this would be repaid him— and that his promise to avert any future court pressure should be recorded and sent to him for perusal. Within two years he married a daughter of the former mayor Sir Richard Gresham, another mercer, and it was perhaps Gresham money which enabled Thynne, in association with Thomas Throckmorton I*, to pay £4,340 to the augmentations for the lands in Gloucestershire, Herefordshire, Lincolnshire and Yorkshire which were granted to himself, his wife and his heirs on 19 May 1549.[12]

Thynne's successful diligence in feathering his own nest, if wholly in keeping with the spirit of the age, remains the least commendable feature of his service with Somerset. Sir William Paget's verdict notwithstanding, there is little or nothing to support the view of Thynne as a grey eminence who wielded a pernicious influence on his master: he appears rather in the light of the hard working man of affairs struggling to keep abreast of the mass of business created by the Protector's multifarious concerns. One of these in particular engaged Thynne's interest and attention. A correspondence conducted between November 1548 and June 1549 shows him in charge of the Protector's plans to supersede the old Seymour house of Wolf Hall by a more palatial seat, on one of two nearby hills known as Bedwyn Brail. At the same time work was begun on Thynne's own mansion at Longleat, which was largely burned down in 1567, only to be rebuilt. Thynne, who may have been his own architect, showed at least as great an enthusiasm for Somerset's building projects as did the Protector: indeed, his neighbour William Darrell of Littlecote was later to charge him with 'infecting his master's head with plats and forms and many a subtle thing'.[13]

Thynne's Membership of the Parliament of 1547 is hedged by doubts similar to those attaching to his earlier elections. The only certain evidence of it is the appearance of his name, with that of Henry Clifford, on the revised version of the Crown Office list which was prepared for the fourth session of the Parliament in January 1552. As Salisbury, the city which Thynne and Clifford are there shown as representing, had on 26 Sept. 1547 elected to this Parliament two of its own citizens, Robert Griffith and William Webbe II (qq.v.), it has to be asked when and in what circumstances these two were superseded. Since both of them outlived the Parliament, and there is no trace of a by-election on any other score, the change may be presumed to have taken place before the Parliament assembled. The intrusion of Thynne is probably to be explained by his absence in Scotland, with the Protector, at the time of the election: if on their return early in October it was to find all the Wiltshire seats, including Marlborough, already bespoke, Somerset could well have decided to dragoon Salisbury into releasing one of its places for his steward. Much the same thing had happened there two years earlier and of the men displaced Webbe, at least, is likely to have abetted rather than opposed the repetition of that episode.[14]

It is not to be supposed that, with so much of the Protector's business passing through his hands, to which was added in 1548–9 the shrievalty of Somerset and Dorset, Thynne was a regular attendant or active participant in the Commons, and his name does not occur in the Journal during this Parliament. He was, in any case, to suffer two forced exclusions from the House which together spanned the whole of the third and fourth sessions. Two days after Somerset's arrest at Windsor on 11 Oct. 1549, Thynne was sent to the Tower with William Grey II*, (Sir) Thomas Smith I*, (Sir) Michael Stanhope* and Edward Wolf, these being the duke's 'principal instruments and counsellors . . . in the affairs of his ill government'. On 28 Nov. he told his interrogators that he had disapproved of Somerset's extravagant building operations as the Protector was always short of money, but denied all knowledge of corruption or sinister political designs. In the following February he was placed in stricter confinement, but received leave of absence for one month on 17 Apr. and a pardon on 5 Aug., when all his goods and offices were restored; he then told

Cecil that he wished to resign his stewardship. In the summer of 1551 he remonstrated with Somerset after being denied the mastership of the game in Bagley woods in favour of Charles, 8th Baron Stourton, and on 3 Oct. he was rebuked for harshly imprisoning a younger poacher who had married a kinswoman of the duchess. He may have been trying to hold aloof from Somerset's party at court, for at the time of the duke's second arrest he was in Wiltshire; none the less he was again put in the Tower on 16 Oct. 1551, although in November his wife was permitted to enjoy his goods and three months later, after the duke's execution, to visit her husband. Like other Seymour partisans whose lives were spared, Thynne had to part with his offices and much of his property; on 19 June 1552 he undertook to surrender his packership of London under penalty of 1,000 marks (although he was to hold it again under Elizabeth), and five days later his lease of the Savoy hospital was restored to the duchy of Lancaster. After this he retired to Wiltshire, where he joined John Berwick in trying to secure provision for the disinherited heir, Edward Seymour.[15]

A man of great wealth, Thynne had been fortunate to escape so lightly; during his first spell in the Tower he had been forced to enter into a bond of £6,000, whereas the four men arrested with him had been rated at £3,000 apiece. He had incurred a good deal of enmity. In Wiltshire he had offended Sir Henry Long*, who claimed that Somerset and his steward had deprived him of rights in Vastern park, and perhaps also (Sir) William Sharington*, whose temporary disgrace for embezzlement in 1549 had led Thynne to agitate for repayment of a debt. As sheriff of Somerset and master to John Hartgill, Thynne had tried to make peace at an early stage in the quarrel between Baron Stourton and John's father, William Hartgill*. Stourton was a dangerous man to cross, for he was nephew to Somerset's triumphant rival the Earl of Warwick. In an action for slander after Mary's accession, Thynne was to declare that he and (Sir) John Bonham* had not dared to bring help to the new Queen lest Stourton should rifle their houses, 'as he once did mine when I was at Windsor with the King before the Duke of Somerset's apprehension'. At court one of Somerset's own intimates, Paget, had long been a detractor: reporting in 1545 that he had pressed Hertford's private affairs with the King, Paget remarked that the details could be explained by Thynne, adding 'Mary! Methinks I smell he looks to have somewhat more. You wot what.', a hint that Thynne needed bribing. In July 1549 Paget had complained to (Sir) William Petre* of Thynne's dishonesty and greed, with the warning that 'there is no one thing whereof his grace hath need to take such heed as that man's proceedings'.[16]

Fortunately for Thynne's prospects Paget, who had changed sides in time to escape the first attack on Somerset, was arrested and disgraced during the second in 1551. Thynne was also helped perhaps by his rich marriage and city connexions, which enabled him to account for his gains, and by the services rendered to Warwick by his brother-in-law Thomas Gresham in the Netherlands. Among other useful friendships were those with William Cecil and Sir William Paulet, Marquess of Winchester, both of whom survived Somerset's fall: Cecil was now a neighbour of Thynne's at Cannon Row, Westminster, and it was from his 'loving friend' Thynne that in December 1552 Winchester sought details of Somerset's property in order to help the heir.[17]

As late as 19 Oct. 1552 his lawyer Humphrey Moseley* reported to Thynne from the court that he was the subject of ominous talk, including the rumour that he was to be returned to the Tower. It is no surprise, therefore, that Thynne is not known to have procured his own re-election to the Parliament summoned by Warwick, now Duke of Northumberland, for March 1553. His support was, however, solicited by Moseley at Marlborough or, failing that, for another Wiltshire seat which he hoped the sheriff, Sir William Sharington, would provide at Thynne's request. Moseley was to be disappointed, but whether because his patron lacked the influence needed to place him cannot be known: Thynne's relations with Sharington seem to have become amicable again—a few months later, on the eve of his death, Sharington would reply courteously to Thynne's request for the loan of a mason from Lacock—and he may have given his support to other aspirants, such as his future associate Gabriel Pleydell, who was returned for Wootton Bassett.[18]

Thynne responded to Queen Mary's orders of 19 July 1553 by proclaiming her at Warminster, where he was high steward. In doing so, he again incurred the wrath of Baron Stourton, who claimed to have a prior commission as the Queen's lieutenant but whose agent was brushed aside. On 22 July Thynne, with Sir John Bonham, Sir James Stumpe* and Sir William Wroughton, informed Mary that she had been duly proclaimed and on 24 July they asked about Stourton's claim to wield special authority. The Queen's order of the following day that they should remain in their own counties told them where their duty lay, and to Stourton's accusations that he was a traitor and a flatterer Thynne retorted, 'Master have I had none but the

King's majesty since the death of the Duke of Somerset'. On 20 Sept. Stourton informed the sheriff that the Queen would not have 'such spotted persons' as Bonham and Thynne elected to Parliament; whether or not this denunciation was responsible for their absence from the parliamentary ranks under Mary, the epithet provoked a suit for slander in which Moseley acted as Thynne's counsel. In January 1554, with Stourton's newfound prestige declining, Moseley advised his client to reach a settlement privately, leaving Bonham in the lurch, but it is not known whether the case was settled before Stourton destroyed himself by murdering the Hartgills.[19]

Thynne's exclusion from public employment under Mary, and by contrast his avoidance of serious subversion, mean that save in one important respect the chronicle of his life during the reign holds little of political interest. He had sued out a pardon on 13 Oct. 1553 and in the following January he was ordered to entertain Philip of Spain if that prince should land at a western port. To judge from Thynne's correspondence with the Protector's widow, and later with his son, he remained genuinely attached to the house of Seymour and he must have welcomed the Queen's restoration of its estates to the duchess on behalf of the young Edward Seymour. Although Thynne was not implicated in the conspiracies against the Marian regime which brought trouble to so many of his west-country neighbours, he was undoubtedly a marked man on account of his loyalty to Princess Elizabeth, with whom he maintained during these hazardous years a regular correspondence through (Sir) Thomas Parry*. In 1555, when she was asserting her right to choose her own household officers, Elizabeth designated Thynne as her comptroller, but it is unlikely that he was ever allowed to function in this capacity. He gave final proof of his support by offering, on the eve of her accession, to place troops at Elizabeth's disposal, thereby repudiating his own claim of three years earlier, in connexion with the feud between Hartgill and Stourton, 'I never meddle in any man's matter but mine own'.[20]

Although Elizabeth's accession brought Thynne no notable preferment, the 22 years of life which remained to him were to be marked by much activity, as well at court and Parliament as in his county, and great prosperity, evinced above all at Longleat. He died in May 1580. His widow married Carew Ralegh[†].

[1] J. Waylen, Marlborough, 521. [2] Ibid. [3] Hatfield 207. [4] Aged 4 in 1517, The Gen. n.s. xi. 194; Wilts. Vis. Peds. (Harl. Soc. cv, cvi), 192; CPR, 1547-8, p. 331; PCC 31 Populwell; HMC Hatfield, i. 325; DNB. [5] LP Hen. VIII, ix; HMC Bath, iv. 340; CSP Dom. 1547-80, pp. 29, 341; City of London RO, Guildhall, rep. 11, ff. 367-7v; 16, ff. 477-7v; Lansd. 19, f. 208; Stowe 571, f. 11v; Wilts. Arch. Mag.

viii. 311; xiv. 201, 204; *CPR*, 1548–9, p. 135; 1560–3, pp. 443, 523; 1563–6, pp. 28, 42; *Two Taxation Lists* (Wilts. Arch. Soc. recs. br. x), 138; SP12/121, 132; *VCH Wilts.* v. 89. ⁶ *DNB* (Thynne, William); Hoare, *Wilts.* Heytesbury, 63; *LP Hen. VIII*, iv, xvi, xxi; PCC 17 Alen. ⁷ SP1/98, f. 89; *HMC Bath*, iv. 340; G. Anstruther, *Vaux of Harrowden*, 53; *LP Hen. VIII*, xii; C1/908/37–41. ⁸ *LP Hen. VIII*, xiv–xvi. ⁹ Ibid. xix; *Wilts. Arch. Mag.* xiv. 17. ¹⁰ Waylen, 521; *HMC Bath*, iv. 129. ¹¹ C219/18C/140; E101/423/12, ff. 8, 12. ¹² City of London RO, rep. 11, ff. 365–5v, 367–7v; List of mercers (T/S Mercers Hall), 491; *CPR*, 1547–8, pp. 97, 331–2; 1548–9, pp. 51, 329; PCC 31 Populwell. ¹³ *Wilts. Arch. Mag.* xiv. 260; xv. 178–86; J. Lees–Milne, *Tudor Renaissance*, 54–59; J. Summerson, *Architecture in Britain 1530–1830*, pp. 45–47, 62; M. Girouard, *Robert Smythson*, 52. ¹⁴ Hatfield 207; Salisbury corp. ledger B, f. 301v. ¹⁵ M. L. Bush, *Govt. Pol. Somerset*, 89; *APC*, ii. 343, 393–4; iii. 411, 413, 425–6, 490; iv. 72, 78, 82, 84, 86; *CPR*, 1549–51, p. 297; *CSP Dom.* 1547–80, p. 29; *HMC Bath*, iv. 112, 114; City of London RO, rep. 15, ff. 516v, 517; 16, ff. 9–9v; *HMC Hatfield*, i. 95–96; *Wilts. Arch. Mag.* xv. 186–7; B. L. Beer, 'Sir William Paget and the Protectorate, 1547–9', *Ohio Academy of Hist. Newsletter*, ii. 2–9. ¹⁶ *APC*, ii, 398; *HMC Hatfield*, i. 48, 50; *Wilts Arch. Mag.* viii. 268 et passim; xviii. 260; SP1/205, f. 106; Tytler, *Edw. VI and Mary*, i. 190. ¹⁷ *Vis. Salop* (Harl. Soc. xxix), 461; *HMC Bath*, iv. 135. ¹⁸ C. Read, *Mr. Sec. Cecil and Q. Eliz.* 57, 67; *Wilts. Arch. Mag.* xv. 186–7; Bath mss, Thynne pprs. 2, ff. 167–8v, 176; Lees–Milne, 54–55. ¹⁹ *Wilts. Arch. Mag* viii. 310–21. ²⁰ *APC*, iv. 417; *Wilts. Arch. Mag.* viii. 322; xv. 187–8, 193–4; xviii. 18; Bath mss, Thynne pprs. 2, ff. 192–3v, 198–9v, 216–17v, 224–5v, 227–8v, 234–8v, 243–4v; *CPR*, 1553–4, p. 438; Hoare, 63, 64; *VCH Wilts.* v. 115.

T.F.T.B.

TICHBORNE, Nicholas (by 1508–55), of Tichborne, Hants.

HAMPSHIRE 1553 (Oct.)

b. by 1508, 1st s. of Nicholas Tichborne† of Tichborne and London by Anne, da. of Robert White of South Warnborough, Hants. *educ.* I. Temple. *m.* (1) by 1529, Julian, da. and coh. of Robert Fenrother of London, 1s. 3da.; (2) c.1540, Elizabeth, sis. and h. of James, Thomas and William Rithe of Totford, Hants, 6s. inc. Benjamin† 4da. *suc.* fa. 1540 or later.¹
Butler, I. Temple 1541–5.
Escheator, Hants and Wilts. 1536–7, 1544–5; j.p. Hants 1547–*d.*; sheriff 1547–8, 1553–4; commr. chantries, Berks. and Hants 1548, relief, Hants 1550, proclamations 1551, goods of churches and fraternities 1553.²

The Tichborne family had held the Hampshire manor of that name since the 12th century and throughout that time had served the neighbouring see of Winchester. Nicholas Tichborne's father did not die, as has often been stated, in or before 1513 but survived until at least 1540; there is, however, little risk of confusion between father and son, whose recorded careers hardly overlapped either at the Inner Temple or in their county. It was the 'young Mr. Nicholas' whose thanks for favours John Kingsmill conveyed to Thomas Wriothesley after visiting Tichborne in 1538 and whom in the following year he advised Wriothesley to have summoned to the Parliament then in session to act as 'an indifferent man' in the contention between Wriothesley and Gardiner. The Nicholas Tichborne assessed for the subsidy of 1541 on goods worth £40 in Bassinghaw ward, London, was probably also the son, whose first marriage had been to an alderman's daughter, and it was almost certainly he who bought

the Hampshire manor of Merifield from the crown in 1543.³

The war with France saw Tichborne engaged in the campaign for Boulogne and after its capture in the supply of troops from Hampshire for its garrison. When in 1545 the French raided the Isle of Wight he and his younger brother mustered and led 160 men to the defence of Portsmouth. His service in the field may have yielded him a seat in Henry VIII's last Parliament, for which the names of the knights for Hampshire are lost, and it is possible, although unlikely, that he was the second knight in that of March 1553, whose name is also unknown. In 1547 it was his neighbour Sir Henry Seymour and his uncle Thomas White II who were elected, while he began his first shrievalty. On Mary's accession, and with Gardiner restored to favour, he joined White in representing the shire, and but for his second shrievalty he might have done so again in either or both of the Parliaments of 1554. Although his Latin speech of welcome to the Queen and her new consort on their passage through Hampshire in July 1554 is to be taken as an official, and not necessarily a personal, statement of belief, there is no reason to doubt that Tichborne shared the Catholicism of his patrons and kinsmen or that he transmitted it to his children.⁴

Tichborne made his will on 15 May 1555 and died eight days later. He asked to be buried in the parish church, provided for his wife and children, and named Sir Thomas White overseer. His goods were valued for probate at £656. His 25 year-old heir Francis did not long survive him and in 1571 the Tichborne lands passed to the next son Benjamin.⁵

¹ Date of birth estimated from marriage. *Vis. Hants* (Harl. Soc. lxiv), 82, 125–6; Mill Stephenson, *Mon. Brasses*, 166. ² *CPR*, 1547–8, p. 84; 1548–9, p. 136; 1550–3, p. 142; 1553, p. 358; NRA 10665 (Hants RO, Kingsmill ms 1223). ³ Wilkes, *Hants*, ii. 17; *VCH Hants*, iii. 337; *HP*, ed. Wedgwood, 1439–1509 (Biogs.), 855–6; *Cal. I.T. Recs.* i. 1 et passim; *LP Hen. VIII*, iii, v, x, xiii–xv, xviii; E179/144/120. ⁴ *LP Hen. VIII*, xix, xx; Wilkes, ii. 293; M. A. R. Graves, 'The Tudor House of Lords 1547–58' (Otago Univ. Ph.D. thesis, 1974), ii. 201; J. E. Paul, 'Hants recusants in the reign of Eliz. I' (Southampton Univ. Ph.D. thesis, 1958), passim. ⁵ Hants RO, B wills 1555; C142/106/58; *CPR*, 1555–7, pp. 4–5, 148.

A.D.K.H.

TIMPERLEY, Thomas (1523/24–94), of Hintlesham, Suff. and Flitcham, Norf.

BRAMBER 1553 (Oct.)
GREAT YARMOUTH 1563

b. 1523/24, 1st s. of William Timperley of Hintlesham by Margaret, da. (prob. illegit.) of Thomas Howard, 3rd Duke of Norfolk; bro. of William†. *m.* (1) by 26 Sept. 1557, Audrey, da. of (Sir) Nicholas Hare* of Bruisyard, Suff., 2s. 7da.; ?(2) Catherine. *suc.* fa. 1 Apr. 1528.¹
Comptroller, the household of Thomas, 4th Duke of

Norfolk by 1569; receiver, Suff., for 4th Duke of Norfolk by 1572, for Philip, 13th Earl of Arundel by 1589.[2]

When Thomas Timperley's father died in 1528 he became the ward of his maternal grandfather the 3rd Duke of Norfolk. Thenceforward his fortunes mirrored those of the Howard family. He had scarcely come of age and succeeded to his patrimony when disaster struck that house, and he presumably spent the next six years in obscurity on his Suffolk estates. In 1551 he came to the Exchequer to show proof that his ancestors had held a court leet at Hintlesham since the reign of Edward I.[3]

In July 1553 Timperley was one of those who rallied to Queen Mary at Framlingham, and he was later to receive an annuity of £20 from the crown. His return to the Queen's first Parliament he owed to Norfolk, who promptly reasserted control at Bramber; the other Member was the duke's friend (Sir) John Baker I*. Timperley might have been expected to sit again under Mary, especially in view of his marriage to a daughter of the master of the rolls, the duke's old follower Sir Nicholas Hare: his failure to do so is perhaps a measure of the competition for places at the disposal of the new duke.[4]

Timperley's career under Elizabeth was to be impaired by his own and his children's recusancy but he was still a prosperous landowner when he died on 13 Jan. 1594.[5]

[1] Date of birth estimated from age at fa.'s i.p.m., C142/49/15. G. H. Ryan and L. J. Redstone, *Timperley of Hintlesham*, tables i, ii; *Vis. Suff.* ed. Metcalfe, 38; Copinger, *Suff. Manors.* vi. 55–57; PCC Maynwaryng. [2] Add. 19152, f. 53v; Arundel castle ms G1/7; Egerton 2074, f. 84. [3] *LP Hen. VIII*, iv; Ryan and Redstone, 31; N. Williams, *Thomas Howard, 4th Duke of Norfolk*, 106; A. H. Smith, *County and Ct.* 25, 38. [4] *APC*, iv. 429–32; E405/121/64. [5] Ryan and Redstone, 37; PCC 60 Dixy.

R.J.W.S.

TINGLEDEN (DINGLEDEN), John (by 1520–51), of Reigate, Surr.

GATTON 1547*

b. by 1520, 1st s. of Henry Tingleden of Reigate by Joan, da. of Thomas Hynde of London. *m.* Mary, da. of John Gille of Wyddial, Herts., 1s. 1da. *suc.* fa. 15 Aug. 1521.[1]
Commr. relief, Surr. 1550.[2]

Although John Tingleden was of gentle birth, his family's pedigree is not recorded in the visitation of Surrey taken in 1530. His grandfather Richard Tingleden had sat for Southwark in the Parliament of 1467, and John Tingleden, Member for Reigate in that of 1449, was doubtless his great-grandfather. Henry Tingleden, a justice of the peace from 1514 until his death, appears to have enjoyed greater standing in the county than his son was to attain.[3]

When Henry Tingleden made his will in 1521 he directed that his son John should receive his inheritance at the age of 18; it consisted of property in Southwark, worth altogether £26 6s.4d. a year, and the manor of Frenches in Reigate. Joan Tingleden took as her second husband John Palmer* of Angmering, Sussex, who may have been responsible for John Tingleden's upbringing. In 1529 Tingleden shared £60 with his brother Thomas and half-brother John Palmer under their grandfather's will. Almost nothing is known of his career, but he may have been a lawyer: both his father and his son were members of Gray's Inn and Tingleden could have begun his studies there before 1521, when the admission register begins. He doubtless owed his return for Gatton in 1547 to the patron of the borough, Sir Roger Copley, to whom he was related through his great-grandmother Elizabeth Shelley: part of his manor of Frenches lay in the parish of Gatton. His fellow-Member Richard Shelley was a kinsman and Copley's brother-in-law: his stepfather John Palmer was one of the knights for Sussex. Tingleden's death between 18 Aug. 1551, when he made his will, and the following 27 Oct., when probate was granted, created a vacancy for the fourth session of the Parliament which was to be filled by Thomas Guildford, another relative of the Copleys.[4]

Tingleden's will opens with a long religious preamble in which he proclaimed his faith in the Trinity and trusted to God's 'mercy that he through the merits of Christ's passion, my only saviour and mediator, will now perform his promise unto me'. He asked to be buried in Reigate church 'before my wife's seat there as she doth use to sit', and where a brass once recorded the deaths of his parents. He granted to his wife a life interest in the property which was already her jointure, consisting of the manor of Frenches worth £10 a year, tenements in Southwark called the *Black Heart* and a house there also worth £10 a year; the remainder of this portion of his property he granted to his son Charles and in default of heirs, in turn to his daughter Margaret, his nephew, and his godson Tingleden, the younger son of John Millicent* of Linton, Cambridgeshire. Tingleden had other property in Southwark, worth altogether £21 4s. a year, which his son was to receive at the age of 18, and of which his wife was to have the custody in the meantime unless she remarried. He asked for a sermon at his burial and a dole for the poor. After remembering friends, relatives and servants he divided £300 'in stock' equally between his wife, son and daughter. He appointed his wife executrix and John Millicent, (Sir) Thomas Saunders* and James Skinner overseers. His widow took as her second husband

Nicholas Pope of Buxted, Sussex, by whom she had seven more children.[5]

[1] Date of birth estimated from fa.'s death and from his having a younger brother. Surr. archdeaconry ct. 158 Mathewe; *Misc. Gen. et Her.* v. 26–27; *Vis. Suss.* (Harl. Soc. liii), 99; PCC 30 Bucke. [2] *CPR*, 1553, p. 357. [3] *LP Hen. VIII*, i–iii; St.Ch.2/24/29. [4] PCC 23 Jankyn. [5] PCC 30 Bucke; *Vis. Surr.* (Harl. Soc. xliii), 112; *Vis. Suss.* 99.

S.R.J.

TIRRELL *see* **TYRRELL**

TIRWHIT *see* **TYRWHITT**

TOLPAT, Peter (by 1526–63/64), of Chichester, Suss.

CHICHESTER 1558

b. by 1526. *m.* by 1555, Anne, da. and h. of William Huntlowe ?of Dorset, wid. of Ralph Dunning (*d.*1544), of Chichester, *d.s.p.*[1]
  Bailiff, Chichester 1557, mayor 1559–60.[2]

Nothing has come to light about Peter Tolpat's origin or upbringing. He may have been a kinsman of the Thomas Tolpat of Singleton and William Tolpat of Petworth who were assessed for subsidy in 1525 at £2 and £3 in goods respectively. In his will he was to mention three brothers, William, Robert and Richard, and a nephew John, but as none of these has been traced he must be accounted an exception to the family's insignificance. This distinction he may have owed to his marriage to the widow of a local surgeon and cousin to a London haberdasher, whose property in Hayes and West Wickham, Kent, she received about 1553. Himself a mercer, in 1547 Tolpat leased a tenement in South Street, Chichester from the dean and chapter.[3]

Tolpat's return to the last Marian Parliament followed an election dispute between the corporation and the commoners. As John Sherwin† recalled the episode in the course of a Star Chamber suit nearly 30 years later,

in the last Parliament holden in Queen Mary's time, the commoners and the baser sort did of a will make choice in the guildhall of one Roger Drue, then a commoner and no free citizen or enfranchised of the said city.

The Member elected by the commoners had to be either a citizen or a person whom the corporation was willing to admit to the freedom before his election was confirmed. On this occasion the corporation found Drue unacceptable and in his stead chose Tolpat, who had just completed a year as bailiff. The dispute echoed that of 1541 when the commoners had chosen Robert Bowyer I* as mayor, but what lay behind it is not known. With his fellow-Member Lawrence Ardren, Tolpat was presumably involved in the bill for the removal of weirs in Chichester harbour which passed the Commons but was lost in the Lords, doubtless at the instigation of the bishop whose weirs it threatened.[4]

It was Ardren and another colleague, John Digons*, whom Tolpat named as two of the overseers of his will of 7 Sept. 1563. Among a number of modest legacies he gave 1*s.* to the cathedral, 40*s.* to the poor and 1*s.* each to the four serjeants of the city. Without a child of his own, he left the lease of his house, after his wife's death, to his nephew John, a wedding gift of £10 to the step-daughter who lived with him, and 20*s.* each to his three sisters. The will was proved on 31 Mar. 1564.[5]

[1] Date of birth estimated from first reference. C1/1366/77; W. Suss. RO, wills 5, f. 21v. [2] W. Suss, RO, wills 9, f. 184v; A. Hay, *Chichester*, 569. [3] *Suss. Rec. Soc.* lvi. 23, 35; lviii. 13, 42; W. Suss. RO, wills 2, f. 44v; 5, f. 21v; PCC 13 Pynnyng; C1/1366/77. [4] St.Ch.5/C23/37; Neale, *Commons*, 261–2; *CJ*, i. 49–50. [5] W. Suss. RO, wills 2, f. 44v.

R.J.W.S.

TOOKE, William (1507/8–88), of Bishops Hatfield, Herts. and London.

HORSHAM 1554 (Nov.)

b. 1507/8, 1st s. of Ralph Tooke of Goddington, Kent by Alice, da. of William Meggs of Canterbury, Kent. *educ.* I. Temple, adm. Feb. 1520. *m.* 1532, Alice, da. of Robert Barley of Bibbesworth Hall, Herts., 9s. 3da.[1]
  Commr. sewers, Kent 1539, benevolence for rebuilding St. Paul's, Herts. 1564; auditor, ct. of wards 1544–*d.*; j.p. Herts. 1558/59, q. 1561–*d.*[2]

Born into a junior branch of a Kentish family, William Tooke was to marry into a Hertfordshire one and to settle in that county, where he bought the manors of Popes and Essendon near Hatfield. He spent upwards of half a century in wardship administration; his memorial brass in Essendon church records his 44 years as auditor of the court of wards, but before he became joint holder of that office with Sir John Peryent in 1544 he had served as Peryent's clerk for at least eight years. Becoming sole auditor in 1551, he was to be succeeded by his son Walter and his grandson John, and the office was still in the family when the court was dissolved in 1646. He also began the process, continued by his descendants, of purchasing wardships himself; between 1544 and 1559 he received 14 such grants.[3]

Tooke's election to the Parliament of November 1554 is of interest both because it was his only one and because it ignored the crown's request for the return of resident Members. The borough of Horsham belonged to the Howard patrimony but in the autumn of 1554 the 4th Duke of Norfolk was himself a royal ward, a circumstance which suggests that Tooke owed his nomination to his office, as his fellow-Member John Purvey—another Hertfordshire man and one with whom Tooke was to be allied by marriage—almost certainly did to his post in the duchy of Lancaster. Such sponsorship would have enabled these two strangers to sit for Horsham, and since they did not quit the Parliament before its dissolution the government lost nothing by their intrusion. For neither of them, however, was there any future at Horsham, but whereas Purvey found seats elsewhere Tooke was not re-elected.

Although he lived to be 80, Tooke was survived by his widow and by seven of his nine sons. By his will of 15 Nov. 1588 his heir Walter, after his debts were paid and his accounts audited, was to have the manor of Popes and, subject to his wife's life interest, the other Hertfordshire lands. Tooke died on 4 Dec. 1588.[4]

[1] Aged 80 at death. *Vis. Herts.* (Harl. Soc. xxii), 99; Clutterbuck, *Herts.* ii. 134, 351; *CPR*, 1553–4, p. 468. [2] *LP Hen. VIII*, xiv, xix; *CPR*, 1560–3, p. 438; 1563–6, p. 123; H. E. Bell, *Ct. of Wards*, 24. [3] *VCH Herts.* iii. 103; *CPR*, 1547–8, pp. 20, 64; 1550–3, p. 230; 1553–4, p. 229; 1554–5, p. 290; 1555–7, p. 486; 1558–60, pp. 1, 33; 1563–6, pp. 110, 430; 1572–5, p. 163; *LP Hen. VIII*, xvi, xix, xxi; Bell, 24–25; J. Hurstfield, *Queen's Wards*, 227; *HMC Hatfield*, i. 147. [4] PCC 51 Leicester, 16 Kidd; C142/246/124.

R.J.W.S.

TOWNSHEND, Sir Roger (by 1478–1551), of Raynham, Norf.

NORFOLK 1529, ?1536,[1] 1542[2]

b. by 1478, 1st s. of Sir Roger Townshend† of Raynham by 2nd w. Eleanor, da. of William Lunsford of Lunsford, Suss. *educ.* L. Inn, adm. 1496. *m.* ?(1) Amy, da. of William Brewes of Wenham, Suff., 6s. 2da.; (2) Anne. *suc.* fa. 9 Nov. 1493. Kntd. 1518/22.[3]

J.p. Norf. 1501–13, 1524–d.; sheriff, Norf. and Suff. 1511–12, 1518–19, Jan.–Nov. 1526; commr. subsidy, Norf. 1512, 1514, 1515, 1523, 1524, for survey of monasteries 1537, benevolence, Norf. and Norwich 1544/45, chantries, Norf., Suff., Norwich, Ipswich, Yarmouth 1546, Norf., Suff., Norwich 1548, relief, Norf., Norwich, Yarmouth 1550; other commissions 1504–47; councillor to hear causes in ct. of requests 1528/29; knight of the body by 1533; jt. lt. Norf. Apr. 1551.[4]

The son of a distinguished lawyer, Roger Townshend was himself bred to the law but did not make much headway in that profession. From his mother's death in 1499, when he obtained possession of all his father's estates, he probably devoted himself mainly to his lands and local affairs. He served against the French in 1512 and 1513, in which year he provided a force of 30 men, and at the time of the northern rebellion he was called upon to supply 50 men to wait upon the King; but he found his real *métier* in the administration of his shire, especially during the upheaval of the Reformation. His later pre-eminence there makes his absence from the commission of the peace for some ten years before 1524 somewhat surprising; it may have had some connexion with the pardon he sued out on 3 July 1514.[5]

In 1536 Townshend was consulted by the 3rd Duke of Norfolk as to the probable yield of the subsidy in that county and throughout the late 1530s he was in constant correspondence with Cromwell, giving news of any disaffection, heresy and treason, and of the progress of the Dissolution. 'Would that the King had three or four such as Mr. Townshend in every shire', wrote the Duke of Norfolk in 1538. In 1528–9 Townshend had been one of the councillors hearing cases in the court of requests and he was still being called King's Councillor as late as 1549. The new reign saw no cessation of his activities: on 2 Feb. 1547 he was one of four gentlemen whom the Privy Council bade secure East Anglia and four years later, only a few months before his death, he was one of three commissioned to act as lieutenants of Norfolk.[6]

During the half century of his public activity Townshend did not neglect his own interests. The 20 manors which he had inherited were valued in his father's inquisition post mortem at just under £100 a year, but in a *valor* of 1500–2 he himself estimated his landed income at £255. He added some properties before 1536 but it was after the Dissolution that he made his greatest acquisitions: between 1536 and 1541 he bought or obtained by exchange at least six manors and much other land including the possessions of several chantries and religious houses. His aim seems to have been to consolidate his holdings round his chief manor at Raynham and he eventually owned a score of manors within a ten-mile radius as well as a number of others only a little further away.[7]

Townshend was a man of sufficient resources to have secured his election as senior knight of the shire from 1529, but as an increasingly valued servant of the crown he could also have counted on official support. Although the names of the knights for Norfolk in the Parliament of 1536 have been lost, Townshend's appears with those of three other lawyers on the dorse of an Act for continuing expiring laws passed in that Parliament, and he may thus be taken as having been re-elected in accordance with the King's general request for the return of the previous Members. Similarly in 1542, when a defective indenture leaves the identity of only one knight known, and that uncertainly, Townshend was one of four Members whose support was solicited on 31 Jan. 1542 by the common council of London for a bill to cleanse the Fleet ditch. In the intervening Parliament, that of 1539, it was his son-in-law, Edmund Wyndham, who had been returned at the King's behest.[8]

By the end of the Parliament of 1542 Townshend was an elderly man, and although he would remain active until the end he had already begun to provide for the future of his family. In 1537–8 he settled a number of estates on himself and his wife in survivorship with remainder to his heir: this transaction may have accompanied a second marriage of which there is no mention in the pedigrees and which has perhaps been obscured by the similarity of the names 'Amie' and 'Anne'. As early as 1511 he had settled four manors on his eldest son John and his wife, in 1537 he allotted considerable estates to his grandson Richard on marriage, and between 1536 and 1550 he provided for his younger sons: but although his children were so numerous his estates were to yield an ample heritage. His lands were valued in his inquisition at £308, a nominal figure of which well over two thirds descended to his heir.[9]

Townshend had seen both his eldest son and his grandson die before him when he came to make his will on 31 July 1551, and his heir apparent was his six year old great-grandson, another Roger Townshend†. He asked to be buried at Raynham alongside his wife Amy, and made a number of religious and charitable bequests. He divided his plate between his heir and his four surviving sons and left flocks of sheep to certain of his children and grandchildren. His sons George and Thomas, who were to share his books, were named executors and were accordingly to hold lands in trust for the heir, and his supervisor was his other son-in-law Sir Henry Bedingfield*. Townshend died on 25 Nov. 1551 and his will was proved on 10 May 1552.[10]

[1] House of Lords RO, Original Acts 28 Hen. VIII, no. 9.　[2] Indenture defaced, only 'Roger T . . .' surviving, C219/18B/54; City of London RO, Guildhall, rep. 10, f. 242v.　[3] Date of birth estimated from age at parents' i.p.m.s, *CIPM Hen. VII*, i. 492; ii. 302. *Vis. Norf.* (Norf. Arch.), i. 306; *LP Hen. VIII*, iii.　[4] *CPR*, 1494–1509, pp. 361, 408, 474, 560, 652; 1547–8, pp. 72, 75, 76, 87; 1548–9, p. 136; 1553, pp. 356, 361–2; *LP Hen. VIII*, i–v, vii, viii, xii–xvi, xviii, xx, xxi; *Statutes*, iii. 81, 115, 173; Lansd. 12(57), ff. 124–30; *APC*, iii. 259.　[5] *CIPM Hen. VII*, ii. 302; *LP Hen. VIII*, i, xiv; C67/62, m. 1.　[6] *LP Hen. VIII*, xi–xiii; Elton, *Policy and Police*, 17, 82, 144–5, 342; Lansd. 12(57), ff. 124–30; *CPR*, 1548–9, p. 308; *APC*, ii. 10–11; iii. 259.　[7] Add. 41139; Wards 7/6/68.　[8] House of Lords RO, Original Acts 28 Hen. VIII, no. 9; City of London RO, rep. 10, f. 242v.　[9] Wards 7/6/68.　[10] Norwich consist. ct. 31 Lyncolne; Wards 7/6/68.

R.V.

TRACY, Richard (by 1501–69), of Stanway, Glos.

WOOTTON BASSETT　1529

b. by 1501, 2nd s. of William Tracy of Toddington by Margaret, da. of Thomas Throckmorton of Warws. *educ.* Oxf. adm. 27 June 1515, determined 1516; I. Temple, adm. 6 July 1519. *m.* by 1547, Barbara, da. of Thomas Lucy of Charlecote, Warws. by Elizabeth, da. of Sir Richard Empson† of Easton Neston, Northants., 3s. 3da.[1]

Master of the revels, I. Temple 1519, butler 1530–4, steward 1535–7, gov. 1549–50.

J.p. Worcs. 1537–47, Glos. 1547, 1558/59–*d.*; commr. musters, Worcs. 1546, chantries, Glos.,

Bristol and Gloucester 1548, relief, Worcs. 1550; escheator, Glos. 1547–8; sheriff 1560–1.[2]

Richard Tracy's background and early life doubtless resembled in most respects those of many young men of similar lineage. His family was an old established one in Gloucestershire, which its members had served both locally and at Westminster, his father a justice of the peace and sheriff. A younger son, Richard Tracy spent some time at Oxford before entering the Inner Temple, where if he made no mark on the professional side he was to work his way up as an administrator to the rank of governor.[3]

The borough of Wootton Bassett, for which Tracy was returned to the Parliament of 1529, was to be represented by many men from across the nearby border, but his home near Winchcomb was rather distant for him to be accounted a local man: the same was true of his fellow-Member, Walter Winston, who lived at Randwick near Stroud. Like two other Wiltshire boroughs, Devizes and Marlborough, Wootton Bassett formed part of the jointure of successive queens consort and this court connexion probably explains the appearance among its Members of men who had little, if any, personal connexion with it. In the case of Tracy, the names of possible patrons include those of Sir Edward Baynton, a local magnate who besides securing his own election for the shire may have been influential in other boroughs, and Sir John Brydges, who was returned for Gloucestershire and whose marriage connexions with Tracy probably assisted his election. If religious sympathy entered into the matter, Baynton's incipient Protestantism would have made him a natural patron for the son of so doughty a reformist as William Tracy.[4]

The elder Tracy's death on 10 Oct. 1530 started a chain of events which were to have a profound effect on his son. The dead man had made a will in which he explicitly refused to bequeath anything 'for that intent that any man shall say or do to help my soul', a provision which, when the will came to be proved, was referred to the Convocation of Canterbury and condemned as heretical on 23 Mar. 1531. Thereupon Dr. Thomas Parker, chancellor of Worcester, not only exhumed Tracy's body, as he had been instructed to do, but burnt it at the stake, for which he needed, but did not obtain, the writ *de heretico comburendo*. The fine of £300 imposed on Parker was some retribution for this gruesome affair but the Church itself was to be the greatest loser. Tracy became a Protestant hero and near-martyr, and his will—or what purported to be it— was circulated among the faithful and was published with a commentary by William Tyndale: even the orthodox Robert Joseph admitted that 'Tracy has done more harm to the Christian religion in his death than by his pestiferous contentions before'.[5]

Filial piety and reforming zeal combined to make Richard Tracy the protagonist in his father's cause —his elder brother is never mentioned—and from his vantage-points of the Temple and Parliament he organized his campaign. He had been present in Convocation when the verdict was given and it would be interesting to know if he tried to interest the Commons either in this or in its sequel. All that is known is that on 15 Jan. 1533, shortly before setting out for London to attend the fifth session (which began on 4 Feb.) he wrote, presumably from Gloucestershire, to an unnamed friend, recounting the story and promising to explain the situation to Cromwell who, he had heard, was commissioned to investigate. Whether Cromwell was brought into the affair, or whether, as some versions suggest, even the King took it up, does not appear. Cromwell was of assistance to Tracy in other spheres and helped him to obtain several properties and leases: on 16 Feb., during the fifth session, the abbot of Tewkesbury agreed to the minister's suggestion to grant him the manor of Stanway, which immediately became his home. Tracy's name appears in several of Cromwell's memoranda, and it is evident that the two men were close. Nothing else has come to light about his part in the work of the Parliament. Presumably he served for Wootton Bassett in the following one, that of June 1536, when the King asked for the re-election of the previous Members, and perhaps again in 1539 and 1542, for which Parliaments the names of the borough's Members are lost.[6]

When in the autumn of 1536 the north rebelled, Tracy was one of those gentlemen in the west on whose loyalty the King felt he could rely, but in the event Tracy's allegiance was never put to the test. In the following year he was named to the bench for Worcestershire, where he owned more land than in his home county, and from then on he cut a figure in local affairs, especially in religious matters for which he earned the praise of Bishop Latimer. In 1538 he served on the commission to examine a relic belonging to Hailes abbey which was adjudged spurious and entrusted to his care, and later in the same year he was nominated, but not pricked, sheriff of Worcestershire, being passed over in favour of Robert Acton*. His friendship with Cromwell led to his occasional presence at court and it was perhaps on such a visit that he witnessed the reception of Anne of Cleves. The fall of the minister did not harm Tracy's career, although in the 1540s no trace of his presence at court has been found.[7]

Tracy's lasting fame rests not so much on his efforts to redeem his father's name as on his literary output. In 1535 he sent Cromwell a discourse, which may have been of his own composing, on the evils of making lawyers bishops and the need to choose suitable preachers. His first known work, *The profe and declaration of thys proposition: Faith alone iustifieth*, dates from five years later; it was dedicated to Henry VIII, to whom he described himself as the 'most simple of this your realm and yet one of the lively members of this your civil and politic body'. Two more tracts, *Of the Preparation to the Crosse and to Death* dedicated to Cromwell in 1540 and *The Supplycation to our most Soueraigne Lorde Kyng Henry the Eyght* published four years later, are usually considered Tracy's work and gained him some popularity. Their reformist bias was not welcomed by the government and in July 1546 his publications were banned, together with those of other Protestant authors. On the accession of Edward VI this ban lapsed, and in 1548 Tracy published *A most godly enstruction and lesson* and *A bryef and short declaration made wherebye every Chrysten Man may knowe what is a Sacrament*, in which he opposed transubstantiation. His purpose was didactic, and according to his sympathisers he observed in his own life the principles that he advocated. His reputation as 'an earnest favourer of all good and godly learning' was generally praised, particularly by his protégé Bartholomew Traheron*.[8]

The year 1551 was an unhappy one for Tracy. On 10 May his friend Robert Keilway II* was imprisoned in the Fleet for having concealed 'a seditious and lewd message' from him, and a week later Tracy was himself committed to the Tower. There he remained until February 1552 when the attorney-general and John Throckmorton I* were ordered to examine him, but he was not released until the following 17 Nov. and even then he was ordered to appear weekly before the Council. This episode has been thought to have resulted from Tracy's unfavourable estimate of the Earl of Warwick, but it may be more than a coincidence that several years later Tracy had to defend his title to a manor against one John Throckmorton. His religious views were to bring him to the notice of the Council during Mary's reign, when he was removed from the bench for both Gloucestershire and Worcestershire. His avowed intention to conform met with some incredulity, and the Queen's doubts were confirmed in September 1555 when the Council rebuked him for his behaviour towards Bishop Brooks of Gloucester. On this occasion Tracy reiterated his avowal and he probably did conform as no more is heard of his opposition and he is not known to have gone into exile: he was to be in trouble with the Council once more before the reign was out, but this was for refusing to contribute towards the forced loan of 1557. He must nevertheless have welcomed the advent of Elizabeth: he was restored to his place on the bench and in 1560 pricked sheriff of Gloucestershire. All the same, the new religious settlement was to disappoint him and in 1565 he protested against the retention of a crucifix in the Queen's chapel and warned Cecil of the dangers of idolatry.[9]

In his brief will, made on 6 Mar. 1569, Tracy provided from a debt owing to him the marriage portions of his three daughters, Hester, Susan and Judith, whose baptismal names, like his sons', reflect his devotion to the Bible. His part of the lands of Clifford priory and certain unspecified lands recently purchased from the 1st Earl of Pembroke he devised upon his younger sons, Samuel and Nathaniel; he appointed his eldest son Paul executor and his cousin George Stretford overseer. Tracy died two days later, and the will was proved in the following month.[10]

[1] Date of birth estimated from education. *DNB*; Emden, *Biog. Reg. Univ. Oxf. 1501–40*, p. 573; C142/48/109, 52/52, 150/131; *Vis. Glos.* Harl. Soc. xxi), 165–7; *Vis. Warws.* (Harl. Soc. xii), 111, 287; NRA 6336, p. 8; *CPR*, 1547–8, p. 48; PCC 8 Babington. [2] *LP Hen. VIII*, xii–xvii, xx, xxi; *CPR*, 1547–8 to 1563–6 passim. [3] Leland, *Itin.* ed. Smith, ii. 56; v. 155; *LP Hen. VIII*, i. [4] *Vis. Glos.* 16, 236. [5] Tyndale, *Works* (Parker Soc.), iii. 269–73; D. Wilkins, *Concilia*, iii. 724–5; Strype, *Annals*, i(2), 198; Lansd. 979, f. 96; A. G. Dickens, *Eng. Ref.* 96; *Letter Bk. of Robert Joseph* (Oxf. Hist. Soc. n.s. xix), 101; *Bristol and Glos. Arch. Soc. Trans.* xc. 146–7. [6] *LP Hen. VIII*, vi–ix, xii; Leland, ii. 53. [7] *LP Hen. VIII*, xi–xiv. [8] Ibid. ix; *Orig. Letters* (Parker Soc.), 613; Dickens, 233; *Tudor R. Proclamations* ed. Hughes and Larkin, i. 373–6. [9] *APC*, iii. 220, 272–3, 482; iv. 172; v. 145, 181; vi. 45; Harl. 249. f. 40; *Vis. Warws.* (Harl. Soc. xii), 111; *VCH Glos.* viii. 255; Dyer, *Reps.* ii. 127; Strype, i(2), 198–9. [10] PCC 8 Babington; C142/150/131.

E.McI.

TRAHERON, Bartholomew (by 1518–58 or later).

BARNSTAPLE 1547[1]

b. by 1518, ?s. of George Traheron of Herefs. *educ.* Oxf. by 1532. *m.* 1542, at least 1da.[2]

Writer of letters patent under the great seal and examiner of letters patent 22 Apr. 1547–1 Dec. 1549; keeper, King's library at Westminster 14 Dec. 1549–22 Oct. 1553; commr. eccles. laws 1551; dean, Chichester Jan.–Dec. 1552; prebendary, St. George's chapel, Windsor castle 10 Jan. 1553.[3]

When Bartholomew Traheron's parents died leaving him a young child 'destitute', Richard Tracy* 'conceived a fatherly affection' towards him and adopted him, financing his studies at Oxford and afterwards on the Continent. The influence of the Protestant Tracy was decisive in Traheron's development, as Traheron acknowledged in dedicating to him a translation of *The most excellent workes of chirurgerye made and set forth by maister John Vigon, head chirurgie of our tyme in Italy*:

Traheron wrote that Tracy had 'earnestly exhorted me to forsake the puddles of sophisters and to fetch water from the pure fountains of the scripture'. In 1532 Traheron, described as an 'old disciple', was reported to the authorities at Oxford as having been in contact with the suspected heretic John Frith. Following this disclosure one of Traheron's companions recanted but he himself preferred to quit the university for the Continent: he remained abroad for five years, travelling mostly in Germany and Italy and attending various universities. It was from Strasbourg that in 1538 he encouraged his brother Thomas to embrace the reformed faith.[4]

Believing that Henry VIII intended to complete the Reformation in England, Traheron returned at the beginning of 1539 and by early March was found employment in the service of Cromwell. A year later he was reporting on the religious changes which had been accomplished and on the friendly disposition of Chancellor Audley towards him and Henry Bullinger, but the fall of Cromwell heralded a period of disappointment and discomfort from which he finally escaped by going abroad again in 1546. Four years earlier he had married the daughter of a man who 'followed godly doctrine', but her portion was so meagre that he had to subsist by teaching. His condition was alleviated when, shortly before his departure, he was granted three rectories in St. Asaph's diocese on the recommendation of Chancellor Wriothesley. At Geneva in 1546 Traheron met Calvin and was converted to his views. He was thinking of staying at Geneva when Henry VIII's death brought him a summons to return: he bade Calvin farewell with the words, 'I must follow where fortune leads me. I pray you therefore, though we are far separated in person, we may yet be united in spirit'. His first appointment was to two minor clerkships.[5]

The man responsible for these and for Traheron's election for Barnstaple in 1547 was probably John Cheke*, the King's tutor. The two men held similar religious views and moved in the same circles: it was Cheke who afterwards recommended Traheron to Roger Ascham as his successor in the keepership of the royal library and to the Council as a tutor for the young Duke of Suffolk. From the outset of the Parliament Traheron campaigned vigorously for the reform of doctrine. In the first session he attacked Thomas Smith I* for his 'lukewarmness', and during the second, as Cheke's father-in-law put it, he made it his duty to see 'that there should be no ambiguity in the reformation of the Lord's supper, but it was not in his power to bring over his old fellow-citizens to his views.' Traheron followed the progress of the debate both in and out of Parliament and reported it all to Bullinger in a series of letters. After the end of the third session Traheron was one of the civilians named to the commission for the overhaul of the canon law. During the prorogations he pursued his studies at Oxford and read Greek.[6]

On the death of Suffolk in July 1551 Cecil suggested to Traheron that he would be of value in the Church, and on 29 Sept. he was nominated to the deanery of Chichester. The cathedral chapter resented this intrusion of a layman and so obstructed him that he asked leave to resign. Although the Council found him another appointment at Windsor he had evidently become a nuisance, and his denunciation of covetousness and pride in high places cost him the backing which might have brought him a seat in the second Edwardian Parliament.[7]

Traheron had hailed Edward VI as the young Josiah and had relished his reign. For such a man the accession of Mary was a disaster; he soon resigned his librarianship and went into exile at Frankfurt, where he supported Richard Cox against John Knox. After Knox's expulsion by the English congregation Traheron was appointed reader in theology at the new university there: later he went to Wesel where he continued his lectures, several of which were published, among them *A warning to England to repente and to turn to god from idolatries and poperie by the terrible example of Calece given the 7 of March Anno C.1558*. That Traheron did not return to England at Elizabeth's accession and that no more books were published under his name after 1558 implies that he died either in that year or shortly afterwards.[8]

[1] C219/282/2; Hatfield 207. [2] Date of birth estimated from education. Emden, *Biog. Reg. Univ. Oxf. 1501–40*, pp. 573–4; *DNB*; D. G. C. Elwes, *Castles of W. Suss.* 156; *LP Hen. VIII*, xvii. [3] *CPR*, 1547–8, p. 250; 1549–51, pp. 8, 74; 1550–3, pp. 114, 408; 1553, p. 8; 1553–4, p. 284. [4] B. Traheron, *Ad Thomam Fratrem Paraenesis* (1538) unpaginated; Lansd. 2, f. 9; *Narr. Ref.* (Cam. Soc. lxxvii), 32–33; Strype, *Eccles. Memorials* i(1), 581, 420; *Orig. Letters 1537–58* (Parker Soc.), 608. [5] *Orig. Letters*, 316–17, 328, 626; *LP Hen. VIII*, xiv, xv, xvii, xxi; M. L. Robertson, 'Cromwell's servants' (Univ. California Los Angeles Ph.D. thesis, 1975), 574–5. [6] *Orig. Letters*, 265, 319–23, 431, 465; Harl. 6989, f.141; W. K. Jordan, *Edw. VI*, i. 176, 322, 340; ii. 61; Strype, *Cheke*, 87; *APC*, iii. 382; *Lit. Rems. Edw. VI*, p.i. [7] *APC*, iii. 377; *CSP Dom.* 1547–80, pp. 38, 49; Lansd. 2(60), f. 135; Dickens, *Eng. Ref.* 256. [8] *Orig. Letters*, 755–63; Strype, *Eccles. Memorials*, iii(1), 415; *Cranmer*, 450, 514.

A.D.K.H.

TREDENECK, John (by 1508–66), of Tredinnick in St. Breock, Cornw.

LOSTWITHIEL	1529
HELSTON	1559

b. by 1508, 1st s. of Christopher Tredeneck of Tredinnick by Jane, da. and coh. of John Gosse. *m.* Frances, da. of one Sutton of Lincoln, Lincs. 2s. 1da. *suc.* fa. 1531/32.[1]

Commr. relief Cornw. 1550; j.p. 1547, 1558/59–*d.*[2]

John Tredeneck's forbears had long been seated at the place from which they took their name. His father was a figure of standing in Cornwall who served on the county bench from 1515 until his death and was pricked sheriff in 1530. Tredeneck had his first experience of Parliament during his father's lifetime, and doubtless his election at Lostwithiel, a borough situated about 14 miles from his home, was achieved with paternal support, but as he took precedence over a local gentleman, Richard Bryan *alias* Croker, he may have been the duchy nominee for the constituency: his brother-in-law, Henry Pyne, who entered the House at the same time, had a link with the steward of the duchy and the warden of the stannaries, the Marquess of Exeter. Tredeneck was presumably chosen to sit for Lostwithiel again in 1536 in compliance with the King's request that the previous Members should be re-elected, but he is not known to have reappeared in the Commons until after the accession of Elizabeth, although in 1545 he attended the election of the knights of the shire at the county court. It seems likely that his earlier Membership had yielded him a wife, his marriage into the Sutton family of Lincoln being best explained as a consequence of his association in the House with Vincent Grantham of that city, whose first wife was also a Sutton.[3]

The long intermission in Tredeneck's parliamentary career may have been due as much to personal as to political considerations. He did not hesitate to take the law into his own hands, being not unfairly described as 'a busy man and a troublous among his neighbours'. In December 1531 he abetted a raid by his father on some property, four years later he joined his brother-in-law, John Carminowe*, in stealing cattle, and in 1543 he abducted a ward. On the other hand, whereas some of his kinsmen supported the western rebellion in 1549, he remained loyal to the crown, a decision which perhaps influenced Queen Mary when she removed him from the bench. His ventures in trade and mining do not always appear to have prospered: after he and his partners (one of them John Thacker* of Hull) in the export of wool had failed to pay their customs the lands of one of the group were confiscated in 1549, and as members of a syndicate to exploit recently discovered mines in the south-west he and another were obliged to go to Chancery in 1563 to obtain their share of the profits. Tredeneck sued out a general pardon in 1559 and died seven years later, being buried at St. Breock on 20 June 1566.[4]

[1] Presumed to be of age at election. *Vis. Cornw.* ed. Vivian, 457–8;

PCC 22 Thower. ² *CPR*, 1547-8, p. 82; 1553, p. 351. ³ *Paroch. Hist. Cornw.* i. 130; *LP Hen. VIII*, ii; C219/18/15. ⁴ St.Ch.2/22/73, 24/141, 150, 28/58; *APC*, iii. 222; vi. 118; *CPR*, 1553-4, p. 502; C3/36/45.

J.J.G.

TREFFRY, Thomas I (c. 1490–1564), of Place, nr. Fowey and St. Kew, Cornw.

BODMIN   1529
?CORNWALL   1554 (Nov.)

b. c.1490, 1st s. of Thomas Treffry of Place by Janet, da. and h. of William Dawe of Plymouth, Devon. *m.* settlement 29 Sept. 1505, Elizabeth, da. of John Killigrew of Penryn, Cornw., at least 1s. 2da. *suc.* fa. by 1510.[1]

Subsidy collector, Cornw. 1523–4; gent. usher, the chamber by 1533; collector of customs, Fowey and Plymouth 28 June 1533–41; j.p. Cornw. 1533–53, 1558/59; reeve, Lostwithiel, Cornw. 1538–9; capt. St. Mawes castle 1541–53; commr. relief, Cornw. 1550, goods of churches and fraternities 1553.[2]

Thomas Treffry, who was descended from a family of Fowey merchants which had grown rich in the later middle ages, liked to think of himself as a man who had grown poor in the service of the crown. As early as 1536 he informed Cromwell that for 26 years he had maintained the defence of Fowey largely at his own expense. In 1540 he complained that his office in the customs had not only involved him in tiresome travelling (during which he had been hurt by a horse) but also cost him 100 marks, and he expressed a wish to exchange it for the captaincy of the royal fort then being built on the east side of Falmouth haven: his request was granted but the drain on his resources continued, with St. Mawes castle being finished only at considerable cost to himself. His work in local government added to his outgoings and in the 1540s the war with France squeezed him dry: besides paying for a contingent of soldiers in the campaign of 1544, he lent money to equip the *Falcon Lisle* for the navy, a loan which he was to claim some years later had yet to be repaid, and on top of this he had to raise money to ransom his son who fell into enemy hands.[3]

A still more crushing blow fell on 21 Sept. 1553, when Treffry was removed from his captaincy, supposedly as a punishment for attending a 'general assize' in Cornwall at which Jane Grey was proclaimed Queen. Fearing both the pecuniary and political consequences of his dismissal he besought Queen Mary to allow him 'to spend the residue of his time in the said room and office and not to be forced now in his old days to change his habitation', a plea which she understandably ignored: his Protestantism apart, it would have been imprudent to leave such a stronghold to the command of 'a man drawn in years, as 60 or above'. His place was taken

by the younger and, from the Queen's point of view, more reliable Thomas Arundell*, whom Treffry later sued for trespass. He also lost his place on the county bench.[4]

Apart from the time that he spent at St. Mawes, Treffry seems to have passed most of his life in his native town. It was as the principal inhabitant of Fowey, newly emancipated from tutelage to the priory of Tywardreath, that in 1536 he approached Cromwell for its incorporation as a borough: the attempt was unsuccessful and it was not until 1571 that Fowey first returned Members to Parliament, and 13 years later still that Treffry's grandson William Treffry went to Westminster as one of them. In 1529 he himself had had to look elsewhere. The nearest parliamentary borough was Lostwithiel, but although he once served as reeve there Treffry is not known to have been one of its Members. In 1529 he must have used his kinship with the Luccombe family of Bodmin to secure a seat: his fellow-Member Gilbert Flamank was also related to the Luccombes as well as being the heir apparent of a leading townsman, but Treffry took the senior place, perhaps because one of his forbears had sat for the borough in the 15th century. He and Flamank probably represented Bodmin again in the Parliament of June 1536, in compliance with the King's request that the previous Members should be re-elected. Treffry may have sat for the town in the two following Parliaments, those of 1539 and 1542, for which the names do not survive, but in 1545 one Thomas Treffry 'junior', presumably a kinsman although not a son, was elected.[5]

It could have been either the older or the younger Thomas Treffry who was returned as knight of the shire to Mary's third Parliament. Both could claim kinship with the sheriff, Sir John Arundell of Trerice. If it was the older one his current disfavour with authority would have given his election the flavour of a challenge to the government. Unlike his fellow-knight Henry Chiverton, the Member concerned was not among those found absent without leave when the House was called early in 1555. During the closing years of Mary's reign the elder Treffry was entrusted with matters relating to the coastal defences of Cornwall and the Scilly Isles, but it was not until the accession of Elizabeth that he was restored to the bench. He died on 24 or 31 Jan. 1564 and was buried in Fowey church: a monument was erected to his memory in the church of St. Kew. At his death his lands in Cornwall passed to his son John, who had married a daughter of Reginald Mohun*.[6]

¹ Aged '57 or thereabouts' in 1547 and '60 or above' in 1553. J. Maclean, *Trigg Minor*, ii. 251–3; Req. 2/25/190; C1/451/20–22,

582/36; St.Ch.2/16/23; 3/3/14. ² E179/87/134, m. 1, 282, m. 4; LP Hen. VIII, vi, x, xv; CPR, 1550–3, p. 393; 1553, p. 351; Req. 2/25/190; Duchy Cornw. RO, 220. ³ A. L. Rowse, Tudor Cornw. 76, 228, 251–2; Leland, Itin. ed. Smith, i. 203; LP Hen. VIII, xi, xv, xviii, xix, xxi; Req. 2/25/190; Bodmin Reg. ed. Wallis, 295; CPR, 1550–3, pp. 141, 423; APC, v. 213; vi. 116–17; C3/36/45. ⁴ Req. 2/25/190; CPR, 1555–7, p. 430. ⁵ LP Hen. VIII, xi. ⁶ APC, vi. 116–17; Maclean, ii. 106, 148, 252–3.

J.J.G.

TREFFRY, Thomas II

BODMIN 1545

?m. Elizabeth, da. of James Erisey (*d.*1522).[1]

It was as Thomas Treffry 'junior' that the senior Member for Bodmin was returned to the Parliament of 1545, a suffix which serves to distinguish him from Thomas Treffry I. What the relationship between the two was remains unknown. The last Parliament of Henry VIII's reign was originally to have met early in 1545 but not long after the writs of summons went out its opening was postponed until the autumn. In Cornwall the two knights for the shire were chosen at a county court held in January but the elections for the boroughs were not held until later in the year, the last being that for Bodmin on 26 Sept. The Members returned for the Cornish boroughs were young and (as far as we know) new to the House. The majority of them were connected with either the sheriff Sir Richard Grenville* or the receiver-general for the duchy of Cornwall Sir Thomas Arundell*, but no link between these two and either of the Treffrys is known. The lord lieutenant in the west, Sir John Russell*, Baron Russell, visited Devon and Cornwall during the summer to inspect fortifications and while doing so he presumably met the elder Treffry, who commanded one of the castles overlooking Falmouth harbour, for he brought this castle's lack of ordnance to the notice of the Privy Council. The elder Treffry had himself sat for Bodmin in the Parliament of 1529 (and perhaps in more than one of its successors), so that he could have been instrumental in his namesake's election, with Russell probably having the final word. No other trace of the younger Treffry has been found unless he was the servant of Chancellor Wriothesley who during 1546 carried messages between Brussels and London. There is also the possibility that he was the knight of the shire returned with Henry Chiverton (the other Member for Bodmin in 1545) to the third Parliament of Mary's reign.[2]

¹ *Vis. Cornw.* ed. Vivian, 154–5. ² C219/18C/16; LP Hen. VIII, xx, xxi.

S.T.B.

TREGONWELL, Sir John (by 1498–1565), of Milton Abbas, Dorset.

SCARBOROUGH 1553 (Oct.)[1]

b. by 1498. *educ.* London Coll., Oxf. by Nov. 1512, BCL 30 June 1516, DCL 21 July 1522; adv. Doctors' Commons 9 Dec. 1522. *m.* (1) ?Elizabeth Bruce; (2) Elizabeth, da. of Sir John Keilway of Rockbourne, Hants, wid. of Robert Martin of Athelhampton, Dorset; at least 1s. 2da. Kntd. 2 Oct. 1553.[2]

Principal, Vine Hall or Peckwater Inn, Oxf. in 1530; commr. piracy 1527, to receive and examine papal bulls 1536, relief, Dorset 1550, appeal of Bp. Bonner Aug. 1553; other commissions from 1534; envoy, the Netherlands 1532, France 1545; principal judge, ct. of Admiralty by 1535, re-apptd. Aug. 1540; master in Chancery by 1536; receiver of petitions in the Lords, Parlts. of 1536, 1539, 1542, Oct. 1553, Nov. 1554, 1555 and 1558; canon and prebendary of Westminster in 1553; sheriff, Som. and Dorset 1553–4; PC Feb. 1555–?58; j.p.q. Dorset 1558/59–*d.*; collector for loan 1562.[3]

John Tregonwell's parentage has not been established and may have been humble. Between 1512, when he appears as a student of civil law at Oxford, and 1530, when he was succeeded as principal of Peckwater Inn by William Petre*, his progress at the university was scarcely affected by demands from outside it, but his entry into practice at the court of Admiralty was quickly followed by his employment by the crown in the matter of the divorce and other, chiefly diplomatic, tasks. In April 1533 he supervised the proceedings of convocation and a year later his expectation of the mastership of the rolls was dashed by Cromwell's appropriation of the office, but by 1535 he was principal judge in the Admiralty as well as a master in Chancery. He played a part in the proceedings against Sir Thomas More, Anne Boleyn and the rebels of 1536.[4]

Tregonwell is chiefly remembered for his part in the dissolution of the monasteries. In April 1533 he had been instrumental in the election of an abbot of Tewkesbury, and he was one of the three men, Cromwell being another, to whom a draft commission to visit monasteries and churches was addressed before the close of 1534. After his visitation of Oxford university in September 1535 Tregonwell's work lay mainly in the south-west, including his own county. He has been called perhaps the most reliable and the most independent of the visitors, one who was prepared to plead for a house which he judged deserving, but he was also among the first to compete for the spoils. His importunity seems to have yielded only a lease of the nunnery of St. Giles at Flamstead, Hertfordshire, and even then the manor was soon afterwards granted to Sir Richard Page. Tregonwell's chief acquisition, Milton Abbas, cost him £1000 in February 1540; to this he and John Southcote of Bodmin (presumably his nephew) added in October 1544 other properties, also mainly in Dorset, for a total of nearly £960, although some of these they promptly resold. Tregonwell's advent in Dorset offended John Horsey*, from whom he looked for protection to Cromwell, but the friction may not have lasted since both men were asked by Sir Giles Strangways I* to assist in the execution of his will. When he married (probably as his second wife) the widow of a Dorset squire Tregonwell linked himself with some of the county's leading families.[5]

As a master in Chancery Tregonwell was four times commissioned to hear cases in the chancellor's stead, in 1544 and 1547 under Wriothesley (who on the second occasion was dismissed for issuing the commission without warrant), in 1550 under Rich, and in 1555 after the death of Gardiner; in the last two commissions he was joined with his son-in-law Sir Richard Rede. It was in virtue of the same office that Tregonwell was appointed a receiver of petitions in the House of Lords in three of Henry VIII's Parliaments and four of Mary's, but he is only known to have sat once in the Commons, in the first Marian Parliament. His election on that occasion for Scarborough, revealed by a copy of the Crown Office list, must be ascribed to government influence, although he had a local connexion through the archdeacon of the East Riding, John Dakins, with whom he had been an executor for Bishop Knight of Bath and Wells. Tregonwell's enjoyment of the Queen's favour was shown by the knighthood conferred on him at her coronation, by his appointment as sheriff while Parliament was sitting, and later by his admission to the Privy Council.[6]

Tregonwell was named to two committees appointed by the Commons to determine whether Alexander Nowell and John Foster II* were eligible to sit there. His choice for the first committee, appointed on 12 Oct. 1553, goes far towards answering two questions about Tregonwell, whether he was in orders and whether he had sat in Parliament before. The nature of the disability urged against Nowell and Foster, namely, their clerical status, would surely have ruled out anyone open to the same objection, and no evidence has been found to support Froude's statement that Tregonwell's prebend at Westminster called into question his own right to sit. (By the same token, it must have been as a lay holder that he was granted the Cornish living of St. Issey and the rectory of Hope All Saints, Kent.) The business of the committee also called for parliamentary experience, and with five of its six members able between them to recall every Parliament since 1539 it would have been strange if Tregonwell had been the sole newcomer; the many gaps in the roll of Members of these Parliaments make it possible that he had sat in more than one of them and his official standing could have

led to his nomination for almost any borough amenable to government influence.[7]

What part Tregonwell played in this committee remains unknown, but after it had reached a decision in Nowell's case he was the only one of its members to be named to the further one charged with considering Foster's. This was a smaller and more specialised group, consisting of three civil lawyers, and Tregonwell was evidently included in it to maintain continuity. Unlike its precursor it left no further trace in the Commons Journal, so that Foster (who was a kinsman by marriage of Tregonwell) presumably kept his seat. On the day this committee was appointed Tregonwell had a bill for the repairing of Sherborne causeway committed to him after its second reading.[8]

Tregonwell's shrievalty may have prevented his re-election to both the Parliaments of 1554, but although eligible thereafter he was not to sit again in the Commons; it may be that his regular appointment as a receiver of petitions in the Lords was a deterrent, although this duty he discharged concurrently with his Membership in October 1553. Neither before nor after 1558 would religion have been a stumbling-block; he had not opposed the Marian Restoration, but he was to be made a justice of the peace under Elizabeth. That he remained a Catholic is evident from his will of 3 Dec. 1563, with its invocation of the prayers of the Virgin Mary and all the company of heaven, and its requirement that the recipients of a charitable bequest should pray for the souls of the testator, of Bishop Knight and of all Christians. Tregonwell named as executors his wife and his grandson and heir, another John, and as overseers his brother-in-law Sir William Keilway, his son-in-law Sir Richard Rede, his nephew John Southcote II*, his kinsmen Nicholas Martin and John Wadham, and William Straken. He also asked his 'especial approved good friend' Sir William Petre to assist with good counsel; Tregonwell had been continuously associated with Petre for more than 30 years.[9]

Tregonwell died at Milton Abbas on 13 Jan. 1565 and was buried in the abbey church, where his monument remains. His grandson, who became the ward of Sir Arthur Champernon*, had licence to enter on the inheritance in July 1571. A Dorset kinsman, George Turberville, wrote of Tregonwell's death,

Now Cornwall thou may'st crake
And Dorset thou may'st cry
For the one hath bred, the other lost
Tregonwell suddenly.[10]

[1] Bodl. e Museo 17.   [2] Date of birth estimated from education. Emden, *Biog. Reg. Univ. Oxf. 1501-40*, pp. 575-6; *Vis. Dorset* (Harl. Soc. xx), 92-93; Hutchins, *Dorset*, i. 161; PCC 17 Morrison; J. H.

Bettey, 'Sir John Tregonwell of Milton Abbey', *Procs. Dorset. Nat. Hist. and Arch. Soc.* xc. 295–302; *DNB.* ³ Oxf. Univ. Arch. T/S cal. chancellor's ct. reg. EEE, p. 174 (f. 228); *LP Hen. VIII,* iv–vii, xi, xiv, xv, xx; *CPR,* 1550–3, p. 142; 1553, p. 352; 1553–4, p. 75; 1554–5, p. 106; 1560–3, p. 436; 1563–6, pp. 21, 37, 42; *LJ,* i. 84, 103, 165, 447, 464, 492, 513; *APC,* v. 96; Osborn coll. Yale Univ. Lib. 71.6.41. ⁴ A. L. Rowse, *Tudor Cornw.* 187; *LP Hen. VIII,* v–viii, xii, xv, xx, xxi; *Narr. Ref.* (Cam. Soc. lxxvii), 220; *APC,* i. 352; C. Sturge, *Cuthbert Tunstal,* 248–9; Elton, *Tudor Rev. in Govt.* 122, 131, 133; *Policy and Police,* 343, 404. ⁵ *LP Hen. VIII,* vi viii, x, xi, xiii–xv, xix, xxi, add.; Rowse, 188–91; D. Knowles, *Rel. Orders in Eng.* iii. 273, 284, 292; *VCH Herts.* ii. 196. ⁶ *LP Hen. VIII,* xix; *CPR,* 1549–51, p. 346; 1555–7, p. 53; *APC,* ii. 51; W. K. Jordan, *Edw. VI,* i. 70; P. M. Hembry, *Bps. Bath and Wells 1540–1640,* p. 78. ⁷ *CJ,* i. 27, 29; J. A. Froude, *Hist. Eng.* (rev. ed.), v. 283; Emden, 575–6. ⁸ *CJ,* i. 29. ⁹ PCC 17 Morrison; F. G. Emmison, *Tudor Sec.* 4n, 41, 45, 56; R. Lloyd, *Dorset Elizabethans,* 90 seq. ¹⁰ C142/144/157; *RCHM Dorset,* iii. 188; Newman and Pevsner, *Dorset,* 288; *CPR,* 1563–6, p. 484; 1569–72, p. 287; Lloyd, 139–40.

A.D.

TRELAWNY, John (1503/4–63), of Poole in Menheniot, Cornw.

LISKEARD   1553 (Mar.)
CORNWALL   1559, 1563*

b. 1503/4, 1st s. of Walter Trelawny of Poole by Isabella, da. of John Toose of Taunton, Som. *m.* (1) by 1533, Margery, da. and h. of Thomas Llamellyn of Lanteglos by Fowey, Cornw. 1s.; (2) Lore, da. and coh. of Henry Trecarrel of Trecarrell, Cornw. 2s. *suc.* fa. 1518, coh. of Edward Courtenay, Earl of Devon, 18 Sept. 1556.¹
Sheriff, Cornw. 1546–7, 1560–1; commr. relief 1550, loan 1557–8; j.p. 1558/59–*d.*²

The senior Member for Liskeard in March 1553, described in the indenture as 'the younger, esquire', has been identified as John Trelawny of Poole (*d.* 1563) rather than his son John born about 1533. The suffix 'younger' was presumably used to distinguish the father from an older kinsman and namesake descended from a great-uncle of his. Trelawny obtained his return at Liskeard as a local gentleman with some property in the town, but he may have been helped by his kinship with the sheriff, Reginald Mohun*, and also supported by his friend, Henry Chiverton, one of the knights for Cornwall on this occasion.³

The Trelawnys were Cornish landowners of ancient lineage dating from before the Norman Conquest. Following his father's death in 1518 the wardship of John Trelawny was in the gift of his kinsman Sir Hugh Courtenay, but it is not known who acquired it. Apart from the details of his first marriage nothing has come to light about his career before being pricked sheriff for the first time when in his early 40s. Thereafter he played a part in the administration of Cornwall. On inheriting extensive lands in the south-west in 1556 as one of the four coheirs of the Earl of Devon his own status there rose accordingly. His return as a knight of the shire twice under Elizabeth reflected this improvement.

He died on 29 Sept. 1563 and was buried at Menheniot.⁴

¹ Aged 52 in 1556, *Vis. Cornw.* (Harl. Soc. ix), 229, 475–6. *Vis. Cornw.* ed. Vivian, 475–6; *Vis. Som.* (Harl. Soc. xi), 111; *Devon and Cornw. N. and Q.* xxiii. 292–3. ² *APC,* vi. 118; *CPR,* 1553, p. 351; 1560–3, p. 435. ³ C142/138/24; Gilbert, *Cornw.* i. 548, n. 1. ⁴ Gilbert, 546–9; *LP Hen. VIII,* i; Leland, *Itin.* ed. Smith, i. 209; *CSP Dom.* 1547–80, p. 71; *APC,* vi. 118, 226; C3/36/45; 142/138/24; *CPR,* 1557–8, pp. 6–7.

J.J.G./M.K.D.

TRENCHARD, Christopher (by 1520–43/44).

DORCHESTER   1542*

b. by 1520, 2nd s. of Sir Thomas Trenchard of Wolveton, Dorset, by 2nd w. Anne, da. of Sir Thomas Delalynd; bro. of Richard*.¹

Trenchard and his younger brother Richard were doubtless returned for Dorchester through the influence of their father the high steward of the borough. Christopher's death was reported not long after the opening of the third session and the writ for a by-election to replace him was issued nearly two weeks later on 27 Jan. 1544.²

¹ Date of birth estimated from younger brother's. *Misc. Gen. et Her.* (ser. 4), ii. 101; Hutchins, *Dorset,* iii. 326. ² C. H. Mayo, *Recs. Dorchester,* 320; C219/18B/22–23.

H.M.

TRENCHARD, Richard (by 1521–60), of North Bradley, Wilts.

DORCHESTER   1542¹

b. by 1521, 3rd s. of Sir Thomas Trenchard and bro. of Christopher*. *m.* by 1556, Catherine, da. of Sir John Kingsmill of Sydmonton, Hants, 1s.²

Richard Trenchard's father settled on him a manor in the Isle of Wight and another in Wiltshire: to this inheritance he added by purchase the manor of Cuttridge in North Bradley, Wiltshire, which became his residence. He died on 31 May 1560, leaving a son of nearly four, and his widow was granted letters of administration of his estate on the following 10 June.³

¹ C219/18B/22. ² Presumed to be of age at election. *Misc. Gen. et Her.* (ser. 4), ii. 101; Mill Stephenson, *Mon. Brasses,* 162; Hutchins, *Dorset,* iii. 326; NRA 10665 (Hants RO, Kingsmill ms 1300); E150/1000/2. ³ C. H. Mayo, *Recs. Dorchester,* 320; PCC 20 Coode; C142/131/182; E150/1000/2; *PCC Admins.* ed. Glencross, i. 8.

H.M.

TRENCREKE, Robert (by 1524–94), of Treworgan in St. Erme, Cornw.

TRURO   1545, 1547¹

b. by 1524, s. of Robert Trencreke of Treworgan. *educ.* L. Inn, adm. 31 Oct. 1541, called 1547. *m.* by Jan. 1556, Avis, da. of (?Thomas) Kingdon of Trehunsey in Quethiock, 2da.²
Commr. gaol delivery, Launceston castle, Cornw. 1555; j.p. Cornw. 1558/59–*d.*; reeve, Moresk, Cornw. 1560–1; recorder, Truro temp. Eliz.³

Robert Trencreke stood on the threshold of his career as a lawyer in his native county when he was returned for Truro on two successive occasions in the 1540s. His family home was only three miles from the borough, but he probably owed the opportunity to serve for it in Parliament not so much to his own connexions as to his senior at Lincoln's Inn, Sir Thomas Arundell*, who was receiver-general for the duchy of Cornwall. Arundell's execution in 1552 deprived Trencreke of a parliamentary patron, and despite his success as a lawyer and his marriage to an heiress he is not known to have sat again. He was one of the electors when Henry Chiverton, perhaps already his brother-in-law, was chosen knight of the shire for the third time in February 1555. In 1556 he and Chiverton divided the Kingdon inheritance between them. Trencreke's legal practice flourished and his services were retained by numerous gentle families and several corporations. He was appointed to the county bench at the accession of Elizabeth, subscribed to the oath of supremacy in 1569 and established himself as a leading figure in local administration. He left no male heir at his death on 24 Dec. 1594 when his property passed to his two daughters, Jane Penwarne and Catherine Polwhele. His body was buried at St. Erme where a monument was erected to his memory, inscribed with these words:

Let him who has the key of Heaven go seek
This wonderful man Mr. Bob Trencreke.[4]

[1] Hatfield 207.   [2] Presumed to be of age at election. *Paroch. Hist. Cornw.* i. 345; *Vis. Cornw.* ed. Vivian, 370, 376, 537; Truro mus. HK12/27.   [3] Duchy Cornw. RO, 133, m. 11; 501, m. 1; *Jnl. R. Inst. Cornw.*, xiv. 210; *CPR*, 1554–5, p. 106; 1563–6, p. 20; 1569–72, p. 223.   [4] C3/148/90; 219/20/21; *CPR*, 1553–4 to 1569–72 passim; *APC*, xi. 148; SP12/60, ff. 83v–84; St.Ch.3/6/29; Cornw. RO, Liskeard accts. 1575–6, m. 2v; Truro mus. HK12/27; J. Allen, Liskeard, 274; *Paroch. Hist. Cornw.* i. 345; *Jnl. R. Inst. Cornw.* xiv. 210.

J.J.G.

TRENGOVE, John

HELSTON 1547[1]

John Trengove, the junior Member for one of the coinage towns in Cornwall in the Parliament of 1547, was probably a relative of Henry Trengove *alias* Nance*, clerk of the coinage. The clerk had a son named John, a student at Lincoln's Inn in the late 1540s, who only attained his majority at the turn of the decade. As Trengove's Membership is known only from the Crown Office list revised for the last session of the Parliament in 1552, the aspiring lawyer may well have entered the Parliament at a by-election, but if he was the Member the returning officer seems to have used the *alias* rarely used by himself. The lawyer had a namesake, a tinner who brought tin to the coinages held at Truro

in 1550 and 1551, and notwithstanding his obscurity his trade and links suggest that he was the Member.[2]

[1] Hatfield 207.   [2] *Vis. Cornw.* ed. Vivian, 485; *CPR*, 1563–6, p. 398; *Black Bk. L. Inn*, i. 288, 291, 296; *L.I. Adm. Reg.* i. 56; C142/134/184; NRA 5960, p. 443; E101/273/20, m. 10v; 274/16, m. 1.

J.J.G.

TRENGOVE *alias* NANCE, Henry (by 1521–61), of Nance in Illogan, Cornw.

HELSTON 1553 (Oct.)

b. by 1521, 2nd s. of Alexander Trengove of Nance by Margaret, da. and h. of Henry Gilly of Cornw. *m.* Cheston, da. of Henry Nanspan of Pulsack in Phillack, 1s.[1]

Clerk of the coinage, Cornw. by 1542–*d.*; bailiff, Tywarnhayle stannary by 1547–54.[2]

Henry Nance, as he was generally known, succeeded his father at Nance, the family property situated some ten miles north of Helston, although he had an elder brother Richard, one of whose daughters married John Courtenay* and later Thomas Arundell*. He was one of the three clerks of the coinage: the other clerks, John Caplyn* and Thomas Carnsew, held their offices under the receiver-general of the duchy and the comptroller of the coinage, but Nance was responsible to Sir William Godolphin, vice-warden of the stannaries and the leading landowner in west Cornwall. In 1543 Nance and Carnsew were accused of fraudulent behaviour in the exercise of their offices. John Grenville*, who drew on information provided by William Chambers*, submitted a memorandum to the Privy Council regarding 'certain deceitful peising of tin' in Cornwall. He alleged that, when weighing their own tin and that of their 'secret friends', the two clerks used a false balance which made the tin appear to be lighter than it was with the result that 'the King's majesty loseth the third penny, which amounteth near to the sum of £160 loss every coinage, and at some coinages the king's highness doth lose the one half of his grace's duty by that false means'. In their reply Nance and Carnsew stated that the charge arose from a misunderstanding of the procedure of the Cornish coinage. They claimed that it had long been the custom to weigh the tin first with the 'King's beam' and then with the 'merchants' beam': the first figure was the official one for purposes of taxation and the second was an unofficial one which was recorded at the request of those wishing to sell their tin in the market. After further investigations Nance was evidently acquitted since he continued to exercise his clerkship until his death.[3]

In February 1553 Nance was one of the freeholders present at the election of Godolphin's eldest son and Henry Chiverton to the second Edwardian Parliament, and in the following autumn he himself took the second place for Helston, one of the coinage boroughs (where he owned some property) in the first Marian Parliament. He is not one of the Members known to have opposed the reunion with Rome. Three years later Nance was outlawed for failing to settle a debt, but on surrendering himself to the Fleet he was pardoned this misdemeanour. He lived to witness the accession of Elizabeth and died on 10 Nov. 1561 seised of over 2,400 acres which passed to his son John, married to a daughter of Sir John Arundell of Trerice.[4]

[1] Date of birth estimated from first reference. *Vis. Cornw.* ed. Vivian, 485. [2] St.Ch.2/31/161; Duchy Cornw. RO, 224, m. 3; information from G. Haslam. [3] C142/134/184; St.Ch.2/31/161. [4] C142/134/184; 219/20/21; *CPR*, 1555-7, pp. 426-7.

J.J.G.

TRENTHAM, Richard (by 1515-47), of Shrewsbury, Salop and Trentham, Staffs.

SHROPSHIRE 1536[1]

b. by 1515, s. of Thomas Trentham* of Shrewsbury by Elizabeth, da. of Sir Richard Corbet† of Moreton Corbet, Salop. *m.* by 1537, Mary, da. of David Ireland of Shrewsbury, 1s. Thomas† 5da.[2]
Esquire of the Household by Nov. 1537; cupbearer, household of Prince Edward by 1544.[3]

The evidence for the return of a 'Mr. Trentham' as one of the knights for Shropshire in 1536 is contained in the letter in which Lady Catherine Blount complained to Cromwell that her son George Blount (q.v.) had been tricked out of election. In view of the King's request that on this occasion the previous Members should be returned, the contest between Blount and Trentham presumably means that whoever had sat with Sir Thomas Cornwall in the later sessions of the Parliament of 1529 was either dead or incapacitated and thus a vacancy arose. Of members of the Trentham family the one most likely to have filled it was Richard Trentham. A son of Thomas Trentham, the Member for Shrewsbury in 1512 and 1515, Richard Trentham entered the royal household (as did his brother Robert) and may have enjoyed government support at an election held in the shire with which he was identified both through his forbears and through his marriage; his kinship with the Corbet family, of whom his cousin Roger Corbet was almost certainly re-elected for Truro in 1536, would in any case have gone far towards ensuring his election.[4]

Trentham was not re-elected in 1539 and is unlikely to have been three years later, when the Shropshire names are unknown, for by then he had established himself in Staffordshire; he did not,

however, part with all his Shropshire lands, as John Leland implies. In November 1537 he was granted a lease of the lands of Trentham priory, and two years later he received the reversion of Rochester abbey, also in Staffordshire, *partim emptione partim largitione regis.* It was as of Trentham that in 1544 he arranged a marriage between his sister and Edmund Foxe*, a leading figure at Ludlow; in the same year he was in the vanguard of the army in France. He died on 1 Jan. 1547, leaving as heir his nine year-old son Thomas whose wardship was acquired in the following November by Sir Philip Draycott*. By his will made on 20 Dec. 1546 he had provided for his wife and children and named among the executors his 'cousins' Andrew Corbet* and Richard Corbet*, and his brothers-in-law Edmund Foxe and Edward Hosier*.[5]

[1] *LP Hen. VIII*, x. 1063. [2] Presumed to be of age at election. *Wm. Salt Arch. Soc.* iii(2), 140-1; *Staffs. Peds.* (Harl. Soc. lxiii), 224; Add. 6276, f. 22v; C142/85/47; PCC 29 Alen. [3] *LP Hen. VIII*, xiii; *Wm. Salt Arch. Soc.* iii(2), 140; E179/69/31. [4] *LP Hen. VIII*, x; *Trans. Salop Arch. Soc.* (ser. 3), iii. 380. [5] *LP Hen. VIII*, xiii, xiv, xix; *VCH Staffs.* iii. 250; Leland, *Itin.* ed. Smith, iii. 66; PCC 29 Alen; C142/85/47; *CPR*, 1547-8, p. 65.

A.H.

TRENTHAM, Thomas (by 1487-?1519), of Shrewsbury.

SHREWSBURY 1512,[1] 1515[2]

b. by 1487, s. of Thomas Trentham of Shrewsbury by Catherine, da. of John Marshall of Hurst, nr. Clun. *m.* Elizabeth, da. of Sir Richard Corbet† of Moreton Corbet, 2s. inc. Richard* 5da.[3]
Burgess (common councilman), Shrewsbury by 1508, rest. Sept. 1511, bailiff 1512-13, 1516-17, coroner 1515-16.[4]

Thomas Trentham's ancestors had prospered in trade at Shrewsbury and by the end of the 15th century his family was connected with many of the leading figures in the town and county. His two sons were to make their careers in the Household with the help of their Corbet kin but he seems to have followed his own father into drapery. As a young man he kept company with a group deemed troublemakers by the Shrewsbury authorities and for his part in releasing a prisoner from the town gaol he was briefly deprived of his burgess-ship: complaints were also lodged against him in the Star Chamber of riotous behaviour, assault and keeping 17 of his wayward companions in food, clothes and money. His burgess-ship was restored to him when his father was made bailiff for a fourth time, and his reinstatement was followed by his election several months later to Henry VIII's second Parliament with Thomas Kynaston, who was a kinsman by marriage and at the time serving with Trentham's father as bailiff. That it was Trentham and not his father and namesake who was returned in 1512 is established by the Member's designation 'junior'. He succeeded his father as bailiff and in this capacity he witnessed a transfer of property in the town shortly before departing under the command of the 4th Earl of Shrewsbury for the French campaign of 1513 while the Parliament stood prorogued. In 1514 he and Kynaston each received £6 10s. for the final session of the Parliament: they were said to have set out eight days after its reconvening and to have returned on the day of the dissolution. Later in the year the town complied with the King's request for the re-election of the previous Members and recorded the result of the election on the back of the King's letter.[5]

According to the town chronicle compiled under Elizabeth, Trentham died during his second term as bailiff within two or three days of the election of his replacement in 1517, but both he and his father were still alive two years later when as a resident of the castle ward Thomas Trentham junior contributed 4s. towards his own wages for the Parliament of 1515. This is the last trace of either Thomas Trentham found at Shrewsbury. However, there are grounds for thinking that the son predeceased the father. A bearer of their name living in London, whose will was made on 4 Oct. 1518 and proved on 10 June 1519, left a wife Elizabeth with Corbet relatives and five daughters with baptismal names identical with those of Thomas Trentham junior's daughters, and although no sons are mentioned he is thus presumably to be identified with the Member. After asking for burial in All Hallows' churchyard in London and providing for his wife and daughters he named his wife, John Latton* and Richard Mainwaring executors and the Earl of Shrewsbury, William Egerton and 'young' Roger Corbet* supervisors. The Thomas Trentham who was the subject with several other Shropshiremen of a writ of *diem clausit extremum* issued on 8 May 1529 was perhaps the Member's father.[6]

¹ Shrewsbury Guildhall 985. ² H. Owen and J. B. Blakeway, *Shrewsbury*, i. 319. ³ Date of birth estimated from first reference. *Wm. Salt Arch. Soc.* iii(2), 140; *Staffs. Peds.* (Harl. Soc. lxiii), 224; *Vis. Salop* (Harl. Soc. xxviii), 136, 192; (ibid. xxix), 323, 483. ⁴ Shrewsbury Guildhall 66, f. unnumbered; Owen and Blakeway, 530. ⁵ *HP*, ed. Wedgwood 1439–1509 (Biogs.), 869; *Trans. Salop Arch. Soc.* (ser. 1), viii. 398; (ser. 4), xviii. 66; liv. 187; St.Ch.2/16/ 57–62, 21/199, 200; *LP Hen. VIII*, i; Owen and Blakeway, i. 549. ⁶ Shrewsbury sch. Taylor ms 35, f. 13v; Shrewsbury Guildhall 986; PCC 17 Ayloffe; *LP Hen. VIII*, iv.

M.B.

TRESHAM, George (by 1519–55 or later), of Newton-in-the-Willows, Northants.

NORTHAMPTON 1553 (Mar.)

b. by 1519, 2nd s. of Richard Tresham by Isabel, da. of Fulke Woodhull of Thenford. *m.* disp. 26 May 1540, Elizabeth, da. of one Savage, *s.p.*[1]

Gent. waiter, household of Prince Edward by 1545–7.[2]

The identity of the George Tresham returned for Northampton with William Chauncy to the second Parliament of Edward VI's reign is not easy to establish. He was doubtless a member of the well known local family where George was a baptismal name favoured for younger sons, at least two of its bearers being active in the early 1550s. The son of Sir Thomas Tresham* who in 1551 shared a grant of ex-monastic land with his father was a cousin to one of the knights for the shire, Robert Lane, but in 1553 he was only in his second year of study at Gray's Inn. Little else has come to light about him: as his father was an executor of Bishop Chamber's will he is probably to be identified with the man who in 1555 accompanied Sir Thomas Tresham to the bishop's funeral, and in 1559 he received a legacy of £100 from his father. The Member, however, is more likely to have been a distant, and more elderly, relative who did not share the Catholicism of the senior branch of the family and who had held a post in Edward VI's household before the King's accession: one of his relations, Robert Saunders, sat in the Parliament for Brackley.[3]

George Tresham inherited the former Mulsho domicile at Newton but he seems to have made no mark until his marriage with the last abbess of the Minories in London. It was evidently a profitable match for he soon began to enlarge his inheritance by purchase and lease, sometimes in partnership with Paul Darrell† and Edmund Twyneho*, and in 1544 he exchanged her pension for the rectories of Great and Little Newton which seven years later he sold to a brother of his kinsman and namesake. On different occasions Sir Thomas Wriothesley and Queen Catherine Parr wrote on his behalf to the chancellor of the court of augmentations, and it was perhaps as a result of their intervention that he obtained some properties so favourably: in 1551 the evaluation of several sales to him were shown to be 'imperfect' and he paid the difference. Some of the land thus acquired was in Northampton and this presumably qualified him for election there. Nothing is known about his part in the House, but after the dissolution a dispute arising from his lease of a rabbit-warren on the outskirts of the town was referred to the mayor for arbitration. Tresham is last glimpsed in November 1555 when he leased various properties at Kingthorpe near Northampton. Most of his lands passed eventually into the possession of his nephew Maurice Tresham, who made Newton one of his own homes.[4]

¹ Date of birth estimated from marriage. *Vis. Northants.*, ed. Metcalfe, 50–51; *Fac. Off. Reg. 1534–49*, ed. Chambers, 216.

[2] *LP Hen. VIII*, xx; Royal 7 C16, f. 94; LC2/2, f. 53v. [3] *Vis. Northants.* 201; *CPR*, 1550-3, pp. 200-3; PCC 25 Ketchyn, 19 Chaynay; *Machyn's Diary* (Cam. Soc. xlii), 348; Emden, *Biog. Reg. Univ. Oxf. 1501-40*, pp. 576-7; *Northants. Past and Present*, v. 91-93. [4] *LP Hen. VIII*, xv, xvi, xix-xxi; Bridges, *Northants.* i. 521, 551, 563; ii. 310 seq.; *CPR*, 1548-9, p. 170; 1549-51, p. 130; 1554-5, p. 51; 1555-7, pp. 108-9; 1566-9, pp. 252, 332, 373; W. C. Richardson, *Ct. Augmentations*, 422n; E315/223, f. 21, 224, f. 500; C1/1386/54-60; St.Ch.3/2/17; *Recs. Northampton*, ed. Cox and Markham, ii. 130-1.

S.M.T.

TRESHAM, Sir Thomas (by 1500-59), of Rushton, Northants.

NORTHAMPTONSHIRE	1539,[1] 1542
LANCASTER	1553 (Oct.)
NORTHAMPTONSHIRE	1554 (Apr.), 1554 (Nov.)

b. by 1500, 1st s. of John Tresham of Rushton by Isabel, da. and coh. of Sir James Harington of Hornby, Lancs. *m.* Anne, da. and coh. of Sir William Parr*, Lord Parr of Horton, 3s. 1da.; (2) Lettice, da. of Sir Thomas Peniston of Hawridge, Bucks., wid. of Robert Knollys (*d.*1521) of Rotherfield Greys, Oxon. and Sir Robert Lee (*d.*1539) of Quarrendon, Bucks. *suc.* fa. 1521. Kntd. by 1524.[2]

Sheriff, Northants. 1524–Jan. 1526, 1539–40, 1555–6; j.p. 1531–*d.*; commr. tenths of spiritualities 1535, musters 1539, 1542, 1546, benevolence 1544/45, relief 1550, goods of churches and fraternities 1553; other commissions 1527–54; esquire of the body by 1533; grand prior, order of St. John of Jerusalem Nov. 1557–*d.*[3]

Sir Thomas Tresham's grandson said of his ancestors that they were 'dignified with many noble offices and advancements'. Tresham's own father made little mark outside Northamptonshire, but he himself followed a career reminiscent of his great-grandfather William[†] and grandfather Sir Thomas[†] but without their violent ends. Pricked sheriff within three years of succeeding to his patrimony, and put on the bench not long after, he combined local management with attendance at court and military service. He helped to suppress the Pilgrimage of Grace in 1536 and Ket's rebellion in 1549.[4]

Tresham's first known election for Northamptonshire answered to his own standing in the county but was also doubtless assisted by his father-in-law and fellow-knight in 1539, Sir William Parr. In the Parliament of 1542, to which Parr was not returned for the county, Tresham replaced him as senior knight. The names of the Members for 1545 are lost. Parr's death two years later and Tresham's own Catholicism presumably account for his failure to be re-elected under Edward VI. After his proclamation of Mary as Queen during the succession crisis of 1553 he might have been expected to reappear as one of the knights for the shire in the first Parliament of her reign, when the senior Member was his kinsman Sir John Fermor, but he found a place at Lancaster, where his name is inserted in the

indenture in a different hand. If his support of the Queen was not in itself sufficient to procure him a nomination, he could claim the interest of Edward Stanley, 3rd Earl of Derby, a distant kinsman and a fellow-landowner in both Lancashire and Northamptonshire. During this Parliament one of Tresham's servants was granted privilege from an action for debt on 21 Nov. 1553. Tresham again sat for Northamptonshire in the two Parliaments of 1554 but did not do so in that of 1555, the year in which he was pricked sheriff for the third time. His appointment to the grand priorship of the order of St. John gave him a seat in the Lords in the Parliament of 1558, but within a week of its assembly he obtained leave of absence. Summoned to the Lords again in 1559 he perhaps thought it expedient not to attend and named Archbishop Heath as his proxy, but he may already have been a sick man as he died on the following 1 Mar. (not 8 Mar., as stated in his inquisition post mortem) and was buried on 16 Mar. with much pomp at Rushton, where a monument was erected to his memory. During February one of his servants, an Italian from Mantua, observed that Tresham would 'remain a good Christian, as he always was at the time of the other schism, but he will remain in the country, and will observe the old rite secretly'. By his will of 28 Nov. 1557 made on entering religion he had provided for his family and had amongst others named Sir George Gifford* and Sir Robert Tyrwhitt I* executors and William Cordell* supervisor. His 15 year-old grandson and heir, also Thomas, was later to become a leading Elizabethan recusant.[5]

[1] E159/319, brev. ret. Mich. r. [1–2]. [2] Of age at fa.'s death. M. E. Finch, *Five Northants. Fams.* (Northants. Rec. Soc. xix), ped. at end of vol.; *Vis. Northants.* ed. Metcalfe, 180-1. [3] *LP Hen. VIII*, ii, iv, v, viii, xi-xiv, xvi, xvii, xx, xxi; *CPR*, 1547 8, p. 87; 1550-3, pp. 141, 395; 1553, pp. 356; 1553-4, pp. 22, 29; 1554-5, pp. 106, 109; 1557-8, p. 313; *Machyn's Diary* (Cam. Soc. xlii), 159. [4] Finch, 66-67; *LP Hen. VIII*, xii, xiv, xv, xix; *APC*, i. 488; ii. 325; iv. 310; v. 9, 30, 161; *CPR*, 1550-3, p. 200; *CSP Ven.* 1558-80, p. 31; *CSP Dom.* 1547-80, pp. 100, 101. [5] C142/124/144; 219/21/86; *Northants. Past and Present*, v. 90-93; *Chron. Q. Jane and Q. Mary* (Cam. Soc. xlviii), 12, 13; *CJ*, i. 30; M. A. R. Graves 'The Tudor House of Lords 1547-8' (Otago Univ. Ph.D. thesis 1974), 238'; *LJ*, i. 514, 541; *CSP Ven.* 1558-80, pp. 31, 46; Finch, 68-69; PCC 19 Chaynay; St.Ch.2/23/34. *Machyn's Diary*, 192; Bridges, *Northants.* ii. 72; Pevsner and Cherry, *Northants.* 397.

S.M.T.

TREVANION, John (by 1483-1539 or later), of Dartmouth, Devon.

DARTMOUTH	1529

b. by 1483, prob. 2nd s. of John Trevanion of Trevanion, Cornw. by Janet, da. of Thomas Treffry of Fowey, Cornw. *m.* by July 1510, Joan, wid. of Richard Holland (*d.*1506) of Dartmouth, at least 1s.; ?(2) Radegund, da. of John Somaster of Widecombe, Devon.[1]

Mayor, Dartmouth 1512-13, 1518-19, 1537-8, 1538-9, 2nd bailiff 1537-8; commr. subsidy, Devon

1512; ?gent. usher in 1526; ?reeve, Grampound, Cornw. 1529–30; ?comptroller of customs, Plymouth and Fowey by 1537.[2]

John Trevanion was doubtless a member of the family of Caerhayes, Cornwall, and although his place in its pedigree is not certain he is taken to have been the younger brother (and an executor) of Sir William Trevanion, a gentleman usher of the Household who died in 1518. Of his career before he came to Dartmouth nothing is known but as he was to be elected mayor in 1512 he must by then have spent some years in the town, where he had perhaps established himself either shortly before or at the time of his marriage to the widow of a prominent townsman.[3]

Trevanion was probably a merchant, as were his wife's first husband and brothers-in-law: in 1523 and 1524 he was to be assessed for subsidy at £100 in goods. Whether he was also the gentleman usher 'out of wages' named in a household list of 1526 it is hard to say, although as the brother and nephew of two men who did enjoy that status he may well have emulated them. It was therefore as a considerable figure in Dartmouth, and perhaps as a minor one at court, that he was elected one of the town's Members to the Parliament of 1529: his fellow-Member was his nephew by marriage William Holland, and he had an uncle in the House in Thomas Treffry I. Trevanion, unlike Holland, was to see that Parliament through to its end and was therefore almost certainly re-elected to its successor of June 1536, in accordance with the King's request for the return of the previous Members; but, again unlike Holland, he was not returned thereafter. Although both were paid by the town for their service, Trevanion appears to have received much more than Holland, at least for some sessions. Thus after sharing £2 9s. with Holland in respect of the first session, Trevanion was paid £17 4s.4d. for his attendance between 1531 and 1533, against £7 2s. for Holland; as the maximum amount payable for the four sessions of these years, calculated at the standard rate of 2s. a day and including days of travel, amounted to rather more than £25, Trevanion was recompensed either at that rate for two thirds of the days involved or at a lower one for a larger total of days. It is tempting, if risky, to think that such disparate payments bore some relation to the length of time each Member spent at Westminster. Of Trevanion's part in the proceedings there nothing is known.[4]

It was during Trevanion's mayoralty in 1538 that there occurred the attempted assault on William Holland which the mayor and his brethren took to the Star Chamber. Trevanion is last met with in the town records in 1539: a list of the common council in 1541 does not include his name. Whether his disappearance was due to death or to removal elsewhere turns upon the identification of the John Trevanion whose comptrollership of customs at Plymouth and Fowey exempted him from serving in the French campaign of 1544. That a Trevanion should have held this office is not surprising, for the leading figure at Fowey, and the customs collector there and at Plymouth until 1541, was Thomas Treffy I; what is not clear is whether the post was held by Trevanion himself or by his son and namesake, unless its re-grant in November 1550 to 'John Trevanion gentleman', may be taken to mean that it was then given to the son after being held by the father. In the same way, the John Trevanion who about this time married Radegund Somaster could have been either the father, if his first wife was dead, or his son (the second alternative being the more likely in view of a reference to John Travanion 'junior' in connexion with Thomas Vowell's* marriage to Radegund's mother about 1537), as could the man of the name who was buried in Saltash in 1564. In view of the elder Trevanion's advancing years, perhaps all these later references should be applied to his son, and his own death be presumed to have occurred in or shortly after 1539.[5]

[1] Date of birth estimated from first reference, 1504, J. Maclean, *Trigg Minor*, ii. 247n. *Vis. Cornw.* (Harl. Soc. ix), 239–40; H. R. Watkin, *Pre-Reformation Dartmouth*, 241; *Vis. Devon*, ed. Vivian, 695. [2] Exeter city lib. Dartmouth ms 1982, ff. 8, 69v; Watkin, 187; St.Ch.2/12/115; Duchy Cornw. rec.-gen. accts. 29–30 Hen. VIII 220/12a; *Statutes*, iii. 80; *LP Hen. VIII*, iv, xix; E122/116/8; information from G. Haslam. [3] PCC 20 Ayloffe, 14 Adeane. [4] L. M. Nicholls, 'Trading communities of Totnes and Dartmouth late 15th and early 16th centuries' (Exeter Univ. M.A. thesis, 1960), 14; *LP Hen. VIII*, iv; Exeter city lib. Dartmouth ms 2002, f. 48v; Watkin, 767–8. [5] St.Ch.2/12/115; Exeter city lib. Dartmouth ms 2003, f. 6; *LP Hen. VIII*, xix; *CPR*, 1553, p. 346; C142/73/36; *Vis. Cornw.* ed. Vivian, 501.

R.V.

TREW, Simon (by 1515–52), of Cambridge.

CAMBRIDGE 1545[1]

b. by 1515.[2]

Alderman, Cambridge, mayor 1536–7; j.p. Cambs. 1539–45; commr. sewers, Cambs., Hunts., Lincs., Northants. 1540, musters, Cambs. 1541; serjeant-at-arms July 1550–*d.*[3]

Although his family is not mentioned in the visitations of Cambridgeshire, Simon Trew must have been of gentle birth to have achieved the office of serjeant-at-arms. Moreover, he was the only Cambridge townsman of this period, apart from Thomas Brakyn*, to serve on the county commission of the peace. He was a loyal supporter of the town in its disputes with the university and when elected mayor he refused to take the accustomed oath binding him to uphold the university's privileges. The corporation wrote to Cromwell on 29 Sept. 1536, Trew's first day of office, justifying this refusal by reference to a supposed alteration of the oath ceremony which Cromwell and the town's high steward, the 3rd Duke of Norfolk, were said to have intended. Cromwell had written to the corporation several times during the previous years, mainly about the townsmen's refusal to allow the university authorities to exercise their rights at Sturbridge fair. Trew evidently aggravated the situation and further letters from Cromwell were followed by a royal letter of 29 Aug. 1537, from which it appears that the only notice the corporation had taken of the minister's remonstrances was to send Trew and others to London 'to have had countermandment of some things in the said letters contained'.[4]

As a commissioner for musters in 1541 Trew attempted to muster the scholars of the university which earned him a further rebuke from the Council. He served with two billmen in the French campaign of 1544 but apparently returned from the war more belligerent than he had gone; on 22 Oct. 1546, as deputy for the absent mayor, Trew 'refused with his brethren that two aldermen and four burgesses should take any oath at the vice-chancellor's hands'. On 1 Nov. the Council ordered the townsmen to adhere to precedent in the matter of the oath, but agreed to hear their objections to the custom, a reasonable condition that was 'received with some stomach'. The town was defeated but not cowed, as the university's articles of complaint of 18 Dec. show; the first complaint alleged that at the last meeting of both sides:

> There was such inordinate unseemly and uncharitable facing and craking of the vice-chancellor, especially by Mr. [Robert] Chapman*, Mr. Trew and Mr. [Edward] Slegge*, that it seemed rather to tend unto a sedition threatening . . . than any other meeting of reasonable men.[5]

After this clash Trew seems to have played less part in Cambridge affairs; his appointment as serjeant-at-arms, in which capacity he joined his municipal colleague Edward Slegge, clearly kept him away from the town, at least to begin with. In July 1550 he was designated 'the King's servant' and a month later was paid £20 'by way of the King's reward for his good attendance at the court'. No will or inquisition post mortem has been found but he died before 28 Sept. 1552, when his post of serjeant-at-arms, vacated by his death, was conferred on another.[6]

¹ C. H. Cooper, *Cambridge Annals*, i. 422. ² Date of birth estimated from first reference. ³ F. Blomefield, *Coll. Cant.* 224; *LP Hen. VIII*, xiii, xiv, xvi, xvii, xx; *CPR*, 1549–51, pp. 291–2; 1550–3, p. 409. ⁴ Cooper, i. 384–5, 388–90; Stowe 669, f. 1. ⁵ J. Lamb, *Letters from ms Lib. of C.C.C. Cambridge*, 41, 73–74; *LP Hen. VIII*, xvi, xix, xxi; Cooper, i. 441–3. ⁶ *CPR*, 1549–51, pp. 291–2; 1550–3, p. 409; *APC*, iii. 102.

D.F.C.

TREWYNNARD, James (c. 1505–72 or later), of Budock, Cornw.

LISKEARD	1529
NEWPORT IUXTA LAUNCESTON	1547[1]
PENRYN	1554 (Nov.)

b. c.1505, yr. s. of James Trewynnard of Trewinnard by Philippa; bro. of William*. *m.* (1), 1da.; (2) c.1559, Philippa, da. and coh. of Nicholas Carminowe of Trenowth, wid. of Hugh Boscawen of Tregothnan, *s.p.*[2]

Dep. capt. Pendennis castle, Cornw. by 1552.[3]

James Trewynnard was in his twenties when he was returned to Parliament as the senior Member for Liskeard. At the time of his election he was probably a student attending an inn of court, perhaps Lincoln's Inn since it was the one favoured by Cornishmen: there is no record of his admission to an inn, but in 1544, when he appeared as counsel in a case at the Truro general sessions, he was described as 'a man greatly studied in the laws of the realm'. His father, who was apparently not long dead in 1529, may have been a dependant of the receiver-general of the duchy of Cornwall, Sir John Arundell, whose support for his master was the subject of a complaint in the court of requests early in the reign of Henry VIII; it was presumably to Arundell that the young Trewynnard was indebted for his first seat. In the spring of 1536 the King asked that those who had sat in the Parliament of 1529 should be re-elected to its successor, and Liskeard probably returned Trewynnard and his fellow Henry Pyne for a second time.[4]

While he was in London, Trewynnard frequented that haunt of lawyers, the church of St. Dunstan in the West, Fleet Street, and a conversation which he had there with a priest on Sunday 26 Mar. 1536 (during the last session of the Parliament of 1529) about a benefice in the presentation of Lady Russell later became the subject of litigation. Trewynnard and his brother William obtained a lease of this benefice from Lady Russell, and his connexion with the wife of the lord warden of the stannaries and high steward of the duchy of Cornwall helps to explain Trewynnard's election to Parliament in 1547 and 1554: the same patron may also have favoured his return in 1539 and 1542, two Parliaments for which the names of nearly all the Cornish Members are lost. He had no known personal link with the borough which he and Reginald Mohun represented in 1547, but at Penryn he was a man of some importance, living at nearby Budock and being deputy captain of the royal fort commanding the marine approach to the town; his election there, unlike his fellow Thomas Mathew's, accorded with Queen Mary's request that Members should be local men. Unlike Mathew again, Trewynnard was not one of those prosecuted in the King's bench for leaving this Parliament early and without permission. That he did not sit in the Commons again is perhaps to be explained by the death in the following spring of the 1st Earl of Bedford, who as Baron Russell had probably used his great influence on Trewynnard's behalf.[5]

His experience at Pendennis was doubtless of use to Trewynnard when in 1560 he was appointed to survey St. Michael's Mount: he had probably resigned the post on his marriage to Philippa Boscawen as he went to live with her at Tregothnan higher up the Fal estuary. Soon after this marriage he became involved in a bitter dispute with his stepson John Boscawen and the young man's guardian John Carminowe* over some livestock. Matters came to a head on 8 Feb. 1560 when there was a skirmish between the two parties, in which Trewynnard was injured and his companion Carew Courtenay was killed. Following his wife's death Trewynnard gave up living at Tregothnan and appears to have left Cornwall for a time; in 1564 or not long afterwards, as James Trewynnard of the county of Devon, he brought an action against Thomas Herle* regarding lands in Kenwyn and elsewhere in the neighbourhood of Truro. Herle was a nephew of Trewynnard's late wife and the lands in question appear to have formed part of the property divided between the elder Nicholas Carminowe's coheirs Elizabeth Herle and Philippa Trewynnard; as Herle pointed out, Trewynnard had no claim to any part of this inheritance. Five years later Herle had further cause for complaint against Trewynnard who had entered his property at Killifreth in Kenwyn and had carried off 100 gallons of black tin. By this date Trewynnard was probably living at Kenwyn, where on 6 Oct. 1572 he contributed to the subsidy on an assessment of lands worth £5 a year. His activities in his last years are not easily distinguishable from those of his nephew and namesake, but he probably died in the 1570s. His heir appears to have been his daughter Jane, who married Thomas Harris *alias* Roscrow.[6]

[1] Hatfield 207. [2] Aged '38 or thereabouts' in 1543, St.Ch.2/31/161. *Vis. Cornw.* ed. Vivian, 47, 408; Req.2/10/30; C3/31/86; 142/138/13. [3] Stowe 571, f. 45v. [4] *LP Hen. VIII*, iii.; C1/1110/5; 142/78/42; Req. 2/3/88; St.Ch.2/18/71. [5] Req.2/10/30; E179/87/172. [6] *CPR*, 1558–60, p. 319; St.Ch.5/T18/4, T22/31, H77/33; *Vis. Cornw.* 47, 205, 408; C3/178/1; E179/88/229, m. 2v.

J.J.G.

TREWYNNARD, William (by 1495–1549), of Trewinnard, Cornw.

HELSTON 1542[1]

b. by 1495, prob. 1st s. of James Trewynnard of Trewinnard by Philippa; bro. of James*. *m.* (1) by 1530, Jane, wid. of Robert Shilston, 2s. 1da.; (2) Thomasin, da. of Sir Thomas Stukely of Affeton in East Worlington, Devon, wid. of John Bere (*d*.1531) of Huntsham, Devon. *suc.* fa. by 1530.[2]

William Trewynnard was probably the eldest son of a small landed proprietor who seems to have been a dependant of the Arundells of Lanherne. On his father's death he succeeded to the family home at Trewinnard, some ten miles from Helston, but most of his father's lands were left in the dower of his mother and became the subject of a suit made to Chancellor Audley by a Cornishman, John Skewys. Skewys pressed his claims on Trewynnard who presumably to evade them sought election to the Parliament of 1542. Trewynnard was sued successfully by Skewys in the King's bench for the recovery of a debt of £74 15s., and a writ was issued for his arrest until he had satisfied Skewys's claims. Sir Hugh Trevanion, sheriff of Cornwall (1542–3) was unable to serve this writ on Trewynnard (who could not be discovered in the county although he had been present at the Helston coinage in the autumn of 1542) so he returned it to the court, and on 13 June 1543 Skewys obtained a second writ which led Trewynnard to deliver himself to the sheriff. Trewynnard did not comply any further with the court's orders and remained in custody. When Richard Chamond* succeeded Trevanion as sheriff, Trewynnard was transferred to his keeping. The third session of the Parliament opened on 14 Jan. 1544 and a writ of privilege was issued on 21 Feb. whereby a month later on 20 Mar., only eight days before the dissolution, Trewynnard was released by Chamond. Skewys died soon afterwards and after his executors had failed to obtain redress against Chamond in the King's bench (the sum involved being now £84 15s., to include damages) the matter was brought before Chancellor Wriothesley. Trewynnard's subsequent release raised the question 'whether he was discharged by the order of the common law . . . or no' but as 'the parties desired to have the matter determined without further trouble' and as Trewynnard 'ought not in conscience to be discharged', Wriothesley ruled on 7 June 1546 that he should pay the executors £66 13s.4d.[3]

Trewynnard, a practising lawyer, was himself a frequent, if not a compulsive, litigant, a trait which he seems to have shared with his father. The actions brought against him by his relatives, neighbours, and business associates (who included John Giles*) during the last 20 years of his life were largely for debt. Early in 1549 he was obliged to pawn plate and jewellery to meet creditors. Later that year during the western uprising his lands were ravaged and his goods despoiled by the rebels. He took refuge at St. Michael's Mount, but in an attack on the island he received 'a great hurt and mortal wound'. He died intestate; the administration of his estate was granted to his son Matthew and his brother James.[4]

[1] C78/1, no. 36. [2] Aged '48 years and above' in 1543, St.Ch.2/31/161. St.Ch.5/T34/32; C1/448/46, 1074/61; Req.2/10/30; *Vis. Devon* ed. Vivian, 60, 340. [3] C1/1074/61, 1111/34; 78/1, no. 36; 142/78/42; *LP Hen. VIII*, iii; St.Ch.2/31/161; 5/T22/12; Hatsell, *Precedents*, i. 59–65; J. Dyer, *Reps.* (1794), i. 59b–61b; PCC 8 Pynnyng. [4] C1/448/46, 581/88, 995/38–39, 1164/32, 1233/5, 1476/44; St.Ch. 5/T34/32.

J.J.G.

TRIGGES, Robert (by 1508–50/51), of St. Peter's, Chichester, Suss. and Chawton, Hants.

CHICHESTER 1529

b. by 1508. *m.* Margaret (?Spring), 1s.[1]
Recorder, Chichester by 1534–*d.*; servant of the 9th Lord la Warr by 1539.[2]

No trace of Robert Trigges has been found before he took the senior place for Chichester in the Parliament of 1529, being presumably already the city's recorder. He may have been helped at the election by the 9th Lord la Warr, a Sussex magnate, with whom he was associated during the 1530s. Nothing is known about Trigges's part in this Parliament, but presumably he sat in its successor, that of 1536, in compliance with the King's request for the re-election of the previous Members, and he may have done so again in 1539 and 1545, for which Parliaments Chichester's returns are lost.

In July 1537 Trigges leased Mundham rectory from the crown, and was also in 1550 a tenant of lands in the same district. A tendency to deal in property on a bigger scale is reflected in Trigges's purchase from Lord la Warr in 1542, with Lawrence Stoughton, of manors in Dorset, Sussex and Wiltshire, and several tenements in Hampshire. He was a sick man when in 1548–9 he made his will at Chawton. After remembering a kinswoman and two of his servants he left all his property to his wife, whom he named sole executrix, with Thomas Carpenter* and William Stapleton as overseers. He seems to have recovered as in August 1550 he leased the mansion house of Waltham prebend, which he sold not long after to Walter Roynon* for £56. The will was proved on 31 Jan. 1551.[3]

[1] Presumed to be of age at election. W. Suss. RO, wills, 7, f. 145v; C1/1478/50–51. [2] *Suss. N. and Q.* xiii. 82; *Suss. Rec. Soc.* lvi. 1–6; SP2/5, f. 206v. [3] *LP Hen. VIII*, xiii; *CPR*, 1548–9, p. 381; *Suss. Rec. Soc.* xix. 45; C1/1478/50–51; W. Suss. RO wills, 7, f. 145v.

R.J.W.S.

TROTT, Thomas (by 1483–1524 or later), of Bodmin, Cornw.

BODMIN 1515[1]

b. by 1483.[2]
Commr. subsidy, Cornw. 1514, Bodmin 1515, 1523, 1524; ?servant of Catherine, dowager Countess of Devon in 1524.[3]

Thomas Trott came from one of the leading families in Bodmin. The first glimpse of him is during the winter of 1503–4 when he was paid 20*d.* by the mayor for an unspecified task performed about the time of the parliamentary election there. Ten years later he was appointed to the commission to supervise the collection of a tax granted in the last session of the Parliament of 1512; the inclusion of his name points to his Membership of the Commons which had agreed to the grant, an inference which is borne out by his appearance in the next Parliament, the third of Henry VIII's reign, when the King had asked for the return of the previous Members. Trott received some money towards his expenses together with John Flamank and served on the subsidy commission following the Parliament. It is possible that he was re-elected in 1523, as in that year and in 1524 he was reappointed subsidy commissioner. No further trace of him has been found.[4]

[1] *HP*, ed. Wedgwood 1439–1509 (Biogs.), 877 and (Reg.), 592 are almost certainly in error in ascribing a parliamentary career to Trott under Henry VII. J. Maclean, *Trigg Minor*, i. 224, 243, citing the lost town records, gives his name as Thomas Nott. [2] Date of birth estimated from first reference. [3] *Statutes*, iii. 113, 175; *LP Hen. VIII*, iii, iv; E36/223 ex inf. W. Harwood. [4] *HP*, ed. Wedgwood 1439–1509 (Biogs.), 876–7; Maclean, i. 224, 235–6; Lysons, *Magna Britannia*, iii. 32.

J.J.G.

TROTTER, Hugh (by 1504–35/36).

BRIDGWATER 1529*

b. by 1504, ?s. of Richard Trotter of Bridgwater, Som. *m.* 1525, Margery, da. of John Drew† of Bridgwater, wid. of Thomas Lyte of Lytes Cary, Som.[1]
Collector of customs, Bridgwater by 1526–*d.*; escheator, Som. and Dorset 1535–*d.*; auditor, commission for tenths of spiritualities, Som. 1535.[2]

Hugh Trotter may have been a son or grandson of Richard and Denise Trotter who were living in Bridgwater in 1469: his own marriage allied him with one of the main families of the town and also with Sir Nicholas Wadham, the junior knight for Somerset in 1529. He was thus well placed when an opportunity to sit in Parliament arose through the recent appointment of the recorder of Bridgwater, Baldwin Malet, as solicitor-general, an office which precluded him from election. Both Trotter and his fellow-Member Henry Thornton were, or were to become, customs officials, while Trotter's close association with his neighbour Sir Andrew Luttrell, who in 1538 was to provide for an obit in Bridgwater for himself, his parents and Trotter, could hardly fail to have been an advantage, Luttrell being sheriff of Somerset and Dorset at the time of the election.[3]

Trotter died intestate at some time between his appointment as escheator in November 1535 and the following 7 Apr., when Alexander Popham* was granted the office; the date of his replacement in it, a week before the end of the last session of the Parliament, suggests that Trotter died during that session. On his deathbed he stated that he would have none but Cromwell as his executor. After Edward North* had reported to Thomas Rush* that Trotter had been worth £400 and that there was money concealed in his study, Cromwell sent his servant Thomas Parry* to Bridgwater to wind up his estate, to settle his accounts as customer and to stop his stepson Thomas Lyte from removing such property as might be the King's. Parry was to become involved in a chancery suit with Lyte over the administration.[4]

¹ Date of birth estimated from marriage. *Bridgwater Bor. Archives*, v. (Som. Rec. Soc. lxx), 2–3; *Som. Arch. and Nat. Hist. Soc. Proc.* xxxviii. 32; Collinson, *Som.* iii. 193; E130/911/1. ² E122/27/10, 200/1; *LP Hen. VIII*, viii. ³ *Bridgwater Bor. Archives*, v. 2–3; Bridgwater corp. ms 1437; *LP Hen. VIII*, i-iv; T. G. Jacks, *Wadham College*, 27–28; PCC 19 Dyngeley, 15 Spert. ⁴ *LP Hen. VIII*, ix; C1/1139/49–50; *Som. and Dorset N. and Q.* vii. 111.

A.D.K.H.

TUDOLL (TUDBOLD), John (by 1485–1548), of Lyme Regis, Dorset.

?LYME REGIS 1529*[1]

b. by 1485, ?s. of John Tudoll of Lyme Regis. *m.* Alice, 1da.[2]

Among 'the twelve for the King', Lyme Regis 1506, 1508, affeeror 1506, 1508, mayor 1531–2, 1539–40, 1543–4.[3]

The John Tudoll who was granted a burgage tenement and admitted a freeman of Lyme in October 1506 is to be distinguished from a namesake who was bailiff in 1499 and one of 'the twelve for the King' in 1504, and who is likely to have been his father. The admission of the younger John Tudoll's brother William to the freedom in May 1508 strengthens the view that these years saw the advent of a new generation of the family in the affairs of the town. A partial gap in the municipal records between 1508 and 1560 makes it difficult to trace the career of either brother but both were to prosper in trade and to serve the town as mayor. Although we need not take too literally his fellow-townsman Thomas Batyn's description of John Tudoll in a chancery bill as 'a man of great might and power', he was clearly a man of local importance and one who was involved in recurrent litigation.[4]

It is probable, but not certain, that John Tudoll sat in the Parliament of 1529 as one of the Members for Lyme Regis. If he did so, it was presumably as a replacement for John Pyne, one of the two men returned for the town in 1529. Pyne was dead by the summer of 1532 and the vacancy was probably filled, as seems to have been the general practice, in time for the opening of the fifth session on 4 Feb. 1533. It is included in the list of vacant seats drawn up by or for Cromwell in this connexion, with the name of William Symonds as that of the suggested new Member. Symonds is probably to be identified with a minor household official and customs administrator whose father was John Simon* of Exeter, but there is no evidence that he was by-elected for Lyme. On the other hand, certain facts point towards Tudoll as Pyne's successor. In a letter to Cromwell which, although undated, may be ascribed to 1533, he wrote that he had been in London 'since the beginning of the Parliament' (by which he probably meant the opening of the fifth session) without having received any payment from the town: he also made flattering reference, in terms which suggest that he had himself heard them, to Cromwell's 'many good words in the parliament house for the commonwealth of all the whole realm'. Lastly, the debt of £59 8s.3d. to Tudoll (of which £11 18s.3d. was outstanding) which the town acknowledged in October 1536 may well have included a payment towards his parliamentary expenses since 1533.[5]

Suggestive as these items are, they fall short of proof, especially when certain others are brought into the reckoning. Chief among these is the document recording that, on 15 Apr. 1532, Tudoll was 'elected and chosen' by the inhabitants of Lyme to plead on their behalf to the King and Council for the town's necessities, and that they undertook to repay whatever sums he should disburse in 'promises or gifts of payment' in his mission even if it were to prove unsuccessful. Why the town should have taken this step is not clear: its timing implies that it was connected with the new parliamentary session which had begun on 10 Apr.: with Pyne already dead and Thomas Burgh as its sole Member, Lyme perhaps judged it necessary to appoint Tudoll, then mayor, as a special attorney. The only glimpse of his discharge of his mission is contained in the letter to Cromwell already cited, the purpose of which was to secure the minister's support, although he may also have been instrumental in winning the goodwill of Thomas Arundell*, an ex-sheriff of Somerset and Dorset, who also addressed Cromwell on the town's behalf. The campaign was to be a long drawn-out one, but it was so far successful that on 15 Jan. 1535 a patent granted Lyme Regis an annual payment of £20 for ten years. The town's indebtedness to Tudoll for his services was acknowledged in

October 1536 by its gift to him of 13s.4d. a year during the term of the royal grant and of a further 6s.8d. a year for life.[6]

It thus appears that when, between the fourth and fifth sessions, the vacancy came to be filled, Tudoll was already prosecuting the town's suit. In the circumstances, he would have been the obvious person to elect, and the tone of his letter to Cromwell is consistent with his having sat as Lyme's second Member from February 1533. In that event he is likely to have been returned again to the Parliament of 1536. There remains, however, the possibility that it was in a non-parliamentary capacity that Tudoll conducted his mission, and that the second seat was filled by another, perhaps Cromwell's *protégé* William Symonds.

With two further terms as mayor ahead of him, Tudoll was to remain a leading local figure until his death in 1548. On 9 Oct. of that year he both made his will and died. He left two houses, one leased from Lord Cobham, as almshouses, and the rest of his property in Lyme to John Hassard and Agnes his wife, with remainder to Tudoll's daughter Thomasin, except for some which was to pass to Tudoll's brother William. Thomasin was also to have another house, then in the holding of John Mallock*. She was at that time married to William Beaumont and was already the widow of John Strowbridge and mother of another John Strowbridge*. She later married William Pole, whose second wife was Catherine, sister of John Popham; both Pole and Popham were to serve the borough in later Parliaments. Tudoll's brother William made his will three years later, and asked to be buried in the parish church 'as nigh unto my brother John Tudbold as convenient'.[7]

[1] *LP Hen. VIII*, add. i. 911 citing SP1/238, pt. 3, f. 233.   [2] Date of birth estimated from first reference. C1/696/9; Lyme Regis recs. N23/2, no. 6.   [3] Lyme Regis recs. B1/2 passim; D3/1, ff. 11–11v; G1/2, no. 1; N23/2, no. 13; C1/696/9, 858/19.   [4] Lyme Regis recs. B1/2 passim; D3/1, f. 12; C1/696/9, 711/53–54; St.Ch.2/30/125.   [5] *LP Hen. VIII*, vii. 56 citing SP1/82, ff. 59–62; add. i. 911; Lyme Regis recs. D3/1, f. 2v.   [6] Lyme Regis recs. D3/1, ff. 3, 5; *LP Hen. VIII*, vi, viii; add. i. 911.   [7] Lyme Regis recs. N23/2, no. 16; PCC 6 Tashe.

S.T.B.

TULL, John (by 1522–54/59), of London.

WOOTTON BASSETT   1554 (Apr.)
OLD SARUM   1554 (Nov.)

b. by 1522, prob. yr. s. of Richard Tull of London. *m*. at least 1s.[1]

John Tull may have sprung from the Berkshire family which was later to produce the noted agriculturalist, but he lived and worked in London as did his father and his brother Richard, a clothworker. His father was probably the Richard Tull, draper, who in 1545 joined Nicholas Bacon* in buying property at Kingswood, Wiltshire, and he himself became free of the Company by apprenticeship in 1543 and was probably the assistant present at Sir William Roche's* funeral in 1549. In 1553 he was a tenant of one John Lambert in the parish of St. Mary Bothaw, but six years earlier the court of aldermen had given him a ten-year lease of the city tenement long occupied by his father. This they had done on the recommendation of the Protector Somerset and the Earl of Warwick. What claim Tull, or his father, had to such powerful patronage has not transpired: neither is known to have held office or been connected with the court.[2]

Tull was a member of the 'New Hanse' of the Merchant Adventurers, that is, he had gained admission to the Company by paying the entrance fee of 10 marks prescribed by the Act of 1497 (12 Hen. VII, c.7). It was his championship of this group against the 'Old Hanse', those who had acquired membership by apprenticeship or patrimony, which landed him in trouble in the spring of 1553. Among the bills debated in the Parliament of March 1553 was one to put an end to the New Hanse by the repeal of the Act of 1497. This threat to their rights propelled Tull and others into a campaign which included petitioning Chancellor Goodrich. Whether the rejection of the bill on its third reading in the Commons owed anything to their opposition is not known, but they found further cause for complaint when two months later the government dragooned the Old Hanse into making it a loan repayable on unfavourable terms at Antwerp. On 30 May the Council reprimanded the New Hanse for its unruly behaviour and sent Tull and his associate John Dymoke to the Fleet until they should submit to the Company and earn its request for their discharge. How long they remained there is unknown, but they were probably released before or upon the accession of Mary six weeks later.[3]

It was doubtless with the object of continuing his campaign that Tull procured his election to the second and third of the new Queen's Parliaments. At both Wootton Bassett and Old Sarum he must have enjoyed influential support, which may have come from a court figure like Sir William Paget or William Herbert I*, Earl of Pembroke, or from someone reviving his earlier patronage by Somerset. What followed is recounted in a memorial, probably of 1566, advocating the repeal of the Act of 1497. This describes how Tull and his associates

did in the reign of Queen Mary exhibit another slanderous bill against the said defendants [the Company] in a Parliament then holden being in effect the substance of the former bill ... and the said defendants making answer thereunto in writing and presenting it to the said Parliament the same being there read and considered the said complainants' bill was rejected and dashed.

According to the Journal the only bill on the subject introduced while Tull was a Member was the one read on 20 Nov. 1554 'for merchants of the Old Hanse and New Hanse to be one Company and to pay 15 marks at their admittance'. Although the Journal gives no hint of its fate, the disappearance of this bill after a single reading was tantamount to its rejection. If it was the bill introduced by Tull and his supporters, they were evidently prepared to see the entrance fee raised in the interest of securing equality between the New Hanse and the Old.[4]

Although Tull did not compromise himself by quitting this Parliament without leave, he was not to return to the Commons. He did not long survive to do so, for the only further reference found to him is in his brother Richard's will of 30 June 1559, where he is described as deceased. The will also reveals that he had a son Francis. Since Tull could not have married before 1543, the Francis Tull whom he had addressed as his servant when sending a bill of exchange to Antwerp on 15 May 1553—two weeks before he was imprisoned—must have been an older member of the family.[5]

[1] Date of birth estimated from admission as freeman. *London IPMs* (Brit. Rec. Soc.), i. 207. [2] *CPR*, 1569–72, p. 161; P. Boyd, *Roll of Drapers' Co.*, 187; A. H. Johnson, *Company of Drapers*, ii. 102, 187; *London IPMs*, i. 134; City of London RO, Guildhall, rep. 11, f. 362. [3] *LJ*, i. 439–41; *CJ*, i. 25, 26, 40; G. Unwin, *Studies in Econ. Hist.* ed. Tawney, 147, 169–70; W. E. Lingelbach, *Internal Organization of Merchant Adventurers*, 16–18; *APC*, iv. 275; Harl. 597, f. 211. [4] On the return of 20 Mar. 1554 for Wootton Bassett the name 'John Tull of London merchant' is inserted in a different hand, C219/22/102, 103. On the Crown Office list for the Parliament of November 1554 the name 'John Tull' was originally copied in error as 'John Story', Huntington Lib. Hastings mss Parl. pprs. Harl. 597, f. 213. [5] *London IPMs*, i. 207. O. de Smedt, *De Engelse Natie te Antwerpen*, ii. 447 and n, 563.

E. McI.

TUNKS, John

CRICKLADE 1554 (Apr.)

John Tunks was one of the servants of (Sir) Edmund Brydges*, later 2nd Baron Chandos, who figure in a Star Chamber case brought by Anthony Daston during the reign of Edward VI. They were accused with their master and some of his kinsmen of poaching, trespass, murder and contempt of the council in the marches of Wales, and Tunks was reported to have said that he 'would threaten all the lords and men of worship in the county so that the case would not be fairly heard'. The outcome is unknown but it is clear that Tunks must have owed his return for Cricklade to the influence of the Brydges family.

St.Ch.3/5/21.

E. McI.

TURGEYS, John

CALNE 1529

This Member has not been identified, and all that can be offered is a choice of families and backgrounds from which he may have sprung.

First for consideration is the family of Turges Melcombe (afterwards Melcombe Horsey) in Dorset which combined gentility with a court connexion. It produced, in successive generations, a Member of Parliament in Richard Turges, who died in 1504, and a justice of the peace and gentleman usher to Henry VII in his son Robert, who died in 1518. Although Robert Turges left no issue, his heir being his 40 year-old sister Elizabeth, married to John Horsey (who thus came to give his name to the family manor), the mention of a William Turges of Dorset as a gentleman usher in the Eltham ordinances of 1526 and as under almoner suggests that the family continued to be represented in the royal service. If the Member for Calne in 1529 also belonged to it, his election might thus be attributed to court influence, although the fact that John Horsey, Elizabeth Turges's son, was knight of the shire for Dorset in the same Parliament might have had some bearing on the matter. It was perhaps a branch of the Turges family of Dorset which later in the century lived at Semley, and the Donheads, across the Wiltshire border from Shaftesbury, but neither seems to have been connected with their namesakes of Petworth in Sussex. The John Horsey who was sheriff of Wiltshire at the time of the election, although he shared arms and thus doubtless ancestry with his Dorset namesake, is not known to have stood in any other relationship with him: a minor gentleman, who lived at Marden south-east of Devizes, he may be thought unlikely to have intervened.[1]

With nothing to connect any of these people with Calne, the Member is to be sought closer to that town, either as a resident or in association with a local patron. His fellow, William Crowche, probably owed his election to Sir Henry Long* of Draycot Cerne, and the possibility that Long nominated both Members raises the question whether the surname 'Turgeys' may not be mythical. Although the name is unmistakably so written on the Crown Office list for this Parliament, that list survives only in a copy made in 1532; thus 'Turgeys' could have resulted from a misreading of 'Curteys', a name of much wider currency in Wiltshire and one which is found in connexion with the Long dynasty. Although none of the several men of the time named John Curteys can be so connected, one Henry Curteys was a collector, under Sir Henry Long and Sir Edward

Darrell*, of the benevolence of 1523, and Griffin Curteys, who was to sit for Calne in 1547, was in Long's service by 1542.[2]

[1] *CIPM Hen. VII*, ii. 845; Hutchins, *Dorset*, iv. 367; Leland, *Itin.* ed. Smith, iv. 108; *VCH Hants*, iv. 63; *Vis. Dorset* (Harl. Soc. xx), 58–59; *LP Hen. VIII*, i, iv, xix; C142/33/74; PCC 16 Thower; *Wilts. Arch. Soc. recs. br.* x. 41, 137, 153; Wilts. RO, archdeaconry of Salisbury wills 1584–90, f. 93; *Suss. Rec. Soc.* xliii. 311; lvi. 36; *Al. Cant.* i(4), 273; Hoare, *Wilts.* S. Damerham, 67. [2] *VCH Wilts.* vii. 58; viii. 173; Hoare, 60–61; *LP Hen. VIII*, i, iii, iv, vi, xv, xix; Foxe, *Acts and Mons.* v. 446; *Al. Ox.* i. 363; *G.I. Adm.* 7; List of mercers (T/S Mercers' Hall), 330.

T.F.T.B.

TURNER, William (by 1512–68), of Kew, Surr., Wells, Som. and London.

LUDGERSHALL 1547[1]

b. by 1512, s. of (?William) Turner of Morpeth, Northumb. *educ.* ?Morpeth, ?Newcastle-upon-Tyne; Pembroke, Camb. adm. 1526, BA 1529/30, fellow 1530, MA 1533; Bologna or Ferrara MD c.1542. *m.* by 1540, Jane, da. of George Auder of Cambridge, Cambs., ?wid. of one Cage of Pakenham, Suff., 1s. Peter† 2da.[2]

Jt. treasurer, Pembroke, Camb. 1532, sen. treasurer 1538; ?servant of William Claybrook, archdeacon of Worcester by 1533, of Bp. Fox of Hereford by 1535; clerk, the Prince's council chamber, Westminster 25 June 1543–*d.*; physician to Edward Seymour, Duke of Somerset 1547–52; prebendary of Botevant, York Feb. 1550–2; dean, Wells 24 Mar. 1551–53/54, June 1560–*d.*; rector, Wedmore, Som. 1563–*d.*[3]

William Turner was almost certainly a native of Morpeth. John Strype's belief that he was is borne out by his own references to 'Northumberland where I uttered my first infant wail' and to 'my people at Morpeth'. There had been Turners at Morpeth since the mid 14th century but of William Turner's immediate forbears nothing has been discovered beyond his own remarks suggesting that either his father or a kinsman was a tanner. Although not mentioned in the wills of either Sir Thomas Wentworth I*, 1st Lord Wentworth, who died in 1551, or of his father Sir Richard, Turner was a protégé of that family; in dedicating the second part of his *Herbal* to Sir Thomas Wentworth II*, 2nd Lord Wentworth, in 1562 he asked 'who hath deserved better to have my book of herbs to be given to him than he whose father with his yearly exhibition did help me, being student in Cambridge of physic and philosophy?', and in one of his treatises Turner mentions having seen wood spurge in the Wentworths' park at Nettlestead. It is not clear how Turner first came to the notice of the family, whose main estates lay in Lincolnshire and Suffolk, although it had branches in Yorkshire. Perhaps his advancement was in some way connected with that of Nicholas Ridley, a younger son of the Ridleys of Unthank Hall in western Northumberland, who after schooling at Newcastle-upon-Tyne was admitted to Pembroke Hall about ten years before Turner entered that college, where he was to become Ridley's pupil and friend.[4]

Before Ridley's return to Cambridge from the Continent in 1528–9 Turner was tutored by George Folbery, the instructor of the King's illegitimate son the Duke of Richmond. He also came under the influence of Hugh Latimer and the early reformers, with the result that his name was coupled by Strype with those of Ridley, Edmund Grindal, John Bradford and other 'eminent professors of sincere religion, that came up students from the northern parts'. *A Comparison betwene the Olde Learnynge and the Newe*, translated by Turner from the Latin, appeared in 1537, to be followed by a short religious book *Unio Dissidentium*, dedicated to Lord Wentworth, and an alphabetical catalogue of plants, *Libellus de re Herbaria*, in 1538. Although Turner is not known to have left the university before 1540, he may already have ventured further afield: in a letter to Cromwell dated only 12 Apr. but belonging to between 1530 and 1533, on his discussion of the King's marriage with German theologians, a William Turner referred to his service with the Cambridge civilian William Claybrook, reminded Cromwell of a promise made at Winchester, and asked for a benefice. Claybrook's membership of the court which annulled the marriage, and Turner's claim to have been 'writing continually in the King's cause of matrimony without any profit', make clear that it was the same man who, following Claybrook's death in 1534, entered the service of Edward Fox, bishop of Hereford, another leading figure in the divorce proceedings.[5]

On 15 Apr. 1536 Turner was ordained deacon at Lincoln and during the following year he received a licence to preach. It was perhaps his preaching which caused him to be brought before Stephen Gardiner, who abused him as a heretic 'because I wore a cloak and hat after the new fashion': this was the beginning of the feud between the two, who were soon to vilify each other in sermons and in print. Turner's later outspokenness against celibacy suggests that he had entertained hopes of a career in the Church but had been denied it by his marriage: perhaps, like John Foster II*, he married when the King was expected to allow clerical marriage and was caught by the royal change of mind. Turner thought himself endangered by Cromwell's fall and in June 1540 he and his wife passed through Calais on an extensive tour of the Continent. Turner visited northern Italy, where he studied medicine at Bologna and Ferrara, as well as Switzerland, the Rhineland and the Netherlands, meeting leading divines, philosophers and botanists, collecting specimens of plants and compiling the first part of the *Herbal* which he published on his return. While abroad he was appointed clerk of the Prince's chamber at Westminster (where the records of the duchy of Cornwall were kept), and it was perhaps as a mark of gratitude that he dedicated to the King *The Huntyng and fyndyng out of the Romysh Foxe . . . hyd among the bysshoppes of Englande*, published at Basle in September 1543 under the pseudonym of 'William Wraghton', and to Prince Edward the *Avium praecipuarum* published at Cologne in 1544. The second of these was a systematic attempt to identify the birds described by Aristotle and Pliny, but the first was less innocuous, with its warning to the temporal lords and the burgesses of Parliament against Gardiner, 'this lying limb of the devil': its date of publication shows that it was meant to be read in England before the opening of the final session (1544) of the Parliament then in being. A further diatribe against Gardiner in 1545, *The Rescuyng of the Romyshe Fox*, was followed by a proclamation on 8 July 1546 banning the English works of Turner and other reformers.[6]

On the King's death Turner was summoned back from the Continent by the Protector Somerset, whose physician he became. In 1551 he was to complain about his lack of freedom in Somerset's service —'For these three years and a half I have had no more liberty but bare three weeks to bestow upon the seeking of herbs and marking the places they do grow'—but it was to the Protector that he dedicated *The Names of Herbes in Greke, Latin, Englishe, Dutch and Frenche* (1548). Somerset was clearly responsible for Turner's election to the Parliament of 1547: that he sat for Ludgershall is known only from the list of Members revised in 1551, the return being lost, but in his assumed guise of the Hunter in *The Huntyng of the Romyshe Wolfe* (?1554) he claimed to have been a Member for five years, that is, throughout the Parliament. He had entered the Commons hoping that the Reformation would soon be completed, but he was to be disillusioned: 'In all my time (although there were some good Acts for the establishing of religion) yet there was always some that either sought their own private lucre as the noble, lordly and knightly sheepmasters did . . . or else sought very earnestly the King's profit wherein they intended always to have not the smallest part'. Turner may have had a personal interest in the Act establishing a deanery at Wells (1 Edw. VI, no. 16) which was passed in the first session, as he was later to be appointed to it, and he doubtless welcomed the Act allowing clerical marriage (2 and 3 Edw. VI, c.21). His plea for the distribution of chantry lands to the benefit of the Church, the advancement of education and the relief of the poor fell on deaf ears both in the House and outside. His disenchantment with Parliament and his colleagues there is voiced in *A New Book of Spirituall Physic* (1555). He derided the notion that learning was unnecessary for gentlemen, pointing out that they

> must oft times go to the Parliament and there they must entreat of matters concerning the glory of God and the commonwealth, and sometimes matters of heritage and of lands and goods are treated there. Sometime men are appeached of heresy and sometime of treason, so that they that are of Parliament are both counsellors and judges.
>
> If gentlemen remain wilfully ignorant and suffer themselves to be led whithersoever it shall please their blind guides to lead them, they may as well tarry at home as come to the parliament house to sit there, except they will either sleep or else tell the clock while learned men dispute the matters that are in contention, as I have seen some gentlemen of the first head do when I was a burgess of late of the Lower House.

As an example of the measures which engaged his fellow-Members' interest he cited one 'made for the destruction of rooks which destroyed the corn', that is, the Act for the maintenance and increase of tillage and corn (5 and 6 Edw. VI, c.5) passed during the last session. This allusion, coupled with the appearance of his name on the list of Members for that session, shows that he continued to sit in the House after his master's execution.[7]

Membership of Parliament had lessened neither Turner's addiction to theology nor his eagerness for advancement. In 1548 he attacked conservative doctrine in *A New Dialogue wherein is contayned an Examination of the Messe*, and later in the reign he refuted heresy in *A Preservative or triacle agaynst the poyson of Pelagius*. On 11 June 1549 he told Cecil that a kinsman of the Wentworths, Archbishop Holgate, had asked him to go to Yorkshire, but that he preferred Hampshire as the Protector had suggested, if a suitable living could be found. A week after the prorogation of the third session of the Parliament on 1 Feb. 1550 he received a prebend in York minster, but his translation to the north was brief: in the summer the Privy Council ordered the fellows of Oriel College, Oxford, to accept him as master, and in September he was in London petitioning for the presidency of Magdalen, if the archdeaconry of the East Riding should be bestowed elsewhere. At the end of November he wrote bitterly of his failure to secure either the mastership or the presidency and threatened to go to Germany to finish his *Herbal*. On 26 Mar. 1551 he was presented to the deanery of Wells and granted a licence for non-residence to enable him to preach the gospel.[8]

Turner was not ordained priest until 21 Dec. 1552, some eight months after the dissolution of Parliament. His title to the deanery was a shaky one.

His conservative precursor John Goodman had been deprived by Bishop Barlow after acquiring the prebend of Wiveliscombe, which was held to be incompatible with the deanery, but Turner knew that Cranmer doubted the legality of Goodman's deprivation. In May 1551 Turner was complaining of obstruction by the canons, who favoured Goodman, and in the following year Goodman brought an action against him in Chancery. The accession of Mary was followed by Barlow's deprivation for marriage and Goodman's reinstatement, but by then Turner had left England, perhaps as early as September 1553 with the Polish reformer John à Lasco, whom he had earlier introduced to Somerset. In Germany he resumed his botanical studies and fulminated against Catholicism; at home his writings were again outlawed on 13 June 1555.[9]

A New Book of Spirituall Physic was published on 20 Feb. 1555 but may have been written over a year earlier, as the ten noblemen to whom it was dedicated included the Dukes of Norfolk and Suffolk. After defending the divorce of Catherine of Aragon, Turner inveighed against his old enemy Gardiner and all priests: 'Whatsoever man ye shall see, with a great bald plate on his crown and wearing woman's clothes . . . take him for a poxy whoremaster of Rome'. Laymen who had waxed fat on the spoils of the Church fared little better; they were swollen with greed like victims of dropsy, a disease which occurred 'for the most part in the crowish start ups and not so much in the right and old nobility', although even Henry VIII had succumbed to it with his 'devilish and abominable Act of First Fruits and Tenths'. Turner's indignation was fanned by his recollection of how these grasping men had not scrupled 'to beg drink from such poor men as I am, when as I had but £74 to spend in the year, my first fruits yet unpaid'.[10]

On Elizabeth's accession Turner returned to England, where his writings had attracted wide attention. On 10 Sept. 1559 he preached at St. Paul's before a large congregation. Early in 1560 a commission under Archbishop Parker recommended his restoration to Wells, and in July the Queen confirmed his licence for non-residence. He was forced none the less to bring a civil action to secure his reinstatement, after which Goodman's further challenge in the courts was met by a royal order that Turner should enjoy the deanery pending a final decision in the case, which lapsed on Goodman's death in December 1562. Earlier in that year the second part of the *Herbal* was printed at Cologne; it set the seal on Turner's reputation as a botanist, even though it contained such invective as the attack upon 'those dark doctors . . . which suddenly

like to toadstools start up physicians within two or three years' study'.[11]

From the stronghold of the deanery Turner proclaimed his brand of Puritanism: he railed at the episcopacy, condemned an adulterer to do penance in a priest's cap and trained his dog to snatch cornered caps from the heads of prelates. His own bishop protested to Cecil and in March 1564 he was suspended for nonconformity, although allowed to retain the title of dean and the income of the office. On 26 Feb. 1567, burdened with 'continual sickness and weakness', he made his will, dividing the bulk of his goods between his wife and children. He died on 7 July 1568 at the Crutched Friars in London and was buried in St. Olave's, Hart Street, where he was commemorated in a tablet set up by his widow, who became the wife of Richard Cox, bishop of Ely. The third part of the *Herbal*, with a dedication to the Queen, appeared in the year of Turner's death, but the survey of the fishes of the British Isles which was announced in its preface did not survive the author.[12]

[1] Hatfield 207. [2] Date of birth estimated from education. *DNB*; *PCC* 14 Babington, 4 Butts; C. E. Raven, *Eng. Naturalists from Neckham to Ray*, 52–53. [3] *Al. Cant.* i(4), 277; *LP Hen. VIII*, ix, x; information from Dr. G. Haslam; Le Neve, *Fasti*, iii (1854), 176; Strype, *Cranmer*, i. 394; *CPR, 1550–3*, p. 51; *1560–3*, p. 575; P. M. Hembry, *Bps. Bath and Wells, 1540–1640*, p. 122; *HMC 10th Rep.* iii. 240. [4] *PCC* 14 Babington; Raven, 49; W. Turner, *Libellus de re Herberia* (1538)—as with nearly all Turner's publications the pagination varies from volume to volume so references are only given to the work; *Avium praecipuarum* (1544); *Facsimiles* (Ray Soc. 1965), passim; Strype, *Cranmer*, i. 394; Hodgson, *Northumb.* i. 458–61. [5] Strype, *Parker*, i. 13; *Grindal*, 7; *Annals Ref.* i(1), 199; *LP Hen. VIII*, ix, x. [6] Raven, 72, 86; *Avium praecipuarum; A new bk. of Spirituall Physic* (1555); *Tudor R. Proclamations* ed. Hughes and Larkin, i. 373–6; J. F. M. Hoeniger, *The Development of Nat. Hist. in Tudor Eng.* (Folger booklets on Tudor and Stuart civilization, 1969), 32; G. E. Fussell, 'William Turner, the father of Eng. botany', *Estate Mag.* xxxvii. 367–70; *LP Hen. VIII*, xxi; M. L. Bush, *Govt. Pol. Somerset*, 104. [7] Bush, 3, 66, 68–69, 104–8; R. Pineas, 'William Turner and Ref. Politics', *Bibliothèque d'Humanisme et Renaissance*, xxxvii. 193–200; Hatfield 207; Raven, 96–110; W. K. Jordan, *Edw. VI*, i. 135; Strype, *Eccles. Memorials*, iii(1), 235; Turner, *The Huntyng of the Romyshe Wolfe* (?1554). [8] Jordan, i. 332, 341; ii. 332–4, 368–70; *CSP Dom.* 1547–80, pp. 18, 29, 31; *APC*, iii. 63; *CPR, 1560–3*, pp. 51, 161. [9] Strype, *Cranmer*, ii(2), 62; *VCH Som.* ii. 37–38; *CSP Dom.* 1547–80, pp. 32–33; Hembry, 118, 121–2; C. H. Garrett, *Marian Exiles*, 314–15. [10] Foxe, *Acts and Mons.* vii. 127. [11] Strype, *Annals Ref.* i(1), 199; *HMC 10th Rep.* iii. 233, 240; *VCH Som.* ii. 39–40; Raven, 115. [12] *CPR*, 1566–9, p. 79; 1569–72, p. 2; *PCC* 14 Babington.

T.F.T.B./A.D.K.H.

TURPIN, George (1529–83), of Knaptoft, Leics. and London.

LEICESTERSHIRE 1554 (Nov.), 1563, 1572

b. 1529, posth. s. of John Turpin (*d.*18 Jan. 1529) of Knaptoft by Rose, da. of Richard Ruthall of Moulsoe, Bucks. *m.* Frances, da. of (Sir) Robert Lane* of Horton, Northants. 1s. William† 1da. *suc.* bro. 1551. Kntd. 21 Aug. 1566.[1]

Commr. of oyer and terminer, Leics. 1554, eccles. causes, dioceses of Lincoln and Peterborough 1571, Lincoln 1575, musters, Leicester 1573, 1577, 1580; j.p. Leics. 1558/59, q. 1561–*d.*; steward, crown lands, Leics. 1561–9; sheriff, Warws. and Leics. 1565–6, Leics. 1574–5.[2]

The Turpins had been established at Knaptoft for nearly a century since acquiring the estate by marriage with an heiress: they had enclosed and improved the village and become prominent in the county. George Turpin's father also held lands elsewhere in the midlands, and his mother, a niece of Thomas Ruthall, bishop of Durham, had brought a substantial dowry with her.[3]

Turpin's early life is obscure, but on the pardon roll of 1554 he is described as 'alias of London', and his appointment to the commission of oyer and terminer in that year implies that he had received some legal training. He had succeeded his brother as head of the family in 1551 and his marriage to the daughter of a Northamptonshire man may have followed shortly afterwards. He also enjoyed influential connexions within his own county: Thomas Farnham* was to bequeath him, as a near and very dear kinsman, some personal property, and through Farnham and his cousin Francis Farnham* these connexions extended to the Caves and the Nevilles of Holt, while Nicholas Beaumont†, with whom Turpin shared the supervision of the estate which Thomas Farnham left to his daughter Catherine, remained an associate until the two men quarrelled dramatically. It was presumably on the strength of their support that Turpin achieved the junior knighthood of the shire in the third Marian Parliament, despite his relative youth.[4]

Turpin's active public career under Elizabeth was to include Membership of two Parliaments and varied service in his county. He died in 1583.

[1] Nichols, Leics. iv. 225; C142/49/2, 5, 59, 103/26. [2] CPR, 1554-5, p. 151; 1569-72, pp. 17, 277-8; 1572-5, p. 552; HMC 8th Rep. pt. 1 (1881), 416-17. [3] C142/49/2. [4] CPR, 1553-4, p. 415; 1558-60, p. 279; PCC 24 Street; Quorndon Recs. ed. Farnham, 253 seq.

S.M.T.

TUSSER (TYSSARD), Andrew (by 1524–59 or later) of London and Frisby-on-the-Wreak, Leics.

MITCHELL   1554 (Apr.), 1554 (Nov.)

b. by 1524, 2nd s. of William Tusser of London and Rivenhall, Essex by 1st w. Dorothy, da. of Thomas Smith of Rivenhall; bro. of Clement*.[1]

Andrew Tusser was evidently a lawyer, but where he received his training is unknown. As a younger son he received only 40 marks under his father's will of 1545 and his prospects of advancement were probably as poor as those for the other members of his family until the accession of Mary. In the spring of 1554 he entered Parliament with his brother Clement, who may have introduced him to Mitchell, and in the following autumn, when Clement sat for a different constituency, he reappeared for the same borough. Tusser was not himself among the

Members found absent when the House was called early in 1555 but he acted as attorney for Edmund Plowden, one of those proceeded against in the King's bench for this dereliction. If Tusser had hoped to find a place in 1555, he was to be disappointed, for he did not sit again. It may have been he, or one of his brothers, who by having Thomas Mynd* arrested during this Parliament secured a mention in the Journal. This breach of privilege, if committed by an ex-Member, would assuredly have told against his subsequent election, as doubtless did his Catholicism after the death of Mary.[2]

In 1556 Tusser and his brother Thomas were accused in the court of requests of depriving Margaret Bishop of property in Frisby-on-the-Wreak. Whatever the outcome of the case, Tusser continued to live at Frisby, and in 1559 it was as a resident there that he sued out a general pardon. This is the last glimpse we have of him: he may have been dead or have left Frisby by 1571 when its inhabitants were assessed for subsidy.[3]

[1] Date of birth estimated from younger brother Thomas's, DNB (Tusser, Thomas). Vis. Essex (Harl. Soc. xiii), 117; PCC 7 Coode. [2] PCC 7 Coode; KB27/1180; CJ, i. 44. [3] Req.2/25/90; CPR, 1558-60, p. 205; E179/134/204.

J.J.G.

TUSSER (TYSSARD), Clement (by 1520–61 or later), of Rivenhall, Essex.

MITCHELL   1554 (Apr.)
CAMELFORD   1554 (Nov.)

b. by 1520, 1st s. of William Tusser of London and Rivenhall by 1st w. Dorothy, da. of Thomas Smith of Rivenhall; bro. of Andrew*. *educ.* Strand Inn, adm. by 1541. *m.* Ursula Pittes of London, 2s. 1da. *suc.* fa. by 26 Mar. 1550.[1]

Coroner, Essex by Dec. 1557–61 or later.[2]

Clement Tusser's brother Thomas claimed in his *Five Hundreth Pointes of Good Husbandry* that he was 'of lineage good, of gentle blood', but the family does not seem to have been of much account in Essex until the 16th century. Its fortunes took an upward turn on the marriage of William Tusser with a sister of Clement Smith* through whom the Tussers made connexion with the Seymours. Clement Tusser may have been intended to follow his father as an officer of the central administration. He received a legal education at one of the inns of chancery, but evidently neither his training nor his connexions led to employment in the capital, although they were to prove their worth in a series of disputes in which he and his father became involved: in 1541 John Gates* tried to impose his rights at Rivenhall and in the trouble that followed Tusser was abducted by several of Gates's men.[3]

The fall of the Protector, and the death not long

afterwards of Clement Smith, probably ruined Tusser's prospect of advancement while Edward VI remained King, but with the accession of Mary his Catholic background ceased to be a handicap. He was returned successively for two Cornish boroughs: on the first occasion he sat with his younger brother Andrew and took the senior place, but on the second when both were again elected, they sat for different boroughs and Tusser had to be content with the second seat. Although Tusser was a stranger to Cornwall, he had a cousin in the duchy who lived variously at Truro (not far from Mitchell) and St. Mabyn (not far from Camelford). Yet Tusser probably owed his nomination to an Essex neighbour, Sir Edward Waldegrave*, who although he had relinquished the receiver-generalship of the duchy to John Cosworth*, still wielded influence in Cornwall. Tusser did not sit again but he, or one of his brothers, may have been the 'Tussard' who had Thomas Mynd* arrested during the Parliament of 1555 and was accordingly ordered by the House to pay the serjeant's expenses and to withdraw the action. This breach of privilege, if committed by an ex-Member, would assuredly have told against his subsequent election, as doubtless did Tusser's faith after the death of Mary.[4]

During the late 1550s Tusser was active in local affairs and it was 'in consideration of his service' that in the spring of 1558 he obtained the reversion of a lease at Tollesbury, Essex. He sued out a pardon at the accession of Elizabeth and two years later he received a confirmation of his family's arms. The last certain trace found of him dates from the summer of 1561, when he was still active as coroner. He was not assessed towards the subsidy at Riven-hall in 1567, but seven years later his Cornish cousin left Tusser £20 under his will, and as he did not change this bequest before his own death in 1574, Tusser may have outlived him.[5]

[1] Date of birth estimated from first reference. *Vis. Essex* (Harl. Soc. xiii), 117, 174; PCC 7 Coode. [2] *CPR*, 1557–8, p. 324. [3] *Last Will of Thomas Tusser*, ed. Clark, 11; *DNB* (Tusser, Thomas); Req.2/3/53; St.Ch.2/6/8–16. [4] C219/23/30; *CJ*, i.44; F. Rose-Troup, *Western Rebellion*, 420–1; PCC 19 Langley. [5] *CPR*, 1557–8, p. 296; 1558–60, p. 198; 1560–3, p. 202; *Grantees of Arms* (Harl. Soc. lxvi), 259; E179/110/419, m. 2v; PCC 19 Langley.

J.J.G.

TWYNE, John (1507/8–81), of Canterbury, and Preston, nr. Wingham, Kent.

CANTERBURY 1553 (Oct.), 1554 (Apr.)

b. 1507/8, 1st s. of William Twyne of Bullington, Hants. *educ.* Oxf. BCL 31 Jan. 1525. *m.* (1) 1525, Alice (*d.*20 Oct. 1567), da. of William Peper of Canterbury, 4s. 3da.; (2) 14 Nov. 1568, Margaret Carpenter of Canterbury.[1]

Common councilman, Canterbury 1539–47, 1548–50, sheriff 1544–5, alderman 1550–62, mayor 1553–4.[2]

In 1538 John Twyne of Canterbury, gentleman, was admitted to the freedom of the city by right of his marriage to a freeman's daughter. As she was to die in October 1567 in the 43rd year of the marriage, this must have taken place in the year in which Twyne became a bachelor of civil law. The marriage debarred Twyne from the priesthood which might otherwise have followed his ordination as acolyte in 1521, and he remained in this minor order during his 16 years' residence, probably as a schoolmaster, in St. Augustine's abbey, Canterbury, and his 20 years as headmaster of the King's School founded in 1542. Successful and prosperous in pedagogy, Twyne made his chief reputation as antiquarian and archaeologist; his *De Rebus Albionicis*, edited by his son in 1590, has been called 'perhaps the earliest attempt at anything like a scientific inquiry into the origins of British history'.[3]

Twyne's civic career, which began after the dissolution of the abbey, was a chequered one. Dismissed from the common council in November 1547, he was reinstated in the following August and in July 1550 elected alderman. On 18 May 1553 the mayor of Canterbury was ordered by the Privy Council to send him up; his offence is not revealed, but the prominence he was soon to attain suggests that he may have championed Mary's claim to the throne. The first year of her reign saw him elected mayor and twice returned to Parliament. His fellow-Member, William Coppyn, was an ex-mayor and former doorkeeper of the abbey. No payment of parliamentary wages to either of them was entered in the city's accounts, but on 10 Apr. 1554 the burmote agreed that a sum of £12 'before this time delivered to Mr. Twyne and Mr. Coppyn . . . should by writ be levied of the commonalty and repaid again into the chamber'. Between the two Parliaments Canterbury held firm during Wyatt's rebellion—a service recorded to Twyne's credit, alongside his ability to make his pupils speak Latin, in the epitaph which he almost certainly wrote for himself —and this may have prompted the instruction given to him and Coppyn on their return to Westminster to 'make suit for the Queen's park in the name of the whole commonalty'.[4]

Twyne was not to sit in the Commons again and he appears to have received no preferment from the crown unless he was the John Twyne, BCL, admitted to the prebend of Llandygwy in Brecon on 3 Nov. 1558. Yet it was probably not only his 'riot and drunkenness' and his holding of civic office which incurred Archbishop Parker's displeasure at the visitation of 1560. His vacating of the headship in 1560 was followed in May 1562 by his dismissal as alderman and another appearance before the Privy

Council. Two of the other five aldermen ejected with him were known enemies of the Elizabethan settlement and Twyne himself was described as 'a very conjurer'. How far he had retracted the alleged 'heresy' of the lectures he had once delivered at Cranmer's direction it is hard to say, but his aspersions on Henry VIII, Foxe and Parker could not have helped, even though he had given manuscripts to the archbishop's library, some of them from the abbey, and was in 1560 keeper of one of the archiepiscopal woods. By 1568 Twyne was living at Preston, near Wingham, Kent, although he probably retained the property in St. Paul's parish, Canterbury, which he had bought in 1539. An autograph will in Latin of 27 Mar. 1580 is in the archives of Corpus Christi College, Oxford. He was buried in St. Paul's on 30 Nov. 1581.[5]

[1] He described himself as 58 in Sept. 1566, C. E. Woodruff and H. J. Cape, *King's School, Canterbury*, 60, although in January 1576 he claimed to be over 74, Lansd. 21, f. 111. *Vis. Kent* (Harl. Soc. lxxv), 41; Emden, *Biog. Reg. Univ. Oxf. 1501–40*, pp. 582–3; *Reg. St. Peter's, Canterbury*, ed. Cowper, 76; *Canterbury Mar. Lic.* ed. Cowper. [2] Canterbury burmote bk. passim. [3] *Freemen of Canterbury*, ed. Cowper, col. 159; Wood, *Ath. Ox.* ed. Bliss, i. 463; Emden, 582; Woodruff and Cape, 56–76; R. B. Ferguson, 'John Twyne: a Tudor humanist and the problem of legend', *Jnl. of Brit. Studies*, ix(1), 24–44. [4] Canterbury burmote bk. ff. 37, 41, 83v, 84v; *APC*, iv. 105; *DNB* repeats the error made by Hasted, *Kent*, iv. 53 that Twyne had sat in the Parliament of March 1553; W. Somner, *Antiqs. Canterbury*, i. app. 70. [5] Emden, 582–3; T. Tanner, *Bibl. Britannica-Hibernica*, 729; Canterbury burmote bk. ff. 145, 151; *APC*, vii. 105; *LP Hen. VIII*, vii, xiv; M. R. James, *Cat. Mss Corpus Christi Coll. Camb.* i. pp. xxii, 358; Lambeth Pal. lib. ct. rolls 1401; *Reg. St. Paul's, Canterbury* ed. Cowper, 205.

H.M.

TWYNEHO (TWINIO, TWYNE), Edmund (by 1518–77), of Watton at Stone, Herts.

LICHFIELD 1547[1]
OLD SARUM 1554 (Apr.)

b. by 1518; poss. bro. of William†. *m.* by 1555, Elizabeth, da. of Thomas Munden of Watton at Stone, wid. of Robert Burgoyne (*d.*1546), of Sutton, Beds., Watton at Stone and London.[2]

Bailiff, Hardwick and eight other manors, Herefs. 1546; servant of the Lords Paget 1546–70 or later; surveyor, duchy of Lancaster, south parts 28 Feb. 1548–*d.*; j.p. Herts. 1561, q. 1562–*d.*; commr. benevolence Herts. 1564.[3]

The origins of Edmund Twyneho are obscure, but he almost certainly came of a minor family in the west country, a member of which, seated at Shipton Sollars, Gloucestershire, married into a Hertfordshire family after Twyneho's own marriage with an heiress of the same county. His career seems to have begun in the service of Burton abbey, Staffordshire, before its dissolution in 1539; the Exchequer later paid him a pension of 100s. for an office he had once held there, and it was in 1546, when Sir William Paget acquired much of the abbey's property, that Twyneho entered Paget's service. In 1545 he and George Tresham* bought various properties in the midlands from the crown for £868: Tresham was evidently the principal in the transaction, for he kept the lands not sold immediately, and Twyneho's role in it may have been connected with his skill as a surveyor.[4]

Twyneho's return to the first Parliament of Edward VI's reign was doubtless the work of Paget. The city of Lichfield enlisted Paget's aid to secure a charter of incorporation when its form of government was threatened by the abolition of the guilds, but before the charter was granted in 1548 the city was re-enfranchised. Both the Members then elected were dependants of Paget, and both obtained surveyorships in the duchy of Lancaster during his chancellorship. Although nothing has come to light about Twyneho's part in the Commons, he doubtless supported the private Act (3 and 4 Edw. VI, no. 25) of the third session enabling his master to acquire the churchyard at West Drayton in exchange for other property. By the second Parliament of the reign Paget was under a cloud and Twyneho is not known to have been re-elected, but with Paget's recovery under Mary he reappeared in the Parliament of April 1554, in which his master was one of the government's spokesmen in the Lords. Twyneho's fellow-Member Richard Cupper was another of Paget's entourage, and it appears that they were intruded at Old Sarum, their names being added to the indenture in a different hand and Twyneho's inserted over an erasure.[5]

Twyneho's marriage brought him a house and position in Hertfordshire and later a place on the bench there, but it was also to bring him some trouble: his wife's first husband had been an auditor in the court of augmentations and the collection of money due to him was to vex her and Twyneho. This was offset by the smoothness of his relations with Paget, whom he continued to serve at a fee of 100s. a year and under whose will, of which he was an overseer, he received a covered gilt bowl. That was not the end of his service with the family, the last reference found to him in its papers coming in 1570 when he surveyed several manors in Staffordshire. He was presumably misnamed 'John Twyneo, esquire' when described by Bishop Bentham of Lincoln as a 'hinderer of religion' in 1564, there being no man of that christian name then serving as a justice for Hertfordshire, but if he was a Catholic he was not removed from the bench where he continued to serve until his death. He died at some time after Christmas 1576 when his last quarterly fee was paid by the duchy of Lancaster, and probably by 25 Apr. 1577 when his surveyorship was granted to another. If he made a will it has not been traced, and it is not known whether he had offspring.[6]

[1] Hatfield 207. [2] Date of birth estimated from service to Burton abbey. *CPR*, 1555–7, p. 63; *Vis. Beds.* (Harl. Soc. xix), 87; PCC 14 Alen; *Wm. Salt Arch. Soc.* xii. 257. [3] *LP Hen. VIII*, xxi; Staffs. RO, E.P.C.2/2, no. 6, f. 1; Somerville, *Duchy*, i. 447; *Rep. R. Comm. of 1552* (Archs. of Brit. Hist. and Culture iii), 105–6; *CPR*, 1560–3, pp. 438, 577; 1563–6, pp. 23, 123; 1569–72, p. 225. [4] *Vis. Glos.* (Harl. Soc. xxi), 262–3; *Vis. Herts.* (Harl. Soc. xxii), 11; *Vis. Som.* ed. Metcalfe, 132; Dugdale, *Monasticon Anglicanum*, iii. 34–35; Staffs. RO, EPC2/2, no. 6, f. 1; information from C. J. Harrison; *LP Hen. VIII*, xx. [5] J. C. Wedgwood, *Staffs. Parlt. Hist.* (Wm. Salt Arch. Soc.), i. 327; C219/22/91; *Wilts. N. and Q.* viii. 392–5, 483; *VCH Wilts.* viii. 104. [6] *VCH Herts.* iii. 162–3; W. C. Richardson, *Ct. Augmentations*, 55; *CPR*, 1555–7, p. 63; *Cam. Misc.* ix(3), 30; xxv. 139; PCC 27 Chayre; Somerville, i. 447; Staffs. RO, EPC2/2, no. 20, f. 54; *Staffs. Rec. Soc.* 1939, pp. 153–5, 157.

E.McI.

TYLCOCK (TYLLOCK, TRILLCOCK), William (1503/4-78), of Oxford.

OXFORD 1554 (Nov.)

b. 1503/4. *m.* Marian, at least 2da.[1]
Chamberlain, Oxford 1542–3, bailiff 1545–6, 1548–9, subsidy collector 1547, assistant to mayor 1554, coroner 1556, 1568, mayor 1556–7, 1560–1, 1568–9, 1575–6, alderman 1557–62, by 1574–*d.*[2]

William Tylcock's origins and parentage are unknown. No one of the name was assessed for subsidy at Oxford in 1524 or 1525 and Tylcock himself was over 30 when he was admitted to the freedom as a baker in 1536–7.[3]

Tylcock was one of ten freemen authorized to sell plate and purchase lands on behalf of the city in 1550 and in the following year he shared the oversight of two fairs with John Wayte, later his fellow-Member. Among similar services, in November 1551 Tylcock was commissioned with Edward Glynton* to negotiate a renewal of the city's charter and in 1554 he was appointed with Wayte to instruct counsel in a suit between the city and George Owen*. As mayor, he presided at the council on 15 Apr. 1557 when Wayte, gaoled for embezzlement, made his submission. He was among the richer citizens, being assessed for subsidy on goods worth £16 in 1543, 1544 and 1547, £12 in 1550, £15 in 1551 and £20 in 1559.[4]

Tylcock's return to Mary's third Parliament was a natural step in his civic career. One of the Members found absent without leave when the House was called early in 1555, he was informed against for this dereliction in the King's bench during the Easter term. He was distrained 40s. on failing to appear, secured a postponement of his case in 1556 and was fined 53s. 4d. in the Hilary term of 1558, when John Barton* and Richard Williams* stood surety for him. These proceedings did not prevent his being elected mayor for the first time in September 1556.[5]

Tylcock was often engaged in more personal disputes, which may have helped to prevent his re-election to Parliament. In 1545 he had been summoned before the city council with William Frere,

father of Edward Frere*, and Maurice Vaughan, all of whom were bound over for £20 each and ordered to submit their quarrels to arbitration. Soon after the end of his first term as mayor, he was sued in the court of requests by Philip Forman for alleged abuse of his authority. Under the terms of the bequest made by Thomas Mallinson* to the city, Tylcock was to have the use of the sum of £200 for ten years. The money was to be used for 'setting the poor people of the city at work' in the clothing industry and Tylcock was also to take over Mallinson's three apprentices. Apart from this no indication has been found that Tylcock, described as a gentleman in the records of the King's bench, followed any other trade than that of baker, save that, like many other leading Oxford freemen, he owned a brewhouse. Mallinson and Tylcock quarrelled shortly before the former's death. Tylcock was obliged to bring a chancery suit to recover the sum of £76 13s. 4d. owed to Mallinson. Later the city itself took action against Tylcock, arranging on 7 Sept. 1562 for a letter of attorney to be made out against him concerning the bequest.[6]

Disgrace had already overtaken Tylcock, 'sometime alderman', since on 19 June 1562 he had been expelled from the council for supporting John Cumber in his disobedience. Tylcock must have hastened to make his peace, for on 16 Sept. it was agreed that his readmittance should be discussed again at Christmas. He had returned to civic life by 1568, when he again became mayor. He continued as a leading citizen for the next ten years and was sent to speak before the Privy Council in October 1574, when the city was at odds with the university. Wood records that Tylcock was involved in an extension of this dispute at the end of his life, when he and Ralph Flaxney* were pronounced contumacious and Richard Williams was excommunicated for refusing to take the annual oath to the vice-chancellor.[7]

Tylcock died on 22 June 1578 and was buried on the same day in the church of St. Thomas. In his will, made on 25 Mar. 1577 and proved on 7 Nov. 1578, he laid down that his widow and executrix should cover the grave 'with such stones as I have already for that purpose provided' within six months of his burial: she was to apply one half year's rent of his brewhouse by the Castle Gate to this use. She was to receive a life interest in this brewhouse, a meadow behind Osney and a farm at Combe. Various kinsmen were remembered, including two men described as the testator's sons-in-law. The city of Oxford was to receive a silver gilt salt and Richard Williams a scarlet cloak.[8]

[1] Aged 74 at death according to MI, *Antiqs. Oxf.* iii. (Oxf. Hist.

Soc. xxxvii), 193. Bodl. wills Oxon. 186, f. 23. ² *Oxf. Recs.* 167, 178, 192, 219, 261, 268, 280, 289, 293, 325, 357, 376; E179/162/244; *CPR*, 1566–9, p. 316. ³ *Antiqs. Oxf.* iii. 193; *Oxf. Recs.* 149. ⁴ *Oxf. Recs.* 203–4, 209–10, 222, 228, 264; *Oxon. Rec. Soc.* i. 76; E179/162/224, 229, 261, 282, 289, 318. ⁵ KB27/1176–7, 1185. ⁶ *Oxf. Recs.* 149, 176, 293; Req. 2/133/21; C1/1475/39; Bodl. wills Oxon. 181, ff. 199–200v. ⁷ *Oxf. Recs.* 289, 294, 325, 357, 375–6; PCC 23 Sheffelde; *APC*, viii. 305; ix. 352–3; A. Wood, *Hist. and Antiqs. Oxf. Univ.* (1796), 186. ⁸ *Antiqs. Oxf.* iii. 193, 261; Bodl. wills Oxon. 186, f. 23.

T.F.T.B.

TYLDESLEY, Thurstan (by 1495–1554), of Tyldesley and Wardley Hall, nr. Worsley, Lancs.

LANCASHIRE 1547

b. by 1495, 1st s. of Thomas Tyldesley of Tyldesley and Wardley Hall by Anne, da. of Sir Alexander (?William) Radcliffe of Ordsall. *m.* (1) Parnell, da. of Geoffrey Shakerley of Shakerley, at least 2s. 1da.; (2) Jane, ?da. of Sir Richard Langton of Newton, ?wid. of Thomas Rigmayden of Wedacre, 1s. 3da. *suc.* fa. 1495.[1]

Commr. subsidy, Lancs. 1512, 1523, ?1543, relief 1550; other commissions 1526–*d.*; j.p. 1523–*d.*; receiver, 3rd Earl of Derby's lands in Cheshire, Cumb., Flints., I. o. M., Lincs., Westmld., Yorks. and the Welsh marches by 1523–*d.*, receiver-gen. I. o. M. by 1532; trustee, Manchester g.s. 1525; dep. master forester, Amounderness and dep. keeper, Myerscough by 1531–*d.*[2]

The Tyldesley family had been seated at Tyldesley since the early 13th century and had acquired Wardley Hall about a hundred years later. Thurstan Tyldesley is said to have rebuilt Wardley Hall during the reign of Edward VI. As his father before him, he entered the service of the Stanley earls of Derby. He is first noticed as the earl's receiver in several counties in 1523, during the minority of the 3rd Earl, but his will shows that he had been in the family's service since 1516 or earlier. He served under the earl's command in the suppression of the Pilgrimage of Grace, when he led a band of 224 of his own tenants. In September 1537 the earl told Cromwell, that he had left his servant Thurstan Tyldesley in London to be his suitor in various causes and asked the minister to be Tyldesley's 'good lord' in a dispute with Sir Richard Brereton. Six months later Tyldesley was still, or again, about Cromwell, seeking the stewardship of the lands of Whalley abbey for his master: either for his own purpose or else the earl's he had compiled a survey of the abbey's property shortly after its suppression. His application in 1538 for one of the abbey's manors failed but in 1540 he bought some of its lands, and three years later he acted as feoffee to Robert Holt of Studley, Lancashire, with regard to other former Whalley lands.[3]

Tyldesley's election as a knight for Lancashire in 1547 was presumably sponsored by the Earl of Derby, with a kinsman and neighbour of his, Sir Alexander Radcliffe, the sheriff, acting as inter-

mediary. Nothing is known of his part in the work of the House but it is likely that he followed his master in opposing the bill for uniformity during its passage through Parliament in the winter of 1548–9. (His brother Richard had been a Carthusian at Sheen.) His name appears incorrectly on the list of Members revised for the final session in 1552 as 'Tristram Tyldesley miles'. He had made his will on 1 Sept. 1547, presumably in anticipation of being returned to Parliament, providing for his wife and family and naming his wife and son Edward executors and the Earl of Derby and Sir William Paget among the supervisors. He confirmed the will on 24 June 1552 and died two years later. An inventory of his goods was taken on 4 July 1554 and his son and heir Thomas had licence to enter on his inheritance in the following December.[4]

¹ Date of birth estimated from fa.'s death. *Vis. Lancs.* (Chetham Soc. lxxxi), 44; (lxxxii), 101; J. B. Watson, 'Lancs. gentry 1529–58' (London Univ. M.A. thesis, 1959), 517. ² *LP Hen. VIII*, iii; Watson, 518; *Statutes*, iii. 87; *Lancs. and Cheshire Rec. Soc.* xxxv. 7, 177–8; lxvii. 117; *CPR*, 1553, p. 360; Somerville, *Duchy*, i. 506–7; R. Cunliffe Shaw, *R. Forest of Lancaster*, 198, 200; NRA 13506, p. 185. ³ Chetham Soc. xix. 51n; Watson, 117–18, 123; *LP Hen. VIII*, iii, xi, xiii, xv, xvi, xviii, add. ⁴ *LJ*, ii. 80; C. Haigh, *Ref. and Resistance in Tudor Lancs.*, 65; Hatfield 207; Chetham Soc. xxxiii. 97–114; *CPR*, 1554–5, p. 1.

A.D.

TYNDALE, Thomas (1528/33–71), of London, Ludgrave, Mdx. and Thornbury, Glos.

MARLBOROUGH 1554 (Apr.)

b. 1528/33, 1st s. of Edward Tyndale of Pull Court, Worcs. ?by 2nd w. Joan, da. of William Lawrence. ?*educ.* Clifford's Inn. *m.* by Feb. 1556, Avice, da. of William Body of London, prob. 2s. 1da. *suc.* fa. by 1546.[1]

Auditor, ct. augmentations, N. Wales ?1551–4; j.p.q. Glos. 1561–*d.*[2]

Thomas Tyndale was under age at the death of his father, who had served both the crown and the abbey of Tewkesbury and who lived at Pull Court, near Upton-on-Severn, a property which he had leased from the abbey. The elder Tyndale's brother William was the translator and martyr. Of Thomas Tyndale's early career nothing has come to light save his brief tenure of the auditorship of North Wales for the court of augmentations. This office he had presumably acquired on the death of his brother-in-law John Perte* in or shortly before 1551, and the relatively small annuity of £50 granted to him when the court was dissolved three years later thus answered to his recent recruitment.[3]

Tyndale's election to the Parliament of April 1554 may not have been unconnected with that reform. Although the principle of compensation for loss of office had already been conceded, it was not until 4 May 1554, the day before the Parliament ended, that the chancellor was empowered to take surrender of the offices concerned and to fix the amounts to be paid for them. Like his fellow-auditor Matthew Colthurst and Colthurst's deputy Henry Leke, Tyndale may have reckoned that a seat in the Commons would strengthen his hand if it came to bargaining. He also resembled Colthurst and Leke in sitting for a Wiltshire borough and in almost certainly owing his nomination to William Herbert I*, 1st Earl of Pembroke. He was linked with Pembroke through the earl's follower William Clerke*, whose marriage to the widowed Anne Perte made him Tyndale's brother-in-law. Pembroke for his part may well have persuaded Marlborough to elect Tyndale and his other nominee Owen Gwyn by promising that they would forgo their wages, something which Tyndale's domicile in London, reflected in his recent general pardon, would have cost him little to concede.[4]

Tyndale was not to be re-elected under Mary or to be employed by her government, perhaps because of the Protestantism which he was to manifest in his will and which may have been strengthened by his uncle's example. At the beginning of Elizabeth's reign he was living at Ludgrave in Middlesex, on an estate formerly held by John Perte and since his death acquired by the Earl of Pembroke and William Clerke, but he soon returned to Gloucestershire, where between 1565 and 1568 he acquired Eastwood Park at Thornbury and other properties; his standing in the shire was recognized by his appointment to the bench. It was, however, in London that Tyndale died on 28 Apr. 1571. From his will of the previous day, in which he commended his soul to Christ 'by whose death and passion I only trust to be saved and by none other means', it appears that his wife Avice and their son Edward were already buried at Thornbury, where he and his daughter Elizabeth were to be laid with them under a single gravestone, and that his sole surviving child was the Thomas Tyndale, 'now abiding beyond the seas', for whom he provided a yearly allowance until he should succeed to the lands at the age of 30. Tyndale's 'mothers in law' Joan Tyndale and Agnes Body, his brothers and sisters and a string of nieces and nephews were given legacies ranging from £10 to £100, and £10 was to go to the poor and £20 to repair the highways. The executors were Tyndale's brothers-in-law William Clerke and Richard Trotman, his 'trusty servant, John Davies, and Richard Stevens of Eastington. Originally buried in St. Gabriel's, Fenchurch Street, Tyndale's body was exhumed for reburial at Thornbury.[5]

[1] Presumed to be of age at election; less than 12 on 17 Aug. 1540, PCC 21 Alen. Rudder, *Glos*. 756; B. W. Greenfield, *Gen. Tyndale Fam*. unpaginated; PCC 10 Wrastley, 19 Holney. [2] W. C. Richard-

son, *Ct. Augmentations*, 258, 280; *CPR*, 1560-3, p. 437; 1563-6, p. 22; 1569-72, p. 225. [3] B. W. Greenfield, *Notes rel. to Fam. of Tyndale*, 1-6; *VCH Worcs*. iv. 47; *DNB* (Tyndale, William). [4] Richardson, 254; *CPR*, 1554-5, p. 355. [5] *CPR*, 1558-60, p. 150; 1563-6, p. 224; *Vis. Glos*. (Harl. Soc. xxi), 263; PCC 19 Holney; Mill Stephenson, *Mon. Brasses*, 155; Rudder, 756.

T.F.T.B.

TYNDALE, William (by 1512-58), of Bristol, Glos.

BRISTOL   1558*

b. by 1512. *m*. (1) by 1545, Maud; (2) by 1547, Jane; at least 1s. 2da.[1]
     Sheriff, Bristol 1547-8, alderman by 1550-*d*., auditor chamberlain's accts. 1551-2.[2]

William Tyndale was born in Lincolnshire but settled in Bristol where following his admission as a freeman in 1538-9 he combined trade in wool with a civic career. Although not known to have been an official of the staple, he was responsible in 1533 for the seizure of Gascon wine for the non-payment of customs at Bristol. During the 1530s and 1540s he carried out numerous tasks on behalf of the corporation. With a house on the Quay he was assessed at £30 on goods towards the subsidy in 1545 and 1547.[3]

Tyndale's Membership of the Parliament of 1538 was the culmination of his career. Nothing is known about his work in the House but on 18 Sept. 1558 he was paid £5 6s. as wages for the first session. Five days before he had made his will providing for his wife, children and kin in Lincolnshire, and he was to die shortly afterwards, probably before the opening of the second session, since his name is marked 'mortuus' on the Crown Office list for the Parliament. His death is also reflected in the Bristol chamberlain's accounts for the year ending Michaelmas 1559 where neither he nor his executors made any payments for the several properties which he leased from the corporation.[4]

[1] Date of birth estimated from first reference. Bristol AO, 04352/292 et passim; 0422/i. 106; PCC 60 Noodes, 7 Chaynay. [2] *Bristol and Glos. Arch. Soc. Trans*. xxvi. 136; Bristol AO, 04026/3/506, 5/104; 04027/12. [3] *Cal. Bristol Apprentices*, i. (Bristol Rec. Soc. xiv), 55; Bristol AO, 04026/2/186, 279, 3/182 et passim; E179/114/269, 272; PCC 60 Noodes, 7 Chaynay; *LP Hen. VIII*, vii. [4] C193/32/2; PCC 6 Noodes, 7 Chaynay; Bristol AO, 04026/5/204, 323 et passim.

A.D.K.H.

TYRRELL, Edmund (by 1513-76), of Rawreth and Ramsden Barrington, Essex.

MALDON   1554 (Apr.), 1558

b. by 1513, 1st s. of Jasper Tyrrell by Anne, da. of one Goodinge or Goring of Suff. *m*. by 1543, Susan Cooke, 4da. *suc*. gd.-fa. 28 Sept. 1543.[1]
     Parker, Ramsden Barrington by 1553; bailiff and parker, St. Osyth, Essex Nov. 1553; j.p. Essex 1554-58/59; various commissions from 1554; gent. at arms by Dec. 1558-*d*.[2]

Edmund Tyrrell came of a cadet branch of one of

the oldest and most prolific of Essex families. He was assessed for the subsidy of 1545 among the residents of Ramsden Bell House at £20 a year in lands, although two years earlier he had inherited from his grandfather William property worth nearly thrice that figure. In 1536 he took a 21-year lease of the rectory and tithes of Hockley, Essex, from Barking abbey, renewing it in 1553 and 1567. By 1543, and probably somewhat earlier, he had married Susan Cooke; she is said to have been of Gidea Hall and thus a kinswoman, although not apparently a daughter, of Sir Anthony Cooke*.[3]

Tyrrell's career was bound up with two personal relationships, his service with William Parr, Marquess of Northampton, and his friendship with (Sir) William Petre*. It was as a 'beloved servant' that between 1539 and 1543 Tyrrell received, with his wife, an annuity of £6 13s.4d. from Parr, probably in return for his assistance with the extensive lands in Essex which Parr received from the crown and through his marriage. That Tyrrell did not make his mark during the years of Parr's ascendancy may be attributed, especially after 1547, to their contrasting attitudes in religion, but their connexion appears to have survived the stresses of the age. As a Member of Mary's second Parliament Tyrrell probably helped to secure the passage of the Act (1 Mary st.3, no.—) which restored Parr in blood, and his own appointment, or retention, in the royal household at Elizabeth's accession coincided with Parr's recovery of his marquessate.[4]

With Petre, his kinsman by marriage, Tyrrell maintained a friendship which eventually led each to invoke the other's assistance in his will, Petre being the first to die and to be mourned by the survivor. Among the friends they had in common were Anthony Browne II*, who also remembered Tyrrell in his will, and George White*, an overseer of Tyrrell's. Tyrrell's Membership was but part of his abundant service to the Marian regime; after helping to defeat Wyatt's rebels he waged war on heresy in his own shire with a brutal efficiency which made his reputation in the eyes of the Queen and Council but blackened it for posterity. He perhaps owed it to the patronage of Parr and Petre that the coming of Elizabeth brought him no heavier penalty than the cost of his general pardon and the loss of his seat on the Essex bench.[5]

By his will of 5 Oct. 1576, revising an earlier one, Tyrrell replaced Sir William Petre as trustee for Thomas Tyrrell, his eldest daughter Thomasine Tyrrell's son who was to succeed to the inheritance. Of the two other daughters mentioned Susan received 1,000 marks. It appears that on the following 6 Nov., when on his deathbed, at Whitstable,

Kent, Tyrrell made a further will, the discrepancies between it and the earlier one being the subject of a court sentence.[6]

[1] Date of birth estimated from age at grandfather's i.p.m., C142/71/98. *Vis. Essex* (Harl. Soc. xiii), 111; Mill Stephenson, *Mon. Brasses*, 130; F. Chancellor, *Anct. Sepul. Mons. of Essex*, 170, 173; P. Benton, *Rochford*, 100 concludes that Susan Cooke came from Kent. [2] Stowe 571, f. 50; *CPR*, 1553-4, pp. 19, 27, 328; 1554-5, p. 107; 1563-6, pp. 122-3; Essex RO, Q/SR1-14, 67-68; Lansd. 3, f. 198; LC 2/4(2); E407/1/1-8. [3] PCC 33 Carew; E315/225, ff. 1 and v; *CPR*, 1566-9, p. 139. [4] E403/2450, f. 10; 101/520/9. [5] F. G. Emmison, *Tudor Sec.* 22, 26, 127-8, 252, 290, 292; PCC 33 Carew, 20 Stonard; *Chron. Q. Jane and Q. Mary* (Cam. Soc. xlviii), 188; *APC*, v. 63, 172; vi. 54, 237; *CPR*, 1553-4, p.328; 1558-60, p. 237; Foxe, *Acts and Mons.* vii. 329; viii. 385-6; Strype, *Eccles. Memorials*, iii(1), 440, 553; J. E. Oxley *Ref. in Essex*, 205-36 passim. [6] PCC 33 Carew, 30 Bakon; C142/176/48; information from W. J. Tighe.

D.F.C.

TYRRELL, Maurice (by 1520-63 or later).

PETERBOROUGH   1555
LEICESTER   1558

b. by 1520, yr. s. of Sir John Tyrrell (*d.*1541) of Little Warley, Essex by 2nd w. Anne, da. of Sir Edward Norris of Yattendon, Berks.[1]

Maurice Tyrrell was a younger son in a cadet branch of one of the most distinguished of Essex families and must have owed his return to Parliament to his family connexions. (Sir) William Petre* married his sister Gertrude and Petre's brother Richard, a prebendary of Peterborough, could have secured his return there. Yet the fact that Tyrrell was to oppose one of the government's bills in the Parliament of 1555 suggests that he entered the House under less Catholic auspices. His half-sister Elizabeth Hopton married Andrew Nowell*, feodary of Leicestershire, Northamptonshire and other counties, and one of the feoffees named in the marriage settlement of April 1551 was John Campanett, then or shortly afterwards a Member for Peterborough. Campanett himself may have been related to the Tyrrells through his marriage to Margaret Lynne, Sir John Tyrrell's first wife having been a Lynne of Southwick, Northamptonshire. Nowell's feoffees also included George Lynne† and another Lynne kinsman, William Gardiner*, and this relationship with Gardiner could have enabled Maurice Tyrrell to call upon the influence in Peterborough of Francis Russell*, 2nd Earl of Bedford, whose patronage, during his absence abroad, seems to have been wielded by Sir William Cecil.[2]

Despite his show of opposition in 1555, Tyrrell was returned again in 1558, this time for Leicester. In a borough which formed part of the duchy of Lancaster honor of Leicester, it cannot have told against Tyrrell that he was a kinsman of the Marian chancellors Sir Robert Rochester* and Sir Edward Waldegrave* (who, although not appointed until

22 Jan. 1558, was probably exercising the office beforehand); he may also have enjoyed the support of Sir Edward Hastings*, receiver of Leicester honor and town clerk, who was related to his family, while George Sherard, junior knight for Leicestershire in this Parliament, was another kinsman.[3]

Little else has been discovered about Tyrrell. His father, in a will of 28 Feb. 1541, left him 5 marks a year for life and a sum of £20, and his mother, in hers of 17 July 1552 which was proved ten years later, bequeathed him most of her goods and chattels and appointed him one of her two executors. The Essex pedigrees derive all those of Sir John Tyrrell's children whom they list from Anne Norris, the sole wife they name, but Maurice, the one Tyrrell mentioned in his mother's will, may have been her only child by that marriage. Maurice Tyrrell was also an executor and witness of Andrew Nowell's will and survived to prove it on 4 Feb. 1563. This is the last reference found to him.[4]

[1] Apparently of age at fa.'s death. *Vis. Essex* (Harl. Soc. xiii), 115, 301; *Vis. Northants.* ed. Metcalfe, 35. [2] F. G. Emmison, *Tudor Sec.* 22; Le Neve, *Fasti* (1854), ii. 543; Guildford mus. Loseley 1331/2; *CPR*, 1550-3, p. 85. [3] *Vis. Essex* and *Tristram*, 113; *Vis. Northants.* (Harl. Soc. lxxxvii), 154; *Vis. Leics.* (Harl. Soc. ii), 10, 88. [4] PCC 25 Alenger, 28 Streat, 6 Chayre; *Trans. Essex Arch. Soc.* iii. 92-93, 179-80.

A.D.

TYRWHITT, Marmaduke (1533/34-1600), of Scotter, Lincs.

GREAT GRIMSBY 1558

b. 1533/34, 4th s. of Sir William Tyrwhitt of Scotter by Isabel, da. of William Girlington of Normanby; bro. of Sir Robert II* and Tristram[†]. *m.* c.1560, Ellen, da. of Lionel Reresby of Thrybergh, Yorks., 5s. 6da.[1]
   Commr. sewers, Lincs. 1564, eccles. causes, dioceses of Lincoln and Peterborough 1571, Lincoln 1575; j.p. Lincs. (Lindsey) 1569, q. 1573/74-93.[2]

Marmaduke Tyrwhitt probably owed his election for Grimsby to the influence of his family, as Ambrose Sutton, who married his sister, may also have done in the spring of 1554. It was certainly Tyrwhitt's elder brother Sir Robert who extinguished his hope of re-election there in January 1559; when Sir Robert Tyrwhitt asked the borough to give a nomination to the 9th Lord Clinton he added, 'and for my brother Marmaduke, I have stayed him that he shall make no further suit to you for the same'.[3]

Tyrwhitt's appointment in 1571 as an ecclesiastical commissioner in two dioceses implies that he received some legal training, as does his receipt two-and-a-half years earlier of a writ empowering him and a common pleas judge to accept the surrender of the clerkship of Lincoln castle. His relationship by marriage with Christopher Wray*,

whose dispute of 1586-7 with Richard Topcliffe[†] over the tithes of Corringham he was one of those commissioned to settle, is also suggestive of a legal connexion, as is perhaps his presiding over his own manorial court at Bottesford, Lincolnshire, in October 1591. It is, however, in civil dress that he is depicted, with his wife, five sons and six daughters, on his memorial brass at Scotter, which states that he died on 21 Jan. 1600 aged 66 and that he had been married for almost 40 years.[4]

[1] Aged 66 at death. *Lincs. Peds.* (Harl. Soc. lii), 1017; Mill Stephenson, *Mon. Brasses*, 290. [2] *CPR*, 1563-6, p. 40; 1569-72, pp. 225, 277-8; 1572-5, pp. 551-2. [3] Great Grimsby AO, letters. [4] *CPR*, 1566-9, p. 248; *APC*, xiv. 242, 301, 303; *Archaeologia*, i. 381.

T.M.H.

TYRWHITT, Philip (c.1510-58), of Barton upon Humber, Lincs.

LINCOLNSHIRE 1554 (Nov.)

b. c.1510, 3rd s. of Sir Robert Tyrwhitt (*d.*1548), of Kettleby by Maud, da. of Sir Robert Tailboys[†], *de jure* 8th Lord Kyme, of Kyme; bro. of Sir Robert I*. *m.* by 1532, Margaret, da. of Edward Barnaby of Barton upon Humber, 4s. 6da.[1]
   J.p. Lincs. (Lindsey) 1547-54; commr. sewers, Lincs. 1547, Cambs., Hunts., I. of Ely, Lincs., Northants., and Notts. 1555, relief, Lincs. (Lindsey) 1550.[2]

Philip Tyrwhitt appears not to have pursued a profession or sought public employment, although his choice by John Bellow* in 1547 and Sir Anthony Neville* ten years later as a trustee for family settlements may mean that he had some legal training. With other members of his family he was caught up in the Lincolnshire rising of 1536, his father being coerced into momentary support of the rebels and he himself described by one of them as a 'captain of the commons of Louth'. Like his father, he must have cleared himself without delay: in January 1537 Sir Ralph Ellerker* sent for him to accompany Sir William Askew* and 100 men to Hull, and later in that year he was one of the grand jury for the trial of Lords Darcy and Hussey. In 1541 he served in the same capacity for Culpeper and Dereham.[3]

It was doubtless his marriage which led Tyrwhitt to settle at Barton, where he was domiciled when he sued out a general pardon at the accession of Mary. His knighthood of the shire in the Queen's third Parliament he presumably owed to the standing of his family: his elder brother had gained it in 1545 and his nephew had done so twice since. He was to be one of the three Lincolnshire Members—another being his kinsman Thomas Constable, sitting for Grimsby—who quitted the Parliament without leave before its dissolution and who were prosecuted for that dereliction. After being dis-

trained once for non-appearance, he was fined
53s.4d. in Hilary term 1556, his sureties being his
brother Sir Robert and Thomas Tyrwhitt of the
Middle Temple. Beyond the fact of the fine there is
nothing to indicate whether he had left the Parliament in protest or had decided to spend Christmas
at home.[4]

Tyrwhitt made his will on 21 Sept. 1558 and died
in the following November. His son Edward, then
rising 25, inherited a modest estate in South
Somercotes, and his widow was to have all his leases
for life and the use of the parsonage of Barton for
12 years as a home for the younger children. Three
sons and four unmarried daughters were given sums
ranging from £50 to £120, and there were gifts to
five churches and for the repair of highways. The
will was proved on behalf of the widow and heir on
18 Jan. 1559.[5]

[1] Date of birth estimated from elder brother's. *Lincs. Peds.* (Harl.
Soc. lii), 1019–21; R. P. Tyrwhitt, *Fam. Tyrwhitt*, 17–21; PCC
30 Welles. [2] *CPR*, 1547–8, pp. 78, 86; 1553, p. 355; 1553–4, p. 21;
1554–5, p. 109. [3] *CPR*, 1547–8, pp. 200, 212; 1555–7, p. 344;
LP Hen. VIII, xi, xii, xvi. [4] *CPR*, 1553–4, p. 439; KB27/1176,
1177. [5] C142/121/111; PCC 30 Welles.

M.K.D.

TYRWHITT, Sir Robert I (by 1504–72), of
Mortlake, Surr. and Leighton Bromswold, Hunts.

LINCOLNSHIRE   1545
HUNTINGDONSHIRE   1554 (Apr.), 1559

b. by 1504, 2nd s. of Sir Robert Tyrwhitt, and bro. of
Philip*. *m.* (1) Bridget, da. and h. of Sir John Wiltshire
of Stone Castle, Kent, wid. of Sir Richard Wingfield of
Kimbolton, Hunts. and (Sir) Nicholas Harvey*
(*d.*1532) of Ickworth, Suff.; (2) by 1540, Elizabeth, da.
of Sir Goddard Oxenbridge of Brede, Suss. at least
1da. *d.v.p.* Kntd. 1543.[1]

Esquire of the body by 1525; chamberlain, Berwick-
upon-Tweed, Northumb. 13 Sept. 1525; j.p. Hunts.
1536, 1544, 1554–*d*., Lincs. (Lindsey) 1538, Northants.
1554, Beds. 1558/59–*d*.; keeper, manor of Dytton,
Bucks. 1536; sheriff, Lincs. 1540–1, Cambs. and
Hunts. 1557–8; master of the hunt, Mortlake, Surr.
1540; gent. the privy chamber by 1540; commr.
ordnance 1541, 1553, benevolence, Surr. 1544/45,
relief, Hunts., Northants. 1550, goods of churches and
fraternities, Hunts. 1553, subsidy, Hunts. 1563, eccles.
causes, dioceses of Lincoln and Peterborough 1571;
servant, household of Queen Catherine Parr July
1543–8, master of the horse by 1544, steward by 1547;
constable, Kimbolton castle, Hunts. 1544; steward,
duchy of Lancaster, Higham Ferrers, Northants. by
1546; steward, unknown property for Thomas
Seymour, Baron Seymour of Sudeley by 1548; jt. (with
Thomas Audley II*) ld. lt. Hunts. in 1551; numerous
other minor offices.[2]

Of old Lincolnshire stock, Robert Tyrwhitt
inherited a tradition of service to the crown: his
grandfather had been a knight of the body and his
father, who received his knighthood at Tournai, was
an outstanding figure in his shire. Through his
mother Tyrwhitt could claim to be linked by marriage with Henry VIII's mistress Elizabeth Blount
and their son the Duke of Richmond.[3]

Tyrwhitt was brought up at court. An esquire of
the body by 1525, he was an early and large recipient
of monastic lands, especially in his own shire:
between 1536 and 1547 he acquired some two
dozen grants and leases from the augmentations.
His first acquisition had been the dissolved monastery of Stainfield in Lincolnshire, which was
suppressed on the orders of the King despite a
recent decision in favour of its exemption. It was
such episodes which provoked the Lincolnshire
rebellion. Tyrwhitt's father was one of the subsidy
commissioners first attacked by the rebels, and as
soon as news reached the court he himself was
despatched with orders for John Hussey*, Lord
Hussey. His part in the suppression of the rebellion
and of the Pilgrimage of Grace is scarcely to be
disentangled from that of his many namesakes. The
dissolution of Stainfield was promptly carried
through, and after leasing them in 1537 Tyrwhitt
was granted the house, site and 662 acres of land in
fee in the following year.[4]

By 1540 Tyrwhitt's advance at court saw him
promoted to be a gentleman of the privy chamber
and acting vice-chamberlain on the King's side. He
survived a rebuke by the Privy Council in September 1540 for being one of those guilty of causing a
disturbance in the presence chamber, and he was
given custody of several royal properties previously
under Cromwell's charge. Among them was the
house at Mortlake, Surrey, where he and his wife,
a gentlewoman of the Queen's privy chamber,
were later to reside. His position was greatly
strengthened when his cousin by marriage became
Henry VIII's last Queen: it was about this time that
he was knighted and by 1544 he was Catherine's
master of the horse. In that year he had charge of the
transportation of ordnance for the campaign in
France, where he served with Sir Edward Baynton*
who remembered him with a legacy. Tyrwhitt was
himself an executor of the will which John Hasilwood* made early in the same year.[5]

Tyrwhitt was elected first knight for Lincolnshire
to the Parliament of 1545, being styled 'junior' on
the return to distinguish him from his father who
was to die in 1548. His father had probably preceded him in the House, being one of three Lincoln-
shiremen suggested in 1532 or 1533 to fill two
vacancies there and one of the two apparently
preferred by Cromwell. It was, howeve., in
Huntingdonshire that Tyrwhitt was to settle. In
1548 he bought Leighton Bromswold, a prebendal
manor of Lincoln cathedral, with 2,400 acres of

land, pasture and marsh, and thereafter he added further property in Huntingdonshire while disposing of much of his monastic land in Lincolnshire and elsewhere; thus in 1550 he sold part of the Thornton college property to his nephew, Sir Robert Tyrwhitt II*, and five years later bought over 5,000 acres at Woodwalton, Huntingdonshire. When in 1553 he was sued by some of his tenants for enclosing he agreed to their demand, saying that 'as he was a true Christian man and knight', he would 'help to pluck up [the hedges] with his own hands'. He was also the defendant in property disputes before the Star Chamber and the court of the duchy of Lancaster.[6]

Tyrwhitt and his wife remained in attendance on Catherine Parr after the death of Henry VIII and so became involved with her new husband Thomas Seymour. Lady Tyrwhitt witnessed Seymour's neglect of Catherine during the last year of her life, and after her death told the story to the Privy Council. Thus in January 1549 the Council, alarmed at Seymour's wooing of Princess Elizabeth, sent the Tyrwhitts to Hatfield as overseers to the princess in place of Catherine Astley and Thomas Parry*, who were suspected of promoting Seymour's cause. At the Council's direction Tyrwhitt questioned the princess about Seymour while Lady Tyrwhitt plied her with 'good advices . . . especially in such matters as [the Council] appointed'. Although the Tyrwhitts treated her gently Elizabeth never forgave them their part in the affair. Lady Tyrwhitt was a devout woman of Puritan tendencies who may have been unwelcome to the young princess on several grounds. Her husband once told Thomas Seymour that she was 'not sane [sound] in divinity, but she was half a Scripture woman'. She was the author of *Morning and Euening praiers with diuers Psalmes Himnes and Meditations* (1574).[7]

Shortly after the interlude at Hatfield House, Tyrwhitt was appointed joint lord lieutenant of Huntingdonshire. He may have been elected senior knight for Huntingdonshire in the Parliament of March 1553. The original return is torn and the name of the senior knight lost, but the circumstances point to his election. Since 1544 he had controlled the wardship of Kimbolton, the traditional stronghold of electoral power in the county, and after his purchase of Leighton Bromswold in 1548 he was a leading landowner; he was one of the lords lieutenant and there was no one of his stature to oppose him; and lastly, his co-lieutenant Audley took the junior seat and his client Simon Throckmorton* heads the list of electors on the indenture.[8]

It is not known what part Tyrwhitt played in the succession crisis of July 1553, but at the end of that year he and Audley took the field against the rebels in Kent, presumably in their capacity as lieutenants, although only Audley, a soldier by profession, was given a reward. Tyrwhitt sat in only one of Mary's Parliaments, that of April 1554. He may have thought it prudent not to court embarrassment. When in Easter term 1555 his brother Philip Tyrwhitt was informed against in the King's bench for having left Parliament without leave, Tyrwhitt stood surety for him. In the following year Tyrwhitt's lease of Mortlake was revoked by the crown and the house was handed over to Cardinal Pole. The shrievalty which he began in November 1557 could have been intended both to discipline him and perhaps to make it difficult for him to sit in the Parliament which was summoned immediately afterwards.[9]

The accession of Elizabeth did not herald Tyrwhitt's return to favour by reason of the Queen's grudge against him. After sitting in her first Parliament he led a retired life at Leighton Bromswold, where he died on 10 May 1572.[10]

[1] Date of birth estimated from first reference. *Lincs. Peds.* (Harl. Soc. lii), 1019–20; *LP Hen. VIII*, xv. [2] *LP Hen. VIII*, iv, v, x, xii, xiii, xvi, xviii–xxi; *CPR*, 1550–3, p. 394; 1553, pp. 186,354,356,414; 1553–4, p. 20; 1560–3, pp. 433–4, 437–8; 1560–3, pp. 18, 22, 24, 40, 41; 1569–72, pp. 222, 277–8; *APC*, iii. 259; iv. 49, 277; vii. 248; Stowe 571, f. 60; Somerville, *Duchy*, i. 590; E101/426/2, f. 6; 163/12/17, nos. 38, 51, 54; *HMC Hatfield*, i. 443; *VCH Northants.* iii. 69. [3] *HP*, ed. Wedgwood, 1439–1509 (Biogs.), 891; *LP Hen. VIII*, ii, iv, x. [4] *LP Hen. VIII*, xi, xiii–xx; *HMC Bath*, iv. 3; *CPR*, 1547–8, p. 172; *DKR*, x(2), 292–3; M. H. and R. Dodds, *Pilgrimage of Grace*, i. 109–10. [5] *LP Hen. VIII*, xii–xvi, xviii–xxi; R. P. Tyrwhitt, *Fam. Tyrwhitt*, 17, 106; *VCH Northants.* iii. 69; *APC*, i. 169; PCC 6, 28 Pynnyng. [6] C219/18C/58v; *LP Hen. VIII*, vii. 56 citing SP1/82, ff. 59–62; *Cal. Feet of Fines, Hunts.* ed. Turner, 138, 144, 146; *CPR*, 1549–51, p. 232; *VCH Hunts.* iii. 89; St.Ch. 4/2/13; *Ducatus Lanc.* ii(3), 316. [7] *Coll. State Pprs.* ed. Haynes, 70–108. [8] *LP Hen. VIII*, xix; *APC*, iii. 14; iv. 49, 277; *CPR*, 1550–3, p. 77; C219/20/59. [9] *Chron. Q. Jane and Q. Mary* (Cam. Soc. xlviii), 187; KB27/1177; *CPR*, 1557–8, pp. 69–70. [10] Tyrwhitt, 22; Pevsner, *Beds., Hunts. and Peterborough*, 283.

T.M.H.

TYRWHITT, Sir Robert II (c.1510–81), of Kettleby, Lincs.

LINCOLNSHIRE 1553 (Mar.),[1] 1554 (Apr.), 1558

b. c.1510, 1st s. of Sir William Tyrwhitt (*d.*19 Mar. 1541) of Scotter by Isabel, da. of William Girlington of Normanby; bro. of Marmaduke* and Tristram†. *m.* by 1531, Elizabeth, da. and h. of Sir Thomas Oxenbridge of Etchingham, Suss., 9s. inc. William* 13da. *suc.* gdfa. 4 July 1548. Kntd. by 16 Feb. 1553.[2]

J.p. Lincs. (Lindsey) 1547–?*d.*; commr. relief, Lincs. (Lindsey) and Lincoln 1550, goods of churches and fraternities, Lincs. (Lindsey) 1553, subsidy 1563; other commissions 1547–78; jt. (with Sir Edward Dymoke* and Sir William Willoughby*, Baron Willoughby of Parham) ld. lt. Lincs. May 1559; sheriff 1559–60.[3]

According to his grandfather's inquisition Robert Tyrwhitt was aged 22 years and more in July 1548, but since his eldest son William (q.v.) was of age by 1552 this must have been a conventional underestimate; his family chronology also suggests that he was born a good deal earlier, probably about 1510. It was under the tutelage of his uncle Sir Robert Tyrwhitt I* that he spent part of his youth as a henchman at court. He did not follow his uncle in making a career there but confined himself to the affairs of his county and the management of the lands which he inherited from his grandfather and those, said to be worth £140 a year, brought by the Sussex heiress whom he married. He does not appear to have fought in the wars of the 1540s and his knighthood, the date of which is unknown, was probably conferred to gratify his uncle. His three elections as knight of the shire within a five-year period attest his own and his family's standing, and it may have been only his comparative youth which excluded him from the first place. As a lifelong Catholic he must have found the second Edwardian Parliament less congenial than either of his two Marian ones, and he was not to sit in any of Elizabeth's. He did, however, intervene in the election of 1559 at Grimsby, where he asked for one nomination to be given to the 9th Lord Clinton and dissuaded his brother Marmaduke from seeking a seat.[4]

Under Elizabeth, although adjudged a 'hinderer of the true religion', Tyrwhitt was retained on the bench at least until 1579. Whether it was he or his uncle who led 237 followers against the northern rebels of 1569 is not known. It was only towards the end of his life that he and his children were harried for their recusancy. He himself had a spell in the Fleet, where in September 1580 he was allowed his wife's company and access to the gardens for his health, and when he died on 16 Nov. 1581 two of his sons were released from prison to attend the funeral. Yet the will which he made five days before his death shows that recusancy had not impoverished him. Of his numerous children five younger sons received annuities of £40, a married daughter £30 and two unmarried ones £800 each; his grandsons Marmaduke Constable and Richard Fitzwilliam had £100 each and his various grand-daughters £266 13s.4d. between them, a niece £40, a godson 40 marks and two other young kinsmen smaller sums. The residuary legatees were Tyrwhitt's wife and grandson Robert Tyrwhitt; the executors his wife, his sons-in-law Philip Constable and William Fitzwilliam, and his cousin John Monson; and the supervisors Lord Burghley and the 3rd Earl of Rutland. Tyrwhitt was buried at Bigby, Lincolnshire, in a tomb of white alabaster surmounted by busts of himself and his wife.[5]

[1] Christian name missing from torn indenture (C219/20/77) but styled knight and described as 'junior'. [2] Date of birth estimated from family history. *Lincs. Peds.* (Harl. Soc. lii), 1019–20; *CPR,*

1549–51, p. 232; 1550–3, p. 395; R. P. Tyrwhitt, *Fam. Tyrwhitt*, 30. [3] *CPR*, 1547–8, pp. 75, 77, 78, 86; 1549–51, p. 67; 1550–3, p. 395; 1553, pp. 355, 361, 414; 1553–4, p. 21; 1554–5, pp. 106, 109, 110; 1555–7, pp. 371–2; 1560–3, p. 439; 1563–6, pp. 40, 42; 1569–72, pp. 221, 222, 225; *APC*, vii. 284; *HMC Hatfield*, ii. 209; Lansd. 8, ff. 77–82; *CSP Dom.* 1547–80, p. 108. [4] C142/87/22; Leland, *Itin.* ed. Smith, ii. 15–16; *CPR*, 1549–51, p. 232; Tyrwhitt, 110–12; *HMC 14th Rep. VIII*, 255. [5] *Cam. Misc.* ix(3), 27; Lansd. 207(c), f.398v; *APC*, xii. 49–318 passim; xiii. 75–446 passim; PCC 1 Tirwhite; Tyrwhitt, 29–30, 110–12.

T.M.H.

TYRWHITT, William (by 1531–91), of Twigmoor and Kettleby, Lincs.

HUNTINGDON   1553 (Mar.)

b. by 1531, 1st s. of Sir Robert Tyrwhitt II* of Kettleby by Elizabeth, da. and h. of Sir Thomas Oxenbridge of Etchingham, Suss. *m.* settlement 1 Sept. 1576, Elizabeth, da. of Peter Frescheville of Staveley, Notts., 5s. 4da. *suc.* fa. 16 Nov. 1581.[1]

The identity of the William Tyrwhitt, gentleman, returned for Huntingdon with Thomas Maria Wingfield to Edward VI's second Parliament is not easy to establish. He must have been a member of the Lincolnshire family, which favoured the baptismal name William equally with Robert, and his election was almost certainly the work of Sir Robert Tyrwhitt I* who had settled in Huntingdon-shire on marrying Wingfield's mother. There is a remote possibility that William Tyrwhitt was a son of this Sir Robert Tyrwhitt, who predeceased his father and of whom no other trace has been found. It is known, however, that Sir Robert was uncle to at least two Williams and great-uncle to another. Of his nephews, the son of Sir William Tyrwhitt of Scotter was a clerk in holy orders who held the prebend of Brampton in Lincoln cathedral until his death in 1555, and the other was a younger son of Philip Tyrwhitt* of Barton upon Humber who received £50 under his father's will in 1558; the great-nephew was the eldest son of the Sir Robert Tyrwhitt of Kettleby who was returned to the Parliament of March 1553 for Lincolnshire. It was this great-nephew, then described as 'William Tyrwhitt esquire, a young gentleman, son and heir apparent of Sir Robert Tyrwhitt of Lincolnshire, a man of great power in those parts', who was involved in an action over lands in Lincolnshire said to have been sold to him unlawfully in or before 1552. He may thus be thought to have come of age recently and to have been eligible for the seat at Huntingdon early in 1553, and he is therefore taken to have been the Member. His father stood close to his great-uncle, his uncle Tristram was to be chosen for the town in 1571, and his younger brothers were to be beneficiaries under the great-uncle's will a year later.[2]

From his marriage until the death of his father Tyrwhitt lived at Twigmoor. In June 1580 he was suspected of Catholicism and committed to the Tower where he remained until set free 12 months later on bail of £300 and a promise to take instruction 'in the truth of the gospel'. A complaint by Bishop Cooper of Lincoln about his part in dissuading friends from conforming with the Anglican settlement led to his committal to the Fleet, from where in November 1581 he was released for his father's funeral. It was discovered that while in the Fleet he had heard mass and this revelation decided an already doubtful Queen against naming him to the Lincolnshire bench upon which his forbears had served since the 14th century. He remained under surveillance for the remaining ten years of his life and although not recommitted to prison he was rarely allowed to visit Lincolnshire. It was while there winding up his mother's affairs that he died on 18 July 1591. By his will made two months earlier he asked to be buried near his father's grave in Bigby church and instructed his executors to sell various lands, including his manor of Fillingham, to provide legacies for his children.[3]

[1] Date of birth estimated from first reference. *Lincs. Peds.* (Harl. Soc. lii), 1019; C142/169/10, 231/65. [2] C219/20/60; R. P. Tyrwhitt, *Fam. Tyrwhitt*, passim; PCC 30 Welles, 1 Tirwhite; Le Neve, *Fasti*, ii. 118; *LP Hen. VIII*, xvii, xix; St.Ch.3/3/72. [3] *CPR*, 1572–5, p. 391; *APC*, xii–xviii, xx passim; *CSP Dom.* 1547–80, p. 280; 1581–90, pp. 46, 145, 280; *Cath. Rec. Soc.* v. 27, 28; G. Anstruther, *Seminary Priests*, i. 9; C142/231/65; PCC 21 Sainberbe.

M.K.D.

TYRWHITT, Sir William (by 1458–1522), of Kettleby, Lincs.

LINCOLNSHIRE   1491
?GREAT GRIMSBY   1510[1]

b. by 1458, 1st s. of Sir Robert Tyrwhitt of Kettleby by Jane, da. of Richard Waterton† of Great Corringham. *m.* by 1476, Anne, da. of Sir Robert Constable† of Somerby, Lincs. and Flamborough, Yorks., 2s. 3da. *suc.* fa. 1457/58. Kntd. 16 June 1487, banneret 17 June 1497.[2]

Sheriff, Lincs. 1481–2, 1494–5, 1500–1, 1517–18; esquire of the body by 1482, knight by 1491; j.p. Lincs. (Lindsey) 1483–*d.*; commr. array, Lincs. 1484, musters 1488, subsidy 1504, 1512, 1514, 1515, enclosures 1517; other commissions 1482–*d.*; keeper, manor of Swallowfield, Berks. 1 Mar. 1485; steward, lordship of Caistor, Lincs. 1484, bailiff 1491; steward, duchy of Lancaster, Lincs. 4 Mar. 1499–*d.*, Castle Donington, Leics. 27 June 1504–*d.*; steward, manor of Barton upon Humber, Lincs. 1509–*d.*[3]

A descendant of the judge Sir Robert Tyrwhitt, Sir William Tyrwhitt combined shire administration with duties at court in a career which spanned five reigns. After a spell in London in 1509 to attend the funeral of Henry VII and the coronation he returned to Lincolnshire, where he received orders to investigate the disturbances which had caused the postponement of the shire election to the first Parliament of the reign. He seems to have used the opportunity afforded by the inquiry to promote his own candidature. Eight days before the assembly of Parliament the corporation of Grimsby complied with his request to set aside their own election and to send a blank indenture to him at Lincoln, to the intent

> that it shall be lawful to Sir William Tyrwhitt, knight, [? to admit] Sir Robert Wingfield, knight, for to be burgess of the Parliament for the town with himself or else to admit . . . the said Sir Robert Wingfield . . . with John Heneage†.

The two bearers of the indenture were instructed to obtain from Tyrwhitt a bond indemnifying the town from charges arising from this interference with the election and releasing it from payment of wages to the Members returned. At the same time the townsmen decided to share the expenses of those burgesses riding at the call of Tyrwhitt to Lincoln for the election of the knights of the shire 'or for any other cause that the mayor do for pleasure of the said Sir William Tyrwhitt'. The most acceptable interpretation of these manoeuvres is that Tyrwhitt hoped to be elected for the shire but wished to keep open a line of retreat in the form of a seat for Grimsby. Since the result of the shire election is not known, and the records at Grimsby afford no further clue, it cannot be said whether Tyrwhitt sat for Lincolnshire or Grimsby, and therefore whether Heneage did so for the town. The possibility that Tyrwhitt was a knight of the shire in the next two Parliaments, for which the names are lost, is strengthened by the inclusion of his name among the commissioners to supervise the collection of the subsidies which they granted.[4]

In 1512 Tyrwhitt served as a captain under Sir William Sandys in the French campaign. He stayed in England when a year later the King went to Tournai and the maintenance of law and order in Lincolnshire was entrusted to him on the eve of Flodden. His closing years saw no diminution of activity and in 1520 he accompanied the King to the Field of Cloth of Gold. He died apparently intestate on 10 Apr. 1522, leaving as heir his son Sir Robert aged 46 years and more, and was buried in Lincoln cathedral.[5]

[1] Great Grimsby AO, oldest ct. bk. f. 224. [2] Date of birth estimated from fa.'s death. *Lincs. Peds.* (Harl. Soc. lii), 1019; *Vis. Lincs.* ed. Metcalfe, 69; *Vis. Yorks.* (Harl. Soc. xvi), 65; R. P. Tyrwhitt, *Fam. Tyrwhitt*, 17; E150/556/23. [3] *CPR*, 1476–85 to 1494–1509 passim; *CFR*, 1471–85, pp. 274–5; *LP Rich. III and Hen. VII*, i. 410; ii. 291; *LP Hen. VIII*, i–iii; *Rot. Parl.* vi. 539–40; *Statutes*, iii. 89, 119, 172; *Domesday of Inclosures*, ed. Leadam, i. 84, 248, 255; Somerville, *Duchy*, i. 573, 577. [4] *DNB* (Tyrwhitt, Sir Robert); *LP Hen. VIII*, i; Great Grimsby AO, oldest ct. bk. ff. 223v–4; *HMC 14th Rep. VIII*, 274. [5] *LP Hen. VIII*, i–iii; E150/556/23; Tyrwhitt, 17.

T.M.H.

TYSAR, John (by 1516–?75), of Sandwich, Kent.

SANDWICH   1554 (Nov.), 1559

b. by 1516. *m.* Margaret, sis. of John Sulyard, at least 2s. 2da.[1]

Constable of the 7th ward, Sandwich 1540–2, common councilman (St. Peter's parish) 1542–7, (St. Clement's parish) 1547–8, (unknown parish) 1548–9, treasurer 1542–3, jurat 1549–?*d.*, mayor 1553–4, 1567–8, keeper of the common chest and of the orphans when mayor; bailiff to Yarmouth 1556; speaker of the Brotherhood of the Cinque Ports 1568.[2]

John Tysar was admitted to the freedom of Sandwich on 6 Dec. 1537, having been an apprentice in the town; his sureties included John Lee III*. Described as a grocer in 1543, he was fined 5*s*. in 1547 for selling candles above the price set by the clerk of the market. In the six months beginning October 1554 he shipped 245 quarters of wheat and 60 quarters of malt to London and 25 quarters of malt to Calais; these were all carried in other men's vessels, but Tysar had a 60-ton ship of his own which was hired by the town for nine days in September 1555 as part of the fleet which transported King Philip to Calais.[3]

Tysar's first known involvement in parliamentary matters was his commission on 11 Sept. 1553 to visit the lord warden, Sir Thomas Cheyne*, with regard to the choice of the town's Members in the forthcoming Parliament; in the event Sandwich made an unsuccessful attempt to defy Cheyne by re-electing Thomas Menys. When on 23 Oct. 1554 Tysar was himself chosen with the usual wages, he being then mayor in place of the disqualified Simon Linch*, Cheyne allowed his election to stand but overrode William Lathebury's. Both Tysar and the warden's nominee Nicholas Crispe were among the Members of this Parliament who quitted it without leave before its dissolution; summoned before the King's bench in the following Easter term to answer to this dereliction Tysar failed to appear, but as no further action was taken against him he was presumably not considered a serious offender. He could not so lightly disregard the summons which brought him and four others of Sandwich before the Privy Council on 12 Nov. 1557. This arose out of a letter sent from the town to the warden who evidently found it offensive enough to warrant a complaint to the Council, and it was as one of those chiefly to blame that Tysar made his appearance. Neither the subject of the letter nor the outcome of the affair is known but coming as it did shortly before the election to the last Marian Parliament the episode may help to explain why on this occasion Tysar was an unsuccessful candidate. If the two were connected, Tysar's exclusion is more likely to have been due to prudence than to hostility, for 12 months

later, with Cheyne recently dead, he was elected to Elizabeth's first Parliament and also chosen to attend the coronation where he was one of those holding the canopy over the Queen.[4]

Tysar's refusal to serve as bailiff to Yarmouth in 1557, which cost him a fine of 50*s*., may also have been connected with his setback in that year; it was his only evasion of duty in more than 30 years of service to the town, including 16 attendances at Brotherhood meetings at Romney. He made his will, which has a Protestant ring, on 15 Apr. 1575 and probably died in the course of that year.[5]

[1] Date of birth estimated from admission as freeman. PCC 45 Tirwhite. [2] Sandwich old red bk. 1527–51, passim; little black bk. passim; new red bk. 1568–81, passim; *Cinque Ports White and Black Bks.* (Kent Arch. Soc. recs. br. xix), 275. [3] Sandwich old red bk. ff. 95v, 155v, 203v–4; little black bk. f. 73; E122/131/8. [4] Sandwich little black bk. ff. 35, 37v, 55v, 122v, 136; KB 29/188 rot. 48; *APC*, vi. 189, 199. [5] *Cinque Ports White and Black Bks.* 257; PCC 45 Tirwhite.

H.M.

TYSSARD *see* **TUSSER**

UNDERHILL, Edward (1512–76 or later), of Hunningham and Baginton, Warws. and Limehouse, Mdx.

TAVISTOCK   1553 (Mar.)

b. 1512, 1st s. of Thomas Underhill (*d.*Sept. 1518/June 1520) of Hunningham by Anne, da. of Robert Winter of Huddington, Worcs. *m.* lic. 17 Nov. 1546, Joan, da. of Thomas Peryns or Speryn of London, wid. of Richard Downes (*d.*1545) of Greenwich, Kent, 5s. 7da. *suc.* ?gdfa. 29 Nov. 1518.[1]

Gent.-at-arms 1544–54, 1558–?*d.*[2]

Man-at-arms and 'hot gospeller', Edward Underhill achieved earthly immortality by leaving a sparkling account of the most hazardous phase of his career. That he emerged so little damaged was due in no small part to his advantages of birth and connexion. The uncle who in 1527 obtained his wardship was William Underhill, a former clerk of the Commons, and his mother's father took as his second wife a daughter of Sir George Throckmorton*. When Underhill was before the Privy Council he could remind Secretary Bourne that Bourne's father 'was beholden unto my uncle Winter'; his cousin Gilbert Winter was a gentleman usher to Princess Elizabeth; and he owed his release from Newgate to another cousin, John Throckmorton I*.[3]

Gravitating to the court, Underhill at first led a dissolute life as one of the gambling set which included Sir Ralph Bagnall*; this probably explains the sale of much of his inheritance, although he denied Bourne's accusation to that effect, ascribing his impoverishment to the cost of his service with the crown. He was not, as he himself claimed, one of the original band of gentlemen pensioners formed in 1540, nor did he ever achieve that prestigious status; he was one of the gentlemen-at-arms added to the corps during the French war. It was on the recommendation of (Sir) Richard Cromwell *alias* Williams*, with whom he served in 1543, that in the following year Underhill joined the King's personal troop and took part in the Boulogne campaign. He was to return to that town in 1549, when he was comptroller of ordnance in the 2nd Earl of Huntingdon's expedition for its relief.[4]

Underhill's description of his lute-playing for Huntingdon at Calais, interspersed with religious argumentation with the earl's brother Sir Edward Hastings*, shows that he was by then imbued with both the radical views and the proselytizing zeal for which he became notorious. 'Even in King Edward's time', he was afterwards to write, 'I became odious unto most men, and many times in danger of my life amongst them', but until 1553 not only was the religious tide with him but he had powerful protectors from the Duke of Northumberland downwards. Among these were Sir John Russell*, 1st Earl of Bedford, and his son Francis*, Lord Russell, whom, from his home at Limehouse, Underhill helped to save from drowning in the Thames. It was without doubt the Russells who procured Underhill a seat for Tavistock in the Parliament of March 1553, although the fact that Sir Edward Rogers, who preceded him there, had been his commanding officer in 1544 must also have told in his favour. Regrettably, Underhill has nothing to say of his brief Membership of the Commons, in which it is hard to believe that he held his tongue.

Underhill stood close to Northumberland—the Earl of Arundel said that he was 'always tutting' in the duke's ear—and it was during her brief reign that Jane Grey was one of the godparents of his newborn son. Although he did not bear arms against Mary, he rashly published a ballad against popery on the day after she was proclaimed in London. Arrested at Limehouse on 3 Aug. by Sir William Garrard*, he was brought before the Privy Council and underwent the examination so vividly, if partially, recounted in his narrative. Of the 11 Councillors present the Earl of Bedford, who presided, and the 2nd Earl of Sussex, whose son Sir Humphrey Radcliffe* was lieutenant of the pensioners, could be expected to sympathize with Underhill, while the 12th Earl of Arundel and the secretary were clearly hostile. Two days later he was sent to Newgate, where he remained until 5 Sept., the order for his release having apparently taken two weeks to produce that result. Francis Russell sent him money while he was in prison.[5]

Upon the approach of Wyatt's rebels in February 1554 Underhill succeeded, after one rebuff, in taking his place alongside the gentlemen pensioners. He did so despite the fact that on the previous 4 Oct. his place as a gentleman-at-arms had been given to another. He even succeeded in serving at the royal marriage in the following July, but with the onset of persecution he withdrew with his family to Warwickshire after having had his books bricked up at Limehouse. He appears to have incurred no further trouble for his opinions. In 1555-7 he received considerable property under the wills of his brother Ralph and his aunt Jane Winter: this included Stoneleigh grange, which he sold, and Baginton, which he made his home and where, after being licensed to alienate lands and the advowson there in 1568, he is last mentioned in 1576. Included as a gentleman-at-arms in a list of Elizabeth's household compiled in 1558, he was assessed as a member of the household for the subsidy of 1566 but is not known to have returned to court.[6]

[1] Aged eight years and more at grandfather's i.p.m. 30 Oct. 1520, C142/35/70; '64 years or very nigh the same' on 19 Nov. 1576, C24/126/F. J. H. Morrison, *Underhills of Warws.* 28-31, 38, 43-44, 46-47; *Vis. Warws.* (Harl. Soc. xii), 31; *DNB.* [2] *CPR, 1553-4*, pp. 198-9; Lansd. 3(89), f. 198; E179/69/82; 407/1/2, 3. [3] *Narr. Ref.* (Cam. Soc. lxxvii), 132-71; *LP Hen. VIII*, i, iv. [4] R. C. Braddock, 'R. Household, 1540-60' (Northwestern Univ. Ph.D. thesis, 1971), 76-79; *Narr. Ref.* 136. [5] *CPR, 1553-4*, p. 324. [6] Ibid. pp. 198-9; 1566-9, p. 304; *VCH Warws.* vi. 24, 25, 235; Morrison, 52; Lansd. 3(89), f. 198; E179/69/82; 407/1/2, 3.

R.V.

UNTON (UMPTON), Edward (1534-82), of Wadley, Berks.; Langley, Oxon. and London.

MALMESBURY 1554 (Nov.)
OXFORDSHIRE 1563*
BERKSHIRE 1572

b. ?May 1534, 1st s. of Sir Alexander Unton of Chequers, Bucks. and Wadley by 2nd w. Cecily, da. of Edward Bulstrode of Hedgerley, Bucks.; bro. of Henry*. *educ.* I. Temple, adm. 3 Feb. 1551. *m.* 29 Apr. 1555, Anne, da. of Edward Seymour, Duke of Somerset, wid. of John Dudley, 2nd Earl of Warwick (*d.*21 Oct. 1554), 5s. inc. Edward† and Henry† 2da. *suc.* fa. 17 Dec. 1547. KB 15 Jan. 1559.[1]

Keeper, Malvern chase, Worcs. and Cornbury park, Oxon.; commr. musters, Berks. 1560, 1569, muster of horses, Oxon. 1565, 1580; j.p. Berks., Oxon. 1561–*d.*; sheriff, Berks. 1567-8.[2]

Edward Unton's family was not an ancient one. His grandfather Thomas Unton†, the first to achieve prominence, obtained a grant of arms under Henry VIII, was living at Wadley near Faringdon by 1514, and was knighted at the coronation of Anne Boleyn. His father's first wife was the elder daughter and coheir presumptive of John Bourchier, 2nd Lord Berners. Alexander Unton added to the lands around Faringdon by buying the manor of Wyke and died holding the manors of Sheepbridge,

Berkshire, Aston Rowant, Oxfordshire, and Stoken-church and Chequers, Buckinghamshire, and other lands in all three counties. There were also small estates, appurtenances of Sheepbridge, in Wiltshire and others in the Isle of Wight, claimed by Sir Alexander as heir to his childless younger brother Thomas, who had died in 1542; Edward Unton was to bring a suit in the court of requests against Morgan Cottesmore, the uncle of Thomas's widow, over lands in the Isle of Wight, and was to establish his right to at least part of the property there.[3]

In July 1548 the wardship of Edward Unton was granted to his mother with £20 a year from the manor of Wyke. Three years later he followed his father to the Inner Temple, where he was excused all offices for a fine of 40s. By February 1553 his mother had married Robert Keilway II*, formerly legal adviser to the Protector Somerset and still surveyor-general of the court of wards, who had been an overseer of Sir Alexander Unton's will. Keilway, a Wiltshireman, may have helped to procure both Edward Unton's return for Malmesbury while still under age and his younger brother's for Heytesbury: Keilway had been an overseer of and a beneficiary under the will of Sir Edward Baynton*, a former steward of Malmesbury abbey, whose daughter and widow had successively married Sir James Stumpe* of Malmesbury. The Unton brothers could also claim kinship through the Hyde family of South Denchworth, Berkshire, with the sheriff of Wiltshire, John Erneley (either the Elizabethan knight of the shire for Wiltshire of that name or his father); in 1542 Thomas Unton had appointed his 'uncle' William Hyde* and his 'cousin' John Erneley overseers of his will. A more distant kinsman, Sir Maurice Denys, for whom Keilway had probably acted as feoffee, sat for Malmesbury in 1547.[4]

In Easter term 1555, as Edward 'Umpton' of London, Unton was prosecuted in the King's bench for having been absent from Parliament without licence early in January 1555. In Michaelmas term of the same year he appeared in person and was allowed to make his answer in Hilary term. There was no further process until 1558 when he was fined 53s.4d. It was also in 1555 that Unton married the late Protector's daughter, six months after the death of her previous husband, who had been heir to the attainted Duke of Northumberland; the marriage was presumably arranged by his stepfather Keilway. The ceremony took place quietly at Hatford church, near Wadley, and seems to have given no offence to the crown since Unton was licensed to enter on his inheritance a month later. On the other hand, the marriage may have

been concealed: on 11 Nov. the Privy Council ordered the warden of the Fleet to bring 'Mr. Umpton' before it and he was not discharged until 18 Dec. His 'secession', his marriage or his Protestant sympathies may explain Unton's failure to sit again under Mary, although this may have been due to nothing more than his youth. Whatever the official attitude to his marriage, the crown later granted Unton's wife, who continued to be styled Countess of Warwick, a life interest in many of the lands which had been forfeited by her first husband and his father. In May 1558 the manor of Coombe and other property in Warwickshire was leased to Robert Keilway during Anne's life for an annual rent of £198; these payments, together with the reversion of the lands, were granted to Anne herself three days later. Further surrenders of royal claim on the Warwick land were to be made under Elizabeth, whose favour Unton enjoyed. He died on 16 Sept. 1582 and was buried at Faringdon.[5]

[1] Date of birth estimated from age at fa.'s i.p.m., Wards 7/4/21, 29, 42. J. G. Nichols, *Unton Inventories*, pp. xxx–xxxii, xxxv–ix, xlv–ix; *DNB* (Unton, Sir Henry); *Vis. Berks.* (Harl. Soc. lvii), 222. [2] Nichols, pp. xlii, xliv; *CSP Dom.* 1547–80, pp. 156, 340, 690; *APC,* vii. 251. [3] Nichols, pp. xvii, xxi–ii, xxx–xxxiii; *VCH Berks.* iii. 271; iv. 494; *VCH Oxon.* viii. 21–22; *VCH Bucks.* iii. 97, 99; *VCH Hants,* v. 193–4, 207; PCC 30 Populwell; Req. 2/8/263. [4] *CPR,* 1547–8, p. 321; 1553, p. 112; *Cal. I. T. Recs.* i. 159; PCC 30 Populwell, 28 Pynnyng, 20 Spert; Nichols, pp. xx, xxv–viii; *Vis. Berks.* (Harl. Soc. lvi), 100. [5] KB27/1176, 1188; Nichols, pp. xxxvii, lxxii; *CPR,* 1554–5, p. 14; 1557–8, pp. 103, 289; *APC,* v. 193, 205; C142/203/61; Pevsner, *Berks.* 140.

T.F.T.B.

UNTON (UMPTON), Henry (?1535–55 or later), of ?Aston Rowant, Oxon., and East Hanney, Berks.

HEYTESBURY 1554 (Nov.)

b. ?1535, 2nd s. of Sir Alexander Unton of Chequers, Bucks. and Wadley, Berks. by 2nd w. Cecily, da. of Edward Bulstrode of Hedgerley, Bucks.; bro. of Edward*. *educ.* ?Peterhouse, Camb. adm. Mich. 1547. prob. *unm., s.p.*[1]

The suggested identification of this Member rests upon the concurrent election of Unton's brother Edward for Malmesbury and the access which both enjoyed to local patronage. Their stepfather Robert Keilway II* was prominent in Wiltshire and the sheriff at the time was John Erneley with whom they were linked in marriage through the Hyde family of Denchworth; of particular significance for the younger Unton's election is the fact that the bailiff of Heytesbury, William Button II*, was a kinsman and associate of William Hyde*.

Unlike his brother (but not his uncle Edmund Ashfield), Unton was not prosecuted in the King's bench for being absent when the House was called early in 1555. Since the brothers could have been expected to act together, it may be that this circumstance, taken in conjunction with the silence which descends on the younger one, implies that he died during or shortly after the Parliament and was for that reason omitted from the list of those proceeded against. He is not mentioned in his brothers' wills of 1563 and 1581 or in the account of Sir Edward Unton's funeral in 1582.[2]

¹ Date of birth estimated from elder brother's. Wards 7/4/21, 29, 42; PCC 30 Populwell; *Vis. Berks.* (Harl. Soc. lvii), 222; *Vis. Bucks.* (ibid. lviii), 149.   ² PCC 35 Tirwhite, 4 Morrison; J. G. Nichols, *Unton Inventories*, pp. xxiv, xlv.

R.L.D.

UVEDALE (EVEDALE, UDALL, WOODALL), John (by 1482–1549), of Marrick, Yorks.

?Berwick-upon-Tweed   1529*[1]

b. by 1482, s. of Juliana Skoore (Scory) of Banwell, Som. *m.* da. of one Brightman, 1s. 1da.[2]

Clerk in the signet office 1503–?25; clerk of the pells, the receipt of the Exchequer 1516–*d.*; keeper, Brasted park, Kent by 1521; sec. to Duke of Richmond Aug. 1525–36, to Queen Anne Boleyn June 1533–6, to the council in the north Jan. 1537–*d.*; clerk of the signet in N. and S. Wales 1533; j.p. Yorks. (E., N. and W. Ridings) 1538–?*d.*; commr. for suppression of monasteries, Yorks. 1539; treasurer for the garrisons in the north, Aug. 1542–Jan. 1544, Oct. 1545–*d.*[3]

The view that John Uvedale was by-elected for Berwick to the Parliament begun in 1529 rests on a conjunction of circumstances. From at least the spring of 1532 one of the Berwick seats had been vacant through the death of John Cooper and the replacement is likely to have been made, as many others are known to have been, in time for the opening of the fifth session in the following February. Because no evidence of a by-election at Berwick survives, and as the borough does not appear on a list of vacancies, with suggestions for filling them, which Cromwell compiled about this time, any suggestion as to the identity of its new Member must be tentative, but Uvedale may be thought a likely choice. His Membership from at least 1534 is established by the inclusion of his name (in the form 'John evedalle') in another list drawn up by Cromwell, probably in December of that year, and thought to be of Members who had a particular, but unknown, connexion with the treasons bill then on its passage through Parliament; his official standing makes it certain that he had been brought into the Commons as a nominee of the government; and his employment in the north would have made his by-election at the border town an appropriate method of doing so. Once in the House Uvedale is also likely to have stayed there, and this he could have done as a Member for Berwick, not only in 1536, when the King asked that the previous Members should be returned, but in any or all of the three following

Parliaments, those of 1539, 1542 and 1545, for which the names of one or both of the Berwick Members are lost. He was, however, in the north during at least part of the third session of the Parliament of 1539.[4]

All that is known of Uvedale's parentage comes from the will of Juliana Skoore of Banwell, Somerset, who in 1542 left all her goods to George, son of Thomas Woodall, assigning his 'governance' during nonage to her son John Uvedale, one of the King's council in the north, whom she also appointed principal overseer. The identity of Juliana Skoore is not known: her first husband, John Uvedale's father, may have come from the family of Woodhall or Woodfall of Churchill by Banwell. Uvedale, in his own will, referred to 'my brother's bastard son George Uvedale'. Although he always signed himself Uvedale, John Uvedale's surname was often spelled as Woodall, especially by the 3rd Duke of Norfolk and other members of the council in the north. The Yorkshire family of Uvedale had given rise in the 13th century to two lines, one of which settled in Hampshire. If Uvedale sprang from either of these he probably owed his advancement to his Hampshire kinsmen: both Sir William Uvedale† of Wickham and his brother Henry†, who moved to Crichel in Dorset, were of the King's privy chamber and the first of them was for many years a member of the council in the marches of Wales.[5]

In addition to his work in the signet office, Uvedale succeeded Robert Blackwell as clerk of the pells at the Exchequer; this post he may have owed to the 2nd Duke of Norfolk, the lord treasurer, to whose will of 1520 he was a witness. As writer of the tallies and pells he was assessed for the subsidy of 1523 on goods worth £40; later in his career he executed this office through his son-in-law Gilbert Claydon. His ability brought Uvedale to the notice of the King and Wolsey, and in 1525 he was one of the group of trusted men chosen to conduct affairs in the north under the young Duke of Richmond. He became Richmond's secretary and remained a member of his council until the duke's death, although in 1528 he was brought to court by Wolsey to put his views on Irish policy before the King: earlier in that year the council in the north objected to his keeping the profits of an office which his deputy John Bretton had earned. Within a few years Uvedale was called on to serve other members of the royal family: in the spring of 1533 Cromwell sent from Calais a bill for the King's signature to his appointment as secretary to Anne Boleyn, and when in the following autumn he and others, including Cromwell, were granted leases of lead mines in Dartmoor forest he was styled 'the Queen's secretary'.[6]

The unrest in the north which culminated in the Pilgrimage of Grace led to the re-establishment of the King's council there in January 1536, under the lieutenancy of the 3rd Duke of Norfolk and with wider powers than before. Uvedale was reappointed as its secretary and made keeper of a new, specially designed, signet; he was to spend the rest of his life in the varied responsibilities arising from this office. In May 1537 he was sent with Anthony Rous* to survey Bridlington and Jervaulx abbeys. He assisted Norfolk in the examination of seditious persons in 1537 and 1538, being appointed to special commissions for the indictment of treason as well as to the commissions of the peace in these and later years. In October 1537 Chancellor Audley suggested to the King that the president and secretary of the council in the north should take recognizances either jointly or separately and offered, with Cromwell's assent, to make Uvedale a master in Chancery. For his part, Uvedale was by no means satisfied with his position: writing to thank Cromwell for his 'recent advancement' he nevertheless complained that the income was insufficient to ensure him qualified assistants, and two months later this 'old, true and steadfast friend' of the minister made an unsuccessful plea for some post under the King or Prince Edward. In 1539 Uvedale was appointed a commissioner to take the surrenders of five priories in Yorkshire, and in the next year that of the hospital of St. James in Northallerton. The wide interests arising out of his work were reflected in two letters to Cromwell in the spring of 1540: in the first he enclosed his draft of a bill to curb malt production at York, with the request that it should be corrected and 'preferred', and in the second he reminded the minister that when recently in London he had moved him 'to be a mean to the King' that all bishops should be enjoined to set up in cathedral and collegiate churches 'two or three bibles, as seemly and as ornately as they can deck them, with seats and forms for men of all ages to read and study on them'.[7]

Uvedale does not appear to have speculated in monastic property, but he found at Marrick a site for his own residence and in January 1538 he asked Cromwell to obtain for him a lease of the house, demesne and parsonage. He did not acquire it without some difficulty: writing as 'your oldest disciple' to thank Cromwell for the present of a stallion in April 1540, he sent William Strickland his servant for help in obtaining the lease which chancellor of augmentations had delayed, although he had passed other leases to persons who 'were of contrary opinions in the late commotions'. A 21-year lease was not issued until June 1541, and Uvedale had to wait another four years before attaining ownership.[8]

The preparation for the war against Scotland in 1542 laid on Uvedale the arduous duties of treasurer and paymaster of the forces under Norfolk's command. While remaining secretary and a member of the council, his clerkship was by the King's instructions committed during his absence to a man chosen by the president. He continued as sole treasurer until this office was split in preparation for an invasion of greater magnitude in the spring of 1544; in February (Sir) Ralph Sadler* was sent north to become high treasurer, leaving to Uvedale the title of under treasurer. His work, involving the distribution of large sums of money, was made more difficult by the constant shortage of coin to meet all demands. To save expense, the Earl of Hertford's advice to end Sadler's appointment was carried out in October 1545 and Uvedale again became sole treasurer. He remained in harness until his death on 20 Oct. 1549, although more than a year earlier he had written of his great age and grievous illness.[9]

Uvedale had acquired certain right in land, leases, mines and fees, which by his will of 24 Oct. 1546 he left to his son Avery, together with goods and jewels. To his daughter Ursula, wife of Gilbert Claydon, he bequeathed a large herd of cattle and sheep, and to his 'brother' Thomas Brightman a turquoise ring and an ambling horse. The will was proved on 2 Mar. 1550 by his son Avery, who was then aged 24 and more and who in the pardon roll of October 1553 was described as of Marrick *alias* of the Middle Temple.[10]

[1] LP Hen. VIII, vii. 1522(ii) citing SP1/87, f. 106v. [2] Date of birth estimated from first reference. Coll. Top. et Gen. v. 244, 253; PCC 6 Coode. [3] DNB; LP Hen. VIII, ii, iv–vii, xi–xvii, xix–xxi; Eliz. Govt. and Soc. ed. Bindoff, Hurstfield and Williams, 219; SP 1/29, f. 179; CSP Dom. 1601–3, Add. 1547–65, pp. 383–4; R. R. Reid, King's Council in the North, 102, 104, 150; CPR, 1547–8, p. 92. [4] LP Hen. VIII, vii. 1522(ii) citing SP 1/87, f. 106v; xv. [5] Coll. Top. et Gen. v. 240–6; PCC 6 Coode; E178/1966, f. 17; Surr. Arch. Colls. iii. 63–192 passim; Vis. Dorset ed. Colby and Rylands, 33–34; Hutchins, Dorset, iii. 144–5; Req.2/67/70. [6] LP Hen. VIII, ii, iv, vi, xv; Eliz. Govt. and Soc. 219; SP Hen. VIII, ii. 136–40; iv. passim; Test. Vet. ed. Nicolas, 604; Cal. I.T. Recs. i. 464; Cam. Misc. iii(4), pp. xxiv, lxx. [7] LP Hen. VIII, xii, xiv, xv, add; Reid, 150, 254 and n; SP Hen. VIII, iv. passim; Merriman, Letters, Thos. Cromwell, ii. 99; Elton, The Tudor Constitution, 203; Reform and Renewal, 26, 78. [8] LP Hen. VIII, xv, xviii; PCC 6 Coode. [9] LP Hen. VIII, xvii–xxi; P. H. Williams, The Tudor Regime, 90; APC, i–ii passim; SP Hen VIII, iv. passim; CSP Dom. 1601–3, Add. 1547–65, pp. 383–4; Wards 7/5/67; Hamilton Pprs. ed. Bain, ii. 605–6, 608, 612, 733; HMC Bath, iv. 73. [10] LP Hen. VIII, iv; PCC 6 Coode; CPR, 1553–4, p. 442; Req.2/22/4.

M.K.D.

VACHELL, Oliver (c.1518–64), of Buriton, nr. Petersfield, Hants and North Marston, Bucks.

HINDON 1553 (Oct.)

TAUNTON 1554 (Apr.)

b. c.1518, yr. s. of Thomas Vachell of Coley, Berks. by 2nd w. Margaret; half-bro. of Thomas Vachell I*. m.

by 25 Aug. 1537, Margaret, da. of Richard Norton of East Tisted, Hants, 2s. 4da.[1]

Gent. household of Stephen Gardiner, bp. of Winchester by 1537–55.[2]

It was certainly to Stephen Gardiner that Oliver Vachell owed his two elections for the bishop's boroughs. He had married the sister of one of Gardiner's advisers, John Norton*. In 1541 or 1542 he became bailiff of the episcopal manor of Bishop's Waltham, Hampshire, and remained so until his death; he enjoyed the same office at Havant during the 1550s. A fluent French speaker, he accompanied Gardiner on missions abroad and sometimes carried despatches to England. He deposed in favour of his master at Gardiner's trial in 1551 and was left £20 in his will. Like others of Gardiner's servants he seems to have remained a Catholic: his eldest son was to be a recusant, as was his nephew Thomas Vachell II*.[3]

Vachell inherited the manor of North Marston in Buckinghamshire; he also acquired, perhaps through his marriage, property near Petersfield which, during his service with Gardiner, he probably made his home. He died on 24 May 1564, his wife surviving him. No will has been found.[4]

[1] Aged 'a little over 19' in 1538, *LP Hen. VIII*, xiii. *Vis. Bucks.* ed. Metcalfe, 44; I. and A. C. Vachell, *Vachell Fam.* 148–9; C142/142/109. [2] *LP Hen. VIII*, xii. [3] Eccles. 2/155883–4, 155900; *LP Hen. VIII*, xii, xiii; Foxe, *Acts and Mons.* vi. 136; *Letters of Stephen Gardiner* ed. Muller, 80, 159; PCC 3 Noodes; Vachell, 148–9. [4] *LP Hen. VIII*, xx; C142/142/109.

R.V.

VACHELL, Thomas I (by 1500–53), of Coley, Berks.

READING 1529, 1536,[1] ?1539,[2] 1542, 1545,[3] 1553 (Oct.)

b. by 1500, 1st s. of Thomas Vachell of Coley by 1st w. Elizabeth, da. and coh. of William Cockworthy of Yarnscombe, Devon; half-bro. of Oliver Vachell*. *educ.* M. Temple, adm. 8 Feb. 1518. *m.* by 1521, Agnes, da. of William Justice* of Southampton, Hants and Reading, Berks., 4s. inc. Thomas II* 5da.[4]

Commr. subsidy, Reading 1523, 1524, relief Berks. 1550, goods of churches and fraternities 1553; other commissions 1527–51; escheator, Oxon. and Berks. 1534–5, 1545–6; j.p. Berks. 1536–44; steward, duchy of Lancaster, manors of Ascot and Deddington, Oxon. 1537–*d.*; dep. steward, Reading 1539; overseer, lands formerly of Reading abbey and Leominster priory, and bailiff, Reading 1540; victualler, Calais and Boulogne 1544–5.[5]

The family of Vachell had lived in Berkshire since the early 13th century, holding land at and near Reading. The shire had sent a Vachell to Parliament in 1324 and 1329, and Reading another in 1388, but by Thomas Vachell's time the tradition of public service had failed, his father having apparently taken no part in affairs.[6]

Despite the family's long connexion with Reading, Vachell was a country gentleman, not a townsman, and his return to Parliament in 1529 for a borough which generally chose its Members from among its own governing group implies that he, and perhaps also his fellow, John Raymond I, were imposed upon it from outside. If Vachell was a court nominee, there is no indication why this youngish man, with no known household connexion or public office, should have enjoyed such support: his association with Cromwell, even if it predated the minister's rise to power, could hardly have been of service in 1529. As a 'King's man', too, Vachell would have given less than complete satisfaction in the House. His name occurs in a list of Members drawn up early in 1533 and believed to indicate those, or some of those, who opposed the bill in restraint of appeals to Rome. The fact that Vachell's name is linked with those of several other men from Berkshire, or connected with that county, besides hinting at a measure of co-ordination, suggests that one source of opposition to the bill was fear of commercial reprisals abroad damaging to two of the country's staple occupations, sheep-rearing and cloth-making: it was probably Vachell's interest in pasture farming which in the following session got him involved in a bill limiting the size of flocks, his name being one of seven appearing on the dorse of the resulting Act. Its reappearance in a list of Members written by Cromwell on the back of a letter of December 1534 is harder to explain. From the character of this list the Members concerned appear to have been connected in a particular way with the treasons bill then passing through Parliament. At least six of those named had appeared on the list associated with the bill in restraint of appeals, and four of them belonged to the 'Berkshire group' discernible in that list: thus Vachell reappears in the company of some likely opponents of the treasons bill, but whether he is to be reckoned as one of them, or as one of its presumed supporters who make up the majority of the newly named Members, it is impossible to say.[7]

Vachell's restiveness—if such it was—in 1533–4 did not prevent his regular employment by Cromwell as a local watchdog. In November 1534 he reported to Cromwell that, as directed, he had been to Oxford to inquire into enclosures, and some two years later Sir George Throckmorton*, riding to confer with Sir William Essex*, met 'one Fachell' hastening to report to authority the circulation of seditious pamphlets, whose origin was investigated in December 1536 by a commission of which Vachell was a member. Vachell was rewarded for these services, first by the grant of the stewardship of two duchy of Lancaster manors, and then by being made Cromwell's deputy in the high steward-ship of Reading, an office to which Abbot Cook had appointed the minister late in 1538. Cook's gesture did not save his abbey from suppression or himself from execution, and Vachell played a part in both episodes. In September 1539 Sir William Peniston, a neighbouring landowner who claimed to have been granted the abbey, wrote in alarm to Cromwell on hearing that the deputy steward was seeking a certain wood and fishing rights. In February 1540 Vachell was granted 20 marks a year as overseer of the abbey's former lands and a further ten as bailiff of the town. Two months later he was disputing with a rival claimant the same office at Leominster, where John Hillesley* was acting as his deputy: it is not known how either this dispute or the one with Peniston was resolved. In August 1543 Vachell bought various of the abbey's lands for £127 and in the next year he obtained a 21-year lease of further ones. Additional income no doubt accrued from his supervision of a residence which the King started to build on the site of the abbey about 1541 and from his custodianship of Reading gaol.[8]

His activities and acquisitions did not endear Vachell to the men of Reading. The town had elected him and Raymond to Parliament again in 1536, doubtless in deference to the King's call for the return of their former Members, and probably it returned Vachell at least for a third time in 1539, when the election indenture, in common with nearly every other, is lost. The fact that this last election is not mentioned in the borough records (a unique occurrence during the century) is given point by the corporation's resolution of 11 Apr. that in future at least one of the town's Members should be a burgess, that is, presumably, a member of the merchants' guild. Such a protest could only have followed the return of two 'strangers', one of them almost certainly Vachell, who was however to continue as one of Reading's Members in subsequent Parlia-ments. In 1542 he was joined with a townsman, Richard Justice, and in 1545, the resolution of 1539 notwithstanding, with a 'stranger' in Cromwell's former protégé Roger Amyce; then, after missing the next two Parliaments, he attended his last in October 1553 with John Bell, another townsman.[9]

Vachell's unpopularity in Reading manifested itself in September 1539, when the corporation asked Cromwell to excuse the mayor-elect, Richard Justice, from having the oath administered to him by the deputy steward who, they declared, was not their friend. Cromwell insisted on this procedure and on 9 Oct. Vachell sat in the great hall of the former abbey to confirm the election; he did so twice more before the new charter of 1542 admitted the corporation's claim that the oath should be administered by the retiring mayor. When in August 1540, after Cromwell's fall, the King and Council paid a visit to Reading, the deputy steward was himself examined about complaints of the town's loss of liberties, but the continuing record of his services and rewards shows that Vachell was scarcely affected by the fate of his patron. He may have had friends in the conservative camp as his half-brother Oliver was a servant of Stephen Gardiner. The affair of the Windsor martyrs gave Vachell an opportunity to establish himself as an upholder of the Six Articles. Having been com-missioned with Richard Ward I* in 1543 to search for heretical books at Windsor, he was among those appointed to try the persons thus discovered: during the trial he intervened against one of the defendants, John Marbeck, who was nevertheless the only one to be pardoned, and at the end of it, although the most junior of the justices present, he passed sentence with the words, 'It must be done. One must do it. And if no man will, then will I'. The conservatism in religion thus displayed may explain the intermission in his parliamentary career during the reign of Edward VI as well as Queen Mary's grant of a pension of £10 a year for life 'for service at Framlingham', although the recipient of this reward may have been his son and namesake, who was already of age. That it was he, however, and not this son, who sat in the Queen's first Parliament is suggested by the fact that his death on 9 Dec. 1553, three days after that Parliament ended, took place in London.[10]

In the will which he had made on 20 Aug. 1551, at a time of religious uncertainty, Vachell gave no hint of his own doctrinal position. He also mentioned by name only his son Thomas, sole executor and sole witness, whom he nevertheless exhorted 'to be good to his brethren and sisters'. He asked to be buried in St. Mary's, Reading, where several members of his family had been baptized. His wife, who predeceased him, was probably the Agnes Vachell buried in the same church on 20 Oct. 1544.[11]

[1] *Reading Recs.* i. 166–7. [2] C. Coates, *Reading*, app. xiii. [3] *Reading Recs.* i. 191–2. [4] Date of birth estimated from marriage. *Berks. Arch. Jnl.* xl. 83–84; *Quarterly Jnl. Berks. Arch. Soc.* iii. 2–4; I. and A. C. Vachell, *Vachell Fam.* 32–33, 147–9. [5] *LP Hen. VIII*, iii, iv, viii, xi, xiii, xv, xvi, xviii, xx, xxi; *CPR*, 1547–8, pp. 75, 77; 1550–3, p. 142; 1553, pp. 351, 413; Somerville, *Duchy*, i. 631; *Reading Recs.* i. 172; R. R. Tighe and J. E. Davis, *Windsor Annals*, i. 544–5. [6] I. and A. C. Vachell, passim; *Reading MPs*, 20. [7] *LP Hen. VIII*, iv; vii. 1522(ii) citing SP1/87, f. 106v; ix. 1077 citing SP1/99, p. 234; House of Lords RO, Original Acts, 25 Hen. VIII, no. 13. [8] *LP Hen. VIII*, vii, xi–xv, xviii, xix; Elton, *Policy and Police*, 75; J. B. Hurry, *Reading Abbey*, 43, 135; *CPR*, 1553–4, p. 57. [9] *Reading Recs.* i. 172. [10] *LP Hen. VIII*, xii–xv; *Reading*

Recs. i. 172; Foxe, *Acts and Mons.* v. 474, 490–1; Tighe and Davis, i. 544–5; Lansd. 156 (28), f. 93; C142/100/3; E150/820/6. 11 PCC 25 Tashe; *Reg. St. Mary's Reading*, ed. Craw⁴urd, i. 1–4; ii. 89.

T.F.T.B.

VACHELL, Thomas II (by 1528–1610), of Coley, Berks.

READING 1555

b. by 1528, 1st s. of Thomas Vachell I* of Coley by Agnes, da. of William Justice* of Southampton, Hants and Reading, Berks. *m.* 5 Sept. 1546, Catherine, da. of Thomas Rede of Barton Court, nr. Abingdon, Berks., 1da. *suc.* fa. 9 Dec. 1553.[1]

J.p.q. Berks. 1554; commr. to survey lands taken by crown, diocese of Salisbury 1560, sewers, Bucks., Oxon. and Berks. 1567.[2]

Either Thomas Vachell or his father was awarded an annuity of £10 for services to Queen Mary at Framlingham, and when in May 1554 the son had licence to enter on his inheritance he had already been appointed to the quorum on the commission of the peace. In the following year he was returned for the borough which his father had long dominated. He may also have enjoyed the patronage of Sir Francis Englefield*, whose father had named the elder Vachell an executor of his will and who was now chief steward of Reading. Vachell's Catholicism, however, meant the virtual end of his career on the accession of Elizabeth.[3]

In 1585 Vachell was summoned in Oxfordshire (where his wife had brought him two manors at Ipsden) to furnish two light horse or £50 and replied that 'he hath always been charged in Berkshire in all services towards the queen's majesty'. In August 1588 Michael Blount* of Mapledurham, Oxfordshire, where Vachell owned land, was ordered as sheriff of that shire to arrest Vachell after vestments and apparently also books belonging to him had been found at Tilehurst, Berkshire. At about this time also his goods and chattels and two thirds of his lands in Berkshire and Oxfordshire were seized. On 16 July 1599 Sir Francis Knollys† and others raided Ufton Court, Berkshire, home of Francis Perkins, son-in-law of another Reading Member, Edmund Plowden, and seized £1,484 in gold, plate valued at £200 and precious chains and other valuables belonging to Vachell. Vachell was one of those to whom Plowden entrusted the control of his daughter Mary's dowry, and he was involved in the quarrel between Plowden's family and Sir Francis Englefield's nephew and namesake and, although not apparently committed to either side, was described by Andrew Blunden, Plowden's nephew, as one that 'loveth the house of Englefield as his own house'.[4]

As late as 9 Feb. 1609 a grant was made of the profits of Vachell's recusancy. By that time he had long been living at Ipsden in the care of his sister Anne, widow of Edmund Montague. He died there on 3 May 1610 but was buried in St. Mary's, Reading. His wife had presumably long been dead and their only daughter, Anne, had in 1565 been buried in St. Mary's at the age of 16. His heir was his nephew Sir Thomas Vachell, who had already in 1603 been granted the property seized by Knollys and who was later to marry Knollys's daughter Lettice. Sir Thomas Vachell was licensed to succeed to his uncle's lands in Burghfield, Mapledurham, Reading, Shinfield, Sulhampstead Abbot, Sulhampstead Banister and Tilehurst but in 1612 charged Anne Montague with exercising undue influence over her brother and with retaining a will. Members of the family continued to represent Reading into the 18th century.[5]

[1] Date of birth estimated from age at fa.'s i.p.m., C142/100/3; E150/820/6. *Quarterly Jnl. Berks. Arch. Soc.* iii. 32–34. [2] *CPR*, 1553–4, p. 17; 1558–60, p. 423; 1569–72, p. 219. [3] Lansd. 156(28), f. 93; *CPR*, 1553–4, p. 377; PCC 11 Dyngeley. [4] *Recs. Eng. Catholics*, ed. Knox, 300; SP 12/183/33; *APC*, xvi. 214, 218; Lansd. 61, art. 30; *Cath. Rec. Soc.* xviii. 7, 252; lvii. 2, 121; lxi. passim; *CSP Dom. Add.* 1580–1625, p. 424; *Recusant Hist.* xii. 102 seq.; PCC 54 Brudenell; *Trans. Salop Arch. Soc.* (ser. 2), ix. 137. [5] Add. 34765, f. 29v; C142/325/172; *Churchwarden's Accts. St. Mary's Reading, 1550–1662*, ed. Garry, 93, 110; *Register St. Mary's Reading*, ed. Crawfurd, i. 4.

T.F.T.B.

VALENTINE, John (by 1502–58/59), of Ipswich, Suff.

ORFORD 1523[1]

b. by 1502. *m.* Margaret, wid., 1s. 1da.[2]

?Member, household of Cardinal Wolsey; jt. customer, Ipswich by 1530–*d.*, portman by 1558.[3]

John Valentine was presumably the man of that name who succeeded Thomas Rush* as customer of Ipswich and was connected with the local family of Sone. Francis Sone, who was later to sit for Orford, and whom Valentine in his will called 'cousin', was the son of the John Sone from whom Valentine acquired a moiety of the manor of Campsea, Suffolk, in September 1545. It is likely, too, that Valentine was the man who figures in an undated list of members of Wolsey's household. That one of the Members for Orford in 1523 bore his name is known from evidence given in an exchequer suit of 1554 relating to rights in the town. A merchant from Dunwich recalled that 'one Valentine' and a Lincolnshire man whose name he did not remember had been returned for Orford in 1523. As the Lincolnshire man was the nominee of the 11th Lord Willoughby, Valentine may have been of the town's own choosing, but if he was one of Wolsey's servants his election was doubtless at the cardinal's prompting, with Rush acting as intermediary.[4]

The surname was an uncommon one at the time, and Valentine's early career remains obscure. Whatever his connexion with Orford, it was at Ipswich that he was to spend the greater part of his life. In 1545 his subsidy assessment in the east ward of that town was on lands worth £30. When making his will on 22 Sept. 1558 he described himself as portman of Ipswich but he apparently held no other municipal office. He also claimed gentility but whether by birth or advancement is not known. He provided for his wife and children, remembered several kinsmen and named his wife and Francis Sone executors and his parish priest supervisor. The will was proved on 4 May 1559.[5]

[1] E111/48. [2] Presumed to be of age at election. Suff. archdeaconry ct. bk. 18, f. 207. [3] E122/53/19, 54/3; 179/69/9; Select Cases in Star Chamber (Selden Soc. xxv), 280; Stowe 571, f. 8; Suff. archdeaconry ct. bk. 18, f. 207. [4] LP Hen. VIII, vi, xx, xxi; E111/48. [5] E179/181/270; Suff. archdeaconry ct. bk. 18, f. 207.

M.K.D.

VANE (FANE), Sir Ralph (by 1510-52), of Hadlow, nr. Tonbridge, Kent.

CONSTITUENCY UNKNOWN   1547*[1]

b. by 1510, o.s. of Henry Vane of Hadlow by Alice Fisher of Hadlow. *m.* by 1540, Elizabeth, da. and h. of Roland Brydges* of Clerkenwell, Mdx. and The Ley, Weobley, Herefs., *s.p. suc.* fa. 1533. Kntd. 30 Sept. 1544, kt. banneret 18/25 Sept. 1547.[2]

Servant of Cromwell by 1531; gent. pens. 1540, lt. by 1545–*d.*; chief gov. Cage and Postern parks, Kent, and Tonbridge warrens 1542; keeper, North Leigh park, Kent 1546; j.p. Kent 1547; commr. sewers 1540, chantries 1548, relief 1550.[3]

Sir Ralph Vane's Membership of the Parliament of 1547 is known from a reference in the Journal, recording that on 14 Jan. 1549 privilege was granted to John Keysar, 'servant to Sir Ralph Vane'. His name does not occur on the list of Members for the final session in 1552, although he was only indicted of treason the day before its opening and he was not executed until a month later. Presumably he was replaced as a Member shortly after his arrest in the previous autumn. His attainder was confirmed by an Act (5 and 6 Edw. VI, no. 37) passed before the dissolution. His constituency remains a matter for speculation but as one close to the Protector Somerset with experience of court and war he could have been found a place almost anywhere.[4]

Sprung from a family established at Tonbridge, Vane inherited a house and other property at Hadlow. As a young man he attached himself to Cromwell who in 1538 recommended his transfer to the royal service. During Wyatt's embassy to

Charles V between 1537 and 1540 Vane was several times the bearer of despatches between the minister and the ambassador. Named to the King's new bodyguard early in 1540 he attended the reception of Anne of Cleves at Blackheath. Unharmed by the palace revolution which destroyed Cromwell he kept his post in the Household and obtained two manors and three rectories in Kent in 1541 and the lease of demesne lands at Hadlow a year later. He served in the continental campaigns of 1543 and 1544, being knighted by Henry VIII at the fall of Boulogne, and was then charged with three others to hire mercenaries in Germany for the army. After being relieved of that task he travelled to the Netherlands to help raise the money to pay the mercenaries.[5]

It was presumably as a gentleman pensioner involved in the war effort that Vane became familiar with the Earl of Hertford, later the Protector Somerset. As one of Henry VIII's executors Somerset designated him as one of the unnamed royal servants to be beneficiaries under the King's will, and as a consequence in October 1547 Vane received a new grant of the rectory at Hadlow, with that of Tonbridge, as well as several manors. He attended the obsequies in memory of the King, was put on the Kent bench in the spring and went with Somerset to Scotland in the summer, capturing the Earl of Huntley at Pinkie and being made a knight banneret at Roxburgh. In reward for capturing Huntley and other services in Scotland he received somewhat belatedly in July 1550 the former chapel and college of St. Stephen, Westminster (save for the upper chapel already given by Edward VI to the Commons for its use) and various of the college properties. Nothing has been discovered about his part in the *coup d'état* against Somerset in 1549 but when Somerset was arrested in October 1551 Vane fled. Found hiding under straw in a Lambeth stable and taken to the Tower with other adherents of Somerset he was accused of conspiring to kill the Earl of Warwick, with whom he was at variance over rights at Postern in Kent. Condemned of felony in treason in January 1552, although protesting his innocence like a 'ruffian', he was hanged on Tower Hill on the 26th of the following month.[6]

[1] CJ, i. 6. [2] Date of birth estimated from first reference. PCC 4 Hogen; Vis. Kent (Harl. Soc. lxxv), 43; LP Hen. VIII, xvi, xvii, xix. [3] M. L. Robertson, 'Cromwell's servants' (Univ. California Los Angeles Ph.D. thesis, 1975), 484–5; LP Hen. VIII, v, xiii, xv–xvii, xix–xxi; E179/69/62, 63, ex inf. W. J. Tighe; CPR, 1547–8, pp. 85, 233; 1548–9, p. 135; 1553, p. 355. [4] CJ, i. 6; Hatfield 207. [5] PCC 4 Hogen; LP Hen. VIII, v, xii, xiii, xv–xx. [6] CPR, 1547–8, p. 175; 1550–3, p. 12; Lit. Rems. Edw. VI, 219, 353, 391 and n.; LC2/2, f. 41v; W. K. Jordan, Edw. VI, i. 64; ii. 64, 80, 85, 87–88, 110; APC, iii. 244–6, 279, 296; B. L. Beer, Northumberland, 116; CSP Dom. 1547–80, p. 4; Rymer, Foedera, vi(3), 216; Machyn's Diary (Cam. Soc. xlii), 10, 15; DKR, iv(2), 230–2; Wards 7/6/26.

P.S.E.

VAUGHAN, Charles (by 1529–74 or later), of Hergest, Herefs.

RADNORSHIRE 1553 (Oct.)

b. by 1529, 1st s. of James Vaughan of Hergest by Elizabeth, da. of Sir Edward Croft of Croft Castle. *m.* (1) by 1550, Elizabeth, da. of Sir James Baskerville of Eardisley, 1s. 1da.; (2) by 1552, Margaret, da. of Sir William Vaughan of Porthaml, Brec., wid. of Roger Vaughan of Clyro, Rad., 5s. 4da. *suc.* fa. 1550 or later.[1]

Commr. subsidy, Rad. 1558; j.p. Herefs. 1558/59–73/74, Rad. 1558/59–64.[2]

Like its namesake of Porthaml, the Vaughan family of Hergest, near Kington, was descended from Roger Vaughan of Bredwardine, Hereford-shire, who fell at Agincourt. Charles Vaughan had already married, as his second wife, one of his cousins of Porthaml when in 1552 the pair appeared at the Radnorshire great sessions. His election in the next year to the first Marian Parliament may have followed the death of his father, an active local official last met with as a relief commissioner in December 1550. Vaughan's return for Radnorshire is explained both by geography—Hergest lies on the border of that county and his wife's former home at Clyro within it—and by the resulting connexions: his brother-in-law Richard Blike was returned for the shire in 1547 and for its Boroughs in 1555. More striking is the fact that, alone among occupants of Welsh seats, Vaughan was noted as having 'stood for the true religion', that is, as having opposed the restoration of Catholicism. Whence he had derived his nonconformity can only be guessed at, but it may be recalled that his first cousin (Sir) James Croft* was to be implicated in Wyatt's rebellion. Although there is nothing to suggest that Vaughan would have joined Croft's projected rising in Hereford-shire, he had doubtless incurred enough disfavour to forfeit the chance of re-election or of local advancement. Not until Elizabeth's accession was he to be made a justice of the peace.[3]

In 1564 Vaughan obtained part of the lordship of Ismynydd in Radnorshire and four years later he applied for a lease of Colwyn forest in the same county. The last reference found to him is his reappointment to the Herefordshire bench in 1573/74. The Charles Vaughan who was elected to the Parliament of 1572 for Shaftesbury was his distant cousin of the Bredwardine line, a servant of the earls of Pembroke who settled in Dorset and died in 1597.[4]

[1] Date of birth estimated from first marriage. Dwnn, *Vis. Wales*, i. 258; *Vis. Herefs.* ed. Weaver, 5, 21, 97; *Hist. Kington* (anon.), 223. [2] E179/224/568; *CPR*, 1560–3, pp. 438, 445; 1563–6, pp. 23, 29; 1569–72, p. 225. [3] *Hist. Kington*, 216–17; *DWB* (Vaughan fam. of Hergest); *CPR*, 1547–8, p. 84; 1553, p. 364; NLW ms Wales 26/8, m. 10v; Bodl. e Museo 17. [4] *Augmentations* (Univ. Wales Bd. of Celtic Studies, Hist. and Law ser. xiii), 523, 525.

P.S.E.

VAUGHAN, John I (by 1512–77), of Sutton Place, Surr., Sutton-upon-Derwent, Yorks. and London.

?HEREFORDSHIRE	1542
HORSHAM	1547*
SURREY	1547*[1]
PETERSFIELD	1553 (Mar.), 1554 (Apr.), 1554 (Nov.)
BLETCHINGLEY	1555
HEDON	1559
NORTHUMBERLAND	1563
DARTMOUTH	1571
GRANTHAM	1572*

b. by 1512, yr. s. of Thomas Vaughan of Porthaml, Brec. by Elizabeth, da. of Henry Miles *alias* Parry of Newcourt in Bacton, Herefs. *m.* 1548/49, Anne, da. and h. of Sir Christopher Pickering of Killington, Westmld. and Escrick, Yorks., wid. of Sir Francis Weston and of Sir Henry Knyvet of Charlton, Wilts., 2s. 2da.[2]

Page of the chamber by 1533, sewer by 1538; steward, Pembridge, Herefs. 1533–*d.*, Penrith, Cumb. 1559–*d.*, Galtres forest, Yorks. 1564–*d.*, keeper, Cawood park, Yorks. 1568, chief steward, crown lands, Yorks. (E. Riding) 1572, Cumb. and Westmld. n.d.; j.p. Surr. by 1555, Yorks. (E., N and W. Ridings) 1558/59–*d.*, Cumb. 1569–*d.*, custos rot. Yorks. (E. Riding) by 1566; member, council in the north Dec. 1558–*d.*; sheriff, Yorks. 1559–60; commr. eccles. causes, province of York from 1561, musters, Surr. from c.1576.[3]

John Vaughan came of a junior branch of the Vaughan family of Porthaml and his relatives included Blanche Parry, Queen Elizabeth's gentle-woman, Sir Roger Vaughan*, (Sir) Thomas Parry* and Sir William Cecil. The last named once corrected in his own hand a pedigree showing the degrees of their relationship.[4]

Vaughan's entry into the royal household cannot be dated with certainty, but it is probable that the John Vaughan who served as a groom of the chamber for the first 25 years of Henry VIII's reign was an older namesake (and perhaps kinsman), and that Vaughan himself began as a page of the chamber not long before the grant to him in that capacity in September 1533 of the stewardship of Pembridge and three other Herefordshire manors. This strengthening of his links with Herefordshire, to which his mother belonged and to which his home at Talgarth was adjacent, would help to identify him as the first knight for that shire in 1542 if, as the compilers of the *Official Return* accepted, the now illegible return bore his name and that of James Croft. To his local standing he could have added his position at court and his cousinship with the sheriff, Sir Richard Vaughan. Whether he was re-elected for the shire to the succeeding Parliament is not known, the Herefordshire names being lost, but thereafter he was to achieve a life-long Membership by way of seats elsewhere. His return for Horsham to the Parliament of 1547 (when his name appears on the indenture over an erasure) he presumably owed to Admiral Seymour, who then held the barony of Bramber in which the borough lay. Vaughan may have attracted Seymour's notice at court or have been recommended to him either by one of his kinsmen, Cecil or Thomas Parry, or by his fellow-Member Andrew Baynton. Some years earlier Baynton had accompanied Sir Henry Knyvet on an embassy to Ratisbon and within a further two years Vaughan was to marry Knyvet's widow. She was the heir to great estates in Middlesex and the north, and during the minority of her eldest son Henry Weston*, she and Vaughan lived at the Weston seat, Sutton Place in Surrey.[5]

Vaughan thus became one of the leading gentlemen in that county, and although in August 1549 Henry Polsted* unsuccessfully recommended him to Cecil for appointment to the Surrey bench he was soon to gain a greater distinction. Both the knights of the shire for Surrey died during the Parliament of 1547, Sir Anthony Browne in April 1548 and Sir Christopher More in August 1549. Browne was evidently replaced by Sir Thomas Cawarden, whose name stands first for the shire on the list of Members as revised in 1551–2, but of a successor to More nothing is heard before 1 Feb. 1552, when the Council sent a writ for a by-election with an instruction to the sheriff, Robert Oxenbridge*, to 'prefer' (Sir) Thomas Saunders*. This recommendation notwithstanding it was presumably Vaughan who was returned and took the vacant seat during the last session. It is, however, likely that he replaced not More, but More's immediate successor (whose identity is unknown), for it would otherwise be hard to explain the holding of the by-election after the opening of the session and after a lapse of two-and-a-half years since More's death. No by-election is known for Horsham.[6]

The Council seems not to have taken amiss this rejection of its recommendation, for at the election to the Parliament of March 1553 it was prepared to support—the letter concerned survives only in draft—both Vaughan and Cawarden. This time, however, Vaughan was passed over, although he managed to find a seat at his stepson's newly enfranchised borough of Petersfield. Henry Weston was still under age and Vaughan probably needed backing, which was perhaps supplied by William Paulet, Marquess of Winchester, a local magnate who was also master of the wards: he may have already become a relation by marriage of his fellow-Member, Sir Anthony Browne, who was also a

kinsman of the Duke of Northumberland. Vaughan himself could hardly have controlled the borough in his stepson's name, for although they were to share its representation in the two Parliaments of 1554, with Vaughan taking the senior seat, he did not sit in the first Parliament of the reign. In 1555 he was returned for Bletchingley, a borough controlled by his former colleague Cawarden: his name may have been inserted in the indenture in a different hand from that of the document. He was not among the Members who 'seceded' from the Parliament of November 1554 but he opposed a government bill in that of 1555. A few months later Vaughan, whose Protestant sympathies were to be apparent in the succeeding reign, was questioned about his relations with Henry Dudley, Henry Peckham* and others who had been proclaimed traitors: he denied having had any communication with them. This opposition to the Marian regime may have prevented Vaughan's sitting in the last Parliament of the reign.[7]

On the accession of Elizabeth, Vaughan was appointed a member of the council in the north, and thereafter spent the greater part of his time in Yorkshire, living at Escrick, one of the estates of his wife's inheritance, until he bought the manor of Sutton-upon-Derwent in 1563. He died on 25 June 1577.[8]

[1] Hatfield 207. [2] Date of birth estimated from first reference. Yorks. Peds. (Harl. Soc. xcvi), 405–6; Vis. Yorks. (Harl. Soc. xvi), 251; Glover's Vis. Yorks. ed. Foster, 120–1; Vis. Herefs. ed. Weaver, 4; Jones, Brec. iv. 43, 271; Gen. Vaughan of Tretower ed. Vaughan; C. A. Bradford, Blanche Parry, 11; Harl. 2141, f. 200. [3] LP Hen. VIII, vi, xiii, xiv, xvi, xvii, xx; CPR, 1558–60, p. 36; 1560–3, pp. 170–1; 1563–6, pp. 86, 256; 1566–9, pp. 172–3; 1569–72, pp. 223–4, 364; 1572–5, pp. 168–9, 468; Lansd. 10(17), f. 84; R. R. Reid, King's Council in the North, 493; SP11/5, f. 45. [4] SP13/Case H. no. 10. [5] LP Hen. VIII, vi, viii; C219/18B/33, 19/108; CPR, 1553–4, p. 229. [6] SP10/8/48; APC, iii. 470–1. [7] Royal 18 C, xxiv, f. 290v; C219/24/153; Guildford mus. Loseley 1331/2; SP11/8/56. [8] CPR, 1558–60, p. 207; 1560–3, p. 581; C142/177/58.

P.H.

VAUGHAN, John II (by 1525–74), of Kidwelly, Carmarthen and Golden Grove, Carm.

CARMARTHEN BOROUGHS   1558, ?1571
CARMARTHENSHIRE   1572*

b. by 1525, 1st s. of Hugh Vaughan of Kidwelly by 1st w. Jane, da. of Morris ab Owen of Bryn-y-Beirdd, Llandeilo, Carm. and Upton Castle, Pemb. m. Catherine, da. of Henry Morgan of Muddlescwm, Carm., 2s. Henry† and Walter†; at least 6s. 5da. illegit. suc. fa. 1532/40.[1]

Bailiff, Carmarthen in 1553, mayor 1554–5, 1563–4, alderman in 1555; receiver, duchy of Lancaster, Kidwelly 10 Mar. 1554–d.; j.p.q. Carm. 1558/59–d.; commr. subsidy 1560, piracy 1565; customer, Milford Haven, Pemb. 1560–d.; steward, Cilgerran, Pemb. 26 Sept. 1560–d.; sheriff, Carm. 1562–3; bailiff, coroner, escheator and town clerk, Kidwelly by 1572.[2]

The family of Vaughan of Golden Grove was of illegitimate descent from the medieval princes of

Powys. John Vaughan's father was the first of the line to settle in Carmarthenshire, where he married the daughter of a Lancastrian supporter who was second cousin to Sir Rhys ap Thomas of Dynevor; on the execution in 1531 of Sir Rhys's grandson and heir Rhys ap Gruffyd he was appointed bailiff and rent collector of the Dynevor lands in the lordship of Kidwelly.[3]

John Vaughan himself took advantage of the dispersal of the Dynevor estates: in 1546 he obtained a lease of the manor of Dryslwyn at a rent of £10 10s. and acquired tenements, mills and rents in the commote of Is-Cennen. Then living at Kidwelly, he was also a notable figure at Carmarthen, where in 1550 he was included in the commission issued to the mayor and leading townsmen to levy the borough's fee-farm. To his leading place in the officialdom of both towns he was to add the customership of Milford Haven and a share in county administration. Pardoned on the accession of Mary as a resident of Carmarthen, he was one of those imprisoned in the Fleet in 1556 for having attacked the deputies of the crown searcher, Thomas Phaer*, as they were confiscating an illegal cargo in Carmarthen harbour. Phaer was to be one of his fellow-Members in the Parliament of 1558.[4]

In his later years a notorious smuggler-in-chief, Vaughan died in 1574.[5]

[1] Date of birth estimated from first reference. Dwnn, *Vis. Wales*, i. 214; *W. Wales Hist. Soc. recs.* i. 58; *Trans. Cymmrod. Soc. 1963*, pp. 96–102; PCC 26 Martyn. [2] *Cal. Sheriffs etc. of Carmarthen* (NLW ms 5586B), 9–10; C219/24/234; Lloyd, *Carm.* ii. 467; Somerville, *Duchy*, i. 643; *CPR*, 1563–6, p. 332; E178/3345, m. 9; *APC*, vii. 285. [3] *DWB*; *Trans. Cymmrod. Soc. 1963*, pp. 96–102; *LP Hen. VIII*, iv, v. [4] E315/230, ff. 81v, 161, 192v; SC6/Hen. VIII, 5590, m. IV. [5] E178/3345; *Trans. Cymmrod. Soc. p.* 102.

P.S.E.

VAUGHAN, Rhys I (by 1523–80/82), of Cors-y-Gedol in Llanddwywe, Merion.

MERIONETH 1545

> *b.* by 1523, 1st s. of William Vaughan of Cors-y-Gedol, Merion. and Cilgerran, Pemb. by Margaret, da. of Sir William Perrot of Haroldston, Pemb. *m.* Gwen, da. of Gruffydd ap William ap Madog Fychan, 3s. 4da. *suc.* fa. ?by 1544.[1]
> Sheriff, Merion. 1547–8, Nov. 1555, 1556–7; commr. relief 1550, subsidy 1556; j.p. 1558/59–*d.*; escheator 1566–7.[2]

Rhys Vaughan's pedigree can be traced back to Osbwrn Wyddel, an Irishman who settled in west Merioneth and married the heiress of Cors-y-Gedol, a ward of Prince Llewelyn the Great. More recently the family was notable for its support of the Lancastrian cause: Rhys Vaughan's grandfather helped to defend Harlech castle against the Yorkists and is said to have built the *Ty Gwŷn* at Barmouth to facilitate a Lancastrian invasion. Both Jasper and

Henry Tudor are believed to have sought refuge at the Vaughan home at Cors-y-Gedol. No such dramatic interest attaches to the life of Rhys Vaughan, who seems to have been a quiet country squire, although his replacement of the murdered Lewis ab Owen* as sheriff in 1555 could have stirred ancestral memories. His election to the Parliament of 1545, at the outset of his career in local administration, was perhaps the work of his neighbour Edward Stanley I* as sheriff. Vaughan had presumably been a justice of the peace for some time before his appearance on the commission of 1558/59; in 1575 his area of jurisdiction was defined as the commote of Ardudwy, where he had been assessed for subsidy in Mary's reign on lands worth £5 a year. In the muster of June 1571 he supplied one light horseman, so ranking equal with the other leading gentlemen of Merioneth. He was a sick man on 8 Aug. 1580 when he made his will. After asking to be buried in Llanddwywe church and leaving 3s.8d. to Bangor cathedral he provided for his wife, sons and kin. The will was proved by his executors, his sons Richard and Robert, on 6 Mar. 1582.[3]

[1] Date of birth estimated from return to Parliament in December 1544. Dwnn, *Vis. Wales*, ii. 218–19. [2] *CPR*, 1553, p. 363; 1560–3, p. 447; E179/222/323; R. Flenley, *Cal. Reg. Council, Marches of Wales*, 135, 212. [3] *DWB* (Osbwrn Wyddel; Vaughan fam. of Cors-y-Gedol); W.W.E.W. 'The Vaughans of Cors-y-Gedol', *Arch. Camb.* (ser. 4), vi. 1–16; E. R. Jones, *Barmouth*, 184; Flenley, 74, 135; E179/222/323; PCC 14 Rowe.

P.S.E.

VAUGHAN, Rhys II (by 1532–74 or later), of Builth Wells, Brec.

BRECONSHIRE 1554 (Nov.)[1]

> *b.* by 1532.[2]
> Sheriff, Brec. 1558–9.

Rhys Vaughan was probably a kinsman of Sir Roger Vaughan, whose election as knight for Breconshire to the Parliament of March 1553 he attended and whom he was to replace 18 months later after Vaughan's two re-elections. His own election he may have owed as much to the 1st Earl of Pembroke as lord of Builth and to the 12th Earl of Arundel as to local connexions. A copy of the list of Members of the third Marian Parliament bears a note that 'Ll[?oydd] Gryffith brought the return for Brecknok from my l[ord] steward'. The returns for both the shire and the Boroughs are lost, but they had presumably been sewn together by the sheriff according to custom and sent to Arundel as lord steward of the Household for transmission to Chancery. Nothing has been found to link Arundel with the sheriff, John Lloyd, or with either Vaughan or the Member for the Boroughs, Meredydd Games. Unlike Games, Vaughan was not one of those who quitted the Parliament before its dissolution, and this may have conduced to his re-election to the next Parliament, that of 1555, for which the name of the knight for Breconshire is lost. It was perhaps his stay in London which led Vaughan and Thomas Jenkin to borrow from Lewis Vaughan of London, a servant of the 1st Baron Rich; after they had returned home their creditor petitioned in Chancery for repayment, but with what result is not known. Vaughan was pricked as the first Elizabethan sheriff of Breconshire and as such he returned two of his kinsmen to the Parliament of 1559. All that is known of the rest of his life is that during March 1574 an information was laid in the Exchequer about his alleged forcible entry into the demesne of Builth castle.[3]

[1] Huntington Lib. Hastings mss Parl. pprs.   [2] Date of birth estimated from first reference.   [3] C1/1479/33; 219/20/176; Huntington Lib. Hastings mss Parl. pprs.; E159/366, Easter 260.

P.S.E.

VAUGHAN, Robert I (by 1524–75 or later), of Presteigne, Rad.

NEW RADNOR BOROUGHS 1554 (Apr.), 1554 (Nov.),[1] 1559

b. by 1524, poss. s. of William Vaughan of Glasbury. *?m.*, at least 1s.[2]

J.p. Rad. 1558/59–73/74 or later; sheriff ?1562–3, 1567–8.

Robert Vaughan is not easily distinguished from his namesakes in the area and elsewhere, but there are grounds for identifying him with Robert Vaughan of Presteigne. The sheriff who returned him to both Parliaments of 1554 was John Bradshaw I*, who had made Presteigne his second home after Ludlow, and the knights for Radnorshire on each occasion were linked by marriage with branches of the Vaughan family, the sheriff's son John Bradshaw II with the Vaughans of Clyro, Radnorshire, and John Knill with those of Hergest, Herefordshire. No connexion has been established between Vaughan and Robert Vaughan II, who was returned to the Parliament of November 1554 for Grampound.

Vaughan was assessed at Presteigne for the subsidy of 1545 on goods worth £6 and for that of 1558 on lands worth £2 a year. As a justice in Radnorshire he was to be accounted by the bishop of Hereford in 1564 'a poor man' and only a lukewarm supporter of Protestantism. If it was he who was sheriff in 1562–3 his description as of Glasbury makes it likely that he was the son of William Vaughan of Glasbury, a commissioner for the assessment of the relief in Radnorshire under Edward VI. He was an executor of his brother Richard Vaughan's will of 28 Sept. 1559, which included the bequest of a house in St. David Street, Presteigne, to his son William; he was also mentioned in the will of Lewis ap David of Old Radnor in connexion with a lease. The only litigation Vaughan is known to have been involved in was a chancery case of Mary's reign, when he was defendant in a dispute over lands in Painscastle.[3]

There are glimpses of Vaughan's further career until 1575, after which nothing has been found about him.

[1] Huntington Lib. Hastings mss Parl. pprs.   [2] Date of birth estimated from first reference.   [3] E179/224/546, 568; *Cam. Misc.* ix(3), 17; *CPR*, 1553, p. 419; *Trans. Rad. Hist. Soc.* xxviii. 15, xxx. 56; C1/1367/41; R. Flenley, *Cal. Reg. Council, Marches of Wales*, 75, 136.

P.S.E.

VAUGHAN, Robert II

GRAMPOUND 1554 (Nov.)

The Robert Vaughan who sat for Grampound in Mary's third Parliament has not been identified. He is almost certainly to be distinguished from Robert Vaughan I, elected on the same occasion for New Radnor Boroughs; a double return for these widely separated constituencies is improbable and there is no trace of a by-election at either. Yet unlike his Radnor colleague, who was a local man, the Member for Grampound had no known link with that borough, a circumstance reflected in the fact that both his own name and his fellow-Member George Tadlowe's were inserted on the indenture in a different hand from that of the document. Tadlowe is thought to have enjoyed the patronage of William Paulet, Marquess of Winchester, and Winchester's relative by marriage the 12th Earl of Arundel, and to have come in for Grampound through the influence of the Arundells of Lanherne. Although no connexion along these lines can be inferred for Vaughan, he could have enjoyed one of his own. If he was the clerk to Oliver Leder*, the Six Clerk in Chancery, who under his master's authority penned a new charter for London in 1547, he might have been sponsored by (Sir) Walter Mildmay*, for besides being Leder's colleague in the duchy of Lancaster Mildmay was an official in the duchy of Cornwall. Vaughan's identification with the chancery clerk would also be suggestive of a family relationship with Stephen Vaughan*, who since 1545 had held the clerkship of faculties in Chancery jointly with John Griffith *alias* Vaughan, perhaps another relative, and this in turn give rise to the supposition that Robert Vaughan was the merchant taylor of that name, this being Stephen Vaughan's own company. If, like Stephen Vaughan, Robert Vaughan was a tradesman-turned-official he could have sought professional status by entering an inn of court and thus have been the man of that name admitted to Gray's Inn in 1548. He is not mentioned in Stephen Vaughan's will of 1549 or in Sir Oliver Leder's of 1554.[1]

If Vaughan thus shared a London background with Tadlowe, a haberdasher who rendered political services to the City, his interests may also have touched Tadlowe's at another point. This turns upon whether he was the Robert Vaughan who wrote the prologue and epilogue of the *Dyalogue defensyve for women agaynst malycyous detractoures* (1542), although perhaps not the poem itself which has been attributed to Robert Burdett (q.v.). Neither the provenance of this work, nor Vaughan's contribution to it, yields clues to his identity, for the 'Mistress Arthur Hardberde' to whom he addressed it remains a mere, if intriguing, name, and the Margaret Vernon whose name he worked into it as an acrostic, although readily identifiable as the first wife of the 'King of the Peak', is probably there on Burdett's account rather than Vaughan's. Yet the resemblance between his role and Tadlowe's encouragement of Ralph Robinson is in favour of their having been associated in other activities. No further reference to Robert Vaughan has been found to add to the few and uncertain ones here assembled.[2]

[1] City of London RO, Guildhall, rep. 11, ff. 361v, 367v. [2] *HL Bull.* ii. 165–72; F. L. Utley, *The Crooked Rib*, 255–6, 272–3; *N. and Q.* ccxxi. 537–9; *The Arundel-Harington Ms* ed. Hughey, i. 302–3; ii. 411–12; information from Dr. Mary L. Robertson of the Huntington Lib.

A.D.K.H.

VAUGHAN, Sir Roger (by 1522–71), of Porthaml, Talgarth, Brec.

BRECONSHIRE	1553 (Mar.),[1] 1553 (Oct.), 1554 (Apr.), 1559
BRECON BOROUGHS	1563
BRECONSHIRE	1571

b. by 1522, 1st s. of Sir William Vaughan of Porthaml by Catherine, da. of Jenkin Havard of Brec. *m.* (1) Catherine, da. of (Sir) George Herbert* of Swansea, Glam., 5s. inc. Rowland†; (2) Eleanor, da. of Henry Somerset, 2nd Earl of Worcester. *suc.* fa. 1546 or later. Kntd. 1551.[2]

J.p. Brec. 1543, 1555, q. 1558/59–?*d*.; commr. relief, Brec. 1550, goods of churches and fraternities, Brec. and Herefs. 1553, felons, Herefs. 1555, armour, Brec. 1569, musters 1570; chancellor and receiver, lordships of Brecon and Hay, Cantref Selyf, Pencelli and Alexanderstone, Brec. July 1546–*d*.; sheriff, Brec. 1551–2; steward, lordships of Huntington and Kington, Herefs. May 1554–*d*.; custos rot. Brec. by 1559.[3]

The Vaughan family of Porthaml was a cadet branch of the Vaughans of Tretower, Breconshire, themselves an offshoot of the line established at Bredwardine, Herefordshire, by the Sir Roger Vaughan who was killed at Agincourt. It was this Sir Roger's great-great-grandson Sir William Vaughan who gave importance to the Talgarth branch by his leasing of the lordship of Dinas in 1529 and his appointment in 1538 as chancellor and receiver of the lordships of Brecon and Hay, in the hands of the crown since the attainder of the 3rd Duke of Buckingham. This office Sir William Vaughan surrendered in 1546 in favour of his heir Roger. He seems to have died soon afterwards, leaving the younger Vaughan to maintain the family's progress.[4]

Vaughan was helped to do so by his marriage to a niece of William Herbert I,* 1st Earl of Pembroke. He may have served under Herbert against the western rebels in 1549, and he was probably knighted in October 1551 on the occasion of Herbert's ennoblement and before his own shrievalty. As a past sheriff he was a suitable choice for the knighthood of the shire in March 1553, but Pembroke presumably lent him support as president of the council in the marches; three Herberts were returned to this Parliament, two in Montgomeryshire and another for Wenlock, as were Vaughan's near kinsman John Vaughan II, his cousin from Tretower Thomas Parry and possibly also his brother-in-law David Evans. Vaughan is unlikely to have been called upon to declare himself in the succession crisis of the following July and the pardon which he sued out from Queen Mary was probably a conventional safeguard. Re-elected to the first two Parliaments of the reign, he did not oppose the initial measures towards the restoration of Catholicism (as did his brother-in-law Charles Vaughan) and he was given local office and included in the new commission of the peace. In 1557 he commanded 250 men in the French campaign under the Earl of Pembroke.[5]

Vaughan's father had acquired the wardship of the coheirs of Henry Miles *alias* Parry of Newcourt in Bacton, Herefordshire (brother-in-law to John Vaughan II); Sir Roger Vaughan evidently used this as one of his residences for it was as of Porthaml and Newcourt that he received a general pardon at Elizabeth's accession. He sat in the first three Elizabethan Parliaments and died a few days after the last of them ended, on 6 June 1571. His widow married Sir Henry Jones*.[6]

[1] Only the christian name remains on the indenture, C219/20/176. [2] Date of birth estimated from first reference. Jones, *Brec.* iii. 43; Dwnn, *Vis. Wales*, i. 189; *DWB*; *CPR*, 1553, pp. 364, 376. (Vaughan fam. of Porthaml). [3] C193/12/1; SP11/5/6; 12/17, ff. 18–20; *CPR*, 1550–3, p. 394; 1553, pp. 364, 414, 419; 1553–4, p. 161; E179/219/38; *APC*, v. 135; *CSP Dom.* 1547–80, p. 176; R. Flenley, *Cal. Reg. Council, Marches of Wales*, 60, 69; *LP Hen. VIII*, xxi. [4] Jones, ii. 193; *LP Hen. VIII*, xiii, xxi. [5] *CPR*, 1553–4, p. 430; *HMC Foljambe*, 6. [6] *CPR*, 1558–60, p. 207; Wards 7/14/91.

P.S.E.

VAUGHAN, Stephen (by 1502–49), of St. Mary-le-Bow, London.

LANCASTER 1547*

b. by 1502. *m.* (1) by 1536, Margery Gwyneth (*d.*16 Sept. 1544), 1s. 2da.; (2) lic. 27 Apr. 1546, Margery, wid. of Henry Brinklow of London.[1]

Servant of Cromwell by 1524; King's factor, the Netherlands c.1530–46; writer of the King's books 1531; clerk of dispensations and faculties in Chancery 1534–*d.*; pres. of the English factory at Antwerp 1534; commr. to survey the King's jewels 1535; gov. Merchant Adventurers, Bergen op Zoom, Holland 1538–?45; ambassador to the Netherlands Sept. 1538–Jan. 1542; under treasurer, Tower II mint 25 Mar. 1544–*d.*[2]

Stephen Vaughan is thought to have been the son of a London mercer of moderate status. Nothing is known of his education unless he attended St. Paul's school. He was no linguist and was later in life to regret the inadequacy of his own education compared with the cultural background of the European diplomats with whom he was sent to negotiate. His career as a royal factor and emissary developed from his business training and force of character.[3]

It was as a successful merchant adventurer trading in the Netherlands that Vaughan must have become known to Cromwell, through whom he undertook various services for Henry VIII and, at least on one occasion, for Wolsey. He was mentioned by Cromwell in a letter as early as 1523: it was Cromwell who intervened to stop charges of heresy against him in 1529. By 1530 Vaughan, while still conducting private affairs, had become factor and intelligence agent of Cromwell and the King. At the end of that year he was engaged in an effort to return William Tyndale to favour and recruit him into the King's service. This mission was apparently undertaken on Vaughan's own initiative and his reluctance to abandon it brought him temporarily under censure from the King and Cromwell. But in July 1531 he secured his first official appointment, that of writer of the King's books, vacant through the death of Thomas Hall whose clerkship at the hanaper was taken over by Cromwell for himself.[4]

During the next decade Vaughan was selected for four important missions about which he sent lengthy reports to England. In December 1532 he journeyed to Paris and Lyons to discover French reactions to English foreign policy, especially concerning the King's divorce. In July of the following year he was in Germany to sound the political attitudes of the Lutheran princes. Between December 1533 and the autumn of 1535 he was occupied with the affairs of the merchant adventurers as crown agent in the Netherlands. In September 1535

he travelled on a short mission to deliver £5,000 to the English ambassadors in Denmark. He acquired the full rank of ambassador in September three years later when sent to the court of the Dowager Queen Mary of Hungary in the Netherlands. Chosen on account of his status with the merchant adventurers, he accompanied Thomas Wriothesley and Sir Edward Carne*, who were both recalled when war threatened in March 1539. Vaughan was left to carry on the mission and at the end of the year he entertained Anne of Cleves at Antwerp and accompanied her to England.[5]

In reward for his services, in July 1533 Vaughan had received an annuity of £20, back-dated to the previous year. This was followed in 1534 by the grant of a clerkship in Chancery, to be held *in absentia*, for which in May 1545 he was to secure a new patent to himself jointly with John Griffith *alias* Vaughan. Cromwell, who described Vaughan in 1529 as 'sometime my servant' and who trusted him sufficiently to appoint him an executor, procured for him a grant of the priory of St. Mary Spital in Shoreditch. In 1541 Vaughan was assessed for the subsidy in the parish of St. Botolph, London, at £66 13s.4d. in lands and fees.[6]

Vaughan's grasp of finance was fully used in government service especially when he was the King's sole financial agent abroad from 1544 to 1546. He was involved in raising mercenary troops for the French war and in borrowing large sums of money through Florentine and other bankers, notably Jasper Ducci and the house of Fugger. Letters to Paget and Wriothesley in 1545 and 1546 describe his search for a suitable second wife, whom he married at Calais because the King refused permission for him to leave his business and go to London; early in 1547 Queen Catherine Parr's debts included £116 to Stephen Vaughan, 'husband of [Margery] Vaughan, late your grace's silk woman'. The end of the French war brought Vaughan's usefulness to an end and with failing health he asked to return to England. Early in 1546 he tried, unsuccessfully, to obtain the treasurership of the chamber which was given to Sir William Cavendish*. About 1547 he was listed among those who, having possessions to the yearly value of £40 or more, had not compounded for knighthood.[7]

Vaughan's absence abroad had prevented him from taking up his responsibilities as under treasurer at the Tower mint and even on his return he did not do so until after the death of Thomas Knight (1 Feb. 1548), whose appointment in July 1545 as under treasurer to control the second mint in the Tower had made Vaughan's office a sinecure. His general pardon obtained on 22 Jan. 1549 (during the second session of the Parliament of 1547) showed that he still held his posts at the Chancery and mint. It was probably as a government official that he had been elected to Parliament for the duchy borough of Lancaster in the autumn of 1547, especially since his fellow-Member was Sir Thomas Chaloner, a teller of the Exchequer and clerk of the Privy Council. The chancellor of the duchy of Lancaster, Sir William Paget, who doubtless nominated Vaughan, had been in continuous correspondence with him during the 1540s.[8]

Vaughan died in London during the third session of Parliament on 25 Dec. 1549, thus causing a by-election at which William Ward I was chosen. By will dated 16 Dec. Vaughan left his soul to the Trinity and his body to be buried in the church of St. Mary-le-Bow. He bequeathed rings to a number of his friends and colleagues including Sir Martin Bowes*, Sir John Mason*, (Sir) Ralph Sadler*, and his two supervisors Thomas Lodge, citizen and grocer, and John Griffith *alias* Vaughan. One third of his goods were left to Stephen, Anne and Jane, Vaughan's children by his first wife. He left rents of £26 6s.8d. to his second wife, as well as his house at St. Mary Spital for nine years. His property consisted of tenements, shops and land in London and its suburbs which were to be held for his heir Stephen, then aged 12 and more. The will was proved on 26 Feb. 1550 by Vaughan's executor and brother-in-law John Gwyneth, clerk. Vaughan's widow married George Rolle* and on his death Sir Leonard Chamberlain*.[9]

[1] Date of birth estimated from first reference. *London IPMs* (Brit. Rec. Soc.), i. 87, 178; W. C. Richardson, 'Stephen Vaughan, financial agent of Hen. VIII', *Louisiana State Univ. Studies, soc. science ser.* iii. 21–23, 85 n. 29; *DNB.* [2] Merriman, *Letters Thos. Cromwell*, i. 362; *LP Hen. VIII*, v, vii, xiii, xix; *CPR*, 1548–9, p. 161; Richardson, 18, 19; *Brit. Numismatic Jnl.* xlv. 70. [3] Richardson, 38. [4] Richardson, 25–34 et passim; M. L. Robertson, 'Cromwell's servants' (Univ. California Los Angeles Ph.D. thesis, 1975), 578–9; Elton, *Reform and Renewal*, 38–41; *Reform and Reformation*, 129; *LP Hen. VIII*, v. [5] Richardson, passim; *LP Hen. VIII*, v–xiv; Elton, *Reform and Reformation*, 185. [6] Merriman, 60, 63, 362; *CPR*, 1550–3, p. 153; Richardson, 15; E179/144/120; *LP Hen. VIII*, xvii. [7] Richardson, 15, 20–22, 45–76; *APC*, i. passim; C. E. Challis, *The Tudor Coinage*, 180; SC 6, Edw. VI/726; SP10/2, f. 97. [8] Challis, 86–89; *Brit. Numismatic Jnl.* xxxvii. 93–97; *CPR*, 1548–9, p. 161. [9] *London IPMs*, i. 87, 178; Hatfield 207; PCC 5 Coode; C1/1319/9–14; City of London RO, Guildhall, rep. 12(1), f.251v; 12(2), ff. 349, 351; 13(1), ff. 154v, 235v; 14, f. 109v.

M.K.D.

VAUGHAN, Thomas (by 1479–1543), of Dover, Kent.

DOVER 1523,[1] 1539[2]

b. by 1479. *m.* 2da.[3]

Jurat, Dover for every year for which records survive from 1500 to *d.*, bailiff 15 Dec. 1503–*d.*, mayor 1515–16, 1518–19, 1527–8, 1532–3; bailiff to Yarmouth 1519.[4]

In his pardon of 28 June 1510 Thomas Vaughan is described as 'of Dover, Crick in lordship of Chepstow, and London, soldier of Calais, bailiff of Dover, yeoman or waterbailiff', but of his background in Monmouthshire and London or his previous service at Calais nothing has come to light. To his 40-year tenure of the crown office of bailiff of Dover he was to add a variety of martial and municipal services. During the French war of 1513–15 he both provided and captained ships and received gunpowder for the defence of the town; between 1519 and 1521 he performed similar services and in 1520 he saw the King embark for the Field of Cloth of Gold; in June 1524 he took the muster of the lord warden's retinue on its departure for France. The onset of war in 1542 found him a captain under the command of the warden; he had earlier been one of those charged with viewing the works at Dover harbour. The owner or tenant of property in various wards of the town, Vaughan represented Dover at several Brotherhoods between 1502 and 1528 and took part in such missions as that of 1516 to the warden about Sandwich's dispute with the other ports over a sum of £44 and another of 1521 in connexion with a *quo warranto* inquiry. In September 1536 the Brotherhood chose him to administer the oath to the new warden, Sir Thomas Cheyne*, if Thomas Wingfield* was not present to do so.[5]

Save in the unlikely event of his having been the Member in 1510 whose name is lost, Vaughan was first elected for Dover in 1523. The writ, issued on 23 Jan. and received by the town from the warden on 20 Feb., was accompanied by a royal letter requiring the election of 'discreet, expert and sufficient persons' who were resident and had held municipal office. These criteria were fully met by both Vaughan and his fellow-Member Robert Nethersole, but their attendance was to prove less satisfactory: they did not leave Dover until 19 Apr., four days after Parliament opened, and Nethersole alone appears to have attended the second session after the three-week prorogation in late May and early June. Vaughan's absence, which may have been excused by a call to share in the preparations for the invasion of France, relieved the town of part of its burden of wages. Given 3s.4d. when he set out (on a hired horse for which the town paid 20d. and accompanied by one John Fuller, whose journey cost the town a further 4s.), and welcomed home with 16d. worth of wine, he was eventually paid £3 15s., the sum due for his 35 days of attendance and travel, against twice that amount paid to Nethersole. Even so, Dover was compelled to levy a tax to recoup this expenditure, after fruitless appeals to Folkestone, Faversham and the Isle of Thanet, as 'limbs' of the port, for contributions. Vaughan was to achieve a better attendance at his only other Parliament, that of 1539. Elected with John Payntor on 23 Mar., he was present for 36 days out of the 56 of the first two sessions, for which he was paid £4 4s., and for 63 out of the 73 of the third, receiving £6 6s.[6]

By his will, made on 22 July 1543 and proved on the following 2 Oct., Vaughan left his lands and the residue of his goods to his brother William, who was to have the custody of his daughters Catherine and Christian until they came of age. To them and to a certain Thomas Vaughan he left 5 marks a year for life. His brother was to be his executor and the vicar of Northbourne the overseer. As one of the witnesses was the vicar of Ripple, which like North-bourne lies nearer to Deal than Dover, Vaughan appears to have ended his life in that neighbourhood.[7]

[1] Add. 29618, f. 187. [2] Ibid. f. 316. [3] Date of birth estimated from first reference. Canterbury prob. reg. A23, f. 96. [4] Add. 29617-18 passim; Egerton 2092-4 passim; *CPR*, 1494-1509, p. 335; *LP Hen. VIII*, i; *Cinque Ports White and Black Bks.* (Kent Arch. Soc. recs. br. xix), 176. [5] *LP Hen. VIII*, i, iii, iv, vii, xv, xvi, xviii, xix, add.; Stowe 146, f. 86; Add. 29618, f. 139; Egerton 2093, ff. 4-18 passim, 49, 146v; *Cinque Ports White and Black Bks.* 128-205 passim. [6] Add. 29618, ff. 187-92v, 199v, 312v, 316; Egerton 2092, ff. 461, 538. [7] Canterbury prob. reg. A23, f. 96.

P.H.

VAUX, Sir Nicholas (c.1460-1523), of Great Harrowden, Northants.

?NORTHAMPTONSHIRE 1515[1]

b. c.1460, o. s. of Sir William Vaux of Great Harrow-den by Catherine, da. of Gregory Penison or Peniston of Coursello, Provence. *m.* (1) Elizabeth, da. of Henry, 5th Lord FitzHugh, wid. of Sir William Parr† (*d.*1483/84) of Kendal, Westmld., 3da.; (2) 1507/8, Anne, da. and coh. of Sir Thomas Green of Boughton and Greens-Norton, Northants., 2s. 3da. *suc.* fa. 4 May 1471. Kntd. 16 June 1487, banneret 17 June 1497; *cr.* Baron Vaux 27 Apr. 1523.[2]

Steward, Olney and Newport Pagnell, Bucks. 1485; numerous other stewardships; j.p. Northants. 1485–*d.*; commr. musters 1488, subsidy 1512, 1515; sheriff 1495–6, 1501–2, 1516–17; constable, Rockingham castle, Northants. 1502; lt. Guisnes 8 July 1502–*d.*; knight of the body 1508.[3]

Nicholas Vaux's mother, an attendant on Queen Margaret of Anjou, remained constant to her mistress when others forsook the Lancastrian cause. Her husband, whom she had married not long before she obtained her letters of denization, was slain at the battle of Tewkesbury after which he was attainted and his property forfeited, but not even his death shook Catherine Vaux's loyalty: she stayed by the Queen during her imprisonment in the Tower and on Margaret's release in 1476 went with her into exile (as she had done earlier in the 1460s), living with her until her death six years later. Catherine's two children did not share either her

confinement or her travels abroad; instead, Nicholas Vaux was brought up in the household of Margaret, Countess of Richmond, without charge even though Edward IV restored two manors to the family for the maintenance of him and his sister.[4]

Catherine's devotion was rewarded after the triumph of Henry VII at Bosworth, where Nicholas Vaux, as a protégé of Margaret Beaufort, probably fought under her husband Lord Stanley; the petition for the reversal of the attainder on Vaux's father and the forfeiture of his property was accepted by the King in the Parliament of 1485, and not long after Vaux was named to the commission of the peace for his home county. He fought for the King at Stoke and Blackheath, being knighted on the field for his service in both battles. Not only was he active and diligent in local government but he was also frequently at court attending all the great state occasions at home and abroad until his death; in 1511 he entertained Henry VIII at Harrowden. It was as a soldier and diplomat, however, that he made his mark. Given the important command at Guisnes, he distinguished himself during the Tournai campaign in 1513 and then in the missions (he had had some earlier experiences in negotiating, chiefly with Burgundy) to the French King about the English withdrawal and the several royal marriage treaties. Later, he was one of the devisers of the Field of Cloth of Gold. His sister had also benefited from the change of dynasty: she entered the royal household, became governess to Henry VII's daughters and married successively Sir Richard Guildford† and the father of Sir Nicholas Poyntz*.[5]

Vaux was a natural candidate for election to Parliament, although in the absence of so many returns for the early Tudor period he is known to have been a Member only in 1515 when he and Sir John Hussey took a memorandum on certain Acts from the Commons up to the Lords. Presumably he sat for his own shire on this occasion as he was afterwards appointed to the Northamptonshire commission for the subsidy which he had helped to grant.[6]

In October 1522 Sir William Sandys reported that Vaux was laid 'very sore' at Calais. Evidently he recovered sufficiently to return to England where in the following year he was summoned to the Upper House as a baron, apparently after the Parliament had opened at the Blackfriars. He did not survive the first session, dying on 14 May at the hospital of St. John, Clerkenwell. Three days previously he had made a will by which he provided for his children and servants and left the residue of his estate to his executors, who included Sir Henry

Guildford*, George Throckmorton* and Richard Knightley*; among the supervisors he appointed Henry Marney†, Lord Marny, and Sir William Parr*. He was presumably buried at the Blackfriars, which of his three choices for interment was the nearest.[7]

[1] LJ, i. 46. [2] Birth follows Wood, Ath. Ox. ed Bliss, i. 41; G. Anstruther, Vaux of Harrowden, 2, 489; CP; EHR, lxxxvii. 82, 99. [3] CPR, 1485–94, pp. 279, 495; 1494–1509, pp. 255, 550, 552; CCR, 1500–9, nos. 99, 131–2; LP Hen. VIII, i; Statutes, iii. 88, 169. [4] Anstruther, 4–7; CPR, 1452–61, p. 342; 1476–85, p. 94. [5] Anstruther, 7–31; LP Rich. III and Hen. VII (Rolls Ser. xxiv), i. 403, 410; ii. 87, 291; LP Hen. VIII, i–iii; Rutland Pprs. (Cam. Soc. xxi), 31, 45; C. G. Cruickshank, Army Royal, 58; Chron. Calais (Cam. Soc. xxv), 3, 86. [6] LJ, i. 46; Statutes, iii. 169. [7] Anstruther, 37; LP Hen. VIII, iii; Orig. Letters, ed. Ellis (1st ser.), i. 223; PCC 11 Bodfelde.

A.D.K.H.

VAVASOUR, Sir William (1514–66), of Hazlewood, Yorks.

YORKSHIRE 1553 (Oct.)

b. 20 Nov. 1514, 1st s. of John Vavasour of Hazlewood by Anne, da. of Henry, 6th Lord Scrope of Bolton. m. by 1537, Elizabeth, da. of Anthony Calverley ?of Calverley, at least 6s. 5da. suc. fa. 11 Aug. 1524. Kntd. 11 May 1544.[1]
J.p. Yorks. (W. Riding) 1542–d., (E. Riding) 1561–d.; commr. benevolence, Yorks. (W. Riding) 1544/45, relief 1550, goods of churches and fraternities 1553, castles and enclosure of borders 1555; other commissions 1555–65; sheriff, Yorks. 1548–9, 1563–4; member, council in the north Sept. 1553–d.; capt. Berwick-upon-Tweed, Northumb. Mar. (patent 21 May) 1555–Aug. 1556; ?master of ordnance in the north 1557.[2]

Of a family reputedly settled at Hazlewood, near Bolton abbey, from the time of the Conqueror, William Vavasour succeeded to his inheritance at the age of nine and was in his 25th year when he had livery. He was nominated but not pricked as sheriff in 1543, 1546 and 1547, served in the Scottish campaign of 1544 as captain of 98 men and was knighted at Leith. In the following March he was one of the captains appointed to garrison the borders, his contingent of 100 consisting of his own and Sir Nicholas Fairfax's* men. He saw service during the civil commotions of 1549, being rewarded with 100 crowns for his part in suppressing 'the rebels of the north', and in March 1550, during his first shrievalty, he was granted £60 'for certain expenses'.[3]
Vavasour came to the fore under Mary, being appointed to the council in the north and made captain of Berwick, although after holding the captaincy for little more than a year he surrendered it to Thomas Wharton I,* 1st Baron Wharton. In expressing its pleasure that he had yielded to Wharton's demand the Privy Council promised Vavasour a seat on the council in the north. In July 1557 he was thought fit to be master of the ordnance in the north and in September 1558 was

one of those who received thanks for their exploits at Coldingham. His election as knight of the shire at the opening of the reign had doubtless been promoted by the president of the council in the north, the 5th Earl of Shrewsbury, and made easier by the Catholicism which kept him, and all his fellow-Members from Yorkshire, out of the ranks of those who opposed the Marian Restoration. That he did not sit again under Mary probably reflects the competition for seats from more powerful figures like Wharton.[4]

Vavasour accommodated himself sufficiently to the Elizabethan regime to be retained on the council in the north and to be pricked sheriff in 1563, but as one who in the following year was judged 'no favourer' of the Anglican settlement could have had little future in public life when he died on 29 May 1566. By his will of the previous 10 Dec. he had directed that he should be buried 'without pomp' at Hazlewood and had named as executors his wife, eldest son and brother Christopher. The son John, aged 28 and more, had licence to enter on the inheritance on 8 Nov. 1566.[5]

[1] Date of birth given at declaration of age, C142/57/79. Vis. Yorks. (Harl. Soc. xvi), 330; Dugdale's Vis. Yorks. ed. Clay, ii. 226–7; Gooder, Parlty. Rep. Yorks. ii. 12–13; LP Hen. VIII, xix. [2] LP Hen. VIII, xvi, xvii, xx; CPR, 1547–8, p. 92; 1550–3, p. 394; 1553, pp. 328, 353, 414; 1553–4, p. 26; 1554–5, p. 111, 299; 1555–7, p. 54; 1560–3, pp. 187–8, 436; 1563–6, pp. 21, 123–4; 1569–72, p. 216; R. R. Reid, King's Council in the North, 493; APC, v. 109, 317; vi. 123. According to LP Hen. VIII, xx Vavasour was pricked sheriff in Nov. 1545 but PRO Lists, ix. 163 gives Sir Christopher Danby*. [3] J. J. Cartwright, Chaps. Yorks. Hist. 367; LP Hen. VIII, iv, xiv, xviii–xxi; HMC Bath, iv. 58, 66, 70, 72; CPR, 1553, p. 316; APC, ii. 354, 407. [4] APC, v. 109, 122, 124, 288, 309, 317; vi. 123, 396; Reid, 181. [5] Cam. Misc. ix(3), 70; Leeds Phil. and Lit. Soc. Procs. x(6), 192–3, 218, 226–7; C142/144/135; York wills 19, f. 401; CPR, 1563–6, p. 530.

L.M.K./A.D.

VENABLES, Sir Thomas (by 1513–80), of Kinderton, Cheshire.

CHESHIRE 1553 (Mar.), 1563

b. by 1513, 1st s. of Sir William Venables of Kinderton by Eleanor, da. and coh. of Richard Cotton of Ridware, Staffs. m. Maud, da. of Sir Robert Needham of Shavington, Salop, 3s. 3da. suc. fa. 31 July 1540. Kntd. 11 May 1544.[1]
Chamberlain, Middlewich, Cheshire 1540–72; j.p. Cheshire 1543–7, q. 1561–d.; sheriff 1544–5, 1556–7; commr. benevolence, Chester 1544/45, musters, Cheshire 1545, 1548, relief 1550, goods of churches and fraternities 1553; gent. of the chamber to Prince Edward by 1547.[2]

Thomas Venables came of a family settled in Cheshire since the Norman Conquest. On his father's death in July 1540 he inherited lands valued by the inquisition at £166 a year. He also quickly took his place in local administration: he was nominated (but not pricked) as sheriff in 1542, brought on to the bench in the following year and made sheriff in 1544. He had first served in the field when he led a contingent under the 3rd Earl of Derby in Lancashire during the Pilgrimage of Grace. In 1544 he took part in the Earl of Hertford's invasion of Scotland and was knighted at Leith, but when in the following April the 5th Earl of Shrewsbury appointed him to lead 3,000 men against the Scots he excused himself on the grounds that the King had appointed him sheriff of Cheshire 'during pleasure' and that he was also commissioned in the marches of Wales to organize coastal defence.[3]

Venables made his entry at court before the death of Henry VIII, whose funeral he attended as a gentleman of the chamber to Prince Edward; he retained his status in the Household until at least 1558, when he was listed as an 'old pensioner'. His standing at court and in the county explains his election to the Parliament of March 1553: he sat with Sir Thomas Holcroft, with whom he had been knighted in 1544 and whose association with the Duke of Northumberland's supporter Sir Richard Cotton* he also shared. With his Catholic leanings (which may help to explain why he had not been pricked sheriff when nominated in the three previous years) Venables could hardly have found this a congenial experience, but he was not above acquiring, as soon as the Parliament was over, 11 salthouses in Middlewich and Nantwich, Cheshire, all former monastic properties, for which he paid £236. His absence from the Commons under Mary did not reflect any estrangement from her government, which he served in his county and which granted him a renewal for 21 years of his father's lease of the town of Middlewich and the office of chamberlain there. By its terms no free burgess of the town could be made without the consent of the lessee and of the lord treasurer. On its expiry, the lease was granted by Elizabeth to another.[4]

Venables sat in Elizabeth's second Parliament and despite an unfavourable report on his religious outlook in 1564 he was retained as a justice until his death on 19 July 1580.[5]

[1] Date of birth estimated from age at fa.'s i.p.m., Ches. 3/67/24. *Vis. Cheshire* (Harl. Soc. xviii), 229; (lix), 241; Ormerod, *Cheshire*, iii. 195–200; *LP Hen. VIII*, xix. [2] R. H. Morris, *Chester*, 154; *LP Hen. VIII*, xx, xxi; *CPR*, 1547–8, p. 81; 1553, p. 360; 1554–5, pp. 168–9; 1560–3, p. 444; 1563–6, p. 28; 1566–9, p. 179; *CSP Dom.* 1547–80, p. 6; LC2/2, f. 53v; Royal 7, cxvi, f. 94; Lansd. 3(89), f. 194. [3] Ormerod, iii. 187, 195; *LP Hen. VIII*, xi, xvii, xix, xx; *HMC Bath*, iv. 66. [4] *CPR*, 1553, pp. 199, 349, 376, 387; 1554–5, pp. 168–9; 1557–8, p. 453. [5] *Cam. Misc.* ix(3), 76; Ormerod, iii. 196.

P.S.E.

VENTRIS, Thomas (by 1526–81), of Cambridge.

CAMBRIDGE 1558, 1559

b. by 1526, prob. 2nd s. of Robert Ventris of Cambridge by Agnes. *m.* Joan, 3s.[1]

Treasurer, Cambridge 1547, common councilman 1552, mayor 1559–60, alderman by 1561; commr. gaol delivery 1561.[2]

There were at least two Cambridgeshire men of this name at the time but the more likely of them to have been mayor and Member was the Cambridge man whose father Robert made a will in 1541 as a privileged person entitled to have it proved in the vice-chancellor's court. Thomas Ventris was for some time vintner to the university, but he lost the appointment to John Edmonds[†] because of 'his ingratitude to the university in denying that he was beholding to the university for that licence to sell wine there'. By the reign of Elizabeth he probably did not need the university's custom, for the borough treasurers' accounts show that he supplied all the presents of wine given to noblemen, counsel and others by the corporation as well as that consumed by municipal officers themselves. In later life he also dealt in foodstuffs.[3]

It was probably this Thomas Ventris who leased Cambridge property formerly owned by the Austin friars. In 1549 Ventris was described as a former master of the Cambridge merchant guild, then abolished; he went to London in 1555 as one of the borough's spokesmen in its dispute with the university, but otherwise he did not take a leading part in borough affairs until the reign of Elizabeth. He was probably related to John Ventris, a Marian exile, and in 1564 was himself described by the bishop of Ely as a 'godly' justice. He left no will to confirm this opinion but died intestate late in 1581, administration of his estate being granted to his wife and sons.[4]

[1] Date of birth estimated from first reference. Camb. Univ. Arch. vice-chancellor's ct. wills, 1, f. 63; PCC admons. act bk. 1581–95, f. 21; Req.2/124/16. [2] C. H. Cooper, *Cambridge Annals*, ii. 22, 66; F. Blomefield, *Coll. Cant.* 225; *CPR*, 1560–3, p. 406. [3] *Vis. Cambs.* (Harl. Soc. xli), 53; Cooper, ii. 205, 427; Downing Coll. Camb. Bowtell mss Liber Rationalis 1510–60 passim; Req.2/288/28. [4] *LP Hen. VIII*, xix; Cooper, ii. 47, 97; C. H. Garrett, *Marian Exiles*, 317–18; *Cam. Misc.* ix(3), 25; Req.2/124/16; PCC admons. act bk. 1581–95, f. 21.

D.F.C.

VERNEY, Edmund (1528–58), of Pendley in Tring, Herts.

BUCKINGHAMSHIRE 1553 (Mar.), 1555

b. 25 July 1528, 1st s. of Sir Ralph Verney of Pendley by Elizabeth, da. of Edmund Bray, 1st Lord Bray, of Eaton Bray, Beds.; bro. of Francis*. *m.* (1) 1546, Dorothy, da. of Sir Edmund Peckham* of Denham, Bucks.; (2) by 1555, Alice ?Knyvet. *suc.* fa. April 1546.[1]

The Verney family can be traced in Buckinghamshire from the 13th century, but its earliest property at Middle Claydon was acquired by the first Sir Ralph Verney[†] about 1467 and the house at Pendley across the Hertfordshire border by his son Sir

John†. Thereafter the family continued to prosper although its successive heads were short-lived; the fourth Sir Ralph was 37 when he died in April 1546 leaving the 18 year-old Edmund as the eldest of his ten children. Of a landed estate valued at £330 a year Edmund Verney inherited one third, including the manors of Pendley and Claydon (leased by the Giffords), a flock of 900 ewes and the household goods at Pendley. His wardship, first acquired by the 2nd Earl of Rutland was bought in 1546 by Sir Edmund Peckham; the resulting marriage with Dorothy Peckham ended with her death in child-birth in May 1547 but her father retained custody of the property until November 1549. Verney's second wife was almost certainly a Knyvet; in October 1551 he granted the site of Pendley manor to Anthony Knyvet, after whose execution for treason four years later a bond given him by Verney in 1553 was transferred to Richard Knyvet, and in a property settlement made by Richard Knyvet in 1556 Verney's wife Alice was one of the remainder-men.[2]

From the outset of their careers Verney and his brother Francis moved in Protestant circles. It was probably their uncle the 2nd Lord Bray, who introduced them at court, and a more distant kinsman, John Dudley, the later Duke of North-umberland, passed most of the month of July 1548 at Pendley. In May 1551 the two Verneys were among the large entourage accompanying the Marquess of Northampton on his embassy to France; in the same year Northampton became lord lieutenant of Buckinghamshire. These connexions explain both their return to the Parliament of March 1553, in which Edmund Verney sat for Buckinghamshire and his brother (probably) for Buckingham, and Edmund's support of Northumberland in the struggle for the succession later that year. For this misadventure he was at first ordered to remain at home and later, it appears, fined £100, before suing out a general pardon.[3]

For any pair of brothers to be elected together as knights of a shire was rare indeed. The Verneys, besides being young and untried in local adminis-tration, must have been unwelcome to authority by reason of their views and associations. Yet together they represented Buckinghamshire in 1555, voting with the opposition led by Sir Anthony Kingston, and after the dissolution becoming involved in the Dudley conspiracy. The date of Edmund Verney's arrest is not known, but he was being interrogated in May 1556 and he was indicted of treason at Guildhall on 11 June. He remained in prison for almost a year and was not pardoned until 12 July 1557.[4]

Verney died on 13 Dec. 1558. His place of burial is unknown and he left no will, but his affairs were in order, for in February 1554 he had made an indenture with Reginald Bray of Pavenham, Bedfordshire, and Thomas Pigott of Quainton, Buckinghamshire, settling his property upon him-self and his heirs in tail male. Dying childless, he was succeeded by his younger brother, another Edmund, then aged 22 and more, who received licence to enter his lands in May 1559, although letters of administration were not granted to John Simpson of Pendley until 17 June 1563.[5]

[1] Date of birth given in fa.'s i.p.m., C142/74/2. *Vis. Bucks.* ed. Metcalfe, 10; *Verney Pprs.* (Cam. Soc. lvi), 57, 67; *CPR, 1555-7,* p. 88. [2] *Verney Pprs.* pp. xiv, 12-57, 79; *VCH Bucks.* iv. 33; *CPR, 1547-8,* p. 249; 1548-9, p. 339; 1550-3, p. 216; 1554-5, p. 287; 1555-7, p. 88; Browne Willis, *Bucks.* 154; Wards 9/149, f. 160; 9/153, Bucks. 38 Hen. VIII. [3] *CSP Dom.* 1547-80, p. 9; *HMC 2nd Rep.* 101-2; *HMC 3rd Rep.* 239; *CSP For.* 1547-53, p. 123; *APC,* iii. 259; iv. 416; *CPR, 1553-4,* p. 444. [4] Guildford mus. Loseley 1331/2; *Verney Pprs.* 72-73; *CPR, 1555-7,* p. 539; 1557-8, pp. 81-82; D. M. Loades, *Two Tudor Conspiracies,* 210-35 passim, 267. [5] *CPR, 1558-60,* p. 73; E150/51/10; *Verney Pprs.* 78.

M.K.D.

VERNEY, Francis (1531/34-59), of Salden in Mursley, Bucks. and London.

?BUCKINGHAM   1553 (Mar.)
BUCKINGHAMSHIRE   1555

b. 1531/34, 4th s. of Sir Ralph Verney, and bro. of Edmund*. ?*m.* lic. 2 Apr. 1548, Margaret, da. of Sir Nicholas Vaux*, 1st Lord Vaux of Harrowden, wid. of Sir Francis Pulteney of Misterton, Leics.[1]
Sewer, the chamber by 1547-*d.*; member, house-hold of Princess Elizabeth in 1554.[2]

Francis Verney received under his father's will of 1543 lands worth £10 a year for life, and his education and welfare by good marriage or 'other promotion' were entrusted to his father's uncle Robert Verney and to his mother's kinsmen Urian Brereton and Reginald Bray.[3]

In 1547 Verney attended the funeral of Henry VIII. Four years later he joined his eldest brother Edmund and their uncle the 2nd Lord Bray in the entourage accompanying the Marquess of North-ampton to France. The brothers could have owed their return to the Parliament of March 1553, in which Edmund sat as knight of the shire for Buckinghamshire, to a more distant kinsman, the Duke of Northumberland. (It is just possible that the Member for Buckingham was not the young courtier but his uncle and namesake, an esquire of the body.) The younger Francis Verney is not known to have followed the lead of his elder brother and their uncle Bray in supporting Northumberland during the summer of 1553. Less than 12 months later, however, after Verney had joined the house-hold of Princess Elizabeth, Sir Henry Bedingfield* informed the Council of a meeting at Woodstock,

Oxfordshire, between Verney and a servant of the late Duke of Suffolk and cited Sir Leonard Chamberlain's* judgment that 'if there be any practice of ill within all England, this Verney is privy to it'. Later in 1554 Verney was employed to carry the princess's letters to the Council and (although this was not disclosed until 1556) was supposedly privy to a plot to kill Mary and Philip.[4]

Verney was indicted of treason after the Dudley conspiracy, and, unlike his brother, he was brought to trial, convicted and sentenced to death. He was reprieved and eventually pardoned on 10 Apr. 1557. He survived to attend the coronation of Elizabeth and was probably the gentleman buried at St. Andrew's, Holborn on 6 Feb. 1559, for from the following July new leases were made of lands at Salden 'late of Francis Verney, deceased and attainted of treason'. He and his brother Edmund were perhaps victims of the prevailing epidemic.[5]

[1] Date of birth estimated from eldest brother's and from election as knight of the shire. *Verney Pprs.* (Cam. Soc. lvi), 53–54, 78; *Fac. Off. Reg. 1534–49* ed. Chambers, 310; G. Anstruther, *Vaux of Harrowden*, 2, 489. [2] LC2/2, f. 75, 4/3, p. 108. [3] *Verney Pprs.* 12–57. [4] *Lit. Rems. Edw. VI*, 582; LC2/2, f. 62v; *Norf. Arch.* iv. 177, 194, 196; F. A. Mumby, *The Girlhood of Elizabeth*, 168, 175, 177; D. M. Loades, *Two Tudor Conspiracies*, 143. [5] Guildford mus. Loseley 1331/2; *Verney Pprs.* 72; *CPR, 1555–7*, pp. 539–40; *1557–8*, pp. 81–82; *APC*, vi. 74; City of London RO, Guildhall 6673/1(68); *CPR, 1558–60*, pp. 113, 276, 393.

M.K.D.

VERNON, George (by 1518–65), of Haddon, Derbys.

DERBYSHIRE 1542

b. by 1518, 1st s. of Richard Vernon of Haddon, by Margaret, da. of Sir Robert Dymoke of Scrivelsby, Lincs. *educ.* Magdalen, Oxf.; G. Inn, adm. 1537. *m.* (1) Margaret, da. of Sir George Tailboys, *de jure* 9th Lord Kyme, wid. of Philip Bullock; (2) Maud, da. of Sir Ralph Longford of Longford, Derbys., 2da. *suc.* fa. Aug. 1517. KB 20 Feb. 1547.[1]

J.p. Derbys. 1539–*d.*; commr. musters 1539, array 1546, chantries 1546, relief 1550.[2]

The Vernon family was established at Haddon by the 14th century and its members were to attain prominence both locally and at court during the 15th. Following the early death of his father George Vernon's wardship, and the custody of his lands in Westmorland, were granted in April 1522 to Wolsey, Sir William Tyrwhitt*, Lady (Elizabeth) Tailboys and her son Gilbert*, and he was married to one of the Tailboys daughters; but it was his uncle Sir John Vernon who administered the bulk of his inheritance and advised him during his early years 'in all his causes and his great affairs'. After Oxford and a spell at Grays Inn, Vernon followed his uncle, then serving as a councillor in the marches, and remained in the elder man's service until his death early in 1545.[3]

It was during these years that Vernon had his only experience of the Commons. In possession since 1536 of wide lands centred on Nether Haddon and Bakewell in the hundred of High Peak, and a justice of the peace of more than three years' standing, he could expect to follow those of his forbears who had sat for the shire; the name of his fellow-knight is lost. Made a knight at Edward VI's coronation, Vernon was one of those claimed by Sir William Paget to have been included in the first, but not the second, list of those whom Henry VIII had intended to create barons. In the event he was never even raised to the quorum of the commission or pricked sheriff; the fact that he was nominated for the office nine times between 1543 and 1552 implies that he was *persona non grata*, although on what ground it is impossible to say. He was one of the three Derbyshire gentlemen who refused to comply with Mary's demand for a forced loan of £100 in 1557, and although the receiver, Sir John Porte*, solicited the 5th Earl of Shrewsbury's help, it is unknown whether or not they ultimately contributed. In 1564 Bishop Bentham, an ardent reformer, rated Vernon 'a great justice [in] religion as in all other things', but he died before he could be transferred to the quorum. Renowned 'for his magnificence . . . for his kind reception of all good men, and his hospitality', he was dubbed the 'King of the Peak'.[4]

The last of his line, Vernon probably suffered from ill-health for several years before his death on 31 Aug. 1565. His heirs were his two daughters, Margaret, the wife of Sir Thomas Stanley*, and the celebrated Dorothy, who had married John Manners†. By his will of 18 Aug. 1565 he bequeathed six Derbyshire manors and two in Staffordshire to his wife for life. His executors were to take the profits of his manor of Kibblestone, in Staffordshire, and two Cheshire manors for 16 years after his decease to pay his debts, funeral expenses and the fulfilment of his will, which included among numerous bequests the provision of one gold chain worth £20 to his godson, Gilbert Talbot†, the future Earl of Shrewsbury, 'as a remembrance of my good will towards him'. His wife, his son-in-law John Manners, his brother-in-law Nicholas Longford† and his 'loving neighbours and faithful friends' Thomas Sutton* and Richard Wennesley† were each to receive £20 for their services as executors, while his 'right worshipful friends' (Sir) John Zouche II* and (Sir) Francis Leke* were each to have a horse. Vernon was buried in Bakewell church where a large table tomb in the centre of the Vernon chapel bears the recumbent effigies of himself, clothed in plate armour, and his two wives.[5]

[1] Date of birth estimated from first commission. *Vis. Salop* (Harl. Soc. xxix), 471; C142/41/19, 43, 42/133, 143/44, 144/70, 98; *HMC Rutland*, i. 76. [2] *LP Hen. VIII*, xiv–xvi, xviii, xx, xxi; *CPR*, 1547–8, p. 82; 1553, p. 352; 1553–4, p. 18; 1560–3, p. 435; 1563–6, p. 20. [3] *Brit. Arch. Assoc. Jnl.* n.s. vi. 143 seq.; *HP*, ed. Wedgwood 1439–1509 (Biogs.), 907–8; *LP Hen. VIII*, iii, xv; *Derbys. Arch. Soc. Jnl.* x. 76, 83. [4] *LP Hen. VIII*, x; *CPR*, 1558–60, p. 201; C142/33/35, 34/117, 40/5, 41/19, 43, 42/133, 204/93; E150/13/1; *APC*, ii. 16; Strype, *Eccles. Memorials*, iii(2), 78–79; *Wealth and Power*, ed. Ives, Knecht and Scarisbrick, 89; *HMC Shrewsbury and Talbot*, ii. 47; Hatfield mss Cecil pprs. M485/60 (*Cam. Misc.* ix(3), 44 misreads 'jester' for 'justice'); *Derbys. Arch. Soc. Jnl.* x. 83. [5] *HMC Shrewsbury and Talbot*, ii. 35; C142/144/170; *CPR*, 1563–6, pp. 489, 491; PCC 28 Morrison; J. C. Cox, *Derbys. Churches*, ii. 20–21.

C.J.B.

VERNON, Henry (by 1523–69), of Sudbury, Derbys.

LICHFIELD 1554 (Apr.)
DERBYSHIRE 1554 (Nov.)[1]

b. by 1523, s. of Sir John Vernon of Sudbury by Helen, da. and coh. of Sir John Montgomery of Cubley. *m.* 3 May 1547, Margaret, da. and coh. of Humphrey Swynnerton* of Swynnerton and Hilton, Staffs., 2s. 3da. *suc.* fa. 4 Feb. 1545.[2]
J.p.q. Derbys. 1558/59–?d., Staffs. 1564.[3]

Born into a cadet branch of the celebrated family of Haddon, Henry Vernon inherited considerable lands in Derbyshire, including the manor and lordship of Sudbury, and in Staffordshire, where his wife added the manor of Hilton on her father's death in 1562.[4]

It was presumably to his own and his father's marriage connexions that Vernon owed his election for Lichfield to Mary's second Parliament. Patronage at Lichfield lay with William, Lord Paget, whose favour Vernon could have secured through his father-in-law, himself returned to that Parliament for Stafford, or his uncle Sir Thomas Giffard, knight of the shire in the previous one. For the knighthood of his own shire in the next Parliament Vernon need have looked no further than his cousin (Sir) George Vernon*, the 'King of the Peak', who had probably been brought up with him at Sudbury. Both Vernon and his fellow-knight Sir Peter Frescheville quitted this Parliament without leave before its dissolution, as did the two Members for Derby. Prosecuted in the King's bench in the following Easter term, Vernon and Frescheville shared the experience of being repeatedly distrained for non-appearance until they both made appearance in Hilary term 1557 and were given days in the following term to answer. A year later they were each fined £4. Vernon was also in trouble in 1555 for his excessive apparel and his escort of liveried retainers at the assizes and sessions of the peace. In 1556 he took part in the trial of Joan Waste for heresy.[5]

The only mentions of Vernon in connexion with the wars of his time appear to be his receipt of money for men sent to France in 1544 and his summons to lead 200 men to Scotland early in 1560. By then he had been put on the Derbyshire bench but he may have been removed after being judged 'an adversary of religion' in 1564. In his will of 1 Mar. 1568 he bequeathed to his younger son Henry, for whom his wife was to hold it until Henry became 18, the lease of Hazlebadge in the Peak granted to his father by Sir George Vernon, although a servant later accused Margaret Vernon of substituting Henry's name for his elder brother John's at this point in the will as well as of similarly defrauding the eldest daughter of a bequest of 500 marks. Vernon divided his library equally between the sons. He died on 29 Sept. 1569. There is no trace of the monument which he charged his executors, his wife, Sir Humphrey Bradbourne* and Serjeant Richard Harpur, to erect in the chancel of Sudbury church.[6]

[1] Huntington Lib. Hastings mss Parl. pprs. [2] Date of birth estimated from first reference. *Vis. Salop* (Harl. Soc. xxix), 472; J. C. Wedgwood, *Staffs. Parl. Hist.* (Wm. Salt Arch. Soc.), i. 305n, 341–2; *LP Hen. VIII*, iii; Lichfield consist. ct. wills 26; PCC 24 Sheffelde. [3] *CPR*, 1560–3, p. 435; 1563–6, pp. 21, 26, 42. [4] *Derbys. Arch. Soc. Jnl.* x. 79–80, 84. [5] KB27/1176–81, 1185; E159/334 Pas. r. 118, Hil. r. 39; Foxe, *Acts and Mons.* viii. 247. [6] *LP Hen. VIII*, xi, xiv, xix; *HMC Shrewsbury and Talbot*, ii. 83; *Cam. Misc.* ix(3), 42–43; PCC 24 Sheffelde; C142/153/23, 245/87; E150/771a/2; Wards 7/12/86; J. C. Cox, *Derbys. Churches*, iii. 321–4.

C.J.B.

VERNON, Thomas (by 1532–56).

SHROPSHIRE 1553 (Mar.)

b. by 1532, 2nd s. of Thomas Vernon of Stokesay, Salop by Anne, da. and coh. of Sir John Ludlow of Stokesay. *m.* Dorothy, da. of Sir Francis Lovell of Barton Bendish and East Harling, Norf. 2s.[1]

As a grandson of Henry Vernon of Haddon, who married a daughter of the 5th Earl of Shrewsbury, Thomas Vernon was first cousin to George Vernon* and Henry Vernon*. When returned to the Parliament of March 1553 he was styled 'junior' to distinguish him from his father and namesake, who was three times sheriff of Shropshire and who was to outlive the son. Vernon's return on that occasion is probably to be attributed to the council in the marches. If he was a lawyer by training—and both his own family and the one into which he married were represented at various inns of court—he could have been the man of his name who acted as attorney to John Dudley, Earl of Warwick, in 1548 during Warwick's presidency of the council, and thus have been Dudley's nominee; he also had a family connexion with the council through his uncle Sir John Vernon and his home was near Ludlow. However sponsored, Vernon may have had a personal interest in a seat in the Commons at this time. Following the death in 1551 of Edward, last Baron

Grey of Powis, Vernon and (another) cousin George claimed the barony as sons of the coheirs of Sir John Ludlow by his wife Anne, whose mother Elizabeth, they claimed, had been a daughter of Sir Richard Grey, the last Baron Powis's great-grandfather. The claim was disputed by Edward Kynaston and also involved the Vernons in litigation with John Herbert, whose Membership of the Parliaments of March 1553 and 1555—and perhaps even Francis Kynaston's of that of April 1554— may have been connected with the affair. Despite an unfavourable decision in Chancery in 1554, the Vernon claim was to be pursued by Thomas Vernon's son Henry under Elizabeth and was to be revived for the last time in 1800.[2]

There survives an inquisition post mortem of a Thomas Vernon of Shropshire who died on 4 June 1556. He left a son named Henry, aged seven, and the probability that he was the Member is increased by his having held no lands in chief, a situation consistent with the survival of his father, who was thus doubtless the Thomas Vernon who died on 5 Mar. 1562 and was buried at Stokesay. In November 1564 the wardship of Henry Vernon, son of the younger and heir of the elder Thomas Vernon, was granted to Bridget, Countess of Rutland.[3]

[1] Presumed to be of age at election. *Vis. Salop* (Harl. Soc. xxix), 471–2. [2] *LP Hen. VIII*, ii, viii–xiii, xv, xviii; Add. 6276, f. 22v; A. Collins, *Procs. Precedents and Arguments concerning Baronies by Writ* (1734), 397 seq.; *CP*, vi. 697–8; *VCH Salop*, ii. 94; *ECP*, x. 63; *Chancery* (Univ. Wales Bd. of Celtic Studies, Hist. and Law ser. iii), 152–3. [3] C142/108/119; *Salop Par. Regs. Diocese of Hereford*, xvii; *CPR*, 1563–6, p. 92.

A.H.

VICARS, Robert (by 1486–1517), of Great Grimsby, Lincs.

GREAT GRIMSBY 1512[1]

b. by 1486. *m.* Mary, 1ch.[2]

Bailiff, Great Grimsby in 1507, member of mayor's council by 1510–*d.*, coroner in 1512, chamberlain in 1513.[3]

Robert Vicars was doubtless related to William Vicars, who was mayor of Grimsby five times between 1490 and 1503 and who issued several orders for reforming the governance of the borough; but if this William Vicars is to be identified with the William Wikers of Grimsby who died in 1506 there is no mention of a Robert in his will. Nothing is known of Robert Vicars's career beyond his municipal record and his description in his will as a merchant. His election to the Parliament of 1512 with George Barnardiston may have been a gesture by the town against the interference which had reversed its previous one, when Vicars had been one of the electors whose choice was superseded. If so, the fact that both he and Barnardiston were to be replaced three years later, despite the King's

request for the re-election of the previous Members, could have been similarly prompted, for Barnardiston's replacement, William Hatcliffe, looks like a court nominee, and the corporation may well have decided that if one of its seats could thus be filled in breach of the general recommendation the other should also. Whether finance entered into the matter is not clear, for it is not known whether Vicars had served for more or less than the 12*d.* a day accepted by his replacement, the mayor Philip Hamby. Vicars's business took him periodically to London, and it was while there that he fell ill and made his will on 13 Aug. 1517. After asking to be buried in the church of St. Dunstan in the East if he died in London, he named his wife sole legatee and executrix and asked his 'brother, the parson of Bramston [?Branston, Lincolnshire]' to help her to execute the will, which was proved on the following 16 Dec.[4]

[1] Great Grimsby AO, oldest ct. bk. f. 223. [2] Date of birth estimated from first reference. PCC 1 Ayloffe. [3] Great Grimsby AO, oldest ct. bk. ff. 61, 93v, 145v, 146, 159v, 163v, 221v. [4] PCC 17 Adeane, 1 Ayloffe; *HMC 14th Rep. VIII*, 241–2, 258, 268, 273, 289; Great Grimsby AO, f. 224.

T.M.H.

VILLERS, Sir John (1485/86–1544), of Brooksby, Leics.

LEICESTERSHIRE 1539[1]

b. 1485/86, o.s. of Sir John Villers of Brooksby by Agnes, da. of John Digby of Coleshill, Warws. *m.* by 1520, Elizabeth, da. of John Winger of London, 1da.; 1s. illegit. *suc.* fa. 29 Sept. 1506. Kntd. 1515/19.[2]

Commr. subsidy, Leics. 1512, 1514, 1515, 1523, 1524, musters, 1539; other commissions 1530–*d.*; j.p. Leics. 1514–*d.*; sheriff, Leics. and Warws. 1531–2, 1537–8; knight of the body by 1532–33 or later.[3]

The family of Villers, or Villiers as it was later called, had been established in Leicestershire, with its principal seat at Brooksby, since at least the 13th century. John Villers had livery of his father's lands in December 1507; they comprised the family's main property in Leicestershire worth £95 a year, manors and lands in Lincolnshire valued at £25 a year, and further lands in Northamptonshire and Warwickshire. Shortly after his father's death Villers was bound in £100 to pay 500 marks to the crown by five annual instalments, but the recognizance was discharged in 1517 with £300 still due to the crown. He took part in the funeral obsequies for Henry VII, and was among those regularly summoned by the new King to such state occasions as the Field of Cloth of Gold and the meeting with Charles V at Gravelines in 1520. In the autumn of 1522 he served in the Picardy campaign. He returned to France ten years later for Henry VIII's meeting with Francis I at Calais.[4]

As a leading gentleman of his county Villers had been appointed a justice of the peace in 1514 and remained on the commission for the rest of his life; his name appeared first on the sheriff roll as early as 1512, although he was not pricked sheriff until 1531. He was to develop into one of the most active and reliable servants of the government in the county. One of the special commissioners appointed to try the Lincolnshire rebels in March 1537, he played his part with zeal, if not relish: as Sir William Parr* reported to Cromwell, 'until . . . executions were done at Horncastle and Louth . . . Sir John Villers and Sir John Markham would in no wise depart'. In the following January Villers was one of three commissioned by Cromwell to take and imprison the vicar of Sproxton, Leicestershire, who was suspected of sedition.[5]

Villers for his part, it appears, was not without blame for the prevalent disorder. A number of complaints against him of lawless behaviour have survived. In one from the 1520s Thomas Grey, 3rd Marquess of Dorset, reporting to Wolsey on the disturbed state of the county, cited Villers's behaviour as a bad example. Dorset's brother Leonard had had two tame harts killed by Villers's servants, and when Villers was indicted for his part in the affair

> [he] who was wont to ride with eight or nine horses at the most came to town with 26 or 30 well weaponed and himself a sword and buckler by his side who never used to ride with one before and set him down upon the bench the said sword and buckler by his side facing and braving the quest with his adherents so that justice could take no place.

It may have been this incident which called for the pardon granted to Sir John and William Villers in July 1529. A fellow-executor of Villers, suing him in the Star Chamber in 1539, alleged misappropriation of the deceased's goods and continual lawlessness by Villers and his servants, which was never punished owing to his power in the county.[6]

The Greys were one of the two leading noble families in Leicestershire, and Villers's hostility to them implies that he adhered to their rivals the Hastings, although there is no known alliance or other close connexion between him and that family, nor would Villers have needed its patronage, even if it had not been in temporary eclipse, to secure his return to the Parliament of 1539. Of more value was his friendship with the 1st Earl of Rutland, for his fellow-knight, John Digby, was, or was soon to become, a servant of Rutland. (Like Digby, Villers may have already sat in Parliament, for it is not known who had sat for the county in 1536.) If Villers had needed government backing, he could doubtless have counted on the support of Cromwell, for whom he had performed much service. Of his

role in the Parliament which was to witness the minister's downfall nothing is known; it was during the prorogation between the second and third sessions that he was present at the reception of Anne of Cleves in January 1540.[7]

Although he was steward of Croxton Ferrial abbey and of Old Dalby commandery, Villers does not appear to have profited from the dissolution of the monasteries to add to his lands in Leicestershire or elsewhere. When his uncle Christopher Villers died childless in 1537, there accrued to him as the heir the manors of Great Cowdon and Kilby, and other land in Leicestershire, which he was to settle on his illegitimate son John Twyford *alias* Villers for life. In 1544 he was charged with raising troops for the French campaign where he himself served in the vanguard with 110 of his own men. He died soon after his return from France, on 8 Dec. 1544. Since he had no legitimate son, his heir was his only daughter, but he had settled much of his property in his lifetime on his younger brothers and their issue. One brother, George, thus acquired the principal Villers manors of Brooksby and Howby; another, William, was the grandfather of George Villiers, Duke of Buckingham and favourite of James I.[8]

Villers had made his will on 24 May 1544, before going to France. After a number of charitable gifts, he left a house to Elizabeth Twyford, mother of his illegitimate son, and divided up the rest of his lands between his daughter and his brothers and sisters. He left 'to my good lord my lord chief justice', Edward Montagu, a neighbour of Villers in North-amptonshire, 'my basin and ewer of silver and my best gelding', and asked him to bring up John Twyford *alias* Villers, for whom 'my mind and will is that he be continually kept at his learning first to have his grammar and afterwards the laws of this realm'. After a number of other gifts in the will and in a codicil of 27 Nov. 1544, Villers left the residue of his goods to his brother George, whom he named sole executor.[9]

¹ E159/319, brev. ret. Mich. r. [1–2].   ² Date of birth estimated from age at fa.'s i.p.m., *CIPM Hen. VII*, iii. 329–30 and from livery of inheritance. Harl. 7178, f. 17; PCC 21 Pynnyng.   ³ *Statutes*, iii. 84, 115, 168; *LP Hen. VIII*, i–v, viii, xiv, xvi; Nichols, *Leics.* iii(1) 192; *HMC Bath*, iv. 2.   ⁴ *Leics. Arch. and Hist. Soc.* xxii. 261; Harl. 7178, f. 1; *CPR*, 1494–1509, p. 566; *CCR*, 1500–9, no. 673; *LP Hen. VIII*, i–iv; *Chron. Calais* (Cam. Soc. xxxv), 32; *HMC Bath*. iv. 2.   ⁵ *LP Hen. VIII*, i, xii, xiii; Elton, *Policy and Police*, 340, ⁶ *LP Hen. VIII*, i, iii, iv; St.Ch.2/24/274.   ⁷ *LP Hen. VIII*, xv; *HMC Rutland*, i. 25; iv. 292.   ⁸ *Trans. Leics. Arch. and Hist. Soc.* xxii. 261; xli. 16; Nichols, iii(1) 192–3, 198; *LP Hen. VIII*, xvi, xix. ⁹ PCC 21 Pynnyng.

D.F.C.

VINCENT, George (by 1493-1566), of Peckleton, Leics.

LEICESTERSHIRE 1558

b. by 1493, 1st s. of Richard Vincent of Messingham, Lincs. by Anne, da. and h. of William Grimsby of Lincoln, Lincs. *educ.* I. Temple, adm. 1519. *m.* (1) by 1517, Jane, da. of William Story of Sleaford, Lincs., 7s. 2da.; (2) by 1542, Anne, da. of Richard Radcliffe, wid. of Roger Lache of Daventry, Northants.; (3) Amy, da. of Peter Colles of Preston Capes, Northants., 2s. 1da. *suc.* fa. bef. 1515.[1]

J.p. Leics. 1538–*d.*; commr. subsidy 1542, benevolence 1544/45, relief 1550, goods of churches and fraternities 1553; escheator, Warws. and Leics. 1543–4, 1549–50; bailiff, Leics. lands formerly of Sheen abbey 1538–53; dep. forester, Leics. 1562.[2]

George Vincent's grandfather, who was heir to a line of unimportant north country gentry, had moved to Lincolnshire on marrying a minor heiress. In the next generation, Richard Vincent further improved the family position by marrying Anne Grimsby, who not only inherited her father's estates after her brother's death but was also coheir through her mother to an important Leicestershire family, the Motons of Peckleton. It was this inheritance which not only provided George Vincent with the bulk of his estates but also brought him into contact with powerful if distant connexions.

Vincent was admitted to the Inner Temple in 1519, but his exemption in the following year from keeping vacation or holding office suggests that he wanted to acquire, rather later in life than usual, the smattering of law, and perhaps the other accomplishments, useful to a gentleman. He was, indeed, already involved, and would long continue, in litigation. Some time before 1515 Robert Brudenell sued Vincent's mother in Chancery over an alleged bargain relating to her manor of Peckleton which she and her second husband were refusing to complete; the action evidently failed, for George Vincent kept possession. In 1517 the death of Philippa Heroy, who had held Peckleton as a free tenement in the right of her first husband Robert Moton, brought her son-in-law John Harington I* into conflict with George Vincent and his cousin Germain Poole, who were named as her heirs in the inquisition post mortem. The case, which appears to have turned on the nature of the entail of the manor, went against Harington, for in 1547 Vincent and Poole summoned him in the common pleas to deliver seisin and they both held a moiety of the manor at their deaths.[3]

The Harington affair might have been expected to evoke a conciliatory intervention by Sir Richard Sacheverell*: he had arranged Harington's marriage with his ward Elizabeth Moton and had doubtless also had a hand in Vincent's marriage with his niece Jane Story. In the upshot Sacheverell appears to have promoted the Vincents' interest, for George Vincent remained his adherent and as such sided with the Hastings faction in its long struggle against the Greys: Vincent was Sacheverell's principal agent in the harrying of Reginald Grey and his ultimate ejection from the manor of Barwell, and when in 1534 Sacheverell came to make his will George and Jane Vincent were among the principal beneficiaries.[4]

In middle life Vincent emerged as an active local administrator, his regular inclusion in commissions of oyer and terminer, and of gaol delivery, doubtless owing something to his acquaintance with the law. In 1544 he was one of the Leicestershire gentry who led a contingent in the vanguard against France. It was not, however, until 1558, and then for the only time, that he was returned to Parliament. He sat as first knight of the shire with George Sherard, who may have owed his nomination to the 2nd Earl of Rutland; Vincent himself presumably relied on his Hastings connexion and may have benefited by the elevation of Sir Edward Hastings* to the peerage and the disappearance, perhaps through illness, from the parliamentary scene of Sir Thomas Hastings*. Of his role in the Commons nothing is known.[5]

Vincent had taken advantage of the Dissolution to consolidate his estate. His purchase of Potters Marston from the crown in 1540 had probably been financed in part by a loan and was followed two years later by the sale of the undisputed portion of his Moton inheritance. In 1553 he acquired the unexpired lease of Germain Poole's half of Peckleton. By his will, made on 8 Feb. 1565, he left all his property to his eldest son Edward, subject to certain annuities for the younger children. (One of his daughters by his first marriage had married William Faunt, his immediate precursor as knight of the shire.) The will throws little light on his personality or on his religion, in which he had been returned as 'indifferent' in 1564. Vincent died on 3 Jan. 1566.[6]

¹ Date of birth estimated from i.p.m. of Philippa Heroy, *Peckleton Manor* ed. Farnham, 42, but said to be aged 80 at death, *Vis. Leics.* (Harl. Soc. ii), 80–82. ² E315/265; *LP Hen. VIII*, xiii–xv, xx; *CPR*, 1553, pp. 356, 414; 1558–60, p. 279; 1560–3, p. 439; 1563–6, p. 241; Somerville, *Duchy*, i. 568. ³ *Cal. I.T. Recs.* i. 47, 83; C1/290/35, 415/6, 1129/18–24; *Peckleton Manor*, 42; G. F. Farnham, *Leics. Med. Peds.* 63. ⁴ *Peckleton Manor*, 45 seq.; *HMC Hastings*, i. 50; St.Ch.2/16/314 seq.; PCC 15 Hogen. ⁵ *LP Hen. VIII*, xiv, xv, xix; *PPC*, vii. 235; *Quorndon Recs.* ed. Farnham, 200, 202; *CPR*, 1553, p. 358; 1553–4, p. 371; 1558–60, p. 279; *APC*, ii. 446; iv. 371. ⁶ *Peckleton Manor*, 42; *CPR*, 1553, p. 395; 1563–6, p. 497; PCC 5 Crymes; *Cam. Misc.* ix(3), 30; C142/144/97.

S.M.T.

VOWELL, Thomas (by 1499–1544), of Fowelscombe, Devon.

PLYMOUTH 1529

b. by 1499, 1st s. of Richard Vowell of Fowelscombe by 1st w. Blanche. *m.* (1) 1518, Mary, da. of Richard Hals of Keynedon, Sherford, 2s. 4da.; (2) Maud

Bevill, 3s.; (3) settlement 1537, Jane, da. of Nicholas Dillon of Bratton Fleming, wid. of John Somaster (*d.*1535) of Painsford. *suc.* fa. 6 Oct. 1525.[1]

It is easier to identify Thomas Vowell than to trace his career. He came of a family settled some miles east of Plymouth and had succeeded to his inheritance some four years before he was returned to Parliament for that borough in his early thirties.

Vowell's election on that occasion gives point to the questions posed by his career. The standing he enjoyed in the neighbourhood is likely to have been augmented by the favour of the sheriff Sir Peter Edgecombe*, for Vowell's stepmother came of that prominent family; but such local advantages would have been outweighed by favour at court, and this too he may have enjoyed. The progress of a gentleman usher of his name can be traced through a series of grants between 1522 and 1543, and some of these, like the custody of lands in Plymouth and Exeter and the reversion of the harbourmastership of the duchy of Cornwall, would have befitted a Member for Plymouth. When and how Vowell, if it was he, obtained the ushership is not known—perhaps he owed this to the Edgecombe connexion—but it may have been before October 1514, when a 'Thomas Vowell of Ringwood, Hampshire, *alias* of Fowelscombe, Devon, Westminster or Greenwich, gentleman', sued out a pardon.[2]

A connexion of quite another kind is glimpsed by way of Vowell's fellow-Member John Pollard, a leading figure at the Middle Temple, the inn which had recently furnished Plymouth with two of its Members. There were two Middle Templars at this time named Vowell: the elder one had been admitted in 1501 and rose to be bencher in 1517 and reader in 1517 and 1524, the younger was admitted in 1525 and is not heard of again. As both are lacking christian names in the records of the inn their relationship, if any, with Thomas Vowell can only be guessed at, but the coincidence of Richard Vowell's death in 1525 with both the disappearance of the elder and the advent of the younger Templar makes it tempting to identify the two with the father and son from Fowelscombe. In any case Vowell may be thought to have had a link with Pollard at the Middle Temple as well as in Devon.[3]

They were certainly to be linked in the minds of at least some of their constituents, although not in respect of their cost to the borough. Whereas Pollard appears to have received only the 13s.4d. which he originally agreed to, the total of £23 1s. paid to Vowell for the first four sessions represented the standard rate of 2s. a day (and not the 16d. on which its first instalment of 40s. had been calculated) for almost the whole of the 224 days involved: he had also had a special payment when he rode with James Horswell*, probably in 1530, to lay before the lord chief justice the town's charter and other documents in its dispute with the lord admiral. By January 1535, however, both Members had fallen out so badly with a faction on the town council as to provoke a complaint to Cromwell against 'certain seditious persons', including the two Members, 'men without substance and unfit to rule this town': matters even reached the point where 'Vowell and his adherents' were reported as having planned to bring a *quo warranto* suit against the town. (This episode is curiously reminiscent of one which had occurred nearly 20 years before, when a Thomas Vowell—whether or not the Member cannot be established—'would have indicted the mayor's deputy, the constables and other persons of the town' at the Exeter assizes.) The dispute thus begun was to outlast this Parliament, but the Members presumably carried too much weight at court to be compromised by it, and when a new one was called for June 1536 Pollard was almost certainly re-elected, and probably Vowell also, in accordance with the King's request for the return of the previous Members. The sole indication of Vowell's part in the proceedings of the Commons is his inclusion on a list of Members whose names Cromwell wrote on the back of a letter of December 1534: the Members concerned are thought to have had a particular connexion with the treasons bill then passing through Parliament, perhaps as forming a committee, but since they range from leading crown officials to men who may have had objections to the bill nothing can be inferred as to Vowell's attitude to the measure, although if he was a gentleman usher he might be regarded as belonging to the 'official' element in the group.[4]

In March 1537 Vowell had a lease of the dissolved Augustinian priory of Cornworthy, near Totnes: it is the only indication found of his having benefited from the Dissolution. His own property, some of it in the same area, had involved him in a number of lawsuits, the last of them dating from the chancellorship of Audley, that is, between 1538 and 1544. He died on 17 Dec. 1544, apparently intestate, but, as the inquisition shows, possessed of lands in various parishes between the rivers Dart and Erme. A year-and-a-half later a gentleman usher of his name was granted a licence to export Gascon wine: this cannot have been a posthumous reward to the Member, for it was made in respect of munitions consumed 'in chasing of the galleys', an episode of July 1545 in the war with France. Unless it was this grantee who had held the ushership for upwards of 20 years, his tenure of it must have overlapped or succeeded the

Member's: in either case he could well have been Vowell's eldest son by his second marriage.[5]

[1] Date of birth estimated from age at fa.'s i.p.m., C142/43/57, 73/36. *Vis. Devon*, ed. Colby, 104; *Vis. Devon*, ed. Vivian, 284, 695; C1/623/44–47, 796/7–10. [2] *Vis. Devon*, ed. Colby, 104; *LP Hen. VIII*, i, iii, vi, viii, xii, xvi, xviii. [3] *M.T. Adm.* i. 4, 18; *M.T. Recs.* i. 2, 15, 50, 51, 73. [4] Plymouth receivers' acct. bk. 1515–16, 1529–30, 1530–1, 1531–2, 1532–3, 1534–5; *LP Hen. VIII*, vii. 1522(ii) citing SP1/87, f. 106v; viii. [5] *LP Hen. VIII*, xiii, xxi; C1/623/44–47, 796/7–10, 914/33–34, 1083/40–42; 142/73/36; J. A. Williamson, *Tudor Age*, 183–4.

R.V.

VOWELL *see also* **HOOKER** *alias* **VOWELL**

WAAD, Armagil (by 1518–68), of London and Hampstead, Mdx.

CHIPPING WYCOMBE 1547

b. by 1518. *educ.* (?Magdalen), Oxf. BA 23 Jan. 1532. *m.* (1) Alice, da. of Richard Patten *alias* Wainfleet of London, wid. of Thomas Searle (*d.*1540/41) of London, 17ch. inc. Thomas[†] and Sir William[†]; (2) Anne, da. of Thomas Marbury of London, wid. of Edward Bradley (*d.* Aug./Oct. 1558) of London, 3ch.[1]

 Servant of Henry, Lord Mautravers, by 1540; clerk of the council, Calais 26 Nov. 1540–24 Sept. 1546; collector and receiver of customs and tolls, Newnham bridge, Calais 17 Apr. 1545; clerk of the Privy Council June 1547–?July 1553; j.p. Mdx. 1561–*d.*; commr. benevolence for St. Paul's cathedral 1564, sewers, Kent and Suss. 1564.[2]

According to the inscription on his tombstone in Hampstead church composed by his son William, Armagil Waad came of a Yorkshire family; the fact that he was to be granted arms shows that his forbears were of humbler stock. It is said that his mother's maiden name was Comyn and his birthplace Kilnsey in the East Riding. The records of Magdalen College do not bear out Anthony Wood's version of his period at Oxford, and if he attended an inn of court its identity is unknown: it could have been the Middle Temple during the period for which the records are missing, or Gray's Inn where he was later to build a chamber to which his descendants were admitted from 1565 onwards. A childhood on the Holderness peninsula may have given Waad a taste for the sea which led him to join Hore's voyage to North America from April to October 1536. From his connexion with this expedition, but without other foundation, Waad was later to be called 'the English Columbus'. Although he was to pursue a public career, he remained closely connected through both his marriages with the merchant community of London; the merchant brothers John and Otwell Johnson called him their 'old and assured friend' and his brother-in-law William Patten published Waad's 'epigram made upon the citizens' receiving of his grace' the Protector Somerset in his *Expedicion into Scotland*.[3]

Waad's introduction to court perhaps came through Sir Richard Gresham*, who acquired land in Kilnsey at the Dissolution, and his progress may have been influenced by his knowledge of languages, including Spanish. He was in the service of Lord Mautravers, deputy governor of Calais, when in November 1540 Mautravers sought leave for him to compound for the vacant clerkship of the council there, and it was again Mautravers who in September 1543 recommended him for the French secretaryship at Calais after his two years' experience as assistant in that office. Waad's clerkship was granted to another from 25 Sept. 1546 and a month later he returned to London, where he at once reported his arrival to Sir William Paget.[4]

By the following summer Waad had become third clerk of the Privy Council, although during his first year of office he did not receive a regular fee. His election to the ensuing Parliament was a by-product of his appointment, his three fellows in the clerkship, Thomas Chaloner, William Honing and Thomas Smith I, all finding seats in it. The choice of Chipping Wycombe may have been determined by either Sir John Russell*, Baron Russell or Sir Edmund Peckham*, both of them influential in Buckinghamshire. Waad's fellow-Member Thomas Fisher was secretary to the Protector Somerset.[5]

In April 1548, when the clerks, now reduced to three, had their fees reviewed. Waad was granted 50 marks a year from the previous 24 June. Under Edward VI he was twice confirmed in office, rising in the process to the first clerkship, and in 1550 he was given an annuity of 200 marks for services to the present and former King. On four occasions during 1550 and 1551, as deputy to the clerk of the Parliaments Sir John Mason*, Waad read out the commission for the prorogation. He appears to have remained clerk of the Privy Council until the death of Edward VI, the last reference to him in its minutes being dated 13 June 1553. If he sat in the Parliament of March 1553, as did his fellow-clerk William Thomas, it must have been for a constituency for which the names are lost.[6]

It was probably on religious grounds that Waad, who was later to be considered a favourer of the Elizabethan settlement, lost his office and was given no other employment under Mary. He sued out a general pardon on 3 Nov. 1553 as of London and Soulbury, Buckinghamshire, and he continued to receive an annuity of £100. Granted Milton Grange, Bedfordshire, in October 1554, by 1559 he had leased property in Belsize, near Hampstead, Middlesex, which then became his home. Soon after Elizabeth's accession Waad addressed to Cecil a long discourse on 'the distresses of the Commonwealth and the means to remedy them'. His activities from that time reflected his varied interests. In April 1559 he was sent on a mission to the Duke of Holstein to treat for increased facilities for English merchants and to offer Elizabeth's aid against the free cities of the duchy. Three years later he was in Rye, Sussex, mustering 600 men for service at Dieppe and looking into the possibilities of support for the Huguenots. His commission to survey watercourses near Rye harbour resulted in his request, with others, for a grant of neighbouring salt marshes. In 1565 he obtained with William Herle a 30 years' monopoly for making sulphur and growing plants for oil for use in the cloth industry, and in the following year he was appointed to interrogate Cornelius de Lannoy, an alchemist, in connexion with the manufacture of gold.[7]

Waad died on 20 June 1568, and was buried in Hampstead church, in the chancel near the tomb of his first wife. By a will made some seven years earlier he left to a younger son Thomas his chamber in Gray's Inn and tenements in Golding Lane. He named his eldest son William executor and among the overseers were John Southcote II* and Thomas Wilbraham†. The will was proved on 5 Feb. 1569.[8]

[1] Date of birth estimated from education. Emden, *Biog. Reg. Univ. Oxf. 1501-40*, p. 598. *DNB*; PCC 6 Lyon, 20 Alenger, 34 Pynnyng, 59 Noodes; C1/1085/4. [2] *LP Hen. VIII*, xvi, xx, xxi; P. T. J. Morgan,'The govt. of Calais 1485-1558' (Oxf. Univ. D.Phil. thesis, 1966), 304; *Rep. R. Comm. of 1552* (Archs. of Brit. Hist. and Culture iii), 19; *APC*, ii-iv passim; *CPR*, 1563-6, pp. 24, 38, 126. [3] PCC 6 Lyon; *G.I. Adm.* 34, 42, 117; Fuller, *Worthies*, iii. 418; D. E. Hoak, *The King's Council in the Reign of Edw. VI*, 163; *Tudor Tracts* ed. Pollard, 63. [4] *LP Hen. VIII*, xvi, xviii, xxi. [5] *APC*, ii-iv passim. [6] *CPR*, 1547-8, p. 381; 1548-9, p. 3; 1549-51, pp. 188, 306; 1550-3, p. 285; E405/117, ff. 13v, 38, 40; Add. 30198, f. 10; Stowe 571, f. 21; *L7*, i. 390-3; Hoak, 271-2. [7] *Cam. Misc.* ix(3), 60; *Fac. Off. Reg. 1534-49* ed. Chambers, 309; PCC 6 Lyon; Lansd. 156(28), f. 96; *CPR*, 1553-4, p. 452; 1554-5, p. 311; 1558-60, p. 158; 1560-3, pp. 410, 505, 581; 1563-6, pp. 110, 235-6; E405/121, ff. 12v, 73; SP12/1/66; *CSP Dom.* 1547-70 passim; 1601-3, *Add.* 1547-65, p. 529; *CSP For.* 1558-9, nos. 531, 541, 1099; 1561-2, no. 346; 1562 passim. [8] PCC 6 Lyon.

M.K.D.

WADHAM, John (by 1520-84), of Catherston Leweston, Dorset.

MELCOMBE REGIS 1553 (Mar.)[1]
WEYMOUTH 1554 (Apr.)

b. by 1520, s. of John Wadham of Catherston Leweston by 1st w. Mary, da. of John Farringdon of Devon. *educ.* I. Temple, adm. May 1533. *m.* by 1545, Margaret, da. of Nicholas Willoughby of Turners Puddle, Dorset, 4s. 3da. *suc.* fa. 10 May 1558.[2]

Capt. Sandsfoot castle, Dorset 9 Aug. 1550; recorder, Lyme Regis, Dorset 1558-*d.*[3]

John Wadham received a legal education but he is to be distinguished from an older namesake (perhaps his cousin of Merrifield, Somerset) who studied civil law at Oxford; he does not appear to have practised as a lawyer although he was to succeed his father in the recordership of Lyme

Regis. Presumably he gained some military experience during the 1540s before being appointed to one of the royal forts protecting Portland harbour, a command which made him a figure of authority in the neighbouring ports of Melcombe Regis and Weymouth. On his election for Melcombe in the spring of 1553 he discharged the borough of any payment for his parliamentary service and he probably did the same at Weymouth in the following year. Whether or no by his own choice, he was not to sit again for either borough although he kept his command until his death. After he inherited the family estates his interests in the neighbourhood of Bridport and Lyme absorbed most of his attention.[4]

In his will, dated 12 Jan. 1584, he composed the following inscription for his tombstone:

Here lieth John Wadham of Catherston, esquire, who was during his life time captain of the Queen's majesty's castle of Sandsfoot besides Weymouth in this county of Dorset and also recorder of Lyme Regis, whose soul God rest to his good will and pleasure Amen.

With the addition of the date of his death, 14 Mar. 1584, this was engraved on a brass plate in the church of Whitechurch Canonicorum. Wadham left 20s. each to the master gunner at Sandsfoot and all the garrison, 20s. to Richard Carpenter, town clerk of Lyme Regis, and £20 each to his younger sons. He left his eldest son and executor George Wadham burgages in Bridport, Charmouth, Dorchester, Lyme and Wareham, and named as overseers his 'cousins', Thomas Hannam†, Thomas Molyns the elder, William Pole*, Nicholas Wadham and his servant William Crocker.[5]

[1] Weymouth and Melcombe Regis mss Sherren pprs. 15. [2] Date of birth estimated from age at fa.'s i.p.m., C142/116/20. Hutchins, *Dorset*, ii. 216; C142/203/73. [3] LR6/12/2; Hutchins, ii. 267. [4] Emden, *Biog. Reg. Univ. Oxf. 1501-40*, p. 599; Lyme Regis ct. bk. 1578-84, ff. 164, 250; fugitive pieces, 2, no. 38; 3, no. 2; finance, 1, p. 15; Weymouth and Melcombe Regis mss Sherren pprs. 15; Bridport doom bk. 260. [5] PCC 2 Watson; Hutchins, ii. 267; Newman and Pevsner, *Dorset*, 460; C142/203/73.

H.M.

WADHAM, Sir Nicholas (by 1472-1542), of Merrifield, nr. Ilton, Som.

SOMERSET 1529

b. by 1472, 1st s. of Sir John Wadham of Merrifield by Elizabeth, da. of Hugh Stukeley. *m.* (1) Joan, da. of Robert Hill† of Halsway, Som. and Bridport, Dorset; (2) Margaret, da. of John Seymour of Wolf Hall, Wilts.; (3) by June 1517, Isabel, da. of Thomas Baynham of Clearwell, Glos., wid. of Sir Giles Brydges (*d.*1511) of Coberley, Glos.; (4) Joan, da. of Richard Lyte, wid. of William Walton; 5s. 2da. *suc.* fa. 20 Apr. 1502. Kntd. 18 Feb. 1504.[1]

Sheriff, Som. and Dorset 1498-9, 1534-5, Devon 1501-2, 1514-15, Wilts. 1516-17; esquire of the body by 1503; j.p. Som. 1503-*d.*, Hants 1515, Dorset 1521, western counties 1540; capt. I. o. W. May 1509-20;

commr. array, Hants 1511, musters, Southampton 1512, Portsmouth 1514, subsidy, Hants, Som. 1512, Som. 1514, 1515, 1524; v.-adm. 1522.[2]

Sir Nicholas Wadham's life was divided between the court and the west country, with an interlude in the Isle of Wight. Pricked sheriff before succeeding to the headship of his family and put on the bench not long after he was active in island administration before being appointed governor there by Henry VIII. Although he is not known to have fought in the French and Scottish campaigns of 1512 and 1513 he helped to muster troops at Southampton and Portsmouth. In 1520, the year that he surrendered his governorship, he went with the King to the meetings with Francis I and Charles V. Four years later he received an honorary admission to the Middle Temple.[3]

Elected to the Parliament of 1529, he came to stand well with Cromwell and, no doubt, was a good servant to the King. Presumably he was re-elected in 1536 in compliance with the general request for the return of the previous Members, when his presence as one of Queen Jane Seymour's alliance would have further commended him to the regime. After an interval of 35 years he again became sheriff of Somerset and Dorset, although he seems to have left all the duties to the under sheriff. In October 1535 he asked Cromwell if he could be pricked again, so as not to lose many of the potential profits of the office, but the request was refused. During the next five years he corresponded intermittently with Cromwell (who had taken his son into his household), asking for his long and faithful service to be mentioned to the King, and hoping for some reward. He seems to have got little but further duties: in 1540 he was placed on several judicial commissions in the west. He died in the middle of this flurry of activity on 5 Mar. 1542.[4]

Wadham had made his will on 25 Nov. 1539. To his fourth wife he left the plate, apparel and goods that she had brought to their marriage, together with much of his own jewellery and plate, livestock and corn. To each of his three younger sons then living he bequeathed a horse and a sum of £100. Most of the remainder of his goods he ordered to be sold to pay his debts and legacies. He named (Sir) Hugh Paulet* and William Portman* among the executors and Sir William Stourton*, 7th Baron Stourton, and Richard Pollard* supervisors. None of his property outside Somerset is mentioned in this testament, which was proved 31 Jan. 1543.[5]

[1] Date of birth estimated from age at fa.'s i.p.m., CIPM Hen. VII, iii. 295. Collinson, Som. i. 48; Hutchins, Dorset, ii. 216; Vis. Som. ed. Weaver, 84; LP Hen. VIII, iii. [2] CPR, 1494–1509, p. 316; LP Hen. VIII, i–xvi; VCH Hants, v. 223; CCR, 1500–9, p. 358. [3] CPR, 1494–1509, pp. 322, 455, 580; CCR, 1500–9, pp. 134, 345; VCH Hants, v. 223, 229, 233; LP Hen. VIII, i; M.T. Adm. i. 12.

[4] C1/924/1; LP Hen. VIII, ix-xv; Elton, Policy and Police, 109–10; M. L. Robertson, 'Cromwell's servants' (Univ. California Los Angeles Ph.D. thesis, 1975), 580; E150/182/3. [5] PCC 15 Spert.

R.V.

WAINFLEET, Thomas (by 1463–1515), of Canterbury, Kent.

CANTERBURY 1512[1]

b. by 1463, s. of Thomas Wainfleet of Canterbury. ?unm. 1s. illegit.[2]
Common councilman, Canterbury by 1500, alderman by 1504, mayor 1514–15; commr. gaol delivery 1510, 1513, subsidy 1512, 1514, 1515.[3]

Thomas Wainfleet, taverner, was admitted to the freedom of Canterbury in 1484 as the son of a freeman. He was not made chamberlain, the customary first step in civic promotion, but otherwise his career followed the normal pattern. He was early employed on city business, being one of those sent to London in 1501 to seek legal advice on a pardon of £300 forfeited by Canterbury in a dispute with the prior of Christchurch over a market-site. When, early in August, the delegation failed to find the city's usual counsel because it was vacation time but met the recorder of London (Sir Robert Sheffield*) at Lord Daubeney's house, the members 'besought him to speed them for the time of the forfeit passed not three days, which answered that he was sore occupied and might not intend it so shortly, where we took him 6s.8d., and then he bade us wait on him on the morrow in the Temple'. The next day they breakfasted the recorder's men in Fleet Street and in the afternoon, 'when Master Recorder had contrived the bill and corrected it', they gave him 6s.8d. 'for his reward'. The matter was then referred to the King's Council, with what result is not known.[4]

As a Member of the Parliament of 1512 Wainfleet was paid £3 10s. 8d. parliamentary wages and journey money by the chamberlains of 1512–13; the number of days was not recorded but at 16d. a day he must have been present nearly every day of the second session. (The accounts for 1511–12, in which wages for the first session were presumably entered, are missing.) In 1514 Wainfleet received 40s. for 30 days at the third session, apparently without any allowance for travelling. With his fellow-Member John Hales I* he had presumably promoted the unsuccessful bill concerning the mayor and aldermen of Canterbury which was read in the Lords in March 1512. By the time of the next election he was himself mayor, and this may explain why, unlike Hales, he was not returned again in accordance with the King's request for the re-election of the previous Members. He did not survive his year of office, receiving only £5 of his mayoral fee of £10 13s.4d. and being replaced by his brother-in-law Thomas Fokes. On 19 Sept. 1515 Thomas Wainfleet, vintner, was admitted a freeman of Canterbury without payment

> not for that he was the son of Thomas Wainfleet, freeman of the said city and late mayor, because the said Thomas the son was *inlegittime procreate*, but at the special request of Mr. Thomas Fokes then mayor and with the consent of the whole court of burmote for the very zeal and love that Mr. Mayor, the aldermen and common council hold unto the said Thomas Wainfleet the father.[5]

[1] Canterbury chamberlains' accts. 1512–13. [2] Date of birth estimated from admission as freeman, *Freemen of Canterbury*, ed. Cowper, cols. 89, 326. [3] Canterbury burmote rolls 1500, 1504, 1509; chamberlains' accts. 1514–15; *LP Hen. VIII*, i; *Statutes*, iii. 79, 112, 168. [4] Canterbury chamberlains' accts. 1500–1; *HMC 9th Rep.* pt. i. 147. [5] Canterbury chamberlains' accts. 1512–13, 1513–14, 1514–15; *LJ*, i. 15, 17; *Freemen of Canterbury*, cols. 120, 326; *HMC 9th Rep.* pt. i. 150.

H.M.

WALDEGRAVE, Sir Edward (1516/17–61), of Sudbury, Suff. and Borley, Essex.

WILTSHIRE	1553 (Oct.)[1]
SOMERSET	1554 (Apr.), 1554 (Nov.)[2]
ESSEX	1558

b. 1516/17, 1st s. of John Waldegrave of Essex by Laura, da. of John Rochester of Terling, Essex. *m.* by 1551, Frances, da. of Sir Edward Neville of Aldington, Kent, 2s. 3da. *suc.* fa. 6 Oct. 1543, gdfa. 1545. Kntd. 2 Oct. 1553.[3]

Gent. household of Princess Mary by Aug. 1551–July 1553; PC Aug. 1553–17 Nov. 1558; commr. augmentations 1553, heresy 1557; bailiff, manor of Havering-atte-Bower, Essex Oct. 1553; keeper, great wardrobe 28 Oct. 1553–20 July 1559; jt. (with John Cosworth*) receiver-gen. duchy of Cornwall 4 Nov. 1553–Feb. 1554; j.p.q. Essex 1554–58/59, Suff. 1554; steward, Clare honor, duchy of Lancaster, 18 Mar. 1554–d., chancellor 22 Jan.–25 Dec. 1558.[4]

Edward Waldegrave was a kinsman of Sir William Waldegrave*. His grandfather had added to his Suffolk property in and near Sudbury the lands of his wife in Somerset. Waldegrave seems not to have held a post before the death of his father and grandfather, and he is not to be confused with a namesake, one of Prince Edward's servants who was found guilty of concealing Catherine Howard's pre-marital indiscretions. At his grandfather's death he was living at Sudbury with his mother but probably soon afterwards joined his uncle, Robert Rochester* in the household of Princess Mary.[5]

By 1551 Waldegrave had become one of Mary's chief advisers. In August of that year he, Sir Francis Englefield* and Rochester were summoned before the Privy Council, accused of encouraging Mary's Catholicism and ordered to prevent the celebration of mass in her household. Mary forbade them to carry out this order and sent them back with a letter for Edward VI. When the Council repeated its instructions on 22 Aug. they refused to obey and were committed to the Tower. After two months' imprisonment Waldegrave, who had contracted a quartan ague, was removed to a house outside the Tower, but he was not liberated until the following March. On 14 Apr. 1552 he and the others were allowed to return to their mistress.[6]

On Mary's accession Waldegrave was rewarded with a Privy Councillorship and the keepership of the great wardrobe; he also received a number of local offices in Essex and was put on the commission to compound for fines with supporters of Jane Grey. He was knighted at the coronation in October and sat as knight of the shire for Wiltshire, where he had little (if any) land, in the Parliament which followed. In the Privy Council there was latent hostility between those who had suffered for their faith and loyalty and the 'politiques' who had held office and prospered during the Protestant ascendancy. This antagonism became mingled with the dispute over the Queen's marriage. In the early autumn Waldegrave argued strongly against the proposed Spanish alliance, claiming that it would mean war with France. The Queen was impressed but the arrival of the new imperial ambassador stiffened her resistance to Stephen Gardiner's advocacy of the Courtenay match. In the struggle that followed Waldegrave played a leading part. At the beginning of November, possibly during a temporary ascendancy of Gardiner's party, it was rumoured that he would succeed the Marquess of Winchester as treasurer; this proved unfounded although on 4 Nov. he shared a grant of the receiver-generalship of the duchy of Cornwall. On 8 Nov. the ambassador reported that Waldegrave and his associates were wavering, but it was soon clear that he was mistaken because a few days later the Commons began to prepare an address to persuade Mary to marry an Englishman. Waldegrave and Sir Edward Hastings* seem to have been instrumental in this, and the ambassador suspected that Gardiner was also privy to the plan. As it became increasingly clear that the Queen was set on marrying Philip, many dropped their opposition, but Waldegrave remained 'entirely for Courtenay' and spoke openly of leaving the Queen's service, to be told that she would have no one in her Council or Household who opposed her on such an issue. By Christmas he had realised that further protest was useless: Wyatt's rebellion made continued support for Courtenay impossible, though the two remained on friendly terms and Waldegrave was one of the earl's trustees during his exile. Waldegrave was still regarded with suspicion by the ambassador who believed that his efforts in the early months of 1554 to expedite Cardinal Pole's return to England were really aimed at preventing the marriage with Philip.[7]

By April 1554 the marriage was assured and Waldegrave's opposition was soothed by a promise of a pension of 500 crowns. He remained in his offices and in the Privy Council, although there was an unsuccessful attempt in the following November to reduce its membership by removing Courtenay's former supporters. He was assiduous in attendance, and served on the committee dealing with financial matters. During 1557–8 he was put on the important commissions to increase the royal revenue. In January 1558 he at last reached high office, succeeding his uncle as chancellor of the duchy of Lancaster.[8]

Waldegrave's position at court and on the Council was buttressed by great landed wealth, which he took every opportunity to extend. In June 1546 he added to his ancestral estates the manor of Borley, Essex, where he made his chief home, and during the next ten years paid some thousands of pounds to the crown for lands and leases of lands in Devon, Essex, Kent, Somerset and Suffolk. Although his main seat was in Essex, his largest agglomeration of property was in north Somerset, where he owned some 15 manors at his death. As two senior Councillors, Sir William Petre and Rochester, were returned as knights of the shire for Essex throughout most of Mary's reign, he had to turn elsewhere for a seat. He used his connexions with the duchies of Cornwall and Lancaster to favour others, but appears to have relied on his position at court and his standing in Somerset to secure a knighthood of the shire there. Since that county, however, had returned two Protestants to Mary's first Parliament, when Waldegrave sat for Wiltshire, it may have done so again in 1555, thus forcing Waldegrave either to retreat to a borough seat or to forgo one altogether. By 1558 Rochester was dead, and Waldegrave was at last returned for Essex: he took a bill up from the Commons to the Lords shortly before the first session closed on 7 Mar. 1558.[9]

On the accession of Elizabeth, Waldegrave was dismissed from the Council and before July 1559 he had surrendered nearly all his offices. He did not conform to the Elizabethan religious settlement; in April 1561 he and his wife were indicted at Brentwood, Essex, on charges of hearing mass and harbouring priests, and in June they were convicted at Westminster. Waldegrave, who had been confined to the Tower since April, fell ill soon afterwards, died on 1 Sept., and was buried there two days later. His widow took as her second husband Lord Chidiock Paulet*.[10]

Waldegrave had made his will on 14 Sept. 1559. He left his wife a life interest in the greater part of his lands and named her executrix, but a few days before his death, when he confirmed the will, he provided that in the event of her death Anthony Browne II*, Sir Francis Englefield, John Throckmorton I* and (with Browne's approval) Sir Thomas Cornwallis* should take her place and hold the lands in trust for his children.[11]

[1] Bodl. e. Museo 17. [2] Huntington Lib. Hastings mss Parl. pprs. [3] Aged 44 at death, Morant, *Essex*, i. 182. *Vis. Essex* (Harl. Soc. xiii), 119; C142/68/58; PCC 43 Pynnyng. [4] *APC*, iii. 333; iv. 318; vi. 429; *CPR*, 1553–4, pp. 19–393 passim; 1555–7, pp. 281, 312–13, 315; 1557–8, p. 73, 211; Somerville, *Duchy*, i. 602. [5] *CIPM Hen. VII*, i. 111–12; ii. 51–52; *LP Hen. VIII*, xvi; PCC 43 Pynnyng. [6] *APC*, iii. 333–508 passim; H. F. M. Prescott, *Mary Tudor*, 153–5, 159; W. K. Jordan, *Edw. VI*, ii. 263; *CSP Span.* 1550–2, pp. 356–8. [7] *CPR*, 1553–4, pp. 75–76; *CSP Span.* 1553, pp. 263–471 passim; 1554, pp. 90, 152–3, 295; *CSP Dom.* 1547–80, pp. 68, 71; E. H. Harbison, *Rival Ambassadors at Ct. of Q. Mary*, p. 89 seq.; Prescott, 214, 217, 261; D. M. Loades, *Two Tudor Conspiracies*, 8, 15, 176. [8] *CSP Span.* 1554, pp. 101, 316; 1554–8, p. 369; *CPR*, 1555–7, p. 312 seq.; 1557–8, p. 71 seq.; Prescott, 281. [9] *LP Hen. VIII*, xxi; *CPR*, 1547–8, p. 178; 1553–4, pp. 136, 319; 1555–7, p. 185; 1557–8, p. 171 seq.; C142/133/130; PCC 29 Loftes; *CJ*, i. 50. [10] *CSP Dom.* 1547–80, pp. 173–4, 176, 179, 183, 185; *CSP Span.* 1558–70, p. 288; *Machyn's Diary* (Cam. Soc. xxxii), 256, 266. [11] PCC 29 Loftes.

R.V.

WALDEGRAVE, Sir William (1507–54), of Smallbridge in Bures, Suff.

SUFFOLK 1545

b. 2 Aug. 1507, 1st s. of Sir George Waldegrave of Smallbridge by Anne, da. of Sir Robert Drury I* of Hawstead. *m.* settlement 7 July 1528, Juliana, da. of Sir John Raynsford of Bradfield, Essex, 1s. William† 4da. *suc.* fa. 8 July 1528. Kntd. 25 May 1533.[1]

J.p. Suff. ?1531, 1532–*d.*; commr. tenths of spiritualities 1535, coastal defence 1539, relief 1550, goods of churches and fraternities 1553; other commissions 1534–*d.*; sheriff, Norf. and Suff. 1550–1.[2]

William Waldegrave was born and brought up at his maternal grandfather's house in Suffolk. The deaths within the space of 14 months of his paternal grandfather Sir William Waldegrave and his own father left him heir to one of the handsomest patrimonies at the age of a few weeks short of 21. The marriage contracted for him by his father while dying strengthened his connexions in the region and added to his property. From thenceforward he combined local administration with attendance at court and military service. Knighted at the coronation of Anne Boleyn he headed the commission to take the oath of succession in Suffolk. In the autumn of 1536 he was one of a group of men who the 3rd Duke of Norfolk believed would quell any rising in Suffolk. Two years later he approached Cromwell about help in obtaining an unspecified reward from the King, but nothing came of this, perhaps because later in the same year he told the minister about his troubled conscience over enforcing the injunctions for divine service to be said in English. Nothwithstanding his 'great heartburning' he remained on the bench and in 1539 he was ordered to attend the reception of Anne of Cleves.[3]

In 1542 Waldegrave served under the Duke of Norfolk's command against the Scots and two years later he captained 60 of his own men in the French campaign. His election to the Parliament of 1545 reflected this recent military experience as much as his own standing in Suffolk and may have been promoted by his uncle Sir William Drury* as sheriff. Of his part in the Parliament nothing has come to light but during the prorogation he was present at the reception of the Admiral of France at Greenwich. Although he was not to be re-elected, early in January 1553 the Council considered him for nomination with Sir William Drury as knights for Suffolk in the forthcoming Parliament but in the event nominated Sir Henry Bedingfield* with Drury. Following Edward VI's death in the summer Cecil listed Waldegrave among potential supporters of Queen Jane but on being summoned to Kenninghall by Mary on 8 July he joined the princess in her successful bid for the throne. Later he heard the indictments in Suffolk against Jane's adherents.[4]

While on a visit to Calais late in 1554, perhaps in connexion with the arrival of Cardinal Pole, Waldegrave fell sick. By his will made on 8 Nov. he asked to be buried in the graveyard of St. Mary's church there, provided for his wife and children and remembered his mother and other kin. He died on the following 12 Dec., and the will was proved by the executors in October 1555 a week before they renounced the administration in favour of the widow. A monument to his memory was placed in Bures church near the tombs of his ancestors and an inscription in the church of St. Mary, Sudbury.[5]

[1] Date of birth given in proof of age, C142/48/142. *Vis. Norf.* (Harl. Soc. xxxii), 298–9; *Vis. Essex* (Harl. Soc. xiii), 96, 121; *Vis. Suff.* ed. Metcalfe, 75; PCC 29, 36 Porch; *LP Hen. VIII*, vi; E150/630/7; *Procs. Suff. Inst. Arch.* iv. 357–66. [2] *LP Hen. VIII*, v, vii, viii, xii–xiv, xviii, xx; C193/12/1, f. 33; E371/300, m. 48; *CPR*, 1547–8, p. 89; 1553, pp. 358, 415; 1553–4, p. 24; 1554–5, pp. 151, 158. [3] Copinger, *Suff. Manors*, i. 51–54, 351; ii. 285; iv. 61, 313; v. 45, 275; Add. 19154, ff. 36–77; 34651, ff. 3–20; *Suff. Green Bks.* x. 19, 299, 338; *LP Hen. VIII*, vi, vii, xi, xiii–xv; Elton, *Policy and Police*, 258–9. [4] *LP Hen. VIII*, xvii, xix, xxi; Lansd. 3(19), f. 36; 103, ff. 1–2; *Chron. Q. Jane and Q. Mary* (Cam. Soc. xlviii), 175; *APC*, iv. 300; *CPR*, 1553–4, p. 224; 1554–5. p. 43, 151, 158. [5] PCC 34 More; C142/104/92; Copinger, i. 54; J. Weever, *Funeral Monuments*, 484.

M.K.D.

WALKER, Alexander

LICHFIELD 1547*[1]

The identity of Alexander Walker has not been established. It was following the death of William Layton in July 1551 that he came to sit with Edmund Twyneho for Lichfield in the last session of the Parliament of 1547. Both Layton and Twyneho had owed their election to William, 1st Lord Paget, but during the autumn of 1551 Paget's fortunes slumped with the overthrow of the Duke of Somerset and his own imprisonment. If the by-election had been held before October, Paget would presumably have had the nomination, but it is not clear who is likely to have intervened thereafter, although Bishop Sampson may have done so.

It has proved impossible to place Alexander Walker among the Staffordshire families of that surname. He may be identifiable with a 'Mr. Walker' mentioned in a letter written from Lichfield on 20 Mar. 1545 by Randall Mainwaring* to Ralph Leftwiche. The writer reported that this Mr. Walker had told Humphrey Mainwaring of his surprise at the passing of a certain order, the nature of which is not indicated, and had promised to send a servant of his own with one of Leftwiche's to (Sir) Nicholas Hare*, then justice of Chester and Flint: Walker also intended to refer the matter personally to Bishop Sampson as president of the council in the marches. However, this man is more likely to have been Richard Walker, a servant and executor of the previous president Bishop Lee and archdeacon of Stafford for 20 years until his death in 1567.[2]

Several Alexander Walkers can be traced living in London during the middle years of the 16th century. All but one of these men were of Scottish origin and of rather humble circumstances. The exception was a merchant taylor, about whom little is known beyond his will, which he made as a sick man on 7 Mar. 1558. After asking to be buried in the church of St. Dunstan-in-the-East, he provided for his wife and children. He left his house in Bread Street to his wife whom he made sole executrix and appointed Edward Dicher as overseer. The will was proved before the end of March 1559, but Walker had presumably been buried at St. Dunstan's before 16 Nov. 1558, the day on which the first surviving burial register begins. A business connexion between Lord Paget and another merchant taylor Simon Lowe *alias* Fyfield who was himself to sit for another Staffordshire borough during Mary's reign, suggests that it was this Alexander Walker who was Member for Lichfield in 1552.[3]

[1] Hatfield 207. [2] *Wm. Salt. Arch. Soc.* v(2), 297; J. C. Wedgwood, *Staffs. Parl. Hist.* (Wm. Salt Arch. Soc.), i. 327; *LP Hen. VIII*, add.; T. Harwood, *Lichfield*, 211. [3] *LP Hen. VIII*, xvi, xix; *CPR*, 1550–3, p. 307; 1560–3, p. 63; PCC 13 Noodes.

A.D.

WALLIS, James (by 1523–88), of Grantham, Lincs.

GRANTHAM 1553 (Oct.)

b. by 1523. *m.* by 1548, 3s. 3da.[1]
Alderman, Grantham in 1557.[2]

James Wallis was a trader in flax and a merchant of the staple who in 1544 was assessed for the subsidy at Grantham on goods worth £30. He presumably owed his election to the eclipse of Sir William Cecil at the beginning of Mary's reign, which enabled the town to choose a resident as its other Member after accommodating the 2nd Earl of Rutland by re-electing Sir Edward Warner. Unlike Warner, Wallis did not oppose the initial measures to restore Catholicism. After the fall of Calais he was licensed to ship wool to Bruges. He was in London on business when on 27 Apr. 1577 he made his will. After asking to be buried near wherever he died, he ordered his debts to be paid and his goods and property to be divided equally among his six children. He also remembered his servants and granddaughters and named his sons Harry and Robert executors. He died at Grantham on 13 Nov. 1588, when he was succeeded by his eldest son John upon whom he had settled his property in the town four years before, and his will was proved at Lincoln in December.[3]

[1] Date of birth estimated from first reference. C142/277/166; Lincs. RO, Lincoln consist. ct. 1578/88. [2] B. Street, Grantham, 123. [3] E179/137/376; CPR, 1557-8, p. 301; 1558-60, p. 25; Lincs. RO, Lincoln consist. ct. 1578/88; C142/277/166.

T.M.H.

WALPOLE, John (by 1522-57), of Harpley, Norf.

LYNN 1553 (Mar.), 1553 (Oct.)[1]

b. by 1522, 2nd s. of Henry Walpole of Harpley by Margaret, da. and coh. of Gilbert Holtoft of Whaplode, Lincs. educ. G. Inn, adm. 1536. m. 1543, Catherine, da. of Edmund Knyvet of Ashwellthorpe, Norf., 1s. 5da.[2]
Collector for serjeants' feast, G. Inn 1548, Lent reader 1549, double reader 1555.[3]
J.p. Norf. 1547, q. 1554; commr. relief, Norf. 1550; other commissions 1551-5; of counsel to Lynn 29 Aug. 1550-6, recorder 8 Aug. 1556-d.; serjeant-at-law 1555; recorder, Norwich 18 Aug. 1556-d.[4]

John Walpole was a lawyer who would doubtless have become a judge but who died, a serjeant of two years' standing, within 15 months of his succeeding Thomas Gawdy I* (who also died before his time) as recorder of Lynn and Norwich. Married to a Knyvet, and brought into shire administration under Edward VI, he was probably the 'Master Walpoole' who in 1549 was the Protector Somerset's master of requests; the position had earlier been held by Cecil, who had followed Walpole at Gray's Inn.[5]
Walpole was already a legal counsellor to Lynn when he became one of its Members, but his first return for the borough was not without complications. On 20 Jan. 1553 the town chose Thomas Waters (q.v.) to partner Sir Richard Corbet, yet it

is Corbet and Walpole who appear on the return, Walpole's name being inserted over an erasure. Tempting as it is to see in this an example of the Duke of Northumberland's interference in the composition of the House, no reason has been found for such favouring of Walpole beyond the marriage connexion he had recently acquired with the Dudleys through his cousin John Walpole of Houghton, himself cousin and heir to Amy Robsart. Walpole can scarcely have appeared more dependable than Waters, who when the crisis came was to stand by the duke, whereas Walpole seems to have held aloof. Again, if it was at Northumberland's bidding that Walpole displaced Waters, the town's decision eight months later, after the duke's overthrow, to send both of them to Mary's first Parliament would be hard to explain. It is thus to some unknown circumstance within the town (which had witnessed similar incidents before) rather than to pressure from outside that the change should probably be ascribed.[6]

Walpole was one of the Members who 'stood for the true religion' against the restoration of Catholicism, but neither his professional nor his public career was affected. Nor was his steady accumulation of land in Norfolk, chiefly around Harpley and partly from monastic sources. It was in London, probably at one or other Serjeants' Inn, that he died on 1 or 2 Nov. 1557; he may have succumbed to the epidemic of that year. By his detailed will of 1 Nov. he gave his wife a life interest in certain lands and goods provided she did not remarry. Of the lands which were to pass to the heir, one third would be enjoyed by the crown during his minority and the remainder were to be used to support the other children. Walpole besought his two supervisors, Bishop Thirlby and serjeant John Prideaux*, to help his executors secure the wardship and left £20 to the master of the wards, Sir Francis Englefield*, 'for his favour and preferment to be had therein'; in the upshot, his servant Thomas Skarlett, an executor who later married the widow, secured a share in the wardship. Among other bequests Walpole left his books and robes to his son. His funeral at St. Dunstan in the West was attended by 200 lawyers, including all the judges and serjeants. The will was proved on 11 Feb. 1558 and the heir, William Walpole, had licence to enter on 26 June 1566.[7]

[1] Lynn congregation bk. 5, f. 192v; Bodl. e Museo 17. [2] Date of birth estimated from education. Vis. Norf. (Norf. Arch.), i. 365, 372. [3] Dugdale, Origines Juridiciales, 137, 293. [4] CPR, 1547-8, p. 87; 1550-3, p. 286; 1553, p. 357; 1553-4, p. 22; 1554-5, pp. 59, 108, 111; Lynn congregation bk. 5, ff. 136v, 151, 170, 211v, 228, 247, 279, 301v; Norwich ass. procs. 3, ff. 26v, 27, 32v, 37. [5] EHR, lxx. 604 and n. 1. [6] Lynn congregation bk. 5, f. 188v; C219/20/83; Vis. Norf. i. 365. [7] Bodl. e Museo 17; C142/114/2; PCC 6 Noodes;

Vis. Norf. i. 452; *CPR*, 1558–60, p. 329; 1563–6, p. 525; *Machyn's Diary* (Cam. Soc. xlii), 156.
                                                          R.V.

WALSHE, John (by 1517–72), of Cathanger, Som. and Bethnal Green, Mdx.

CRICKLADE	1547[1]
BRISTOL	1553 (Mar.), 1553 (Oct.), 1554 (Apr.), 1554 (Nov.),[2] 1555
SOMERSET	1558
BRISTOL	1559, 1563*

b. by 1517, 1st s. of John Walshe of Cathanger by 1st w. Joan, da. of John Broke of Bristol, Glos.; half-bro. of Thomas Walshe*. *educ.* M. Temple. *m.* by 1538, 1da.[3]

Bencher, M. Temple 1554–9, Lent reader 1555, 1559.

Justice, Card., Carm., Pemb. 6 May 1551; recorder, Bristol 1552–?71; member, council in the marches of Wales 1553; j.p. Glos., Herefs., Salop, Som., Worcs. and Welsh counties 1554–58/59, six northern counties 1562; serjeant-at-law 19 Apr. 1559; j.c.p. 10 Feb. 1563; c.j. Lancaster 1563.[4]

John Walshe, who is to be distinguished from several namesakes resident in Gloucestershire, Warwickshire and Worcestershire, came from a minor Somerset family. In the heralds' visitations for Gloucestershire and Somerset he appears to have been confused with one of his namesakes, Sir John Walshe of Little Sodbury, Gloucestershire, leaving the identity of his wife uncertain. Walshe's father may be identifiable with an early 16th century Middle Templar, as the Member subsequently entered the same inn. In doing so, Walshe was following in the steps of his maternal grandfather and his uncle David Broke*, and like them he became a serjeant. It is clear that Walshe owed his early advancement to his uncle, whom he succeeded as justice of Cardigan, Carmarthen and Pembroke and who secured his appointment as recorder of Bristol.[5]

Walshe's return for Cricklade was probably arranged by Broke as the brother-in-law of Sir John Brydges* whose parliamentary patronage is discernible in the borough during this period. No connexion between Walshe and Admiral Seymour, who held the manor by right of his wife Catherine Parr, is known; but Walshe's daughter was married by 1556 to one of the Protector Somerset's sons by his repudiated first wife, and this relationship, if it had been established or foreshadowed by 1547, might have entered into the matter. In the third session of the Parliament of 1547, after the *coup* against the Protector, a proviso in the bill for patentees was committed to Walshe and Robert Broke on 26 Dec. 1549, and in 1550 he and Thomas

Gawdy I* acted as attorneys in Chancery for Bishop Barlow of Bath.[6]

On becoming recorder of Bristol Walshe was assured of the city's senior seat and he was to fill it in seven out of the next eight Parliaments; only in 1558 did he exchange it for the knighthood for Somerset. Both in 1555 and 1558 Walshe had bills committed to him in the House, one for punishing procurers of murder on 30 Nov. 1555, and two others, for tithes on waste ground and against the abduction of young women, on 28 Jan. and 12 Feb. 1558; he was also appointed with three fellow-Members to investigate the grants for sanctuary at Westminster.[7]

Elizabeth at her accession confirmed Walshe in his appointments and later made him a judge. He made his will on 3 Feb. 1572 and died nine days later.[8]

[1] Hatfield 207. [2] Huntington Lib. Hastings mss Parl. pprs. [3] Date of birth estimated from marriage. Collinson, *Som.* i. 41–42; *Vis. Som.* ed. Weaver, 86; *Vis. Glos.* (Harl. Soc. xxi), 134, 204–5. [4] *CPR*, 1550–3, p. 54; 1553–4, pp. 19–24; 1560–3, pp. 435–45, 469; Stowe 571, f. 196; *Machyn's Diary* (Cam. Soc. xlii), 373; Somerville, *Duchy*, i. 471; Bristol AO, 04026/5/189. [5] E. W. Ives, 'Some aspects of the legal profession in the 15th and early 16th centuries', (Birmingham Univ. Ph.D. thesis, 1955), iii. [6] *CJ*, i. 14; *CPR*, 1549–51, p. 222; C142/162/156. [7] *CJ*, i. 46–47, 49. [8] PCC 18 Daper; C142/162/156.
                                                          A.D.K.H.

WALSHE, Thomas (by 1537–72/79), of Stowey, Som.

BRIDPORT	1558

b. by 1537, s. of John Walshe of Cathanger by 2nd w. Margaret, da. of John Clawse (Claveshey); half-bro. of John Walshe*. *m.* Julian, da. of one Richards, wid. of Baldwin Sandford (*d.*1571/72) of Winsford.[1]

Thomas Walshe's father is said to have retired to Muchelney abbey, Somerset, after the death of his first wife and to have married his second wife after being expelled for rape and degraded from his orders. Whether or not there was any truth in the story, there seems to have been no ill feeling between the Member and his half-brother John, who in his will of 1572 admonished his heir not to disturb Walshe in the lands appointed to him in Curry Mallet, Fivehead, Stowey and Wrantage.[2]

There is no evidence that Walshe was a lawyer, but he seems to have owed his seat in Parliament to legal connexions. His half-brother, who was chosen a knight for Somerset in 1558, belonged to the Middle Temple; so did John Hippesley, his fellow-Member. Neither Hippesley nor Walshe had any direct connexion with Bridport: their link with the borough was probably through John Popham*, also of the Middle Temple, the brother-in-law of William Pole* (and more distantly related by marriage to Thomas Walshe himself) and John Walshe's successor as recorder of Bristol.[3]

Nothing has been discovered about Thomas Walshe during his remaining years. He died without making a will and administration of his estate was granted to his widow on 5 Feb. 1579.[4]

[1] Presumed to be of age at election. *Vis. Som.* ed. Weaver, 87; PCC 6 Daper. [2] Collinson, *Som.* i. 41–42; PCC 18 Daper. [3] *Vis. Som.* ed. Weaver, 15. [4] *PCC Admins.* ed. Glencross, ii. 111.

H.M.

WALSHE see also **WELSCHE, WELSHE**

WALSINGHAM, Sir Edmund (by 1480–1550), of Scadbury, Chislehurst, Kent.

SURREY 1545

b. by 1480, 1st s. of James Walsingham of Scadbury by Eleanor, da. and event. coh. of Walter Writtle† of Bobbingworth, Essex. *m.* (1) by 1510, Catherine, da. and h. of John Gunter of Chilworth, Surr. and Brecon, Brec., wid. of Henry Morgan of Pencoed, Mon., 4s. inc. Thomas† 4da.; (2) by 1543, Anne, da. of Edward Jerningham of Somerleyton, Suff., wid. of Lord Edward Grey (*d.* by 1517), ?of one Berkeley, of Henry Barley* (*d.*12 Nov. 1529) of Albury, Herts., and of Sir Robert Drury I* (*d.*2 Mar. 1535) of Hawstead, Suff., *s.p.* Kntd. 13 Sept. 1513; *suc.* fa. 10 Dec. 1540.[1]

J.p. Surr. 1514, Kent 1547; sewer in 1521; lt. Tower 1521–43; commr. subsidy, Surr. 1523, 1524, ordnance in Tower 1533, 1536, musters, Surr. 1544, benevolence, Surr. Southwark 1544/45; other commissions Essex, Kent, Surr. and London 1525–*d.*; vicechamberlain, household of Queen Catherine Parr by 1544.[2]

Edmund Walsingham's surname suggests that his forbears came from Norfolk, but the only known ones were a prosperous cordwainer of London followed by vintners who bought property in Chislehurst and elsewhere in Kent. His father was prominent in that county, which he helped to represent at the Field of Cloth of Gold; another of James Walsingham's sons William, father of the illustrious Sir Francis†, was a lawyer who also served in local administration. On his mother's side, Edmund Walsingham was first cousin to Sir Robert Rochester*.[3]

A witness to the will of John Gunter of Chilworth in 1510, and thus probably by then a married man, Walsingham was knighted on Flodden Field by the Earl of Surrey in whose retinue he travelled homewards. His next few years at court culminated in his attendance on the King at the Field of Cloth of Gold and at Gravelines in 1520, and early in 1521 he was appointed lieutenant of the Tower in succession to Sir Richard Cholmley. In the same year he was made free of the Mercers' Company, probably in recognition of his new standing in the City; his naming as one of the feoffees of a mercer in 1529 suggests a continuing connexion with the Company.[4]

By Henry VIII's reign the office of constable of the Tower had become a dignity and the lieutenant was the resident head of that institution. After 1539, when a new house was built for the lieutenant, the only exit from the Belfry, where many of the prisoners were kept, was through this house. Walsingham was responsible for their custody and was their channel of communication with the outside world. During his 22 years in office Walsingham had charge of a host of prisoners, many of them famous, the majority obscure, and perhaps inevitably he acquired a reputation for rigour. Bishop Fisher complained of the harsh treatment he received, and the Countess of Salisbury suffered horribly from cold during her winter there; even the Council in London remonstrated that unless the Duchess of Norfolk and others arraigned with her were given some liberty within the Tower they could not long survive. Yet Walsingham could point to such episodes as his leniency towards the condemned prisoner Alice Tankerfelde, to whom at one of his own daughters' intercession he allowed freedom from irons and frequent visits from a trusted servant, only to have the servant engineer an attempted escape. To one reputed example of his lingering humanity, his braving of the King's displeasure by his refusal to stretch Anne Askew further on the rack, he could lay no claim, for it was his successor Sir Anthony Knyvet who was the lieutenant concerned. But to an old friend like Sir Thomas More he could offer 'such poor cheer as he had', to Cromwell's 'gentle chaplain, Curtoyse by name', he allowed the privilege of saying mass every day, and to John Frith he gave freedom from irons and scope for his 'pleasant tongue'.[5]

For his own part Walsingham prospered materially. In addition to his salary of £100 he made a handsome profit out of prisoners. The state made generous allowances for the illustrious among them: Walsingham was allowed £14 10s. a month for the board of Viscount Lisle and £26 13s.4d. every two months for the diets of the Countess of Salisbury, the Marquess of Exeter and Lord Montagu, but these payments the lieutenant and his officers treated as perquisites and the offenders were expected to pay their own costs and upon release or execution to leave their goods behind. The resulting income fed Walsingham's steady acquisition of landed property both in Kent and Surrey. In 1531 he had acquired the reversion or remainder of a lease of Gomshall Towerhill, Surrey, from the abbey of St. Mary Graces near the Tower at an annual rent of £19; in the following year he was granted by Newark priory a 40-year lease of the parish church of St. Martha together with its rectory at an annual rent of 26s. 8d.; and in 1534 he negotiated a 40-year lease with the same priory of the parsonage and church of Ewell, the term to run from 1542 at £13 a year. These three leases were confirmed by the court of augmentations in 1539. Walsingham later took a 99-year lease of the manor of Tyting, Surrey, from the bishop of Exeter and another of the manor of Stanground in Huntingdonshire, previously belonging to the abbey of Thorney. In 1539 the King rewarded his services by granting him Gomshall Towerhill in fee simple as well as nine houses in London; Gomshall Towerhill he was to sell in 1549 for £600. Walsingham also increased his inheritance in Kent, notably by acquiring from (Sir) Robert Southwell* the manors of Swanton Court, West Peckham and Yokes, all adjacent to the Scadbury estate.[6]

If Walsingham's landed interest in Surrey qualified him for the knighthood of that shire in the Parliament of 1545, while his association at court with his fellow-knight Sir Anthony Browne and the marriage of one of his daughters to Thomas Saunders* gave him powerful local support, he probably owed his election principally to the Queen, whose vice-chamberlain he became within a year of his departure from the Tower in 1543. He thus joined the sizeable group of her officers who sat in the last Parliament of the reign. He also rubbed shoulders in the House with men whom he had met in quite other circumstances: with Sir Nicholas Hare, who had once been his prisoner, and with such relatives and friends of other former prisoners as Sir Marmaduke Constable II*, who had tried in vain to save his father, or Richard Heywood and William Roper, of the circle of Sir Thomas More. That Walsingham, unlike Browne, was not to be re-elected in 1547 is perhaps a reflection of Queen Catherine's loss of influence, although his approaching death may have cast its shadow before.

Walsingham made his will on 7 Feb. 1550 and died three days later; the will was proved on 8 Nov. 1550. He asked to be buried in 'the tomb within the chapel where myself have usually sitten', that is, the Scadbury chapel which had probably been built by his grandfather Thomas. He left 12s. a year to the 24 poorest householders in Chislehurst, Footscray and St. Paul's Cray, and 40s. for repairs to bridges and highways in Chislehurst. He had goods and rich estates to bequeath and his son Thomas was the main beneficiary, the remainder of the lands going to his nephew Francis. To a kinsman 'William', whose surname is left a blank but who is elsewhere referred to as William Thwaites, he left his leases of the manors of Stanground and Tyting, and he appointed his son-in-law Sir Thomas Saunders the youth's guardian, providing an annuity of £7 and profits of lands in Wales for his education and upbringing. He left the bulk of his household goods at Yokes to his wife for her lifetime with remainder to his daughters, his 'brother Ayloff's' children and his 'kinsman' William if his son should die without heirs; his wife was to keep the lease of her house in the Blackfriars and all her personal property there which she had brought to the marriage. He made bequests of money and goods to several of his servants, appointed his son Thomas his executor and named as overseers his wife and two of his sons-in-law, Sir Thomas Saunders and Sir Thomas Barnardiston.[7]

[1] Date of birth estimated from family history. LP Hen. VIII, xviii; Vis. Kent (Harl. Soc. lxxiv), 20; Vis. Surr. (ibid. xliii), 11, 33; Vis. Suss. (ibid. liii), 59; Arch. Cant. xiii. 390, 401; E. A. Webb, G. W. Miller and J. Beckwith, Chislehurst, 119, 125; PCC 27 Alenger; DNB. [2] LP Hen. VIII, i-iv, vi, x, xiii-xvi, xix, xx, add.; E371/303; CPR, 1547-8, pp. 79, 85; Manning and Bray, Surr. iii. 664. [3] Chislehurst, 111-19; C. Read, Walsingham, i. 3 seq. [4] O. M. Heath, Notes on Hist. of St. Martha's, 30; LP Hen. VIII, i-iii; Chislehurst, 121; Acts Ct. of Mercers' Co. ed. Lyell and Watney, 537. [5] H. Dixon, Her Majesty's Tower, i. 48, 68; Chislehurst, 33; LP Hen. VIII, iv-viii, xi-xiv, xvi, xviii, xix; Roper, Life of More (EETS cxcvii), 77. [6] LP Hen. VIII, v, viii, xiv-xvi, xviii, xx, xxi; Surr. Feet of Fines 1509-58 (Surr. Rec. Soc. xix), 91; C142/91/30; E315/100/279, 279v, 280; VCH Surr. iii. 105n, 116; VCH Hunts. 213; Guildford mus. Loseley 85/13/165-7; Manning and Bray, ii. 119; PCC 25 Coode; Hasted, Kent, v. 60, 85. [7] PCC 25 Coode; C142/91/30.

S.R.J.

WALTER, William (d.1555), of Horley, Oxon.

BUCKINGHAM 1553 (Oct.)

m. Jane, 1da.[1]
J.p. Bucks. 1547-54; commr. relief 1550.[2]

The identity of William Walter 'armiger' is not easy to establish, but he was presumably the justice of the peace active in Buckinghamshire affairs under Edward VI and Mary. His designation suggests an origin in a Cambridgeshire family with property throughout the south-east midlands, almost certainly in a cadet line. Of the three namesakes traceable in the mid 16th century two were sprung from this family as in all likelihood was the third. The first, born in London, appears to have taken up the law and settled in Gloucestershire where he died in January 1559: the second, born in Northamptonshire in 1509, became clerk to the Attorney-general William Whorwood*, and lived at Wimbledon, Surrey, until his death in 1587: while the third, a resident at Horley in Oxfordshire died in 1555. The legal attainments of the first two would have qualified either for a place on the Buckinghamshire bench but no reason has been discovered for their removal or for their failure to become magistrates in their own counties, whereas the death of the Oxfordshire man occurring about the time of the disappearance of the name of the justice from the *liber pacis* creates a strong presumption that he was the justice. His domicile at Horley further suggests that he was the Member, for Horley although some 18 miles from Buckingham formed with it and King's Sutton the prebend of Sutton-cum-Buckingham in the diocese of Lincoln. This connexion with Buckingham could explain why Walter took precedence on the election indenture over Edward Gifford, whose family seems to have had a lien on the borough. Neither Walter nor Gifford opposed the reunion with Rome. By a will dated only 1555 and proved in October that year Walter asked for burial at Horley and provided for his wife (the sole executrix) and daughter.[3]

[1] Bucks. RO, D/A/WE/8, f. 137.   [2] *CPR*, 1547–8, p. 81; 1553, p. 351; 1553–4, p. 17.   [3] C142/48/120, 118/60; 219/21/11; *Vis. Cambs.* (Harl. Soc. xli), 19; PCC 30 Blamyr, 9 Holder, 13 Adeane, 26 Porch, 29 Wrastley; *CIPM Hen. VII*, ii. 752; *L. I. Adm.* i. 43; *Cal. I.T. Recs.* i. 110; Req.2/17/115; *Vis. Glos.* (Harl. Soc. xxi), 4; *LP Hen. VIII*, xviii; Gloucester consist. ct. wills 1559; *VCH Bucks.* i. 344.

                               M.K.D.

WALTON, James (1479/80–1546/50), of Preston, Lancs.

PRESTON 1529

b. 1479/80, s. of James Walton of Preston by Ellen. *m.* Alice, a widow. *suc.* fa. by 1499.[1]

   Bailiff, Preston 1515–16, mayor 1526–7, ?1532–3, ?1533–4, 1545–6, alderman by 1542.[2]

The Waltons had probably taken their name from Walton-le-Dale, two miles from Preston. A John de Walton and his son Richard were freemen of the borough in 1397, and when it began to return Members again in 1529, after a long interval without representation, James Walton was a natural, though probably not an undisputed, choice to be one of them.[3]

A reconstruction of Walton's career involves its disentanglement from that of a younger namesake and probable kinsman. In November 1527 the elder Walton brought an action in the duchy of Lancaster court in which he claimed that, at the end of his term of office as mayor, Sir Richard Houghton* and his faction had prevented the lawful election of his successor and had imposed their own candidate Nicholas Banaster. Houghton's party, on the other hand, maintained that Walton had tried to foist William Wall on the town. Walton was able to prove his case and by February 1528 Christopher Haydock, who was to be Walton's fellow-Member, had

been appointed mayor and in November 1528 articles for 'the good rule' of Preston were drawn up by agreement between James Walton and Henry Clifton on behalf of the town and Audley on behalf of the duchy.[4]

At some time after October 1534 Walton brought a further action against Houghton, whom he accused of unlawfully retaining various freemen of Preston and outsiders 'to the intent to have all the rule and governance there'. He listed those so retained, including James Walton the younger, and claimed that since his coming to London Houghton had tried to unseat him and replace him by one Alexander Clayton, then bailiff. Describing the reasons for this malice, Walton revealed that his agreed parliamentary wage was 16*d.* a day and that his stepdaughter was Houghton's mistress. He went on to describe how James Walton the younger and others had been indicted on 5 Nov. 1534 for attempting another unlawful mayoral election on 3 Oct. 1534 and subsequent days. There is no evidence to suggest that Walton received less countenance and protection from the authorities on this occasion than in 1528. Although he is marked 'mortuus' on the list of Members drawn up about 1532 and Preston included in the list of vacancies drawn up shortly afterwards, Walton certainly did not die during the Parliament; both he and his namesake were aldermen of the guild in 1542 and he was mayor again in 1545. He could therefore have been re-elected in 1536, in accordance with the King's request for the return of the previous Members, and could also have sat in the two following Parliaments, for which the names of the Preston Members are unknown.[5]

It is not clear which of the Waltons was mayor in 1532 and 1533 but it was the younger who was mayor in 1551. In 1536 a James Walton was one of two persons, described as the earl's servants, sent by Edward Stanley, 3rd Earl of Derby, to advise and command the rebels beyond Lancaster to disperse; this was probably the younger man, whose master Houghton was active in support of Derby during the Pilgrimage of Grace. The date of the elder James Walton's death is a matter of inference. In the regnal year 5 Edward VI, probably in 1551, his widow Alice brought an action against James Walton, then mayor, for having on 20 Apr. 1550 riotously entered the messuage and garden in Preston which, she alleged, her husband had leased from the dean and canons of New College, Newark, but which James the younger claimed to have inherited from his father, here named Richard. The elder Walton had bequeathed the lease to Alice with remainder to his 'cousin' James Walton, who was perhaps a son of Thomas Walton of Bermondsey, Surrey.[6]

[1] Aged 52 in January 1532, DL3/24/W6b. Pedigrees in *VCH Lancs.* vii. 101n and H. Fishwick, *Preston,* 337, supplemented by the duchy cases cited. For discussion of questions arising out of these cases we are indebted to Prof. Margaret Hastings. [2] NRA 5791, p. 21; Fishwick, 77. [3] Fishwick, 337; J. B. Watson, 'Lancs. gentry, 1529–58' (London Univ. M.A. thesis, 1959), 569. [4] DL1/6/W9, 11, 11a, 19/B1; Fishwick, 38–45. [5] DL1/6/W11; 26/12/4; Fishwick, 45, 368. [6] *LP Hen. VIII,* xi; DL1/6/W10b; 3/59/W1; *VCH Lancs.* vii. 101n.

L.M.K./A.D.

WALWYN John (by 1520–66 or later), of Aylesbury, Bucks.

AYLESBURY 1554 (Nov.)[1]

b. by 1520, 1st s. of Edmund Walwyn of Thornborough by Anne, da. of Thomas Green of Greens-Norton, Northants. *m.* (1) Alice, da. of William Falkener of Quarrendon, Bucks., 3s. 2da.; (2) Joan, da. of John Hokeley of Bromwich, Staffs., 3s.; (3) Joan, da of Robert Cook of Tandridge, Surr., 2s. 1da.[2] Bailiff, Aylesbury Jan.–Sept. 1554.[3]

Walwyn's family was of marcher origin but his father settled in Buckinghamshire. The career traditionally pursued by his family was that of estate administration. Through his mother Walwyn was connected with the noble families of Parr and Vaux. Apart from his descent and marriages all that has been discovered about Walwyn relates to Aylesbury where following his mother's death he took up a copyhold in 1541. Named the town's first bailiff in its charter granted by Mary in January 1554 he returned its first two Members to Parliament several months later and was himself returned in the autumn. He was the only townsman to sit for Aylesbury in the century and his election with William Rice, a household officer with local affiliations, was presumably in compliance with the Queen's call for residents. Neither Member was found to be absent without leave when the House was called early in January 1555. Walwyn is last glimpsed in August 1566 when he and a merchant let land and crops in Aylesbury for a term of six years.[4]

[1] Huntington Lib. Hastings mss Parl. pprs. [2] Date of birth estimated from first reference. *Vis. Bucks.* ed. Metcalfe, 45; Harl. 1533. [3] *CPR,* 1553–4, p. 46. [4] C. Rawcliffe, *The Staffords, Earls of Stafford and Dukes of Buckingham, 1394–1521,* pp. 200, 210–231, 245, 248; Somerville, *Duchy,* i. 441; M. L. Robertson, 'Cromwell's servants' (Univ. California Los Angeles Ph.D. thesis, 1975), 581–2; NRA 7372, nos. 498373, 498388, 499832, 501407; C219/22/9; Bucks. RO, D/LE 1/22.

M.K.D.

WARCOP, Thomas (by 1525–89), of Smardale, Westmld.

WESTMORLAND 1547, 1553 (Oct.), 1554 (Apr.), 1554 (Nov.),[1] 1559, 1571, 1572, 1584, 1586, 1589

b. by 1525, 1st s. of John Warcop of Smardale, by Anne, da. of Geoffrey Lancaster of Crake Trees. *m.* Anne, da. of Rowland Thornborough of Hampsfield, Lancs., 2da. *suc.* fa. 1561/62.[2]

Esquire of the body in 1546; gent. pens. by 1552–*d.*; gov. Kirkby Stephen g.s. 1565; capt. Carlisle castle Sept. 1568–*d.*; j.p. Westmld. 1573/74–*d.*, q. by 1579; commr. for pirates' goods 1588.[3]

The Warcops were tenants by military service of the Clifford family, but Thomas Warcop could also have looked for his preferment to Thomas Wharton*, 1st Baron Wharton, whose mother was a Warcop of Smardale. Wharton was captain-general of Carlisle (although Warcop does not seem to have been appointed to office there until after his kinsman's death) and Warcop was a governor of the school Wharton founded at Kirkby Stephen, but as he was also on good terms with Wharton's successor at Carlisle, the 9th Lord Scrope, whose mother was a Clifford, he may not have been affected by Wharton's quarrel with that family. His election as knight for Westmorland to four of the seven Parliaments called between 1547 and 1558 (and to six of the first seven called thereafter) certainly betokens his general acceptance by his neighbours as well as his standing at court. While knight for the first time he and another Member Thomas Jolye (q.v.) were sued in the court of common pleas for money owed to a Londoner, but with what result is not known.[4]

Warcop is first mentioned at court early in 1552 when he took part in two jousts before the King, in the second of which he took the side of 'youth' against 'riches'. He may already have seen real warfare against the Scots in 1542, and he was to be in the field in 1569, although then as a messenger between Scrope and the government rather than as a soldier. In the meantime he had prospered as a courtier. On 9 Feb. 1546 he obtained a lease of the tithes of Warcop rectory for 21 years. He conveyed this lease to his father before December 1560, when John Warcop made his will leaving it to his sons Reynold and John: the statement in the will that the lease had been granted in 1546 to Thomas Warcop, 'esquire for the body of the same late King', furnishes the evidence for Warcop's entry into the Household by that date. On 10 June 1550 he obtained a lease for 21 years of the subsidy or custom of merchandise in Cumberland, with some reservations, at a rent of £13 6s.8d. Later grants included a licence to export 1,500 quarters of wheat, a venture which ended disastrously owing to French piracy, and four wardships: one of the wards was Warcop's nephew James Leyburn, son of Warcop's sister Elizabeth and grandson of Sir James Leyburn, Member for Westmorland in 1542 and 1545.[5]

In 1564 Bishop Best of Carlisle named Thomas Warcop among gentlemen of Westmorland 'very good in religion' and fit to be made justices of the peace; as within a few years he was to become one, Bishop Barnes's description of him in October 1570 as an enemy of religion seems to have been disregarded and may have been unjustified. He lived to see his ex-ward James Leyburn executed as a Catholic traitor in 1583, but he had ceased to be responsible for the young man in 1567, when he sold the wardship to his sister. It is not known whether he was related to the Thomas Warcop of Winston, Durham, who was executed for harbouring priests in 1597. Warcop's own children, his daughters and coheirs Agnes and Frances, married respectively Talbot Bowes†, of a strongly Protestant family, and John Dalston*, who succeeded his father-in-law as captain of Carlisle in 1589. Warcop died on 25 Mar. 1589.[6]

[1] Huntington Lib. Hastings mss Parl. pprs. [2] Date of birth estimated from first certain reference. *Vis. Westmld.* ed. Bridges, 10; *Vis. Northern Counties* (Surtees Soc. xli), 100–1; *Vis. Yorks.* (Harl. Soc. xvi), 334; Nicolson and Burn, *Westmld. and Cumb.* i. 554; PCC 21 Loftes. [3] PCC 21 Loftes; E179/69/63, 64; E407/1/1–19; LC2/4/2; *CPR*, 1563–6, p. 367; 1566–9, p. 200; *APC*, xvi. 385. [4] M. E. James, *Change and Continuity in Tudor North* (Borthwick Pprs. xxvii), 13, 48; *Northern Hist.* i. 52–53, 55n; *CPR*, 1563–6, p. 367; *Cal. Border Pprs.* i. 95, 155; CP 40/1142, r. 719. [5] *Lit. Rems. Edw. VI*, 384, 388; *LP Hen. VIII*, xvii, xxi; *HMC Hatfield*, i. 442; *CSP Dom.* 1547–80, p. 352; *Add.* 1566–79, pp. 88, 148, 167; PCC 21 Loftes; *CPR*, 1553, p. 344; 1555–7, p. 512; 1558–60, pp. 14, 327; 1560–3, p. 122; 1569–72, pp. 177, 448; *APC*, ix. 71–72; *CSP For.* 1579–80, pp. 13–14. [6] *Cam. Misc.* ix(3), 51; *Cath. Rec. Soc.* xxii, 117; J. H. Pollen, *Acts of Eng. Martyrs*, 212–18; *CPR*, 1560–3, p. 122; Strype, *Annals*, iv. 426; *HMC Hatfield*, vii. 230, 300; *CSP Dom. Add.* 1580–1625, p. 290; C142/222/8.

A.D.

WARD, Henry (by 1519–56), of Gray's Inn, London and Kirby Bedon and Postwick, Norf.

NORWICH 1554 (Apr.)

b. by 1519, 1st s. of Robert Ward of Kirby Bedon by Alice, da. of Sir Giles Capell of London. *educ.* G. Inn, adm. 1539. *m.* by 1540, Margaret, da. of William Uggs of Pockthorpe by Norwich, Norf., 5s. 2da.[1]
   Autumn reader, G. Inn 1549.[2]
   Common clerk, Norwich May 1542–May 1553; j.p. Norf. 1542–*d.*, q. 1554; commr. relief 1550.[3]

Henry Ward came of a family of lesser Norfolk gentry. He had probably begun his legal training before his admission to Gray's Inn in 1539, for in that year Cromwell recommended him for the office of town clerk of Norwich as a man well learned in the law. Among Cromwell's accounts for 1537–8 are various payments to and from Richard Cromwell *alias* Williams* 'at Mr. Warde's house', including one for a horse taken to 'Harry Warde' by Richard. Despite the minister's support Ward did not immediately obtain the post at Norwich, the city answering that it preferred a local man to a stranger. As Ward's home was close to Norwich, this may mean that he had spent his early life elsewhere, probably in London. This shortcoming he

remedied on 15 Jan. 1540, when as 'Henry Ward gentleman, *legis peritus*, mercer' he was admitted to the freedom of Norwich, being excused all offices. His election as common clerk followed on 3 May 1542.[4]

During the next ten years Ward combined his professional career at Gray's Inn with his service at Norwich and his share in the administration of Norfolk. A connexion between him and the 9th Lord Clinton is reflected in the pardon granted to them jointly in June 1548 for offences ranging from heresies and lollardies to the conversion of arable land to pasture. It was doubtless the last of these for which they sought immunity, under the threat of the enclosure commission about to be issued, and the inclusion of heresy may be dismissed as a piece of common form; Ward had probably been involved in Clinton's amassing of lands as well as acquiring some for himself. Since 1543 he had bought three Norfolk manors, valued in his inquisition at £42, as well as several smaller properties, but his largest purchase was to follow in the autumn of 1555, when he paid Sir Thomas Holles nearly £3,000 for former possessions of Flitcham abbey and others in the neighbourhood—a bad bargain this, as unknown to Ward the lands had been seized by Holles's creditors and all he obtained was the reversion.[5]

Ward had ceased to be common clerk of Norwich when he was elected to Mary's second Parliament, but there is no reason to doubt that he was the city's own choice, perhaps to compensate him for having been passed over before. It was in this Parliament that a bill for the manufacture of russells in Norwich was given three readings in the Commons. Ward had then only two years to live, for he died on 8 May 1556. In the will which he had made at Gray's Inn as a sick man on the previous 25 Feb., after pleading indebtedness as his reason for not giving legacies, he supplemented what he had already done for his wife and children by dividing his property among them. He made his wife sole executrix and asked her to have a mass and dirge said for him at each of her four manors; as supervisors he named John Stubbes (perhaps the father of John Stubbe† the Puritan), and two of his colleagues at Gray's Inn, John Birch and his 'gentle gossip' Robert Flint. (If Flint was the Member for Thirsk in the Parliament of 1547, he could have been a link in Ward's connexion with Clinton.) The will was proved on 6 May 1557 and in the following November the widow was granted the wardship of the 15 year-old heir Edward and an annuity from the Flitcham property for his maintenance.[6]

[1] Date of birth estimated from marriage. *Vis. Norf.* (Harl. Soc. xxxii), 305–6; C142/108/73. [2] Dugdale, *Origines Juridiciales*, 293.

[3] Norwich ass. procs. 2, f. 169 et passim; *LP Hen. VIII*, xvii, xx; *CPR*, 1547–8, p. 87; 1553, p. 357; 1553–4, p. 22. [4] *Blomefield, Norf.* v. 451; *LP Hen. VIII*, xiv; Norwich old free bk. ff. 134v, 137v. [5] *CPR*, 1547–8, pp. 18, 359; 1553–4, p. 362; 1555–7, p. 212; *LP Hen. VIII*, xviii; C142/108/73; Blomefield, viii. 413. [6] *CJ*, i. 33–34; C142/108/73; PCC 12 Wrastley; *CPR*, 1557–8, pp. 3–4.

R.V.

WARD, Richard I (by 1511–78), of Hurst, Berks.

NEW WINDSOR 1542, 1547, 1553 (Mar.), 1553 (Oct.), 1554 (Apr.), 1554 (Nov.), 1555

BERKSHIRE 1571

b. by 1511, o. s. of Thomas Ward I* of Winkfield by Maud, da. of Thomas More of Bourton, Bucks. *educ.* Eton c.1520–5; scholar, King's, Camb. 1525. *m.* by 1539, Colubra (*d.*1574), da. of William Flambert or Lambert of Chertsey, Surr., 8s. 9da. (at least 2s. 4da. *d.v.p.*). *suc.* fa. July 1538.[1]

Clerk of the scullery by 1532, of the poultry by 1537, second clerk of the spicery by 1540, first clerk 1549–56; clerk of the green cloth by 1565; porter of the outer gate and keeper of the armoury, Windsor castle 1538–*d.*; bailiff, liberties of Bray and Cookham, Berks. 1540–64; commr. subsidy, New Windsor 1540, 1560, 1571, relief, Berks. 1550, goods of churches and fraternities 1553; other commissions 1543–*d.*; escheator, Oxon. and Berks. 1542–3; j.p. Berks. 1543–*d.*, Wilts. 1574; cofferer, the Household ?Oct. 1558–1 Jan. 1559, 1567–*d.*; receiver, duchy of Lancaster, former lands of Furness abbey in Cumb., Lancs., Yorks. 1559.[2]

In November 1537 two offices held by Thomas Ward at Windsor castle, together with an annuity of £5, were granted in reversion to his son. Richard Ward appears to have been an only child and was probably unmarried when the father made his will on 20 July 1538, four days before his death. By that time Richard Ward had already spent several years in the royal household, and was poised for advancement.[3]

Ward was quick to consolidate his estates in Berkshire. His father had leased the manor of Hurst from Abingdon abbey in 1519 and on his death had been succeeded as tenant by Edmund Ashfield*. On 7 May 1539 Richard Ward and his heirs were granted the manor of Hurst for a rent of £4 10s. as he, his wife and his mother-in-law had surrendered to the crown their manor of Stannards at Chobham, with other lands in Surrey. The estates of Abingdon abbey were now in the King's hands but this exchange was resisted by Ashfield, who had secured the reversion of Thomas Ward's lease from the last abbot in 1537; some four years after his father's death, Ward brought a suit in Chancery against Ashfield for molestation. About 1547 he had to go to law again over Hurst, this time against Sir John Norris, who claimed some of the premises as his own freehold: this suit Ward brought in the court of requests on the grounds that his official duties prevented him from successfully invoking the com-

mon law and that since Norris was 'so allied and friended in the said county of Berks.' a fair trial was impossible there.[4]

Perhaps Ward first entered Parliament in 1539, when the Members for Windsor are not known, for his fellow-Member in 1542 was William Symonds, who had been his father's colleague in 1529 and may himself have sat in 1539. There is nothing surprising in the election of Ward, who enjoyed the triple advantage of his parentage, his offices at the castle and his estates near the town; he probably sat again in 1545. Although he never held municipal office, the chamberlain of Windsor recorded on 15 Oct. 1539 that 6s.8d. had been 'received of Master Ward for being brother of this hall'; no other royal servant who sat for the town is known to have enjoyed this distinction.[5]

What is remarkable is that six out of the eight Parliaments in which Ward is known to have sat (or eight out of nine if he did sit in 1545 when his experience of victualling the French campaign of the previous year would have made him an invaluable addition to the House) were consecutive and that they witnessed so many revolutionary changes. Although re-elected for Windsor in 1558 he was replaced six days before the assembly by William Hanley: the reason for this substitution is not known but it ended a monopoly of one of the town's seats stretching back 16 years. When he was re-elected in 1571 it was as one of the knights for Berkshire. Nothing has come to light about his part in the House before the accession of Elizabeth save that he was found to be absent without leave at the call early in January 1555. Informed against in the King's bench for this dereliction in the following Easter term, he was distrained 69s.8d. for repeated non-appearance and fined 53s.4d. in Easter term 1558 when his sureties were two yeomen from his manor of Hurst.[6]

Ward added regularly to his landed wealth. He and a Lincolnshire merchant of the staple jointly paid £263 in April 1540 for ex-monastic lands in Berkshire and Lincolnshire. Annual payments to Ward by the chamberlains of Windsor, between 1541 and 1545, of £6 13s.4d. 'for debt for Underour' presumably represent instalments for the manor of Windsor Underour, which had been granted to his father and sold by Ward himself to the corporation. In 1549 he and another paid £629 for property in Berkshire, Cambridgeshire and Essex, and a year later he and his wife received the Berkshire rectory of White Waltham, formerly granted to Thomas Weldon*, in exchange for two messuages at Clewer and New Windsor. Sixteen months later, he and John Norris* leased the manor and park of Yate,

Gloucestershire, for 21 years, and in 1556 Ward also held the manor of Waltham St. Lawrence, where in 1566 he was to buy the rectory from the Lovelace family.[7]

Although Elizabeth did not at first confirm Ward in his temporary appointment as cofferer of the Household at her accession, she had accorded him the post by 1567. Ward made his will on 5 Nov. 1577 and died on 11 Feb. 1578.[8]

[1] Date of birth estimated from first reference, *Eton Coll. Reg.* ed. Sterry, 350. *LP Hen. VIII*, xiv; *Vis. Berks.* (Harl. Soc. lvi), 57; Mill Stephenson, *Mon. Brasses*, 22. [2] *HMC Bath*, iv. 6; *LP Hen. VIII*, xii, xvi, xviii–xxi; *CPR*, 1547–8, p. 81; 1553, pp. 351, 413; 1553–4, p. 17; 1555–7, p. 404; 1558–60, p. 423; 1563–6, pp. 20, 28, 39, 169–70, 184, 257, 488; 1569–72, pp. 29, 31, 219–21, 223; 1572–5, p. 522; Req.2/7/108; *APC*, iv. 227; Somerville, *Duchy*, i. 497; E179/73/153, 74/217, 233; 351/1795, mm. 20–37; Foxe, *Acts and Mons.* v. 474; information from Dr. R. C. Braddock. [3] *LP Hen. VIII*, xiii; PCC 21 Dyngeley; E150/809/1. [4] *LP Hen. VIII*, xiv; *VCH Surr.* iii. 416; Req.2/7/108; C1/1086/12. [5] Windsor recs. Wi/FA c. 1, f. 43. [6] *LP Hen. VIII*, xix; KB27/1176–86. [7] *LP Hen. VIII*, xv; Windsor recs. Wi/FA c. 1, ff. 45v, 46v, 47, 48v, 49; *VCH Berks.* iii. 66, 176, 181, 183; *CPR*, 1548–9, pp. 423–5; 1549–51, p. 424; 1557–8, p. 404. [8] PCC 20 Langley; C142/180/6.

T.F.T.B.

WARD, Richard II (by 1517–70/71), of Derby.

DERBY 1555

b. by 1517, prob. 2nd s. of Thomas Ward II* of Derby by Joan. *m.* Margaret, 5s. 2da.[1]

1st bailiff, Derby 1547–8, 1555–6, 1563–4.[2]

The identity of Richard Ward as the son of Thomas Ward II is established by comparison of their wills. An ironmonger by trade, Ward claimed in a suit brought against him between 1553 and 1555 over the title to a shop, garden and barn in Derby that he was a mere tenant at will of the premises, which he had occupied for 17 years. He also held some of the property included in the royal grant to the town of May 1554 and he may have had land at Wilborne in the shire.[3]

Ward's single spell in Parliament came during his second term as bailiff. It may be an indication of his attitude towards the Marian regime that, whereas both Members for the town in the previous Parliament were to be fined for quitting it before its dissolution, neither Ward nor his fellow-Member William Allestry is found on the list of those who followed Sir Anthony Kingston in opposing one of the government's bills. Twelve months later it fell to Ward to attend the trial of the blind heretic Joan Waste and with William Bainbridge* to execute the writ for her burning. Their share in her martyrdom seems to have provoked no hostility towards them after 1558, for although Ward, unlike Bainbridge, did not sit in an Elizabethan Parliament, he was elected bailiff again in 1563. The accusation made in June 1556 that he had instigated his servants to seize tithe hay in Derby perhaps reflected less on

Ward than on his accuser, the notorious trouble-maker John Sharpe who had once similarly attacked Ward's father.[4]

Ward's will, drawn up on 19 Nov. 1570, was proved on 20 Apr. in the following year. He asked to be buried near his father in St. Peter's church, Derby, and bequeathed lands, tenements and mills in the town to each of his five sons. He named his wife Margaret and heir Thomas his executors, and his brother John Ward, parson of Blore, Staffordshire, one of his four overseers. In the inventory made after his death his goods were valued at £132 11s.8d.[5]

[1] Date of birth estimated from his evidence in suit of 1553/55. Lichfield consist. ct. wills 48, 141. [2] W. Hutton, *Derby*, 80–81. [3] Lichfield consist. ct. wills 48, 141; St.Ch.4/4/23; C1/1385/43–44; *CPR*, 1549–51, p. 78; 1553–4, p. 245. [4] Guildford mus. Loseley 1331/2; R. Simpson, *Derby*, 662–70; St.Ch.4/4/23. [5] Lichfield consist. ct. will 141.

C.J.B.

WARD, Thomas I (by 1488–1538), of Winkfield, Berks.

NEW WINDSOR 1529

b. by 1488, 1st s. of Thomas Ward by Elizabeth, da. of William Cunnington of Hunts. *m.* c.1505, Maud, da. of Thomas More of Bourton, Bucks., 1s. Richard Ward I*.[1]

Yeoman harbinger by 1509–*d.*; jt. porter, Wallingford castle, Berks, 1511, sole 1520–*d.*; porter of the outer gate, Windsor castle 1515–*d.*, comptroller of works, Nov. 1528–*d.*, keeper of the butts and keeper of the armoury by 1532–*d.*; bailiff, manor of Amersham, Bucks. 1522; commr. subsidy, Berks. 1523, 1524; j.p. 1526–*d.*; escheator, Oxon. and Berks. 1531–2; steward, former lands of Wallingford priory 1531.[2]

Thomas Ward's father and namesake was himself the third son of Sir Christopher Ward of Givendale, Yorkshire, whose pedigree has been traced back to the end of the 12th century. Nothing certain is known about Thomas the elder, who presumably moved south and may have been the gentleman and mercer of London who sued out a pardon on 6 June 1509. His son is first mentioned in the same year, when he attended both the funeral of Henry VII and the coronation of Henry VIII as a yeoman harbinger.[3]

Thomas Ward the younger prospered from the beginning of the reign. On 1 Mar. 1511 he was granted 13 tenements and gardens in Holborn, and on 3 Nov. 1514 he received an annuity of £5 for life out of the lordship of Denbigh. He was taxed as a member of the royal household, his goods being valued at £41 in 1524, and occasionally he received special gifts, such as a New Year's present in 1533 and a 'reward' of £20 three months later. Ward's main income, however, came from his numerous offices. In spite of these, there is little evidence of his investing in land. He is described as a resident of Winkfield only in a lease of November 1537, when he secured 150 acres of the manor of Holcombe in Oxfordshire, but he had leased the Berkshire manor of Hurst from Abingdon abbey in 1518 and he was granted Windsor Underour on the suppression of Reading abbey. An inquisition taken at Reading on 8 Oct. 1538 found that Ward had property at White Waltham, Windsor, Winkfield and Worth; when he spoke in his will of furnishings 'in the chambers at Windsor' he may have meant lodgings in the castle rather than a house in the town.[4]

With his ancestry, his royal offices and his country properties, Ward was more prominent in the county than in Windsor. A Robert Ward appears low down on the subsidy assessments for the town in 1524 and 1525, with goods valued at 20s., but the surname is not mentioned in any municipal records and Thomas Ward cannot be classed as a townsman. His return to the Parliament of 1529 therefore marked a change from earlier practice under Henry VIII, except perhaps in 1523 when it is not known who sat for Windsor. Ward was probably nominated by or on behalf of the King, who sent for several parliamentary writs while at Windsor castle in September 1529 and who can hardly have overlooked the town beside the castle. The choice was balanced by that of the townsman William Symonds. Windsor's Members in the Parliament of June 1536 are again unknown but it would have been in accordance with the King's wish for the men of 1529 to be returned again. Symonds was to sit in 1542, after Ward's death, and Ward himself remained in favour, for in May 1536 the bishop of Lincoln urged Cromwell to appoint him a justice of the peace in Buckinghamshire as well as in Berkshire. Of Ward's part in the proceedings of the House there is only one dubious glimpse. The name 'Thomas Warde' occurs in a list of Members compiled by Cromwell probably in December 1534 and believed to indicate those having a particular connexion, possibly as a committee, with the treasons bill then on its way through Parliament. Whether the Member thus designated was Thomas Ward of Windsor or his namesake of Derby it seems impossible to determine: either would have suited a list which included both 'official' names and those of Members without court connexion.[5]

Ward made his will on 20 July 1538, acknowledging the royal supremacy but making elaborate and traditional arrangements for his funeral and masses at Winkfield church. Numerous household servants were left sums ranging from 3s.4d. to 26s.8d., while among the recipients of black gowns were his chaplain Richard Gibson, and Thomas* and Edward

Weldon. He provided for his son Richard, made his wife residuary legatee and sole executrix and named John Norris* supervisor. Ward died four days after making the will, leaving Richard to succeed to many of his offices and to start his own long parliamentary career.[6]

[1] Date of birth estimated from first reference. *Vis. Berks.* (Harl. Soc. lvi), 12, 57; PCC 21 Dyngeley. [2] *LP Hen. VIII*, i–v, viii, xiii, xxi; *The King's Works*, iii. 415. [3] *Yorks. Peds.* (Harl. Soc. xcvi), 433; *LP Hen. VIII*, i. [4] *LP Hen. VIII*, i, iii–vi, xii, xiii; C1/1086/12; *VCH Berks.* iii. 66; E150/809/1. [5] E179/73/30, 137; *LP Hen. VIII*, iv; vii, 1522 (ii) citing SP1/87, f. 106v; x. [6] PCC 21 Dyngeley; E150/809/1.

T.F.T.B.

WARD, Thomas II (by 1499–1563), of Derby.

DERBY 1529

b. by 1499. *m.* (1) Joan, 2s. prob. inc. Richard II*; (2) 3s. 4da.[1]

2nd bailiff, Derby 1528–9, 1536–7, 1st bailiff 1544–5, 1552–3; commr. goods of churches and fraternities 1553.[2]

Thomas Ward of Derby is readily distinguishable from his namesake who sat for Windsor in the Parliament of 1529 but less readily from those others who lived nearer him. There was a Ward family, which included more than one Thomas, in the neighbourhood of Bingham, near Nottingham, and another at Carlton Curlieu in Leicestershire: in the absence of information on his parentage and early life it is fruitless to try to link him with, or separate him from, any family in the region.[3]

Ward was elected to Parliament towards the close of his first term as a bailiff of Derby. The junior of the two officers so styled who exercised the functions of mayor, he was presumably a townsman of standing, although nothing has come to light about his earlier life save his participation as feoffee to a use which may have been set up shortly before 1520; if this transaction is correctly dated, Ward was at least 30 years old when he took his seat in the Commons. At such an age, and occupying such a place in municipal life, he was a natural choice for this service, and there is less call to speculate about his election than there is about his fellow-Member Henry Ainsworth's. Both were to see this Parliament through to its end, and having done so they were probably re-elected to its brief successor of June 1536 in accordance with the King's general request for the return of the previous Members: either or both may even have reappeared in 1539, when again the names of the Members for Derby, in common with those for nearly all boroughs, are lost. Of Ward's part in the proceedings of the Commons there is only a single, and dubious, glimpse. The name 'Thomas Warde' occurs in a list of some 50 Members written by Cromwell on the back of a letter of December 1534, but without indication which Member is intended. The make-up of the list does not help. Believed to denote Members having a particular connexion with the treasons bill then passing through Parliament, perhaps as belonging to a committee, the list comprises men likely to have taken varying attitudes towards that measure: it contains an 'official' element into which the Windsor Member would have fitted easily but also an assortment of representatives of provincial towns which could have included his namesake from Derby. Which of the two was involved it seems impossible to determine.[4]

Ward's career after he ceased to sit in Parliament is relatively well documented. In 1552 he appears as a tenant of ex-monastic property in the town, and in 1546 and 1549 as holding ex-chantry lands at Kirk Hallam (where his name is also inscribed on a church bell) and elsewhere, as a member of a group which included his parliamentary colleague Henry Ainsworth. He also figures in litigation in both a personal and a public capacity. In 1545 he was one of the objects of a 'seditious attempt' by John Sharpe and a number of other freemen of Derby to disfranchise him, his fellow-bailiff William Buckley, and the recorder Thomas Sutton*, and to make Sharpe a freeman. In May 1546 Sharpe launched another attack on Ward, this time in the Exchequer: Ward appeared by attorney to deny the charge, one of keeping a dicing house, but after a jury had been summoned no further process is recorded. Ward was perhaps not guiltless in this or another matter for the same charge had been brought against him in the previous year and in July 1546 he was accused of forestalling. Ward was also taken to Chancery for his action as bailiff in arresting a London vintner for alleged failure to pay for some lead he had bought of a Derbyshire man. Finally, he was one of the defendants in a suit brought before the court of requests by George Liversage of Warwickshire, who claimed that Ward had dispossessed him and sought to disinherit him of property in Derby which Ward held as a feoffee to a use created by his father, a dyer in the town.[5]

The Thomas Ward of Derby who died in 1563 was almost certainly the Member. He appointed two of his sons, John and Richard, as his executors and his two sons-in-law, John Heather and Thomas Brockhouse, as his overseers. William Buckley was one of the Derby men who compiled the inventory of his goods, which were valued at £251.[6]

[1] Date of birth estimated from first reference. Lichfield consist. ct. will 48. [2] W. Hutton, *Derby*, 79–80; Stowe 5(141), ff. 59–69. [3] *Test. Ebor.* vi (Surtees Soc. cvi), 20; *Old Notts.* ii. 95–96, 100; *Vis. Leics.* (Harl. Soc. ii), 83, 87. [4] Req.2/59/3; *LP Hen. VIII*, vii. 1522 (ii) citing SP1/87, f. 106v. [5] *LP Hen. VIII*, xx; *CPR*, 1549–51, p. 92; 1550–3, p. 366; 1553, p. 246; *APC*, i. 304; St.Ch.2/25/11, 129;

E159/324/rec. Hil. r. 37, 325/rec. East. r. 32, rec. Trin. r. 27; C1/1118/51; 2/L8/17; Req.2/59/3. [6] Lichfield consist. ct. will 48.

C.J.B.

WARD, William I

LANCASTER 1547*[1]

William Ward, styled 'armiger', was returned for Lancaster to the Parliament of 1547 at a by-election held after the death of Stephen Vaughan on 25 Dec. 1549. During the last session of the Parliament he obtained a writ of privilege out of Chancery without first securing a warrant for it from the House of Commons and on 22 Feb. 1552 his misdemeanour was referred by the House to four Members, Sir Robert Bowes, Sir Nicholas Hare, Sir John Mason and Richard Morgan, although with what result is not known. Ward had presumably been the nominee at Lancaster of Sir William Paget, then chancellor of the duchy of Lancaster. He may have been the man of that name employed to write accounts for the duchy at some time between 1525 and 1547, and either he or a namesake was by 1567 a servant of the Paget family, becoming receiver-general to Thomas, 4th Lord Paget, by 1572 and remaining in the family's service at least until 1596. All that has been discovered of the receiver-general's personal history is that he had a nephew Richard who was a member of King's College, Cambridge, in 1593. The name is a common one in Staffordshire, William Paget's adopted shire, and elsewhere. On 19 Dec. 1541 one William Ward of Monks Heath, Cheshire, gentleman, who gave his age as 47 or thereabouts, made a deposition in the dispute over the division of the property of Lawrence Starkey, who had sat for Lancaster in the Parliament of 1529, and in 1568 a namesake received a lease for 21 years of lands in Carnforth and Ashton, Lancashire. There is nothing to suggest that Ward was, or was connected with, the William Ward who sat for Morpeth and Carlisle.[2]

[1] Hatfield 207. [2] *CJ*, i. 18; Somerville, *Duchy*, i. 460; NRA 0010, pp. 169–248 passim; *Lichfield Wills* (Brit. Rec. Soc. Ltd. Index Lib. vii), 112; J. B. Watson, 'Lancs. gentry 1529–58' (London Univ. MA thesis, 1959), 542, 544, 568–9; *Trans. Hist. Soc. Lancs. and Cheshire*, lxxiii. 206; *CPR*, 1566–9, p. 380.

A.D.K.H.

WARD, William II

MORPETH 1553 (Oct.), 1554 (Apr.), 1554 (Nov.)[1]
CARLISLE 1555
MORPETH 1559, 1563

William Ward, who may have come from a family which can be traced at Morpeth between 1366 and 1505, presumably owed his five elections there and his one at Carlisle to William, 3rd Lord Dacre, lord of Morpeth and warden of the west marches, which were administered from Carlisle. In the indenture for October 1553 Ward's name was inserted in a different hand from that of the document. On the Crown Office lists for that Parliament and for November 1554 he was described as a gentleman, but he is almost certainly to be distinguished from the William Ward 'armiger' who had earlier sat for Lancaster.[2]

Ward may have been the William Ward to whom in 1561 Lord Dacre's daughter Dorothy, widow of Sir Thomas Windsor*, left a grey mare and £3 6s.8d. He was perhaps also the London gentleman who in 1548 and 1549 made three extensive purchases of church lands of which the second, made with Richard Venables, a serjeant-at-arms, included property in Bristo and Skelton, Cumberland, and Appleby, Westmorland; a further parcel of Skelton land was bought a few months later by Thomas Dalston* of Carlisle and his kinsman William Denton*, a Londoner of Cumberland origin who was to owe his parliamentary career to the patronage of Anthony Browne*, Viscount Montagu and, by 1558, son-in-law of Lord Dacre.[3]

Ward was re-elected twice in the reign of Elizabeth before the death of Lord Dacre in November 1563. The date of his own death is unknown.

[1] Huntington Lib. Hastings mss Parl. pprs. supplies the christian name missing from the damaged indenture, C219/23/96; Hodgson, *Northumb.* ii(2), 531 gives the christian name as Robert. [2] Hodgson, ii(2), 492-5, 497-500, 505, 531; C219/21/115; Bodl. e Museo 17. [3] *N. Country Wills*, ii (Surtees Soc. cxxi), 32-34; *CPR*, 1548-9, pp. 47-50, 222, 324-9, 410-17; *Trans. Cumb. and Westmld. Antiq. and Arch. Soc.* n.s. lx. 77, 94; lxii. 147, 157.

M.J.T.

WAREN *see* WARREN

WARNECOMBE (WARMECOMBE), James (by 1523–81), of Ivington, Herefs.

LUDLOW	1554 (Nov.)
LEOMINSTER	1555
HEREFORDSHIRE	1563
HEREFORD	1571, 1572*

b. by 1523, 2nd s. of Richard Warnecombe* (*d.* 17 Nov. 1547) of Ivington, Lugwardine and Hereford by 2nd w. Anne, da. of Richard Bromwich of Hereford; bro. of John*. *educ.* I. Temple, adm. 3 July 1537, called. *m.* (1) by 1548, Eleanor Hyett, *s.p.*; (2) 24 July 1567, Mary, da. of John Cornwall of Burford, Salop, *s.p.*[1]

V.-justice of Chester 1545; escheator, Herefs. and the marches 1548-9; commr. relief, Herefs. 1550, to survey lands of bpric. of Hereford 1559, musters, Herefs. by 1573; recorder, Ludlow 1551-63; standing counsel to Leominster by 1552; j.p. Herefs. 1554-*d.*, q. by 1569; collector for loan, Herefs. 1562; mayor, Hereford 1571-2, 1578-9; dep. justice, Brec. circuit 1575; sheriff, Herefs. 1576-7.[2]

As a member of the Inner Temple James Warnecombe was chosen marshal for Christmas seven times between 1542 and 1559, but he usually defaulted and was fined. His absences were doubtless connected with his discharge of the offices which he accumulated from 1545 and his succession to the headship of the family on his brother's death in 1552. One of the exceptions occurred in 1554 when Warnecombe's Membership of the third Marian Parliament kept him in London over Christmas. His election to that Parliament for Ludlow, with the town clerk John Allsop, may have owed something to the Queen's directive for the return of resident borough Members, for although Warnecombe made his home at Ivington, near Leominster, he was recorder of Ludlow and a familiar figure there. Unlike Allsop, he did not quit this Parliament prematurely without leave, nor during its successor, in which he sat for his neighbouring borough of Leominster, was he to be included among the Members who opposed one of the government's bills. Made a justice for Herefordshire in 1554, he probably acquiesced in rather than enthused over the restoration of Catholicism, for ten years later he was to be adjudged a 'favourer' of the Anglican settlement. Under Elizabeth his career focussed on his native city and shire, for both of which he was returned to Parliament. He died childless and intestate on 21 Feb. 1581.[3]

[1] Date of birth estimated from education. *Vis. Herefs.* ed. Weaver, 71; C142/86/94; *Cal. I.T. Recs.* i. 116. [2] Ormerod, *Cheshire*, i. 65; *CPR*, 1553, p. 354; 1553-4, p. 20; 1558-60, pp. 31, 422; 1569-72, p. 225; Lansd. 56, ff. 168 seq.; *Trans. Salop Arch. Soc.* (ser. 2), xi. 313-14; G. F. Townsend, *Leominster*, 77-78, 292; Osborn coll. Yale Univ. Lib. 71.6.41; Duncumb, *Herefs.* i. 367; *Cal. Hereford Docs.* ed. Macray, 31; W. R. Williams, *Welsh Judges*, 70. [3] *Cal. I.T. Recs.* i. 132, 133, 137, 139, 140, 169, 172, 175, 199, 202, 203; *Cam. Misc.* ix(3), 14; C142/199/90; PCC admons. act bk. 1581, ff. 4v, 6.

A.H.

WARNECOMBE (WARMECOMBE), John (1516/18–52), of Lugwardine and Hereford.

HEREFORD	1547*[1]

b. 1516/18, 1st s. of Richard Warnecombe*, and bro. of James*. *m.* c.1543, Jane, da. of John Scudamore* of Holme Lacy, 1da. *suc.* fa. 17 Nov. 1547.[2]

Town clerk, Hereford 1547, mayor 1548-9; commr. relief, Herefs. 1550, goods of churches and fraternities 1553.[3]

The eldest son of a town clerk and mayor of Hereford who had represented the city in at least two Parliaments, John Warnecombe was to follow a trodden path, but as he died less than five years after his father there is little to recount of him. First met with in June 1542, when with Hugh Gebons* and others he witnessed a confession there, Warnecombe succeeded his father as town clerk in

1547 and as mayor in the following year. He also appears to have served the bishop of Hereford: it was before him as the bishop's steward that a court and view of frankpledge was held at Bishop's Castle in October 1549. In 1550 and 1551 he was one of those nominated for the shrievalty but he was not pricked. His opportunity of following his father in the House of Commons came with the death of William Berkeley: as this cannot have taken place before 23 Apr. 1551 Warnecombe sat only in the final session, which opened in January 1552, and his name appears accordingly in the list of Members as revised on that occasion.[4]

Warnecombe made his will on 22 Sept. 1552, asking for no special place of burial. He left 10s. for the repair of Hereford cathedral, 6s.8d. to the vicar of Lugwardine for forgotten tithes, and 6s.8d. to the vicar of All Hallows; other bequests included £4 to his brother James Warnecombe, and £5 to each of the unmarried daughters (save one who had £10) of his uncle Thomas Bromwich*. His dwelling house in Hereford Warnecombe left to his father-in-law John Scudamore. To his wife he gave two parts of his manor of Lugwardine for life, on condition that she should not remarry without the permission of her father, her brother, her brother-in-law and Thomas Bromwich: otherwise her interest would pass to the daughter and heir Joan. The executors of the will were Jane and John Scudamore, and the overseers James Warnecombe and Thomas Bromwich. One of the witnesses was Stephen Parry*. Warnecombe died two days after making the will, leaving the eight year-old Joan, who became a royal ward. The will was proved on 2 Dec. 1552 but the devising of two parts of Lugwardine to the widow was judged illegal, and she was charged with trespass, to be pardoned and licensed to enter in February 1553 for a fine of £22: she later married William Devereux*.[5]

[1] Hatfield 207. [2] Date of birth estimated from parents' marriage and age at fa.'s i.p.m., C142/86/94. *Vis. Herefs.* ed. Weaver, 63, 71; Wards 7/6/113. [3] R. Johnson, *Anct. Customs, Hereford,* 237; Duncumb, *Herefs.* i. 366; *CPR, 1550–3,* p. 394; 1553, p. 354. [4] Hereford pub. lib., Hereford city muniments 942, ff. 52–53; NRA 16218, no. 676; *CPR, 1553,* pp. 348, 375. [5] PCC 33 Powell; Wards 7/6/113; *CPR, 1553,* p. 17.

P.S.E.

WARNECOMBE (WARMECOMBE), Richard (by 1494–1547), of Ivington, Lugwardine and Hereford.

HEREFORD 1529, 1542

b. by 1494, s. of John Warnecombe of Hereford. *m.* (1) Margaret, da. of Richard Phillips of Hereford; (2) disp. 27 Dec. 1515, Anne, da. of Richard Bromwich of Hereford, wid. of Richard Jones of Bullinghope, 3s. inc. James* and John* 6da.[1]

Town clerk, Hereford by 1518, alderman by 1525–*d.,*

mayor 1525–6, 1540–1; commr. subsidy, Herefs. 1515, musters 1539, 1542; other commissions 1538–*d.*; servant of bp. of Hereford by 1528, dep. steward in 1535; escheator, Herefs. and the marches 1532–3, 1543–Jan. 1545; j.p. Herefs. 1538–*d.*; custos rot. c.1547.[2]

Richard Warnecombe combined civic office in Hereford with service to the bishopric and, in his later years, to the crown. Both his marriages were within the civic circle: his father-in-law by the first of them served at least six terms as mayor and his brother-in-law by the second was to do so in 1546–7.[3]

Warnecombe's parliamentary career was almost certainly longer than is conveyed by his two known attendances at Westminster. It may be taken that both he and Thomas Havard were re-elected in the spring of 1536, when the King asked for the return of all Members of the previous Parliament, and their reappearance in 1542 makes it likely that they had both sat in 1539 and were to do so again in 1545, two Parliaments for which the names of the city's representatives are lost: these were the years of Warnecombe's entry into county administration and of his consequent increase in local stature. By the time of the election to the Parliament of 1547, however, Warnecombe was a sick man, and he died within two weeks of its opening. Of his role in the House of Commons nothing is known, but whereas Thomas Havard, a staunch Catholic, may have been troubled by the Henrician Reformation, Warnecombe's association with the bishopric perhaps kept him more easily in step with royal policy.

Warnecombe's importance in the episcopal administration is illustrated by the part he played in the successive transmissions of the bishopric: when Edward Fox was appointed in 1535 it was through Warnecombe and John Scudamore* that he arranged the business side of the matter, and on his death in 1538 Warnecombe and Archdeacon Richard Sparkford (later to be an overseer of Warnecombe's will) were commissioned to make the survey. Warnecombe doubtless prospered in this service, receiving several leases of episcopal lands at Shelwick, Warham and elsewhere, and it may have been his profits as 'steward in fee' that in 1540 enabled him to purchase from Sir John Brydges* the manor of Lugwardine, a few miles from Hereford. He was also by 1542 seised of half the manor of Bradbury.[4]

Warnecombe died on 17 Nov. 1547. By his will, made on the previous 28 Sept., he had asked to be buried in Hereford cathedral. Of his three sons the youngest, Richard, was still under age, and of his six daughters three were married (Alice to James Croft*) and one was under age. Warnecombe named as his executors all three of his sons, and as overseers John Scudamore, the dean of Hereford Hugh Curwen, the mayor Thomas Bromwich*, and the archdeacon of Shropshire Richard Sparkford. The will, which was proved on 9 Feb. 1548, bears a note that on 26 Feb. 1593, the executors being dead, administration was granted to Thomas Wigmore†, Alice Warnecombe's son by her first husband.[5]

¹ Date of birth estimated from second marriage. *Vis. Herefs.* ed. Weaver, 71; PCC 3 Populwell; *Reg. Ricardi Mayew* (Cant. and York Soc. xxvii), 220; Duncumb, *Herefs.* i. 567. ² C1/414/28; 193/12/1; Duncumb, i. 366; *Statutes*, iii. 171; *LP Hen, VIII*, xiii–xviii, xx, xxi; *CPR*, 1547–8, pp. 75, 77; *Reg. Caroli Bothe* (Cant. and York Soc. xxviii), pp. xiii, 201, 240. ³ Duncumb, i. 366. ⁴ *LP Hen. VIII*, ix, xiii, xv; Duncumb, i. 502–13; *Reg. Caroli Bothe*, 242, 284, 377; Wards 7/6/113. ⁵ C142/86/94; PCC 3 Populwell; *CPR*, 1547–8, p. 266.

L.M.K./M.K.D.

WARNER, Sir Edward (1511–65), of Polsteadhall and Plumstead, Norf.

GRANTHAM	1545, 1547, 1553 (Mar.),[1] 1553 (Oct.)
GREAT GRIMSBY	1559
NORFOLK	1563*

b. 1511, yr. s. of Henry Warner of Besthorpe by Mary, da. of John Blennerhassett of Frenze; bro. of Robert*. *m.* (1) Elizabeth (*d.*1560), da. of Thomas Brooke, 8th Lord Cobham, wid. of Sir Thomas Wyatt I* (*d.*1542) of Allington Castle, Kent, 3s. all *d. inf.*; (2) Audrey, da. and h. of William Hare of Beeston, Norf., wid. of Thomas Hobart of Plumstead, *s.p.* Kntd. 18 May 1544.[2]

Member, King's household by 1537, sewer by 1545, esquire of the body by 1552; constable, Clitheroe castle, Lancs. 1542; lt. the Tower Oct. 1552–July 1553, jt. (with Sir Thomas Cawarden*) Nov. 1558–63; commr. to investigate office of master of Ordnance 1553, musters, Mdx. in 1559; master, St. Katharine's hospital and steward, East Smithfield 1560; j.p. Mdx. 1561–*d.*, Norf. 1564; collector for loan, Mdx. 1562; steward for William Paget, 1st Lord Paget, unknown property.[3]

A younger son of a Norfolk gentleman, Edward Warner was a professional soldier and household official. Described in 1536–7 as of the Household in a minor augmentations grant of Nottinghamshire property, he became an active dealer in monastic property, selling or exchanging nearly as much as he bought. In one of these transactions, the purchase of the Carmelite friary at Burnham, Norfolk, in 1541, his name is associated for the first time with that of his future brother-in-law George, 9th Lord Cobham.[4]

Warner is listed in the army for the Netherlands in 1543, and his service in the Scottish campaign of the following year brought him a knighthood: in this campaign one of his commanders was his future parliamentary patron, the 2nd Earl of Rutland. In 1546 he was examined about the Earl of Surrey's alleged treasonable statements but could give no information at first hand. On 8 May 1546 he was himself brought before the Privy Council for

'indiscreet talking of Scripture matters' but was dismissed on promising to amend: it was a foretaste of his later radicalism.[5]

With the accession of Edward VI, Warner advanced rapidly. He received a £50 annuity for his services to the late King and a wardship carrying an annuity of £22, while in a series of transactions with other purchasers he acquired a share in monastic and chantry lands worth between £3,000 and £4,000. He was also granted a licence to eat flesh in Lent for life, perhaps a token of his developing Protestantism. In 1549 he took the field as marshal against Ket's rebellion and in 1552 his military prowess was rewarded with the lieutenancy of the Tower. It is slightly surprising that the Duke of Northumberland should have entrusted him with this key post, as Warner had become an intimate of the ex-Protector Somerset's loyal colleague Lord Paget, whose house he visited 15 times between December 1550 and March 1551 and again as late as 6 Sept. 1551, only a month before Somerset's arrest.[6]

Warner had begun to represent the borough of Grantham in Henry VIII's last Parliament. He may have owed something at first to his brother Robert's service with Catherine Parr, who held the manor of Grantham, but his immediate patron was the 2nd Earl of Rutland, as is made clear by a letter from the burgesses of Grantham to William Cecil in February 1553, when Cecil had asked for the nomination of both Members: they 'most gladly' granted Cecil one seat, but the other they had already committed to their former Member Warner, 'at the special suit of the Earl of Rutland ... from which agreement, made at the instance of so noble a man, we cannot with our honesties digress'. Rutland seems to have been heir to the Hussey influence at Grantham, and was to marry a daughter of John Hussey*, Lord Hussey. His connexion with Warner had apparently begun at court and in the field and had been strengthened by their common attachment to extreme Protestantism. Warner's marriage to a daughter of Lord Cobham had also made him a figure of some standing.[7]

In the crisis of July 1553 Warner held the Tower for Northumberland, and Mary's triumph brought his immediate dismissal from the lieutenancy. He was, however, re-elected for Grantham to Mary's first Parliament, where he was one of those who 'stood for the true religion', that is, for Protestantism. The outbreak of Wyatt's rebellion inevitably cast Warner under suspicion. On 23 Jan. 1554 he was denounced to Gardiner by the Spanish ambassador for plotting against the Tower and two days later he was arrested with the Marquess of Northampton, a relation by marriage who was staying at his house by

Carter Lane. Within six months Warner had sunk from lieutenant of the Tower to prisoner there, but his punishment was not to be severe: he was not put on trial, his wife continued to receive the revenues of his lands, and on 18 Jan. 1555 he and several other prisoners were ceremonially released, with 'a great shooting of guns'. At first bound in a recognizance of £300, he received his pardon on 2 July. He was to survive the Marian period with no worse damage than the loss of a few of his monastic lands, and before the end of the reign he was even employed under Sir Thomas Tresham* in a survey of the Isle of Wight.[8]

On Elizabeth's accession Warner was restored to the lieutenancy of the Tower, and re-entered Parliament, although not for Grantham. After his leniency in dealing with prisoners, among them Lady Catherine Grey, had led to his dismissal and another short imprisonment while the Parliament in which he sat as knight of the shire was in session, he spent his last years in pleasant retirement in Norfolk. In the summer of 1565 he travelled to continental spas for his health, but on 7 Nov. he died. His will of 22 Oct. ordained a funeral 'with as little pomp as may be' and mentioned a collection of law books and chronicles.[9]

[1] Lansd. 3, f. 75. [2] Warner's elder brother was born in 1510 and Warner himself was 54 at death, Mill Stephenson, *Mon. Brasses*, 360. *Vis. Norf.* (Norf. Arch. Soc.), i. 18; *Vis. Norf.* (Harl. Soc. xxxii), 308–9; *LP Hen. VIII*, xix; *DNB*. [3] *LP Hen. VIII*, xiii, xx; *CPR*, 1550–3, p. 300; 1553, p. 186; 1560–3, p. 440; 1563–6, pp. 24–25; Somerville, *Duchy*, i. 499; *APC*, iv. 156, 422; *East London Pprs.* viii. 69–72; *CSP Dom.* 1547–80, p. 150; Osborn coll. Yale Univ. Lib. 71–6–41; Staffs. RO, EPC2/2, no. 20, f. 1 ex inf. C. J. Harrison. [4] *LP Hen. VIII*, xiii, xiv, xvi. [5] Ibid. xviii, xix, xxi; *APC*, i. 411. [6] *CPR*, 1547–8, pp. 210, 272; 1548–9, pp. 215, 267; 1549–51, pp. 236, 307; 1550–3, p. 300; Strype, *Eccles. Memorials*, ii(2), 15, 110, 242, 402; Greater London RO (Mdx. section), Anglesey muniments, deposit acc. 446/H.13; Staffs. RO, EPC1/1, f. 13 ex inf. Harrison; *APC*, iv. 156. [7] Lansd. 3, f. 75. [8] Bodl. e Museo 17; *CSP Span.* 1554, p. 42; *APC*, iv. 422; v. 35, 90; Wriothesley's Chron. ii (Cam. Soc. n.s. xx), 107; *Trevelyan Pprs.* ii (Cam. Soc. lxxxiv), 36; *Machyn's Diary* (Cam. Soc. xlii), 80; *CPR*, 1554–5, p. 293; 1555–7, p. 113; D. M. Loades, *Two Tudor Conspiracies*, 16, 57, 95–96, 125; *CSP Dom.* 1547–80, p. 100. [9] *HMC Hatfield*, i. 261, 264; *Parker Corresp.* (Parker Soc.), 121–2; C7, i. 64; Lansd. 7, f. 68; *CSP Dom.* 1601–3, Add. 1547–65, p. 571; E150/658/3; PCC 12 Crymes.

T.M.H.

WARNER, Robert (1510–75), of London and Cranleigh, Surr.

CHIPPENHAM   1545
WILTON   1547[1]
DOWNTON   1553 (Mar.)[2]
BOSSINEY   1559

b. ?Apr. 1510, 1st s. of Henry Warner of Besthorpe, and bro. of Sir Edward*. *m.* (1) by 1550, Cecily, da. of Walter Marshe of London, wid. of William Harding of Cranleigh, 1s. Henry† 1da.; (2) Anne, da. of Sir Humphrey Wingfield* of Brantham, Suff., wid. of Alexander Newton (*d*.1566 or later). *suc.* fa. 26 Apr. 1519, bro. Sir Edward 7 Nov. 1565.[3]
?Servant of 1st Earl of Sussex by 1538; servant of Queen Catherine Parr by 1544, particular receiver of

her lands in Hunts. and Northants. by 1545–8, first sewer in her household by 1546–7 or later; particular receiver of Thomas Seymour, Baron Seymour of Sudeley's lands in Hunts. and Northants. by 1548; sewer by 1556–8 or later; commr. subsidy, Surr. 1559, Norf. 1569; j.p. Surr. 1561–4.[4]

Although there were others of the name, including a wealthy London draper, Robert Warner may be identified with the gentleman from Norfolk. It was probably he who in 1538 as a servant of the Earl of Sussex wrote to the earl's son, Lord Fitzwalter, reporting the news from London, and he may even have been brought up in the household of Sussex, who owned the manor of Attleborough, adjacent to Besthorpe; in the same year Fitzwalter married Warner's cousin Anne Calthrope. By 1544 Warner had apparently exchanged Sussex's service for that of the Queen and in September of that year was employed to carry a letter to the King in France. Although there was a Northamptonshire family of Warner it was probably the Member who became particular receiver of the Queen's lands in that county. As a member of her household, he was assessed for the subsidy in 1545 on £20 a year in lands and in 1546 on £40. The office of first sewer carried a wage of about £3 a quarter; the second of the two sewers at this time was Nicholas Throckmorton*, who became a close friend of Warner's brother Sir Edward. John Bonham, Warner's fellow-Member for Chippenham (where Warner's name was inserted in the return, possibly in a different hand from that of the document), may also have been a servant of Queen Catherine and both could have owed their return to her predominant influence in the borough. The Queen's brother-in-law (Sir) William Herbert I*, later 1st Earl of Pembroke, for whose borough of Wilton Warner was to sit in 1547, also perhaps lent a hand. Robert Watson, Warner's fellow-Member in 1547, may have been a Norfolk man and accordingly indebted to Warner for his introduction to the earl. Warner's re-election to the following Parliament early in 1553 was presumably the work of the earl, perhaps acting through Bishop Ponet, the patron of Downton.[5]

On 28 Jan. 1551 Warner's son Henry was born in Milk Street, London. His godparents were the 2nd Earl of Rutland, (Sir) Walter Mildmay* and the Duchess of Richmond. In May 1556 a Robert Warner was trustee for Warwickshire lands of Sir Robert Tyrwhitt I*, another erstwhile member of Catherine Parr's household. A year later Warner received confirmation of his purchase from his brother-in-law John Marshe* of the wardship of his stepdaughters Catherine and Helen Harding. Warner's own daughter Elizabeth was born in August 1557 at Cranleigh, where he had apparently taken up residence after his marriage to Cecily Marshe. Elizabeth's godparents were William More II* of Loseley, Lady Clinton and Elizabeth Polsted. Warner's stepdaughter Catherine married Richard Onslow* in 1559 and her sister Helen married first Richard Knyvet and then Thomas Browne† of Betchworth Castle, Surrey.[6]

Either through the Earl of Pembroke or another of his circle of high-ranking acquaintances Warner had obtained preferment in the Household by the middle of Mary's reign, and it was as a member of the Household that he attended the Queen's funeral in 1558. Warner's choice of godparents for his children and his return to Parliament on Elizabeth's accession suggest that he shared the Protestant views of his brother and his brother-in-law Marshe, although he was to play surprisingly little part in affairs under Elizabeth. He settled in Norfolk after his brother's death and died on 7 Oct. 1575, having made his will in the previous August.[7]

[1]Hatfield 207. [2] C219/330/35 ex inf. Margaret Condon. [3] Date of birth estimated from age at fa.'s and bro.'s i.p.ms, C142/34/30, 143/67. *Vis. Norf.* (Harl. Soc. xxxii); 308–9; *Misc. Gen. et Her.* (ser. 2), iv. 90–91; PCC 6 Arundell. [4] *LP Hen. VIII*, xiii, xx; E115/413/33, 430/94, 433/118; 163/12/17, nos. 30, 38, 51, 54; 315/340, ff. 5v, 52, 68v; SC6 Edw. VI/726, ff. 7, A1; *CPR*, 1560–3, p. 441; 1563–6, p. 26. [5] *LP Hen. VIII*, xiii, xix, xx; E179/69/47, 48; C219/18C/142. [6] *Misc. Gen. et Her.* (ser. 2), iv. 90–91; *CPR*, 1555–7, pp. 88, 397. [7] LC2/4/2; PCC 44 Pyckering.

D.F.C.

WARREN, Christopher (by 1512–71), of Coventry, Warws.

COVENTRY 1545, 1547

b. by 1512, 1st s. of Thomas Warren of Coventry prob. by Elizabeth, da. of John Stanfield. *m.* Catherine, da. of John Coxon of Coventry, 2s. *suc.* fa. 1527.[1]
   Warden, Coventry 1533–4, sheriff or bailiff 1537–8, mayor 1542–3, alderman by 1544.[2]

From his father, who was mayor of Coventry in 1518, Christopher Warren inherited wealth and standing in the city. A draper like his father, he traded on a large scale and for more than 30 years he was one of the city's busiest officials. When representatives were to be sent to London, when action was needed on a lease, when a house was needed for the Earl of Warwick to lodge in for the night, Warren was the man called upon. Not that he was universally liked. During his mayoralty there were numerous prosecutions under the Act of Six Articles and some of those prosecuted sued Warren for proceeding against them out of revenge for their testimony in the trial of the vicar of St. Michael's. The result of the case is unknown but there are other suggestions that Warren was apt to be harsh and vindictive; Foxe records that the martyr Robert Glover ascribed his death sentence to Warren's 'cruel seeking'. Yet his mayoralty also conduced to the public welfare:

the city cross, erected with funds specially entrusted to him, was completed and monastic property acquired. The money for this undertaking was mainly provided by Sir Thomas White, a London merchant, who intended to bestow the income from the property to charitable uses. Warren and his fellows on the city council entered into a trust bond and he and Henry Over *alias* Waver* were the two principally concerned in all the subsequent negotiations with White. As trustees of the money which was still during White's lifetime at his own disposal, they disbursed it at his command and were thus his agents in much of the preliminary negotiation for the purchase of the site of St. John's College, Oxford, and in the establishment of the college.[3]

Warren attended both sessions of the Parliament of 1545, although the payment of £3 4s. for the 32 days of the first was made to him on 12 Dec., 12 days before its end; for the 17 days of the second he received full payment and an allowance of a further three days at the rate of 2s. a day. He seems to have become less regular in his attendance during the following Parliament, receiving £3 18s. for 39 days towards the end of the first session and £5 16s. in full payment of all his costs a month before the close of the second, and sharing £6 11s. with his fellow-Member Henry Porter at the beginning of the third. The larger payment made to Porter for the first session (£6 8s. for 64 days, 13 longer than it lasted) suggests that it was he who took the lead in the city's opposition to the bill for the dissolution of the chantries and guilds. It was Warren, however, who at about this time consulted George Willoughby* on civic business. The bill 'for the city of Coventry' introduced during the second session was clearly intended to settle a related matter, the fate of Bond's hospital, but it proceeded no further than its second reading, being abandoned after Thomas Bond (q.v.) had given evidence. Warren was active in the prosecution of the city's claim on the lands in Chancery which resulted in a compromise whereby part of the property was to be vested in trustees to be named by Warren.[4]

When in 1554 the Duke of Suffolk was brought as a prisoner to Coventry on his way to his death in London he was confined in Warren's house. Warren continued to be one of Coventry's leading citizens until his death; he travelled to London on its business, attended council meetings and surpervised the city lands. From 1554 onwards, despite the fact that he sold the city land worth £6, he was considerably in its debt as well as owing several smaller sums to private individuals. This probably reflects no decrease in his prosperity: at about this time he was arranging a wealthy match for his eldest son and in

1565 he endowed the vicar of St. Michael's with an annuity of £6 a year. He died on 18 June 1571 possessed of a grange in Binley and property within the city of Coventry which descended to his grandson William. His younger son and namesake became in his turn a leading citizen of Coventry.[5]

[1] Date of birth estimated from first civic appointment. T. W. Whitley, *Parly. Rep. Coventry*, 38 (mistaken in crediting Warren with Membership of the Parliament of 1539); C142/275/225; Shakespeare Birthplace Trust, Gregory Hood collection 152; Coventry statute merchant rolls 48, 51. [2] *Coventry Leet Bk.* (EETS cxxxiv), ii. 714, 727, 767; *LP Hen. VIII*, xix. [3] C1/1483/15; Foxe, *Acts and Mons.* vi. 620; *LP Hen. VIII*, xvii; St.Ch.2/3/61; Coventry mayors' accts. 1542–61, pp. 3, 12, 13, 17, 21, 26, 28, 37, 38, 42, 43, 45, 49, 55, 58, 59, 62–64, 70, 496, 503; Cheylesmore early rental A.11 unpaginated; B. Poole, *Coventry*, 292–3; E314/16; St. John's Coll. muniments xix. 3–5; C. M. Clode, *Early Hist. Merchant Taylors*, ii. [4] Coventry mayors' accts. 1542–61, pp. 30, 35, 43, 49, 494; *APC*, ii. 193–5; W. K. Jordan, *Edw. VI*, ii. 184–5; *CJ*, i. 5–7; *VCH Warws.* ii. 112; C1/1209/52, 1471/10–14. [5] D. M. Loades, *Two Tudor Conspiracies*, 100; *VCH Warws.* vi. 36; *LP Hen. VIII*, xix; *Dugdale Soc. Pubs.* ii. 52, 137; C142/162/180, 275/225; *CPR*, 1569–72, p. 365; Coventry mayors' accts. 1542–61, pp. 70, 404, 406–8, 509; treasurers' payments, pp. 3, 5, 7, 13; statute merchant rolls 41, 42, 44, 48, 51, 53; council bk. 1555–1628, pp. 15–125 passim.

S.M.T.

WARREN, John (by 1488–1547), of Dover, Kent.

DOVER 1510,[1] 1512,[2] 1515,[3] 1529, 1536,[4] 1542,[5] 1545[6]

b. by 1488, 1st s. of William Warren† of Dover by w. Joan. *m.* Jane, da. of John Monninges of Swanton, 2s. inc. Thomas* 2da. *suc.* fa. 1506.[7]

Jurat, Dover 1509–*d.*, mayor 1525–6, 1536–7, 1540–1; commr. subsidy 1514, 1523, 1524; bailiff to Yarmouth 1533[8].

Three successive heads of the Warren family of Dover were Members for this, the leading, Cinque Port, and between them they attended 12 Parliaments spread over more than 80 years. Longest to serve was John Warren, of the second generation, who sat in seven out of Henry VIII's nine Parliaments, beginning with the first and ending with the last.

Warren's municipal career, which was also conterminous with the King's reign, followed the customary pattern and for a time at least he also enjoyed official status at Dover castle, where in 1514 he received gunpowder as deputy to John Copledike, lieutenant to the lord warden Sir Edward Guildford*. In the previous year he had become involved in the ports' struggle to secure their exemption from subsidy; he was offered 2s. a day in wages (evidently in continuation of his current parliamentary allowance) 'for the withstanding of the subsidy if it be demanded' and promised the loan of the ports' charter for use in the campaign. When appointed a subsidy commissioner in the following year he was instructed by the Brotherhood to lodge any money collected by 1 May with nominees of the lord warden who would hold it until the dispute was settled. In 1516 he and Robert Sparrow* of Winchelsea reported their efforts in the matter: they were paid £3 each and were allowed £5 4s.4d. for disbursements to 'learned men' in the court of Exchequer. Warren was put on subsidy commissions again in 1523 and 1524 but whether or how he discharged the duty is not known. The issue appears to have concerned him for the last time in 1541 when the ports again fought the case in the Exchequer and Warren helped to secure a ruling that subsidy collectors were not to enter pending the outcome of the suit in that court.[9]

A variety of other matters came his way. During his first Parliament he had obtained a confirmation of the Dover charter, in 1516 the Brotherhood appointed him to sue Sandwich for wrongfully detaining a sum of £44, and four years later he and others were deputed to discuss with the lord warden the maritime service owed by the ports, a charge which led him to pay a two weeks' visit to Calais in company with the town clerk of Dover. Then from about 1530, after the partial destruction of one of its embankments, the problem of saving Dover harbour became an endemic one. In April 1532, on leaving to attend the fourth session of the current Parliament, Warren took with him money for payment of learned counsel who were 'suing for the haven'; a 'plat of Dover haven' is mentioned among Cromwell's remembrances of that year, and on the eve of the minister's fall eight years later Warren was one of those charged with informing him about a new quay.[10]

There was thus much to absorb Warren's attention during his frequent spells in the capital and as these multiplied they must in turn have increased his value as a representative. Why he missed the Parliament of 1523, with its swingeing subsidy exaction, does not appear, but in 1539 he probably declined election for the same 'certain causes' which he pleaded in the following July to secure his discharge from another mission as bailiff to Yarmouth. His sojourns in London—not necessarily to be equated with attendances in the House—and his remuneration for them can be traced with unusual precision in the borough records. Corresponding closely with the duration of the sessions concerned (travelling time being always included) the numbers of days' service with which Warren was credited show that he could have been present throughout almost every session. To this rule there was one notable exception, the third session of the Parliament of 1529. It was not until 25 Jan. 1532 that Warren set out from Dover to attend a session which had begun ten days earlier; then both he and his fellow-Member Robert Nethersole were home from 10 to 17 Feb.; and finally Warren himself was again home by 21 Mar., a week before the session ended on Maundy Thursday. Thus out of its 74 days he must have attended on less than 50, and he was to be a week late for the next session. This is so far below his usual standard of availability, if not attendance, as to invite speculation on its cause. Among a number of possible explanations is the onset of that epidemic disease which was to kill several of Warren's fellow-Members in the spring and summer of 1532 and from which he may have sought temporary refuge. Yet it is not without interest that by withdrawing before the end of the session Warren missed the climax of the battle over the annates bill and almost certainly spared himself what could have been a chastening experience, that of being counted when the King himself came down and 'divided' the Commons on this contentious measure. It must be added that if Warren's absenteeism at this juncture owed anything to scruples over royal policy, his resumption of more regular attendance thereafter seems to imply that these were quickly overcome and did not manifest themselves again.[11]

There is nothing of doctrinal import in the will which Warren made on 7 May 1547, presumably on his death-bed as it was proved a month later; he simply asked to be buried near his father in St. Peter's church, Dover. His movable goods and houses at Dover and Ripple, Kent—the latter held on lease first from St. Augustine's, Canterbury, and later from the archbishop—he left to his wife, with remainder to his son Thomas, both being named executors. One daughter, Battell, received a tenement in Dover, the other, Elizabeth, who married the son of Richard Fyneux†, was not mentioned. The eldest son John had died in 1545-6.[12]

[1] Add. 29618, f. 25.   [2] Ibid. f. 53v.   [3] Ibid. f. 101v.   [4] Ibid. f. 300v.   [5] Ibid. f. 335.   [6] Ibid. f. 393.   [7] Date of birth estimated from first reference. Vis. Kent (Harl. Soc. lxxv), 45.   [8] Add. 29618 passim; Egerton 2092-3 passim; LP Hen. VIII, i, iii, iv.   [9] LP Hen. VIII, i; K. M. E. Murray, Const. Hist. of Cinque Ports, 219-23; Cinque Ports White and Black Bks. (Kent Arch. Soc. recs. br. xix), 143, 150, 155, 161; Cinque Ports white bk. ff. 142, 154v.   [10] Add. 29618, ff. 25, 137v; Cinque Ports White and Black Bks. 165, 180; LP Hen. VIII, v; Egerton 2093, f. 191v.   [11] Cinque Ports white bk. f. 229v; Add. 29618 passim. Warren claimed (and was paid, normally at 2s. a day) for the following numbers of days per session, the sessional figures being added in brackets 1514, 50 (41); 1515, 63 (60) and 44 (41); 1532, 85 (108); 1533, 63 (63); 1534, 70 (75) and 31 (46); 1536, 81 (70); 1542, 70 (76); 1543, 83 (111); 1545, 39 (32).   [12] Canterbury prob. reg. C21, ff. 57-58, Act I, f. 63v; LP Hen. VIII, xvii; Vis. Kent, 128.

P.H.

WARREN, Thomas (by 1513-91), of Dover and Ripple, Kent.

Dover 1547,[1] 1555, 1559, 1563, 1572

b. by 1513, 2nd but o. surv. s. of John Warren* of Dover by Jane, da. of John Monninges of Swanton. m. Christian Close of Calais, at least 1s. suc. fa. 1547.[2] Councilman and chamberlain, Dover 1547-8, jurat

for every year for which records survive from Sept. 1551 to 1557, mayor 1548-9, 1549-50, 1557-8, 1574-5; bailiff to Yarmouth 1553.[3]

Thomas Warren, whose father and grandfather had both sat in Parliament for Dover, himself became an important local figure. He first represented the port at the Brotherhood in 1534 and is next heard of as clerk of call at the building of Sandgate castle in 1539. He appears to have played a leading part in the controversies in the port during the reigns of Edward VI and Mary, although the details have not survived. In June 1549 he arbitrated in a dispute between Thomas Portway* and John Bodending.[4]

According to a local historian, Warren was elected mayor in September 1550 but removed from office by order of the Privy Council in January 1551 and replaced by Portway; in the Dover hundred court book, however, Portway appears as mayor on 17 Oct. 1550. On 24 May 1553 Warren was cited to appear, with Robert Nethersole*, in a case brought against them by a widow, Anne White. When other writs were sent on 3 June and 13 Sept. the mayor returned that he was 'not within our jurisdiction', yet on 17 Sept. he was appointed canopy bearer at the coronation and two days later he was one of those who indemnified the port against the legal consequences of setting aside the parliamentary election of Thomas Colly and Portway two days before. In December 1553 Colly and Warren were each bound in £20 to keep the peace with one another and in January 1554 both were fined for misbehaviour before the mayor and jurats. A month later Warren and others appeared before the Privy Council to answer the charge that the port had given passive support to Wyatt's rebellion. On 22 July 1554 Robert Nethersole was cited to answer certain charges made by Warren, who was himself summoned on 8 Sept. to answer further charges made by the widow White. In 1556 Warren and a Mr. Foxley were paid £11 as solicitors appointed by the port, probably in connexion with the new charter then granted. The last reference to Warren in the town books of Dover occurs on 21 Sept. 1577. He probably then retired to Ripple where he was living when he made his will on 11 Apr. 1591. It was proved on the following 16 June.[5]

The town books are missing for the early years of the reign of Edward VI but Warren's attendance at the Parliament of 1547 can be followed in the municipal accounts. He and Joseph Beverley presented their account for 54 days' attendance at the first session from 2 Nov. to 25 Dec. 1547, and for this they were allowed £10 16s. at a rate of 2s. a day each: they had also paid 4s. to the clerk of the crown for the return, 4s. to the serjeant for placing them and 5s. to the keeper of the door, and they themselves expected 10s. for 'penning of a book concerning the passage'. In this accounting year Warren was paid £4 of what was due to him. On 23 Nov. 1548 he rode again to London to attend the second session which opened the next day: remaining there for 36 days, he arrived home on 26 Dec. He went back to London on 4 Jan. and stayed there for 70 days, arriving in Dover again on 16 Mar., two days after the session ended. For this attendance he received £10 12s., with a further payment of 34s.6d. outstanding from the year before. On 17 Dec. 1549 both Members came away from the third session which had opened on 4 Nov. and Beverley, who alone seems to have received wages for this session, went up again early in January. It was Beverley who set out first for the final session, leaving on 23 Jan. 1552, the day that it opened, and taking with them 'our charter to go the Parliament'; Warren followed on 6 Feb. and after his return he was paid on 7 May for 64 days' attendance, at the rate of 2s. a day, a total of £6 8s., with another 2s. for placing.[6]

[1] Hatfield 207. [2] Date of birth estimated from first reference. *Vis. Kent* (Harl. Soc. lxxv), 45; *Chron. Calais* (Cam. Soc. xxxv), 39. [3] Dover accts. 1547–58, ff. 34, 63, 92; hundred ct. bk. 1545–58, ff. 88, 116; Egerton 2094, f. 171; 2095, passim; *Cinque Ports White and Black Bks.* (Kent Arch. Soc. recs. br. xix), 240, 242, 248, 256, 300, 307. [4] *Cinque Ports White and Black Bks.* 218; *LP Hen. VIII*, xiv; Egerton 2093, f. 136. [5] J. Bavington Jones, *Dover Annals*, 244, 297; Dover hundred ct. bk. 1545–58, f. 192; accts. 1547–58, ff. 220v, 302; Egerton 2094, ff. 79, 89, 90v, 92, 95, 109v, 110, 223–4; 2095, f. 4; *APC*, iv. 393; Canterbury prob. reg. A48, f. 243. [6] Dover accts. 1547–58, ff. 53, 61, 85v, 114, 150v, 163–4.

P.H.

WASTFIELD, Edward (by 1523–71 or later), of Draycot Cerne, Wilts.

CALNE 1554 (Nov.), 1555

b. by 1523.[1]
Petty collector of subsidy, hundred of Chippenham in 1549–50, 1552.[2]

In May 1544 Edward Wastfield joined a hunting party led by Robert Long* whose members were subsequently sued in the Star Chamber for trespass in the park of Castle Combe, Wiltshire. He acted as collector when Sir Henry Long*, Robert's father, was a commissioner for the subsidy, was described in 1550 as a yeoman of Draycot Cerne, where the Longs had their residence, and witnessed Sir Henry Long's will on 4 Oct. 1556. It was to this family that he evidently owed his return for Calne. Nothing is known of his role in Parliament save that he was neither a 'seceder' from the Parliament of November 1554 nor one of those listed as having opposed a government bill in its successor. His end is equally obscure; all that has been discovered about him after 1558 is that on 19 May 1561 he received a crown lease for 21 years of lands in Langley, and that ten years later, presumably while he was still alive, the reversion of this lease was granted to the 9th Lord Scrope.[3]

[1] Date of birth estimated from first reference. [2] E179/198/256a, 265, 267. [3] St.Ch.2/30/149; E179/198/256a; PCC 17 Ketchyn; *CPR*, 1569–72, p. 310.

T.F.T.B.

WATERS, Thomas (by 1495–1563/64), of Lynn, Norf.

LYNN 1539,[1] 1542, 1553 (Oct.), 1554 (Apr.), 1554 (Nov.), 1555, 1558, 1559

b. by 1495. *m.* prob. da. of William Coningsby* of Lynn, 2s. 1da.[2]
Alderman, Lynn 1525–63, mayor 1535–6, 1551–2, June–Sept. 1558; commr. relief, Norf. 1550; other commissions, Norf. and Lynn 1541–59.[3]

Thomas Waters had more than one contemporary namesake at Lynn, but his record as an alderman and the repeated mention of him in the congregation books leave little doubt that it was he who sat in Parliament for the town eight times in 20 years. Born in Cambridgeshire, he was styled 'merchant' when he bought his freedom at Lynn in 1519, six years after his brother John had done so. Within six years he became an alderman and within a further ten he was elected to his first mayoralty. He had by then already been involved in the contest with the bishop of Norwich over jurisdiction in the town and as mayor he negotiated with the crown for the charter of 1537. In that year he also gave evidence in London on the conflicting claims to the stewardship between William Hastings and the Duke of Suffolk. With the coming of war in 1542 he combined the roles of merchant and town official in the service of the crown, purveying victuals for the armies in France and Scotland and equipping warships and advancing money for their crews, while being increasingly used in civil administration; among his services to the town were the handling in 1544–5, in partnership with Thomas Miller*, of the purchase of the four dissolved friaries there (he himself putting up part of the sum in exchange for the site of the Blackfriars), a share in the collection of the fee-farm for the year 1548–9 and official missions to London in 1551–2.[4]

Waters's election to the Parliaments of 1539 and 1542 followed his first mayoralty and were perhaps also promoted by his marriage to a daughter of the recorder William Coningsby: at his second election he and Thomas Miller were each given £10 to spend on municipal business. His omission from the next two Parliaments was in keeping with Lynn's custom of choosing a man on two successive occasions and then replacing him, but if the town had had its way Waters would have next sat in the Parliament of March 1553. On 20 Jan. the congregation chose Sir Richard Corbet and Waters, now styled 'gentleman', but when the sheriff made his return Waters's name was replaced by John Walpole's. It is tempting to see in this unexplained intervention the hand of the Duke of Northumberland, who interfered extensively with elections to this Parliament, but if it was Northumberland's doing his motive is not wholly clear. Walpole, a rising lawyer, would have been acceptable to the duke both as a relation by marriage and as a Protestant, and to the town as its standing counsel. It was Waters who with William Overend* was to be fined for his alleged complicity with Sir Robert Dudley* in engaging Lynn's support of Jane Grey. The penalty was offset by the town's support of the two men: not only did the corporation raise a large part of their fine until countermanded by the Council but it re-elected both of them to Parliament, Overend once and Waters without a break throughout the reign. Whether on principle or out of prudence Waters does not appear to have aligned himself with the opposition in the Commons. Unlike Walpole he was not among those who 'stood for the true religion' in the first Marian Parliament and in the fourth his name is not to be found, as is his fellow-Member Sir Nicholas Lestrange's, on the list of opponents of one of the government's bills. Even his inclusion among the Members who were prosecuted in the King's bench for their withdrawal from the third Parliament before its dissolution probably means no more than that he had gone home for Christmas and not returned, for whereas Sir Thomas Moyle, his fellow-Member on that occasion, was distrained for non-appearance in answer to his summons for the same offence there is no record of proceedings against Waters as there would surely have been if he had been held contumacious. Unfortunately, evidence of payment of Waters's wages, which might have thrown light on the episode, is missing for this Parliament; when in January 1558 he received £10 13s. 11d. in this respect it was probably in discharge of his bill for the 50 days of the Parliament of 1555, belatedly and on the eve of his departure for its successor. On this occasion the town gave the 4th Duke of Norfolk the nomination of one Member and exercised its choice of the other in favour of Waters.[5]

Waters's parliamentary career was to end in 1559 but he remained active in local affairs until within a short time of his death late in 1563 or early in 1564.[6]

[1] Lynn congregation bk. 4, f. 320. [2] Aged 60 and more in 1555, HCA 13/10, f. 76v. PCC 13 Alenger, 17 Stevenson. [3] Lynn congregation bks. 4 and 5 passim; LP Hen. VIII, xvi, xx; CPR, 1553, p. 357; 1554-5, pp. 108, 111; 1558-60, p. 32. [4] Lynn Freemen

(Norf. Arch), 78, 81; PCC 10 Alen; Lynn congregation bk. 4, ff. 252v, 261, 268, 274v, 302, 304v, 307, 310v, 312; 5, ff. 11, 147v; chamberlains' accts. 1551-2; LP Hen. VIII, xvii-xx; APC, i. 79, 93, 123, 148, 199, 325; E351/130, 198; CPR, 1549-51, p. 344. [5] Lynn congregation bk. 4, f. 337v; 5, ff. 181v, 192v, 222, 227v, 308, 324v; APC, iv. 416; KB27/1176. [6] PCC 17 Stevenson.

R.V.

WATERTON, Thomas I (by 1501–58), of Walton and Sandal, Yorks.

YORKSHIRE 1542*

b. by 1501, o. s. of Sir Robert Waterton of Walton and Sandal by Muriel, da. of John Leeke of Sutton in the Dale, Derbys. m. (1) by 1526, Joan, da. of Sir Richard Tempest* of Bracewell and Bowling, Yorks., 5s. inc. Thomas II* 7da.; (2) 1549, Agnes, da. of John Cheyne of Drayton Beauchamp, Bucks., wid. of Edward Restwold (d.June 1547) of The Vache, Bucks., ?s.p. suc. fa. 26 Feb. 1541. Kntd. 11 May 1544.[1]

J.p. Yorks. (W. Riding) 1539-45; commr. benevolence 1544/45, relief 1550; sheriff, Yorks. 1553-4.[2]

The Waterton family was an ancient one of Lincolnshire origin; it had come to Walton through the marriage of Richard Waterton†. The earliest references to Thomas Waterton show him enjoying the support of his father-in-law Sir Richard Tempest. In 1532-4 Tempest backed his claim to the wardship of Edward, son and heir of Joscelyn Percy of Beverley and grandson of Henry, 4th Earl of Northumberland. The nine year-old Edward had been married to Waterton's daughter Elizabeth, a match which his uncle Sir William Percy called 'a sorry bargain, his blood considered'. Since a Waterton was a fit bride for a Percy, the complaint may echo a traditional hostility between the families. The dispute was eventually settled in Waterton's favour, and of the children of the marriage one, Alan Percy, was to sit for Beverley in the Parliament of 1604 and his younger brother Thomas to be connected with that Parliament in a less conventional way. In June 1542 Waterton was granted another wardship, that of Thomas Pilkington, whom he married to his daughter Rosamund.[3]

Nothing has come to light about Waterton's conduct during the rebellion of 1536 but unlike his father-in-law he seems to have emerged from it uncompromised and within three years he was named to the West Riding bench. From 1542 he was engaged in the Scottish war. In May 1544 he had command of 100 men and was knighted by the Earl of Hertford at Leith. In the following March he was among the captains appointed to garrison the borders but at the end of April (Sir) Robert Bowes* reported that he wished to return home on weighty private business. It was Bowes, then a prisoner of the Scots, whom he had replaced as a knight for Yorkshire in the Parliament of 1542, to which he was returned on 5 Feb. 1543, only a week before Bowes's release; he presumably attended the remainder of the second session and the third early in 1544. The sheriff who returned him, Sir Thomas Tempest, was either his brother-in-law or the more distant relative who had sat for Newcastle-upon-Tyne in 1529. The names of the Yorkshire knights in the next Parliament are lost, but Waterton was probably not re-elected as he would then have superseded Bowes, returned on this occasion for Newcastle-upon-Tyne. It is also unlikely that Waterton was the first knight of the shire in March 1553, whose christian name 'Thomas' alone survives on the indenture; his four nominations as sheriff between 1548 and 1551 without being pricked, and his subsequent choice as the first Marian sheriff, alike argue against his choice for that Parliament. As sheriff at the election for Mary's second Parliament he doubtless had a hand in his son's adoption for Thirsk.[4]

Waterton may have owed his second marriage into a Buckinghamshire family to the Tempest connexions with that county. The marriage allied Waterton with the Peckham family, and it was with Sir Edmund*, Sir Robert*, Henry* and George Peckham, and Sir Francis Hastings of Fenwick, Yorkshire, that in 1555 he received a lease for 21 years of certain lands of Richard Bunny* in Yorkshire, lands which he had himself seized into the hands of the crown when sheriff.[5]

Waterton died apparently intestate on 28 July 1558.[6]

[1] Date of birth estimated from age at fa.'s i.p.m., C142/63/58. Glover's Vis. Yorks. ed. Foster, 105; Yorks. Arch. Jnl. xxx. ped. bet. pp. 418 and 419; Gooder, Parlty. Rep. Yorks. ii. 4; VCH Bucks. iii. 188; Misc. Gen. et Her. ii. 134–5. [2] LP Hen. VIII, xiv–xvii, xx; CPR, 1553, p. 353. [3] Yorks. Arch. Jnl. xxx. 349, 371, 391, 397; LP Hen. VIII, v–vii, xvii, add.; G. Brenan, House of Percy, ii. 99, 370–1; DNB (Percy, Thomas). [4] LP Hen. VIII, xvii, xix, xx; HMC Bath, iv. 58, 66, 72, 92; CPR, 1553, pp. 328, 338, 348, 375. [5] Vis. Yorks. (Harl. Soc. xvi), 314; CPR, 1550–3, p. 427; 1554–5, pp. 294–5. [6] C142/116/38.

L.M.K./A.D.

WATERTON, Thomas II (by 1526–75).

THIRSK 1554 (Apr.)
YORKSHIRE 1572*

b. by 1526, 2nd but 1st surv. s. of (Sir) Thomas Waterton I* of Walton and Sandal, Yorks, by Joan, da. of Sir Richard Tempest* of Bracewell and Bowling, Yorks. educ. G. Inn, adm. 1544. m. by 1552, Beatrice, da. and event. coh. of Edward Restwold of The Vache, Bucks., 2s. 3da. suc. fa. 28 July 1558.[1]

J.p.q. Yorks. (W. Riding) 1561–d.; commr. eccles. causes, province of York 1573.[2]

It was clearly to his father, who was sheriff of Yorkshire at the time, that Thomas Waterton owed his election for Thirsk to Mary's second Parliament. The nomination was probably made by the 3rd Earl of Derby, lord of the borough, with whom Waterton could claim a family relationship through the Fleet-

woods, and court influence could have been brought to bear through another of his kinsmen by marriage, Sir Edmund Peckham*. Waterton's membership of Gray's Inn and marriage to Beatrice Restwold of Buckinghamshire may have given him a southern domicile at the time of his election, although after his father's death he was to appear on the pardon roll of 1559 as of Corringham, Lincolnshire, and Walton, Yorkshire. To judge from his religious outlook in later life he is likely to have welcomed the Marian restoration. He was not to sit in Parliament again until a few years before his death on 5 Nov. 1575.[3]

[1] Date of birth estimated from age at fa.'s i.p.m., C142/116/38. Glover's Vis. Yorks. ed. Foster, 104–5; Yorks. Arch. Jnl. xxx. 398–404. [2] CPR, 1569–72, p. 224; 1572–5, pp. 168–9. [3] VCH Yorks. (N. Riding), ii. 63; VCH Bucks. ii. 256; iii. 188; Vis. Bucks. (Harl. Soc. lviii), 153; CPR, 1558–60, p. 149; J. T. Cliffe, Yorks. Gentry, 168; C142/173/55.

A.D.

WATKIN, William

PEMBROKE BOROUGHS 1558

William Watkin has not been identified. The suggestion that he was the son and heir of Lewis Watkins (q.v.) has little to commend it, for this bearer of the name appears to have been well under age at the time of the election concerned. A William Watkyn appears on the muster roll of Narberth, Pembrokeshire, in 1539 and another, or the same one, was reeve of nearby Templeton seven years later. Since Narberth lies not far from Pembroke either or both of these could have been the Watkyn William, burgess of Pembroke, who was assessed there for subsidy in 1544 on goods valued at £19. Somewhat further afield. the 3rd Earl of Worcester's lordship of Pennard, in the Gower peninsula, had a reeve named William Watkin in 1551–2.

Williams, Parlty. Hist. Wales, 160; Pemb. Recs. (Cymmrod. rec. ser. vii), ii. 103, 116; E179/223/422; Augmentations (Univ. Wales Bd. of Celtic Studies, Hist. and Law ser. xiii), 214–15; NRA 12101, vi. 50.

P.S.E.

WATKINS (AP GWATKYN, GWATKYN), Lewis (by 1511–47/48), of Llangorse, Brec. and Upton, Pemb.

PEMBROKE BOROUGHS 1545

b. by 1511. m. by 1542, Elizabeth (or Isabella), da. of Sir Edmund Tame, 3s. 1da.[1]

Yeoman of the guard by 1532–40; serjeant-at-arms 13 July 1540–d.; receiver and bailiff, lordships of Cilsain, Carm., Angle, Burton, Carew and Upton, Pemb. 1 Mar. 1543–?d.; customer and butler, ports of Haverfordwest, Pembroke and Tenby, Pemb. 11 Dec. 1544–d.; bailiff, lordship of Rowse within the lordship of Haverfordwest 11 Dec. 1544–d.; escheator, Brec. Jan.–Nov. 1545.[2]

Returned to Parliament under the English form

of his name, Lewis Watkins came from Llangorse, Breconshire, and was known in Wales as 'ap Gwatkyn' or 'Gwatkyn'. A yeoman of the guard from at least 1532, Watkins was designated one of the yeoman ushers at the coronation of Anne Boleyn and one of the surveyors at the dresser to wait on the lord mayor of London, who was to sit on the Queen's left. In July 1540 he was made a serjeant-at-arms, and it was in this capacity that he accompanied the King on the campaign of 1544, although the ten archers and ten billmen who followed him were recruited from his own tenants in Pembrokeshire. His association with that shire, begun by his leasing of land and tenements at Upton about 1541, was progressively strengthened by his appointment as receiver and bailiff of one lordship in Carmarthenshire and four in Pembrokeshire and as customer of the ports of Haverfordwest, Pembroke and Tenby, and bailiff of the lordship of Rowse.[3]

It was on 10 Jan. 1545 that Watkins was elected for Pembroke Boroughs to the Parliament which, first summoned to meet in that month, was postponed until the following November. During the interval he had the unique, if unenviable, distinction of being the only Member-elect to be convicted of murder. In August he and three others—a labourer of Llangorse named Richard ap Watkin, John Thomas ap Ieuan and Watkin ap Philip—slew Roger ap Watkin of Llangorse with an arrow. This was loosed by Watkin ap Philip, but the three others were also sentenced to death as accessories and only the intervention of the Privy Council on 2 Oct. stayed the execution of Watkins, while allowing Richard ap Watkin to go to his death. On the following day the Council noted that Watkins had been granted a pardon with full restitution of goods, and the pardon was enrolled on 12 Oct. Whether it had taken more than the customary financial consideration to save Watkins, and if so by whom it was wielded, remain unanswered questions, as is whether he took his seat in the House. If he did, it was as one not completely out of the wood, for six months later the Privy Council was notified that although the King had pardoned Lewis Watkins

> of the murder of Roger ap Watkins . . . the wife of the said Roger did not cease to prosecute the appeal; his Majesty's pleasure was that by such good means as they [the council in the marches] could best devise they should see her pacified, and to stay the matter from proceeding to any further issue, so as the woman may be contented, and yet the law not seem to be impeached.[4]

Watkins made his will on 7 Dec. 1547, asking to be buried in the church at Nash, near Upton, Pembrokeshire. He left his serjeant's mace to his eldest son William, who was a minor; the best part

of his goods, and all his lands at Llangorse, Breconshire, he left to his wife and executrix. The stock at Llangorse numbered over 100 horses and cattle, and 400 sheep. The will was proved on 6 May 1548, but Watkins was dead by 28 Feb. when his office of serjeant-at-arms was granted to another. An inquisition taken belatedly at Brecon in 1562 showed that Watkins had held in that shire the capital messuage of Llangorse and 45 acres of land attached, with some three acres of meadow elsewhere, worth altogether 25s. a year.[5]

[1] Date of birth estimated from first reference. *LP Hen. VIII*, xxi; *Pemb. Recs.* (Cymmrod rec. ser. vii), iii. 184; PCC 6 Populwell. [2] *LP Hen. VIII*, v, vi, xv, xviii, xx; *Pemb. Recs.* iii. 204–5; LC2/2/376. [3] *LP Hen. VIII*, vi; *Pemb. Recs.* iii. 76, 184, 204. [4] *LP Hen. VIII*, xx; *APC*, i. 252–3, 411. [5] PCC 6 Populwell; *CPR*, 1548–9, pp. 133, 224; C142/134/171 incorrectly gives the date of Watkins's death as 20 Mar. 1546, the error occurring presumably because the i.p.m. was taken so long after his death.

P.S.E.

WATKINS, Richard (by 1507–50), of London and Hunstrete, Som.

?BRAMBER 1542
BRIDPORT 1545

b. by 1507, 5th s. of Walter Vaughan of Bredwardine, Herefs. by Jenett Owgan. *educ.* Oxf. BA 1525, BCL by 1530, MA 1535. *m.* by 1531, Etheldreda, da. of Robert or Thomas Coker of Mappowder, Dorset, 3s. 2da.[1] Notary, ct. arches 1528, proctor by Nov. 1532; prothonotary 1533–*d.*; collector of customs, Bristol by Aug. 1535–47; registrar, ct. admiralty from 1540–*d.*[2]

Richard Watkins's full name was Richard Watkins Vaughan but he customarily used the shorter form. He started his career in the service of his kinsman William Edwards, one of Wolsey's secretaries, probably as a tutor. While at Louvain in March 1528 Watkins received the offer of an appointment in England which he modestly thought too great for his powers. This was evidently the notaryship from which his subsequent career developed: the earliest known document which he attested was the foundation charter of Wolsey's college at Ipswich dated 3 July 1528.[3]

In 1529 Watkins was appointed a notary for the proceedings in the King's divorce, and for the next four years 'the great matter' dominated his life. His efforts on the King's behalf brought him to the notice of Cromwell who in 1534 favoured his appointment as the bishop of Salisbury's registrar against that of a servant of his own, John Price*. To compensate Watkins for being passed over for this office (which he had been promised by the bishop, Lorenzo Campeggio, presumably to win him over in the divorce proceedings), Cromwell obliged Price to pay him £20 a year until he should receive the customership of Bristol; this post Watkins had obtained by August 1535, when he was licensed to perform his duties by deputy. His standing with Cromwell encouraged his kinsman Edwards to ask his intercession with the minister for a benefice.[4]

In the 1530s Watkins lived in London, signing his attestations variously at the Temple, 'in his gallery near Charing Cross', or 'at his house in St. Faith's parish'. In 1543 he bought three manors in Somerset and a house at Box, Wiltshire; for these he should have paid nearly £1,145, but the crown remitted £200. Watkins made one of the Somerset manors, Hunstrete, his country home, leaving all his household stuff there to his son and heir when he died.[5]

The indenture returned for Bramber in 1542 is mutilated and of the second Member's name only 'Ric'm Wa...' remains. Watkins was almost certainly the man elected since his deputy at Bristol, John Gilmyn, was chosen for the borough in the following Parliament when he himself found a place at Bridport. Bramber was a borough controlled by the 3rd Duke of Norfolk, to whom as treasurer Watkins was responsible at Bristol, and Bridport probably came his way because of his admiralty position, with his friend Christopher Smith* perhaps acting as an intermediary.[6]

A married man, whose eldest son was born in 1531, Watkins cannot have been a priest. His styling of himself in 1530 as *clericus landavensis diocesis* and in 1535, when he supplicated for his MA, as a secular chaplain, must mean that he had taken minor orders. On other occasions he described himself as gentleman, although when he made his will on 20 July 1548 it was as 'Richard Watkins Vaughan, prothonotary'. He asked his wife to bind herself in 300 marks for the faithful performance of the will to Clement Smith*, Dr. Baugh, archdeacon of Surrey, David Baugh, and William Vaughan, Watkins's nephew. His three sons were to be 'found and brought up in grammar first, and in writing schools, and after in the law or literal science or otherwise at the discretion of their schoolmaster in grammar', and he left all his books to 'such one of my sons as will apply his learning therein'. One-third of his lands he devised to his heir, the other two-thirds, including lands in Stepney and a manor in Monmouth, he left to his wife and younger children. Watkins died in late April 1550 when his son and heir Polydore was 18 years old. In the following November his widow obtained the wardship of Polydore, who three years later was licensed to enter upon his inheritance.[7]

[1] Date of birth estimated from first appointment. *The Gen.* n.s. iii. 175; Rymer, *Foedera*, vi(2), 142; PCC 12 Coode; Emden, *Biog. Reg. Univ. Oxf. 1501-40*, p. 708; *Vis. Dorset* ed. Colby and Rylands, 7. [2] *LP Hen. VIII*, iv-vi, ix, xv; *CPR*, 1553, p. 314; E122/22/1, 199/3. [3] *LP Hen. VIII*, iv. [4] Ibid. iv-vii, ix. [5] Ibid. iv-v, xviii; PCC 12 Coode. [6] C219/18B/95; E122/22/1; *LP Hen. VIII*, xviii;

PCC 12 Coode. [7] C142/91/53, 92/81; Rymer, vi(2), 142; St.Ch. 2/23/31; PCC 12 Coode; *CPR*, 1549-51, p. 209; 1553-4, p. 376.

H.M.

WATSON, John, of Newcastle-upon-Tyne, Northumb. and Lincoln's Inn, London.

?BERWICK-UPON-TWEED   1547[1]
?MORPETH   1553 (Oct.)
NEWCASTLE-UPON-TYNE   1554 (Nov.)[2]

?s. of John Watson of Newcastle-upon-Tyne. *educ.* L. Inn, adm. 29 May 1550.[3]

A John Watson sat for each of the Northumbrian boroughs in three of the Parliaments summoned between 1547 and 1554, but whether the name covers one, two or even three individuals has not been established.

Least difficult to trace is the Member for Newcastle in the Parliament of November 1554. Named on the torn indenture as '[blank] Watson, gentleman, of Lincoln's Inn', he is given the christian name 'Johannes' on a copy of the Crown Office list. He was clearly the John Watson admitted to the inn on 29 May 1550 and, with no one else of his surname found there during these years, doubtless also the 'Mr. Watson' elected escheator of the inn for the year 1552-3. His appearance on the pardon roll of 1559 as 'of Lincoln's Inn ... *alias* late of Newcastle-upon-Tyne' shows that his affiliation with that town was not limited to his election there. So much might have been inferred from the preponderance of townsmen among Newcastle's Members, especially as Watson had been elected to a Parliament which the Queen wished to see composed of such Members. He was almost certainly related to the John Watson who was the town's sheriff in 1523 and to another who was sheriff in 1567 and mayor in 1574, but he is scarcely to be identified with the second of these, who had made his way as a merchant adventurer while the Member followed the law—this is probably why the election indenture contains the distinguishing suffix. He cannot be certainly traced among the several John Watsons who lived and died at Newcastle during the last quarter of the century nor among those in or near London.[4]

Whether Watson had already sat for Berwick is partly a question of chronology. His name as that of the town's second Member in the Parliament of 1547 is known only from the list compiled before the opening of its final session in January 1552, so that its bearer may either have sat from the beginning or have been by-elected. Since Watson is unlikely to have gained a seat before he entered his inn, his identification with the Member for Berwick presupposes a by-election there in or after 1550, a hypothesis which accords well with the suggestion that George Willoughby (q.v.) had been one of that town's Members; by then his London domicile could have commended him as a suitable replacement. Failing him, no eligible namesake has been found. There were Watsons at Berwick, but after the Thomas Watson who was one of the Twelve at the earliest recorded guild meeting in 1506 none of them appears to have made any mark in the town, while the contemporary John Watsons in the county seem equally insignificant.[5]

Whoever sat for Berwick in this Parliament could have done so in either or both of its successors of 1553, for which the names of the Members are lost. It was to the second of them that Morpeth elected a John Watson as its senior Member. This was the first occasion on which the borough made a return, and the presumption is that patronage lay with its lord, the 3rd Lord Dacre of Gilsland; the second Member in October 1553, William Ward II, was almost certainly his nominee. Although John Watson of Lincoln's Inn had no known connexion with Dacre or with Morpeth, another member (or ex-member) of the inn, Cuthbert Horsley (q.v.), who was himself to sit for both Newcastle and Morpeth, as well as for the shire, could have promoted his election there. As at Berwick there is no local John Watson who invites consideration, although a family of that name had furnished the town with a bailiff half a century before and would do so again after a similar lapse of time.[6]

[1] Hatfield 207. [2] The christian name missing from the torn indenture (C219/23/174), is supplied from Huntington Lib. Hastings mss Parl. pprs. [3] *Vis. Northumb.* ed. Foster, 122. [4] *Black Bk. L. Inn*, i. 304; *CPR*, 1558-60, p. 162; J. Brand, *Newcastle*, ii. 444, 446; *Newcastle Merchant Adventurers* i (Surtees Soc. xciii), 93; ii (ibid. ci), 199; *Wills and Inventories*. iii (ibid. cxii), 61-62, 94, 147, 164; PCC 3 Brudenell, 24 Dixy, 82 Montague, 22 Tirwhite, 9 Wrastley. [5] J. Scott, *Berwick*, 259, 456, 458, 460; *Northumb. Co. Hist.* ii. 38; xv. 320. [6] *Arch. Ael.* (ser. 4), xiv. 61, 65.

M.J.T.

WATSON, Robert (by 1515-55/59), of Norwich, Norf.

WILTON 1547[1]

b. by 1515. *m.* (2) Elizabeth; at least 1s.[2]
?Steward of Abp. Cranmer c.1547; canon, Norwich May 1549-51.[3]

Robert Watson's identity is doubtful. He was not among the townsmen assessed for subsidy at Wilton in 1547 and he had no known links with (Sir) William Herbert I*, who had been granted the lordship of Wilton three years before and was to become Earl of Pembroke in 1551. He is not listed among the earl's tenants early in Elizabeth's reign, and he is mentioned neither in Pembroke's will nor among those who attended his funeral in April 1570. The only Robert Watson of any prominence at

this time was a native of Norwich, who became steward to Archbishop Cranmer early in Edward VI's reign. Described by Strype as 'a great civilian', he is unlikely to have been the man of that name admitted to Gray's Inn in 1533. It was presumably he who was granted a canonry in Norwich cathedral in May 1549, although a twice-married layman, and he was probably also the Mr. Watson to whom a royal commission 'for reformation of divers things' was brought on 13 July 1549, the day after Ket's men encamped on Mousehold Heath; during the following weeks Robert Watson, described as 'a new preacher', was one of those who urged moderation on the rebels, with some success. If elected for Wilton he was doubtless nominated for that borough by Herbert as a favour to the archbishop; his fellow-Member, Robert Warner, may also have had a hand in the matter, for he too came from Norfolk and later had property in Norwich. The canon had resigned his stall by 4 Oct. 1551, perhaps because he was already in trouble at Norwich for his extreme Protestant opinions, but this would not have affected his place in the Commons.[4]

The ex-canon appears to have been arrested for heresy early in Mary's reign. On 17 Feb. 1554 the Privy Council ordered the mayor and aldermen of Norwich to deliver Robert Watson to the chancellor of the diocese, and he remained in custody for nearly 16 months. He won his freedom by publishing his belief in the doctrine of transubstantiation, only to be threatened with re-arrest after the dean and others had accused him of casuistry. Friends helped him to escape from the country and in November 1555 he described his imprisonment and its sequel in the *Aetiologia*; it is not clear where this pamphlet was written nor where it was first published, but it seems to have appeared abroad during the following year.[5]

The will of Robert Watson 'late of Norwich' must have been made on the eve of his arrest, if not in prison itself, for it is dated 10 Feb. 1554. In it he committed his soul to Christ, by whose merits 'I most constantly believe that I am redeemed and saved', and bequeathed to his wife Elizabeth all the goods which he had left in her custody, as well as a house in St. Martin's parish by the palace gate. The sum of 40s. was set aside 'for the debt of my son young John at Cambridge to Dr. Parker or to the college, which though my son had evil deserved of me yet I will have yet paid'; the son must have been one of the two men named John Watson who had matriculated in 1550 from Corpus Christi College, whose master was the future archbishop, himself a native of Norwich. Small gifts of clothing were made to Robert Watson's friends at Norwich, and Thomas

Beaumont (either the Elizabethan Member for Norwich or his father) and Ellis Bate were appointed executors. Nothing is known of the testator after 1555 but it is probable that he died in exile, since the will was proved on 30 June 1559.[6]

[1] Hatfield 207. [2] Date of birth estimated from that of son who matriculated in 1550. *DNB*; PCC 31 Chaynay. [3] Strype, *Cranmer*, i. 610; *CPR*, 1548–9, p. 178; 1550–3, p. 53. [4] Strype, i. 610; F. W. Russell, *Kett's Rebellion*, 38–40. [5] *APC*, iv. 394; Strype, i. 610–11; C. H. Garrett, *Marian Exiles*, 322–3. [6] PCC 31 Chaynay; *Al. Cant.* i(4), 348.

T.F.T.B.

WATSON, William (by 1513–68), of York.

YORK 1553 (Mar.),[1] 1559, 1563

b. by 1513.[2]
   Constable, Merchant Guild York 1536–8, gov. 1547–8, 1566–7; chamberlain 1536–7, sheriff 1541–2, alderman Mar. 1543, mayor 1547–8, 1566–7; commr. for offences against Acts of Uniformity and Supremacy, York province 1561.[3]

William Watson was already established as a merchant when admitted to the freedom of York during the year 1533–4. After his term as chamberlain he was fined and imprisoned for non-payment of arrears due from his recent office. He lived in the parish of St. Michael, Ousebridge End, where in 1546 and 1547 he was assessed for subsidy on goods worth £50 and 100 marks respectively. In a chancery suit over a deal in lead brought against him by a London goldsmith between 1544 and 1558 he was described as 'a man of much wealth and substance and greatly borne and maintained, friended and allied' in York.[4]

When elected to the Parliament of March 1553 Watson and William Holme were given lengthy instructions from the corporation on such matters of local concern as the conditions for the sale of wool, cloth and leather. On their return they recommended an approach to the Duke of Northumberland for a reduction in the city's liability for tax, a subject which was to recur on both his subsequent elections. A 'favourer' of the Anglican settlement, he died between 18 Oct. and 19 Nov. 1568, the dates of the making and proving of his will.[5]

[1] *York Civic Recs.* v (Yorks. Arch. Soc. rec. ser. cx), 87. [2] Date of birth estimated from admission as freeman. [3] *Reg. Freemen, York*, i (Surtees Soc. xcvi), 252, 255, 266; *York Mercers and Merchant Adventurers* (Surtees Soc. cxxix), 140, 323–4; *CPR*, 1560–3, pp. 170–1. [4] *York Mercers*, 135; *York Civic Recs.* iv (Yorks. Arch. Soc. rec. ser. cviii), 22, 23; E179/217/110, 111; C1/1276/17–19. [5] *York Civic Recs.* v. 87–88; *Cam. Misc.* ix(3), 72; York wills 18, f. 18.

D.M.P./M.K.D.

WAVER see OVER alias WAVER

WAYTE, John (by 1522–78 or later), of Oxford.

OXFORD 1553 (Oct.), 1554 (Nov.), 1555

b. by 1522, ?*m.* at least 1s.[1]

Bailiff, Oxford 1552–3, assistant to mayor 1554–7, 1562–78, mayor 1555–6, 1561–2.[2]

John Wayte was almost certainly of Oxford origin. One namesake was sub-warden of Merton College in 1508 and another was a fellow of Queen's by 1534; a Thomas Wayte was among the Oxford councilmen between 1518 and 1522; a Robert Wayte was assessed for subsidy in St. Martin's parish on goods worth £5 in 1525, and both a Roger Waytes and an Elizabeth Wayte were so assessed in 1543, the year of John Wayte's first appearance on a subsidy roll. The John Wayte admitted as a freeman in 1537–8 was described as a painter, whereas the man presumed to have been the Member was called a haberdasher in 1557, 1569–70 and 1574–5; there was also a relatively long interval of 14 or 15 years between the admission of the freeman and his appointment as a bailiff. There may thus have been two contemporaries so named in Oxford. His later history suggests that it was the Member who in 1551 was accused in the chancellor's court of drawing a wood knife against James Neyland: William Aubrey II* of New Inn Hall was one of the witnesses against him.[3]

Wayte undertook all the usual duties of a leading resident. He was an overseer of the city's fairs with William Tylcock* in 1551 and of Port Meadow with Ralph Flaxney*, Edward Glynton*, Thomas Mallinson* and others in the following year. The way to the mayoralty was opened by a decision to elect eight assistants in 1554 and to make these new officials, as well as the five aldermen, eligible for election. Wayte became mayor at Michaelmas 1555 and during his term it was agreed that he and any other assistant chosen for the mayoralty should thereafter enjoy the privileges of an alderman. He had ranked for some time among the richer citizens, being assessed for subsidy on goods valued at £8 in 1543 and at £18 in 1544, 1545, 1547, 1550 and 1551.[4]

The date of Wayte's first mayoralty identifies him more closely than any other Member for Oxford with the persecution of heretics. He was responsible, by virtue of his office, for the safe-keeping of Bishops Latimer and Ridley, and of Archbishop Cranmer, who had been brought to Oxford in March 1554. The mayor and other leading citizens presided with Sir John Williams*, Lord Williams of Thame, at the burning of the two bishops on 16 Oct. 1555 and of Cranmer on 20 Mar. 1556. Wayte is also unusual in having been returned to Parliament by the city three times during Mary's reign. This is a further sign that he was regarded as a good Catholic and it is probable that his election was sponsored by Williams, who is thought to have been high steward of Oxford from 1553.[5]

Williams may have rewarded Wayte's zeal, for the two men had dealings over the site of St. Mary's college, a former house of Austin canons which had continued as an ordinary hall of residence until it passed into unknown hands in or about 1547. It seems that Williams eventually acquired control and that he allowed Wayte to occupy the premises, for in 1556 the university complained to Cardinal Pole and others that Wayte was despoiling the property. He must have been ordered to desist, as on 8 Oct. 1556 the city council agreed to disallow a bargain previously made with Wayte over some timber and slate belonging to St. Mary's college which he had bought from Williams.[6]

Wayte's career is remarkable for its vicissitudes. On 17 Feb. 1557 the city decided to accept the verdict of its auditors on an account submitted by him, perhaps as a former mayor or perhaps in connexion with St. Mary's college. In April he was taken from prison to make his submission in the council chamber before the recorder Sir John Pollard* and the mayor William Tylcock. He admitted a debt of £42 4s.7d., paid 44s.7d. for his immediate discharge and promised to pay the rest within eight years. Evidently he received special treatment, for it was resolved at the same time that no future defaulter could expect prompt release or permission to pay by instalments. The councilmen may have been made to show leniency against their will, for on 30 Apr. they decided to exclude Wayte from their number until his suit for readmittance should be approved.[7]

Wayte's fortunes revived under Elizabeth. It seems that he again enjoyed powerful patronage, since the council agreed on 18 Sept. 1561 that the total number of 13 citizens eligible for the mayoralty should be raised to 15 and that Wayte should be one of the two new assistants. The decision was taken at a meeting attended by the new high steward, Francis Russell*, 2nd Earl of Bedford, and when the number was again reduced to 13 in the following September, Wayte continued as an assistant, being chosen mayor a few days later. His wealth may have dwindled after his disgrace, since he was assessed for subsidy at £12 in 1559, but on 1 Apr. 1568 he was able to contribute 10s. towards a lottery, as did every other leading citizen.[8]

If Wayte showed unusual resource in rehabilitating himself so quickly, ingenuity was to prove his undoing. He engaged in a lawsuit with a fellow-citizen Edmund Bennet, feared an adverse decision in the mayor's court and matriculated so as to claim the protection of the university. Relations between town and gown being particularly strained during the 1570s, this move had unexpected repercussions.

Proceedings were stayed in the mayor's court while Bennet secured three writs against his opponent in the King's bench, so that the city was faced with the choice of infringing the privileges of the university or of disobeying the Queen's judges. The citizens appealed to Bedford's successor as high steward (Sir) Francis Knollys* who spoke to the Earl of Leicester, chancellor of the university, and on 4 June 1576 Leicester advised the vice-chancellor to remit the case to the mayor. This had so little effect that on 22 June 1578 the Privy Council told the lord chief justice to stay Bennet's proceedings and excuse the mayor, while a week later the vice-chancellor was rebuked for having admitted Wayte without due consideration. The university itself seems to have been deceived, for when both litigants were summoned before the justices at Burford, Wayte could not produce his instrument of privilege and on 23 July the Privy Council ordered a special inquiry to see if it had been lawfully obtained. The result of this investigation is not known but in any event Wayte could hardly have continued as a city councilman. On 31 July it was assumed that he had forfeited his rights as a citizen.[9]

It is difficult to determine what happened to Wayte thereafter. A Mr. Wayte is said to have reported the treasonable words of one Yates to Dr. Yeldard, then vice-chancellor. A marginal note to the report points out that although Yeldard was vice-chancellor in 1580, he may have been deputy vice-chancellor earlier. Anthony Wood notes a memorial to the Member in All Saints church, but without giving dates, and one of 1587 to a John Wayte whom he identifies as the Member's son. If this is correct, the Member may have been the John Wayte of Oxford, gentleman, who made a modest and fairly uninformative will on 24 Feb. 1589 which was proved on 5 or 6 May 1589.[10]

[1] Date of birth estimated from first certain reference. *Antiqs. Oxf.* iii. (Oxf. Hist. Soc. xxxvii), 148. [2] *Oxf. Recs.* 212, 219, 227, 266, 282, 297, 397. [3] Oxf. Univ. Arch. T/S cal. chancellor's ct. reg. F, p. 76; GG, p. 81; Emden, *Biog. Reg. Univ. Oxf. 1501–40*, pp. 611–12; *Oxf. Recs.* 20, 32, 151, 264, 332, 376. [4] *Oxf. Recs.* 204, 211, 219, 227, 256; E179/162/224, 229, 240, 261, 282, 289. [5] *APC*, v. 17, 77, 233; Foxe, *Acts and Mons.* vii. 547, 549; viii. 84. [6] *Antiqs. Oxf.* ii. (Oxf. Hist. Soc. xvii), 228–9, 232–5, 241–3; *Oxf. Recs.* 261, 263. [7] *Oxf. Recs.* 264–6. [8] Ibid. 282–3, 295, 297, 321; E179/162/318. [9] *APC*, x. 259–60, 264, 291; *Oxf. Recs.* 380, 396, 397. [10] Oxf. Univ. Arch. B27, p. 4; *Antiqs. Oxf.* iii. 148; Bodl. wills Oxon. 187, ff. 297–8.

T.F.T.B.

WEARE (WEYER, WARRE) *alias* BROWNE, Robert (by 1512–70), of Marlborough, Wilts.

MARLBOROUGH 1553 (Oct.)

b. by 1512, ?s. of John or Thomas Weare of Marlborough. *m.* Agnes, ?da. of William Pierse of Langley, 1s. 4da.[1]

Member, mayor's council, Marlborough by 1538, mayor 1539-40, 1552-3, 1562-3 and in four later years.[2]

A senior and a junior Robert Weare were freemen of Marlborough in 1532-3, when the elder of them was one of the mayor's 24 councilmen, and again in 1537-8, by which time both men had joined the council; thereafter only one, presumably the younger, appears in the town records. From 1540 he is found with the *alias* Browne already attached to Thomas and John Weare, freemen in 1524-5, so that he is more likely to have been the son of one of these than of his older namesake.[3]

Weare was assessed for subsidy in 1540 at 20s. on goods worth £40, figures exceeded only by three other inhabitants, and when he contributed 40s. towards the benevolence in 1545 Geoffrey Daniell* alone paid more; by 1551, when Weare was required to pay 40s. on goods worth £40, he and Robert Bithway* were the most highly taxed men in Marlborough. Always described as resident there, and long prominent in borough affairs, Weare is not known to have followed a trade or profession or to have served either the crown or a local magnate, but he prospered sufficiently to be styled gentleman in later life and to become the first of his family to appear in the heralds' visitations. In April 1549 he partnered John Knight I* in paying £613 for chantry property in Berkshire, London and Oxfordshire, of which his share may well have included the lands of two former chantries in St. Mary's church, Marlborough, but the purchaser of the Wiltshire manor of Nettleton in 1551 was probably a namesake. In 1560 he was licensed to alienate a tenement and shop in Marlborough to William Daniell*, and between 1561 and 1568 he paid fines ranging from £60 and £400 for acquiring property in Marlborough and Preshute and the manor of Great Poulton near Cirencester.[4]

Weare's only known link with the house of Seymour was as the tenant of Barton, near Marlborough, which at the time he made his will he was renting from the 1st Earl of Hertford, while with the other neighbouring magnate, William Herbert I*, 1st Earl of Pembroke, he seems to have had no connexion. His election with Bithway on 28 Sept. 1553 to Mary's first Parliament may thus be taken to mark one of the occasions when Marlborough, helped by the hiatus in both Seymour and Herbert influence, chose two townsmen instead of the customary nominees. For each of them it was to be a solitary event, and neither took the liberty of opposing the initial measures to restore Catholicism.

Weare's will of 2 Sept. 1565 provided that all his property in Marlborough, Mildenhall and Poulton, Wiltshire, was to go to his wife Agnes for life or for so long as she remained a widow, then to their son Richard Weare *alias* Browne, and after his death to his three sons Thomas, Clement and Richard the younger. Weare's grandchildren by his four daughters, were each to receive £3 6s. 8d., as were all the children of Richard the elder except a daughter Agnes, who was left £40. The residue was to go to the widow, who if she remarried would receive £200, and to Richard; they were named executors, and the overseers were John Allen, William Drury and Thomas Stephens. Weare died on 26 Oct. 1570 and his will was proved on the following 22 Nov. His seven terms as mayor were commemorated by a brass, now lost, in the church of SS. Peter and Paul, and his line was continued among the local gentry by the descendants of his grandson Clement.[5]

[1] Date of birth estimated from first reference. *Vis. Berks.* (Harl. Soc. lvi), 138; PCC 37 Lyon. [2] Marlborough corp. gen. entry bk. 1537-8, f. 1; 1542-3, f. 2; *Bor. of Marlborough Guide*, 7; Mill Stephenson, *Mon. Brasses*, 590. [3] Marlborough corp. gen. entry bk. 1524-5, f. 2; 1532-3, f. 1; 1537-8, f. 1; 1542-3, f. 2; E179/197/185, 203. [4] *LP Hen. VIII*, xiii; E179/197/185, 198/257; *Two Taxation Lists* (Wilts. Arch. Soc. recs. br. x), 25; *CPR*, 1548-9, pp. 425-7; 1550-3, p. 74; 1560-3, p. 52; *Wilts. N. and Q.* v. 25, 354; vi. 232-3. [5] PCC 37 Lyon; *Wilts. N. and Q.* vi. 233-4; *Wilts. Arch. Mag.* xxxiv. 199-200.

T.F.T.B.

WEBBE, George (by 1509-56), of Canterbury, Kent.

CANTERBURY 1553 (Mar.)[1]

b. by 1509. *m.* (1) by 1531, Anne (*d.*1551), 6s. inc. Anthony† 6da.; (2) Margaret.[2]
Common councilman, Canterbury by 1537, sheriff 1537-8, alderman 1540, mayor 1552-3; commr. goods of churches and fraternities 1553.[3]

George Webbe's admission in 1532 to the freedom of Canterbury by redemption shows that he was not the son of a freeman, and it was as a recent arrival there that he had paid a fee to the corporation in the previous two years to ply his trade. If it was his widow who gave John Webbe (q.v.) the ring which its recipient later bequeathed to her, George and John Webbe are to be thought of as kinsmen, perhaps brothers, and probably natives of Sandwich.

By profession a mercer, Webbe engaged in the corn trade, being one of the regrators who in 1540 were reported to be buying up all the grain in Kent. Such dealings evidently did not affect his civic progress, for it was in December 1540 that he was made an alderman of Westgate ward; three months earlier he had been fined £10 for failing to attend a burmote to which he had been specially summoned. In keeping with the city's readiness to elect its mayor to Parliament, Webbe's one short spell in the Commons came during his mayoral year. His name is missing from the torn return, and neither the election itself nor, owing to the loss of the accounts for 1552–3, any payment of wages is recorded in the city archives. Webbe cannot be identified with any particular attitude in politics or religion, unless his purchase of confiscated church goods in 1553 reflects an acceptance of that act of spoliation.[4]

Styling himself alderman of Canterbury and of the parish of St. Andrew, Webbe made his will on 23 Aug. 1556, asking to be buried in the cathedral. To his wife, Margaret, he left the lease of the house in which he lived, his new house at Fordwich and a tenement and lands in the parish of Monkton; after her death the house at Fordwich was to go to his son Anthony and the land in Monkton to be equally divided between two other sons, both named Thomas. Two more sons, Erasmus and Stephen, received a tenement each and lands in Fordwich and Westbere, and a sixth, George, £6 13s.4d. out of a lease in Westcliffe. Each of Webbe's six daughters was to have £20 on marriage or at the age of 21, the first four also receiving a goblet apiece and the two youngest a 'bunkyne'. The residue of all his goods went to his wife, whom he named executrix. The will was witnessed by two aldermen of Canterbury, Thomas Frenche and Henry Alday, and by the common clerk, George Toftes; it was proved on 18 Nov. 1556.[5]

[1] Canterbury burmote bk. 1542–78, f. 75v. [2] Date of birth estimated from first reference. *Reg. St. George, Canterbury*, ed. Cowper, 168; Canterbury prob. reg. A32, f. 151. [3] *Freemen of Canterbury*, ed. Cowper, 308; Canterbury burmote bk. passim; *Arch. Cant.* xiv. 318. [4] *Intrantes of Canterbury*, ed. Cowper, 193; *LP Hen. VIII*, ix; Canterbury burmote bk.; *Arch. Cant.* xiv. 320. [5] Canterbury prob. reg. A32, f. 151.

H.M.

WEBBE, James (by 1528–57), of Devizes, Wilts.

DEVIZES 1555

b. by 1528, s. of Richard Webbe. *m.* Wilhelmina, wid., at least 2s.[1]

James Webbe does not seem to have been related to the rich merchant family of Salisbury. He was assessed for subsidy in 1549, 1551 and 1553, each time on goods worth £10, in the parish of St. John's, Devizes, and in 1553 he was among the townsmen who certified that the tax had been collected. In July 1556 a James Webbe was one of four bakers who were each fined 20d. for some offence against the constitutions of the borough; this was presumably an otherwise obscure namesake, since the Member seems to have been a prosperous tanner who was to leave his son Thomas 'my vessels, knives and other tools that belongeth to the occupation of tanner's craft', with a quantity of skins and leather.[2]

It is uncertain whether Webbe was active in borough affairs, since no records of Devizes from before 1555 have survived. Of his brief parliamentary career all that is known is that he is not among those Members listed as having opposed a government bill. When his fellow-Member Thomas Hull was elected deputy to the mayor on 8 Oct. 1557, Webbe was promised the mayoralty for the following year, but on the first day of the following month he died. He had made his will on 28 Oct., asking to be buried in St. John's church. The principal legatees were his sons Thomas and Jeremy, but until they attained the age of 20 his wife and executrix was to enjoy the property. Webbe's father and 'brother' (?brother-in-law) Richard Wyllys were appointed overseers and Thomas Hull was among the witnesses.[3]

[1] Date of birth estimated from first reference. Wilts. RO, bishop's act bk. 1559. [2] E179/198/255b, 258, 261a; B. H. Cunnington, *Annals Devizes*, ii. 111. [3] Wilts. RO, bishop's act bk. 1559; Cunnington, i. p. xviii.

T.F.T.B.

WEBBE, John (by 1516–56/57), of London and Faversham, Kent.

DOVER 1553 (Oct.),[1] 1554 (Apr.), 1554 (Nov.)

b. 1516, prob. s. of John Webbe of Sandwich, Kent, by Joan, da. of John Hobard* of Sandwich. *educ.* ?Oxf. BA 1514; L. Inn. *m.* Alice, 1s.[2]

Steward, Faversham by 1537, auditor 1540–4, jurat in 1555, mayor 1556–*d.*; j.p. Kent 1554–*d.*; commr. heretical books 1556, crown lands 1556.[3]

John Webbe was almost certainly the son of the John Webbe of Sandwich whose widow Joan married Thomas Wingfield*, and thus probably a kinsman of Bennet Webb, mayor of Sandwich in 1488–9 and one of its Members in 1495. It is likely that George Webbe, who sat for Canterbury in March 1553, was another kinsman; to whom the Mistress Webbe of Canterbury, widow, to whom John Webbe bequeathed the ring which she herself had sent him, was doubtless George Webbe's wife, and the uncle and cousin, both named Henry Alday, who received articles of clothing belonged to a leading Canterbury family, one of them being the alderman who witnessed George Webbe's will. The city also furnished the background to John Webbe's long association with William Roper*. The two may have been contemporaries at Oxford, where Roper is thought to have studied and a John Webbe took his BA in July 1514, and were almost certainly so at Lincoln's Inn; although no record survives of his admission Webbe was probably the steward of the inn who in 1553 was allowed to have a clerk in commons at 20d. a week—perhaps one of the two clerks mentioned in Webbe's will—and who in 1555 was given leave to exchange chambers with 'Mr. Hale', another name redolent of Canterbury. Roper was to recall in his life of Sir Thomas More that Webbe and Richard Heywood* were present at More's trial and reported the proceedings to him. For the next 20 years Webbe and Roper, whom in his will Webbe called his master, were to be associated in a variety of contexts, in feoffments of Roper's manors, at Faversham where they were stewards in succession, with Webbe seemingly deputizing for Roper in 1552–3, and in branches of county administration. Another Kent figure with whom Webbe had much to do was Cyriak Petyt (q.v.). It was with Petyt and another that in 1554 he arraigned certain rebels to whom Dover had given passive support; later in the same year the two purchased the remainder of a lease at Boughton under Blean formerly held by Sir James Hales, a transaction which gave rise to the famous lawsuit of *Hales v. Petyt*.[4]

Webbe owed his three returns for Dover to the lord warden of the Cinque Ports, Sir Thomas Cheyne*. At the first election Cheyne set aside the port's choice of Thomas Portway* and Thomas Colly* in favour of Webbe and Joseph Beverley, clerk of Dover castle, with the result that the mayor and jurats had to indemnify the commonalty for this breach of electoral law. Although there was no repetition of this on the next two occasions, when Webbe was nominated by Cheyne and his fellow-Members seem to have been chosen by the port itself, the probability that on the first of them Webbe was also nominated for Rye may reflect some initial reluctance by Dover to accept him again. The warden's support of Webbe, and Dover's acquiescence in it, may have been influenced by his standing at Faversham, which as a 'limb' of the Cinque Ports had formerly claimed a share in the election of Members and which had seen another of its leading figures, Thomas Ardern, returned for Sandwich in 1547. An entry in the Dover accounts for July 1554 of the payment to Webbe of 40s., 'in part of payment of his parliament wages which he received of the town of Faversham', suggests that the port, having paid Webbe and Beverley a total of £13 for their attendance in the previous autumn, persuaded Faversham to meet some of the costs of Webbe's Membership in the spring of 1554. Whether or by which town he was paid for his third Parliament does not appear, the Dover accounts for the year 1554–5 being lost. Of Webbe's part in the proceedings of the Commons nothing is known save that he did not oppose the restoration of Catholicism in the first Marian Parliament or depart prematurely and without leave from the third.[5]

Having been passed over by Cheyne in 1555, Webbe was dead before Mary summoned her last Parliament. In his will of 28 Dec. 1556, which he made as a sick man, he left to his executors the choice of a burial place but asked that if it were in London the funeral should be attended by Father Peryn 'and his company', the members of the Dominican priory of St. Bartholomew, Smithfield, that Prior Peryn should preach a sermon and that the community should celebrate a trental of masses; he also provided for commemorative masses at Faversham, with gifts to the poor. To his wife he left his goods and landed property, including his interest in Ospringe parsonage at Faversham, and the custody of their son Germain. The only child mentioned, Germain was the godson of Webbe's 'gossip' Germain Cioll, who was to retain all Webbe's money for delivery to the son when he became 25, taking £100 for himself and £50 for his son John Cioll. (Germain Cioll was at this time the owner of Crosby Place in St. Helen's Bishopsgate, once the home of Sir Thomas More, and since Webbe left a gift to the curate of 'St. Ellyns' he was probably a neighbour of Cioll in that parish.) Among Webbe's other provision for his relatives, friends and servants were gifts to the three executors, William Roper, William Rastell* and Richard Heywood, and to the two overseers, Germain Cioll and Cyriak Petyt, and the disposition of his books, the religious ones going to Roper's chaplains Mr. Wade and Mr. Wells, and the legal ones to Webbe's two clerks Richard Best and John Ewer. The will was proved on 9 Mar. 1557.[6]

[1] Bodl. e Museo 17. [2] Date of birth estimated from first certain reference. Emden, *Biog. Reg. Univ. Oxf. 1501–40*, p. 612; Canterbury prob. reg. A18, f. 270; PCC 8 Wrastley. [3] Faversham wardmote bk. ff. 34–38v, 62v, 68, 70; *CPR*, 1553–4, p. 21; 1555–7, p. 24; 1557–8, p. 398. [4] PCC 8 Wrastley; Roper, *Life of More* (EETS cxcvii), 96; C142/181/122; Faversham wardmote bk. ff. 43–112 passim; *APC*, v. 18; *CPR*, 1554–5, p. 102. [5] Egerton 2094, ff. 81, 89, 90v; Dover accts. 1547–58, ff. 238–9. [6] PCC 8 Wrastley; *DNB* (Peryn, William).

P.H.

WEBBE, William I (by 1508–c.47), of Huntingdon.

HUNTINGDON 1529

b. by 1508. *m.* Elizabeth.[1]

The junior Member for Huntingdon in 1529 remains a shadowy figure. Perhaps descended from Simon Webbe, a bailiff of Huntingdon who died in 1497, he makes occasional appearances in the affairs of the town. In 1532 he was one of the witnesses—and among the few of these who wrote their own names—to its agreement with the King on the appointment of a new incumbent at the Hospital of St. John; five years later he was involved in Huntingdon's dispute with Cambridge over its claim, as part of the duchy of Lancaster, to be free of toll on horses laden with wool, a claim which the mayor of Cambridge declared to be 'imagined by the procurement of William Webbe'.[2]

The election of 1529 is the only one held during the reigns of the first two Tudors for which the names of the Members for Huntingdon survive: this fact, combined with the paucity of the borough's records, limits comment on that election largely to speculation. As a duchy of Lancaster borough Huntingdon might have been expected to return at least one nominee, and the senior Member, Thomas Hall II, appears to answer this description. If the town was able to claim the second seat for itself, Webbe is to be regarded as its choice, although with a Webbe family living ten miles away at Kimbolton, home of Sir Richard Wingfield, chancellor of the duchy until his death in 1525, he too may have enjoyed duchy support: nothing has come to light, however, to connect either Hall or Webbe specifically with Sir Thomas More, Wingfield's successor and chancellor at the time of the election. Of Webbe's role in the proceedings of the Parliament nothing is known, for although his name occurs on a list of Members drawn up by Cromwell late in 1534, it is likely to have been his namesake of Salisbury who was meant to figure there.[3]

Webbe was probably returned again in 1536, in accordance with the King's request for the re-election of the previous Members, and he may have sat in any or all of the three remaining Parliaments of the reign. That he did so in 1542 is the more likely from the inclusion of a proviso in the Act of 1543 (34 and 35 Hen. VIII, c.26) reorganizing the government of Wales: this allowed William Webbe to go on collecting, under a lease of 1 May 1542, dues of 1d. on large and ½d. on small cloths produced in the Welsh shires and Monmouthshire. The possibility that the beneficiary of this clause was not the Member for Huntingdon but a namesake, notably the well known merchant of Salisbury William Webbe II*, is practically excluded by the evidence relating to the lease given in a chancery suit brought between 1547 and 1551: by that time the lessee himself was dead, and his widow was being sued for payment of an annuity of 5 marks a year due to John Clerke of London for his 'friendship' in helping Webbe to obtain the lease. Thus, although either Webbe of Salisbury or Webbe of Huntingdon might well have extended his interest in wool and cloth to cover the Welsh alnage, the former is ruled out of consideration as having lived until 1554, whereas nothing more is heard of the latter after the limiting dates of this suit.[4]

[1] Presumed to be of age at election. C1/1276/47.   [2] Add. 3340;

E. Griffith, *Huntingdon Recs.* 82; Hunts. RO, Huntingdon box 1; Hunts. bor. recs. 135/1; DL1/21/L16.   [3] *VCH Hunts.* iii. 82; E179/122/100; *LP Hen. VIII*, vii. 1522(ii) citing SP1/87, f. 106v.   [4] C1/1276/47.

M.K.D.

WEBBE, William II (by 1499-1554), of Salisbury, Wilts.

SALISBURY   1529, 1536[1]

b. by 1499, o. s. of William Webbe *alias* Kellowe* of Salisbury by 1st w. Joan. *m.* by 1534, Catherine, da. of John Abarough* of Salisbury, 2s. John† and William† 6da. *suc.* fa. July/Aug. 1523.[2]

Member of the Forty-Eight, Salisbury 1520, of the Twenty-Four 1523, auditor 1528, 1538, 1541, 1545, 1551, mayor 1533-4, 1553-4; assistant for the Synxon mart of the Merchant Adventurers 1523; j.p. Salisbury 1540; commr. goods of churches and fraternities 1553.[3]

A merchant like his father, William Webbe early acquired experience in overseas trade, being appointed by the general court of the Merchant Adventurers in February 1523 one of the 14 assistants for the following Synxon or Whitsun mart in the Netherlands. In 1540 he was employing a factor at San Lucar in southern Spain. He was probably one of the eight merchants whom the Earl of Hertford allowed in April 1544, during the war with France, to export 1,000 tons of cloth to Jersey, where unarmed French ships would collect it in exchange for canvas. He also dealt in tin in association with Peter Martin* and John Melhuish*.[4]

In 1523 Webbe was assessed for subsidy in the Market ward of Salisbury on goods worth £100, his father's goods being valued at 15 times that figure; two years later, after his father's death, his goods were valued at £400, in 1547 at £500, in 1550 and 1551 at £300 and in 1552 at £200, sums which although modest by his father's standard were far higher than those recorded for any of his contemporaries, even Thomas Chaffyn I* never topping £180. Webbe's pre-eminence is also reflected in the £400 which he lent to the King in 1542 (the next largest sum of £40 being lent by Chaffyn) and in his high contribution to a benevolence in 1545. Unlike his father, he had clearly sunk much of his wealth in land. Although he continued to live chiefly in Salisbury, where he left his dwelling house to his elder son John, he acquired the nearby manor of Odstock in 1540. He was also a freeholder of Wilton and in 1524 he bought a 50-year lease from the bishop of Salisbury of manorial rights at West Lavington, near Devizes. In Hampshire he owned at the time of his death the manor of Stockbridge and property at Andover, as well as the estates which he had bought from Sir John Rogers* in 1544, no doubt when his daughter Elizabeth married into the Rogers family. In Cornwall he held property at Fawton on the river Fowey and elsewhere, over which he brought a suit in Chancery before Lord Audley alleging detention of deeds and which were presumably the lands in that county mentioned but not specified in his will.[5]

Among apparently unrelated namesakes from whom Webbe is to be distinguished is the Member for Huntingdon in the Parliament of 1529 who was almost certainly the William Webbe named in a proviso to the Act of 1543 (34 and 35 Hen. VIII, c.26) for the government of Wales. His wealth makes it likely, however, that it was Webbe of Salisbury who joined William Breton of London in paying £1,332 for the manors of Bushton, Wiltshire, previously held by Admiral Seymour and of Wolferlow, Herefordshire, together with rectories in Suffolk and other former monastic properties: this grant, made on 24 Feb. 1553, was followed by the sale of Wolferlow on the next day and of Bushton on 20 Mar.[6]

It is remarkable that Webbe, with his widespread property and business activities, played such a full part in affairs at Salisbury. He was not particularly prominent in the city's struggle with the reforming bishop Nicholas Shaxton but on 21 Jan. 1538 he was one of four citizens who were commissioned to present their fellows' case before the Privy Council. His stake in the freedom of Salisbury was soon demonstrated in a chancery suit before Audley, when Webbe complained that he could not hope for justice in the bishop's court against three chaplains of the cathedral who had forcibly entered his property after asserting that he was merely the tenant and that he owed arrears of rent amounting to £8.[7]

In returning William Webbe and Thomas Chaffyn to the Parliament of 1529 Salisbury chose two men who already ranked as its wealthiest citizens. As prorogation followed prorogation, and session succeeded session, the city doubtless began to wonder, as did other municipalities, how it was to pay the mounting bill for parliamentary wages. By June 1535, when Webbe presented his writ *de expensis*, the seven sessions ending in the previous December had lasted 407 days and his claim for £43 8s. thus represented payment for maximum attendance as well as an allowance for travel and perhaps for incidental expenses at Westminster. The corporation finding it hard to raise such a sum, Webbe 'of his goodness' remitted the £3 8s. and agreed to take the £40 by instalments of 20 marks a year. The final session of the Parliament lasted for 69 days and its successor of 1536, to which Webbe was also returned (though without Chaffyn, despite the King's request for the previous Members),

another 40; as he was not elected in 1539 the 'burgess money' mentioned on 3 Dec. of that year, when he remitted £7 10s. and agreed to accept the rest in two payments of £13 16s.8d., must include either arrears or payment for additional services.[8]

Of Webbe's part in the House which, to judge from his wages bill, he attended so assiduously there are two unclear and tantalizing glimpses. His name occurs, next to Thomas Chaffyn's, in a list of Members probably dating from the session of 1533. If, as has been suggested, this is a list compiled by Cromwell of actual or potential opponents of the bill in restraint of appeals, Webbe and his fellow-Member are probably to be reckoned among the woolmen and clothiers who feared repercussions on the cloth trade. The other possible reference to Webbe arises from the appearance of his name on a further list, dating from the winter of 1534. Although the Member concerned may have been his namesake of Huntingdon, the fact that this later list includes several of the names occurring on the earlier one makes it likely that Webbe of Salisbury is again intended: if so, he is to be thought of as one of the seemingly recalcitrant Members who, with a group of more reliable ones, appear to have been especially connected with the treasons bill then passing through the House, perhaps as belonging to a committee on it.[9]

Webbe was not elected to any of the three remaining Parliaments of Henry VIII's reign, but on 26 Sept. 1547 he and Robert Griffith* were chosen by Salisbury to attend the first Parliament called in the name of Edward VI. It is, however, open to serious doubt whether they sat in this Parliament. There is no reference to any claim for expenses, and the debt of £20 due to him for his 'burgess-ship' which Webbe was to remit in his will could have represented a sum outstanding from his earlier claims. There are, moreover, alternative names to consider. On the copy of the Crown Office list of Members which was annotated in preparation for the final session in 1552 the names of the Members for Salisbury are given as Sir John Thynne and Henry Clifford. As both Webbe and Griffith outlived the Parliament they can scarcely have been replaced at by-elections; rather, if Thynne and Clifford are to be accepted as the Members, they must be thought of as having supplanted the two local men from the outset. What gives colour to this supposition is the happenings at Salisbury at both the previous election and the following one. In 1545 Edmund Gawen and Robert Keilway II* were replaced by two 'outsiders', Thomas Gawdy I and John Story and in the spring of 1553 the Earl of Pembroke nominated George Penruddock and John

Beckingham. It would be wrong, however, to conclude that Webbe was dragooned (whatever may have been the case with Griffith) into withdrawal in 1547, for throughout these years he appears to have acted as a kind of election agent at Salisbury. It was he who had 'managed' the return of Charles Bulkeley, another outsider, to the Parliament of 1542, and in March 1553, when he was mayor, he undertook to pay the parliamentary wages of Pembroke's two nominees if the earl himself should fail to pay them. He is therefore more likely to have abetted than to have opposed his own, and Griffith's, supersession in 1547.[10]

Whether Webbe's collaboration with Pembroke reflects more than a personal tie between them it is hard to tell since little is known of Webbe's religious outlook or political affiliation. His descendants, the Webbe baronets of Odstock, were to be recusants and his will contains a number of traditional bequests. Modest alms were to be distributed to the poor at his funeral, his 'month's mind' and his 'year's mind', annuities of 20s. went to two chantries in St. Thomas's church and a further 20s. 'to the maintenance of clerks and singing men' there. Webbe also bequeathed to the church a number of vestments which he had bought as a commissioner under Edward VI, perhaps for safe keeping in the hope that Catholicism would be restored.[11]

The will, which he made on 22 Jan. 1554, provides further evidence of Webbe's large fortune. Charitable gifts included £100 to the mayor of Salisbury to 'maintain clothiers and other young occupiers', £20 to the Trinity hospital, £40 for the repair of highways and £5 for unpaid tithes to St. Thomas's church, where he asked to be buried. His ample provision for his family included dowries of 500 marks each for his three unmarried daughters. Among further bequests he left black gowns to Robert Eyre* and his wife, and 40s. a year to John Hooper* 'for his pains taking in keeping of courts upon my lands according as he hath heretofore accustomed'. The executors were Webbe's two sons and his sons-in-law Thomas Bingley and Robert Rogers. The overseers were (Sir) Thomas White II* of South Warnborough, John White of London, Matthew Haviland, another son-in-law, and Edward Courteys, Webbe's 'servant', who was betrothed to his daughter Annys; each of these was to receive £100 and a mourning gown. The curate of St. Thomas's, Thomas Chaffyn, Robert Eyre, John Hooper and Thomas St. Barbe acted as witnesses to the will, which must therefore have been made at Salisbury and which was proved on 22 Feb. 1554.

¹ Salisbury corp. ledger B, f. 281. ² Date of birth estimated from first reference. Salisbury corp. ledger B, f. 244; *Wilts. Vis. Peds.*

(Harl. Soc. cv, cvi), 208; C1/810/58–62; PCC 12 Bodfelde. ³ Ledger B, ff. 244, 253v, 263, 276v, 287v, 294, 300, 307v, 309; *Acts Ct. of Mercers' Co.* ed. Lyell and Watney, 557; *LP Hen. VIII*, xv, xxi; *CPR*, 1553, p. 416. ⁴ *VCH Wilts.* vi. 127–8; PCC 12 Bodfelde; E122/121/7–8, 122/4–5, 7, 21, 123/2, 207/2, 6; *Acts Ct. of Mercers' Co.* pp. xv, 557; C1/1186/14; *LP Hen. VIII*, xix. ⁵ PCC 12 Bodfelde, 26 Tashe; E179/197/154, 240, 198/256, 260, 262, 259/16, 19; *Two Taxation Lists* (Wilts. Arch. Soc. recs. br. x), 38; *Wilts. N. and Q.* iii. 88; vi. 24; vii. 200; *Pembroke Survey* (Roxburghe Club cliv), 181, 183–5, 202–4; *VCH Hants*, iii. 414–15; iv. 473, 656–7; C1/1091/8–9; Elton, *Policy and Police*, 10–11. ⁶ C1/917/21–22, 1276/47–48; 142/99/41; *VCH Hants*, vii. 14, 25; *CPR*, 1553, pp. 109 160–2, 275. ⁷ Ledger B, ff. 272v, 286; *LP Hen. VIII*, vi, xiii; C1/1088/20–21; Elton, 100–107. ⁸ Ledger B, ff. 277v, 279v, 292v, 310v. ⁹ *LP Hen. VIII*, vii. 1522(ii) citing SP1/87, f.106v; ix. 1077 citing SP1/99, p. 234; xii. ¹⁰ Hatfield 207; ledger B, ff. 281, 294v, 301v, 310v. ¹¹ *VCH Wilts.* iii. 88–89; PCC 26 Tashe.

T.F.T.B.

WEBBE, William III, of Warwick Castle, Warws.

WARWICK 1542[1]

The junior Member for Warwick in the Parliament of 1542 was almost certainly the William Webbe of Warwick Castle who pastured 30 of the King's stud mares on Sir Nicholas Strelley's land in 1544–45. He was evidently of a family which served in the royal stable and which included both Robert Webbe, yeoman of the stud, who in 1531 was appointed keeper or mower of meadows in the lordship of Warwick and who held a lease from the town of the parsonage of St. Nicholas, and Henry Webbe, who attended Henry VIII's funeral as an equerry of the stable. William Webbe's most likely patron was Sir John Dudley, later Earl of Warwick and already joint constable of Warwick castle, whose younger brother Andrew Dudley* was an equerry of the stable by 1544, but he may also have enjoyed the favour of Sir Thomas Wriothesley, bailiff of Warwick, whose deputy John Ray was an associate of Robert Webbe. Moreover, his fellow-Member Clement Throckmorton, a younger son in a locally influential family, was later to serve in the household of Queen Catherine Parr with a Henry Webbe. If, as seems likely, William Webbe is to be distinguished from an obscure resident of Long Lawford, Warwickshire, who made his will in February 1559, nothing further has come to light about him.[2]

¹ C219/18B/101; *OR* gives the surname as 'Webbere'. ² *LP Hen. VIII*, v, xx; *VCH Warws.* v. 475–7; Warwick accts. 1546–69, mm. IV, 7v, IIV, 28; SC6/Hen. VIII/3700, 3706, 3713; LC2/2, ff. 34, 36; 4/1, f. 21V; E179/69/27, 48; Lichfield consist. ct. wills 1559, f. 165.

S.M.T.

WEBBE alias KELLOWE, William (by 1466–1523), of Salisbury, Wilts.

SALISBURY 1504, 1510[1]

b. by 1466. *m.* (1) Joan, wid. of one Stone ?of Salisbury, 1s. William Webbe II* 1da.; (2) Edith, wid. of Robert Long (*d.* 1501) of Steeple Ashton and of one Morgan; (3) Joan.[2]

Member of the Forty-Eight, Salisbury by 1487, of

the Twenty-Four 1487, jt. keeper of the keys 1488, constable, Market ward 1488, assessor 1492, 1498, city 1497, auditor 1495, 1497–1500, 1504, 1506–7, 1509, 1513, 1517–18, 1521, mayor 1495–6, 1511–12, 1513–14, 1522–d.; commr. subsidy 1496, 1512, 1514, 1515.[3]

According to a statement in his will, William Webbe was christened in the church of St. Lawrence at Shaftesbury. His parentage is unknown, but his use of the *alias* 'Kellowe' in his will raises the possibility that he was an illegitimate offspring of one of the Keilway family of Dorset and thus perhaps related in blood to Robert Keilway I*. If Webbe was a bastard it did not impede his progress, for by the end of the 15th century he had become one of the richest merchants of Salisbury. He may have started his career in Southampton, an important outlet for the Wiltshire cloth trade, where he built the so-called Church House in Crane Street; in 1509 a pardon was issued to John Stone of Salisbury and William James of Southampton and Salisbury, factors and attorneys of Thomas Coke I*, William Hawkins and William Webbe. Poole was probably another port through which Webbe exported his goods, since both his son and grandson did so, while his daughter married a merchant of that town.[4]

Webbe performed many special duties for the corporation of Salisbury and during his second mayoralty he presided over the compilation of rules for public order to be approved by the King's justices. His first three terms as mayor ended by his being paid £17, £19 12s.5d. and £18 4s.8d. respectively, of which £10 was for his pension and the remainder for other charges. He appears to have been reluctant to undertake a fourth term, perhaps because of failing health, for his election on 2 Nov. 1522 was followed three days later by a resolution that 'for various considerations' he need not hold the office again.[5]

Webbe and Coke claimed payment at the statutory rate of 2s. a day for their service in the Parliament of 1504 but when both men were re-elected on 2 Jan. 1510 they were promised only 1s. a day. It was not customary for the mayor of Salisbury to be returned to Parliament, and this may explain why Webbe was not chosen when these reduced wages were again offered in 1512.[6]

Webbe made his will on 13 July 1523, describing himself as 'William Kellowe or William Webbe of the city of New Sarum, mercer and merchant' and asking to be buried in the church of St. Thomas, where his three wives already lay. He made bequests to his daughter Cecily, the wife of Thomas White of Poole, and her three children, as well as to the children of his second wife by her two earlier

marriages. The chief beneficiary and sole executor was his son William who received a dwelling house, shop, warehouses and five tenements 'by the water lane in Castle Street' at Salisbury. Thomas White and another 'son-in-law', John Stone, were named overseers, with £10 and £5 apiece. Webbe died some three months before the close of his mayoralty, for the will was proved on 14 Aug. and his death was noted when the assembly met to elect a successor five days later.[7]

[1] Salisbury corp. ledger B, f. 220v. [2] Date of birth estimated from first reference. Hutchins, *Dorset*, iii. 298; PCC 12 Bodfelde, 48 Blamyr. [3] Ledger B, ff. 162v, 164v, 165v, 166, 177, 191, 192, 198, 198v, 201, 201v, 203, 204v, 212v, 215, 217, 219v, 224v, 229, 229v, 239, 241, 247v, 250v; *Rot. Parl.* vi. 518; *Statutes*, iii. 80, 113, 117. [4] PCC 10, 12 Bodfelde; *VCH Wilts.* vi. 126–8; *CPR, 1494–1509*, p. 526; A. A. Ruddock, *Italian Merchants and Shipping in Southampton, 1270–1600* (Soton Rec. Ser. i), 145; *LP Hen. VIII*, i. [5] Ledger B, ff. 169, 173v, 174v, 181v, 192v, 195, 200, 209, 224, 225, 226, 227, 231v, 250v, 251. [6] Ibid. ff. 211v, 212, 220v, 225. [7] PCC 12 Bodfelde, 30 Hogen; ledger B, f. 252v.

T.F.T.B.

WEKYS, William

OLD SARUM 1553 (Mar.)[1]

The William Wekys, armiger, returned for Old Sarum to the Parliament of March 1553 has not been identified. His claim to gentility makes it likely that he belonged to one of the several families named Weekes or Wykes to be found in the west country, but he cannot be placed with confidence in their pedigrees. He may well have been the William Wykes included in a group headed 'knights and lords' sons' in the issue of cloth for the funeral of Henry VIII but there seems to be no reason to identify him with the William Wykys admitted a bachelor of civil law at Oxford in 1532. The only other bearer of the name whose career can be glimpsed or surmised is the William Weekes admitted to the freedom of the Drapers' Company in 1542. Perhaps a kinsman of the 'Master Weekes', described by Hakluyt as a west-country gentleman worth 500 marks a year, who had accompanied the disastrous Newfoundland voyage of 1536, the draper is last heard of making his will in the Canary Islands on 20 Oct. 1561. His claim to wages of £3 due to him as purser of the ship *John the Baptist* 'for half the voyage' may mean that he had only recently come to the islands in her and did not belong to the English merchant community there; his wife Margery, to whom he left all his goods, houses and lands, was then living in the London parish of St. Catherine Cree. The will is registered as having been proved on 3 Nov. 1562, but in January 1566 administration was granted to Weekes's brothers Edward and Francis.[2]

The most likely patron at Old Sarum was William Herbert I,* 1st Earl of Pembroke. Either the courtier or the draper could have been associated with the earl, the draper through Pembroke's interest in overseas enterprise, but there may have been a more direct connexion: in July 1557 the Privy Council ordered Pembroke, then campaigning in France, to send over four men accused of robbery, two of whom, Thomas Cobham and one Wykes, were his own servants. If, as may be thought likely, Pembroke had recruited a servant of this name from the Salisbury family which was to produce Anthony † and Christopher Weekes†, the Member may also have come from its ranks, perhaps as a migrant from further west.[3]

[1] C219/282/9; *HMC Hatfield*, xv. 386. [2] Atkins, *Glos.* 207; *Bristol and Glos. Arch. Soc. Trans.* xlix, 287, 291, 294–5; Leland, *Itin.* ed Smith, vii(2), 72; *Vis. Som.* (Harl. Soc. xi), 120; *Vis. Devon* ed Vivian, 117, 511, 767, 825; C142/29/87, 33/87, 43/49, 73/30, 79/268, 270, 92/83, 96/30, 167/96; Emden, *Biog. Reg. Univ. Oxf. 1501–40*, p. 644; LC2/2, f. 66v; P. Boyd, *Roll of Drapers' Co.* 196; Hakluyt, *Principal Voyages* (1904), viii. 36–38; PCC 28 Street; *PCC Admins.* ed Glencross, i. 66. [3] *APC*, vi. 127, 134.

E.McI.

WELBORED *see* CORNELIUS *alias* JOHNSON *alias* WELBORED

WELCHE, Arthur

DUNHEVED 1554 (Apr.)

The election indenture for Dunheved to the second Marian Parliament does not survive, and the name of the junior Member is known only from a list of Members, where it appears as 'Arthurus Welche'. Since no one so named has been traced, other than a townsman of Morpeth who sat in the Parliament of 1563, the possibility has to be envisaged that the name was either mis-spelt on the indenture or wrongly copied onto the list. In the case of the christian name the most likely substitution would have been that of 'Arthurus' for 'Anthonius', whereas for the surname no such simple variant presents itself.

Three men of the time named Anthony Welsh can be distinguished, an exchequer clerk, a younger son in the family of Little Sodbury, Gloucestershire, and this one's kinsman a Monmouthshire gentleman. The first had business dealings with the court of augmentations, where the Mildmay brothers Thomas* and Walter* were auditors, a capacity in which they also served the duchy of Cornwall, but his claim to consideration is weakened by the absence of any reference to him after 1543. The second was to succeed his father Maurice Welshe of Little Sodbury for a few months in 1556, but as a youngster of 22 at the time of the election he would have needed patronage or connexion of which no trace has been found. Finally, Anthony Welshe of Llanwarne, Herefordshire, and Dinham, Mon-

mouthshire, who might have enjoyed such an advantage through his contemporary at the Inner Temple Thomas Williams II*, an associate of the Edgecombe family and the 1st Earl of Bedford, is all but excluded from consideration on the score of his having been sheriff of Monmouthshire during the year concerned.

LP Hen. VIII, xiii, xv–xxi; *Vis. Glos.* (Harl. Soc. xxi), 266 *Bristol and Glos. Arch. Soc. Trans.* xxi. 19; C142/60/23, 109/71, 77, 134/219; *CPR*, 1553, pp. 360, 418; 1558–60, p. 188; 1560–3, pp. 144, 598; PCC 5 Peter.

S.T.B.

WELCHE *see also* WELSCHE, WELSHE

WELDON, Edward (*d*.1551), of Bray, Berks.

NEW WINDSOR 1547*

1st s. of Hugh Weldon of Horsleydown, Surr. *m.* Isabel, da. of one Beake of Haddenham, Bucks., 2s. 3da.[1]

?Surveyor of the dresser by 1544–45 or later.[2]

Edward Weldon is apt to be confused with an uncle and namesake who served in the Household but who seems to have died in or shortly after 1541. It was presumably the younger man who was surveyor of the dresser during the mid 1540s.[3]

Weldon was certainly associated with another uncle, Thomas Weldon of Cookham, Berkshire, also of the Household, who sat for Berkshire in 1542 and became high steward of Windsor in April 1548, and to whose influence he may well have owed his own election to the Parliament of 1547. He was returned with Richard Ward I,* another household officer, with whose family the Weldons had long been close. The land purchase which established Edward Weldon as a landowner near Windsor was that of the manor of Shottesbrook, for which he and his uncle Thomas paid £963 to the court of augmentations in 1548. It included the site of the late college of St. John the Baptist, whose church was henceforth to serve as the parish church of Shottesbrook, as well as the rectories of Ashampstead and Basildon, and lands at Cookham and in the London parish of St. Edmund, Lombard Street. At an unknown date, Weldon also acquired the manor of Cresswell, near Bray, where he was living when he made his will.[4]

The probate copy of Weldon's will is dated 1 Oct. 1552, but as he added a codicil on 12 May 1551 and died on 25 May, this must be an error, probably for 1550. He commended his soul to the Trinity, 'firmly believing that at the last and general day of judgement I shall rise in my flesh and receive and have everlasting life', but he left the place and manner of his burial to the executors. His wife Isabel was given the lease of Cresswell for 20 years, on condition that she provided for their sons Thomas and Edward until they became 15 and also for their daughters Joan, Cecily and Edith. She was then left two thirds of Shottesbrook and its adjacent property for 21 years and required, if she were with child, to give it £100 on its coming of age. She and Richard Randall* of the Inner Temple were named executors of the will but Randall's name was struck out in the codicil, to which, however, he was a witness. The will was not proved until 1555, by which time Isabel and Randall were married, but the custody and marriage of Weldon's heir was granted on 20 June 1552 to Thomas Weldon, who had been appointed overseer. Weldon was replaced in the final session (1552) of the Parliament of 1547 by Thomas Little, a neighbour of his at Bray.[5]

[1] *Vis. Berks.* (Harl. Soc. lvi), 139–40; PCC 31 More. [2] *LP Hen VIII*, xx. [3] R. C. Braddock, 'R. household, 1540–60' (Northwestern Univ. Ph.D. thesis, 1971), 133–4, with additional information from Dr. Braddock; Hasted, *Kent*, ii. 411; *Vis. Northants.* (Harl. Soc. lxxxvii), 234–8. [4] *CPR*, 1547–8, pp. 404–5. [5] PCC 31 More; C142/93/4; *LP Hen. VIII*, xv; *CPR*, 1550–3, p. 227.

T.F.T.B.

WELDON, Thomas (by 1499–1567), of Cookham, Berks.

BERKSHIRE 1542
NEW WINDSOR 1559

b. by 1499, 3rd s. of Hugh Weldon. *m.* (1) by 1538, Cecily; (2) Anne; 5s. 2da.[1]

Cofferer's clerk in 1520; third clerk of kitchen by Mar. 1526, second clerk by 1532, chief clerk by 1538–40; keeper of the houses in upper bailey, Windsor castle 1538–*d.*, of the butts by 1539–*d.*, of leads 1540–*d.*, of the keys by 1553; first master, the Household 1540, cofferer 1552–30 Sept. 1553, by 14 Dec. 1558–*d.*; steward, manors of Cookham and Bray, Berks. 1541–*d*;. j.p. Berks. 1543–*d.* q. by 1554, j.p. Wilts. 1558/59–*d.*; commr. benevolence, Berks. 1544/45, subsidy 1546, 1563, relief, Berks. and Windsor 1550, goods of churches and fraternities 1553; other commissions 1541–64; high steward, Windsor Apr. 1548–Sept. 1563; keeper, the great wardrobe 1559.[2]

The Weldons, who claimed descent from a Northumberland family, rose by service in the royal household. Hugh Weldon, a sewer to Henry VIII, placed his second son Edward in the service of John Shirley, then cofferer, in 1509. A clerk of the green cloth by 1518, Edward Weldon was granted a lease of the manor of Swanscombe, Kent, in 1540 and was to be followed on the board of green cloth by his son Anthony who established his line at Swanscombe. Meanwhile, Thomas Weldon was leasing the demesne lands of Chertsey abbey in 1535 and is first mentioned as a clerk of the kitchen when licensed to shoot with a long bow at Bray, in Berkshire, on 7 Feb. 1536. By 1540 he had overtaken his brother, being first master of the Household with Edward as third master.[3]

Cromwell may have been responsible for this promotion, for his reforms of the Household in 1539 were aimed at unifying the administration of the court by making the four masters of the Household act as links between the cofferer and the clerks of the green cloth. The fall of Cromwell did not halt Weldon's progress, which entered a new stage with his return to the Parliament of 1542 for Berkshire, a county in which he now held a great deal of property and to which he may have been drawn by Sir Richard Weston*, chief steward of Chertsey abbey by 1534, whom he succeeded as steward of Bray and Cookham. It had a brief setback in March 1543, when he was summoned before the Council, found guilty of maintaining an offender against the Six Articles, Anthony Peirson, and sent to the Fleet; Peirson was one of the Windsor Martyrs, but his abettors in the Household were pardoned in September 1543. In 1544 Weldon was ordered to muster with the Berkshire gentry and went to France as a captain, and two years later he and John Norris* were paid for conducting 40 men from Berkshire to Dover.[4]

When in 1552 he succeeded John Ryther* as cofferer of the Household, Weldon became responsible for the day-to-day financing, and so for the smooth running, of that institution. The cofferer's annual account ended in September, so that Weldon's first full year of office was completed under Mary. He was then superseded, for Sir Richard Freeston's accounts follow, but for a time the government still made use of him, perhaps to test his loyalty. His appointment as a commissioner of oyer and terminer on 2 May 1554 was followed at the end of the month by a letter to 'Mr. Weldon' and one John Dodge at Southampton, telling them to greet the Spanish Marques de las Navas on behalf of the Council; on 5 June, presumably as steward of Windsor, he was ordered to set a seditious slanderer in the pillory. After this Weldon lapsed into obscurity until at Elizabeth's accession he was reappointed cofferer, being jointly responsible with Richard Ward I* for the account of 1558–9. He was to remain cofferer until his death.[5]

Weldon had started to acquire property with a reversion of some London tenements in the parish of St. Giles without Cripplegate in 1538. At about the same time he received the rectory of Bisham, Berkshire, where Henry VIII had briefly contemplated resettling the monks of Chertsey, and in September 1538 he and his wife Cecily were granted the manor and advowson of White Waltham, also in Berkshire and once the property of Chertsey abbey. Ten years later he and his nephew Edward Weldon* paid £963 for the site of the college of St. John the

Baptist, Shottesbrook, Berkshire, with which came the manor and advowson there, the rectories of Ashampstead and Basildon, and lands at Cookham and in the parish of St. Edmund in Lombard Street, London, at a total rent of £49 10s. a year. In December 1551, a month after his nephew's death, Weldon secured the manor of Woolstone, Berkshire, at a rent of £17 14s., and in July 1563 he and Thomas Gardiner* paid £844 for the reversion of Pangbourne manor.[6]

Weldon's Protestantism was therefore profitable. The only acquisition which brought him any trouble seems to have been Woolstone, which had belonged to St. Swithin's priory, Winchester, and then to the Protector's brother Admiral Seymour; an alleged lease by the prior forced Weldon to sue the occupants in the court of requests. Difficulty also arose over the only property which he is known to have inherited, from his eldest brother Hugh, who had a tenement in what is now Cannon Street, London: in 1546 Hugh Weldon's son Edward had to promise to pay £20 arrears of rent to the court of augmentations and at about the same time Thomas Weldon was pursued for an annuity of 40s. assigned on the tenement to the nunnery of Ankerwyke, Buckinghamshire, and so now due to the crown.[7]

Weldon made his will on 6 Mar. 1566 and died on 2 Mar. 1567.[8]

[1] Date of birth estimated from first reference. *Vis. Northants.* (Harl. Soc. lxxxvii), 234–8; Hasted, *Kent,* ii. 411; *LP Hen. VIII,* xiii; PCC 5 Babington. [2] R. C. Braddock, 'R. household, 1540–60' (Northwestern Univ. Ph.D. thesis, 1971), 133–4 and additional information from Dr. Braddock; E179/69/23; 351/1795/6, 11–19; LC2/4/2; PCC 13 Jankyn; *CSP Dom.* 1547–80, p. 146; *LP Hen. VIII,* x, xiii–xvi, xviii, xx, xxi; Bodl. Ashmole 1176, f. 41v; Stowe 571, f. 59–59v; *CPR,* 1547–8, p. 81; 1550–3, pp. 142, 393–4; 1553, pp. 351, 362, 413, 416; 1553–4, pp. 17, 28; 1560–3, pp. 343, 443; 1563–6, pp. 20, 28, 39, 184, 488; Lansd. 8, f. 77. [3] Braddock, 133–4; *Surr. Rec. Soc.* xii. p. liv; *LP Hen. VIII,* x. [4] Elton, *Tudor Rev. in Govt.* 393; *LP Hen. VIII,* xviii, xix, xxi. [5] *CPR,* 1550–3, p. 227; 1553–4, p. 28; Elton, 390; E351/1795/6, 7, 11–19; *APC,* v. 28, 33. [6] *CPR,* 1547–8, pp. 404–5; 1550–3, p. 112; 1560–3, pp. 351, 614; *LP Hen. VIII,* xii, xiii, xvi, xvii; *VCH Berks.* iii. 127. [7] Req.2/18/1–3, 10, 4/244, 5/106; *LP Hen. VIII,* xiv, xv, xxi; Lansd. 3, ff. 29v, 150. [8] PCC 5 Babington; E150/824/1.

T.F.T.B.

WELLES, Alexander (by 1514–58), of Rye, Suss.

RYE 1545,[1] 1547[2]

b. by 1514. *m.* Joan, 1da.[3]
    Common clerk, Rye 1535–6, 1539–40, 1550, 1551–57, Winchelsea 1538, 1541–42; jurat, Rye 1544–58, mayor 1557–8; bailiff to Yarmouth 1555.[4]

Alexander Welles presumably had some legal training, for the common clerk of Rye also served as the town's recorder. He seems also to have been a plumber with an interest in iron-founding and in the supply of building materials. Much of his time was evidently spent on municipal business: he went to Romney to the Brotherhood of the Cinque Ports 17 times between 1535 and 1558, generally as part

of the delegation from Rye but three times as town (or common) clerk of Winchelsea. He also attended Guestlings and on 27 Apr. 1557 he was chosen at one of them to be Rye's solicitor with George Reynolds* to answer a writ of *quo warranto* directed to the Cinque Ports.[5]

If Welles's Membership of Parliament appears a natural extension of his local career, its timing may have owed something to his association with Sir Thomas Seymour II* and his lieutenant in the Ordnance office Francis Fleming*, under whom Welles took charge of the guns defending the town in the spring of 1545. For attending the Parliament of that year he and his fellow-Member Robert Wymond shared a payment of £12 (the full amount due at the standard rate) and in May 1546 Welles was also paid £2 'for the soliciting of the subsidy', that is, for ensuring that the customary proviso exempting the inhabitants of the Cinque Ports was included in the Subsidy Act. In the following Parliament, the first of Edward VI's reign, he sat with George Reynolds. During the second session both Members were active on the town's behalf. They petitioned the Protector, consulted the clerk of the Commons, the King's attorney, John Hales II*, and others on various matters, and obtained an exempting proviso for the town in the Relief Act (2 and 3 Edw. VI, c.36); they also paid for three bills to be drawn and copied, of which that for the towns of Rye and Winchelsea and for the casting of ballast into the Camber was enacted (2 and 3 Edw. VI, c.30), the second for the levying of fines in the Cinque Ports failed in the Lords and the third for iron mills does not appear to have been introduced. In the last session Welles paid 8s. to 'the clerk of the parliament house for a promise to take recognizances for keeping tippling houses', presumably in connexion with the bill passed for keepers of alehouses (5 and 6 Edw. VI, c.25), and £3 10s. for fish given to the learned counsel and other officers in the parliament house 'to make friends to speak for the . . . ports' in a matter no longer identifiable. Record of payments of wages to Welles survives for all but the opening session.[6]

It is almost certain that Rye re-elected Welles to the following Parliament but was over-ridden. On 10 Apr. 1553 he and Robert Wood were paid £3 'for the riding up and down to the Parliament' but on the following day Richard Fletcher and John Holmes I were paid £6 6s. for attending it. Although Fletcher and Holmes were clearly the Members returned, a list of burgesses for the Cinque Ports compiled from the collections of a 17th-century lieutenant of Dover Castle shows Welles and Wood as Rye's Members for this Parliament. That they were the town's own choice but were superseded by nominees of the lord warden, Sir Thomas Cheyne*, is borne out by his interference at Romney which resulted in a similar discrepancy between the names occurring on the later compilation and the name (only one survives) on the return.[7]

In 1537 Welles had been accused of heresy by the parish priest of Rye William Inold, being charged with saying that the blood of Christ was sufficient for salvation without any sacrament of unction. He denied the accusation, but when he came to make his will he renounced the doctrine of the mass by declaring his trust in the merits of Christ's passion and the offering of His precious blood 'once for all'. A year after his denial he and another townsman took up to Cromwell books and papers found in Inold's house. About the same time the bishop of Chichester was relieved to hear that Welles had not tried to sing any service openly in English and asked him to forbear such novelties until the King's pleasure was known. So enthusiastic a reformer must have welcomed the legislation carried during his second Membership. He and George Reynolds supervised the destruction of the painted glass and wall paintings in the parish church, 'cleansing the chancel from popery', and the provision of prayer books and a communion table. It is understandable that the accession of Mary saw the disappearance of Welles from the Commons.[8]

In August 1557 Welles was chosen mayor in defiance of an order from the Council for the re-election of George Reynolds; he was called before the Council although not dismissed from office. Two months later he was again summoned before the Council, and this time committed to the Fleet, 'for his refusal to appear before the commissioners for the loan [in Sussex] when they sent for him'; not long afterwards he was discharged, 'having a good lesson given him to beware of the like disobedience hereafter'. His stand for the exemption of Rye from loans as well as from subsidies seems nevertheless to have been successful: in January 1558 the Council thanked him and the jurats for their 'towardness' in providing ships (the traditional reason for the ports' exemption from taxation) and told them that in return the Queen would take no money from them by way of loan.[9]

Welles was re-elected mayor in 1558 but died before the end of the year. By the will which he made on 21 Sept. 1558 he left to the mayor and jurats 'all my books remaining at the vicarage', to be used by the vicars of Rye for ever, and to Robert Jackson, his successor as common clerk, 'all my papers, books and precedents in my closet'. He left to his wife all his lands and tenements for life and the custody of their grandson Alexander Sheppard until he was seven,

and to his grandson much of his household stuff and his cisterns and pipes of lead, his 'tons, coolbacks [coolers] and horsemills'. As executrix he named his wife and as overseer Robert Bennet, jurat of Rye. George Reynolds was one of the witnesses to the will which was proved on 28 Nov. 1558.[10]

[1] Rye chamberlains' accts. 5, f. 122. [2] Ibid. 5, ff. 184, 185v; Hatfield 207. [3] Date of birth estimated from first reference. PCC 1 Welles; Vis. Kent (Harl. Soc. lxxv), 111. [4] Rye chamberlains' accts. 5, 6 passim; Cinque Ports White and Black Bks. (Kent Arch. Soc. recs. br. xix), 219, 223-4, 229, 233, 242, 252, 256. [5] Rye chamberlains' accts. 5, f. 110v; Cinque Ports White and Black Bks. 219-56 passim. [6] APC, i. 163; Rye chamberlains' accts. 5, ff. 106v, 110v, 122, 123, 126v, 144v, 184, 185v, 186, 190, 218, 218v, 219, 222, 6. f. 39; Rye churchwardens' accts. 1513-70, f. 114. [7] Rye chamberlains' accts. 6, f. 56; Add. 34150. [8] SP1/113, f. 108v; LP Hen. VIII, xi, xiii; Elton, Policy and Police, 20, 86-90; PCC 1 Welles; Rye churchwardens' accts. 1513-70, f. 114. [9] APC, vi. 112, 166, 182, 185, 188, 238; Rye chamberlains' accts. 6, f. 165v. [10] PCC 1 Welles.

H.M.

WELLES, Humphrey (by 1502-65), of Hoar Cross, Staffs.

NEWCASTLE-UNDER-LYME 1545

b. by 1502, 1st s. of John Welles of Hoar Cross by Anne, da. (?illegit.) of John Fitzherbert of Norbury, Derbys. educ. I. Temple, adm. 1 Mar. 1522. m. by 1533, Mary, da. of William Chetwynd of Ingestre, Staffs., s.p. suc. fa. 4 May 1528.[1]

J.p. Staffs. 1538-d.; commr. musters 1539, relief 1550; other commissions 1539-51; escheator 1543-4, 1551-2, 1556-7; custos rot. in 1553; sheriff 1559-60; ?clerk of the summons, Exchequer by 1546; ?clerk, Tower I mint 1557-d.[2]

Humphrey Welles had both an uncle and a nephew who were namesakes and his career is not always easy to distinguish from theirs. That he was the Humphrey Welles admitted to the Inner Temple on 1 Mar. 1522 may be inferred from the fact that the sponsor was Thomas Bonham*, who as receiver-general of the duchy of Lancaster could have been expected to patronize the nephew of a duchy bailiff in the honor of Tutbury. Welles's start is also likely to have been smoothed by his kinship through his mother with Sir Anthony Fitzherbert, who became a judge in 1522: Fitzherbert probably belonged to Gray's Inn, as did his eldest son Thomas*, but a younger son William* was to attain prominence at the Inner Temple.[3]

Welles himself does not appear to have practised law but to have made his way as an administrator. He probably took service with a magnate although with whom is not clear. He could have been the servant whom Cromwell recommended for the King's service in 1538, and the result may have been a post in the Exchequer. At the shire election for Mary's first Parliament he and Sir George Griffith* were to try unsuccessfully to have the 1st Baron Stafford's son Sir Henry Stafford* elected. As Griffith and Thomas Fitzherbert had been returned for the shire on the occasion of Welles's own election for Newcastle-under-Lyme, it may be that Welles was then dependent on Lord Stafford and that he owed his adoption at Newcastle, a borough with which he had no known connexion, to that magnate's support: his fellow-Member Henry Broke was Griffith's brother-in-law. Another possible patron was William Paget. In 1563 Paget had a servant named 'Wellys' who had been with him for 19 years, that is, from the first years of Paget's establishment in Staffordshire; the appearance of Welles in November 1545 as Paget's deputy in connexion with the secretary's acquisition of Burton abbey may thus have come early in a long association, with Welles's Membership as one of its first results. A further possible connexion turns on the identification of Welles with the holder of a clerkship of the summons before the death of Henry VIII; it was almost certainly this official who was the servant of Sir Robert Southwell*, master of the rolls, admitted in 1548 to the freedom of London as a member of the Fishmongers' Company. Less doubt attaches to the identity of the clerk of the mint at the Tower, for when this office, which had been granted to Humphrey Welles in March 1557, was filled in 1569 it was with the fees due since the death of its holder.[4]

After having been restored to the Staffordshire bench under Elizabeth, and recommended by his bishop for retention in 1564 as 'better learned than the rest', Welles had died on 9 Sept. 1565, leaving property at Hoar Cross and over a dozen other parishes in Staffordshire. The heir was his brother Robert, whose age was given as over 40. Welles also held a lease of some houses in Fetter Lane, London. His will, made on 31 Aug. 1564, and proved at Lichfield on 29 Jan. 1566, mentioned property in Staffordshire which he had been administering for the daughters of a deceased brother Richard: he settled his own 'burgess lands at Newborough' on the same nieces. There were small bequests for the repair of seven bridges, including those at Tutbury and Yoxall; 5s. to poor prisoners in Stafford gaol; and 40s. to be divided among the poor of Abbots Bromley, Newborough, Tutbury and Yoxall. After legacies to a number of relatives, including his aunt, the widow of Sir Philip Draycott*, Welles left the residue of his goods to his wife and executrix. An inventory valued his property at £632. He was buried, as he had asked to be, under an alabaster monument in Yoxall church. Since the heir died childless, the lands descended to the younger Humphrey, son of Richard Welles.[5]

[1] Date of birth estimated from age at fa.'s i.p.m., *Wm. Salt Arch. Soc.* ii(2), 131; (ser. 3), 1912, p. 170; J. C. Wedgwood, *Staffs. Parl. Hist.* (Wm. Salt Arch. Soc.), i. 287 and n, 294n, 318–19; *Staffs. Rec.*

Soc. (ser. 4), viii, 172; Erdeswick, *Staffs.* 271n. [2] *LP Hen. VIII*, xiii, xiv, xviii, xx; *Wm. Salt Arch. Soc.* (ser. 3), 1912, p. 320; 1917, pp. 318–19; *Staffs. Rec. Soc.* 1938, p. 45; *EHR*, lxxviii. 228; *CPR*, 1547–8, p. 89; 1550–3, p. 142; 1553, p. 357; 1553–4, p. 24; 1555–7, p. 468; 1560–3, p. 442; 1563–6, pp. 41–42; 1566–9, p. 405; E405/115, m. 7; Stowe 571, f. 6; *Brit. Numismatic Jnl.* xlv. 70. [3] Somerville, *Duchy*, i. 548. [4] *LP Hen. VIII*, xiii; M. L. Robertson, 'Cromwell's servants' (Univ. California Los Angeles Ph.D. thesis, 1975), 585; *EHR*, lxxviii. 227–9; T. Pape, *Newcastle-under-Lyme*, 38; Staffs. RO, E.C.P. 2/2, no. 6, f. 1 ex inf. C. J. Harrison; *Staffs. Rec. Soc.* 1937, p. 187; City of London RO, Guildhall, rep. 11, f. 405; *CPR*, 1566–9, p. 405. [5] *Cam. Misc.* ix(3), 42–43; C142/143/41; *Wm. Salt. Arch Soc.* ii(2), 130–1; iii(2), 146; (ser. 3), 1917, p. 318n; *LP Hen. VIII*, xix; *CPR*, 1548–9, p. 391; 1554–5, p. 326; Pevsner, *Staffs.* 330.

N.M.F.

WELLES, John (by 1485–1515/18), of New Windsor, Berks.

NEW WINDSOR　1510,[1]　1512,[2]　1515[3]

b. by 1485, prob. *d.s.p.*[4]
　　Commr. gaol delivery, Windsor 1506, subsidy 1515; warden, guild of the Holy Trinity bef. 1511.[5]

Little has come to light about John Welles save that he had close ties with Windsor, at any rate during his later years. He probably lived there, to judge from his inclusion in the commission of gaol delivery in 1506 and from the pardon of 1511 to his successors as wardens of the guild of the Holy Trinity, a body identical in all but name with the town council. That Welles had property in the town is shown by the petition which his executor William Gretham addressed to Wolsey in Chancery before May 1518 claiming a tenement and various goods belonging to Welles, worth £10 a year, which had been seized by the mayor and bailiffs to meet unpaid debts.[6]

No widow or other relative is mentioned in Gretham's suit, so that it is unlikely that the Member left children, although his name was preserved at Windsor by an 18 year-old of the town admitted to King's College, Cambridge, as a scholar from Eton in 1547 and by men included in subsidy assessments there under Elizabeth. Among contemporaries elsewhere were an alderman of Norwich and a Staffordshire gentleman, as well as an official of the royal household who had sat for Bodmin in 1491. The presumed identification of this last with John Welles of Windsor appears to rest on his association in a grant of 1489 with a John Dalyland who was Welles's fellow warden of the Holy Trinity at Windsor, but Dalyland's name does not appear in that grant.[7]

The Members for Windsor in the first three Parliaments of Henry VIII are known only from a book of chamberlains' accounts or from transcriptions of these and other records, now lost, made by Elias Ashmole in the 17th century. Ashmole names Welles as a Member of the Parliament of 1510 with William Pury. His Membership of the next Parliament is attested both by Ashmole and by the chamberlains' accounts, which on 13 Jan. 1514 record the payment to Welles and Thomas Rider of 40s. for their expenses. It is not clear whether each was paid that sum, but if so the payment probably related to the second session of this Parliament, which lasted from 4 Nov. to 20 Dec. 1512. Ashmole records a further payment of 40s. to Rider and Welles during the sixth year of the reign (April 1514 to April 1515), while the chamberlains' accounts for that year include payments to them of 29s.6d., and 10s.4d.; these could equally well have been for either the third session of the Parliament of 1512 (23 Jan. to 4 Mar. 1514) or the first session of the next one (5 Feb. to 5 Apr. 1515). A surer sign that Rider and Welles had sat in both Parliaments is a sum of 14s. given to Rider and Welles 'in full payment', ascribed by Ashmole to the seventh year of the reign but entered in the chamberlains' accounts of the following year. Unless other payments went unrecorded it seems that the Members were given instalments at irregular intervals and that their remuneration fell far below the statutory rate of 2s. a day, not even reaching the reduced rate of 1s. which seems to have become established at Windsor by Mary's reign.[8]

[1] R. R. Tighe and J. E. Davis, *Windsor Annals*, i. 500. [2] Ibid. i. 465; Windsor recs. Wi/FA c.1, f. 6v. [3] Tighe and Davis, i. 474; Windsor recs. Wi/FA c.1, ff. 7v, 9v. [4] Date of birth estimated from first reference. C1/413/57. [5] CPR, 1494–1509, p. 487; Windsor Wi/FA c.1, f. 7; LP Hen. VIII, i. [6] VCH Berks. iii. 59–60; C1/413/57. [7] E179/74/217, 221, 233; HP ed. Wedgwood, 1439–1509 (Biogs.), 929; LP Hen. VIII, i; CPR, 1485–94, p. 293. [8] Tighe and Davis, i. 500; Bodl. Ashmole 1126, f. 23; Windsor recs. Wi/FA c.1, ff. 6v, 7v, 9v.

T.F.T.B.

WELPLEY, Thomas (c.1483–1534 or later), of Bath, Som.

BATH 1529

b. c.1483.[1]
Alderman, Bath by 1530, mayor c.1530.[2]

Thomas Welpley was a flourishing clothier in the last of the great days of the Bath cloth industry. (Whether he was related to George Whelplay, the London haberdasher turned professional informer, is not known.) He was assessed, as a parishioner of St. Michael's, Bath, for the subsidy of 1524 at £25 on goods, a sum well below that of the three most important Bath clothiers but one of the larger ones in the city. His election to Parliament was a natural extension of his civic career.[3]

In a Star Chamber case of 1534 Welpley deposed to the violent and threatening behaviour of William Crowche*, who had caused many quarrels and affrays among the citizens. His colleague in Parliament, John Bird, alleged that Crowche had been the

cause of Welpley's departure from Bath to Salisbury: he had used 'to make cloth and set the people of the said city in work' but had been so troubled by Crowche that he had left Bath, to his own and his workpeople's loss. It is probable, however, that deeper causes were behind Welpley's move. Writing about 1540 Leland remarked of the cloth industry at Bath that since the death of three great clothiers of the 1520s 'it hath somewhat decayed'. The centre of the broadcloth industry was moving east to Salisbury and its environs, and Welpley may have been swimming with the economic tide. He has not been traced at Salisbury or elsewhere, but his departure from Bath presumably means that he was not re-elected there in 1536 when the King asked for the return of the previous Members.[4]

[1] Aged 51 'or thereabouts' in 1534, Som. Rec. Soc. xxvii. 147. [2] Som. Rec. Soc. xxvii. 147. [3] Elton, St. Ch. Stories, 80–112; E179/142/1. [4] Som. Rec. Soc. xxvii. 146–7; Leland, Itin. ed. Smith, i. 143; G. D. Ramsay, The Wilts. Woollen Industry, 22–23.

R.V.

WELSBORNE, John (by 1498–1548), of Fulwell, Oxon. and London.

OXFORDSHIRE 1539[1]

b. by 1498, s. of Thomas Welsborne (?of Chipping Wycombe, Bucks.) by Margery, da. of Thomas Poure of Bletchingdon, Oxon. educ. ?Eton 1494; ?King's, Camb. 1498. m. lic. 1 Feb. 1546, Elizabeth, da. of one Lawrence of Fulwell, 2s.; 1s. illegit. Kntd. 30 Sept. 1544.[2]
Groom, the privy chamber June 1519, page in May 1520, gent. June 1530–d.; esquire of the body July 1528; receiver, duchy of Lancaster, honor of Pontefract, surveyor and collector, Knaresborough May 1520–July 1526; comptroller of customs, port of Bristol 1523; ambassador to King of France 1529–30; keeper of writs and rolls, ct. c.p. June 1532–d.; ranger, Groveley forest, Wilts. Oct. 1527; steward, former lands of Abingdon abbey Dec. 1539; various stewardships, Berks., Northants. and Oxon. 1538–d.; j.p. Northants. 1539–d., Berks. and Oxon. 1541–d.; commr. musters, Oxon. 1539, Berks. 1546, benevolence, Berks. 1544/45, chantries, Berks. and Hants 1546.[3]

The names of both John Welsborne's parents are known and the identity of his mother is clear, but it is not certain that his father was the Thomas Welsborne of Chipping Wycombe who had sat for that borough in 1478. If he was, Welsborne followed his father and grandfather into the royal household. Nothing certain is known of him before his appointment as a groom of the privy chamber in June 1519, although he may have been the Eton scholar of 1494.[4]

Successively groom, page and gentleman of the privy chamber, Welsborne received many leases, grants and appointments. In July 1521 he was granted the reversion to the keepership of the writs and rolls in the court of common pleas, the court of which his uncle Sir Robert Brudenell had recently become chief justice. The grant and the relationship to Brudenell and other leading lawyers might suggest that Welsborne had received a legal education at a time when there are gaps in the records of the inns of court, but the office, to which he did not succeed until June 1532 after the death of the holder Thomas Bonham*, could be exercised by deputy and a chancery case in which Welsborne later engaged over a sublease of Beckley Park, Oxfordshire, arising out of the deficiencies of a lease drawn up by himself, casts doubt on his legal knowledge. The office of customs comptroller in Bristol was granted to him in July 1523 with special licence to exercise it by deputy.[5]

In November 1529 Welsborne was named one of two commissioners to take an inventory of the possessions of the college founded by Cardinal Wolsey at Ipswich. It must therefore have been after this that he was sent as ambassador to the French King. Only two of his letters to Henry VIII have survived, one dating from May and the other from July 1530. It was in October 1530 that Sir Francis Bryan* succeeded Welsborne as ambassador resident with Francis I, but he may have begun to act some months earlier, for in July he wrote from Angoulême to the King on the same day as Welsborne. The shortness of Welsborne's embassy and the absence of his name from the diplomatic correspondence of the time suggest that he made little mark. He was probably overshadowed by Thomas Boleyn, Earl of Wiltshire, whom he calls his 'fellow'; Wiltshire had been sent on a special mission to France, Italy and the Emperor in connexion with the King's divorce, and was doubtless more in the King's confidence. Welsborne's inconspicuousness may have owed something to the ill-health and lack of funds which he complained of, but there is nothing to suggest that he was entrusted with business of any importance.[6]

In July 1532 Cromwell unsuccessfully recommended his 'very friend and fellow' Welsborne for the lease of Mixbury, Oxfordshire, a possession of Osney abbey. A few years later, after he had obtained a lease of Fulwell manor, Welsborne begged Cromwell to arrange for the next abbot to surrender the lordship of Mixbury and Fulwell to the King for regrant to himself, because 'it is liever to me than thrice the value thereof in any place in England'. In the event, Welsborne was not to obtain the two manors in fee simple until July 1541, when Cromwell was dead and the abbey's entire property was in the King's hands.[7]

Welsborne continued to serve at court, receiving regular New Year's gifts and attending such state occasions as the meeting with Francis I in October 1532, the christening of Prince Edward in October 1537 and the reception of Anne of Cleves in January 1540. He was mentioned in a letter of 1535 as one of the abbot of Abingdon's friends, and it was perhaps as such that he was made keeper of the site and lands of the abbey after its surrender to the crown in February 1538. He took charge of the destruction of the buildings and the removal of the lead, stone and other materials as well as the upkeep of the landed property pending the negotiation of new leases. Although his reports are void of religious or aesthetic scruple, his letters to Thomas Wriothesley, his 'bed-fellow' at court, show him in a more pleasing light than the continual begging letters to Cromwell. One of his duties was to replace the abbey's hospitality to the town; he estimated the cost of this at between £6 and £7 a week and reported the townsmen's satisfaction at his way of dispensing it.[8]

Welsborne had probably lived at Fulwell from the late 1520s; it lies in Oxfordshire, but on the border with Northamptonshire, the county in which he first became a justice of the peace. In the same year, 1539, he was returned as a knight of the shire for Oxfordshire with William Fermor. He probably owed this to his position at court and the patronage of Cromwell rather than to his local standing, although on his mother's side he was related to many neighbouring families. Between 1539 and his death Welsborne served on a number of commissions in Berkshire, no doubt in virtue of his stewardship of Abingdon and his property there. He continued to acquire leases and offices, among the former being a 21-year lease of East Grange in Pipewell, Northamptonshire; he subsequently became keeper of the site and lands of the dissolved abbey there.[9]

By 1543 Welsborne was a justice of the peace for three counties. He was appointed to raise 100 men for the French war in 1544, and served in 'the King's battle' with the relatively large retinue of 20 archers and 80 billmen. Eighty of these footmen remained with him in attendance on the King at Boulogne, where he was knighted on 30 Sept. 1544. He was assessed for the last subsidy of Henry VIII's reign, collected under Edward VI, on the sizeable figure of £200 in lands. He sued out a pardon at the accession and retained his post in the privy chamber. Re-appointed to his three commissions of the peace in May 1547, he died on 11 Apr. 1548, having made his will three weeks earlier.[10]

Welsborne had married—so far as is known for the first time—in February 1546. Inquisitions held in Yorkshire (where besides his duchy offices he had been granted lands formerly Viscount Lovel's) and Oxfordshire after his death gave his son and heir John's age as two years and two days, which if correct placed his birth barely two months after the marriage. The principal manors were to go to John, subject to the widow's life interest, with remainder to the second son Edward; the widow was also to continue to provide for an older but evidently illegitimate son Arthur, 'and to use him as she will her own'. Anthony Arden or Ardern, the testator's servant, received his lease of the duchy of Lancaster manor of Kirtlington. John Eyston received bequests including 'all such books as I have in my house at London'. This was presumably John Eyston of the family of East Hendred, Berkshire: either he or his son and namesake later married Jane Yate, then the widow of Welsborne's brother, Oliver. Eyston was asked, together with Sir Maurice Berkeley* and George Gifford*, who received small bequests, to assist the testator's wife as sole executrix. She later married Edward Chamberlain II* and after his death Richard Hussey*.[11]

[1] E159/319, brev. ret. Mich. r [1–2]. [2] Date of birth estimated from first certain reference. *Vis. Oxon.* (Harl. Soc. v), 209; *Vis. Berks.* (Harl. Soc. lvii), 224; *Marr. Lics. Fac. Off.* (Harl. Soc. xxiv), 6; *LP Hen. VIII*, xix. [3] *LP Hen. VIII*, iii–v, xiii–xxi; *CPR*, 1547–8, pp. 81, 87, 88; 1553–4, p. 62; Somerville, *Duchy*, i. 517, 526. [4] *Bucks. Recs.* vii. 393–4; PCC 16 Holder. [5] *LP Hen. VIII*, iii; M. Hastings, *Ct. Common Pleas in 15th Cent. Eng.* 133–6; C1/1087/16. [6] *LP Hen. VIII*, iv. [7] Ibid. v, xvi; SP1/72, f. 47, 126, f. 16; *VCH Oxon.* vi. 254. [8] HMC Bath, iv. 2; *LP Hen. VIII*, ix, xii; Browne Willis, *Mitred Abbeys*, i. 2; W. C. Richardson, *Ct. Augmentations*, 290; SP1/129, ff. 53, 126, 193, 221; 7, ff. 70, 71–73; Elton, *Policy and Police*, 79. [9] *LP Hen. VIII*, xiii, xiv, xvi, xvii; SP1/130, f. 95. [10] *LP Hen. VIII*, xviii, xix, xxi; E115/429/42; *CPR*, 1547–8, pp. 81, 87, 88; 1548–9, p. 148. [11] Wards 7/4/59 bis.; *LP Hen. VIII*, iv; PCC 16 Populwell; A. L. Humphreys, *East Hendred*, 103; *VCH Oxon.* vi. 222–3, 254. An incised slab set up in Mixbury church to Welsborne and his family has since been destroyed: the details of family history recorded from it by Rawlinson are clearly wrong, *Oxon Rec. Soc.* iv. 218; *VCH Oxon.* vi. 261.

D.F.C.

WELSCHE, Richard

DORCHESTER 1542*

On 18 Feb. 1544 'Richard Welsche' was elected a Member for Dorchester in place of Christopher Trenchard who had died. No one of that name is known to have had any personal link with the town, but Welsche may have been a kinsman of its high steward, Sir Thomas Trenchard, since the arms of Fyloll were quartered with those of Walshe (Welsche) during the 16th century and Trenchard's mother was a Fyloll. He could have been the Richard Walshe of Pilton, Devon, who made his will on 24 Dec. 1550 leaving household stuff and money to his only daughter, married to Robert Salusbury, and his stepson and daughter; the will was proved by his widow on 29 Apr. 1551. He was probably a relative of John Walshe*, who was connected by marriage with the Salusburys of Denbighshire and later in his

life with the Fylolls. One or other men of his name lived at Berkeley, Gloucestershire, in the 1530s, acquired the reversion to a manor in Herefordshire in 1544, and rented a chamber in the parish of St. Botolph without Aldgate in 1549.

C1/921/8–11; 219/18B/23; *Vis. Dorset* ed. Colby and Rylands, 39; Hutchins, *Dorset*, iii. 326; C. H. Mayo, *Recs. Dorchester*, 320; PCC 12 Bucke, 18 Daper; *LP Hen. VIII*, xiv, xix; *CPR*, 1549–51, p. 144.

H.M.

WELSCHE *see also* WALSHE, WELSHE

WELSHE (WALSHE), Hugh (by 1503–64), of Hereford.

HEREFORD 1553 (Mar.)[1]

b. by 1503. *m.* by 1524, Sybil (?Rees), at least 3s. 5da.[2] Mayor, Hereford 1531–2, 1537–8, 1544–5, 1554–5, alderman by 1559; commr. gaol delivery 1540.[3]

The parentage of Hugh Welshe has not been established but he could have belonged to the Gloucestershire family of that name and have been a kinsman of Anthony Welshe*. By trade a mercer (although also called scrivener by a local historian), he was assessed for subsidy in 1546 on goods worth £130. He also acquired considerable landed property in the shire. In or before 1542 he bought the manor of Lyre Ocle from Sir Philip Hoby* (who married the widow of Walter Walsh of Abberley, Worcestershire), two years later he added Sutton manor and in 1545 he and his son-in-law Thomas Smith paid £745 for Mansell and other properties; later he acquired moieties of two other manors.[4]

Welshe is known to have sat in only one Parliament, and that some 20 years after the first of his four mayoralties. During that time the city's representation appears to have rested with Thomas Havard and Richard Warnecombe and unless Welshe was elected in 1539, when the names are lost, it appears that he had to wait his turn until the beginning of 1553, when Havard, then mayor, probably stood down. Neither his choice on that occasion, nor his failure to secure re-election under Mary, need imply that he did not share Havard's conservatism in religion: he was to be mayor again in 1554–5 when his son-in-law Hugh Gebons was returned to the Parliament of 1555. In this respect the will which he made on 30 Nov. 1562 is unrevealing. He asked to be buried in Hereford cathedral 'nigh as convenient may be to the burial of my sons Richard and John' and left 3s.4d. for the repair of the cathedral and 2s. for forgotten tithes to the vicar of All Hallows, Hereford, besides sums for the poor and sick and for prisoners. He mentioned his three married daughters Elizabeth, Catherine and Anne, and one seemingly unmarried daughter

Margery, who was left an annuity of £8. He bequeathed to his wife Sybil his dwelling house in Hereford, another house in the city and some lands. The executors were his son and heir Edward and his sons-in-law Thomas Smith and Robert Saxsey, and the overseers a 'brother' Rowland Rees and another son-in-law William Cole. The will was proved on 27 Nov. 1565; the delay in doing so seems to have arisen from a doubt as to its eligibility to be proved in the prerogative court of Canterbury. Welshe died on 10 Jan. 1564, possessed of lands in the shire valued at more than £96 a year. Edward Welshe was then aged 39 years and more, and had a son Hugh for whose education the testator had made provision.[5]

[1] Hereford pub. lib., city muniments, bag 2 ex inf. Dr. M. G. Price. [2] Date of birth estimated from marriage. PCC 31 Morrison. [3] R. Johnson, *Anct. Customs, Hereford*, 233; *CPR*, 1558-60, p. 173; *LP Hen. VIII*, xv. [4] *Vis. Glos.* (Harl. Soc. xxi), 266; E179/117/162; *LP Hen. VIII*, xvii, xix, xx; *CPR*, 1553, p. 117; 1555-7, p. 497; Duncumb, *Herefs.* i. 126-7. [5] *HMC 13th Rep. IV*, 325; *CPR*, 1558-60, p. 173; 1563-6, p. 8; PCC 31 Morrison; Wards 7/10/60.

P.S.E.

WELSHE *see also* WALSHE, WELSCHE

WELSHOT, John (by 1473-1518/19), of Wells, Som.

WELLS 1510[1]

b. by 1473. *m.* by 1494, Isabel, 2s. 1da.[2]
Keeper, church goods, Wells 1499-1500, guild of the Holy Trinity 1503-4, altar of St. Catherine 1515-17, rent collector 1505-6, constable 1505-7, auditor 1507-d., member of the Twenty-Four by Oct. 1507-d., master 1509-10, 1515-16.[3]

The antecedents of John Welshot are obscure. He may have sprung from the family of that name in Bristol, but his only known relative, apart from his immediate kin, was his uncle Thomas Cornish, suffragan bishop of Tenos and precentor of Bath and Wells, who made him an executor of his will in 1513 and left him two tenements to found a chantry in the parish church of St. Cuthbert.[4]

Welshot was admitted to the freedom of Wells in 1494 without payment of a fine because he was married to the daughter of a burgess, and thereafter he stood surety for a number of other freemen. With Bishop Cornish and two others he was appointed executor of John Tyler† in 1512. Doubtless preoccupied with his own trade as a mercer, he did not at first readily accept civic office. In 1501 he would not pay the 20s. exacted for his refusal to become collector of the town rents. He swore that he had never wished to become a freeman and threatened to bring the matter before the King's Council. Such was his obstinacy that this item in the city's act book was subsequently struck through and a note added

that Welshot had been pardoned: and although this was followed by an ordinance that in future no one should be elected to the Twenty-Four unless he had previously acted as rent collector, Welshot's payment in the following year of 6s.8d. of the 20s. demanded led to the decision that service as chamberlain or rent collector should not be a condition of membership of the governing body. Welshot's own record during the next few years appears to reflect a change of heart in the matter. It was during his first term as master that he was elected to Parliament with John Mawdley I*, who had been master in the previous year. They were paid at the city's usual rate of 12d. a day 'and no more'. Both were replaced in the following two Parliaments and Welshot died before another was called.[5]

In his will of 26 Apr. 1518 Welshot made a number of religious bequests and provided money for obits at two altars in the parish church, where he wished to be buried near the altar of St. Catherine; he also left the commonalty a house and land in Wedmore for another obit. To his wife he bequeathed plate and £100 in money, together with land at Congresbury, a tucking mill and a tenement in Wells, all of which were to pass to his son William after her death; all other land, doubtless including long leases of the *Catherine Wheel* in the High Street and of property in Biddisham which Welshot had acquired in 1509 and 1511, went to William, who was named an executor with his mother. He left much plate and household ware, with sums of money, to this son and to another son and a daughter John and Julian, and to John a gold ring with a T surmounted by crown. John Coke of London, merchant taylor, and John Bonar of Wells, two of the overseers of the will, were appointed to act for the heir until he came of age. The will was proved on behalf of the widow on 16 June 1519, but the second probate was not obtained by William Welshot until 10 May 1532.[6]

[1] Wells act bk. 2, p. 258. [2] Date of birth estimated from admission as freeman. PCC 18 Ayloffe; *HMC Wells*, ii. 213. [3] Wells act bk. 2, pp. 213-91 passim. [4] PCC 12 Stokton, 18 Fetiplace, 30 Powell, 18 Ayloffe. [5] PCC 15 Fetiplace; *Wells City Chs.* (Som. Rec. Soc. xlvi), 162-3, 165, 167; Wells act bk. 2, pp. 204-91 passim. [6] PCC 18 Ayloffe; *HMC Wells*, ii. 213, ch. 736; Wells act bk. 2, p. 291.

M.K.D.

WENDON, John (by 1514-54), of Boston, Lincs.

BOSTON 1547[1]

b. by 1514. *m.* ?Alice, at least 2s. 1 da.[2]
Alderman, Boston 1545-d., mayor 1548-9; commr. sewers 1550; chief subsidy collector, wapentake of Skirbeck, Lincs. 1545, Boston 1546.[3]

John Wendon was probably a native of Boston, but nothing is known of his ancestry. He is to be distinguished from the John Wendons, father and son, of St. Mary Colchurch, London, of whom the elder, a grocer, died in 1543 and the younger was still alive in the reign of Elizabeth. In 1535 he sent Cromwell a fat swan and a fat crane, perhaps on behalf of the town, which had earlier sent similar gifts to Wolsey. Wendon was one of the most substantial men in Boston and, along with Nicholas Robertson, an important member of the staple of the town, he took the lead in drawing up a book of articles for incorporation. On 14 May 1545, when the charter was granted incorporating Boston as a borough with a mayor and 12 aldermen, Wendon was named one of the aldermen; according to the terms of the charter, the appointment was for life. On the following 9 Sept. he paid £4 to the court of augmentations on behalf of the corporation for some local property. In 1545–6 he was deputed by the subsidy commissioners for the parts of Holland as chief collector in the wapentake of Skirbeck, including Boston; his own assessment was 40s. on £30 in goods.[4]

The Parliament of 1547 was the first to be summoned after Boston had received its charter and the first to which it is known to have returned Members. Wendon probably sat in it from the outset, although the original return is lost and the Members for Boston are known only from a list revised in 1552. The other Member was William Naunton, a nominee of the Duchess of Suffolk, but no such influence from outside was necessary to the election of so prominent a townsman. During the life of the Parliament, which was not dissolved until 15 Apr. 1552, Wendon and Robertson acted on behalf of the corporation as the defendants in a protracted Star Chamber suit concerning the guild property which Boston had annexed at the time of its charter. The Journal is silent as to Wendon's role in the Commons but he was doubtless active in furthering a bill for the re-edifying of homes in Boston which was introduced in the fourth session but which failed of enactment. In 1548 he was elected mayor, in accordance with the town's decision to elect mayors from the list of original aldermen in the order in which they were named in the charter.[5]

Wendon made his will on 18 Nov. 1554 and it was proved on 3 Feb. 1555 in the consistory court of Lincoln. He asked to be buried in St. Botulph's, Boston, near to his wife. His will mentions some books in his study and his probate inventory, taken on 20 Dec. 1554, a pair of clavicords. His son and residuary legatee Nicholas may have been the Anglican rector, archdeacon and canon who later became a seminary priest.[6]

[1] Hatfield 207. [2] Date of birth estimated from first reference.

Lincoln consist. ct. wills 1554–6, ff. 182–2 v; G. Anstruther, *Seminary Priests*, i. 375. [3] *LP Hen. VIII*, xx; P. Thompson, *Boston*, 303, 454; Allen, *Lincs.* i. 234; E179/137/409, 430. [4] *LP Hen. VIII*, iv, viii, xviii, xx, xxi; *CPR*, 1548–9, p. 349; 1549–51, p. 198; 1557–8, pp. 9, 235; 1558–60, p. 379; PCC 21 Spert; St.Ch.3/8/18; E179/137/409, 430. [5] St.Ch.3/5/11, 8/18; *CJ*, i. 17; SP10/11/16; Thompson, 454. [6] Lincoln consist. ct. wills 1554–6, ff. 182–2 v; Anstruther, i. 375.

T.M.H.

WENDY, Thomas (1498/99–1560), of Haslingfield and Cambridge, Cambs. and London.

ST. ALBANS 1554 (Apr.)
CAMBRIDGESHIRE 1555

b. 1498/99, 2nd s. of John Wendy of Clare, Suff. *educ.* Gonville, Camb., BA 1518/19, MA 1522, MD 1526/27; Ferrara bef. 1527. *m.* (1) by 1541, Margaret, ?da. of one Butler, *s.p.*; (2) 13 June 1552, Margaret, da. of John Porter of London, wid. of Thomas Atkins of London.[1]

Physician to Queen Catherine Parr by Oct. 1546–8, to Henry VIII by 1547, to Edward VI 1547–53, to Mary 1553–8, to Elizabeth 1558–d.; fellow, college of physicians 22 Dec. 1551, elect 1552; pres. Gonville bef. 1559; j.p. Cambs. 1547, q. by 1554–d.; commr. to visit Eton and Cambridge Univ. 1548, goods of churches and fraternities, Cambridge 1550, 1553, relief, Cambridge and Cambs. 1550.[2]

Thomas Wendy came of a Suffolk yeoman family, whose earlier provenance, as its name suggests, was probably Wendy in Cambridgeshire. The modesty of his origin is attested by the bequests in Wendy's will 'to my poor kinsfolk in Suffolk'. After taking his arts degree in 1522 Wendy probably studied medicine at Ferrara until 1527, when he was again at Cambridge; he had leave of absence for the year 1527–8, perhaps for the purpose of further foreign travel. Another bequest in Wendy's will seems to reflect early experience of Venice: he gave 'to one Aurelius of Venice whose father was called Battista a bookbinder sometime dwelling in Venice aforesaid at the sign of the Anchor in the Mercerie a sovereign of two angels if he be living'. Wendy was a fellow of Gonville Hall for his whole adult life and its president at some date before the rule of Dr. Caius began in 1559. No doubt his connexion with the university determined his choice of Haslingfield, Cambridgeshire, as his principal residence; he does not seem to have been active in university life, however, and obtained in 1538–9 licence dispensing him from lecturing in medicine or the arts except at his option.[3]

Wendy's medical practice was lucrative, his patients being drawn largely from the peerage or the royal family. His services were retained by Henry Percy, 5th Earl of Northumberland as early as July 1534, when he obtained an annuity of £3 6s.8d. from Fountains abbey, Yorkshire, the grant being made at the instance of the earl, a benefactor of the abbey. Wendy was employed by Northumberland in a number of other capacities. In March 1535 he executed with the earl a deed transferring the Percy lands in Sussex to the crown. He carried a number of letters from the earl to Cromwell in 1536 and 1537 and attended him at Hackney in his last illness in June 1537. Wendy also received from the earl an annuity of £40 and a lease of two Yorkshire manors granted in March 1535 and still subsisting in 1559; this lease was virtually a gift for term of years, since the manors were valued in 1535 at £41 4s. a year and the annual rent payable by Wendy was a mere 6s.8d. The earl also tried unsuccessfully to secure Wendy grants of ex-monastic lands at Ickleton and Royston, Cambridgeshire. Wendy remembered the earl with gratitude and left his nephew Thomas Percy*, 1st Earl of the new creation, in his will a silver ewer and basin 'in remembrance of such benefits which I have received at the hands of my very good lord and late master the late earl of Northumberland his uncle'.[4]

Wendy bought the manor and advowson of Haslingfield in June 1541 and settled it on himself and his wife, the feoffees including William Paget. The two men seem to have had a long friendship. Paget sent both his sons to Gonville Hall, where they must have come under Wendy's influence; it is even possible that Wendy introduced Paget to his wife, for he bequeathed Lady Paget his lands at Coton and Whitwell, Cambridgeshire, 'as a poor token of the good will which I have ever borne to her lady-ship and in remembrance that in that place she had her first acquaintance with my lord her husband'. Wendy may have shared Paget's early Protestant sympathies; he is said by Foxe to have helped frustrate a scheme by Chancellor Wriothesley and Stephen Gardiner to have Queen Catherine Parr condemned for heresy, and Gonville Hall was at that time known as a stronghold of the reformers. Wendy was summoned to court in March 1546, perhaps to attend on the Queen; he was appointed her physician before October 1546, when he received a further grant of Haslingfield land, in return for the surrender of his £40 annuity from Northumberland. Most of the Percy lands were by then vested in the crown, which thus obtained exoneration from the payment of Wendy's annuity. Paget may have helped Wendy to this royal appointment, which in turn led to his being made physician to the King, whom he attended in his last illness; in that capacity he witnessed the King's will, under which he received a legacy of £100. William Butts, physician to Henry VIII until his death in November 1545, was a fellow of Gonville Hall and may have recommended Wendy to the King.[5]

Wendy was re-appointed royal physician for life in March 1547. In the same year he began his public service, which comprised numerous commissions in Cambridgeshire and elsewhere. The tempo of his land purchases increased; in September 1547 he took a 30-year lease of the bishop of Hereford's mansion adjoining Old Fish Street in London. He purchased, in January 1549, the fee simple in numerous ex-chantry lands in Cambridgeshire and Essex. In May 1550 there followed a similar purchase of two manors and an advowson in Cambridgeshire, worth £55 a year; the Privy Council ordered the chancellor of the court of augmentations to complete the sale for £400 cash and—an unusual concession—to accept the rest of the £1,118 purchase price by instalments over four years. Wendy's last important purchase in Edward VI's reign brought him the manors of Ditton Valence, Cambridgeshire, and Kingsbury, Hertfordshire—his only known connexion with the latter county. The terms were even more favourable this time, for Wendy paid only £72 10s. to the crown for lands valued at £33 12s.6d. a year, or in capital value, at 20 years' purchase, at more than £600, the difference being treated as a gift to Wendy by the crown in consideration of his services. Wendy's remaining large purchases (in the following reign) may be noted here: in September 1553 he had licence to buy from the 9th Lord Clinton the conventual buildings of Barnwell priory, Cambridgeshire, and in October 1558 he paid the crown £300 for the fee simple in the manor of Chatteris, in the same county. On one occasion he was accused by Edward Slegge* of making an improper use of his influence to obtain an augmentations grant of Cambridgeshire lands.[6]

The generally poor health of the monarchs whom he served from 1546 onwards must have redounded to Wendy's advantage. His election to the second and fourth Marian Parliaments was doubtless the result of royal nomination, for, whatever his religious views, he was hardly likely to act or vote in Parliament in a way repugnant to a sovereign on whom he depended so entirely and with whom he was in such frequent and intimate contact. To his first seat, St. Albans, Wendy may have been helped by Paget and by the young Henry Parker, a former student at Gonville Hall, son of Sir Henry Parker*. The Parkers were a family of standing and influence in Hertfordshire and their backing, combined with the royal support, must have sufficed to obtain Wendy his election although it is possible that his first wife was related to another leading Hertfordshire family, the Butlers of Watton at Stone. Moreover, John Maynard, first steward of St. Albans and one of its Members in the previous and succeeding Parliaments, had a 61-year lease of the timber and wood of Wendy's manor of Kingsbury in February 1556, perhaps in reward for his support of Wendy's candidature. By 1555 Wendy was a considerable landowner in his adoptive county of Cambridge; this fact and his standing in the university city must have offset his modest birth. Although he had been active earlier in connexion with the Act touching the incorporation of physicians (1 Mary st.2, c.9), he is not known to have played any such part when himself a Member although he doubtless lent his support to the Act 'that purveyors shall not take victuals within five miles of Cambridge and Oxford' (2 and 3 Phil. and Mary, c.15), which principally affected the universities and their students.[7]

Wendy attended Queen Mary on her deathbed, as he had her father and brother. He sued out a pardon on the accession of Elizabeth, was reappointed royal physician, but died in London on 11 May 1560 and was buried at Haslingfield 16 days later. By a will made earlier in the year he provided 40s. for annual distribution to the poor of Haslingfield 'to pray for my soul and for the soul of my first wife'. Most of his lands, including six manors in Cambridgeshire, Essex and Hertfordshire, went, after a life interest to his wife, to his nephew and eventual heir Thomas Wendy; there were remainders in favour of a stepson of Wendy's and two of Paget's sons. Gonville and Caius College was left Haslingfield rectory, and directed to let it to Wendy's nephew for £10 a year. In addition to Lord and Lady Paget and the Earl of Northumberland he also remembered Anthony Browne II*, (Sir) Henry Percy*, Sir Humphrey Radcliffe* and Richard Weston*. Wendy left the residue of his personal estate to his 'right entirely beloved wife', appointing her sole executrix, and naming four assistants or overseers. One of these was 'my friend Mr. Nicholas Purslow* of the Inner Temple of London', to whom Wendy left £10 and a piece of plate 'in some part of recompense for his great pains taking for me in many of my causes and matters'. His immediate heir was his brother, John, then aged 50.[8]

[1] Aged 61 at death, W. Munk, *Roll of R. Coll. of Physicians*, i. 50. *N. and Q.* cc. 278, 329; J. Venn, *Gonville and Caius Biog. Hist.* i. 24; PCC 35 Mellershe; *Vis. Cambs.* (Harl. Soc. xli), 40; *DNB*. [2] *LP Hen. VIII*, viii, xxi; Munk, i. 50; *CPR*, 1547–8, pp. 81, 102, 369; 1550–3, p. 395; 1553, pp. 352, 362, 417; 1553–4, pp. 17, 28; 1558–60, p. 177. [3] *Luard Mems.* (ser. 3), *Grace Bk. B.* ii. 134, 140, *Grace Bk.*, 230, 340. [4] *LP Hen. VIII*, viii, xi, xii; PCC 35 Mellershe; E403/2448, ff. 59v, 60; J. M. W. Bean, *Estates of the Percy Fam. 1416–1537*, pp. 145–6. [5] *LP Hen. VIII*, xvi, xxi; Foxe, *Acts and Mons.* v. 557–9; Venn, 17. [6] *CPR*, 1547–8, pp. 102, 321–4; 1549–51, p. 339; 1550–3, p. 405; 1553, p. 197; 1553–4, p. 353; 1557–8, pp. 450–1; *APC*, ii. 432; E405/212; St.Ch.4/2/54; C1/1382/25. [7] Venn, 28; G. Clark, *R. Coll. of Physicians*, i. 72. [8] Munk, 50; *CPR*, 1558–60, p. 177; *Machyn's Diary* (Cam. Soc. xlii), 235–6; PCC 35 Mellershe; E150/104/6; *VCH Cambs.* iv. 105.

D.F.C.

WENMAN, Richard (1524–73), of Witney, Oxon.

NORTHAMPTON 1547

b. April 1524, 1st s. of Sir Thomas Wenman* of Witney by Ursula, da. and h. of Thomas Gifford of Twyford, Bucks. *educ.* ? Corpus, Oxf. 1540/41. *m.* by 1547, Isabel, da. and event. coh. of Sir John Williams*, Lord Williams of Thame, 3s. inc. Thomas[†] 2 or 3da. *suc.* fa. 8 Aug. 1557. Kntd. 6 Sept. 1566.[1]

J.p. Oxon. 1561–d.; sheriff, Oxon. and Berks. 1563–4, Oxon. 1571–2.

Richard Wenman's father held a lease of the parsonage at Evenley, Northamptonshire, and would inherit Hellidon from the Giffords, while his family's relationship and association with the Fermors, another family of Witney origin which had risen largely through the wool trade, brought him into alliance with the predominant group in the shire. The Wenmans' own continued interest in the wool trade may also have given Richard a link with Northampton itself, but he probably owed his return to the Parliament of 1547 for a borough which at this period customarily chose residents to the influence of his father-in-law. Sir John Williams, who himself sat in this Parliament for Oxfordshire, secured the return of his eldest son Henry for Northamptonshire and probably contributed to that of his other son-in-law Henry Norris for Berkshire: like Wenman, both were inexperienced youngsters. Norris was himself further related to Wenman through the marriage of his aunt Elizabeth Norris of Yattendon, Berkshire, to William Fermor*.[2]

Nothing is known of Wenman's role in the Commons and little of his life thereafter. His father-in-law rallied to Mary in the succession crisis of 1553 and his father (who had suffered outlawry earlier in the same year) was knighted on the day after the coronation, but Richard Wenman was not to sit in Parliament again either in this or the succeeding reign, when his appointment to the commission of the peace and two shrievalties presumably signalized his succession to his parents' lands and, through his wife, to a moiety of the Williams inheritance. In 1564 the archbishop of Canterbury reported on the Oxfordshire gentry but could do no more than list those, including Wenman, who had been commended to him with the observation, 'I know them not'. Wenman received his own knighthood during the Queen's visit to his brother-in-law Norris's house at Rycote. He died in March 1573 leaving the estates which he had consolidated by judicious sale and purchase to his eldest son Thomas, then aged 25. His widow erected a monument to him in Twyford church, Buckinghamshire and later married Richard Huddlestone of Little Haseley, Oxfordshire.[3]

[1] Date of birth estimated from age at fa.'s i.p.m., E150/821/14-15. *Vis. Oxon.* (Harl. Soc. v), 178-9; F. G. Lee, *Thame*, 433-6; Lipscomb, *Bucks.* iii. 136; Corpus visus bk. (unpaginated). [2] Bridges, *Northants.* i. 167; *APC*, iv. 243; Baker, *Northants.* i. 396-7. [3] *APC*, iv. 243; *VCH Bucks.* iv. 255; *Cam. Soc.* ix(3), 81; J. Nichols, *Progresses Eliz.* i. 250; C142/163/5; *CPR*, 1553-4, p. 374; 1558-60, pp. 73, 448; 1560-3, p. 134; 1569-72, p. 139; Lipscomb, iii. 136; *VCH Oxon.* vii. 177; Pevsner, *Bucks.* 271.

S.M.T.

WENMAN, Sir Thomas (by 1504-57), of Witney, Oxon.

OXFORDSHIRE 1555

b. by 1504, 1st s. of Richard Wenman of Witney by Anne, da. of John Bushe of Northleach, Glos. *educ.* I. Temple, adm. 1523. *m.* by 1523, Ursula, da. and h. of Thomas Gifford of Twyford, Bucks., 6s. inc. Richard* 3 da. *suc.* fa. 4 Oct. 1534. Kntd. 2 Oct. 1553.[1]
Commr. tenths of spiritualities, Oxon. 1535, musters 1542, relief 1550; j.p. 1536-*d.*; escheator, Oxon. and Berks. Jan.-Nov. 1539.[2]

Sir Thomas Wenman's father was a prosperous Witney clothier and merchant of the staple, the family name being traditionally derived from the wains in which the cloth was driven to London. Wenman inherited a manor at Caswell, besides Witney park and many burgages in Witney town, and his father also left him 2,000 marks in a will remarkable for its lengthy and detailed arrangement for alms and masses. A provision for masses to be said at Eton suggests that Wenman may have been educated there, as were at least two of his descendants later in the century. He was admitted to the Inner Temple during the Lent vacation of 1523 but exempted from all offices and licensed to absent himself at pleasure.[3]

At about this time he increased the property and dignity of his family (his mother was a yeoman's daughter and his father had been granted arms only in 1509) by his marriage to the daughter of Thomas Gifford, into whose estates he entered in 1551. Between 1542 and 1546 Wenman purchased manors at Dymock and Little Rissington, Gloucestershire, and Eaton Hastings, Berkshire, acquisitions in lands which must have offset his family's losses in goods when Calais fell in 1558. Although never chosen sheriff, he played a leading part in county affairs. He was one of the Oxfordshire gentlemen on whose aid the government intended to call at the time of the Pilgrimage of Grace, and he provided ten footmen for the vanguard of the army in France in 1544. In 1539 he was appointed to attend the reception of Anne of Cleves and in 1546 that of the Admiral of France.[4]

A sign of Wenman's standing in the county was the marriage of his son Richard to one of the two daughters and eventual coheirs of Sir John Williams*. Williams played a leading role in securing the succession of Mary and the force which he raised to that end probably included Wenman, who was knighted on the day after Mary's coronation. Like Williams, Wenman had a personal grudge against the Dudleys for in 1551 Sir Andrew Dudley* had been granted lands in Oxfordshire including the borough of Witney, thus becoming Wenman's landlord and the most powerful personage in the region where Wenman had been pre-eminent. It may well have been against Dudley or his brother the Duke of Northumberland that Wenman directed the 'slanderous reports' for which he was summoned before the Privy Council in the winter of 1551 and outlawed early in 1553. Wenman was returned as senior knight of the shire in 1555 in succession to Williams who had been raised to the peerage in 1554, and another kinsman by marriage, Sir Leonard Chamberlain, who was occupied as governor of Guernsey; the sheriff, Sir Richard Brydges*, was also a distant kinsman by marriage. Wenman died on 8 Aug. 1557.[5]

[1] Date of birth estimated from age at fa.'s i.p.m., E150/805/2. *Vis. Oxon.* (Harl. Soc. v), 178-9; F. G. Lee, *Thame Church*, 433-6; E150/821/14-15. [2] *Oxf. Recs.* 130; *LP Hen. VIII*, xv, xvii; *CPR*, 1547-8, pp. 75, 77; 1553, p. 357. [3] Lee, 439; *CPR*, 1494-1509, p. 510; PCC 21 Hogen. [4] *LP Hen. VIII*, i, xi, xiv, xvii, xix, xxi; Lee, 433; *CPR*, 1550-3, p. 39. [5] *CPR*, 1550-3, pp. 153-4; *APC*, iii. 428; iv. 97, 130, 141, 175, 187, 208, 243; W. K. Jordan, *Edw. VI*, ii. 433; E150/821/14-15.

A.H.

WENTWORTH, Michael (by 1512-58), of Whitley, Yorks., Mendham, Suff. and Cannon Row, Westminster, Mdx.

MIDHURST 1554 (Apr.)

b. by 1512, 2nd s. of Thomas Wentworth of Wentworth Woodhouse, Yorks. by Beatrice, da. of Sir Richard Woodruffe of Woolley, Yorks. *m.* (1) by 1542, Isabella (b. 1524), da. and h. of Percival Whitley of Whitley, 3s. 5da.; (2) July/Nov. 1556, Agnes, wid. of Roger More of Bicester, Oxon. and Thomas Curzon of Waterperry, Oxon., *s.p.*[1]
Clerk of the kitchen by 1533, chief clerk 1540; master of the Household by Aug. 1546-Jan. 1558, cofferer Jan. 1558-*d.*; steward, Langton in the Wold, Yorks. 1536, Catton and Pocklington, Yorks. 1540, Castle Sowerby, Penrith and Scotby, Cumb. 1542; gen. receiver and surveyor, Eye and Westhorpe, Suff. and other crown lands 1545.[2]

A well connected younger son, Michael Wentworth probably owed his steady rise in the royal household to his kinship with Sir Thomas Wentworth I*, 1st Lord Wentworth, himself a follower of the Duke of Suffolk. First mentioned as clerk of the kitchen at the coronation of Anne Boleyn, whom he was appointed to attend at the banquet 'to see that nothing be embezzled' from the dressers, Wentworth was promoted to the chief clerkship in the re-organization of 1540, when Suffolk became head of the Household as lord great master. Four years later, when Suffolk commanded the army which captured Boulogne, Wentworth led the household contingent which accompanied the King and he spent most of the summer in the field. Suffolk's death in August 1545 was followed by Wentworth's appointment as general receiver of the lands in Suffolk and else-where which the duke had ceded to the King in 1536, and within a year he had become one of the three masters of the Household.[3]

It was in the duke's, and Lord Wentworth's, shire that Wentworth was to make his own main invest-ment in land; he did not add to the lands in York-shire which his first wife brought to their marriage but he acquired the site and some of the lands of Mendham priory, and several manors in Essex. His second wife, who had previously married in succes-sion two of Wentworth's colleagues in the House-hold, brought him lands in Oxfordshire, a London house, and the wardship of her young children. Wentworth's last purchase was of a large house in Cannon Row, adjoining Whitehall, for which he paid £600 in February 1558. This followed im-mediately upon, and may have been connected with, his final promotion, to the post of cofferer of the Household.[4]

Wentworth's election to Mary's second Parlia-ment was clearly a by-product of his official career. The borough of Midhurst belonged to Wentworth's distant kinsman (Sir) Anthony Browne I*, to whom he could have been recommended by more than one of his associates: by Browne's grandfather Sir John Gage*, the lord chamberlain, by Gage's son James, the second master of the Household, or by Edward Shelley, the third master, another Sussex man. (In the next Parliament, and again in 1558, one of the Members for Midhust was another household official, Thomas Harvey, whom Wentworth called 'cousin' and appointed to oversee his will.) Went-worth's Membership of this brief Parliament has left no trace but his official standing and future promotion imply that he supported the government. One of his fellow-Members was Leonard West (q.v.), whose dispute with William Gascoigne, a kinsman of both, he sought to compose in 1555.[5]

Wentworth died on 13 or 20 Oct. 1558; the inquisitions taken on his lands give different dates, but the earlier one perhaps agrees better with his burial in St. Margaret's, Westminster, on 23 Oct., performed with much ceremonial and attended by many of the Queen's servants. By his will of 12 Oct. Wentworth had bequeathed to his wife Agnes the greater part of his lands in Essex, Oxfordshire,

Suffolk and Yorkshire, with the profits from the sale of wool and of coal from his mines in the north; to his heir Thomas, then aged 17, all the goods in his mansions in Suffolk and Cannon Row; and to his younger sons Michael and Henry the profit of the alnagership at York. His five daughters were each to receive £100 on marriage, with a further £100 going to whichever of them married his ward Richard Freeston, the son of his predecessor as cofferer. He named as executors his nephew Thomas Wentworth (whose grandson was to become 1st Earl of Strafford) and Nicholas Denham and as the second overseer his brother Thomas.[6]

[1] Date of birth estimated from first reference. *Vis. Yorks.* (Harl. Soc. xvi), 346; PCC 9 Powell, 26 More, 2 Welles; *Surtees Soc.* cvi. 241; *CPR*, 1555-7, p. 508; *Vis. Oxon.* (Harl. Soc. v), 56; *Misc. Gen. et Her.* (ser. 3), i. 209; E150/249/12, 14, 653/6; Leeds univ. lib. Wentworth-Woolley M41-43 ex inf. Dr. C. E. Challis. [2] *LP Hen. VIII*, vi, x, xvi, xvii, xix, xx; *Yorks. Arch. Soc. rec. ser.* lxiii. 129n. [3] R. C. Braddock, 'R. household, c.1540-60' (Northwestern Univ. Ph.D. thesis, 1971), 50-51, 94; *LP Hen. VIII*, xix, xx. [4] *CPR*, 1550-3, p. 380; 1553-4, p. 203; 1554-5, p. 325; 1557-8, pp. 257, 425, 442; PCC 9 Powell, 26 More. [5] PCC 2 Welles; Req.1/10, f. 15v; 2/23/110, f. 20. [6] E150/249/12, 653/6; *Machyn's Diary* (Cam. Soc. xlii), 176-7; PCC 2 Welles.

R.J.W.S.

WENTWORTH, Sir Thomas I (by 1500-51), of Nettlestead, Suff. and Westminster, Mdx.

SUFFOLK 1529*

b. by 1500, 1st s. of Sir Richard Wentworth, *de jure* 5th Lord le Despenser, of Nettlestead, by Anne, da. of Sir James Tyrrell† of Gipping, Suff. *m.* by 1524, Margaret da. of Sir Adrian Fortescue of Shirburn and Stonor, Oxon., 8s. inc. Sir Thomas II* 9da. Kntd. 1 Nov. 1523; *suc.* fa. 17 Oct. 1528; *cr.* Lord Wentworth of Nettlestead 2 Dec. 1529.[1]

J.p. Suff. 1523-*d.*; commr. subsidy 1523, 1524, coastal defence 1539, benevolence 1544/45, musters 1546, relief, London, Suff., royal household 1550; other commissions, Suff. and eastern counties 1534-45; member, household of Duke of Suffolk by 1524-?8; PC by 7 Aug. 1549; chamberlain, the Household Feb. 1550-*d.*[2]

Thomas Wentworth's family, whose ancestors were of Wentworth Woodhouse, Yorkshire, had acquired Nettlestead by a mid 15th century marriage with the Despensers: his father Sir Richard, who served twice as sheriff of Norfolk and Suffolk, also owned land in Cambridgeshire, Essex, Kent, Lincolnshire and Yorkshire. The first known reference to Thomas Wentworth concerns his service in 1523 under the Duke of Suffolk in the French campaign, when he was knighted at the surrender of Roye. He may have been already a member of Suffolk's household, for in the following year, as a commissioner for the subsidy levied upon it, he returned himself second on the list with an assess-ment of £50.[3]

On the death of his father in 1528 Wentworth succeeded to Nettlestead with five other Suffolk manors lying northwest of Ipswich, and five manors in Yorkshire; he was also to enjoy rights in Kentish and Lincolnshire property after feoffees had taken the profits for ten years. The following year saw his only known return to Parliament, although he may have sat in 1523, when the names of the Suffolk knights of the shire are lost. Returned in the autumn of 1529, he was not to sit in the Commons for more than a few weeks after the Parliament opened on 3 Nov.; one of the four Members elevated to baronies, perhaps *par parole*, early in the session, he took his seat in the Lords on 2 Dec. Three years later Cromwell put forward Arthur Hopton (q.v.) as Wentworth's replacement in the Commons, but the outcome of the by-election is not known. The Thomas Wentworth, whose nomination as one of the knights for Yorkshire was passed over in favour of Sir John Neville II* at the same time, was a distant kinsman.[4]

Wentworth may have owed his ennoblement to his close association with the Duke of Suffolk. His attendance in the Lords was erratic until the accession of Edward VI, and he was absent from the House for an entire session in 1533 and while the attainder of his father-in-law was under review in 1539. Little has come to light about his part in its proceedings. In 1529 he was one of the signatories to the draft of a measure to resolve problems arising from uses. He signed six Acts passed during the third session of the Parliament of 1547 and the bill assuring lands to the city of London which was to be enacted a year after his death. His career was to show him as a constant supporter of government policies, whatever their religious implications. In 1530 he was one of those who signed the letter to Clement VII asking for the pope's consent to the royal divorce. He took part in the impeachment of both the Queens and all the noblemen brought to trial from 1536 onwards. His decision against Anne Boleyn may not have been without bias as he was a cousin of Jane Seymour. On the outbreak of rebellion in the summer of 1536 he was ordered to attend the King with 100 of his men and in the following October the 3rd Duke of Norfolk asked the King to empower Wentworth 'to take the chief rule' in Suffolk during his own absence in the north. A year later he attended the christening of Prince Edward, handing the water to the godfathers, Cranmer and Norfolk. Present at the reception of Anne of Cleves in January 1540, he was host to the King and Catherine Howard at Nettlestead later in the same year. In 1543 he campaigned in the Netherlands and in 1544 in France.[5]

From 1523, when Wentworth had first been put on the Suffolk bench, he was in local management.

It was perhaps in return for some favour from Cromwell that in 1531 Wentworth gave him an annuity of £5 from the manor of Nettlestead. He corresponded on a number of topics with Cromwell, to whom he was to write as late as February 1540, 'I shall not fail to favour whomsoever you shall hereafter command me to befriend'. In 1538 a certain William Lawrence reported to the minister that Wentworth had helped in the secret transport of an image of the Virgin Mary by ship to London and that he had done much good in quietening controversies in Ipswich, ordering their instigators to reform and to 'speak the sincere gospel'. In the same year Wentworth himself wrote to Cromwell, as founder in blood of the Greyfriars of Ipswich, to object to the friars' sale of their plate and jewels: the order, he declared, was 'neither stock nor graft which the heavenly Father had planted, but only a hypocritical seed planted of . . . the bishop of Rome', adding that he had purchased the site of the priory for himself and his heirs. Wentworth's religious views influenced the careers of two men who were to become notable Protestant preachers and writers. It was at his request that in 1538 the parishioners of St. Lawrence, Ipswich, appointed the newly ordained Thomas Becon as priest of the chantry of Edmund Daundy*; Wentworth described Becon to Cromwell as a man 'well learned, a true preacher of the word of God, a great setter forth . . . of the King's most just and lawful title of supremacy, approved by God's word'. John Bale, later a prebendary of Canterbury and bishop of Ossory, must have known Wentworth while a friar in Ipswich; in his writings he acknowledged that Wentworth had brought about his conversion. Wentworth's official attitude towards dissent may have caused him some heart searchings, and Foxe was probably right when he described, in his account of the trial of two Protestant martyrs at Ipswich in 1545, how after giving judgment for burning Wentworth 'did shroud himself behind one of the posts of the gallery and wept' during its execution.[6]

With the succession of Edward VI Wentworth could look forward to advancement as a kinsman of the Protector Somerset and a friend of reform. In accordance with the late King's wishes he received the stewardship of all the lands of the bishop of Ely in Norfolk and Suffolk; he was also given temporary custody of the younger children of the Earl of Surrey. When the crisis came in 1549, however, it was not Somerset but the Earl of Warwick whom Wentworth followed. He accompanied the Marquess of Northampton in the first attempt to suppress Ket's rebellion and he sat on the commission which subsequently tried prisoners at Yarmouth. He was admitted to the Privy Council somewhat earlier than his first recorded appearance at its meeting of 9 Oct. 1549, for on the previous 7 Aug. he had joined with Somerset and others in signing a letter to the mayor of Southampton about a prize court case, but his allegiance to Warwick is proved by his inclusion among the six lords appointed on 15 Oct. to be governors of the King's person and education. He was also made one of a quorum of two among the group of Councillors responsible for the finances of the Household and the army, a commitment which was to be followed by his appointment as chamberlain of the Household in succession to the 12th Earl of Arundel, who had sided with Somerset. He held this post for little more than a year before his death in 1551.[7]

Wentworth had shown no personal interest in acquiring monastic property, except for the Blackfriars at Ipswich and a lease for 21 years from March 1537 of Newsom manor in Lincolnshire. In April 1550 he was granted the lordships and manors of Hackney and Stepney, valued at over £245 yearly, and two months later, in recognition of his service under two monarchs, the former abbot's house at Westminster. He died in the palace at Westminster on 3 Mar. 1551 and was buried in great state in the abbey. According to Edward VI all but one of his 17 children survived Wentworth. By a will made on 16 May 1544 he had left marriage portions of 200 marks to his nine daughters and £10 yearly to his seven younger sons on their majority. These bequests were payable from manors in Lincolnshire and Yorkshire. Wentworth left to his wife for life all the manors (unspecified) which he had acquired from Nicholas Astley, clerk, and a share of all household goods except plate. He directed that some of his property in Ipswich should be sold to pay off a mortgage on lands in Kent. Any ambiguities in the will were to be referred to James Hales, serjeant-at-law. It was proved on 27 Nov. 1551 by Wentworth's eldest son Thomas, the executorship having been renounced by the widow and John Gosnold*. A drawing by Holbein and several portraits of Wentworth survive.[8]

[1] Date of birth estimated from age at fa.'s i.p.m., C142/49/8, 60. *DNB*; *CP*; *LP Hen. VIII*, iii; W. L. Rutton, *Three Branches of the Fam. Wentworth*, 24–35. [2] E179/69/4–6; 371/300, r. 47; Burnet, *Hist. Ref.* iii. 321, 333; *Lit. Rems. Edw. VI*, 248–9; D. E. Hoak, *The King's Council in the Reign of Edw. VI*, 270; *LP Hen. VIII*, iii–v, vii, xii–xiv, xviii, xx, xxi; *CPR*, 1547–8, p. 89; 1553, pp. 358, 360–1, 363. [3] C142/49/8, 31, 60, 50/71, 149, 151; *LP Hen. VIII*, iii, iv; E179/64/4–6. [4] PCC 40 Porch; C142/49/8, 31, 50/71, 151; E150/631/5; *LP Hen. VIII*, iv; vii. 56 citing SP1/82, ff. 59–62; x, xvi, xx, xxi. [5] *LP Hen. VIII*, iii, iv, x, xiv, xvi, xix; *LJ*, i. 59–388; M. A. R. Graves, 'The Tudor House of Lords 1547–58' (Otago Univ. Ph.D. thesis, 1974), ii. 357; House of Lords RO, Original Acts 3 and 4 Edw. VI, nos. 22–25, 29, 31; 5 Edw. VI, no. 28. [6] *LP Hen. VIII*, iv–vi, viii, xi–xv, add; *DNB* (Becon, Thomas; Bale, John); *Sel. Works of John Bale* (Parker Soc.) pp. vii, viii; Fox, *Acts and Mons.* v. 530–2. [7] *APC*, ii. 19, 28, 337, 344 et passim; Hoak, 50–51, 53,

82, 100; W. K. Jordan, *Edw. VI*, i. 64, 363; ii. 20, 34; Burnet, ii. 244; iii. 321, 333; v. 12; *Letters 15th and 16th Cents.* (Soton Rec. Soc.), 72; M. Dewar, *Sir Thomas Smith*, 60–61; F. W. Russell, *Kett's Rebellion*, 87, 152; *CPR*, 1548–9, pp. 250–1; 1549–51, p. 420; 1550–3, p. 26; *Wriothesley's Chron.* ii (Cam. Soc. n.s. xx), 33; Foxe, v. 708–9; vi. 5, 95. [8] *LP Hen. VIII*, xiii, xiv; *CPR*, 1549–51, pp. 331, 404; Rutton, 30, 32, 34–35; *Machyn's Diary* (Cam. Soc. xlii), 314; PCC 35 Bucke; E150/648/18; *Holbein* (The Queen's Gallery, Buckingham Palace 1978–9), 55–57; R. C. Strong, *Tudor and Jacobean Portraits*, 325–7.

M.K.D.

WENTWORTH, Sir Thomas II (by 1525–84), of Nettlestead, Suff., Westminster and Stepney, Mdx.

SUFFOLK 1547*

b. by 1525, 1st s. of Sir Thomas Wentworth I*, 1st Lord Wentworth. *educ.* ?St. John's, Camb. *m.* (1) settlement 9 Feb. 1546, Mary (*d.* 1554), da. of Sir John Wentworth of Gosfield, Essex, *s.p.*; (2) by 1556, Anne or Agnes (*d.* 1574), da. of Henry Wentworth of Mountnessing, Essex, 2s. 1da.; ?(3). Kntd. 28 Sept. 1547; *suc.* fa. as 2nd Lord Wentworth 3 Mar. 1551.[1] Jt. ld. lt. Suff. 1552–3, 1560–1, Norf. and Suff. 1569; trier of petitions in the Lords, Parlts. of Mar. 1553, 1563, 1571; PC 21 Aug. 1553–8; dep. Calais Dec. 1553–Jan. 1558; j.p. Suff. 1554, q. 1558/59–?*d.*, Mdx. 1561, q. 1577–?*d.*; commr. goods of churches and fraternities Suff. 1553; other commissions, Essex, Suff., and eastern counties 1564–*d.*[2]

Thomas Wentworth is said to have been educated at St. John's College, Cambridge, leaving without a degree, and to have shown early promise as a soldier. He may have served under his father in the campaigns of 1543 and 1544, but he is first certainly glimpsed in the army led by his kinsman the Protector Somerset against the Scots in 1547, when he was knighted in the camp at Roxburgh. His return to the Parliament which assembled a month-and-a-half later reflected his kinship with Edward VI, and was presumably abetted by his father, the most influential peer in Suffolk after the downfall of the 3rd Duke of Norfolk. Nothing is known about his part in the work of the Commons before the death of his father during the third prorogation left him heir to a peerage and a place in the Lords. His cousin Sir Thomas Cornwallis replaced him in the Commons as one of the knights for Suffolk during the last session of the Parliament.[3]

Wentworth attended 14 out of the 25 sittings of the Parliament of March 1553 and three months later he witnessed the device settling the crown on Jane Grey. As joint lord lieutenant of Suffolk he was expected to support Jane but in the event he joined Princess Mary, to whom he swore allegiance on 17 July. For his decisive part in securing Suffolk for her during the succession crisis Mary made him a Privy Councillor in August and deputy of Calais before the end of the year. The imperial ambassador Renard considered Wentworth 'rather lightweight, young and inexperienced', and his term at Calais was a testing and unrewarding time. Censured for failing to suppress Protestantism in the town he was not given adequate support to maintain its defences. He misjudged the seriousness of the French attack early in 1558 and on the fall of the town he was taken prisoner. While in captivity he was indicted on 2 July 1558 for his ineptitude and his estates were ordered to be sequestered. After his ransom and return to England in March 1559, he was arraigned for high treason on 22 Apr. but 'quit himself, thanks be to God, and [was] clean delivered'. Although acquitted of treason and restored to his lands, he was not renamed to the Privy Council by Elizabeth, but many local issues were entrusted to him by the Queen. He bettered his father's somewhat poor record of attendance in the Lords, but after being present for the prorogation on 20 Oct. 1580 he missed the short session in 1581. He died intestate at Stepney on 13 Jan. 1584 and administration of his goods was granted five days later to his son Henry.[4]

[1] Date of birth estimated from age at fa.'s i.p.m., E150/648/18. *DNB*; *CP*; W. L. Rutton, *Three Branches of the Fam. Wentworth*, 39–52, 143–201. [2] *APC*, iv. 50, 277, 323; vi. 85; J. Daus, *A Hundred Sermons on the Apocalypse by H. Bullinger* (1861), dedication; G. S. Thomson, *Lds. Lts.* 50; *LJ*, i. 430, 581, 667; P. T. J. Morgan, 'The govt. of Calais, 1485–1558' (Oxf. Univ. D. Phil. thesis, 1966), 294; *CPR*, 1553–4, pp. 24, 67; 1560–3, pp. 439, 442; 1563–6, pp. 130, 141, 221–2; 1569–72, pp. 217–18. [3] Cooper, *Ath. Cant.* i. 484; M. A. R. Graves, 'The Tudor House of Lords, 1547–58' (Otago Univ. Ph.D. thesis, 1974), ii. 357–8. [4] *LJ*, i. 394–751; ii. 9–52; *Lit. Rems. Edw. VI*, 371; *CPR*, 1550–3, pp. 141, 347, 395; 1553–4, p. 67; 1558–60 to 1566–9 passim; *APC*, iv–xi pssaim; xiii. 352; *DKR*, iv. 234–8, 259; Foxe, *Acts and Mons.* vi. 538, 540, 768; H. F. M. Prescott, *Mary Tudor*, 357, 360–9; *CSP For.* 1553–8, pp. 310, 321 et passim; *CSP Span.* 1554–8, pp. xxi–xxii, 144, 229, 320 et passim; *CSP Dom.* 1547–80, passim; *CSP Ven.* 1557–8, pp. 1444–5; *Zurich Letters* (Parker Soc.), 99; C142/204/155(2); PCC admons. 1584, f. 91.

M.K.D.

WERER *see* **WEARE** *alias* **BROWNE**

WEST, Leonard (by 1518–78), of Burghwallis, Yorks.

NEW SHOREHAM 1554 (Apr.)

b. by 1518, 3rd s. of Thomas West, 8th Lord la Warr, by 2nd w. Eleanor, da. of Roger Copley of Roughey, Suss. and Gatton, Surr. m. by 1540, Barbara, da. of Sir William Gascoigne of Gawthorpe, Yorks., 3s. 4da.[1]

The youngest of Lord la Warr's sons, Leonard West was bequeathed the manors of Hasilden and Sutton Mandeville, Wiltshire, and Bradell, Dorset, although they were to remain with his mother until he became 18. In 1539 he sold Bradell, and the impression of financial difficulty is strengthened by (Sir) William Shelley's* decision, when adding a codicil to his will of 1548, to remit all West's debts to him. West was included as a remainderman in the Act of 1540 (32 Hen. VIII, c.74) confirming an exchange of lands between his half-brother the 9th Lord la Warr and the King. In 1552 he benefited by the will of his brother-in-law Thomas Gascoigne, whose dislike of his own brother and affection for his sister led him to leave the Yorkshire manors of Burghwallis and Thorpe to the Wests in the event of his dying childless. On Gascoigne's death West braved the brother's threat to murder one of West's servants, who was to support the will for probate, by reading it twice in the courtyard at Burghwallis before taking possession, and when after his departure the brother turned out his servants he brought the dispute before the court of requests. In November 1555, after an intervention on the brother's behalf by his kinsman Michael Wentworth*, the court awarded Burghwallis to West and remitted the claim to Thorpe to judgment at common law.[2]

It may have been in the interest of furthering his cause that West obtained a seat in the Parliament of April 1554 (one of his fellow-Members being Wentworth), although as one who styled himself the Queen's servant and who was to help bear the canopy at her funeral he could have received a royal recommendation. The opening at Shoreham he owed to his half-brother, joint lord lieutenant of Sussex, who on this occasion nominated both Members, presumably by arrangement with the aged 3rd Duke of Norfolk, the customary patron. La Warr's death in the following autumn probably cost West the chance of re-election, and with his right to Burghwallis established in the following year he lost that inducement to seek it. A 'Mr. West' was among the patentees of the 3rd Duke of Norfolk who on 9 Nov. 1555 'exhibited a bill for their assurance' in the Commons and were granted a copy of the bill enabling the 4th Duke to dispose of his lands notwithstanding his minority, but this may have been Leonard West's nephew William. After 1558 he is scarcely heard of, having presumably settled at Burghwallis which he continued to hold until his death on 17 June 1578.[3]

[1] Date of birth estimated from first land transaction. Comber, *Suss. Genealogies* (Lewes), 306. [2] PCC 2 Porch, 41 Hogen, 25 Populwell, 10 Ketchyn; *Suss. Rec. Soc.* xxix. 38; *LP Hen. VIII*, xv; CP40/1102/9, m.7; Req. 1/10, ff. 15v–17; 2/23/110. [3] SP12/1, f. 71; *CJ*, i. 43; *CPR*, 1569–72, pp. 358–9; E150/266/107.

R.J.W.S.

WESTCLIFF, John (by 1466–1524), of Sandwich, Kent.

SANDWICH 1504, 1510,[1] 1512,[2] 1515[3]

b. by 1466 m. Elizabeth.[4]
Common councilman, Sandwich (St. Peter's parish) 1487–93, auditor 1488, 1491, 1499, 1501, 1514, 1517, common clerk 1493–7, jurat 1497–?d., mayor 1500–1,

1504-5, 1508-9, 1510-11, 1520-1, 1522-3, keeper of the common chest and of the orphans when mayor and 1502, 1503-4; bailiff to Yarmouth 1499, 1509; burgess to the Shepway 1509; collector of customs, Sandwich by 1513-18; commr. subsidy 1514, 1523.[5]

Although no trace has been found of his legal education, John Westcliff was probably a lawyer. The office of common (or town) clerk of Sandwich, to which he was elected in 1493, then entailed duties comparable to those performed later by the recorder, and when in 1516 the Brotherhood of the Cinque Ports agreed to send two 'learned men' to negotiate with the mayor and aldermen of London, the choice fell on Westcliff and the town clerk of Rye.[6]

During his first Parliament Westcliff petitioned Henry VII for a patent authorizing Sandwich to hold two free fairs each year and his success in this matter presumably conduced to his regular re-election. On 24 Dec. 1509, after having earlier been chosen to go to the coronation, he was elected to the Parliament called for the following January, on 5 Jan. 1512 to the Parliament of February 1512, and on 12 Jan. 1515 to the Parliament of February 1515; this last re-election also accorded with the King's request for the return of the previous Members. At the session of 1514 a subsidy was granted (5 Hen. VIII, c.17), to be levied 'as well within liberties as without', any usage to the contrary notwithstanding. Although the Act as passed contained a proviso exempting the Cinque Ports, this was only inserted under pressure from their Members. During the session Westcliff and his fellow-Member John Hobard reported to Sandwich by letter and were authorized by the mayor, jurats and commonalty 'to do as other of the five ports therein shall do by the advice of their counsel and the favour of' the lord warden, the 5th Lord Bergavenny. On 15 Mar., after the Parliament had ended, the townsmen assembled again to hear of 'the good expedition' of their members; the arguments used for the exemption of the Cinque Ports were then read, 'for which considerations the said ports be discharged of the said subsidy by a special proviso in the Act'. None the less, in that or the following month a warrant was sent to the chancellor to name commissioners for the subsidy in Kent, among whom Westcliff was one for Sandwich; when he was reappointed in 1523, again for Sandwich, the name of the town (as of a number of others) was struck out.[7]

In this as in other matters the ports acted together. Westcliff represented Sandwich at their Brotherhood some 45 times between 1487 and 1524; he was chosen to administer the oath to the new lord warden in 1509; and he was frequently employed in negotiations for the ports. Toward the end of his life his service received special recognition. In July 1521 the Brotherhood granted him an annuity of 40s. for life. It was more than his own town did. When in May 1519, nearly four years after his last attendance at Parliament, he asked for 20 marks of his wages still unpaid, he was told to bring in 'a due reckoning of his said demand or else not to be allowed for the same'; he was also asked for an account of the money raised from the inhabitants for the suit of the two free markets—the suit which he had successfully concluded nearly 15 years before—and questioned on his liability for £4 10s. owing to the town by a man for whom he had stood surety. The accounts are defective and it is not known whether Westcliff received his money.[8]

Westcliff was six times mayor of Sandwich, more often than any other 16th-century mayor. It seems that in December 1512 he did not want to remain a jurat, but in January he was sworn in at the request of the whole commons. In October 1516 the mayor and jurats went to his home, where he lay ill, and recorded his and his wife Elizabeth's grant of all their tenements in Sandwich to Thomas Clifford of Canterbury and two others, who were evidently feoffees. At this time Westcliff was collector of customs in Sandwich and the adjacent ports. His only surviving ledger runs from Michaelmas 1513 to Michaelmas 1514; he received his pardon and release as collector on 23 Nov. 1518. Five months earlier John Lee III* had been banished from the town for a year and a day for striking Westcliff and another jurat, after an altercation in which Lee refused to doff his cap. The dispute may have arisen from Westcliff's promise to deliver to Lee, on behalf of Thomas Wingfield*, a sure estate in law for a tenement which he had bought from Wingfield. Although Lee was a troublemaker, Westcliff seems to have provoked the quarrel, whereas his earlier scuffle with John Somer* was probably of Somer's making.[9]

It was as of St. Clement's parish, Sandwich, that Westcliff made his will on 23 Mar. 1524, asking to be buried in the parish church of St. Peter, where Edmund Westcliff and other friends of his were buried. He left to his wife Elizabeth all his lands and tenements in Sandwich and elsewhere in Kent in fee simple, to give and sell at her pleasure; she was also to be the residuary legatee and executrix. The will was proved on 11 Apr.; the year is not given but it is registered among wills proved in 1524. From this, and from the fact that he was ill when he made it, one may infer that he died during that year, a conclusion borne out by his omission from the list of jurats of December 1524. His appointment as a subsidy collector in 1524, and a summons to his executors in 1535 to answer for his collection of the subsidy instalment payable in February 1527, may thus merely indicate a bureaucratic time-lag.[10]

[1] Sandwich white bk. f. 176. [2] Ibid. f. 191v. [3] Ibid. f. 231v. [4] Date of birth estimated from first reference. Canterbury prob. reg. A16, f. 178. [5] Sandwich old black bk., white bk. passim; *Cinque Ports White and Black Bks.* (Kent Arch. Soc. recs. br. xix), 124, 144; E122/130/2; *LP Hen. VIII*, i–iii. [6] Sandwich white bk. f. 24v; *Cinque Ports White and Black Bks.* 163. [7] Sandwich white bk. ff. 116, 124, 126v, 127, 170v, 176, 191v, 222–4, 231v; *CPR, 1494 1509*, p. 402. [8] *Cinque Ports White and Black Bks.* 97–189 passim; Sandwich white bk. f. 268. [9] W. Boys, *Sandwich* (1792), 418–19; Sandwich white bk. ff. 205v, 242, 244, 257v, 259. [10] Canterbury prob. reg. A16, f. 178; *LP Hen. VIII*, iv; Egerton 2093, ff. 131v–2.

R.J.K.

WESTON, Henry (1534/35–92), of Sutton Place, Surr.

PETERSFIELD 1554 (Apr.), 1554 (Nov.), 1555, 1558, 1559, 1563
SURREY 1571
PETERSFIELD 1584

b. 1534/35, s. of Sir Francis Weston by Anne, da. and h. of Sir Christopher Pickering of Killington, Westmld. and Escrick, Yorks.; half-bro. of Henry[†] and Thomas Knyvet[†]. *m.* (1) 1559, Dorothy, da. of Sir Thomas Arundell* of Shaftesbury, Dorset and Wardour Castle, Wilts., 2s. inc. Richard[†] 1da.; (2) Elizabeth, da. of Sir Francis Lovell of Harling, Norf., wid. of Henry Repps (*d.* 1566) of West Walton, Norf., *s.p.* suc. fa. 17 May 1536, gdfa. 7 Aug. 1541. KB 15 Jan. 1559.[1]

J.p. Surr. 1558/59–*d.*, Norf. 1577–9 or later, I. of Ely 1577–9, 1583/86; sheriff, Surr. 1568–9; commr. musters 1574.[2]

Henry Weston was not yet two years old when his father was executed for alleged intimacy with Queen Anne Boleyn. Twelve days later, on 28 May 1536, his grandfather Sir Richard Weston* enfeoffed (Sir) Christopher More* and two others of most of his lands, which were immediately regranted to himself and his wife with remainder to Henry Weston. The arrangement was confirmed five years later in Sir Richard Weston's will, with a proviso against the contingency that Henry Weston's taint in blood would bar his succession. The young Weston was to be restored in blood by an Act (2 and 3 Edw. VI, no. 45) passed in 1549 while he was still a minor. Since there is no evidence that his wardship had been granted away it may be concluded that he remained in the custody of the court of wards and that the master, William Paulet, Baron St. John, took this young neighbour under his wing. Paulet almost certainly had a hand in the bill restoring Weston in blood, which in the Commons would have been sponsored by Weston's second stepfather John Vaughan I*, and he is likely to have been responsible for the restoration of Petersfield as a parliamentary borough in 1547.[3]

Although he did not live near Petersfield but at Sutton Place, the house built by his grandfather in Surrey, it was for the Hampshire borough, also acquired by Sir Richard Weston, that Weston was to sit in every Parliament summoned from his 20th year until he became a knight of the shire in 1571. Before he came of age he yielded place to his fellow-Members, his stepfather Vaughan and the local Christopher Rithe, but thereafter he took the senior seat. The 'Mr. Weston' to whom a treasons bill was committed on 7 Dec. 1554 was almost certainly Richard Weston, then one of the Members for Lancaster. Henry Weston is said to have been at Calais when on 8 Jan. 1558 it was taken by the French: if this is true, he may not have been released by his captors in time for the opening of the last Parliament of Mary's reign two weeks later.[4]

Weston died on 11 Apr. 1592.[5]

[1] Date of birth estimated from age at grandfather's ipm, C142/65/30, 66/73, 77, 80, 67/166. *Vis. Surr.* (Harl. Soc. xliii), 8; *Vis. Norf.* (Harl. Soc. xxxii), 191; *Vis. Norf.* (Norf. Arch.), i. 196; PCC 19 Populwell, 100 Cope. [2] *CSP Dom.* 1547–80, p. 485. [3] *DNB* (Weston, Francis); PCC 13 Spert, 19 Populwell. [4] *CJ*, i. 39; F. Harrison, *Sutton Place*, 88; *Vis. Surr.* 8. [5] C142/235/90.

P.H.

WESTON, Richard (by 1527–72), of the Middle Temple, London and Roxwell, Essex.

LOSTWITHIEL 1553 (Mar.)
SALTASH 1553 (Oct.)
LANCASTER 1554 (Nov.)
MALDON 1555

b. by 1527, prob. 3rd s. of Richard Weston of Colchester, Essex. *educ.* M. Temple. *m.* (1) Weburgh, da. of Anthony Catesby of Whiston, Northants., wid. of Richard Jenour* (*d.* 1548) of Great Dunmow, Essex, 1s. 1da.; (2) 1552/55, Margaret, da. of Eustace Burneby, wid. of Thomas Addington, 1s. 2da.; (3) July 1566, Elizabeth, da. of Thomas Lovett of Astwell, Northants., wid. of Anthony Cave of Chicheley, Bucks. and John Newdigate* (*d.* 1565) of Harefield, Mdx.[1]

Bencher and Autumn reader, M. Temple 1554.

Commr. relief, Essex 1550, eccles. causes 1572; other commissions 1552–*d.*; j.p. Essex 1554–*d.*, Maldon 1556–9, q. Cornw., Devon, Dorset, Hants, Som., Wilts. 1564, Bucks., Devon 1569; solicitor-gen. Nov. 1557–Feb. 1559; member, council of 16th Earl of Oxford by 1558; serjeant-at-law Jan. 1559; Queen's serjeant Feb. 1559; j.c.p. Oct. 1559–*d.*; receiver of petitions in the Lords, Parlts. of 1563, 1571 and 1572.[2]

Richard Weston's grandson Richard Weston[†] became Earl of Portland under Charles I and inspired the fabrication of a pedigree tracing his grandfather's descent from the Staffordshire family of Weston and a Neville of Westmorland. Weston's real ancestry is uncertain. He was probably a grandson of William Weston, mercer of London, who died in 1515 leaving four sons, of whom one, Richard, settled in Colchester, where he died in 1541 or 1542, styling himself gentleman and leaving three sons under age, the youngest named Richard. Richard Weston of Colchester left legacies to his 'most singular good lord and master' Chancellor Audley and to John Lucas*, to whom he also committed the upbringing of his second son John. Both Audley and Lucas were members of the Inner Temple, but the younger Richard Weston was apparently to follow his stepfather Jerome Gilbert to the Middle Temple.[3]

The date of Weston's admission there is unknown but in July 1548 he was counsel to Admiral Seymour who ordered him to obtain the opinions of 'such lawyers as be of long continuance in study of the law and in estimation therefore', phrases which imply that Weston was still junior in the law and was perhaps appointed in vacation time in the absence of older counsel. In November 1550, he purchased the wardship of Andrew Jenour, the heir of Richard Jenour, whose widow Weston had married. His appointment to the commission of gaol delivery in 1552 was an early one, as was that of his friend and associate Anthony Browne II*, and his inclusion in the commission of the peace two years later, coming equally soon for one who did not belong to a leading county family, may be attributed either to his legal gifts or to his Catholic sympathies. In April 1553 Browne and Weston jointly purchased land around Finchingfield, Essex, and in Bedfordshire and Northamptonshire for £893; a month later they sold the land outside Essex. In January 1555 Weston bought for £280 the manor of Skreens in Roxwell, which he was to make his principal seat. He made further purchases of Essex lands in July 1558 and October 1560.[4]

Weston sat three times for boroughs in the duchies of Cornwall and Lancaster. In the returns for Saltash and Lancaster his name is inserted in a different hand; in the case of the two Cornish boroughs his nomination may have owed something to Browne, whose earliest parliamentary seat had also been Lostwithiel, but his return for Lancaster implies the favour of Sir Robert Rochester*, chancellor of the duchy, who appears to have been instrumental in bringing a number of his Essex neighbours into the House by way of duchy seats. It was almost certainly Richard Weston, and not the young Henry Weston, Member for Petersfield, to whom a treasons bill was committed on 7 Dec. 1554. He was one of the four or five Essex justices who received the Council's instructions on the enforcement of the statutes against heresy; unlike Browne, however, Weston does not figure in the pages of Foxe as a leading persecutor of Essex Protestants.

It is possible that he, rather than Robert Weston* of Lichfield, was the Weston described with Rochester and others in a polemic published before 16 Aug. 1553 as 'hardened and detestable papists', but it is more likely that this was the Hugh Weston who was installed as dean of Westminster in September 1553. Richard Weston sat for Maldon in the Parliament of 1555 and must have been the 'Mr. Weston counsellor' to whom the borough was paying 20s. a year by 1552, a sum increased to 40s. by 1557, no doubt owing his election principally to being the borough's counsel, although he may have been recommended by the Earl of Oxford. In 1556 Weston was appointed one of the justices of the Maldon borough courts, but the appointment may have been an honorary one, for his name does not appear among those of the sitting justices in the surviving records of the courts. In May 1557 the Privy Council appointed Weston and another lawyer to draw a bill 'for the quieting of some disorders that lately have arisen in the town of Newcastle', disorders perhaps connected with the town's dispute with the bishop of Durham over episcopal lands. Six months later Weston became solicitor-general; in that capacity he served on many commissions for the trial of disputes in Cornwall and elsewhere during the reign of Mary and, in December 1557, on the commission of inquiry into matters of currency and foreign trade. He was summoned to Parliament in 1558 *virtute officii*, receiving a writ of assistance and carrying bills and messages from the Lords to the Commons on at least eight occasions; and he was a receiver of petitions in the Lords in the Parliaments of 1563, 1571 and 1572.[5]

On 13 Feb. 1559 Weston was called to the degree of serjeant-at-law and in the following October he was appointed a justice of the common pleas. He remained a justice of this court until his death on 6 July 1572. In a will made two days earlier he had asked to be buried in Writtle church in 'a plain tomb of marble made without curiosity ... my funeral to be seemly and convenient without pomp'. He provided for his wife and children and named as executor his elder son Jerome Weston and as overseers John Pinchon† and John Glascock of Writtle. The will was proved on the following 29 July.[6]

[1] Date of birth estimated from first certain reference. *Vis. Essex* (Harl. Soc. xiii), 319; *Trans. Essex Arch. Soc.* n.s. ix. 56 seq.; R. E. C. Waters, *Chester of Chicheley*, i. 93–96; PCC 25 Populwell; C142/160/35; Essex RO, D/ABW39/51. [2] *CPR*, 1553–4, pp. 19, 27, 31–32; 1554–5, pp. 104–5, 107; 1557–8, pp. 65, 72; 1558–60, pp. 18, 104; 1563–6, pp. 20–22, 26–28, 37, 41–43, 104–5, 123, 332, 490; 1566–9, pp. 131, 441; 1569–72, pp. 35, 219–24, 431, 441; E159/337, r. 244; Essex RO, D/B3/1/5, ff. 1, 12, 29; information from Susan Flower; *LJ*, i. 580, 667, 703. [3] Morant, *Essex*, ii. 71, 171; *Colchester Oath Bk.* ed. Benham, 162; Essex RO, D/ABW39/51; PCC 31 Fetiplace; *Essex Rev.* xlviii. 37. [4] *HMC Hatfield*, i. 55; *Coll. State Pprs.* ed. Haynes, 73–74; *CPR*, 1549–51, p. 208; 1550–3, p. 419; 1553, pp. 145, 210, 353; 1554–5, p. 227; 1557–8, p. 464; 1558–60, p. 261; C142/160/35; *Essex Rev.* xxviii. 31–33;

CP25(2)/70/580, f. 28. [5] C218/1; 219/21/21, 23/72; CJ, i. 39, 48–52; APC, vi. 90; vii. passim; CSP Span. 1553, p. 174; Essex RO, D/B3/1/5, f.1, 3/243, 244, 247; CPR, 1557–8, pp. 65, 72; LJ, i. 580, 667, 703. [6] PCC 26 Daper.

D.F.C.

WESTON, Sir Richard (c. 1465–1541), of Sutton Place, Surr.

BERKSHIRE 1529

b. c. 1465, 1st s. of Edmund Weston of Boston, Lincs. by Catherine, da. of Robert Cammel of Fiddleford, Dorset. m. by 1502, Anne, da. of Oliver Sandys of Shere, Surr., 1s. 2da. suc. fa. ?by 1505. Kntd. 3 Jan. 1518.[1]

Keeper, Sunninghill park, Berks, and forester, Windsor forest 1503–d.; groom, the chamber by 1505; keeper, Castle Cornet, Guernsey 1506; steward, manors of Bray and Cookham, Berks. 1507–d., Stratfield Mortimer, Berks. and lt. Windsor castle and forest 1508–d.; other minor offices 1504–d.; esquire of the body 1509, knight 1518; gov. Guernsey and neighbouring islands 1509–d., jt. (with s.) 1533–6; j.p. Berks. 1510–d., Kent 1518, Surr. 1524–d.; keeper of swans on Thames 1517–d.; jt. master or surveyor of wards 1518–21, sole 1521–6; cup bearer, the Household 1521; commr. subsidy, Berks. 1523, 1524, tenths of spiritualities, Surr. 1535; other commissions, Berks., Calais, Kent, London and Surr. 1505–39; treasurer, Calais 1525–8; Councillor 'for matter in law' 1526; under treasurer, Exchequer 1528–d.; chief steward, Chertsey abbey by 1534–5.[2]

The Westons of Sutton first appear in the early 16th century. No relationship has been established between them and an old Surrey family of that name but they were kinsmen of the Westons of Prested Hall, Essex, a family which, on acquiring the earldom of Portland in 1632, would be provided with a pedigree reaching back to the reign of Henry I. Edmund Weston had been appointed joint captain, keeper and governor of Guernsey, of Castle Cornet and of the lesser Channel Islands, in 1485, while his younger brother, John, was prior of the Knights of St. John in England from 1476 to 1489. The elder Weston was probably dead by 1505, when his wife Catherine became the coheir of her brother William, the last of the Cammels of Shapwick in Dorset. It was the young Richard Weston who had made an agreement with William Cammel by which the Dorset manors of Kentleworth and West Parley were to come to him on the death of Cammel's widow, although in 1547 West Parley was to be claimed from Weston's widow by the descendant of a cousin of Cammel.[3]

Weston probably rose in the service of Henry VII's queen, Elizabeth of York. A man of his name was paid £4 10s. in 1502 for buying 'harnesses of girdles' for her overseas, and the Mistress Anne Weston who was one of her gentlewomen may well have been the daughter of Oliver Sandys whom Weston married about this time. Sandys had a very distant connexion with Sir William Sandys, who in November 1506 joined Richard Weston in a recognizance for £100 to the King shortly before Weston was given the custody of Castle Cornet in succession to his father.[4]

Weston's presence at the old King's funeral, at the coronation, and thereafter at practically every great ceremony for the next 30 years, was accompanied by more substantial service. Already keeper of Cornet, in May 1509 Weston succeeded to the governorship of Guernsey and all the other posts held by his father and Thomas Martin, who was now also dead. At least two wardships were granted to him that summer and in August 1510 he received a two-year licence to ship merchandise free of customs on any vessel not exceeding 150 tons through the Straits of Gibraltar. Weston then went to fight the Moors with Thomas, Lord Darcy, but he was in Guernsey by May 1513 and in the following March he was granted for 40 years the alnage of woollen cloth at Presteigne, Radnorshire. Later in 1514 he attended the marriage of Henry VIII's sister Mary to Louis XII, and in 1518 he formed part of an embassy to France to arrange the betrothal of the young Princess Mary to the Dauphin.[5]

In 1518 Weston was appointed to join the aged Sir Thomas Lovell I* as master of the wards, at a time when the royal rights of wardship were being exploited more thoroughly than before. Weston soon took full charge and seems to have sought to control the indiscriminate sale of wardships and leasing of wards' lands, while also strengthening the supervision of escheators. When Sir Edward Belknap succeeded Lovell in December 1520 a new patent described him and Weston not as 'masters' but as 'surveyors, governors, keepers and sellers' of wards, a title which brought more prestige to their office; at the same time, they were empowered to consult members of the Council on legal problems arising from their work. As a general surveyor of crown lands Belknap was experienced but preoccupied, so that Weston continued to exercise control both before and after his colleague's death in March 1521. Success fed ambition, for in September 1555 Wolsey told the King that Weston had offered to surrender his post, or its annuity of £100, in return for the stewardship of the duchy of Lancaster. The cardinal supported this request, since the stewardship would be more suitable than the chancellorship of the duchy, but instead Weston succeeded Sir William Sandys, now Lord Sandys, as treasurer of Calais.[6]

Weston cannot be detected as a policy-maker at any stage of his long career and Wolsey's letter of 1525 suggests that he was merely an able servant who deserved some reward. It is true that in May 1519 a reaction against the King's young advisers had led to changes in the Household, whereupon Sir Thomas Boleyn reported Weston to be among the new men of influence, but the dubiousness of such advancement appears from Hall's description of Weston and three other 'sad and ancient knights', appointed to the King's chamber at the Council's request, whose solemnity in dancing incurred the mockery of their master and of the younger courtiers. Ironically, if not altogether surprisingly, Weston's only son Francis, who became a royal page in 1525, was to furnish a classic example of the attractive young courtier whose meteoric and undeserved rise ended in tragedy.[7]

At Calais, Weston seems at first to have co-operated with Sandys, who was now captain of Guisnes, in the thankless tasks of keeping the defences in order, supplying victuals and paying the garrisons, but in 1528 he withheld the wages of Sandys and his retinue and had to be ordered by Wolsey to allow for the money, which had already been spent on repairs. It was always difficult to raise revenue from the Company of the Staple, which was supposed to help bear the military expenses, and Weston complained to the government about this and the weight of Sandys's demands. He did not neglect his own family, for on 12 Apr. he asked Wolsey to further the promotion of his younger brother Sir William Weston, then turcopolier, if the illness of the prior of the Knights of St. John proved fatal; the prior died and Sir William Weston duly became the last head of the order in England before the Dissolution. Weston himself was sometimes absent during his treasurership, and after becoming under treasurer at the Exchequer was for a time torn between London and Calais: in January 1529 he was at Calais but anxious to be gone 'on account of the term', but in April his absence from a commission for the repair of the defences deprived it of a quorum.[8]

On 12 July 1529 Weston joined the Dukes of Norfolk and Suffolk and others as witnesses against a dispensation exhibited by Queen Catherine; this and his past services made it likely that he would be a useful Member of Parliament, experienced and respected, yet pliable. Weston's main property now lay in Surrey but he had sat on more commissions in Berkshire, where he also held most of his local offices, and it was for Berkshire that he was returned in 1529, perhaps not for the first time. His fellow-Member (who was also a relative) was another veteran, Sir William Essex, but one less cautious in his political friendships. The King is not known to have intervened in the election for Berkshire, but he was at Windsor when the writs for several other

counties were sent for, so that both Essex and Weston were probably royal nominees.[9]

In 1530 Weston married his son to Anne Pickering, sole heir of Sir Christopher Pickering of Killington, Westmorland, who had been his ward for 11 years. Francis Weston was now outbidding his father as a recipient of royal gifts and in 1533, at the time of Anne Boleyn's coronation, he too was knighted. His father played host to Henry VIII at Sutton Place, and later in the same year a new grant invested father and son with the governorship of Guernsey, but on 4 May 1536 the younger Weston was arrested on a charge of being the Queen's lover and two weeks later he was beheaded, despite his family's attempts to save him.[10]

The father's fortunes were not affected by the tragedy. It is not known whether he sat in the Parliament which followed, in accordance with the King's general request, but on the outbreak of the Lincolnshire rebellion he was included in a list of Surrey gentry who were to attend the King; his quota of 150 men was larger than that of any of his neighbours save Sir Nicholas Carew*. He was also named to advise Queen Jane Seymour, and a year later he attended first the christening of Prince Edward and then the Queen's funeral. After a gap of several years he resumed local duties in 1538 and he was asked to sit as a knight of the shire for Surrey in 1539. Sir William Fitzwilliam I*, Earl of Southampton, on his way to arrange the elections in Hampshire and Sussex, wrote to Cromwell on 14 Mar. that he had stayed with Weston, who was very sick and had refused a seat in Parliament, although promising to further the return of the earl's half-brother and Sir Matthew Browne. Weston was then expecting to die, but he was well enough to greet Anne of Cleves in January 1540.[11]

Weston's first acquisition of land had been the Berkshire manor of Ufton Pole in 1510, but his chief possession and monument was Sutton Place, near Guildford. The manor of Sutton, previously joined with that of Woking, had been granted in fee to Weston in 1521. While in France from 1518 to 1519 Weston had journeyed down the Loire to see the Dauphin, and his travels bore fruit in the palatial home which he built a few years later by the River Wey, on the site of the ruined manor. The building, with its perpendicular forms overlaid with Italian ornament, bears little resemblance to any other courtier's house of the 1520s, and it ranks with the vanished Nonsuch as a landmark in the introduction of renaissance ideas. Its nearness to several royal residences (and to Wolsey's house at Esher) made it convenient for a rich courtier, while it was also hard by Clandon, where Weston had a house as early as

1516; in May 1530 he was licensed to empark lands at Clandon and Merrow, thereby creating Clandon park. Also at Merrow were three manors held by the Knights of St. John, and on the dissolution of the order in 1540 one of these, Temple Court, was granted to Weston. He had numerous sources of income from keeperships and stewardships, apart from his lands: as knight of the body he enjoyed £100 a year, and as master or surveyor of the wards he drew a further £100 as well as the yield of many lucrative wardships. An inventory of goods at Clandon and Sutton, drawn up by his executors, valued the plate at £144, while the sumptuous furnishings included a 'great carpet to lay under the King's feet'.[12]

Weston made a short will on 16 May and died on 7 Aug. 1541. He began with the traditional bequest of his soul to the Virgin Mary and the saints and did not refer to the royal supremacy. He asked to be laid in Holy Trinity church, Guildford, where in 1540 he had endowed a chantry for 20 years, but there is no trace of his tomb among those of his descendants. He named as executors his wife, the Earl of Southampton and the lord high admiral, Sir John Russell*, Baron Russell, and as overseer (Sir) Christopher More*. In accordance with the terms of an enfeoffment which he had made to More and others on 29 May 1536, soon after his son's execution, he bequeathed his lands to Anne for life and then to his seven year-old grandson Henry Weston*. His daughters Margaret and Catherine had married Sir Walter Denys* and Sir John Rogers*, and 'for lack of the said Henry', who was not restored in blood until 1549, the lands were to be divided equally between their eldest sons, Richard Denys* and Richard Rogers†.[13]

[1] Date of birth given in F. Harrison, Sutton Place, 34. Vis. Surr. (Harl. Soc. xliii), 7; Hutchins, Dorset, ii. 166; Privy Purse Expenses of Elizabeth of York ed. Nicolas, 23; Vis. Cumb. (Harl. Soc. vii), 19; PCC 13 Spert; CIPM Hen. VII, iii. 318; DNB. [2] LP Hen. VIII, i–vi, viii, xiii, xiv, xvi, add.; W. C. Richardson, Tudor Chamber Admin. 487; Elton, Tudor Rev. in Govt. 108; CPR, 1494–1509, pp. 343, 412–13, 416, 456, 525, 560, 585; CCR, 1500–9, p. 255; Manning and Bray, Surr. iii. 218; VCH Surr. iii. 88. [3] VCH Surr. i. 387; iii. 347–8, 361, 368; CIPM Hen. VII, i. 162; iii. 318; Harrison, 34; Hutchins, ii. 166, 439; C1/1168/71–75. [4] Privy Purse Expenses of Elizabeth of York, 23, 84, 99; Harrison, 34, 38, 64; Manning and Bray, i. 524; Vis. Cumb. 19; CCR, 1500–9, p. 255. [5] LP Hen. VIII, i, ii; Harrison, 40–41. [6] H. E. Bell, Ct. of Wards and Liveries, 10; Richardson, 287–90; LP Hen. VIII, iv. [7] LP Hen. VIII, iii; Hall, Chron. 598–9; Harrison, 42, 48. [8] LP Hen. VIII, iv. [9] Ibid. iv. [10] R. E. C. Waters, Chester Fam. of Chicheley, i. 260; LP Hen. VIII, v, vi. [11] LP Hen. VIII, xi, xii, xiv. [12] Ibid. i–iv, xiii, xvi, add.; Harrison, 1, 28–29, 41, app. iv; Nairn and Pevsner, Surr. 32; VCH Surr. iii. 348, 358, 368, 384–6; Manning and Bray, iii. 218. [13] PCC 13 Spert; VCH Surr. iii. 567–8; C142/67/166; E150/812/4.

T.F.T.B.

WESTON, Robert (by 1522–73), of Lichfield, Staffs.

EXETER	1553 (Mar.)
LICHFIELD	1558, 1559

b. by 1522, 3rd s. of John Weston of Weeford, Staffs. by Cecily, da. of Ralph Neville and sis. of Ralph, 4th Earl of Westmorland; bro. of James†. educ. All Souls, Oxf., fellow 1536, law dean 1538; BCL 1538, DCL 1556; adv. Doctors' Commons 1 Oct. 1556. m. Alice, da. of Richard Jenyns or Jennings of Great Barr, Staffs., 1s. 3da.[1]

Principal, Broadgates Hall, Oxf. 1546–9; vicar-gen. Lichfield diocese in 1550; chancellor, Exeter diocese 1551–3, Lichfield diocese by 1564; dean of arches 11 Jan. 1560–67; commr. visit diocese of Lichfield 1560, to enforce Acts of Uniformity and Supremacy 1562, [I] 1568, England 1571, piracy 1564; master in Chancery by 1563; ld. chancellor and ld. justice [I] 1567; dean, St. Patrick's, Dublin 11 June 1567–d, Wells 30 June 1570–d.[2]

It was on the recommendation of Sir Thomas Wriothesley that in May 1546 Robert Weston was appointed deputy to John Story* in the regius professorship of civil law at Oxford; in the same year he became principal of Broadgates Hall, as Story had earlier been. Unlike Story, whose Catholicism drove him abroad in 1549, Weston accepted the Edwardian Reformation and remained at his post; in November 1550 John ab Ulmis reported during his visit to Oxford that he found Weston 'a man of pleasing elocution and considerable erudition'.[3]

It was Weston's appointment late in 1551 as chancellor to the new bishop of Exeter, Miles Coverdale, which linked him with that city and so led to his Membership of the Parliament of March 1553. The corporation preserved the rule that only freemen could be elected by admitting Weston on 13 Feb. 'at the instance of the Twenty-Four for divers considerations'. Weston's interlude at Exeter came to an end when in the following September Coverdale was deprived, but his future at Oxford was secured by his renewal as deputy professor on the appointment of William Aubrey II* to the chair. After taking his doctorate in July 1556 he became an advocate at Doctors' Commons and practised in the court of Canterbury. His election to the Parliaments of 1558 and 1559 may not have been unconnected with his profession, which could have involved work for the ecclesiastical authorities at Lichfield, although the bishop himself, a zealous Catholic, would hardly have viewed with favour a man of Weston's religious record. His local ties and residence in the city, strengthened by his marriage into a prominent Lichfield family, doubtless conduced to his adoption, and he must have been known to the borough's patron William, Lord Paget, although no connexion has been traced between him and Paget such as those which accounted for the election of his fellow-Members Richard Cupper and Henry Paget. He is to be distinguished from the 'Dr. Weston' who spent the greater part of 1558 in the Tower; this was Hugh Weston, successively dean of Westminster and Windsor who was deprived and imprisoned for immorality.[4]

Weston's considerable attainments were recognized by Elizabeth who entrusted him with key posts in the administration of Ireland. He died in Dublin on 30 May 1573.[5]

[1] Date of birth estimated from education. Erdeswick, *Staffs.* 164; *Wm. Salt Arch. Soc.* iii(2), 29n; *CP* (1887), viii. 112; Foss, *Judges*, v. 543. Although the published pedigrees disagree as to whether Cecily Neville was Weston's mother or grandmother, what little is known about Cecily establishes her identity with Weston's mother. PCC 25 Peter; *N. and Q.* (ser. 4), iv. 367; Emden, *Biog. Reg. Univ. Oxf. 1501–40*, p. 618. [2] Emden, 618; J. Vowell *alias* Hooker, *Bps. of Exeter*, 43; *Cam. Misc.* ix(3), 46–47; *CPR*, 1560–3, pp. 279–80; 1566–9, pp. 27, 173; 1569–72, pp. 2, 440–2; Strype, *Parker*, i(1), 152; *CSP For.* 1558–9, p. 287; 1561–2, p. 127; *CSP Dom.* 1547–80, p. 24; *Add.* 1566–79, p. 525; *CSP Ire.* 1509–73, pp. 294, 335–6. [3] *LP Hen. VIII*, xxi; *CPR*, 1553–4, p. 395; *Rep. R. Comm. of 1552* (Archs. of Brit. Hist. and Culture iii), 81. [4] D. H. Pill, 'The diocese of Exeter under Bp. Veysey' (Exeter Univ. M.A. thesis, 1963), 346; Exeter mayor's ct. bk. 1545–57, f. 321; *Exeter Freemen* (Devon and Cornw. Rec. Soc. extra ser. i), 79; *Trans. Dev. Assoc.* lvi. 206–7; lxii. 221; *CPR*, 1553–4, p. 395; J. C. Wedgwood, *Staffs. Parlt. Hist.* (Wm. Salt Arch. Soc.), i. 352; E179/178/168; *DNB* (Weston, Hugh). [5] M. Mason, *St. Patrick's, Dublin*, 166–7, app. liv.

A.D.K.H.

WESTWOOD, Hugh (by 1500–59), of Chedworth, Glos.

WOOTTON BASSETT 1545

b. by 1500. *m.* (1) by 1521, Agnes; (2) Jane, da. of Sir Alexander Baynham of Westbury-on-Severn, wid. of Robert Wye (*d.* 1544) of Lipyeate, Som.; 1s. illegit.[1]

Queen's collector of rents, Marlborough, Wilts. in 1534 and 1544–5; j.p. Glos. 1547, q. 1554–*d.*; commr. relief 1550, goods of churches and fraternities 1553; other commissions, Glos. and Worcs. 1554–8; escheator, Glos. 1550–1.[2]

Hugh Westwood's parentage has not been established. There seems to be no reason to connect him with the Worcestershire family of that name and he may have been of relatively humble origin. First appearing in 1521 as the grantee, with his wife Agnes, of a crown lease for 21 years of the demesne lands of Chedworth, a lease which they exchanged for a similar one in 1532 and again in 1543, Westwood also held a lease from Tewkesbury abbey of neighbouring Coln St. Denis which, after that manor and Calcot had been granted at the Dissolution to William Sharington*, he converted into a freehold by purchase from Sharington in 1543. That Westwood was linked—although in what way does not appear—with the Tame family of Fairford is shown by his receipt of bequests from both Sir Edmund Tame the elder and the younger: in 1534 the first of them left him a life interest in tenements at Tewkesbury and ten years later the second bequeathed him a lease of Chedworth parsonage. Shortly before his death the younger Tame was also licensed to alienate the manor of Swindon, Wiltshire, to Westwood and Maurice Denys*. The Tames had made their fortune from Cotswold wool, and Westwood was to do the same: it has been calculated that at his death he had upwards of 6,000 acres of grazing land and he was to bequeath at least 1,300 sheep.[3]

Westwood lived to enjoy other powerful connexions. As a collector of rents at Marlborough for Queens Anne Boleyn and Catherine Parr he was associated with Sir John Brydges*, who besides being his near neighbour at Coberley would also become his kinsman when Westwood married Jane Baynham, Brydges's first cousin. It could scarcely have been other than Brydges's influence which procured Westwood's election for Wootton Bassett in 1545, his fellow-Member being Brydges's son Edmund. (For either or both of them it could have been a re-election, since the names for the borough for the two previous Parliaments are unknown.) Westwood is not known to have sat again, but he might have been one of those whom the contemporary observer had in mind in describing how 'the ears of the great sheepmasters do hang upon this House' when there was any question of limiting their activities by legislation.[4]

Westwood died on 21 Oct. 1559. Where John Tame had applied the profits of the fleece to Fairford church, Westwood focussed his philanthropy upon education. By his will of 1 May 1559 he endowed a grammar school at Northleach, which lies a few miles north-east of Chedworth; the trustees included Edmund Brydges, by then the 2nd Baron Chandos, (Sir) Nicholas Arnold*, Henry Hodgkins*, Sir Giles Poole* and (Sir) Thomas Throckmorton I*. His other principal charity was the foundation of an almshouse at Bibury, where in 1552 he had bought the manor from William Herbert I*, 1st Earl of Pembroke. In the absence of legitimate offspring the bulk of his lands and goods passed to his nephew Robert Westwood; his widow received the manor of Arlingham, on the banks of the Severn (which she had probably brought to the marriage), with cattle, sheep and household goods, and an illegitimate son Hugh, his child by Anne Hughes, was left 100 sheep, farm implements and an annuity of £6 13s.4d. The executors were his wife and his nephew Robert Westwood, and the overseers Henry Hodgkins and Thomas Watson; the will was proved on 5 Apr. 1560.[5]

[1] Date of birth estimated from first reference. *LP Hen. VIII*, iii; A. C. Painter, 'Hugh Westwood', *Bristol and Glos. Arch. Soc. Trans.* liv. 85–105. [2] *LP Hen. VIII*, vii, xix, xx; *CPR*, 1547–8, p. 84; 1550–3, p. 394; 1553, pp. 354, 414; 1553–4, p. 19; 1554–5, pp. 106–7; 1557–8, pp. 364–5; *APC*, vi. 93; *Bristol and Glos. Arch. Soc. Trans.* xxiii. 67. [3] *LP Hen. VIII*, iii, v, xvii–xix; *VCH Glos.* viii. 29; Painter, 86, 87, 93; PCC 23 Mellershe. [4] *LP Hen. VIII*, vii, xix, xx; *Bristol and Glos. Arch. Soc. Trans.* vi. 184–5. [5] C142/126/80; PCC 23 Mellershe; *CPR*, 1550–3, p. 246; Rudder, *Glos.* 232–3.

E.McI.

WHALLEY, Richard (1498/99–1583), of Kirton, Welbeck and Sibthorpe, Notts. and Wimbledon, Surr.

SCARBOROUGH 1547
EAST GRINSTEAD 1554 (Apr.)
NOTTINGHAMSHIRE 1554 (Nov.), 1555

b. 1498/99, o.s. of Thomas Whalley of Kirton, by 2nd w. Elizabeth, da. of John Strelley of Woodborough, Notts. *educ.* St. John's, Camb. *m.* (1) Laura, da. of Thomas Brockman or Brookman of Essex, 5 ch.; (2) by 1540, Ursula, 13 ch.; (3) Barbara, 7 ch.[1] J.p. Yorks. (N. Riding) 1538–47, (E. Riding) 1547–50, Notts. 1543, 1554, q. 1558/59; commr. musters, Yorks. (N. Riding) 1539, chantries, Yorks., Hull and York 1546, 1548, relief, Notts., Yorks. (E. Riding) 1550; comptroller, household of 1st Earl of Rutland Dec. 1540–Nov. 1541; receiver, ct. augmentations Yorks. 1545–June 1552; esquire of the body by 1545; jt. keeper, castle and parks at Wressell and bailiwick, E. Riding 1546; chamberlain, household of Duke of Somerset by 1547.[2]

Richard Whalley's great-grandfather held land in Darlaston in Staffordshire but moved to Nottinghamshire after his marriage to the heiress of Thomas Leke of Kirton in that shire, and established his family at Kirton.[3]

After a spell at Cambridge, Whalley entered the household of Sir Thomas Lovell I*: he was one of the young gentlemen mentioned in Lovell's will of 10 Dec. 1522 and at the funeral in 1524. Nothing has been discovered about him from that time until his appearance on the North Riding commission of the peace in 1538: on both this and the commission for the following year his is the last name, so that he was probably a newcomer. It was a namesake, probably of Dalby in the North Riding, who entered Gray's Inn in 1529 and died in 1560 after serving for a year as attorney to the council in the north. Whalley is said to have surveyed religious houses in Leicestershire in 1536 with John Beaumont*, but his name does not appear on the relevant commission; he did, however, examine certain lands in that county in which his son Hugh, one of Cromwell's servants, was interested and he encouraged him to purchase them.[4]

Whalley was himself to acquire substantial monastic estates in Nottinghamshire. Outstanding among them was the abbey of Welbeck, which he purchased in February 1539. In the following year he bought Hardwick Grange and other property in Hardwick, Osberton and Worksop, and acquired the grain rent from the lessee of Gringley rectory. Two years later he wrote to John Gates* asking him to further his suit for other properties, to the value of 100 marks a year; although he claimed that these were only 'mean lands', incapable of improvement, and desirable only because they intermingled with his estates, he considered them valuable enough to send Gates a gold chain and to offer him 100 marks if he could secure the King's favour. Apparently Whalley was unsuccessful in this case, and it was not until 1545 that he received a further grant, the reversion of the college, wardenry and chantry of St. Mary of Sibthorpe and other property there after the death (which took place in 1550) of Thomas Magnus, archdeacon of the East Riding. In 1546 Whalley bought the rectory and advowson of Car Colston, together with lands in Carlton, Cromwell and Sutton, from John Bellow* and Robert Bigod, the large-scale dealers in such properties. The grant of a valuable wardship in Yorkshire in 1548 closes his list of acquisitions until Elizabeth's accession.[5]

The reign of Edward VI saw the climax of Whalley's career. He became chamberlain of the Duke of Somerset's household and was intimately involved in the Protector's affairs: he is even said to have been related by marriage to his master. He also dealt with large sums of crown money, some to be employed at Boulogne in the summer of 1549. It was presumably with Somerset's support that Whalley was returned for Scarborough to the Parliament of 1547, although as augmentations receiver in Yorkshire he was well known in the county. He acquired a house at Wimbledon for which William Cecil had unsuccessfully sued. It appears from a letter of Cecil's to (Sir) John Thynne* that Cecil expected Whalley to succeed to one or other of Sir Anthony Denny's* offices on Denny's death in September 1549; if there were any such expectation it was doubtless prevented by Somerset's fall a month later.[6]

Whalley was among those of the duke's adherents who were imprisoned after the *coup* of October 1549. He had certainly been in the duke's confidence in the days preceding his arrest. When Somerset travelled to Windsor with the King, Whalley and the duchess removed several coffers of goods from London to Whalley's house at Wimbledon, and the duke instructed Whalley to comfort his wife during the crisis which was to follow. Released on a bond of 1,000 marks in January 1550, a few days before the duke, Whalley was instructed to pay his colleagues in the household: the clerk comptroller, John Raves, later complained that Whalley had embezzled £60 owing to him. With Somerset's restoration to his estates in June 1550 the Earl of Warwick set out to win over some of his rival's adherents, and with Whalley he seems to have been momentarily successful. In a letter to Cecil of this time Whalley echoed Warwick's charge that Somerset had acted arrogantly and said that the majority of the Council agreed. After exhorting Cecil not to leave Somerset 'until you so thoroughly persuade him to some better consideration of his proceedings', he went on: 'and for what his lordship [Warwick] is my very good lord, and hath friendly promised his help in the furtherance of my suit, I heartily pray you fail not to remember the same'. A few days later the Council gave Whalley leave to purchase lands of the King valued at £50 a year.[7]

Whalley's defection did not last and within a few months he was intriguing for Somerset's restoration to power. In February 1551 the King noted in his journal that Whalley had been arrested and examined 'for persuading divers nobles of the realm to make the Duke of Somerset protector at the next Parliament': this, the King wrote, was affirmed by the 2nd Earl of Rutland, who had exposed Whalley's intentions in a debate with him before the Council. (Sir) Francis Leke* was also called as a witness. Whalley was committed to the Fleet but was released in April. Six months later Somerset's arrest was followed by Whalley's, and the 5th Earl of Shrewsbury was asked for a detailed account of a conversation with him the previous summer. It was probably under the threat of a treason charge that Whalley, 'a busy headed man anxious to be set on work', became a principal witness against Somerset at the trial in December, but after the execution he was kept in the Tower for several months, with occasional visits from his wife and his brother Walter, who was deputizing for him in the receivership of Yorkshire. In June 1552 the King wrote that he had confessed 'how he lent my money upon gain and lucre . . . how he bought mine own land with my money, how in his account he had made many false suggestions, how at the time of fall of money he borrowed divers sums of money and had allowance for it after . . . the whole sum £2,000'. Like Sir John Thynne and Sir Thomas Holcroft*, Whalley was deprived of his public office, and all three were released in June 1552.[8]

Whalley had missed two sessions of Parliament through imprisonment and he may even have been deprived of his seat. On the list of Members revised in preparation for the final session, which opened in January 1552, the name of the first Member for Scarborough is given as Edward Whalley. This must be a copyist's error, for not only has no one of that name been found who could conceivably have been by-elected to the seat but Richard Whalley, if deprived, would hardly have been replaced by a namesake. Yet the error itself is an ambiguous one. If it lies in the christian name, Richard Whalley is shown to have kept his seat, his enforced absence from it notwithstanding, whereas if the surname is wrong, he must have lost

it. Of the two possibilities the first may be judged the more likely, for Whalley's continued, if nominal, Membership would have been consistent with the experience of Somerset's other followers in the House.[9]

While in prison Whalley encouraged Richard Eden in his experiments in transmutation. He himself could certainly have done with a new source of wealth for his affairs were in confusion. He had mortgaged three Nottinghamshire manors to his fellow-Member Sir Maurice Denys, but his imprisonment prevented him from redeeming them at the agreed time while Denys protested that the lands were worth £40 a year less than Whalley had claimed: early in Mary's reign Denys was still seeking the £3,000 he claimed by default. Whalley's neighbours also seized one of his wards, whose return was ordered by the Council in June 1552. The position was made worse by his fourth and longest imprisonment which began in August 1552. Ostensibly for peculation, it was probably a political sanction: it was brought to an end within a few days of Mary's accession by the order which also freed the bishops of Durham and London.[10]

Whalley was never again of political account, but he was to resume his interrupted career in Parliament. Unable to regain his receivership in Yorkshire, he was no longer a justice of the peace there and had to look for a seat elsewhere. His election to the Parliament of April 1554 for East Grinstead, a duchy of Lancaster borough, he probably owed to his association with Sir Thomas Holcroft who was acting with the 12th Earl of Arundel early in 1554 and himself sat on this occasion for the earl's borough of Arundel. As steward of the duchy lands in Sussex, the earl could have procured Whalley his seat, with the chancellor of the duchy, Sir Robert Rochester*, perhaps agreeable because Whalley's first wife had probably been a kinswoman of his. Whalley's final achievement was his knighthood of the shire for Nottinghamshire in the next two Parliaments. To his own standing in the county, where he concentrated his energies after withdrawing from Yorkshire, he was probably able to add the support of the 2nd Earl of Rutland, whose father he had served and who was again on friendly terms with Whalley after having testified against him in 1551. Whalley can scarcely have sought election out of enthusiasm for the Marian Restoration, for Strype records that during 'Queen Mary's dismal days' he entertained the scholar William Ford, 'a great enemy of papism in Oxford', at his home at Welbeck. He is not likely to have overlooked the degree of financial protection which Membership conferred by way of freedom from arrest for debt, for his financial embarrassment, which his plethora of children did nothing to relieve, outlasted his political misadventures.[11]

It was probably to relieve his position that in 1559 Whalley seems to have contemplated the sale of Welbeck abbey: a licence to alienate the property to a London clothworker was apparently not used, perhaps because about the same time he negotiated the provision of 1,000 tons of wood for Berwick from his forest there. He continued to supply large quantities of timber to the crown; in 1565 the Queen had 3,000 tons of it in Whalley's charge, much of it waiting at the coast for shipment to Berwick. By the time he made his will in October 1583 he had evidently made plans for the settlement of his property. The lease of the manor of Welbeck devolved upon his son-in-law (Sir) John Zouche II* according to indentures which Whalley and his son Thomas made with Zouche, who entered into bonds to perform Whalley's will. Whalley specified the manner in which his daughter Anne was to receive the £300 he had previously assigned to her and referred to a further indenture by which he had granted to James Couper and William Poule his movable goods, chattels, leases and jewels for a purpose specified in the indenture, saving the third part reserved to the use of his wife and executrix, which she was to use to pay the wages of household servants, to fulfil bequests and if possible to augment the portions he had assigned to three of his daughters. Whalley died on 23 Nov. 1583 and was buried in Screveton church. Thomas Whalley had died shortly before his father who was therefore succeeded by his grandson Richard, a knight of the shire in the Parliament of 1597.[12]

[1] Aged 84 at death according to MI, J. T. Godfrey, *Notts. Churches: Hundred of Bingham*, 391. *Vis. Notts.* (Harl. Soc. iv), 116–17; *Vis. Essex* (Harl. Soc. xiii), 161; *DNB*. [2] *LP Hen. VIII*, xiii–xv, xviii, xx, xxi; *CPR*, 1547–8, p. 92; 1548–9, p. 136; 1553, pp. 353, 357; 1553–4, p. 22; 1563–6, p. 38; *HMC Rutland*, iv. 307; SP12/2, f. 53; *HMC Bath*, iv. 338; *Rep. R. Comm. of 1552* (Archs. of Brit. Hist. and Culture iii), 55. [3] *Vis. Notts.* 117. [4] PCC 27 Jankyn; *LP Hen. VIII*, iv, xiii; *G. I. Adm.* 7; *CSP For.* 1560–1, p. 385; *VCH Yorks.* (*N. Riding*), ii. 125; Lansd. 1218, f. 13v. [5] *LP Hen. VIII*, xiv, xv, xx, xxi, add.; *CPR*, 1547–8, p. 308. [6] SP10/6/35; *APC*, ii. 303, 323; Bath mss, Thynne pprs. 2, f. 116. [7] *Orig. Letters* ed. Ellis (ser. 1), ii. 175; SP10/9/42, 52; C1/1377/24, 1482/60; Tytler, *Edw. VI and Mary*, i. 276; ii. 21–24; *APC*, ii. 372; iii. 59; W. K. Jordan, *Edw. VI*, ii. 75. [8] Burnet, *Hist. Ref.* v. 31, 76; *APC*, iii. 215, 248, 398, 459; iv. 31, 72, 82, 201; SP10/14/37; E. Lodge, *Illustrations*, i. 170; Harl. 2194, f. 20v; Jordan, ii. 79–80. [9] Hatfield 207. [10] *Bull. IHR*, xlv. 308–15; *APC*, iv. 90, 126, 176, 234, 312; R. Ruding, *Annals of Coinage*, i. 177. [11] *APC*, v. 238; *Vis. Essex*, 161; Strype, *Eccles. Memorials*, iii(1), 277. [12] *CPR*, 1558–60, p. 8; 1560–3, pp. 30–31; *APC*, vii. 59; *CSP For.* 1562, p. 425; 1564–5, pp. 310, 329; NRA 5959, p. 58; York wills 23, f. 159; Godfrey, 391.

C.J.B./R.J.W.S.

WHARTON, Charles

BERWICK-UPON-TWEED 1555

Charles Wharton was clearly a kinsman of Thomas Wharton I* 1st Baron Wharton, who became captain of Berwick shortly before the summoning of Mary's fourth Parliament and whose son and namesake was returned to that Parliament for Northumberland. Although he is not to be found in the pedigree of either the main line or of the cadet branch at Kirkby Thore, Wharton could have been the 1st Lord Wharton's son, his omission from the latter's will of July 1568 perhaps implying that he was by then dead and his absence from among the children shown on Wharton's tomb reflecting either the same circumstance or his possible illegitimacy. Dubious light is cast on his identity by four inquisitions post mortem taken at Appleby on 20 Jan. 1591 according to which a Charles Wharton of Orton had died on 7 June 1548 leaving four daughters, Anne Thornborough, Elizabeth and Isabel Birkbeck, and Jane Wharton, who at the time of the inquisition were aged either 40 years and more or 42 years and more. The property concerned was a fourth part of a messuage, with its appurtenances, worth 16s.8d. a year and had been held of Thomas Warcop* as of his manor of Orton. It is reasonable to infer that these inquisitions were prompted by Warcop's death in 1589 and that Wharton's daughters were interested by reason of a marriage connexion between their father and Warcop. The only connexion traced is that which had made the 1st Baron Wharton great-uncle to Thomas Warcop, but the fact that what was in question in 1591 was a fourth part suggests that the property concerned may have been divided between four of Thomas Warcop's sisters, one of whose shares passed to Wharton by marriage; it is not without interest that three of Wharton's daughters bore the same christian names as three of Warcop's. More difficult to explain is the date 7 June 1548 given for this Charles Wharton's death, which would make him a predecessor of the Member although, in the light of the daughters' approximate dates of birth, almost certainly not his father. It is easier to believe that there were not two men of the name but only one, whose date of death was wrongly stated on the inquisitions, perhaps by the miscopying of the regnal year '2 Elizabeth' (1559–60) as '2 Edward VI' (1548–9). This would make it possible to identify the subject of the inquisitions not only with the Member but with the namesake who served as one of four commissioners appointed by Baron Wharton in 1560 to effect a redistribution of holdings in Ravenstonedale near Kirkby Stephen.

Vis. of the North, i (Surtees Soc. cxxii), 7; E. R. Wharton, *Whartons*, 23; J. Scott, *Berwick*, 459, 473; *Trans. Cumb. and Westmld. Antiq. and Arch. Soc.* i. 233; iv. 240; n.s. ii. 262–3; Nicolson and Burn, *Westmld. and Cumb.* i. 377–8; C142/277/239, 261, 263, 280.

M.J.T.

WHARTON, Thomas I (c. 1495–1568), of Wharton and Nateby, Westmld. and Healaugh, Yorks.

APPLEBY 1529
?CUMBERLAND 1542

b. c. 1495, 1st s. of Thomas Wharton of Wharton and Nateby by Agnes, da. of Reginald Warcop of Smardale, Westmld. *m.* (1) bef. 4 July 1518, Eleanor, da. of Sir Brian Stapleton of Wighill, Yorks., at least 2s. inc. Thomas II* 2 da.; (2) 18 Nov. 1561, Anne, da. of Francis Talbot, 5th Earl of Shrewsbury, wid. of John, 2nd Lord Bray. *suc.* fa. c. 1520. Kntd. 1527/30 June 1531; *cr.* Baron Wharton of Wharton 18 Feb./ 5 Mar. 1544.[1]

Servant of 5th Earl of Northumberland; j.p. Westmld. 1524–d., Northumb. 1532–d., Yorks. (E. Riding) 1532, northern circuit 1540, Yorks. 1554–d.; sheriff, Cumb. 1529–30, 1535–6, 1539–40; comptroller under Earl of Northumberland in marches 1533; dep. warden, west marches, steward, Carlisle and Wetherall priories and Holme abbey 28 June 1537, warden, west marches 1 Feb. 1544–17 Apr. 1549, dep. warden, marches 31 July 1552, warden, middle marches, keeper, Redesdale and Tyndale, capt. Berwick-upon-Tweed, constable, Alnwick and chief steward, Hexham 30 July 1555, warden, east marches and steward, Rothbury 16 Dec. 1555, jt. warden, east and middle marches 2–9 Aug. 1557; gov. and capt.-gen. Carlisle 1541; member, council in the north c. Jan. 1545; steward, lands formerly of Furness abbey by Mar. 1545; jt. (with s. Thomas) steward, manor of Preston, Yorks. 20 Jan. 1546; commr. relief, Cumb., Westmld., Yorks. 1550, goods of churches and fraternities, York 1553, border defences 1555, unlawful congregations, northern counties 1561, eccles. causes, province of York 1561; other commissions 1531–d.; keeper, Berwick-upon-Tweed 16 Aug. 1556–Dec. 1557; councillor assistant to lt.-gen. in north 1560.[2]

The Whartons were minor Westmorland gentry, tenants and followers of the Cliffords, but Thomas Wharton's father had also served the crown. The date of his death is unknown but his son became a ward of the 10th Lord Clifford, who sold the wardship for 200 marks. The young Wharton next appears as a soldier, taking part in 1522 in a raid into Scotland, and then in the household of Henry Percy, 5th Earl of Northumberland. His service with Percy, perhaps a result of his marriage to a Stapleton, was to bring him vast rewards from a master who described him in 1534 as 'mine one hand'. In May 1528 the earl appointed Wharton comptroller of his household and steward of the Percy lordships of Healaugh and Tadcaster in the West Riding, offices which Wharton held for life. They were followed in October 1530 by the stewardship of the lordships of Eskdale and Wasdale, the constableship of Egremont castle and the lieutenancy of Cockermouth. In granting Wharton these offices, which were to pass to his heirs, Northumberland transferred to him much of the Percy power in Cumberland: with them went

several manors in that shire (all at a rent which was not only low in itself but was to be partly paid by the earl himself in the shape of an annuity out of it to Wharton of 100 marks) as well as several properties in Yorkshire. Northumberland's liberality to Wharton and others, notably Sir Reynold Carnaby, has usually been regarded as feckless, but it has recently been suggested that he may have been seeking to perpetuate Percy influence in the face of the crown's apparent intention to destroy the family. Although Wharton became increasingly a King's man he did not break with the earl, who died in 1537, and he and his kinsman Carnaby remained friends, Wharton being supervisor of Carnaby's will and obtaining the wardship of his daughters.[3]

Wharton's entry into the service of the Percy family had not meant a break with the Cliffords and it was evidently to Henry Clifford, 1st Earl of Cumberland, who was Northumberland's brother-in-law, that he owed his return in 1529 for Appleby, a borough for which three of his forbears had sat a century before. His election was straightway followed by his being pricked sheriff of Cumberland. Of his role in the Commons the only glimpse is provided by his inclusion in a list of Members drawn up by Cromwell on the back of a letter of December 1534: those listed are thought to have had a particular connexion, perhaps as a committee, with the treasons bill then on its passage through Parliament. Wharton was probably returned again in 1536, in accordance with the King's general request for the re-election of the previous Members, and perhaps also in 1539, when the Members for Appleby are unknown. The return for Cumberland to the Parliament of 1542 survives, but in a damaged form: what is left of it suggests that both Wharton and his son, then barely of age, were returned for the shire.[4]

The northern rising of 1536 was a landmark in Wharton's career. He did not join the rebels but as an opponent of the 3rd Lord Dacre became one of their targets. Yet he was not among those who vigorously opposed the rebels from the start: in effect, he went into hiding, either from fear or because he was torn in his loyalties between the crown and the Percys, and early in 1537 the Earl of Cumberland linked him with Sir Thomas Curwen and Sir William Musgrave* as men who had been in jeopardy during the rising. He redeemed his reputation by bestirring himself in the final work of suppression, and in June 1537 he was appointed deputy warden of the west marches. The 3rd Duke of Norfolk had opposed any such appointment on the ground that only a nobleman was adequate to the task; Cumberland accordingly remained warden until 1542, but it was in name only, for the King met Norfolk's argument with a flat refusal to accept the service of none but lords. (Some years later Norfolk's grandson would also object to Wharton's being made warden of the west marches, but this time it was because Wharton, albeit wise and experienced, was at deadly feud with the Master of Maxwell.) Wharton himself, writing to Cromwell in September 1537, claimed that whereas in the late Lord Dacre's day the cry had been 'A Dacre, a Dacre', and afterwards 'A Clifford, a Clifford' and still 'A Dacre, a Dacre', now it was only 'A King, a King'; six years later he suggested that the King should obtain, by exchange or otherwise, the border lordships of Burgh, Gilsland and Greystoke. Although he had owed his start to Northumberland, Wharton came to personify the Tudor hostility to the overmighty northern families, Cliffords, Dacres and Percys. He himself was closely linked with two other families similarly placed, the Curwens and the Musgraves. Sir Thomas Curwen, whom the Duke of Norfolk called Wharton's greatest and most trusted friend, took as his second wife Wharton's sister and in 1534 his son Henry* was contracted to Wharton's daughter Agnes: when that arrangement fell through Agnes married Sir Richard Musgrave*, Wharton's ward whose mother had been Elizabeth Curwen.[5]

Wharton had sometimes to take orders from a magnate like Seymour, Earl of Hertford, Talbot, Earl of Shrewsbury, or Dudley, Duke of Northumberland, but for the most part he was supreme in one or other of the marches. Bishop Holgate wrote of his good service and hoped that his neighbours' disdain would not upset him. When, after his victory at Solway Moss, he became warden of the west marches Wharton was raised to the peerage along with his colleague Eure: their patents were delivered to them by Hertford at Newcastle-upon-Tyne on 18 Mar. 1544, so that if Wharton was then knight of the shire for Cumberland he was an absentee during the third session of the Parliament. The northern nobility did not welcome the newcomer to their ranks. He ceased to stand well with the Cliffords and when in 1549 Richard Musgrave brought in a bill to deprive the Earl of Cumberland of his hereditary shrievalty of Westmorland it was said that this 'could not be otherwise than by the procurement of the Lord Wharton'; later the Privy Council had to intervene annually to prevent Wharton and Cumberland quarrelling over the Kirkby Stephen fair. Dacre was another source of trouble, and although in 1551 the Council with great difficulty brought him and Wharton to shake hands they had to go through the ceremony again, this time with Cumberland present, three-and-a-half years later. In September

1557 Wharton reported to the 5th Earl of Shrewsbury that Cumberland had seized his goods at Wharton for debt and that he would prefer a formal complaint. The upshot was the introduction in Mary's last Parliament of a bill to punish the 'lewd misdemeanours of certain of the Earl of Cumberland's servants and tenants towards my Lord Wharton', which however did not get beyond its first reading in the Lords on 3 Feb. 1558. Wharton appears not to have sat in the Lords until the reign of Edward VI, being evidently unable or unwilling to delegate his authority on the borders. On 5 Oct. 1547, and again a week later, he wrote asking whether he should leave his 'weighty charge' by obeying his writ of summons to the King's first Parliament and was finally instructed by the Protector Somerset to stay in the north. He was present during the second and third sessions of this Parliament and thereafter attended as often as the duties of his various offices allowed. He was one of the peers who tried Somerset. His dissentient votes include two against measures allowing the marriage of priests and one against the bill for abolishing images but he did not, as is sometimes stated, vote against the second Act of Uniformity; this belonged to the fourth session, for which he had received licence to remain in the north and at which he appointed the Duke of Northumberland as his proxy.[6]

Wharton profited from service to the King as he had from service to the Earl of Northumberland. It has been estimated that at the height of his prosperity he was receiving between £600 and £700 a year in fees, although this total may have included the £100 which his son had as master of the Queen's henchmen. He also received large grants of land, chiefly monastic but including some of the confiscated estates of Sir Francis Bigod*. Ravenstonedale in Westmorland was one of these and Wharton later added to his unpopularity by emparking it: according to the family history he was so hated by the common people that he was forced to quit his Westmorland estates for Healaugh in Yorkshire.[7]

Wharton was a pillar of border government throughout the changes in religious policy: towards the end of his life he was even named to several commissions for enforcing the Elizabethan settlement, although he had ceased to attend the Lords. In 1559 he named as his proxies in the Lords, Edward North*, 1st Lord North and Edward Hastings*, Baron Hastings of Loughborough, and in 1563 and 1566 the 6th Earl of Shrewsbury. His own sympathies seem to have been conservative, for in his will, made on 18 July 1568 and proved on 7 Apr. 1570, he invoked the prayers of 'the Blessed

Virgin Mary and all the holy company in heaven'. As supervisors he appointed three earls, Pembroke, Shrewsbury and Sussex, and his cousin Sir George Bowes†, a Puritan who had also married into the Talbot family, and as executors his son Thomas and Bowes's brother Robert†. His widow made her will in 1582, using the same religious formula and appointing the Catholic John Talbot† of Grafton one of her executors. Wharton died on 23 Aug. 1568 and was buried, as he had asked to be, at Healaugh: there is also a monument to him and his two wives at Kirkby Stephen, where he had founded a school.[8]

[1] Date of birth given in *CP. Vis. of the North*, i (Surtees Soc. cxxii), 7; *Vis. N. Counties* (Surtees Soc. xli), 99; *DNB*. [2] M. E. James, *Change and Continuity in Tudor North* (Borthwick Pprs. xxvii), passim; *LP Hen. VIII*, iv, v, vii–ix, xi–xx, add.; *CPR*, 1547–8 to 1563–6 passim; *CSP Scot.* 1547–63, p. 191; H. Pease, *Ld. Wardens*, 199; Somerville, *Duchy*, i. 510; R. R. Reid, *King's Council in the North*, 19n, 116, 163, 173, 176. [3] Nicolson and Burn, *Westmld. and Cumb.* i. 557–9; M. E. James, *Change and Continuity in Tudor North*, passim, *A Tudor Magnate and the Tudor State* (Borthwick Pprs. xxx), 20n; *LP Hen. VIII*, iii, xii; J. M. W. Bean, *Estates of Percy Fam.* 66n, 146; *Northumb. Co. Hist.* x. 399, 401, 409. [4] *LP Hen. VIII*, v; vii. 1522(ii) citing SP1/87, f.106v; C219/18B/15. [5] *LP Hen. VIII*, xi, xii, xviii; R. B. Smith, *Land and Politics*, 172–3; *HMC Hatfield*, i. 199–200, 229, 235; *CSP Scot.* 1547–63, p. 487. [6] *LP Hen. VIII*, xiv; *CP*, xii(2), App. D, 14–17; *Clifford Letters* (Surtees Soc. clxxii), 102; *APC*, ii. 553; iii. 499; iv. 56, 271; v. 13, 43, 86–87; vi. 18; vii. 10; *LJ*, i. 316 et passim; M. A. R. Graves, 'The Tudor House of Lords 1547–58' (Otago Univ. Ph.D. thesis, 1974), ii. 359–62; *DKR*, iv. app. ii. 230; *HMC Shrewsbury and Talbot*, ii. 6–90 passim; *HMC Bath*, iv. 35–74 passim. [7] *Trans. Cumb. and Westmld. Antiq. and Arch. Soc.* n.s. ii. 400–1; E. R. Wharton, *Whartons*, 25; *Arch. Jnl.* cii. 134. [8] *Trans. Cumb. and Westmld. Antiq. and Arch. Soc.* iv. 206, 240–2; *LJ*, i. 541, 580, 624.

A.D.

WHARTON, Thomas II (1520–72), of Wharton and Nateby, Westmld., Beaulieu *alias* New Hall, Essex and Westminster, Mdx.

?CUMBERLAND	1542[1]
CUMBERLAND	1545, 1547, 1553 (Oct.)
HEDON	1554 (Apr.)
YORKSHIRE	1554 (Nov.)[2]
NORTHUMBERLAND	1555
NORTHUMBERLAND or YORKSHIRE	1558

b. 1520, 1st s. of Thomas Wharton I*, 1st Baron Wharton, of Wharton and Nateby, Westmld. and Healaugh, Yorks. by 1st w. *m.* May 1547, Anne, da. of Robert Radcliffe, 1st Earl of Sussex, by Margaret, da. of Thomas Stanley, 2nd Earl of Derby, 2s. 3da. Kntd. 23 Sept. 1545; *suc.* fa. as 2nd Baron Wharton 23 Aug. 1568.[3]

Jt. (with fa.) steward, manor of Preston, Yorks. Jan. 1546; j.p. Cumb. 1547, q. 1554–58/59, Westmld. 1547, q. 1554–58/59, 1564, Yorks. (W. Riding) 1547; sheriff, Cumb. 1547–8; commr. chantries, Cumb., Westmld. and Carlisle 1548, relief from aliens, Cumb. 1550; ?steward, Princess Mary's household by 1552; PC by Aug. 1553–8; member, council in the north Sept. 1553–Apr. 1561; master of henchmen 26 Oct. 1553–Dec. 1558; chief steward, crown lands Yorks. (E. Riding) Oct. 1553–?*d.*; steward, manor of Beverley, Yorks. Oct. 1553; bailiff, clerk of the court and chief steward, manor and honor of Beaulieu, Essex June 1558.[4]

Thomas Wharton the younger is first mentioned, when aged about 16, during the Pilgrimage of Grace. The rebels came to the family house in Kirkby Stephen, Westmorland, seeking his father, but on finding that he had fled they took Wharton prisoner; what befell the young man at their hands is not known. By November 1542 he had entered the service of Sir Anthony Browne*, a leading courtier who saw much service in the north in the period after the Pilgrimage. In the same month he was engaged in border raids in which he continued to figure prominently. He was also employed by his father who was deputy warden of the west marches; in 1543 he conveyed letters on Scottish matters to the Duke of Suffolk at Newcastle. Later in the same year his father petitioned Suffolk for the stewardship of Furness and Sheriff Hutton for his son, whom he described as 'Mr. Brown's servant', but Wharton is not known to have been granted them. The suggestion that in May 1544 he was attending Browne in France is not supported by evidence. Between February and April of that year he had been engaged in border raids but a reference in a despatch of 8 Nov. to Wharton's repairing to court may imply that he was briefly absent from the north about that time. It may have been in part for military services that he was knighted in 1545 by the Earl of Hertford at Norham castle after Hertford had been in Scotland for two weeks.[5]

Wharton's parliamentary career had probably begun in 1542. The return for Cumberland to the Parliament of that year survives in a damaged condition: all that is legible is the name 'Thomas Wharton' followed by the incomplete christian name 'Thomas'. Although he was then barely of age, it is likely that the second name is that of the younger Wharton and that his father was the senior knight. In view of his activity on the border the younger Wharton could hardly have given full attendance, especially during the third session. No uncertainty attaches to his Membership of the next Parliament, that of 1545: he was elected on 27 Jan. senior knight of the shire, being styled on the indenture 'Thomas Wharton esquire son and heir of Thomas Lord Wharton lord warden of the west marches of England towards Scotland'. He was to profit in a small way from the two fallen interests of the north, the Percys and the monasteries, for in January 1546, in addition to the stewardship of Preston manor in Yorkshire which had previously belonged to the 5th Earl of Northumberland, he received, again jointly with his father, the lands of St. Bees in Cumberland, a dependent cell of St. Mary's, York.[6]

The first year of Edward VI's reign was a busy

one for Wharton. In March 1547 his father asked the Protector Somerset for permission to be present at his wedding, 'concluded by your pleasure', at Lady Derby's house a month after Easter: the reward of £100 for good service in the north which was granted by warrant in the same month has the air of a wedding present. Later in the year he was put on the commission of the peace in three counties, was pricked sheriff of Cumberland and was re-elected senior knight of the shire in the first Parliament of the new reign. Twice during the year he was sent by his father to bring border business before Somerset and the Council, on the second occasion when he was 'about to attend Parliament'. He had earlier led a foray into Annandale and Niths-dale and in 1548 he burnt and devastated the lands of the Irwins. On the day before this exploit he was ordered by his father to hang some Scots outside Carlisle, one of them a Maxwell of the prominent west march family; the resulting feud between Whartons and Maxwells later led the 4th Duke of Norfolk to consider his father as unsuitable for the wardenship of the west marches.[7]

Nothing seems to be known about the next four years of Wharton's career or how he came to unite his fortunes with those of Princess Mary: it may have been in part through the connexion with his brother-in-law the 2nd Earl of Sussex who was one of the first to declare for Mary as Queen. Wharton had entered her service by September 1552, when Bishop Ridley visited Mary at Hunsdon and was 'gently entertained' by him and other of her officers: later he became the object of Ridley's attack upon the religious practices of the princess's household. Wharton's attachment to Mary cannot have commended him to the Duke of Northumberland. It is noteworthy that, unless he found a seat for the first time outside Cumberland, Wharton was not elected to the second Edwardian Parliament, which was called at Northumberland's behest, although he sat in every other Parliament from 1545 to 1558 and was knight of the shire for Cumberland in 1545, 1547 and October 1553.[8]

Throughout the crisis of 1553 Wharton's loyalty to Mary never wavered. On 12 July it was reported to the Council, then at the Tower with Jane Grey, that Wharton and several other prominent men were with Mary at Kenninghall; later he followed her to Framlingham castle. His fidelity found quick recognition when she became Queen; he became a Privy Councillor on or before 21 Aug. 1553 and in October master of the Queen's henchmen with an annual fee of £100. He was the only member appointed to the council in the north in September 1553 whose selection may have been prompted by Mary's desire

to reward loyalty when such loyalty had been dangerous. He also acquired from the crown grants of office and property in Yorkshire.[9]

Wharton was a regular attendant at meetings of Mary's Privy Council. When Gardiner wrote to Secretary Petre, three days after the outbreak of Wyatt's rebellion, about the arrest of John Harington II*, he added a postscript that 'Master [written over 'Sir'] Wharton shall tell you the rest'. Certain border affairs were entrusted to him. In June 1554 he was to examine with others matters concerning the marshal of Berwick, and in November 1555 the dispute between Sir Robert Brandling (q.v.) and Sir John Widdrington was committed to him and other prominent men. It is probable that Wharton favoured the Queen's marriage to Philip of Spain. In July 1554 he accompanied the 12th Earl of Arundel to Southampton when Philip was invested with the Garter on his arrival there, and in 1555 Philip became godfather to Wharton's son and heir. Wharton was a pensioner of Spain and it was probably the Spanish ambassador Feria who, after Mary's death, described him as 'a good man, harmless; he is retiring'. In June 1555 Wharton was present at the trial of Bishop Hooper.[10]

Wharton was sent north in July 1557 when the border was threatened by Scottish incursions; 600 horsemen and 400 archers were levied under him for strengthening the east and middle marches, and he was again responsible to his father as warden of the marches. On 12 Aug. 1557 Wharton was noted as being at Berwick with Thomas Percy*, 1st Earl of Northumberland. Favours continued to be bestowed upon him. He was licensed to retain 30 persons besides those in his household and pardoned for his offences against the Act of Retainers. In July 1558 in addition to the grant of the stewardship of Beaulieu he had the keepership of the capital mansion and the parks there and was also appointed bailiff. He was further engaged in augmenting his estates: in 1558 he bought from Thomas Gravesend* and Richard Day of London ex-monastic property at Thorpe Underwood in Yorkshire. Wharton's nearness to the Queen is indicated by his status as a witness to her will in March 1558. He was present at her funeral, as was his wife, who was probably one of the ladies of the privy chamber.[11]

Wharton was elected to every one of Mary's Parliaments. His return for Hedon in April 1554, instead of Cumberland, reflected the shift of his interest and influence to the court and to Yorkshire, and especially his stewardship of crown lands in the East Riding. This was the only break in Wharton's successive knighthoods of the shire. His next election, for Yorkshire, answered to his own and his family's property there, his local offices and his membership of the council in the north. (As steward of the crown's manor at Beverley he was presumably interested in the bill uniting the three manors there which failed after a single reading in the Commons on 6 Dec. 1554.) In Northumberland, however, for which he sat in 1555, he had no standing of his own and his election must be attributed to the influence of his father, who was by then a key figure in the county, being warden of the middle marches, captain of Berwick, constable of Alnwick castle and chief steward of Hexham: it may have been a younger brother Charles who sat in this Parliament for Berwick. At his last election Wharton seems to have had the unusual distinction of being returned for two shires, Northumberland and Yorkshire. Which of them he sat for is not known: there is no trace of a by-election, although there was ample time for one to be held before the second session. For someone of his parliamentary experience Wharton appears to have made little mark in the Commons: the only indication of his part there is his employment to carry bills to the Lords, which he did on 23 Nov. 1553 and 7 Mar. 1558.[12]

Under Elizabeth, Wharton quickly fell into disfavour and was removed from office. He openly defied the new religious settlement and in June 1561 he and his wife were among the Catholics indicted at Brentwood, Essex, for hearing mass and other offences. Committed to the Tower, he petitioned the Queen for release and pardon, saying that he had been ill, his wife had died and there was domestic disharmony; by July he had submitted. In July 1564, however, the bishop of Carlisle reported that Wharton was still 'evil of religion'. During the rising of 1569 he had a fall from a horse from which he nearly died, but before this accident he had done nothing towards checking the rebellion and he was said to have an 'affection for the cause'.[13]

Having succeeded his father in 1568, Wharton took his seat in the Lords at the opening of the Parliament of 1571 and thereafter was regular in his attendance until his death during the first session of the following Parliament. He made his last appearance on 11 June 1572 and died three days later at his house in Cannon Row, Westminster. He was buried in Westminster abbey. He left considerable property in Cumberland, Yorkshire and Westmorland, and perhaps some in Durham, where his father had lands at Castletown and Trimdon. Administration of his estates was granted on 28 Feb. 1579 and again on 3 Feb. 1637.[14]

[1] C219/18B/15. [2] Huntington Lib. Hastings mss Parl. pprs. [3] Date of birth given in CP. E. R. Wharton, *Whartons*, 26; *Vis. of the North* (Surtees Soc. cxxxiii), 184; *Machyn's Diary* (Cam. Soc. xlii), 384; *Essex Rev.* i. 219; *CSP Dom.* 1601–3, *Add.* 1547–65,

p. 321; *DNB.* [4] *LP Hen. VIII*, xxi; Foxe, *Acts and Mons.* vi. 354–5; *APC*, iv. 323; vii. 34; D. M. Gladish, *Tudor Privy Council*, 142; R. R. Reid, *King's Council in the North*, 493; *CPR*, 1547–8, p. 82; 1548–9, p. 136; 1553, p. 364; 1553–4, pp. 18, 25, 277, 393; 1554–5, p. 110; 1557–8, p. 293; 1560–3, pp. 187–8; Lansd. 104(14), ff. 33–34; *CSP Dom.* 1601–3, *Add.* 1547–65, p. 567. [5] *LP Hen. VIII*, xii, xvii–xix. [6] Ibid. xxi. [7] *APC*, ii. 175; *CSP Dom.* 1601–3, *Add.* 1547–65, pp. 321, 330, 338, 372, 374. [8] Foxe, vi. 354–5; H. F. M. Prescott, *Mary Tudor*, 161. [9] *Chron. Q. Jane and Q. Mary* (Cam. Soc. xlviii), 4; *APC*, iv. 53; Lansd. 156(28), f. 102v; *CPR*, 1553–4, pp. 277, 296, 393; Reid, 181. [10] *APC*, iv. 53, 311 et passim; v. 45, 193; *Letters of Stephen Gardiner* ed. Muller, 460; *CSP Span.* 1554–8, pp. 1, 374, 454–5; Wharton, 26–27; Strype, *Eccles. Memorials*, iii(1), 286. [11] *APC*, vi. 114–15, 120, 125, 131–2; *CSP Dom.* 1601–3, *Add.* 1547–65, pp. 413, 455, 457; Strype, iii(2), 83, 162; *HMC Shrewsbury and Talbot*, ii. 58–76 passim; *CPR*, 1555–7, p. 281; 1557–8, pp. 293, 403–4; *Privy Purse Expenses of Princess Mary 1536–44* ed. Madden, app. iv, p. cci; LC2/4/2; Lansd. 14(1), f.2. [12] J. Scott, *Berwick*, 473; *Arch. Ael.* (ser. 4), xiv. 64; *CJ*, i. 31, 39, 51. [13] *APC*, vii. 34; *Essex Recusant*, iii. 1–21; *CSP Dom.* 1547–80, pp. 152, 171, 173–4, 176, 179–80; 1598–1601, p. 505; 1601–3, *Add.* 1547–65, p. 510; *CSP Dom. Add.* 1566–79, pp. 112, 120, 137–9, 164, 225, 413; *CSP Span.* 1558–67, p. 208; *Cath. Rec. Soc.* i. 45, 50, 51; *Machyn's Diary*, 259, 384; *Cam. Misc.* ix(3), 51; *Surtees Soc.* cxxxiv. 97. He did not, as stated in Browne Willis, *Notitia Parliamentaria*, iii. 65, sit for Northumb. in 1559. [14] *LJ*, i. 668–721 passim; J. Nichols, *Progresses Eliz.* i. 307; *HMC 4th Rep.* 179; C142/163/30; *CPR*, 1566–9, pp. 376, 417; 1569–72, p. 318; *PCC Admins.* ed. Glencross, ii. 112.

M.J.T.

WHAYTE *see* **WAYTE**

WHEATCROFT, William (by 1517–?58), of Rendlesham and Ipswich, Suff.

IPSWICH 1558*

b. by 1517. *m.* by 1538, at least 1s.[1]
Common clerk, Ipswich Sept. 1547–?58.[2]

According to the will of his grandson Henry Wheatcroft, proved in July 1616, William Wheatcroft had migrated to Suffolk 'with his special friends the Lord and Lady Willoughby from Lincolnshire'. Wheatcroft is first glimpsed in 1545 when he was assessed for the benevolence at Rendlesham on lands worth £12. Two years later he was made common clerk at Ipswich but another two elapsed before he bought a house there to enable him to carry out the duties of his office with less inconvenience to himself. About the same time the dowager Lady Willoughby sent his son William to Cambridge and Oxford with her grandsons Henry Brandon, 2nd Duke of Suffolk, and his younger brother; she is said to have paid £80 in one year towards young Wheatcroft's expenses.[3]

As a municipal officer of 11 years' standing Wheatcroft was well qualified to sit for Ipswich in the Parliament of 1558. The Journal does not mention him, but the substitution of 'Withepoll' for his name on the list of Members in use during the second session suggests that he died during the course of the Parliament. This inference is further borne out by the disappearance of his name as town clerk about the same time. A namesake, presumably his son, is mentioned in May 1562 as 'now town clerk'.[4]

¹ Date of birth estimated from marriage. Add. 37230. ² N. Bacon, *Annals Ipswich*, 228–51 passim. ³ PCC 76 Cope; Bacon, 228; E179/181/253; CP25(2)/41/281, no. 26, 63/510, nos. 40, 44; 40/1143, m. 4. ⁴ Ipswich treasurers' accts. 1557–8, 1559–60; Bacon, 249, 253, 260, 262, 265, 284; William Salt Lib. SMS 264; Add. 37230, ff. 1, 50, 51; Norwich consist. ct. 248 Moyse *alias* Spicer; E378/358, m. 143; Copinger, *Suff. Manors*, v. 112.

M.K.D.

WHEATLEY, Robert (by 1517–58 or later), of Cumb. and London.

APPLEBY 1545, 1547
CARLISLE 1554 (Apr.), 1554 (Nov.)
MORPETH 1558

b. by 1517. *educ.* ?M. Temple. *m.* at least 2 da.¹

Little trace has been found of Robert Wheatley. Styled 'gentleman' on each of his returns, he was perhaps a member of a minor family found in several northern counties: his daughter Anne was to marry into its most important branch at Woolley in Yorkshire. He may have been a lawyer, although the 'Mr. Wheteley' found at the Middle Temple during the 1550s and 1560s is more likely to have been William Wheatley of Little Walsingham, Norfolk, a master of the bench there. A connexion with the law might explain both Robert Wheatley's presence in London in 1538, when he leased Silloth grange in Cumberland for 21 years, and his recurrent election to Parliament from 1545, for which he probably had the support of William, 3rd Lord Dacre, an influential figure in the boroughs concerned. In addition to his known elections he could have been returned for Appleby to the Parliament of March 1553 for which the names are missing. He may have been one of the 'friends' mentioned by his fellow-Member Thomas Jolye (q.v.) who on 5 Jan. 1549 opposed the bill to deprive the 2nd Earl of Cumberland of his hereditary shrievalty.²

¹ Date of birth estimated from first reference. *Fam. Min. Gent.* (Harl. Soc. xxxiii), 596. ² C219/18C/131, 19/118, 23/36; *M.T. Recs.* i. 115, 123, 153, 164, 210, 213; *M.T. Adm.* i. 19; *LP Hen. VIII*, xiii; *CPR*, 1555–7, pp. 321–2; *Trans. Cumb. and Westmld. Antiq. and Arch. Soc.* n.s. lix. 100; *Clifford Letters* (Surtees Soc. clxxii), 101–3.

M.J.T.

WHEELER, Thomas (by 1513–74), of Dorking, Surr. and Ludlow, Salop.

LUDLOW 1539,¹ 1545, 1553 (Mar.), 1553 (Oct.)

b. by 1513, 4th s. of William Wheeler of Dorking. *educ.* ?I. Temple, adm. 2 Nov. 1529. *m.* (1) Juliana Passey of Ludlow, *s.p.*; (2) Anne, da. of William Foxe* of Ludlow, *s.p.*; (3) by 1565, Elizabeth, da. of Thomas Barnaby of Bockleton, Worcs., 1s. 3da.²

Steward, palmers' guild, Ludlow 1534; bailiff 1538–9, 1542–3, 1554–5, 1565–6; commr. musters 1542.³

It is not clear how a member of a little known Surrey family made his way to Ludlow, where he must have arrived before 1534, but if he was the Thomas Wheeler of Clement's Inn admitted to the Inner Temple in November 1529 he could have gone there to practise in the court of the marches, perhaps with the encouragement of Charles Foxe*, who probably entered the inn at about the same time. Once established at Ludlow, Wheeler strengthened his position by two advantageous marriages, to the sister or daughter of John Passey* and to the daughter of William Foxe and sister of Edmund* and Charles Foxe, and he was to pass the rest of his life as one of the elite of the town. During his first term as bailiff he became marginally involved, through his part in the arrest of John Cragge, parson of Ludlow, in the complex struggle for the property of Wigmore abbey between Bishop Rowland Lee, president of the council in the marches, his kinsman John Bradshaw I*, Thomas Croft* and probably the Foxe family.⁴

Among Members for Ludlow between 1523 and 1558 Wheeler ranks equal first with Charles Foxe in his total of elections. For his first Parliament, in which he sat with Foxe, the borough paid Wheeler £8 6s.3d.; this sum included expenses in connexion with one of Ludlow's dissolved friaries, among them the cost of breakfasting 'Mr. Lyster', presumably the chief baron of the Exchequer, so that the rate for attending three sessions totalling 166 days was somewhat less than 1s. a day. No other evidence survives of payments to Wheeler, who like Foxe may have owed his re-elections in part to his willingness to forgo them. His recurrent Membership has left no trace on the Commons Journal and he was not one of those who in the first Marian Parliament 'stood for the true religion' against the restoration of Catholicism. There is no obvious reason for his disappearance from the House thereafter, although as Charles Foxe was not to sit again for Ludlow the two may together have held aloof, or been excluded, from re-election.⁵

Wheeler made his will on 21 Apr. 1568. 'Trusting only in the merits and glorious passion of [Christ's] blood-shedding to be saved', he made bequests to Ludlow church and Hereford cathedral. The will, witnessed by Thomas Blashefild*, mentions Wheeler's purchase of a property in Shropshire from (Sir) Edward Littleton*, with whom there is a little more evidence that he was connected, and of another in Herefordshire; he also seems to have acquired certain tithes and a lease of chantry property in Ludlow. Wheeler was buried on 15 July 1574 and the will was proved on the following 2 Dec. He left his third wife, the mother of all his children, as sole executrix, and his only son Humphrey (possibly the Humphry Wheler who sat for Droitwich in 1601), then about eight years old, as heir.[6]

[1] Salop RO, Ludlow bailiffs' accts. 1540–1, where the 'Mr. Wheeler' mentioned is taken to be Thomas Wheeler. [2] Date of birth estimated from first certain reference. *Vis. Salop* (Harl. Soc. xxix), 496–7; *Vis. Worcs.* (Harl. Soc. xxvii), 13–14; PCC 46 Martyn. [3] *Trans. Salop Arch. Soc.* (ser. 2), vii. 11; Bodl. Gough Salop 1, ff. 276–7v; *LP Hen. VIII*, xvii. [4] *Cal. I.T. Recs.* i. 94; *LP Hen. VIII*, xiii; Elton, *Policy and Police*, 351. [5] Ludlow bailiffs' accts. 1540–1. [6] PCC 46 Martyn; Ludlow bailiffs' accts. 1547–8; *CPR*, 1548–9, pp. 349–50; *Trans. Salop Arch. Soc.* (ser. 2), vii. 11.

A.H.

WHITE, George (c. 1530–84), of Hutton, Essex.

LIVERPOOL   1558

b. c. 1530, 1st s. of Richard White of Hutton by Margaret, da. of (?Sir) Nicholas Strelley of Strelley, Notts. *educ.* ?Eton *c.* 1541; ?King's, Camb. adm. Aug. 1545, BA 1549/50, fellow 1548–50; I. Temple adm. Feb. 1552. *m.* by 1560, Catherine, da. of William Strode of Newnham in Plympton St. Mary, Devon, 4s. 1da.[1]
?Gent. waiter in 1558; escheator, Essex and Herts. 1563–4.[2]

The Whites of Hutton were a cadet branch of the family of that name of South Warnborough, Hampshire. George White probably owed his seat in Lancashire to Sir Edward Waldegrave*, who although not yet officially chancellor of the duchy of Lancaster had probably been in control of most of its administration since the death in November 1557 of his uncle Sir Robert Rochester*. White's aunt, Susan Tonge, was first lady of the bedchamber to Queen Mary and in touch with Waldegrave and other prominent figures, including (Sir) William Petre*, to whom the Whites were related by marriage. The grant of the petty customs of Poole for life on 23 Apr. 1555, in consideration of service, to George White, styled 'esquire' and 'the King and Queen's servant', could relate to a member of the White family of Poole, which however does not seem to have included a George at this time; but it was almost certainly George White of Hutton who had received an annuity of £20 for his service at Framlingham at the beginning of the reign and who attended the Queen's funeral as a gentleman waiter.[3]

Susan Tonge (who was commonly known as 'Mrs. Clarentius' or even simply 'Clarentius', her husband having been Clarenceux king of arms) had licence at about the time her nephew was sitting for Liverpool to enfeoff Sir Francis Englefield*, a kinsman of the Whites of South Warnborough, Sir Edward Waldegrave and others with four manors in Essex, to her use during her lifetime and with remainder to her nephews, of whom George was to receive Rivenhall and Runwell, John was to have

Chingford Paul and Humphrey Chingford Comitis. Although she did not die until about 1566, the brothers seem to have acquired the disposition of the properties before then: on 26 Apr. 1560 George White was licensed to alienate Runwell to two trustees and in 1562 John White conveyed Chingford Paul to his brother George, who three years later passed it to his other brother Humphrey, then described as citizen and merchant taylor of London. George White also acquired the manor of Thundersley in Essex which his aunt had been given by Edward VI in 1553.[4]

The George White who is mentioned as a merchant of the staple between 1558 and 1560 was probably not the Member. There were also a namesake in Essex who died only six months before George White of Hutton and had also held land in Thundersley, one who sold property in Suffolk in 1561 and another who acquired some in Buckinghamshire in 1570.[5]

Although his wife, a sister of Richard Strode II*, came from a seemingly Protestant family and although he did not suffer with Waldegrave and other Essex gentlemen in Elizabeth's reign, White was probably a Catholic. His aunt went overseas for a short while soon after Elizabeth's accession; his brother Humphrey was later described as 'a conveyor of letters and messages to and from her majesty's evil disposed subjects . . . beyond the seas'; and ten years after his death his eldest son Richard and his third son George were questioned about religion. Richard White married Mary, daughter of Edmund Plowden*, and their second son was the famous secular priest Thomas White *alias* Blacklow.[6]

White made his will shortly before his death on 13 June 1584. He left Hutton to his wife for 40 years on condition that she remained unmarried, and £200 to each of his sons, the eldest of whom was aged 24. Sir Edmund Huddleston and Thomas Tyrrell, both of Catholic families, were each to receive a gold ring. Thomas Tyrrell was perhaps the grandson and heir of Edmund Tyrrell*, of whose will White had been an overseer. White was buried in Hutton church where a memorial brass survives.[7]

[1] Date of birth estimated from probable education. *Vis. Essex* (Harl. Soc. xiii), 321–2, 521; H. Curtis, *Whyte or White Peds.* 20–22; *N. and Q.* clxxi. 167–8, 182; *Vis. Devon* ed. Colby, 196. [2] LC2/4/2. [3] *Essex Rev.* I. 94–98; M. Noble, *Coll. of Arms*, 115–17; F. G. Emmison, *Tudor Sec.* 118, 124, 127, 180, 219; *CPR*, 1554–5, p. 298; Lansd. 156, f. 93. [4] *CPR*, 1553, p. 28; 1557–8, p. 50; 1558–60, p. 365; 1560–3, p. 380; 1563–6, p. 305. [5] *CPR*, 1557–8, p. 301; 1558–60, pp. 25, 412; 1560–3, p. 200; 1569–72, p. 144; PCC 21 Watson; C142/203/77. Yet another George White, curate of Bradwell, Essex and perhaps the Etonian, had died between 26 Mar. 1559 and 2 May 1561, PCC 15 Loftes. [6] *Cath. Rec. Soc.* i. 45; xxii. 123; SP12/248/111; 15/11/45; *APC*, ix. 269; *Al. Cant.* iv. 386. [7] *Essex Recusant*, x. 100–1; C142/204/132; PCC 33 Carew; Mill Stephenson, *Mon. Brasses*, 123.

A.D.

WHITE, Giles (1512/13–74), of Winchester, Hants.

WINCHESTER 1558

b. 1512/13. *m.* Thomasin, 4s. 3da.
Bailiff, Winchester 1552–3, mayor 1557–8, 1565–6.[1]

Giles White was active in city affairs from 1542, when he became a freeman of Winchester, being often employed on civic business in London, Salisbury and Southampton. A linen draper and mercer, he also had some legal knowledge: in 1551 he was licensed to plead in the town court, in 1564 he was described by Bishop Horne as 'White towards the law', and he bequeathed 'all my books of the law' to his son Giles. His election to Parliament occurred during his first term as mayor.[2]

White testified at the trial of Bishop Gardiner in 1551 that he had been present at the bishop's first sermon after his release from the Fleet prison: he assured the court that Gardiner had stressed the importance of obedience, and that he himself had 'no affection but as truth requireth'. Together with other supporters of Gardiner he was listed among 'mislikers of religion of the chief authority' at Winchester in 1564.[3]

In October 1572 White was steward of the manor of Twyford near Winchester, the property of Sir Henry Seymour*. By his will, drawn up in October 1571, he left all his goods to his wife, with gifts of money amounting to £116 to his children. He died on 25 May 1574.[4]

[1] Aged 38 in 1551, Foxe, *Acts and Mons.* vi. 210. Hants RO, wills B1574; Stowe 846, f. 4v. [2] *Black Bk. of Winchester*, ed. Bird, 168, 185; Hants RO, Winchester chamberlains' accts.; wills B1574; E179/174/313; *Cam. Misc.* ix (3), 56. [3] Foxe, vi. 210; *Cam. Misc.* ix (3), 56. [4] C2/Eliz. I/B.26/63; Hants RO, wills B1574; Winchester ledger bk. 2, f. 266.

P.H./A.B.R.

WHITE, Henry (1531/32–70), of South Warnborough, Hants, and London.

REIGATE 1554 (Apr.)
DOWNTON 1555

b. 1531/32, 1st s. of Thomas White II*, and bro. of Thomas IV*. *educ.* I. Temple, adm. 20 May 1549. *m.* 30 May 1554, Bridget, da. and event. coh. of Henry Bradshaw of Halton, Bucks., 3da. *suc.* fa. 2 Nov. 1566.[1] Jt. constable, Farnham castle, Surr. 20 Jan. 1545–*d.*[2]

The Henry White who sat for Downton in 1555 was unquestionably either the brother[3] or the son of the treasurer of the bishopric of Winchester to which that borough belonged. What is less clear is which of the two did so and whether he or his namesake had previously sat for Reigate. That it was the younger man (whose particulars appear above) who sat for Downton may be inferred from the fact that his younger brother Thomas IV sat for the borough in

1555 and the father would hardly have nominated him had the elder brother not been provided with a seat. The question which of the two namesakes had been returned for Reigate 18 months earlier is slightly complicated by the appearance of their name twice on the list of Members of that Parliament, where besides being entered against Reigate it originally stood against the neighbouring borough of Gatton but was afterwards crossed out and replaced by Thomas Gatacre's. Although this is probably to be regarded as a copyist's error, it could mean that the Henry White in question had been returned for both boroughs and had chosen Reigate. There would be no difficulty in explaining the younger Henry White's return at Gatton, since the patron there, Lady Copley, had a disposition to choose her son's contemporaries. If only the seat at Reigate is in question, it may be thought that (Sir) Thomas White II would have approached the patron, Lord William Howard, more readily and with better prospect on his son's behalf than on his brother's, especially as he was then setting up the younger Henry in preparation for his marriage. On these, admittedly slight, grounds it is concluded that this Henry White sat in successive Parliaments for Reigate and Downton. Of his role in them nothing is known save that he is not to be found on the list of those who in December 1555 voted against one of the government's bills.[4]

Like his uncle, the younger Henry White was specially admitted to the Inner Temple and thus makes no further appearance in its records, but from the settlement which preceded his marriage to a daughter of Henry Bradshaw, chief baron of the Exchequer and a member of the inn, it is clear that he was adequately set up, with an immediate provision of lands worth £13 a year and the prospect of receiving nearly as much again on the death of his father and mother. Since his wife was soon to add to the joint resources her share of the lands in Buckinghamshire and Oxfordshire inherited by her brother Benedict, whose death had followed quickly upon his father's, White had less reason to lament his own father's decision to divide the bulk of his lands among his numerous progeny. He may have settled in London, where his maternal uncle Sir John White † became sheriff in 1556 and mayor in 1563. It was as of London, gentleman, that he made his will on 5 Feb. 1570, asking to be buried in St. Martin's Ludgate. He left £30 as a marriage portion to each of his three daughters and the residue of his goods to two of his brothers, both named Stephen, whom he named executors, with Sir John White as overseer. He died two days after making the will, which was proved on 8 Jan. 1571. His widow married Thomas Fermor*.[5]

[1] Date of birth estimated from age at fa.'s i.p.m., C142/145/9. *Vis. Hants* (Harl. Soc. lxiv), 81–82; E150/1005/6; C142/157/91; PCC 6 Holney. [2] Manning and Bray, *Surr.* iii. 136. [3] *Cal. I.T. Recs.* i. 16–144 passim; PCC 25 Populwell, 4 Stonard. [4] C193/23/1, f. 3v. [5] *CPR*, 1554–5, p. 14; PCC 6 Holney; C142/157/91 where White's date of death is given in error as 7 Feb. 13 Eliz. (1571).

S.R.J.

WHITE, Richard (by 1509–58), of York.

YORK 1554 (Apr.)

b. by 1509. *m.* Elizabeth, *d.s.p.*[1]

Keeper, guild of SS. Christopher and George, York c. 1533; junior chamberlain 1537–8, sheriff 1544–5, member of the Twenty-Four 1545, alderman 1549–*d.*, mayor 1552–3; royal receiver and chantry commr. 1548.[2]

Richard White was born at Edlingham in Northumberland but his parentage has not been traced. It was as a tailor that he became a freeman of York in 1529–30, and by 1551 he was master of the tailors' and drapers' guild. He lived in the wealthy parish of St. Michael-le-Belfrey, where in 1546 he was assessed for subsidy on £40 in goods (raised in the following year to £50), being by this criterion one of the richest laymen in York; for at least the last dozen years of his life he dwelt in a timbered house adjoining the minster gate leased from the dean and chapter. His election on 8 Mar. 1554 to Mary's second Parliament came in the 17th year of his civic career. While attending it he and John Beane secured a renewal of the city's charter, caused action to be taken against infringers of its citizens' exemption from tolls, and were approached by the Vintners' Company for help in the unsuccessful attempt to repeal the Edwardian Licensing Act (7 Edw. VI, c.5).[3]

White made his will on 8 Aug. 1558. Asking to be buried 'honestly' according to his degree, he made provision for a perpetual obit in Belfrey church, twice-weekly prayers for his soul and the perpetual maintenance of a lamp before the sacrament in the church. The residue of his estate was to go to charity and to his kinsfolk at the discretion of his executrix, his wife Elizabeth, and supervisors, Alderman Richard Goldthorpe[†] and John Shelito, notary. By two codicils of 12 Sept. 1558 he made additional arrangements, including the replacement of Shelito, who had died, by Thomas Standeven, one of the Twenty-Four. The will shows him as owner or lessor of lands and tithes at various places, and the inquisition on his York property lists ten houses and several closes in his ownership and the leases of his dwelling-house and of half the Tailors' Hall. White died on 1 Nov. 1558, perhaps of the epidemic then severe in the city, and was buried in the minster. His heir was a nine year-old niece Elizabeth White. The will was not proved until 3 Dec. 1563.[4]

[1] Date of birth estimated from admission to freedom. York wills, dean and chapter's ct. 5, f. 14; C142/122/51. [2] *Reg. Freemen, York*, i (Surtees Soc. xcvi), 249; York archs. B12–22 passim; *York Civic Recs.* iv (Yorks. Arch. Soc. rec. ser. cviii), 181; v (ibid. cx), 4. [3] York wills, dean and chapter's ct. 5, f. 14; York pub. lib. R. H. Skaife ms civic officials, iii. 830; *Reg. Freemen, York*, i. 249; *York Civic Recs.* iv. 20, 181–2; v. 4, 57–58, 71–86, 102–6; York archs. B19, f. 92v; C142/122/51; E179/217/110, 111; York dean and chapter archs. Wb, ff. 35, 138; *Reg. Corpus Christi Guild, York* (Surtees Soc. lvii), 300n; *Guildhall Studies in London Hist.* i. 48–49. [4] York wills, dean and chapter's ct. 5, f. 14 (the will is dated 1556 but the first codicil corrects this to 1558); C142/122/51.

D.M.P.

WHITE, Robert (1518/19–65), of Christchurch and Moyles Court in Ellingham, Hants.

POOLE 1555

b. 1518/19, 1st s. of Henry White of London by Audrey, da. and coh. of Robert Fenrother of London. *m.* by 1543, Catherine, da. of George Barrett of Belhus in Aveley, Essex, 1s. William[†] 7da. *suc.*fa. 1535.[1]

J.p. Hants, 1553–58/59.[2]

Robert White's father, who had been an eminent lawyer and under sheriff of London, entrusted his property in Hampshire, Kent and Middlesex to the executors of his will to keep his children in a manner suitable to their station and to send his sons 'to school and to court' as they thought fit. The wardship of Robert White was acquired in 1538 by a rising lawyer William Thornhill*. White may have followed his father, his uncles John Kirton[†] and Nicholas Tichborne[†], and his guardian in receiving a legal education, although there is no trace of him at an inn of court and he is not known to have practised as a lawyer. His patrimony consisted of two manors in Eling, a moiety of the manor of Bednam in Alverstoke and other lands in Hampshire including Milford near Christchurch; he also inherited through his mother a lease of the manor of Notting Hill with land in Chelsea, Kensington and Paddington, a valuable property which he exchanged with the King in 1543 for land in Hampshire, and a tenement in St. Dunstan in the East, London. He appears to have preferred the life of a country gentleman to residence in the capital since nearly all that has been discovered about him refers to the management of his Hampshire estate which he enlarged by several purchases, notably that of Christchurch priory in 1548, and consolidated by exchanges; the remainder of his inheritance in and around London he sold off gradually.[3]

Queen Mary asked that 'such as be grave men, and of good and honest behaviour and conversation, and especially of Catholic religion' should be chosen for the fourth Parliament of her reign, and in electing White as its senior Member Poole respected her wishes. As far as is known, he had no personal link with the borough, for which his former guardian Thornhill had sat in the Parliament of 1529, even though his main residence was not a dozen miles away, but his kinship with (Sir) Thomas White II* gave him a connexion with John Paulet, Lord St. John, steward of the royal manor of which Poole was a 'member'. Unlike his partner John Phelips, White did not join the opposition to a government bill.

After Elizabeth's accession White was removed from the Hampshire bench, and nothing more has come to light about him before his death on 30 Jan. 1565. He had made his will on the previous 15 Nov. as an adherent of 'the true Catholic faith of Christ.' He directed that £6 be given to the poor of Christ-church and 6s.8d. to each of the four London gaols, while several servants were left sums varying from 10s. to 40s. He bequeathed to his daughters £100 each on marriage, to his sister Elizabeth, widow of Sir John Godsalve*, a ring and a gelding, and to Sir John Berkeley† a piece of silver; five marks each went to his supervisors, Chidiock Paulet* and Edward Barrett, a brother-in-law. At the inquisition following his death White's house, which had 23 rooms in addition to outhouses and stables, was valued at £795.[4]

¹ Date of birth estimated from age at fa.'s i.p.m., C142/57/8. PCC 37 Hogen, 19, 36 Bodfelde; *Vis. Essex* (Harl. Soc. xiii), 145–6; *N. and Q.* clxxi. 148–51; C142/142/88; *LP Hen. VIII*, xviii. ² *APC*, iv. 347; *CPR*, 1553–4, p. 19. ³ *Cal. I.T. Recs.* i. 16 passim; W. C. Richardson, *Ct. Augmentations*, 63; *Cal. Ct. Hustings Wills* ed. Sharpe, ii(2), 630–1; PCC 26 Hogen; *N. and Q.* clxxi. 150; C142/57/8; *DKR*, x(2), 297; *CPR*, 1547–8 to 1557–8 passim; *LP Hen. VIII*, xviii; *VCH Hants*, iii. 193, 204; iv. 119, 554, 565. ⁴ *HMC 13th Rep. IV*, 320; PCC 4 Stonard, 17 Tashe; *N. and Q.* clxxi. 148, 151, 167; *CPR*, 1563–6, p. 236; Hants RO, wills B1564/65; C142/142/88.

M.K.D.

WHITE, Thomas I (by 1500–42), of Coventry, Warws. and Bristol, Glos.

BRISTOL 1539[1]

b. by 1500. *m.* by 1530, Christine (*d.* 1546), wid. of one Perkins, 1da.[2]

?Warden, guild of Holy Trinity, Coventry 1509, master 1524; ?sheriff, Coventry 1514–15, jury member 1516–22, 1524–6, mayor 1523–4; mayor, Bristol 1530–1, alderman by 1536; commr. examine preaching 1537.[3]

There were at least three Thomas Whites living at Bristol during the 1530s, a merchant, a pinner and a mariner. Neither the pinner nor the mariner was a man of substance or standing, whereas the merchant was rich (his widow's goods being assessed at £100 in 1545), prominent in the town and a client of Cromwell; he is therefore taken as the Member. Reference in his will to his property in Coventry suggests his identification with a merchant of Coventry who shared a lease dated November 1524 of the 'prise' wine within the port, and with a mayor of Coventry admitted to the freedom of Bristol in

1525–6 and simultaneously amerced £20 for the privilege of not being pricked sheriff. After 1526 the name of Thomas White merchant *alias* fishmonger disappears from the records of Coventry.[4]

White, who lived in Broad Street, Bristol, was rewarded with £37 6s.8d. by the King in 1536 when he built the *Mary Bryde*, which he intended 'to set to the utter parts with commodities of this realm'; a second vessel, the *Mary James*, he was to leave to his daughter. The proceeds of his business enabled him to buy property in Dyrham and Hinton, Gloucestershire.[5]

When on account of plague in the town the King stayed at Thornbury castle, Gloucestershire, in 1535, White was one of several Bristolians received there by Cromwell. Official correspondence between the two survives, with White frequently advocating the interests of the corporation, and Cromwell chose him as one of the arbitrators (the others being David Broke and Sir William Kingston and his son Anthony, all three, like White, subsequently returned to the Parliament of 1539) in a long-standing dispute between Bristol and Tewkesbury. White must have been absent from part of the second session of that Parliament, one of his letters to Cromwell being dated 22 June 1539 at Bristol, but he received his wages in full for attending the third session.[6]

White was already a sick man when he made his will on 10 Sept. 1542; it was proved on 12 Oct. He made several charitable bequests, for the mainten-ance of almshouses, for the repair of the All Hallows' and St. John's pipes, and for the erection in the cathedral of a screen removed from the dissolved White Friars in Bristol. He was buried, as he had asked to be, in the crypt of St. John the Baptist's church. His daughter married one Thomas Harris, perhaps a kinsman of David Harris*.[7]

¹ Bristol AO, 04026/2/335; E159/319, brev. ret. Mich. r. [1–2]. ² Date of birth estimated from trading activity. PCC 9 Spert, 20 Alen; *Cal. Bristol Apprentice Bk.* i (Bristol Rec. Soc. xiv), 39, 83, 193; *Gt. Red. Bk. Bristol*, iii (Bristol Rec. Soc. xvi), 130–3. ³ *Coventry Leet Bk.* (EETS cxxxviii), 624–92; *Recs. Guild Coventry*, ii (Dugdale Soc. xix), 168; *Bristol and Glos. Arch. Soc. Trans.* xix. 130–1; xxvi. 135; *Ricart's Cal.* (Cam. Soc. n.s v), 51; Bristol AO, 04027/1/a–1, 219. ⁴ *Cal. Bristol Apprentice Bk.* i. 199; PCC 9 Spert; *Coventry Leet Bk.* 624 seq.; B. Poole, *Coventry*, 371; *Recs. Guild Coventry*, ii. 168; *LP Hen. VIII*, xviii; Bristol AO, 0427/8v; E179/114/269. ⁵ *LP Hen. VIII*, add; E179/114/269; PCC 9 Spert. ⁶ *LP Hen. VIII*, viii–xiv; Bristol AO, 04719/unnumbered, temp. 26 Hen. VIII; 04026/2/335. ⁷ *LP Hen. VIII*, xiv; *Gt. Red. Bk Bristol*, i (Bristol Rec. Soc. iv), 162–5; *Bristol and Glos. Arch. Soc. Trans.* xxvii. 125.

A.D.K.H.

WHITE, Thomas II (1507–66), of South Warn-borough, Hants.

HAMPSHIRE 1547, 1553 (Oct.), 1554 (Apr.), 1554 (Nov.),[1] 1555, 1558, 1559

b. 25 Mar. 1507, 1st s. of Robert White of South

Warnborough by Elizabeth, da. of Sir Thomas Englefield* of Englefield, Berks. *educ.* I. Temple, called. *m.* by 1532, Agnes, da. of Robert White of Farnham, Surr., 14s. inc. Henry* and Thomas IV* 6da. *suc.* fa. 2 Mar. 1521. Kntd. 2 Oct. 1553.[2]

Bencher, I. Temple by 1555, gov. 1557.

Treasurer, bpric. of Winchester 1538–*d.*; keeper, Farnham castle, Surr. 1540–*d.*; jt. (with Thomas Wriothesley) clerk of the crown and King's attorney KB 1542–50, sole 1550–9; commr. contribution, Hants 1546, relief 1550, goods of churches and fraternities 1553; j.p. Hants 1547, q. 1554; master of requests Aug. 1553–?58.[3]

White came of a well-connected family with lands in Hampshire, Kent and Surrey. At his father's death in 1521 he was nearly 14 years old, and his wardship was granted to John Morris*. As Morris was later to hold minor office under the bishop of Winchester at Farnham, he may have commended White to Bishop Gardiner; another possible sponsor was Thomas Wriothesley, with whom in 1538 White was to be granted the reversion to William Fermor's* offices in the King's bench. White was appointed Gardiner's treasurer at Michaelmas 1538 and held the post throughout the bishop's arrest, trial and deprivation; he was himself questioned during the proceedings but his deposition has not survived. White next served Gardiner's successor John Ponet, on whose surrender of most of the episcopal lands to the King his fee of £13 6s.8d. a year as treasurer and surveyor was reduced to £8 17s.9d. At Mary's accession, with Ponet deprived and Gardiner restored and given the great seal, White's fortunes revived: in August 1553 he was made a master of requests and two months later he was knighted at the coronation. Although White must have felt Gardiner's death in 1555 personally—he was a chief mourner at both the burial at Southwark and the subsequent re-interment at Winchester—the appointment of his own brother-in-law as Gardiner's successor in the see confirmed his position and his services were used both locally and at the centre: in 1556 he served on a commission concerning pirates arrested at Southampton and in 1557 made investigations into allegations against Sir John Allen, a former chancellor of Ireland.[4]

White's return as knight of the shire for every Parliament between 1547 and 1559 save perhaps one, that of March 1553 (for which only the name of one of the knights, Sir Richard Cotton, is known), while doubtless owing something to his personal standing in the county, for which he was nominated as sheriff four times between 1545 and 1552, although never pricked, must be chiefly ascribed to his official position. This was also true of his election to Elizabeth's first Parliament: when he was returned, probably early in January 1559, the bishop

was still in office although under house arrest following his funeral sermon for Queen Mary. By this time his Catholicism, and his identification with the Marian regime, were already bringing White's public career to an end. He made his will on 21 Feb. 1564. He had increased the family estate by the purchase of former monastic lands in Hampshire. One of his executors was Chidiock Paulet*, his son-in-law and successor in the treasurership. White died in London on 2 Nov. 1566 and was buried at South Warnborough.[5]

[1] Huntington Lib. Hastings mss Parl. pprs.   [2] Date of birth given at fa.'s i.p.m., C142/37/82, 127. *Vis. Hants* (Harl. Soc. lxiv), 82; *VCH Hants*, iii. 380; C142/145/9.   [3] Eccles. 2/155881, 155883, 155903; *LP Hen. VIII*, xiii, xvii, xxi; *CPR*, 1553, pp. 358, 416; 1558–60, p. 107; *APC*, iv. 324.   [4] Eccles. 2/155874, 155881; *LP Hen. VIII*, xiii; Foxe, *Acts. and Mons.* vi. 130; *CPR*, 1550–3, p. 179; *APC*, v. 335; vi. 105; Lansd. 156, f. 103; *Machyn's Diary* (Cam. Soc. xlii), 335; *Letters of Stephen Gardiner* ed. Muller, 507, 511, 514.   [5] *LP Hen. VIII*, xviii, xx, xxi; *CPR*, 1553, pp. 316, 387; PCC 4 Stonard; C142/145/9; *VCH Hants*, iii. 380; Pevsner and Lloyd, *Hants*, 603–4.

H.M.

WHITE, Thomas III (by 1517–90), of Fittleford in Sturminster Newton, Dorset.

POOLE   1553 (Mar.)[1]

b. by 1517, 1st s. of Thomas White of Poole. *m.* by 1560, Anne, da. of John Williams of Winterbourne Herrington, 2s. 2da. *suc.* fa. 28 Dec. 1556.[2]

Bailiff, Poole 1545–6, mayor 1551–2; subsidy collector, hundred of Puddletown 1557.[3]

In 1553 there were two Thomas Whites in Poole either of whom could have been returned to Parliament. The senior of them, who derived his wealth from trade in cloth, lead and other goods, and was assessed for the subsidy of 1547 on lands worth £50, had served as mayor three times between 1531 and 1545. His son and partner in the business had been chosen mayor in 1551 at the age of 34.[4]

Thomas White senior was described by Thomas Hancock, the reforming minister of St. James's, Poole, as 'old Thomas White, a great rich merchant and ringleader of the papists'; he had opposed Hancock's preaching on the eucharist with the words, 'Come from him, good people. He came from the devil and teacheth unto you devilish doctrine'. White afterwards set up the high altar removed from the parish church in his own house so that Catholics could hear mass. So notorious a dissident is unlikely to have prevailed in an election dominated by the opposing forces. The letter sent on this occasion by the Privy Council to the sheriff of Dorset does not survive, but the county was strongly Protestant, the sheriff Sir John Rogers* a supporter of the Duke of Northumberland and the butler of Poole (Sir) John Gates* the duke's henchman. Although less is known about the younger man's religious outlook than about his father's, it was

presumably not so rigid as to offset his local standing. After the brief Parliament was over he and his
fellow-Member William Newman were paid
£4 3s.4d. between them for the balance of their
charges.[5]

On his father's death White inherited land in
Dorset, Somerset, Hampshire and Wiltshire. He
also had the use of two chambers, a counting house
and cellar in the family house at Poole bequeathed
for life to his stepmother Christian. He was sole
executor of his father's will and he had licence to
enter his lands on 4 July 1557. Described in the
pardon roll of 1559 as merchant of Poole, White had
in fact attained gentle status and in the same year
he received a grant of arms as White of Fittleford.
Little is known of his later life; in 1563 he still had
property in Poole, paying 2s.2d. rent for a house,
gardens and tenements. He lived until 21 Dec. 1590,
when his inheritance passed to his son Thomas,
aged 30. By her will of 24 Apr. 1592 his widow Anne
asked to be buried beside him in the aisle of the
church at Sturminster Newton.[6]

[1] Poole rec. bk. 1, p. 85.   [2] Date of birth estimated from age at
fa.'s i.p.m., C142/107/15. Hutchins, *Dorset*, iv. 341; PCC 23
Wrastley, 56 Scott.   [3] Poole rec. bk. 1, pp. 72, 82; *APC*, vi. 161.
[4] Poole rec. bk. 1, pp. 55, 63, 72, 82; E122/121/7, 8, 122/4, 7, 21,
123/2, 207/2, 6, 222/5; 179/104/174.   [5] *Narr. Ref.* (Cam. Soc. lxxvii),
77–82; H. P. Smith, *Poole*, ii. 58; Poole rec. bk. 1, p. 85.   [6] PCC 23
Wrastley, 16 Welles, 56 Scott; C. H. Mayo, *Shastonian Recs.* 81;
CPR, 1555–7, p. 374; 1558–60, p. 182; *CSP Dom.* 1547–80, p. 131;
Poole recs. envelope 11; C142/228/36; Hutchins, iv. 341.

M.K.D.

WHITE, Thomas IV (1532/34–58), of the Middle Temple, London and Downton, Wilts.

DOWNTON   1555, 1558

b. 1532/34, 2nd s. of Thomas White II* and
bro. of Henry*. *educ.* Winchester, adm. 1543; M.
Temple. *m.* by 1551, Anne, da. of Stephen Kirton
of London, 1s. John†.[1]

Thomas White was a scholar of Winchester when
his maternal uncle John White was warden of the
college, and the subsequent choice of the Middle
Temple as his inn instead of the Inner Temple, his
family's inn for three generations, was probably
determined by his kinship with one of its recent
luminaries Sir Thomas Englefield. He himself was to
achieve nothing more there than repeated election
as master of the revels. His marriage to a daughter
of Stephen Kirton, a merchant taylor and alderman
of London, accorded with what seems to have been
the family practice of making alliances within a
circle of relatives; his younger brother Richard
married another daughter of Kirton, who was their
father's first cousin. White's return for Downton to
the last two Marian Parliaments was the work of
successive bishops of Winchester, Stephen Gardiner
and John White; his father served both of them as

treasurer, and the second was his uncle, the ex-
warden of the college. In 1555 his fellow-Member
was either his elder brother Henry or, less probably,
his uncle of the same name; neither of the Whites is
found on the list of those who voted against one of
the government's bills.[2]

White made his will on 1 Sept. 1558. Although
its long and pious preamble might suggest that he
felt the approach of death, his direction that he
should be buried where he should chance to die and
his provision for such other children as he should
happen to have imply that what moved him
was the risk attaching to his return to London for
the approaching parliamentary session. It was to this
danger that he probably succumbed, for whereas on
3 Nov., two days before the session began, he was
again elected master of the revels at his inn, this was
afterwards rescinded by the addition of 'mortuus'
to the entry. It is thus likely that he died either
during the two weeks of the session, or shortly
before or after it; his will was not to be proved until
20 May 1559. Describing himself as of Downton,
where he was lessee of the parsonage, he left 40s.
to its parish church and 20s. to South Warnborough
church and asked for a dirge and masses at his burial
and his month's mind, and the same at his old
school, to which he gave £5 and a present of grain.
His wife, who must have brought a substantial
dowry to the marriage, was to have £500 in money
and jewels, as he had agreed with her mother when
they married, and a life interest in the Downton
property. He set aside another property for the
maintenance of his son John and created an entail,
in the event of failure of the direct line, through his
numerous brothers and sisters. The executors were
his father, mother and uncle the bishop.[3]

[1] Date of birth estimated from elder brother's and from presump-
tion that he was of age at election. *Vis. Hants* (Harl. Soc. lxiv),
81–82; *Winchester Scholars*, ed. Kirby, 124; PCC 15 Chaynay;
Vis. London (Harl. Soc. cix, cx), 4n.   [2] *DNB* (White, John); *M.T.
Recs.* i. 94–118 passim; Beaven, *Aldermen of London*, i. 32; PCC 17
Tashe.   [3] PCC 15 Chaynay; *M.T. Recs.* i. 118.

S.R.J.

WHITLEY see WHEATLEY

WHORWOOD (HORWOOD), William (by 1505–45), of the Middle Temple, London and Putney, Surr.

DOWNTON   1529

b. by 1505, 2nd or 3rd s. of John Whorwood of Compton, Staffs. by Elizabeth, da. of Richard Corbyn of
Kingswinford, Staffs. *educ.* M. Temple, adm. 2 Nov.
1519. *m.* (1) ?1527, Cassandra, da. of Sir Edward Grey
of Enville, Staffs., 1 da.; (2) by 1537, Margaret, da. of
(Sir) Richard Broke* of London, 1da.[1]

Under treasurer, M. Temple 1524, bencher 1537,
Autumn reader 1537.

J.p. Staffs. 1531–d., Surr., Worcs. 1538–d., Derbys. 1541–d., Warws. 1542–d., Lincs. (Holland and Kesteven) 1543, (Lindsey) 1544, Northants. 1543, Notts. 1543–d., Rutland 1543, Leics. 1544; other commissions 1530–d.; solicitor-gen. 1536–40; attorney-gen. 1540–d.[2]

William Whorwood's descent has been traced only to his grandfather but the family seems to have been settled in south-west Staffordshire by at least the early 15th century; its seat in Compton is described in the inquisition of William Whorwood's brother as 'la Horewode alias le Halowes'.[3]

Admitted to the Middle Temple in 1519, Whorwood soon built up a successful practice: in 1524 he is named, with John Baldwin*, in the funeral accounts of Sir Thomas Lovell I* as among 'our counsel', and in 1527 he gave advice to Anne Rede, niece of Archbishop Warham, in a suit concerning her jointure. He also held office at the inn, one of his duties being that of receiver of moneys for the roll of serjeants-at-law in 1521, a year which saw the creation of ten serjeants, three of them from the Middle Temple. By 1526 he was of sufficient account for the mayor and aldermen of London to nominate him, with Thomas Audley and Richard Rich, for the office of common serjeant: all were passed over in favour of a royal nominee.[4]

It was probably in 1527 that Whorwood married a daughter of Sir Edward Grey, the head of an old Staffordshire family: Whorwood's elder brother John also married one of Grey's daughters. On 24 Jan. 1527 Sir Giles Greville of Wick, Worcestershire, who was probably related by marriage to the Redes, wrote to Henry Gold, Archbishop Warham's chaplain, that his proposal for Whorwood was presumably foreclosed as 'he is toward marriage in another place'; as Warham had confidence in Whorwood and favoured him, Greville, who had been comptroller of Princess Mary's household and chamberlain of South Wales, declared his intention of entrusting him with his legal affairs.[5]

It is not clear whether Wolsey, who held the see of Winchester in commendam, exercised parliamentary patronage in 1529 in the borough of Downton, one of three which belonged to the bishopric. Although he was already in disgrace when the elections were held, both the Members for Hindon, and Nicholas Hare, Whorwood's fellow-Member at Downton, were clients of his and may have been his nominees. Yet at the third borough, Taunton, Cromwell's return was arranged by Sir William Paulet, the steward of the bishopric, and it may be that Whorwood's return for Downton owed something to William Portman, Cromwell's fellow-Member at Taunton, who was prominent at Whorwood's own inn. Whether Archbishop War-

ham had any hand in his choice is not known, but the fact that of the six Members returned for the Winchester boroughs five were lawyers of some standing seems to imply that the legal connexions involved were decisive.

In the final session of the Parliament Whorwood was one of four Members, all lawyers, who signed the Act for the heirs of Sir Hugh Dutton (27 Hen. VIII, c.43). He succeeded Sir Richard Rich as solicitor-general on 13 Apr. 1536, one day before the close of the Parliament. His status in the next Parliament, which met seven weeks later, is not wholly clear. In the light of the King's request for the re-election of the previous Members he might have been expected to sit for Downton again, but the omission of his name from a list of the bishop of Winchester's three boroughs accompanied by names thought to be those of Cromwell's nominees for election there is all but proof that Whorwood was not re-elected for Downton. Save for the remote contingency of his transfer elsewhere it thus seems that he did not re-appear in the Commons. In that case, the payment to him of £26 13s.4d. 'for his pains in the time of the Parliament', if it implies his attendance, must mean that he was present in the Lords. This would have accorded with precedent, for Rich had sat there as solicitor-general from 1533 to 1536 although, like Whorwood, he is not known to have been summoned by writ of assistance. With the calling of the next Parliament in 1539 the position is clarified: Whorwood received a writ of assistance, as he was to do again in 1542. Whether any significance attaches to his position on the list of those so summoned—he was placed fifth among the judges, and before Attorney-General Baker—is a matter for argument. As the first solicitor-general to be included he may have been arbitrarily placed; from 1542 the two law-officers were regularly to be placed next to each other. In July 1539 Whorwood and the attorney-general were paid £30 each, with £6 13s.4d. to be shared among their clerks, 'for their pains in penning and writing of sundry Acts'. Of the Acts which Whorwood may have helped to draft in the Parliament of 1539 the most noteworthy were those for the Six Articles, for proclamations and for the dissolution of the monasteries.[6]

Whorwood's upward progress from 1536 is an interesting commentary on the solitary pointer to his attitude on the great issue of the breach with Rome. This is the inclusion of his name on a list of Members drawn up by Cromwell early in 1533. If, as is thought, this list records the names of those who opposed the bill in restraint of appeals, the appearance of Whorwood's among them implies that, at this stage at least, he was out of step with royal policy. He was not the only lawyer listed, his name being preceded by that of Thomas Polsted and followed by that of Thomas Bromley I*. The fact that, like Whorwood, both of these were to go on to office—Bromley to the coif and the bench—shows that their aberration, if such it was, did them no lasting damage. In Whorwood's case, it may not be without significance that his preferment began only after the death of Catherine of Aragon, an event which may have helped to reconcile him to the new order, although his appointment three years later as executor by John Stokesley, the conservative bishop of London, suggests his continued attachment to the old.[7]

In 1530 Whorwood had been appointed a commissioner of gaol delivery and in the following year he was included on the commission of the peace for his native county. So began the appointments to such commissions which were to multiply as his status rose and he was required to travel further afield to enforce obedience to the crown. After a rising in Somerset in April 1536 he and John Hynde* were paid £50 'for executing of rebels in the west'. Two months after the close of the Parliament of 1536 Whorwood wrote to Cromwell and Sir Thomas Kitson from Staffordshire about a dispute over the late Lord Berners's lands in the county. In March 1537 he served as a commissioner of oyer and terminer against the Lincolnshire rebels, and in a letter to the King Sir William Parr* praised the way in which Hynde and Whorwood had handled an awkward prisoner. At the trial of those implicated in the Pilgrimage of Grace, Whorwood conducted the prosecution against Nicholas Tempest and the prior of Bridlington.[8]

Some further indication of Whorwood's private practice is contained in his receipt for 10s. from Richard Catesby* for his half-year's fee for 1534 and in the household accounts of Sir Thomas Heneage for 1534–40, which include a payment to Whorwood of 7s.9d. for his counsel. With legal office came other patronage: in 1537 the city of London granted the solicitor-general an annuity of four marks 'as long as he shall be friendly to this City'. In July 1540 Whorwood succeeded Cromwell as chief steward of the lands of Vale Royal abbey in Cheshire: the ex-abbot was a namesake and perhaps a relative of his. In the following February Whorwood, by now attorney-general, joined Audley and Rich in examining witnesses against the knight porter of Calais; later that year he helped to take an inventory of the goods belonging to the Duchess of Norfolk and Lord William Howard in their houses at Lambeth, and he was appointed by the Council to give evidence against Howard and his wife at their trial. After the King had approved the petition of the borough of Reading for incorporation in 1542, it was passed to Sir John Baker and Whorwood for their further consideration. In the following year Whorwood was appointed to a commission for the sale of crown lands.[9]

The revenue courts frequently needed extra legal advice and Whorwood was paid handsomely for his services: thus in 1539 he and Baker received £64 16s. from the augmentations for advice and in July 1543 Whorwood was paid £33 6s.8d. for drawing indentures. In 1544 he was put on the establishment of the court of surveyors at a salary of £6 13s.4d. It was probably on account of this connexion with the augmentations, rather than his attorney-generalship, that he signed 11 Acts concerned with lands during the Parliament of 1542. He took advantage of his position to acquire lands throughout the west midlands. He may have obtained his house at Putney through his second marriage, for his wife's father Sir Richard Broke had bequeathed 20s. to the churchwardens of Putney. In 1538 Whorwood was included on the commission of the peace for Surrey, and in 1543 he was expected to supply six foot soldiers from the county for the war against France. In 1544 his contribution to the 'aid' for the war was £100.[10]

On 27 May 1545, the day before his death, Whorwood made a brief will. He bequeathed 100 marks to his servants in his house at Putney and £100 to be divided between his nephews, nieces and his brother Richard, who was a priest. His executors were to be his wife Margaret, his brother-in-law William Grey I* and a servant. The will was proved on 9 June 1545, and Whorwood was buried in Putney church, where a brass was erected to his memory. On the following Christmas Eve, Hugh Meire wrote from the parsonage at Rosthorne, Cheshire, of which he was presumably the incumbent, to three eminent lawyers, Henry Bradshaw, Edward Griffin and John Sewster, under the mistaken impression that Whorwood had either not made a will or that he had not been mentally capable of doing so. He proceeded to describe the making of a will, which he himself had written 'upon a cupboard, standing by the bedside', and gave details of its contents which tally with those of the will as proved. The episode lacks explanation.[11]

Whorwood's heirs were his two daughters, both of them minors. John Dudley, Viscount Lisle must quickly have acquired the wardship of Anne, the elder daughter, for by March 1546 she had married his son Ambrose Dudley. A month after her death in 1552 Lisle, now Duke of Northumberland, acquired the wardship of the younger daughter,

Margaret, which in February 1553 passed to his son-in-law Sir Henry Sidney*. She was to marry Thomas Throckmorton II*.[12]

[1] Date of birth estimated from education. *Wm. Salt. Arch. Soc.* v(2), 311; Shaw, *Staffs.* ii. 230; C142/102/78; *LP Hen. VIII,* xii. [2] *LP Hen. VIII,* iv, v, x-xviii, xx. [3] Shaw, ii. 230, 264-7; C142/46/26. [4] *LP Hen. VIII,* iv; *M.T. Recs.* i. 63, 65, 76; Foss, *Judges,* v. 102. [5] *LP Hen. VIII,* iv, v. [6] House of Lords RO, Original Acts, 27 Hen. VIII, no. 53; *LP Hen. VIII,* x. 40(ii) citing Cott. Otho C10, f. 218; xi. 381; xiv; C218/1; Rymer, *Foedera,* vi(3), 74. [7] *LP Hen. VIII,* ix. 1077 citing SP1/99, p. 234; xiv. [8] Ibid. xi-xiii; M. H. and R. Dodds, *Pilgrimage of Grace,* ii. 212. [9] *LP Hen. VIII,* vii, xiv, xvi-xviii; City of London RO, Guildhall, rep. 10, f. 7. [10] W. C. Richardson, *Ct. Augmentations,* 389; *LP Hen. VIII,* xii-xix; C142/73/72, 102/78, 89; E150/1153/9; PCC 3 Jankyn; House of Lords RO, Original Acts, 33 Hen. VIII, no. 44; 34 and 35 Hen. VIII, nos. 29, 32, 36, 39, 42, 43, 45; 35 Hen. VIII, nos. 19, 20, 23. [11] PCC 30 Pynnyng; Mill Stephenson, *Mon. Brasses,* 494; *LP Hen. VIII,* xx. [12] C142/102/78; *CP,* xii(2), 402; *CPR,* 1553, p. 1; *CSP Dom.* 1547-80, p. 41.

S.R.J.

WIGHTMAN, William (by 1517-80), of Harrow-on-the-Hill, Mdx.

MIDHURST	1547
WILTON	1553 (Mar.)[1]
POOLE	1554 (Apr.)
CARMARTHEN BOROUGHS	1555
LUDGERSHALL	1559
WILTON	1563, 1571

b. by 1517, 1st s. of Richard Wightman of Coventry, Warws. by Elizabeth, da. of Humphrey Purcell of Wolverhampton, Staffs. *m.* Audrey, da. of (?Thomas) Dering, 5da.[2]

Clerk to Sir Anthony Browne* by 1547-8; sec. to Thomas Seymour, Baron Seymour of Sudeley by Sept. 1548-9; teller of the change of coin, Tower mint 31 Jan. 1551-*d.*; jt. (with John Perte*) receiver ct. augmentations, S. Wales by 1551, sole 1552-4; receiver, Exchequer, Wales 1554-*d.*; j.p.q. Mdx. 1569-*d.*[3]

William Wightman's youth and early career lay in Coventry, where his father, a capper by trade, was a civic official who rose to be sheriff in 1552-3. The first glimpse of Wightman comes in 1538 when he was appointed with three others to enforce a decree against fouling the city's ditch. In the following decade he entered the service of Sir Anthony Browne, and it was doubtless to Browne as lord of Midhurst that he owed his seat in the first Edwardian Parliament—and perhaps in 1545, for which Parliament the borough's return is lost; his marriage into the Dering family, if it had been celebrated or arranged by the autumn of 1547, may have helped as Nicholas Dering had earlier sat for the borough. Browne died in the spring of 1548 (having mentioned Wightman in his will) but within a few months Wightman secured a post in the household of the young King's uncle, Admiral Seymour. It was Wightman who suggested that the dispute between the admiral and his brother the Protector over the ownership of Catherine Parr's jewels should be referred to Parliament. On 17 Jan. 1549 Seymour

was committed to the Tower for intriguing against his brother, and Wightman too was arrested. Under examination he protested that he had tried to dissuade Seymour, 'but it prevailed nothing . . . for if he had once conceived opinion by his own persuasions, neither lawyer nor other could turn him'. Wightman escaped his master's fate but had difficulty in countering the statements 'cursedly invented and maliciously uttered' by Seymour until in May he threw himself upon the Protector's mercy and was cleared. He probably missed most of the second session (1548-9) of the Parliament of 1547, although his testimony in the House during the passage of Seymour's attainder would have been acceptable. He soon found a new patron in Seymour's brother-in-law (Sir) William Herbert I*, with whose house the rest of his career was to be linked.[4]

In 1550 Herbert served as chief commissioner for the mints and the standard of gold, and almost certainly secured the tellership at the Tower for Wightman. There followed a receivership in South Wales when Herbert became Earl of Pembroke, and on the earl's appointment as commander of the expedition against France in 1557 he made Wightman treasurer of the army 'having special trust and confidence in the wisdom and fidelity of you, with your experience of matters of account'. It was chiefly as a nominee of Pembroke and his son the 2nd earl that Wightman sat in Parliament from 1553; Wilton, where in the spring of 1553 his name was inserted on the indenture in a different hand, was Pembroke's home, Poole yielded to his authority as vice-admiral in Dorset, Carmarthen knew him as constable of its castle, and Ludgershall lay some 15 miles from Wilton. To supplement this pervasive patronage Wightman had connexions of his own, as at Carmarthen where he enjoyed both official standing and the friendship of Thomas Phaer*.[5]

In 1552 Wightman had acquired property in Harrow where he made his home; he leased land in several counties, mostly in Wales, but he continued to live at Harrow until his death and it was there that he was buried on 1 Feb. 1580.[6]

[1] C219/282/10. [2] Date of birth estimated from first reference. *Mdx. Peds.* (Harl. Soc. lxv), 34; D. Lysons, *Environs of London,* ii. 571. [3] PCC 10 Coode; *Coll. State Pprs.* ed. Haynes, 68-71; Tytler, *Edw. VI and Mary,* i. 168-73; Egerton 2545, f. 25; W. C. Richardson, *Ct. Augmentations,* 281; *Brit. Numismatic Jnl.* xlv. 71; *CPR,* 1550-3, p. 108; 1569-72, p. 226. [4] *Coventry Leet Bk.* (EETS cxxxiv), i. 228; ii. 728-812 passim; PCC 10 Coode; *Coll. State Pprs.* 68-71; Tytler, 168-73. [5] *CPR,* 1550-3, p. 108; HMC Foljambe, 4. [6] Lysons, ii. 571; PCC 9 Arundell, 59 Lewyn; *Reg. St. Mary's Harrow,* i. 101.

R.J.W.S.

WIGSTON, Roger (1482/83-1542), of Wolston, Warws.

LEICESTER	1523[1]
COVENTRY	1529, ?1536, 1539,[2] 1542*

b. 1482/83, yst. s. of John Wigston[†] of Leicester, Leics. by Elizabeth, da. of one Gillot. *educ.* I. Temple, adm. 1514. *m.* by 1509, Christian, da. and coh. of Edward Langley, wid. of William Pye, 2s. inc. William* 4da.[3]

Commr. subsidy, Leicester 1515, Coventry 1523, 1524, enclosures, midlands 1517, for survey of monasteries, Warws. 1536, loan 1542; receiver, Beaumont lands 1516–30; jt. (with Sir John Dauntesey*) receiver-gen., wards' lands Feb. 1518–Oct. 1520; j.p. Warws. 1522–*d.*, Salop and Staffs. 1536–*d.*, Worcs., Glos. 1537–*d.*, Herefs. 1538–*d.*, Cheshire 1539–*d.*; recorder, Coventry by 1524–41; receiver, duchy of Lancaster, Tutbury honor, surveyor and receiver, Castle Donington 1528–42; gen. surveyor, King's woods 1530; member, council in the marches of Wales 1534; solicitor, Kenilworth abbey, Warws. and St. Mary's college, Warwick by 1536; steward, Pinley priory, Warws. by 1536; sheriff, Warws. and Leics. 1541–2.[4]

Of the several strands which were to be interwoven in Roger Wigston's varied career, two were contributed by his forbears: commerce and civic authority. The Wigstons had been leading merchants in Leicester for nearly a century and by his time the filling of the mayoralty from its ranks had become 'something of a family tradition'.[5]

Wigston's father, himself twice mayor of Leicester, also had interests in Coventry and these he probably left to his youngest son, together with a legacy of money. The young man followed an elder brother into the Company of the Staple, of which he became mayor at least once and would be listed, before his death, one of the two dozen outstanding merchants. Besides producing wool from his own estate at Wolston, the impropriate rectory which he leased from the Coventry Charterhouse, he also bought it for export, at times with borrowed money: in a letter dated only 27 July, he sought a loan from his brother Thomas, a priest of Newark, 'for now is the chief time of all the year for me to occupy that poor stock that I have or can make for buying of wool', and his brother William died his creditor for £86.[6]

Less traditionally, Wigston also undertook a different apprenticeship, to the law. His admission to the Inner Temple, when he was about 30 years of age, was sponsored by Ralph Swillington*, recorder of Leicester, and he must have learned enough law to qualify him for his own recordership of Coventry. More important, it was probably this channel which led, within two years, to his entry into the King's service and, within a further two, to the receiver-generalship of the wards. From 1517, when he served on Wolsey's enclosure commission, he was increasingly called upon for such investigatory and administrative duties. Public recognition in its turn fostered private practice: a string of religious

houses in Leicestershire and Warwickshire retained his services as counsel and from 1530 he is found writing to Cromwell on their behalf. As recorder of Coventry from 1524 he handled much of the city's litigation, including disputes with the crown arising out of the Dissolution. Then in 1533 he became a member of the newly reorganized council in the marches; its president was Rowland Lee, Wigston's own bishop at Coventry, who doubtless had something to do with the appointment.[7]

To this mounting activity Wigston was to add regular Membership of the Commons. He is first known to have sat there in 1523 as the second Member for Leicester, but he could have done so in 1515 (when he was a subsidy commissioner), especially if he was then residing in the Temple and so unlikely to expect parliamentary wages. If Wigston's name is almost enough to account for his adoption by Leicester, his successive returns for Coventry from 1529 were as clearly a by-product of his recordership. (It is only the Parliament of 1536 for which, in the absence of returns, Wigston's Membership remains uncertain, although highly probable in the light of the King's request for the return of the Members of the previous Parliament.) Of the part he played in the Commons there is only one tiny indication, the appearance of his name among a list of seven on the dorse of an Act passed during the first session of 1534: the purpose of the Act, to limit the number of sheep owned by any individual, explains Wigston's connexion with it, presumably as an expert scrutineer, but whether his self-interest is reflected in the watering-down clauses which weakened its effect must remain a speculation. Among other Acts passed during his Membership which touched his interests and must have engaged his attention were those of 1534 concerning Wales and the marches (26 Hen. VIII, cc.4–6, 11, 12). In 1535 Wigston was involved in a piece of electioneering: as he reported to Cromwell, the death of Sir Edward Ferrers, one of the knights for Warwickshire, had given rise to intrigues among the freeholders about the consequent by-election and it was necessary for Cromwell to make known his wishes if, as Wigston understood, 'it is your mind to have the house furnished with good and discreet men'. The outcome of this episode is unknown as no trace of the by-election survives. A similar opportunity was to present itself in 1541, when Wigston was sheriff of Warwickshire and Leicestershire at the time of the elections to Parliament. His own return for Coventry, although technically invalid, was not without precedent, and may have been part of the arrangement by which he gave up the recordership. What influence, if any, he wielded in the two counties of his bailiwick is difficult, if not impossible, to discern: the names of the knights for Warwickshire are lost, and of those for Leicester-shire the only one known is that of Sir Richard Manners, who as steward of the honor of Leicester and brother of the 1st Earl of Rutland can have needed no support. (If the other was Thomas Brokesby (q.v.), Wigston may have been of assistance.) Wigston's own Membership was to be cut short by his death, but he does not appear to have been replaced until the session of 1544, when his successor as recorder, Edward Saunders, took the seat.[8]

Wigston's attitude towards the religious changes of his later years is not easy to determine. The revelation, in the course of heresy proceedings staged in the diocese of Coventry and Lichfield in 1511–12, that 'master Wyggeston', perhaps Roger Wigston's father or uncle, had 'fine books of heresy' in his possession is an interesting glimpse of a possible Lollard background; but there is no corresponding hint of reform about Wigston himself. When John London, the monastic spoliator, visited him in 1539 he found Wigston much esteemed and resorted to in the shire and his children a great credit to him, all his sons and sons-in-law being in the King's service. London added that Wigston had accepted the Dissolution without protest and had served as a commissioner, despite his personal connexion with several houses and his part in the foundation of the Wyggeston hospital. The recipient of several leases of crown property down to 1530, Wigston appears to have had no grants of monastic property and even failed to get his lease of Wolston renewed. The impression left is of a man who accepted rather than welcomed what was going on.[9]

When he died on 27 Nov. 1542 Wigston held a respectable amount of property: there were Bredon, Dalby and Hathern in Leicestershire, and in Warwickshire the manor of Nethercot, land in Rugby, and various leases, notably that of the priory of Pinley, where his sister had been prioress. Most of this property he left to his elder son after making provision for his wife and small bequests to servants and relatives, for his daughters were already married (one of them was later to marry Edward Aglionby II* as her third husband), and his younger son, a priest. He was buried in Wolston church as he had asked to be.[10]

[1] Leicester Recs. ed. Bateson, iii. 23. [2] E159/319, brev. ret. Mich. r. [1–2]. [3] Aged 36 in 1519, Pollard mss in custody of HP. A. H. Thompson, Wyggeston Hospital Recs. p. xiv; LP Hen. VIII, iii, xiii; Vis. Warws. (Harl. Soc. xii), 37; PCC 15 Spert. [4] LP Hen. VIII, ii–iv, vii, x–xii, xvii, add.; Statutes, iii. 169; E179/123/120, 133/120; H. E. Bell, Ct. of Wards and Liveries, 10; Somerville, Duchy, i. 544; Coventry Leet Bk. (EETS cxxxiv), ii. passim; Val. Eccles. iv. 5n; Leicester Recs. iii. 34. [5] VCH Leics. iv. 27 seq. [6] Thompson, pp. xiii, xiv, 44, 51–52; LP Hen. VIII, v, add. [7] Cal.

I.T. Recs. i. 30; LP Hen. VIII, iii–vii, ix, xi–xvi, xxi; Wealth and Power, ed. Ives, Knecht and Scarisbrick, 57, 58. [8] House of Lords RO, Original Acts, 25 Hen. VIII, no. 13; Agrarian Hist. England and Wales, iv. ed. Thirsk, 217; LP Hen. VIII, vii; Coventry mayors' accts. 1542–61, p. 4. [9] Jnl. Eccles. Hist. xiv. 162–3; LP Hen. VIII, iv, vii. [10] PCC 15 Spert; C142/69/73, 82.

S.M.T.

WIGSTON, William (by 1509–77), of Wolston, Warws.

LEICESTER	1539[1]
WARWICKSHIRE	1554 (Apr.), 1554 (Nov.), 1555

b. by 1509, 1st s. of Roger Wigston*. educ. prob. I. Temple. m. by 1536, Elizabeth, da. of Sir Robert Peyton of Isleham, Cambs., 4s. 7da. suc. fa. 27 Nov. 1542. Kntd. 19 Oct. 1553.[2]

Commr. subsidy, Leicester 1540, relief, Warws. 1550, loan 1557, musters 1569, Coventry 1573, 1577; receiver, duchy of Lancaster, Tutbury honor 1542–76; escheator, Warws. and Leics. 1544–5; j.p. Warws. 1547–d., Leics. 1547–53; sheriff, Warws. and Leics. 1551–2, 1557–8; recorder, Warwick 1554–72.[3]

Dr. John London, in a rare panegyric, praised Roger Wigston for the upbringing of his children: they were loyal and obedient subjects and the sons and sons-in-law were all in public service. Yet William Wigston was never to become as active an official as his father: he held several under steward-ships of crown lands but did not rise much higher. His later employment on commissions of oyer and terminer and as recorder of Warwick implies a legal education and it is all but certain, since both his father and his son belonged to the Inner Temple, that he was the Wigston chosen as marshal there for Christmas 1539 but afterwards fined £5 for refusal, and the 'Wigston, the elder, knight' who was steward for Christmas on several occasions from 1555.[4]

Wigston was probably the 'young Wigston' who attended the reception of Anne of Cleves, but from his father's death he was chiefly employed in local duties. In 1544 he was at first ordered to lead his tenants in the army against France but later exempted from this duty as receiver of Tutbury. A grant of crown land which he received about this time may have been, at least in part, a reward for service. Under Edward VI his appointment to commissions was less frequent, but it was then that he served his first term as sheriff. The recognizance which he gave for Thomas Fisher*, fined £1,000 for his part in the alleged conspiracy of the Duke of Somerset, was probably of no political significance.[5]

Wigston's parliamentary career had begun in 1539, when he was returned for the borough of Leicester. His father, who sat in this Parliament for Coventry, was then at the height of his influence and it was evidently enough to carry the day, aided perhaps by a recommendation from John Beaumont, recorder of Leicester and Wigston's fellow-Member, who was also a senior colleague of his at the Inner Temple. This early start was to be followed by a long intermission, for unless the evidence of an intervening election has been lost it was not until April 1554 that Wigston reappeared in the House. His election as one of the knights for Warwickshire —and as senior knight ahead of the powerful Sir Fulke Greville—seems to imply that his fortunes had risen with the accession of Queen Mary. Although not a Member of the Parliament of the previous autumn, he had been knighted shortly after it opened and his new status, although by no means *de rigueur* for the representation of the shire, may have smoothed his ascent to it. Yet he was not to give the government unswerving support. Re-elected for Warwickshire to the Parliament of November 1554 (although this time as second string to Greville), he was one of the Members who were prosecuted for absenting themselves from its closing days. The fact that, unlike some of the individuals concerned, Wigston did not see the case dropped but was still being distrained for non-appearance at the close of the reign may mean that he was one of the 'real' culprits and not an inadvertent offender. This would give added interest to both his re-election to the Parliament of 1555 and such indication as survives of his alignment there. During the lifetime of that Parliament, and for a year or more after its dissolution, the series of distraints already commenced against Wigston was suspended. If this was an olive branch he may have responded to it by holding aloof from the opposition led by Sir Anthony Kingston, for his name does not appear on the list (which admittedly seems to be incomplete) of Members voting against a government bill in December 1555. The final twist to this obscure story comes with Wigston's second term as sheriff in 1557–8. This not only debarred him from sitting in Mary's last Parliament (unless he was prepared to repeat his father's illegality of 1541) but made him responsible for levying distraints upon himself.[6]

Wigston was to survive Elizabeth's accession by 20 years, but without sitting in any of her Parliaments. As the first holder, until he surrendered it in 1572, of the recordership of Warwick established in 1554 he might have been expected to be returned by that borough even if the knighthood of the shire was no longer within his reach. It may be, therefore, that he had had enough of Parliament, and even of London and Westminster, finding satisfaction in his local round as magistrate and squire. In matters religious he was adjudged 'indifferent' by his bishop in 1564; as the bishop was reporting the verdict of Edward Aglionby II*, Wigston's brother-in-law,

the view may be taken as well informed although not necessarily impartial. As recorder he seems to have been moderate and humane: in a dispute between William Powell, a rebellious townsman, and the town oligarchy he first examined the charter and then decided in favour of the corporation, but also 'earnestly entreated the bailiff to pardon the offence, which was committed through ignorance', a course which was reluctantly followed.[7]

Wigston lived to see all his surviving daughters suitably married and all his younger sons provided for. Himself the heir to both his father and his uncle William Wigston†, he had taken the opportunity provided by the Dissolution to acquire, by judicious purchase and sale, a group of compact properties, Belgrave in Leicestershire and Pinley and Wolston in Warwickshire. The inventory of his goods and chattels came to £209. He made his will on 21 Sept. 1577 and died six days later, being buried as he desired in Wolston church.[8]

[1] C60/352, mm. 17–18. [2] Date of birth estimated from age at fa.'s i.p.m., C142/69/82. *Vis. Warws.* (Harl. Soc. xii), 37–38; C142/183/95. [3] C60/352, m. 18; *CPR*, 1553, p. 360; 1554–5, pp. 18–21; *CSP Dom.* 1547–80, pp. 95, 339; *Coventry Recs.* ed. Jeaffreson, 36, 37; Stowe 571, f. 143; *Black Bk. of Warwick*, ed. Kemp, 14, 86; Somerville, *Duchy*, i. 544; *VCH Warws.* iii. 493. [4] *LP Hen. VIII*, xiv; *CPR*, 1553–4, p. 29; *Cal. I.T. Recs.* i. 123, 134, 186. [5] Shakespeare Birthplace Trust Archer ms 35, f. 20; *LP Hen. VIII*, xiv, xix, xx, add.; *CPR*, 1553, pp. 360, 408. [6] *APC*, v. 101; KB27/1176, 1178–9, 1186–8. [7] *Black Bk. of Warwick*, 14, 86; *Cam. Misc.* ix(3), 45–46; Lansd. 8, f. 81; *CPR*, 1558–60, p. 423; *CSP Dom.* 1547–80, pp. 339, 343. [8] *VCH Warws.* ii. 83; iii. 119, 151; v. 211; vi. 73, 271, 280; *LP Hen. VIII*, xix–xxi; *CPR*, 1550–3, p. 104; 1553–4, p. 366; 1555–7, pp. 310–11; Index to CP 40 Easter 38 Hen. VIII, m. 6v; *Lichfield Wills* (Brit. Rec. Soc. vii), 374; C142/183/95.

S.M.T.

WILBRAHAM (WILBRAM), Richard (by 1504–58), of Woodhey, Cheshire.

TAVISTOCK	1553 (Oct.)
CHESHIRE	1554 (Apr.), 1554 (Nov.), 1555

b. by 1504, 2nd s. of William Wilbraham of Woodhey by Ellen, da. of Philip Egerton of Cheshire. *m.* Dorothy, da. of Richard Grosvenor of Eaton, at least 1s. *suc.* bro. 3 July 1558.[1]

Clerk of kitchen and of spicery, household of Princess Mary in 1525, clerk comptroller by 1533, gent. usher in 1536; member, household of Queen Catherine Parr 1547; keeper, Shotwick park, Cheshire 1548–*d.*, Kenninghall park, Norf. in 1552–3; master of jewel house 1553–*d.*; butler, duchy of Lancaster, Lancs. 14 Nov. 1553–*d.*; bailiff, manor of Walsall, Staffs. 30 Nov. 1553; commr. accts. 1555, 1557, sale of crown lands 1557; sheriff, Cheshire 1555–6.[2]

A younger son who came into the family inheritance on his brother's death a month before his own, Richard Wilbraham was a lifelong servant of Mary Tudor. First recorded as an officer of her household on its establishment at Ludlow, he had risen to be clerk comptroller when in May 1533 the princess asked Cromwell to excuse his father, then nearly 80, from travelling from Cheshire to receive a knighthood. Later in the same year the 3rd Duke of Norfolk replaced Wilbraham in the post by one Richard Tomes, a move which the Duke of Suffolk and others believed had so affronted the princess and her mother that they advised Norfolk to rescind it. Wilbraham is included as clerk comptroller in a roll of Mary's household dating from October 1533 and three years later he appears as one of her gentlemen ushers. Both he and his wife received gifts from the princess. He presumably remained in her entourage, the place which he obtained in Queen Catherine Parr's household being perhaps an extension of his role in the princess's at a time when Mary regularly visited her stepmother. It was during these years that Wilbraham acquired some of the property of Combermere abbey, including the houses and saltworks at Nantwich for which he paid £228 in 1546.[3]

It is not known whether Wilbraham shared in the harassment of Mary's servants under Edward VI, but his services were rewarded on her accession by the mastership of the jewel house and grants of local office. He was also found a place in her first Parliament for Tavistock, a borough controlled by the 1st Earl of Bedford, who presumably transmitted to it a nomination by the Queen herself or by Sir Robert Rochester*, Wilbraham's chief as comptroller of the Household. His return to the next three Parliaments as one of the knights for Cheshire he must again have owed to his standing at court. Predictably, his name is not to be found on any of the lists of Members opposing the government. It was while he was attending the Parliament of 1555 that he was pricked sheriff of Cheshire. The marks of royal favour might have been expected to include a knighthood, but the precedent of his father's evasion of the order perhaps stood in his way.

Wilbraham's absence from the last Parliament of the reign may not have been unconnected with the premonition which led him in February 1558 to secure the wardship of his four year-old son Thomas for his wife, her father and his own kinsman Sir Rowland Hill*, and his eminent friend (Sir) William Cordell*. He was to survive this transaction by only six months, dying on 6 or 7 Aug. 1558. In his will of the previous 25 July he had invoked the prayers of the Blessed Virgin and the company of saints and asked to be buried in Acton church near his father under a marble slab which he hoped would elicit the prayers of its beholders. He made provision for a priest who would say a requiem mass for his family on every 17 Aug. with the children of Acton parish whom he was also to teach, and left money for church repairs, for a canopy over the sacrament and for the poor.

His other bequests included that of 'a long wood knife gilt sometime King Henry VIII's' to his son Thomas. The executors were his wife, his sister Elizabeth Whitmore and his 'cousins' William Liversage and Thomas Clutton. The Thomas Wilbraham[†] who became attorney of the court of wards in 1571 and his nephew Sir Roger Wilbraham, the diarist, were also distant cousins. Wilbraham's widow married Henry Savile*.[4]

[1] Date of birth estimated from first reference. Ormerod, *Cheshire*, iii. 377–9; *Vis. Cheshire* (Harl. Soc. xviii), 249. [2] *LP Hen. VIII*, iv, vi, x; *Privy Purse Expenses of Princess Mary 1536–44*, ed. Madden, 12, 52, 73; *CPR*, 1553–4, p. 83; 1554–5, pp. 11, 343; 1555–7, pp. 314–15; 1557–8, p. 14; 1558–60, p. 64; *APC*, ii. 85; iv. 361, 425; v. 37; E179/69/47; Ormerod, iii. 378; Stowe 571, f. 52; Somerville, *Duchy*, i. 491. [3] *LP Hen. VIII*, vi, x, xix, xxi; *Privy Purse Expenses*, 52, 184; E179/69/47. [4] *CPR*, 1557–8, p. 178; C142/124/176; Ormerod, iii. 378; *Chetham Soc.* xxxiii. 85–90.

P.S.E.

WILD, Thomas (by 1508–59), of The Ford and Worcester, Worcs.

WORCESTER 1547*,[1] 1558

b. by 1508, s. of Simon Wild of The Ford. *m.* (1) by 1529, Alice, da. of Robert Ledington of Worcester, 1s. 2da.; (2) Eleanor, da. and coh. of George Wall of Droitwich, 2s. inc. George[†] 1da.[2]

Chamberlain, Worcester 1545–6, bailiff 1547–8, bridgemaster 1554–5, member of the Twenty-Four 1555, auditor 1555–6.[3]

A clothier who was probably the second of his family and trade to settle and prosper in Worcester, Thomas Wild was elected to the Parliament of 1547 to replace John Braughing who had died about Whitsuntide 1551. He attended most of the last session which opened on 23 Jan. 1552, receiving on 28 Apr. a payment of £7 6s. for 73 days at the customary rate of 2s. a day. Re-elected to the Parliament of 1558, he and his fellow-Member Robert Youle set out on 16 Jan., four days before the opening of the first session, returning on 11 Mar., four days after its close, and receiving payment accordingly 'over and above other charges allowed' by the city. It was in this Parliament that Worcester's repeated efforts to secure the amendment of an Edwardian statute regulating the cloth trade finally succeeded (6 Edw. VI, c.6; 4 and 5 Phil. and Mary, c.5) and it may well have been in this connexion that Wild was accused of slandering John Marshe, one of the Members for London, by saying 'that he had unburdened the clothiers from the search of cloths and laid it upon the buyers'. On 18 Feb. the House committed the matter to the consideration of Sir John Baker and Mr. Mason, probably Robert Mason who sat for Ludlow rather than Sir John Mason.[4]

Wild shared with Youle an interest in the Worcester free school, and while attending Parliament together either in 1552 or in 1558 they procured from the crown £6 a year for its master. In his will of 19 May 1558 Wild bequeathed Little Pitchcroft and four-and-a-half acres in Great Pitchcroft to re-establish the school 'for the bringing up of youth in their ABC, matins and evensong and other learning'. The extract thus preserved in the city records is the only trace found of Wild's will. Besides the property there mentioned, in 1544 he had bought the hospital of St. Wulfstan in Worcester, known as the Commandery, from Richard Morison* for £498. In 1551 he joined with Youle and others to purchase Trinity Hall, Worcester, and in the same year with Hugh Wild, perhaps his brother, to buy a manor in Bromsgrove: in 1559 Hugh Wild conveyed his interest to Wild and Wild's eldest son Robert. Wild died on 11 Aug. 1559 and Robert, then in his 30s, had licence to enter on his lands in the following June. Wild's goods were valued by inventory at £700 and his house, the Commandery, had 31 rooms, one of them containing 20 feather beds.[5]

[1] Hatfield 207. [2] Date of birth estimated from marriage. *Vis. Worcs.* (Harl. Soc. xxvii), 151. [3] Worcester Guildhall, audit of accts. 1540–1600; Nash, *Worcs.* ii. app. cxii; A. F. Leach, *Early Educ. in Worcester* (Worcs. Hist. Soc. 1913), 178; *CPR*, 1554–5, p. 81. [4] A. D. Dyer, *Worcester in 16th Cent.*, 187; Worcester Guildhall, chamber order bk. 1540–1601, ff. 43v, 72v; *CJ*, i. 49. [5] Leach, pp. xxxv, 198–9, 217; *VCH Worcs.* ii. 293; iii. 26; iv. 392, 479; *LP Hen. VIII*, xix; *CPR*, 1550–3, p. 217; 1553, p. 108; 1558–60, pp. 271, 448; C142/128/94; Dyer, 101.

A.D.

WILFORD, Sir James (by 1517–50), of Hartridge, Kent.

BARNSTAPLE 1547*[1]

b. by 1517, 1st s. of Thomas Wilford of Hartridge by 1st w. Elizabeth, da. of Walter Culpeper of Bedgebury; half-bro. of Thomas Wilford†. *m.* by 1543, Joyce, da. of John Barrett of Belhus in Aveley, Essex, 1s. 2da. Kntd. 28 Sept. 1547.[2]

Provost-marshal of the army against Scotland 1547; capt. Lauder Apr.–June 1548, Haddington June 1548–early 1549; keeper, Little Park, Otford, Kent, and steward, manor of Gravesend, Kent 2 Feb. 1550–*d.*[3]

James Wilford's family, originally of Devon stock, had settled in Kent only at the beginning of the 16th century. His grandfather, after whom he was named, had prospered as a merchant taylor in London and his uncle Nicholas Wilford had sat for the City in 1542. His father acquired lands in Kent but aspirations to gentility did not lead him to break with London, where he continued to figure with his brothers.[4]

Wilford was considered by Cromwell in 1538 for a post as daily waiter in his household. Whatever the decision, Cromwell's downfall did not harm Wilford, who by 1542 had obtained a minor (unspecified) post in the royal service. In that year he and his lifelong friend Thomas Wyatt* were pardoned for an assault and robbery, but the outbreak of war in 1544 gave him a more legitimate outlet: he was included in the Kent musters and served with distinction in the campaign which led to the fall of Boulogne. Two years later the Council recommended his appointment as Adrian Poynings's lieutenant in the citadel there, but he refused to serve under Poynings. This was not held against him and Henry VIII rewarded him with an annuity worth £50 and the Protector Somerset with the provost-marshalship in the army against Scotland in 1547. His valour at the battle of Pinkie, where he 'placed himself with the foremost of the foreward', confirmed Somerset's esteem for Wilford and earned him a knighthood.[5]

It was doubtless on Somerset's recommendation that Wilford was elected at Barnstaple with Bartholomew Traheron, even if his family's origin was of some help. Although almost certainly chosen in his absence, he returned south with the army and may be expected to have spoken during the first session on the need to press the war to a conclusion. After the prorogation he raised troops in London to that end, and by 22 Feb. 1548 he was on his way back to Scotland, where he took up a command at Lauder. In April his services were enlisted by the 13th Lord Grey de Wilton towards the capture of Haddington, and on its fall Grey proposed him as its governor. Neither Grey nor Somerset was to be disappointed, for Wilford—'such a one as was able to make a cowardly beast a courageous man'—held Haddington, ill manned, badly fortified and plague stricken, almost without help for close on a year, and the garrison lost heart only after his capture by the French during an ill-advised attack on Dunbar. When it was learnt that he had fallen ill Grey persuaded the Council to secure his release by an exchange: his condition on arrival at York in November 1549 was described as 'very weak'. He had missed the second session of the Parliament and his failing health probably prevented him from resuming his place during the third: his wife remained in constant attendance on him, a boy was employed to assist her, and his affairs were managed by his brothers and brothers-in-law. He nevertheless interested himself in Sir Thomas Wyatt's scheme to establish a militia by Act of Parliament to preserve England from Catholicism: he also availed himself of the privilege of the House to have a servant freed from arrest.[6]

When Wilford made his will on 18 Nov. 1550 he was living in the Crutched Friars, London, at a house belonging to Sir Thomas Wyatt. After remembering his father and kinsmen, he provided for his wife and children, left some 'white harness' to Sir Philip Hoby* and asked his 'good friend' (Sir) John Baker I* to placate his father if he objected to the terms of the will. As executors Wilford appointed his wife, father and brothers, and Wyatt and Baker, the last being also a witness. He was buried on 24 Nov. near his grandfather at Little Bartholomew's beside St. Anthony's, the funeral oration being preached by Miles Coverdale. His widow took as her second husband Thomas Stanley*, and Sir Arthur Champernon replaced him in the Commons for the final session. A portrait shows Wilford standing in front of a view of Haddington.[7]

[1] C219/282/2.   [2] Date of birth estimated from first reference. *Vis. Kent* (Harl. Soc. xlii), 53; (lxxiv), 22; (lxxv), 46–47; *Vis. Essex* (Harl. Soc. xiii), 322; *DNB*; *The Gen.* iv. 1–5; C142/100/50.   [3] W. Patten, *The Expedicion into Scotland* (1548), unpaginated; *APC*, ii. 379; *CPR*, 1548–9, p. 226.   [4] *The Gen.* iv. 1–5; *Arch. Cant.* xxxviii. 26; xlviii. 36–37.   [5] M. L. Robertson, 'Cromwell's servants' (Univ. California Los Angeles Ph.D. thesis, 1975), 587; *LP Hen. VIII*, xiii, xvii, xxi; Patten.   [6] *HMC Bath*, iv. 336; information from Julianna Marker; *CSP Scot.* i. passim; *APC*, ii. 160, 170; W. K. Jordan, *Edw. VI.* i. 274, 276, 285, 287–90; *Life of Ld. Grey of Wilton* (Cam. Soc. xl), 46–47; M. H. Merriman, 'Eng. and Fr. intervention in Scot. 1543–50' (London Univ. Ph.D. thesis, 1975), 323–4; U. Fulwell, *The flower of fame* (1575), 50–51, 54; *Lit. Rems. Edw. VI*, 224; *HMC Rutland*, iv. 194, 196–7; PCC 28 Coode; *Pprs. Geo. Wyatt* (Cam. Soc. ser. 4, v), 57; *CJ*, i. 15.   [7] PCC 28 Coode; *Machyn's Diary* (Cam. Soc. xlii), 3; information from Dr. R. C. Strong.

A.D.K.H.

WILFORD, Nicholas (c. 1495–1551), of London and Wandsworth, Surr.

LONDON   1542

b. c. 1495, 5th s. of James Wilford of London by Elizabeth, da. of John Bettenham of Pluckley, Kent. *m.* 1529, Elizabeth, da. of Thomas Gale, 4s. 5da.[1]
Auditor, London 1545–7.[2]

Nicholas Wilford's father, a merchant taylor and alderman of London, gave each of his five younger sons 500 marks before making his will in 1526. Nicholas Wilford also became a merchant taylor and first engaged in the Spanish trade. In 1527 he was a substantial merchant in Bilbao, but in that year the ominous political situation caused him and other English merchants in Spain to arrange to send home all their possessions; they themselves probably returned to England soon after. Wilford had presumably been importing Spanish wool; later he was to export cloth from London.[3]

Wilford settled in his father's parish of St. Bartholomew the Less; in 1536 he was one of the 'substantial inhabitants' there appointed as collectors of the subsidy and five years later his own goods were assessed at 1,000 marks. In or after 1540 he moved to the parish of St. George, Botolph Lane, when his wife inherited her parents' property there, a capital tenement with four smaller houses and adjacent shops held of a chantry in the cathedral. It was probably from the Gales that he also acquired his

lands in Wandsworth, where Thomas Gale had left £20 for the repair of highways and his wife was buried; Wilford himself was a parishioner there from at least 1546, when the churchwardens' accounts begin.[4]

Wilford's election by the commonalty of London to the Parliament of 1542, seemingly unremarkable in itself, acquires interest from an episode which took place a week before the Parliament opened. On 9 Jan. 1542 one of his elder brothers, alderman Robert Wilford, was accused before his fellow-aldermen of being a 'maintainer' of the pope. As a son-in-law of Richard Fermor (q.v.), who had been convicted of a similar offence 18 months before but had since been pardoned, Robert Wilford was an obvious target; yet the timing of the accusation suggests that it was intended to compromise his brother, while the fact that the commonalty's other choice on this occasion, John Sturgeon, seems to have had Protestant leanings raises the possibility that religion had played some part in the election. Of Nicholas Wilford's beliefs there is no indication, but the episode seems to have damaged neither him nor his brother. The only glimpse of Wilford's role in the Parliament is the unexciting one of his being asked by the City in February 1544 to strive to prevent the passage of a bill 'against merchants for packing of woollen cloths, the surmise whereof is that they do usually pack money, both silver and gold, in their said cloths': the bill did not pass the Commons. With Sturgeon he had been named a commissioner in the Act for the partition of Wapping marsh (35 Hen. VIII, c.9).[5]

Wilford made his will on 3 Aug. 1551, asking to be buried 'without pomp or vain glory' in the church of St. George in Botolph Lane, beside his father-in-law. According to the custom of London he left one third of his goods to his widow, his executrix, one third to be divided among his children and the remaining third to be spent on his legacies. He left £10 for the poor of the hospital of St. Bartholomew in Smithfield, of which he was a governor, and £6 13s.4d. to the Merchant Taylors' Company, with many small bequests to friends and relatives. All his freehold lands in Surrey and elsewhere in England, unspecified, he left to his widow and her heirs for ever, and his lands in customary or copyhold tenure to her for life with remainder to their eldest son. Wilford was buried in St. George's, where a monument later commemorated him and his wife. The will was proved on 24 Aug. 1551.[6]

[1] Date of birth estimated from family history. *Vis. Surr.* (Harl. Soc. xliii), 141–2; *Surr. Arch. Colls.* vii. 309; *The Gen.* iv. 1–5; PCC 20 Alenger.   [2] City of London RO, Guildhall, jnl. 15, ff. 176, 267.   [3] PCC 13 Porch; *LP Hen. VIII*, iv; G. Connell-Smith, *Forerunners of Drake*, 8; E122/82/7, 167/1 ex inf. Prof. P. Ramsey.   [4] City of

London RO, rep. 9, ff. 157v–8; E179/144/120; *CPR*, 1548–9, p. 4182
PCC 20 Alenger, 4 Alen; *Surr. Arch. Colls.* xv. 82, 84, 89, 92;
[5] City of London RO, rep. 10, f. 236v; 11, f. 38. [6] PCC 22 Bucke;
City of London RO, rep. 12(1), f. 141; *Stow's Survey of London*,
i. 210.

H.M.

WILKES, Thomas (by 1508–36/37), of Chippen-ham, Wilts.

CHIPPENHAM 1529

b. by 1508. *m.* Edith, at least 1s.[1]

Thomas Wilkes was presumably the Chippenham 'yeoman' of that name who figures in two actions brought before the court of requests in 1537 and 1538 by Geoffrey Daniell* and his wife Margaret: save for his Membership in 1529 and collectorship of the revenues of Monkton Farleigh priory before its dissolution in February 1536, everything that has come to light about Wilkes is drawn from these suits. In 1531 Margaret Daniell, then the widow of Richard Hitchcock, had sold wool worth £36 to Nicholas Taylor, a Gloucestershire clothier, who was to pay the money to Thomas Wilkes to the use of Margaret's children. This Taylor claimed to have done, and although Wilkes had since died his brother John admitted as much in his deposition of May 1538. The Daniells accordingly claimed the amount from Wilkes's executors, his widow and son John, who replied, as did Edith Wilkes's second husband Richard ap Harry, by denying knowledge of the transaction: which party prevailed is not known. Wilkes presumably lived long enough to be re-elected to the Parliament of 1536, in accordance with the King's request for the return of the previous Members, but on the evidence of the lawsuit of 1537–8 he did not long survive it.[2]

[1] Presumed to be of age at election. Req.2/10/208.   [2] Req.2/3/153,
10/208; *VCH Wilts.* iii. 266; *Val. Eccles.* ii. 144.

T.F.T.B.

WILKINSON, Thomas (by 1477–1535/37), of Kingston-upon-Hull, Yorks.

KINGSTON-UPON-HULL 1512,[1] 1515[2]

b. by 1477. *m.* (1) Margaret; (2) Alice; (3) Elizabeth; at least 2da. prob. by 1st w.[3]
     Chamberlain, Kingston-upon-Hull 1498–9, sheriff 1501–2, mayor 1507–8, 1520–1, 1527–8; commr. gaol delivery 1508, 1509, 1511, subsidy 1512, 1515, 1523, 1524.[4]

A draper by trade, Thomas Wilkinson was among the substantial townsmen of Hull who were assessed in 1524 for subsidy at £20 or more. Elected to the Parliament of 1512 after having served his first mayoralty, he was re-elected to its successor in accordance with the King's request for the return of the previous Members and may have sat again in 1523, when the names of the Hull Members are lost.

In 1532 he conveyed four houses in Kirk Lane (where he had acquired a tenement in 1507) to the corporation as endowment for a chantry, but the will in which he confirmed this arrangement was not drawn up until 7 May 1535 or proved until 3 Oct. 1537. He asked to be buried in the south aisle of Holy Trinity church beside his first wife. To his third wife Elizabeth he left a life interest in the property destined to support the chantry and made her executrix and residuary legatee. The overseers were his sons-in-law Thomas Dalton and William Knowles, both prominent residents of Hull and the first the father of the Marian Member of the same name.[5]

[1] Kingston-upon-Hull chamberlains' roll 3 Hen. VIII. [2] Ibid
6 Hen. VIII. [3] Date of birth estimated from first reference. York
wills 11, f. 259. [4] L. M. Stanewell, *Cal. Anct. Deeds, Kingston-upon-Hull*, M479(56); T. Gent, *Kingston-upon-Hull* (1735), 106,
108, 109; *CPR*, 1494–1509, pp. 560, 580, 628; *LP Hen. VIII*, i, iii,
iv; *Statutes*, iii. 85, 175. [5] Stanewell, D491–2, 558–9; *VCH Yorks.*
(*E. Riding*), i. 159, 288; J. Tickell, *Kingston-upon-Hull* (1798),
801n; York wills 11, f. 259.

M.K.D.

WILLIAMS, George (by 1521–56), of Denton, Lincs.

GRANTHAM 1555

b. by 1521, 1st s. of William Williams of Stamford by Elizabeth, da .of John Upton. *educ.* L. Inn, adm. 8 Feb. 1535. *m.* (1) by 1539, Alice Cony of Bassingthorpe, 2s. 5da.; (2) 1551/55, Rose, 2da. *suc.* fa. by 1538.[1]
     J.p. Lincs. (Kesteven) 1554; commr. sewers, Cambs., Hunts., Isle of Ely, Lincs., Northants, Notts. 1555.[2]

After a legal education George Williams took service with William Cecil. He had probably done so by July 1549, when he bought from Cecil and Lawrence Eresby (or Irby) for £261 the manors of Hungerton and Wyville, formerly belonging to the chantry called 'Curteys' in Grantham church; the property, which Cecil and Eresby had themselves just acquired from the crown, lay at Denton (which Williams made his home), Harlaxton, Hungerton and Wyville, all to the southwest of Grantham. Williams seems to have managed Cecil's Lincoln-shire properties, writing to him in 1551 about repairs to a church at Ewerby and tithes at Thorpe Waterville (Northamptonshire), and in 1552 about the purchase of land at Barholm and about guild property at Baston which he thought that Cecil could claim in right of his ward Arthur Hall[†]. The last of these provoked a Star Chamber suit after Williams had tried to intimidate the escheator, among his opponents being Edmund Hall*, a rival claimant, and George Foster*, who wanted to maintain the guild. In the same year Williams conveyed to Cecil a complaint by Cecil's father about a grant of lands, and in 1554 his activities included receiving rents and debts and reporting arrears, describing the abuse of woods at Pickworth by servants of (Sir) William Hussey II*, and attending a 'great sale' at Grimsthorpe.[3]

Williams clearly owed his election at Grantham to the patronage of Cecil, who was himself returned senior knight of the shire. Although he had sufficiently commended himself to the Marian regime to be put on the Kesteven bench, Williams was among those who in this Parliament opposed one of the government's bills. Within eight months of doing so he was dead (2 Aug. 1556), perhaps unexpectedly, as he left no will. Letters of administration were granted to his 16 year-old heir Richard, whose wardship was acquired by John Allen, not the Member for Stamford who had died in 1554 but perhaps his son of the same name.[4]

[1] Date of birth estimated from education. *Lincs. Peds.* (Harl. Soc. lii), 1083. [2] *CPR*, 1553-4, p. 21; 1554-5, p. 109. [3] Ibid. 1549-51, p. 59; 1553-4, p. 380; NRA 8679 (Lincoln AO, Pearson-Gregory pprs. 1/81, 84, 85, 88; 2/12 no. 1/1); *CSP Dom.* 1547-80, pp. 35-38, 45-47, 62-64, 69. [4] Guildford mus. Loseley 1331/2; C142/110/98; *CPR*, 1555-7, p. 526.

T.M.H.

WILLIAMS, Gruffydd (by 1512-49 or later), of New Carmarthen, Carm.

CARMARTHEN BOROUGHS 1542, 1545

b. by 1512.[1]
Bailiff, Carmarthen 1533-4, mayor 1548-9.[2]

A prominent townsman of Carmarthen, Gruffydd Williams was assessed for the subsidy in 1544 as of King's Street, New Carmarthen; his goods were said to be worth £30 6s.8d. He was one of the freemen named in Carmarthen's new charter of 1546, but after his term as mayor no further trace has been found of him.[3]

[1] Date of birth estimated from first reference. [2] *Principality of Wales: S. Wales* (Univ. Wales Bd. of Celtic Studies, Hist. and Law ser. xxvi), 346-7; Lloyd, *Carm.* ii. 467; C. Spurrell, *Carmarthen*, 174. [3] E179/264/1; *LP Hen. VIII*, xxi.

P.S.E.

WILLIAMS, Henry (1524/26-51), of Alderton, Northants.

NORTHAMPTONSHIRE 1547*

b. 1524/26, 1st s. of Sir John Williams*, Lord Williams of Thame, by Elizabeth, da. and coh. of Thomas Bledlow of Bledlow, Bucks. *m.* Anne, da. of Henry Stafford, 1st Baron Stafford, *s.p.*[1]

Henry Williams undoubtedly owed his knighthood of the shire for Northamptonshire in 1547 to the influence of his father who was present at the election: the father owned or was steward of several manors in the southern part of the county, and himself sat in this Parliament for Oxfordshire. When returned, the son was young and inexperienced; he

may have been the Henry Williams of the stable who served in the army against France in 1544 but he had played no part in civil affairs, so that it was doubtless his father who as 'Mr. Williams' had several bills committed to him. In August 1548 Henry Williams and his younger brother Francis were in Padua, but he may have returned to England in time for the second session of the Parliament as in October he was named an overseer of the will of Robert Burdett*. He died of the sweating sickness and was buried in London on 20 Aug. 1551, 'with banners of arms, coats of armour and four dozen escutcheons'. His brother's death in the same epidemic left their father without a male heir. An epitaph on Henry Williams was written by Thomas Norton (q.v.). It is not known who replaced him in the House.[2]

[1] Date of birth estimated from election and date of parents' marriage. Dugdale, *Warws.* 394. [2] C219/19/70; *LP Hen. VIII*, xix; *CJ*, i. 2, 14; *Cam. Misc.* x(2), 8; Lichfield consist. ct. wills 1549, f. 5; *Machyn's Diary* (Cam. Soc. xlii), 8; Strype, *Eccles. Memorials*, ii (1), 494.

S.M.T.

WILLIAMS, James (by 1514-82 or later), of Pant Hoel and Trelech-a'r-Bettws, Carm.

CARDIGANSHIRE 1553 (Mar.), 1554 (Nov.)[1]

b. by 1514, 1st s. of William ap John Thomas of Trelech by Margaret, da. of Hywel ap Jenkin. *m.* Elizabeth, da. of John Bowen of Pentre Ieuan, Pemb., at least 1s. *suc.* fa. by 1544. Kntd. 19 Oct. 1553.[2]
Steward, lordship of Narberth, Pemb. in 1535; commr. tenths of spiritualities, St. David's diocese 1535, musters, Narberth 1539, Card. 1569, benevolence, Carm. 1544/45, relief 1549-50, goods of churches and fraternities 1553; j.p. Card. c. 1543, 1555, q. 1558/59-61, Carm. 1543, 1558/59, 1562, 1572, q. 1573/74-82; sheriff, Carm. 1544-5, 1568-9, Pemb. 1555-6; burgess, Carmarthen, Carm. 1546.[3]

James Williams came from Trelech, near Carmarthen, but his wife's family lived in north Pembrokeshire, close to Cardigan, and he was to be active in the three newly formed counties of southwest Wales. One of the town council of Carmarthen under the charter of 1546, and assessed there for subsidy in 1549 on goods worth £30, he was among the first justices appointed in both Carmarthenshire and Cardiganshire and was twice sheriff of Carmarthenshire and once of Pembrokeshire. Some sidelights are cast on his career by his own and others' resort to law. In 1543 or 1544, as a newly appointed justice, he complained to Chancellor Audley of the levy of forced loans in Carmarthenshire and Pembrokeshire. If Williams's speedy appointment as sheriff owed anything to this episode, a complaint against him in this capacity of detaining the money paid by a debtor whom he had arrested, and a further one of refusing to quit a mill belonging to Dr. John Vaughan, suggest that his own conduct was not beyond reproach. The chancery suit brought against him under Edward VI by David Owen Philip for occupying Llanbedwy parsonage in Carmarthenshire in the name of Edmund Powell, an Oxfordshire man and probably the Member for Ludgershall, sounds like an echo of the forced loans affair, while his attachment in 1550 to appear before the Pembrokeshire great sessions for slandering Roger Barlow, brother of the former bishop of St. David's, shows that he shared the local hostility to these intruders.[4]

Williams's two elections for Cardiganshire are probably to be explained by his local connexions. The first took place during the shrievalty of Owen Gwyn (perhaps the Member for Marlborough) and was accompanied by the return of Edward ap Hywel for the Cardigan Boroughs; the second occurred when (Sir) Henry Jones I* was sheriff and coincided with the election of John Gwyn for the Boroughs. As Jones had himself sat with Williams in the earlier Parliament, when he was knight for Carmarthenshire, he may have promoted Williams's re-election in his capacity as sheriff, especially as both hailed from Carmarthenshire. Jones and Williams were also to be knighted on the same day, 19 Oct. 1553; the first was then sitting in Parliament while the second was not, but the tempting speculation that Williams had gone to London as the defeated candidate who would challenge the validity of John Price II's (q.v.) return to that Parliament for Cardiganshire can scarcely be reconciled with Price's re-election to its successor after Jones had become sheriff. Of Williams's part in the proceedings of the Commons all that is known is that he was not among the Members who quitted the Parliament prematurely and without leave.

Williams's continued activity in county administration under Mary and Elizabeth implies that he was conformable to their differing regimes. In 1575 he was described as resident in the commote of Elvet, Carmarthenshire, but in 1570 he had mustered with one demilance and two light horsemen in Cardiganshire. He probably died shortly after his last appearance on the commission of the peace in 1582.[5]

[1] Huntington Lib. Hastings mss Parl. pprs. [2] Date of birth estimated from first reference. J. Buckley, *Gen. of Carm. Sheriffs*, 8; C1/1081/43. [3] *LP Hen. VIII*, viii, xiv, xxi; *CPR*, 1553, pp. 364, 419; 1560–3, p. 445; R. Flenley, *Cal. Reg. Council, Marches of Wales*, 69; C193/12/1; E179/220/96, 263/35; St.Ch.2/26/303; SP11/5/6. [4] *LP Hen. VIII*, viii, xiv, xxi; C1/1081/43, 1146/15, 1281/43, 1313/48; 193/12; E179/264/1; St.Ch.2/26/303; NLW ms Wales 25/8; *Augmentations* (Univ. Wales Bd. of Celtic Studies, Hist. and Law ser. xiii), 40, 166; *Chancery* (ibid. iii), 55, misreading Edward for Edmund Powell; *W. Wales Hist. Recs.* iii. 117–22. [5] J. Allen, *Sheriffs Pemb.* 9; Flenley, 74, 139.

P.S.E.

WILLIAMS, John (by 1518–57/58), of Langton Herring, Dorset.

WEYMOUTH 1554 (Apr.)

b. by 1518. *m.* Anne, 1da.[1]

John Williams bought the lease of Langton in 1539 from Sir John Rogers* for £100 but sold it soon afterwards, with the farmstock, for £300. In 1543 its purchaser, Edward Clement, sold to Williams 700 sheep which they agreed were to be pastured at Langton free for one year; Clement also sold or agreed to sell to him property in Shaftesbury and lands in Wiltshire. These transactions brought both parties into Chancery as complainants, Williams asserting that he had never received his sheep, Clement alleging partiality by Williams's attorney Christopher Hole*. The lease of Langton reverted to Williams and when he made his will, on 7 Oct. 1557, he left it to his wife during her widowhood and then to his nephew and executor Henry Williams. The will was proved on 13 May 1558. Three years later Henry Williams was granted a pardon of outlawry incurred as its executor. The widow married as her second husband Clement Hyett*.[2]

As Williams's home lay five miles north-west of Weymouth, it was presumably as a local gentleman that he was returned to Parliament early in 1554, but if Hole was still under sheriff of Dorset his Membership may have been promoted by Hole, who himself was returned for Dorchester. Nothing is known about Williams's part in the work of the House. As a freeholder he helped choose the knights of the shire in 1555. He was never put on the Dorset bench, the John Williams who appears on commissions of the peace from 1537 to 1547 being his more eminent namesake of Winterbourne Herringston.[3]

[1] Date of birth estimated from first reference. PCC 21 Noodes. [2] C1/1092/52, 1110/21; C. H. Mayo, *Shastonian Recs.* 81–82; PCC 21 Noodes; *CPR*, 1560–3, p. 21. [3] C219/24/50.

H.M.

WILLIAMS, Sir John (by 1503–59), of Rycote and Thame, Oxon.

OXFORDSHIRE 1542, 1547, 1553 (Mar.), 1553 (Oct.)

b. by 1503, 2nd surv. s. of Sir John Williams† of Burghfield, Berks. by Isabel, da. and coh. of Richard More of Burghfield. *m.* (1) by July 1524, Elizabeth (*d.* 25 Oct. 1556), da. and coh. of Thomas Bledlow of Bledlow, Bucks., wid. of Andrew Edmonds (*d.* 23 June 1523) of Cressing Temple, Essex, 3s. inc. Henry* 2da.; (2) settlement 19 Apr. 1557, Margaret, da. of Thomas Wentworth*, 1st Lord Wentworth, of Nettlestead, Suff., 1da. Kntd. 15 Nov. 1538/28 June 1539; *cr.* Lord Williams of Thame 1554.[1]

?Chancery official by 1526; clerk of the King's

jewels 8 May 1530, jt. (with Thomas Cromwell) master c. Jan. 1535, sole 1540–44; receiver, lands formerly of 3rd Duke of Buckingham Mar. 1531, Thame abbey by 1535; j.p. Bucks. 1535, Oxon. 1535–7, 1542–7 or later, Berks. 1544, Northants. 1554; sheriff, Oxon. and Berks. 1538–9, 1544–5, Sept.–Nov. 1553; visitor of monasteries 1538; commr. subsidy, Oxon. 1540, benevolence 1544/45, chantries, Northants., Oxon., Rutland 1546, 1548, of Admiralty in Nov. 1547, relief, Berks., Oxon., Northants. 1550, musters, Salop, Staffs., Warws. 1559; steward, manors of Grafton and Hartwell, Northants. Feb. 1540, Easton Neston, Northants. 1542; master of cygnets in Thames Mar. 1542; treasurer, ct. augmentations Mar. 1544–Jan. 1554; high steward, Oxford ?by 1553; chamberlain to King Philip Apr. 1554–8; trier of petitions in the Lords, Parlts. of Nov. 1554, 1555 and 1559; pres. council in the marches of Wales Feb. 1559–*d*.[2]

John Williams was of Welsh descent. His father was the first of the line to anglicize his name and probably the first to seek his fortune in England. He was a kinsman of Morgan Williams who married Cromwell's sister, a relationship which must have helped his son in his early career: in 1535 Gregory Cromwell* wrote to his own father from Rycote that he had been splendidly entertained by all the neighbourhood, especially by Williams. In 1544 Sir Richard Cromwell *alias* Williams*, Morgan Williams's son, left Sir John Williams two of his best horses.[3]

It is not certain which of the family first became established in the region of Thame. John Williams's sister Anne married William King, of Thame, and by 1535 another sister was prioress of Studley, but it was Williams's own marriage which was probably decisive, for Bledlow is only five miles from Thame. The marriage, to the widow of an important Londoner, also suggests that by 1524 Williams was a royal servant with London connexions; these may have included Sir John Dauntesey*, his neighbour at Thame.[4]

In 1536 Williams increased his reputation by his prompt and effective action against the Lincolnshire rebellion. In 1537 he was commissioned to investigate allegations against the abbots of Eynsham and Osney and to sit with Dauntesey to hear charges of sedition at Thame. Although he was probably responsible for the reprieve of Studley in that year, he was assiduous in receiving the surrender of monasteries and particularly, as master of the jewels, in ransacking their shrines. Early in 1538 he took 5,000 marks' worth of gold and silver from Bury St. Edmunds; between 7 and 11 Mar. he stripped Abingdon and was reported to have left 100 barge-loads of spoils at the waterside; and at three o'clock on a Saturday morning in September, he and two others 'made an end' of the shrine of St. Swithun at

Winchester, taking the trouble to 'sweep away all the rotten bones called relics' lest the citizens think that they came only for the treasure. In the previous May he and Thomas Lee I* had taken the surrender of Woburn, where he heard accusations of treason against the abbot and eventually became the receiver of the property. In Oxfordshire he took the surrenders of Eynsham, Godstow, Osney, Studley and Thame, that of Studley from his own sister. Between 1542 and 1557 he pulled down and sold the materials of Gloucester Hall, Oxford.[5]

The abbot of Thame was Anne Williams's brother-in-law Robert King, for whom Williams had secured the abbacy of Osney *in commendam* in 1537 and who in 1541 became bishop of Thame and Osney and in 1545 first bishop of Oxford, no doubt with Williams's continued assistance. If he could look after a relative in this way, Williams was able to do much more for himself. He had begun by securing a 21-year lease of the crown's demesne lands at Grafton, Northamptonshire, in 1528 and the reversion of lands at Upper Winchendon, Buckinghamshire, four years later. With the Dissolution there began an impressive series of grants and purchases. He had already bought the house at Rycote, which became his chief seat, from Giles Heron* and had secured an interest in the estates of Thame abbey. His possession of Rycote was confirmed by an Act of 1539 (31 Hen. VIII, c.19), introduced into the Lords by Williams himself, and reaffirmed in the following year by a proviso to Heron's Act of attainder (32 Hen. VIII, c.58). In 1538 he purchased Wytham, Berkshire, from Leonard Chamberlain* and began to form a second cluster of properties west of Oxford, while his purchase of a manor in Monmouthshire may reflect some awareness of his origins. In Cripplegate, London, he purchased the priory of Elsingspital for some £530 and up to 1547 he made five further purchases, in conjunction with other speculators, of monastic lands to a total value of about £8,000, much of which was resold. At the beginning of Edward VI's reign he bought the abbeys of Thame and Notley, near Thame, from the Duke of Somerset and Sir William Paget. His last major purchase was that of the priory of Marlow in 1555.[6]

The fall of Cromwell does not seem to have affected Williams's position, save in making him sole master of the jewels. On 26 Aug. 1540 the Privy Council met at Rycote and a week later it added his name to the Oxfordshire subsidy commission. In 1544 he was licensed to retain ten men in addition to his household servants and was listed as the captain of 20 archers and 40 billmen in the King's battle of the army against France. His career in royal administration culminated in his appointment as treasurer of the augmentations in 1544 with a yearly salary of £320.[7]

Williams is first known to have been elected to the Parliament of 1542, although he could have sat for a borough in its precursor of 1539, for which most of the returns are lost. His shrievalty doubtless excluded him from the last Parliament of the reign, but he was to sit in the three summoned before his ennoblement. It was presumably he rather than his son Henry, knight of the shire for Northamptonshire, who as Mr. Williams had a bill concerning sheriffs committed to him after its second reading on 8 Dec. 1547, and certainly he to whom one concerning tithes and another on regrators and forestallers were committed during the second session of that Parliament on 22 Feb. and 1 Mar. 1549. In the third session he was doubtless the recipient of a bill to encourage husbandry, first read on 4 Jan. 1550, and another for putting away old service books after its second reading ten days later. On 21 Jan. 1549 he secured privilege for his servant Anthony Butler*. He was himself an unpopular landlord and a victim of the rising in Oxfordshire in the summer of 1549 when the commons 'disparked his park(s) . . . and killed all the deer' at Rycote and Thame. It is not surprising, therefore, in view of Somerset's alleged leniency to the rebels, that Williams was one of the three ordered to Windsor in October 1549 to 'protect' the King and arrest Somerset.[8]

In October 1551 the imperial ambassador reported that Williams himself had been arrested, an act which, since Williams possessed a huge amount of livestock and was loathed by the people, was meant to show that the Duke of Northumberland wanted to ease the people's burdens. There is no other evidence of the arrest before 8 Apr. 1552, when the Privy Council ordered the warden of the Fleet prison to receive him and to allow none to converse with him. By 25 Apr. the confinement was affecting his health and he was allowed to exercise and to be visited by his family and friends; the ill-health seems to have persisted, for on the Crown Office list of the Parliament of October 1553 he is described as 'infirmus'. According to the King's journal, Williams had disobeyed an order not to pay pensions without the Council's foreknowledge, and it was for 'lack of doing his duty in his office' that he made his humble submission on 22 May 1552, when he was released. The Privy Council continued to issue warrants to Williams throughout his imprisonment. There is little reason to question the official version of his offence, although his unpopularity may have made him a target, and there are other pointers to his having fallen short of even the far from rigor-

ous standards of the time. Only in May 1552 were his accounts as master of the jewels cleared, and in Mary's reign he was to be in trouble over his augmentations accounts. On 5 June 1556 he was charged with a debt of £2,500; he promised to pay within a fortnight but five days later, in consideration of his service, he was pardoned all arrears both as master of the jewels and treasurer of augmentations. At the end of Edward VI's reign these arrears had already stood at over £28,000. Despite the pardon, the Privy Council was still discussing Williams's accounts in May 1558.[9]

The Council recommended to the sheriff of Oxfordshire and Berkshire that Williams should be returned for Oxfordshire to the Parliament of March 1553, but he had to yield first place to Northumberland's brother Sir Andrew Dudley, whose recent acquisitions in the county were making him a threat to Williams's local preponderance. On grounds of self-interest Williams might therefore have been expected to go over to Mary and in the event he sprang to her support with the alacrity he had shown in 1536 and with the same reward for himself. He is said to have raised 6,000 men, including cavalry recruited among the peasantry, and the news of the response to his summons was believed to have had a decisive effect on the Council in London. On 22 July he was ordered to dismiss his men and to wait upon the Queen who continued to employ him in a military role; on 12 Aug. 1553 he and Leonard Chamberlain were given £2,000, on 14 Aug. 400 lances and 500 corselets and on the 15th six field pieces. In the following February he was commanded to provide 100 horse and 100 foot for the Queen's retinue.[10]

He discharged the office of sheriff of Oxfordshire and Berkshire for a few weeks in the autumn of 1553 and Mary thereafter treated him as her henchman in Oxfordshire. In this capacity he was involved in the custody and execution of Cranmer, Latimer and Ridley, and the safe-keeping of Princess Elizabeth. On 19 May 1554 he joined Sir Henry Bedingfield* and Sir Leonard Chamberlain to escort Elizabeth from the Tower to Woodstock. It is not clear either that he was ever in sole charge of her, or that he was replaced by Bedingfield for his leniency, but he gained a lasting reputation for kindness to Elizabeth on her journeys to and from Woodstock. On both occasions he entertained her at Rycote and, according to Foxe, protested that he would die for her if necessary and clashed with Bedingfield over the respect he paid her. There is some likelihood,therefore, that he was the 'Lord William' reported by the imperial ambassador in March 1555 to be conspiring with Elizabeth and plotting to marry her to

Courtenay. Williams's favourable reputation with Protestants is also clear from Foxe's report of his treatment of the condemned bishops, whom he conducted to Oxford from the Tower in March 1554 and at whose executions he presided in October 1555 and March 1556. The rumour is therefore intelligible which is reported to have been rife in September 1554, that the see of Canterbury 'was given to a Spanish friar; and the Lord Williams was out of his chamberlainship, and Secretary Petre out of his office'.[11]

There is no evidence that Williams ever betrayed his allegiance to Mary and he remained in favour throughout the reign. In April 1554 he was summoned to Parliament as Lord Williams of Thame; this was in part to compensate him for his loss of office when the court of augmentations was dissolved and in part to give him the dignity necessary to his new office of chamberlain to King Philip. It was he who with the 12th Earl of Arundel met Philip at the gates of Southampton on 20 July 1554. On losing his augmentations office Williams was granted an annuity of £320, and in March 1554 he received a gift of 200 crowns from the Queen and in July a pension of 1,000 crowns from the King. He was fairly regular in his attendance in the Lords throughout the remainder of the reign and had several bills committed to him in the Parliaments of April 1554 and 1555, including one to confirm the articles of the Spanish marriage. In 1555 he was one of four peers who voted against a bill 'for the keeping of milch kine' and the sole dissenter from a bill for the repeal of an Act of 1497 concerning merchant adventurers (12 Hen. VII, c.6); in 1558 he was again the sole dissenter from a bill to cancel import licences for French or Gascon wines.[12]

With Elizabeth on the throne Williams's ability to keep on good terms with all parties once more paid him well. One of his servants brought the Queen's proclamation to Oxford, and he was one of the lords appointed to attend Elizabeth from Hatfield to London. Two months later he was appointed president of the council in the marches of Wales, but by the following March he was seriously ill and before he was able to make any impression on the marches he died at Ludlow on 14 Oct. 1559. Only at the very end of his life is there a suggestion that he was other than a leading example of the profiteer from the religious revolution: in his last illness he received into his house for a period Bishop Jewel, once vicar of Sunningwell, near Oxford, where Williams had an estate, and in 1559 just returned from exile.[13]

Williams was buried with great pomp at Thame on 15 Nov. 1559, and his tomb remains in the church. His sons having predeceased him, the barony became extinct and the heirs to his property were his sons-in-law Henry Norris* and Richard Wenman*. To his wife Williams left several manors, his house at Elsingspital and cups given by the Queen, the Duchess of Norfolk and Francis Russell*, 2nd Earl of Bedford, at the christening of one of her children; she later married in turn William Drury* and James Croft†. To Bedford he left his personal armour and to Sir Robert Dudley* a black mare called 'Maud Mullford which mare I take to be the best mare in England'. Several rectories were assigned for the endowment of a free school at Thame and provision was also made for the restoration of the footway between Oxford and Botley and the support of Botley road upon stone arches: a bill for the amendment of causeways and highways had been committed to Mr. Williams, either Sir John or Thomas Williams I*, a Member for Oxford, in the Parliament of October 1553. The executors included Sir Walter Mildmay* and the supervisors the Earl of Bedford and Sir William Cecil.[14]

[1] Date of birth estimated from marriage. *DNB*; *CP*; N. J. O'Conor, *Godes peace and the Queenes*; *Vis. Hants* (Harl. Soc. lxiv), 39–40; *Vis. Berks.* (Harl. Soc. lvi), 55; PCC 28 Bennett; F. G. Lee, *Thame Church*, 414–18; Strype, *Eccles. Memorials*, iii(1), 507. [2] *Rep. R. Comm. of 1552* (Archs. of Brit. Hist. and Culture iii), 5, 75, 78; Lee, 410; *LP Hen. VIII*, iii–v, viii, x, xv, xvii–xxi; Elton, *Tudor Rev. in Govt.* 100; *Machyn's Diary* (Cam. Soc. xlii), 59; *LJ*, i. 465, 492, 542; C. A. J. Skeel, *Council in the Marches of Wales*, 84–85; *CPR*, 1548–9, p. 137; 1553, pp. 351, 356–7; *CSP Dom.* 1547–80, p. 139; *Val. Eccles.* ii. 213–14; *Oxf. Recs.* 220, 225–6, 258–60, 266–7; NCA 14/2. [3] *LP Hen. VIII*, ix, xx. [4] Lee, 385; *Val. Eccles.* ii. 186. [5] *LP Hen. VIII*, xi–xiv; *VCH Oxon.* iii. 298, 306. [6] *LP Hen. VIII*, iv, v, xiii–xxi, add.; *DNB* (King, Robert); *LJ*, i. 112, 136; *VCH Berks.* iv. 399, 429; *CPR*, 1547–8, p. 208; 1550–3, pp. 11, 51, 85; 1555–7, p. 212; M. C. Rosenfield, 'The disposal of the property of London monastic houses' (London Univ. Ph.D. thesis, 1961), 312, 313. [7] *Wriothesley's Chron.* i (Cam. Soc. n.s. xi), 133; *PPC*, vii. 12; *LP Hen. VIII*, xvi, xvii, xix, xxi. [8] *CJ*, i. 2, 6, 8, 9, 14; A. F. Pollard, *Eng. under Somerset*, 227–8; *Cam. Misc.* xii. 18; *APC*, ii. 342; W. K. Jordan, *Edw. VI*, i. 520. [9] *CSP Span.* 1550–2, p. 389; *APC*, iv. 16–17, 26, 54; v. 279; vi. 319; Bodl. e Museo 17; *Lit. Rems. Edw. VI*, 421–2; *LP Hen. VIII*, xxi; Strype, ii(2), 76, 257; *CPR*, 1553–4, p. 264; 1555–7, p. 72; W. C. Richardson, *Tudor Chamber Admin.* 436. [10] Strype, ii(2), 66; *CSP Span.* 1553, p. 107; *Narr. Ref.* (Cam. Soc. lxxvii), 80; *Chron. Q. Jane and Q. Mary* (Cam. Soc. xlviii), 9, 12; *APC*, iv. 301, 310, 316, 318, 320, 392. [11] *APC*, iv. 406; vi. 101, 180; *CPR*, 1553–4, p. 27; *Wriothesley's Chron.* ii (Cam. Soc. n.s. xx), 116; Strype, iii(1), 22; *Machyn's Diary*, 37, 57; *Chron. Q. Jane and Q. Mary*, 76, 82; *CSP Span.* 1554–8, pp. 145, 148; *Narr. Ref.* 228; Foxe, *Acts and Mons.* vi. 439, 553; vii. 549–50; viii. 83, 90, 606, 614–15, 619; *Norf. Arch.* iv. 151–4. [12] Richardson, 330; Strype, iii(1), 186; *APC*, v. 31; *CSP Span.* 1554, pp. 158, 266, 297, 315; 1554–8, pp. 374, 456; 1558–67, pp. 59, 66; Foxe, vi. 554; M. A. R. Graves, 'The Tudor House of Lords 1547–58', (Otago Univ. Ph.D. thesis, 1974), ii. 362. [13] *Oxf. Recs.* 276; Strype, *Annals*, i(1), 192; (2), 391; *CSP Dom.* 1547–80, p. 126; *VCH Berks.* iv. 424; *DNB* (Jewel, John). [14] *Machyn's Diary*, 217, 377; Lee, 427–30, 457; Strype, *Eccles Memorials*, ii(1), 494; *CPR*, 1558–60, p. 448; PCC 11 Mellershe; *CJ*, i. 31.

A.H.

WILLIAMS, Philip (by 1519–58 or later), of Ipswich, Suff.

IPSWICH 1558

b. by 1519, prob. 3rd s. of Francis Williams.[1]
Chamberlain, Ipswich 1550–1, treasurer 1557–8.[2]

Philip Williams was one of three brothers of

Welsh descent living in Ipswich. Their father was the first of the family to adopt the surname Williams but the circumstances of its migration to East Anglia have not come to light. Williams himself first appears in 1540 when he was fined 6s.8d. by the corporation for 'colouring foreigners' goods'. He evidently prospered as a merchant and in 1545 he was assessed for the subsidy on £20 in goods as a resident of the west ward. Five years later he began the brief municipal career which culminated in his election when treasurer to the Parliament of 1558; he remitted half his parliamentary 'fee'. These are the last references found to him unless he is to be identified with the Philip Williams *alias* Footman who in May 1556 had given evidence against 'such as favoured the gospel at Ipswich' and who early in Elizabeth's reign had a house in St. Mary Tower, Churchgate there. According to the visitation pedigree, Williams died without issue.[3]

[1] Date of birth estimated from first reference. *Vis. Essex* (Harl. Soc. xiii), 524. [2] N. Bacon, *Annals Ipswich*, 232, 248. [3] Bacon, 216, 251; E179/181/270; Foxe, *Acts and Mons.* viii. 598; Ipswich treasurers' accts. 1559–60.

J.P.

WILLIAMS, Richard (by 1516–79), of Oxford.

OXFORD 1558

b. by 1516. *m.* Joan (?Barton, sis. of John Barton*), *s.p.*[1]

Chamberlain, Oxford 1547–8, bailiff 1550–1, key keeper 1554, 1557, assistant to mayor 1557, subsidy collector 1559, mayor Mar.–Sept. 1565, 1571–2, 1578–*d.*, coroner 1568, alderman 1578–*d.*[2]

There were several men of this name in Oxford including in the previous generation two Johns, a brewer and a glover, either of whom might have been Richard Williams's father. No relationship has been established between Richard and Thomas Williams I*, and neither man mentions the other in his will.[3]

Richard Williams was admitted a freeman in 1536–7 and assessed for subsidy on goods valued at £6 in 1543, 1544 and 1547, at £12 in 1551 and at £9 in 1559. These assessments were low compared with those of other citizens who were returned to Parliament, although in 1568 Williams paid 10s. towards a lottery, as did all the other leading freemen. His property acquisitions also suggest that he became more prosperous in his later years. He occupied a garden belonging to Christ Church in St. Aldate's parish in 1548; leased an orchard for 21 years at an annual rent of 26s.8d. in 1565; with Roger Taylor[†] leased the site of the former Greyfriars in October 1571 for 1,500 years; was the tenant of a fishery near the former Blackfriars in 1573/74; and, with his wife, leased a 'great garden' for 21 years in 1576.

Designated 'generosus' on his return to Parliament and 'gentleman' in a grant of 1568, Williams was a baker by trade. When all 11 bakers of the city subscribed towards a 'load horse' in 1572, he gave 5s., the second largest sum.[4]

Williams was as active as any of his fellows in the city's service. In 1554 and 1555 he was appointed to lease the stands of St. Frideswide's fair. In 1562 he was among those who visited the son of Dr. George Owen* at Godstow to settle a dispute over Port Meadow, and in the following April he was ordered to inspect the road which was being made there. When the mayor and his 12 assistants, with 24 associates, voted in a secret ballot for the new mayor in September 1562, the candidates with most support proved to be Ralph Flaxney* and Richard Williams, of whom the first was chosen. In March 1565 Williams was elected mayor in place of William Matthew, who had died in office: it was the first of his three terms, the last being cut short by his own death. On 22 Jan. 1579 he joined the deputy vice-chancellor and others, including Thomas Williams, in licensing the city's alehouse-keepers.[5]

Richard Williams's fellow-Member John Barton was also his brother-in-law: Barton probably married Joan Williams. Both men stood surety for their precursor William Tylcock when he was fined 53s.4d. in Hilary term 1558 for having departed from the Parliament of November 1554 without licence, and Tylcock and Williams were supervisors and witnesses of Barton's will.[6]

The customs of Oxford allowed the mayor to make one of his sons a freeman for a gilded penny. On 9 Sept. 1572 Williams, who had no children, was offered the chance to prefer one of his kinsmen or else a servant named Evans for 4s.6d. and on 20 Aug. 1579 it was agreed that he could prefer anyone for a total fee of 14s. He made his will on 27 Jan. 1579. His charitable bequests included £20 to the Oxford charity known as Dame Margaret Northern's coffer and two silver tankards and a dozen silver spoons to the city. Several members of the Barton and Sutton families were among the beneficiaries and the executors and residuary legatees were William Frere[†], Joan Atkinson, widow of John Barton and described as the testator's sister, and Robert and Agnes Sutton. The date of probate is not known but, according to Wood, Williams was buried on 21 Sept. 1579 and brass effigies of him and his wife were placed in St. Aldate's church.[7]

[1] Date of birth estimated from admission as freeman. *Antiqs. Oxf.* iii. (Oxf. Hist. Soc. xxxvii), 130. [2] *Oxf. Recs.* 189, 203, 227, 266, 308, 324, 338, 394, 398; *Oxf. City Docs.* (Oxf. Hist. Soc. xviii), 113; *CPR*, 1566–9, p. 316. [3] *Oxf. Recs.* 58, 103, 174, 189, 204, 220, 349. [4] Ibid. 149, 300, 309, 321, 347, 355, 378; E179/162/224, 229, 261, 289, 318; *Liber Albus Civ. Oxon.* ed. Ellis, nos. 355, 362; *Surv. Oxf.* ii. (Oxf. Hist. Soc. n.s. xx), 1–2. [5] *Oxf. Recs.* 222, 228, 262, 294,

296, 303, 308, 375, 399. ⁶ KB27/1185; PCC 23 Sheffelde. ⁷ *Oxf. Recs.* 208, 342, 404; Bodl. wills Oxon. 186, ff. 105–6; *Antiqs. Oxf.* iii. 130.

T.F.T.B.

WILLIAMS, Thomas I (by 1518–79/90), of Oxford.

OXFORD   1553 (Oct.)

b. by 1518. *m.* (1) by 1539, Elizabeth; (2) Margaret; 6s. 2da.[1]

Subsidy collector, Oxford 1544, bailiff 1546–7, assistant to mayor 1554, key keeper 1555, 1556, alderman 1557–*d.*, mayor 1557–8, 1565–6, 1576–7.[2]

According to the visitation of Oxfordshire, Thomas Williams was of Dorset origin. There is no indication that he was related to his colleague Richard Williams*. He appears on a list of 'privileged persons which came to be freemen' as 'Thomas Williams a mercer and innholder servant to London', presumably John London of New College, the monastic visitor. It is possible, therefore, that he was the Thomas Williams who on several occasions in 1538 and 1539 was appointed attorney to receive and deliver the premises of monastic houses which had surrendered to London, and he was probably the Thomas Williams, yeoman, who, with his wife Elizabeth, obtained the lease of a messuage from New College in June 1541. He was present when an inventory of church goods was taken at Osney on 19 May 1545.[3]

Williams was assessed for the subsidy in November 1543, paying 8*s.* on goods worth £12 in the north-west ward of Oxford. His goods were again valued at £12 in 1544, 1547 and 1550, at £13 in 1551 and at £20 in 1559; he paid 10*s.* towards a lottery on 1 Apr. 1568, as did other leading citizens. In 1547 he was again described as a mercer but six years later he was appointed one of three vintners for the city, in accordance with the Act of that year (7 Edw. VI, c.5); on 22 Jan. 1579 he joined the deputy vice-chancellor, the mayor and others in licensing the city's alehouse-keepers.[4]

Williams was entrusted with several such special duties. He was given custody of the armoury in 1548, and with Thomas Mallinson* he was among those who were to draw up indentures for a new fulling mill in 1555. He was paid 20*s.* on 1 Dec. 1565, during his second mayoralty, for charges in London, and in the following August received Queen Elizabeth on her visit to Oxford. On 19 Oct. 1574 he was one of those selected to attend the mayor before the Privy Council in connexion with a series of far-ranging disputes with the university.[5]

Williams's Membership of Mary's first Parliament was a natural step in his civic progression. Nothing is known for certain of his role in the House but on 22 Nov. 1553 a bill for the amendment of causeways and highways was committed to a Mr. Williams,

either the Oxford Member or Sir John Williams; two years later Sir Humphrey Radcliffe secured privilege for one of his servants arrested at the suit of one T. Williams. Williams was not among the Members of the Parliament of October 1553 who opposed the initial measures towards the restoration of Catholicism, and while this is not conclusive evidence as to his sympathies at the time these became apparent shortly before his death. In 1577 he was included in a return of Catholics in Oxford with his wife, his son Alexander and his daughter Anne, then the wife of Dr. Roger Marbeck, a physician and former provost of Oriel. Williams himself, although a church-goer, was described as 'a common receiver of professed enemies' among the Catholic gentry of Oxfordshire and was said to be worth 1,000 marks. Moreover, his will, undated but proved on 29 Jan. 1580, establishes that he was the father of Thomas Williams, one of the earliest English Jesuits, to whom he left 'if he be alive £10 if the laws of the realm will permit it'. His lease of the *Star* inn was to go to Alexander after the death of his wife Margaret or when she should cease to dwell there. He left an embroidered pall to the city, £5 to the poor of Oxford, an angel apiece to John Kennall, archdeacon of Oxford, and Thomas Glasier, rector of Exeter College 'to make merry among the fellows'. He owed his son John £6 13*s.*8*d.* 'which he paid for the redeeming of certain books that his brother Ralph Williams sold of Mr. London's which he must restore to be laid up with the rest of Mr. London's books'. Ralph had joined his brother Thomas in exile by 1581 and another brother, Edward, was by 1594 in the service of Cardinal Allen, having formerly been in that of Ralph Sheldon†. Williams named his wife Margaret residuary legatee and executrix. She was buried in St. Thomas's church on 8 June 1585.[6]

[1] Date of birth estimated from marriage. *Surv. Oxf.* ii. (Oxf. Hist. Soc. n.s. xx), 159; H. Foley, *Jesuit Recs.* iv. 572; Bodl. wills Oxon. 186, ff. 113–14. [2] E179/162/229; *Oxf. Recs.* 188, 219, 260, 261, 268, 313, 383. [3] *Vis. Oxon.* (Harl. Soc. v), 312; Oxf. Univ. Arch. B27, p. 2; *LP Hen. VIII*, xiii, xiv; *Surv. Oxf.* ii. 159; *Oxon. Rec. Soc.* i. 135. [4] E179/162/224, 229, 261, 282, 289, 318; *Oxf. Recs.* 270, 321, 400; *Liber Albus Civ. Oxon.* ed. Ellis, no. 354. [5] *Oxf. Recs.* 192, 224, 294, 299, 313, 314, 357, 362–5; *APC*, viii. 305, 376–86; ix. 350, 352–3. [6] *CJ*, i. 31, 42; *Cath. Rec. Soc.* xxii. 97–98, 101, 112–13; *DNB* (Marbeck, Roger); Bodl. wills Oxon. 186, ff. 113–14; Foley, iv. 572; SP12/150/95, 249/64, 92, 96; *Recusant Hist.* xiii. 299–300; *Worcs. Recusant*, xxv. 2–4; *Antiqs. Oxf.* iii. (Oxf. Hist. Soc. xxxvii), 250, 252.

T.F.T.B.

WILLIAMS, Thomas II (1513/14–66), of Stowford in Harford, Devon.

BODMIN	1555
SALTASH	1558
TAVISTOCK	1559
EXETER	1563*

b. 1513/14, 1st s. of Adam Williams of Stowford by

Alice, da. and h. of Thomas Prideaux of Ashburton. *educ.* I. Temple, adm. 14 Nov. 1539, called. *m.* Emmeline, da. and coh. of William Cruwys of Chudleigh, at least 2s. 3da.[1]

Attendant on reader, I. Temple 1556, 1557, 1560, Lent reader 1558, 1561.

Attorney, Plymouth 1546–*d.*; feodary, Devon and Exeter in 1559; j.p.q. Devon 1558/9–*d.*[2]

Speaker of House of Commons 1563.

Thomas Williams followed in his father's footsteps and became a lawyer whose council was retained by the principal towns in south Devon. His father, who obtained a grant of arms in 1538, had enjoyed the favour of the Edgecombe family and Williams, 'a man of rare gifts and excellently learned in the laws', was probably indebted for his return to the last two Parliaments of Mary's reign to (Sir) Richard Edgecombe*. Edgecombe owned property in the neighbourhood of Bodmin, Saltash lay between his two houses at Mount Edgcumbe and Cotehele, and in 1555 the sheriff Sir John Arundell* was his brother-in-law. Unlike Edgecombe's son Peter, a Member for Totnes, the Protestant Williams followed Sir Anthony Kingston in opposition to a government bill in the Parliament of 1555. Possibly he enjoyed the support of Francis Russell*, 2nd Earl of Bedford, on both occasions since his brother-in-law John Belfield had long been in the service of the Russell family.[3]

Williams was able to enlarge his Devonshire patrimony, his chief purchase being the manors of Ugborough, and together with his kinsman Roger Prideaux* he speculated on the land market. The death of Mary enabled him to take a more active part in local government, and under the new regime his career blossomed. His appointment as Speaker was universally welcomed, but he died during his tenure of the office on 1 July 1566, leaving two sons 'both of them thriftless'.[4]

[1] Aged 52 at death according to MI. *Vis. Devon* ed. Vivian, 789; *DNB*. [2] Plymouth receiver's acct. bk. 1546–7, 1547–8 et passim; Wards 9/104, f. 152v; *CPR*, 1560–3, p. 435; 1563–6, p. 42. [3] *Cal. I.T. Recs.* i. 461; *Grantees of Arms* (Harl. Soc. lxvi), 280; *Som. Med. Wills* (Som. Rec. Soc. xxi), 149–50; Plymouth receiver's acct. bk. 1546–7, 1547–8 et passim; Exeter act bk. 3, p. 131; C1/1343/44, 1418/62; W. Pole, *Description of Devonshire* (1791), 320; PCC 25 Coode; Guildford mus. Loseley 1331/2. [4] *CPR*, 1550–3, pp. 17–18; PRO T/S, 'Cal. deeds enrolled in CP 1547–55', pp. 114, 250; Devon RO, Tingey mss; C142/147/197; Pole, 320.

J.J.G.

WILLIAMS, William Wynn (by 1500–59), of Cochwillan, Caern.

CAERNARVONSHIRE 1558

b. by 1500, 1st s. of William ap Gruffydd ap Robin of Cochwillan by Angharad, da. of Dafydd ab Ifan of Cryniarth and Hendwr, Merion. *m.* Lowri, da. of Henry Salusbury of Llanrhaiadr, Denb., 6s. 4da. *suc.* fa. by 1500.[1]

Commr. tenths of spiritualities, Bangor and St. Asaph dioceses 1535, relief, Caern. 1550; sheriff 1541–2, 1546–7; j.p. 1555.[2]

The Williams family of Cochwillan, founded by William Wynn Williams's great-grandfather, was linked with the Wynns of Gwydir, John Wynn ap Meredydd* being Williams's nephew. A supporter of the Tudor cause, Williams's father had been made sheriff of the old 'county' of Caernarvon in 1485 and granted denizenship in the following year.[3]

Williams was presumably the William ap William whom Edward Gruffydd of Penrhyn reported to Cromwell in 1534 as having vexed him before the royal commissioners. As William Gruffydd *alias* Williams he was sheriff in 1541–2 and as William Williams *alias* Gruffydd he had a second term in 1546–7, but the William ap William esquire who served in 1552–3 is more likely to have been his son, from whom he was sometimes distinguished by the suffix 'senior', as on the plea roll of the Caernarvonshire great sessions in the time of Edward VI. He was then assessed on lands worth £10 a year in the commote of Uchaf, and at about the same time he was sued by one James ap Robert over lands in the lordship of Bangor.[4]

In 1555 Williams was one of the Caernarvonshire gentlemen, his nephew John Wyn ap Hugh* and John Wyn ap Meredydd being among them, to whom the council in the marches recommended Sir Rhys Gruffydd (q.v.) as knight of the shire; Gruffydd was married to a great-niece of Williams. His own return at the next election, despite his age, is the less hard to credit in the light of his eldest son's death some months earlier and of his nephew John Wynn ap Meredydd's shrievalty until shortly before the election. It was to this nephew that he was to write not long before his own death in 1559 describing himself as 'old and stricken in age'; the hope which he expressed that 'your sons and mine shall be loving together' was not to be realized, his heir William Williams and John Wynn† of Gwydir proving the worst of enemies.[5]

[1] Date of birth estimated from fa.'s death. Griffith, *Peds.* 186, with dating errors; Dwnn, *Vis. Wales*, ii. 86–87 and n; *DWB* app. (Williams fam.). [2] *LP Hen. VIII*, viii; *CPR*, 1553, p. 363. [3] *CPR*, 1485–94, p. 55. [4] *LP Hen. VIII*, vii, xx; UCNW Penrhyn ms 63; NLW ms Wales 20/4, m. 92; E179/264/24; C1/1283/2. [5] NLW Add. ms 464/E19; ms 9051E; *Cal. Wynn (of Gwydir) Pprs. 1515–1690*, p. 3; *DWB* app. mentions Williams's will but this has not been located from the references there given.

P.S.E.

WILLIAMS see also CROMWELL *alias* WILLIAMS

WILLIAMS *alias* SCOTT, John (by 1519–61 or later), of Bedford.

BEDFORD 1554 (Nov.)

b. by 1519. *m.* Dorothy, at least 3s.[1]

Mayor, Bedford 1546–7, 1549–50, 1551–2.[2]

A grant to John Gostwick*, early in 1540, of houses and land in Bedfordshire included 'a meadow called Hanchurche mead, now in the tenure of John Scott', the name by which John Williams alias Scott appears to have been usually known early in his career. By the time of his first mayoralty he was using either name, or both, but from about 1549 he seems to have dropped the use of Scott. No reason for these changes is known: possibly he claimed some relationship with John Williams*, later Lord Williams of Thame, whose brother-in-law Gerard Harvey alias Smart sat for Bedford in 1547.[3]

Whether or not he was related to Williams of Thame, they had at least one activity in common, speculation in monastic lands. The source of the Bedford man's capital is unknown, but he may have acquired it by legal practice. It was in the mid 1540s that Williams made his largest acquisitions of property. Perhaps the John Williams who in October 1544 bought unspecified crown land to the value of nearly £80, he was certainly the John Williams alias Scott of Bedford who in the following year paid £254 for ex-monastic property in the town. Several of the houses involved were in the tenancy of William Bourne*. Another was the old schoolhouse in School Lane, later Mill Street. During Williams's first mayoralty the church of St. Peter Dunstable in Bedford was demolished and he used part of the materials to repair the school. With other stone and rubble from the church he made 'a large and pleasant place before his door where he dwelt at that time to bait bull and bear'. It was also during his first mayoralty that Williams brought an action against William Johnson I* when the latter tried to obtain wages from the borough for the Parliaments of 1539 and 1542.[4]

Williams has been identified, it appears correctly, as the legal adviser to the town on the status of the hospital of St. John, declared by the Edwardian government to have been a chantry. In or soon after 1561 the town won the case, and Queen Elizabeth revoked the grant made to one John Farnham. But Williams was alleged to have retained in his hands all the title deeds and other legal documents concerning the hospital: after his death the corporation brought a lawsuit for possession against his widow and sons. The matter became more complicated since Williams had apparently bought up, in his son's name, John Farnham's dubious right to the hospital.[5]

No will or inquisition post mortem has been found for Williams. He was probably dead by 1566, his name not appearing among the ex-mayors who were 'associate to' the existing holder of the office when Bedford received a confirmation of its arms in that year.[6]

[1] Date of birth estimated from first reference. Vis. Beds. (Harl. Soc. xix), 72; information from G. D. Gilmore; C. F. Farrar, Old Bedford, 159 seq.; Reps. Charity Commrs. xxxii(2), 574–89. [2] Bedford yr. bk. ex. inf. G. D. Gilmore. [3] LP Hen. VIII, xv. [4] Ibid. xix, xx; C. F. Farrar, Bedford Charity, 2–3; Godber, Beds. 194–5; Beds. Hist. Rec. Soc. xxxvi. 16 and n, 18; C24/27. [5] Farrar, Old Bedford, 159 seq.; Reps. Charity Commrs. xxxii(2), 574–89. [6] Vis. Beds. 72.

N.M.F.

WILLOUGHBY, Christopher (by 1508–70), of West Knoyle, Wilts.

WILTON 1545
WILTSHIRE 1554 (Nov.)[1]

b. by 1508, illegit. s. of Sir William Willoughby† of Turners Puddle, Dorset. educ. ?L. Inn, adm. 12 Feb. 1528, m. (1) Alice, wid. of one Bulstrode; (2) by 1547, Isabel, da. of Nicholas Wykes* of Dodington, Glos., wid. of John Ringwood of Sherfield English, Hants, 4s. 4da.[2]

Escheator, Hants and Wilts. 1529–30, 1557–8; steward of hospice and gen. receiver, Wilton abbey by 1533–5 or later; j.p. Wilts. 1543–?d.; commr. relief 1550; other commissions 1544–68.[3]

Christopher Willoughby's father was the younger brother of Robert Willoughby, whom Henry VII created Lord Willoughby de Broke. Christopher Willoughby was thus a natural cousin of the 2nd Lord, whose many offices in Wiltshire included the stewardship of the borough and manor of Wilton. He was also a nephew of Cecily Willoughby, abbess of Wilton until 1528, although if she introduced him to its service she quickly turned against him. When in March 1533 the prioress complained to the Council of the damage done to the house, while it had been without a head, by the bishop of Salisbury's vicar-general Dr. Hilley, the grievances included his appointment of Willoughby as receiver general and steward of the hospice in spite of Willoughby's expulsion by Abbess Cecily and subsequent rejection by her successor. Willoughby appears to have fared better under Cecily Bodenham, who was elected abbess in the following year and who in March 1537 leased him the manor of Knoyle Odierne or West Knoyle. The valor ecclesiasticus shows that he still held office in 1535 with fees amounting to 56s.8d. a year; it also names a Robert Willoughby as auditor. Christian Willoughby, a nun who received a pension when Wilton was dissolved in 1539, may have been the sister to whom Willoughby was to leave £6 13s.4d. in his will.[4]

In December 1543 Willoughby paid £842 for the manors of Baverstock and Fovant and the reversion of a house at Fovant then belonging to the ex-abbess; Baverstock he was to retain, but Fovent he immediately disposed of to Sir Edward Baynton*. At this time he was being harassed at West Knoyle by its new landlord, John Marvyn*, whose depredations and eventual denial of the validity of the abbey's lease Willoughby made the subject of two Star Chamber actions; the result of these is unknown, but their practical outcome was that in November 1545 Marvyn took out a licence to alienate the manor to Willoughby. From the coincidence of this transaction with the meeting of the Parliament in which Willoughby was one of the Members for Wilton it may be inferred that he had sought election with the object of promoting his cause. (He could have sat in the previous Parliament, although not for Wilton, which furnishes one of the two exceptions—the other is Salisbury—to the loss of all the Wiltshire names on that occasion.) Willoughby can hardly have secured the Wilton seat without the consent of Sir William Herbert, who already controlled the borough and himself sat in this Parliament as a knight of the shire, so that although Willoughby is not known to have been connected with Herbert otherwise than as a tenant they had presumably been on good terms at the time of the election. Whether they remained so when the Parliament met is open to question, for in September 1545 Willoughby was the ringleader in the destruction of a fulling mill at Wilton belonging to Henry Creed (q.v.), who declared in the ensuing Star Chamber case that Willoughby had ignored repeated demands by Herbert to make reparation.[5]

It is therefore less surprising that Willoughby was not to sit again for Wilton—especially as the borough seal was to be lost while in his custody—than that nine years afterwards he carried off a knighthood of the shire. Since Herbert, by then Earl of Pembroke, had in the meantime strengthened his hold on the county he must at least have acquiesced in Willoughby's election, but what conduced to it is not clear beyond his dozen years of service in local administration and his marriage to the daughter of a Gloucestershire neighbour who had sat in the previous Parliament. His attitude towards the Catholic restoration was perhaps the same as his bishop was to diagnose ten years later, that he was 'no hinderer'.[6]

Willoughby made his will at West Knoyle on 24 Nov. 1570, committing his soul to the Trinity and asking to be buried in the parish church. His chief concern was to alter the disposition of his lands in favour of the eldest son Henry, while reserving certain goods and annuities of £20 apiece to two younger sons, John and Christopher. The widow was left £16 a year from Baverstock and lands at Motcombe, in north Dorset, with a sum of £20, furnishings and plate, and accommodation in the house at Knoyle; she was also given the custody of

two unmarried daughters, Anne and Jane, each of whom was to have £300 at the age of 21 or on marriage. Other beneficiaries included Willoughby's married daughter Mary Preston, and his brother Henry, sister Christian and cousin John Willoughby of the Inner Temple. He named his son Henry executor, and Lawrence Hyde†, John Willoughby and a nephew Thomas St. Barbe overseers. The statement that Willoughby's children were all born of his second marriage is supported by the inquisition taken on 24 Feb. 1571, when it was found that the heir was aged 23 at his father's death at the end of the previous November.[7]

[1] Huntington Lib. Hastings mss Parl. pprs. [2] Date of birth estimated from first reference. *LP Hen. VIII*, xxi; *Wilts. Vis. Peds.* (Harl. Soc. cv, cvi), 216–17; *VCH Hants*, iv. 510. [3] *LP Hen. VIII*, xviii, xx, xxi; *CPR*, 1547–8, p. 91; 1553, p. 359; 1553–4, pp. 25, 28; 1560–3, pp. 443, 494; 1563–6, pp. 28, 38, 39, 42; 1566–9, p. 205; *VCH Wilts*. ii. 239. [4] *CP*, xii(2), 683–9; *CPR*, 1494–1509, p. 311; *VCH Wilts*. iii. 239–41; *LP Hen. VIII*, vi, xxi; *Wilts. Arch. Mag.* xxviii. 305–6; St.Ch.2/23/32; *Val. Eccles.* ii. 112. [5] *VCH Wilts*. iii. 240; vi. 21, 24, 36–37; *LP Hen. VIII*, xviii, xx; St.Ch.2/21/32, 102, 34/15; *Pembroke Survey* (Roxburghe Club cliv), i. 40, 71, 290, 294, 296–7. [6] *Cam. Misc.* ix(3), 38. [7] PCC 23 Holney; C142/159/81; *CPR*, 1569–72, p. 244.

T.F.T.B.

WILLOUGHBY, George (by 1515–50), of the Inner Temple, London, Elmley Castle and Netherton, Worcs.

CONSTITUENCY UNKNOWN 1547*[1]

b. by 1515, illegit. s. of Robert, 2nd Lord Willoughby de Broke by Joan Pye of ?Chippenham, Wilts. *educ.* I. Temple. *m.* by 1544, Anne, da. of Thomas Huncks of Radbroke, Glos., wid. of Thomas Lyttleton, 2s. 3da.[2]

Auditor, I. Temple 1536, 1546–7, bencher 1546, attendant on reader 1547, 1549, Autumn reader 1548, Lent reader 1549.

?Servant, household of Cardinal Wolsey by 1523; j.p. Worcs. 1538–*d.*, Cheshire, Herefs., Mon., Warws., Salop 1547; commr. oyer and terminer, Oxford circuit 1539, 1543, 1544, musters, Worcs. 1539, subsidy 1543, chantries, Herefs., Worcs. 1548; escheator, Worcs. 1541–2, 1545–6; attorney, council in the marches of Wales 28 Apr. 1546–*d.*; particular receiver, Queen Catherine Parr, Herefs. and Worcs. by 1547–8; member, council of John Dudley, Earl of Warwick by 1547; ?serjeant-at-law by 1550.[3]

The Commons Journal records that on 19 Jan. 1549 a bill for buying of wool was committed after its first reading to 'Mr. Wyllaby' and that a week later 'Mr. Willoughby' and Thomas Gawdy I were similarly entrusted with a bill for captains and soldiers. This is the only evidence that the Parliament then in session included a Member named Willoughby. His identification with George Willoughby of Netherton is suggested by one fact and one probability: he must have died before the end of 1551, when the revised list of Members of this Parliament was drawn up, and he probably had the grounding in law which was the customary qualification of Members to whom bills were committed. George Willoughby died on 8 Aug. 1550 and he was a member of the Inner Temple, as was his associate in the committal of the second bill, Thomas Gawdy.[4]

Willoughby was one of the bastard sons of the 2nd Lord Willoughby de Broke. In 1521 his father left him £56 13s.4d. for his 'promotion and living', to be paid when he reached the age of 24. It is possible that Lord Willoughby had already obtained for him a place in Cardinal Wolsey's household, where a George Willoughby was assessed for subsidy during the early 1520s, on one occasion paying £5, and a transition from Wolsey's service to Cromwell's may be reflected in a letter of 1536 from John Pye to Cromwell recommending his 'nephew' George Willoughby 'who is, I think, extremely dealt with'. It was in this year that Willoughby took his first upward step at the Inner Temple, where he continued to make steady progress: according to a family tradition he was called to be serjeant shortly before his death, but this lacks confirmation. Lord Willoughby had provided for his mother's maintenance with a small estate in Somerset, and this eventually passed to Willoughby, but it was in Worcestershire that he settled, presumably on his marriage to Anne Huncks. The couple first occupied a lodging in Elmley Castle but were forcibly ejected by Urian Brereton, keeper of the adjoining park, who claimed it as a perquisite. By 1547 Willoughby had made his home at Netherton and in November 1549 he leased the manor from the dean and chapter of Worcester.[5]

Willoughby's appointment as attorney to the council in the marches of Wales answered to his progress in his profession and his standing in the region: he was probably helped to it by Queen Catherine Parr and by John Dudley, Earl of Warwick, for both of whom he acted. Willoughby became a member of Warwick's council and dealt with him in land, acquiring from him the reversion of a Gloucestershire manor in June 1547 and two more manors in Gloucestershire and one in Worcestershire in January 1550. If it was at Warwick's nomination that Willoughby was returned to the Parliament of 1547 a number of seats would have been available: as lieutenant of all northern counties in that year Warwick could have placed him in a northern borough, perhaps Berwick-upon-Tweed where the earl was stationed early in October, or as a member of the council in the marches he may have procured a Welsh seat. Another possibility is that Catherine Parr had Willoughby returned for one of her Wiltshire boroughs: it was with a Wiltshireman, Robert Long*, that on the day of the prorogation he acquired from Warwick a wood in Morville, Shrop-

shire. During the first session Willoughby sued out a general pardon.[6]

Willoughby made his will early in August 1550, the probate copy being erroneously dated as of after his death: the phrase 'if I die of this visitation' shows him to have fallen victim to the current epidemic. Leaving his place of burial to his wife's discretion, he provided for her, his children and kinsmen, and all servants of more than a year's standing. He appointed his wife sole executrix, and his father-in-law and brother-in-law overseers of the will, which was proved on the following 7 Sept. Willoughby died at Netherton on 8 Aug., leaving as his heir a six year-old boy; his widow, who acquired the wardship in the following year, married as her third husband Francis Bulstrode*.[7]

[1] *CJ*, i. 6, 7. [2] Date of birth estimated from auditorship at I. Temple. *Vis. Worcs.* (Harl. Soc. xxvii), 82, 119; Wards 7/5/122, 129, 6/88; PCC 20 Coode. [3] E179/200/145, 200/unnumbered; 315/340, f. 7v; *LP Hen. VIII*, xiii–xxi; *CPR*, 1547–8, pp. 75, 77, 82, 84, 87, 88, 90, 91; 1548–9, p. 137; 1549–51, p. 299; SC6, Edw. VI/726; Coventry mayors' accts. 1542–61, p. 43; *Habington's Worcs.* (Worcs. Hist. Soc. 1895), i. 455. [4] *CJ*, i. 6, 7; Hatfield 207. [5] PCC 21 Maynwaryng; Dugdale, *Baronage* (1676), ii. 88; E179/69/8, 200/unnumbered; *LP Hen. VIII*, x, xii, xiv–xxi; *Habington's Worcs.* i. 455; *VCH Worcs.* iii. 327, 341; iv. 61, 64; *CPR*, 1547–8 to 1550–3 passim. [6] *CPR*, 1547–8, p. 199; 1548–9, p. 167; 1549–51, p. 61. [7] PCC 20 Coode; Wards 7/5/122, 129, 6/88; *CPR*, 1550–1, p. 108.

P.S.E./A.D.K.H.

WILLOUGHBY, Leonard (by 1509–60), of Turners Puddle, Dorset.

WAREHAM 1553 (Oct.)

b. by 1509, 1st s. of Nicholas Willoughby of Turners Puddle by Robegia, da. of William Satchfield. *m.* (1) settlement 3 Sept. 1533, Mary, da. of John Turberville of Bere Regis, 6da.; (2) by Mar. 1559, Margaret, da. of William Thornhill* of Thornhill in Stalbridge. *suc.* fa. 10 June 1542.[1]

Leonard Willoughby was the head of a minor gentle family seated about seven miles from Wareham. He had property on the outskirts of Wareham and an annuity of £10 out of the dissolved priory there but he probably owed his election to Mary's first Parliament to the influence of his brother-in-law James Turberville, an associate of Stephen Gardiner and soon to be chosen bishop of Exeter. Another brother-in-law John Wadham* was captain of a royal fort near Portland. Neither Willoughby nor his fellow-member Thomas Phelips opposed the initial measures towards the restoration of Catholicism in this Parliament but, unlike Phelips, Willoughby was not to sit again. He made his will on 1 Apr. 1560 and died on the following 13 June. Most of his lands lay in and around Turners Puddle but he also had property in Devon and Cornwall which he left to his unmarried daughters. He named as executor his brother John Willoughby, who was heir to Turners Puddle. He was buried at Bere Regis.[2]

[1] Date of birth estimated from age at fa.'s i.p.m., C142/68/38. *Cat. Anct. Deeds*, v. 12338, 12589, 12984; C142/125/12; *Vis. Dorset* ed Colby and Rylands, 14. [2] *CPR*, 1553-4, p. 123; Hutchins, *Dorset*, i. 153, 211-12; *DNB* (Turberville, James); PCC 56 Mellershe; C142/125/12.

H.M.

WILLOUGHBY, Sir William (c.1515-70), of Minting, Lincs. and Parham, Suff.

LINCOLNSHIRE 1545

b. c. 1515, s. of Sir Christopher Willoughby of Parham by Elizabeth, da. of Sir George Tailboys, *de jure* 9th Lord Kyme. *educ.* ?Oxf. BA 1526. *m.* (1) by 1536, Elizabeth (*d.* Dec. 1555 or later), da. of Sir Thomas Heneage of Hainton, Lincs., 1s. 1da.; (2) settlement 20 Aug. 1559, Margaret, da. of Robert Garneys of Kenton, Suff., wid. of Walter Devereux (*d.* 17 Sept. 1558), 1st Viscount Hereford, *s.p. suc.* fa. July 1538/Oct. 1540. Kntd. ?16 Jan. 1542; *cr.* Baron Willoughby of Parham 20 Feb. 1547.[1]

J.p. Lincs. (Lindsey) 1539-47 or later, q. Lincs. (Holland, Kesteven and Lindsey) by 1558/59-*d.*, Suff. 1561-*d.*; esquire of the body by 1545; commr. musters, Lincs. 1546, chantries, Lincs., Boston and Lincoln 1546, goods of churches and fraternities, Calais 1553; ld. lt. Lincs. 1549, 1557-10 Oct. 1558, jt. (with Sir Edward Dymoke* and Sir Robert Tyrwhitt II*) May 1559; dep. Calais 6 Oct. 1550-Oct. 1552; trier of petitions in the Lords, Parlts. of Mar. 1553, Oct. 1553, ?Apr. 1554, Nov. 1554, 1555, 1559, 1563; chief steward in north parts, duchy of Lancaster 22 Aug. 1553-*d.*[2]

Sir William Willoughby's father was a younger brother of William, 11th Lord Willoughby, who died in 1526 leaving no male heir. Lord Willoughby had settled lands worth 300 marks on his brother at the time of Christopher Willoughby's marriage to Elizabeth Tailboys but had died before the lands were transferred; his widow contested the transaction and the Duke of Suffolk inherited the dispute when he married Lord Willoughby's daughter Catherine. It was eventually settled by an Act (27 Hen. VIII, c.40) which divided the lands between the claimants.[3]

Willoughby was almost certainly the William Willoughby who was serving the Duke of Richmond at the time of Richmond's death in 1536; his uncle Gilbert Tailboys*, 1st Lord Tailboys, had married Richmond's mother Elizabeth Blount. By that time Willoughby himself had probably married Elizabeth Heneage. He seems to have kept an unblemished record during the rebellion of 1536 and three years later he was put on the Lincolnshire bench. This may have coincided both with the death of his father and with his first election to Parliament, for although the names of the knights for Lincolnshire are known—one of them being John Heneage—those for both Grantham and Grimsby are lost. Three years later three out of those four names are again unknown and with them those of the shire, to

which Willoughby could already have laid claim; his knighting in that year would have been an appropriate sequel to election. By the close of 1544, when the next Parliament was summoned, he had added to this royal recognition a place in the Household and, in all probability, service in the Boulogne campaign, for which he was called upon to furnish 10 archers and 40 billmen; his fellow-knight was his kinsman by marriage Sir Robert Tyrwhitt I*, and his brother-in-law Edmund Hall sat for Grantham.[4]

Willoughby had no further opportunity to sit in the Commons, for on 20 Feb. 1547 he was one of the four knights raised to the peerage, ostensibly in accordance with the intentions of the late King. The choice of Willoughby may have been a personal one of Henry VIII's, although it has been suggested that either or both of his relatives the Duchess of Suffolk and Sir Thomas Heneage could have intervened in his favour. That the duchess did so is hardly to be reconciled with her later complaint to Cecil that 'her barony was gone from her and her heirs' through her cousin's elevation, and the suffix 'of Parham' may have been meant to distinguish the new creation from the barony of Eresby, which Willoughby himself is said to have requested. Heneage, for his part, could not but have welcomed the honour: with no son of his own, he evidently looked to his son-in-law to maintain the house, as was shown when in 1553 Willoughby secured the reversion of his office of chief steward (northern parts) to the duchy of Lancaster.[5]

In 1548 Willoughby's name was put forward by John Brende* as one of those qualified to take command of the army in the north, but the Protector Somerset did not act upon the suggestion. Ket's rebellion in the following year gave him the chance to display his martial skill, and his service with John Dudley, Earl of Warwick, bore fruit in his appointment as deputy of Calais after Warwick had displaced the Protector. His two-year term at Calais was vexed by a quarrel over jurisdiction with Warwick's brother Andrew Dudley*, who was captain of Guisnes, and ended with the recall of both men. Although he signed the instrument settling the crown on Jane Grey his part in the succession crisis is not clear: on Queen Mary's entry into London he was placed under house arrest, but at the coronation he escorted the Queen to the ceremony and a year later he greeted Philip of Spain at Southampton. For the remaining 16 years of his life he was active in Lincolnshire and Suffolk and he received several letters of thanks from Mary and Elizabeth, although in 1569 the 3rd Earl of Sussex deplored his inability to stop his men from looting after the northern rising.[6]

Willoughby was exemplary in his attendance in the House of Lords. Even when he obtained leave of absence during the third session of the Parliament of 1547 he attended two thirds of the sittings, and his duties at Calais did not prevent him from attending almost daily during the final session in 1552, when he secured a proviso preserving his rights in the Act (5 and 6 Edw. VI, no. 37) for the Duke of Somerset's lands. Early in 1555 he introduced a bill into the Lords confirming his title to the Duchess of Suffolk's inheritance if she died childless. When on 9 Jan. her advisers asked to see the settlement on which Willoughby's claims rested, he made an appearance in the Commons, protesting that the 'duchess's counsel having no warrant ought not to be heard'. The committee of the House charged with scrutinizing the settlement reported that several of the manors included in the bill were not named in the settlement, and when several days later the bill was read for a third time it was defeated by 120 votes to 73. The manor of Orford could have been one of the properties in question; in spite of his uncertain title and signs of hostility towards him in the town, many of the Members returned for Orford until his death evidently enjoyed his support.[7]

By his will made at Doncaster on 10 Dec. 1569 Willoughby provided for his wife Margaret, daughter Mary and son Charles, and remembered several relatives. He named Mary executrix, or in case of her refusal his 'cousin' Christopher Heydon* and Christopher Wray*, and if they refused his cousin William Fitzwilliam and Anthony Butler*. On 21 July 1570 his brother-in-law Edmund Hall told Cecil that Willoughby was 'very sick and in great peril of life, much desiring to see me and indisposed to perfect his will until I came'. Willoughby died nine days later at Minting and was buried in accordance with his wishes at Parham on 15 Aug.[8]

[1] Date of birth estimated from marriage of parents in 1512 and from career. CP; Add. 19155, ff. 203 seq.; PCC 25 Martyn; Emden, Biog. Reg. Univ. Oxf. 1501–40, p. 632. [2] LP Hen. VIII, xiv, xvi, xx, xxi; CPR, 1547–8 to 1569–72 passim; P. T. J. Morgan, 'The govt. of Calais, 1485–1558' (Oxf. Univ. D. Phil. thesis, 1966), 294; LJ, i. 430, 447, 464, 492, 513, 542, 581; Somerville, Duchy, i. 424; G. S. Thomson, Lds. Lts. 42, 48; M. L. Bush, Govt. Pol. Somerset, 127 n. 1. [3] LP Hen. VIII, vii; A. Collins, Procs. Precedents and Arguments . . . concerning Baronies by Writ (1734), 4. [4] LP Hen. VIII, xi, xix. [5] Elton, Reform and Reformation, 337; Wealth and Power ed. Ives, Knecht and Scarisbrick, 88–90, 96; W. K. Jordan, Edw. VI, i. 65, 100; APC, ii. 16, 18, 35; CSP Dom. 1601–3, Add. 1547–65, p. 320; Collins, 4. [6] Jordan, i. 290, 489, 491; ii. 125; Bush, 87 n. 25, 94, 127 n. 1; APC, iii. passim; iv. 416; CSP Dom. 1547–80, p. 108; 1601–3, Add. 1547–65, p. 401; CSP Dom. Add. 1566–79, pp. 87, 88, 91, 161, 177, 178; S. T. Bindoff, Ket's Rebellion 1549 (Hist. Assoc. gen. ser. xii), 6; B. L. Beer, Northumberland, 128–9; CSP For. 1547–53, pp. 111, 357; 1553–8, p. 107; 1558–9, p. 327. [7] HMC Bath, iv. 335–6, 344; M. A. R. Graves, 'The Tudor House of Lords, 1547–58' (Otago Univ. Ph.D. thesis, 1974), 363–6; LJ, i. 290, 665; CJ, i. 41. [8] PCC 25 Martyn; CSP Dom. Add. 1566–79, p. 307; C142/157/122.

A.D.

WILSON, Egion (by 1530–63/67), of Redland, Glos.

GRAMPOUND 1553 (Mar.)[1]

b. by 1530, 4th s. of Edward Wilson of Over Staveley, Westmld., by Anne, da. of Miles Godmount of the Ashes in Staveley Godmount, Kendal, Westmld. m. by 1552, Dorothy, da. and h. of Thomas Hall of Redland, prob. 2s. 1da.[2]

Egion Wilson came from a gentle family of small consequence in Westmorland. The poverty of the region and the number of his father's offspring (both in and out of wedlock), must have compelled him to seek his own fortune, which he did as a soldier and victualler in the armies of Edward VI and Mary. While serving the first of these monarchs he fell into the hands of the French but was released when peace was concluded in 1551 and awarded £8 in compensation by the Privy Council. He then joined the retinue of the deputy of Berwick-upon-Tweed, Sir Nicholas Strelley, and it was as of London and Berwick that on 18 Dec. 1552 he obtained a protection from the King in his capacity as supplier of the town and garrison.[3]

The circumstances of Wilson's return to the Parliament of March 1553 are obscure. He was elected for a duchy of Cornwell borough with which he had no personal tie, and unless he was to serve for Berwick under Mary (when the names of its Members are lost), this was his only spell in the Commons. It is possible that he was in financial difficulties and sought a temporary respite from creditors: while the Parliament was in session a servant of his was arrested and on 21 Mar. the House issued a writ of privilege for his release. As a military man he may have been known to Sir John Russell*, 1st Earl of Bedford, the high steward of the duchy, or else have been recommended to the earl by the Duke of Northumberland.[4]

Wilson married a Gloucestershire heiress who brought him a home near Bristol and an estate in the west country worth £70 a year. He appears to have settled at Redland soon after his wife's death but the war of 1557 saw him back in the field: in August 1558 he was described by a cousin, who bequeathed him a lease, as 'being in [the] wars'. The last known trace of Wilson dates from five years later, when he sued out a pardon after surrendering to outlawry for not answering a charge of trespass. He must have died within the next four years, as Redland passed to a Miles Wilson, gentleman, either his son or his nephew, who made his will there on 12 Apr. 1567.[5]

[1] His name appears as 'Egi'em Welson' on the election indenture, C219/20/26, but this was incorrectly extended as 'Egidius (i.e. Giles) Wilson' in OR. [2] Date of birth estimated from first reference. Vis. Yorks. (Harl. Soc. xvi), 354; PCC 32 Stonard. [3] Vis. Yorks. 354; PCC 9 Alen; APC, iii. 290; CPR, 1553, p. 413. [4] CJ, i. 25. [5] Bristol and Glos. Arch. Soc. Trans. liii. 210; CPR, 1563–6, p. 288; PCC 57 Noodes, 32 Stonard.

A.D.K.H.

WINCHCOMBE, John (by 1519–74), of Bucklebury and Thatcham, Berks.

READING	1553 (Mar.)
LUDGERSHALL	1554 (Apr.), 1555
WOOTTON BASSETT	1571

b. by 1519, 1st s. of John Winchcombe *alias* Small-wood* of Newbury prob. by 1st w. *m.* by 1550, Helen, da. of Thomas St. Loe, 3s. 1da. *suc.* fa. 2 Dec. 1557.[1] Commr. musters, Berks. 1546, relief 1550, goods of churches and fraternities 1553; other commissions 1563–70; escheator, Oxon. and Berks. 1552–3, 1560–1; j.p.q. Berks. 1558/59–*d.*; sheriff 1571–2.[2]

John Winchcombe's early career is not always distinguishable from that of his father. It was clearly the son who was the 'young Mr. Wynch-combe' sent in February and March 1539 from Newbury as a confidential messenger to Cromwell by Miles Coverdale. The message concerned the suppression of papal books and it may be that such employment is early evidence of Winchcombe's attachment to the cause of reform. It was probably the father who was on the Berkshire bench in 1547 but it could have been either the father or the son who in 1551 served on the commission to execute the proclamation for victuals. The corporation journal establishes that it was the younger man who was returned for Reading to the Parliament of March 1553. The family seems to have had no property in the town but at this time one of the Members was customarily a local gentleman. The elder Winch-combe's religious conservatism makes it probable that he and not his son was rewarded for 'service at Framlingham' and was appointed a commissioner of gaol delivery by Mary. There is, however, no evidence that the younger Winchcombe opposed government policy when he sat in two Marian Parliaments for Ludgershall. His patron (Sir) Richard Brydges*, the keeper of that borough, was an old family friend; Winchcombe's father lived at Newbury as had Sir Richard's father, Henry Brydges*, whose will the elder Winchcombe had witnessed in 1538; and one of the two Winchcombes was associated with Sir Richard in a property transaction.[3]

Winchcombe's Protestantism undoubtedly recom-mended him to the Elizabethan government although he was to sit in Parliament only once more, again for a Wiltshire constituency. He died on 28 Feb. 1574.[4]

[1] Date of birth estimated from age at fa.'s death, E150/822/5; C142/111/10. *Vis. Berks.* (Harl. Soc. lvii), 233; Ashmole, *Berks.* iii. 300; A. L. Humphreys, *Bucklebury*, ped. opp. p. 310. [2] *LP Hen. VIII*, xxi; *CPR*, 1553, pp. 351, 386, 413; 1560–3, pp. 434, 523; 1563–6, pp. 20, 38–39; 1569–72, pp. 219, 221, 223. [3] *Remains, Miles Coverdale* (Parker Soc. 1846), 500, 502; Humphreys, 304–5; *CPR*, 1547–8, p. 81; 1550–3, p. 142; 1553–4, p. 34; *Reading Recs.* i. 231; Lansd. 156(28), f. 94; PCC 24 Dyngeley; C142/124/191. [4] *Cam. Misc.* ix(3), 38–39; C142/168/2; E150/828/8.

T.F.T.B./R.L.D.

WINCHCOMBE *alias* **SMALLWOOD, John** (1488/89–1557), of Newbury, Berks.

GREAT BEDWYN	1545
CRICKLADE	1547[1]

b. 1488/89, 1st s. of John Smallwood *alias* Winch-combe of Newbury, prob. by 2nd w. Joan. *m.* (1) Jane or Elizabeth; (2) Christian; 3s. inc. John Winch-combe* 1 da. *suc.* fa. 15 Feb. 1520.[2] J.p. Berks. 1541–?47; commr. benevolence 1544/45, relief 1550, ?to execute proclamation for victuals 1551, ?gaol delivery, Oxford castle 1553.[3]

John Winchcombe's father was the renowned 'Jack of Newbury', whom Fuller called 'the most considerable clothier (without fancy and fiction) England ever beheld', and who described himself in his will of 1520 as John Smallwood the elder *alias* John Winchcombe. He probably originated from Winchcombe, Gloucestershire, where the name Smallwood appears in the parish registers. Accord-ing to Thomas Deloney, of whose *Pleasant History of John Winchcombe* he is the hero, 'Jack of New-bury' came into a flourishing business by marrying his master's widow, gave employment to 1,054 persons, and having led a contingent of 150 to the battle of Flodden and entertained Henry VIII at his house, headed a deputation of clothiers to the same King.[4]

If stories of the father are more impressive, the achievements of the son are better documented and show the esteem in which the family's products were held. In 1539 Cromwell ordered 1,000 pieces of kerseys from Winchcombe, while in 1544 Stephen Vaughan* wrote to the Council that 'if your honours send hither Winchcombe's kerseys they will, with great gains, make great heaps of money'. Between 1538 and 1544, at least, they were in great demand in Antwerp and the Levant and were used as the standard by which the quality of other kerseys was assessed. In both 1538 and 1539 rumours of a possible truce with the Turks created such demands for Winchcombe's kerseys that merchants agreed to sell them only on condition that the customer purchased a stipulated proportion of other kerseys; such shortages were evidently not due to low pro-duction for of 2,106 kersey cloths sent by land to Morando in Ancona between January 1539 and October 1544, 640 were Winchcombe's. In 1547 William Damsell* at Antwerp came to the notable conclusion that although there was 'wondrous little profit to be had presently in cloths or kerseys, it shall be best to have hither 1,000 of Winchcombe's kerseys'. The status of Winchcombe among clothiers is evident from his success in 1541, with others unnamed, in securing the suspension of the

Act of 1536 (27 Hen. VIII, c.12) regulating the manufacture of woollen cloth.[5]

The only lands mentioned by Winchcombe's father in his will were those which he held of the 'college of Windsor', and since there is no evidence of an inquisition post mortem, it may be that Thomas Deloney was largely correct in assuming that his lands were his looms and his only rents those from the backs of sheep. The son, however, invested heavily in land. In 1540 he bought the manors of Bucklebury and Thatcham and other property formerly of Reading abbey from the crown for £2,620; in 1542 he obtained a lease of Farnborough manor, Berkshire, and six years later he purchased further Berkshire lands for £1,068. In February 1548 he appointed feoffees, including Edmund Plowden*, to hold some of these lands to the eventual use of his heirs and in 1555 he further settled the manors of Bucklebury and Thatcham on his eldest son. In 1536 Winchcombe had been one of those to whom it was proposed to write for aid against the rebels in the north, but it was probably his acquisition of land that conferred on him the normal duties of a gentleman: he was selected for Anne of Cleves's train at her reception in 1540, appointed to the commission of the peace in 1541, and listed to supply men for the armies in the Netherlands in 1543 and France in 1544. His estate was given official recognition when in October 1549 he was granted a coat of arms. It was undoubtedly this elevation which occasioned the painting of his portrait, once thought to be of his father.[6]

Winchcombe is first known to have been returned to Parliament in 1545, but he may have sat in one or more of the earlier Parliaments of the reign for which no returns survive. (Deloney's mention of his father as Member for Newbury may be dismissed as fictional, if for no other reason than that Newbury was not a parliamentary borough.) Bedwyn, for which he was returned with John Seymour I in 1545, lay in the heart of Edward Seymour's territory in Wiltshire; the future Protector is said to have lodged at Winchcombe's house in 1537, and the two men must have been well known to each other. Seymour influence probably secured his return for Cricklade in 1547 when Admiral Seymour held the manor in right of his wife Catherine Parr, but he may also have owed something to the patronage of Sir John Brydges*, as did his fellow-Member John Walshe. Winchcombe had witnessed the will of his neighbour Henry Brydges* in 1538 and his son was to be returned to two Marian Parliaments for Ludgershall, a borough then controlled by (Sir) Richard Brydges*. In the absence of nearly all the returns for Wiltshire to the Parliament of March

1553 it is not known whether Winchcombe sat again; his son was returned to that Parliament for Reading, but in view of the father's advancing age, and perhaps his connexion with the Seymours, it is unlikely that he did so.[7]

Whereas the son was a Protestant, the father seems on the evidence of his will to have been at least conservative in religion, which makes it more likely that it was the father who was granted a pension of £10 a year by Mary for 'service at Framlingham', and was both commissioner of gaol delivery at Oxford castle in 1553 and a visitor at the trial of Julins Palmer at Newbury in 1556. If Foxe's report of Palmer's trial is accurate Winchcombe's part virtually amounted to the recommendation 'take pity on thy golden years, and pleasant flowers of lusty youth, before it is too late'.[8]

Winchcombe died on 2 Dec. 1557, perhaps a victim of the epidemic: he had made a will on that day which was proved on 23 May 1558. He made ample provision for his second wife and the bequests of movables to her and to other members of his family show him to have been a man of considerable wealth. He left £50 against any debts he might have, £800 in cash to the members of his family and £50 to be distributed among the poor. For six years the residue of the sum put aside for his obit masses was to be 'delivered unto and for the exhibition of John Deale's two sons in Oxford'. Half of any remaining goods was to go to his heir John, the other half to be divided between his younger sons Thomas and Henry. Winchcombe was buried in Newbury church on 8 Dec. 1557 and at the inquisition taken in 1558 the annual value of his lands was given as £158.[9]

[1] Hatfield 207 where his name is altered from 'Warmecombe'. [2] Aged 61 in 1550 according to inscription on portrait, *Exhibition of House of Tudor*, annoted by H. A. Grueber, p. 65. PCC 27 Ayloffe, 26 Noodes; *Vis. Berks.* (Harl. Soc. lvii), 233; S. Barfield, *Thatcham*, ii. 304; *DNB*. [3] *LP Hen. VIII*, xvi, xviii, xx; *CPR*, 1547-8, p. 81; 1550-3, p. 142; 1553, p. 351; 1553-4, p. 34. [4] Ashmole, *Berks.* iii. 300; Fuller, *Worthies*, i. 137; *VCH Berks.* iv. 149; PCC 27 Ayloffe; W. Money, *Newbury*, 192; *Popular Hist. Newbury*, 25; T. Deloney, *Pleasant Hist. John Winchcombe* (Everyman 1929), 19, 23-27, 50-51. [5] *LP Hen. VIII*, xiv, xvi, xix; *VCH Berks.* iv. 138; *Econ. Hist. Rev.* vii. 57-62; J. Burnley, *Wool and Woolcombing*, 69; *PPC*, vii. 156. [6] PCC 27 Ayloffe; Deloney, 28; *LP Hen. VIII*, xi, xiv, xv, xvii-xix, xxi; *CPR*, 1548-9, pp. 89, 90; Barfield, ii. 273-4, 300-2, 322-3; *Vis. Berks.* 232; *VCH Berks.* iii. 292; Lysons, *Magna Britannia*, i(2), 320. [7] Deloney, 53, 68; Money, *Popular Hist. Newbury*, 27; PCC 24 Dyngeley; C142/124/191. [8] PCC 26 Noodes; Lansd. 156(28), f. 94; *CPR*, 1553-4, p. 34; Foxe, *Acts and Mons.* viii, 214. [9] C142/111/10; PCC 26 Noodes; Money, *Newbury*, 211; *Popular Hist. Newbury*, 148.

R.L.D.

WINDSOR, Sir Andrew (c. 1467–1543), of Stanwell, Mdx.

CONSTITUENCY UNKNOWN 1510[1]
BUCKINGHAMSHIRE 1529*

b. c. 1467, 2nd but 1st surv. s. of Thomas Windsor† of

Stanwell by Elizabeth, da. and coh. of John Andrews[†] of Baylham, Suff. *educ.* M. Temple. *m.* c. 1485, Elizabeth, da. of William Blount[†], 4s. inc. Thomas* and William* 3da. *suc.* fa. 29 Sept. 1485, KB 23 June 1509; *cr.* Lord Windsor by 1 Dec. 1529.[2]

Bencher, M. Temple bef. 1500.

J.p. Hants 1502–15, Mdx. 1505–*d.*, Bucks. 1507–*d.*, Berks. 1509–15, Suss. 1526–9; commr. subsidy, Bucks. 1503, 1512, 1514, 1515, 1524, 1534, Mdx. 1503, 1512, 1514, 1515, New Windsor 1512, Berks. 1514, 1515, 1524, Hants 1524, enclosures, Berks., Beds., Bucks., Leics., Northants., Oxon., Warws. 1517, loan, Mdx. 1522, 1524; other commissions 1500–*d.*; steward, 3rd Duke of Buckingham's lands, Hants Mar. 1504, Northants. c. 1510, Beds. and Bucks. by Feb. 1514; various stewardships, Bucks., Essex, London and Mdx. 1505–*d.*; keeper, great wardrobe 1506–*d.*; high steward, New Windsor by 1510–*d.*; custos rot. Bucks. ?by 1527; trier of petitions in the Lords, Parlt. of 1542.[3]

The family of Windsor was descended from William Fitzother, who had the manor of Stanwell at the time of Domesday Book: constable of Windsor castle, he held his manor of that fortress, whence his descendants acquired their royal-sounding name. Thomas Windsor, Sir Andrew's father, who was made constable of the castle by Richard III, forfeited his lands after Bosworth but had them restored on 22 Sept. 1485, one week before his death. The inquisitions then taken show that the 18 year-old Andrew inherited lands in Berkshire, Buckinghamshire, Hampshire, Middlesex and Surrey.[4]

The Windsors quickly recovered from their association with Richard III. A ten-year lease of the farm of Cold Kennington manor, Middlesex, granted to Thomas Windsor just before his death, was renewed for his widow and her eldest son in November 1485. In July 1486 Lady Elizabeth was given possession of Stanwell and its dependencies, which her husband had vested in feoffees for her and their heirs. By 1489 she had married Sir Robert Lytton[†], who became keeper of the wardrobe in 1492 and who, with Andrew Windsor and others, was granted the presentation to the next vacant canonry at St. Stephen's, Westminster, in 1493. When Lytton died, his stepson succeeded him as keeper of the wardrobe, during good behaviour and with effect from 20 Apr. 1506; at the same time, or soon afterwards, Windsor was granted an annuity of £300. He had already acted as feoffee for Henry VII, in a land transaction with Syon abbey in 1504, as well as for his brother-in-law Edmund Dudley[†], whom he partnered in at least one wardship and several land settlements. In a will made just before his execution in 1510, Dudley appointed Windsor one of the guardians of his son Jerome.[5]

The fall of Dudley did not impede Windsor's advancement: he continued as keeper of the wardrobe, was knighted at the coronation of Henry VIII, and a month later sued out a pardon for himself and his wife. In 1512 he was appointed to the retinue of Sir William Sandys and in June 1513 received £60,000 as treasurer of the middle ward of the royal army; he landed at Calais with the King on 30 June and was paid on the army's dismissal in November. As keeper of the wardrobe he was concerned with all the ceremonies of state, at several of which his attendance is recorded. He witnessed the marriage of Princess Mary to Louis XII in 1514, signed the peace and marriage treaties with France in 1518, and two years later accompanied the King to the Field of Cloth of Gold. On 1 Sept. 1524 he was at Blackheath to greet the papal envoy, who was bearing Henry VIII the gift of a sacred rose.[6]

Little is known of Andrew Windsor's career in the House of Commons. His election to Henry VIII's first Parliament may be inferred from an entry in the Windsor borough records, copied in the 17th century, which credited him, as high steward of the town, with the insertion of a clause of local interest in the Act passed by that Parliament allocating funds to the royal household (1 Hen. VIII, c.16): this proviso he is more likely to have secured from within than from outside the House, which also passed a companion Act (c.17) regulating payments to him as keeper of the great wardrobe. His Membership of the Parliaments of 1512 and 1515 is more hypothetical, being suggested only by his service on subsidy commissions in these years for Berkshire, Buckinghamshire, Middlesex and Windsor, but there is a stronger presumption that he sat again in 1523 as that Parliament passed both a private Act (14 and 15 Hen. VIII, c.31), which he doubtless initiated, enabling him and his brother Anthony to retain stewardships granted to them by the 3rd Duke of Buckingham, and a public one (14 and 15 Hen. VIII, c.19) amending the provisions of the Act of 1510 relating to the Household. Provisos were also added on behalf of the brothers to the Act attainting Buckingham (14 and 15 Hen. VIII, c.20) and to another private Act (14 and 15 Hen. VIII, c.27) protecting the interests of Sir John Marney*, 2nd Baron Marny.[7]

Windsor seems to have accommodated himself to Wolsey, and his connexion with Buckingham, like his earlier attachment to Dudley, left him unscathed when the duke perished in 1521. There had, it is true, been one awkward, even dangerous, moment some four years before that tragedy. It was in August 1517 that an affray between Windsor's servants and those of Serjeant Thomas Piggott, over their masters' rival claims to a ward, provoked

Wolsey's celebrated threat 'to see them learn the new law of the Star Chamber', a lesson which would be the more salutary in that both offenders were 'learned in the temporal law'. In Windsor's case, however, the lesson was to have a reassuring sequel, for two years later he was chosen by Wolsey as one of the commissioners in the cardinal's enlarged court of requests, and in 1526 he was made a councillor 'for matter in law'. None the less, Windsor's next great advancement was to follow, not precede, the fall of Wolsey. His election in 1529 as knight of the shire for Buckinghamshire, with Sir John Russell, was clearly a product of royal intervention, since the writ for Buckinghamshire was among those called for from Wolsey by the King when he lay at Windsor that summer: it is likely enough that as high steward of the borough Sir Andrew was at hand to receive the nomination. Parliament opened on 4 Nov., but Windsor's Membership of the Commons was soon terminated by his creation as a baron, probably by patent, and his admission to the House of Lords on 1 Dec. He was to attend there regularly for the rest of his life and in the process to partake in the condemnation of many of his peers. There is no warrant for the suggestion that his eldest surviving son William, who had been returned to this Parliament for Wycombe in Buckinghamshire, may have opted to follow him into the Upper House: no such privilege was available to the son of a baron, and William Windsor was to join the Lords only after his father's death. Windsor was probably replaced in the Commons by Sir Francis Bryan (q.v.), for whom he had earlier bought the wardship of Henry Fortescue (q.v.).[8]

Windsor's attitude to the upheavals of his later years seems to have been that of a wary conservative. He joined the spiritual and temporal lords who wrote to the pope in July 1530, beseeching him to further the King's divorce lest worse should follow. He received Anne Boleyn at the Tower on the eve of her coronation and did not scruple to offer Cromwell £40 a year, with a gold collar worth £100, if the secretary would help him to obtain some unnamed but evidently lucrative office. In December 1535 Thomas Bedyll, one of Cromwell's monastic visitors to Syon abbey, reported ambiguously that Lord Windsor had sent for him and his colleague 'and laboured much for the converting of his sister and some of his kinswomen here'. As there were one or two defiant inmates at Syon, Windsor may have feared for his sister Margaret, who had been its prioress for some 20 years, and for her sake have appealed personally to the royal agents to proceed gently. Syon eventually passed to the King in December 1539, seemingly without a surrender, and

its nuns became the most highly paid of all those who received pensions, Margaret Windsor's being £100 a year. Meanwhile, her brother had contributed to a subsidy for crushing the northern rising and been included in a list, annotated by Cromwell, of peers who were to punish the rebels. He was among those summoned to attend Queen Jane Seymour in 1536, he escorted Sir John Russell when his former fellow-Member was raised to the peerage in March 1539, and he greeted Anne of Cleves at Blackheath on 3 Jan. 1540. Yet his long and varied services did not bring Windsor the Garter. He had first been proposed by the 2nd Marquess of Dorset as early as 1523, was backed by the Dukes of Norfolk and Suffolk in 1525 and was repeatedly nominated thereafter. The two dukes usually favoured him and often a majority of the knights added their voices, as did Russell (who was admitted within a month of becoming a peer) on two occasions in 1541, but the King persistently ignored him, preferring to leave a vacancy.[9]

Windsor for his part did not fit easily into the new England of his maturity. He was often in the law courts, and while it was common enough to be grasping and litigious, Windsor went beyond the norm in high-handedness, even if he was dealing with the powerful. When he seized the lands of a widow's son, he apparently ignored a letter in her favour from Cromwell. He would have preferred similar short cuts in dealing with the city of London, after its attempts to make the King's tenants of the wardrobe keep watch like other citizens or to infringe their liberties in other ways. Detained at Stanwell by an ague, the 70 year-old keeper asked Cromwell to restrain the mayor, adding that there had been a time when such usurpations 'would have weighed to a forfeiture of the liberties of the City'.[10]

During his long career Windsor added considerably to his inheritance. Near Stanwell he acquired the manor of Poyle from the family of that name; in Buckinghamshire he bought the manor of Bradenham in or after 1505, and that of Weston Turville some time after 1512; and in Surrey he added the manor and advowson of Headley in or after 1526. A conservative temperament did not inhibit him from sharing in the spoils of the monasteries. In August 1539 he was granted the reversion of the house and site of Ankerwyke priory, Buckinghamshire, with its property in that county and in Middlesex and Surrey, the rectory and other property at 'Wyllasham' (probably Willingham), Suffolk, and the advowson of Stanwell, which had belonged to Chertsey abbey.[11]

All Windsor's estate arrangements were shattered, however, when towards the end of 1541 the King dined at Stanwell and, on leaving, declared that he wanted Windsor's ancestral home. Tradition ascribes this demand to the King's wish to bind his nobility to the Dissolution—in this case surely an unnecessary precaution—and adds that the protesting owner was forced to leave at once, although he had laid in his Christmas provisions. Be that as it may, on 14 Mar. 1542 Windsor parted with all his lands at Stanwell, and its dependencies elsewhere, in exchange for £2,197 and a string of ex-monastic estates scattered over Buckinghamshire, Gloucestershire, Surrey, Sussex, Wiltshire, Worcestershire, Westminster and London. The only lands in Middlesex were the manors of Cranford and Le Mote. Windsor sold the London property to Sir William Stourton*, 7th Baron Stourton, in November 1542, but in the following April, after his death, he was assigned a further annuity of £40 from some more Gloucestershire and Wiltshire property formerly belonging to Syon.[12]

The loss of his home notwithstanding, Windsor described himself as of Stanwell when he made his will on 26 Mar. 1543. He acknowledged the royal supremacy but made the traditional bequest of his soul to God, the Virgin Mary and the holy company of heaven, and asked to be buried next to his wife in the church at Hounslow. There followed elaborate directions for the funeral, the distribution of alms, a month's mind and an obit for 14 years on the anniversary of his father's death, all in addition to the chantries which he had founded at Dorney and Stanwell. His eldest son George had died in 1520, so that the heir was his second son Sir William, who was to have all his mother's plate and goods, while a younger son Edmund was left all the household goods at Stoke Poges and another, Thomas, those from the testator's chambers at London and Stanwell. The three daughters Elizabeth, Anne and Edith had already been provided for on their marriages to Sir Peter Vavasour, Roger Corbet* and George Ludlow, but many other smaller bequests were made to Windsor's sons, grandchildren and the heirs of his brother, Sir Anthony, while his sister Margaret, the late prioress of Syon, was given £80 a year from the manor of Cranford. The executors were Sir William and Edward Windsor, Chancellor Audley, who was given £50, and (Sir) John Baker I*, who received £30 6s.8d.; the 3rd Duke of Norfolk and Sir Anthony Windsor, as overseers, were left £40 and £10 respectively.[13]

Windsor died on 30 Mar. 1543 and was buried at Hounslow. His 44 year-old heir was granted livery of the lands on 11 June and the will was proved on 31 July.[14]

¹ R. R. Tighe and J. E. Davis, *Windsor Annals*, i. 500. ² Date of

birth estimated from age at fa.'s i.p.m.s, *CIPM Hen. VII*, i. 12, 16, 28, 29. *CP*; PCC 23 Spert. ³ *CPR*, 1494–1509, pp. 209, 470, 487, 560, 592, 632, 650; *LP Hen. VIII*, i–v, vii, viii, x–xix; St.Ch.2/33/58; *Rot. Parl.* vi. 517, 540; *Statutes*, iii. 82, 83, 86, 116, 118, 171, 173; *LJ*, i. pp. 165, lxviii, lxxi, lxxii, cxliv; Tighe and Davis, i. 500; SP1/29/170, 174, 178; *VCH Bucks*. iii. 90; M. C. Rosenfield, 'The disposal of the property of London monastic houses' (London Univ. Ph.D. thesis, 1961), 34; *Guildhall Misc.* iii. 166, 172; G. J. Aungier, *Syon Monastery*, 446; *Val. Eccles.* i. 397, 402; *Chron. Calais* (Cam. Soc. xxxv), 13; C. Rawcliffe, *The Staffords, Earls of Stafford and Dukes of Buckingham 1394–1521*, pp. 203, 204, 211. ⁴ *VCH Mdx.* iii. 37; *CIPM Hen. VII*, i. 12, 28, 29; *Test. Vet.* 352–6; Copinger, *Suff. Manors*, ii. 297. ⁵ *CFR*, 1485–1509, pp. 11, 26; *CCR*, 1485–1500, p. 8; 1500–9, pp. 50, 102, 235, 239, 252, 286; *CIPM Hen. VII*, i. 497; *CPR*, 1485–94, p. 430; 1494–1509, pp. 354, 396, 470, 542; *LP Hen. VIII*, i, ii. ⁶ *LP Hen. VIII*, i–iv; *Chron. Calais*, 13. ⁷ Tighe and Davis, i. 500; *Statutes*, iii. 12; *LJ*, i. p. cxlvi. ⁸ *LP Hen. VIII*, ii, iv; Pollard, *Wolsey* (1953), 73 and n. 1; *Bull. IHR*, ix. 39. ⁹ *LP Hen. VIII*, iv, vi, viii, ix, xi, xii, xiv–xvi; Aungier, 81, 89; F. A. Gasquet, *Hen. VIII and the Eng. Monasteries*, 441; J. Anstis, *Reg. Order of Garter*, i. 363–422. ¹⁰ C1/456/34; St.Ch.2/7/41–42; *LP Hen. VIII*, ii, xi, xiii. ¹¹ *VCH Mdx.* iii. 39; *VCH Bucks.* ii. 367–8; iii. 36; *VCH Surr.* iii. 291, 293; *LP Hen. VIII*, xiv. ¹² Dugdale, *Baronage* (1676), ii. 308; *LP Hen. VIII*, xvii, xviii. ¹³ PCC 23 Spert. ¹⁴ Manning and Bray, *Surr.* ii. 639; *LP Hen. VIII*, xviii.

T.F.T.B.

WINDSOR, Thomas (by 1517–c. 67), of Bentley, Hants, and London.

REIGATE 1555

b. by 1517, 4th but 3rd surv. s. of Sir Andrew Windsor*, 1st Lord Windsor, and bro. of William*. *m.* by 1538, Mary, da. and h. of Thomas Beckingham of London and Buscot, Berks., 5s. 4da.[1]

?Serjeant-at-arms in 1544; carver to King Philip June 1554.[2]

Thomas Windsor might have been expected to follow his father and three brothers at the Middle Temple, but although his admission could have been obscured by a gap in the records there is no other indication that he belonged to the inn or practised law; such career as he had lay in the royal household, where he appears to have been for a time a serjeant-at-arms. It was probably his nephew and namesake who accompanied an embassy to France in 1546, but the younger Windsor died in 1552 and it was the uncle who in 1554 was seconded as a carver to the suite of King Philip. A modest beneficiary in lands and goods under his father's will, Windsor made an advantageous marriage which in 1551 put him in possession of several Berkshire manors and the arrears of income from them for about 16 years; by 1547 he also had a lease of the bishop of Winchester's manor of Bentley. It was his nephew who two years later leased ex-church property in Darlington, but in 1553 Windsor paid £1,000 for a manor at Iver, Buckinghamshire, and also leased South Mimms, Middlesex, from another nephew. During his later years he seems to have overstretched his resources: when he died he still owed £400 for the last lease and he had mortgaged the Iver property for £1,000.[3]

At the beginning of Mary's reign Windsor was granted an annuity of £10 for 'service at Framlingham' and his election for Reigate is sufficiently explained by his position at court. The borough was normally controlled by the Howard family, represented there at this time by Lord William Howard, whose cousin Sir George Howard* had been appointed with Windsor to Philip's household. As a Member of this Parliament Windsor is not named among those who opposed one of the government's bills.[4]

Windsor died intestate and in December 1567 his widow was given the administration of his property. She herself died in May 1574, and her will and inquisition indicate that she was a woman of some wealth and standing. The heir Andrew was aged 36 and more at his mother's death. The second son Miles, of Corpus Christi College, Oxford, was to be described as 'a tolerable Latin poet, but a better orator', and his 'popish affections' were to lead to his withdrawal from the university.[5]

[1] Date of birth estimated from marriage. *Vis. Surr.* (Harl. Soc. xliii), 186; *PCC Admins.* ed. Glencross, i. 82; PCC 21, 46 Martyn. [2] *LP Hen. VIII*, xix; *CSP Span.* 1554, p. 297. [3] PCC 23 Spert; *LP Hen. VIII*, xxi; *VCH Berks.* iii. 283, 480; iv. 538; *VCH Bucks.* iii. 290; *VCH Hants*, iv. 27–28; Eccles. 2/155888A, 155897; *CPR*, 1550–3, p.45; 1563–6, pp. 150–1; C142/146/188, 170/7; Req.2/35/101. [4] Lansd. 156(28), f. 90. [5] *PCC Admins.* i. 82; PCC 21 Martyn; C3/146/5; 142/146/188, 170/7; Wood, *Ath. Ox.* ed. Bliss, ii. 358.

S.R.J.

WINDSOR, Sir Thomas (by 1523–52), of Princes Risborough, Bucks.

BUCKINGHAMSHIRE 1547*

b. by 1523, 2nd but 1st surv. s. of William Windsor*, 2nd Lord Windsor, by 1st w. *educ.* M. Temple. *m.* 29 Nov. 1544, Dorothy, da. of William, 3rd Lord Dacre, 1da. KB 20 Feb. 1547.[1]

Feodary, duchy of Lancaster, Beds. and Bucks. in May 1544, in Feb. 1548.[2]

Thomas Windsor probably spent some time at the Middle Temple, where his father and grandfather had both been benchers, but the loss of the admission records for the period in question leaves this uncertain. He doubtless obtained the feodaryship of the duchy of Lancaster at the suit of his father, who held the office before him. His marriage late in 1544 to a daughter of Lord Dacre may mean that he took part in the Scottish campaign of the previous summer, in which Dacre had fought, and he was probably the Thomas Windsor who accompanied the embassy to France in 1546. With a number of other peers' sons he was knighted at the coronation of Edward VI. At the court festivities at Christmas 1551, the last he was to see, he was one of the eight councillors to the lord of misrule, George Ferrers*.[3]

It was the death of Sir Anthony Lee in November 1549 which left vacant the knighthood of the shire filled by Windsor. His choice is not hard to explain. As a peer's son he was a suitable colleague for young

Francis Russell, he was doubtless favoured by the sheriff, Russell's father-in-law Sir John St. John*, and if the Earl of Warwick, newly come to power, interested himself in the matter he may have looked kindly on the grandson of the 1st Lord Windsor, his own father's associate and brother-in-law. The election writ is dated 24 Dec. 1549 and the indenture 8 Jan. 1550, so that Windsor entered the House halfway through the third session. Nothing is known of the part which he played there.[4]

Windsor was a sick man when he drew up his will on 8 Nov. 1552 and he died in the following month. He is thought to have been buried at Bradenham: a year later his 'month's mind' was held in the county with fitting pomp of heraldry. By his short will Windsor left to his wife his lease of Princes Risborough and that of Darlington, Durham, which he had obtained early in 1549: after her death they were to pass to his daughter and sole heir Anne. His executors, his wife and uncle Edmund Windsor, proved the will on 16 Jan. 1553.[5]

[1] Date of birth estimated from first reference. *CP*, xii(2), 797. [2] Somerville, *Duchy*, i. 592. [3] *HMC Bath*, iv. 58–72 passim; *LP Hen. VIII*, xxi; *Lit. Rems. Edw. VI*, 382n. [4] C219/19/10. [5] PCC 1 Tashe; *Machyn's Diary* (Cam. Soc. xlii), 29; *CPR*, 1563–6, pp. 150–1.

M.K.D.

WINDSOR, William (by 1499–1558), of Bradenham, Bucks.

CHIPPING WYCOMBE 1529

b. by 1499, 2nd but 1st surv. s. of Sir Andrew Windsor*, 1st Lord Windsor, and bro. of Thomas*. *educ.* ?M. Temple. *m.* (1) by 1527, Margaret, da. of William Sambourne of Fernham in Shrivenham, Berks., at least 5s. inc. Sir Thomas* 1da.; (2) by Mar. 1554, Elizabeth, da. of Peter Cowdray of Herriard, Hants, wid. of Richard Paulet (*d.* by 1515), 1s. 1da. KB 30 May 1533; *suc.* fa. as 2nd Lord Windsor 30 Mar. 1543.[1]

Bencher, M. Temple by 1553.

Member, the Household 1520; j.p. Bucks. 1530–*d.*, Mdx. 1544, commr. benevolence, Bucks. 1544/45, musters 1546, relief 1550, loan 1557; other commissions, Bucks. and London 1535–*d.*; feodary, duchy of Lancaster, Beds. and Bucks. 12 July 1535–45; sheriff, Beds. and Bucks. 1537–8.[2]

William Windsor was probably educated at the Middle Temple, of which his father was a bencher. If so, his admission may have dated from about 1513, the year in which his younger brother Edmund was admitted: 40 years later he held a bencher's chamber. By 1520, when the death of his elder brother George made him the heir, he was receiving half-yearly wages of £6 13s.4d. as one of the royal household, and in December of that year he was at Enfield with the King when instructed by his father to wait on Wolsey after conveying horses to Calais for Francis I. After serving on local commissions for some years, he was nominated for the sheriffdom of Bedfordshire and Buckinghamshire in 1536 but was not chosen until the following year: he was by then domiciled at his father's manor of Bradenham, whence he wrote to Cromwell arguing a point of procedure relating to the office.[3]

Windsor had undoubtedly owed his election for Chipping Wycombe in 1529 to the influence of his father, who was himself probably the royal nominee with another courtier, Sir John Russell, for the knighthood of the shire. Both Windsor and his fellow-Member Robert Dormer appear on a list, drawn up by Cromwell in the spring of 1533 and believed to be of Members opposed to the bill in restraint of appeals. Presumably he was re-elected in 1536 in compliance with the general directive for the return of the previous Members, and perhaps again three years later when the names of the Wycombe Members are lost.[4]

In June 1543 Windsor received livery of his inheritance on the death of his father: he also dealt with some accounts for the great wardrobe, presumably as the executor. He was present at the signing of the treaty with Charles V, and in 1544 he served with the rearguard of the army against France, having contributed £1,000 to the loan for the war. At the funeral of Henry VIII he carried the standard of the lion and he was to be a chief mourner at that of Edward VI.[5]

Windsor signed the device settling the crown on Jane Grey, but soon joined the magnates who proclaimed Queen Mary in Buckinghamshire. On 22 July 1553 he, Sir Edward Hastings* and Sir Edmund Peckham* were ordered to dismiss their troops and join Mary at Framlingham. Windsor died on 20 Aug. 1558 leaving to his eldest surviving son and heir Sir Edward Windsor, aged 26, a rich inheritance of lands in 14 counties. In his will of 10 Aug. he had asked to be buried according to his 'degree and estate' at Bradenham, where he had built a new manor house, or at Hounslow, Middlesex, beside his parents. His London house in Cripplegate called Windsor Place he left to his widow with remainder to his next male heir. He made provision for the education of his son William at Oxford or at one of the inns of court or of chancery, and for Philip and Elizabeth, his children by his second wife: Philip was to receive from Bradenham three christening cups including one given to him by his godfather King Philip. Among the executors and overseers of the will, which was proved on 10 Dec. 1558, were Windsor's kinsmen by marriage William Paulet, 1st Marquess of Winchester, Lord Chidiock Paulet* and Sir

George Paulet, as well as William Roper* and (Sir) Thomas White II*.[6]

[1] Date of birth estimated from age at fa.'s i.p.m., C142/68/28. [2] *LP Hen. VIII*, iii–vi, viii, xi, xiv, xvii, xx, xxi; Somerville, *Duchy*, i. 592; *APC*, v. 50, 243; vi. 186; *CPR*, 1547–8, p. 81; 1550–3, p. 141; 1553, p. 351; 1553–4, pp. 17, 28; 1555–7, p. 281. [3] *M.T. Bench Bk.* 50, 65–66; *M.T. Adm.* i. 8; *M.T. Recs.* i. 93; *LP Hen. VIII*, iii, xi, xiii; *VCH Bucks.* iii. 36. [4] *LP Hen. VIII*, ix. 1077 citing SP1/99, p. 234. [5] *LP Hen. VIII*, xviii, xix; Strype, *Eccles. Memorials*, ii(1), 123, 132; *Lit. Rems. Edw. VI*, pp. ccxl, 491–2; Burnet, *Hist. Ref.* ii. 168, 176, 250, 321, 324; *LJ*, i. 411; M. A. R. Graves, 'The Tudor House of Lords 1547–58' (Otago Univ. Ph.D. thesis, 1974), ii. 366–8. [6] *Chron. Q. Jane and Q. Mary* (Cam. Soc. xlviii), 8; *APC*, iv. 301; PCC 12 Welles; C142/115/57; *Machyn's Diary* (Cam. Soc. xlii), 172.

M.K.D.

WINGFIELD, Sir Anthony (by 1488–1552), of Letheringham, Suff.

SUFFOLK	1529, 1539,[1] ?1542
HORSHAM	1545
SUFFOLK	1547

b. by 1488, 1st s. of Sir John Wingfield of Letheringham by Anne, da. of John Tuchet, 6th Lord Audley. *m.* by 1528, Elizabeth, da. of Sir George Vere, 7s. inc. Sir Robert† 3da. *suc.* fa. Mar./July 1509. Kntd. 25 Sept. 1513; KG nom. 23 Apr. inst. 22 May 1541.[2] Esquire of the body by 1509; j.p. Suff. 1510–*d.*; commr. subsidy 1512, 1514, 1515, 1523, 1524, dissolution of monasteries 1536, benevolence 1544/45, relief, Suff., London, royal household 1550, goods of churches and fraternities, Suff. 1552; other commissions 1525–*d.*; sheriff, Norf. and Suff. 1515–16; PC 1539–*d.*; v.-chamberlain, the Household 1539–2 Feb. 1550, comptroller by 2 Feb. 1550–*d.*; capt. the guard 1539; member, council of Boulogne 1544; constable Denbigh castle, Denb., steward, lordship of Denbigh, chancellor and chamberlain, Denb. Dec. 1549; chamberlain, receipt of the Exchequer 1550; jt. ld. lt. Suff. 1552.[3]

As an esquire of the body Anthony Wingfield was present at the funeral of Henry VII, but it was the new King's first war which brought him advancement. In 1512 he served in the *Dragon* of Greenwich with his kinsman Sir Charles Brandon and Sir John Seymour* under the captaincy of Sir William Sidney, and in the following year his part in the capture of Tournai brought him a knighthood. Pricked sheriff of Norfolk and Suffolk in November 1513, he was 'discharged' and shortly afterwards succeeded by Thomas Gebon: the reason may have been that he was required either at court or with one of his uncles abroad, but two years later he served his term in the office. He was present at the Field of Cloth of Gold and also went with the King to Gravelines for the meeting with Charles V. He served in the campaign of 1523 under Brandon, now Duke of Suffolk, who was afterwards to use him in the suppression of the Lincolnshire rebellion in 1536. He last took the field in 1544 against the French: he commanded 500 men at the capture of Boulogne and was made a member of the council there, but he did not remain abroad for long.[4]

Like his prominent kinsmen Wingfield was more than a soldier: to long service in the administration of his county he was to add from 1539 responsibilities in the royal household and a seat on the Privy Council. Well placed to profit from the Dissolution, he purchased the lands of Campsea priory and those of Letheringham and Woodbridge, was appointed steward of the college at Worcester and in 1546 became keeper of the former abbey of Bury St. Edmunds. Other lands, this time in Essex, came to him after the attainder of Thomas Culpeper, but these he parted with almost immediately. In the last year of the reign he was in debt to the King and surrendered several manors in lieu of payment, but this evidently did not tell against him, for in the King's will he was named an assistant executor and bequeathed £200. In the royal funeral procession he led the guard.[5]

During the Protectorate of Somerset, Wingfield was a member of the Council but he appears to have attended less frequently than he had hitherto done. Whether this reflected a lack of sympathy with the new regime does not appear, but with the outbreak of rebellion in 1549 Wingfield was to prove a strenuous and successful upholder of law and order in his county and the experience must have helped to align him with the revolt against Somerset which followed. It was he whom the Council despatched on 10 Oct. to Windsor to arrest Somerset and his adherents, an operation which he conducted without a hitch: four days later he escorted his prisoner from Windsor to the Tower. He was rewarded with offices in the Household and the Exchequer and with the constableship of Denbigh castle.[6]

Wingfield regularly sat for his county in Parliament. His earliest known election dates from 1529, when he was returned first knight of the shire with Sir Thomas Wentworth I*. Both were followers of the Duke of Suffolk and Wingfield probably took precedence as the elder, but it was no mean achievement, for not only was Wentworth to be ennobled before the year was out but Wingfield's uncle Humphrey, the future Speaker, was to appear in the same House in the inferior role of Member for Yarmouth. Nothing is known of Wingfield's part in the proceedings of this Parliament, but it was perhaps during its first session that he, his brother-in-law Edmund Knightley* and Knightley's brother Richard* were assaulted in Cheapside. Presumably he sat for Suffolk again in the following Parliament, that of 1536, when the King asked for the re-election of the previous Members. He was to do so in 1539, when in the course of the second session he was the

bearer of several bills, including the bill dissolving the greater monasteries, from the Commons to the Lords, and perhaps again in 1542, for which Parliament only the name of one of the knights of the shire for Suffolk remains: of the other all that is known is his style 'the right worshipful', which would accord with Wingfield's status as a Councillor. In December 1544, while presumably at Boulogne, he was returned for Horsham, a borough controlled by his kinsman the 3rd Duke of Norfolk. It is possible that Wingfield, sensing that his current duties at Boulogne were an obstacle to re-election for Suffolk, asked for the duke's help in obtaining a place elsewhere or alternatively that the duke, perhaps anxious to promote the election of Arthur Hopton, offered to compensate Wingfield if to facilitate Hopton's election he forwent his own. The opening of the Parliament of 1545 was postponed from January until the following autumn and when it assembled Wingfield, who had long since ceased attending the council at Boulogne, took his place in the House, on 23 Dec. taking three bills up to the Lords.[7]

The Parliament of 1547 was to be Wingfield's last and once more he appeared as knight of the shire for Suffolk: it was also, to judge from the Commons Journal, the one which kept him most busy. Bills were committed to him which dealt with the export of bell-metal (14 Dec. 1548), the buying of pensions (19 Dec. 1548), regrators (30 Jan., 11, 12 Nov. 24 Dec. 1549 and 3 Jan. 1550), the forestalling of herring in Lowestoft Roads (12 Nov. 1549), farms (6 Dec. 1549), the ownership of sheep and farms and the export of corn, leather, cheese and tallow (6 Dec. 1549). The third session also saw him deliver bills to the Lords and append his signature to the Acts for the general pardon, the restitution of Sir William Hussey, the acquisition of a churchyard at West Drayton by Sir William Paget, and the fine and ransom of the Duke of Somerset. In February 1549 and in February and March 1552 the House granted privilege to servants of Wingfield but on the last occasion revoked the grant made to Hugh Flood after receiving a petition against it. Flood's escape from custody and recapture engaged the attention of the House and of Wingfield himself for several days.[8]

On the list of Members of this Parliament, as revised in the winter of 1551–2, Wingfield is marked 'mortuus', but he survived its dissolution by four months, dying on 15 Aug. 1552 at the house of his friend (Sir) John Gates* at Bethnal Green. He had made his will two days earlier, providing for his family and servants, and naming as executors his wife and his second but eldest surviving son Robert, and as supervisor Sir Thomas Wentworth II*, 2nd

Lord Wentworth. He was buried at Stepney on 21 Aug.[9]

[1] E159/319, brev. ret. Mich. r. [1–2]. [2] Date of birth estimated from first reference. DNB; Vis. Suff. ed. Metcalfe, 79; LP Hen. VIII, i, iv, xvi; CPR, 1494–1509, p. 457; J. M. Wingfield, Some Recs. Wingfield Fam., 32; M. E. Wingfield, Visct. Powerscourt, Muniments of Wingfield, 3–4, 30. [3] LP Hen. VIII, i–iv, viii, xi, xiii, xix, xx; Statutes, iii. 83, 116, 172; CPR, 1547–8, p. 89; 1549–51, pp. 163, 291; 1550–3, p. 395; 1553, pp. 358, 360, 363; APC, iv. 50; D. E. Hoak, The King's Council in the Reign of Edw. VI, 47, 49, 51, 79, 270. [4] LP Hen. VIII, i, iii, xi, xix. [5] Ibid. xi, xvi, xvii, xxi; SP10/1, f. 73. [6] APC, ii. 342; SP10/9, f. 82; W. K. Jordan, Edw. VI, i. 88, 446–7, 520–1; Hoak, 44, 69, 195, 252; M. L. Bush, Govt. Pol. Somerset, 97. [7] C219/18B/82; LJ, i. 125, 281. [8] CJ, i. 5, 7, 11–16, 18, 20–23; Jordan, ii. 336; House of Lords RO, Original Acts, 3 and 4 Edw. VI, nos. 24, 25, 30, 31. [9] Hatfield 207; Machyn's Diary (Cam. Soc. xlii), 23–24, 326; C142/98/65 (giving date of death as 20 Aug.).

R.J.W.S.

WINGFIELD, Humphrey (by 1481–1545), of Brantham and Ipswich, Suff.

IPSWICH	1523[1]
GREAT YARMOUTH	1529, 1542[2]

b. by 1481, 12th s. of Sir John Wingfield[†] of Letheringham, by Elizabeth, da. of Sir Lewis John[†] of West Horndon, Essex; bro. of Sir Robert* and Thomas. *educ.* G. Inn, called. *m.* by 1512, Anne (*d.* by Jan. 1537), da. and h. of Sir John Wiseman of Great Canfield, Essex, wid. of Gregory Edgar, 2s. at least 1da. Kntd. 1533.[3]

Lent reader, G. Inn 1517.

J.p. Suff. 1504–?*d.*, Essex 1509–?*d*, Norf. 1540; of counsel to Ipswich 1507, Great Yarmouth 1520; commr. subsidy, Essex 1512, Suff. 1512, 1514, 1523, 1524, Ipswich 1523, 1524, legal profession in London 1523, for survey of monasteries, Norf. and Suff. 1536, benevolence 1544/45; other commissions 1503–*d*.; dep. chief steward, duchy of Lancaster, south parts 1512–*d*.; chamberlain, household of Duchess of Suffolk 1515; sheriff, Norf. and Suff. 1520–1; bailiff, manor of Framsden, Suff. 1529–*d*.; member, council of 15th Earl of Oxford by 1532.[4]

Speaker of House of Commons Feb. 1533–6.

Humphrey Wingfield was an infant when his father died in 1481, but the name of his guardian has not been found. A member of Gray's Inn, his readership of 1517 there was his second—the date of the first is unrecorded—and by the time he gave it his name appears regularly as attorney to his relative Charles Brandon, Duke of Suffolk. His first known court appointment was in the household of Suffolk's duchess, the King's sister. In 1518 he was listed as one of the barristers regularly pleading at Westminster. He had a reputation for humanism, and Roger Ascham paid tribute to 'this worshipful man [who] hath ever loved and used to have many children brought up in learning in his house, amongst whom I myself was one'. He had come to Wolsey's notice about 1515, perhaps because of his frequent missions to the minister on Suffolk's behalf: in July of the following year the duke reminded Wolsey of his promise to make Wingfield custos rotulorum for Suffolk, a post for which he

was qualified by residence, his main seat being at Brantham near Ipswich, where in 1524 he was assessed for the subsidy on £130 in goods.[5]

Wingfield is first known to have sat in Parliament in 1523, when he and Sir Thomas Rush were returned for Ipswich; the town records note that both Members came in person and were sworn freemen. Although Wingfield's appointment as legal counsel to the borough may have sufficed to procure him the seat, he could have relied on the support of both Suffolk and Wolsey, with whom he was in high favour during these years. In 1528 Dean Capon, writing to Wolsey about the building of the cardinal's college at Ipswich, described himself as 'much bound' to Wingfield for his assistance with the project. In the following June Wolsey chose Wingfield as one of a commission of 21 lawyers to hear cases in Chancery. Before the year was out he sought to make use of Wingfield's legal ability himself. Accused of *praemunire*, he attempted to secure the exemption of his college from its penalties, and Wingfield was one of the seven lawyers whom he retained as being 'the best counsel' for this purpose. In July 1530, however, when Dean Capon was writing to the cardinal that he was not hopeful in the matter, Wingfield was appointed one of the commissioners to inquire into Wolsey's possessions in Suffolk, and in September the commission, which sat at Woodbridge, declared that his conviction meant the forfeiture of all the college lands to the King.[6]

In 1529 Wingfield was elected for Great Yarmouth, another borough which he served as legal counsellor. Nothing is known of his role in the House during the first four sessions, but in February 1533 he was chosen Speaker in succession to Sir Thomas Audley. Although Wingfield is often said to have been the first Speaker who was not a knight of the shire when elected to the chair, not only is the evidence in other cases too scanty to warrant such a statement but it is not impossible that Wingfield had replaced Sir Thomas Wentworth I*, who had vacated a seat for Suffolk on being a peer in December 1529; no by-election is known either for the shire or for Yarmouth. According to Chapuys, the King knighted Wingfield, after receiving the Commons' presentation of their new Speaker, in a colourful ceremony witnessed by the papal nuncio and the French ambassador; Wingfield is styled 'knight' in the account of the prorogation in March 1534. Although his Speakership coincided with the breach with Rome and the legislation concerned with the supersession of Catherine of Aragon by Anne Boleyn, only scattered references have survived to his personal part in the proceedings of the House. On 5 Mar. 1534 he addressed the King on behalf of the Commons, protesting against measures passed by Convocation—a prelude to the Act for the submission of the clergy (25 Hen. VIII, c.19), passed soon afterwards. His eloquent oration on 30 Mar. the same year, when presenting bills for the royal signature, is noted in the Lords Journal. He apparently received the usual fee of £100 a session, but the only other payment to him noted was £50 'for his reward' in March 1533. However, in June 1537 he received a valuable grant of former monastic property in Dedham, Essex and Creppinghall in Stutton, Suffolk, perhaps in recognition of his work in Parliament. He had almost certainly been re-elected in 1536 in accordance with the King's general request for the return of the previous Members and may have been so in 1539, but his only known Membership subsequent to his Speakership was in 1542, again for Great Yarmouth, which at the close of the Parliament made him a token payment of 20s.; in January 1545 he seems to have been elected once more for the borough but to have immediately yielded place to Sir William Woodhouse, presumably on the ground of ill-health.[7]

In January 1533 and May 1535 Wingfield acted for Audley in legal disputes. In 1536 he was appointed a commissioner for the survey of monasteries and was also one of the local gentlemen named to keep order in Suffolk during the northern rebellion. He was himself steward or under steward of several religious houses in Suffolk and in 1538 he shared with Sir Thomas Rush in a lease of lands formerly of Holy Trinity priory, Ipswich. In 1537 he had asked Cromwell to intercede on his behalf in a dispute over the settlement for a marriage between his daughter and a nephew of the bishop of Norwich; he said that he had lost half his living by the death of his wife and claimed that had it not been for the land granted him by the King in January he would have had 'to begin the world again'. Wingfield took part in the examination or trial of various East Anglian dissidents. He was one of the knights appointed to receive Anne of Cleves in 1540 and three years later he was called upon to provide ten men for the army in France.[8]

By his will of 13 Mar. 1543 Wingfield left most of his property in Essex and Suffolk to his son and executor Robert who was, however, to share a house in Ipswich with his sister Anne and her husband Alexander Newton. Wingfield died on 23 Oct. 1545 and the will was proved on 26 Nov. 1546.[9]

[1] Ipswich ct. bk. 8, p. 116. [2] OR gives 'Humfridus Wy(nne)'. The deed of return (C219/18B/55) has only the christian name. [3] Date of birth estimated from father's death. N. Bacon, Annals Ipswich, 179n.; Vis. Suff. ed. Metcalfe, 80, 176; LP Hen. VIII, vi; C142/72/74;

Wards 7/2/71; J. A. Manning, Lives of Speakers, 181; DNB. [4] E.W. Ives, 'Some aspects of the legal profession in the late 15th and early 16th centuries' (London Univ. Ph.D. thesis, 1955), 11–13; C193/12/1; Statutes, iii. 83, 84, 116, 173; Ipswich ct. bk. 8, p. 54; Bacon, 179n.; Gt. Yarmouth chamberlains' rolls, 1519–41 passim; CPR, 1494–1509, pp. 305, 447, 560, 660; LP Hen. VIII, i, iii–v, viii, xi–xvi, xviii, xx; LJ, i. 82; information from Susan Flower and G. Haslam. [5] J. K. McConica, Eng. Humanists and Reformation Politics, 207; LP Hen. VIII, ii, iii; Suff. Green Bks. x. 307. [6] Bacon, 198; Ipswich ct. bk. 8, p. 116; LP Hen. VIII, iv. [7] Manning, 179–80; P. Laundy, Office of Speaker, 160–1; J. S. Roskell, The Commons and their Speakers, 1376–1523, p. vii; S. E. Lehmberg, Ref. Parl., 171, 199, 213, 247; LP Hen. VIII, iv, vi, vii, x, xii; LJ, i. 82; Gt. Yarmouth Assembly Minutes (Norf. Rec. Soc. xxxix), 50, 60–61. [8] LP Hen. VIII, vi, viii, x, xi–xv. [9] PCC 23 Alen; C142/72/74.

J.P.

WINGFIELD, Jacques (c. 1519–87), of Stone Castle, Kent and St. Giles-in-the-Fields, Mdx.

TAUNTON 1553 (Oct.)

b. c. 1519, 3rd s. of Sir Richard Wingfield of Kimbolton, Hunts. by 2nd w. Bridget, da. of Sir John Wiltshire of Stone Castle; bro. of Thomas Maria*.[1]

Gent. household of Stephen Gardiner, bp. of Winchester 1531–55; master of the ordnance, Ireland c. 1558–d.; constable, Dublin castle c. 1558–Jan. 1586; member, council of Ireland 1559–62, of Munster 26 Apr. 1587; commr. eccles. causes, Ireland 1568; sewers Kent 1568.[2]

Jacques Wingfield's early life was probably spent in Calais and he is said to have spoken excellent French. He entered Gardiner's household in 1531 (his uncle Lewis had been comptroller of Bishop Fox's household) and it is as the bishop's servant that he appears during the next 24 years. He was in Paris with Gardiner in 1538, when Germain Gardiner described him as popular at the French Court, though an outspoken defender of England, and he again accompanied Gardiner on foreign missions in 1546–7. From 1540 he was bailiff of the episcopal manor of Bishops Sutton, Hampshire, and from 1551 of Farnham, Surrey. Clearly it was on Gardiner's nomination that he sat in Mary's first Parliament for Taunton, another manor of the see of Winchester. Wingfield had remained faithful to Gardiner during the bishop's imprisonment under Edward VI; he continually pleaded with the Duke of Somerset for Gardiner's release and was named one of his proctors at the trial of 1551, in which he deposed as to the numbers and quality of Gardiner's household and to his master's loyalty.[3]

The death of Gardiner (who left him £40) ended the first phase of Wingfield's career. The remainder of his life centred on Ireland. In May 1556 he arrived at Dublin with the lord deputy Sir Thomas Radcliffe*; he was sent home in the following year, probably to fetch more troops, for he returned early in 1558 with 400 men, and by November had obtained the offices of master of the ordnance and constable of Dublin castle. His ignominious defeat by Shane O'Neill in a skirmish in 1561 led Queen Elizabeth to order his removal from all his offices, but through the intercession of Radcliffe (now 3rd Earl of Sussex) and Cecil he was allowed to keep them, and though on bad terms with some of the deputies who succeeded Sussex he did so until his death. Sir John Perrot* complained in 1586 that Wingfield was too old and had been four years in England, but in that year he secured large grants of land in the Munster Plantation for himself and his family. He went back to Ireland but died soon afterwards, between April and September 1587. His will, in the name of 'James Wingfield esquire of St. Giles's parish, London', was proved in the prerogative court of Ireland, and letters of administration for his English property were granted at Lambeth on 6 Sept. 1587.[4]

[1] Aged 19 or under in February 1538. *Vis. Hunts.* (Cam. Soc. xliii), 131. [2] Foxe, *Acts and Mons.* vi. 197; *CSP Carew*, 1515-74, p. 278; *CSP Ire.* 1509-73, p. 158; 1585-8, pp. 41, 313; *APC*, xv. 33; *CPR*, 1566-9, pp. 173-4; 1569-72, p. 220. [3] *LP Hen. VIII*, xiii, xxi; Eccles. 2/155883-4, 155889, 155898; Foxe, vi. 120, 197-9, 250. [4] PCC 3 Noodes; *CSP Carew*, 1515-74, pp. 257, 278, 299; *CSP Ire.* 1509-73, p. 147 passim; 1574-85, p. 584; 1585-8, pp. 17-407 passim; SP63/3, f. 100; A. Vicars, *Index to Prerogative Wills of Ireland*, 501; PCC admons. act. bk. 1587-92, f. 30.

R.V.

WINGFIELD, Sir Richard (c. 1510-57/59), of Portsmouth, Hants.

PORTSMOUTH 1553 (Mar.)

b. c. 1510, s. of Lewis Wingfield of Bishops Sutton by da. of one Macwilliam of Suff. *m.* Christian, da. of Sir William Fitzwilliam of Gains Park, Essex, and Milton, Northants., at least 1s. Kntd. 30 Sept. 1544.[1]

Capt. *Morian* 1546, *Swallow* 1557; paymaster, Portsmouth 1548-54, capt. 1551-4; commr. goods of churches and fraternities, Hants 1553; burgess, Portsmouth by 1553-4.[2]

Richard Wingfield's father, the ninth son of Sir John Wingfield[†] of Letheringham, Suffolk, was comptroller of the household of the bishop of Winchester, from whom he had a lease of the manor of Bishops Sutton. Lewis Wingfield died in or before 1526, leaving Richard a goblet and the reversion of Sutton after it had been applied to the upbringing of his brother, or stepbrother, Robert. No further trace of Wingfield has been found until 1544, when he was one of those knighted for his part in the capture of Boulogne. Shortly afterwards he was taken prisoner when the French were repulsed 'in their camisado out of Base Boulogne'. Released after 17 months and on the payment of a large ransom, he came home bearing a letter of recommendation to the King from the council at Boulogne. He was promptly made captain of the *Morian* and saw action in the Channel.[3]

It was probably at about this time that Wingfield married and became brother-in-law to Sir William Fitzwilliam II*. Of greater significance locally was his sister Anne's marriage to Anthony Pound, whose

family owed a tenurial service at Portsmouth castle and was prominent in the town; Pound's own sister was the wife of Ralph Henslowe, one of Wingfield's successors as Member for Portsmouth. Wingfield probably owed his appointment at Portsmouth to John Dudley, Earl of Warwick, the admiral under whom he had served at sea. It was almost certainly Warwick, by then Duke of Northumberland, who procured the return of John Chaderton and Wingfield to the Parliament of March 1553 (in Wingfield's case perhaps with the approval of his relative the 9th Lord Clinton, the current admiral), but there is no indication that either of them supported Northumberland in the succession crisis of the following summer. Although Wingfield, who in 1551 had succeeded Sir Thomas Radcliffe, Lord Fitzwalter (another Member of that Parliament) as captain of Portsmouth, was to be relieved of both his posts early in Mary's reign, he received a handsome annuity of £100 for his past services and went to sea again in 1557 as captain of the *Swallow*.[4]

Wingfield's end is obscure. In June 1559 his widow Christian was granted an annuity of £40 from the previous March, so that he probably died in 1558 or early 1559; he could have died at sea or fallen victim to the epidemic of the time. His eldest, or perhaps only, son Richard, born about 1550, was to see long military service in Ireland and to be created Viscount Powerscourt in 1618.[5]

[1] Date of birth estimated from family history. *Vis. Hunts.* (Cam. Soc. xliii), 129; *LP Hen. VIII*, xix. [2] *LP Hen. VIII*, xxi; SP11/11, f. 79; *APC*, ii. 198, 216, 221, 223; iii. 37, 106, 261, 293, 321; iv. 37, 47, 67, 104, 106, 180, 213; *CPR*, 1550-3, p. 395; 1553, p. 415; C210/20/106, 21/138, 22/76; CP40/1142, r. 719. [3] *LP Hen. VIII*, i, xix-xxi; Hants RO, wills R. [4] *CPR*, 1554-5, p. 72; SP11/11, f. 79. [5] *CPR*, 1558-60, p. 101.

P.H.

WINGFIELD, Sir Robert (c. 1470-1539), of London and Calais.

GREAT GRIMSBY 1510[1]

b. c. 1470, ?7th s. of Sir John Wingfield[†] of Letheringham, Suff. by Elizabeth, da. of Sir Lewis John[†] of West Horndon, Essex; bro. of Humphrey* and Thomas*. *m.* (1) by 1497, Eleanor, da. of Sir William Raynsford of Bradfield, Essex; (2) lic. 4 July 1519, Joan, illegit. da. of Sir Edward Poynings* of Westenhanger, Kent, wid. of Thomas Clinton *alias* Fiennes, 8th Lord Clinton (*d.* 7 Aug. 1517), *s.p.* Kntd. by 2 July 1509.[2]

Usher, the chamber by 1505; bailiff, honor of Eye, Suff., and constable of Eye castle 2 July 1509; bailiff, manors of Syleham and Veale, Suff. 10 Apr. 1510; knight of the body by 1511; Councillor in 1511; jt. marshal of Calais 6 Aug. 1513-20, lt. of the castle ?1523-6, dep. 1526-31, mayor in 1534.[3]

Robert Wingfield's family had been seated at Letheringham since the 14th century, and by the late 15th had come to prominence in Suffolk, being linked by marriage with the Audleys, de la Poles, Waldegraves and Woodvilles. His father, a leading figure in central and local government, had 12 sons, of whom the best known, besides Robert, were Sir Humphrey and Sir Richard. Generally reckoned to have been the 7th son, Wingfield was brought up by Anne, Lady Scrope of Bolton, his aunt by her former marriage, and he doubtless followed her husband, the 5th Lord, in transferring his allegiance from the house of York to that of Tudor. In 1492 he and Scrope were included in the army raised for war with France, and in the troubled year 1497, while Scrope helped to raise the siege of Norham castle, Wingfield served with his brother Richard against the Cornish rebels. If he was the Robert Wingfield of London, gentleman, pardoned for non-appearance for debt in 1499 and put under bond to the King in 1501 he was by then domiciled in the capital.[4]

In March 1505 the two brothers arrived as pilgrims in Rome, perhaps on the journey which took Wingfield to Jerusalem and yielded him the title 'knight of the Holy Sepulchre'. He was by then an usher of the chamber, being so styled while at Rome, and the English knighthood which he enjoyed by 1509 may have been given him by Henry VII. The 'Wingfield' who returned to England in January 1508 from a mission to the Emperor was probably his brother Edward who had been sent thither in the previous year, but Wingfield may have accompanied him, and before September 1509 he was himself despatched to the same court. In the previous July he had been granted for life a rent of £20 payable by William, 11th Lord Willoughby, from the castle, town and manor of Orford, with arrears from 1501, and on 6 Sept. he was made constable of Eye castle. It was between his return from this mission and his despatch to the Emperor again early in 1510 that Wingfield had his only known spell in the Commons. The circumstances of his nomination for Grimsby by Sir William Tyrwhitt (q.v.) are not wholly clear, but the choice of a borough relatively remote from his own territory implies that Wingfield was a royal nominee, with Tyrwhitt acting as the go-between.[5]

During the next 16 years Wingfield was employed almost continuously in diplomacy, for which he was qualified by linguistic and scholarly attainments but handicapped by defects of personality and outlook. In 1516 his credulity in dealing with Maximilian, his duplicity towards his colleague Richard Pace, and his 'vainglorious' and 'undiscreet' despatches drew stinging rebukes from both Wolsey and the King. His confidence that everything would

turn out for the best if only England trusted the Emperor led to his being nicknamed 'Summer shall be green' in Pace's despatches to Wolsey. His hatred of the French seems at times to have blinded him to all other considerations. In 1517 he published, under the title *Nobilissima Disceptatio super dignitate et magnitudine Regnorum Britannici et Gallici*, the debates at the Council of Constance in 1416 when the French had maintained that the English were not a sufficient nation to be represented at the Council; the English reply, remarked Wingfield in his preface, made plain that 'whether in arms or in faith ... the English nation always surpassed the French, nor could it be judged inferior in the dignity and antiquity of its inhabitants, the size and greatness of its lands, or the character and learning of its people'. The book was printed in Louvain by Theodoricus Martinus (Thierry Martens), Erasmus's printer, who had just completed the first edition of More's *Utopia*. Wingfield must have felt keen disappointment that he never attained his country's highest honour: between 1523 and 1536 he was nominated six times for the Garter but without success.[6]

Wingfield's closing years were passed chiefly at Calais. He had held office there since 1513, and in 1515 he was the King's first choice as governor but was passed over. After serving for five years as deputy he became involved in protracted controversy with his successors the 2nd Lord Berners and Viscount Lisle. The issues included his lease of a large area outside the town which, formerly a marsh, he drained and built upon, thereby weakening the town's defence. When Wingfield became mayor the dispute broadened into one between his and the deputy's jurisdictions. It came before the Parliament of 1536 in the form of a bill for the revocation of Wingfield's lease. This passed the Commons (in which his brother Thomas was a Member and another, Humphrey, the ex-Speaker, was almost certainly sitting) but was evidently dropped in favour of a settlement: on 25 July, shortly after the the dissolution, Wingfield surrendered his lease and seven months later was granted lands at Guisnes. He was to remain at odds with Lisle and the Calais administration until his death.[7]

Wingfield made his will on 25 Mar. 1538, and died on 18 Mar. 1539, the will being proved eight months later. He left no issue, but was survived by his wife Joan, to whom he left his house near the Boulogne gate, and other property at Calais. Wingfield had been an opponent of the Lutherans for most of his life, but less than a month before his death he wrote to Henry VIII praising the Reformation and stating that he would not for all the world have died in his former ignorance. In one of his many surviving letters and despatches, which mirror his wit, learning and goodwill, as well as his failings, he reviewed his many years of service and mused on his

> white hairs, which I have gotten in the cold snowy mountains, which have the power to make all hares and partridges that dwell among them white, where my beard (which I have promised to bear to our Lady of Walsingham, an God give me the life) is wax so white, that whilst I shall wear it I need none other mean to cause women [to] rejoice little in my company.[8]

[1] Great Grimsby AO, oldest ct. bk. f. 224. [2] Date of birth estimated from family history. *DNB*; P. Buckland, 'Sir Robert and Sir Richard Wingfield' (Birmingham Univ. MA thesis, 1968); *CP*, iii. 317; M. E. Wingfield, Visct. Powerscourt, *Muniments of Wingfield*, 3. [3] *Coll. Top. et Gen.* v. 66; *LP Hen. VIII*, i–vii; P. T. J. Morgan, 'The govt. of Calais, 1485–1558' (Oxf. Univ. D. Phil. thesis, 1966), 295, 298, 301. [4] *Test. Vet.* ed. Nicolas, 435–6; P. Vergil, *Anglica Historia* (Cam. Soc. ser. 3, lxxiv), 52n, 94n; *CPR*, 1494–1509, p. 183; *CCR*, 1500–9, no. 11. [5] *Coll. Top. et Gen.* v. 66–67; J. Anstis, *Reg. Order of Garter*, 229; *LP Hen. VIII*, i; B. Andreas, *Historia Regis Henrici Septimi* (Rolls ser. x), 108; Great Grimsby AO, oldest ct. bk. f. 224 indifferently summarised in *HMC 14th Rep. VIII*, 274. [6] *LP Hen. VIII*, i–iv; C. G. Cruickshank, *Eng. Occupation of Tournai, 1513–19*, pp. 3, 41; Anstis, 363–401 passim. [7] *The King's Works*, iii. 345–6, 349, 373; *LP Hen. VIII*, ii, iv–xi. [8] *HMC Bath*, iv. 2, 24; PCC 33 Dyngeley; *LP Hen. VIII*, ii, xiv.

T.M.H.

WINGFIELD, Thomas (c. 1475–1548/51), of Sandwich, Kent.

SANDWICH 1529*,[1] 1536[2]

b. c. 1475, ?8th s. of Sir John Wingfield† of Letheringham, Suff. by Elizabeth, da. of Sir Lewis John† of West Horndon, Essex; bro. of Humphrey* and Sir Robert*. *m.* Joan, da. of John Hobard* of Sandwich, wid. of John Webbe of Sandwich, *d.s.p.*[3]

Comptroller of customs, port of Sandwich 2 Mar. 1515–42 or 43, gauger from 1546; jurat, Sandwich 1519–23, 1534–48, auditor 1519, 1522; bailiff to Yarmouth 1521; commr. subsidy, Sandwich 1523, Kent 1524, gaol delivery, Canterbury 1525; burgess to the Shepway 1534, 1536; comptroller of the King's works, Dover 1536–40; paymaster of the King's works in the Downs 1539; capt. Deal castle 1540.[4]

Thomas Wingfield's official connexion with Sandwich seems to have begun with his appointment as comptroller of customs there in 1515. By then he must have been about 40—his father had died in 1481—but of his earlier life nothing has been discovered. His marriage to the widow of the previous comptroller, a freeman of Sandwich, qualified him for the freedom of the port, which he received on 10 Dec. 1517, the four jurats who stood surety for him being John Cock I*, Thomas Godard, John Hobard and John Westcliffe*. His own first spell as a jurat was cut short when in 1523 he and Richard Taylor were dismissed 'by assent of all the whole commonalty'. No reason for this action was recorded in the town book, but from other entries it appears that Wingfield was disliked. In 1517 a man had been committed to gaol for calling him a 'false and untrue gentleman', and in 1525 a local tailor went further

by proclaiming 'that Wingfield had set up certain arms in the church which if they were his he was a traitor, for he knew never none that did give such a bar in his arms unless he were a traitor'; this was accompanied by a somewhat confused accusation which included references to 'Mr. Wingfield's wench', and together they cost the tailor seven years' banishment from the port. More significant was the assembly's resolution of December 1526 that if Wingfield would not pay his town dues as other freemen did he would at the next general assembly forfeit his freedom for ever without redemption. The threat was not implemented, but it helps to explain why for the time being Wingfield played no part in the government of the town, although he was still comptroller at the port. He was also sparingly employed during this period by the central government.[5]

This ten-year exclusion was brought to an unexpected end when on 29 Dec. 1533 the whole commonalty of Sandwich elected Wingfield one of its Members of Parliament in place of John Boys, who had died in the previous March; on the following 2 July 1534 he was readmitted a jurat. What lay behind this *volte face* is not clear, but there must have been pressure from outside. Wingfield came from a powerful family—one of his younger brothers, Humphrey Wingfield, had recently been elected Speaker—but neither this brother nor two others, Sir Richard and Sir Robert mentioned him in their wills, detailed though these were. If family influence is to be discounted, it may be conjectured that Cromwell intervened in the course of his systematic filling of vacancies: the surviving Member, Vincent Engeham, was perhaps already revealing the conservative outlook which was to show later, and a court nomination would redress the balance. By contrast, Wingfield's re-election in 1536 was due, as were those of all known Members for the Cinque Ports, to the King's request for the return of the previous Members, and in common with them it reflects no interest in the individual case.[6]

Wingfield was paid by Sandwich for his parliamentary service, but as the accounts are defective the full amount of his wages is not known. In 1534 he and Vincent Engeham received £12, evidently for attending the sixth session. In February 1535 the town officers reviewed all the accounts and agreed that Wingfield was owed 30s. for attendance in Parliament and 15s. for town business; they decided to pay him 40s. out of the box of 'bonne pens', or beer money, and when a few days later the box was opened he was given this sum 'upon his parliament wages' and he remitted the balance. Finally, on

12 May 1538 he was paid 18s., the residue of the wages owing to him for the Parliament of 1536.[7]

In 1534 Wingfield resumed the attendances at the Brotherhood of the Cinque Ports which he had begun in 1520 but which had been interrupted in 1523 by his dismissal from the juratship. In July 1534 the Brotherhood agreed that Thomas Wingfield should give the oath at the court of Shepway to George Boleyn, Lord Rochford, the new lord warden of the Cinque Ports, and two years later he was again chosen to perform this ceremony when Sir Thomas Cheyne* assumed office. Five months earlier, in April 1536, he had been appointed comptroller of the works at Dover, a town of which he had been a freeman since September 1515. On him fell the responsibility for clearing the entrance to Dover haven and building the new defence works there, a task which went forward amid bickering between the local officials and under reproof from above at their incessant demands for money. This harrying did not affect Wingfield's tenure of office, which lasted until 1540, when he became captain of the 'great castle at the Downs', that is, Deal castle.[8]

Soon after this Wingfield gave up the comptrollership at Sandwich; his last extant controlment roll runs to Michaelmas 1542 and the first of his successor begins 12 months later. On the outbreak of war with France he was made victualler of the King's ships and from November 1545 was stationed at Dover to convey letters and execute orders: as King's commissioner he drew 6s.8d. a day from October 1545 to February 1546 and 10s. a day from February to April 1546, when the appointment came to an end. On hearing that he was to be discharged, the admiral, John Dudley, Viscount Lisle, wrote to Sir William Paget that he thought Wingfield 'one of the meetest men, both for experience and diligence, that is to be placed here', a notable tribute to a man then approaching 70. His age did not deter him from accepting, in the following November, a lease for 21 years from Michaelmas 1547 of the office of gauger in the port of Sandwich at a rent of 3s.8d. with 4d. increment. The re-granting of this lease on the same terms to Francis Wilford in March 1551 provides a terminal date for Wingfield's death: his captaincy of Deal castle was also filled by another appointment that year. As his name is missing from the list of Sandwich jurats from December 1548, his death took place within this two-year period and probably towards the end of it. He appears to have died intestate.[9]

[1] Sandwich old red bk. f. 51v. [2] Ibid. f. 80. [3] Date of birth estimated from father's death and position in family. Vis. Hunts. (Cam. Soc. xliii), 126; Vis. Suff. ed. Metcalfe, 80, 176; Sandwich white bk. f. 257v; PCC 6 Holder. [4] Sandwich white bk., old red bk. passim; LP Hen. VIII, ii–iv, x, xiv–xvi, xxi; E122/130/14, 15; Add. 29618, f. 112; Cinque Ports White and Black Bks. (Kent Arch. Soc.

recs. br. xix), 179–84, 188, 195, 218, 221–2, 229. [5] LP Hen. VIII, ii; Sandwich white bk. ff. 252, 255, 271v, 323, 351–2, 367. [6] Sandwich old red bk. ff. 51v, 56v; PCC 3 Alen, 33 Dyngeley, 3 Porch. [7] Sandwich treasurers' accts. SA/FA t. 30, 32; old red bk. f. 64. [8] Cinque Ports White and Black Bks. 218, 221; Egerton 2092, f. 356; LP Hen. VIII, x, xi, xiv–xvi; Add. 29618, f. 112. [9] E122/130/14, 15; LP Hen. VIII, xviii, xix, xxi; APC, i. 265–6, 381; CPR, 1553, p. 374; J. Laker, Deal, 118.

H.M.

WINGFIELD, Thomas Maria (?1516–57), of Stoneley, Hunts. and London.

HUNTINGDON   1553 (Mar.), 1553 (Oct.), 1554 (Apr.)

HUNTINGDONSHIRE   1555

b. ?1516, 2nd s. of Sir Richard Wingfield of Kimbolton by 2nd w. Bridget, da. and h. of Sir John Wiltshire of Stone Castle, Kent; bro. of Jacques*. educ. Oxf. BA 1534. m. (1) Margaret (d. 1546), wid. of James Cole and William Sabine* (d. Apr. 1543) of Ipswich, Suff.; (2) by 1550, Margaret, da. of Edward Kaye of Woodsome, Yorks., at least 2s. inc. Edward Maria†.[1] Rector, Warrington, Lancs. 6 Dec. 1527–8 Nov. 1537; j.p. Hunts. 1554, commr. sewers, Cambs., Hunts., I. of Ely, Lincs., Northants., Notts. 1555.[2]

The herald who registered the Wingfield pedigree in 1613 enshrined the legend that Thomas Maria Wingfield had been 'so christened by Queen Mary and Cardinal Pole'. Unacceptable as it stands, since Mary was a near-contemporary of Wingfield, the derivation was not wholly fictitious: Wingfield's godmother was almost certainly Mary, Queen of France, a relative of Sir Richard Wingfield both through his marriage to her great-aunt and through hers to Charles Brandon, Duke of Suffolk, and the cardinal-godfather was doubtless Thomas Wolsey, the elder Wingfield's diplomatic chief.[3]

Wingfield's widowed mother married in succession (Sir) Nicholas Harvey* and Sir Robert Tyrwhitt I*, whose standing at court was matched by her own as an intimate of Anne Boleyn; the 'young Wingfield' who served at the coronation of 1533 was either Thomas Maria or his elder brother. At that time Wingfield was in the midst of what looks like a false start in his career: in December 1527 he had been made rector of Warrington. It was his uncle Humphrey Wingfield* and a clerk named Robert Brown who had presented this 11 year-old to the benefice, and they had done so in virtue of a grant from his father, the former chancellor of the duchy who had been dead two years. Wingfield was to retain the rectory, which was doubtless intended to finance his education, until December 1537, when his resignation of it may have marked his coming of age and his decision to forgo the ecclesiastical career planned for him. He had by then taken his degree at Oxford and he is not met with again until 1545, when he was assessed for subsidy at 20s. on landed property at Ipswich; his uncle Sir Humphrey, who died in that year, had long been a leading figure in the town, and Wingfield's marriage to William Sabine's widow may have been a cause or an effect of his own sojourn there. One consequence of the marriage was a rift with his stepson Ambrose Cole, whom he accused in Chancery of slander and robbery.[4]

By 1552 Wingfield had remarried and returned to Huntingdonshire, where he settled at Stoneley, near Kimbolton, on property which he bought from Oliver Leder*. Kimbolton itself was in the custody of his stepfather Sir Robert Tyrwhitt, one of the two lords lieutenant of the county. Wingfield's election to four of the next five Parliaments argues an interest in politics and religion of which there is no earlier trace in his career. First returned for Huntingdon, a duchy of Lancaster borough, with his cousin William Tyrwhitt, at a time when Sir Robert Tyrwhitt stood well with the Duke of Northumberland's confidant Sir John Gates*, the chancellor of the duchy, he twice retained the seat after Mary's accession and the advent of a new chancellor in Sir Robert Rochester*. His brother Jacques was a faithful servant of Stephen Gardiner, and Wingfield did not compromise himself by opposing the restoration of Catholicism, but his association with the leading dissidents in the shire could not have commended him to the court, and he was probably one of those whom the government sought to exclude, and in his case successfully, by the directive of October 1554 for the election of resident Catholics. If on this occasion Wingfield hoped for promotion to the knighthood of the shire he was disappointed, although his brother-in-law William Lawrence II* was more fortunate, but in the following year he took the senior place; his stepfather Tyrwhitt attended the election which was presided over by his neighbour Sir Oliver Leder as sheriff. Wingfield's parliamentary swansong was the vote which he gave against one of the government's bills.[5]

During these years Wingfield engaged in several small property transactions around Stoneley, prosecuted a chancery suit concerning a parsonage in Bedfordshire, and joined with his stepfather to buy more than 5,000 acres at Wood Walton, Huntingdonshire. Like his father and elder brother, Wingfield died prematurely and suddenly. The will which he made on 14 Aug. 1557, the day before he died, is known from its citation in the inquisition post mortem of the following 7 June. His wife was to have two thirds of his lands during the minority of the heir Edward Maria.[6]

[1] Date of birth estimated from elder brother's in 1514 and from his

resignation of Warrington rectory in 1537. *Vis. Hunts.* (Cam. Soc. xliii), 33, 131; *Vis. Northants.* ed. Metcalfe, 16; PCC 16 Alen; Emden, *Biog. Reg. Univ. Oxf. 1501–40*, p. 632; CP 40/1142, r. 471. [2] Emden, 632; *CPR, 1553–4*, pp. 20, 35; 1554–5, p. 109. [3] *Vis. Hunts.* 131. [4] *LP Hen. VIII*, vi; *VCH Lancs.* iii. 311 and n; C. Haigh, *Ref. and Resistance in Tudor Lancs.* 24–25; E179/181/270; C1/1391/88, 89. [5] *VCH Hunts.* ii. 365; iii. 81; C219/24/80; Guildford mus. Loseley 1331/2. [6] *Cal. Feet of Fines, Hunts.* ed. Turner, 143, 146; *CPR*, 1550–3, p. 271; 1553–4, p. 349; C1/1482/104; E150/102/3, 315/222/10.

T.M.H.

WINSTON, Walter (by 1502–40 or later), of Randwick, Glos.

WOOTTON BASSETT 1529

b. by 1502. *m.* Margaret, sis. and h. of Thomas Baynham (*d.* Mar./Apr. 1529) of Bristol.[1]
Escheator, Glos. 1523–4, 1538–9.

Little has come to light about Walter Winston, a Gloucestershire man of gentle birth. The pedigrees of his family contain numerous errors, but it is evident from other sources that he was well connected in the west and that he could count among his kinsmen David Broke*, Sir John Brydges* and Richard Tracy*. It was with Tracy that Winston was returned to Parliament for a north Wiltshire borough, but presumably he owed his place in the Commons not so much to Tracy as to Brydges, who was powerful in the locality and who was at the same time elected one of the knights for Gloucestershire. Winston may have hoped that his own presence at Westminster would aid his executorship of Thomas Baynham's will: he had proved the will in the spring of 1529, but his efforts to obtain Baynham's plate had been rebuffed by James Cliff of Gloucester to whom Baynham had entrusted it, so that between late 1529 and early 1532 he petitioned More as chancellor for redress. Whether he succeeded is not known, but he doubtless had the support of Brydges, one of Baynham's feoffees, and perhaps also of another of them, the courtier and soldier Sir Anthony Poyntz. Nothing is known of Winston's role in the proceedings of the House. He may have served for Wootton Bassett in the following Parliament, that of June 1536, when the King asked for the re-election of the previous Members, and perhaps again in 1539 and 1542, Parliaments for which the names of its Members are also lost.[2]

Winston's two terms as escheator suggest that he had received a legal education but his name has not been traced in the records of any inn of court. In a chancery case brought in 1540 he was accused of wrongfully dispossessing Anthony Cole of Gloucester of property in the town and at Stanton, a village in north Gloucestershire: he replied that he had purchased the disputed properties of one of Cole's cousins. This is the last certain reference found to Winston but he may have been the Walter Winston who with a wife Margaret is mentioned in a deed of 1551 as holding land in the neighbourhood of Chippenham.[3]

[1] Date of birth estimated from first reference. PCC 4 Jankyn; C1/693/13. [2] *Vis. Glos.* (Harl. Soc. xxi), 16, 236; Fosbroke, *Glos.* i. 305; *Bristol and Glos. Arch. Soc. Trans.* vi. 184–6; PCC 4 Jankyn; C1/693/13, 969/45–48. [3] C1/969/45–48; *Wilts. N. and Q.* iv. 29.

E. McI.

WISEMAN, John (by 1515–58), of Great Canfield, Essex.

MALDON 1554 (Nov.)
EAST GRINSTEAD 1555

b. by 1515, 1st s. of William Wiseman by Mary Glascock of Essex. *educ.* ?I. Temple, adm. 7 May 1525. *m.* Agnes, da. of (?Ralph) Josselyn of Essex, at least 3s. inc. Robert[†] 1da.[1]

Servant of 15th Earl of Oxford, member, council of 16th Earl by 1542, auditor to 16th Earl in 1542; auditor, ct. augmentations Cheshire, Derbys., Lincs. and Notts. 12 May 1536–4 May 1544, Kent, Surr., Suss. in 1552–3; j.p. Essex 1554–*d.*[2]

There can be little doubt that the John Wiseman who sat in the third and fourth Marian Parliaments was the augmentations official of that name. As one of the auditors of that court from its establishment in 1536 until its dissolution in 1554 Wiseman had served for eight years under Sir Richard Rich and, after an interval, for a further five under Sir Richard Sackville*. The influence wielded by these two ex-chancellors of the court at Maldon and East Grinstead respectively points to this former subordinate as the Member for those boroughs in turn. At East Grinstead Wiseman probably had as his fellow-Member another auditor of the augmentations in William Barnes I*.

Wiseman had two contemporary namesakes with whom he is liable to be confused. The first, an Essex justice of the peace who lived at Felstead, may have sprung from the family of Thornham in Suffolk which had furnished that shire with one of its knights in the Parliament of 1491; this John Wiseman died in January 1559 leaving a wife Joan and a son and heir Thomas. The other made his career in London, where he was for 26 years secondary of the Compter in Bread Street; he also had a son Thomas, who married one of the daughters of Stephen Vaughan*. If John Wiseman of the augmentations, who himself settled at Great Canfield, is distinguishable from his neighbour at Felstead by their differing domiciles, marital histories and dates of death, his identification with the Londoner can scarcely be entertained in view of the seeming incompatibility of their offices. Of the three, the future auditor is most likely to have been

the member of the Inner Temple since he alone was to be regularly styled esquire.[3]

Wiseman was to combine his duties for the augmentations with service to successive earls of Oxford. How early he became associated with the 15th Earl is not known, but it could have been with Oxford's support that he obtained the auditorship. (Still more useful would have been the favour of Rich which he is likely to have enjoyed as a kinsman of Rich's servant William Glascock.) His standing with the 16th Earl is reflected in the dispute of 1542 between his cousin Thomas Josselyn and the earl over the keepership of Stansted Mountfitchet park; he and one 'Ryve' (probably John Ryther*, another of Oxford's servants who was to name Wiseman an executor) handled the earl's case, and not even the intervention of Josselyn's brother-in-law John Gates* seems to have affected the issue. It was from Oxford that Wiseman leased the manor of Great Canfield in February 1546 and in the following year bought the park. His other acquisitions included Ringmere grange in Suffolk from the Duke of Suffolk, Little Maplestead in Essex from George Harper (probably the Member of that name), and a string of ex-monastic properties in Leicestershire, the last doubtless a dividend of his auditorship. He continued to extend and consolidate his landed position after he exchanged that office for a pension of £133 6s.8d.; in May 1557 he had a grant of the manor of Middle Lavant, Sussex, and among his last purchases was the parsonage of Great Canfield from one of the Cecils.[4]

Wiseman was evidently on his deathbed when he made his will on 12 Aug. 1558, for it was proved 13 days later. The will distributed his lands, which it catalogued in detail, between his heir John and his younger sons Thomas and Robert, bestowed 200 marks and £20 towards marriage on his daughter Clement, and provided for his wife, who was the executrix, relatives and servants.[5]

[1] Date of birth estimated from first appointment. *Vis. Essex* (Harl. Soc. xiii), 326, 529; PCC 38 Noodes. [2] *LP Hen. VIII*, add.; Essex RO, D/DPr/140, 141; information from Susan Flower; W. C. Richardson, *Ct. Augmentations*, 55–56, 59n, 81–82, 100n, 240 and n, 258, 267 and n, 339, 494; Stowe 571, f. 9v; *CSP Dom.* 1601–3, *Add.* 1547–65, p. 408; *CPR*, 1553–4, p. 19. [3] *Vis. Suff.* ed. Metcalfe, 210; *LP Hen. VIII*, i–iv, vi, xiii, xviii, xix; *CPR*, 1547–8, p. 83; 1549–51, p. 199; 1553–4, p. 19; 1554–5, pp. 107, 115, 354; 1555–7, p. 434; 1558–60, pp. 363, 365; PCC 8 Mellershe; City of London RO, Guildhall, rep. 4, ff. 170, 170v; 5, f. 181; 10, ff. 178, 238, 238v; 11, ff. 19, 27, 246v; 12(1), f. 199v; 13(2), f. 293; SP10/5/18, f. 76. [4] *LP Hen. VIII*, xi–xvii, xix–xxi, add.; *CPR*, 1547–8 to 1558–60 passim; C1/1381/32, 33; Lansd. 156(28), f. 108v. [5] PCC 38 Noodes; C142/118/48.

S.M.T./R.J.W.S.

WITHYPOLL, Edmund (1510/13–82), of London; Walthamstow, Essex; and Christchurch, Ipswich, Suff.

IPSWICH 1558*[1]

b. 1510/13, 1st s. of Paul Withypoll* of London and Walthamstow by Anne, da. of Robert Curzon of Brightwell, Suff. *m*. c. 1535, Elizabeth, da. of Thomas Hynde of London, 12s. 7da. *suc*. fa. 3 June 1547.[2]

J.p. Suff. 1561–*d*.; commr. sewers 1566; sheriff, Norf. and Suff. 1570–1.[3]

On the list of Members in use during the second session of the Parliament of 1558 the surname of William Wheatcroft, who had been returned on 13 Dec. 1557, is struck through and replaced by 'Withepoll'. Wheatcroft had presumably died during the Parliament, although he is not marked 'mortuus', and 'Withepoll' is taken to have been Edmund Withypoll, a leading figure in Ipswich and recently an associate of Sir John Sulyard who had sat for the town twice earlier in the reign. Either Sulyard or his kinsman Sir Thomas Cornwallis* (later a feoffee and relative of Withypoll himself) could have secured him the nomination.[4]

Withypoll was educated by Thomas Lupset, rector of St. Martin's, Ludgate, who taught his pupil Latin but no Greek and who fostered in him a lasting love of scholarship; Christchurch, Withypoll's Ipswich house, was adorned with Latin inscriptions, and he translated some verses of Robert Norton, the preacher of Ipswich, which were printed at the end of Gabriel Harvey's *Two other very commendable letters* (1580). In 1529 Lupset wrote for and dedicated to Withypoll *An exhortation to yonge men*, published in 1535, in which he encouraged his former pupil to read the New Testament, Chrysostom, Jerome, Erasmus's *Enchiridion*, Xenophon's *Oecominia* in a Latin translation and the works of other leading classical authors, ending:

> if you will proceed in virtue; the which is only the thing, that maketh a man both happy in this world and also blessed in the world to come. Believe you my counsel, and use the same, or else hereafter you will peradventure bewail your negligence. Fare you well.[5]

Withypoll at first followed in the footsteps of his father, becoming a merchant and a money-lender. In 1534 he was assessed at 16*d*. for the land which he held at Walthamstow. Six years later he bought land in Shropshire from his uncle, John Withypoll*. In 1544 he participated in the siege and capture of Boulogne where on 25 Sept. he took from the church of Notre Dame a copy of Cicero's *Epistolae*. In December 1545 he was pardoned at Queen Catherine Parr's suit for the manslaughter of William Mathew, a serving man of Lowhall, Walthamstow. No further details have come to light concerning this incident but it may have influenced Withypoll's migration to Ipswich, where his father had acquired some former monastic property from Sir Thomas Pope* in 1544 and where, after the son had been

licensed to enter upon his lands on 1 Feb. 1548, he began the construction of Christchurch.[6]

Thereafter Withypoll became chiefly concerned with the administration and expansion by purchase of his property and the affairs of his adopted shire, into the principal families of which his children married. He none the less continued to lend money and those in his debt included the 12th Earl of Arundel, the 9th Lord Clinton and Sir Thomas Gerard†. At the beginning of the reign of Mary he paid a composition of £10 to avoid knighthood. He carried on numerous disputes with the corporation of Ipswich, but no permanent ill will seems to have resulted and his failure to sit again for the town is perhaps attributable to the loss of influence of his patrons Cornwallis and Sulyard. During the summer of 1558 Withypoll incurred the displeasure of the Privy Council, who wrote on 8 Aug. ordering him to explain his failure to supply demi-lances at the musters.[7]

On 6 Apr. 1568 Withypoll wrote a lengthy will which was replaced by a shorter one on 1 May 1582 in which he left instructions for his burial in St. Margaret's, Ipswich, provided for the division of his property, made various bequests, and left the residue to his 18 year-old grandson, Paul, as his eldest son had predeceased him. He died at Christchurch on the following 16 May and was buried five days later in accordance with his wishes.[8]

[1] Wm. Salt Lib. SMS 264. [2] Date of birth estimated from parents' marriage and first subsidy assessment. *Walthamstow Antiq. Soc.* xxxiv. app. [3] *CPR*, 1550–3, p. 113; 1560–3, p. 442; 1563–6, p. 27; 1569–72, pp. 217, 434. [4] Wm. Salt Lib. SMS 264; *Walthamstow Antiq. Soc.* xxxiv. 15, 21–22, 25, 29, 45, 48, 60; PCC 21 Tirwhite. [5] *Walthamstow Antiq. Soc.* xxxiv. 52–53. [6] Ibid. 18, 20–22, 42–45, 47; DKR, ix. 301; LP Hen. VIII, xx. [7] *Walthamstow Antiq. Soc.* xxxiv. 45–47; CPR, 1550–3, p. 232; 15–557, p. 496; 1569–72, p. 316; CSP Dom. 1601–3, Add. 1547–65, p. 437; APC, v. 105; vi. 369. [8] Pevsner, *Suff.* 269; PCC 52 Sheffelde, 21 Tirwhite; C142/197/78.

A.D.K.H.

WITHYPOLL, John (*b*. by 1483), of Malmesbury, Wilts.

BOSSINEY 1547[1]

b. by 1483, 1st s. of John Withypoll of Bristol, Glos. by Alison, da. and h. of John a Gaunt of Cardiff, Glam.; bro. of Paul*. *m*. Alice, 2da.[2]

Bailiff, Malmesbury hundred by 1510.[3]

John Withypoll remains an obscure figure overshadowed by his brother. He followed his father's example and became a merchant, possibly trading from Bristol with Spain and Portugal. Although he retained his links with Bristol, he settled in Malmesbury presumably to take advantage of the town's flourishing cloth industry. He obtained a minor post in local administration and on the accession of Henry VIII he sued out a general pardon. Few traces have been found of his activities in later life, but doubtless he benefited from Paul Withypoll's success and from his numerous connexions. He appears to have married well as his wife owned property in her own right, some of which she sold during the early 1540s.[4]

Withypoll's election, when in his sixties, for a newly enfranchised Cornish borough would be more readily explained if he had already sat for Malmesbury, which he could have done, the returns for that borough being lost for the four previous Parliaments. In that case his appearance for Bossiney could be looked upon as a by-product of the election at Malmesbury in 1547 of two leading figures, Sir Maurice Denys and William Stumpe, and his consequent quest of a seat elsewhere. That he found one at Bossiney is probably to be ascribed to Sir Thomas Arundell*, the receiver-general for the duchy of Cornwall, who could add to his earlier association with Malmesbury abbey his nearness to Queen Catherine Parr. Withypoll, unlike Arundell, survived the Parliament but nothing further has come to light about him.

[1] Hatfield 207.   [2] Date of birth estimated from younger brother's. *Walthamstow Antiq. Soc.* xxxiv. 101; *CPR*, 1547–8, p. 194.   [3] *LP Hen. VIII*, i.   [4] *Walthamstow Antiq. Soc.* xxxiv. 13, 42.

A.D.K.H.

WITHYPOLL, Paul (by 1485–1547), of London and Walthamstow, Essex.

LONDON   1529, 1539,[1] 1545

b. by 1485, 3rd s. of John Withypoll of Bristol, Glos. and bro. of John*. *m.* 21 Jan. 1510, Anne, da. of Robert Curzon of Brightwell, Suff., wid. of William Freville of Little Shelford, Cambs. and of William Reede of Boston, Lincs., 3s. inc. Edmund* 1 da.[2]

Warden, Merchant Taylors' Co. 1513–14, 1516–17, 1520–1, master 1523–4; auditor, London 1521–3; gov. Merchant Adventurers 1526.[3]

The Withypoll family took its name from the village in Shropshire, near Cleobury Mortimer. Paul Withypoll's grandfather lived there, but his father became a merchant of Bristol, trading to Spain and Portugal, and he himself entered the Spanish trade but transferred his residence to London. By 1506 he was exporting considerable quantities of cloth and importing in return chiefly oil and soap: during a visit to Cadiz in or before 1524 he invested his former apprentice, Robert Thorne, with powers of attorney. He also traded to Crete and, nearer home, 'studied' merchandising in the Netherlands to such effect that in 1532 he was described by Stephen Vaughan* as knowing more about it 'than any merchant [be]longing to all the Adventurers'.[4]

Withypoll's knowledge was drawn upon by the common council of London in 1518 when he and others drew up a 'declaration of the lawful buying and selling of woollen cloths'. During the years that followed his services were frequently in demand by both the corporation and the Merchant Adventurers. Thus in 1520 he was among those deputed by the general court of the Merchant Adventurers to frame regulations 'for men's attornies and apprentices that go over the sea for their masters'; in 1521 he served on a committee to advise the common council on new rates for the admission of freemen to the City; and in 1522 he was authorized to assess Londoners for the loan of £20,000 to the King. When a Parliament was called in 1523 the Merchant Adventurers commissioned him 'to devise such articles as should be thought necessary for the company' and the mayor and aldermen 'to devise what things be most necessary and behoveful for the common weal of this City, to be moved at this next Parliament'.[5]

Although ready enough to discharge such tasks as a leading merchant and a common councilman, Withypoll refused to become an alderman. In 1525 he was one of four candidates in the ward of Billingsgate, but the nominations were rejected by the mayor and aldermen on the ground that the nominees were not worth enough in goods. This disability seems to have been only a first line of defence for Withypoll, which the court of aldermen immediately turned by altering the qualification from £1,000 in goods to 2,000 marks in goods and purchased lands combined, a move to prevent evasion of office by the conversion of movables into landed property. On 27 Jan. 1527 Withypoll was again nominated, and this time elected, for the ward of Farringdon Within, but two weeks later the court of aldermen received a request from the King that he should be exempted. Such intervention being against the liberties of the City, Wolsey's support was enlisted in defence of free election, but when the cardinal arranged for the mayor, Sir Thomas Seymour I*, and a deputation of aldermen to wait on the King at Greenwich they failed to move him from his purpose. For a year no further action was taken: then early in February 1528 Withypoll, having 'had a sparing of all that time till now', was ordered either to accept the aldermanship or to obtain his discharge by swearing that his goods and lands were together worth less than 2,000 marks. He refused to do either and was committed to Newgate for his contempt. At the beginning of March he again appeared before the court of aldermen and was given the opportunity of compounding for his discharge. This was the compromise eventually adopted, and on 27 May he was exempted from the aldermanship and all other offices within the City on payment of a fine of £100.[6]

The King's insistence is not surprising, for

Withypoll had long been in favour at court. As early as 1515 he had obtained letters patent exempting him from jury service, and at some time after 1521 the mayor and aldermen were warned that failure to respect this privilege would entail a fine of £1,000. In 1524 Withypoll was one of four merchants to whom Wolsey committed the hearing of a mercantile dispute, in 1527 the cardinal appointed him to arbitrate in another case, and in 1529 he and Cromwell heard a further dispute between two London merchants. Withypoll had known Cromwell since at least 1526, when they appear to have been already on good terms, and was thus able to rely on continued support against pressure from the City.[7]

It is a tribute to Withypoll that his behaviour had not forfeited the esteem of his fellows. To Thomas Lupset, writing in 1529, he was 'that sort of man, the which hath by long approved honesty purchased him a good name, and is thereby beloved and regarded of good men', and in 1538 the corporation was itself to bury the dispute by exempting him, as 'a man of high discretion and great experience', from constraints laid upon those who had refused to become aldermen. He had by then served his first, and probably also his second, term as one of the City's Members of Parliament: elected in 1529 by the commonalty, he was probably returned again in 1536, when the names of the London Members are unknown but the King had asked that the previous House should be re-elected. Withypoll was soon active as a Member. In his first session he was associated with Cromwell and three others in the examination of a bill to prevent debtors defaulting under cover of the King's protection, a measure which had been proposed to the court of aldermen by the Mercers' Company shortly before the opening of Parliament. Early in the fifth session, on 13 Feb. 1533, the recorder of London reported to the court of aldermen 'that Mr. Bowyer and Mr. Withypoll desired him to draw a bill to be exhibited to the Parliament house to corroborate and confirm the court of requests used in this City'; to this proposal the aldermen agreed, although no such Act was passed. In the last session Withypoll was one of the 'setters forth' of a statute for the true making of woollen cloths (27 Hen. VIII, c.12).[8]

Withypoll may also have been involved in an attempt to persuade the King to remit the question of his divorce to a general council of the Church in return for a grant of £200,000. The imperial ambassador, reporting this move on 10 Apr. 1533, ascribed it especially to 'one who represents this city of London, who was once in Spain and is one of my most intimate and familiar friends'. The only one of London's Members of this Parliament known to

have been in Spain was Withypoll, and while his religious views were probably conservative (he put his son to school under Thomas Lupset, then rector of St. Martin's, Ludgate), they may well have been combined, in the shaping of his attitude on this issue, with the apprehensions entertained by many merchants as to the effect on the cloth trade of possible retaliation by the Emperor. It was not Withypoll, however, but his fellow-Member William Bowyer whose name appears on a list drawn up about this time by Cromwell and thought to record the names of Members who opposed the bill in restraint of appeals.[9]

Withypoll's Membership of the Parliament of 1539 is established through his involvement in the collection of the subsidy granted in the second session: the Subsidy Act (32 Hen. VIII, c.50) empowered the knights of the shire and some borough Members to appoint the collectors of the grant, and on 4 Aug. 1540 Withypoll and the other Members for London were sent a letter asking for their nominees. He was not elected to the next Parliament, but on 14 Mar. 1542, towards the close of its first session, he and three other merchants were assigned by the court of aldermen to meet 'them of the parliament house that have the hearing of the matter of tithes to be paid by the citizens of this City to their curates, and to assist them therein with their good advice and counsel'; three days later the same four, accompanied this time by the recorder, Sir Roger Cholmley*, were appointed to meet in Sir John Baker's* chamber at the Temple 'for the matter of tithes'. This vexed question was revived in the Parliament of 1545, in which Withypoll again sat as a Member for the City and which passed an Act (37 Hen. VIII, c.12) giving statutory recognition to an award to be made by commissioners, leaving details to be settled later. Before this Parliament opened the London Members had been instructed by the court of aldermen to prepare their programme and in particular to introduce two bills, one binding all inhabitants to contribute to the City's charges and the other resuming all liberties within London into the King's hands preparatory to their incorporation into the City. Neither bill passed the Commons.[10]

Withypoll had been assessed for the subsidy of 1523 at £500 in goods. In the assessment of the subsidy of 1534 his freehold lands were valued at £20 a year and those he held in right of his wife at £28; although his goods were then valued at only 300 marks he was called upon to contribute 2,000 marks to the loan of 1535 or 1536. He lived in the parish of St. Laurence Pountney but had property elsewhere in the City: in 1512 he had bought a tenement and wharf in St. Martin Vintry and in 1520 two messuages in St. Andrew Undershaft and St. Botolph. He also acquired considerable estates outside London. He already owned property in Walthamstow when in 1538 he bought the manor of Higham Banstead, to the north of that town, from Giles Heron*. In 1544 he received a large grant of lands in the same district, comprising the manors of Walthamstow Tony and Mark and the rectory manor of Walthamstow (for which he paid £1,381), as well as Netherholme manor in Clifton, Worcestershire. Two years later he was licensed to sell Walthamstow Tony to Sir Ralph Sadler* and bought instead the house, site and possessions of the dissolved priory of Holy Trinity, Ipswich, where his son made his home. He also acquired several properties in Lincolnshire, and in 1542 he bought a messuage and land in the parish of Cleobury Mortimer, Shropshire.[11]

Withypoll died at his London house on 3 June 1547. He had made his will nearly five years before, leaving his goods to be divided between his wife, his son and heir Edmund, and his apprentices and servants, and appointing Edmund executor. The day before he died he added a short codicil to the will, which was proved on 8 June 1547. In 1514 Withypoll had been portrayed as the donor of a triptych by Antonio de Solario.[12]

[1] E159/319, brev. ret. Mich. r. [1–2]. [2] Date of birth estimated from first reference. *Walthamstow Antiq. Soc.* xxxiv. 13–15. [3] H. L. Hopkinson, *Anct. Recs. of Merchant Taylors*, 116–17; City of London RO, Guildhall, jnl. 12, ff. 137, 194v; *Acts Ct. of Mercers' Co.* ed. Lyell and Watney, 731. [4] *Walthamstow Antiq. Soc.* xxxiv. 13–14; E122/79/12, 80/4, 5, 81/8, 82/3 ex inf. Prof. P. Ramsey; G. Connell-Smith, *Forerunners of Drake*, 229; *LP Hen. VIII*, add.; G. Schanz, *Englische Handelspolitik*, ii. 253. [5] City of London RO, jnl. 11, ff. 366v–7; 12, ff. 118v, 188; rep. 4, ff. 84v, 145; *Acts Ct. of Mercers' Co.* 501, 559–60. [6] City of London RO, rep. 7, ff. 39v, 45v–46, 162, 171v, 172, 172v, 174v, 179, 179v, 180, 180v, 240, 240v, 243v, 260, 261v; jnl. 13, ff. 61v–62. [7] *LP Hen. VIII*, ii, iv, vi, add. [8] T. Lupset, *An exhortation to yonge men* (1535), unpaginated; City of London RO, jnl. 14, f. 113v; rep. 8, f. 274; *LP Hen. VIII*, add.; Mercers' Co. acts of ct. 1527–60, f. 24v; *PPC*, vii. 156. [9] *CSP Span.* 1531–3, p. 628; *LP Hen. VIII*, vi; *Walthamstow Antiq. Soc.* xxxiv. 40. [10] E159/319, brev. ret. Mich. r. [1–2]; 371/309, r. 61(i); City of London RO, jnl. 14, f. 238; rep. 10, ff. 250, 251v; 11, ff. 220v, 222v. [11] E179/251/15b; SP1/33, f. 21; Cott. Cleop. F6, f. 344v; *Walthamstow Antiq. Soc.* xxxiv. 16, 18, 20–21; *LP Hen. VIII*, xix, xxi. [12] C142/84/52; PCC 38 Alen; M. Davies, *Earlier Ital. Schs.* (Nat. Gall. Cats. 2nd ed.), 492–3.

H.M.

WODDE *see* **AT WODE**

WODHOWSE *see* **WOODHOUSE**

WOGAN (HOGAN, OGAN, OWGAN), John (c.1480–1557), of Wiston, Pemb.

PEMBROKESHIRE　1545, 1553 (Oct.)

b. c. 1480, 1st s. of Sir John Wogan of Wiston by Anne, da. of Sir Thomas Vaughan†. *m.* Jane, da. and h. of William Philip ap Gwilym of Stone Hall, 4s. 12da. *suc.* fa. 1483, Kntd. c. 1547.[1]

Gent. usher by 1513–30 or later; bailiff errant,

lordship of Haverfordwest Dec. 1520; jt. rhaglaw (or constable), Card. 18 Aug. 1524; bailiff, Rowse, Pemb. 24 Jan. 1525; commr. for division of shires 1536, relief, Card., Carm., Mon. and Pemb. 1550, goods of churches and fraternities, Card. and Pemb. 1553, subsidy, Pemb. 1555; sheriff, Card. 1541–2, Pemb. 1542–3, 1553–4; burgess, Cardigan, Card. in 1553; j.p. Glos., Herefs., Salop and Worcs. 1554, Card. 1555.[2]

John Wogan, of the Wiston branch of the old Pembrokeshire family of that name, was the son and grandson of namesakes who had died for the Lancastrian cause. First met with in the royal service in 1513, when as a gentleman usher he served as a captain in the French campaign, he had in December 1510 been granted a life annuity of £2 by the borough of Haverfordwest. When, many years later, Wogan sued in the court of requests for two-and-a-half years' arrears of this annuity, the borough contended that it had been granted on condition that he lived there and gave counsel, which he had done for only three years before moving elsewhere. The complaint, if true, implies that from 1513 Wogan resided mainly at court, where he is glimpsed at the Field of Cloth of Gold in 1520 and at Eltham in 1526, and that the local offices granted to him by the crown had not brought him home. He doubtless spent more time there after the Union, when he served three terms as sheriff and was charged with a variety of other duties in his own shire and its neighbours.[3]

Wogan was first returned for Pembrokeshire by a sheriff who was his brother-in-law. Whether he enjoyed a similar advantage at his re-election in the autumn of 1553 does not appear, but he was to be pricked sheriff again while sitting in this Parliament and in the course of the next year he twice returned his son-in-law Arnold Butler. Of Wogan's part in the Commons nothing is known save that in Mary's first Parliament he did not oppose the restoration of Catholicism. He made his will on 20 Aug. 1557. He asked to be buried at Wiston. The fact that he called his wife Anne may mean that he had married again; he made her sole executrix and left her all his goods. The will was witnessed by his sons-in-law Arnold Butler and Thomas Cathern* (mistranscribed in the register as Laugherne) and was proved on 8 Nov. 1557. Wogan had died four days after making it, leaving his grandson, another John Wogan†, heir to large estates in Cardiganshire and Pembrokeshire.[4]

[1] Date of birth estimated from that of mother, *HP*, ed. Wedgwood, 1439–1509 (Biogs.), 902, and from father's death. Dwnn, *Vis. Wales*, i. 107–8; *CPR*, 1476–85, pp. 387, 412; *W. Wales Hist. Recs.* vi. 196, 199–200. [2] *DWB* (Wogan fams.); *LP Hen. VIII*, i, iii, iv, xv; G. Owen, *Taylors Cussion*, ii. 34d; *CPR*, 1553, pp. 360, 364, 404, 418–19; 1553–4, pp. 19, 20, 23, 25; C60/370; 219/21/215; SP11/5/6. [3] Req.2/10/238. [4] PCC 45 Wrastley; C142/113/3, 114/19.

P.S.E.

WOOD, George (by 1526–58), of the Inner Temple, London and Balterley, Staffs.

FLINTSHIRE 1547[1]

b. by 1526, prob. 1st s. of Humphrey Wood of Balterley by Elizabeth, da. of Thomas Rance. *educ.* I. Temple. *m.* by 1548, Margaret, da. of Richard Grosvenor of Eaton, Cheshire, wid. of Ralph Birkenhead of Crowton, Cheshire, 1da.[2]

Steward, reader's dinner, I. Temple 1548, bencher by 20 Nov. 1552, attendant upon reader 1554, auditor for treasurer 1550–4, Summer reader 1555, Lent 1556.

Serjeant-at-law 1555; justice, Anglesey, Caern. and Merion. 26 Apr. 1555, Chester and Flint 2 Apr. 1558.[3]

George Wood came of a family which had resided in Staffordshire since the reign of Edward III. Although his early death led to his omission from its pedigree he was almost certainly an eldest son, and the Robert Wood of Balterley whose wardship he purchased in 1547, and who followed him at the Inner Temple in the next year, may thus have been his nephew.[4]

After a career at the Inner Temple which can be traced from 1548 Wood was made a serjeant and a Welsh judge in 1555. To his own family's interest in Flintshire, reflected in the grant of 5 July 1547 by which in addition to the wardship of Robert Wood he was given by the court of wards an annuity of 5 marks out of the capital messuage of Hall Wood and other properties in the county, he added the yield of his marriage into the family of Grosvenor of Eaton, Cheshire, which had a stake in Flintshire. It was also to this alliance that Wood may have owed his seat in the Parliament of 1547. Since his Membership is known only from the list of Members as revised for the opening of the session of January 1552 he could have been returned either at the outset or at a by-election, and in the latter case it would be tempting to link his return with the shrievalty of his brother-in-law Richard Grosvenor in 1551. By that time, too, John Pollard*, whom Wood was to succeed as justice of Chester and Flint in 1558, had joined the council in the marches and from that vantage point could have given Wood support. A less likely source of influence would have been William, Lord Paget, who in 1550 had obtained the wardship of Wood's nephew Thomas Grosvenor, for by the close of 1551 Paget was in disgrace with the faction in power.[5]

Wood was ill when he made his will on 28 Apr. 1558: he asked to be buried 'after a Christian sort without vain glory or pomp'. His lands in England he left to his younger brother Thomas and in default to his other brother Richard, and those in Denbighshire and Flintshire to his daughter Mary. He gave a ring to Sir Henry Delves*. According to the inquisitions post mortem his lands in Flintshire were worth £10 3s.4d. and those at Balterley a mere 24s. a year. Wood died on 23 June 1558. His widow married John Molyneux of Melling near Maghull in Lancashire.[6]

[1] Hatfield 207. [2] Date of birth estimated from first reference. *Wm. Salt Arch. Soc.* v(2), 325–6; *Vis. Cheshire* (Harl. Soc. xviii), 108; (lix), 115, 138; *Vis. Lancs.* (Chetham Soc. lxxxi), 100; Harl. 6159; Wards 7/10/96. [3] *CPR,* 1554–5, pp. 59, 278; 1557–8, p. 311; W. R. Williams, *Welsh Judges,* 31. [4] *LP Hen. VIII,* xxi. [5] *CPR,* 1547–8, p. 13; Ormerod, *Cheshire,* ii(2), 836, 842. [6] PCC 36 Noodes; Wards 7/10/96, 102/26; C142/121/157.

P.S.E.

WOODHOUSE, Sir Thomas (by 1514–72), of Waxham and Great Yarmouth, Norf.

GREAT YARMOUTH 1558, 1559

b. by 1514, 1st s. of John Woodhouse of Waxham by Alice, da. of William Croftes of Wyston; bro. of Sir William*. *educ.* ?L. Inn, adm. 12 Mar. 1525. *m.* Margaret, da. of William Stubbert, wid. of one Wymer of Scottow, *s.p.*; 1da. illegit. *suc.* fa. prob. by 1533. Kntd. 10 Nov. 1549.[1]

Escheator, Norf. and Suff. 1535–6; collector subsidy, Norf. 1540; j.p. 1542–54, q. 1558/59–*d.*; jt. v.-adm. Norf. and Suff. 1543–*d.*; commr. of Admiralty in Nov. 1547, relief, Norf. 1550; sheriff, Norf. and Suff. 1553–4, 1563–4.[2]

Thomas Woodhouse came of a Norfolk family related only distantly, if at all, to that established at Kimberley. Little trace has been found of his early career but he may be presumed to have augmented his modest patrimony by becoming a merchant and shipowner. From 1542 he was busily and lucratively engaged, generally in partnership with Thomas Waters*, as victualler of royal armies and garrisons at home and abroad. Although at one time the Privy Council suspected him of giving 'overmuch regard' to 'his own commodities', no serious charges against Woodhouse of either inefficiency or malpractice have survived. In 1542 one Henry Dowe of Friesland accused him of buying a ship from pirates who had stolen it from Dowe and of refusing the rightful owner any redress, and in 1546 the Council ordered him and Robert Turcok of Waxham to appear before the commissioners inquiring into the losses from piracy of 'subjects of both sides'.[3]

The yield of his various enterprises Woodhouse invested in land. In 1533, when he wrote to Cromwell from Waxham asking that a summons to appear before the Council should be respited, he probably owned only the manor of Waxham and properties in Stalham and neighbouring parishes, but between the Dissolution and 1550 he made extensive acquisitions on and near the coast. In 1546 he paid over £1,400 for Bromholm priory and its possessions, and two years later added £1,000 worth of chantry lands in Norfolk. His inquisition post mortem lists over 20 manors and other properties in that county.[4]

Woodhouse's growing importance on land and at sea was reflected in his official progress: he became successively escheator, justice of the peace, vice-admiral and sheriff. Himself inclined towards Protestantism, he appears to have accommodated himself without difficulty to each regime. During Ket's rebellion he and Sir Thomas Clere successfully defended Yarmouth against attack. After the rebellion had been suppressed he informed the Council through his brother that, while his neighbours were clamouring for redress, he had not sought compensation for his heavy losses of sheep, cattle and corn and that all he asked was to be put on the commission of oyer and terminer 'that I be not forgotten, for then I shall lose my credit in the county'. Although this plea does not seem to have prevailed, the knighthood conferred on Woodhouse in the following November must have solaced him. But for his brother's superior claim Woodhouse would probably have been elected for Yarmouth to the second Edwardian Parliament. As it was, the appearance of his name, accompanied by the note 'to stand for Yarmouth', on a list of men in different counties dating from 1553 and thought to be of those expected to rally support for Queen Jane, implies that the Duke of Northumberland looked to him to secure that port, of which Northumberland was high steward. There is nothing to suggest that Woodhouse declared for Jane, and his choice as Mary's first sheriff of Norfolk and Suffolk shows that the new government trusted him. He continued to serve it throughout the reign and with the coming of war in 1557 he was put in charge of the defence of Yarmouth. His ascendancy in the town doubtless smoothed his election to the Parliaments of 1558 and 1559, in both of which his brother found seats elsewhere, although he probably shared the support given to his fellow-Member William Barker by the 4th Duke of Norfolk, to whom on the first occasion he was charged by the town to report his election.[5]

Woodhouse died on 21 Jan. 1572 leaving only an illegitimate daughter, and his heir was his brother's son Henry Woodhouse†.[6]

[1] Date of birth estimated from first office. *Vis. Norf.* (Harl. Soc. xxxii), 320–1; *LP Hen. VIII*, vi. [2] E179/150/293; *Norf. Rec. Soc.* i. 7; *LP Hen. VIII*, xvii, xviii, xx; *CPR*, 1547–8, p. 87; 1553, p. 357; 1554–5, p. 56; HCA 14/2, 25/1, 5; *CSP Dom.* 1547–80, p. 22; *EHR*, xxiii. 747. [3] *Bronnen tot de Geschiedenis van den Handel met Engeland, Schotland en Ierland*, ed. Smit, ii. 812; *APC*, i. 123, 325; ii. 78, 207; vi. 109; *LP Hen. VIII*, xvii. [4] *LP Hen. VIII*, vi, xx; *CPR*, 1548–9, p. 112; 1549–51, p. 322; 1550–3, p. 29; 1553, p. 401; 1554–5 passim; Blomefield, *Norf.* i. 459; ii. 191, 534, 552; v. 56; ix. 334, 342, 352; xi. 75; C142/161/116. [5] *Cam. Misc.* ix(3), 58; F. W. Russell, *Kett's Rebellion*, 46, 151–3; W. K. Jordan, *Edw. VI*, ii. 491; H. Manship, *Gt. Yarmouth*, 88–9, 92, 147, 156 seq., 259, 325; Lansd. 103, ff. 1–2; *CSP Dom.* 1547–80, pp. 22, 141; *APC*, vi. 109; Add. 23012, p. 69; Gt. Yarmouth ass. bk. A, ff. 19v, 32v, 104v, 113v, 115, 115v, 150, 180,

213; A. H. Smith, *County and Ct.* 38. [6] C142/161/116; Pevsner, *N.-E. Norf. and Norwich*, 338.

N.M.F.

WOODHOUSE, Sir William (by 1517–64), of Hickling, Norf.

GREAT YARMOUTH	1545, 1547, 1553 (Mar.)
NORFOLK	1558
NORWICH	1559
NORFOLK	1563*

b. by 1517, 2nd s. of John Woodhouse of Waxham, and bro. of Sir Thomas*. *m.* (1) Anne, da. of Henry Repps of Thorpe Market, 2s. inc. Henry† 2da.; (2) settlement 11 Nov. 1552, Elizabeth, da. and h. of Sir Philip Calthrope of Erwarton, Suff., wid. of Sir Henry Parker* of Morley Hall and Hingham, Norf. and Furneux Pelham, Herts., 2s. 2da. Kntd. 13 May 1544.[1]

Escheator, Norf. and Suff. 1538–9; bailiff, manor of Gaywood and receiver of King's rents, Lynn, Norf. 1541; jt. v.-adm. Norf. and Suff. 1543–63; master of naval ordnance 1545–52; lt.-adm. Dec. 1552–*d.*; keeper, Queenborough castle, Kent *c.* 1546–50; commr. of Admiralty in Nov. 1547, relief, Norf. 1550; j.p. 1554–*d.*; custos rot. 1561–*d.*[2]

William Woodhouse was one of the most distinguished and active naval commanders during and after the Henrician reconstruction of the navy. Born the younger son of a Norfolk gentleman, he found advancement through service to the King. Its long coastline and busy intercourse with the Continent made Norfolk a nursery of seamen, and Woodhouse probably took to the sea from his youth. He may have been the William Woodhouse who was a prisoner in Scotland in the early months of 1535, but if so he was back in England by November of that year. By May 1541, when granted various offices in and near Lynn, he was the 'King's servant' and was to remain so for life.[3]

In September 1542 Woodhouse commanded the *Primrose* and in the following February was appointed admiral of four ships in the North Sea with which he probably saw action and took prizes: by November 1543 he was in charge of ten ships at Portsmouth waiting to attack the French fishing grounds. Made vice-admiral of the fleet which accompanied the Earl of Hertford's expedition to Scotland in 1544, he was knighted at Leith in May. He returned south at the same time as Hertford, and between July and November he commanded the fleet in the Channel and at Boulogne under Sir Thomas Seymour II: on 30 Nov. Seymour was ordered to send him and John Winter to report to the Council. In August 1545 he was again with the fleet at Portsmouth but reported to be very sick. In January 1546 the admiral, Viscount Lisle, wrote to Sir William Paget that if Sir Thomas Clere were appointed to a certain office he thought Woodhouse 'meet for his place, who may take charge of the artillery of the ships withal and so save a fee': Paget himself recommended Woodhouse to the King through Sir William Petre*—'not that I gain one penny from it, but because he is his majesty's good servant'—and on 24 Apr. 1546 Woodhouse was formally appointed master of the ordnance to the navy. He was the first holder of the office and a member of the Admiralty Board set up at this time under Sir Thomas Clere, who was made lieutenant of the Admiralty.[4]

Woodhouse continued to serve afloat: he was with the Channel fleet in March 1546, when he was again reported to be very ill, and in the following summer he was vice-admiral of the fleet against Scotland. Following the death of Sir Thomas Clere he was appointed lieutenant of the Admiralty. On the outbreak of war in 1557 he was appointed to the command of the Channel fleet with orders to assist at Calais and Dunkirk but was unable to avert the fall of Calais. Pardoned in January 1559 as 'vice-admiral general of the fleet', he was again sent to sea in 1562 with instructions to clear the Channel of pirates and to watch the French coast. This was his last active service, although he probably continued with the other duties of his office.[5]

Woodhouse was well but not excessively rewarded for his 20 years of service. His two admiralty posts brought in salaries of 100 marks and £100 plus allowances, he received several grants of land and he was granted licences to import and export goods. He seems to have been a keen businessman as well as a good sailor, and he built up a considerable landed estate. In November 1535 it was reported to Cromwell that Woodhouse had anticipated the Dissolution by agreeing with the prior of Ingham to buy the priory's possessions, to the annoyance of Edward Calthrope, heir of the priory's founder, who offered Cromwell £100 to prevent the transaction. Woodhouse kept the lands, and in April 1542 made a profitable exchange with the bishop of Norwich by which he obtained the priory of Hickling with Hickling manor and other lands. In April 1545 he had a grant of numerous manors and lands in Norfolk and Suffolk formerly of Heringby college and in March 1550 he joined with his brother Sir Thomas Woodhouse to buy chantry lands in Norfolk valued at £36 10s. a year. In April 1542 he had obtained a 21-year lease of the Black Friars house in Yarmouth. A number of his acquisitions he later re-sold, and when he remarried he settled ten manors and other lands on himself and his wife for life with remainder to his heirs. Apart from these and two manors which he bequeathed to his stepsons Edward and William Parker, he left the rever-

sion of all the rest of his lands to his eldest son by Elizabeth Calthrope. Like his brother, he was a founder-member of the Russia Company and it is likely that he engaged in other commercial ventures.[6]

His periods at sea and on official duty doubtless kept Woodhouse away from Norfolk for long spells and it was not until February 1554 that he was put on the commission of the peace: he had been named to few previous commissions and was never sheriff. In 1549 he and Sir Nicholas Lestrange* had been forced by Ket's rebels to leave hostages in their hands but were themselves released: it is possible that they had supported the Protector Somerset's action against enclosure—Lestrange was certainly suspected of sympathy with the rebels—and although Thomas Woodhouse helped to put down the rising he showed no desire for revenge. Yet Woodhouse was to benefit from Somerset's fall, being no less trusted by the Duke of Northumberland, to whom as Viscount Lisle he had been beholden for his naval promotion. He seems to have shown little enthusiasm in either politics or religion, serving the government of the day and prospering under every ruler from Henry VIII to Elizabeth. The William Woodhouse arrested at Lynn in July 1553 as a follower of Sir Robert Dudley* was certainly a different person.[7]

Woodhouse's parliamentary career falls into two phases; each of them saw him sit in three successive Parliaments but they were separated by another four. If this pattern shows any correspondence with that of his life at sea, it is in the coincidence of his Membership with his active service, not the reverse, and it seems to follow that he was most needed, or felt himself to be most needed, in the Commons when he was also busiest in his profession. His first constituency, Yarmouth, was certainly a suitable one for a sailor who was also a local man. In so far as he required patronage he could have looked to successive admirals, in 1545 Lisle, in 1547 Thomas Seymour (who was also high steward of the borough) and in March 1553 the 9th Lord Clinton, with Lisle, now Duke of Northumberland and a vigorous electioneer, also at hand. It is true that at his first election Woodhouse seems to have been only a second choice, the town assembly first choosing Sir Humphrey Wingfield*, who presumably withdrew, perhaps because of the onset of the illness which was to kill him that year; but no similar doubt attaches to the next two occasions. It was for his 'gentleness to this town showed and hereafter to be showed' that in 1550 the borough made Woodhouse a gift of 500 ling and 100 cod. The phraseology suggests that the 'gentleness' may have extended to an agreed reduction of the wages payable to Woodhouse, for in December 1553 he was given 50 ling 'for certain money due to him for burgess-ship' after having been paid £5 by the chamberlain for an unspecified reason in the previous June.[8]

There is no reason to connect Woodhouse's absence from the first four Marian Parliaments with the Catholic Restoration. At the elections to the Parliament of November 1554 he was approached by the 2nd Earl of Sussex, on behalf of the Queen, to lend his support to the crown's nominees. Yarmouth may have been closed to Woodhouse by the town's restriction, perhaps in deference to the government's wishes, of its representation to townsmen, and elsewhere the 4th Duke of Norfolk, to whom Woodhouse had probably yet to commend himself, was beginning to reassert the patronage lost during his grandfather's eclipse under Edward VI. For the first four years of the reign, moreover, the country was at peace: it was not until the outbreak of war in 1557 again focussed attention on the army and navy that Woodhouse reappeared in the Commons, this time as a knight of the shire. By then he had established the close connexion with the duke which he was to maintain for the rest of his life. On a copy of the list of Members of this Parliament Woodhouse's name is one of those marked with a circle.[9]

Woodhouse died on 22 Nov. 1564.[10]

[1] Date of birth estimated from first office. *Vis. Norf.* (Harl. Soc. xxxii), 320; *CPR, 1550-3*, pp. 272, 329; E150/648/2; PCC 6 Morrison; *LP Hen. VIII*, xix. [2] *LP Hen. VIII*, xvii, xxi; *EHR*, xxiii. 747; *CPR, 1549-51*, p. 308; 1550-3, p. 403; 1553, p. 356; 1553-4, p. 22; *Mariner's Mirror*, xiv. 30, 42-43, 51; HCA 14/2. [3] *LP Hen. VIII*, viii, ix, xvii. [4] *APC*, i. 60, 344; *LP Hen. VIII*, xviii-xxi; *Mariner's Mirror*, xiv. 42-43. [5] *LP Hen. VIII*, xxi; *CSP Scot.* i. 14; *APC*, ii. 415; iii. 37, 77; vi. 233, 236; vii. 82; *CPR*, 1557-8, p. 193; 1558-60, p. 176; *CSP Dom.* 1547-80, p. 203. [6] *LP Hen. VIII*, ix, xi, xvii, xx; *APC*, iv. 250; *CPR*, 1547-8, p. 373; 1548-9, p. 86; 1549-51, p. 308; 1550-3, p. 29; 1554-5, p. 56; 1560-3, pp. 103, 338; E150/648/2; PCC 6 Morrison. [7] F. W. Russell, *Kett's Rebellion*, 209; Tytler, *Edw. VI and Mary*, i. 195; *APC*, iv. 305. [8] C. J. Palmer, *Gt. Yarmouth*, 197; Gt. Yarmouth ass. bk. A, ff. 3, 77v, 102v. [9] Strype, *Cranmer*, i. 493-4; A. Hassell Smith, *County and Ct.* 39, 41; Wm. Salt Lib. SMS 264. [10] E150/648/2.

R.V.

WOODLEAF, Robert (by 1516–93), of Aylesbury and Great Missenden, Bucks.

CHIPPING WYCOMBE 1558

b. by 1516, ?s. of Robert Woodleaf of Henley, Oxon. *educ.* I. Temple. *m.* (1) Jane, da. of Robert Smith, *s.p.*; (2) 25 Nov. 1557, Anne, da. of Sir Robert Drury II* of Hedgerley and Chalfont St. Peter, Bucks., 4s. 2da.[1]

Alderman, Aylesbury 1554.[2]

The Robert Woodleaf returned for Chipping Wycombe in 1558 was undoubtedly the man of that name who had just married into the important south Buckinghamshire family of Drury. According to the one known pedigree he was the son of a Nicholas Woodleaf, but since the only Nicholas Woodleaf who has been traced died at Henley in 1510 leaving gowns and chattels to a second son Robert he is

more likely to have been the Member's grandfather. Admitted a freeman of Henley by fine in 1498, Nicholas Woodleaf had become one of the two bailiffs of the borough; a man of moderate wealth whose trade or profession is not known, he may have been related to William Woodleaf, a London mercer and father-in-law of John Purvey*, since this name is also found at Henley.[3]

Robert Woodleaf was an attorney in the common pleas and his connexion with Buckinghamshire may have arisen from his membership of the Inner Temple. In 1537 he stood surety at the inn for John Cheyne, of the Buckinghamshire family allied by marriage with Sir Edmund Peckham*, and by 1552 he was holding property in Aylesbury, a borough dominated by another Inner Templar, Thomas Pakington. When Aylesbury obtained its charter of incorporation in January 1554 Woodleaf was named one of its first aldermen. In 1557, on the eve of his marriage to Anne Drury, he settled upon the two of them and their heirs the manor or farm of Peterley in Great Missenden, which he had acquired six years earlier. It was to this nexus of relationships that he must have owed his return for Chipping Wycombe, a borough controlled during Mary's reign by Peckham.[4]

Woodleaf was not appointed to the local bench and presumably devoted himself to his professional and domestic concerns. In 1577 he was given permission, as a fellow of the Inner Temple, to build rooms there 'in the great garden' for the use of himself and any of his sons for life, paying all dues. He died on 7 Jan. 1593 and was succeeded by his son Dru, aged 21 and more. The Great Missenden property is the only one mentioned in the inquisition. No will or administration of goods has been found.[5]

[1] Date of birth estimated from first reference. Harl. 1533, f. 86v; PCC 35 Bennett; *Bucks. Par. Reg. Mar.* ed. Phillimore and Gurney, iv. 107. [2] *CPR*, 1553-4, p. 46. [3] PCC 35 Bennett; *Oxon. Rec. Soc.* xli. 121 passim; *Acts. Ct. of Mercers' Co.* ed. Lyell and Watney, 738, 762, 768. [4] CP40/1142, r. 491; *Cal. I.T. Recs.* i. 119, 203; NRA 7372, nos. 499833, 499844, 501380; *CPR*, 1550-3, p. 415; 1553, p. 106; 1553-4, p. 46; *VCH Bucks.* ii. 350. [5] *Cal. I.T. Recs.* i. 291, 334; C142/234/34.

M.K.D.

WOOTTON see WOTTON

WORLICH (WOORLEDGE, WORLEGE, WORLYGE), Thomas (by 1520–92 or later), of Alconbury, Hunts.

HUNTINGDON 1555

b. by 1520. *m.* Jane, da. of Sir Richard Wingfield of Kimbolton, Hunts., prob. at least 4s. 1da.[1]

Commr. to enforce Acts of Supremacy and Uniformity, dioceses of Lincoln and Peterborough 1571, 1575; j.p. Hunts. 1575-92/93.[2]

Thomas Worlich first emerges clearly in the 1540s. In November 1541 he was granted a 21-year lease of Alconbury rectory and it was as of Alconbury that in 1546 he was assessed for subsidy at 26s.8d. on goods valued at £20. His origin and early life are matter for speculation. It is reasonable to assume that he belonged to the family of which one branch was settled at Everton and Potton, near Sandy in Bedfordshire, and another at Wickhambrook, Suffolk. If, as one visitation has it, his daughter Honor married Charles Worlich of the Suffolk line he may be thought to have sprung from the other, yet it could have been at Wickhambrook that he first met Stephen Gardiner, who came from nearby Bury St. Edmunds and whose protégé George Eden* was to become a land-holder at Wickhambrook. Worlich's other principal connexion, with the Wingfields of Kimbolton, may have been of independent origin. The marriage which sealed it could well have coincided with his settlement at Alconbury, for Jane Wingfield was probably born about the time her father died in 1525 and may have given birth to her first son about 1544. Of the education which qualified Worlich to be the recipient of Gardiner's library no trace has been found; he appears to have sent four sons to Cambridge but not to have gone to either university himself, and his name does not occur at an inn of court, although his son Francis probably entered the Inner Temple. Early dependence upon the Wingfields might have taken him to Calais, and there is a remote chance that he was the Thomas Warley who served Viscount Lisle, the deputy, for a number of years before being discharged, with a reward of 13s.4d., when Lisle's household was dissolved in 1540. Alternatively, he could have joined his future brother-in-law Jacques Wingfield* in service with Gardiner and perhaps have accompanied the bishop on his missions abroad.[3]

Worlich was not among Gardiner's dependants who testified at the trial in 1551 nor does his name occur in the evidence then given. If Gardiner, by then a dying man, had a hand in Worlich's election in 1555, it was presumably the Wingfields who procured him the seat for Huntingdon; Thomas Maria Wingfield had recently sat three times for the borough and it may have been Wingfield's promotion to the knighthood of the shire which gave Worlich his chance there. Unlike his brother-in-law Worlich is not listed among the Members who voted against one of the government's bills; the division concerned took place within a month of Gardiner's death and Worlich may either have acted out of respect for the chancellor's memory or perhaps have been engaged in collecting his legacy of all Gardiner's 'humanity

and law books'. It is unlikely that he shared Gardiner's beliefs, for in 1564 his bishop was to commend him to the Privy Council as 'earnest in religion and fit to be trusted', and in 1571 and 1575 he was to be named to the commission for enforcing the Acts of Supremacy and Uniformity in the dioceses of Lincoln and Peterborough. In 1558 he and seven others had been commissioned to investigate breaches of Acts governing the making of cloth and leather. Worlich is not known to have made a will and his date of death has not been discovered.[4]

[1] Date of birth estimated from first reference. *Vis. Hunts.* (Cam. Soc. xliii), 131; *Vis. Suff.* ed. Metcalfe, 107; *Al. Cant.* iv. 448. [2] *CPR*, 1569-72, p. 277; 1572-5, p. 552. [3] *LP Hen. VIII*, vii, x-xv, xvii; E179/122/136; PCC 10 Adeane, 11 Bucke; *Cal. Feet of Fines, Hunts.* ed. Turner, 124, 128; *Cal. I.T. Recs.* i. 235. [4] PCC 3 Noodes; *Cam. Misc.* ix(3), 29; *CPR*, 1557-8, p. 148.

M.K.D.

WORSLEY, Ralph (by 1464–1529 or later), of Hamworthy and Wimborne Minster, Dorset.

POOLE 1512[1]

b. by 1464, ?s. of John Worsley of Dorset. *m.* by 1507, Ellen.[2]

Bailiff, duchy of Lancaster, hundreds of Holt and Kingston Lacy, Dorset 1485–1511, Bradbury by 1496–1511; searcher, port of Poole 1493.[3]

Ralph Worsley was returned for Poole with another port official, Richard Phelips, and both men received 20s. each for 'their labours' during the first session. Presumably he sat for the borough again in 1515 since the King asked for the re-election of the same Members, but there is no evidence that he did so thereafter, although he could have chosen again with Phelips in 1523, when the names of the Members are lost.

Worsley had obtained a local appointment in the duchy of Lancaster at the accession of Henry VII and in the following decade he secured several leases from the duchy and the lucrative searchership at Poole, an office in which he was twice confirmed. During 1496 he and his servants were accused of misconduct and embezzlement, and it was perhaps for this reason that he sued out a pardon on 4 June of that year as Ralph Worsley 'gentleman . . . of Wimborne Minster . . . *alias* of Hamworthy . . . late of Canford, Dorset'. No further complaint appears to have been made in respect of his duchy office, which he retained for a further 15 years and which was later shared by a namesake (perhaps a son) with Sir John Russell*, although he did receive a second (general) pardon in 1510. He was still searcher at Poole in June 1529 when he made a small personal gift to Cardinal Wolsey; this is the last certain reference to him.[4]

The christian name Ralph was a popular one with

the Worsley family of Lancashire, and the allocation of the many references to Worsley or to his namesakes is difficult. He was presumably related to that family, as in 1507 he disposed of some property near Wigan and three years later he was pardoned as of Hamworthy, Wimborne, Holt and Wigan. He could have been the son of John Worsley, customer of Poole in 1466, and a kinsman of Christopher Worsley of Tarrant Launceston, Dorset, sheriff of Somerset and Dorset, who died in 1471.[5]

[1] Poole rec. bk. 1, p. 26. [2] Date of birth estimated from first reference. *Lancs. Fines* (Lancs. Rec. Soc. xlvi), 162–3. [3] Somerville, *Duchy*, i. 629; *CFR*, 1485–1509, no. 451. [4] Poole rec. bk. 1, p. 26. Somerville, i. 629–30; C67/55, m. 2; *CFR*, 1485–1509, no. 451; *CCR*, 1500–9, no. 978; *LP Hen. VIII*, i–iv; St.Ch.3/8/50. [5] *CFR*, 1461–71, p. 181; Hutchins, *Dorset*, iii. 574; *LP Hen. VIII*, ii; *Lancs. Fines*, 162–3.

M.K.D.

WORSLEY, Richard (by 1517–65), of Appuldurcombe in Godshill, I.o.W.

HAMPSHIRE 1539[1]

b. by 1517, 1st s. of Sir James Worsley of Appuldurcombe by Anne, da. and h. of Sir John Leigh of More, Dorset. *m.* Ursula, da. of Henry St. Barbe of Som., 2s. *suc.* fa. 4 Sept. 1538.[2]
Capt. I.o.W. 1540–53, 1560–*d.*, Carisbrooke castle 1544–53, 1560–*d.*; chamberlain or particular receiver, ct. gen. surveyors of the King's lands by 1545; comptroller of customs, Southampton 1560; j.p. Hants 1547–54 or later, q. by 1558/59–*d.*; commr. benevolence 1544/45, chantries, Berks., Hants and I.o.W. 1546, relief, Hants and I.o.W. 1550, goods of churches and fraternities 1553; other commissions 1551–*d.*[3]

Richard Worsley's father, who came of the Lancashire family and was a kinsman of Sir Robert Worsley*, crowned a career in the royal household by becoming captain of the Isle of Wight, a position he was the better able to support by reason of his marriage to a local heiress. It was almost certainly the eldest of Sir James Worsley's sons whom Cromwell took into service in 1531, for six years later Richard Worsley was entrusted with financial business with Gregory Cromwell and it was for him that in 1538 the minister asked the prior of Sheen, apparently without success, for the advowson of Godshill. This was shortly before Sir James Worsley's death brought Worsley into his inheritance and Cromwell himself into the vacant captaincy of the island, with Worsley probably acting as his deputy. The King and Cromwell are said to have visited the family seat of Appuldurcombe in Godshill.[4]

It was as 'Mr. Worsley' that Cromwell recommended Worsley, then in his early twenties, as Thomas Wriothesley's fellow-knight for Hampshire in the Parliament of 1539, when his first choice of John Kingsmill lapsed because Kingsmill was sheriff.

Both were elected and so were destined to witness at close quarters the destruction of their patron in the following year. For Worsley, whose favour the town of Southampton engaged at this time with a gift of oranges and lemons, while the borough of Yarmouth sought his aid against customs evaders, the fall of Cromwell was followed by his own succession to the captaincy of Wight; he also became the particular receiver for the region, probably from the establishment of the court of general surveyors in 1542. His military competence was put to the test with the French landing on the island in 1545; he seems to have emerged with credit and he was much involved with the construction of Yarmouth castle and other defences built shortly afterwards. He had not been re-elected with Wriothesley to the Parliament of 1542 and is unlikely to have been to its successor of 1545, for which the Hampshire names are lost; to the memory of his precocious appearance in 1539 would doubtless have been added the argument that his place was on the island.[5]

Worsley's replacement as captain in the autumn of 1553 need not imply that the Marian government lacked confidence in him—he was retained on the commission of the peace—and it was his successor William Girling who was to come under suspicion at the time of the Dudley conspiracy. The next captain, William Paulet, 1st Marquess of Winchester, resigned the office in 1560, whereupon Worsley was reappointed for life, being at the same time relieved of his obligation to reside at Southampton as customs comptroller since he was 'now to serve the Queen elsewhere'; he was indeed engaged during these years in surveying the defences of Portsmouth and the Channel Islands. By his will of 28 Dec. 1564 he asked to be buried at Godshill, near his grandfather, left the manor of Appuldurcombe to his wife during her widowhood and provided for his two infant sons. His numerous minor bequests included a piece of unicorn's horn to Sir William Pickering* and a gelding to John Astley*. Worsley died on 12 May 1565 and a monument to him was erected at Godshill by his brother. Both his sons were killed on 6 Sept. 1567 in an explosion at the gatehouse at Appuldurcombe. Their mother married as her second husband Sir Francis Walsingham†, who fought and won a law suit with Worsley's brother and executor about the inheritance. The family was to produce several later Members, including Sir Richard Worsley, the historian of the Isle of Wight.[6]

[1] *LP Hen. VIII*, xiv(1), 662 citing SP1/146, pp. 237–40; E159/319, brev. ret. Mich. r. [1–2]. [2] Date of birth estimated from age at fa.'s i.p.m., C142/83/179. *Vis. Hants* (Harl. Soc. lxiv), 23. [3] Worsley, *I.o.W.* app. no. xxxvii; *LP Hen. VIII*, xix–xxi; *CPR*, 1547–8, p. 84; 1548–9, p. 57; 1550–3, p. 142; 1553, pp. 358, 362, 415, 417; 1553–4, pp. 19, 286; 1558–60, pp. 291, 461; 1560–3, passim; *APC*, i. 86, 87; Stowe 571, ff. 45, 56. [4] *LP Hen. VIII*, iii, v, xii, xiii; Worsley, 92.

[5] M. L. Robertson, 'Cromwell's servants' (Univ. California Los Angeles, Ph.D. thesis, 1975), 589–90; *LP Hen. VIII*, xiv; Soton RO, stewards' bk. 1539–40; *VCH Hants*, v. 287n, 289. [6] *CPR*, 1553–4, p. 286; 1558–60, pp. 291, 461; 1563–6, pp. 435–7; PCC 23 Morrison; C142/124/156, 141/21; *VCH Hants*, v. 171; *Oglander Mems.* ed. Long, 155; C. Read, *Walsingham*, i. 29, 229; Pevsner and Lloyd, *Hants and I.o.W.* 747.

P.H.

WORSLEY, Sir Robert (by 1512–85), of Booths, Lancs.

LANCASHIRE 1553 (Mar.)*, 1559

b. by 1512, 1st s. of Robert Worsley of Booths by Alice, da. and coh. of Hamlet Massey of Rixton. *m.* by 1533, Alice, da. of Thurstan Tyldesley* of Tyldesley and Wardley Hall, nr. Worsley, 1s. Robert[†]; 3s. illegit. *suc.* gdfa. 1533. Kntd. 11 May 1544.[1]

J.p. Lancs. from *c.* 1540; sheriff Dec. 1548–Nov. 1549, 1559–60; dep. lt.; commr. eccles. causes, diocese of Chester 1562.[2]

The manor of Booths, which Robert Worsley inherited from his grandfather, also Robert, in 1533, had been in the possession of his family since the 14th century. Although he acquired further property in Lancashire and Yorkshire, his own son Robert was later forced to sell many of his Lancashire estates, including Booths. He himself was assessed at 30*s.* for £30 in lands in the subsidy roll for Salford Hundred in 1541.[3]

Worsley joined the 3rd Earl of Derby with 63 men in 1536 and continued to perform military services. In April 1544, as captain of 100 men, he received £21 conduct money from Manchester to Newcastle and £16 16*s.*8*d.* coat money: on 11 May he was knighted by the Earl of Hertford at Leith. In 1556 he was appointed with Edward Tyldesley to command 200 archers and on 18 Dec. 1557 the Privy Council agreed to move the Queen to give him £20 in reward for the good service he had done in the north 'and in consideration he had more soldiers than he was allowed for'. He was a commander in Salford Hundred in 1553, 1556 and 1569. He was by-elected to Edward VI's second Parliament in place of Sir Richard Houghton who was, or was said to be, too ill to sit: two returns were made, of which the first, dated 6 Feb. 1553, bore both Worsley's and Houghton's names (both written over erasures) as well as Thomas Butler I's as junior knight, and the second, dated 13 Mar., Worsley's alone as replacing Houghton's. Since the Parliament had opened on 1 Mar. and was to end on the 31st, Worsley's attendance at it must have been brief.[4]

One of Worsley's landed acquisitions was Upholland priory near Wigan, which he obtained from Sir John Holcroft* in 1546–7; it may have been in exchange that Worsley conveyed his interest in Pennington to Holcroft. Worsley had been one of those who joined Sir Thomas Langton* in an attempt to control the mayoral election in Wigan in 1539. Later, as sheriff of Lancashire, he engaged in several lawsuits with Miles Gerard, mayor of Wigan, and others, who claimed that the mayor should sit as a justice of the peace at sessions in Wigan. His son Robert and his fellow-Member in 1559, Sir John Atherton, were among his other opponents at law.[5]

The younger Robert was Worsley's son by Alice Tyldesley, whom he had married by 1533, but by September 1547, when Thurstan Tyldesley made his will, Worsley had repudiated her in favour of Margaret Beetham. As so often with the Lancashire gentry, the status of this second union is uncertain.[6]

Worsley died in 1585 and was buried at Eccles in December: no will or inquisition post mortem has been found.[7]

[1] Of age at grandfather's death, *VCH Lancs.* iv. 383. *Vis. Lancs.* (Chetham Soc. lxxxi), 131; (lxxxviii), 340; (xcviii), 81; *Chetham Soc.* xxxiii. 100–1. [2] J. B. Watson, 'Lancs. gentry 1529–58' (London Univ. M.A. thesis, 1959), 538; *VCH Lancs.* ii. 98; *CPR*, 1560–3, pp. 280–1; *Chetham Soc.* l. 131n. [3] *VCH Lancs.* iv. 382–3; *VCH Yorks.* (N. Riding), i. 506–8; *Lancs. and Cheshire Rec. Soc.* xii. 141. [4] *LP Hen. VIII*, xi, xix; HMC Kenyon, 587; *APC*, vi. 217; *VCH Lancs.* ii. 220; Watson, 527; C219/20/66, 67. [5] *LP Hen. VIII*, xxi; *VCH Lancs.* iii. 428, 442; iv. 383n; Watson, 526; *Chetham Soc.* n.s. xv. 108; *Ducatus Lanc.* ii. 224, 231, 237; iii. 100. [6] *Chetham Soc.* xxxiii. 100–1. [7] *VCH Lancs.* iv. 383n.

A.D.

WORTH, Roger (by 1504–64), of Barnstaple, Devon.

BARNSTAPLE 1553 (Oct.)

b. by 1504, 2nd s. of Oates Worth (*d.* 1504) of Compton Pole by Alice, da. of John Milleton of Meavy. *m.* by 1539, Joan, da. of Henry Drew of Barnstaple, 3s. 7da.[1] Mayor, Barnstaple 1549–50.[2]

A younger son in a cadet branch of the family settled at Worth in Devon, Roger Worth had namesakes in the service of Viscount Lisle and the 2nd Lord Daubeney. Himself a merchant, he was assessed at 10*s.* for the subsidies of 1540 and later years; in 1546 he came to the notice of the Privy Council as one of the purchasers of goods taken by privateers. In the previous year he had shared with John Goddisland* and another in leasing the 'lathstedes' in the town, the pyx of the market-toll and the annual fair; in 1550 he leased property which had belonged to a chantry in the parish church.[3]

Worth's services to the town included the entertaining of successive recorders and other visitors and riding to the recorder on business. It was with the future recorder (and his probable relative by marriage) Robert Carey that he was returned to the first Marian Parliament, in which neither of them opposed the restoration of Catholicism. Worth was buried in Barnstaple church on 4 Oct. 1564. His will, which was proved on the following 27 July, was one of those in the Exeter probate registry destroyed in an air raid in 1942.[4]

[1] Date of birth estimated from fa.'s death. *Vis. Devon*, ed. Colby, 212–13; N. Devon Athenaeum, Barnstaple D. Drake ms 'MPs Barnstaple', 25. [2] J. B. Gribble, *Barnstaple*, 201. [3] *LP Hen. VIII*, x–xii, xx; *APC*, i. 426–7; N. Devon Athenaeum 3972, ff. 47, 49–50. [4] *CPR*, 1548–9, p. 380; *Barnstaple Wills*, ed. Beckerlegge, 1816; E179/97/214.

A.D.K.H.

WOTTON, John (by 1523–55 or later), of Totnes and Great Englebourne, Devon.

TOTNES 1553 (Mar.), 1553 (Oct.)

b. by 1523, 1st s. of William Wotton of Harberton and Great Englebourne by da. of one Holcomb. *m.* by 1544, Agnes, da. of (?Thomas) Hackwell of Totnes, 5s. 3da. *suc.* fa. 1554/55.[1]
Mayor, Totnes 1552–3.[2]

Although they founded an armorial family, little trace has been found of William Wotton, a clothier of Harberton near Totnes, and his son John, a merchant of that town. Together they paid £324 in September 1546 for a lease of the neighbouring manor of Great Englebourne, formerly owned by Buckfast abbey, which then became the family seat. By then John Wotton was involved with Christopher Savery* and others in the privateering exploits of the ships *George* and *Trynitie*, built and equipped at Totnes, a business in which Wotton was again licensed to engage in 1549. It was with Savery that he was elected, while mayor, to both Parliaments of 1553. All that is known of his part in the Commons is that he did not oppose the Marian restoration of Catholicism. His sale of a house in Totnes on 21 Dec. 1555 is the last reference found to him.[3]

[1] Date of birth estimated from marriage. *Vis. Devon* (Harl. Soc. vi), 316; *Vis. Devon*, ed. Vivian, 811; *Western Antiq.* ix. 152; PCC 20 More. [2] *Western Antiq.* ix. 152; C210/21/43. [3] *LP Hen. VIII*, xxi; *DKR*, x. 302; *Devon Monastic Lands* (Devon and Cornw. Rec. Soc. n.s. i), 91–92; Totnes charters; deeds; R. M. S. Tugwood, 'Piracy and privateering from Dartmouth and Kingswear, 1540–58' (London Univ. M.A. thesis, 1953), 142, 146.

A.D.K.H.

WOTTON, Thomas (by 1521–87), of Boughton Place, Boughton Malherbe, Kent.

WEST LOOE 1547[1]

b. by 1521, 1st s. of Sir Edward Wotton of Boughton Place by Dorothy, da. of Sir Robert Rede; bro. of William*. *educ.* L. Inn, adm. 7 Feb. 1541. *m.* (1) by 1545, Elizabeth, da. of Sir John Rudston of London, 6s. inc. Edward[†] 3da.; (2) settlement 12 Apr. 1565, Eleanor, da. of William Finch of the Moat, Kent, wid. of Robert Morton, 2s. *suc.* fa. 8 Nov. 1551.[2]
Commr. heresies, Kent 1552, goods of churches and fraternities 1553, Rochester bridge 1561, 1571, 1574, piracy 1565, offences against the Acts of Uniformity and Supremacy 1572; sheriff 1558–9, 1578–9; j.p.q. 1558/59–*d.*; custos rot. 1561–*d.*[3]

Thomas Wotton was described by Izaak Walton as 'a man of great modesty, of a plain and single heart, of an ancient freedom and integrity of mind, . . . of great learning, religion and wealth'. He came from a Kentish family which stood high in the esteem of the crown: his father was prominent at the court of Henry VIII, a beneficiary under the King's will and a Privy Councillor and treasurer of Calais under Edward VI, and his uncle successively an ambassador, Privy Councillor and secretary of state. With the exception of his single (known) appearance at Westminster, Wotton did not try to emulate them: he was of a retiring disposition and rarely visited either the court or the capital, but as a landlord and magistrate he showed exemplary diligence.[4]

Wotton spent some time at Lincoln's Inn, presumably to round off his education since he is not known to have been called or to have practised; while a student at the inn he occupied a house in the nearby parish of St. Foster's, Gutter Lane. His marriage, which may have taken place before he left it, was one of a series between his family and the Rudstons, his father having married the widow of Sir John Rudston and his sister being the wife of Robert Rudston*.[5]

Wotton's return in 1547 for a newly enfranchised Cornish town was doubtless arranged by his father, with help from another Privy Councillor, Sir John Russell*, Baron Russell, an honorary member of Lincoln's Inn and lord lieutenant in the west. The Journal contains no reference to Wotton, but he missed some of the first session conveying treasure to his father in Calais and in the second he may have interested himself in the Act for gavelkind (2 and 3 Edw. VI, no. 40), which was to his benefit as an eldest son. He doubtless acted for his father and uncle during their absences abroad, and early in 1549 he wrote a letter of advice to the Protector which, coming from one of so little experience, probably offended its recipient. By the next Parliament, that of March 1553, Wotton's father was dead; his uncle was in favour with the Duke of Northumberland, but in the absence of so many returns it is not known whether he sat again, although his younger brother did. In the previous autumn he had been nominated, but not pricked, sheriff, and he was promised a knighthood of the Bath which the King did not live to confer. Wotton's Protestantism did not commend him to Mary. On 16 Jan. 1554 he was summoned before the Council, perhaps in connexion with Sir Thomas Wyatt II's* plot, and five days later he was committed to the Fleet 'for obstinate standing in matters of religion'. His uncle interceded with the Queen on his behalf and averted harsher punishment. It is not known how long Wotton stayed in custody and nothing has come to light about his career during the rest of the reign.[6]

With Elizabeth on the throne Wotton emerged as a figure of importance in Kent. As her first sheriff he received in 1559 a letter from (Sir) Henry Crispe* 'touching the tranquillity of the realm' which he sent on to Cecil. In 1564 his religious beliefs were approved by Archbishop Parker, and his efforts to defend extreme Protestants and to extirpate recusancy show where his heart lay. In 1573 the Queen visited Boughton Place and offered him a knighthood, which he declined. Wotton is chiefly remembered as the patron of William Lambarde†, whose *Perambulation of Kent* (1576) was dedicated to him; as a young man he had been similarly associated with *The Christian state of matrimony* (1543) translated by Miles Coverdale, and later in life Edward Dering dedicated to him *The sparing restraint* (1568). Wotton made his will on 8 Jan. 1587. He left £400 and some furniture to his wife, provided she quitclaimed her interest in the Wotton estates to his son Edward. He remembered various members of his family and his friends (Sir) Roger Manwood II* and Thomas Temple, and appointed as executors his son Edward, his brother-in-law Robert Rudston and his nephew William Cromer†. He died three days later and was buried in Boughton church, where a monument was erected to his memory.[7]

[1] Hatfield 207. [2] Date of birth estimated from age at fa.'s i.p.m., C142/93/113. *Vis. Kent* (Harl. Soc. lxxiv), 21-22; (lxxv), 78-79; CPR, 1563-6, p. 196. [3] CPR, 1550-3 to 1572-5 passim; APC, vii. 382. [4] Izaak Walton, *Reliquiae Wottoniane* (1685), sig. b. 4; DNB (Wotton, Sir Edward and Sir Nicholas). [5] LP Hen. VIII, xvii. [6] APC, ii. 148; iv. 351; PCC 33 Bucke; *Thomas Wotton's Letter Bk.* 1574-86 ed. Eland, 13-14; CPR, 1553, p. 387; Foxe, *Acts and Mons.* vi. 413; Walton, sig. b. 4. [7] *Arch. Cant.* xii. 417-18; lxxxii. 124; *Cam. Misc.* ix (3), 57; CSP Dom. 1547-80, pp. 560, 685; 1581-90, p. 80; APC, vii. 31, 37, 382; xii. 161; *Cantium*, ii. 43; Strype, *Annals Ref.* i(2), 272; ii(1), 44, 465; *Parker*, 339; PCC 4 Spencer; C142/215/263; J. Newman, *W. Kent and the Weald*, 167.

A.D.K.H.

WOTTON, William (by 1532-56), of London.

MAIDSTONE 1553 (Mar.)
GATTON 1554 (Nov.)

b. by 1532, 2nd s. of Sir Edward Wotton of Boughton Place, Boughton Malherbe, Kent, and bro. of Thomas*. *educ.* L. Inn, adm. 17 Dec. 1547. *m.* Mary, da. of Sir John Dannett of Merstham, Surr., prob. *s.p.*[1]

William Wotton received only £20 a year under his father's will in 1551, and that on condition of his renouncing any claim to the family lands, which the reform of gavelkind in 1539 (31 Hen. VIII, c.3) had enabled his father to preserve from division. Unlike his elder brother's, Wotton's admission to Lincoln's Inn was thus doubtless seen as the prelude to a career in law or government and his youthful entry to the Commons as a step in his progress. The opportunity was—or appeared to be—presented by the enfranchisement of Maidstone. The borough had been incorporated in July 1549, and although the charter then granted made no mention of its parliamentary representation Maidstone elected and the sheriff returned two Members to the Parliament of March 1553. The initiative could have come from the town itself, in the belief that it was entitled to them, from the sheriff Sir John Guildford* or someone close to the Duke of Northumberland, or even from Northumberland himself, and any one of these could have nominated Wotton to one of the seats, Maidstone because of his local standing, Guildford by reason of a marriage connexion, and Northumberland in recognition of the support he had received from Wotton's father; Wotton was also related to Jane Grey through an aunt who had married the 2nd Marquess of Dorset. The fact that the second Member John Salveyn belonged to Lincoln's Inn but lacked any known connexion with Kent suggests that he was brought in under Wotton's wing.[2]

The election did not go unchallenged. On 21 Mar., three weeks after the opening of Parliament, the Commons deputed two Members, Robert Broke and Richard Morgan, to examine the Maidstone charter and ordered Salveyn and Wotton to withdraw pending the result of their inquiry. There is no evidence that they reported during the remaining ten days of the Parliament, but when Guildford made his second return as sheriff six months later Maidstone was omitted; it was not represented again until 1563. Wotton, unlike Salveyn, was to be re-elected. His seat for Gatton in November 1554 he owed to Lady Copley, who herself returned him and her son Thomas, and whose preference for relatives he exemplified by being not only her first cousin once removed but also the husband, or husband-to-be, of another cousin of both in Mary Dannett, sister of a recent Member for Gatton.[3]

In his will of 28 Sept. 1556 Wotton described himself as of London, but as one of the witnesses was the parson of Boughton Malherbe it was probably there that he died. He left all his possessions to his wife, with a remainder in the lands to his brother Thomas, in return for the surrender of her jointure of £30 a year; he named her executrix and his brother supervisor; there is no mention of children. The will was proved on the following 1 Dec.[4]

[1] Presumed to be of age at election. *Vis. Kent* (Harl. Soc. lxxv), 78-79. [2] PCC 33 Bucke; C142/93/113, 117. [3] CJ, i. 25; *Vis. Leics.* (Harl. Soc. ii), 64; *Vis. Suss.* (Harl. Soc. liii), 36-37. [4] PCC 24 Ketchyn.

H.M.

WRASTLEY (WRESTLEY), Robert

CHIPPENHAM 1553 (Oct.)

This Member has not been identified. His surname is spelled clearly 'Wrastlay' in the return and

'Wrastley' on the Crown Office list. He is named first in the return and is styled 'gentleman', whereas his fellow-Member Henry Goldney *alias* Fernell is described as a yeoman. Neither was marked among those who 'stood for the true religion' in the Parliament. As Goldney was to be appointed first bailiff in the charter of incorporation granted to Chippenham on 2 May 1554 it would be strange if the gentleman who had taken precedence over him eight months earlier was the Robert 'Wrotesley' named in the charter as one of the 12 burgesses who were to assist Goldney, yet the municipal accounts mention payments of 20s. in 1566 and 1570 to a Joan Wrestley, who was assessed for subsidy as a widow in 1571. No one else of the name is recorded earlier at Chippenham, but a John Wrastley became bailiff there in 1586.[1]

There was a John Wrastley of Sutton Benger, Wiltshire, who died late in 1556, and a Henry Wrastley of Salisbury who made his will in 1559; both described themselves as gentlemen but neither seems to have had a kinsman called Robert or any connexion with Chippenham. A man who might have been the Member was Robert Wrasteling, 'trusty friend', executor and residuary legatee of Richard Manchester, clerk. Manchester made his will when dying at the Savoy on 20 Oct. 1541 and shortly afterwards Wrasteling was sued by Charles Belfeld for goods worth at least £80, which Manchester was alleged to have obtained by posing as the executor of Ralph Belfeld. The case required depositions from several acquaintances of the dead men, including a gentleman of the King's wardrobe; Ralph Belfeld himself had been secretary to the 3rd Duke of Norfolk and Richard Manchester a chaplain to Sir John Russell* and a canon of Exeter. Wrasteling's own position or residence is not stated, but he may thus have had connexions at court which later could have helped to bring him into Parliament.[2]

[1] C219/21/178; Bodl. e Museo 17; *CPR*, 1553-4, p. 104; *Chippenham Recs.* ed. Goldney, 262, 337-9, 342; E179/198/287. [2] PCC 1 Wrastley, 2 Streat, 10 Lyon, 4 Spert; Req.2/4/221; Le Neve, *Fasti* ed. Hardy, ix. 65; *LP Hen. VIII*, v, vii.

T.F.T.B.

WRAY, Christopher (1521/22–92), of Lincoln's Inn, London and Glentworth, Lincs.

BOROUGHBRIDGE	1553 (Oct.), 1554 (Apr.), 1554 (Nov.),[1] 1555, 1558
GREAT GRIMSBY	1563
LUDGERSHALL	1571

b. 1521/22, 3rd s. of Thomas Wray of Yorks. by Joan, da. of Robert Jackson of Gatenby, Bedale, Yorks. *educ.* Buckingham (Magdalene), Camb.; L. Inn, adm. 6 Feb. 1545, called 1550. *m.* Anne, da. of Nicholas Girlington of Normanby, Yorks., wid. of Robert

Brocklesby (*d.* 3 Apr. 1557) of Glentworth, 1s. William† 4da. Kntd. 6 Nov. 1574.[2]

Lent reader, L. Inn 1563, 1567, treasurer 1565–6.[3] J.p.q. Lincs. (Lindsey) 1558/59–*d.*, (Kesteven) 1562–*d.*, (Holland) 1569–*d.*, Hunts. 1577–*d.*; steward, manor of Wetherby, Yorks. Jan. 1559–63; of counsel to Lincoln c. 1559, to Henry Neville, 5th Earl of Westmorland by 1562; serjeant-at-law Easter 1567, Queen's serjeant 18 June 1567; justice of assize, Yorks. 31 May 1570; 2nd justice of Lancaster 13 June 1570; j.K.B. 14 May 1572; l.c.j. 8 Nov. 1574; commr. eccles. causes, diocese of Lincoln 1575, to visit Oxf. univ. 1577; custos rot. Hunts. 1579; receiver of petitions in the Lords, Parlts. of 1584, 1586, 1589; eccles. commr. 1589.[4]

Speaker of House of Commons 1571.

Christopher Wray was a younger son in an undistinguished Yorkshire family, though of more reputable descent than was suggested by Richard Topcliffe† in 1584. He had not progressed far in his legal career when he was first returned for Boroughbridge and his re-election there to every Parliament of Mary's reign—on each occasion with a different partner—implies that he enjoyed a special advantage with regard to the borough. What this was is by no means clear. If, as may be presumed, Boroughbridge was re-enfranchised at the beginning of Mary's reign with the object of adding to the ranks of government supporters, the two most likely sources of nominations would have been the duchy of Lancaster, within whose honor of Knaresborough the borough lay, and the council in the north, which wielded general patronage in Yorkshire. Wray is not known to have been connected with either the successive chancellors of the duchy, Sir Robert Rochester* and Sir Edward Waldegrave*, or the president of the council, the 5th Earl of Shrewsbury, nor is there any indication that the 2nd Earl of Cumberland, as steward of the honor, extended to Wray the support which he gave to at least one of the other Members. It is thus probably Wray's combination of local and professional links which explains his hold on the seat. Among the first is to be noted his mother's bequest in 1562 of her 'goods and chattels at Aldborough, and all the corn growing in the fields there'; if these had come to her either from her own family or from her first marriage they would have given Wray a standing in the manor and parish of which Boroughbridge was a part. On the professional side, it could scarcely be fortuitous that three of Wray's fellow-Members belonged to his inn, which also supplied Members for some other Yorkshire boroughs. Through that institution, and through his own marriage, Wray was associated with relatives and friends of Sir Thomas More, and the presumption of his own Catholicism is borne out by the absence of his name from among those who offered any opposition in the Commons to the

Marian Restoration. His only mention in the Journal is as receiving for scrutiny a bill concerning exigents and proclamations on 29 Jan. 1558.[5]

Wray's progress under Elizabeth was to carry him to the Speakership in 1571 and to a long and distinguished tenure of the office of lord chief justice. He died on 7 May 1592.

[1] Huntington Lib. Hastings mss Parl. pprs. [2] Aged 70 at death. *Lincs. Peds.* (Harl. Soc. l), 176; (lv), 1322; Req.2/42/62; C. Dalton, *Wrays of Glentworth*, i. 58, 60; *DNB.* [3] Dugdale, *Origines Juridiciales*, 252–3. [4] *CPR*, 1560–3 to 1572–5 passim; *CSP Dom.* 1547–80, p. 543; J. W. F. Hill, *Tudor and Stuart Lincoln*, 70; Great Grimsby AO, letter of Francis Ayscough 1562; Somerville, *Duchy*, i. 473; *LJ*, ii. 61, 113, 145. [5] *CSP Dom.* 1581–90, p. 207; *Richmondshire Wills* (Surtees Soc. xxvi), 159; PCC 47 Harrington ptd. *N. Country Wills*, ii (Surtees Soc. cxxi), 142–6; *CJ*, i. 48.

A.D.

WRIGHT, George (by 1516–57), of London.

BEDFORD   1547
WALLINGFORD   1553 (Mar.), 1553 (Oct.)

b. by 1516. *m.* by 1543, Dorothy, 1s.[1]
Clerk in ct. augmentations by 1537, surveyor and receiver of purchased lands 1544–7, receiver for Beds., Berks., Bucks. and Oxon. 1547–54; commr. chantries, Beds. and Bucks. 1546, relief, Bucks. 1550; j.p. Bucks. 1554.[2]

Nothing is known for certain of the origins of George Wright. He was probably a kinsman of Edmund Wright[†] of Burnt Bradfield, Suffolk, with whom he engaged in land transactions, but in view of his election for Bedford he may also have been the George Wright described by a plaintiff in the court of requests under Mary as a relative of William Wigge, a yeoman of Milton (possibly Milton Bryant), Bedfordshire. He is first mentioned in 1537 as being paid by the court of augmentations for engrossing documents, and it was as a 'servant' or clerk to the chancellor of the court, Sir Richard Rich, that he afterwards received many small sums. On 15 May 1544 he was promoted to the twin offices of surveyor and receiver of exchanged and purchased lands in succession to Geoffrey Chamber. This position, which exempted Wright from attending the King in France that year, he retained until the re-organization of 1547, when he secured a local receivership which he held until the court was abolished.[3]

Wright's first recorded land transactions were made in 1541, when he was licensed to acquire property at Walsham, in Norfolk, and in 1543, when he added a sheepfold at Gaywood in the same county. More significant was his purchase two years later, with Edmund Wright, of Westerdale manor, Yorkshire, and other monastic property there and in Lincolnshire, for £478. In May 1547 the same pair, now both described as 'gentlemen', were allowed to sell a farm in Lincolnshire: this was the first of

several moves by George to concentrate his property in the area of his receivership, while himself continuing to live in London at least until 1550, when Westerdale was sold. He is not known to have held any property in the town of Bedford, which provided his first parliamentary seat, but he was granted some former monastic lands around Leighton Buzzard, at a rent of £7 16s. a year, in April 1553.[4]

It was thus as an 'outsider' that he was returned in 1547. The fact that his fellow-Member was Gerard Harvey *alias* Smart, brother-in-law to Sir John Williams*, Wright's superior in the augmentations, suggests that he owed the seat to this connexion, perhaps with the local assistance of Sir Francis Bryan*, recorder of Bedford. The connexion with Wallingford, Wright's second seat, seems not dissimilar. In December 1549 he and one Eustace Moon paid £412 for properties which included tithes at South Moreton, Berkshire, the rectory of East Claydon, Buckinghamshire, and the lordship and manor of Wycombe; the last of these had belonged to the college of St. Nicholas, Wallingford, but as Wright sold it later in the same year no connexion with the town can have resulted. In its absence, a patron must again be presumed. Bryan, who had died in 1550, had been constable of Wallingford castle, and he and Thomas Parry, Wright's fellow-Member in March 1553, had married the widows of the brothers Fortescue, while Williams, the sheriff of Oxfordshire and Berkshire at the time of Wright's second return in September 1553, was later to marry Sir Adrian Fortescue's granddaughter.[5]

Wright seems to have been flexible in religion, which is consonant with his presence in the second Parliament of Edward VI and the first of Mary. In April 1553 the Privy Council ordered him and Ralph Lee to cross-examine the churchwardens and parishioners of Radnage, Buckinghamshire, over the words of a parson who had hopefully predicted that the old ceremonies would soon be restored; by contrast, in May 1554 Sir Henry Bedingfield* reported to the Council on Wright's interrogation of a suspect servant who had fled from Princess Elizabeth's household at Woodstock. No will survives to throw light on Wright's beliefs. He died on 1 Aug. 1557, leaving a 13 year-old son William and a widow Dorothy, who in the following year was granted a new lease of some property which her husband had rented at Old Windsor. The boy's wardship, and a small annuity, were given in 1561 to his mother, who had remarried.[6]

[1] Date of birth estimated from first reference. *CPR*, 1557–8, p. 128; C142/111/4. [2] *HMC 8th Rep.* pt. 2 (1881), 23–24; W. C. Richardson, *Ct. Augmentations*, 53–54, 281, 493; E315/218/61, 126; Stowe 571, ff. 6–7v, 10v; *LP Hen. VIII*, xx; *CPR*, 1553, p. 351; 1553–4, p. 17. [3] Req.2/47/46; *LP Hen. VIII*, xvi, xviii–xx; Richardson, 53–54. [4] *LP Hen. VIII*, xvi, xviii, xx; *CPR*, 1547–8, p. 164; 1549–51, p. 321;

1553, p. 138. ⁵ *CPR*, 1549–51, pp. 68, 354. ⁶ *APC*, iv. 252, 254; *Norf. Arch.* iv. 162; C142/111/4; *CPR*, 1557–8, p. 128; 1560–3, p. 167.

T.F.T.B.

WRIGHT, William (by 1482–1543), of York.

YORK 1515[1]

b. by 1482, s. of William Wright of York. *m.* Ursula Joye or Jone, of Riccall, ch.[2]

Member, Corpus Christi guild, York 1503, senior chamberlain 1509–10, sheriff 1511–12, member of the Twenty-Four 1512, master, merchant guild 1512–14, alderman 1514–*d.*, mayor 1518–19, 1535–6; master, York archiepiscopal mint 1523.[3]

William Wright was the son of a York notary of the same name who died about 1523. He became a York freeman, as a merchant and notary, in 1508–9. Ten years later, he was living as a married man in the parish of Holy Trinity, King's Court, but the lay subsidy of 1524 shows that he had then returned to his father's parish of St. Michael-le-Belfrey, perhaps after his father's death. By 1539 he had moved again, to the parish of St. Martin, Coney Street, where he remained until his death. Little has come to light about Wright's life apart from his civic career. Presumably starting in trade, since he was a member of the York merchants' guild until 1529 at least, in 1523 he contracted with Wolsey to become, at a rent of £5 a year, master and worker of silver moneys at the archbishop's mint. It is not clear how long he held this office, which by 1529 seems to have passed to George Gale*, but he had other strings to his bow: there was his profession of notary—he so described himself in his will—and perhaps the business of moneylending. His assessment of £16 in goods for the subsidy of 1524 carries a note that he was 'decayed since the first levy by trusting of his goods to divers persons—£24, whereof he trusteth to be paid'.[4]

Wright rose rapidly in civic responsibility. He became senior chamberlain only a year after taking up his freedom, was at once entrusted with a mission to the Earl of Surrey in London and within five more years had risen to the bench of aldermen, on which he served nearly 30. Shortly after his election as alderman he was chosen to partner Alan Staveley in Parliament and when the city belatedly received the King's letter requiring the re-election of the previous Members only Staveley was replaced, by the veteran William Nelson, perhaps because Thomas Drawswerd, Nelson's former colleague, was the mayor-designate. Nelson and Wright were instructed to transact city business in London, which included appearing before the Exchequer. In 1518 Wright was the first mayor to be elected by the new method prescribed by letters patent of 1517, with ordinary citizens barred from the election. During his second term, in 1535–6, there was a great legal battle with the archbishop over the Bishopfields, common fields adjoining the city. An alderman until his death in 1543, in the previous year he was displaced as a warden through 'impotency'.[5]

Wright made his will on 10 Apr. 1543, bequeathing his soul to the Trinity, the Virgin, St. Peter and all saints, and asking for burial in his parish church of St. Martin, Coney Street. It was an unusually brief will for an alderman, merely stipulating that his wife and children should have their thirds of his goods according to custom; even the number of children is not mentioned. He made his wife residuary legatee for the health of his soul and ended, 'God send us all to be merry in Heaven, Amen. And my wife and children grace well to do, and my servants good masters'. The will was proved on 19 June 1543.[6]

¹ *York Civic Recs.* iii (Yorks. Arch. Soc. rec. ser. cvi), 45–46. ² Date of birth estimated from first reference. *Reg. Corpus Christi Guild, York* (Surtees Soc. lvii), 159n. ³ *Reg. Corpus Christi Guild, York.* 159, 219; *Reg. Freemen, York*, i (Surtees Soc. xcvi), 32; York archs. B 9–17 passim; C. Caine, *Archiepiscopal Coins of York*, 59–61. ⁴ *Reg. Corpus Christi Guild, York*, 159n; York chapter archs. L2(5)a, f. 134; *Reg. Freemen, York*, i. 232; *Test. Ebor.* iii (Surtees Soc. xlv), 370; *Yorks. Arch. Jnl.* iv. 170; *LP Hen. VIII*, xiv; *York Mercers and Merchant Adventurers* (Surtees Soc. cxxix), 130, 323; York wills 11, f. 680v; C. E. Challis, *The Tudor Coinage*, 40, 76, 311. ⁵ *York Civic Recs.* iii. 27–28, 45–46, 66–67, 171–4; York archs. B9, ff. 78, 94; 16, f. 18v. ⁶ York wills 11, f. 680v.

D.M.P.

WRIOTHESLEY, Thomas (1505–50), of Micheldever and Titchfield, Hants and Lincoln Place, London.

HAMPSHIRE 1539,[1] 1542*

b. 21 Dec. 1505, 1st s. of William Writh *alias* Wriothesley of London by Agnes, da. of James Drayton of London. *educ.* St. Paul's; Trinity Hall, Camb. *m.* by 1533, Jane, da. of William Cheyne of Chesham Bois, Bucks., 3s. 5da. *suc.* fa. 1513. Kntd. 18 Apr. 1540; KG nom. 23 Apr., inst. 17 May 1545; *cr.* Baron Wriothesley 1 Jan. 1544, Earl of Southampton 16 Feb. 1547.[2]

Clerk, the signet by May 1530–Apr. 1540; bailiff, manors of Snitterfield and Warwick, Warws. 29 Aug. 1535–*d.*; engraver, Tower mint 29 May 1536–31 Mar. 1544; constable, Donnington castle, Berks. 21 July 1536, Southampton castle, Hants 7 Jan. 1541–*d.*, Christchurch castle 20 Feb. 1541–*d.*, Portchester castle 28 Oct. 1542–*d.*; j.p. Hants 1538–46 or later; jt. ambassador to the Queen of Hungary Sept. 1538–Mar. 1539; principal sec. to the King Apr. 1540–Apr. 1544; PC Apr. 1540—Mar. 1547, rest. early 1548–?*d.*; steward, manors of Christchurch and Ringwood, Hants 20 Feb. 1541, forfeited lands of Margaret, Countess of Salisbury 28 Oct. 1542; jt. (with Thomas White II*) clerk of the crown and King's attorney KB 1542–*d.*; commr. loan, London 1542, array, six southern counties 1545, contribution, London 1546; chamberlain, receipt of the Exchequer 28 Jan. 1543–?*d.*; high steward, borough of Andover, Hants 14 May 1543; treasurer of the wars Jan.–Apr.

1544; ld. keeper of the great seal 22 Apr.–3 May 1544; ld. chancellor 3 May 1544–6 Mar. 1547.[3]

Thomas Wriothesley came of a line of heralds: his paternal grandfather John Writh was Garter King of arms, his father William Writh *alias* Wriothesley York herald, his uncle Sir Thomas Writh *alias* Wriothesley John Writh's successor as Garter, and his cousin, the chronicler Charles Wriothesley, Windsor herald. It was his uncle Sir Thomas who on appointment as Garter adopted the surname Wriothesley in preference to Writh, and the example was followed by others in the family.[4]

When his father died the care of the eight year-old Wriothesley was shared between his mother and uncle who seems to have encouraged him to follow his great-grandfather William Writh[†] into the law. A contemporary of John Leland and William Paget at St. Paul's, he studied civil law at Cambridge with Paget under the supervision of Stephen Gardiner, perhaps at the expense of Thomas Boleyn. Wriothesley is not known to have graduated but he seems to have followed Gardiner into the service of Cardinal Wolsey. There he met Thomas Cromwell whom as early as 1524 he was to call master. Since his early advancement was evidently the work of Gardiner his assurance of obedience to Cromwell in 1524 was perhaps merely a formal courtesy, but it could signify a spell at an inn of chancery under the tutelage of Cromwell before admission to Gray's Inn in 1534, which accords well with his later career. By 1529 he was clerk to Gardiner's kinsman, the cofferer of the Household, Edmund Peckham*, but within a year he had been named as one of the clerks of the signet, presumably by Gardiner as the King's secretary, and had taken up residence in Gardiner's house.[5]

Wriothesley probably ingratiated himself with Henry VIII by his diligence in the King's great matter. It was on the recommendation of Cromwell that in 1531 he received an annuity out of St. Mary's abbey, York. Late in 1532 he was sent abroad as a bearer of despatches, and he was to fulfil several similar missions before Gardiner's resignation as secretary. He continued as clerk of the signet under Cromwell, who used him as a personal representative in the privy seal office. His emergence as a spokesman of anti-clericalism, and his proposal to use ex-monastic land to endow hospitals, to support a standing army, and to provide funds for poor relief, won him commendation from Cromwell but alienated him from Gardiner, who was later to regret the loss of their former friendship.

After supervising the demolition of St. Swithin's shrine at Winchester in 1538 Wriothesley was sent as ambassador to the Regent of the Netherlands for the abortive marriage negotiation between the King and the Duchess of Milan. Given leave to depart from Brussels on 19 Mar. 1539, he returned to receive news of his election as knight of the shire for Hampshire from the sheriff John Kingsmill. Cromwell had nominated him, and the cellarer of the Household, Richard Hill of Hartley Wintney, had rallied his neighbours and tenants to ensure Wriothesley's return, with the other nominee Richard Worsley, against opposition from Gardiner. Kingsmill also asked Wriothesley to remind Cromwell of the promise made to him about his own return to the Parliament and went on to commend John Dale (q.v.), who 'says he will follow your advice if it please you to get him [a] place'. Before the Parliament assembled Wriothesley went down to Hampshire where he upheld the King's religious policy. In mid April William Petre* advised him 'to make himself strong against Parliament' but a week later he had not returned to London although he was daily expected. Of his part in this Parliament all that has come to light is that, on his appointment with Ralph Sadler* as principal secretary, the King set aside the recent Act (31 Hen. VIII, c.10) requiring the secretary to attend in the Lords by allowing them to sit alternate weeks in the Commons 'where they now have places'.[6]

Early in the third session Wriothesley was knighted at the time of Cromwell's ennoblement, and the minister's subsequent fall might well have brought him down also; thus his omission, in favour of his kinsman Richard Lyster, from the list of Members charged with supervising the collection of the subsidy could have been a reflection of his weakened position rather than a concession to his preoccupations as senior secretary. He is thought by some to have been the 'secret friend' of Gardiner who was accused by an anonymous writer of duplicity towards Cromwell, but his identification with the man whom the minister had trusted 'as brother to brother' is dubious. He was certainly active in the annulment of the Cleves marriage which under Cromwell he had helped to promote, but this may have been prompted by the danger which he was thought to be in by the imperial ambassador. He weathered the charges brought against him by Walter Chandler* and others, and kept his place on the Council. His inquiry into Catherine Howard's indiscretions was followed by his re-election for Hampshire to the Parliament which attainted her. During the first session he was instructed to report to the King on a debate on Irish affairs in the Lords, and in that and the next he signed the Acts for the manor of Blewbury in Berkshire and for the naturalization of Thomas Brandling's children. His elevation to the peerage on the eve of the final session presumably caused a by-election, but it is not known who took his place in the Commons. He was admitted to the Lords on the third day of the session and until he became immersed in the preparations for war he attended there regularly.[7]

On Audley's death Wriothesley was made lord keeper and shortly afterwards chancellor. His diverse activities during the last three years of the reign, especially in raising revenue, earned praise from the King and many others: even Sir Richard Morison*, who disliked him, admitted that he was 'an earnest follower of whatever he took in hand, and very seldom did miss where wit and travail were able to bring his purpose'. He was responsible for summoning the Parliament of 1545 and its repeated postponement greatly exercised him. Evidence of his influence at the elections is scanty, but John Fryer clearly owed his Membership for Portsmouth to being Wriothesley's physician. It fell to him to open the Parliament, to preside over the Lords and to pronounce prorogation and dissolution. During the first session he obtained a private Act (37 Hen. VIII, c.26) confirming an exchange of lands between the Earl of Hertford, the bishop of Salisbury and himself. Henry VIII attended the prorogation and once Wriothesley had finished speaking the King reminded the assembly:

> Although my chancellor for the time being hath before this time used very eloquently and substantially to make answer to such ovations, yet he is not able to open and set forth my mind and meaning, and the secrets of my heart in so plain and ample manner as I myself am and can do.

He was one of the panel empowered to sign Acts on the King's behalf during the second session: the only measure on which its members were apparently unanimous was that for the attainder of the Earl of Surrey, and Wriothesley's defence of Chancery against the proposal to unite the court of general surveyors with the augmentations almost certainly accounts for the delay in its engrossment before being sent to the Commons on the eve of dissolution. He wept when before dissolving the Parliament he announced the King's death.[8]

Under Henry VIII's will Wriothesley was named an executor, and according to the testimony of secretary Paget as to the King's intentions he was to receive £500 and an earldom. Edward VI reinvested him in the chancellorship but the mutual dislike between him and the Duke of Somerset, his opposition to the Protectorate and his championship of his own court provoked his dismissal. The allegations of incompetence and transgression of authority brought against him in the Council by certain unnamed

common lawyers, although not substantiated before the tribunal which degraded him, have given rise to the tradition that he was unsuited to the office. After a period of confinement to his London house he was given his liberty but not restored to the Council. Thus freed from public commitments, he was able to devote himself to his own and his county's affairs, and he seems to have played a more prominent part in the Hampshire elections of 1547 than previously. His own appearance at the opening of the Parliament was commented upon by the imperial ambassador. He attended the first session almost daily, having four bills committed to him, one being for the erection of a new court of Chancery for ecclesiastical causes which came to nothing, and taking part in the conference between both Houses for the repeal of the heresy laws. He was equally regular in the second session, when he at first opposed the Act of Uniformity (2 and 3 Edw. VI, c.1) but 'lost his constancy in the end and agreed to everything' shortly before being reinstated in the Council. During the second prorogation he was ruthless in preventing the spread of insurrection from the south-west to Hampshire and his discontent at Somerset's handling of the affair combined with his personal dislike of the Protector made him a ready accomplice in the Earl of Warwick's *coup* of October 1549.[9]

The resulting transformation of Wriothesley's position elicited John Ponet's comment, 'Wriothesley that before was banished the court is lodged with his wife and son next to the King. Every man repaireth to Wriothesley, honoureth Wriothesley, sueth unto Wriothesley and all things [are] done by his advice.' He did not long enjoy this ascendancy. In the summer he had excused himself through ill-health from joining in the embassy to negotiate peace with France; by the autumn he was worse and in November he was said to be dying. He seems to have attended only nine days of the third session of the Parliament of 1547, all in the first two months of its sitting, but he was one of the signatories to the Act for the fine and ransom of the Duke of Somerset which was introduced into Parliament only in the third month. In January 1550, after a three months' absence from the Council, he was asked to clarify a legal point and in February he was advised 'to keep his house and not depart thence'. In March the imperial ambassador reported an improvement in his condition but that Wriothesley wished rather 'to be under the earth than upon it'. Reports of his imminent death continued for another three months but it was not until 30 July that he died, and then amid rumours of suicide. He was buried four days later in St. Andrew's Holborn, where the funeral sermon was preached by Bishop Hooper of Gloucester. His corpse was later transferred to Titchfield.[10]

By his will, made on 21 July 1550, Wriothesley left his collar of garters to the King and a cup each to Princess Mary and Elizabeth. After providing for his wife and children he remembered his son-in-law Sir Thomas Radcliffe*, Lord Fitzwalter, and other relatives including his sister the wife of Oliver Lawrence*, 'cousins' William Honing* and John Hungerford*, and the children of Nicholas Cutler* as well as his friend Sir Richard Southwell*, his ward Anthony Rush[†] and his surveyor Thomas Wroth*. He named Sir Edmund Peckham, Sir Thomas Pope* and Sir William Stanford* among the executors and Sir William Petre supervisor. Two codicils added on 23 and 24 July dealt with aspects of the division of the extensive lands that he had obtained in Hampshire and elsewhere which had been overlooked in earlier settlements.[11]

The wardship of Wriothesley's four year-old son Henry was acquired by William Herbert*, Earl of Pembroke. The 2nd Earl of Southampton grew up a notorious Catholic and three of his sisters married into Catholic families, but Wriothesley himself was almost certainly a Protestant. The part he played in the examination of Anne Askew and Dr. Crome was by order of the Council and Gardiner was critical of his attitude as chancellor long before John Foxe described the sufferings of the martyrs. Because Wriothesley grew up a 'man to purge the cankered and rusty hearts from their old superstitions' his early friendship with Gardiner did not last, but the esteem in which Cranmer came to hold him must have provided some compensation. There seems to be no reason to mistrust the acknowledgements of his part in some conversions, for he maintained several Protestants and paid Richard Cox a pension as an exile during the 1540s. His vitriolic attack upon the papacy on taking the oath as chancellor had not been required of him by the King and was not to be repeated by his successors, but it accords well with his choice of Hooper to preach at his funeral. A drawing of Wriothesley by Holbein survives.[12]

[1] LP Hen. VIII, xiv(1), 662 citing SP1/146, pp. 237–40; E159/319, brev. ret. Mich. r. [1–2]. [2] Date of birth given in Ald. Ch. 16194. This biography rests on C. J. Adams 'Tudor minister: Sir Thomas Wriothesley' (Manchester Univ. M.A. thesis, 1970). [3] Brit. Numismatic Jnl. xlv. 71–72; NRA 8800, pt. i. no. 158; LP Hen. VIII, xiii. [4] A. Wagner, Heralds of England, 129, 146–7; Heralds and Heraldry, 86. [5] M. L. Robertson, 'Cromwell's servants' (Univ. California Los Angeles Ph.D. thesis, 1975), 591–3. [6] LP Hen. VIII, xiv; Elton, Tudor Constitution, 121–3, 292; Policy and Police, 369–70. [7] E159/319, brev. ret. Mich. r. [1–2]; Vis. Hants (Harl. Soc. lxiv), 45; Elton, 'Thomas Cromwell's decline and fall', Studies in Tudor and Stuart Pol. and Govt. i. 189–230; Bull IHR, vi. 22; House of Lords RO, Original Acts, 33Hen. VIII, no. 40, 34 and 35 Hen. VIII, no. 41. [8] LP Hen. VIII, xx; Tudor Men and Institutions, ed. Slavin, 49–69. [9] Wealth and Power, ed. Ives, Knecht and Scarisbrick, 88, 90, 96; A. J. Slavin, 'The fall of Lord Chancellor Wriothesley', Albion, vii. 265–86; M. A. R. Graves, 'The Tudor House of Lords 1547–58' (Otago Univ. Ph.D. thesis, 1974), ii. 289–90. [10] Graves, ii. 290; House of Lords RO, Original Acts, 3 and 4 Edw. VI, no. 31. [11] PCC 13 Bucke; L. Stone, Fam. and Fortune, 209–11. [12] CP, xii(1),

126–7; CPR, 1549–51, p. 300; Holbein (The Queen's Gallery, Buckingham Palace 1978–79), 12.

A.D.K.H.

WROTH, Robert (1488/89–1535), of Durants, Enfield, Mdx.

MIDDLESEX 1529*

b. 1488/89, 2nd but 1st surv. s. of John Wroth of Durants by Joan. educ. G. Inn. m. by 1517, Jane, da. of Sir Thomas Haute of Kent, wid. of Thomas Goodere of Hadley, Herts., 4s. inc. Thomas* 2da. suc. fa. 23 Aug. 1517.[1]

J.p. Mdx. 1522–d.; commr. subsidy 1523, 1524; other commissions, Herts., London and Mdx. 1525–d.; steward, manor of Cheshunt, Herts. 1524–d.; attorney-gen. duchy of Lancaster 1531–d., steward, Savoy manor 1532–d., Herts. and Mdx. 1534–d.; steward, Finsbury, Mdx. 1532–d.; jt. (with Thomas Cromwell) steward, Westminster abbey 1534–d.; steward, manor of Edmonton, Mdx. Feb. 1535–d.[2]

Robert Wroth was in his late twenties when he inherited the manor of Durants, in Enfield, which had been the family residence since the early 15th century, with the greater part of his father's lands in Essex, Hertfordshire, Middlesex and Somerset. In 1518 he was granted livery of the lands in Somerset, Richard Hawkes* entering into bond with him for the payment of what was due to the crown.[3]

Wroth had been educated at Gray's Inn, where he was elected Autumn reader in 1528 but did not read, and it was through the law that he made his way in the world. He was retained as counsel by his influential neighbour Sir Thomas Lovell I*, from whom shortly before Lovell's death in 1524 he was given the reversion of the stewardship of Cheshunt, and whose will included a bequest to him of a silver cup and £5: the young gentlemen then in Lovell's household included Wroth's stepson Francis Goodere*. Wroth's most important appointment was as attorney-general of the duchy of Lancaster in 1531; his other offices included stewardships of lands belonging to the city of London and to the crown. Several of his forbears had been knights of the shire for Middlesex, and as a rising lawyer Wroth was probably able to add crown support to his own claim to be returned as senior knight in 1529 and may have had a hand in the choice of his colleague Hawkes. He became a friend of Cromwell whom he advised in 1532 on a point of law; on 14 Feb. 1534 Cromwell and Wroth were jointly appointed to the stewardship of Westminster abbey, an office which Cromwell had held alone since the previous September. Wroth's name was included in a list drawn up by the minister on the back of a letter of December 1534 and thought to be of Members with a particular but unknown interest in the treasons bill then on its passage through Parliament.[4]

Wroth died in his mid forties and while still a Member of the Parliament of 1529, in which he is not known to have been replaced for the last session. He made his will on 8 May 1535, 'every day looking for the messenger of God', who summoned him three days later. He bequeathed his best grey horse to Cromwell and a black colt to Sir William Fitz-william I*, his chief in the duchy of Lancaster, while two thirds of all his lands went to his wife for the education of his children 'in virtue and learning'. In accordance with the will Wroth's ward Edward Lewknor* married his daughter Dorothy.[5]

[1] Date of birth estimated from age at fa.'s i.p.m.s, C142/32/31, 83, 57/7, 33. PCC 36 Hogen, 16 Pyckering correcting visitation peds. as *Vis. Essex* (Harl. Soc. xiii), 132; *LP Hen. VIII*, ii; D. O. Pam, *Protestant Gentlemen: the Wroths of Enfield and Loughton* (Edmonton Hundred Hist. Soc. occasional ppr. n.s. xxv), passim. [2] *LP Hen. VIII*, iii, iv, viii; Somerville, *Duchy*, i. 407; Somerville, *The Savoy*, 235; City of London RO, Guildhall, rep. 8, f. 233; Westminster abbey, reg. 3, f. 298v. [3] W. Robinson, *Enfield*, i. 143; *LP Hen. VIII*, ii. [4] *G.I. Adm.* 2; Dugdale, *Origines Juridiciales*, 292; *LP Hen. VIII*, iii–v, vii, viii; *HMC Rutland*, iv. 260; PCC 27 Jankyn; Westminster abbey, reg. 3, ff. 288, 298v. [5] PCC 36 Hogen; C142/57/7, 33; *LP Hen. VIII*, xi.

H.M.

WROTH, Thomas (1518–73), of Durants, Enfield, Mdx. and London.

MIDDLESEX 1545, 1547[1], 1553 (Mar.), 1559, 1563

b. 1518, o.s. of Robert Wroth*, and half-bro. of Francis Goodere*. *educ.* St. John's, Camb.; G. Inn, adm. 1536. *m.* 1538, Mary, da. of Richard Rich, 1st Baron Rich, 7s. inc. John†, Richard† and Robert† 7da. *suc.* fa. 11 May 1535. Kntd. 22 Feb. 1547.[2]

Gent. usher, the chamber to Prince Edward 1541–7; gent., the privy chamber 1547–9, principal gent. 1549–53; standard bearer Jan.–Nov. 1549; commr. relief, Mdx. 1550, goods of churches and fraternities 1553, subsidy 1563, musters 1569, benevolence, Essex, Mdx. 1564, eccles. causes 1572; other commissions 1540–70; bailiff, manors of Enfield 1550–*d.*, Ware, Herts. 1551–3; jt. ld. lt. Mdx. 1551, 1552, 1553; keeper, Syon house and steward, lordship of Isleworth, Mdx. 1552–3; steward, manors of Elsing and Worcesters in Enfield 1553–9, Edmonton, Mdx. 1553–*d.*; master forester, Enfield chase 1553–9, woodward 1564–6; j.p.q. Mdx. 1558/59–*d.*, Essex 1561–*d.*; keeper, manor of Elsing 1560–*d.*; special commr. to consult with ld. dep. on govt. of Ireland 1562; custos rot. Mdx. by 1564–*d.*[3]

In October 1536 the wardship of Thomas Wroth was granted to Cromwell who had been a friend of his father. He was then 18 years old and negotiations for his marriage opened in the following year with an offer by Sir Brian Tuke of one of his daughters. This came to nothing, but in 1538 Cromwell sold the marriage to Sir Richard Rich for 300 marks and Wroth married Rich's third daughter Mary. In April 1540 he was granted livery of the lands which had descended to him from his father: a month later he increased this substantial inheritance by purchasing lands in Hertfordshire and Middlesex from Cromwell and Rich, the commissioners for the sale

of crown lands. After the fall of Cromwell he obtained a lease of the minister's manor of Highbury, Middlesex, and in 1544 he bought a manor in Hertfordshire.[4]

Wroth was appointed a gentleman usher to Prince Edward in October 1541 and began a career in the royal service which presumably accounts for his earlier appearances in Parliament and for his knighthood. In 1547 he was sent north to congratulate the Protector Somerset on the victory at Pinkie and two years later he was appointed standard bearer during the minority of Sir Anthony Browne*. On the fall of Somerset he was promoted to be one of the four principal gentlemen of the privy chamber, of whom at least two were to be continually attendant upon the King: their salaries were raised from £50 to £100 'in consideration of the singular care and travail that they should have about his majesty's person'. Besides his duties about the King he was employed on special commissions for the better execution of penal laws, for the recovery of outstanding debts to the crown and for the reform of the revenue courts. He was rewarded for his services by appointment to a number of offices in the administration of crown lands and by the grant of four manors in Essex, three in Middlesex, one in Somerset and two in Sussex; the reversion to two monastic houses, which he also received, he re-sold within two or three years.[5]

Although Wroth signed the letters patent of 7 June 1553 devising the crown to Jane Grey and also attended the King on his deathbed, he took no part in the attempt to force the King's supposed will upon the country. He helped to proclaim Mary Queen in Cheapside on 19 July but a week later he was sent to the Tower: he was not held in prison for long and on 9 Oct. 1553 he was granted a general pardon. Early in the following year he was suspected of complicity in the rising of Henry Grey, Duke of Suffolk. He was approached by the conspirators and although he refused to join them Stephen Gardiner advised his arrest. He fled overseas, arriving at Padua with Sir John Cheke* in July 1554, and remained abroad for the rest of the reign, first in Italy and from 1555 at Strasbourg. In August 1556 a messenger from the Queen arrived to recall him to England, but Wroth managed to hide from him and when the messenger had left he applied to the magistrate of Strasbourg for a residence permit. This was renewed in 1557, when he declared that he was an exile for the sake of religion, and again in 1558. Directly the news of Mary's death reached him Wroth set out for home, leaving Strasbourg on 20 Dec. 1558.[6]

The ascendancy which Wroth and other exiles had hoped for in the England of Elizabeth was not vouchsafed them. Wroth recovered few of his lost offices and became a country gentleman rather than a courtier until his death on 9 Oct. 1573.[7]

[1] Hatfield 207. [2] Aged 17 and more at fa.'s death, C142/57/7, 33, and 32 or thereabouts at Gardiner's trial in 1551, Foxe, *Acts and Mons.* vi. 148. PCC 36 Hogen, 16 Pyckering; D. O. Pam, *Protestant Gentlemen: the Wroths of Enfield and Loughton* (Edmonton Hundred Hist. Soc. occasional ppr. n.s. xxv), passim; *DNB;* C142/171/97. [3] W. C. Richardson, *Ct. Augmentations,* 470; *LP Hen. VIII,* xvi, xvii, xxi; *APC,* ii–iv passim; *CPR,* 1549–51 to 1569–72 passim; Somerville, *Duchy,* i. 612–13; *CSP Dom.* 1547–80, p. 40; *CSP Ire.* 1509–73, pp. 230, 246. [4] *LP Hen. VIII,* xi, xii, xiv–xvi, xix; M. L. Robertson, 'Cromwell's servants' (Univ. California Los Angeles Ph.D. thesis, 1975), 593. [5] *LP Hen. VIII,* xxi; W. K. Jordan, *Edw. VI,* ii. 20; *Lit. Rems. Edw. VI,* 224, 403, 469, 499–501; *Rep. R. Comm. of 1552* (Archs. of Brit. Hist. and Culture iii), pp. xxvi, 76, 82; Richardson, 198; Elton, *Tudor Rev. in Govt.* 230; *VCH Mdx.* ii. 30–31; iii. 103; iv. 114. [6] Jordan, ii. 519; *Chron. Q. Jane and Q. Mary* (Cam. Soc. xlviii), 100, 182, 184; *Grey Friars Chron.* (Cam. Soc. liii), 81; Pam, 6; *CPR,* 1553–4, p. 436; D. M. Loades, *Two Tudor Conspiracies,* 27, 263; *CSP For.* 1553–8, p. 112; *Cam. Misc.* x(2) 116–19; C. H. Garrett, *Marian Exiles,* 345–6; *Zurich Letters 1558–79* (Parker Soc.), 3–6. [7] C142/171/97.

H.M.

WROUGHTON, Sir William (1509/10–59), of Broad Hinton, Wilts.

WILTSHIRE 1547,[1] 1554 (Apr.)

b. 1509/10, o.s. of William Wroughton of Broad Hinton by Anne, da. of Sir William Norris[†] of Yattendon, Berks. *m.* (1) Elizabeth, da. of George Twyneho of Keyford by Frome, Som., *s.p.*; (2) by 1540, Eleanor, da. of Edward Lewknor of Kingston Buci, Suss., 4s. inc. James[†] and Thomas[†] 3da. *suc.* gdfa. 4 Aug. 1515. Kntd. 11 May 1544.[2]

Lt. and chief forester, Chute forest, Wilts. 1542; j.p. Wilts. 1543–7, 1558/59; commr. musters 1546, chantries, Wilts. and Salisbury 1548, relief, Wilts. 1550, goods of churches and fraternities 1553; other commissions 1544–54.[3]

His father's early death left William Wroughton the heir to his grandfather, Sir Christopher Wroughton[†], who died in 1515 possessed of the ancestral manor of Broad Hinton, near Swindon, and numerous estates in Gloucestershire, Somerset and Wiltshire. In the following year Sir John Seymour[*] paid £500 for Wroughton's wardship and on coming of age the heir was licensed to enter on 30 Mar. 1531. His mother married Sir John Baldwin[*], who died in October 1545, whereupon Seymour's son the Earl of Hertford tried to have her placed in Wroughton's care, since she had for long been 'abstracted of her wits'.[4]

When musters were taken in 1539 Wroughton and his servants accounted for 13 men in the hundred of Ramsbury. Since he was among the esquires appointed to welcome Anne of Cleves, his wife may have been the Mistress Wroughton listed among the ladies of the Queen's household in 1540. Four years later he joined Hertford on his Scottish campaign and was paid for conducting 100 men from York to Newcastle before being knighted by the earl at Leith. Wroughton was a victim of ill-health: in 1546 he was noted as 'sick' on a list of gentry who were to attend the court during the embassy of the Admiral of France, and in November 1548 he was to be absent from Parliament with an attack of his 'old disease of the colic and stone'.[5]

It is not clear how closely the Wroughtons were related to the Seymours, but Hertford described Wroughton as kinsman when seeking for him the custody of his mother. The relationship and their service together may have led Hertford, when Protector and Duke of Somerset, to promote his return as a knight of the shire to the Parliament of 1547. His presence on several local commissions, in particular those concerned with the spoliation of the Church, suggests that Wroughton was ready to serve both Somerset and the more extreme reformers who displaced him, but he was passed over three times in succession for the shrievalty and he is not known to have bought any monastic or chantry lands, despite Aubrey's statement that he built a new mansion at Broad Hinton from the stones of Bradenstoke abbey.[6]

On 22 July 1553 Wroughton joined with (Sir) John Bonham[*], Sir James Stumpe[*] and (Sir) John Thynne[*] (who was to marry his daughter Dorothy), in a declaration of allegiance to Queen Mary and three days later they were thanked for their service and instructed to remain in Wiltshire. Wroughton does not seem to have been involved in the subsequent quarrel between Thynne and Charles, 8th Baron Stourton. Although he was elected with Sir John Marvyn to Mary's second Parliament, he is rarely mentioned during her reign. He may have been returned with the support of Sir William Herbert, formerly his fellow-Member and now Earl of Pembroke, whose tenant at 'Montour' he was at the time of his death. After interfering in defence of some unnamed retainers who had been implicated in a robbery, he was committed to close custody in the Fleet on 4 Nov. 1556 and at the end of the month was forced to enter into a bond of 2,000 marks for his good behaviour: in the previous September his wife's nephew Edward Lewknor[*] had died in the Tower while awaiting execution for his part in the Dudley conspiracy. Wroughton may have been kept out of Mary's later Parliaments by this offence and perhaps also by his health; while he was in the Fleet the warden had been ordered to allow him the freedom of the prison on account of his sickness.[7]

Wroughton made his will on 10 Sept. 1558, committing his soul to 'Jesus Christ, my Redeemer' and asking for burial wherever it should please his executors. The widow was to have all his lands in Broad Hinton, Hinton Columbine, Medbourne and Woodhill, Wiltshire, for life, as her agreed jointure, although the rectories of Broad Hinton and Wroughton were to pass respectively to their first and second sons, Thomas and George, when they should come of age. Thomas also received livestock and some specified jewellery, and shared plate and household goods with his mother; George and a third son William were each to have 20 marks a year from the rectory of Wroughton or, if the title should be held invalid, from lands at Beversbrook. Further lands and £100 were left to the youngest son James, and £200 apiece to two daughters, Dorothy and Anne; a third daughter, recorded by Aubrey from the memorial in Broad Hinton church, must have died young, since there is no other reference to her. The widow, who was left £100 and the residue, was appointed executrix, with Thomas Wroughton as co-executor and 'my brother Hassett', that is, John Blennerhasset* (he and Wroughton had married half-sisters), John Erneley†, Richard Kingsmill† and John St. John*, as overseers. An inquisition taken on 18 Sept. 1559 found that Wroughton had died on 4 Sept. and that his eldest son, whose wardship was granted to John Berwick*, was then aged 19. His widow married Sir Giles Poole*.[8]

[1] Hatfield 207.   [2] Date of birth estimated from age at grandfather's i.p.m., C142/30/27. *Aubrey, Wilts. Topog. Colls.* ed. Jackson, 336; *Wilts. Vis. Peds.* (Harl. Soc. cv, cvi), 219; *Vis. Som.* ed. Weaver, 132; *Vis. Dorset* (Harl. Soc. xx), 95; E150/999/24; *LP Hen. VIII,* xix. [3] *LP Hen. VIII,* xvii, xx, xxi; *CPR,* 1547-8, p. 91; 1548-9, p. 135; 1550-3, pp. 142, 396; 1553, pp. 359, 415; 1553-4, p. 28. [4] C142/30/27, 118(2), 119; Index 10217(1), f. 2v; *LP Hen. VIII,* ii, v, xx. [5] *LP Hen. VIII,* xiv, xv, xix, xxi; Bath mss, Thynne pprs. 2, f. 33. [6] *LP Hen. VIII,* xx; *CPR,* 1553, pp. 339, 349, 376; *Aubrey,* 189. [7] Bath mss, Thynne pprs. 2, ff. 184-5v; *Wilts. Arch. Mag.* viii. 311-12; E150/999/24; *APC,* vi. 15, 17, 25. [8] PCC 6 Street; *Aubrey,* 336; Comber, *Suss. Genealogies (Lewes),* 159; *CPR,* 1560-3, p. 23.

T.F.T.B.

WYATT, Sir Thomas I (by 1504-42), of Allington Castle, Kent.

KENT 1542*

b. by 1504, 1st s. of Sir Henry Wyatt of Allington Castle by Anne, da. of John Skinner† of Reigate, Surr. *educ.* St. John's, Camb. BA 1518, MA 1520. *m.* by 1521, Elizabeth, da. of Thomas Brooke, 8th Lord Cobham, 1s. Sir Thomas II*; 2s. illegit. by Elizabeth, da. of Sir Edward Darrell* of Littlecote, Wilts.; 1 da. (?illegit.). Kntd. ?28 Mar. 1535. *suc.* fa. 10 Nov. 1536.[1]

Esquire of the body by 1524; clerk of the King's jewels 21 Oct. 1524; marshal, Calais by Sept. 1529-24 Nov. 1530; sewer extraordinary by 1533; sheriff, Kent 1536-7; ambassador to the Emperor 1537-40; Councillor by 1540-*d.*; commr. sewers, Kent 1540; steward, manor of Maidstone, Kent Mar. 1542.[2]

Sir Henry Wyatt was treasurer of the chamber and his son, after taking a degree at Cambridge, began his career in the royal household whence he quickly moved into diplomacy. Early in 1526 he accompanied Sir Thomas Cheyne* on an embassy to France, returning briefly to England in May with letters to the King and Wolsey, which he supplemented from his own observations, and a commen-

dation from Cheyne. His next mission arose, so tradition has it, from his having met Sir John Russell* sailing down the Thames on his way to Italy on the King's service and having offered to accompany him. They travelled to Rome together and were ceremoniously received by the pope. Then as they set out for Venice, Russell's horse fell and he had to return to Rome with a broken leg, responsibility for their mission devolving upon Wyatt. On his way home from Venice, wanting to see the country he visited Ferrara; although he had a safe conduct from the duke he was captured by the Spaniards but managed to escape. Wyatt was next briefly marshal of Calais. A list of officers there, probably dating from 1528, includes his name, and it was as marshal that in September 1529 he was granted a licence to import wine and woad from France; but his patent of appointment was not issued until June 1530 and in November he was replaced by Sir Edward Ryngeley*.[3]

In 1533 Wyatt attended the coronation of Anne Boleyn, acting as chief ewerer in the place of his father. According to Nicholas Harpsfield it was believed that Anne had been Wyatt's mistress and that Wyatt had confessed as much to Henry VIII, who although taken aback had merely bound him to secrecy. The story receives some colour from Wyatt's sudden imprisonment in May 1536 when Anne's infidelities were officially proclaimed. At one point it was rumoured that Wyatt would die with her other alleged lovers, but probably it was never intended that he should be more than a reserve witness against her. On 10 May Cromwell wrote a reassuring letter to Sir Henry Wyatt, who in June received his son home at Allington, advising him—so he assured Cromwell—to obey the King and treat the minister as a father, although both Sir Henry, and Thomas himself after the event, considered that his fault lay less in disobeying human authority than in flouting the law of God.[4]

Cromwell did much for Wyatt in the next few years when he was in need of friends. Although not ostracized by the King, whom later in 1536 he was called on to attend and to support with men against the rebels in the north, Wyatt never rose to high office or wielded power in England. He was a Councillor, but whether he often attended is doubtful; his presence is not recorded in the register kept from 1540. He is not known to have been justice of the peace in Kent, although he had a year as sheriff and he was named to a commission of sewers.[5]

In these years, however, Wyatt was much abroad, returning home on visits in 1538 and 1539 and for good in May 1540. In January 1537 Henry VIII decided to send him as resident ambassador to the

Emperor and in March he was given his instructions. Wyatt's harping on this reversal of fortune— 'Was not that a pretty sending of me ambassador to the Emperor, first to put me into the Tower and then forthwith to send me hither?'—was one of the complaints made against him by Bishop Bonner, who was joined with him in the embassy in 1538. The fall of Cromwell undermined Wyatt's position and on 17 Jan. 1541, some months after he had completed his embassy and been rewarded by an exchange of lands with the King, confirmed by a private Act (32 Hen. VIII, c.77), he was arrested and led, bound, to the Tower. The affair created a great stir. The French ambassador described Wyatt as a courtier, one of the richest gentlemen in England, very popular, although no one now dared speak up for him, and considered that this, his third visit to the Tower—the writer was probably including Wyatt's brief imprisonment in the Fleet in May 1534 for a riot in London—was likely to be his last, since Cromwell's enemies were determined to bring him down. Wyatt vehemently denied the most serious charge, of treasonable correspondence with Cardinal Pole, and defended himself with wit and spirit. Yet formally he submitted himself to the King's mercy and in March 1541 was pardoned for the treason which it seems unlikely that he ever committed: far from being a supporter of Catholicism Wyatt declared that he had been in trouble with the Spanish Inquisition, and after his death he was mourned as a zealous Protestant.[6]

Wyatt soon recovered from this crisis, as he had in 1536. It was rumoured in April 1541 that he had been appointed to command 300 horse at Calais and in August 1542 that he would be captain and vice-admiral of the fleet prepared for action against France. In fact he seems to have spent these 18 months at Allington Castle, which he made more splendid by the addition of a long gallery and more comfortable with panelling and fire places and a new kitchen. In December 1541 he was elected knight of the shire for Kent, and in the following month was appointed bailiff of the manor of South Frith and given the manor of Bayhall, Kent; in March 1542, described as the King's servant, he was granted, with the stewardship of the manor of Maidstone, three ex-monastic properties, including the Carmelite priory at Aylesford, Kent, in exchange for other lands in the county. In 1540 he had been much occupied in the preparation of private bills for the confirmation of his estate and his exchange of lands with the King (31 Hen. VIII, c.28; 32 Hen. VIII, cc.75, 77) but nothing is known of his role in the House during his Membership.[7]

In the autumn of 1542 Wyatt was sent to meet the imperial ambassador at Falmouth and escort him to London. On the way there he died at the home of Sir John Horsey* at Clifton Maybank in Dorset, and he was buried in the Horsey vault in Sherborne abbey on 11 Oct. He was lamented as a friend and poet by the Earl of Surrey, who with him popularized the sonnet in England, and by John Leland. Two drawings and several paintings of Wyatt survive. His widow, from whom he had separated about 1525, married Sir Edward Warner*.[8]

[1] Date of birth estimated from education. *DNB*; *Works of Henry Howard, Earl of Surrey and Sir Thomas Wyatt* ed. Nott, ii. ped.; *Pprs. Geo. Wyatt* (Cam. Soc. ser. 4, v), 5, 6; C142/65/90, 82/64; *LP Hen. VIII*, xviii, xix; *Trans. Cumb. and Westmld. Antiq. and Arch. Soc.* n.s. xxv. 135; information from Dr. D. R. Starkey; *Jnl. Eng. and Germanic Philology*, lx. 268–72. [2] *LP Hen. VIII*, ii, iv, v, xi, xvi, xvii; P. T. J. Morgan, 'The govt. of Calais, 1485–1558' (Oxf. Univ. D.Phil. thesis, 1966), 295; *Works*, ii. p. lxxiv. [3] *LP Hen. VIII*, iv; *Gent. Mag.* 1850(ii), 237; *CSP Ven.* 1527–33, no. 50. [4] *LP Hen. VIII*, vi, x, xiii; N. Harpsfield, *A Treatise on the Pretended Divorce* (Cam. Soc. n.s. xxi), 253. [5] *LP Hen. VIII*, xi, xvi. [6] Ibid. vii, xii–xvi; *Gent. Mag.* 1850(i), 565–8. [7] *LP Hen. VIII*, xv–xvii; *Arch. Cant.* xxviii. 355–6. [8] *LP Hen. VIII*, xvi, xvii; *Works*, i.p. lxxiv; R. C. Strong, *Tudor and Jacobean Portraits*, 338–9; Holbein (The Queen's Gallery, Buckingham Palace 1978–9), 119–21; Harl. 6157, f. 10.

H.M.

WYATT, Sir Thomas II (by 1521–54), of Allington Castle, Kent.

KENT 1547[1]

b. by 1521, o.s. of Sir Thomas Wyatt I*. *m.* settlement Mar. 1537, Jane, da. and coh. of Sir William Haute of Bishopsbourne, Kent, 6s. 4da. *suc.* fa. 11 Oct. 1542. Kntd. Jan./May 1545.[2]

Capt. of Bas Boulogne 1545–6; j.p. Kent 1547; commr. relief 1550, goods of churches and fraternities 1553; sheriff 1550–1.[3]

Thomas Wyatt had only recently come of age when his father died in October 1542; a letter from the elder Wyatt in Spain, written in 1537 or 1538, is endorsed in what appears to be a 16th-century hand, 'to his son, then 15 years old'. The father exhorted the son, who was already married, to live contentedly with his wife—something Sir Thomas himself had failed to do—and in general to follow the good example of his grandfather rather than the past behaviour of his father; in another letter he advised the study of moral philosophy. Although Sir Thomas Wyatt stood well with Cromwell, the Thomas Wyatt who entered the minister's household about this time was probably not his son but a namesake, possibly a distant kinsman of Barking, Essex. Wyatt himself was a wild young man, pardoned for robbery in November 1542 and imprisoned in the Tower in April 1543 for eating meat on Fridays and fast days (for which he pleaded a licence) and rioting in London with the Earl of Surrey, a charge which he first denied and then admitted. He was released early in May and a month later was given an outlet for his energies in levying men for the war against France.[4]

Wyatt grasped eagerly at the prospect of active service. Commissioned to lead 100 foot soldiers of the vanguard, he must have acquitted himself well since in November 1544 he was put in charge of part of the garrison of Boulogne and early in 1545 promoted to be captain of Bas Boulogne and member of the council of the town. He remained there for the rest of the year. Writing to Sir William Petre* in December 1545, Secretary Paget recommended him to the King's service. Already a good keeper of discipline and capable of devising sound schemes of fortification, he would, Paget declared, develop with time and experience into a very able soldier; Paget's only misgiving was lest Wyatt should have inherited his father's weakness of 'too strong opinion', but he judged him a wise young man for his age. A few days later the Earl of Surrey wrote to the King in the same vein: Wyatt was anxious to pay a visit home and Surrey begged leave for him to report on the progress of the campaign.[5]

Early in the New Year Wyatt was back in Boulogne, taking part in a raid which cost the English heavy losses. Although unhurt on this occasion, he was wounded at some other time. In March 1546 the Earl of Hertford arrived in Calais and ordered Wyatt and the surveyor of works at Boulogne to sound the harbour of Ambleteuse; they reported considerable silting. In April Wyatt took part in the survey of Boulogne and joined Hertford in the 'camp near to Newhaven' by the old port of Ambleteuse. He badly wanted to be given the command of the fortress built there and was indeed appointed its captain by Hertford, but in June news came from England that the King had chosen William Stourton*, 7th Baron Stourton; disappointed, Wyatt sought leave to return home. In the following March he was licensed to grant the house of the Crutched Friars in London, which his father had received from Henry VIII, to Admiral Seymour and (Sir) William Sharington*. He sat in Edward VI's first Parliament as a knight of the shire for Kent.[6]

Early in Edward's reign Wyatt and others submitted a general scheme for the establishment of a militia to the Protector Somerset and some of the Council. Although approved in principle, the scheme was not carried further, 'either for the newness of the thing', Wyatt's son George later explained, 'or for that it was not at that season thought so convenient to have the subjects armed, whereof the greater numbers were evil affected to the religion then professed, or for that some division then being amongst those that bore the sway, some hindered

that the other liked of'. Wyatt and his friends, who included Sir James Croft*, Sir William Pickering*, Robert Rudston* and Sir James Wilford*, thereupon prepared a more detailed plan 'to be tendered and viewed over by the then lord Protector's grace to have been established by Parliament'. According to his son, Wyatt's own contribution, of which two fragments survive, was based upon his observations of military practice 'in Italy, Germany and France and especially amongst the Switzers', travels which have not been recorded elsewhere. The proposals again came to nothing but at about the same time Wyatt demonstrated the effectiveness of his ideas by leading the local gentry in the suppression of disorders which broke out in Kent during May 1549. It may have been in part for this service that in June 1550 he was granted the manor of Maidstone, of which his father had been steward. In November 1550 the French ambassador asked that 'some one man of trust' might be sent over to Calais to assist the English commissioners in negotiating with France ways of avoiding further quarrels over the boundaries. It had already been decided to send Wyatt to advise the deputy and council of Calais, and on 11 Nov. he was appointed to join in the negotiations. It was only a short visit; on 16 Nov. the Privy Council ordered him to return and a fortnight later he was said to be too ill to take part in the negotiations.[7]

Whatever Wyatt's private thoughts on the accession of Mary he supported her (so he later claimed) against the Duke of Northumberland; certainly by 19 July 1553 he had proclaimed her Queen. But the news of the Spanish marriage, announced on 15 Jan. 1554, was more than he could endure. Although the Queen instructed Sir Thomas Cornwallis* and Sir Edward Hastings* to explain the situation, and offered to arrange a conference with him, it was to no avail. Declaring that 100 Spaniards had already landed at Dover, he called on the people of Kent to follow him and save England from the foreigners and the Queen from her advisers. This proclamation was read at Maidstone and other places on 25 Jan. and the rebellion began. Wyatt had an early success at Rochester against the 3rd Duke of Norfolk, took Cooling Castle, the home of his uncle the 9th Lord Cobham, with little difficulty, and marched on London. But there his fortunes changed. The Londoners would not support him, and after several days of indecision the final assault on the City failed; Wyatt was taken prisoner at Temple Bar and quickly lodged in the Tower. Five weeks later he was brought to trial and pleaded guilty to high treason but protested that he never intended harm to the Queen herself. On 11 Apr. he was beheaded on Tower Hill, maintaining on the scaffold that Princess

Elizabeth, the Earl of Devon and others were innocent of any part in the uprising. He also besought Secretary Bourne to intercede with the Queen for his wife and children; and although Bourne made no reply at the time, Mary in June 1554 granted Wyatt's widow an annuity of 200 marks and in December 1555 she restored some of Wyatt's lands. In the meantime a bill confirming Wyatt's attainder had failed in the Commons when on 5 May 1554 an amendment from the Lords was rejected, but in the following Parliament a bill to the same effect had been enacted (1 and 2 Phil. and Mary no. 21).[8]

[1] Hatfield 207. [2] Date of birth estimated from age at fa.'s i.p.m., C142/65/90. *Works of Henry Howard, Earl of Surrey and Sir Thomas Wyatt the elder* ed. Nott, ii. ped.; *LP Hen. VIII*, xx; *CPR*, 1555–7, p. 159; *DNB*. [3] *LP Hen. VIII*, xx, xxi; *CPR*, 1547–8, p. 85; 1553, pp. 355, 414. [4] *LP Hen. VIII*, xiii, xvii, xviii; M. L. Robertson, 'Cromwell's servants' (Univ. California Los Angeles Ph.D. thesis, 1975), 594; *PPC*, vii. 104–5, 125–6, 142. [5] *LP Hen. VIII*, xix, xx. [6] Ibid. xxi; *State Trials* ed. Howell, i. 862; *CPR*, 1547–8, p. 3. [7] BM Loan 15/17, 23 ptd. incorrectly *Pprs. Geo. Wyatt* (Cam. Soc. ser. 4, v), 53 seq; D. E. Hoak, *The King's Council in the Reign of Edw. VI*, 199–200; W. K. Jordan, *Edw. VI*, i. 446; ii. 125; *CPR*, 1549–51, p. 337; *APC*, iii. 147, 152, 156, 157. [8] Add. 33230, f. 21; *State Trials*, i. 861–3; *CSP Dom.* 1547–80, p. 56; *Loseley Mss* ed. Kempe, 127; J. Proctor, *The historie of Wyates rebellion (An Eng. Garner*, ed. Arber, viii), passim; D. M. Loades, *Two Tudor Conspiracies*, passim; *Pprs. Geo. Wyatt*, 9–11; *DKR*, iv(2), 24–25; *Chron. Q. Jane and Q. Mary* (Cam. Soc. xlviii), 72–73; *CPR*, 1553–4, p. 275; 1555–7, p. 159; *CJ*, i. 35, 36, 41.

H.M.

WYBURGH, Thomas (by 1460–1531 or later), of Maldon, Essex.

MALDON 1523[1]

b. by 1460.[2]

Warden, Maldon 1481, constable 1489, chamberlain 1492, bailiff 1493–5, 1497–8, 1499–1500, 1503–4, 1510–11, 1512–13, 1516–17, 1518, 1522–4, 1527–8, 1529–30, 1531; commr. subsidy, Maldon 1523, Essex 1524.[3]

The only native and office-holder of Maldon known to have sat for the borough in Parliament during the early Tudor period, Thomas Wyburgh clearly owed his election to his 40 years of municipal service. No evidence has been found that he was paid parliamentary wages, although his fellow-Member John Bozom was, exceptionally, given 40s. His assessment of £260 for the subsidy which he helped to grant—more than double the next largest and far exceeding those of most of his fellow-townsmen—shows that Wyburgh could afford to meet his own costs, and this may mean that he had been elected to the Parliaments of 1512 and 1515, for each of which the name of only one Member has survived. In 1515 the Maldon court book records the admission of John Strangman to the freedom following his election, and its silence in respect of the other Member implies that he was already a freeman.[4]

No trace has been found of Wyburgh's parentage and little of his personal affairs. In 1511 he pur-

chased 24 acres of land at Bradwell-near-the-Sea for £20. He was joint defendant in 1526 or 1527 in a suit in the court of requests for recovery of land at Tillingham, Essex, which he claimed to have quietly enjoyed for over 43 years; the abbot of Waltham, who was commissioned to hear the case, reported that the plaintiff did not pursue the action. The frequency of Wyburgh's mention in the borough records until 1531 makes its disappearance thereafter all but proof of his death at about that time, while the fact that it does not recur in a further generation implies that he left no son or at least none who remained in the town.[5]

[1] Essex RO, D/B3/1/2, f. 98v. [2] Date of birth estimated from first reference. [3] Essex RO, D/B3/1/2, ff. 39v–108 passim; D/DHt/ TI/24, 32; *LP Hen. VIII*, iii, iv. [4] E179/108/148; Essex RO, D/B3/1/2, f. 78; D/B3/3/229. [5] *Essex Feet of Fines*, iv. ed. Reaney and Fitch, 121; Req.2/13/106.

D.F.C.

WYETHE *see* **WYTHE**

WYGSTON *see* **WIGSTON**

WYKES, Nicholas (by 1488–1558), of Dodington, Glos.

GLOUCESTERSHIRE 1554 (Apr.)

b. by 1488, 1st s. of Edmund Wykes of Dodington and Dursley by Elizabeth, da. of Thomas Norton of Bristol. *m.* (1) c. 1508, Elizabeth, da. of Sir Robert Poyntz of Iron Acton by Margaret, illegit. da. of Anthony Wydevill, 2nd Earl Rivers, 6s. 2da.; (2) by 1555, Anne. *suc.* fa. 21 Nov. 1514.[1]

Gent. waiter to Prince Henry 1511; commr. subsidy, Glos. 1524, relief, Glos., Bristol 1550; j.p. Glos. 1531–?*d.*; comptroller of customs, Bristol 1542–5; escheator, Glos. 1544–5; sheriff 1544–5, 1554–5.[2]

Nicholas Wykes's grandfather and father were probably the John and Edmund Wykes admitted to Lincoln's Inn in 1465 and 1486. Whatever his calling, Edmund Wykes secured an important match for his son with the daughter of Sir Robert Poyntz, vice-chamberlain to Catherine of Aragon. Edmund Wykes left to his son the modest family estates in Gloucestershire, two manors in Somerset and four tenements in Bristol obtained through his marriage into the Norton family.[3]

Wykes doubtless secured his post at court through the influence of his wife's family. His sister-in-law Elizabeth Poyntz was nurse to the infant Prince Henry and after the prince's death Wykes may have continued in the Queen's household under his father-in-law. Although he was distantly related to the royal family, Wykes appears to have led an unspectacular life as a country landowner. In 1527 he obtained the grant of a market and two fairs at

Dursley, but his chief dwelling was at Dodington, where according to Leland he restored the house from material brought from the ruins of Dursley castle. Having possessions to the yearly value of £40 or more, he is listed among those who had not compounded for knighthood in 1547. As sheriff in that year he returned his nephew Sir Nicholas Poyntz and Sir Anthony Kingston to Parliament and in 1555 he did the same for Kingston and Sir Nicholas Arnold. His own election to the second Parliament of Mary's reign was a natural extension of his local career. Nothing is known about his part in the House.[4]

Wykes died on 21 Apr. 1558. By his will, written in his own hand on 10 Mar. 1556 although he was a sick man, he asked to be buried near the high altar in Dodington church. He left pieces of land or small sums of money to his five surviving sons and two daughters, and he appointed his son William executor. His heir was his grandson Robert, aged 30 and more, the son of John Wykes who had predeceased him.[5]

[1] Date of birth estimated from age at fa.'s i.p.m., C142/29/87, 98. *Bristol and Glos. Arch. Soc. Trans.* ix. 275–6; *CPR*, 1554–5, p. 139. [2] *LP Hen. VIII*, i, iv, v, viii, xii, xvi, xvii, xx, xxi; *CPR*, 1553, pp. 354, 361; E122/21/6, 15. [3] *CIPM Hen. VII*, i. 68; C142/29/87, 96, 98. [4] *LP Hen. VIII*, i, iv, xiii, xvii, xix; Leland, *Itin.* ed Smith, viii. 130; x. 94; SP10/2/97. [5] PCC 27 Noodes; C142/113/48.

M.K.D.

WYKES, Thomas, of Moreton Jeffries, Herefs.

LEOMINSTER 1554 (Nov.)

1st s. of William Wykes of Moreton Jeffries by Margaret, da. of Thomas ap Henry of Poston in Vowchurch. *m.* (1) Mary, da. of William Nicholas, 1s. 1da.; (2) Elizabeth, da. of Richard Abingdon of Brockhampton, 5s. 4da.[1]

The Thomas Wykes, gentleman, who was returned for Leominster to Mary's third Parliament was almost certainly the head of the family settled at Moreton Jeffries, which lies some ten miles distant from both Leominster and Hereford; none of his various namesakes elsewhere, including one mentioned in the will of Nicholas Wykes* of Dodington, Gloucestershire, appears to have had any connexion with Herefordshire or the marches. What little has come to light about Wykes is mainly derived from his involvement in two lawsuits. The first was a Star Chamber suit brought in the reign of Henry VIII by Thomas ap Harry against William and Thomas Wykes, James Bromwich clerk, William Herford and James Garreway, for kidnapping his cousin George and taking him into Wales. If, as is likely, the plaintiff was the Thomas ap Harry who died in December 1522, the case can be assigned to the early years of the reign, a conclusion which is borne out by the appearance among the defendants of Thomas

Wykes's father. That William Wykes died about 1530 is suggested by his son's testimony in the second suit, brought in Chancery by Richard Pauncefoot between 1547 and 1551: to Pauncefoot's complaint that Wykes was evading arbitration in a dispute between them over the ownership of a messuage and 60 acres at Moreton Jeffries, Wykes replied that these had descended 60 years before from his grandfather to his father, who then held them for 28 years before he himself succeeded. This he had certainly done by 1542, when he alone appears in the Herefordshire muster book as responsible for the accoutrements of five archers and three billmen.[2]

Wykes was therefore well advanced in years when he attended his only Parliament. His return for Leominster, a borough which had twice elected his grandfather, but with which he himself had no clear connexion, is probably to be attributed to the influence of Sir John Price*, secretary to the council in the marches and sheriff of Herefordshire at the time of the election; his fellow-Member Nicholas Depden almost certainly had council support, as had the two previous Members, John Evans and Lewis Jones. No link has been found between Wykes and Price save the nearness of their residences, although the fact that Price had married a granddaughter of Henry Wykes of Putney is suggestive of a family relationship. Wykes was not among the Members who quitted this Parliament without leave before its dissolution. This piece of negative evidence is the last trace found of him. His second son Richard was to be killed at Le Havre in 1563.[3]

[1] *Vis. Herefs.* ed. Weaver, 78–79. [2] PCC 27 Noodes; St.Ch.2/30/45; *Vis. Herefs.* 4; C1/1253/9–11; *LP Hen. VIII*, xvii. [3] *HP*, ed. Wedgwood, 1439–1509 (Biogs.), 927; *Vis. Herefs.* 79.

P.S.E.

WYMOND, Robert (by 1508–49), of Rye, Suss· and Goudhurst, Kent.

RYE 1545[1]

b. by 1508, 3rd s. of Robert Wymond (*d.* 1510) of Rye by Joan. *m.* Dorothy, 2s. 1da.[2]
Chamberlain, Rye 1537–8, jurat 1538–9, 1541–3, 1544–8; bailiff to Yarmouth 1540.[3]

Robert Wymond came of a line of merchants but his own occupation has not been traced. In 1533 he and a fellow-townsman told Cromwell of a conversation in which the parish priest William Inold had upheld papal supremacy and of rumours following the King's marriage to Anne Boleyn that excommunication would help the Emperor and the Danes to conquer England. Four years later he himself denied charges of heresy brought by Inold. Several of his friends and colleagues were similarly accused at the same time, among them William Mede*, whose executor he became in 1543, and Alexander Welles, his fellow-Member.[4]

All that is known of Wymond's attendance at the Parliament of 1545 is that he and Welles received between them £12 paid in three instalments for their expenses and that Wymond had a further 2s. after the King's death. He was related, perhaps only by marriage, to John Eston who sat in the same Parliament for Wigan. It is possible that he was re-elected to the next Parliament and even that he attended its first session. He and Alexander Welles are named as the Members for Rye on a list compiled from the collections of a 17th-century lieutenant of Dover Castle, whereas the town paid Welles and George Reynolds for their attendance from the opening of the second session in November 1548. Unless the list in question made the mistake of repeating the names from the previous Parliament, the discrepancy is best resolved by assuming that Wymond was elected with Welles but then superseded by Reynolds. Although intervention by the warden of the Cinque Ports, Sir Thomas Cheyne*, cannot be excluded, with Wymond's election being overruled at the outset, he may have retired of his own accord, and in this case the more likely time would have been before the opening of the second session. His re-election as a jurat on 26 Aug. 1548 was quickly followed by his replacement on the score of ill-health, and even if he had been willing to discharge his parliamentary duty the town's marked preference for Members who were jurats might have told against his retention.[5]

Wymond made his will on 27 May 1549. He asked to be buried at Goudhurst and gave his wife a life interest in all his property in Rye and elsewhere in Sussex, out of which she was to maintain their sons William and Robert until they reached 15. He left to his daughter Alice £20 on marriage to be raised from his goods and named his wife residuary legatee and sole executrix. The will was proved on 24 Sept. 1549.[6]

[1] Rye chamberlains' accts. 5, f. 122. [2] Date of birth estimated from father's death and from his having two younger brothers, PCC 28 Bennett. Canterbury prob. reg. A. 26, ff. 266v–267. [3] Rye chamberlains' accts. 4, 5 passim; Cinque Ports White and Black Bks. (Kent Arch. Soc. recs. br. xix), 224. [4] Cinque Ports White and Black Bks. passim; LP Hen. VIII, vi, xi; SP1/79, ff. 23v–24, 113, ff. 106v–109; Elton, Policy and Police, 20, 86–90; Lewes archdeaconry ct. wills bk. A. 1, f. 44. [5] Rye chamberlains' accts. 5, ff. 122, 123, 144v, 145v, 167v; PCC 8 Powell; Add. 34150. [6] Rye chamberlains' accts. 5, f. 167v; Canterbury prob. reg. A. 26, ff. 266v–267.

H.M.

WYN see also **GWYN, WYNN, WYNN AP MEREDYDD**

WYN AP HUGH, John (by 1525–76), of Bodvel in Llannor, Caern.

CAERNARVONSHIRE 1553 (Mar.), 1571

b. by 1525, 1st s. of Hugh ap John ap Madog of Bodvel by Catherine, da. of Henry Salusbury of Llanrhaiadr, Denb. m. Elizabeth, da. of Sir John Puleston* of Caernarvon, Caern. and Bersham, Denb., 3s. inc. Hugh Gwyn alias Bodvel[†] 1da.; 1s. illegit.[1] Jt. (with David Lloyd ap Thomas*) bailiff of Pwllheli and constable, commote of Gafflogion, Caern. in 1546; sheriff, Caern. 1550–1, 1559–60; commr. relief 1550, goods of churches and fraternities 1553, loan 1557, piracy 1565, tanneries 1574; j.p. 1550–d.[2]

John Wyn ap Hugh's family, which later took the surname Bodvel, was of ancient Welsh descent. The earliest trace found of him is in the quarter sessions records of Caernarvonshire, where in 1546 he appears with David Lloyd ap Thomas as bailiff of Pwllheli and constable of the commote of Gafflogion. According to Sir John Wynn[†] of Gwydir he bore the standard at the defeat of the Norfolk rebels at Dussindale in August 1549, where although unhorsed and wounded, 'yet he upheld the great standard of England'. It is not clear whether this honour had fallen to Wyn as a personal follower of the victor John Dudley, Earl of Warwick, or as one of the household troops, but the episode marked the beginning of his rise to prominence. Nominated as sheriff in the following autumn, he was pricked a year later and in the meantime was granted a 21-year lease of townships and lands in the Llŷn peninsula near the family residence. Three years later the earl, by then Duke of Northumberland, was licensed to grant him Bardsey Island and the former abbot of Bardsey's house at Aberdaron. Sir John Wyn claimed that the grant made mention of its recipient's valour in the field, but the licence as enrolled does not do so. What is suggestive is its date, 15 Apr. 1553, for this was two weeks after the close of the Parliament of the previous month in which Wyn ap Hugh had sat as knight of the shire. Sir John Puleston, Wyn's father-in-law, had been steward of the lands of Bardsey abbey until his death in 1551, so that Wyn seems to have used his Membership to extract the grant from Northumberland, who for his part may have seen in it a means of ensuring Wyn's support.[3]

Whether Wyn gave the duke any support is not known, but after he had sued out a pardon from Mary he served her in his shire, and although not re-elected to any of her Parliaments he was one of the Caernarvonshire gentlemen, John Wynn ap Meredydd* and William Wynn Williams* among them, to whom the council in the marches recommended Sir Rhys Gruffydd (q.v.) as knight of the shire in 1555. Under Elizabeth Wyn was to be brought into the Star Chamber for his alleged use of Bardsey as an entrepôt for the spoils of piracy, but he sat in one further Parliament before his death in 1576.[4]

[1] Date of birth estimated from first reference. Griffith, *Peds.* 171; Dwnn, *Vis. Wales*, ii. 174; PCC 30 Carew. [2] *Cal. Caern. Q. Sess. Recs.* ed. Williams, passim; *CPR*, 1553, pp. 363, 419; *Cal. Wynn (of Gwydir) Pprs. 1515–1690*, p. 4; *APC*, vii. 286; R. Flenley, *Cal. Reg. Council, Marches of Wales*, 127, 134. [3] *DWB* (Bodvel fam.); *Cal. Caern. Q. Sess. Recs.* 31–32; J. Wynn, *Gwydir Fam.* ed. Llwyd, 120–1; *CPR*, 1553, pp. 109, 339, 363; 1566–9, p. 74. [4] *CPR*, 1554–5, p. 357; *Cal. Wynn (of Gwydir) Pprs. 1515–1690*, p. 3; St.Ch.5/J 18/1; C. Roberts, 'Piracy in Caern. and Anglesey', *Trans. Caern. Hist. Soc.* xxi. 45–49; PCC 30 Carew.

P.S.E.

WYNDE, John (by 1482–1515 or later), ?of Ramsey, Hunts.

HUNTINGDONSHIRE 1510[1]

b. by 1482. ?*m.* settlement Sept./Oct. 1503, Dorothy, da. of Robert Castell of East Hatley, Cambs., wid. of James Caldecote (*d.* 27 Jan. 1501) of Thundersley, Essex.[2]

Commr. sewers, Cambs., Norf. 1503, Cambs., Hunts., Leics., Northants. 1515, subsidy, Hunts. 1512, 1514, 1515; j.p. Hunts. 1504–14 or later.[3]

John Wynde's Membership of the first Parliament of Henry VIII's reign is known from an information laid by him in February 1511 against the ex-sheriff of Cambridgeshire and Huntingdonshire, Francis Hasilden. He alleged that Hasilden had collected the sum of £16 due to Wynde and his fellow-knight John Taylard for their wages and travelling expenses but had ignored repeated requests to hand it over to them, thus forfeiting £20 to the crown and £10 to Wynde, besides being liable to Wynde for 10 marks incurred in bringing the action. A day to hear the case was fixed in late April but the hearing was twice postponed and after 30 May nothing more is heard of it. Wynde may well have been re-elected to the next two Parliaments, for which the names of the Huntingdonshire knights are unknown, as he was named to the commissions charged with supervising the collection of the subsidies then granted.[4]

Apart from this episode and his role in Huntingdonshire little has come to light about Wynde, whose origins are as obscure as his end. Doubtless belonging to the Fenland family which can be traced back to the early 14th century, he probably followed in its tradition of service to local monasteries. A bearer of his name was bailiff to Ramsey abbey in 1509, and either this man or a namesake was the 'John Wynde junior of Ramsey, gentleman' who six years earlier had been named feoffee of property in St. Ives and not long afterwards acquired land at Ramsey. The Member's connexion with Ramsey is suggested by his having asked for payment there when suing out his writ *de expensis*, while the links between Ramsey abbey and the Castell family of East Hatley in Cambridgeshire make it likely that he was the second husband of Dorothy Castell. Wynde is last found on commissions for Huntingdonshire in 1515 and his absence from the subsidy commission of 1523 seems

to imply that he was dead by that year. He could have been the John Wynde accused in 1520–1 of dispossessing the rightful owners of four houses and 55 acres in Godmanchester, but this was more probably the namesake (perhaps son) who became comptroller of the mint at York in 1545 and died nine years later.[5]

[1] E13/187, m. 30. [2] Date of birth estimated from first reference. *Feet of Fines, Cambs.* ed. Palmer, 127; *CIPM Hen. VII*, ii. 611, 624; *Vis. Cambs.* (Harl. Soc. xli), 42. [3] *CPR*, 1494–1509, pp. 322, 359, 507, 627, 644; *LP Hen. VIII*, i, ii; *Statutes*, iii. 82, 115, 175. [4] E13/187, m. 30. [5] *Early Hunts. Lay Subsidy Rolls* (Subsidia Mediaevalia viii), 166; *LP Hen. VIII*, i, xxi; *CCR*, 1500–9, no. 386; *Feet of Fines, Hunts.* ed. Turner, 114, 116, 121, 124–5, 130, 182; *Brit. Numismatic Jnl.* xlv. 72; PCC 29 Tashe.

M.K.D.

WYNDHAM, Edmund (by 1496–1569), of Felbrigg, Norf.

NORFOLK 1539,[1] 1559

b. by 1496, 1st s. of Sir Thomas Wyndham of Felbrigg by 1st w. Eleanor, da. of Richard Scrope of Upsall, Yorks. *m.* by Oct. 1521, Susan, da. of Sir Roger Townshend* of Raynham, Norf., 3s. inc. Francis† 3da.; 1da. illegit. *suc.* fa. 29 Apr. 1522. Kntd. Feb./May 1543.[2]

Commr. subsidy, Norf. 1523, tenths of spiritualities 1535, benevolence 1544/45, relief 1550, goods of churches and fraternities 1553, to enforce Acts of Supremacy and Uniformity 1559, eccles. causes 1569; servant, household of Cardinal Wolsey by 1525; j.p. Norf. 1532–54, q. 1558/59–*d.*; sheriff, Norf. and Suff. 1537–8, 1545–6, 1549–50; dep. lt. Norf. 1559, jt. (with Sir Christopher Heydon*) ld. lt. 1560.[3]

Edmund Wyndham was the son of a member of the Council related to the Howard dukes of Norfolk. It was doubtless his father's closeness to Wolsey which accounts for Wyndham's entry into the cardinal's household, although no trace of him has been found there until three years after his father's death. His extensive inheritance in East Anglia was burdened with the provision made by his father for his stepmother and half-brothers and sisters, so that during the 1520s he had an income of barely £100 a year. He was not compromised by Wolsey's fall, and the subsequent winding-up of trusts for relatives enabled him to resume the place in Norfolk enjoyed by his forbears since the mid 15th century.[4]

In 1532 Wyndham went in the 3rd Duke of Norfolk's suite to Calais for Henry VIII's meeting with Francis I and later moved on to Paris with the duke's son and the King's illegitimate son Richmond, presumably staying with them at the French court until their return to England a year later. Although ordered to join the King at Ampthill during the northern rebellion in 1536, he is not known to have served in its suppression. His standing as a 'cousin' of the duke and his association with Cromwell since their service with Wolsey are sufficient to account for his nomination, with his step-sister's husband Richard Southwell, for the knighthood of the shire in 1539, but he was also doubtless supported by his father-in-law Sir Roger Townshend; unlike Southwell, he did not have to meet the challenge of Sir Edmund Knyvet (q.v.), one of his father's ex-wards. Nothing has come to light about Wyndham's part in this Parliament, but during the prorogation of 1539 he attended the duke at the reception of Anne of Cleves and after the dissolution he and Southwell were instructed about the collection of the subsidy they had helped to grant.[5]

In 1542 Wyndham served under Norfolk on the Scottish border and two years later at the siege of Boulogne; during 1545 he saw action at sea. With the fall of the Howards he seems to have confined himself to his own and his county's affairs. In 1549 he tried to dissuade Ket and his supporters from rebellion, but 'had not . . . his horsemanship been better than his rhetoric, himself had not departed the place'; as sheriff after Ket's overthrow he had the task of restoring order in the shire. During the succession crisis of 1553 he attempted, at least momentarily, to rally support for Jane Grey. On 18 July Mary's Council ordered the mobilization of parts of Norfolk, notwithstanding directions by Sir Christopher Heydon and Wyndham to the contrary, and summoned the pair to her headquarters: a week later they were ordered to come to London and to stay there during the Council's pleasure. Like Heydon, Wyndham evidently soon repented and was forgiven; he was named to the commission at Norwich to try those who had refused to submit to Mary, and clearly he stood well with the old duke.[6]

Although Wyndham remained active in local affairs under Mary it was only at the accession of Elizabeth that he reappeared in Parliament. He remained a client of the Howards and an important figure in Norfolk until his death on 23 July 1569.[7]

[1] LP Hen. VIII, xiv(1), 808 citing SP1/150/160–1; E159/319, brev. ret. Mich. r. [1–2]. [2] Date of birth estimated from age at fa.'s i.p.m., C142/38/16. Vis. Norf. (Harl. Soc. xxxii), 324; H. A. Wyndham, A Fam. Hist. 1410–1688; the Wyndhams of Norf. and Som. 28–44; PCC 3 Bodfelde; LP Hen. VIII, xx. [3] LP Hen. VIII, iii, v, xv, xx; CPR, 1550–3, p. 396; 1553, pp. 356, 416; 1563–6, p. 25; CSP Dom. 1547–80, p. 329; E179/60/9–10; Norwich chamberlains' acct. bk. 1551–67, f. 176. [4] Wyndham, 22–44; Blomefield, Norf. viii. 113; C142/38/14, 16; E179/60/9–10; PCC 3 Bodfelde; LP Hen. VIII, v. [5] Wyndham, 90; Somerville, Duchy, i. 595; LP Hen. VIII, xi, xiii, xiv; E159/319, brev. ret. Mich. r. [1–2]. [6] LP Hen. VIII, xvii, xix, xxi, add; Wyndham, 92–94; Blomefield, iii. 224; F. W. Russell, Kett's Rebellion, 30; APC, iv. 296, 416; v. 109. [7] APC, vi. 109; A. Hassell Smith, County and Ct. 39, 127, 176, 355; Cam. Misc. ix(3), 58; E150/661/13.

R.V.

WYNN, Morris (by 1526–81), of Gwydir, Caern.

CAERNARVONSHIRE   1553 (Oct.), 1554 (Apr.), 1563

b. by 1526, 1st s. of John Wynn ap Meredydd* of Dolwyddelan and Gwydir by Ellen, da. of Morris ap John ap Meredydd of Clenennau; bro. of John Gwynne[†] and Robert Wynn[†]. m. (1) by Sept. 1551, Sian, da. of Sir Richard Bulkeley (d. 1547) of Beaumaris, Anglesey, 3s. inc. Ellis[†] and John[†] 5da.; (2) Anne, da. of Edward Greville of Milcote, Warws., 1da.; (3) c. 1570, Catherine (d. Aug. 1591), da. and h. of Tudor ap Robert of Berain, Denb. and Penmynydd, Anglesey, wid. of John Salusbury and Richard Clough of Bachegraig, Tremeirchion, Flints., 3s. 1da. suc. fa. 1559.[1]

Commr. goods of churches and fraternities, Caern. 1553, piracy 1565, subsidy 1570, victuals 1574, tanneries 1574; escheator 1553–4; sheriff 1554–5, 1569–70, 1577–8; j.p. Caern., Merion. 1555–d., Denb. 1575; custos rot. Caern. by 1562–d.[2]

Morris Wynn was the first member of his family to stabilise its surname as Wynn. He was probably in his late twenties when he began to follow his father into public office, although as early as 1547 he had been one of the witnesses to the shire election and in 1551 he was charged by Sir Richard Bulkeley*, then or soon to be his brother-in-law, to act in the name of the lord admiral with regard to a wreck off Harlech, Merioneth. His election as knight of the shire to the first two Marian Parliaments followed closely on his father's discharge of that duty and his first shrievalty preceded his father's second. He was not among those who in the Parliament of October 1553 'stood for the true religion' against the initial measures of Catholic restoration. Brought on to the bench in Caernarvonshire and Merioneth in 1555 he made his first recorded appearance at the Caernarvonshire quarter sessions in 1558. It was probably the office of custos rotulorum for Merioneth which his brother Robert tried to secure for him during the vacancy in the lord chancellorship following the death of Gardiner, for their father continued to hold that office in Caernarvonshire until his death.[3]

Wynn did not attain the prestige enjoyed by his father, but after his death in 1581 his son Sir John Wynn of Gwydir was to bring fresh lustre to the family.[4]

[1] Date of birth estimated from first reference. Dwnn, Vis. Wales, ii. 159; Griffith, Peds. 280–1; J. Wynn, Gwydir Fam. ed. Llwyd, table iii. [2] CPR, 1553, p. 410; 1560–3, p. 446; 1563–6, p. 31; APC, viii. 286; E179/200/145; R. Flenley, Cal. Reg. Council, Marches of Wales, 109, 127, 132, 134–5. [3] C219/19/109; Cal. Wynn (of Gwydir) Pprs. 1515–1690, pp. 3–4; Cal. Caern. Q. Sess. Recs. ed. Williams, 206. [4] PCC 19 Darcy.

P.S.E.

WYNN AP MEREDYDD, John (by 1494–1559), of Dolwyddelan and Gwydir, Caern.

CAERNARVONSHIRE   ?1542, 1547*[1]

b. by 1494, 1st surv. s. of Meredydd ap Ieuan ap Robert of Dolwyddelan and Gwydir by 1st w. Alice, da. of William ap Gruffydd ap Robin of Cochwillan. m. Ellen, da. of Morris ap John ap Meredydd of Clenennau, 5s. inc. John Gwynne†, Morris Wynn* and Robert Wynn† 2da. *suc.* fa. 1525.[2]

Commr. tenths of spiritualities, Bangor diocese 1535, subsidy, Caern. 1543, benevolence 1544/45, surveillance of N. Wales coast 1544-5, relief, Caern. 1550, goods of churches and fraternities, Caern. and Merion. 1553, loan, Caern. 1557; j.p. Caern., Merion. 1543-*d.*; custos rot. Merion. in 1543, Caern. by 1550-*d.*; sheriff, Caern. 1544-5, 1556-7; steward, former lands of Beddgelert priory, Conway abbey, and the order of St. John of Jerusalem, Caern. c. 1550.[3]

The Wynn family of Gwydir was one of the great families of Tudor Wales. Of ancient descent from Owain Gwynedd, son of Gryffydd ap Cynan, the house of Gwydir was established by John Wynn's father, who purchased the lease of Dolwyddelan castle about 1489 and the family home at Gwydir about the turn of the century.[4]

The earliest reference found to Wynn is a letter of 1515 to him from Mary, Duchess of Suffolk, sister of Henry VIII, whose husband was chamberlain of North Wales; it contained a request to him to give her servant any merlins from these parts. After this tantalizing early glimpse, he is hardly caught sight of again before the Union: in 1530 he renewed the lease of the vills of Dolwyddelan, Gwydir and Trefriw at an annual rent of £19 4s.8d.[5]

It was almost certainly Wynn who was returned for the shire to the Parliament of 1542: although only the name John survives on the dorse of the writ and on the sheriff's schedule, he is the most likely man to have had the honour of first representing the shire in Parliament, especially as John Puleston, who might have made a bid for it, was elected for Caernarvon Boroughs on the same occasion. Wynn was one of the first justices of the peace in Caernarvonshire and a member of the quorum; in 1543 he was also custos rotulorum in Merioneth. It was to him that, on the eve of the parliamentary election of 1542, Bishop Lee and Sir Nicholas Hare* of the council in the marches wrote to recommend Richard Mytton* for election in Merioneth, but Wynn's kinsman, Edward Stanley I, carried the day. Wynn was a brother-in-law and ally of John Puleston, whom as sheriff he returned to Parliament in 1545. It is not surprising, therefore, that when early in 1551 Puleston died while knight for Caernarvonshire in the next Parliament, Wynn was by-elected in his place. His name appears on the list of Members revised in preparation for the final session in January 1552, so that he may be presumed to have taken his seat then. He was not to sit again, probably because of his advancing years, but he saw to it that his heir Morris Wynn did so twice and he was one of the local gentlemen to whom the council in the marches successfully recommended Sir Rhys Gruffydd for election in 1555. His local ascendancy

owed something to the support of the 1st Earl of Pembroke, whom one member of his family called his truest friend. He sued out a general pardon at the accession of both Mary and Elizabeth, and from 1555 he rebuilt Gwydir.[6]

Wynn made his will on 14 June 1557, asking to be buried in Bangor cathedral. He left 20s. for the repair of Llanrwst church and a weekly sum of 1s. to be divided equally between the 'poor folks' of the parish every Sunday for a year. His wife was to have all the goods and chattels, some livestock and half the household stuff, the other half going to his heir Morris Wynn, who was also given some livestock and £40 in cash; three other sons and his daughter Margaret received livestock. The executors of the will were his wife and their sons Morris and John. Wynn survived its making by two years, dying on 9 July 1559; the will was proved on the following 23 Aug. An elegy was written by Sion Brwynog.[7]

[1] Hatfield 207.   [2] Date of birth estimated from first reference. Dwnn, *Vis. Wales*, ii. 158-9 and n; Griffith, *Peds.* 280-1.   [3] *LP Hen. VIII*, viii; *Cal. Wynn (of Gwydir) Pprs. 1515-1690*, pp. 2, 4; *CPR, 1553*, pp. 363, 419; E179/220/140; *Cal. Caern. Q. Sess. Recs.* ed. Williams, passim; C193/12/1; SP11/5/6.   [4] *DWB* (Wynn fam. of Gwydir).   [5] *Cal. Wynn (of Gwydir) Pprs. 1515-1690*, p. 1; *LP Hen. VIII*, iv.   [6] *Cal. Wynn (of Gwydir) Pprs. 1515-1690*, pp. 1, 3, 4; *CPR, 1553-4*, p. 356; *1557-8*, p. 265; *1558-60*, p. 160.   [7] PCC 39 Chaynay; *HMC Welsh*, i(1), 208.

P.S.E.

WYRLEY (WORLEY), Mark (c.1500-55 or later), of Lichfield, Staffs.

LICHFIELD   1553 (Mar.), 1554 (Nov.)

b. c. 1500, 2nd s. of Cornelius Wyrley of Handsworth by Clare, da. and h. of John Sheldon of Rowley Regis.[1]

Bailiff, Lichfield by 1541, 1548-9; commr. chantries 1553.[2]

Mark Wyrley may have had legal training, for when in 1538 his master John Vernon was pricked sheriff of Staffordshire Wyrley was appointed his under sheriff; whether this was overruled by Cromwell's alternative recommendation is not known. By January 1541, when he brought a charge of riot and assault at Lichfield into the Star Chamber, Wyrley was one of the bailiffs of the city, and on Lichfield's receipt of its first charter in July 1548 he was named one of the bailiffs until the following year. No other ex-bailiff was to sit for Lichfield until 1584, so that Wyrley must have owed his two elections less to that qualification than to his personal standing and connexions. Nothing has been found to link him with William Lord Paget, who usually wielded patronage there but whose temporary eclipse may have weakened his hold when Wyrley was first elected. The most likely source of support is indicated by Wyrley's fellow-Member on that occasion: William Fitzherbert's sister-in-law was the wife of Henry Vernon who was to sit for the city in the spring of 1554. Although as a Member of Mary's third Parliament Wyrley absented himself before the dissolution and was summoned to appear in the King's bench, he was not proceeded against further as were Henry Vernon, then one of the knights for Derbyshire, and Matthew Cradock, returned for Stafford. This could mean either that he was not regarded as contumacious or that he did not long survive the initial summons, which is the last reference found to him. His omission from the subsidy list for Lichfield in 1559 gives some colour to the second possibility.[3]

[1] Elder brother died 24 Feb. 1562 aged 63. J. C. Wedgwood, *Staffs. Parl. Hist.* (Wm. Salt Arch. Soc.), i. 332; *Wm. Salt Arch. Soc.* iii(2), 154. [2] *Wm. Salt Arch. Soc.* (ser. 3), 1913, pp. 137–8; 1915, p. 403. [3] *LP Hen. VIII*, xiii; *Wm. Salt Arch. Soc.* (ser. 3), 1913, pp. 137–8; *CPR*, 1547–8, p. 386; KB29/188 rot. 48; E179/177/137, 178/168.

A.D.K.H.

WYTHE, Robert (?1523–86), of Droitwich, Worcs. and the Inner Temple, London.

DROITWICH 1554 (Nov.),[1] 1555, 1558, 1559, 1563

b. ?1523, 2nd s. of John Wythe of Droitwich by Isabel, da. of John More. *educ.* I. Temple, adm. 5 Feb. 1551. Prob. unm.[2]
Autumn reader, I. Temple 1565, Lent 1572, treasurer 1576–7, bencher by 1580.
J.p.q. Worcs. 1573/74–*d.*

It is not certain whether the same Robert Wythe was returned for Droitwich at three successive elections under Mary: on the second occasion he is styled on the indenture 'junior, gentleman' and on the third 'de interiori Templ[o]'. Whether or not these descriptions are mutually exclusive, each implies the existence of at least one namesake and this is confirmed by the presence among the voters at the third election of a Robert Wythe who cannot also have been the man elected. To the uncertainty thus created the first of the three indentures adds its quota by surviving in so damaged a state that only the christian name Robert and the initial 'W' of a surname are legible, and all trace of a style, if there was one, has been lost: fortunately, the name appears intact on the Crown Office list, where it has 'generosus' appended. It is thus possible, if unlikely, that three namesakes were elected in turn, each distinguished by the appropriate suffix; less improbable that the man returned on the first two occasions was the voter on the third, when his namesake was elected; and not impossible that the same man was elected three times running, although differently styled on the second and third occasions.[3]

Of only one Robert Wythe, the Inner Templar returned to the Parliament of 1558, has it proved possible to sketch a life-story. A second son in an established family of Droitwich (from whose second syllable, formerly in itself the designation of the town, its name may have been derived), he was given a special admission to the inn in 1551 and can be traced there as office-holder, reader and bencher, with a chamber in Fig Tree court, until his death; himself childless, he secured the special admission of his nephews Robert and Thomas Wythe. His election in the autumn of 1554 as the junior of the borough's first two Members since 1311 would have satisfied Queen Mary's preference for residents, without burdening him with the problem of accommodation during the Parliament. Unlike his fellow-Member George Newport he was not among those found absent without leave when the House was called early in 1555. In Mary's fourth Parliament, which met later that year, neither Newport nor Wythe followed the lead of Sir Anthony Kingston in opposing a government bill.[4]

Wythe died on 24 Dec. 1586 and was buried at Droitwich. His property in London, Middlesex, the marches and Wales passed to his brother John on condition that John looked after their sister and her children.[5]

[1] Little of Wythe's name, which is listed in Huntington Lib. Hastings mss Parl. pprs., remains on the indenture, C219/23/138. [2] Aged 63 at death according to MI. *Vis. Worcs.* (Harl. Soc. xxvii), 150; *VCH Worcs.* iii. 86. [3] C193/32/2; 219/23/138, 24/173, 25/125; Huntington Lib. Hastings mss Parl. pprs. [4] *Cal. I.T. Recs.* i. 309, 311, 340, 344. [5] PCC 3 Spencer; *Habington's Worcs.* (Worcs. Hist. Soc. 1895), i. 482.

M.K.D.

WYTHE, Thomas (by 1479–1521/22), of Wisbech, Cambs. and Lynn, Norf.

LYNN 1512,[1] 1515[2]

b. by 1479, s. of John Wythe of Eye, Suff. *m.* (1) by 1500, 3da.; (2) by 13 May 1510, Joan, wid. of John Palmer of Lynn, *s.p.*[3]
Chamberlain, Lynn 1507–8, jurat 1510–20, mayor 1510–11, 1511–12, j.p. 1512; commr. sewers, Fen districts of Ely and Norf. 1508, Cambs., Lincs. and Northants. 1515, Norf. 1517; dep. constable and clerk, Wisbech castle by 1509.[4]

Thomas Wythe was born at Eye in Suffolk but his forbears may have included the several burgesses of that name found at Lynn in the 14th and 15th centuries; his own connexion with the town perhaps sprang from his second marriage, to the widow of an ex-mayor. There is no reason to connect him with the family of Droitwich, Worcestershire, which was to produce Robert Wythe*.[5]

Wythe was styled merchant or gentleman when he sued out a pardon in 1509, but his association with Sir James Hobart[†], the attorney-general and Councillor, whose deputy he was at Wisbech castle by that time, may imply a legal training of which no trace has been found. Such a background could also have qualified Wythe for his concurrent service to the bishop of Ely as steward of the episcopal lands in Freebridge and Wisbech hundreds. It was 'by the service of the bishop of Ely' that he excused himself from sitting for Lynn when first elected there on 2 Jan. 1510: the fact that the bishop was James Stanley, son of the 1st Earl of Derby and stepbrother of the late King, must have strengthened Wythe's hand, although the townsman who had been elected with him also contrived to be discharged. Wythe was not to persist in his objection. Having begun his municipal career in 1507 in the customary office of chamberlain, he was made a jurat in August 1510 and immediately elected mayor. Re-elected in the following year, he was in office when chosen for the Parliament of 1512. Neither on this occasion, nor three years later when he was again returned in compliance with the King's request for the re-election of the previous Members, is there any indication that he demurred. Both the bishop and Hobart, who received a writ of assistance, sat in the Lords in the first of these Parliaments, and Hobart in the second. No reference has been found to Wythe's being paid parliamentary wages.[6]

In his will of 28 July 1521 Wythe mentions no property in Lynn but he appears to have had considerable lands in and around Wisbech, in Eye and in Norfolk. These he left for 20 years to two priests as feoffees and then to his grandchildren in tail; he named three daughters, each of whom had at least one son. He made bequests to a number of churches and, as befitted a servant of Bishop Stanley, showed a concern for education, leaving £5 a year for 20 years to provide a grammar master to teach poor children in Wisbech and making elaborate provision for the schooling of his grandchildren. After money had been left for obits and to the Trinity guild of Wisbech, the residue went to the executors, Dr. Thomas Pell, Thomas Dunbolt and Wythe's son-in-law Thomas Prentyse, for the performance of the will, which was proved on 24 May 1522. Wythe does not appear on the jurat list of Lynn for September 1521 and was probably dead by that time.[7]

[1] Lynn congregation bk. 4, f. 115v. [2] Ibid. f. 151. [3] Date of birth estimated from marriage. PCC 24 Maynwaryng; *LP Hen. VIII*, i. [4] Lynn congregation bk. 4, ff. 80, 83v, 104, 112; *LP Hen. VIII*, i, ii; *CPR*, 1494–1509, p. 581. [5] PCC 24 Maynwaryng; *Lynn Freemen* (Norf. Arch.), 8–45 passim; Lynn congregation bk. 2 passim. [6] *LP Hen. VIII*, i; Lynn congregation bk. 4, ff. 97v, 98, 115v, 151. [7] PCC 24 Maynwaryng.

R.V.

WYVILL, Marmaduke (by 1496–1558), of Little Burton, Yorks.

RIPON 1553 (Oct.)

b. by 1496, s. of Robert Wyvill of Little Burton by Anne, da. of Sir John Norton of Norton Conyers. *m.* (1) by 1517, Agnes, da. and coh. of Sir Ralph Fitzrandolph (Fitzrandell) of Spennithorne, 4s.; (2) by 1541, Margery or Margaret, da. of Sir Robert Aske of Aughton, wid. of Sir Roger Bellingham; (3) Dorothy, da. of Sir Brian Hastings of Fenwick, wid. of Sir William St. Quintin of Harpham, 1da. *suc.* fa. 24 Sept. 1527.[1]

Commr. tenths of spiritualities, Yorks. 1535, musters, Yorks. (N. Riding) 1539, benevolence 1544/45; j.p. Yorks. (N. Riding) 1536–d.[2]

Marmaduke Wyvill's lands at Burton in the North Riding came to him partly through inheritance and partly through his marriage to Agnes Fitzrandolph, one of the four daughters of Elizabeth, sister and coheir of the 10th and last Lord Scrope of Masham; he and his wife had livery of her share of the Scrope property four years after he had succeeded his father at Little Burton. His second marriage appears to have made him the brother-in-law of Christopher and Robert Aske. Although its date is unknown this marriage probably took place before 4 May 1537, for on that date Wyvill was granted a pardon in connexion with the recent rebellion, a transaction not difficult to understand if one of his brothers-in-law was then awaiting trial and execution. That Wyvill was not further compromised by the connexion is shown by his retention on the North Riding bench and his subsequent employment on other commissions; on the contrary, Margaret Aske's descent from the 9th Lord Clifford was to bring him favours from that powerful clan such as the annuity of £13 6s.8d. granted to him and his wife by her cousin Sir Thomas Clifford in November 1541. It was from George Clifford* and Michael Welbore that Wyvill acquired various ex-monastic properties in Yorkshire in May 1545; to these he was to add others in May 1553.[3]

Wyvill remained a justice of the peace under Edward VI and Mary, but his only other intervention in public life appears to have been in the first Marian Parliament. His return as one of the first two Members for Ripon may be attributed to his many connexions—with the Earls of Cumberland (steward of the honor of Knaresborough) and Shrewsbury (president of the council in the north) and with the locally influential families of Norton and Staveley. What his attitude was towards the Catholic restoration cannot be deduced from the list of Members who opposed it in the Commons, since Ripon is one of the three boroughs omitted from that list. It would be surprising, however, if he had done so, and the explanation of his absence from the later Parliaments of the reign is to be sought elsewhere; he may, for instance, have been preoccupied with the defence of his property which in 1555 brought him into litigation with Sir Christopher Danby*, another partaker in the Scrope inheritance.[4]

In his will, made on 8 Aug. (the day of his death) and proved on 26 Aug. 1558, Wyvill provided for his third wife, asked to be buried in Masham church and appointed his four sons executors and his cousin Richard Norton supervisor. Christopher, the eldest son, was then aged 40 and more.[5]

[1] Date of birth estimated from age at fa.'s i.p.m., C142/51/78. *Vis. Yorks.* (Harl. Soc. xvi), 8, 356–7, 372–3; *Glover's Vis. Yorks.* ed. Foster, 380; *Yorks. Arch. Jnl.* xviii. 373; xxviii. 47; T. D. Whitaker, *Richmondshire*, i. ped. bet. pp. 322–3. [2] *LP Hen. VIII*, viii, x, xii–xvi, xx; *CPR*, 1547–8, p. 92; 1553–4, p. 26. [3] *VCH Yorks.* (*N. Riding*), i. 234, 259, 264, 266, 326, 336n; NRA 13480 (N. Riding RO, Wyvill of Burton Agnes mss 16/6); *Yorks. Arch. Jnl.* xviii. 373; *LP Hen. VIII*, xx; *CPR*, 1553, p. 132. [4] NRA 13480 (N. Riding RO, Wyvill of Burton Agnes mss 10). [5] York wills 15(2), f. 292; C142/116/51.

A.D.

YATES, William (by 1505-58/59), of Lincoln.

LINCOLN 1545

b. by 1505, ?s. of John Yates of Lincoln. *m.* Elizabeth, 2s.[1]

Sheriff, Lincoln 1526–7, alderman by 1539, mayor 1539–40, 1549–50, graceman, St. Mary's guild by Nov. 1545.[2]

William Yates's parentage has not been established, but he was probably a kinsman of the John Yates whose name occurs in assessments made at Lincoln early in the reign of Henry VIII. It was presumably at the beginning of his civic career that Yates was elected sheriff of Lincoln in 1526.

In December 1541 Yates served on the grand jury which presented Thomas Culpeper and Francis Dereham for misconduct with the Queen at Lincoln, and in the following year he was one of the aldermen who supplicated to the King against the heavy charges to the city of the fee-farm and of fifteenths and tenths. His prominence in the negotiations over the fee-farm may have contributed to Yates's election to the Parliament of 1545; the city had certainly expected its Members in the previous Parliament to set forward this business. Another reason could have been the threat to the guilds. At the time of his election Yates may already have been serving as graceman of St. Mary's guild, and when the common council voted to use the guild plate to meet the expenses of the negotiations over the fee-farm Yates (although he was one of the persons to be paid) refused to yield up the plate until a brief detention in the guildhall and the threat of a fine led him to change his mind. When the plate was finally sold, he received £24 13s.4d. from the proceeds, one of several payments made to him in the 1540s for negotiations over the fee-farm. On 14 Nov. 1545, a week before the delayed opening of Parliament, he signed the final deed of surrender when the city took

over all of the guild's lands and properties in an attempt to avoid losses through its expected dissolution by statute. Yates was nominated for Parliament again in 1547, but in the face of three influential candidates he polled only four votes out of 84. That this was no measure of his standing in the city, however, was shown by his election as mayor for the second time in 1549.[3]

In 1545 Yates was listed as a tenant of John Bellow* and John Broxholme at Austin Friars, just outside Newport Arch, but in his will, made on 20 Oct. 1558 and proved on 4 Mar. 1559, he asked to be buried in the parish of St. Swithin. At the time of his death both his children were still minors. One of his bequests was to cause trouble in the city in 1561 when the corporation had to sue his nephew and executor, Martin Mason, for £100 left as a fund to be loaned to Lincoln craftsmen.[4]

[1] Date of birth estimated from first reference. Lincoln min. bk. 1511–42, ff. 13v–14; PCC 48 Welles. [2] *Associated Architectural Societies' Reps. and Pprs.* xxxix. 243, 245; *HMC 14th Rep. VIII*, 39–40. [3] *LP Hen. VIII*, xvi; *HMC 14th Rep. VIII*, 37, 39–41; J. W. F. Hill, *Tudor and Stuart Lincoln*, 53–56. [4] *LP Hen. VIII*, xx; PCC 48 Welles; *HMC 14th Rep. VIII*, 52.

T.M.H.

YAXLEY, Francis (by 1528-65), of Yaxley, Suff.

DUNWICH 1553 (Mar.)
STAMFORD 1555
SALTASH 1558

b. by 1528, 1st s. of Richard Yaxley of Mellis by Anne, da. of Roger Austin of Earl Soham. *educ.* G. Inn, adm. 1553. *m.* Margaret, da. of Sir Henry Hastings of Braunstone, Leics., *s.p.*[1]

Servant of William Cecil by 1546; clerk of signet by 1557.[2]

Francis Yaxley belonged to a younger branch of a family which had been established for some generations at Yaxley Hall near Eye and Mellis. His father was related to John Yaxley†, a serjeant-at-law, whose descendants continued at Yaxley until the 18th century. His uncle Robert Yaxley was a founder-member of the college of physicians and may have introduced the young Francis to William Cecil. Described as 'Cecil's Yaxley', he was said to reverence his master 'as though he were his father'.[3]

Yaxley's employment in public service began before Cecil's appointment as secretary, for in September 1548 he was reimbursed for money paid to nine Italian mercenaries. In the following June he was reporting court news to Cecil from Greenwich and about a year later, in furtherance of his diplomatic education, he was sent to join the embassy of Peter Vannes in Italy, whence he conducted a correspondence with Cecil and with Vannes, from whom he received some letters in Latin. Returning to England in November 1552, he passed through

Speyer where at a great banquet the Elector Palatine made him his cupbearer. From England Yaxley continued his correspondence with Italian diplomats, especially Girolamo Spagna who wrote to him concerning the Italian wars. At about this time he entered Gray's Inn, but in April 1553 he was sent to join Nicholas Wotton, the ambassador at the French court. Before he set out the Duke of Northumberland 'used him very gently', gave him 10 crowns and asked him to send news from France. Two days after his arrival Yaxley wrote to Cecil that he was doubtful about complying with the duke's request without Cecil's advice.[4]

With such patronage Yaxley can have had little difficulty in entering Parliament, although there is no evidence of intervention in the Dunwich election early in 1553; as a member of a Suffolk landed family, Yaxley was a likely Member for a borough which often returned local gentlemen. He may have been in France during Mary's first two Parliaments but in October 1554 he sent Cecil news from the court and a copy of the Queen's letter to the sheriffs 'for the better election of knights and burgesses'. If this gesture was intended to procure him a seat it failed, but in 1555 he sat on Cecil's nomination for Stamford. Unlike his partner Francis Thorneff, Yaxley does not appear on the list of Members who followed Sir Anthony Kingston's lead in voting against one of the government's bills, but both Members were presumably involved with the bill for the town and river of Stamford which passed both Houses but was not enacted. Yaxley's return for Saltash in 1558 was probably the work of the steward of the duchy of Cornwall, his kinsman (Sir) Edward Hastings*, although he could claim some connexion with the locality; in 1549 he had obtained from the crown a 21-year lease of the lordship and manor of Calliland, less than 15 miles from Saltash. On one of the lists of Members for the Parliament of 1558 his name is marked with a circle.[5]

Yaxley may have served an apprenticeship as an under clerk of the signet; he was not named among the five clerks who were present at the funeral of Edward VI, but in April 1555 he obtained a grant of the next vacancy. He was occupying the clerkship by March 1557, for in that month he drew up, with William Honing* and two others, articles for the conduct of their business and the sharing of fees. (His description in two private deeds shortly afterwards as clerk of the privy seal was presumably a slip, since by this date the clerkships concerned were separate offices). He does not appear to have been much interested in acquiring landed property: the manor of Brooke, Norfolk, of which he obtained a grant with his father in May 1557, was almost

immediately transferred to two local men. It may have been for the time he spent at the French court in the summer of 1557 that in October he received a 21-year lease of the manor of Thorndon near Yaxley 'in consideration of his service' to the King and Queen.[6]

Under Elizabeth the course of Yaxley's life was to change. As a clerk of the signet he had attended Mary's funeral but he was not present at the coronation and the belief that he retained his clerkship is open to question, although during the next few years his help was solicited by such men as Sir Thomas Cornwallis* and Sir Thomas Wharton II*. According to the Spanish ambassador he was a good Catholic who combined a love of intrigue with an inability to keep secrets. In January 1561 he was imprisoned for babbling about the Queen's affair with Sir Robert Dudley* and later that year he was said to be advocating her marriage to the King of Sweden. More dangerous was his connexion with the Countess of Lennox, which involved him in the conspiracy to marry her son Lord Darnley to Mary, Queen of Scots; he was summoned before the Privy Council in February 1562 and consigned to the Tower, the articles against the countess being partly based on his confession. He was still in the Tower when examined again by the Council in January 1563 but was at large by August 1565; in the following month, after a brief visit to the Netherlands, he established himself at the Scottish court. Here he boasted of his knowledge of affairs in England, France, Spain and Italy, claiming to know many gentlemen 'of good power' who were ready to follow Philip II if England's religion could be altered. He became the secretary and confidant of Darnley and was sufficiently trusted by Mary to be sent on a mission to Philip, suitably provided with plate and jewels. On the return voyage towards the end of October 1565 his ship was wrecked in the North Sea; his body, cast up on Holy Island, was taken to Yaxley for burial according to his wish.[7]

Yaxley had made his will on 3 July 1561. He left his title to Yaxley Hall and lands which he had bought in Braiseworth, Eye, Thornham and Yaxley to his father, with remainder to William, son of his cousin Richard Yaxley, and his lease of the manor of Thorndon to another cousin, George Waller. He left remembrance rings to 15 persons including Sir Thomas Cornwallis and Sir John Sulyard* and their wives; a sum of £100 owed him by the merchant John Isham was to go towards payment of the legacies. The executors were to have been the testator's uncle Sir Christopher Yaxley, his cousins George Waller and Thomas Sherman, and Robert Thrower, who was to receive two grey geldings, but the will does not appear to have been proved and letters of administration were taken out by Yaxley's father on 4 Mar. 1566.[8]

[1] Date of birth estimated from grant of 1549. *Vis. Suff.* ed. Metcalfe, 83; *DNB.* [2] *CPR,* 1554–5, p. 279. [3] CP 25(2) 41/280, no. 25; Lansd. 118, f. 35v.; *CSP For.* 1547–53, p. 228. [4] *APC,* ii. 221; Bath mss, Thynne pprs. 2, ff. 140, 140v.; *HMC Hatfield,* i. 74, 118, 121; *CSP For.* 1547–53, pp. 52, 62, 228, 230, 237, 242; 1553–8, pp. 2, 15, 25, 323. [5] Lansd. 3, f. 92; *CJ,* i. 44, 45; Add. 19156, ff. 313–20; *CPR,* 1553–4, p. 250; William Salt Lib. SMS 264. [6] LC2/4/1, f. 19; *CPR,* 1555–7, pp. 397, 432; 1557–8, p. 125; *Statutes,* iii. 542–4; H. C. Maxwell-Lyte, *Great Seal,* 38. [7] LC2/4/2; *CSP Dom.* 1547–80, pp. 131, 149, 157, 194, 201; 1601–3 *Add.* 1547–65, p. 509; *CSP For.* 1562, pp. 13–15; 1564–5, pp. 437, 439, 444, 461–2, 467, 469, 484, 505, 519; 1566–8, pp. 6, 40; *APC,* vii. 136; Lansd. 5, f. 109; Froude, *Hist. Eng.,* vi. 541–2; vii. 359–64. [8] Lansd. 5, f. 109; *PCC Admins.* ed. Glencross, i. 67.

M.K.D.

YELVERTON, William (by 1505–86), of Rougham, Norf.

LYNN 1558*

b. by 1505, 1st s. of William Yelverton of Rougham by Margaret, da. of one Garnon of London. *educ.* G. Inn. *m.* (1) by 1526, Anne, da. of Sir Henry Farmer of East Barsham, Norf., 5s. inc. Christopher† 4da.; (2) Jane, da. of Edmund Cokett of Ampton, Suff., 3s. 2da. *suc.* fa. 1541.[1]
    Autumn reader, G. Inn 1534.[2]
    J.p. Norf. 1538–53, q. 1555–69, 1579–86; commr. relief 1550; other commissions 1537–86; recorder, Lynn June 1558–61.[3]

William Yelverton belonged to a dynasty of lawyers. Entering Gray's Inn about 1520, he was Autumn reader in 1534 but paid a fine of £20 for not reading in Lent 1541. From 1537 he joined his father on commissions in Norfolk, and with intervals he was to serve on the county bench for nearly half-a-century. Appointed counsel to Lynn in August 1542, he appears to have been retained in that capacity, at a fee of 20s. a year, with a break between 1552 and 1556, until he succeeded Ambrose Gilberd* as recorder in June 1558; when he relinquished this office in December 1561 the borough granted him a fee of 40s. a year for life in return for his counsel. One of his perquisites had been the town's grant to him and his wife in 1551 of water into their house in St. James's End for the term of their lives.[4]

Yelverton sat in only one Parliament, and then for a single brief session: on 30 Sept. 1558 he was elected to replace Gilberd in Mary's last Parliament, which met again for 13 days before the Queen's death. He had been elected, so it appears, as the second Member for Lynn to the Parliament of 1545, only to be superseded by Thomas Miller. This episode, and the fact that after his fleeting appearance in 1558 Yelverton was not re-elected to the succeeding Parliament suggests that some inhibition was at work to exclude him, although whether on his part or the town's cannot be said. It may be that his marriage to the daughter of a wealthy London

merchant who had settled in the county predisposed Yelverton to spend his time there and to concentrate upon acquiring property, which he did on a considerable scale. In 1564 the bishop of Norwich included him among the Norfolk justices who were 'very well affected' to the Anglican settlement. Of the will which he is said to have made on 30 Dec. 1582 only some indications appear in his inquisition post mortem, and it was evidently not proved, his death on 12 Aug. 1586 being followed by the issue of letters of administration to his third son Christopher, the future Speaker. His heir Henry was then a man of 59. A brass in Rougham church commemorated Yelverton and his wives and children.[5]

[1] Date of birth estimated from marriage. *Vis. Norf.* (Harl. Soc. xxxii), 328–9; *Test. Vet.* ed. Nicolas, 716. [2] Dugdale, *Origines Juridiciales,* 292–3. [3] *LP Hen. VIII,* xii, xiv–xvii, xx; *CPR,* 1547–8, pp. 75, 76, 79, 87; 1553, p. 357; 1560–3, p. 440; 1563–6, pp. 25, 199; 1569–72, pp. 216–17; Lynn congregation bk. 5, ff. 316v, 369. [4] Lynn congregation bk. 4, f. 344; 5, ff. 16v–369 passim. [5] Ibid. 5, ff. 24, 320v; Blomefield, *Norf.* viii. 444–9; x. 31–36; *Cam. Misc.* ix(3), 58; C142/219/91; PCC admons. act bk. 1586, f. 181; A. H. Smith, *County and Ct.* 356, 359; Pevsner, *N.-W. and S. Norf.* 296.

R.V.

YEO (YAWE, YOWE), Hugh (by 1499–1548), of Braunton, Devon.

BARNSTAPLE 1529

b. by 1499, 1st s. of John Yeo of Hatherleigh by Joan, da. of Thomas Asshe of Brampton. *educ.* M. Temple, adm. 9 Feb. 1517. *m.* by 1520, Alice, da. of John Pyke, 3s. 1da.[1]
    J.p. Devon by 1535–*d.*; commr. tenths of spiritualities, Devon and Exeter 1535, oyer and terminer, Devon 1540, subsidy 1540, 1543; under steward and auditor of Pilton, Devon, for bp. of Exeter.[2]

When his mill at Braunton was the subject of a chancery suit Hugh Yeo professed himself 'loath to be in trouble with the law', a disclaimer which accords ill with his reputation as a man learned in that science: the mayor and corporation of Barnstaple retained his counsel for upwards of 20 years until his death and he acted for Lady Lisle in her protracted dispute with the 2nd Lord Daubeney and her other estate business. Yeo was less wide of the mark in deprecating his kinship and 'ability', for although he was of gentle birth his family was of small standing and in the main poorly connected: if it was by marrying a kinswoman that he acquired the manor of Little Buckland, and his residence at Fairlinch in the parish of Braunton, his brother William, an Inner Templar, did better for himself with Audrey Stukley, daughter of a recorder of Barnstaple.[3]

It was doubtless to Sir Thomas Stukley, who had held that office for the three years preceding, that Yeo owed his election in 1529. Having seen this protracted Parliament through, he was probably returned again in 1536, when the King issued a general request for the re-election of the previous Members, and may even have sat in 1539, when the names of both Members are also lost, and in 1542, when only one name has survived. Of his part in the proceedings of the Commons nothing is known. He was made a justice of the peace by 1535 and it was as such that in July of that year he and Humphrey Prideaux tried to eject the abbot of Hartland. It must have been either then or in an earlier summer that he had a deer from Viscount Lisle's park at Umberleigh; in the next few years, when he was busy with her affairs, Yeo would thank Lady Lisle for other presents. Yet he does not seem to have acquired further property; it was doubtless as an agent that in May 1542 he was joined with John Prideaux, probably the future Member for Plymouth and Devon, in a recovery against the 2nd Earl of Bath for Spitchwick park, Widecombe. For the subsidy of 1540 he was assessed at the modest figure of 30s.[4]

Yeo died on 25 Oct. 1548 and was buried in the church at Braunton three days later. He appears to have left no will, but at the inquisition held at Exeter on 2 Oct. 1550 his 30 year-old son William was found to be his heir. Leonard Yeo, Member for Totnes in 1555 and 1558, was a kinsman, although the relationship is not clear.[5]

¹ Date of birth estimated from marriage. *Vis. Devon* ed. Colby, 218; N. Devon Athenaeum, Barnstaple, D. Drake ms 'MPs Barnstaple', 21. ² *LP Hen. VIII*, viii, xv; E179/97/214, 98/255; D. H. Pill, 'The diocese of Exeter under Bp. Veysey' (Exeter Univ. M.A. thesis,1963),199. ³ C1/1013/6,1038/48–9,1093/15;St.Ch.2/27/126; N. Devon Athenaeum, 3972, ff. 33v, 36, 40(3), 50(2); D. Drake ms op. cit. 21; *LP Hen. VIII*, vi, viii, xii, xiii, add.; M. L. Bush, 'Lisle-Seymour Land Disputes', *Hist. Jnl.* ix. 255–74; PCC 29 Dyngeley. ⁴ *LP Hen. VIII*, vi, viii, xii, xiii; L. Snell, *Suppression of Rel. Foundations Devon and Cornw.* 67; NRA 6042, p. 20; E179/97/214. ⁵ C142/90/62; N. Devon Athenaeum, D. Drake ms op. cit. 21.

L.M.K./A.D.K.H.

YEO, Leonard (by 1512–86), of London and Totnes, Devon.

TOTNES 1555, 1558, 1559

b. by 1512, 2nd *s.* of Nicholas Yeo of Heanton Satchville by Joan, da. of Richard Lybbe of Tavistock. *m.* (1) ?27 Oct. 1534, Arminell, da. of Christopher Beresford of London, wid. of John Broke (*d.* 1533) of London, at least 1s. 2da.; (2) Denise, da. of William Dotyn of Harberton, Devon.[1]
Mayor, Totnes 1558–9, 1570–1.[2]

Although Leonard Yeo came of a gentle family long settled in north Devon, he was born at Tavistock. His apprenticeship to the London mercer John Broke was perhaps arranged by his uncle Richard Lybbe*, helped by another kinsman Hugh Yeo*. Admitted to the Mercers' Company in 1533, Yeo soon married his former master's widow, from whom he had already acquired much of her husband's stock and property. As executrix she entrusted

him with the administration of Broke's possessions and made him guardian of his stepchildren, who however did not take to the situation. Until Broke's heir came of age Yeo occupied his house called the *Unicorn* on Cheapside. In 1542 he bought land at Halstock in Devon and by 1553 he was the lessee of the castle ditch at Totnes from Sir Richard Edgecombe* and of other property in the town from the corporation.[3]

Yeo's association with Edgecombe probably conduced to his return for Totnes, where in 1555 his fellow-Member was Edgecombe's son Peter, although he could also claim kinship with James Bassett, one of the knights of the shire. The borough appears to have raised the question of his municipal status, for three days after the Parliament of 1555 was dissolved the common council of London agreed to give him a certificate of his freedom for presentation at Totnes 'provided the said Yeo shall be quietly permitted ... to enjoy the liberties of the town by reason of his said freedom here'. This evidently settled the matter; Yeo was to be re-elected to the next two Parliaments and in the autumn of 1558 he began his first mayoralty. In the Parliament of that year Bassett was again one of the knights for Devon, and Bernard Smith, whose niece Yeo's son George was to marry in 1561, was the other Member for Totnes. All that is known about Yeo's part in the House is that in 1555 he did not join the opposition headed by Sir Anthony Kingston to one of the government's bills.[4]

Yeo later settled at Exeter, where he died on 30 May 1586, his goods being valued for probate at £1,090.[5]

¹ Date of birth estimated from admission to Mercers' Company. *Vis. Devon*, ed. Colby, 217; PCC 21 Holgrave, 51 Windsor; NRA 5984 (Devon RO, 312M/FY 35, 37–40, 44, 67); Req.2/124/59; *Vis. Devon*, ed. Vivian, 834–5 compounds the errors in *Vis. Devon* (Harl. Soc. vi), 324. ² *Trans. Dev. Assoc.* xxxii. 438; *Western Antiq.* ix. 152. ³ List of Mercers (T/S, Mercers' Hall), 567; NRA 5984 (citing Devon RO, 312M/FY 37–41, 44, 45, 59, TY 283–6; 9834 (Surr. RO, 87/16/ 36–39); Req.2/124/59; *Devon Monastic Lands* (Devon and Cornw. Rec. Soc. i), 29; Devon RO, 1579/25, r. 1555–2v. ⁴ City of London RO, Guildhall, rep. 13(ii), f. 354; NRA 5984 (Devon RO, 312M/TY 301). ⁵ PCC 51 Windsor; Wards 7/21/183; *Devon Inventories* (Devon and Cornw. Rec. Soc. n.s. xi), 4–5.

D.F.C.

YOULE, Robert (c.1497–1561), of Worcester.

WORCESTER 1547, 1554 (Nov.), 1555, 1558

b. c. 1497. *m.* (1) Eleanor; (2) Margaret, wid.; 3da. prob. by 1st *w.*[1]
Auditor, Worcester 1544, 1550–1, 1555–6, chamberlain 1545–6, alderman 1547–8, 1553–4, 1559–60, bailiff 1546–7, 1548–9, 1552–3, 1558–9, bridgemaster 1553–4, member of the Twenty-Four 1555; gov. Worcester free sch. and almshouses Feb. 1561.[2]

Robert Youle came to Worcester at about the age of 12 and prospered there as a clothier. One of several of his trade who in May 1551 purchased the Trinity Hall in the parish of St. Nicholas, Youle gave his share to the company of weavers, walkers and clothiers of the city which had been meeting in the hall for some years; his grandson Robert Rowland *alias* Steyner was later to make a final transference of the property to the company.[3]

Youle sat for Worcester in four Parliaments and payments to him are recorded in respect of each of them. He was paid at the customary rate of 2s. a day for the whole of the fourth session of the Parliament of 1547, for the entire Parliaments of November 1554 (when his fellow-Member Edward Brogden, although prosecuted as a 'seceder', received the same amount) and 1555, and for the first session of that of 1558: on the last occasion the payment was 'over and above other charges allowed by this council'. Youle also received £4 4s. in 1546–7 for negotiations 'in the lord chancellor's court', £5 in 1555–6 'which he paid to Mr. Lord to enrol the charter in the Exchequer' and an unspecified amount in 1558 for his expenses 'in his suit for the redress of the weight of cloths'. Worcester made repeated efforts to secure the amendment of a recent statute (6 Edw. VI, c.6) regulating the cloth trade before succeeding in the Parliament of 1558 (4 and 5 Phil. and Mary, c.5): a bill touching the making of Worcester cloths was introduced in 1555 but proceeded no further than its first reading. Youle was not among those who opposed a government bill in the Parliament of 1555: on the contrary, Catholic zeal may account for the harsh treatment which, according to Foxe, he had meted out during his first term as bailiff to John Davis, a boy not 12 years of age, whom he imprisoned as a heretic and shackled with 'a pair of bolts, so that he could not lift up his small legs'.[4]

Against such alleged inhumanity must be set Youle's beneficence, especially in education. He and his fellow-Member for the last session of the Parliament of 1547 and again in 1558, Thomas Wild, shared an interest in the Worcester free school and while attending one or other of these Parliaments they obtained a crown grant of £6 a year for the master. Youle had already helped to procure him an increase of salary and on another occasion he lent the city the money to pay it. Later he made the school a gift of lands worth £13 6s.8d. a year and when it was refounded in 1561 he was one of the first governors. He left the school a further £100 in his will of 5 Nov. 1560. Although the preamble to the will does not contain the traditional Catholic formula, the master and boys were required to come yearly to Youle's grave in Worcester cathedral to pray for his soul and those of his family and all Christians. Youle bequeathed 500 marks and property in Worcester to

his wife. His three daughters were all married, Anne to John Rowland *alias* Steyner, Alice to Brian Chamberlain and Eleanor to John Walsgrove *alias* Fleet, and each had at least one child: these shared some £800 and various properties in Worcester and elsewhere in the county. There were smaller bequests to other relations and, in addition to the school's £100, a gift of certain tenements to the use of the poor and provision for them of £30 at his burial, £20 at his month's mind and £20 at his year's mind. The Worcestershire historian Habington was to call Youle 'as worthy and charitable a citizen as his time produced'. His son-in-law John Rowland was executor and the overseers were Thomas Walsgrove (probably Youle's grandson, who was to sit for Worcester in the Parliament of 1571), Alice Fleet and Brian Chamberlain. It is not known when Youle died but he was appointed a governor of the free school in February 1561 and his will was proved on the following 17 Sept.[5]

[1] Aged '62 or thereabouts' in October 1559, A. F. Leach, *Early Educ. in Worcester* (Worcs. Hist. Soc. 1913), 197. PCC 29 Loftes. [2] Worcester Guildhall, audit of accts. 1540–1600, unpaginated; Leach, 186; *CPR*, 1554–5, p. 81; 1558–60, p. 271; 1560–3, p. 215. Nash, *Worcs*. ii. app. cxii gives Richard Gowle as low bailiff in 1546 but the indenture for 1547 (C219/19/133) identifies him as Robert Youle. [3] Leach, 197; *VCH Worcs*. ii. 287, 293. [4] Worcester Guildhall, chamber order bk. 1540–1601, ff. 43v, 54, 62, 72v; audit of accts. 1540–1600; *CJ*, i. 43; Foxe, *Acts and Mons*. viii. 554–5. [5] Leach, pp. xxxi–xxxii, xxxiv, 181, 197, 199, 205, 218, 220; *VCH Worcs*. iv. 478–80, 491–2; PCC 29 Loftes; *Habington's Worcs*. (Worcs. Hist. Soc. 1899), ii. 425.

A.D.

YOUNG, John (by 1519–89), of Bristol, Glos., London and Melbury Sampford, Dorset.

OLD SARUM	1547[1]
PLYMOUTH	1555
DEVIZES	1559
WEST LOOE	1563
OLD SARUM	1571

b. by 1519, 1st (surv.) s. of Hugh Young of Bristol and Castle Combe, Wilts. by Alice. *m.* c. 1563, Joan, da. of John Wadham of Merrifield, Som., wid. of Sir Giles Strangways II* (*d.* 11 Apr. 1562) of Melbury Sampford, 1s. 2da. *suc.* fa. 7 Jan. 1534. Kntd. 21 Aug. 1574.[2]

?Sewer, the chamber by 1546; collector of customs, Bristol Mar. 1559; sheriff, Dorset 1569–70; j.p.q. Dorset and Som. 1573/74–*d*., ?Wilts. 1583–*d*.; keeper, Castle Cary park, Som. and Melbury park, Dorset.[3]

It was probably the same John Young who sat in five Parliaments and for four boroughs in all between 1547 and 1571. A Bristolian who inherited his patrimony while still under age, he is first met with as a servant of Edward Seymour, Earl of Hertford, who as constable of Bristol castle (in survivorship with his father) from 1517 and steward of the city from 1544 exercised a powerful attraction there. It was to Hertford that Young doubtless owed the post in the royal household which he appears to have been holding by 1546 and the seat in Parliament for Old Sarum which he secured either in the following year or perhaps at a by-election later. In 1548 he travelled in Italy, whence he corresponded with his master, now Duke of Somerset: while there he may have met William Thomas, who was to become his fellow-Member for Old Sarum by the last session of the Parliament. In July 1549 he was sent by the Privy Council with letters to the west country at the time of the rebellion. Of his fortunes during the decline and downfall of his master nothing has come to light, but he emerged from it early in 1552 as the recipient of a crown annuity of £150. At what point Young had detached himself from Seymour is unknown, but he seems to have transferred his allegiance to William Herbert*, 1st Earl of Pembroke. The transition was a natural one, for Pembroke was Seymour's successor at Bristol as well as in Wiltshire: Young could also claim kinship with the earl's first wife Anne Parr, Queen Catherine's sister.[4]

Young was probably the man of that name whose arrest was ordered in February 1554, doubtless on suspicion of complicity in Wyatt's rebellion. He must have cleared himself for he was soon released, but 18 months later he was still engaged in controversy with Charles, 8th Baron Stourton over the return of goods seized at the time of his arrest. These tribulations did not prevent his return for Plymouth to the fourth Parliament of the reign. His patron is unknown but Young was apparently a distant kinsman of George Ferrers, another courtier who had survived the fall of Somerset; William Baldwin, a friend of Ferrers and co-author of *A myrroure for magistrates*, later dedicated one of his works to Young, who may also have known Ferrers's other friend and fellow-Member for Plymouth Thomas Sternhold. (It is unlikely that Young was the man of his name who was elected to this Parliament by Rye but was passed over by the lord warden in favour of John Holmes I (q.v.).) Young opposed one of the government's bills in this Parliament and was named by John Daniell as having been present when the 'opposition' group met to arrange its tactics. The six other men named by Daniell were connected by various ties of blood, friendship or common experience and four of them were from Devon, including Sir Arthur Champernon* whose family had influence in Plymouth. Young was the only one of the seven not involved in the Dudley conspiracy of the following year. If this was a sign of his renewed allegiance to Pembroke, who had chosen to remain loyal to the Marian government, he had to wait until the following reign for his reward.[5]

Young was returned to the Parliament of 1559 for

Devizes, presumably on Pembroke's nomination, and shortly afterwards he was appointed collector of customs at Bristol. Within a few years he married the widow of Sir Giles Strangways, who had likewise voted against the crown in the Parliament of 1555 and who had been named an executor by Sir William Courtenay II,* one of the Members named by Daniell. If he was also the John Young who received £40 by the will of Sir James Stumpe, this bequest may also reflect a similar community of outlook and experience, for Stumpe too had opposed the crown in 1555. Although he was to sit twice more in Parliament, Young seems to have passed the remainder of his life largely in the west, building the large house on the site of the Carmelite friary in Bristol where he died on 4 Sept. 1589.[6]

[1] Hatfield 207. [2] Date of birth estimated from age at fa.'s i.p.m., *Bristol and Glos. Arch. Soc. Trans.* xv. 227–45; *Vis. Dorset* (Harl. Soc. xx), 86; *CPR*, 1558–60, p. 215. [3] *LP Hen. VIII*, xxi; *CPR*, 1558–60, p. 49; St.Ch.5/Y1/9, 38. [4] *CP*, xii(1), 60; Bristol AO, 04721/295; *CSP Dom.* 1547–80, p. 11; *VCH Wilts.* v. 115; *APC*, ii. 163, 306, 539; *CPR*, 1550–3, p. 386; *HP* ed. Wedgwood, 1439–1509 (Biogs.), 661, 980. [5] *APC*, iv. 401; v. 56–57, 151, 160; F. B. Williams, *Index of Dedications*, 206; Guildford mus. Loseley 1331/2; SP11/8/35. [6] Prob. 10/34; PCC 23 Chayre, 93 Leicester; C142/222/51.

R.V.

YOWE *see* **YEO**

ZOUCHE, John I (c.1515–85), of Ansty, Wilts.

HINDON   1547*[1]
SHAFTESBURY   1559

b. c. 1515, yr. s. of John, 8th Lord Zouche, of Harringworth, Northants., prob. by 1st w. Dorothy, da. of Sir William Capell* of London. *m.* by 1545, Catherine, da. of Sir George St. Leger of Annery in Monkleigh, Devon, wid. of George Courtenay of Powderham, Devon, 3 or 4s. inc. Francis†. Kntd. 10 Nov. 1549.[2]

Esquire of the body extraordinary by 1533; gent. pens. 1540; steward and bailiff, duchy of Cornwall manor of Mere, Wilts., keeper, Mere park 1539–*d.*; warden, Gillingham forest and bailiff, town and manor of Gillingham, Dorset 1539–*d.*; bailiff for Thomas Seymour, Baron Seymour of Sudeley, unknown property by 1548; j.p. Wilts. 1558/59–*d.*; sheriff 1559–60; commr. musters 1573; other commissions 1551–68.[3]

As the son of a peer and the nephew of Sir William Paulet, later Marquess of Winchester, John Zouche was well placed to gain entry to the court. He and two other courtiers, George Carew* and Edward Rogers*, appear in Cromwell's remembrances for 1536 in connexion with a bond for £60, and later in the same year he and Rogers were granted a licence to import Toulouse woad and Gascon wine.[4]

Zouche probably owed his appointment early in 1539 to duchy of Cornwall offices at Mere, formerly held by the attainted Marquess of Exeter, to another kinsman, Sir Thomas Arundell*, receiver-general of the duchy, while those that he secured shortly afterwards at Gillingham, a few miles across the Dorset border, may have accrued to him through another family connexion, their former holder, John Rogers. These two offices were to involve Zouche in a Star Chamber dispute with William Grimston*, a former servant of Sir John Rogers. Zouche was included in the King's new bodyguard, the 'spears', or gentlemen pensioners, and was one of the esquires who greeted Anne of Cleves. The manor of Encombe, Dorset, granted to him in May 1540, he immediately alienated to Sir Thomas Arundell, but the manor and rectory of Ansty, which he leased in April 1541 was to become his chief residence; he received a life grant of it later in the same year and in 1546 he was granted it in tail male in return for his services and £100. In 1543 he was one of an evidently Protestant group, including Sir Edward Baynton* and Gawain Carew*, summoned before the Privy Council for eating flesh in Lent.[5]

Zouch was knighted at Westminster six days after the opening of the third session of the Parliament of 1547. He appears on the Crown Office list drawn up for the fourth session as having replaced John Story at Hindon, which lies a few miles from Ansty. Story had been committed to the Tower on 24 Jan. 1549 and had been there for the remainder of the second session; Zouche could therefore have taken his place either during that session or at the opening of the third. Hindon was one of the bishop of Winchester's boroughs, but with Bishop Gardiner also in the Tower Zouche may have owed his return to his uncle Paulet who was steward of the bishopric. He probably enjoyed the support of his neighbour Sir William Herbert*, soon to be created Earl of Pembroke, from whose home at Wilton he wrote in January 1552 to persuade the commissioners for the sale of crown property to retain Mere: it was presumably Pembroke who was to sponsor his later return for Shaftesbury. With such patrons, his advent in Parliament was in keeping with the downfall of the Protector Somerset; his brother Richard, who succeeded their father in August 1550, was to serve as a commissioner for Somerset's trial. Zouche himself was to benefit from the execution in 1552 of Sir Thomas Arundell, whose manor of Tisbury, Wiltshire, he was to obtain on a 30-year lease. The return for Hindon to Edward VI's last Parliament is missing, but in view of Zouche's standing and connexions it is not unlikely that he was re-elected.[6]

In the pardon which he sued out in October 1553 Zouche was described as of Ansty, 'alias Queen's servant', and he retained a position in the royal household throughout Mary's reign. In 1551 he had been granted a life annuity of 200 marks to take effect from the death of Elizabeth Zouche, formerly abbess of Shaftesbury and presumably a kinswoman; he surrendered the patent in 1555 in exchange for a life annuity of £100. In 1557 he made a similar exchange of an annuity of £43 from Charles, 8th Baron Stourton, recently attainted of felony, for a life interest in his offices at Mere. He did not, however, reappear in Parliament during the reign, although his stepson Sir William Courtenay II was one of the most prominent of the opposition in the Parliament of 1555.[7]

Although he had stayed out of trouble Zouche doubtless welcomed Elizabeth's accession. He was pricked sheriff of his county in 1559 and in 1564 he was described, like Sir John Thynne*, as 'a furtherer earnest in religion'. Zouche was to remain an active administrator in his county until his death on 30 May 1585.[8]

[1] Hatfield 207. [2] Date of birth estimated from family history and career. PCC 13 Holder; E150/939/1; Hoare, *Wilts.* Alderbury, 207; *DNB* (Zouche, Richard); *CP*, xii (2), 948; C142/209/44; *Lit. Rems. Edw. VI*, p. cccvii. [3] *LP Hen. VIII*, ii, xiv, xv, xix, xx; E163/12/17, nos. 37, 50, 54; *CPR*, 1550–3, p. 142; 1558–60, pp. 86, 103; 1563–6, pp. 39, 42, 260; 1569–72, p. 219; *CSP Dom.* 1547–80, p. 464. [4] *LP Hen. VIII*, x, xi, xiv. [5] Ibid. xiv–xvii, xxi; *CPR*, 1558–60, p. 86; St.Ch.2/16/351–9; *APC*, i. 114. [6] Hatfield 207; *Wilts. Arch. Mag.* xxix. 241; *APC*, iv. 5; *CPR*, 1553–4, p. 340. [7] *CPR*, 1553–4, p. 413; 1554–5, p. 172; 1557–8, p. 312. [8] *Cam. Misc.* ix(3), 36; C142/209/44.

S.R.J.

ZOUCHE, John II (1534–86), of Codnor, Derbys.

DERBYSHIRE 1558

b. 27 Aug. 1534, 1st s. of George Zouche of Codnor by Anne, da. of Sir John Gaynsford of Crowhurst, Surr. *educ.* St. John's, Camb. matric. Easter 1549; ?G. Inn, adm. 1552. *m.* Eleanor, da. of Richard Whalley* of Kirton, Welbeck and Sibthorpe, Notts. and Wimbledon, Surr. 3s. inc. John† 1da. *suc.* fa. 30 Aug. 1556. KB 15 Jan. 1559.[1]

J.p. Derbys. 1558/59–*d.*, q. by 1569; sheriff, Notts. and Derbys. 1561–2, Derbys. 1571–2, 1580–1; commr. musters 1569, 1573, 1577, subsidy 1581; other commissions 1564–*d.*; dep. lt. 1585–*d.*[2]

John Zouche of Codnor came of a cadet branch of the noble family seated at Harrington, Northamptonshire. His father was a gentleman pensioner 1540–c.1544. Zouche had livery of his lands in May 1557, so that his election as knight of the shire at the close of the year, when still in his early twenties, was an early recognition of his emergence; in this he resembled his fellow-Member Godfrey Foljambe, who although some years older had yet to succeed to his patrimony. If, as is likely, Zouche was one of the executors of Sir John St. John's* will of April 1558, he was probably already connected with St. John's son-in-law Francis Russell*, 2nd Earl of Bedford, who 20 years later was to recommend him as custos rotulorum of Derbyshire; his cousin Thomas Randolph, who sat with him in the Commons, was a protégé of the earl.[3]

The accession of Elizabeth brought Zouche the knighthood of the Bath, membership of the Derbyshire bench and his first shrievalty. His acceptability to the new regime was confirmed by a favourable judgment from his bishop in 1564 and by his choice in June 1569 to assist the 6th Earl of Shrewsbury, who was ill, in his custody of Mary Queen of Scots at South Wingfield. This episode may have helped to turn Shrewsbury against Zouche, whom the earl later denounced as both a troublemaker and a mishandler of public funds, and whom he appointed his joint deputy lieutenant in 1585 only 'to please others'; Zouche's failure to succeed Sir Francis Leke* as custos rotulorum in 1580, despite the Queen's promise to that effect, also owed something to Shrewsbury's intervention. A further cause of dissension with his neighbours was the leading part which Zouche played in the exploitation of the Derbyshire lead deposits. If he sought election to any of the early Elizabethan Parliaments these various enmities clearly balked him, but as sheriff of Derbyshire he made the return in 1572 and 12 years later he and John Harpur† sought to engineer the defeat of Sir Charles Cavendish†.[4]

Zouche died on 19 June 1586. In 1566 he had sued out a licence to alienate the manor and castle of Codnor, other Derbyshire manors, and lands in Northamptonshire and Yorkshire, but in the inquisition taken in September 1586 he is recorded as holding these Derbyshire properties, which are said to have been sold by a descendant in 1634. By his will of 6 May 1586 Zouche bequeathed all his lands, apart from the remaining years of a lease in a Nottinghamshire parsonage, to his wife and his eldest son John, whom he appointed executor. He named as supervisors his friends John Harpur, Ralph Sacheverell and Michael Willoughby.[5]

[1] Date of birth given at fa.'s i.p.m., C142/109/18. *Vis. Surr.* (Harl. Soc. xliii), 12, 91–93; *The Gen.* n.s. viii. 180; Harl. 5809, f. 7; *CPR, 1555–7*, p. 248; *1563–6*, p. 399. [2] *CPR, 1563–6*, pp. 38, 42, 114, 489, 491; *1569–72*, p. 223; *1572–5*, pp. 146, 153; *CSP Dom. 1547–80*, pp. 341, 346, 460; *HMC Rutland*, i. 112, 126, 168, 176, 190, 214. [3] *CPR, 1555–7*, p. 248; *HMC Rutland*, i. 120; information from W. J. Tighe. [4] *Machyn's Diary* (Cam. Soc. xlii), 370; *APC*, ix. 374; x. 115–270 passim; xi. 350; xii. 357; *CPR, 1558–60*, p. 165; *CSP Dom. 1547–80*, p. 470; *1581–90*, p. 74; *CSP For. 1561–2*, p. 635; *CSP Scot.* ed. Thorpe, *1589–1603*, pp. 876–7, 975; *HMC 6th Rep.* 450; *HMC Hatfield*, ii. 150; *HMC Rutland*, i. 120–1, 176; *HMC Shrewsbury and Talbot*, ii. 92–375 passim; *Cam. Misc.* ix(3), 43; Strype, *Annals*, ii(2), 138–9; M. B. Donald, *Eliz. Monopolies*, 148–75, 201–7. [5] C142/210/90(1); Wards 7/21/179; *CPR, 1563–6*, p. 362; PCC 31 Windsor.

C.J.B.